Algebra 2

Common Core

Randall I. Charles
Basia Hall
Dan Kennedy
Allan E. Bellman
Sadie Chavis Bragg
William G. Handlin
Stuart J. Murphy
Grant Wiggins

PEARSON

Boston, Massachusetts • Chandler, Arizona • Glenview, Illinois • Hoboken, New Jersey

Acknowledgments appear on page 1160, which constitutes an extension of this copyright page.

Copyright © 2015 Pearson Education, Inc., or its affiliates. All Rights Reserved. Printed in the United States of America. This publication is protected by copyright, and permission should be obtained from the publisher prior to any prohibited reproduction, storage in a retrieval system, or transmission in any form or by any means, electronic, mechanical, photocopying, recording, or likewise. For information regarding permissions, write to Rights Management & Contracts, Pearson Education, Inc., 221 River Street, Hoboken, New Jersey 07030.

PEARSON

ISBN-13: 978-0-13-328116-3
ISBN-10:   0-13-328116-7
4 5 6 7 8 9 10 V057 18 17 16 15 14

Contents *in Brief*

Welcome to *Pearson Algebra 2 Common Core Edition* student book. Throughout this textbook, you will find content that has been developed to cover many of the High School Standards for Mathematical Content and all of the Standards for Mathematical Practice. The End-of-Course Assessment provides students with practice with all of the Standards for Mathematical Content listed on pages xx to xxiii.

Series *Authors*

Randall I. Charles, Ph.D., is Professor Emeritus in the Department of Mathematics and Computer Science at San Jose State University, San Jose, California. He began his career as a high school mathematics teacher, and he was a mathematics supervisor for five years. Dr. Charles has been a member of several NCTM committees and is the former Vice President of the National Council of Supervisors of Mathematics. Much of his writing and research has been in the area of problem solving. He has authored more than 90 mathematics textbooks for kindergarten through college.

Dan Kennedy, Ph.D., is a classroom teacher and the Lupton Distinguished Professor of Mathematics at the Baylor School in Chattanooga, Tennessee. A frequent speaker at professional meetings on the subject of mathematics education reform, Dr. Kennedy has conducted more than 50 workshops and institutes for high school teachers. He is coauthor of textbooks in calculus and precalculus, and from 1990 to 1994, he chaired the College Board's AP Calculus Development Committee. He is a 1992 Tandy Technology Scholar and a 1995 Presidential Award winner.

Basia Hall currently serves as Manager of Instructional Programs for the Houston Independent School District. With 33 years of teaching experience, Ms. Hall has served as a department chair, instructional supervisor, school improvement facilitator, and professional development trainer. She has developed curricula for Algebra 1, Geometry, and Algebra 2 and co-developed the Texas state mathematics standards. A 1992 Presidential Awardee, Ms. Hall is past president of the Texas Association of Supervisors of Mathematics and is a state representative for the National Council of Supervisors of Mathematics (NCSM).

Consulting *Authors*

Stuart J. Murphy is a visual learning author and consultant. He is a champion of helping students develop learning skills so they become more successful students. He is the author of *MathStart,* a series of children's books that presents mathematical concepts in the context of stories and *I See I Learn,* a Pre-Kindergarten and Kindergarten learning initiative that focuses on social and emotional skills. A graduate of the Rhode Island School of Design, he has worked extensively in educational publishing and has been on the authorship teams of a number of elementary and high school mathematics programs. He is a frequent presenter at meetings of the National Council of Teachers of Mathematics, the International Reading Association, and other professional organizations.

Grant Wiggins, Ed.D., is the President of Authentic Education in Hopewell, New Jersey. He earned his B.A. from St. John's College in Annapolis and his Ed.D. from Harvard University. Dr. Wiggins consults with schools, districts, and state education departments on a variety of reform matters; organizes conferences and workshops; and develops print materials and Web resources on curricular change. He is perhaps best known for being the coauthor, with Jay McTighe, of *Understanding by Design* and *The Understanding by Design Handbook*[1], the award-winning and highly successful materials on curriculum published by ASCD. His work has been supported by the Pew Charitable Trusts, the Geraldine R. Dodge Foundation, and the National Science Foundation.

[1] ASCD, publisher of "The Understanding by Design Handbook" coauthored by Grant Wiggins and registered owner of the trademark "Understanding by Design," has not authorized or sponsored this work and is in no way affiliated with Pearson or its products.

Program *Authors*

Algebra 1 and Algebra 2

Allan E. Bellman, Ph.D., is an Associate Professor of Mathematics Education at the University of Mississippi. He previously taught at the University of California, Davis for 12 years and in public school in Montgomery County, Maryland for 31. He has been an instructor for both the Woodrow Wilson National Fellowship Foundation and the Texas Instruments' T^3 program. Dr. Bellman has a expertise in the use of technology in education and assessment-driven instruction, and speaks frequently on these topics. He was a 1992 Tandy Technology Scholar and has twice been listed in Who's Who Among America's Teachers.

Sadie Chavis Bragg, Ed.D., is Senior Vice President of Academic Affairs and professor of mathematics at the Borough of Manhattan Community College of the City University of New York. She is a past president of the American Mathematical Association of Two-Year Colleges (AMATYC). In recognition of her service to the field of mathematics locally, statewide, nationally, and internationally, she was awarded AMATYC's most prestigious award, the Mathematics Excellence Award for 2010. Dr. Bragg has coauthored more than 50 mathematics textbooks for kindergarten through college.

William G. Handlin, Sr., is a classroom teacher and Department Chair of Mathematics and former Department Chair of Technology Applications at Spring Woods High School in Houston, Texas. Awarded Life Membership in the Texas Congress of Parents and Teachers for his contributions to the well-being of children, Mr. Handlin is also a frequent workshop and seminar leader in professional meetings.

Geometry

Laurie E. Bass is a classroom teacher at the 9–12 division of the Ethical Culture Fieldston School in Riverdale, New York. A classroom teacher for more than 30 years, Ms. Bass has a wide base of teaching experience, ranging from Grade 6 through Advanced Placement Calculus. She was the recipient of a 2000 Honorable Mention for the Radio Shack National Teacher Awards. She has been a contributing writer for a number of publications, including software-based activities for the Algebra 1 classroom. Among her areas of special interest are cooperative learning for high school students and geometry exploration on the computer. Ms. Bass is a frequent presenter at local, regional, and national conferences.

Art Johnson, Ed.D., is a professor of mathematics education at Boston University. He is a mathematics educator with 32 years of public school teaching experience, a frequent speaker and workshop leader, and the recipient of a number of awards: the Tandy Prize for Teaching Excellence, the Presidential Award for Excellence in Mathematics Teaching, and New Hampshire Teacher of the Year. He was also profiled by the Disney Corporation in the American Teacher of the Year Program. Dr. Johnson has contributed 18 articles to NCTM journals and has authored over 50 books on various aspects of mathematics.

Reviewers *National*

From the *Authors*

Welcome

Math is a powerful tool with far-reaching applications throughout your life. We have designed a unique and engaging program that will enable you to tap into the power of mathematics and mathematical reasoning. This award-winning program has been developed to align fully to the Common Core State Standards.

Developing mathematical skills and problem-solving strategies is an ongoing process—a journey both inside and outside the classroom. This course is designed to help make sense of the mathematics you encounter in and out of class each day and to help you develop mathematical proficiency.

You will learn important mathematical principles. You will also learn how the principles are connected to one another and to what you already know. You will learn to solve problems and learn the reasoning that lies behind your solutions. You will also develop the key mathematical practices of the Common Core State Standards.

Each chapter begins with the "big ideas" of the chapter and some essential questions that you will learn to answer. Through this question-and-answer process you will develop your ability to analyze problems independently and solve them in different applications.

Your skills and confidence will increase through practice and review. Work through the problems so you understand the concepts and methods presented and the thinking behind them. Then do the exercises. Ask yourself how new concepts relate to old ones. Make the connections!

Everyone needs help sometimes. You will find that this program has built-in opportunities, both in this text and online, to get help whenever you need it.

This course will also help you succeed on the tests you take in class and on other tests like the SAT, ACT, and state exams. The practice exercises in each lesson will prepare you for the format and content of such tests. No surprises!

The problem-solving and reasoning habits and skills you develop in this program will serve you in all your studies and in your daily life. They will prepare you for future success not only as a student, but also as a member of a changing technological society.

Best wishes,

Dan Kennedy   Randy Charles.   Basia Hall

Allan E. Bellman   Sadie C. Bragg   William G. Handlin

Laurie E. Bass   Art Johnson   Stuart J. Murphy

PowerAlgebra.com

Welcome to Algebra 2. *Pearson Algebra 2 Common Core Edition* is part of a blended digital and print environment for the study of high school mathematics. Take some time to look through the features of our mathematics program, starting with **PowerAlgebra.com,** the site of the digital features of the program.

Hi, I'm Darius. My friends and I will be showing you the great features of Pearson Algebra 2 Common Core Edition program.

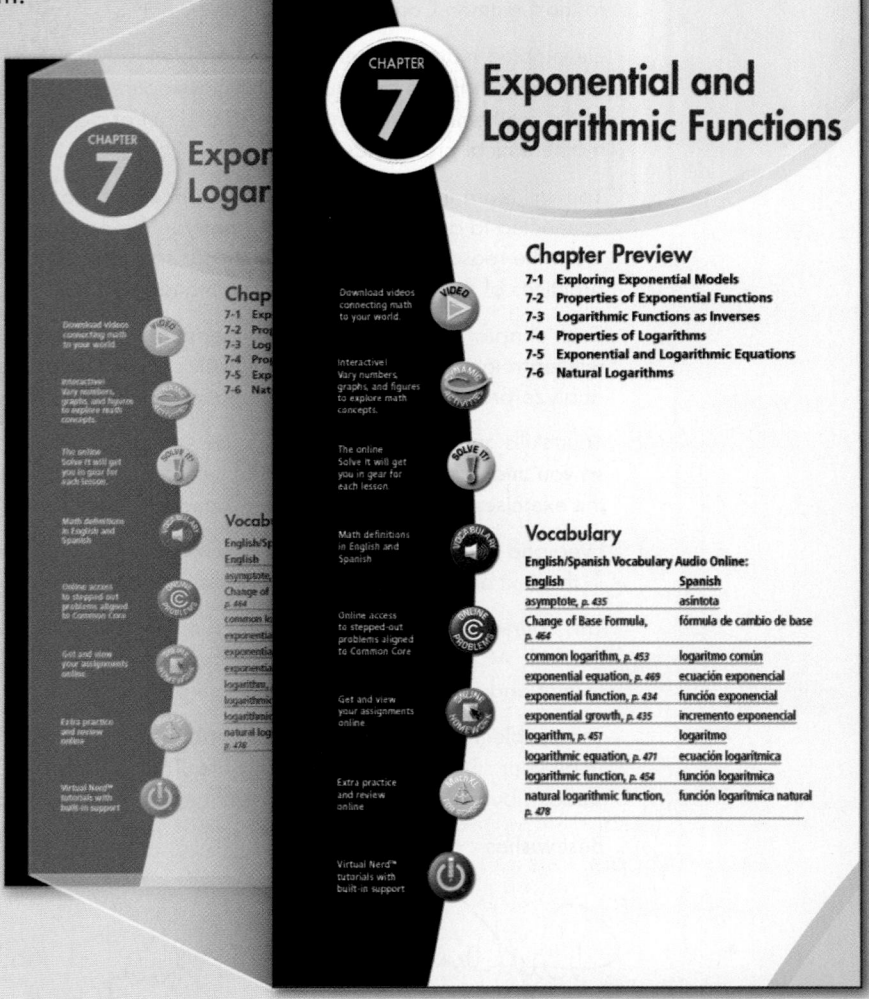

CHAPTER 7

Exponential and Logarithmic Functions

Chapter Preview
7-1   **Exploring Exponential Models**
7-2   **Properties of Exponential Functions**
7-3   **Logarithmic Functions as Inverses**
7-4   **Properties of Logarithms**
7-5   **Exponential and Logarithmic Equations**
7-6   **Natural Logarithms**

Download videos connecting math to your world.

Interactive! Vary numbers, graphs, and figures to explore math concepts.

The online Solve It will get you in gear for each lesson.

Math definitions in English and Spanish

Online access to stepped-out problems aligned to Common Core

Get and view your assignments online

Extra practice and review online

Virtual Nerd™ tutorials with built-in support

Vocabulary

English/Spanish Vocabulary Audio Online:

English	Spanish
asymptote, p. 435	asíntota
Change of Base Formula, p. 464	fórmula de cambio de base
common logarithm, p. 453	logaritmo común
exponential equation, p. 469	ecuación exponencial
exponential function, p. 434	función exponencial
exponential growth, p. 435	incremento exponencial
logarithm, p. 451	logaritmo
logarithmic equation, p. 471	ecuación logarítmica
logarithmic function, p. 454	función logarítmica
natural logarithmic function, p. 478	función logarítmica natural

On each **Chapter Opener,** you will find a listing of the online features of the program. Look for these buttons throughout the lessons.

Big *Ideas*

We start with **Big Ideas.** Each chapter is organized around Big Ideas that convey the key mathematics concepts you will be studying in the program. Take a look at the Big Ideas on pages xxiv and xxv.

The Common Core State Standards have a similar organizing structure. They begin with **Conceptual Categories,** such as Algebra or Functions. Within each category are **domains** and **clusters.**

Common Core State Standards

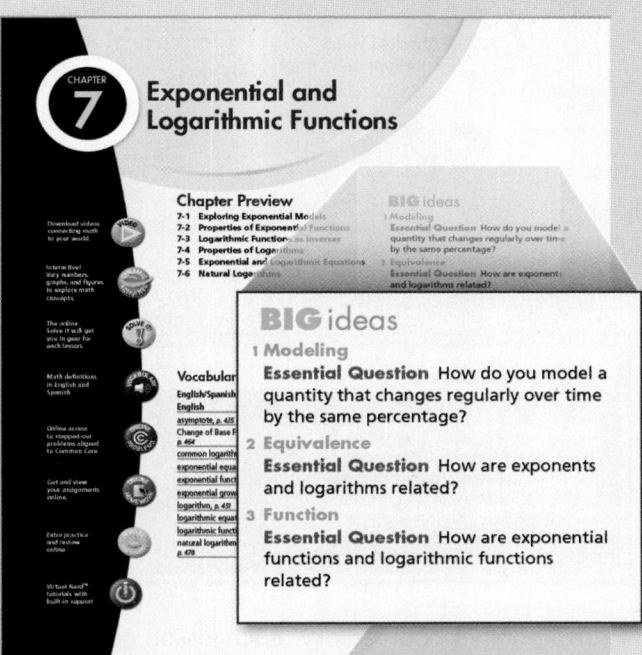

BIG ideas

1 Modeling
Essential Question How do you model a quantity that changes regularly over time by the same percentage?

2 Equivalence
Essential Question How are exponents and logarithms related?

3 Function
Essential Question How are exponential functions and logarithmic functions related?

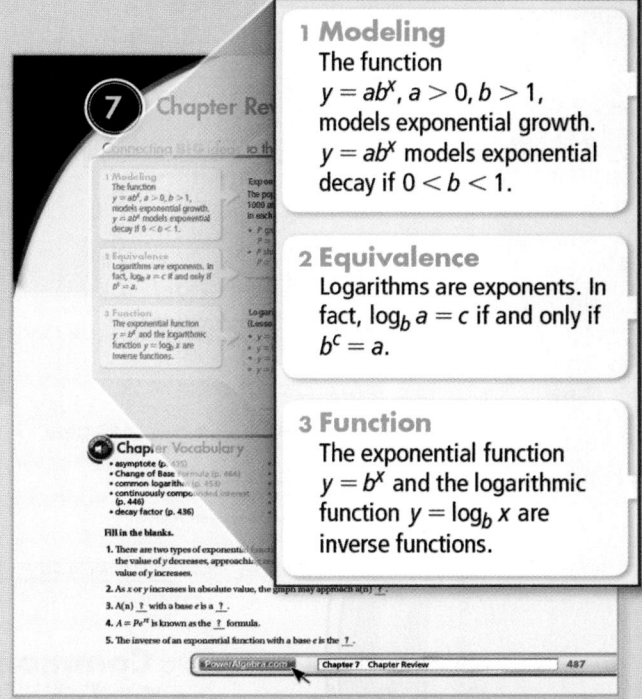

1 Modeling
The function $y = ab^x$, $a > 0$, $b > 1$, models exponential growth. $y = ab^x$ models exponential decay if $0 < b < 1$.

2 Equivalence
Logarithms are exponents. In fact, $\log_b a = c$ if and only if $b^c = a$.

3 Function
The exponential function $y = b^x$ and the logarithmic function $y = \log_b x$ are inverse functions.

The **Big Ideas** are organizing ideas for all of the lessons in the program. At the beginning of each chapter, we'll tell you which Big Ideas you'll be studying. We'll also present an **Essential Question** for each Big Idea.

In the **Chapter Review** at the end of the chapter, you'll find an answer to the Essential Question for each Big Idea. We'll also remind you of the lesson(s) where you studied the concepts that support the Big Ideas.

Exploring *Concepts*

The lessons offer many opportunities to explore concepts in different contexts and through different media.

> Hi, I'm Serena. I never have to power down when I am in math class now.

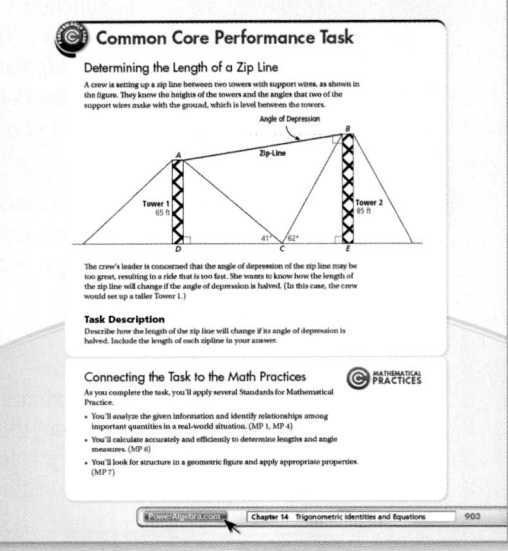

For each chapter, there is a **Common Core Performance Task** that you will work on throughout the chapter. See pages xii and xiii for more information.

Here's another cool feature. Each lesson opens with a **Solve It,** a problem that helps you connect what you know to an important concept in the lesson. Do you notice how the Solve It frame looks like it comes from a computer? That's because all of the Solve Its can be found at **PowerAlgebra.com.**

The **Standards for Mathematical Practice** describe processes, practices, and habits of mind of mathematically proficient students. Many of the features in *Pearson Algebra 2 Common Core Edition* help you develop proficiency in math.

Developing Mathematical Proficiency

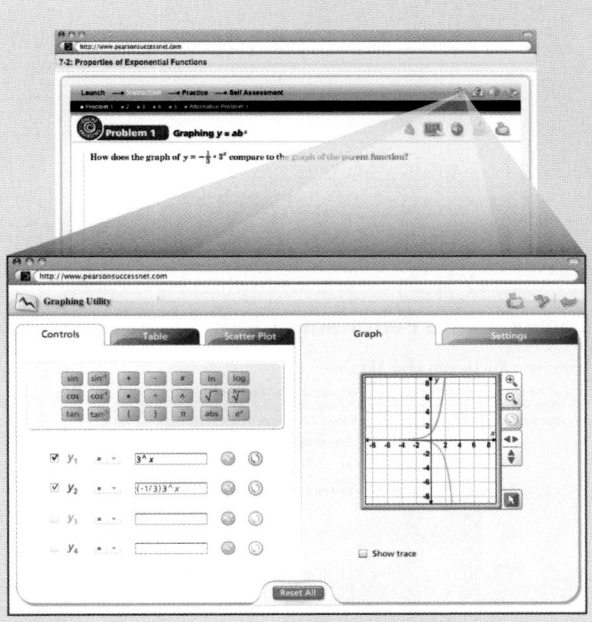

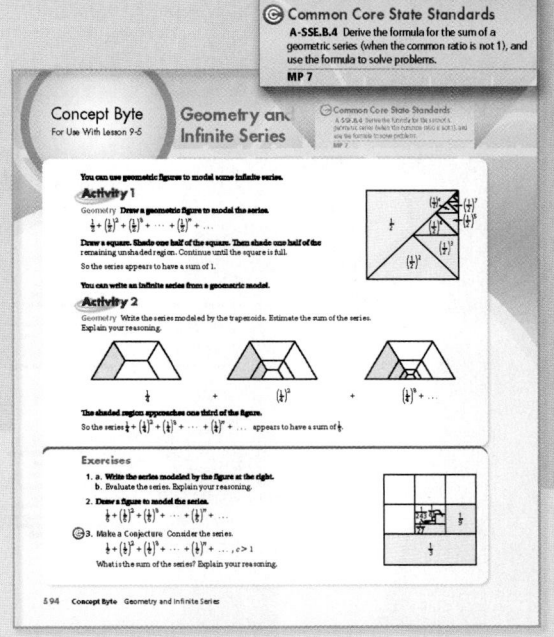

Want to do some more exploring? Try the **Math Tools** at **PowerAlgebra.com.** Click on this icon to access these tools: Graphing Utility, Number Line, Algebra Tiles, and 2D and 3D Geometric Constructor. With the Math Tools, you can continue to explore the concepts presented in the lesson.

Try a **Concept Byte!** In a Concept Byte, you might explore technology, do a hands-on activity, or try a challenging extension. The text in the top right corner of the first page of a lesson or Concept Byte tells you the **Standards for Mathematical Content** and the **Standards for Mathematical Practice** that you will be studying.

Solving *Problems*

Pearson Algebra 2 Common Core Edition includes many opportunities to build on and strengthen your problem-solving abilities. In each chapter, you'll work through a multi-part Performance Task.

> Hi, I'm Maya. These Common Core Performance Tasks will help you become a proficient problem solver.

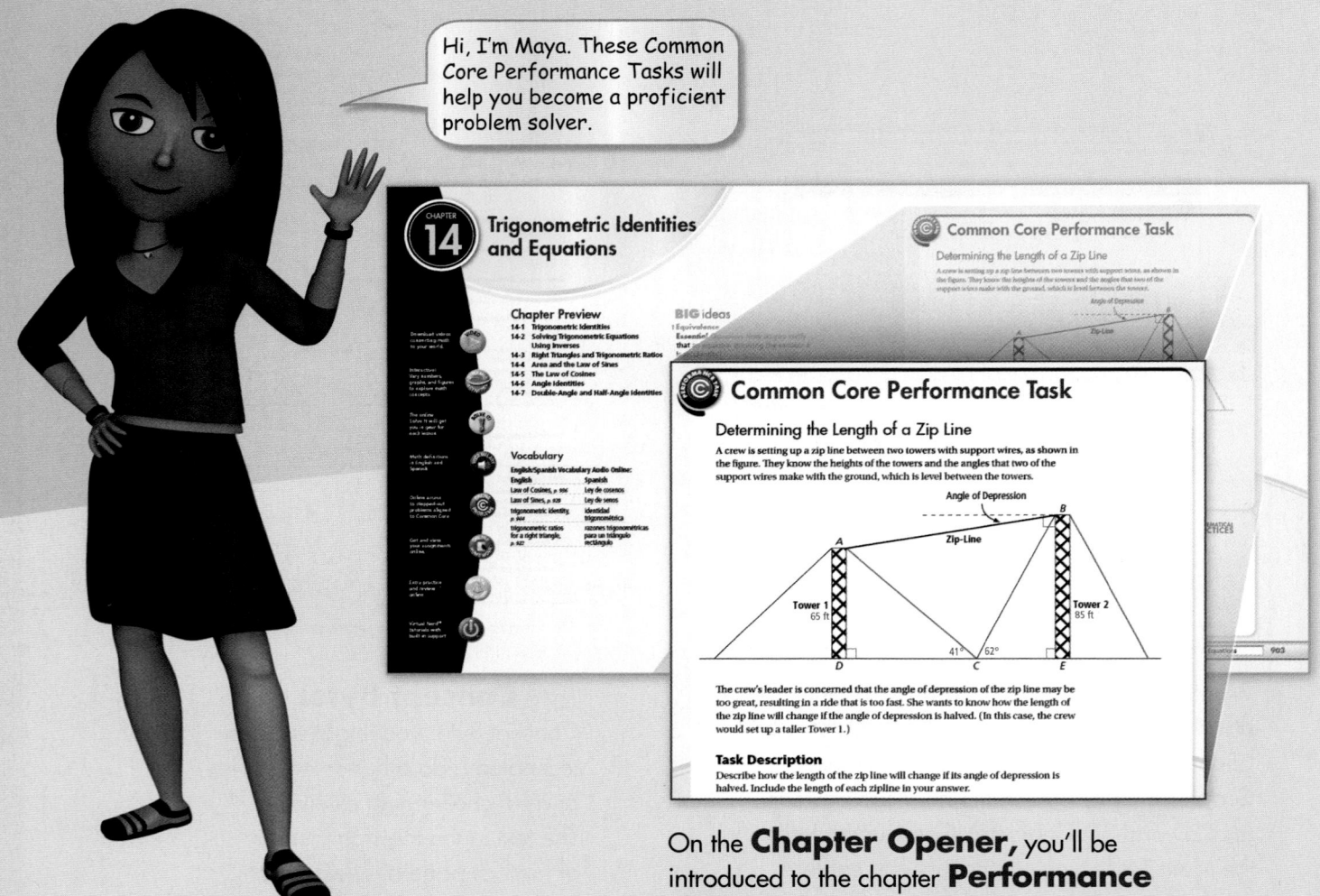

On the **Chapter Opener,** you'll be introduced to the chapter **Performance Task.** You'll start to make sense of the problem and think about solution plans.

Proficient Problem Solvers make sense of problem situations, develop workable solution plans, model the problem situation with mathematics, and communicate their thinking clearly.

Developing Proficiency with Problem Solving

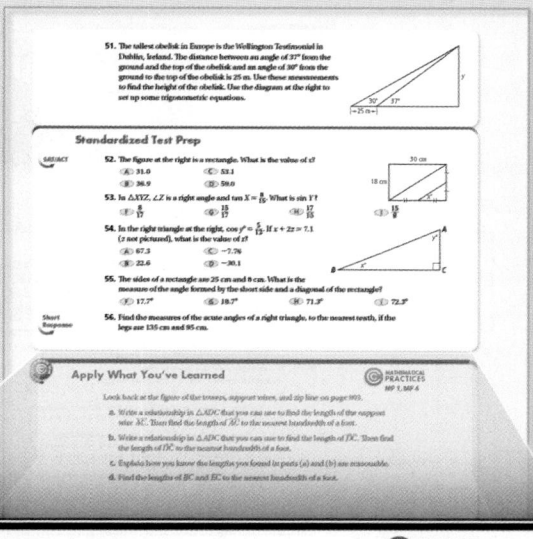

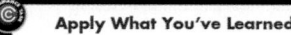

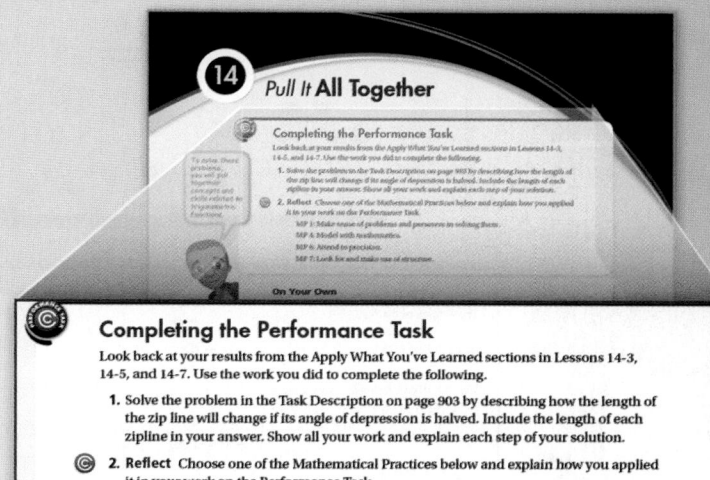

Apply What You've Learned

MATHEMATICAL PRACTICES
MP 1, MP 4

Look back at the figure of the towers, support wires, and zip line on page 903.

a. Write a relationship in $\triangle ADC$ that you can use to find the length of the support wire $\overline{AC}$. Then find the length of $\overline{AC}$ to the nearest hundredth of a foot.

b. Write a relationship in $\triangle ADC$ that you can use to find the length of $\overline{DC}$. Then find the length of $\overline{DC}$ to the nearest hundredth of a foot.

c. Explain how you know the lengths you found in parts (a) and (b) are reasonable.

d. Find the lengths of $\overline{BC}$ and $\overline{EC}$ to the nearest hundredth of a foot.

Throughout the chapter, you will **Apply What You've Learned** to solve problems that relate to the Performance Task. You'll be asked to reason quantitatively and model with mathematics.

Completing the Performance Task

Look back at your results from the Apply What You've Learned sections in Lessons 14-3, 14-5, and 14-7. Use the work you did to complete the following.

1. Solve the problem in the Task Description on page 903 by describing how the length of the zip line will change if its angle of depression is halved. Include the length of each zipline in your answer. Show all your work and explain each step of your solution.

2. **Reflect** Choose one of the Mathematical Practices below and explain how you applied it in your work on the Performance Task.

   MP 1: Make sense of problems and persevere in solving them.

   MP 4: Model with mathematics.

   MP 6: Attend to precision.

   MP 7: Look for and make use of structure.

In the **Pull It All Together** at the end of the chapter, you will use the concepts and skills presented throughout the chapter to solve the Performance Task. Then you'll have another Task to solve **On Your Own.**

Thinking *Mathematically*

Mathematical reasoning is the key to making sense of math and solving problems. Throughout the program you'll learn strategies to develop mathematical reasoning habits.

Hello, I'm Tyler. These Think-Write and Know-Need-Plan boxes help me plan my work.

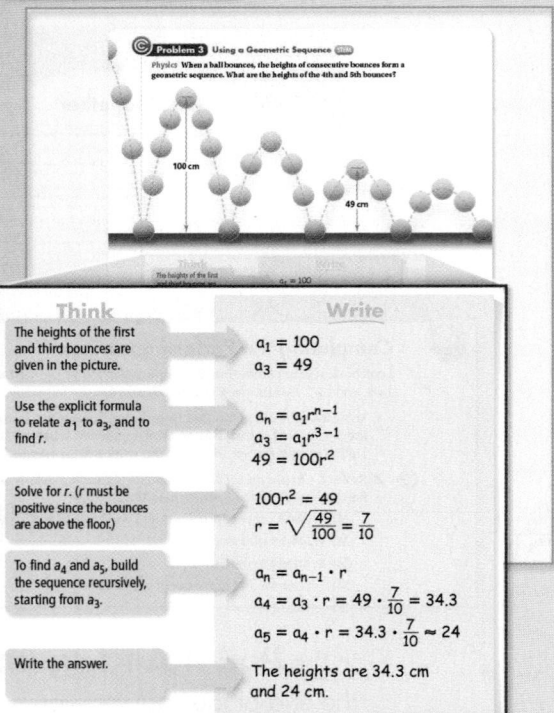

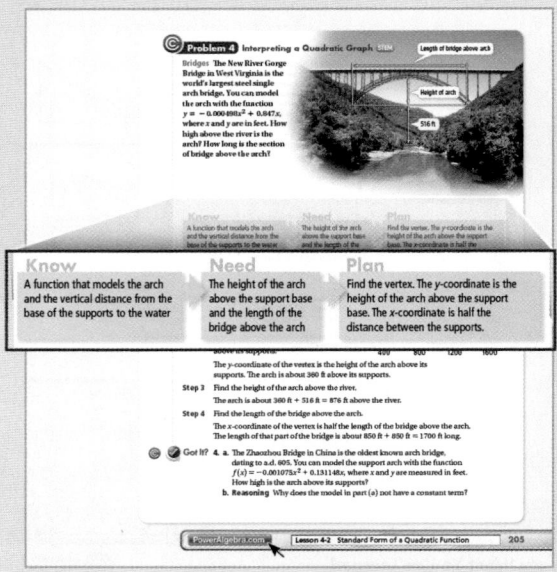

The worked-out problems include call-outs that reveal the strategies and reasoning behind the solution. The **Think-Write** problems model the thinking behind each step of a solution.

Also, look for the boxes labeled **Plan** and **Think.**

Other worked-out problems model a problem-solving plan that includes the steps of stating what you **Know,** identifying what you **Need,** and developing a **Plan.**

The **Standards for Mathematical Practice** emphasize sense-making, reasoning, and critical reasoning. Many features in *Pearson Algebra 2 Common Core Edition* provide opportunities for you to develop these skills and dispositions.

Standards for Mathematical Practice

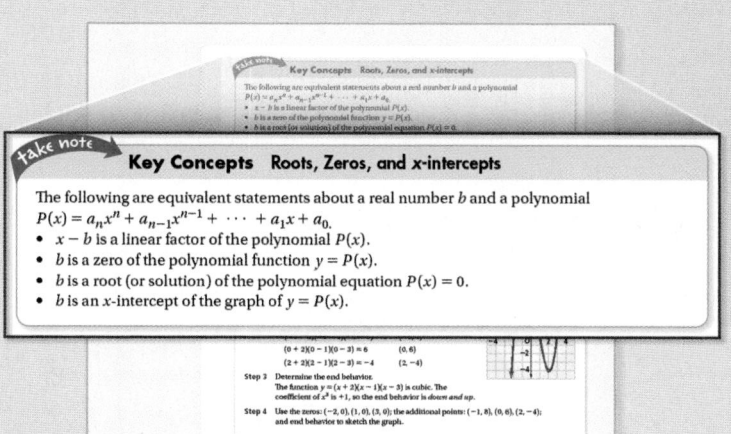

take note

Key Concepts   Roots, Zeros, and *x*-intercepts

The following are equivalent statements about a real number b and a polynomial $P(x) = a_n x^n + a_{n-1} x^{n-1} + \cdots + a_1 x + a_0.$
- $x - b$ is a linear factor of the polynomial $P(x)$.
- b is a zero of the polynomial function $y = P(x)$.
- b is a root (or solution) of the polynomial equation $P(x) = 0$.
- b is an *x*-intercept of the graph of $y = P(x)$.

A **Take Note** box highlights key concepts in a lesson. You can use these boxes to review concepts throughout the year.

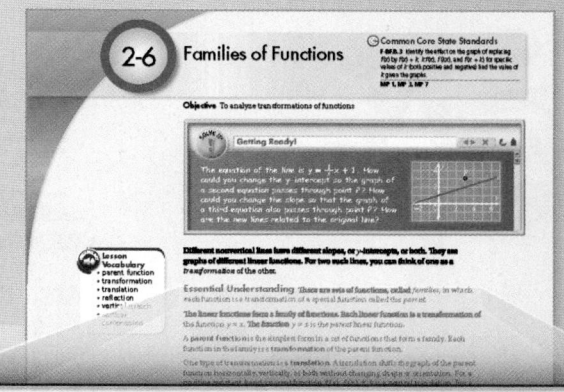

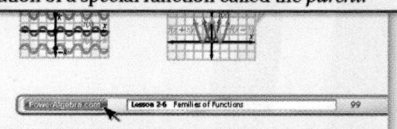

Essential Understanding There are sets of functions, called *families*, in which each function is a transformation of a special function called the *parent*.

Part of thinking mathematically is making sense of the concepts that are being presented. The **Essential Understandings** help you build a framework for the Big Ideas.

Practice *Makes Perfect*

Ask any professional and you'll be told that the one requirement for becoming an expert is practice, practice, practice. *Pearson Algebra 2 Common Core Edition* offers rich and varied exercises to help you become proficient with the mathematics.

Hello, I'm Anya. I can leave my book at school and still get my homework done. All of the lessons are at PowerAlgebra.com

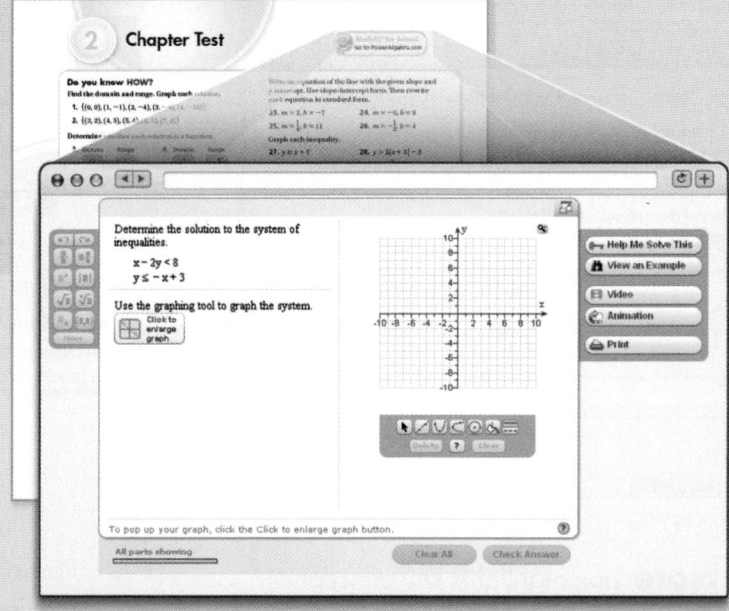

Want more practice? Look for this icon in your book. Check out all of the opportunities in **MathXL® for School.** Your teacher can assign you some practice exercises or you can choose some on your own. And you'll know right away if you got the right answer!

Acing *the Test*

Doing well on tests, whether they are chapter tests or state assessments, depends on a deep understanding of math concepts, fluency with calculations and computations, and strong problem-solving abilities.

All of these opportunities for practice help you prepare for assessments throughout the year, including the assessments to measure your proficiency with the Common Core State Standards.

Assessing the Common Core State Standards

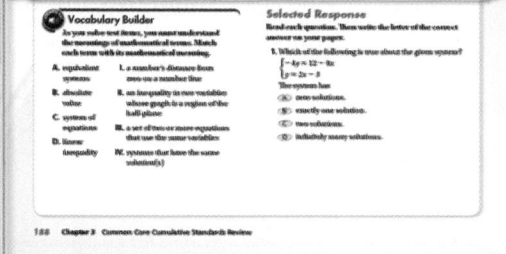

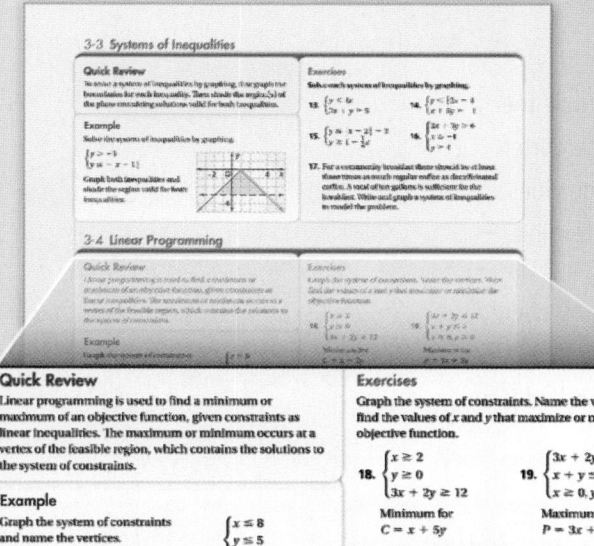

Quick Review

Linear programming is used to find a minimum or maximum of an objective function, given constraints as linear inequalities. The maximum or minimum occurs at a vertex of the feasible region, which contains the solutions to the system of constraints.

Example

Graph the system of constraints and name the vertices.
$$\begin{cases} x \le 8 \\ y \le 5 \\ x \ge 0, y \ge 0 \end{cases}$$
Objective function: $P = 2x + y$

Graph the inequalities and shade the area satisfying all inequalities.

The vertices of the feasible region are $(0, 0)$, $(0, 5)$, $(8, 5)$, and $(8, 0)$.

Evaluate the objective function at each vertex:

Exercises

Graph the system of constraints. Name the vertices. Then find the values of x and y that maximize or minimize the objective function.

18. $\begin{cases} x \ge 2 \\ y \ge 0 \\ 3x + 2y \ge 12 \end{cases}$ 19. $\begin{cases} 3x + 2y \le 12 \\ x + y \le 5 \\ x \ge 0, y \ge 0 \end{cases}$

Minimum for
$C = x + 5y$

Maximum for
$P = 3x + 5y$

20. A lunch stand makes \$.75 profit on each chef's salad and \$1.20 profit on each Caesar salad. On a typical weekday, it sells between 40 and 60 chef's salads and between 35 and 50 Caesar salads. The total number sold has never exceeded 100 salads. How many of each type should be prepared in order to maximize profit?

At the end of the chapter, you'll find a **Quick Review** of the concepts in the chapter and a few examples and exercises so you can check your skill at solving problems related to the concepts.

In the Cumulative Standards Review at the end of the chapter, you'll also find **Tips for Success,** reminders to help with problem solving. We include problems of all different formats and types so you can feel comfortable with any test item on your state assessment.

Standards *for Mathematical Practice*

The **Common Core State Standards** are made of two separate, but equally important sets of standards:

- **Standards** *for Mathematical Content*
- **Standards** *for Mathematical Practice*

The **Math Content Standards** are grade-specific, while the **Math Practices Standards** are the same from Kindergarten through High School. The **Math Practices** describe qualities and habits of mind that strong mathematical thinkers exhibit.

The eight **Standards for Mathematical Practice,** numbered 1 through 8, can be put into the four groups shown on this page and the next. Included with the statement of each standard is a description of what the Math Practice means for you.

Making Sense of and Solving Problems

1. Make sense of problems and persevere in solving them.

When you make sense of problems, you can explain the meaning of the problem, and you are able to find an entry point to its solution and plan a solution pathway. You can look at a problem and analyze givens, constraints, relationships, and goals. You can think of similar problems or can break the problem into easier-to-solve problems. You are able to track your progress as you work through the solution and check your answer using a different method. As you work through your solution, you frequently check whether the results you are getting make sense.

6. Attend to precision.

You attend to precision when you communicate clearly and precisely the approach you used to solve a problem, and you also understand the approaches that your classmates used. You identify the meaning of symbols that you use, you specify units of measure, and you include labels on the axes of graphs. Your answers are expressed with the appropriate degree of accuracy. You are able to give clear, concise definitions of math terms.

Reasoning and Communicating

2. Reason abstractly and quantitatively.

As a strong math thinker and problem solver, you are able to make sense of quantities in problem situations. You can both represent a problem situation using symbols or equations and explain what the symbols or equations represent in relationship to the problem situation. As you represent a situation symbolically or mathematically, you can explain the meaning of the quantities.

3. Construct viable arguments and critique the reasoning of others.

You are able to communicate clearly and convincingly about your solutions to problems. You can build sound mathematical arguments, drawing on definitions, assumptions, or established solutions. You can develop and explore conjectures about mathematical situations. You make use of examples and counterexamples to support your arguments and justify your conclusions. You respond clearly and logically to the positions and conclusions of your classmates, and are able to compare two arguments, identifying any flaws in logic or reasoning that the arguments may contain. You can ask useful questions to clarify or improve the argument of a classmate.

Representing and Connecting

4. Model with mathematics.

As a strong math thinker, you are able to use mathematics to represent a problem situation and can make connections between a real-world problem situation and mathematics. You see the applicability of mathematics to everyday problems. You can explain how geometry can be used to solve a carpentry problem or algebra to solve a proportional relationship problem. You can define and map relationships among quantities in a problem, using appropriate tools to do so. You are able to analyze the relationships and draw conclusions.

5. Use appropriate tools strategically.

As you develop models to match a given problem situation, you are able to strategize about which tools would be most helpful to use to solve the problem. You consider all tools, from paper and pencil to protractors and rulers, to calculators and software applications. You can articulate the appropriateness of different tools and recognize which would best serve your needs for a given problem. You are especially insightful about technology tools and use them in ways that deepen or extend your understanding of concepts. You also make use of mental tools, such as estimation, to determine the reasonableness of a solution.

Seeing Structure and Generalizing

7. Look for and make use of structure.

You are able to go beyond simply solving problems, to see the structure of the mathematics in these problems, and to generalize mathematical principles from this structure. You are able to see complicated expressions or equations as single objects, or a being composed of many parts.

8. Look for and express regularity in repeated reasoning.

You notice when calculations are repeated and can uncover both general methods and shortcuts for solving similar problems. You continually evaluate the reasonableness of your solutions as you solve problems arising in daily life.

Standards for *Mathematical Content*
Algebra 2

Hi, I'm Max. Here is a list of many of the Common Core State Standards that you will study this year. Mastering these topics will help you be ready for your state assessment.

Number and Quantity

The Real Number System

Extend the properties of exponents to rational exponents

N-RN.A.1   Explain how the definition of the meaning of rational exponents follows from extending the properties of integer exponents to those values, allowing for a notation for radicals in terms of rational exponents.

N-RN.A.2   Rewrite expressions involving radicals and rational exponents using the properties of exponents.

Quantities

Reason quantitatively and use units to solve problems

N-Q.A.2   Define appropriate quantities for the purpose of descriptive modeling.

The Complex Number System

Perform arithmetic operations with complex numbers

N-CN.A.1   Know there is a complex number i such that $i^2 = -1$, and every complex number has the form $a + bi$ with a and b real.

N-CN.A.2   Use the relation $i^2 = -1$ and the commutative, associative, and distributive properties to add, subtract, and multiply complex numbers.

Use complex numbers in polynomial identities and equations.

N-CN.C.7   Solve quadratic equations with real coefficients that have complex solutions.

Algebra

Seeing Structure in Expressions

Interpret the structure of expressions

A-SSE.A.2   Use the structure of an expression to identify ways to rewrite it.

Write expressions in equivalent forms to solve problems

A-SSE.B.3   Choose and produce an equivalent form of an expression to reveal and explain properties of the quantity represented by the expression.

A-SSE.B.3c   Use the properties of exponents to transform expressions for exponential functions.

A-SSE.B.4   Derive the formula for the sum of a finite geometric series (when the common ratio is not 1), and use the formula to solve problems.

Arithmetic with Polynomials and Rational Expressions

Understand the relationship between zeros and factors of polynomial

A-APR.B.2   Know and apply the Remainder Theorem: For a polynomial $p(x)$ and a number a, the remainder on division by $x - a$ is $p(a)$, so $p(a) = 0$ if and only if $(x - a)$ is a factor of $p(x)$.

A-APR.B.3   Identify zeros of polynomials when suitable factorizations are available, and use the zeros to construct a rough graph of the function defined by the polynomial.

Use polynomial identities to solve problems

A-APR.C.4   Prove polynomial identities and use them to describe numerical relationships.

Rewrite rational expressions

A-APR.D.6   Rewrite simple rational expressions in different forms; write $a(x)/b(x)$ in the form $q(x) + r(x)/b(x)$, where $a(x)$, $b(x)$, $q(x)$, and $r(x)$ are polynomials with the degree of $r(x)$ less than the degree of $b(x)$, using inspection, long division, or, for the more complicated examples, a computer algebra system.

Creating Equations

Create equations that describe numbers or relationships

A-CED.A.1   Create equations and inequalities in one variable and use them to solve problems. *Include equations arising from linear and quadratic functions, and simple rational and exponential functions.*

Reasoning with Equations and Inequalities

Understand solving equations as a process of reasoning and explain the reasoning

A-REI.A.1   Explain each step in solving a simple equation as following from the equality of numbers asserted at the previous step, starting from the assumption that the original equation has a solution. Construct a viable argument to justify a solution method.

A-REI.A.2   Solve simple rational and radical equations in one variable, and give examples showing how extraneous solutions may arise.

Solve equations and Inequalities in one variable

A-REI.B.4   Solve quadratic equations in one variable.

A-REI.B.4b   Solve quadratic equations by inspection (e.g., for $x^2 = 49$), taking square roots, completing the square, the quadratic formula and factoring, as appropriate to the initial form of the equation. Recognize when the quadratic formula gives complex solutions and write them as $a \pm bi$ for real numbers a and b.

Solve systems of equations

A-REI.C.6   Solve systems of linear equations exactly and approximately (e.g., with graphs), focusing on pairs of linear equations in two variables.

A-REI.C.7   Solve a simple system consisting of a linear equation and a quadratic equation in two variables algebraically and graphically.

Represent and solve equations and inequalities graphically

A-REI.D.11   Explain why the *x*-coordinates of the points where the graphs of the equations $y = f(x)$ and $y = g(x)$ intersect are the solutions of the equation $f(x) = g(x)$; find the solutions approximately, e.g., using technology to graph the functions, make tables of values, or find successive approximations. Include cases where $f(x)$ and/or $g(x)$ are linear, polynomial, rational, absolute value, exponential, and logarithmic functions.

Functions

Interpreting Functions

Understand the concept of a function and use function notation

F-IF.A.3   Recognize that sequences are functions, sometimes defined recursively, whose domain is a subset of the integers.

Interpret functions that arise in applications in terms of the context

F-IF.B.4   For a function that models a relationship between two quantities, interpret key features of graphs and tables in terms of the quantities, and sketch graphs showing key features given a verbal description of the relationship. *Key features include: intercepts; intervals where the function is increasing, decreasing, positive, or negative; relative maximums and minimums; symmetries; end behavior; and periodicity.*

F-IF.B.6   Calculate and interpret the average rate of change of a function (presented symbolically or as a table) over a specified interval. Estimate the rate of change from a graph.

Analyze functions using different representations

F-IF.C.7   Graph functions expressed symbolically and show key features of the graph, by hand in simple cases and using technology for more complicated cases.

F-IF.C.7c   Graph polynomial functions, identifying zeros when suitable factorizations are available, and showing end behavior.

F-IF.C.7e   Graph exponential and logarithmic functions, showing intercepts and end behavior, and trigonometric functions, showing period, midline, and amplitude.

F-IF.C.8   Write a function defined by an expression in different but equivalent forms to reveal and explain different properties of the function.

Look at the domain titles and cluster descriptions in bold to get a good idea of the topics you'll study this year.

F-IF.C.8b Write a function defined by an expression in different but equivalent forms to reveal and explain different properties of the function. Use the properties of exponents to interpret expressions for exponential functions.

F-IF.C.9 Compare properties of two functions each represented in a different way (algebraically, graphically, numerically in tables, or by verbal descriptions)

Building Functions

Build a function that models a relationship between two quantities

F-BF.A.1 Write a function that describes a relationship between two quantities.

F-BF.A.1a Determine an explicit expression, a recursive process, or steps for calculation from a context.

F-BF.A.1b Combine standard function types using arithmetic operations.

F-BF.A.2 Write arithmetic and geometric sequences both recursively and with an explicit formula, use them to model situations, and translate between the two forms.

Build new functions from existing functions

F-BF.B.3 Identify the effect on the graph of replacing $f(x)$ by $f(x) + k$, $k\,f(x)$, $f(kx)$, and $f(x + k)$ for specific values of k (both positive and negative); find the value of k given the graphs. Experiment with cases and illustrate an explanation of the effects on the graph using technology. *Include recognizing even and odd functions from their graphs and algebraic expressions for them.*

F-BF.B.4 Find inverse functions.

F-BF.B.4a Solve an equation of the form $f(x) = c$ for a simple function f that has an inverse and write an expression for the inverse.

Linear and Exponential Models

Construct and compare linear and exponential models and solve problems

F-LE.A.2 Construct linear and exponential functions, including arithmetic and geometric sequences, given a graph, a description of a relationship, or two input-output pairs (include reading these from a table).

F-LE.A.4 For exponential models, express as a logarithm the solution to $ab^{ct} = d$ where a, c, and d are numbers and the base b is 2, 10, or e; evaluate the logarithm using technology.

Interpret expressions for functions in terms of the situation they model

F-LE.B.5 Interpret the parameters in a linear or exponential function in terms of a context.

Trigonometric Functions

Extend the domain of trigonometric functions using the unit circle

F-TF.A.1 Understand radian measure of an angle as the length of the arc on the unit circle subtended by the angle.

F-TF.A.2 Explain how the unit circle in the coordinate plane enables the extension of trigonometric functions to all real numbers, interpreted as radian measures of angles traversed counterclockwise around the unit circle.

Model periodic phenomena with trigonometric functions

F-TF.B.5 Choose trigonometric functions to model periodic phenomena with specified amplitude, frequency, and midline.

Prove and apply trigonometric identities

F-TF.C.8 Prove the Pythagorean identity $\sin^2(\theta) + \cos^2(\theta) = 1$ and use it to find $\sin\theta$, $\cos\theta$, or $\tan\theta$ given $\sin\theta$, $\cos\theta$, or $\tan\theta$ and the quadrant of the angle.

Geometry

Expressing Geometric Properties with Equations

Translate between the geometric description and the equation for a conic section

G.GPE.2 Derive the equation of a parabola given a focus and directrix.

Statistics and Probability

Interpreting Categorical and Quantitative Data

Summarize, represent, and interpret data on a single count or measurement variable

S-ID.A.4   Use the mean and standard deviation of a data set to fit it to a normal distribution and to estimate population percentages. Recognize that there are data sets for which such a procedure is not appropriate. Use calculators, spreadsheets, and tables to estimate areas under the normal curve.

S-ID.A.6   Represent data on two quantitative variables on a scatter plot, and describe how the variables are related.

S-ID.A.6a   Fit a function to the data; use functions fitted to data to solve problems in the context of the data. Use given functions or choose a function suggested by the context. Emphasize linear and exponential models.

Making Inferences and Justifying Conclusions

Understand and evaluate random processes underlying statistical experiments

S-IC.A.1   Understand statistics as a process for making inferences to be made about population parameters based on a random sample from that population.

S-IC.A.2   Decide if a specified model is consistent with results from a given data-generating process, e.g., using simulation.

Make inferences and justify conclusions from sample surveys, experiments, and observational studies

S-IC.B.3   Recognize the purposes of and differences among sample surveys, experiments, and observational studies; explain how randomization relates to each.

S-IC.B.4   Use data from a sample survey to estimate a population mean or proportion; develop a margin of error through the use of simulation models for random sampling.

S-IC.B.5   Use data from a randomized experiment to compare two treatments; use simulations to decide if differences between parameters are significant.

S-IC.B.6   Evaluate reports based on data.

Conditional Probability and the Rules of Probability

Understand independence and conditional probability and use them to interpret data

S-CP.A.1   Describe events as subsets of a sample space (the set of outcomes) using characteristics (or categories) of the outcomes, or as unions, intersections, or complements of other events ("or," "and," "not").

S-CP.A.2   Understand that two events A and B are independent if the probability of A and B occurring together is the product of their probabilities, and use this characterization to determine if they are independent.

S-CP.A.3   Understand the conditional probability of A given B as $P(A$ and $B)/P(B)$, and interpret independence of A and B as saying that the conditional probability of A given B is the same as the probability of A, and the conditional probability of B given A is the same as the probability of B.

S-CP.A.4   Construct and interpret two-way frequency tables of data when two categories are associated with each object being classified. Use the two-way table as a sample space to decide if events are independent and to approximate conditional probabilities.

S-CP.A.5   Recognize and explain the concepts of conditional probability and independence in everyday language and everyday situations.

Use the rules of probability to compute probabilities of compound events in a uniform probability model

S-CP.B.6   Find the conditional probability of A given B as the fraction of B's outcomes that also belong to A, and interpret the answer in terms of the model.

S-CP.B.7   Apply the Addition Rule, $P(A$ or $B) = P(A) + P(B) - P(A$ and $B)$, and interpret the answer in terms of the model.

BIGideas

These Big Ideas are the organizing ideas for the study of important areas of mathematics: algebra, geometry, and statistics.

Stay connected! These Big Ideas will help you understand how the math you study in high school fits together.

Algebra

Properties
- In the transition from arithmetic to algebra, attention shifts from arithmetic operations (addition, subtraction, multiplication, and division) to use of the *properties* of these operations.
- All of the facts of arithmetic and algebra follow from certain properties.

Variable
- Quantities are used to form expressions, equations, and inequalities.
- An expression refers to a quantity but does not make a statement about it. An equation (or an inequality) is a statement about the quantities it mentions.
- Using variables in place of numbers in equations (or inequalities) allows the statement of relationships among numbers that are unknown or unspecified.

Equivalence
- A single quantity may be represented by many different expressions.
- The facts about a quantity may be expressed by many different equations (or inequalities).

Solving Equations & Inequalities
- Solving an equation is the process of rewriting the equation to make what it says about its variable(s) as simple as possible.
- Properties of numbers and equality can be used to transform an equation (or inequality) into equivalent, simpler equations (or inequalities) in order to find solutions.
- Useful information about equations and inequalities (including solutions) can be found by analyzing graphs or tables.
- The numbers and types of solutions vary predictably, based on the type of equation.

Proportionality
- Two quantities are *proportional* if they have the same ratio in each instance where they are measured together.
- Two quantities are *inversely proportional* if they have the same product in each instance where they are measured together.

Function
- A function is a relationship between variables in which each value of the input variable is associated with a unique value of the output variable.
- Functions can be represented in a variety of ways, such as graphs, tables, equations, or words. Each representation is particularly useful in certain situations.
- Some important families of functions are developed through transformations of the simplest form of the function.
- New functions can be made from other functions by applying arithmetic operations or by applying one function to the output of another.

Modeling
- Many real-world mathematical problems can be represented algebraically. These representations can lead to algebraic solutions.
- A function that models a real-world situation can be used to make estimates or predictions about future occurrences.

Statistics and Probability

Data Collection and Analysis
- Sampling techniques are used to gather data from real-world situations. If the data are representative of the larger population, inferences can be made about that population.
- Biased sampling techniques yield data unlikely to be representative of the larger population.
- Sets of numerical data are described using measures of central tendency and dispersion.

Data Representation
- The most appropriate data representations depend on the type of data—quantitative or qualitative, and univariate or bivariate.
- Line plots, box plots, and histograms are different ways to show distribution of data over a possible range of values.

Probability
- Probability expresses the likelihood that a particular event will occur.
- Data can be used to calculate an experimental probability, and mathematical properties can be used to determine a theoretical probability.
- Either experimental or theoretical probability can be used to make predictions or decisions about future events.
- Various counting methods can be used to develop theoretical probabilities.

Geometry

Visualization
- Visualization can help you see the relationships between two figures and connect properties of real objects with two-dimensional drawings of these objects.

Transformations
- Transformations are mathematical functions that model relationships with figures.
- Transformations may be described geometrically or by coordinates.
- Symmetries of figures may be defined and classified by transformations.

Measurement
- Some attributes of geometric figures, such as length, area, volume, and angle measure, are measurable. Units are used to describe these attributes.

Reasoning & Proof
- Definitions establish meanings and remove possible misunderstanding.
- Other truths are more complex and difficult to see. It is often possible to verify complex truths by reasoning from simpler ones using deductive reasoning.

Similarity
- Two geometric figures are similar when corresponding lengths are proportional and corresponding angles are congruent.
- Areas of similar figures are proportional to the squares of their corresponding lengths.
- Volumes of similar figures are proportional to the cubes of their corresponding lengths.

Coordinate Geometry
- A coordinate system on a line is a number line on which points are labeled, corresponding to the real numbers.
- A coordinate system in a plane is formed by two perpendicular number lines, called the x- and y-axes, and the quadrants they form. The coordinate plane can be used to graph many functions.
- It is possible to verify some complex truths using deductive reasoning in combination with the distance, midpoint, and slope formulas.

1

Expressions, Equations, and Inequalities

Chapters 1 & 2

Algebra
Seeing Structure in Expressions
Interpret the structure of expressions
Creating Equations
Create equations that describe numbers or relationships

Functions
Interpreting Functions
Interpret functions that arise in applications in terms of the context
Analyze functions using different representations
Building Functions
Build a function that models a relationship between two quantities

2 Functions, Equations, and Graphs

Visual See It!

Reasoning Try It!

Practice Do It!

3 Linear Systems

Chapters 3 & 4

Number and Quantity
The Complex Number System
    Perform arithmetic operations with complex numbers
    Use complex numbers in polynomial identities and equations
Functions
Interpreting Functions
    Interpret functions that arise in applications in terms of the context
    Analyze functions using different representations
Building Functions
    Build new functions from existing functions

Algebra
Seeing Structure in Expressions
    Interpret the structure of expressions
Arithmetic with Polynomials and Rational Expressions
    Understand the relationship between zeros and factors of polynomials
Creating Equations
    Create equations that describe numbers or relationships
Reasoning with Equations and Inequalities
    Solve systems of equations
    Represent and solve equations and inequalities graphically

4 Quadratic Functions and Equations

Visual See It!

Reasoning Try It!

Practice Do It!

5

Polynomials and Polynomial Functions

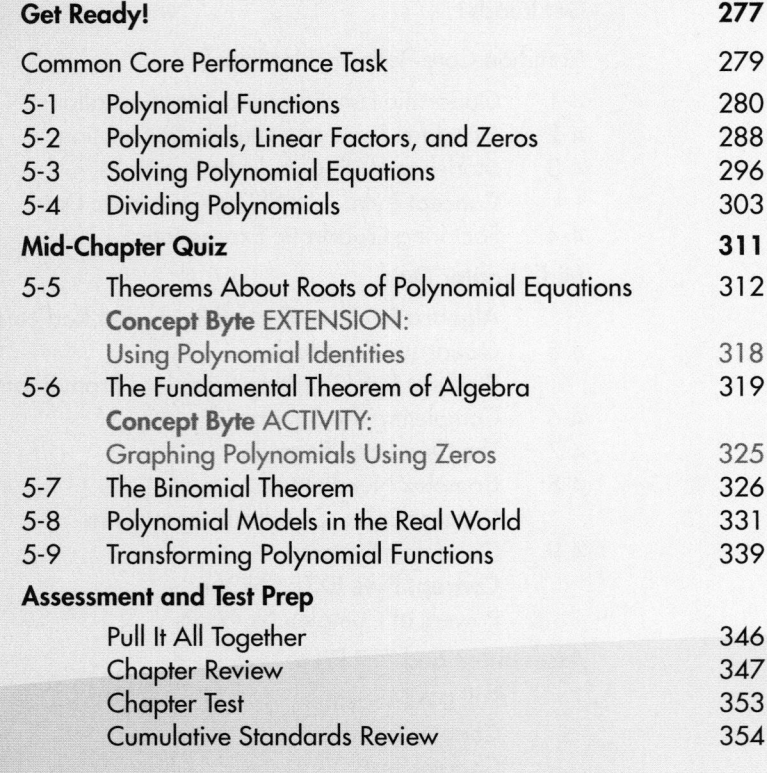

Chapters 5 & 6

Number and Quantity
The Complex Number System
    Use complex numbers in polynomial identities and equations
Functions
Interpreting Functions
    Interpret functions that arise in applications in terms of the context
    Analyze functions using different representations
Building Functions
    Build a function that models a relationship between two quantities
    Build new functions from existing functions

Algebra
Seeing Structure in Expressions
    Interpret the structure of expressions
Creating Equations
    Create equations that describe numbers or relationships
Arithmetic with Polynomials and Rational Expressions
    Understand the relationship between zeros and factors of polynomials
    Use polynomial identities to solve problems

6 Radical Functions and Rational Exponents

Visual See It!

Reasoning Try It!

Practice Do It!

7

Exponential and Logarithmic Functions

Chapters 7 & 8

Algebra

Seeing Structure in Expressions
Interpret the structure of expressions

Creating Equations
Create equations that describe numbers or relationships

Arithmetic with Polynomials and Rational Expressions
Rewrite rational expressions

Reasoning with Equations and Inequalities
Represent and solve equations and inequalities graphically

Functions

Interpreting Functions
Analyze functions using different representations

Building Functions
Build a function that models a relationship between two quantities
Build new functions from existing functions

Linear and Exponential Models
Construct and compare linear and exponential models and solve problems

8 Rational Functions

Visual See It!

Reasoning Try It!

Practice Do It!

9

Sequences and Series

Chapters 9 & 10

Algebra
Seeing Structure in Expressions
   Write expressions in equivalent forms to solve problems
Functions
Interpreting Functions
   Understand the concept of a function and use function notation
   Analyze functions using different representations

Geometry
Expressing Geometric Properties with Equations
   Translate between the geometric description and the equation
   for a conic section

10 Quadratic Relations and Conic Sections

Visual See It!

Reasoning Try It!

Practice Do It!

11

Probability and Statistics

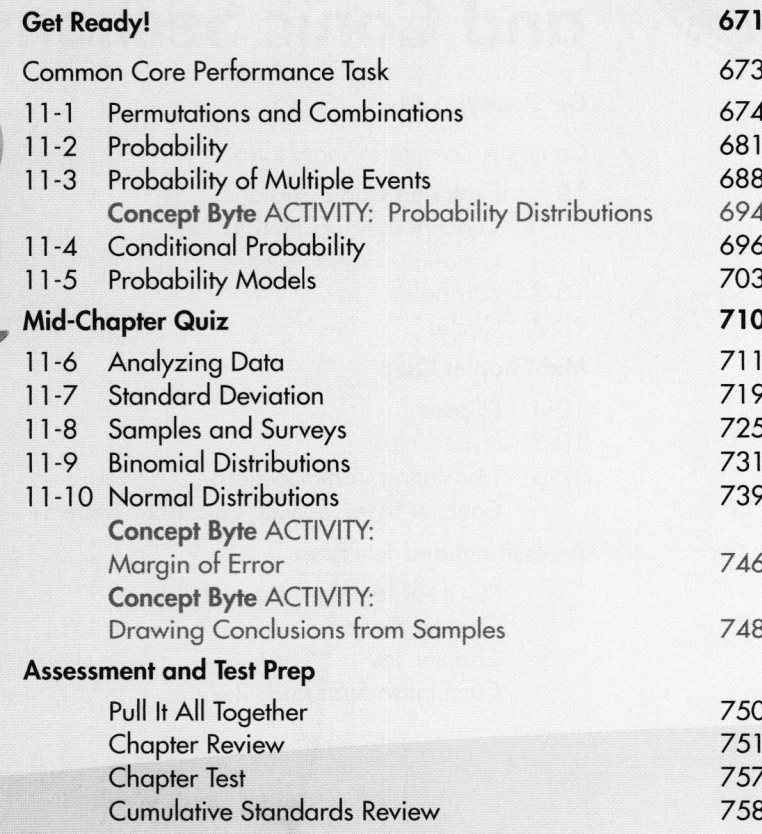

Chapters 11 & 12

Number and Quantity
Vector and Matrix Quantities
Represent and model with vector quantities
Perform operations on vectors
Perform operations on matrices and use matrices in applications

Statistics and Probability
Interpreting Categorical and Quantitative Data
Summarize, represent, and interpret data on a single count or measurement variable

Making Inferences and Justifying Conclusions
Understand and evaluate random processes underlying statistical experiments
Make inferences and justify conclusions from sample surveys, experiments, and observational studies

Conditional Probability and the Rules of Probability
Understand independence and conditional probability and use them to interpret data
Use the rules of probability to compute probabilities of compound events in a uniform probability model

Use Probability to Make Decisions
Use probability to evaluate outcomes of decisions

12 Matrices

Visual See It!

Reasoning Try It!

Practice Do It!

13

Periodic Functions and Trigonometry

Functions
Interpreting Functions
  Interpret functions that arise in applications in terms of the context
  Analyze functions using different representations
Trigonometric Functions
  Extend the domain of trigonometric functions using the unit circle
  Model periodic phenomena with trigonometric functions
  Prove and apply trigonometric identities

Geometry
Similarity, Right Triangles, and Trigonometry
  Define trigonometric ratios and solve problems involving right triangles
  Apply trigonometry to general triangles

Chapters 13 & 14

14 Trigonometric Identities and Equations

Visual **See It!**

Reasoning **Try It!**

Practice **Do It!**

Entry-Level Assessment

Multiple Choice

Read each question. Then write the letter of the correct answer on your paper.

1. Let $A = \{1, 2, 3, 4\}$ be a set in the universe $U = \{1, 2, 3, 4, 5, 6, 7, 8\}$. What is the complement of A?

- **A** $\{2, 3\}$
- **B** $\{5, 6, 7, 8\}$
- **C** $\{1, 2, 3, 4\}$
- **D** $\{2, 3, 7, 8\}$

2. Solve $x^2 + 2x - 3 = 0$ by factoring.

- **F** $x = -3$ and $x = 1$
- **G** $x = -1$ and $x = 3$
- **H** $x = 0$
- **I** $x = -3$ and $x = 0$

3. Simplify $\dfrac{3a^2b^3 - 12a^4b^3 + 6a^4b^2}{3a^2b}$.

- **A** $b^2 - 4a^2b^2 + 2a^2b$
- **B** $a^2b - 4a^2b^2 + 2a^2b$
- **C** $3b^2 - 12a^2b + 6b^2$
- **D** $3ab^2 - 4a^2b + 2ab^2$

4. Which relation is not a function?

- **F** $\{(1, -5), (2, 4), (1, -4)\}$
- **G** $\{(1, -5), (2, 4), (3, -3)\}$
- **H** $\{(1, -5), (2, 4), (3, 2)\}$
- **I** $\{(1, -5), (2, 4), (3, -4)\}$

5. In the diagram, m and n are parallel.

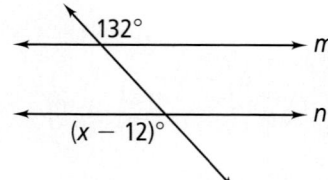

What is the value of x?

- **A** 36
- **B** 60
- **C** 120
- **D** 144

6. Solve $2(1 - 2w) = 4w + 18$.

- **F** -4
- **G** -2
- **H** 8
- **I** 16

7. Which of the following lines is perpendicular to the line $3x + y = 2$?

- **A** $y = 3x + 4$
- **B** $y = \frac{1}{3}x - 2$
- **C** $y = -3x + 3$
- **D** $y = -\frac{1}{3}x + 1$

8. If $y = 1$, then $(x + 5) \cdot y = x + 5$. Which property supports this statement?

- **F** Inverse Property of Multiplication
- **G** Identity Property of Multiplication
- **H** Associative Property of Addition
- **I** Commutative Property of Addition

9.

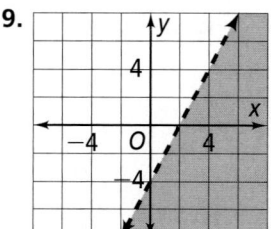

Which inequality does the graph represent?

- **A** $y < 2x - 4$
- **B** $y > -4x + 2$
- **C** $y > 2x - 4$
- **D** $y < -4x + 2$

10. The area of a trapezoid is $A = \frac{1}{2}h(b_1 + b_2)$. Solve for b_1.

- **F** $b_1 = \dfrac{2A - b_2}{h}$
- **G** $b_1 = \dfrac{2A - h}{b_2}$
- **H** $b_1 = \dfrac{2A}{h} - b_2$
- **I** $b_1 = 2A - b_2$

11. Let $\overleftrightarrow{AB}$ be parallel to $\overleftrightarrow{CD}$, with $A(-2, 3)$, $B(1, 4)$, and $C(1, 2)$. Which of the following could be the coordinates of point D?

Ⓐ $(4, 1)$ Ⓒ $(-2, 3)$

Ⓑ $(-2, -1)$ Ⓓ $(4, 3)$

12. Solve $3 \geq 4g - 5 \geq -1$.

Ⓕ $-\frac{3}{2} \leq g \leq 2$ Ⓗ $-4 \leq g \leq 8$

Ⓖ $-1 \leq g \leq \frac{3}{4}$ Ⓘ $1 \leq g \leq 2$

13. Which is *not* a solution of $5(2x + 4) \geq 2(x + 34)$?

Ⓐ 48 Ⓒ 6

Ⓑ 8 Ⓓ 3

14. Factor $6x^2 - 216$.

Ⓕ $6(x - 6)(x + 6)$

Ⓖ $(6x - 36)(6x + 36)$

Ⓗ $6(x - 6)$

Ⓘ $6(x - 36)(x + 6)$

15. Mike and Jane leave their home on bikes traveling in opposite directions on a straight road. Mike rides 5 mi/h faster than Jane. After 4 h they are 124 mi apart. At what rate does Mike ride his bike?

Ⓐ 5 mi/h   Ⓒ 18 mi/h

Ⓑ 13 mi/h   Ⓓ 31 mi/h

16. What is the point-slope form for the equation of the line in the graph?

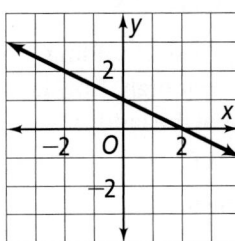

Ⓕ $y - 2 = \frac{3}{2}(x + 2)$

Ⓖ $y - 2 = \frac{1}{2}(x + 2)$

Ⓗ $y - 2 = -\frac{1}{2}(x + 2)$

Ⓘ $y - 2 = -\frac{2}{3}(x + 2)$

17. A rectangular photograph is being enlarged to poster size by making both the length and width six times as large as the original. How many times as large as the area of the original photograph is the area of the poster?

Ⓐ $\frac{1}{6}$ Ⓒ 12

Ⓑ 6   Ⓓ 36

18. A rectangle has a length of $2x + 3$ and a width of $x - 4$. Find the area of the rectangle.

Ⓕ $2x^2 - 12$

Ⓖ $2x^2 - 8x$

Ⓗ $2x^2 - 5x - 12$

Ⓘ $2x^2 - 11x - 12$

19. What is the y-intercept of the line that passes through the points $(-4, 4)$ and $(2, -5)$?

Ⓐ -2 Ⓒ $\frac{3}{2}$

Ⓑ $-\frac{3}{2}$ Ⓓ 2

20. Which of the following is equivalent to $\sqrt{2}(\sqrt{6} - 4)$?

Ⓕ $\sqrt{12} - 4$ Ⓗ $\sqrt{12} - 8$

Ⓖ $2\sqrt{3} - 2\sqrt{2}$ Ⓘ $2\sqrt{3} - 4\sqrt{2}$

21. Which of the following represents the system shown in the graph?

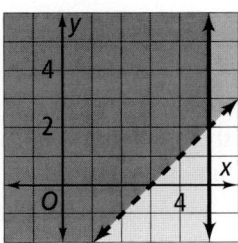

Ⓐ $\begin{cases} y = x - 3 \\ x \geq 5 \end{cases}$ Ⓒ $\begin{cases} y < x - 3 \\ x = 5 \end{cases}$

Ⓑ $\begin{cases} y \leq x - 3 \\ x > 5 \end{cases}$ Ⓓ $\begin{cases} y > x - 3 \\ x \leq 5 \end{cases}$

22. Which of the following equations represents the line that is parallel to the line $y = 5x + 2$ and that passes through the point $(1, -3)$?

Ⓕ $y = -5x + 2$ Ⓗ $y = \frac{1}{5}x - 8$

Ⓖ $y = 5x + 8$ Ⓘ $y = 5x - 8$

23. Which equation represents a line that would be perpendicular to a second line with a slope of $\frac{1}{5}$?

- **A** $y = -5x + 2$
- **B** $y = -\frac{1}{5}x + 3$
- **C** $y = 5x - 2$
- **D** $5y + x = 2$

24. $\triangle ABC$ is similar to $\triangle DEF$.

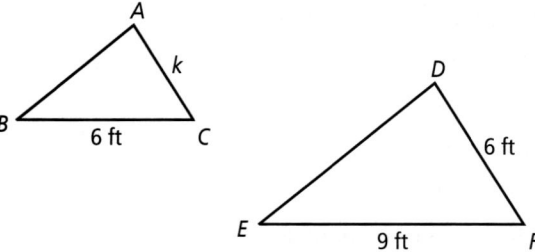

What is the value of k?

- **F** 3 ft
- **H** 6 ft
- **G** 4 ft
- **I** 9 ft

25. Solve the equation using the Quadratic Formula.
$$6x^2 - 10x + 3 = 0$$

- **A** $\frac{5 \pm \sqrt{7}}{6}$
- **B** $\frac{3 \pm \sqrt{5}}{6}$
- **C** -2 and 5
- **D** $\frac{3}{4}$ and $\frac{2}{3}$

26. A rectangle in the coordinate plane has vertices $(3, 2)$, $(8, 2)$, $(3, 6)$, and $(8, 6)$. Which of the following sets of vertices describes a rectangle that is congruent to this one?

- **F** $(3, -2), (3, -8), (5, -8), (5, -2)$
- **G** $(-2, -4), (-2, -8), (3, -8), (3, -4)$
- **H** $(0, 0), (5, 0), (5, 5), (0, 5)$
- **I** $(-3, 2), (1, 2), (1, 6), (-3, 6)$

27. Simplify the expression below.
$$(-6y^{-4})^5$$

- **A** $7776y^{20}$
- **C** $-7776y^{20}$
- **B** $\frac{7776}{y^{20}}$
- **D** $-\frac{7776}{y^{20}}$

28. What is the solution to $\frac{2n + 8}{3} = \frac{n + 7}{2}$?

- **F** -9
- **H** 5
- **G** -1
- **I** 13

29. Solve the system of equations below.
$$\begin{cases} 3x + y = -7 \\ 4x - y = -14 \end{cases}$$

- **A** $(-3, 2)$
- **C** $(-3, -2)$
- **B** $(3, 2)$
- **D** no solution

30. Which of the following is equivalent to $\frac{2x - 12}{x^2 - 2x - 24}$?

- **F** $\frac{2}{x + 4}$
- **H** $\frac{1}{x^2 - 2}$
- **G** $\frac{1}{x + 2}$
- **I** $\frac{2x - 3}{x - 6}$

31. What is (are) the solution(s) of the graphed function when the value of the function is 0?

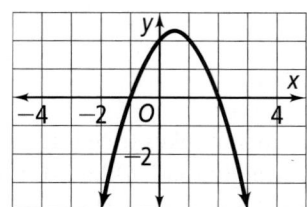

- **A** -1 and 2
- **C** 2
- **B** 1 and -2
- **D** 2.2

32. Which of the following is true?

- **F** $\sqrt{85} < 9$
- **H** $\sqrt{\frac{16}{25}} > \sqrt{\frac{16}{4}}$
- **G** $8 < \sqrt{62}$
- **I** $\sqrt{121} < \sqrt{144}$

33. A firefighter leans a 30-ft ladder against a building in order to reach a window that is 24 ft high. How far away from the building is the base of the ladder?

- **A** 18 ft
- **C** 24 ft
- **B** 20 ft
- **D** 30 ft

34. What is the number of x-intercepts of the parabola with equation $y = 6x^2 - 4x - 3$?

- **F** 0
- **H** 2
- **G** 1
- **I** 3

Get Ready!

Skills
Handbook,
page 973

◆ Adding Rational Numbers

Find each sum.

1. $6 + (-6)$
2. $-8 + 6$
3. $5.31 + (-7.40)$
4. $-1.95 + 10$

5. $7\frac{3}{4} + \left(-8\frac{1}{2}\right)$
6. $-2\frac{1}{3} + 3\frac{1}{4}$
7. $6\frac{2}{5} + 4\frac{3}{10}$
8. $-1\frac{5}{6} + 5\frac{1}{3}$

Skills
Handbook,
page 973

◆ Subtracting Rational Numbers

Find each difference.

9. $-28 - 14$
10. $61 - (-11)$
11. $-16 - (-25)$
12. $-6.2 - 3.6$

13. $-5\frac{2}{3} - \left(-2\frac{1}{3}\right)$
14. $-2\frac{1}{4} - 3\frac{1}{4}$
15. $2\frac{2}{3} - 7\frac{1}{3}$
16. $\frac{5}{2} - \frac{13}{4}$

Skills
Handbook,
page 973

◆ Multiplying and Dividing Rational Numbers

Find each product or quotient.

17. $-3 \cdot 7$
18. $-2.1 \cdot (-3.5)$
19. $-\frac{2}{3} \div 4$
20. $-\frac{3}{8} \div \frac{5}{8}$

Skills
Handbook,
page 975

◆ Using the Order of Operations

Simplify each expression.

21. $8 \cdot (-3) + 4$
22. $3 \cdot 4 - 8 \div 2$
23. $1 \div 2^2 - 0.54 + 1.26$

24. $9 \div (-3) - 2$
25. $5(3 \cdot 5 - 4)$
26. $1 - (1 - 5)^2 \div (-8)$

©27. Reasoning Why don't the expressions $3 + 5^2 \cdot 3 \div 15$ and $(3 + 5^2) \cdot 3 \div 15$
yield the same answer?

Looking Ahead Vocabulary

28. The current of a river flows north at a *constant* rate. What is the constant in the
mathematical expression $3x + 5y + 3$?

29. Before signing a contract, you must review the *terms* and conditions of the contract.
How many terms are there in the surface area formula below?

$$2(\ell w + wh + h\ell)$$

30. Engineers *evaluate* the efficiency of the memory and speed of a computer. What
does evaluate mean in mathematics?

31. Smiling is a facial *expression* of happiness or contentment. In math, what is the
expression that represents the quotient of 3 and 3 less than a number?

CHAPTER 1

Expressions, Equations, and Inequalities

Download videos connecting math to your world.

Interactive! Vary numbers, graphs, and figures to explore math concepts.

The online Solve It will get you in gear for each lesson.

Math definitions in English and Spanish

Online access to stepped-out problems aligned to Common Core

Get and view your assignments online.

Extra practice and review online

Virtual Nerd™ tutorials with built-in support

Chapter Preview

1-1 Patterns and Expressions
1-2 Properties of Real Numbers
1-3 Algebraic Expressions
1-4 Solving Equations
1-5 Solving Inequalities
1-6 Absolute Value Equations and Inequalities

Vocabulary

English/Spanish Vocabulary Audio Online:

English	Spanish
absolute value, *p. 41*	valor absoluto
algebraic expression, *p. 5*	expresión algebraica
compound inequality, *p. 36*	desigualdad compuesta
like terms, *p. 21*	términos semejantes
literal equation, *p. 29*	ecuación literal
term, *p. 20*	término
variable, *p. 5*	variable

BIG ideas

1 Variable
Essential Question How do variables help you model real-world situations?

2 Properties
Essential Question How can you use the properties of real numbers to simplify algebraic expressions?

3 Solving Equations and Inequalities
Essential Question How do you solve an equation or inequality?

 DOMAINS
• Seeing Structure in Expressions
• Creating Equations

Common Core Performance Task

Where's My Car?

Cody leaves his friend Mia's house and drives along the road shown in the diagram below. Somewhere between Mia's house and the restaurant, Cody's car runs out of gas.

Cody has an empty gas can in his car, but he does not want to leave the car unattended. Cody calls Mia, who drives to Cody's car to pick up his gas can. She then drives to the gas station that is located on the same road. After Mia fills the gas can, she drives back to Cody's car. She gives Cody the gas can, and then drives to the restaurant along the same road to meet another friend for lunch. When she reaches the restaurant, Mia has driven a total of 34 mi.

Task Description

Determine how far Cody is from Mia's house when his car runs out of gas. Find all possible distances.

Connecting the Task to the Math Practices

As you complete the task, you'll apply several Standards for Mathematical Practice.

- You'll draw diagrams to help you make sense of the problem. (MP 1)
- You'll assign a variable to an unknown distance and use your variable to write expressions that represent other distances. (MP 2)
- You'll model the problem situation with an equation. (MP 4)

1-1 Patterns and Expressions

Common Core State Standards

A-SSE.B.3 Choose and produce an equivalent form of an expression to reveal and explain properties of the quantity represented by the expression.

MP 1, MP 2, MP 3, MP 7

Objective To identify and describe patterns

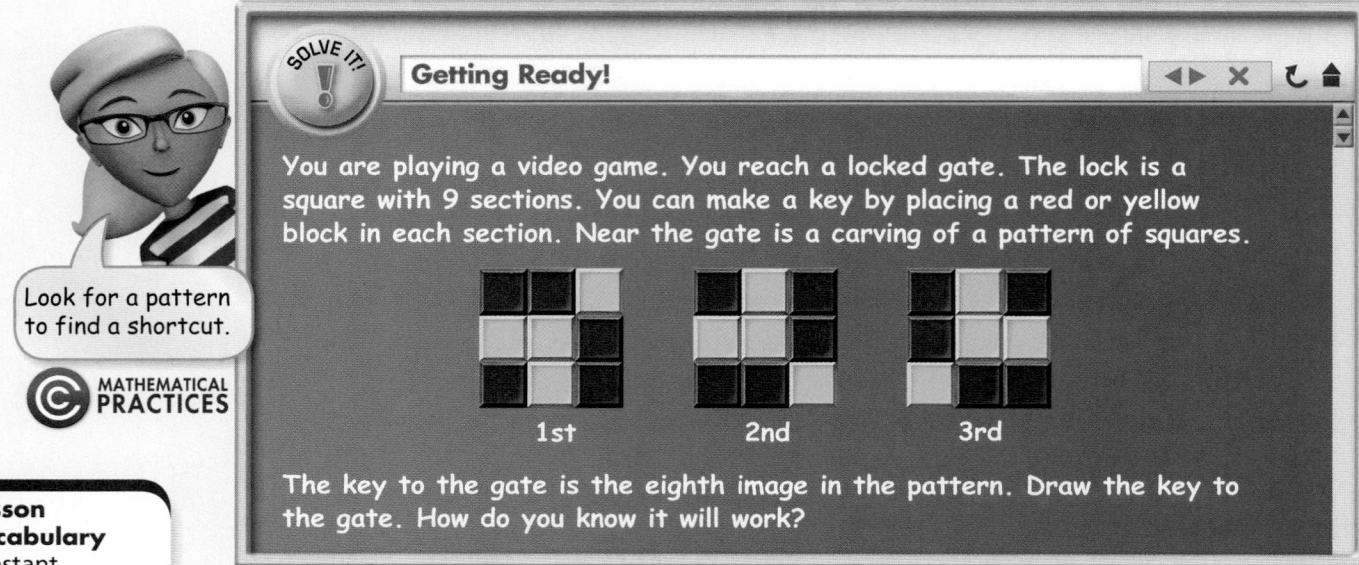

SOLVE IT!

Look for a pattern to find a shortcut.

MATHEMATICAL PRACTICES

Getting Ready!

You are playing a video game. You reach a locked gate. The lock is a square with 9 sections. You can make a key by placing a red or yellow block in each section. Near the gate is a carving of a pattern of squares.

1st   2nd   3rd

The key to the gate is the eighth image in the pattern. Draw the key to the gate. How do you know it will work?

Lesson Vocabulary
- constant
- variable quantity
- variable
- numerical expression
- algebraic expression

In the Solve It, you identified and used a geometric pattern. In this lesson, you will identify patterns in pictures, tables, and graphs and describe them using numbers and variables.

Essential Understanding You can represent some patterns using diagrams, words, numbers, or algebraic expressions.

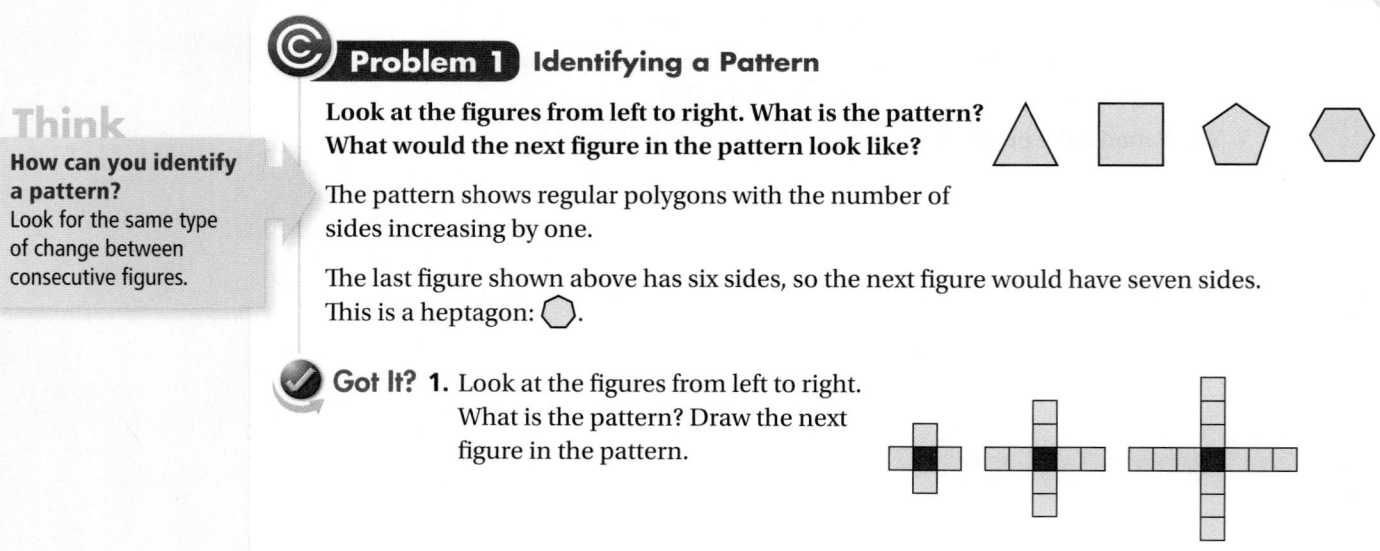

Problem 1 Identifying a Pattern

Think

How can you identify a pattern?
Look for the same type of change between consecutive figures.

Look at the figures from left to right. What is the pattern? What would the next figure in the pattern look like?

The pattern shows regular polygons with the number of sides increasing by one.

The last figure shown above has six sides, so the next figure would have seven sides. This is a heptagon: ⬡.

Got It? 1. Look at the figures from left to right. What is the pattern? Draw the next figure in the pattern.

A mathematical *quantity* is anything that can be measured or counted. The *value* of the quantity is its measure or the number of items that are counted. Quantities whose values do not change are called **constants**. In other situations, the value of a quantity can change. Quantities whose values change or vary are called **variable quantities**.

take note

Key Concepts   Variables and Expressions

Definition	Examples	
A **variable** is a symbol, usually a letter, that represents one or more numbers.	n	x
A **numerical expression** is a mathematical phrase that contains numbers and operation symbols.	$3 + 5$	$(8 - 2) + 5$
An **algebraic expression** is a mathematical phrase that contains one or more variables.	$3n + 5$	$(8x - 2) + 5n$

Tables are a convenient way to organize data and discover patterns. They work much like an "input/output" machine: a machine that takes one value as an input, processes it, and gives a value as an output. A process column in the table provides a way to understand what happens to the input values.

© **Problem 2** **Expressing a Pattern With Algebra**

Use a pattern to answer each question.

Ⓐ **How many toothpicks are in the 20th figure?**

Use a table. Look for a pattern that relates the figure number to the number of toothpicks.

Figure Number (Input)	Process Column	Number of Toothpicks (Output)
1	1(4)	4
2	2(4)	8
3	3(4)	12
⋮	⋮	⋮
n	▪	▪

To get the output, multiply the input by 4.

Pattern: Multiply the figure number by 4 to get the number of toothpicks. So, there are $20(4) = 80$ toothpicks in the 20th figure.

Ⓑ **What is an expression that describes the number of toothpicks in the *n*th figure?**

Use the pattern from part (A). There are $4n$ toothpicks in the *n*th figure.

Think

What would the process look like for the *n*th row?
Multiply the figure number, *n*, by 4.

✓ **Got It?**   **2.** How many tiles are in the 25th figure in this pattern? Show a table of values with a process column.

 **Problem 3** Using a Graph

Aquarium You want to set up an aquarium and need to determine what size tank to buy. The graph shows tank sizes using a rule that relates the capacity of the tank to the combined lengths of the fish it can hold.

If you want five 2-in. platys, four 1-in. guppies, and a 3-in. loach, which is the smallest capacity tank you can buy: 15-gallon, 20-gallon, or 25-gallon? Use a table to find the answer.

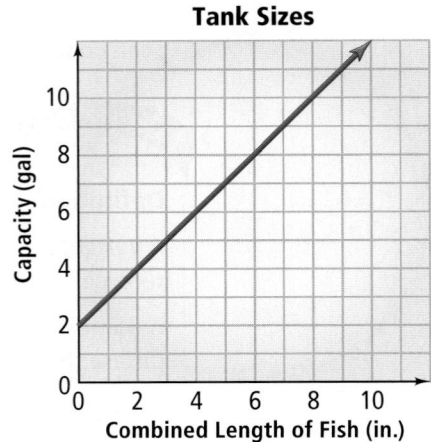

Tank Sizes

Plan

How can you use the given graph?
You can use the graph to make a table and find a pattern relating capacity and combined fish length.

Think

Choose some points on the graph.

Make a table using the input and output values shown in the ordered pairs.
Find a pattern in the process column. Each output is 2 more than the corresponding input.

You want 5 platys, 4 guppies, and 1 loach. So, you will have a total of 17 in. of fish. Find the output when the input is 17.

Write the answer in words.

Write

(0, 2), (5, 7), (10, 12)

Input	Process Column	Output
0	0 + 2	2
5	5 + 2	7
10	10 + 2	12

output = input + 2
= 17 + 2
= 19

You need to buy the 20-gal tank.

  Got It? **3.** The graph at the right shows the total cost of platys at the aquarium shop. Use a table to answer the questions.
  a. How much do six platys cost?
  b. How much do ten platys cost?
  c. **Reasoning** Why is the graph in Problem 3 a line while the graph at the right is a set of points?

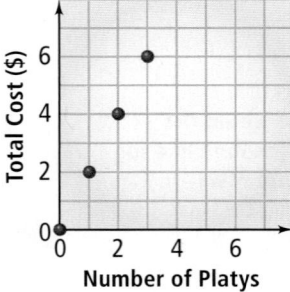

Cost of Platys

Lesson Check

Do you know HOW?

Describe a rule for each pattern.

1. 35, 70, 105, 140, . . .

2.
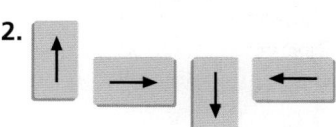

Make a table to represent each pattern. Use a process column.

3. 2, 4, 6, 8, . . .

4.

Do you UNDERSTAND?

5. Explain the strategy you use to identify a pattern.

6. Compare and Contrast How are tables of values like pictorial representations? How are they different?

7. Error Analysis Your friend looks for a pattern in the table below and claims that the output equals the input divided by 2. Is your friend correct? Explain.

Input	3	6.8	8	10	25
Output	2	3.4	4	5	12.5

Practice and Problem-Solving Exercises  MATHEMATICAL PRACTICES

Ⓐ Practice   Describe each pattern using words. Draw the next likely figure in each pattern.   ◀ **See Problem 1.**

8.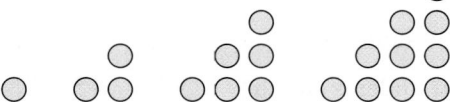

9.

10.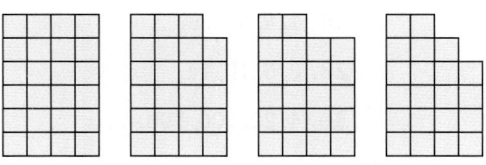

11.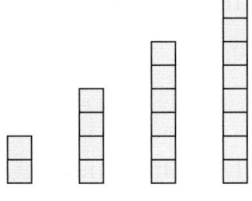

Make a table with a process column to represent each pattern. Write an expression for the number of tiles or circles in the *n*th figure.   ◀ **See Problem 2.**

12.

13.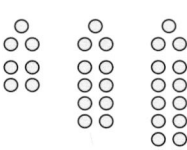

14.

15.

Copy and complete each table. Include a process column.

16.

Input	Output
1	0
2	1
3	2
4	3
5	■
6	■
⋮	⋮
n	■

17.

Input	Output
1	3
2	4
3	5
4	6
5	■
6	■
⋮	⋮
n	■

18.

Input	Output
1	−3
2	−6
3	−9
4	−12
5	■
6	■
⋮	⋮
n	■

Identify a pattern by making a table. Include a process column.

◀ See Problem 3.

19.

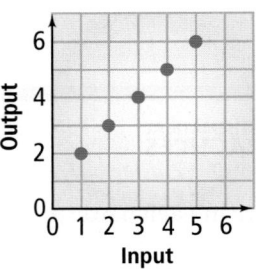

20.

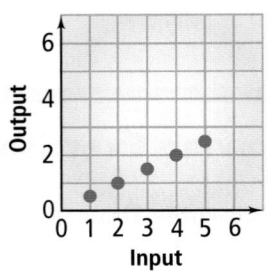

21.

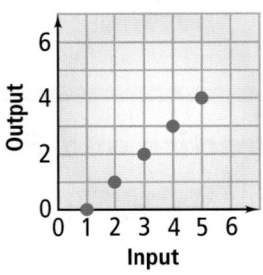

The graph shows the number of bottles of water needed for students going on a field trip.

22. How many bottles of water are needed if 5 students attend?

23. How many bottles of water are needed if 20 students attend?

24. How many bottles of water are needed if n students attend?

Class Field Trip

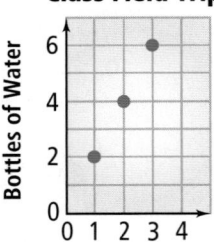

B Apply

Identify a pattern and find the next three numbers in the pattern.

25. 6, 12, 18, 24, . . .

26. 1, 4, 3, 6, 5, . . .

27. 3, 6, 10, 15, . . .

28. 2, 6, 10, 14, . . .

29. 1, 3, 9, 27, 81, . . .

30. 4, 20, 100, 500, . . .

31. Identify a pattern and draw the next three figures in the pattern.

 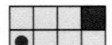 

Ⓒ 32. Open-Ended Write a rule so that for every input, the output is an even number.

33. Think About a Plan A moving company sells different sizes of boxes as shown. The extra-large box is one size larger than the third box shown. What is its volume?
- Identify a pattern of the dimension changes.
- What is the formula for the volume of a rectangular prism?

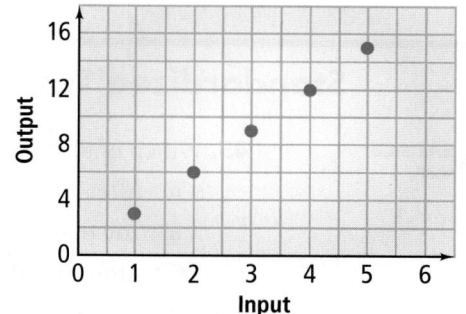

12 in. 12 in. 16 in.
16 in. 16 in. 16 in.
20 in. 20 in. 16 in.

34. Use the graph shown.
 a. Identify a pattern of the graph by making a table of the inputs and outputs.
 b. What are the outputs for inputs 6, 7, and 8?

35. Collecting Jay has a rare baseball card collection. He currently owns 10 baseball cards. Each month, he purchases a new card for his collection. Write a model to represent the number of cards in Jay's collection after n months.

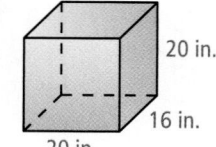

36. Use the figures below.

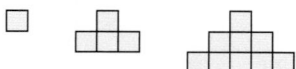

 a. Draw the next two figures.
 b. Copy and complete the table to find the number of squares in each figure.
 c. What is the number of squares in the nth figure? Explain your reasoning.

Figure (Input)	Process Column	Number of Squares (Output)
1	■	■
2	■	■
3	■	■
4	■	■
5	■	■

Copy and complete each table.

37.

Input	Output
1	5
2	9
3	13
4	17
5	■
⋮	⋮
n	■

38.

Input	Output
1	2
2	−3
3	−8
4	−13
5	■
⋮	⋮
n	■

39.

Input	Output
1	3
2	−1
3	−5
4	−9
5	■
⋮	⋮
n	■

Challenge

40. Open-Ended Write the first five numbers of two different patterns in which 12 is the third number.

41. Reasoning For the past 4 years, Jesse has grown 3 inches each year. He is now 15 years old and is 5 feet 6 inches tall. He predicts that when he is 20 years old, he will be 6 feet 9 inches tall. What would you tell Jesse about his prediction?

42. This pattern shows the first five steps in constructing the Sierpinski Triangle. Use a pattern to describe the figures.

Standardized Test Prep

SAT/ACT

43. Which of the following is the best statement about the graph?

Ⓐ After 4 weeks, the plant will be 7 inches tall.

Ⓑ The plant was 1 inch tall at the beginning of the experiment.

Ⓒ After 2 weeks, the plant was 3 inches tall.

Ⓓ After 6 weeks, the plant will be 8 inches tall.

Plant Growth

44. Which is the 7th number in this pattern?

$$8, 13, 18, 23, \ldots$$

Ⓕ 28

Ⓖ 33

Ⓗ 38

Ⓘ 43

Short Response

45. Look at the pattern shown.

$$144, 72, 36, \ldots$$

a. What is a rule for the pattern?

b. What is the first non-integer number in this pattern?

Mixed Review

Simplify each expression.

◀ See p. 975.

46. $3.6 + (-1.7)$

47. $1.2 - 5$

48. $(-3)(-9)$

49. $0(-8)$

50. $-2.8 \div 7$

51. $-35 \div (-5)$

Get Ready! **To prepare for Lesson 1-2, do Exercises 52–57.**

Write each number as a percent.

◀ See p. 972.

52. 0.5

53. 0.25

54. $\frac{1}{3}$

55. $1\frac{2}{5}$

56. 1.72

57. 1.23

1-2 Properties of Real Numbers

© **Common Core State Standards**

Reviews N-RN.B.3 Explain why the sum or product of two rational numbers is rational; that the sum of a rational number and an irrational number is irrational, and that the product of a nonzero rational number and an irrational number is irrational.

MP 1, MP 3, MP 6

Objectives To graph and order real numbers
To identify properties of real numbers

SOLVE IT!

Getting Ready!

You use emoticons in text messages to help you communicate.

Here are six emoticons. How can you describe a set that includes five of the emoticons but not the sixth?

Lesson Vocabulary
• opposite
• additive inverse
• reciprocal
• multiplicative inverse

In the Solve It, you classified sets of emoticons. In this lesson, you will classify real numbers into special subsets.

Essential Understanding The set of real numbers has several special subsets related in particular ways.

Algebra involves operations on and relations among numbers, including real numbers and imaginary numbers. (You will learn about imaginary numbers in Chapter 4.) Rational numbers and irrational numbers form the set of real numbers.

You can graph every real number as a point on the number line.

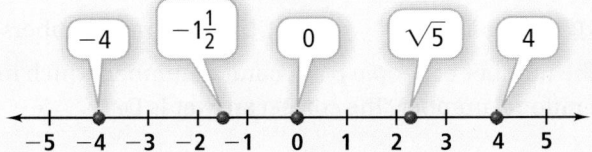

The diagram shows how subsets of the real numbers are related.

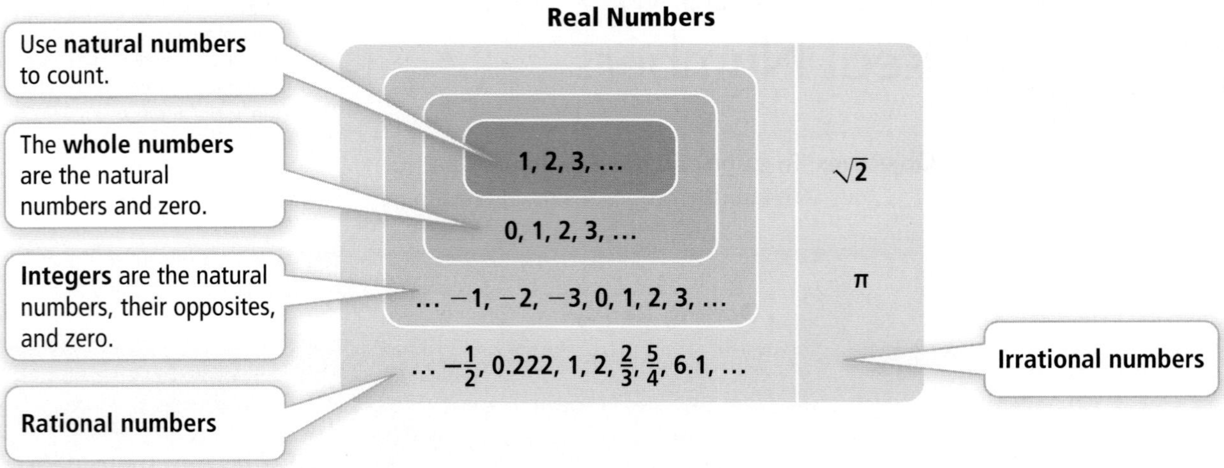

Real Numbers

Use **natural numbers** to count.

The **whole numbers** are the natural numbers and zero.

1, 2, 3, …

0, 1, 2, 3, …

Integers are the natural numbers, their opposites, and zero.

… −1, −2, −3, 0, 1, 2, 3, …

$\sqrt{2}$

π

… −$\frac{1}{2}$, 0.222, 1, 2, $\frac{2}{3}$, $\frac{5}{4}$, 6.1, …

Irrational numbers

Rational numbers

Rational numbers
- are all numbers you can write as a quotient of integers $\frac{a}{b}$, $b \neq 0$.
- include terminating decimals. For example, $\frac{1}{8} = 0.125$.
- include repeating decimals. For example, $\frac{1}{3} = 0.\overline{3}$.

Irrational numbers
- have decimal representations that neither terminate nor repeat. For example, $\sqrt{2} = 1.414213\ldots$.
- cannot be written as quotients of integers.

You classify a variable by naming the subset that gives you the most information about the numbers the variable represents.

 **Problem 1** **Classifying a Variable**

Multiple Choice Your school is sponsoring a charity race. Which set of numbers does not contain the number of people p who participate in the race?

Ⓐ natural numbers   Ⓒ rational numbers

Ⓑ integers   Ⓓ irrational numbers

The number of people p is a natural number, which means that it is also an integer and a rational number. The correct answer is D.

Think

What are some examples of possible values of p?
The number of people p must be represented by a whole number. Determine which other sets of numbers include the whole numbers.

Got It? **1.** In Problem 1, if each participant made a donation d of $15.50 to a local charity, which subset of real numbers best describes the amount of money raised?

Problem 2 Graphing Numbers on the Number Line

Plan

How do you graph a number on the number line?
If the number is an integer, determine whether it is positive or negative. If it's not an integer, determine which integer it's closest to.

What is the graph of the numbers $-\frac{5}{2}$, $\sqrt{2}$, and $2.\overline{6}$?

Since $-\frac{5}{2} = -2\frac{1}{2}$, $-\frac{5}{2}$ is between -3 and -2.

Use a calculator. $\sqrt{2} \approx 1.4$.

Think: $2.\overline{6} = 2\frac{2}{3}$.

$$\begin{array}{c}\underset{-3\ -2\ -1\quad 0\quad 1\quad 2\quad 3}{\longleftrightarrow}\end{array}$$

Got It? **2.** What is the graph of the numbers $\sqrt{3}$, $-1.\overline{4}$, and $\frac{1}{3}$?

The number line is helpful for ordering several real numbers. For two numbers, however, it is easier to show order, or compare, using one of the inequality symbols $>$ or $<$.

 Problem 3 Ordering Real Numbers

Think

Why compare $\sqrt{17}$ to the square root of a perfect square?
It makes it easier to determine which two integers $\sqrt{17}$ is between.

How do $\sqrt{17}$ and 3.8 compare? Use $>$ or $<$.

Compare both numbers to $\sqrt{16}$.

$\quad \sqrt{16} < \sqrt{17} \qquad$ 16 is less than 17.

$\quad 3.8 \ < \sqrt{16} \qquad \sqrt{16} = 4$ and $3.8 < 4$.

Therefore, $3.8 < \sqrt{17}$, or $\sqrt{17} > 3.8$.

Check Use a calculator.

$\quad \sqrt{17} \approx 4.123$

$\quad 3.8 < 4.123$ ✔

 Got It? **3. a.** How do $\sqrt{26}$ and 6.25 compare? Use $>$ or $<$.
  b. Reasoning Let a, b, and c be real numbers such that $a < b$ and $b < c$. How do a and c compare? Explain.

Essential Understanding The properties of real numbers are relationships that are true for all real numbers (except, in one case, zero).

One property of real numbers excludes a single number, zero. Zero is the *additive identity* for the real numbers, and zero is the one real number that has no *multiplicative inverse*.

The **opposite** or **additive inverse** of any number a is $-a$.

The sum of a number and its opposite is 0, the additive identity.

Examples $\quad 12 + (-12) = 0 \qquad\qquad -7 + 7 = 0$

The **reciprocal** or **multiplicative inverse** of any nonzero number a is $\frac{1}{a}$.

The product of a number and its reciprocal is 1, the multiplicative identity.

Examples $\quad 8\left(\frac{1}{8}\right) = 1 \qquad\qquad -5\left(-\frac{1}{5}\right) = 1$

take note

Properties Properties of Real Numbers

Let a, b, and c represent real numbers.

Property	Addition	Multiplication
Closure	$a + b$ is a real number.	ab is a real number.
Commutative	$a + b = b + a$	$ab = ba$
Associative	$(a + b) + c = a + (b + c)$	$(ab)c = a(bc)$
Identity	$a + 0 = a, 0 + a = a$ 0 is the additive identity.	$a \cdot 1 = a, 1 \cdot a = a$ 1 is the multiplicative identity.
Inverse	$a + (-a) = 0$	$a \cdot \frac{1}{a} = 1, a \neq 0$
Distributive	$a(b + c) = ab + ac$	

Ⓒ **Problem 4** **Identifying Properties of Real Numbers**

Plan

How can you analyze an equation?

Determine whether it

- uses addition or multiplication
- reorders or regroups the numbers
- uses an identity

Which property does the equation illustrate?

A $\left(-\frac{2}{3}\right)\left(-\frac{3}{2}\right) = 1$

The product of the numbers is 1.

Inverse Property of Multiplication

B $(3 \cdot 4) \cdot 5 = (4 \cdot 3) \cdot 5$

The equation reorders 3 and 4.

Commutative Property of Multiplication

Ⓒ **Got It?** **4. a.** Which property does the equation $3(g + h) + 2g = (3g + 3h) + 2g$ illustrate?

b. Reasoning Use properties of real numbers to show that $a + [3 + (-a)] = 3$. Justify each step of your solution.

Lesson Check

Do you know HOW?

Write an example from daily life that uses each type of real number.

1. whole numbers

2. integers

3. rational numbers

Identify the property illustrated by the equation.

4. $5 + (-5) = 0$

5. $2 \cdot (4 \cdot 5) = (2 \cdot 4) \cdot 5$

Do you UNDERSTAND?

6. Vocabulary Identify another name for a reciprocal.

7. Compare and Contrast How is the Additive Identity Property similar to the Multiplicative Identity Property? How is it different?

8. Reasoning There are grouping symbols in the equation $(5 + w) + 8 = (w + 5) + 8$, but it does not illustrate the Associative Property of Addition. Explain.

9. Give an example of a number that is not a rational number. Explain why it is not rational.

  ## Practice and Problem-Solving Exercises

A Practice Classify each variable according to the set of numbers that best describes its values.

See Problem 1.

10. the number of times n a ball bounces; the height h from which the ball is dropped

11. the year y; the median selling price p for a house that year

12. the circumference C of a circle found by using the formula $C = 2\pi r$

Graph each number on a number line.

See Problem 2.

13. 0 **14.** $-\sqrt{24}$ **15.** -2 **16.** $2\frac{1}{2}$ **17.** $-4\frac{2}{3}$

18. 3.5 **19.** -1.4 **20.** $\sqrt{10}$ **21.** $-2\frac{1}{5}$ **22.** 4.8

Compare the two numbers. Use $>$ or $<$.

See Problem 3.

23. $16, \sqrt{16}$ **24.** $-4, -\sqrt{4}$ **25.** $\sqrt{5}, \sqrt{7}$

26. $-\sqrt{3}, -\sqrt{5}$ **27.** $5, \sqrt{22}$ **28.** $-\sqrt{38}, 6$

29. $4, \sqrt{12}$ **30.** $-8, \sqrt{70}$ **31.** $\sqrt{63}, 7.5$

32. $4.7, \sqrt{26}$ **33.** $\sqrt{75}, 9$ **34.** $12, -\sqrt{150}$

Name the property of real numbers illustrated by each equation.

See Problem 4.

35. $\pi(a + b) = \pi a + \pi b$ **36.** $-10 + 4 = 4 + (-10)$

37. $\left(2\sqrt{7}\right) \cdot \sqrt{3} = 2\left(\sqrt{7} \cdot \sqrt{3}\right)$ **38.** $29 \cdot \pi = \pi \cdot 29$

39. $-\sqrt{5} + 0 = -\sqrt{5}$ **40.** $\frac{4}{7} \cdot \frac{7}{4} = 1$

Estimate the numbers graphed at the labeled points.

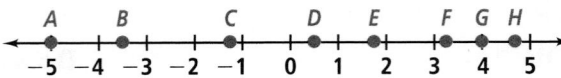

41. point A **42.** point B **43.** point C **44.** point D

45. point E **46.** point F **47.** point G **48.** point H

49. Think About a Plan A cube-shaped jewelry box has a surface area of 300 square inches. What are the dimensions of the jewelry box?
- Write an algebraic expression to find the total surface area of a cube. What is the surface area of one side of a cube?
- How is the side length of a square related to its area?

50. Error Analysis A student labeled the points on the number line as shown. Explain the student's error.

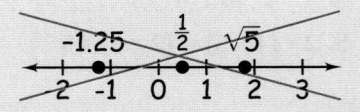

STEM Science The formula $I = \sqrt{\dfrac{W}{R}}$ gives the electric current I in amperes that flows through an appliance, where W is the power in watts and R is the resistance in ohms. Which set of numbers best describes the value of I for the given values of W and R?

51. $W = 100, R = 25$ **52.** $W = 100, R = 5$ **53.** $W = 500, R = 100$

54. $W = 50, R = 200$ **55.** $W = 250, R = 100$ **56.** $W = 240, R = 100$

Write the numbers in decreasing order.

57. $1, -3, -\sqrt{2}, 8, \dfrac{1}{3}$ **58.** $\sqrt{14}, \dfrac{5}{2}, -\dfrac{9}{16}, 1, 11$ **59.** $-17, -0.06, -3\sqrt{3}, 5.73, \dfrac{1}{4}$

Reasoning An example is a *counterexample* to a general statement if it makes the statement false. Show that each of the following statements is false by finding a counterexample.

60. The reciprocal of each natural number is a natural number.

61. The opposite of each whole number is a whole number.

62. There is no integer that has a reciprocal that is an integer.

63. The product of two irrational numbers is an irrational number.

64. All square roots are irrational numbers.

65. Writing Write an example of each of the 11 properties of real numbers shown on page 14.

66. Restaurant Five friends each ordered a sandwich and a drink at a restaurant. Each sandwich costs the same amount and each drink costs the same amount. What are two ways to compute the bill? What property of real numbers is illustrated by the two methods?

67. Open-Ended Write an algebraic problem that requires the use of the real-number properties to solve. Then solve the problem.

68. Writing Are there two integers with a product of -12 and a sum of -3? Explain.

69. Your friend used the Distributive Property and got the expression $5x + 10y - 35$. What algebraic expression could your friend have started with?

70. Geometry π is an irrational number you can use to calculate the circumference or area of a circle.
   a. Find the value of π on your calculator. Can you obtain an exact representation? Explain.
   b. The value of π is often represented as $\frac{22}{7}$. How does this representation compare to the decimal representation your calculator gives using the π key?

71. Does zero have a multiplicative inverse? Explain.

Standardized Test Prep

SAT/ACT

72. Which of the following shows the numbers π, $\sqrt{8}$, and 3.5 in the correct order from greatest to least?

   (A) π, $\sqrt{8}$, 3.5   (B) 3.5, π, $\sqrt{8}$ (C) $\sqrt{8}$, π, 3.5   (D) $\sqrt{8}$, 3.5, π

73. Which of the following is the best statement about the graph?
   (F) A 400-minute plan costs $40.
   (G) A 100-minute plan costs $10.
   (H) A 1000-minute plan costs $110.
   (I) A 200-minute plan costs $35.

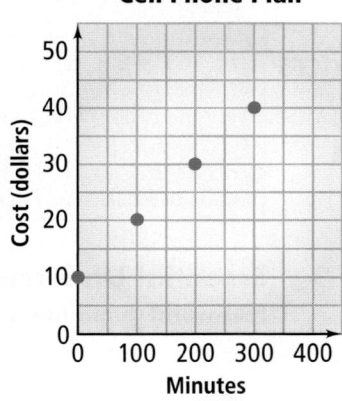

Cell Phone Plan

Short Response

74. Why is the opposite of the reciprocal of 5 the same as the reciprocal of the opposite of 5?

 ## Apply What You've Learned

MATHEMATICAL PRACTICES

MP 1

Look back at the information on page 3 about Cody's car running out of gas.

   a. Copy the diagram shown on page 3. Place a point C along the line at a point where Cody's car could be when it runs out of gas. Draw as many diagrams as needed to show the possible locations of Cody's car relative to the locations of Mia's house, the gas station, and the restaurant.

   b. How many diagrams did you draw in part (a)? Explain why you needed that number of diagrams to account for all possible locations of Cody's car relative to the other three locations.

1-3 Algebraic Expressions

 Common Core State Standards

Reviews A-SSE.A.1a Interpret parts of an expression, such as terms, factors, and coefficients. **Also reviews A-SSE.B.3**

MP 1, MP 2, MP 3

Objectives To evaluate algebraic expressions
To simplify algebraic expressions

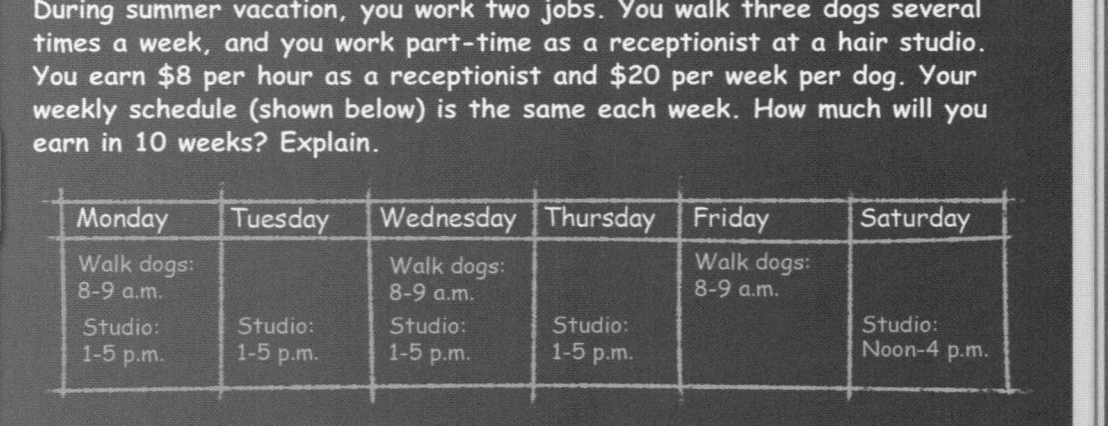

SOLVE IT!

Getting Ready!

During summer vacation, you work two jobs. You walk three dogs several times a week, and you work part-time as a receptionist at a hair studio. You earn $8 per hour as a receptionist and $20 per week per dog. Your weekly schedule (shown below) is the same each week. How much will you earn in 10 weeks? Explain.

Ten weeks is a long time! Perhaps you can solve a simpler problem first.

 **MATHEMATICAL PRACTICES**

Monday	Tuesday	Wednesday	Thursday	Friday	Saturday
Walk dogs: 8-9 a.m.		Walk dogs: 8-9 a.m.		Walk dogs: 8-9 a.m.	
Studio: 1-5 p.m.	Studio: 1-5 p.m.	Studio: 1-5 p.m.	Studio: 1-5 p.m.		Studio: Noon-4 p.m.

 **Lesson Vocabulary**
- evaluate
- term
- coefficient
- constant term
- like terms

Essential Understanding You can represent some mathematical phrases and real-world quantities using algebraic expressions.

Think

What does "seven fewer than t" mean?
"Seven fewer than t" means your answer will be less than t.

 Problem 1 Modeling Words With an Algebraic Expression

Multiple Choice Which algebraic expression models the word phrase *seven fewer than a number t*?

A. $t + 7$ B. $-7t$ C. $t - 7$ D. $7 - t$

"Seven fewer than" suggests subtraction. Begin with the number t and subtract 7. This can be represented by the expression $t - 7$. The correct answer is C.

 Got It? 1. Which algebraic expression models the word phrase *two times the sum of a and b*?

F. $a + b$ H. $2(a + b)$

G. $2a + b$ I. $a + 2b$

To model a situation with an algebraic expression, do the following:
- Identify the actions that suggest operations.
- Define one or more variables to represent the unknown(s).
- Represent the actions using the variables and the operations.

 Problem 2 **Modeling a Situation**

Savings **You start with $20 and save $6 each week. What algebraic expression models the total amount you save?**

Plan

How can you identify the variable?
Determine which quantity is unknown.

Relate	starting amount	plus	amount saved	times	number of weeks

Define Let w = the number of weeks.

Write	20	+	6	•	w

The expression $20 + 6w$ models the situation.

✓ **Got It?** **2.** You had $150, but you are spending $2 each day. What algebraic expression models this situation?

To **evaluate** an algebraic expression, substitute a number for each variable in the expression. Then simplify using the order of operations.

 Problem 3 **Evaluating Algebraic Expressions**

What is the value of the expression for the given values of the variables?

Plan

What operations should you start with?
Do operations that occur in grouping symbols first. Parentheses are grouping symbols.

Ⓐ $7(a + 4) + 3b - 8$ for $a = -4$ and $b = 5$

$7(-4 + 4) + 3(5) - 8$	Substitute the value for each variable.
$= 7(0) + 3(5) - 8$	Perform operations within grouping symbols.
$= 0 + 15 - 8$	Multiply.
$= 15 - 8$	Add and subtract from left to right.
$= 7$	

Ⓑ $\frac{x}{2} + y^2$ for $x = 1$ and $y = \frac{1}{2}$

$\frac{1}{2} + \left(\frac{1}{2}\right)^2$	Substitute the value for each variable.
$= \frac{1}{2} + \frac{1}{4}$	Simplify the power.
$= \frac{3}{4}$	Add.

 ✓ **Got It?** **3. a.** What is the value of the expression $\frac{2(x^2 - y^2)}{3}$ for $x = 6$ and $y = -3$?
b. Reasoning Will the value of the expression change if the parentheses are removed? Explain.

Problem 4 **Writing and Evaluating an Expression**

Sports In football, a touchdown (TD) is worth six points, an extra-point kick (EPK) one point, and a field goal (FG) three points. What algebraic expression models the total number of points that a football team scores in a game, assuming each scoring play is one of the three given types? Suppose a football team scores 3 touchdowns, 2 extra-point kicks, and 4 field goals. How many points did the team score?

Know	Need	Plan
• Number of points each scoring play is worth • Number of each type of score	• Algebraic expression to model points scored • Total number of points scored	• Determine the variables. • Write an expression. • Evaluate the expression.

Think

How many points come from touchdowns?
The number of points from touchdowns is six times the number of touchdowns.

Relate   points per TD · number of TDs + points per EPK · number of EPKs + points per FG · number of FGs

Define   Let t = the number of touchdowns.
Let k = the number of extra-point kicks.
Let f = the number of field goals.

Write   6 · t + 1 · k + 3 · f

The expression $6t + 1k + 3f$ models the team's total score.

The football team scores 3 touchdowns, 2 extra-point kicks, and 4 field goals, so $t = 3$, $k = 2$, and $f = 4$.

$6(3) + 1(2) + 3(4)$ Substitute the value for each variable.
$= 18 + 2 + 12$ Multiply.
$= 32$ Add.

The team scored 32 points.

 Got It? **4.** In basketball, teams can score by making two-point shots, three-point shots, and one-point free throws. What algebraic expression models the total number of points that a basketball team scores in a game? If a team makes 10 two-point shots, 5 three-point shots, and 7 free throws, how many points does it score in all?

An expression that is a number, a variable, or the product of a number and one or more variables is a **term**. A **coefficient** is the numerical factor of a term. A **constant term** is a term with no variables. You can add terms to form longer expressions. The expression below has three terms.

$$-4ax + 7w - 6$$

coefficients
The numerical coefficient of $-4ax$ is -4.

constant term
Think of $7w - 6$ as $7w + (-6)$.
The constant term is -6.

Like terms have the same variables raised to the same powers.

$$3x^2 + 5x^2 + 9y^3z + 2yz - 4y^3z$$

like terms   like terms

You can simplify an algebraic expression that has like terms. You combine like terms using the properties of real numbers (Lesson 1-2). An expression and its simplified form are equivalent. Their values are equal for all values of their variables.

take note

Concept Summary   Properties for Simplifying Algebraic Expressions

Let a, b, and c represent real numbers.

Definition of Subtraction	$a - b = a + (-b)$
Definition of Division	$a \div b = \dfrac{a}{b} = a \cdot \dfrac{1}{b}, \ b \neq 0$
Distributive Property for Subtraction	$a(b - c) = ab - ac$
Multiplication by 0	$0 \cdot a = 0$
Multiplication by -1	$-1 \cdot a = -a$
Opposite of a Sum	$-(a + b) = -a + (-b) = -a - b$
Opposite of a Difference	$-(a - b) = -a + b = b - a$
Opposite of a Product	$-(ab) = -a \cdot b = a \cdot (-b)$
Opposite of an Opposite	$-(-a) = a$

Problem 5   Simplifying Algebraic Expressions

Combine like terms. What is a simpler form of each expression?

Think

Are $7x^2$ and $3y^2$ like terms?
No; they have different variables.

A $7x^2 + 3y^2 + 2y^2 - 4x^2$

$7x^2 + 3y^2 + 2y^2 - 4x^2$ Identify like terms.

$= 7x^2 - 4x^2 + 3y^2 + 2y^2$ Commutative Property of Addition

$= (7 - 4)x^2 + (3 + 2)y^2$ Distributive Property

$= 3x^2 + 5y^2$ Combine like terms.

B $-(3k + m) + 2(k - 4m)$

$-3k - m + 2k - 8m$ Opposite of a Sum and Distributive Property

$= -k - 9m$ Combine like terms.

Got It? **5.** Combine like terms. What is a simpler form of each expression?
    a. $-4j^2 - 7k + 5j + j^2$ **b.** $-(8a + 3b) + 10(2a - 5b)$

Lesson Check

Do you know HOW?

Write an algebraic expression that models each word phrase.

1. the quotient of the sum of 2 and a number b, and 3

2. the sum of the product of a number k and 4, and a number m

Evaluate each algebraic expression for $x = 3$ and $y = -2$.

3. $2x - 3y$ **4.** $5x + y$

5. $y - x$ **6.** $x + 4y$

Do you UNDERSTAND?

 7. Error Analysis A student simplified the expression as shown.

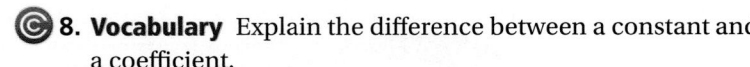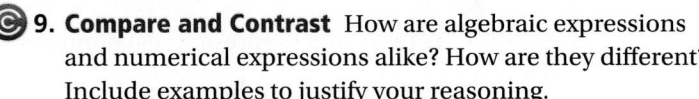
$$3p^2q + 2p - (5q + p - 2p^2q) = q^2p + 3p - 5q$$

Identify the errors and correct them.

8. Vocabulary Explain the difference between a constant and a coefficient.

9. Compare and Contrast How are algebraic expressions and numerical expressions alike? How are they different? Include examples to justify your reasoning.

Practice and Problem-Solving Exercises

 Practice

Write an algebraic expression that models each word phrase.   ◀ **See Problem 1.**

10. four more than a number b

11. the product of 8 and the sum of a number x and 3

12. the quotient of the difference between 5 and a number n, and 2

Write an algebraic expression that models each situation.   ◀ **See Problem 2.**

13. Jenny had \$130, but she is spending \$10 per week.

14. The piggy bank contained \$25, and \$1.50 is added each day.

15. You had 250 minutes left on your cell phone, and you talk an hour a week.

Evaluate each expression for the given values of the variables.   ◀ **See Problem 3.**

16. $4a + 7b + 3a - 2b + 2a$; $a = -5$ and $b = 3$

17. $-k^2 - (3k - 5n) + 4n$; $k = -1$ and $n = -2$

18. $-5(x + 2y) + 15(x + 2y)$; $x = 7$ and $y = -7$

19. $4(2m - n) - 3(2m - n)$; $m = -15$ and $n = -18$

STEM **Physics** The expression $16t^2$ models the distance in feet that an object falls during the first t seconds after being dropped. What is the distance the object falls during each time?

20. 0.25 second   **21.** 0.5 second   **22.** 2 seconds   **23.** 10 seconds

Investing The expression $1000(1.1)^t$ represents the value of a $1000 investment that earns 10% interest per year, compounded annually for t years. What is the value of a $1000 investment at the end of each period?

24. 2 years   **25.** 3 years   **26.** 4 years   **27.** 5 years

Write an algebraic expression to model the total score in each situation. Then evaluate the expression to find the total score.

 **See Problem 4.**

28. In the first set, the volleyball team made only 8 shots worth one point each.

29. In the last baseball game, there were two 3-run home runs and 4 hits that each scored 2 runs.

Simplify by combining like terms.

 **See Problem 5.**

30. $5a - a$ **31.** $5 + 10s - 8s$ **32.** $-5a - 4a + b$

33. $2a + 3b + 4a$ **34.** $6r + 3s + 2s + 4r$ **35.** $0.5x - x$

36. $7b - (3a - 8b)$ **37.** $5 + (4g - 7)$ **38.** $-(3x - 4y) + x$

 **Apply**

Evaluate each expression for the given value of the variable.

39. $x + 2x - x - 1; x = 2$ **40.** $2z + 3 + 5 - 3z; z = -3$ **41.** $3(2a + 5) + 2(3 - a); a = 4$

42. $\dfrac{5(2k - 3) - 3(k + 4)}{3k + 2}; k = -2$ **43.** $y^2 + 3; y = \sqrt{7}$ **44.** $5c^3 - 6c^2 - 2c; c = -5$

45. Think About a Plan Tran's truck gets very poor gas mileage. If Tran pays $84 to fill his truck with gas and is able to drive m miles on a full tank, what expression shows his gas cost per mile?
- What operation does "per" indicate?
- Check your expression by substituting 200 miles for m. Does your answer make sense?

Simplify by combining like terms.

46. $-a^2 + 2b^2 + \frac{1}{4}a^2$ **47.** $x + \dfrac{x^2}{2} + 2x^2 - x$ **48.** $\dfrac{y^2}{4} + \dfrac{y}{3} + \dfrac{y^2}{3} - \dfrac{y}{5}$

49. $-(2x + y) - 2(-x - y)$ **50.** $x(3 - y) + y(x + 6)$ **51.** $\frac{1}{2}(x^2 - y^2) - \frac{5}{2}(x^2 - y^2)$

Write an algebraic expression to model each situation.

52. Class Project The freshman class will be selling carnations as a class project. What is the class's income after it pays the florist a flat fee of $200 and sells x carnations for $2 each?

53. Jobs You have a summer job at a car wash. You earn $8.50 per hour and are expected to pay a one-time fee of $15 for the uniform. If you work x hours per week, how much will you make during the first week?

54. Reasoning Suppose you need to subtract a from b but mistakenly subtract b from a instead. How is the answer you get related to the correct answer? Explain.

55. Error Analysis John simplified the expression as shown. Is his work correct? Explain.

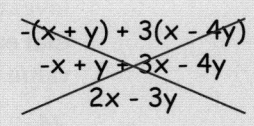

$-(x + y) + 3(x - 4y)$
$-x + y + 3x - 4y$
$2x - 3y$

56. Open-Ended Write an example of an algebraic expression that has a nonnegative value regardless of the value of the variable.

Name the property of real numbers illustrated by the equation.

57. $2(s - t) = 2s - 2t$

58. $-[-(x - 10)] = x - 10$

59. $-(2t - 11) = 11 - 2t$

60. $-(a - b) = (-1)(a - b)$

Challenge

61. Simplify $2(b - a) + 5(b - a)$ and justify each step in your simplification.

62. a. Evaluate the expression $2(2x^2 - x) - 3(x^2 - x) + x^2 - x$ for $x = 3$. Do *not* simplify the expression before evaluating it.

    b. Simplify the expression in part (a) and then evaluate your answer for $x = 3$.

    c. Writing Explain why the values in parts (a) and (b) should be the same.

Apply What You've Learned

Look back at the information on page 3 about Mia helping her friend Cody after Cody's car runs out of gas.

In the Apply What You've Learned in Lesson 1-2, you drew diagrams to show possible locations of Cody's car when it runs out of gas. Choose one of these diagrams to use for parts (a)–(d) below.

    a. Assign a variable to one unknown distance in your diagram.

Use your variable from part (a) to write an algebraic expression for each of the following distances.

    b. the distance Mia drove from her house to Cody's car

    c. the distance Mia drove between the time she picked up Cody's gas can and the time she delivered the full gas can to Cody

    d. the distance Mia drove to the restaurant after leaving Cody

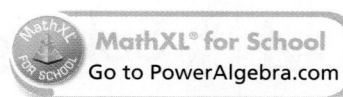
Do you know HOW?

1. Draw the next figure in the pattern.

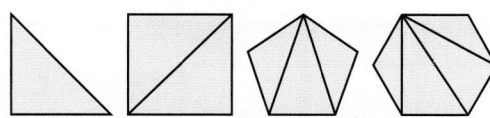

Identify a pattern and find the next number in the pattern.

2. $-405, -135, -45, -15, \ldots$

3. $\frac{2x}{3}, \frac{x}{3}, \frac{x}{6}, \frac{x}{12}, \ldots$

4. $101, 92, 83, 74, \ldots$

5. $0.4, 1.2, 3.6, 10.8, \ldots$

Name the property of real numbers illustrated by the equation.

6. $7(x - y) = 7x - 7y$

7. $\sqrt{7} \cdot 1 = \sqrt{7}$

8. $-2 \cdot \left(-\frac{1}{2}\right) = 1$

9. $2.3(3.4 \cdot 12.9) = (2.3 \cdot 3.4)(12.9)$

Write an algebraic expression to model each word phrase.

10. eight times the sum of a and b

11. four more than the product of x and y

12. six less than the quotient of d and g

13. ten less than twice the product of s and t

Simplify each expression.

14. $-x^2 + 2y - 3x^2 + 10$

15. $-2(d + 2e) + 5(3d - 8e)$

16. $-(a + 2b) + 4(a + 2b) - 2(a + 2b)$

17. $-3x + 14x + 7x^2 - 3x + 4x(x + 1)$

Identify a pattern by making a table of the inputs and outputs. Include a process column.

18.

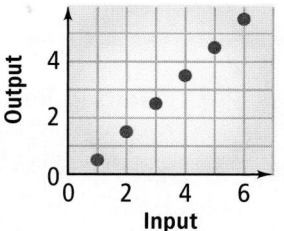

19.

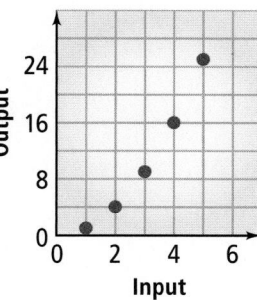

Evaluate each expression for $a = 4$, $b = -3$, and $c = 10$.

20. $7a - 5b$

21. $4a + b - |2c|$

22. $|a - b - c^2|$

Write an algebraic expression to model each situation.

23. You have 16 tomatoes, and your tomato plants produce 5 tomatoes each day.

24. Your car's gas tank holds 25 gallons, and you use 1.5 gallons of gas each day.

Do you UNDERSTAND?

25. Writing Explain why every integer is also a rational number.

26. Reasoning What expression describes the number of squares in the nth figure?

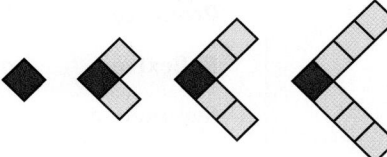

27. Reasoning Is there a Closure Property of Subtraction that applies to whole numbers? Explain.

1-4 Solving Equations

© Common Core State Standards

A-CED.A.1 Create equations and inequalities in one variable and use them to solve problems. **Also A-CED.A.4**

MP 1, MP 2, MP 3, MP 4, MP 6

Objectives To solve equations

To solve problems by writing equations

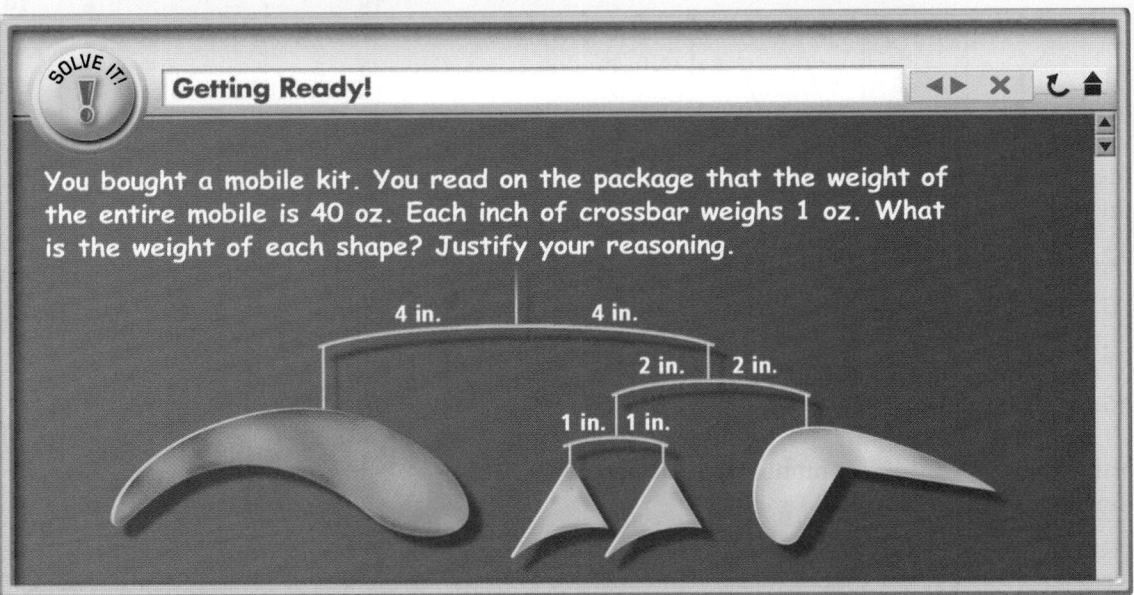

SOLVE IT!

Getting Ready!

You bought a mobile kit. You read on the package that the weight of the entire mobile is 40 oz. Each inch of crossbar weighs 1 oz. What is the weight of each shape? Justify your reasoning.

4 in.   4 in.

2 in.   2 in.

1 in.   1 in.

An **equation** is a statement that two expressions are equal. In this lesson you will use equations to model and solve problems.

Essential Understanding You can use the properties of equality and inverse operations to solve equations.

Lesson Vocabulary

- equation
- solution of an equation
- inverse operations
- identity
- literal equation

take note

Properties Properties of Equality

Assume a, b, and c represent real numbers.

Property	Definition	Example
Reflexive	$a = a$	$5 = 5$
Symmetric	If $a = b$, then $b = a$.	If $\frac{1}{2} = 0.5$, then $0.5 = \frac{1}{2}$.
Transitive	If $a = b$ and $b = c$, then $a = c$.	If $2.5 = 2\frac{1}{2}$ and $2\frac{1}{2} = \frac{5}{2}$, then $2.5 = \frac{5}{2}$.
Substitution	If $a = b$, then you can replace a with b and vice versa.	If $a = b$ and $9 + a = 15$, then $9 + b = 15$.

Properties   Properties of Equality, Continued

Assume a, b, and c represent real numbers.

Property	Definition	Example
Addition	If $a = b$, then $a + c = b + c$.	If $x = 12$, then $x + 3 = 12 + 3$.
Subtraction	If $a = b$, then $a - c = b - c$.	If $x = 12$, then $x - 3 = 12 - 3$.
Multiplication	If $a = b$, then $a \cdot c = b \cdot c$.	If $x = 12$, then $x \cdot 3 = 12 \cdot 3$.
Division	If $a = b$, then $a \div c = b \div c$ (with $c \neq 0$).	If $x = 12$, then $x \div 3 = 12 \div 3$.

Solving an equation that contains a variable means finding all values of the variable that make the equation true. Such a value is a **solution of the equation**. To find a solution, isolate the variable on one side of the equation using *inverse operations*.

Inverse operations are operations that "undo" each other. Addition and subtraction have this inverse relationship, as do multiplication and division.

 Problem 1 Solving a One-Step Equation

What is the solution of $x + 4 = -12$?

> Subtraction is the inverse operation of addition, so subtract 4 from each side.

$$x + 4 = -12$$
$$x + 4 - 4 = -12 - 4 \qquad \text{Subtraction Property of Equality}$$
$$x = -16 \qquad \text{Simplify.}$$

Check $\quad -16 + 4 \stackrel{?}{=} -12$

$$-12 = -12 ✔$$

 Got It? **1.** What is the solution of $12b = 18$?

 Problem 2 Solving a Multi-Step Equation

What is the solution of $-27 + 6y = 3(y - 3)$?

$$-27 + 6y = 3(y - 3)$$
$$-27 + 6y = 3y - 9 \qquad \text{Distributive Property}$$
$$6y = 3y + 18 \qquad \text{Add 27 to each side.}$$
$$3y = 18 \qquad \text{Subtract } 3y \text{ from each side.}$$
$$y = 6 \qquad \text{Divide each side by 3.}$$

GRIDDED RESPONSE

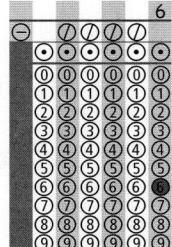

Got It? **2.** What is the solution of $3(2x - 1) - 2(3x + 4) = 11x$?

Problem 3 Using an Equation to Solve a Problem

Flowers "Flower carpets" incorporate hundreds of thousands of brightly-colored flowers as well as grass, tree bark, and sometimes fountains to form intricate designs and motifs. The flower carpet shown here, from Grand Place in Brussels, Belgium, has a perimeter of 200 meters. What are the dimensions of the flower carpet?

Plan

How can you relate the dimensions to the perimeter?
Use the formula for the perimeter of a rectangle.

Relate 2 · ⟨ width ⟩ plus 2 · ⟨ length ⟩ equals ⟨ perimeter ⟩

Define Let ⟨ x ⟩ = the width.

Then ⟨ $3x$ ⟩ = the length.

Write 2 · ⟨ x ⟩ + 2 · ⟨ $3x$ ⟩ = ⟨ 200 ⟩

$2x + 2 \cdot 3x = 200$

$2x + 6x = 200$ Multiply.

$8x = 200$ Combine like terms.

$\dfrac{8x}{8} = \dfrac{200}{8}$ Divide each side by 8.

$x = 25$ Simplify.

Find the length: $3x = 3 \cdot 25 = 75$.

The width is 25 meters. The length is 75 meters.

 Got It? 3. Suppose the flower carpet from Problem 3 had a perimeter of 320 meters. What would the dimensions of the flower carpet be?

An equation does not always have one solution. An equation has no solution if no value of the variable makes the equation true. An equation that is true for every value of the variable is an **identity**.

Essential Understanding Sometimes, no value of the variable makes an equation true. For identities, all values of the variable make the equation true.

Think

What does it mean for an equation to be sometimes true?
An equation is sometimes true if it is true for some, but not all, values of the variable.

 Problem 4 Equations With No Solution and Identities

Is the equation *always, sometimes,* or *never* true?

Ⓐ $11 + 3x - 7 = 6x + 5 - 3x$

$$4 + 3x = 3x + 5$$

$$4 = 5 \quad \boxed{\text{Never true!}}$$

The last equation is not true, so no value of x makes the first two equations true. The original equation has no solution. It is never true.

Ⓑ $6x + 5 - 2x = 4 + 4x + 1$

$$4x + 5 = 4x + 5$$

$$4x = 4x$$

$$0 = 0 ✔ \quad \boxed{\text{Always true!}}$$

The last equation is true, so any value of x makes the first three equations true. The original equation is always true. It is an identity.

Got It? **4.** Is the equation *always, sometimes,* or *never* true?

    a. $7x + 6 - 4x = 12 + 3x - 8$ **b.** $2x + 3(x - 4) = 2(2x - 6) + x$

A **literal equation** is an equation that uses at least two different letters as variables. You can solve a literal equation for any one of its variables by using the properties of equality. You solve for a variable "in terms of" the other variables.

 Problem 5 Solving a Literal Equation

The equation $C = \frac{5}{9}(F - 32)$ relates temperatures in degrees Fahrenheit F and degrees Celsius C. What is F in terms of C?

Plan

How do you solve a literal equation for one of its variables?
Use inverse operations to isolate the indicated variable.

$$C = \frac{5}{9}(F - 32)$$

$$\frac{9}{5}C = F - 32 \qquad \text{Multiply each side by } \frac{9}{5}.$$

$$\frac{9}{5}C + 32 = F \qquad \text{Add 32 to each side.}$$

$$F = \frac{9}{5}C + 32 \qquad \text{Symmetric Property}$$

 Got It? **5. a.** The equation $K = C + 273$ relates temperatures kelvins K and degrees Celsius C. What is C in terms of K?

    b. Reasoning Is the equation relating temperatures in kelvins and degrees Celsius *always, sometimes,* or *never* true? Explain your answer.

Lesson Check

Do you know HOW?

Solve each equation.

1. $w - 15 = 8.2$

2. $\frac{x}{3} = -30$

3. $2y - 1 = y + 11$

Solve each equation for k.

4. $r - 2k = 15$

5. $6k - 2z = 12$

6. $4k + h = -2k - 14$

Do you UNDERSTAND?

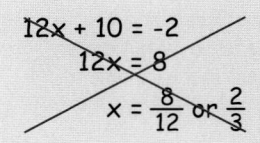

7. Vocabulary Explain what it means to find a solution of an equation.

8. Reasoning Suppose you solve an equation and find that your school needs 4.3 buses for a class trip. Explain how to interpret this solution.

9. Error Analysis Find the error(s) in the steps shown.

12x + 10 = -2
12x = 8
x = $\frac{8}{12}$ or $\frac{2}{3}$

Practice and Problem-Solving Exercises

 **Practice** Solve each equation.

See Problem 1.

10. $h - 12 = 6$ **11.** $-\frac{x}{3} = 27$ **12.** $4t = 48$ **13.** $22 + r = 36$

Solve each equation. Check your answer.

See Problem 2.

14. $7w + 2 = 3w + 94$ **15.** $15 - g = 23 - 2g$ **16.** $43 - 3d = d + 9$

17. $5y + 1.8 = 4y - 3.2$ **18.** $6a - 5 = 4a + 2$ **19.** $7y + 4 = 3 - 2y$

20. $5c - 9 = 8 - 2c$ **21.** $4y - 8 - 2y + 5 = 0$ **22.** $6(n - 4) = 3n$

23. $2 - 3(x + 4) = 8$ **24.** $5(2 - g) = 0$ **25.** $2(x + 4) = 8$

Write an equation to solve each problem.

See Problem 3.

26. Bus Travel Two buses leave Houston at the same time and travel in opposite directions. One bus averages 55 mi/h and the other bus averages 45 mi/h. When will they be 400 mi apart?

27. Aviation Two planes left an airport at noon. One flew east and the other flew west at twice the speed. After 3 hours the planes were 2700 mi apart. How fast was each plane flying?

28. Geometry The length of a rectangle is 3 cm greater than its width. The perimeter is 24 cm. What are the dimensions of the rectangle?

Determine whether the equation is *always*, *sometimes*, or *never* true.

See Problem 4.

29. $5x + 3 - 2x = 7x + 3$ **30.** $2(5x + 4) = 10x + 6$

31. $\frac{2}{3}x + 4 = 2x$ **32.** $6x - 12 + 2x = 3 + 8x - 15$

Solve each formula for the indicated variable.

 See Problem 5.

33. $A = \frac{1}{2}bh$, for h **34.** $s = \frac{1}{2}gt^2$, for g **35.** $V = lwh$, for w **36.** $I = prt$, for r

Solve each equation for x.

37. $ax + bx = c$ **38.** $\frac{x}{a} - 5 = b$ **39.** $\frac{x-2}{2} = m + n$ **40.** $\frac{2}{5}(x + 1) = g$

 **Apply**   **Solve each equation.**

41. $0.2(x + 3) - 4(2x - 3) = 0.9$ **42.** $12 - 3(2w + 1) = 7w - 3(7 + w)$

43. $(m - 2) - 5 = 8 - 2(m - 4)$ **44.** $7(a + 1) - 3a = 5 + 4(2a - 1)$

 45. Think About a Plan The measures of an angle and its complement differ by 22°. What are the measures of the angles?
- What is true about the sum of the measures of an angle and its complement?
- When modeling the problem with an equation, how can you algebraically represent that the two angle measures differ by 22°?

Solve each formula for the indicated variable.

46. $R(r_1 + r_2) = r_1 r_2$, for R **47.** $A = \frac{1}{2}h(b_1 + b_2)$, for b_2 **48.** $S = 2\pi r^2 + 2\pi rh$, for h

49. $h = vt - 5t^2$, for v **50.** $v = s^2 + \frac{1}{2}sh$, for h **51.** $R(r_1 + r_2) = r_1 r_2$, for r_2

 52. Writing Suppose you write and solve an equation to determine the amount of money m you have in your bank account after several weeks. You find that $m = -36$. What does this solution mean?

53. Geometry The measure of the supplement of an angle is 20° more than three times the measure of the original angle. Find the measures of the angles.

54. Find 4 consecutive odd integers with a sum of 184.

Solve each equation for x.

55. $c(x + 2) - 5 = b(x - 3)$ **56.** $a(3tx - 2b) = c(dx - 2)$ **57.** $b(5px - 3c) = a(qx - 4)$

58. $\frac{a}{b}(2x - 12) = \frac{c}{d}$ **59.** $\frac{3ax}{5} - 4c = \frac{ax}{5}$ **60.** $\frac{a-c}{x-a} = m$

Write an equation to solve each problem.

61. Swimming A city park is opening a new swimming pool. You can pay a daily entrance fee of $3 or purchase a membership for the 12-week summer season for $82 and pay only $1 per day to swim. How many days would you have to swim to make the membership worthwhile?

STEM 62. Rocket The first stage of a rocket burns 28 s longer than the second stage. If the total burning time for both stages is 152 s, how long does each stage burn?

63. Error Analysis Your friend says that the equations shown are two ways to write the same formula. Is your friend correct? Explain your answer.

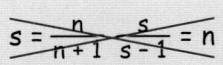

 **Challenge**

64. Assume that a, b, and c are integers and $a \neq 0$.

    a. Proof Prove that the solution of the linear equation $ax - b = c$ must be a rational number.

     b. Writing Describe the values of a, b, and c for which the solutions of $ax^2 + b = c$ are rational.

65. A tortoise crawling at a rate of 0.1 mi/h passes a resting hare. The hare wants to rest another 30 min before chasing the tortoise at a rate of 5 mi/h. How many feet must the hare run to catch the tortoise?

Apply What You've Learned

 **MATHEMATICAL PRACTICES**

MP 4

Look back at the information on page 3 about Mia helping her friend Cody after Cody's car runs out of gas. In the Apply What You've Learned in Lesson 1-2, you thought about the possible locations of Cody's car when it runs out of gas.

Suppose Cody runs out of gas between the gas station and the restaurant. Let x represent the distance between Cody's car and the gas station. Choose from the following numbers and expressions to complete the equation below. The equation represents the relationship among the distances Mia drives.

9	11	20	34
$2x$	x	$9 + x$	$x - 9$
$9 - x$	$x + 11$	$x - 11$	$11 - x$

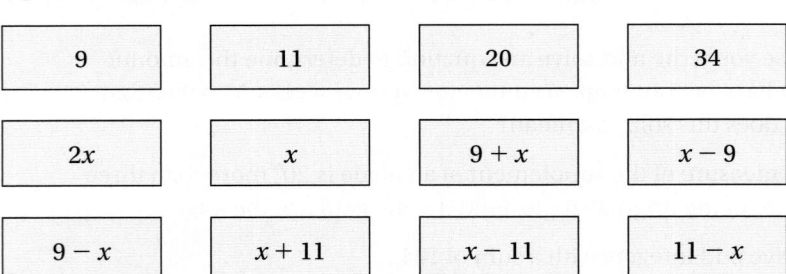

a. ___?___ + **b.** ___?___ + **c.** ___?___ = **d.** ___?___

from Mia's house to Cody's car   from Cody's car to gas station, then back to Cody's car   from Cody's car to the restaurant   total distance Mia drives

1-5 Solving Inequalities

Common Core State Standards

A-CED.A.1 Create equations and inequalities in one variable and use them to solve problems.

MP 1, MP 3, MP 4, MP 7

Objectives To solve and graph inequalities
To write and solve compound inequalities

Getting Ready!

You want to download some new songs on your MP3 player. Each song will use about 4.3 MB of space. The amount of storage space on your MP3 player is shown at the right. At most how many songs can you download? Explain. (Hint: 1 GB = 1000 MB)

7.8 GB free of 19.5 GB

Does your answer make sense? Check it using a different method.

MATHEMATICAL PRACTICES

Words like "at most" and "at least" suggest a relationship in which two quantities may not be equal. You can represent such a relationship with a mathematical inequality.

Essential Understanding Just as you use properties of equality to solve equations, you can use properties of inequality to solve inequalities.

Lesson Vocabulary
• compound inequality

take note

Key Concept Writing and Graphing Inequalities

Inequality	Word Sentence	Graph
$x > 4$	x is greater than 4.	number line from −1 to 5, open dot at 4, shaded right
$x \geq 4$	x is greater than or equal to 4.	number line from −1 to 5, closed dot at 4, shaded right
$x < 4$	x is less than 4.	number line from −1 to 5, open dot at 4, shaded left
$x \leq 4$	x is less than or equal to 4.	number line from −1 to 5, closed dot at 4, shaded left

In the graphs above, the point at 4 is a boundary point because it separates the graph of the inequality from the rest of the number line. An open dot at 4 means that 4 *is not* a solution. A closed dot at 4 means that 4 *is* a solution.

Problem 1 Writing an Inequality From a Sentence

What inequality represents the sentence, "5 fewer than a number is at least 12."?

5 fewer than a number is at least 12.

"Fewer" indicates subtraction.   "At least" indicates greater than or equal to.

$x - 5 \geq 12$

Got It? 1. What inequality represents the sentence, "The quotient of a number and 3 is no more than 15."?

Plan

How can you translate a sentence into an inequality?
Look for key words, such as "at least" or "greater than."

The solutions of an inequality are the numbers that make it true. The properties you use for solving inequalities are similar to the properties you use for solving equations. However, when you multiply or divide each side of an inequality by a negative number, you must reverse the inequality symbol.

take note

Properties Properties of Inequalities

Let a, b, c, and d represent real numbers.

Property	Definition	Example
Transitive	If $a > b$ and $b > c$, then $a > c$.	$5 > 3$ and $3 > 1$, so $5 > 1$
Addition	If $a > b$, then $a + c > b + c$.	$4 > 2$, so $4 + 1 > 2 + 1$
Subtraction	If $a > b$, then $a - c > b - c$.	$7 > 4$, so $7 - 3 > 4 - 3$
Multiplication	If $a > b$ and $c > 0$, then $ac > bc$.	$6 > 5$ and $3 > 0$, so $6(3) > 5(3)$
	If $a > b$ and $c < 0$, then $ac < bc$.	$3 > 2$ and $-4 < 0$, so $3(-4) < 2(-4)$
Division	If $a > b$ and $c > 0$, then $\frac{a}{c} > \frac{b}{c}$.	$9 > 3$ and $3 > 0$, so $\frac{9}{3} > \frac{3}{3}$
	If $a > b$ and $c < 0$, then $\frac{a}{c} < \frac{b}{c}$.	$12 > 6$ and $-6 < 0$, so $\frac{12}{-6} < \frac{6}{-6}$

Here's Why It Works The steps below show that if $a > b$, then $-a < -b$. Therefore, you need to reverse the inequality symbol when multiplying each side of the inequality $a > b$ by -1.

$$a > b$$
$$a - b > 0 \qquad \text{Subtract } b \text{ from each side.}$$
$$-b - (-a) > 0 \qquad a - b = -b + a = -b - (-a).$$
$$-b > -a \qquad \text{Add } -a \text{ to each side.}$$
$$-a < -b \qquad \text{Rewrite the inequality with } -a \text{ on the left side.}$$

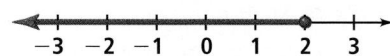

Problem 2 Solving and Graphing an Inequality

What is the solution of $-3(2x - 5) + 1 \geq 4$? Graph the solution.

$$-3(2x - 5) + 1 \geq 4$$

$-6x + 15 + 1 \geq 4$	Distributive Property
$-6x + 16 \geq 4$	Simplify.
$-6x \geq -12$	Subtraction Property of Inequality
$x \leq 2$	Divide each side by -6. Reverse the inequality symbol.

```
◄──┼──┼──┼──┼──┼──●──┼──►
  -3 -2 -1  0  1  2  3
```

 Got It? 2. What is the solution of $-2(x + 9) + 5 \geq 3$? Graph the solution.

Plan

How is solving an inequality like solving an equation?
You isolate the variable by doing the same things to each side of the inequality.

Problem 3 Using an Inequality

Movie Rentals A movie rental company offers two subscription plans. You can pay $36 a month and rent as many movies as desired, or you can pay $15 a month and $1.50 to rent each movie. How many movies must you rent in a month for the first plan to cost less than the second plan?

Plan

How will an inequality help answer this question?
The cost of the first plan must be less than the cost of the second plan, so an inequality can be used to determine the number of movies.

Think

Assign a variable.

Write an expression for the cost of each plan for a month.

The first plan must cost less than the second plan.

Solve.

Write the answer in words.

Write

Let n = the number of movie rentals in one month.

first plan: 36
second plan: 15 + 1.5n

36 < 15 + 1.5n

21 < 1.5n
14 < n

You must rent more than 14 movies in a month for the first plan to cost less .

 Got It? 3. A digital music service offers two subscription plans. The first has a $9 membership fee and charges $1 per download. The second has a $25 membership fee and charges $.50 per download. How many songs must you download for the second plan to cost less than the first plan?

Problem 4 No Solution or All Real Numbers as Solutions

Is the inequality *always*, *sometimes*, or *never* true?

A $-2(3x + 1) > -6x + 7$

$$-6x - 2 > -6x + 7 \quad \text{Distributive Property}$$

$$-2 > 7 \quad \text{Add } 6x \text{ to each side.}$$

The last inequality $-2 > 7$ is false, so $-2(3x + 1) > -6x + 7$ is always false. It has no solution, so it is never true.

B $5(2x - 3) - 7x \le 3x + 8$

$$10x - 15 - 7x \le 3x + 8 \quad \text{Distributive Property}$$

$$3x - 15 \le 3x + 8 \quad \text{Combine like terms.}$$

$$-15 \le 8 \quad \text{Subtract } 3x \text{ from each side.}$$

The inequality $-15 \le 8$ is true, so $5(2x - 3) - 7x \le 3x + 8$ is always true. All real numbers are solutions.

Think

How did you determine that an *equation* has no solution?
If you solve an equation and obtain a false statement, then the equation has no solution.

 Got It? **4.** Is $4(2x - 3) < 8(x + 1)$ *always*, *sometimes*, or *never* true?

You can join two inequalities with the word *and* or the word *or* to form a **compound inequality**. To solve a compound inequality containing *and*, find all values of the variable that make both inequalities true.

Think

How do you graph a compound inequality with *and*?
Find the intersection of the solutions of the two inequalities.

 Problem 5 Solving an *And* Inequality

What is the solution of $7 < 2x + 1$ and $3x \le 18$? Graph the solution.

$$7 < 2x + 1 \quad \text{and} \quad 3x \le 18$$

$$3 < x \quad \text{and} \quad x \le 6 \quad \text{Solve each inequality.}$$

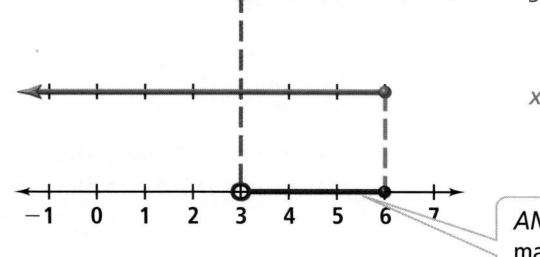

AND means that a solution makes *BOTH* inequalities true.

  Got It? **5. a.** What is the solution of $5 \le 3x - 1$ and $2x < 12$? Graph the solution.

       b. Reasoning Is the compound inequality in Problem 5 *always*, *sometimes*, or *never* true? Explain your reasoning.

You can collapse a compound *and* inequality, like $5 < x + 1$ and $x + 1 < 13$, into a simpler form, $5 < x + 1 < 13$. You read $5 < x + 1 < 13$ as "$x + 1$ is greater than 5 and less than 13."

To solve a compound inequality containing *or*, find all values of the variable that make at least one of the inequalities true.

Problem 6 Solving an *Or* Inequality

 Think
How does the solution to an *or* inequality differ from the solution to an *and* inequality?
The solution to an *or* inequality includes all of the solutions of each inequality, not just the solutions of both inequalities.

What is the solution of $7 + k \geq 6$ or $8 + k < 3$? Graph the solution.

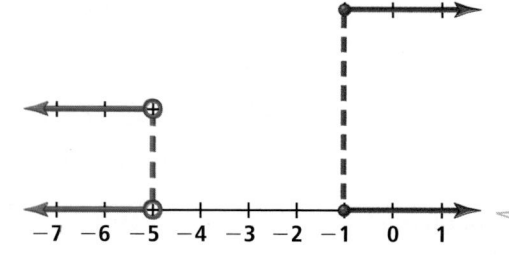

$$7 + k \geq 6 \quad \text{or} \quad 8 + k < 3$$
$$k \geq -1 \quad \text{or} \quad k < -5 \qquad \text{Subtraction Property of Inequality}$$

$k \geq -1$

$k < -5$

 OR means that a solution makes EITHER inequality true.

Got It? **6.** What is the solution of each compound inequality? Graph the solution.
  a. $7w + 3 > 11$ or $4w - 1 < -13$ **b.** $16 < 5x + 1$ or $3x + 9 < 6$

Lesson Check

Do you know HOW?

Write an inequality that represents each sentence.

1. Rachel's hair is at least as long as Julia's.

2. The wind speeds of tropical storms are at least 40 mi/h, but less than 74 mi/h.

Solve each inequality. Graph the solution.

3. $-4(3x + 2) \geq 16$

4. $3 < 5x - 2 < 7$

5. $7x - 3 > 18$ or $3x - 2 \leq -2$

Do you UNDERSTAND? MATHEMATICAL PRACTICES

6. Reasoning Make up an example to help explain why you must reverse the inequality symbol when you multiply or divide by a negative number.

7. Compare and Contrast Describe how the properties of inequality are similar to the properties of equality and how they differ.

8. Write an inequality for which the solution is the set of all real numbers.

9. Error Analysis Your classmate says that you cannot write a compound inequality that has no solution. Do you agree? If so, explain why. If not, give a counterexample.

Practice and Problem-Solving Exercises

 MATHEMATICAL PRACTICES

 **Practice**

Write the inequality that represents the sentence.

See Problem 1.

10. The sum of a number and 5 is less than -7.

11. The product of a number and 8 is at least 25.

12. Six less than a number is greater than 54.

13. The quotient of a number and 12 is no more than 6.

Solve each inequality. Graph the solution.

See Problem 2.

14. $-12 \geq 24x$

15. $-7k < 63$

16. $8a - 15 > 73$

17. $57 - 4t \geq 13$

18. $-18 - 5y \geq 52$

19. $14 - 4y \geq 38$

20. $4(x + 3) \leq 44$

21. $2(m - 3) + 7 < 21$

22. $4(n - 2) - 6 > 18$

23. $-2(w + 4) + 9 < -11$

Solve each problem by writing an inequality.

 See Problem 3.

24. The length of a picture frame is 3 in. greater than the width. The perimeter is less than 52 in. Describe the dimensions of the frame.

25. The lengths of the sides of a triangle are in the ratio 5 : 6 : 7. Describe the length of the longest side if the perimeter is less than 54 cm.

26. Find the lesser of two consecutive integers with a sum greater than 16.

27. The cost of a field trip is $220 plus $7 per student. If the school can spend at most $500, how many students can go on the field trip?

Is the inequality *always, sometimes,* or *never* true?

See Problem 4.

28. $9(x + 2) > 9(x - 3)$

29. $6x - 13 < 6(x - 2)$

30. $-6(2x - 10) + 12x \leq 180$

31. $-7(3x - 7) + 21x \geq 50$

32. $3 + 5x < 5(x + 1)$

33. $2(x + 6) < 30$

34. $4x - 8 > 1 + 4(x + 3)$

35. $9x + 2(2 + x) < 5 + 9x$

Solve each compound inequality. Graph the solution.

 See Problems 5 and 6.

36. $2x > -10$ and $9x < 18$

37. $3x \geq -12$ and $8x \leq 16$

38. $6x \geq -24$ and $9x < 54$

39. $7x > -35$ and $5x \leq 30$

40. $4x < 16$ or $12x > 144$

41. $3x \geq 3$ or $9x < 54$

42. $8x > -32$ or $-6x \geq 48$

43. $9x \leq -27$ or $4x \geq 36$

44. Think About a Plan The diagram shows the scores in seconds of a skater's first three trials in a speed-skating event. What is the maximum time she can score on her last trial so that her average time on all four trials is under 36 seconds?

- What do you need to find an average?
- What inequality can you use to model the situation?

Solve each inequality. Graph the solution.

45. $2 - 3z \geq 7(8 - 2z) + 12$

46. $6(x - 2.5) \geq 8 - 6(3.5 + x)$

47. $\frac{2}{3}(x - 12) \leq x + 8$

48. $\frac{3}{5}(x - 12) > x - 24$

49. $3[4x - (2x - 7)] < 2(3x - 5)$

50. $6[5y - (3y - 1)] \geq 4(3y - 7)$

51. Grades Your math test scores are 68, 78, 90, and 91. What is the lowest score you can earn on the next test and still achieve an average of at least 85?

52. Chemistry The pH level of a popular shampoo is between 6.0 and 6.5 inclusive. What compound inequality shows the pH levels of this shampoo? Graph the solution.

53. Geometry The sum of the lengths of any two sides of a triangle is greater than the length of the third side. In $\triangle ABC$, $BC = 4$ and $AC = 8 - AB$. What can you conclude about AB?

54. Writing Write a word problem that can be solved using $25 + 0.5x \leq 60$.

55. Error Analysis A classmate solved the inequality $\frac{1}{2}(y - 16) \geq y + 2$ as shown. Prove that his answer is incorrect by checking a number that is less than -20. (Select a number that makes the computation easy.) What was his error?

$$\frac{1}{2}(y - 16) \geq y + 2$$
$$\frac{1}{2}y - 8 \geq y + 2$$
$$-10 \geq \frac{1}{2}y$$
$$-20 \leq y$$

56. Construction A contractor estimated that her expenses for a construction project would be between $700,000 and $750,000. She has already spent $496,000. How much more can she spend and remain within her estimate?

Justifying Steps Justify each step by identifying the property used.

57. $3x \leq 4(x - 1) - 8$

$3x \leq 4x - 4 - 8$

$3x \leq 4x - 12$

$-x \leq -12$

$x \geq 12$

58. $\frac{1}{2}(y + 3) > \frac{1}{3}(4 - y)$

$3(y + 3) > 2(4 - y)$

$3y + 9 > 8 - 2y$

$5y + 9 > 8$

$5y > -1$

$y > -0.2$

Solve each compound inequality. Graph the solution.

59. $-6 < 2x - 4 < 12$

60. $4x \leq 12$ and $-7x \leq 21$

61. $15x > 30$ or $18x < -36$

 **Challenge** **Open-Ended** Write an inequality with a solution that matches the graph. At least two steps should be needed to solve your inequality.

62.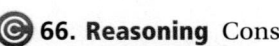
-4 -3 -2 -1 0 1 2 3 4

63.
-4 -3 -2 -1 0 1 2 3 4

64.
-4 -3 -2 -1 0 1 2 3 4

65.
-4 -3 -2 -1 0 1 2 3 4

Ⓒ **66. Reasoning** Consider the compound inequality $x < 8$ and $x > a$.
  a. Are there any values of a such that all real numbers are solutions of the compound inequality? If so, what are they?
  b. Are there any values of a such that no real numbers are solutions of the compound inequality? If so, what are they?
  c. Repeat parts (a) and (b) for the compound inequality $x < 8$ or $x > a$.

Standardized Test Prep

SAT/ACT

67. What is the solution of $1 < 2x + 3 < 9$?

   Ⓐ $-1 > x < 2$ Ⓑ $2 < x < 3$ Ⓒ $-1 < x < 2$ Ⓓ $-1 < x < 3$

68. Which expression best represents the value of x in $y = mx + b$?

   Ⓕ $\dfrac{b - y}{m}$ Ⓖ $\dfrac{y + b}{m}$ Ⓗ $m(y - b)$ Ⓘ $\dfrac{y - b}{m}$

69. The hourly rate of a waiter is $4 plus tips. On a particular day, the waiter worked 8 hours and received more than $150 in pay. Which could be the amount of tips the waiter received?

   Ⓐ $18.75   Ⓑ $32   Ⓒ $118   Ⓓ $120.75

Extended Response

70. Solve $3(x - 2) + 8 = 12$. Identify each property of real numbers or equality you use.

Mixed Review

Simplify each expression.   ◀ See Lesson 1-3.

71. $(2a - 4) + (5a + 9)$ **72.** $3(x + 3y) - 5(x - y)$

73. $\frac{1}{3}(b + 12) - \frac{1}{4}(b + 12)$ **74.** $0.4(k - 0.1) + 0.5(3.3 - k)$

Get Ready!   To prepare for Lesson 1-6, do Exercises 75–78.

Solve each equation. Check your answers.   ◀ See Lesson 1-4.

75. $7x - 6(11 - 2x) = 10$ **76.** $10x - 7 = 2(13 + 5x)$

77. $4y - \frac{1}{10} = 3y + \frac{4}{5}$ **78.** $0.4x + 1.18 = -3.1(2 - 0.01x)$

1-6 Absolute Value Equations and Inequalities

© **Common Core State Standards**

A-SSE.A.1b Interpret complicated expressions by viewing one or more of their parts as a single entity.
A-CED.A.1 Create equations and inequalities in one variable and use them to solve problems.
MP 1, MP 3

Objective To write and solve equations and inequalities involving absolute value

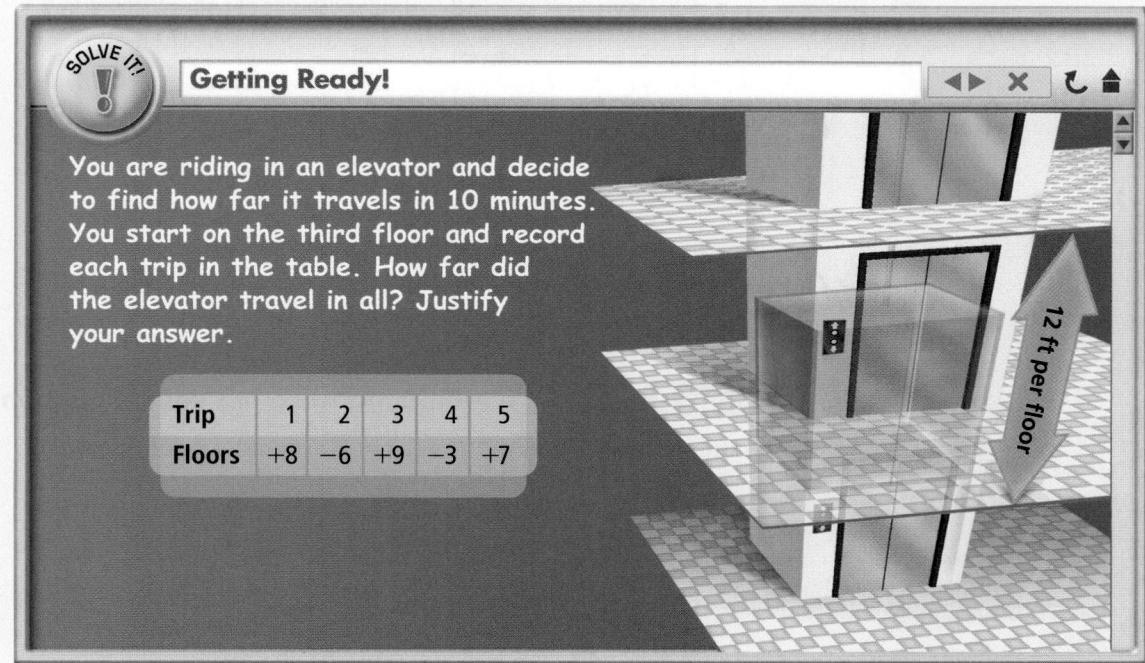

SOLVE IT!

Getting Ready!

You are riding in an elevator and decide to find how far it travels in 10 minutes. You start on the third floor and record each trip in the table. How far did the elevator travel in all? Justify your answer.

Trip	1	2	3	4	5
Floors	+8	−6	+9	−3	+7

12 ft per floor

In the Solve It, signed numbers represent distance and direction. Sometimes, only the size of a number (its *absolute value*), not the direction, is important.

Essential Understanding An absolute value quantity is nonnegative. Since opposites have the same absolute value, an absolute value equation can have two solutions.

Lesson Vocabulary
• absolute value
• extraneous solution

take note

Key Concept Absolute Value

Definition	Numbers	Symbols
The **absolute value** of a real number x, written $|x|$, is its distance from zero on the number line.	$|4| = 4$ $|-4| = 4$	$|x| = x$, if $x \geq 0$ $|x| = -x$, if $x < 0$

An absolute value equation has a variable within the absolute value sign. For example, $|x| = 5$. Here, the value of x can be 5 or −5 since $|5|$ and $|-5|$ both equal 5.

> Both 5 and −5 are 5 units from 0.

$$-6\ -5\ -4\ -3\ -2\ -1\ \ 0\ \ 1\ \ 2\ \ 3\ \ 4\ \ 5\ \ 6$$

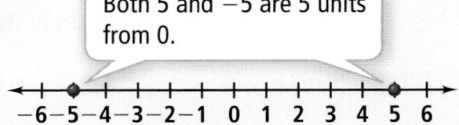

Problem 1 Solving an Absolute Value Equation

What is the solution of $|2x - 1| = 5$? Graph the solution.

$|2x - 1| = 5$

$2x - 1 = 5$ or $2x - 1 = -5$ Rewrite as two equations.
    $2x - 1$ could be 5 or -5.

$2x = 6$ | $2x = -4$ Add 1 to each side of both equations.

$x = 3$ or $x = -2$ Divide each side of both equations by 2.

Check $|2(3) - 1| \stackrel{?}{=} 5$ $|2(-2) - 1| \stackrel{?}{=} 5$

$|6 - 1| \stackrel{?}{=} 5$ $|-4 - 1| \stackrel{?}{=} 5$

$|5| = 5$ ✔ $|-5| = 5$ ✔

✅ **Got It?** **1.** What is the solution of $|3x + 2| = 4$? Graph the solution.

 Problem 2 Solving a Multi-Step Absolute Value Equation

Plan

Is there a simpler way to think of this problem?
Solving
$3|x + 2| - 1 = 8$
is similar to solving
$3y - 1 = 8$.

What is the solution of $3|x + 2| - 1 = 8$? Graph the solution.

$3|x + 2| - 1 = 8$

$3|x + 2| = 9$ Add 1 to each side.

$|x + 2| = 3$ Divide each side by 3.

$x + 2 = 3$ or $x + 2 = -3$ Rewrite as two equations.

$x = 1$ or $x = -5$ Subtract 2 from each side of both equations.

Check $3|(1) + 2| - 1 \stackrel{?}{=} 8$ $3|(-5) + 2| - 1 \stackrel{?}{=} 8$

$3|3| - 1 \stackrel{?}{=} 8$ $3|-3| - 1 \stackrel{?}{=} 8$

$8 = 8$ ✔ $8 = 8$ ✔

✅ **Got It?** **2.** What is the solution of $2|x + 9| + 3 = 7$? Graph the solution.

Distance from 0 on the number line cannot be negative. Therefore, some absolute value equations, such as $|x| = -5$, have no solution. It is important to check the possible solutions of an absolute value equation. One or more of the possible solutions may be *extraneous*.

An **extraneous solution** is a solution derived from an original equation that is *not* a solution of the original equation.

Problem 3 Checking for Extraneous Solutions

Think

Can you solve this the same way as you solved Problem 1?
Yes, let $3x + 2$ equal $4x + 5$ and $-(4x + 5)$.

What is the solution of $|3x + 2| = 4x + 5$? Check for extraneous solutions.

$$|3x + 2| = 4x + 5$$

$3x + 2 = 4x + 5$ or $3x + 2 = -(4x + 5)$ Rewrite as two equations.

$-x = 3$ $\qquad\qquad$ $3x + 2 = -4x - 5$ Solve each equation.

$\qquad\qquad\qquad\qquad$ $7x = -7$

$x = -3$ or $x = -1$

Check $|3(-3) + 2| \overset{?}{=} 4(-3) + 5$ $\qquad$ $|3(-1) + 2| \overset{?}{=} 4(-1) + 5$

$\qquad\quad |-9 + 2| \overset{?}{=} -12 + 5$ $\qquad\qquad$ $|-3 + 2| \overset{?}{=} -4 + 5$

$\qquad\qquad\quad |-7| \neq -7$ ✗ $\qquad\qquad\qquad$ $|-1| = 1$ ✔

Since $x = -3$ does not satisfy the original equation, -3 is an extraneous solution. The only solution to the equation is $x = -1$.

Got It? **3.** What is the solution of $|5x - 2| = 7x + 14$? Check for extraneous solutions.

The solutions of the absolute value inequality $|x| < 5$ include values greater than -5 *and* less than 5. This is the compound inequality $x > -5$ *and* $x < 5$, which you can write as $-5 < x < 5$. So, $|x| < 5$ means x is between -5 and 5.

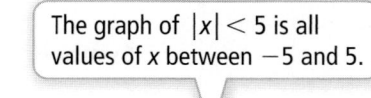
The graph of $|x| < 5$ is all values of x between -5 and 5.

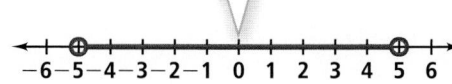
$-6\ -5\ -4\ -3\ -2\ -1\ \ 0\ \ 1\ \ 2\ \ 3\ \ 4\ \ 5\ \ 6$

Essential Understanding You can write an absolute value inequality as a compound inequality without absolute value symbols.

 Problem 4 Solving the Absolute Value Inequality $|A| < b$

Plan

Is this an *and* problem or an *or* problem?
$2x - 1$ is less than 5 and greater than -5. It is an *and* problem.

What is the solution of $|2x - 1| < 5$? Graph the solution.

$$|2x - 1| < 5$$

$-5 < 2x - 1 < 5$ $2x - 1$ is between -5 and 5.

$\qquad -4 < 2x < 6$ Add 1 to each part.

$\qquad -2 < x < 3$ Divide each part by 2.

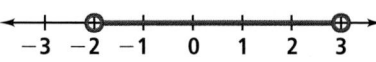
$-3\quad -2\quad -1\quad 0\quad 1\quad 2\quad 3$

Got It? **4.** What is the solution of $|3x - 4| \leq 8$? Graph the solution.

$|x| < 5$ means x is between -5 and 5. So, $|x| > 5$ means x is outside the interval from -5 to 5. You can say $x < -5$ *or* $x > 5$.

Ⓒ Problem 5 Solving the Absolute Value Inequality $|A| \geq b$

What is the solution of $|2x + 4| \geq 6$? Graph the solution.

$$|2x + 4| \geq 6$$

$2x + 4 \leq -6$ or $\quad 2x + 4 \geq 6$	Rewrite as a compound inequality.
$2x \leq -10$ $\qquad\qquad 2x \geq 2$	Subtract 4 from each side of both inequalities.
$x \leq -5$ or $\qquad\quad x \geq 1$	Divide each side of both inequalities by 2.

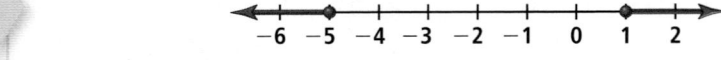

Think

How do you determine the boundary points?
To find the boundary points, find the solutions of the related equation.

✔ **Got It?** **5. a.** What is the solution of $|5x + 10| > 15$? Graph the solution.
  Ⓒ **b. Reasoning** Without solving $|x - 3| \geq 2$, describe the graph of its solution.

---

take note

Concept Summary   Solutions of Absolute Value Statements

Symbols	Definition	Graph
$|x| = a$	The distance from x to 0 is a units.	$x = -a$ or $x = a$
$|x| < a$ $(|x| \leq a)$	The distance from x to 0 is less than a units.	$-a < x < a$ $x > -a$ and $x < a$
$|x| > a$ $(|x| \geq a)$	The distance from x to 0 is greater than a units.	$x < -a$ or $x > a$

A manufactured item's actual measurements and its target measurements can differ by a certain amount, called *tolerance*. Tolerance is one half the difference of the maximum and minimum acceptable values. You can use absolute value inequalities to describe tolerance.

Problem 6 Using an Absolute Value Inequality

Car Racing In car racing, a car must meet specific dimensions to enter a race. Officials use a template to ensure these specifications are met. What absolute value inequality describes heights of the model of race car shown within the indicated tolerance?

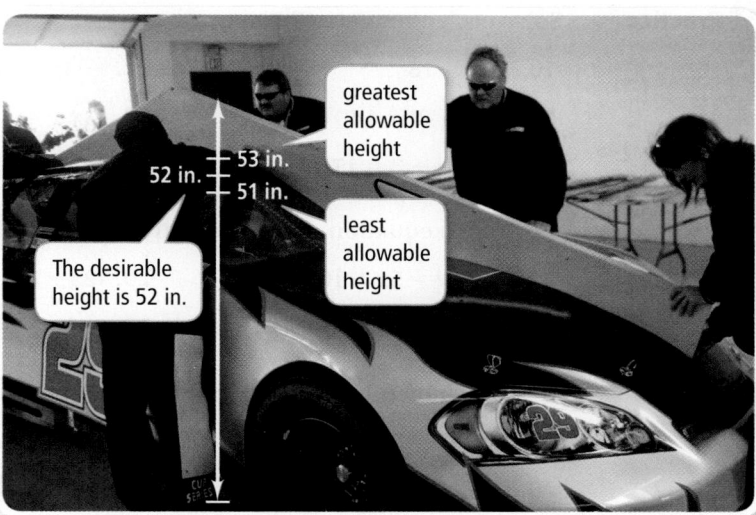

greatest allowable height

52 in.

53 in.
51 in.

least allowable height

The desirable height is 52 in.

Plan

How does *tolerance* relate to an inequality?
Tolerance allows the height to differ from a desired height by no less and no more than a small amount.

$\frac{53-51}{2} = \frac{2}{2} = 1$ Find the tolerance.

$-1 \le h - 52 \le 1$ Use h for the height of the race car. Write a compound inequality.

$|h - 52| \le 1$ Rewrite as an absolute value inequality.

 Got It? **6.** Suppose the least allowable height of the race car in Problem 6 was 52 in. and the desirable height was 52.5 in. What absolute value inequality describes heights of the model of race car shown within the indicated tolerance?

 Lesson Check

Do you know HOW?

Solve each equation. Check your answers.

1. $|-6x| = 24$

2. $|2x + 8| - 4 = 12$

3. $|x - 2| = 4x + 8$

Solve each inequality. Graph the solution.

4. $|2x + 2| - 5 < 15$

5. $|4x - 6| \ge 10$

Do you UNDERSTAND? MATHEMATICAL PRACTICES

© **6. Vocabulary** Explain what it means for a solution of an equation to be extraneous.

© **7. Reasoning** When is the absolute value of a number equal to the number itself?

8. Give an example of a compound inequality that has no solution.

© **9. Compare and Contrast** Describe how absolute value equations and inequalities are like linear equations and inequalities and how they differ.

Practice and Problem-Solving Exercises

MATHEMATICAL
PRACTICES

See Problems 1 and 2.

 **Practice**

Solve each equation. Check your answers.

10. $|3x| = 18$

11. $|-4x| = 32$

12. $|x - 3| = 9$

13. $2|3x - 2| = 14$

14. $|3x + 4| = -3$

15. $|2x - 3| = -1$

16. $|x + 4| + 3 = 17$

17. $|y - 5| - 2 = 10$

18. $|4 - z| - 10 = 1$

Solve each equation. Check for extraneous solutions.

See Problem 3.

19. $|x - 1| = 5x + 10$

20. $|2z - 3| = 4z - 1$

21. $|3x + 5| = 5x + 2$

22. $|2y - 4| = 12$

23. $3|4w - 1| - 5 = 10$

24. $|2x + 5| = 3x + 4$

Solve each inequality. Graph the solution.

See Problem 4.

25. $3|y - 9| < 27$

26. $|6y - 2| + 4 < 22$

27. $|3x - 6| + 3 < 15$

28. $\frac{1}{4}|x - 3| + 2 < 1$

29. $4|2w + 3| - 7 \le 9$

30. $3|5t - 1| + 9 \le 23$

Solve each inequality. Graph the solution.

See Problem 5.

31. $|x + 3| > 9$

32. $|x - 5| \ge 8$

33. $|y - 3| \ge 12$

34. $|2x + 1| \ge -9$

35. $3|2x - 1| \ge 21$

36. $|3z| - 4 > 8$

Write each compound inequality as an absolute value inequality.

See Problem 6.

37. $1.3 \le h \le 1.5$

38. $50 \le k \le 51$

39. $27.25 \le C \le 27.75$

40. $50 \le b \le 55$

41. $1200 \le m \le 1300$

42. $0.1187 \le d \le 0.1190$

B Apply

Solve each equation.

43. $-|4 - 8b| = 12$

44. $4|3x + 4| = 4x + 8$

45. $|3x - 1| + 10 = 25$

46. $\frac{1}{2}|3c + 5| = 6c + 4$

47. $5|6 - 5x| = 15x - 35$

48. $7|8 - 3h| = 21h - 49$

49. $2|3x - 7| = 10x - 8$

50. $6|2x + 5| = 6x + 24$

51. $\frac{1}{4}|4x + 7| = 8x + 16$

52. $\frac{2}{3}|3x - 6| = 4(x - 2)$

Ⓒ 53. Think About a Plan The circumference of a basketball for college women must be from 28.5 in. to 29.0 in. What absolute value inequality represents the circumference of the ball?
- What is the tolerance?
- What is the inequality without using absolute value?

Write an absolute value equation or inequality to describe each graph.

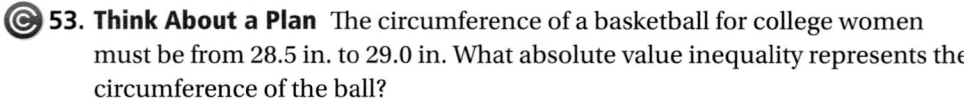

54.

55.

56.

Solve each inequality. Graph the solutions.

57. $|3x - 4| + 5 \le 27$

58. $|2x + 3| - 6 \ge 7$

59. $-2|x + 4| < 22$

60. $2|4t - 1| + 6 > 20$

61. $|3z + 15| \ge 0$

62. $|-2x + 1| > 2$

63. $\frac{1}{9}|5x - 3| - 3 \ge 2$

64. $\frac{1}{11}|2x - 4| + 10 \le 11$

65. $\left|\frac{x - 3}{2}\right| + 2 < 6$

66. $\left|\frac{x + 5}{3}\right| - 3 > 6$

Ⓒ **67. Writing** Describe the differences in the graphs of $|x| < a$ and $|x| > a$, where a is a positive real number.

Ⓒ **68. Open-Ended** Write an absolute value inequality for which every real number is a solution. Write an absolute value inequality that has no solution.

Write an absolute value inequality to represent each situation.

69. Cooking Suppose you used an oven thermometer while baking and discovered that the oven temperature varied between $+5$ and -5 degrees from the setting. If your oven is set to 350°, let t be the actual temperature.

70. Time Workers at a hardware store take their morning break no earlier than 10 A.M. and no later than noon. Let c represent the time the workers take their break.

71. Climate A friend is planning a trip to Alaska. He purchased a coat that is recommended for outdoor temperatures from $-15°F$ to $45°F$. Let t represent the temperature for which the coat is intended.

Write an absolute value inequality and a compound inequality for each length x with the given tolerance.

72. a length of 36.80 mm with a tolerance of 0.05 mm

73. a length of 9.55 mm with a tolerance of 0.02 mm

74. a length of 100 yd with a tolerance of 4 in.

Is the absolute value inequality or equation *always*, *sometimes*, or *never* true? Explain.

75. $|x| = -6$

76. $-8 > |x|$

77. $|x| = x$

78. $|x| + |x| = 2x$

79. $|x + 2| = x + 2$

80. $(|x|)^2 < x^2$

Ⓒ **81. Error Analysis** A classmate wrote the solution to the inequality $|-4x + 1| > 3$ as shown. Describe and correct the error.

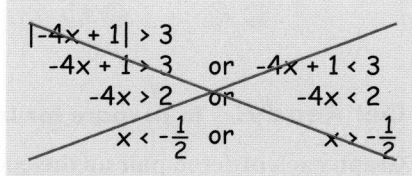

Challenge Solve each equation for x.

82. $|ax| - b = c$

83. $|cx - d| = ab$

84. $a|bx - c| = d$

Graph each solution.

85. $|x| \geq 5$ and $|x| \leq 6$

86. $|x| \geq 6$ or $|x| < 5$

87. $|x - 5| \leq x$

© **88. Writing** Describe the difference between solving $|x + 3| > 4$ and $|x + 3| < 4$.

© **89. Reasoning** How can you determine whether an absolute value inequality is equivalent to a compound inequality joined by the word *and* or one joined by the word *or*?

Standardized Test Prep

GRIDDED RESPONSE

SAT/ACT

90. What is the positive solution of $|3x + 8| = 19$?

91. If p is an integer, what is the least possible value of p in the following inequality?

$$|3p - 5| \leq 7$$

92. In wood shop, you have to drill a hole that is 2 inches deep into a wood panel. The tolerance for drilling a hole is described by the inequality $|t - 2| \leq 0.125$. What is the shallowest hole allowed?

93. The normal thickness of a metal structure is shown. It expands to 6.54 centimeters when heated and shrinks to 6.46 centimeters when cooled down. What is the maximum amount in cm that the thickness of the structure can deviate from its normal thickness?

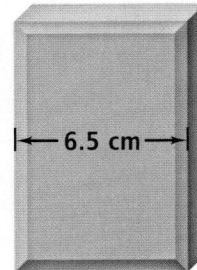

$\longleftarrow$ 6.5 cm $\longrightarrow$

Mixed Review

Solve each inequality. Graph the solution.

See Lesson 1-5.

94. $5y - 10 < 20$

95. $15(4s + 1) < 23$

96. $4a + 6 > 2a + 14$

Describe each pattern using words. Draw the next figure in each pattern.

See Lesson 1-1.

97.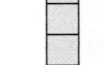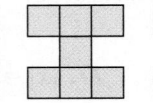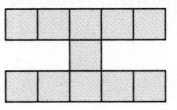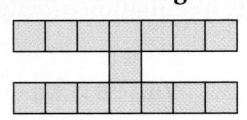

98.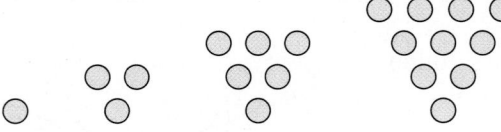

Get Ready! **To prepare for Lesson 2-1, do Exercises 99–102.**

See p. 977.

Graph each ordered pair on the coordinate plane.

99. $(-4, -8)$

100. $(3, 6)$

101. $(0, 0)$

102. $(-1, 3)$

Pull It **All Together**

Completing the Performance Task

Look back at your results from the Apply What You've Learned sections in Lessons 1-2, 1-3, and 1-4. Use the work you did to complete the following.

These problems will challenge you to pull together many concepts and skills of algebra that you have learned.

1. Solve the problem in the Task Description on page 3 by determining how far Cody is from Mia's house when his car runs out of gas. Find all possible distances. Show all your work and explain each step of your solution.

2. Reflect Choose one of the Mathematical Practices below and explain how you applied it in your work on the Performance Task.

MP 1: Make sense of problems and persevere in solving them.

MP 2: Reason abstractly and quantitatively.

MP 4: Model with mathematics.

On Your Own

Christine drives her car for her sales job. Her company allows her to drive no more than 50 mi per day.

On Tuesday, Christine drives to a business meeting 15 mi from her house. On her way, she realizes she left her laptop computer at home and must drive back to get it. After attending the business meeting, Christine drives to a client's office 8 mi down the road from the location of the business meeting, as shown in the diagram below. After meeting with her client, Christine drives home, returning by the same road.

Christine's House	Business Meeting	Client's Office
●—————————————	●—————————	●
15 mi	8 mi	

a. Write and simplify an algebraic expression that models the total distance Christine drives by the time she reaches her client's office. Be sure to tell what your variable represents.

b. In order for Christine not to exceed her company's daily mileage limit, what is the greatest distance she can drive before she turns around to go back for her laptop?

Chapter Review

1

Connecting **BIG** ideas and Answering Essential Questions

1 Variable
You can use variables to represent variable quantities in real-world situations and in patterns.

Patterns and Expressions (Lesson 1-1)
$$6, 12, 18, 24, \ldots\ 6n$$
$$8, 9, 10, 11, \ldots\ (n + 7)$$

Algebraic Expressions (Lesson 1-3)
$$6n$$
$$n + 7$$
$$5x - x = (5 - 1)x$$
$$a + 0 = a$$
$$h + k = k + h$$

2 Properties
The properties that apply to real numbers also apply to variables that represent them.

Properties of Real Numbers (Lesson 1-2)
$$4(6 - 1) = 4(6) - 4(1)$$
$$23 + 0 = 23$$
$$5 + 12 = 12 + 5$$

3 Solving Equations and Inequalities
You can use properties of numbers and equality (or inequality) to solve an equation (or inequality) by finding increasingly simpler equations (or inequalities) which have the same solution as the original equation (or inequality).

Solving Equations and Inequalities (Lessons 1-4 and 1-5)
$$4x - 1 = 5 \qquad 7 > -3h - 2$$
$$4x = 6 \qquad\ \ 9 > -3h$$
$$x = \tfrac{3}{2} \qquad\ \ -3 < h$$

Absolute Value Equations and Inequalities (Lesson 1-6)
$$|2b + 7| = 15$$
$$2b + 7 = 15 \quad \text{or} \quad 2b + 7 = -15$$
$$2b = 8 \qquad\qquad\ 2b = -22$$
$$b = 4 \quad \text{or} \qquad\ b = -11$$

Chapter Vocabulary

- absolute value (p. 41)
- additive inverse (p. 14)
- algebraic expression (p. 5)
- coefficient (p. 20)
- compound inequality (p. 36)
- constant (p. 5)
- constant term (p. 20)
- equation (p. 26)

- evaluate (p. 19)
- extraneous solution (p. 42)
- identity (p. 28)
- inverse operations (p. 27)
- like terms (p. 21)
- literal equation (p. 29)
- multiplicative inverse (p. 14)

- numerical expression (p. 5)
- opposite (p. 14)
- reciprocal (p. 14)
- solution of an equation (p. 27)
- term (p. 20)
- variable (p. 5)
- variable quantity (p. 5)

Choose the correct term to complete each sentence.

1. The ? makes an equation true.

2. A number's distance from zero on the number line is its ? .

3. ? is another name for the multiplicative inverse of a number.

4. A pair of inequalities joined by *and* or *or* are called a ? .

1-1 Patterns and Expressions

Quick Review

You can represent patterns using words, diagrams, numbers, and **algebraic expressions**. You can identify a pattern by looking for the same type of change between consecutive figures or numbers. It often helps to make a table.

Example

Identify a pattern by making a table of inputs and outputs. Include a process column. 7, 14, 21, 28, 35, . . .

Input	Process Column	Output
1	$1 \cdot 7$	7
2	$2 \cdot 7$	14
3	$3 \cdot 7$	21
$\vdots$	$\vdots$	$\vdots$
n	$n \cdot 7$	$7n$

The nth output is $7n$.

Exercises

Identify a pattern and find the next three numbers in the pattern.

5. 5, 10, 15, 20, . . .

6. 3, 4, 5, 6, . . .

Copy and complete the table. Then find the output when the input is n.

7.

Input	Output
1	9
2	10
3	11
4	■
$\vdots$	$\vdots$
n	■

8.

Input	Output
1	19
2	38
3	57
4	■
$\vdots$	$\vdots$
n	■

9. Finance If you put $20 in your savings account each week, how much have you saved after n weeks?

1-2 Properties of Real Numbers

Quick Review

The natural numbers, whole numbers, integers, rational numbers, and irrational numbers are all subsets of the real numbers.

You can use properties such as the ones listed below to simplify and evaluate expressions.

Commutative Properties	$-3 + 5 = 5 + (-3)$
	$2 \times 9 = 9 \times 2$
Associative Properties	$3 + (5 + 7) = (3 + 5) + 7$
	$4 \times (8 \times 11) = (4 \times 8) \times 11$
Distributive Property	$5(7 + 9) = 5(7) + 5(9)$

Example

Identify the property illustrated by the equation.

$4 \cdot x = x \cdot 4$ — Commutative Property of Multiplication

Exercises

Name the subset(s) of real numbers to which each number belongs.

10. 8.1π

11. -79

12. $\sqrt{121}$

13. $12\frac{7}{8}$

Compare the two numbers. Use $<$ or $>$.

14. $-\sqrt{60}, -8$

15. $5, \sqrt{32}$

Name the property of real numbers illustrated by each equation.

16. $\frac{9}{4} \cdot \frac{4}{9} = 1$

17. $\left(8 \cdot \frac{1}{3}\right) \cdot 12 = 8 \cdot \left(\frac{1}{3} \cdot 12\right)$

1-3, 1-4, and 1-5 Expressions, Equations, and Inequalities

Quick Review

You **evaluate** an algebraic expression by substituting numbers for the variables. You simplify an algebraic expression by combining **like terms**. To find the **solution of an equation** or inequality, use the properties of equality or inequality. Some **equations** and inequalities are true for all real numbers, and some have no solution.

Example

Evaluate $3(x - 4) + 2x - x^2$ for $x = 6$.

$3(6 - 4) + 2(6) - 6^2$	Substitute.
$= 3(2) + 2(6) - 6^2$	Simplify inside parentheses.
$= 6 + 12 - 36$	Multiply.
$= 18 - 36$	Add.
$= -18$	Subtract.

Exercises

18. Evaluate $3t(t + 2) - 3t^2$ for $t = 19$.

19. Simplify $-(3a - 2b) - 3(-a - b)$.

Solve each equation. Check your answer.

20. $2x - 5 = 17$

21. $3(x + 1) = 9 + 2x$

Solve each inequality. Graph the solution.

22. $4 - 5z \geq 2$

23. $2(5 - 3x) < x - 4(3 - x)$

Solve each compound inequality. Graph the solution.

24. $10 \geq 7 + 3x$ and $9 - 4x \leq 1$

25. $3 \geq 2x$ or $x - 4 > 2$

Write an equation to solve the problem.

26. Geometry The length and width of a rectangle are in the ratio $5 : 3$. The perimeter of the rectangle is 32 cm. Find the length and width.

1-6 Absolute Value Equations and Inequalities

Quick Review

To rewrite an equation or inequality that involves the **absolute value** of an algebraic expression, you must consider both cases of the definition of absolute value.

Example

Solve $|3x - 5| = 4 + 2x$. Check for extraneous solutions.

$3x - 5 = 4 + 2x$ or $3x - 5 = -(4 + 2x)$

$$3x - 5 = -4 - 2x$$
$$5x = 1$$

$x = 9$ or $x = \frac{1}{5}$

Check $|3(9) - 5| \stackrel{?}{=} 4 + 2(9)$ $\quad$ $\left|3\left(\frac{1}{5}\right) - 5\right| \stackrel{?}{=} 4 + 2\left(\frac{1}{5}\right)$

$|27 - 5| \stackrel{?}{=} 22$ $\qquad\qquad$ $\left|\frac{3}{5} - 5\right| \stackrel{?}{=} 4 + \frac{2}{5}$

$|22| = 22$ ✔ $\qquad\qquad$ $\left|-\frac{22}{5}\right| = \frac{22}{5}$ ✔

Exercises

Solve each equation. Check for extraneous solutions.

27. $|2x + 8| = 3x + 7$

28. $|x - 4| + 3 = 1$

29. $3|x + 10| = 6$

30. $2|x - 7| = x - 8$

Solve each inequality. Graph the solution.

31. $|3x - 2| + 4 \leq 7$

32. $4|y - 9| > 36$

33. $|7x| + 3 \leq 21$

34. $\frac{1}{2}|x + 2| > 6$

35. The specification for a length x is 43.6 cm with a tolerance of 0.1 cm. Write the specification as an absolute value inequality.

Chapter Test

Do you know HOW?

Evaluate each expression for $x = 5$.

1. $\frac{5}{3}(3x - 6) - (6 - 4x)$

2. $3(x^2 - 4) + 7(x - 2)$

3. $x - 2x + 3x - 4x + 5x$

Simplify each expression.

4. $a^2 + a + a^2$

5. $2x + 3y - 5x + 2y$

6. $5(a - 2b) - 3(a - 2b)$

7. $3[2(x - 3) + 2] + 5(x - 3)$

Solve each equation.

8. $4y - 6 = 2y + 8$

9. $3(2z + 1) = 35$

10. $5(3w - 2) - 7 = 23$

11. $t - 2(3 - 2t) = 2t + 9$

12. $5(s - 12) - 24 = 3(s + 2)$

13. The lateral surface area of a cylinder is given by the formula $S = 2\pi rh$. Solve the equation for r.

14. **Savings** Briana and her sister Molly both want to buy the same model bicycle. Briana needs $73 more before she can afford the bike. Molly needs $65 more. If they combine their money, they will have just enough to buy one bicycle that they could share. What is the cost of the bicycle?

15. **Musical** There is only one freshman in the cast of a high school musical. There are 6 sophomores and 11 juniors. One third of the cast are seniors. How many seniors are in the musical?

Determine whether each equation is *always*, *sometimes*, or *never* true.

16. $2x + 7 - x = 3 + x + 4$

17. $5a - 1 - 3a = 2a + 1$

Solve each equation or inequality. Graph the solution.

18. $3x + 17 \geq 5$

19. $25 - 2x < 11$

20. $\frac{3}{8}x < -6$ or $5x > 2$

21. $2 < 10 - 4d < 6$

22. $4 - x = |2 - 3x|$

23. $5|3w + 2| - 3 > 7$

Do you UNDERSTAND?

24. Writing Describe the relationships among these sets of numbers: natural numbers, whole numbers, integers, rational numbers, irrational numbers, and real numbers.

25. Reasoning Justify each step by identifying the property used.

$$
\begin{aligned}
t + 5(t + 1) &= t + (5t + 5) \\
&= (t + 5t) + 5 \\
&= (1t + 5t) + 5 \\
&= (1 + 5)t + 5 \\
&= 6t + 5
\end{aligned}
$$

26. Reasoning The first four figures of a pattern are shown.

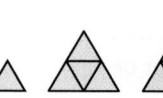

Describe the tenth figure in the pattern.

TIPS FOR SUCCESS

Some questions on tests ask you to write a short response. To get full credit for an answer, you must give the correct answer (including appropriate units, if applicable) and justify your reasoning or show your work. Read the sample question at the right. Then follow the tips to answer it.

TIP 1

Think about the total cost to make a batch of muffins.

Short Response Your school is having a bake sale to raise money for a field trip. The ingredients for each batch of bran muffins cost $3.25, and the cost for the energy to bake them is $.50. You plan to sell each batch for $5.

Write an expression to represent the total amount of money your school will have after selling n batches of muffins. Evaluate your expression for 25 batches. Show your work.

TIP 2

You need to make a profit in the bake sale in order to raise money. Consider the total sales and the cost to make the muffins. What operation do you use to find the profit?

Think It Through

It costs $3.25 + $.50 = $3.75 to bake each batch. The school makes $5 − ($3.75) = $1.25 after selling one batch. So, it makes $1.25n$ after selling n batches. It earns $1.25(25) = $31.25 after selling 25 batches. This answer is complete and earns full credit.

Vocabulary Builder

As you solve test items, you must understand the meanings of mathematical terms. Match each term with its mathematical meaning.

A. inequality

B. compound inequality

C. extraneous solution

D. expression

E. equation

I. a mathematical sentence that contains $>, <, \geq, \leq,$ or $\neq$

II. a solution of an equation derived from an original equation but not a solution of the original equation

III. a pair of inequalities joined by *and* or *or*

IV. a mathematical sentence that contains an equals sign

V. a mathematical phrase that uses numbers, variables, and operational symbols

Selected Response

Read each question. Then write the letter of the correct answer on your paper.

1. A person receives a salary of $600 a month and a 10% commission of all sales made. Which expression can be used to find the person's income when the sales amount is x?

    A) $x + 600$

    B) $600 - 0.10x$

    C) $10x + 600$

    D) $0.10x + 600$

2. Which expression can be used to find the next term of the sequence 1, 4, 9, 16, . . . ?

    F) $2n$

    G) $n + 3$

    H) $n^2 + 1$

    I) n^2

3. Which inequality has a solution that matches the graph below?

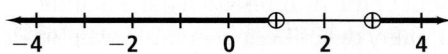

- Ⓐ $|x - 2| - 3 > -2$
- Ⓑ $|x - 2| < -5$
- Ⓒ $|x + 2| + 3 < 2$
- Ⓓ $|x + 4| + 2 > 1$

4. A worker is taking boxes of nails on an elevator. Each box weighs 54 lb, and the worker weighs 170 lb. The elevator has a weight limit of 2500 lb. Which inequality describes the number of boxes b that he can safely take on each trip?

- Ⓕ $54b - 170 \leq 2500$
- Ⓖ $54b + 170 \leq 2500$
- Ⓗ $54(b - 170) \leq 2500$
- Ⓘ $54(b + 170) \leq 2500$

5. An electrical circuit is connected in series as shown. The total voltage V can be calculated by using the equation shown, where I is the total current and R is the resistance across the circuit. $\left(Hint: 1\text{A} = 1\frac{\text{volt}}{\text{ohm}} \right)$

$$V = I(R_1 + R_2 + R_3)$$

$R_1 = 10\ \Omega \quad R_2$

$I = 2\ \text{A}$
$V = 120\ \text{V}$

$R_3 = 35\ \Omega$

A = amperes
V = volts
Ω = ohms

What is the value of R_2?

- Ⓐ $15\ \Omega$
- Ⓒ $60\ \Omega$
- Ⓑ $45\ \Omega$
- Ⓓ $75\ \Omega$

6. Solve $3(x - 2) + 4 \geq -3x + 1$.

- Ⓕ $x \geq -3$
- Ⓗ $x \geq \frac{3}{2}$
- Ⓖ $x \geq \frac{1}{2}$
- Ⓘ $x \leq 3$

7. You used an oven thermometer while baking and found out that the oven temperature varied between $+7$ degrees and -7 degrees from the setting. If your oven is set to 325°F, let t be the actual temperature. What is the absolute value inequality that represents this situation?

- Ⓐ $|t - 325| \geq 7$
- Ⓑ $|t - 325| < 7$
- Ⓒ $|t - 7| \leq 325$
- Ⓓ $|t - 325| \leq 7$

8. A designer is designing a handbag. The height of the handbag must be between 16 in. and 18 in. The desirable height is 17 in. Which absolute value inequality represents the height of the handbag?

- Ⓕ $|h - 16| \leq 1$
- Ⓗ $|h - 17| \geq 2$
- Ⓖ $|h - 17| \leq 1$
- Ⓘ $|h - 18| \geq 2$

9. A company makes gift boxes in different sizes following the pattern shown below. What is the volume of the fourth gift box to the nearest cubic inch?

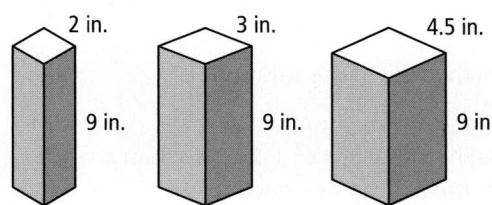

2 in.   3 in.   4.5 in.

9 in.   9 in.   9 in.

- Ⓐ 324 in.³
- Ⓑ 352 in.³
- Ⓒ 376 in.³
- Ⓓ 410 in.³

10. How many negative solutions does $2|3x - 6| \leq 6$ have?

- Ⓕ 0
- Ⓗ 2
- Ⓖ 1
- Ⓘ infinitely many

11. For which value of a does $4 = a + |x - 4|$ have no solution?

- Ⓐ -6
- Ⓒ 4
- Ⓑ 0
- Ⓓ 6

Constructed Response

12. The graph shows the amount of paint needed (in gallons) to paint the walls (in square feet) of an office building.

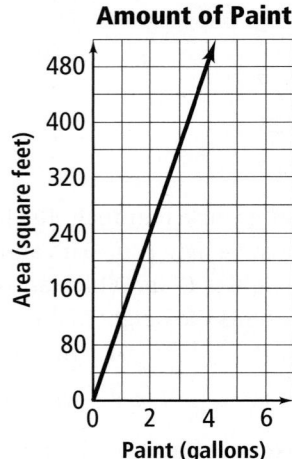

Amount of Paint

The pattern can be represented by $y = 120x$. How many gallons of paint will be needed to paint 900 square feet?

13. What is the sum of the solutions of $|2x + 4| - 6 = 8$?

14. What is the value of $4x^2 + 2x - 1$ when $x = \frac{3}{4}$? Express the answer as a decimal.

15. The cost for taking a taxi is $1.80 plus $.10 per eighth of a mile. What is the cost of a ride that is 4.5 miles long?

16. What is the coefficient of b in the simplified form of the expression $-8(a - 3b) + 2(-a + 4b + 1)$?

17. The expression $21 + 0.5n$ describes the length in inches of a baby n months old. How long is the baby at 6 months?

18. A new 10-lb dumbbell will pass inspection if it is between 9.95 lb and 10.05 lb. What is the tolerance of the weight of the dumbbell? What absolute value inequality describes acceptable weights of the dumbbell within an indicated tolerance? Show all work.

19. Is $7\sqrt{56}$ rational or irrational? Explain.

Extended Response

20. A trapezoidal deck has dimensions as shown.

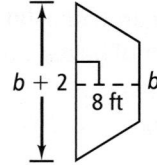

a. What is a formula for the area of this trapezoid?

b. Rearrange the formula so that it is solved for b. Show all work.

c. What is the longer base length if the area is 88 square feet (ft^2)?

21. The two cylinders below have identical bases.

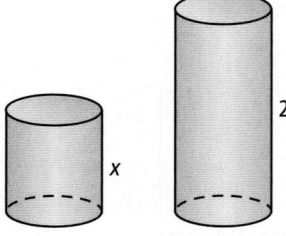

a. Write an equation for the volume of each cylinder in terms of x.

b. Solve each equation you wrote in (a) for x. Show all work.

c. Compare the volume of the shorter cylinder with the volume of the taller cylinder.

Get Ready!

Lesson 1-3 ◆ ## Simplifying Expressions

Simplify by combining like terms.

1. $7s - s$ **2.** $3a + b + a$ **3.** $xy - y + x$

4. $0.5g + g$ **5.** $4t - (t + 3t)$ **6.** $b - 2(1 + c - b)$

7. $5f - (5d - f)$ **8.** $2(h + 2g) - (g - h)$ **9.** $-(3z - 5) + z$

10. $(2 - d)g - 3d(4 + g)$ **11.** $5v - 3(2 - v)$ **12.** $7t - 3s(2 + t) + s$

Lesson 1-4 ◆ ## Solving Equations

Solve each equation.

13. $4 + x = -52$ **14.** $-y + 13 = -67$ **15.** $12 = 2 - k$

16. $3x = -72$ **17.** $\frac{h}{5} = 215$ **18.** $64 = 4 + 12g$

19. $5 - 4t = 12$ **20.** $7x - 9 = x$ **21.** $3(w - 8) = 36$

22. $-10p = 2(p - 12)$ **23.** $3(2 - c) = -(c + 4)$ **24.** $7 + b = 11(b - 3)$

Lesson 1-6 ◆ ## Solving Absolute Value Inequalities

Solve each absolute value inequality. Graph the solution.

25. $|x - 3| < 5$ **26.** $|2a - 1| \geq 2a + 1$ **27.** $|3x + 4| > -4x - 3$

28. $|3x + 1| + 1 > 12$ **29.** $3|d - 4| \leq 13 - d$ **30.** $-\frac{1}{3}|f + 3| + 2 \geq -5$

 # Looking Ahead Vocabulary

31. A person's field of study is often called that person's *domain*. If your domain is American history, what topics might you be interested in?

32. When is a person's height likely to show a greater *rate of change,* from 1 to 2 years of age or from 30 to 31 years of age? Explain.

33. When you look in the mirror, you see your *reflection*. How does the image in the mirror differ from the way other people see you? How is it the same?

34. The boundaries of a country determine the limit of the country's land. How does an inequality form a *boundary* on a number line?

CHAPTER 2

Functions, Equations, and Graphs

Download videos connecting math to your world.

Interactive! Vary numbers, graphs, and figures to explore math concepts.

The online Solve It will get you in gear for each lesson.

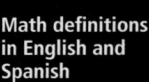

Math definitions in English and Spanish

Online access to stepped-out problems aligned to Common Core

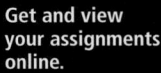

Get and view your assignments online.

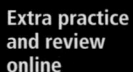

Extra practice and review online

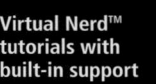 

Virtual Nerd™ tutorials with built-in support

Chapter Preview

Vocabulary

English/Spanish Vocabulary Audio Online:

English	Spanish
correlation, *p. 92*	correlación
direct variation, *p. 68*	variación directa
domain, *p. 61*	dominio
function, *p. 62*	función
linear equation, *p. 75*	ecuación lineal
range, *p. 61*	rango
relation, *p. 60*	relación
slope, *p. 74*	pendiente

BIG ideas

1 Equivalence
Essential Question Does it matter which form of a linear equation you use?

2 Function
Essential Question How do you use transformations to help graph absolute value functions?

3 Modeling
Essential Question How can you model data with a linear function?

 DOMAINS
- Interpreting Functions
- Building Functions
- Creating Equations

Common Core Performance Task

Road Maintenance

A county's Department of Transportation is repainting the lane lines on Main Street. Several streets that intersect Main Street are shown in the diagram below.

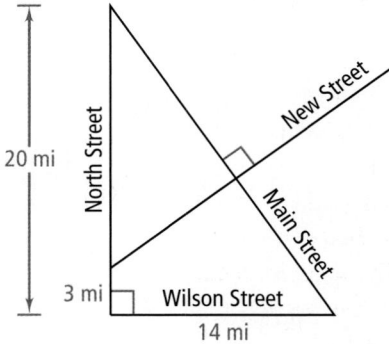

At 1 P.M., the work crew starts at the intersection of New Street and Main Street and moves toward the intersection of Main Street and Wilson Street, painting lane lines at an average speed of 5 mi/h. The work crew will take its afternoon break when it is 3 mi from the intersection of Main Street and Wilson Street.

Task Description

Determine what time the work crew will take its afternoon break.

Connecting the Task to the Math Practices

MATHEMATICAL PRACTICES

As you complete the task, you'll apply these Standards for Mathematical Practice.

- You'll use a coordinate plane to model the streets in the diagram. (MP 4)
- You'll write equations of lines to represent streets, and you will write and interpret a function modeling a distance that changes over time. (MP 2)

2-1 Relations and Functions

Common Core State Standards

Reviews F-IF.A.1 Understand that a function . . . assigns to each element of the domain exactly one element of the range. **Also Reviews F-IF.A.2**

MP 1, MP 3, MP 4

Objectives To graph relations
To identify functions

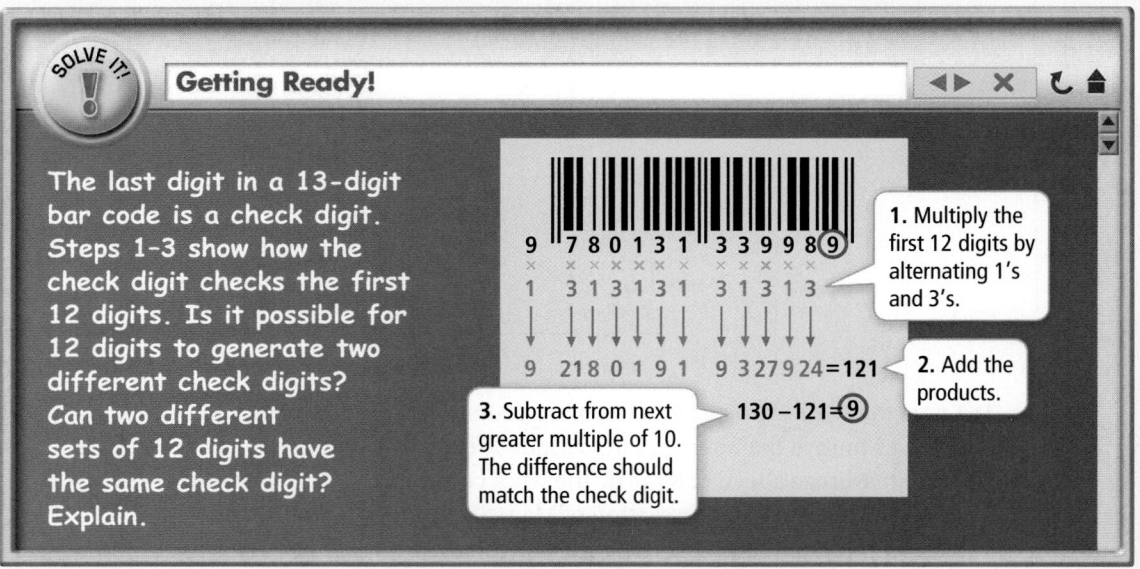

SOLVE IT!

Getting Ready!

The last digit in a 13-digit bar code is a check digit. Steps 1–3 show how the check digit checks the first 12 digits. Is it possible for 12 digits to generate two different check digits? Can two different sets of 12 digits have the same check digit? Explain.

9 780131 339989

1 313131 313133

9 218 0 1 9 1 9 3 27 9 24 = 121

1. Multiply the first 12 digits by alternating 1's and 3's.

2. Add the products.

3. Subtract from next greater multiple of 10. The difference should match the check digit.

130 − 121 = 9

You can use mappings to describe relationships between sets of numbers.

Essential Understanding A pairing of items from two sets is special if each item from one set pairs with exactly one item from the second set.

A **relation** is a set of pairs of input and output values. You can represent a relation in four different ways as shown below.

Lesson Vocabulary
- relation
- domain
- range
- function
- vertical-line test
- function rule
- function notation
- independent variable
- dependent variable

take note

Key Concept Four Ways to Represent Relations

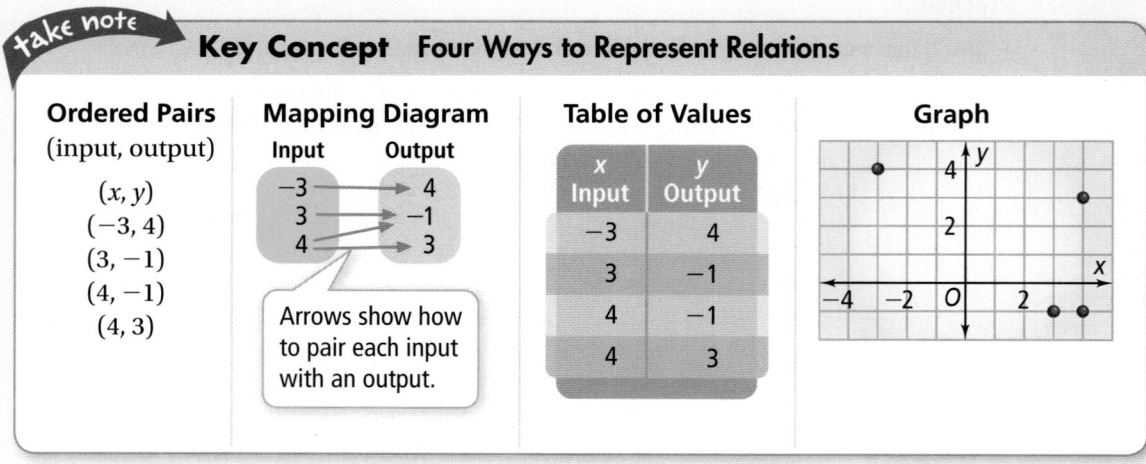

Ordered Pairs
(input, output)

(x, y)
$(-3, 4)$
$(3, -1)$
$(4, -1)$
$(4, 3)$

Mapping Diagram

Input   Output

−3 → 4
3 → −1
4 → 3

Arrows show how to pair each input with an output.

Table of Values

x Input	y Output
−3	4
3	−1
4	−1
4	3

Graph

Problem 1 Representing a Relation

Skydiving When skydivers jump out of an airplane, they experience free fall. The photos show various heights of a skydiver at different times during free fall, ignoring air resistance. How can you represent this relation in four different ways?

(0 seconds, 10,000 ft)

(8 seconds, 8976 feet)

(12 seconds, 7696 feet)

(4 seconds, 9744 ft)

(16 seconds, 5904 feet)

Think

What is the input? The output?
The input is the time. The output is the height above the ground.

Mapping Diagram

Input		Output
0	→	10,000
4	→	9744
8	→	8976
12	→	7696
16	→	5904

Ordered Pairs

$\{(0, 10{,}000),$
$(4, 9744),$
$(8, 8976),$
$(12, 7696),$
$(16, 5904)\}$

Table of Values

Time (s)	Height (ft)
0	10,000
4	9744
8	8976
12	7696
16	5904

Each time value represents an input, which is paired with its corresponding output value (height).

Graph

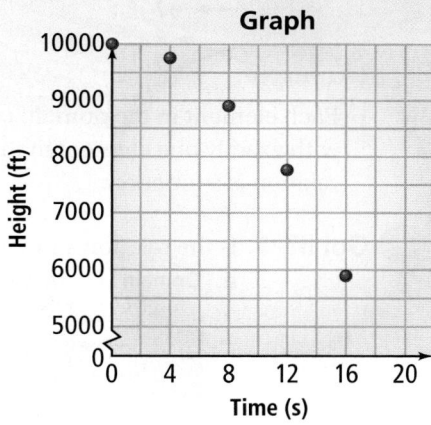

Got It? **1.** The monthly average water temperature of the Gulf of Mexico in Key West, Florida varies during the year. In January, the average water temperature is 69°F, in February, 70°F, in March, 75°F, and in April, 78°F. How can you represent this relation in four different ways?

The **domain** of a relation is the set of inputs, also called x-coordinates, of the ordered pairs. The **range** is the set of outputs, also called y-coordinates, of the ordered pairs.

Think

How could you use the mapping diagram in Problem 1 to find the domain and range?
The *input* corresponds to the domain of the relation. The *output* corresponds to the range.

© **Problem 2** Finding Domain and Range

Use the relation from Problem 1. What are the domain and range of the relation?

The relation is $\{(0, 10{,}000), (4, 9744), (8, 8976), (12, 7696), (16, 5904)\}$.

The domain is the set of x-coordinates. $\quad\{0, 4, 8, 12, 16\}$

The range is the set of y-coordinates. $\quad\{10{,}000, 9744, 8976, 7696, 5904\}$

✓ **Got It? 2.** What are the domain and range of this relation?
$$\{(-3, 14), (0, 7), (2, 0), (9, -18), (23, -99)\}$$

A **function** is a relation in which each element of the domain corresponds with exactly one element of the range.

Plan

How can you use a mapping diagram to determine whether a relation is a function?
A function has only one arrow from each element of the domain.

© **Problem 3** Identifying Functions

Is the relation a function?

A Domain   Range

-3 → -2
0 ⤬ 1
4 → 7

Each element in the domain corresponds with exactly one element in the range. This relation is a function.

B $\{(4, -1), (8, 6), (1, -1), (6, 6), (4, 1)\}$

Each x-coordinate must correspond to only one y-coordinate. The x-coordinate 4 corresponds to -1 and 1. The relation is *not* a function.

© ✓ **Got It? 3.** Is the relation a function?

a. Domain   Range

2 → -3
3 ⤬ -1
4 → 3
6 → 6

b. $\{(-7, 14), (9, -7), (14, 7), (7, 14)\}$

c. Reasoning How does a mapping diagram of a relation that is not a function differ from a mapping diagram of a function?

You can use the *vertical-line test* to determine whether a relation is a function. The **vertical-line test** states that if a vertical line passes through more than one point on the graph of a relation, then the relation is *not* a function.

Here's Why It Works If a vertical line passes through a graph at more than one point, there is more than one value in the range that corresponds to one value in the domain.

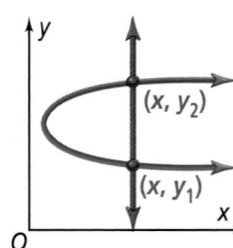

Problem 4 Using the Vertical-Line Test

Use the vertical-line test. Which graph(s) represent functions?

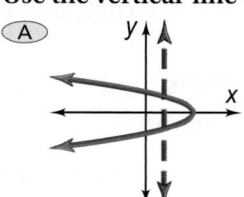 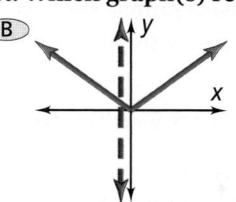 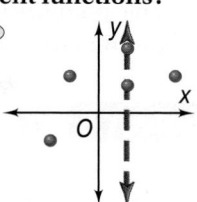

Think

Is a relation a function if it passes through the y-axis twice?
No; the y-axis is a vertical line so the relation fails the vertical-line test.

Graphs A and C fail the vertical-line test because for each graph, a vertical line passes through more than one point. They do not represent functions. Graph B does not fail the vertical-line test so it represents a function.

 Got It? 4. Use the vertical-line test. Which graph(s) represent functions?

a. 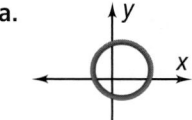   b. 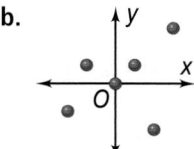   c.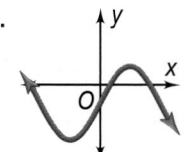

A **function rule** is an equation that represents an output value in terms of an input value. You can write a function rule in **function notation**. Shown below are examples of function rules.

$$y = 3x + 2 \qquad f(x) = 3x + 2 \qquad f(1) = 3(1) + 2$$

Output | Input

Read as "*f* of *x*" or "function *f* of *x*."

"*f* of 1" is the output when 1 is the input.

The **independent variable**, *x*, represents the input of the function. The **dependent variable**, *f(x)*, represents the output of the function. It is called the dependent variable because its value depends on the input value.

 Problem 5 Using Function Notation

For $f(x) = -2x + 5$, what is the output for the inputs, -3, 0, and $\frac{1}{4}$?

Plan

How do you find the output?
Substitute the input into the function rule and simplify.

x Input	Function Rule $f(x) = -2x + 5$	f(x) Output
−3	$f(-3) = -2(-3) + 5$	11
0	$f(0) = -2(0) + 5$	5
$\frac{1}{4}$	$f\left(\frac{1}{4}\right) = -2\left(\frac{1}{4}\right) + 5$	$4\frac{1}{2}$

 Got It? 5. For $f(x) = -4x + 1$, what is the output for the given input?

    a. -2 **b.** 0 **c.** 5

To model a real-world situation using a function rule, you need to identify the dependent and independent quantities. One way to describe the dependence of a variable quantity is to use a phrase such as, "distance is a function of time." This means that distance *depends* on time.

 Problem 6 Writing and Evaluating a Function

Ticket Price Tickets to a concert are available online for $35 each plus a handling fee of $2.50. The total cost is a function of the number of tickets bought. What function rule models the cost of the concert tickets? Evaluate the function for 4 tickets.

Think

Why is cost the dependent quantity?
Cost is dependent because the cost depends on the number of tickets bought.

Cost is the dependent quantity and the number of tickets is the independent quantity.

Relate | Total cost | is | cost per ticket | times | number of tickets bought | plus | handling fee |

Define Let t = number of tickets bought.

Let $C(t)$ = the total cost.

Write | $C(t)$ | = | 35 | $\cdot$ | t | + | 2.50 |

$C(t) = 35t + 2.50$

$C(4) = 35 \cdot 4 + 2.50$ Substitute 4 for t.

$= 142.50$ Simplify.

The cost of 4 tickets is $142.50.

Got It? 6. You are buying bottles of a sports drink for a softball team. Each bottle costs $1.19. What function rule models the total cost of a purchase? Evaluate the function for 15 bottles.

Lesson Check

Do you know HOW?

List the domain and range of each relation.

1. $\{(3, -2), (4, 4), (0, -2), (4, 1), (3, 2)\}$

2. $\{(0, 4), (4, 0), (-3, -4), (-4, -3)\}$

Determine whether each relation is a function.

3. $\{(3, -8), (-9, 1), (3, 2), (-4, 1), (-11, -2)\}$

4. $\{(1, 1), (2, 0), (3, 1), (4, 3), (0, 2)\}$

Do you UNDERSTAND? MATHEMATICAL PRACTICES

5. Vocabulary Can you have a relation that is not a function? Can you have a function that is not a relation? Explain.

6. Error Analysis Your friend writes, "In a function, every vertical line must intersect the graph in exactly one point." Explain your friend's error and rewrite the statement so that it is correct.

7. Reasoning Why is there no horizontal-line test for functions?

 **Practice**

Every year, the Rock and Roll Hall of Fame and Museum inducts legendary musicians and musical acts to the Hall. The table shows the number of inductees for each year.

◀ **See Problems 1 and 2.**

8. Represent the data using each of the following:
   a. a mapping diagram
   b. ordered pairs
   c. a graph on the coordinate plane

9. What are the domain and range of this relation?

Rock and Roll Hall of Fame Inductees

Year	Number of Inductees	Year	Number of Inductees
2001	11	2004	8
2002	8	2005	7
2003	9	2006	6

SOURCE: Rock and Roll Hall of Fame

Determine whether each relation is a function.

◀ **See Problem 3.**

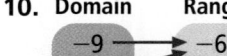

10.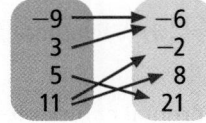
11.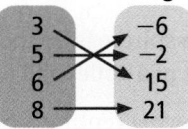
12.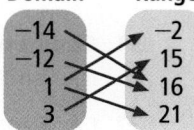

13. $\{(3, -9), (11, 21), (121, 34), (34, 1), (23, 45)\}$

Use the vertical-line test to determine whether each graph represents a function.

◀ **See Problem 4.**

14.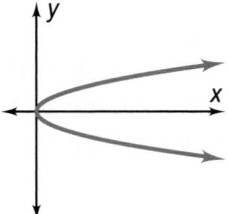
15.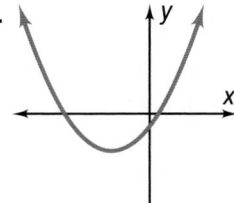
16.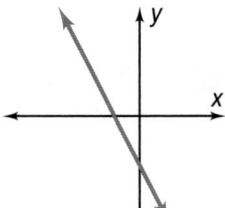

Evaluate each function for the given value of x, and write the input x and output $f(x)$ as an ordered pair.

◀ **See Problem 5.**

17. $f(x) = 17x + 3$ for $x = 4$

18. $f(x) = -\frac{2x + 1}{3}$ for $x = -5$

19. $f(x) = 2x - 33$ for $x = 9$

20. $f(x) = -9x - 2$ for $x = 7$

21. $f(x) = \frac{7}{3}x - 9$ for $x = 3$

22. $f(x) = -\frac{12x}{5}$ for $x = -1$

23. $f(x) = 11x - 11$ for $x = -11$

24. $f(x) = \frac{2}{9}x - \frac{9}{2}$ for $x = 9$

Write a function rule to model the cost per month of a long-distance cell phone calling plan. Then evaluate the function for the given number of minutes.

◀ **See Problem 6.**

25. Monthly service fee: $4.52
    Rate: $.12 per minute
    Minutes used: 250

26. Monthly service fee: $3.12
    Rate: $.18 per minute
    Minutes used: 175

27. Think About a Plan A cube is a solid figure with six square faces. If the edges of a cube have length 1.5 cm, what is the surface area of the cube?
- What is the relationship between the length of the edges and the area of each face?
- What is the relationship between the area of one face and the surface area of the whole cube?

28. Geometry Suppose you have a box with a 4 × 4-in. square base and variable height h. The surface area of this box is a function of its height. Write a function to represent the surface area. Evaluate the function for $h = 6.5$ in.

Find the domain and range of each relation, and determine whether it is a function.

29.

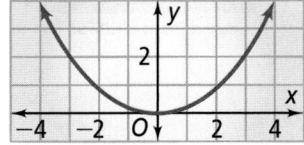

30.

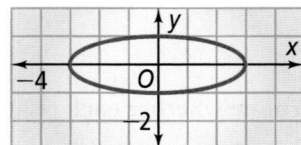

31. Geometry The volume of a sphere is a function of its radius, $V = \frac{4}{3}\pi r^3$. Evaluate the function for the volume of a volleyball with radius 10.5 cm.

32. Car Rental You are considering renting a car from two different rental companies. Proxy car rental company charges \$.32 per mile plus an \$18 surcharge. YourPal rental company charges \$.36 per mile plus a \$12 surcharge.
a. Write a function that shows the cost of renting a car from Proxy.
b. Write a function that shows the cost of renting a car from YourPal.
c. Which company offers the better deal for an 820-mile trip?

STEM **33. Temperature** The relation between degrees Fahrenheit F and degrees Celsius C is described by the function $F = \frac{9}{5}C + 32$. In the following ordered pairs, the first element is degrees Celsius and the second element is its equivalent in degrees Fahrenheit. Find the unknown measure in each ordered pair.

a. $(43, m)$ **b.** $(-12, n)$ **c.** $(p, 12)$ **d.** $(q, 19)$

34. Reasoning Suppose a function pairs items from set A with items from set B. You can say that the function maps *into* set B. If the function uses every item from set B, the function maps *onto* set B. Does each function below map the set of whole numbers *into* or *onto* the set of whole numbers?
a. Function f doubles every number.
b. Function g maps every number to 1 more than that number.
c. Function h maps every number to itself.
d. Function j maps every number to its square.

 Challenge

35. Reasoning Given the functions $f(x) = 3x - 21$ and $g(x) = 3x + 21$, show that the function $f(x) - g(x)$ is a constant for all the values of x.

Determine whether y is a function of x. Explain.

36. $y = \frac{3}{x} - 11$ **37.** $y^2 = 3x - 7$ **38.** $x^2 = 3y + y$

39. Chemistry The time required for a certain chemical reaction is related to the amount of catalyst present during the reaction. The domain of the relation is the number of grains of catalyst, and the range is the number of seconds required for a fixed amount of the chemical to react. The table shows the data from several reactions.

a. Is the relation a function?

b. If the domain and range were interchanged, would the relation be a function? Explain.

Catalyst and Reaction Time

Number of Grains	Number of Seconds
2.0	180
2.5	6
2.7	0.05
2.9	0.001
3.0	6
3.1	15
3.2	37
3.3	176

Standardized Test Prep

SAT/ACT

40. If $f(x) = -3x + 7$ and $g(x) = -7x + 3$, what is the value of $f(-3) - g(3)$?

Ⓐ 40　　　　　Ⓑ 34　　　　　Ⓒ 8　　　　　Ⓓ -8

41. What is the formula for the volume of a cylinder, $V = \pi r^2 h$, solved for h?

Ⓕ $h = \dfrac{r^2}{\pi V}$　　　Ⓖ $h = \dfrac{\pi V}{r^2}$　　　Ⓗ $h = \dfrac{V}{\pi r^2}$　　　Ⓘ $h = \dfrac{\pi r^2}{V}$

42. Which of the following statements are true?

I.　$-(-6) = 6$ and $-(-4) > -4$　　　　III.　$5 + 6 = 11$ or $9 - 2 = 11$

II.　$-(-4) < 4$ or $-10 > 10 - 10$　　　　IV.　$17 > 2$ or $6 < 9$

Ⓐ I and II only　　　Ⓑ I, II, and III only　　　Ⓒ I, III, and IV only　　　Ⓓ III and IV only

Short Response

43. What are the numbers 1.9, $\frac{5}{4}$, -1.2, and $\sqrt{3}$ in order from greatest to least?

Mixed Review

Solve each equation or inequality.　　　　　◀ **See Lessons 1-5 and 1-6.**

44. $|3x + 9| = 11$　　　**45.** $19 + |x - 1| = 33$　　　**46.** $2 - 3x < 11$

47. $5x - 3 \le 12 - 5x$　　　**48.** $|2x| + 4 < 7$　　　**49.** $4x + 6 \ge -6$

Get Ready!　To prepare for Lesson 2-2, do Exercises 50–52.　　　◀ **See Lesson 1-4.**

Solve each equation for y.

50. $12y = 3x$　　　**51.** $-10y = 5x$　　　**52.** $\frac{3}{4}y = 15x$

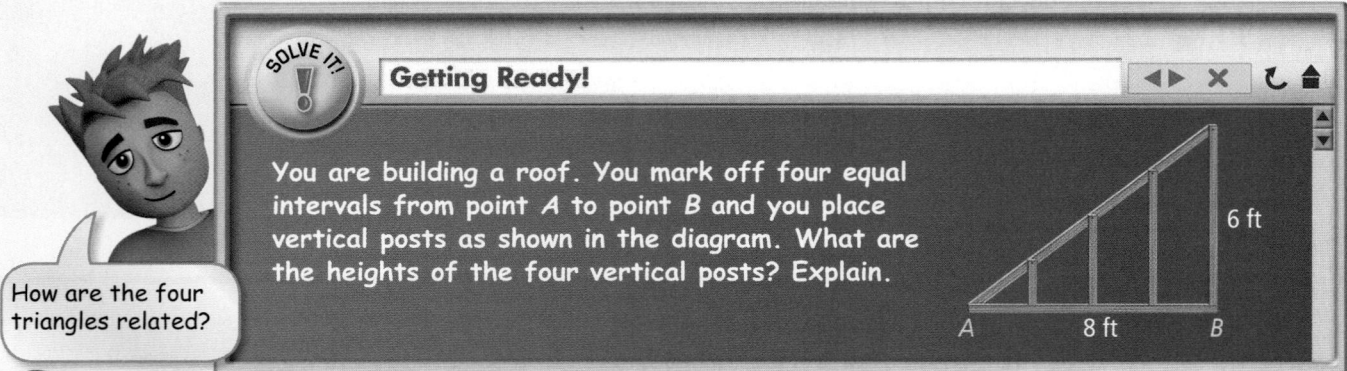

2-2 Direct Variation

© Common Core State Standards

A-CED.A.2 Create equations in two or more variables to represent relationships between quantities; graph equations on coordinate axes with labels and scales.
Also F-BF.A.1

MP 1, MP 3, MP 4

Objective To write and interpret direct variation equations

SOLVE IT!

Getting Ready!

You are building a roof. You mark off four equal intervals from point *A* to point *B* and you place vertical posts as shown in the diagram. What are the heights of the four vertical posts? Explain.

6 ft

A   8 ft   *B*

How are the four triangles related?

MATHEMATICAL PRACTICES

The post heights in the Solve It satisfy a relationship called *direct variation*.

Lesson Vocabulary
• direct variation
• constant of variation

Essential Understanding Some quantities are in a relationship where the ratio of corresponding values is constant.

You can write a formula for a **direct variation** function as $y = kx$, or $\frac{y}{x} = k$, where $k \neq 0$. x represents input values, and y represents output values. The formula $\frac{y}{x} = k$ says that, except for $(0, 0)$, the ratio of all output-input pairs equals the constant k, the **constant of variation**.

© Problem 1 **Identifying Direct Variation From Tables**

For each function, determine whether y varies directly with x. If so, what is the constant of variation and the function rule?

A

x	y
1	2
3	6
4	8

B

x	y
1	4
2	8
3	11

Think

How do you find the constant of variation?
The constant of variation is the ratio of any y-value to the corresponding x-value.

$\frac{y}{x} = \frac{2}{1} = \frac{6}{3} = \frac{8}{4} = 2$,

so y varies directly with x.

The constant of variation is 2.
The function rule is $y = 2x$.

$\frac{y}{x} = \frac{4}{1} = \frac{8}{2} \neq \frac{11}{3}$

so $\frac{y}{x}$ is *not* constant.

y does *not* vary directly with x.

Got It? **1.** For each function, determine whether y varies directly with x. If so, what are the constant of variation and the function rule?

a.

x	3	2	1
y	−21	−14	−7

b.

x	2	3	6
y	5	7	13

 Problem 2 Identifying Direct Variation From Equations

For each function, determine whether y varies directly with x. If so, what is the constant of variation?

A $3y = 7x$

Divide each side of the equation $3y = 7x$ by 3 to get $y = \frac{7}{3}x$. Since you can write the equation in the form $y = kx$, y varies directly with x. The constant of variation is $\frac{7}{3}$.

B $7y = 14x + 7$

Divide each side of the equation $7y = 14x + 7$ by 7 to get $y = 2x + 1$. Since you cannot write the equation in the form $y = kx$, y does not vary directly with x.

Think

How is the form of this function different from the function in part (A)?
This function includes a nonzero constant term.

 Got It? **2.** For each function, determine whether y varies directly with x. If so, what is the constant of variation?

a. $5x + 3y = 0$ **b.** $y = \frac{x}{9}$

In a direct variation, $\frac{y}{x}$ is the same for all pairs of data where $x \ne 0$. So, $\frac{y_1}{x_1} = \frac{y_2}{x_2}$ is true for the ordered pairs (x_1, y_1) and (x_2, y_2), where neither x_1 nor x_2 is zero.

 Problem 3 Using a Proportion to Solve a Direct Variation

Suppose y varies directly with x, and $y = 9$ when $x = -15$. What is y when $x = 21$?

Know

y varies directly with x.
$\frac{y}{x}$ is constant.

Need

The value of y when x is 21.

Plan

Use two forms of $\frac{y}{x}$ in a proportion.

$\dfrac{9}{-15} = \dfrac{y}{21}$ In a direct variation, $\frac{y}{x}$ is constant.

$9(21) = -15(y)$ Write the cross products.

$\dfrac{9(21)}{-15} = \dfrac{-15y}{-15}$ Divide each side by −15.

$-12.6 = y$ Simplify.

So y is −12.6 when x is 21.

 Got It? **3.** Suppose y varies directly with x, and $y = 15$ when $x = 3$. What is y when $x = 12$?

Problem 4 Using Direct Variation to Solve a Problem

Think

Could you use the method in Problem 3 to solve this problem?
Yes; you could solve this problem by using the proportion $\frac{c_1}{s_1} = \frac{c_2}{s_2}$.

A salesperson's commission varies directly with sales. For $1000 in sales, the commission is $85. What is the commission for $2300 in sales?

Step 1 Use $y = kx$ to find k.

Let $c =$ commission.
Let $s =$ sales.

$c = k(s)$ ◁ Commission varies directly with sales, so it is the dependent variable.

$85 = k(1000)$

$0.085 = k$

Step 2 Write the direct variation for the situation and find the commission when sales = $2300.

$c = k(s)$

$c = 0.085(s)$ Write the direct variation using k.

$c = 0.085(2300)$ Substitute 2300 for s.

$c = 195.5$ Simplify.

The commission for $2300 in sales is $195.50.

  Got It? **4. a.** The number of Calories varies directly with the mass of cheese. If 50 grams of cheese contain 200 Calories, how many Calories are in 70 grams of cheese?

     b. Reasoning If y^2 varies directly with x^2, does that mean y must vary directly with x? Explain.

The graph of a direct variation function is always a line through the origin.

 Problem 5 Graphing Direct Variation Equations

Think

What x-values should you use to make a table of values?
The constant of variation is a fraction. Use multiples of the denominator for x. This ensures integer values for y.

What is the graph of each direct variation equation?

Ⓐ $y = \frac{3}{4}x$ Ⓑ $y = -2x$

x	y
4	3
8	6
12	9

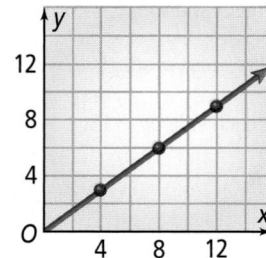

x	y
-2	4
-1	2
1	-2

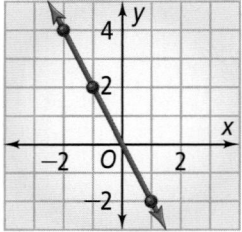

 Got It? **5.** What is the graph of each direct variation equation?

     a. $y = -\frac{2}{3}x$ **b.** $y = 3x$

Lesson Check

Do you know HOW?

1. Write a function rule for the direct variation in the table.

Identify the constant of variation.

2. $y = \frac{3}{2}x$

3. $4y - 5x = 0$

x	y
2	−1
4	−2
6	−3

Do you UNDERSTAND?

4. Vocabulary Explain what it means for two variables to be directly related.

5. Reasoning Explain why the graph of a direct variation function always passes through the origin.

6. Give an example of a function that represents a direct variation.

Practice and Problem-Solving Exercises

A Practice

For each function, determine whether y varies directly with x. If so, find the constant of variation and write the function rule.

◀ See Problem 1.

7.

x	y
2	14
3	21
5	35

8.

x	y
27	9
30	10
60	20

9.

x	y
11	22
16	32
7	42

10.

x	y
3	9
4	10
5	11

Determine whether y varies directly with x. If so, find the constant of variation.

◀ See Problem 2.

11. $y = 12x$

12. $y = 6x$

13. $y = -2x$

14. $y = 4x + 1$

15. $y = 4x - 3$

16. $y = -5x$

17. $y - 6x = 0$

18. $y + 3 = -3x$

For Exercises 19–24, y varies directly with x.

◀ See Problem 3.

19. If $y = 4$ when $x = -2$, find x when $y = 6$.

20. If $y = 6$ when $x = 2$, find x when $y = 12$.

21. If $y = 7$ when $x = 2$, find x when $y = 3$.

22. If $y = 5$ when $x = -3$, find x when $y = -1$.

23. If $y = -7$ when $x = -3$, find y when $x = 9$.

24. If $y = 25$ when $x = 15$, find y when $x = 6$.

25. Distance For a given speed, the distance traveled varies directly with the time. Kate's school is 5 miles away from her home and it takes her 10 minutes to reach the school. If Josh lives 2 miles from school and travels at the same speed as Kate, how long will it take him to reach the school?

◀ See Problem 4.

26. Conservation A dripping faucet wastes a cup of water if it drips for three minutes. The amount of water wasted varies directly with the amount of time the faucet drips. How long will it take for the faucet to waste $4\frac{1}{2}$ cups of water?

Make a table of x- and y-values and use it to graph the direct variation equation.

 See Problem 5.

27. $x = \left(-\frac{1}{3}\right)y$

28. $y = -9x$

29. $x = y$

B Apply

Determine whether y varies directly with x. If so, find the constant of variation and write the function rule.

30.

x	y
1	−2
3	−8
5	14

31.

x	y
9	6
12	8
15	10

32.

x	y
4	1
6	2
8	3

33.

x	y
23	24
55	56
66	67

34. Think About a Plan Suppose you make a 4-minute local call using a calling card and are charged 7.6 cents. The cost of a local call varies directly with the length of the call. How much more will it cost to make a 30-minute local call?
- Which quantity is the dependent quantity?
- How does the word "more" affect the method needed to solve the problem?

Write and graph a direct variation equation that passes through each point.

35. $(1, 2)$

36. $(-3, -7)$

37. $(2, -9)$

38. $(-0.1, 50)$

39. $(-5, -3)$

40. $(9, -1)$

41. $(7, 2)$

42. $(-3, 14)$

For Exercises 43–46, y varies directly with x.

43. If $y = \frac{1}{2}$ when $x = 4$, find y when $x = 5$.

44. If $y = \frac{3}{4}$ when $x = \frac{1}{2}$, find y when $x = 3$.

45. If $y = \frac{5}{3}$ when $x = \frac{3}{4}$, find x when $y = \frac{1}{2}$.

46. If $y = -\frac{5}{8}$ when $x = \frac{3}{2}$, find x when $y = \frac{2}{5}$.

47. Reasoning Explain why you cannot answer the following question.
If $y = 0$ when $x = 0$, what is x when $y = 13$?

Open-Ended Choose a value of k within the given range. Then write and graph a direct variation function using your value for k.

48. $0 < k < 1$

49. $3 < k < 4.5$

50. $-1 < k < -\frac{1}{2}$

51. Error Analysis Identify the error in the statement shown at the right.

> If y varies directly with x², and y = 2 when x = 4, then y = 3 when x = 9.

52. Sports The number of rotations of a bicycle wheel varies directly with the number of pedal strokes. Suppose that in the bicycle's lowest gear, 6 pedal strokes move the cyclist about 357 in. In the same gear, how many pedal strokes are needed to move 100 ft?

53. Writing Suppose you use the origin to test whether a linear equation is a direct variation function. Does this method work? Support your answer with an example.

In Exercises 54–55, *y* varies directly with *x*. Explain your answer.

54. If *x* is doubled, what happens to *y*? **55.** If *x* is divided by 7, what happens to *y*?

56. If *z* varies directly with the product of *x* and *y* ($z = kxy$), then *z* is said to vary jointly with *x* and *y*.

    a. Geometry The area of a triangle varies jointly with its base and height. What is the constant of variation?

    b. Suppose *q* varies jointly with *v* and *s*, and *q* = 24 when *v* = 2 and *s* = 3. Find *q* when *v* = 4 and *s* = 2.

    c. Reasoning Suppose *z* varies jointly with *x* and *y*, and *x* varies directly with *w*. Show that *z* varies jointly with *w* and *y*.

Standardized Test Prep

SAT/ACT

57. A speed of 75 mi/h is equal to a speed of 110 ft/s. To the nearest mile per hour, what is the speed of an aircraft traveling at a speed of 1600 ft/s?

58. What number is a solution to both $|x - 3| = 2$ and $|9 - x| = 8$?

59. If $f(x) = 7 - 3x$ and $g(x) = 3x - 7$, what is the value of $f(1) + g(1)$?

60. Look at the pattern. How many circles are in the 6th figure of this pattern?

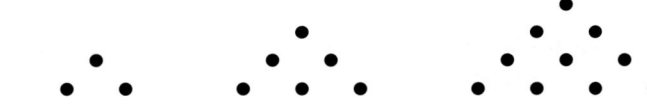

61. What is the solution of $4(x - 5) + x = 8x - 10 - x$?

Mixed Review

Graph each relation. Find the domain and range. ◀ See Lesson 2-1.

62. $\{(0, 1), (1, -3), (-2, -3), (3, -3)\}$ **63.** $\{(4, 0), (7, 0), (4, -1), (7, -1)\}$

64. $\{(1, -2), (2, -1), (4, 1), (5, 2)\}$ **65.** $\{(1, 7), (2, 8), (3, 9), (4, 10)\}$

Identify a pattern and find the next three numbers in the pattern. ◀ See Lesson 1-1.

66. 8, 16, 24, 32, . . . **67.** 5, 3, 1, −1, . . .

68. 144, 132, 120, 108, . . . **69.** 30, 45, 60, 75, . . .

Get Ready! To prepare for Lesson 2-3, do Exercises 70–73.

Evaluate each expression for $x = -2, 0, 1,$ **and 4.** ◀ See Lesson 1-3.

70. $\frac{2}{3}x + 7$ **71.** $\frac{3}{5}x - 2$ **72.** $3x + 1$ **73.** $\frac{1}{2}x - 8$

2-3 Linear Functions and Slope-Intercept Form

 Common Core State Standards

A-CED.A.2 Create equations in two or more variables to represent relationships between quantities; graph equations on coordinate axes with labels and scales.

Also F-IF.B.4, F-LE.B.5

MP 1, MP 3, MP 4

Objectives To graph linear equations
To write equations of lines

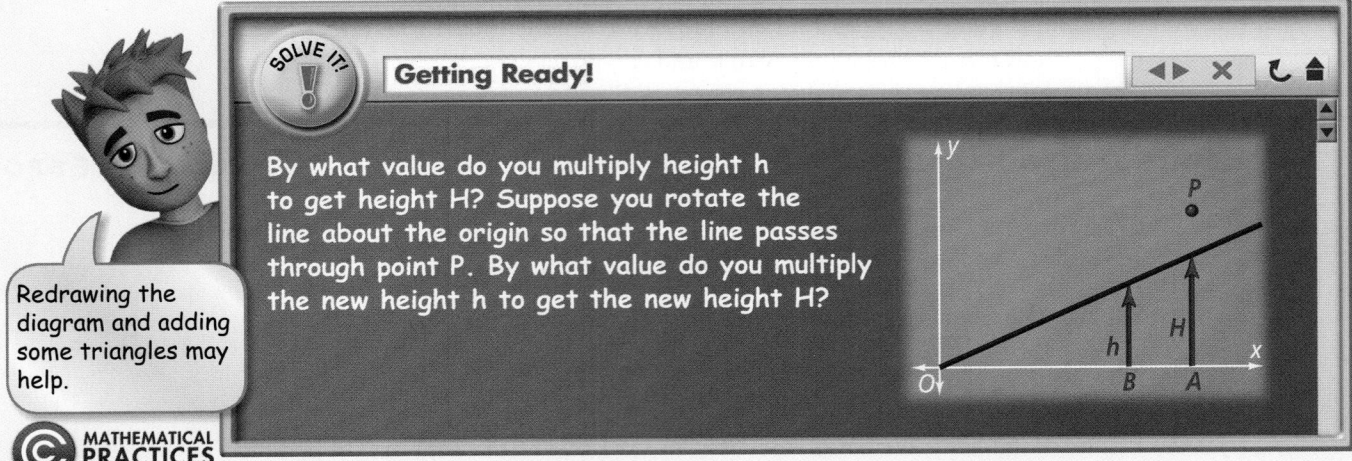

SOLVE IT!

Getting Ready!

By what value do you multiply height h to get height H? Suppose you rotate the line about the origin so that the line passes through point P. By what value do you multiply the new height h to get the new height H?

Redrawing the diagram and adding some triangles may help.

MATHEMATICAL PRACTICES

Lesson Vocabulary

- slope
- linear function
- linear equation
- y-intercept
- x-intercept
- slope-intercept form

You can describe movement in a coordinate plane by describing how far you need to move vertically and how far you need to move horizontally to get from one point to another point.

Essential Understanding Consider a nonvertical line in the coordinate plane. If you move from any point on the line to any other point on the line, the ratio of the vertical change to the horizontal change is constant. That constant ratio is the slope of the line.

The **slope** of a nonvertical line is the ratio of the vertical change to the horizontal change between two points. You can calculate slope by finding the ratio of the difference in the y-coordinates to the difference in the x-coordinates for any two points on the line.

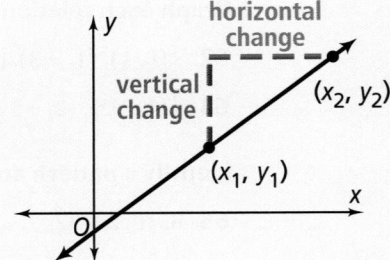

take note

Key Concept Slope

The slope of a nonvertical line through points (x_1, y_1) and (x_2, y_2) is the ratio of the vertical change to the corresponding horizontal change.

$$\text{slope} = \frac{\text{vertical change (rise)}}{\text{horizontal change (run)}} = \frac{y_2 - y_1}{x_2 - x_1}, \text{ where } x_2 - x_1 \neq 0$$

 **Problem 1** Finding Slope

What is the slope of the line that passes through the given points?

Ⓐ $(-3, 7)$ and $(-2, 4)$

$$m = \frac{y_2 - y_1}{x_2 - x_1} = \frac{4 - 7}{-2 - (-3)} = \frac{-3}{1}$$

The slope of the line that passes through $(-3, 7)$ and $(-2, 4)$ is $\frac{-3}{1}$ or -3.

Ⓑ $(3, 1)$ and $(-4, 1)$

$$m = \frac{y_2 - y_1}{x_2 - x_1} = \frac{1 - 1}{-4 - 3} = \frac{0}{-7} = 0$$

The slope of the line that passes through $(3, 1)$ and $(-4, 1)$ is $\frac{0}{-7}$ or 0.

Ⓒ $(7, -3)$ and $(7, 1)$

$$m = \frac{y_2 - y_1}{x_2 - x_1} = \frac{1 - (-3)}{7 - 7} = \frac{4}{0}$$

Division by zero is undefined, so slope is undefined for the line that passes through $(7, -3)$ and $(7, 1)$.

Got It? **1.** What is the slope of the line that passes through the given points?

    a. $(5, 4)$ and $(8, 1)$ **b.** $(2, 2)$ and $(-2, -2)$ **c.** $(9, 3)$ and $(9, -4)$

    d. Reasoning Use the slope formula to show in part (a) that it does not matter which point you choose for (x_1, y_1).

 Concept Summary Slope of a Line

Positive Slope	Negative Slope	Zero Slope	Undefined Slope
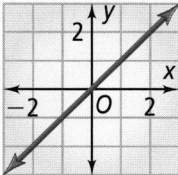	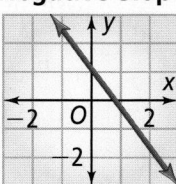	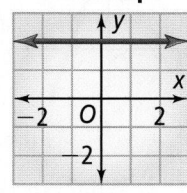	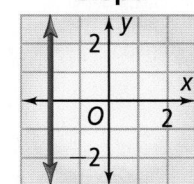
Line rises from left to right	Line falls from left to right	Horizontal line	Vertical line

A function whose graph is a line is a **linear function**. You can represent a linear function with a **linear equation**, such as $y = 6x - 4$. A solution of a linear equation is any ordered pair (x, y) that makes the equation true.

A special form of a linear equation is called *slope-intercept form*.

An *intercept* of a line is a point where a line crosses an axis. The **y-intercept** of a nonvertical line is the point at which the line crosses the y-axis. The **x-intercept** of a nonhorizontal line is the point at which the line crosses the x-axis.

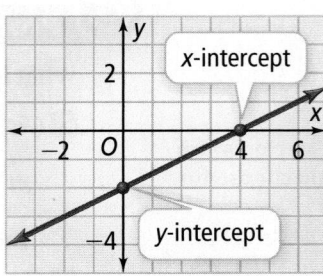

---

take note

Key Concept   Slope-Intercept Form

The **slope-intercept form** of an equation of a line is $y = mx + b$, where m is the slope of the line and $(0, b)$ is the y-intercept.

© **Problem 2** **Writing Linear Equations**

What is an equation of each line?

A $m = \frac{1}{5}$ and the y-intercept is $(0, -3)$

$y = mx + b$ Use the slope-intercept form.

$y = \frac{1}{5}x + (-3)$ Substitute $m = \frac{1}{5}$ and $b = -3$.

$y = \frac{1}{5}x - 3$ Simplify.

Plan

What information do you need from the graph?
You need the y-intercept and another point to find the slope.

B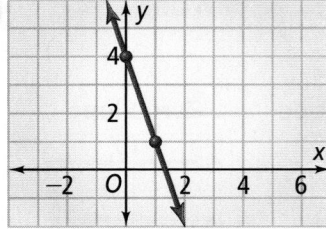

Look at the line shown in the graph. The y-intercept is the point where the line crosses the y-axis, $(0, 4)$, so $b = 4$.

Use the second point $(1, 1)$ to find the slope.

$m = \dfrac{y_2 - y_1}{x_2 - x_1} = \dfrac{1 - 4}{1 - 0} = -3.$

So, $y = -3x + 4$.

© **✓ Got It?** **2.** What is an equation of each line?

    a. $m = 6$, y-intercept is $(0, 5)$

    b.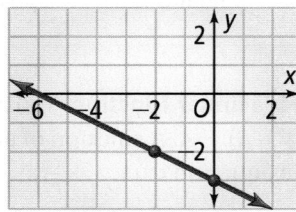

    c. Reasoning Using the graph from part (b), do you get a different equation if you use $(-6, 0)$ and the y-intercept to find the slope of the line? Explain.

You can rewrite a linear equation in slope–intercept form by solving for y.

Problem 3 Writing Equations in Slope-Intercept Form

Write the equation in slope-intercept form. What are the slope and y-intercept?

Ⓐ $5x - 4y = 16$

$$-4y = -5x + 16 \qquad \text{Subtract } 5x \text{ from each side.}$$

$$\frac{-4y}{-4} = \frac{-5x}{-4} + \frac{16}{-4} \qquad \text{Divide each side by } -4.$$

$$y = \frac{5}{4}x - 4 \qquad \text{Compare the equation with } y = mx + b$$

The slope $m = \frac{5}{4}$. The y-intercept is $(0, -4)$.

Ⓑ $-\frac{3}{4}x + \frac{1}{2}y = -1$

$$\frac{1}{2}y = \frac{3}{4}x - 1 \qquad \text{Add } \frac{3}{4}x \text{ to each side.}$$

$$y = \frac{3}{2}x - 2 \qquad \text{Multiply each side by 2.}$$

The slope $m = \frac{3}{2}$. The y-intercept is $(0, -2)$.

Think

Is there another way to solve this problem?
Yes; clear the fractions by multiplying all terms by 4, the LCM of the denominators.

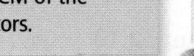 **Got It?** **3.** Write the equation in slope-intercept form. What are the slope and y-intercept?

    a. $3x + 2y = 18$ **b.** $-7x - 5y = 35$

Problem 4 Graphing a Linear Equation

What is the graph of $-2x + y = 1$?

Know	Need	Plan
• The equation of a line	Two points to draw the line	• Write the equation in slope-intercept form. • Plot the y-intercept. • Use the slope to find a second point. • Draw a line through the two points.

Write the equation in slope-intercept form.

$$-2x + y = 1$$
$$y = 2x + 1$$

The slope is 2 and the y-intercept is $(0, 1)$.

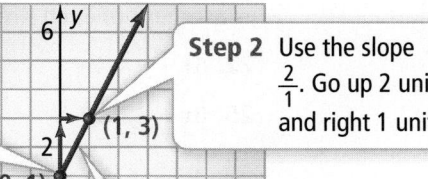

Step 1 Plot the y-intercept.

Step 2 Use the slope $\frac{2}{1}$. Go up 2 units and right 1 unit.

Step 3 Draw a line through the two points.

 Got It? **4.** What is the graph of $4x - 7y = 14$?

Lesson Check

Do you know HOW?

Write each equation in slope-intercept form.

1. $x - 2y + 3 = 1$

2. $-4x + 3y = 1$

What is the slope of the line passing through the following points?

3. $(2, 4)$ and $(4, 2)$

4. $(-1, -3)$ and $(3, 1)$

Do you UNDERSTAND?

5. Vocabulary What is a y-intercept? How is a y-intercept different from an x-intercept?

6. Explain why the slope of a vertical line is called "undefined."

7. Error Analysis A classmate found the slope between two points. What error did she make?

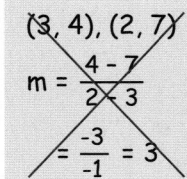

Practice and Problem-Solving Exercises

 **Practice**   Find the slope of the line through each pair of points.   ◀ **See Problem 1.**

8. $(1, 6)$ and $(8, -1)$ **9.** $(-3, 9)$ and $(0, 3)$ **10.** $(0, 0)$ and $(2, 6)$

11. $(-4, -3)$ and $(7, 1)$ **12.** $(-2, -1)$ and $(8, -3)$ **13.** $(1, 2)$ and $(2, 3)$

14. $(2, 7)$ and $(-3, 11)$ **15.** $(-3, 5)$ and $(4, 5)$ **16.** $(-5, -7)$ and $(0, 10)$

Write an equation for each line.   ◀ **See Problem 2.**

17. $m = 3$ and the y-intercept is $(0, 2)$.

19. $m = \frac{5}{6}$ and the y-intercept is $(0, 12)$.

20. $m = 0$ and the y-intercept is $(0, -2)$.

21. $m = -5$ and the y-intercept is $(0, -7)$.

18.

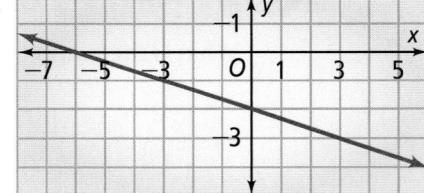

Write each equation in slope-intercept form. Then find the slope and y-intercept of each line.   ◀ **See Problem 3.**

22. $5x + y = 4$ **23.** $-3x + 2y = 7$ **24.** $-\frac{1}{2}x - y = \frac{3}{4}$

25. $8x + 6y = 5$ **26.** $9x - 2y = 10$ **27.** $y = 7$

Graph each equation.   ◀ **See Problem 4.**

28. $y = 2x$ **29.** $y = -3x - 1$ **30.** $y = 3x - 2$

31. $y = -4x + 5$ **32.** $5x - 2y = -4$ **33.** $-2x + 5y = -10$

34. $y - 3 = -2x$ **35.** $y + 4 = -3x$ **36.** $-y + 5 = -2x$

B Apply

Graph each equation.

37. $y = -\frac{1}{2}x - \frac{3}{2}$

38. $y = -2x + 3$

39. $y = -x + 7$

40. $3y - 2x = -12$

41. $4x + 5y = 20$

42. $4x - 3y = -6$

43. $\frac{2}{3}x + \frac{y}{3} = -\frac{1}{3}$

44. $x = 5$

45. $2.4 = -3.6x - 0.4y$

46. Think About a Plan Suppose the equation $y = 12 + 10x$ models the amount of money in your wallet, where y is the total in dollars and x is the number of weeks from today. If you graphed this equation, what would the slope represent in the situation? Explain.

- Is the equation in slope-intercept form?
- What units make sense for the slope?

Find the slope and y-intercept of each line.

47.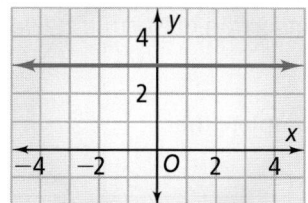

48.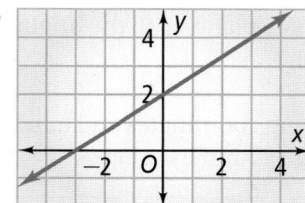

49.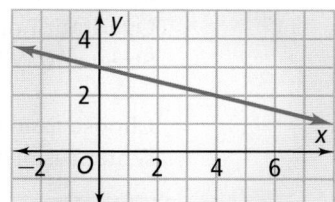

Find the slope and y-intercept of each line.

50. $y = 0.4 - 0.8x$

51. $x = -3$

52. $y = 0$

53. $-\frac{1}{3}x - \frac{2}{3}y = \frac{5}{3}$

54. $-Ax + By = -C$

55. $\frac{A}{D}x + \frac{B}{D}y = \frac{C}{D}$

56. The equation $d = 4 - \frac{1}{15}t$ represents your distance from home d for each minute you walk t.

a. If you graphed this equation, what would the slope represent? What would the constant term 4 represent? Explain.

b. Are you walking towards or away from your home? Explain.

57. Reasoning Use the graph to find the slope between the following points on the line.

a. P and Q **b.** Q and S

c. S and P **d.** R and Q

e. Make a conjecture based on your answers to parts (a)–(d).

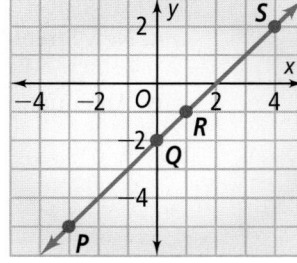

58. Error Analysis A classmate says that the graph of $3y - 2x = 5$ has a slope of 2. What mistake did he make?

Find the slope of the line through each pair of points.

59. $\left(\frac{3}{2}, -\frac{1}{2}\right)$ and $\left(-\frac{2}{3}, \frac{1}{3}\right)$

60. $\left(-\frac{1}{2}, -\frac{1}{2}\right)$ and $(-3, -4)$

61. $\left(0, -\frac{1}{2}\right)$ and $\left(\frac{7}{5}, 10\right)$

62. You can find the equation of a line through two points even if one point is not the
y-intercept.
- Find the slope *m* of the line passing through the two points.
- Using either point, substitute for *x*, *y*, and *m* into $y = mx + b$.
- Solve for *b* and rewrite $y = mx + b$ for the values of *m* and *b*.

Write an equation in slope-intercept form for the line passing through each
pair of points.

a. (2, 5) and (6, 7) **b.** (−4, 16) and (3, −5) **c.** (−2, 17) and (2, 1)

Apply What You've Learned

MP 4

Look back at the information on page 59 about the work crew that is painting
lane lines on Main Street. Copy the diagram of the streets and place it in
Quadrant 1 of a coordinate plane, with the origin at the intersection of North
Street and Wilson Street.

Choose from the following coordinates and equations to complete the
sentences below. Explain your reasoning.

(0, 14)	(14, 0)	(0, 20)	(20, 0)	(0, 3)
(3, 0)	(0, 17)	(14, 20)	$y = -\frac{10}{7}x + 17$	$y = \frac{7}{10}x + 17$
$y = \frac{10}{7}x + 20$	$y = -\frac{10}{7}x + 20$	$y = -\frac{7}{10}x + 20$	$y = \frac{7}{10}x + 20$	$y = -\frac{7}{10}x + 17$

a. North Street and Main Street intersect at ? .

b. Wilson Street and Main Street intersect at ? .

c. New Street intersects North Street at ? .

d. An equation of the line that represents Main Street is ? .

More About Linear Equations

© Common Core State Standards

F-IF.C.9 Compare properties of two functions each represented in a different way . . . **Also F-IF.A.2, F-IF.C.8, A-CED.A.2, F-LE.B.5**

MP 1, MP 3, MP 7

Objective To write an equation of a line given its slope and a point on the line

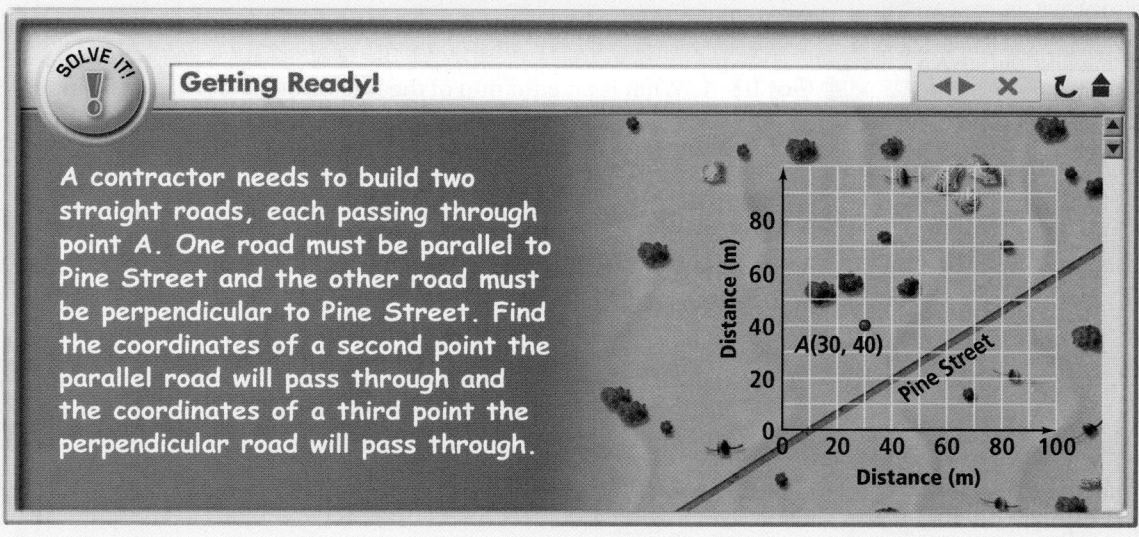

Getting Ready!

A contractor needs to build two straight roads, each passing through point A. One road must be parallel to Pine Street and the other road must be perpendicular to Pine Street. Find the coordinates of a second point the parallel road will pass through and the coordinates of a third point the perpendicular road will pass through.

Lesson Vocabulary
- point-slope form
- standard form of a linear equation
- parallel lines
- perpendicular lines

If you travel along a line that is parallel to a given line, you will stay the same distance from the given line. If you travel along a line that is perpendicular to a given line, you will travel either toward or away from the given line along the most direct path.

Essential Understanding The slopes of two lines in the same plane indicate how the lines are related.

Given the slope and y-intercept, you can write the equation of a line in slope-intercept form. You can also write the equation of a line in *point-slope form*.

> **take note**
>
> **Key Concept** Point-Slope Form
>
> The equation of a line in **point-slope form** through point (x_1, y_1) with slope m:
> $$y - y_1 = m(x - x_1)$$

Here's Why It Works By substituting the general point (x, y), for (x_2, y_2) in the slope formula, you can rewrite the slope formula in point-slope form.

$$m = \frac{y_2 - y_1}{x_2 - x_1} = \frac{y - y_1}{x - x_1}$$

$$m(x - x_1) = \frac{y - y_1}{x - x_1}(x - x_1)$$

$$m(x - x_1) = y - y_1$$

$$y - y_1 = m(x - x_1)$$

Plan

Is slope-intercept or point-slope form more helpful for writing this equation?

Since the slope and a point (not the y-intercept) are given, point-slope form is more helpful.

Problem 1 Writing an Equation Given a Point and the Slope

A line passes through $(-5, 2)$ with slope $\frac{3}{5}$. What is an equation of the line?

$$y - y_1 = m(x - x_1) \qquad \text{Use point-slope form.}$$

$$y - 2 = \frac{3}{5}[x - (-5)] \qquad \text{Substitute } m = \frac{3}{5} \text{ and } (x_1, y_1) = (-5, 2).$$

$$y - 2 = \frac{3}{5}(x + 5) \qquad \text{Simplify.}$$

An equation for the line is $y - 2 = \frac{3}{5}(x + 5)$.

✓ **Got It? 1.** What is an equation of the line through $(7, -1)$ with slope -3?

Problem 2 Writing an Equation Given Two Points

A line passes through $(3, 2)$ and $(5, 8)$. What is an equation of the line in point-slope form?

Know	Need	Plan
Two points	An equation written in point-slope form	Substitute the slope and either point in the point-slope form.

Think

Does it matter which point you substitute into point-slope form?

No; you can choose either point as (x_1, y_1).

Let $(x_1, y_1) = (3, 2)$ and $(x_2, y_2) = (5, 8)$.

$$m = \frac{8 - 2}{5 - 3} = \frac{6}{2} = 3 \qquad \text{Substitute into the slope formula and simplify.}$$

$$y - 2 = 3(x - 3) \qquad \text{Substitute into point-slope form.}$$

✓ **Got It? 2. a.** A line passes through $(-5, 0)$ and $(0, 7)$. What is an equation of the line in point-slope form?

    b. Reasoning What is another equation in point-slope form of the line through the points $(-5, 0)$ and $(0, 7)$? Explain.

Another form of the equation of a line is *standard form*, in which the sum of the x and y terms are set equal to a constant. When possible, you write the coefficients of x and y and the constant term as integers.

Key Concept Standard Form of a Linear Equation

A **standard form of a linear equation** is $Ax + By = C$, where A, B, and C are real numbers and A and B are not *both* zero.

Problem 3 Writing an Equation in Standard Form

What is an equation of the line $y = \frac{3}{4}x - 5$ in standard form? Use integer coefficients.

Think

How can you rewrite the equation using only integer values?
Multiply each side of the equation by the least common denominator of all fraction coefficients.

$$y = \frac{3}{4}x - 5$$

$$-\frac{3}{4}x + y = -5 \qquad \text{Subtract } \frac{3}{4}x \text{ from each side.}$$

$$-3x + 4y = -20 \qquad \text{Multiply each side by 4.}$$

 Got It? **3.** What is an equation of the line $y = 9.1x + 3.6$ in standard form?

take note **Concept Summary** **Writing Equations of Lines**

Slope-Intercept Form	**Point-Slope Form**	**Standard Form**
$y = mx + b$	$y - y_1 = m(x - x_1)$	$Ax + By = C$
Use this form when you know the slope and the y-intercept.	Use this form when you know the slope and a point, or when you know two points.	A, B, and C are real numbers. A and B cannot both be zero.

You can graph an equation in standard form quickly by determining the x- and y-intercepts and then drawing the line through them.

 Problem 4 Graphing an Equation Using Intercepts

Think

Why set $x = 0$ to find the y-intercept?
The x-coordinate of any point on the y-axis is zero.

What are the intercepts of $3x + 5y = 15$? Graph the equation.

Set $x = 0$ to find the y-intercept.

$$3(0) + 5y = 15$$

$$5y = 15$$

$$y = 3$$

Set $y = 0$ to find the x-intercept.

$$3x + 5(0) = 15$$

$$3x = 15$$

$$x = 5$$

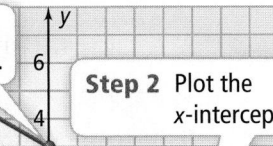

Step 1 Plot the y-intercept: (0, 3).

Step 2 Plot the x-intercept: (5, 0).

Step 3 Draw a line through the intercepts.

 Got It? **4.** What are the intercepts of $2x - 4y = 8$? Graph the equation.

Problem 5 **Drawing and Interpreting a Linear Graph** STEM

Biology The number of times a cricket chirps per minute depends on the temperature. The number of chirps in 2 seconds for two temperatures are shown at the bottom right.

A **What graph models the situation?**

First, find the number of chirps per minute.

$$40°F: \ 30(0) = 0$$
$$93°F: \ 30(8) = 240$$

Let x = temperature in degrees Fahrenheit.
Let y = number of times a cricket chirps.

Plot (40,0) and (93, 240).
Draw a line through the points.

B **What is an equation of the line in standard form?**

$$m = \frac{240 - 0}{93 - 40}$$ Use the slope formula $m = \frac{y_2 - y_1}{x_2 - x_1}$.

$$= \frac{240}{53} \approx 4.5$$ Subtract and simplify.

$$y - y_1 = m(x - x_1)$$ Use point-slope form.

$$y - 0 = 4.5(x - 40)$$ Substitute one of the points: (40, 0).

$$y = 4.5x - 180$$ Simplify.

$$4.5x - y = 180$$ Write in standard form.

C **If the temperature is 70°F, how many times would a cricket be expected to chirp in one minute?**

Let $x = 70$.

$$y = 4.5x - 180$$ Use an equation from part (b).

$$y = 4.5(70) - 180$$ Substitute.

$$y = 135$$ Simplify.

If the temperature is 70°F, the cricket would be expected to chirp 135 times in one minute.

Think

How can you find the number of chirps in a minute given the number of chirps in 2 seconds?

There are 60 seconds in 1 minute. Multiply the number of chirps in 2 seconds by $\frac{60}{2}$ or 30.

Cricket Chirping

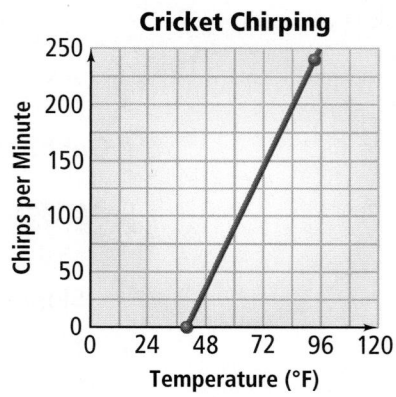

0 chirps

2 seconds

8 chirps

Got It? **5.** The office manager of a small office ordered 140 packs of printer paper. Based on average daily use, she knows that the paper will last about 80 days.

a. What graph represents this situation?

b. What is the equation of the line in standard form?

c. How many packs of printer paper should the manager expect to have after 30 days?

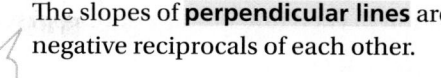

Key Concepts Parallel and Perpendicular Lines

The slopes of **parallel lines** are equal.

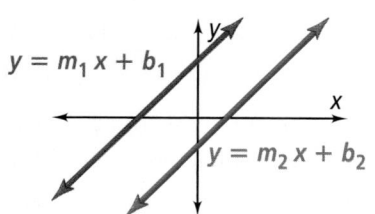

$y = m_1 x + b_1$

x

$y = m_2 x + b_2$

$m_1 = m_2$

$b_1 \neq b_2$

No line can be vertical.

The slopes of **perpendicular lines** are negative reciprocals of each other.

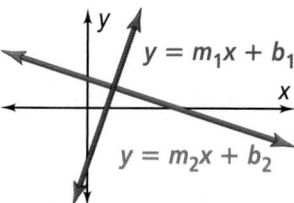

$y = m_1 x + b_1$

x

$y = m_2 x + b_2$

$m_1 \cdot m_2 = -1$

$m_1 = -\dfrac{1}{m_2}$

$m_2 = -\dfrac{1}{m_1}$

m_1 and m_2 are negative reciprocals of each other.

Problem 6 Writing Equations of Parallel and Perpendicular Lines

What is the equation of each line in slope-intercept form?

A **the line parallel to $y = 6x - 2$ through $(1, -3)$**

Identify the slope, use point-slope form, and rewrite in slope-intercept form.

$m = 6$	Parallel lines have the same slope. The slope of the line with equation $y = 6x - 2$ is 6.
$y - y_1 = m(x - x_1)$	Point-slope form
$y - (-3) = 6(x - 1)$	Substitute 6 for m and $(1, -3)$ for (x_1, y_1).
$y + 3 = 6x - 6$	Distributive Property
$y = 6x - 9$	Write in slope-intercept form.

B **the line perpendicular to $y = -4x + \frac{2}{3}$ through $(8, 5)$**

Identify the slope, use point-slope form, and rewrite in slope-intercept form.

$m = -\dfrac{1}{-4} = \dfrac{1}{4}$	The slopes of perpendicular lines are negative reciprocals.
$y - y_1 = m(x - x_1)$	Point-slope form
$y - 5 = \dfrac{1}{4}(x - 8)$	Substitute $\frac{1}{4}$ for m and $(8, 5)$ for (x_1, y_1).
$y - 5 = \dfrac{1}{4}x - 2$	Distributive Property
$y = \dfrac{1}{4}x + 3$	Write in slope-intercept form.

Plan

How can you find the slope of a perpendicular line?
Slopes of perpendicular lines are negative reciprocals, so use the equation $m_1 = -\dfrac{1}{m_2}$.

 **Got It?** **6.** What is the equation of each line in slope-intercept form?

  a. the line parallel to $4x + 2y = 7$ through $(4, -2)$

  b. the line perpendicular to $y = \frac{2}{3}x - 1$ through $(0, 6)$

Lesson Check

Do you know HOW?

Write an equation of each line in slope-intercept form.

1. slope -3; through $(1, -4)$

2. slope $\frac{1}{2}$; through $(2, 3)$

3. What are the intercepts of $3x + y = 6$? Graph the equation.

Write an equation of each line in standard form.

4. the line parallel to $y = -3x + 4$ through $(0, -1)$

5. the line perpendicular to $-2x + 3y = 9$ through $(-1, -3)$

Do you UNDERSTAND? MATHEMATICAL PRACTICES

6. Vocabulary Tell whether each equation is in slope-intercept, point-slope, or standard form.

   a. $y + 2 = -2(x - 1)$ **b.** $y = -\frac{1}{4}x + 9$

   c. $-x - 2y = 1$ **d.** $y - 3 = 4x$

7. Which form would you use to write the equation of a line if you knew its slope and x-intercept? Explain.

8. If the intercepts of a line are $(a, 0)$ and $(0, b)$, what is the slope of the line?

9. Error Analysis Your friend says the line $y = -2x + 3$ is perpendicular to the line $x + 2y = 8$. Do you agree? Explain.

Practice and Problem-Solving Exercises  MATHEMATICAL PRACTICES

 **Practice**

Write an equation of each line.   ● **See Problem 1.**

10. slope $= 3$; through $(1, 5)$ **11.** slope $= \frac{5}{6}$; through $(22, 12)$ **12.** slope $= -\frac{3}{5}$; through $(-4, 0)$

13. slope $= 0$; through $(4, -2)$ **14.** slope $= -1$; through $(-3, 5)$ **15.** slope $= 5$; through $(0, 2)$

Write in point-slope form an equation of the line through each pair of points.   ● **See Problem 2.**

16. $(-10, 3)$ and $(-2, -5)$ **17.** $(1, 0)$ and $(5, 5)$ **18.** $(-4, 10)$ and $(-6, 15)$

19. $(0, -1)$ and $(3, -5)$ **20.** $(7, 11)$ and $(13, 17)$ **21.** $(1, 9)$ and $(6, 2)$

Write an equation of each line in standard form with integer coefficients.   ● **See Problem 3.**

22. $y = \frac{1}{2}x - 2$ **23.** $y = -7x - 9$ **24.** $y = -\frac{3}{5}x + 3$ **25.** $y = 4.2x + 7.9$

Find the intercepts and graph each line.   ● **See Problem 4.**

26. $x - 4y = -4$ **27.** $2x + 5y = -10$ **28.** $-3x + 2y = 6$ **29.** $5x + 7y = 14$

Write and graph an equation to represent each situation.   ● **See Problem 5.**

30. You put 15 gallons of gasoline in your car. You know that this amount of gasoline will allow you to drive about 450 miles.

31. A meal plan lets students buy \$20 meal cards. Each meal card lasts about 8 days.

Write the equation of the line through each point. Use slope-intercept form.   ● **See Problem 6.**

32. $(1, -1)$; parallel to $y = \frac{2}{5}x - 3$ **33.** $(-3, 1)$; perpendicular to $y = -\frac{2}{5}x - 4$

34. $(-7, 10)$; parallel to $2x - 3y = -3$ **35.** $(-2, 1)$; perpendicular to $3x + y = 1$

B Apply

Graph each equation.

36. $3x + 5y = 12$ 　　　　**37.** $y = \frac{2}{3}x + 4$ 　　　　**38.** $x + 3 = 0$

39. $3y - x = -6$ 　　　　**40.** $y + 3 = 3$ 　　　　**41.** $2x - \frac{3}{2}y = -3$

Write an equation of the line through each pair of points. Use point-slope form.

42. $\left(\frac{3}{2}, -\frac{1}{2}\right)$ and $\left(-\frac{2}{3}, \frac{1}{3}\right)$ 　　**43.** $\left(-\frac{1}{2}, -\frac{1}{2}\right)$ and $(-3, -4)$ 　　**44.** $\left(0, \frac{1}{2}\right)$ and $\left(\frac{5}{7}, 0\right)$

45. Think About a Plan Write an equation for the line shown here.
Each interval is 1 unit.
- What do you know from the graph?
- Which form of the equation of a line could you use with the information you have?

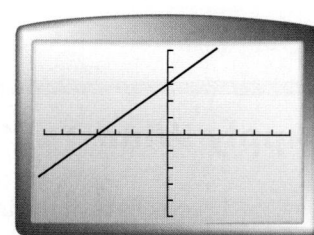

Write an equation for each line. Each interval is 1 unit.

46. 　　　　　　　　　　　　　　　　**47.**

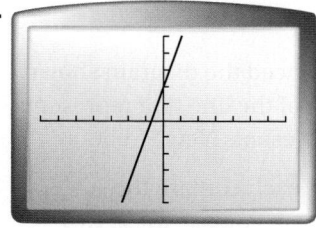 　　　　　　　　　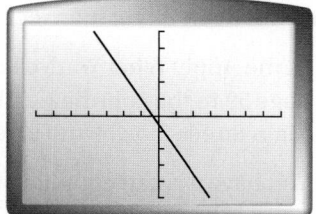

48. The equation $5x - 2y = -6$ and the table each represent linear functions. Which has the greater slope? Explain.

x	−2	−1	0	1	2
y	1	3	5	7	9

49. a. Write the point-slope form of the line that passes through $A(-3, 12)$ and $B(9, -4)$. Use point A in the equation.
b. Write the point-slope form of the same line using point B in the equation.
c. Rewrite each equation in standard form. What do you notice?

Write an equation for each line. Then graph the line.

50. $m = 0$, through $(5, -1)$ 　　　　　　**51.** $m = -\frac{3}{2}$, through $(0, -1)$

52. Reasoning Suppose lines ℓ_1 and ℓ_2 intersect at the origin. Also, ℓ_1 has slope $\frac{y}{x}$ $(x > 0, y > 0)$ and ℓ_2 has slope $-\frac{x}{y}$. Then ℓ_1 contains (x, y) and ℓ_2 contains $(-y, x)$.
a. Explain why the two right triangles are congruent.
b. Complete each equation about the angle measures a, b, c, and d.
　　$a = \blacksquare$ 　　　　　　$c = \blacksquare$
　　$a + c = \blacksquare$ 　　　　$b + d = \blacksquare$
c. What must be true about $a + b$? Why?
d. What must be true about ℓ_1 and ℓ_2? Why?

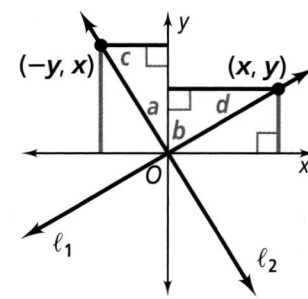

Points that are on the same line are *collinear*. Use the definition of slope to determine whether the given points are collinear.

53. $(-2, 6), (0, 2), (1, 0)$ **54.** $(3, -5), (-3, 3), (0, 2)$

55. Geometry Prove that the triangle with vertices $(3, 5)$, $(-2, 6)$, and $(1, 3)$ is a right triangle.

56. Geometry Prove that the quadrilateral with vertices $(2, 5)$, $(4, 8)$, $(7, 6)$, and $(5, 3)$ is a rectangle.

Apply What You've Learned

MATHEMATICAL
PRACTICES
MP 2

Look back at the information on page 59 about the work crew that is painting lane lines on Main Street. Note that the diagram on page 59 shows that New Street and Main Street intersect at a right angle.

a. In the Apply What You've Learned in Lesson 2-3, you placed the diagram shown on page 59 in the coordinate plane and wrote an equation of the line that represents Main Street. Now, write an equation of the line that represents New Street.

b. You have written equations in x and y for two lines that each contain the intersection point of Main Street and New Street. How can you use these two equations to write an equation that involves only x?

c. Solve the equation you wrote in part (b). Round your answer to the nearest tenth of a mile.

d. The solution you found in part (d) is the x-coordinate of the intersection point of Main Street and New Street. Find the y-coordinate. Round your answer to the nearest tenth of a mile.

e. Find the distance from the intersection of Main Street and New Street to the intersection of Main Street and Wilson Road. Round your answer to the nearest tenth of a mile. (*Hint:* Use the Distance Formula.)

f. Let d represent the distance, in miles, along Main Street that the work crew still needs to paint. Find a function rule that expresses d in terms of the time t, in hours, since 1 P.M. Interpret each coefficient or constant in the function rule in terms of the problem situation.

2 Mid-Chapter Quiz

Do you know HOW?

Determine whether each relation is a function.

1.

x	y
3	7
4	2
3	2
5	1

2.

x	y
1	1
2	2
3	3
4	4

Find the x- and y-intercepts of each line.

3. $x - 3y = 9$

4. $y = 7x + 5$

5. $y = 6x$

6. $-4x + y = 10$

Write the equation of each line in slope-intercept form and identify the slope.

7. $2x - y = 9$

8. $4x = 2 + y$

9. $5y = -3x - 10$

10. $4x + 6y = 12$

Write an equation of each line in standard form with integer coefficients.

11. the line through $(2, 3)$ and $(4, 5)$

12. the line through $(-4, 6)$ and $(2, -2)$

13. the line through $(-4, 2)$ with slope 3

14. the line through $(1, 2)$ with slope $\frac{4}{5}$

15. a line through $(3, 1)$ with slope 0

16. a line with slope of $\frac{2}{3}$ and y-intercept $(0, 5)$

17. $2y = -4x - 12$

18. $\frac{2}{3}x + 3 = 6y - 15$

Write an equation of each line in point-slope form.

19. $(-4, 2)$ and $(-3, 5)$

20. $(0, 0)$ and $(-4, -5)$

21. $(-4, -3)$ and $(2, 7)$

Graph each equation.

22. $2y = 4x + 8$

23. $2x - 3y = 6$

24. $4y - x = 16$

For each function, determine whether y varies directly with x. If so, identify the constant of variation.

25. $2y = 3x$

26. $4y - 7x = 0$

27. $y + \frac{3}{4}x = 12$

Do you UNDERSTAND?

28. a. A group of friends is going to the movies. Each ticket costs $8.00. Write an equation to model the total cost of the group's tickets.

b. Graph the equation. Explain what the x- and y-intercepts represent.

c. What would be the cost for 12 tickets?

d. Writing Could the domain include fractions? Explain.

29. Which line is perpendicular to $3x + 2y = 6$?

Ⓐ $4x - 6y = 3$ Ⓒ $2x + 3y = 12$

Ⓑ $y = -\frac{3}{2}x + 4$ Ⓓ $y = \frac{3}{2}x + 1$

30. Reasoning Why is the slope of a vertical line undefined?

31. Suppose $m = 25 - 0.15n$ describes the amount of money remaining on a $25 phone card m, as a function of the number of minutes of calls you make n. What are a reasonable domain and range?

Concept Byte

Piecewise Functions

For Use With Lesson 2-4

 Common Core State Standards

F-IF.C.7b Graph . . . piecewise-defined functions, including step functions and absolute value functions.

MP 5

Recall from Lesson 1-6 that $|x|$, the absolute value of x, is the distance of x from zero. When $x \geq 0$, $|x| = x$. When $x < 0$, $|x| = -x$. The absolute value function is an example of a *piecewise function*. A **piecewise function** has different rules for different parts of its domain.

Example 1

Graph the absolute value function $f(x) = \begin{cases} x, & \text{for } x \geq 0 \\ -x, & \text{for } x < 0 \end{cases}$.

Graph each piece separately.

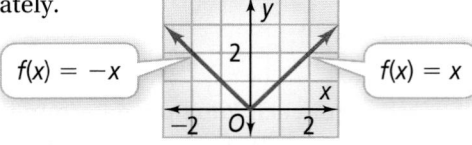

Example 2

Use a graphing calculator to graph the function $f(x) = \begin{cases} -2x + 3, & \text{if } x < 2 \\ x - 1, & \text{if } x \geq 2 \end{cases}$.

Define the function $f(x)$. Use the brackets from the math expression templates to enter the piecewise function.

Enter the rules for the two branches. Set $f_1(x) = f(x)$ and graph.

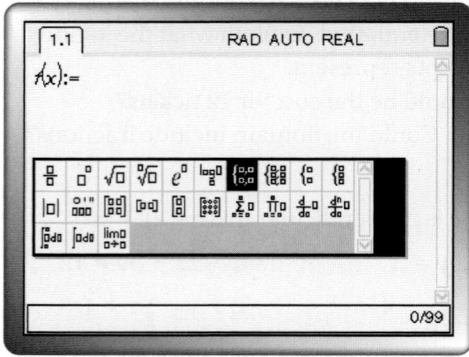

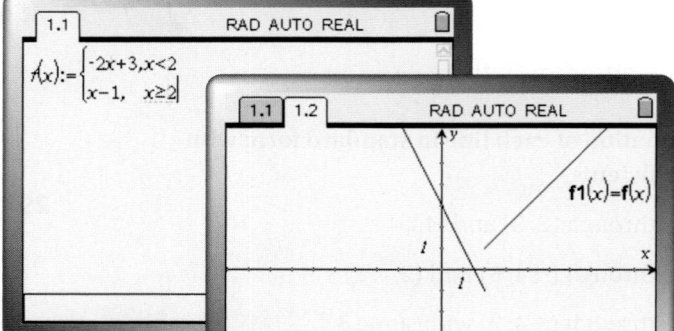

Step functions are piecewise functions. A **step function** pairs every number in an interval with a single value. The graph of a step function can look like the steps of a staircase. One step function is the **greatest integer function** $y = [x]$, where $[x]$ represents the greatest integer less than or equal to x.

Example 3

What is the graph of the function $f(x) = [x]$?

Each piece of the graph is a horizontal segment that is missing its right endpoint. The open circle indicates that the right endpoint is not part of the graph.

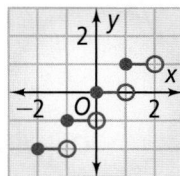

Given a piecewise function in one form, you can represent it in each of the other forms, including a table, graph, algebraic function, or verbal statement.

Example 4

Media Postage You want to mail a book that weighs 2.5 lb. The table lists postage for a book weighing up to 3 lb. Define and graph the media-postage function. How much will you pay in postage?

$$f(x) = \begin{cases} 2.23, & \text{for } 0 < x \le 1 \\ 2.58, & \text{for } 1 < x \le 2 \\ 2.93, & \text{for } 2 < x \le 3 \end{cases}$$

Since $2 < 2.5 \le 3$, you will pay $2.93.

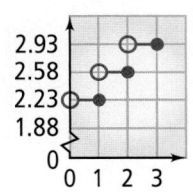

Media Postage

Weight (lb)	Price ($)
$x \le 1$	2.23
$1 < x \le 2$	2.58
$2 < x \le 3$	2.93

Example 5

What piecewise function represents the graph?

Piece 1 When $x \le -2$, the rule is $f(x) = 2x + 6$.

Piece 2 When $-2 < x \le 0$, the rule is $f(x) = -2x - 2$.

Piece 3 When $x > 0$, the rule is $f(x) = 3x - 2$.

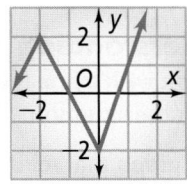

$$f(x) = \begin{cases} 2x + 6, & \text{for } x \le -2 \\ -2x - 2, & \text{for } -2 < x \le 0 \\ 3x - 2, & \text{for } x > 0 \end{cases}$$

Exercises

1. Graph the sign function. $f(x) = \begin{cases} -1, & \text{for } x < 0 \\ 0, & \text{for } x = 0 \\ 1, & \text{for } x > 0 \end{cases}$.

2. Graph the function $f(x) = $ the least integer greater than x.
3. What piecewise function represents the graph at the right?
4. **Postage** In 2008, first-class letter postage was $.42 for up to one ounce and $.17 for each additional ounce up to 3.5 oz. Graph this postage function.

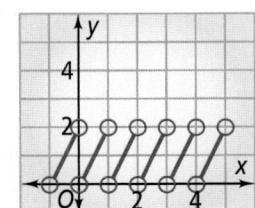

2-5 Using Linear Models

Common Core State Standards

F-IF.B.4 For a function that models a relationship between two quantities, interpret key features of graphs . . . and sketch graphs showing key features . . .
Also A-CED.A.2, F-IF.B.6

MP 1, MP 3, MP 4, MP 5

Objectives To write linear equations that model real-world data
To make predictions from linear models

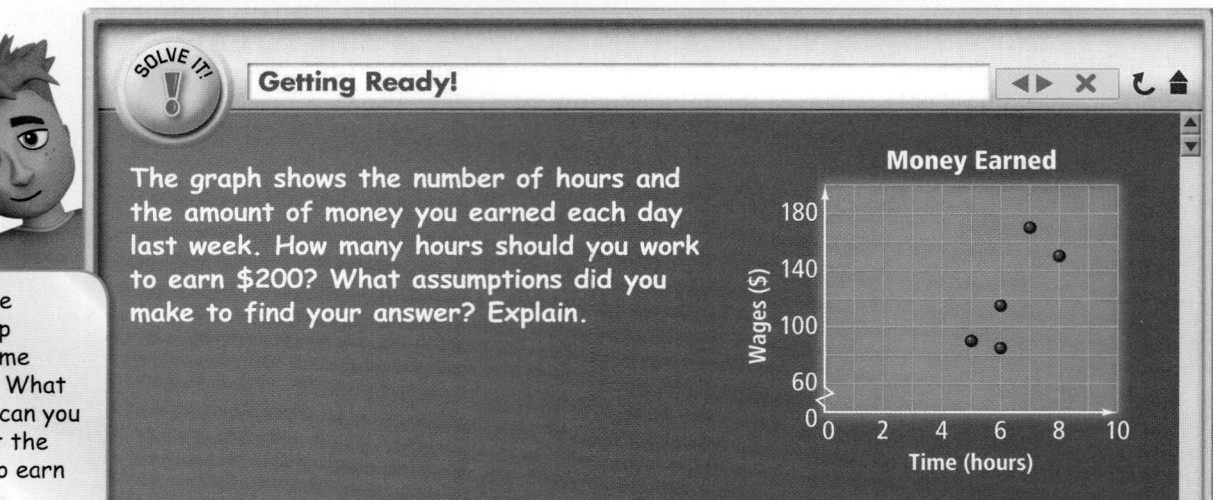

SOLVE IT!

Getting Ready!

The graph shows the number of hours and the amount of money you earned each day last week. How many hours should you work to earn $200? What assumptions did you make to find your answer? Explain.

Analyze the relationship between time and wages. What conclusion can you draw about the best way to earn money?

MATHEMATICAL PRACTICES

Graphs of data pairs for a real-world situation rarely fall in a line. Their arrangement, however, can suggest a relationship that you can model with a linear function.

Essential Understanding Sometimes it is possible to model data from a real-world situation with a linear equation. You can then use the equation to draw conclusions about the situation.

Lesson Vocabulary
• scatter plot
• correlation
• line of best fit
• correlation coefficient

A **scatter plot** is a graph that relates two sets of data by plotting the data as ordered pairs. You can use a scatter plot to determine the strength of the relationship, or **correlation**, between data sets. The closer the data points fall along a line,

• the stronger the relationship and
• the stronger the positive or negative correlation

between the two variables.

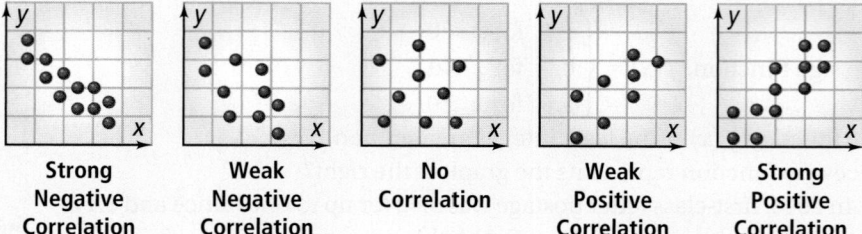

Strong Negative Correlation — Weak Negative Correlation — No Correlation — Weak Positive Correlation — Strong Positive Correlation

Problem 1 Using a Scatter Plot

Utilities The table lists average monthly temperatures and electricity costs for a Texas home in 2008. The table displays the values rounded to the nearest whole number. Make a scatter plot. How would you describe the correlation?

Average Temperatures and Electricity Costs

Month	Average Temp. (°F)	Electricity Bill ($)	Month	Average Temp. (°F)	Electricity Bill ($)
January	61	150	July	84	255
February	58	139	August	85	245
March	67	172	September	81	210
April	75	205	October	76	183
May	79	170	November	65	132
June	83	234	December	58	110

Plan

Which variable is the independent variable?
Temperature does not depend on the electric bill, so temperature is the independent variable.

Step 1 Make a scatter plot.

Step 2 Describe the correlation.

As the temperature increases, the electricity cost also increases. The points are relatively tightly clustered around a line. There is a strong positive correlation between temperature and electricity cost.

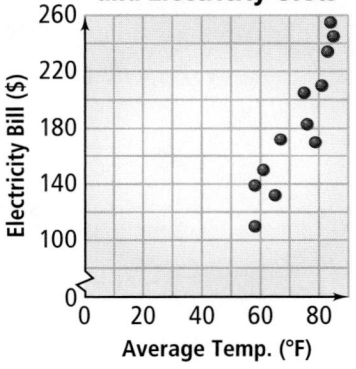

Average Temperatures and Electricity Costs

 Got It? **1. a.** The table shows the numbers of hours students spent online the day before a test and the scores on the test. Make a scatter plot. How would you describe the correlation?

   b. Reasoning Using the graph from Problem 1, how much would you expect to pay for electricity if the average temperature was 70°F? Explain.

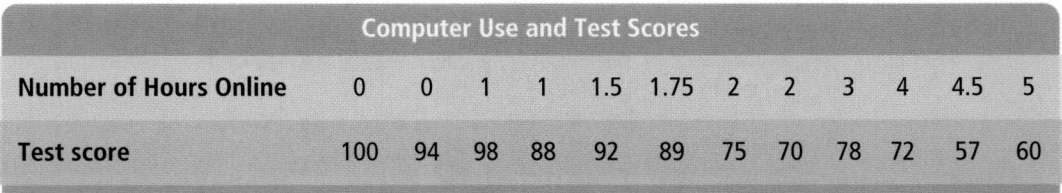

Computer Use and Test Scores

Number of Hours Online	0	0	1	1	1.5	1.75	2	2	3	4	4.5	5
Test score	100	94	98	88	92	89	75	70	78	72	57	60

A *trend line* is a line that approximates the relationship between the variables, or data sets, of a scatter plot. You can use a trend line to make predictions from the data. In a previous lesson you learned how to use two points to write the equation of a line to model a real-world problem. You can use this method to write the equation of a trend line.

Problem 2 Writing the Equation of a Trend Line

Finance The table shows the median home prices in Florida. What is the equation of a trend line that models a relationship between time and home prices? Use the equation to predict the median home price in 2020.

Florida Median Home Prices							
Year	1940	1950	1960	1970	1980	1990	2000
Median Price ($)	23,100	40,100	58,100	57,600	89,300	98,500	105,500

Know

Seven data points

Need

The equation of a trend line

Plan

- Plot the given points.
- Find a trend line.
- Write the equation.

Step 1 Make a scatter plot. Let $x = 0$ correspond to 1940.

Step 2 Sketch a trend line.

Step 3 Choose two points on the trend line, (10, 40,000) and (55, 110,000). Use slope-intercept form to write an equation for the line.
$y = 1556x + 24{,}440$

Step 4 Use the equation to predict the median home price in 2020.

$y = 1556(80) + 24{,}440 = 148{,}920$

Based on the trend line, the median home price in 2020 will be around $149,000.

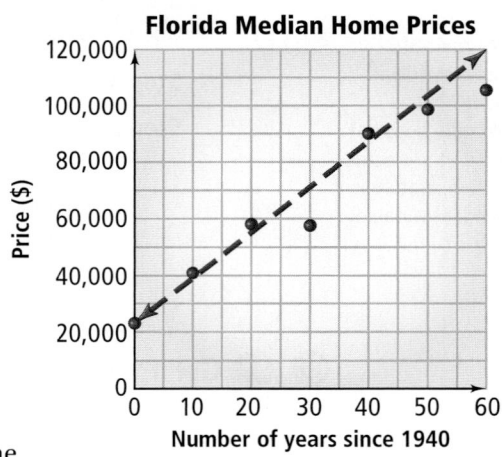

Florida Median Home Prices

 Got It? **2.** The table shows median home prices in California. What is an equation for a trend line that models the relationship between time and home prices?

California Median Home Prices							
Year	1940	1950	1960	1970	1980	1990	2000
Median Price ($)	36,700	57,900	74,400	88,700	167,300	249,800	211,500

The trend line that gives the most accurate model of related data is the **line of best fit**. One method for finding a line of best fit is *linear regression*. You can use the **LinReg** function on your graphing calculator to find the line of best fit. The **correlation coefficient**, r, indicates the strength of the correlation. The closer r is to 1 or -1, the more closely the data resembles a line and the more accurate your model is likely to be.

Problem 3 Finding the Line of Best Fit

Food You research the average cost of whole milk for several recent years to look for trends. The table shows your data.

Cost of Whole Milk						
Year	1998	2000	2002	2004	2006	2008
Average cost for one gallon ($)	2.65	2.89	3.00	3.01	3.20	3.77

SOURCE: U.S. Department of Agriculture

A What is the equation for the line of best fit? How accurate is your line of best fit?

Step 1
Use the **STAT** feature to enter the data in your graphing calculator. Enter the x-values (year) in **L1** and the y-values (price) in **L2**. Let 1997 = year 0.

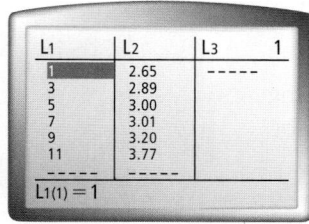

Step 2
Use **LinReg** to find the linear regression line of best fit for the data.

$$y = 0.09x + 2.53$$

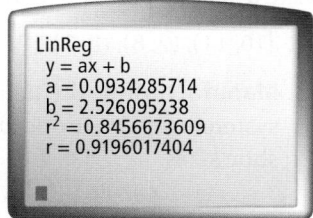

The correlation coefficient, r, is approximately 0.92. Since r is close to 1, the line of best fit is quite accurate.

B Based on your linear model, how much would you expect to pay for a gallon of whole milk in 2020?

$y = 0.09x + 2.53$	Use the line of best fit.
$y = 0.09(23) + 2.53$	Substitute 23 for x.
$y = 4.60$	

In 2020, you would expect to pay about $4.60 for a gallon of whole milk.

Think

What factors could affect the accuracy of your prediction?
Predictions based on strongly correlated data are likely to be more reliable than predictions based on weakly correlated data.

Got It? **3.** The table lists the cost of 2% milk. Use a scatter plot to find the equation of the line of best fit. Based on your linear model, how much would you expect to pay for a gallon of 2% milk in 2025?

Cost of 2% Milk						
Year	1998	2000	2002	2004	2006	2008
Average cost for one gallon ($)	2.57	2.83	2.93	2.93	3.10	3.71

SOURCE: U.S. Department of Agriculture

Lesson Check

Do you know HOW?

Make a scatter plot of each set of points and describe the correlation.

1. $\{(1.2, 1), (2.5, 6), (2.5, 7.5), (4.1, 11), (7.9, 19)\}$

2. $\{(1, 55), (2, 38), (3, 54), (4, 37), (5, 53), (6, 40),$
   $(7, 53), (8, 36)\}$

3. Make a scatter plot for the following set of points. Describe the correlation and sketch a trend line.
   $\{(2, 58), (6, 105), (8, 88), (8, 118), (12, 117),$
   $(16, 137), (20, 157), (20, 169)\}$

Do you UNDERSTAND?

 4. **Writing** How can you determine whether two variables x and y for a real-life situation are correlated?

5. Do you think a trend line on a graph is always the same as the line of best fit? Why or why not?

6. **Compare and Contrast** What is the difference between a positive correlation and a negative correlation? How might you relate positive correlation with direct variation?

Practice and Problem-Solving Exercises

 **Practice**

Make a scatter plot and describe the correlation.

See Problem 1.

7. $\{(0, 11), (2, 8), (3, 7), (7, 2), (8, 0)\}$

8. **Manufacturing** The table shows the numbering system used in Europe and the United States for shoe sizes.

Shoe Sizes						
U.S. Size	1	3	5	7	9	11
European Size	31	34	36	39	41	44

Write the equation of a trend line.

See Problem 2.

9. $\{(-10, 3), (-5, 1), (-1, -4), (3, -7), (12, -12)\}$

10. $\{(-15, 8), (-8, 7), (-3, 0), (0, 0), (7, -3)\}$

11. The table shows the number of hours you studied before your eight math tests and your percent score on each test.

Studying Hours and Test Score								
Number of Hours	8	5	12	10	2	9	11	14
Score (%)	75	62	80	85	35	70	82	95

12. **a. Food Production** The table below shows pork production in China from 2000 to 2007. Use a calculator to find the line of best fit.

   b. Use your linear model to predict how many metric tons of pork will be produced in 2025.

   c. Use your linear model to predict when production is likely to reach 100,000 metric tons.

See Problem 3.

Pork Production in China								
Year	2000	2001	2002	2003	2004	2005	2006	2007
Production (metric tons)	40,475	42,010	43,413	45,331	47,177	50,254	52,407	54,491

SOURCE: USDA Foreign Agricultural Service GAIN Report

 **Apply**

ⓒ 13. Think About a Plan The table shows the relationship between the production and the export of rice in Vietnam from 1985 to 2005.

Rice Production and Export					
Production (1000 tonnes)	15,875	19,225	24,964	32,554	35,600
Export (1000 tonnes)	59	1624	1988	3400	5100

SOURCE: International Rice Research Institute

How much rice would you expect Vietnam to export in 2015 if the production that year is 42,250,000 tonnes?
- How can you use a scatter plot to find a linear model?
- How can you use your model to make a prediction?

ⓒ 14. Nutrition The table shows the relationship between Calories and fat in various fast-food hamburgers.

Fast Food Calories									
Restaurant	A	B	C	D	E	F	G	H	I
Number of Calories	720	530	510	500	305	410	440	320	598
Grams of fat	46	30	27	26	13	20	25	13	26

a. Find the line of best fit for the relationship between Calories and fat.
b. How much fat would you expect a 330-Calorie hamburger to have?
c. Error Analysis Which estimate is *not* reasonable: 10 g of fat for a 200-Calorie hamburger or 36 g of fat for a 660-Calorie hamburger? Explain.

ⓒ Reasoning For any correlation, people often assume that change in one quantity *causes* change in the second quantity. This is not always true. For each situation, do you think that change in the first quantity causes change in the second quantity? What else may have affected the change in the second quantity?

15. number of miles driven and fuel expenses

16. the size of a car's engine and the number of passengers it is designed for

17. a person's age and the number of cassette tapes he or she owns

ⓒ 18. Data Analysis The table shows population and licensed driver statistics from a recent year.
   a. Make a scatter plot.
   b. Draw a trend line.
   c. The population of Michigan was approximately 10 million that year. About how many licensed drivers lived in Michigan that year?
   d. Writing Is the correlation between population and number of licensed drivers strong or weak? Explain.

Licensed Drivers

State	Population (millions)	Number of Drivers (millions)
Arkansas	2.8	2.0
Illinois	12.8	8.1
Kansas	2.8	2.0
Massachusetts	6.4	4.7
Pennsylvania	12.4	8.5
Texas	23.5	14.9

19. Social Studies The table shows per capita revenues and expenditures for selected states for a recent year.

  a. Show the data on a scatter plot. Draw a trend line.

  b. If a state collected revenue of $3000 per capita, how much would you expect it to spend per capita?

  c. Ohio spent $5142 per capita during that year. According to your model, how much did it collect in taxes per capita?

  d. In that same year, New Jersey collected $5825 per capita in taxes and spent $5348 per capita. Does this information follow the trend? Explain.

Per Capita Revenue and Expenditure

State	Per Capita Revenue ($)	Per Capita Expenditure ($)
Arizona	4144	3789
Georgia	3904	3834
Maryland	5109	4557
Mississippi	5292	4871
New Mexico	6205	5793
Nevada	4345	3723
New York	7081	6891
Texas	4030	3442
Utah	5439	4459

Standardized Test Prep

SAT/ACT

20. What is the equation of the line shown in the graph?

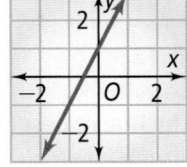

Ⓐ $y = -2x + 2$ Ⓒ $y = 2x + 1$

Ⓑ $y = 2x$ Ⓓ $y = 2x + 2$

21. Shauna drove 75 miles in 3 hours at a constant speed. How many miles did she drive in 2 hours?

Ⓕ 25 miles   Ⓖ 50 miles   Ⓗ 75 miles   Ⓘ 100 miles

22. Which equation does NOT represent a direct variation?

Ⓐ $y = x$ Ⓒ $2x - y = 0$

Ⓑ $2x - y = 5$ Ⓓ $2x - 5y = 0$

Short Response

23. The line $(y - 1) = \frac{2}{3}(x + 1)$ contains point $(a, -3)$. What is the value of a? Show your work.

Mixed Review

Graph the following linear equations.   ◀ See Lesson 2-3.

24. $y = -7.5x + 11$ **25.** $-\frac{2}{9}x - \frac{5}{9}y = 10$ **26.** $5x - 4y = 3$

Write the equation of each line in standard form.   ◀ See Lesson 2-4.

27. slope = 2; (2, 6)   **28.** slope = -1; (-3, 3)   **29.** slope = 0; (0, 2)

Get Ready! To prepare for Lesson 2-6, do Exercises 30–32.

Graph each pair of functions on the same coordinate plane.   ◀ See Lesson 2-3.

30. $y = -x$; $y = x$ **31.** $y = x + 1$; $y = 2x - 1$ **32.** $y = -\frac{1}{4}x$; $y = -\frac{1}{4}x + 2$

2-6 Families of Functions

© Common Core State Standards

F-BF.B.3 Identify the effect on the graph of replacing $f(x)$ by $f(x) + k$, $k\,f(x)$, $f(kx)$, and $f(x + k)$ for specific values of k (both positive and negative) find the value of k given the graphs.

MP 1, MP 3, MP 7

Objective To analyze transformations of functions

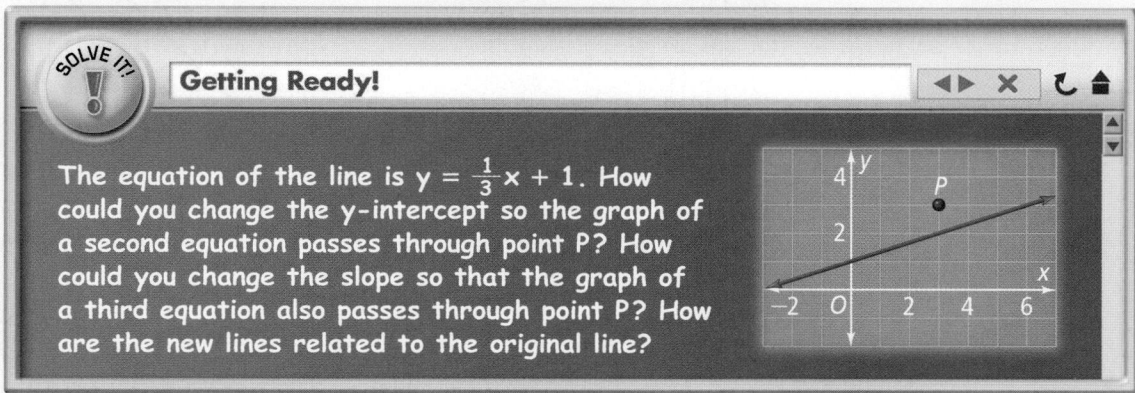

SOLVE IT!

Getting Ready!

The equation of the line is $y = \frac{1}{3}x + 1$. How could you change the y-intercept so the graph of a second equation passes through point P? How could you change the slope so that the graph of a third equation also passes through point P? How are the new lines related to the original line?

Lesson Vocabulary

- parent function
- transformation
- translation
- reflection
- vertical stretch
- vertical compression

Different nonvertical lines have different slopes, or y-intercepts, or both. They are graphs of different linear functions. For two such lines, you can think of one as a *transformation* of the other.

Essential Understanding There are sets of functions, called *families*, in which each function is a transformation of a special function called the *parent*.

The linear functions form a family of functions. Each linear function is a transformation of the function $y = x$. The function $y = x$ is the *parent* linear function.

A **parent function** is the simplest form in a set of functions that form a family. Each function in the family is a **transformation** of the parent function.

One type of transformation is a **translation**. A translation shifts the graph of the parent function horizontally, vertically, or both without changing shape or orientation. For a positive constant k and a parent function $f(x)$, $f(x) \pm k$ is a vertical translation. For a positive constant h, $f(x \pm h)$ is a horizontal translation.

> Adding k to the outputs shifts the graph up.

> Subtracting h from the inputs shifts the graph right.

Vertical Translation

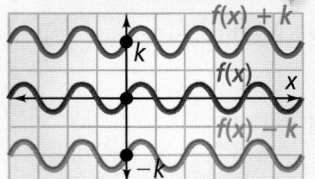

Horizontal Translation

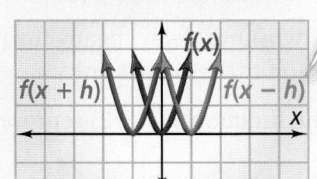

Plan

What is one way
to compare two
functions?
Use a table to compare
their values.

Problem 1 Vertical Translation

A How are the functions $y = x$ and $y = x - 2$ related? How are their graphs related?

Make a table of values.

Draw their graphs.

x	y = x	y = x − 2
−2	−2	−4
−1	−1	−3
0	0	−2
1	1	−1
2	2	0

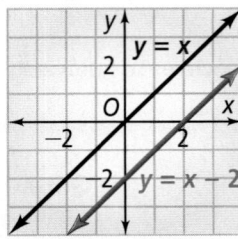

Each output for $y = x - 2$ is two less than the corresponding output for $y = x$.

The graph of $y = x - 2$ is the graph of $y = x$ translated down two units.

B What is the graph of $y = x^2 - 1$ translated up 5 units?

Translate the graph of $y = x^2 - 1$ up 5 units to get the blue parabola. The equation of the blue parabola is $y = x^2 + 4$.

Check Every value in the $y = x^2 + 4$ column is 5 greater than the corresponding value in the $y = x^2 - 1$ column.

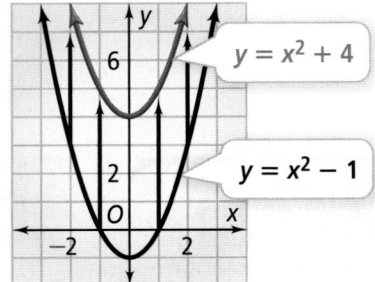

x	y = x² − 1	y = x² + 4
−2	3	8
−1	0	5
0	−1	4
1	0	5
2	3	8

Got It? **1. a.** How are the functions $y = 2x$ and $y = 2x - 3$ related? How are their graphs related?

 b. What is the graph of $y = 3x$ translated up 2 units?

Problem 2 Horizontal Translation

Think

If the time of the
flight is later, why do
you subtract rather
than add in $f(x - 2)$?
The y-values of
the delayed flight
correspond to x-values
2 hours *earlier* than the
delayed flight.

The graph shows the projected altitude $f(x)$ of an airplane scheduled to depart an airport at noon. If the plane leaves two hours late, what function represents this transformation?

A two-hour delay means the plane leaves at 2 P.M. This shifts the graph to the right 2 units.

The function $f(x - 2)$ represents this transformation.

Airplane Altitude

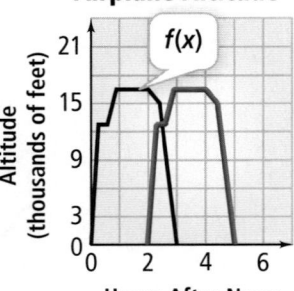

Got It? **2.** Suppose the flight leaves 30 minutes early. What function represents this transformation?

A **reflection** flips the graph of a function across a line, such as the *x*- or *y*-axis. Each point on the graph of the reflected function is the same distance from the line of reflection as its corresponding point on the graph of the original function.

When you reflect a graph in the *y*-axis, the *x*-values change signs and the *y*-values stay the same.

When you reflect a graph in the *x*-axis, the *x*-values stay the same and the *y*-values change signs.

For a function $f(x)$, the reflection in the *y*-axis is $f(-x)$ and the reflection in the *x*-axis is $-f(x)$.

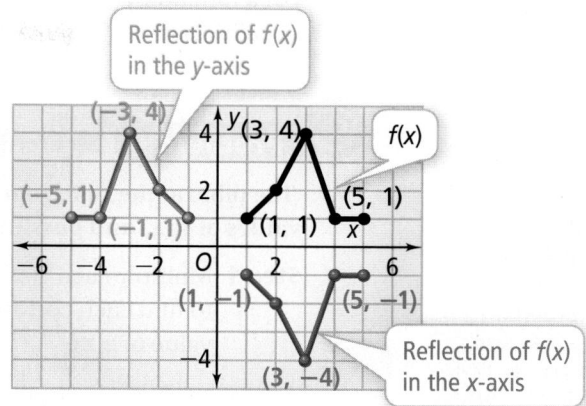

Problem 3 Reflecting a Function Algebraically

Let $g(x)$ be the reflection of $f(x) = 3x + 3$ in the *y*-axis. What is a function rule for $g(x)$?

Think

For a reflection in the *y*-axis, change the sign of *x*.

Evaluate $f(-x)$ and simplify.

You can check by graphing $f(x)$ and $g(x)$.

Write

$g(x) = f(-x)$

$g(x) = f(-x)$
$\quad = 3(-x) + 3$
$g(x) = -3x + 3$

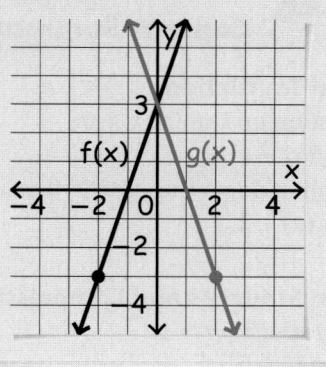

Got It? 3. Let $h(x)$ be the reflection of $f(x) = 3x + 3$ in the *x*-axis. What is a function rule for $h(x)$?

A **vertical stretch** multiplies all y-values of a function by the same factor greater than 1. A **vertical compression** reduces all y-values of a function by the same factor between 0 and 1. For a function $f(x)$ and a constant a, $y = af(x)$ is a vertical stretch when $a > 1$ and a vertical compression when $0 < a < 1$.

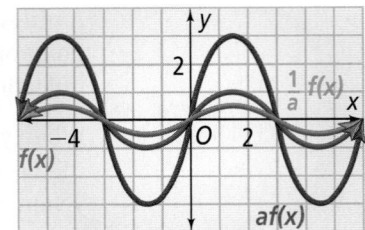

Ⓒ **Problem 4** Stretching and Compressing a Function

The table at the right represents the function $f(x)$. What are corresponding values of $g(x)$ and possible graphs for the transformation $g(x) = 3f(x)$?

x	f(x)
−5	2
−2	2
0	−3
3	1
5	−2

Think

Is this a vertical stretch or compression?
3 is greater than 1, so this is a vertical stretch.

Step 1 Multiply each value of $f(x)$ by 3 to find each corresponding value of $g(x)$.

x	f(x)	3f(x)	g(x)
−5	2	3(2)	6
−2	2	3(2)	6
0	−3	3(−3)	−9
3	1	3(1)	3
5	−2	3(−2)	−6

Step 2 Use the values from the table in Step 1. Draw simple graphs for $f(x)$ and $g(x)$.

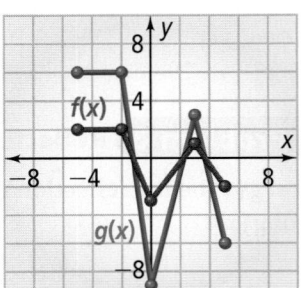

Ⓒ ✓ **Got It?** **4. a.** For the function $f(x)$ shown in Problem 4, what are the corresponding table and graph for the transformation $h(x) = \frac{1}{3}f(x)$?

   b. Reasoning If several transformations are applied to a graph, will changing the order of transformations change the resulting graph? Explain.

---

take note   **Concept Summary**   **Transformations of $f(x)$**

Vertical Translations
Translation up k units, $k > 0$
$$y = f(x) + k$$
Translation down k units, $k > 0$
$$y = f(x) - k$$

Horizontal Translations
Translation right h units, $h > 0$
$$y = f(x - h)$$
Translation left h units, $h > 0$
$$y = f(x + h)$$

Vertical Stretches and Compressions
Vertical stretch, $a > 1$
$$y = a f(x)$$
Vertical compression, $0 < a < 1$
$$y = a f(x)$$

Reflections
In the x-axis
$$y = -f(x)$$
In the y-axis
$$y = f(-x)$$

Problem 5 Combining Transformations

A The graph of $g(x)$ is the graph of $f(x) = 4x$ compressed vertically by the factor $\frac{1}{2}$ and then reflected in the y-axis. What is a function rule for $g(x)$?

$\frac{1}{2}(4x) = 2x$ Compress $f(x)$.

$2(-x) = -2x$ Reflect the new function in the y-axis.

The function rule is $g(x) = -2x$.

B What transformations change the graph of $f(x)$ to the graph of $g(x)$?

$f(x) = 2x^2 \qquad g(x) = 6x^2 - 1$

Think

How can you write $g(x)$ in terms of $f(x)$?
Factor out 3 from the $6x^2$ term.

$g(x) = 6x^2 - 1$

$= 3(2x^2) - 1$

$= 3(f(x)) - 1$

The graph of $g(x)$ is the graph of $f(x)$ stretched vertically by a factor of 3 and then translated down 1 unit.

Got It? **5. a.** The graph of $g(x)$ is the graph of $f(x) = x$ stretched vertically by a factor of 2 and then translated down 3 units. What is the function rule for $g(x)$?

b. What transformations change the graph of $f(x) = x^2$ to the graph of $g(x) = (x + 4)^2 - 2$?

 Lesson Check

Do you know HOW?

Describe the transformation of the parent function $f(x)$.

1. $g(x) = f(x) + 6$

2. $h(x) = 0.25f(x)$

3. $j(x) = f(x - 4)$

4. $k(x) = f(-x)$

The graph of $f(x) = -2x$ is shown. Describe and graph each transformation.

5. $g(x) = f(x + 1) - 2$

6. $h(x) = 2f(x) + 1$

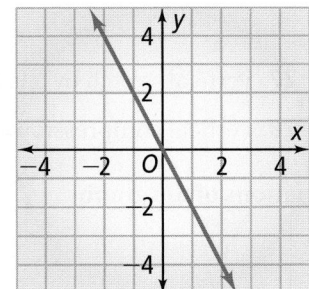

Do you UNDERSTAND?  MATHEMATICAL PRACTICES

7. Compare and Contrast The graph shows $f(x) = 0.5x - 1$.

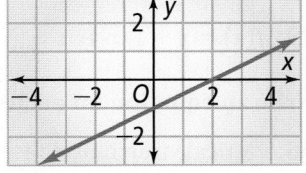

Graph $g(x)$ by translating $f(x)$ up 2 units and then stretching it vertically by the factor 2. Graph $h(x)$ by stretching $f(x)$ vertically by the factor 2 and then translating it up 2 units. Compare the graphs of $g(x)$ and $h(x)$.

8. Reasoning Can you give an example of a function for which a horizontal translation gives the same resulting graph as a vertical translation? Explain.

9. Find a new function $g(x)$ transformed from $f(x) = -x - 2$ such that $g(x)$ is perpendicular to $f(x)$.

Practice and Problem-Solving Exercises

MATHEMATICAL PRACTICES

 **Practice**

How is each function related to $y = x$? Graph the function by translating the parent function.

◀ See Problem 1.

10. $y = x - 3$

11. $y = x + 4.5$

12. $y = x + 1.5$

Make a table of values for $f(x)$ after the given translation.

13. 3 units up

x	f(x)
−2	3
0	1
1	−2
3	−1

14. 1 unit down

x	f(x)
−1	1
0	0
2	−4
3	2

15. 4 units up

x	f(x)
−3	1
−1	−2
1	0
4	3

Write an equation for each vertical translation of $y = f(x)$.

16. $\frac{2}{3}$ unit down

17. 4 units up

18. 2 units up

For each function, identify the horizontal translation of the parent function, $f(x) = x^2$. Then graph the function.

◀ See Problems 2 and 3.

19. $y = (x - 4)^2$

20. $y = (x + 1)^2$

21. $y = (x + 3)^2$

22. The graph of the function $f(x)$ is shown at the right.
   a. Make a table of values for $f(x)$ and $f(x + 3)$.
   b. Graph $f(x)$ and $f(x + 3)$ on the same coordinate grid.

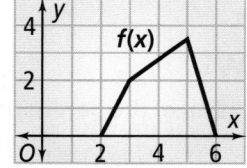

Write the function rule for each function reflected in the given axis.

23. $f(x) = x + 1$; x-axis

24. $f(x) = 3x$; y-axis

25. $f(x) = 2x - 4$; x-axis

Write an equation for each transformation of $y = x$.

◀ See Problem 4.

26. vertical stretch by a factor of 4

27. vertical stretch by a factor of 2

28. vertical compression by a factor of $\frac{1}{2}$

29. vertical compression by a factor of $\frac{1}{4}$

Write the function rule $g(x)$ after the given transformations of the graph of $f(x) = 4x$.

◀ See Problem 5.

30. translation up 5 units; reflection in the x-axis

31. reflection in the y-axis; vertical compression by a factor of $\frac{1}{8}$

Describe the transformations of $f(x)$ that produce $g(x)$.

32. $f(x) = \frac{x}{2}$; $g(x) = -2x + 4$

33. $f(x) = 3x$; $g(x) = \left(\frac{3x}{4} - 2\right)$

 **Apply**

34. Think About a Plan Suppose you are playing with a yo-yo during a school talent show. The string is 3 ft long and you hold your hand 4 ft above the stage. The stage is 3.5 ft above the floor of the auditorium. Make a graph of the yo-yo's distance from the auditorium floor with respect to time during the show.
   • How could you graph the position of the yo-yo with respect to the stage, if you let time $t = 0$ when you start your routine?
   • How could you transform this graph to show the position with respect to the auditorium floor?

35. If someone started to take a video of your yo-yo routine when you were introduced, 10 seconds before you actually started, what transformation would you have to make to your graph to match their video?

Write the equations for $f(x)$ and $g(x)$. Then identify the reflection that transforms the graph of $f(x)$ to the graph of $g(x)$.

36. 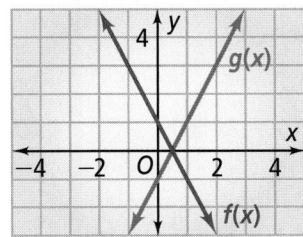   **37.** 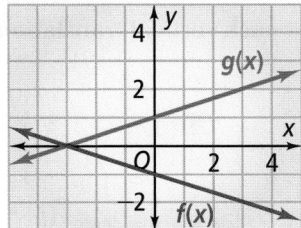   **38.**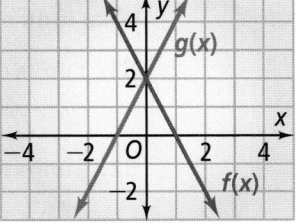

39. Open-Ended Draw a figure in Quadrant I. Use a translation to move your figure into Quadrant III. Describe your translation.

40. Writing The graph of $f(x)$ is shown at the right. Suppose each transformation of $f(x)$ results in the given functions.
   i. vertical translation; $g(x)$
   ii. reflection in the x-axis; $h(x)$
   iii. vertical stretch; $k(x)$,
   iv. horizontal translation; $m(x)$
   a. Describe how the domain and range of the four new functions compare with the domain and range of $f(x)$.
   b. Reasoning Do you think these effects on the domain and range of the original function hold true for all functions? Explain.

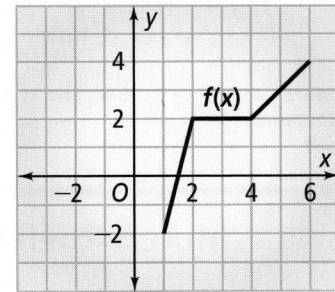

Graph each pair of functions on the same coordinate plane. Describe a transformation that changes $f(x)$ to $g(x)$.

41. $f(x) = x + 1; g(x) = x - 5$ **42.** $f(x) = -x + 3; g(x) = x - 4$

43. $f(x) = x - 3; g(x) = x + 1$ **44.** $f(x) = -x - 1; g(x) = -x + 2$

45. Error Analysis Your friend wrote the transformations shown to describe how to change the graph of $f(x) = x^2$ to the graph of $g(x) = 2(x + 1)^2 - 3$. Explain the error and give the correct transformations.

> • ~~shift vertically 1 unit up~~
> • ~~shift horizontally 2 units right~~
> • ~~shift vertically 3 units down~~

Using the graph of the function $f(x)$ shown, sketch the graph of each transformed function.

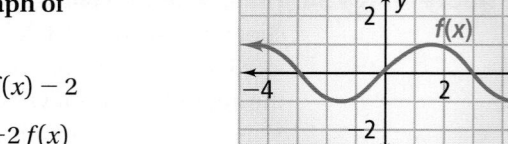

46. $f(x + 1)$

47. $f(x) - 2$

48. $f(x + 2) + 1$

49. $-2f(x)$

50. Graph all of the following functions in the same viewing window. After you enter each new function, view its graph.

  i. $y = x^2$ ii. $y = x^2 + 2$ iii. $y = (x + 2)^2$ iv. $y = (x - 1)^2 - 4$ v. $y = -x^2 - 2$

  Based on your results, make a sketch of the graph of $f(x) = -(x + 2)^2 + 1$ and check your prediction on your calculator.

Standardized Test Prep

SAT/ACT

What is an equation for each vertical translation of $y = 2x - 1$?

51. 3 units down

  (A) $y = 2x - 7$ (B) $y = 2x + 2$ (C) $y = 2x + 5$ (D) $y = 2x - 4$

52. $\frac{3}{5}$ units up

  (F) $y = 2x - \frac{2}{5}$ (G) $y = 2x - \frac{11}{5}$ (H) $y = 2x - \frac{8}{5}$ (I) $y = 2x + \frac{1}{5}$

53. What is the slope of the line in the graph at the right?

  (A) $-\frac{5}{2}$ (C) $\frac{2}{5}$

  (B) $-\frac{2}{5}$ (D) $\frac{5}{2}$

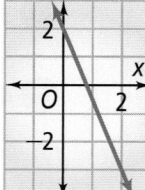

Short Response

54. The weight of a gold bar varies directly with its volume. If a 40 cm³ bar weighs 772 grams, how much will a 100 cm³ bar weigh?

Mixed Review

55. A musician's manager keeps track of the ticket prices and the attendance at recent performances. Use a graphing calculator to determine the equation of the line of best fit for the given data.

🔵 **See Lesson 2-5.**

| Ticket Prices($) | 41.00 | 41.50 | 42.00 | 43.00 | 43.50 | 44.00 | 44.50 | 45.00 | 45.00 | 47.00 |
| Number Sold | 256 | 276 | 250 | 241 | 210 | 235 | 195 | 194 | 205 | 180 |

Get Ready! **To prepare for Lesson 2-7, do Exercises 56–58.**

Solve each absolute value equation.

🔵 **See Lesson 1-6.**

56. $|x - 3| + 2 = 7$

57. $|2x + 1| - 14 = 9$

58. $\frac{1}{3}|5x - 3| = 6$

2-7 Absolute Value Functions and Graphs

Common Core State Standards

F-BF.B.3 Identify the effect on the graph of replacing $f(x)$ by $f(x) + k$, $k\,f(x)$, $f(kx)$, and $f(x + k)$ for specific values of k ... find the value of k given the graphs. **Also F-IF.C.7b**

MP 1, MP 3, MP 5

Objective To graph absolute value functions

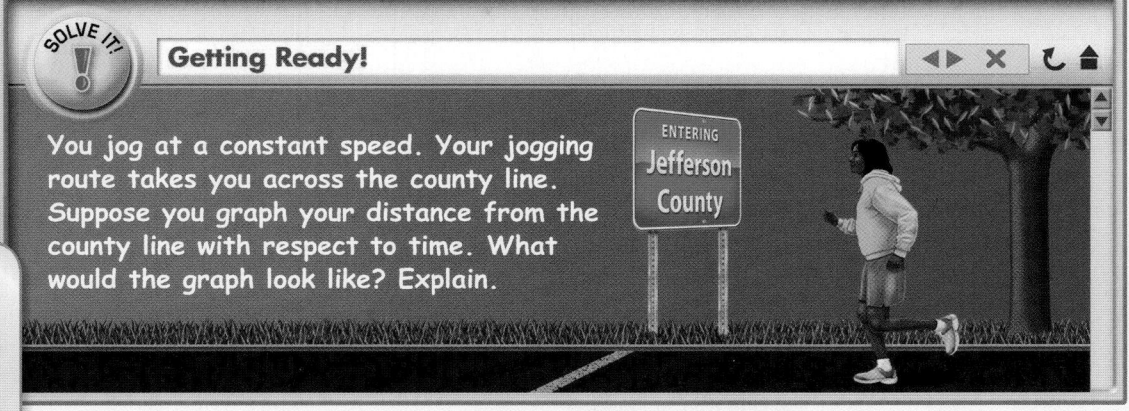

SOLVE IT!

Getting Ready!

You jog at a constant speed. Your jogging route takes you across the county line. Suppose you graph your distance from the county line with respect to time. What would the graph look like? Explain.

ENTERING Jefferson County

Think about how the distance changes before and after you cross the county line. Can a distance ever be negative?

MATHEMATICAL PRACTICES

There is a family of functions related to the one you represented in the Solve It.

Essential Understanding Just as the absolute value of x is its distance from 0, the absolute value of $f(x)$, or $|f(x)|$, gives the distance from the line $y = 0$ for each value of $f(x)$.

The simplest example of an **absolute value function** is $f(x) = |x|$. The graph of the absolute value of a linear function in two variables is V-shaped and symmetric about a vertical line called the **axis of symmetry**. Such a graph has either a single maximum point or a single minimum point, called the **vertex**.

Lesson Vocabulary
- absolute value function
- axis of symmetry
- vertex

Key Concept Absolute Value Parent Function $f(x) = |x|$

Table	Function	Graph

Table

x	$y = |x|$
-3	3
-2	2
-1	1
0	0
1	1
2	2
3	3

Function

$$f(x) = \begin{cases} |x| = x, \text{ when } x \geq 0 \\ |x| = -x, \text{ when } x < 0 \end{cases}$$

Graph

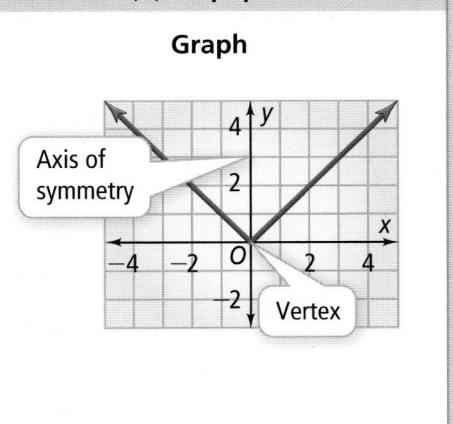

Axis of symmetry

Vertex

 **Problem 1** Graphing an Absolute Value Function

What is the graph of the absolute value function $y = |x| - 4$? How is this graph different from the graph of the parent function $f(x) = |x|$?

Think

Make a table of values and graph the function.

Write

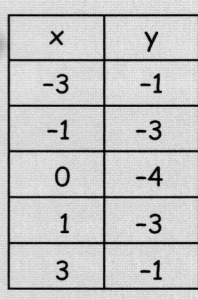

x	y
-3	-1
-1	-3
0	-4
1	-3
3	-1

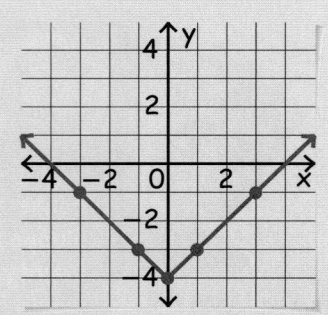

Use the location of the vertex to see how the graph has been translated. The parent function was not multiplied by a number, so the graph wasn't stretched, compressed, or reflected.

Since the vertex is at $(0, -4)$, you translated the graph of $y = |x|$ down 4 units.

  Got It? **1. a.** What is the graph of the function $y = |x| + 2$? How is this graph different from the parent function?

b. Reasoning Do transformations of the form $y = |x| + k$ affect the axis of symmetry? Explain.

The transformations you studied in Lesson 2-6 also apply to absolute value functions.

take note

Key Concept   The Family of Absolute Value Functions

Parent Function $y = |x|$

Vertical Translation	**Horizontal Translation**
Translation up k units, $k > 0$ $\quad y = |x| + k$	Translation right h units, $h > 0$ $\quad y = |x - h|$
Translation down k units, $k > 0$ $\quad y = |x| - k$	Translation left h units, $h > 0$ $\quad y = |x + h|$
Vertical Stretch and Compression	**Reflection**
Vertical stretch, $a > 1$ $\quad y = a|x|$	In the x-axis $\quad y = -|x|$
Vertical compression, $0 < a < 1$ $\quad y = a|x|$	In the y-axis $\quad y = |-x|$

Problem 2 Combining Translations

Multiple Choice Which of the following is the graph of $y = |x + 2| + 3$?

Ⓐ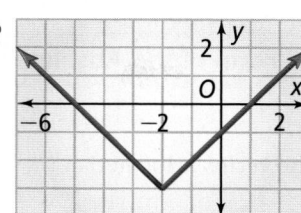

Ⓒ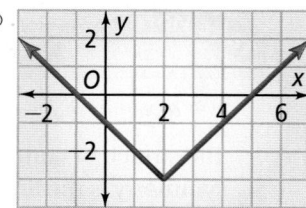

Ⓑ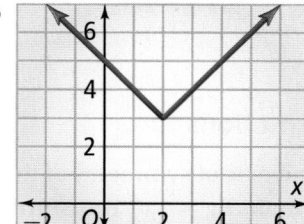

Ⓓ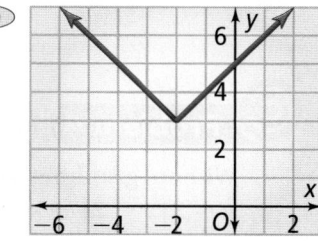

Think

Can you eliminate any answers after this comparison?
Only choices A and D show translations of $y = |x|$ to the left.

Compare $y = |x + 2| + 3$ to each form, $y = |x + h|$ and $y = |x| + k$.

$y = |x + h|$ The parent function, $y = |x|$, is translated left 2 units.

$y = |x| + k$ The parent function, $y = |x|$, is translated up 3 units.

The parent function $y = |x|$ is translated left 2 units and up 3 units. The vertex will be at $(-2, 3)$. The correct choice is D.

 Got It? 2. What is the graph of the function $y = |x - 2| + 1$?

The right branch of the graph of $y = |x|$ has slope 1. The graph of $y = a|x|$, $a > 0$, is a stretch or compression of the graph of $y = |x|$. Its right branch has slope a. The graph of $y = -a|x|$ is a reflection of $y = a|x|$ in the x-axis and its right branch has slope $-a$.

 Problem 3 Vertical Stretch and Compression

What is the graph of $y = \frac{1}{2}|x|$?

The graph is a vertical compression of the graph of $f(x) = |x|$ by the factor $\frac{1}{2}$. Graph the right branch and use symmetry to graph the left branch.

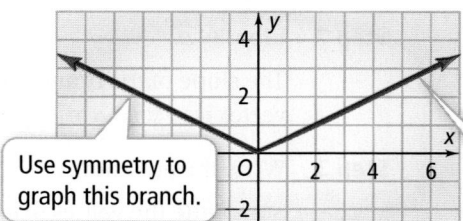

Use symmetry to graph this branch.

Starting at $(0, 0)$, graph $y = \frac{1}{2}x$.

 Got It? 3. What is the graph of each function?

      a. $y = 2|x|$ **b.** $y = -\frac{2}{3}|x|$

You can combine the equations for stretches and compressions with the equations for translations to write a general form for absolute value functions.

Key Concept General Form of the Absolute Value Function

$y = a|x - h| + k$

The stretch or compression factor is $|a|$, the vertex is located at (h, k), and the axis of symmetry is the line $x = h$.

Problem 4 Identifying Transformations

Plan

To what should you compare
$y = 3|x - 2| + 4$?
Compare it to the general form,
$y = a|x - h| + k$.

Without graphing, what are the vertex and axis of symmetry of the graph of $y = 3|x - 2| + 4$? How is the parent function $y = |x|$ transformed?

Compare $y = 3|x - 2| + 4$ with the general form $y = a|x - h| + k$.

$a = 3, h = 2$, and $k = 4$.

The vertex is $(2, 4)$ and the axis of symmetry is $x = 2$.

The parent function $y = |x|$ is translated 2 units to the right, vertically stretched by the factor 3, and translated 4 units up.

Check Check by graphing the equation on a graphing calculator.

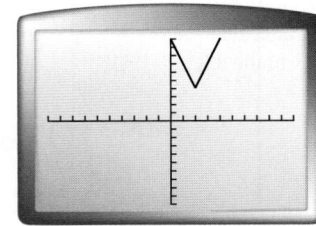

✓ **Got It? 4.** What are the vertex and axis of symmetry of $y = -2|x - 1| - 3$? How is $y = |x|$ transformed?

Problem 5 Writing an Absolute Value Function

What is the equation of the absolute value function?

Think

What does the graph tell you about a?
The upside-down V suggests that $a < 0$.

Step 1 Identify the vertex.

The vertex is at $(-1, 4)$, so $h = -1$ and $k = 4$.

Step 2 Identify a.

The slope of the branch to the right of the vertex is $-\frac{1}{3}$, so $a = -\frac{1}{3}$.

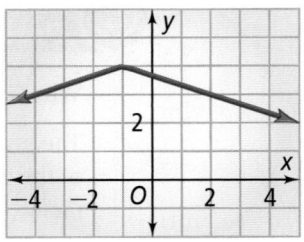

Step 3 Write the equation.

Substitute the values of a, h, and k into the general form $y = a|x - h| + k$.
The equation that describes the graph is $y = -\frac{1}{3}|x + 1| + 4$.

✓ **Got It? 5.** What is the equation of the absolute value function?

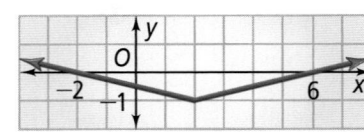

Lesson Check

Do you know HOW?

Find the vertex and the axis of symmetry of the graph of each function.

1. $y = 2|x + 4| - 3$ **2.** $y = |-x - 3| + 9$

Determine if each function is a vertical stretch or vertical compression of the parent function $y = |x|$.

3. $y = -\frac{7}{2}|x|$ **4.** $y = \frac{3}{2}|x|$

Do you UNDERSTAND?

5. Is it true that without making a graph of an absolute value function, you can describe its position in the coordinate plane? Explain with an example.

6. Write two absolute value functions such that they have a common vertex in Quadrant III and one is the reflection of the other in a horizontal line.

7. Compare and Contrast How is the graph of $y = x$ different from the graph of $y = |x|$?

 **Practice and Problem-Solving Exercises**

 **Practice**

Make a table of values for each equation. Then graph the equation.   📍 **See Problems 1 and 2.**

8. $y = |x| + 1$ **9.** $y = |x| - 1$ **10.** $y = |x| - 3$

11. $y = |x + 2|$ **12.** $y = |x + 4|$ **13.** $y = |x + 5|$

14. $y = |x - 1| + 3$ **15.** $y = |x + 6| - 1$ **16.** $y = |x - 5| + 4$

Graph each equation. Then describe the transformation from the parent function $f(x) = |x|$.   📍 **See Problem 3.**

17. $y = 3|x|$ **18.** $y = -\frac{1}{2}|x|$ **19.** $y = -2|x|$

20. $y = \frac{1}{3}|x|$ **21.** $y = \frac{3}{2}|x|$ **22.** $y = -\frac{3}{4}|x|$

Without graphing, identify the vertex, axis of symmetry, and transformations from the parent function $f(x) = |x|$.   📍 **See Problem 4.**

23. $y = |x + 2| - 4$ **24.** $y = \frac{3}{2}|x - 6|$ **25.** $y = 3|x + 6|$

26. $y = 4 - |x + 2|$ **27.** $y = -|x - 5|$ **28.** $y = |x - 2| - 6$

Write an absolute value equation for each graph.   📍 **See Problem 5.**

29.

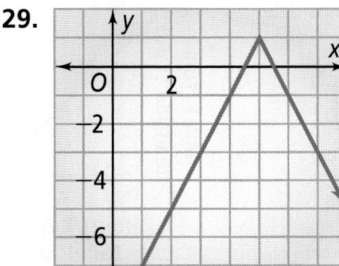

30.

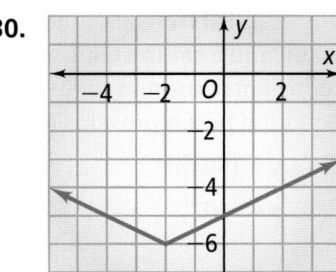

 **Apply**

31. Think About a Plan Graph $y = -2|x + 3| + 4$. List the x- and y-intercepts, if any.
- What is the vertex?
- What does y equal at the x-intercept(s)? What does x equal at the y-intercept(s)?

32. Graph $y = 4|x - 3| + 1$. List the vertex and the x- and y-intercepts, if any.

33. Error Analysis A classmate says that the graphs of $y = -3|x|$ and $y = |-3x|$ are identical. Graph each function and explain why your classmate is not correct.

34. Graph each pair of equations on the same coordinate grid.

  a. $y = 2|x + 1|; y = |2x + 1|$ **b.** $y = 5|x - 2|; y = |5x - 2|$

  c. Reasoning Explain why each pair of graphs in parts (a) and (b) are different.

35. The graphs of the absolute value functions $f(x)$ and $g(x)$ are given.

  a. Describe a series of transformations that you can use to transform $f(x)$ into $g(x)$.

  b. Reasoning If you change the order of the transformations you found in part(a), could you still transform $f(x)$ into $g(x)$? Explain.

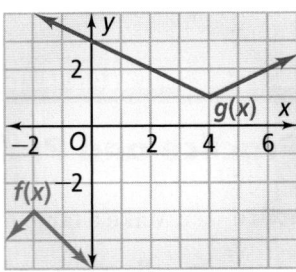

Graph each absolute value equation.

36. $y = \left|-\frac{1}{4}x - 1\right|$ **37.** $y = \left|\frac{5}{2}x - 2\right|$ **38.** $y = \left|\frac{3}{2}x + 2\right|$

39. $y = |3x - 6| + 1$ **40.** $y = -|x - 3|$ **41.** $y = |2x + 6|$

42. $y = 2|x + 2| - 3$ **43.** $y = 6 - |3x|$ **44.** $y = 6 - |3x + 1|$

45. a. Graph the equations $f(x) = -\frac{1}{2}|x - 3|$ and $g(x) = \left|-\frac{1}{2}(x - 3)\right|$ on the same set of axes.

  b. Writing Describe the similarities and differences in the graphs.

46. a. Use a graphing calculator. Graph $y_1 = k|x|$ and $y_2 = |kx|$ for some positive value of k.

  b. Graph $y_1 = k|x|$ and $y_2 = |kx|$ for some negative value of k.

  c. What conclusion can you make about the graphs of $y_1 = k|x|$ and $y_2 = |kx|$?

 **Challenge**   **Graph each absolute value equation.**

47. $y = |3x| - \frac{x}{3}$ **48.** $y = \frac{1}{2}|x| + 4|x - 1|$ **49.** $y = |2x| + |x - 4|$

50. The graph at the right models the distance between a roadside stand and a car traveling at a constant speed. The x-axis represents time and the y-axis represents distance. Which equation best represents the relation shown in the graph?

  Ⓐ $y = |60x|$ Ⓒ $y = |x| + 60$

  Ⓑ $y = |40x|$ Ⓓ $y = |x| + 40$

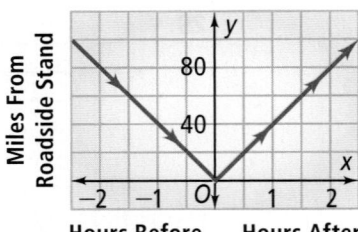

Standardized Test Prep

SAT/ACT

51. The graph shows which equation?

  Ⓐ $y = |3x - 1| + 2$ Ⓒ $y = |x - 1| - 2$

  Ⓑ $y = |x - 1| + 2$ Ⓓ $y = |3x - 3| - 2$

52. How are the graphs of $y = 2x$ and $y = 2x + 2$ related?

  Ⓕ The graph of $y = 2x + 2$ is the graph of $y = 2x$ translated down two units.

  Ⓖ The graph of $y = 2x + 2$ is the graph of $y = 2x$ translated up two units.

  Ⓗ The graph of $y = 2x + 2$ is the graph of $y = 2x$ translated to the left two units.

  Ⓘ The graph of $y = 2x + 2$ is the graph of $y = 2x$ translated to the right two units.

53. What is the equation of a line parallel to $y = x$ that passes through the point $(0, 1)$?

  Ⓐ $y = x + 1$ Ⓒ $y = x - 1$

  Ⓑ $y = 2x + 2$ Ⓓ $y = -x$

Short Response

54. Is $|y| = x$ a function? Explain.

Mixed Review

Write an equation for each transformation of the graph of $y = x + 2$.  **See Lesson 2-6.**

55. 2 units up, 3 units right

56. vertical compression by a factor of $\frac{1}{2}$, reflection in the y-axis

Write the function rule for each function reflected in the given axis.

57. $f(x) = x - 7$; y-axis   **58.** $f(x) = 2x - 6$; y-axis   **59.** $f(x) = 4 + x$; x-axis

Find a trend line for each scatter plot. Write the equation for each trend line. **See Lesson 2-5.**

60. 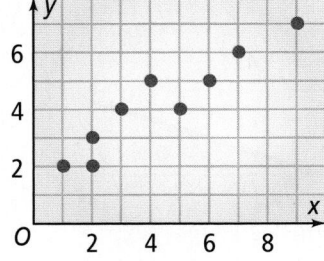   **61.**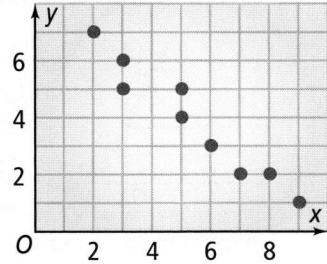

Get Ready! **To prepare for Lesson 2-8, do Exercises 62–64.**

Solve each inequality. Graph the solution on a number line. **See Lesson 1-5.**

62. $12p \leq 15$ **63.** $4 + t > 17$ **64.** $5 - 2t \geq 11$

2-8 Two-Variable Inequalities

Common Core State Standards

A-CED.A.2 Create equations in two or more variables to represent relationships between quantities; graph equations on coordinate axes with labels and scales.
Also F-IF.C.7b
MP 1, MP 3, MP 4, MP 5, MP 7

Objective To graph two-variable inequalities

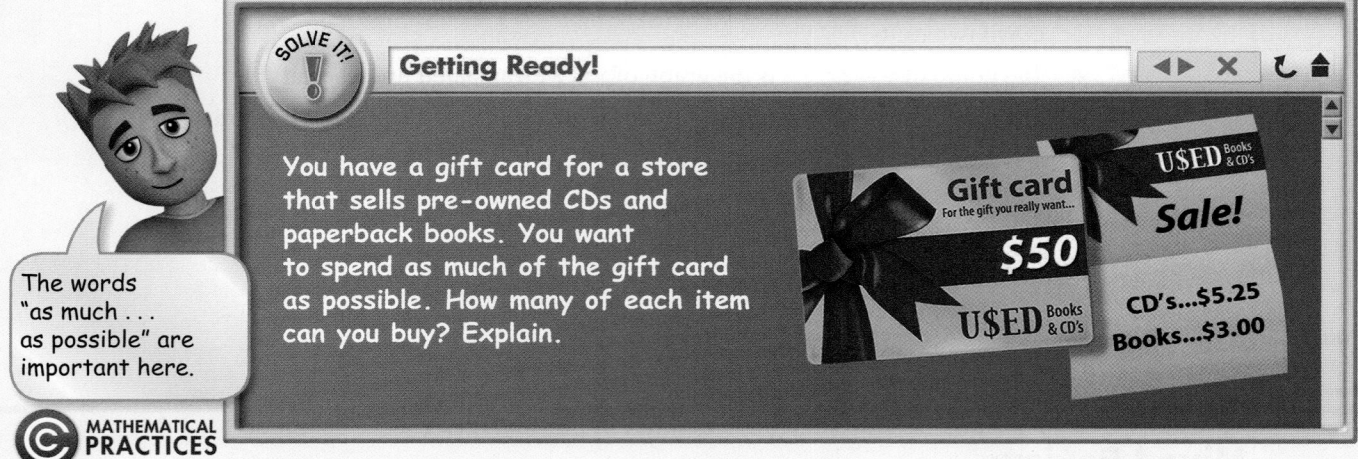

The words "as much . . . as possible" are important here.

MATHEMATICAL PRACTICES

In some situations you need to compare quantities. You can use inequalities for situations that involve these relationships: *less than, less than or equal to, greater than,* and *greater than or equal to.*

Essential Understanding Graphing an inequality in two variables is similar to graphing a line. The graph of a linear inequality contains all points on one side of the line and may or may not include the points on the line.

A **linear inequality** is an inequality in two variables whose graph is a region of the coordinate plane bounded by a line. This line is the **boundary** of the graph. The boundary separates the coordinate plane into two **half-planes**, one of which consists of solutions of the inequality.

Lesson Vocabulary
- linear inequality
- boundary
- half-plane
- test point

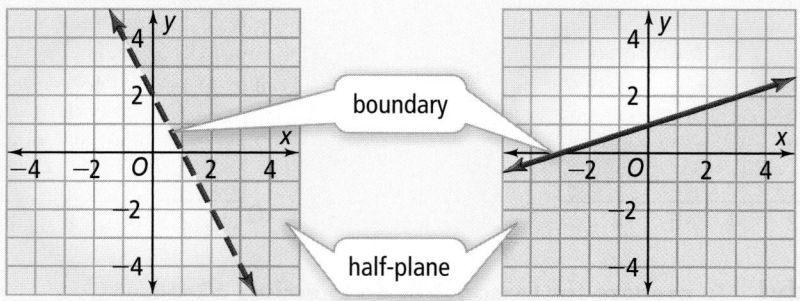

To determine which half-plane to shade, pick a **test point** that is *not* on the boundary. Check whether that point satisfies the inequality. If it does, shade the half-plane that includes the test point. If not, shade the other half-plane. The origin, (0, 0), is usually an easy test point as long as it is not on the boundary.

 **Problem 1** Graphing Linear Inequalities

What is the graph of each inequality?

A $y > 3x - 1$

Step 1
Graph the boundary line $y = 3x - 1$. Use a dashed boundary line because the inequality is *greater than*, and the points on the line do not satisfy the inequality.

Step 2
Choose a test point, (0, 0). Substitute $x = 0$ and $y = 0$ into $y > 3x - 1$.
$$0 > 3(0) - 1$$
$$0 > -1$$
Since $0 > -1$ is true, shade the half plane that includes (0, 0).

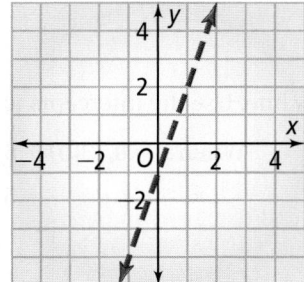

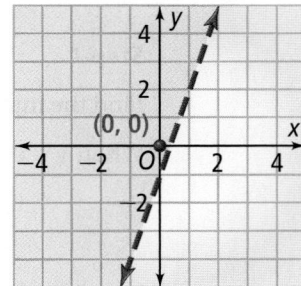

B $y \leq 3x - 1$

The boundary line is again $y = 3x - 1$, but it is solid because the inequality is less than or *equal to*.

Shade the region opposite the region shaded above (for $>$) because the inequality is *less than* or equal to.

You can also check the point (0, 0).

$$0 \leq 3(0) - 1$$

$$0 \leq -1$$

Since $0 \leq -1$ is false, (0, 0) is not part of the solution.

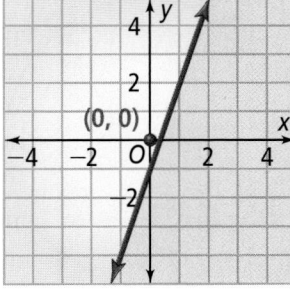

Plan

Can you use the graph of $y > 3x - 1$ to help graph $y \leq 3x - 1$?
If you shaded above the line for $y > 3x - 1$, then shade below the line for $y \leq 3x - 1$.

Got It? **1.** What is the graph of each inequality?
    a. $y \geq -2x + 1$ **b.** $y < -2x + 1$

You can also inspect inequalities solved for y, such as $y > mx + b$ to determine which half-plane describes the solution. Since y describes vertical position, the solution of $y > mx + b$ will be *above* the boundary line. The solution of $y < mx + b$ will be *below* the boundary line.

Problem 2 Using a Linear Inequality

Entertainment The map shows the number of tickets needed for small or large rides at the fair. You do not want to spend more than $15 on tickets. How many small or large rides can you ride?

Think

What are the unknowns?
The unknowns are the number of small rides and the number of large rides you can get on.

You can buy 60 tickets with $15.

Relate the number of tickets for small rides   plus   the number of tickets for large rides   is less than or equal to   60

Define Let x = the number of small rides.

Let y = the number of large rides.

Write $3x$ + $5y$ ≤   60

Step 1

Find the intercepts of the boundary line. Use the intercepts to graph the boundary line.

When $y = 0$, $3x + 5(0) = 60$.

$$3x = 60$$
$$x = 20$$

When $x = 0$, $3(0) + 5y = 60$.

$$5y = 60$$
$$y = 12$$

Graph the line that connects the intercepts $(20, 0)$ and $(0, 12)$. Since the inequality is ≤, use a solid boundary line.

Step 2

The region above the boundary line represents combinations of rides that require more than 60 tickets. You purchased a *finite* number of tickets, 60, so you will not be able to go on an infinite number of rides. Shade the region below the boundary line.

The number of small rides x and the number of large rides y are whole numbers. In math, such a situation is called *discrete*. All points with whole number coordinates in the shaded region represent possible combinations of small and large rides.

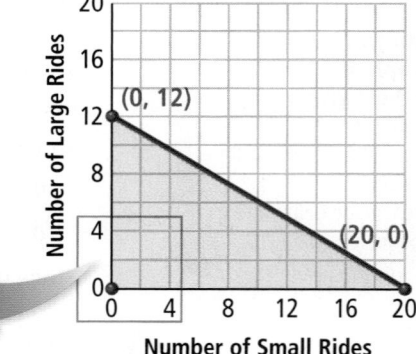

Got It? 2. a. Suppose that you decide to spend no more than $30 for tickets. What are the possible combinations of small and large rides that you can ride now? Use a graph to find your answer.

b. Reasoning Why did the graph of the solution in Problem 2 only include Quadrant I?

You can graph two-variable absolute value inequalities in the same way that you graph linear inequalities.

 Problem 3 Graphing an Absolute Value Inequality

What is the graph of $1 - y < |x + 2|$?

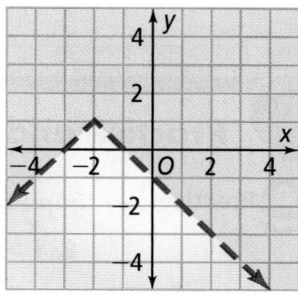

$1 - y < |x + 2|$

$-y < |x + 2| - 1$ Subtract 1 from each side.

$y > -|x + 2| + 1$ Multiply both sides by -1.

The graph of $y = -|x + 2| + 1$ is the graph of $y = |x|$, reflected in the x-axis and translated left 2 units and up 1 unit.

Since the inequality is solved for y and $y > -|x + 2| + 1$, shade the region above the boundary.

 Got It? 3. What is the graph of $y - 4 \geq 2|x - 1|$?

You can use the transformations discussed in previous lessons to help draw the boundary graphs more quickly. You can also use them to write an inequality based on a graph.

 Problem 4 Writing an Inequality Based on a Graph

What inequality does this graph represent?

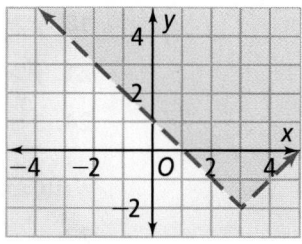

The boundary is the graph of the absolute value function $y = |x|$, translated. The vertex of $y = |x|$ is translated to $(3, -2)$, so the boundary is the graph of $y = |x - 3| - 2$.

The solution is shaded above the boundary, so the inequality is either $>$ or $\geq$. Since the boundary is a dashed line, the correct inequality is $y > |x - 3| - 2$.

 **Got It? 4. a.** What inequality does this graph represent?

    b. Reasoning You can tell from looking at the inequality $y > 5x - 3$ to shade above the boundary line to represent the solution. Can you use the same technique to show the solution of an inequality like $2x - y > 1$? Explain.

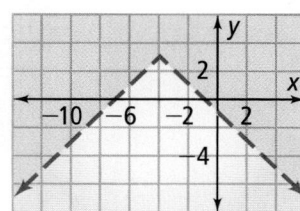

Lesson Check

Do you know HOW?

What is the graph of each inequality?

1. $9y \le 12x$

2. $7x + y \ge 8$

What is the graph of each absolute value inequality?

3. $y \le |x + 1|$

4. $y \ge |2x - 3|$

Do you UNDERSTAND?

5. Do the points on the boundary line of the graph of an inequality help determine the shaded area of the graph? Explain.

6. Compare and Contrast How is graphing a linear inequality in two variables different from graphing a linear equation in two variables?

7. Reasoning Is the ordered pair $\left(\frac{3}{4}, 0\right)$ a solution of $3x + y > 3$? Explain.

Practice and Problem-Solving Exercises

 **Practice**   **Graph each inequality.**   See Problem 1.

8. $y > 2x + 1$ **9.** $y < 3$ **10.** $x \le 0$

11. $y \le x - 5$ **12.** $2x + 3y \ge 12$ **13.** $2y \ge 4x - 6$

14. $3x - 2y \le 9$ **15.** $-y < 2x + 2$ **16.** $5 - y \ge x$

17. Cooking The time needed to roast a chicken depends on its weight. Allow at least 20 min/lb for a chicken weighing as much as 6 lb. Allow at least 15 min/lb for a chicken weighing more than 6 lb.   See Problem 2.
  a. Write two inequalities to represent the time needed to roast a chicken.
  b. Graph the inequalities.

Graph each absolute value inequality.   See Problem 3.

18. $y \ge |2x - 1|$ **19.** $y \le |3x| + 1$ **20.** $y \le |4 - x|$

21. $y > |-x + 4| + 1$ **22.** $y - 7 > |x + 2|$ **23.** $y + 2 \le \left|\frac{1}{2}x\right|$

24. $3 - y \ge -|x - 4|$ **25.** $1 - y < |2x - 3|$ **26.** $y + 3 \le |3x| - 1$

Write an inequality for each graph. The equation for the boundary line is given.   See Problem 4.

27. $y = -x - 2$ **28.** $5x + 3y = 9$ **29.** $2y = |2x + 6|$

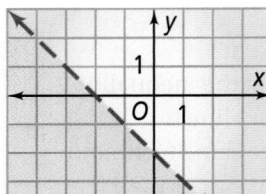   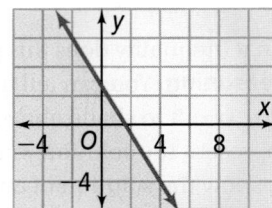   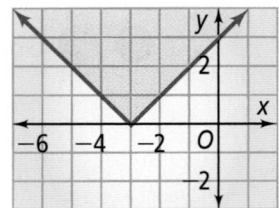

Graph each inequality on a coordinate plane.

30. $5x - 2y \geq -10$ **31.** $2x - 5y < -10$ **32.** $\frac{3}{4}x + \frac{2}{3}y > \frac{5}{2}$ **33.** $3(x - 2) + 2y \leq 6$

34. $|x - 1| > y + 7$ **35.** $y - |2x| \leq 21$ **36.** $\frac{2}{3}x + 2 \leq \frac{2}{9}y$ **37.** $0.25y - 1.5x \geq -4$

38. Think About a Plan The graph at the right relates the number of hours you spend on the phone to the number of hours you spend studying per week. Describe the domain for this situation. Write an inequality for the graph.

- What is the least amount of time you can spend on the phone per week? What is the most?
- What is the least amount of time you can spend studying per week? What is the most?
- What is the greatest amount of time you can spend either on the phone or studying per week?

Time per Week

Write an inequality for each graph.

39.
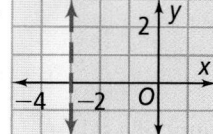

40.
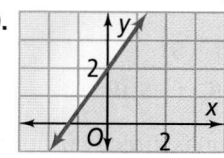

41.
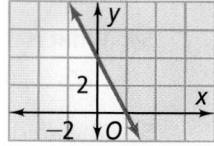

42.
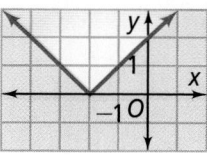

43.
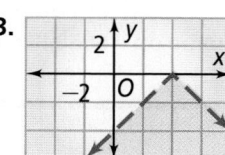

44.
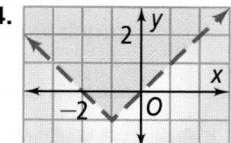

45. Which graph best represents the solution of the inequality $y \geq 2|x - 1| - 2$?

Ⓐ 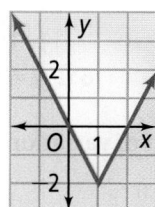   Ⓑ 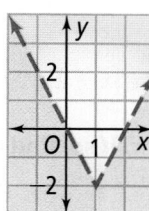   Ⓒ 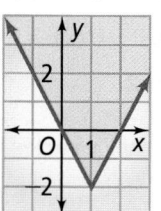   Ⓓ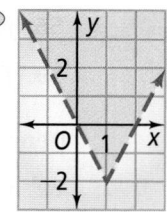

46. The graph at the right relates the amount of gas in the tank of your car to the distance you can drive.
- **a.** Describe the domain for this situation.
- **b.** Why does the graph stop?
- **c.** Why is only the first quadrant shown?
- **d. Reasoning** Would every point in the solution region be a solution?
- **e.** Write an inequality for the graph.
- **f.** What does the coefficient of x represent?

Miles to Travel

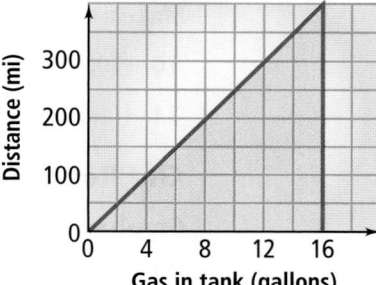

 **Challenge**

47. Writing When you graph an inequality, you can often use the point $(0, 0)$ to test which side of the boundary line to shade. Describe a situation in which you could not use $(0, 0)$ as a test point.

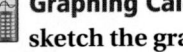 **Graphing Calculator** Graph each inequality on a graphing calculator. Then sketch the graph.

48. $y \le |x + 1| - |x - 1|$

49. $y > |x| + |x + 3|$

50. $y < |x - 3| - |x + 3|$

51. $y < 7 - |x - 4| + |x|$

Standardized Test Prep

SAT/ACT

52. Suppose y varies directly with x. If x is 30 when y is 10, what is x when y is 9?

Ⓐ 3   Ⓑ 27   Ⓒ 29   Ⓓ $\frac{300}{9}$

53. Which equation represents a line with slope -2 and y-intercept 3?

Ⓕ $3y = x - 2$ Ⓖ $3y = -2x + 1$ Ⓗ $y = 2x - 3$ Ⓘ $y = -2x + 3$

54. What is the vertex of $y = |x| - 5$?

Ⓐ $(5, 0)$ Ⓑ $(-5, 0)$ Ⓒ $(0, 5)$ Ⓓ $(0, -5)$

Extended Response

55. The amount of a commission is directly proportional to the amount of a sale. A realtor received a commission of $48,000 on the sale of an $800,000 house. How much would the commission be on a $650,000 house?

Mixed Review

Graph each function by translating its parent function.   ◀ **See Lesson 2-7.**

56. $y = |2x + 5|$

57. $y = |x| - 3$

58. $f(x) = |x + 6|$

59. $f(x) = |x| - 2$

60. $y = |x + 2|$

61. $y = |x - 1| + 5$

Determine whether y varies directly with x. If so, find the constant of variation.   ◀ **See Lesson 2-2.**

62. $y = x + 1$

63. $y = 100x$

64. $5x + y = 0$

65. $y - 2 = 2x$

66. $x = \frac{y}{3}$

67. $-4 = y - x$

68. $y = -10x$

69. $xy = 1$

Make a scatter plot and describe the correlation.   ◀ **See Lesson 2-5.**

70. $\{(0, 6), (1, 4), (2, 4), (4, 1), (5, 0)\}$

71. $\{(-10, 5), (-5, -5), (-2, 0), (0, 3), (5, -2)\}$

Get Ready! To prepare for Lesson 3-1, do Exercises 72–74.

Graph each equation. Use one coordinate plane for all three graphs.   ◀ **See Lesson 2-3.**

72. $3x - y = 2$

73. $3x - y = -2$

74. $x + 3y = -2$

Completing the Performance Task

Look back at your results from the Apply What You've Learned sections in Lessons 2-3 and 2-4. Use the work you did to complete the following.

> To solve these problems, you will pull together concepts about equivalence, linear functions and modeling. Show your work and justify your reasoning.

1. Solve the problem in the Task Description on page 59 by determining what time the work crew will take its afternoon break. Show all your work and explain each step of your solution.

 2. Reflect Choose one of the Mathematical Practices below and explain how you applied it in your work on the Performance Task.

MP 2: Reason abstractly and quantitatively.

MP 4: Model with mathematics.

On Your Own

The diagram from page 59 is shown again below. The county's Department of Transportation is planning the construction of another road, to be called Oak Street. Oak Street will begin at North Street, 30 miles north of Wilson Street. *Note:* North Street continues north, beyond its intersection with Main Street. Oak Street will be parallel to Main Street.

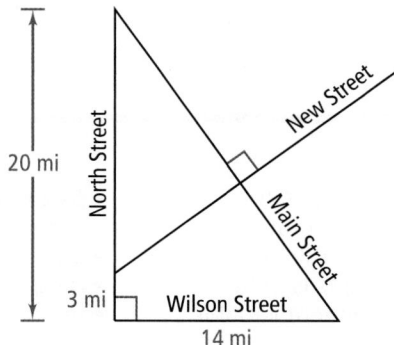

Determine how far the intersection of Oak Street and New Street will be from the intersection of Main Street and New Street.

2 Chapter Review

Connecting BIG ideas and Answering the Essential Questions

1 Equivalence
You can use either slope-intercept, point-slope, or standard form to represent linear functions. (You can transform one version to another as needed.)

Slope-Intercept Form (Lesson 2-3)
$y = mx + b$
$y = 2x - 1$

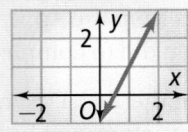

More Linear Equations (Lesson 2-4)
$y - y_1 = m(x - x_1)$ $Ax + By = C$
$y - 5 = 2(x - 3)$ $2x - y = 1$

2 Function
You can use the values of a, h, and k in the form $y = a|x - h| + k$ to determine how the parent function $y = |x|$ has been transformed.

Families of Functions (Lesson 2-6)
$f(x) + k$ vertical translation
$f(x - h)$ horizontal translation
$af(x)$ stretch or compression
$-f(x)$ reflection in the x-axis
$f(-x)$ reflection in the y-axis

Absolute Value Functions and Graphs (Lesson 2-7)
Parent: $y = |x|$
General form:
$y = a|x - h| + k$
vertex: (h, k)

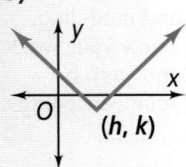

3 Modeling
You can use the equation of a trend line or line of best fit to model data that cluster in a linear pattern.

Using Linear Models (Lesson 2-5)
Positive correlation   Trend Line

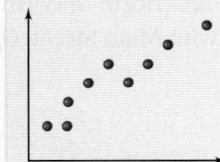 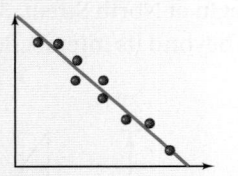

🔊 Chapter Vocabulary

- absolute value function (p. 107)
- axis of symmetry (p. 107)
- boundary (p. 114)
- constant of variation (p. 68)
- correlation (p. 92)
- correlation coefficient (p. 94)
- dependent variable (p. 63)
- direct variation (p. 68)
- domain (p. 61)

- function (p. 62)
- function notation (p. 63)
- function rule (p. 63)
- half-plane (p. 114)
- independent variable (p. 63)
- line of best fit (p. 94)
- linear equation (p. 75)
- linear function (p. 75)
- linear inequality (p. 114)
- parallel lines (p. 85)

- parent function (p. 99)
- perpendicular lines (p. 85)
- point-slope form (p. 81)
- range (p. 61)
- reflection (p. 101)
- relation (p. 60)
- scatter plot (p. 92)
- slope (p. 74)
- slope-intercept form (p. 76)
- standard form of a linear equation (p. 82)

- test point (p. 115)
- transformation (p. 99)
- translation (p. 99)
- vertex (p. 107)
- vertical compression (p. 102)
- vertical stretch (p. 102)
- vertical-line test (p. 62)
- x-intercept (p. 76)
- y-intercept (p. 76)

Choose the correct term to complete each sentence.

1. The graph of a function is (*always*/*sometimes*) a line.

2. The equation $y - 5 = 3(x + 2)$ is in (*point-slope*/*slope-intercept*) form.

2-1 Relations and Functions

Quick Review

A **relation** is a set of ordered pairs. The **domain** of a relation is the set of x-coordinates. The **range** is the set of y-coordinates. When each element of the domain is paired with exactly one element of the range, the relation is a **function**.

Example

Determine whether the relation is a function. Find the domain and range.

$$\{(5, 0), (8, 1), (1, 3), (5, 2), (3, 8)\}$$

In this relation, the x-coordinate 5 is paired with both 0 and 2. This relation is not a function.

The domain is the set of x-coordinates, which is $\{5, 8, 1, 3\}$.

The range is the set of y-coordinates, which is $\{0, 1, 3, 2, 8\}$.

Exercises

Determine whether each relation is a function. Find the domain and range.

3. $\{(10, 2), (-10, 2), (6, 4), (5, 3), (-6, 7)\}$

4. $\{(4, 5), (1, 5), (3, 8), (4, 6), (10, 12)\}$

5. 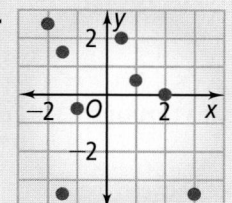   **6.**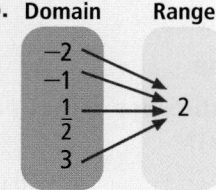

For each function, find $f(-2)$, $f(-0.5)$, and $f(3)$.

7. $f(x) = -x + 4$ **8.** $f(x) = \frac{3}{8}x - 3$

2-2 Direct Variation

Quick Review

A linear equation of the form $y = kx$, $k \neq 0$, represents **direct variation**. The **constant of variation** is k. You can use proportions to solve direct variation problems.

Example

In the table, determine whether y varies directly with x. If so, what is the constant of variation and the function rule?

x	y
2	6
3	9
8	24

$\frac{6}{2} = \frac{9}{3} = \frac{24}{8} = 3$, so y varies directly with x, and the constant of variation is 3.

The function rule is $y = 3x$.

Exercises

For each function, determine whether y varies directly with x. If so, find the constant of variation and write the function rule.

9.
x	y
-2	3
1	4
2	7

10.
x	y
4	5
6	9
10	17

11.
x	y
1	1
2	2
5	5

For each function, y varies directly with x. Find each constant of variation. Then find the value of y when $x = -0.3$.

12. $y = 2$ when $x = -\frac{1}{2}$ **13.** $y = \frac{2}{3}$ when $x = 0.2$

14. $y = 7$ when $x = 2$ **15.** $y = 4$ when $x = -3$

2-3 Linear Functions and Slope-Intercept Form

Quick Review

The graph of a **linear function** is a line. You can represent a linear function with a **linear equation**. Given two points on a line, the **slope** of the line is the ratio of the change in the y-coordinates to the change in the corresponding x-coordinates. The slope is the coefficient of x when you write a linear equation in **slope-intercept form**.

Example

What is the slope of the line that passes through (3, 5) and (−1, −2)?

$$m = \frac{y_2 - y_1}{x_2 - x_1}$$
Find the difference between the coordinates.

$$= \frac{5 - (-2)}{3 - (-1)} = \frac{7}{4}$$
Simplify.

Exercises

Identify the slope of the line that passes through the given points.

16. $(1, 3)$ and $(6, 1)$ **17.** $(4, 4)$ and $(-2, -3)$

18. $(3, 2)$ and $(-3, -2)$ **19.** $(5, 2)$ and $(-4, 6)$

Write an equation for each line in slope-intercept form.

20. slope $= -3$ and the y-intercept is $(0, 4)$

21. slope $= \frac{1}{2}$ and the y-intercept is $(0, 6)$

Rewrite each equation in slope-intercept form. Graph each line.

22. $4x - 2y = 3$ **23.** $-4x + 6y = 18$

24. $3y + 3x = 15$ **25.** $3y + x = 5$

2-4 More About Linear Equations

Quick Review

You write the equation of a line in **point-slope form** when you have a point and the slope or when you have two points. The **standard form** of an equation has both variables and no constants on the left side.

When two lines have the same slope, they are **parallel**. When two lines have slopes that are negative reciprocals of each other, they are **perpendicular**.

Example

Write an equation in standard form for the line with a slope of 2, going through (1, 6).

$$y - 6 = 2(x - 1)$$
Write the equation in point-slope form, substituting the given point and slope.

$$y = 2x - 2 + 6$$
Simplify.

$$-2x + y = 4$$
Write in standard form.

Exercises

Write an equation for each line in point-slope form and then convert it to standard form.

26. slope $= -3$, through $(4, 0)$

27. slope $= 5$, through $(1, -1)$

28. through $(0, 0)$ and $(3, -7)$

29. through $(2, 3)$ and $(3, 5)$

30. a. Write an equation of the line parallel to $x + 2y = 6$ through $(8, 3)$.
    b. Write an equation of the line perpendicular to $x + 2y = 6$ through $(8, 3)$.
    c. Graph the three lines on the same coordinate plane.

2-5 Using Linear Models

Quick Review

You can use a **scatter plot** to show relationships between data sets. You can make predictions using a trend line, which approximates the relationship between two data sets. The most accurate trend line is a **line of best fit**.

Example

Draw a scatter plot of the data. Is a linear model reasonable? If so, predict the value of y when $x = 9$.

$$\{(0, 6), (1, 7), (2, 5), (3, 4), (4, 2), (5, 1)\}$$

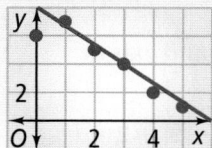

The points are close to the line $y = -\frac{4}{3}x + 8$, so a linear model is reasonable. When $x = 9$,

$$y = -\frac{4}{3}(9) + 8$$
$$= -4$$

Exercises

Draw a scatter plot of each set of data. Decide whether a linear model is reasonable. If so, describe the correlation. Then draw a trend line and write its equation. Predict the value of y when x is 15.

31. $\{(3, 5), (4, 7), (5, 9), (7, 10), (8, 10), (9, 11), (10, 13)\}$

32. $\{(6, 15.5), (7, 14.0), (8, 13.0), (9, 12.5), (10, 12.0), (11, 11.5), (12, 10.0)\}$

33.

x	0	3	6	9	12
y	17.5	35.4	50.5	60.6	66.3

2-6 Families of Functions

Quick Review

A **parent function** is the simplest form of a function in a family of functions. Each member is a **transformation** of the parent function.

Translations shift the graph horizontally, vertically, or both. A **reflection** flips the graph over a line of symmetry. **Vertical stretches** and **compressions** change the shape of the graph by a factor.

Example

Write the equation of the transformation of the graph of $f(x) = x^2$ translated 3 units up, vertically stretched by a factor of 6, and reflected across the y-axis.

$y = x^2 + 3$	Translated 3 units up.
$y = 6(x^2 + 3)$	Vertically stretched.
$y = 6(-x)^2 + 18$	Reflected across the y-axis.
$y = 6x^2 + 18$	

Exercises

Write the equation for the transformation of the graph of $y = f(x)$.

34. translated 2 units left, 7 units down

35. translated 5 units right, reflected across the x-axis

36. translated 3 units up, reflected across the y-axis

Describe the transformation(s) of the parent function $f(x)$.

37. $g(x) = f(x) - 4$

38. $h(x) = 12f(x) + 2$

39. $k(x) = -2f(-x)$

2-7 Absolute Value Functions and Graphs

Quick Review

The **absolute value function** $y = |x|$ is the **parent function** for the family of functions of the form $y = a|x - h| + k$. The maximum or minimum point of the graph is the vertex of the graph.

$y = 2|x + 3| + 1$
$a = 2, h = -3, k = 1$
- Vertex is at $(-3, 1)$
- Translated left 3 units
- Stretched by a factor of 2
- Translated up 1 unit

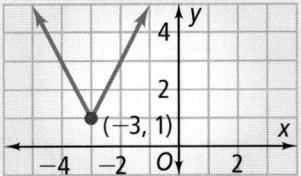

Example

Write an equation for the translation of the graph $y = |x|$ up 5 units.

Because the graph is translated up, k is positive, so the equation of the translated graph is $y = |x| + 5$.

Exercises

Write an equation for each translation of the graph of $y = |x|$.

40. up 4 units, right 2 units   **41.** vertex $(-3, 0)$

42. vertex $(5, 2)$ **43.** vertex $(4, 1)$

Graph each function.

44. $f(x) = |x| - 8$ **45.** $f(x) = 2|x - 5|$

46. $y = -\frac{1}{4}|x - 2| + 3$ **47.** $y = -2|x + 1| - 1$

Without graphing, identify the vertex and axis of symmetry of each function.

48. $y = 2|x - 4|$ **49.** $y = -|x| + 2$

2-8 Two Variable Inequalities

Quick Review

An inequality describes a region of the coordinate plane that has a **boundary**. To graph an inequality involving two variables, first graph the boundary. Then determine which side of the boundary contains the solutions. Points on a dashed boundary are not solutions. Points on a solid boundary are solutions.

Example

Graph the inequality $y \geq 2x + 3$.

Graph the solid boundary line $y = 2x + 3$.

Since y is *greater than* $2x + 3$, shade above the boundary.

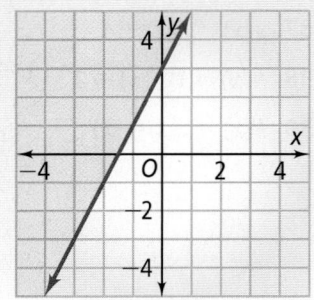

Exercises

Graph each inequality.

50. $y \geq -2$ **51.** $y < 3x + 1$

52. $y < -|x - 5|$ **53.** $y > |2x + 1|$

54. Transportation An air cargo plane can transport as many as 15 regular shipping containers. One super-size container takes up the space of 3 regular containers.
   a. Write an inequality to model the number of regular and super-size containers the plane can transport.
   b. Describe the domain and range.
   c. Graph the inequality you wrote in part (a).

55. Open-Ended Write an absolute value inequality with a solid boundary that only has solutions below the x-axis.

Chapter Test

Do you know HOW?

Find the domain and range. Graph each relation.

1. $\{(0, 0), (1, -1), (2, -4), (3, -9), (4, -16)\}$

2. $\{(3, 2), (4, 3), (5, 4), (6, 5), (7, 6)\}$

Determine whether each relation is a function.

3.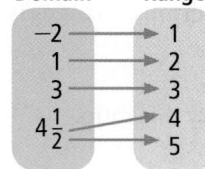

4.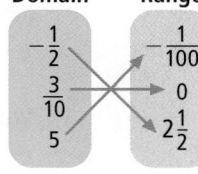

Suppose $f(x) = 2x - 5$ **and** $g(x) = |-3x - 1|$. **Find each value.**

5. $f(3)$ **6.** $f(1) + g(2)$ **7.** $g(0)$

8. $g(2) - f(0)$ **9.** $f(-1) - g(3)$ **10.** $2g(-4)$

Find the slope of each line.

11. through $(3, 5)$, parallel to $y = 5x - 1$

12. through $(-0.5, 0.5)$, perpendicular to $y = -2x - 4$

Write an equation of the line in standard form with the given slope through the given point.

13. slope $= -3$, $(0, 0)$ **14.** slope $= \frac{2}{5}$, $(6, 7)$

15. slope $= 4$, $(-2, -5)$ **16.** slope $= -0.5$, $(0, 6)$

Write an equation of the line in point-slope form through each pair of points.

17. $(0, 0)$ and $(-4, 7)$ **18.** $(-1, -6)$ and $(-2, 10)$

19. $(3, 0)$ and $(-1, -2)$ **20.** $(9, 5)$ and $(8, 2)$

For each direct variation, find the constant of variation. Then find the value of y when $x = -0.5$.

21. $y = 4$ when $x = 0.5$ **22.** $y = 2$ when $x = 3$

Write an equation of the line with the given slope and y-intercept. Use slope-intercept form. Then rewrite each equation in standard form.

23. $m = 3$, $b = -7$ **24.** $m = -6$, $b = 9$

25. $m = \frac{1}{4}$, $b = 11$ **26.** $m = -\frac{1}{2}$, $b = 4$

Graph each inequality.

27. $y \geq x + 7$ **28.** $y > 2|x + 3| - 3$

29. $4x - 3y < 2$ **30.** $y \leq -\frac{1}{2}|x + 2| - 3$

Do you UNDERSTAND?

Ⓒ 31. Open-Ended Graph a relation that is *not* a function. Find its domain and range.

Ⓒ 32. Writing Explain how point-slope form is related to the formula for slope.

Describe each transformation of the parent function $y = |x|$. Then, graph each function.

33. $y = |x| - 4$ **34.** $y = |x - 1| - 5$

35. $y = -|x + 4| + 3$ **36.** $y = 2|x + 1|$

Ⓒ 37. Recreation The table displays the amounts the Jackson family spent on vacations during the years 2000–2009.

Family Vacations

Year	Cost	Year	Cost
2000	$1750	2005	$2750
2001	$1750	2006	$3200
2002	$2000	2007	$2900
2003	$2200	2008	$3100
2004	$2700	2009	$3300

a. Make a scatter plot of the data.

b. Draw a trend line. Write its equation.

c. Estimate the amount the Jackson family will spend on vacations in 2015.

d. Writing Explain how to use a trend line to make a prediction.

Common Core Cumulative Standards Review

 **ASSESSMENT**

TIPS FOR SUCCESS

Some problems require you to use direct variation to solve for an unknown quantity. Read the question at the right. Then follow the tips to answer the sample question.

TIP 1

Some problems give more information than you need. Decide what information you need to answer the question.

A salad dressing recipe calls for $1\frac{1}{3}$ cups of buttermilk, 1 egg, $\frac{1}{2}$ cup of orange juice, and 1 tablespoon of lemon juice. Dan plans to use 2 cups of buttermilk instead. How much orange juice should he use?

- (A) $\frac{3}{8}$ cup
- (B) $\frac{3}{4}$ cup
- (C) $1\frac{1}{6}$ cup
- (D) $1\frac{1}{3}$ cup

TIP 2

Use some of the information to find k, the constant of variation in $y = kx$.

Think It Through

The ratio that shows how the amount of buttermilk changes is
$$k = \frac{2}{1\frac{1}{3}}.$$

You can simplify this ratio.
$$2 \div \frac{4}{3} = \frac{2}{1} \cdot \frac{3}{4} = \frac{3}{2}$$

Use $k = \frac{3}{2}$ in the direct variation equation $y = \frac{3}{2}x$.
Let x represent the original amount of orange juice.
$$y = \frac{3}{2}x = \frac{3}{2} \cdot \frac{1}{2} = \frac{3}{4}$$

The correct answer is B.

Vocabulary Builder

As you solve test items, you must understand the meanings of mathematical terms. Match each term with its mathematical meaning.

A. linear function

B. direct variation

C. range

D. translation

I. the set of all outputs, or y-coordinates, of a relation

II. a transformation that shifts a graph horizontally, vertically, or both

III. a function that can be written in the form $y = mx + b$

IV. a function that can be written in the form $y = kx$, $k \neq 0$

Selected Response

Read each question. Then write the letter of the correct answer on your paper.

1. Which of the following absolute value inequalities has no solutions in Quadrant IV?

- (A) $y + 2 \geq |x - 3|$
- (B) $y > 3 - |5 - x|$
- (C) $y - 1 > |2x + 6|$
- (D) $y \leq |4x| - 7$

2. For which value of b would the equation $3|x - 2| = bx - 6$ have infinitely many solutions?

- (F) -6
- (G) 3
- (H) -3
- (I) 6

3. A meteorologist predicts the daily high and low temperatures as 91°F and 69°F. If t represents the temperature, then this situation can be described with the inequality $69 \leq t \leq 91$. Which of the following absolute value inequalities is an equivalent way of expressing this?

- Ⓐ $69 \leq |t| \leq 91$
- Ⓑ $|t - 80| \leq 11$
- Ⓒ $|t - 69| \leq 91$
- Ⓓ $|t - 11| \leq 80$

4. Which inequality has a solution that matches the graph below?

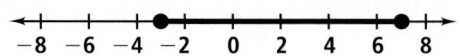

- Ⓕ $|x - 2| - 3 \geq 2$
- Ⓖ $|x - 2| - 3 \leq 2$
- Ⓗ $|x - 3| + 2 \geq 7$
- Ⓘ $|x - 3| + 2 \leq 7$

5. Which inequality best describes the graph?

- Ⓐ $y \leq \frac{1}{2}|x + 1| - 1$
- Ⓑ $y \geq \frac{1}{2}|x - 1| - 1$
- Ⓒ $y \leq \frac{1}{2}|x - 1| - 1$
- Ⓓ $y \geq \frac{1}{2}|x + 1| - 1$

6. Which relation is a function?

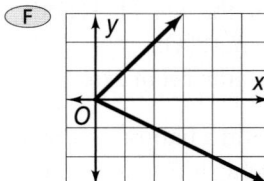 Ⓕ

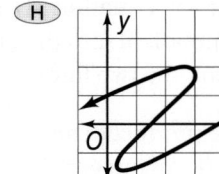 Ⓗ

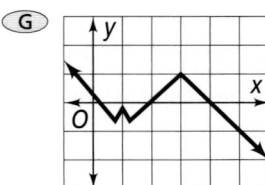 Ⓖ

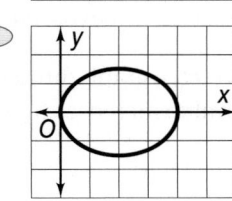 Ⓘ

7. For $f(x) = 2x - 3$ find $f\left(-\frac{1}{4}\right)$.

- Ⓐ $-\frac{3}{2}$
- Ⓑ -2
- Ⓒ $2\frac{1}{2}$
- Ⓓ $-\frac{7}{2}$

8. Which equation is graphed?

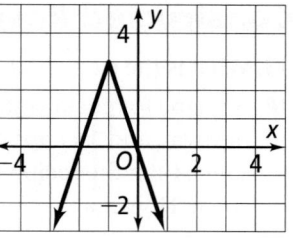

- Ⓕ $y = -3|x + 1| + 3$
- Ⓖ $y = 3|x + 1| + 3$
- Ⓗ $y = -3|x - 1| + 3$
- Ⓘ $y = 3|x + 1| - 3$

9. Which describes the translation of $y = |x - 3| + 5$?

- Ⓐ $y = |x|$ translated 3 units left and 5 units up
- Ⓑ $y = |x|$ translated 3 units right and 5 units up
- Ⓒ $y = |x|$ translated 5 units left and 3 units up
- Ⓓ $y = |x|$ translated 5 units right and 3 units up

10. If a rate of speed r is constant, then distance, rate, and time are related by the direct variation equation $d = rt$, where d represents distance and t represents time. If $r = 30$ miles per hour, which of the following best describes the graph of $d = rt$?

- Ⓕ A straight line through the point $(0, 0)$
- Ⓖ A straight line through the point $(0, 30)$
- Ⓗ A parabola through the point $(0, 0)$
- Ⓘ A parabola through the point $(0, 30)$

11. Which function has the graph shown?

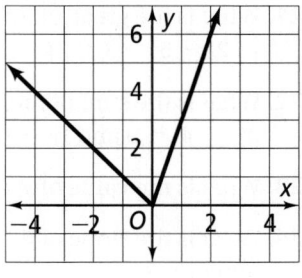

- Ⓐ $f(x) = \begin{cases} -x, \, x < 0 \\ 3x, \, x \geq 0 \end{cases}$
- Ⓑ $f(x) = \begin{cases} x, \, x < 0 \\ -3x, \, x \geq 0 \end{cases}$
- Ⓒ $f(x) = \begin{cases} x, \, x > 0 \\ -3x, \, x \leq 0 \end{cases}$
- Ⓓ $f(x) = \begin{cases} -x, \, x > 0 \\ 3x, \, x \leq 0 \end{cases}$

12. Which equation has the same graph as
$$f(x) = \begin{cases} \frac{1}{3}x, \quad x > 6 \\ -\frac{1}{3}x + 4, \, x \leq 6 \end{cases}?$$

- Ⓕ $f(x) = -\frac{1}{3}|x - 6| + 4$
- Ⓖ $f(x) = \frac{1}{3}x$
- Ⓗ $f(x) = \frac{1}{3}|x - 6| + 2$
- Ⓘ $f(x) = -\frac{1}{3}x + 10$

Constructed Response

13. What is the slope of the line $5y + 3 = \frac{2}{5}x$?

14. A recipe for custard sauce calls for 6 egg yolks, $\frac{2}{3}$ cup of sugar, and $1\frac{1}{2}$ cups of hot milk. Chelsea needs more sauce than the recipe yields. She plans to use 1 cup of sugar. How many cups of hot milk should she use?

15. What is the y-coordinate of the point through which the graph of every direct variation passes?

16. Six members of the math club will participate in a regional competition. A processing fee of $15 is added to the registration cost. If the math coach sends in a check for $87, how much does he pay for each registration?

17. What is the y-coordinate of the y-intercept of the line $4x + 3y = 12$?

18. If $4(x + 2) - 2(x - 10) = 0$, what is the value of x?

19. Mr. Wong traveled 45 miles on a business trip. The cost to rent a car is $30.00 plus $.75 per mile. How much did Mr. Wong pay for the car rental?

20. In the expression $38 + 27y$, which number is a coefficient?

21. What is the greatest integer solution of $|-2x - 5| - 3 \le 2$?

22. What is the sum of the solutions of $3|y - 4| = 9$ and $|y - 4| = 3$?

23. What is the value of x in the equation $6(x - 4) = 3x$?

24. What is the slope of the line represented by the function $3x - 2y = -12$?

25. What is $f(-3)$ for the function $f(x) = -3x + 6$?

26. What is the y-coordinate of the y-intercept of the line?

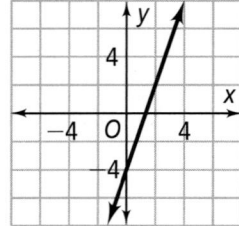

27. Matt drove at a steady speed during the first morning of his road trip. The table shows data about his driving.

Time Driving (hours) t	Total Distance (miles) d
1.5	87
2.25	130.5
3	174

Determine whether distance d varies directly with time t. If so, what are the constant of variation and the function rule?

28. Find $f(-3)$, $f(0)$, and $f(1)$ for the function $f(x) = \frac{2}{5}x - 2$.

29. Graph $y < |x + 3|$. Identify the parent function of the boundary and describe the translation.

30. Suppose y varies directly with x, and $y = 2$ when $x = -2$. Find the constant of variation. Then find the value of x when $y = 3$.

31. The points $(-3, 2)$, $(-1, 3)$, $(0, 0)$, $(-2, -1)$ represent a function. What are the domain and range?

Extended Response

32. a. Write an equation of the line through $(-2, 6)$ with slope 2.
   b. Write an equation of the line through $(1, 1)$ and perpendicular to the line in part (a).
   c. Graph the two lines on the same set of axes.

33. Will the product of an integer and a natural number always be an integer? Why or why not? Justify your answer with two examples.

34. Sketch a graph through the point $(1, 1)$ such that as an x-value increases by 2, the y-value decreases by 3.

Get Ready!

CHAPTER

3

Lesson 1-3   **Evaluating Algebraic Expressions**

Evaluate each expression for the given values of the variables.

1. $9t + 6(2v - t) - 7v$; $t = 1$ and $v = 5$

2. $11(a + 2b) + 2(a - 2b)$; $a = -3$ and $b = 4$

3. $\frac{3}{5}d + \frac{1}{10}h - \frac{7}{10}d - \frac{4}{5}h$; $d = 5$ and $h = 10$

4. $12\left(\frac{3}{4}x - \frac{1}{2}y\right) - 6\left(\frac{1}{2}x - \frac{3}{4}y\right)$; $x = 2$ and $y = -2$

Lesson 2-3   **Writing Linear Equations in Slope-Intercept Form**

Write the equation of each line in slope-intercept form.

5. $2x - 4y = 10$ **6.** $3y + 9 = -6x$ **7.** $y - 5x = 16$ **8.** $-7 - y = -3x$

9. $\frac{x}{6} - \frac{5}{12}y = \frac{5}{8}$ **10.** $4x = y - 11$ **11.** $2y = -12x - 16$ **12.** $\frac{y}{9} + \frac{x}{3} = 2$

Lesson 2-3   **Graphing Linear Equations**

Graph each equation.

13. $3x = y - 1$ **14.** $x - 5y = 10$ **15.** $12 + 2y = 3x$ **16.** $y = 4x$

Lesson 2-8   **Graphing Inequalities**

Graph each inequality.

17. $4y \le 24x$ **18.** $y \ge 2|x - 1.5|$ **19.** $x + 5y \ge 20$ **20.** $y > |x + 6| - 2$

 Looking Ahead Vocabulary

21. A *system* of mountains is a group of mountains that share similar geographic and geological features. What are some mountain systems in the United States?

22. Two things are *consistent* if they are in agreement with each other. What does it mean for your actions to be consistent with your words?

23. How many books does Jeff own if he has more than 14 books? Describe the number of books that Jeff owns if you add the *constraint* that he owns fewer than his sister, who owns 19 books.

CHAPTER 3

Linear Systems

Download videos connecting math to your world.

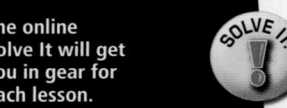

Interactive! Vary numbers, graphs, and figures to explore math concepts.

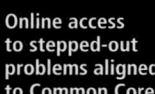

The online Solve It will get you in gear for each lesson.

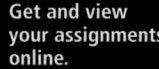

Math definitions in English and Spanish

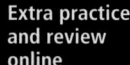

Online access to stepped-out problems aligned to Common Core

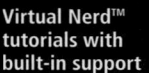

Get and view your assignments online.

Extra practice and review online

Virtual Nerd™ tutorials with built-in support

Chapter Preview

Vocabulary

English/Spanish Vocabulary Audio Online:

BIG ideas

1 Function
Essential Question How does representing functions graphically help you solve a system of equations?

2 Equivalence
Essential Question How does writing equivalent equations help you solve a system of equations?

3 Solving Equations and Inequalities
Essential Question How are the properties of equality used in the matrix solution of a system of equations?

DOMAINS

• Creating Equations
• Reasoning with Equations and Inequalities

Common Core Performance Task

Planning a Triathlon

Sophia is in charge of planning an annual triathlon in her city. The triathlon will consist of three distinct sections, as described below.

Section 1: A swim across a part of Sunset Lake

Section 2: A bicycle ride through the new city park

Section 3: A run through downtown that ends at City Hall

The organizing committee for the triathlon asks Sophia to follow these criteria:

- Elite athletes should be able to finish in 2 hours.

- The distance of the swim is $\frac{1}{5}$ the distance of the run.

- The entire course covers a distance of 28 miles.

Sophia does some research on top triathlon finish times. She finds that, on average, elite athletes are able to swim at about 3 mi/h, bicycle at about 20 mi/h, and run at about 10 mi/h. Sophia needs to determine a triathlon course based on these rates.

Task Description
Plan the triathlon by determining the distance for each part of the course.

Connecting the Task to the Math Practices

MATHEMATICAL PRACTICES

As you complete the task, you'll apply several Standards for Mathematical Practice.

- You'll use a table and a graph to solve a related problem. (MP 5)

- You'll reason abstractly to write algebraic representations of parts of the triathlon. (MP 2)

- You'll use a system of linear equations to model the three criteria for the triathlon. (MP 4)

3-1 Solving Systems Using Tables and Graphs

Common Core State Standards

A-CED.A.2 Create equations in two or more variables to represent relationships between quantities; graph equations on coordinate axes with labels and scales.

Also A-REI.C.6, A-CED.D.11, A-CED.A.3

MP 1, MP 2, MP 3, MP 4, MP 5

Objective To solve a linear system using a graph or a table

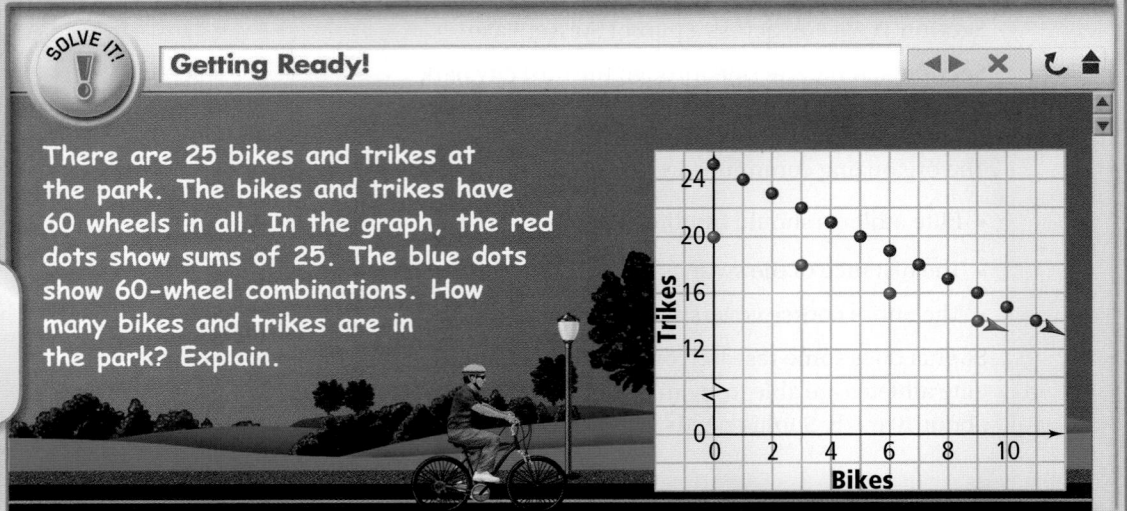

Getting Ready!

There are 25 bikes and trikes at the park. The bikes and trikes have 60 wheels in all. In the graph, the red dots show sums of 25. The blue dots show 60-wheel combinations. How many bikes and trikes are in the park? Explain.

If there were only 2 bikes and 2 trikes how many wheels would there be?

MATHEMATICAL PRACTICES

Lesson Vocabulary
• system of equations
• linear system
• solution of a system
• inconsistent system
• consistent system
• independent system
• dependent system

When you have two or more related unknowns, you may be able to represent their relationship with a **system of equations**—a set of two or more equations.

Essential Understanding To solve a system of equations, find a set of values that replace the variables in the equations and make each equation true.

A **linear system** consists of linear equations. A **solution of a system** is a set of values for the variables that makes all the equations true. You can solve a system of equations graphically or by using tables.

How can you use a graph to find the solution of a system?
Find the point where the two lines intersect.

Problem 1 Using a Graph or Table to Solve a System

What is the solution of the system? $\begin{cases} -3x + 2y = 8 \\ x + 2y = -8 \end{cases}$

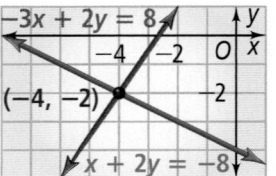

Method 1 Graph the equations. The point of intersection appears to be $(-4, -2)$.

Check by substituting the values into both equations.

$$-3x + 2y = 8 \qquad\qquad x + 2y = -8$$

$$-3(-4) + 2(-2) = 8 ✔ \qquad -4 + 2(-2) = -8 ✔$$

Both equations are true so $(-4, -2)$ is the solution of the system.

Method 2 Use a table. Write the equations in slope-intercept form.

$$-3x + 2y = 8 \qquad\qquad x + 2y = -8$$
$$2y = 3x + 8 \qquad\qquad 2y = -x - 8$$
$$y_1 = \frac{3}{2}x + 4 \qquad\qquad y_2 = -\frac{1}{2}x - 4$$

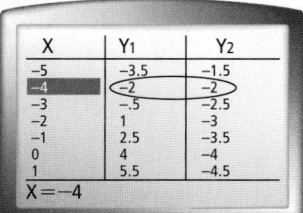

X	Y₁	Y₂
−5	−3.5	−1.5
−4	−2	−2
−3	−.5	−2.5
−2	1	−3
−1	2.5	−3.5
0	4	−4
1	5.5	−4.5

X = −4

Enter the equations in the **Y=** screen as **Y1** and **Y2**.
View the table. Adjust the x-values until you see $y_1 = y_2$.

When $x = -4$, both y_1 and y_2 equal -2. So, $(-4, -2)$ is the solution of the system.

 Got It? **1.** What is the solution of the system? $\begin{cases} x - 2y = 4 \\ 3x + y = 5 \end{cases}$

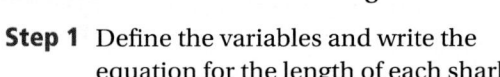 **Problem 2** Using a Table to Solve a Problem **STEM**

GREENLAND SHARK
Growth rate: 0.75 cm/yr
Birth length: 37 cm

Biology The diagrams show the birth lengths and growth rates of two species of shark. If the growth rates stay the same, at what age would a Spiny Dogfish and a Greenland shark be the same length?

Step 1 Define the variables and write the equation for the length of each shark.

Let x = age in years.
Let y = length in centimeters.

Length of Greenland: $y_1 = 0.75x + 37$
Length of Spiny Dogfish: $y_2 = 1.5x + 22$

SPINY DOGFISH SHARK
Growth rate: 1.5 cm/yr
Birth length: 22 cm

Think

How can you use slope-intercept form to write each equation?
Use the growth rate for m and the length at birth for b.

Step 2 Use the table to solve the problem.

List x-values until the corresponding y-values match.

The sharks will be the same length when they are 20 years old.

Shark Length in cm

Age	Greenland	Spiny Dogfish
x	$y_1 = 0.75x + 37$	$y_2 = 1.5x + 22$
15	48.25	44.5
16	49	46
⋮	⋮	⋮
20	52	52

 Got It? **2. a.** If the growth rates continue, how long will each shark be when it is 25 years old?

b. Reasoning Explain why growth rates for these sharks may not continue indefinitely.

Problem 3 Using Linear Regression

Population The table shows the populations of the New York City and Los Angeles metropolitan regions from the census reports for 1950 through 2000. Assuming these linear trends continue, when will the populations of these regions be equal? What will that population be?

Populations of New York City and Los Angeles Metropolitan Regions (1950–2000)

	1950	1960	1970	1980	1990	2000
New York City	12,911,994	14,759,429	16,178,700	16,121,297	18,087,251	21,199,865
Los Angeles	4,367,911	6,742,696	7,032,075	11,497,568	14,531,529	16,373,645

SOURCE: U.S. Census Bureau

Know	**Need**	**Plan**
Population data for two regions	The point in time when their populations will be the same	• Use a calculator to find linear regression models. • Plot the models. • Find the point of intersection.

Enter all the numbers as millions, rounded to the nearest hundred thousand. For example, enter 12,911,994 as 12.9.

Step 1 Enter the data into lists on your calculator.
L1: number of years since 1950
L2: New York City populations
L3: Los Angeles populations

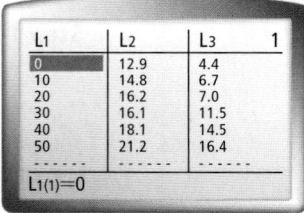

Step 2 Use **LinReg(ax + b)** to find lines of best fit.
Use **L1** and **L2** for New York City.
Use **L1** and **L3** for Los Angeles.

Step 3 Graph the linear regression lines.
Use the **Intersect** feature.

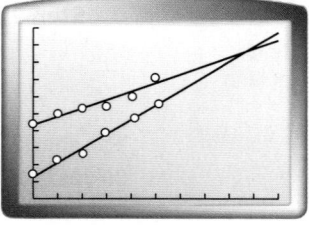

Think

What does x represent?
The x-value is the number of years *since* the zero year.

The x-value of the point of intersection is about 87, which represents the year 2037. The data suggest that the populations of the New York City and Los Angeles metropolitan regions will each be about 25.6 million in 2037.

Got It? 3. The table shows the populations of the San Diego and Detroit metropolitan regions. When were the populations of these regions equal? What was that population?

Populations of San Diego and Detroit Metropolitan Regions (1950–2000)

	1950	1960	1970	1980	1990	2000
San Diego	334,387	573,224	696,769	875,538	1,110,549	1,223,400
Detroit	1,849,568	1,670,144	1,511,482	1,203,339	1,027,974	951,270

SOURCE: U.S. Census Bureau

You can classify a system of two linear equations by the number of solutions.

A **consistent system** has at least one solution.

Consistent system — Independent / Dependent

An **independent system** has one solution.

A **dependent system** has infinitely many solutions.

An **inconsistent system** has no solution.

Inconsistent system

The graphs for an inconsistent system are parallel lines. So, there are no solutions. For a dependent system, the two equations represent the same line.

take note

Concept Summary   Graphical Solutions of Linear Systems

Intersecting Lines	Coinciding Lines	Parallel Lines
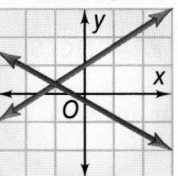	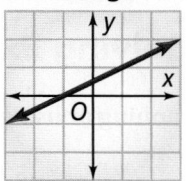	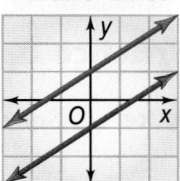
one solution	infinitely many solutions	no solution
Consistent	Consistent	Inconsistent
Independent	Dependent	

© **Problem 4**   **Classifying a System Without Graphing**

Without graphing, is the system *independent*, *dependent*, or *inconsistent*?

$$\begin{cases} 4y - 2x = 6 \\ 8y = 4x - 12 \end{cases}$$

Plan

What should you compare to classify the system?
Compare the slopes and *y*-intercepts of each line.

Rewrite each equation in slope-intercept form. Compare slopes and *y*-intercepts.

$4y - 2x = 6$ $\qquad\qquad$ $8y = 4x - 12$

$y = \frac{1}{2}x + \frac{3}{2}$ $\qquad\qquad$ $y = \frac{1}{2}x - \frac{3}{2}$

$m = \frac{1}{2};$ *y*-intercept is $\frac{3}{2}$ $\qquad$ $m = \frac{1}{2};$ *y*-intercept is $-\frac{3}{2}$

The slopes are equal and the *y*-intercepts are different. The lines are different but parallel. The system is inconsistent.

✓ **Got It?**   **4.** Without graphing, is each system *independent*, *dependent*, or *inconsistent*?

a. $\begin{cases} -3x + y = 4 \\ x - \frac{1}{3}y = 1 \end{cases}$ $\qquad$ b. $\begin{cases} 2x + 3y = 1 \\ 4x + y = -3 \end{cases}$ $\qquad$ c. $\begin{cases} y = 2x - 3 \\ 6x - 3y = 9 \end{cases}$

Lesson Check

Do you know HOW?

Solve each system of equations by graphing. Check your solution.

1. $\begin{cases} y = x - 1 \\ y = -x + 3 \end{cases}$

2. $\begin{cases} 2x + y = 4 \\ x - y = 2 \end{cases}$

3. You bought a total of 6 pens and pencils for $4. If each pen costs $1 and each pencil costs $.50, how many pens and pencils did you buy?

Do you UNDERSTAND?

4. **Vocabulary** Is it possible for a system of equations to be both independent and inconsistent? Explain.

5. **Open-Ended** Write a system of linear equations that has no solution.

6. **Reasoning** In a system of linear equations, the slope of one line is the negative reciprocal of the slope of the other line. Is this system *independent*, *dependent*, or *inconsistent*? Explain.

Practice and Problem-Solving Exercises

 **Practice**

Solve each system by graphing or using a table. Check your answers.

◀ See Problem 1.

7. $\begin{cases} y = x - 2 \\ y = -2x + 7 \end{cases}$

8. $\begin{cases} y = -x + 3 \\ y = \frac{3}{2}x - 2 \end{cases}$

9. $\begin{cases} 2x + 4y = 12 \\ x + y = 2 \end{cases}$

10. $\begin{cases} x = -3 \\ y = 5 \end{cases}$

11. $\begin{cases} 2x - 2y = 4 \\ y - x = 6 \end{cases}$

12. $\begin{cases} 3x + y = 5 \\ x - y = 7 \end{cases}$

Write and solve a system of equations for each situation. Check your answers.

◀ See Problem 2.

13. A store sells small notebooks for $8 and large notebooks for $10. If you buy 6 notebooks and spend $56, how many of each size notebook did you buy?

14. A shop has one-pound bags of peanuts for $2 and three-pound bags of peanuts for $5.50. If you buy 5 bags and spend $17, how many of each size bag did you buy?

Graphing Calculator Find linear models for each set of data. In what year will the two quantities be equal?

◀ See Problem 3.

15.

U.S. Life Expectancy at Birth (1970–2000)

Year	1970	1975	1980	1985	1990	1995	2000
Men (years)	67.1	68.8	70.0	71.1	71.8	72.5	74.3
Women (years)	74.7	76.6	77.4	78.2	78.8	78.9	79.7

SOURCE: U.S. Census Bureau

16.

Annual U.S. Consumption of Vegetables

Year	1980	1985	1990	1995	1998	1999	2000
Broccoli (lb/person)	1.5	2.6	3.4	4.3	5.1	6.5	6.1
Cucumbers (lb/person)	3.9	4.4	4.7	5.6	6.5	6.8	6.4

SOURCE: U.S. Census Bureau

Without graphing, classify each system as *independent*, *dependent*, or *inconsistent*.

◀ **See Problem 4.**

17. $\begin{cases} 7x - y = 6 \\ -7x + y = -6 \end{cases}$

18. $\begin{cases} -3x + y = 4 \\ x - \frac{1}{3}y = 1 \end{cases}$

19. $\begin{cases} 4x + 8y = 12 \\ x + 2y = -3 \end{cases}$

20. $\begin{cases} y = 2x - 1 \\ y = -2x + 5 \end{cases}$

21. $\begin{cases} x = 6 \\ y = -2 \end{cases}$

22. $\begin{cases} 2y = 5x + 6 \\ -10x + 4y = 8 \end{cases}$

23. $\begin{cases} x - 3y = 2 \\ 4x - 12y = 8 \end{cases}$

24. $\begin{cases} y - x = 0 \\ y = -x \end{cases}$

25. $\begin{cases} 2y - x = 4 \\ \frac{1}{2}x + y = 2 \end{cases}$

26. $\begin{cases} x + 4y = 12 \\ 2x - 8y = 4 \end{cases}$

27. $\begin{cases} 4x + 8y = -6 \\ 6x + 12y = -9 \end{cases}$

28. $\begin{cases} 4y - 2x = 6 \\ 8y = 4x - 12 \end{cases}$

 **Apply**

Graph and solve each system.

29. $\begin{cases} 3 = 4y + x \\ 4y = -x + 3 \end{cases}$

30. $\begin{cases} y = \frac{1}{2}x + \frac{1}{2} \\ y = \frac{1}{4}x + \frac{3}{2} \end{cases}$

31. $\begin{cases} 3x + 6y - 12 = 0 \\ x + 2y = 8 \end{cases}$

32. $\begin{cases} 3x = -5y + 4 \\ 250 + 150x = 300y \end{cases}$

33. $\begin{cases} y = -\frac{1}{2}x + 8 \\ y = 2x - 6 \end{cases}$

34. $\begin{cases} x + 3y = 6 \\ 6y + 2x = 12 \end{cases}$

Without graphing, classify each system as *independent*, *dependent*, or *inconsistent*.

35. $\begin{cases} 3x - 2y = 8 \\ 4y = 6x - 5 \end{cases}$

36. $\begin{cases} 2x + 8y = 6 \\ x = -4y + 3 \end{cases}$

37. $\begin{cases} 3m = -5n + 4 \\ n - \frac{6}{5} = -\frac{3}{5}m \end{cases}$

ⓒ **38. Reasoning** Find the solution of the system of equations $f(x) = 3x - 1$ and $g(x) = |x - 3|$. Explain why the x-coordinates of the points where the graphs of the equations $y = f(x)$ and $y = g(x)$ intersect are solutions of $3x - 1 = |x - 3|$.

ⓒ **39. Think About a Plan** You and a friend are both reading a book. You read 2 pages each minute and have already read 55 pages. Your friend reads 3 pages each minute and has already read 35 pages. Graph and solve a system of equations to find when the two of you will have read the same number of pages. Since the number of pages you have read depends on how long you have been reading, let x represent the number of minutes it takes to read y pages.
  - How can you describe the relationship between x and y for you?
  - How can you describe the relationship between x and y for your friend?
  - How can a graph help you solve this problem?

ⓒ **40. Sports** You can choose between two tennis courts at two university campuses to learn how to play tennis. One campus charges $25 per hour. The other campus charges $20 per hour plus a one-time registration fee of $10.
  a. Write a system of equations to represent the cost c for h hours of court use at each campus.
  b. Graphing Calculator Find the number of hours for which the costs are the same.
  c. Reasoning If you want to practice for a total of 10 hours, which university campus should you choose? Explain.

41. Error Analysis Your friend used a graphing calculator to solve a system of linear equations, shown below. After using the **TABLE** feature, your friend says that the system has no solution. Explain what your friend did wrong. What is the solution of the system?

X	Y₁	Y₂
−4	14	10
−3	12	8.5
−2	10	7
−1	8	5.5
0	6	4
1	4	2.5
2	2	1

X=2

$$2x + y = 6 \qquad\qquad 3x + 2y = 8$$
$$y = 6 - 2x$$
$$y = \frac{8 - 3x}{2}$$

42. Reasoning Is it possible for an inconsistent linear system to contain two lines with the same y-intercept? Explain.

43. Writing Summarize the possible relationships for the y-intercepts, slopes, and number of solutions in a system of two linear equations in two variables.

Reasoning Determine whether each statement is *always, sometimes,* or *never* true for the following system.

$$\begin{cases} y = x + 3 \\ y = mx + b \end{cases}$$

44. If $m = 1$, the system has no solution.

45. If $b = 3$, the system has exactly one solution.

46. If $m \neq 1$, the system has no solution.

47. If $m \neq 1$ and $b = 2$, the system has infinitely many solutions.

 **Challenge**   **Open-Ended** Write a second equation for each system so that the system will have the indicated number of solutions.

48. infinite number of solutions

$$\begin{cases} \dfrac{x}{4} + \dfrac{y}{3} = 1 \\ \underline{\quad ? \quad} \end{cases}$$

49. no solutions

$$\begin{cases} 5x + 2y = 10 \\ \underline{\quad ? \quad} \end{cases}$$

50. Write a system of linear equations with the solution set $\{(x, y) \mid y = 5x + 2\}$.

51. Reasoning What relationship exists between the equations in a dependent system?

52. Economics Research shows that in a certain market only 2000 widgets can be sold at $8 each, but if the price is reduced to $3, then 10,000 can be sold.
  a. Let p represent price and n represent the number of widgets. Identify the independent and dependent variables.
  b. Write a linear equation that relates price and the quantity demanded. This type of equation is called a *demand* equation.
  c. A shop can make 2000 widgets for $5 each and 20,000 widgets for $2 each. Use this information to write a linear equation that relates price and the quantity supplied. This type of equation is called a *supply* equation.
  d. Find the equilibrium point where supply is equal to demand. Explain the meaning of the coordinates of this point within the context of the exercise.

Standardized Test Prep

53. Which graph shows the solution of the following system? $\begin{cases} 4x + y = 1 \\ x + 4y = -11 \end{cases}$

Ⓐ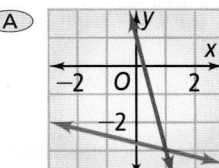

Ⓑ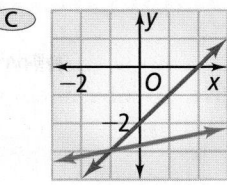

Ⓒ

Ⓓ

54. Which is the equation of a line that is perpendicular to the line in the graph?

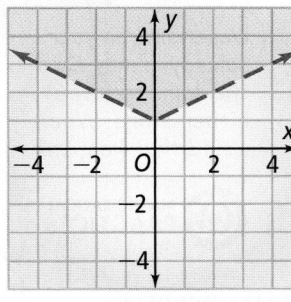

Ⓕ $y = -3x + 2$

Ⓖ $y = \frac{1}{3}x + 5$

Ⓗ $y = -\frac{1}{3}x - 4$

Ⓘ $y = 3x - 1$

55. Which inequality represents the graph at the right?

Ⓐ $y \geq \frac{1}{2}|x| + 1$

Ⓑ $y \leq \frac{1}{2}|x| + 1$

Ⓒ $y > \frac{1}{2}|x| + 1$

Ⓓ $y < \frac{1}{2}|x| + 1$

Extended Response

56. Amy ordered prints of a total of 6 photographs in two different sizes, 5 × 7 and 4 × 6, from an online site. She paid $7.50 for her order. The cost of a 5 × 7 print is $1.75 and the cost of a 4 × 6 print is $.25. Explain how to solve a system of equations using tables to find the number of 4 × 6 prints Amy ordered.

Apply What You've Learned

MATHEMATICAL PRACTICES

MP 5

William and Maggie are competing in a triathlon like the one described on page 133. Maggie begins the bicycle portion of the triathlon half an hour ahead of William, and rides at a rate of 12 mi/h. William rides at a rate of 18 mi/h.

a. If the bicycle portion of the race is long enough, can William catch up with Maggie? Explain your answer.

b. Use a table to find how much time it takes William to catch up with Maggie.

c. Write a system of equations to model William's and Maggie's bicycle portions of the triathlon.

d. Graph the system of equations.

e. Does your graph give the same amount of time for William to catch up with Maggie as the table from part (b)? Explain how each tool is used to find the amount of time.

f. After how many miles will William catch up with Maggie?

3-2 Solving Systems Algebraically

 Common Core State Standards

A-REI.C.6 Solve systems of linear equations exactly and approximately (e.g., with graphs), focusing on pairs of linear equations in two variables. **Also A-REI.C.5, A-CED.A.2**

MP 1, MP 2, MP 3

Objective To solve linear systems algebraically

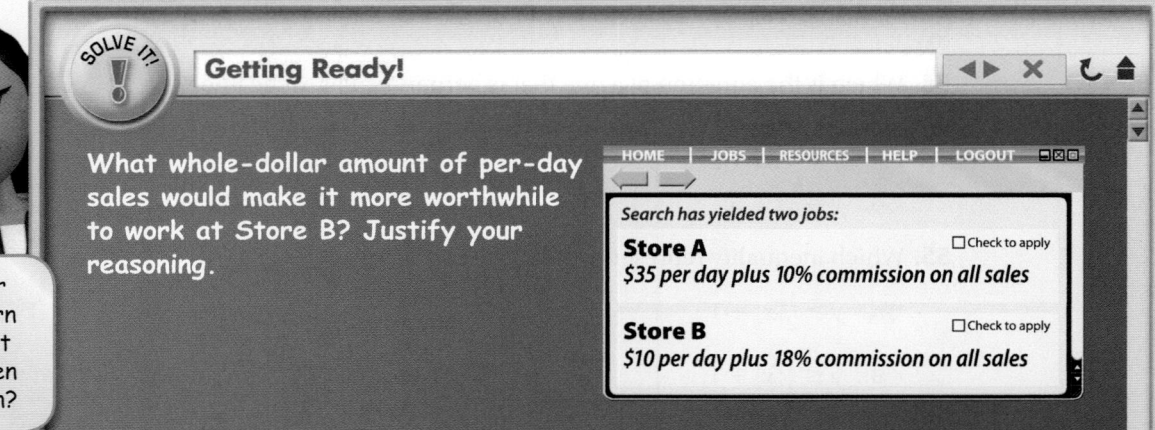

SOLVE IT!

Getting Ready!

What whole-dollar amount of per-day sales would make it more worthwhile to work at Store B? Justify your reasoning.

Depending on your sales, you may earn the same money at either store. When would that happen?

HOME | JOBS | RESOURCES | HELP | LOGOUT

Search has yielded two jobs:

Store A   ☐ Check to apply
$35 per day plus 10% commission on all sales

Store B   ☐ Check to apply
$10 per day plus 18% commission on all sales

MATHEMATICAL PRACTICES

When you try to solve a system of equations by graphing, the coordinates of the point of intersection may not be obvious.

Lesson Vocabulary
• equivalent systems

Essential Understanding You can solve a system of equations by writing equivalent systems until the value of one variable is clear. Then substitute to find the value(s) of the other variable(s).

You can use the substitution method to solve a system of equations when it is easy to isolate one of the variables. After isolating the variable, substitute for that variable in the other equation. Then solve for the other variable.

 **Problem 1** Solving by Substitution

What is the solution of the system of equations? $\begin{cases} 3x + 4y = 12 \\ 2x + y = 10 \end{cases}$

Think

Which variable should you solve for first?
In the second equation, the coefficient of y is 1. It is the easiest variable to isolate.

Step 1

Solve one equation for one of the variables.

$2x + y = 10$
$y = -2x + 10$

Step 2

Substitute the expression for y in the other equation. Solve for x.

$3x + 4y = 12$
$3x + 4(-2x + 10) = 12$
$3x - 8x + 40 = 12$
$x = 5.6$

Step 3

Substitute the value for x into one of the original equations. Solve for y.

$2x + y = 10$
$2(5.6) + y = 10$
$11.2 + y = 10$
$y = -1.2$

The solution is $(5.6, -1.2)$.

Got It? 1. What is the solution of the system of equations? $\begin{cases} x + 3y = 5 \\ -2x - 4y = -5 \end{cases}$

Problem 2 **Using Substitution to Solve a Problem**

Music A music store offers piano lessons at a discount for customers buying new pianos. The costs for lessons and a one-time fee for materials (including music books, CDs, software, etc.) are shown in the advertisement. What is the cost of each lesson and the one-time fee for materials?

Piano Lessons♪

6 Lessons:	12 Lessons:
$300	**$480**

(Prices include one-time fee)

Relate 6 · [cost of one lesson] + [one-time fee] = $300

12 · [cost of one lesson] + [one-time fee] = $480

Define Let [c] = the cost of one lesson.

Let [f] = the one-time fee.

Write $\begin{cases} 6 \cdot [c] + [f] = 300 \\ 12 \cdot [c] + [f] = 480 \end{cases}$

$6c + f = 300$ Choose one equation. Solve for f in terms of c.

$f = 300 - 6c$

$12c + (300 - 6c) = 480$ Substitute the expression for f into the other equation, $12c + f = 480$. Solve for c.

$c = 30$

$6(30) + f = 300$ Substitute the value of c into one of the equations. Solve for f.

$f = 120$

Think

Which equation should you use to find f?
Use the equation with numbers that are easier to work with.

Check Substitute $c = 30$ and $f = 120$ in the original equations.

$6c + f = 300$ $12c + f = 480$

$6(30) + 120 \stackrel{?}{=} 300$ $12(30) + 120 \stackrel{?}{=} 480$

$180 + 120 \stackrel{?}{=} 300$ $360 + 120 \stackrel{?}{=} 480$

$300 = 300$ ✔ $480 = 480$ ✔

The cost of each lesson is $30. The one-time fee for materials is $120.

 Got It? 2. An online music company offers 15 downloads for $19.75 and 40 downloads for $43.50. Each price includes the same one-time registration fee. What is the cost of each download and the registration fee?

You can use the Addition Property of Equality to solve a system of equations. If you add a pair of additive inverses or subtract identical terms, you can eliminate a variable.

Problem 3 Solving by Elimination

What is the solution of the system of equations? $\begin{cases} 4x + 2y = 9 \\ -4x + 3y = 16 \end{cases}$

Think

How can you use the Addition Property of Equality?
Since $-4x + 3y$ is equal to 16, you can add the same value to each side of $4x + 2y = 9$.

$4x + 2y = 9$

$\underline{-4x + 3y = 16}$ One equation has $4x$ and the other has $-4x$. Add to eliminate the variable x.

$5y = 25$

$y = 5$ Solve for y.

$4x + 2y = 9$ Choose one of the original equations.

$4x + 2(5) = 9$ Substitute for y.

$4x = -1$ Solve for x.

$x = -\frac{1}{4}$

The solution is $\left(-\frac{1}{4}, 5\right)$.

 Got It? 3. What is the solution of the system of equations? $\begin{cases} -2x + 8y = -8 \\ 5x - 8y = 20 \end{cases}$

When you multiply each side of one or both equations in a system by the same nonzero number, the new system and the original system have the same solutions. The two systems are called **equivalent systems**. You can use this method to make additive inverses.

 Problem 4 Solving an Equivalent System

What is the solution of the system of equations? $\begin{array}{l} ① \\ ② \end{array}\begin{cases} 2x + 7y = 4 \\ 3x + 5y = -5 \end{cases}$

Think

By multiplying ① by 3 and ② by -2, the x-terms become opposites, and you can eliminate them. Add ③ and ④. Solve for y.

Write

① $2x + 7y = 4$ ③ $\quad 6x + 21y = 12$

② $3x + 5y = -5$ ④ $\underline{-6x - 10y = 10}$

$\qquad\qquad\qquad\qquad\qquad 11y = 22$

$\qquad\qquad\qquad\qquad\qquad\quad y = 2$

Now that you know the value of y, use either equation to find x.

① $2x + 7(2) = 4$

$2x + 14 = 4$

$2x = -10$

$x = -5$

The solution is $(-5, 2)$.

Got It? **4.** **a.** What is the solution of this system of equations? $\begin{cases} 3x + 7y = 15 \\ 5x + 2y = -4 \end{cases}$

b. Reasoning In Problem 4, you found that $y = 2$. Substitute this value into equation ② instead of equation ①. Do you still get the same value for x? Explain why.

Solving a system algebraically does not always provide a unique solution. Sometimes you get infinitely many solutions. Sometimes you get no solutions.

 Problem 5 Solving Systems Without Unique Solutions

Think

How are the two equations in this system related?
Multiplying both sides of the first equation by -1 results in the second equation.

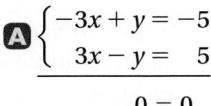

What are the solutions of the following systems? Explain.

A $\begin{cases} -3x + y = -5 \\ 3x - y = 5 \end{cases}$

$0 = 0$

Elimination gives an equation that is always true. The two equations in the system represent the same line. This is a dependent system with infinitely many solutions.

B $\begin{cases} 4x - 6y = 6 \\ -4x + 6y = 10 \end{cases}$

$0 = 16$

Elimination gives an equation that is always false. The two equations in the system represent parallel lines. This is an inconsistent system. It has no solutions.

 Got It? **5.** What are the solutions of the following systems? Explain.

a. $\begin{cases} -x + y = -2 \\ 2x - 2y = 0 \end{cases}$

b. $\begin{cases} 4x + y = 6 \\ 12x + 3y = 18 \end{cases}$

 Lesson Check

Do you know HOW?

Solve each system by substitution.

1. $\begin{cases} 3x + 5y = 13 \\ 2x + y = 4 \end{cases}$

2. $\begin{cases} 2x - 3y = 6 \\ x + y = -12 \end{cases}$

Solve each system by elimination.

3. $\begin{cases} 2x + 3y = 7 \\ -2x + 5y = 1 \end{cases}$

4. $\begin{cases} x + 2y = -1 \\ x - y = 8 \end{cases}$

5. $\begin{cases} x - y = -4 \\ 3x + 2y = 7 \end{cases}$

6. $\begin{cases} 3x + 4y = 10 \\ 2x + 3y = 7 \end{cases}$

Do you UNDERSTAND?  MATHEMATICAL PRACTICES

7. Vocabulary Give an example of two equivalent systems.

8. Compare and Contrast Explain how the substitution method of solving a system of equations differs from the elimination method.

9. Writing A café sells a regular cup of coffee for $1 and a large cup for $1.50. Melissa and her friends buy 5 cups of coffee and spend a total of $6. Explain how to write and solve a system of equations to find the number of large cups of coffee they bought.

Practice and Problem-Solving Exercises
MATHEMATICAL PRACTICES

 **Practice** Solve each system by substitution. Check your answers.

See Problem 1.

10. $\begin{cases} 4x + 2y = 7 \\ y = 5x \end{cases}$

11. $\begin{cases} 3c + 2d = 2 \\ d = 4 \end{cases}$

12. $\begin{cases} x + 12y = 68 \\ x = 8y - 12 \end{cases}$

13. $\begin{cases} 4p + 2q = 8 \\ q = 2p + 1 \end{cases}$

14. $\begin{cases} x + 3y = 7 \\ 2x - 4y = 24 \end{cases}$

15. $\begin{cases} x + 6y = 2 \\ 5x + 4y = 36 \end{cases}$

16. $\begin{cases} t = 2r + 3 \\ 5r - 4t = 6 \end{cases}$

17. $\begin{cases} y = 2x - 1 \\ 3x - y = -1 \end{cases}$

18. $\begin{cases} r + s = -12 \\ 4r - 6s = 12 \end{cases}$

19. Money A student has some $1 bills and $5 bills in his wallet. He has a total of 15 bills that are worth $47. How many of each type of bill does he have?

See Problem 2.

20. A student took 60 minutes to answer a combination of 20 multiple-choice and extended-response questions. She took 2 minutes to answer each multiple-choice question and 6 minutes to answer each extended-response question.
   a. Write a system of equations to model the relationship between the number of multiple choice questions m and the number of extended-response questions r.
   b. How many of each type of question was on the test?

21. Transportation A youth group with 26 members is going skiing. Each of the five chaperones will drive a van or sedan. The vans can seat seven people, and the sedans can seat five people. Assuming there are no empty seats, how many of each type of vehicle could transport all 31 people to the ski area in one trip?

Solve each system by elimination.

See Problem 3.

22. $\begin{cases} x + y = 12 \\ x - y = 2 \end{cases}$

23. $\begin{cases} x + 2y = 10 \\ x + y = 6 \end{cases}$

24. $\begin{cases} 3a + 4b = 9 \\ -3a - 2b = -3 \end{cases}$

25. $\begin{cases} 4x + 2y = 4 \\ 6x + 2y = 8 \end{cases}$

26. $\begin{cases} 2w + 5y = -24 \\ 3w - 5y = 14 \end{cases}$

27. $\begin{cases} 3u + 3v = 15 \\ -2u + 3v = -5 \end{cases}$

28. $\begin{cases} 3x + 2y = 6 \\ 3x + 3 = y \end{cases}$

29. $\begin{cases} 5x - y = 4 \\ 2x - y = 1 \end{cases}$

30. $\begin{cases} 2r + s = 3 \\ 4r - s = 9 \end{cases}$

Solve each system by elimination.

See Problems 4 and 5.

31. $\begin{cases} 4x - 6y = -26 \\ -2x + 3y = 13 \end{cases}$

32. $\begin{cases} 9a - 3d = 3 \\ -3a + d = -1 \end{cases}$

33. $\begin{cases} 2a + 3b = 12 \\ 5a - b = 13 \end{cases}$

34. $\begin{cases} 2x - 3y = 6 \\ 6x - 9y = 9 \end{cases}$

35. $\begin{cases} 20x + 5y = 120 \\ 10x + 7.5y = 80 \end{cases}$

36. $\begin{cases} 6x - 2y = 11 \\ -9x + 3y = 16 \end{cases}$

37. $\begin{cases} 2x - 3y = -1 \\ 3x + 4y = 8 \end{cases}$

38. $\begin{cases} 5x - 2y = -19 \\ 2x + 3y = 0 \end{cases}$

39. $\begin{cases} r + 3s = 7 \\ 2r - s = 7 \end{cases}$

40. $\begin{cases} y = 4 - x \\ 3x + y = 6 \end{cases}$

41. $\begin{cases} 3x + 2y = 10 \\ 6x + 4y = 15 \end{cases}$

42. $\begin{cases} 3m + 4n = -13 \\ 5m + 6n = -19 \end{cases}$

 **Apply**

43. Think About a Plan Suppose you have a part-time job delivering packages. Your employer pays you a flat rate of $9.50 per hour. You discover that a competitor pays employees $2 per hour plus $3 per delivery. How many deliveries would the competitor's employees have to make in four hours to earn the same pay you earn in a four-hour shift?
- How can you write a system of equations to model this situation?
- Which method should you use to solve the system?
- How can you interpret the solution in the context of the problem?

Solve each system.

44. $\begin{cases} 5x + y = 0 \\ 5x + 2y = 30 \end{cases}$

45. $\begin{cases} 2m = -4n - 4 \\ 3m + 5n = -3 \end{cases}$

46. $\begin{cases} 7x + 2y = -8 \\ 8y = 4x \end{cases}$

47. $\begin{cases} 2m + 4n = 10 \\ 3m + 5n = 11 \end{cases}$

48. $\begin{cases} -6 = 3x - 6y \\ 4x = 4 + 5y \end{cases}$

49. $\begin{cases} \dfrac{x}{3} + \dfrac{4y}{3} = 300 \\ 3x - 4y = 300 \end{cases}$

50. $\begin{cases} 0.02a - 1.5b = 4 \\ 0.5b - 0.02a = 1.8 \end{cases}$

51. $\begin{cases} 4y = 2x \\ 2x + y = \dfrac{x}{2} + 1 \end{cases}$

52. $\begin{cases} \dfrac{1}{2}x + \dfrac{2}{3}y = 1 \\ \dfrac{3}{4}x - \dfrac{1}{3}y = 2 \end{cases}$

53. Error Analysis Identify and correct the error shown in finding the solution of $\begin{cases} 3x - 4y = 14 \\ x + y = -7 \end{cases}$ using substitution.

$x + y = -7$
$y = -7 - x$

$3x - 4y = 14$
$3x - 4(-7 - x) = 14$
$3x - 28 + 4x = 14$
$-x - 28 = 14$
$x = -42$

$y = -7 - (-42)$
$y = 35$

54. Break-Even Point Jenny's Bakery sells carrot muffins at $2 each. The electricity to run the oven is $120 per day and the cost of making one carrot muffin is $1.40. How many muffins need to be sold each day to break even?

55. Open-Ended Write a system of equations in which both equations must be multiplied by a number other than 1 or −1 before using elimination. Solve the system.

STEM 56. Chemistry A scientist wants to make 6 milliliters of a 30% sulfuric acid solution. The solution is to be made from a combination of a 20% sulfuric acid solution and a 50% sulfuric acid solution. How many milliliters of each solution must be combined to make the 30% solution?

57. Writing Explain how you decide whether to use substitution or elimination to solve a system.

58. The equation $3x - 4y = 2$ and which equation below form a system with no solutions?

Ⓐ $2y = 1.5x - 2$

Ⓒ $3x + 4y = 2$

Ⓑ $2y = 1.5x - 1$

Ⓓ $4y - 3x = -2$

For each system, choose the method of solving that seems easier to use. Explain why you made each choice. Solve each system.

59. $\begin{cases} 3x - y = 5 \\ y = 4x + 2 \end{cases}$

60. $\begin{cases} 2x - 3y = 4 \\ 2x - 5y = -6 \end{cases}$

61. $\begin{cases} 6x - 3y = 3 \\ 5x - 5y = 10 \end{cases}$

 **Challenge** 62. **Entertainment** In the final round of a singing competition, the audience voted for one of the two finalists, Luke or Sean. Luke received 25% more votes than Sean received. Altogether, the two finalists received 5175 votes. How many votes did Luke receive?

 63. **Weather** The equation $F = \frac{9}{5}C + 32$ relates temperatures on the Celsius and Fahrenheit scales. Does any temperature have the same number reading on both scales? If so, what is the number?

Find the value of a that makes each system a dependent system.

64. $\begin{cases} y = 3x + a \\ 3x - y = 2 \end{cases}$

65. $\begin{cases} 3y = 2x \\ 6y - a - 4x = 0 \end{cases}$

66. $\begin{cases} y = \frac{x}{2} + 4 \\ 2y - x = a \end{cases}$

Standardized Test Prep

SAT/ACT 67. What is the slope of the line at the right?

68. What is the x-value of the solution of $\begin{cases} x + y = 7 \\ 3x - 2y = 11 \end{cases}$?

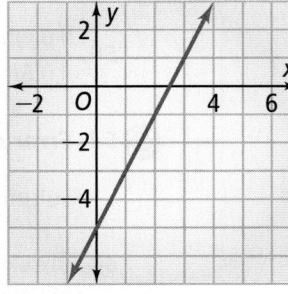

69. Solve $9(x + 7) - 6(x - 3) = 99$. What is the value of x?

70. Georgia has only dimes and quarters in her bag. She has a total of 18 coins that are worth $3. How many more dimes than quarters does she have?

71. The graph of $g(x)$ is a horizontal translation of $f(x) = 2|x + 1| + 3$, 5 units to the right. What is the x-value of the vertex of $g(x)$?

Apply What You've Learned

 **MATHEMATICAL PRACTICES**
MP 2

In the Apply What You've Learned in Lesson 3-1, you created a system of equations and solved the system graphically. Now, you will start to create a system of three linear equations to represent the criteria in the problem on page 133.

a. Write an equation that models the distances of all parts of the triathlon.

b. Write an equation modeling the relationship between the distances of the swim and the run of the triathlon.

c. Use substitution to write a new equation that models the distance of all parts of the triathlon, and solve it for the distance for the bicycle ride.

3-3 Systems of Inequalities

© Common Core State Standards

A-REI.D.12 Graph . . . the solution set to a system of linear inequalities in two variables as the intersection of the corresponding half-planes. **Also A-REI.C.6, A-CED.A.3**

MP 1, MP 2, MP 3, MP 4, MP 7

Objective To solve systems of linear inequalities

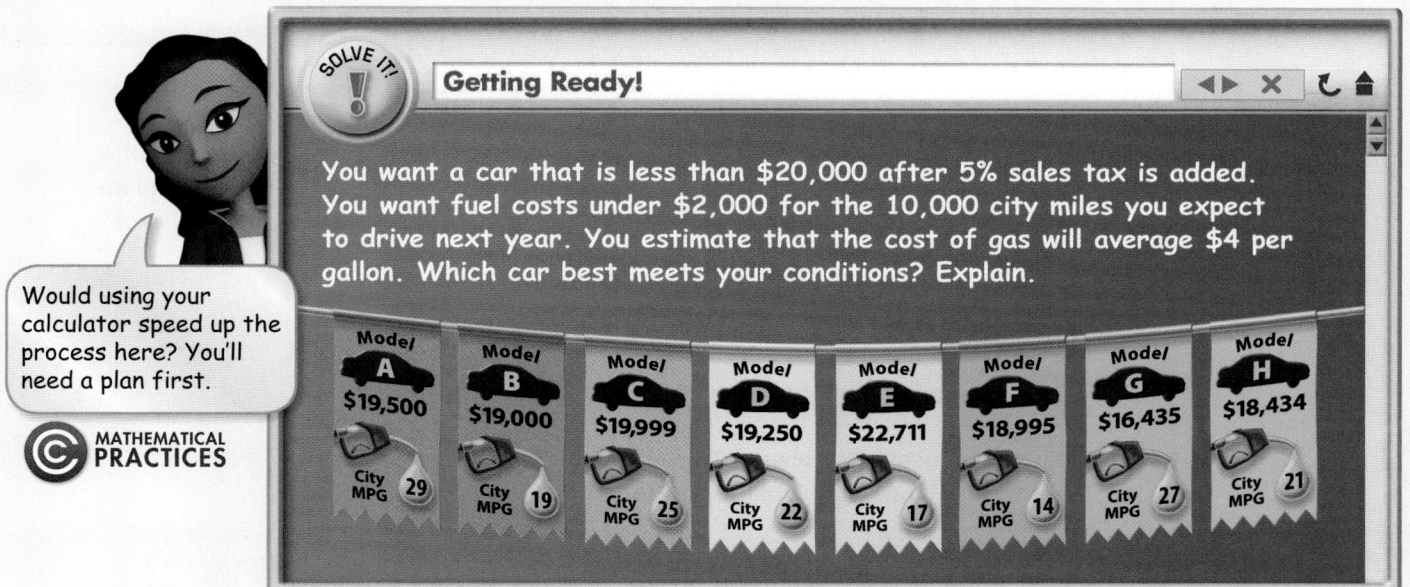

SOLVE IT!

Getting Ready!

You want a car that is less than $20,000 after 5% sales tax is added. You want fuel costs under $2,000 for the 10,000 city miles you expect to drive next year. You estimate that the cost of gas will average $4 per gallon. Which car best meets your conditions? Explain.

Would using your calculator speed up the process here? You'll need a plan first.

© MATHEMATICAL PRACTICES

Model	Price	City MPG
A	$19,500	29
B	$19,000	19
C	$19,999	25
D	$19,250	22
E	$22,711	17
F	$18,995	14
G	$16,435	27
H	$18,434	21

An inequality and a system of inequalities can each have many solutions. A solution of a system of inequalities is a solution for each inequality in the system.

Essential Understanding You can solve a system of inequalities in more than one way. Graphing the solution is usually the most appropriate method. The solution is the set of all points that are solutions of each inequality in the system.

© Problem 1 Solving a System by Using a Table

Assume that g and m are whole numbers. What is the solution of the system of inequalities? $\begin{cases} g + m \geq 6 \\ 5g + 2m \leq 20 \end{cases}$

Make a table of values for g and m that satisfy the second inequality. The values for g and m must be whole numbers.

If $g = 0$, then $5(0) + 2m \leq 20$, and $m \leq 10$.
If $m = 0$, then $5g + 2(0) \leq 20$, and $g \leq 4$.

g	m
0	0, 1, 2, 3, 4, 5, 6, 7, 8, 9, 10
1	0, 1, 2, 3, 4, 5, 6, 7
2	0, 1, 2, 3, 4, 5
3	0, 1, 2
4	0

Plan

Which inequality should you use to build a table?
The first inequality has an infinite number of whole number solutions. The second one has a finite number of solutions. Use the second inequality.

In the table, highlight each pair of values that satisfies the first inequality. The highlighted pairs are the solutions of both inequalities.

g	m
0	0, 1, 2, 3, 4, 5, 6, 7, 8, 9, 10
1	0, 1, 2, 3, 4, 5, 6, 7
2	0, 1, 2, 3, 4, 5
3	0, 1, 2
4	0

 Got It? **1.** Assume that x and y are whole numbers. What is the solution of the system of inequalities?
$$\begin{cases} x + y > 4 \\ 3x + 7y \le 21 \end{cases}$$

You can solve a system of linear inequalities by graphing. Recall that when the variables of a linear inequality represent real numbers, a graphed solution consists of a half-plane and possibly its boundary line. Thus, for two inequalities, the solution is the overlap of the two half-planes.

© Problem 2 Solving a System by Graphing

What is the solution of the system of inequalities? $\begin{cases} 2x - y \ge -3 \\ y \ge -\frac{1}{2}x + 1 \end{cases}$

Graph each inequality. Rewrite $2x - y \ge -3$ in slope-intercept form as $y \le 2x + 3$. The overlap is the solution of the system.

Plan

How can you be sure to shade the correct half-planes?
If the inequality is in slope-intercept form, shade above the boundary if $y >$ or $y \ge$ and shade below the boundary if $y <$ or $y \le$. If not, use a test point.

$y \le 2x + 3$

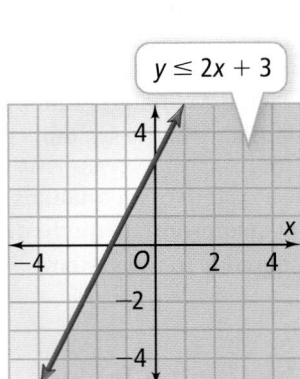

$y \ge -\frac{1}{2}x + 1$

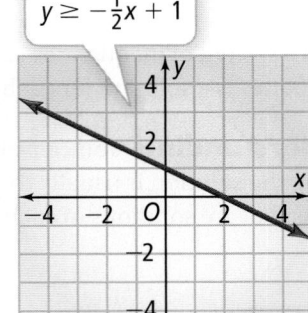

$\begin{cases} 2x - y \ge -3 \\ y \ge -\frac{1}{2}x + 1 \end{cases}$

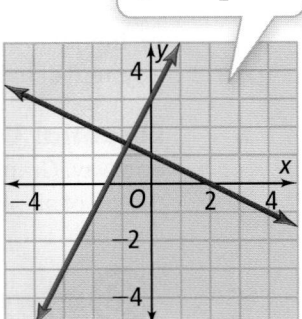

Check Pick a point in the overlap region, such as $(0, 2)$, and check it in both inequalities of the system.

$2x - y \ge -3 \qquad y \ge \frac{1}{2}x + 1$

$2(0) - 2 \ge -3 \qquad 2 \ge \frac{1}{2}(0) + 1$

$-2 \ge -3 ✔ \qquad 2 \ge 1 ✔$

 Got It? **2.** What is the solution of the system of inequalities? $\begin{cases} x + 2y \le 4 \\ y \ge -x - 1 \end{cases}$

Sometimes, you can model a real situation with a system of linear inequalities. Solutions to real-world problems are often whole numbers, so only certain points in the region of overlap will solve the problem.

Problem 3 Using a System of Inequalities

Fundraising Your city's cultural center is sponsoring a concert to raise at least $30,000 for the city's Youth Services. Tickets are $20 for balcony seats and $30 for orchestra seats. If the center has 500 orchestra seats, how many of each type of seat must they sell?

Know	Need	Plan
Must raise at least $30,000. There are at most 500 orchestra seats.	The possible sales of balcony and orchestra seats	• Model the problem with a system of inequalities. • Graph the inequalities on your calculator.

Relate $20 \cdot$ balcony seats $+ 30 \cdot$ orchestra seats $\geq 30,000$

orchestra seats ≤ 500

Define   Let x = the number of balcony seats sold.

Let y = the number of orchestra seats sold.

Write $20 \cdot x + 30 \cdot y \geq 30,000$

$y \leq 500$

Rewrite $20x + 30y \geq 30,000$ in slope intercept form as $y \geq -\frac{2}{3}x + 1000$.

The system of inequalities is $\begin{cases} y \geq -\frac{2}{3}x + 1000 \\ y \leq 500 \end{cases}$.

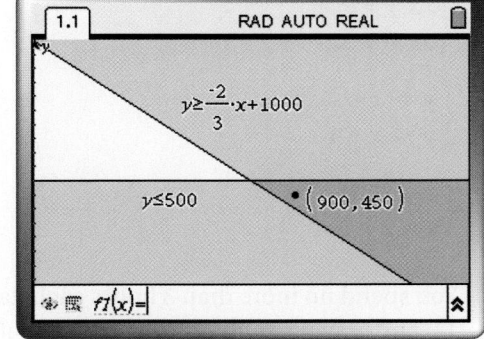

Use your graphing calculator to graph the inequalities. The solution is the overlap.

Test a point. If the cultural center sells 900 balcony and 450 orchestra tickets, will the Youth Services meet its goal?

$20(900) + 30(450) \overset{?}{\geq} 30,000$ $450 \overset{?}{\leq} 500$

$18,000 + 13,250 \overset{?}{\geq} 30,000$ $450 \leq 500$ ✔

$31,250 \geq 30,000$ ✔

Because the number of seats must be a whole number, only the points in the overlap that represent whole numbers are solutions.

Think

What do points in the overlap represent?
The points represent combinations of balcony and orchestra seats that have a total value of at least $30,000.

Got It?   3. A pizza parlor charges $1 for each vegetable topping and $2 for each meat topping. You want at least five toppings on your pizza. You have $10 to spend on toppings. How many of each type of topping can you get on your pizza?

A system of inequalities can include nonlinear inequalities. You can also solve these systems graphically.

 **Problem 4** **Solving a Linear/Absolute-Value System**

What is the solution of the system of inequalities? $\begin{cases} y \leq 3 \\ y \geq |x - 1| \end{cases}$

Graph each inequality.

$y \leq 3$

$y \geq |x - 1|$

$\begin{cases} y \leq 3 \\ y \geq |x - 1| \end{cases}$

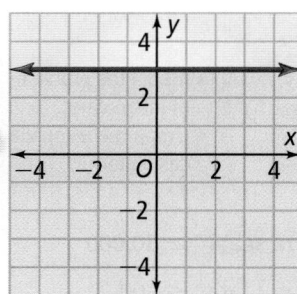

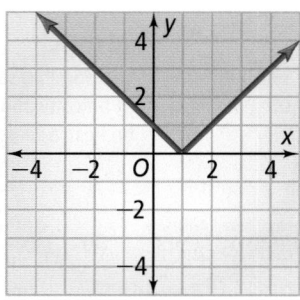

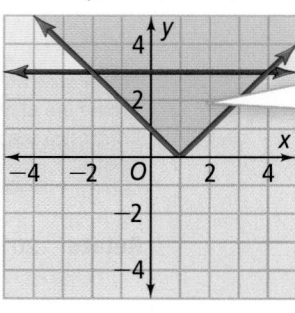

The region of overlap represents the solution.

Think

Why is the shape of the overlap different from that of a system of linear inequalities?
The overlap is not formed by 2 half-planes so it is more varied in shape.

 Got It? **4.** What is the solution of the system of inequalities? $\begin{cases} y < -\frac{1}{3}x + 1 \\ y > 2|x - 1| \end{cases}$

 Lesson Check

Do you know HOW?

Solve each system of inequalities by graphing.

1. $\begin{cases} x + y \geq 2 \\ 2x + y \leq 5 \end{cases}$

2. $\begin{cases} y > x \\ y < x + 1 \end{cases}$

3. $\begin{cases} y \geq -3x - 1 \\ y < x + 2 \end{cases}$

4. You spend no more than 3 hours each day watching TV and playing football. You play football for at least 1 hour each day. What are the possible numbers of hours you can spend on each activity in one day?

Do you UNDERSTAND?  **MATHEMATICAL PRACTICES**

5. Reasoning Is the solution of a system of linear inequalities the union or intersection of the solutions of the two inequalities? Justify your answer.

6. Compare and Contrast Explain how the graphical solution of a system of inequalities is different from the graphical solution of a system of equations.

7. Error Analysis Describe and correct the error made in solving this system of inequalities.

$\begin{cases} y < \frac{1}{2}x - 1 \\ y > -3x + 3 \end{cases}$

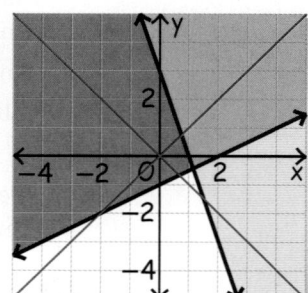

Practice and Problem-Solving Exercises

MATHEMATICAL PRACTICES

 **Practice**

Find all whole number solutions of each system using a table.

See Problem 1.

8. $\begin{cases} y + 3x \leq 8 \\ y - 3 > 2x \end{cases}$

9. $\begin{cases} x + y < 8 \\ 3x \leq y + 6 \end{cases}$

10. $\begin{cases} y \geq x + 2 \\ 3y < -6x + 6 \end{cases}$

Solve each system of inequalities by graphing.

See Problem 2.

11. $\begin{cases} y \leq 2x + 2 \\ y < -x + 1 \end{cases}$

12. $\begin{cases} y > -2 \\ x < 1 \end{cases}$

13. $\begin{cases} y \leq 3 \\ y \leq \frac{1}{2}x + 1 \end{cases}$

14. $\begin{cases} y \leq 3x + 1 \\ -6x + 2y > 5 \end{cases}$

15. $\begin{cases} x + 2y \leq 10 \\ x + y \leq 3 \end{cases}$

16. $\begin{cases} -x - y \leq 2 \\ y - 2x > 1 \end{cases}$

17. $\begin{cases} y > -2x \\ 2x - y \geq 2 \end{cases}$

18. $\begin{cases} c \geq d - 3 \\ c < \frac{1}{2}d + 3 \end{cases}$

19. $\begin{cases} 2x + y < 1 \\ y > -2x + 3 \end{cases}$

20. You want to decorate a party hall with a total of at least 40 red and yellow balloons, with a minimum of 25 yellow balloons. Write and graph a system of inequalities to model the situation.

See Problem 3.

21. A gardener wants to plant at least 50 tulips and rose plants in a garden, but no more than 20 rose plants. Write and graph a system of inequalities to model the situation.

Solve each system of inequalities by graphing.

See Problem 4.

22. $\begin{cases} y > 4 \\ y < |x - 1| \end{cases}$

23. $\begin{cases} y < -\frac{1}{3}x + 1 \\ y > |2x - 1| \end{cases}$

24. $\begin{cases} y > x - 2 \\ y \geq |x + 2| \end{cases}$

25. $\begin{cases} y \leq -\frac{4}{3}x \\ y \geq -|x| \end{cases}$

26. $\begin{cases} 3y < -x - 1 \\ y \leq |x + 1| \end{cases}$

27. $\begin{cases} y > -2 \\ y \leq -|x - 3| \end{cases}$

28. $\begin{cases} -2y < 4x + 2 \\ y > |2x + 1| \end{cases}$

29. $\begin{cases} -x \geq 4 - y \\ y \geq |3x - 6| \end{cases}$

30. $\begin{cases} y \leq x - 4 \\ y > |x - 6| \end{cases}$

 **Apply**

©️ 31. Think About a Plan The food pyramid suggests that you eat 4–6 servings of fruits and vegetables a day for a healthy diet. It also says that the number of servings of vegetables should be greater than the number of servings of fruits. Find the number of servings of fruits and vegetables that could make a healthy diet. Use whole numbers only.
- How can you write two inequalities that model the information in the problem?
- How can you use a graph to find combinations of fruits and vegetable servings that may help in having a healthy diet?

32. **College Admissions** An entrance exam has two sections, a verbal section and a mathematics section. You can score a maximum of 1600 points. For admission, the school of your choice requires a math score of at least 600. Write a system of inequalities to model scores that meet the school's requirements. Then solve the system by graphing.

33. Open-Ended Write and graph a system of inequalities for which the solution is bounded by a dashed vertical line and a solid horizontal line.

34. Writing Explain how you determine where to shade when solving a system of inequalities.

35. Given a system of two linear inequalities, explain how you can pick test points in the plane to determine where to shade the solution set.

In Exercises 36–45, identify the inequalities A, B, and C for which the given ordered pair is a solution.

A. $x + y \leq 2$

B. $y \leq \frac{3}{2}x - 1$

C. $y > -\frac{1}{3}x - 2$

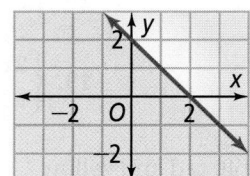
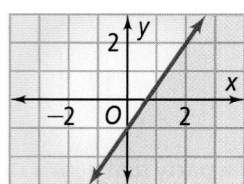
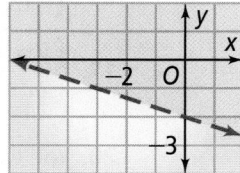

36. $(0, 0)$ **37.** $(-2, -5)$ **38.** $(-2, 0)$ **39.** $(0, -2)$ **40.** $(-15, 15)$

41. $(3, 2)$ **42.** $(2, 0)$ **43.** $(-6, 0)$ **44.** $(4, -1)$ **45.** $(-8, -11)$

Solve each system of inequalities by graphing.

46. $\begin{cases} x + y < 8 \\ x \geq 0 \\ y \geq 0 \end{cases}$

47. $\begin{cases} 2y - 4x \leq 0 \\ x \geq 0 \\ y \geq 0 \end{cases}$

48. $\begin{cases} y \geq -2x + 4 \\ x > -3 \\ y \geq 1 \end{cases}$

49. $\begin{cases} y \leq \frac{2}{3}x + 2 \\ y \geq |x| + 2 \end{cases}$

50. $\begin{cases} y < x - 1 \\ y > -|x - 2| + 1 \end{cases}$

51. $\begin{cases} 2x + y \leq 3 \\ y > |x + 3| - 2 \end{cases}$

52. $\begin{cases} y < |x - 1| + 2 \\ x \geq 0 \end{cases}$

53. $\begin{cases} y > |x - 1| + 1 \\ y \leq -|x - 3| + 4 \end{cases}$

54. $\begin{cases} y \leq |x| - 2 \\ y \leq |x| + 2 \end{cases}$

C Challenge **Geometry** Write a system of inequalities to describe each shaded figure.

55.
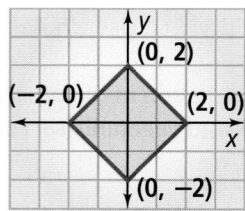

56.
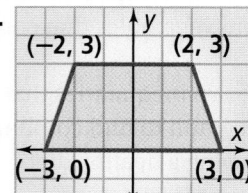

57.
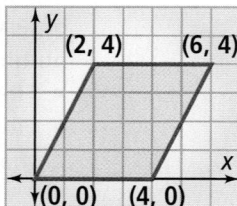

58. a. Graph the "bowtie" inequality, $|y| \leq |x|$.
   b. Write a system of inequalities to describe the graph shown at the right.

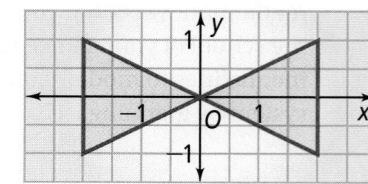

Standardized Test Prep

SAT/ACT

59. Which system of inequalities is shown in the graph?

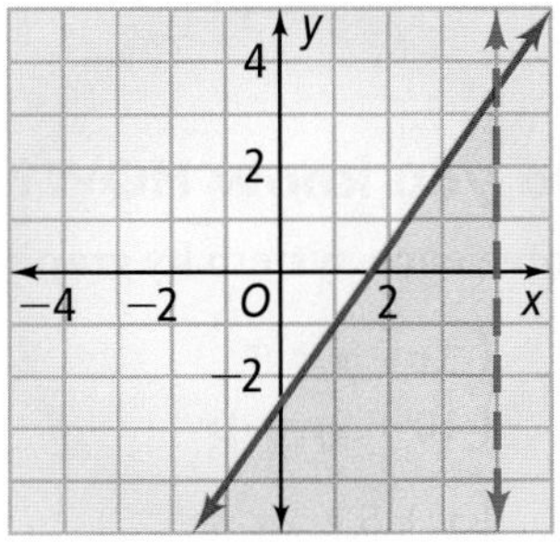

Ⓐ $\begin{cases} x \geq 4 \\ 3x - 2y > 5 \end{cases}$

Ⓑ $\begin{cases} x > 4 \\ 3x - 2y \leq 5 \end{cases}$

Ⓒ $\begin{cases} x < 4 \\ 3x - 2y \geq 5 \end{cases}$

Ⓓ $\begin{cases} x \leq 4 \\ 3x - 2y < 5 \end{cases}$

60. What is the equation of the line that passes through the point $(4, -3)$ and has slope $\frac{1}{2}$?

Ⓕ $y = \frac{1}{2}x + 3$

Ⓖ $y = \frac{1}{2}x - 1$

Ⓗ $y = \frac{1}{2}x - 5$

Ⓘ $y = x - \frac{1}{2}$

61. Which equation is a vertical translation of $y = -5x$?

Ⓐ $y = -\frac{5}{2}x$

Ⓑ $y = -5x + 2$

Ⓒ $y = -10x$

Ⓓ $y = 5x - 2$

Short Response

62. The cost of renting a pool at an aquatic center is either \$30 per hour or \$20 per hour with a \$40 non-refundable deposit. For how many hours is the cost of renting a pool the same for both plans?

Mixed Review

Solve each system by elimination or substitution.

See Lesson 3-2.

63. $\begin{cases} y = 3x + 1 \\ 2x - y = 8 \end{cases}$

64. $\begin{cases} 3x + y = 4 \\ 2x - 4y = 7 \end{cases}$

65. $\begin{cases} -x + 5y = 3 \\ 2x - 10y = 4 \end{cases}$

66. $\begin{cases} 2x + 4y = -8 \\ -5x + 4y = 6 \end{cases}$

67. $\begin{cases} y - 3 = x \\ 4x + y = -2 \end{cases}$

68. $\begin{cases} 2 = 4y - 3x \\ 5x = 2y - 3 \end{cases}$

Get Ready! To prepare for Lesson 3-4, do Exercises 69–72.

Write an ordered pair that is a solution of each system of inequalities.

See Lesson 3-3.

69. $\begin{cases} x + y > 2 \\ 3x + 2y \leq 6 \end{cases}$

70. $\begin{cases} 2y > 4 \\ 3x + 4y \leq 14 \end{cases}$

71. $\begin{cases} x \geq 2 \\ 5x + 2y \leq 9 \end{cases}$

72. $\begin{cases} x + 3y < 6 \\ y < x \end{cases}$

MathXL® for School
Go to PowerAlgebra.com

Do you know HOW?

Solve each system by graphing.

1. $\begin{cases} 3x - y = 8 \\ 10 + 2y = 4x \end{cases}$

2. $\begin{cases} y + 5 = 2x \\ 3y + 6x = -3 \end{cases}$

3. $\begin{cases} 14x - 2y = 6 \\ 6y - 9x = 15 \end{cases}$

Without graphing, classify each system as independent, dependent, or inconsistent.

4. $\begin{cases} 3y + 2x = 12 \\ 36 - 9y = -6x \end{cases}$

5. $\begin{cases} -2y = 20 - 2x \\ 3y - 6x = -30 \end{cases}$

6. $\begin{cases} 15x = 10y - 20 \\ 18 + 9x = 6y \end{cases}$

Solve each system by substitution.

7. $\begin{cases} 5m - n = 7 \\ 3 + 3n = 6m \end{cases}$

8. $\begin{cases} 4y - 6 = 2x \\ y - 3x = 9 \end{cases}$

9. $\begin{cases} 3u + 8 = 4v \\ 24v = 6 - 3u \end{cases}$

Solve each system by elimination.

10. $\begin{cases} 5c - 4t = 8 \\ 14 + 4t = 3c \end{cases}$

11. $\begin{cases} 8y + 10 = 6x \\ 8y - 4x = -12 \end{cases}$

12. $\begin{cases} 11 - 2c = 3d \\ 2c - 7d = -9 \end{cases}$

Graph the solutions to each of the following systems.

13. $\begin{cases} y < 2 + 3x \\ y \geq |x - 3| \end{cases}$

14. $\begin{cases} 2x + y > 7 \\ x < 4 \\ y \leq 5 \end{cases}$

Do you UNDERSTAND?

15. Which equation below combines with the equation $-4x + 6y = 3$ to form a system with an infinite number of solutions?

 Ⓐ $0.5 + x = 1.5y$

 Ⓑ $0.75 + 2x = 1.5y$

 Ⓒ $0.5 + 2x = 1.5y$

 Ⓓ $0.75 + x = 1.5y$

16. Write a system of inequalities to describe the shaded region.

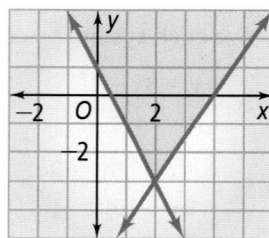

17. An ordinary refrigerator costs $503 and has an estimated annual operating cost of $92. An energy-efficient model costs $615 with an estimated annual operating cost of $64. Write a system of equations to represent this situation.
 a. What is the solution of the system?
 b. What does the solution mean?
 c. Which model would you choose for your family? Why?

Ⓒ **18. Writing** Explain how to classify a linear system as independent, dependent, or inconsistent without graphing.

Linear Programming

Common Core State Standards

A-CED.A.3 Represent constraints by equations or inequalities, and by systems of equations and/or inequalities, and interpret solutions as viable or nonviable options in a modeling context.

MP 1, MP 3, MP 4

Objective To solve problems using linear programming

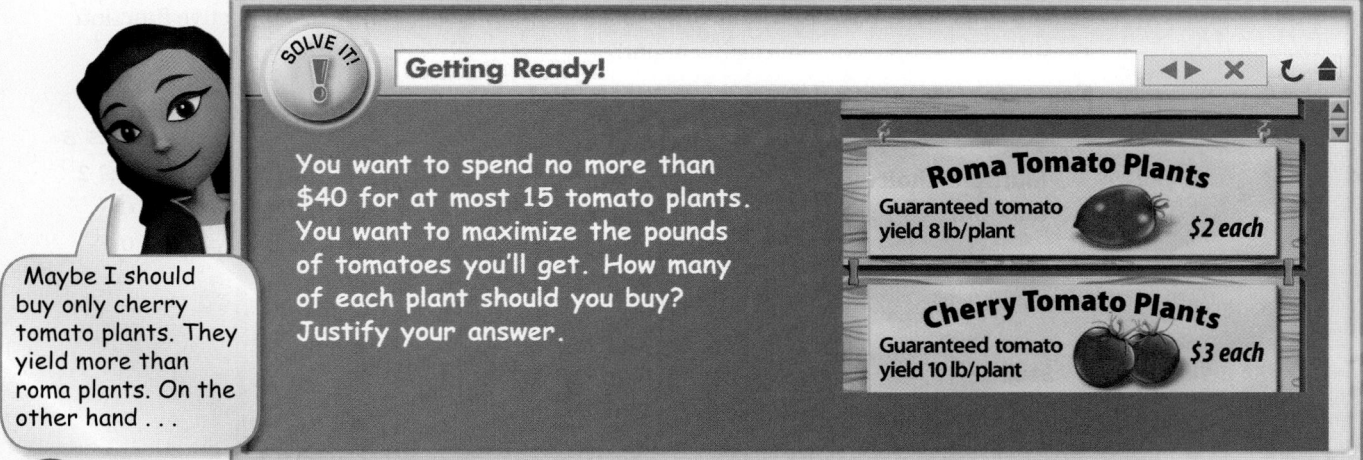

SOLVE IT!

Getting Ready!

You want to spend no more than $40 for at most 15 tomato plants. You want to maximize the pounds of tomatoes you'll get. How many of each plant should you buy? Justify your answer.

Roma Tomato Plants
Guaranteed tomato yield 8 lb/plant   **$2 each**

Cherry Tomato Plants
Guaranteed tomato yield 10 lb/plant   **$3 each**

Maybe I should buy only cherry tomato plants. They yield more than roma plants. On the other hand . . .

MATHEMATICAL PRACTICES

In the Solve It, you maximized your tomato production given some limits, or **constraints**. **Linear programming** is a method for finding a minimum or maximum value of some quantity, given a set of constraints.

Essential Understanding Some real-world problems involve multiple linear relationships. Linear programming accounts for all of these linear relationships and gives the solution to the problem.

The constraints in a linear programming situation form a system of inequalities, like the one at the right. The graph of the system is the **feasible region**. It contains all the points that satisfy all the constraints.

$$\begin{cases} x \geq 2 \\ y \geq 3 \\ y \leq 6 \\ x + y \leq 10 \end{cases}$$

Feasible Region

The quantity you are trying to maximize or minimize is modeled with an **objective function**. Often this quantity is cost or profit. Suppose the objective function is $C = 2x + y$.

Graphs of the objective function for various values of C are parallel lines. Lines closer to the origin represent smaller values of C.

The graphs of the equations $7 = 2x + y$ and $17 = 2x + y$ intersect the feasible region at $(2, 3)$ and $(7, 3)$. These vertices of the feasible represent the least and the greatest values for the objective function.

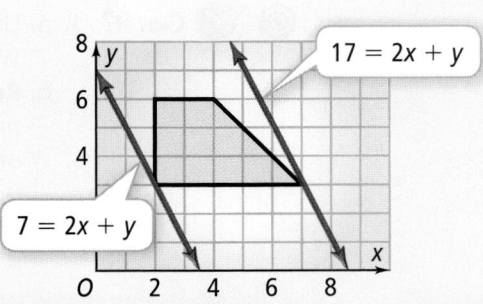

$17 = 2x + y$

$7 = 2x + y$

Key Concept Vertex Principle of Linear Programming

If there is a maximum or a minimum value of the linear objective function, it occurs at one or more vertices of the feasible region.

You can solve a problem using linear programming by testing in the objective function all of the vertices of the feasible region.

 Problem 1 Testing Vertices

Multiple Choice What point in the feasible region maximizes P for the objective function $P = 2x + y$?

$$\text{Constraints} \begin{cases} x + 2y \le 5 \\ x - y \le 2 \\ x \ge 0 \\ y \ge 0 \end{cases}$$

Ⓐ $(2, 0)$ Ⓑ $(0, 0)$ Ⓒ $(3, 1)$ Ⓓ $(0, 2.5)$

Think

What quadrant will the feasible region be in?
The constraints $x \ge 0$ and $y \ge 0$ indicate the first quadrant.

Step 1

Graph the inequalities.

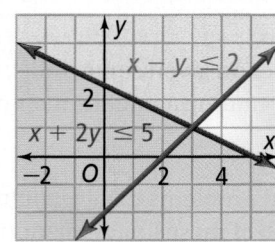

Step 2

Form the feasible region.

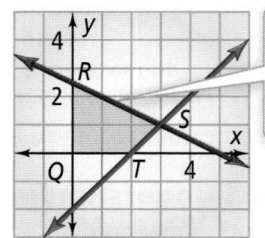

The intersections of the boundaries are the vertices of the feasible region.

Step 3

Find the coordinates of each vertex.

$Q\,(0, 0)$

$R\,(0, 2.5)$

$S\,(3, 1)$

$T\,(2, 0)$

Step 4

Evaluate P at each vertex.

$P = 2(0) + 0 = 0$

$P = 2(0) + 2.5 = 2.5$

$P = 2(3) + 1 = 7$ Maximum Value

$P = 2(2) + 0 = 4$

P has a maximum value of 7 when $x = 3$ and $y = 1$. The correct choice is C.

  Got It? **1. a.** Use the constraints in Problem 1 with the objective function $P = x + 3y$. What values of x and y maximize P?
  b. **Reasoning** Can an objective function $P = ax + by + c$ have (the same) maximum value at all four vertex points Q, R, S, and T? At points R and S only? Explain using examples.

 **Problem 2** Using Linear Programming to Maximize Profit

Business You are screen-printing T-shirts and sweatshirts to sell at the Polk County Blues Festival and are working with the following constraints.

- You have at most 20 hours to make shirts.
- You want to spend no more than $600 on supplies.
- You want to have at least 50 items to sell.

Blues Festival

1-Color T-shirt
Takes 10 minutes to make
Supplies cost $4
Profit $6

3-Color Sweatshirt
Takes 30 minutes to make
Supplies cost $20
Profit $20

How many T-shirts and how many sweatshirts should you make to maximize your profit? How much is the maximum profit?

Organize the information in a table.

Write the constraints and the objective function.

Constraints: $\begin{cases} 10x + 30y \le 1200 \\ x + y \ge 50 \\ 4x + 20y \le 600 \\ x \ge 0 \\ y \ge 0 \end{cases}$

	T-Shirts, x	Sweatshirts, y	Total
Minutes	$10x$	$30y$	1200
Number	x	y	50
Cost	$4x$	$20y$	600
Profit	$6x$	$20y$	$6x + 20y$

Objective Function: $P = 6x + 20y$

Step 1

Graph the constraints to form the feasible region.

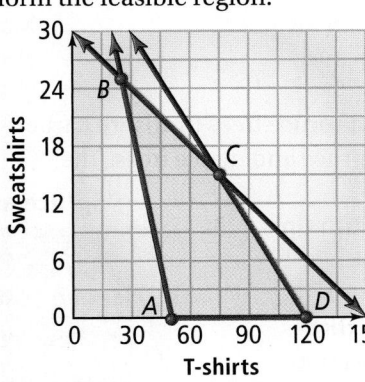

Step 2

Find the coordinates of each vertex.

$A(50, 0)$

$B(25, 25)$

$C(75, 15)$

$D(120, 0)$

Step 3

Evaluate P.

$P = 6(50) + 20(0) = 300$

$P = 6(25) + 20(25) = 650$

$P = 6(75) + 20(15) = 750$

$P = 6(120) + 20(0) = 720$

 Think

How do you find the coordinates of the vertices if they are hard to read off the graph?
Solve the system of equations related to the lines that intersect to form the vertex.

You can maximize your profit by selling 75 T-shirts and 15 sweatshirts. The maximum profit is $750.

✔ **Got It?** **2.** If it took you 20 minutes to make a sweatshirt, how many of each type of shirt should you make to maximize your profit?

Lesson Check

Do you know HOW?

Graph each system of inequalities.

1. $\begin{cases} x + y \le 6 \\ x \ge 0 \\ y \ge 0 \end{cases}$

2. $\begin{cases} 2x - y \le 4 \\ x \ge 0 \\ y \ge 0 \end{cases}$

3. $\begin{cases} x + 2y \le 10 \\ x \ge 1 \\ y \ge 2 \end{cases}$

4. $\begin{cases} 2x + 3y \le 18 \\ 0 \le x \le 5 \\ 0 \le y \le 4 \end{cases}$

Graph each system of constraints. Then name the vertices of the feasible region.

5. $\begin{cases} x \le 5 \\ y \le 4 \\ x \ge 0 \\ y \ge 0 \end{cases}$

6. $\begin{cases} x + y \le 8 \\ y \ge 5 \\ x \ge 0 \end{cases}$

Do you UNDERSTAND?

7. Vocabulary Explain why the inequalities of a linear programming problem are called constraints. *Hint*: Use the definition of *constraint* as part of your answer.

8. Compare and Contrast What are some similarities between solving a linear programming problem and solving a system of linear inequalities? What are some differences?

9. Open-Ended Write a system of constraints whose graphs determine a trapezoid. Write an objective function and evaluate it at each vertex.

Practice and Problem-Solving Exercises

 **Practice** Graph each system of constraints. Name all vertices. Then find the values of x and y that maximize or minimize the objective function.

See Problem 1.

10. $\begin{cases} x + y \le 8 \\ 2x + y \le 10 \\ x \ge 0 \\ y \ge 0 \end{cases}$

Maximum for
$N = 100x + 40y$

11. $\begin{cases} x + 2y \ge 8 \\ x \ge 2 \\ y \ge 0 \end{cases}$

Minimum for
$C = x + 3y$

12. $\begin{cases} 2 \le x \le 6 \\ 1 \le y \le 5 \\ x + y \le 8 \end{cases}$

Maximum for
$P = 3x + 2y$

13. Air Quality A city wants to plant maple and spruce trees to absorb carbon dioxide It has $2100 to spend on planting spruce and maple trees. The city has 45,000 ft^2 available for planting.

See Problem 2.

   a. Use the data from the table. Write the constraints for the situation.
   b. Write the objective function.
   c. Graph the feasible region and find the vertices.
   d. How many of each tree should the city plant to maximize carbon dioxide absorption?

Spruce and Maple Tree Data

	Spruce	Maple
Planting Cost	$30	$40
Area Required	600 ft^2	900 ft^2
Carbon Dioxide Absorption	650 lb/yr	300 lb/yr

SOURCE: Auburn University and Anderson Associates

 **Apply**

Ⓒ **14. Think About a Plan** A biologist is developing two new strains of bacteria. Each sample of Type I bacteria produces four new viable bacteria, and each sample of Type II produces three new viable bacteria. Altogether, at least 240 new viable bacteria must be produced. At least 30, but not more than 60, of the original samples must be Type I. Not more than 70 of the original samples can be Type II. A sample of Type I costs $5 and a sample of Type II costs $7. How many samples of Type II bacteria should the biologist use to minimize the cost?
- What are the unknowns?
- What constraints do you get from each condition in the problem?
- Are there any implicit constraints?

Ⓒ **15. Error Analysis** Your friend is trying to find the maximum value of $P = -x + 3y$ subject to the following constraints.

$$\begin{cases} y \le -2x + 6 \\ y \le x + 3 \\ x \ge 0, y \ge 0 \end{cases}$$

What error did your friend make? What is the correct solution?

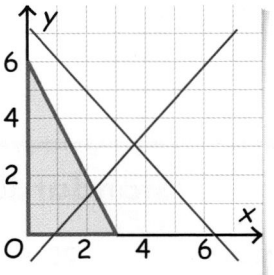

16. Cooking Baking a tray of corn muffins takes 4 cups of milk and 3 cups of wheat flour. Baking a tray of bran muffins takes 2 cups of milk and 3 cups of wheat flour. A baker has 16 cups of milk and 15 cups of wheat flour. He makes $3 profit per tray of corn muffins and $2 profit per tray of bran muffins. How many trays of each type of muffin should the baker make to maximize his profit?

Graph each system of constraints. Name all vertices. Then find the values of x and y that maximize or minimize the objective function. Find the maximum or minimum value.

17. $\begin{cases} 3x + y \le 7 \\ x + 2y \le 9 \\ x \ge 0, y \ge 0 \end{cases}$
Maximum for
$P = 2x + y$

18. $\begin{cases} 25 \le x \le 75 \\ y \le 110 \\ 8x + 6y \ge 720 \end{cases}$
Minimum for
$C = 8x + 5y$

19. $\begin{cases} x + y \le 11 \\ 2y \ge x \\ x \ge 0, y \ge 0 \end{cases}$
Maximum for
$P = 3x + 2y$

20. $\begin{cases} 2x + y \le 300 \\ x + y \le 200 \\ x \ge 0, y \ge 0 \end{cases}$
Maximum for
$P = x + 2y$

21. $\begin{cases} 5x + y \ge 10 \\ x + y \le 6 \\ x + 4y \ge 12 \\ x \ge 0, y \ge 0 \end{cases}$
Minimum for
$C = 10{,}000x + 20{,}000y$

22. $\begin{cases} 6 \le x + y \le 13 \\ x \ge 3 \\ y \ge 1 \end{cases}$
Maximum for
$P = 4x + 3y$

 **Challenge**

23. A vertex of a feasible region does not always have whole-number coordinates. Sometimes you may need to round coordinates to find the solution. Using the objective function and the constraints at the right, find the whole-number values of x and y that minimize C. Then find C for those values of x and y.

$$C = 6x + 9y$$
$$\begin{cases} x + 2y \geq 50 \\ 2x + y \geq 60 \\ x \geq 0, y \geq 0 \end{cases}$$

24. Reasoning Sometimes two corners of a graph both yield the maximum profit. In this case, many other points may also yield the maximum profit. Evaluate the profit formula $P = x + 2y$ for the graph shown. Find four points that yield the maximum profit.

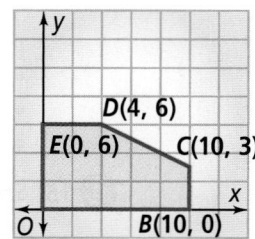

SAT/ACT

25. Solve the equation $\frac{1}{2}(a + b) = c$ for b.

(A) $b = \frac{1}{2}c - a$ (B) $b = 2a - c$ (C) $b = 2c - a$ (D) $b = 2ca$

26. Which is the graph of $y \leq |x - 3|$?

(F) 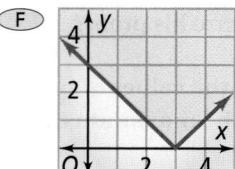   (G) 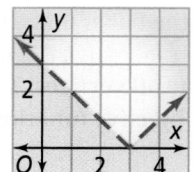   (H) 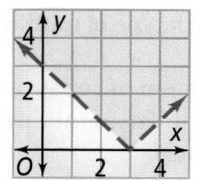   (I)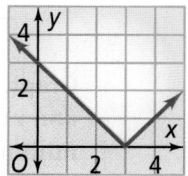

Short Response

27. What are the vertices of the feasible region bounded by the constraints at the right?

$$\begin{cases} x + y \leq 3 \\ 2x + y \leq 4 \\ x \geq 0, y \geq 0 \end{cases}$$

Mixed Review

Solve each system of inequalities by graphing.

See Lesson 3-3.

28. $\begin{cases} y < -2x + 8 \\ 3y \geq 4x - 6 \end{cases}$ **29.** $\begin{cases} x - 2y \geq 11 \\ 5x + 4y < 27 \end{cases}$ **30.** $\begin{cases} 2x + 6y > 12 \\ 3x + 9y \leq 27 \end{cases}$

Evaluate each expression for $a = 3$ and $b = -5$.

See Lesson 1-3.

31. $2a + b$ **32.** $-4 + 2ab$ **33.** $3(a - b)$ **34.** $b(2b - a)$

Get Ready!   To prepare for Lesson 3-5, do Exercises 35–37.

Find the x- and y-intercepts of the graph of each linear equation.

See Lesson 2-4.

35. $y = 2x + 6$ **36.** $2x + 9y = 36$ **37.** $y = x - 1$

Linear Programming

 Common Core State Standards

A-CED.A.3 Represent constraints by equations or inequalities, and by systems of equations and/or inequalities, and interpret solutions as viable or nonviable options in a modeling context.

MP 5

You can solve linear programming problems using your graphing calculator.

Activity

Find the values of x and y that will maximize the objective function $P = 13x + 2y$ for the constraints at the right. What is the value of P at this maximum point?

$$\begin{cases} -3x + 2y \le 8 \\ -8x + y \ge -48 \\ x \ge 0, y \ge 0 \end{cases}$$

Step 1 Rewrite the first two inequalities to isolate y. Enter the inequalities.

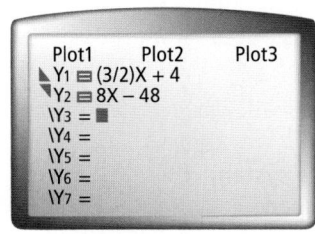

Step 2 Use the **VALUE** option of **CALC** to find the upper left vertex. Press 0 **enter**.

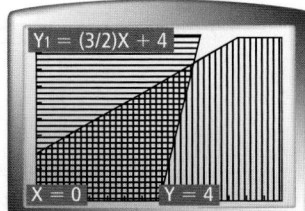

Step 3 Enter the objective function on the home screen. Press **enter** for the value of P at the vertex.

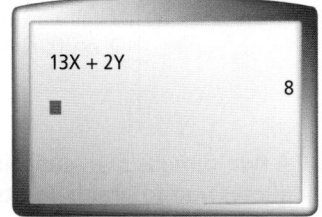

Step 4 Use the **INTERSECT** option of **CALC** to find the upper right vertex. Go to the home screen and press **enter** for the value of P.

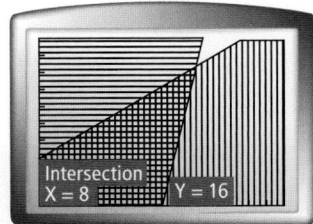

Step 5 Use the **ZERO** option of **CALC** to find the lower right vertex. Go to the home screen and press **enter** for the value of P. The objective function has a value of 0 when the vertex is at the origin. The maximum value of P is 136.

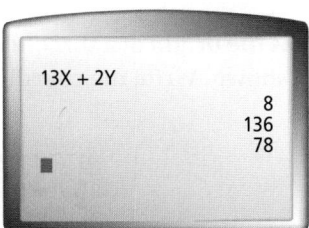

Exercises

Find the values of x and y that maximize or minimize the objective function.

1. $\begin{cases} 4x + 3y \ge 30 \\ x + 3y \ge 21 \\ x \ge 0, y \ge 0 \end{cases}$

Minimum for
$C = 5x + 8y$

2. $\begin{cases} 3x + 5y \ge 35 \\ 2x + y \le 14 \\ x \ge 0, y \ge 0 \end{cases}$

Maximum for
$P = 3x + 2y$

3. $\begin{cases} x + y \ge 8 \\ x + 5y \ge 20 \\ x \ge 0, y \ge 2 \end{cases}$

Minimum for
$C = 3x + 4y$

4. $\begin{cases} x + 2y \le 24 \\ 3x + 2y \le 34 \\ 3x + y \le 29 \\ x \ge 0 \end{cases}$

Maximum for
$P = 2x + 3y$

Graphs in Three Dimensions

 Common Core State Standards

Extends A-REI.C.6 Solve systems of linear equations exactly and approximately (e.g., with graphs), focusing on pairs of linear equations in two variables.

MP 4

To describe positions in space, you need a three-dimensional coordinate system. You have learned to graph on an *xy*-coordinate plane using ordered pairs. Adding a third axis, the *z*-axis, to the *xy*-coordinate plane creates **coordinate space**. In coordinate space you graph points using **ordered triples** of the form (x, y, z).

Points in a Plane

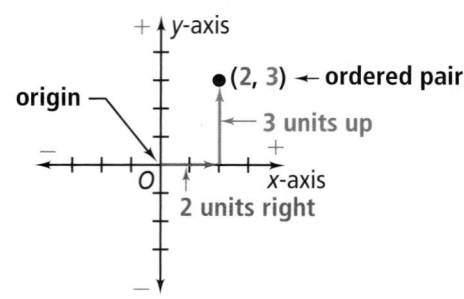

A two-dimensional coordinate system allows you to graph points in a plane.

Points in Space

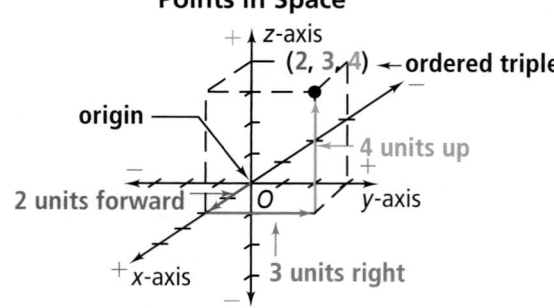

A three-dimensional coordinate system allows you to graph points in space.

In the coordinate plane, point $(2, 3)$ is two units right and three units up from the origin. In coordinate space, point $(2, 3, 4)$ is two units forward, three units right, and four units up.

Activity 1

Define one corner of your classroom as the origin of a three-dimensional coordinate system like the classroom shown. Write the coordinates of each item in your coordinate system.

1. each corner of your classroom

2. each corner of your desk

3. one corner of the blackboard

4. the clock

5. the waste-paper basket

6. Pick 3 items in your classroom and write the coordinates of each.

An equation in two variables represents a line in a plane. An equation in three variables represents a plane in space.

Activity 2

Given the following equation in three variables, draw the plane in a coordinate space. $x + 2y - z = 6$

7. Let $x = 0$. Graph the resulting equation in the yz plane.

8. Let $y = 0$. Graph the resulting equation in the xz plane.

From geometry you know that two lines determine a plane.

9. Sketch the plane $x + 2y - z = 6$.
(If you need help, find a third line by letting $z = 0$ and then graph the resulting equation in the xy plane.)

Activity 3

Two equations in three variables represent two planes in space.

10. Draw the two planes determined by the following equations:
$2x + 3y - z = 12$
$2x - 4y + z = 8$

11. Describe the intersection of the two planes above.

Exercises

Find the coordinates of each point in the diagram.

12. A **13.** B **14.** C

15. D **16.** E **17.** F

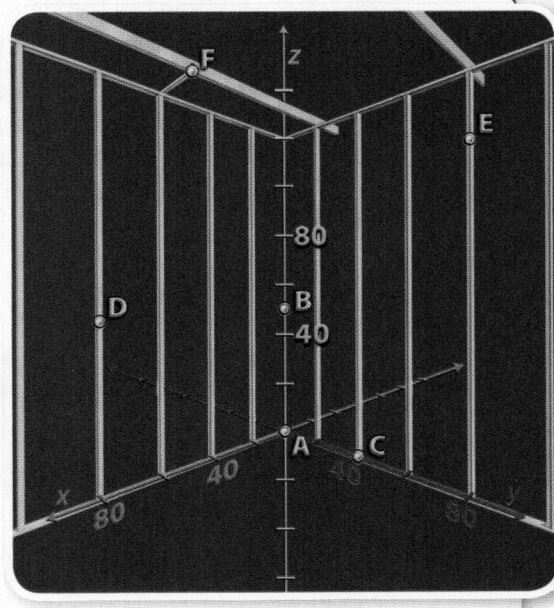

Sketch the graph of each equation.

18. $x - y - 4z = 8$ **19.** $x + y + z = 2$

20. $-3x + 5y + 10z = 15$ **21.** $6x + 6y - 12z = 36$

Graph the following pairs of equations in the same coordinate space and describe their intersection, if any.

22. $-x + 3y + z = 6$ **23.** $-2x - 3y + 5z = 7$
$-3x + 5y - 2z = 60$ $2x - 3y - 4z = -4$

3-5 Systems With Three Variables

© **Common Core State Standards**

Extends A-REI.C.6 Solve systems of linear equations exactly and approximately (e.g., with graphs), focusing on pairs of linear equations in two variables.

MP 1, MP 3

Objectives To solve systems in three variables using elimination
To solve systems in three variables using substitution

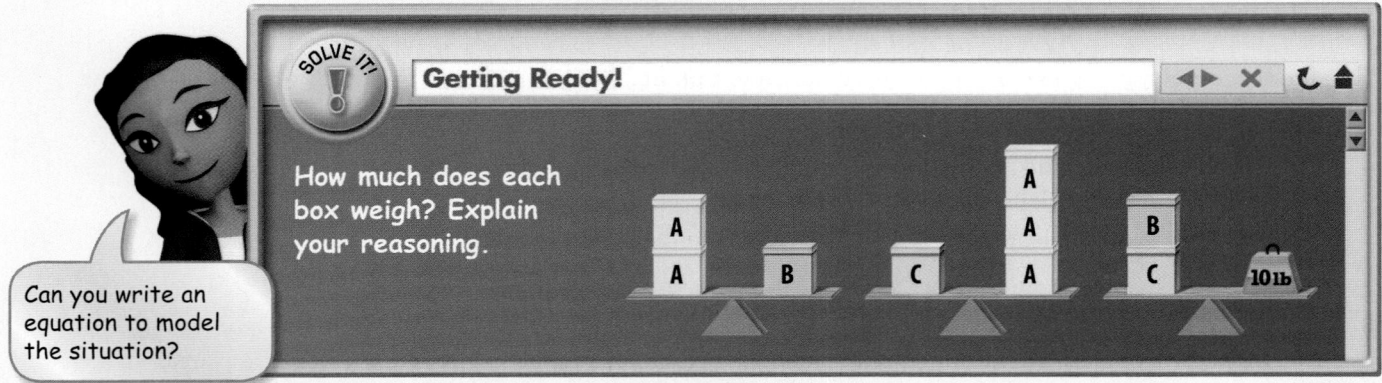

SOLVE IT!

Getting Ready!

How much does each box weigh? Explain your reasoning.

Can you write an equation to model the situation?

© **MATHEMATICAL PRACTICES**

You can represent three relationships involving three unknowns with a system of equations.

Essential Understanding To solve systems of three equations in three variables, you can use some of the same algebraic methods you used to solve systems of two equations in two variables.

You can represent systems of equations in three variables as graphs in three dimensions. The graph of an equation of the form $Ax + By + Cz = D$, where A, B, and C are not all zero, is a plane. You can show the solutions of a three-variable system graphically as the intersection of planes.

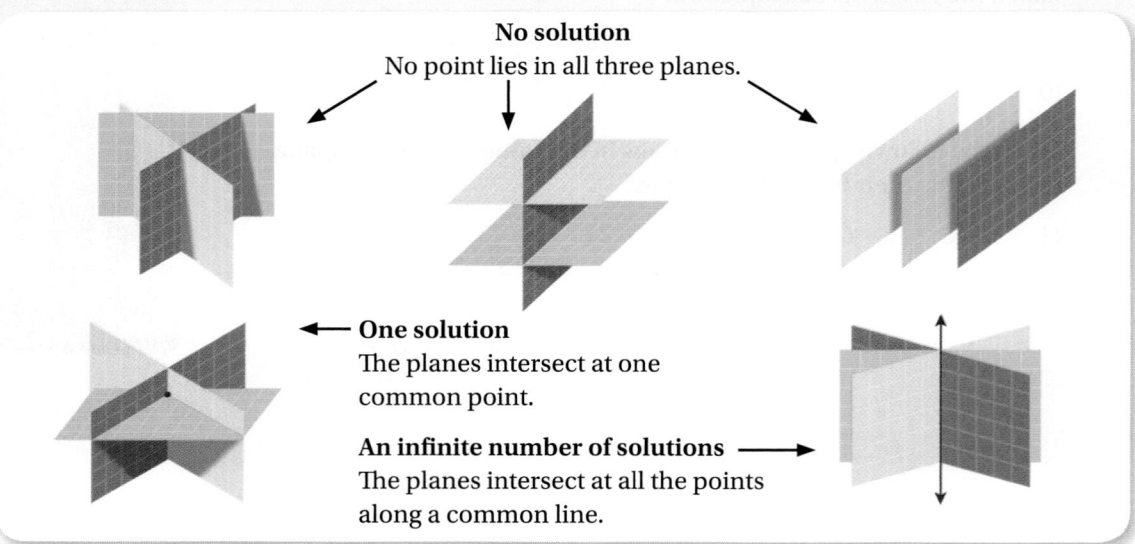

No solution
No point lies in all three planes.

One solution
The planes intersect at one common point.

An infinite number of solutions
The planes intersect at all the points along a common line.

You can use the elimination and substitution methods to solve a system of three equations in three variables by working with the equations in pairs. You will use one of the equations *twice*. When one point represents the solution of a system of equations in three variables, write it as an ordered triple (x, y, z).

Problem 1 Solving a System Using Elimination

What is the solution of the system? Use elimination.
The equations are numbered to make the procedure
easy to follow.

$$① \begin{cases} 2x - y + z = 4 \\ ② \quad x + 3y - z = 11 \\ ③ \quad 4x + y - z = 14 \end{cases}$$

Think

Which variable do you eliminate first?
Eliminate the variable for which the process requires the fewest steps.

Step 1 Pair the equations to eliminate z. Then you will have two equations in x and y.

Add.

$$\begin{array}{ll} ① & 2x - y + z = 4 \\ ② & \underline{x + 3y - z = 11} \\ ④ & 3x + 2y = 15 \end{array}$$

Subtract.

$$\begin{array}{ll} ② & x + 3y - z = 11 \\ ③ & \underline{4x + y - z = 14} \\ ⑤ & -3x + 2y = -3 \end{array}$$

Step 2 Write the two new equations as a system. Solve for x and y.

Add and solve for y.

$$\begin{array}{ll} ④ & 3x + 2y = 15 \\ ⑤ & \underline{-3x + 2y = -3} \\ & 4y = 12 \\ & y = 3 \end{array}$$

Substitute $y = 3$ and solve for x.

$$\begin{array}{ll} ④ & 3x + 2y = 15 \\ & 3x + 2(3) = 15 \\ & 3x = 9 \\ & x = 3 \end{array}$$

Think

Does it matter which equation you substitute into to find z?
No, you can substitute into any of the original three equations.

Step 3 Solve for z. Substitute the values of x and y into one of the original equations.

$$\begin{array}{lll} ① & 2x - y + z = 4 & \text{Use equation } ①. \\ & 2(3) - 3 + z = 4 & \text{Substitute.} \\ & 6 - 3 + z = 4 & \text{Simplify.} \\ & z = 1 & \text{Solve for } z. \end{array}$$

Step 4 Write the solution as an ordered triple. The solution is $(3, 3, 1)$.

 Got It? **1.** What is the solution of the system? Use elimination. Check your answer in all three original equations.

$$\begin{cases} x - y + z = -1 \\ x + y + 3z = -3 \\ 2x - y + 2z = 0 \end{cases}$$

You can apply the method in Problem 1 to most systems of three equations in three variables. You may need to multiply in one, two, or all three equations by one, two, or three nonzero numbers. Your goal is to obtain a system—equivalent to the original system—with coefficients that allow for the easy elimination of variables.

Problem 2 Solving an Equivalent System

What is the solution of the system? Use elimination.

$$①\begin{cases} x + y + 2z = 3 \\ ②\ 2x + y + 3z = 7 \\ ③\ -x - 2y + z = 10 \end{cases}$$

Think

You are trying to get two equations in x and z. Multiply ① so you can add it to ② and eliminate y. Do the same with ② and ③.

Write

$$①\begin{cases} x + y + 2z = 3 \\ ②\ 2x + y + 3z = 7 \end{cases} \longrightarrow$$

$$\begin{array}{r} -x - y - 2z = -3 \\ 2x + y + 3z = 7 \\ \hline ④ \quad x + z = 4 \end{array}$$

$$②\begin{cases} 2x + y + 3z = 7 \\ ③\ -x - 2y + z = 10 \end{cases} \longrightarrow$$

$$\begin{array}{r} 4x + 2y + 6z = 14 \\ -x - 2y + z = 10 \\ \hline ⑤ \quad 3x + 7z = 24 \end{array}$$

Multiply ④ so you can add it to ⑤ and eliminate x.

$$④\begin{cases} x + z = 4 \\ ⑤\ 3x + 7z = 24 \end{cases} \longrightarrow$$

$$\begin{array}{r} -3x - 3z = -12 \\ 3x + 7z = 24 \\ \hline 4z = 12 \\ z = 3 \end{array}$$

Substitute $z = 3$ into ④. Solve for x.

$$x + 3 = 4$$
$$x = 1$$

Substitute the values for x and z into ① to find y. Check the answer in the three original equations.

$$x + y + 2z = 3$$
$$1 + y + 2(3) = 3$$
$$y = -4$$

The solution is $(1, -4, 3)$.

Check
$$1 + (-4) + 2(3) = 3 \quad ✔$$
$$2(1) + (-4) + 3(3) = 7 \quad ✔$$
$$-(1) - 2(-4) + 3 = 10 \quad ✔$$

Got It? **2. a.** What is the solution of the system? Use elimination.
b. Reasoning Could you have used elimination in another way? Explain.

$$\begin{cases} x - 2y + 3z = 12 \\ 2x - y - 2z = 5 \\ 2x + 2y - z = 4 \end{cases}$$

Here is a graphical representation of the solution of Problem 2. The graphs are enclosed in a 10-by-10-by-10 cube with the origin of the coordinate axes at the center.

The graphs of equations ①, ②, and ③, are planes ①, ②, and ③, respectively.

Each pair of planes intersects in a line. The three lines intersect in $(1, -4, 3)$, the solution of the system.

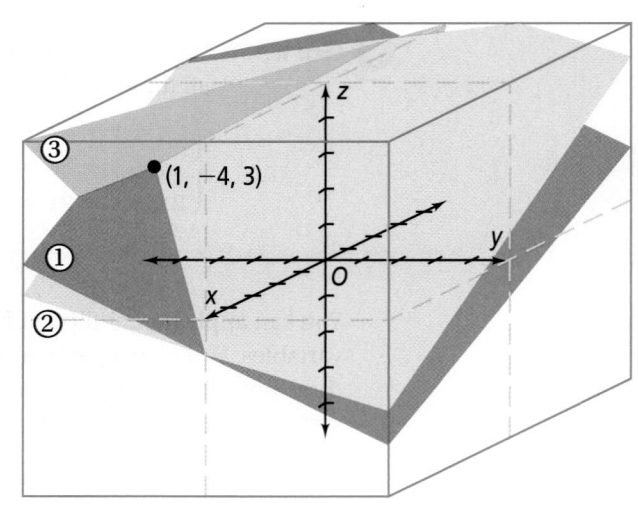

You can also use substitution to solve a system of three equations. Substitution is the best method to use when you can easily solve one of the equations for a single variable.

Problem 3 Solving a System Using Substitution

Multiple Choice What is the x-value in the solution of the system?

$$①\begin{cases} 2x + 3y - 2z = -1 \\ ②\quad x + 5y = 9 \\ ③\quad 4z - 5x = 4 \end{cases}$$

(A) 1   (C) 6

(B) 4   (D) 10

Think

Which equation should you solve for one of its variables?
Look for an equation that has a variable with coefficient 1.

Step 1 Choose equation ②. Solve for x.

② $x + 5y = 9$
       $x = 9 - 5y$

Step 2 Substitute the expression for x into equations ① and ③ and simplify.

①   ③
$\quad 2x + 3y - 2z = -1$ $\quad 4z - 5x = 4$
$2(9 - 5y) + 3y - 2z = -1$ $4z - 5(9 - 5y) = 4$
$18 - 10y + 3y - 2z = -1$ $4z - 45 + 25y = 4$
$\quad 18 - 7y - 2z = -1$ $\quad 4z + 25y = 49$
④ $\quad -7y - 2z = -19$ ⑤ $\quad 25y + 4z = 49$

Step 3 Write the two new equations as a system. Solve for y and z.

④ $\begin{cases} -7y - 2z = -19 \\ ⑤ \quad 25y + 4z = 49 \end{cases}$
  $\quad -14y - 4z = -38$ Multiply by 2.
  $\quad \underline{25y + 4z = 49}$ Then add.
  $\qquad\qquad 11y = 11$
  $\qquad\qquad\quad y = 1$

④ $-7y - 2z = -19$
   $-7(1) - 2z = -19$ Substitute the value of y into ④.
   $\quad -2z = -12$
   $\qquad z = 6$

Step 4 Use one of the original equations to solve for x.

② $x + 5y = 9$
   $x + 5(1) = 9$ Substitute the value of y into ②.
   $\quad x = 4$

The solution of the system is $(4, 1, 6)$, and $x = 4$.

The correct answer is B.

Got It? 3. a. What is the solution of the system? Use substitution.

$$\begin{cases} x - 2y + z = -4 \\ -4x + y - 2z = 1 \\ 2x + 2y - z = 10 \end{cases}$$

b. Reasoning In Problem 3, was it necessary to find the value of z to solve the problem? Explain.

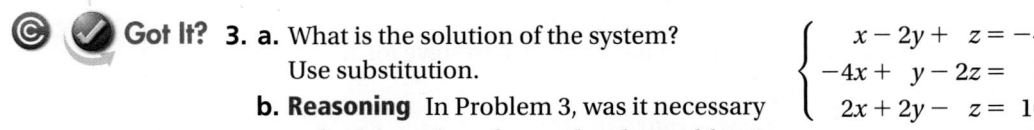

Problem 4 Solving a Real-World Problem

Business You manage a clothing store and budget $6000 to restock 200 shirts. You can buy T-shirts for $12 each, polo shirts for $24 each, and rugby shirts for $36 each. If you want to have twice as many rugby shirts as polo shirts, how many of each type of shirt should you buy?

Relate T-shirts + polo shirts + rugby shirts = 200

rugby shirts = 2 · polo shirts

12 · T-shirts + 24 · polo shirts + 36 · rugby shirts = 6000

Think

How many unknowns are there?
There are three unknowns: the number of each type of shirt.

Define Let x = the number of T-shirts.

Let y = the number of polo shirts.

Let z = the number of rugby shirts.

Write
$$\begin{cases} ① & x + y + z = 200 \\ ② & z = 2 \cdot y \\ ③ & 12 \cdot x + 24 \cdot y + 36 \cdot z = 6000 \end{cases}$$

Step 1 Since 12 is a common factor of all the terms in equation ③, write a simpler equivalent equation.

③ $\begin{cases} 12x + 24y + 36z = 6000 \\ x + 2y + 3z = 500 \end{cases}$ Divide by 12.
④

Step 2 Substitute $2y$ for z in equations ① and ④. Simplify to find equations ⑤ and ⑥.

① $\quad x + y + z = 200$ $\qquad$ ④ $\quad x + 2y + 3z = 500$
$\quad x + y + (2y) = 200$ $\qquad\quad x + 2y + 3(2y) = 500$
⑤ $\qquad x + 3y = 200$ $\qquad$ ⑥ $\qquad x + 8y = 500$

Step 3 Write ⑤ and ⑥ as a system. Solve for x and y.

⑤ $\begin{cases} x + 3y = 200 \\ x + 8y = 500 \end{cases}$ $\qquad$ $\begin{aligned} -x - 3y &= -200 \quad \text{Multiply by } -1. \\ x + 8y &= 500 \quad \text{Then add.} \\ \hline 5y &= 300 \\ y &= 60 \end{aligned}$
⑥

⑤ $\qquad x + 3y = 200$
$\qquad x + 3(60) = 200$ $\quad$ Substitute the value of y into ⑤.
$\qquad\qquad x = 20$

Step 4 Substitute the value of y in ② and solve for z.

② $z = 2y$
$\quad z = 2(60) = 120$

You should buy 20 T-shirts, 60 polo shirts, and 120 rugby shirts.

 Got It? **4.** Suppose you want to have the same number of T-shirts as polo shirts. Buying 200 shirts with a budget of $5400, how many of each shirt should you buy?

Lesson Check

Do you know HOW?

Solve each system.

1. $\begin{cases} 2y - 3z = 0 \\ x + 3y = -4 \\ 3x + 4y = 3 \end{cases}$

2. $\begin{cases} 3x + y - 2z = 22 \\ x + 5y + z = 4 \\ x = -3z \end{cases}$

3. $\begin{cases} 2x + 3y - 2z = 1 \\ -x - y + 2z = 5 \\ 3x + 2y - 3z = -6 \end{cases}$

4. $\begin{cases} 2x - y + z = -2 \\ x + 3y - z = 10 \\ x + 2z = -8 \end{cases}$

Do you UNDERSTAND?

5. Reasoning How do you decide whether substitution is the best method to solve a system in three variables?

6. Error Analysis A classmate says that the system consisting of $x = 0$, $y = 0$, and $z = 0$ has no solution. Explain the student's error.

7. Writing How many solutions does this system have? Explain your answer in terms of intersecting planes. (*Hint:* Is the system dependent? inconsistent?)

① $\begin{cases} 2x - 3y + z = 5 \\ 2x - 3y + z = -2 \\ -4x + 6y - 2z = 10 \end{cases}$
②
③

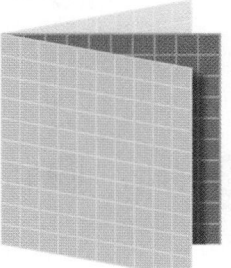

8. The graph of a system is shown. How many solutions does this system have? Explain.

Practice and Problem-Solving Exercises

A Practice   Solve each system by elimination. Check your answers.   ◀ See Problems 1 and 2.

9. $\begin{cases} x - y + z = -1 \\ x + y + 3z = -3 \\ 2x - y + 2z = 0 \end{cases}$

10. $\begin{cases} x - y - 2z = 4 \\ -x + 2y + z = 1 \\ -x + y - 3z = 11 \end{cases}$

11. $\begin{cases} -2x + y - z = 2 \\ -x - 3y + z = -10 \\ 3x + 6z = -24 \end{cases}$

12. $\begin{cases} a + b + c = -3 \\ 3b - c = 4 \\ 2a - b - 2c = -5 \end{cases}$

13. $\begin{cases} 6q - r + 2s = 8 \\ 2q + 3r - s = -9 \\ 4q + 2r + 5s = 1 \end{cases}$

14. $\begin{cases} x - y + 2z = -7 \\ y + z = 1 \\ x = 2y + 3z \end{cases}$

15. $\begin{cases} 3x + 3y + 6z = 9 \\ 2x + y + 3z = 7 \\ x + 2y - z = -10 \end{cases}$

16. $\begin{cases} 3x - y + z = 3 \\ x + y + 2z = 4 \\ x + 2y + z = 4 \end{cases}$

17. $\begin{cases} x - 2y + 3z = 12 \\ 2x - y - 2z = 5 \\ 2x + 2y - z = 4 \end{cases}$

18. $\begin{cases} x + 2y = 2 \\ 2x + 3y - z = -9 \\ 4x + 2y + 5z = 1 \end{cases}$

19. $\begin{cases} 3x + 2y + 2z = -2 \\ 2x + y - z = -2 \\ x - 3y + z = 0 \end{cases}$

20. $\begin{cases} x + 4y - 5z = -7 \\ 3x + 2y + 3z = 7 \\ 2x + y + 5z = 8 \end{cases}$

Solve each system by substitution. Check your answers.  See Problems 3 and 4.

21. $\begin{cases} x + 2y + 3z = 6 \\ \quad\quad y + 2z = 0 \\ \quad\quad\quad\quad z = 2 \end{cases}$

22. $\begin{cases} 3a + b + c = 7 \\ a + 3b - c = 13 \\ b = 2a - 1 \end{cases}$

23. $\begin{cases} 5r - 4s - 3t = 3 \\ t = s + r \\ r = 3s + 1 \end{cases}$

24. $\begin{cases} 13 = 3x - y \\ 4y - 3x + 2z = -3 \\ z = 2x - 4y \end{cases}$

25. $\begin{cases} x + 3y - z = -4 \\ 2x - y + 2z = 13 \\ 3x - 2y - z = -9 \end{cases}$

26. $\begin{cases} x - 4y + z = 6 \\ 2x + 5y - z = 7 \\ 2x - y - z = 1 \end{cases}$

27. $\begin{cases} x - y + 2z = 7 \\ 2x + y + z = 8 \\ x \quad\quad - z = 5 \end{cases}$

28. $\begin{cases} x + y + z = 2 \\ x \quad\quad + 2z = 5 \\ 2x + y - z = -1 \end{cases}$

29. $\begin{cases} 5x - y + z = 4 \\ x + 2y - z = 5 \\ 2x + 3y - 3z = 5 \end{cases}$

STEM 30. Manufacturing In a factory there are three machines, A, B, and C. When all three machines are working, they produce 287 bolts per hour. When only machines A and C are working, they produce 197 bolts per hour. When only machines A and B are working, they produce 202 bolts per hour. How many bolts can each machine produce per hour?

Ⓑ Apply Ⓒ **31. Think About a Plan** In triangle PQR, the measure of angle Q is three times the measure of angle P. The measure of angle R is $20°$ more than the measure of angle P. Find the measure of each angle.
- What are the unknowns in this problem?
- What system of equations represents this situation?
- Which method of solving looks easier for this problem?

32. Sports A stadium has 49,000 seats. Seats sell for $25 in Section A, $20 in Section B, and $15 in Section C. The number of seats in Section A equals the total number of seats in Sections B and C. Suppose the stadium takes in $1,052,000 from each sold-out event. How many seats does each section hold?

Solve each system using any method.

33. $\begin{cases} x - 3y + 2z = 11 \\ -x + 4y + 3z = 5 \\ 2x - 2y - 4z = 2 \end{cases}$

34. $\begin{cases} x + 2y + z = 4 \\ 2x - y + 4z = -8 \\ -3x + y - 2z = -1 \end{cases}$

35. $\begin{cases} 4x - y + 2z = -6 \\ -2x + 3y - z = 8 \\ 2y + 3z = -5 \end{cases}$

36. $\begin{cases} 4a + 2b + c = 2 \\ 5a - 3b + 2c = 17 \\ a - 5b = 3 \end{cases}$

37. $\begin{cases} 4x - 2y + 5z = 6 \\ 3x + 3y + 8z = 4 \\ x - 5y - 3z = 5 \end{cases}$

38. $\begin{cases} 2\ell + 2w + h = 72 \\ \ell = 3w \\ h = 2w \end{cases}$

39. $\begin{cases} 6x + y - 4z = -8 \\ \frac{y}{4} - \frac{z}{6} = 0 \\ 2x \quad\quad - z = -2 \end{cases}$

40. $\begin{cases} 4y + 2x = 6 - 3z \\ x + z - 2y = -5 \\ x - 2z = 3y - 7 \end{cases}$

41. $\begin{cases} 4x - y + z = -5 \\ -x + y - z = 5 \\ 2x - z - 1 = y \end{cases}$

42. Finance A worker received a $10,000 bonus and decided to split it among three different accounts. He placed part in a savings account paying 4.5% per year, twice as much in government bonds paying 5%, and the rest in a mutual fund that returned 4%. His income from these investments after one year was $455. How much did the worker place in each account?

 **Challenge**

43. **Open-Ended** Write your own system with three variables. Begin by choosing the solution. Then write three equations that are true for your solution. Use elimination to solve the system.

44. **Geometry** Refer to the regular five-pointed star at the right. Write and solve a system of three equations to find the measure of each labeled angle.

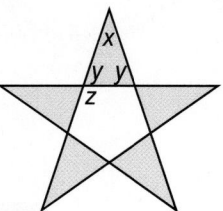

45. **Geometry** In the regular polyhedron described below, all faces are congruent polygons. Use a system of three linear equations to find the numbers of vertices, edges, and faces.

Every face has five edges and every edge is shared by two faces. Every face has five vertices and every vertex is shared by three faces. The sum of the number of vertices and faces is two more than the number of edges.

Apply What You've Learned

MATHEMATICAL PRACTICES
MP 4

In the Apply What You've Learned section in Lesson 3-2, you represented some of the criteria given on page 133 using equations in three variables. Now, you will create another equation needed to solve the problem. Choose from the following words and equations to complete the sentences below.

multiply	substitution	three
a graph	divide	two
$\frac{x}{3} + \frac{y}{20} + \frac{z}{10} = 2$	elimination	$x + y + z = 28$

a. If a distance traveled is given in *miles*, then you should ? by the rate in *miles per hour* to find the time traveled in *hours*.

b. To create a system of equations in three variables that you can solve, you need to write at least ? equations.

c. The equation ? models the time in hours each section of the triathlon takes an elite athlete to complete.

3-6 Solving Systems Using Matrices

 Common Core State Standards

A-REI.C.8 Represent a system of linear equations as a single matrix equation in a vector variable.

MP 1, MP 2, MP 3, MP 5

Objectives To represent a system of linear equations with a matrix
To solve a system of linear equations using matrices

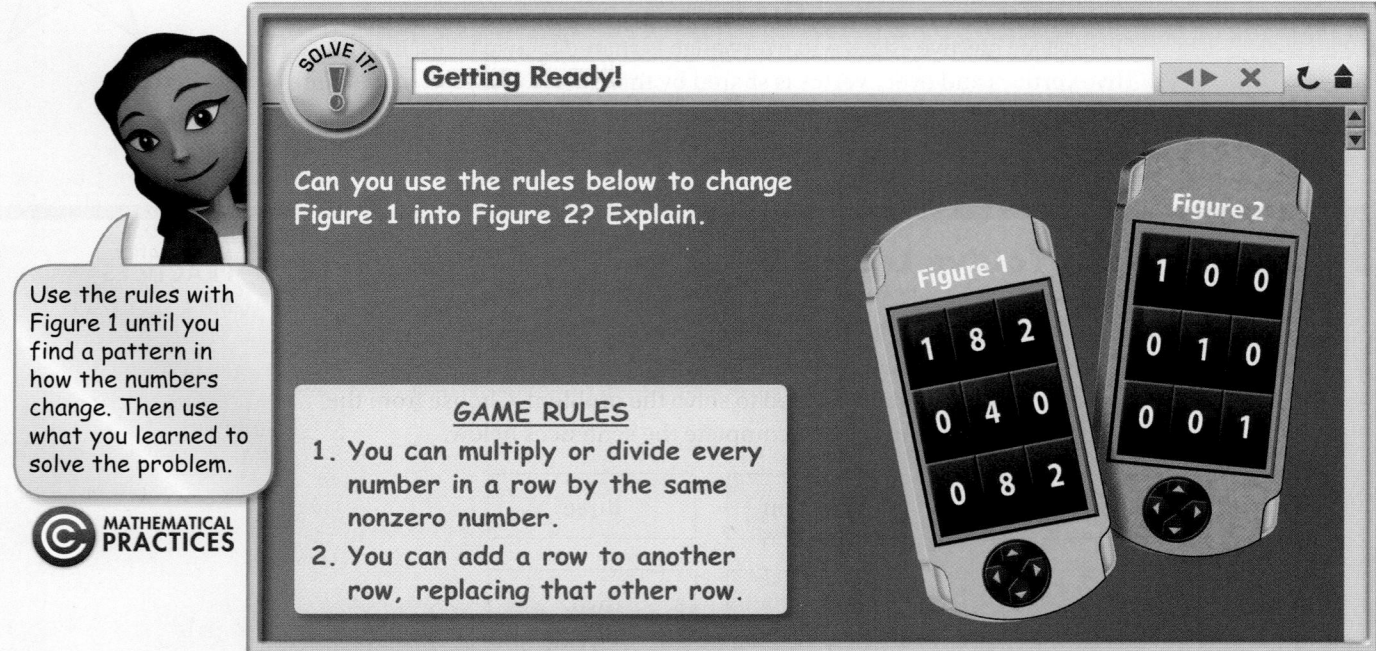

Getting Ready!

Can you use the rules below to change Figure 1 into Figure 2? Explain.

Use the rules with Figure 1 until you find a pattern in how the numbers change. Then use what you learned to solve the problem.

 **MATHEMATICAL PRACTICES**

GAME RULES

1. You can multiply or divide every number in a row by the same nonzero number.

2. You can add a row to another row, replacing that other row.

Figure 1

1	8	2
0	4	0
0	8	2

Figure 2

1	0	0
0	1	0
0	0	1

Lesson Vocabulary
• matrix
• matrix element
• row operation

An array of numbers, such as each of those suggested by the tile arrangements in the Solve It, is a matrix.

Essential Understanding You can use a *matrix* to represent and solve a system of equations without writing the variables.

A **matrix** is a rectangular array of numbers. You usually display the array within brackets. The dimensions of a matrix are the numbers of rows and columns in the array.

3 columns
$$A = \begin{bmatrix} 2 & 4 & 1 \\ 6 & 5 & 3 \end{bmatrix} \quad 2 \text{ rows}$$

Matrix A has 2 rows and 3 columns and is a 2×3 matrix, read "2 by 3." You can write it as A or $A_{2 \times 3}$.

Each number in a matrix is a **matrix element**. You can identify a matrix element by its row and column numbers. In matrix A, a_{12} is the element in row 1 and column 2. a_{12} is the element 4.

Problem 1 Identifying a Matrix Element

What is element a_{23} in matrix A?

$$A = \begin{bmatrix} 4 & -9 & 17 & 1 \\ 0 & 5 & 8 & 6 \\ -3 & -2 & 10 & 0 \end{bmatrix}$$

A_{23} is in Row 2 and Column 3.

a_{23} is 8.

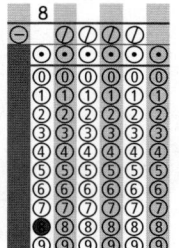

Got It? 1. What is element a_{13} in matrix A?

You can represent a system of equations efficiently with a matrix. Each matrix row represents an equation. The last matrix column shows the constants to the right of the equal signs. Each of the other columns shows the coefficients of one of the variables.

System of Equations

$$\begin{array}{rcrcr} x & + & 3y & = & 7 \\ 3x & + & y & = & -8 \end{array}$$

| x-coefficients | y-coefficients | constants |

Matrix

$$\begin{bmatrix} 1 & 3 & | & 7 \\ 3 & 1 & | & -8 \end{bmatrix}$$

The 1's are coefficients of x and y.

Draw a vertical bar to replace the equal signs and separate the coefficients from the constants.

 Problem 2 Representing Systems With Matrices

How can you represent the system of equations with a matrix?

A $\begin{cases} 2x + y = 9 \\ x - 6y = -1 \end{cases}$

The matrix $\begin{bmatrix} 2 & 1 & | & 9 \\ 1 & -6 & | & -1 \end{bmatrix}$ represents the system above.

B $\begin{cases} x - 3y + z = 6 \\ x + 3z = 12 \\ y = -5x + 1 \end{cases}$

Step 1 Write each equation in the same variable order. Line up the variables. Leave space where a coefficient is 0.

$$\begin{cases} x - 3y + z = 6 \\ x + 3z = 12 \\ 5x + y = 1 \end{cases}$$

Step 2 Write the matrix using the coefficients and constants. Notice the 1's and 0's.

$$\begin{bmatrix} 1 & -3 & 1 & | & 6 \\ 1 & 0 & 3 & | & 12 \\ 5 & 1 & 0 & | & 1 \end{bmatrix}$$

Got It? 2. How can you represent the system of equations with a matrix?

a. $\begin{cases} -4x - 2y = 7 \\ 3x + y = -5 \end{cases}$

b. $\begin{cases} 4x - y + 2z = 1 \\ y + 5z = 20 \\ 2x = -y + 7 \end{cases}$

Problem 3 Writing a System From a Matrix

What linear system of equations does this matrix represent? $\begin{bmatrix} 5 & 2 & | & 7 \\ 0 & 1 & | & 9 \end{bmatrix}$

Think

Each row shows coefficient-coefficient-constant of one equation.

Simplify. Write the system.

Write

$5x + 2y = 7$

$0x + 1y = 9$

$\begin{cases} 5x + 2y = 7 \\ y = 9 \end{cases}$

 Got It? 3. What linear system does $\begin{bmatrix} 2 & 0 & | & 6 \\ 5 & -2 & | & 1 \end{bmatrix}$ represent?

You can use a matrix that represents a system of equations to solve the system. In this way, you do not have to write the variables. To solve the system using the matrix, use the steps for solving by elimination. Each step is a **row operation**.

Your goal is to use row operations to get a matrix in the form $\begin{bmatrix} 1 & 0 & | & a \\ 0 & 1 & | & b \end{bmatrix}$ or $\begin{bmatrix} 1 & 0 & 0 & | & a \\ 0 & 1 & 0 & | & b \\ 0 & 0 & 1 & | & c \end{bmatrix}$

Notice that the first matrix represents the system $x = a$, $y = b$, which then will be the solution of a system of two equations in two unknowns. The second matrix represents the system $x = a$, $y = b$, and $z = c$.

take note

Key Concept Row Operations

Switch any two rows.	$\begin{bmatrix} 2 & -1 & 3 \\ 3 & 2 & 5 \end{bmatrix}$ becomes $\begin{bmatrix} 3 & 2 & 5 \\ 2 & -1 & 3 \end{bmatrix}$
Multiply a row by a constant.	$\begin{bmatrix} 3 & 2 & 5 \\ 2 & -1 & 3 \end{bmatrix}$ becomes $\begin{bmatrix} 3 & 2 & 5 \\ 2 \cdot 2 & -1 \cdot 2 & 3 \cdot 2 \end{bmatrix} = \begin{bmatrix} 3 & 2 & 5 \\ 4 & -2 & 6 \end{bmatrix}$
Add one row to another.	$\begin{bmatrix} 3 & 2 & 5 \\ 4 & -2 & 6 \end{bmatrix}$ becomes $\begin{bmatrix} 3+4 & 2-2 & 5+6 \\ 4 & -2 & 6 \end{bmatrix} = \begin{bmatrix} 7 & 0 & 11 \\ 4 & -2 & 6 \end{bmatrix}$

Combine any of these steps.

Think

How is solving a system using row operations similar to using elimination?
You use the same steps but the variables don't appear in the matrices.

What is the solution of the system? $\begin{cases} x + 4y = -1 \\ 2x + 5y = 4 \end{cases}$

$\begin{bmatrix} 1 & 4 & | & -1 \\ 2 & 5 & | & 4 \end{bmatrix}$

Write the matrix for the system.

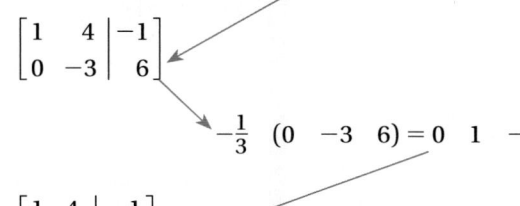

$\begin{array}{ccc} -2 & (1 & 4 & -1) \\ + & 2 & 5 & 4 \\ \hline & 0 & -3 & 6 \end{array}$

Multiply Row 1 by -2. Add to Row 2. Replace Row 2 with the sum. Write the new matrix.

$\begin{bmatrix} 1 & 4 & | & -1 \\ 0 & -3 & | & 6 \end{bmatrix}$

$-\dfrac{1}{3}(0 \quad -3 \quad 6) = 0 \quad 1 \quad -2$

Multiply Row 2 by $-\dfrac{1}{3}$. Write the new matrix.

$\begin{bmatrix} 1 & 4 & | & -1 \\ 0 & 1 & | & -2 \end{bmatrix}$

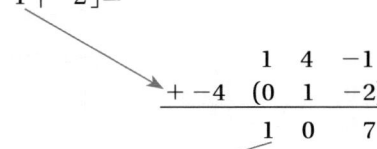

$\begin{array}{ccc} & 1 & 4 & -1 \\ + -4 & (0 & 1 & -2) \\ \hline & 1 & 0 & 7 \end{array}$

Multiply Row 2 by -4. Add to Row 1. Replace Row 1 with the sum. Write the new matrix.

$\begin{bmatrix} 1 & 0 & | & 7 \\ 0 & 1 & | & -2 \end{bmatrix}$

The solution to the system is $(7, -2)$.

Check

$x + 4y = -1$	$2x + 5y = 4$	Use the original equations.
$7 + 4(-2) \stackrel{?}{=} -1$	$2(7) + 5(-2) \stackrel{?}{=} 4$	Substitute.
$7 + (-8) \stackrel{?}{=} -1$	$14 + (-10) \stackrel{?}{=} 4$	Multiply.
$-1 = -1$ ✔	$4 = 4$ ✔	Simplify.

 ✓ **Got It?** **4. a.** What is the solution of the system? $\begin{cases} 9x - 2y = 5 \\ 3x + 7y = 17 \end{cases}$

    b. Reasoning Which method is more similar to solving a system using row operations: *elimination* or *substitution*? Justify your reasoning.

Matrices that represent the solution of a system are in *reduced row echelon form*. Many calculators have a **rref** (reduced row echelon form) function for working with matrices. This function will do all the row operations for you. You can use **rref** to solve a system of equations.

Problem 5 Using a Calculator to Solve a Linear System

What is the solution of the system of equations? $\begin{cases} 2a + 3b - c = 1 \\ -4a + 9b + 2c = 8 \\ -2a + 2c = 3 \end{cases}$

Think

How do you enter missing variables into a matrix?
If a variable is not present in an equation, enter its coefficient as 0 in the matrix.

Step 1 Enter the system into a calculator as a matrix.

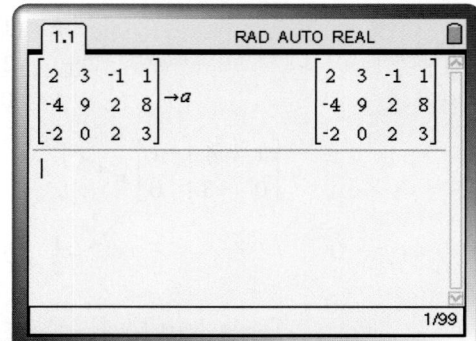

Step 2 Apply the **rref()** function to the matrix. Put the matrix elements in fraction form if some are not integers.

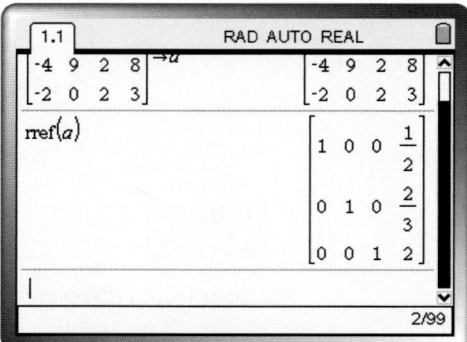

Step 3 List the solution.

The solution of the system is $a = \frac{1}{2}$, $b = \frac{2}{3}$, $c = 2$.

Check

$2a + 3b - c = 1$	$-4a + 9b + 2c = 8$	$-2a + 2c = 3$
$2\left(\frac{1}{2}\right) + 3\left(\frac{2}{3}\right) - 2 \stackrel{?}{=} 1$	$-4\left(\frac{1}{2}\right) + 9\left(\frac{2}{3}\right) + 2(2) \stackrel{?}{=} 8$	$-2\left(\frac{1}{2}\right) + 2(2) \stackrel{?}{=} 3$
$1 + 2 - 2 \stackrel{?}{=} 1$	$-2 + 6 + 4 \stackrel{?}{=} 8$	$-1 + 4 \stackrel{?}{=} 3$
$1 = 1$ ✔	$8 = 8$ ✔	$3 = 3$ ✔

 Got It? 5. What is the solution of the system of equations?

$$\begin{cases} a + 4b + 6c = 21 \\ 2a - 2b + c = 4 \\ - 8b + c = -1 \end{cases}$$

Lesson Check

Do you know HOW?

State the dimensions of each matrix.

1. $\begin{bmatrix} 2 \\ 5 \end{bmatrix}$

2. $\left[\begin{array}{ccc|c} 6 & 9 & 0 & 3 \\ 4 & 6 & 2 & 7 \end{array}\right]$

Write a matrix to represent each system.

3. $\begin{cases} 3a + 5b = 0 \\ a + b = 2 \end{cases}$

4. $\begin{cases} x + 3y - z = 2 \\ x + 2z = 8 \\ 2y - z = 1 \end{cases}$

Do you UNDERSTAND?

5. How many elements are in a 4×4 matrix?

6. Writing Using Matrix A in Problem 1, describe the difference in identifying element a_{21} and element a_{12}.

7. Open-Ended Write a situation that can be modeled by the matrix. $\left[\begin{array}{cc|c} 4 & 2 & 8 \\ 0 & 1 & 2 \end{array}\right]$

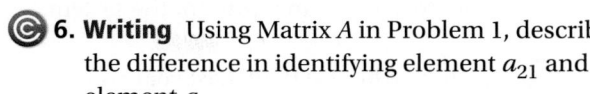 **Practice and Problem-Solving Exercises**

Ⓐ Practice   Identify the indicated element. $\quad A = \begin{bmatrix} 3 & 12 & 6 \\ 1 & 0 & 9 \\ 8 & 7 & 4 \end{bmatrix}$ **See Problem 1.**

8. a_{32} **9.** a_{21} **10.** a_{13} **11.** a_{31}

Write a matrix to represent each system.   **See Problem 2.**

12. $\begin{cases} x + 2y = 11 \\ 2x + 3y = 18 \end{cases}$ **13.** $\begin{cases} 3x + 2y = 16 \\ y = 5 \end{cases}$ **14.** $\begin{cases} 2a - 3b = 6 \\ a + b = 2 \end{cases}$

15. $\begin{cases} r - s + t = 150 \\ 2r + t = 425 \\ s + 3t = 0 \end{cases}$ **16.** $\begin{cases} y = 3x - 7 \\ x = 2 \end{cases}$ **17.** $\begin{cases} x - y + z = 0 \\ x - 2y - z = 5 \\ 2x - y + 2z = 8 \end{cases}$

Write the system of equations represented by each matrix.   **See Problem 3.**

18. $\left[\begin{array}{cc|c} 1 & 0 & 4 \\ 0 & 1 & -6 \end{array}\right]$ **19.** $\left[\begin{array}{cc|c} 5 & 1 & -3 \\ -2 & 2 & 4 \end{array}\right]$ **20.** $\left[\begin{array}{cc|c} -1 & 2 & -6 \\ 1 & 1 & 7 \end{array}\right]$

21. $\left[\begin{array}{ccc|c} 2 & 1 & 1 & 1 \\ 1 & 1 & 1 & 2 \\ 1 & -1 & 1 & -2 \end{array}\right]$ **22.** $\left[\begin{array}{ccc|c} 0 & 1 & 2 & 4 \\ -2 & 3 & 6 & 9 \\ 1 & 0 & 1 & 3 \end{array}\right]$ **23.** $\left[\begin{array}{ccc|c} 5 & 2 & 1 & 5 \\ 4 & 1 & 2 & 8 \\ 1 & 3 & -6 & 2 \end{array}\right]$

Solve the system of equations using a matrix.   **See Problems 4 and 5.**

24. $\begin{cases} x + 3y = 5 \\ x + 4y = 6 \end{cases}$ **25.** $\begin{cases} p - 3q = -1 \\ -5p + 16q = 5 \end{cases}$ **26.** $\begin{cases} 300x - y = 130 \\ 200x + y = 120 \end{cases}$

27. $\begin{cases} x + 3y = 22 \\ 2x - y = 2 \end{cases}$ **28.** $\begin{cases} x + 3y = 6 \\ 2x + 4y = 12 \end{cases}$ **29.** $\begin{cases} x + y = 5 \\ -2x + 4y = 8 \end{cases}$

 **Apply**

30. Business A manufacturer sells pencils and erasers in packages. The price of a package of five erasers and two pencils is $.23. The price of a package of seven erasers and five pencils is $.41. Write a system of equations to represent this situation. Then write a matrix to represent the system.

31. Think About a Plan Last year your town invested a total of $25,000 into two separate funds. The return on one fund was 4% and the return on the other was 6%. If the town earned a total of $1300 in interest, how much money was invested in each fund?
- What variables will you use? What will they represent?
- What equations can you write to model this situation?
- How can you use a matrix to solve this system?

 Graphing Calculator Solve each system.

32. $\begin{cases} x + y + z = 2 \\ 2y - 2z = 2 \\ x - 3z = 1 \end{cases}$

33. $\begin{cases} x - y + z = 3 \\ x + 3z = 6 \\ y - 2z = -1 \end{cases}$

34. $\begin{cases} x + y + z = -1 \\ 3x + 4y - z = 8 \\ 6x + 8y - 2z = 16 \end{cases}$

35. $\begin{cases} x - y + 3z = 9 \\ x + 2z = 3 \\ 2x + 2y + z = 10 \end{cases}$

36. $\begin{cases} 2x + 3y + z = 13 \\ 5x - 2y - 4z = 7 \\ 4x + 5y + 3z = 25 \end{cases}$

37. $\begin{cases} -2w + x + y = 0 \\ -w + 2x - y + z = 1 \\ -2w + 3x + 3y + 2z = 6 \\ w + x + 2y + z = 5 \end{cases}$

38. Snacks Suppose you want to fill nine 1-lb tins with a snack mix. You have $15 and plan to buy almonds for $2.45 per lb, hazelnuts for $1.85 per lb, and raisins for $.80 per lb. You want the mix to contain an equal amount of almonds and hazelnuts and twice as much of the nuts as the raisins by weight.
   a. Writing Explain how each equation to the right relates to the problem. What does each variable represent?
   b. Solve the system.
   c. How many of each ingredient should you buy?

$\begin{cases} x + y + z = 9 \\ 2.45x + 1.85y + 0.8z = 15 \\ x + y = 2z \end{cases}$

39. Geometry The coordinates (x, y) of a point in a plane are the solution of the system $\begin{cases} 2x + 3y = 13 \\ 5x + 7y = 31 \end{cases}$. Find the coordinates of the point.

40. Error Analysis A classmate writes the matrix at the right to represent a system and says that the solution is $x = 2$, $y = 0$. Explain your classmate's error and describe how to correct it.

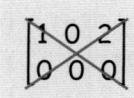

41. Paint A hardware store mixes paints in a ratio of two parts red to six parts yellow to make two gallons of pumpkin orange. A ratio of five parts red to three parts yellow makes two gallons of pepper red. A gallon of pumpkin orange sells for $25, and a gallon of pepper red sells for $28. Find the cost of 1 quart of red paint and the cost of 1 quart of yellow paint.

Open-Ended Complete each system for the given number of solutions.

42. infinitely many

$$\begin{cases} x + y = 7 \\ 2x + 2y = \blacksquare \end{cases}$$

43. one solution

$$\begin{cases} x + y + z = 7 \\ y + z = \blacksquare \\ z = \blacksquare \end{cases}$$

44. no solution

$$\begin{cases} x + y + z = 7 \\ y + z = \blacksquare \\ y + z = \blacksquare \end{cases}$$

Solve the system of equations using a matrix. (Hint: Start by substituting $m = \frac{1}{x}$ and $n = \frac{1}{y}$.)

45. $\begin{cases} \frac{4}{x} + \frac{1}{y} = 1 \\ \frac{8}{x} + \frac{4}{y} = 3 \end{cases}$

46. $\begin{cases} \frac{4}{x} - \frac{2}{y} = 1 \\ \frac{10}{x} + \frac{20}{y} = 0 \end{cases}$

47. $\begin{cases} \frac{7}{x} + \frac{3}{y} = 5 \\ \frac{2}{x} + \frac{1}{y} = -1 \end{cases}$

Standardized Test Prep

48. Which equation represents a line with a slope of $\frac{1}{2}$ and a y-intercept of $\frac{3}{4}$?

Ⓐ $y = \frac{1}{2}x - \frac{3}{4}$ Ⓑ $y = \frac{3}{4}x - \frac{1}{2}$ Ⓒ $y = \frac{1}{2}x + \frac{3}{4}$ Ⓓ $y = \frac{3}{4}x + \frac{1}{2}$

49. Which graph best represents the solution of the inequality $y \le 2|x - 1| - 4$?

Ⓕ 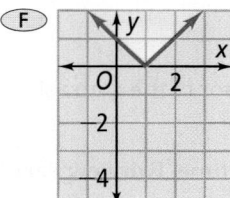 Ⓖ 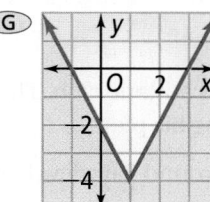 Ⓗ 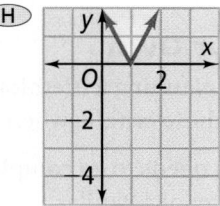 Ⓘ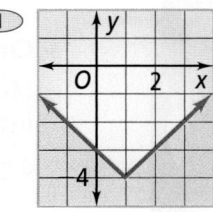

50. At what point do the graphs of the equations $y = 7x - 3$ and $-6x + y = 2$ intersect?

Mixed Review

Solve each inequality. Graph the solution.

See Lesson 1-5.

51. $12 \ge 2(4x + 1) + 22$ **52.** $2x - (3x + 5) \le 30$ **53.** $4x + 5 - 3x \le 2x + 1$

Solve each equation. Check your answers.

See Lesson 1-6.

54. $|2y - 3| = 12$ **55.** $|4x| = 40$ **56.** $|2y - 4| = 16$

Get Ready! To prepare for Lesson 4-1, do Exercises 57 and 58.

Write an equation for each transformation of $y = x$.

See Lesson 2-6.

57. vertical stretch by a factor of 2. **58.** vertical compression by a factor of $\frac{1}{3}$

3

Pull It **All Together**

Completing the Performance Task

Look back at your results from the Apply What You've Learned sections in Lessons 3-1, 3-2, and 3-5. Use the work you did to complete the following.

To solve these problems, you will pull together concepts and skills related to solving a system of linear equations.

1. Solve the problem in the Task Description on page 133 by determining the distance for each part of the course. Show all your work and explain each step of your solution.

2. Reflect Choose one of the Mathematical Practices below and explain how you applied it in your work on the Performance Task.

MP 2: Reason abstractly and quantitatively.

MP 4: Model with mathematics.

MP 5: Use appropriate tools strategically.

On Your Own

Manny is planning a triathlon for his athletic club. The director of the club asks Manny to follow these criteria when creating his plan.

- The run needs to go completely around Fairview Park one time. Fairview Park has a perimeter of 4.2 miles.

- The entire triathlon should cover a distance of 21 miles.

- The bicycle part of the triathlon should be 20 times the distance of the swim.

Manny finds that, on average, the members of his athletic club are able to swim about 2 mi/h, bicycle about 20 mi/h, and run about 7 mi/h.

a. What are the distances of each part of the triathlon?

b. On average, how long will it take a member of Manny's athletic club to complete the course?

3 Chapter Review

Connecting BIG ideas and Answering the Essential Questions

1 Function
Find a point of intersection (x, y) of the graphs of functions f and g and you have found a solution of the system $y = f(x)$, $y = g(x)$.

Solving Systems Using Tables and Graphs (Lesson 3-1)
$$\begin{cases} y = -2x + 3 \\ y = 2x - 1 \end{cases}$$

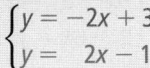

The solution is $(1, 1)$.

Systems of Inequalities and Linear Programming (Lessons 3-3 and 3-4)
$$\begin{cases} y > -2x + 3 \\ y \le 2x - 1 \end{cases}$$

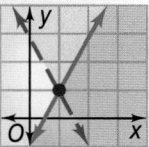

2 Equivalence
If the equations of two systems are equivalent, then a solution of the system that is easier to solve is also a solution of the more difficult system.

Solving Systems Algebraically (Lesson 3-2)
$$\begin{cases} -y = -x + 2 \\ 3y = 2x - 2 \end{cases}$$

$$\begin{array}{rcl} -2y &=& -2x + 4 \\ 3y &=& 2x - 2 \\ \hline y &=& 2 \end{array}$$

$3(2) = 2x - 2 \quad \rightarrow \quad x = 4$

The solution is $x = 4$, $y = 2$

Systems With Three Variables (Lesson 3-5)
$$\begin{cases} -2x + y + z = -3 \\ 2x - y + z = -1 \\ -2x, -y - z = -1 \end{cases}$$

$x = 1$, $y = 1$, $z = -2$

3 Solving Equations and Inequalities
The matrix row operations of adding rows and multiplying a row by a constant are equivalent to addition and multiplication properties of equality.

Solving Systems Using Matrices (Lesson 3-6)
$$\left[\begin{array}{cc|c} -2 & 3 & 1 \\ 2 & -1 & 1 \end{array}\right]$$
$$\left[\begin{array}{cc|c} 1 & 0 & 1 \\ 0 & 1 & 1 \end{array}\right] \quad \rightarrow \quad x = 1, y = 1$$

Chapter Vocabulary

- consistent system (p. 137)
- constraint (p. 157)
- dependent system (p. 137)
- equivalent systems (p. 144)
- feasible region (p. 157)
- inconsistent system (p. 137)
- independent system (p. 137)
- linear programming (p. 157)
- linear system (p. 134)
- matrix (p. 174)
- matrix element (p. 174)
- objective function (p. 157)
- row operation (p. 176)
- solution of a system (p. 134)
- system of equations (p. 134)

Fill in the blank.

1. A consistent system with exactly one solution is a(n) _____.

2. _____ is a method for finding a minimum or maximum value, given a system of limits called _____.

3-1 Solving Systems Using Tables and Graphs

Quick Review

A **system of equations** has two or more equations. Points of intersection are solutions. A **linear system** has linear equations. A **consistent system** can be **dependent**, with infinitely many solutions, or **independent**, with one solution. An **inconsistent system** has no solution.

Example

Solve the system $\begin{cases} 3x + 2y = 4 \\ 2x - 4y = 8 \end{cases}$

Graph the equations.

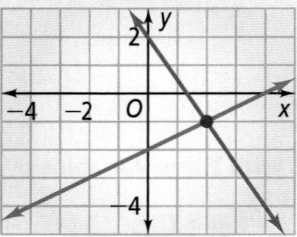

The only solution, where the lines intersect, is $(2, -1)$.

Exercises

Without graphing, classify each system of equations as *independent*, *dependent*, or *inconsistent*. Solve independent systems by graphing.

3. $\begin{cases} 6x - 2y = 2 \\ 2 + 6x = y \end{cases}$

4. $\begin{cases} 5 - y = 2x \\ 6x - 15 = -3y \end{cases}$

5. $\begin{cases} 6y + 2x = 8 \\ 12y + 4x = 4 \end{cases}$

6. $\begin{cases} 1.5 + 3x = 0.5y \\ 6 - 2y = -12x \end{cases}$

7. $\begin{cases} 2 - 0.25x = 0.5y \\ -1.5y = 1.5x - 3 \end{cases}$

8. $\begin{cases} 1 + y = x \\ x + y = 1 \end{cases}$

9. For $7.52, you purchased 8 pens and highlighters from a local bookstore. Each highlighter cost $1.09 and each pen cost $.69. How many pens did you buy?

3-2 Solving Systems Algebraically

Quick Review

To solve an independent system by substitution, solve one equation for a variable. Then substitute that expression into the other equation and solve for the remaining variable. To solve by elimination, add two equations with additive inverses as coefficients to eliminate one variable and solve for the other. In both cases you solve for one of the variables and use substitution to solve for the remaining variable.

Example

Solve $\begin{cases} 10 - y = 4x \\ x = 4 + 0.5y \end{cases}$ by substitution.

Substitute for x: $10 - y = 4(4 + 0.5y) = 16 + 2y$.

Solve for y: $y = -2$.

Substitute into the first equation:

$10 - (-2) = 4x$.

Solve for x: $x = 3$. The solution is $(3, -2)$.

Exercises

Solve each system by substitution.

10. $\begin{cases} x - 2y = 3 \\ 3x + y = -5 \end{cases}$

11. $\begin{cases} 14x - 35 = 7y \\ -25 - 6x = 5y \end{cases}$

Solve each system by elimination.

12. $\begin{cases} 11 - 5y = 2x \\ 5y + 3 = -9x \end{cases}$

13. $\begin{cases} 2x + 3y = 4 \\ 4x + 6y = 9 \end{cases}$

14. Roast beef has 25 g of protein and 11 g of calcium per serving. A serving of mashed potatoes has 2 g of protein and 25 g of calcium. How many servings of each are needed to supply exactly 29 g of protein and 61 g of calcium?

3-3 Systems of Inequalities

Quick Review

To solve a system of inequalities by graphing, first graph the boundaries for each inequality. Then shade the region(s) of the plane containing solutions valid for both inequalities.

Example

Solve the system of inequalities by graphing.

$$\begin{cases} y > -3 \\ y \le -|x-1| \end{cases}$$

Graph both inequalities and shade the region valid for both inequalities.

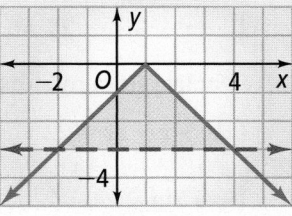

Exercises

Solve each system of inequalities by graphing.

15. $\begin{cases} y < 4x \\ 3x + y \ge 5 \end{cases}$

16. $\begin{cases} y < |2x - 4| \\ x + 5y \ge -1 \end{cases}$

17. $\begin{cases} y \le |x + 2| - 3 \\ y \ge 1 + \frac{1}{4}x \end{cases}$

18. $\begin{cases} 2x + 3y > 6 \\ x \le -1 \\ y \ge 4 \end{cases}$

19. For a community breakfast there should be at least three times as much regular coffee as decaffeinated coffee. A total of ten gallons is sufficient for the breakfast. Write and graph a system of inequalities to model the problem.

3-4 Linear Programming

Quick Review

Linear programming is used to find a minimum or maximum of an **objective function**, given **constraints** as linear inequalities. The maximum or minimum occurs at a vertex of the **feasible region**, which contains the solutions to the system of constraints.

Example

Graph the system of constraints and name the vertices.

Objective function: $P = 2x + y$

$$\begin{cases} x \le 8 \\ y \le 5 \\ x \ge 0, y \ge 0 \end{cases}$$

Graph the inequalities and shade the area satisfying all inequalities.

The vertices of the feasible region are (0, 0), (0, 5), (8, 5), and (8, 0).

Evaluate the objective function at each vertex:

$2(0) + 0 = 0$ $\qquad$ $2(0) + 5 = 5$

$2(8) + 5 = 21$ $\qquad$ $2(8) + 0 = 16$

The maximum value occurs at (8, 5).

Exercises

Graph the system of constraints. Name the vertices. Then find the values of x and y that maximize or minimize the objective function.

20. $\begin{cases} x \ge 2 \\ y \ge 0 \\ 3x + 2y \ge 12 \end{cases}$

Minimum for
$C = x + 5y$

21. $\begin{cases} 3x + 2y \le 12 \\ x + y \le 5 \\ x \ge 0, y \ge 0 \end{cases}$

Maximum for
$P = 3x + 5y$

22. A lunch stand makes $.75 profit on each chef's salad and $1.20 profit on each Caesar salad. On a typical weekday, it sells between 40 and 60 chef's salads and between 35 and 50 Caesar salads. The total number sold has never exceeded 100 salads. How many of each type should be prepared in order to maximize profit?

3-5 Systems With Three Variables

Quick Review

To solve a system of three equations, either pair two equations and eliminate the same variable from both equations, using one equation twice, or choose an equation, solve for one variable, and substitute the expression for that variable into the other two equations. Then, solve the remaining system.

Example

Solve by elimination. $\begin{array}{ll} ① \\ ② \\ ③ \end{array} \begin{cases} x + y + z = 10 \\ 2x - y + z = 9 \\ -3x + 2y + 2z = 5 \end{cases}$

Add equations ① and ② to eliminate y.　④ $3x + 2z = 19$

Add 2 times ② to ③ to eliminate y.　⑤ $x + 4z = 23$

Add -3 times ⑤ to ④ to eliminate x.　$z = 5$

Substitute $z = 5$ into ⑤.　$x = 3$

Substitute $z = 5$ and $x = 3$ into ① or ②.　$y = 2$

The solution to the system is $(3, 2, 5)$.

Exercises

Solve each system by elimination.

23. $\begin{cases} x + y - 2z = 8 \\ 5x - 3y + z = -6 \\ -2x - y + 4z = -13 \end{cases}$

24. $\begin{cases} -x + y + 2z = -5 \\ 5x + 4y - 4z = 4 \\ x - 3y - 2z = 3 \end{cases}$

Solve each system by substitution.

25. $\begin{cases} 3x + y - 2z = 22 \\ x + 5y + z = 4 \\ x = -3z \end{cases}$

26. $\begin{cases} x + 2y + z = 14 \\ y = z + 1 \\ x = -3z + 6 \end{cases}$

3-6 Solving Systems Using Matrices

Quick Review

A **matrix** can represent a system of equations where each row stands for a different equation. The columns contain the coefficients of the variables and the constants.

Example

Solve using a matrix. $\begin{cases} 6x + 3y = -15 \\ 2x + 4y = 10 \end{cases}$

Enter coefficients as matrix elements $\begin{bmatrix} 6 & 3 & | & -15 \\ 2 & 4 & | & 10 \end{bmatrix}$.

Divide the first row by 3 to get $\begin{bmatrix} 2 & 1 & | & -5 \\ 2 & 4 & | & 10 \end{bmatrix}$. Subtract the

first row from the second row to get $\begin{bmatrix} 2 & 1 & | & -5 \\ 0 & 3 & | & 15 \end{bmatrix}$. Multiply

the second row by $\frac{1}{3}$ to get $\begin{bmatrix} 2 & 1 & | & -5 \\ 0 & 1 & | & 5 \end{bmatrix}$. Subtract the second

row from the first row to get $\begin{bmatrix} 2 & 0 & | & -10 \\ 0 & 1 & | & 5 \end{bmatrix}$. Divide the first row

by 2 to get $\begin{bmatrix} 1 & 0 & | & -5 \\ 0 & 1 & | & 5 \end{bmatrix}$. The solution to the system is $(-5, 5)$.

Exercises

Solve each system using a matrix.

27. $\begin{cases} 4x - 12y = -1 \\ 6x + 4y = 4 \end{cases}$

28. $\begin{cases} 7x + 2y = 5 \\ 13x + 14y = -1 \end{cases}$

29. $\begin{cases} -5x + 3y + 4z = 2 \\ 3x - y - z = 4 \\ x - 6y - 5z = -4 \end{cases}$

30. $\begin{cases} x + y + z = 4 \\ 2x - y + z = 5 \\ x + y - 2z = 13 \end{cases}$

Do you know HOW?

Without graphing, classify each system. Then find the solution to each system using a graph.

1. $\begin{cases} y = 5x - 2 \\ y = x + 4 \end{cases}$

2. $\begin{cases} 3x + 2y = 9 \\ 3x + 2y = 4 \end{cases}$

Solve the system by substitution.

3. $\begin{cases} 0.3x - y = 0 \\ y = 2 + 0.25x \end{cases}$

Solve the system by elimination.

4. $\begin{cases} 4x - 2y = 3 \\ y - 2x = -\frac{3}{2} \end{cases}$

5. $\begin{cases} 3x + 4y = 9 \\ 2x + y = 6 \end{cases}$

Graph the solution of each system.

6. $\begin{cases} 2x + y < 3 \\ x < y + 3 \end{cases}$

7. $\begin{cases} |x + 3| > y \\ y > 2x - 1 \end{cases}$

Graph the system of constraints. Identify all vertices. Then find the values of x and y that maximize or minimize the objective function.

8. $\begin{cases} x \leq 5 \\ y \leq 4 \\ x \geq 0 \\ y \geq 0 \end{cases}$

Maximum for $P = 2x + y$

Solve each system.

9. $\begin{cases} x - y + z = 0 \\ 3x - 2y + 6z = 9 \\ -x + y - 2z = -2 \end{cases}$

10. $\begin{cases} 2x + y + z = 8 \\ x + 2y - z = -5 \\ z = 2x - y \end{cases}$

Do you UNDERSTAND?

Write a matrix that represents the system. Then solve the system. Tell what method you used and why.

11. $\begin{cases} -a + 4b + 2c = -8 \\ 3a + b - 4c = 9 \\ b = -1 \end{cases}$

12. **Sales** A pizza shop makes $1.50 on each small pizza and $2.15 on each large pizza. On a typical Friday, it sells between 70 and 90 small pizzas and between 100 and 140 large pizzas. The shop can make no more than 210 pizzas in a day. How many of each size pizza must be sold in order to maximize profit?

13. **Investing** Your teacher invested $5000 in three funds. After a year they had $5450. The growth fund had a return rate of 12%, the income fund had a return rate of 8%, and the money market fund had a return rate of 5%. Your teacher invested twice as much in the income fund as in the money market fund. How much money was invested in each fund?

14. **Writing** Describe how to identify situations in which substitution may be the best method for solving a system of equations.

15. **Open-Ended** Write a system of constraints whose graph is a parallelogram.

3 Common Core Cumulative Standards Review

Some problems require the selection of an appropriate representation (concrete, pictorial, graphical, verbal, or symbolic) to find a solution.

TIP 1

Make a drawing.

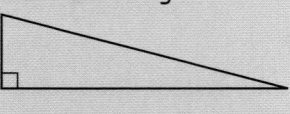

One angle of a right triangle measures 90°. The measure of the second angle is 5 times the measure of the third. What are the measures of these angles?

Ⓐ 30° and 60°

Ⓑ 30° and 150°

Ⓒ 15° and 75°

Ⓓ 20° and 100°

TIP 2

Write a system:
$$x + y + 90 = 180$$
$$x = 5y$$

Think It Through

A triangle can have only one right angle, so the other two angles must each have a measure less than 90°. Use x and y to represent the unknown angles.

$$x = 5y$$
$$5y + y + 90 = 180$$
$$6y + 90 = 180$$
$$6y = 90$$
$$y = 15, x = 75$$

The correct answer is C.

Vocabulary Builder

As you solve test items, you must understand the meanings of mathematical terms. Match each term with its mathematical meaning.

A. equivalent systems

B. absolute value

C. system of equations

D. linear inequality

I. a number's distance from zero on a number line

II. an inequality in two variables whose graph is a region of the half-plane

III. a set of two or more equations that use the same variables

IV. systems that have the same solution(s)

Selected Response

Read each question. Then write the letter of the correct answer on your paper.

1. Which of the following is true about the given system?
$$\begin{cases} -4y = 12 - 8x \\ y = 2x - 3 \end{cases}$$
The system has

Ⓐ zero solutions.

Ⓑ exactly one solution.

Ⓒ two solutions.

Ⓓ infinitely many solutions.

2. Which is the graph of $y = -|x - 2| + 1$?

F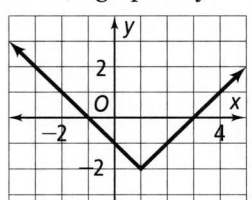

H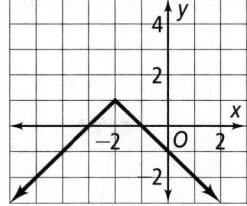

G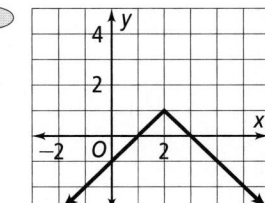

I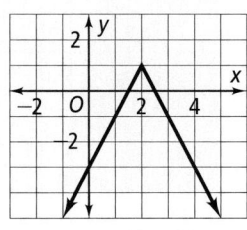

3. Which graph represents the solution of the inequality $|3x + 12| \geq 3$?

A

B

C

D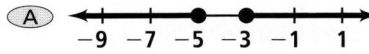

4. Josea wants to solve the system using substitution.

$$\begin{cases} x = -2y + 4 \\ 2x - 3y = 5 \end{cases}$$

Which of the following is the best way for Josea to proceed?

F Solve the first equation for y, then substitute into the second equation.

G Solve the second equation for y, then substitute into the first equation.

H Substitute $-2y + 4$ for x in the second equation.

I Substitute $-2y + 4$ for y in the second equation.

5. A board must be cut so that its length is 40.50 cm. The tolerance is 0.25 cm. Which inequality describes the allowable lengths for the board?

A $|x - 0.25| \leq 40.50$

B $|x + 0.25| \leq 40.50$

C $|x - 40.50| \leq 0.25$

D $|x - 0.25| \leq 40.75$

6. Which graph shows the solution to the given system?

$$\begin{cases} \frac{1}{2}x - y = 1 \\ x = 3 \end{cases}$$

F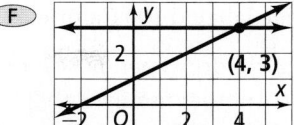

H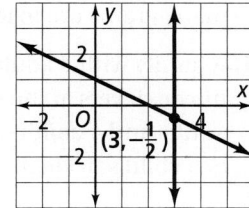

G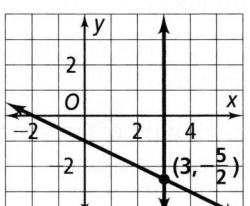

I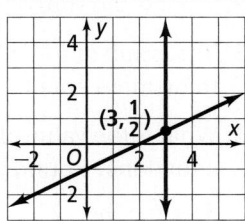

7. The formula for the area of a trapezoid is $A = \frac{h}{2}(b_1 + b_2)$. Solve this equation for b_2.

A $b_2 = \frac{2A}{hb_1}$

C $b_2 = \frac{2A}{h - b_1}$

B $b_2 = \frac{2A}{h} - b_1$

D $b_2 = \frac{2A}{h + b_1}$

8. What is the equation of the line that passes through $(-2, 4)$ and $(2, 7)$?

F $y - 7 = \frac{3}{4}(x + 2)$

H $y - 7 = \frac{3}{4}(x - 2)$

G $y + 7 = \frac{3}{4}(x - 2)$

I $y - 2 = \frac{3}{4}(x - 7)$

9. Which of the following describes the translation of $y = |x|$ to $y = |x + 2| - 1$?

A $y = |x|$ translated 2 units to the left and 1 unit down

B $y = |x|$ translated 2 units to the right and 1 unit down

C $y = |x|$ translated 1 unit to the left and 2 units down

D $y = |x|$ translated 1 unit to the right and 2 units down

Constructed Response

10. The nutrition label on a package of crackers shows there are 80 Calories in 16 grams of crackers. How many grams are in a package labeled 100 Calories?

11. A family with 4 adults and 3 children spends $47 for movie tickets at the theater. Another family with 2 adults and 4 children spends $36. What is the price of a child's ticket in dollars?

12. What is the sum of the solutions of $|5 - 3x| = x + 1$?

13. The graph of $y = x$ is translated up two units. What is the x-intercept of the new graph?

14. What is the value of x in the solution of the system of equations? Round your answer to the nearest tenth.
$$\begin{cases} 5x = -3y - 7 \\ 5y = -4x - 7 \end{cases}$$

15. What is the slope of the line $3y - 4 = \frac{1}{2}x$?

16. The line $(y - 2) = \frac{2}{7}(x - 1)$ contains point $(a, 4)$. What is the value of a?

17. An ice cream shop has regular mix-ins for $.50 each and premium mix-ins for $1 each. You have $2.50 to spend on mix-ins, and you want at least 4 mix-ins. How many of each type of mix-in can you get in your ice cream?

18. Solve the following system by graphing.
$$\begin{cases} y < \frac{1}{3}x + 1 \\ y \le \frac{2}{3}x + 4 \end{cases}$$

19. Find $f(-4)$, $f(0)$, and $f(3)$ for the function $f(x) = \frac{1}{4}x + 2$.

20. How can you use the graphs of $f(x) = -|3x| + 6$ and $g(x) = 2x + 1$ to find the solutions of $-|3x| + 6 = 2x + 1$?

21. The equation of line m is $y = 3x - 1$. What is the equation of a line that goes through the point $(3, -2)$ and is perpendicular to line m? Show your work.

22. The graph below shows the boundaries for the system of linear inequalities.
$$\begin{cases} y \le 0.5x + 5 \\ y \le -5x - 6 \end{cases}$$

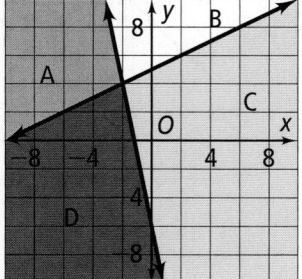

a. Of the shaded areas A, B, C and D, which area represents a solution to the first inequality but not the second?

b. Which represents a solution to the second inequality but not the first?

c. Which represents a solution to both inequalities?

d. Which represents a solution to neither inequality?

Extended Response

23. Jenna is trying to break her school's record for doing the most push-ups in ten minutes. The current record holder did 350 push-ups in ten minutes. The table shows the number of push-ups Jenna completed in the first 6 minutes.
   a. Draw a scatter plot and find the line of best fit.
   b. Will Jenna beat the current record? Justify your reasoning.

Time (min)	1	2	3	4	5	6
Number of push-ups	37	70	99	132	169	207

Get Ready!

Lesson 1-4 ◀ **Solving Linear Equations**

Solve each equation. Check your answer.

1. $9x - 16 = 8 + 5x$

2. $4(y + 2) + 1 = -5(3 - 2y)$

Lesson 1-6 ◀ **Solving Absolute Value Inequalities**

Solve each inequality. Graph the solution.

3. $|6x - 12| + 6 < 30$

4. $6|4y - 2| \geq 42$

Lesson 2-3 ◀ **Writing and Graphing Equations in Slope-Intercept Form**

Graph the line passing through the given points. Then write its equation in slope-intercept form.

5. $(1, -1)$ and $(3, 17)$

6. $(2, 9)$ and $(6, 11)$

Lesson 2-6 ◀ **Identifying Translations**

Identify each horizontal and vertical translation of the parent function $y = |x|$.

7. $y = |x - 4| + 2$

8. $y = |x + 10| - 3$

Lesson 3-2 ◀ **Solving Systems of Equations**

Solve each system of equations by substitution.

9. $\begin{cases} 2x + 6y = 14 \\ 4x - 8y = 48 \end{cases}$

10. $\begin{cases} x + 2y = -18 \\ 2x - 4y = 12 \end{cases}$

 Looking Ahead Vocabulary

11. A *form* is a document with blank spaces to fill in. What types of forms might you use?

12. Something is *imaginary* if it has no factual reality. What are some examples of imaginary items?

13. Many items have a specific *function*, or purpose for use. What is the function of a pencil?

Quadratic Functions and Equations

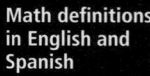
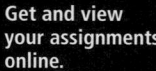
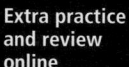
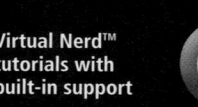
Chapter Preview

Vocabulary

English/Spanish Vocabulary Audio Online:

BIG ideas

1 Equivalence
Essential Question What are the advantages of a quadratic function in vertex form? In standard form?

2 Function
Essential Question How is any quadratic function related to the parent quadratic function $y = x^2$?

3 Solving Equations and Inequalities
Essential Question How are the real solutions of a quadratic equation related to the graph of the related quadratic function?

 DOMAINS

- Interpreting Functions
- Creating Equations
- The Complex Number System

Common Core Performance Task

Maximizing Profit

Victor runs a small sandwich shop. He plans to sell a new brand of chips, which he is able to buy at a cost of $.30 per bag. Victor needs to decide the price he will charge customers for a bag of chips.

Another sandwich shop sells the same brand of chips. The shop owner tells Victor that the number of bags of chips she sold increased when she lowered her selling price. The table below shows her data.

Average Weekly Sales of Chips

Number of Bags Sold	Selling Price per Bag
150	$1.00
190	$.90
250	$.75
350	$.50

Victor wants to price the bags of chips so that he maximizes his profit.

Task Description

Find all possible prices Victor can charge for a bag of chips in order to make a profit, and determine the price he should charge to maximize his profit.

Connecting the Task to the Math Practices

MATHEMATICAL PRACTICES

As you complete the task, you'll apply several Standards for Mathematical Practice.

- You'll model the situation with functions for selling price, cost, revenue, and profit. (MP 4)
- You'll use connections between the profit function's equation and its graph to give you information about the situation. (MP 1)
- You'll find the zeros of the profit function and interpret them in terms of the situation. (MP 2)

4-1

Quadratic Functions and Transformations

© **Common Core State Standards**

F-BF.B.3 Identify the effect on the graph of replacing $f(x)$ by $f(x) + k$, $k\,f(x)$, $f(kx)$, and $f(x + k)$ for specific values of k . . . find the value of k given the graphs. **Also A-CED.A.1, F-IF.B.4, F-IF.B.6**

MP 1, MP 2, MP 3, MP 4, MP 7

Objective To identify and graph quadratic functions

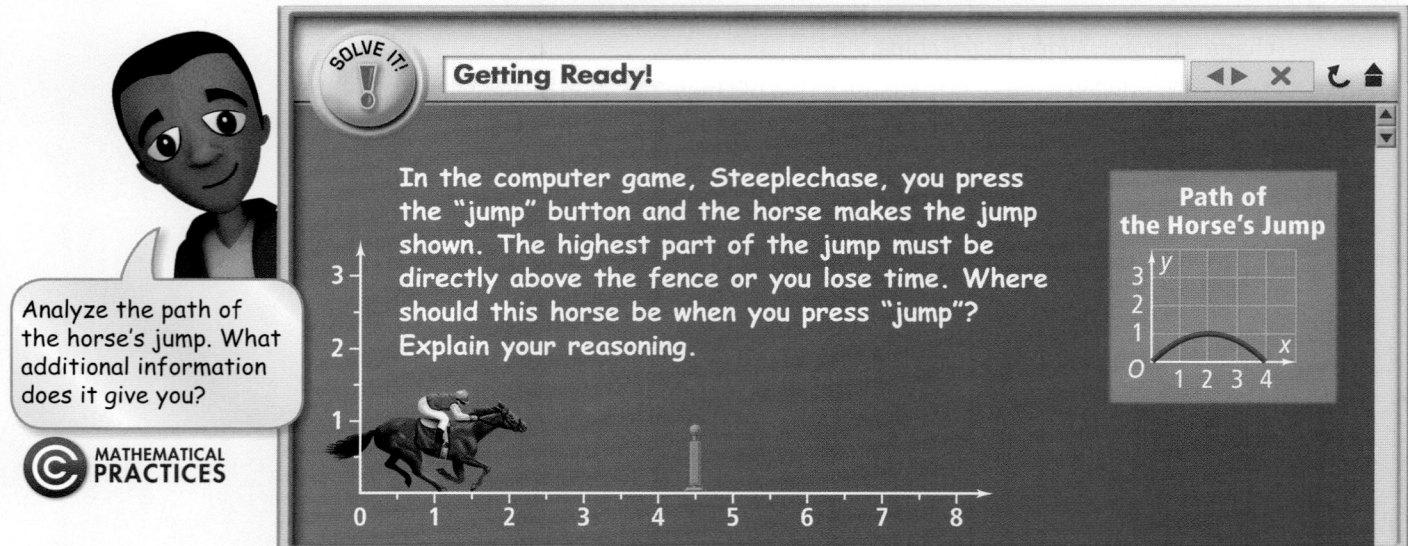

SOLVE IT!

Getting Ready!

In the computer game, Steeplechase, you press the "jump" button and the horse makes the jump shown. The highest part of the jump must be directly above the fence or you lose time. Where should this horse be when you press "jump"? Explain your reasoning.

Path of the Horse's Jump

Analyze the path of the horse's jump. What additional information does it give you?

© MATHEMATICAL PRACTICES

In the Solve It, you used the *parabolic* shape of the horse's jump. A **parabola** is the graph of a **quadratic function**, which you can write in the form $f(x) = ax^2 + bx + c$, where $a \neq 0$.

Essential Understanding The graph of any quadratic function is a transformation of the graph of the parent quadratic function, $y = x^2$.

The **vertex form** of a quadratic function is $f(x) = a(x - h)^2 + k$, where $a \neq 0$. The **axis of symmetry** is a line that divides the parabola into two mirror images. The equation of the axis of symmetry is $x = h$. The **vertex of the parabola** is (h, k), the intersection of the parabola and its axis of symmetry.

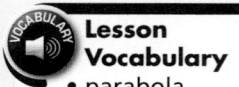

Lesson Vocabulary

- parabola
- quadratic function
- vertex form
- axis of symmetry
- vertex of the parabola
- minimum value
- maximum value

take note

Key Concept The Parent Quadratic Function

The parent quadratic function is $f(x) = x^2$. Its graph is the parabola shown. The axis of symmetry is $x = 0$. The vertex is $(0, 0)$.

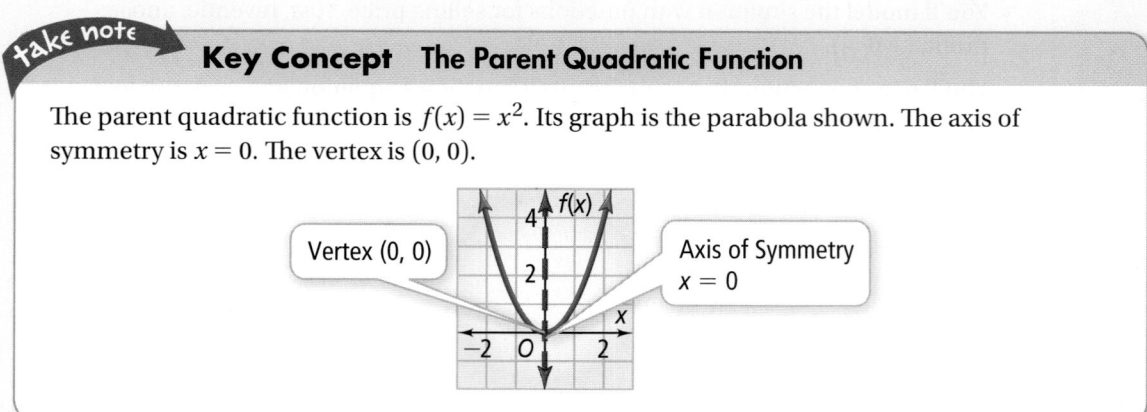

Vertex (0, 0)

Axis of Symmetry $x = 0$

Plan

How do you choose points to plot?
Choose the vertex and two points on one side of the axis of symmetry that give integer values of $f(x)$.

Problem 1 **Graphing a Function of the Form** $f(x) = ax^2$

What is the graph of $f(x) = \frac{1}{2}x^2$**?**

Step 1 Plot the vertex $(0, 0)$. Draw the axis of symmetry, $x = 0$.

Step 2 Find and plot two points on one side of the axis of symmetry.

x	$f(x) = \frac{1}{2}x^2$	$(x, f(x))$
0	$\frac{1}{2}(0)^2 = 0$	$(0, 0)$
2	$\frac{1}{2}(2)^2 = 2$	$(2, 2)$
4	$\frac{1}{2}(4)^2 = 8$	$(4, 8)$

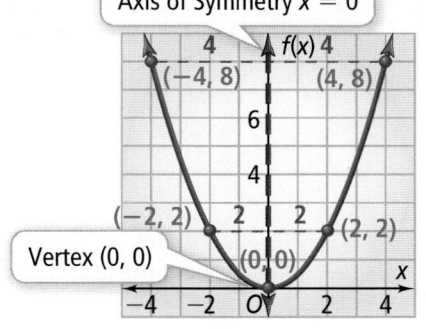

Step 3 Plot the corresponding points on the other side of the axis of symmetry.

Step 4 Sketch the curve.

 Got It? **1. a.** What is the graph of $f(x) = -\frac{1}{3}x^2$?

b. Reasoning What can you say about the graph of the function $f(x) = ax^2$ if a is a negative number? Explain.

Graphs of $y = ax^2$ and $y = -ax^2$ are reflections of each other across the x-axis. Increasing $|a|$ stretches the graph vertically and narrows it horizontally. Decreasing $|a|$ compresses the graph vertically and widens it horizontally.

take note

Key Concept **Reflection, Stretch, and Compression**

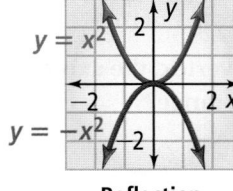

Reflection,
a and $-a$

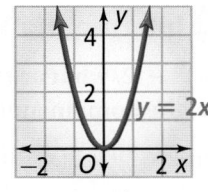

Stretch,
$a > 1$

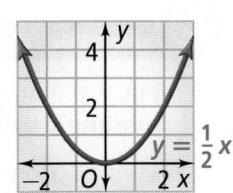

Compression,
$0 < a < 1$

If $a > 0$, the parabola opens upward. The y-coordinate of the vertex is the **minimum value** of the function. If $a < 0$, the parabola opens downward. The y-coordinate of the vertex is the **maximum value** of the function.

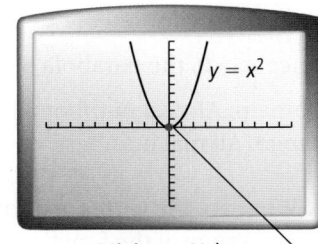

Minimum Value   Vertex

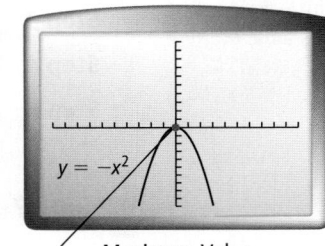

Maximum Value

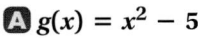 **Problem 2** Graphing Translations of $f(x) = x^2$

Graph each function. How is each graph a translation of $f(x) = x^2$?

Think

How does $g(x)$ differ from $f(x)$?
For each value of x, the value of $g(x)$ is 5 less than the value of $f(x)$.

A $g(x) = x^2 - 5$

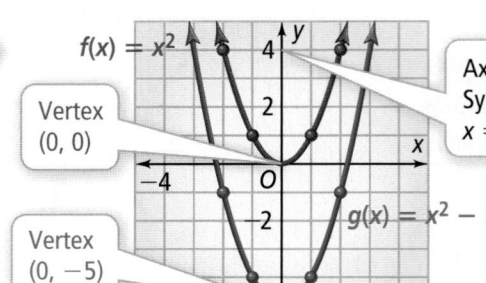

B $h(x) = (x - 4)^2$

Vertex (4, 0)

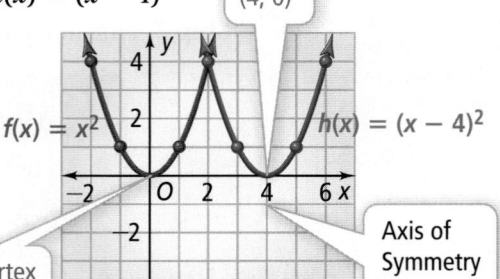

Translate the graph of f down 5 units to get the graph of $g(x) = x^2 - 5$.

Translate the graph of f to the right 4 units to get the graph of $h(x) = (x - 4)^2$.

 Got It? 2. Graph each function. How is it a translation of $f(x) = x^2$?

    a. $g(x) = x^2 + 3$ **b.** $h(x) = (x + 1)^2$

The vertex form, $f(x) = a(x - h)^2 + k$, gives you information about the graph of f without drawing the graph. If $a > 0$, k is the minimum value of the function. If $a < 0$, k is the maximum value.

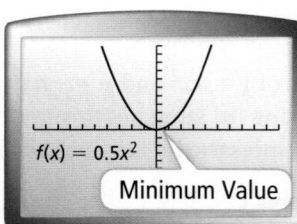

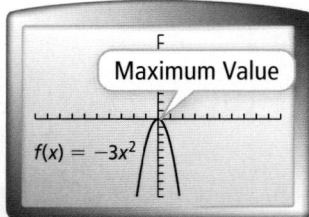

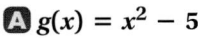 **Problem 3** Interpreting Vertex Form

Plan

How do you use vertex form?
Compare
$y = 3(x - 4)^2 - 2$
to vertex form
$y = a(x - h)^2 + k$
to find values for a, h, and k.

For $y = 3(x - 4)^2 - 2$, what are the vertex, the axis of symmetry, the maximum or minimum value, the domain and the range?

Step 1 Compare: $y = 3(x - 4)^2 - 2$
                        $y = a(x - h)^2 + k$

Step 2 The vertex is $(h, k) = (4, -2)$.

Step 3 The axis of symmetry is $x = h$, or $x = 4$.

Step 4 Since $a > 0$, the parabola opens upward. $k = -2$ is the minimum value.

Step 5 Domain: All real numbers. There is no restriction on the value of x.
          Range: All real numbers ≥ -2, since the minimum value of the function is -2.

 Got It? 3. What are the vertex, axis of symmetry, minimum or maximum, and domain and range of the function $y = -2(x + 1)^2 + 4$?

You can use the vertex form of a quadratic function, $f(x) = a(x - h)^2 + k$, to transform the graph of the parent function $f(x) = x^2$.

- Stretch or compress the graph of $f(x) = x^2$ vertically by the factor $|a|$.
- If $a < 0$, reflect the graph across the x-axis.
- Shift the graph $|h|$ units horizontally and $|k|$ units vertically.

take note

Key Concept   Translation of the Parabola

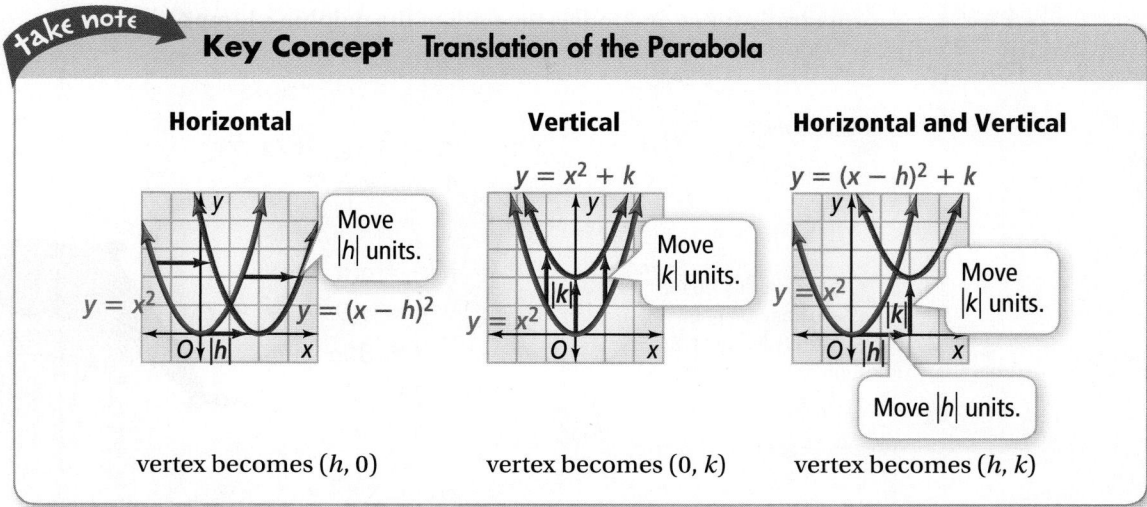

Horizontal

$y = (x - h)^2$

$y = x^2$

Move $|h|$ units.

vertex becomes $(h, 0)$

Vertical

$y = x^2 + k$

$y = x^2$

Move $|k|$ units.

vertex becomes $(0, k)$

Horizontal and Vertical

$y = (x - h)^2 + k$

$y = x^2$

Move $|k|$ units.

Move $|h|$ units.

vertex becomes (h, k)

© **Problem 4**   Using Vertex Form

A What is the graph of $f(x) = -2(x - 1)^2 + 3$?

Plan

What do the values of a, h, and k tell you about the graph?
The graph is a stretched reflection of $y = x^2$, shifted 1 unit right and 3 units up.

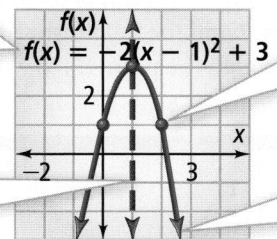

Step 1 Identify the constants $a = -2$, $h = 1$, and $k = 3$. Because $a < 0$, the parabola opens downward.

$f(x) = -2(x - 1)^2 + 3$

Step 2 Plot the vertex $(h, k) = (1, 3)$ and draw the axis of symmetry $x = 1$.

Step 3 Plot two points. $f(2) = -2(2 - 1)^2 + 3 = 1$. Plot $(2, 1)$ and the symmetric point $(0, 1)$.

Step 4 Sketch the curve.

B **Multiple Choice** What steps transform the graph of $y = x^2$ to $y = -2(x + 1)^2 + 3$?

Ⓐ Reflect across the x-axis, stretch by the factor 2, translate 1 unit to the right and 3 units up.

Ⓑ Stretch by the factor 2, translate 1 unit to the right and 3 units up.

Ⓒ Reflect across the x-axis, translate 1 unit to the left and 3 units up.

Ⓓ Stretch by the factor 2, reflect across the x-axis, translate 1 unit to the left and 3 units up.

The correct choice is D.

✓ **Got It?** **4.** What steps transform the graph of $y = x^2$ to $y = 2(x + 2)^2 - 5$?

You can use the vertex form of a quadratic function to model a real-world situation.

 Problem 5 **Writing a Quadratic Function in Vertex Form**

Nature The picture shows the jump of a dolphin. What quadratic function models the path of the dolphin's jump?

Think

What is the vertex?

Choose another point, $(9, 4)$, from the path. Substitute in the vertex form.

Solve for a.

Substitute in the vertex form.

Write

The vertex is $(3, 7)$.
$h = 3, k = 7$

$f(x) = a(x - h)^2 + k$
$4 = a(9 - 3)^2 + 7$
$4 = 36a + 7$
$-3 = 36a$
$a = -\frac{1}{12}$

$f(x) = -\frac{1}{12}(x - 3)^2 + 7$ models the path of the dolphin's jump.

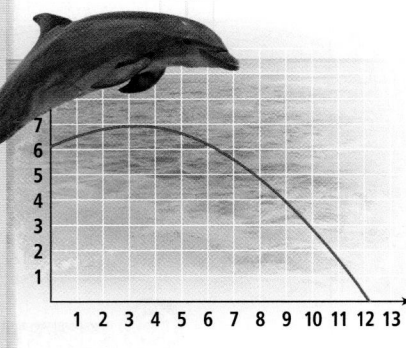

 Got It? **5.** Suppose the path of the jump changes so that the axis of symmetry becomes $x = 2$ and the height stays the same. If the path of the jump also passes through the point $(5, 5)$, what quadratic function would model this path?

 Lesson Check

Do you know HOW?

1. Graph the function $f(x) = -3x^2$.

2. Determine whether the function $f(x) = 0.25 (2x - 15)^2 + 150$ has a maximum or a minimum value.

3. Rewrite $y = -2x^2 + 35$ in vertex form.

Do you UNDERSTAND?  **MATHEMATICAL PRACTICES**

4. Vocabulary When does the graph of a quadratic function have a minimum value?

5. Reasoning Is $y = 0(x - 4)^2 + 3$ a quadratic function? Explain.

6. Compare and Contrast Describe the differences between the graphs of $y = (x + 6)^2$ and $y = (x - 6)^2 + 7$.

Practice and Problem-Solving Exercises  MATHEMATICAL PRACTICES

Graph each function.

See Problem 1.

7. $y = -x^2$ **8.** $f(x) = 5x^2$ **9.** $y = \frac{2}{5}x^2$ **10.** $y = 2x^2$

11. $f(x) = 2\frac{1}{4}x^2$ **12.** $y = -\frac{4}{9}x^2$ **13.** $y = -7x^2$ **14.** $f(x) = 3\frac{2}{5}x^2$

Graph each function. Describe how it was translated from $f(x) = x^2$.

See Problem 2.

15. $f(x) = x^2 + 3$ **16.** $f(x) = (x - 2)^2$ **17.** $f(x) = x^2 - 6$ **18.** $f(x) = (x + 3)^2$

19. $f(x) = x^2 - 9$ **20.** $f(x) = (x + 5)^2$ **21.** $f(x) = x^2 + 1.5$ **22.** $f(x) = (x - 2.5)^2$

Identify the vertex, the axis of symmetry, the maximum or minimum value, and the domain and the range of each function.

See Problem 3.

23. $y = -1.5(x + 20)^2$ **24.** $f(x) = 0.1(x - 3.2)^2$ **25.** $f(x) = 24(x + 5.5)^2$

26. $y = 0.0035(x + 1)^2 - 1$ **27.** $f(x) = -(x - 4)^2 - 25$ **28.** $y = (x - 125)^2 + 125$

Graph each function. Identify the axis of symmetry.

 See Problem 4.

29. $f(x) = (x - 1)^2 + 2$ **30.** $y = (x + 3)^2 - 4$ **31.** $f(x) = 2(x - 2)^2 + 5$

32. $y = -3(x + 7)^2 - 8$ **33.** $y = -(x - 1)^2 + 4$ **34.** $f(x) = -(x - 7)^2 + 10$

Write a quadratic function to model each graph.

See Problem 5.

35. 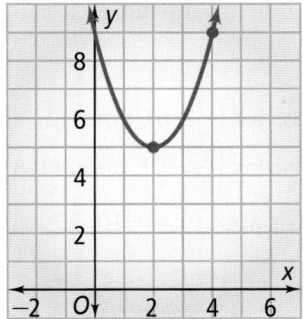   **36.** 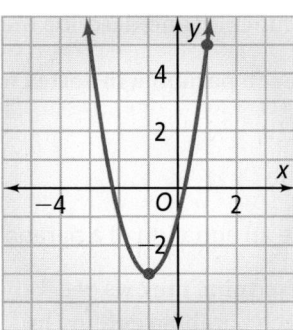   **37.**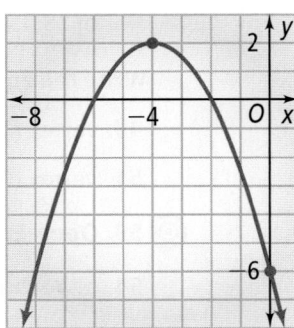

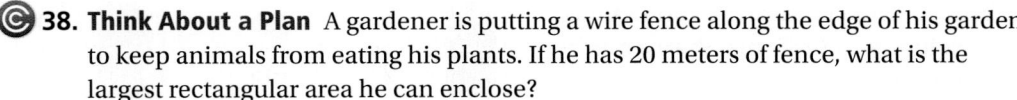 **Apply**

38. Think About a Plan A gardener is putting a wire fence along the edge of his garden to keep animals from eating his plants. If he has 20 meters of fence, what is the largest rectangular area he can enclose?

- To find the area of a rectangle, what two quantities do you need? Choose one to be your variable and write the other in terms of this variable.
- How can a graph help you solve this problem?
- What quadratic function represents the area of the garden?

STEM 39. Manufacturing The equation for the cost in dollars of producing computer chips is $C = 0.000015x^2 - 0.03x + 35$, where x is the number of chips produced. Find the number of chips that minimizes the cost. What is the cost for that number of chips?

In Chapter 2, you graphed absolute value functions as transformations of their parent function $y = |x|$. Similarly, you can graph a quadratic function as a transformation of the parent function $y = x^2$. Graph the following pairs of functions on the same set of axes. Determine how they are similar and how they are different.

40. $y = -|x - 2| + 1; y = -(x - 2)^2 + 1$

41. $y = 3|x + 1| - 2; y = 3(x + 1)^2 - 2$

42. $y = -2|x| + 4; y = -2x^2 + 4$

43. $y = |x + 3|; y = (x + 3)^2$

Describe how to transform the parent function $y = x^2$ to the graph of each function below. Graph both functions on the same axes.

44. $y = -2(x - 1)^2$

45. $y = -2(x + 1)^2 + 1$

46. $y = -0.25x^2 + 3$

 47. You can find the rate of change for an interval between two points of a function by finding the slope between the points. Use the graph to find the y-value for each x-value. Then find the rate of change for each interval.

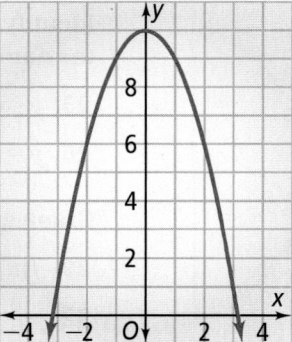

    a. $(0, \blacksquare)$ and $(1, \blacksquare)$

    b. $(1, \blacksquare)$ and $(2, \blacksquare)$

    c. $(2, \blacksquare)$ and $(3, \blacksquare)$

    d. Reasoning. What do you notice about the rate of change as the interval gets further away from the vertex?

    e. Would your answer to part (d) change if the intervals were on the left side of the graph? Explain.

48. Write a quadratic function to represent the areas of all rectangles with a perimeter of 36 ft. Graph the function and describe the rectangle that has the largest area.

Write the equation of each parabola in vertex form.

49. vertex $(1, 2)$, point $(2, -5)$

50. vertex $(-3, 6)$, point $(1, -2)$

51. vertex $(0, 5)$, point $(1, -2)$

52. vertex $\left(\frac{1}{4}, -\frac{3}{2}\right)$, point $(1, 3)$

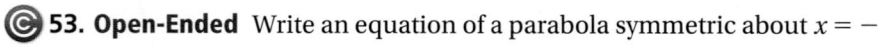 **53. Open-Ended** Write an equation of a parabola symmetric about $x = -10$.

54. a. Technology Determine the axis of symmetry for each parabola defined by the spreadsheet values at the right.

    b. How could you use the spreadsheet columns to verify that the axes of symmetry are correct?

    c. What functions in vertex form model the data?

    Check that the axes of symmetry are correct.

	A	B
1	X1	Y1
2	1	-35
3	2	-15
4	3	-3
5	4	1
6	5	-3

	A	B
1	X2	Y2
2	1	10
3	2	2
4	3	2
5	4	10
6	5	26

Determine a and k so the given points are on the graph of the function.

55. $(0, 1), (2, 1); y = a(x - 1)^2 + k$

56. $(-3, 2), (0, 11); y = a(x + 2)^2 + k$

57. $(1, 11), (2, -19); y = a(x + 1)^2 + k$

58. $(-2, 6), (3, 1); y = a(x - 3)^2 + k$

59. a. In the function $y = ax^2 + bx + c$, c represents the y-intercept. Find the value of the y-intercept in the function $y = a(x - h)^2 + k$.
   b. Under what conditions does k represent the y-intercept?

Find the quadratic function $y = a(x - h)^2$ whose graph passes through the given points.

60. $(-2, 1)$ and $(2, 1)$

61. $(-5, 2)$ and $(-1, 2)$

62. $(-1, -4)$ and $(7, -4)$

63. $(2, -1)$ and $(4, 0)$

64. $(-2, 18)$ and $(1, 0)$

65. $(1, -64)$ and $(-3, 0)$

Standardized Test Prep

66. One parabola at the right has the equation $y = (x - 4)^2 + 2$. Which equation represents the second parabola?

Ⓐ $y = -(x - 4)^2 + 2$

Ⓒ $y = (x + 4)^2 - 2$

Ⓑ $y = (-x - 4)^2 + 2$

Ⓓ $y = -(x + 4)^2 - 2$

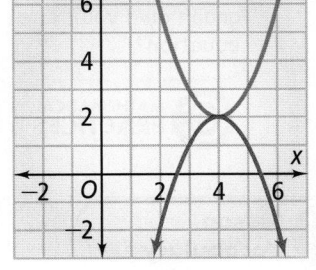

67. Which system has the unique solution $(1, 4)$?

Ⓕ $\begin{cases} y = x - 3 \\ x + y = 5 \end{cases}$

Ⓗ $\begin{cases} x + y = 5 \\ y = -x + 3 \end{cases}$

Ⓖ $\begin{cases} y = -x + 5 \\ x - y = -3 \end{cases}$

Ⓘ $\begin{cases} -x + y = 3 \\ 2x - 2y = -6 \end{cases}$

68. What is the formula for the surface area of a right circular cylinder, $S = 2\pi r h + 2\pi r^2$, solved for h?

Ⓐ $h = \dfrac{S}{4\pi r}$

Ⓑ $h = \dfrac{S}{2\pi r^2}$

Ⓒ $h = \dfrac{S}{2\pi r} - r$

Ⓓ $h = r - \dfrac{S}{2\pi r}$

69. An athletic club has 225 feet of fencing to enclose a tennis court. What quadratic function can be used to find the maximum area of the tennis court? Find the maximum area, and the lengths of the sides of the resulting fence.

Mixed Review

Solve each system of equations using a matrix.

◀ **See Lesson 3-6.**

70. $\begin{cases} 3x - y = 7 \\ 2x + 2y = 10 \end{cases}$

71. $\begin{cases} 2x + 5y = 10 \\ -3x + y = 36 \end{cases}$

72. $\begin{cases} 3x + y - 2z = -3 \\ x - 3y - z = -2 \\ 2x + 2y + 3z = 11 \end{cases}$

Get Ready! **To prepare for Lesson 4-2, do Exercises 73–75.**

Find the vertex of the graph of each function.

◀ **See Lesson 2-7.**

73. $y = -2|x|$

74. $y = |-x - 1|$

75. $y = 5|x - 5|$

4-2 Standard Form of a Quadratic Function

@ **Common Core State Standards**

A-CED.A.2 Create equations in two or more variables . . . graph equations on coordinate axes with labels and scales. **Also F-IF.B.4, F-IF.B.6, F-IF.C.8, F-IF.C.9**

MP 1, MP 3, MP 4

Objective To graph quadratic functions written in standard form

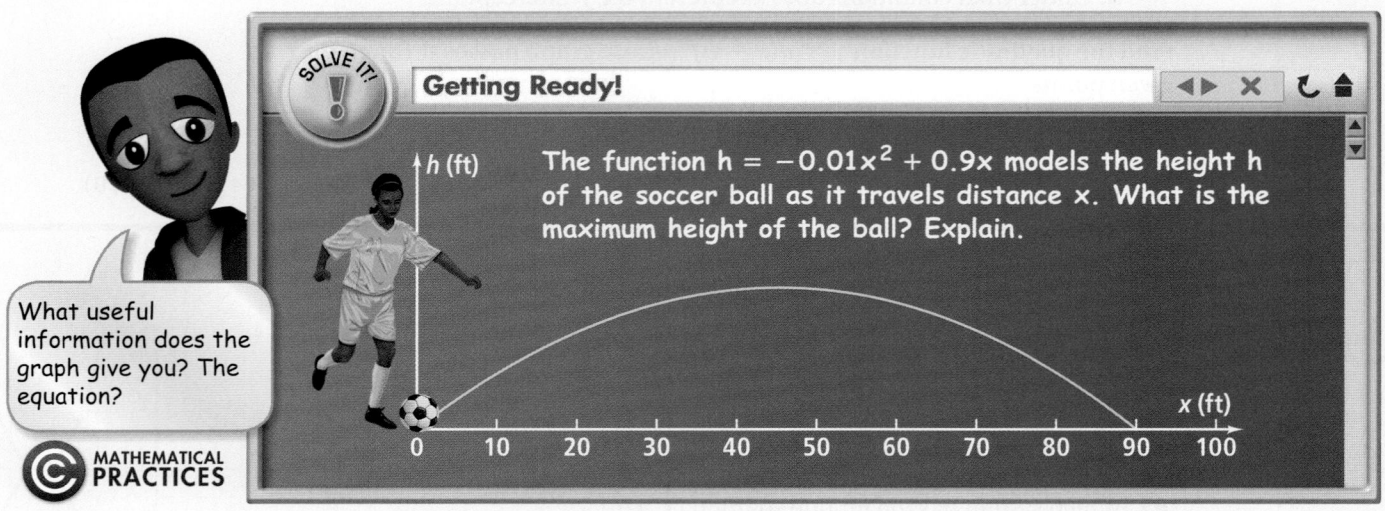

SOLVE IT!

Getting Ready!

The function $h = -0.01x^2 + 0.9x$ models the height h of the soccer ball as it travels distance x. What is the maximum height of the ball? Explain.

What useful information does the graph give you? The equation?

@ **MATHEMATICAL PRACTICES**

VOCABULARY

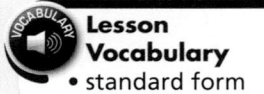

Lesson Vocabulary
• standard form

In Lesson 4-1, you worked with quadratic functions written in vertex form. Now you will use quadratic functions in *standard form*. The **standard form** of a quadratic function is $f(x) = ax^2 + bx + c$, where $a \neq 0$.

Essential Understanding For any quadratic function $f(x) = ax^2 + bx + c$, the values of a, b, and c provide key information about its graph.

You can find information about the graph of a quadratic function (such as the vertex) easily from the vertex form. Such information is "hidden" in standard form. However, standard form is easier to enter into a graphing calculator.

@ **Problem 1** Finding the Features of a Quadratic Function

Graphing Calculator What are the vertex, the axis of symmetry, the maximum or minimum value, and the range of $y = 2x^2 + 8x - 2$?

Plan

How can you use a calculator to find the features of a quadratic function in standard form?
Graph the function. Then use the **CALC** and **TABLE** features.

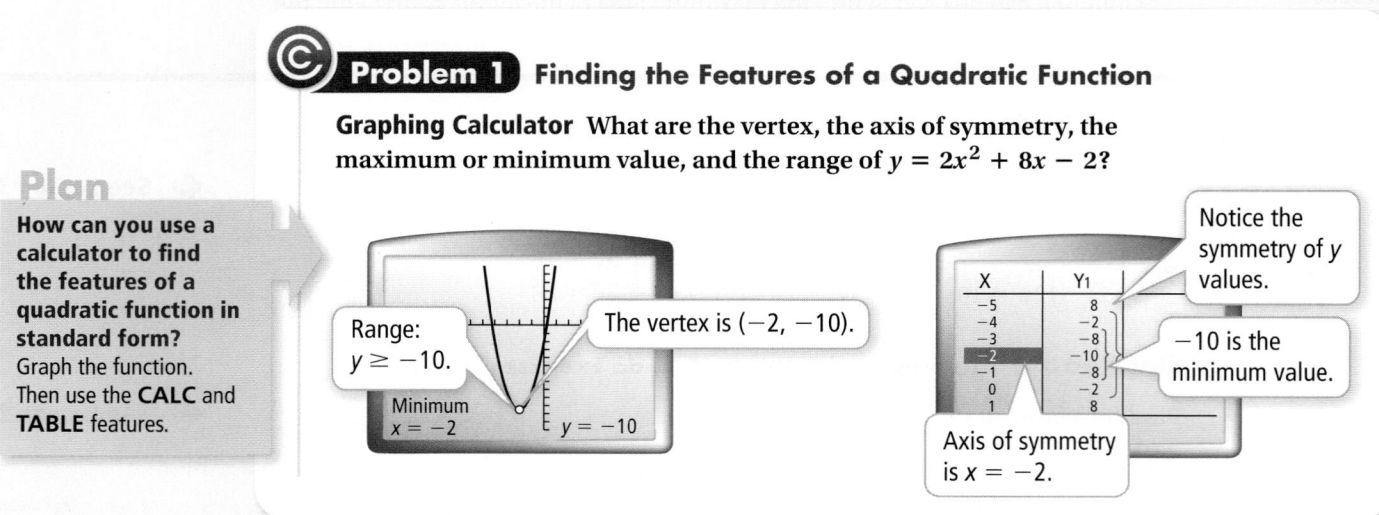

Range: $y \geq -10$.

The vertex is $(-2, -10)$.

Minimum $x = -2$

$y = -10$

Notice the symmetry of y values.

X	Y1
−5	8
−4	−2
−3	−8
−2	−10
−1	−8
0	−2
1	8

−10 is the minimum value.

Axis of symmetry is $x = -2$.

Got It? **1.** What are the vertex, axis of symmetry, maximum or minimum value, and range of $y = -3x^2 - 4x + 6$?

You can find information about the quadratic function $f(x) = ax^2 + bx + c$ from the coefficients a and b, and from the constant term c.

take note

Properties   Quadratic Function in Standard Form

- The graph of $f(x) = ax^2 + bx + c$, $a \neq 0$, is a parabola.
- If $a > 0$, the parabola opens upward. If $a < 0$, the parabola opens downward.
- The axis of symmetry is the line $x = -\dfrac{b}{2a}$.
- The x-coordinate of the vertex is $-\dfrac{b}{2a}$. The y-coordinate of the vertex is the y-value of the function for $x = -\dfrac{b}{2a}$, or $y = f\left(-\dfrac{b}{2a}\right)$.
- The y-intercept is $(0, c)$.

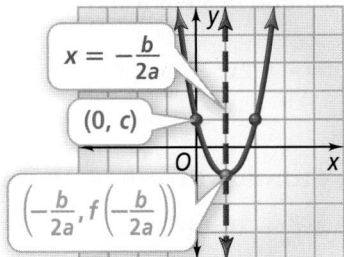

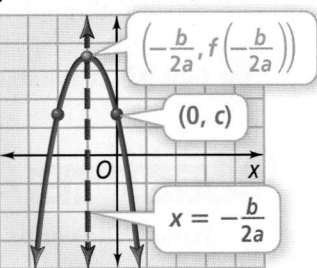

Here's Why It Works You can expand the vertex form of a quadratic function to determine properties of the graph of a quadratic function written in standard form.

$$f(x) = a(x - h)^2 + k$$
$$= a(x^2 - 2hx + h^2) + k$$
$$= ax^2 - 2ahx + ah^2 + k$$
$$= ax^2 + (-2ah)x + (ah^2 + k)$$

Compare to the standard form, $f(x) = ax^2 + bx + c$.

$a = a$ *a in standard form is the same as a in vertex form.*

$b = -2ah$

$-\dfrac{b}{2a} = h$ *Solve for h.*

Since, $h = -\dfrac{b}{2a}$, the axis of symmetry is $x = -\dfrac{b}{2a}$ and the vertex is $(h, k) = \left(-\dfrac{b}{2a}, f\left(-\dfrac{b}{2a}\right)\right)$.

Problem 2 Graphing a Function of the Form $y = ax^2 + bx + c$

What is the graph of $y = x^2 + 2x + 3$?

Step 1 Identify a, b, and c.
$a = 1$, $b = 2$, $c = 3$

Think

How can you use the axis of symmetry?
The entire curve on one side of the axis is the mirror image of the curve on the other side.

Step 2 The axis of symmetry is $x = -\frac{b}{2a}$.
$$x = -\frac{2}{2(1)}$$
Lightly sketch the line $x = -1$.

Step 3 The x-coordinate of the vertex is also $-\frac{b}{2a}$, or -1.

The y-coordinate is
$y = (-1)^2 + 2(-1) + 3 = 2$.

Plot the vertex $(-1, 2)$.

Step 4 Since $c = 3$, the y-intercept is $(0, 3)$. The reflection of $(0, 3)$ across $x = -1$ is $(-2, 3)$. Plot both points.

Step 5 $a > 0$ confirms that the graph opens upward. Draw a smooth curve through the points you found in Steps 3 and 4.

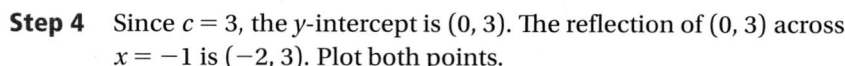

Got It? 2. What is the graph of $y = -2x^2 + 2x - 5$?

 Problem 3 Converting Standard Form to Vertex Form

Plan

How do you find h, k, and a?
Find the vertex. This gives you h and k. The value for a is the same in both forms.

What is the vertex form of $y = 2x^2 + 10x + 7$?

$y = 2x^2 + 10x + 7$ Identify a and b.

$x = -\frac{b}{2a}$ Find the x-coordinate of the vertex.

$= -\frac{10}{2(2)}$

$= -2.5$

$y = 2(-2.5)^2 + 10(-2.5) + 7$ Substitute $x = -2.5$ into the equation.

$= -5.5$

The vertex is $(-2.5, -5.5)$.

$y = a(x - h)^2 + k$ Write the vertex form.

$y = 2[x - (-2.5)]^2 + (-5.5)$ Substitute $a = 2$, $h = -2.5$, $k = -5.5$.

$y = 2(x + 2.5)^2 - 5.5$ Simplify.

The vertex form is $y = 2(x + 2.5)^2 - 5.5$.

Got It? 3. What is the vertex form of $y = -x^2 + 4x - 5$?

Problem 4 **Interpreting a Quadratic Graph** STEM

Length of bridge above arch

Height of arch

516 ft

Bridges The New River Gorge Bridge in West Virginia is the world's largest steel single arch bridge. You can model the arch with the function $y = -0.000498x^2 + 0.847x$, where x and y are in feet. How high above the river is the arch? How long is the section of bridge above the arch?

Know

A function that models the arch and the vertical distance from the base of the supports to the water

Need

The height of the arch above the support base and the length of the bridge above the arch

Plan

Find the vertex. The y-coordinate is the height of the arch above the support base. The x-coordinate is half the distance between the supports.

Think

How can you tell that the quadratic function has a maximum value?
Since $a < 0$, the graph of the function opens down. The function has a maximum value.

Step 1 Find the vertex of the arch.

$$x = -\frac{b}{2a} = -\frac{0.847}{2(-0.000498)} \approx 850$$

$$y = -0.000498(850)^2 + 0.847(850) \approx 360$$

The vertex is about (850, 360).

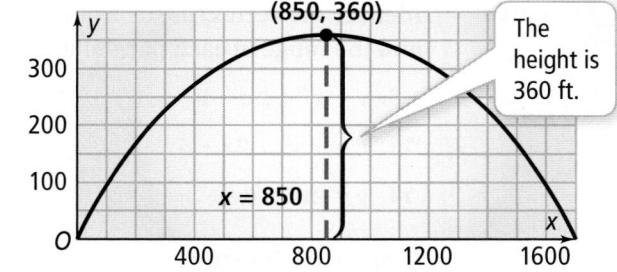

(850, 360)

The height is 360 ft.

$x = 850$

Step 2 Find the height of the arch above its supports.

The y-coordinate of the vertex is the height of the arch above its supports. The arch is about 360 ft above its supports.

Step 3 Find the height of the arch above the river.

The arch is about 360 ft + 516 ft = 876 ft above the river.

Step 4 Find the length of the bridge above the arch.

The x-coordinate of the vertex is half the length of the bridge above the arch. The length of that part of the bridge is about 850 ft + 850 ft = 1700 ft long.

Got It? **4. a.** The Zhaozhou Bridge in China is the one of the oldest known arch bridges, dating to A.D. 605. You can model the support arch with the function $f(x) = -0.001075x^2 + 0.131148x$, where x and y are measured in feet. How high is the arch above its supports?
b. Reasoning Why does the model in part (a) not have a constant term?

Lesson Check

Do you know HOW?

1. Identify the vertex, axis of symmetry, and the maximum or minimum value of the parabola at the right.

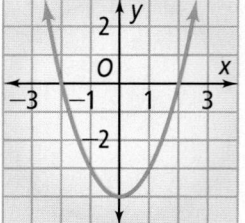

Graph each function.

2. $y = x^2 - 2x + 4$

3. $y = -x^2 - 3x + 6$

Write each function in vertex form.

4. $y = x^2 - 2x + 9$

5. $y = -x^2 + 3x - 1$

Do you UNDERSTAND?  MATHEMATICAL PRACTICES

 6. **Error Analysis** A student graphed the function $y = 2x^2 - 4x - 3$. Find and correct the error.

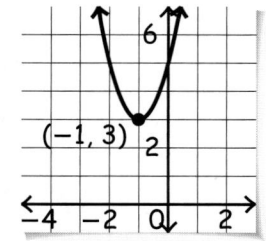

7. **Compare and Contrast** Explain the difference between finding the vertex of a function written in vertex form and finding the vertex of a function written in standard form.

Practice and Problem-Solving Exercises MATHEMATICAL PRACTICES

 **Practice**

Identify the vertex, the axis of symmetry, the maximum or minimum value, and the range of each parabola.

 See Problem 1.

8. $y = x^2 + 2x + 1$

9. $y = -x^2 + 2x + 1$

10. $y = x^2 + 4x + 1$

11. $y = -x^2 + 2x + 5$

12. $y = 3x^2 - 4x - 2$

13. $y = -2x^2 - 3x + 4$

14. $y = 2x^2 - 6x + 3$

15. $y = -x^2 - x$

16. $y = 2x^2 + 5$

Graph each function.

See Problem 2.

17. $y = x^2 + 6x + 9$

18. $y = -x^2 - 3x + 6$

19. $y = 2x^2 + 4x$

20. $y = 4x^2 - 12x + 9$

21. $y = -6x^2 - 12x - 1$

22. $y = -\frac{3}{4}x^2 + 6x + 6$

23. $y = 3x^2 - 12x + 10$

24. $y = \frac{1}{2}x^2 + 2x - 8$

25. $y = -4x^2 - 24x - 36$

Write each function in vertex form.

See Problem 3.

26. $y = x^2 - 4x + 6$

27. $y = x^2 + 2x + 5$

28. $y = 4x^2 + 7x$

29. $y = 2x^2 - 5x + 12$

30. $y = -2x^2 + 8x + 3$

31. $y = \frac{9}{4}x^2 + 3x - 1$

32. **Economics** A model for a company's revenue from selling a software package is $R = -2.5p^2 + 500p$, where p is the price in dollars of the software. What price will maximize revenue? Find the maximum revenue.

See Problem 4.

Sketch each parabola using the given information.

33. vertex $(3, 6)$, y-intercept 2

34. vertex $(-1, -4)$, y-intercept 3

35. vertex $(0, 5)$, point $(1, -2)$

36. vertex $(2, 3)$, point $(6, 9)$

37. Think About a Plan Suppose you work for a packaging company and are designing a box that has a rectangular bottom with a perimeter of 36 cm. The box must be 4 cm high. What dimensions give the maximum volume?
- How can you model the volume of the box with a quadratic function?
- What information can you get from the function to find the maximum volume?

38. Landscaping A town is planning a playground. It wants to fence in a rectangular space using an existing wall. What is the greatest area it can fence in using 100 ft of donated fencing?

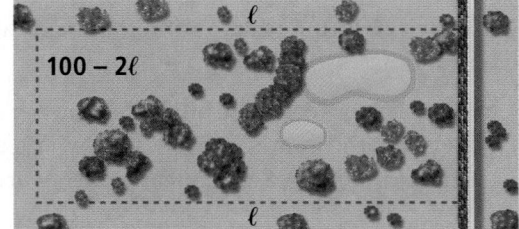

For each function, the vertex of the function's graph is given. Find the unknown coefficients.

39. $y = x^2 + bx + c$; $(3, -4)$

40. $y = -3x^2 + bx + c$; $(1, 0)$

41. $y = ax^2 + 10x + c$; $(-5, -27)$

42. $y = c - ax^2 - 2x$; $(-1, 3)$

STEM **43. Physics** The height of a projectile fired straight up in the air with an initial velocity of 64 ft/s is $h = 64t - 16t^2$, where h is height in feet and t is time in seconds. The table represents the data for another projectile. Which projectile goes higher? How much higher?

Time (t)	Height (h)
0.5	20
1	32
1.5	36
2	32

44. A student says that the graph of $y = ax^2 + bx + c$ gets wider as a increases.
- **a. Error Analysis** Use examples to show that the student is wrong.
- **b. Writing** Summarize the relationship between $|a|$ and the width of the graph of $y = ax^2 + bx + c$.

For each function, find the y-intercept.

45. $y = (x - 1)^2 + 2$

46. $y = -3(x + 2)^2 - 4$

47. $y = -\frac{2}{3}(x - 9)^2$

48. Use the functions $f(x) = 4x + 3$ and $g(x) = \frac{1}{2}x^2 + 2$ to answer parts (a)–(c).
- **a.** Which function has a greater rate of change from $x = 0$ to $x = 1$?
- **b.** Which function has a greater rate of change from $x = 2$ and $x = 3$?
- **c.** Does $g(x)$ ever have a greater rate of change than $f(x)$? Explain.

 **Challenge** For each function, the vertex of the function's graph is given. Find a and b.

49. $y = ax^2 + bx - 27; (2, -3)$ **50.** $y = ax^2 + bx + 5; (-1, 4)$

51. $y = ax^2 + bx + 8; (2, -4)$ **52.** $y = ax^2 + bx; (-3, 2)$

53. Sketch the parabola with an axis of symmetry $x = 2$, y-intercept 1, and point $(3, 2.5)$.

 ## Apply What You've Learned

 MATHEMATICAL
PRACTICES
MP 4

Look back at the information about the sandwich shops and at the table of data on page 193.

a. Victor plans to use the other shop owner's data to determine the relationship between the number of bags sold, x, and the selling price, s. Does the other shop owner's data set appear to be linear? Explain.

b. Write an equation that models the data in the table. This is Victor's selling-price function.

You can use the following relationship to construct a function that models Victor's profit from selling x bags of chips.

$$\text{Profit} = \text{Revenue} - \text{Cost}$$
$$P(x) = R(x) - C(x)$$

c. Write an equation for Victor's cost function $C(x)$.

d. Victor's revenue will be the selling price times the number of bags sold. Use your result from part (b) to write and simplify an equation for Victor's revenue function $R(x)$.

e. Use your results from parts (c) and (d) to write an equation for Victor's profit function $P(x)$.

f. You have now written four functions. Which functions are linear functions and which are quadratic functions?

Modeling With Quadratic Functions

 Common Core State Standards

F-IF.B.5 Relate the domain of a function to its graph and, where applicable, to the quantitative relationship it describes. **Also F-IF.B.4**

MP 1, MP 3, MP 4

Objective To model data with quadratic functions

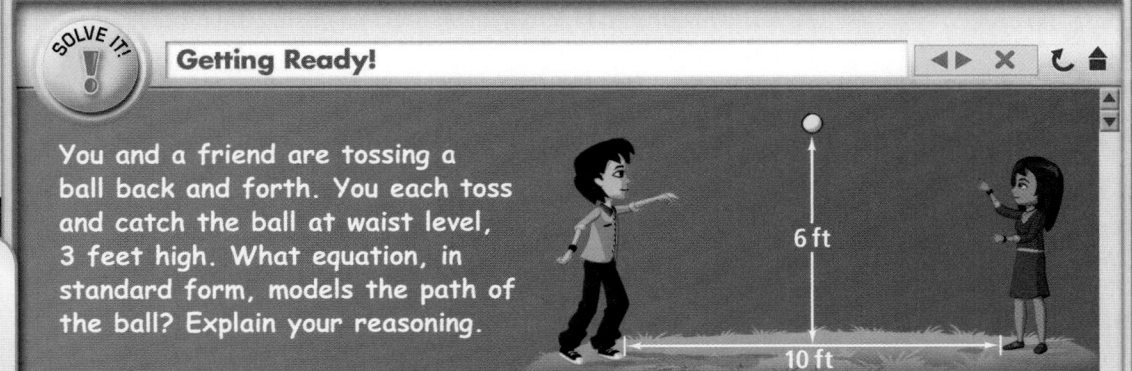

Try making a sketch of the path of the ball based on what you know about projectile motion.

When you know the vertex and a point on a parabola, you can use vertex form to write an equation of the parabola. If you do not know the vertex, you can use standard form and any three points of the parabola to find an equation.

Essential Understanding Three noncollinear points, no two of which are in line vertically, are on the graph of exactly one quadratic function.

Problem 1 Writing an Equation of a Parabola

A parabola contains the points $(0, 0)$, $(-1, -2)$, and $(1, 6)$. What is the equation of this parabola in standard form?

Substitute the (x, y) values into $y = ax^2 + bx + c$ to write a system of equations.

Use $(0, 0)$.	Use $(-1, -2)$.	Use $(1, 6)$.
$y = ax^2 + bx + c$	$y = ax^2 + bx + c$	$y = ax^2 + bx + c$
$0 = a(0)^2 + b(0) + c$	$-2 = a(-1)^2 + b(-1) + c$	$6 = a(1)^2 + b(1) + c$
$0 = c$	$-2 = a - b + c$	$6 = a + b + c$

Since $c = 0$, the resulting system has two variables. $\begin{cases} a - b = -2 \\ a + b = 6 \end{cases}$

Use elimination. $a = 2$ and $b = 4$.

Substitute $a = 2$, $b = 4$, and $c = 0$ into standard form: $y = 2x^2 + 4x + 0$.

$y = 2x^2 + 4x$ is the equation of the parabola that contains the given points.

Plan

How do you use the 3 given points?
Use them to write a system of 3 equations. Solve the system to get a, b, and c.

✓ **Got It?** **1.** What is the equation of a parabola containing the points $(0, 0)$, $(1, -2)$, and $(-1, -4)$?

 **Problem 2** Comparing Quadratic Models STEM

Physics Campers at an aerospace camp launch rockets on the last day of camp. The path of Rocket 1 is modeled by the equation $h = -16t^2 + 150t + 1$ where t is time in seconds and h is the distance from the ground. The path of Rocket 2 is modeled by the graph at the right. Which rocket flew higher?

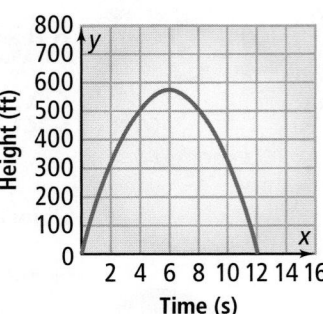

Think

What property of the quadratic tells you how high the rocket flew?
The parabolas model the rockets' paths, so the maximums of each parabola describe how high the rockets flew.

Find the maximum height of each rocket by using the models of their paths.

Rocket 1

The maximum height of Rocket 1 is at the vertex of the parabola.

$$-\frac{b}{2a}, f\left(-\frac{b}{2a}\right)$$ Use the vertex formula.

$$-\frac{150}{2(-16)}, f\left(-\frac{150}{2(-16)}\right)$$ $a = -16, b = 150$

$(4.7, 352.6)$ Simplify.

The maximum height of Rocket 1 is 352.6 feet.

Rocket 2

The maximum height of Rocket 2 is at the vertex of the parabola.

You can use the graph to find the approximate maximum height of the rocket.

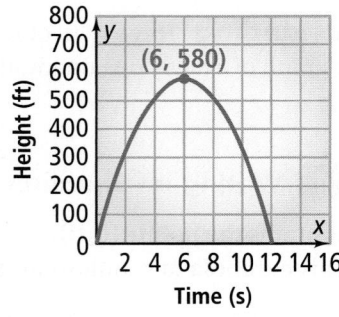

The maximum height of Rocket 2 is at about 580 feet.

Rocket 2 flew higher than Rocket 1.

  Got It? 2. a. Which rocket stayed in the air longer?
  b. What is the reasonable domain and range for each quadratic model?
  c. Reasoning Describe what the domains tell you about each of the models and why the domains for the models are different.

When more than three data points suggest a quadratic function, you can use the quadratic regression feature of a graphing calculator to find a quadratic model.

© **Problem 3** Using Quadratic Regression

The table shows a meteorologist's predicted temperatures for an October day in Sacramento, California.

Sacramento, CA

Time	Predicted Temperature (°F)
8 A.M.	52
10 A.M.	64
12 P.M.	72
2 P.M.	78
4 P.M.	81
6 P.M.	76

Think

How do you write times using a 24-hour clock?
Add 12 to the number of hours past noon. So, 2 P.M. is 14:00 in the 24-hour clock.

A What is a quadratic model for this data?

Step 1 Enter the data. Use the 24-hour clock to represent times after noon.

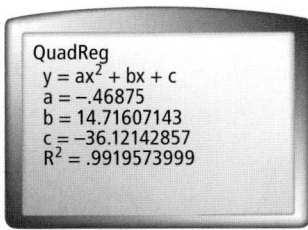

Step 2 Use **QuadReg.**

QuadReg
$y = ax^2 + bx + c$
$a = -.46875$
$b = 14.71607143$
$c = -36.12142857$
$R^2 = .9919573999$

Step 3 Graph the data and the function.

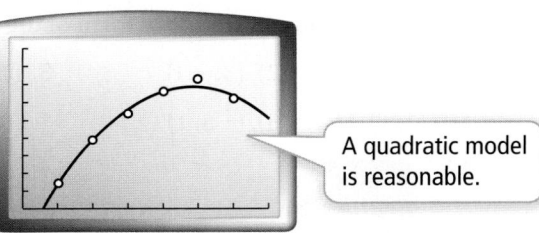

A quadratic model is reasonable.

A quadratic model for temperature is $y = -0.469x^2 + 14.716x - 36.121$.

B Use your model to predict the high temperature for the day. At what time does the high temperature occur?

Use the **Maximum** feature or tables.

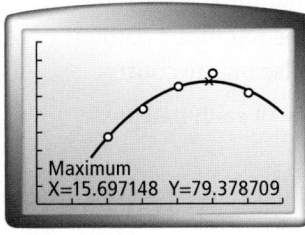

Maximum
X=15.697148 Y=79.378709

X	Y1
15.4	79.337
15.5	79.36
15.6	79.374
15.7	79.379
15.8	79.374
15.9	79.359
16	79.336

Y1=79.3787053571

16 represents 4 P.M. The maximum occurs at approximately 15.7, or about 3:42 P.M.

Predict the high temperature for the day to be 79.4°F at about 3:42 P.M.

Got It? 3. The table shows a meteorologist's predicted temperatures for a summer day in Denver, Colorado. What is a quadratic model for this data? Predict the high temperature for the day. At what time does the high temperature occur?

Denver, CO

Time	Predicted Temperature (°F)
6 A.M.	63
9 A.M.	76
12 P.M.	86
3 P.M.	89
6 P.M.	85
9 P.M.	76

Lesson Check

Do you know HOW?

Find a quadratic function that includes each set of values.

1. $(1, 0), (2, -3), (3, -10)$

2.

x	−2	−1	0	1	2
y	3.5	3.5	7.5	15.5	27.5

3.

x	−2	−1	0	1
y	−41.5	−25.5	−13.5	−5.5

Do you UNDERSTAND?

4. Compare and Contrast How do you know whether to perform a linear regression or a quadratic regression for a given set of data?

5. Reasoning Explain how you can determine which of the quadratic functions in Exercise 1 and Exercise 2 attains the greatest values.

6. Error Analysis Your classmate says he can write the equation of a quadratic function that passes through the points $(3, 4)$, $(5, -2)$, and $(3, 0)$. Explain his error.

Practice and Problem-Solving Exercises

 **Practice**   Find an equation in standard form of the parabola passing through the points.   See Problem 1.

7. $(1, -2), (2, -2), (3, -4)$ **8.** $(1, -2), (2, -4), (3, -4)$ **9.** $(-1, 6), (1, 4), (2, 9)$

10. $(1, 1), (-1, -3), (-3, 1)$ **11.** $(3, -6), (1, -2), (6, 3)$ **12.** $(-2, 9), (-4, 5), (1, 0)$

13.

x	f(x)
−1	−1
1	3
2	8

14.

x	f(x)
−1	17
1	17
2	8

15.

x	f(x)
−1	−4
1	−2
2	−4

16. A player throws a basketball toward a hoop. The basketball follows a parabolic path that can be modeled by the equation $y = -0.125x^2 + 1.84x + 6$. The table models the parabolic path of another basketball thrown from somewhere else on the court.

If the center of the hoop is located at $(12, 10)$, will each ball pass through the hoop?

See Problems 2 and 3.

x	y
2	10
4	12
10	12

STEM **17. Physics** A man throws a ball off the top of a building and records the height of the ball at different times, as shown in the table.
 a. Find a quadratic model for the data.
 b. Use the model to estimate the height of the ball at 2.5 seconds.
 c. What is the ball's maximum height?

Height of a Ball

Time (s)	Height (ft)
0	46
1	63
2	48
3	1

 **Apply**

Determine whether a quadratic model exists for each set of values. If so, write the model.

18. $f(-2) = 16, f(0) = 0, f(1) = 4$ **19.** $f(0) = 5, f(2) = 3, f(-1) = 0$

20. $f(-1) = -4, f(1) = -2, f(2) = -1$ **21.** $f(-2) = 7, f(0) = 1, f(2) = 0$

22. a. Geometry Copy and complete the table. It shows the total number of segments whose endpoints are chosen from x points, no three of which are collinear.

Number of points, x	2	3	■	■
Number of segments, y	1	3	■	■

b. Write a quadratic model for the data.

c. Predict the number of segments that can be drawn using 10 points.

23. Think About a Plan The table shows the height of a column of water as it drains from its container. Use a quadratic model of this data to estimate the water level at 30 seconds.
- What system of equations can you use to solve this problem?
- How can you determine if your answer is reasonable?

Water Levels

Elapsed Time (s)	Water Level (mm)
0	120
20	83
40	50

24. A parabola contains the points $(-1, 8)$, $(0, 4)$, and $(1, 2)$. Name another point also on the parabola.

25. a. Postal Rates Find a quadratic model for the data. Use 1981 as year 0.

Price of First-Class Stamp								
Year	1981	1991	1995	1999	2001	2006	2007	2008
Price (cents)	18	29	32	33	34	39	41	42

SOURCE: United States Postal Service

b. Describe a reasonable domain and range for your model. (*Hint*: This is a discrete, real situation.)

c. Estimation Estimate when first-class postage was 37 cents.

d. Use your model to predict when first-class postage will be 50 cents. Explain why your prediction may not be valid.

26. Road Safety The table and graph below give the stopping distances of an automobile for dry and wet road conditions.

Speed (mi/h)			0	20	30	40	50
Stopping Distance on Dry Roadway (ft)			0	40	75	120	175

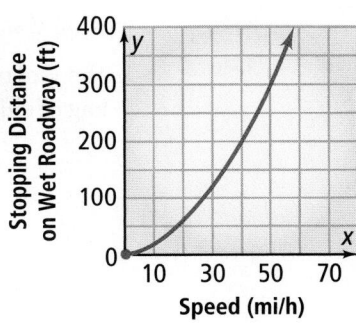

a. Find a quadratic model for the stopping distance of an automobile for each type of road condition.

b. Writing Use your models to compare the stopping distance of an automobile traveling at 65 mph on dry and wet road conditions.

 **Challenge**

27. a. A parabola contains the points $(0, -4)$, $(2, 4)$, and $(4, 4)$. Find the vertex.
    b. Reasoning What is the minimum number of data points you need to find a single quadratic model for a data set? Explain.

28. A model for the height of an arrow shot into the air is $h(t) = -16t^2 + 72t + 5$, where t is time and h is height. Without graphing, answer the following questions.
   a. What can you learn by finding the graph's intercept with the h-axis?
   b. What can you learn by finding the graph's intercept(s) with the t-axis?

Apply What You've Learned

 **MATHEMATICAL PRACTICES**

MP 1

Look back at the information about Victor's sandwich shop on page 193 and at the equations you wrote in the Apply What You've Learned in Lesson 4-2.

From your work in Lesson 4-2, you know that the following function models Victor's profit for selling x bags of chips at selling price s.

$$P(x) = -0.0025x^2 + 1.075x$$

Select all of the following that are true about the function $y = P(x)$ and its graph. Explain your reasoning.

A. The graph is a parabola that opens up and the function has a maximum value.

B. The graph is a parabola that opens down and the function has a maximum value.

C. The graph is a parabola that opens up and the function has a minimum value.

D. The equation of the axis of symmetry is $y = 215$.

E. The x-coordinate of the vertex is 215.

F. The x-coordinate of the vertex is -215.

G. The x-coordinate of the vertex is 430.

H. The x-coordinate of the vertex represents the number of bags of chips Victor should sell to maximize his profit.

I. The y-coordinate of the vertex represents the number of bags of chips Victor should sell to maximize his profit.

J. The y-coordinate of the vertex represents the price Victor should charge for a bag of chips in order to maximize his profit.

Identifying Quadratic Data

 Common Core State Standards

F-IF.B.6 Calculate and interpret the average rate of change of a function . . . Estimate the rate of change from a graph.

MP 7

You can identify perfect quadratic data when x-values are evenly spaced using the pattern in the differences between y-values.

Example

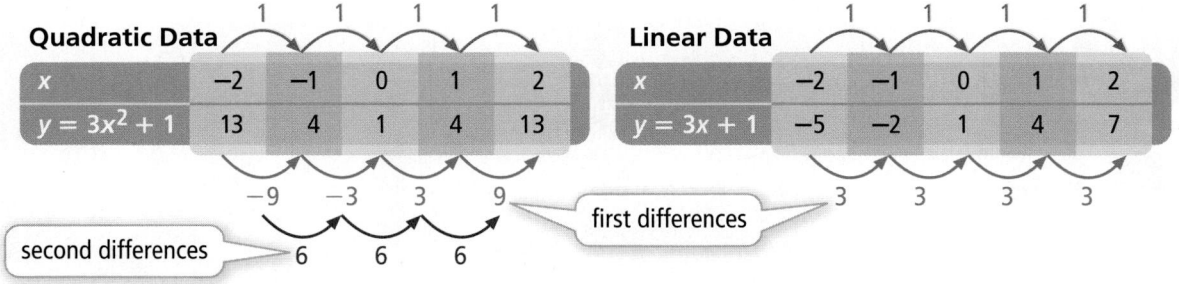

Quadratic Data

x	-2	-1	0	1	2
$y = 3x^2 + 1$	13	4	1	4	13

Linear Data

x	-2	-1	0	1	2
$y = 3x + 1$	-5	-2	1	4	7

For linear data, the *first* differences of adjacent y-values are constant.
For quadratic data, the *second* differences are constant and not equal to 0.

Exercises

Determine if each data set represents perfect quadratic data.

1.

x	1	2	3	4	5	6	7
y	6	12	22	36	54	76	102

2.

x	-2	-1	0	1	2	3	4
y	-8	-1	0	1	8	27	64

© 3. Reasoning Can you use the method above to determine if a data set represents perfect linear or quadratic data if the x-values are *not* evenly spaced? Explain.

4. Recall that the average rate of change over any interval of a function is the slope of the line segment joining the endpoints of the interval.

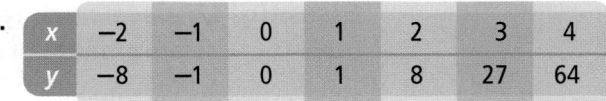

x	-4	-2	0	2	4
y	16	4	0	4	16

    a. The table indicates points on a quadratic function. Use the table to find the average rate of change between the vertex and each of the other points in the table.

    b. As one of the endpoints gets further away from the vertex, what do you notice about the average rate of change?

4-4 Factoring Quadratic Expressions

Common Core State Standards
A-SSE.A.2 Use the structure of an expression to identify ways to rewrite it.
MP 1, MP 3, MP 4

Objectives To find common and binomial factors of quadratic expressions
To factor special quadratic expressions

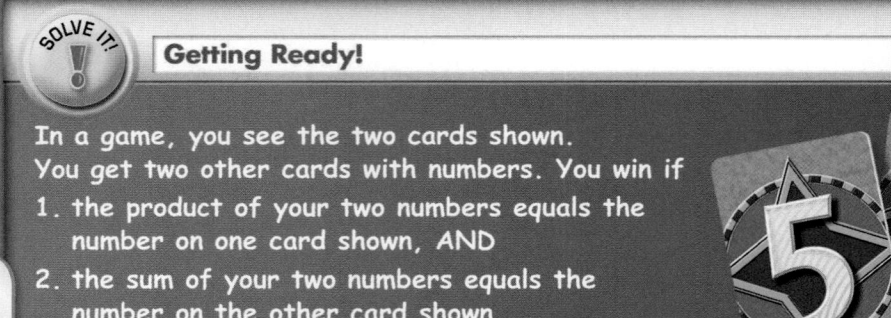

Getting Ready!

In a game, you see the two cards shown.
You get two other cards with numbers. You win if
1. the product of your two numbers equals the number on one card shown, AND
2. the sum of your two numbers equals the number on the other card shown.
What should your two cards be for you to win the game? Is there more than one answer? Explain.

If you have cards numbered 1 to 50, could you play the game with <u>any</u> two cards?

Factors of a given number are numbers that have a product equal to the given number. Factors of a given expression are expressions that have a product equal to the given expression. **Factoring** is rewriting an expression as a product of its factors.

Essential Understanding You can factor many quadratic trinomials $(ax^2 + bx + c)$ into products of two binomials.

You can use the Distributive Property or the FOIL method to multiply two binomials. You can use FOIL in reverse to help you factor.

Lesson Vocabulary
- factoring
- greatest common factor (GCF) of an expression
- perfect square trinomial
- difference of two squares

$$(x + 4)(x + 2) = (x + 4)(x) + (x + 4)(2) \quad \text{Use the Distributive Property.}$$
$$= x(x) + 4(x) + x(2) + 4(2)$$
$$= x^2 + 6x + 8$$

$(x + 4)(x + 2) = x(x) + x(2) + 4(x) + 4(2)$ F: First; O: Outer; I: Inner; L: Last
$$= x^2 + 6x + 8$$

To factor $x^2 + 6x + 8$, think of FOIL in reverse. Find two binomials for which the first terms have the product x^2, the products of the outer and inner terms have the sum $6x$, and the last terms have the product 8.

$$x^2 + 6x + 8 = (x + 4)(x + 2)$$

When you factor, a table of the different possible factors of the constant term may be helpful.

 **Problem 1** Factoring $ax^2 + bx + c$ when $a = \pm1$

What is the expression in factored form?

Plan

How can you make a table to find factors?
Use the first row to list sets of factors of the constant. Use the second row to find the sum of each set of factors.

A $x^2 + 9x + 20$

Step 1 Find factors of 20 with sum 9.

Since both 20 and 9 are positive, both factors are positive.

Factors of 20	1, 20	2, 10	4, 5
Sum of factors	21	12	9

Step 2 Use the factors you found. Write the expression as the product of two binomials.

$$x^2 + 9x + 20 = (x + 4)(x + 5) \quad \text{Use the factors 4 and 5.}$$

B $x^2 + 14x - 72$

Step 1 Find factors of -72 with sum 14.

Since $c < 0$, one factor is positive and the other is negative.
Since $b > 0$, the factor with greater absolute value is positive.

Factors of –72	–1, 72	–2, 36	–3, 24	–4, 18	–6, 12	–8, 9
Sum of factors	71	34	21	14	6	1

Step 2 Use the factors you found, -4 and 18. Write
$x^2 + 14x - 72 = (x - 4)(x + 18)$.

C $-x^2 + 13x - 12$

Think

Will factoring out −1 change the answer?
No; because the final factored expression will include −1 as a factor.

Step 1 Rewrite the expression to show a trinomial with leading coefficient 1.

$$-(x^2 - 13x + 12) \quad \text{Factor out } -1.$$

Step 2 Find factors of 12 with sum -13.

Since $c > 0$, both factors have the same sign.
Since $b < 0$, both factors must be negative.

Factors of 12	–1, –12	–2, –6	–3, –4
Sum of factors	–13	–8	–7

Step 3 Use the factors you found, -1 and -12. Write
$-x^2 + 13x - 12 = -(x^2 - 13x + 12) = -(x - 1)(x - 12)$.

Got It? 1. What is the expression in factored form?

    a. $x^2 + 14x + 40$ **b.** $x^2 - 11x + 30$ **c.** $-x^2 + 14x + 32$

The **greatest common factor (GCF) of an expression** is a common factor of the terms in the expression. It is the common factor with the greatest coefficient and the greatest exponent. You can factor any expression that has a GCF not equal to 1.

 Problem 2 Finding Common Factors

What is the expression in factored form?

Plan

Should you factor out a number, a variable, or both?
Both; the two terms have numerical and variable common factors.

Ⓐ $6n^2 + 9n$

$$6n^2 + 9n = 3n(2n) + 3n(3)$$ Factor out the GCF, $3n$.

$$= 3n(2n + 3)$$ Use the Distributive Property.

Ⓑ $4x^2 + 20x - 56$

$$4x^2 + 20x - 56 = 4(x^2) + 4(5x) - 4(14)$$ Factor out the GCF, 4.

$$= 4(x^2 + 5x - 14)$$ Use the Distributive Property.

$$= 4(x - 2)(x + 7)$$ Factor the trinomial.

Got It? 2. What is the expression in factored form?

    a. $7n^2 - 21$ **b.** $9x^2 + 9x - 18$ **c.** $4x^2 + 8x + 12$

To factor a quadratic trinomial of the form $ax^2 + bx + c$ where $a \neq 1$, and there is no common factor, rewrite the middle term, bx, as two terms. The coefficients of these two terms will be factors of ac that have sum b.

 Problem 3 Factoring $ax^2 + bx + c$ when $|a| \neq 1$

What is the expression in factored form?

Ⓐ $2x^2 + 11x + 12$

    Step 1 Since there is no common factor, find ac.

        $$ac = 2(12) = 24$$

    Step 2 Since both b and ac are positive, find positive factors of 24 that have sum 11.

Think

How should you make your table in this case?
Use the first row to list sets of factors of ac. Use the second row as before, to find the sum of each set of factors.

Factors of 24	1, 24	2, 12	3, 8	4, 6
Sum of factors	25	14	11	10

    Step 3 Factor the trinomial as follows.

        $2x^2 + 11x + 12$

        $2x^2 + 3x + 8x + 12$ Rewrite bx. Since $ac = 24$, try 3 and 8 as coefficients of x.

        $x(2x + 3) + 4(2x + 3)$ Find a common factor for the first two terms and another common factor for the last two terms.

        $(x + 4)(2x + 3)$ Rewrite using the Distributive Property.

B $4x^2 - 4x - 3$

Think

Do you need positive or negative factors?
You need one negative factor and one positive factor.

Step 1 Since there is no common factor, rewrite bx as the sum of two terms with coefficients that are factors of ac, and have sum b.

$$ac = 4(-3) = -12$$

Step 2 Since $ac = -12 < 0$, find factors of ac with opposite signs.
Since $b < 0$, the factor with greater absolute value is negative.

Factors of –12	1, –12	2, –6	3, –4
Sum of factors	–11	–4	–1

Step 3 Factor the trinomial as follows.

$$4x^2 - 4x - 3$$

$$4x^2 + 2x - 6x - 3 \qquad \text{Rewrite } bx \text{ using } b = 2 - 6.$$

$$2x(2x + 1) - 3(2x + 1) \qquad \text{Find a common factor for the first two terms and another common factor for the last two terms.}$$

$$(2x - 3)(2x + 1) \qquad \text{Rewrite using the Distributive Property.}$$

Check $(2x - 3)(2x + 1) = 4x^2 + 2x - 6x - 3$

$$= 4x^2 - 4x - 3 \checkmark$$

Got It? 3. What is the expression in factored form? Check your answers.

a. $4x^2 + 7x + 3$ b. $2x^2 - 7x + 6$

c. **Reasoning** Can you factor the expression $2x^2 + 2x + 2$ into a product of two binomials? Explain.

A **perfect square trinomial** is a trinomial that is the square of a binomial. For example, $x^2 + 10x + 25 = (x + 5)^2$ is a perfect square trinomial.

If $ax^2 + bx + c$ is a perfect square trinomial, then ax^2 and c are squares of the terms of the binomial and thus are both positive. bx is twice the product of the terms of the binomial. b is negative if the binomial terms have opposite signs.

Here is another way to represent the two forms of a perfect square trinomial.

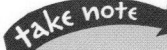 **Key Concept** **Factoring Perfect Square Trinomials**

$$a^2 + 2ab + b^2 = (a + b)^2 \qquad\qquad a^2 - 2ab + b^2 = (a - b)^2$$

 **Problem 4** Factoring a Perfect Square Trinomial

What is $4x^2 - 24x + 36$ in factored form?

Think

Write the expression.

You can do this in one step.

Is the first term a perfect square?
Yes, $4x^2$ is $(2x)^2$.

Is the last term a perfect square?
Yes, 36 is 6^2.

Is the middle term twice the product of 6 and $2x$?
Yes $2 \cdot 6 \cdot 2x = 24x$

There's a minus sign in the middle.
You are done.

You should check.

Write

$4x^2 - 24x + 36$

$(2x - 6)^2$

$(2x - 6)^2 = 4x^2 - 24x + 36$ ✔

 Got It? **4.** What is $64x^2 - 16x + 1$ in factored form?

The expression $a^2 - b^2$ is the **difference of two squares**. There is a pattern to its factors.

take note

Key Concept Factoring a Difference of Two Squares

$$a^2 - b^2 = (a + b)(a - b)$$

Think

How can a binomial be the product of two binomials?
If the outer and inner products of the binomials are opposites, their sum is zero.

 **Problem 5** Factoring a Difference of Two Squares

What is $25x^2 - 49$ in factored form?

$25x^2 - 49 = (5x)^2 - 7^2$ Write as the difference of two squares.

$\qquad\qquad = (5x + 7)(5x - 7)$ Use the pattern for factoring a difference of two squares.

 Got It? **5.** What is $16x^2 - 81$ in factored form?

Lesson Check

Do you know HOW?

Factor each expression.

1. $x^2 + 6x + 8$

2. $x^2 - 13x + 12$

3. $x^2 - 81$

4. $25y^2 - 36$

5. $y^2 - 6y + 9$

6. $4x^2 - 4x + 1$

Find the GCF of each expression.

7. $15x^2 - 25x$

8. $4a^3 + 8a^2$

9. $18b^2 - 12b + 24$

10. $21h^3 + 35h^2 - 28h$

Do you UNDERSTAND?

11. Vocabulary Is $4b^2 - 26b + 169$ a perfect square trinomial? Explain.

12. Compare and Contrast How is factoring a trinomial $ax^2 + bx + c$ when $a \neq 1$ different from factoring a trinomial when $a = 1$? How is it similar?

13. Reasoning Explain how to rewrite the expression $a^2 - 2ab + b^2 - 25$ as the product of two trinomial factors. (*Hint:* Group the first three terms. What type of expression is this?)

Practice and Problem-Solving Exercises

 **Practice**

Factor each expression.

See Problem 1.

14. $x^2 + 3x + 2$

15. $x^2 + 5x + 6$

16. $x^2 + 7x + 10$

17. $x^2 + 10x + 16$

18. $y^2 + 15y + 36$

19. $x^2 + 22x + 40$

20. $x^2 - 3x + 2$

21. $-x^2 + 13x - 12$

22. $-r^2 + 11r - 18$

23. $x^2 - 10x + 24$

24. $d^2 - 12d + 27$

25. $x^2 - 13x + 36$

26. $x^2 - 5x - 14$

27. $-x^2 - x + 20$

28. $-x^2 + 3x + 40$

29. $c^2 + 2c - 63$

30. $x^2 + 10x - 75$

31. $-t^2 + 7t + 44$

Find the GCF of each expression. Then factor the expression.

See Problem 2.

32. $3a^2 + 9$

33. $25b^2 - 20b$

34. $x^2 - 2x$

35. $5t^2 - 5t - 10$

36. $14y^2 + 7y - 21$

37. $27p^2 - 9p + 18$

Factor each expression.

See Problem 3.

38. $3x^2 + 31x + 36$

39. $2x^2 - 19x + 24$

40. $5r^2 + 23r + 26$

41. $2m^2 - 11m + 15$

42. $5t^2 + 28t + 32$

43. $2x^2 - 27x + 36$

44. $3x^2 + 7x - 20$

45. $5y^2 + 12y - 32$

46. $7x^2 - 8x - 12$

Factor each expression that can be factored. For an expression that cannot be factored into a product of two binomials, explain why.

See Problems 4 and 5.

47. $x^2 + 2x + 1$

48. $t^2 - 14t + 49$

49. $k^2 - 18k + 81$

50. $4z^2 - 20z + 25$

51. $4x^2 + 16x + 8$

52. $81z^2 + 36z + 4$

53. $x^2 - 4$

54. $25a^2 - 120a + 144$

55. $81y^2 + 49$

Apply

56. Think About a Plan Suppose you cut a small square from a square sheet of cardboard. Find the sides of one rectangle whose area is equal to the area of the remaining part.
- How can you represent the remaining part as a combination of rectangles with known sides?
- Can you factor the resulting expression?

57. The area in square centimeters of a square area rug is $25x^2 - 10x + 1$. What are the dimensions of the rug in terms of x?

Factor each expression completely.

58. $9x^2 - 36$

59. $18z^2 - 8$

60. $4n^2 - 20n + 24$

61. $64t^2 - 16$

62. $12x^2 + 36x + 27$

63. $3y^2 + 24y + 45$

64. $2a^2 - 16a + 32$

65. $3x^2 - 24x - 27$

66. $-x^2 + 5x - 4$

67. $4x^2 - 22x + 10$

68. $-6z^2 - 600$

69. $-\frac{1}{16}s^2 + 1$

70. a. Multiply $(a + b)(a - b)(a^2 + b^2)$.
   b. Use your result from part (a) to completely factor $81x^4 - 256y^4$.

71. Error Analysis Your friend attempted to factor an expression as shown. Find the error in your friend's work. Then factor the expression correctly.

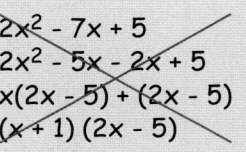

72. Agriculture The area in square feet of a rectangular field is $x^2 - 120x + 3500$. The width, in feet, is $x - 50$. What is the length, in feet?

Find the GCF of each expression. Then factor the expression.

73. $y^2 - y$

74. $ab^2 - b$

75. $10x^2 - 90$

76. $3t^2 - 24t$

77. $2x^2 - 74x + 12$

78. $x^2y^2 + xy$

79. What is the factored form of $4x^2 + 15x - 4$?
   - (A) $(2x + 2)(2x - 2)$
   - (C) $(4x + 1)(x - 4)$
   - (B) $(2x - 4)(2x + 1)$
   - (D) $(4x - 1)(x + 4)$

80. Geometry What is the volume of the shaded pipe with outer radius R, inner radius r, and height h as shown? Express your answer in completely factored form.

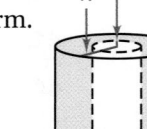

81. Open-Ended Write a quadratic trinomial that you can factor, where $a \neq 1$, $ac > 0$, and $b < 0$. Factor the expression.

82. Writing Explain how to factor $3x^2 + 6x - 72$ completely.

 **Challenge**

Factor each expression completely.

83. $0.25t^2 - 0.16$

84. $8100x^2 - 10{,}000$

85. $(x + 3)^2 + 3(x + 3) - 54$

86. $(x - 2)^2 - 15(x - 2) + 56$

87. $6(x + 5)^2 - 5(x + 5) + 1$

88. $3(2a - 3)^2 + 17(2a - 3) + 10$

89. Reasoning Explain how to factor $4x^4 + 24x^3 + 32x^2$.

Factor each expression completely.

90. $\frac{1}{16}x^4 - y^4$ **91.** $16x^4 - 625y^4$ **92.** $243a^5 - 3a$

93. When the expression $x^2 + bx - 24$ is factored completely, the difference of the factors is 11. Find both factors if it is known that b is negative.

94. Prove that $n^3 - n$ is divisible by 3 for all positive integer values of n.
(*Hint:* Factor the expression completely.)

Standardized Test Prep

SAT/ACT

95. How can you write $(m - 5)(m + 4) + 8$ as a product of two binomials?

    Ⓐ $(m - 1)(m + 8)$ Ⓒ $(m + 8)(m + 8)$

    Ⓑ $(m - 4)(m + 3)$ Ⓓ $(m - 5)(8m + 32)$

96. The graph of a quadratic function has vertex $(7, 6)$. What is the axis of symmetry?

    Ⓕ $x = 6$ Ⓖ $y = 6$ Ⓗ $x = 7$ Ⓘ $y = 7$

Extended Response

97. Suppose you hit a baseball and its flight takes a parabolic path. The height of the ball at certain times appears in the table below.

Time (s)	0.5	0.75	1	1.25
Height (ft)	10	10.5	9	5.5

   a. Find a quadratic model for the ball's height as a function of time.
   b. Write the quadratic function in factored form.

Mixed Review

98. Find a quadratic model for the values in the table.

x	0	5	10	15	20
y	17	39	54	61	61

◀ See Lesson 4-3.

99. Coins The combined mass of a penny, a nickel, and a dime is 9.8 g. Ten nickels and three pennies have the same mass as 25 dimes. Fifty dimes have the same mass as 18 nickels and 10 pennies. Write and solve a system of equations to find the mass of each type of coin.

◀ See Lesson 3-6.

Get Ready!   **To prepare for Lesson 4-5, do Exercises 100–102.**

Graph each function.   ◀ See Lesson 4-2.

100. $y = x^2 - 2x - 5$ **101.** $y = x^2 - 4x + 4$ **102.** $y = -x^2 - 3x + 8$

Do you know HOW?

Graph each function.

1. $y = 4x^2 + 16x + 7$

2. $y = (x + 8)^2 - 3$

3. $y = -(x + 2)^2 - 7$

4. $y = -3x^2 - 2x + 1$

Identify the axis of symmetry, maximum or minimum value, and the domain and range of each function.

5. $y = -x^2 + 6x + 5$

6. $y = \frac{1}{2}(x - 6)^2 + 7$

7. $y = -3(x + 2)^2 + 1$

8. $y = 4x^2 - 8x$

9. Rewrite the equation $y = -3x^2 - 6x - 8$ in vertex form. Identify the vertex and the axis of symmetry of the graph.

Write each expression in factored form.

10. $16 - 2m^2$

11. $-x^2 + 3x$

12. $y^2 - 13y + 12$

13. $k^2 - 5k - 24$

14. $4y^2 - 9$

15. $-10n + 25 + n^2$

16. $2x^2 + 7x + 6$

Find a quadratic model in standard form for each set of values.

17. $(0, 3), (1, 10), (2, 19)$

18. $(0, 0), (1, -5), (2, 0)$

Write the equation of each parabola in vertex form.

19.

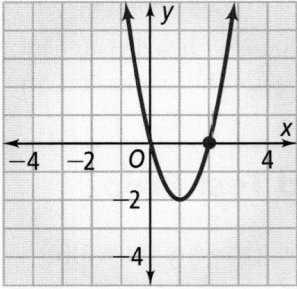

20.

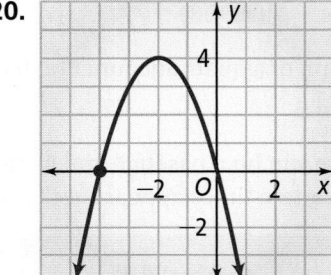

Do you UNDERSTAND?

21. Write the expression $3x^4 - 12x^3 - 36x^2$ in factored form. Explain how you know the expression is completely factored.

Ⓒ **22. Open-Ended** Write the equation of a parabola with a vertex at $(3, 2)$. Name the axis of symmetry and the coordinates of two other points on the graph.

Ⓒ **23. Writing** Explain how to factor $25x^2 - 30x + 9$.

Ⓒ **24. Reasoning** Write the equations of two parabolas that have a common vertex and are reflections of each other across the x-axis.

25. Write the equation of a parabola in standard form and explain how to convert it to vertex form. How would you reverse the process?

26. What is the relationship between the x-intercepts of the graph of a quadratic function and the x-coordinate of the vertex of that graph? Explain how you determined your answer.

Square Roots and Radicals

 Common Core State Standards

Prepares for N-RN.A.2 Rewrite expressions involving radicals and rational exponents using the properties of exponents.

A radical symbol $\sqrt{}$ indicates a square root. In general, $\sqrt{x^2} = |x|$ for all real numbers x.

Square Roots

Multiplication Property of Square Roots

For any numbers $a \geq 0$ and $b \geq 0$,

$$\sqrt{ab} = \sqrt{a} \cdot \sqrt{b}.$$

Division Property of Square Roots

For any numbers $a \geq 0$ and $b > 0$,

$$\sqrt{\frac{a}{b}} = \frac{\sqrt{a}}{\sqrt{b}}.$$

Example

Simplify each expression.

A $\sqrt{50}$

$\sqrt{50} = \sqrt{25} \cdot \sqrt{2}$ Multiplication Property of Square Roots

$\phantom{\sqrt{50}} = 5\sqrt{2}$ Simplify.

B $\sqrt{\frac{5}{11}}$

$\sqrt{\frac{5}{11}} = \frac{\sqrt{5}}{\sqrt{11}}$ Division Property of Square Roots

$\phantom{\sqrt{\frac{5}{11}}} = \frac{\sqrt{5}}{\sqrt{11}} \cdot \frac{\sqrt{11}}{\sqrt{11}}$ Multiply both the numerator and denominator by $\sqrt{11}$.

$\phantom{\sqrt{\frac{5}{11}}} = \frac{\sqrt{55}}{\sqrt{121}}$ Multiplication Property of Square Roots

$\phantom{\sqrt{\frac{5}{11}}} = \frac{\sqrt{55}}{11}$ Simplify.

Exercises

Simplify each radical expression.

1. $\sqrt{18}$ **2.** $\sqrt{75}$ **3.** $-\sqrt{32}$ **4.** $\sqrt{\frac{-5}{7}}$

5. $-\sqrt{\frac{7}{13}}$ **6.** $\sqrt{\frac{3}{15}}$ **7.** $-\sqrt{200}$ **8.** $5\sqrt{320}$

9. $(2\sqrt{27})^2$ **10.** $-\sqrt{10^4}$ **11.** $\sqrt{x^2y^2}$ **12.** $\sqrt{\frac{8}{x^2}}$

13. $-\sqrt{\frac{7x^3}{5x}}$ **14.** $\sqrt{\frac{(-3)^4}{12}}$ **15.** $\sqrt{\frac{200}{28}}$ **16.** $\sqrt{120x}$

4-5 Quadratic Equations

 Common Core State Standards
A-CED.A.1 Create equations and inequalities in one variable and use them to solve problems. **Also A-SSE.A.1a, A-APR.B.3, A-SSE.B.3a**
MP 1, MP 2, MP 3, MP 4, MP 5, MP 8

Objectives To solve quadratic equations by factoring
To solve quadratic equations by graphing

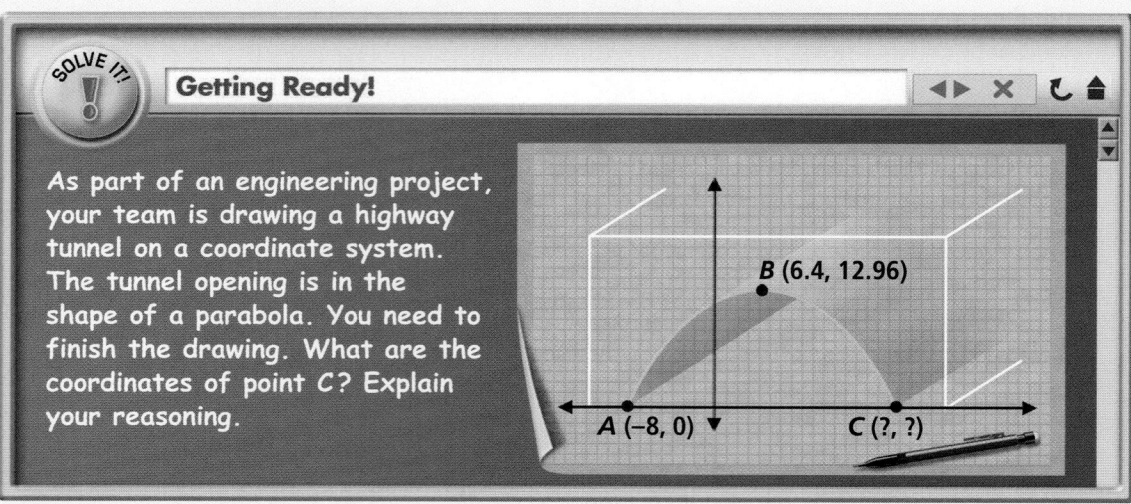

Getting Ready!

As part of an engineering project, your team is drawing a highway tunnel on a coordinate system. The tunnel opening is in the shape of a parabola. You need to finish the drawing. What are the coordinates of point C? Explain your reasoning.

B (6.4, 12.96)

A (−8, 0)   C (?, ?)

 **Lesson Vocabulary**
• zero of a function
• Zero-Product Property

Wherever the graph of a function $f(x)$ intersects the x-axis, $f(x) = 0$. A value of x for which $f(x) = 0$ is a **zero of the function**.

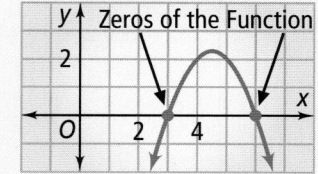

Essential Understanding To find the zeros of a quadratic function $y = ax^2 + bx + c$, solve the related quadratic equation $0 = ax^2 + bx + c$.

You can solve some quadratic equations in standard form by factoring the quadratic expression and using the **Zero-Product Property**.

 take note

Property Zero-Product Property

If $ab = 0$, then $a = 0$ or $b = 0$.

Think
What do you know about the factors of $x^2 − bx + c$?
The product of their constant terms is c. The sum is $−b$.

Problem 1 **Solving a Quadratic Equation by Factoring**

What are the solutions of the quadratic equation $x^2 − 5x + 6 = 0$?

$(x − 2)(x − 3) = 0$ Factor the quadratic expression.

$x − 2 = 0$ or $x − 3 = 0$ Use the Zero-Product Property.

$x = 2$ or $x = 3$ Solve for x.

The solutions are $x = 2$ and $x = 3$.

Got It? **1.** What are the solutions of the quadratic equation $x^2 - 7x = -12$?

 Problem 2 Solving a Quadratic Equation With Tables

What are the solutions of the quadratic equation $5x^2 + 30x + 14 = 2 - 2x$?

$$5x^2 + 30x + 14 = 2 - 2x$$

$$5x^2 + 32x + 12 = 0 \qquad \text{Rewrite in standard form.}$$

Use your calculator's **TABLE** feature to find the zeros.

Think

What should you look for in the calculator table?
Look for x-values for which $y = 0$.

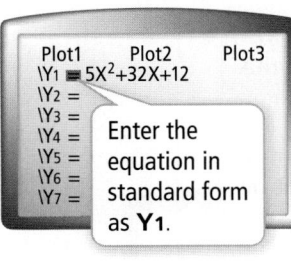

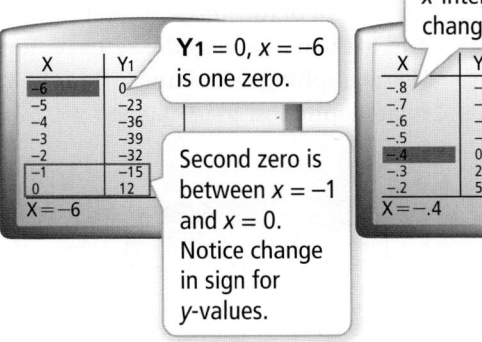

The solutions are $x = -6$ and $x = -0.4$.

 Got It? **2.** What are the solutions of the quadratic equation $4x^2 - 14x + 7 = 4 - x$?

 Problem 3 Solving a Quadratic Equation by Graphing

What are the solutions of the quadratic equation $2x^2 + 7x = 15$?

$$2x^2 + 7x = 15$$

$$2x^2 + 7x - 15 = 0 \qquad \text{Rewrite in standard form.}$$

Plan

How can you use a graph to find the solutions?
Find the zeros of the related quadratic function.

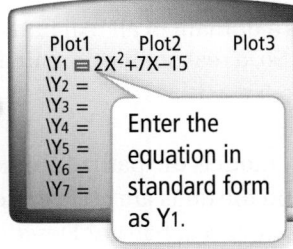

The solutions are $x = -5$ and $x = 1.5$.

 Got It? **3.** What are the solutions of the quadratic equation $x^2 + 2x - 24 = 0$?

$Y_1 = -.029X^2 + .59X$

Problem 4 Using a Quadratic Equation

Competition From the time Mark Twain wrote *The Celebrated Jumping Frog of Calaveras County* in 1865, frog-jumping competitions have been growing in popularity. The graph shows a function modeling the height of one frog's jump, where x is the distance, in feet, from the jump's start.

Think

How can you use a graphing calculator to determine the distance?
Graph the function and locate the point where the graph crosses the x-axis.

A **How far did the frog jump?**

The height of the jump is 0 at the start and end of the jump. Find the zeros of the function. Use a graphing calculator to find the zeros of the related function $y = -0.029x^2 + 0.59x$.

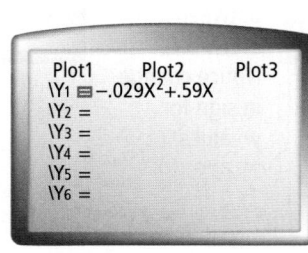

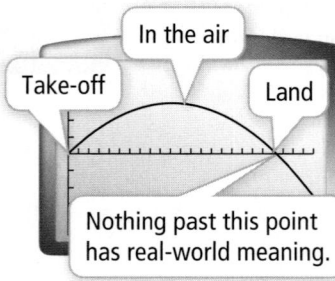

In the air

Take-off

Land

Nothing past this point has real-world meaning.

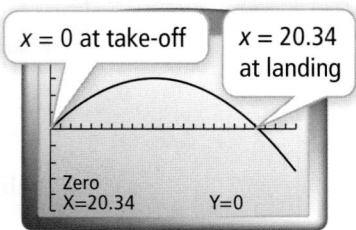

$x = 0$ at take-off

$x = 20.34$ at landing

Zero
X=20.34   Y=0

The frog jumped about 20.34 ft.

B **How high did the frog jump?**

The maximum height of the jump is the maximum value of the function. This occurs midway, at 10.17 ft from the start. Find y for $x = 10.17$.

$$y = -0.029(10.17)^2 + 0.59(10.17) \approx 3.0$$

The frog jumped to a height of about 3.0 ft.

C **What is a reasonable domain and range for such a frog-jumping function?**

While the function $y = -0.029x^2 + 0.59x$ has a domain of all real numbers, actual frog jumping does not allow negative values. So, a reasonable domain for frog-jumping distances is $0 \le x \le 30$. A reasonable range is $0 \le y \le 5$.

  Got It? **4. a.** The function $y = -0.03x^2 + 1.60x$ models the path of a kicked soccer ball. The height is y, the distance is x, and the units are meters. How far does the soccer ball travel? How high does the soccer ball go? Describe a reasonable domain and range for the function.

b. Reasoning Are all domains and ranges reasonable for real-world situations? Explain.

Lesson Check

Do you know HOW?

Solve each equation by factoring.

1. $x^2 - 9 = 0$

2. $x^2 + 13x = -36$

3. $3x^2 - x - 2 = 0$

Solve by graphing.

4. $x^2 - 3x = 6$

5. $2x^2 - x = 11$

Do you UNDERSTAND?

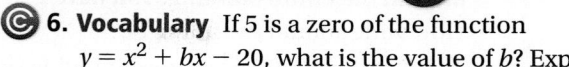 **6. Vocabulary** If 5 is a zero of the function $y = x^2 + bx - 20$, what is the value of b? Explain.

7. Compare and Contrast When is it easier to solve a quadratic equation by factoring than to solve it using a table?

8. Reasoning Using tables, how might you recognize that a quadratic equation likely has exactly one solution? no solutions?

Practice and Problem-Solving Exercises

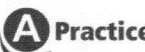 **Practice** Solve each equation by factoring. Check your answers. 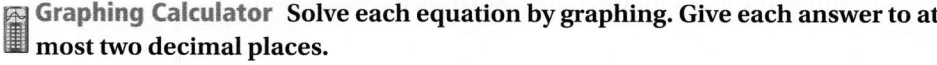 See Problem 1.

9. $x^2 + 6x + 8 = 0$ **10.** $x^2 + 18 = 9x$ **11.** $2x^2 - x = 3$

12. $x^2 - 10x + 25 = 0$ **13.** $2x^2 + 6x = -4$ **14.** $3x^2 = 16x + 12$

15. $x^2 - 4x = 0$ **16.** $6x^2 + 4x = 0$ **17.** $2x^2 = 8x$

Graphing Calculator Solve each equation using tables. Give each answer to at most two decimal places. See Problem 2.

18. $x^2 + 5x + 3 = 0$ **19.** $x^2 - 11x + 24 = 0$ **20.** $x^2 - 7x = 11$

21. $2x^2 - x = 2$ **22.** $x^2 - 16x = 36$ **23.** $x^2 + 6x = 40$

24. $4x^2 = x + 3$ **25.** $5x^2 + x = 4$ **26.** $10x^2 + 3 = 11x$

Graphing Calculator Solve each equation by graphing. Give each answer to at most two decimal places. See Problem 3.

27. $6x^2 = -19x - 15$ **28.** $3x^2 - 5x - 4 = 0$ **29.** $5x^2 - 7x - 3 = 8$

30. $6x^2 + 31x = 12$ **31.** $1 = 4x^2 + 3x$ **32.** $\frac{1}{2}x^2 - x = 8$

33. $x^2 = 4x + 8$ **34.** $x^2 + 4x = 6$ **35.** $2x^2 - 2x - 5 = 0$

STEM 36. Physics The function $h = -16t^2 + 1700$ gives an object's height h, See Problem 4.
in feet, at t seconds.
  a. What does the constant 1700 tell you about the height of the object?
  b. What does the coefficient of t^2 tell you about the direction the object is moving?
  c. When will the object be 1000 ft above the ground?
  d. When will the object be 940 ft above the ground?
  e. What are a reasonable domain and range for the function h?

37. Think About a Plan Suppose you want to put a frame around the painting shown at the right. The frame will be the same width around the entire painting. You have 276 in.^{2} of framing material. How wide should the frame be?

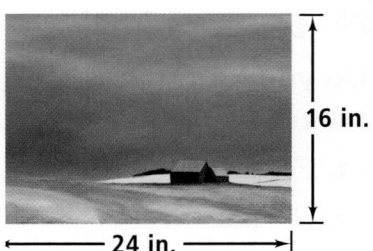

16 in.

24 in.

• What does 276 in.^{2} represent in this situation?
• How can you write the dimensions of the frame using two binomials?

38. The period of a pendulum is the time the pendulum takes to swing back and forth. The function $L = 0.81t^2$ relates the length L in feet of a pendulum to the time t in seconds that it takes to swing back and forth. A convention center has a pendulum that is 90 feet long. Find the period.

39. Landscaping Suppose you have an outdoor pool measuring 25 ft by 10 ft. You want to add a cement walkway around the pool. If the walkway will be 1 ft thick and you have 304 ft^3 of cement, how wide should the walkway be?

40. Error Analysis A classmate solves the quadratic equation as shown. Find and correct the error. What are the correct solutions?

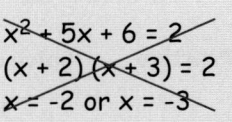

$$x^2 + 5x + 6 = 2$$
$$(x + 2)(x + 3) = 2$$
$$x = -2 \text{ or } x = -3$$

41. Open-Ended Write an equation with the given solutions.
a. 3 and 5   **b.** −3 and 2   **c.** −1 and −6

Solve each equation by factoring, using tables, or by graphing. If necessary, round your answer to the nearest hundredth.

42. $x^2 + 2x = 6 - 6x$ **43.** $6x^2 + 13x + 6 = 0$ **44.** $2x^2 + x - 28 = 0$

45. $2x^2 + 8x = 5x + 20$ **46.** $3x^2 + 7x = 9$ **47.** $2x^2 - 6x = 8$

48. $(x + 3)^2 = 9$ **49.** $x^2 + 4x = 0$ **50.** $x^2 = 8x - 7$

51. $x^2 - 3x = 6$ **52.** $4x^2 + 5x = 4$ **53.** $7x - 3x^2 = -10$

Reasoning The graphs of each pair of functions intersect. Find their points of intersection without using a calculator. (*Hint:* Solve as a system using substitution.)

54. $y = x^2$
$y = -\frac{1}{2}x^2 + \frac{3}{2}x + 3$

55. $y = x^2 - 2$
$y = 3x^2 - 4x - 2$

56. $y = -x^2 + x + 4$
$y = 2x^2 - 6$

C Challenge

57. The equation $x^2 - 10x + 24 = 0$ can be written in factored form as $(x - 4)(x - 6) = 0$. How can you use this fact to find the vertex of the graph of $y = x^2 - 10x + 24$?

58. a. Let $a > 0$. Use algebraic or arithmetic ideas to explain why the lowest point on the graph of $y = a(x - h)^2 + k$ must occur when $x = h$.
b. Suppose that the function in part (a) is $y = a(x - h)^3 + k$. Is your reasoning still valid? Explain.

STEM **59. Physics** When serving in tennis, a player tosses the tennis ball vertically in the air. The height h of the ball after t seconds is given by the quadratic function $h(t) = -5t^2 + 7t$ (the height is measured in meters from the point of the toss).

a. How high in the air does the ball go?

b. Assume that the player hits the ball on its way down when it's 0.6 m above the point of the toss. For how many seconds is the ball in the air between the toss and the serve?

Standardized Test Prep

SAT/ACT

60. What are the solutions of the equation $6x^2 + 9x - 15 = 0$?

Ⓐ $1, -15$ Ⓑ $1, -\frac{5}{2}$ Ⓒ $-1, -5$ Ⓓ $3, \frac{5}{2}$

61. The vertex of a parabola is $(3, 2)$. A second point on the parabola is $(1, 7)$. Which point is also on the parabola?

Ⓕ $(-1, 7)$ Ⓖ $(3, 7)$ Ⓗ $(5, 7)$ Ⓘ $(3, -2)$

62. For which quadratic function is -3 the constant term?

Ⓐ $y = (3x + 1)(-x - 3)$ Ⓒ $f(x) = (x - 3)(x - 3)$

Ⓑ $y = x^2 - 3x + 3$ Ⓓ $g(x) = -3x^2 + 3x + 9$

Short Response

63. What transformations are needed to go from the parent function $f(x) = x^2$ to the new function $g(x) = -3x^2 + 2$? Graph $g(x)$.

Apply What You've Learned

MATHEMATICAL
PRACTICES

MP 2

Look back at the information about Victor's sandwich shop on page 193 and at the equations you wrote in the Apply What You've Learned in Lesson 4-2. Your equations should be equivalent to the ones shown below.

$s = -0.0025x + 1.375$, where x is the number of bags sold at selling price s
$C(x) = 0.3x$
$R(x) = -0.0025x^2 + 1.375x$
$P(x) = -0.0025x^2 + 1.075x$

a. Write the function $P(x) = -0.0025x^2 + 1.075x$ in factored form, and use the factored form to find the zeros of $P(x)$.

b. What information do the zeros you found in part (a) give you about the graph of $P(x) = -0.0025x^2 + 1.075x$?

c. What information do the zeros you found in part (a) give you about Victor's profit?

d. Use the revenue and cost equations you wrote in the Apply What You Learned in Lesson 4-2. For each zero z of the profit function, what should be true about $C(z)$ and $R(z)$? Why? To confirm your answer, evaluate $C(z)$ and $R(z)$ for each zero z.

Concept Byte

For Use With Lesson 4-5

Writing Equations From Roots

© Common Core State Standards

A-CED.A.2 Create equations in two or more variables to represent relationships between quantities; graph equations on coordinate axes with labels and scales.

MP 8

A **root** of an equation is a value that makes the equation true. You can use the Zero-Product Property to write a quadratic function from its zeros or a quadratic equation from its roots.

Activity 1

1. a. Write a nonzero linear function $f(x)$ that has a zero at $x = 3$.
   b. Write a nonzero linear function $g(x)$ that has a zero at $x = 4$.

2. a. For f and g from Exercise 1, write the product function $h(x) = f(x) \cdot g(x)$.
   b. What kind of function is $h(x)$?   **c.** Solve the equation $h(x) = 0$.

© Mental Math **Write a quadratic equation with each pair of values as roots.**

3. 5 and 3   **4.** 2.5 and 4   **5.** −4 and 4   **6.** 5 and 10   **7.** $\frac{3}{2}$ and −2

You can also use zeros or roots to write quadratic expressions in standard form.

Activity 2

8. a. Copy and complete the table. Write the product $(x - a)(x - b)$ in standard form for each pair a and b.
   b. Is there a pattern in the table? Explain.

9. a. If you know the roots, you can write a quadratic function or equation in standard form. Explain how.
   b. Demonstrate your method for each pair of values in Exercises 3–7.

a	b	$a + b$	ab	$(x - a)(x - b)$
4	5	9	20	$x^2 - 9x + 20$
−4	5	1	−20	■
4	−5	■	■	■
−4	−5	■	■	■
−9	−1	■	■	■
−2	7	■	■	■

Exercises

10. Explain how to write a quadratic equation that has −6 as its only root.

11. Describe the family of quadratic functions that have zeros at r and s. Sketch several members of the family in the coordinate plane.

Find the sum and product of the roots for each quadratic equation.

12. $2x^2 + 3x - 2 = 0$ **13.** $x^2 - 2x + 1 = 0$ **14.** $x^2 - 5x + 6 = 0$

Given the sum and product of the roots, write a quadratic equation in standard form.

15. sum = −3, product = −18   **16.** sum = 4, product = 3   **17.** sum = 2, product = $\frac{3}{4}$

4-6 Completing the Square

© **Common Core State Standards**
Reviews A-REI.B.4b Solve quadratic equations by . . . completing the square . . .
MP 1, MP 3, MP 4

Objectives To solve equations by completing the square
To rewrite functions by completing the square

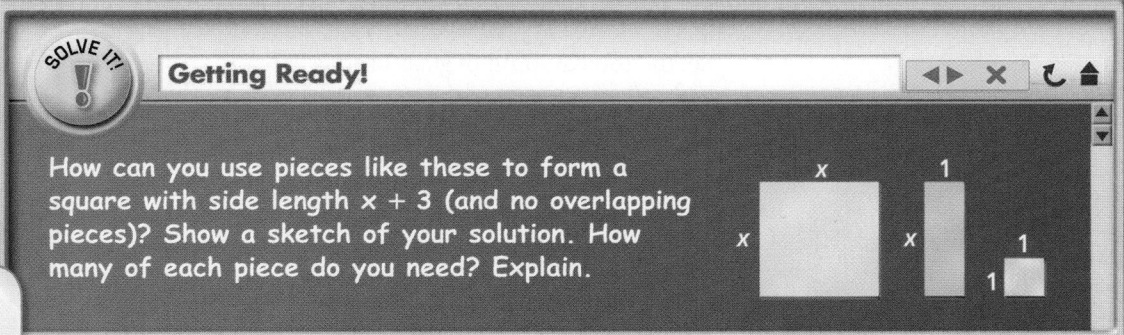

Getting Ready!

How can you use pieces like these to form a square with side length $x + 3$ (and no overlapping pieces)? Show a sketch of your solution. How many of each piece do you need? Explain.

Can you write the area of your square in two ways?

© **MATHEMATICAL PRACTICES** Forming a square with model pieces provides a useful geometric image for completing a square algebraically.

Lesson Vocabulary
• completing the square

Essential Understanding Completing a perfect square trinomial allows you to factor the completed trinomial as the square of a binomial.

You can solve an equation that contains a perfect square by finding square roots. The simplest of this type of equation has the form $ax^2 = c$.

© **Problem 1** Solving by Finding Square Roots

Plan

How is solving this equation like solving a linear equation?
You isolate the variable term.

What is the solution of each equation?

A $4x^2 + 10 = 46$

$4x^2 = 36$ ← Rewrite in $ax^2 = c$ form. →

$\dfrac{4x^2}{4} = \dfrac{36}{4}$ ← Isolate x^2. →

$x^2 = 9$

$x = \pm 3$ ← Find square roots. →

B $3x^2 - 5 = 25$

$3x^2 = 30$

$\dfrac{3x^2}{3} = \dfrac{30}{3}$

$x^2 = 10$

$x = \pm \sqrt{10}$

✓ **Got It?** **1.** What is the solution of each equation?

a. $7x^2 - 10 = 25$

b. $2x^2 + 9 = 13$

Problem 2 Determining Dimensions **STEM**

Architecture While designing a house, an architect used windows like the one shown here. What are the dimensions of the window if it has 2766 square inches of glass?

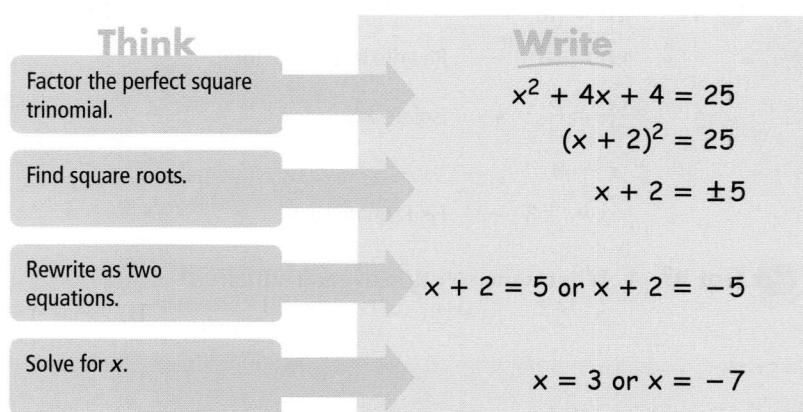

Step 1 Find the area of the window.

The area of the rectangular part is $(2x)(x) = 2x^2$ in.^{2}.

The area of the semicircular part is

$$\tfrac{1}{2}\pi r^2 = \tfrac{1}{2}\pi\left(\tfrac{x}{2}\right)^2 = \tfrac{1}{2}\pi\tfrac{x^2}{4} = \tfrac{\pi}{8}x^2 \text{ in.}^2.$$

So, the total amount of glass used is

$2x^2 + \tfrac{\pi}{8}x^2 = 2766$ in.^{2}.

Step 2 Solve for x.

$$\left(2 + \tfrac{\pi}{8}\right)x^2 = 2766 \qquad \text{Write the equation in } ax^2 = c \text{ form.}$$

$$x^2 = \frac{2766}{2 + \tfrac{\pi}{8}} \qquad \text{Isolate } x^2.$$

$$x \approx \pm 34 \qquad \text{Find square roots. Use a calculator.}$$

Length cannot be negative. So the rectangular portion of the window is 34 in. wide by 68 in. long. The semicircular top has a radius of 17 in.

Think

Is the answer reasonable?
Yes; the rectangular part is about $30 \times 70 = 2100$ in.^{2}. This leaves enough glass for the semicircle.

✔ **Got It?** **2.** The lengths of the sides of a rectangular window have the ratio 1.6 to 1. The area of the window is 2822.4 in.^{2}. What are the window dimensions?

Sometimes an equation shows a perfect square trinomial equal to a constant. To solve, factor the perfect square trinomial into the square of a binomial. Then find square roots.

Problem 3 Solving a Perfect Square Trinomial Equation

What is the solution of $x^2 + 4x + 4 = 25$?

Think	Write
Factor the perfect square trinomial.	$x^2 + 4x + 4 = 25$
	$(x + 2)^2 = 25$
Find square roots.	$x + 2 = \pm 5$
Rewrite as two equations.	$x + 2 = 5$ or $x + 2 = -5$
Solve for x.	$x = 3$ or $x = -7$

✔ **Got It?** **3.** What is the solution of $x^2 - 14x + 49 = 25$?

If $x^2 + bx$ is not part of a perfect square trinomial, you can use the coefficient b to find a constant c so that $x^2 + bx + c$ is a perfect square. When you do this, you are **completing the square**. The diagram models this process.

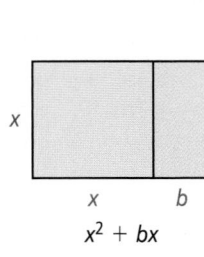 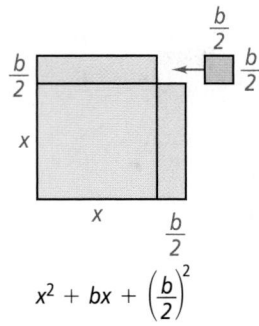 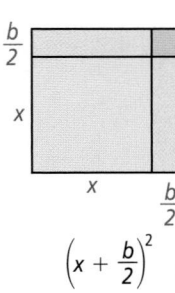

$x^2 + bx$ $\qquad$ $x^2 + bx + \left(\dfrac{b}{2}\right)^2$ $\qquad$ $\left(x + \dfrac{b}{2}\right)^2$

Key Concept Completing the Square

You can form a perfect square trinomial from $x^2 + bx$ by adding $\left(\dfrac{b}{2}\right)^2$.

$$x^2 + bx + \left(\dfrac{b}{2}\right)^2 = \left(x + \dfrac{b}{2}\right)^2$$

 Problem 4 Completing the Square

What value completes the square for $x^2 - 10x$? Justify your answer.

Think

Why do you want a perfect square trinomial?
You can factor a perfect square trinomial into the square of a binomial.

$x^2 - 10x$	Identify b; $b = -10$
$\left(\dfrac{b}{2}\right)^2 = \left(\dfrac{-10}{2}\right)^2 = (-5)^2 = 25$	Find $\left(\dfrac{b}{2}\right)^2$.
$x^2 - 10x + 25$	Add the value of $\left(\dfrac{b}{2}\right)^2$ to complete the square.
$x^2 - 10x + 25 = (x - 5)^2$	Rewrite as the square of a binomial.

  Got It? **4. a.** What value completes the square for $x^2 + 6x$?

b. Reasoning Is it possible for more than one value to complete the square for an expression? Explain.

Key Concept Solving an Equation by Completing the Square

1. Rewrite the equation in the form $x^2 + bx = c$. To do this, get all terms with the variable on one side of the equation and the constant on the other side. Divide all the terms of the equation by the coefficient of x^2 if it is not 1.

2. Complete the square by adding $\left(\dfrac{b}{2}\right)^2$ to each side of the equation.

3. Factor the trinomial.

4. Find square roots.

5. Solve for x.

Problem 5 Solving by Completing the Square

What is the solution of $3x^2 - 12x + 6 = 0$?

$$3x^2 - 12x + 6 = 0$$

$$3x^2 - 12x = -6 \qquad \text{Rewrite. Get all terms with } x \text{ on one side of the equation.}$$

$$\frac{3x^2}{3} - \frac{12x}{3} = \frac{-6}{3} \qquad \text{Divide each side by 3 so the coefficient of } x^2 \text{ will be 1.}$$

$$x^2 - 4x = -2 \qquad \text{Simplify.}$$

$$\left(\frac{b}{2}\right)^2 = \left(\frac{-4}{2}\right)^2 = (-2)^2 = 4 \qquad \text{Find } \left(\frac{b}{2}\right)^2 = 4.$$

$$x^2 - 4x + 4 = -2 + 4 \qquad \text{Add 4 to each side.}$$

$$(x - 2)^2 = 2 \qquad \text{Factor the trinomial.}$$

$$x - 2 = \pm\sqrt{2} \qquad \text{Find square roots.}$$

$$x = 2 \pm \sqrt{2} \qquad \text{Solve for } x.$$

Think

Is there a way to check without a calculator?
Yes; you can check that your solutions are reasonable by estimating.

Check your results on your calculator. Replace x in the original equation with $2 + \sqrt{2}$ and $2 - \sqrt{2}$.

✓ **Got It?** **5.** What is the solution of $2x^2 - x + 3 = x + 9$?

You can complete a square to change a quadratic function to vertex form.

 Problem 6 Writing in Vertex Form

Plan

What should be your first step?
Complete the square.

What is $y = x^2 + 4x - 6$ in vertex form? Name the vertex and y-intercept.

$$y = x^2 + 4x - 6$$

$$y = x^2 + 4x + 2^2 - 6 - 2^2 \qquad \text{Add } \left(\frac{4}{2}\right)^2 = 2^2 \text{ to complete the square. Also, subtract } 2^2$$
$$\text{to leave the function unchanged.}$$

$$y = (x + 2)^2 - 6 - 2^2 \qquad \text{Factor the perfect square trinomial.}$$

$$y = (x + 2)^2 - 10 \qquad \text{Simplify.}$$

The vertex is $(-2, -10)$. The y-intercept is $(0, -6)$.

Check with a graphing calculator.

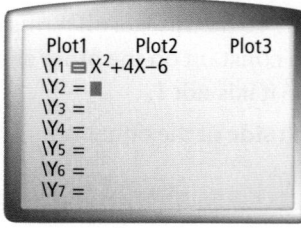 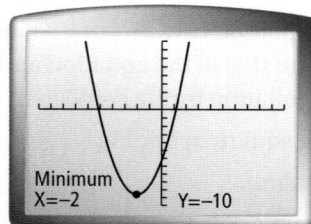 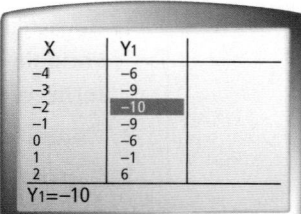

✓ **Got It?** **6.** What is $y = x^2 + 3x - 6$ in vertex form? Name the vertex and y-intercept.

Lesson Check

Do you know HOW?

Solve each equation by finding square roots.

1. $2x^2 = 72$

2. $6x^2 = 54$

Complete the square.

3. $x^2 + 2x + \blacksquare$

4. $x^2 + 10x + \blacksquare$

5. $x^2 - 4x + \blacksquare$

6. $x^2 + 12x + \blacksquare$

7. $x^2 + 100x + \blacksquare$

8. $x^2 - 32x + \blacksquare$

Do you UNDERSTAND?

 9. Vocabulary Explain the process of completing the square.

10. How can you rewrite the equation $x^2 + 12x + 5 = 3$ so the left side of the equation is in the form $(x + a)^2$?

 11. Error Analysis Your friend completed the square and wrote the expression shown. Explain your friend's error and write the expression correctly.

$$x^2 - 14x + 36$$
$$x^2 - 14x + 49 + 36$$
$$(x - 7)^2 + 36$$

Practice and Problem-Solving Exercises

 Solve each equation by finding square roots.

◀ See Problem 1.

12. $5x^2 = 80$

13. $x^2 - 4 = 0$

14. $2x^2 = 32$

15. $9x^2 = 25$

16. $3x^2 - 15 = 0$

17. $5x^2 - 40 = 0$

18. Fitness A rectangular swimming pool is 6 ft deep. One side of the pool is 2.5 times longer than the other. The amount of water needed to fill the swimming pool is 2160 cubic feet. Find the dimensions of the pool.

◀ See Problem 2.

Solve each equation.

◀ See Problem 3.

19. $x^2 + 6x + 9 = 1$

20. $x^2 - 4x + 4 = 100$

21. $x^2 - 2x + 1 = 4$

22. $x^2 + 8x + 16 = \frac{16}{9}$

23. $4x^2 + 4x + 1 = 49$

24. $x^2 - 12x + 36 = 25$

25. $25x^2 + 10x + 1 = 9$

26. $x^2 - 30x + 225 = 400$

27. $9x^2 + 24x + 16 = 36$

Complete the square.

◀ See Problem 4.

28. $x^2 + 18x + \blacksquare$

29. $x^2 - x + \blacksquare$

30. $x^2 - 24x + \blacksquare$

31. $x^2 + 20x + \blacksquare$

32. $m^2 - 3m + \blacksquare$

33. $x^2 + 4x + \blacksquare$

Solve each quadratic equation by completing the square.

◀ See Problem 5.

34. $x^2 + 6x - 3 = 0$

35. $x^2 - 12x + 7 = 0$

36. $x^2 + 4x + 2 = 0$

37. $x^2 - 2x = 5$

38. $x^2 + 8x = 11$

39. $x^2 + 12 = 10x$

40. $x^2 - 3x = x - 1$

41. $x^2 + 2 = 6x + 4$

42. $2x^2 + 2x - 5 = x^2$

43. $4x^2 + 10x - 3 = 0$

44. $9x^2 - 12x - 2 = 0$

45. $25x^2 + 30x = 12$

Rewrite each equation in vertex form.

◀ **See Problem 6.**

46. $y = x^2 + 4x + 1$ **47.** $y = 2x^2 - 8x + 1$ **48.** $y = -x^2 - 2x + 3$

49. $y = x^2 + 4x - 7$ **50.** $y = 2x^2 - 6x - 1$ **51.** $y = -x^2 + 4x - 1$

 **Apply**   Ⓖ **52. Think About a Plan** The area of the rectangle shown is 80 square inches. What is the value of x?

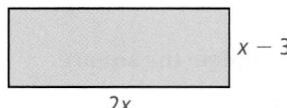

- How can you write an equation to represent 80 in terms of x?
- How can you find the value of x by completing the square?

Find the value of k that would make the left side of each equation a perfect square trinomial.

53. $x^2 + kx + 25 = 0$ **54.** $x^2 - kx + 100 = 0$ **55.** $x^2 - kx + 121 = 0$

56. $x^2 + kx + 64 = 0$ **57.** $x^2 - kx + 81 = 0$ **58.** $25x^2 - kx + 1 = 0$

59. $x^2 + kx + \frac{1}{4} = 0$ **60.** $9x^2 - kx + 4 = 0$ **61.** $36x^2 - kx + 49 = 0$

62. Geometry The table shows some possible dimensions of rectangles with a perimeter of 100 units. Copy and complete the table.
   a. Plot the points (width, area). Find a model for the data set.
   b. What is another point in the data set? Use it to verify your model.
   c. What is a reasonable domain for this function? Explain.
   d. Find the maximum possible area. What dimensions yield this area?
   e. Find a function for area in terms of width without using the table. Do you get the same model as in part (a)? Explain.

Width	Length	Area
1	49	49
2	48	■
3	■	■
4	■	■
5	■	■

Solve each quadratic equation by completing the square.

63. $x^2 + 5x - 3 = 0$ **64.** $x^2 + 3x = 2$

65. $x^2 - x = 5$ **66.** $x^2 + x - 1 = 0$

67. $3x^2 - 4x = 2$ **68.** $5x^2 - x = 4$

69. $x^2 + \frac{3}{4}x = \frac{1}{2}$ **70.** $2x^2 - \frac{1}{2}x = \frac{1}{8}$

71. $3x^2 + x = \frac{2}{3}$ **72.** $-x^2 + 2x + 4 = 0$

73. $-x^2 - 6x = 2$ **74.** $-0.25x^2 - 0.6x + 0.3 = 0$

75. Football The quadratic function $h = -0.01x^2 + 1.18x + 2$ models the height of a punted football. The horizontal distance in feet from the point of impact with the kicker's foot is x, and h is the height of the ball in feet.
   a. Write the function in vertex form. What is the maximum height of the punt?
   b. The nearest defensive player is 5 ft horizontally from the point of impact. How high must the player reach to block the punt?
   c. Suppose the ball was not blocked but continued on its path. How far down the field would the ball go before it hit the ground?

Challenge

Solve for x in terms of a.

76. $2x^2 - ax = 6a^2$

77. $3x^2 + ax = a^2$

78. $2a^2x^2 - 8ax = -6$

79. $4a^2x^2 + 8ax + 3 = 0$

80. $3x^2 + ax^2 = 9x + 9a$

81. $6a^2x^2 - 11ax = 10$

82. Solve $x^2 = (6\sqrt{2})x + 7$ by completing the square.

Rewrite each equation in vertex form. Then find the vertex of the graph.

83. $y = -4x^2 - 5x + 3$

84. $y = \frac{1}{2}x^2 - 5x + 12$

85. $y = -\frac{1}{5}x^2 + \frac{4}{5}x + \frac{11}{5}$

Standardized Test Prep

SAT/ACT

86. The graph of which inequality has its vertex at $\left(2\frac{1}{2}, -5\right)$?

Ⓐ $y < |2x - 5| + 5$

Ⓒ $y > |2x + 5| - 5$

Ⓑ $y < |2x + 5| - 5$

Ⓓ $y > |2x - 5| - 5$

87. Which number is a solution of $|9 - x| = 9 + x$?

Ⓕ -3 Ⓖ 0 Ⓗ 3 Ⓘ 6

88. Joanne tosses an apple seed on the ground. It travels along a parabola with the equation $y = -x^2 + 4$. Assume the seed was thrown from a height of 4 ft. How many feet away from Joanne will the apple seed land?

Ⓐ 1 ft   Ⓑ 2 ft   Ⓒ 4 ft   Ⓓ 8 ft

Extended Response

89. List the steps for solving the equation $x^2 - 9 = -8x$ by the completing the square method. Explain each step.

Mixed Review

Solve each equation by factoring. Check your answers.

                                    ◀ See Lesson 4-5.

90. $2x^2 - 3x + 1 = 0$

91. $x^2 - 4 = -3x$

92. $16 + 22x = 3x^2$

Determine whether a quadratic model exists for each set of values. If so, write the model.

                                    ◀ See Lesson 4-3.

93. $(-4, 3), (-3, 3), (-2, 4)$

94. $\left(-1, \frac{1}{2}\right), (0, 2), (2, 2)$

95. $(0, 2), (1, 0), (2, 4)$

Solve each system by elimination.

                                    ◀ See Lesson 3-2.

96. $\begin{cases} 2x + y = 4 \\ 3x - y = 6 \end{cases}$

97. $\begin{cases} 2x + y = 7 \\ -2x + 5y = -1 \end{cases}$

98. $\begin{cases} 2x + 4y = 10 \\ 3x + 5y = 14 \end{cases}$

Get Ready!   **To prepare for Lesson 4-7, do Exercises 99–100.**

Evaluate each expression for the given values of the variables.

                                    ◀ See Lesson 1-3.

99. $b^2 - 4ac$; $a = 1, b = 6, c = 3$

100. $b^2 - 4ac$; $a = -5, b = 2, c = 4$

The Quadratic Formula

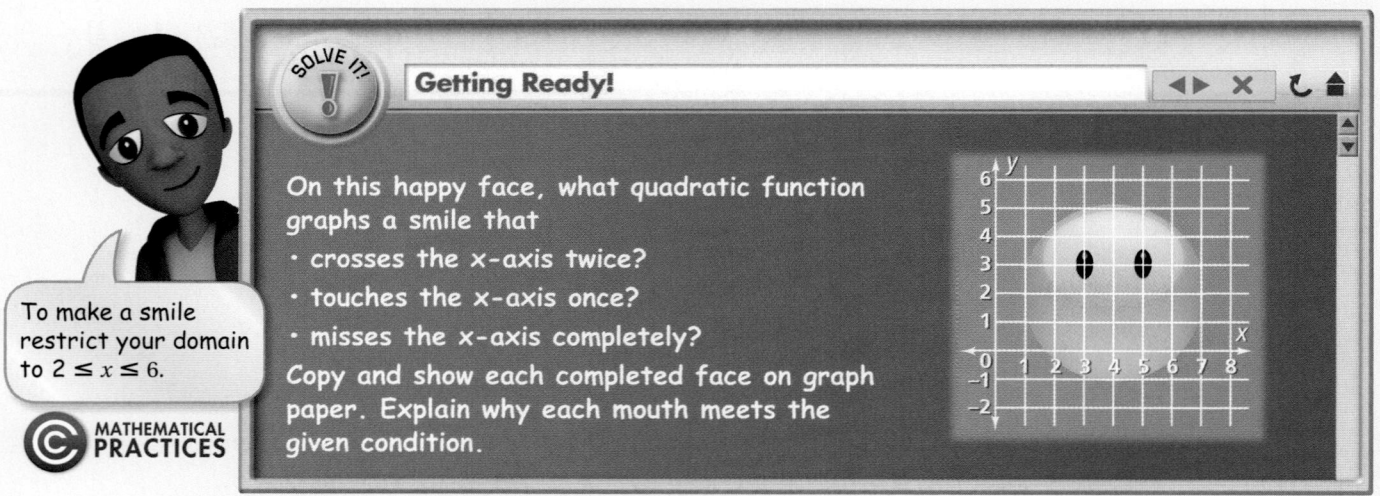

4-7 The Quadratic Formula

Common Core State Standards

Reviews A-REI.B.4b Solve quadratic equations by . . . the quadratic formula . . .

MP 1, MP 2, MP 3, MP 4, MP 8

Objectives To solve quadratic equations using the Quadratic Formula
To determine the number of solutions by using the discriminant

SOLVE IT!

Getting Ready!

On this happy face, what quadratic function graphs a smile that
• crosses the x-axis twice?
• touches the x-axis once?
• misses the x-axis completely?
Copy and show each completed face on graph paper. Explain why each mouth meets the given condition.

To make a smile restrict your domain to $2 \leq x \leq 6$.

MATHEMATICAL PRACTICES

Another way to solve a quadratic equation $ax^2 + bx + c = 0$ is by completing a square and then factoring.

Lesson Vocabulary
• Quadratic Formula
• discriminant

Essential Understanding You can solve a quadratic equation $ax^2 + bx + c = 0$ in more than one way. In general, you can find a formula that gives values of x in terms of a, b, and c.

Here's how to solve $ax^2 + bx + c = 0$ to get the *Quadratic Formula*.

$$ax^2 + bx + c = 0$$

$$x^2 + \frac{b}{a}x + \frac{c}{a} = 0 \qquad \text{Divide each side by } a.$$

$$x^2 + \frac{b}{a}x = -\frac{c}{a} \qquad \text{Rewrite so all terms containing } x \text{ are on one side.}$$

$$x^2 + \frac{b}{a}x + \left(\frac{b}{2a}\right)^2 = \left(\frac{b}{2a}\right)^2 - \frac{c}{a} \qquad \text{Complete the square.}$$

$$\left(x + \frac{b}{2a}\right)^2 = \frac{b^2 - 4ac}{4a^2} \qquad \text{Factor the perfect square trinomial. Also, simplify.}$$

$$x + \frac{b}{2a} = \pm \sqrt{\frac{b^2 - 4ac}{4a^2}} \qquad \text{Find square roots.}$$

$$x = -\frac{b}{2a} \pm \frac{\sqrt{b^2 - 4ac}}{2a} \qquad \text{Solve for } x. \text{ Also, simplify the radical.}$$

$$x = \frac{-b \pm \sqrt{b^2 - 4ac}}{2a} \qquad \text{Simplify.}$$

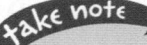

Key Concept   The Quadratic Formula

To solve the quadratic equation $ax^2 + bx + c = 0$, use the **Quadratic Formula**.

$$x = \frac{-b \pm \sqrt{b^2 - 4ac}}{2a}$$

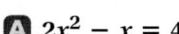 **Problem 1** Using the Quadratic Formula

What are the solutions? Use the Quadratic Formula.

A $2x^2 - x = 4$

Plan

Should you write the equation in standard form?
Yes; write the equation in standard form to identify *a*, *b*, and *c*.

$2x^2 - x = 4$

$2x^2 - x - 4 = 0$ \hspace{2em} Write in standard form.

$\quad a = 2, b = -1, c = -4$ \hspace{2em} Find the values of *a*, *b*, and *c*.

$x = \dfrac{-b \pm \sqrt{b^2 - 4ac}}{2a}$ \hspace{2em} Write the Quadratic Formula.

$\quad = \dfrac{-(-1) \pm \sqrt{(-1)^2 - 4(2)(-4)}}{2(2)}$ \hspace{1em} Substitute for *a*, *b*, and *c*.

$\quad = \dfrac{1 \pm \sqrt{33}}{4}$ \hspace{2em} Simplify.

$\quad = \dfrac{1 + \sqrt{33}}{4}$ or $\dfrac{1 - \sqrt{33}}{4}$

Check Use a graphing calculator to graph
$y = 2x^2 - x - 4$. The *x*-intercepts are about
$-1.186 \approx \dfrac{1 - \sqrt{33}}{4}$ and $1.686 \approx \dfrac{1 + \sqrt{33}}{4}$, as
expected.

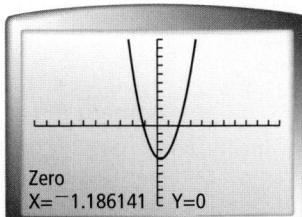

Zero
X=⁻1.186141   Y=0

B $x^2 + 6x + 9 = 0$

$x^2 + 6x + 9 = 0$

$\quad a = 1, b = 6, \ c = 9$ \hspace{1em} Find the values of *a*, *b*, and *c*.

$x = \dfrac{-6 \pm \sqrt{6^2 - 4(1)(9)}}{2(1)}$ \hspace{1em} Substitute into $\dfrac{-b \pm \sqrt{b^2 - 4ac}}{2a}$.

$\quad = \dfrac{-6 \pm \sqrt{36 - 36}}{2}$ \hspace{1em} Simplify.

$\quad = \dfrac{-6 \pm \sqrt{0}}{2}$

$\quad = -3$

Think

Why is there only one solution?
Because if you add or subtract zero you get the same number.

 Got It? 1. What are the solutions? Use the Quadratic Formula.

\hspace{3em} **a.** $x^2 + 4x = -4$ \hspace{6em} **b.** $x^2 + 4x - 3 = 0$

 **Problem 2** Applying the Quadratic Formula

Fundraising Your school's jazz band is selling CDs as a fundraiser. The total profit p depends on the amount x that your band charges for each CD. The equation $p = -x^2 + 48x - 300$ models the profit of the fundraiser. What is the least amount, in dollars, you can charge for a CD to make a profit of $200?

$$p = -x^2 + 48x - 300$$

$$200 = -x^2 + 48x - 300 \qquad \text{Substitute 200 for } p.$$

$$0 = -x^2 + 48x - 500 \qquad \text{Write the equation in standard form.}$$

$$a = -1, b = 48, c = -500 \qquad \text{Find the values of } a, b, \text{ and } c.$$

$$x = \frac{-48 \pm \sqrt{48^2 - 4(-1)(-500)}}{2(-1)} \qquad \text{Substitute into } \frac{-b \pm \sqrt{b^2 - 4ac}}{2a}.$$

$$x = \frac{-48 \pm \sqrt{304}}{-2} \qquad \text{Simplify.}$$

$$x \approx 15.282 \text{ or } x \approx 32.717 \qquad \text{Use a calculator.}$$

The least amount you can charge is $15.29 for each CD to make a profit of $200.

The answer is 15.29.

Think

Does it make sense that two different prices can yield the same profit?

Yes. You can generate a given profit either by selling many CDs at a low price, or fewer CDs at a high price.

 Got It? 2. a. In Problem 2, what is the least amount you can charge for each CD to make a $100 profit?

b. Reasoning Would a negative profit make sense in this problem? Explain.

A quadratic equation can have two real solutions ($x^2 = 4$), one real solution ($x^2 = 0$), or no real solutions ($x^2 = -4$). In the Quadratic Formula, the value under the radical symbol, $b^2 - 4ac$, tells you how many real-number solutions exist.

In Problem 1(a), $b^2 - 4ac > 0$ and there are two real solutions. In Problem 1(b), $b^2 - 4ac = 0$ and there is only one real solution.

take note

Key Concept Discriminant

The **discriminant** of a quadratic equation in the form $ax^2 + bx + c = 0$ is the value of the expression $b^2 - 4ac$.

$$x = \frac{-b \pm \sqrt{b^2 - 4ac}}{2a} \leftarrow \text{discriminant}$$

Discriminants and Solutions of Quadratic Equations		
Value of the Discriminant	**Number of Solutions for $ax^2 + bx + c = 0$**	**x-intercepts of Graph of Related Function $y = ax^2 + bx + c$**
$b^2 - 4ac > 0$	two real solutions	two x-intercepts 
$b^2 - 4ac = 0$	one real solution	one x-intercept
$b^2 - 4ac < 0$	no real solutions	no x-intercepts

Problem 3 Using the Discriminant

What is the number of real solutions of $-2x^2 - 3x + 5 = 0$?

Think

Find the values of a, b, and c.

Evaluate $b^2 - 4ac$.

Interpret the discriminant.

Write

$a = -2, b = -3, c = 5$

$b^2 - 4ac = (-3)^2 - 4(-2)(5)$
$= 49$

The discriminant is positive. The equation has two real solutions.

Got It? **3.** What is the number of real solutions of each equation?

a. $2x^2 - 3x + 7 = 0$ **b.** $x^2 = 6x + 5$

Problem 4 Using the Discriminant to Solve a Problem (STEM)

Projectile Motion You hit a golf ball into the air from a height of 1 in. above the ground with an initial vertical velocity of 85 ft/s. The function $h = -16t^2 + 85t + \frac{1}{12}$ models the height, in feet, of the ball at time t, in seconds. Will the ball reach a height of 115 ft?

Plan

What value should you substitute for h?
You are trying to determine whether the ball will reach 115 ft. Replace h with 115.

$$h = -16t^2 + 85t + \frac{1}{12}$$

$$115 = -16t^2 + 85t + \frac{1}{12} \qquad \text{Substitute 115 for } h.$$

$$0 = -16t^2 + 85t - 114\tfrac{11}{12} \qquad \text{Write the equation in standard form.}$$

$$a = -16, b = 85, c = -114\tfrac{11}{12} \qquad \text{Find the values of } a, b, \text{ and } c.$$

$$b^2 - 4ac = 85^2 - 4(-16)\left(-114\tfrac{11}{12}\right) \qquad \text{Evaluate the discriminant.}$$

$$= 7225 - 7354\tfrac{2}{3} \qquad \text{Simplify.}$$

$$= -129\tfrac{2}{3}$$

The discriminant is negative. The equation $115 = -16t^2 + 85t + \frac{1}{12}$ has no real solutions. The golf ball will not reach a height of 115 feet.

  Got It? **4. Reasoning** Without solving an equation, will the golf ball in Problem 4 reach a height of 110 ft? Explain.

 Lesson Check

Do you know HOW?

Solve each equation using the Quadratic Formula.

1. $x^2 - 5x - 7 = 0$

2. $x^2 + 3x - 13 = 0$

3. $2x^2 - 5x - 3 = 0$

4. $3x^2 - 4x + 3 = 0$

Find the discriminant of each quadratic equation. Determine the number of real solutions.

5. $-x^2 + 2x - 9 = 0$

6. $x^2 + 17x + 4 = 0$

7. $x^2 - 6x + 9 = 0$

Do you UNDERSTAND?

© **8. Reasoning** For what values of k does the equation $x^2 + kx + 9 = 0$ have one real solution? two real solutions?

© **9. Error Analysis** Your friend concluded that because two discriminants are equal, the solutions to the two equations are the same. Explain your friend's error. Give an example of two quadratic equations that disprove this conclusion.

© **10. Reasoning** If one quadratic equation has a positive discriminant, and another quadratic equation has a discriminant equal to 0, can the two quadratic equations share a solution? Explain why or why not. If so, give two quadratic equations that meet this criterion.

Practice and Problem-Solving Exercises  MATHEMATICAL PRACTICES

 **Practice**   **Solve each equation using the Quadratic Formula.**   See Problem 1.

11. $x^2 - 4x + 3 = 0$

12. $x^2 + 8x + 12 = 0$

13. $2x^2 + 5x = 7$

14. $3x^2 + 2x - 1 = 0$

15. $x^2 + 10x = -25$

16. $2x^2 - 5 = -3x$

17. $x^2 = 3x - 1$

18. $6x - 5 = -x^2$

19. $3x^2 = 2(2x + 1)$

20. $2x(x - 1) = 3$

21. $x(x - 5) = -4$

22. $12x + 9x^2 = 5$

23. Fundraising Your class is selling boxes of flower seeds as a fundraiser. The total   See Problem 2. profit p depends on the amount x that your class charges for each box of seeds. The equation $p = -0.5x^2 + 25x - 150$ models the profit of the fundraiser. What's the smallest amount, in dollars, that you can charge and make a profit of at least $125?

24. Baking Your local bakery sells more bagels when it reduces prices, but then its profit changes. The function $y = -1000x^2 + 1100x - 2.5$ models the bakery's daily profit in dollars, from selling bagels, where x is the price of a bagel in dollars. What's the highest price the bakery can charge, in dollars, and make a profit of at least $200?

Evaluate the discriminant for each equation. Determine the number of real   See Problem 3. **solutions.**

25. $x^2 + 4x + 5 = 0$

26. $x^2 - 4x - 5 = 0$

27. $-4x^2 + 20x - 25 = 0$

28. $-2x^2 + x - 28 = 0$

29. $2x^2 + 7x - 15 = 0$

30. $6x^2 - 2x + 5 = 0$

31. $-2x^2 + 7x = 6$

32. $x^2 - 12x + 36 = 0$

33. $x^2 + 8x = -16$

34. $3x^2 + x = -3$

35. $x + 2 = -3x^2$

36. $12x(x + 1) = -3$

37. Business The weekly revenue for a company is $r = -3p^2 + 60p + 1060$,   See Problem 4. where p is the price of the company's product. Use the discriminant to find whether there is a price for which the weekly revenue would be $1500.

 38. Physics The equation $h = 80t - 16t^2$ models the height h in feet reached in t seconds by an object propelled straight up from the ground at a speed of 80 ft/s. Use the discriminant to find whether the object will ever reach a height of 90 ft.

 **Apply**   ⓒ **39. Think About a Plan** The area of a rectangle is 36 in.^{2}. The perimeter of the rectangle is 36 in. What are the dimensions of the rectangle to the nearest hundredth of an inch?

- How can you write an equation using one variable to find the dimensions of the rectangle?
- How can the discriminant of the equation help you solve the problem?

ⓒ **40. Writing** Summarize how to use the discriminant to analyze the types of solutions of a quadratic equation.

Solve each equation using any method. When necessary, round real solutions to the nearest hundredth.

41. $6x^2 - 5x - 1 = 0$

42. $7x^2 - x - 12 = 0$

43. $5x^2 + 8x - 11 = 0$

44. $4x^2 + 4x = 22$

45. $2x^2 - 1 = 5x$

46. $2x^2 + x = \frac{1}{2}$

47. $x^2 = 11x - 10$

48. $5x^2 = 210x$

49. $4x^2 + 4x = 3$

50. $2x^2 + 4x = 10$

51. $x^2 - 3x - 8 = 0$

52. $-3x^2 + 147 = 0$

53. $x^2 + 8x = 4$

54. $4x^2 - 4x - 3 = 0$

55. $x^2 = 11 - 6x$

 56. Air Pollution The function $y = 0.4409x^2 - 5.1724x + 99.0321$ models the emissions of carbon monoxide in the United States since 1987, where y represents the amount of carbon monoxide released in a year in millions of tons, and $x = 0$ represents the year 1987.
  a. How can you use a graph to estimate the year in which more than 100 million tons of carbon monoxide were released into the air?
  b. How can you use the Quadratic Formula to estimate the year in which more than 100 million tons of carbon monoxide were released into the air?
  c. Which method do you prefer? Explain why.

57. Sports A diver dives from a 10 m springboard. The equation $f(t) = -4.9t^2 + 4t + 10$ models her height above the pool at time t in seconds. At what time does she enter the water?

Without graphing, determine how many x-intercepts each function has.

58. $y = -2x^2 + 3x - 1$

59. $y = 0.25x^2 + 2x + 4$

60. $y = x^2 + 3x + 5$

61. $y = -x^2 + 3x + 10$

62. $y = 3x^2 - 10x + 6$

63. $y = 10x^2 + 13x - 3$

64. $y = x^2 + 17x - 2$

65. $y = -5x^2 - 4x + 3$

66. $y = 7x^2 - 2x + 9$

 67. Reasoning Determine the value(s) of k for which $3x^2 + kx + 12 = 0$ has each type of solution.
  a. no real solutions
  b. exactly one real solution
  c. two real solutions

68. Use the discriminant to match each function with its graph.
  a. $f(x) = x^2 - 4x + 2$
  b. $f(x) = x^2 - 4x + 4$
  c. $f(x) = x^2 - 4x + 6$

I. 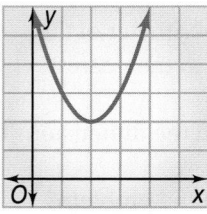   **II.** 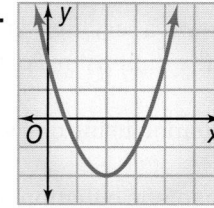   **III.**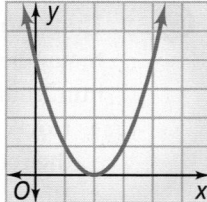

69. a. Geometry Write an equation to find the dimensions of a square that has the same area as a circle with a radius of 10 cm.
  b. Find the length of a side of the square, to the nearest hundredth centimeter.

Write a quadratic equation with the given solutions.

70. $\dfrac{3 + \sqrt{5}}{2}, \dfrac{3 - \sqrt{5}}{2}$

71. $\dfrac{-5 + \sqrt{13}}{2}, \dfrac{-5 - \sqrt{13}}{2}$

72. $\dfrac{-5 + \sqrt{17}}{4}, \dfrac{-5 - \sqrt{17}}{4}$

Solve each equation.

73. $\left|5 - 2x^2\right| = 5$

74. $\left|x^2 - 4x\right| = 3$

75. $\left|x^2 + 4x + 3\right| = 8$

76. Use the Quadratic Formula to prove each statement.
  a. The sum of the solutions of the quadratic equation $ax^2 + bx + c = 0$ is $-\dfrac{b}{a}$.
  b. The product of the solutions of the quadratic equation $ax^2 + bx + c = 0$ is $\dfrac{c}{a}$.

77. Explain the meaning of the value $\dfrac{\sqrt{b^2 - 4ac}}{2a}$ in terms of the graph of the standard quadratic function $y = ax^2 + bx + c$.

Standardized Test Prep

SAT/ACT

78. How many different real solutions are there for $2x^2 - 3x + 5 = 0$?

79. What is the y-value of the y-intercept of the quadratic function $y = 2(x + 2)^2 - 5$?

80. What is the x-value in the solution to the system $\begin{cases} 3x + y = -7 \\ 2x - 2y = -10 \end{cases}$?

81. The graph of the system of inequalities $\begin{cases} y \le \frac{1}{2}x + 3 \\ y \ge 6x - 30 \\ x \ge 0 \\ y \ge 0 \end{cases}$ is shown at the right.

What is the maximum value of the function $P = 3x - 4y$ for the (x, y) pairs in the bounded region shown?

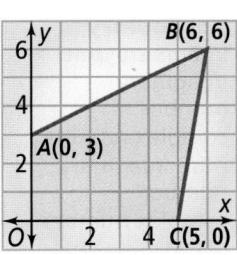

Mixed Review

Solve each equation by completing the square.

See Lesson 4-6.

82. $x^2 - 8x - 20 = 0$

83. $2y^2 = 4y - 1$

84. $x^2 - 3x - 8 = 0$

Simplify by combining like terms.

See Lesson 1-3.

85. $z^2 + 8z^2 - 2z + 5z$

86. $4k - x - 3k + 5x$

87. $4y - (2y + 3x) - 5x$

Get Ready! To prepare for Lesson 4-8, do Exercises 88–90.

See p. 981.

Simplify each expression.

88. $\sqrt{(-2)^2 + 8^2}$

89. $\sqrt{3^2 + 4^2}$

90. $\sqrt{5^2 + (-12)^2}$

Complex Numbers

© **Common Core State Standards**

N-CN.A.1 Know there is a complex number i such that $i^2 = -1$, and every complex number has the form $a = bi$ with a and b real. **Also N-CN.A.2, N-CN.C.7, N-CN.C.8**

MP 1, MP 2, MP 3, MP 6

Objectives To identify, graph, and perform operations with complex numbers
To find complex number solutions of quadratic equations

Once you find the pattern in the boxes, finding a^{99} becomes simple.

MATHEMATICAL PRACTICES

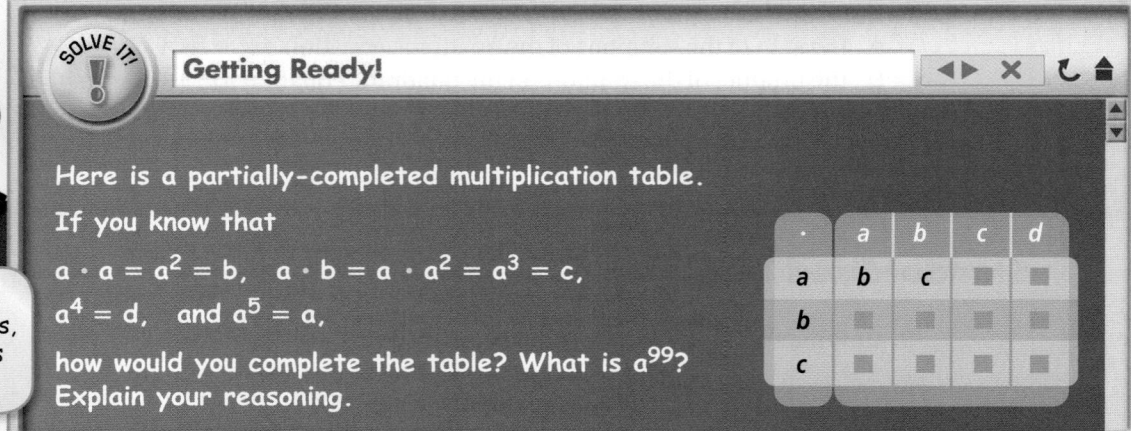

Getting Ready!

Here is a partially-completed multiplication table.
If you know that

$a \cdot a = a^2 = b$, $a \cdot b = a \cdot a^2 = a^3 = c$,

$a^4 = d$, and $a^5 = a$,

how would you complete the table? What is a^{99}?
Explain your reasoning.

·	a	b	c	d
a	b	c	■	■
b	■	■	■	■
c	■	■	■	■

Lesson Vocabulary
- imaginary unit
- imaginary number
- complex number
- pure imaginary number
- complex number plane
- absolute value of a complex number
- complex conjugates

In Chapter 1, you learned about different subsets of real numbers. The set of real numbers is itself a subset of a larger set of numbers, the *complex numbers*. Curiously, the complex numbers include a number like a in the Solve It. Its fifth power is itself.

Essential Understanding The complex numbers are based on a number whose square is -1.

The **imaginary unit** i is the complex number whose square is -1. So, $i^2 = -1$, and $i = \sqrt{-1}$.

> **Key Concept** Square Root of a Negative Real Number
>
> **Algebra**
> For any positive number a,
> $\sqrt{-a} = \sqrt{-1 \cdot a} = \sqrt{-1} \cdot \sqrt{a} = i\sqrt{a}.$
>
> **Example**
> $\sqrt{-5} = i\sqrt{5}$
>
> Note that $(\sqrt{-5})^2 = (i\sqrt{5})^2 = i^2(\sqrt{5})^2 = -1 \cdot 5 = -5$ (not 5).

Think

Is $\sqrt{-18}$ a real number?
No. There is no real number that when multiplied by itself gives -18. You must use the imaginary unit i to write $\sqrt{-18}$.

Problem 1 Simplifying a Number Using i

How do you write $\sqrt{-18}$ by using the imaginary unit i?

$$\sqrt{-18} = \sqrt{-1 \cdot 18}$$
$$= \sqrt{-1} \cdot \sqrt{18} \qquad \text{Multiplication Property of Square Roots}$$
$$= i \cdot \sqrt{18} \qquad \text{Definition of } i$$
$$= i \cdot 3\sqrt{2} \qquad \text{Simplify.}$$
$$= 3i\sqrt{2}$$

  Got It? **1.** How do you write each number in parts (a)-(c) by using the imaginary unit i?

    a. $\sqrt{-12}$ **b.** $\sqrt{-25}$ **c.** $\sqrt{-7}$

    d. Reasoning Explain why $\sqrt{-64} \neq -\sqrt{64}$.

An **imaginary number** is any number of the form $a + bi$, where a and b are real numbers and $b \neq 0$. Imaginary numbers and real numbers together make up the set of *complex numbers*.

---

take note

Key Concept   Complex Numbers

You can write a **complex number** in the form $a + bi$, where a and b are real numbers.

If $b = 0$, the number $a + bi$ is a real number.

If $a = 0$ and $b \neq 0$, the number $a + bi$ is a **pure imaginary number**.

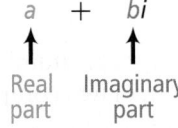

a + bi

Real part   Imaginary part

Complex Numbers ($a + bi$)

Real Numbers ($a + 0i$)	Imaginary Numbers ($a + bi$, $b \neq 0$)
	Pure Imaginary Numbers ($0 + bi$, $b \neq 0$)

In the **complex number plane**, the point (a, b) represents the complex number $a + bi$. To graph a complex number, locate the real part on the horizontal axis and the imaginary part on the vertical axis.

The **absolute value of a complex number** is its distance from the origin in the complex plane.

$$|a + bi| = \sqrt{a^2 + b^2}$$

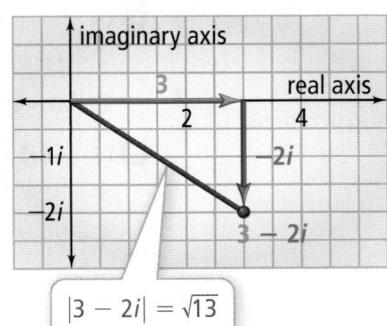

$|3 - 2i| = \sqrt{13}$

Problem 2 Graphing in the Complex Number Plane

What are the graph and absolute value of each number?

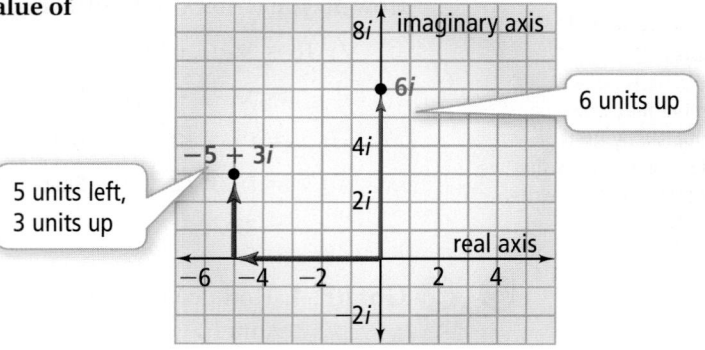

A $-5 + 3i$

$$|-5 + 3i| = \sqrt{(-5)^2 + 3^2}$$
$$= \sqrt{34}$$

B $6i$

$$|6i| = |0 + 6i|$$
$$= \sqrt{0^2 + 6^2}$$
$$= \sqrt{36}$$
$$= 6$$

 Think

Where is a pure imaginary number in the complex plane?
The real part of a pure imaginary number is 0. The number must be on the imaginary axis.

 Got It? **2.** What are the graph and absolute value of each number?

a. $5 - i$ **b.** $-3 - 2i$ **c.** $1 + 4i$

Essential Understanding You can define operations on the set of complex numbers so that when you restrict the operations to the subset of real numbers, you get the familiar operations on the real numbers.

To add or subtract complex numbers, combine the real parts and the imaginary parts separately. If the sum of two complex numbers is 0, or $0 + 0i$, then each number is the opposite, or additive inverse, of the other. The associative and commutative properties apply to complex numbers as well.

 Problem 3 Adding and Subtracting Complex Numbers

What is each sum or difference?

Plan

How is adding complex numbers similar to adding algebraic expressions?
Adding the real parts and imaginary parts separately is like adding like terms.

A $(4 - 3i) + (-4 + 3i)$

$4 + (-4) + (-3i) + 3i$ Use the commutative and associative properties.

$0 + 0 = 0$ $4 - 3i$ and $-4 + 3i$ are additive inverses.

B $(5 - 3i) - (-2 + 4i)$

$5 - 3i + 2 - 4i$ To subtract, add the opposite.

$5 + 2 - 3i - 4i$ Use the commutative and associative properties.

$7 - 7i$ Simplify.

 Got It? **3.** What is each sum or difference?

a. $(7 - 2i) + (-3 + i)$ **b.** $(1 + 5i) - (3 - 2i)$

c. $(8 + 6i) - (8 - 6i)$ **d.** $(-3 + 9i) + (3 + 9i)$

You multiply complex numbers $a + bi$ and $c + di$ as you would multiply binomials. For imaginary parts bi and di, $(bi)(di) = bd(i)^2 = bd(-1) = -bd$.

 Problem 4 Multiplying Complex Numbers

What is each product?

A $(3i)(-5 + 2i)$

$\quad -15i + 6i^2$ Distributive Property

$\quad -15i + 6(-1)$ Substitute -1 for i^2.

$\quad -6 - 15i$ Simplify.

Think

How do you multiply two binomials?
Multiply each term of one binomial by each term of the other binomial.

B $(4 + 3i)(-1 - 2i)$

$\quad -4 - 8i - 3i - 6i^2$

$\quad -4 - 8i - 3i - 6(-1)$

$\quad 2 - 11i$

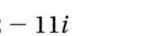 Substitute -1 for i^2.

C $(-6 + i)(-6 - i)$

$\quad 36 + 6i - 6i - i^2$

$\quad 36 + 6i - 6i - (-1)$

$\quad 37$

 Got It? 4. What is each product?

    a. $(7i)(3i)$ **b.** $(2 - 3i)(4 + 5i)$ **c.** $(-4 + 5i)(-4 - 5i)$

In Problem 4(c), the product is a real number. Number pairs of the form $a + bi$ and $a - bi$ are **complex conjugates**. The product of complex conjugates is a real number.

$$(a + bi)(a - bi) = a^2 - (bi)^2 = a^2 - b^2 i^2 = a^2 - b^2(-1) = a^2 + b^2$$

You can use complex conjugates to simplify quotients of complex numbers.

 Problem 5 Dividing Complex Numbers

What is each quotient?

Plan

What is the goal?
Write the quotient in the form $a + bi$.

A $\dfrac{9 + 12i}{3i}$

$\quad \dfrac{9 + 12i}{3i} \cdot \dfrac{-3i}{-3i}$

$\quad \dfrac{-27i - 36i^2}{-9i^2}$

$\quad \dfrac{-27i - 36(-1)}{-9(-1)}$

$\quad \dfrac{36 - 27i}{9}$

$\quad 4 - 3i$

Multiply numerator and denominator by the complex conjugate of the denominator.

Substitute -1 for i^2.

B $\dfrac{2 + 3i}{1 - 4i}$

$\quad \dfrac{2 + 3i}{1 - 4i} \cdot \dfrac{1 + 4i}{1 + 4i}$

$\quad \dfrac{2 + 8i + 3i + 12i^2}{1 + 4i - 4i - 16i^2}$

$\quad \dfrac{2 + 8i + 3i + 12(-1)}{1 + 4i - 4i - 16(-1)}$

$\quad \dfrac{-10 + 11i}{17}$

$\quad -\dfrac{10}{17} + \dfrac{11}{17}i$

 Got It? 5. What is each quotient?

    a. $\dfrac{5 - 2i}{3 + 4i}$ **b.** $\dfrac{4 - i}{6i}$ **c.** $\dfrac{8 - 7i}{8 + 7i}$

 **Problem 6** Factoring Using Complex Conjugates

Think

Is the expression factorable using real numbers?
No. Look for factors using complex numbers.

What is the factored form of $2x^2 + 32$?

$2x^2 + 32$

$2(x^2 + 16)$ Factor out the GCF.

$2(x + 4i)(x - 4i)$ Use $a^2 + b^2 = (a + bi)(a - bi)$ to factor $(x^2 + 16)$.

Check

$2(x^2 + 4xi - 4xi - 16i^2)$ Multiply the binomials.

$2(x^2 - 16(-1))$ $i^2 = -1$

$2(x^2 + 16)$ Simplify within the binomial.

$2x^2 + 32$ Multiply.

 Got It? 6. What are the factored forms of each expression?

     a. $5x^2 + 20$ **b.** $x^2 + 81$

Essential Understanding Every quadratic equation has complex number solutions (that sometimes are real numbers).

 **Problem 7** Finding Imaginary Solutions

What are the solutions of $2x^2 - 3x + 5 = 0$?

Think

Use the Quadratic Formula with $a = 2, b = -3$, and $c = 5$.

Simplify.

Write

$x = \dfrac{-b \pm \sqrt{b^2 - 4ac}}{2a}$

$= \dfrac{-(-3) \pm \sqrt{(-3)^2 - 4(2)(5)}}{2(2)}$

$= \dfrac{3 \pm \sqrt{9 - 40}}{4}$

$= \dfrac{3 \pm \sqrt{-31}}{4}$

$= \dfrac{3}{4} \pm \dfrac{\sqrt{31}}{4} i$

 Got It? 7. What are the solutions of each equation?

     a. $3x^2 - x + 2 = 0$ **b.** $x^2 - 4x + 5 = 0$

Lesson Check

Do you know HOW?

1. Simplify $\sqrt{-75}$ by using the imaginary number i.

2. Find the absolute value of $4 - 3i$.

3. Find the complex factors of $x^2 + 16$. Check your answers.

Simplify each expression.

4. $(4 - 2i) - (-3 + i)$

5. $(2 + i)(4 - 5i)$

Do you UNDERSTAND?

6. **Vocabulary** Explain the difference between the additive inverse of a complex number and a complex conjugate.

7. **Error Analysis** Describe and correct the error made in simplifying the expression $(4 - 7i)(4 + 7i)$.

$(4 - 7i)(4 + 7i) = 16 + 28i - 28i + 49i^2$
$= 16 - 49$
$= -33$

Practice and Problem-Solving Exercises

 **Practice**

Simplify each number by using the imaginary number i. *See Problem 1.*

8. $\sqrt{-4}$ 9. $\sqrt{-7}$ 10. $\sqrt{-15}$ 11. $\sqrt{-81}$ 12. $\sqrt{-50}$

Plot each complex number and find its absolute value. *See Problem 2.*

13. $2i$ 14. $5 + 12i$ 15. $2 - 2i$ 16. $1 - 4i$ 17. $3 - 6i$

Simplify each expression. *See Problems 3 and 4.*

18. $(2 + 4i) + (4 - i)$ 19. $(-3 - 5i) + (4 - 2i)$ 20. $(7 + 9i) + (-5i)$

21. $(12 + 5i) - (2 - i)$ 22. $(-6 - 7i) - (1 + 3i)$ 23. $(8 + i)(2 + 7i)$

24. $(-6 - 5i)(1 + 3i)$ 25. $(-6i)^2$ 26. $(9 + 4i)^2$

Write each quotient as a complex number. *See Problem 5.*

27. $\dfrac{3 - 2i}{5i}$ 28. $\dfrac{-2i}{1 + i}$ 29. $\dfrac{4 - 3i}{-1 - 4i}$

30. $\dfrac{i + 2}{i - 2}$ 31. $\dfrac{4}{2 - 3i}$ 32. $\dfrac{3 + 2i}{(1 + i)^2}$

Find the factored forms of each expression. Check your answer. *See Problem 6.*

33. $x^2 + 25$ 34. $x^2 + 1$ 35. $3s^2 + 75$

36. $x^2 + \dfrac{1}{4}$ 37. $4b^2 + 1$ 38. $-9x^2 - 100$

Find all solutions to each quadratic equation. *See Problem 7.*

39. $x^2 + 2x + 3 = 0$ 40. $-3x^2 + x - 3 = 0$ 41. $2x^2 - 4x + 7 = 0$

42. $x^2 - 2x + 2 = 0$ 43. $x^2 + 5 = 4x$ 44. $2x(x - 3) = -5$

45. a. Name the complex number represented by each point on the graph at the right.
  b. Find the additive inverse of each number.
  c. Find the complex conjugate of each number.
  d. Find the absolute value of each number.

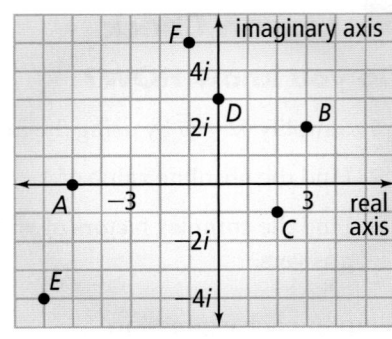

46. Think About a Plan In the complex number plane, what geometric figure describes the complex numbers with absolute value 10?
  • What does the absolute value of a complex number represent?
  • How can you use the complex number plane to solve this problem?

47. Solve $(x + 3i)(x - 3i) = 34$.

Simplify each expression.

48. $(8i)(4i)(-9i)$

49. $(2 + \sqrt{-1}) + (-3 + \sqrt{-16})$

50. $(4 + \sqrt{-9}) + (6 - \sqrt{-49})$

51. $(10 + \sqrt{-9}) - (2 + \sqrt{-25})$

52. $(8 - \sqrt{-1}) - (-3 + \sqrt{-16})$

53. $2i(5 - 3i)$

54. $-5(1 + 2i) + 3i(3 - 4i)$

55. $(3 + \sqrt{-4})(4 + \sqrt{-1})$

56. Open-Ended In the equation $x^2 - 6x + c = 0$, find values of c that will give:
  a. two real solutions   **b.** two imaginary solutions   **c.** one real solution

57. A student wrote the numbers 1, 5, $1 + 3i$, and $4 + 3i$ to represent the vertices of a quadrilateral in the complex number plane. What type of quadrilateral has these vertices?

The multiplicative inverse of a complex number z is $\frac{1}{z}$ where $z \neq 0$. Find the multiplicative inverse, or reciprocal, of each complex number. Then use complex conjugates to simplify. Check each answer by multiplying it by the original number.

58. $2 + 5i$

59. $8 - 12i$

60. $a + bi$

Find the sum and product of the roots of each equation.

61. $x^2 - 2x + 3 = 0$

62. $5x^2 + 2x + 1 = 0$

63. $-2x^2 + 3x - 3 = 0$

For $ax^2 + bx + c = 0$, the sum of the roots is $-\frac{b}{a}$ and the product of the roots is $\frac{c}{a}$. Find a quadratic equation for each pair of roots. Assume $a = 1$.

64. $-6i$ and $6i$

65. $2 + 5i$ and $2 - 5i$

66. $4 - 3i$ and $4 + 3i$

Two complex numbers $a + bi$ and $c + di$ are equal when $a = c$ and $b = d$. Solve each equation for x and y.

67. $2x + 3yi = -14 + 9i$

68. $3x + 19i = 16 - 8yi$

69. $-14 - 3i = 2x + yi$

 **Challenge**

70. Show that the product of any complex number $a + bi$ and its complex conjugate is a real number.

71. For what real values of x and y is $(x + yi)^2$ an imaginary number?

 72. Reasoning True or false: The conjugate of the additive inverse of a complex number is equal to the additive inverse of the conjugate of that complex number. Explain your answer.

Standardized Test Prep

SAT/ACT

73. How can you rewrite the expression $(8 - 5i)^2$ in the form $a + bi$?

Ⓐ $39 + 80i$ Ⓑ $39 - 80i$ Ⓒ $69 + 80i$ Ⓓ $69 - 80i$

74. How many solutions does the quadratic equation $4x^2 - 12x + 9 = 0$ have?

Ⓕ two real solutions   Ⓗ two imaginary solutions

Ⓖ one real solution   Ⓘ one imaginary solution

75. What are the solutions of $3x^2 - 2x - 4 = 0$?

Ⓐ $\dfrac{1 \pm \sqrt{13}}{3}$ Ⓑ $\dfrac{1 \pm i\sqrt{11}}{3}$ Ⓒ $\dfrac{-1 \pm \sqrt{13}}{3}$ Ⓓ $\dfrac{-1 \pm i\sqrt{11}}{3}$

Short Response

76. Using factoring, what are all four solutions to $x^4 - 16 = 0$? Show your work.

Mixed Review

Solve each equation using the Quadratic Formula.   ◀ See Lesson 4-7.

77. $2x^2 + 3x - 4 = 0$ **78.** $4x^2 + x = 1$ **79.** $x^2 = -7x - 8$

Graph each function. Identify the axis of symmetry.   ◀ See Lesson 4-1.

80. $y = -2(x + 1)^2 - 3$ **81.** $y = \frac{1}{2}(x - 4)^2 + 1$ **82.** $y = 3(x - 1)^2 - 5$

Write an equation for each line.   ◀ See Lesson 2-3.

83. $m = 3$ and the y-intercept is -4 **84.** $m = -0.5$ and the y-intercept is -2

85. $m = -7$ and the y-intercept is 10 **86.** $m = 2$ and the y-intercept is 8

Get Ready! To prepare for Lesson 4-9, do Exercises 87–89.   ◀ See Lesson 3-3.

Solve each system of inequalities by graphing.

87. $\begin{cases} y < 2x + 4 \\ y \geq |x - 3| + 2 \end{cases}$ **88.** $\begin{cases} y > -x \\ y < -|x + 1| \end{cases}$ **89.** $\begin{cases} y \leq |x| + 2 \\ y \geq -\frac{1}{2}x + 4 \end{cases}$

Quadratic Inequalities

 Common Core State Standards

A-APR.B.3 Identify zeros of polynomials when suitable factorizations are available, and use the zeros to construct a rough graph of the function defined by the polynomial.

MP 3

To solve some quadratic inequalities, relate the quadratic expression to 0 and factor. To determine the sign of each factor, use what you know about multiplying positive and negative numbers.

Example 1

Solve each inequality algebraically.

a. $2x^2 - 14x < 0$

$2x(x - 7) < 0$ Factor.

$2x > 0$ and $(x - 7) < 0$, or $2x < 0$ and $(x - 7) > 0$ The product is negative, so the two factors must have *different* signs.

$x > 0$ and $x < 7$, or $x < 0$ and $x > 7$ Simplify.

$0 < x < 7$ No value can be both greater than 7 *and* less than 0.

b. $2x^2 - 14x > 0$

$2x(x - 7) > 0$ Factor.

$2x > 0$ and $(x - 7) > 0$, or $2x < 0$ and $(x - 7) < 0$ The product is positive, so the two factors must have the *same* signs.

$x > 0$ and $x > 7$, or $x < 0$ and $x < 7$ Simplify.

$x > 7$ or $x < 0$ A value that is greater than both 0 *and* 7 is always greater than 7. A value that is less than both 0 *and* 7 is always less than 0.

You can use a table to solve inequalities by analyzing the values of y around 0.

Activity

Use a table to find the solutions of $x^2 - 6x + 5 < 0$.

1. What happens to the value of y when $0 \le x \le 6$?
2. Does this make sense when you think of the shape of the graph of $y = x^2 - 6x + 5$? Explain.
3. What x-values in the table make the inequality $x^2 - 6x + 5 < 0$ true?
4. What are the solutions of $x^2 - 6x + 5 < 0$?

x	y
0	5
1	0
2	-3
3	-4
4	-3
5	0
6	5

You can determine the solution of a quadratic inequality based on how many times and where the graph of the related function crosses the x-axis. The graph could open upward or downward, and could intersect the x-axis at 0, 1, or 2 points.

You can solve inequalities of the form $ax^2 + bx + c > 0$ or $ax^2 + bx + c < 0$ by graphing the corresponding function and seeing where the graph is above or below the x-axis.

Example 2

Find the solution sets for $\frac{1}{4}(x - 2)^2 - 1 > 0$ and $\frac{1}{4}(x - 2)^2 - 1 < 0$.

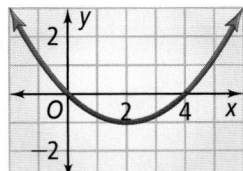

The solution set for $\frac{1}{4}(x - 2)^2 - 1 > 0$ is all x-values of points on the parabola that lie above the x-axis.

$$x < 0 \text{ or } x > 4$$

The solution set for $\frac{1}{4}(x - 2)^2 - 1 < 0$ is all x-values of points on the parabola that lie below the x-axis.

$$0 < x < 4$$

Example 3

Solve $-2x^2 - 8x - 6 < 0$.

Think: Since the coefficient of x^2 is less than zero, the graph of $y = -2x^2 - 8x - 6$ opens downward.

Solve: Find where $-2x^2 - 8x - 6$ equals 0.

$$-2x^2 - 8x - 6 = 0$$
$$-2(x^2 + 4x + 3) = 0$$
$$-2(x + 3)(x + 1) = 0$$
$$x = -3 \text{ or } x = -1$$

The graph of $y = -2x^2 - 8x - 6$ opens down and crosses the x-axis at $x = -3$ and $x = -1$. The solution of $-2x^2 - 8x - 6 < 0$ is $x < -3$ or $x > -1$.

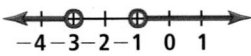

Exercises

5. Solve each inequality. Graph your solution on a number line.

   a. $x^2 < 36$
   b. $x^2 - 9 > 0$
   c. $x^2 < -4$
   d. $x^2 - 3x - 18 > 0$

6. How can you use the graph of $y = 3x - 4$ to solve the linear inequality $3x - 4 < 0$? Graph the solution.

7. How can you solve the absolute value inequality $|-3x + 4| > 0$?

8. Example 2 shows two possible graphs for a quadratic inequality. What other possibilities are there?

9. Describe the graphs of possible solutions of $ax^3 + bx^2 + cx + d > 0$.

4-9

Quadratic Systems

Ⓒ **Common Core State Standards**

A-CED.A.3 Represent constraints by equations or inequalities, and by systems of equations and/or inequalities, and interpret solutions as viable or nonviable options in a modeling context. **Also A-REI.C.7, A-REI.D.11**

MP 1, MP 2, MP 3, MP 4

Objectives To solve and graph systems of linear and quadratic equations
To solve and graph systems of quadratic inequalities

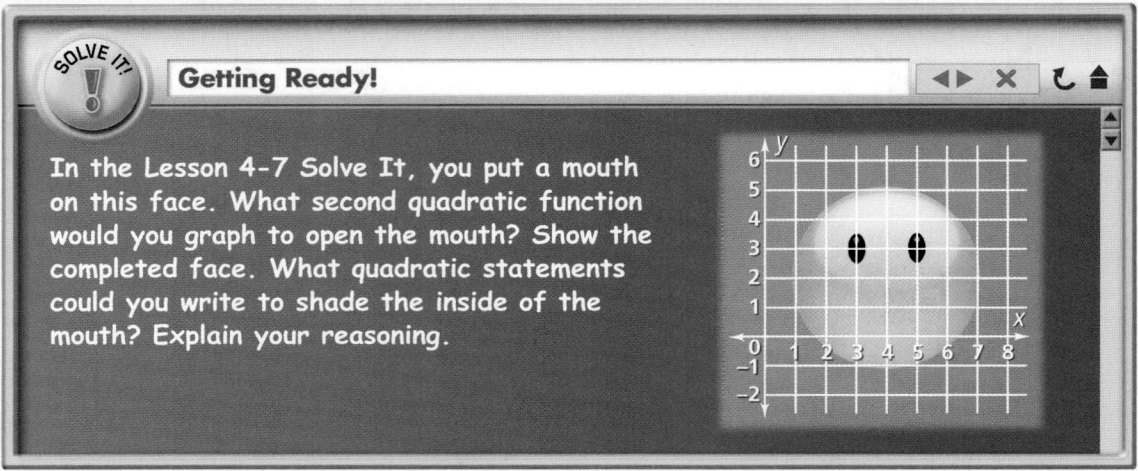

Getting Ready!

In the Lesson 4-7 Solve It, you put a mouth on this face. What second quadratic function would you graph to open the mouth? Show the completed face. What quadratic statements could you write to shade the inside of the mouth? Explain your reasoning.

By drawing a second parabola in the Solve It, you created a quadratic system.

Essential Understanding You can solve systems involving quadratic equations using methods similar to the ones used to solve systems of linear equations.

The points where the graphs of the equations intersect represent the solutions of a system.

take note

Key Concept Solutions of a Linear-Quadratic System

A system of one quadratic equation and one linear equation can have two solutions, one solution, or no solution.

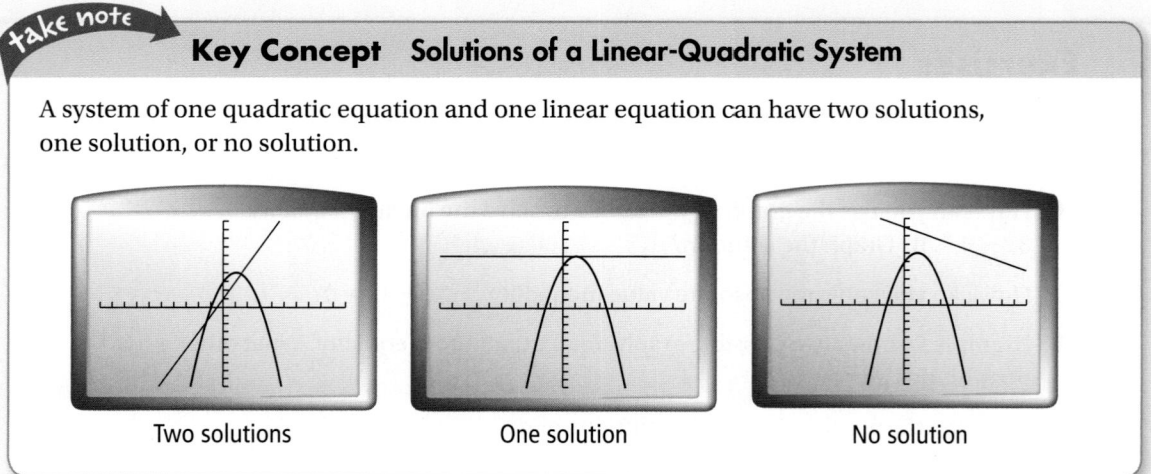

Two solutions   One solution   No solution

Problem 1 Solving a Linear-Quadratic System by Graphing

Multiple Choice Which numbers are y-values of the solutions of the system of equations?

$$\begin{cases} y = -x^2 + 5x + 6 \\ y = x + 6 \end{cases}$$

Ⓐ 4 only   Ⓑ 6 only   Ⓒ 4 and 6   Ⓓ 6 and 10

Plan

How can you graph these two equations?
Use slope-intercept form to graph the linear equation. Make a table of values to graph the quadratic equation.

Graph the equations. Find their intersections.

The solutions appear to be $(0, 6)$ and $(4, 10)$.

Check

$$y = -x^2 + 5x + 6 \qquad\qquad y = x + 6$$
$$6 \overset{?}{=} -(0)^2 + 5(0) + 6 \qquad 6 \overset{?}{=} 0 + 6$$
$$6 = 6 ✔ \qquad\qquad\qquad 6 = 6 ✔$$

$$y = -x^2 + 5x + 6 \qquad\qquad y = x + 6$$
$$10 \overset{?}{=} -(4)^2 + 5(4) + 6 \qquad 10 \overset{?}{=} 4 + 6$$
$$10 = 10 ✔ \qquad\qquad\qquad 10 = 10 ✔$$

The y-values of the solutions are 6 and 10, choice D.

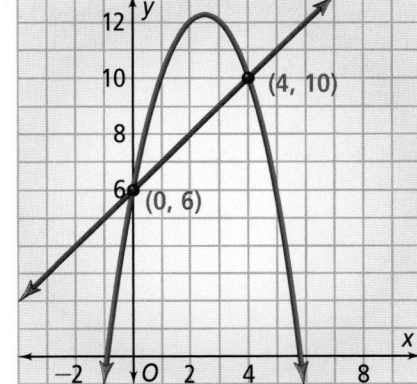

 Got It? 1. What is the solution of the system? $\begin{cases} y = x^2 + 6x + 9 \\ y = x + 3 \end{cases}$

 Problem 2 Solving a Linear-Quadratic System Using Substitution

What is the solution of the system of equations? $\begin{cases} y = -x^2 - x + 6 \\ y = x + 3 \end{cases}$

Think

Substitute $x + 3$ for y in the quadratic equation.

Write in standard form.

Factor. Solve for x.

Substitute for x in $y = x + 3$.

Write

$$x + 3 = -x^2 - x + 6$$

$$x^2 + 2x - 3 = 0$$

$$(x - 1)(x + 3) = 0$$
$$x = 1 \text{ or } x = -3$$

$$x = 1 \rightarrow y = 1 + 3 = 4$$
$$x = -3 \rightarrow y = -3 + 3 = 0$$
The solutions are $(1, 4)$ and $(-3, 0)$.

 Got It? 2. What is the solution of the system? $\begin{cases} y = -x^2 - 3x + 10 \\ y = x + 5 \end{cases}$

You can solve quadratic–quadratic systems using the same methods you used for linear–quadratic systems.

 Problem 3 Solving a Quadratic System of Equations

Plan

Which variable should you substitute for?
You can substitute for either variable, but substituting for y results in a simple equation.

What is the solution of the system? $\begin{cases} y = -x^2 - x + 12 \\ y = x^2 + 7x + 12 \end{cases}$

Method 1 Use substitution.

Substitute $y = -x^2 - x + 12$ for y in the second equation. Solve for x.

$$-x^2 - x + 12 = x^2 + 7x + 12 \quad \text{Substitute for } y.$$

$$-2x^2 - 8x = 0 \quad \text{Write in standard form.}$$

$$-2x(x + 4) = 0 \quad \text{Factor.}$$

$$x = 0 \text{ or } x = -4 \quad \text{Solve for } x.$$

Substitute each value of x into either equation. Solve for y.

$$y = x^2 + 7x + 12 \qquad\qquad y = x^2 + 7x + 12$$

$$y = (0)^2 + 7(0) + 12 \qquad\quad y = (-4)^2 + 7(-4) + 12$$

$$y = 0 + 0 + 12 = 12 \qquad\quad y = 16 - 28 + 12 = 0$$

The solutions are $(0, 12)$ and $(-4, 0)$.

Method 2 Graph the equations.

Use a graphing calculator.
Define functions Y_1 and Y_2.

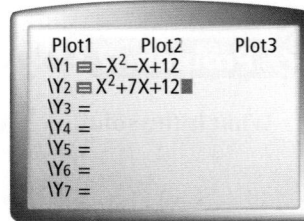

Use the **INTERSECT** feature to find the points of intersection.

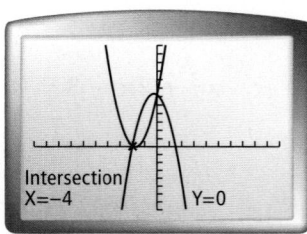 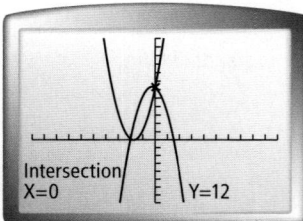

The solutions are $(-4, 0)$ and $(0, 12)$.

✔ **Got It?** **3.** What is the solution of each system of equations?

a. $\begin{cases} y = x^2 - 4x + 5 \\ y = -x^2 + 5 \end{cases}$
 b. $\begin{cases} y = x^2 - 4x + 5 \\ y = -x^2 - 5 \end{cases}$

You can use the techniques for solving a linear system of inequalities to solve a quadratic system of inequalities.

 Problem 4 Solving a Quadratic System of Inequalities

What is the solution of the system of inequalities? $\begin{cases} y < -x^2 - 9x - 2 \\ y > x^2 - 2 \end{cases}$

Plan

How can you find the solution?
Graph each inequality and find the region where the graphs overlap.

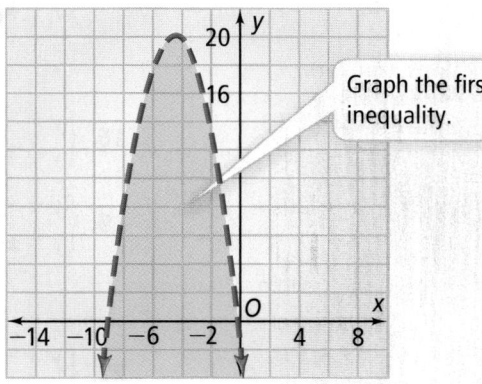

Graph the first inequality.

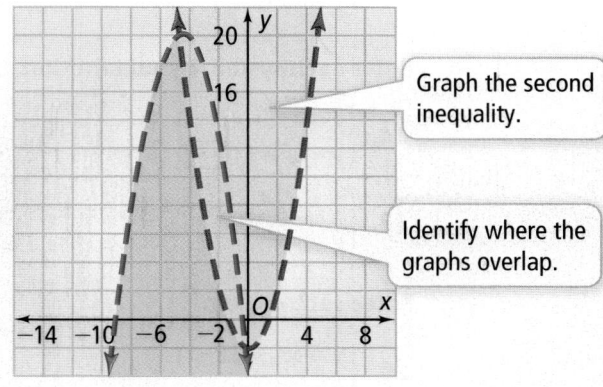

Graph the second inequality.

Identify where the graphs overlap.

The solution of this system is the region where the graphs overlap. The region contains no boundary points.

Got It? **4. a.** What is the solution of this system of inequalities? $\begin{cases} y \le -x^2 - 4x + 3 \\ y > x^2 + 3 \end{cases}$

b. Reasoning How many solutions can a system of inequalities have?

 Lesson Check

Do you know HOW?

Solve each system by substitution.

1. $\begin{cases} y = x^2 - 2x + 3 \\ y = x + 1 \end{cases}$

2. $\begin{cases} y = 2x^2 - 5x + 2 \\ y = x - 2 \end{cases}$

3. $\begin{cases} y = x^2 - 3x - 3 \\ y = -2x^2 - x + 5 \end{cases}$

Solve each system by graphing.

4. $\begin{cases} y > 2x^2 + x + 3 \\ y < -x^2 - 4x + 1 \end{cases}$

5. $\begin{cases} y > -3x^2 - 6x + 1 \\ y < -2x^2 - 3x + 5 \end{cases}$

Do you UNDERSTAND? MATHEMATICAL PRACTICES

6. Compare and Contrast How are solving systems of two linear equations or inequalities and solving systems of two quadratic equations or inequalities alike? How are they different?

7. Reasoning How many points of intersection can graphs of the following types of functions have? Draw graphs to justify your answers.
  a. a linear function and a quadratic function
  b. two quadratic functions
  c. a quadratic function and an absolute value function (*Hint:* Graph $y = x^2$ and $y = |x|$ together. Can you transform one of the graphs slightly to increase the number of intersections?)

Practice and Problem-Solving Exercises  MATHEMATICAL PRACTICES

 **Practice**

Solve each system by graphing. Check your answers.

◀ **See Problem 1.**

8. $\begin{cases} y = -x^2 + 2x + 1 \\ y = 2x + 1 \end{cases}$

9. $\begin{cases} y = x^2 - 2x + 1 \\ y = 2x + 1 \end{cases}$

10. $\begin{cases} y = x^2 - x + 3 \\ y = -2x + 5 \end{cases}$

11. $\begin{cases} y = 2x^2 + 3x + 1 \\ y = -2x + 1 \end{cases}$

12. $\begin{cases} y = -x^2 - 3x + 2 \\ y = x + 6 \end{cases}$

13. $\begin{cases} y = -x^2 - 2x - 2 \\ y = x - 4 \end{cases}$

Solve each system by substitution. Check your answers.

◀ **See Problem 2.**

14. $\begin{cases} y = x^2 + 4x + 1 \\ y = x + 1 \end{cases}$

15. $\begin{cases} y = -x^2 + 2x + 10 \\ y = x + 4 \end{cases}$

16. $\begin{cases} y = -x^2 + x - 1 \\ y = -x - 1 \end{cases}$

17. $\begin{cases} y = 2x^2 - 3x - 1 \\ y = x - 3 \end{cases}$

18. $\begin{cases} y = x^2 - 3x - 20 \\ y = -x - 5 \end{cases}$

19. $\begin{cases} y = -x^2 - 5x - 1 \\ y = x + 2 \end{cases}$

Solve each system.

◀ **See Problem 3.**

20. $\begin{cases} y = x^2 + 5x + 1 \\ y = x^2 + 2x + 1 \end{cases}$

21. $\begin{cases} y = x^2 - 2x - 1 \\ y = -x^2 - 2x - 1 \end{cases}$

22. $\begin{cases} y = -x^2 - 3x - 2 \\ y = x^2 + 3x + 2 \end{cases}$

23. $\begin{cases} y = -x^2 - x - 3 \\ y = 2x^2 - 2x - 3 \end{cases}$

24. $\begin{cases} y = -3x^2 - x + 2 \\ y = x^2 + 2x + 1 \end{cases}$

25. $\begin{cases} y = x^2 + 2x + 1 \\ y = x^2 + 2x - 1 \end{cases}$

Solve each system by graphing.

◀ **See Problem 4.**

26. $\begin{cases} y > x^2 + 2x \\ y > x^2 - 1 \end{cases}$

27. $\begin{cases} y > x^2 - 3x \\ y < 2x^2 - 3x \end{cases}$

28. $\begin{cases} y < -x^2 - 3x \\ y > x^2 - 1 \end{cases}$

 **Apply**

29. Think About a Plan A manufacturer is making cardboard boxes by cutting out four equal squares from the corners of the rectangular piece of cardboard and then folding the remaining part into a box. The length of the cardboard piece is 1 in. longer than its width. The manufacturer can cut out either 3×3 in. squares, or 4×4 in. squares. Find the dimensions of the cardboard for which the volume of the boxes produced by both methods will be the same.
- How can you represent the volume of the box using one variable?
- What system of equations can you write?
- Which method can you use to solve the system?

30. Open-Ended Can you solve the system of equations shown by graphing? Justify your answer. Can you solve this system using another method? If so, solve the system and explain why you chose that method.

$\begin{cases} x = y^2 + 2y + 1 \\ y = x - 4 \end{cases}$

Solve each system by substitution.

31. $\begin{cases} x + y = 3 \\ y = x^2 - 8x - 9 \end{cases}$

32. $\begin{cases} y - 2x = x + 5 \\ y + 1 = x^2 + 5x + 3 \end{cases}$

33. $\begin{cases} y - \frac{1}{2}x^2 = 1 + 3x \\ y + \frac{1}{2}x^2 = x \end{cases}$

34. $\begin{cases} x + y - 2 = 0 \\ x^2 + y - 8 = 0 \end{cases}$

35. $\begin{cases} x^2 - y = x + 4 \\ x - 1 = y + 3 \end{cases}$

36. $\begin{cases} 2y = y - x^2 + 1 \\ y = x^2 - 5x - 2 \end{cases}$

Graph the solution to each set of inequalities.

37. $\begin{cases} y < -3x^2 + 1 \\ y > x^2 - x - 5 \end{cases}$

38. $\begin{cases} y < 3x^2 + 2x + 1 \\ y > 2x^2 - x + 1 \end{cases}$

39. $\begin{cases} y > x^2 - 5x + 4 \\ y > x^2 + 3x + 2 \end{cases}$

Ⓒ 40. Error Analysis A classmate graphed the system of inequalities and concluded that because the shaded regions do not intersect, there are no solutions to the system. Describe and correct the error.

$\begin{cases} y \le x^2 - 4x + 6 \\ y \ge x^2 - 4x + 2 \end{cases}$

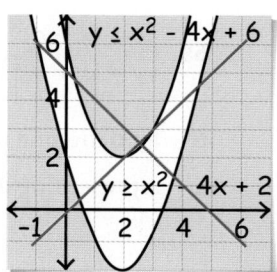

Solve each system.

41. $\begin{cases} y = 3x^2 - 2x - 1 \\ y = x - 1 \end{cases}$

42. $\begin{cases} y = -x^2 + x - 5 \\ y = x - 5 \end{cases}$

43. $\begin{cases} y = x^2 - 3x - 2 \\ y = 4x + 28 \end{cases}$

44. $\begin{cases} y = \frac{1}{2}x^2 + 4x + 4 \\ y = -4x + 12\frac{1}{2} \end{cases}$

45. $\begin{cases} y = -\frac{3}{4}x^2 - 4x \\ y = 3x + 8 \end{cases}$

46. $\begin{cases} y = -\frac{1}{4}x^2 + x + 1 \\ y = x - 4 \end{cases}$

47. Business A company's weekly revenue R is given by the formula $R = -p^2 + 30p$, where p is the price of the company's product. The company is considering hiring a distributor, which will cost the company $4p + 25$ per week.
  a. Use a system of equations to find the values of the price p for which the product will still remain profitable if they hire this distributor.
  b. Which value of p will maximize the profit after including the distributor cost?

Solve each system.

48. $\begin{cases} y = 5x^2 + 9x + 4 \\ y = -5x + 3 \end{cases}$

49. $\begin{cases} y = -7x^2 - 9x + 6 \\ y = \frac{1}{2}x + 11 \end{cases}$

50. $\begin{cases} y = x^2 + 3x + 6 \\ y = -x + 2 \end{cases}$

51. $\begin{cases} y = -4x^2 + 7x + 1 \\ y = 3x + 2 \end{cases}$

Ⓒ 52. Reasoning Sketch the graphs of $y = 2x^2 + 4x - 5$ and $y = x^2 + 2x - 3$. Change these equations into inequalities so the system has solutions that comprise:
  a. two non-overlapping regions
  b. one bounded region

Solve the systems by graphing. For each system indicate one point in the solution set.

53. $\begin{cases} y < x^2 - 1 \\ y > 3x^2 - 3 \end{cases}$

54. $\begin{cases} y > x^2 \\ y < -x^2 + 1 \end{cases}$

55. $\begin{cases} y > (x - 3)^2 + 4 \\ y < -(x - 3)^2 + 5 \end{cases}$

Ⓒ Challenge

56. Find a value of a for which the line $y = x + a$ separates the parabolas $y = x^2 - 3x + 2$ and $y = -x^2 + 8x - 15$.

Determine whether the following systems *always, sometimes,* or *never* have solutions. (Assume that different letters refer to unequal constants.) Explain.

57. $\begin{cases} y = x^2 + c \\ y = x^2 + d \end{cases}$

58. $\begin{cases} y = ax^2 + c \\ y = bx^2 + c \end{cases}$

59. $\begin{cases} y = (x + a)^2 \\ y = (x + b)^2 \end{cases}$

60. $\begin{cases} y = a(x + m)^2 + c \\ y = b(x + n)^2 + d \end{cases}$

61. Find the side of the square with vertical and horizontal sides inscribed in the region representing the solution of the system $\begin{cases} y \le -x^2 + 1 \\ y \ge x^2 - 1 \end{cases}$.

Standardized Test Prep

SAT/ACT

62. How many solutions does the system have? $\begin{cases} y = -\frac{1}{4}x^2 - 2x \\ y = x^2 + \frac{3}{4} \end{cases}$

    Ⓐ 0   Ⓑ 1   Ⓒ 2   Ⓓ 3

63. Which expression is equivalent to $(-3 + 2i)(2 - 3i)$?

    Ⓕ $13i$ Ⓖ 12 Ⓗ $12 + 13i$ Ⓘ -12

64. Which expression is equivalent to $(2 - 7i) \div (2i)^3$?

    Ⓐ $\frac{7}{8} - \frac{1}{4}i$ Ⓑ $\frac{1}{4} - \frac{7}{8}i$ Ⓒ $\frac{7}{8} + \frac{1}{4}i$ Ⓓ $\frac{1}{4} + \frac{7}{8}i$

Short Response

65. Solve the equation $-3x^2 + 5x + 4 = 0$. Show your work.

Mixed Review

Find the sum or difference.

See Lesson 4-8.

66. $(1 - i) + (-5 + 4i)$ **67.** $(3 + 4i) - (-4 - 3i)$ **68.** $(1 + i) + (2 + 2i)$

Solve each equation using the Quadratic Formula.

See Lesson 4-7.

69. $2m^2 + 5m + 3 = 0$ **70.** $p^2 - 4p + 3 = 0$ **71.** $25x^2 - 30x + 9 = 0$

Rewrite each equation in vertex form.

See Lesson 4-6.

72. $y = -k^2 + 4k + 6$ **73.** $y = x^2 + 6x + 1$ **74.** $y = 2n^2 - 8n - 3$

Get Ready! To prepare for Lesson 5-1, do Exercises 75–77.

Simplify by combining like terms.

See Lesson 1-3.

75. $3q + 9q - q$ **76.** $-2ab^2 + 2a^2b + 3ab^2$ **77.** $-4y^2 + 2y + 3y^2$

Powers of Complex Numbers

© **Common Core State Standards**

Extends N-CN.A.2 Use the relation $i^2 = -1$ and the commutative, associative, and distributive properties to add, subtract, and multiply . . .

MP 5

You can use the rules for multiplying complex numbers to find powers of complex numbers.

Example 1

Compute and graph $(2i)^n$, for $n = 0, 1, 2,$ and 3.

n	$(2i)^n$
0	$(2i)^0 = 1$
1	$(2i)^1 = 2i$
2	$(2i)^2 = 4i^2 = 4(-1) = -4$
3	$(2i)^3 = 8i^3 = 8(i^2 \cdot i) = 8(-1 \cdot i) = -8i$

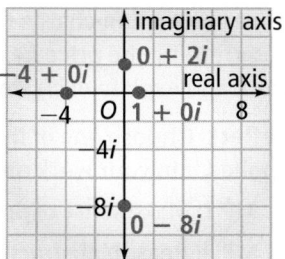

Example 2

Compute and graph $(2 - 3i)^n$, for $n = 0, 1, 2,$ and 3.

n	$(2 - 3i)^n$
0	$(2 - 3i)^0 = 1$
1	$(2 - 3i)^1 = 2 - 3i$
2	$(2 - 3i)^2 = 4 - 6i - 6i + 9i^2 = 4 - 12i + 9(-1) = -5 - 12i$
3	$(2 - 3i)^3 = -10 - 24i + 15i + 36i^2 = -10 - 9i + 36(-1) = -46 - 9i$

Exercises

1. Based on the graph in Example 1, predict the location of $(2i)^5$.

2. Compute and graph $(-3i)^n$ for $n = 0, 1, 2,$ and 3.

3. **a.** Connect the points from the graph in Example 1 with a smooth curve. Estimate $(2i)^{\frac{1}{2}}$.

   b. Use a graphing calculator to compute $(2i)^{\frac{1}{2}}$. Does it fall on the curve? Was it close to your estimate?

4. Use a graphing calculator to find values of $(2 - 3i)^n$ for $n = 0.5, 1.5,$ and 2.5. Copy the graph and add these points.

5. Compute and graph $(3 - 4i)^n$ for $n = 0, 1, 2,$ and 3.

Pull It **All Together**

Completing the Performance Task

Look back at your results from the Apply What You've Learned sections in Lessons 4-2, 4-3, and 4-5. Use the work you did to complete the following.

1. Solve the problem in the Task Description on page 193 by finding all possible prices Victor can charge for a bag of chips in order to make a profit, and determining the price he should charge to maximize his profit. Show all your work and explain each step of your solution.

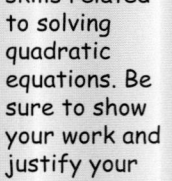 **2. Reflect** Choose one of the Mathematical Practices below and explain how you applied it in your work on the Performance Task.

    MP 1: Make sense of problems and persevere in solving them.

    MP 2: Reason abstractly and quantitatively.

    MP 4: Model with mathematics.

On Your Own

At his sandwich shop, Victor charges customers $5.00 for a sandwich, and sells an average of 300 sandwiches per week. He wonders if lowering his selling price will increase his sandwich sales. One week, Victor offers sandwiches at $3.00 instead of $5.00. That week, he sells 500 sandwiches.

Victor's cost per sandwich is $1.50. He assumes a linear relationship between the selling price per sandwich and the number of sandwiches sold per week.

a. Determine the greatest price Victor can charge and still make a profit.

b. Determine Victor's maximum weekly profit from sandwich sales and the selling price that gives him that profit.

Chapter Review

Connecting BIG ideas and Answering the Essential Questions

1 Equivalence

Vertex form of a quadratic function shows the vertex of the parabola. Standard form is "calculator ready." Both forms give additional information.

The Different Forms of a Quadratic Function (Lessons 4-1 and 4-2)

$y = 2(x - 1)^2 + 3$ has vertex $(1, 3)$ and opens upward $(2 > 0)$.

$y = -2x^2 + 4x + 1$ has vertex with x-coordinate $-\frac{4}{2(-2)} = 1$ and opens downward $(-2 < 0)$.

Each has axis of symmetry $x = 1$.
Each is a stretch of $y = x^2$ by the factor 2.

Modeling With Quadratics (Lessons 4-3 and 4-9)

$y = -16x^2 + 12x + 4$ can model the height y in feet reached by the coin tossed by the referee before the game. x represents time in seconds.

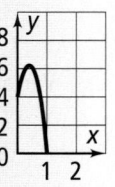

2 Function

Any quadratic function is possibly a stretch or compression, a reflection, and a translation of $y = x^2$.

3 Solving Equations and Inequalities

The real solutions of a quadratic equation show the zeros of the related quadratic function and the x-intercepts of its graph.

Helpful Aids for Solving Quadratic Equations (Lessons 4-4, 4-6, 4-8)

Factor a quadratic: $-16x^2 + 12x + 4$
$$= -4(4x + 1)(x - 1)$$
Complete the square: $x^2 + 4x + 1$
$$= x^2 + 4x + \left(\frac{4}{2}\right)^2 + 1 - \left(\frac{4}{2}\right)^2$$
$$= (x + 2)^2 - 3$$
Complex numbers: $x^2 + 1 = (x + i)(x - i)$
where $i = \sqrt{-1}$.

Solving Quadratic Equations (Lessons 4-5, 4-7)

$-16x^2 + 12x + 4 = 0$ $\longrightarrow$
$-4(4x + 1)(x - 1) = 0$ $\longrightarrow$
$x = -\frac{1}{4}$ or $x = 1$.

$-2x^2 + 4x + 1 = 0$ $\longrightarrow$
$x = \dfrac{-4 \pm \sqrt{4^2 - 4(-2)(1)}}{2(-2)}$ $\longrightarrow$
$x = 1 + \dfrac{\sqrt{6}}{2}$ or $x = 1 - \dfrac{\sqrt{6}}{2}$.

Chapter Vocabulary

- absolute value of a complex number (p. 249)
- axis of symmetry (p. 194)
- completing the square (p. 235)
- complex conjugate (p. 251)
- complex number (p. 249)
- complex number plane (p. 249)
- difference of two squares (p. 220)
- discriminant (p. 242)
- factoring (p. 216)
- greatest common factor (p. 218)
- imaginary number (p. 249)
- imaginary unit (p. 248)
- maximum value (p. 195)
- minimum value (p. 195)
- parabola (p. 194)
- perfect square trinomial (p. 219)
- pure imaginary number (p. 249)
- quadratic formula (p. 240)
- quadratic function (p. 194)
- standard form (p. 202)
- vertex form (p. 194)
- vertex of the parabola (p. 194)
- zero of a function (p. 226)
- zero product property (p. 226)

Choose the correct term to complete each sentence.

1. To solve an equation by factoring, the equation should first be written in (standard form/vertex form).

2. The value of $b^2 - 4ac$ for the equation $ax^2 + bx + c = 0$ is called the (discriminant/difference of two squares).

3. The number $a + bi$, where $b = 0$, is an example of a(n)(imaginary/complex) number.

4-1 Quadratic Functions and Transformations

Quick Review

You can write every **quadratic function** in the form $f(x) = ax^2 + bx + c$, where $a \neq 0$. A **parabola** is the graph of a quadratic function. Every parabola has a vertex and an axis of symmetry. Shown below is the graph of the quadratic parent function $f(x) = x^2$.

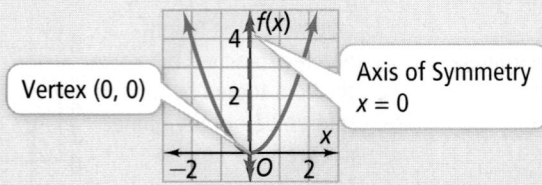

The **vertex form** of a quadratic function is

$f(x) = a(x - h)^2 + k$, where $a \neq 0$. The vertex of the parabola formed by a quadratic function is (h, k).

If $a > 0$, k is the **minimum value** of the function.

If $a < 0$, k is the **maximum value** of the function. The axis of symmetry is given by $x = h$.

Example

What is the vertex, axis of symmetry, maximum or minimum, and domain and range of the function
$f(x) = 5(x - 7)^2 + 2$?

$a = 5, h = 7, k = 2$	Identify a, h, and k.
vertex: $(7, 2)$	Find the vertex: (h, k).
axis of symmetry: $x = 7$	The axis of symmetry is at $x = h$.
$k = 2$ is a minimum	Since $a > 0$, k is a minimum.
domain: all real numbers	There are no restrictions on x.
range: $y \geq 2$.	Since the minimum is 2, $y \geq 2$.

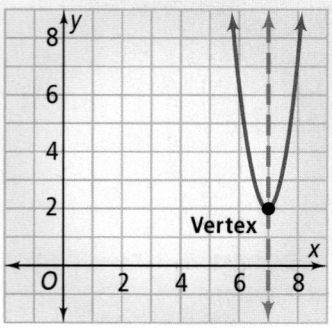

Exercises

Identify the vertex, axis of symmetry, maximum or minimum, and domain and range of each function.

4. $f(x) = 4(x + 2)^2 - 6$

5. $f(x) = -(x - 3)^2 + 2$

6. $f(x) = 10(x - 1)^2 + 5$

7. $f(x) = 2(x + 9)^2 - 4$

Graph each function. Describe each transformation of the parent function $f(x) = x^2$.

8. $f(x) = x^2 + 4$

9. $f(x) = (x - 9)^2 + 2$

10. $f(x) = \frac{1}{2}(x + 1)^2 - 5$

Write the equation of each parabola in vertex form.

11.

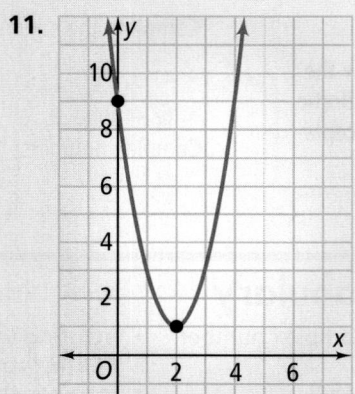

12.

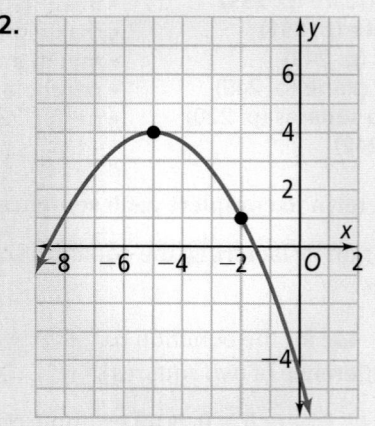

4-2 Standard Form of a Quadratic Function

Quick Review

The **standard form** of a quadratic function is
$f(x) = ax^2 + bx + c$, where $a \neq 0$. When $a > 0$, the parabola opens up. When $a < 0$, the parabola opens down.

The axis of symmetry is the line $x = -\frac{b}{2a}$. The vertex is $\left(-\frac{b}{2a}, f\left(-\frac{b}{2a}\right)\right)$, and the y-intercept is $(0, c)$.

Example

What are the vertex, the axis of symmetry and y-intercept of the graph of the function $f(x) = x^2 - 6x + 8$?

axis of symmetry: $x = -\left(\frac{-6}{2(1)}\right) = 3$

vertex: $(3, -1)$

y-intercept: $(0, 8)$

Exercises

Graph each function.

13. $f(x) = x^2 + 6x + 5$ **14.** $f(x) = x^2 - 7x - 18$

15. $f(x) = x^2 - 7x + 12$ **16.** $f(x) = x^2 - 9$

Write each function in vertex form.

17. $f(x) = 4x^2 - 8x + 2$ **18.** $f(x) = x^2 - 8x + 12$

19. $f(x) = 8x^2 + 8x - 12$ **20.** $f(x) = -2x^2 - 6x + 10$

21. Physics The equation $h = -16t^2 + 32t + 9$ gives the height of a ball, h, in feet above the ground, at t seconds after the ball is thrown upward. How many seconds after the ball is thrown will it reach its maximum height? What is its maximum height?

4-3 Modeling With Quadratic Functions

Quick Review

You can use quadratic functions to model real world data. You can find a quadratic function to model data that passes through any three non-collinear points given that no two of the points lie on a vertical line.

Example

Find the equation of the parabola that passes through the points $(-2, 8)$, $(0, -2)$, and $(1, 2)$.

$y = ax^2 + bx + c$	Use the standard form of a quadratic function.
$\begin{cases} 8 = a(-2)^2 + b(-2) + c \\ -2 = a(0)^2 + b(0) + c \\ 2 = a(1)^2 + b(1) + c \end{cases}$	Substitute the (x, y) values to write a system of equations.
$\begin{cases} 4a - 2b + c = 8 \\ c = -2 \\ a + b + c = 2 \end{cases}$	
$a = 3, b = 1, c = -2$	Solve the system of equations.
$y = 3x^2 + x - 2$	Substitute a, b, and c to find the quadratic function.

Exercises

Find the equation of the parabola that passes through each set of points.

22. $(0, 5), (2, -3), (-1, 12)$

23. $(2, 0), (3, -2), (1, -2)$

24. $(4, 10), (0, -18), (-2, -20)$

25. $(0, -7), (7, -14), (-3, -19)$

26. Track and Field The table shows the height of a javelin as it is thrown and travels across a horizontal distance. Use your calculator to find a quadratic model to represent the path of the javelin.

Distance (m)	Height (m)
5	2
18	5
33	8
55	6
68	4
74	3

4-4 Factoring Quadratic Expressions

Quick Review

To factor an expression of the form $ax^2 + bx + c$, when $a \neq 1$, you find numbers that have the product ac and sum b. You can also factor an expression using the FOIL method in reverse or by finding the greatest common factor (GCF).

Example

Factor the expression $5x^2 + 13x + 6$.

$ac = (5)(6) = 30$	Find ac.
$30 = 1 \cdot 30 = 2 \cdot 15 = 3 \cdot 10 = 5 \cdot 6$	Find the factors of ac.
$b = 13 = 3 + 10$	Find two factors that sum to b.
$5x^2 + 10x + 3x + 6$	Rewrite bx.
$5x(x + 2) + 3(x + 2)$	Find the common factors.
$(5x + 3)(x + 2)$	Rewrite using the Distributive Property.

Exercises

Factor each expression.

27. $x^2 - 8x + 12$ **28.** $3x^2 + 11x - 20$

29. $-4x^2 + 14x - 6$ **30.** $x^2 + 14x + 40$

Factor each perfect square trinomial.

31. $x^2 - 14x + 49$ **32.** $9x^2 + 30x + 25$

Factor each difference of two squares.

33. $36x^2 - 16$ **34.** $25x^2 - 4$

Find the GCF of each expression. Then factor each expression.

35. $6x^2 - 24x$ **36.** $-14x^2 - 49$

4-5 Solving Quadratic Equations

Quick Review

The **zeros** of a quadratic function are the solutions of the related quadratic equation. You can find the zeros from a table or from the x-intercepts of the parabola that is the graph of the function. You can also find them by **factoring** the **standard form of a quadratic equation**, $ax^2 + bx + c = 0$, and using the **Zero-Product Property**.

Example

Solve $2x^2 + 6x = 8$ by factoring.

$2x^2 + 6x - 8 = 0$	Rewrite the equation in standard form.
$2(x^2 + 3x - 4) = 0$	Factor out the GCF, 2.
$2(x + 4)(x - 1) = 0$	Factor the quadratic expression.
$2(x + 4) = 0$ or $x - 1 = 0$	Use the Zero-Product Property.
$x = -4$ or $x = 1$	Solve.

Exercises

Solve each equation by factoring.

37. $x^2 = 4x + 12$ **38.** $2x^2 - 3x - 14 = 0$

39. $x^2 + 2x = 8$ **40.** $x^2 + 7x = 18$

Solve each equation by graphing.

41. $5x^2 + 8x - 13 = 0$ **42.** $9 - 4x = 2x^2$

43. $x^2 - x = 1$ **44.** $x^2 - 2x - 4 = 0$

Solve each equation by using a table.

45. $x^2 - 6x + 8 = 0$ **46.** $9x - 14 = 3x^2$

47. $x^2 - 5x + 2 = 0$ **48.** $2x^2 - 12x = -16$

4-6 Completing the Square

Quick Review

If you cannot solve a quadratic equation by factoring, you can use **completing the square**. You write one side as a perfect square trinomial and then take square roots. You can also convert a quadratic function from standard form to vertex form by completing the square.

Example

Solve $x^2 + 6x - 7 = 0$ by completing the square.

$x^2 + 6x = 7$	Rewrite the equation so the constant is by itself.
$\left(\frac{b}{2}\right)^2 = \left(\frac{6}{2}\right)^2 = 3^2 = 9$	Find $\left(\frac{b}{2}\right)^2$.
$x^2 + 6x + 9 = 7 + 9$	Add $\left(\frac{b}{2}\right)^2$ to each side.
$(x + 3)^2 = 16$	Factor and simplify.
$x + 3 = \pm 4$	Take the square root of each side.
$x = 1$ or $x = -7$	Solve for x.

Exercises

Solve each equation by finding square roots.

49. $4x^2 = 16$

50. $4x^2 - 20 = 0$

51. $5x^2 - 45 = 0$

52. $3x^2 = 36$

What values complete each square?

53. $x^2 - 6x$

54. $x^2 + 3x$

Solve each equation by completing the square.

55. $x^2 + 8x + 6 = 0$

56. $x^2 - 10x = 13$

57. $9x^2 + 6x + 1 = 4$

58. $x^2 - 2x + 4 = 0$

59. $x^2 + 3x = -25$

60. $4x^2 - x - 3 = 0$

4-7 The Quadratic Formula

Quick Review

You can solve a quadratic equation in the form $ax^2 + bx + c = 0$ by using the **Quadratic Formula**, $x = \frac{-b \pm \sqrt{b^2 - 4ac}}{2a}$. The **discriminant** of a quadratic equation in standard form is the value of the expression $b^2 - 4ac$. You can use it to find the quantity and type of solutions of a quadratic equation.

Example

Use the Quadratic Formula to solve $2x^2 - 6x = -3$.

$2x^2 - 6x + 3 = 0$	Write the equation in standard form.
$a = 2, b = -6, c = 3$	Identify a, b, and c.
$x = \frac{-(-6) \pm \sqrt{(-6)^2 - 4(2)(3)}}{2(2)}$	Substitute a, b, and c into the quadratic formula.
$x = \frac{6 \pm \sqrt{12}}{4} = \frac{3 \pm \sqrt{3}}{2}$	Simplify.

Exercises

Solve each equation using the quadratic formula.

61. $3x^2 + 5x = 8$

62. $x^2 = 6x - 9$

63. $x(x - 3) = 4$

64. $5x^2 - 7x - 3 = 0$

Determine the discriminant of each equation. How many real solutions does each equation have?

65. $4x^2 - 2x = 10$

66. $x^2 - 5x + 7 = 0$

67. $3x^2 + 3 = 6x$

68. $7 - 3x = 8x^2$

69. Gardening Margaret is planning a rectangular garden. Its length is 4 ft less than twice its width. Its area is 170 ft^2. What are the dimensions of the garden?

4-8 Complex Numbers

Quick Review

A **complex number** is written in the form $a + bi$, where a and b are real numbers, and i is equal to $\sqrt{-1}$. If $b = 0$, $a + bi$ is a real number. If $b \neq 0$, $a + bi$ is an **imaginary number**. You can use the Quadratic Formula or completing the square to find the imaginary solutions of quadratic equations.

Example

Use the Quadratic Formula to solve $3x^2 - 4x + 2 = 0$.

$x = \dfrac{-(-4) \pm \sqrt{(-4)^2 - 4(3)(2)}}{2(3)}$ Enter a, b, and c into the quadratic formula.

$x = \dfrac{4 \pm \sqrt{16 - 24}}{6} = \dfrac{4 \pm \sqrt{-8}}{6}$ Simplify.

$x = \dfrac{2}{3} \pm \dfrac{\sqrt{2}}{3}i$ Write the solutions.

Exercises

Simplify each expression using the imaginary unit i.

70. $\sqrt{-24}$ **71.** $\sqrt{-2} - 3$

72. $(4 + \sqrt{-25})(\sqrt{-100})$ **73.** $2\sqrt{-24} + 6$

Simplify each expression.

74. $(9 + 7i) - (6 - 2i)$ **75.** $(3 + 11i) + (10 + 9i)$

76. $(1 - 9i)(3 + 2i)$ **77.** $(3i)^2 - 3(1 + 5i)$

78. $\dfrac{4 - 6i}{2i}$ **79.** $\dfrac{2 - 3i}{1 + 5i}$

Solve each equation.

80. $x^2 + 9 = 0$ **81.** $5x^2 - 2x + 1 = 0$

82. $-x^2 + 4x = 10$ **83.** $7x^2 + 8x = -6$

4-9 Quadratic Systems

Quick Review

A system of quadratic equations can be solved by substitution or by graphing. You can use these methods to solve a linear–quadratic system or a quadratic–quadratic system. Use graphing to solve a quadratic system of inequalities.

Example

Use substitution to solve $\begin{cases} y = 2x^2 + 2x - 10 \\ y = x^2 + 5x - 6 \end{cases}$.

$2x^2 + 2x - 10 = x^2 + 5x - 6$ Substitute for y.

$x^2 - 3x - 4 = 0$ Rewrite in standard form.

$(x + 1)(x - 4) = 0$ Factor.

$x = -1$ or $x = 4$ Solve for x.

$y = (-1)^2 + 5(-1) - 6 = -10$ Substitute for x then solve for y.

$y = (4)^2 + 5(4) - 6 = 30$

$(-1, -10)$ and $(4, 30)$ Write solutions as ordered pairs.

Exercises

Solve each system by substitution.

84. $\begin{cases} y = x^2 - 7x - 6 \\ y = 8 - 2x \end{cases}$

85. $\begin{cases} y = -x^2 - 2x + 8 \\ y = x^2 - 8x - 12 \end{cases}$

Solve each system by graphing.

86. $\begin{cases} y = -x^2 - 10x + 12 \\ y = x^2 - 6x - 18 \end{cases}$

87. $\begin{cases} y = x^2 - x - 18 \\ y = 2x + 3 \end{cases}$

Solve each system of inequalities.

88. $\begin{cases} y < x + 4 \\ y \geq x^2 + 2x + 2 \end{cases}$

89. $\begin{cases} y > 3x^2 - 10x - 8 \\ y < x^2 - 5x + 4 \end{cases}$

Do you know HOW?

Sketch a graph of the quadratic function with the given vertex and through the given point. Then write the equation of the parabola in vertex form and describe how the function was transformed from the parent function $y = x^2$.

1. vertex $(0, 0)$, point $(-3, 3)$

2. vertex $(1, 5)$, point $(2, 1)$

Graph each quadratic function. Identify the axis of symmetry, the vertex, and the domain and the range of each function.

3. $y = x^2 - 7$

4. $y = x^2 + 2x + 6$

5. $y = -x^2 + 5x - 3$

Simplify each expression.

6. $\sqrt{-16}$

7. $4\sqrt{-9} - 2$

8. $(2 + 3i)(8 - 5i)$

9. $(-3 + 2i) - (6 + i)$

10. $\frac{4 + 2i}{2 - i}$

Factor each expression completely.

11. $2y^2 - 8y$

12. $3x^2 + 8x - 3$

13. $9w^2 - 30w + 25$

Solve each quadratic equation.

14. $x^2 - 25 = 0$

15. $x^2 - 2x + 3 = 0$

16. $x^2 - 8x = -6$

Solve the following systems of equations.

17. $\begin{cases} y = 3x^2 - x + 1 \\ y = 3x^2 + x - 1 \end{cases}$

18. $\begin{cases} y = -x^2 + 2x - 3 \\ y = 4x - 3 \end{cases}$

Solve the following systems of inequalities.

19. $\begin{cases} y > 2x^2 + 5x + 1 \\ y < -2x^2 - 5x - 1 \end{cases}$

20. $\begin{cases} y < x^2 - x + 2 \\ y > x^2 - 1 \end{cases}$

Evaluate the discriminant of each equation. How many real and imaginary solutions does each have?

21. $x^2 + 6x - 7 = 0$

22. $3x^2 - x + 3 = 0$

23. $-4x^2 - 4x + 1 = 0$

Do you UNDERSTAND?

© **24. Writing** Compare graphing a number on the complex plane to graphing a point on the coordinate plane. How are they similar? How are they different?

© **25. Open-Ended** Sketch the graph of a quadratic function $f(x) = ax^2 + bx + c$ that has no real zeros. How does this relate to the solutions of the related equation $ax^2 + bx + c = 0$?

STEM **26. Physics** A model for the path of a toy rocket is given by $h = 68t - 4.9t^2$, where h is the altitude in meters and t is the time in seconds. Explain how to find both the maximum altitude of the rocket and how long it takes to reach that altitude.

27. How many solutions are possible for:
   a. a system of two quadratic equations?
   b. a system of two quadratic inequalities?
   Explain your answers.

Common Core Cumulative Standards Review

 **ASSESSMENT**

TIPS FOR SUCCESS

Some questions on tests require that you model a word problem with a quadratic function.

TIP 1

To identify the function, use what you already know. You know that the perimeter of a rectangle is $2(\ell + w)$ and the area is $\ell \cdot w$.

Roy has a 400 foot roll of wire. He wants to use it to fence in a rectangular area. What is the maximum area of the enclosed space?

  Ⓐ 20,000 square feet

  Ⓑ 10,000 square feet

  Ⓒ 200 square feet

  Ⓓ 100 square feet

TIP 2

Use the information from the problem. The perimeter is 400, so $2(\ell + w) = 400$. Solve for w: $w = 200 - \ell$.

Think It Through

Substitute for w in the area formula:
$$A = f(\ell) = \ell \cdot (200 - \ell)$$
$$= -\ell^2 + 200\ell.$$

The maximum value is the y-coordinate of the vertex,
$$f\left(-\frac{b}{2a}\right) = f(100) = 10{,}000.$$
So, the maximum area Roy can enclose is 10,000 square feet.

The correct answer is B.

Vocabulary Builder

As you solve test items, you must understand the meanings of mathematical terms. Match each term with its mathematical meaning.

A. axis of symmetry

B. discriminant

C. imaginary number

D. Zero-Product Property

E. parabola

F. perfect square trinomial

G. completing the square

I. value of $b^2 - 4ac$ for the equation $ax^2 + bx + c = 0$

II. If $ab = 0$, then $a = 0$ or $b = 0$.

III. line that divides a parabola into two parts that are mirror images

IV. $a + bi$, a and b are real numbers and $b \neq 0$

V. square of a binomial

VI. process of finding the last term to make a perfect square trinomial

VII. graph of a quadratic function

Selected Response

Read each question. Then write the letter of the correct answer on your paper.

1. Which equation is equivalent to $x^2 + 24x + 100 = -46$?

  Ⓐ $(x + 12)^2 = -2$

  Ⓑ $(x - 12)^2 = -2$

  Ⓒ $(x - 12)^2 = 2$

  Ⓓ $(x + 12)^2 = 2$

2. What is the solution of the following system of equations?

$$2x - y = 4$$
$$3x + y = 1$$

  Ⓕ $(-1, 2)$

  Ⓖ $(1, -2)$

  Ⓗ $(2, 1)$

  Ⓘ $(-2, 1)$

3. What are the factors of the quadratic function graphed below?

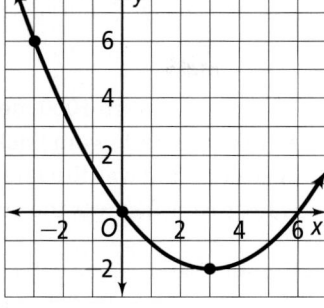

- (A) $(x + 3)$ and $(x + 2)$
- (B) x and $(x - 6)$
- (C) x and $(x + 6)$
- (D) $(x - 3)$ and $(x + 2)$

4. Which equation has $-1 \pm i$ as its solution?

- (F) $x^2 - 2x - 2 = 0$
- (G) $2x^2 - 2x - 1 = 0$
- (H) $2x^2 + 2x + 1 = 0$
- (I) $x^2 + 2x + 2 = 0$

5. What are the solutions of $|3x - 5| = 2$?

- (A) $x = -1$ and $x = \frac{7}{3}$
- (B) $x = 1$ and $x = \frac{7}{3}$
- (C) $x = 1$ and $x = \frac{1}{5}$
- (D) $x = -1$ and $x = \frac{1}{5}$

6. What is the transformation of the graph of $y = (x + 3)^2 - 2$ from its parent function $y = x^2$?

- (F) 3 units left and 2 units down
- (G) 3 units right and 2 units up
- (H) 6 units right and 2 units up
- (I) 2 units left and 3 units down

7. What is the axis of symmetry for the graph of the quadratic equation $y = -3x^2 - 12 + 12x$?

- (A) $x = -2$
- (B) $x = 2$
- (C) $x = 12$
- (D) $x = -12$

8. What are the domain and range of the function graphed below?

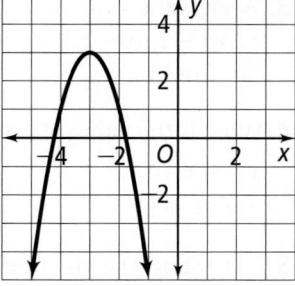

- (F) Domain: All real numbers
  Range: All real numbers ≤ 3
- (G) Domain: All real numbers
  Range: All real numbers ≥ 3
- (H) Domain: All real numbers between -5 and -1
  Range: All real numbers ≤ 3
- (I) Domain: All real numbers between -5 and -1
  Range: All real numbers ≥ 3

9. The formula for the total surface area of a regular right pentagonal prism is $A = ap + pH$. Solve this equation for p.

- (A) $p = \frac{a + H}{A}$
- (B) $p = \frac{A}{a + H}$
- (C) $p = A - \frac{a}{H}$
- (D) $p = \frac{H - a}{A}$

10. What is the solution of $\begin{cases} -y = 3x - 1 \\ 2y = -x - 2 \end{cases}$?

- (F) $x = 20, y = -11$
- (G) $x = \frac{4}{5}, y = -\frac{7}{5}$
- (H) $x = -20, y = 11$
- (I) $x = -\frac{4}{5}, y = \frac{7}{5}$

11. Which system of inequalities is graphed below?

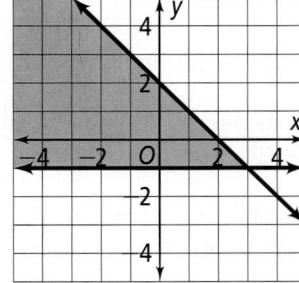

- (A) $\begin{cases} y \leq -1 \\ y + x \geq 2 \end{cases}$
- (B) $\begin{cases} y \geq -1 \\ y + x \leq 2 \end{cases}$
- (C) $\begin{cases} y < 1 \\ y + x > -2 \end{cases}$
- (D) $\begin{cases} y > 1 \\ y + x < -2 \end{cases}$

12. What is the vertex of $y = -2|x + 4| - 5$?

- (F) $(-2, -5)$
- (G) $(-4, -5)$
- (H) $(4, -5)$
- (I) $(2, -5)$

Selected Response

13. What is the sum of the solutions of the equation $1.5x^2 - 2.5x - 1.5 = 0$? Round to the nearest hundredth.

14. What is the value of y in the system of equations?

$x + y = 10$

$y = 2x + 1$

15. Zeroy and Darius shop at the mall during the special sale extravaganza. Zeroy spends $120 on 3 pairs of pants and 4 shirts. Darius buys 2 pairs of pants and 3 shirts and spends $85. What is the price of one shirt?

16. What is the sum of the solutions of $|5x - 4| = 8 - x$?

17. Suppose y varies directly with x, and $y = -4$ when $x = 5$. What is the constant of variation?

18. Molly is making a punch for the school picnic. The recipe calls for $\frac{3}{4}$ quart of lemonade, 3 cups of cranberry juice, 4 cans of orange juice concentrate, and 5 cups of water. If Molly uses $1\frac{2}{5}$ quarts of lemonade, how many cups of cranberry juice will she need?

19. What is the value of $3x^2 - 5x + 7$ when $x = \frac{2}{5}$? Express the answer as a decimal.

20. What is the real part of $(11 + 10i)(2 + 3i)$?

21. How many imaginary roots does $2x^2 + 3x - 5 = 0$ have?

22. What is the product of $(4 + 3i)(4 - 3i)$?

23. What is the greatest integer solution of $|2x + 3| - 4 \le 0$?

24. What is the coefficient of the x-term of the factorization of $25x^2 + 20x + 4$?

25. A piggy bank contains $2.40 in nickels and dimes. If there are 33 coins in all, how many nickels are there?

26. What are the solutions of the system? Solve by graphing.

$y = x^2 - x - 2$

$y = -x + 2$

27. A swimmer swam 1000 meters downstream in 15 minutes and swam back in 30 minutes against the current. What was the rate of the swimmer in still water? How fast was the current?

28. Claudia has a rectangular flowerbed. She decided that the original width w, in feet, was too small, so she increased the width by 3 feet. She also changed the length to be 1 foot less than twice the original width. What is an expression that represents the area of the new flower bed?

29. Explain how you would graph $y + 4 < 2|x - 3|$ on a coordinate grid.

Extended Response

30. A hat company is designing a one-size-fits-all hat with a strap in the back that makes the hat smaller or larger. Head sizes normally range from 51 to 64 centimeters. What absolute value inequality models the different sizes of the hat? Graph the solution.

31. Robby decided to earn extra money by making and selling brownies and cookies. He had space in his oven to make at most 80 brownies and cookies. Each brownie cost $.10 to make and each cookie cost $.05 to make. He had $6 to spend on ingredients.
   a. Write a system of inequalities to represent the situation.
   b. Graph the system, choose one point in the feasible region, and explain what the point means in terms of the problem.
   c. If Robby makes a profit of $.25 on each brownie and $.20 on each cookie, how many of each dessert should he make to maximize his profit?

Get Ready!

Lesson 4-2 ◆ **Graphing Quadratic Functions**

Graph each function.

1. $f(x) = x^2 - 8x + 7$ **2.** $f(x) = -\frac{1}{2}x^2 - 4x - 4$ **3.** $f(x) = x^2 + 4x + 4$

Lesson 4-3 ◆ **Writing Equations of Parabolas**

Write in standard form the equation of the parabola passing through the given points.

4. $(-1, -6), (-3, -4), (2, 6)$ **5.** $(3, 4), (-2, 9), (2, 1)$ **6.** $(-5, -8), (4, -8), (-3, 6)$

Lesson 4-5 ◆ **Solving Quadratic Equations by Graphing**

Solve each equation by graphing. Round to the nearest hundredth.

7. $1 = 4x^2 + 3x$ **8.** $\frac{1}{2}x^2 + x - 14 = 0$ **9.** $5x^2 + 30x = 12$

Lesson 4-5 ◆ **Solving Quadratic Equations by Factoring**

Solve each equation by factoring.

10. $x^2 - x - 20 = 0$ **11.** $x^2 + 6x - 27 = 0$ **12.** $3x^2 - 9x + 6 = 0$

Lesson 4-7 ◆ **Finding the Number and Type of Solutions**

Evaluate the discriminant of each equation. Tell how many solutions each equation has and whether the solutions are real or imaginary.

13. $x^2 - 12x + 30 = 0$ **14.** $-4x^2 + 20x - 25 = 0$ **15.** $2x^2 = 8x - 8$

Looking Ahead Vocabulary

16. A *turning point* is a place where a graph changes direction. Suppose you start hiking north on a winding trail, and the trail makes a turn and heads south, and then north again. If you make a total of 3 of these 180 degree turns, in which direction will you be hiking after the last turn?

17. A *relative maximum* is the greatest value in a region. The highest point in Maine is Mt. Katahdin at 5267 ft. How might that compare to the highest point in the United States? What might the relative maximum of a graph be?

18. A contraction is a shortened form of a word or phrase. The expanded form of the contraction "don't" is "do not." You can *expand* a math phrase by multiplying it out. For example, $(x - 2)^2 = (x - 2)(x - 2) = x^2 - 4x + 4$. Expand $(2x + 1)^2$.

CHAPTER 5

Polynomials and Polynomial Functions

Chapter Preview

BIG ideas

1 Function

Essential Question What does the degree of a polynomial tell you about its related polynomial function?

2 Equivalence

Essential Question For a polynomial function, how are factors, zeros, and x-intercepts related?

3 Solving Equations and Inequalities

Essential Question For a polynomial equation, how are factors and roots related?

Vocabulary

English/Spanish Vocabulary Audio Online:

English	Spanish
end behavior, *p. 282*	comportamiento extremo
monomial, *p. 280*	monomio
multiplicity, *p. 291*	multiplicidad
Pascal's Triangle, *p. 327*	Triángulo de Pascal
polynomial function, *p. 280*	función polinomial
relative maximum, *p. 291*	máximo relativo
relative minimum, *p. 291*	mínimo relativo
standard form of a polynomial function, *p. 281*	forma normal de una función polinomial
synthetic division, *p. 306*	división sintética
turning point, *p. 282*	punto de giro

 DOMAINS

- Interpreting Functions
- Arithmetic with Polynomials and Rational Expressions
- The Complex Number System

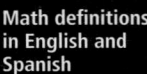
Download videos connecting math to your world.

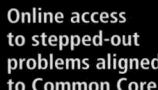
Interactive! Vary numbers, graphs, and figures to explore math concepts.

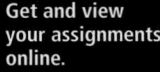
The online Solve It will get you in gear for each lesson.

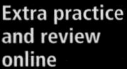
Math definitions in English and Spanish

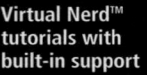
Online access to stepped-out problems aligned to Common Core

Get and view your assignments online.

Extra practice and review online

Virtual Nerd™ tutorials with built-in support

Common Core Performance Task

Determining the Dimensions of a Diorama

A diorama is a three-dimensional model of a scene in which small figures and objects are arranged against a background. Dioramas are often displayed in rectangular boxes with open fronts.

Eliana wants to make a diorama for an art contest. She starts with a rectangular sheet of cardboard that is 12 in. long and 8 in. wide. She plans to make the diorama box by cutting identical squares from the corners and folding the sides to create a box with an open front, as shown below.

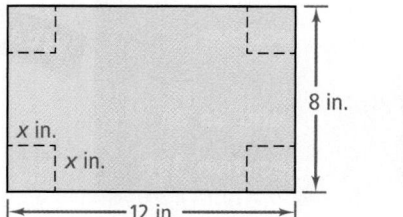
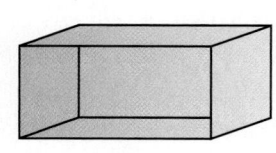

The art contest is accepting entries for miniature dioramas, requiring the volume to be no more than 36 in.^{3}. Eliana wants her diorama box to have the maximum allowable volume.

Task Description

Determine all possible dimensions Eliana can use for a diorama box with volume 36 in.^{3}. Round dimensions to the nearest hundredth of an inch.

Connecting the Task to the Math Practices

MATHEMATICAL PRACTICES

As you complete the task, you'll apply several Standards for Mathematical Practice.

- You'll analyze the given information and write a function that models the volume of the diorama box. (MP 4)

- You'll graph the volume function and think about which points of the graph correspond to possible volumes of the diorama box. (MP 1)

- You'll look for and use structure in a polynomial to find the real roots of an equation. (MP 7)

5-1 Polynomial Functions

© **Common Core State Standards**

F-IF.C.7c Graph polynomial functions, identifying zeros when suitable factorizations are available and showing end behavior. **Also A-SSE.A.1a**

MP 1, MP 2, MP 3, MP 5

Objectives To classify polynomials
To graph polynomial functions and describe end behavior

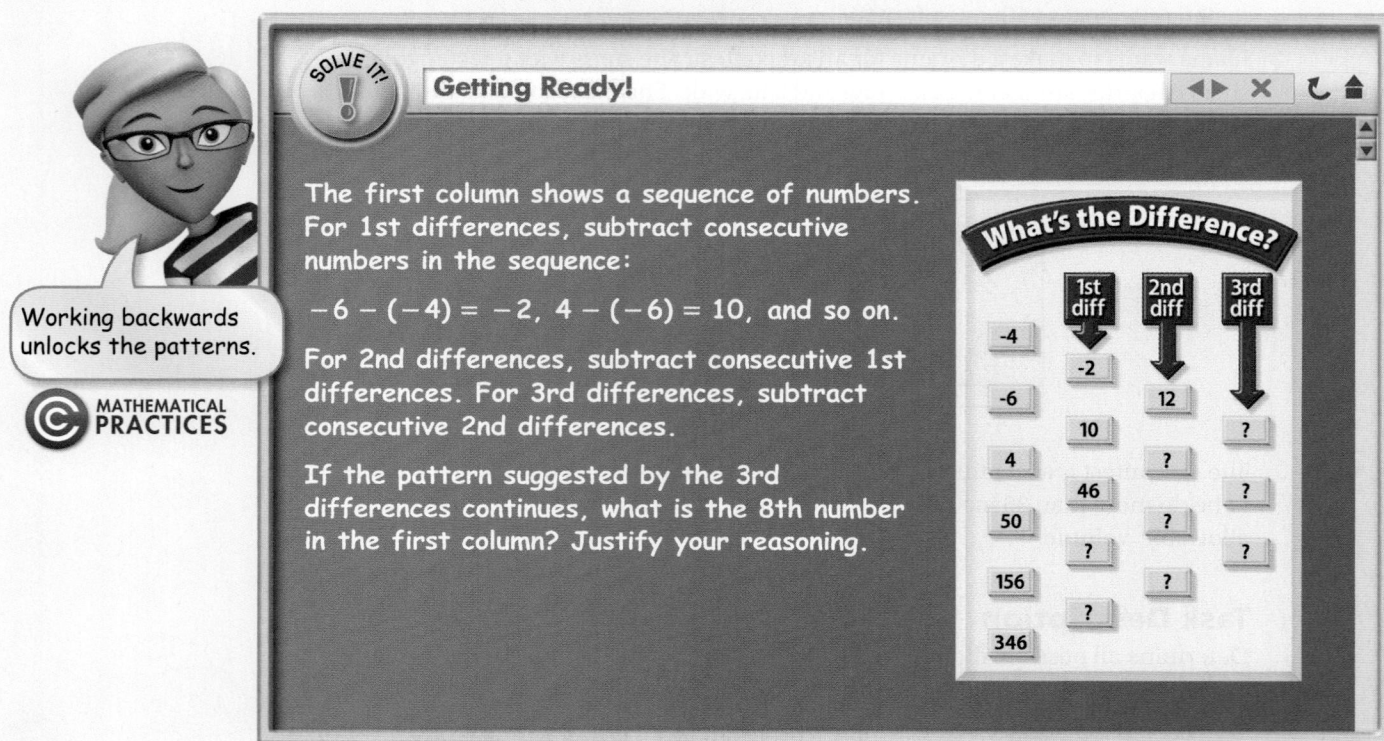

SOLVE IT!

Getting Ready!

◄► ✕ ↻ ⬆

The first column shows a sequence of numbers. For 1st differences, subtract consecutive numbers in the sequence:

$-6 - (-4) = -2$, $4 - (-6) = 10$, and so on.

For 2nd differences, subtract consecutive 1st differences. For 3rd differences, subtract consecutive 2nd differences.

If the pattern suggested by the 3rd differences continues, what is the 8th number in the first column? Justify your reasoning.

What's the Difference?

	1st diff	2nd diff	3rd diff
-4			
	-2		
-6		12	
	10		?
4		?	
	46		?
50		?	
	?		?
156		?	
	?		
346			

Working backwards unlocks the patterns.

MATHEMATICAL **PRACTICES**

Lesson Vocabulary
- monomial
- degree of a monomial
- polynomial
- degree of a polynomial
- polynomial function
- standard form of a polynomial function
- turning point
- end behavior

The sequence of numbers in the first column above are values of a particular *polynomial function*. For such a sequence, you can use patterns of 1st differences, 2nd differences, 3rd differences, and so on, to learn more about the polynomial function.

Essential Understanding A polynomial function has distinguishing "behaviors." You can look at its algebraic form and know something about its graph. You can look at its graph and know something about its algebraic form.

A **monomial** is a real number, a variable, or a product of a real number and one or more variables with whole-number exponents. The **degree of a monomial** in one variable is the exponent of the variable. A **polynomial** is a monomial or a sum of monomials. The **degree of a polynomial** in one variable is the greatest degree among its monomial terms.

A polynomial with the variable x defines a **polynomial function** of x. The degree of the polynomial function is the same as the degree of the polynomial.

Key Concept Standard Form of a Polynomial Function

The **standard form of a polynomial function** arranges the terms by degree in descending numerical order.

A polynomial function $P(x)$ in standard form is

$$P(x) = a_n x^n + a_{n-1} x^{n-1} + \cdots + a_1 x + a_0,$$

where n is a nonnegative integer and $a_n, \ldots, a_0$ are real numbers.

$$P(x) = 4x^3 + 3x^2 + 5x - 2$$

| Cubic term | Quadratic term | Linear term | Constant term |

You can classify a polynomial by its degree or by its number of terms. Polynomials of degrees zero through five have specific names, as shown in this table.

Degree	Name Using Degree	Polynomial Example	Number of Terms	Name Using Number of Terms
0	constant	5	1	monomial
1	linear	$x + 4$	2	binomial
2	quadratic	$4x^2$	1	monomial
3	cubic	$4x^3 - 2x^2 + x$	3	trinomial
4	quartic	$2x^4 + 5x^2$	2	binomial
5	quintic	$-x^5 + 4x^2 + 2x + 1$	4	polynomial of 4 terms

 Problem 1 Classifying Polynomials

Write each polynomial in standard form. What is the classification of each polynomial by degree? by number of terms?

Ⓐ $3x + 9x^2 + 5$

$9x^2 + 3x + 5$

The polynomial has degree 2 and 3 terms. It is a quadratic trinomial.

Ⓑ $4x - 6x^2 + x^4 + 10x^2 - 12$

$x^4 + 4x^2 + 4x - 12$

The polynomial has degree 4 and 4 terms. It is a quartic polynomial of 4 terms.

Think

How do you write a polynomial in standard form?
Combine like terms if possible. Then, write the terms with their degrees in descending order.

 Got It? 1. Write each polynomial in standard form. What is the classification of each by degree? by number of terms?

a. $3x^3 - x + 5x^4$

b. $3 - 4x^5 + 2x^2 + 10$

The degree of a polynomial function affects the shape of its graph and determines the maximum number of **turning points**, or places where the graph changes direction. It also affects the **end behavior**, or the directions of the graph to the far left and to the far right.

The table below shows you examples of polynomial functions and the four types of end behavior. The table also shows intervals where the functions are increasing and decreasing. A function is *increasing* when the y-values increase as x-values increase. A function is *decreasing* when the y-values decrease as x-values increase.

take note

Key Concept Polynomial Functions

$y = 4x^4 + 6x^3 - x$

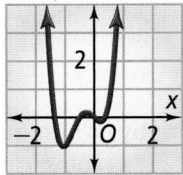

End Behavior: Up and Up

Turning Points: $(-1.07, -1.04)$, $(-0.27, 0.17)$, and $(0.22, -0.15)$

The function is decreasing when $x < -1.07$ and $-0.27 < x < 0.22$. The function increases when $-1.07 < x < -0.27$ and $x > 0.22$.

$y = -x^2 + 2x$

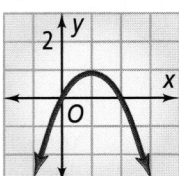

End Behavior: Down and Down

Turning Point: $(1, 1)$

The function is increasing when $x < 1$ and is decreasing when $x > 1$.

$y = x^3$

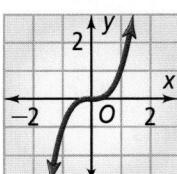

End Behavior: Down and Up

Zero turning points.

The function is increasing for all x.

$y = -x^3 + 2x$

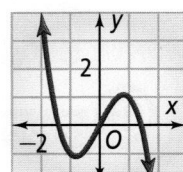

End Behavior: Up and Down

Turning Points: $(-0.82, -1.09)$ and $(0.82, 1.09)$

The function is decreasing when $x < -0.82$ and when $x > 0.82$. The function is increasing when $-0.82 < x < 0.82$.

You can determine the end behavior of a polynomial function of degree n from the leading term ax^n of the standard form.

End Behavior of a Polynomial Function With Leading Term ax^n

	n Even ($n \neq 0$)	n Odd
a Positive	Up and Up	Down and Up
a Negative	Down and Down	Up and Down

In general, the graph of a polynomial function of degree n ($n \geq 1$) has at most $n - 1$ turning points. The graph of a polynomial function of odd degree has an even number of turning points. The graph of a polynomial function of even degree has an odd number of turning points.

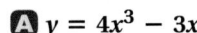 **Problem 2** Describing End Behavior of Polynomial Functions

Consider the leading term of each polynomial function. What is the end behavior of the graph? Check your answer with a graphing calculator.

Think

What do a and n represent?
a is the coefficient of the leading term. n is the exponent of the leading term.

A $y = 4x^3 - 3x$

The leading term is $4x^3$. Since n is odd and a is positive, the end behavior is down and up.

B $y = -2x^4 + 8x^3 - 8x^2 + 2$

The leading term is $-2x^4$. Since n is even and a is negative, the end behavior is down and down.

 Got It? 2. Consider the leading term of $y = -4x^3 + 2x^2 + 7$. What is the end behavior of the graph?

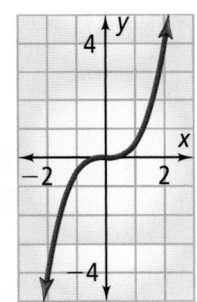 **Problem 3** Graphing Cubic Functions

What is the graph of each cubic function? Describe the graph, including end behavior, turning points, and increasing/decreasing intervals.

A $y = \frac{1}{2}x^3$

B $y = 3x - x^3$

Plan

How can you graph a polynomial function?
Make a table of values to help you sketch the middle part of the graph. Use what you know about end behavior to sketch the ends of the graph.

Step 1

x	y
-2	-4
-1	-0.5
0	0
1	0.5
2	4

Step 2

Step 1

x	y
-2	2
-1	-2
0	0
1	2
2	-2

Step 2

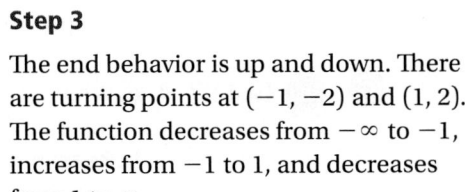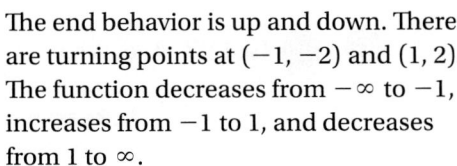

Step 3

The end behavior is down and up. There are no turning points. The function increases from $-\infty$ to ∞.

Step 3

The end behavior is up and down. There are turning points at $(-1, -2)$ and $(1, 2)$. The function decreases from $-\infty$ to -1, increases from -1 to 1, and decreases from 1 to ∞.

 Got It? 3. What is the graph of each cubic function? Describe the graph.

a. $y = -x^3 + 2x^2 - x - 2$

b. $y = x^3 - 1$

Suppose you are given a set of polynomial function outputs. You know that their inputs are an ordered set of x-values in which consecutive x-values differ by a constant. By analyzing the differences of consecutive y-values, it is possible to determine the least-degree polynomial function that could generate the data.

If the first differences are constant, the function is linear. If the second differences (but not the first) are constant, the function is quadratic. If the third differences (but not the second) are constant, the function is cubic, and so on.

Problem 4 Using Differences to Determine Degree

What is the degree of the polynomial function that generates the data shown at the right?

x	y
−3	−1
−2	−7
−1	−3
0	5
1	11
2	9
3	−7

Know

A set of polynomial function values

Need

Degree of the polynomial function

Plan

Check first differences of y-values. Then check second differences, third differences, and so on until they are constant.

Think

How do you find the second differences?
Subtract the consecutive first differences.

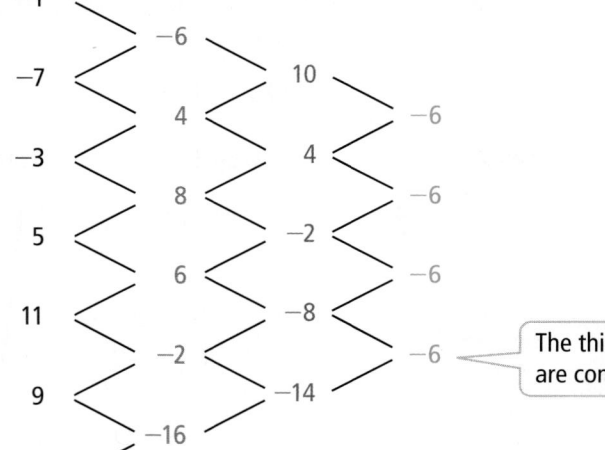

The third differences are constant.

The degree of the polynomial function is 3.

  Got It? **4. a.** What is the degree of the polynomial function that generates the data shown at the right?

b. Reasoning What is an example of a polynomial function whose fifth differences are constant but whose fourth differences are not constant?

x	y
−3	23
−2	−16
−1	−15
0	−10
1	−13
2	−12
3	29

Lesson Check

Do you know HOW?

Classify each polynomial by degree and by number of terms.

1. $5x^3$

2. $6x^2 + 4x - 2$

Write each polynomial in standard form.

3. $7x + 3 + 5x^2$

4. $-3 + 9x$

Do you UNDERSTAND?

 **5. Vocabulary** Describe the end behavior of the graph of $y = -2x^7 - 8x$.

6. Reasoning Can the graph of a polynomial function be a straight line? If so, give an example.

7. Error Analysis Your friend claims the graph of the function $y = 4x^3 + 4$ has only one turning point. Describe the error your friend made and give the correct number of turning points.

Practice and Problem-Solving Exercises

 **Practice**

Write each polynomial in standard form. Then classify it by degree and by number of terms.

See Problem 1.

8. $7x + 3x + 5$

9. $5 - 3x$

10. $2m^2 - 3 + 7m$

11. $-x^3 + x^4 + x$

12. $-4p + 3p + 2p^2$

13. $5a^2 + 3a^3 + 1$

14. $-x^5$

15. $3 + 12x^4$

16. $6x^3 - x^3$

17. $7x^3 - 10x^3 + x^3$

18. $4x + 5x^2 + 8$

19. $x^2 - x^4 + 2x^2$

Determine the end behavior of the graph of each polynomial function.

See Problem 2.

20. $y = -7x^3 + 8x^2 + x$

21. $y = -3x + 6x^2 - 1$

22. $y = 1 - 4x - 6x^3 - 15x^6$

23. $y = 8x^{11} - 2x^9 + 3x^6 + 4$

24. $y = -x^5 - 15x^7 - 4x^9$

25. $y = -3 - 6x^5 - 9x^8$

26. $y = x^4 - 7x^2 + 3$

27. $y = -8x^7 + 16x^6 + 9$

28. $y = -14x^6 + 11x^5 - 11$

29. $y = -x^3 - x^2 + 3$

30. $y = x^3 - 14x - 4$

31. $y = 5 - 17x^7 + 9x^{10}$

Describe the shape of the graph of each cubic function including end behavior, turning points, and increasing/decreasing intervals.

See Problem 3.

32. $y = 3x^3 - x - 3$

33. $y = -9x^3 - 2x^2 + 5x + 3$

34. $y = 10x^3 + 9$

35. $y = 3x^3$

36. $y = -4x^3 - 5x^2$

37. $y = 8x^3$

Determine the degree of the polynomial function with the given data.

See Problem 4.

38.

x	-2	-1	0	1	2
y	16	7	2	1	4

39.

x	-2	-1	0	1	2
y	-15	-9	-9	-9	-3

 **Apply**

40. Think About a Plan The data shows the power generated by a wind turbine. The *x* column gives the wind speed in meters per second. The *y* column gives the power generated in kilowatts. What is the degree of the polynomial function that models the data?

x	y
5	10
6	17.28
7	27.44
8	40.96
9	58.32

- What are the first differences of the *y*-values?
- What are the second differences of the *y*-values?
- When are the differences constant?

Classify each polynomial by degree and by number of terms. Simplify first if necessary.

41. $a^2 + a^3 - 4a^4$ **42.** 7 **43.** $2x(3x)$

44. $(2a - 5)(a^2 - 1)$ **45.** $(-8d^3 - 7) + (-d^3 - 6)$ **46.** $b(b - 3)^2$

Determine the sign of the leading coefficient and the least possible degree of the polynomial function for each graph.

47.
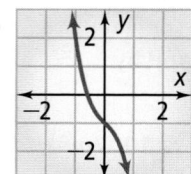

48.
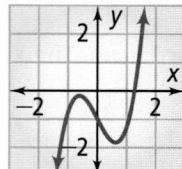

49.
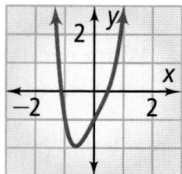

50. Open-Ended Write an equation for a polynomial function that has three turning points and end behavior up and up.

51. Show that the third differences of a polynomial function of degree 3 are nonzero and constant. First, use $f(x) = x^3 - 3x^2 - 2x - 6$. Then show third differences are nonzero and constant for $f(x) = ax^3 + bx^2 + cx + d, a \neq 0$.

52. Reasoning Suppose that a function pairs elements from set *A* with elements from set *B*. A function is called *onto* if it pairs every element in *B* with at least one element in *A*. For each type of polynomial function, and for each set *B*, determine whether the function is *always*, *sometimes*, or *never* onto.
   a. linear; $B =$ all real numbers
   b. quadratic; $B =$ all real numbers
   c. quadratic; $B =$ all real numbers greater than or equal to 4
   d. cubic; $B =$ all real numbers

53. Make a table of second differences for each polynomial function. Using your tables, make a conjecture about the second differences of quadratic functions.
   a. $y = 2x^2$ **b.** $y = 5x^2$ **c.** $y = 5x^2 - 2$
   d. $y = 7x^2$ **e.** $y = 7x^2 + 1$ **f.** $y = 7x^2 + 3x + 1$

54. a. Write the equation for the volume of a box with a length that is 5 in. less than its width and a height that is 3 in. less than its width.
   b. Graph the equation.
   c. For which interval(s) does the graph increase?
   d. For which interval(s) does the graph decrease?

Challenge

55. Copy and complete the table, which shows the first and second differences in y-values for consecutive x-values for a polynomial function of degree 2.

56. The outputs for a certain function are 1, 2, 4, 8, 16, 32, and so on.
   a. Find the first differences of this function.
   b. Find the second differences of this function.
   c. Find the tenth differences of this function.
   d. Can you find a polynomial function that matches the original outputs? Explain your reasoning.

57. Reasoning A cubic polynomial function f has leading coefficient 2 and constant term 7. If $f(1) = 7$ and $f(2) = 9$, what is $f(-2)$? Explain how you found your answer.

x	y	1st diff.	2nd diff.
−3	14	−8	2
−2	6	▪	2
−1	▪	−4	2
0	−4	−2	2
1	▪	0	2
2	−6	▪	
3	▪		

Apply What You've Learned

Look back at the information given on page 279 about the diorama Eliana plans to make for an art contest. The diagrams of the sheet of cardboard and the finished box are shown again below.

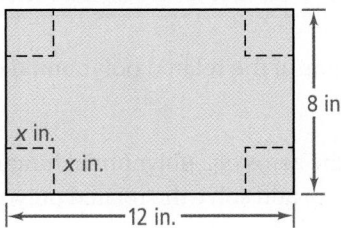

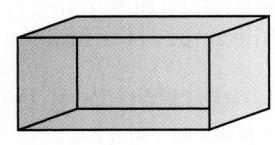

a. In the diagram, x represents the side length of the squares Eliana will cut from each corner. Which dimension of the diorama box does x represent: the length or the width of the back of the box, or the depth of the box from front to back?

b. Write expressions for the length and width of the back of the diorama box. Use your expressions to find a polynomial in standard form that represents the area of the back of the box. Classify the polynomial by degree and by number of terms.

c. Write a function $V(x)$ for the volume of the diorama box as a polynomial in standard form. Classify the polynomial function by degree and by number of terms.

d. Without graphing $y = V(x)$, describe the end behavior of the graph of the function $y = V(x)$. Explain.

e. Describe how you could identify which points on a graph of $y = V(x)$ correspond to a volume of 36 in.^{3}.

5-2 Polynomials, Linear Factors, and Zeros

Common Core State Standards

F-IF.C.7c Graph polynomial functions, identifying zeros when suitable factorizations are available and showing end behavior. **Also A-APR.B.3**

MP 1, MP 2, MP 3, MP 4, MP 5

Objectives To analyze the factored form of a polynomial
To write a polynomial function from its zeros

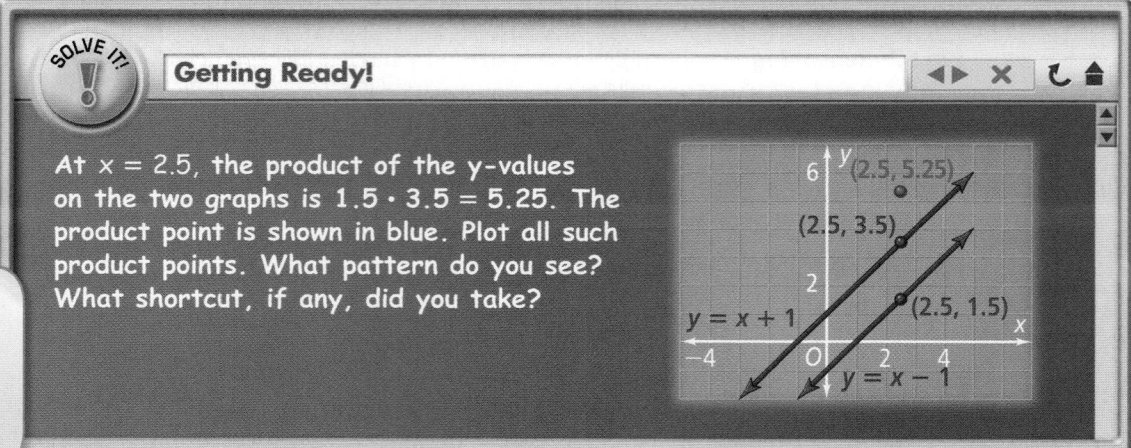

Getting Ready!

At $x = 2.5$, the product of the y-values on the two graphs is $1.5 \cdot 3.5 = 5.25$. The product point is shown in blue. Plot all such product points. What pattern do you see? What shortcut, if any, did you take?

You plot <u>all</u> points based on the pattern. If you calculate for every point, you'll never get done.

MATHEMATICAL PRACTICES If $P(x)$ is a polynomial function, the solutions of the related polynomial equation $P(x) = 0$ are the zeros of the function.

Lesson Vocabulary
• Factor Theorem
• multiple zero
• multiplicity
• relative maximum
• relative minimum

Essential Understanding Finding the zeros of a polynomial function will help you factor the polynomial, graph the function, and solve the related polynomial equation.

In Chapter 4, you solved a quadratic equation of the form $x^2 + bx + c = 0$ by factoring. You wrote it using *linear factors* in the form $(x - r_1)(x - r_2) = 0$. Then you applied the Zero-Product Property to find the solutions $x = r_1$ and $x = r_2$. You can solve some polynomial equations $a_n x^n + a_{n-1} x^{n-1} + \cdots + a_0 = 0$ in much the same way.

Plan

How do you write the factored form of a polynomial?
Write the polynomial as a product of factors. Make sure each factor cannot be factored any further.

Problem 1 **Writing a Polynomial in Factored Form**

What is the factored form of $x^3 - 2x^2 - 15x$?

$$x^3 - 2x^2 - 15x = x(x^2 - 2x - 15) \qquad \text{Factor out the GCF, } x.$$
$$= x(x - 5)(x + 3) \qquad \text{Factor } x^2 - 2x - 15.$$

Check $x(x - 5)(x + 3) = x(x^2 - 2x - 15) \qquad$ Multiply $(x - 5)(x + 3)$.
$$= x^3 - 2x^2 - 15x \quad ✔ \qquad \text{Distributive Property}$$

Got It? **1.** What is the factored form of $x^3 - x^2 - 12x$?

Key Concepts   Roots, Zeros, and *x*-intercepts

The following are equivalent statements about a real number b and a polynomial
$P(x) = a_n x^n + a_{n-1} x^{n-1} + \cdots + a_1 x + a_0.$
- $x - b$ is a linear factor of the polynomial $P(x)$.
- b is a zero of the polynomial function $y = P(x)$.
- b is a root (or solution) of the polynomial equation $P(x) = 0$.
- b is an x-intercept of the graph of $y = P(x)$.

 Problem 2   Finding Zeros of a Polynomial Function

What are the zeros of $y = (x + 2)(x - 1)(x - 3)$? Graph the function.

Know

Polynomial function

Need
- Zeros
- Additional points
- End behavior

Plan
- Use the Zero-Product Property to find zeros.
- Find points between the zeros.
- Sketch the graph.

Think

Does knowing the zeros of a function give you enough information to sketch it?
No; several different cubic functions could pass through $(-2, 0)$, $(1, 0)$, and $(3,0)$.

Step 1   Use the Zero-Product Property to find the zeros.

$$(x + 2)(x - 1)(x - 3) = 0$$

so $x + 2 = 0$ or $x - 1 = 0$ or $x - 3 = 0.$
The zeros of the function are -2, 1, and 3.

Step 2   Find points for x-values between the zeros.
Evaluate $y = (x + 2)(x - 1)(x - 3)$ for $x = -1, 0,$ and 2.

$(-1 + 2)(-1 - 1)(-1 - 3) = 8$ $(-1, 8)$

$(0 + 2)(0 - 1)(0 - 3) = 6$ $(0, 6)$

$(2 + 2)(2 - 1)(2 - 3) = -4$ $(2, -4)$

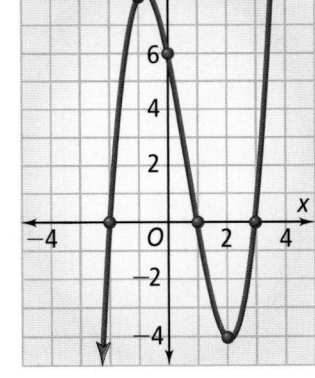

Step 3   Determine the end behavior.
The function $y = (x + 2)(x - 1)(x - 3)$ is cubic. The coefficient of x^3 is $+1$, so the end behavior is *down and up*.

Step 4   Use the zeros: $(-2, 0)$, $(1, 0)$, $(3, 0)$; the additional points: $(-1, 8)$, $(0, 6)$, $(2, -4)$; and end behavior to sketch the graph.

 Got It?   **2.** What are the zeros of $y = x(x - 3)(x + 5)$? Graph the function.

The Factor Theorem describes the relationship between the linear factors of a polynomial and the zeros of a polynomial.

 take note

Theorem   Factor Theorem

The expression $x - a$ is a factor of a polynomial if and only if the value a is a zero of the related polynomial function.

© **Problem 3** Writing a Polynomial Function From Its Zeros

Plan

How can you use the zeros to find the function?
By the Factor Theorem, a is a zero means that $x - a$ is a factor of the related polynomial.

A **What is a cubic polynomial function in standard form with zeros -2, 2, and 3?**

$$\begin{array}{ccc} -2 & 2 & 3 \\ \downarrow & \downarrow & \downarrow \end{array}$$ -2, 2, and 3 are zeros.

$$f(x) = (x + 2)(x - 2)(x - 3)$$ Write a linear factor for each zero.

$$= (x + 2)(x^2 - 5x + 6)$$ Multiply $(x-2)$ and $(x-3)$.

$$= x(x^2 - 5x + 6) + 2(x^2 - 5x + 6)$$ Distributive Property

$$= x^3 - 5x^2 + 6x + 2x^2 - 10x + 12$$ Distributive Property

$$= x^3 - 3x^2 - 4x + 12$$ Simplify.

The cubic polynomial $f(x) = x^3 - 3x^2 - 4x + 12$ has zeros -2, 2, and 3.

B **What is a quartic polynomial function in standard form with zeros -2, -2, 2, and 3?**

$$\begin{array}{cccc} -2 & -2 & 2 & 3 \\ \downarrow & \downarrow & \downarrow & \downarrow \end{array}$$ -2, -2, 2, and 3 are zeros.

$$g(x) = (x + 2)(x + 2)(x - 2)(x - 3)$$ Write a linear factor for each zero.

$$= x^4 - x^3 - 10x^2 + 4x + 24$$ Simplify.

The quartic polynomial $g(x) = x^4 - x^3 - 10x^2 + 4x + 24$ has zeros -2, -2, 2, and 3.

C **Graph both functions. How do the graphs differ? How are they similar?**

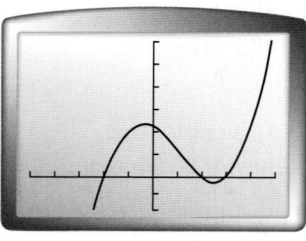 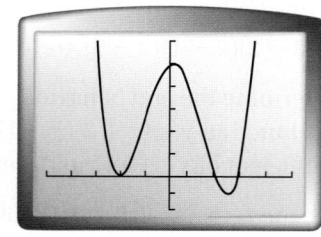

Both screens:
x-scale: 1
y-scale: 5

Both graphs have x-intercepts at -2, 2, and 3. The cubic has down-and-up end behavior. The quartic has up-and-up end behavior.

The cubic function has two turning points, and it crosses the x-axis at -2. The quartic function touches the x-axis at -2 but does not cross it. The quartic function has three turning points.

© **Got It? 3. a.** What is a quadratic polynomial function with zeros 3 and -3?
        b. What is a cubic polynomial function with zeros 3, 3, and -3?
        c. Reasoning Graph both functions. How do the graphs differ? How are they similar?

You can write the polynomial functions in Problem 3 in factored form as $f(x) = (x + 2)(x - 2)(x - 3)$ and $g(x) = (x + 2)^2(x - 2)(x - 3)$. In $g(x)$ the repeated linear factor $x + 2$ makes -2 a **multiple zero**.

In particular, since the linear factor $x + 2$ appears twice, you can say that -2 is a zero of **multiplicity** 2. In general, *a is a zero of multiplicity n* means that $x - a$ appears n times as a factor.

take note

Key Concept   How Multiple Zeros Affect a Graph

If a is a zero of multiplicity n in the polynomial function $y = P(x)$, then the behavior of the graph at the x-intercept a will be close to linear if $n = 1$, close to quadratic if $n = 2$, close to cubic if $n = 3$, and so on.

Problem 4 Finding the Multiplicity of a Zero

What are the zeros of $f(x) = x^4 - 2x^3 - 8x^2$? What are their multiplicities? How does the graph behave at these zeros?

$$f(x) = x^4 - 2x^3 - 8x^2$$
$$= x^2(x^2 - 2x - 8) \qquad \text{Factor out the GCF, } x^2.$$
$$= x^2(x + 2)(x - 4) \qquad \text{Factor } (x^2 - 2x - 8).$$

Think

How can you find the multiplicities?
Factor the polynomial. Find the number of times each linear factor appears.

Since $x^2 = (x - 0)^2$, the number 0 is a zero of multiplicity 2. The numbers -2 and 4 are zeros of multiplicity 1.

The graph looks close to linear at the x-intercepts -2 and 4. It resembles a parabola at the x-intercept 0.

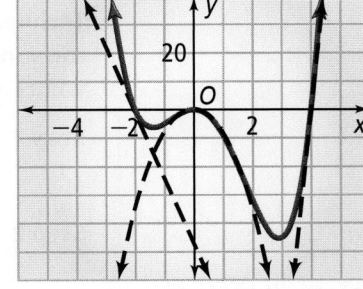

Got It? 4. What are the zeros of $f(x) = x^3 - 4x^2 + 4x$? What are their multiplicities? How does the graph behave at these zeros?

If the graph of a polynomial function has several turning points, the function can have a **relative maximum** and a **relative minimum**. A relative maximum is the value of the function at an up-to-down turning point. A relative minimum is the value of the function at a down-to-up turning point.

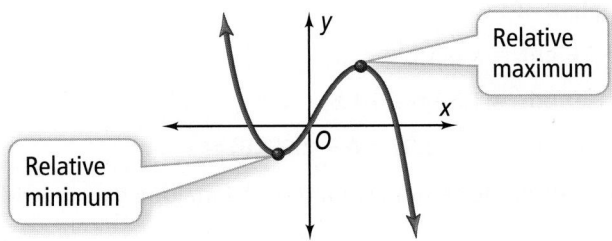

Relative maximum

Relative minimum

Problem 5 Identifying a Relative Maximum and Minimum

Think

How is a relative maximum different from a maximum at the vertex of a parabola?
A relative maximum is the greatest y-value in the "neighborhood" of its x-value. The maximum at the vertex of a parabola is the greatest y-value for *all* x-values.

What are the relative maximum and minimum of $f(x) = x^3 + 3x^2 - 24x$?

Use a graphing calculator to find a relative maximum and a relative minimum.

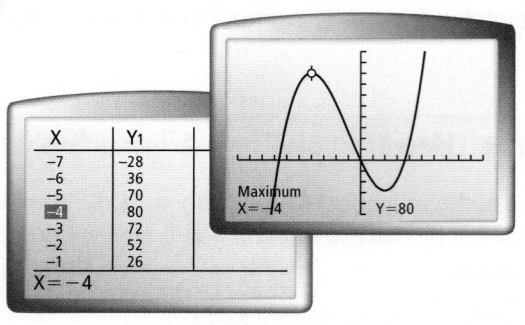

Relative maximum

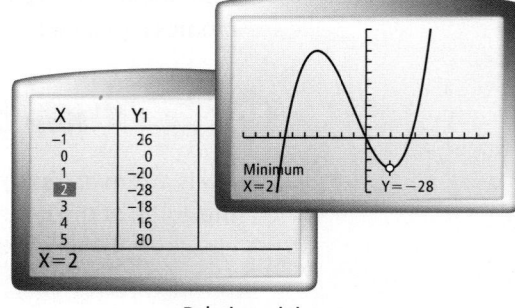

Relative minimum

The relative maximum is 80 at $x = -4$ and the relative minimum is -28 at $x = 2$.

 Got It? **5.** What are the relative maximum and minimum of $f(x) = 3x^3 + x^2 - 5x$?

Problem 6 Using a Polynomial Function to Maximize Volume

Technology The design of a digital box camera maximizes the volume while keeping the sum of the dimensions at 6 inches. If the length must be 1.5 times the height, what should each dimension be?

Step 1 Define a variable x.

> Let $x =$ the height of the camera.

Step 2 Determine length and width.

> length $= 1.5x$; width $= 6 - (x + 1.5x) = 6 - 2.5x$

Think

What is the formula for the volume of a "box"?
$V = \ell wh$

Step 3 Model the volume.

$$V = (\text{length})(\text{width})(\text{height}) = (1.5x)(6 - 2.5x)(x)$$
$$= -3.75x^3 + 9x^2$$

Step 4 Graph the polynomial function. Use the **MAXIMUM** feature to find that the maximum volume is 7.68 in.^{3} for a height of 1.6 in.

> height $= x = 1.6$
>
> length $= 1.5x = 1.5(1.6) = 2.4$
>
> width $= 6 - 2.5x = 6 - 2.5(1.6) = 2$

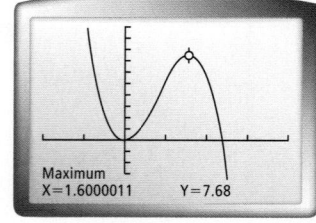

The dimensions of the camera should be 2.4 in. long by 2 in. wide by 1.6 in. high.

 Got It? **6.** What is the maximum volume of the camera in Problem 6, if the sum of the dimensions is at most 4 inches?

Lesson Check

Do you know HOW?

Find the zeros of each function.

1. $y = x(x - 6)$

2. $y = (x + 4)(x - 5)$

3. $y = (x + 12)(x - 9)(x - 7)$

4. Write a polynomial function in standard form with zeros -1, 1, and 0.

Do you UNDERSTAND?

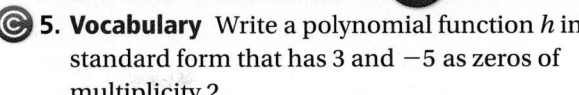 **5. Vocabulary** Write a polynomial function h in standard form that has 3 and -5 as zeros of multiplicity 2.

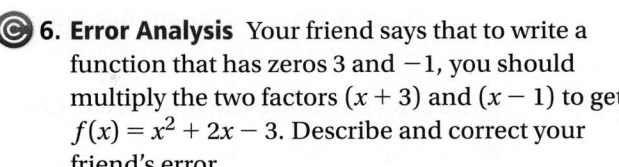 **6. Error Analysis** Your friend says that to write a function that has zeros 3 and -1, you should multiply the two factors $(x + 3)$ and $(x - 1)$ to get $f(x) = x^2 + 2x - 3$. Describe and correct your friend's error.

Practice and Problem-Solving Exercises

 **Practice** Write each polynomial in factored form. Check by multiplication. **See Problem 1.**

7. $x^3 + 7x^2 + 10x$ **8.** $x^3 - 7x^2 - 18x$ **9.** $x^3 - 4x^2 - 21x$

10. $x^3 - 36x$ **11.** $x^3 + 8x^2 + 16x$ **12.** $9x^3 + 6x^2 - 3x$

Find the zeros of each function. Then graph the function. **See Problem 2.**

13. $y = (x - 1)(x + 2)$ **14.** $y = (x - 2)(x + 9)$ **15.** $y = x(x + 5)(x - 8)$

16. $y = (x + 1)(x - 2)(x - 3)$ **17.** $y = (x + 1)(x - 1)(x - 2)$ **18.** $y = x(x + 2)(x + 3)$

Write a polynomial function in standard form with the given zeros. **See Problem 3.**

19. $x = 5, 6, 7$ **20.** $x = -2, 0, 1$ **21.** $x = -5, -5, 1$ **22.** $x = 3, 3, 3$

23. $x = 1, -1, -2$ **24.** $x = 0, 4, -\frac{1}{2}$ **25.** $x = 0, 0, 2, 3$ **26.** $x = -1, -2, -3, -4$

Find the zeros of each function. State the multiplicity of multiple zeros. **See Problem 4.**

27. $y = (x + 3)^3$ **28.** $y = x(x - 1)^3$

29. $y = 2x^3 + x^2 - x$ **30.** $y = 3x^3 - 3x$

31. $y = (x - 4)^2$ **32.** $y = (x - 2)^2(x - 1)$

33. $y = (2x + 3)(x - 1)^2$ **34.** $y = (x + 1)^2(x - 1)(x - 2)$

Find the relative maximum and relative minimum of the graph of each function. **See Problem 5.**

35. $f(x) = x^3 + 4x^2 - 5x$ **36.** $f(x) = -x^3 + 16x^2 - 76x + 96$

37. $f(x) = -4x^3 + 12x^2 + 4x - 12$ **38.** $f(x) = x^3 - 7x^2 + 7x + 15$

STEM **39. Metalwork** A metalworker wants to make an open box from a sheet of metal, by cutting equal squares from each corner as shown.

a. Write expressions for the length, width, and height of the open box.

b. Use your expressions from part (a) to write a function for the volume of the box. (*Hint:* Write the function in factored form.)

c. Graph the function. Then find the maximum volume of the box and the side length of the cut-out squares that generates this volume.

See Problem 6.

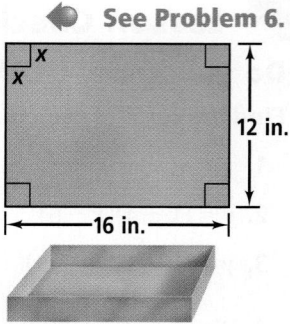

B Apply **Write each function in factored form. Check by multiplication.**

40. $y = 3x^3 - 27x^2 + 24x$ **41.** $y = -2x^3 - 2x^2 + 40x$ **42.** $y = x^4 + 3x^3 - 4x^2$

43. Think About a Plan A storage company needs to design a new storage box that has twice the volume of its largest box. Its largest box is 5 ft long, 4 ft wide, and 3 ft high. The new box must be formed by increasing each dimension by the same amount. Find the increase in each dimension.

- How can you write the dimensions of the new storage box as polynomial expressions?
- How can you use the volume of the current largest box to find the volume of the new box?

STEM **44. Carpentry** A carpenter hollowed out the interior of a block of wood as shown at the right.

a. Express the volume of the original block and the volume of the wood removed as polynomials in factored form.

b. What polynomial represents the volume of the wood remaining?

45. Geometry A rectangular box is $2x + 3$ units long, $2x - 3$ units wide, and $3x$ units high. What is its volume, expressed as a polynomial?

46. Measurement The volume in cubic feet of a CD holder can be expressed as $V(x) = -x^3 - x^2 + 6x$, or, when factored, as the product of its three dimensions. The depth is expressed as $2 - x$. Assume that the height is greater than the width.

a. Factor the polynomial to find linear expressions for the height and the width.

b. Graph the function. Find the x-intercepts. What do they represent?

c. What is a realistic domain for the function?

d. What is the maximum volume of the CD holder?

Find the relative maximum, relative minimum, and zeros of each function.

47. $y = 2x^3 - 23x^2 + 78x - 72$ **48.** $y = 8x^3 - 10x^2 - x - 3$ **49.** $y = (x + 1)^4 - 1$

50. Open-Ended Write a polynomial function with the following features: it has three distinct zeros; one of the zeros is 1; another zero has a multiplicity of 2.

51. Writing Explain how the graph of a polynomial function can help you factor the polynomial.

For each function, determine the zeros. State the multiplicity of any multiple zeros.

52. $f(x) = x^3 - 36x$ **53.** $y = (x + 1)(x - 4)(3 - 2x)$ **54.** $y = (x + 7)(5x + 2)(x - 6)^2$

 **Challenge** 55. Find a fourth-degree polynomial function with zeros 1, -1, i, and $-i$. Write the function in factored form.

 56. **a.** Compare the graphs of $y = (x + 1)(x + 2)(x + 3)$ and $y = (x - 1)(x - 2)(x - 3)$. What transformation could you use to describe the change from one graph to the other?

b. Compare the graphs of $y = (x + 1)(x + 3)(x + 7)$ and $y = (x - 1)(x - 3)(x - 7)$. Does the transformation that you chose in part (a) still hold true? Explain.

c. Make a Conjecture What transformation could you use to describe the effect of changing the signs of the zeros of a polynomial function?

 ## Apply What You've Learned

 MATHEMATICAL PRACTICES
MP 1

Look back at the information about the diorama box Eliana plans to make using the rectangular sheet of cardboard shown on page 279. In the Apply What You've Learned in Lesson 5-1, you wrote a polynomial function $V(x)$ in standard form for the volume of the diorama box.

Write the function $V(x)$ in factored form and then graph $y = V(x)$. Select all of the following that are true. Explain your reasoning.

A. $V(x) = (12 - 2x)(8 - 2x)x$

B. $V(x) = 4x(6 - x)(4 - x)$

C. $V(x) = -4x(x - 6)(x - 4)$

D. The zeros of $y = V(x)$ correspond to values of x that result in a diorama box with volume 36 in.^{3}.

E. The graph of $y = V(x)$ crosses the x-axis at $(0, 0)$, $(4, 0)$, and $(6, 0)$.

F. The graph of $y = V(x)$ shows that there is only one value of x for which the volume of the diorama box will be 36 in.^{3}.

G. The graph of $y = V(x)$ has a turning point between $x = 0$ and $x = 4$.

H. The only portion of the graph that represents the possible volumes of Eliana's diorama box is the portion for which $0 < x < 4$.

Solving Polynomial Equations

Common Core State Standards

A-REI.D.11 Explain why the *x*-coordinates of the points where the graphs of the equations $y = f(x)$ and $y = g(x)$ intersect are the solutions of the equation $f(x) = g(x)$ ... **Also A-SSE.A.2**

MP 1, MP 2, MP 3, MP 5, MP 6

Objectives To solve polynomial equations by factoring
To solve polynomial equations by graphing

Getting Ready!

Can you arrange all of these pieces to make a rectangle with no pieces overlapping and no gaps? If you can, make a sketch. If you cannot, explain why.

I count 2 pieces with area x^2, 11 with area x, and 12 with area 1. The rectangle would have the same total area.

MATHEMATICAL PRACTICES

Factoring a polynomial like $ax^2 + bx + c$ can help you solve a polynomial equation like $ax^2 + bx + c = 0$.

Lesson Vocabulary

- sum of cubes
- difference of cubes

Essential Understanding If $(x - a)$ is a factor of a polynomial, then the polynomial has value 0 when $x = a$. If a is a real number, then the graph of the polynomial has $(a, 0)$ as an x-intercept.

To solve a polynomial equation by factoring:

1. Write the equation in the form $P(x) = 0$ for some polynomial function P.
2. Factor $P(x)$. Use the Zero Product Property to find the roots.

Plan

What does it mean if x is a common factor of every term in $P(x)$?
You can write $P(x)$ as $xQ(x)$, so 0 will be a solution of $P(x) = 0$.

 Problem 1 **Solving Polynomial Equations Using Factors**

What are the real or imaginary solutions of each polynomial equation?

A $2x^3 - 5x^2 = 3x$

$2x^3 - 5x^2 - 3x = 0$ Rewrite in the form $P(x) = 0$.

$x(2x^2 - 5x - 3) = 0$ Factor out the GCF, x.

$x(2x + 1)(x - 3) = 0$ Factor $2x^2 - 5x - 3$.

$x = 0$ or $2x + 1 = 0$ or $x - 3 = 0$ Zero Product Property

$x = 0$ $x = -\frac{1}{2}$ $x = 3$ Solve each equation for x.

The solutions are 0, $-\frac{1}{2}$, and 3.

B $3x^4 + 12x^2 = 6x^3$

$3x^4 - 6x^3 + 12x^2 = 0$ Rewrite in the form $P(x) = 0$.

$x^4 - 2x^3 + 4x^2 = 0$ Multiply by $\frac{1}{3}$ to simplify.

$x^2(x^2 - 2x + 4) = 0$ Factor out the GCF, x^2.

$x^2 = 0$ or $x^2 - 2x + 4 = 0$ Zero Product Property

Think

How will the solution be similar to the solution of the equation in part (a)?
Both equations have 0 as a solution, but here it will have a multiplicity of 2.

> Use the Quadratic Formula to solve $x^2 - 2x + 4 = 0$. Substitute $a = 1$, $b = -2$, and $c = 4$.

$x = 0$ $\Bigg|$ $x = \dfrac{-(-2) \pm \sqrt{(-2)^2 - 4(1)(4)}}{2(1)}$

$x = \dfrac{2 \pm \sqrt{-12}}{2} = \dfrac{2 \pm 2i\sqrt{3}}{2} = 1 \pm i\sqrt{3}$

The solutions are 0, $1 + i\sqrt{3}$, and $1 - i\sqrt{3}$.

 Got It? 1. What are the real or imaginary solutions of each equation?
    a. $(x^2 - 1)(x^2 + 4) = 0$ **b.** $x^5 + 4x^3 = 5x^4 - 2x^3$

---

take note

Concept Summary   Polynomial Factoring Techniques

Techniques	Examples
Factoring out the GCF Factor out the greatest common factor of all the terms.	$15x^4 - 20x^3 + 35x^2$ $= 5x^2(3x^2 - 4x + 7)$
Quadratic Trinomials For $ax^2 + bx + c$, find factors with product ac and sum b.	$6x^2 + 11x - 10$ $= (3x - 2)(2x + 5)$
Perfect Square Trinomials $a^2 + 2ab + b^2 = (a + b)^2$ $a^2 - 2ab + b^2 = (a - b)^2$	$x^2 + 10x + 25 = (x + 5)^2$ $x^2 - 10x + 25 = (x - 5)^2$
Difference of Squares $a^2 - b^2 = (a + b)(a - b)$	$4x^2 - 15 = (2x + \sqrt{15})(2x - \sqrt{15})$
Factoring by Grouping $ax + ay + bx + by$ $= a(x + y) + b(x + y)$ $= (a + b)(x + y)$	$x^3 + 2x^2 - 3x - 6$ $= x^2(x + 2) + (-3)(x + 2)$ $= (x^2 - 3)(x + 2)$
Sum or Difference of Cubes $a^3 + b^3 = (a + b)(a^2 - ab + b^2)$ $a^3 - b^3 = (a - b)(a^2 + ab + b^2)$	$8x^3 + 1 = (2x + 1)(4x^2 - 2x + 1)$ $8x^3 - 1 = (2x - 1)(4x^2 + 2x + 1)$

The sum and difference of cubes is a new factoring technique.

Here's Why It Works Factoring $a^3 + b^3 = (a + b)(a^2 - ab + b^2)$:

$$a^3 + b^3 = a^3 + a^2b - a^2b - ab^2 + ab^2 + b^3 \qquad \text{Add 0.}$$
$$= a^2(a + b) - ab(a + b) + b^2(a + b) \qquad \text{Factor out } a^2, -ab, \text{ and } b^2.$$
$$= (a + b)(a^2 - ab + b^2) \qquad \text{Factor out } (a + b).$$

For $a^3 - b^3 = (a - b)(a^2 + ab + b^2)$, you can follow steps similar to those above, or you can factor $a^3 - b^3$ as the sum of cubes $a^3 + (-b)^3$.

© **Problem 2** **Solving Polynomial Equations by Factoring**

What are the real or imaginary solutions of each polynomial equation?

Think

How can you write the polynomial in quadratic form?
Write in terms of x^2:
$(x^2)^2 - 3(x^2) - 4 = 0$,
which shows the factorable quadratic form
$a^2 - 3a - 4 = 0$.

Ⓐ $x^4 - 3x^2 = 4$

$$x^4 - 3x^2 - 4 = 0 \qquad \text{Rewrite in the form } P(x) = 0.$$
$$a^2 - 3a - 4 = 0 \qquad \text{Let } a = x^2.$$
$$(a - 4)(a + 1) = 0 \qquad \text{Factor.}$$
$$(x^2 - 4)(x^2 + 1) = 0 \qquad \text{Replace } a \text{ with } x^2.$$
$$(x + 2)(x - 2)(x^2 + 1) = 0 \qquad \text{Factor } x^2 - 4 \text{ as a difference of squares.}$$

It follows from the Zero Product Property that $x = 2$, $x = -2$, or $x^2 = -1$.
Solving $x^2 = -1$ yields two imaginary roots: $x = i$ or $x = -i$.

Check Graph the related function $y = x^4 - 3x^2 - 4$.

The graph shows zeros at $x = 2$ and $x = -2$. It also shows three turning points. This means that there are imaginary roots, which do not appear on the graph.

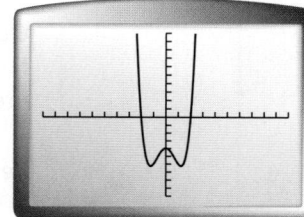

Ⓑ $x^3 = 1$

$$x^3 - 1 = 0 \qquad \text{Rewrite in the form } P(x) = 0.$$
$$(x - 1)(x^2 + x + 1) = 0 \qquad \text{Factor the difference of cubes.}$$

It follows from the Zero Product Property that $x = 1$ or $x^2 + x + 1 = 0$.
Use the Quadratic Formula to solve $x^2 + x + 1 = 0$.

$$x = \frac{-(1) \pm \sqrt{(1)^2 - 4(1)(1)}}{2(1)} = \frac{-1 \pm \sqrt{-3}}{2} = \frac{-1 \pm i\sqrt{3}}{2}$$

The three solutions of $x^3 = 1$ are 1, $-\frac{1}{2} + i\frac{\sqrt{3}}{2}$, and $-\frac{1}{2} - i\frac{\sqrt{3}}{2}$.

 Got It? 2. What are the real or imaginary solutions of each polynomial equation?

    a. $x^4 = 16$ **b.** $x^3 = 8x - 2x^2$ **c.** $x(x^2 + 8) = 8(x + 1)$

While factoring is an effective way to solve a polynomial equation, you can also find the real roots quickly by using a graphing calculator.

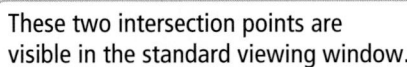 **Problem 3** Finding Real Roots by Graphing

What are the real solutions of the equation $x^3 + 5 = 4x^2 + x$?

Plan

Why is it helpful to graph Y_1 and Y_2?
The values of x for which $Y_1 = Y_2$ are the solutions of the original equation.

Method 1 Graph $Y_1 = x^3 + 5$ and $Y_2 = 4x^2 + x$. Use the **INTERSECT** feature to find the x-values of the points of intersection.

These two intersection points are visible in the standard viewing window.

You must adjust the window to obtain this point of intersection.

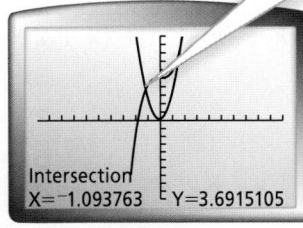
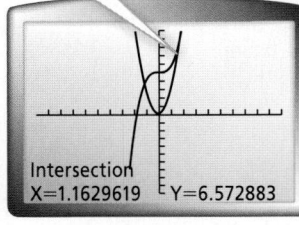
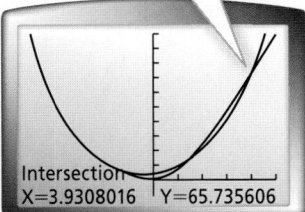

Approximate solutions are $x = -1.09$, $x = 1.16$, and $x = 3.93$.

Method 2 Rewrite the equation as $x^3 - 4x^2 - x + 5 = 0$. Graph the related function $y = x^3 - 4x^2 - x + 5$. Use the **ZERO** feature.

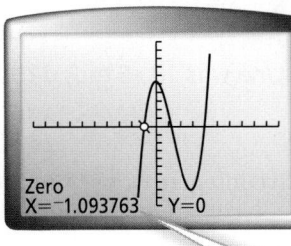
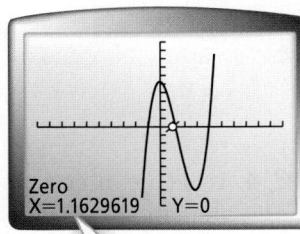
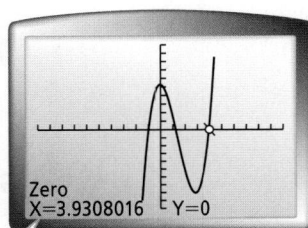

The solutions are the same as identified using Method 1.

Approximate solutions are $x = -1.09$, $x = 1.16$, and $x = 3.93$.

Check Verify the solutions by showing that they satisfy the original equation. Show values of $y_1 = x^3 + 5$ and $y_2 = 4x^2 + x$ in a table.

The solution checks.

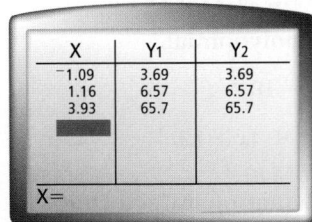

Got It? 3. a. What are the real solutions of the equation $x^3 + x^2 = x - 1$?

　b. Reasoning In Problem 3, which method seems to be an easier and more reliable way to find the solutions of an equation? Explain.

 **Problem 4** Modeling a Problem Situation

Close friends Stacy, Una, and Amir were all born on July 4. Stacy is one year younger than Una. Una is two years younger than Amir. On July 4, 2010, the product of their ages was 2300 more than the sum of their ages. How old was each friend on that day?

Think

Write

Define variables.

> Let x = Una's age on July 4, 2010.
> Stacy's age = x − 1.
> Amir's age = x + 2.

Write an equation. Simplify and change it to $P(x) = 0$ form.

> $$\overbrace{x + (x - 1) + (x + 2)}^{\text{Sum of ages}} + 2300 = \overbrace{x(x - 1)(x + 2)}^{\text{Product of ages}}$$
> $$3x + 2301 = x(x^2 + x - 2)$$
> $$3x + 2301 = x^3 + x^2 - 2x$$
> $$x^3 + x^2 - 5x - 2301 = 0$$

Only real solutions make sense, so graphing $y_1 = P(x)$ should show any real solution that exists. Use the **ZERO** feature.

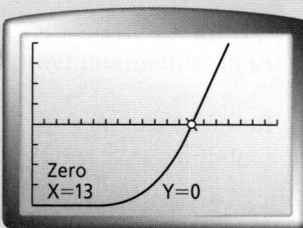

x = 13

Zero
X=13   Y=0

Write the answer.

> Una was 13, Stacy 12, and Amir 15.

 Got It? **4.** What are three consecutive integers whose product is 480 more than their sum?

 Lesson Check

Do you know HOW?

Factor each polynomial.

1. $x^2 - 3x - 18$

2. $x^3 - 27$

3. $x^3 + 3x^2 + 4x + 12$

4. $x^4 - 2^4$

Solve each equation by factoring.

5. $2x^2 + 7x - 4 = 0$

6. $2x^3 + 2x^2 - 4x = 0$

Do you UNDERSTAND?  MATHEMATICAL PRACTICES

7. Vocabulary Identify each expression as a sum of cubes, difference of cubes, or difference of squares.

a. $x^2 - 64$ **b.** $x^3 + 8$

c. $x^3 - 125$ **d.** $x^2 - 81$

8. Reasoning Which method of solving polynomial equations will not identify the imaginary roots? Explain.

9. Reasoning Show two different ways to find the real roots of the polynomial equation $0 = x^6 - x^2$. Show your steps.

Practice and Problem-Solving Exercises

 **MATHEMATICAL PRACTICES**

 **Practice**

Find the real or imaginary solutions of each equation by factoring.

◀ **See Problems 1 and 2.**

10. $x^3 + 64 = 0$

11. $x^3 - 1000 = 0$

12. $125x^3 - 27 = 0$

13. $64x^3 - 1 = 0$

14. $x^3 + 2x^2 + 5x + 10 = 0$

15. $6x^2 + 13x - 5 = 0$

16. $0 = x^3 - 27$

17. $0 = x^3 - 64$

18. $8x^3 = 1$

19. $64x^3 = -8$

20. $x^4 - 10x^2 = -9$

21. $x^4 - 8x^2 = -16$

22. $x^4 - 12x^2 = 64$

23. $x^4 + 7x^2 = 18$

24. $x^4 + 4x^2 = 12$

Find the real solutions of each equation by graphing.

◀ **See Problem 3.**

25. $x^3 - 4x^2 - 7x = -10$

26. $3x^3 - 6x^2 - 9x = 0$

27. $4x^3 - 8x^2 + 4x = 0$

28. $6x^2 = 48x$

29. $x^3 + 3x^2 + 2x = 0$

30. $2x^3 + 5x^2 = 7x$

31. $4x^3 = 4x^2 + 3x$

32. $2x^4 - 5x^3 - 3x^2 = 0$

33. $x^2 - 8x + 7 = 0$

34. $x^4 - 4x^3 - x^2 + 16x = 12$

35. $x^3 - x^2 - 16x = 20$

36. $3x^3 + 12x^2 - 3x = 12$

📱 **Graphing Calculator** **Write an equation to model each situation. Then solve each equation by graphing.**

◀ **See Problem 4.**

37. The Johnson twins were born two years after their older sister. This year, the product of the three siblings' ages is exactly 4558 more than the sum of their ages. How old are the twins?

38. The product of three consecutive integers is 210. What are the numbers?

 **Apply**

Solve each equation.

39. $x^3 + 13x = 10x^2$

40. $x^3 - 6x^2 + 6x = 0$

41. $12x^3 = 60x^2 + 75x$

42. $125x^3 + 216 = 0$

43. $81x^3 - 192 = 0$

44. $x^4 - 64 = 0$

45. $-2x^4 - 100 = 0$

46. $27 = -x^4 - 12x^2$

47. $x^5 - 5x^3 + 4x = 0$

48. $5x^3 = 5x^2 + 12x$

49. $x^3 + x^2 + x + 1 = 0$

50. $x^3 + 1 = x^2 + x$

ⓒ **51. Think About a Plan** The width of a plastic storage box is 1 ft longer than the height. The length is 4 ft longer than the height. The volume is 36 ft³. What are the dimensions of the box?
- What is the formula for the volume of a rectangular prism?
- What variable expressions represent the length, height, and width?
- What equation represents the volume of the plastic storage box?

ⓒ **52. Error Analysis** A student claims that 1, 2, 3, and 4 are the zeros of a cubic polynomial function. Explain why the student is mistaken.

53. Geometry The width of a box is 2 m less than the length. The height is 1 m less than the length. The volume is 60 m³. What is the length of the box?

Graph each function to find the zeros. Rewrite the function with the polynomial in factored form.

54. $y = 2x^2 + 3x - 5$ **55.** $y = x^4 - 10x^2 + 9$ **56.** $y = x^3 - 3x^2 + 4$

57. Open-Ended To solve a polynomial equation, you can use any combination of graphing, factoring, and the Quadratic Formula. Write and solve an equation to illustrate each method.

 **Challenge**

58. The geometric figure at the right has volume $a^3 + b^3$. You can split it into three rectangular blocks (including the long one with side $a + b$). Explain how to use this figure to prove the factoring formula for the sum of cubes, $a^3 + b^3 = (a + b)(a^2 - ab + b^2)$.

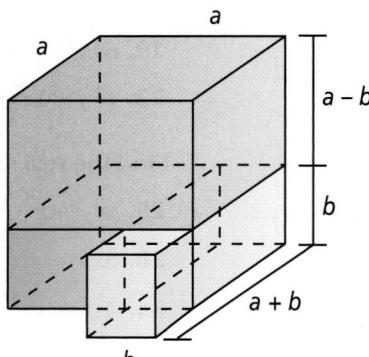

59. Open-Ended Find equations for two different polynomial functions whose zeros include -12, 0, $\frac{1}{4}$, and $\frac{1}{6}$.

60. What are the complex solutions of $x^5 + x^3 + 2x = 2x^4 + x^2 + 1$?

Standardized Test Prep

SAT/ACT

61. Which value is NOT a solution to the equation $x^4 - 3x^2 - 54 = 0$?

   Ⓐ -3 Ⓑ 3 Ⓒ $-3i$ Ⓓ $-i\sqrt{6}$

62. Ava drove 3 hours at 45 miles per hour. How many miles did she drive?

   Ⓕ 45 miles   Ⓖ 48 miles   Ⓗ 90 miles   Ⓘ 135 miles

63. Which polynomial has the complex roots $1 + i\sqrt{2}$ and $1 - i\sqrt{2}$?

   Ⓐ $x^2 + 2x + 3$ Ⓑ $x^2 - 2x + 3$ Ⓒ $x^2 + 2x - 3$ Ⓓ $x^2 - 2x - 3$

Short Response

64. Sam has only quarters and dimes in his pocket. He has a total of 12 coins, totaling $1.95. How many of each coin does Sam have?

Mixed Review

Write each polynomial in factored form. Check by multiplication.   ◆ *See Lesson 5-2.*

65. $3x^2 - 18x + 24$ **66.** $2x^4 + 6x^3 - 18x^2 - 54x$ **67.** $x^4 - 4x^3 - 5x^2$

Solve each equation by factoring. Check your answers.   ◆ *See Lesson 4-5.*

68. $x^2 - 4x = 12$ **69.** $x^2 + 1 = 37$ **70.** $2x^2 - 5x - 3 = 0$

Get Ready!   **To prepare for Lesson 5-4, do Exercises 71 and 72.**

Evaluate each expression for the given values of the variables.   ◆ *See Lesson 1-3.*

71. $\dfrac{16(x - 4)(y - 2)}{4(x - 3)y}$; $x = 1$ and $y = -2$ **72.** $\dfrac{2(x + 5)y}{10(x - 4)(y - 2)}$; $x = 1$ and $y = -2$

5-4 Dividing Polynomials

© **Common Core State Standards**

A-APR.B.2 Know and apply the Remainder Theorem: For a polynomial $p(x)$ and a number a, the remainder on division by $x - a$ is $p(a)$, so $p(a) = 0$ if and only if $(x - a)$ is a factor of $p(x)$. **Also A-APR.A.1, A-APR.D.6**

MP 1, MP 2, MP 3, MP 6, MP 7

Objectives To divide polynomials using long division
To divide polynomials using synthetic division

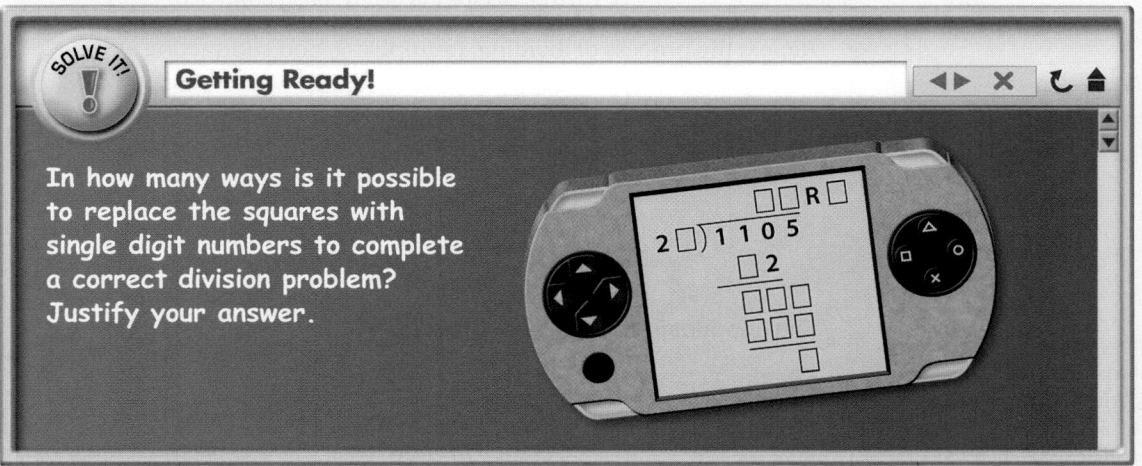

SOLVE IT!

Getting Ready!

In how many ways is it possible to replace the squares with single digit numbers to complete a correct division problem? Justify your answer.

Lesson Vocabulary
• synthetic division
• Remainder Theorem

Long division is one of many methods you can use to divide whole numbers.

Essential Understanding You can divide polynomials using steps that are similar to the long-division steps that you use to divide whole numbers.

When you try to factor a polynomial, you are trying to find a divisor of the polynomial that gives a quotient (the other factor) and remainder 0. This suggests that being able to divide one polynomial by another could help you factor polynomials.

Numerical long division and polynomial long division are similar.

Numerical Long Division		Polynomial Long Division	

$$\begin{array}{r} 32 \\ 21\overline{)672} \\ 63 \\ \hline 42 \\ 42 \\ \hline 0 \end{array}$$

21 divides into
67 3 times
21 divides into
42 2 times

$$\begin{array}{r} 3x + 2 \\ 2x + 1\overline{)6x^2 + 7x + 2} \\ 6x^2 + 3x \\ \hline 4x + 2 \\ 4x + 2 \\ \hline 0 \end{array}$$

$(2x + 1)$ divides into
$(6x^2 + 7x)$ $3x$ times
$(2x + 1)$ divides into
$(4x + 2)$ 2 times

The remainder from each division above is 0, so 21 is a factor of 672 and $2x + 1$ is a factor of $6x^2 + 7x + 2$.

Problem 1 **Using Polynomial Long Division**

Use polynomial long division to divide $4x^2 + 23x - 16$ by $x + 5$. What is the quotient and remainder?

$$
\begin{array}{r}
4x \\
x + 5 \overline{)4x^2 + 23x - 16} \\
\underline{4x^2 + 20x} \\
3x - 16
\end{array}
$$

Divide: $\frac{4x^2}{x} = 4x$.
Multiply: $4x(x + 5) = 4x^2 + 20x$.
Subtract to get $3x$. Bring down -16.

Repeat the process of dividing, multiplying, and subtracting.

$$
\begin{array}{r}
4x \ + 3 \\
x + 5 \overline{)4x^2 + 23x - 16} \\
\underline{4x^2 + 20x} \\
3x - 16 \\
\underline{3x + 15} \\
-31
\end{array}
$$

Divide: $\frac{3x}{x} = 3$
Multiply: $3(x + 5) = 3x + 15$.
Subtract to get -31.

The quotient is $4x + 3$ with remainder -31. ◁ You can say: $4x + 3$, R -31.

Think

How can you check your result?
Show that
(divisor)(quotient) + remainder = dividend.

Check

$(x + 5)(4x + 3) - 31 = (4x^2 + 3x + 20x + 15) - 31$ Multiply $(x + 5)(4x + 3)$.
$= 4x^2 + 23x - 16$ ✔   Simplify.

✅ **Got It?** **1.** Use polynomial long division to divide $3x^2 - 29x + 56$ by $x - 7$. What is the quotient and remainder?

---

 take note

Key Concept   The Division Algorithm for Polynomials

You can divide polynomial $P(x)$ by polynomial $D(x)$ to get polynomial quotient $Q(x)$ and polynomial remainder $R(x)$. The result is $P(x) = D(x)Q(x) + R(x)$.

$$
\begin{array}{r}
Q(x) \\
D(x) \overline{)P(x)} \\
\cdot \\
\cdot \\
\cdot \\
\overline{R(x)}
\end{array}
$$

If $R(x) = 0$, then $P(x) = D(x)Q(x)$ and $D(x)$ and $Q(x)$ are factors of $P(x)$.

To use long division, $P(x)$ and $D(x)$ should be in standard form with zero coefficients where appropriate. The process stops when the degree of the remainder, $R(x)$, is less than the degree of the divisor, $D(x)$.

Problem 2 Checking Factors

A Is $x^2 + 1$ a factor of $3x^4 - 4x^3 + 12x^2 + 5$?

$$
\begin{array}{r}
3x^2 - 4x + 9 \\
x^2 + 0x + 1\overline{)3x^4 - 4x^3 + 12x^2 + 0x + 5} \\
\underline{3x^4 + 0x^3 + 3x^2} \\
-4x^3 + 9x^2 + 0x \\
\underline{-4x^3 + 0x^2 - 4x} \\
9x^2 + 4x + 5 \\
\underline{9x^2 + 0x + 9} \\
4x - 4
\end{array}
$$

Include 0x terms.

> The degree of the remainder is less than the degree of the divisor. Stop!

The remainder is not zero. $x^2 + 1$ is not a factor of $3x^4 - 4x^3 + 12x^2 + 5$.

Plan

Can you use the Factor Theorem to help answer this question?
Yes; recall that if $P(a) = 0$, then $x - a$ is a factor of $P(x)$.

B Is $x - 2$ a factor of $P(x) = x^5 - 32$? If it is, write $P(x)$ as a product of two factors.

Step 1 Use the Factor Theorem to determine if $x - 2$ is a factor of $x^5 - 32$.

$$P(2) = 2^5 - 32$$
$$= 32 - 32$$
$$= 0$$

Since $P(2) = 0$, $x - 2$ is a factor of $P(x)$.

Step 2 Use polynomial long division to find the other factor.

$$
\begin{array}{r}
x^4 + 2x^3 + 4x^2 + 8x + 16 \\
x - 2\overline{)x^5 + 0x^4 + 0x^3 + 0x^2 + 0x - 32} \\
\underline{x^5 - 2x^4} \\
2x^4 + 0x^3 \\
\underline{2x^4 - 4x^3} \\
4x^3 + 0x^2 \\
\underline{4x^3 - 8x^2} \\
8x^2 + 0x \\
\underline{8x^2 - 16x} \\
16x - 32 \\
\underline{16x - 32} \\
0
\end{array}
$$

$$P(x) = (x - 2)(x^4 + 2x^3 + 4x^2 + 8x + 16)$$

  Got It? 2. a. Is $x^4 - 1$ a factor of $P(x) = x^5 + 5x^4 - x - 5$? If it is, write $P(x)$ as a product of two factors.

b. Reasoning Use the fact that $12 \cdot 31 = 372$ to write $3x^2 + 7x + 2$ as the product of two factors.

Synthetic division simplifies the long-division process for dividing by a linear expression $x - a$. To use synthetic division, write the coefficients (including zeros) of the polynomial in standard form. Omit all variables and exponents. For the divisor, reverse the sign (use a). This allows you to add instead of subtract throughout the process.

Ⓒ Problem 3 Using Synthetic Division

Use synthetic division to divide $x^3 - 14x^2 + 51x - 54$ by $x + 2$. What is the quotient and remainder?

Think

To divide by $x + 2$ what number do you use for the synthetic divisor?

$x + 2 = x - (-2)$ so use -2.

Step 1   Reverse the sign of $+2$. Write the coefficients of the polynomial.

$$-2 \, \rfloor \, \underline{1 \quad -14 \quad 51 \quad -54}$$

Step 2   Bring down the first coefficient.

$$\begin{array}{r|rrrr} -2 & 1 & -14 & 51 & -54 \\ \hline & 1 \end{array}$$

Step 3   Multiply the coefficient by the divisor. Add to the next coefficient.

$$\begin{array}{r|rrrr} -2 & 1 & -14 & 51 & -54 \\ & & -2 \\ \hline & 1 & -16 \end{array}$$

Step 4   Continue multiplying and adding through the last coefficient.

$$\begin{array}{r|rrrr} -2 & 1 & -14 & 51 & -54 \\ & & -2 & 32 & -166 \\ \hline & 1 & -16 & 83 & -220 \end{array}$$

The quotient is $x^2 - 16x + 83$, R -220.

✓ **Got It?**   **3.** Use synthetic division to divide $x^3 - 57x + 56$ by $x - 7$. What is the quotient and remainder?

Ⓒ Problem 4 Using Synthetic Division to Solve a Problem

Crafts The polynomial $x^3 + 7x^2 - 38x - 240$ expresses the volume, in cubic inches, of the shadow box shown.

Ⓐ What are the dimensions of the box? (*Hint:* The length is greater than the height (or depth).)

Plan

How can you use the picture to help solve the problem?

The picture gives the width of the box. Remember for a rectangular prism, $V = \ell \times w \times h$.

$$\begin{array}{r|rrrr} -5 & 1 & 7 & -38 & -240 \\ & & -5 & -10 & 240 \\ \hline & 1 & 2 & -48 & 0 \end{array}$$

$x^2 + 2x - 48 = (x - 6)(x + 8)$

So, $x^3 + 7x^2 - 38x - 240 = (x + 5)(x^2 + 2x - 48)$
$$= (x + 5)(x - 6)(x + 8)$$

The length, width, and height (or depth) of the box are $(x + 8)$ in., $(x + 5)$ in., and $(x - 6)$ in., respectively.

$x + 5$

B **If the width of the box is 15 in., what are the other two dimensions?**

The width of the box is $x + 5$. So if $x + 5 = 15$, then $x = 10$.

Substitute for x to find the length and height (or depth).

Length: $x + 8 = 10 + 8 = 18$ in.
Height: $x - 6 = 10 - 6 = 4$ in.

 **Got It?** **4.** If the polynomial $x^3 + 6x^2 + 11x + 6$ expresses the volume, in cubic inches, of the box, and the width is $(x + 1)$ in., what are the dimensions of the box?

The **Remainder Theorem** provides a quick way to find the remainder of a polynomial long-division problem.

take note

> ### Theorem   The Remainder Theorem
>
> If you divide a polynomial $P(x)$ of degree $n \geq 1$ by $x - a$, then the remainder is $P(a)$.

Here's Why It Works When you divide polynomial $P(x)$ by $D(x)$, you find $P(x) = D(x)Q(x) + R(x)$.

$P(x) = (x - a)Q(x) + R(x)$ Substitute $(x - a)$ for $D(x)$.
$P(a) = (a - a)Q(a) + R(a)$ Evaluate $P(a)$. Substitute a for x.
$\quad\ = R(a)$ Simplify.

© **Problem 5** **Evaluating a Polynomial**   GRIDDED RESPONSE

Think

Is there a way to find $P(3)$ without substituting?
Use synthetic division. $P(3)$ is the remainder.

Given that $P(x) = x^5 - 2x^3 - x^2 + 2$, what is $P(3)$?

By the Remainder Theorem, $P(3)$ is the remainder when you divide $P(x)$ by $x - 3$.

```
3 | 1   0   -2   -1    0     2
  |     3    9   21   60   180
    1   3    7   20   60   182
```

$P(3) = 182$.

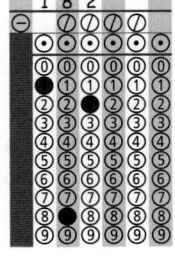

 Got It? **5.** Given that $P(x) = x^5 - 3x^4 - 28x^3 + 5x + 20$, what is $P(-4)$?

Lesson Check

Do you know HOW?

Divide using any method.

1. $(2x^2 + 7x + 11) \div (x + 2)$

2. $(x^3 + 5x^2 + 11x + 15) \div (x + 3)$

3. $(x^3 - x^2 - 4x + 4) \div (x - 2)$

4. $(4x^3 + 21x^2 - x - 24) \div (x + 5)$

5. $(9x^3 - 15x^2 + 4x) \div (x - 3)$

Do you UNDERSTAND?

6. Reasoning A polynomial $P(x)$ is divided by a binomial $x - a$. The remainder is 0. What conclusion can you draw? Explain.

7. Writing Explain why it is important to have the terms of both polynomials written in descending order of degree before dividing.

8. Open-Ended Write a polynomial division that has a quotient of $x + 3$ and a remainder of 2.

Practice and Problem-Solving Exercises

 Divide using long division. Check your answers. ◀ **See Problem 1.**

9. $(x^2 - 3x - 40) \div (x + 5)$

10. $(3x^2 + 7x - 20) \div (x + 4)$

11. $(x^3 + 3x^2 - x + 2) \div (x - 1)$

12. $(2x^3 - 3x^2 - 18x - 8) \div (x - 4)$

13. $(3x^3 + 9x^2 + 8x + 4) \div (x + 2)$

14. $(9x^2 - 21x - 20) \div (x - 1)$

15. $(x^2 - 7x + 10) \div (x + 3)$

16. $(x^3 - 13x - 12) \div (x - 4)$

Determine whether each binomial is a factor of $x^3 + 4x^2 + x - 6$. ◀ **See Problem 2.**

17. $x + 1$　　　　**18.** $x + 2$　　　　**19.** $x + 3$　　　　**20.** $x - 3$

Divide using synthetic division. ◀ **See Problem 3.**

21. $(x^3 + 3x^2 - x - 3) \div (x - 1)$

22. $(x^3 - 4x^2 + 6x - 4) \div (x - 2)$

23. $(x^3 - 7x^2 - 7x + 20) \div (x + 4)$

24. $(x^3 - 3x^2 - 5x - 25) \div (x - 5)$

25. $(x^2 + 3) \div (x - 1)$

26. $(3x^3 + 17x^2 + 21x - 9) \div (x + 3)$

27. $(x^3 + 27) \div (x + 3)$

28. $(6x^2 - 8x - 2) \div (x - 1)$

Use synthetic division and the given factor to completely factor each polynomial function. ◀ **See Problem 4.**

29. $y = x^3 + 2x^2 - 5x - 6;\ (x + 1)$

30. $y = x^3 - 4x^2 - 9x + 36;\ (x + 3)$

31. Geometry The volume, in cubic inches, of the decorative box shown can be expressed as the product of the lengths of its sides as $V(x) = x^3 + x^2 - 6x$. What linear expressions with integer coefficients represent the length and height of the box?

x

Use synthetic division and the Remainder Theorem to find $P(a)$. ◀ See Problem 5.

32. $P(x) = x^3 + 4x^2 - 8x - 6; a = -2$ **33.** $P(x) = x^3 + 4x^2 + 4x; a = -2$

34. $P(x) = x^3 - 7x^2 + 15x - 9; a = 3$ **35.** $P(x) = x^3 + 7x^2 + 4x; a = -2$

36. $P(x) = 6x^3 - x^2 + 4x + 3; a = 3$ **37.** $P(x) = 2x^3 - x^2 + 10x + 5; a = \frac{1}{2}$

38. $P(x) = 2x^3 + 4x^2 - 10x - 9; a = 3$ **39.** $P(x) = 2x^4 + 6x^3 + 5x^2 - 45; a = -3$

 **Apply**

ⓒ 40. Think About a Plan Your friend multiplies $x + 4$ by a quadratic polynomial and gets the result $x^3 - 3x^2 - 24x + 30$. The teacher says that everything is correct except for the constant term. Find the quadratic polynomial that your friend used. What is the correct result of multiplication?
- What does the fact that all the terms except for the constant are correct tell you?
- How can polynomial division help you solve this problem?
- What is the connection between the remainder of the division and your friend's error?

ⓒ 41. Error Analysis A student used synthetic division to divide $x^3 - x^2 - 2x$ by $x + 1$. Describe and correct the error shown.

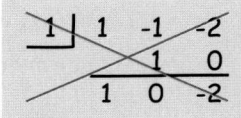

ⓒ 42. Reasoning When a polynomial is divided by $(x - 5)$, the quotient is $5x^2 + 3x + 12$ with remainder 7. Find the polynomial.

43. Geometry The expression $\frac{1}{3}(x^3 + 5x^2 + 8x + 4)$ represents the volume of a square pyramid. The expression $x + 1$ represents the height of the pyramid. What expression represents the side length of the base? (*Hint:* The formula for the volume of a pyramid is $V = \frac{1}{3}Bh$.)

Divide.

44. $\left(2x^3 + 9x^2 + 14x + 5\right) \div (2x + 1)$ **45.** $\left(x^4 + 3x^2 + x + 4\right) \div (x + 3)$

46. $\left(x^5 + 1\right) \div (x + 1)$ **47.** $\left(x^4 + 4x^3 - x - 4\right) \div (x^3 - 1)$

48. $\left(3x^4 - 5x^3 + 2x^2 + 3x - 2\right) \div (3x - 2)$

Determine whether each binomial is a factor of $x^3 + x^2 - 16x - 16$.

49. $x + 2$ **50.** $x - 4$ **51.** $x + 1$ **52.** $x - 1$

Use synthetic division to determine whether each binomial is a factor of $3x^3 + 10x^2 - x - 12$.

53. $x + 3$ **54.** $x - 1$ **55.** $x + 2$ **56.** $x - 4$

Divide using synthetic division.

57. $\left(x^4 - 2x^3 + x^2 + x - 1\right) \div (x - 1)$ **58.** $\left(x^4 + 3x^3 + 3x^2 + 4x + 3\right) \div (x + 1)$

59. $\left(x^4 + 3x^3 + 7x^2 + 26x + 15\right) \div (x + 3)$ **60.** $\left(x^4 - 6x^2 - 27\right) \div (x + 2)$

61. $\left(x^4 - 5x^2 + 4x + 12\right) \div (x + 2)$ **62.** $\left(x^4 - \frac{9}{2}x^3 + 3x^2 - \frac{1}{2}x\right) \div \left(x - \frac{1}{2}\right)$

 **Challenge**

63. Reasoning Divide. Look for patterns in your answers.
a. $(x^2 - 1) \div (x - 1)$ b. $(x^3 - 1) \div (x - 1)$ c. $(x^4 - 1) \div (x - 1)$
d. Using the patterns, factor $x^5 - 1$.

64. Reasoning The remainder from the division of the polynomial $x^3 + ax^2 + 2ax + 5$ by $x + 1$ is 3. Find a.

65. Use synthetic division to find $(x^2 + 4) \div (x - 2i)$.

66. Writing Suppose 3, -1, and 5 are zeros of a cubic polynomial function $f(x)$. What is the sign of $f(1) \cdot f(4)$? (*Hint:* Sketch the graph; consider all possibilities.)

Standardized Test Prep

SAT/ACT

67. What is the remainder when $x^2 - 5x + 7$ is divided by $x + 1$?
    (A) 1   (B) 3   (C) 11   (D) 13

68. What is the least degree of a polynomial that has a zero of multiplicity 3 at 1, a zero of multiplicity 1 at 0, and a zero of multiplicity 2 at 2?
    (F) 3   (G) 4   (H) 5   (I) 6

69. The equation $y = 0.17x$ represents your weight, in pounds, on the Moon y in relation to your weight on Earth x. If Al weighs 130 lb on Earth, what would he weigh on the Moon?
    (A) 22.1 lb   (B) 92.3 lb   (C) 130 lb   (D) 764.7 lb

Extended Response

70. The formula for the area of a circle is $A = \pi r^2$. Solve the equation for r. If the area of a circle is 78.5 cm^2, what is the radius? Use 3.14 for π.

Mixed Review

Find the real solutions of each equation by factoring.   ◀ **See Lesson 5-3.**

71. $x^3 + 2x^2 + x = 0$ **72.** $2x^4 - 2x^3 + 2x^2 = 2x$ **73.** $5x^5 = 125x^3$

Solve each equation using the Quadratic Formula.   ◀ **See Lesson 4-7.**

74. $x^2 + 3x - 2 = 0$ **75.** $2x^2 + 4x - 4 = 0$ **76.** $7x^2 - 2x - 5 = 0$

77. $x^2 - 5x = -5$ **78.** $x^2 - 6x = -7$ **79.** $x^2 + 7x + 11 = 0$

Find the solution of each system by graphing.   ◀ **See Lesson 3-3.**

80. $\begin{cases} y < 2x + 3 \\ y > -x \end{cases}$ **81.** $\begin{cases} y > x - 4 \\ y > 4 - \frac{1}{3}x \end{cases}$ **82.** $\begin{cases} y < -|x| + 3 \\ y > x + 1 \end{cases}$

Get Ready!   To prepare for Lesson 5-5, do Exercises 83–85.

Simplify each expression.   ◀ **See Lesson 4-8.**

83. $(-4i)(6i)$ **84.** $(2 + i)(2 - i)$ **85.** $(4 - 3i)(5 + i)$

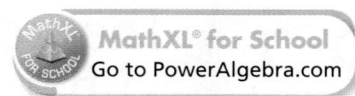
Do you know HOW?

For each polynomial function, describe the end behavior of its graph.

1. $f(x) = x^8 - 8x^4 + 6x^2$

2. $f(x) = -x^4 - x^3 + 1$

3. $f(x) = x^7 - 3x^5 - 5x^3$

4. What is the degree of the function that generates the data shown?

x	y
−3	159
−2	29
−1	−1
0	−3
1	−1
2	29
3	159

Find all the solutions of each equation by factoring.

5. $x^3 - 5x^2 = 36x$

6. $27x^3 = 8$

7. $x^4 - 20x^2 + 64 = 0$

8. $x^3 + 125 = 0$

9. Use the Remainder Theorem and synthetic division to find $P(4)$ for $P(x) = 2x^4 - 3x^2 + 4x - 1$.

You have several boxes with the same dimensions. They have a combined volume of $2x^4 + 4x^3 - 18x^2 - 4x + 16$. Determine whether each binomial below could represent the number of boxes you have.

10. $x - 1$

11. $x + 2$

12. $2x + 8$

Write each polynomial in standard form. Then classify it by degree and number of terms.

13. $-2x^3 + 6 - x^3 + 5x$

14. $3(x - 1)(x + 4)$

Describe the shape of the graph of each cubic function by determining the end behavior and number of turning points.

15. $y = -5x^3$

16. $y = 3x^3 + 4x^2 + 2x - 1$

Do you UNDERSTAND?

Ⓒ **17.** You buy one container each of strawberries, blueberries, and cherries. Cherries are $1 more per container than blueberries, which are $1 more per container than strawberries. The product of the 3 individual prices is 5 times the total cost of one container of each fruit.
   a. Write a polynomial function to model the cost of your purchase.
   b. Graph to find the price of each container.
   c. Writing Explain how you used the graph to find the prices.

Ⓒ **18.** A cylinder has a radius of $3x - 2$ and a height of $3 - 2x$.
   a. Use 3.14 as π and graph the equation for the volume.
   b. Find the relative maximum.
   c. Reasoning What kind of limitation on the radius would make your answer in part (b) the maximum possible volume?

Ⓒ **19. Open-Ended** Write a polynomial function in factored form with at least three zeros that are negative, one of which has multiplicity 2.

5-5 Theorems About Roots of Polynomial Equations

Common Core State Standards

N-CN.C.7 Solve quadratic equations with real coefficients that have complex solutions. **Also N-CN.C.8**

MP 1, MP 2, MP 3, MP 4, MP 8

Objectives To solve equations using the Rational Root Theorem
To use the Conjugate Root Theorem

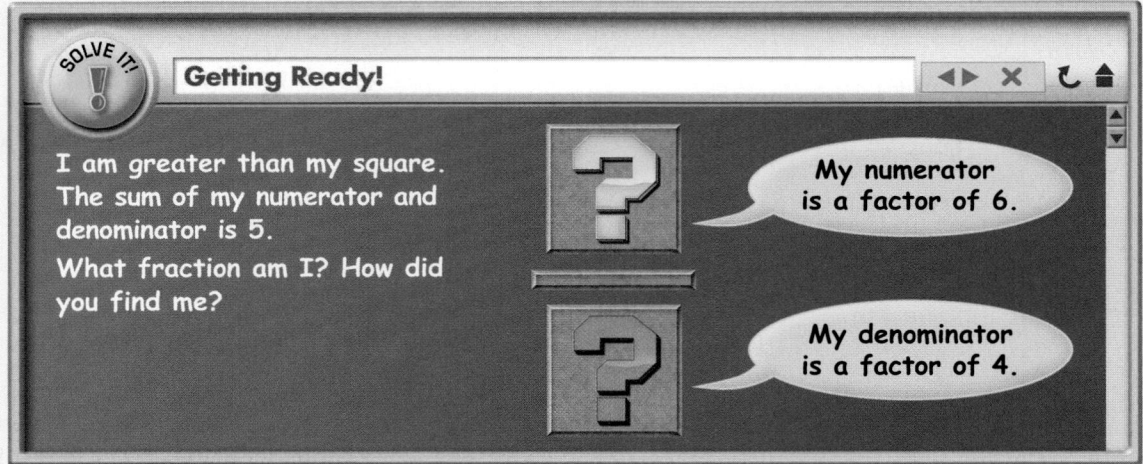

Getting Ready!

I am greater than my square. The sum of my numerator and denominator is 5.
What fraction am I? How did you find me?

My numerator is a factor of 6.

My denominator is a factor of 4.

Lesson Vocabulary
- Rational Root Theorem
- Conjugate Root Theorem
- Descartes' Rule of Signs

Factoring the polynomial $P(x) = a_n x^n + a_{n-1} x^{n-1} + \cdots + a_1 x + a_0$ can be challenging, especially when both a_n and a_0 have many factors.

Essential Understanding The factors of the numbers a_n and a_0 in $P(x) = a_n x^n + a_{n-1} x^{n-1} + \cdots + a_1 x + a_0$ can help you factor $P(x)$ and solve the equation $P(x) = 0$.

One way to find a root of the polynomial equation $P(x) = 0$ is to guess and check. This is inefficient unless there is a way to minimize the number of guesses, or possible roots. The **Rational Root Theorem** does just that.

take note

Theorem Rational Root Theorem

Let $P(x) = a_n x^n + a_{n-1} x^{n-1} + \cdots + a_1 x + a_0$ be a polynomial with integer coefficients. There are a limited number of possible roots of $P(x) = 0$:

- Integer roots must be factors of a_0.
- Rational roots must have reduced form $\frac{p}{q}$ where p is an integer factor of a_0 and q is an integer factor of a_n.

Factors of the leading coefficient:
$\pm 1, \pm 3, \pm 7,$ and $\pm 21.$

$21x^2 + 29x + 10 = 0$

$x^2 + \frac{29}{21}x + \frac{10}{21} = 0$

Factors of the constant term:
$\pm 1, \pm 2, \pm 5,$ and $\pm 10.$

$\left(x + \frac{2}{3}\right)\left(x + \frac{5}{7}\right) = 0$

The roots are $-\frac{2}{3}$ and $-\frac{5}{7}$.

Plan

What information can you get from the equation?
The equation gives you the leading coefficient and the constant term.

 Problem 1 Finding a Rational Root

What are the rational roots of $2x^3 - x^2 + 2x + 5 = 0$?

The only possible rational roots have the form $\dfrac{\text{factor of constant term}}{\text{factor of leading coefficient}}$.

The constant factors are ± 1, ± 5. The leading coefficient factors are ± 1, ± 2.
The only possible rational roots are ± 1, ± 5, $\pm \frac{1}{2}$, $\pm \frac{5}{2}$.

The table shows the values of the function $y = P(x)$ for the possible roots.

x	1	-1	5	-5	$\frac{1}{2}$	$-\frac{1}{2}$	$\frac{5}{2}$	$-\frac{5}{2}$
$P(x)$	8	0	240	-280	6	$\frac{7}{2}$	35	$-\frac{75}{2}$

The only rational root of $2x^3 - x^2 + 2x + 5 = 0$ is -1.

 Got It? 1. What are the rational roots of $3x^3 + 7x^2 + 6x - 8 = 0$?

Once you find one root, use synthetic division to factor the polynomial. Continue finding roots and dividing until you have a second-degree polynomial. Use the Quadratic Formula to find the remaining roots.

© **Problem 2** Using the Rational Root Theorem

What are the rational roots of $15x^3 - 32x^2 + 3x + 2 = 0$?

Know	Need	Plan
Coefficients and the constant term of the polynomial	The roots of the polynomial equation	• Find one root. • Factor until you get a quadratic. • Use the Quadratic Formula to find the other roots.

Step 1 The constant term factors are ± 1 and ± 2. The leading coefficient factors are ± 1, ± 3, ± 5, and ± 15.

Step 2 The possible rational roots are: ± 1, ± 2, $\pm \frac{1}{3}$, $\pm \frac{2}{3}$, $\pm \frac{1}{5}$, $\pm \frac{2}{5}$, $\pm \frac{1}{15}$, and $\pm \frac{2}{15}$.

Step 3 Test each possible rational root in $15x^3 - 32x^2 + 3x + 2$ until you find a root.
Test 1: $15(1)^3 - 32(1)^2 + 3(1) + 2 = -12 \neq 0$

Test 2: $15(2)^3 - 32(2)^2 + 3(2) + 2 = 0$ So 2 is a root.

Step 4 Factor the polynomial by using synthetic division:
$P(x) = (x - 2)(15x^2 - 2x - 1)$.

$$
\begin{array}{r|rrrr}
2 & 15 & -32 & 3 & 2 \\
  &   & 30 & -4 & -2 \\
\hline
  & 15 & -2 & -1 & 0
\end{array}
$$

Step 5 Since $15x^2 - 2x - 1 = (5x + 1)(3x - 1)$, the other roots are $-\frac{1}{5}$ and $\frac{1}{3}$.

The rational roots of $15x^3 - 32x^2 + 3x + 2 = 0$ are 2, $-\frac{1}{5}$, and $\frac{1}{3}$.

 Got It? 2. What are the rational roots of $2x^3 + x^2 - 7x - 6 = 0$?

Recall from Lesson 4-8 that the complex numbers $a + bi$ and $a - bi$ are conjugates. Similarly, the irrational numbers $a + \sqrt{b}$ and $a - \sqrt{b}$ are conjugates. If a complex number or an irrational number is a root of a polynomial equation with rational coefficients, so is its conjugate.

take note

Theorem Conjugate Root Theorem

If $P(x)$ is a polynomial with *rational* coefficients, then irrational roots of $P(x) = 0$ that have the form $a + \sqrt{b}$ occur in conjugate pairs. That is, if $a + \sqrt{b}$ is an irrational root with a and b rational, then $a - \sqrt{b}$ is also a root.

If $P(x)$ is a polynomial with *real* coefficients, then the complex roots of $P(x) = 0$ occur in conjugate pairs. That is, if $a + bi$ is a complex root with a and b real, then $a - bi$ is also a root.

 Problem 3 Using the Conjugate Root Theorem to Identify Roots

Think

Do you have real coefficients?
All rational numbers are real numbers. Therefore the rational coefficients are real coefficients.

A quartic polynomial $P(x)$ has rational coefficients. If $\sqrt{2}$ and $1 + i$ are roots of $P(x) = 0$, what are the two other roots?

Since $P(x)$ has rational coefficients and $0 + \sqrt{2}$ is a root of $P(x) = 0$, it follows from the Conjugate Root Theorem that $0 - \sqrt{2}$ is also a root.

Since $P(x)$ has real coefficients and $1 + i$ is a root of $P(x) = 0$, it follows that $1 - i$ is also a root.

The two other roots are $-\sqrt{2}$ and $1 - i$.

Got It? 3. A cubic polynomial $P(x)$ has real coefficients. If $3 - 2i$ and $\frac{5}{2}$ are two roots of $P(x) = 0$, what is one additional root?

 Problem 4 Using Conjugates to Construct a Polynomial

Think

Does the Conjugate Root Theorem apply to -4?
No; the theorem does not apply because -4 is neither irrational nor imaginary.

Multiple Choice What is a third-degree polynomial function $y = P(x)$ with rational coefficients so that $P(x) = 0$ has roots -4 and $2i$?

Ⓐ $P(x) = x^3 - 2x^2 - 16x + 32$ Ⓒ $P(x) = x^3 + 4x^2 + 4x + 16$

Ⓑ $P(x) = x^3 - 4x^2 + 4x - 16$ Ⓓ $P(x) = x^3 + 4x^2 - 4x - 16$

Since $2i$ is a root, then $-2i$ is also a root.

$P(x) = (x + 2i)(x - 2i)(x + 4)$ Write the polynomial function.

$\quad = (x^2 + 4)(x + 4)$ Multiply the complex conjugates.

$\quad = x^3 + 4x^2 + 4x + 16$ Write the polynomial function in standard form.

The equation $x^3 + 4x^2 + 4x + 16 = 0$ has rational coefficients and has roots -4 and $2i$. The correct answer is C.

Got It? 4. What quartic polynomial equation has roots $2 - 3i$, 8, 2?

The French mathematician René Descartes (1596–1650) recognized a connection between the roots of a polynomial equation and the $+$ and $-$ signs of the standard form.

 take note

Theorem   Descartes' Rule of Signs

Let $P(x)$ be a polynomial with real coefficients written in standard form.

- The number of positive real roots of $P(x) = 0$ is either equal to the number of sign changes between consecutive coefficients of $P(x)$ or is less than that by an even number.

- The number of negative real roots of $P(x) = 0$ is either equal to the number of sign changes between consecutive coefficients of $P(-x)$ or is less than that by an even number.

In both cases, count multiple roots according to their multiplicity.

 Problem 5   Using Descartes' Rule of Signs

What does Descartes' Rule of Signs tell you about the real roots of $x^3 - x^2 + 1 = 0$?

Think

Why can't there be zero negative real roots?
The number of negative roots is equal to 1 or is less than 1 by an even number. Zero is less than 1 by an odd number.

There are two sign changes, $+$ to $-$ and $-$ to $+$.
Therefore, there are either 0 or 2 positive real roots.

$P(-x) = (-x)^3 - (-x)^2 + 1 = -x^3 - x^2 + 1 = 0$ has
only one sign change $-$ to $+$. There is one negative real root.

Recall that graphs of cubic functions have zero or two turning points. Because the graph already shows two turning points, it will not change direction again. So there are no positive real roots.

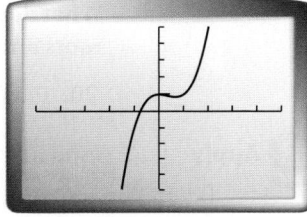

 **Got It?   5. a.** What does Descartes' Rule of Signs tell you about the real roots of
$2x^4 - x^3 + 3x^2 - 1 = 0$?

b. Reasoning Can you confirm real and complex roots graphically? Explain.

 Lesson Check

Do you know HOW?

Use the Rational Root Theorem to list all possible rational roots for each equation.

1. $x^2 + x - 2 = 0$

2. $2x^3 - x^2 - 6 = 0$

3. $3x^4 + 2x^2 - 12 = 0$

Write a polynomial function with rational coefficients so that $P(x) = 0$ has the given roots.

4. 5 and 9   **5.** -4 and $2i$

Do you UNDERSTAND? 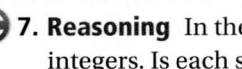 MATHEMATICAL PRACTICES

6. Vocabulary Give an example of a conjugate pair.

7. Reasoning In the statements below, r and s represent integers. Is each statement *always*, *sometimes*, or *never* true? Explain.
a. A root of the equation
$3x^3 + rx^2 + sx + 8 = 0$ could be 5.
b. A root of the equation
$3x^3 + rx^2 + sx + 8 = 0$ could be -2.

8. Error Analysis A student claims that $-4i$ is the only imaginary root of a polynomial equation that has real coefficients. What is the student's mistake?

Practice and Problem-Solving Exercises  MATHEMATICAL PRACTICES

 **Practice**

Use the Rational Root Theorem to list all possible rational roots for each equation. Then find any actual rational roots.

 **See Problems 1 and 2.**

9. $x^3 - 4x + 1 = 0$

10. $x^3 + 2x - 9 = 0$

11. $2x^3 - 5x + 4 = 0$

12. $3x^3 + 9x - 6 = 0$

13. $4x^3 + 2x - 12 = 0$

14. $6x^3 + 2x - 18 = 0$

15. $7x^3 - x^2 + 4x + 10 = 0$

16. $8x^3 + 2x^2 - 5x + 1 = 0$

17. $10x^3 - 7x^2 + x - 10 = 0$

A polynomial function $P(x)$ with rational coefficients has the given roots. Find two additional roots of $P(x) = 0$.

 **See Problem 3.**

18. $-2i$ and $\sqrt{10}$

19. $14 - \sqrt{2}$ and $-6i$

20. i and $7 + 8i$

21. $-\sqrt{3}$ and $5 - \sqrt{11}$

Write a polynomial function with rational coefficients so that $P(x) = 0$ has the given roots.

 **See Problem 4.**

22. 7 and 12

23. -9 and -15

24. $-10i$

25. $3i + 9$

26. 4, 16, and $1 + 19i$

27. $13i$ and $5 + 10i$

28. $11 - 2i$ and $8 + 13i$

29. $17 - 4i$ and $12 + 5i$

What does Descartes' Rule of Signs say about the number of positive real roots and negative real roots for each polynomial function?

 **See Problem 5.**

30. $P(x) = x^2 + 5x + 6$

31. $P(x) = 9x^3 - 4x^2 + 10$

32. $P(x) = 8x^3 + 2x^2 - 14x + 5$

 **Apply**

Find all rational roots for $P(x) = 0$.

33. $P(x) = 2x^3 - 5x^2 + x - 1$

34. $P(x) = 6x^4 - 13x^3 + 13x^2 - 39x - 15$

35. $P(x) = 7x^3 - x^2 - 5x + 14$

36. $P(x) = 3x^4 - 7x^3 + 10x^2 - x + 12$

37. $P(x) = 6x^4 - 7x^2 - 3$

38. $P(x) = 2x^3 - 3x^2 - 8x + 12$

Write a polynomial function $P(x)$ with rational coefficients so that $P(x) = 0$ has the given roots.

39. -6, 3, and $-15i$

40. $4 + \sqrt{5}$ and $8i$

41. $-5 - 7i$ and $2 - \sqrt{11}$

42. Think About a Plan You are building a square pyramid out of clay and want the height to be 0.5 cm shorter than twice the length of each side of the base. If you have 18 cm³ of clay, what is the greatest height you could use for your pyramid?
  - How can drawing a diagram help you solve this problem?
  - What is the formula for the volume of a pyramid?
  - What equation can you solve to find the height of the pyramid?

43. Error Analysis Your friend is using Descartes' Rule of Signs to find the number of negative real roots of $x^3 + x^2 + x + 1 = 0$. Describe and correct the error.

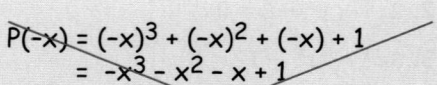

$P(-x) = (-x)^3 + (-x)^2 + (-x) + 1$
$= -x^3 - x^2 - x + 1$

Because there is only one sign change in $P(-x)$, there must be one negative real root.

44. Reasoning A quartic equation with integer coefficients has two real roots and one imaginary root. Explain why the fourth root must be imaginary.

45. Gardening A gardener is designing a new garden in the shape of a trapezoid. She wants the shorter base to be twice the height and the longer base to be 4 feet longer than the shorter base. If she has enough topsoil to create a 60 ft^2 garden, what dimensions should she use for the garden?

46. Open-Ended Write a fourth-degree polynomial equation with integer coefficients that has two irrational roots and two imaginary roots.

 Challenge
47. **a.** Find a polynomial equation in which $1 + \sqrt{2}$ is the only root.
  b. Find a polynomial equation with root $1 + \sqrt{2}$ of multiplicity 2.
  c. Find c such that $1 + \sqrt{2}$ is a root of $x^2 - 2x + c = 0$.

48. **a.** Using *real* and *imaginary* as types of roots, list all possible combinations of root type for a fourth-degree polynomial equation.
  b. Repeat the process for a fifth-degree polynomial equation.
  c. **Make a Conjecture** Make a conjecture about the number of real roots of an odd-degree polynomial equation.

49. Writing A student states that $2 + \sqrt{3}$ is a root of $x^2 - 2x - (3 + 2\sqrt{3}) = 0$. The student claims that $2 - \sqrt{3}$ is another root of the equation by the Conjugate Root Theorem. Explain how you would respond to the student.

Apply What You've Learned

MATHEMATICAL
PRACTICES
MP 7

Look back at the information about the diorama box Eliana plans to make using the rectangular sheet of cardboard shown on page 279. In the Apply What You've Learned in Lesson 5-1, you wrote a polynomial function $V(x)$ in standard form for the volume of Eliana's diorama box. You graphed this function in the Apply What You've Learned in Lesson 5-2.

a. Use your volume function to write an equation that you can solve to find the possible side lengths of the squares Eliana will cut from each corner.

b. Rewrite your equation from part (a) as an equation in the form $P(x) = 0$, where $P(x)$ is a polynomial in standard form.

c. Find all the real roots of $P(x) = 0$.

Using Polynomial Identities

© **Common Core State Standards**

A-APR.C.4 Prove polynomial identities and use them to describe numerical relationships.

MP 7

You can use what you know about polynomial identities to discover relationships among numbers.

Example

Use polynomial identities to prove that the sum of the cubes of any two consecutive positive integers is odd.

You can represent any two consecutive positive integers as n and $n + 1$, where n is a positive integer. Use the formula for factoring the sum of two cubes.

$$a^3 + b^3 = (a + b)\left(a^2 - ab + b^2\right)$$

$$= (n + (n + 1))\left(n^2 - n(n + 1) + (n + 1)^2\right) \quad \text{Substitute } n \text{ for } a \text{ and } n + 1 \text{ for } b.$$

$$= (2n + 1)\left(n^2 - n^2 - n + n^2 + 2n + 1\right) \quad \text{Simplify.}$$

$$= (2n + 1)\left(n^2 + n + 1\right)$$

$$= 2n^3 + 2n^2 + 2n + n^2 + n + 1$$

$$= 2n^3 + 3n^2 + 3n + 1$$

You know that $2n^3$ is always even because it has a factor of 2.

If n is even, then $3n^2$ is even and $3n$ is even. So $2n^3 + 3n^2 + 3n$ is even, and $2n^3 + 3n^2 + 3n + 1$ is odd, because it is 1 more than an even number.

If n is odd, then $3n^2$ is odd and $3n$ is odd. The sum of two odd integers is always even. So $2n^3 + 3n^2 + 3n$ is even, and $2n^3 + 3n^2 + 3n + 1$ is odd, because it is 1 more than an even number.

Therefore, $n^3 + (n + 1)^3$ is always odd for consecutive positive integers.

Exercises

1. Use polynomial identities to prove that the difference of the squares of any two consecutive integers is odd.

2. a. Prove that for any two positive consecutive integers a and b, where $a > b$, $a^3 - b^3 = a^2 + ab + b^2$.

  b. Prove that the difference of the cubes of two consecutive positive integers is always odd.

3. Prove that the square of the sum of two consecutive positive integers is odd.

4. Prove that the reciprocals of any two consecutive integers have a product that is equal to the reciprocal of the smaller integer minus the reciprocal of the larger integer.

5. Use the identity $n^3 - n = n(n - 1)(n + 1)$ to prove that 6 is a factor of $n^3 - n$ for all integers n. (*Hint:* n, $n - 1$, and $n + 1$ are consecutive integers.)

5-6 The Fundamental Theorem of Algebra

Common Core State Standards

N-CN.C.7 Solve quadratic equations with real coefficients that have complex solutions. **Also N-CN.C.8, N-CN.C.9, A-APR.B.3**

MP 1, MP 2, MP 3, MP 4

Objective To use the Fundamental Theorem of Algebra to solve polynomial equations with complex solutions

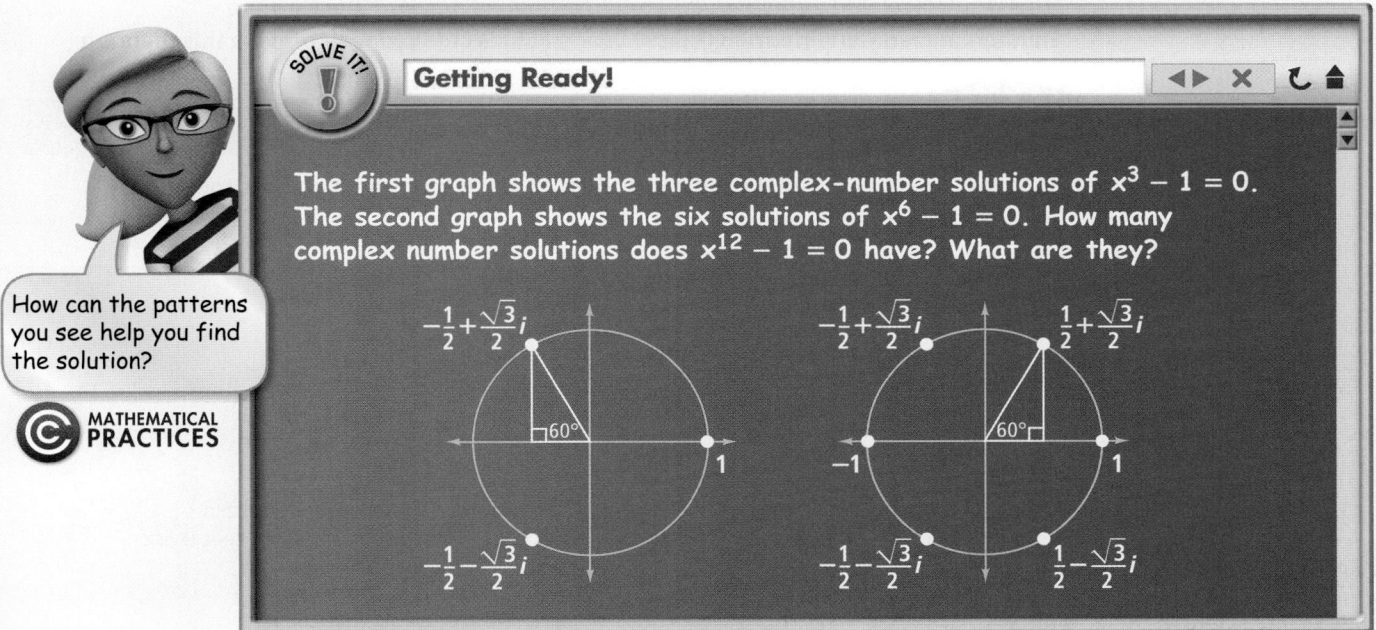

SOLVE IT!

Getting Ready!

The first graph shows the three complex-number solutions of $x^3 - 1 = 0$. The second graph shows the six solutions of $x^6 - 1 = 0$. How many complex number solutions does $x^{12} - 1 = 0$ have? What are they?

How can the patterns you see help you find the solution?

MATHEMATICAL PRACTICES

Lesson Vocabulary
• Fundamental Theorem of Algebra

You can factor any polynomial of degree n into n linear factors, but sometimes the factors will involve imaginary numbers.

Essential Understanding The degree of a polynomial equation tells you how many roots the equation has.

It is easy to see graphically that every polynomial function of degree 1 has a single zero, the x-intercept. However, there appear to be three possibilities for polynomials of degree 2. They correspond to these three graphs:

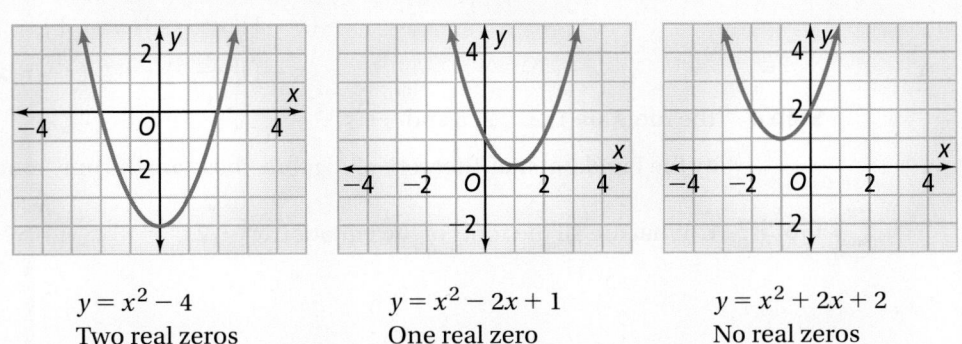

$y = x^2 - 4$
Two real zeros

$y = x^2 - 2x + 1$
One real zero

$y = x^2 + 2x + 2$
No real zeros

However, by factoring, you can see that each related equation has two roots.

$$x^2 - 4 = (x - 2)(x + 2) = 0$$ *two* real roots, 2 and -2

$$x^2 - 2x + 1 = (x - 1)(x - 1) = 0$$ a root of multiplicity *two* at 1

$$x^2 + 2x + 2 = (x - (-1 + i))(x - (-1 - i)) = 0$$ *two* complex roots, $-1 + i$ and $-1 - i$

Every quadratic polynomial equation has two roots, every cubic polynomial equation has three roots, and so on.

This result is related to the *Fundamental Theorem of Algebra*. The German mathematician Carl Friedrich Gauss (1777–1855) is credited with proving this theorem.

take note

Theorem   The Fundamental Theorem of Algebra

If $P(x)$ is a polynomial of degree $n \geq 1$, then $P(x) = 0$ has exactly n roots, including multiple and complex roots.

Problem 1   Using the Fundamental Theorem of Algebra

What are all the roots of $x^5 - x^4 - 3x^3 + 3x^2 - 4x + 4 = 0$?

Know

The polynomial equation has degree 5.
There are 5 roots.

Need

The zeros of the function

Plan

Use the Rational Root and Factor Theorems, synthetic division, and factoring.

Step 1   The polynomial is in standard form. The possible rational roots are $\pm 1, \pm 2, \pm 4$.

Step 2   Evaluate the related polynomial function for $x = 1$. Since $P(1) = 0$, 1 is a root and $x - 1$ is a factor. Use synthetic division to factor out $x - 1$:

$$
\begin{array}{r|rrrrrr}
1 & 1 & -1 & -3 & 3 & -4 & 4 \\
  &   & 1 & 0 & -3 & 0 & -4 \\
\hline
  & 1 & 0 & -3 & 0 & -4 & 0 \\
\end{array}
$$

Think

How many linear factors will there be?
If there are five roots, there must be five linear factors.

Step 3   Continue factoring until you have five linear factors.

$$x^5 - x^4 - 3x^3 + 3x^2 - 4x + 4 = (x - 1)(x^4 - 3x^2 - 4)$$

$$= (x - 1)(x^2 - 4)(x^2 + 1)$$

$$= (x - 1)(x - 2)(x + 2)(x - i)(x + i)$$

Step 4   The roots are 1, 2, -2, i, and $-i$.

By the Fundamental Theorem of Algebra, these are the only roots.

 Got It?   **1.** What are all the roots of the equation $x^4 + 2x^3 = 13x^2 - 10x$?

Problem 2 **Finding All the Zeros of a Polynomial Function**

What are the zeros of $f(x) = x^4 + x^3 - 7x^2 - 9x - 18$?

Step 1 Use a graphing calculator to find any real roots. The graph of $y = x^4 + x^3 - 7x^2 - 9x - 18$ shows real zeros at $x = -3$ and $x = 3$.

Think

Does the graph show all of the real roots?
Yes; the graphs of quartic functions have one or three turning points. Since the graph shows three turning points, it will not turn again to cross the x-axis a third time.

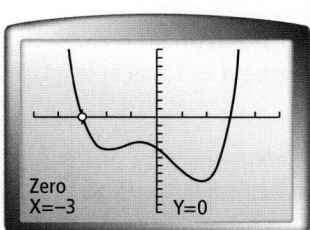

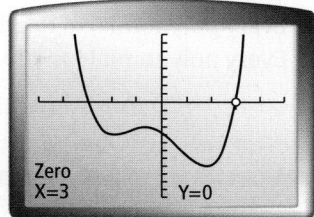

Step 2 Factor out the linear factors $x + 3$ and $x - 3$. Use synthetic division twice.

$$\begin{array}{r|rrrrr} -3 & 1 & 1 & -7 & -9 & -18 \\ & & -3 & 6 & 3 & 18 \\ \hline & 1 & -2 & -1 & -6 & 0 \end{array} \qquad \begin{array}{r|rrrr} 3 & 1 & -2 & -1 & -6 \\ & & 3 & 3 & 6 \\ \hline & 1 & 1 & 2 & 0 \end{array}$$

$$\begin{aligned} x^4 + x^3 - 7x^2 - 9x - 18 &= (x + 3)\left(x^3 - 2x^2 - x - 6\right) \\ &= (x + 3)(x - 3)\left(x^2 + x + 2\right) \end{aligned}$$

Step 3 Use the Quadratic Formula. Find the complex roots of $x^2 + x + 2 = 0$.

$a = 1, b = 1, c = 2$ 　Identify the values of a, b, and c.

$\dfrac{-1 \pm \sqrt{1^2 - 4(1)(2)}}{2(1)}$ 　Substitute.

$\dfrac{-1 \pm \sqrt{-7}}{2}$ 　Simplify.

The complex roots are $\dfrac{-1 + i\sqrt{7}}{2}$ and $\dfrac{-1 - i\sqrt{7}}{2}$.

Step 4 The four zeros of the function are -3, 3, $\dfrac{-1 + i\sqrt{7}}{2}$, and $\dfrac{-1 - i\sqrt{7}}{2}$.

By the Fundamental Theorem of Algebra, there can be no other zeros.

  Got It? **2. a.** What are all the zeros of the function $g(x) = 2x^4 - 3x^3 - x - 6$?
　　b. Reasoning The graph of
　　　$f(x) = x^5 + 4x^4 - 3x^3 - 12x^2 - 4x - 4$ is shown
　　　at the right.
　　　i. Use the turning points to explain why the graph does
　　　　NOT show all of the real zeros of the function.
　　　ii. The graph of $g(x) = f(x) + 4$ is a translation of the graph
　　　　of f up 4 units. How many real zeros of g will the graph
　　　　of g show? Explain.

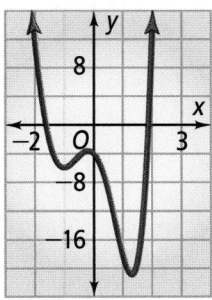

Concept Summary   The Fundamental Theorem of Algebra

Here are equivalent ways to state the Fundamental Theorem of Algebra. You can use any one of these statements to prove the others.

- Every polynomial equation of degree $n \geq 1$ has exactly n roots, including multiple and complex roots.
- Every polynomial of degree $n \geq 1$ has n linear factors.
- Every polynomial function of degree $n \geq 1$ has at least one complex zero.

Lesson Check

Do you know HOW?

Find the number of roots for each equation.

1. $5x^4 + 12x^3 - x^2 + 3x + 5 = 0$

2. $-x^{14} - x^8 - x + 7 = 0$

Find all the zeros for each function.

3. $y = x^3 - 5x^2 + 16x - 80$

4. $y = x^4 - 2x^3 + x^2 - 2x$

Do you UNDERSTAND?

5. Vocabulary Given a polynomial equation of degree n, explain how you determine the number of roots of the equation.

6. Open-Ended Write a polynomial function of degree 4 with rational coefficients and two complex zeros of multiplicity 2.

7. Writing Describe when to use synthetic division and when to use the Quadratic Formula to determine the linear factors of a polynomial.

Practice and Problem-Solving Exercises

 **Practice**   Without using a calculator, find all the roots of each equation.   ◀ See Problem 1.

8. $x^3 - 3x^2 + x - 3 = 0$

9. $x^3 + x^2 + 4x + 4 = 0$

10. $x^3 + 4x^2 + x - 6 = 0$

11. $x^3 - 5x^2 + 2x + 8 = 0$

12. $x^4 + 4x^3 + 7x^2 + 16x + 12 = 0$

13. $x^4 - 4x^3 + x^2 + 12x - 12 = 0$

14. $x^5 + 3x^3 - 4x = 0$

15. $x^5 - 8x^3 - 9x = 0$

Find all the zeros of each function.   ◀ See Problem 2.

16. $y = 2x^3 + x^2 + 1$

17. $f(x) = x^3 - 3x^2 + x - 3$

18. $g(x) = x^3 - 5x^2 + 5x - 4$

19. $y = x^3 - 2x^2 - 3x + 6$

20. $y = x^4 - 6x^2 + 8$

21. $f(x) = x^4 - 3x^2 - 4$

22. $y = x^3 - 3x^2 - 9x$

23. $y = x^3 + 6x^2 + x + 6$

24. $y = x^4 + 3x^3 + x^2 - 12x - 20$

25. $y = x^4 + x^3 - 15x^2 - 16x - 16$

For each equation, state the number of complex roots, the possible number of real roots, and the possible rational roots.

26. $2x^4 - x^3 + 2x^2 + 5x - 26 = 0$

27. $x^5 - x^3 - 11x^2 + 9x + 18 = 0$

28. $-12 + x + 10x^2 + 3x^3 = 0$

29. $4x^6 - x^5 - 24 = 0$

Find all the zeros of each function.

30. $y = x^3 - 4x^2 + 9x - 36$

31. $f(x) = x^3 + 2x^2 - 5x - 10$

32. $y = 2x^3 - 3x^2 - 18x - 8$

33. $y = 3x^3 - 7x^2 - 14x + 24$

34. $g(x) = x^3 - 4x^2 - x + 22$

35. $y = x^3 - x^2 - 3x - 9$

36. $y = x^4 - x^3 - 5x^2 - x - 6$

37. $y = 2x^4 + 3x^3 - 17x^2 - 27x - 9$

38. Think About a Plan A polynomial function, $f(x) = x^4 - 5x^3 - 28x^2 + 188x - 240$, is used to model a new roller coaster section. The loading zone will be placed at one of the zeros. The function has a zero at 5. What are the possible locations for the loading zone?
  • Can you determine how many zeros you need to find?
  • How can you use polynomial division?
  • What other methods can be helpful?

STEM 39. Bridges A twist in a river can be modeled by the function $f(x) = \frac{1}{3}x^3 + \frac{1}{2}x^2 - x$, $-3 \le x \le 2$. A city wants to build a road that goes directly along the x-axis. How many bridges would it have to build?

40. Error Analysis Maurice says: "Every linear function has exactly one zero. It follows from the Fundamental Theorem of Algebra." Cheryl disagrees. "What about the linear function $y = 2$?" she asks. "Its graph is a line, but it has no x-intercept." Whose reasoning is incorrect? Where is the flaw?

Determine whether each of the following statements is *always*, *sometimes*, or *never* true.

41. A polynomial function with real coefficient has real zeros.

42. Polynomial functions with complex coefficients have one complex zero.

43. A polynomial function that does not intercept the x-axis has complex roots only.

44. Reasoning A 4th-degree polynomial function has zeros at 3 and $5 - i$. Can $4 + i$ also be a zero of the function? Explain your reasoning.

45. Open-Ended Write a polynomial function that has four possible rational zeros but no actual rational zeros.

46. Reasoning Show that the Fundamental Theorem of Algebra must be true for all quadratic polynomial functions.

 **Challenge**

47. Use the Fundamental Theorem of Algebra and the Conjugate Root Theorem to show that any odd degree polynomial equation with real coefficients has at least one real root.

48. Reasoning What is the maximum number of points of intersection between the graphs of a quartic and a quintic polynomial function?

49. Reasoning What is the least possible degree of a polynomial with rational coefficients, leading coefficient 1, constant term 5, and zeros at $\sqrt{2}$ and $\sqrt{3}$? Show that such a polynomial has a rational zero and indicate this zero.

Standardized Test Prep

SAT/ACT

50. How many roots does $f(x) = x^4 + 5x^3 + 3x^2 + 2x + 6$ have?

   Ⓐ 5   Ⓑ 4   Ⓒ 3   Ⓓ 2

51. Which translation takes $y = |x + 2| - 1$ to $y = |x| + 2$?

   Ⓕ 2 units right, 3 units down   Ⓗ 2 units left, 3 units up

   Ⓖ 2 units right, 3 units up   Ⓘ 2 units left, 3 units down

52. What is the factored form of the expression $x^4 - 3x^3 + 2x^2$?

   Ⓐ $x^2(x - 1)(x + 2)$ Ⓒ $x^2(x + 1)(x - 2)$

   Ⓑ $x^2(x + 1)(x + 2)$ Ⓓ $x^2(x - 1)(x - 2)$

Short Response

53. How would you test whether $(2, -2)$ is a solution of the system? $\begin{cases} y < -2x + 3 \\ y \geq x - 4 \end{cases}$

Mixed Review

54. Find a fourth-degree polynomial equation with real coefficients that has $2i$ and $-3 + i$ as roots.

   ◀ See Lesson 5-5.

Solve each equation using the Quadratic Formula.

   ◀ See Lesson 4-7.

55. $x^2 - 6x + 1 = 0$ **56.** $2x^2 + 5x = -9$ **57.** $2(x^2 + 2) = 3x$

Determine whether a quadratic model exists for each set of values. If so, write the model.

   ◀ See Lesson 4-3.

58. $f(-1) = 0, f(2) = 3, f(1) = 4$ **59.** $f(-4) = 11, f(-5) = 5, f(-6) = 3$

Get Ready!   **To prepare for Lesson 5-7, do Exercises 60–65.**

   ◀ See Lesson 4-2.

Write each polynomial in standard form.

60. $(x + 1)^3$ **61.** $(x - 3)^3$ **62.** $(x - 2)^4$

63. $(x - 1)^2$ **64.** $(x + 5)^3$ **65.** $(4 - x)^3$

Graphing Polynomials Using Zeros

© **Common Core State Standards**
A-APR.B.3 Identify zeros of polynomials when suitable factorizations are available, and use the zeros to construct a rough graph of the function defined by the polynomial.
MP 7

In this activity you will learn how to sketch the graph of a polynomial function by using the zeros, turning points, and end behavior.

Example

Sketch the graph of the function $f(x) = (x - 3)(x + 1)(x - 2)$.

Step 1 Identify the zeros and plot them on a coordinate grid.

$$f(x) = (x - 3)(x + 1)(x - 2)$$

$$0 = (x - 3)(x + 1)(x - 2)$$

$0 = x - 3$	or	$0 = x + 1$	or	$0 = x - 2$
$3 = x$		$-1 = x$		$2 = x$

The function has zeros at $(3, 0)$, $(-1, 0)$, and $(2, 0)$.

Step 2 Determine whether the polynomial is positive or negative over each interval.

To determine whether $f(x)$ is positive or negative over the interval $x < -1$, choose an x-value within the interval. Let $x = -2$. Then evaluate $f(-2)$.

$$f(-2) = (-2 - 3)(-2 + 1)(-2 - 2) = (-5)(-1)(-4) = -20$$

$f(x)$ is negative over the interval $x < -1$.

Repeat the process for the intervals $-1 < x < 2$, $2 < x < 3$, and $x > 3$.

Interval	x	$f(x)$
$x < -1$	-2	-20
$-1 < x < 2$	0	6
$2 < x < 3$	2.5	-0.875
$x > 3$	4	10

Step 3 Sketch the graph.

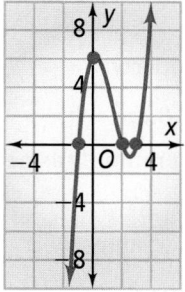

Exercises

Sketch a graph of each function. Check your answer using a graphing calculator.

1. $h(x) = (x + 6)(x - 7)$

2. $g(x) = (x + 1)(x - 3)(x - 5)$

3. $p(x) = x(x + 4)(x - 4)$

4. $h(x) = (x + 2)(x - 3)(x + 1)(x - 1)$

5. $f(x) = x^4 - 8x^2 + 16$

6. $k(x) = x^4 - 10x^2 + 9$

5-7 The Binomial Theorem

© **Common Core State Standards**

A-APR.C.5 Know and apply the Binomial Theorem for the expansion of $(x + y)^n$ in powers of x and y for a positive integer n, where x and y are any numbers, with coefficients determined for example by Pascal's Triangle.

MP 1, MP 3, MP 8

Objectives To expand a binomial using Pascal's Triangle
To use the Binomial Theorem

When counting seems complicated, it helps to be systematic.

MATHEMATICAL PRACTICES

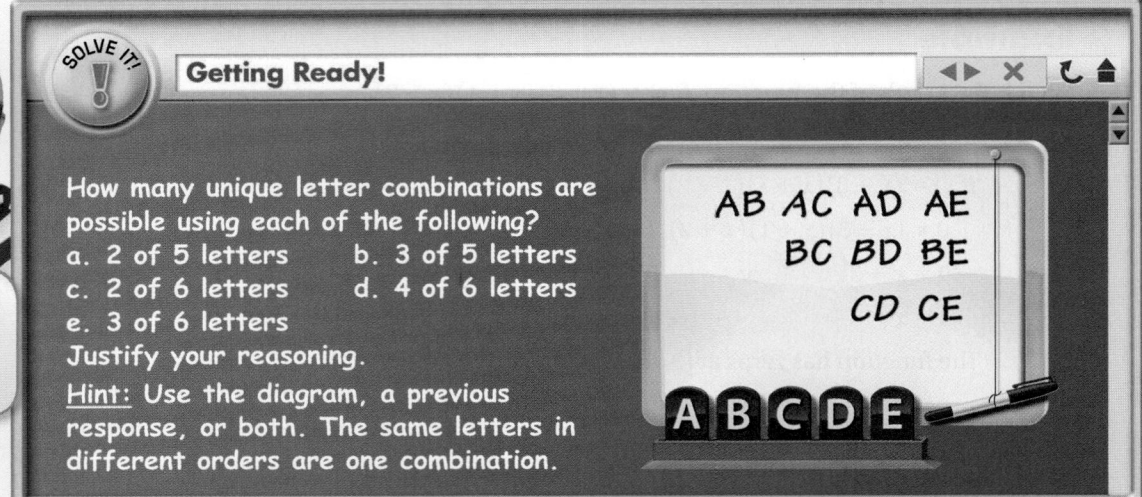

SOLVE IT!

Getting Ready!

How many unique letter combinations are possible using each of the following?
a. 2 of 5 letters   b. 3 of 5 letters
c. 2 of 6 letters   d. 4 of 6 letters
e. 3 of 6 letters
Justify your reasoning.

<u>Hint:</u> Use the diagram, a previous response, or both. The same letters in different orders are one combination.

AB AC AD AE
BC BD BE
CD CE

A B C D E

Lesson Vocabulary
• expand
• Pascal's Triangle
• Binomial Theorem

There is a connection between the triangular pattern of numbers in the Solve It and the expansion of $(a + b)^n$.

Essential Understanding You can use a pattern of coefficients and the pattern

$a^n, a^{n-1}b, a^{n-2}b^2, \ldots, a^2b^{n-2}, ab^{n-1}, b^n$ to write the expansion of $(a + b)^n$.

You can *expand* $(a + b)^3$ using the Distributive Property.

$(a + b)^3 = (a + b)(a + b)(a + b) = a^3 + 3a^2b + 3ab^2 + b^3$

To **expand** the power of a binomial in general, first multiply as needed. Then write the polynomial in standard form.

Consider the expansions of $(a + b)^n$ for the first few values of n:

Row	Power	Expanded Form	Coefficients Only
0	$(a + b)^0$	1	1
1	$(a + b)^1$	$1a^1 + 1b^1$	1 1
2	$(a + b)^2$	$1a^2 + 2a^1b^1 + 1b^2$	1 2 1
3	$(a + b)^3$	$1a^3 + 3a^2b^1 + 3a^1b^2 + 1b^3$	1 3 3 1
4	$(a + b)^4$	$1a^4 + 4a^3b^1 + 6a^2b^2 + 4a^1b^3 + 1b^4$	1 4 6 4 1

The "coefficients only" column matches the numbers in *Pascal's Triangle*. **Pascal's Triangle**, named for the French mathematician Blaise Pascal (1623–1662), is a triangular array of numbers in which the first and last number of each row is 1. Each of the other numbers in the row is the sum of the two numbers above it.

For example, to generate row 5, use the sums of the adjacent elements in the row above it.

Row   **Pascal's Triangle**

0   1

1   1   1

2   1   2   1

3   1   3   3   1

4   1   4   6   4   1

5   1   5   10   10   5   1

6   1   6   15   20   15   6   1

7   1   7   21   35   35   21   7   1

8   1   8   28   56   70   56   28   8   1

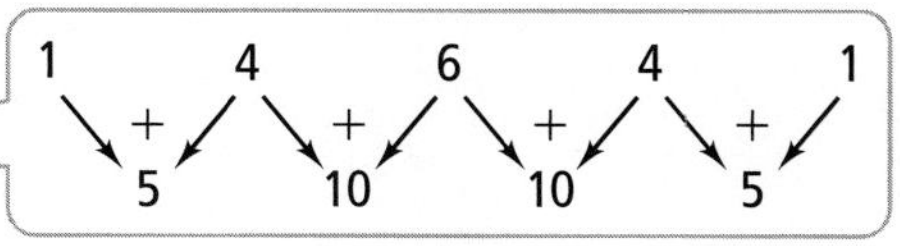

Callout (row 4 to row 5):

1   4   6   4   1
   +   +   +   +
   5   10   10   5

Problem 1   Using Pascal's Triangle

What is the expansion of $(a + b)^6$? Use Pascal's Triangle.

Plan

What row of Pascal's Triangle should you use for this expansion?

The expression is raised to the 6th power so use the 6th row.

The exponents for *a* begin with 6 and decrease to 0.

$$1a^6b^0 + 6a^5b^1 + 15a^4b^2 + 20a^3b^3 + 15a^2b^4 + 6a^1b^5 + 1a^0b^6$$

The exponents for *b* begin with 0 and increase to 6.

$$(a + b)^6 = a^6 + 6a^5b + 15a^4b^2 + 20a^3b^3 + 15a^2b^4 + 6ab^5 + b^6.$$

Got It?   **1.** What is the expansion of $(a + b)^8$? Use Pascal's Triangle.

The **Binomial Theorem** gives a general formula for expanding a binomial.

take note

Theorem   Binomial Theorem

For every positive integer *n*,

$$(a + b)^n = P_0a^n + P_1a^{n-1}b + P_2a^{n-2}b^2 + \cdots + P_{n-1}ab^{n-1} + P_nb^n$$

where $P_0, P_1, \ldots, P_n$ are the numbers in the *n*th row of Pascal's Triangle.

When you use the Binomial Theorem to expand $(x - 2)^4$, $a = x$ and $b = -2$. To expand a binomial such as $(3x - 2)^5$, $a = 3x$ so remember that $a^4 = (3x)^4$ not $3x^4$.

 Problem 2 Expanding a Binomial

What is the expansion of $(3x - 2)^5$? Use the Binomial Theorem.

Think

For $(3x - 2)^5$, use the 5th row of Pascal's Triangle.

The Binomial Theorem uses a binomial sum.

Apply the Binomial Theorem.

Simplify.

Write

Pascal's Triangle

```
        1
      1   1
    1   2   1
  1   3   3   1
1   4   6   4   1
1   5   10   10   5   1
```

$(3x - 2)^5 = (3x + (-2))^5$

$= (3x)^5 + 5(3x)^4(-2)^1 + 10(3x)^3(-2)^2$
$\quad + 10(3x)^2(-2)^3 + 5(3x)^1(-2)^4 + 1(-2)^5$

$= 243x^5 - 810x^4 + 1080x^3 - 720x^2 + 240x - 32$

Got It? 2. a. What is the expansion of $(2x - 3)^4$? Use the Binomial Theorem.
   b. Reasoning Consider the following:

$$11^0 = 1 \quad 11^1 = 11 \quad 11^2 = 121 \quad 11^3 = 1331 \quad 11^4 = 14{,}641$$

   Why do these powers of 11 have digits that mirror Pascal's Triangle?

Lesson Check

Do you know HOW?

Use Pascal's Triangle to expand each binomial.

1. $(x + a)^3$

2. $(x - 2)^5$

3. $(2x + 4)^2$

4. $(3a - 2)^3$

Do you UNDERSTAND?  MATHEMATICAL PRACTICES

5. Vocabulary Tell whether each expression can be expanded using the Binomial Theorem.
   a. $(2a - 6)^4$ **b.** $(5x^2 + 1)^5$ **c.** $(x^2 - 3x - 4)^3$

6. Writing Describe the relationship between Pascal's Triangle and the Binomial Theorem.

7. Reasoning Using Pascal's Triangle, determine the number of terms in the expansion of $(x + a)^{12}$. How many terms are there in the expansion of $(x + a)^n$?

Practice and Problem-Solving Exercises

MATHEMATICAL PRACTICES

**Practice**

Expand each binomial.

⬤ See Problems 1 and 2.

8. $(x - y)^3$ **9.** $(a + 2)^4$ **10.** $(6 + a)^6$ **11.** $(x - 5)^3$

12. $(y + 1)^8$ **13.** $(x + 2)^{10}$ **14.** $(b - 4)^7$ **15.** $(b + 3)^9$

16. $(2x - y)^7$ **17.** $(a + 3b)^4$ **18.** $(4x + 2)^6$ **19.** $(4 - x)^8$

20. $(4x + 5)^2$ **21.** $(3a - 7)^3$ **22.** $(2a + 16)^6$ **23.** $(3y - 11)^4$

**Apply**

ⓒ **24. Think About a Plan** The side length of a cube is $\left(x^2 - \frac{1}{2}\right)$. Determine the volume of the cube.
- Rewrite the binomial as a sum.
- Consider $(a + b)^n$. Identify a and b in the given binomial.
- Which row of Pascal's Triangle can be used to expand the binomial?

25. In the expansion of $(2m - 3n)^9$, one of the terms contains m^3.
- **a.** What is the exponent of n in this term?
- **b.** What is the coefficient of this term?

Find the specified term of each binomial expansion.

26. Fourth term of $(x + 2)^5$ **27.** Third term of $(x - 3)^6$

28. Third term of $(3x - 1)^5$ **29.** Fifth term of $(a + 5b^2)^4$

ⓒ **30. Reasoning** Explain why the coefficients in the expansion of $(x + 2y)^3$ do not match the numbers in the 3rd row of Pascal's Triangle.

ⓒ **31. Compare and Contrast** What are the benefits and challenges of using the Binomial Theorem when expanding $(2x + 3)^2$? Using FOIL? Which method would you choose when expanding $(2x + 3)^6$? Why?

Expand each binomial.

32. $(2x - 2y)^6$ **33.** $(x^2 + 4)^{10}$ **34.** $(x^2 - y^2)^3$ **35.** $(a - b^2)^5$

36. $(3x + 8y)^3$ **37.** $(4x - 7y)^4$ **38.** $(7a + 2y)^{10}$ **39.** $(4x^3 + 2y^2)^6$

40. $(3b - 36)^7$ **41.** $(5a + 2b)^3$ **42.** $(b^2 - 2)^8$ **43.** $(-2y^2 + x)^5$

44. Geometry The side length of a cube is given by the expression $(2x + 8)$. Write a binomial power for the area of a face of the cube and for the volume of the cube. Then use the Binomial Theorem to expand and rewrite the powers in standard form.

ⓒ **45. Writing** Explain why the terms of $(x - y)^n$ have alternating positive and negative signs.

ⓒ **46. Error Analysis** A student expands $(3x - 8)^4$ as shown below. Describe and correct the student's error.

$$(3x - 8)^4 = (3x)^4 + 4(3x)^3(-8) + 6(3x)^2(-8)^2 + 4(3x)(-8)^3 + (-8)^4$$
$$= 3x^4 - 96x^3 + 1152x^2 - 6144x + 4096$$

 **Challenge**

Use the Binomial Theorem to expand each complex expression.

47. $(7 + \sqrt{-16})^5$ **48.** $(\sqrt{-81} - 3)^3$ **49.** $(x^2 - i)^7$

50. The first term in the expansion of a binomial $(ax + by)^n$ is $1024x^{10}$. Find a and n.

51. Determine the coefficient of x^7y in the expansion of $\left(\frac{1}{2}x + \frac{1}{4}y\right)^8$.

52. a. Expand $(1 + i)^4$.
    b. Verify that $1 - i$ is a fourth root of -4 by repeating the process in part (a) for $(1 - i)^4$.

53. Verify that $-1 + \sqrt{3}i$ is a cube root of 8 by expanding $(-1 + \sqrt{3}i)^3$.

Standardized Test Prep

SAT/ACT

54. What is the fourth term in the expansion of $(2a + 4b)^5$?

    Ⓐ $256a^4b$ Ⓑ $768a^3b^2$ Ⓒ $2560a^2b^3$ Ⓓ $2048ab^4$

55. Suppose y varies directly with x. If x is 30 when y is 10, what is x when y is 9?

    Ⓕ 3   Ⓖ 27   Ⓗ 29   Ⓘ $\frac{300}{9}$

56. Which of following is a root of $9x^2 - 30x + 25 = 0$?

    Ⓐ $x = \frac{3}{5}$ Ⓑ $x = \frac{5}{3}$ Ⓒ $x = -\frac{5}{3}$ Ⓓ $x = -\frac{3}{5}$

Extended Response

57. One company charges a monthly fee of \$7.95 and \$2.25 per hour for Internet access. Another company does not charge a monthly fee, but charges \$2.75 per hour for Internet access. Write a system of equations to represent the cost c for t hours of access in one month for each company. Then find how many hours of use it will take for the costs to be equal.

Mixed Review

Find all the roots of each equation.   ◀ *See Lesson 5-6.*

58. $x^4 + 7x^3 + 20x^2 + 29x + 15 = 0$ **59.** $x^5 - x^4 + 10x^3 - 10x^2 + 9x - 9 = 0$

60. $2x^3 + 11x^2 + 14x + 8 = 0$ **61.** $x^4 - x^3 + 6x^2 - 13x + 7 = 0$

Simplify each expression.   ◀ *See Lesson 4-8.*

62. $(5i - 4)(-2i + 7)$ **63.** $(-3i)(20i)(10i)$

64. $\frac{-6 - 2i}{3 + i}$ **65.** $\frac{11i + 9}{2 - i}$

Get Ready! To prepare for Lesson 5-8, do Exercises 66–68.

Write each polynomial in standard form. Then classify it by degree and by number of terms.   ◀ *See Lesson 5-1.*

66. $5x^2 - x + 2x^3 + 9$ **67.** $1 + 4x - 7x^2$ **68.** $-9x^2 + x - 3x^3 - 8 + 12x^4$

5-8 Polynomial Models in the Real World

 Common Core State Standards

F-IF.B.5 Relate the domain of a function to its graph and, where applicable, to the quantitative relationship it describes. **Also F-IF.B.4, F-IF.B.6**

MP 1, MP 3, MP 4, MP 5

Objective To fit data to linear, quadratic, cubic, or quartic models

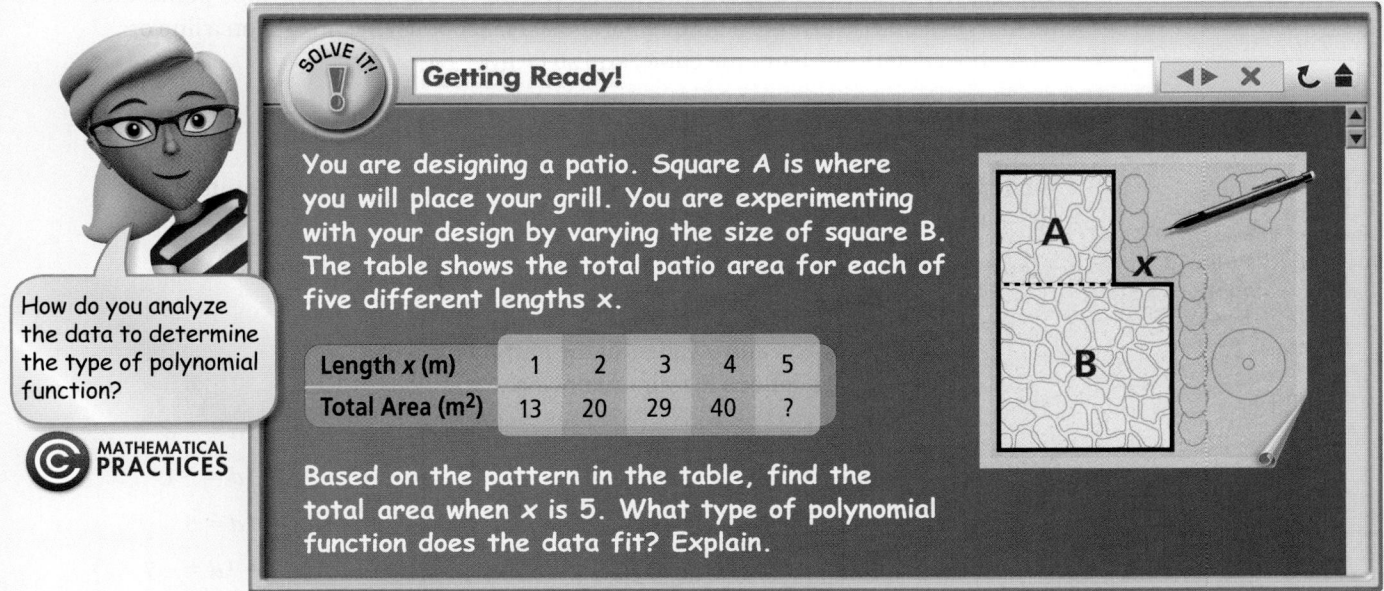

SOLVE IT!

Getting Ready!

How do you analyze the data to determine the type of polynomial function?

MATHEMATICAL PRACTICES

You are designing a patio. Square A is where you will place your grill. You are experimenting with your design by varying the size of square B. The table shows the total patio area for each of five different lengths x.

Length x (m)	1	2	3	4	5
Total Area (m²)	13	20	29	40	?

Based on the pattern in the table, find the total area when x is 5. What type of polynomial function does the data fit? Explain.

Polynomial functions can be degree 0 (constant), degree 1 (linear), degree 2 (quadratic), degree 3 (cubic), and so on.

Essential Understanding You can use polynomial functions to model many real-world situations. The behavior of the graphs of polynomial functions of different degrees can suggest what type of polynomial will best fit a particular data set.

You can use a graphing calculator to help you find functions that model the data in the table shown here.

Enter the data into calculator lists **L1** and **L2**. Use three different regressions: **LINREG**, **QUADREG**, and **CUBICREG**.

Graph each regression function and the scatter plot of the data in the same window. For this data, the cubic function appears to be a perfect fit.

x	y
0	10.1
5	2.8
10	8.1
15	16.0
20	17.8

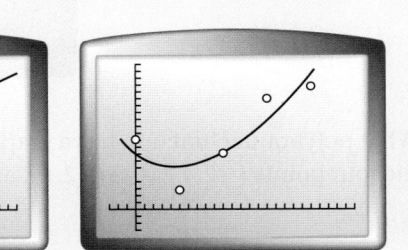

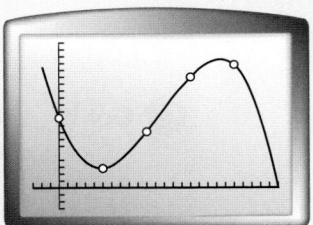

Key Concept The (n + 1) Point Principle

For any set of $n + 1$ points in the coordinate plane that pass the vertical line test, there is a unique polynomial of degree at most n that fits the points perfectly.

This principle confirms that any two points determine a unique line. Three points that are not on a line determine a unique parabola. Four points that are not on a line or a parabola determine a unique cubic, and so forth.

Problem 1 Using A Polynomial Function to Model Data

What polynomial function has a graph that passes through the four points $(0, -3), (1, -1), (2, 5),$ and $(-1, -7)$?

Plan

How can you use the four points to find a system of equations?
Substitute each point into a polynomial function.

Step 1 By the $(n + 1)$ Point Principle, there is a cubic polynomial $y = ax^3 + bx^2 + cx + d$ that fits the points perfectly.

Substitute the x- and y-values of the four points to get four linear equations in four unknowns.

$$-3 = a(0)^3 + b(0)^2 + c(0) + d \qquad 0a + 0b + 0c + 1d = -3$$
$$-1 = a(1)^3 + b(1)^2 + c(1) + d \qquad 1a + 1b + 1c + 1d = -1$$
$$5 = a(2)^3 + b(2)^2 + c(2) + d \qquad 8a + 4b + 2c + 1d = 5$$
$$-7 = a(-1)^3 + b(-1)^2 + c(-1) + d \qquad -1a + 1b - 1c + 1d = -7$$

Step 2 Write the system in augmented matrix form. Use the **RREF()** function to find the coefficient values a, b, c, and d.

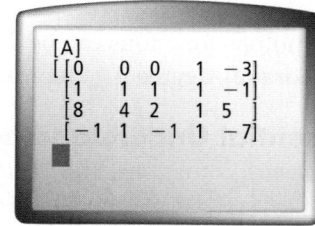
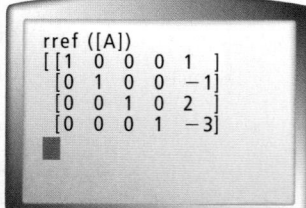

Step 3 $a = 1, b = -1, c = 2,$ and $d = -3$. The polynomial function is $y = x^3 - x^2 + 2x - 3$.

Check Use **CUBICREG** with the four given points.

The solution checks.

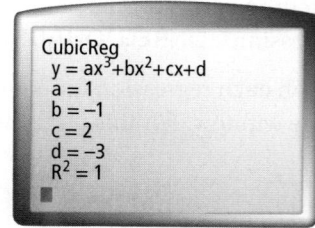
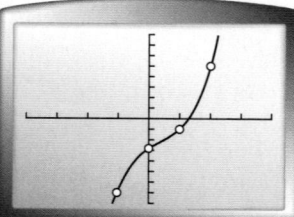

Got It? **1.** What polynomial function has a graph that passes through the four points $(-2, 1), (0, 5), (2, 9),$ and $(3, 36)$?

Problem 2 Modeling Data STEM

Food Production The chart shows how much milk Wisconsin dairy farms produced in 1955, 1980, and 2005. What linear model best fits this data? Use the model to estimate milk production in 2000.

Milk Production (in billions of lbs)

1955	1980	2005
16.5	22.4	22.9

Think

What data should you enter?
Enter the years, after 1900, and billions of pounds of milk produced.

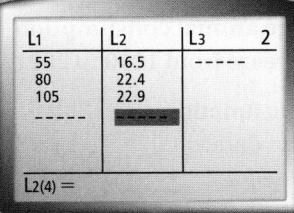

L1	L2	L3	2
55	16.5	-----	
80	22.4		
105	22.9		
-----	-----		

L2(4) =

```
LinReg
y=ax+b
a=.128
b=10.36
r²=.8082083662
r=.8990040969
```

Enter the data. Let *x* represent years after 1900. Let *y* represent pounds of milk.

Use **LINREG** to find a linear model: $f(x) = 0.128x + 10.36$. Notice the value of r^2.

Show the scatter plot of the data and a graph of $f(x)$.

The closer r^2 is to 1, the better the fit.

Use the model to estimate milk production in 2000.

$$f(100) = 0.128(100) + 10.36 \approx 23.2$$

In 2000, Wisconsin produced about 23.2 billion pounds of milk.

 Got It? 2. Use the linear model. Estimate Wisconsin milk production in 1995.

Problem 3 Comparing Models STEM

Food Production The graph shows the quadratic model for the milk production data in Problem 2. The quadratic model fits the data points exactly because of the $(n + 1)$ Point Principle. Given that both models are good fits, which seems more likely to represent milk production over time?

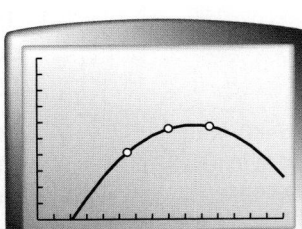

Think

Is the quadratic model reasonable?
No; the quadratic model will show milk production eventually decreasing to below zero.

Linear Model: This model continually rises.

Quadratic Model: This model has down-and-down end behavior. It shows slowing growth, a turning point, and then a decline, eventually to 0 and negative values.

Despite the R^2 value of 1 for the quadratic model, the linear model is more likely to represent milk production over time since it shows a continuing increase.

 Got It? 3. If four data points were given, would a cubic function be the best model for the data? Explain your answer.

When deciding whether a model is reliable, it is important to consider the source of the data. Data generated by a law of physics or a geometric formula will have a mathematical model that fits the data and yields accurate predictions. With other data, such as sales records, you can approximate the data only within, or close to, the domain over which it was generated.

Using a model to predict a y-value "outside" the domain of a data set is *extrapolation*. Estimating within the domain is *interpolation*. Interpolation usually yields reliable estimates. Extrapolation becomes less reliable as you move farther away from the data.

Problem 4 Using Interpolation and Extrapolation

Cheese Consumption The table shows average annual consumption of cheese per person in the U. S. for selected years from 1910 to 2001.

A Use **CUBICREG**. Model the data with a cubic function. Graph the function with a scatter plot of the data.

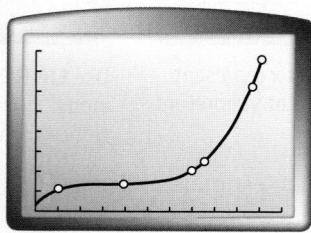

CubicReg
$y = ax^3+bx^2+cx+d$
$a = 9.242151E^-5$
$b = ^-.0095843361$
$c = .3106497055$
$d = 1.802125648$
$R^2 = .9976342$

Cheese Consumption

Year	Pounds Consumed
1910	4
1940	5
1970	8
1975	10
1995	25
2001	30

SOURCE: U.S. Department of Agriculture

Since R^2 is close to 1, the fit is good. The cubic model is approximately
$y = 0.0000924x^3 - 0.00958x^2 + 0.311x + 1.802$.

B Use the model to estimate cheese consumption for 1980, 2000, and 2012. In which estimate do you have the most confidence? The least confidence? Explain.

Use the cubic model from part A to estimate the cheese consumption for each year:

1980: 12.6 lb of cheese per person
2000: 29.4 lb of cheese per person
2012: 46.2 lb of cheese per person

You can be confident in interpolating the estimates for 1980 (**Y1(80)**) and 2000 (**Y1(100)**) because the cheese consumption fits the pattern of increase shown in the table. You should have the least confidence in the extrapolated 2012 (**Y1(112)**) estimate because the cubic model increases so quickly beyond 2001.

Y1 (80)
     12.63416396
Y1 (100)
     29.44524491
Y1 (112)
     46.21454748

Got It? **4. a.** Use **LINREG** to find a linear model for cheese consumption. Graph it with a scatter plot.

   b. Reasoning Use the model to estimate consumption for 1980, 2000, and 2012. In which of these estimates do you have the most confidence? The least confidence? Explain.

Lesson Check

Do you know HOW?

Determine which type of model best fits each set of points.

1. $(-2, -1)$, $(0, 3)$, and $(2, 7)$

2. $(0, 3)$, $(3, 4)$, and $(5, 6)$

3. $(2, 3)$, $(4, 2)$, $(6, 4)$, and $(8, 5)$

4. $(-5, 6)$, $(-4, 3)$, $(0, 2)$, $(2, 4)$, and $(5, 10)$

Do you UNDERSTAND?

MATHEMATICAL
PRACTICES

5. **Vocabulary** Explain which form of estimation, interpolation or extrapolation, is more reliable.

6. **Reasoning** Is it possible to create a cubic function that passes through $(0, 0)$, $(-1, 1)$, $(-2, 2)$, and $(-3, 9)$? Explain.

7. **Writing** The R^2 value for a quartic model is 0.94561. The R^2 value for a cubic model of the same data is 0.99817. Which model seems to show a better fit? Explain.

Practice and Problem-Solving Exercises

MATHEMATICAL
PRACTICES

 **Practice**   Find a polynomial function whose graph passes through each set of points.

◀ **See Problem 1.**

8. $(0, 5)$ and $(2, -13)$

9. $(-2, -4)$ and $(8, 1)$

10. $(-5, 14)$ and $(1, -16)$

11. $(7, 13)$, $(10, -11)$, and $(0, 4)$

12. $(-2, -16)$, $(3, 11)$, and $(0, 2)$

13. $(-1, 8)$, $(5, -4)$, and $(7, 8)$

14. $(-1, -15)$, $(1, -7)$, and $(6, -22)$

15. $(-1, 9)$, $(0, 6)$, $(1, 5)$, and $(2, 18)$

For each set of data, compare two models and determine which one better fits the data. Which model seems more likely to represent each set of data over time?

◀ **See Problems 2 and 3.**

16. **U.S. Federal Spending**

Year	Total (billions $)
1965	630
1980	1300
1995	1950
2005	2650

17. **World Population**

Year	Average Growth Rate (%)
1972	1.96
1982	1.73
1992	1.5
2002	1.22

18. **U.S. Homes**

Year	Average Sale Price (thousands $)
1990	149
1995	158
2000	207

19. **U.S. Crude Oil and Petroleum**

Month (2008)	Products Supplied (millions of barrels/day)
2	19.782
4	19.768
6	19.553

Use your models from Exercises 16-19 to make predictions.

 **See Problem 4.**

20. Estimate total U.S. federal spending for 1990 and 2010.

21. Estimate the average annual growth rate of the world population for 1950, 1988, and 2010.

22. Estimate the average sale price of homes sold in the United States for 1985, 1999, and 2020.

23. Estimate the number of barrels of crude oil and petroleum supplied per day for January, March, and October of 2008.

B Apply

Find a cubic and a quartic model for each set of values. Explain why one models the data better.

24.

x	−2	−1	0	2	3
y	−25	−4	3	23	40

25.

x	−2	−1	0	1	2
y	−65	−14	−4	2	90

Find a polynomial function whose graph passes through the points.

26. $(−14, 14), (−10, 0), (0, −1), (8, 0)$, and $(12, 4)$

27. $(−3, −50), (−2, −4), (−1, 10), (0, 7)$, and $(2, −23)$

© 28. Think About a Plan The table at the right shows the amount of carbon dioxide in Earth's atmosphere for selected years. Predict the amount of carbon dioxide in Earth's atmosphere in 2022. How confident are you in your prediction?
• How can you plot the data? (*Hint:* Let x equal the years after 1900.)
• What polynomial model should you use?

Year	CO_2 in atmosphere (ppm)
1968	324.14
1983	343.91
1998	367.68
2003	376.68
2008	385.60

Source: The Weather Channel

Find a cubic model for each set of values. Then use the regression coefficient of each model to determine whether the model is a good fit.

29. $(−5, −60), (−1, −5), (0, 0.5), (1, 8), (5, 17), (10, 32)$

30. $(8, −101), (−1, 10), (−8, 47), (−10, 59)$

31. Air Travel The table shows the percent of on-time flights for selected years. Find a polynomial function to model the data. Use 1998 as Year 0.

Year	1998	2000	2002	2004	2006
On-time Flights (%)	77.20	72.59	82.14	78.08	75.45

Source: U.S. Bureau of Transportation Statistics

© 32. Writing Explain two ways to find a polynomial function to model a given set of data.

33. Error Analysis The table at the right shows the number of students enrolled in a high school personal finance course. A student says that a cubic model would best fit the data based on the $(n + 1)$ Point Principle. Explain why a quadratic model might be more appropriate.

Year	Number of Students Enrolled
2000	50
2004	65
2008	94
2010	110

34. Compare and Contrast The table shows the United States gross domestic product for selected years. Construct curves using cubic regression and quartic regression to model the data. Which curve seems most likely to model gross domestic product over the years?

Year	1960	1970	1980	1990	2000
GDP (billions $)	526.4	1038.5	2789.5	5803.1	9817.0

35. The table below shows the percentage of the U.S. labor force in unions for selected years between 1955 and 2005.

Year	1955	1960	1965	1970	1975	1980	1985	1990	1995	2000	2005
%	33.2	31.4	28.4	27.3	25.5	21.9	18.0	16.1	14.9	13.5	12.5

    a. What is the average rate of change between 1955 and 1965? Between 1975 and 1985?

    b. Make a scatter plot of the data. Which kind of polynomial model seems to be most appropriate?

    c. Use a graphing calculator to find the type of model from part (b).

    d. Use the model you found in part (c) to predict the percent of the labor force in unions in the year 2020.

    e. Reasoning Do you have much confidence in this prediction? Explain.

Challenge

36. Your friend's teacher showed the class a graph of a cubic polynomial in the ZDecimal window, which is $[-4.7, 4.7]$ by $[-3.1, 3.1]$. She then challenged the class to find the polynomial *without using cubic regression on their calculators*, and your friend succeeded. Follow your friend's steps and see if you can find the polynomial.

    a. The graph resembles a parabola with vertex $(2, 0)$ near $x = 2$. Find the equation in standard form for that parabola.

    b. Find the equation of a line in slope-intercept form through $(-2, 0)$ with slope 1. Multiply the linear expression by the quadratic expression from part (a) to get a cubic. (Leave it in factored form.) Graph the cubic function. What do you notice about the zeros and the y-intercept of the cubic function?

    c. Multiply the cubic by a constant to change the y-intercept to 2. Graph the function to see if you've found the right polynomial. What is the function?

37. The graph at the right is that of a certain quartic polynomial in the ZDecimal window, which is $[-4.7, 4.7]$ by $[-3.1, 3.1]$. Find the equation of the quartic *without using quartic regression on your calculator*. You may leave it in factored form.

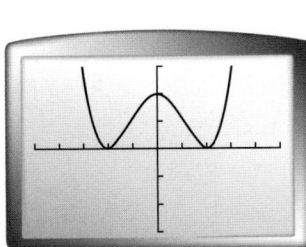

Standardized Test Prep

38. The table shows the time it takes a computer program to run, given the number of files used as input. Using a cubic model, what do you predict the run time will be if the input consists of 1000 files?

Files	Time(s)
100	0.5
200	0.9
300	3.5
400	8.2
500	14.8

39. Suppose you hit a ball and its flight follows the graph of $f(x) = -16x^2 + 20x + 3$. How many seconds will it take for the ball to hit the ground? Round your answer to the nearest second.

40. What is the multiplicity of the zeros of $y = 16x^2 - 8x + 1$?

41. What is the slope of the line shown?

42. What is the degree of the polynomial function $y = -9x^3 - 5x^2 - 2x^5 + 4x + x^4 + 1$?

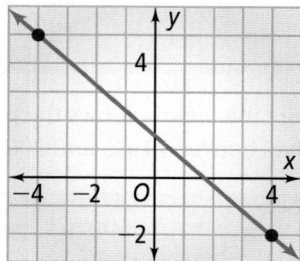

Mixed Review

Expand each binomial.

$\qquad\qquad\qquad\qquad\qquad\qquad\qquad\qquad\qquad$ See Lesson 5-7.

43. $(2x + 3)^5$

44. $(11x - 1)^3$

45. $(8 - 3x)^4$

46. $(4 + 9x)^3$

Write each compound inequality as an absolute value inequality.

$\qquad\qquad\qquad\qquad\qquad\qquad\qquad\qquad\qquad$ See Lesson 1-6.

47. $7 < x < 9$

48. $\frac{1}{4} \le x \le \frac{1}{2}$

49. $1.7 < y < 3.9$

50. $500 < t < 1000$

Solve each formula for the indicated variable.

$\qquad\qquad\qquad\qquad\qquad\qquad\qquad\qquad\qquad$ See Lesson 1-4.

51. $A = s^2$, for s

52. $P = 2(l + w)$, for l

53. $C = 2\pi r$, for r

54. $A = bh$, for b

Get Ready!   To prepare for Lesson 5-9, do Exercises 55–58.

Graph each function.

$\qquad\qquad\qquad\qquad\qquad\qquad\qquad\qquad\qquad$ See Lesson 4-1.

55. $y = x^2$

56. $y = -4x^2$

57. $y = x^2 + 3$

58. $y = -7x^2 - 1$

5-9

Transforming Polynomial Functions

© **Common Core State Standards**

F-BF.B.3 Identify the effect on the graph of replacing $f(x)$ by $f(x) + k$, $k f(x)$, $f(kx)$, and $f(x + k)$ for specific values of k (both positive and negative) find the value of k given the graphs. **Also F-IF.C.7c, F-IF.C.8, F-IF.C.9**

MP 1, MP 2, MP 3, MP 4, MP 7

Objective To apply transformations to graphs of polynomials

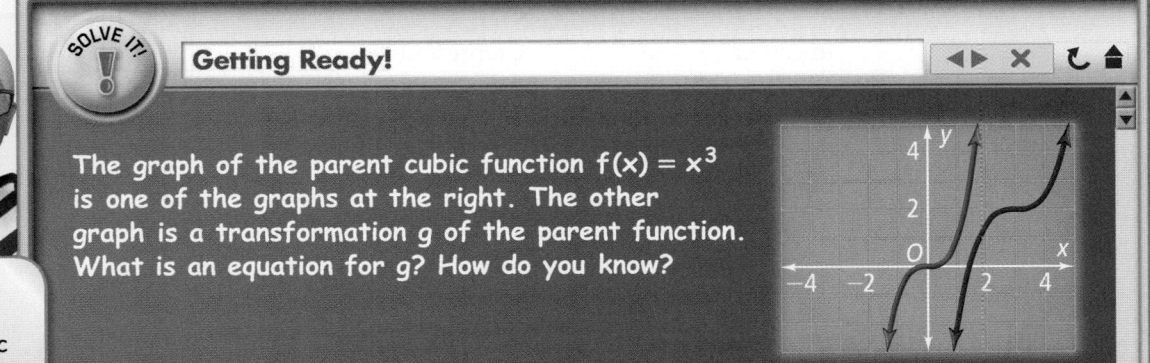

SOLVE IT!

Getting Ready!   ◄► ✕ ↻ ▲

The graph of the parent cubic function $f(x) = x^3$ is one of the graphs at the right. The other graph is a transformation g of the parent function. What is an equation for g? How do you know?

Remember you transformed the graphs of quadratic and absolute value functions.

© **MATHEMATICAL PRACTICES**

Recall that you can obtain the graph of any quadratic function from the graph of the parent quadratic function, $y = x^2$, using one or more basic transformations. You will find that this is not true of cubic functions.

Lesson Vocabulary
• power function
• constant of proportionality

Essential Understanding The graph of the function $y = af(x - h) + k$ is a vertical stretch or compression by the factor $|a|$, a horizontal shift of h units, and a vertical shift of k units of the graph of $y = f(x)$.

© **Problem 1**   **Transforming $y = x^3$**

What is an equation of the graph of $y = x^3$ under a vertical compression by the factor $\frac{1}{2}$ followed by a reflection across the x-axis, a horizontal translation 3 units to the right, and then a vertical translation 2 units up?

Step 1 Multiply by $\frac{1}{2}$ to compress.

$$y = x^3 \qquad \longrightarrow \qquad y = \frac{1}{2}x^3$$

Step 2 Multiply by -1 to reflect.

$$y = \frac{1}{2}x^3 \qquad \longrightarrow \qquad y = -\frac{1}{2}x^3$$

Think

How is translating this cubic function like translating a quadratic function?
In each case you replace x with $x - h$ to translate h units to the right.

Step 3 Replace x with $x - 3$ to translate horizontally.

$$y = -\frac{1}{2}x^3 \qquad \longrightarrow \qquad y = -\frac{1}{2}(x - 3)^3$$

Step 4 Add 2 to translate vertically.

$$y = -\frac{1}{2}(x - 3)^3 \qquad \longrightarrow \qquad y = -\frac{1}{2}(x - 3)^3 + 2$$

Got It? **1.** What is an equation of the graph of $y = x^3$ under a vertical stretch by the factor 2 followed by a horizontal translation 3 units to the left and then a vertical translation 4 units down?

The graph shows $y = x^3$ and the graphs that result from the transformations in Problem 1.

In general, $y = a(x - h)^3 + k$ represents all of the cubic functions you can obtain by stretching, compressing, reflecting, or translating the cubic parent function $y = x^3$.

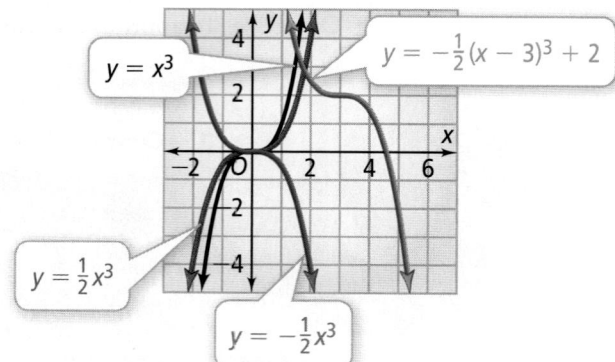

$y = x^3$

$y = -\frac{1}{2}(x - 3)^3 + 2$

$y = \frac{1}{2}x^3$

$y = -\frac{1}{2}x^3$

 Problem 2 **Finding Zeros of a Transformed Cubic Function**

Multiple Choice If a, h, and k are real numbers and $a \neq 0$, how many distinct real zeros does $y = -a(x - h)^3 + k$ have?

Ⓐ 0   **Ⓑ** 1   **Ⓒ** 2   **Ⓓ** 3

Plan

How can you find the zeros of a function?
Set the function equal to 0 and solve for x.

$-a(x - h)^3 + k = 0$ x is a zero means it is an x-intercept, so $y = 0$.

$-a(x - h)^3 = -k$ Subtract k from each side.

$(x - h)^3 = \frac{k}{a}$ Divide each side by $-a$.

$x - h = \sqrt[3]{\frac{k}{a}}$ Take the cube root of each side.

$x = \sqrt[3]{\frac{k}{a}} + h$ Solve for x.

Disregarding multiplicities, the function has a single real zero. The correct answer is B.

 Got It? **2.** What are all the real zeros of the function $y = 3(x - 1)^3 + 6$?

Problems 1 and 2 together illustrate that the graph of an "offspring" function of the parent cubic function $y = x^3$ has only one x-intercept.

The graph of the cubic function $y = x^3 - 2x^2 - 5x + 6$ has three x-intercepts. You cannot obtain this function or others like it by transforming the parent cubic function $y = x^3$ using stretches, reflections, and translations.

Similarly, some quartic functions are simple transformations of $y = x^4$ and some are not.

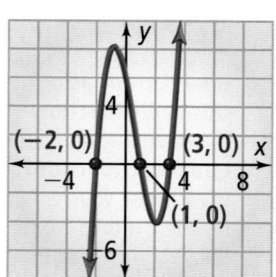

$(-2, 0)$

$(3, 0)$

$(1, 0)$

Problem 3 Constructing a Quartic Function with Two Real Zeros

What is a quartic function with only two real zeros, $x = 5$ and $x = 9$?

Method 1 Use transformations.

First, find a quartic with zeros at ± 2.
Translate the basic quartic 16 units down:
$y = x^4 \rightarrow y = x^4 - 16$

9 is 7 units to the right of 2.
Translate 7 units to the right.
$y = x^4 - 16 \rightarrow y = (x - 7)^4 - 16$

$y = x^4$

$y = x^4 - 16$ $\quad$ $y = (x - 7)^4 - 16$

A quartic function with its only real zeros at 5 and 9 is
$y = (x - 7)^4 - 16$.

Method 2 Use algebraic methods.

$$y = (x - 5)(x - 9) \cdot Q(x)$$
$$= (x - 5)(x - 9)(x^2 + 1)$$
$$= (x^2 - 14x + 45)(x^2 + 1)$$
$$= x^4 - 14x^3 + 46x^2 - 14x + 45$$

Make $Q(x)$ a quadratic with no real zeros.

Another quartic function with its only real zeros at
5 and 9 is $y = x^4 - 14x^3 + 46x^2 - 14x + 45$.

Think

What should you use for $Q(x)$?
Choose $Q(x)$ to be a quadratic with no real zeros. Keep it simple, such as $x^2 + 1$.

  Got It? **3. a.** What is a quartic function $f(x)$ with only two real zeros, $x = 0$ and $x = 6$?
b. Reasoning Does the quartic function $-f(x)$ have the same zeros? Explain.

The "offspring" of the parent function $y = x^4$ is a subfamily of all quartic polynomials. This subfamily consists of quartics of the form $y = a(x - h)^4 + k$. These functions also belong to another category of polynomials, and in this category you can generate families as usual.

take note

Key Concept Power Functions

Definition	**Examples**
A **power function** is a function of the form $y = a \cdot x^b$, where a and b are nonzero real numbers.	$y = 0.5x^6$ $\qquad$ $y = \frac{1}{2}x^2$ $y = -4x^{\frac{2}{3}}$ $\qquad$ $y = x^{0.25}$

If the exponent b in $y = ax^b$ is a positive integer, the function is also a *monomial function*.

If $y = ax^b$ describes y as a power function of x, then y *varies directly with*, or is *proportional to*, the bth power of x. The constant a is the **constant of proportionality**. Power functions arise in many real-world contexts related to the concept of direct variation, which you studied in Chapter 2.

Wind
8 m/s

Electric Power
600 kW

Problem 4 Modeling With a Power Function (STEM)

Wind-Generated Power Wind farms are a source of renewable energy found around the world. The power P (in kilowatts) generated by a wind turbine varies directly as the cube of the wind speed v (in meters per second). The picture shows the power output of one turbine at one wind speed. To the nearest kilowatt, how much power does this turbine generate in a 10 m/s wind?

Think

How is this problem like the direct variation you studied in Chapter 2?
With the direct variation, $y = kx$, you use a first power. Here you use a third power.

The formula for P as a power function of v is $P = a \cdot v^3$. From the picture, $P = 600$ when $v = 8$, or $600 = a \cdot 8^3$. Solve for a.

$$600 = a \cdot 8^3 \qquad \text{Use values of } P \text{ and } v \text{ to find } a.$$

$$600 = 512a$$

$$a \approx 1.1719$$

$$P \approx 1.1719v^3 \qquad \text{Use the value of } a \text{ in the original formula.}$$

$$P \approx 1.1719 \cdot 10^3 = 1171.9 \qquad \text{Substitute 10 for } v \text{ and simplify.}$$

This turbine generates about 1172 kW of power in a 10 m/s wind.

 Got It? **4.** Another turbine generates 210 kW of power in a 12 mi/h wind. How much power does this turbine generate in a 20 mi/h wind?

 Lesson Check

Do you know HOW?

Find all the real zeros of each function.

1. $y = -(x + 3)^3 + 1$

2. $y = -8(x - 5)^3 - 64$

3. $y = \frac{9}{2}(x - 1)^3 + \frac{4}{3}$

Do you UNDERSTAND?

4. Vocabulary Is the function $y = 4x^3 + 5$ an example of a power function? Explain.

5. Error Analysis Your friend says that he has found a way to transform the graph of $y = x^3$ to obtain three real roots. Using the graph of the function, explain why this is impossible.

6. Compare and Contrast How are the graphs of $y = x^3$ and $y = 4x^3$ alike? How are they different? What transformation was used to get the second equation?

Practice and Problem-Solving Exercises

MATHEMATICAL PRACTICES

 **Practice**

Determine the cubic function that is obtained from the parent function $y = x^3$ after each sequence of transformations.

See Problem 1.

7. a vertical stretch by a factor of 3;
a reflection across the x-axis;
a vertical translation 2 units up;
and a horizontal translation 1 unit right

8. a vertical stretch by a factor of 2;
a vertical translation 4 units up;
and a horizontal translation 3 units left

9. a reflection across the y-axis;
a vertical translation 1 unit down;
and a horizontal translation 5 units left

10. a vertical translation 3 units down;
and a horizontal translation 2 units right

11. a vertical stretch by a factor of 3;
a reflection across the y-axis;
a vertical translation $\frac{3}{4}$ unit up;
and a horizontal translation $\frac{1}{2}$ unit left

12. a vertical stretch by a factor of $\frac{5}{3}$;
a reflection across the x-axis;
a vertical translation 4 units down;
and a horizontal translation 3 units right

Find all the real zeros of each function.

See Problem 2.

13. $y = -27(x - 2)^3 + 8$

14. $y = -\frac{1}{8}(x - 7)^3 - 8$

15. $y = -3\left(x + \frac{4}{5}\right)^3 + \frac{8}{9}$

16. $y = -16(x + 3)^3 + 9$

17. $y = 4(x - 1)^3 + 10$

18. $y = 2(x + 5)^3 + 10$

Find a quartic function with the given x-values as its only real zeros.

See Problem 3.

19. $x = 2$ and $x = -1$

20. $x = -3$ and $x = -4$

21. $x = -1$ and $x = 3$

22. $x = 4$ and $x = 2$

23. $x = -4$ and $x = -1$

24. $x = -3$ and $x = 2$

25. Cooking The number of pepperoni slices that Kim puts on a pizza varies directly as the square of the diameter of the pizza. If she puts 15 slices on a 10" diameter pizza, how many slices should she put on a 16" diameter pizza?

See Problem 4.

26. Volume The amount of water that a spherical tank can hold varies directly as the cube of its radius. If a tank with radius 7.5 ft holds 1767 ft^3 of water, how much water can a tank with radius 16 ft hold?

 **Apply**

27. Think About a Plan The kinetic energy generated by a 5 lb ball is represented by the formula $K = \frac{1}{2}(5)v^2$. If the ball is thrown with a velocity of 6 ft/sec, how much kinetic energy is generated?
- What does 5 represent in the function?
- What number should you substitute for v?

Determine whether each function can be obtained from the parent function, $y = x^n$, using basic transformations. If so, describe the sequence of transformations.

28. $y = -4x^3$

29. $y = 2(x - 3)^2 + 5$

30. $y = x^3 - x$

31. $y = x^2 - 8x + 7$

Determine the transformations that were used to change the graph of the parent function $y = x^3$ to each of the following graphs.

32.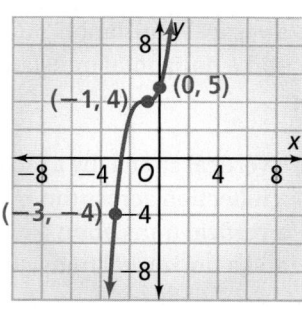

33.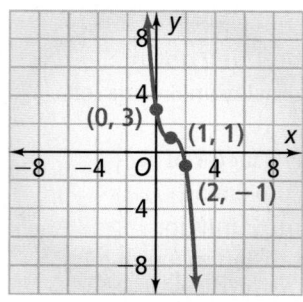

34.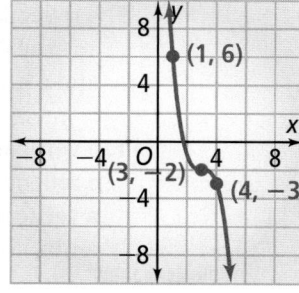

35.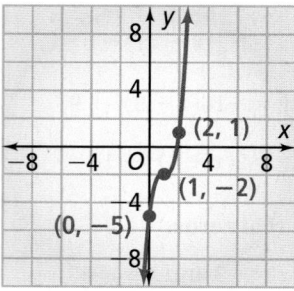

36.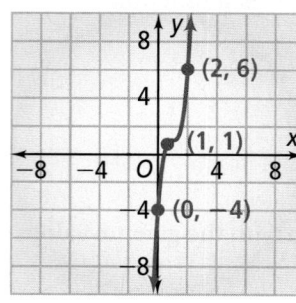

37.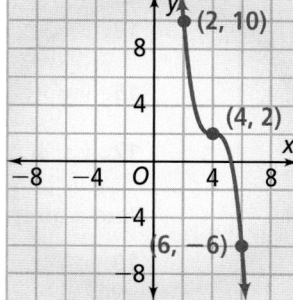

38. Compare the function $y = 3x^3$ to the function shown in the graph at the right. Which function has a greater vertical stretch factor? Explain.

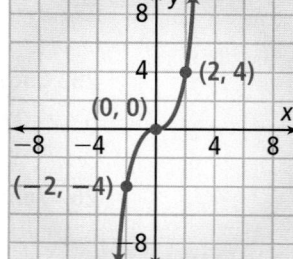

STEM 39. Physics The formula $K = \frac{1}{2}mv^2$ represents the kinetic energy of an object. If the kinetic energy of a ball is 10 lb-ft^2/s^2 when it is thrown with a velocity of 4 ft/s, how much kinetic energy is generated if the ball is thrown with a velocity of 8 ft/s?

© 40. Reasoning Explain why the basic transformations of the parent function $y = x^5$ will only generate functions that can be written in the form $y = a(x - h)^5 + k$.

© 41. Reasoning Explain why some quartic polynomials cannot be written in the form $y = a(x - h)^4 + k$. Give two examples.

42. Reasoning Find a sequence of basic transformations by which the polynomial function $y = 2x^3 - 6x^2 + 6x + 5$ can be derived from the cubic function $y = x^3$.

 43. Physics For a constant resistance R (in ohms), the power P (in watts) dissipated across two terminals of a battery varies directly as the square of the current I (in amps). If a battery connected in a circuit dissipates 24 watts of power for 2 amps of current flow, how much power would be dissipated when the current flow is 5 amps?

44. Writing Give an argument that shows that *every* polynomial family of degree $n > 2$ contains polynomials that cannot be generated from the basic function $y = x^n$ by using stretches, compressions, reflections, and translations.

Standardized Test Prep

Use the graph to answer questions 45–47.

45. Which equation does the graph represent?

Ⓐ $y = (x + 2)^2 - 1$ Ⓒ $y = (x - 2)^2 + 1$

Ⓑ $y = (x - 2)^2 - 1$ Ⓓ $y = (x - 2)^4 - 1$

46. If $y = f(x)$ is an equation for the graph, what are factors of $f(x)$?

Ⓕ $(x - 1)$ and $(x + 3)$ Ⓗ $(x + 1)$ and $(x - 3)$

Ⓖ $(x - 1)$ and $(x - 3)$ Ⓘ $(x + 1)$ and $(x + 3)$

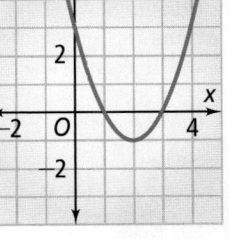

Short Response

47. If $y = ax^2 + bx + c$ is an equation for the graph, what type of number is its discriminant?

Mixed Review

Find a polynomial function whose graph passes through the given points.   🔵 **See Lesson 5-8.**

48. $(-1, 4), (0, -2), (1, -2), (2, -8)$ **49.** $(-2, -17), (0, -3), (1, -5), (3, 63)$

Write an equation of each line.   🔵 **See Lesson 2-4.**

50. slope $= -\frac{4}{5}$; through $(-1, 4)$ **51.** slope $= -3$; through $(2, -1)$

Determine whether each relation is a function.   🔵 **See Lesson 2-1.**

52. $\{(0, -1), (-1, 3), (2, 3), (-3, 3)\}$ **53.** $\{(-4, 0), (-7, 0), (-4, 1), (-7, 1)\}$

Get Ready! **To prepare for Lesson 6-1, do Exercises 54–56.**

Factor each expression.   🔵 **See Lesson 5-2.**

54. $x^{10} + x^2$ **55.** $x^4 - y^4$ **56.** $169x^6y^{12} - 13x^3y^6$

Pull It All Together

Completing the Performance Task

Look back at your results from the Apply What You've Learned sections in Lessons 5-1, 5-2, and 5-5. Use the work you did to complete the following.

1. Solve the problem in the Task Description on page 279 by determining all possible dimensions Eliana can use for a diorama box with volume 36 in.^{3}. Round dimensions to the nearest hundredth of an inch. Show all your work and explain each step of your solution.

 2. Reflect Choose one of the Mathematical Practices below and explain how you applied it in your work on the Performance Task.

> MP 1: Make sense of problems and persevere in solving them.
>
> MP 4: Model with mathematics.
>
> MP 7: Look for and make use of structure.

> To solve these problems, you will pull together concepts and skills related to working with polynomials and their related functions and equations.

On Your Own

After finishing her miniature diorama for the art contest, Eliana decides to make another diorama. Her new diorama will be inside a wooden box, as shown in the figure below. Eliana orders a wooden box online with sides and back panel that are 1 in. thick. The outside length is twice as long as the outside width and outside depth. According to the information Eliana finds online, the interior of the box has a volume of 96 in.^{3}.

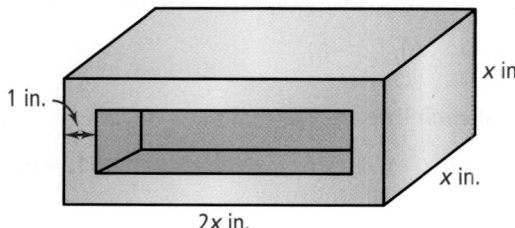

1 in.

x in.

x in.

$2x$ in.

a. Determine all possible outside dimensions of the box.

b. Explain how you know that you found all possible answers in part (a).

Connecting **BIG** ideas and Answering the Essential Questions

1 Function
A polynomial of degree n has n linear factors. The graph of the related function crosses the x-axis an even or odd number of times depending on whether n is even or odd.

Polynomial Functions, Zeros, and Linear Factors (Lessons 5-1 and 5-2)
$y = 2x^3 + 7x^2 - 9$ has 3 linear factors $(x + 3)$, $(2x + 3)$, $(x - 1)$; it crosses the x-axis 3 times—at $(-3, 0)$, $(-\frac{3}{2}, 0)$, and $(1, 0)$. Its end behavior is down and up.

2 Equivalence
$(x - a)$ is a linear factor if and only if a is a zero, and if and only if $(a, 0)$ is an x-intercept when a is a real number.

Solving Polynomial Equations (Lesson 5-3)
$2x^3 + 7x^2 - 9 = 0$ has factored form $(x + 3)(2x + 3)(x - 1) = 0$. It has 3 roots or solutions, $x = -3$, $x = -\frac{3}{2}$, and $x = 1$.

Theorems About Roots of Polynomial Equations (Lesson 5-5)
$P(x) = 2x^3 + 7x^2 - 9$ and $Q(x) = 2x^3 + 5x^2 + 9$ each have degree 3 so $P(x) = 0$ and $Q(x) = 0$ each have 3 complex roots.
Each has ± 1, ± 3, ± 9, $\pm\frac{1}{2}$, $\pm\frac{3}{2}$, $\pm\frac{9}{2}$ as its possible rational roots.
$P(-3) = 0$, so $x + 3$ is a factor of $2x^3 + 7x^2 - 9$.
$Q(-3) = 0$, so $x + 3$ is a factor of $2x^3 + 5x^2 + 9$.

3 Solving Equations and Inequalities
$(x - a)$ is a linear factor if and only if a is a root of the related polynomial equation.

The Fundamental Theorem of Algebra (Lesson 5-6)
$2x^3 + 5x^2 + 9 = 0$ has factored form $(x + 3)(2x^2 - x + 3) = 0$. It has 3 roots or solutions, $x = -3$, $x = \frac{1}{4} - \frac{\sqrt{23}}{4}i$, and $x = \frac{1}{4} + \frac{\sqrt{23}}{4}i$.

Chapter Vocabulary

- Binomial Theorem (p. 327)
- Conjugate Root Theorem (p. 314)
- constant of proportionality (p. 341)
- degree of a monomial (p. 280)
- degree of a polynomial (p. 280)
- Descartes' Rule of Signs (p. 315)
- difference of cubes (p. 297)
- end behavior (p. 282)
- expand a binomial (p. 326)
- Factor Theorem (p. 290)

- Fundamental Theorem of Algebra (p. 320)
- monomial (p. 280)
- multiple zero (p. 291)
- multiplicity (p. 291)
- Pascal's Triangle (p. 327)
- polynomial (p. 280)
- polynomial function (p. 280)
- power function (p. 341)
- Rational Root Theorem (p. 312)

- relative maximum (p. 291)
- relative minimum (p. 291)
- Remainder Theorem (p. 307)
- standard form of a polynomial function (p. 281)
- sum of cubes (p. 297)
- synthetic division (p. 306)
- turning point (p. 282)

Match each vocabulary term with the description that best fits it.

1. Conjugate Root Theorem
2. Fundamental Theorem of Algebra
3. Rational Root Theorem
4. Remainder Theorem

A. determines $P(a)$ by dividing the polynomial by $x - a$
B. the degree equals the number of roots
C. minimizes guessing fraction and integer solutions
D. complex numbers as roots come in pairs

5-1 Polynomial Functions

Quick Review

The **standard form of a polynomial function** is $P(x) = a_n x^n + a_{n-1} x^{n-1} + \cdots + a_1 x + a_0$, where n is a nonnegative integer and the coefficients are real numbers. A **polynomial function** is classified by degree. Its degree is the highest degree among its monomial term(s). The degree determines the possible number of **turning points** in the graph and the **end behavior** of the graph.

Example

Write the polynomial function in standard form and classify it by degree. How many terms does it have? What are the possible numbers of turning points of the graph of $P(x)$ given the degree of the polynomial?

$$P(x) = -4x^2 + x^4$$

Standard form arranges the terms by decreasing exponents, or $P(x) = x^4 - 4x^2$. Its degree is 4, so $x^4 - 4x^2$ is a quartic binomial. It has two terms. The graph of a quartic polynomial function can have either one or three turning points.

Exercises

Write each polynomial function in standard form, classify it by degree, and determine the end behavior of its graph.

5. $y = 12 - x^4$

6. $y = x^2 + 7 - x$

7. $y = 2x^3 - 6x + 3x^2 - x^4 + 12$

8. $y = 2x^2 + 8 - 4x + x^3$

9. $y = 10 - 3x^3 + 3x^2 + x^4$

10. If the volume of a cube can be represented by a polynomial of degree 9, what is the degree of the polynomial that represents each side length?

11. A polynomial function $P(x)$ has degree n. If n is even, is the number of turning points of the graph of $P(x)$ even or odd? What can you say about the number of turning points if n is odd?

5-2 Polynomials, Linear Factors, and Zeros

Quick Review

For any real number a and polynomial $P(x)$, if $x - a$ is a **factor** of $P(x)$, then a is:

- a **zero** of $y = P(x)$,
- a **root** (or **solution**) of $P(x) = 0$, and
- an **x-intercept** of the graph of $y = P(x)$.

If a is a **multiple zero**, its **multiplicity** is the same as the number of times $x - a$ appears as a factor.

A turning point is a **relative maximum** or **relative minimum** of a polynomial function.

Example

Find the zeros for $y = 3x^3 - 6x^2 + 3x$ and state the multiplicity of any multiple zeros.

$y = 3x(x^2 - 2x + 1)$ Factor out the GCF, $3x$.

$y = 3x(x - 1)(x - 1)$ Factor the quadratic.

The zeros are 0, and 1 with multiplicity 2.

Exercises

Write a polynomial function with the given zeros.

12. $x = -1, -1, 6$ **13.** $x = -1, 0, 2$

14. $x = 1, 2, 3$ **15.** $x = -2, 1, 4$

Find the zeros of each function. State the multiplicity of any multiple zeros.

16. $y = 3x(x + 2)^3$ **17.** $y = x^4 - 8x^2 + 16$

18. $y = 4x^3 - 2x^2 - 2x$ **19.** $y = (x - 5)(x + 2)^2$

Use a graphing calculator to find the relative maximum, relative minimum, and zeros of each function.

20. $y = x^4 - 5x^3 + 5x^2 - 3$

21. $y = 5x^3 + x^2 - 9x + 4$

22. $y = x^4 - 4x - 1$

23. $y = x^3 - 3x^2 - 3x - 4$

5-3 Solving Polynomial Equations

Quick Review

One way to solve a polynomial equation is by factoring. First write the equation in the form $P(x) = 0$, where $P(x)$ is the polynomial. Then factor the polynomial. Last, use the Zero-Product Property to find the solutions, or roots. The solutions may be real or imaginary. Real solutions and approximations of irrational solutions can also be found by using a graphing calculator.

Example

Solve $x^3 + 4x^2 = 12x$ by factoring.

$x^3 + 4x^2 - 12x = 0$	Subtract 12x from each side.
$x(x - 2)(x + 6) = 0$	Factor the left side.
$x = 0, x - 2 = 0, x + 6 = 0$	Zero Product Property
$x = 0, x = 2, x = -6$	Solve each equation.

The solutions are 0, 2, and −6.

Exercises

Find the real or imaginary solutions of each equation by factoring.

24. $x^2 - 11x = -24$ **25.** $4x^2 = -4x - 1$

26. $3x^3 + 3x^2 = 27x$ **27.** $2x^2 + 3 = 4x$

Find the real roots of each equation by graphing.

28. $x^4 + 3x^2 - 2x + 5 = 0$

29. $x^2 + 3 = x^3 - 5$

30. The height and width of a rectangular prism are each 2 inches shorter than the length of the prism. The volume of the prism is 40 cubic inches. Approximate the dimensions of the prism to the nearest hundredth.

5-4 Dividing Polynomials

Quick Review

You can divide a polynomial by one of its factors to find another factor. When you divide by a linear factor, you can simplify this division by writing only the coefficients of each term. This is called **synthetic division**. The **Remainder Theorem** says that $P(a)$ is the remainder when you divide $P(x)$ by $x - a$.

Example

Let $P(x) = 3x^2 - 13x + 15$. What is $P(3)$?

According to the Remainder Theorem, $P(3)$ is the remainder when you divide $P(x)$ by $x - 3$.

$$\begin{array}{r|rrr} 3 & 3 & -13 & 15 \\ & & 9 & -12 \\ \hline & 3 & -4 & 3 \end{array}$$

Put the opposite of the constant in the divisor at the top left.

The quotient is $3x - 4$ with remainder 3, so $P(3) = 3$.

Exercises

Divide using long division. Check your answers.

31. $(x^3 + 7x^2 + 15x + 9) \div (x + 1)$

32. $(2x^3 - 7x^2 - 7x + 13) \div (x - 4)$

Determine whether each binomial is a factor of $x^3 + x^2 - 10x + 8$.

33. $x - 2$ **34.** $x - 4$

Divide using synthetic division.

35. $(x^3 + 5x^2 - x - 5) \div (x + 5)$

36. $(2x^3 + 14x^2 - 58x) \div (x + 10)$

37. $(5x^3 + 8x^2 - 60) \div (x - 2)$

Use the Remainder Theorem to determine the value of $P(a)$.

38. $P(x) = 2x^3 + 5x^2 + 7x - 4, a = -2$

39. $P(x) = x^3 - 4x^2 + 2x + 3, a = 1$

Quick Review

The **Rational Root Theorem** gives a way to determine the possible roots of a polynomial equation $P(x) = 0$. If the coefficients of $P(x)$ are all integers, then every root of the equation can be written in the form $\frac{p}{q}$, where p is a factor of the constant term and q is a factor of the leading coefficient.

The **Conjugate Root Theorem** states that if $P(x)$ is a polynomial with rational coefficients, then irrational roots that have the form $a + \sqrt{b}$ and imaginary roots of $P(x) = 0$ come in conjugate pairs. Therefore, if $a + \sqrt{b}$ is an irrational root, where a and b are rational, then $a - \sqrt{b}$ is also a root. Likewise, if $a + bi$ is a root, where a and b are real and i is the imaginary unit, then $a - bi$ is also a root.

Descartes' Rule of Signs gives a way to determine the possible number of positive and negative real roots by analyzing the signs of the coefficients. The number of positive real roots is equal to the number of sign changes in consecutive coefficients of $P(x)$, or is less than that by an even number. The number of negative real roots is equal to the number of sign changes in consecutive coefficients of $P(-x)$, or is less than that by an even number.

Example

Find the rational roots of $P(x) = 0$ if $P(x) = 2x^3 - 4x^2 - 10x + 12$.

List the possible roots: $\pm\frac{1}{2}, \pm1, \pm\frac{3}{2}, \pm2, \pm3, \pm4, \pm6, \pm12$.
Use synthetic division to test roots.

$$
\begin{array}{r|rrrr}
3 & 2 & -4 & -10 & 12 \\
  &   & 6 & 6 & -12 \\
\hline
  & 2 & 2 & -4 & 0
\end{array}
$$

So $x - 3$ and $(2x^2 + 2x - 4)$ are factors of $P(x)$.
$$P(x) = (x - 3)(2x^2 + 2x - 4)$$

Factor the quadratic.
$$P(x) = 2(x - 3)(x + 2)(x - 1)$$

Solve $2(x - 3)(x + 2)(x - 1) = 0$.
$$x = 3, \ x = -2, \text{ or } x = 1$$

The rational roots are 3, −2, and 1.

Exercises

List the possible rational roots of $P(x)$ given by the Rational Root Theorem.

40. $P(x) = x^3 + 4x^2 - 10x + 6$

41. $P(x) = 3x^3 - x^2 - 7x + 2$

42. $P(x) = 4x^4 - 2x^3 + x^2 - 12$

43. $P(x) = 3x^4 - 4x^3 - x^2 - 7$

Find any rational roots of $P(x)$.

44. $P(x) = x^3 + 2x^2 + 4x + 21$

45. $P(x) = x^3 + 5x^2 + x + 5$

46. $P(x) = 2x^3 + 7x^2 - 5x - 4$

47. $P(x) = 3x^4 + 2x^3 - 9x^2 + 4$

A polynomial $P(x)$ has rational coefficients. Name additional roots of $P(x)$ given the following roots.

48. $1 - i$ and 5

49. $5 + \sqrt{3}$ and $-\sqrt{2}$

50. $-3i$ and $7i$

51. $-2 + \sqrt{11}$ and $-4 - 6i$

Write a polynomial function with the given roots.

52. 7 and 10

53. −3 and $5i$

54. $6 - i$

55. $3 + i$, 2, and −4

Determine the possible number of positive real zeros and negative real zeros for each polynomial function given by Descartes' Rule of Signs.

56. $P(x) = 5x^3 + 7x^2 - 2x - 1$

57. $P(x) = -3x^3 + 11x^2 + 12x - 8$

58. $P(x) = 6x^4 - x^3 + 5x^2 - x + 9$

59. $P(x) = -x^4 - 3x^3 - 8x^2 + 2x - 14$

5-6 The Fundamental Theorem of Algebra

Quick Review

The **Fundamental Theorem of Algebra** states that if $P(x)$ is a polynomial of degree n, where $n \geq 1$, then $P(x) = 0$ has exactly n roots. This includes multiple and complex roots.

Example

Use the Fundamental Theorem of Algebra to determine the number of roots for $x^4 + 2x^2 - 3 = 0$.

Because the polynomial is of degree 4, it has 4 roots.

Exercises

Find the number of roots for each equation.

60. $x^3 - 2x + 5 = 0$

61. $2 - x^4 + x^2 = 0$

62. $-x^5 - 6 = 0$

63. $5x^4 - 7x^6 + 2x^3 + 8x^2 + 4x - 11 = 0$

Find all the zeros for each function.

64. $P(x) = x^3 + 5x^2 - 4x - 2$

65. $P(x) = x^4 - 4x^3 - x^2 + 20x - 20$

66. $P(x) = 2x^3 - 3x^2 + 3x - 2$

67. $P(x) = x^4 - 4x^3 - 16x^2 + 21x + 18$

5-7 The Binomial Theorem

Quick Review

Rows 0–5 of Pascal's Triangle are shown below.

$$
\begin{array}{ccccccccccc}
 & & & & & 1 & & & & & \\
 & & & & 1 & & 1 & & & & \\
 & & & 1 & & 2 & & 1 & & & \\
 & & 1 & & 3 & & 3 & & 1 & & \\
 & 1 & & 4 & & 6 & & 4 & & 1 & \\
1 & & 5 & & 10 & & 10 & & 5 & & 1
\end{array}
$$

The **Binomial Theorem** uses Pascal's Triangle to expand binomial powers. For a positive integer n, $(a + b)^n = P_0 a^n + P_1 a^{n-1}b + P_2 a^{n-2}b^2 + \cdots + P_{n-1}ab^{n-1} + P_n b^n$, where $P_0, P_1, \ldots, P_n$ are the coefficients of the nth row of Pascal's Triangle.

Example

Use the Binomial Theorem to expand $(2x + 3)^3$.

$(2x + 3)^3$

$= 1(2x)^3 + 3(2x)^2(3) + 3(2x)(3)^2 + 1(3)^3$

$= 8x^3 + 36x^2 + 54x + 27$

Exercises

68. How many numbers are in the eighth row of Pascal's Triangle?

69. List the numbers in the eighth row of Pascal's Triangle.

70. How many numbers are in the fifteenth row of Pascal's Triangle?

71. What is the third number in the fifteenth row of Pascal's Triangle?

Use the Binomial Theorem to expand each binomial.

72. $(x + 9)^3$ **73.** $(b + 2)^4$

74. $(3a + 1)^3$ **75.** $(x - 5)^3$

76. $(x - 2y)^3$ **77.** $(3a + 4b)^5$

78. $(x + 1)^6$ **79.** $(2x - 1)^6$

Find the coefficient of the x^2 term in each binomial expansion.

80. $(3x + 4)^3$ **81.** $(ax - c)^4$

5-8 Polynomial Models in the Real World

Quick Review

A data set can be modeled by a polynomial function. Methods of finding a model that fits the data include the $(n + 1)$ Point Principle and **regression**. Linear, quadratic, cubic, and quartic regressions can be performed on a graphing calculator. A higher R^2 value means a better fit. Once the equation that models the data is known, it can be used to make predictions.

Example

For the data set $(8, 30)$, $(10, 45)$, and $(11, 65)$, predict y when $x = 15$.

Enter 8, 10, and 11 in **L1** and 30, 45, and 65 in **L2**. Choose **LINREG** to find the regression model $y \approx 11.071x - 60.357$. The r^2 value is about 0.928.

Now try **QUADREG**. The model is $y \approx 4.17x^2 - 67.5x + 303.3$ with an R^2 value of 1. Assuming the model makes sense in context, it fits the data better.

Using the quadratic model, when $x = 15$, $y \approx 228.3$.

Exercises

82. Write a polynomial function whose graph passes through $(0, 5)$, $(2, 10)$, and $(1, 4)$. Use a regression to check your answer.

83. Find a linear, a quadratic, and a cubic model for the data. Which model best fits the data?

x	3	8	15	21
y	7	11	26	44

84. Use **CUBICREG** to model the data below. Then use the model to estimate the population in 2008. Let x be the number of years after 2000.

Year	2004	2007	2009	2010
Population	457	910	1244	1315

5-9 Transforming Polynomial Functions

Quick Review

A polynomial function can be transformed into other polynomial functions using stretches, reflections, and translations. The monomial function $y = ax^b$ is called a **power function**.

Example

This is the graph of a cubic function. Determine which sequence of transformations you can apply to the graph of the parent function $y = x^3$ to get this graph. Write an equation for the graph.

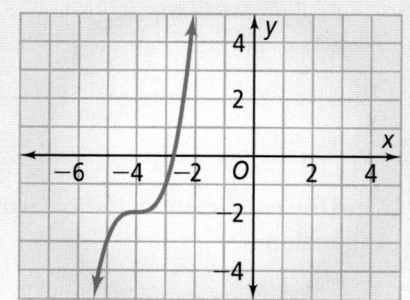

Translate the parent function 4 units left and 2 units down: $y = (x + 4)^3 - 2$.

Exercises

Determine the cubic function obtained from the parent function $y = x^3$ after each sequence of transformations.

85. a reflection across the x-axis;
a translation 1 unit up;
and a translation 2 units right

86. a vertical stretch by a factor of 6;
and a translation 3 units left

87. Find a quartic function whose only real zeros are 4 and 6.

88. The parent power function $y = x^5$ is translated 3 units up and is compressed by the factor 0.3. Write the function.

Do you know HOW?

Write each polynomial function in standard form. Then classify it by degree and by number of terms and describe its end behavior.

1. $y = 3x^2 - 7x^4 + 9 - x^4$

2. $y = 2x(x^2 - 3)(x^2 + 2)$

3. $y = (t - 2)(t + 1)(t + 1)$

Write a polynomial function for each set of zeros.

4. $x = 1, 2, \frac{3}{5}$

5. $x = \sqrt{2}, -i$

6. $x = 3 + i, -1 - \sqrt{5}$

Find the quotient and remainder.

7. $(x^2 + 3x - 4) \div (x - 1)$

8. $(x^3 + 7x^2 - 5x - 6) \div (x + 2)$

9. $(2x^3 + 9x^2 + 11x + 3) \div (2x + 3)$

For each equation, state the number of complex roots, the possible number of real roots, and the possible rational roots.

10. $3x^4 + 5x^3 - 2x^2 + x - 9 = 0$

11. $x^7 - 2x^5 - 4x^3 - 2x - 1 = 0$

For each equation, find all the roots.

12. $3x^4 - 11x^3 + 15x^2 - 9x + 2 = 0$

13. $x^3 - x^2 - x - 2 = 0$

14. One x-intercept of the graph of the cubic function $f(x) = x^3 - 2x^2 - 111x - 108$ is -9. What are the other zeros?

Use synthetic division and the Remainder Theorem to find $P(a)$.

15. $P(x) = 6x^4 + 19x^3 - 2x^2 - 44x - 24; a = -\frac{2}{3}$

16. $P(x) = x^4 + 3x^3 - 7x^2 - 9x + 12; a = 3$

17. $P(x) = x^3 + 3x^2 - 5x - 4; a = -1$

Expand each binomial.

18. $(x + z)^5$

19. $(1 - 2t)^2$

20. Graph and write the equation of the cubic function that is obtained from the parent function $y = x^3$ after this sequence of transformations: vertical stretch by a factor of 2, reflection across the x-axis, translation 3 units down and 4 units right.

Do you UNDERSTAND?

STEM 21. **Physics** You take measurements of the distance traveled by an object that is increasing its speed at a constant rate. The distance traveled as a function of time can be modeled by a quadratic function.
   a. Write a quadratic function that models distances of 10 ft at 1 sec, 30 ft at 2 sec, and 100 ft at 4 sec.
   b. Find the zeros of the function.
   c. **Reasoning** Describe what each zero represents for this real-world situation.

 22. **Writing** For the polynomial $x^6 - 64$, could you apply the Difference of Cubes? Difference of Squares? Explain your answers.

23. The number of pairs of shoes Emily buys varies directly as the square of the area of the floor of her closet. If she could fit 12 pairs of shoes when her closet was 10 square feet, how many pairs of shoes will she fit when the area of her closet floor is 18 square feet?

TIPS FOR SUCCESS

Some problems require you to simplify expressions that contain imaginary numbers.

TIP 1

When multiplying binomials, you should use the Distributive Property.

Which expression is equivalent to $(3 - 4i)(2 + i)$?

- (A) $2 - 5i$
- (B) $2 + 5i$
- (C) $10 - 5i$
- (D) $10 + 5i$

TIP 2

Recall that $i^2 = -1$.

Think It Through

$(3 - 4i)(2 + i)$

$= 6 + 3i - 8i - 4i^2$

$= 6 - 5i - 4(-1)$

$= 10 - 5i$

The correct answer is C.

Vocabulary Review

As you solve test items, you must understand the meanings of mathematical terms. Match each term with its mathematical meaning.

A. multiplicity

B. synthetic division

C. Conjugate Root Theorem

D. relative maximum

E. polynomial

I. the process of dividing a polynomial by a linear factor, omitting all variables and exponents

II. if $a + bi$ is an irrational root where a and b are real numbers, then $a - bi$ is also a root

III. a monomial or the sum of monomials

IV. the greatest y-value in a region of a graph

V. the number of times a zero is repeated in a polynomial function

Selected Response

Read each question. Then write the letter of the correct answer on your paper.

1. Which statement is true about this system of linear equations?

$$\begin{cases} 3x - 4y = 12 \\ 6x - 8y = 12 \end{cases}$$

- (A) The solution is $(0, -1)$.
- (B) The solution is $(8, 4)$.
- (C) There is no solution because the lines are parallel.
- (D) There are infinitely many solutions because the lines are coinciding.

2. Which of the following statements is *never* true about a quartic function?

- (F) The end behavior of the function is up and up.
- (G) The function has 4 zeros.
- (H) The function has 4 turning points.
- (I) The function has complex roots.

3. Tia deposited x dollars in a bank account that paid 4% interest. She also deposited y dollars in a bank account that paid 8% interest. The system below represents one year's interest on Tia's deposits.

$$\begin{cases} 0.04x + 0.08y = 240 \\ \quad\;\; 0.04x = 0.08y \end{cases}$$

Based on the solution of the system of equations, which of the following can you conclude?

- Ⓐ Tia deposited $3000 in each account, and the amounts of interest earned were $240 and $120.

- Ⓑ Tia deposited $3000 in each account, and the amount of interest earned in each account was $120.

- Ⓒ The deposit amounts were $3000 and $1500, and the amounts of interest earned in each account were $240 and $120.

- Ⓓ The deposit amounts were $3000 and $1500, and the amount of interest earned in each account was $120.

4. The total area of the parallelogram below is $4x^4 + 3x^3 - 14x^2 + 33x - 35$. Which of the following expressions best represents the length of the base of the parallelogram? (*Hint:* $A = bh$)

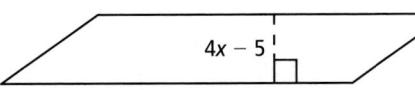

$4x - 5$

- Ⓕ $x^3 + 2x^2 - x + 7$
- Ⓖ $x^3 - 2x^2 + x - 7$
- Ⓗ $4x^4 + 3x^3 - 14x^2 + 33x - 7$
- Ⓘ $x^3 + 5x^2 - x + 5$

5. Which point corresponds to a zero of the function $f(x) = x^2 + 2x - 15$?

- Ⓐ $(0, -15)$ Ⓒ $(-5, 0)$
- Ⓑ $(5, 0)$ Ⓓ $(-3, 0)$

6. Solve the equation $x^2 + 3w = P$ for x.

- Ⓕ $x = P - 3w$ Ⓗ $x = \pm\sqrt{P - 3w}$
- Ⓖ $x = \pm\sqrt{\frac{P}{3w}}$ Ⓘ $x = \pm\sqrt{P + 3w}$

7. A bridge supported by a parabolic arch spans a stream of water 180 feet wide. There must be a clearance of at least 40 feet over a 100-foot channel in the middle of the stream. The origin is placed at water level directly below the center of the arch. Which equation best represents the situation?

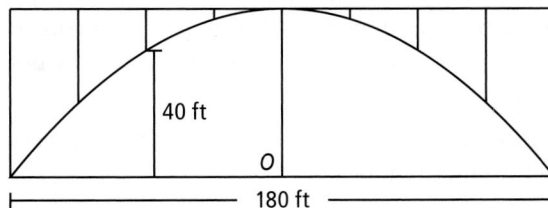

40 ft

O

180 ft

- Ⓐ $y = 140(x + 180)(x - 180)$
- Ⓑ $y = -\frac{1}{140}(x + 90)(x - 90)$
- Ⓒ $y = -\frac{1}{140}(x + 40)(x - 40)$
- Ⓓ $y = 140(x + 40)(x - 40)$

8. Sofia has $25 in her savings account. She plans to deposit between $5 and $10 each week into her account. On the graph, line m represents a deposit of exactly $5 per week and line n represents a deposit of exactly $10 per week.

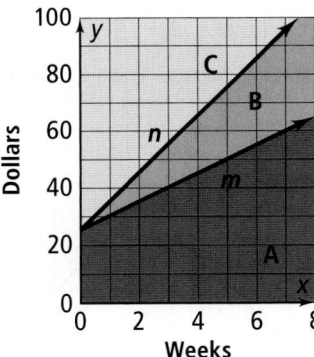

If Sofia deposits between $5 and $10 per week, which region on the graph represents all possible balances in her account?

- Ⓕ A   Ⓗ C
- Ⓖ B   Ⓘ A and C combined

Constructed Response

9. The power created by a wind turbine varies directly as the cube of the wind speed in miles per hour. A turbine with 30% efficiency spinning in a 50 mile per hour wind can be expected to produce approximately 10,000 watts of electricity. How many watts would the same turbine produce in a 25-mile-per-hour wind? If necessary, round your answer to the nearest whole number.

10. One root of a cubic equation is $2i$. How many real roots does the equation have?

11. What is the value of the real part of the sum of $(6 + 4i)$ and $(5 - i)$?

12. If the solutions of an equation are -1, 2, and 5, what is the sum of the zeros of the related function?

13. Assume y varies directly with x. If $y = -3$ when $x = -\frac{2}{5}$, what is x when y is 45?

14. What is the x-coordinate of the point where a relative maximum of $g(x) = -2x^3 + 6x^2 - 10$ occurs?

15. Using a graph, find the real zero of the function $y = 2x^3 - 2x^2 + x - 1$.

16. How many imaginary roots does $x^2 - 5x + 10 = 0$ have?

17. What is the product of $(2 + i)(2 - i)$?

18. Write the equation represented by the graph. Show your work.

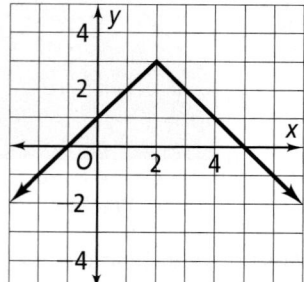

19. Solve the absolute value inequality $-2\left|x - 3\right| \le -16$. Show your work.

20. The graph shows line m and point P. Write the equation of a line n that goes through point P and is perpendicular to line m. Show your work.

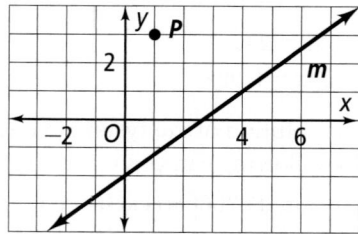

21. A cat ran around part of a telephone pole on a path modeled by the equation $y = -x^2 + 4x - 1$. Graph the cat's path in the first quadrant. If the pole is at $(2, 0)$, at what point is the cat furthest from the pole?

22. Solve the equation $x^2 - 7x = 8$.

Extended Response

23. Use the graph to answer the questions below.

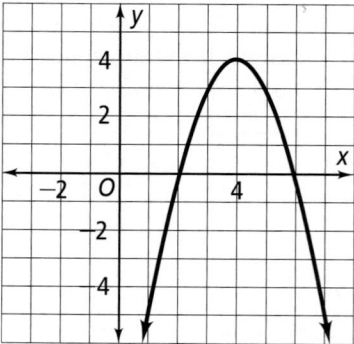

a. Describe the sequence of transformations that would take the graph of the parent function $y = x^2$ to the graph shown.

b. Identify the zeros of the function represented in the graph and explain your reasoning.

c. Write the equation of the function in the graph.

d. Explain how you could check to see that the equation is correct.

Get Ready!

Lessons 2-1
and 4-1

◀ Finding the Domain and Range of Functions

Find the domain and range of each function.

1. $\{(1, 2), (2, 3), (3, 4), (4, 5)\}$ **2.** $\{(1, 2), (2, 2), (3, 2), (4, 2)\}$

3. $f(x) = (x - 4)^2 - 8$ **4.** $f(x) = 2x^2 + 3$

Lesson 4-1

◀ Graphing Quadratic Functions

Graph each function.

5. $y = 2x^2 - 4$ **6.** $y = -3(x^2 + 1)$ **7.** $y = \frac{1}{2}(x - 3)^2 + 1$

Lesson 4-4

◀ Multiplying Binomials

Multiply.

8. $(3y - 2)(y - 4)$ **9.** $(7a + 10)(7a - 10)$ **10.** $(x - 3)(x + 6)(x + 1)$

Lessons 4-5
and 5-3

◀ Solving by Factoring

Solve each equation by factoring.

11. $x^2 - 5x - 14 = 0$ **12.** $2x^2 - 11x + 15 = 0$ **13.** $3x^2 + 10x - 8 = 0$

14. $12x^2 - 12x + 3 = 0$ **15.** $8x^2 - 98 = 0$ **16.** $x^4 - 14x^2 + 49 = 0$

Looking Ahead Vocabulary

17. Combining two or more elements forms composite chemical mixtures. In some cases, if you change the order in which you mix two chemicals, it can produce very different results. A *composite function* is made by combining two functions. If you are buying a $60 shirt and there is a 50% off sale and you have a $10 coupon, does it make a difference which discount is applied first?

18. One-to-one relationships describe situations where people are matched with unique identifiers, such as their social security numbers. A function is a relation that matches *x*-values to *y*-values. What do you suppose a *one-to-one function* is?

19. In an orchestra, the principal player is chosen among all the other musicians that play a certain instrument to sit in the first chair and lead his section. In math, what do you suppose a *principal root* is?

CHAPTER

6

Radical Functions and Rational Exponents

Download videos connecting math to your world.

Interactive! Vary numbers, graphs, and figures to explore math concepts.

The online Solve It will get you in gear for each lesson.

Math definitions in English and Spanish

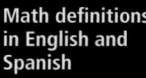

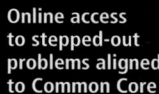

Online access to stepped-out problems aligned to Common Core

Get and view your assignments online.

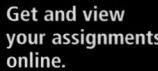

Extra practice and review online

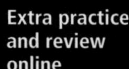

Virtual Nerd™ tutorials with built-in support

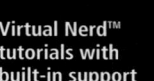 

Chapter Preview

Vocabulary

English/Spanish Vocabulary Audio Online:

English	Spanish
composite function, *p. 399*	función compuesta
inverse function, *p. 405*	función inversa
*n*th root, *p. 361*	raíz *n*-ésima
principal root, *p. 361*	raíz principal
radical equation, *p. 390*	ecuación radical
radicand, *p. 362*	radicando
rational exponent, *p. 382*	exponente racional
rationalize the denominator, *p. 369*	racionalizar el denominador
square root equation, *p. 390*	ecuación de raíz cuadrada
square root function, *p. 415*	función de raíz cuadrada

BIG ideas

1 Equivalence
Essential Question To simplify the *n*th root of an expression, what must be true about the expression?

2 Solving Equations and Inequalities
Essential Question When you square each side of an equation, is the resulting equation equivalent to the original?

3 Function
Essential Question How are a function and its inverse function related?

 DOMAINS
• Seeing Structure in Expressions
• Interpreting Functions
• Reasoning with Equations and Inequalities

Common Core Performance Task

Analyzing the Dimensions of a Yacht

America's Cup is the name of both an international yacht race and the trophy that is awarded to the winner. To compete in America's Cup, a yacht must meet certain standards of design and construction. The inequality below describes one of the rules for the yachts.

$$\frac{L + 1.25S^{\frac{1}{2}} - 9.8D^{\frac{1}{3}}}{0.686} \le 24$$

In the inequality, L is the boat's length (in meters), S is the sail area (in square meters), and D is the displacement (in cubic meters). Displacement is the volume of the boat that is underwater. Yacht designers try to make the value of the left side of the inequality as close to 24 as possible.

The table below lists data on the AC45 Wingsail Catamaran, a yacht that was built to compete in the 2013 America's Cup. You are going to design a new yacht that will satisfy the America's Cup rule and have twice the length and twice the sail area of the AC45.

AC45 Wingsail Catamaran	
Length	13.45 meters
Sail Area	93.7 square meters
Displacement	1.3 cubic meters

Task Description

Verify that the AC45 Wingsail Catamaran satisfies the America's Cup rule, and find all possible displacements for your new yacht.

Connecting the Task to the Math Practices

MATHEMATICAL PRACTICES

As you complete the task, you'll apply several Standards for Mathematical Practice.

- You'll write the America's Cup rule using a radical expression and then estimate the value of the expression for the AC45. (MP 2)

- You'll write a function and describe how to use it to analyze the displacement of the new yacht. (MP 6)

- You'll use a calculator to graph a function that models the rule for the new yacht. (MP 4, MP 5)

Properties of Exponents

© **Common Core State Standards**

Prepares for N-RN.A.1 Explain how the definition of the meaning of rational exponents follows from extending the properties of integer exponents to those values, allowing for a notation for radicals in terms of rational exponents.

MP 8

Exponents indicate powers. The table below lists the properties of exponents. Assume that no denominator is equal to zero and that m and n are integers.

take note

Properties Properties of Exponents

- $a^0 = 1, a \neq 0$
- $\dfrac{a^m}{a^n} = a^{m-n}$

- $a^{-n} = \dfrac{1}{a^n}$
- $(ab)^n = a^n b^n$
- $(a^m)^n = a^{mn}$

- $a^m \cdot a^n = a^{m+n}$
- $\left(\dfrac{a}{b}\right)^n = \dfrac{a^n}{b^n}$

Example

Simplify and rewrite each expression using only positive exponents.

a. $(5a^3)(-3a^{-4})$

$(5a^3)(-3a^{-4}) = 5(-3)a^{(3+(-4))}$

$= -15a^{-1}$

$= \dfrac{-15}{a}$, or $-\dfrac{15}{a}$

b. $(-4x^{-3}y^5)^2$

$(-4x^{-3}y^5)^2 = (-4)^2(x^{-3})^2(y^5)^2$

$= 16x^{-6}y^{10}$

$= \dfrac{16y^{10}}{x^6}$

c. $\dfrac{4ab^6c^3}{a^5bc^3}$

$\dfrac{4ab^6c^3}{a^5bc^3} = 4a^{(1-5)}b^{(6-1)}c^{(3-3)}$

$= 4a^{-4}b^5c^0$

$= \dfrac{4b^5}{a^4}$

Exercises

Simplify each expression. Use only positive exponents.

1. $(2a^3)(5a^4)$

2. $(-3x^2)(-4x^{-2})$

3. $(3x^2y^3)^2$

4. $(3x^{-4}y^3)^2$

5. $\dfrac{4a^8}{2a^4}$

6. $\dfrac{12x^5y^3}{4x^{-1}}$

7. $\dfrac{(6x^3)^0}{3xy^2}$

8. $\left(\dfrac{2x^4}{3}\right)^3$

9. $(-4m^2n^3)(2mn)$

10. $(2x^3y^7)^{-2}$

11. $\dfrac{(3r^{-2}s^3t^0)^{-3}}{3rs}$

12. $(h^7k^3)^0$

13. $\dfrac{r^2s^4t^6}{r^3s^4t^{-6}}$

14. $\dfrac{x^2y}{4} \cdot \dfrac{16x}{y}$

15. $(s^4t)^2(st)$

16. $\left(\dfrac{1}{h^{-2}}\right)^{-1} \cdot h^3$

17. $\dfrac{1}{a^2b^{-3}}(a^2b^{-3})^{-1}$

18. $\left(\dfrac{r^{-1}s^2t^{-3}}{r^{-2}s^0t^1}\right)^{-1}$

© **19. Reasoning** Your friend tells you that $(k^2)^{-5} = -k^{10}$. Did she apply the properties of exponents correctly? Explain why or why not.

Roots and Radical Expressions

 Common Core State Standards

A-SSE.A.2 Use the structure of an expression to identify ways to rewrite it.

MP 1, MP 2, MP 3, MP 4

Objective To find nth roots

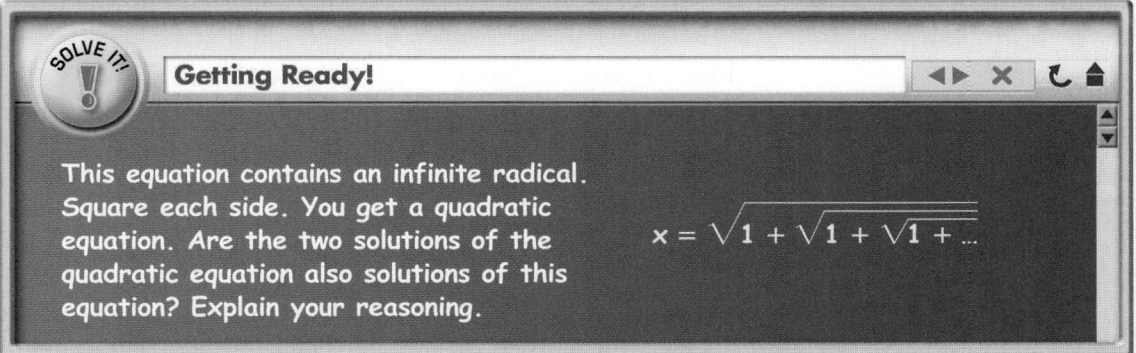

Getting Ready!

This equation contains an infinite radical. Square each side. You get a quadratic equation. Are the two solutions of the quadratic equation also solutions of this equation? Explain your reasoning.

$$x = \sqrt{1 + \sqrt{1 + \sqrt{1 + \ldots}}}$$

Lesson Vocabulary

- nth root
- principal root
- radicand
- index

In Chapter 5, you used *root* to represent a solution of an equation. For example, 2 is a root of the equation $x^3 = 8$. For such a simple power equation, you can simply refer to 2 as a cube root of 8.

Essential Understanding Corresponding to every power, there is a root. For example, just as there are squares (second powers), there are square roots. Just as there are cubes (third powers), there are cube roots, and so on.

$5^2 = 25$	5 is a square root of 25.
$5^3 = 125$	5 is a cube root of 125.
$5^4 = 625$	5 is a fourth root of 625.
$5^5 = 3125$	5 is a fifth root of 3125.

This pattern suggests a definition of an nth root.

take note

Key Concept The nth Root

If $a^n = b$, with a and b real numbers and n a positive integer, then a is an **nth root** of b.

If n is odd...

there is one real nth root of b, denoted in radical form as $\sqrt[n]{b}$.

If n is even...

- and b is positive, there are two real nth roots of b. The positive root is the **principal root** (or principal nth root) and its symbol is $\sqrt[n]{b}$. The negative root is its opposite, or $-\sqrt[n]{b}$.
- and b is negative, there are no real nth roots of b.

The only nth root of 0 is 0.

You use a radical sign to indicate a root. The number under the radical sign is the **radicand**. The **index** gives the degree of the root.

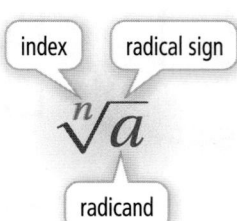

index   radical sign

$$\sqrt[n]{a}$$

radicand

Problem 1 Finding All Real Roots

Ⓐ What are the real cube roots of 0.008, -1000, and $\frac{1}{27}$?

$0.008 = (0.2)^3$ 0.2 is the only real cube root of 0.008.

$-1000 = (-10)^3$ -10 is the only real cube root of -1000.

$\frac{1}{27} = \left(\frac{1}{3}\right)^3$ $\frac{1}{3}$ is the only real cube root of $\frac{1}{27}$.

Ⓑ What are the real fourth roots of 1, -0.0001, and $\frac{16}{81}$?

Since 1 is positive, there are two real fourth roots.

$1 = 1^4$ 1 is a real fourth root of 1.

$1 = (-1)^4$ -1 is the other real fourth root of 1.

Since -0.0001 is negative, there are no real fourth roots of -0.0001.

Since $\frac{16}{81}$ is positive, there are two real fourth roots.

$\frac{16}{81} = \left(\frac{2}{3}\right)^4$ $\frac{2}{3}$ is a real fourth root of $\frac{16}{81}$.

$\frac{16}{81} = \left(-\frac{2}{3}\right)^4$ $-\frac{2}{3}$ is the other real fourth root of $\frac{16}{81}$.

Got It? 1. a. What are the real fifth roots of 0, -1, and 32?

       b. What are the real square roots of 0.01, -1, and $\frac{36}{121}$?

       c. Reasoning Explain why a negative real number b has no real nth roots if n is even.

Plan

How many real cube roots are there?
A cube root is the same as a third root, and 3 is odd. So there is only one real cube root of a number.

According to the Fundamental Theorem of Algebra, $x^4 - 1 = 0$ has four roots, only two of which are real. In this chapter, the focus is on real roots only.

Problem 2 Finding Roots

What is each real-number root?

Ⓐ $\sqrt[3]{-8}$

$(-2)^3 = -8$

So, $\sqrt[3]{-8} = -2$.

Ⓑ $\sqrt{0.04}$

$(0.2)^2 = 0.04$

So, $\sqrt{0.04} = 0.2$.

> $(-0.2)^2 = 0.04$ also, but $\sqrt{0.04}$ represents the positive square root.

Ⓒ $\sqrt[4]{-1}$

There is no real root because there is no real number whose fourth power is -1.

Ⓓ $\sqrt{(-2)^2}$

$\sqrt{(-2)^2} = \sqrt{4} = 2$.

Plan

How can you find a cube root?
Work backwards. Find a number whose cube is the radicand.

Got It? **2.** What is each real-number root?

    a. $\sqrt[3]{-27}$ **b.** $\sqrt[4]{-81}$ **c.** $\sqrt{(-7)^2}$ **d.** $\sqrt{-49}$

It is tempting to conclude that $\sqrt[n]{a^n} = a$ for all real numbers a, but part (d) of Problem 2 shows that this is not the case. If n is even, then $\sqrt[n]{a^n}$ is positive even if a itself is negative.

take note

Property   *n*th Roots of *n*th Powers

For any real number a, $\sqrt[n]{a^n} = \begin{cases} a \text{ if } n \text{ is odd} \\ |a| \text{ if } n \text{ is even} \end{cases}$

It is easy to overlook this rule for simplifying radicals. It is particularly important that you remember it when the radicand contains a variable expression. You must *include* the absolute value when n is even, and you must *omit* it when n is odd.

Ⓒ **Problem 3** **Simplifying Radical Expressions**

What is a simpler form of each radical expression?

Ⓐ $\sqrt{16x^8}$

$$\sqrt{16x^8} = \sqrt{4^2(x^4)^2} = \sqrt{(4x^4)^2} = |4x^4| = 4x^4$$

You need to include absolute value symbols because the index of a square root is 2, which is even. However, $|4x^4| = 4x^4$ because x^4 is always nonnegative.

Ⓑ $\sqrt[3]{a^6b^9}$

$$\sqrt[3]{a^6b^9} = \sqrt[3]{(a^2)^3(b^3)^3} = \sqrt[3]{(a^2b^3)^3} = a^2b^3$$

The index is odd, so you cannot include absolute value symbols here.

Ⓒ $\sqrt[4]{x^8y^{12}}$

$$\sqrt[4]{x^8y^{12}} = \sqrt[4]{(x^2)^4(y^3)^4} = \sqrt[4]{(x^2y^3)^4} = x^2|y^3|$$

The index is even. The absolute value symbols ensure that the root is positive when y^3 is negative. Absolute value symbols are not needed for x^2 since x^2 is always nonnegative.

 Got It? **3.** What is the simplified form of each radical expression?

    a. $\sqrt{81x^4}$ **b.** $\sqrt[3]{a^{12}b^{15}}$ **c.** $\sqrt[4]{x^{12}y^{16}}$

Plan

How can you get started?
You're simplifying a square root, so use properties of exponents to write the *entire* radicand as a perfect square.

 **Problem 4** **Using a Radical Expression**

Academics Some teachers adjust test scores when a test is difficult. One teacher's formula for adjusting scores is $A = 10\sqrt{R}$, where A is the adjusted score and R is the raw score. If the raw scores on one test range from 36 to 90, what is the range of the adjusted scores?

Think

You have to adjust the lowest raw score and the highest raw score.

The other adjusted scores must be between the lowest and highest adjusted scores.

Write

$10\sqrt{36} = 10(6) = 60$

$10\sqrt{90} \approx 10(9.487) = 94.87 \approx 95$

The adjusted scores range from 60 to 95.

 Got It? **4.** In Problem 4, what are the adjusted scores for raw scores of 0 and 100?

 ## Lesson Check

Do you know HOW?

Find all the real square roots of each number.

1. 25   **2.** 0.16   **3.** -64

Simplify each radical expression.

4. $\sqrt{9b^2}$ **5.** $\sqrt{a^8 b^{18}}$ **6.** $\sqrt[3]{-125a^3}$

Do you UNDERSTAND?  MATHEMATICAL PRACTICES

7. Error Analysis A student said the only fourth root of 16 is 2. Describe and correct his error.

8. Vocabulary Explain the difference between a real root and the principal root.

9. Reasoning A number has only one real nth root. What can you conclude about the index n?

 ## Practice and Problem-Solving Exercises  MATHEMATICAL PRACTICES

 **Practice**   Find all the real square roots of each number.   ◀ See Problem 1.

10. 225   **11.** 0.0049   **12.** $-\frac{1}{121}$ **13.** $\frac{64}{169}$

Find all the real cube roots of each number.

14. -64 **15.** 0.125   **16.** $-\frac{27}{216}$ **17.** 0.000343

Find all the real fourth roots of each number.

18. 16   **19.** -16 **20.** 0.0081   **21.** $\frac{10,000}{81}$

Find each real root.

See Problem 2.

22. $\sqrt{36}$ **23.** $\sqrt{0.25}$ **24.** $-\sqrt[3]{64}$ **25.** $\sqrt[3]{-27}$

Simplify each radical expression. Use absolute value symbols when needed.

See Problem 3.

26. $\sqrt{16x^2}$ **27.** $\sqrt[3]{27y^6}$ **28.** $\sqrt[4]{x^{20}y^{28}}$ **29.** $\sqrt[5]{32y^{10}}$

30. Grades In many classes, a passing test grade is 70. Using the formula $A = 10\sqrt{R}$, what raw score would a student need to get a passing grade after her score is adjusted?

See Problem 4.

 **Apply**

Find the two real solutions of each equation.

31. $x^2 = 100$ **32.** $x^4 = 1$ **33.** $x^2 = 0.25$ **34.** $x^4 = \frac{16}{81}$

35. Think About a Plan The radius of a spherical balloon can be expressed as $r = \sqrt[3]{\frac{3V}{4\pi}}$ inches, where r is the radius and V is the volume of the balloon in cubic inches. If air is pumped to inflate the balloon from 500 cubic inches to 800 cubic inches, by how many inches has the radius of the balloon increased?
- What was the radius of the balloon originally?
- What was the radius after inflating the balloon to 800 cubic inches?
- How can you use the two radii to find the amount of increase?

 36. Electricity The voltage V of an audio system's speaker can be represented by $V = 4\sqrt{P}$, where P is the power of the speaker. An engineer wants to design a speaker with 400 watts of power. What will the voltage be?

 37. Boat Building Boat builders share an old rule of thumb for sailboats. The maximum speed K in knots is 1.35 times the square root of the length L in feet of the boat's waterline.
- **a.** A customer is planning to order a sailboat with a maximum speed of 12 knots. How long should the waterline be?
- **b.** How much longer would the waterline have to be to achieve a maximum speed of 15 knots?

Simplify each radical expression. Use absolute value symbols when needed.

38. $\sqrt[3]{0.125}$ **39.** $\sqrt[3]{\frac{8}{216}}$ **40.** $\sqrt[4]{0.0016}$ **41.** $\sqrt[4]{\frac{1}{256}}$ **42.** $\sqrt[4]{16c^4}$

43. Open-Ended Write three radical expressions that simplify to $-2x^2$.

44. Reasoning For what positive integers n is each of the statements true?
- **a.** If $x^n = b$, then x is an nth root of b.
- **b.** If $x^n = b$, then $x = \sqrt[n]{b}$.

Is each equation *always*, *sometimes*, or *never* true? Explain your answer.

45. $\sqrt{x^4} = x^2$ **46.** $\sqrt{x^6} = x^3$ **47.** $\sqrt[3]{x^8} = x^2$ **48.** $\sqrt[3]{x^3} = |x|$

Challenge Simplify each radical expression if n is even, and then if n is odd.

49. $\sqrt[n]{m^n}$ **50.** $\sqrt[n]{m^{2n}}$ **51.** $\sqrt[n]{m^{3n}}$ **52.** $\sqrt[n]{m^{4n}}$

53. Reasoning How many square roots of integers are in the interval between 24 and 25?

54. Reasoning The square root of a positive integer is either a positive integer or an irrational number. Is this a true statement or not? Explain your reasoning.

55. Geometry Without using a calculator, determine which is greater: the altitude of an equilateral triangle with side 8 or the diagonal of a square with side 5. Show your work.

Standardized Test Prep

SAT/ACT

56. Which equation has more than one real-number solution?

    Ⓐ $x^2 = 0$ Ⓑ $x^2 = 1$ Ⓒ $x^2 = -1$ Ⓓ $x^3 = -1$

57. According to the Rational Root Theorem, which of the following is NOT a possible root of the polynomial equation $7x^5 + 3x^2 - 4x + 21 = 0$?

    Ⓕ $\frac{1}{7}$ Ⓖ $\frac{1}{3}$ Ⓗ 3   Ⓘ 7

58. The fuse of a three-break firework rocket is programmed to ignite three times with 2-second intervals between the ignitions. When the rocket is shot vertically in the air, its height h in feet after t seconds is given by the formula $h(t) = -5t^2 + 70t$. At how many seconds after the shot should the firework technician set the timer of the first ignition to make the second ignition occur when the rocket is at its highest point?

    Ⓐ 3   Ⓑ 9   Ⓒ 5   Ⓓ 7

Extended Response

59. Write a system of equations to find a cubic polynomial that goes through $(-3, -35)$, $(0, 1)$, $(2, 3)$, and $(4, 7)$.

Mixed Review

Determine the cubic function that is obtained from the parent function $y = x^3$ after each sequence of transformations.   ◀ **See Lesson 5-9.**

60. translation up 3 units and to the left 2 units

61. vertical compression by a factor of $\frac{1}{2}$, translation down 2 units

Solve each equation by using the Quadratic Formula.   ◀ **See Lesson 4-7.**

62. $-4x^2 + 7x - 3 = 0$ **63.** $3x^2 - 5x + 3 = 0$ **64.** $36x^2 - 132x + 121 = 0$

Get Ready!   To prepare for Lesson 6-2, do Exercises 65–67.

Simplify each algebraic expression.   ◀ **See Lesson 1-3.**

65. $\dfrac{14x^7y^9}{7x^4y^6}$ **66.** $\dfrac{3abc}{9b}$ **67.** $\dfrac{20x}{5x^3}$

6-2 Multiplying and Dividing Radical Expressions

© **Common Core State Standards**

A-SSE.A.2 Use the structure of an expression to identify ways to rewrite it.

MP 1, MP 2, MP 3, MP 4

Objective To multiply and divide radical expressions

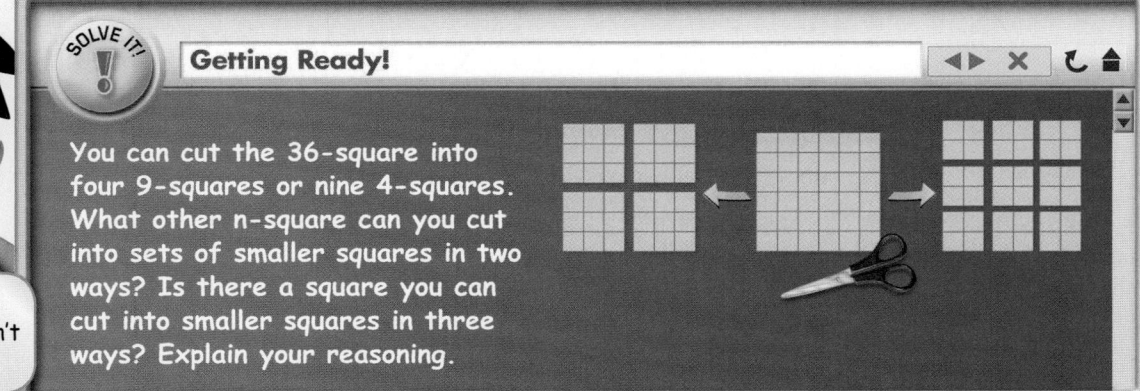

SOLVE IT!

Getting Ready!

You can cut the 36-square into four 9-squares or nine 4-squares. What other n-square can you cut into sets of smaller squares in two ways? Is there a square you can cut into smaller squares in three ways? Explain your reasoning.

Cutting *n*-squares into 1-squares doesn't count.

MATHEMATICAL PRACTICES

Lesson Vocabulary
- simplest form of a radical
- rationalize the denominator

Knowing the perfect squares greater than 1 (namely, 4, 9, 16, and so on) will help you simplify some radical expressions.

Essential Understanding You can simplify a radical expression when the exponent of one factor of the radicand is a multiple of the radical's index.

You can simplify the product of powers that have the same exponent. Similarly, you can simplify the product of radicals that have the same index.

Same Exponent	Same Index
$2^2 \cdot 3^2 = (2 \cdot 3)^2$	$\sqrt{2} \cdot \sqrt{3} = \sqrt{2 \cdot 3}$
$4^3 \cdot 5^3 = (4 \cdot 5)^3$	$\sqrt[3]{4} \cdot \sqrt[3]{5} = \sqrt[3]{4 \cdot 5}$

take note

Property Combining Radical Expressions: Products

If $\sqrt[n]{a}$ and $\sqrt[n]{b}$ are real numbers, then $\sqrt[n]{a} \cdot \sqrt[n]{b} = \sqrt[n]{ab}$.

© **Problem 1** Multiplying Radical Expressions

Plan

What allows you to use the property for multiplying radicals?
The radicals must be real numbers. The indexes must be the same.

Can you simplify the product of the radical expressions? Explain.

Ⓐ $\sqrt[3]{6} \cdot \sqrt{2}$

No. The indexes are different. The property above does not apply.

Ⓑ $\sqrt[3]{-4} \cdot \sqrt[3]{2}$

Yes. $\sqrt[3]{-4} \cdot \sqrt[3]{2} = \sqrt[3]{-4(2)} = \sqrt[3]{-8} = -2$.

Got It? 1. Can you simplify the product of the radical expressions? Explain.

 a. $\sqrt[4]{7} \cdot \sqrt[5]{7}$ **b.** $\sqrt[5]{-5} \cdot \sqrt[5]{-2}$

If the radicand of $\sqrt[n]{a}$ has a perfect nth power among its factors, you can *reduce* the radical. If you reduce a radical as much as possible, the radical is in **simplest form**. For example, consider $\sqrt{24}$ and $\sqrt[3]{24}$.

$$\sqrt{24} = \sqrt{4 \cdot 6} = \sqrt{2^2 \cdot 6} = \sqrt{2^2} \cdot \sqrt{6} = 2\sqrt{6} \qquad 2\sqrt{6} \text{ is in simplest form.}$$

$$\sqrt[3]{24} = \sqrt[3]{8 \cdot 3} = \sqrt[3]{2^3 \cdot 3} = \sqrt[3]{2^3} \cdot \sqrt[3]{3} = 2\sqrt[3]{3} \qquad 2\sqrt[3]{3} \text{ is in simplest form.}$$

 Problem 2 Simplifying a Radical Expression

Think

How do you know when you are done simplifying?
You are done when the radicand contains no perfect cube factors.

What is the simplest form of $\sqrt[3]{54x^5}$?

$$\sqrt[3]{54x^5} = \sqrt[3]{3^3 \cdot 2 \cdot x^2 \cdot x^3} \qquad \text{Find all perfect cube factors.}$$

$$= \sqrt[3]{3^3 x^3} \cdot \sqrt[3]{2x^2} \qquad \sqrt[n]{ab} = \sqrt[n]{a} \cdot \sqrt[n]{b}$$

$$= 3x\sqrt[3]{2x^2} \qquad \text{Simplify.}$$

Got It? 2. What is the simplest form of $\sqrt[3]{128x^7}$?

Problem 2 involves simplifying a cube root, so absolute value symbols are not needed. Remember that to combine $\sqrt[n]{a}$ and $\sqrt[n]{b}$ by multiplication, both radical expressions must be real numbers.

 Problem 3 Simplifying a Product

What is the simplest form of $\sqrt{72x^3y^2} \cdot \sqrt{10xy^3}$?

Think

You need to multiply the radicands and find the perfect square factors.

Now find square roots. Since $\sqrt{72x^3y^2}$ and $\sqrt{10xy^3}$ must be real numbers, x and y are nonnegative, so no absolute value symbols are needed.

Write

$$\sqrt{72x^3y^2} \cdot \sqrt{10xy^3} = \sqrt{(72x^3y^2)(10xy^3)}$$

$$= \sqrt{720x^4y^5}$$

$$= \sqrt{12^2(5)(x^2)^2(y^2)^2y}$$

$$= \sqrt{12^2(x^2)^2(y^2)^2} \cdot \sqrt{5y}$$

$$= 12|x^2y^2| \cdot \sqrt{5y}$$

$$= 12x^2y^2\sqrt{5y}$$

The simplest form is $12x^2y^2\sqrt{5y}$.

 Got It? 3. What is the simplest form of $\sqrt{45x^5y^3} \cdot \sqrt{35xy^4}$?

Since you define division in terms of multiplication, you can extend the property for multiplying radical expressions. If the indexes are the same, you can write a quotient of roots as a root of a quotient.

Multiplying	Dividing
$\sqrt{2} \cdot \sqrt{3} = \sqrt{2 \cdot 3}$	$\dfrac{\sqrt{2}}{\sqrt{3}} = \sqrt{\dfrac{2}{3}}$
$\sqrt[3]{4} \cdot \sqrt[3]{5} = \sqrt[3]{4 \cdot 5}$	$\dfrac{\sqrt[3]{4}}{\sqrt[3]{5}} = \sqrt[3]{\dfrac{4}{5}}$

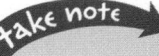 take note

Property   Combining Radical Expressions: Quotients

If $\sqrt[n]{a}$ and $\sqrt[n]{b}$ are real numbers and $b \neq 0$, then $\dfrac{\sqrt[n]{a}}{\sqrt[n]{b}} = \sqrt[n]{\dfrac{a}{b}}$.

 Problem 4   Dividing Radical Expressions

What is the simplest form of the quotient?

Think

Do you need to include absolute value symbols?
No. Both the divisor and dividend already require that x be nonnegative.

A $\dfrac{\sqrt{18x^5}}{\sqrt{2x^3}}$

$$\dfrac{\sqrt{18x^5}}{\sqrt{2x^3}} = \sqrt{\dfrac{18x^5}{2x^3}}$$
$$= \sqrt{9x^2}$$
$$= 3x$$

B $\dfrac{\sqrt[3]{162y^5}}{\sqrt[3]{3y^2}}$

$$\dfrac{\sqrt[3]{162y^5}}{\sqrt[3]{3y^2}} = \sqrt[3]{\dfrac{162y^5}{3y^2}}$$
$$= \sqrt[3]{54y^3}$$
$$= \sqrt[3]{27y^3} \cdot \sqrt[3]{2}$$
$$= \sqrt[3]{3^3y^3} \cdot \sqrt[3]{2}$$
$$= 3y\sqrt[3]{2}$$

  Got It?   4. a. What is the simplest form of $\dfrac{\sqrt{50x^6}}{\sqrt{2x^4}}$?

b. Reasoning Can you simplify the expression in Problem 4(a) by first simplifying $\sqrt{18x^5}$ and $\sqrt{2x^3}$? Explain.

Another way to simplify a radical expression is to **rationalize the denominator**. You rewrite the expression so that there are no radicals in any denominator and no denominator in any radical.

Multiply by 1.

$$\dfrac{1}{\sqrt{2}} = \dfrac{1}{\sqrt{2}}\left(\dfrac{\sqrt{2}}{\sqrt{2}}\right) = \dfrac{\sqrt{2}}{2}$$ The product of $\sqrt{2}$ and itself is a rational number, 2.

© Problem 5 **Rationalizing the Denominator**

Multiple Choice What is the simplest form of $\sqrt[3]{\dfrac{5x^2}{12y^2z}}$?

A $\dfrac{\sqrt[3]{90x^2yz^2}}{6yz}$ B $\dfrac{\sqrt[3]{5x^2}}{\sqrt[3]{12y^2z}}$ C $\dfrac{5\sqrt[3]{x^2yz^2}}{yz}$ D $5\sqrt[3]{x^2z}$

Think

How do you choose what to multiply by?
Choose a cube root with a radicand that will make each factor of the radicand in the denominator a perfect cube.

$\sqrt[3]{\dfrac{5x^2}{12y^2z}} = \dfrac{\sqrt[3]{5x^2}}{\sqrt[3]{2^2 \cdot 3y^2z}}$

The radicand in the denominator needs 2, 3^2, y, and z^2 to make the factors perfect cubes.

$= \dfrac{\sqrt[3]{5x^2}}{\sqrt[3]{2^2 \cdot 3y^2z}} \cdot \dfrac{\sqrt[3]{2 \cdot 3^2yz^2}}{\sqrt[3]{2 \cdot 3^2yz^2}}$

Multiply the numerator and denominator by $\sqrt[3]{2 \cdot 3^2yz^2}$.

$= \dfrac{\sqrt[3]{90x^2yz^2}}{\sqrt[3]{2^3 \cdot 3^3y^3z^3}}$

$= \dfrac{\sqrt[3]{90x^2yz^2}}{2 \cdot 3yz}$ Simplify.

$= \dfrac{\sqrt[3]{90x^2yz^2}}{6yz}$

The correct answer is A.

© ✓ **Got It? 5. a.** What is the simplest form of $\dfrac{\sqrt[3]{7x}}{\sqrt[3]{5y^2}}$?

    b. Reasoning Which choice in Problem 5 could be eliminated immediately? Explain your reasoning.

✓ **Lesson Check**

Do you know HOW?

Multiply, if possible. Then simplify.

1. $\sqrt{2} \cdot \sqrt{5}$

2. $\sqrt[3]{-27} \cdot \sqrt[3]{4}$

3. $\sqrt[3]{2} \cdot \sqrt[2]{7}$

4. $\sqrt{3} \cdot \sqrt{-4}$

Divide and simplify.

5. $\dfrac{\sqrt[3]{15x^2}}{\sqrt[3]{5x}}$

6. $\dfrac{\sqrt{21x^{10}}}{\sqrt{7x^5}}$

Do you UNDERSTAND? © **MATHEMATICAL PRACTICES**

© **7. Vocabulary** Write the simplest form of $\sqrt[3]{32x^4}$.

© **8. Reasoning** For what values of x is $\sqrt{-4x^3}$ real? Justify your reasoning.

© **9. Error Analysis** Explain the error in this simplification of radical expressions.

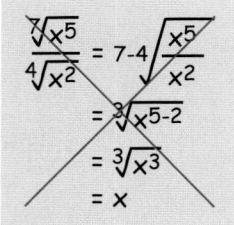

$$\dfrac{\sqrt[7]{x^5}}{\sqrt[4]{x^2}} = {}^{7\text{-}4}\sqrt{\dfrac{x^5}{x^2}}$$
$$= \sqrt[3]{x^{5\text{-}2}}$$
$$= \sqrt[3]{x^3}$$
$$= x$$

 **Practice**

Multiply, if possible. Then simplify.

See Problem 1.

10. $\sqrt{8} \cdot \sqrt{32}$

11. $\sqrt[3]{4} \cdot \sqrt[3]{16}$

12. $\sqrt[3]{9} \cdot \sqrt[3]{-81}$

13. $\sqrt[4]{8} \cdot \sqrt[3]{32}$

14. $\sqrt{-5} \cdot \sqrt{5}$

15. $\sqrt[3]{-5} \cdot \sqrt[3]{-25}$

16. $\sqrt[3]{9} \cdot \sqrt[3]{-24}$

17. $\sqrt[3]{-12} \cdot \sqrt[3]{-18}$

18. $\sqrt{50} \cdot \sqrt{75}$

Simplify.

See Problem 2.

19. $\sqrt{20x^3}$

20. $\sqrt[3]{81x^3}$

21. $\sqrt{50x^5}$

22. $\sqrt[3]{32a^5}$

23. $\sqrt[3]{54y^{10}}$

24. $\sqrt{200a^6b^7}$

25. $\sqrt[3]{-250x^6y^5}$

26. $\sqrt[4]{64x^3y^6}$

27. $\sqrt[5]{-32x^6y^7}$

Multiply and simplify.

See Problem 3.

28. $\sqrt[3]{6} \cdot \sqrt[3]{16}$

29. $\sqrt{8y^5} \cdot \sqrt{40y^2}$

30. $\sqrt{8x^5} \cdot \sqrt{3x}$

31. $4\sqrt{2x} \cdot 5\sqrt{6xy^2}$

32. $3\sqrt[3]{5y^3} \cdot 2\sqrt[3]{50y^4}$

33. $-\sqrt[3]{2x^2y^2} \cdot 2\sqrt[3]{15x^5y}$

34. $\sqrt[4]{81x^5y^4} \cdot \sqrt[4]{32x^3y}$

35. $2\sqrt[3]{2xy^2} \cdot \sqrt[3]{4x^2y^5}$

36. $3\sqrt[4]{18a^9} \cdot \sqrt[4]{6ab^2}$

Divide and simplify.

See Problem 4.

37. $\dfrac{\sqrt{500}}{\sqrt{5}}$

38. $\dfrac{\sqrt{48x^3}}{\sqrt{3xy^2}}$

39. $\dfrac{\sqrt{56x^5y^5}}{\sqrt{7xy}}$

40. $\dfrac{\sqrt[3]{250x^7y^3}}{\sqrt[3]{2x^2y}}$

41. $\dfrac{\sqrt[3]{48x^3y^2}}{\sqrt[3]{6x^4y}}$

42. $\dfrac{\sqrt{20ab}}{\sqrt{45a^2b^3}}$

Rationalize the denominator of each expression.

See Problem 5.

43. $\dfrac{\sqrt{x}}{\sqrt{2}}$

44. $\dfrac{\sqrt{5}}{\sqrt{8x}}$

45. $\dfrac{\sqrt[3]{x}}{\sqrt[3]{2}}$

46. $\sqrt[3]{\dfrac{5}{3x}}$

47. $\dfrac{\sqrt[4]{2}}{\sqrt[4]{5}}$

48. $\dfrac{15\sqrt{60x^5}}{3\sqrt{12x}}$

49. $\dfrac{\sqrt{3xy^2}}{\sqrt{5xy^3}}$

50. $\dfrac{\sqrt{5x^4y}}{\sqrt{2x^2y^3}}$

51. $\dfrac{\sqrt[3]{12ab^3c^2}}{\sqrt[3]{10a^3bc}}$

 **Apply**

© **52. Think About a Plan** The formula $t = \sqrt{\dfrac{2s}{a}}$ shows the time t that any vehicle takes to travel a distance s at a constant acceleration a, starting from rest. What is the difference in time between a car accelerating at 16 m/s^2 and one accelerating at 25 m/s^2 for a distance of 200 m?

- What is the time that a car accelerating at 16 m/s^2 takes to travel 200 m?
- What is the time that a car accelerating at 25 m/s^2 takes to travel 200 m?

53. Geometry The base of a triangle is $\sqrt{18}$ cm and its height is $\sqrt{8}$ cm. Find its area.

STEM **54. Physics** The formula $F = \frac{mv^2}{r}$ gives the centripetal force F of an object of mass m moving along a circle of radius r, where v is the tangential velocity of the object. Solve the formula for v. Rationalize the denominator.

STEM **55. Satellites** The circular velocity v in miles per hour of a satellite orbiting Earth is given by the formula $v = \sqrt{\frac{1.24 \times 10^{12}}{r}}$, where r is the distance in miles from the satellite to the center of Earth. How much greater is the velocity of a satellite orbiting at an altitude of 100 mi than the velocity of a satellite orbiting at an altitude of 200 mi? (The radius of Earth is 3950 mi.)

56. a. Simplify $\frac{\sqrt{2} + \sqrt{3}}{\sqrt{45}}$ by multiplying the numerator and denominator by $\sqrt{75}$.

b. Simplify the expression in (a) by multiplying by $\sqrt{3}$ instead of $\sqrt{75}$.

c. Explain how you would simplify $\frac{\sqrt{2} + \sqrt{3}}{\sqrt{98}}$.

Simplify each expression. Rationalize all denominators.

57. $\sqrt{5} \cdot \sqrt{50}$

58. $\sqrt[3]{4} \cdot \sqrt[3]{80}$

59. $\sqrt{x^5 y^5} \cdot 3\sqrt{2x^7 y^6}$

60. $5\sqrt{2xy^6} \cdot 2\sqrt{2x^3 y}$

61. $\sqrt{2}(\sqrt{50} + 7)$

62. $\sqrt{5}(\sqrt{5} + \sqrt{15})$

63. $\frac{\sqrt{5x^4}}{\sqrt{2x^2 y^3}}$

64. $\frac{5\sqrt{2}}{3\sqrt{7x}}$

65. $\frac{1}{\sqrt[3]{9x}}$

66. $\frac{10}{\sqrt[3]{5x^2}}$

67. $\frac{\sqrt[3]{14}}{\sqrt[3]{7x^2 y}}$

68. $\frac{3\sqrt{11x^3 y}}{-2\sqrt{12x^4 y}}$

STEM **69. Physics** The mass m of an object is $\sqrt{80}$ g and its volume V is $\sqrt{5}$ cm³. Use the formula $D = \frac{m}{V}$ to find the density D of the object.

Ⓒ **70. Writing** Does $\sqrt{x^3} = \sqrt[3]{x^2}$ for *all*, *some*, or *no* values of x? Explain.

Ⓒ **71. Open-Ended** Of the equivalent expressions $\sqrt{\frac{2}{3}}, \frac{\sqrt{2}}{\sqrt{3}}$ and $\frac{\sqrt{6}}{3}$, which do you prefer to use for finding a decimal approximation with a calculator? Justify your reasoning.

Ⓒ **72. Error Analysis** Explain the error in this simplification of radical expressions.

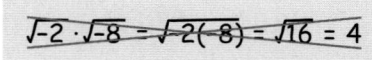

Determine whether each expression is *always*, *sometimes*, or *never* a real number. Assume that x can be any real number.

73. $\sqrt[3]{-x^2}$

74. $\sqrt{-x^2}$

75. $\sqrt{-x}$

 **Challenge** **Simplify each expression. Rationalize all denominators.**

76. $\sqrt{\sqrt{16x^4 y^4}}$

77. $\sqrt{\sqrt[3]{8000}}$

78. $\sqrt[6]{\frac{y^{-3}}{x^{-4}}}$

Ⓒ **79. Reasoning** When $\sqrt{x^a y^b}$ is simplified, the result is $\frac{1}{x^c y^{3d}}$, where c and d are positive integers. Express a in terms of c, and b in terms of d.

SAT/ACT

80. What is the simplified form of the expression $\frac{3}{\sqrt{18xy^2}}$ if x and y are positive?

Ⓐ $\frac{\sqrt{2x}}{2xy}$ Ⓑ $\frac{\sqrt{2y}}{2xy}$ Ⓒ $\frac{\sqrt{54xy^2}}{2xy}$ Ⓓ $\frac{\sqrt{27xy^2}}{2xy}$

81. What are the solutions, in simplest form, of the quadratic equation
$3x^2 + 6x - 5 = 0$?

Ⓕ $\frac{-6 \pm \sqrt{96}}{6}$ Ⓖ $\frac{-6 \pm i\sqrt{24}}{6}$ Ⓗ $\frac{-3 \pm 2\sqrt{6}}{3}$ Ⓘ $\frac{-3 \pm i\sqrt{6}}{3}$

82. Which inequality is shown by the graph at the right?

Ⓐ $y \geq \frac{2}{3}|x - 1| - 2$ Ⓒ $y \geq \frac{3}{2}|x - 1| - 2$

Ⓑ $y \geq \frac{2}{3}|x - 2| - 1$ Ⓓ $y \geq |\frac{2}{3}x - 1| - 2$

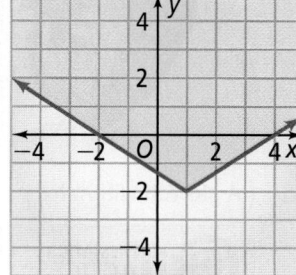

83. A triangle has the dimensions shown below.

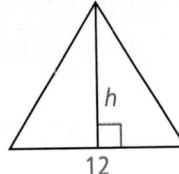

What is the height of a triangle with equal area but a base of 36?

Ⓕ $\frac{h}{3}$ Ⓖ $\frac{2h}{3}$ Ⓗ $2h$ Ⓘ $3h$

Short Response

84. Find the axis of symmetry of the graph of the function $y = -2x^2 - 5x + 4$. Show your work.

Mixed Review

Simplify each radical expression. Use absolute value symbols when needed. ◀ See Lesson 6-1.

85. $\sqrt{121a^{90}}$ **86.** $\sqrt{81c^{48}d^{64}}$ **87.** $\sqrt[3]{64a^{81}}$ **88.** $\sqrt[5]{32y^{25}}$

Divide using synthetic division. ◀ See Lesson 5-4.

89. $(y^3 - 64) \div (y + 4)$ **90.** $(6a^3 + a^2 - a + 4) \div (a + 1)$

Complete each square. ◀ See Lesson 4-6.

91. $x^2 + 10x + \blacksquare$ **92.** $x^2 - 10x + \blacksquare$ **93.** $x^2 + 11x + \blacksquare$ **94.** $x^2 - 11x + \blacksquare$

Get Ready! To prepare for Lesson 6-3, do Exercises 95–98.

Write each quotient as a complex number in the form $a \pm bi$. ◀ See Lesson 4-8.

95. $\frac{2}{3 - i}$ **96.** $\frac{5}{2 + 3i}$ **97.** $\frac{4}{4 + i}$ **98.** $\frac{-1}{7 - 5i}$

6-3 Binomial Radical Expressions

© **Common Core State Standards**
A-SSE.A.2 Use the structure of an expression to identify ways to rewrite it.
MP 1, MP 2, MP 3, MP 4

Objective To add and subtract radical expressions

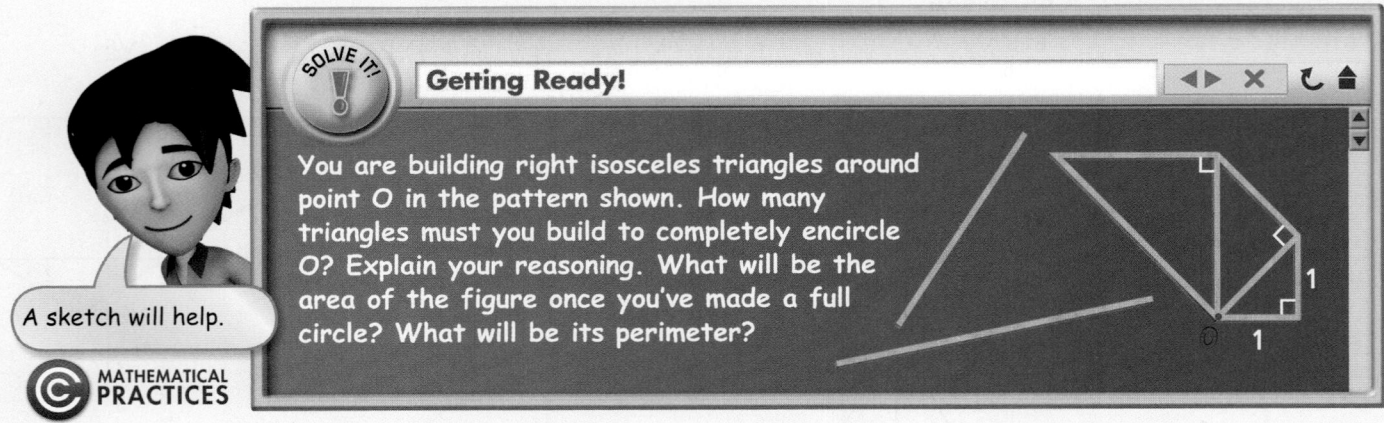

SOLVE IT!

Getting Ready!

You are building right isosceles triangles around point O in the pattern shown. How many triangles must you build to completely encircle O? Explain your reasoning. What will be the area of the figure once you've made a full circle? What will be its perimeter?

A sketch will help.

© MATHEMATICAL PRACTICES

Lesson Vocabulary
• like radicals

Like radicals are radical expressions that have the same index and radicand.

Essential Understanding You can combine like radicals using properties of real numbers.

Here is how you can combine like radicals using the Distributive Property.

Like Radicals With Numbers	Like Radicals With Variables
$\sqrt{2} + 3\sqrt{2} = 4\sqrt{2}$	$\sqrt{5xy} + 8\sqrt{5xy} = 9\sqrt{5xy}$
$\sqrt[3]{7} - 5\sqrt[3]{7} = -4\sqrt[3]{7}$	$\sqrt[3]{9x^2y} - 8\sqrt[3]{9x^2y} = -7\sqrt[3]{9x^2y}$

take note

Property Combining Radical Expressions: Sums and Differences

Use the Distributive Property to add or subtract like radicals.

$$a\sqrt[n]{x} + b\sqrt[n]{x} = (a + b)\sqrt[n]{x} \qquad\qquad a\sqrt[n]{x} - b\sqrt[n]{x} = (a - b)\sqrt[n]{x}$$

Combining radical expressions is different from *adding* them. The sum of any two real numbers is a real number, so you can add $\sqrt{2}$ and $\sqrt{3}$ to get the real number $\sqrt{2} + \sqrt{3}$. However, you cannot *combine* the result into a single radical, so $\sqrt{2} + \sqrt{3} \neq \sqrt{5}$.

$$
\begin{array}{ll}
\sqrt{2} \approx 1.414 & \sqrt{5} \approx 2.236 \\
\underline{+ \sqrt{3} \approx 1.732} & \\
\sqrt{2} + \sqrt{3} \approx 3.146 & \neq 2.236
\end{array}
$$

Problem 1 Adding and Subtracting Radical Expressions

What is the simplified form of each expression?

Ⓐ $3\sqrt{5x} - 2\sqrt{5x}$

$$3\sqrt{5x} - 2\sqrt{5x} = (3-2)\sqrt{5x} \quad \text{Distributive Property}$$
$$= \sqrt{5x} \qquad\qquad \text{Simplify.}$$

Ⓑ $6x^2\sqrt{7} + 4x\sqrt{5}$

The radicands are different. You cannot combine the expressions.

Ⓒ $12\sqrt[3]{7xy} - 8\sqrt[5]{7xy}$

The indexes are different. You cannot combine the expressions.

Think

Can you always simplify a radical sum?
No. The radicands and the indexes must be the same.

Got It? **1.** What is the simplified form of each expression?

a. $7\sqrt[3]{5} - 4\sqrt{5}$ **b.** $3x\sqrt{xy} + 4x\sqrt{xy}$ **c.** $17\sqrt[5]{3x^2} - 15\sqrt[5]{3x^2}$

Problem 2 Using Radical Expressions STEM

Architecture In the stained-glass window design, the side of each small square is 5 in. Find the perimeter of the window to the nearest tenth of an inch.

Length of the diagonal of a square with side s: $s\sqrt{2}$.
Length of the diagonal of each 5-inch square: $5\sqrt{2}$.

Length of the window: $\quad l = 3(5\sqrt{2}) = 15\sqrt{2}$
Width of the window: $\quad w = 2(5\sqrt{2}) = 10\sqrt{2}$

Perimeter $= 2l + 2w$

$$= 2(15\sqrt{2}) + 2(10\sqrt{2}) \quad \begin{array}{l}\text{Substitute for length}\\ \text{and width.}\end{array}$$
$$= 30\sqrt{2} + 20\sqrt{2} \qquad\quad \text{Simplify.}$$
$$= 50\sqrt{2} \qquad\qquad\qquad \text{Distributive Property}$$
$$\approx 70.7 \qquad\qquad\qquad \text{Use a calculator to approximate.}$$

The perimeter of the window is about 70.7 inches.

Think

Does it make sense that you have a radical expression as the answer?
Yes, because perimeter is a linear measure, and there is no squaring in the calculations.

Got It? **2. a.** Find the perimeter of the window if the side of each small square is 6 in.

b. Reasoning Describe a different sequence of steps which you could use to compute the perimeter of the window.

When you have a sum or difference of radical expressions, you should simplify each expression so that you can find all the like radicals.

Problem 3 Simplifying Before Adding or Subtracting

What is the simplest form of the expression? $\sqrt{12} + \sqrt{75} - \sqrt{3}$

Think

To simplify each radical expression, factor each radicand.

These are like radicals. Combine them. Remember $\sqrt{3} = 1\sqrt{3}$.

Write

$\sqrt{12} + \sqrt{75} - \sqrt{3}$

$= \sqrt{4 \cdot 3} + \sqrt{25 \cdot 3} - \sqrt{3}$

$= \sqrt{2^2 \cdot 3} + \sqrt{5^2 \cdot 3} - \sqrt{3}$

$= \sqrt{2^2}\sqrt{3} + \sqrt{5^2}\sqrt{3} - \sqrt{3}$

$= 2\sqrt{3} + 5\sqrt{3} - \sqrt{3}$

$= 6\sqrt{3}$

Got It? 3. What is the simplest form of the expression? $\sqrt[3]{250} + \sqrt[3]{54} - \sqrt[3]{16}$

You can use the FOIL method to multiply binomials that have radical expressions. Remember that the FOIL method ensures that you multiply each term of one binomial by each term of the other.

Problem 4 Multiplying Binomial Radical Expressions

What is the product of each radical expression?

Plan

How do you multiply two binomials?
Use the FOIL method:
First, **O**uter, **I**nner, **L**ast.
Then simplify.

A $(4 + 2\sqrt{2})(5 + 4\sqrt{2})$

$(4 + 2\sqrt{2})(5 + 4\sqrt{2})$

$= 4 \cdot 5 + 4 \cdot 4\sqrt{2} + 2\sqrt{2} \cdot 5 + 2\sqrt{2} \cdot 4\sqrt{2}$ Distribute.

$= 20 + 16\sqrt{2} + 10\sqrt{2} + 16$ Multiply.

$= 36 + 26\sqrt{2}$ Combine like radicals.

B $(3 - \sqrt{7})(5 + \sqrt{7})$

$(3 - \sqrt{7})(5 + \sqrt{7})$

$= 3 \cdot 5 + 3\sqrt{7} - \sqrt{7} \cdot 5 - \sqrt{7} \cdot \sqrt{7}$ Distribute.

$= 15 - 2\sqrt{7} - 7$ Multiply and combine like radicals.

$= 8 - 2\sqrt{7}$ Simplify.

Got It? 4. What is the product $(3 + 2\sqrt{5})(2 + 4\sqrt{5})$?

Conjugates are expressions, like $\sqrt{a} + \sqrt{b}$ and $\sqrt{a} - \sqrt{b}$, that differ only in the signs of the second terms. When a and b are rational numbers, the product of two radical conjugates is a rational number.

 **Problem 5** Multiplying Conjugates

Think

Where have you seen conjugates before?
The complex number $a + bi$ has a conjugate, $a - bi$. Multiplying them results in a number with no imaginary part.

What is the product $(5 - \sqrt{7})(5 + \sqrt{7})$?

$$(5 - \sqrt{7})(5 + \sqrt{7}) = 5 \cdot 5 + 5\sqrt{7} - 5\sqrt{7} - (\sqrt{7})^2 \quad \text{Distribute.}$$
$$= 25 - 7 \qquad\qquad\qquad \text{Simplify.}$$
$$= 18$$

 Got It? 5. What is each product?

a. $(6 - \sqrt{12})(6 + \sqrt{12})$ 　　　　　　**b.** $(3 + \sqrt{8})(3 - \sqrt{8})$

Sometimes a denominator is a sum or difference involving radicals. If the radical expressions are square roots, you can rationalize the denominator by multiplying the numerator and the denominator by the conjugate of the denominator.

 Problem 6 Rationalizing the Denominator

Think

What is a rationalized denominator?
A rationalized denominator contains no radicals.

How can you write the expression with a rationalized denominator?

$$\frac{3\sqrt{2}}{\sqrt{5} - \sqrt{2}}$$

$$\frac{3\sqrt{2}}{\sqrt{5} - \sqrt{2}} = \frac{3\sqrt{2}}{\sqrt{5} - \sqrt{2}} \cdot \frac{\sqrt{5} + \sqrt{2}}{\sqrt{5} + \sqrt{2}} \quad \text{Multiply. Use the conjugate of the denominator.}$$

$$= \frac{3\sqrt{2}(\sqrt{5} + \sqrt{2})}{(\sqrt{5})^2 - (\sqrt{2})^2} \quad \text{The radicals in the denominator cancel out.}$$

$$= \frac{3(\sqrt{2} \cdot \sqrt{5} + \sqrt{2} \cdot \sqrt{2})}{5 - 2} \quad \text{Distribute } \sqrt{2} \text{ in the numerator.}$$

$$= \frac{3(\sqrt{10} + 2)}{3} \quad \text{Simplify.}$$

$$= \sqrt{10} + 2$$

Got It? 6. How can you write the expression with a rationalized denominator?

a. $\dfrac{2\sqrt{7}}{\sqrt{3} - \sqrt{5}}$ 　　　　　　**b.** $\dfrac{4x}{3 - \sqrt{6}}$

c. Reasoning Suppose you were going to rationalize the denominator of $\dfrac{1 - \sqrt{8}}{2 - \sqrt{8}}$. Would you simplify $\sqrt{8}$ before or after rationalizing? Explain your answer.

Lesson Check

Do you know HOW?

Simplify if possible.

1. $10\sqrt{6} + 2\sqrt{6}$

2. $3\sqrt{2} + 4\sqrt[3]{2}$

3. $8\sqrt{3x} - 5\sqrt{3x}$

4. $5\sqrt{3} + \sqrt{12}$

Multiply.

5. $(4 + \sqrt{3})(4 - \sqrt{3})$

6. $(5 + 2\sqrt{5})(7 + 4\sqrt{5})$

7. $(2 + 3\sqrt{2})(1 - 3\sqrt{2})$

Do you UNDERSTAND?

8. Vocabulary Determine whether each of the following is a pair of like radicals. If so, add them.
   a. $3x\sqrt{11}$ and $3x\sqrt{10}$
   b. $2\sqrt{3xy}$ and $7\sqrt{3xy}$
   c. $12\sqrt{13y}$ and $12\sqrt{6y}$

9. Compare and Contrast How are the processes of multiplying radical expressions and multiplying polynomial expressions alike? How are the processes different?

Practice and Problem-Solving Exercises

 Simplify if possible.

◀ See Problem 1.

10. $5\sqrt{6} + \sqrt{6}$

11. $6\sqrt[3]{3} - 2\sqrt[3]{3}$

12. $4\sqrt{3} + 4\sqrt[3]{3}$

13. $3\sqrt{x} - 5\sqrt{x}$

14. $14\sqrt{x} + 3\sqrt{y}$

15. $7\sqrt[3]{x^2} - 2\sqrt[3]{x^2}$

16. The design of a garden path uses stone pieces shaped as squares with a side length of 15 in. Find the length of the path.

◀ See Problem 2.

Simplify.

◀ See Problem 3.

17. $6\sqrt{18} + 3\sqrt{50}$

18. $14\sqrt{20} - 3\sqrt{125}$

19. $\sqrt{18} + \sqrt{32}$

20. $\sqrt[3]{54} + \sqrt[3]{16}$

21. $3\sqrt[3]{81} - 2\sqrt[3]{54}$

22. $\sqrt[4]{32} + \sqrt[4]{48}$

Multiply.

◀ See Problem 4.

23. $(3 + \sqrt{5})(1 + \sqrt{5})$

24. $(2 + \sqrt{7})(1 + 3\sqrt{7})$

25. $(3 - 4\sqrt{2})(5 - 6\sqrt{2})$

26. $(\sqrt{3} + \sqrt{5})^2$

27. $(\sqrt{13} + 6)^2$

28. $(2\sqrt{5} + 3\sqrt{2})^2$

Multiply each pair of conjugates.

◀ See Problem 5.

29. $(5 - \sqrt{11})(5 + \sqrt{11})$

30. $(4 - 2\sqrt{3})(4 + 2\sqrt{3})$

31. $(2\sqrt{6} + 8)(2\sqrt{6} - 8)$

32. $(\sqrt{3} + \sqrt{5})(\sqrt{3} - \sqrt{5})$

Rationalize each denominator. Simplify your answer.

◀ See Problem 6.

33. $\dfrac{4}{1 + \sqrt{3}}$

34. $\dfrac{4}{3\sqrt{3} - 2}$

35. $\dfrac{5 + \sqrt{3}}{2 - \sqrt{3}}$

36. $\dfrac{3 + \sqrt{8}}{2 - 2\sqrt{8}}$

© **37. Think About a Plan** The design on a parquet floor, shown at the right, is made of equilateral triangles. The side of a large triangle is 6 in., and the side of a small triangle is 3 in. Find the total area of the design to the nearest tenth of a square inch.

- How many large and how many small triangles form the design?
- Can you express the area of an equilateral triangle through its side?

Simplify.

38. $\sqrt{72} + \sqrt{32} + \sqrt{18}$

39. $\sqrt{75} + 2\sqrt{48} - 5\sqrt{3}$

40. $5\sqrt{32x} + 4\sqrt{98x}$

41. $\sqrt{75} - 4\sqrt{18} + 2\sqrt{32}$

42. $4\sqrt{216y^2} + 3\sqrt{54y^2}$

43. $3\sqrt[3]{16} - 4\sqrt[3]{54} + \sqrt[3]{128}$

44. $(1 + \sqrt{72})(5 + \sqrt{2})$

45. $(\sqrt{3} - \sqrt{7})(\sqrt{3} + 2\sqrt{7})$

46. $(\sqrt{y} + \sqrt{2})(\sqrt{y} - 7\sqrt{2})$

47. $(\sqrt{12} + \sqrt{72})^2$

48. $(\sqrt{1.25} - \sqrt{1.8})(\sqrt{5} + \sqrt{0.2})$

49. $(\sqrt{a+1} + \sqrt{a-1})(\sqrt{a+1} - \sqrt{a-1})$

© **50. Error Analysis** Describe and correct the error made while simplifying the expression $\dfrac{3 + \sqrt{2}}{3 - \sqrt{2}}$.

$$\frac{3 + \sqrt{2}}{3 - \sqrt{2}} = \frac{3 + \sqrt{2}}{3 - \sqrt{2}} \cdot \frac{3 + \sqrt{2}}{3 + \sqrt{2}}$$

$$= \frac{3^2 + (\sqrt{2})^2}{3^2 - (\sqrt{2})^2} = \frac{9 + 2}{9 - 2} = \frac{11}{7}$$

STEM **51. Chemistry** A scientist found that x grams of Metal A is completely oxidized in $2x\sqrt{3}$ seconds and x grams of Metal B is completely oxidized in $6x\sqrt{3}$ seconds. How much faster is Metal A oxidized than Metal B?

© **52. Reasoning** Describe the possible values of a such that $\sqrt{72} + \sqrt{a}$ simplifies to a single term.

© **53. Writing** Discuss the advantages and disadvantages of first simplifying $\sqrt{72} + \sqrt{32} + \sqrt{18}$ in order to estimate its decimal value.

54. Geometry Show that a right triangle with legs of lengths $\sqrt{2} - 1$ and $\sqrt{2} + 1$ is similar to a right triangle with legs of lengths $6 - \sqrt{32}$ and 2.

© **55. Open-Ended** Find two pairs of conjugates with a product of 3.

Rationalize the denominators and simplify.

56. $\dfrac{4 + \sqrt{27}}{2 - 3\sqrt{27}}$

57. $\dfrac{4 + \sqrt{6}}{\sqrt{2} + \sqrt{3}}$

58. $\dfrac{5 - \sqrt{21}}{\sqrt{3} - \sqrt{7}}$

59. $\dfrac{\sqrt{44x^2}}{\sqrt{11} + 3}$

60. $\dfrac{\sqrt{2} + \sqrt{6}}{\sqrt{1.5} + \sqrt{0.5}}$

61. $\dfrac{\sqrt{27} - \sqrt{5}}{\sqrt{15} - 3}$

62. $\dfrac{4 + \sqrt[3]{2}}{\sqrt[3]{2}}$

63. $\dfrac{5 + \sqrt[4]{x}}{\sqrt[4]{x}}$

64. $\dfrac{4 - 2\sqrt[3]{6}}{\sqrt[3]{4}}$

 **Challenge**

Add or subtract.

65. $\dfrac{1}{1-\sqrt{5}}+\dfrac{1}{1+\sqrt{5}}$

66. $\dfrac{4}{\sqrt{5}-\sqrt{3}}-\dfrac{4}{\sqrt{5}+\sqrt{3}}$

67. For what values of a and b does $\sqrt{a}+\sqrt{b}=\sqrt{a+b}$?

68. In the expression $\sqrt[n]{x^m}$, m and n are positive integers and x is a real number. The expression can be simplified.
  a. If $x>0$, what are the possible values for m and n?
  b. If $x<0$, what are the possible values for m and n?
  c. If $x<0$, and an absolute value symbol is needed in the simplified expression, what are the possible values of m and n?

Standardized Test Prep

GRIDDED RESPONSE

SAT/ACT

69. What is the value of the expression $(5-2\sqrt{3})(5+2\sqrt{3})$?

70. What is the value of z in the solution of the system of equations below?

$$\begin{cases} 2x-3y+\ z=\ \ 6 \\ -x+\ y-2z=-5 \\ 3x-\ y-3z=-7 \end{cases}$$

71. What is the y-value of the y-intercept of the line $5x-7y=-15$?

72. What is the slope of a line perpendicular to the line $2x+5y=10$?

73. What is the value of p for which the equation $x^2-12x+4p=0$ has exactly one real root?

Mixed Review

Simplify each expression. Rationalize all denominators.

 See Lesson 6-2.

74. $\sqrt[3]{3}\cdot\sqrt[3]{18}$

75. $\sqrt[3]{\dfrac{4}{0.5x}}$

76. $\dfrac{\sqrt{32}}{\sqrt{2}}$

77. $\dfrac{\sqrt{216}}{\sqrt{6}}$

78. $\sqrt[3]{2x^2}\cdot\sqrt[3]{4x}$

79. $\sqrt{7x}\cdot\sqrt{14x^3}$

80. $\sqrt{3x}\cdot\sqrt{5x}$

81. $\sqrt{9x^2}\cdot\sqrt{25x^2}$

Find the real and imaginary solutions of each equation.

See Lesson 5-3.

82. $2x^3-16=0$

83. $x^3+1000=0$

84. $125x^3-1=0$

85. $x^4-14x^2+49=0$

86. $25x^4-40x^2+16=0$

87. $81x^4-1=0$

Get Ready! **To prepare for Lesson 6-4, do Exercises 88–91.**

Simplify.

See p. 978.

88. $(x^2)^3$

89. $(pq)^5$

90. $(2^4)(2^5)$

91. $(3^{-2})(3^5)$

Rational Exponents

 Common Core State Standards

N-RN.A.2 Rewrite expressions involving radicals and rational exponents using the properties of exponents.
Also reviews N-RN.A.1

MP 1, MP 3, MP 4

Objective To simplify expressions with rational exponents

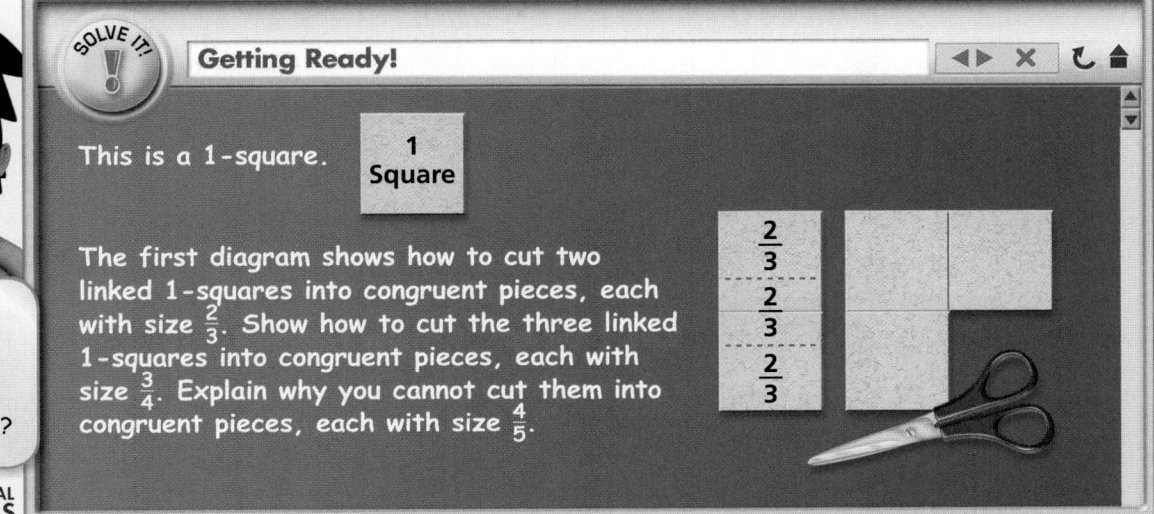

It is easy to cut one 1-square into congruent pieces each with size $\frac{1}{2}$. How about size $\frac{1}{5}$?

MATHEMATICAL PRACTICES

Lesson Vocabulary
• rational exponent

If $a^x = \sqrt[4]{a^3}$, then by definition, $a^x \cdot a^x \cdot a^x \cdot a^x = a^3$. By adding exponents, $a^{4x} = a^3$, then $4x = 3$. So x is $\frac{3}{4}$. This suggests an alternative notation for radical expressions in which, for example, $\sqrt[4]{a^3} = a^{\frac{3}{4}}$.

Essential Understanding You can write a radical expression in an equivalent form using a fractional (rational) exponent instead of a radical sign.

In general, $\sqrt[n]{x} = x^{\frac{1}{n}}$ for any positive integer n. Like the radical form, the exponent form indicates the principal root.

$$\sqrt{36} = 36^{\frac{1}{2}} \qquad \sqrt[3]{64} = 64^{\frac{1}{3}} \qquad \sqrt[4]{16} = 16^{\frac{1}{4}}$$

Problem 1 Simplifying Expressions with Rational Exponents

Think

What does the denominator of the fractional exponent represent?
The denominator of the fraction is the index of the radical.

What is the simplified form of each expression?

A $216^{\frac{1}{3}}$

$216^{\frac{1}{3}} = \sqrt[3]{216}$ ⟵ Rewrite as radicals.

$= \sqrt[3]{6^3}$

$= 6$

B $7^{\frac{1}{2}} \cdot 7^{\frac{1}{2}}$

$7^{\frac{1}{2}} \cdot 7^{\frac{1}{2}} = \sqrt{7} \cdot \sqrt{7}$

$= \sqrt{7 \cdot 7}$

$= \sqrt{7^2}$

$= 7$

You can also solve this problem by adding the exponents.

$7^{\frac{1}{2}} \cdot 7^{\frac{1}{2}} = 7^{\frac{1}{2}+\frac{1}{2}} = 7^1 = 7$

C $5^{\frac{1}{4}} \cdot 125^{\frac{1}{4}}$

$$5^{\frac{1}{4}} \cdot 125^{\frac{1}{4}} = \sqrt[4]{5} \cdot \sqrt[4]{125} \qquad \text{Rewrite as radicals.}$$

$$= \sqrt[4]{5 \cdot 125} \qquad \text{Property for multiplying radical expressions}$$

$$= \sqrt[4]{625} \qquad \text{Multiply.}$$

$$= \sqrt[4]{5^4} \qquad \text{Rewrite the radicand.}$$

$$= 5 \qquad \text{Simplify.}$$

 Got It? **1.** What is the simplified form of each expression?

    a. $64^{\frac{1}{2}}$ **b.** $11^{\frac{1}{2}} \cdot 11^{\frac{1}{2}}$ **c.** $3^{\frac{1}{2}} \cdot 12^{\frac{1}{2}}$

If $\sqrt[n]{x} = x^{\frac{1}{n}}$, it follows from the Laws of Exponents that for all real numbers $\sqrt[n]{x^m} = (x^m)^{\frac{1}{n}} = \left(x^{\frac{1}{n}}\right)^m = \left(\sqrt[n]{x}\right)^m$. This leads to the definition of a rational exponent.

take note →

> ## Key Concept Rational Exponent
>
> If the nth root of a is a real number, m is an integer, and $\frac{m}{n}$ is in lowest terms, then
>
> $$a^{\frac{1}{n}} = \sqrt[n]{a} \text{ and } a^{\frac{m}{n}} = \sqrt[n]{a^m} = (\sqrt[n]{a})^m. \qquad \text{If } m \text{ is negative, } a \neq 0.$$

 Problem 2 **Converting Between Exponential and Radical Forms**

Think

Does the fraction $\frac{3}{7}$ first need to be simplified?
No. The fraction is already in lowest terms.

A What are $x^{\frac{3}{7}}$ and $y^{-3.5}$ in radical form?

$$x^{\frac{3}{7}} = \sqrt[7]{x^3} \text{ or } \left(\sqrt[7]{x}\right)^3$$

$$y^{-3.5} = y^{-\frac{7}{2}}$$

$$= \frac{1}{y^{\frac{7}{2}}}$$

$$= \frac{1}{\sqrt{y^7}} = \frac{1}{\sqrt{y^6 y}} = \frac{1}{y^3\sqrt{y}} \text{ or } \frac{\sqrt{y}}{y^4}$$

B What are $\sqrt{a^5}$ and $\left(\sqrt[5]{b}\right)^3$ in exponential form?

$$\sqrt{a^5} = (a^5)^{\frac{1}{2}} = a^{\frac{5}{2}}$$

$$\left(\sqrt[5]{b}\right)^3 = \left(b^{\frac{1}{5}}\right)^3 = b^{\frac{3}{5}}$$

  Got It? **2. a.** What are the expressions $w^{-\frac{5}{8}}$ and $w^{0.2}$ in radical form?

    b. What are the expressions $\sqrt[4]{x^3}$ and $\left(\sqrt[5]{y}\right)^4$ in exponential form?

    c. Reasoning Refer to the definition of rational exponent. Explain the need for the restriction that $a \neq 0$ if m is negative.

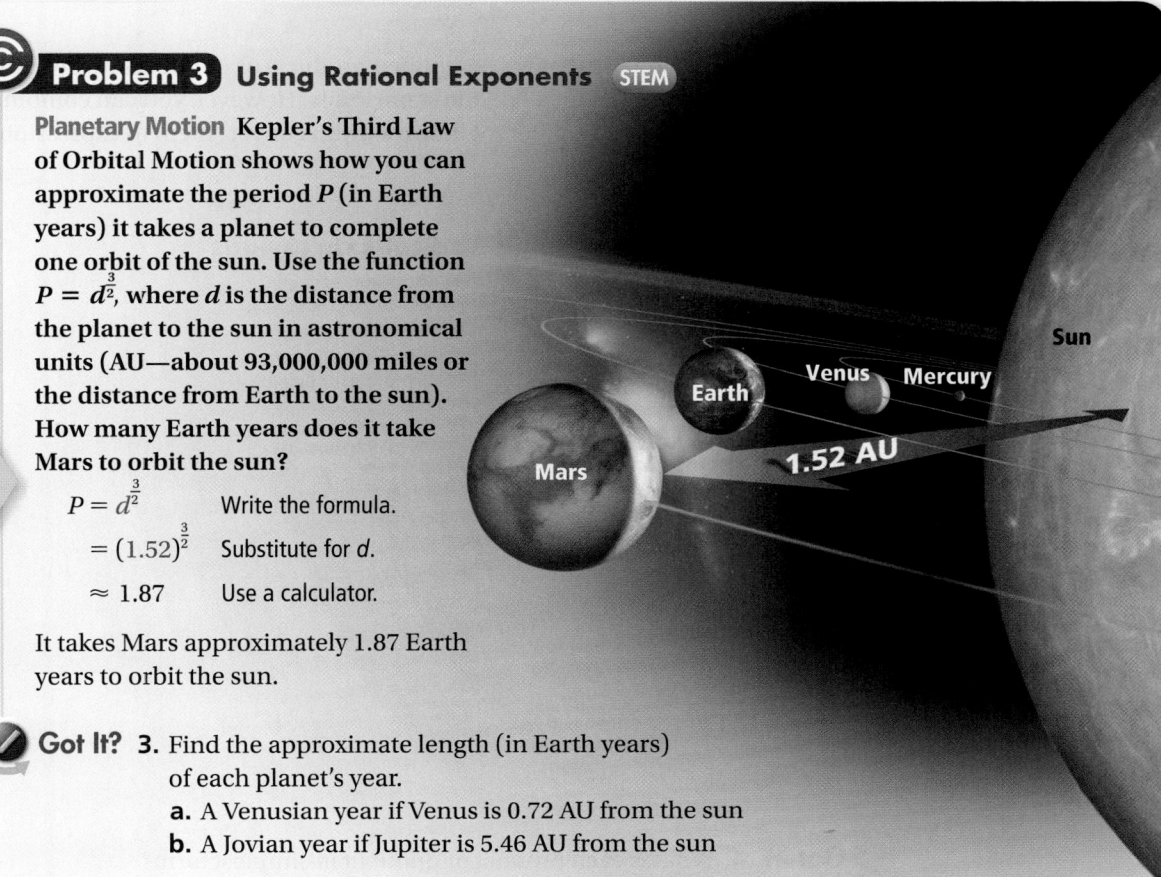

Problem 3 Using Rational Exponents STEM

Planetary Motion Kepler's Third Law of Orbital Motion shows how you can approximate the period P (in Earth years) it takes a planet to complete one orbit of the sun. Use the function $P = d^{\frac{3}{2}}$, where d is the distance from the planet to the sun in astronomical units (AU—about 93,000,000 miles or the distance from Earth to the sun). How many Earth years does it take Mars to orbit the sun?

$$P = d^{\frac{3}{2}} \qquad \text{Write the formula.}$$
$$= (1.52)^{\frac{3}{2}} \qquad \text{Substitute for } d.$$
$$\approx 1.87 \qquad \text{Use a calculator.}$$

It takes Mars approximately 1.87 Earth years to orbit the sun.

Sun

Venus **Mercury**

Earth

1.52 AU

Mars

Plan

How can you find a $\frac{3}{2}$ power on a calculator?
You can use ∧ (3 ÷ 2).
You can also cube the number and then take the square root, or take the square root then cube.

✓ **Got It?** **3.** Find the approximate length (in Earth years) of each planet's year.
   a. A Venusian year if Venus is 0.72 AU from the sun
   b. A Jovian year if Jupiter is 5.46 AU from the sun

All the properties of integer exponents apply to rational exponents.

take note

Properties Properties of Rational Exponents

Let m and n represent rational numbers. Assume that no denominator equals 0.

Property	Example	Property	Example
$a^m \cdot a^n = a^{m+n}$	$8^{\frac{1}{3}} \cdot 8^{\frac{2}{3}} = 8^{\frac{1}{3}+\frac{2}{3}} = 8^1 = 8$	$a^{-m} = \dfrac{1}{a^m}$	$9^{-\frac{1}{2}} = \dfrac{1}{9^{\frac{1}{2}}} = \dfrac{1}{3}$
$(a^m)^n = a^{mn}$	$\left(5^{\frac{1}{2}}\right)^4 = 5^{\frac{1}{2}\cdot 4} = 5^2 = 25$	$\dfrac{a^m}{a^n} = a^{m-n}$	$\dfrac{7^{\frac{3}{2}}}{7^{\frac{1}{2}}} = 7^{\frac{3}{2}-\frac{1}{2}} = 7^1 = 7$
$(ab)^m = a^m b^m$	$(4 \cdot 5)^{\frac{1}{2}} = 4^{\frac{1}{2}} \cdot 5^{\frac{1}{2}} = 2 \cdot 5^{\frac{1}{2}}$	$\left(\dfrac{a}{b}\right)^m = \dfrac{a^m}{b^m}$	$\left(\dfrac{5}{27}\right)^{\frac{1}{3}} = \dfrac{5^{\frac{1}{3}}}{27^{\frac{1}{3}}} = \dfrac{5^{\frac{1}{3}}}{3}$

Recall from Lesson 6-2 that you simplified products or quotients involving radical expressions only when they had the same index. However, you can combine radical expressions with different indexes if you convert them to expressions with rational exponents.

 Problem 4 Combining Radical Expressions

What is $\dfrac{\sqrt[4]{x^3}}{\sqrt[8]{x^2}}$ in simplest form?

Think

Write

The radicands are different, but both are powers of the same variable. Write the expressions using exponents.

$$\dfrac{\sqrt[4]{x^3}}{\sqrt[8]{x^2}} = \dfrac{x^{\frac{3}{4}}}{x^{\frac{2}{8}}}$$

Use the division property for exponents. Subtract the exponents.

$$= x^{\frac{3}{4} - \frac{2}{8}}$$

$$= x^{\frac{3}{4} - \frac{1}{4}}$$

Simplify, and write in either exponential or radical form.

$$= x^{\frac{1}{2}} = \sqrt{x}$$

✓ **Got It?** **4.** What is each product or quotient in simplest form?

a. $\sqrt{3}\left(\sqrt[4]{3}\right)$ **b.** $\dfrac{\sqrt{x^3}}{\sqrt[3]{x^2}}$ **c.** $\sqrt{7}\left(\sqrt[3]{7}\right)$

You can simplify a number with a rational exponent by using the properties of exponents or by converting the expression to a radical expression.

Ⓒ **Problem 5** Simplifying Numbers With Rational Exponents

What is each number in simplest form?

Ⓐ $16^{-2.5}$

Plan

What is the first step?
Rewrite the decimal exponent as a fraction in lowest terms.

Method 1

$$16^{-2.5} = 16^{-\frac{5}{2}}$$

$$= \left(2^4\right)^{-\frac{5}{2}}$$

$$= 2^{4 \cdot -\frac{5}{2}}$$

$$= 2^{-10}$$

$$= \dfrac{1}{2^{10}} = \dfrac{1}{1024}$$

Method 2

$$16^{-2.5} = 16^{-\frac{5}{2}}$$

$$= \dfrac{1}{16^{\frac{5}{2}}}$$

$$= \dfrac{1}{\left(\sqrt{16}\right)^5}$$

$$= \dfrac{1}{4^5}$$

$$= \dfrac{1}{1024}$$

B $(-32)^{\frac{4}{5}}$

Method 1

$(-32)^{\frac{4}{5}} = \left((-2)^5\right)^{\frac{4}{5}}$

$= (-2)^{5 \cdot \frac{4}{5}}$

$= (-2)^4$

$= 16$

Method 2

$(-32)^{\frac{4}{5}} = \left(\sqrt[5]{-32}\right)^4$

$= \left(\sqrt[5]{(-2)^5}\right)^4$

$= (-2)^4$

$= 16$

 Got It? 5. What is each number in simplest form?

a. $32^{-\frac{3}{5}}$ **b.** $16^{\frac{3}{4}}$ **c.** $9^{-3.5}$

To write an expression with rational exponents in simplest form, write every exponent as a positive number.

 Problem 6 Writing Expressions in Simplest Form

What is each expression in simplest form?

A $\left(-8x\sqrt{xy}\right)^{\frac{2}{3}}$

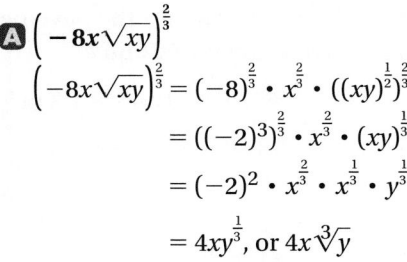

$\left(-8x\sqrt{xy}\right)^{\frac{2}{3}} = (-8)^{\frac{2}{3}} \cdot x^{\frac{2}{3}} \cdot ((xy)^{\frac{1}{2}})^{\frac{2}{3}}$

$= ((-2)^3)^{\frac{2}{3}} \cdot x^{\frac{2}{3}} \cdot (xy)^{\frac{1}{3}}$

$= (-2)^2 \cdot x^{\frac{2}{3}} \cdot x^{\frac{1}{3}} \cdot y^{\frac{1}{3}}$

$= 4xy^{\frac{1}{3}}$, or $4x\sqrt[3]{y}$

B $\left(16y^{-8}\right)^{-\frac{3}{4}}$

$\left(16y^{-8}\right)^{-\frac{3}{4}} = 16^{-\frac{3}{4}} \cdot y^{-8 \cdot -\frac{3}{4}}$

$= (2^4)^{-\frac{3}{4}} \cdot y^6$

$= 2^{-3}y^6$

$= \frac{y^6}{8}$

 Got It? 6. What is each expression in simplest form?

a. $(8x^{15})^{-\frac{1}{3}}$ **b.** $\left(9x\sqrt[4]{y}\right)^{\frac{3}{2}}$

 Lesson Check

Do you know HOW?

Simplify each expression.

1. $125^{\frac{1}{3}}$ **2.** $5^{\frac{1}{2}} \cdot 5^{\frac{1}{2}}$

3. $25^{-\frac{3}{2}}$ **4.** $4^{-3.5}$

5. $\sqrt{11}\left(\sqrt[4]{11}\right)$ **6.** $\frac{\sqrt[3]{x}}{\sqrt[6]{x^5}}$

Do you UNDERSTAND?  MATHEMATICAL PRACTICES

7. Open-Ended Find a nonzero number q such that $q(1 - 2^{\frac{1}{2}})$ is a rational number. Explain.

8. Error Analysis Explain why this simplification is incorrect.

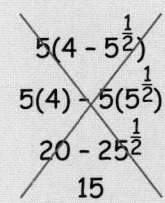

$5(4 - 5^{\frac{1}{2}})$

$5(4) - 5(5^{\frac{1}{2}})$

$20 - 25^{\frac{1}{2}}$

15

9. Reasoning Explain why $(-64)^{\frac{1}{3}} = -64^{\frac{1}{3}}$ but $(-64)^{\frac{1}{2}} \neq -64^{\frac{1}{2}}$.

Practice and Problem-Solving Exercises

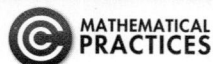
MATHEMATICAL PRACTICES

See Problem 1.

**Practice**

Simplify each expression.

10. $36^{\frac{1}{2}}$

11. $27^{\frac{1}{3}}$

12. $49^{\frac{1}{2}}$

13. $10^{\frac{1}{2}} \cdot 10^{\frac{1}{2}}$

14. $(-3)^{\frac{1}{3}} \cdot (-3)^{\frac{1}{3}} \cdot (-3)^{\frac{1}{3}}$

15. $7^{\frac{1}{2}} \cdot 21^{\frac{1}{2}}$

16. $2^{\frac{1}{2}} \cdot 32^{\frac{1}{2}}$

17. $3^{\frac{1}{3}} \cdot 9^{\frac{1}{3}}$

18. $3^{\frac{1}{4}} \cdot 27^{\frac{1}{4}}$

Write each expression in radical form.

See Problem 2.

19. $x^{\frac{1}{6}}$

20. $x^{\frac{1}{5}}$

21. $x^{\frac{2}{7}}$

22. $y^{\frac{2}{5}}$

23. $y^{-\frac{9}{8}}$

24. $t^{-\frac{3}{4}}$

25. $x^{1.5}$

26. $y^{1.2}$

Write each expression in exponential form.

27. $\sqrt{-10}$

28. $\sqrt{7x^3}$

29. $\sqrt{(7x)^3}$

30. $(\sqrt{7x})^3$

31. $\sqrt[3]{a^2}$

32. $(\sqrt[3]{a})^2$

33. $\sqrt[4]{c^2}$

34. $\sqrt[3]{(5xy)^6}$

Optimal Height The optimal height h of the letters of a message printed on pavement is given by the formula $h = \frac{0.00252d^{2.27}}{e}$. Here d is the distance of the driver from the letters and e is the height of the driver's eye above the pavement. All of the distances are in meters. Find h for the given values of d and e.

See Problem 3.

35. $d = 100$ m, $e = 1.2$ m

36. $d = 50$ m, $e = 1.2$ m

37. $d = 50$ m, $e = 2.3$ m

38. $d = 25$ m, $e = 2.3$ m

Find each product or quotient.

See Problem 4.

39. $(\sqrt[4]{6})(\sqrt[3]{6})$

40. $\frac{\sqrt[9]{y^3}}{\sqrt[3]{y^9}}$

41. $\sqrt{5} \cdot \sqrt[5]{5}$

42. $\sqrt[7]{7} \cdot \sqrt[3]{7}$

43. $\frac{\sqrt[6]{4}}{\sqrt[3]{4}}$

44. $\sqrt[4]{18} \cdot \sqrt{12}$

45. $\frac{\sqrt{6}}{\sqrt[3]{36}}$

46. $\frac{\sqrt{x^4y}}{\sqrt[4]{x^2y^8}}$

Simplify each number.

See Problem 5.

47. $8^{\frac{2}{3}}$

48. $64^{\frac{2}{3}} 64^{\frac{2}{3}}$

49. $(-8)^{\frac{2}{3}}$

50. $(-32)^{\frac{6}{5}}$

51. $(32)^{-\frac{4}{5}}$

52. $4^{1.5}$

53. $16^{1.5}$

54. $10,000^{0.75}$

Write each expression in simplest form.

See Problem 6.

55. $\left(x^{\frac{2}{3}}\right)^{-3}$

56. $\left(x^{-\frac{4}{7}}\right)^7$

57. $\left(3x^{\frac{2}{3}}\right)^{-1}$

58. $5\left(x^{\frac{2}{3}}\right)^{-1}$

59. $\left(-27x^{-9}\right)^{\frac{1}{3}}$

60. $\left(-32y^{15}\right)^{\frac{1}{5}}$

61. $\left(x^{\frac{1}{2}}y^{-\frac{2}{3}}\right)^{-6}$

62. $\left(x^{\frac{2}{3}}y^{-\frac{1}{6}}\right)^{-12}$

63. $\left(\frac{x^3}{x^{-1}}\right)^{-\frac{1}{4}}$

64. $\left(\frac{x^2}{x^{-11}}\right)^{\frac{1}{3}}$

65. $\left(\frac{x^{\frac{1}{4}}}{y^{-\frac{3}{4}}}\right)^{12}$

66. $\left(\frac{x^{-\frac{2}{3}}}{y^{-\frac{1}{3}}}\right)^{15}$

Ⓒ 67. Think About a Plan The ratio R of radioactive carbon to nonradioactive carbon left in a sample of an organism that died T years ago can be approximated by the formula $R = A(2.7)^{-\frac{T}{8033}}$. Here A is the ratio of radioactive carbon to nonradioactive carbon in the living organism. What percent of A is left after 2000 years? After 4000 years? After 8000 years?
- What are the known and unknown values?
- How can you use the properties of exponents to solve this problem?

68. The expression $0.036m^{\frac{3}{4}}$ is used in the study of fluids. Which best represents the value of the expression for $m = 46 \times 10^4$?

Ⓐ 636   Ⓑ 1460   Ⓒ 1660   Ⓓ 16,600

Simplify each number.

69. $(-343)^{\frac{1}{3}}$ **70.** $(-243)^{\frac{1}{5}}$ **71.** $32^{1.2}$

72. $243^{1.2}$ **73.** $64^{3.5}$ **74.** $100^{4.5}$

75. $-(-27)^{-\frac{4}{3}}$ **76.** $\dfrac{1000^{\frac{4}{3}}}{100^{\frac{3}{2}}}$ **77.** $25^{\frac{3}{2}}$

STEM 78. Science A desktop world globe has a volume of about 1386 cubic inches. The radius of Earth is approximately equal to the radius of the globe raised to the 10th power. Find the radius of Earth. (*Hint:* Use the formula $V = \frac{4}{3}\pi r^3$ for the volume of a sphere.)

Simplify each expression.

79. $x^{\frac{2}{7}} \cdot x^{\frac{3}{14}}$ **80.** $y^{\frac{1}{2}} \cdot y^{\frac{3}{10}}$ **81.** $x^{\frac{3}{5}} \div x^{\frac{3}{10}}$

82. $y^{\frac{5}{7}} \div y^{\frac{3}{14}}$ **83.** $\dfrac{x^{\frac{2}{3}} y^{-\frac{1}{4}}}{x^{\frac{1}{2}} y^{-\frac{1}{2}}}$ **84.** $\dfrac{x^{\frac{1}{2}} y^{-\frac{1}{3}}}{x^{\frac{3}{4}} y^{\frac{1}{2}}}$

85. $\left(\dfrac{16x^{14}}{81y^{18}}\right)^{\frac{1}{2}}$ **86.** $\left(\dfrac{81y^{16}}{16x^{12}}\right)^{\frac{1}{2}}$ **87.** $\left(\dfrac{8x^6}{27y^9}\right)^{\frac{1}{3}}$

Ⓒ 88. Open-Ended Find three nonzero numbers a such that $a\left(4 + 5^{\frac{1}{2}}\right)$ is a rational number. Can a itself be a rational number? Explain.

Ⓒ 89. a. Reasoning Show that $\sqrt[4]{x^2} = \sqrt{x}$ by using the definition of fourth root.

    b. Reasoning Show that $\sqrt[4]{x^2} = \sqrt{x}$ by rewriting $\sqrt[4]{x^2}$ in exponential form.

90. Simplify $4^{\frac{1}{2}} \cdot 4^{\frac{1}{2}}$ using the following methods. Show all your work.
    a. Use the properties of exponents.
    b. Simplify each term in the product, then multiply.
    c. Convert to radical form, then simplify.

 **Challenge** You can define the rules for irrational exponents so that they have the same properties as rational exponents. Use those properties to simplify each expression.

91. $\left(7^{\sqrt{2}}\right)^{\sqrt{2}}$

92. $\dfrac{3^{3+\sqrt{5}}}{3^{1+\sqrt{5}}}$

93. $\dfrac{x^{4\pi}}{x^{2\pi}}$

94. $5^{2\sqrt{3}} \cdot 25^{-\sqrt{3}}$

95. $9^{\frac{1}{\sqrt{2}}}$

96. $\left(3^{2+\sqrt{2}}\right)^{2-\sqrt{2}}$

 97. Weather Using data for the effect of temperature and wind on an exposed face, the National Weather Service uses the following formula to determine wind chill.

$$\text{Wind Chill Index} = 35.74 + 0.6215T - 35.75V^{0.16} + 0.4275TV^{0.16}$$

T is the temperature in degrees Fahrenheit and V is the velocity of the wind in miles per hour. Frostbite occurs in about 15 minutes when the wind chill index is -20. Find the wind velocity that produces a wind chill index of -20 when the temperature is 5°F.

SAT/ACT

98. What is the simplified value of $\left(\frac{1}{64}\right)^{-\frac{1}{6}}$?

99. What positive value of b makes $9x^2 - bx + 4$ a perfect square trinomial?

100. How many real roots does the cubic polynomial equation $x^3 - 7x^2 + 13x - 4 = 0$ have?

101. What is the y-value of the y-intercept of the graph of $f(x) = 4|x - 2| - 5$?

 ## Apply What You've Learned

 **MATHEMATICAL PRACTICES**

MP 2

Look back at the rule for America's Cup yachts given on page 359.

a. Write the expression on the left side of the rule in radical form.

b. What is the unit of measure associated with each variable in the expression? What is the unit associated with the expression as a whole? Explain.

c. Estimate the value of the expression for the AC45 Wingsail Catamaran detailed on page 359. Show your work and explain how you chose values for the length, sail area, and displacement to make the calculation easier.

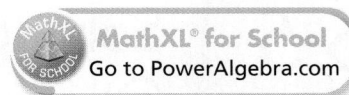

Do you know HOW?

Find all the real square roots of each number.

1. 100

2. 0.49

Simplify each radical expression. Use absolute value symbols when needed.

3. $\sqrt{36x^2}$

4. $\sqrt[3]{0.008y^3x^6}$

Simplify.

5. $\sqrt{50x^4y^8}$

6. $\sqrt[4]{32m^7n^9}$

Multiply and simplify.

7. $6\sqrt{4x^2} \cdot 2\sqrt{9x^2y^2}$

8. $\sqrt[3]{9} \cdot \sqrt[3]{9}$

9. $\sqrt[4]{16x^8} \cdot \sqrt[4]{x^{14}}$

Divide and simplify.

10. $\dfrac{\sqrt{36x^4}}{\sqrt{9x^6}}$

11. $\dfrac{\sqrt[3]{64x^9y^3}}{\sqrt[3]{8x^3}}$

Simplify. Rationalize all denominators.

12. $10\sqrt[3]{81} - 8\sqrt[3]{24}$

13. $\dfrac{4 + \sqrt{12}}{4 - \sqrt{12}}$

14. $\sqrt{48} - 3\sqrt{27} + 2\sqrt{75}$

15. $(3 + \sqrt{63})(1 + \sqrt{7})$

16. $\dfrac{\sqrt{x}}{\sqrt{6y^3}}$

Write each expression in exponential form.

17. $-\sqrt{17}$

18. $\sqrt[3]{y^8}$

Write each expression in radical form.

19. $m^{\frac{3}{7}}$

20. $y^{-\frac{4}{3}}$

Simplify each expression.

21. $(-27)^{\frac{2}{3}}$

22. $(16)^{\frac{3}{4}}$

Write each expression in simplest form.

23. $7\sqrt[3]{2x} - 3\sqrt[3]{2x}$

24. $2\sqrt{32x^2} + 3\sqrt{72x^2}$

25. $\sqrt[3]{125x^6} - \sqrt[3]{27x^6}$

26. $\sqrt[4]{7} - \sqrt[3]{7}$

27. $(\sqrt{y} - \sqrt{3})(\sqrt{y} + 2\sqrt{3})$

28. $\left(16x^{\frac{1}{4}}y^{\frac{3}{4}}\right)^{-4}$

29. $\left(\dfrac{x^{\frac{1}{3}}}{y^{\frac{2}{3}}}\right)^9$

30. $\left(\dfrac{x^{-10}}{x^5}\right)^{\frac{2}{5}}$

31. The radius of a circle can be expressed as $r = \sqrt{\dfrac{A}{\pi}}$ inches where r is the radius and A is the area of the circle. If the area of a circle is 169π in.^{2}, what is its radius?

Do you UNDERSTAND?

32. What are the real roots of $\sqrt{-16}$? Explain.

© 33. Error Analysis Identify the error in this statement.
$$\frac{\sqrt[3]{x}}{\sqrt[3]{y}} \cdot \frac{\sqrt[3]{y}}{\sqrt[3]{y}} = \frac{\sqrt[3]{xy}}{y}$$

© 34. Reasoning If $0^{\frac{2}{3}} = 0$, why is $0^{-\frac{2}{3}}$ undefined?

35. Given that x and y are integers, explain why the product of $x + \sqrt{y}$ and its conjugate will always be an integer.

© 36. Reasoning Explain why $(-8)^{\frac{1}{2}} \neq -(8)^{\frac{1}{2}}$, but $(-27)^{\frac{1}{3}} = -(27)^{\frac{1}{3}}$.

6-5 Solving Square Root and Other Radical Equations

Common Core State Standards

A-REI.A.2 Solve simple rational and radical equations in one variable, and . . . show how extraneous solutions may arise. **Also A-CED.A.4**

MP 1, MP 2, MP 3, MP 4

Objective To solve square root and other radical equations

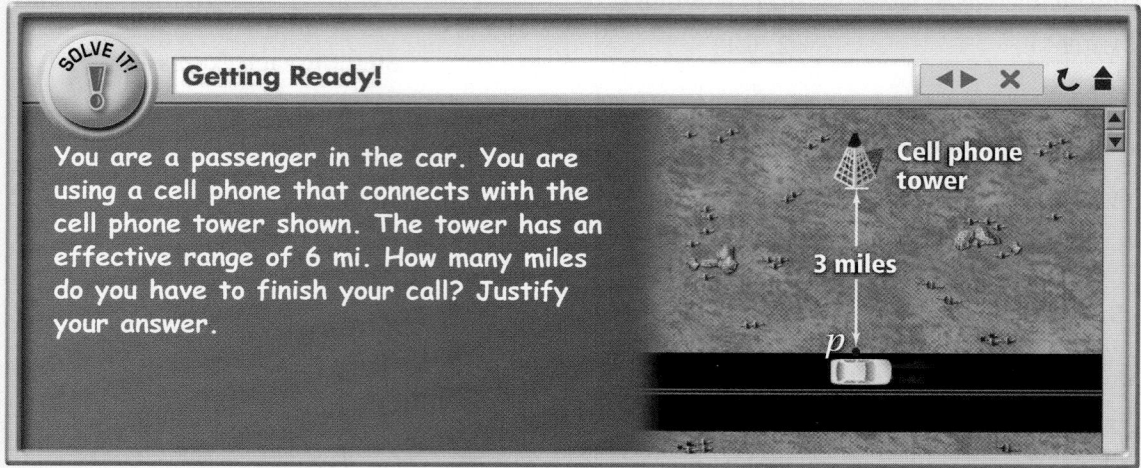

Getting Ready!

You are a passenger in the car. You are using a cell phone that connects with the cell phone tower shown. The tower has an effective range of 6 mi. How many miles do you have to finish your call? Justify your answer.

Cell phone tower

3 miles

p

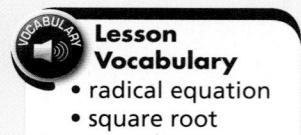
Lesson Vocabulary
• radical equation
• square root equation

A **radical equation** is an equation that has a variable in a radicand or a variable with a rational exponent. If the radical has index 2, the equation is a **square root equation**. In this lesson, assume that all radicals and expressions with rational exponents represent real numbers.

Essential Understanding Solving a square root equation may require that you square each side of the equation. This can introduce extraneous solutions.

To solve a radical equation, isolate the radical on one side of the equation. Then raise each side to the power suggested by the index.

Problem 1 Solving a Square Root Equation

What is the solution of $3 + \sqrt{2x - 3} = 8$?

$$3 + \sqrt{2x - 3} = 8$$
$$\sqrt{2x - 3} = 5 \qquad \text{Isolate the radical expression.}$$
$$(\sqrt{2x - 3})^2 = 5^2 \qquad \text{Square each side.}$$
$$2x - 3 = 25$$
$$2x = 28 \qquad \text{Add 3 to each side.}$$
$$x = 14 \qquad \text{Divide each side by 2.}$$

Think

Do you need to introduce a ± sign here?
No, when you take the square root of each side of an equation you do, but here you are squaring both sides of the equation.

Check

$$3 + \sqrt{2x - 3} = 8 \qquad \text{Write the original equation.}$$

$$3 + \sqrt{2(14) - 3} \stackrel{?}{=} 8 \qquad \text{Substitute 14 for } x.$$

$$3 + \sqrt{25} \stackrel{?}{=} 8 \qquad \text{Simplify.}$$

$$3 + 5 \stackrel{?}{=} 8$$

$$8 = 8 \ \checkmark$$

Got It? **1.** What is the solution of $\sqrt{4x + 1} - 5 = 0$?

To solve equations of the form $x^{\frac{m}{n}} = k$, raise each side of the equation to the power $\frac{n}{m}$, the reciprocal of $\frac{m}{n}$. If either m or n is even, then $\left(x^{\frac{m}{n}}\right)^{\frac{n}{m}} = |x|$.

 Problem 2 Solving Other Radical Equations

A What is the solution of $3(x + 1)^{\frac{2}{3}} = 12$?

Know	Need	Plan
• The equation • The power of the exponential expression	Solution of the equation	• Isolate the exponential expression. • Use the inverse of the power to simplify and solve the equation.

Think

How can you get rid of the rational exponent?
Raise each side to the reciprocal power.

$$3(x + 1)^{\frac{2}{3}} = 12$$

$$(x + 1)^{\frac{2}{3}} = 4 \qquad \text{Divide each side by 3.}$$

$$\left((x + 1)^{\frac{2}{3}}\right)^{\frac{3}{2}} = 4^{\frac{3}{2}} \qquad \text{Raise each side to the } \frac{3}{2} \text{ power.}$$

$$(x + 1)^{\frac{6}{6}} = 4^{\frac{3}{2}}$$

$$|x + 1| = 8 \qquad \boxed{\text{Since the numerator of } \frac{2}{3} \text{ is even, } (x^{\frac{2}{3}})^{\frac{3}{2}} = |x|}$$

$$x + 1 = \pm 8$$

$$x = 7 \text{ or } x = -9$$

The solutions are 7 and -9.

Check

$$3(x + 1)^{\frac{2}{3}} = 12 \qquad\qquad 3(x + 1)^{\frac{2}{3}} = 12$$

$$3(7 + 1)^{\frac{2}{3}} \stackrel{?}{=} 12 \qquad\qquad 3(-9 + 1)^{\frac{2}{3}} \stackrel{?}{=} 12$$

$$3(2^3)^{\frac{2}{3}} \stackrel{?}{=} 12 \qquad\qquad 3((-2)^3)^{\frac{2}{3}} \stackrel{?}{=} 12$$

$$3(2)^2 \stackrel{?}{=} 12 \qquad\qquad 3(-2)^2 \stackrel{?}{=} 12$$

$$12 = 12 \ \checkmark \qquad\qquad 12 = 12 \ \checkmark$$

B What is the solution of $3\sqrt[5]{(x+1)^3} + 1 = 25$?

$$3\sqrt[5]{(x+1)^3} + 1 = 25$$

$$3(x+1)^{\frac{3}{5}} + 1 = 25 \qquad \text{Rewrite the radical using a rational exponent.}$$

$$3(x+1)^{\frac{3}{5}} = 24 \qquad \text{Subtract 1 from each side.}$$

$$(x+1)^{\frac{3}{5}} = 8 \qquad \text{Divide each side by 3.}$$

$$((x+1)^{\frac{3}{5}})^{\frac{5}{3}} = 8^{\frac{5}{3}} \qquad \text{Raise each side to the } \frac{5}{3} \text{ power.}$$

$$x + 1 = 32 \qquad \text{Simplify.}$$

$$x = 31 \qquad \text{Subtract 1 from each side.}$$

The solution is 31.

 Got It? 2. What are the solution(s) of $2(x+3)^{\frac{2}{3}} = 8$?

Think

Why is isolating the variable important?
If you raise each side of $3\sqrt[5]{(x+1)^3} + 1 = 25$ to the $\frac{5}{3}$ power you will end up with a more complicated equation, not a simpler one.

 Problem 3 **Using Radical Equations** **STEM**

Earth Science For Meteor Crater in Arizona, the formula $d = 2\sqrt[3]{\dfrac{V}{0.3}}$ relates the diameter d of the rim (in meters) to the volume V (in cubic meters). What is the volume of Meteor Crater? (All values are approximate.)

— 1.2 km —

$$d = 2\sqrt[3]{\frac{V}{0.3}}$$

$$\frac{d}{2} = \sqrt[3]{\frac{V}{0.3}} \qquad \text{Solve for } V. \text{ First divide each side by 2.}$$

$$\left(\frac{d}{2}\right)^3 = \frac{V}{0.3} \qquad \text{Cube each side.}$$

$$0.3\left(\frac{d}{2}\right)^3 = V \qquad \text{Multiply each side by 0.3.}$$

$$0.3\left(\frac{1200}{2}\right)^3 = V \qquad \text{Substitute 1200 for } d.$$

$$64,800,000 = V \qquad \text{Simplify.}$$

The volume of Meteor Crater is about 64,800,000 m³.

Think

What is the diameter in meters?
$1.2\ km = 1.2 \times 1000\ m$.

 Got It? 3. Suppose the diameter of a similarly shaped crater is 1 km. What is the volume of the crater? Use the formula given in Problem 3.

When you raise each side of an equation to a power, it is possible to introduce extraneous solutions. Therefore, it becomes very important that you check all solutions in the original equation. A correct solution will give a true statement. An extraneous solution will give a false statement.

 Problem 4 Checking for Extraneous Solutions

What is the solution of $\sqrt{x+7} - 5 = x$? Check your results.

Think

How do you square a binomial?
Use the formula,
$(a+b)^2 = a^2 + 2ab + b^2$.

$$\sqrt{x+7} - 5 = x$$

$$\sqrt{x+7} = x + 5 \qquad \text{Isolate the radical.}$$

$$\left(\sqrt{x+7}\right)^2 = (x+5)^2 \qquad \text{Square each side.}$$

$$x + 7 = x^2 + 10x + 25 \qquad \text{Simplify.}$$

$$0 = x^2 + 9x + 18 \qquad \text{Combine like terms.}$$

$$0 = (x+3)(x+6) \qquad \text{Factor.}$$

$$x = -3 \text{ or } x = -6 \qquad \text{Zero-Product Property}$$

Check

$$\sqrt{x+7} - 5 = x$$
$$\sqrt{-3+7} - 5 \overset{?}{=} -3$$
$$\sqrt{4} - 5 \overset{?}{=} -3$$
$$2 - 5 \overset{?}{=} -3$$
$$-3 = -3 ✔$$

The only solution is -3.

$$\sqrt{x+7} - 5 = x$$
$$\sqrt{-6+7} - 5 \overset{?}{=} -6$$
$$\sqrt{1} - 5 \overset{?}{=} -6$$
$$1 - 5 \overset{?}{=} -6$$
$$-4 \neq -6$$

false

 Got It? **4. a.** What is the solution of $\sqrt{5x-1} + 3 = x$? Check your results.
   b. Reasoning When should you check for extraneous solutions? Explain.

In this lesson you studied algebraic methods of solving square root and radical equations. In Lesson 6-8 you will study the graphs of square root functions. These graphs can help you find solutions and identify extraneous solutions.

The calculator screen shows the graphs **Y1 = $\sqrt{(x + 7)}$ − 5** and **Y2 = x.** From the graph, it is clear that -3 is a solution of $\sqrt{x+7} - 5 = x$, and -6 is not a solution.

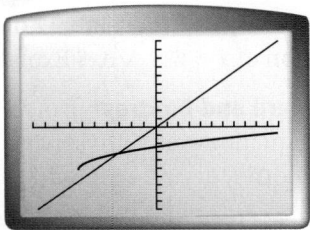

If an equation contains two radical expressions (or two terms with rational exponents), isolate one of the radicals (or one of the terms), then eliminate it (or its rational exponent). Isolate the more complicated radical expression first. In the resulting equation, simplify the expressions before you eliminate the second radical.

 Problem 5 Solving an Equation With Two Radicals

What is the solution of $\sqrt{2x + 1} - \sqrt{x} = 1$?

Plan

Which radical expression should you isolate first?
Isolate the more complicated radical first, $\sqrt{2x + 1}$.

$$\sqrt{2x + 1} - \sqrt{x} = 1$$

$$\sqrt{2x + 1} = \sqrt{x} + 1 \qquad \text{Isolate the more complicated radical.}$$

$$(\sqrt{2x + 1})^2 = (\sqrt{x} + 1)^2 \qquad \text{Square each side.}$$

$$2x + 1 = x + 2\sqrt{x} + 1$$

$$x = 2\sqrt{x} \qquad \text{Isolate } 2\sqrt{x}.$$

$$x^2 = (2\sqrt{x})^2 \qquad \text{Square each side.}$$

$$x^2 = 4x$$

$$x^2 - 4x = 0 \qquad \text{Subtract } 4x \text{ from each side.}$$

$$x(x - 4) = 0 \qquad \text{Factor.}$$

$$x = 0 \text{ or } x = 4 \qquad \text{Zero-Product Property}$$

Check

$$\sqrt{2x + 1} - \sqrt{x} = 1 \qquad\qquad \sqrt{2x + 1} - \sqrt{x} = 1$$

$$\sqrt{2(0) + 1} - \sqrt{0} \stackrel{?}{=} 1 \qquad\qquad \sqrt{2(4) + 1} - \sqrt{4} \stackrel{?}{=} 1$$

$$\sqrt{1} - 0 \stackrel{?}{=} 1 \qquad\qquad\qquad \sqrt{9} - \sqrt{4} \stackrel{?}{=} 1$$

$$1 - 0 \stackrel{?}{=} 1 \qquad\qquad\qquad\quad 3 - 2 \stackrel{?}{=} 1$$

$$1 = 1 \checkmark \qquad\qquad\qquad\qquad 1 = 1 \checkmark$$

The solutions are 0 and 4.

Got It? **5.** What is the solution of $\sqrt{5x + 4} - \sqrt{x} = 4$?

Lesson Check

Do you know HOW?

Solve. Check for extraneous solutions.

1. $\sqrt{4x - 23} - 3 = 2$ **2.** $-\sqrt[3]{x} + 3 = 0$

3. $5\sqrt{x} + 7 = 8$ **4.** $3\sqrt{x} = 6$

5. $5 - 2\sqrt{x} = 3$ **6.** $\sqrt[3]{x} = 8$

Do you UNDERSTAND?  MATHEMATICAL PRACTICES

 7. Vocabulary Which value, 12 or 3, is an extraneous solution of $x - 6 = \sqrt{3x}$? Explain your reasoning.

 8. Compare and Contrast How is solving a square root equation similar to solving an absolute value equation? How is it different?

Practice and Problem-Solving Exercises

MATHEMATICAL PRACTICES

 **Practice**

Solve.

⬤ See Problem 1.

9. $3\sqrt{x} + 3 = 15$

10. $4\sqrt{x} - 1 = 3$

11. $\sqrt{x + 3} = 5$

12. $\sqrt{x + 1} = 4$

13. $\sqrt{2x - 1} = 3$

14. $\sqrt{x + 2} - 2 = 0$

15. $\sqrt{3x + 4} = 4$

16. $\sqrt{2x + 3} - 7 = 0$

17. $\sqrt{6 - 3x} - 2 = 0$

Solve.

⬤ See Problem 2.

18. $(x + 5)^{\frac{2}{3}} = 4$

19. $(x + 2)^{\frac{2}{3}} = 9$

20. $3(x - 2)^{\frac{3}{4}} = 24$

21. $3(x + 3)^{\frac{3}{4}} = 81$

22. $(x + 1)^{\frac{3}{2}} - 2 = 25$

23. $3 + (4 - x)^{\frac{3}{2}} = 11$

24. Volume A spherical water tank holds 9000 ft^3 of water. What is the diameter of the tank? $\left(Hint: \frac{1}{6}\, d^3\pi = V\right)$

⬤ See Problem 3.

 25. Hydraulics The formula $\frac{\pi d^2 v}{4} = Q$ models the diameter of a pipe where Q is the maximum flow of water in a pipe, and v is the velocity of the water. What is the diameter of a pipe that allows a maximum flow of 30 ft^3/min of water flowing at a velocity of 400 ft/min? Round your answer to the nearest inch.

Solve. Check for extraneous solutions.

⬤ See Problem 4.

26. $\sqrt{3x + 7} = x - 1$

27. $(5 - x)^{\frac{1}{2}} = x + 1$

28. $\sqrt{-3x - 5} = x + 3$

29. $\sqrt{11x + 3} - 2x = 0$

30. $(5x - 4)^{\frac{1}{2}} - x = 0$

31. $\sqrt{3x + 13} - 5 = x$

32. $\sqrt{x + 7} + 5 = x$

33. $(x + 3)^{\frac{1}{2}} - 1 = x$

34. $\sqrt{x + 7} - x = 1$

Solve. Check for extraneous solutions.

⬤ See Problem 5.

35. $\sqrt{3x} = \sqrt{x + 6}$

36. $(2x)^{\frac{1}{2}} = (x + 5)^{\frac{1}{2}}$

37. $(7x + 6)^{\frac{1}{2}} - (9 + 4x)^{\frac{1}{2}} = 0$

38. $\sqrt{3x + 2} - \sqrt{2x + 7} = 0$

39. $(x + 5)^{\frac{1}{2}} - (5 - 2x)^{\frac{1}{4}} = 0$

40. $(x - 2)^{\frac{1}{2}} - (28 - 2x)^{\frac{1}{4}} = 0$

41. $\sqrt{5 - x} - \sqrt{x} = 1$

42. $\sqrt{3x + 1} - \sqrt{x + 1} = 2$

43. $\sqrt{2x + 6} - \sqrt{x - 1} = 2$

44. $\sqrt{3 - x} + \sqrt{x + 2} = 3$

 **Apply**

© **45. Think About a Plan** A hexagonal tray of vegetables has an area of 450 cm^2. What is the length of each side of the hexagon?
- What is the area of the triangle at the bottom in terms of the side length?
- How can you use the diagram at the right to find the formula for the area of the hexagon? (*Hint:* Six triangles make one hexagon.)

46. Traffic Signs A stop sign is a regular octagon, formed by cutting triangles off the corners of a square. If a stop sign measures 36 in. from top to bottom, what is the length of each side?

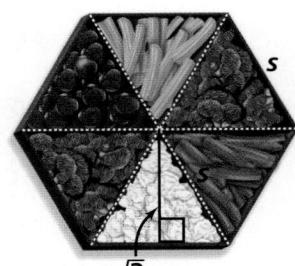

s

$\dfrac{s\sqrt{3}}{2}$

47. Mental Math What is the solution? $\sqrt{x+11} = 4$

48. You can find the area A of a square whose side is s units with the formula $A = s^2$. What is the best estimate for the side of a square with an area of 32 m^2?

- **A** 4.2 m
- **B** 5.7 m
- **C** 8.0 m
- **D** 16 m

Solve. Check for extraneous solutions.

49. $3\sqrt{2x} - 3 = 9$

50. $2(2x)^{\frac{1}{3}} + 1 = 5$

51. $\sqrt{2x-1} - 3 = 0$

52. $(2x+3)^{\frac{1}{2}} - 7 = 0$

53. $\sqrt{x^2+3} = x+1$

54. $(2x+3)^{\frac{3}{4}} - 3 = 5$

55. $2(x-1)^{\frac{4}{3}} + 4 = 36$

56. $x^{\frac{1}{2}} - (x-5)^{\frac{1}{2}} = 2$

57. $\sqrt{x} = \sqrt{x-8} + 2$

58. $(x-3)^{\frac{2}{3}} = x - 7$

59. Error Analysis A student said that 4 and 1 are the solutions of the problem shown. Describe and correct the student's error.

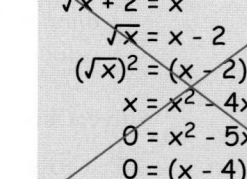
$\sqrt{x} + 2 = x$
$\sqrt{x} = x - 2$
$(\sqrt{x})^2 = (x-2)^2$
$x = x^2 - 4x + 4$
$0 = x^2 - 5x + 4$
$0 = (x-4)(x-1)$

STEM 60. Physics The velocity v of an object dropped from a tall building is given by the formula $v = \sqrt{64d}$, where d is the distance the object has dropped. Solve the formula for d.

61. Open-Ended Write an equation that has two radical expressions and no real roots.

62. Reasoning You have solved equations containing square roots by squaring each side. You were using the property that if $a = b$ then $a^2 = b^2$. Show that the following statements are *not* true for all real numbers.
a. If $a^2 = b^2$ then $a = b$.
b. If $a \le b$ then $a^2 \le b^2$.

63. A teacher asked students why it is necessary to check for extraneous roots when squaring both sides of the equation. Which of the following answers is the best? Is this answer complete? Explain.
- **A** Because the squared equation can have negative roots.
- **B** Because squaring is multiplication, and any multiplication is a potential source of extraneous roots.
- **C** Because when you square both sides of the equation $a = b$, you add to the solution set the roots of the equation $a = -b$.
- **D** Because any operation with an equation may result in extraneous roots.

Solve. Check for extraneous solutions.

64. $\sqrt{x+1} + \sqrt{2x} = \sqrt{5x+3}$

65. $\sqrt{x + \sqrt{2x}} = \sqrt{2x}$

66. $\sqrt{x + \sqrt{2x}} = 2$

67. $\sqrt{\sqrt{x+25}} = \sqrt{x+5}$

Challenge

68. Reasoning Devise a plan to find the value of x.

$$x = \sqrt{2 + \sqrt{2 + \sqrt{2 + \cdots}}}$$

For each set of values, determine which is greater without using a calculator.

69. $\sqrt{6}$ or $\sqrt{2} + 1$

70. $\sqrt{3} + \sqrt{11}$ or 5

71. $\sqrt{10}$ or $\sqrt{2} + \sqrt{3}$

72. $\sqrt{19} + \sqrt{3}$ or $\sqrt{5} + \sqrt{13}$

Standardized Test Prep

73. What is the solution of $(x + 2)^{\frac{3}{4}} = 27$?

Ⓐ $x = 27$ Ⓑ $x = 79$ Ⓒ $x = 81$ Ⓓ $x = 83$

74. A problem on a test asked students to solve a fifth-degree polynomial equation with rational coefficients. Adam found the following roots: -11.5, $\sqrt{2}$, $\frac{2i + 6}{2}$, $-\sqrt{2}$ and $3 - i$. His teacher wrote that four of these roots are correct, and one is incorrect. Which root is incorrect?

Ⓕ -11.5 Ⓖ $\sqrt{2}$ Ⓗ $\frac{2i + 6}{2}$ Ⓘ $3 - i$

75. Which expression represents the solution of the equation $\frac{x}{y} = \frac{c}{a + b}$ solved for a?

Ⓐ $\frac{c}{b} - \frac{x}{y}$ Ⓑ $\frac{yc}{a + b}$ Ⓒ $\frac{yc}{x} + b$ Ⓓ $\frac{yc - xb}{x}$

Short Response

76. To rationalize the denominator of $\sqrt[4]{\frac{4}{25}}$, by what number would you multiply the numerator and denominator of the fraction?

 ## Apply What You've Learned

 **MATHEMATICAL PRACTICES**

MP 6

Look back at the information on page 359 about the America's Cup rule and the dimensions for the new yacht you are designing. In the Apply What You've Learned in Lesson 6-4, you wrote the expression on the left side of the America's Cup rule in radical form. Now, you will use this form of the expression to write a function $f(D)$ that gives the value of the expression for the new yacht in terms of the displacement D.

a. To write the function, what variables will you replace with specific values? What are those values?

b. Write and simplify the function.

c. Describe how you could use the function to write and solve an equation to find the displacement that makes the value of the left side of the America's Cup rule exactly 24.

6-6 Function Operations

© **Common Core State Standards**

F-BF.A.1b Combine standard function types using arithmetic operations.

F-BF.A.1c Compose functions.

MP 1, MP 2, MP 3, MP 4

Objectives To add, subtract, multiply, and divide functions
To find the composite of two functions

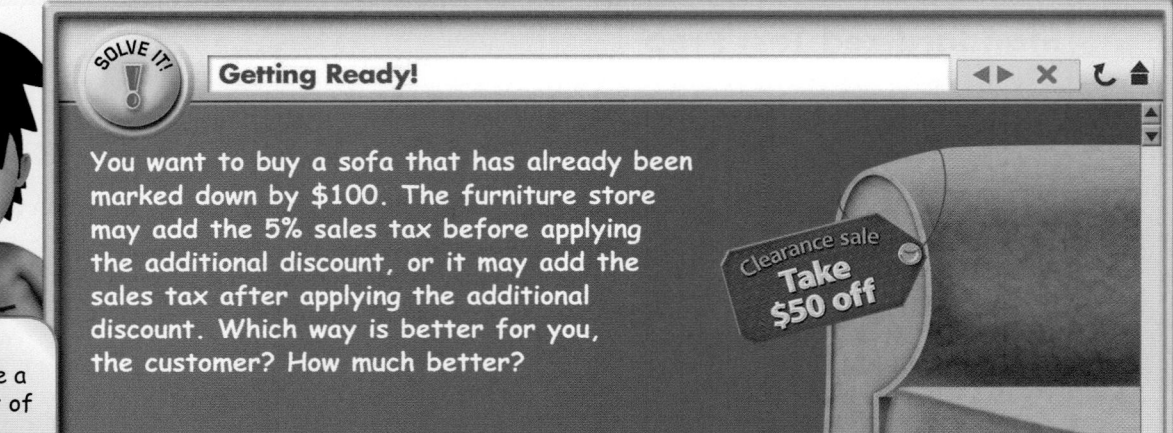

Getting Ready!

You want to buy a sofa that has already been marked down by $100. The furniture store may add the 5% sales tax before applying the additional discount, or it may add the sales tax after applying the additional discount. Which way is better for you, the customer? How much better?

Solve a simpler problem first. Use a value for the cost of the sofa.

Clearance sale
Take $50 off

The final cost of the sofa in the Solve It involves two functions: one that gives an additional discount and one that multiplies to find the sales tax.

Lesson Vocabulary
• composite function

Essential Understanding You can add, subtract, multiply, and divide functions based on how you perform these operations for real numbers. One difference, however, is that you must consider the domain of each function.

---

take note

Key Concepts   Function Operations

Addition	$(f + g)(x) = f(x) + g(x)$
Subtraction	$(f - g)(x) = f(x) - g(x)$
Multiplication	$(f \cdot g)(x) = f(x) \cdot g(x)$
Division	$\left(\dfrac{f}{g}\right)(x) = \dfrac{f(x)}{g(x)}, g(x) \neq 0$

The domains of the sum, difference, product, and quotient functions consist of the *x*-values that are in the domains of *both f* and *g*. Also, the domain of the quotient function does not contain any *x*-value for which $g(x) = 0$.

Problem 1 Adding and Subtracting Functions

Let $f(x) = 4x + 7$ and $g(x) = \sqrt{x} + x$. What are $f + g$ and $f - g$? What are their domains?

$$(f + g)(x) = f(x) + g(x) = (4x + 7) + (\sqrt{x} + x) = 5x + \sqrt{x} + 7$$

$$(f - g)(x) = f(x) - g(x) = (4x + 7) - (\sqrt{x} + x) = 3x - \sqrt{x} + 7$$

Think

What determines the domain of g?
Because there is a square root of x, x must be ≥ 0.

The domain of f is the set of all real numbers. The domain of g is all $x \geq 0$. The domain of both $f + g$ and $f - g$ is the set of numbers common to the domains of both f and g, which is all $x \geq 0$.

 Got It? 1. Let $f(x) = 2x^2 + 8$ and $g(x) = x - 3$. What are $f + g$ and $f - g$? What are their domains?

 Problem 2 Multiplying and Dividing Functions

Let $f(x) = x^2 - 9$ and $g(x) = x + 3$. What are $f \cdot g$ and $\frac{f}{g}$ and their domains?

$$(f \cdot g)(x) = f(x) \cdot g(x) = (x^2 - 9)(x + 3)$$
$$= x^3 + 3x^2 - 9x - 27$$

$$\left(\frac{f}{g}\right)(x) = \frac{f(x)}{g(x)} = \frac{x^2 - 9}{x + 3} = \frac{(x - 3)(x + 3)}{x + 3} = x - 3, x \neq -3$$

Think

Is the domain of $\frac{f}{g}$ the domain of $x - 3$?
No; the fraction can only be simplified and the function is only defined when $g(x) \neq -3$.

The domain of both f and g is the set of real numbers, so the domain of $f \cdot g$ is also the set of real numbers.

The domain of $\frac{f}{g}$ is the set of all real numbers except $x \neq -3$, because $g(-3) = 0$. The definition of $\frac{f}{g}$ requires that you consider the zero denominator in the *original* expression for $\frac{f(x)}{g(x)}$ despite the fact that the simplified form has the domain all real numbers.

 Got It? 2. Let $f(x) = 3x^2 - 11x - 4$ and $g(x) = 3x + 1$. What are $f \cdot g$ and $\frac{f}{g}$ and their domains?

The diagram shows what happens when you apply one function $g(x)$ after another function $f(x)$.

The output from the first function becomes the input for the second function. When you combine two functions as in the diagram, you form a **composite function**.

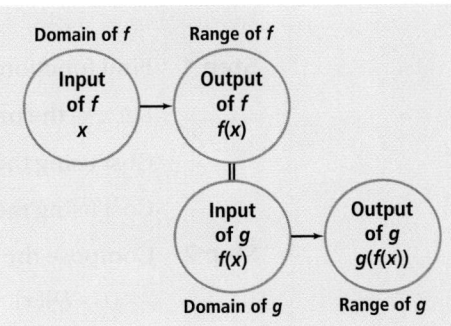

Key Concept Composition of Functions

The composition of function g with function f is written as $g \circ f$ and is defined as $(g \circ f)(x) = g(f(x))$. The domain of $g \circ f$ consists of the x-values in the domain of f for which $f(x)$ is in the domain of g.

$(g \circ f)(x) = g(f(x))$ **1.** Evaluate $f(x)$ first.

                    2. Then use $f(x)$ as the input for g.

Function composition is not commutative since $f(g(x))$ does not always equal $g(f(x))$.

Problem 3 **Composing Functions**

GRIDDED RESPONSE

Let $f(x) = x - 5$ and $g(x) = x^2$. What is $(g \circ f)(-3)$?

Think

Which function is substituted into the other?

Use $f(x)$ as the input for g.

Method 1

$$(g \circ f)(x) = g(f(x))$$
$$= g(x - 5) = (x - 5)^2$$
$$(g \circ f)(-3) = (-3 - 5)^2$$
$$= (-8)^2$$
$$= 64$$

Method 2

$$(g \circ f)(-3) = g(f(-3))$$
$$= g(-3 - 5)$$
$$= g(-8)$$
$$= (-8)^2$$
$$= 64$$

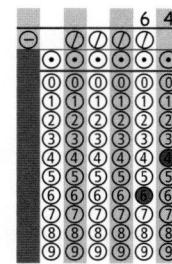

Got It? **3.** What is $(f \circ g)(-3)$ for the functions f and g defined in Problem 3?

Problem 4 **Using Composite Functions**

You have a coupon good for $5 off the price of any large pizza. You also get a 10% discount on any pizza if you show your student ID. How much more would you pay for a large pizza if the cashier applies the coupon first?

Know	Need	Plan
The coupon value and the discount rate	The difference between the results of applying the discount or coupon first	• Compose two functions in two ways. • Then find the difference in their results.

Step 1 Find functions C and D that model the cost of a large pizza.

Let $x =$ the price of a large pizza.

Cost using the coupon: $C(x) = x - 5$

Cost using the 10% discount: $D(x) = x - 0.1x = 0.9x$

Step 2 Compose the functions to apply the discount and then the coupon.

$$(C \circ D)(x) = C(D(x)) \qquad \text{Apply the discount, } D(x), \text{ first.}$$
$$= C(0.9x) = 0.9x - 5$$

Step 3 Compose the functions to apply the coupon and then the discount.

$$(D \circ C)(x) = D(C(x)) \quad \text{Apply the coupon, } C(x), \text{ first.}$$

$$= D(x - 5) = 0.9(x - 5) = 0.9x - 4.5$$

Step 4 Subtract the functions to find how much more you would pay if the cashier applies the coupon first.

$$(D \circ C)(x) - (C \circ D)(x) = (0.9x - 4.5) - (0.9x - 5)$$

$$= -4.5 + 5$$

$$= 0.5$$

You pay $.50 more if the cashier applies the coupon first.

  Got It? **4.** A store is offering a 15% discount on all items. Also, employees get a 20% employee discount. Write composite functions

    a. to model taking the 15% discount and then the 20% discount.

    b. to model taking the 20% discount and then the 15% discount.

    c. Reasoning If you were an employee, which discount would you take first? Why?

 ## Lesson Check

Do you know HOW?

Let $f(x) = 3x - 2$ and $g(x) = x^2 + 1$. Perform each function operation.

1. $(f \cdot g)(x)$ **2.** $(f - g)(x)$

3. $(f \circ g)(x)$ **4.** $f(x) + g(x)$

5. $g(x) - f(x)$ **6.** $f(x) - g(x)$

Do you UNDERSTAND?

7. Error Analysis Your friend used some simple functions and found that $(f \circ g)(x) = (g \circ f)(x)$, and concluded that function composition is commutative. Give an example to show that your friend is mistaken.

8. Open-Ended Find two functions f and g such that $f(g(x)) = x$ for all real numbers x.

 ## Practice and Problem-Solving Exercises

 **Practice**   Let $f(x) = 7x + 5$ and $g(x) = x^2$. Perform each function operation and then find the domain of the result.    **See Problems 1 and 2.**

    9. $(f + g)(x)$ **10.** $(f - g)(x)$ **11.** $(g - f)(x)$

    12. $(f \cdot g)(x)$ **13.** $\frac{f}{g}(x)$ **14.** $\frac{g}{f}(x)$

Let $f(x) = 2 - x$ and $g(x) = \frac{1}{x}$. Perform each function operation and then find the domain of the result.

    15. $(f + g)(x)$ **16.** $(f - g)(x)$ **17.** $(g - f)(x)$

    18. $(f \cdot g)(x)$ **19.** $\frac{f}{g}(x)$ **20.** $\frac{g}{f}(x)$

Let $f(x) = 2x^2 + x - 3$ and $g(x) = x - 1$. Perform each function operation and then find the domain.

21. $(f + g)(x)$

22. $(f - g)(x)$

23. $(g - f)(x)$

24. $(f \cdot g)(x)$

25. $\dfrac{f}{g}(x)$

26. $\dfrac{g}{f}(x)$

Let $g(x) = 2x$ and $h(x) = x^2 + 4$. Find each value or expression.

See Problem 3.

27. $(h \circ g)(1)$

28. $(h \circ g)(-5)$

29. $(h \circ g)(-2)$

30. $(g \circ h)(-2)$

31. $(g \circ h)(0)$

32. $(g \circ h)(a)$

33. $(g \circ g)(a)$

34. $(h \circ h)(a)$

35. $(h \circ g)(a)$

Let $f(x) = x^2$ and $g(x) = x - 3$. Find each value or expression.

36. $(g \circ f)(-2)$

37. $(f \circ g)(-2)$

38. $(g \circ f)(0)$

39. $(f \circ g)(0)$

40. $(g \circ f)(3.5)$

41. $(f \circ g)(3.5)$

42. $(f \circ g)(a)$

43. $(g \circ f)(-a)$

44. $(f \circ g)(-a)$

45. Sales A computer store offers a 5% discount off the list price x for any computer bought with cash, rather than put on credit. At the same time, the manufacturer offers a \$200 rebate for each purchase of a computer.

See Problem 4.

   a. Write a function $f(x)$ to represent the price after the cash discount.
   b. Write a function $g(x)$ to represent the price after the \$200 rebate.
   c. Suppose the list price of a computer is \$1500. Use a composite function to find the price of the computer if the discount is applied before the rebate.
   d. Suppose the list price of a computer is \$1500. Use a composite function to find the price of the computer if the rebate is applied before the discount.

46. Economics Suppose the function $f(x) = 0.15x$ represents the number of U.S. dollars equivalent to x Chinese yuan and the function $g(y) = 14.07y$ represents the number of Mexican pesos equivalent to y U.S. dollars.

   a. Write a composite function that represents the number of Mexican pesos equivalent to x Chinese yuan.
   b. Find the value in Mexican pesos of an item that costs 15 Chinese yuan.

Let $f(x) = 2x + 5$ and $g(x) = x^2 - 3x + 2$. Perform each function operation and then find the domain.

47. $f(x) + g(x)$

48. $3f(x) - 2$

49. $g(x) - f(x)$

50. $-2g(x) + f(x)$

51. $f(x) - g(x) + 10$

52. $4f(x) + 2g(x)$

53. $-f(x) + 4g(x)$

54. $f(x) - 2g(x)$

55. $f(x) \cdot g(x)$

56. $-3f(x) \cdot g(x)$

57. $\dfrac{f(x)}{g(x)}$

58. $\dfrac{5f(x)}{g(x)}$

59. Think About a Plan A craftsman makes and sells violins. The function $I(x) = 5995x$ represents the income in dollars from selling x violins. The function $P(y) = y - 100{,}000$ represents his profit in dollars if he makes an income of y dollars. What is the profit from selling 30 violins?
- How can you write a composite function to represent the craftsman's profit?
- How can you use the composite function to find the profit earned when he sells 30 violins?

60. Suppose your teacher offers to give the whole class a bonus if everyone passes the next math test. The teacher says she will give everyone a 10-point bonus and increase everyone's grade by 9% of their score.
a. You earned a 75 on the test. Would you rather have the 10-point bonus first and then the 9% increase, or the 9% increase first and then the 10-point bonus?
b. Reasoning Is this the best plan for all students? Explain.

61. Sales A salesperson earns a 3% bonus on weekly sales over $5000. Consider the following functions.

$$g(x) = 0.03x \qquad\qquad h(x) = x - 5000$$

a. Explain what each function above represents.
b. Which composition, $(h \circ g)(x)$ or $(g \circ h)(x)$, represents the weekly bonus? Explain.

62. If $(f \circ g)(x) = x^2 - 6x + 8$ and $g(x) = x - 3$, what is $f(x)$?

Let $g(x) = 3x + 2$ and $f(x) = \dfrac{x-2}{3}$. Find each value.

63. $f(g(1))$ **64.** $g(f(-4))$ **65.** $f(g(0))$ **66.** $g(f(2))$

67. $g(g(0))$ **68.** $(g \circ g)(1)$ **69.** $(f \circ g)(-2)$ **70.** $(f \circ f)(0)$

71. Geometry You toss a pebble into a pool of water and watch the circular ripples radiate outward. You find that the function $r(x) = 12.5x$ describes the radius r, in inches, of a circle x seconds after it was formed. The function $A(x) = \pi x^2$ describes the area A of a circle with radius x.
a. Find $(A \circ r)(x)$ when $x = 2$. Interpret your answer.
b. Find the area of a circle 4 seconds after it was formed.

For each pair of functions, find $f(g(x))$ and $g(f(x))$.

72. $f(x) = 3x,\, g(x) = x^2$ **73.** $f(x) = x + 3,\, g(x) = x - 5$

74. $f(x) = 3x^2 + 2,\, g(x) = 2x$ **75.** $f(x) = \dfrac{x-3}{2},\, g(x) = 2x - 3$

76. $f(x) = -x - 7,\, g(x) = 4x$ **77.** $f(x) = \dfrac{x+5}{2},\, g(x) = x^2$

78. Open-Ended Write a function rule that approximates each value.
a. The amount you save is a percent of what you earn. (You choose the percent.)
b. The amount you earn depends on how many hours you work. (You choose the hourly wage.)
c. Write and simplify a composite function that expresses your savings as a function of the number of hours you work. Interpret your results.

Let $f(x) = x^4 + 2x^3 - 5x^2 - 10x$ and $g(x) = x^3 - 3x^2 - 5x + 15$. Perform each function operation and simplify, and then find the domain.

79. $f(x) \cdot g(x)$

80. $\dfrac{f(x)}{g(x)}$

81. $\dfrac{g(x)}{f(x)}$

Find each composition of functions. Simplify your answer.

82. Let $f(x) = \frac{1}{x}$. Find $f(f(f(x)))$.

83. Let $f(x) = 2x - 3$. Find $\dfrac{f(1 + h) - f(1)}{h}$, $h \neq 0$.

84. Let $f(x) = 4x - 1$. Find $\dfrac{f(a + h) - f(a)}{h}$, $h \neq 0$.

85. Let $f(x) = 4x^2 - 1$. Find $\dfrac{f(a + h) - f(a)}{h}$, $h \neq 0$.

Standardized Test Prep

86. Let $f(x) = x + 5$ and $g(x) = x^2 - 25$. What is the domain of $\frac{f}{g}(x)$?

Ⓐ All real numbers

Ⓒ All real numbers except -5

Ⓑ All real numbers except 5

Ⓓ All real numbers except -5 and 5

87. Let $g(x) = x - 3$ and $h(x) = x^2 + 6$. What is $(h \circ g)(1)$?

Ⓕ -14

Ⓖ 4

Ⓗ 10

Ⓘ 15

88. Which number is a solution of $|3 - 2x| < 5$?

Ⓐ -6

Ⓑ -1

Ⓒ 2

Ⓓ 4

89. What is the coefficient of the x^3y^4 term in the expansion of $(3x - y)^7$? Show your work.

Mixed Review

Solve. Check for extraneous solutions.

◀ See Lesson 6-5.

90. $\sqrt{x^2 + 3} = x + 1$

91. $x + 8 = \left(x^2 + 16\right)^{\frac{1}{2}}$

92. $\sqrt{x^2 + 9} = x + 1$

93. $\left(x^2 - 9\right)^{\frac{1}{2}} - x = -3$

94. $\sqrt{x^2 + 12} - 2 = x$

95. $(3x)^{\frac{1}{2}} = (x + 6)^{\frac{1}{2}}$

Expand each binomial.

◀ See Lesson 5-7.

96. $(x + 4)^8$

97. $(x + y)^6$

98. $(2x - y)^4$

99. $(2x - 3y)^7$

100. $(9 - 2x)^5$

101. $(4x - y)^5$

102. $\left(x^2 + x\right)^4$

103. $\left(x^2 + 2y^3\right)^6$

Get Ready! To prepare for Lesson 6-7, do Exercises 104–106.

Graph and solve each system.

◀ See Lesson 3-1.

104. $\begin{cases} y = x - 6 \\ y = x + 6 \end{cases}$

105. $\begin{cases} y = 0.5x + 1 \\ y = 2x - 2 \end{cases}$

106. $\begin{cases} y = \dfrac{x + 4}{5} \\ y = 5x - 4 \end{cases}$

6-7 Inverse Relations and Functions

Common Core State Standards
F-BF.B.4a Solve an equation of the form $f(x) = c$ for a simple function f that has an inverse and write an expression for the inverse. **Also F-BF.B.4c**
MP 1, MP 2, MP 3

Objective To find the inverse of a relation or function

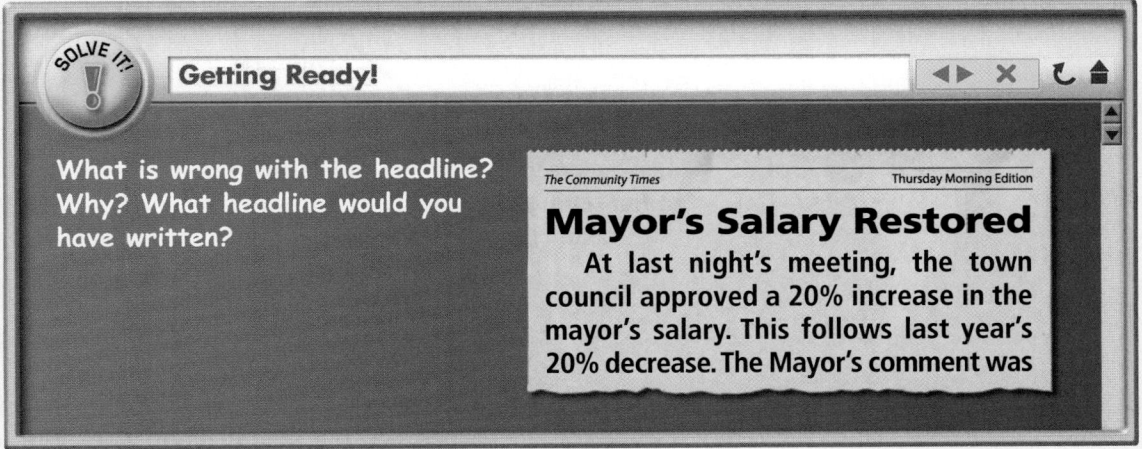

Getting Ready!

What is wrong with the headline? Why? What headline would you have written?

The Community Times — Thursday Morning Edition

Mayor's Salary Restored

At last night's meeting, the town council approved a 20% increase in the mayor's salary. This follows last year's 20% decrease. The Mayor's comment was

Lesson Vocabulary
• inverse relation
• inverse function
• one-to-one function

If a relation pairs element a of its domain to element b of its range, the **inverse relation** pairs b with a. So, if (a, b) is an ordered pair of a relation, then (b, a) is an ordered pair of its inverse. If both a relation and its inverse happen to be functions, they are **inverse functions**.

Essential Understanding The inverse of a function may or may not be a function.

This diagram shows a relation r (a function) and its inverse (not a function). The range of the relation is the domain of the inverse. The domain of the relation is the range of the inverse.

	Relation r		Inverse of r	
	Domain	Range	Domain	Range
	1.2	1	1	1.2
	1.4			1.4
	1.6	2	2	1.6
	1.9			1.9

Problem 1 Finding the Inverse of a Relation

Think

(0, −1) is in *s*. How do you find the corresponding pair in the inverse of *s*?
Switch the coordinates. (−1, 0) is in the inverse of *s*.

A What is the inverse of relation *s*?

Relation *s*

x	y
0	−1
2	0
3	2
4	3

Switch the *x*- and *y*-values to get the inverse. →

Inverse of Relation *s*

x	y
−1	0
0	2
2	3
3	4

B What are the graphs of *s* and its inverse?

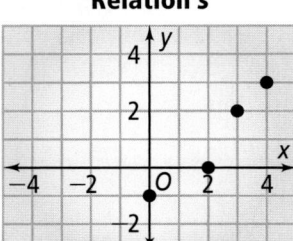

Relation *s*

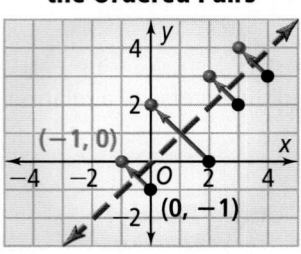

Reversing
the Ordered Pairs

$(-1, 0)$
$(0, -1)$

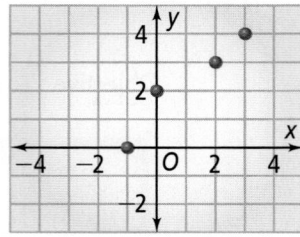

Inverse of *s*

Got It? **1.** **a.** What are the graphs of *t* and its inverse?
b. Reasoning Is *t* a function? Is the inverse
of *t* a function? Explain.

Relation *t*

x	0	1	2	3
y	−5	−4	−3	−3

As shown in Problem 1, the graphs of a relation and its inverse are the reflections of each other in the line $y = x$. If you describe a relation or function by an equation in *x* and *y*, you can switch *x* and *y* to get an equation for the inverse.

Problem 2 Finding an Equation for the Inverse

Think

Why do you solve for *y*?
If you solve the equation for *y*, you can use it to easily generate ordered pairs that are part of the inverse relation.

What is the inverse of the relation described by $y = x^2 - 1$?

$$y = x^2 - 1$$

$$x = y^2 - 1 \quad \text{Switch } x \text{ and } y.$$

$$x + 1 = y^2 \quad \text{Add 1 to each side.}$$

$$\pm \sqrt{x + 1} = y \quad \text{Find the square root of each side to solve for } y.$$

Got It? **2.** What is the inverse of $y = 2x + 8$?

Problem 3 Graphing a Relation and Its Inverse

Think

What does the graph of $y = x^2 - 1$ look like?
The graph of $y = x^2 - 1$ is a translation of $y = x^2$ down one unit.

What are the graphs of $y = x^2 - 1$ and its inverse, $y = \pm \sqrt{x + 1}$?

The graph of $y = x^2 - 1$ is a parabola that opens upward with vertex $(0, -1)$. The graph of the inverse is the reflection of the parabola in the line $y = x$.

Got It? **3.** What are the graphs of $y = 2x + 8$ and its inverse?

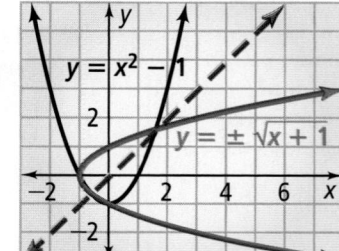

$y = x^2 - 1$

$y = \pm \sqrt{x + 1}$

The inverse of a function f is denoted by f^{-1}. You read f^{-1} as "the inverse of f" or as "f inverse." The notation $f(x)$ is used for functions, but the relation f^{-1} may not even be a function.

© **Problem 4** **Finding an Inverse Function**

Consider the function $f(x) = \sqrt{x-2}$.

A What are the domain and range of f?

The radicand cannot be negative, so the numbers $x \geq 2$ make up the domain. The principal square root is nonnegative, so the numbers $y \geq 0$ make up the range.

B What is f^{-1}, the inverse of f?

$$f(x) = \sqrt{x-2}$$

$y = \sqrt{x-2}$	Rewrite the equation using y.
$x = \sqrt{y-2}$	Switch x and y. Since x equals a principal square root, $x \geq 0$.
$x^2 = y - 2$	Square both sides.
$y = x^2 + 2$	Solve for y.

So, $f^{-1}(x) = x^2 + 2$, for $x \geq 0$.

C What are the domain and range of f^{-1}?

Think

How could a graph help you check your answer?
You could graph f^{-1} and see whether the graph passes the vertical line test. If it does, f^{-1} is a function.

Part (b) shows that the domain of f^{-1} is the range of f—the numbers $x \geq 0$. Since $x^2 \geq 0$, $x^2 + 2 \geq 2$. Therefore, the numbers $y \geq 2$ make up the range of f^{-1}. Note that the range of f^{-1} is the same as the domain of f.

D Is f^{-1} a function? Explain.

For each x in the domain ($x \geq 0$) of f^{-1}, there is only one value of y in the range. So $f^{-1}(x) = x^2 + 2$, $x \geq 0$, is a function.

✓ **Got It?** **4.** Let $g(x) = 6 - 4x$.

a. What are the domain and range of g?
b. What is the inverse of g?
c. What are the domain and range of g^{-1}?
d. Is g^{-1} a function? Explain.

Functions that model real-world behavior are often expressed as formulas with meaningful variables, like $A = \pi r^2$ for the area of a circle. Strictly speaking, the inverse formula would be $r^2 = \pi A$, but this expresses a false relationship between A and r. It is better to leave the variables in place and solve for r as a function of A.

$A = \pi r^2$	Original formula.
$r = \sqrt{\frac{A}{\pi}}$	Same formula, but inversely expressed.

Problem 5 Finding the Inverse of a Formula

The function $d = 4.9t^2$ represents the distance d, in meters, that an object falls in t seconds due to Earth's gravity. Find the inverse of this function. How long, in seconds, does it take for the cliff diver shown to reach the water below?

Think

Why shouldn't you interchange the variables?
Interchanging the variables leads to a false relationship between distance and time.

$d = 4.9t^2$

$t^2 = \dfrac{d}{4.9}$ Solve for t. Do not switch the variables.

$t = \sqrt{\dfrac{d}{4.9}}$ Time must be nonnegative.

$= \sqrt{\dfrac{24}{4.9}}$ Substitute 24 for d.

≈ 2.2 Use a calculator.

It will take about 2.2 seconds for the diver to reach the water.

24 meters

 Got It? **5.** The function $d = \dfrac{v^2}{19.6}$ relates the distance d, in meters, that an object has fallen to its velocity v, in meters per second. Find the inverse of this function. What is the velocity of the cliff diver in meters per second as he enters the water?

You know that for any function f, each x-value in the domain corresponds to exactly one y-value in the range. For a **one-to-one function**, it is also true that each y-value in the range corresponds to exactly one x-value in the domain. A one-to-one function f has an inverse f^{-1} that is also a function. If f maps a to b, then f^{-1} must map b to a.

Domain of f   **Range of f**
Range of f^{-1}   **Domain of f^{-1}**

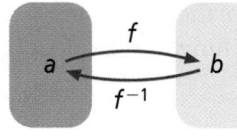

Key Concept **Composition of Inverse Functions**

If f and f^{-1} are inverse functions, then

$(f^{-1} \circ f)(x) = x$ and $(f \circ f^{-1})(x) = x$ for x in the domains of f and f^{-1}, respectively.

This says that the composition of a function and its inverse is essentially the identity function, $id(x) = x$, or $y = x$.

Problem 6 Composing Inverse Functions

For $f(x) = \frac{1}{x-1}$, what is each of the following?

Ⓐ $f^{-1}(x)$

$$f(x) = \frac{1}{x-1}$$

$$y = \frac{1}{x-1} \qquad \text{Rewrite the equation using } y.$$

$$x = \frac{1}{y-1} \qquad \text{Switch } x \text{ and } y.$$

$$x(y-1) = 1 \qquad \text{Solve for } y.$$

$$y - 1 = \frac{1}{x}$$

$$y = \frac{1}{x} + 1$$

So $f^{-1}(x) = \frac{1}{x} + 1$.

Think

Is this a function?
Yes. For each value of x, there is only one value for y.

Ⓑ $(f \circ f^{-1})(1)$

$$(f \circ f^{-1})(1) = f(f^{-1}(1))$$

$$= f\left(\frac{1}{1} + 1\right)$$

$$= f(2)$$

$$= \frac{1}{2-1} = 1$$

Ⓒ $(f^{-1} \circ f)(1)$

$$(f^{-1} \circ f)(1) = f^{-1}(f(1))$$

$$= f^{-1}\left(\frac{1}{1-1}\right)$$

$$= f^{-1}\left(\frac{1}{0}\right) \quad \boxed{\text{undefined}}$$

1 is not in the domain of f. Therefore $(f^{-1} \circ f)(1)$ does not exist.

Got It? **6.** Let $g(x) = \frac{4}{x+2}$. What is each of the following?
    a. $g^{-1}(x)$ **b.** $(g \circ g^{-1})(0)$ **c.** $(g^{-1} \circ g)(0)$

 Lesson Check

Do you know HOW?

Find the inverse of each function. Is the inverse a function?

1. $f(x) = 4x + 3$

2. $f(x) = x^2 - 1$

3. $f(x) = (x+1)^2$

4. For $h(x) = -\frac{1}{x+2}$, find:
    a. $h^{-1}(x)$
    b. $h^{-1}(4)$
    c. Value of x for which the equality $(h \circ h^{-1})(x) = x$ does not hold.

Do you UNDERSTAND? MATHEMATICAL PRACTICES

Ⓒ 5. Vocabulary Does every function have an inverse which is a function? Does every relation have an inverse which is a relation?

Ⓒ 6. Reasoning A function consists of the pairs $(2, 3)$, $(x, 4)$, and $(5, 6)$. What values, if any, may x not assume?

Ⓒ 7. Error Analysis A classmate says that $(f \circ g)^{-1}(x) = (f^{-1} \circ g^{-1})(x)$. Show that this is incorrect by finding examples of $f(x)$ and $g(x)$ for which the equation does not hold.

Practice and Problem-Solving Exercises

MATHEMATICAL PRACTICES

 Practice

See Problem 1.

See Problem 2.

See Problem 3.

See Problem 4.

See Problem 5.

See Problem 6.

Find the inverse of each relation. Graph the given relation and its inverse.

8.

x	y
1	0
2	1
3	0
4	2

9.

x	y
1	0
2	1
3	2
4	3

10.

x	y
0	0
1	1
2	4
3	9

11.

x	y
−3	2
−2	2
−1	2
0	2

Find the inverse of each function. Is the inverse a function?

12. $y = 3x + 1$

13. $y = 2x - 1$

14. $y = 4 - 3x$

15. $y = 5 - 2x^2$

16. $y = x^2 + 4$

17. $y = 3x^2 - 5$

18. $y = (x - 8)^2$

19. $y = (3x - 4)^2$

20. $y = (1 - 2x)^2 + 5$

Graph each relation and its inverse.

21. $y = 2x - 3$

22. $y = 3 - 7x$

23. $y = -x$

24. $y = 3x^2$

25. $y = -x^2$

26. $y = 4x^2 - 2$

27. $y = (x - 1)^2$

28. $y = (2 - x)^2$

29. $y = (3 - 2x)^2 - 1$

For each function, find the inverse and the domain and range of the function and its inverse. Determine whether the inverse is a function.

30. $f(x) = 3x + 4$

31. $f(x) = \sqrt{x - 5}$

32. $f(x) = \sqrt{x + 7}$

33. $f(x) = \sqrt{-2x + 3}$

34. $f(x) = 2x^2 + 2$

35. $f(x) = -x^2 + 1$

36. Temperature The formula for converting from Celsius to Fahrenheit temperatures is $F = \frac{9}{5}C + 32$.

    a. Find the inverse of the formula. Is the inverse a function?

    b. Use the inverse to find the Celsius temperature that corresponds to 25°F.

37. Geometry The formula for the volume of a sphere is $V = \frac{4}{3}\pi r^3$.

    a. Find the inverse of the formula. Is the inverse a function?

    b. Use the inverse to find the radius of a sphere that has a volume of 35,000 ft³.

For Exercises 38–41, $f(x) = 10x - 10$. Find each value.

38. $(f^{-1} \circ f)(10)$

39. $(f \circ f^{-1})(-10)$

40. $(f^{-1} \circ f)(0.2)$

41. $(f \circ f^{-1})(d)$

 **Apply**

Find the inverse of each function. Is the inverse a function?

42. $f(x) = x^3$

43. $f(x) = x^4$

44. $f(x) = \dfrac{2x^2}{5} + 1$

45. $f(x) = 1.5x^2 - 4$

46. $f(x) = \dfrac{3x^2}{4}$

47. $f(x) = \sqrt{2x - 1} + 3$

48. Think About a Plan The velocity of the water that flows from an opening at the base of a tank depends on the height of water above the opening. The function $v(x) = \sqrt{2gx}$ models the velocity v in feet per second where g, the acceleration due to gravity, is about $32\ \text{ft/s}^2$ and x is the height in feet of the water. What is the depth of water when the flow is 40 ft/s, and when the flow is 20 ft/s?
- How can you use inverse functions to help you find the answer?
- What restrictions are on the domain of $v(x)$? of $v^{-1}(x)$?

49. Let $f(x) = 3x^2 - 4$ and $g(x) = x - 2$. Calculate $(f \circ g^{-1})(x)$ for $x = -3$.

50. Writing Explain how you can find the range of the inverse of $f(x) = \sqrt{x - 1}$ without finding the inverse itself.

For each function, find the inverse and the domain and range of the function and its inverse. Determine whether the inverse is a function.

51. $f(x) = -\sqrt{x}$

52. $f(x) = \sqrt{x} + 3$

53. $f(x) = \sqrt{-x + 3}$

54. $f(x) = \sqrt{x + 2}$

55. $f(x) = \dfrac{x^2}{2}$

56. $f(x) = \dfrac{1}{x^2}$

57. $f(x) = (x - 4)^2$

58. $f(x) = (7 - x)^2$

59. $f(x) = \dfrac{1}{(x + 1)^2}$

60. $f(x) = 4 - 2\sqrt{x}$

61. $f(x) = \dfrac{3}{\sqrt{x}}$

62. $f(x) = \dfrac{1}{\sqrt{-2x}}$

63. a. Open-Ended Copy the mapping diagram at the right. Complete it by writing members of the domain and range and connecting them with arrows so that r is a function and r^{-1} is not a function.
b. Repeat part (a) so that r is not a function and r^{-1} is a function.

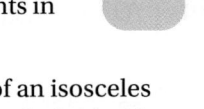

Relation *r*

Domain   Range

64. Reasoning Relation r has one element in its domain and two elements in its range. Is r a function? Is the inverse of r a function? Explain.

65. Geometry Write a function that gives the length of the hypotenuse of an isosceles right triangle with side length s. Evaluate the inverse of the function to find the side length of an isosceles right triangle with a hypotenuse of 6 in.

66. For the function $f(x) = \sqrt[3]{2x}$, find $f^{-1}(x)$. Then determine the value of x when $f(x) = 16$.

67. Reasoning To determine if the inverse of function f is also a function, you can use a *horizontal line test*. It says that if no horizontal line intersects the graph of the function f in more than one point, then the inverse of f is a function.
a. Explain why the horizontal line test works.
b. The graph of a polynomial function passes through the points $(-1, 1)$, $(0, 4)$ and $(2, 3)$. Can its inverse be a function?

C **Challenge**   Find the inverse of each function. Is the inverse a function?

68. $f(x) = \frac{1}{5}x^3$

69. $f(x) = \sqrt[3]{x-5}$

70. $f(x) = \frac{\sqrt[3]{x}}{3}$

71. $f(x) = (x-2)^3$

72. $f(x) = \sqrt[4]{x}$

73. $f(x) = 1.2x^4$

74. Function $f(x)$ is defined the following way:
- if x is an integer, then $f(x) = x + 1$;
- for all other x, $f(x) = x + 2$.

Is the inverse of $f(x)$ a function? Explain.

Standardized Test Prep

SAT/ACT

75. Which pair of words makes this sentence FALSE?
The product of two ____(I)____ numbers is always a (n) ____(II)____ number.

Ⓐ (I) complex; (II) complex

Ⓒ (I) rational; (II) real

Ⓑ (I) real; (II) complex

Ⓓ (I) imaginary; (II) imaginary

76. If $f(x) = x + 1$ and $g(x) = x^2 - 3x - 4$, what is $(f \circ g)(x)$?

Ⓕ $x^2 - 3x - 3$ Ⓖ $x^2 - x - 6$ Ⓗ $x^2 - x$ Ⓘ $x^2 - x - 3$

77. What is the simplified form of $\left(a^{\frac{2}{3}} b^{\frac{3}{4}}\right)^2$?

Ⓐ $a^{\frac{4}{9}} b^{\frac{9}{16}}$ Ⓑ $a^{\frac{4}{3}} b^{\frac{3}{2}}$ Ⓒ ab Ⓓ $(ab)^{\frac{17}{6}}$

Extended Response

78. Let $f(x) = (x+1)^2 - 2$. Find the x- and y-intercepts of $f(x)$ and the inverse of $f(x)$. Is the inverse a function?

Mixed Review

Let $f(x) = 4x$, $g(x) = \frac{1}{2}x + 7$, and $h(x) = -2x + 4$. Perform each function operation.

◀ See Lesson 6-6.

79. $(g \circ f)(x)$

80. $(h \circ g)(x)$

81. $h(x) + g(x)$

82. $f(x) \cdot g(x)$

83. $(f \circ g)(x) + h(x)$

84. $(f \circ g)(x)$

Find each real root.

◀ See Lesson 6-1.

85. $-\sqrt[4]{16}$

86. $\sqrt[4]{-16}$

87. $\sqrt[5]{243}$

88. $-\sqrt[5]{243}$

89. $\sqrt[5]{-243}$

90. $\sqrt[3]{0.064}$

91. $\sqrt[4]{810,000}$

92. $\sqrt[4]{\frac{1}{160,000}}$

Get Ready!   **To prepare for Lesson 6-8, do Exercises 93–95.**

Graph each function.

◀ See Lesson 4-1.

93. $y = -x^2 - 1$

94. $y = -(x+1)^2 + 1$

95. $y = 3x^2 + 3$

Graphing Inverses

Common Core State Standards

Extends F-BF.B.4a Solve an equation of the form $f(x) = c$ for a simple function f that has an inverse and write an expression for the inverse.

MP 5

You can graph inverses of functions on a graphing calculator by using the **DrawInv** feature or by using parametric equations. It takes more keystrokes to set up parametric equations, but once you do you can easily change from one function to another and quickly see the graphs of the new function and its inverse.

MATHEMATICAL PRACTICES

Activity

Graph $y = 0.3x^2 + 1$ and its inverse.

Method 1 Use the **DrawInv** feature.

Step 1 Press (y=) and enter the equation. Press (zoom) 5 to see a graph of the function with equal x- and y-intervals.

Step 2 Press (2nd) (draw) 8. You will see **DrawInv** followed by a flashing cursor. Select equation Y_1 by pressing (vars) ▷ 1 1. Press (enter) to see the graph of the function and its inverse.

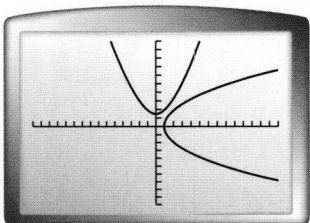

Method 2 Use parametric equations.

Step 1 Set to parametric mode. Press (mode), select **Par**, and press (2nd) (quit).

Step 2 Enter the given equation in parametric form. Press (y=) and enter the equations $X_{1T} = T$ and $Y_{1T} = .3T^2 + 1$.

Step 3 Now use $X_{2T} = Y_{1T}$ and $Y_{2T} = X_{1T}$ to interchange the x- and y-values of the first parametric equation. Press (y=) and move the cursor to follow $X_{2T} =$. Select Y_{1T} by pressing (vars) ▷ 2 2. Enter the equation $Y_{2T} = X_{1T}$ in a similar fashion.

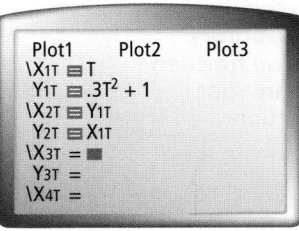

Plot1   Plot2   Plot3
\X₁ᴛ ▤ T
Y₁ᴛ ▤ .3T² + 1
\X₂ᴛ ▤ Y₁ᴛ
Y₂ᴛ ▤ X₁ᴛ
\X₃ᴛ = ■
Y₃ᴛ =
\X₄ᴛ =

Step 4 Press (zoom) 5. Adjust the **Window** so that **Tmin** and **Tmax** approximately agree with **Xmin** and **Xmax**. Press (graph) to see the graph of the function and its inverse.

Exercises

Graph each function and its inverse with a graphing calculator. Then sketch the graphs.

1. $y = x^2 - 5$ **2.** $y = (x - 3)^2$ **3.** $y = 0.01x^4$ **4.** $y = 0.5x^3 - 3$

ⓒ **5. Writing** Change the parametric equation $X_{2T} = Y_{1T}$ in Method 2, Step 3 to $X_{2T} = -Y_{1T}$. Describe the graph that results.

6. Explain how once you set up parametric equations, you can change from one function to another and quickly see the graphs of the new function and its inverse.

6-8 Graphing Radical Functions

© **Common Core State Standards**

F-IF.C.7b Graph square root *and* cube root functions . . .
F-IF.C.8 Write a function defined by an expression in different but equivalent forms . . .

MP 1, MP 2, MP 3, MP 4, MP 5

Objective To graph square root and other radical functions

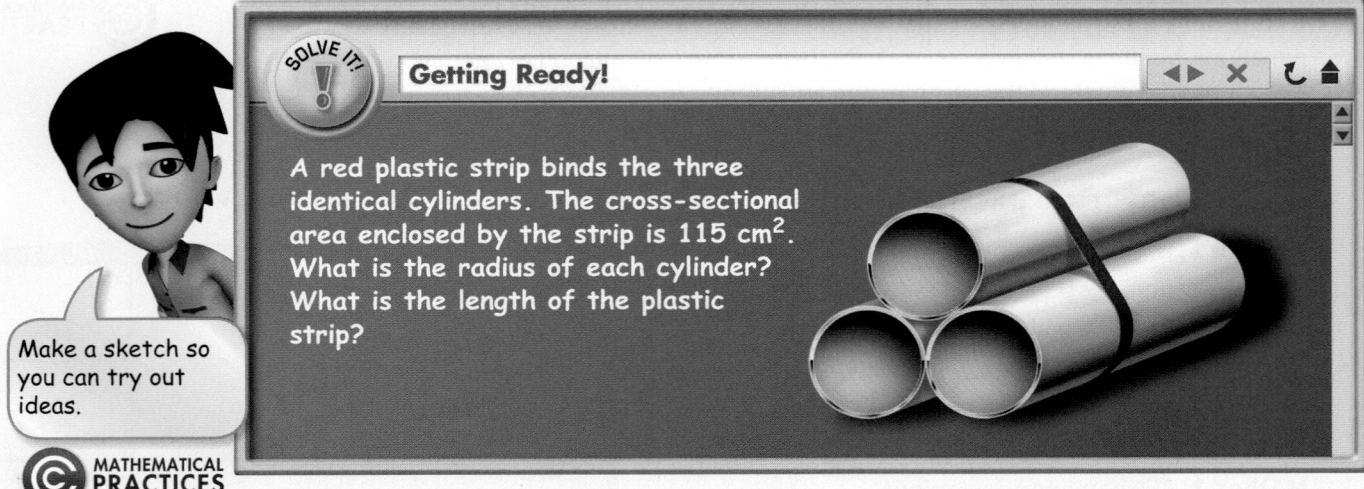

Getting Ready!

A red plastic strip binds the three identical cylinders. The cross-sectional area enclosed by the strip is 115 cm². What is the radius of each cylinder? What is the length of the plastic strip?

Make a sketch so you can try out ideas.

MATHEMATICAL PRACTICES

The formula $A = \pi r^2$ shows that area is a quadratic function of the radius of a circle. The formula $r = \frac{1}{\sqrt{\pi}} \sqrt{A}$ shows that the radius of a circle is a square root function of the area.

Essential Understanding A square root function is the inverse of a quadratic function that has a restricted domain.

A horizontal line can intersect the graph of $f(x) = x^2$ in two points—where $f(-2) = f(2)$, for example. Thus, a vertical line can intersect the graph of f^{-1} in two points. f^{-1} is *not* a function because it fails the vertical line test.

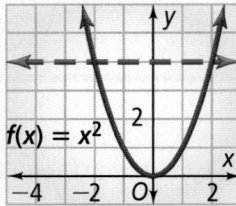

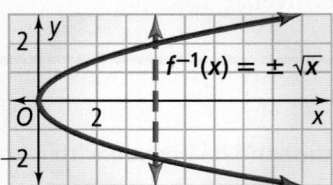

However, you can restrict the domain of f so that the inverse of the restricted function is a function.

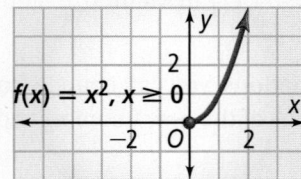

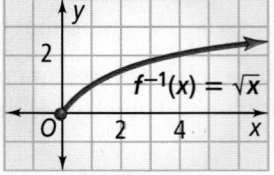

Inverses of the power functions $y = x^n$ (with domains restricted as needed) form parent functions $y = \sqrt[n]{x}$ for families of **radical functions**. In particular, $f(x) = \sqrt{x}$ is the parent for the family of **square root functions**. Members of this family have the general form $f(x) = a\sqrt{x - h} + k$.

take note

Key Concepts   Families of Radical Functions

	Square Root	Radical
Parent function:	$y = \sqrt{x}$	$y = \sqrt[n]{x}$
Reflection in x-axis:	$y = -\sqrt{x}$	$y = -\sqrt[n]{x}$
Stretch ($a > 1$), shrink ($0 < a < 1$) by the factor a:	$y = a\sqrt{x}$	$y = a\sqrt[n]{x}$
Translation: Horizontal by h Vertical by k	$y = \sqrt{x - h} + k$	$y = \sqrt[n]{x - h} + k$

© **Problem 1** Translating a Square Root Function Vertically

What are the graphs of $y = \sqrt{x} - 2$ and $y = \sqrt{x} + 1$?

Think

How is $y = \sqrt{x} + k$ related to the parent function $y = \sqrt{x}$?
It is related to the parent function in the same way that $y = f(x) + k$ is related to $y = f(x)$. It is a vertical translation of k units.

The graph of $y = \sqrt{x} - 2$ is the graph of $y = \sqrt{x}$ shifted down 2 units.

The graph of $y = \sqrt{x} + 1$ is the graph of $y = \sqrt{x}$ shifted up 1 unit.

The domains of both functions are the set of nonnegative numbers, but their ranges differ.

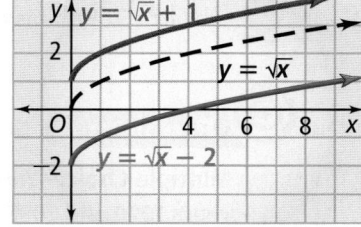

✓ **Got It?** **1.** What are the graphs of $y = \sqrt{x} + 2$ and $y = \sqrt{x} - 3$?

© **Problem 2** Translating a Square Root Function Horizontally

What are the graphs of $y = \sqrt{x + 4}$ and $y = \sqrt{x - 1}$?

Think

How is $y = \sqrt{x - h}$ related to the parent function $y = \sqrt{x}$?
It is a horizontal translation of h units.

The graph of $y = \sqrt{x + 4}$ is the graph of $y = \sqrt{x}$ shifted left 4 units.

The graph of $y = \sqrt{x - 1}$ is the graph of $y = \sqrt{x}$ shifted right 1 unit.

The ranges of both functions are the set of nonnegative numbers, but their domains differ.

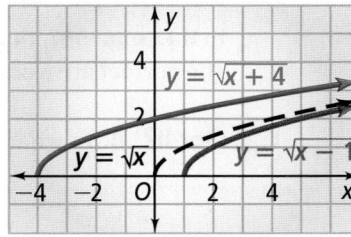

✓ **Got It?** **2.** What are the graphs of $y = \sqrt{x - 3}$ and $y = \sqrt{x + 2}$?

Recall from Lesson 2-7 that for any transformation, $y = af(x - h) + k$ of the parent function $f(x)$, a indicates a vertical stretch or shrink.

Similarly, for the combined transformation $y = a\sqrt{x - h} + k$, a indicates a vertical stretch ($|a| > 1$) or shrink ($|a| < 1$). A negative value of a indicates a reflection in the x-axis.

© **Problem 3** Graphing a Square Root Function

Think
What would be good points to choose?
Points that have integer x- and y-coordinates.

What is the graph of $y = -\frac{1}{2}\sqrt{x - 3} + 1$?

Step 1 Choose several points from the parent function $y = \sqrt{x}$.

Step 2 Multiply the y-coordinates by $a = -\frac{1}{2}$. This shrinks the parent graph vertically by the factor $\frac{1}{2}$ and reflects the result in the x-axis.

Step 3 The values of h and k give the horizontal and vertical translations. Translate the graph from Step 2 to the right 3 units and up 1 unit.

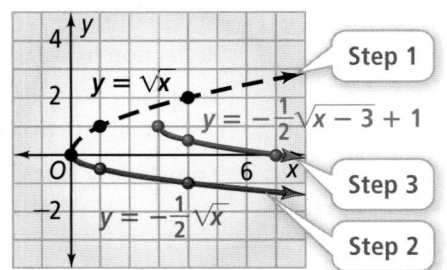

 Got It? 3. What is the graph of $y = 3\sqrt{x + 2} - 4$?

© **Problem 4** Solving a Radical Equation by Graphing

Multiple Choice You can model the population P of Corpus Christi, Texas, between the years 1970 and 2005 by the radical function $P(x) = 75{,}000\sqrt[3]{x - 1950}$, where x is the year. Using this model, in what year was the population of Corpus Christi 250,000?

   Ⓐ 1980   Ⓑ 1983   Ⓒ 1987   Ⓓ 1990

Think
How can you rewrite a radical function using an exponent?
You can write a radical function $y = \sqrt[n]{x}$ as $y = x^{\frac{1}{n}}$.

For $P = 250{,}000$, solve the equation $250{,}000 = 75{,}000\sqrt[3]{x - 1950}$.

Graph **Y1 = 75000(X − 1950)^(1/3)** and **Y2 = 250000**. Adjust the window to find where the graphs intersect.

Use the **INTERSECT** feature to find the x-coordinate of the intersection.

In the year 1987, the population of Corpus Christi was 250,000. The correct answer is C.

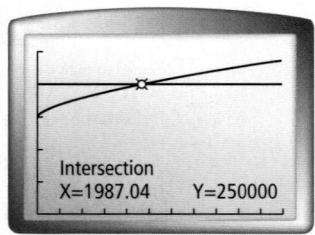

 Got It? 4. In what year was the population of Corpus Christi 275,000?

Problem 4 uses a transformation of $y = \sqrt[3]{x}$. The function $f(x) = \sqrt[3]{x}$ is the inverse of $g(x) = x^3$. Unlike $y = \sqrt{x}$, the domain and range of $f(x) = \sqrt[3]{x}$ are all real numbers.

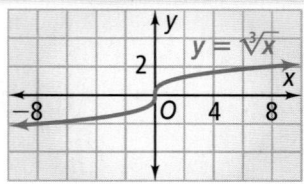

The patterns for graphing square root functions apply to other radical functions.

Problem 5 Graphing a Cube Root Function

Plan

How is
$y = a\sqrt[n]{x - h} + k$
related to its parent function?
a stretches or shrinks the parent function and *h* and *k* translate it horizontally and vertically.

What is the graph of $y = 2\sqrt[3]{x + 1} - 4$**?**

Step 1 Graph the parent function, $y = \sqrt[3]{x}$.

Step 2 Multiply the *y*-coordinates by 2. This stretches the graph vertically.

Step 3 Translate the graph from step 2, 1 unit to the left and 4 units down.

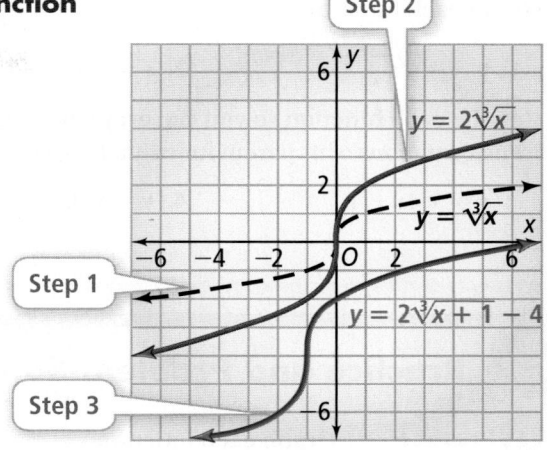

Got It? 5. What is the graph of
$y = 3 - \frac{1}{2}\sqrt[3]{x - 2}$?

You can graph functions of the form $y = \sqrt[n]{bx + c}$ using transformations, if you can simplify the radicand so that *x* has a coefficient of 1. This is also true for functions in the form $y = a\sqrt[n]{bx + c} + k$.

Problem 6 Rewriting a Radical Function

How can you rewrite $y = \sqrt{9x + 18}$ **so you can graph it using transformations? Describe the graph.**

Think

The form $y = a\sqrt{x}$ shows the stretch or shrink. Factor to get $x - h$ in the radicand.

Find the square root of 9. Now, you have the form $y = a\sqrt{x - h}$ that you can graph using transformations.

Write

$y = \sqrt{9x + 18}$

$y = \sqrt{9(x + 2)}$

$y = \sqrt{9(x - (-2))}$

$y = 3\sqrt{x - (-2)}$

The graph of $y = \sqrt{9x + 18}$ is the graph of $y = 3\sqrt{x}$ translated 2 units to the left.

Got It? 6. a. How can you rewrite $y = \sqrt[3]{8x + 32} - 2$ so you can graph it using transformations? Describe the graph.

  b. Reasoning Describe the graph of $y = |9x + 18|$ by rewriting it in the form $y = a|x - h|$. How is this similar to rewriting $y = \sqrt{9x + 18}$ in Problem 6?

Lesson Check

Do you know HOW?

Graph each function.

1. $y = -\sqrt{x} + 3$

2. $y = -\sqrt[3]{x} + 5$

Rewrite each function so you can graph it using transformations of its parent function. Describe the graph.

3. $y = \sqrt{4x - 4}$

4. $y = \sqrt[3]{8x + 16}$

Do you UNDERSTAND?

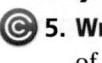 **5. Writing** Explain the effect that a has on the graph of $y = a\sqrt{x}$. How does this compare to its effect on other functions you have studied?

6. Error Analysis Your friend states that the graph of the function $g(x) = \sqrt{-x - 1}$ is a reflection of the graph of the function $f(x) = -\sqrt{x + 1}$ across the x-axis. Describe your friend's error.

Practice and Problem-Solving Exercises

A Practice

Graph each function.

See Problems 1 and 2.

7. $y = \sqrt{x} + 1$ **8.** $y = \sqrt{x} - 2$ **9.** $y = \sqrt{x} - 4$ **10.** $y = \sqrt{x} + 5$

11. $y = \sqrt{x - 3}$ **12.** $y = \sqrt{x + 1}$ **13.** $y = \sqrt{x + 6}$ **14.** $y = \sqrt{x - 4}$

Graph each function.

See Problem 3.

15. $y = 3\sqrt{x}$ **16.** $y = -\sqrt{x - 1}$ **17.** $y = -5\sqrt{x + 2}$

18. $y = -0.5\sqrt{x} + 3$ **19.** $y = \frac{1}{2}\sqrt{x + 2} - 1$ **20.** $y = 3\sqrt{x + 1} + 4$

Solve each square root equation by graphing. Round the answer to the nearest hundredth, if necessary. If there is no solution, explain why.

See Problem 4.

21. $\sqrt{x - 3} = 12$ **22.** $\sqrt{2x - 3} = 4$ **23.** $\sqrt{2x + 5} = \sqrt{2 - x}$

24. Landscaping A sprinkler can water between 1 and 130 square yards of a lawn. The length L in inches of rotating pipe needed to water A square yards is given by the function $L = 117.75\sqrt{A}$.

 a. Graph the equation on your calculator. Make a sketch of the graph.

 b. How much area can be watered if the length of the pipe is 500, 800, or 1300 inches long?

Graph each function.

See Problem 5.

25. $y = \sqrt[3]{x} + 5$ **26.** $y = \sqrt[3]{x} - 4$ **27.** $y = \sqrt[3]{x + 2} - 7$

28. $y = -\sqrt[3]{x + 3} - 1$ **29.** $y = 2\sqrt[3]{x - 6} - 9$ **30.** $y = \frac{1}{2}\sqrt[3]{x - 1} + 3$

Rewrite each function to make it easy to graph using transformations of its parent function. Describe the graph.

See Problem 6.

31. $y = \sqrt{9x - 9}$ **32.** $y = -\sqrt{16x + 32}$ **33.** $y = -2\sqrt{4x + 16}$

34. $y = \sqrt[3]{64x + 128}$ **35.** $y = \sqrt{25x + 125} - 3$ **36.** $y = \sqrt[3]{8x - 24} + 1$

B Apply

© 37. **Think About a Plan** The time t in seconds for a pendulum to complete one full cycle is given by the function $t = 1.11 \sqrt{l}$, where l is the length of the pendulum in feet. How long is a pendulum that takes 4.5 seconds to complete one full cycle? 6 seconds to complete one full cycle? Round your answers to the nearest hundredth.
- How can you use a graph to approximate the length of a pendulum?
- How can you check your answers algebraically?

Graph each function. Find the domain and range.

38. $y = 4 \sqrt[3]{x - 2} + 1$ 39. $y = \frac{1}{2}\sqrt{x - 1} + 3$ 40. $y = 3\sqrt[3]{x - 6} + 2$

41. Suppose that a function pairs elements from set A with elements from set B. Recall that a function is called *onto* if every element in B is paired with at least one element in A.
   a. The graph shows a transformation of $y = \sqrt{x}$. Write the function.
   b. What are the domain and range of the function?
   c. For the domain, is the function onto the set of nonnegative real numbers? Explain.

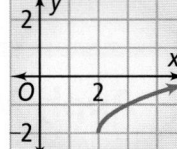

© 42. **Open-Ended** Write a radical function such that for its domain, the function is onto the set of real numbers such that $y \le 3$.

Rewrite each function to make it easy to graph using transformations of its parent function. Describe the graph.

43. $y = \sqrt{25x - 100} - 1$ 44. $y = \sqrt{36x + 108} + 4$ 45. $y = -\sqrt[3]{8x - 2}$

46. $y = \sqrt{\dfrac{x-1}{4}} - 2$ 47. $y = 10 - \sqrt[3]{\dfrac{x+3}{27}}$ 48. $y = \sqrt{\dfrac{x}{9} + 1} + 5$

📱 **Graphing Calculator** Solve the following radical equations.

49. $2\sqrt{x} = \sqrt{(x + 1)}$ 50. $\sqrt{(x + 3)} = 4\sqrt{(x)} - 2$ 51. $\sqrt[3]{x - 1} = \sqrt{x} - 1$

52. a. Solve $3 - \sqrt{(x - 3)} = x$ algebraically.
   b. Solve the equation from part (a) graphically.
   c. What do you notice about your answer to part (a) compared to your answer to part (b)?

STEM 53. **Electronics** The size of a computer monitor is given as the length of the screen's diagonal d in inches. The equation $d = \frac{5}{6}\sqrt{3A}$ models the length of a diagonal of a monitor screen with area A in square inches.
   a. Graph the equation on your calculator.
   b. Suppose you want to buy a new monitor with a screen that is twice the area of your old screen. Your old screen has a diagonal of 15 inches. What will be the diagonal of your new screen?

STEM 54. **Physics** You can model time t, in seconds, an object takes to reach the ground falling from height H, in meters, by $t(H) = \sqrt{\dfrac{2H}{g}}$. The value of g is 9.81 m/s². If an object takes 7 seconds to fall to the ground, what was its initial height?

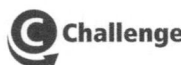

Challenge **Rewrite each function to make it easy to graph using transformations of its parent function. Describe the graph. Find the domain and range of each function.**

55. $y = -\sqrt{2(4x - 3)}$ **56.** $y = \sqrt{3x - 5} + 6$ **57.** $y = -3 - \sqrt{12x + 18}$

58. a. Graph $y = \sqrt{-x}$, $y = \sqrt{1 - x}$, and $y = \sqrt{2 - x}$.

b. Make a Conjecture How does the graph of $y = \sqrt{h - x}$ differ from the graph of $y = \sqrt{x - h}$?

59. For what positive integers n are the domain and range of $y = \sqrt[n]{x}$ the set of real numbers? Assume that x is a real number.

PERFORMANCE TASK

Apply What You've Learned

MATHEMATICAL PRACTICES
MP 4, MP 5

In the Apply What You've Learned in Lesson 6-5, you wrote a function $f(D)$ for the new yacht, described on page 359. The function gives the value of the expression on the left side of the America's Cup rule for any displacement D. Use a graphing calculator to graph this function. Select all of the following that are true. Explain your reasoning.

A. For any viewing window, the graph of $f(D)$ lies entirely above the x-axis.

B. In the context of this real-world situation, the relevant domain of the function is all real numbers.

C. As the value of D increases, the value of $f(D)$ decreases.

D. The graph of the function intersects the horizontal line $y = 24$ at exactly one point.

E. The graph shows that when $D = 10$, $f(D)$ is less than 24.

F. The graph shows that a displacement of 30 cubic meters is one possible displacement for the new yacht.

Pull It **All Together**

To solve these problems, you will pull together concepts and skills related to roots and radical functions.

Completing the Performance Task

Look back at your results from the Apply What You've Learned sections in Lessons 6-4, 6-5, and 6-8. Use the work you did to complete the following.

1. Solve the problem in the Task Description on page 359 by verifying that the AC45 Wingsail Catamaran satisfies the America's Cup rule, and by finding the possible displacements for your yacht. Show all your work and explain each step of your solution.

2. **Reflect** Choose one of the Mathematical Practices below and explain how you applied it in your work on the Performance Task.

   MP 2: Reason abstractly and quantitatively.

   MP 4: Model with mathematics.

   MP 5: Use appropriate tools strategically.

   MP 6: Attend to precision.

On Your Own

A yacht designer is considering the dimensions shown below for a new yacht called the SailSmart Catamaran.

SailSmart Catamaran	
Length	17.35 meters
Sail Area	97.5 square meters
Displacement	2.1 cubic meters

a. Does the SailSmart Catamaran satisfy the rule on page 359? Explain.

b. The designer would like to change only the sail area so that the value of the expression on the left side of the rule is at least 20 but no more than 24. Determine a range of sail areas the designer could use to meet this goal.

Connecting BIG ideas and Answering the Essential Questions

1 Equivalence
You can simplify the *n*th root of an expression that contains an *n*th power as a factor.

$$\sqrt[n]{x^n} = x^{\frac{n}{n}} = \begin{cases} x, & n \text{ odd} \\ |x|, & n \text{ even} \end{cases}$$

Radical Expressions and Rational Exponents (Lessons 6-1, 6-2 and 6-4)

$$\sqrt[3]{-8x^5} \cdot \sqrt[3]{x^2} = \sqrt[3]{-8x^7}$$
$$= \sqrt[3]{(-2)^3 x^6 \cdot x}$$
$$= -2x^2 \sqrt[3]{x}$$

$$(-8x^5)^{\frac{1}{3}} (x^2)^{\frac{1}{3}} = (-8x^7)^{\frac{1}{3}}$$
$$= ((-2)^3 \cdot x^6 \cdot x)^{\frac{1}{3}}$$
$$= -2x^2 x^{\frac{1}{3}}$$

Solving Square Root Equations (Lesson 6-5)

$$x - 2 = \sqrt{x}$$
$$x^2 - 4x + 4 = x$$
$$x^2 - 5x + 4 = 0$$
$$(x - 4)(x - 1) = 0$$
$$x = 4 \text{ or } x = 1$$
$$4 - 2 = \sqrt{4} \checkmark$$
$$1 - 2 \neq \sqrt{1} \text{ ✗}$$

2 Solving Equations and Inequalities
When you square each side of an equation, the resulting equation may have more solutions than the original equation.

Inverse Relations and Functions (Lesson 6-7)
The inverse of $y = \sqrt{x} + 2, x \geq 0, y \geq 2$ is $x = \sqrt{y} + 2$, or $\sqrt{y} = x - 2$, or $y = (x - 2)^2, y \geq 0, x \geq 2$.

3 Function
If f and f^{-1} are inverse functions and if one maps a to b, then the other maps b to a, i.e.,

$$(f \circ f^{-1})(a) = (f^{-1} \circ f)(a)$$
$$= a.$$

Graphing Radical Functions (Lesson 6-8)

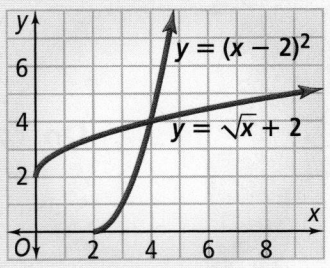

Chapter Vocabulary

- composite function (p. 399)
- index (p. 362)
- inverse function (p. 405)
- inverse relation (p. 405)
- like radicals (p. 374)
- *n*th root (p. 361)

- one-to-one function (p. 408)
- principal root (p. 361)
- radical equation (p. 390)
- radical function (p. 415)
- radicand (p. 362)
- rational exponent (p. 382)

- rationalize the denominator (p. 369)
- simplest form of a radical (p. 368)
- square root equation (p. 390)
- square root function (p. 415)

Choose the correct term to complete each sentence.

1. The number under a radical sign is called the (index/radicand).

2. (Radical functions/Inverse functions) are of the form $f(x) = \sqrt[n]{x}$.

3. A radical expression can always be rewritten using a(n) (rational exponent/inverse relation).

4. When two functions are combined so the range of one becomes the domain of the other, the resulting function is called a (square root function/composite function).

6-1 Roots and Radical Expressions

Quick Review

You can simplify a radical expression by finding the roots. The **principal root** of a number with two real roots is the positive root. The principal **nth root** of b is written as $\sqrt[n]{b}$, where b is the **radicand** and n is the **index** of the radical expression.

For any real number a, $\sqrt[n]{a^n} = \begin{cases} a \text{ if } n \text{ is odd} \\ |a| \text{ if } n \text{ is even} \end{cases}$.

Example

What is the simplified form of $\sqrt{36x^6}$?

$\sqrt{6^2 x^6}$ Find the root of the integer.

$= \sqrt{6^2(x^3)^2}$ Find the root of the variable.

$= 6|x^3|$ Take the square root of each term. Since the index is even, include the absolute value symbol to ensure that the root is positive even when x^3 is negative.

Exercises

Find each real root.

5. $\sqrt{25}$ **6.** $\sqrt{0.49}$

7. $\sqrt[3]{-8}$ **8.** $-\sqrt[3]{8}$

Simplify each radical expression. Use absolute value symbols when needed.

9. $\sqrt{81x^2}$ **10.** $\sqrt[3]{64x^6}$

11. $\sqrt[4]{16x^{12}}$ **12.** $\sqrt[5]{0.00032x^5}$

13. $\sqrt{\dfrac{9x^4}{36}}$ **14.** $\sqrt[3]{125x^6y^9}$

6-2 Multiplying and Dividing Radical Expressions

Quick Review

If $\sqrt[n]{a}$ and $\sqrt[n]{b}$ are real numbers, then

$\left(\sqrt[n]{a}\right)\left(\sqrt[n]{b}\right) = \sqrt[n]{ab}$, and, if $b \neq 0$, then $\dfrac{\sqrt[n]{a}}{\sqrt[n]{b}} = \sqrt[n]{\dfrac{a}{b}}$.

To **rationalize the denominator** of an expression, rewrite it so that the denominator contains no radical expressions.

Example

What is the simplest form of $\sqrt{32x^2y} \cdot \sqrt{18xy^3}$?

$\sqrt{(32x^2y)(18xy^3)}$ Combine terms.

$= \sqrt{\left(4^2 \cdot 2x^2y\right)\left(3^2 \cdot 2xy^3\right)}$ Factor.

$= \sqrt{4^2 \cdot 3^2 \cdot 2^2x^3y^4}$ Consolidate like terms.

$= \sqrt{4^2 \cdot 3^2 \cdot 2^2(x^2x)(y^2)^2}$ Identify perfect squares.

$= 4 \cdot 3 \cdot 2xy^2 \sqrt{x} = 24xy^2 \sqrt{x}$ Extract perfect squares.

Exercises

Multiply if possible. Then simplify.

15. $\sqrt[3]{9} \cdot \sqrt[3]{3}$ **16.** $\sqrt[3]{-7} \cdot \sqrt[3]{49}$ **17.** $\sqrt{2} \cdot \sqrt{8}$

Multiply and simplify.

18. $\sqrt{8x^2} \cdot \sqrt{2x^2}$ **19.** $5\sqrt[3]{9y^2} \cdot \sqrt[3]{24y}$

Divide and simplify.

20. $\sqrt{\dfrac{128}{8}}$ **21.** $\dfrac{\sqrt[3]{81x^5y^3}}{\sqrt[3]{3x^2}}$ **22.** $\dfrac{\sqrt[4]{162x^4}}{\sqrt[4]{2y^8}}$

Divide. Rationalize all denominators.

23. $\dfrac{\sqrt{8}}{\sqrt{6}}$ **24.** $\dfrac{\sqrt{3x^5}}{8x^2}$ **25.** $\dfrac{\sqrt[3]{6x^2y^4}}{2\sqrt[3]{5x^7y}}$

6-3 Binomial Radical Expressions

Quick Review

Like radicals have the same index and the same radicand. Use the distributive property to add and subtract them. Use the FOIL method to multiply binomial radical expressions. To rationalize a denominator that is a square root binomial, multiply the numerator and denominator by the conjugate of the denominator.

Example

What is the simplified form of $\sqrt{18} + \sqrt{50} - \sqrt{8}$?

$$\sqrt{18} + \sqrt{50} - \sqrt{8}$$
$$= \sqrt{3^2 \cdot 2} + \sqrt{5^2 \cdot 2} - \sqrt{2^2 \cdot 2} \quad \text{Factor.}$$
$$= 3\sqrt{2} + 5\sqrt{2} - 2\sqrt{2} \quad \text{Simplify each radical.}$$
$$= (3 + 5 - 2)\sqrt{2} \quad \text{Combine like terms.}$$
$$= 6\sqrt{2} \quad \text{Simplify.}$$

Exercises

Add or subtract if possible.

26. $10\sqrt{27} - 4\sqrt{12}$

27. $3\sqrt{20x} + 8\sqrt{45x} - 4\sqrt{5x}$

28. $\sqrt[3]{54x^3} - \sqrt[3]{16x^3}$

Multiply.

29. $(3 + \sqrt{2})(4 + \sqrt{2})$

30. $(\sqrt{5} + \sqrt{11})(\sqrt{5} - \sqrt{11})$

31. $(10 + \sqrt{6})(10 - \sqrt{3})$

Divide. Rationalize all denominators.

32. $\dfrac{2 + \sqrt{5}}{\sqrt{5}}$

33. $\dfrac{3 + \sqrt{18}}{1 + \sqrt{8}}$

6-4 Rational Exponents

Quick Review

You can rewrite a radical expression with a rational exponent. By definition, if the nth root of a is a real number and m is an integer, then $a^{\frac{m}{n}} = \sqrt[n]{a^m} = (\sqrt[n]{a})^m$; if m is negative then $a \neq 0$. Rational exponents can be used to simplify radical expressions.

Example

Multiply and simplify $\sqrt{x}(\sqrt[4]{x^3})$.

$$\sqrt{x}(\sqrt[4]{x^3}) = x^{\frac{1}{2}} \cdot x^{\frac{3}{4}} \quad \text{Rewrite with rational exponents.}$$
$$= x^{\frac{5}{4}} \quad \text{Combine exponents.}$$
$$= \sqrt[4]{x^5} \quad \text{Rewrite as a radical expression.}$$

Exercises

Simplify each expression.

34. $25^{\frac{1}{2}}$

35. $81^{\frac{1}{4}}$

36. $16^{\frac{1}{3}} \cdot 4^{\frac{1}{3}}$

37. $5^{\frac{3}{2}} \cdot 5^{\frac{1}{2}}$

Write each expression in simplest form.

38. $\left(x^{\frac{1}{4}}\right)^4$

39. $(-8y^9)^{\frac{1}{3}}$

40. $\left(\sqrt{9xy^2}\right)^4$

41. $\left(x^{\frac{1}{6}} y^{\frac{1}{3}}\right)^{-18}$

42. $\left(\dfrac{x^4}{x^{-1}}\right)^{-\frac{1}{5}}$

43. $\left(\dfrac{x^{\frac{1}{3}}}{y^{-\frac{2}{3}}}\right)^9$

6-5 Solving Square Root and Other Radical Equations

Quick Review

To solve a **radical equation**, you must isolate a radical expression on one side of the equation. You can then rewrite the radical expression using a rational exponent and use the reciprocal of the exponent to solve the equation.

For example, to solve a square root equation, you square each side of the equation. Check all possible solutions in the original equation to eliminate extraneous solutions.

Example

What is the solution of $4(x - 2)^{\frac{2}{3}} = 16$?

$$(x - 2)^{\frac{2}{3}} = 4 \qquad \text{Isolate the radical.}$$

$$((x - 2)^{\frac{2}{3}})^{\frac{3}{2}} = 4^{\frac{3}{2}} \qquad \text{Raise both sides to the } \tfrac{3}{2} \text{ power.}$$

$$(x - 2)^{\frac{6}{6}} = 4^{\frac{3}{2}} \qquad \text{Law of exponents.}$$

$$|x - 2| = 8 \qquad \text{Simplify.}$$

$$x = 10 \text{ or } x = -6 \qquad \text{Solve for } x.$$

Exercises

Solve each equation. Check for extraneous solutions.

44. $2 + \sqrt{x + 5} = 4$

45. $3\sqrt{2x + 6} = 18$

46. $5(3x + 1)^{\frac{1}{4}} = 10$

47. $4(3x - 3)^{\frac{2}{3}} = 36$

48. $\sqrt{3x + 3} - 1 = x$

49. $\sqrt{x + 6} + 2 = x + 6$

50. $\sqrt{5x + 1} - 2\sqrt{x} = 1$

51. $\sqrt{2x + 9} - \sqrt{x} = 3$

52. Electricity The power P, in watts, that a circular solar cell produces and the radius of the cell r in centimeters are related by the square root equation $r = \sqrt{\frac{P}{0.02\pi}}$. About how much power is produced by a cell with a radius of 12 cm?

6-6 Function Operations

Quick Review

When performing function operations, you can use the same rules you used for real numbers, but you must take into consideration the domain and range of each function. The composition of function g with function f is defined as $(g \circ f)(x) = g(f(x))$.

Example

Let $f(x) = x + 3$ and $g(x) = x^2 - 2$. What is $(g \circ f)(-2)$?

$$g(f(-2)) = g((-2) + 3) \qquad \text{Evaluate } f(-2).$$

$$= g(1) \qquad \text{Simplify.}$$

$$= (1)^2 - 2 \qquad \text{Evaluate } g(f(-2)).$$

$$= -1 \qquad \text{Simplify.}$$

Therefore, $(g \circ f)(-2) = -1$.

Exercises

Let $f(x) = x - 4$ and $g(x) = x^2 - 16$. Perform each function operation and then find the domain.

53. $f(x) + g(x)$

54. $g(x) - f(x)$

55. $f(x) \cdot g(x)$

56. $\dfrac{g(x)}{f(x)}$

Let $g(x) = 5x - 2$ and $h(x) = x^2 + 1$. Find the value of each expression.

57. $(h \circ g)(-1)$

58. $(h \circ g)(0)$

59. $(g \circ h)(2)$

60. $(g \circ h)(a)$

61. Discounts A grocery store is offering a 50% discount off a $4.00 box of cereal. You also have a $1.00 off coupon for the same cereal. Use a composite function to show whether it is better to use the coupon before or after the store discount.

6-7 Inverse Relations and Functions

Quick Review

If a relation or a function is described by an equation in x and y, you can interchange x and y to get the inverse. The domain of a function becomes the range of its inverse, and the range of a function becomes the domain of its inverse.

Example

What is the inverse of $f(x) = \sqrt{x - 10}$?

$y = \sqrt{x - 10}$	Rewrite using y.
$x = \sqrt{y - 10}$	Interchange the x and y values.
$x^2 = y - 10$	Square each side.
$y = x^2 + 10$	Solve for y.
$f^{-1}(x) = x^2 + 10$	Write the inverse function.

The domain of $f(x)$ is $x \geq 10$, which means the range of $f^{-1}(x)$ is $y \geq 10$. Also, since the range of $f(x)$ is $y \geq 0$, the domain of $f^{-1}(x)$ is $x \geq 0$.

Exercises

Find the inverse of each function. Determine whether each inverse is a function.

62. $f(x) = 2x^2 - 8$

63. $f(x) = 15 - 3x$

64. $f(x) = \sqrt{x + 6}$

65. $f(x) = (2x - 3)^2$

Graph each function and its inverse. Describe the domain and range of each.

66. $f(x) = 4x - 1$

67. $f(x) = (x + 3)^2$

68. $f(x) = \sqrt{x - 3}$

69. $f(x) = 6 - 5x^2$

70. Geometry The volume of a cube is determined by the formula $V = s^3$, where s is the length of one side. Find the inverse formula. Use it to find the side length of a cube with a volume of 64 ft^3.

6-8 Graphing Radical Functions

Quick Review

The function $f(x) = \sqrt{x}$ is the parent function of the **square root function** $f(x) = a\sqrt{x - h} + k$. The graph of $f(x) = a\sqrt{x}$ is a stretch $(a > 1)$ or a shrink $(0 < a < 1)$ of the parent function. The graph of $f(x) = a\sqrt{x - h} + k$ is a translation h units horizontally and k units vertically of $y = a\sqrt{x}$. The graph of $f(x) = \sqrt[n]{x}$ is transformed by a, h, and k in the same way as the graph of $f(x) = \sqrt{x}$.

Example

Describe the graph of $y = \sqrt{4x + 12}$.

$y = \sqrt{4x + 12}$	
$y = \sqrt{4(x + 3)}$	Factor the polynomial.
$y = 2\sqrt{x + 3}$	Simplify the radical.

The graph of $y = \sqrt{4x + 12}$ is the graph of $y = 2\sqrt{x}$ translated 3 units to the left.

Exercises

Graph each function. Find the domain and range.

71. $y = \sqrt{x} - 5$

72. $y = \sqrt{x + 8}$

73. $y = 5\sqrt{x} + 9$

74. $y = -\sqrt{x - 4}$

75. $y = \sqrt[3]{x + 10}$

76. $y = -\sqrt[3]{x - 2} + 5$

Rewrite each function to make it easy to graph using transformations. Describe each graph.

77. $y = \sqrt{9x - 27} + 4$

78. $y = -3\sqrt{4x - 16}$

79. $y = \sqrt[3]{8x + 24}$

80. $y = \sqrt{\dfrac{x - 4}{4}} + 6$

Solve each equation by graphing.

81. $5 = -\sqrt{x - 3}$

82. $\sqrt{8x - 16} = 2\sqrt{x + 2}$

Do you know HOW?

Simplify each radical expression. Use absolute value symbols when needed.

1. $\sqrt{54x^3y^5}$

2. $\sqrt[3]{-0.027}$

3. $\sqrt[5]{-64x^{14}y^{20}}$

Simplify each expression. Rationalize all denominators.

4. $\sqrt{7x^3} \cdot \sqrt{14x}$

5. $\dfrac{1 - \sqrt{3x}}{\sqrt{6x}}$

6. $\sqrt{48} + 2\sqrt{27} + 5\sqrt{12}$

7. $(3 + 2\sqrt{5})(1 - \sqrt{20})$

8. $4\sqrt{7xz} + 2\sqrt{7xz}$

9. $\dfrac{5\sqrt{2}}{\sqrt{7} - \sqrt{2}}$

Simplify each expression.

10. $(125)^{-\frac{2}{3}}$

11. $x^{\frac{1}{6}} \cdot x^{\frac{1}{3}}$

12. $\left(\dfrac{8x^9y^3}{27x^2y^{12}}\right)^{\frac{2}{3}}$

13. $\sqrt{8x^5} - \sqrt{18x^5}$

Solve each equation. Check for extraneous solutions.

14. $\sqrt{x - 3} = x - 5$

15. $\sqrt{x + 4} = \sqrt{3x}$

16. $2(x - 1)^{\frac{3}{4}} = 16$

17. $\sqrt{x + 3} - 1 = x$

Let $f(x) = x - 2$ and $g(x) = x^2 - 3x + 2$. Perform each function operation and then find the domain.

18. $-2g(x) + f(x)$

19. $-f(x) \cdot g(x)$

20. $\dfrac{g(x)}{f(x)}$

Find each product or quotient.

21. $\sqrt{5}(\sqrt[4]{5})$

22. $\dfrac{\sqrt{x^3}}{\sqrt[5]{x^2}}$

For each pair of functions, find $(g \circ f)(x)$ and $(f \circ g)(x)$.

23. $f(x) = x^2 - 2,\ g(x) = 4x + 1$

24. $f(x) = 2x^2 + x - 7,\ g(x) = -3x - 1$

Find the inverse of each function. Is the inverse a function?

25. $f(x) = (x + 3)^2 + 1$

26. $f(x) = \sqrt{2x + 1}$

27. $g(x) = 3x^3 - 4$

28. $f(x) = \frac{1}{4}x$

Rewrite each function to make it easy to graph using transformations. Describe the graph.

29. $y = \sqrt{16x + 80} - 1$

30. $y = \sqrt{9x + 3}$

Graph. Find the domain and range of each function.

31. $y = 2\sqrt{x} + 3$

32. $y = -\sqrt{2x + 3}$

33. $y = \sqrt{x + 3} - 4$

Do you UNDERSTAND?

ⓒ 34. **Writing** Explain why -108 has no real 6th roots.

ⓒ 35. **Open-Ended** Write a relation that is not a function, but whose inverse is a function.

36. **Measurement** The time t in seconds for a swinging pendulum to complete one full cycle is given by the function $t = 0.2\sqrt{l}$, where l is the length of the pendulum in centimeters. To the nearest tenth, how long is a full cycle if the pendulum is 10 cm long? 20 cm long? How long, in centimeters, is a pendulum that takes 2 seconds for one full cycle?

Common Core Cumulative Standards Review

 ASSESSMENT

Some problems require you to find the inverse of a function.

What is the inverse of the function $y = x^2 + 3$?

- Ⓐ $y = x - 3$
- Ⓑ $y = \pm\sqrt{x - 3}$
- Ⓒ $y = \pm\sqrt{x^2 + 3}$
- Ⓓ $y = (x - 3)^2$

TIP 2

After you interchange x and y, solve for y.

TIP 1

To find the inverse of a function, interchange x and y.

Think It Through

$y = x^2 + 3$
$x = y^2 + 3$
$x - 3 = y^2$
$\pm\sqrt{x - 3} = y$
$y = \pm\sqrt{x - 3}$

The correct answer is B.

Vocabulary Review

As you solve test items, you must understand the meanings of mathematical terms. Match each term with its mathematical meaning.

A. radicand

B. index

C. composite function

D. inverse functions

E. radical function

I. the combination of two functions such that the output from the first becomes the input for the second

II. the degree of a root in a radical expression

III. the number under the radical sign in a radical expression

IV. a function that can be written in the form $f(x) = a\sqrt[n]{x - h} + k$

V. the range of one function is the domain of the other and vice versa

Selected Response

Read each question. Then write the letter of the correct answer on your paper.

1. Find all the roots of $2x^4 + x^3 - 8x^2 - 4x = 0$.
- Ⓐ $x = -2, x = -0.5, x = 0, x = 2$
- Ⓑ $x = -2, x = -0.5, x = 2$
- Ⓒ $x = -2, x = 0.5, x = 0, x = 2$
- Ⓓ $x = -2, x = 0.5, x = 2$

2. Solve the equation $ax^2 + bx + c = 0$ for b.
- Ⓕ $b = -cx - ax^2$
- Ⓗ $b = -(cx - ax^2)$
- Ⓖ $b = \dfrac{-c - ax^2}{x}$
- Ⓘ $b = \dfrac{-(c - ax^2)}{x}$

3. Use the sum of cubes formula to factor $x^3 + 64$.
- Ⓐ $(x + 4)(x^2 - 4x + 4)$
- Ⓑ $(x + 4)(x^2 + 4x + 4)$
- Ⓒ $(x + 4)(x^2 - 4x + 16)$
- Ⓓ $(x + 4)(x^2 + 4x + 16)$

4. The time it takes to copy pages varies directly with the number of pages being copied. The copier at your office can copy 21 color pages per minute and 40 black and white pages per minute. Approximately how long will it take to copy 60 color pages and 35 black and white pages?

  (F) 0.9 minute   (H) 2.9 minutes

  (G) 2.5 minutes   (I) 3.7 minutes

5. Which equation is modeled by the graph?

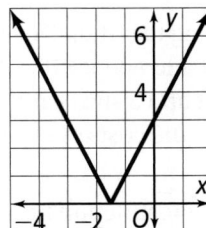

  (A) $y = |2x - 3|$ (C) $y = |2x + 3|$

  (B) $y = 2|x - 3|$ (D) $y = 2|x + 3|$

6. What are the vertex and axis of symmetry for the given parabola?

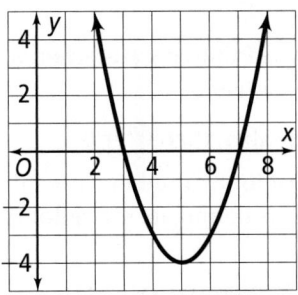

  (F) $(-4, 5), y = 5$

  (G) $(-4, 5), x = 5$

  (H) $(5, -4), y = -4$

  (I) $(5, -4), x = 5$

7. What is the product of $\sqrt[3]{3}$ and $\sqrt[5]{3}$?

  (A) $\sqrt[8]{3}$

  (B) $\sqrt[8]{9}$

  (C) $\sqrt[15]{3^8}$

  (D) $\sqrt[8]{3^{15}}$

8. Solve $7x^2 + 196 = 0$ for x.

  (F) $\pm 4i\sqrt{7}$

  (G) $\pm 4\sqrt{7}$

  (H) $\pm 2i\sqrt{7}$

  (I) $\pm 2\sqrt{7}$

9. Which inequality is modeled by the graph?

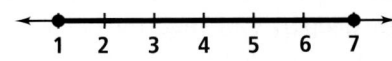

  (A) $k + 1 \le 7$

  (B) $|k + 1| \le 7$

  (C) $k - 4 \le 3$

  (D) $|k - 4| \le 3$

10. What is the solution of the system? $\begin{cases} 4x + 2y = 4 \\ 6x + 2y = 8 \end{cases}$

  (F) $(-2, 2)$

  (G) $(2, -2)$

  (H) $(1, 2)$

  (I) $(-1, 2)$

11. A photographer is promoting three photo specials. How much does it cost for each type of print?

 **One 5x7**
Three 3x5s
One wallet sheet — $25

 **Two 5x7s**
Five 3x5s
One wallet sheet — $42

 **Four 5x7s**
Four 3x5s
Two wallet sheets — $54

  (A) 5×7 costs \$7, 3×5 costs \$5, Wallet costs \$3

  (B) 5×7 costs \$11, 3×5 costs \$7, Wallet costs \$3

  (C) 5×7 costs \$12, 3×5 costs \$11, Wallet costs \$7

  (D) 5×7 costs \$7, 3×5 costs \$5, Wallet costs \$5

12. What is an equivalent form of $\frac{5}{2 + 2i}$?

  (F) $\frac{5}{4i}$ (H) $\frac{5 + 5i}{4}$

  (G) $\frac{10 - 10i}{4 - 4i}$ (I) $\frac{5 - 5i}{4}$

Constructed Response

13. Let $g(x) = x - 3$ and $h(x) = x^2 + 6$. What is $h(1) \times g(1)$?

14. A laptop comes without any programs installed on it. Each program costs \$20 and the laptop you want costs \$319. What is the greatest number of programs you can buy if you want to spend at most \$500 for the laptop?

15. You are building an entertainment center with shelves that are x in. deep by x in. long. The height of the unit will be twice the depth. If the volume of the unit will be 8,192 in.^{3}, what is the height, in inches, of the entertainment center?

16. What is the solution of the equation $x^2 - 24x + 144 = 0$?

17. What is the number of real roots of the equation $2x^2 + 3x = -4$?

18. What is the quotient $\dfrac{\sqrt[3]{8x^6 y^{12}}}{\sqrt{4x^4 y^8}}$?

19. What is the solution of $4 + \sqrt{3x + 5} = 7$?

20. All 385 tickets for a high-school play sold in 10 days. The ticket receipts totaled \$1960. If the cost of a child's ticket was \$4 and the cost of an adult's ticket was \$6, how many adult tickets were sold?

21. What is the x-value of the x-intercept of the graph of $f(x) = x^2 + 4x + 4$?

22. The graph shows a transformation of $f(x) = x^2$. What is an equation of the graph? Explain your answer by using translations of the parent quadratic function.

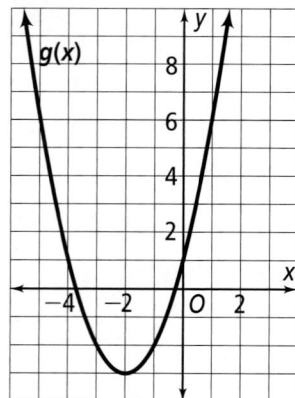

23. The total cost (in cents) of $x + 2$ markers is $x^3 + 5x^2 + 2x - 8$.
  a. Write an expression that models the cost of each marker.
  b. If you buy 7 markers, how much would each marker cost?

24. You are given that $f(x) = x^2 + 4$ and $g(x) = 3x - 1$.
  a. What are the domain and range of $f(x)$ and $g(x)$?
  b. Find $f(x) + g(x)$.
  c. What is the domain of your answer to part (b)?

25. Two friends went shopping together. One friend bought 2 hats and 1 shirt and spent \$70, while the other friend bought 1 hat and 3 shirts and spent \$85. Use a graph to determine the costs of each shirt and hat.

26. A student found that a cubic function has zeros 16 and $1 - 2i$ with a leading coefficient of 3. What is the constant term of this polynomial function with real coefficients?

27. Describe the graph of the polynomial function $f(x) = -x^6 + 3x^5 + 4x - 10$. What is its end behavior?

Decide whether the following statements are *always*, *sometimes*, or *never* true.

28. If n is a real number, then $0^n = 0$.

29. If a and b are rational numbers, then the product of $(a + \sqrt{b})$ and its conjugate is a rational number.

Extended Response

30. An online music store is having a promotion. Customers receive a \$5 rebate if they buy any regular priced CD at \$13 each. They can also receive 15% off if they register as a store member.
  a. What functions model the two discounts?
  b. In which order should the discounts be applied for the customer to receive the greatest discount?
  c. Use your answer from part (b) to determine the amount a customer will save if she buys 5 CDs.

Get Ready!

Lesson 1-3

Evaluating Expressions

Evaluate each expression for $x = -2, 0,$ and 2.

1. 10^{x+1} **2.** $\left(\frac{3}{2}\right)^x$ **3.** -5^{x-2} **4.** $-(3)^{0.5x}$

Lesson 2-5

Using Linear Models

Draw a scatter plot and find the line of best fit for each set of data.

5. $(0, 2), (1, 4), (2, 6.5), (3, 8.5), (4, 10), (5, 12), (6, 14)$

6. $(3, 100), (5, 150), (7, 195), (9, 244), (11, 296), (13, 346), (15, 396)$

Lessons 4-1 and 5-9

Graphing Transformations

Identify the parent function of each equation. Graph each equation as a transformation of its parent function.

7. $y = (x + 5)^2 - 3$ **8.** $y = -2(x - 6)^3$

Lesson 6-4

Simplifying Rational Exponents

Simplify each expression.

9. $\left(x^{\frac{1}{5}}\right)^{10}$ **10.** $\left(-8x^3\right)^{\frac{4}{3}}$

Lesson 6-7

Finding Inverses

Find the inverse of each function. Is the inverse a function?

11. $y = 10 - 2x^2$ **12.** $y = (x + 4)^3 - 1$

Looking Ahead Vocabulary

13. In advertising, the *decay factor* describes how an advertisement loses its effectiveness over time. In math, would you expect a decay factor to increase or decrease the value of *y* as *x* increases?

14. There are many different kinds of growth patterns. Patterns that increase by a constant rate are linear. Patterns that grow *exponentially* increase by an ever-increasing rate. If your allowance doubles each week, does that represent linear growth or exponential growth?

15. The word *asymptote* comes from a Greek word meaning "not falling together." When looking at the end behavior of a function, do you expect the graph to intersect its asymptote?

CHAPTER
7

Exponential and Logarithmic Functions

Download videos
connecting math
to your world.

Interactive!
Vary numbers,
graphs, and figures
to explore math
concepts.

The online
Solve It will get
you in gear for
each lesson.

Math definitions
in English and
Spanish

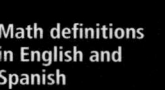

Online access
to stepped-out
problems aligned
to Common Core

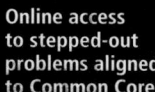

Get and view
your assignments
online.

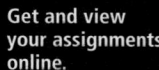

Extra practice
and review
online

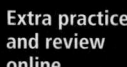

Virtual Nerd™
tutorials with
built-in support

Chapter Preview

7-1 **Exploring Exponential Models**
7-2 **Properties of Exponential Functions**
7-3 **Logarithmic Functions as Inverses**
7-4 **Properties of Logarithms**
7-5 **Exponential and Logarithmic Equations**
7-6 **Natural Logarithms**

Vocabulary

English/Spanish Vocabulary Audio Online:

English	Spanish
asymptote, *p. 435*	asíntota
Change of Base Formula, *p. 464*	fórmula de cambio de base
common logarithm, *p. 453*	logaritmo común
exponential equation, *p. 469*	ecuación exponencial
exponential function, *p. 434*	función exponencial
exponential growth, *p. 435*	incremento exponencial
logarithm, *p. 451*	logaritmo
logarithmic equation, *p. 471*	ecuación logarítmica
logarithmic function, *p. 454*	función logarítmica
natural logarithmic function, *p. 478*	función logarítmica natural

BIG ideas

1 Modeling
Essential Question How do you model a quantity that changes regularly over time by the same percentage?

2 Equivalence
Essential Question How are exponents and logarithms related?

3 Function
Essential Question How are exponential functions and logarithmic functions related?

 DOMAINS
• Linear and Exponential Models
• Creating Equations that Describe Numbers
• Interpreting Functions

Common Core Performance Task

Apparent Magnitudes of Stars

Astronomers refer to the brightness of a star as its *apparent magnitude*. Apparent magnitude is measured on a decreasing scale, meaning that brighter stars have lower apparent magnitudes. For example, Polaris (the North Star) is one of the brighter stars in the night sky and has an apparent magnitude of 1.97, while stars that can barely be seen with the unaided eye have apparent magnitudes of about 6.5. The Sun has an apparent magnitude of -26.74.

Apparent magnitude does not indicate how brightly a star burns. Many stars burn brighter than our Sun, but they appear faint and dim because of their great distance from us.

In the apparent magnitude scale, a decrease of 1 unit corresponds to an increase in brightness by a factor of $\sqrt[5]{100}$. For example, a star of magnitude 3 and a star of magnitude 1 are separated by 2 units on the apparent magnitude scale, so the star of magnitude 1 is $(\sqrt[5]{100})^2$ times (or about 6.3 times) as bright as the star of magnitude 3.

Task Description

Sirius, the brightest star in the night sky, is about 24 times as bright as Polaris. What is the apparent magnitude of Sirius?

Connecting the Task to the Math Practices

As you complete the task, you'll apply several Standards for Mathematical Practice.

- You'll make sense of the information provided and write an exponential function that models the problem situation. (MP 1, MP 2)
- You'll solve an equation algebraically and by using a graph. (MP 5)

7-1 Exploring Exponential Models

Common Core State Standards

F-IF.C.7e Graph exponential . . . functions, showing intercepts and end behavior . . . **Also A-SSE.A.1b, A-CED.A.2, F-IF.C.8**

MP 1, MP 2, MP 3, MP 4, MP 5

Objective To model exponential growth and decay

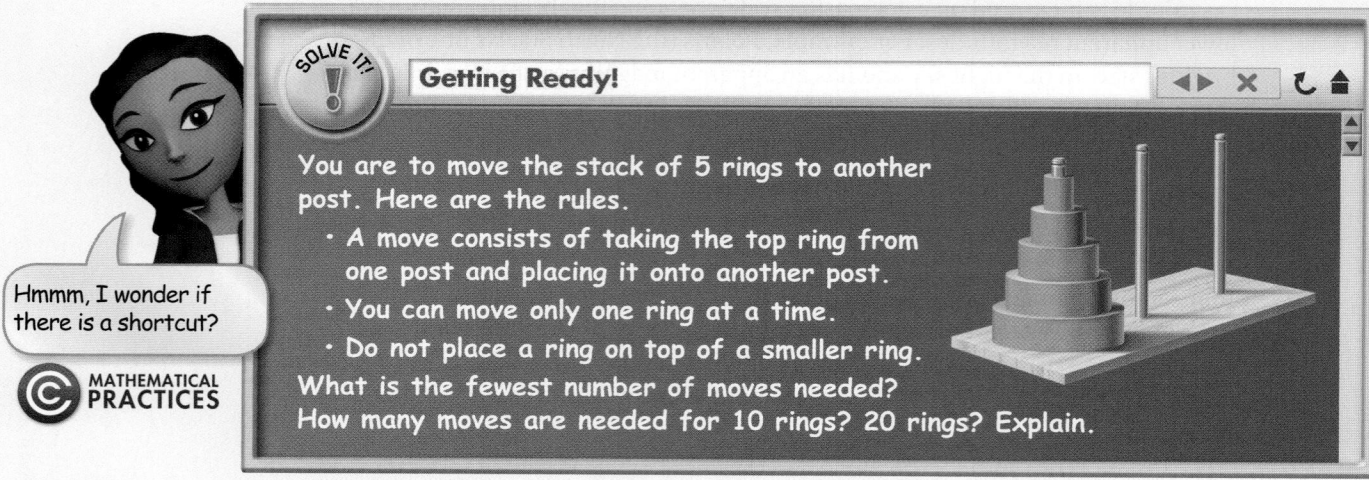

SOLVE IT!

Getting Ready!

You are to move the stack of 5 rings to another post. Here are the rules.

• A move consists of taking the top ring from one post and placing it onto another post.
• You can move only one ring at a time.
• Do not place a ring on top of a smaller ring.

What is the fewest number of moves needed?
How many moves are needed for 10 rings? 20 rings? Explain.

Hmmm, I wonder if there is a shortcut?

MATHEMATICAL PRACTICES

The number of moves needed for additional rings in the Solve It suggests a pattern that approximates repeated multiplication.

Essential Understanding You can represent repeated multiplication with a function of the form $y = ab^x$ where b is a positive number other than 1.

An **exponential function** is a function with the general form $y = ab^x$, $a \neq 0$, with $b > 0$, and $b \neq 1$. In an exponential function, the base b is a constant. The exponent x is the independent variable with domain the set of real numbers.

Lesson Vocabulary

• exponential function
• exponential growth
• exponential decay
• asymptote
• growth factor
• decay factor

Problem 1 Graphing an Exponential Function

What is the graph of $y = 2^x$?

Step 1 Make a table of values.

Plan

How does making a table help you sketch the graph?
The table shows coordinates of several points on the graph.

x	2^x	y
-4	2^{-4}	$\frac{1}{16} = 0.0625$
-3	2^{-3}	$\frac{1}{8} = 0.125$
-2	2^{-2}	$\frac{1}{4} = 0.25$
-1	2^{-1}	$\frac{1}{2} = 0.5$

x	2^x	y
0	2^0	1
1	2^1	2
2	2^2	4
3	2^3	8

Step 2 Plot and connect the points.

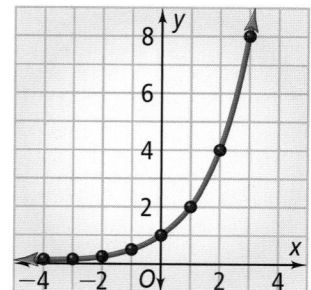

Got It? **1.** What is the graph of each function?

a. $y = 4^x$ **b.** $y = \left(\frac{1}{3}\right)^x$ **c.** $y = 2(3)^x$

d. Reasoning What generalizations can you make about the domain, range, and y-intercepts of these functions?

Two types of exponential behavior are *exponential growth* and *exponential decay*.

For **exponential growth**, as the value of x increases, the value of y increases. For **exponential decay**, as the value of x increases, the value of y decreases, approaching zero.

The exponential functions shown here are *asymptotic* to the x-axis. An **asymptote** is a line that a graph approaches as x or y increases in absolute value.

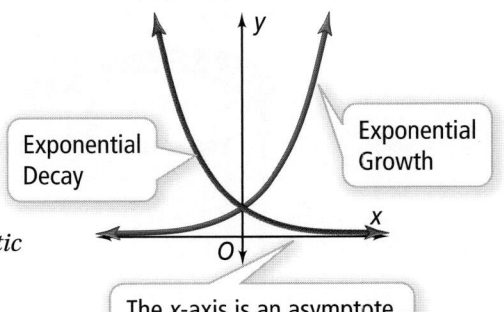

Exponential Decay

Exponential Growth

The x-axis is an asymptote.

take note

Concept Summary Exponential Functions

For the function $y = ab^x$,

- if $a > 0$ and $b > 1$, the function represents exponential growth.
- if $a > 0$ and $0 < b < 1$, the function represents exponential decay.

In either case, the y-intercept is $(0, a)$, the domain is all real numbers, the asymptote is $y = 0$, and the range is $y > 0$.

 Problem 2 **Identifying Exponential Growth and Decay**

Identify each function or situation as an example of exponential growth or decay. What is the y-intercept?

Ⓐ $y = 12(0.95)^x$

Since $0 < b < 1$, the function represents exponential decay. The y-intercept is $(0, a) = (0, 12)$.

Ⓑ $y = 0.25(2)^x$

Since $b > 1$, the function represents exponential growth. The y-intercept is $(0, a) = (0, 0.25)$.

Ⓒ You put $1000 into a college savings account for four years. The account pays 5% interest annually.

The amount of money in the bank grows by 5% annually. It represents exponential growth. The y-intercept is 1000, which is the dollar value of the initial investment.

Think

What quantity does the y-intercept represent?
The y-intercept is the amount of money at $t = 0$, which is the initial investment.

 Got It? **2.** Identify each function or situation as an example of exponential growth or decay. What is the y-intercept?

a. $y = 3\left(4^x\right)$ **b.** $y = 11\left(0.75^x\right)$

c. You put $2000 into a college savings account for four years. The account pays 6% interest annually.

For exponential growth $y = ab^x$, with $b > 1$, the value b is the **growth factor**. A quantity that exhibits exponential growth increases by a constant percentage each time period. The percentage increase r, written as a decimal, is the *rate of increase* or *growth rate*. For exponential growth, $b = 1 + r$.

For exponential decay, $0 < b < 1$ and b is the **decay factor**. The quantity decreases by a constant percentage each time period. The percentage decrease, r, is the *rate of decay*. Usually a rate of decay is expressed as a negative quantity, so $b = 1 + r$.

take note

Key Concept Exponential Growth and Decay

You can model exponential growth or decay with this function.

Amount after t time periods

Rate of growth ($r > 0$) or decay ($r < 0$)

$$A(t) = a(1 + r)^t$$

Initial amount

Number of time periods

For growth or decay to be exponential, a quantity changes by a fixed percentage each time period.

Problem 3 Modeling Exponential Growth

You invested $1000 in a savings account at the end of 6th grade. The account pays 5% annual interest. How much money will be in the account after six years?

Step 1 Determine if an exponential function is a reasonable model.

The money grows at a fixed rate of 5% per year. An exponential model is appropriate.

Step 2 Define the variables and determine the model.

Let t = the number of years since the money was invested.
Let $A(t)$ = the amount in the account after each year.

A reasonable model is $A(t) = a(1 + r)^t$.

Think

What is the growth rate r?
It is the annual interest rate, written as a decimal: $5\% = 0.05$.

Step 3 Use the model to solve the problem.

$\quad A(6) = 1000(1 + 0.05)^6$ Substitute $a = 1000$, $r = 0.05$, and $t = 6$.

$\quad\quad\quad\quad = 1000(1.05)^6$ Simplify.

$\quad\quad\quad\quad \approx \$1340.10$

The account contains $1340.10 after six years.

 Got It? **3.** Suppose you invest $500 in a savings account that pays 3.5% annual interest. How much will be in the account after five years?

 **Problem 4** Using Exponential Growth

Suppose you invest $1000 in a savings account that pays 5% annual interest. If you make no additional deposits or withdrawals, how many years will it take for the account to grow to at least $1500?

Plan

How can you make a table to solve this problem?
Define the variables, write an equation and enter it into a graphing calculator. Then you can inspect a table to find the solution.

Think

Define the variables.

Determine the model.

Make a table using the table feature on a graphing calculator. Find the input when the output is 1500.

The account pays interest only once a year. The balance after the 8th year is not yet $1500.

Write

Let t = the number of years.

Let $A(t)$ = the amount in the account after t years.

$A(t) = 1000(1 + 0.05)^t$
$ = 1000(1.05)^t$

X	Y₁
4	1215.5
5	1276.3
6	1340.1
7	1407.1
8	1477.5
9	1551.3
10	1628.9

Y₁=1551.32821598

The account will not contain $1500 until the ninth year. After nine years, the balance will be $1551.33.

  Got It? 4. a. Suppose you invest $500 in a savings account that pays 3.5% annual interest. When will the account contain at least $650?

b. Reasoning Use the table in Problem 4 to determine when that account will contain at least $1650. Explain.

Exponential functions are often discrete. In Problem 4, interest is paid only once a year. So the graph consists of individual points corresponding to $t = 1, 2, 3$, and so on. It is not continuous. Both the table and the graph show that there is never *exactly* $1500 in the account and that the account will not contain more than $1500 until the ninth year.

To model a discrete situation using an exponential function of the form $y = ab^x$, you need to find the growth or decay factor b. If you know y-values for two consecutive x-values, you can find the rate of change r, and then find b using $r = \dfrac{(y_2 - y_1)}{y_1}$ and $b = 1 + r$.

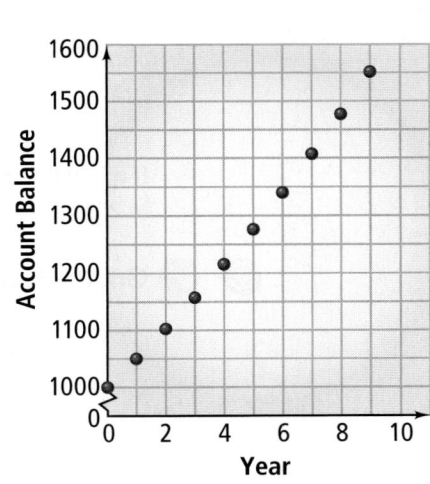

Problem 5 Writing an Exponential Function STEM

Endangered Species The table shows the world population of the Iberian lynx in 2003 and 2004. If this trend continues and the population is decreasing exponentially, how many Iberian lynx will there be in 2014?

Use the general form of the exponential equation, $y = ab^x = a(1 + r)^x$.

Step 1 Define the variables.

Let $x =$ the number of years since 2003.
Let $y =$ the population of the Iberian lynx.

Think

How can you find the value of r?
You can use the populations for two consecutive years to find r.

Step 2 Determine r.

Use the populations for 2003 and 2004.
$$r = \frac{y_2 - y_1}{y_1}$$
$$= \frac{120 - 150}{150}$$
$$= -0.2$$

World Population of Iberian Lynx

Year	2003	2004
Population	150	120

Step 3 Use r to determine b.

$$b = 1 + r = 1 + (-0.2) = 0.8$$

Step 4 Write the model.

$$y = ab^x$$
$$150 = a(0.8)^0 \quad \boxed{\text{Solve for } a \text{ using the initial values } x = 0 \text{ and } y = 150.}$$
$$150 = a$$

The model is $y = 150(0.8)^x$.

Think

How do you find the x-value corresponding to 2014?
The initial x-value corresponds to 2003, so find the difference.

Step 5 Use the model to find the population in 2014.

For the year 2014, $x = 2014 - 2003 = 11$.

$$y = 150(0.8)^x$$
$$= 150(0.8)^{11}$$
$$\approx 13$$

If the 2003–2004 trend continues, there will be approximately 13 Iberian lynx in the wild in 2014.

  Got It? **5. a.** For the model in Problem 5, what will be the world population of Iberian lynx in 2020?

b. Reasoning If you graphed the model in Problem 5, would it ever cross the x-axis? Explain.

Lesson Check

Do you know HOW?

Without graphing, determine whether the function represents exponential growth or exponential decay. Then find the y-intercept.

1. $y = 10(0.45)^x$
2. $y = 0.75(4)^x$

3. $y = 3^x$
4. $y = 0.95^x$

Graph each function.

5. $A(t) = 3(1.04)^t$
6. $A(t) = 7(0.6)^t$

Do you UNDERSTAND?

7. Vocabulary Explain how you can tell if $y = ab^x$ represents exponential growth or exponential decay.

8. Reasoning Identify each function as *linear*, *quadratic*, or *exponential*. Explain your reasoning.
  a. $y = 3(x + 1)^2$
  b. $y = 4(3)^x$
  c. $y = 2x + 5$
  d. $y = 4(0.2)^x + 1$

9. Error Analysis A classmate says that the growth factor of the exponential function $y = 15(0.3)^x$ is 0.3. What is the student's mistake?

Practice and Problem-Solving Exercises

 **Practice**

Graph each function.

 See Problem 1.

10. $y = 6^x$
11. $y = 3(10)^x$
12. $y = 1000(2)^x$
13. $y = 9(3)^x$

14. $f(x) = 2(3)^x$
15. $s(t) = 1.5^t$
16. $y = 8(5)^x$
17. $y = 2^{2x}$

Without graphing, determine whether the function represents exponential growth or exponential decay. Then find the y-intercept.

See Problem 2.

18. $y = 129(1.63)^x$
19. $f(x) = 2(0.65)^x$
20. $y = 12\left(\frac{17}{10}\right)^x$
21. $y = 0.8\left(\frac{1}{8}\right)^x$

22. $f(x) = 4\left(\frac{5}{6}\right)^x$
23. $y = 0.45(3)^x$
24. $y = \frac{1}{100}\left(\frac{4}{3}\right)^x$
25. $f(x) = 2^{-x}$

26. Interest Suppose you deposit $2000 in a savings account that pays interest at an annual rate of 4%. If no money is added or withdrawn from the account, answer the following questions.
  a. How much will be in the account after 3 years?
  b. How much will be in the account after 18 years?
  c. How many years will it take for the account to contain $2500?
  d. How many years will it take for the account to contain $3000?

See Problems 3 and 4.

Write an exponential function to model each situation. Find each amount after the specified time.

 See Problem 5.

27. A population of 120,000 grows 1.2% per year for 15 years.

28. A population of 1,860,000 decreases 1.5% each year for 12 years.

29. a. Sports Before a basketball game, a referee noticed that the ball seemed underinflated. She dropped it from 6 feet and measured the first bounce as 36 inches and the second bounce as 18 inches. Write an exponential function to model the height of the ball.
  b. How high was the ball on its fifth bounce?

 **Apply**

 30. Think About a Plan Your friend invested $1000 in an account that pays 6% annual interest. How much interest will your friend have after her college graduation in 4 years?
- Is an exponential model reasonable for this situation?
- What equation should you use to model this situation?
- Is the solution of the equation the final answer to the problem?

 31. Oceanography The function $y = 20(0.975)^x$ models the intensity of sunlight beneath the surface of the ocean. The output y represents the percent of surface sunlight intensity that reaches a depth of x feet. The model is accurate from about 20 feet to about 600 feet beneath the surface.
- **a.** Find the percent of sunlight 50 feet beneath the surface of the ocean.
- **b.** Find the percent of sunlight at a depth of 370 feet.

 32. Population The population of a certain animal species decreases at a rate of 3.5% per year. You have counted 80 of the animals in the habitat you are studying.
- **a.** Write a function that models the change in the animal population.
- **b. Graphing Calculator** Graph the function. Estimate the number of years until the population first drops below 15 animals.

33. Sports While you are waiting for your tennis partner to show up, you drop your tennis ball from 5 feet. Its rebound was approximately 35 inches on the first bounce and 21.5 inches on the second. What exponential function would be a good model for the bouncing ball?

For each annual rate of change, find the corresponding growth or decay factor.

34. +70%	**35.** +500%	**36.** −75%	**37.** −55%
38. +12.5%	**39.** −0.1%	**40.** +0.1%	**41.** +100%

 **Challenge**

42. Manufacturing The value of an industrial machine has a decay factor of 0.75 per year. After six years, the machine is worth $7500. What was the original value of the machine?

43. Zoology Determine which situation best matches the graph.
- Ⓐ A population of 120 cougars decreases 98.75% yearly.
- Ⓑ A population of 120 cougars increases 1.25% yearly.
- Ⓒ A population of 115 cougars decreases 1.25% yearly.
- Ⓓ A population of 115 cougars decreases 50% yearly.

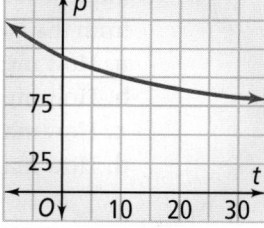

44. Open-Ended Write a problem that could be modeled with $y = 20(1.1)^x$.

45. Reasoning Which function does the graph represent? Explain. (Each interval represents one unit.)
- Ⓐ $y = \left(\frac{1}{3}\right)2^x$
- Ⓑ $y = 2\left(\frac{1}{3}\right)^x$
- Ⓒ $y = -2\left(\frac{1}{3}\right)^x$

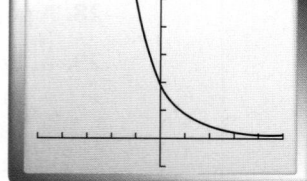

Standardized Test Prep

46. Which function represents the value after x years of a new delivery van that costs $25,000 and depreciates 15% each year?

Ⓐ $y = -15(25{,}000)^x$ Ⓒ $y = 25{,}000(0.85)^x$

Ⓑ $y = 25{,}000(0.15)^x$ Ⓓ $y = 25{,}000(1.15)^x$

47. What is $f(x) = 3x^{\frac{1}{3}}$ for $x = \frac{1}{125}$?

Ⓕ 15   Ⓖ $\frac{3}{5}$ Ⓗ $\frac{\sqrt[3]{3}}{5}$ Ⓘ $5\sqrt[3]{3}$

48. What is the simplified form of $\frac{2+i}{2-i}$?

Ⓐ -1 Ⓑ $\frac{3+4i}{3}$ Ⓒ $\frac{5+4i}{5}$ Ⓓ $\frac{3+4i}{5}$

49. Which graph represents the equation $y = x^2 - x - 2$?

Ⓕ 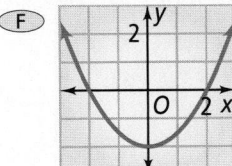   Ⓖ 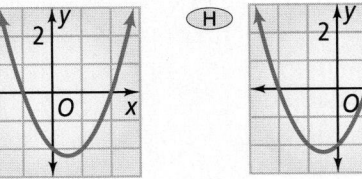   Ⓗ   Ⓘ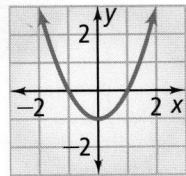

50. You are driving a car when a deer suddenly darts across the road in front of you. Your brain registers the emergency and sends a signal to your foot to hit the brake. The car travels a reaction distance D, in feet, during this time, where D is a function of the speed r, in miles per hour, that the car is traveling when you see the deer, given by $D(r) = \frac{11r + 5}{10}$. Find the inverse and explain what it represents. Is the inverse a function?

Apply What You've Learned

MATHEMATICAL
PRACTICES
MP 1, MP 2

Look back at the information on page 433 about the apparent magnitudes of stars. Suppose Star 1 is separated from Star 2 on the apparent magnitude scale by x, and is y times as bright as Star 2.

a. Write an exponential function relating the variables x and y.

b. Graph the exponential function from part (a).

c. Using properties of exponents, rewrite the function in part (a) as an exponential function with a base of 10. Show your work.

d. Which properties of exponents did you use in part (c) to rewrite the function as an exponential function with a base of 10?

7-2 Properties of Exponential Functions

 Common Core State Standards

F-IF.C.8 Write a function defined by an expression in different but equivalent forms . . . **Also F-IF.C.7e, F-BF.A.1b, A-CED.A.2, A-SSE.A.1b**

MP 1, MP 2, MP 3, MP 4, MP 5, MP 7

Objectives To explore the properties of functions of the form $y = ab^x$
To graph exponential functions that have base e

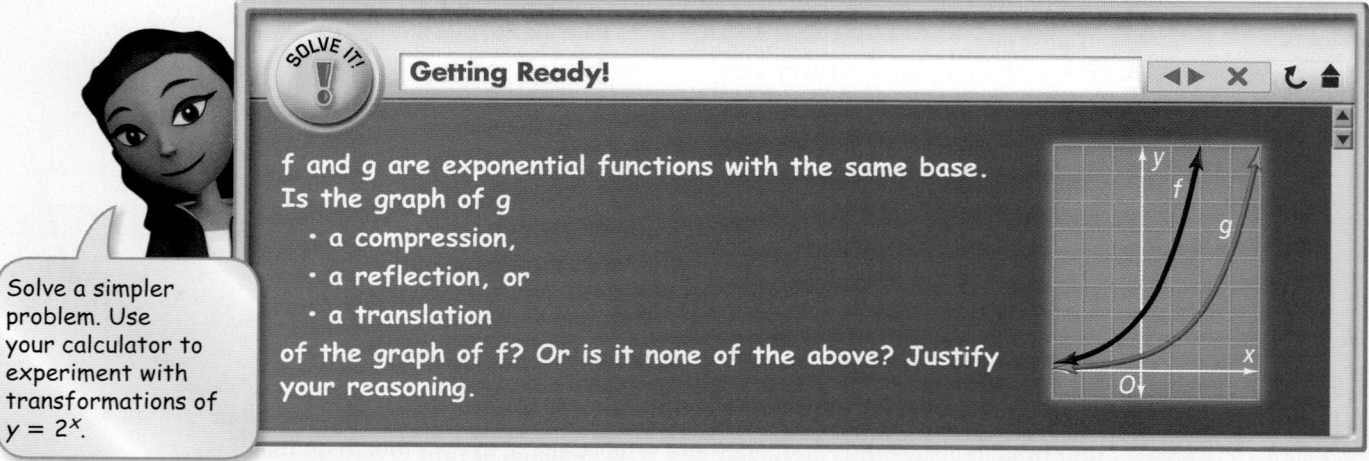

SOLVE IT!

Getting Ready!

f and g are exponential functions with the same base. Is the graph of g
  • a compression,
  • a reflection, or
  • a translation
of the graph of f? Or is it none of the above? Justify your reasoning.

Solve a simpler problem. Use your calculator to experiment with transformations of $y = 2^x$.

MATHEMATICAL PRACTICES You can apply the four types of transformations—stretches, compressions, reflections, and translations—to exponential functions.

Essential Understanding The factor a in $y = ab^x$ can stretch or compress, and possibly reflect the graph of the parent function $y = b^x$.

The graphs of $y = 2^x$ (in red) and $y = 3 \cdot 2^x$ (in blue) are shown. Each y-value of $y = 3 \cdot 2^x$ is 3 times the corresponding y-value of the parent function $y = 2^x$.

Lesson Vocabulary
• natural base exponential function
• continuously compounded interest

x	$y = 2^x$	$y = 3 \cdot 2^x$
-2	$\frac{1}{4}$	$\frac{3}{4}$
-1	$\frac{1}{2}$	$\frac{3}{2}$
0	1	3
1	2	6
2	4	12

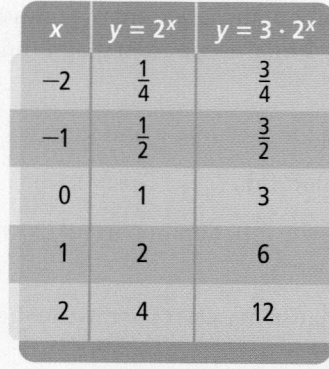

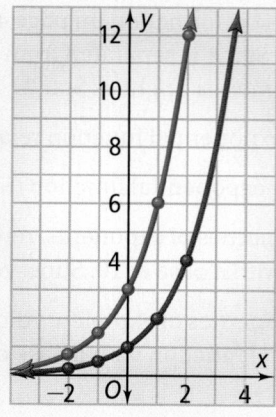

$y = 3 \cdot 2^x$ stretches the graph of the parent function $y = 2^x$ by the factor 3.

Problem 1 Graphing $y = ab^x$

Think

Which x-values should you use to make a table?
Use $x = 0$ and then choose both positive and negative values.

How does the graph of $y = -\frac{1}{3} \cdot 3^x$ compare to the graph of the parent function?

Step 1 Make a table of values.

x	$y = 3^x$	$y = -\frac{1}{3} \cdot 3^x$
-2	$\frac{1}{9}$	$-\frac{1}{27}$
-1	$\frac{1}{3}$	$-\frac{1}{9}$
0	1	$-\frac{1}{3}$
1	3	-1
2	9	-3

Each value is $-\frac{1}{3}$ times the corresponding value of the parent function.

Step 2 Graph the function.

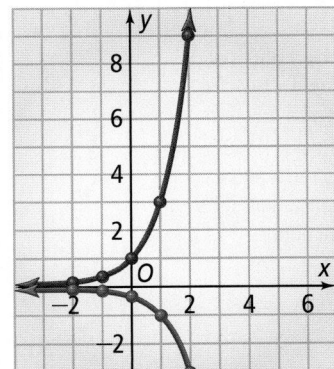

The $-\frac{1}{3}$ in $y = -\frac{1}{3} \cdot 3^x$ reflects the graph of the parent function $y = 3^x$ across the x-axis and compresses it by the factor $\frac{1}{3}$. The domain and asymptote remain unchanged. The y-intercept becomes $-\frac{1}{3}$ and the range becomes $y < 0$.

 Got It? **1.** How does the graph of $y = -0.5 \cdot 5^x$ compare to the graph of the parent function?

A horizontal shift $y = ab^{(x-h)}$ is the same as the vertical stretch or compression $y = (ab^{-h})b^x$. A vertical shift $y = ab^x + k$ also shifts the horizontal asymptote from $y = 0$ to $y = k$.

Problem 2 Translating the Parent Function $y = b^x$

Think

How is the graph of $y = 2^{(x-4)}$ different from the graph of $y = 2^x$?
The graph of $y = 2^{(x-4)}$ is a horizontal translation of $y = 2^x$ to the right 4 units.

How does the graph of each function compare to the graph of the parent function?

A $y = 2^{(x-4)}$

Step 1 Make a table of values of the parent function $y = 2^x$.

x	$y = 2^x$
-2	$\frac{1}{4}$
-1	$\frac{1}{2}$
0	1

x	$y = 2^x$
1	2
2	4
3	8

Step 2 Graph $y = 2^x$ then translate 4 units to the right.

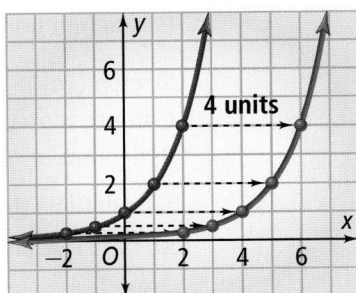

4 units

The $(x - 4)$ in $y = 2^{(x-4)}$ translates the graph of $y = 2^x$ to the right 4 units. The asymptote remains $y = 0$. The y-intercept becomes $\frac{1}{16}$.

B $y = 20\left(\frac{1}{2}\right)^x + 10$

Think

Where have you seen this situation before?
The graph of a function like $y = 20\left(\frac{1}{2}\right)^x + 10$ is both a stretch and a vertical translation of its parent function.

Step 1 Make a table of values for $y = 20\left(\frac{1}{2}\right)^x$.

x	$y = 20 \cdot \left(\frac{1}{2}\right)^x$
-1	40
0	20
1	10
2	5
3	2.5

Step 2 Graph $y = 20\left(\frac{1}{2}\right)^x$, then translate 10 units up.

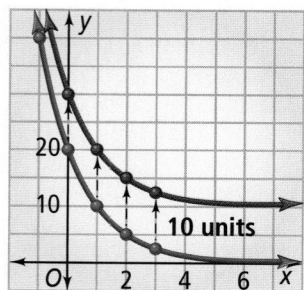

The "+ 10" in $y = 20\left(\frac{1}{2}\right)^x + 10$ translates the graph of $y = 20\left(\frac{1}{2}\right)^x$ up 10 units. It also translates the asymptote, the y-intercept, and the range 10 units up. The asymptote becomes $y = 10$, the y-intercept becomes 30, and the range becomes $y > 10$. The domain is unchanged.

Check Use a graphing calculator to graph $y = 20\left(\frac{1}{2}\right)^x + 10$.

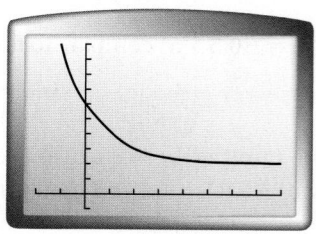

Got It? 2. How does the graph of each function compare to the graph of the parent function?

a. $y = 4^{(x+2)}$

b. $y = 5 \cdot 0.25^x + 5$

take note

Concept Summary   Families of Exponential Functions

Parent function	$y = b^x$
Stretch $\left(\lvert a \rvert > 1\right)$ Compression (Shrink) $(0 < \lvert a \rvert < 1)$ Reflection $(a < 0)$ in x-axis	$y = ab^x$
Translations (horizontal by h; vertical by k)	$y = b^{(x-h)} + k$
All transformations combined	$y = ab^{(x-h)} + k$

 **Problem 3** **Using an Exponential Model** (STEM)

Physics The best temperature to brew coffee is between 195°F and 205°F. Coffee is cool enough to drink at 185°F. The table shows temperature readings from a sample cup of coffee. How long does it take for a cup of coffee to be cool enough to drink? Use an exponential model.

Time (min)	Temp (°F)
0	203
5	177
10	153
15	137
20	121
25	111
30	104

Know
- Set of values
- Best serving temperature

Need
Time it takes for a cup of coffee to become cool enough to drink

Plan
Use an exponential model to find the time it takes for coffee to reach 185°F.

Think

Why does it make sense that a graph of this data would have an asymptote?
The temperature of the hot coffee will get closer and closer to room temperature as it cools, but it cannot cool below room temperature.

Step 1
Plot the data to determine if an exponential model is realistic.

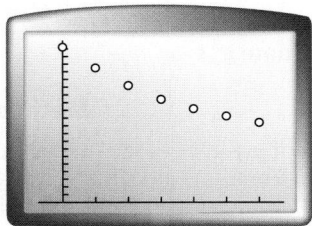

Step 2
The graphing calculator exponential model assumes the asymptote is $y = 0$. Since room temperature is about 68°F, subtract 68 from each temperature value. Calculate the third list by letting **L3 = L2 − 68**.

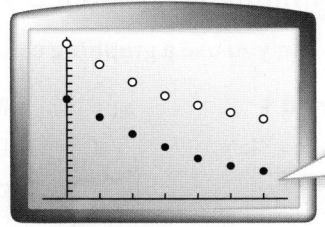

The graphing calculator exponential model assumes the asymptote is $y = 0$.

Step 3
Use the **ExpReg L1**, **L3** function on the transformed data to find an exponential model.

```
ExpReg
y = a*b^x
a = 134.5169825
b = .956011669
r² = .9981659939
r = ˉ.9990825761
```

Step 4
Translate $y = 134.5(0.956)^x$ vertically by 68 units to model the original data. Use the model $y = 134.5 \cdot 0.956^x + 68$ to find how long it takes the coffee to cool to 185°F.

X	Y₁
2.6	187.65
2.7	187.11
2.8	186.58
2.9	186.05
3	185.52
3.1	184.99
3.2	184.46

X=3.1

The coffee takes about 3.1 min to cool to 185°F.

 Got It? **3. a.** Use the exponential model. How long does it take for the coffee to reach a temperature of 100 degrees?

   b. Reasoning In Problem 3, would the model of the exponential data be useful if you did not translate the data by 68 units? Explain.

Up to this point you have worked with rational bases. However, exponential functions can have irrational bases as well. One important irrational base is the number e. The graph of $y = \left(1 + \frac{1}{x}\right)^x$ has an asymptote at $y = e$ or $y \approx 2.71828$.

x	$y = \left(1 + \frac{1}{x}\right)^x$
1	$y = 2$
10	$y \approx 2.594$
100	$y \approx 2.70$
1000	$y \approx 2.717$

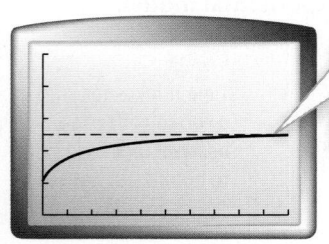

As x approaches infinity the graph approaches the value of e.

Natural base exponential functions are exponential functions with base e. These functions are useful for describing continuous growth or decay. Exponential functions with base e have the same properties as other exponential functions.

Problem 4   Evaluating e^x

Think

After you press the e^x key, what keys should you press?

Press **3**, **)**, and **enter**.

How can you use a graphing calculator to evaluate e^3?

Method 1

Use the e^x key.

```
e^(3)
        20.08553692
```

Method 2

Use the graph of $y = e^x$.

```
Y1=e^(X)
```
X=3   Y=20.085537

Method 3

Use a table of values for $y = e^x$.

X	Y1
0	1
1	2.7183
2	7.3891
3	20.086
4	54.598
5	148.41
6	403.43

Y1=20.086

$e^3 \approx 20.086$

Got It? 4. How can you use a graphing calculator to calculate e^8?

In Lesson 7-1 you studied interest that was compounded annually. The formula for continuously compounded interest uses the number e.

take note

Key Concept   Continuously Compounded Interest

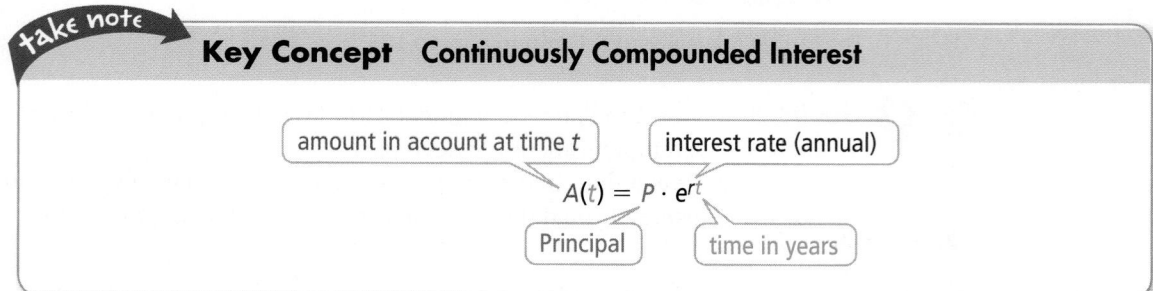

amount in account at time t interest rate (annual)

$$A(t) = P \cdot e^{rt}$$

Principal   time in years

Problem 5 Continuously Compounded Interest   `GRIDDED RESPONSE`

Scholarships Suppose you won a contest at the start of 5th grade that deposited $3000 in an account that pays 5% annual interest compounded continuously. How much will you have in the account when you enter high school 4 years later? Express the answer to the nearest dollar.

Plan

 What is the unknown?
The amount A in the account after 4 years.

$A = P \cdot e^{rt}$

$\quad = 3000e^{(0.05)(4)}$ Substitute values for P, r, and t.

$\quad = 3000e^{0.2}$ Simplify.

$\quad \approx 3664$ Use a calculator. Round to the nearest dollar.

The amount in the account, to the nearest dollar, is $3664.
Write your answer, 3664 in the grid.

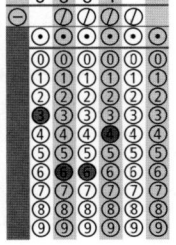

 Got It? 5. About how much will be in the account after 4 years of high school?

 ## Lesson Check

Do you know HOW?

For each function, identify the transformation from the parent function $y = b^x$.

1. $y = -2 \cdot 3^x$

2. $y = \frac{1}{2}(9)^x$

3. $y = 7^{(x-5)}$

4. $y = 5^x + 3$

Do you UNDERSTAND?

5. Vocabulary Is $y = e^{(x+7)}$ a natural base exponential function?

6. Reasoning Is investing $2000 in an account that pays 5% annual interest compounded continuously the same as investing $1000 at 4% and $1000 at 6%, each compounded continuously? Explain.

 ## Practice and Problem-Solving Exercises    MATHEMATICAL PRACTICES

Ⓐ Practice   Graph each function.   ◀ See Problem 1.

7. $y = -5^x$

8. $y = \left(\frac{1}{2}\right)^x$

9. $y = 2(4)^x$

10. $y = -9(3)^x$

11. $y = 3(2)^x$

12. $y = 24\left(\frac{1}{2}\right)^x$

13. $y = -4^x$

14. $y = -\left(\frac{1}{3}\right)^x$

15. $y = 2\left(\frac{3}{2}\right)^x$

Graph each function as a transformation of its parent function.   ◀ See Problem 2.

16. $y = 2^x + 5$

17. $y = 5\left(\frac{1}{3}\right)^x - 8$

18. $y = -(0.3)^{x-2}$

19. $y = -2(5)^{x+3}$

20. $y = 3(2)^{x-1} + 4$

21. $y = -2(3)^{x+1} - 5$

22. Baking A cake recipe says to bake the cake until the center is 180°F, then let the cake cool to 120°F. The table shows temperature readings for the cake.

See Problem 3.

Time (min)	Temp (°F)
0	180
5	126
10	94
15	80
20	73

  a. Given a room temperature of 70°F, what is an exponential model for this data set?
  b. How long does it take the cake to cool to the desired temperature?

 **Graphing Calculator** Use the graph of $y = e^x$ to evaluate each expression to four decimal places.

See Problem 4.

23. e^6　　　　　**24.** e^{-2}　　　　　**25.** e^0　　　　　**26.** $e^{\frac{5}{2}}$　　　　　**27.** e^e

Find the amount in a continuously compounded account for the given conditions.

See Problem 5.

28. principal: $2000
annual interest rate: 5.1%
time: 3 years

29. principal: $400
annual interest rate: 7.6%
time: 1.5 years

30. principal: $950
annual interest rate: 6.5%
time: 10 years

B Apply

C 31. Think About a Plan A student wants to save $8000 for college in five years. How much should be put into an account that pays 5.2% annual interest compounded continuously?
  • What formula should you use?
  • What information do you know?
  • What do you need to find?

32. Investment How long would it take to double your principal in an account that pays 6.5% annual interest compounded continuously?

C 33. Error Analysis A student says that the graph of $f(x) = \left(\frac{1}{3}\right)^{x+2} + 1$ is a shift of the parent function 2 units up and 1 unit to the left. Describe and correct the student's error.

34. Assume that a is positive and $b \geq 1$. Describe the effects of $c > 0$, $c = 0$, and $c < 0$ on the graph of the function $y = ab^{cx}$.

35. Graphing Calculator Using a graphing calculator, graph each of the functions below on the same coordinate grid. What do you notice? Explain why the definition of exponential functions has the constraint that $b \neq 1$.

$y = \left(\frac{1}{2}\right)^x$　　　　$y = \left(\frac{8}{10}\right)^x$　　　　$y = \left(\frac{9}{10}\right)^x$　　　　$y = \left(\frac{99}{100}\right)^x$

STEM 36. Botany The half-life of a radioactive substance is the time it takes for half of the material to decay. Phosphorus-32 is used to study a plant's use of fertilizer. It has a half-life of 14.3 days. Write the exponential decay function for a 50-mg sample. Find the amount of phosphorus-32 remaining after 84 days.

STEM 37. Archaeology Archaeologists use carbon-14, which has a half-life of 5730 years, to determine the age of artifacts in carbon dating. Write the exponential decay function for a 24-mg sample. How much carbon-14 remains after 30 millennia? (*Hint:* 1 millennium = 1000 years)

The parent function for each graph below is of the form $y = ab^x$. Write the parent function. Then write a function for the translation indicated.

38.

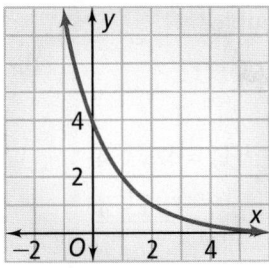

translation: left 4 units, up 3 units

39.

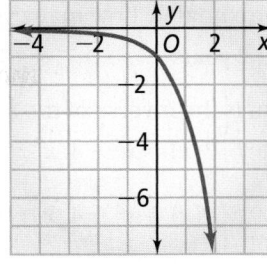

translation: right 8 units, up 2 units

40. Two financial institutions offer different deals to new customers. The first bank offers an interest rate of 3% for the first year and 2% for the next two years. The second bank offers an interest rate of 2.49% for three years. You decide to invest the same amount of principal in each bank. To answer the following, assume you make no withdrawals or deposits during the three-year period.
   a. Write a function that represents the total amount of money in the account in the first bank after three years.
   b. Write a function that represents the total amount of money in the account in the second bank after three years.
   c. Write a function that represents the total amount of money in both accounts at the end of three years.

STEM **41. Physics** At a constant temperature, the atmospheric pressure p in pascals is given by the formula $p = 101.3e^{-0.001h}$, where h is the altitude in meters. What is p at an altitude of 500 m?

Ⓒ **Challenge** **42. Landscaping** A homeowner is planting hedges and begins to dig a 3-ft-deep trench around the perimeter of his property. After the first weekend, the homeowner recruits a friend to help. After every succeeding weekend, each digger recruits another friend. One person can dig 405 ft³ of dirt per weekend. The figure at the right shows the dimensions of the property and the width of the trench.
   a. Geometry Determine the volume of dirt that must be removed for the trench.
   b. Write an exponential function to model the volume of dirt remaining to be shoveled after x weekends. Then, use the model to determine how many weekends it will take to complete the trench.

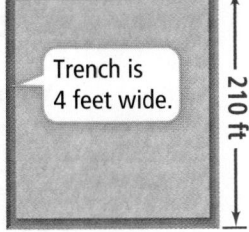

├── 180 ft ──┤

Trench is 4 feet wide.

210 ft

STEM **43. Psychology** Psychologists use an exponential model of the learning process, $f(t) = c(1 - e^{-kt})$, where c is the total number of tasks to be learned, k is the rate of learning, t is time, and $f(t)$ is the number of tasks learned.
   a. Suppose you move to a new school, and you want to learn the names of 25 classmates in your homeroom. If your learning rate for new tasks is 20% per day, how many complete names will you know after 2 days? After 8 days?
   b. Graphing Calculator Graph the function on your graphing calculator. How many days will it take to learn everyone's name? Explain.
   c. Open-Ended Does this function seem to describe your own learning rate? If not, how could you adapt it to reflect your learning rate?

Standardized Test Prep

SAT/ACT

44. A savings account earns 4.62% annual interest, compounded continuously. After approximately how many years will a principal of $500 double?

    Ⓐ 2 years   Ⓑ 10 years   Ⓒ 15 years   Ⓓ 44 years

45. What is the inverse of the function $f(x) = \sqrt{x - 4}$?

    Ⓕ $f^{-1}(x) = x^2 - 4, x \geq 0$ Ⓗ $f^{-1}(x) = \sqrt{x + 4}$

    Ⓖ $f^{-1}(x) = x^2 + 4, x \geq 0$ Ⓘ $f^{-1}(x) = \dfrac{\sqrt{x - 4}}{x - 4}$

In Exercises 46 and 47, let $f(x) = x^2 - 4$ and $g(x) = \dfrac{1}{x + 4}$.

46. What is $(g \circ f)(x)$?

    Ⓐ $\dfrac{1}{x^2}$ Ⓑ $\dfrac{1}{x^2 - 8x + 16} - 4$ Ⓒ $\dfrac{x^2 - 4}{x + 4}$ Ⓓ $x - 4$

47. What is $(f \circ f)(3)$?

    Ⓕ 1   Ⓖ 5   Ⓗ 21   Ⓘ 77

48. What is the equation of the line shown at the right?

    Ⓐ $y = -\dfrac{4}{5}x + 2$ Ⓒ $-4x + 5y = 7$

    Ⓑ $y = \dfrac{5}{4}x - 2$ Ⓓ $4x - 5y = 15$

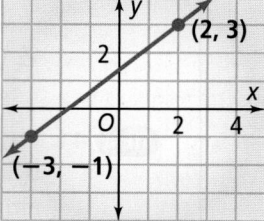

Short Response

49. How much should you invest in an account that pays 6% annual interest compounded continuously if you want exactly $8000 after four years? Show your work.

Mixed Review

Without graphing, determine whether the function represents exponential growth or exponential decay. Then find the *y*-intercept.   ◀ **See Lesson 7-1.**

50. $y = 23(3.03)^x$ **51.** $f(x) = 3(5)^x$

52. $y = 2\left(\dfrac{3}{4}\right)^x$ **53.** $y = 5\left(\dfrac{8}{3}\right)^x$

Simplify.   ◀ **See Lesson 6-3.**

54. $5\sqrt{5} + \sqrt{5}$ **55.** $\sqrt[3]{4} - 2\sqrt[3]{4}$ **56.** $\sqrt{75} + \sqrt{125}$

57. $\sqrt[4]{32} + \sqrt[4]{128}$ **58.** $5\sqrt{3} - 2\sqrt{12}$ **59.** $3\sqrt{63} + \sqrt{28}$

Get Ready!   To prepare for Lesson 7-3, do Exercises 60–62.

Find the inverse of each function. Is the inverse a function?   ◀ **See Lesson 6-7.**

60. $f(x) = 4x - 1$ **61.** $f(x) = x^7$ **62.** $f(x) = 5x^3 + 1$

7-3 Logarithmic Functions as Inverses

 Common Core State Standards

F-BF.B.4a Solve an equation of the form $f(x) = c$ for a simple function f that has an inverse and write . . . the inverse. **Also A-SSE.A.1b, F-IF.C.7e, F-IF.C.8, F-IF.C.9**

MP 1, MP 2, MP 3, MP 4, MP 5

Objectives To write and evaluate logarithmic expressions
To graph logarithmic functions

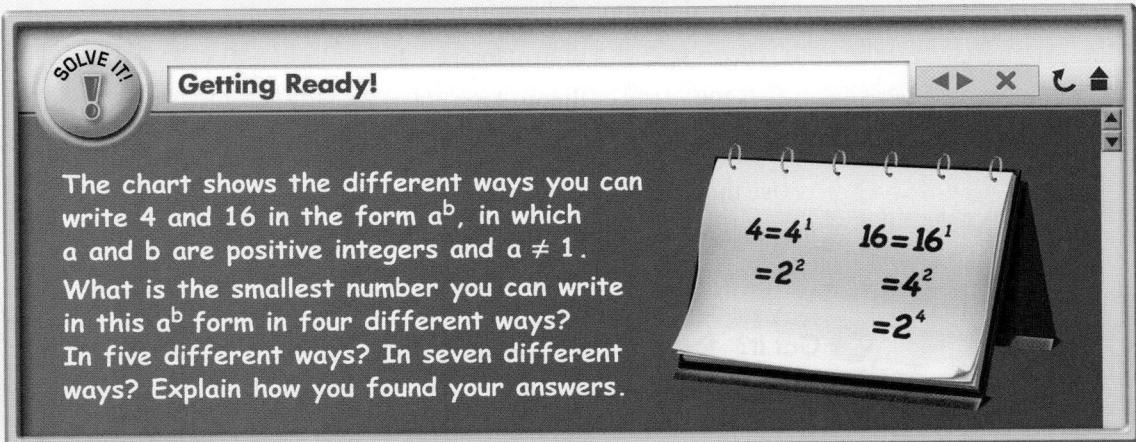

SOLVE IT!

Getting Ready!

The chart shows the different ways you can write 4 and 16 in the form a^b, in which a and b are positive integers and $a \neq 1$. What is the smallest number you can write in this a^b form in four different ways? In five different ways? In seven different ways? Explain how you found your answers.

$$4 = 4^1 \qquad 16 = 16^1$$
$$= 2^2 \qquad = 4^2$$
$$= 2^4$$

Lesson Vocabulary

- logarithm
- logarithmic function
- common logarithm
- logarithmic scale

Many even numbers can be written as power functions with base 2. In this lesson you will find ways to express all numbers as powers of a common base.

Essential Understanding The exponential function $y = b^x$ is one-to-one, so its inverse $x = b^y$ is a function. To express "y as a function of x" for the inverse, write $y = \log_b x$.

take note

Key Concept Logarithm

A **logarithm** base b of a positive number x satisfies the following definition.

For $b > 0$, $b \neq 1$, $\log_b x = y$ if and only if $b^y = x$.

You can read $\log_b x$ as "log base b of x." In other words, the logarithm y is the exponent to which b must be raised to get x.

The exponent y in the expression b^y is the logarithm in the equation $\log_b x = y$. The base b in b^y and the base b in $\log_b x$ are the same. In both, $b \neq 1$ and $b > 0$.

Since $b \neq 1$ and $b > 0$, it follows that $b^y > 0$. Since $b^y = x$ then $x > 0$, so $\log_b x$ is defined only for $x > 0$.

Because $y = b^x$ and $y = \log_b x$ are inverse functions, their compositions map a number a to itself. In other words, $b^{\log_b a} = a$ for $a > 0$ and $\log_b b^a = a$ for all a.

You can use the definition of a logarithm to write exponential equations in logarithmic form.

 Problem 1 Writing Exponential Equations in Logarithmic Form

What is the logarithmic form of each equation?

A $100 = 10^2$

Think

To what power do you raise 10 to get 100?
10 raised to the 2nd power equals 100.

Use the definition of logarithm.

If $x = b^y$ then $\log_b x = y$

If $100 = 10^2$ then $\log_{10} 100 = 2$

B $81 = 3^4$

Use the definition of logarithm.

If $x = b^y$ then $\log_b x = y$

If $81 = 3^4$ then $\log_3 81 = 4$

Got It? **1.** What is the logarithmic form of each equation?

    a. $36 = 6^2$ **b.** $\frac{8}{27} = \left(\frac{2}{3}\right)^3$ **c.** $1 = 3^0$

You can use the exponential form to help you evaluate logarithms.

 Problem 2 Evaluating a Logarithm

Multiple Choice What is the value of $\log_8 32$?

   Ⓐ $\frac{3}{5}$ Ⓑ $\frac{5}{3}$ Ⓒ 3   Ⓓ 5

Plan

How can you use the definition of logarithm to help you find the value of $\log_8 32$?
If $\log_b x = y$ then $x = b^y$, so to what power must you raise 8 to get 32?

$\log_8 32 = x$ Write a logarithmic equation.

$32 = 8^x$ Use the definition of a logarithm to write an exponential equation.

$2^5 = (2^3)^x$ Write each side using base 2.

$2^5 = 2^{3x}$ Power Property of Exponents

$5 = 3x$ Since the bases are the same, the exponents must be equal.

$\frac{5}{3} = x$ Solve for x.

Since $8^{\frac{5}{3}} = 32$, then $\log_8 32 = \frac{5}{3}$.
The correct answer is B.

Got It? **2.** What is the value of each logarithm?

    a. $\log_5 125$ **b.** $\log_4 32$ **c.** $\log_{64} \frac{1}{32}$

A **common logarithm** is a logarithm with base 10. You can write a common logarithm $\log_{10} x$ simply as $\log x$, without showing the 10.

Many measurements of physical phenomena have such a wide range of values that the reported measurements are logarithms (exponents) of the values, not the values themselves. When you use the logarithm of a quantity instead of the quantity, you are using a **logarithmic scale**. The Richter scale is a logarithmic scale. It gives logarithmic measurements of earthquake magnitude.

The Richter Scale

magnitude: + 1

0	1	2	3	4	5	6	7	8	9
E	$E{\cdot}30$	$E{\cdot}30^2$	$E{\cdot}30^3$	$E{\cdot}30^4$	$E{\cdot}30^5$	$E{\cdot}30^6$	$E{\cdot}30^7$	$E{\cdot}30^8$	$E{\cdot}30^9$

energy released: × 30

Problem 3 Using a Logarithmic Scale

In December 2004, an earthquake with magnitude 9.3 on the Richter scale hit off the northwest coast of Sumatra. The diagram shows the magnitude of an earthquake that hit Sumatra in March 2005. The formula $\log \dfrac{I_1}{I_2} = M_1 - M_2$ compares the intensity levels of earthquakes where I is the intensity level determined by a seismograph, and M is the magnitude on a Richter scale. How many times more intense was the December earthquake than the March earthquake?

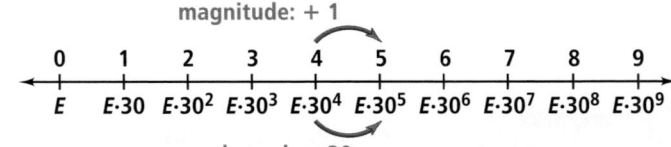

THAILAND

Magnitude 8.7

MALAYSIA

Epicenter, March 2005

Sumatra

INDONESIA

$\log \dfrac{I_1}{I_2} = M_1 - M_2$ — Use the formula.

$\log \dfrac{I_1}{I_2} = 9.3 - 8.7$ — Substitute $M_1 = 9.3$ and $M_2 = 8.7$.

$\log \dfrac{I_1}{I_2} = 0.6$ — Simplify.

$\dfrac{I_1}{I_2} = 10^{0.6}$ — Apply the definition of common logarithm.

≈ 4 — Use a calculator.

Think

What is the base of this logarithm?
This is the common logarithm. It has base 10.

The December earthquake was about 4 times as strong as the one in March.

Got It? 3. In 1995, an earthquake in Mexico registered 8.0 on the Richter scale. In 2001, an earthquake of magnitude 6.8 shook Washington state. How many times more intense was the 1995 earthquake than the 2001 earthquake?

A **logarithmic function** is the inverse of an exponential function. The graph shows $y = 10^x$ and its inverse $y = \log x$. Note that $(0, 1)$ and $(1, 10)$ are on the graph of $y = 10^x$, and that $(1, 0)$ and $(10, 1)$ are on the graph of $y = \log x$.

Recall that the graphs of inverse functions are reflections of each other across the line $y = x$. You can graph $y = \log_b x$ as the inverse of $y = b^x$.

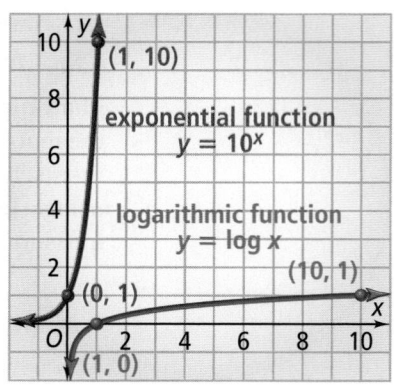

Problem 4 Graphing a Logarithmic Function

What is the graph of $y = \log_3 x$? Describe the domain and range and identify the y-intercept and the asymptote.

$y = \log_3 x$ is the inverse of $y = 3^x$.

Step 1 Graph $y = 3^x$.

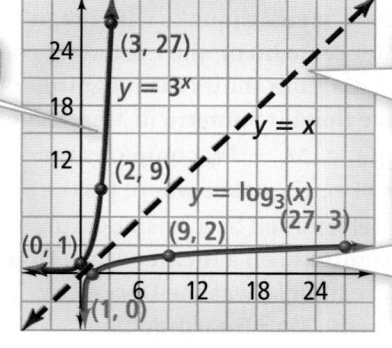

Step 2 Reflecting across the line $y = x$ produces the inverse of $y = 3^x$.

Step 3 Choose a few points on $y = 3^x$ and reverse their coordinates. Plot these new points and graph $y = \log_3 x$.

Think

How are the domain and range of $y = 3^x$ and $y = \log_3 x$ related?
Since they are inverse functions, the domain and range of $y = \log_3 x$ are the same as the *range* and *domain* of $y = 3^x$.

The domain is $x > 0$. The range is all real numbers. There is no y-intercept. The vertical asymptote is $x = 0$.

Got It? **4. a.** What is the graph of $y = \log_4 x$? Describe the domain, range, y-intercept and asymptotes.

b. Reasoning Suppose you use the following table to help you graph $y = \log_2 x$. (Recall that if $y = \log_2 x$, then $2^y = x$.) Copy and complete the table. Explain your answers.

x	$2^y = x$	y
−1	$2^y = -1$	▪
0	$2^y = 0$	▪
1	$2^y = 1$	▪
2	$2^y = 2$	▪

The function $y = \log_b x$ is the parent for a function family. You can graph $y = \log_b (x - h) + k$ by translating the graph of the parent function, $y = \log_b x$, horizontally by h units and vertically by k units. The a in $y = a \log_b x$ indicates a stretch, a compression, and possibly a reflection.

take note

Concept Summary   Families of Logarithmic Functions

Parent functions:	$y = \log_b x, b > 0, b \neq 1$
Stretch ($\|a\| > 1$) Compression (Shrink) ($0 < \|a\| < 1$) Reflection ($a < 0$) in x-axis	$y = a \log_b x$
Translations (horizontal by h; vertical by k)	$y = \log_b (x - h) + k$
All transformations together	$y = a \log_b (x - h) + k$

 Problem 5 Translating $y = \log_b x$

How does the graph of $y = \log_4 (x - 3) + 4$ compare to the graph of the parent function?

Think

How is the function $y = \log_4(x - 3) + 4$ similar to other functions you have seen?

Recall that the graph of $y = f(x - h) + k$ is a vertical and horizontal translation of the parent function, $y = f(x)$.

Step 1

Make a table of values for the parent function. Use the definition of logarithm.

x	$\log_4 x = y \longrightarrow 4^y = x$	y
$\frac{1}{16}$	$4^{-2} = \frac{1}{16}$	-2
$\frac{1}{4}$	$4^{-1} = \frac{1}{4}$	-1
1	$4^0 = 1$	0
4	$4^1 = 4$	1
16	$4^2 = 16$	2

Step 2

Graph the parent function. Shift the graph to the right 3 units and up 4 units to graph $y = \log_4 (x - 3) + 4$.

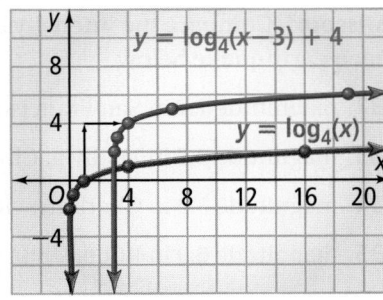

Because $y = \log_4 (x - 3) + 4$ translates the graph of the parent function 3 units to the right, the asymptote changes from $x = 0$ to $x = 3$. The domain changes from $x > 0$ to $x > 3$. The range remains all real numbers.

 Got It? **5.** How does the graph of each function compare to the graph of the parent function?

a. $y = \log_2(x - 3) + 4$ **b.** $y = 5 \log_2 x$

Lesson Check

Do you know HOW?

Write each equation in logarithmic form.

1. $25 = 5^2$ **2.** $64 = 4^3$

3. $243 = 3^5$ **4.** $16 = 2^4$

Evaluate each logarithm.

5. $\log_2 8$ **6.** $\log_9 9$

7. $\log_7 49$ **8.** $\log_2 \frac{1}{4}$

Do you UNDERSTAND?

 9. Vocabulary Determine whether each logarithm is a common logarithm.

   a. $\log_2 4$ **b.** $\log 64$ **c.** $\log_{10} 100$ **d.** $\log_5 5$

10. Reasoning Explain how you could use an inverse function to graph the logarithmic function $y = \log_6 x$.

11. Compare and Contrast Compare the graph of $y = \log_2 (x + 4)$ to the graph of $y = \log_2 x$. How are the graphs alike? How are they different?

 ## Practice and Problem-Solving Exercises

 **Practice**   Write each equation in logarithmic form.   See Problem 1.

   12. $49 = 7^2$ **13.** $10^3 = 1000$ **14.** $625 = 5^4$ **15.** $\frac{1}{10} = 10^{-1}$

   16. $8^2 = 64$ **17.** $4 = \left(\frac{1}{2}\right)^{-2}$ **18.** $\left(\frac{1}{3}\right)^3 = \frac{1}{27}$ **19.** $10^{-2} = 0.01$

Evaluate each logarithm.   See Problem 2.

   20. $\log_2 16$ **21.** $\log_4 2$ **22.** $\log_8 8$ **23.** $\log_4 8$

   24. $\log_2 8$ **25.** $\log_{49} 7$ **26.** $\log_5 (-25)$ **27.** $\log_3 9$

   28. $\log_2 2^5$ **29.** $\log_{\frac{1}{2}} \frac{1}{2}$ **30.** $\log 10{,}000$ **31.** $\log_5 125$

STEM Seismology In 1812, an earthquake of magnitude 7.9 shook New Madrid,   See Problem 3.
Missouri. Compare the intensity level of that earthquake to the intensity level of
each earthquake below.

   32. magnitude 7.7 in San Francisco, California, in 1906

   33. magnitude 9.5 in Valdivia, Chile, in 1960

   34. magnitude 3.2 in Charlottesville, Virginia, in 2001

   35. magnitude 6.9 in Kobe, Japan, in 1995

Graph each function on the same set of axes.   See Problem 4.

   36. $y = \log_2 x$ **37.** $y = 2^x$ **38.** $y = \log_{\frac{1}{2}} x$ **39.** $y = \left(\frac{1}{2}\right)^x$

Describe how the graph of each function compares with the graph of the parent   See Problem 5.
function, $y = \log_b x$.

   40. $y = \log_5 x + 1$ **41.** $y = \log_7 (x - 2)$

   42. $y = \log_3 (x - 5) + 3$ **43.** $y = \log_4 (x + 2) - 1$

44. Think About a Plan The pH of a substance equals $-\log[\text{H}^+]$, where $[\text{H}^+]$ is the concentration of hydrogen ions, and it ranges from 0 to 14. A pH level of 7 is neutral. A level greater than 7 is basic, and a level less than 7 is acidic. The table shows the hydrogen ion concentration $[\text{H}^+]$ for selected foods. Is each food basic or acidic?
- How can you find the pH value of each food?
- What rule can you use to determine if the food is basic or acidic?

STEM **45. Chemistry** Find the concentration of hydrogen ions in seawater, if the pH level of seawater is 8.5.

Approximate [H⁺] of Foods

Food	$[\text{H}^+]$
Apple juice	3.2×10^{-4}
Buttermilk	2.5×10^{-5}
Cream	2.5×10^{-7}
Ketchup	1.3×10^{-4}
Shrimp sauce	7.9×10^{-8}
Strained peas	1.0×10^{-6}

Write each equation in exponential form.

46. $\log_2 128 = 7$ **47.** $\log 0.0001 = -4$ **48.** $\log_6 6 = 1$ **49.** $\log_4 1 = 0$

50. $\log_7 16{,}807 = 5$ **51.** $\log_2 \frac{1}{2} = -1$ **52.** $\log_3 \frac{1}{9} = -2$ **53.** $\log 10 = 1$

Find the greatest integer that is less than the value of the logarithm. Use your calculator to check your answers.

54. $\log 5$ **55.** $\log 0.08$ **56.** $\log 17.52$ **57.** $\log (1.3 \times 10^7)$

58. Compare the graph at the right to the function $y = \log_5 x$. Describe the domain and range and identify the y-intercept of $y = \log_5 x$.

59. Write $5 = \log_{2x+1}(a + b)$ in exponential form.

60. Open-Ended Write a logarithmic function of the form $y = \log_b x$. Find its inverse function. Graph both functions on one set of axes.

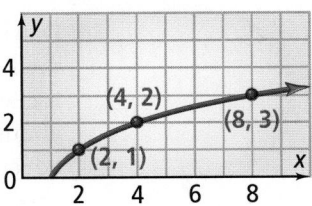

Find the inverse of each function.

61. $y = \log_4 x$ **62.** $y = \log_{0.5} x$ **63.** $y = \log_{10} x$ **64.** $y = \log_2 2x$

65. $y = \log (x + 1)$ **66.** $y = \log 10x$ **67.** $y = \log_2 4x$ **68.** $y = \log (x - 6)$

Graph each logarithmic function.

69. $y = \log 2x$ **70.** $y = 2 \log_2 x$ **71.** $y = \log_4 (2x + 3)$ **72.** $y = \log_3 (x + 5)$

Find the domain and the range of each function.

73. $y = \log_5 x$ **74.** $y = 3 \log x$ **75.** $y = \log_2 (x - 3)$ **76.** $y = 2 \log (x - 2)$

You can write $5^3 = 125$ in logarithmic form using the fact that $\log_b b^x = x$.

$\log_5(5^3) = \log_5(125)$ Apply the log base 5 to each side.

$\qquad 3 = \log_5 125$ Use $\log_b b^x = x$ to simplify.

Use this method to write each equation in logarithmic form. Show your work.

77. $3^4 = 81$ **78.** $x^4 = y$ **79.** $6^8 = a + 1$

Find the least integer greater than each number. Do not use a calculator.

80. $\log_3 38$

81. $\log_{1.5} 2.5$

82. $\log_{\sqrt{7}} \sqrt{50}$

83. $\log_5 \frac{1}{47}$

84. Match each function with the graph of its inverse.

a. $y = \log_3 x$

b. $y = \log_2 4x$

c. $y = \log_{\frac{1}{2}} x$

I.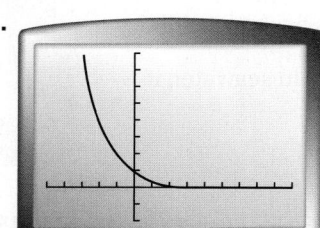

II.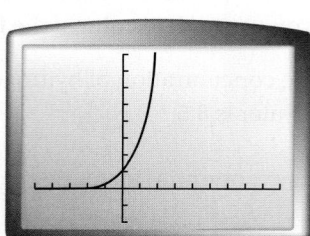

III.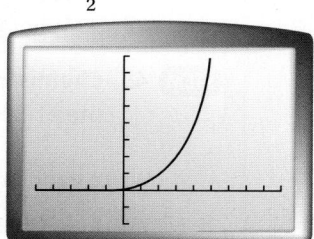

Standardized Test Prep

85. Which is the logarithmic form of the exponential equation $2^3 = 8$?

Ⓐ $\log_8 2 = 3$ Ⓑ $\log_8 3 = 2$ Ⓒ $\log_3 8 = 2$ Ⓓ $\log_2 8 = 3$

86. Dan will begin advertising his video production business online using a pay-per-click method, which charges $30 as an initial fee, plus a fixed amount each time the ad is clicked. Dan estimates that with the cost of 8 cents per click, his ad will be clicked about 150 times per day. Which expression represents Dan's total estimated cost of advertising, in dollars, after x days?

Ⓕ $(30 + 0.08x)150$ Ⓖ $360x$ Ⓗ $30 + 1200x$ Ⓘ $30 + 12x$

87. Which translation takes $y = |x|$ to $y = |x + 3| - 1$?

Ⓐ 3 units right, 1 unit down   Ⓒ 3 units left, 1 unit down

Ⓑ 3 units right, 1 unit up   Ⓓ 3 units left, 1 unit up

88. What is the expression $\sqrt[3]{(\sqrt{a})^7}$ written as a variable raised to a single rational exponent?

Mixed Review

Graph each function.

⬤ **See Lesson 7-2.**

89. $y = 5^x - 100$

90. $y = -10(4)^{x+2}$

91. $y = -27(3)^{x-1} + 9$

Factor each expression.

⬤ **See Lesson 4-4.**

92. $4x^2 - 8x + 3$

93. $4b^2 - 100$

94. $5x^2 + 13x - 6$

Get Ready!   **To prepare for Lesson 7-4, do Exercises 95–98.**

⬤ **See Lesson 1-3.**

Evaluate each expression for the given value of the variable.

95. $x^2 - x$; $x = 2$

96. $x^3 \cdot x^5$; $x = 2$

97. $\frac{x^8}{x^{10}}$; $x = 2$

98. $x^3 + x^2$; $x = 2$

Concept Byte

Use With Lesson 7-3

TECHNOLOGY

Fitting Curves to Data

Common Core State Standards

F-IF.B.4 For a function that models a relationship between two quantities, interpret key features of graphs . . . and sketch graphs showing key features . . .

MP 5

Example 1

Which type of function models the data best—linear, logarithmic, or exponential?

Connect the points with a smooth curve. Since the points do not fall along a line, the function is not linear. The graph appears to approach a horizontal asymptote, so an exponential function models the data best.

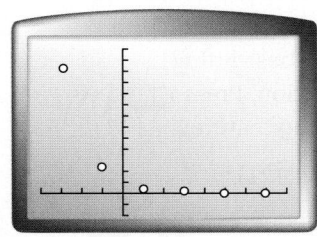 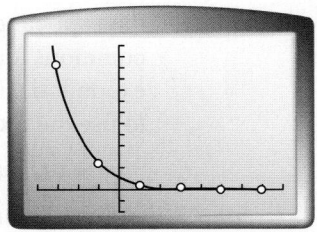

Example 2

Which type of function models the data best—quadratic, logarithmic, or cubic?

Step 1 Press (stat) (enter) to enter the data in lists.

Step 2 Use the (stat plot) feature to draw a scatter plot.

Step 3 If you connect the points with a smooth curve, the end behavior of the graph is up and up. The graph is not cubic or logarithmic, so a quadratic function best models the data.

x	y
0	14
1	7.5
2	4
3	1.8
4	1.8
5	3.9

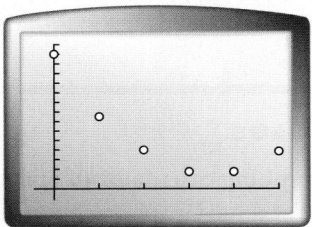

Exercises

1. Which type of function models the data shown in the graphing calculator screen best—*linear, quadratic, logarithmic, cubic,* or *exponential*?

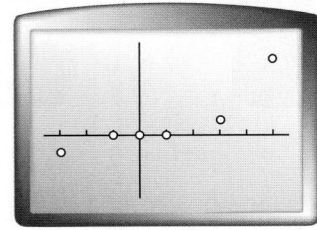

2. Which type of function models the data in the table best—*linear, quadratic, logarithmic, cubic,* or *exponential*?

3. Reasoning Could you use a different model for the data in Exercises 1 and 2? Explain.

x	y
−1	0
1	1.4
3	2.09
5	2.53
7	2.81
9	3.12

Example 3

The table shows the number of bacteria in a culture after the given number of hours. Find a good model for the data. Based on the model, how many bacteria will be in the culture after an additional ten hours?

Hour	Bacteria
1	2205
2	2270
3	2350
4	2653
5	3052
6	3417
7	3890
8	4522
9	5107
10	5724

Step 1 Press (stat) (enter) to enter the data in lists. Use the (stat plot) feature to draw a scatter plot.

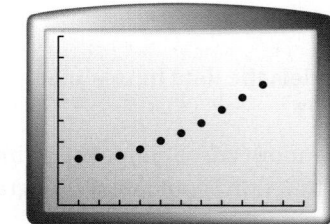

Step 2 Notice from the scatter plot that the data appear exponential. Find the equations for the best-fitting exponential function. Press (stat) ▷ **0** to use the **ExpReg** feature.

$$y = 1779.404(1.121)^x$$

Step 3 Graph the function. Press (y=) (clear) (vars) **5** ▷ ▷ (enter) to enter the **ExpReg** results. Press (graph) to display the function and the scatter plot together. Press (zoom) **9** to automatically adjust the window.

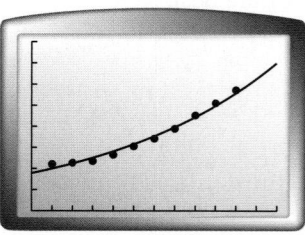

Step 4 In 10 more hours, there will be approximately $y = 1779.404(1.121)^{20} \approx 17{,}474$ bacteria in the culture.

Exercises

Use a graphing calculator to find the exponential or quadratic function that best fits each set of data. Graph each function.

4.

x	y
−1	4.9
0	3.8
1	5.0
2	8.1
3	13.3
4	70.2

5.

x	y
−3	0.1
−1	0.4
1	1.6
3	6.4
5	25.6
7	102.4

6.

x	y
1	3.5
2	2.11
3	1.30
4	0.73
5	0.28
6	0.08

7.

x	y
−1	0.04
0	0.1
1	0.5
2	2.5
3	12.5
4	62.5

© **8. Writing** In Exercise 6 the function appears to level off. Explain why.

9. A savings account begins with $14.00. After 1 year, the account has a balance of $16.24. After 2 years, the account has a balance of $18.84. Assuming no additional deposits or withdrawals are made, find the equation for the best-fitting exponential function to represent the balance of the account after *x* years. How much money will be in the account after 20 years?

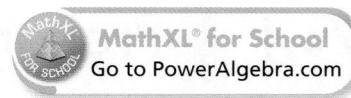
MathXL® for School
Go to PowerAlgebra.com

Do you know HOW?

Determine whether each function is an example of exponential growth or decay. Then find the y-intercept.

1. $y = 100(0.25)^x$ **2.** $y = 0.6\left(\frac{1}{10}\right)^x$ **3.** $y = \frac{7}{8}(18)^x$

Graph each function. Then find the domain, range, and y-intercept.

4. $y = -4(2)^x$ **5.** $y = \frac{1}{4}(10)^x$ **6.** $y = 8(0.25)^x$

7. Investment Suppose you deposit $600 into a savings account that pays 3.9% annual interest. How much will you have in the account after 3 years if no money is added or withdrawn?

8. Depreciation The initial value of a car is $25,000. After one year, the value of the car is $21,250. Write an exponential function to model the expected value of the car. Estimate the value of the car after 5 years.

Graph each function as a transformation of its parent function. Write the parent function.

9. $y = 3^x - 2$ **10.** $y = \frac{1}{2}(5)^{x-1} + 4$

11. $y = -(0.5)^{x+3}$ **12.** $y = -6\left(\frac{3}{4}\right)^x - 10$

Evaluate each expression to four decimal places.

13. e^5 **14.** $e^{\frac{3}{2}}$ **15.** e^{-4}

Find the amount in a continuously compounded account for the given conditions.

16. principal: $500; annual interest rate: 4.9%; time: 2.5 years

17. principal: $6000; annual interest rate: 6.8%; time: 10 years

Write each equation in logarithmic form.

18. $10^4 = 10,000$ **19.** $\frac{1}{4} = 4^{-1}$ **20.** $8 = \left(\frac{1}{2}\right)^{-3}$

Evaluate each logarithm.

21. $\log_8 64$ **22.** $\log_4 (256)$ **23.** $\log_{\frac{1}{5}} 625$

Graph each logarithmic function. Find the domain and range.

24. $y = \log_5 (x - 1)$ **25.** $y = 4 \log x + 5$

26. Crafts For glass to be shaped, its temperature must stay above 1200°F. The temperature of a piece of glass is 2200°F when it comes out of the furnace. The table shows temperature readings for the glass. Write an exponential model for this data set and then find how long it takes for the piece of glass to cool to 1200°F.

Time (min)	Temp (°F)
0	2200
5	1700
10	1275
15	1000
20	850
25	650

Do you UNDERSTAND?

27. Error Analysis A student claims the y-intercept of the graph of the function $y = ab^x$ is the point $(0, b)$. What is the student's mistake? What is the actual y-intercept?

28. Writing Without graphing, how can you tell whether an exponential function represents exponential growth or exponential decay?

29. Compare and Contrast Compare the graph of $y = \log_3 (x + 1)$ to the graph of its inverse $y = 3^x - 1$. How are the graphs alike? How are they different?

30. Vocabulary Explain how the continuously compounded interest formula differs from the annually compounded interest formula.

7-4 Properties of Logarithms

© **Common Core State Standards**

Prepares for F-LE.A.4 For exponential models, express as a logarithm the solution to $ab^{ct} = d$ where a, c, and d are numbers and the base b is 2, 10, or e; evaluate the logarithm using technology.

MP 1, MP 2, MP 3

Objective To use the properties of logarithms

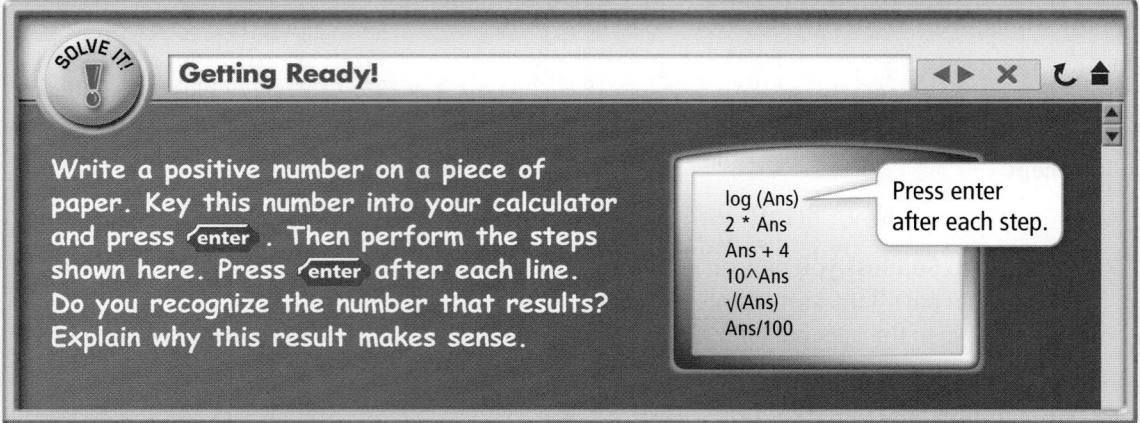

Getting Ready!

Write a positive number on a piece of paper. Key this number into your calculator and press ⟨enter⟩. Then perform the steps shown here. Press ⟨enter⟩ after each line. Do you recognize the number that results? Explain why this result makes sense.

log (Ans)
2 * Ans
Ans + 4
10^Ans
√(Ans)
Ans/100

Press enter after each step.

Lesson Vocabulary
• Change of Base Formula

You can derive the properties of logarithms from the properties of exponents.

Essential Understanding Logarithms and exponents have corresponding properties.

Here's Why It Works You can use a product property of exponents to derive a product property of logarithms.

Let $x = \log_b m$ and $y = \log_b n$.

$m = b^x$ and $n = b^y$	Definition of logarithm
$mn = b^x \cdot b^y$	Write mn as a product of powers.
$mn = b^{x+y}$	Product Property of Exponents
$\log_b mn = x + y$	Definition of logarithm
$\log_b mn = \log_b m + \log_b n$	Substitute for x and y.

take note

Properties   Properties of Logarithms

For any positive numbers m, n, and b where $b \neq 1$, the following properties apply.

Product Property	$\log_b mn = \log_b m + \log_b n$
Quotient Property	$\log_b \frac{m}{n} = \log_b m - \log_b n$
Power Property	$\log_b m^n = n \log_b m$

 **Problem 1** Simplifying Logarithms

What is each expression written as a single logarithm?

A $\log_4 32 - \log_4 2$

$\log_4 32 - \log_4 2 = \log_4 \frac{32}{2}$ Quotient Property of Logarithms

$= \log_4 16$ Divide.

$= \log_4 4^2$ Write 16 as a power of 4.

$= 2$ Simplify.

B $6 \log_2 x + 5 \log_2 y$

$6 \log_2 x + 5 \log_2 y = \log_2 x^6 + \log_2 y^5$ Power Property of Logarithms

$= \log_2 x^6 y^5$ Product Property of Logarithms

Think

What must you do with the numbers that multiply the logarithms?
Apply the Power Property of Logarithms.

 Got It? **1.** What is each expression written as a single logarithm?

    a. $\log_4 5x + \log_4 3x$ **b.** $2 \log_4 6 - \log_4 9$

You can expand a single logarithm to involve the sum or difference of two or more logarithms.

 Problem 2 Expanding Logarithms

What is each logarithm expanded?

A $\log \frac{4x}{y}$

$\log \frac{4x}{y} = \log 4x - \log y$ Quotient Property of Logarithms

$= \log 4 + \log x - \log y$ Product Property of Logarithms

B $\log_9 \frac{x^4}{729}$

Think

Can you apply the Power Property of Logarithms first?
No; the fourth power applies only to x.

$\log_9 \frac{x^4}{729} = \log_9 x^4 - \log_9 729$ Quotient Property of Logarithms

$= 4 \log_9 x - \log_9 729$ Power Property of Logarithms

$= 4 \log_9 x - \log_9 9^3$ Write 729 as a power of 9.

$= 4 \log_9 x - 3$ Simplify.

 Got It? **2.** What is each logarithm expanded?

    a. $\log_3 \frac{250}{37}$ **b.** $\log_3 9x^5$

You have seen logarithms with many bases. The **log** key on a calculator finds $\log_{10}$ of a number. To evaluate a logarithm with any base, use the **Change of Base Formula**.

---

take note

Property   Change of Base Formula

For any positive numbers m, b, and c, with $b \neq 1$ and $c \neq 1$,

$$\log_b m = \frac{\log_c m}{\log_c b}.$$

Here's Why It Works

$$\log_b m = \frac{(\log_b m)(\log_c b)}{\log_c b} \qquad \text{Multiply } \log_b m \text{ by } \frac{\log_c b}{\log_c b} = 1.$$

$$= \frac{\log_c b^{\log_b m}}{\log_c b} \qquad \text{Power Property of Logarithms}$$

$$= \frac{\log_c m}{\log_c b} \qquad b^{\log_b m} = m$$

© **Problem 3**   Using the Change of Base Formula

What is the value of each expression?

A $\log_{81} 27$

Think

What common base has powers that equal 27 and 81?
3; $3^3 = 27$ and $3^4 = 81$.

Method 1   Use a common base.

$$\log_{81} 27 = \frac{\log_3 27}{\log_3 81} \qquad \text{Change of Base Formula}$$

$$= \frac{3}{4} \qquad \text{Simplify.}$$

Method 2   Use a calculator.

$$\log_{81} 27 = \frac{\log 27}{\log 81} \qquad \text{Change of Base Formula}$$

$$= 0.75 \qquad \text{Use a calculator.}$$

Think

What would be a reasonable result?
$5^2 = 25$ and $5^3 = 125$, so $\log_5 36$ should be between 2 and 3.

B $\log_5 36$

$$\log_5 36 = \frac{\log 36}{\log 5} \qquad \text{Change of Base Formula}$$

$$\approx 2.23 \qquad \text{Use a calculator to evaluate.}$$

Got It? **3.** Use the Change of Base Formula. What is the value of each expression?

    a. $\log_8 32$ **b.** $\log_4 18$

 **Problem 4** Using a Logarithmic Scale

Chemistry The pH of a substance equals $-\log[H^+]$, where $[H^+]$ is the concentration of hydrogen ions. $[H^+_a]$ for household ammonia is 10^{-11}. $[H^+_v]$ for vinegar is 6.3×10^{-3}. What is the difference of the pH levels of ammonia and vinegar?

Think	Write
Write the equation for pH.	$pH = -\log[H^+]$
Write the difference of the pH levels.	$-\log[H^+_a] - (-\log[H^+_v])$ $= -\log[H^+_a] + \log[H^+_v]$ $= \log[H^+_v] - \log[H^+_a]$
Substitute values for $[H^+_v]$ and $[H^+_a]$.	$= \log(6.3 \times 10^{-3}) - \log 10^{-11}$
Use the Product Property of Logarithms, and simplify.	$= \log 6.3 + \log 10^{-3} - \log 10^{-11}$ $= \log 6.3 - 3 + 11$
Use a calculator.	≈ 8.8
Write the answer.	The pH level of ammonia is about 8.8 greater than the pH level of vinegar.

Got It? **4. Reasoning** Suppose the hydrogen ion concentration for Substance A is twice that for Substance B. Which substance has the greater pH level? What is the greater pH level minus the lesser pH level? Explain.

Lesson Check

Do you know HOW?

Write each expression as a single logarithm.

1. $\log_4 2 + \log_4 8$

2. $\log_6 24 - \log_6 4$

Expand each logarithm.

3. $\log_3 \frac{x}{y}$ **4.** $\log m^2 n^5$ **5.** $\log_2 \sqrt{x}$

Do you UNDERSTAND?

6. Vocabulary State which property or properties need to be used to write each expression as a single logarithm.

   a. $\log_4 5 + \log_4 5$ **b.** $\log_5 4 - \log_5 6$

7. Reasoning If $\log x = 5$, what is the value of $\frac{1}{x}$?

8. Open-Ended Write $\log 150$ as a sum or difference of two logarithms. Simplify if possible.

Practice and Problem-Solving Exercises

MATHEMATICAL PRACTICES

 **Practice**

Write each expression as a single logarithm.

See Problem 1.

9. $\log 7 + \log 2$

10. $\log_2 9 - \log_2 3$

11. $5 \log 3 + \log 4$

12. $\log 8 - 2 \log 6 + \log 3$

13. $4 \log m - \log n$

14. $\log 5 - k \log 2$

15. $\log_6 5 + \log_6 x$

16. $\log_7 x + \log_7 y - \log_7 z$

17. $\log_3 4 + \log_3 y + \log_3 8x$

Expand each logarithm.

See Problem 2.

18. $\log x^3 y^5$

19. $\log_7 49xyz$

20. $\log_b \frac{b}{x}$

21. $\log a^2$

22. $\log_5 \frac{r}{s}$

23. $\log_3 (2x)^2$

24. $\log_3 7(2x-3)^2$

25. $\log \frac{a^2 b^3}{c^4}$

26. $\log_4 5\sqrt{x}$

27. $\log_8 8\sqrt{3a^5}$

28. $\log_5 \frac{25}{x}$

29. $\log 10m^4 n^{-2}$

Use the Change of Base Formula to evaluate each expression.

See Problem 3.

30. $\log_2 9$

31. $\log_{12} 20$

32. $\log_7 30$

33. $\log_5 10$

34. $\log_4 7$

35. $\log_3 54$

36. $\log_5 62$

37. $\log_3 33$

STEM **38. Science** The concentration of hydrogen ions in household dish detergent is 10^{-12}. What is the pH level of household dish detergent?

See Problem 4.

 Apply

Use the properties of logarithms to evaluate each expression.

39. $\log_2 4 - \log_2 16$

40. $\log_2 96 - \log_2 3$

41. $\log_3 27 - 2\log_3 3$

42. $\log_6 12 + \log_6 3$

43. $\log_4 48 - \frac{1}{2}\log_4 9$

44. $\frac{1}{2}\log_5 15 - \log_5 \sqrt{75}$

45. Think About a Plan The loudness in decibels (dB) of a sound is defined as $10 \log \frac{I}{I_0}$, where I is the intensity of the sound in watts per square meter (W/m^2). I_0, the intensity of a barely audible sound, is equal to $10^{-12}\,\text{W/m}^2$. Town regulations require the loudness of construction work not to exceed 100 dB. Suppose a construction team is blasting rock for a roadway. One explosion has an intensity of $1.65 \times 10^{-2}\,\text{W/m}^2$. Is this explosion in violation of town regulations?
- Which physical value do you need to calculate to answer the question?
- What values should you use for I and I_0?

STEM **46. Construction** The foreman of a construction team puts up a sound barrier that reduces the intensity of the noise by 50%. By how many decibels is the noise reduced? Use the formula $L = 10 \log \frac{I}{I_0}$ to measure loudness. (*Hint:* Find the difference between the expression for loudness for intensity I and the expression for loudness for intensity $0.5I$.)

47. Error Analysis Explain why the expansion at the right of $\log_4 \sqrt{\frac{t}{s}}$ is incorrect. Then do the expansion correctly.

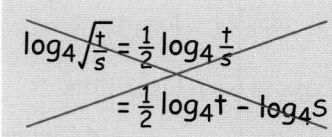

48. Reasoning Can you expand $\log_3 (2x + 1)$? Explain.

49. Writing Explain why $\log (5 \cdot 2) \neq \log 5 \cdot \log 2$.

Determine if each statment is *true* or *false*. Justify your answer.

50. $\log_2 4 + \log_2 8 = 5$

51. $\log_3 \frac{3}{2} = \frac{1}{2} \log_3 3$

52. $\log (x - 2) = \frac{\log x}{\log 2}$

53. $\frac{\log_b x}{\log_b y} = \log_b \frac{x}{y}$

54. $(\log x)^2 = \log x^2$

55. $\log_4 7 - \log_4 3 = \log_4 4$

Write each logarithmic expression as a single logarithm.

56. $\frac{1}{4} \log_3 2 + \frac{1}{4} \log_3 x$

57. $\frac{1}{2} (\log_x 4 + \log_x y) - 3 \log_x z$

58. $x \log_4 m + \frac{1}{y} \log_4 n - \log_4 p$

59. $\left(\frac{2\log_b x}{3} + \frac{3\log_b y}{4} \right) - 5 \log_b z$

Expand each logarithm.

60. $\log \sqrt{\frac{2x}{y}}$

61. $\log \frac{s\sqrt{7}}{t^2}$

62. $\log \left(\frac{2\sqrt{x}}{5} \right)^3$

63. $\log \frac{m^3}{n^4 p^{-2}}$

64. $\log 4 \sqrt{\frac{4r}{s^2}}$

65. $\log_b \frac{\sqrt{x}\sqrt[3]{y^2}}{\sqrt[5]{z^2}}$

66. $\log_4 \frac{\sqrt{x^5 y^7}}{zw^4}$

67. $\log \frac{\sqrt{x^2 - 4}}{(x + 3)^2}$

Write each logarithm as the quotient of two common logarithms. Do not simplify the quotient.

68. $\log_7 2$

69. $\log_3 8$

70. $\log_5 140$

71. $\log_9 3.3$

72. $\log_4 3x$

 **Astronomy** The apparent brightness of stars is measured on a logarithmic scale called magnitude, in which lower numbers mean brighter stars. The relationship between the ratio of apparent brightness of two objects and the difference in their magnitudes is given by the formula $m_2 - m_1 = -2.5 \log \frac{b_2}{b_1}$, where m is the magnitude and b is the apparent brightness.

73. How many times brighter is a magnitude 1.0 star than a magnitude 2.0 star?

74. The star Rigel has a magnitude of 0.12. How many times brighter is Capella than Rigel?

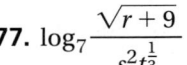 Capella
$m = 0.1$

Challenge

Expand each logarithm.

75. $\log \sqrt{\frac{x\sqrt{2}}{y^2}}$

76. $\log_3 [(xy^{\frac{1}{3}}) + z^2]^3$

77. $\log_7 \frac{\sqrt{r + 9}}{s^2 t^{\frac{1}{3}}}$

Simplify each expression.

78. $\log_3(x + 1) - \log_3(3x^2 - 3x - 6) + \log_3(x - 2)$

79. $\log(a^2 - 10a + 25) + \frac{1}{2} \log\frac{1}{(a - 5)^3} - \log(\sqrt{a - 5})$

Standardized Test Prep

SAT/ACT

80. Which expression is NOT equivalent to $\sqrt[6]{16r^2}$?

Ⓐ $\left(16r^2\right)^{\frac{1}{6}}$ Ⓑ $4r^{\frac{1}{3}}$ Ⓒ $(4r)^{\frac{1}{3}}$ Ⓓ $\sqrt[3]{4r}$

81. Assume that there are no more turning points beyond those shown. Which graph CANNOT be the graph of a fourth degree polynomial?

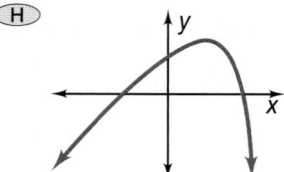

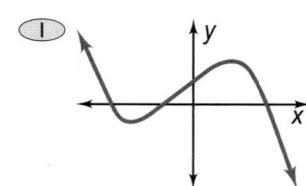

82. A florist is arranging a bouquet of daisies and tulips. He wants twice as many daisies as tulips in the bouquet. If the bouquet contains 24 flowers, how many daisies are in the bouquet?

Ⓐ 8 daisies   Ⓑ 12 daisies   Ⓒ 16 daisies   Ⓓ 24 daisies

Short Response

83. Use the properties of logarithms to write log 18 in four different ways. Name each property you use.

Mixed Review

Write each equation in logarithmic form.   See Lesson 7-3.

84. $49 = 7^2$ **85.** $\frac{1}{4} = 8^{-\frac{2}{3}}$ **86.** $5^{-3} = \frac{1}{125}$

Solve. Check for extraneous solutions.   See Lesson 6-5.

87. $\sqrt[3]{y^4} = 16$ **88.** $\sqrt[3]{7x} - 4 = 0$ **89.** $2\sqrt{w-1} = \sqrt{w+2}$

Write a polynomial function with rational coefficients and the given roots.   See Lesson 5-5.

90. $\sqrt{3}, -5$ **91.** $-i, 4i$ **92.** $-\sqrt{7}, 1 + 2i$

Get Ready!   To prepare for Lesson 7-5, do Exercises 93–95.

Evaluate each logarithm.   See Lesson 7-3.

93. $\log_{12} 144$ **94.** $\log_4 64$ **95.** $\log_{64} 4$

7-5 Exponential and Logarithmic Equations

© **Common Core State Standards**

F-LE.A.4 For exponential models, express as a logarithm the solution to $ab^{ct} = d$ where a, c, and d are numbers and the base b is 2, 10, or e; evaluate the logarithm using technology. **Also A-REI.D.11**

MP 1, MP 3, MP 4, MP 5, MP 7

Objective To solve exponential and logarithmic equations

SOLVE IT!

Getting Ready!

You are a winner on a TV game show. Which prize would you choose? Explain.

Make sure you win the most money.

MATHEMATICAL PRACTICES

Prize A
$10,000
per week

Prize B
1¢ today,
2¢ tomorrow,
4¢ the next day,
and so on,
doubling each day

Lesson Vocabulary
- exponential equation
- logarithmic equation

Any equation that contains the form b^{cx}, such as $a = b^{cx}$ where the exponent includes a variable, is an **exponential equation**.

Essential Understanding You can use logarithms to solve exponential equations. You can use exponents to solve logarithmic equations.

© **Problem 1** Solving an Exponential Equation—Common Base

Multiple Choice What is the solution of $16^{3x} = 8$?

Ⓐ $x = \frac{1}{4}$　　　Ⓑ $x = \frac{3}{7}$　　　Ⓒ $x = 1$　　　Ⓓ $x = 4$

Plan

What common base is appropriate?
2 because 16 and 8 are both powers of 2.

$16^{3x} = 8$

$(2^4)^{3x} = 2^3$　　Rewrite the terms with a common base.

$2^{12x} = 2^3$　　Power Property of Exponents

$12x = 3$　　If two numbers with the same base are equal, their exponents are equal.

$x = \frac{1}{4}$　　Solve and simplify.

The correct answer is A.

Got It? 1. What is the solution of $27^{3x} = 81$?

When bases are not the same, you can solve an exponential equation by taking the logarithm of each side of the equation. If m and n are positive and $m = n$, then $\log m = \log n$.

 Problem 2 Solving an Exponential Equation—Different Bases

What is the solution of $15^{3x} = 285$?

Think

Which property of logarithms will help isolate x?
The rule $\log a^x = x \log a$ moves x out of the exponent position.

$$15^{3x} = 285$$

$$\log 15^{3x} = \log 285 \qquad \text{Take the logarithm of each side.}$$

$$3x \log 15 = \log 285 \qquad \text{Power Property of Logarithms}$$

$$x = \frac{\log 285}{3 \log 15} \qquad \text{Divide each side by } 3 \log 15 \text{ to isolate } x.$$

$$x \approx 0.6958 \qquad \text{Use a calculator.}$$

Check $15^{3x} = 285$

$$15^{3(0.6958)} \approx 285.0840331 \approx 285 \checkmark$$

 Got It? **2. a.** What is the solution of $5^{2x} = 130$?

b. Reasoning Why can't you use the same method you used in Problem 1 to solve Problem 2?

Problem 3 Solving an Exponential Equation With a Graph or Table

What is the solution of $4^{3x} = 6000$?

Method 1 Solve using a graph.

Use a graphing calculator. Graph the equations.

$$Y_1 = 4^{3x}$$

$$Y_2 = 6000$$

Adjust the window to find the point of intersection. The solution is $x \approx 2.09$.

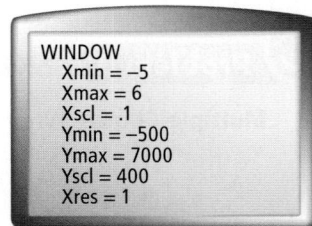

WINDOW
Xmin = −5
Xmax = 6
Xscl = .1
Ymin = −500
Ymax = 7000
Yscl = 400
Xres = 1

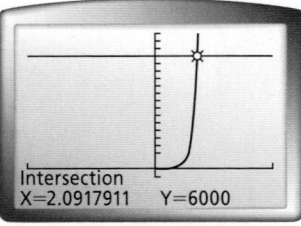

Intersection
X=2.0917911   Y=6000

Method 2 Solve using a table.

Think

How do you choose TblStart and ΔTbl values?
Start with 0 and 1, respectively. Adjust both values as you close in on the solution.

Use the table feature of a graphing calculator. Enter $Y_1 = 4^{3x}$.

Use the **TABLE SETUP** and **ΔTbl** features to locate the x-value that gives the y-value closest to 6000.

The solution is $x \approx 2.09$.

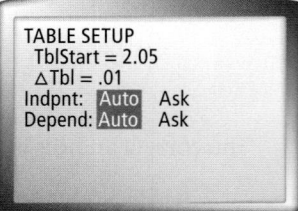

TABLE SETUP
TblStart = 2.05
ΔTbl = .01
Indpnt: Auto Ask
Depend: Auto Ask

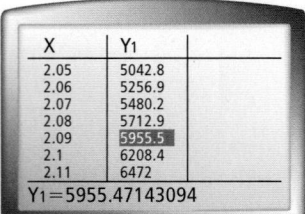

X	Y₁
2.05	5042.8
2.06	5256.9
2.07	5480.2
2.08	5712.9
2.09	5955.5
2.1	6208.4
2.11	6472

Y₁=5955.47143094

 Got It? **3.** What is the solution of each exponential equation? Check your answer.

a. $7^{4x} = 800$ **b.** $5.2^{3x} = 400$

 **Problem 4** **Modeling With an Exponential Equation** STEM

Resource Management Wood is a sustainable, renewable, natural resource when you manage forests properly. Your lumber company has 1,200,000 trees. You plan to harvest 7% of the trees each year. How many years will it take to harvest half of the trees?

Know	Need	Plan
• Number of trees • Rate of decay	Number of years it takes to harvest 600,000 trees	• Write an exponential equation. • Use logarithms to solve the equation.

Think

What equation should you use to model this situation?
Since you are planning to harvest 7% of the trees each year, you should use $y = ab^x$, where b is the decay factor.

Step 1 Is an exponential model reasonable for this situation?

Yes, you are harvesting a fixed percentage each year.

Step 2 Define the variables and determine the model.

Let n = the number of years it takes to harvest half of the trees.

Let $T(n)$ = the number of trees remaining after n years.

A reasonable model is $T(n) = a(b)^n$.

Step 3 Use the model to write an exponential equation.

$T(n) = 600,000$

$a = 1,200,000$

$r = -7\% = -0.07$

$b = 1 + r = 1 + (-0.07) = 0.93$

So, $1,200,000(0.93)^n = 600,000$.

Step 4 Solve the equation. Use logarithms.

$1,200,000(0.93)^n = 600,000$

$0.93^n = \dfrac{600,000}{1,200,000}$ Isolate the term with n.

$\log 0.93^n = \log 0.5$ Take the logarithm of each side.

$n \log 0.93 = \log 0.5$ Power Property of Logarithms

$n = \dfrac{\log 0.5}{\log 0.93}$ Solve for n.

$n \approx 9.55$ Use a calculator.

It will take about 9.55 years to harvest half of the original trees.

 Got It? **4.** After how many years will you have harvested half of the trees if you harvest 5% instead of 7% yearly?

A **logarithmic equation** is an equation that includes one or more logarithms involving a variable.

Problem 5 Solving a Logarithmic Equation

What is the solution of $\log (4x - 3) = 2$?

Method 1 Solve using exponents.

$$\log (4x - 3) = 2$$

$$4x - 3 = 10^2 \qquad \text{Write in exponential form.}$$

$$4x = 103 \qquad \text{Simplify.}$$

$$x = \frac{103}{4} = 25.75 \qquad \text{Solve for } x.$$

Method 2 Solve using a graph.
Graph the equations
$Y_1 = \textbf{LOG (4x} - \textbf{3)}$ and $Y_2 = \textbf{2}$.
Find the point of intersection.
The solution is $x = 25.75$.

Method 3 Solve using a table.
Enter $Y_1 = \textbf{LOG (4x} - \textbf{3)}$.
Use the **TABLE SETUP** feature to find the
x-value that corresponds to a y-value of
2 in the table.
The solution is $x = 25.75$.

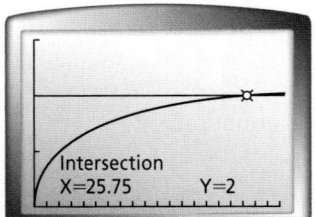

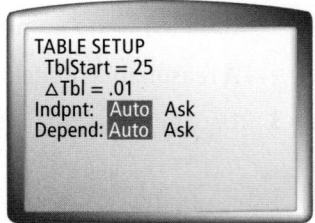

 Got It? **5.** What is the solution of $\log (3 - 2x) = -1$?

Problem 6 Using Logarithmic Properties to Solve an Equation

What is the solution of $\log (x - 3) + \log x = 1$?

$$\log (x - 3) + \log x = 1$$

$$\log ((x - 3)x) = 1 \qquad \text{Product Property of Logarithms}$$

$$(x - 3)x = 10^1 \qquad \text{Write in exponential form.}$$

$$x^2 - 3x - 10 = 0 \qquad \text{Simplify to a quadratic equation in standard form.}$$

$$(x - 5)(x + 2) = 0 \qquad \text{Factor the trinomial.}$$

$$x = 5 \quad \text{or} \quad x = -2 \qquad \text{Solve for } x.$$

Check

$$\log (x - 3) + \log (x) = 1 \qquad\qquad \log (x - 3) + \log (x) = 1$$

$$\log (-2 - 3) + \log (-2) \overset{?}{=} 1 \; \textbf{✗} \qquad \log (5 - 3) + \log (5) \overset{?}{=} 1$$

$$\log 2 + \log 5 \overset{?}{=} 1$$

$$0.3010 + 0.6990 = 1 \; \textbf{✔}$$

If $\log (x - 3) + \log(x) = 1$, $x = 5$.

 Got It? **6.** What is the solution of $\log 6 - \log 3x = -2$?

Lesson Check

Do you know HOW?

Solve each equation.

1. $3^x = 9$

2. $2^{y+1} = 25$

3. $\log 4x = 2$

4. $\log x - \log 2 = 3$

Do you UNDERSTAND?

 MATHEMATICAL PRACTICES

5. Error Analysis Describe and correct the error made in solving the equation.

$$\log_2 x = 2 \log_3 9$$
$$\log_2 x = \log_3 9^2$$
$$x = 9^2$$
$$x = 81$$

6. Reasoning Is it possible for an exponential equation to have no solutions? If so, give an example. If not, explain why.

Practice and Problem-Solving Exercises

 MATHEMATICAL PRACTICES

A  Practice

Solve each equation.

 See Problem 1.

7. $2^x = 8$

8. $3^{2x} = 27$

9. $4^{3x} = 64$

10. $5^{3x} = \frac{1}{125}$

11. $2^{5x+1} = 32$

12. $3^{-2x+2} = 81$

13. $2^{3x} = 4^{x+1}$

14. $3^{x+2} = 27^{2x}$

Solve each equation. Round to the nearest ten-thousandth. Check your answers.

See Problem 2.

15. $2^x = 3$

16. $4^x = 19$

17. $8 + 10^x = 1008$

18. $5 - 3^x = -40$

19. $9^{2y} = 66$

20. $12^{y-2} = 20$

21. $25^{2x+1} = 144$

22. $2^{3x-4} = 5$

Graphing Calculator Solve by graphing. Round to the nearest ten-thousandth.

See Problem 3.

23. $4^{7x} = 250$

24. $5^{3x} = 500$

25. $6^x = 4565$

26. $1.5^x = 356$

Use a table to solve each equation. Round to the nearest hundredth.

27. $2^{x+3} = 512$

28. $3^{x-1} = 72$

29. $6^{2x} = 10$

30. $5^{2x} = 56$

31. The equation $y = 6.72(1.014)^x$ models the world population y, in billions of people, x years after the year 2000. Find the year in which the world population is about 8 billion.

See Problem 4.

Solve each equation. Check your answers.

See Problem 5.

32. $\log 2x = -1$

33. $2 \log x = -1$

34. $\log (3x + 1) = 2$

35. $\log x + 4 = 8$

36. $\log 6x - 3 = -4$

37. $3 \log x = 1.5$

38. $2 \log (x + 1) = 5$

39. $\log (5 - 2x) = 0$

Solve each equation.

See Problem 6.

40. $\log x - \log 3 = 8$

41. $\log 2x + \log x = 11$

42. $2 \log x + \log 4 = 2$

43. $\log 5 - \log 2x = 1$

44. $3 \log x - \log 6 + \log 2.4 = 9$

45. $\log (7x + 1) = \log (x - 2) + 1$

 **Apply**

46. Think About a Plan An earthquake of magnitude 9.1 occurred in 2004 in the Indian Ocean near Indonesia. It was about 74,900 times as strong as the greatest earthquake ever to hit Texas. Find the magnitude of the Texas earthquake. (Remember that an increase of 1.0 on the Richter scale means an earthquake is 30 times stronger.)
- Can you write an exponential or logarithmic equation?
- How does the solution of your equation help you find the magnitude?

47. Consider the equation $2^{\frac{x}{3}} = 80$.
- **a.** Solve the equation by taking the logarithm base 10 of each side.
- **b.** Solve the equation by taking the logarithm base 2 of each side.
- **c. Writing** Compare your result in parts (a) and (b). What are the advantages of each method? Explain.

 48. Seismology An earthquake of magnitude 7.7 occurred in 2001 in Gujarat, India. It was about 4900 times as strong as the greatest earthquake ever to hit Pennsylvania. What is the magnitude of the Pennsylvania earthquake? (*Hint*: Refer to the Richter scale on page 453.)

49. As a town gets smaller, the population of its high school decreases by 6% each year. The senior class has 160 students now. In how many years will it have about 100 students? Write an equation. Then solve the equation without graphing.

Mental Math Solve each equation.

50. $2^x = \frac{1}{2}$

51. $3^x = 27$

52. $\log_9 3 = x$

53. $\log_4 64 = x$

54. $\log_8 2 = x$

55. $10^x = \frac{1}{100}$

56. $\log_7 343 = x$

57. $25^x = \frac{1}{5}$

58. Demography The table below lists the states with the highest and with the lowest population growth rates. Determine in how many years each event can occur. Use the model $P = P_0(1 + r)^x$, where P_0 is population from the table, as of July, 2007; x is the number of years after July, 2007, P is the projected population, and r is the growth rate.
- **a.** Population of Idaho exceeds 2 million.
- **b.** Population of Michigan decreases by 1 million.
- **c.** Population of Nevada doubles.

State	Growth rate (%)	Population (in thousands)	State	Growth rate (%)	Population (in thousands)
1. Nevada	2.93	2,565	46. New York	0.08	19,298
2. Arizona	2.81	6,339	47. Vermont	0.08	621
3. Utah	2.55	2,645	48. Ohio	0.03	11,467
4. Idaho	2.43	1,499	49. Michigan	−0.30	10,072
5. Georgia	2.17	9,545	50. Rhode Island	−0.36	1,058

Source: U.S. Census Bureau

© **59. Open-Ended** Write and solve a logarithmic equation.

© **60. Reasoning** The graphs of $y = 2^{3x}$ and $y = 3^{x+1}$ intersect at approximately (1.1201, 10.2692). What is the solution of $2^{3x} = 3^{x+1}$?

© **61. Reasoning** If $\log 12^{0.5x} = \log 143.6$, then $12^{0.5x} = \underline{\ ?\ }$.

STEM Acoustics In Exercises 62–63, the loudness measured in decibels (dB) is defined by loudness $= 10 \log \frac{I}{I_0}$, where I is the intensity and $I_0 = 10^{-12}$ W/m².

62. The human threshold for pain is 120 dB. Instant perforation of the eardrum occurs at 160 dB.
  a. Find the intensity of each sound.
  b. How many times as intense is the noise that will perforate an eardrum as the noise that causes pain?

63. The noise level inside a convertible driving along the freeway with its top up is 70 dB. With the top down, the noise level is 95 dB.
  a. Find the intensity of the sound with the top up and with the top down.
  b. By what percent does leaving the top up reduce the intensity of the sound?

Solve each equation. If necessary, round to the nearest ten-thousandth.

64. $8^x = 444$

65. $\frac{1}{2}\log x + \log 4 = 2$

66. $4\log_3 2 - 2\log_3 x = 1$

67. $\log x^2 = 2$

68. $9^{2x} = 42$

69. $\log_8 (2x - 1) = \frac{1}{3}$

70. $\log (5x - 4) = 3$

71. $12^{4-x} = 20$

72. $5^{3x} = 125$

73. $\log 4 + 2\log x = 6$

74. $4^{3x} = 77.2$

75. $\log_7 3x = 3$

Use the properties of exponential and logarithmic functions to solve each system. Check your answers.

76. $\begin{cases} y = 2^{x+4} \\ y - 4^{x-1} = 0 \end{cases}$

77. $\begin{cases} 2^{x+y} = 16 \\ 4^{x-y} = 1 \end{cases}$

78. $\begin{cases} \log(2x - y) = 1 \\ \log(x + y) = 3\log 2 \end{cases}$

 **Challenge** **Solve each equation.**

79. $\log_7 (2x - 3)^2 = 2$

80. $\log_2 (x^2 + 2x) = 3$

81. $\frac{3}{2}\log_2 4 - \frac{1}{2}\log_2 x = 3$

STEM 82. Meteorology In the formula $P = P_0\left(\frac{1}{2}\right)^{\frac{h}{4795}}$, P is the atmospheric pressure in millimeters of mercury at elevation h meters above sea level. P_0 is the atmospheric pressure at sea level. If P_0 equals 760 mm, at what elevation is the pressure 42 mm?

STEM **83. Music** The pitch, or frequency, of a piano note is related to its position on the keyboard by the function $F(n) = 440 \cdot 2^{\frac{n}{12}}$, where F is the frequency of the sound waves in cycles per second and n is the number of piano keys above or below Concert A, as shown. If $n = 0$ at Concert A, which of the instruments shown in the diagram can sound notes at the given frequency?

a. 590   **c.** 1440

b. 120   **d.** 2093

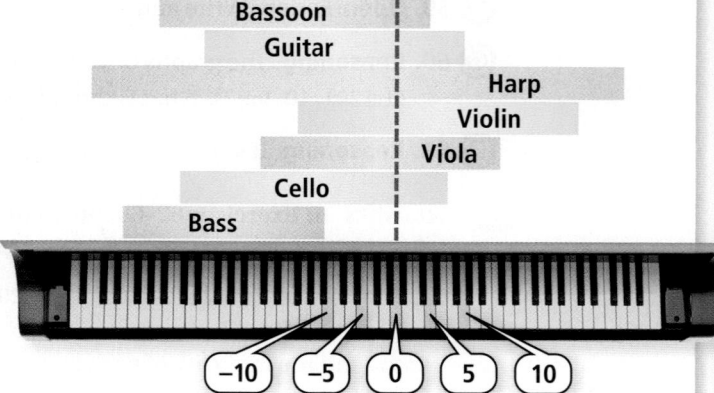

Standardized Test Prep

GRIDDED RESPONSE

SAT/ACT

84. The graph at the right shows the translation of the graph of the parent function $y = |x|$ down 2 units and 3 units to the right. What is the area of the shaded triangle in square units?

85. What does x equal if $\log(1 + 3x) = 3$?

86. Using the change of base formula, what is the value of x for which $\log_9 x = \log_3 5$?

87. The polynomial $x^4 + 3x^3 + 16x^2 - 19x + 8$ is divided by the binomial $x - 1$. What is the coefficient of x^2 in the quotient?

88. What positive value of b makes $x^2 + bx + 81$ a perfect square trinomial?

Apply What You've Learned

MATHEMATICAL PRACTICES

MP 5

Look back at the information on page 433 about apparent magnitudes of stars. In the Apply What You've Learned section in Lesson 7-1, you wrote an exponential function to model the problem on page 433.

a. Use the exponential function you wrote in part (c) on page 441 to write an exponential equation that you can solve for the difference in apparent magnitude between Polaris and Sirius.

b. Explain how to use a graphing calculator to solve the equation you wrote in part (a).

c. Solve the equation algebraically, and use a graphing calculator to check your answer. Round your answer to the nearest hundredth.

Using Logarithms for Exponential Models

© **Common Core State Standards**

F-IF.C.8 Write a function defined by an expression in different but equivalent forms to reveal and explain different properties of the function. **Also F-IF.C.7c**

MP 5

You can transform an exponential function into a linear function by taking the logarithm of each side. Since linear models are easy to recognize, you can then determine whether an exponential function is a good model for a set of values.

MATHEMATICAL PRACTICES

$y = ab^x$ Write the general form of an exponential function.

$\log y = \log ab^x$ Take the logarithm of each side.

$\log y = \log a + x(\log b)$ Use the Product Property and the Power Property.

If $\log b$ and $\log a$ are constants, then $\log y = (\log b)x + \log a$ is a linear equation in slope-intercept form when you plot the points as $(x, \log y)$.

Activity

Determine whether an exponential function is a good model for the values in the table.

x	0	2	4	6	8	10
y	0.5	2	7.8	32	127.9	511.7

Step 1 Enter the values into (stat) lists **L₁** and **L₂**. To enter the values of log y, place the cursor in the heading of **L₃** and press (log) **L₂** (enter).

Step 2 To graph log y, access the (stat plot) feature and press **1**. Then enter **L₃** next to **YLIST:**. Then press (zoom) **9**.

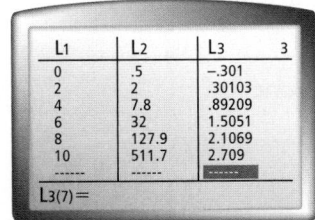

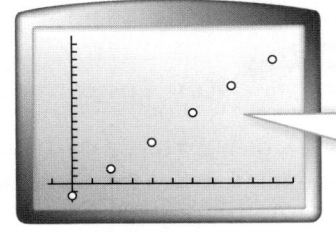

The points $(x, \log y)$ lie on a line, so an exponential model is appropriate.

Step 3 Press (stat) ▷ **0** (enter) to find the exponential function $y = 0.5(2)^x$.

Exercises

For each set of values, determine whether an exponential function is a good model. If so, find the exponential function.

1.

x	1	3	5	7	9
y	6	22	54	102	145

2.

x	−1	0	1	2	3
y	40.2	19.8	9.9	5.1	2.5

© **3. Writing** Explain how you could determine whether a logarithmic function is a good model for a set of data.

Common Core State Standards

F-LE.A.4 For exponential models, express as a logarithm the solution to $ab^{ct} = d$ where a, c, and d are numbers and the base b is 2, 10, or e . . .

MP 1, MP 3, MP 4, MP 5

Objectives To evaluate and simplify natural logarithmic expressions
To solve equations using natural logarithms

What do you know about inverse functions that could help here?

MATHEMATICAL PRACTICES

SOLVE IT!

Getting Ready!

A function f is <u>bounded above</u> if there is some number B that f(x) can never exceed. The exponential function base e shown here is not bounded above. Is the logarithmic function base e bounded above? If so, find a bounding number. If not, explain why.

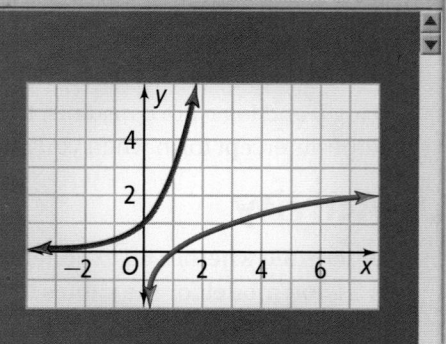

Lesson Vocabulary

• natural logarithmic function

The function $y = e^x$ has an inverse, the **natural logarithmic function**, $y = \log_e x$, or $y = \ln x$.

Essential Understanding The functions $y = e^x$ and $y = \ln x$ are inverse functions. Just as before, this means that if $a = e^b$, then $b = \ln a$, and vice versa.

take note

Key Concept Natural Logarithmic Function

If $y = e^x$, then $x = \log_e y = \ln y$. The natural logarithmic function is the inverse of $x = \ln y$, so you can write it as $y = \ln x$.

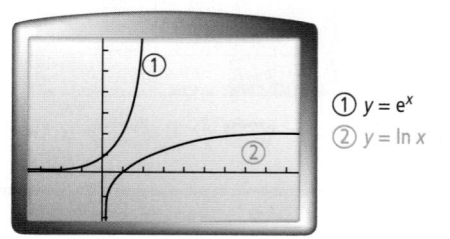

① $y = e^x$
② $y = \ln x$

Plan

Can you use properties of logarithms?
Yes; the properties you studied in Lesson 7-4 apply to logarithms with any base.

Problem 1 Simplifying a Natural Logarithmic Expression

What is $2 \ln 15 - \ln 75$ written as a single natural logarithm?

$2 \ln 15 - \ln 75 = \ln 15^2 - \ln 75$ Power Property of Logarithms

$= \ln \dfrac{15^2}{75}$ Quotient Property of Logarithms

$= \ln 3$ Simplify.

Got It? **1.** What is each expression written as a single natural logarithm?

     a. $\ln 7 + 2 \ln 5$ **b.** $3 \ln x - 2 \ln 2x$ **c.** $3 \ln x + 2 \ln y + \ln 5$

You can use the inverse relationship between the functions $y = \ln x$ and $y = e^x$ to solve certain logarithmic and exponential equations.

Problem 2 Solving a Natural Logarithmic Equation

What are the solutions of $\ln (x - 3)^2 = 4$?

Think

How do you go from logarithmic form to exponential form?
Use the definition of logarithm: $\ln x = y$ if and only if $x = e^y$.

$$\ln (x - 3)^2 = 4$$

$$(x - 3)^2 = e^4 \qquad \text{Rewrite in exponential form.}$$

$$x - 3 = \pm e^2 \qquad \text{Find the square root of each side.}$$

$$x = 3 \pm e^2 \qquad \text{Solve for } x.$$

$$x \approx 10.39 \text{ or } -4.39 \qquad \text{Use a calculator.}$$

Check

$$\ln (10.39 - 3)^2 \overset{?}{=} 4 \qquad \ln (-4.39 - 3)^2 \overset{?}{=} 4$$

$$4.0003 \approx 4 \; ✔ \qquad\qquad 4.0003 \approx 4 \; ✔$$

 Got It? **2.** What are the solutions of each equation? Check your answers.

     a. $\ln x = 2$ **b.** $\ln (3x + 5)^2 = 4$ **c.** $\ln 2x + \ln 3 = 2$

Problem 3 Solving an Exponential Equation

What is the solution of $4e^{2x} + 2 = 16$?

Plan

How can you solve this equation?
First get e^x by itself on one side of the equation. Then rewrite the equation in logarithmic form and solve for x.

$$4e^{2x} + 2 = 16$$

$$4e^{2x} = 14 \qquad \text{Subtract 2 from each side.}$$

$$e^{2x} = 3.5 \qquad \text{Divide each side by 4.}$$

$$2x = \ln 3.5 \qquad \text{Rewrite in logarithmic form.}$$

$$x = \frac{\ln 3.5}{2} \qquad \text{Divide each side by 2.}$$

$$x \approx 0.626 \qquad \text{Use a calculator.}$$

Check

$$4e^{2x} + 2 = 16$$

$$4e^{2(0.626)} + 2 \overset{?}{=} 16$$

$$15.99 \approx 16 \; ✔$$

 Got It? **3.** What is the solution of each equation? Check your answers.

     a. $e^{x-2} = 12$ **b.** $2e^{-x} = 20$ **c.** $e^{3x} + 5 = 15$

Natural logarithms are useful because they help express many relationships in the physical world.

 Problem 4 Using Natural Logarithms STEM

Space A spacecraft can attain a stable orbit 300 km above Earth if it reaches a velocity of 7.7 km/s. The formula for a rocket's maximum velocity v in kilometers per second is $v = -0.0098t + c \ln R$. The booster rocket fires for t seconds and the velocity of the exhaust is c km/s. The ratio of the mass of the rocket filled with fuel to its mass without fuel is R. Suppose the rocket shown in the photo has a mass ratio of 25, a firing time of 100 s and an exhaust velocity as shown. Can the spacecraft attain a stable orbit 300 km above Earth?

Let $R = 25$, $c = 2.8$, and $t = 100$. Find v.

$v = -0.0098t + c \ln R$ Use the formula.

$ = -0.0098(100) + 2.8 \ln 25$ Substitute.

$ \approx -0.98 + 2.8(3.219)$ Use a calculator.

$ \approx 8.0$ Simplify.

The maximum velocity of 8.0 km/s is greater than the 7.7 km/s needed for a stable orbit. Therefore, the spacecraft can attain a stable orbit 300 km above Earth.

 Got It? 4. a. A booster rocket for a spacecraft has a mass ratio of about 15, an exhaust velocity of 2.1 km/s, and a firing time of 30 s. Can the spacecraft achieve a stable orbit 300 km above Earth?

    b. Reasoning Suppose a rocket, as designed, cannot provide enough velocity to achieve a stable orbit. Could alterations to the rocket make a stable orbit achievable? Explain.

 Lesson Check

Do you know HOW?

Write each expression as a single natural logarithm.

1. $4 \ln 3$

2. $\ln 18 - \ln 10$

3. $\ln 3 + \ln 4$

4. $-2 \ln 2$

Solve each equation.

5. $\ln 5x = 4$

6. $\ln (x - 7) = 2$

7. $2 \ln x = 4$

8. $\ln (2 - x) = 1$

Do you UNDERSTAND? MATHEMATICAL PRACTICES

9. Error Analysis Describe the error made in solving the equation. Then find the correct solution.

10. Reasoning Can $\ln 5 + \log_2 10$ be written as a single logarithm? Explain your reasoning.

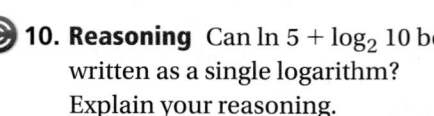

Practice and Problem-Solving Exercises

MATHEMATICAL PRACTICES

 **Practice**

Write each expression as a single natural logarithm.

See Problem 1.

11. $3 \ln 5$

12. $\ln 9 + \ln 2$

13. $\ln 24 - \ln 6$

14. $5 \ln m - 3 \ln n$

15. $\frac{1}{3}(\ln x + \ln y) - 4 \ln z$

16. $\ln a - 2 \ln b + \frac{1}{3}\ln c$

17. $4 \ln 8 + \ln 10$

18. $\ln 3 - 5 \ln 3$

19. $2 \ln 8 - 3 \ln 4$

Solve each equation. Check your answers.

See Problem 2.

20. $\ln 3x = 6$

21. $\ln x = -2$

22. $\ln (4x - 1) = 36$

23. $1.1 + \ln x^2 = 6$

24. $\ln \frac{x-1}{2} = 4$

25. $\ln 4r^2 = 3$

26. $2 \ln 2x^2 = 1$

27. $\ln (2m + 3) = 8$

28. $\ln (t - 1)^2 = 3$

Use natural logarithms to solve each equation.

See Problem 3.

29. $e^x = 18$

30. $e^{\frac{x}{5}} + 4 = 7$

31. $e^{2x} = 12$

32. $e^{\frac{x}{2}} = 5$

33. $e^{x+1} = 30$

34. $e^{2x} = 10$

35. $e^{3x} + 5 = 6$

36. $e^{\frac{x}{9}} - 8 = 6$

37. $7 - 2e^{\frac{x}{2}} = 1$

STEM **Space** For Exercises 38 and 39, use $v = -0.0098t + c \ln R$, where v is the velocity of the rocket, t is the firing time, c is the velocity of the exhaust, and R is the ratio of the mass of the rocket filled with fuel to the mass of the rocket without fuel.

See Problem 4.

38. Find the velocity of a spacecraft whose booster rocket has a mass ratio of 20, an exhaust velocity of 2.7 km/s, and a firing time of 30 s. Can the spacecraft achieve a stable orbit 300 km above Earth?

39. A rocket has a mass ratio of 24 and an exhaust velocity of 2.5 km/s. Determine the minimum firing time for a stable orbit 300 km above Earth.

B **Apply**

© 40. Think About a Plan By measuring the amount of carbon-14 in an object, a paleontologist can determine its approximate age. The amount of carbon-14 in an object is given by $y = ae^{-0.00012t}$, where a is the amount of carbon-14 originally in the object, and t is the age of the object in years. In 2003, a bone believed to be from a dire wolf was found at the La Brea Tar Pits. The bone contains 14% of its original carbon-14. How old is the bone?
- What numbers should you substitute for y and t?
- What properties of logarithms and exponents can you use to solve the equation?

STEM **41. Archaeology** A fossil bone contains 25% of its original carbon-14. What is the approximate age of the bone?

Simplify each expression.

42. $\ln 1$

43. $\frac{\ln e}{4}$

44. $\frac{\ln e^2}{2}$

45. $\ln e^{83}$

46. $\ln e$

47. $\ln e^2$

48. $\ln e^{10}$

49. $10 \ln e$

50. $\ln e^3$

51. $\frac{\ln e^4}{8}$

52. **Error Analysis** A student has broken the natural logarithm key on his calculator, so he decides to use the Change of Base Formula to find ln 100. Explain his error and find the correct answer.

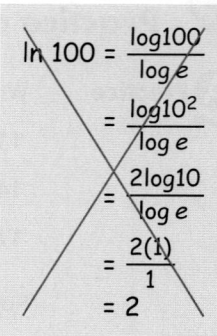

$$\ln 100 = \frac{\log 100}{\log e}$$
$$= \frac{\log 10^2}{\log e}$$
$$= \frac{2\log 10}{\log e}$$
$$= \frac{2(1)}{1}$$
$$= 2$$

53. **Satellite** The battery power available to run a satellite is given by the formula $P = 50\, e^{-\frac{t}{250}}$, where P is power in watts and t is time in days. For how many days can the satellite run if it requires 15 watts of power?

Determine whether each statement is *always*, *sometimes*, or *never* true.

54. $\ln e^x \geq 1$

55. $\ln e^x = \ln e^x + 1$

56. $\ln t = \log_e t$

57. **Space** Use the formula for maximum velocity $v = -0.0098t + c \ln R$. Find the mass ratio of a rocket with an exhaust velocity of 3.1 km/s, a firing time of 50 s, and a maximum shuttle velocity of 6.9 km/s.

Biology The formula $H = \frac{1}{r}(\ln P - \ln A)$ models the number of hours it takes a bacteria culture to decline, where H is the number of hours, r is the rate of decline, P is the initial bacteria population, and A is the reduced bacteria population.

58. A scientist determines that an antibiotic reduces a population of 20,000 bacteria to 5000 in 24 hours. Find the rate of decline caused by the antibiotic.

59. A laboratory assistant tests an antibiotic that causes a rate of decline of 0.14. How long should it take for a population of 8000 bacteria to shrink to 500?

 **Challenge** Solve each equation.

60. $\frac{1}{3}\ln x + \ln 2 - \ln 3 = 3$

61. $\ln(x + 2) - \ln 4 = 3$

62. $2e^{x-2} = e^x + 7$

63. **Error Analysis** Consider the solution to the equation $\ln(x-3)^2 = 4$ at the right. In Problem 2 you saw that there are two solutions to this equation, $3 + e^2$ and $3 - e^2$. Why do you get only one solution using this method?

$$\ln(x-3)^2 = 4$$
$$2\ln(x-3) = 4$$
$$\ln(x-3) = 2$$
$$e^{\ln(x-3)} = e^2$$
$$x - 3 = e^2$$
$$x = e^2 + 3$$

64. **Technology** In 2008, there were about 1.5 billion Internet users. That number is projected to grow to 3.5 billion in 2015.
   a. Let t represent the time, in years, since 2008. Write a function of the form $y = ae^{ct}$ that models the expected growth in the population of Internet users.
   b. In what year were there 2 billion Internet users?
   c. In what year will there be 5 billion Internet users?
   d. Solve your equation for t.
   e. **Writing** Explain how you can use your equation from part (d) to verify your answers to parts (b) and (c).

STEM 65. Physics The function $T(t) = T_r + (T_i - T_r)e^{kt}$ models Newton's Law of Cooling. $T(t)$ is the temperature of a heated substance t minutes after it has been removed from a heat (or cooling) source. T_i is the substance's initial temperature, k is a constant for that substance, and T_r is room temperature.

a. The initial surface temperature of a beef roast is 236°F and room temperature is 72°F. If $k = -0.041$, how long will it take for this roast to cool to 100°F?

b. Graphing Calculator Write and graph an equation that you can use to check your answer to part (a). Use your graph to complete the table below.

Temperature (°F)	225	200	175	150	125	100	75
Minutes Later	▨	▨	▨	▨	▨	▨	▨

Standardized Test Prep

SAT/ACT

66. An investment of $750 will be worth $1500 after 12 years of continuous compounding at a fixed interest rate. What percent is the interest rate?

67. What is $\log 33{,}000 - \log 99 + \log 30$?

68. If $f(x) = 5 - x^2$ and $g(x) = x^2 - 3$, what is $(g \circ f)(6)$?

69. What is the positive root of $y = 2x^2 - 35x - 57$?

70. What is the real part of $3 + 2i$?

71. What is $\dfrac{\sqrt{36}}{\sqrt{4}}$?

Mixed Review

Solve each equation. ◀ **See Lesson 7-5.**

72. $3^{2x} = 6561$

73. $7^x - 2 = 252$

74. $25^{2x+1} = 144$

75. $\log 3x = 4$

76. $\log 5x + 3 = 3.7$

77. $\log 9 - \log x + 1 = 6$

Find the inverse of each function. Is the inverse a function? ◀ **See Lesson 6-7.**

78. $y = 5x + 7$

79. $y = 2x^3 + 10$

80. $y = -x^2 + 5$

81. $y = 3x + 2$

Get Ready! **To prepare for Lesson 8-1, do Exercises 82–84.**

For Exercises 82–84, y varies directly with x. ◀ **See Lesson 2-2.**

82. If $x = 2$ when $y = 4$, find y when $x = 5$.

83. If $x = 1$ when $y = 5$, find y when $x = 3$.

84. If $x = 10$ when $y = 3$, find y when $x = 4$.

Exponential and Logarithmic Inequalities

© Common Core State Standards

A-REI.D.11 Explain why the x-coordinates of the points where the graphs of the equations $y = f(x)$ and $y = g(x)$ intersect are the solutions of the equation $f(x) = g(x) \ldots$

MP 5

You can use the graphing and table capabilities of your calculator to solve problems involving exponential and logarithmic inequalities.

Example 1

Solve $2(3)^{x+4} > 10$ using a graph.

Step 1 Define **Y1** and **Y2**.

Step 2 Make a graph and find the point of intersection.

Step 3 Identify the x-values that make the inequality true.

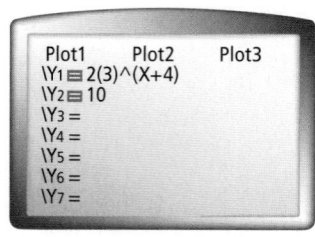

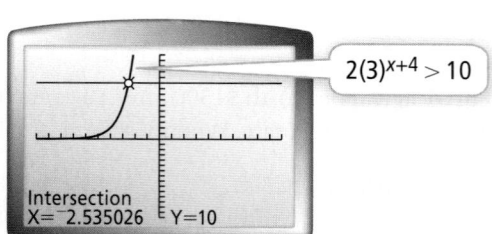

$2(3)^{x+4} > 10$

The solution is $x > -2.535$.

Exercises

Solve each inequality using a graph.

1. $4(3)^{x+1} > 6$

2. $\log x + 3 \log(x - 1) < 4$

3. $3(2)^{x+2} \geq 5$

4. $x + 1 < 12 \log x$

5. $2(3)^{x-4} > 7$

6. $\log x + 2 \log(x - 1) < 1$

7. $4(2)^{x-1} \leq 5$

8. $2 \log x + 4 \log(x + 3) > 3$

9. $5(4)^{x-1} < 2$

STEM **10. Bacteria Growth** Scientists are growing bacteria in a laboratory. They start with a known population of bacteria and measure how long it takes the population to double.

a. Write an exponential function that models the population in Sample A as a function of time in hours.

b. Write an exponential function that models the population in Sample B as a function of time in hours.

c. Write an inequality that models the population in Sample B overtaking the population in Sample A.

d. Use a graphing calculator to solve the inequality in part (c).

Bacteria Population

Sample	Initial Population	Doubling Time (in hours)
Sample A	200,000	1
Sample B	50,000	0.5

© 11. Writing Describe the solution sets to the inequality $x + c < \log x$ as c varies over the real numbers.

Example 2

Solve $\log x + 2 \log(x + 1) < 2$ using a table.

Step 1 Define **Y1** and **Y2**.

Step 2 Make a table and examine the values.

Step 3 Identify the *x*-values that make the inequality true.

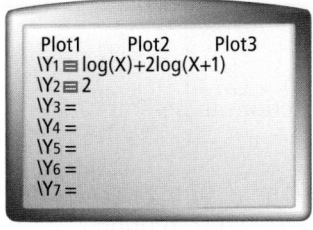

Plot1 Plot2 Plot3
\Y1 ▤ log(X)+2log(X+1)
\Y2 ▤ 2
\Y3 =
\Y4 =
\Y5 =
\Y6 =
\Y7 =

X	Y₁	Y₂
0	ERR.	2
1	.60206	2
2	1.2553	2
3	1.6812	2
4	2	2
5	2.2553	2
6	2.4683	2

X=4

Y₁ < Y₂ for these *x*-values.

The solution is $0 < x < 4$.

Exercises

Solve each inequality using a table.
(Hint: For more accurate results, set ΔTbl = 0.001.)

12. $\log x + \log(x + 1) < 3$

13. $3(2)^{x+1} > 5$

14. $\log x + 5 \log(x - 1) \geq 3$

15. $5(3)^x \leq 2$

16. $3 \log x + \log(x + 2) > 1$

17. $2(4)^{x+3} \leq 8$

Barometric Pressure Average barometric pressure varies with the altitude of a location. The greater the altitude is, the lower the pressure. The altitude A is measured in feet above sea level. The barometric pressure P is measured in inches of mercury (in. Hg). The altitude can be modeled by the function $A(P) = 90,000 - 26,500 \ln P$.

18. What is a reasonable domain of the function? What is the range of the function?

19. Graphing Calculator Use a graphing calculator to make a table of function values. Use **TblStart** = 30 and Δ**Tbl** = −1.

20. Write an equation to find what average pressure the model predicts at sea level, or $A = 0$. Use your table to solve the equation.

21. Kilimanjaro is a mountain in Tanzania that formed from three extinct volcanoes. The base of the mountain is at 3000 ft above sea level. The peak is at 19,340 ft above sea level. On Kilimanjaro, $3000 \leq A(P) \leq 19,340$ is true for the altitude. Write an inequality from which you can find minimum and maximum values of normal barometric pressure on Kilimanjaro. Use a table and solve the inequality for P.

22. Denver, Colorado, is nicknamed the "Mile High City" because its elevation is about 1 mile, or 5280 ft, above sea level. The lowest point in Phoenix, Arizona, is 1117 ft above sea level. Write an inequality that describes the range of $A(P)$ as you drive from Phoenix to Denver. Then solve the inequality for P. (Assume that you never go lower than 1117 ft and you never go higher than 5280 ft.)

Pull It **All Together**

Completing the Performance Task

Look back at your results from the Apply What You've Learned sections in Lessons 7-1 and 7-5. Use the work you did to complete the following.

1. Solve the problem in the Task Description on page 433 by finding the apparent magnitude of Sirius. Show all your work and explain each step of your solution.

 2. Reflect Choose one of the Mathematical Practices below and explain how you applied it in your work on the Performance Task.

> MP 1: Make sense of problems and persevere in solving them.
>
> MP 2: Reason abstractly and quantitatively.
>
> MP 5: Use appropriate tools strategically.

To solve these problems, you will pull together concepts and skills related to exponential functions and logarithms.

On Your Own

Use the information on page 433 about apparent magnitude. The table below shows the apparent magnitudes of several stars in the night sky. One of these stars is 7.8 times as bright as Polaris.

Star	Apparent Magnitude
Betelgeuse	0.43
Vega	0.03
Alpha Centauri	−0.26

a. Write and solve an exponential equation to find the apparent magnitude difference between Polaris and the star that is 7.8 times as bright as Polaris.

b. Which star is 7.8 times as bright as Polaris?

Connecting **BIG** ideas to the Math You've Learned

1 Modeling

The function
$y = ab^x$, $a > 0$, $b > 1$,
models exponential growth.
$y = ab^x$ models exponential
decay if $0 < b < 1$.

2 Equivalence

Logarithms are exponents. In
fact, $\log_b a = c$ if and only if
$b^c = a$.

3 Function

The exponential function
$y = b^x$ and the logarithmic
function $y = \log_b x$ are
inverse functions.

Exponential Models (Lesson 7-1)

The population P is
1000 at the start.
In each time period,

- P grows by 5%.
  $P = 1000(1.05)^t$
- P shrinks by 5%.
  $P = 1000(0.95)^t$

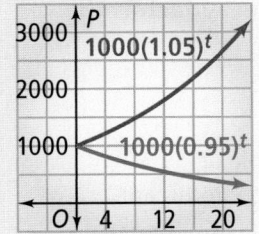

Logarithmic Functions as Inverses (Lesson 7-3)

- $y = 2^x$
- $y = \log_2 x$
- $y = 2^{x-1}$
- $y = (\log_2 x) + 1$

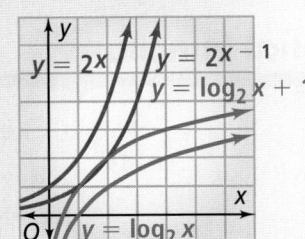

Properties of Logarithms (Lesson 7-4)

$$b^a b^c = b^{a+c}$$
$$\log_b mn = \log_b m + \log_b n$$
$$\frac{b^a}{b^c} = b^{a-c}$$
$$\log_b \frac{m}{n} = \log_b m - \log_b n$$
$$\log_b m^n = n \log_b m$$
$$\log_n m = \frac{\log_b m}{\log_b n}$$

Exponential and Natural Logarithm Equations (Lessons 7-5 and 7-6)

$$e^{x+3} = 4$$
$$e^x \cdot e^3 = 4 \qquad \text{or} \qquad x + 3 = \ln 4$$
$$e^x = \frac{4}{e^3}$$
$$x = \ln \frac{4}{e^3}$$
$$x = \ln 4 - \ln e^3 \qquad x = (\ln 4) - 3$$

Chapter Vocabulary

- asymptote (p. 435)
- Change of Base Formula (p. 464)
- common logarithm (p. 453)
- continuously compounded interest (p. 446)
- decay factor (p. 436)

- exponential decay (p. 435)
- exponential equation (p. 469)
- exponential function (p. 434)
- exponential growth (p. 435)
- growth factor (p. 436)
- logarithm (p. 451)

- logarithmic equation (p. 471)
- logarithmic function (p. 454)
- logarithmic scale (p. 453)
- natural base exponential functions (p. 446)
- natural logarithmic function (p. 478)

Fill in the blanks.

1. There are two types of exponential functions. For __?__ , as the value of x increases, the value of y decreases, approaching zero. For __?__ , as the value of x increases, the value of y increases.

2. As x or y increases in absolute value, the graph may approach a(n) __?__ .

3. A(n) __?__ with a base e is a __?__ .

4. $A = Pe^{rt}$ is known as the __?__ formula.

5. The inverse of an exponential function with a base e is the __?__ .

7-1 Exploring Exponential Models

Quick Review

The general form of an **exponential function** is $y = ab^x$, where x is a real number, $a \neq 0$, $b > 0$, and $b \neq 1$. When $b > 1$, the function models **exponential growth**, and b is the **growth factor**. When $0 < b < 1$, the function models **exponential decay**, and b is the **decay factor**. The y-intercept is $(0, a)$.

Example

Determine whether $y = 2(1.4)^x$ is an example of exponential growth or decay. Then, find the y-intercept.

Since $b = 1.4 > 1$, the function represents exponential growth.

Since $a = 2$, the y-intercept is $(0, 2)$.

Exercises

Determine whether each function is an example of exponential growth or decay. Then, find the y-intercept.

6. $y = 5^x$

7. $y = 2(4)^x$

8. $y = 0.2(3.8)^x$

9. $y = 3(0.25)^x$

10. $y = \frac{25}{7}\left(\frac{7}{5}\right)^x$

11. $y = 0.0015(10)^x$

12. $y = 2.25\left(\frac{1}{3}\right)^x$

13. $y = 0.5\left(\frac{1}{4}\right)^x$

Write a function for each situation. Then find the value of each function after five years. Round to the nearest dollar.

14. A \$12,500 car depreciates 9% each year.

15. A baseball card bought for \$50 increases 3% in value each year.

7-2 Properties of Exponential Functions

Quick Review

Exponential functions can be translated, stretched, compressed, and reflected.

The graph of $y = ab^{x-h} + k$ is the graph of the parent function $y = b^x$ stretched or compressed by a factor $|a|$, reflected across the x-axis if $a < 0$, and translated h units horizontally and k units vertically.

The **continuously compounded interest** formula is $A = Pe^{rt}$, where P is the principal, r is the annual interest rate, and t is time in years.

Example

How does the graph of $y = -3^x + 1$ compare to the graph of the parent function?

The parent function is $y = 3^x$.

Since $a = -1$, the graph is reflected across the x-axis.

Since $k = 1$, it is translated up 1 unit.

Exercises

How does the graph of each function compare to the graph of the parent function?

16. $y = 5(2)^{x+1} + 3$

17. $y = -2\left(\frac{1}{3}\right)^{x-2}$

Find the amount in a continuously compounded account for the given conditions.

18. principal: \$1000
annual interest rate: 4.8%
time: 2 years

19. principal: \$250
annual interest rate: 6.2%
time: 2.5 years

Evaluate each expression to four decimal places.

20. e^{-3}

21. e^{-1}

22. e^5

23. $e^{-\frac{1}{2}}$

7-3 Logarithmic Functions as Inverses

Quick Review

If $x = b^y$, then $\log_b x = y$. The **logarithmic function** is the inverse of the exponential function, so the graphs of the functions are reflections of one another across the line $y = x$. Logarithmic functions can be translated, stretched, compressed, and reflected, as represented by $y = a \log_b(x - h) + k$, similarly to exponential functions. When $b = 10$, the logarithm is called a **common logarithm**, which you can write as $\log x$.

Example

Write $5^{-2} = 0.04$ in logarithmic form.

If $y = b^x$, then $\log_b y = x$.

$y = 0.04$, $b = 5$ and $x = -2$.

So, $\log_5 0.04 = -2$.

Exercises

Write each equation in logarithmic form.

24. $6^2 = 36$ **25.** $2^{-3} = 0.125$

26. $3^3 = 27$ **27.** $10^{-3} = 0.001$

Evaluate each logarithm.

28. $\log_2 64$ **29.** $\log_3 \frac{1}{9}$

30. $\log 0.00001$ **31.** $\log_2 1$

Graph each logarithmic function.

32. $y = \log_3 x$ **33.** $y = \log x + 2$

34. $y = 3 \log_2 (x)$ **35.** $y = \log_5 (x + 1)$

How does the graph of each function compare to the graph of the parent function?

36. $y = 3 \log_4 (x + 1)$ **37.** $y = -\ln x + 2$

7-4 Properties of Logarithms

Quick Review

For any positive numbers, m, n, and b where $b \neq 1$, each of the following statements is true. Each can be used to rewrite a logarithmic expression.

- $\log_b mn = \log_b m + \log_b n$, by the Product Property
- $\log_b \frac{m}{n} = \log_b m - \log_b n$, by the Quotient Property
- $\log_b m^n = n \log_b m$, by the Power Property

Example

Write $2 \log_2 y + \log_2 x$ as a single logarithm. Identify any properties used.

$2 \log_2 y + \log_2 x$

$= \log_2 y^2 + \log_2 x$ Power Property

$= \log_2 xy^2$ Product Property

Exercises

Write each expression as a single logarithm. Identify any properties used.

38. $\log 8 + \log 3$ **39.** $\log_2 5 - \log_2 3$

40. $4 \log_3 x + \log_3 7$ **41.** $\log x - \log y$

42. $\log 5 - 2 \log x$ **43.** $3 \log_4 x + 2 \log_4 x$

Expand each logarithm. State the properties of logarithms used.

44. $\log_4 x^2 y^3$ **45.** $\log 4s^4 t$

46. $\log_3 \frac{2}{x}$ **47.** $\log (x + 3)^2$

48. $\log_2 (2y - 4)^3$ **49.** $\log \frac{z^2}{5}$

Use the Change of Base Formula to evaluate each expression.

50. $\log_2 7$ **51.** $\log_3 10$

7-5 Exponential and Logarithmic Equations

Quick Review

An equation in the form $b^{cx} = a$, where the exponent includes a variable, is called an **exponential equation**. You can solve exponential equations by taking the logarithm of each side of the equation. An equation that includes one or more logarithms involving a variable is called a **logarithmic equation**.

Example

Solve and round to the nearest ten-thousandth.

$$6^{2x} = 75$$

$\log 6^{2x} = \log 75$ Take the logarithm of both sides.

$2x \log 6 = \log 75$ Power Property of Logarithms

$x = \dfrac{\log 75}{2 \log 6}$ Divide both sides by 2 log 6.

$x \approx 1.2048$ Evaluate using a calculator.

Exercises

Solve each equation. Round to the nearest ten-thousandth.

52. $25^{2x} = 125$ **53.** $3^x = 36$

54. $7^{x-3} = 25$ **55.** $5^x + 3 = 12$

56. $\log 3x = 1$ **57.** $\log_2 4x = 5$

58. $\log x = \log 2x^2 - 2$ **59.** $2 \log_3 x = 54$

Solve by graphing. Round to the nearest ten-thousandth.

60. $5^{2x} = 20$ **61.** $3^{7x} = 160$

62. $6^{3x+1} = 215$ **63.** $0.5^x = 0.12$

64. A culture of 10 bacteria is started, and the number of bacteria will double every hour. In about how many hours will there be 3,000,000 bacteria?

7-6 Natural Logarithms

Quick Review

The inverse of $y = e^x$ is the **natural logarithmic function** $y = \log_e x = \ln x$. You solve natural logarithmic equations in the same way as common logarithmic equations.

Example

Use natural logarithms to solve $\ln x - \ln 2 = 3$.

$\ln x - \ln 2 = 3$

$\ln \dfrac{x}{2} = 3$ Quotient Property

$\dfrac{x}{2} = e^3$ Rewrite in exponential form.

$\dfrac{x}{2} \approx 20.0855$ Use a calculator to find e^3.

$x \approx 40.171$ Simplify.

Exercises

Solve each equation. Check your answers.

65. $e^{3x} = 12$

66. $\ln x + \ln (x + 1) = 2$

67. $2 \ln x + 3 \ln 2 = 5$

68. $\ln 4 - \ln x = 2$

69. $4e^{(x-1)} = 64$

70. $3 \ln x + \ln 5 = 7$

71. An initial investment of $350 is worth $429.20 after six years of continuous compounding. Find the annual interest rate.

Do you know HOW?

Determine whether each function is an example of exponential growth or decay. Then find the y-intercept.

1. $y = 3(0.25)^x$ **2.** $y = 2(6)^{-x}$

3. $y = 0.1(10)^x$ **4.** $y = 3e^x$

Describe how the graph of each function is related to the graph of its parent function. Then find the domain, range, and asymptotes.

5. $y = 3^x + 2$

6. $y = \left(\dfrac{1}{2}\right)^{x+1}$

7. $y = -(2)^{x+2}$

Write each equation in logarithmic form.

8. $5^4 = 625$ **9.** $e^0 = 1$

Evaluate each logarithm.

10. $\log_2 8$ **11.** $\log_7 7$

12. $\log_5 \dfrac{1}{125}$ **13.** $\log_{11} 1$

Graph each logarithmic function. Compare each graph to the graph of its parent function. List each function's domain, range, y-intercept, and asymptotes.

14. $y = \log_3 (x - 1)$

15. $y = \dfrac{1}{2}\log_3 (x + 2)$

16. $y = 1 - \log_2 x$

Write each logarithmic expression as a single logarithm.

17. $\log_2 4 + 3 \log_2 9$

18. $3 \log a - 2 \log b$

Expand each logarithm.

19. $\log_7 \dfrac{a}{b}$ **20.** $\log 3x^3 y^2$

Use the properties of logarithms to evaluate each expression.

21. $\log_9 27 - \log_9 9$

22. $2 \log 5 + \log 40$

Solve each equation.

23. $(27)^{3x} = 81$ **24.** $3^{x-1} = 24$

25. $2e^{3x} = 16$ **26.** $2 \log x = -4$

Use the Change of Base Formula to rewrite each expression using common logarithms.

27. $\log_3 16$ **28.** $\log_2 10$

29. $\log_7 8$ **30.** $\log_4 9$

Use the properties of logarithms to simplify and solve each equation. Round to the nearest thousandth.

31. $\ln 2 + \ln x = 1$

32. $\ln (x + 1) + \ln (x - 1) = 4$

33. $\ln (2x - 1)^2 = 7$

34. $3 \ln x - \ln 2 = 4$

Do you UNDERSTAND?

35. Writing Show that solving the equation $3^{2x} = 4$ by taking the common logarithm of each side is equivalent to solving it by taking the logarithm with base 3 of each side.

36. Open-Ended Give an example of an exponential function that models exponential growth and an example of an exponential function that models exponential decay.

37. Investment You put $1500 into an account that pays 7% annual interest compounded continuously. How long will it be before you have $2000 in your account?

TIPS FOR SUCCESS

Some problems ask you to find lengths of arcs or areas of sectors. Read the question at the right. Then follow the tips to answer the sample question.

TIP 1

Draw a diagram

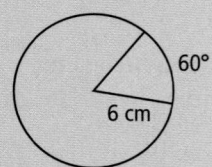

Let $f(x) = \pi x^2$ represent the area of a circle with radius x. Let $g(x) = \frac{60x}{360}$ represent the area of a 60° sector of a circle with area x. A circle with radius 6 centimeters has a sector measuring 60°. What is the area of this sector $(g \circ f)(x)$?

- A 6π cm²
- B 12π cm²
- C 24π cm²
- D 36π cm²

TIP 2

Find $f(x)$ first.
$$f(x) = \pi x^2$$
$$= \pi \cdot 6^2$$
$$= 36\pi$$

Think It Through

$$g(x) = \frac{60x}{360}$$

$$(g \circ f)(x) = \frac{60(36\pi)}{360}$$

$$= \frac{36\pi}{6}$$

$$= 6\pi$$

The correct answer is A.

Vocabulary Builder

As you solve problems, you must understand the meanings of mathematical terms. Match each term with its mathematical meaning.

A. growth factor

B. asymptote

C. logarithmic function

D. exponential equation

I. the inverse of an exponential function

II. a line that a graph approaches as x or y increases in absolute value

III. the value of b in $y = ab^x$, when $b > 1$

IV. an equation of the form $b^{cx} = a$, where the exponent includes a variable

Selected Response

Read each question. Then write the letter of the correct answer on your page.

1. The population of a town is modeled by the equation $P = 16{,}581e^{0.02t}$ where P represents the population t years after 2000. According to the model, what will the population of the town be in 2020?

   - A 16,916
   - B 17,258
   - C 20,252
   - D 24,736

2. If $i = \sqrt{-1}$, then which expression is equal to $9i(13i)$?

   - F -117
   - G $117i$
   - H 117
   - I $-117i$

3. Which expression is equivalent to $\log_5 32$?

   - A $\log 5 + \log 32$
   - B $\log 5 - \log 32$
   - C $(\log 5)(\log 32)$
   - D $\frac{\log 32}{\log 5}$

4. The table shows the height of a ball that was tossed into the air. Which equation best models the relationship between time t and the height of the ball h?

Time (seconds)	0	0.25	0.5	0.75
Height (feet)	4	10.5	15	17.5

- Ⓕ $h = 26t + 4$
- Ⓖ $h = -16t^2 + 30t + 4$
- Ⓗ $h = 4t^2$
- Ⓘ $h = -16t^2 + 4$

5. Which is the graph of $y = 3^x$?

Ⓐ 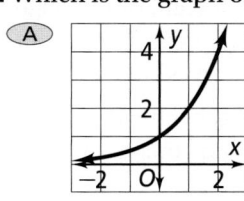   Ⓒ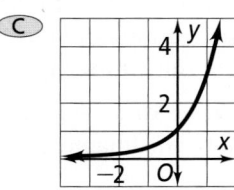

Ⓑ 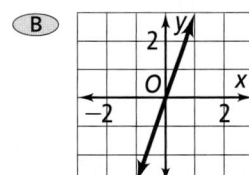   Ⓓ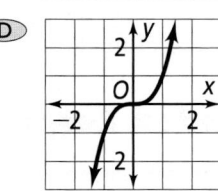

6. Which exponential function is equivalent to $y = \log_3 x$?

- Ⓕ $y = 3^x$
- Ⓖ $y = \frac{x}{3}$
- Ⓗ $y = x^3$
- Ⓘ $x = 3^y$

7. What is the simplest form of the quotient $\dfrac{\sqrt{72x^5y^3z^8}}{\sqrt{3xy^2z^2}}$?

- Ⓐ $\sqrt{24x^4yz^6}$
- Ⓒ $24x^4yz^6$
- Ⓑ $2x^2z^3\sqrt{6y}$
- Ⓓ $12x^2yz^6$

8. Solve the mass energy equivalence formula $e = mc^2$ for c.

- Ⓕ $c = e^2m$
- Ⓗ $c = \sqrt{\frac{e}{m}}$
- Ⓖ $c = \sqrt{\frac{m}{e}}$
- Ⓘ $c = \sqrt{(e - m)}$

9. What is the quotient of $(x^3 + 2x^2 - x + 6) \div (x + 3)$?

- Ⓐ $x^2 + 5x + 14$, R 42
- Ⓒ $x^3 + 5x^2 + 14x + 42$
- Ⓑ $x^2 - x + 2$
- Ⓓ $x^2 + x - 2$

10. On a certain night, a restaurant employs x servers at $25 per hour and y bus persons at $8 per hour. The total hourly cost for the restaurant's 12 employees that night is $249. The following system of equations can be used to find the number of servers and the number of bus persons at work.

$$\begin{cases} 25x + 8y = 249 \\ x + y = 12 \end{cases}$$

Based on the solution of the system of equations, which of the following can you conclude?

- Ⓕ Fewer than 2 bus persons were working.
- Ⓖ More than ten servers were working.
- Ⓗ 50% of the people working were bus persons.
- Ⓘ 75% of the people working were servers.

11. Which polynomial equation has the real roots of -3, 1, 1, and $\frac{3}{2}$?

- Ⓐ $x^4 - \frac{1}{2}x^3 - \frac{13}{2}x^2 + \frac{21}{2}x - \frac{9}{2} = 0$
- Ⓑ $x^4 - \frac{1}{2}x^3 - \frac{17}{2}x^2 - 10x - \frac{9}{2} = 0$
- Ⓒ $x^4 + x^3 - 5x^2 + 3x - \frac{3}{2} = 0$
- Ⓓ $(x - 3)(x + 1)(x + 1)\left(x + \frac{3}{2}\right) = 0$

12. What is the factored form of $2x^3 + 5x^2 - 12x$?

- Ⓕ $x(2x - 3)(x + 4)$
- Ⓗ $x(2x + 4)(x - 3)$
- Ⓖ $(2x^2 - 3)(x + 4)$
- Ⓘ $(2x - 4)(x + 3)$

13. If $f(x) = 5\sqrt[3]{x^2}$ and $g(x) = 3\sqrt[3]{x^2}$, what is $f(x) + g(x)$?

- Ⓐ $8\sqrt[3]{x^2}$
- Ⓑ $8\sqrt[6]{x^2}$
- Ⓒ $8\sqrt[3]{x^4}$
- Ⓓ $8\sqrt[6]{x^4}$

14. What is the equation of the function graphed below?

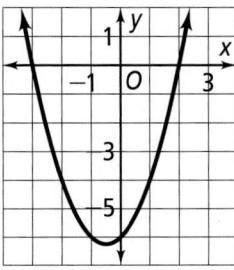

- Ⓕ $y = (x + 2)(x - 3)$
- Ⓗ $y = (x + 3)(x - 2)$
- Ⓖ $y = (x - 6)^2$
- Ⓘ $y = (x - 1)(x + 5)$

Constructed Response

15. What is the solution of the equation $\log_9 x = \log_6 x$?

16. A savings account pays 4.62% annual interest, compounded continuously. After approximately how many years will a principal of $500 double?

17. The graph of a polynomial has x-intercepts at $(-3, 0)$, $(-1, 0)$, and $(1, 0)$. What is the least possible degree of the polynomial?

18. Evaluate $\log_4 8$.

19. Solve $4^{2x} = 32$.

20. How many different real solutions are there for the equation $4x^2 = -4x - 4$?

21. Use the Fundamental Theorem of Algebra to determine the total number of complex zeros of $f(x) = x^2 - 3x^5 + 4x - x^7 - 44$.

22. Solve the following system of equations. What is the x-coordinate of the solution?

$$\begin{cases} y - 3 = x \\ \dfrac{y}{x^2 - 9} = 1 \end{cases}$$

23. What is the solution of $\sqrt{x + 2} = x$?

24. What is the x-intercept of $f(x) = x^3 - x^2 + 1$? Round the answer to the nearest hundredth.

25. What is the maximum y-value of the parabola?

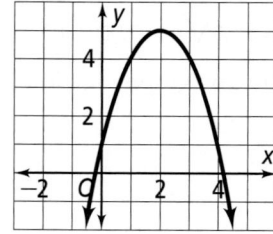

26. What is solution of the equation $-16 = x^2 + 8x$?

27. The graph below is transformation of the radical parent function $y = \sqrt{x}$.

   a. Describe the transformations used to create the graph shown.

   b. What is an equation of the graph shown?

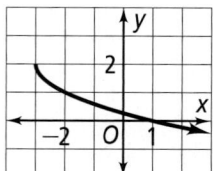

28. Compare the end behaviors of the functions below.

$$f(x) = x^3 + 1 \qquad\qquad g(x) = 5x^2 - 7$$

29. To use an outdoor toddler swing, a child must weigh at least 15 pounds, and can weigh no more than 35 pounds. Draw a graph to model this situation.

30. Can a quadratic equation with real coefficients have exactly one imaginary root? Explain your answer.

31. Graph the function $y = -3(2)^{x+1}$ as a translation of its parent function.

Extended Response

32. A transformation of the parent absolute value function is shown in the graph.

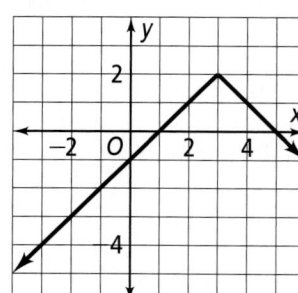

   a. What is the transformation from the parent function $y = |x|$?

   b. Draw the graph of the transformed function after reflecting it across the y-axis and translating it 4 units down.

Get Ready!

Lesson 2-2 ◀ **Using Direct Variation**

For each direct variation, find the constant of variation. Then find the value of y when $x = -3$.

1. $y = 4$ when $x = 3$

2. $y = 1$ when $x = -1.5$

3. $y = -5$ when $x = \frac{3}{2}$

4. $y = -16$ when $x = 7$

Lesson 4-4 ◀ **Factoring Quadratic Expressions**

Factor each expression.

5. $x^2 + x - 6$

6. $4x^2 + 17x + 15$

7. $9x^2 - 25$

8. $x^2 - 12x + 36$

9. $3x^2 + 10x + 8$

10. $x^2 - 5x + 6$

Lesson 4-5 ◀ **Solving Quadratic Equations**

Solve each equation.

11. $x^2 + 7x - 8 = 0$

12. $\frac{1}{4}x^2 + \frac{7}{2}x = -12$

13. $3x^2 = 18x - 24$

14. $9x^2 + 6x = 0$

15. $4x^2 + 16 = 34x$

16. $x^2 - 13x - 30 = 0$

Looking Ahead Vocabulary

17. If you need to drive 30 miles, you have many options. For instance, you can drive 15 miles per hour for 2 hours, 30 miles per hour for 1 hour, or 60 miles per hour for half an hour. Notice that when you double your speed, it takes half as much time to get to your destination. Mathematicians describe this kind of relationship as an *inverse variation*. Why do you suppose they use the word *inverse* to describe it?

18. Suppose you are hiking on a trail and find that the bridge over the river has been washed out, making a gap or *discontinuity* in the trail. Graphs can have gaps too. Sketch what you think a graph with a discontinuity might look like.

CHAPTER 8

Rational Functions

Download videos connecting math to your world.

Interactive! Vary numbers, graphs, and figures to explore math concepts.

The online Solve It will get you in gear for each lesson.

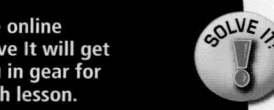

Math definitions in English and Spanish

Online access to stepped-out problems aligned to Common Core

Get and view your assignments online.

Extra practice and review online

Virtual Nerd™ tutorials with built-in support

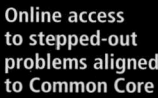
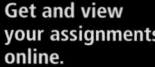
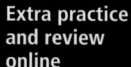
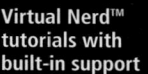

Chapter Preview

Vocabulary

English/Spanish Vocabulary Audio Online:

BIG ideas

1 Proportionality
Essential Question Are two quantities inversely proportional if an increase in one corresponds to a decrease in the other?

2 Function
Essential Question What kinds of asymptotes are possible for a rational function?

3 Equivalence
Essential Question Are a rational expression and its simplified form equivalent?

 DOMAINS
- Arithmetic with Polynomials and Rational Expressions
- Building Functions
- Creating Equations

Common Core Performance Task

Upstream and Downstream

Steve and Sally went canoeing on Red River on a day when the current flowed at 3 mi/h. They left at 8:30 A.M and paddled upstream until they reached Elk Island, where they stopped to have lunch.

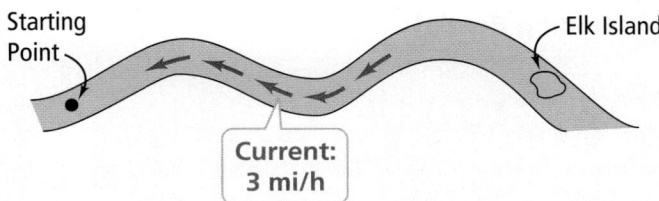

Starting Point

Elk Island

Current: 3 mi/h

After an hour and a half, Steve and Sally got back in their canoe and paddled downstream, returning to their starting point at 4:00 P.M. They paddled a total of 24 mi during the day.

Task Description

How long did it take Steve and Sally to paddle to Elk Island? Assume that Steve and Sally always paddle in such a way as to result in the same speed in still water. Round your answer to the nearest 5 minutes.

Connecting the Task to the Math Practices

MATHEMATICAL PRACTICES

As you complete the task, you'll apply several Standards for Mathematical Practice.

- You'll explore aspects of the problem situation using expressions, functions, and graphs. (MP 1, MP 4)

- You'll find a rational expression that represents the problem situation. (MP 2)

- You'll use more than one method to solve an equation. (MP 1, MP 5)

8-1 Inverse Variation

© Common Core State Standards

A-CED.A.2 Create equations in two or more variables to represent relationships between quantities; graph equations on coordinate axes with labels and scales.
Also A-CED.A.4

MP 1, MP 2, MP 3, MP 4, MP 6

Objectives To recognize and use inverse variation
To use joint and other variations

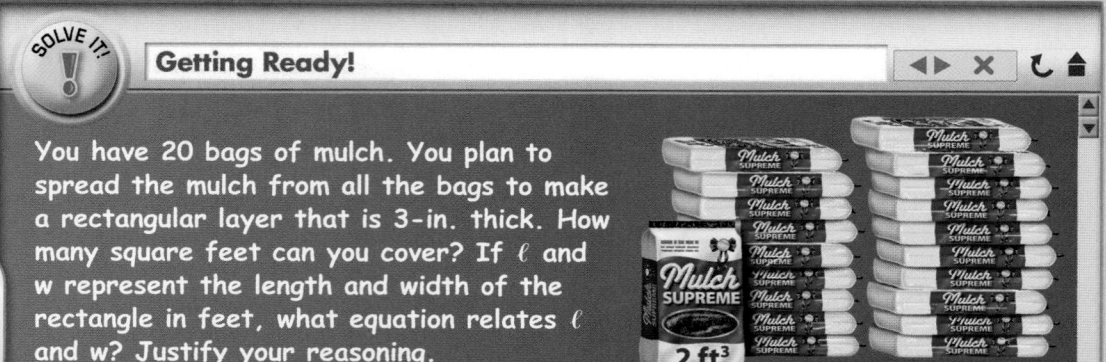

Getting Ready!

You have 20 bags of mulch. You plan to spread the mulch from all the bags to make a rectangular layer that is 3-in. thick. How many square feet can you cover? If ℓ and w represent the length and width of the rectangle in feet, what equation relates ℓ and w? Justify your reasoning.

Solve a simpler problem first. How many square feet will one bag cover?

2 ft³

MATHEMATICAL PRACTICES

Lesson Vocabulary
• inverse variation
• combined variation
• joint variation

Among all rectangles with a given area, the longer the length of one side, the shorter the length of an adjacent side.

Essential Understanding If a product is constant, where the constant is positive, a decrease in the value of one factor must accompany an increase in the value of the other factor.

As an equation, direct variation has the form $y = kx$, where $k \neq 0$. **Inverse variation** can have the form $xy = k$, $y = \frac{k}{x}$, or $x = \frac{k}{y}$, where $k \neq 0$. When two quantities vary inversely, as one quantity increases, the other decreases proportionally. For both inverse and direct variation, k is the constant of variation.

© Problem 1 Identifying Direct and Inverse Variations

Is the relationship between the variables a *direct variation*, an *inverse variation*, or *neither*? Write function models for the direct and inverse variations.

Think

How can you tell if the quantities vary directly or inversely?
If the product of corresponding x- and y-values is constant, they vary inversely. If the ratio of corresponding x- and y-values is constant, they vary directly.

Ⓐ

x	y
2	15
4	7.5
10	3
15	2

As x increases, y decreases. This might be an inverse relationship. A plot confirms that an inverse relationship is possible. Test to see whether xy is constant.

$2 \cdot 15 = 30$ $4 \cdot 7.5 = 30$

$10 \cdot 3 = 30$ $15 \cdot 2 = 30$

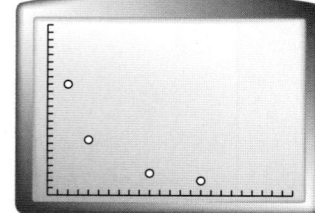

The product of each pair is 30, so $xy = 30$ and y varies inversely with x. The constant of variation is 30 and the function model is $y = \frac{30}{x}$.

Could you model this data with a direct variation?
No; the ratio of corresponding *x*- and *y*-values are not constant.

B

x	y
2	10
4	8
10	3
15	1.5

A plot of the points suggests that an inverse relationship is possible. Test to see whether the products of *x* and *y* are constant.

$2 \cdot 10 = 20$, $4 \cdot 8 = 32$, $10 \cdot 3 = 30$, and $15 \cdot 1.5 = 22.5$

Since the products are not constant, the relationship is not an inverse variation.

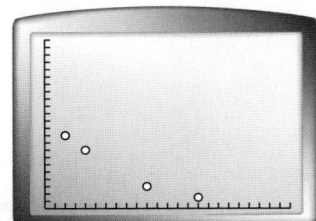

Got It? **1.** Is the relationship between the variables a *direct variation*, an *inverse variation*, or *neither*? Write function models for the direct and inverse variations.

a.

x	y
0.2	8
0.5	20
1.0	40
1.5	60

b.

x	y
0.2	40
0.5	16
1.0	8.0
2.0	4.0

c.

x	y
0.5	40
1.2	12
2	10
2.5	6

© Problem 2 Determining an Inverse Variation

Suppose *x* and *y* vary inversely, and *x* = 4 when *y* = 12.

A What function models the inverse variation?

$y = \dfrac{k}{x}$ Write the general function form for inverse variation.

$12 = \dfrac{k}{4}$ Substitute for *x* and *y*.

$k = 48$ Solve for *k*.

The function is $y = \dfrac{48}{x}$.

Plan

Is it reasonable to connect the points of this function with a smooth curve?
Yes, $\frac{48}{x}$ is defined for every real number except *x* = 0.

B What does the graph of this function look like?

Make a table of values. Sketch a graph.

x	y
3	16
4	12
6	8
8	6
12	4
16	3

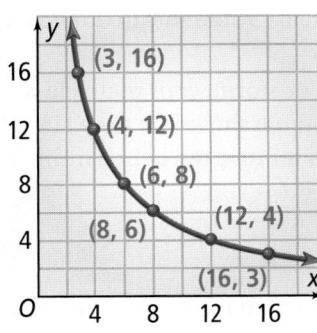

C What is *y* when *x* = 10?

$y = \dfrac{48}{x}$ Write the function.

$y = \dfrac{48}{10}$ Evaluate *y* for *x* = 10.

$y = 4.8$, when *x* = 10.

Got It? **2.** Suppose x and y vary inversely, and $x = 8$ when $y = -7$.

    a. What is the function that models the inverse variation?

    b. What does the graph of this function look like?

    c. What is y when $x = 2$?

© **Problem 3** **Modeling an Inverse Variation**

Your math class has decided to pick up litter each weekend in a local park. Each week there is approximately the same amount of litter. The table shows the number of students who worked each of the first four weeks of the project and the time needed for the pickup.

Park Cleanup Project

Number of students (n)	3	5	12	17
Time in minutes (t)	85	51	21	15

Think

Can you still use inverse variation to model the data if 12 × 21 = 252?
Often, you cannot describe real-life data exactly with a function rule. But 252 is close enough to 255 for inverse variation to still be a good model.

A What function models the data?

Step 1 Investigate the data. The more students who help, the less time the cleanup takes. An inverse variation seems appropriate. If this is an inverse variation, then $nt = k$. From the table, nt (or **L1 · L2**) is almost always 255.

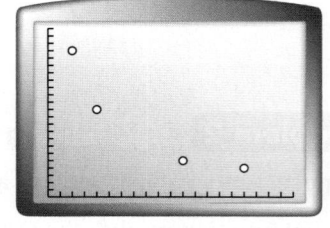
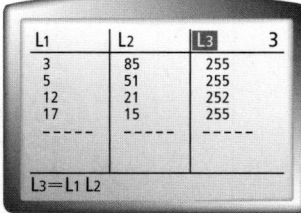

Step 2 Determine the model. $nt = 255$

B How many students should there be to complete the project in at most 30 minutes each week?

$nt = 255$ Use the model from part A.

$n(30) = 255$ Substitute for t.

$n = \dfrac{255}{30} = 8.5$ Solve for n.

There should be at least 9 students to do the job in at most 30 minutes.

 Got It? **3.** After a major storm, your math class volunteers to remove debris from yards. The table shows the time t in minutes that it takes a group of n students to remove the debris from an average-sized yard.

Number of students (n)	1	3	5	14
Time in minutes (t)	225	75	45	16

    a. What function models the time needed to clear the debris from an average-sized yard relative to the number of students who do the work?

    b. How many students should there be to clear debris from an average-sized yard in at most 25 minutes?

You have seen many variation formulas in geometry. Some, like the formula for the perimeter of a square, are simple direct variations. Others, like the volume of a cone, relate three or more variables.

When one quantity varies with respect to two or more quantities, you have a **combined variation**. When one quantity varies directly with two or more quantities, you have **joint variation**. The volume of a cone varies jointly with the area of the base and the height of the cone, $V = kBh$.

take note

Key Concept   Combined Variations

Combined Variation	Equation Form
z varies jointly with x and y.	$z = kxy$
z varies jointly with x and y and inversely with w.	$z = \dfrac{kxy}{w}$
z varies directly with x and inversely with the product wy.	$z = \dfrac{kx}{wy}$

Problem 4   Using Combined Variation

Multiple Choice The number of bags of grass seed n needed to reseed a yard varies directly with the area a to be seeded and inversely with the weight w of a bag of seed. If it takes two 3-lb bags to seed an area of 3600 ft^2, how many 3-lb bags will seed 9000 ft^2?

Ⓐ 3 bags	Ⓑ 4 bags	Ⓒ 5 bags	Ⓓ 6 bags

$n = \dfrac{ka}{w}$ n varies directly with a and inversely with w.

$2 = \dfrac{3600k}{3}$ Substitute for n, a, and w.

$\dfrac{(2)(3)}{3600} = k$ Solve for k.

$k = \dfrac{6}{3600} = \dfrac{1}{600}$ Simplify.

The combined variation equation is $n = \dfrac{a}{600w}$.

$n = \dfrac{a}{600w}$ Use the combined variation equation.

$= \dfrac{9000}{600 \cdot 3}$ Substitute for a and w.

$= 5$

You need five 3-lb bags to seed 9000 ft^2. The correct choice is C.

Plan

How can you write the model?
Write the constant of variation and direct variation variable in the numerator. Write the inverse variation variable in the denominator.

✓ **Got It?**   **4.** The number of bags of mulch you need to cover a planting area varies jointly with the area to be mulched a in square feet and the depth of the mulch d in feet. If you need 10 bags to mulch 120 ft^2 to a depth of 3 in., how many bags do you need to mulch 200 ft^2 to a depth of 4 in.?

Problem 5 Applying Combined Variation

Physics Gravitational potential energy *PE* is a measure of energy. *PE* varies directly with an object's mass *m* and its height *h* in meters above the ground. Physicists use *g* to represent the constant of variation, which is gravity.

The skateboarder in the photo has a mass of 58 kg and a potential energy of 2273.6 joules. What is the gravitational potential energy of a 65-kg skateboarder on the halfpipe shown?

HEIGHT 4 M

Know
- The mass of each skateboarder
- The height of each skateboarder
- The potential energy of the first skateboarder

Need
The potential energy of the second skateboarder

Plan
- Write the variation for potential energy.
- Use the known information to find *g*.
- Then find the potential energy of the second skateboarder.

Step 1 Write the formula for potential energy. Potential energy varies directly with mass and height. $PE = gmh$

Step 2 Use the given data to find *g*.

$$PE = gmh \qquad \text{Potential energy formula}$$

$$\frac{PE}{mh} = g \qquad \text{Solve for } g.$$

$$\frac{2273.6}{(58)(4)} = g \qquad \text{Substitute.}$$

$$9.8 = g \qquad \text{Simplify.}$$

Step 3 Use the formula to find the potential energy of the second skateboarder.

$$PE = 9.8mh \qquad \text{Potential energy formula}$$

$$= 9.8(65)(4) \qquad \text{Evaluate for } m = 65 \text{ and } h = 4.$$

$$= 2548 \qquad \text{Simplify.}$$

The second skateboarder has 2548 joules of potential energy.

  Got It? **5. a.** How much potential energy would a 41-kg diver have standing on a 10-m diving platform?

b. Reasoning An 80-kg diver stands on a 6-m diving platform. At what height should a 40-kg diver stand to have equal potential energy? Do you need to find the potential energy of either diver to solve this? Explain.

Lesson Check

Do you know HOW?

Is the relationship between the variables in each table a *direct variation*, an *inverse variation*, or *neither*? Write equations to model the direct and inverse variations.

1.

x	y
1	6
3	2
12	0.5
15	0.4

2.

u	v
−3	−15
5	25
6	30
16	80

Do you UNDERSTAND?

 MATHEMATICAL PRACTICES

3. Compare and Contrast Describe the difference between direct variation and inverse variation.

4. Writing Describe how the variables in the given equation are related.

$$p = \frac{kqrt}{s}$$

5. Error Analysis A student described the relationship between the variables in the equation below as d varies directly with r and inversely with t. Correct the error in relating the variables.

$$d = \frac{k\sqrt[3]{r}}{t^2}$$

Practice and Problem-Solving Exercises

 **MATHEMATICAL PRACTICES**

Practice

Is the relationship between the values in each table a *direct variation*, an *inverse variation*, or *neither*? Write equations to model the direct and inverse variations.

◀ **See Problem 1.**

6.

x	y
3	15
8	40
10	50
22	110

7.

x	y
3	14
5	8.4
7	6
10.5	4

8.

x	y
0.5	1
2.1	4.2
3.5	7
11	22

9.

x	y
0.1	3
3	0.1
6	0.05
24	0.0125

Suppose that x and y vary inversely. Write a function that models each inverse variation. Graph the function and find y when $x = 10$.

◀ **See Problem 2.**

10. $x = 1$ when $y = 11$

11. $x = -13$ when $y = 100$

12. $x = 1$ when $y = 1$

13. $x = 1$ when $y = 5$

14. $x = 1.2$ when $y = 3$

15. $x = 2.5$ when $y = 100$

16. $x = 20$ when $y = -4$

17. $x = 5$ when $y = -\frac{1}{3}$

18. $x = -\frac{4}{15}$ when $y = -105$

19. Fundraising In a bake sale, you recorded the number of muffins sold and the amount of sales in a table as shown.
 a. What is a function that relates the sales and the number of muffins?
 b. How many muffins would you have to sell to make at least $250.00 in sales?

◀ **See Problem 3.**

Number of muffins (m)	Sales (s)
5	$12.50
8	$20.00
13	$32.50
20	$50.00

20. Painting The number of buckets of paint n needed to paint a fence varies directly with the total area a of the fence and inversely with the amount of paint p in a bucket. It takes three 1-gallon buckets of paint to paint 72 square feet of fence. How many 1-gallon buckets will be needed to paint 90 square feet of fence?

See Problem 4.

STEM **21. Potential Energy** On Earth with a gravitational acceleration g, the potential energy stored in an object varies directly with its mass m and its vertical height h.

See Problem 5.

   a. What is an equation that models the potential energy of a 2-kg skateboard that is sliding down a ramp?

   b. The acceleration due to gravity is $g = -9.8 \text{ m/s}^2$. What is the height of the ramp if the skateboard has a potential energy of $-39.2 \text{ kg m}^2/\text{s}^2$?

 **Apply**

22. Think About a Plan The table shows data about how the life span s of a mammal relates to its heart rate r. The data could be modeled by an equation of the form $rs = k$. Estimate the life span of a cat with a heart rate of 126 beats/min.

- How can you estimate a constant of the inverse variation?
- What expression would you use to find the life span?

Heart Rate and Life Span

Mammal	Heart rate (beats/min)	Life span (min)
Mouse	634	1,576,800
Rabbit	158	6,307,200
Lion	76	13,140,000

Source: *The Handy Science Answer Book*

STEM **23. Physics** The force F of gravity on a rocket varies directly with its mass m and inversely with the square of its distance d from Earth. Write a model for this combined variation. Write an equation to find the mass of the rocket in terms of F and d.

24. The spreadsheet shows data that could be modeled by an equation of the form $PV = k$. Estimate P when $V = 62$.

STEM **25. Chemistry** The formula for the Ideal Gas Law is $PV = nRT$, where P is the pressure in kilopascals (kPA), V is the volume in liters (L), T is the temperature in Kelvin (K), n is the number of moles of gas, and $R = 8.314$ is the universal gas constant.

   a. Write an equation to find the volume in terms of P, n, R, and T.

   b. What volume is needed to store 5 moles of helium gas at 350 K under the pressure 190 kPA?

   c. A 10 L cylinder is filled with hydrogen gas to a pressure of 5000 kPA. The temperature of gas is 300 K. How many moles of hydrogen gas are in the cylinder?

	A	B
1	P	V
2	140.00	100
3	147.30	95
4	155.60	90
5	164.70	85
6	175.00	80
7	186.70	75

Write the function that models each variation. Find z when $x = 4$ and $y = 9$.

26. z varies directly with x and inversely with y. When $x = 6$ and $y = 2$, $z = 15$.

27. z varies jointly with x and y. When $x = 2$ and $y = 3$, $z = 60$.

28. z varies inversely with the product of x and y. When $x = 2$ and $y = 4$, $z = 0.5$.

Each pair of values is from a direct variation. Find the missing value.

29. $(2, 5), (4, y)$ **30.** $(4, 6), (x, 3)$ **31.** $(3, 7), (8, y)$ **32.** $(x, 12), (4, 1.5)$

Each ordered pair is from an inverse variation. Find the constant of variation.

33. $(6, 3)$ **34.** $(0.9, 4)$ **35.** $\left(\frac{3}{8}, \frac{2}{3}\right)$ **36.** $(\sqrt{2}, \sqrt{18})$

Each pair of values is from an inverse variation. Find the missing value.

37. $(2, 5), (4, y)$ **38.** $(4, 6), (x, 3)$ **39.** $(3, 7), (8, y)$ **40.** $(x, 12), (4, 1.5)$

C Challenge **41. Writing** Explain why 0 cannot be in the domain of an inverse variation.

42. Reasoning Suppose that (x_1, y_1) and (x_2, y_2) are values from an inverse variation. Show that $\frac{x_1}{x_2} = \frac{y_2}{y_1}$.

43. Open-Ended The height h of a cylinder varies directly with its volume V and inversely with the square of its radius r. Find at least four ways to change the volume and radius of a cylinder so that its height is quadrupled.

Standardized Test Prep

SAT/ACT

44. Which equation represents inverse variation between x and y?

Ⓐ $x = \frac{y}{z}$　　Ⓑ $x = -\frac{15z}{y}$　　Ⓒ $z = -\frac{15y}{x}$　　Ⓓ $xz = 5y$

45. How can you rewrite the expression $(8 - 5i)^2$ in the form $a + bi$?

Ⓕ $39 + 80i$　　Ⓖ $39 - 80i$　　Ⓗ $89 + 80i$　　Ⓘ $89 - 80i$

46. The height of a ball thrown straight up from the ground with a velocity of 96 ft/s is given by the quadratic function $h(t) = -16t^2 + 96t$. What is the maximum height the ball reaches?

Ⓐ 6 ft　　Ⓑ 128 ft　　Ⓒ 144 ft　　Ⓓ 160 ft

47. Which expression is NOT equivalent to $\sqrt[6]{81x^4y^8}$?

Ⓕ $\left(3xy^2\right)^{\frac{2}{3}}$　　Ⓖ $(3x)^{\frac{2}{3}}y^{\frac{4}{3}}$　　Ⓗ $(3x^2y^2)^{\frac{1}{3}}$　　Ⓘ $\sqrt[3]{9x^2y^4}$

Short Response

48. What is the inverse of $y = 4x^2 + 5$? Is the inverse a function?

Mixed Review

Solve each equation. Check your answers.　　◀ See Lesson 7-6.

49. $\ln 4 + \ln x = 5$　　**50.** $\ln x - \ln 3 = 4$　　**51.** $2\ln x + 3\ln 4 = 4$

Multiply and simplify.　　◀ See Lesson 6-2.

52. $-5\sqrt{6x} \cdot 3\sqrt{6x^3}$　　**53.** $3\sqrt[3]{2x^2} \cdot 7\sqrt[3]{32x^4}$　　**54.** $\sqrt{5x^3} \cdot \sqrt{40xy^7}$

Get Ready!　**To prepare for Lesson 8-2, do Exercises 55–60.**

Graph each equation. Then describe the transformation of the parent function $f(x) = |x|$.　　◀ See Lesson 2-7.

55. $y = |x| + 2$　　**56.** $y = |x + 2|$　　**57.** $y = |x| - 3$

58. $y = |x - 3|$　　**59.** $y = |x + 4| - 5$　　**60.** $y = |x - 10| + 7$

Concept Byte

For Use With Lesson 8-2

TECHNOLOGY

Graphing Rational Functions

 **Common Core State Standards**

F-IF.C.7d Graph rational functions, identifying zeros and asymptotes when suitable factorizations are available, and showing end behavior.

MP 5

You can use your graphing calculator to graph *rational functions* and other members of the reciprocal function family. It is sometimes preferable to use the **DOT** plotting mode rather than **CONNECTED** plotting mode. The **CONNECTED** mode can join branches of a graph that should be separated. Try both modes to get the best graph.

MATHEMATICAL
PRACTICES

Example

Graph $y = \dfrac{4}{x-3} - 1.5$.

Step 1 Press the (mode) key. Scroll down to highlight the word **DOT**. Then press (enter).

Step 2 Enter the function. Use parentheses to enter the denominator accurately.

Step 3 Graph the function.

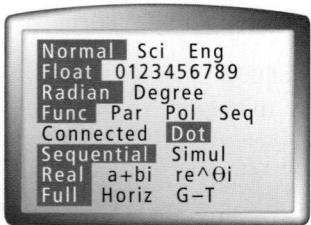

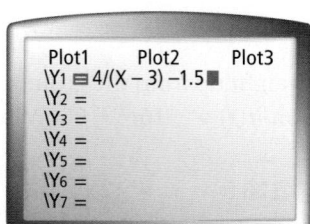

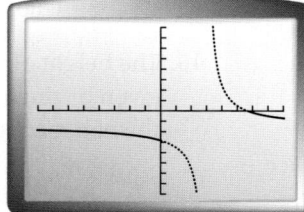

Exercises

1. a. Graph the parent reciprocal function $y = \frac{1}{x}$.
   b. Examine both negative and positive values of x. Describe what happens to the y-values as x approaches zero.
   c. What happens to the y-values as x increases? As x decreases?

2. a. Change the mode on your calculator to **CONNECTED**. Graph the function from the example.
   b. Press (trace) and trace the function. What happens between $x \approx 2.8$ and $x \approx 3.2$?
   c. **Reasoning** How does your graph differ from the graph in the example? Explain the differences.

Use a graphing calculator to graph each function. Then sketch the graph.

3. $y = \frac{7}{x}$

4. $y = \frac{3}{x+4} - 2$

5. $y = \frac{x+2}{(x+1)(x+3)}$

6. $y = \frac{4x+1}{x-3}$

7. $y = \frac{2}{x-2}$

8. $y = \frac{1}{x+2} + 3$

9. $y = \frac{2x}{x+3}$

10. $y = \frac{x^2}{x^2-5}$

11. $y = \frac{20}{x^2+5}$

The Reciprocal Function Family

© Common Core State Standards

F-BF.B.3 Identify the effect on the graph of replacing $f(x)$ by $f(x) + k$, $kf(x)$, $f(kx)$, and $f(x + k)$ for specific values of k . . . **Also A-CED.A.2, A-APR.A.1**

MP 1, MP 2, MP 3, MP 4, MP 5

Objectives To graph reciprocal functions
To graph translations of reciprocal functions

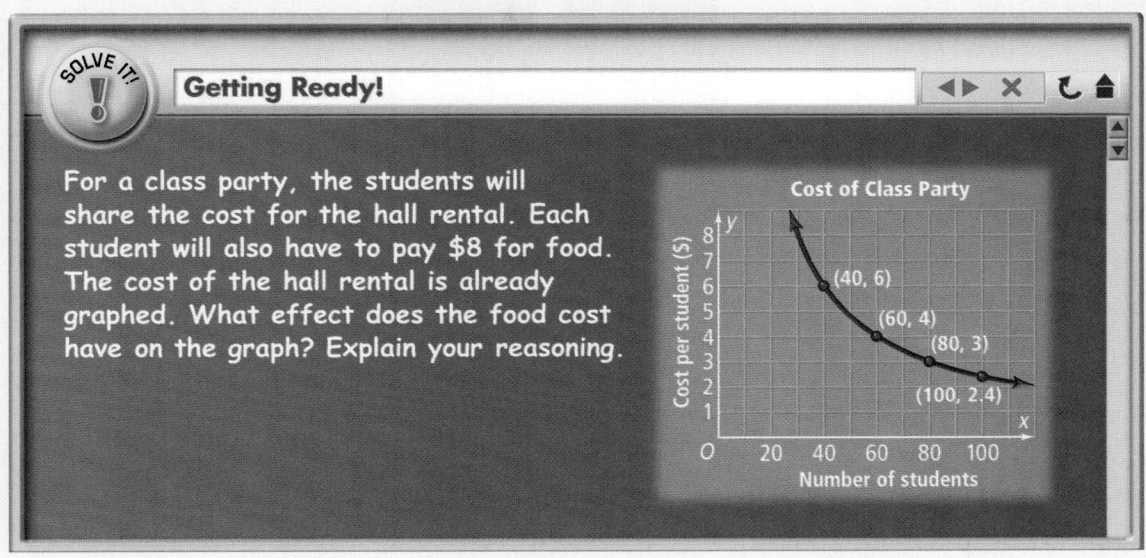

SOLVE IT!

Getting Ready!

For a class party, the students will share the cost for the hall rental. Each student will also have to pay $8 for food. The cost of the hall rental is already graphed. What effect does the food cost have on the graph? Explain your reasoning.

Cost of Class Party

Cost per student ($)

Number of students

(40, 6)
(60, 4)
(80, 3)
(100, 2.4)

Lesson Vocabulary
• reciprocal function
• branch

Functions that model inverse variation have the form $f(x) = \frac{a}{x}$, where $x \neq 0$. They belong to a family whose parent is the **reciprocal function** $f(x) = \frac{1}{x}$, where $x \neq 0$.

Essential Understanding Transformations of the parent reciprocal function include stretches, compressions (or shrinks), reflections, and horizontal and vertical translations.

take note

Key Concept   General Form of the Reciprocal Function Family

The general form of a member of the reciprocal function family is $y = \frac{a}{x - h} + k$, where $x \neq h$.

The inverse variation functions, $y = \frac{a}{x}$, are stretches, shrinks, and reflections of the parent reciprocal function, depending on the value of a.

The graph of the parent reciprocal function $y = \frac{1}{x}$ is shown at the right.

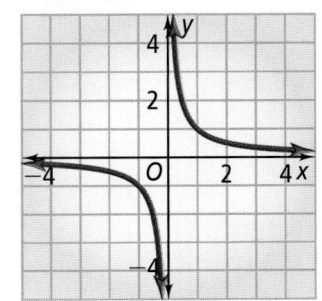

Problem 1 Graphing an Inverse Variation Function

What is the graph of $y = \frac{8}{x}, x \neq 0$? Identify the x- and y-intercepts and the asymptotes of the graph. Also, state the domain and range of the function.

Think

What values should you choose for x?
Choose values of x that divide nicely into 8. Make a table of points that are easy to graph.

Step 1 Make a table of values that includes positive and negative values of x.

Step 2 Graph the points.

x	y	x	y
-16	$-\frac{1}{2}$	$\frac{1}{2}$	16
-8	-1	1	8
-4	-2	2	4
-2	-4	4	2
-1	-8	8	1
$-\frac{1}{2}$	-16	16	$\frac{1}{2}$

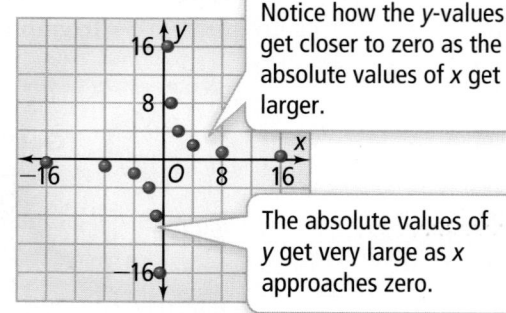

Notice how the y-values get closer to zero as the absolute values of x get larger.

The absolute values of y get very large as x approaches zero.

Step 3 Connect the points with a smooth curve. x cannot be zero, so there is no y-intercept.
The numerator is never zero, so y is never 0.
There is no x-intercept.

The x-axis is a horizontal asymptote.
The y-axis is a vertical asymptote.
Knowing the asymptotes provides you with the basic shape of the graph.
The domain is the set of all real numbers except $x = 0$.
The range is the set of all real numbers except $y = 0$.

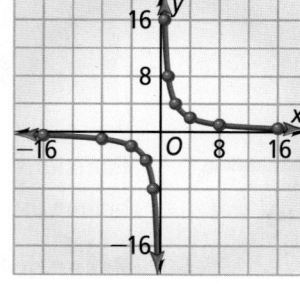

Got It? **1. a.** What is the graph of $y = \frac{12}{x}$? Identify the x- and y-intercepts and the asymptotes of the graph. Also, state the domain and range of the function.

b. Reasoning Would the function $y = \frac{6}{x}$ have the same domain and range as $y = \frac{8}{x}$ or $y = \frac{12}{x}$? Explain.

Each part of the graph of a reciprocal function is a **branch**. The branches of the parent function $y = \frac{1}{x}$ are in Quadrants I and III. Stretches and compressions of the parent function remain in the same quadrants. Reflections are in Quadrants II and IV.

Problem 2 Identifying Reciprocal Function Transformations

For each given value of a, how do the graphs of $y = \frac{1}{x}$ and $y = \frac{a}{x}$ compare? What is the effect of a on the graph?

A $a = 6$

The graph (in red) of $y = \frac{6}{x}$ is a stretch of the graph of $y = \frac{1}{x}$ (in black) by the factor 6.

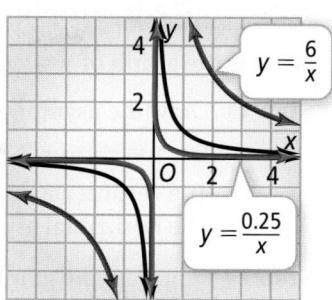

B $a = 0.25$

The graph (in blue) of $y = \frac{0.25}{x}$ is a shrink of the graph of $y = \frac{1}{x}$ (in black) by the factor $\frac{1}{4}$.

Think

How does the negative sign affect the graph?
The y-values have signs that are opposite those in part A. The graph in A reflects across the x-axis.

C $a = -6$

The graph of $y = \frac{-6}{x}$ is the stretch by the factor 6 in part A followed by a reflection across the x-axis.

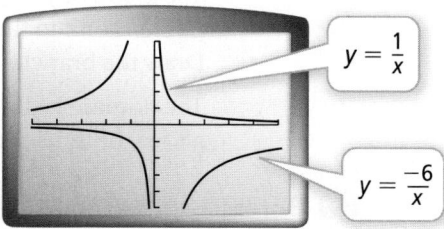

 Got It? **2.** For each given value of a, how do the graphs of $y = \frac{1}{x}$ and $y = \frac{a}{x}$ compare? What is the effect of a on the graph?

a. $a = \frac{1}{2}$ **b.** $a = 2$ **c.** $a = -\frac{1}{2}$

You can translate any reciprocal function horizontally or vertically just as you can other functions.

take note

Key Concept The Reciprocal Function Family

Parent function	$y = \frac{1}{x}, x \neq 0$
Stretch ($\lvert a \rvert > 1$) Shrink ($0 < \lvert a \rvert < 1$) Reflection ($a < 0$) across x-axis	$y = \frac{a}{x}, x \neq 0$
Translation (horizontal by h; vertical by k) with vertical asymptote $x = h$ horizontal asymptote $y = k$	$y = \frac{1}{x - h} + k; x \neq h$
Combined	$y = \frac{a}{x - h} + k; x \neq h$

When you graph a translated reciprocal function, a good first step is to draw the asymptotes.

 Problem 3 **Graphing a Translation**

Think

How do you find the asymptotes?
The asymptotes of $y = \frac{1}{x}$ (the axes) translate 1 unit to the left and 2 units down.

What is the graph of $y = \frac{1}{x+1} - 2$? Identify the domain and range.

Step 1 Draw the asymptotes (red).

For $y = \frac{1}{x+1} - 2$, $h = -1$ and $k = -2$.

The vertical asymptote is $x = -1$.

The horizontal asymptote is $y = -2$.

Step 2 Translate the graph of $y = \frac{1}{x}$.

The graph of $y = \frac{1}{x}$ contains the points $(1, 1)$ and $(-1, -1)$. Translate these points 1 unit to the left and 2 units down to $(0, -1)$ and $(-2, -3)$, respectively. Draw the branches through these points (blue).

The domain is the set of all real numbers except $x = -1$. The range is the set of all real numbers except $y = -2$.

 Got It? **3.** What is the graph of $y = \frac{1}{x-4} + 6$? Identify the domain and range.

If you know the asymptotes of the graph of a reciprocal function and the value of a, you can write the equation of the function.

 Problem 4 **Writing the Equation of a Transformation**

Multiple Choice This graph of a function is a translation of the graph of $y = \frac{2}{x}$. What is an equation for the function?

  Ⓐ $y = \frac{2}{x+3} + 4$ Ⓒ $y = \frac{2}{x-3} + 4$

  Ⓑ $y = \frac{2}{x+3} - 4$ Ⓓ $y = \frac{2}{x-3} - 4$

Plan

How can you get started?
Identify the asymptotes of the graph.

The asymptotes are $x = -3$ and $y = 4$. Thus $h = -3$ and $k = 4$.

$y = \frac{a}{x-h} + k$ Use the general form.

$y = \frac{2}{x-(-3)} + 4$ Substitute for a, h, and k.

$y = \frac{2}{x+3} + 4$ Simplify.

The correct choice is A.

 Got It? **4.** This graph of a function is a translation of the graph of $y = \frac{2}{x}$. What is an equation for the function?

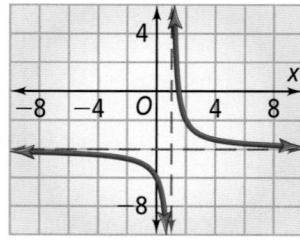

 **Problem 5** Using a Reciprocal Function

Clubs The rowing club is renting a 57-passenger bus for a day trip. The cost of the bus is $750. Five passengers will be chaperones. If the students who attend share the bus cost equally, what function models the cost per student C with respect to the number of students n who attend? What is the domain of the function? How many students must ride the bus to make the cost per student no more than $20?

Know
- The bus holds 57 passengers.
- The bus costs $750.
- Five riders are chaperones who pay nothing for the bus.

Need
- A function for the cost per student
- The number of students needed so that the cost does not exceed $20 per student

Plan
- Write a reciprocal function for the situation.
- Graph the function and solve an inequality using the $20 limit.

To share the cost equally, divide 750 by the number of students, n, who attend.

The function that models the cost per student is $C = \frac{750}{n}$.

The bus has a capacity of 57 passengers and there will be 5 chaperones. The maximum number of students is $57 - 5 = 52$.

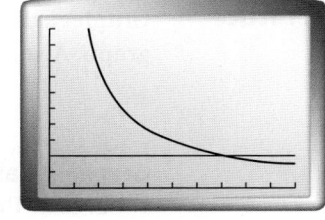

Think

Is the domain $x \leq 52$?
No; the domain is the possible numbers of students, so only positive integers make sense.

The domain is the integers from 1 to 52.

Use a graphing calculator to solve the inequality $\frac{750}{n} \leq 20$. Let $\mathbf{Y1} = \frac{750}{x}$ and $\mathbf{Y2} = 20$.

Change the window dimensions to get a closer look at the graph. Use the **intersect** feature.

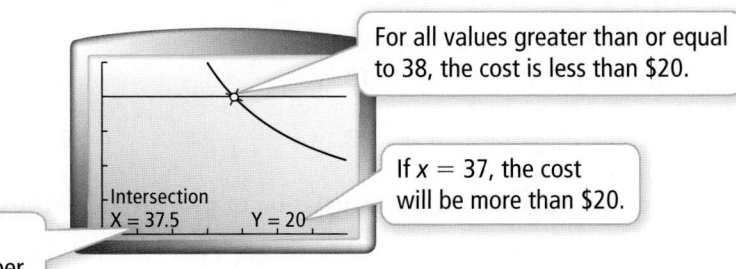

For all values greater than or equal to 38, the cost is less than $20.

If $x = 37$, the cost will be more than $20.

Intersection
X = 37.5   Y = 20

The number of people must be a whole number.

At least 38 students must ride the bus.

 Got It? 5. The junior class is renting a laser tag facility with a capacity of 325 people. The cost for the facility is $1200. The party must have 13 adult chaperones.
   a. If every student who attends shares the facility cost equally, what function models the cost per student C with respect to the number of students n who attend? What is the domain of the function? How many students must attend to make the cost per student no more than $7.50?
   b. The class wants to promote the event by giving away 30 spots to students in a drawing. How does the model change? Now how many paying students must attend so the cost for each is no more than $7.50?

Lesson Check

Do you know HOW?

1. Graph the equation $y = \frac{3}{x}$.

Describe the transformation from the graph of $y = \frac{1}{x}$ to the graph of the given function.

2. $y = \frac{1}{x} + 5$ **3.** $y = \frac{-4}{x}$

4. What are the asymptotes of the graph of $y = \frac{5}{x+2} - 7$?

Do you UNDERSTAND?  MATHEMATICAL PRACTICES

5. Vocabulary What transformation changes the graph of $y = \frac{1}{x}$ into the graph of $y = \frac{1}{2x}$?

6. Open Ended Write an equation of a stretch and a reflection of the graph $y = \frac{1}{x}$ across the x-axis.

7. Writing Explain how you can tell if a function $y = \frac{a}{x}$ is a stretch or compression of the parent function $y = \frac{1}{x}$.

Practice and Problem-Solving Exercises  MATHEMATICAL PRACTICES

A Practice Graph each function. Identify the x- and y-intercepts and the asymptotes of the graph. Also, state the domain and the range of the function.

See Problem 1.

8. $y = \frac{2}{x}$ **9.** $y = \frac{15}{x}$ **10.** $y = \frac{-3}{x}$ **11.** $y = -\frac{10}{x}$ **12.** $y = \frac{10}{x}$

 **Graphing Calculator** Graph the equations $y = \frac{1}{x}$ and $y = \frac{a}{x}$ using the given value of a. Then identify the effect of a on the graph.

See Problem 2.

13. $a = 2$ **14.** $a = -4$ **15.** $a = 0.5$ **16.** $a = 12$ **17.** $a = 0.75$

Sketch the asymptotes and the graph of each function. Identify the domain and range.

See Problem 3.

18. $y = \frac{1}{x} - 3$ **19.** $y = \frac{-2}{x} - 3$ **20.** $y = \frac{1}{x-2} + 5$ **21.** $y = \frac{1}{x-3} + 4$

22. $y = \frac{2}{x+6} - 1$ **23.** $y = \frac{10}{x+1} - 8$ **24.** $y = \frac{1}{x} - 2$ **25.** $y = \frac{-8}{x+5} - 6$

Write an equation for the translation of $y = \frac{2}{x}$ that has the given asymptotes.

See Problem 4.

26. $x = 0$ and $y = 4$ **27.** $x = -2$ and $y = 3$ **28.** $x = 4$ and $y = -8$

 29. Construction The weight P in pounds that a beam can safely carry is inversely proportional to the distance D in feet between the supports of the beam. For a certain type of wooden beam, $P = \frac{9200}{D}$. What distance between supports is needed to carry 1200 lb?

See Problem 5.

B Apply  **30. Think About a Plan** A high school decided to spend $750 on student academic achievement awards. At least 5 awards will be given, they should be equal in value, and each award should not be less than $50. Write and sketch a function that models the relationship between the number a of awards and the cost c of each award. What are the domain and range of the function?
- Which equation describes the relationship between a and c?
- What information can you use to determine the domain and range?

31. Open-Ended Write an equation for a horizontal translation of $y = \frac{2}{x}$. Then write an equation for a vertical translation of $y = \frac{2}{x}$. Identify the horizontal and vertical asymptotes of the graph of each function.

Sketch the graph of each function.

32. $xy = 3$ **33.** $xy + 5 = 0$ **34.** $3xy = 1$ **35.** $5xy = 2$ **36.** $10xy = -4$

37. Writing Explain how knowing the asymptotes of a translation of $y = \frac{1}{x}$ can help you graph the function. Include an example.

38. Multiple Choice The formula $p = \frac{69.1}{a + 2.3}$ models the relationship between atmospheric pressure p in inches of mercury and altitude a in miles.

Use the data shown with the photo. At which location does the model predict the pressure to be about 23.93 in. of mercury? (*Hint:* 1 mi = 5280 ft.)

Ⓐ Sahara Desert

Ⓑ Kalahari Desert

Ⓒ Mt. Kilimanjaro

Ⓓ Vinson Massif

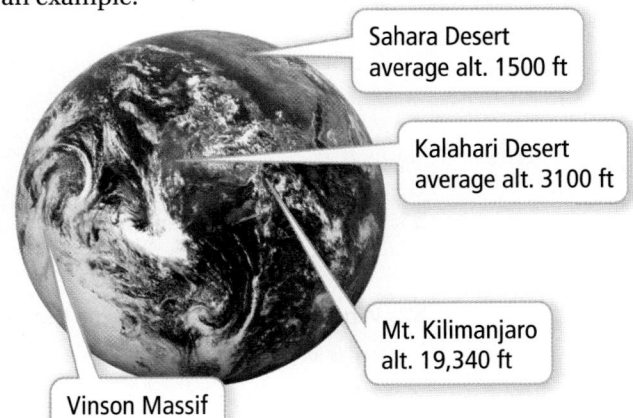

Sahara Desert average alt. 1500 ft

Kalahari Desert average alt. 3100 ft

Mt. Kilimanjaro alt. 19,340 ft

Vinson Massif alt. 16,680 ft

Graphing Calculator Graph each pair of functions. Find the approximate point(s) of intersection.

39. $y = \frac{6}{x-2}, y = 6$ **40.** $y = -\frac{1}{x-3} - 6, y = 6.2$ **41.** $y = \frac{3}{x+1}, y = -4$

42. Reasoning How will the domain and the range of the parent function $y = \frac{1}{x}$ change after the translation of its graph by 3 units up and by 5 units to the left?

43. a. Gasoline Mileage Suppose you drive an average of 10,000 miles each year. Your gasoline mileage (mi/gal) varies inversely with the number of gallons of gasoline you use each year. Write and graph a model for your average mileage m in terms of the gallons g of gasoline used.

b. After you begin driving on the highway more often, you use 50 gal less per year. Write and graph a new model to include this information.

c. Calculate your old and new mileage assuming that you originally used 400 gal of gasoline per year.

Ⓒ Challenge **Reasoning** Compare each pair of graphs and find any points of intersection.

44. $y = \frac{1}{x}$ and $y = \left|\frac{1}{x}\right|$ **45.** $y = \frac{1}{x}$ and $y = \frac{1}{x^2}$ **46.** $y = \left|\frac{1}{x}\right|$ and $y = \frac{1}{x^2}$

47. Find two reciprocal functions such that the minimum distance from the origin to the graph of each function is $4\sqrt{2}$.

48. Write each equation in the form $y = \frac{k}{x-b} + c$, and sketch the graph.

a. $y = \frac{2}{3x - 6}$ **b.** $y = \frac{1}{2 - 4x}$ **c.** $y = \frac{3 - x}{x + 2}$ **d.** $xy - y = 1$

Standardized Test Prep

SAT/ACT

49. What is an equation for the translation of $y = \frac{2}{x}$ that has asymptotes at $x = 3$ and $y = -5$?

    A $y = \frac{2}{x-3} - 5$ **B** $y = \frac{2}{x+3} + 5$ **C** $y = \frac{2}{x+5} - 3$ **D** $y = \frac{2}{x-5} + 3$

50. The graph at the right shows which inequality?

    F $y < -2.5x + 5$ **H** $-2.5x + y < 5$

    G $2.5x + y \geq 5$ **I** $5x + y \leq 5$

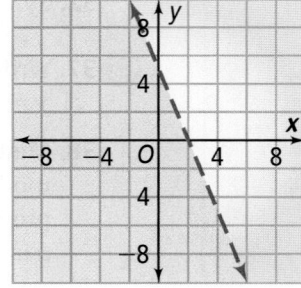

51. If p and q vary inversely, and $p = 10$ when $q = -4$, what is q when $p = -2$?

    A 20 **B** $\frac{4}{5}$ **C** $-\frac{4}{5}$ **D** -20

52. Which equation represents the inverse of the graph at the right?

    F $y = \log_3 x$ **H** $y = \log_x 3$

    G $x = \log_3 y$ **I** $x = \log_y 3$

Short Response

53. What is b if the graph of $y = 27b^x$ includes the point $(-1, 81)$?

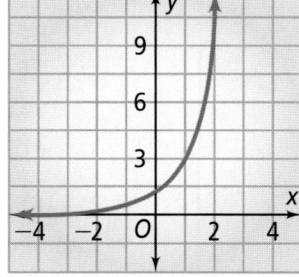

Apply What You've Learned

MATHEMATICAL
PRACTICES

MP 1, MP 4

Look back at the information on page 497 about Steve's and Sally's canoe trip.

   a. How far did Steve and Sally paddle upstream?

   b. How does the 3-mi/h current affect the speed at which Steve and Sally travel while they are paddling upstream?

   c. Let x represent the speed, in miles per hour, that Steve and Sally paddle in still water. Write a function $y = f(x)$ that gives the time y, in hours, that it takes Steve and Sally to paddle to Elk Island. (Hint: Use the formula $d = rt$.)

   d. What are the asymptotes of the graph of the function you wrote in part (c)? Describe the relationship of this function to the parent reciprocal function. Check your answers using a graphing calculator.

   e. What part of the graph has meaning in terms of this situation? Explain. Describe the y-values of the points with x-values that are close to 3 on this part of the graph. Interpret these points of the graph in terms of Steve and Sally's trip to Elk Island.

8-3 Rational Functions and Their Graphs

Common Core State Standards
F-IF.C.7d Graph rational functions, identifying zeros and asymptotes . . ., and showing end behavior.
Also F-BF.A.1b
MP 1, MP 3, MP 4

Objectives To identify properties of rational functions
To graph rational functions

 **Getting Ready!**

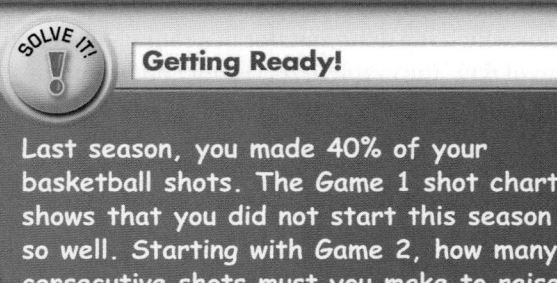

Last season, you made 40% of your basketball shots. The Game 1 shot chart shows that you did not start this season so well. Starting with Game 2, how many consecutive shots must you make to raise this season's percentage to 40%? If you never miss another shot this season, how high can you raise your percentage? Explain your reasoning.

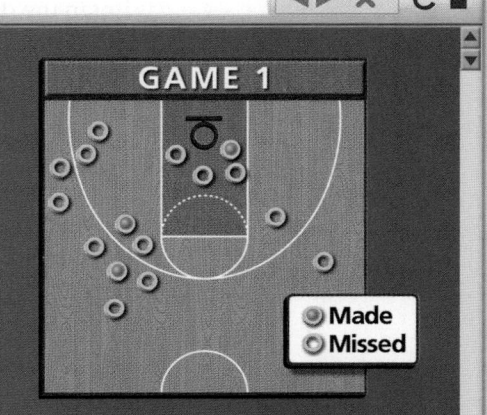

Solve a simpler problem to better understand the situation. Suppose you make baskets in your next two attempts. What will your percentage be?

MATHEMATICAL PRACTICES

You use a ratio of polynomial functions to form a *rational function*, like $y = \frac{x+3}{x+16}$.

Essential Understanding If a function has a polynomial in its denominator, its graph has a gap at each zero of the polynomial. The gap could be a one-point hole in the graph, or it could be the location of a vertical asymptote for the graph.

A **rational function** is a function that you can write in the form $f(x) = \frac{P(x)}{Q(x)}$

where $P(x)$ and $Q(x)$ are polynomial functions. The domain of $f(x)$ is all real numbers except those values for which $Q(x) = 0$.

Here are graphs of three rational functions:

Lesson Vocabulary
- rational function
- continuous graph
- discontinuous graph
- point of discontinuity
- removable discontinuity
- non-removable discontinuity

$y = \dfrac{x^2}{x^2 + 1}$

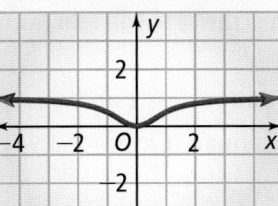

$y = \dfrac{(x+3)(x+2)}{(x+2)}$

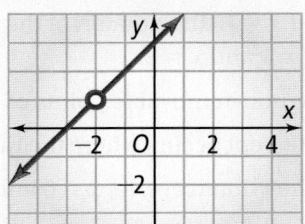

$y = \dfrac{x+4}{x-2}$

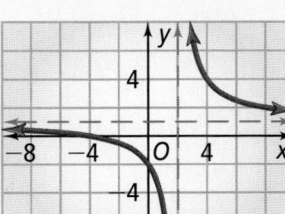

For the first rational function, $y = \frac{x^2}{x^2 + 1}$, there is no value of x that makes the denominator 0. The graph is a **continuous graph** because it has no jumps, breaks, or holes. You can draw the graph and your pencil never leaves the paper.

For the second rational function, $y = \frac{(x + 3)(x + 2)}{x + 2}$, x cannot be -2. For $y = \frac{x + 4}{x - 2}$, x cannot be 2. The second and third graphs are **discontinuous graphs**.

take note

Key Concept Point of Discontinuity

If a is a real number for which the denominator of a rational function $f(x)$ is zero, then a is not in the domain of $f(x)$. The graph of $f(x)$ is not continuous at $x = a$ and the function has a **point of discontinuity** at $x = a$.

The graph of $y = \frac{(x + 3)(x + 2)}{x + 2}$ has a **removable discontinuity** at $x = -2$. The hole in the graph is called a removable discontinuity because you could make the function continuous by redefining it at $x = -2$ so that $f(-2) = 1$.

The graph of $y = \frac{x + 4}{x - 2}$ has a **non-removable discontinuity** at $x = 2$. There is no way to redefine the function at 2 to make the function continuous.

When you are looking for discontinuities, it is helpful to factor the numerator and denominator as a first step. The factors of the denominator will reveal the points of discontinuity. The discontinuity caused by $(x - a)^n$ in the denominator is removable if the numerator also has $(x - a)^n$ as a factor.

 Problem 1 Finding Points of Discontinuity

What are the domain and points of discontinuity of each rational function? Are the points of discontinuity removable or non-removable? What are the x- and y-intercepts?

A $y = \dfrac{x + 3}{x^2 - 4x + 3}$

Factor the numerator and denominator to check for common factors.
$$y = \frac{x + 3}{x^2 - 4x + 3} = \frac{x + 3}{(x - 3)(x - 1)}$$

The function is undefined where $x - 3 = 0$ and where $x - 1 = 0$, at $x = 3$ and $x = 1$. The domain of the function is the set of all real numbers except $x = 1$ and $x = 3$.

There are non-removable points of discontinuity at $x = 1$ and $x = 3$.

The x-intercept occurs where the numerator equals 0, at $x = -3$.

To find the y-intercept, let $x = 0$ and simplify.
$$y = \frac{0 + 3}{(0 - 3)(0 - 1)} = \frac{3}{(-3)(-1)} = \frac{3}{3} = 1$$

Think

Are the discontinuities removable?
There are no common factors in the numerator and denominator. Any discontinuity is non-removable.

B $y = \dfrac{x - 5}{x^2 + 1}$

You cannot factor the numerator or the denominator. Also, there are no values of x that make the denominator 0. The domain of the function is all real numbers, and there are no discontinuities.

The x-intercept occurs where the numerator equals 0, at $x = 5$.

To find the y-intercept, let $x = 0$ and simplify: $y = \dfrac{0 - 5}{0^2 + 1} = \dfrac{-5}{1} = -5$

C $y = \dfrac{x^2 - 3x - 4}{x - 4}$

Factor the numerator and denominator: $y = \dfrac{x^2 - 3x - 4}{x - 4} = \dfrac{(x - 4)(x + 1)}{(x - 4)}$

The function is undefined where $x - 4 = 0$, at $x = 4$. The domain of the function is the set of all real numbers except $x = 4$.

Because $y = x + 1$, except at $x = 4$, there is a removable discontinuity at $x = 4$.

At $x = 4$, $y = x + 1 = 4 + 1 = 5$, so you can redefine the function to remove the discontinuity.

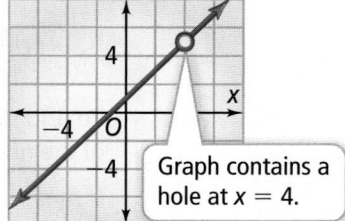

Graph contains a hole at $x = 4$.

$$y = \begin{cases} \dfrac{x^2 - 3x - 4}{x - 4}, & \text{if } x \neq 4 \\ 5, & \text{if } x = 4 \end{cases}$$

The x-intercept occurs where the numerator equals 0, at $x = -1$.

To find the y-intercept, let $x = 0$ and simplify.

$$y = \dfrac{0^2 - 3 \cdot 0 - 4}{0 - 4} = \dfrac{0 - 0 - 4}{-4} = \dfrac{-4}{-4} = 1$$

 Got It? 1. What are the domain and points of discontinuity of the rational function? Are the points of discontinuity *removable* or *non-removable*? What are the x- and y-intercepts of the rational function?

a. $y = \dfrac{1}{x^2 - 16}$ **b.** $y = \dfrac{x^2 - 1}{x^2 + 3}$ **c.** $y = \dfrac{x + 1}{x^2 + 3x + 2}$

In Chapter 7, you learned that an asymptote is a line that a graph approaches as x or y increases in absolute value. If a rational function has a non-removable discontinuity at $x = a$, the graph of the rational function will have a vertical asymptote at $x = a$.

take note

Key Concept   Vertical Asymptotes of Rational Functions

The graph of the rational function $f(x) = \dfrac{P(x)}{Q(x)}$ has a vertical asymptote at each real zero of $Q(x)$ if $P(x)$ and $Q(x)$ have no common zeros. If $P(x)$ and $Q(x)$ have $(x - a)^m$ and $(x - a)^n$ as factors, respectively and $m < n$, then $f(x)$ also has a vertical asymptote at $x = a$.

Problem 2 Finding Vertical Asymptotes

How can you locate a vertical asymptote?
Find factors $x - a$ of the denominator that have no matching factor in the numerator. $x = a$ is a vertical asymptote.

What are the vertical asymptotes for the graph of $y = \dfrac{(x + 1)}{(x - 2)(x - 3)}$?

Since 2 and 3 are zeros of the denominator and neither is a zero of the numerator, the lines $x = 2$ and $x = 3$ are vertical asymptotes.

 Got It? 2. What are the vertical asymptotes for the graph of the rational function?

a. $y = \dfrac{x - 2}{(x - 1)(x + 3)}$ **b.** $y = \dfrac{x - 2}{(x - 2)(x + 3)}$ **c.** $y = \dfrac{x^2 - 1}{x + 1}$

While the graph of a rational function can have any number of vertical asymptotes, it can have no more than one horizontal asymptote.

take note

Key Concept Horizontal Asymptote of a Rational Function

To find the horizontal asymptote of the graph of a rational function, compare the degree of the numerator m to the degree of the denominator n.

If $m < n$, the graph has horizontal asymptote $y = 0$ (the x-axis).

If $m > n$, the graph has no horizontal asymptote.

If $m = n$, the graph has horizontal asymptote $y = \dfrac{a}{b}$ where a is the coefficient of the term of greatest degree in the numerator and b is the coefficient of the term of greatest degree in the denominator.

Problem 3 Finding Horizontal Asymptotes

How can you find the horizontal asymptote when the numerator and denominator have equal degree?
Find the quotient, q, of the leading coefficients of the numerator and denominator. $y = q$ is the horizontal asymptote.

What is the horizontal asymptote for the rational function?

A $y = \dfrac{2x}{x - 3}$

The degree of the numerator and denominator are the same.

The horizontal asymptote is $y = \dfrac{2}{1}$ or $y = 2$.

B $y = \dfrac{x - 2}{x^2 - 2x - 3}$

The degree of the numerator is less than the degree of the denominator. The horizontal asymptote is $y = 0$.

C $y = \dfrac{x^2}{2x - 5}$

The degree of the numerator is greater than the degree of the denominator. There is no horizontal asymptote.

 Got It? 3. What is the horizontal asymptote for the rational function?

a. $y = \dfrac{-2x + 6}{x - 5}$ **b.** $y = \dfrac{x - 1}{x^2 + 4x + 4}$ **c.** $y = \dfrac{x^2 + 2x - 3}{x - 2}$

Essential Understanding You can get a reasonable graph for a rational function by finding all intercepts and asymptotes. Sometimes you will also have to plot a few extra points to get a good sense of the shape of the graph.

Ⓒ Problem 4 Graphing a Rational Function

What is the graph of the rational function $y = \dfrac{x^2 + x - 12}{x^2 - 4}$?

Plan

How can you graph this function?
Find the horizontal and vertical asymptotes and the x- and y-intercepts. Look for holes and find additional points to help get a better sense of the graph.

Think

The degrees of the numerator and denominator are equal.

Factor the numerator and the denominator. They have no common factor. The graph has no holes. It has two vertical asymptotes at the zeros of the denominator.

Find the x- and y-intercepts. The x-intercepts occur where $y = 0$. The y-intercepts occur where $x = 0$.

Find a few more points on the graph.

Graph the asymptotes. Then plot the intercepts and additional points. Use the points to sketch the graph.

Write

$y = \dfrac{x^2 + x - 12}{x^2 - 4}$

horizontal asymptote: $y = \dfrac{1}{1} = 1$

$y = \dfrac{(x + 4)(x - 3)}{(x + 2)(x - 2)}$

vertical asymptotes: $x = -2, x = 2$

When the numerator equals zero, $y = 0$.
x-intercepts: $(-4, 0)$ and $(3, 0)$

$y = \dfrac{(0 + 4)(0 - 3)}{(0 + 2)(0 - 2)} = 3$

y-intercept: $(0, 3)$

More points on the graph:
$\left(-3, -\dfrac{6}{5}\right), (-1, 4), \left(1, \dfrac{10}{3}\right),$ and $\left(4, \dfrac{2}{3}\right)$

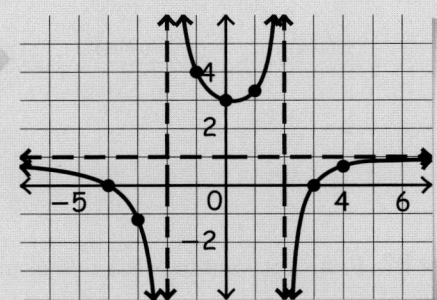

✓ Got It? 4. What is the graph of the rational function $y = \dfrac{x + 3}{x^2 - 6x + 5}$?

 **Problem 5** Using a Rational Function STEM **GRIDDED RESPONSE**

Chemistry You work in a pharmacy that mixes different concentrations of saline solutions for its customers. The pharmacy has a supply of two concentrations, 0.5% and 2%. The function $y = \dfrac{(100)(0.02) + x(0.005)}{100 + x}$ gives the concentration of the saline solution after adding x milliliters of the 0.5% solution to 100 milliliters of the 2% solution. How many milliliters of the 0.5% solution must you add for the combined solution to have a concentration of 0.9%?

Plan

How can you use a calculator to solve the problem?
Graph
$y = \dfrac{(100)(0.02) + x(0.005)}{100 + x}$
and $y = 0.009$ in the calculator and find the point of intersection.

Step 1 Use a graphing calculator to graph $\mathbf{Y1} = \dfrac{(100)(0.02) + x(0.005)}{100 + x}$ and $\mathbf{Y2} = 0.009$.

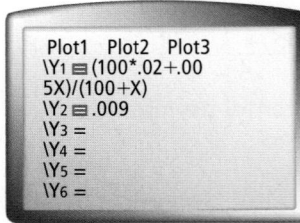
```
Plot1  Plot2  Plot3
\Y1 ▄ (100*.02+.00
5X)/(100+X)
\Y2 ▄ .009
\Y3 =
\Y4 =
\Y5 =
\Y6 =
```

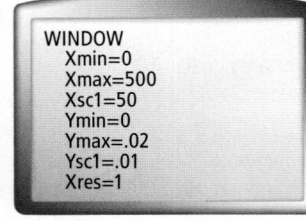
```
WINDOW
Xmin=0
Xmax=500
Xscl=50
Ymin=0
Ymax=.02
Yscl=.01
Xres=1
```

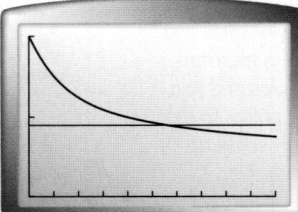

Step 2 Find the point of intersection of the two functions.

Graphic Solution

Table Solution

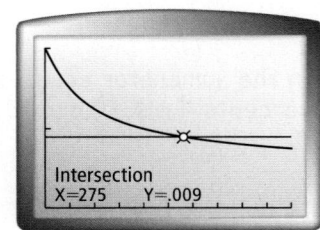

X	Y1	Y2
150	.011	.009
175	.01045	.009
200	.01	.009
225	.00962	.009
250	.00929	.009
275	.009	.009
300	.00875	.009

X=275

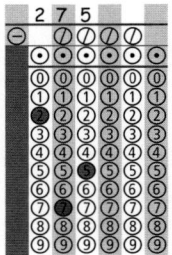

You should add 275 mL of the 0.5% solution to get a 0.9% solution.
Write 275 in the grid.

Check $y = \dfrac{(100)(0.02) + x(0.005)}{100 + x}$

$y \stackrel{?}{=} \dfrac{(100)(0.02) + (275)(0.005)}{100 + 275}$ Substitute 275 for x.

$y \stackrel{?}{=} \dfrac{2 + 1.375}{375}$

$y = 0.009$ ✔

© ✓ **Got It? 5. a.** You want to mix a 10% orange juice drink with 100% pure orange juice to make a 40% orange juice drink. The function $y = \dfrac{(2)(1.0) + x(0.1)}{2 + x}$ gives the concentration y of orange juice in the drink after you add x gallons of the 10% drink to 2 gallons of pure juice. How much of the 10% drink must you add to get a drink that is 40% juice?

b. Reasoning If you wanted a drink that is 80% orange juice, would you need to add half as much as your answer in part (a)? Explain.

Lesson Check

Do you know HOW?

Find any points of discontinuity for each rational function.

1. $y = \dfrac{x + 5}{x^2 + 9x + 20}$

2. $y = \dfrac{x^2 + 2x}{x^2 - 7x - 18}$

3. $y = \dfrac{x - 1}{(x + 1)^2}$

4. $y = \dfrac{x^2 - x - 2}{3x^2 - 7x + 2}$

Find the vertical asymptotes of the graph of each rational function.

5. $y = \dfrac{x - 3}{x + 5}$

6. $y = \dfrac{x - 3}{x^2 + 5x + 6}$

7. $y = \dfrac{2x + 2}{x^2 - 1}$

8. $y = \dfrac{x^2 + 2x + 3}{x^2 + 2x - 3}$

Sketch the graph of each rational function.

9. $y = \dfrac{3x}{x - 4}$

10. $y = \dfrac{x + 3}{(x - 1)(x - 6)}$

Do you UNDERSTAND?

For Exercises 11 and 12, use the following table. The table shows data for a rational function.

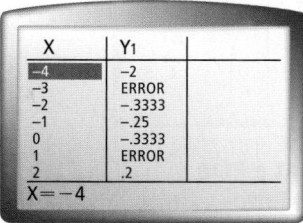

X	Y₁
-4	-2
-3	ERROR
-2	-.3333
-1	-.25
0	-.3333
1	ERROR
2	.2

X=-4

11. What do the **Y1** values for **X = −3** and **X = 1** tell you about the rational function?

ⓒ **12. Reasoning** Assume that there are no more **ERROR** values in the **Y1** column. What is the lowest possible degree of the denominator? Explain how you know.

Practice and Problem-Solving Exercises

 **Practice**   Find the domain, points of discontinuity, and *x*- and *y*-intercepts of each rational function. Determine whether the discontinuities are removable or non-removable.   ◀ **See Problem 1.**

13. $y = \dfrac{2x^2 + 5}{x^2 - 2x}$

14. $y = \dfrac{x^2 + 2x}{x^2 + 2}$

15. $y = \dfrac{3x - 3}{x^2 - 1}$

16. $y = \dfrac{6 - 3x}{x^2 - 5x + 6}$

Find the vertical asymptotes and holes for the graph of each rational function.   ◀ **See Problem 2.**

17. $y = \dfrac{3}{x + 2}$

18. $y = \dfrac{x + 5}{x + 5}$

19. $y = \dfrac{x + 3}{(2x + 3)(x - 1)}$

20. $y = \dfrac{(x + 3)(x - 2)}{(x - 2)(x + 1)}$

21. $y = \dfrac{x^2 - 4}{x + 2}$

22. $y = \dfrac{x + 5}{x^2 + 9}$

Find the horizontal asymptote of the graph of each rational function.   ◀ **See Problem 3.**

23. $y = \dfrac{5}{x + 6}$

24. $y = \dfrac{x + 2}{2x^2 - 4}$

25. $y = \dfrac{x + 1}{x + 5}$

26. $y = \dfrac{x^2 + 2}{2x^2 - 1}$

27. $y = \dfrac{5x^3 + 2x}{2x^5 - 4x^3}$

28. $y = \dfrac{3x - 4}{4x + 1}$

Sketch the graph of each rational function.   ◀ **See Problem 4.**

29. $y = \dfrac{x^2 - 4}{3x - 6}$

30. $y = \dfrac{4x}{x^3 - 4x}$

31. $y = \dfrac{x + 4}{x - 4}$

32. $y = \dfrac{x(x + 1)}{x + 1}$

33. $y = \dfrac{x + 6}{(x - 2)(x + 3)}$

34. $y = \dfrac{3x}{(x + 2)^2}$

STEM **35. Pharmacology** How many milliliters of the 0.5% solution must be added to the 2% solution to get a 0.65% solution? Use the rational function given in Problem 5.   ◀ **See Problem 5.**

Find the vertical and horizontal asymptotes, if any, of the graph of each rational function.

36.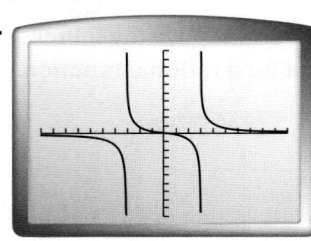

37.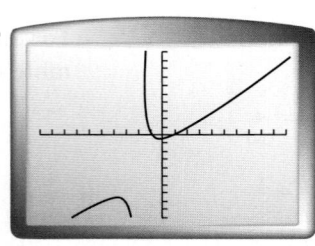

38.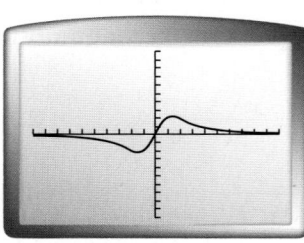

Ⓒ 39. **Think About a Plan** A basketball player has made 21 of her last 30 free throws—a percentage of 70%. How many more consecutive free throws does she need to raise her free throw percentage to 75%?
   • How can you model the player's free throw percentage as a rational function? (*Hint:* Let x = the number of additional free throws needed.)
   • How can a graph help you answer this question?

40. **Grades** A student earns an 82% on her first test. How many consecutive 100% test scores does she need to bring her average up to 95%? Assume that each test has equal impact on the average grade.

Ⓒ 41. **Error Analysis** A student listed the asymptotes of the function $y = \dfrac{x^2 - 3x + 2}{x^2 + 6x + 5}$ as shown at the right. Explain the student's error. What are the correct asymptotes?

vertical asymptotes:
x = 1, x̶ ̶=̶ ̶2̶
horizontal asymptotes:
y̶ ̶=̶ ̶−̶1̶,̶ y = −5

Sketch the graph of each rational function.

42. $y = \dfrac{2x + 3}{x - 5}$

43. $y = \dfrac{x^2 + 6x + 9}{x + 3}$

44. $y = \dfrac{4x^2 - 100}{2x^2 + x - 15}$

45. $y = -\dfrac{x}{(x - 1)^2}$

46. **Business** CDs can be manufactured for $.19 each. The development cost is $210,000. The first 500 discs are samples and will not be sold.
   a. Write a function for the average cost of a disc that is not a sample. Graph the function.
   b. What is the average cost if 5000 discs are produced? If 15,000 discs are produced?
   c. How many discs must be produced to bring the average cost under $10?
   d. What are the vertical and horizontal asymptotes of the graph of the function?

Ⓒ 47. **Writing** Describe the conditions that will produce a rational function with a graph that has no vertical asymptotes.

Ⓒ Challenge

48. **Reasoning** Look for a pattern in the sequence of file folders below.
   a. Write a model for the number of yellow folders $Y(n)$ at each step n.
   b. Write a model for the number of green folders $G(n)$ at each step n.
   c. Write a model for the ratio of $Y(n)$ to $G(n)$. Use it to predict the ratio of yellow folders to green folders in the next figure. Verify your answer.

49. Write a rational function with the following characteristics.

a. Vertical asymptotes at $x = 1$ and $x = -3$, horizontal asymptote at $y = 1$, zeros at 3 and 4

b. Vertical asymptotes at $x = 0$ and $x = 3$, horizontal asymptote at $y = 0$, a zero at -4

c. Vertical asymptotes at $x = -2$ and $x = 2$, horizontal asymptote at $y = 3$, only one zero at -1

Standardized Test Prep

GRIDDED RESPONSE

SAT/ACT

50. What is the x-coordinate of the hole in the graph of $y = \frac{x^2 - 9}{2x^2 - x - 15}$?

51. Suppose z varies directly with x and inversely with y. If z is 1.5 when x is 9 and y is 4, what is z when x is 6 and y is 0.5?

52. What is the y-coordinate of the vertex of the parabola $y = -3(x - 4)^2 + 5$?

53. What is the real solution of $54x^3 - 16 = 0$ written as a fraction?

54. Using the Change of Base Formula, what is the value of $\log_7 15$ rounded to the nearest hundredth?

Mixed Review

Sketch the asymptotes and the graph of each equation. Identify the domain and range. See Lesson 8-2.

55. $y = \frac{3}{x} + 4$ **56.** $y = \frac{2}{x + 3}$ **57.** $y = \frac{-1}{x + 1} + 1$

58. $y = \frac{5}{x - 7} - 3$ **59.** $y = \frac{4}{x}$ **60.** $y = \frac{-2}{x - 1} + 2$

Find the inverse of each function. Determine if the inverse is a function. See Lesson 6-7.

61. $y = 2x - 3$ **62.** $y = 6 - x$ **63.** $y = 2x^2$

64. $y = \frac{x^2}{5}$ **65.** $y = \frac{1}{x + 2}$ **66.** $y = \sqrt{x - 2} + 1$

Solve each inequality. Graph the solution. See Lesson 1-5.

67. $6a - 17 < 47$ **68.** $2(x + 9) \geq 90$ **69.** $5(x - 11) + 13 \geq 47$

70. $6 + y < 3y - 2$ **71.** $49 > 7x + 28$ **72.** $12 - 2b > 3(b - 3) - 4$

Get Ready! To prepare for Lesson 8-4, do Exercises 73–76.

Factor each expression. See Lesson 4-4.

73. $2x^2 - 3x + 1$ **74.** $4x^2 - 9$ **75.** $5x^2 + 6x + 1$ **76.** $10x^2 - 10$

Oblique Asymptotes

Common Core State Standards

Extends F-IF.C.7d Graph rational functions, identifying zeros and asymptotes when suitable factorizations are available, and showing end behavior.

MP 5

In Lesson 8-2, you saw that the graphs of some rational functions have horizontal and vertical asymptotes. The graphs of some rational functions can have *oblique asymptotes*. **Oblique asymptotes** are asymptotes that are neither horizontal nor vertical. These asymptotes only occur in rational functions in which the degree of the numerator is one greater than the degree of the denominator.

MATHEMATICAL PRACTICES

Example 1

Compare the graphs of $y = \dfrac{6x^2 + 1}{3x}$ **and** $y = 2x$ **using a graphing calculator.**

The graph of $y = \dfrac{6x^2 + 1}{3x}$ gets closer to $y = 2x$ as $|x|$ gets increasingly large.

The graph of $y = 2x$ is an oblique asymptote of $y = \dfrac{6x^2 + 1}{3x}$.

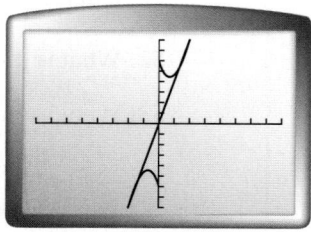

Example 2

Use a spreadsheet to find the differences between $f(x) = \dfrac{6x^2 + 1}{3x}$ **and** $g(x) = 2x$ **for the values from 1 to 10.**

Step 1   Label each column in Row 1.

Step 2   Enter the x-values in column A.

Step 3   Enter the formulas for $f(x)$, $g(x)$, and $f(x) - g(x)$ into cells B2, C2, and D2.

$$B2 = \left(6 \times (A2)^2 + 1\right)/(3 \times A2)$$

$$C2 = 2 \times A2$$

$$D2 = B2 - C2$$

	A	B	C	D	
1	x	f(x) = (6x^2 + 1)/(3x)	g(x) = 2x	f(x) − g(x)	
2	1	2.333	2	0.333	
3	2	4.167	4	0.167	
4	3	6.111	6	0.111	

Step 4   In columns B, C, and D fill the formulas down to find the values of $f(x)$, $g(x)$, and $f(x) - g(x)$ for each corresponding x-value.

As the values of x get larger, the value $6x^2$ becomes much larger than the constant term in the numerator. As a result, the constant term has a smaller effect on the value of the function. So, as x increases, the value of $\dfrac{6x^2 + 1}{3x}$ gets closer to the value of $\dfrac{6x^2}{3x} = 2x$, for $x \neq 0$. The spreadsheet confirms this conclusion by showing that the difference between these two values gets closer to zero as x gets larger.

Sometimes it is not as easy to find the oblique asymptote. For example, the asymptote of $y = \frac{2x^2 - 3x + 3}{x - 2}$ is not $\frac{2x^2}{x}$ or $2x$. You can use polynomial division to find the oblique asymptote of any rational function.

Example 3

Determine the oblique asymptote of $y = \frac{2x^2 - 3x + 3}{x - 2}$.

Divide the numerator by the denominator.

$$
\begin{array}{r}
2x + 1 \\
x - 2 \overline{)\, 2x^2 - 3x + 3} \\
\underline{2x^2 - 4x} \\
x + 3 \\
\underline{x - 2} \\
5
\end{array}
$$

Ignore the remainder. The asymptote is the quotient, $y = 2x + 1$.

Check

Use a graphing calculator to check your answer.

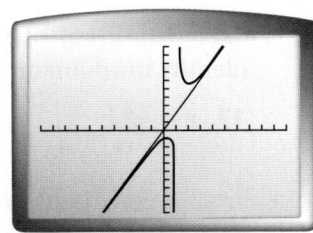

Exercises

Graphing Calculator For each function determine the oblique asymptote. Check with a graphing calculator.

1. $y = \frac{x^2 - 1}{x}$

2. $y = -\frac{2x^2}{3x + 2}$

3. $y = \frac{4 - x^3}{4x^2 - 1}$

4. $y = \frac{2x^4 + 99{,}999}{x^3}$

©5. Technical Writing Write a step-by-step manual for classmates to use so they can use a spreadsheet to explore the differences between $f(x)$ and $g(x)$ as the value of x increases.

$$f(x) = \frac{12x^2 - 7}{3x} \qquad\qquad g(x) = 4x$$

©6. Open-Ended Write three rational functions that have an oblique asymptote of $y = 2x$. Graph to check your work.

Describe the asymptotes of the graph of each function.

7. $f(x) = \frac{2x + 1}{x^2 - 1}$

8. $f(x) = \frac{x^2 - 9}{x + 3}$

9. $f(x) = \frac{5x + 11}{4x + 6}$

10. $f(x) = \frac{4x^2 + x - 3}{7x - 1}$

11. $y = \frac{2x^2 - 7x - 5}{2x + 3}$

12. $y = \frac{6x^2 + 14x + 7}{2x + 3}$

Do you know HOW?

If $z = 30$ when $x = 3$ and $y = 2$, write the function that models the relationship.

1. z varies jointly with x and y.

2. z varies directly with x and inversely with y.

3. z varies inversely with the product of x and y.

Is the relationship between the values in the table a *direct variation*, an *inverse variation*, or *neither*?

4.

x	y
22	104
35	174
48	239
54	269

5.

x	y
2	−4.8
6	−14.4
12	−28.8
19	−45.6

6.

x	y
15	2.4
18	2
20	1.8
45	0.8

Suppose that x and y vary inversely. Write a function that models the inverse variation.

7. $x = 13$ when $y = 17$

8. $x = -12$ when $y = 4$

9. $x = -52$ when $y = \frac{1}{4}$

Explain how the graph of y_2 is related to the graph of y_1.

10. $y_1 = \frac{4}{x}$ and $y_2 = \frac{9}{x}$

11. $y_1 = \frac{1}{x}$ and $y_2 = \frac{1}{x} + 5$

12. $y_1 = \frac{1}{x-1} + 2$ and $y_2 = \frac{1}{x+1} - 2$

Find any holes and vertical or horizontal asymptotes for the graph of each rational function.

13. $y = \dfrac{1}{x^2 + 3x - 10}$

14. $y = \dfrac{x + 2}{(x + 2)(x - 3)}$

15. $y = \dfrac{x - 1}{x^2 - 2x + 1}$

16. $y = \dfrac{5x - 2}{x + 2}$

Sketch the graph of each rational function. Then identify the domain and range.

17. $y = \dfrac{-2}{x}$

18. $y = \dfrac{5}{x + 3} - 4$

19. $y = \dfrac{x^2 - 9}{2x + 6}$

20. $y = \dfrac{3x}{x^3 - x}$

21. $y = \dfrac{x + 3}{x - 3}$

22. $y = \dfrac{x^2 - 2x}{x - 2}$

Do you UNDERSTAND?

Ⓒ **Open-Ended** Write a rational function with the given characteristics.

23. a vertical asymptote at $x = 8$ and a horizontal asymptote at $y = 0$

24. a vertical asymptote at $x = -4$ and a horizontal asymptote at $y = 3$

25. a hole at $x = -5$ and a vertical asymptote at $x = 2$

Ⓒ **26. Reasoning** How many inverse variation functions have (2, 3) as a solution?

Ⓒ **27. Reasoning** The graph of an inverse variation function contains the point (a, b). Using a and b, identify 3 other points on the graph.

Ⓒ **28. Reasoning** Graph the equations $y = \dfrac{x^2 + x - 6}{x^2 - 5x + 6}$ and $y = \dfrac{x + 3}{x - 3}$. Are they equivalent? Explain.

Rational Expressions

 Common Core State Standards

A-SSE.A.2 Use the structure of an expression to identify ways to rewrite it.
A-SSE.A.1b Interpret complicated expressions by viewing one or more of their parts as a single entity.
Also A-SSE.A.1a

MP 1, MP 2, MP 3, MP 4

Objectives To simplify rational expressions
To multiply and divide rational expressions

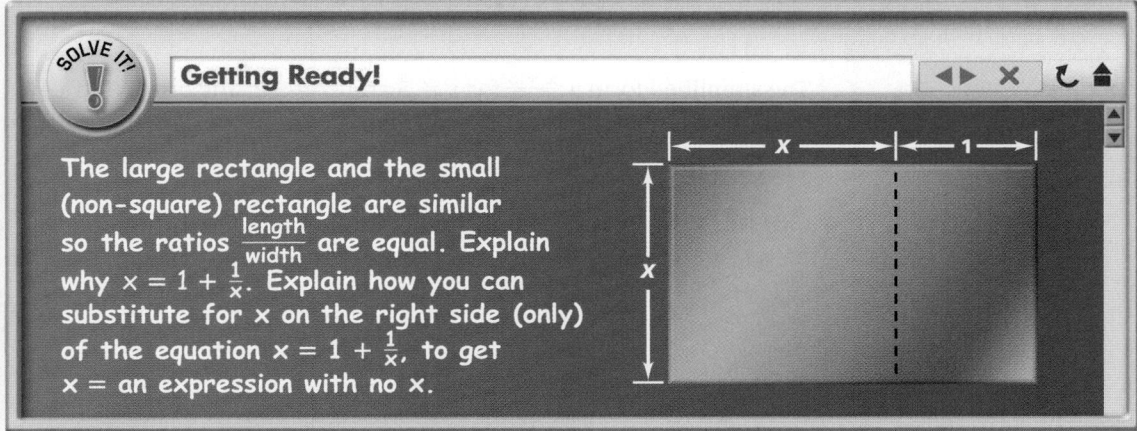

SOLVE IT!

Getting Ready!

The large rectangle and the small (non-square) rectangle are similar so the ratios $\frac{length}{width}$ are equal. Explain why $x = 1 + \frac{1}{x}$. Explain how you can substitute for x on the right side (only) of the equation $x = 1 + \frac{1}{x}$, to get $x =$ an expression with no x.

Lesson Vocabulary
• rational expression
• simplest form

The expression $1 + \frac{1}{x}$ in the Solve It is equivalent to the *rational expression* $\frac{x+1}{x}$. A **rational expression** is the quotient of two polynomials. You will find that, at different times, it is helpful to think of rational expressions as ratios, as fractions, or as quotients.

Essential Understanding You can use much of what you know about multiplying and dividing fractions to multiply and divide rational expressions.

A rational expression is in **simplest form** when its numerator and denominator are polynomials that have no common divisors.

In simplest form	Not in simplest form
$\dfrac{x+1}{x-1}, \dfrac{x^2+3x+2}{x+3}$	$\dfrac{x}{x^2}, \dfrac{3(x-3)}{x-3}, \dfrac{x^2-x-6}{x^2+x-2}$

You simplify a rational expression by dividing out the common factors in the numerator and the denominator. Factoring the numerator and denominator will help you find the common divisors.

A rational expression and any simplified form must have the same domain in order to be equivalent.

$$\frac{x^2-x-6}{x^2+x-2} = \frac{(x-3)(x+2)}{(x-1)(x+2)} \text{ and } \frac{x-3}{x-1}, x \neq -2, \text{ are equivalent.}$$

In the example above, you must exclude -2 from the domain of $\frac{x-3}{x-1}$ because -2 is not in the domain of $\frac{x^2-x-6}{x^2+x-2}$. Note that this restriction is not evident from the simplified expression $\frac{x-3}{x-1}$.

Problem 1 Simplifying a Rational Expression

What is $\frac{x^2 + 7x + 10}{x^2 - 3x - 10}$ in simplest form? State any restrictions on the variable.

$$\frac{x^2 + 7x + 10}{x^2 - 3x - 10} = \frac{(x + 2)(x + 5)}{(x + 2)(x - 5)} \qquad \text{Factor the numerator and denominator.}$$

$$= \frac{\cancel{(x + 2)}(x + 5)}{\cancel{(x + 2)}(x - 5)} \qquad \text{Divide out common factors.}$$

$$= \frac{x + 5}{x - 5} \qquad \text{Simplify.}$$

Think

Is there more than one restriction?
Yes, before you divided the common factors out, $(x + 2)$ was one of the factors of the denominator so $x \neq -2$.

The simplified form is $\frac{x + 5}{x - 5}$ for $x \neq 5$ and $x \neq -2$. The restriction $x \neq -2$ is not evident from the simplified form, but is needed to prevent the denominator of the original expression from being zero.

 Got It? **1.** What is the rational expression in simplest form? State any restrictions on the variables.

a. $\frac{24x^3y^2}{-6x^2y^3}$ **b.** $\frac{x^2 + 2x - 8}{x^2 - 5x + 6}$ **c.** $\frac{12 - 4x}{x^2 - 9}$

You can use what you know about simplifying rational expressions when you multiply and divide them.

 Problem 2 Multiplying Rational Expressions

Plan

How is multiplying rational expressions like multiplying fractions?
To multiply rational expressions, you multiply the numerators and multiply the denominators.

What is the product $\frac{x^2 + x - 6}{x - 5} \cdot \frac{x^2 - 25}{x^2 + 4x + 3}$ in simplest form? State any restrictions on the variable.

$$\frac{x^2 + x - 6}{x - 5} \cdot \frac{x^2 - 25}{x^2 + 4x + 3}$$

$$= \frac{(x + 3)(x - 2)}{x - 5} \cdot \frac{(x + 5)(x - 5)}{(x + 3)(x + 1)} \qquad \text{Factor all polynomials.}$$

$$= \frac{\cancel{(x + 3)}(x - 2)}{\cancel{x - 5}} \cdot \frac{(x + 5)\cancel{(x - 5)}}{\cancel{(x + 3)}(x + 1)} \qquad \text{Divide out common factors.}$$

$$= \frac{(x - 2)(x + 5)}{x + 1} \qquad \text{Simplify.}$$

The product is $\frac{(x - 2)(x + 5)}{x + 1}$ for $x \neq -3$, $x \neq 5$, and $x \neq -1$. The restrictions $x \neq -3$ and $x \neq 5$ are not evident from the simplified form, but are needed to prevent the denominators in the original product from being zero.

 Got It? **2.** What is the product $\frac{2x - 8}{x^2 - 16} \cdot \frac{x^2 + 5x + 4}{x^2 + 8x + 16}$ in simplest form? State any restrictions on the variable.

To divide rational expressions, you multiply by the reciprocal of the divisor, just as you do when you divide rational numbers.

Problem 3 **Dividing Rational Expressions**

What is the quotient $\dfrac{2-x}{x^2+2x+1} \div \dfrac{x^2+3x-10}{x^2-1}$ in simplest form? State any restrictions on the variable.

Plan

How do you start?
Think of division as multiplying by the reciprocal.

Think

To divide, you multiply by the reciprocal.

The expressions may have common factors. So, factor the numerators and denominators.

Factor -1 from $(2 - x)$ to get a second $(x - 2)$.

Divide out common factors.

Rewrite the remaining factors.

Identify the restrictions from the denominator of the simplified expression and from any other denominator used.

Write

$$\dfrac{2-x}{x^2+2x+1} \div \dfrac{x^2+3x-10}{x^2-1}$$

$$= \dfrac{2-x}{x^2+2x+1} \cdot \dfrac{x^2-1}{x^2+3x-10}$$

$$= \dfrac{2-x}{(x+1)(x+1)} \cdot \dfrac{(x+1)(x-1)}{(x+5)(x-2)}$$

$$= \dfrac{-1(x-2)}{(x+1)(x+1)} \cdot \dfrac{(x+1)(x-1)}{(x+5)(x-2)}$$

$$= \dfrac{-1\cancel{(x-2)}}{\cancel{(x+1)}(x+1)} \cdot \dfrac{\cancel{(x+1)}(x-1)}{(x+5)\cancel{(x-2)}}$$

$$= \dfrac{-1(x-1)}{(x+1)(x+5)}$$

$$x \neq -1,\ x \neq -5,\ x \neq 1, \text{ and } x \neq 2$$

Got It? **3. a.** What is the quotient $\dfrac{x^2+5x+4}{x^2+x-12} \div \dfrac{x^2-1}{2x^2-6x}$ in simplest form? State any restrictions on the variable.

b. Reasoning Without doing the calculation, what is greatest number of restrictions the quotient $\dfrac{x^2+8x+7}{x^2-x-12} \div \dfrac{x^2+2x-8}{x^2+13x+24}$ could have? Explain.

Problem 4 Using Rational Expressions to Solve a Problem STEM

Construction Your community is building a park. It wants to fence in a play space for toddlers. It wants the maximum area for a given amount of fencing. Which shape, a square or a circle, provides a more efficient use of fencing?

One measure of efficiency is the ratio of *area fenced* to *fencing used*, or area to perimeter. Which of the two shapes has the greater ratio?

Square		**Circle**
Area $= s^2$	Define area and perimeter.	Area $= \pi r^2$
Perimeter $= 4s$		Perimeter $= 2\pi r$
$s = \dfrac{P}{4}$	Express s and r in terms of a common variable, P.	$r = \dfrac{P}{2\pi}$
$\dfrac{\text{Area}}{\text{Perimeter}} = \dfrac{s^2}{P}$	Write the ratios.	$\dfrac{\text{Area}}{\text{Perimeter}} = \dfrac{\pi r^2}{P}$
$= \dfrac{\left(\frac{P}{4}\right)^2}{P}$	Substitute for s and r.	$= \dfrac{\pi\left(\frac{P}{2\pi}\right)^2}{P}$
$= \dfrac{P}{16}$	Simplify.	$= \dfrac{P}{4\pi}$

Think

How can you compare $\frac{P}{16}$ and $\frac{P}{4\pi}$ without evaluating P?
Since the numerators are the same, the fraction with the smaller denominator is the larger fraction.

Since $\dfrac{P}{4\pi} > \dfrac{P}{16}$, a circle provides a more efficient use of fencing.

Check Assume $P = 40$ ft. The area of the circle is $\pi\left(\frac{40}{2\pi}\right)^2 \approx 127$ ft^2.

The area of the square is $\left(\frac{40}{4}\right)^2 = 100$ ft^2. The area of the circle is greater.

 Got It? **4.** Which shape of play space provides for a more efficient use of fencing, a square or an equilateral triangle? (*Hint:* The area of an equilateral triangle in terms of one side is $\frac{1}{2}(s)\left(\frac{\sqrt{3}}{2}s\right)$. The perimeter of an equilateral triangle is $3s$.)

 Lesson Check

Do you know HOW?

Simplify each rational expression. State any restrictions on the variables.

1. $\dfrac{4z - 12}{8z + 24}$ **2.** $\dfrac{3x - 3}{x^2 - x}$

Multiply or divide. State any restrictions on the variables.

3. $\dfrac{x^2 + 3x - 10}{x^2 + 4x - 12} \cdot \dfrac{3x + 18}{x + 3}$

4. $\dfrac{x^2 - 7x + 10}{x^2 - 8x + 15} \div \dfrac{4 - x^2}{x^2 + 3x - 18}$

Do you UNDERSTAND? MATHEMATICAL PRACTICES

5. Vocabulary Is the equation $y = \dfrac{x + 1}{x^2 + 1}$ in simplest form? Explain how you can tell.

6. Error Analysis A student claims that $x = 2$ is the only solution of the equation $\dfrac{x}{x - 2} = \dfrac{2}{x - 2}$. Is the student correct? Explain.

7. Reasoning The width of the rectangle is $\dfrac{a + 10}{3a + 24}$. Write an expression for the length of the rectangle in simplest form.

$\dfrac{2a + 20}{3a + 15}$ w

ℓ

Practice and Problem-Solving Exercises

MATHEMATICAL PRACTICES

Simplify each rational expression. State any restrictions on the variables.

See Problem 1.

8. $-\dfrac{5x^3y}{15xy^3}$

9. $\dfrac{2x}{4x^2 - 2x}$

10. $\dfrac{6c^2 + 9c}{3c}$

11. $\dfrac{49 - z^2}{z + 7}$

12. $\dfrac{x^2 + 8x + 16}{x^2 - 2x - 24}$

13. $\dfrac{12 - x - x^2}{x^2 - 8x + 15}$

Multiply. State any restrictions on the variables.

See Problem 2.

14. $\dfrac{4x^2}{5y} \cdot \dfrac{7y}{12x^4}$

15. $\dfrac{2x^4}{10y^{-2}} \cdot \dfrac{5y^3}{4x^3}$

16. $\dfrac{8y - 4}{10y - 5} \cdot \dfrac{5y - 15}{3y - 9}$

17. $\dfrac{2x + 12}{3x - 9} \cdot \dfrac{6 - 2x}{3x + 8}$

18. $\dfrac{x^2 - 4}{x^2 - 1} \cdot \dfrac{x + 1}{x^2 + 2x}$

19. $\dfrac{x^2 - 5x + 6}{x^2 - 4} \cdot \dfrac{x^2 + 3x + 2}{x^2 - 2x - 3}$

Divide. State any restrictions on the variables.

See Problem 3.

20. $\dfrac{7x}{4y^3} \div \dfrac{21x^3}{8y}$

21. $\dfrac{3x^3}{5y^2} \div \dfrac{6y^{-3}}{5x^{-5}}$

22. $\dfrac{6x + 6y}{y - x} \div \dfrac{18}{5x - 5y}$

23. $\dfrac{3y - 12}{2y + 4} \div \dfrac{6y - 24}{8 + 4y}$

24. $\dfrac{x^2}{x^2 + 2x + 1} \div \dfrac{3x}{x^2 - 1}$

25. $\dfrac{y^2 - 5y + 6}{y^3} \div \dfrac{y^2 + 3y - 10}{4y^2}$

STEM **26. Industrial Design** A storage tank will have a circular base of radius r and a height of r. The tank can be either cylindrical or hemispherical (half a sphere).

See Problem 4.

   a. Write and simplify an expression for the ratio of the volume of the hemispherical tank to its surface area (including the base). For a sphere, $V = \frac{4}{3}\pi r^3$ and $SA = 4\pi r^2$.

   b. Write and simplify an expression for the ratio of the volume of the cylindrical tank to its surface area (including the bases).

   c. Compare the ratios of volume to surface area for the two tanks.

   d. Compare the volumes of the two tanks.

   e. Describe how you used these ratios to compare the volumes of the two tanks. Which measurement of the tanks determines the volumes?

Apply

Simplify each rational expression. State any restrictions on the variables.

27. $\dfrac{x^2 - 5x - 24}{x^2 - 7x - 30}$

28. $\dfrac{2y^2 + 8y - 24}{2y^2 - 8y + 8}$

29. $\dfrac{xy^3 - 9xy}{12xy^2 + 12xy - 144x}$

30. Open-Ended Write three rational expressions that simplify to $\dfrac{x}{x + 1}$.

31. Think About a Plan A cereal company wants to use the most efficient packaging for their new product. They are considering a cylindrical-shaped box and a cube-shaped box. Compare the ratios of the volume to the surface area of the containers to determine which packaging will be more efficient.
- How can you measure the cereal box's efficiency?
- What formulas will you need to use to solve this problem?

Multiply or divide. State any restrictions on the variables.

32. $\dfrac{6x^3 - 6x^2}{x^4 + 5x^3} \div \dfrac{3x^2 - 15x + 12}{2x^2 + 2x - 40}$

33. $\dfrac{2x^2 - 6x}{x^2 + 18x + 81} \cdot \dfrac{9x + 81}{x^2 - 9}$

34. $\dfrac{x^2 - x - 2}{2x^2 - 5x + 2} \div \dfrac{x^2 - x - 12}{2x^2 + 5x - 3}$

35. $\dfrac{2x^2 + 5x + 2}{4x^2 - 1} \cdot \dfrac{2x^2 + x - 1}{x^2 + x - 2}$

36. a. Reasoning Write a simplified expression for the area of the rectangle at the right.
  b. Which parts of the expression do you analyze to determine the restrictions on a? Explain.
  c. State all restrictions on a.

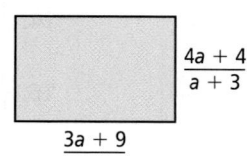

$\dfrac{4a + 4}{a + 3}$

$\dfrac{3a + 9}{2a - 6}$

STEM 37. Manufacturing A toy company is considering a cube or sphere-shaped container for packaging a new product. The height of the cube would equal the diameter of the sphere. Compare the volume-to-surface area ratios of the containers. Which packaging will be more efficient? For a sphere, $SA = 4\pi r^2$.

Decide whether the given statement is *always*, *sometimes*, or *never* true.

38. Rational expressions contain exponents.

39. Rational expressions contain logarithms.

40. Rational expressions are undefined for values of the variables that make the denominator 0.

41. Restrictions on variables change when a rational expression is simplified.

Simplify. State any restrictions on the variables.

42. $\dfrac{(x^2 - x)^2}{x(x - 1)^{-2}(x^2 + 3x - 4)}$

43. $\dfrac{2x + 6}{(x - 1)^{-1}(x^2 + 2x - 3)}$

44. $\dfrac{54x^3 y^{-1}}{3x^{-2} y}$

 **Challenge**

45. a. Reasoning Simplify $\dfrac{(2x^n)^2 - 1}{2x^n - 1}$, where x is an integer and n is a positive integer. (*Hint:* Factor the numerator.)
  b. Use the result from part (a). Which part(s) of the expression can you use to show that the value of the expression is always odd? Explain.

Use the fact that $\dfrac{\frac{a}{b}}{\frac{c}{d}} = \dfrac{a}{b} \div \dfrac{c}{d}$ **to simplify each rational expression. State any restrictions on the variables.**

46. $\dfrac{\frac{8x^2 y}{x + 1}}{\frac{6xy^2}{x + 1}}$

47. $\dfrac{\frac{3a^3 b^3}{a - b}}{\frac{4ab}{b - a}}$

48. $\dfrac{\frac{9m + 6n}{m^2 n^2}}{\frac{12m + 8n}{5m^2}}$

49. $\dfrac{\frac{x^2 - 1}{x^2 - 9}}{\frac{x^2 + 3x - 4}{x^2 + 8x + 15}}$

Standardized Test Prep

SAT/ACT

50. Which function is graphed at the right?

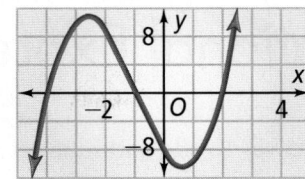

- Ⓐ $y = (x + 4)(x - 1)(x + 2)$
- Ⓑ $y = (x - 4)(x - 1)(x + 2)$
- Ⓒ $y = (x - 4)(x + 1)(x - 2)$
- Ⓓ $y = (x + 4)(x + 1)(x - 2)$

51. Which function generates the table of values at the right?

- Ⓕ $y = \log_{\frac{1}{2}} x$
- Ⓖ $y = -\log_2 x$
- Ⓗ $y = \log_2 x$
- Ⓘ $y = \left(\frac{1}{2}\right)^x$

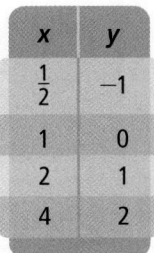

x	y
$\frac{1}{2}$	−1
1	0
2	1
4	2

52. Which expression equals $\dfrac{x}{x^2 - 2x - 3} \cdot \dfrac{2x - 6}{x^2 - 4x + 3}$?

- Ⓐ $\dfrac{2x - 1}{(x - 1)(x + 3)(x + 1)}$
- Ⓑ $\dfrac{2x + 1}{(x - 1)(x + 1)(x - 3)}$
- Ⓒ $\dfrac{2x}{(x - 1)(x + 1)(x - 3)}$
- Ⓓ $\dfrac{2x}{(x + 3)(x - 1)(x + 1)}$

Short Response

53. What is the solution of the equation $3^{-x} = \frac{1}{243}$?

Mixed Review

Find the vertical asymptotes and holes for the graph of each rational function.   ◀ **See Lesson 8-3.**

54. $y = \dfrac{x - 3}{x - 3}$

55. $y = \dfrac{x - 1}{(3x + 2)(x + 1)}$

56. $y = \dfrac{(x - 4)(x + 5)}{(x + 3)(x - 4)}$

Evaluate each logarithm.   ◀ **See Lesson 7-3.**

57. $\log_4 64$

58. $\log_2 \frac{1}{32}$

59. $\log_5 5\sqrt{5}$

60. $\log_{16} 8$

Solve. Check for extraneous solutions.   ◀ **See Lesson 6-5.**

61. $\sqrt{x} - 3 = 4$

62. $\sqrt{x + 1} - 5 = 8$

63. $\sqrt{5x - 3} = \sqrt{2x + 3}$

Get Ready!   To prepare for Lesson 8-5, do Exercises 64–67.

Add or Subtract.   ◀ **See p. 973.**

64. $\frac{5}{19} + \frac{7}{38}$

65. $\frac{2}{15} + \frac{3}{25}$

66. $\frac{7}{24} - \frac{5}{36}$

67. $\frac{11}{12} - \frac{7}{45}$

8-5 Adding and Subtracting Rational Expressions

© **Common Core State Standards**

A-APR.D.7 ... Add, subtract, multiply, and divide rational expressions.

MP 1, MP 3, MP 4

Objective To add and subtract rational expressions

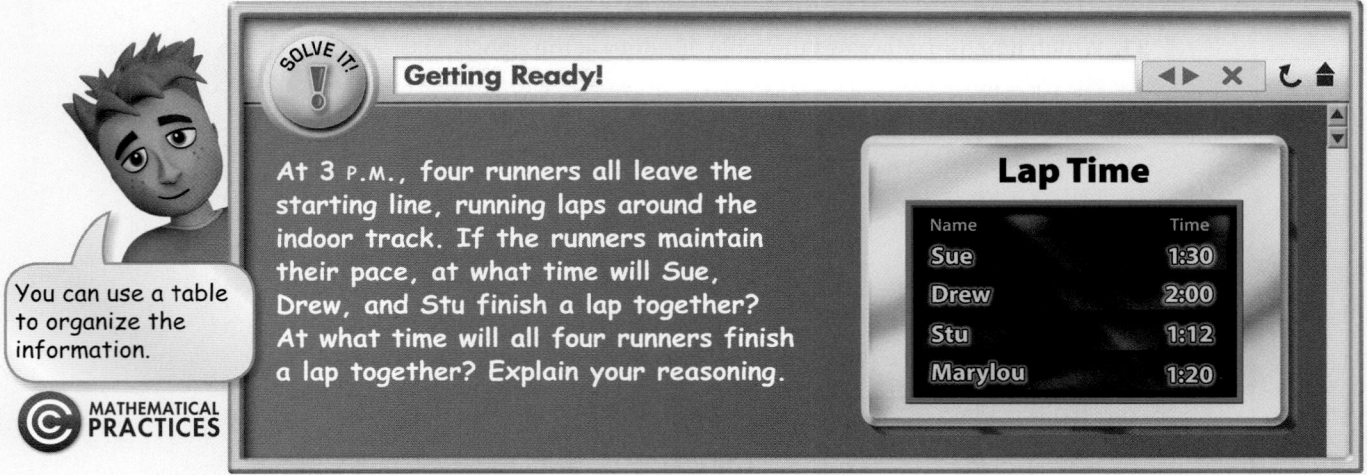

You can use a table to organize the information.

© MATHEMATICAL PRACTICES

Getting Ready!

At 3 P.M., four runners all leave the starting line, running laps around the indoor track. If the runners maintain their pace, at what time will Sue, Drew, and Stu finish a lap together? At what time will all four runners finish a lap together? Explain your reasoning.

Lap Time

Name	Time
Sue	1:30
Drew	2:00
Stu	1:12
Marylou	1:20

Lesson Vocabulary
• complex fraction

You use common multiples of polynomials to add and subtract rational expressions, just as you use common multiples of numbers to add and subtract fractions.

Essential Understanding To operate with rational expressions, you can use much of what you know about operating with fractions.

To add or subtract rational expressions, you first find a common denominator—preferably the least common multiple (LCM) of the denominators.

To find the LCM of several expressions, factor the expressions (numbers or polynomials) completely. The LCM is the product of the prime factors, each raised to the greatest power that occurs in any of the expressions.

How do you determine the exponent of each factor for the LCM?
Use the exponent from the expression that has that factor to the greatest power.

© **Problem 1** Finding the Least Common Multiple

What is the LCM of $12x^2y(x^2 + 2x + 1)$ and $18xy^3(x^2 + 5x + 4)$?

Step 1 Find the prime factors of each expression.

$$12x^2y(x^2 + 2x + 1) = 2^2 \cdot 3x^2y(x + 1)^2$$
$$18xy^3(x^2 + 5x + 4) = 2 \cdot 3^2xy^3(x + 1)(x + 4)$$

Step 2 Write the product of the prime factors, each raised to the greatest power that occurs in either expression.

$$2^2 \cdot 3^2x^2y^3(x + 1)^2(x + 4)$$

The LCM is $2^2 \cdot 3^2x^2y^3(x + 1)^2(x + 4)$, or $36x^2y^3(x + 1)^2(x + 4)$.

Got It? **1.** What is the LCM of the expressions?

    a. $2x + 4$ and $x^2 - x - 6$

    b. $x^2 + 3x - 4$, $x^2 + 2x - 8$, and $x^2 - 4x + 4$

The LCM of the denominators of two rational expressions is also the Least Common Denominator (LCD) of the rational expressions. You can use the LCD to add or subtract the expressions.

Recall how you used the LCD to add fractions.

$$\frac{1}{8} + \frac{1}{10} = \frac{1}{2^3} + \frac{1}{2 \cdot 5} = \frac{1}{2^3}\left(\frac{5}{5}\right) + \frac{1}{2 \cdot 5}\left(\frac{2^2}{2^2}\right) = \frac{5}{40} + \frac{4}{40} = \frac{9}{40}$$

 Problem 2 Adding Rational Expressions

What is the sum of the two rational expressions in simplest form? State any restrictions on the variable. $\dfrac{x}{x - 1} + \dfrac{2x - 1}{x^2 - 3x + 2}$

Plan

How does the LCD help you simplify this sum?
The LCD is $(x - 1)(x - 2)$. Multiply the first expression by $\frac{x-2}{x-2}$ to get a common denominator.

$$\frac{x}{x - 1} + \frac{2x - 1}{x^2 - 3x + 2} = \frac{x}{x - 1} + \frac{2x - 1}{(x - 1)(x - 2)}$$
                          Factor the denominators.

$$= \frac{x}{x - 1} \cdot \frac{x - 2}{x - 2} + \frac{2x - 1}{(x - 1)(x - 2)}$$
                          Rewrite each expression with the LCD.

$$= \frac{x^2 - 2x}{(x - 1)(x - 2)} + \frac{2x - 1}{(x - 1)(x - 2)}$$

$$= \frac{x^2 - 2x + 2x - 1}{(x - 1)(x - 2)}$$
                          Add the numerators. Combine like terms.

$$= \frac{x^2 - 1}{(x - 1)(x - 2)}$$

$$= \frac{(x - 1)(x + 1)}{(x - 1)(x - 2)}$$
                          Factor the numerator and divide out the common factors.

$$= \frac{x + 1}{x - 2}, x \neq 1$$

The sum of the expressions is $\frac{x + 1}{x - 2}$ for $x \neq 1$ and $x \neq 2$.

  Got It? **2.** What is the sum of the two rational expressions in simplest form? State any restrictions on the variable.

    a. $\dfrac{x + 1}{x - 1} + \dfrac{-2}{x^2 - x}$

    b. $\dfrac{x}{x^2 - 4} + \dfrac{1}{x + 2}$

    c. Reasoning Is it possible to add the rational expressions in Problem 2 by finding a common denominator, but not the *least* common denominator? Explain.

What is the difference of the two rational expressions in simplest form? State any restrictions on the variable. $\dfrac{x+2}{x^2-2x} - \dfrac{x+2}{2x-4}$

$$\frac{x+2}{x^2-2x} - \frac{x+2}{2x-4} = \frac{x+2}{x(x-2)} - \frac{x+2}{2(x-2)}$$ Factor the denominators.

The LCD is $2x(x-2)$.

$$= \frac{x+2}{x(x-2)} \cdot \frac{2}{2} - \frac{x+2}{2(x-2)} \cdot \frac{x}{x}$$ Rewrite each expression with the LCD.

$$= \frac{2(x+2)}{2x(x-2)} - \frac{x(x+2)}{2x(x-2)}$$

$$= \frac{2x+4}{2x(x-2)} - \frac{x^2+2x}{2x(x-2)}$$ Simplify the numerators.

$$= \frac{2x+4-(x^2+2x)}{2x(x-2)}$$ Subtract the numerators.

$$= \frac{-x^2+4}{2x(x-2)}$$ Combine like terms.

$$= \frac{-(x^2-4)}{2x(x-2)}$$ Factor -1 from the numerator.

$$= \frac{-(x-2)(x+2)}{2x(x-2)}$$ Factor x^2-4 and divide out the common factors.

$$= \frac{-(x+2)}{2x}$$

The difference is $\dfrac{-(x+2)}{2x}$ for $x \neq 2$ and $x \neq 0$.

 Got It? 3. What is the difference of the two rational expressions in simplest form? State any restrictions on the variable.

a. $\dfrac{x+3}{x-2} - \dfrac{6x-7}{x^2-3x+2}$ **b.** $\dfrac{x-1}{x+5} - \dfrac{x+3}{x^2+6x+5}$

A **complex fraction** is a rational expression that has at least one fraction in its numerator or denominator or both. Here are some examples.

$$\frac{\frac{1}{x}+\frac{1}{y}}{\frac{1}{xy}} \qquad \frac{\frac{x+3}{2}}{\frac{2}{x-4}} \qquad \frac{\frac{x+3}{x^2-2x+1}+\frac{x}{x^2-3x+2}}{\frac{x}{x^2-4x+4}-\frac{2}{x^2-4}}$$

Sometimes you can simplify a complex fraction by multiplying the numerator and the denominator by the LCD of all the rational expressions. You can also simplify them by combining the fractions in the numerator and those in the denominator. Then multiply the new numerator by the reciprocal of the new denominator.

 Problem 4 Simplifying a Complex Fraction

What is a simpler form of the complex fraction?

$$\frac{\frac{1}{x} + \frac{x}{y}}{\frac{1}{y} + 1}$$

Think

What is the LCD of $\frac{1}{x}$, $\frac{x}{y}$, and $\frac{1}{y}$?

The LCD of the rational expressions is xy.

Method 1 Multiply both the numerator and the denominator by the LCD of all the rational expressions and simplify the result.

$$\frac{\frac{1}{x} + \frac{x}{y}}{\frac{1}{y} + 1} = \frac{\left(\frac{1}{x} + \frac{x}{y}\right) \cdot xy}{\left(\frac{1}{y} + 1\right) \cdot xy}$$ Multiply the numerator and the denominator by xy.

$$= \frac{\frac{1}{x} \cdot xy + \frac{x}{y} \cdot xy}{\frac{1}{y} \cdot xy + 1 \cdot xy}$$ Use the Distributive Property.

$$= \frac{y + x^2}{x + xy}$$ Simplify.

Method 2 Combine the expressions in the numerator and those in the denominator. Then multiply the new numerator by the reciprocal of the new denominator.

$$\frac{\frac{1}{x} + \frac{x}{y}}{\frac{1}{y} + 1} = \frac{\frac{1}{x} \cdot \frac{y}{y} + \frac{x}{y} \cdot \frac{x}{x}}{\frac{1}{y} + 1 \cdot \frac{y}{y}}$$ Write equivalent expressions with common denominators.

$$= \frac{\frac{y}{xy} + \frac{x^2}{xy}}{\frac{1}{y} + \frac{y}{y}}$$ Multiply.

$$= \frac{\frac{y + x^2}{xy}}{\frac{1 + y}{y}}$$ Add.

$$= \frac{y + x^2}{xy} \div \frac{1 + y}{y}$$ Divide the numerator fraction by the denominator fraction.

$$= \frac{y + x^2}{xy} \cdot \frac{y}{1 + y}$$ Multiply by the reciprocal.

$$= \frac{y + x^2}{x + xy}$$ Divide out the common factor, y.

Think

How do you divide a fraction by a fraction?

Multiply the numerator by the reciprocal of the denominator.

Got It? **4.** What is a simpler form of the complex fraction?

a. $\dfrac{x}{\frac{1}{x} + \frac{1}{y}}$

b. $\dfrac{\frac{x-2}{x} + \frac{2}{x+1}}{\frac{3}{x-1} - \frac{1}{x+1}}$

Fuel Economy A woman drives an SUV that gets 10 mi/gal (mpg). Her husband drives a hybrid that gets 60 mpg. Every week, they travel the same number of miles. They want to improve their combined mpg. They have two options on how they can improve it.

Option 1: They can tune the SUV and increase its mileage by 1 mpg and keep the hybrid as it is.

Option 2: They can buy a new hybrid that gets 80 mpg and keep the SUV as it is.

Which option will give them a better combined mpg?

Think

The combined gas mileage is total miles divided by total gallons.

Define a variable and describe each option.

The gallons used by each vehicle are $\frac{miles}{mpg}$. Write the variable expressions for each option's combined mpg.

Find the LCD of the fractions in each expression. Multiply the numerator and denominator by the LCD.

Distribute and simplify.

Round the ratios and compare them.

Write

$$\text{combined mpg} = \frac{\text{SUV miles} + \text{Hybrid miles}}{\text{SUV gallons} + \text{Hybrid gallons}}$$

Let x = number of miles each drives in a week.

Option 1

Tuned SUV gets 11 mpg.
Hybrid gets 60 mpg.

$$\frac{x + x}{\frac{x}{11} + \frac{x}{60}}$$

$$\left(\frac{2x}{\frac{x}{11} + \frac{x}{60}}\right) \cdot \left(\frac{660}{660}\right)$$

$$\frac{(2x)(660)}{\left(\frac{x}{11}\right)(660) + \left(\frac{x}{60}\right)(660)}$$

$$= \frac{1320x}{60x + 11x}$$

$$= \frac{1320x}{71x}$$

$$\approx 18.6 \text{ mpg}$$

Option 2

SUV gets 10 mpg.
New hybrid gets 80 mpg.

$$\frac{x + x}{\frac{x}{10} + \frac{x}{80}}$$

$$\left(\frac{2x}{\frac{x}{10} + \frac{x}{80}}\right) \cdot \left(\frac{80}{80}\right)$$

$$\frac{(2x)(80)}{\left(\frac{x}{10}\right)(80) + \left(\frac{x}{80}\right)(80)}$$

$$= \frac{160x}{8x + x}$$

$$= \frac{160x}{9x}$$

$$\approx 17.8 \text{ mpg}$$

Option 1 gives the better combined mpg.

✓ **Got It?** **5.** Suppose Option 3 is to buy a new hybrid that will get double the mileage of the present hybrid. The SUV mileage stays the same. Which of the three options will give the best combined mpg?

Lesson Check

Do you know HOW?

Simplify each sum or difference. State any restrictions on the variables.

1. $\dfrac{a+11}{3a-5} + \dfrac{a-21}{3a-5}$

2. $\dfrac{1}{x^2-4} + \dfrac{6}{x+2}$

3. $\dfrac{m}{3m+6} - \dfrac{4m}{m+2}$

4. $\dfrac{b-4}{b^2+2b-8} - \dfrac{b+2}{b^2-16}$

Do you UNDERSTAND?

5. Error Analysis Describe and correct the error made in simplifying the complex fraction.

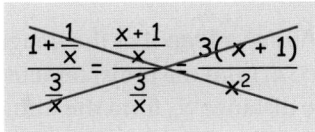

6. Open-Ended Write two rational expressions that simplify to $\dfrac{x+1}{x-5}$.

Practice and Problem-Solving Exercises

Find the least common multiple of each pair of polynomials.

See Problem 1.

7. $9(x+2)(2x-1)$ and $3(x+2)$

8. x^2-1 and x^2+2x+1

9. $5y^2-80$ and $y+4$

10. $x^2-32x-10$ and $2x+10$

Simplify each sum or difference. State any restrictions on the variables.

See Problems 2 and 3.

11. $\dfrac{1}{2x} + \dfrac{1}{2x}$

12. $\dfrac{d-3}{2d+1} + \dfrac{d-1}{2d+1}$

13. $\dfrac{-2}{x} - \dfrac{1}{x}$

14. $\dfrac{-5y}{2y-1} - \dfrac{y+3}{2y-1}$

15. $\dfrac{5y+2}{xy^2} + \dfrac{2x-4}{4xy}$

16. $\dfrac{5x}{x^2-9} + \dfrac{2}{x+4}$

17. $\dfrac{y}{2y+4} - \dfrac{3}{y+2}$

18. $\dfrac{x}{3x+9} - \dfrac{8}{x^2+3x}$

19. $\dfrac{-3x}{x^2-9} + \dfrac{4}{2x-6}$

20. $\dfrac{5x}{x^2-x-6} + \dfrac{4}{x^2+4x+4}$

21. $\dfrac{2x}{x^2-x-2} - \dfrac{4x}{x^2-3x+2}$

Simplify each complex fraction.

See Problem 4.

22. $\dfrac{\frac{1}{x}}{\frac{2}{y}}$

23. $\dfrac{1-\frac{1}{4}}{2-\frac{3}{5}}$

24. $\dfrac{\frac{2}{x+y}}{3}$

25. $\dfrac{\frac{1}{3}}{\frac{3}{b}}$

26. $\dfrac{1}{1+\frac{x}{y}}$

27. $\dfrac{3}{\frac{2}{x}+y}$

28. $\dfrac{\frac{2}{x+y}}{\frac{5}{x+y}}$

29. $\dfrac{\frac{3}{x-4}}{1-\frac{2}{x-4}}$

30. Your car gets 25 mi/gal around town and 30 mi/gal on the highway.

See Problem 5.

  a. If 50% of the miles you drive are on the highway and 50% are around town, what is your overall average miles per gallon?

  b. If 60% of the miles you drive are on the highway and 40% are around town, what is your overall average miles per gallon?

Add or subtract. Simplify where possible. State any restrictions on the variables.

31. $\dfrac{3}{4x} - \dfrac{2}{x^2}$

32. $\dfrac{3}{x+1} + \dfrac{x}{x-1}$

33. $\dfrac{4}{x^2-9} + \dfrac{7}{x+3}$

34. $\dfrac{5x}{x^2-x-6} - \dfrac{4}{x^2+4x+4}$

35. $3x + \dfrac{x^2+5x}{x^2-2}$

36. $\dfrac{5y}{y^2-7y} - \dfrac{4}{2y-14} + \dfrac{9}{y}$

37. Think About a Plan For the image of the overhead projector to be in focus, the distance d_i from the projector lens to the image, the projector lens's focal length f, and the distance d_o from the transparency to the projector lens must satisfy the thin-lens equation $\dfrac{1}{f} = \dfrac{1}{d_i} + \dfrac{1}{d_o}$. What is the focal length of the projector lens if the transparency placed 4 in. from the projector lens is in focus on the screen located 8 ft from the projector lens?
- Can you write the equation for the unknown variable?
- What units would you use for the focal length of the lens?

STEM 38. Optics To read a small font, you use a magnifying lens with the focal length 3 in. How far from the magnifying lens should you place the page if you want to hold the lens at 1 foot from your eyes? Use the thin-lens equation from Exercise 37.

39. Reasoning Does the Closure Property of rational numbers extend to rational expressions? Explain and describe any restrictions on rational expressions.

40. Writing Explain how factoring is used when adding or subtracting rational expressions. Include an example in your explanation.

Simplify each complex fraction.

41. $\dfrac{\frac{2}{x} + \frac{3}{y}}{\frac{-5}{x} + \frac{7}{y}}$

42. $\dfrac{1 + \frac{2}{x}}{2 + \frac{3}{2x}}$

43. $\dfrac{\frac{1}{xy} - \frac{1}{y^2}}{\frac{1}{x^2y} - \frac{1}{xy^2}}$

44. $\dfrac{\frac{2}{x+4} + 2}{1 + \frac{3}{x+4}}$

STEM 45. Harmony The harmonic mean of two numbers a and b equals $\dfrac{2}{\frac{1}{a} + \frac{1}{b}}$. As you vary the length of a violin or guitar string, its pitch changes. If a full-length string is 1 unit long, then many lengths that are simple fractions produce pitches that harmonize, or sound pleasing together. The harmonic mean relates two lengths that produce harmonious sounds. Find the harmonic mean for each pair of string lengths.

a. 1 and $\frac{1}{2}$

b. $\frac{3}{4}$ and $\frac{1}{2}$

c. $\frac{3}{4}$ and $\frac{3}{5}$

d. $\frac{1}{2}$ and $\frac{1}{4}$

 **Challenge**

46. Show that the sum of the reciprocals of three different positive integers is greater than 6 times the reciprocal of their product.

STEM 47. Electricity The resistance of a parallel circuit with 3 bulbs is $\dfrac{1}{\frac{1}{R_1} + \frac{1}{R_2} + \frac{1}{R_3}}$.

a. Find the resistance of a parallel circuit with 3 bulbs that have resistances 5 ohms, 4 ohms, 2.5 ohms.

b. The resistance of a parallel circuit with 3 bulbs is 1.5 ohms. Find the resistances of the bulbs, if two of them have equal resistances, while the resistance of the 3rd is 3 ohms less.

Standardized Test Prep

SAT/ACT

48. Which expression equals $\dfrac{5x}{x^2 - 9} - \dfrac{4x}{x^2 + 5x + 6}$?

Ⓐ $\dfrac{7x}{(x - 3)(x + 3)(x + 2)}$

Ⓒ $\dfrac{x^2 + 22x}{(x - 3)(x + 3)(x + 2)}$

Ⓑ $\dfrac{x^2 - 2x}{(x - 3)(x + 3)(x + 2)}$

Ⓓ $\dfrac{9x^2 - 2x}{(x - 3)(x + 3)(x + 2)}$

49. Which of the relationships is represented by the graph at the right?

Ⓕ $y = \log_4(x - 1) + 5$

Ⓖ $y = \log_4(x - 1) - 2$

Ⓗ $y = \log_4(x + 2) - 2$

Ⓘ $y = \log_4(x - 1) - 1$

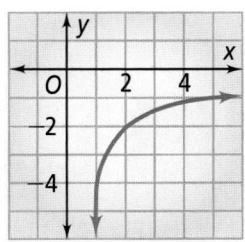

50. What is a simpler form of $\dfrac{\frac{2}{x} - 5}{\frac{6}{x} - 3}$?

Ⓐ $\dfrac{2 - 5x}{6 - 3x}$

Ⓑ $\dfrac{2 + 5x}{6 - 3x}$

Ⓒ $\dfrac{2x - 5}{6x + 3}$

Ⓓ $\dfrac{6 + 3x}{2 - 5x}$

51. What word makes the statement "The domain and range of a(n) _____ function is the set of all real numbers" *sometimes* true?

Ⓕ polynomial

Ⓗ exponential

Ⓖ logarithmic

Ⓘ quadratic

Short Response

52. What is the least common denominator for the rational expressions $\dfrac{1}{x^2 - 5x - 6}$ and $\dfrac{1}{x^2 - 12x + 36}$? Show your work.

Apply What You've Learned

MATHEMATICAL
PRACTICES

MP 2

Look back at the information on page 497 about Steve and Sally's canoe trip. In the Apply What You've Learned in Lesson 8-2, you thought about how the current of the river affects the speed Steve and Sally travel while paddling upstream.

Let x represent the speed, in miles per hour, that Steve and Sally paddle in still water. Select all of the following expressions that represent the total amount of time Steve and Sally spent paddling. Explain your reasoning.

A. $\dfrac{12}{x - 3}$

B. $\dfrac{12}{x - 3} + \dfrac{12}{x}$

C. $\dfrac{12}{x - 3} + \dfrac{12}{x + 3}$

D. $\dfrac{12}{(x - 3)(x + 3)}$

E. $\dfrac{24x}{x^2 - 9}$

F. $\dfrac{24x}{x^2 - 6x - 9}$

Solving Rational Equations

© **Common Core State Standards**

A-APR.D.7 . . . Add, subtract, multiply, and divide rational expressions. **Also A-APR.D.6, A-CED.A.1, A-REI.D.11**

MP 1, MP 2, MP 3, MP 4, MP 5

Objectives To solve rational equations
To use rational equations to solve problems

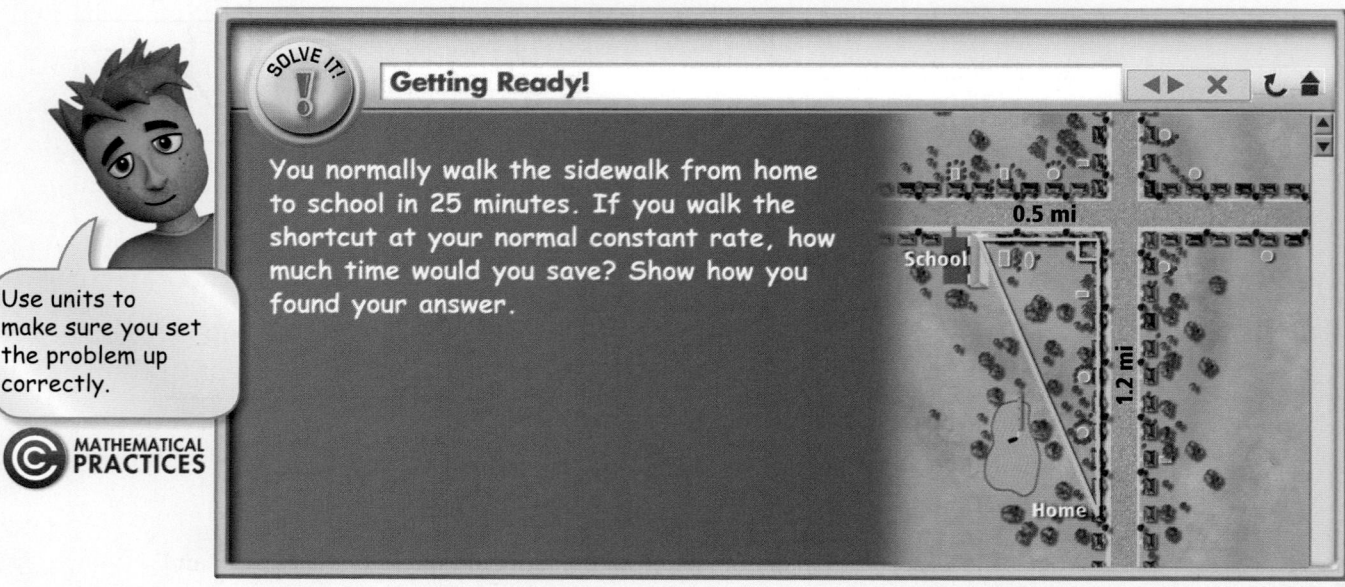

SOLVE IT!

Getting Ready!

You normally walk the sidewalk from home to school in 25 minutes. If you walk the shortcut at your normal constant rate, how much time would you save? Show how you found your answer.

0.5 mi

School

1.2 mi

Home

Use units to make sure you set the problem up correctly.

© **MATHEMATICAL PRACTICES**

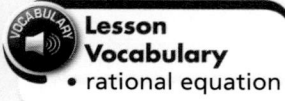

Lesson Vocabulary
• rational equation

Sometimes you can solve a problem using a proportion—an equation involving two rational expressions set equal to each other.

Essential Understanding To solve an equation containing rational expressions, first multiply each side by the least common denominator of the rational expressions. Doing this, however, can introduce extraneous solutions.

A **rational equation** contains at least one rational expression. You can simplify solving a rational equation if you first clear the equation of denominators. You can do this by multiplying by the LCD of the rational expressions in the equation.

Rational Equation	**Not a Rational Equation**
$\dfrac{x}{x+1} + \dfrac{x}{x-1} = \dfrac{2}{x^2-1}$	$x + \dfrac{1}{2} = \dfrac{2}{3}$

Any time you multiply each side of an equation by an algebraic expression, it is possible to introduce an extraneous solution. Recall that an extraneous solution is a solution of the derived equation, but not a solution of the original equation. You must check all solutions in the original equation to confirm that they are indeed solutions.

Problem 1 Solving a Rational Equation

What are the solutions of the rational equation?

A $\dfrac{x}{x-3} + \dfrac{x}{x+3} = \dfrac{2}{x^2-9}$

Think | **Write**

Factor the denominators to find the LCD.

$$\frac{x}{x-3} + \frac{x}{x+3} = \frac{2}{(x-3)(x+3)}$$

Multiply each side by the LCD to clear denominators.

$$(x-3)(x+3)\left[\frac{x}{x-3} + \frac{x}{x+3}\right] = (x-3)(x+3)\frac{2}{(x-3)(x+3)}$$

Now simplify and solve.

$$x^2 + 3x + x^2 - 3x = 2$$
$$2x^2 = 2$$
$$x^2 = 1, \text{ so } x = \pm 1$$

Check whether $x = 1$ or $x = -1$ is extraneous. Use the original equation.

$$\frac{1}{1-3} + \frac{1}{1+3} \stackrel{?}{=} \frac{2}{(1)^2 - 9} \qquad \frac{-1}{-1-3} + \frac{-1}{-1+3} \stackrel{?}{=} \frac{2}{(-1)^2 - 9}$$

$$-\frac{1}{2} + \frac{1}{4} = -\frac{1}{4} \checkmark \qquad\qquad \frac{1}{4} + -\frac{1}{2} = -\frac{1}{4} \checkmark$$

Write the solutions.

The solutions are $x = 1$ and $x = -1$.

Plan

How can you use technology to solve this equation?
You can use a computer algebra system to solve the equation. Calculators have limitations, and you will still need to check for extraneous solutions.

B $\dfrac{x-1}{x^2+3x+2} + \dfrac{2x}{x+2} = \dfrac{x-1}{x+1}$

Use a computer algebra system (CAS) to solve this rational equation.

Step 1 On the Home screen, choose **New Document**. Then select **Add Calculator**.

Step 2 Choose **Menu, Algebra, Solve**.

Step 3 Enter the equation, followed by a comma and x. Then press enter to solve.

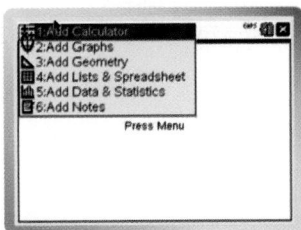 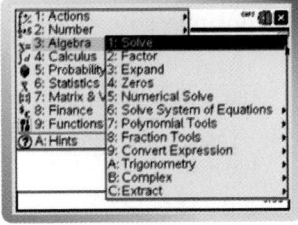 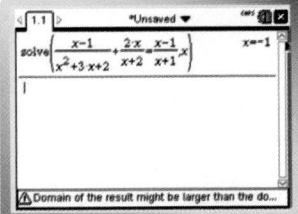

The calculator shows a warning because there may be extraneous solutions. The original equation restricts x so that $x \neq -2$ and $x \neq -1$. There is no solution.

 Got It? **1.** What are the solutions of the rational equation?

a. $\dfrac{x-1}{x+2} = \dfrac{x^2+2x-3}{x+2}$

b. $\dfrac{x}{x+1} + \dfrac{3}{x+4} = \dfrac{x+3}{x+4}$

Problem 2 **Using Rational Equations**

Flight A flight across the U.S. takes longer east to west than it does west to east. Assume that winds are constant in the eastward direction. When flying westward, the headwind decreases the airplane's speed. When flying eastward, the tailwind increases its speed. The time for a round trip shown at the right is $7\frac{3}{4}$h. If the airplane cruises at 480 mi/h, what is the speed of the wind?

1850 mi

Chicago

San Francisco

Let x = the wind speed.

$$\text{Rate} \times \text{Time} = \text{Distance, so Time} = \frac{\text{Distance}}{\text{Rate}}$$

	Distance	Rate	Time
Going west to east	1850	$480 + x$	$\frac{1850}{480 + x}$
Going east to west	1850	$480 - x$	$\frac{1850}{480 - x}$

Total time = Time west to east + Time east to west

$$7.75 = \frac{1850}{480 + x} + \frac{1850}{480 - x}$$

> Multiply both sides by the LCD, $(480 + x)(480 - x)$.

$$(480 + x)(480 - x)\,7.75 = (480 + x)(480 - x)\frac{1850}{480 + x} + (480 + x)(480 - x)\frac{1850}{480 - x}$$

$$7.75(480 + x)(480 - x) = 1850(480 - x) + 1850(480 + x)$$

$$1{,}785{,}600 - 7.75x^2 = 888{,}000 - 1850x + 888{,}000 + 1850x$$

$$-7.75x^2 = -9600$$

$$x^2 = \frac{-9600}{-7.75}$$

$$x \approx \pm 35$$

Wind speed is positive, so $x \approx 35$. The west-to-east wind speed is about 35 mi/h.

Think

If you substitute 35 for x will the equation check exactly?
No; since 35 is an approximation it is likely that the values will be nearly equal, but probably not equal.

Check $7.75 = \frac{1850}{480 + x} + \frac{1850}{480 - x}$

$$7.75 \overset{?}{=} \frac{1850}{480 + 35} + \frac{1850}{480 - 35}$$

$$7.75 \approx 3.6 + 4.2 \ ✔$$

  Got It? **2. a.** You ride your bike to a store, 4 mi away, to pick up things for dinner. When there is no wind, you ride at 10 mi/h. Today your trip to the store and back took 1 hour. What was the speed of the wind today?

b. Reasoning Explain why there is no difference between the travel time to and from the store when there is no wind.

You can also use a graphing calculator to solve a rational equation.

 Problem 3 Using a Graphing Calculator to Solve a Rational Equation

What are the solutions of the rational equation? Use a graphing calculator to solve.

$$\frac{2}{x+2} + \frac{x}{x-2} = 1$$

Plan

How do the graphs of the two sides of the equation help you solve the equation?
The x-values of the points of intersection are the solutions to the equation.

Enter one side of the equation as Y_1. Enter the other side as Y_2.

There appears to be only one intersection point, at $x = 0$.

$Y_1 = Y_2$ when $x = 0$.

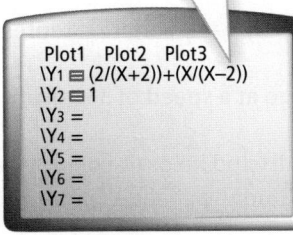
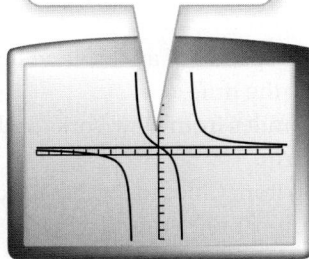
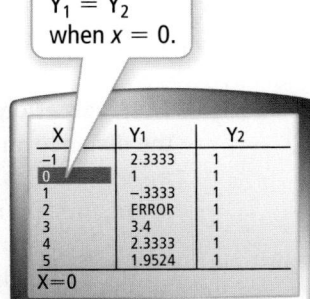

The solution is $x = 0$.

Check $\dfrac{2}{x+2} + \dfrac{x}{x-2} = 1$

$\dfrac{2}{0+2} + \dfrac{0}{0-2} \overset{?}{=} 1$

$1 + 0 = 1$ ✔

 Got It? **3.** What are the solutions of the rational equation $\frac{x+2}{1-2x} = 5$? Use a graphing calculator to solve.

 Lesson Check

Do you know HOW?

Solve each equation. Check each solution.

1. $\dfrac{4}{x-2} = \dfrac{x-1}{x-2}$

2. $\dfrac{2a+1}{6} + \dfrac{a}{2} = \dfrac{a-1}{3}$

3. $\dfrac{2}{n} + \dfrac{n+2}{n+1} = \dfrac{-2}{n^2+n}$

4. Flight If the speed of an airplane is 350 mi/h with a tail wind of 40 mi/h, what is the speed of the plane in still air?

Do you UNDERSTAND? MATHEMATICAL PRACTICES

5. Error Analysis Describe and correct the error made in solving the equation.

$\dfrac{5}{x} + \dfrac{9}{7} = \dfrac{28}{x}$

$\dfrac{14}{x+7} = \dfrac{28}{x}$

$14x = 28(x+7)$

$14x = 28x + 196$

$-196 = 14x$

$-14 = x$

6. Open-Ended Write a rational equation using expressions that have $x^2 - 9$ as their LCD.

7. Reasoning Describe two methods you can use to check whether a solution is extraneous.

Practice and Problem-Solving Exercises  MATHEMATICAL PRACTICES

 **Practice**

Solve each equation. Check each solution. **See Problem 1.**

8. $\frac{1}{4} - x = \frac{x}{8}$

9. $\frac{y}{5} + \frac{y}{2} = 7$

10. $\frac{2x}{3} - \frac{1}{2} = \frac{2x+5}{6}$

11. $\frac{3x-2}{12} - \frac{1}{6} = \frac{1}{6}$

12. $\frac{1}{x} + \frac{x}{2} = \frac{x+4}{2x}$

13. $\frac{11}{3x} - \frac{1}{3} = \frac{-4}{x^2}$

14. $\frac{3}{2x} - \frac{5}{3x} = 2$

15. $\frac{5x}{4} - \frac{3}{x} = \frac{1}{4}$

16. $\frac{2}{y} + \frac{1}{2} = \frac{5}{2y}$

17. $x + \frac{6}{x} = -5$

18. $\frac{1}{4x} - \frac{3}{4} = \frac{7}{x}$

19. $\frac{5}{2x} - \frac{2}{3} = \frac{1}{x} + \frac{5}{6}$

20. Transportation The speed s of an airplane is given by $s = \frac{d}{t}$, where d represents the distance and t is the time. **See Problem 2.**

  a. A plane flies 700 miles from New York to Chicago at a speed of 360 mi/h. Find the time for the trip.

  b. On the return trip from Chicago to New York, a tail wind helps the plane move faster. The total flying time for the round trip is 3.5 h. Find the speed x of the tail wind.

 **Graphing Calculator** **Solve each equation. Check each solution.** **See Problem 3.**

21. $\frac{3}{x} = 5$

22. $\frac{1}{3x} = -2$

23. $\frac{2}{x-1} = 4$

24. $\frac{4}{x+3} = 5$

25. $\frac{5x-2}{x-4} = -3$

26. $\frac{3x-1}{x+2} = 7$

27. $\frac{2}{x} = \frac{x}{2}$

28. $\frac{2}{x+3} = \frac{x-3}{2}$

29. $\frac{2}{x-1} + \frac{3}{x+1} = 4$

Ⓑ Apply

Solve each equation for the given variable.

30. $m = \frac{2E}{V^2}; E$

31. $\frac{c}{E} - \frac{1}{mc} = 0; E$

32. $\frac{m}{F} = \frac{1}{a}; F$

33. $\frac{1}{c} - \frac{c}{a^2 - b^2} = 0; c$

34. $\frac{\ell}{T^2} = \frac{g}{4\pi^2}; T$

35. $\frac{q}{m} = \frac{2V}{B^2 r^2}; B$

Ⓒ 36. Think About a Plan You and a classmate have volunteered to contact every member of your class by phone to inform them of an upcoming event. You can complete the calls in six days if you work alone. Your classmate can complete them in four days. How long will it take to complete the calls working together?

  • If N is the total number of calls, what expression represents the number of calls that you can make per day? What expression represents the number of calls your friend can make per day?

  • What is the expression for the number of days needed to make N calls if you are working together?

37. Storage One pump can fill a tank with oil in 4 hours. A second pump can fill the same tank in 3 hours. If both pumps are used at the same time, how long will they take to fill the tank?

38. Teamwork You can stuff envelopes twice as fast as your friend. Together, you can stuff 6750 envelopes in 4.5 hours. How long would it take each of you working alone to complete the job?

39. Grades On the first four tests of the term your average is 84%. You think you can score 96% on each of the remaining tests. How many consecutive test scores of 96% would you need to bring your average up to 90% for the term?

Ⓒ **40. Error Analysis** Describe and correct the error made in solving the equation.

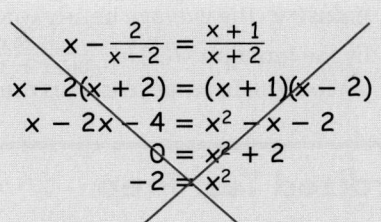

41. Fuel Economy Suppose you drive an average of 15,000 miles per year, and your car gets 24 miles per gallon. Suppose gasoline costs $3.60 a gallon.
  a. How much money do you spend each year on gasoline?
  b. You plan to trade in your car for one that gets x more miles per gallon. Write an expression to represent the new yearly cost of gasoline.
  c. Write an expression to represent your total savings on gasoline per year.
  d. Suppose you can save $600 a year with the new car. How many miles per gallon does the new car get?

STEM **42. Woodworking** A tapered cylinder is made by decreasing the radius of a rod continuously as you move from one end to the other. The rate at which it tapers is the taper per foot. You can calculate the taper per foot using the formula $T = \dfrac{24(R - r)}{L}$. The lengths R, r, and L are measured in inches.

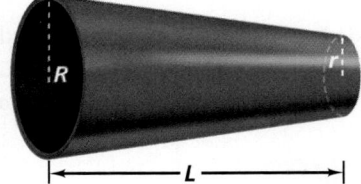

  a. Solve this equation for L.
  b. What is L for $T = 0.75$, 0.85, and 0.95, if $R = 4$ in.; $r = 3$ in.?

Solve each equation. Check each solution.

43. $\dfrac{15}{x} + \dfrac{9x - 7}{x + 2} = 9$

44. $\dfrac{2}{x + 2} - \dfrac{1}{x} = \dfrac{-4}{x(x + 2)}$

45. $\dfrac{1}{b + 1} + \dfrac{1}{b - 1} = \dfrac{2}{b^2 - 1}$

46. $c - \dfrac{c}{3} + \dfrac{c}{5} = 26$

47. $\dfrac{1}{x - 5} = \dfrac{x}{x^2 - 25}$

48. $\dfrac{k}{k + 1} + \dfrac{k}{k - 2} = 2$

49. $\dfrac{5}{x^2 - 7x + 12} - \dfrac{2}{3 - x} = \dfrac{5}{x - 4}$

50. $\dfrac{10}{2y + 8} - \dfrac{7y + 8}{y^2 - 16} = \dfrac{-8}{2y - 8}$

51. $\dfrac{7x + 3}{x^2 - 8x + 15} + \dfrac{3x}{x - 5} = \dfrac{1}{3 - x}$

52. $\dfrac{2}{x + 3} - \dfrac{3}{4 - x} = \dfrac{2x - 2}{x^2 - x - 12}$

Ⓒ **53. Writing** Write and solve a problem that can be modeled by a rational equation.

 **Challenge**

54. Sports An automatic pitching machine can pitch all its baseballs in $1\frac{1}{4}$ hours. One attendant can retrieve all the baseballs pitched by one machine in $3\frac{1}{2}$ hours. At least how many attendants working at the same rate should be hired so that the baseballs from 10 machines are all retrieved in less than 8 hours?

 55. Open-Ended Write a rational equation that has the following.

    a. one solution   **b.** two solutions   **c.** no real solution

STEM **56. Industry** The average hourly wage $H(x)$ of workers in an industry is modeled by the function $H(x) = \frac{16.24x}{0.062x + 39.42}$, where x represents the number of years since 1970. In what year does the model predict that wages will be $25/h?

Standardized Test Prep

 SAT/ACT

57. What is the solution of $x + \frac{1}{x} = -2$?

    Ⓐ $1, -1$ Ⓑ 0 only   Ⓒ $-\frac{1}{2}$ only   Ⓓ -1 only

58. Which of the following is equivalent to $\frac{6\sqrt{24}}{2\sqrt{3}}$?

    Ⓕ $2\sqrt{2}$ Ⓖ $3\sqrt{2}$ Ⓗ $5\sqrt{2}$ Ⓘ $6\sqrt{2}$

59. An investment of $750 will be worth $1500 after 12 years of continuous compounding at a fixed interest rate. What is that interest rate?

    Ⓐ 2.00% Ⓑ 5.78% Ⓒ 6.93% Ⓓ 200%

Extended Response

60. A librarian orders 48 fiction and nonfiction books for the school library. A fiction book costs $15 and a nonfiction book costs $20. The total cost of the order was $900. How many nonfiction books did the librarian order? Show your work.

 ## Apply What You've Learned

MATHEMATICAL
PRACTICES
MP 1, MP 5

Look back at the information on page 497 about Steve and Sally's canoe trip.

    a. How much time did Steve and Sally spend paddling?

    b. In the Apply What You've Learned in Lesson 8-5, you found two expressions that each represent the total amount of time Steve and Sally paddled during their trip, in terms of their paddling speed x. Use one of those expressions and your answer to part (a) to write an equation that you can solve for x.

    c. Describe how to solve the equation you wrote in part (b) with a graphing calculator.

    d. Solve the equation you wrote in part (b). Round your solutions to the nearest hundredth. Check your answer by another method.

    e. Interpret your solutions to the equation in terms of the problem situation.

Concept Byte

For Use With Lesson 8-6

Systems With Rational Equations

Common Core State Standards

Extends A-REI.D.11 Explain why the *x*-coordinates of the points where the graphs of the equations $y = f(x)$ and $y = g(x)$ intersect are the solutions of the equation $f(x) = g(x)$ . . .

MP 1

You can solve systems with rational equations using some of same methods you used with linear systems.

Activity 1

Follow each direction to solve the system $\begin{cases} y = \dfrac{x}{3x - 1} \\ y = \dfrac{1}{x + 1} \end{cases}$.

1. Set the expressions for *y* equal to each other.

2. Solve for *x*.

3. Check your answer by substituting in the original system.

Activity 2

Follow each direction to solve the system $\begin{cases} x - 2 = \dfrac{6}{y} \\ y + 1 = x \end{cases}$.

4. Solve each equation for *y*.

5. Set the resulting expressions equal to each other.

6. Solve for *x*.

7. Check your answer by substituting in the original system.

Exercises

Solve each system.

8. $\begin{cases} \dfrac{y}{x^2 - 4x + 3} = -2 \\ x - 2y = 3 \end{cases}$

9. $\begin{cases} y = \dfrac{1}{x} \\ y = \dfrac{3}{4 - x^2} \end{cases}$

10. $\begin{cases} y = x^2 - 2x - 2 \\ y = \dfrac{x^2 + x - 6}{x + 3} \end{cases}$

11. $\begin{cases} y = \dfrac{x + 2}{x^2 + 3x + 2} + 2 \\ y - 3 = x \end{cases}$

Ⓒ 12. **Reasoning** It is possible for the graph of a system of rational equations to include a point of intersection that is an extraneous solution? Explain.

Rational Inequalities

Common Core State Standards

Extends A-REI.D.11 Explain why the
x-coordinates of the points where the graphs
of the equations $y = f(x)$ and $y = g(x)$
intersect are the solutions of the equation
$f(x) = g(x)$ . . .

MP 5

Consider the rational inequality $\frac{x}{4-x} < 3$.

Activity 1

1. Enter $y_1 = \frac{x}{4-x}$ and $y_2 = 3$ in your graphing calculator. Graph the functions using the settings at the right. Use the calculator's **INTERSECT** feature to find where the two functions are equal. Use the graph to find the solution of the inequality $\frac{x}{4-x} < 3$.

```
WINDOW
 Xmin=-6
 Xmax=12
 Xscl=1
 Ymin=-7
 Ymax=5
 Yscl=1
 Xres=1▪
```

Activity 2

Using the functions you entered in Activity 1, set up the table as shown.

```
TABLE SETUP
 TblStart = -1
 ΔTbl=1
 Indpnt: Auto Ask
 Depend:Auto Ask
```

X	Y₁	Y₂
-1	-.2	3
0	0	3
1	.33333	3
2	1	3
3	3	3
4	ERROR	3
5	-5	3

X=-1

2. Scroll to x-values less than 3. Do they make the inequality true?

3. Scroll to x-values greater than 4. Do they make the inequality true?

4. What happens to the inequality when $x = 3$? When $x = 4$?

5. Change ΔTbl to 0.1. Investigate the inequality between $x = 3$ and $x = 4$.

6. Make a conjecture about the solution of the inequality based on your results in Steps 2–5.

Activity 3

Now use algebra to solve the inequality. You can multiply both sides of a rational inequality by the same algebraic expression just as you have done with equations. But you must keep in mind the properties of inequalities. Consider the first step, multiplying each side by $(4 - x)$.

$$\frac{x}{4-x} < 3$$

$$(4-x)\frac{x}{4-x} < (4-x)3$$

Depending on whether the factor $(4 - x)$ is positive or negative, there are two possible solutions to the inequality.

7. First, consider the case where $4 - x > 0$, or $x < 4$. Justify each step.
Hint: The solution must satisfy both $x < 3$ and $x < 4$.

$$\frac{x}{4 - x} < 3$$

a. $(4 - x)\frac{x}{4 - x} < (4 - x)3$

b. $\qquad x < 12 - 3x$

c. $\qquad 4x < 12$

d. $\qquad x < 3$

8. Combine this result with the given condition $x < 4$. What is the solution for this case?

9. Now consider the case where $4 - x < 0$, or $x > 4$. Justify each step.
Hint: The solution must satisfy both $x > 3$ and $x > 4$.

$$\frac{x}{4 - x} < 3$$

a. $(4 - x)\frac{x}{4 - x} > (4 - x)3$

b. $\qquad x > 12 - 3x$

c. $\qquad 4x > 12$

d. $\qquad x > 3$

10. Combine this result with the given condition $x > 4$. What is the solution for this case?

11. Examine your solutions for Exercises 8 and 10. Now, write the solution of the inequality $\frac{x}{4 - x} < 3$.

Exercises

For Exercises 12–17, solve each inequality graphically and algebraically.

12. $\frac{2}{x - 1} < x$

13. $x + 1 > \frac{x + 5}{x + 2}$

14. $\frac{2x}{(x - 2)(x + 3)} < 1$

15. $\frac{2x + 2}{x - 1} < x + 1$

16. $\frac{x^2 + 1}{x} < 2x$

17. $\frac{x - 1}{x - 2} < \frac{x + 3}{x - 1}$

18. For Exercises 12–17, check your work by using a table to solve each inequality.

The equation $d = rt$ relates the distance d you travel, the time t it takes to travel that distance, and the rate r at which you travel. So the time it takes to travel a distance d at a rate r is $t = \frac{d}{r}$. If you increase your rate by a to $r + a$, then it takes less time, $t = \frac{d}{r + a}$. In fact, the time you save by going at the faster rate is $T = \frac{d}{r} - \frac{d}{r + a}$.

19. a. You normally take a 500-mi trip, averaging 45 mi/h. You want to increase the rate so that you save at least an hour. Write an inequality that describes the situation.

    b. Solve your inequality from part (a).

Pull It **All Together**

> To solve these problems, you will pull together concepts and skills related to rational expressions, functions, and equations.

Completing the Performance Task

Look back at your results from the Apply What You've Learned sections in Lessons 8-2, 8-5, and 8-6. Use the work you did to complete the following.

1. Solve the problem in the Task Description on page 497 by determining how long it took Steve and Sally to paddle to Elk Island. Assume that Steve and Sally always paddle at the same speed. Round your answer to the nearest 5 minutes. Show all your work and explain each step of your solution.

 2. Reflect Choose one of the Mathematical Practices below and explain how you applied it in your work on the Performance Task.

   MP 1: Make sense of problems and persevere in solving them.

   MP 2: Reason abstractly and quantitatively.

   MP 4: Model with mathematics.

   MP 5: Use appropriate tools strategically.

On Your Own

The next time Steve and Sally went on a canoe trip on Red River, the current was flowing at a different rate. This time they left at 8:00 A.M. and returned at 5:30 P.M. They paddled 15 mi downstream and then returned to their starting point by paddling back upstream. They took two 45 min breaks during the day.

Assuming that Steve and Sally paddle at a steady speed of 5 mi/h in still water, what was the speed of Red River's current during Steve and Sally's canoe trip?

Connecting **BIG** ideas and Answering the Essential Questions

1 Proportionality

Quantities x and y are inversely proportional only if growing x by the factor k ($k > 1$) means shrinking y by the factor $\frac{1}{k}$.

Inverse Variation (Lesson 8-1)

Are ℓ and w inversely proportional?
$A = \ell w$
$P = 2\ell + 2w$
- for a constant area—yes
- for a constant perimeter—no

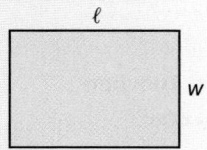

The Reciprocal Function Family (Lesson 8-2)

$A(\ell) = \frac{5}{\ell}$ is a stretch of the graph of $A(\ell) = \frac{1}{\ell}$ by a factor of 5.

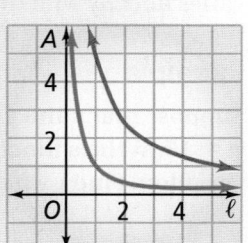

2 Function

A rational function may have no asymptotes, one horizontal or oblique asymptote, and any number of vertical asymptotes.

Rational Functions and Their Graphs (Lesson 8-3)

Asymptotes:
For $y = \frac{2x^2}{x^2 - 9}$
horizontal: $y = 2$
vertical: $x = \pm 3$
For $y = \frac{2x^3 + 6x^2}{x^2 + 1}$
oblique: $y = 2x + 6$.

$y = \frac{x^4 + 5}{x^2 + 1}$ has no asymptotes.

3 Equivalence

$f(x) = \frac{x + a}{x^2 - a^2}$, $x \neq \pm a$,
and $g(x) = \frac{1}{x - a}$, $x \neq \pm a$, are equivalent.

Solving Equations Involving Rational Expressions (Lessons 8-4, 8-5, and 8-6)

$\frac{2x^2}{x^2 - 9} = \frac{x - 6}{x - 3} + \frac{18}{x^2 - 9}$

$\frac{2x^2}{x^2 - 9} = \frac{(x - 6)(x + 3)}{(x - 3)(x + 3)} + \frac{18}{x^2 - 9}$

$2x^2 = x^2 - 3x - 18 + 18$

$x^2 + 3x = 0$

$x(x + 3) = 0$

$x = 0 \checkmark$ or $x = -3$ ✗

Chapter Vocabulary

- branch (p. 508)
- combined variation (p. 501)
- complex fraction (p. 536)
- continuous graph (p. 516)
- discontinuous graph (p. 516)
- inverse variation (p. 498)
- joint variation (p. 501)
- non-removable discontinuity (p. 516)
- oblique asymptote (p. 524)
- point of discontinuity (p. 516)
- rational equation (p. 542)
- rational expression (p. 527)
- rational function (p. 515)
- reciprocal function (p. 507)
- removable discontinuity (p. 516)
- simplest form (p. 527)

Choose the correct term to complete each sentence.

1. When the numerator and denominator of a rational expression are polynomials with no common factors, the rational expression is in __?__ .

2. If a quantity varies directly with one quantity and inversely with another, it is a(n) __?__ .

3. A(n) __?__ has a fraction in its numerator, denominator, or both.

4. If a is a zero of the polynomial denominator of a rational function, the function has a(n) __?__ at $x = a$.

5. A(n) __?__ of the graph of a rational function is one of the continuous pieces of its graph.

8-1 Inverse Variation

Quick Review

An equation in two variables of the form $y = \frac{k}{x}$ or $xy = k$, where $k \neq 0$, is an **inverse variation** with a **constant of variation** k. **Joint variation** describes when one quantity varies directly with two or more other quantities.

Example

Suppose that x and y vary inversely, and $x = 10$ when $y = 15$. Write a function that models the inverse variation. Find y when $x = 6$.

$y = \frac{k}{x}$

$15 = \frac{k}{10}$, so $k = 150$.

The inverse variation is $y = \frac{150}{x}$.

When $x = 6$, $y = \frac{150}{6} = 25$.

Exercises

6. Suppose that x and y vary inversely, and $x = 30$ when $y = 2$. Find y when $x = 5$.

Write a direct or inverse variation equation for each relation.

7.

x	3	4	8
y	24	18	9

8.

x	5	7	9
y	30	42	54

Write the function that models each relationship. Find z when $x = 4$ and $y = 8$.

9. z varies jointly with x and y. When $x = 2$ and $y = 2$, $z = 7$.

10. z varies directly with x and inversely with y. When $x = 5$ and $y = 2$, $z = 10$.

8-2 The Reciprocal Function Family

Quick Review

The graph of a **reciprocal function** has two parts called **branches**. The graph of $y = \frac{k}{x - b} + c$ is a translation of $y = \frac{k}{x}$ by b units horizontally and c units vertically. It has a vertical asymptote at $x = b$ and a horizontal asymptote at $y = c$.

Example

Graph the equation $y = \frac{3}{x - 2} + 1$. Identify the x- and y-intercepts and the asymptotes of the graph.

$b = 2$, so the vertical asymptote is $x = 2$.

$c = 1$, so the horizontal asymptote is $y = 1$.

Translate $y = \frac{3}{x}$ two units to the right and one unit up.

When $y = 0$, $x = -1$.

The x-intercept is $(-1, 0)$.

When $x = 0$, $y = -\frac{1}{2}$.

The y-intercept is $(0, -\frac{1}{2})$.

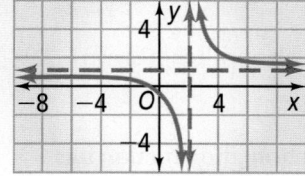

Exercises

Graph each equation. Identify the x- and y-intercepts and the asymptotes of the graph.

11. $y = \frac{1}{x}$

12. $y = \frac{-2}{x^2}$

13. $y = \frac{-1}{x} - 4$

14. $y = \frac{2}{x + 3} - 1$

Write an equation for the translation of $y = \frac{4}{x}$ that has the given asymptotes.

15. $x = 0, y = 3$

16. $x = 2, y = 2$

17. $x = -3, y = -4$

18. $x = 4, y = -3$

8-3 Rational Functions and Their Graphs

Quick Review

The **rational function** $f(x) = \frac{P(x)}{Q(x)}$ has a **point of discontinuity** for each real zero of $Q(x)$.

If $P(x)$ and $Q(x)$ have

- no common factors, then $f(x)$ has a vertical asymptote when $Q(x) = 0$.
- a common real zero a, then there is a hole or a vertical asymptote at $x = a$.
- degree of $P(x)$ < degree of $Q(x)$, then the graph of $f(x)$ has a horizontal asymptote at $y = 0$.
- degree of $P(x)$ = degree of $Q(x)$, then there is a horizontal asymptote at $y = \frac{a}{b}$, where a and b are the coefficients of the terms of greatest degree in $P(x)$ and $Q(x)$, respectively.
- degree of $P(x)$ > degree of $Q(x)$, then there is no horizontal asymptote.

Example

Find any points of discontinuity for the graph of the rational function $y = \frac{2.5}{x + 7}$. Describe any vertical or horizontal asymptotes and any holes.

There is a vertical asymptote at $x = -7$ and a horizontal asymptote at $y = 0$.

Exercises

Find any points of discontinuity for each rational function. Sketch the graph. Describe any vertical or horizontal asymptotes and any holes.

19. $y = \frac{x - 1}{(x + 2)(x - 1)}$

20. $y = \frac{x^3 - 1}{x^2 - 1}$

21. $y = \frac{2x^2 + 3}{x^2 + 2}$

22. The start-up cost of a company is $150,000. It costs $.17 to manufacture each headset. Graph the function that represents the average cost of a headset. How many must be manufactured to result in a cost of less than $5 per headset?

8-4 Rational Expressions

Quick Review

A **rational expression** is in **simplest form** when its numerator and denominator are polynomials that have no common factors.

Example

Simplify the rational expression. State any restrictions on the variable.

$$\frac{2x^2 + 7x + 3}{x - 4} \cdot \frac{x^2 - 16}{x^2 + 8x + 15}$$

$$= \frac{(2x + 1)(x + 3)}{x - 4} \cdot \frac{(x - 4)(x + 4)}{(x + 3)(x + 5)}$$

$$= \frac{(2x + 1)(x + 4)}{x + 5}, x \neq -5, x \neq -3, \text{ and } x \neq 4$$

Exercises

Simplify each rational expression. State any restrictions on the variable.

23. $\frac{x^2 + 10x + 25}{x^2 + 9x + 20}$

24. $\frac{x^2 - 2x - 24}{x^2 + 7x + 12} \cdot \frac{x^2 - 1}{x - 6}$

25. $\frac{4x^2 - 2x}{x^2 + 5x + 4} \div \frac{2x}{x^2 + 2x + 1}$

26. What is the ratio of the volume of a sphere to its surface area?

8-5 Adding and Subtracting Rational Expressions

Quick Review

To add or subtract rational expressions with different denominators, write each expression with the LCD. A fraction that has a fraction in its numerator or denominator or in both is called a **complex fraction**. Sometimes you can simplify a complex fraction by multiplying the numerator and denominator by the LCD of all the rational expressions.

Example

Simplify the complex fraction. $\dfrac{\frac{1}{x} + 3}{\frac{5}{y} + 4}$

$$\frac{\frac{1}{x} + 3}{\frac{5}{y} + 4} = \frac{\left(\frac{1}{x} + 3\right) \cdot xy}{\left(\frac{5}{y} + 4\right) \cdot xy}$$

$$= \frac{\frac{1}{x} \cdot xy + 3 \cdot xy}{\frac{5}{y} \cdot xy + 4 \cdot xy}$$

$$= \frac{y + 3xy}{5x + 4xy}$$

Exercises

Simplify the sum or difference. State any restrictions on the variable.

27. $\dfrac{3x}{x^2 - 4} + \dfrac{6}{x + 2}$

28. $\dfrac{1}{x^2 - 1} - \dfrac{2}{x^2 + 3x}$

Simplify the complex fraction.

29. $\dfrac{2 - \frac{2}{x}}{3 - \frac{1}{x}}$

30. $\dfrac{\frac{1}{x + y}}{4}$

8-6 Solving Rational Equations

Quick Review

Solving a **rational equation** often requires multiplying each side by an algebraic expression. This may introduce extraneous solutions—solutions that solve the derived equation but not the original equation. Check all possible solutions in the original equation.

Example

Solve the equation. Check your solution.

$$\frac{1}{2x} - \frac{2}{5x} = \frac{1}{2}$$

$$10x\left(\frac{1}{2x} - \frac{2}{5x}\right) = 10x\left(\frac{1}{2}\right)$$

$$5 - 4 = 5x$$

$$x = \frac{1}{5}$$

Check $\dfrac{1}{2\left(\frac{1}{5}\right)} - \dfrac{2}{5\left(\frac{1}{5}\right)} = \dfrac{5}{2} - 2 = \dfrac{1}{2}$ ✔

Exercises

Solve each equation. Check your solutions.

31. $\dfrac{1}{x} = \dfrac{5}{x - 4}$

32. $\dfrac{2}{x + 3} - \dfrac{1}{x} = \dfrac{-6}{x(x + 3)}$

33. $\dfrac{1}{2} + \dfrac{x}{6} = \dfrac{18}{x}$

34. You travel 10 mi on your bicycle in the same amount of time it takes your friend to travel 8 mi on his bicycle. If your friend rides his bike 2 mi/h slower than you ride your bike, find the rate at which each of you is traveling.

Do you know HOW?

Write a function that models each variation.

1. $x = 2$ when $y = -8$, and y varies inversely with x.

2. $x = 0.2$ and $y = 3$ when $z = 2$, and z varies jointly with x and y.

3. $x = \frac{1}{3}$, $y = \frac{1}{5}$, and $r = 3$ when $z = \frac{1}{2}$, and z varies directly with x and inversely with the product of r^2 and y.

Is the relationship between the values in each table a *direct variation*, an *inverse variation*, or *neither*? Write equations to model any direct or inverse variations.

4.

x	y
3	6
5	8
7	10
9	12

5.

x	y
4	32
8	16
16	8
32	4

Write and graph an equation of the translation of $y = \frac{7}{x}$ that has the given asymptotes.

6. $x = 1; y = 2$

7. $x = -3; y = -2$

For each rational function, identify any holes or horizontal or vertical asymptotes of the graph.

8. $y = \frac{x+1}{x-1}$

9. $y = \frac{x+3}{x+3}$

10. $y = \frac{x-2}{(x+1)(x-2)}$

11. $y = \frac{2x^2}{x^2-4x}$

12. $y = \frac{1}{x+2} - 3$

13. $y = \frac{x^2+5}{x-5}$

Simplify each complex fraction.

14. $\dfrac{\frac{2}{x}}{1-\frac{1}{y}}$

15. $\dfrac{3-\frac{3}{x}}{\frac{1}{2}-\frac{1}{x}}$

Simplify each rational expression. State any restrictions on the variable.

16. $\dfrac{x^2+7x+12}{x^2-9}$

17. $\dfrac{(x+3)(2x-1)}{x(x+4)} \div \dfrac{(-x-3)(2x+1)}{x}$

18. $\dfrac{x^2-1}{x^2+2x-3} - \dfrac{x+1}{x+3}$

19. $\dfrac{x(x+4)}{x-2} + \dfrac{x-1}{x^2-4}$

Solve each equation. Check your solutions.

20. $\frac{x}{2} = \frac{x+1}{4}$

21. $\frac{3}{x-1} = \frac{4}{3x+2}$

22. $\frac{3x}{x+1} = 0$

23. $\frac{3}{x+1} = \frac{1}{x^2-1}$

24. $\frac{1}{x} + \frac{1}{3} = \frac{6}{x^2}$

25. $\frac{1}{x} + \frac{x}{x+2} = 1$

26. Your neighbor can seal your driveway in 4 hours. Working together, you and your neighbor can seal it in 2.3 hours. How long would it take you to seal it working alone?

Do you UNDERSTAND?

27. **Vocabulary** Describe a situation that represents an inverse variation.

28. **Compare and Contrast** How is simplifying rational expressions similar to simplifying fractions? How is it different?

29. **Writing** When does a discontinuity result in a vertical asymptote? When does it result in a hole in the graph?

30. **Open-Ended** Write a function whose graph has a hole, a vertical asymptote, and a horizontal asymptote.

31. **Reasoning** State any restrictions on the variable in the complex fraction. $\dfrac{\frac{x-3}{x+4}}{\frac{x^2-1}{x}}$

TIPS FOR SUCCESS

Some problems ask you to find the lateral area or the (total) surface area of a three-dimensional figure. Read the sample question at the right. Then follow the tips to answer the question.

What is the approximate lateral area of the cone shown below?

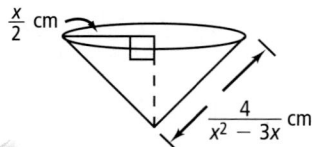

$\frac{x}{2}$ cm

$\frac{4}{x^2 - 3x}$ cm

TIP 2

Use the information from the diagram for the values you need in the formula.

TIP 1

Use the formula for the lateral area of a cone:
$S = \pi r \ell$.

Ⓐ $\frac{3}{x + 3}$ Ⓒ $\frac{3}{x - 3}$

Ⓑ $\frac{6}{x - 3}$ Ⓓ $\frac{6}{x + 3}$

Think It Through

radius: $r = \frac{x}{2}$

slant height: $\ell = \frac{4}{x^2 - 3x}$

$S = \pi r \ell$

$= \pi\left(\frac{x}{2}\right)\left(\frac{4}{x^2 - 3x}\right)$

$= \frac{2\pi}{x - 3}$

Since $\pi \approx 3$, the correct answer is B.

Vocabulary Builder

As you solve test items, you must understand the meanings of mathematical terms. Match each term with its mathematical meaning.

A. joint variation

B. branch

C. point of discontinuity

D. inverse variation

E. reciprocal function

I. a point where the graph of a function breaks into branches

II. each piece of a discontinuous graph

III. a relation represented by an equation of the form $y = \frac{k}{x}$ or $xy = k$, where $k \neq 0$

IV. a function that can be written in the form $f(x) = \frac{a}{x - h} + k$, where $a \neq 0$

V. one variable varies directly with two or more other variables

Selected Response

Read each question. Then write the letter of the correct answer on your paper.

1. Which expression equals $\frac{5x}{x^2 - 9} - \frac{4x}{x^2 + 5x + 6}$?

Ⓐ $\frac{7x}{(x - 3)(x + 3)(x + 2)}$

Ⓑ $\frac{x^2 - 2x}{(x - 3)(x + 3)(x + 2)}$

Ⓒ $\frac{x^2 + 22x}{(x - 3)(x + 3)(x + 2)}$

Ⓓ $\frac{9x^2 - 2x}{(x - 3)(x + 3)(x + 2)}$

2. If x is a real number, for what values of x is the equation $\frac{2x - 8}{4x^{-1}} = \frac{x^2 - 4x}{2}$ true?

Ⓕ all values of x

Ⓖ some values of x

Ⓗ no values of x

Ⓘ impossible to determine

3. Which expression represents the solution to $4^x = 13$?

- Ⓐ $\dfrac{\log 13}{\log 4}$

- Ⓑ $\log_4 + \log_{13}$

- Ⓒ $\dfrac{\log 4}{\log 13}$

- Ⓓ $\log_{13} 4$

4. If $f(x) = x^2$ and $g(x) = x - 1$, which statement is true?

- Ⓕ $f(x) \cdot g(x) = 2x^3 - 1$
- Ⓖ $f(x) - g(x) = x - 1$
- Ⓗ $f(x) - g(x) = x^2 - x + 1$
- Ⓘ $f(x) + g(x) = x^3 - 1$

5. Which expression is a simpler form of the complex fraction $\dfrac{\frac{1}{x} + \frac{3}{y}}{\frac{2}{xy}}$?

- Ⓐ $\dfrac{3xy}{2}$
- Ⓒ $\dfrac{3}{2}$
- Ⓑ $\dfrac{3x + y}{2xy}$
- Ⓓ $\dfrac{3x + y}{2}$

6. Which is the first *incorrect* step in simplifying $\log_9 243$?

Step 1: $\log_9 243 = x$

Step 2: $\qquad 9^x = 243$

Step 3: $\qquad x = 243 \div 9$

Step 4: $\qquad = 27$

- Ⓕ Step 1
- Ⓖ Step 2
- Ⓗ Step 3
- Ⓘ Step 4

7. Which is/are the solution(s) of the equation $\sqrt{2x + 2} = 2x - 4$?

- Ⓐ $x = 3.5$ and $x = 1$
- Ⓑ $x = 3.5$ and $x = -1$
- Ⓒ $x = 3.5$
- Ⓓ $x = 1$

8. Which is the simplest form of the expression?
$$4\sqrt{18x^4} - 3\sqrt{72x^4}$$

- Ⓕ $-6x^2\sqrt{2}$
- Ⓗ -6
- Ⓖ $-6x^2$
- Ⓘ none of the above

9. If $g(x) = x^2 - 4$ and $h(x) = 4x - 6$, which expression is equal to $\left(\frac{g}{h}\right)(x)$?

- Ⓐ $\dfrac{4x - 6}{x^2 - 4}$
- Ⓑ $\dfrac{x^2 - 2}{4x - 3}$
- Ⓒ $x^2 - 4 - (4x - 6)$
- Ⓓ $\dfrac{(x + 2)(x - 2)}{2(2x - 3)}$

10. If $i = \sqrt{-1}$, what is the value of $-i^4$?

- Ⓕ i
- Ⓗ 1
- Ⓖ $-i$
- Ⓘ -1

11. The graph below shows the transformation of the function $f(x) = (x + 3)^2$. Which quadratic function models this graph?

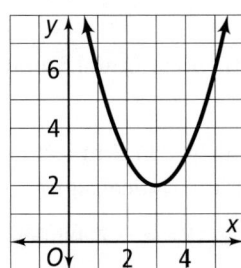

- Ⓐ $f(x) = (x - 1)^2$
- Ⓒ $f(x) = (x - 3)^2 - 2$
- Ⓑ $f(x) = 2(x - 3)^2$
- Ⓓ $f(x) = (x - 3)^2 + 2$

12. What is the solution of $3e^{2x} + 1 = 5$?

- Ⓕ $x \approx 0.131$
- Ⓗ $x \approx 0.187$
- Ⓖ $x \approx 0.151$
- Ⓘ $x \approx 0.144$

Constructed Response

13. Solve for x: $\dfrac{5}{2x-2} = \dfrac{15}{x^2-1}$.

14. Solve for x: $\log(x-3) = 3$.

15. What is the value of the x-coordinate of the solution of the system of equations?
$$\begin{cases} 2x + y = 6 \\ y - 3 = x \end{cases}$$

16. What is the remainder when $x^4 - 3x^2 + 7x + 3$ is divided by $x - 2$?

17. The product of three consecutive even integers is -2688. What is the value of the largest integer?

18. What is the smallest zero of $f(x) = 2x^5 - 4x^2 + 3x + 7$? Round your answer to the nearest hundredth.

19. The matrix below represents a linear system of equations. What is the y-coefficient of the first equation of the system?
$$\begin{bmatrix} 3 & -1 & | & 5 \\ 1 & 2 & | & -1 \end{bmatrix}$$

20. What is the sum of the zeros of the polynomial function $y = x^2 - 4y - 5$?

21. Write the radical expression $\sqrt{50x^5 y^3 z}$ in simplest form. What is the constant value under the radical sign?

22. If $p(x) = 3x^4 - 2x^3 + x^2 - 1$ and $g(x) = x - 2$, what is the remainder of $\dfrac{p(x)}{g(x)}$? Show your work.

23. Solve the equation $\dfrac{2g^2}{d} - c = 3x$ for g. Show your work.

24. Explain how you know that the graph of $f(x) = -x^4 - 3x + 7$ does not have up and down end behavior.

25. Graph $y = 3^{x+2} - 5$.

26. How can the solution of $4^x = 13$ be written as a logarithm?

27. If $g(x) = x^2 - 4$ and $h(x) = 4x - 6$, write an expression equivalent to $\left(\dfrac{g}{h}\right)(x)$ in factored form.

Extended Response

28. Explain how to find an equation for the translation of $y = \dfrac{3}{x}$ that has asymptotes at $x = -13$ and $y = 5$.

29. What is the inverse of $y = x^2 + 15$? Is the inverse a function? Explain.

30. What are the solutions of $3x^2 + 4x + 2 = 0$? Show your work.

31. You are given the equation $y = 2\,|x - 1| + 3$.
   a. Without graphing, what are the vertex and axis of symmetry of this function?
   b. Describe the transformations from the parent function $y = |x|$.
   c. Sketch the graph.

32. Without solving, explain how you know that the equation $\sqrt{3x - 4} + \sqrt{x + 3} = -2$ has no real solutions.

Get Ready!

Lesson 2-1 ◆ **Evaluating Functions**

For each function, find $f(1), f(2), f(3),$ and $f(4).$

1. $f(x) = 2x + 7$ **2.** $f(x) = 5x - 4$

3. $f(x) = 0.2x + 0.7$ **4.** $f(x) = -5x + 3$

5. $f(x) = 4x - \frac{2}{3}$ **6.** $f(x) = -3x - 9$

Lesson 1-1 ◆ **Identifying Mathematical Patterns**

Identify a pattern and find the next three numbers in the pattern.

7. $9, 4, -1, -6, \ldots$ **8.** $1, 2, 4, 8, \ldots$

9. $18, 9, 10, 1, 2, \ldots$ **10.** $7, 10, 13, 16, \ldots$

Lesson 8-5 ◆ **Simplifying Complex Fractions**

Simplify each complex fraction.

11. $\dfrac{1 - \frac{1}{3}}{\frac{1}{2}}$ **12.** $\dfrac{\frac{1}{3} + \frac{1}{6}}{\frac{2}{3}}$ **13.** $\dfrac{1}{1 - \frac{2}{5}}$ **14.** $\dfrac{1 - \frac{3}{8}}{2 + \frac{1}{4}}$

 Looking Ahead Vocabulary

15. Think of a function and evaluate the function for the input numbers 1, 2, 3, 4, and 5. List the five outputs in order. This list is a *sequence* of numbers. The sequence can be infinitely long.

16. Use a linear function to generate a sequence of five numbers. Beginning with the second number, subtract the number that precedes it. Continue doing this until you have found all four differences. Are the results the same? If so, you have discovered that your sequence has a *common difference*.

17. Now use an exponential function to define your sequence. Instead of subtracting, divide each number by the number that precedes it. Do this until you find all four quotients. Are these four results the same? If so, you have discovered that your sequence has a *common ratio*.

Sequences and Series

Chapter Preview

9-1 **Mathematical Patterns**
9-2 **Arithmetic Sequences**
9-3 **Geometric Sequences**
9-4 **Arithmetic Series**
9-5 **Geometric Series**

Vocabulary

English/Spanish Vocabulary Audio Online:

English	Spanish
arithmetic sequence, p. 572	progresión aritmética
arithmetic series, p. 587	serie aritmética
common difference, p. 572	diferencia común
common ratio, p. 580	razón común
converge, p. 598	convergir
diverge, p. 598	divergir
explicit formula, p. 565	fórmula explícita
geometric sequence, p. 580	progresión geométrica
geometric series, p. 595	serie geométrica
limits, p. 589	límites
recursive formula, p. 565	formula recursiva

BIG ideas

1 Variable
Essential Questions How can you represent the terms of a sequence explicitly? How can you represent them recursively?

2 Equivalence
Essential Question What are equivalent explicit and recursive definitions for an arithmetic sequence?

3 Modeling
Essential Questions How can you model a geometric sequence? How can you model its sum?

 DOMAINS
• Seeing Structure in Expressions

Common Core Performance Task

Reconstructing Sales Data

Matthew has a valuable collection of a certain toy car, which is a collector's item. He bought his first toy car in 1994. Since then, the value of the toy car has increased by the same percent each year. A recent edition of a collector's magazine lists the following values for the toy car for the years 2009–2013.

Year	Value of Toy Car
2009	$96.17
2010	$100.02
2011	$104.02
2012	$108.18
2013	$112.51

Over a span of 7 consecutive years, Matthew sold 7 toy cars, with each sale occurring one year after the previous sale and at the published price. His total revenue from the sales was $533.62. However, he cannot remember when he sold the cars, and he is wondering how he can figure this out.

Task Description
Determine the years in which Matthew sold the 7 toy cars.

Connecting the Task to the Math Practices

As you complete the task, you'll apply these Standards for Mathematical Practice.

- You'll use the structure of the sequence of car values to write a formula for the toy car's value in any year. (MP 4, MP 7)

- You'll distinguish between a sequence of numbers and its sum, and choose an appropriate formula to find the value of the first car Matthew sold. (MP 2, MP 6)

9-1 Mathematical Patterns

© **Common Core State Standards**

Prepares for A-SSE.B.4 Derive the formula for the sum of a geometric series (when the common ratio is not 1), and use the formula to solve problems.

MP 1, MP 3, MP 4, MP 7

Objectives To identify mathematical patterns found in a sequence
To use a formula to find the *n*th term of a sequence

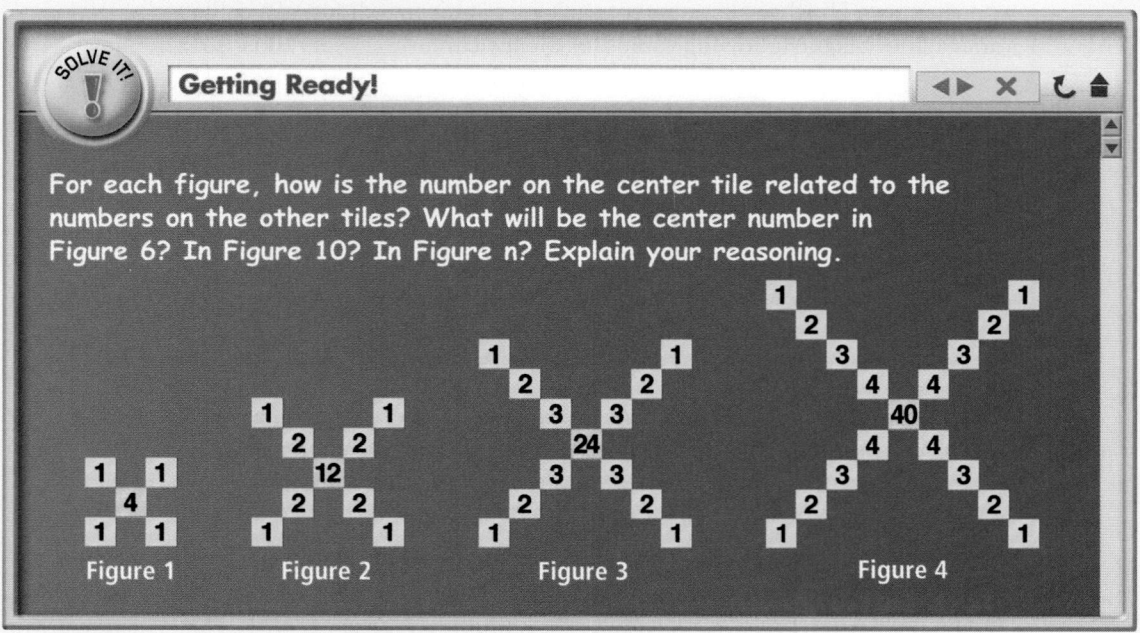

SOLVE IT!

Getting Ready!

For each figure, how is the number on the center tile related to the numbers on the other tiles? What will be the center number in Figure 6? In Figure 10? In Figure n? Explain your reasoning.

Figure 1   Figure 2   Figure 3   Figure 4

Lesson Vocabulary
- sequence
- term of a sequence
- explicit formula
- recursive formula

Sometimes you can state a rule to describe a pattern. At other times, you have to do a bit of work to find a rule.

Essential Understanding If the numbers in a list follow a pattern, you may be able to relate each number in the list to its numerical position in the list with a rule.

A **sequence** is an ordered list of numbers. Each number in a sequence is a **term of a sequence**. You can represent a term of a sequence by using a variable with a subscript number to indicate its position in the sequence. For example, a_5 is the fifth term in the sequence $a_1, a_2, a_3, a_4, \ldots$.

The subscripts of sequence terms are often positive integers starting with 1. If so, you can generalize a term as a_n, the *n*th term in the sequence.

1st term	2nd term	3rd term	. . .	$n - 1$ term	nth term	$n + 1$ term	. . .
↓	↓	↓		↓	↓	↓	
a_1	a_2	a_3	. . . a_{n-1}		a_n	a_{n+1}	. . .

An **explicit formula** describes the nth term of a sequence using the number n.

For example, in the sequence 2, 4, 6, 8, 10, . . . , the nth term is twice the value of n. You write this as $a_n = 2n$. The table shows how to find a_n by substituting the value of n into the explicit formula.

n	nth term
1	$a_1 = 2(1) = 2$
2	$a_2 = 2(2) = 4$
3	$a_3 = 2(3) = 6$
4	$a_4 = 2(4) = 8$

 Problem 1 Generating a Sequence Using an Explicit Formula

Plan

How does the explicit formula help you find the value of a term?
Replace n in the formula with the number of the term. Simplify to find the value of the term.

A sequence has an explicit formula $a_n = 3n - 2$. What are the first 10 terms of this sequence?

$a_n = 3n - 2$ Write the formula.

$a_1 = 3(1) - 2 = 1$ Substitute 1 for n and simplify.

$a_2 = 3(2) - 2 = 4$ Substitute 2 for n and simplify.

You can use a table to organize your work for the remaining terms.

n	a_n	
3	$a_3 = 3(3) - 2 = 7$	Substitute 3 for n and simplify.
4	$a_4 = 3(4) - 2 = 10$	
5	$a_5 = 3(5) - 2 = 13$	And so on.
6	$a_6 = 3(6) - 2 = 16$	
7	$a_7 = 3(7) - 2 = 19$	
8	$a_8 = 3(8) - 2 = 22$	
9	$a_9 = 3(9) - 2 = 25$	
10	$a_{10} = 3(10) - 2 = 28$	

The first ten terms are 1, 4, 7, 10, 13, 16, 19, 22, 25, 28.

 Got It? **1.** A sequence has an explicit formula $a_n = 12n + 3$. What is term a_{12} in the sequence?

Sometimes you can see the pattern in a sequence by comparing each term to the one that came before it. For example, in the sequence 133, 130, 127, 124, . . . , each term after the first term is equal to three less than the previous term.

A recursive definition for this sequence contains two parts.
(a) an initial condition (the value of the first term): $a_1 = 133$
(b) a **recursive formula** (relates each term after the first term to the one before it):
     $a_n = a_{n-1} - 3$, for $n > 1$

 **Problem 2** Writing a Recursive Definition for a Sequence

The number of blocks in a two-dimensional pyramid is a sequence that follows a recursive formula. What is a recursive definition for the sequence?

Think	Write
Count the number of blocks in each pyramid.	1, 3, 6, 10, 15, 21
Subtract consecutive terms to find out what happens from one term to the next.	$a_2 - a_1 = 3 - 1 = 2$ $a_3 - a_2 = 6 - 3 = 3$ $a_4 - a_3 = 10 - 6 = 4$ $a_5 - a_4 = 15 - 10 = 5$ $a_6 - a_5 = 21 - 15 = 6$
Use n to express the relationship between successive terms.	$a_n - a_{n-1} = n$
To write a recursive definition, state the initial condition and the recursive formula.	$a_1 = 1$ and $a_n = a_{n-1} + n.$

 Got It? **2.** What is a recursive definition for each sequence?
(*Hint:* Look for simple addition or multiplication patterns to relate consecutive terms.)
a. 1, 2, 6, 24, 120, 720, . . .
b. 1, 5, 14, 30, 55, . . .

Recursive definitions can be very helpful when you look at a small section of a sequence. However, if you want to know both a_3 and a_{5000} of a sequence, an explicit formula often works better.

 Problem 3 Writing an Explicit Formula for a Sequence

What is the 100th term of the pyramid sequence in Problem 2?

Plan

Why do you use the explicit formula to find a_{100}?
Because starting with a_1, it would take 99 iterations of the formula to get a_{100} using the recursive formula.

To find an explicit formula, expand the first few terms of the pyramid sequence.

a_1	a_2	a_3	a_4	a_5	$\ldots$	a_n
1	$1 + 2$	$1 + 2 + 3$	$1 + 2 + 3 + 4$	$1 + 2 + 3 + 4 + 5$	$\ldots$	$1 + 2 + \ldots + n$
1	3	6	10	15	$\ldots$	■

Therefore,

$$a_n = 1 + 2 + 3 + \cdots + (n - 2) + (n - 1) + n,$$

which you can write as

$$a_n = n + (n - 1) + (n - 2) + \cdots + 3 + 2 + 1.$$

Adding the two previous equations gives the following result:

$$
\begin{aligned}
a_n &= 1 &&+ 2 &&+ 3 &&+ \cdots &&+ (n-2) + (n-1) + n \\
+\, a_n &= n &&+ (n-1) &&+ (n-2) &&+ \cdots &&+\; 3\; + \;2\; + 1 \\
\hline
2a_n &= (n+1) + (n+1) + (n+1) + \cdots + (n+1) + (n+1) + (n+1)
\end{aligned}
$$

$$2a_n = n(n + 1)$$

$$a_n = \tfrac{1}{2}n(n + 1)$$

The explicit formula for this sequence is $a_n = \tfrac{1}{2}n(n + 1)$.

Substitute 100 into the explicit formula to find the 100th term.

$$
\begin{aligned}
a_{100} &= \tfrac{1}{2}(100)(100 + 1) \\
&= \tfrac{1}{2}(100)(101) \\
&= 5050
\end{aligned}
$$

The 100th term is 5050.

  Got It? **3. a.** What is an explicit formula for the sequence 0, 3, 8, 15, 24, $\ldots$? What is the 20th term?

b. Reasoning Why is using an explicit formula often more efficient than using a recursive definition?

 **Problem 4** Using Formulas to Find Terms of a Sequence

Finance Pierre began the year with an unpaid balance of $300 on his credit card. Because he had not read the credit card agreement, he did not realize that the company charged 1.8% interest each month on his unpaid balance, in addition to a $29 penalty in any month he might fail to make a minimum payment. Pierre ignored his credit card bill for 4 consecutive months before finally deciding to pay off the balance. What did he owe after 4 months of non-payment?

Step 1 Write a recursive definition.
Initial condition: $a_0 = 300$ (Use a_0 so that a_1 represents the balance after 1 month.)
Recursive formula: $a_n = 1.018 \cdot a_{n-1} + 29$, for $n > 1$

Think

Why is it helpful to change **FLOAT** to 2?
This problem involves money, so, real-world solutions will only have 2 decimal places.

Step 2 Use a calculator. In the **MODE** menu, change the digit display from **FLOAT** to 2.

Enter 300 in the home screen. Enter the recursive formula **1.018ANS + 29**. Press **enter** for the balance after one month.

Press **enter** three more times until the calculator shows the balance after 4 months.

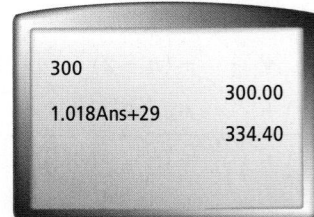

After 4 months, Pierre owes $441.36.

 Got It? **4.** If the credit card company were to allow Pierre to continue making no payments, after how many months would his balance exceed $1000?

 Lesson Check

Do you know HOW?

Find the first five terms of each sequence.

1. $a_n = 5n - 3$

2. $a_n = n^2 - 2n$

3. What is a recursive definition for the sequence 3, 6, 12, 24, . . . ?

4. What is an explicit formula for the sequence 5, 8, 11, 14, . . . ?

Do you UNDERSTAND?  MATHEMATICAL PRACTICES

5. Vocabulary Explain the difference between an explicit formula and a recursive definition. Give an example of each.

6. Error Analysis A student writes that $a_n = 3n + 1$ is an explicit formula for the sequence 1, 4, 7, 10, ... Explain the student's error and write a correct explicit formula for the sequence.

Practice and Problem-Solving Exercises

MATHEMATICAL PRACTICES

 **Practice**

Find the first six terms of each sequence.

◀ **See Problem 1.**

7. $a_n = 3n + 2$ **8.** $a_n = -5n + 1$ **9.** $a_n = \frac{1}{2}n$ **10.** $a_n = n^2 + 1$

11. $a_n = 3n^2 - n$ **12.** $a_n = 2^n - 1$ **13.** $a_n = \frac{1}{2}n^3 - 1$ **14.** $a_n = (-3)^n$

Write a recursive definition for each sequence.

◀ **See Problem 2.**

15. $80, 77, 74, 71, 68, \ldots$ **16.** $4, 8, 16, 32, 64, \ldots$ **17.** $0, 3, 7, 12, 18, \ldots$

18. $1, 4, 7, 10, 13, \ldots$ **19.** $100, 10, 1, 0.1, 0.01, \ldots$ **20.** $\frac{1}{2}, \frac{1}{4}, \frac{1}{8}, \frac{1}{16}, \frac{1}{32}, \ldots$

21. $4, -8, 16, -32, 64, \ldots$ **22.** $1, 2, 6, 24, 120, \ldots$ **23.** $1, 5, 14, 30, \ldots$

Write an explicit formula for each sequence. Find the tenth term.

◀ **See Problem 3.**

24. $4, 5, 6, 7, 8, \ldots$ **25.** $4, 7, 10, 13, 16, \ldots$ **26.** $3, 7, 11, 15, 19, \ldots$

27. $-2\frac{1}{2}, -2, -1\frac{1}{2}, -1, \ldots$ **28.** $1, 4, 9, 16, \ldots$ **29.** $2, 5, 10, 17, 26, \ldots$

30. $\frac{1}{2}, \frac{1}{3}, \frac{1}{4}, \frac{1}{5}, \frac{1}{6}, \ldots$ **31.** $1, 3, 9, 27, \ldots$ **32.** $\frac{1}{2}, -\frac{1}{4}, \frac{1}{8}, -\frac{1}{16}, \ldots$

Find the eighth term of each sequence.

33. $-2, -1, 0, 1, 2, \ldots$ **34.** $43, 41, 39, 37, 35, \ldots$ **35.** $40, 20, 10, 5, \frac{5}{2}, \ldots$

36. $6, 1, -4, -9, \ldots$ **37.** $144, 36, 9, \frac{9}{4}, \ldots$ **38.** $\frac{1}{2}, \frac{1}{4}, \frac{1}{8}, \frac{1}{16}, \frac{1}{32}, \ldots$

39. $2, 1, -2, -7, -14, \ldots$ **40.** $\frac{3}{4}, -\frac{3}{2}, 3, -6, \ldots$ **41.** $2, -\frac{3}{2}, \frac{4}{3}, -\frac{5}{4}, \ldots$

42. Exercise You walk 1 mile the first day of your training, 1.2 miles the second day, 1.6 miles the third day, and 2.4 miles the fourth day. If you continue this pattern, how many miles do you walk the seventh day?

◀ **See Problem 4.**

B Apply

Determine whether each formula is *explicit* or *recursive*. Then find the first five terms of each sequence.

43. $a_n = 2a_{n-1} + 3$, where $a_1 = 3$ **44.** $a_n = \frac{1}{2}(n)(n - 1)$

45. $a_n = (n - 5)(n + 5)$ **46.** $a_n = -3a_{n-1}$, where $a_1 = -2$

47. $a_n = -4n^2 - 2$ **48.** $a_n = 2n^2 + 1$

Use the given rule to write the 4th, 5th, 6th, and 7th terms of each sequence.

49. $a_n = (n + 1)^2$ **50.** $a_n = 2(n - 1)^3$

51. $a_n = \frac{n^2}{n + 1}$ **52.** $a_n = \frac{n + 1}{n + 2}$

53. Think About a Plan You invested money in a company, and each month you receive a payment for your investment. Over the first four months, you received $50, $52, $56, and $62. If this pattern continues, how much do you receive in the tenth month?
- What pattern do you see between consecutive terms?
- Can you write a recursive or explicit formula to describe the pattern?
- How can you use your formula to find the amount you receive in the tenth month?

54. Entertainment Suppose you are building towers of cards with levels as displayed below. Copy and complete the table, assuming the pattern continues.

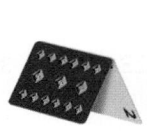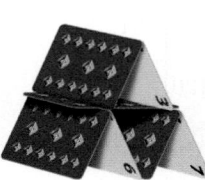

Number of Levels	Cards Needed
1	2
2	7
3	■
4	■
5	■

Find the next two terms in each sequence. Write a formula for the nth term. Identify each formula as *explicit* or *recursive*.

55. 5, 8, 11, 14, 17, . . .   **56.** 3, 6, 12, 24, 48, . . .   **57.** 1, 8, 27, 64, 125, . . .

58. 4, 16, 64, 256, 1024, . . .   **59.** 49, 64, 81, 100, 121, . . .   **60.** −1, 1, −1, 1, −1, 1, . . .

61. −16, −8, −4, −2, . . .   **62.** −75, −68, −61, −54, . . .   **63.** 21, 13, 5, −3, . . .

64. a. Open-Ended Write four terms of a sequence of numbers that you can describe both recursively and explicitly.
  b. Write a recursive definition and an explicit formula for your sequence.
  c. Find the 20th term of the sequence by evaluating one of your formulas. Use the other formula to check your work.

65. Geometry Suppose you are stacking boxes in levels that form squares. The numbers of boxes in successive levels form a sequence. The figure at the right shows the top four levels as viewed from above.
  a. How many boxes of equal size would you need for the next lower level?
  b. How many boxes of equal size would you need to add three levels?
  c. Suppose you are stacking a total of 285 boxes. How many levels will you have?

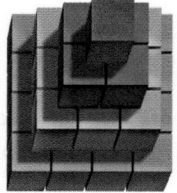

Challenge

66. Geometry The triangular numbers form a sequence. The diagram represents the first three triangular numbers: 1, 3, 6.
  a. Find the fourth and fifth triangular numbers.
  b. Write a recursive formula for the nth triangular number.
  c. Is the explicit formula $a_n = \frac{1}{2}(n^2 + n)$ the correct formula for this sequence? Explain.

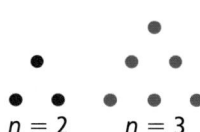

$n = 1$ $n = 2$ $n = 3$

Use each recursive definition to write an explicit formula for the sequence.

67. $a_1 = 10, a_n = 2a_{n-1}$

68. $a_1 = -5, a_n = a_{n-1} - 1$

69. $a_1 = 1, a_n = a_{n-1} + 4$

 70. Finance Use the information in the ad.

    a. Suppose you start a savings account. Write a recursive definition and an explicit formula for the amount of money you would have in the bank at the end of any week.

    b. How much money would you have in the bank after four weeks?

    c. Assume the bank pays interest every four weeks. To calculate your interest, multiply the balance at the end of the four weeks by 0.005. Then, add that amount to your account on the last day of the four-week period. Write a recursive formula for the amount of money you have after each interest payment.

    d. Reasoning What is the bank's annual interest rate?

Standardized Test Prep

GRIDDED RESPONSE

SAT/ACT

71. Scientists determine an object is moving at the rate of $(5 - \sqrt{2})$ ft/s. How many seconds will it take the object to travel 125 ft? Round the answer to the nearest tenth of a second.

72. What is the solution of $\sqrt{4x - 23} - 3 = 2$?

73. Using a calculator, what is the solution of $1080 = 15^{3x-4}$? Round the answer to the nearest hundredth.

74. Using the change of base formula, what is the solution of $\log_5 x = \log_3 20$? Round the answer to the nearest tenth.

75. The battery power available to operate a deep space probe is given by the formula $P = 42e^{-0.005t}$, where P is power in watts and t is time in years. For how many years can the probe run if it requires 35 watts? Round the answer to the nearest tenth year.

Mixed Review

Solve each equation. Check the solution.

See Lesson 8-6.

76. $\dfrac{y}{y+1} = \dfrac{2}{3}$

77. $\dfrac{4}{2a} = \dfrac{5}{a+6}$

78. $\dfrac{3}{b+2} = \dfrac{6}{b-1}$

Find the slope of the line that passes through the two points.

See Lesson 2-3.

79. $(4, 5)$ and $(1, 8)$

80. $(-3, -3)$ and $(2, 2)$

81. $(1, 3)$ and $(4, 9)$

Get Ready! To prepare for Lesson 9-2, do Exercises 82–84.

Identify the pattern and find the next three terms.

See Lesson 1-1.

82. $10, 8, 6, 4, 2, 0, \ldots$

83. $100, 117, 134, 151, 168, \ldots$

84. $\dfrac{5}{7}, \dfrac{8}{7}, \dfrac{11}{7}, 2, \ldots$

© **Common Core State Standards**
F-IF.A.3 Recognize that sequences are functions, sometimes defined recursively, whose domain is a subset of the integers.
MP 1, MP 2, MP 3, MP 4, MP 5, MP 6

Objective To define, identify, and apply arithmetic sequences

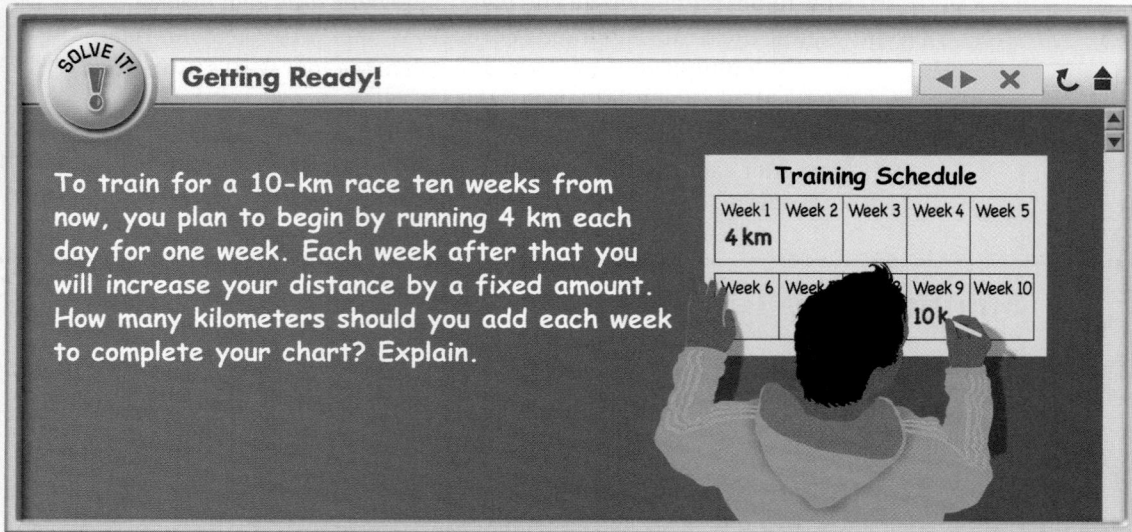

SOLVE IT!

Getting Ready!

To train for a 10-km race ten weeks from now, you plan to begin by running 4 km each day for one week. Each week after that you will increase your distance by a fixed amount. How many kilometers should you add each week to complete your chart? Explain.

Training Schedule

Week 1	Week 2	Week 3	Week 4	Week 5
4 km				

Week 6	Week 7	Week 8	Week 9	Week 10
				10 k

Lesson Vocabulary
• arithmetic sequence
• common difference
• arithmetic mean

It sometimes is helpful to represent a situation with a sequence of numbers. There are different types of numerical sequences.

Essential Understanding In an *arithmetic sequence,* the difference between any two consecutive terms is always the same number. You can build an arithmetic sequence by adding the same number to each term.

An **arithmetic sequence** is a sequence where the difference between consecutive terms is constant. This difference is the **common difference**.

take note

Key Concept   Arithmetic Sequence

An arithmetic sequence with a starting value a and common difference d is a sequence of the form

$$a, a + d, a + 2d, a + 3d, \ldots.$$

A recursive definition for this sequence has two parts:

$a_1 = a$ initial condition

$a_n = a_{n-1} + d$, for $n > 1$ recursive formula

An explicit definition for this sequence is a single formula:

$a_n = a + (n - 1)d$, for $n \geq 1$

Problem 1 Identifying Arithmetic Sequences

Is the sequence an arithmetic sequence?

Ⓐ 3, 6, 9, 12, 15, . . .

Find the differences between consecutive terms.

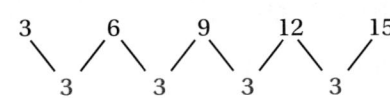

Each difference is 3. The sequence has a common difference. The sequence is an arithmetic sequence.

Ⓑ 1, 4, 9, 16, 25, . . .

Find the difference between consecutive terms.

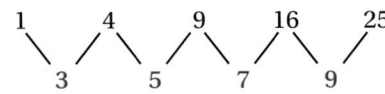

There is no common difference. The sequence is not an arithmetic sequence.

 Got It? **1.** Is the sequence an arithmetic sequence?

    a. 2, 4, 8, 16, . . .   **b.** 1, 5, 9, 13, 17, . . .

Problem 2 Analyzing Arithmetic Sequences

Ⓐ **What is the 100th term of the arithmetic sequence that begins 6, 11, . . . ?**

The first term a is 6. The common difference d is $11 - 6 = 5$.

$$a_n = a + (n - 1)d \quad \text{Use the explicit formula.}$$

$$a_{100} = 6 + (100 - 1)5 \quad \text{Substitute 100 for } n, \text{6 for } a, \text{ and 5 for } d.$$

$$a_{100} = 501 \quad \text{Simplify.}$$

The 100th term is 501.

Ⓑ **What are the second and third terms of the arithmetic sequence 100, ▪, ▪, 82, . . . ?**

The first term a is 100. The fourth term a_4 is 82. There are 3 common differences between 100 and 82.

$$82 = 100 + 3d \quad \text{Add } 3d \text{ to move from 100 to 82.}$$

$$-18 = 3d \quad \text{Solve for } d.$$

$$-6 = d$$

The common difference is -6. The terms are 100, 94, 88, 82, ...

The second and third terms are 94 and 88.

 Got It? **2. a.** What is the 46th term of the arithmetic sequence that begins 3, 5, 7, . . . ?

    b. What are the second and third terms of this arithmetic sequence?

       80, ▪, ▪, 125, . . .

The **arithmetic mean**, or average, of two numbers x and y is $\frac{x+y}{2}$.

In an arithmetic sequence, the middle term of any three consecutive terms is the arithmetic mean of the other two terms.

© **Problem 3** Using the Arithmetic Mean

GRIDDED RESPONSE

What is the missing term of the arithmetic sequence . . . , 15, ■, 59, . . . ?

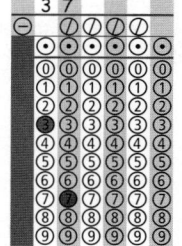

Think
To use the formula for arithmetic mean, what are x and y?
x is 15 and y is 59.

arithmetic mean $= \frac{15+59}{2} = 37$

The missing term is 37.

© ✓ **Got It?** **3. a.** The 9th and 11th terms of an arithmetic sequence are 132 and 98. What is the 10th term?

b. Reasoning If you know the 5th and 6th terms of an arithmetic sequence, how can you find term 7 using the arithmetic mean?

© **Problem 4** Using an Explicit Formula for an Arithmetic Sequence

Sports Arena The numbers of seats in the first 13 rows in a section of an arena form an arithmetic sequence. Rows 1 and 2 are shown in the diagram below. How many seats are in Row 13?

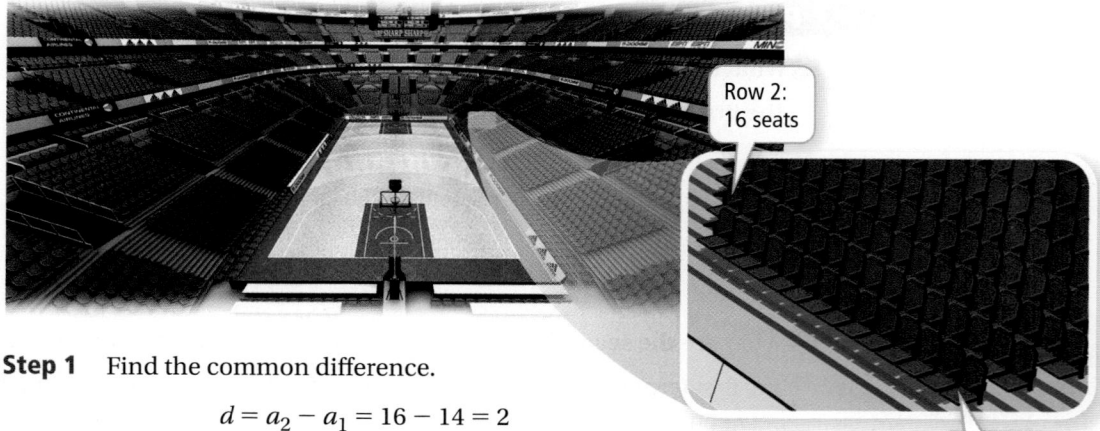

Row 2: 16 seats

Row 1: 14 seats

Plan
What two terms should you use to find the common difference?
Use the consecutive terms given.

Step 1 Find the common difference.

$$d = a_2 - a_1 = 16 - 14 = 2$$

Step 2 Write an explicit formula for the arithmetic sequence.

$a_n = a + (n-1)d$ Use the explicit formula.

$a_{13} = 14 + (13-1)2$ Substitute 13 for n, 14 for a, and 2 for d.

$\quad\;\; = 38$ Simplify.

There are 38 seats in Row 13.

✓ **Got It?** **4.** The numbers of seats in the first 16 rows in a curved section of another arena form an arithmetic sequence. If there are 20 seats in Row 1 and 23 seats in Row 2, how many seats are in Row 16?

Lesson Check

Do you know HOW?

Find the tenth term of each arithmetic sequence.

1. 2, 8, 14, 20, . . .   **2.** 15, 23, 31, . . .

Find the missing term of each arithmetic sequence.

3. . . . 4, ■, 22, . . .   **4.** . . . 25, ■, 53, . . .

Do you UNDERSTAND?

5. Vocabulary Explain what it means for a sequence to be an arithmetic sequence.

6. Open-Ended Give an example of a sequence that is not an arithmetic sequence.

Practice and Problem-Solving Exercises

 **Practice**

Determine whether each sequence is arithmetic. If so, identify the common difference.

See Problem 1.

7. 10, 20, 30, 40, . . .   **8.** 1, 1, 2, 3, 5, 8, . . .   **9.** −21, −18, −15, −12, . . .

10. 97, 86, 75, 64, . . .   **11.** 3, 7, 11, 15, . . .   **12.** 100, 10, 1, 0.1, . . .

Find the 32nd term of each sequence.

See Problem 2.

13. 34, 37, 40, 43, . . .   **14.** −9, −8.7, −8.4, . . .   **15.** 23, 30, 37, 44, . . .

16. 9, 4, −1, −6, −11, . . .   **17.** 0.1, 0.5, 0.9, 1.3, . . .   **18.** 101, 105, 109, 113, . . .

Find the missing term of each arithmetic sequence.

See Problem 3.

19. −15, ■, 1, . . .   **20.** 14, ■, 28, . . .   **21.** . . . 5, ■, 21, . . .

22. . . . 98, ■, 66, . . .   **23.** 25, ■, −10, . . .   **24.** . . . 65, ■, −60, . . .

25. Savings A student deposits the same amount of money into her bank account each week. At the end of the second week she has $30 in her account. At the end of the third week she has $45 in her account. How much will she have in her bank account at the end of the ninth week?

See Problem 4.

 **Apply**

Find the 17th term of each sequence.

26. $a_{16} = 18, d = 5$ **27.** $a_{16} = 21, d = -3$ **28.** $a_{18} = -5, d = 12$

29. $a_{18} = 32, d = -4$ **30.** $a_{16} = \frac{1}{5}, d = \frac{1}{2}$ **31.** $a_{18} = -9, d = -11$

32. Think About a Plan The arithmetic mean of the monthly salaries of two employees is $3210. One employee earns $3470 per month. What is the monthly salary of the other employee?
  - What is the given information and what is the unknown?
  - What equation can you use to find the other monthly salary?

33. Error Analysis A student claims that the next term of the arithmetic sequence 0, 2, 4, . . . is 8. Explain and correct the student's error.

Find the arithmetic mean a_n of the given terms.

34. $a_{n-1} = 7, a_{n+1} = 1$ **35.** $a_{n-1} = 100, a_{n+1} = 140$ **36.** $a_{n-1} = 4, a_{n+1} = -3$

37. $a_{n-1} = 0.3, a_{n+1} = 1.9$ **38.** $a_{n-1} = r, a_{n+1} = s$ **39.** $a_{n-1} = -2x, a_{n+1} = 2x$

40. a. Graphing Calculator Use your calculator to generate an arithmetic sequence with a common difference of -7. How could you use a calculator to find the 6th term? The 8th term? The 20th term?

     b. Reasoning Explain how your answer to part (a) relates to the explicit formula $a_n = a + (n-1)d$.

Write an explicit and a recursive formula for each sequence.

41. 2, 4, 6, 8, 10, ...   **42.** 0, 6, 12, 18, 24, ...   **43.** $-5, -4, -3, -2, -1, \ldots$

44. $-4, -8, -12, -16, -20, \ldots$ **45.** $-5, -3.5, -2, -0.5, 1, \ldots$ **46.** $-32, -20, -8, 4, 16, \ldots$

47. $1, 1\frac{1}{3}, 1\frac{2}{3}, 2, \ldots$ **48.** $0, \frac{1}{8}, \frac{1}{4}, \frac{3}{8}, \ldots$ **49.** $27, 15, 3, -9, -21, \ldots$

50. Reasoning What information do you need to find a term of a sequence using an explicit formula?

51. Writing Describe some advantages and some disadvantages of a recursive formula and an explicit formula. When is it appropriate to use each formula?

52. Transportation Suppose a trolley stops at a certain intersection every 14 min. The first trolley of the day gets to the stop at 6:43 A.M. How long do you have to wait for a trolley if you get to the stop at 8:15 A.M.? At 3:20 P.M.?

Find the missing terms of each arithmetic sequence. (*Hint:* The arithmetic mean of the first and fifth terms is the third term.)

53. $2, a_2, a_3, a_4, -22, \ldots$ **54.** $10, a_2, a_3, a_4, -11.6, \ldots$ **55.** $1, a_2, a_3, a_4, -35, \ldots$

56. $\ldots \frac{13}{5}, a_6, a_7, a_8, \frac{37}{5}, \ldots$ **57.** $17, a_2, a_3, a_4, 17, \ldots$ **58.** $660, a_2, a_3, a_4, 744, \ldots$

59. $\ldots -17, a_4, a_5, a_6, 1, \ldots$ **60.** $\ldots a + 1, a_3, a_4, a_5, a + 17, \ldots$

61. Income The arithmetic mean of the monthly salaries of two people is $4475. One person earns $3895 per month. What is the monthly salary of the other person?

62. Reasoning Suppose you turn the water on in an empty bathtub with vertical sides. After 20 s, the water has reached a level of 1.15 in. You then leave the room. You want to turn the water off when the level in the bathtub is 8.5 in. How many minutes later should you return? (*Hint:* Begin by identifying two terms of an arithmetic sequence.)

 **Challenge**

63. In an arithmetic sequence with $a_1 = 4$ and $d = 9$, which term is 184?

64. In an arithmetic sequence with $a_1 = 2$ and $d = -2$, which term is -82?

65. The arithmetic mean of two terms in an arithmetic sequence is 42. One term is 30. Find the other term.

66. The arithmetic mean of two terms in an arithmetic sequence is -6. One term is -20. Find the other term.

Given two terms of each arithmetic sequence, find a_1 and d.

67. $a_3 = 5$ and $a_5 = 11$ **68.** $a_4 = 8$ and $a_7 = 20$ **69.** $a_3 = 32$ and $a_7 = -8$

70. $a_{10} = 17$ and $a_{14} = 34$ **71.** $a_4 = -34.5$ and $a_5 = -12.5$ **72.** $a_4 = -2.4$ and $a_6 = 2$

Find the indicated term of each arithmetic sequence.

73. $a_1 = k$, $d = k + 4$; a_9 **74.** $a_1 = k + 7$, $d = 2k - 5$; a_{11}

Standardized Test Prep

SAT/ACT

75. The equation $X(t) = t^4 - 5t^2 + 6$ gives the position of a comet relative to a fixed point, measured in millions of miles, at time t, measured in days. Solve the equation $X(t) = 0$. At what times is the position zero?

  Ⓐ 2, 3   Ⓒ ± 2, ± 3

  Ⓑ -2, -3 Ⓓ $\pm\sqrt{2}$, $\pm\sqrt{3}$

76. Simplify $\dfrac{3 - \frac{1}{x}}{\frac{1}{2x} - 5}$.

  Ⓕ $\dfrac{6x - 2}{1 - 10x}$ Ⓗ $\dfrac{4}{1 - 10x}$

  Ⓖ $\dfrac{3x - 1}{1 - 10x}$ Ⓘ $\dfrac{3x - 1}{1 - 5x}$

Extended Response

77. What are all the solutions of $\dfrac{3}{x^2 - 1} + \dfrac{4x}{x + 1} = \dfrac{1.5}{x - 1}$? Show your work.

Mixed Review

Determine whether each formula is *explicit* or *recursive*. Then find the first five terms of each sequence.   ◀ See Lesson 9-1.

78. $a_1 = -2$, $a_n = a_{n-1} - 5$ **79.** $a_n = 3n(n + 1)$

80. $a_n = n^2 - 1$ **81.** $a_1 = -121$, $a_n = a_{n-1} + 13$

Write an equation in point-slope form for each pair of points.   ◀ See Lesson 2-4.

82. $(0, 3)$ and $(3, 11)$ **83.** $(4, 6)$ and $(10, 30)$ **84.** $(1, 10)$ and $(5, 42)$

85. Geometry The formula for volume V of a sphere with radius r is $V = \frac{4}{3}\pi r^3$. Find the radius of a sphere as a function of its volume. Rationalize the denominator.   ◀ See Lesson 6-2.

Get Ready!   To prepare for Lesson 9-3, do Exercises 86–88.

Find the next term in each sequence.   ◀ See Lesson 9-1.

86. 2, 4, 8, 16, . . .   **87.** 1, 5, 25, 125, . . .   **88.** $-1, -3, -9, -27, \ldots$

The Fibonacci Sequence

© **Common Core State Standards**

F-IF.A.3 Recognize that sequences are functions, sometimes defined recursively, whose domain is a subset of the integers.

MP 7

One famous mathematical sequence is the Fibonacci sequence. You can find each term of the sequence using addition, but the sequence is not arithmetic.

Example

The recursive formula for the Fibonacci sequence is $F_n = F_{n-2} + F_{n-1}$, with $F_1 = 1$ and $F_2 = 1$. Using the formula, what are the first five terms of the sequence?

$F_1 = 1$
$F_2 = 1$
$F_3 = F_1 + F_2 = 1 + 1 = 2$
$F_4 = F_2 + F_3 = 1 + 2 = 3$
$F_5 = F_3 + F_4 = 2 + 3 = 5$

The first five terms of the Fibonacci sequence are 1, 1, 2, 3, 5.

Exercises

1. **Nature** The numbers of the Fibonacci sequence are often found in other areas, especially nature. Which term of the Fibonacci sequence does each picture represent?

 a.    b.    c.   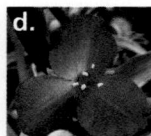 d.

2. Find "diagonals" in Pascal's triangle at the right by starting with the first 1 in each row and moving one row up and one number to the right. For example, the diagonal starting in the fifth row is 1, 3, 1. The diagonal starting in the sixth row is 1, 4, 3. For each diagonal, write the sum of its entries. What pattern do the sums form?

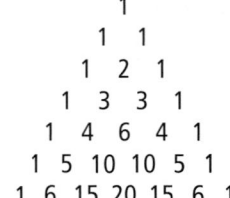

```
          1
        1   1
      1   2   1
    1   3   3   1
  1   4   6   4   1
1   5  10  10   5   1
1  6  15  20  15   6   1
```

© 3. **a.** Generate the first ten terms of the Fibonacci sequence.
   b. Find the sum of the first ten terms of the Fibonacci sequence. Divide the sum by 11. What do you notice?
   c. Open-Ended Choose two numbers other than 1 and 1. Generate a Fibonacci-like sequence from them. Write the first ten terms of your sequence, find the sum, and divide the sum by 11. What do you notice?
   d. Make a Conjecture What is the sum of the first ten terms of any Fibonacci-like sequence?

4. **a.** Study the pattern at the right. Write the next line.
   b. Without calculating, use the pattern to predict the sum of the squares of the first ten terms of the Fibonacci sequence.
   c. Verify the prediction you made in part (b).

$$1^2 + 1^2 = \ \ 2 = 1 \cdot 2$$
$$1^2 + 1^2 + 2^2 = \ \ 6 = 2 \cdot 3$$
$$1^2 + 1^2 + 2^2 + 3^2 = 15 = 3 \cdot 5$$
$$1^2 + 1^2 + 2^2 + 3^2 + 5^2 = 40 = 5 \cdot 8$$

Do you know HOW?

Find the first five terms of each sequence.

1. $a_n = 3n + 1$

2. $a_n = -2n - 1$

3. $a_n = n^2 + 2n$

4. $a_n = 3a_{n-1}$, where $a_1 = 2$

5. $a_n = 5 - a_{n-1}$, where $a_1 = 1$

6. $a_n = a_{n-1} + 2n$, where $a_1 = 1$

Write a recursive definition for each sequence.

7. $2, -4, 8, -16, \ldots$

8. $1, 4, 7, 10, \ldots$

9. $4, 2, 5, 1, 6, \ldots$

Write an explicit formula for each sequence.

10. $2, 4, 8, 16, \ldots$

11. $5, 2, -1, -4, \ldots$

12. $2, 5, 10, 17, \ldots$

Find the ninth and tenth terms of each arithmetic sequence.

13. $1, 8, 15, 22, \ldots$

14. $4, 10, 16, 22, \ldots$

15. $6, 3, 0, -3, \ldots$

Determine whether each sequence is arithmetic. If so, identify the common difference.

16. $1, 3, 9, 27, \ldots$

17. $11, 22, 33, 44, \ldots$

18. $1, -1, -3, -5, -7, \ldots$

19. $0, 2, 5, 9, 14, \ldots$

Find the missing term of each arithmetic sequence.

20. $\ldots, 3, \blacksquare, 17, \ldots$

21. $\ldots, 25, \blacksquare, -15, \ldots$

22. $\ldots, -3, \blacksquare, 8, \ldots$

23. $\ldots, 66, \blacksquare, 48, \ldots$

Find the missing terms of each arithmetic sequence.

24. $4, a_2, a_3, a_4, 32, \ldots$

25. $10, a_2, a_3, a_4, -20, \ldots$

26. $5, a_2, a_3, a_4, 35, \ldots$

Do you UNDERSTAND?

27. **Open-Ended** Write the first four terms of an arithmetic sequence with a common difference of 3 and a third term of 10. Then write both a recursive definition and an explicit formula for this sequence.

28. **Investments** You invested money in a fund and each month you receive a payment for your investment. Over the first four months, you received $50, $52, $55, and $59. If this pattern continues, how much will you receive in the tenth month?
    a. Write a formula to describe this sequence.
    b. Identify your formula as explicit or recursive.
    c. Writing Explain the difference between an explicit formula and a recursive formula. Use your formula from part (a) as part of your explanation.

29. **Open-Ended** Write the first five terms of a sequence that is not an arithmetic sequence. Then give both an explicit and recursive formula to describe this sequence.

30. **Sports** A tennis club charges players a $20 court fee plus a $10 hourly charge with a 5-hour maximum. A posted list of the total charges for 1, 2, 3, 4, or 5 hours forms an arithmetic sequence. What is the first term and what is the common difference?

9-3

Geometric Sequences

© **Common Core State Standards**

Prepares for A-SSE.B.4 Derive the formula for the sum of a geometric series (when the common ratio is not 1), and use the formula to solve problems.

MP 1, MP 2, MP 3, MP 4, MP 6

Objective To define, identify, and apply geometric sequences

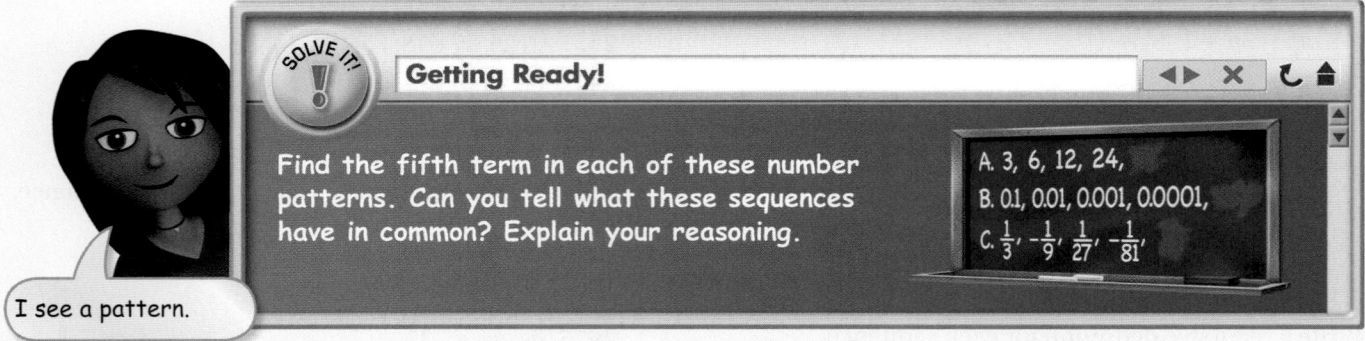

SOLVE IT!

Getting Ready!

Find the fifth term in each of these number patterns. Can you tell what these sequences have in common? Explain your reasoning.

A. 3, 6, 12, 24,

B. 0.1, 0.01, 0.001, 0.0001,

C. $\frac{1}{3}, -\frac{1}{9}, \frac{1}{27}, -\frac{1}{81}$,

I see a pattern.

© **MATHEMATICAL PRACTICES** You build a *geometric sequence* by multiplying each term by a constant.

Essential Understanding In a *geometric sequence*, the ratio of any term to its preceding term is a constant value.

 **Lesson Vocabulary**
• geometric sequence
• common ratio
• geometric mean

take note

Key Concept   Geometric Sequence

A **geometric sequence** with a starting value a and a **common ratio** r is a sequence of the form

$$a, ar, ar^2, ar^3, \ldots$$

A recursive definition for the sequence has two parts:

$a_1 = a$ initial condition
$a_n = a_{n-1} \cdot r$, for $n > 1$ recursive formula

An explicit definition for this sequence is a single formula:

$a_n = a_1 \cdot r^{n-1}$, for $n \geq 1$

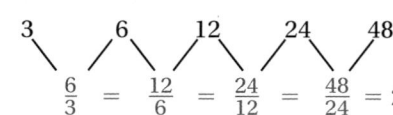 **Problem 1**   **Identifying Geometric Sequences**

Think

How do I find the ratios between consecutive terms?
Divide the second term by the first term, then the third term by the second term, and so on.

Is the sequence geometric? If it is, what are a_1 and r?

Ⓐ 3, 6, 12, 24, 48, . . .

Find the ratios between consecutive terms.

3   6   12   24   48

$$\frac{6}{3} = \frac{12}{6} = \frac{24}{12} = \frac{48}{24} = 2$$

The common ratio is 2. The sequence is geometric with $a_1 = 3$ and $r = 2$.

B 3, 6, 9, 12, 15, . . .

Find the ratio between consecutive terms.

$$3 \quad 6 \quad 9 \quad 12 \quad 15$$

$$\frac{6}{3} \neq \frac{9}{6} \neq \frac{12}{9} \neq \frac{15}{12}$$

The ratios are different. With no common ratio, the sequence is not geometric.

C $3^5, 3^{10}, 3^{15}, 3^{20}, \ldots$

Use the properties of exponents to simplify the ratios of successive terms.

$$3^5 \quad 3^{10} \quad 3^{15} \quad 3^{20}$$

$$\frac{3^{10}}{3^5} = \frac{3^{15}}{3^{10}} = \frac{3^{20}}{3^{15}} = 3^5$$

The common ratio is 3^5. The sequence is geometric with $a_1 = 3^5$ and $r = 3^5$.

Got It? **1.** Is the sequence geometric? If it is, what are a_1 and r?

    a. 2, 4, 8, 16, . . .   **b.** 1, 5, 9, 13, 17, . . .   **c.** $2^3, 2^7, 2^{11}, 2^{15}, \ldots$

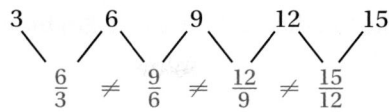 **Problem 2** **Analyzing Geometric Sequences**

What are the indicated terms of the geometric sequence?

A the 10th term of the geometric sequence 4, 12, 36, . . .

The first term a_1 is 4. The common ratio r is $12 \div 4 = 3$.

    $a_n = a_1 r^{n-1}$ Use the explicit formula.

    $a_{10} = 4 \cdot 3^{10-1}$ Substitute 10 for n, 4 for a_1, and 3 for r.

    $a_{10} = 78,732$ Simplify.

The 10th term is 78,732.

Plan

What do you need to find the second term given the first term?
You need the common ratio.

B the second and third terms of the geometric sequence 2, ■, ■, −54, . . .

The first term a_1 is 2. The fourth term a_4 is −54.

    $a_n = a_1 r^{n-1}$ Use the explicit formula.

    $a_4 = 2r^{4-1}$ Substitute 2 for a_1 and 4 for n.

    $-54 = 2r^3$ Substitute −54 for a_4. Simplify.

    $-27 = r^3$ Solve for r.

    $-3 = r$

The common ratio is −3. Begin with 2 and multiply by −3.

    2, −6, 18, −54, . . .

The second and third terms are −6 and 18.

Got It? **2.** What is the 2nd term of the geometric sequence 3, ■, 12, . . . ?

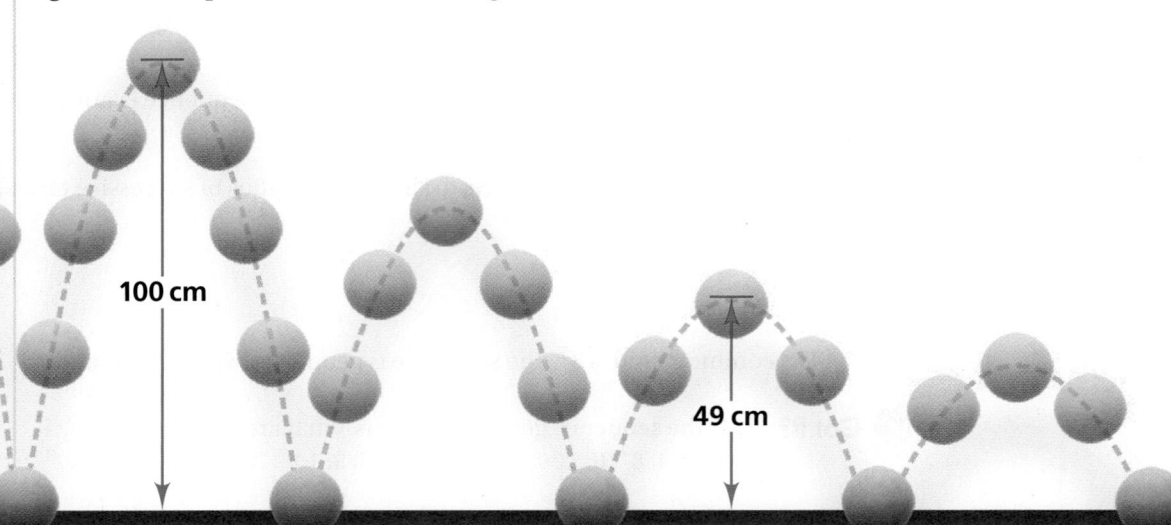

Problem 3 Using a Geometric Sequence STEM

Physics When a ball bounces, the heights of consecutive bounces form a geometric sequence. What are the heights of the 4th and 5th bounces?

100 cm

49 cm

Think

The heights of the first and third bounces are given in the picture.

Use the explicit formula to relate a_1 to a_3, and to find r.

Solve for r. (r must be positive since the bounces are above the floor.)

To find a_4 and a_5, build the sequence recursively, starting from a_3.

Write the answer.

Write

$a_1 = 100$

$a_3 = 49$

$a_n = a_1 r^{n-1}$

$a_3 = a_1 r^{3-1}$

$49 = 100 r^2$

$100 r^2 = 49$

$r = \sqrt{\dfrac{49}{100}} = \dfrac{7}{10}$

$a_n = a_{n-1} \cdot r$

$a_4 = a_3 \cdot r = 49 \cdot \dfrac{7}{10} = 34.3$

$a_5 = a_4 \cdot r = 34.3 \cdot \dfrac{7}{10} \approx 24$

The heights are 34.3 cm and 24 cm.

Got It? 3. a. Reasoning To find the height of the 10th bounce, would you use the recursive or the explicit formula? Explain.

   b. What are the heights of the 6th and 10th bounces?

In a geometric sequence, the square of the middle term of any three consecutive terms is equal to the product of the other two terms. For example, examine the sequence $2, -6, 18, -54, \ldots$.

$$(-6)^2 = 2 \cdot 18 = 36$$
$$2, -6, 18, -54, \ldots$$
$$18^2 = (-6)(-54) = 324$$

In an arithmetic sequence, recall that the middle term of any three consecutive terms is the arithmetic mean of the other two terms.

The **geometric mean** of two positive numbers x and y is $\sqrt{xy}$.

Note that the geometric mean is positive by definition. While there are two possible values for the missing term in the geometric sequence $3, \blacksquare, 12, \ldots$, there is only one geometric mean. The geometric mean is one possible value to fill in the geometric sequence. The opposite of the geometric mean is the other.

Problem 4 Using the Geometric Mean

Multiple Choice What are the possible values of the missing term of the geometric sequence?

$48, \blacksquare, 3, \ldots$

Ⓐ ± 4 Ⓑ ± 9 Ⓒ ± 12 Ⓓ ± 20

Find the geometric mean of 48 and 3.

$$\sqrt{48 \cdot 3} = \sqrt{144}$$
$$= 12$$

Think

Why would this question ask for "possible values" rather than "the value"?

The geometric mean and its opposite are both possible values.

The possible values for the missing term are ± 12. The correct answer choice is C.

 Got It? **4.** The 9th and 11th terms of a geometric sequence are 45 and 80. What are possible values for the 10th term?

 Lesson Check

Do you know HOW?

Determine whether each sequence is geometric. If so, find the common ratio.

1. $5, 10, 15, \ldots$

2. $10, 20, 40, \ldots$

Find the seventh term of each geometric sequence.

3. $1, -3, 9, \ldots$

4. $100, 20, 4, \ldots$

Do you UNDERSTAND? Ⓒ MATHEMATICAL PRACTICES

Ⓒ **5. Error Analysis** To find the third term of the geometric sequence $5, 10, \blacksquare, \blacksquare, 80$, your friend says that there are two possible answers—the geometric mean of 5 and 80, and its opposite. Explain your friend's error.

Ⓒ **6. Compare and Contrast** How is finding a missing term of a geometric sequence using the geometric mean similar to finding a missing term of an arithmetic sequence using the arithmetic mean? How is it different?

Practice and Problem-Solving Exercises

 **MATHEMATICAL PRACTICES**

 **Practice**

Determine whether each sequence is geometric. If so, find the common ratio. **See Problem 1.**

7. $1, 2, 4, 8, \ldots$

8. $1, 2, 3, 4, \ldots$

9. $1, -2, 4, -8, \ldots$

10. $-1, 1, -1, 1, \ldots$

11. $10, 4, 1.6, 0.64, \ldots$

12. $7, 0.7, 0.07, 0.007, \ldots$

13. $18, -6, 2, -\frac{2}{3}, \ldots$

14. $1, \frac{1}{2}, \frac{1}{3}, \frac{1}{4}, \ldots$

15. $10, 15, 22.5, 33.75, \ldots$

16. $2, -10, 50, -250, \ldots$

17. $-1, -6, -36, -216, \ldots$

18. $\frac{1}{2}, \frac{1}{4}, \frac{1}{6}, \frac{1}{8}, \ldots$

Find the eighth term of each geometric sequence. **See Problem 2.**

19. $3, 9, 27, \ldots$

20. $-3, 6, -12, \ldots$

21. $10, 5, 2.5, \ldots$

22. $\frac{2}{3}, \frac{4}{9}, \frac{8}{27}, \ldots$

23. $24, -6, \frac{3}{2}, \ldots$

24. $-30, 7.5, -1.875, \ldots$

STEM **25. Science** When radioactive substances decay, the amount remaining will form a **See Problem 3.** geometric sequence when measured over constant intervals of time. The table shows the amount of Np-240, a radioactive isotope of Neptunium, initially and after 2 hours. What are the amounts left after 1 hour, 3 hours, and 4 hours?

Hours Elapsed	0	1	2	3	4
Grams of Np-240	1244	■	346	■	■

Find the missing term of each geometric sequence. It could be the geometric mean or its opposite.  **See Problem 4.**

26. $5, \blacksquare, 911.25, \ldots$

27. $9180, \blacksquare, 255, \ldots$

28. $\frac{2}{5}, \blacksquare, \frac{8}{45}, \ldots$

29. $3, \blacksquare, 0.75, \ldots$

30. $5, \blacksquare, 2.8125, \ldots$

31. $12, \blacksquare, 3, \ldots$

 **Apply**

Write an explicit formula for each sequence. Then generate the first five terms.

32. $a_1 = 1, r = 0.5$

33. $a_1 = 100, r = -20$

34. $a_1 = 7, r = 1$

35. $a_1 = 1024, r = 0.5$

36. $a_1 = 4, r = 0.1$

37. $a_1 = 10, r = -1$

Identify each sequence as *arithmetic, geometric,* or *neither*. Then find the next two terms.

38. $45, 90, 180, 360, \ldots$

39. $25, 50, 75, 100, \ldots$

40. $3, -3, 3, -3, \ldots$

41. $-5, 10, -20, 40, \ldots$

42. $2, 1, 0.5, 0.25, \ldots$

43. $1, 4, 9, 16, \ldots$

Find the missing terms of each geometric sequence. (*Hint:* The geometric mean of the first and fifth terms is the third term. Some terms might be negative.)

44. $972, \blacksquare, \blacksquare, \blacksquare, 12, \ldots$

45. $2.5, \blacksquare, \blacksquare, \blacksquare, 202.5, \ldots$

46. $12.5, \blacksquare, \blacksquare, \blacksquare, 5.12, \ldots$

47. $-4, \blacksquare, \blacksquare, \blacksquare, -30\frac{3}{8}, \ldots$

48. Think About a Plan Suppose a balloon is filled with 5000 cm³ of helium. It then loses one fourth of its helium each day. How much helium will be left in the balloon at the start of the tenth day?
- How can you write a sequence of numbers to represent this situation?
- Is the sequence arithmetic, geometric, or neither?
- How can you write a formula for this sequence?

49. Athletics During your first week of training for a marathon, you run a total of 10 miles. You increase the distance you run each week by twenty percent. How many miles do you run during your twelfth week of training?

50. a. Open-Ended Choose two positive numbers. Find their geometric mean.
    b. Find the common ratio for a geometric sequence that includes the terms from part (a) as its first three terms.
    c. Find the 9th term of the geometric sequence from part (b).
    d. Find the geometric mean of the term from part (c) and the first term of your sequence. What term of the sequence have you just found?

For the geometric sequence 3, 12, 48, 192, . . . , find the indicated term.

51. 5th term   **52.** 17th term   **53.** 20th term   **54.** nth term

Find the 10th term of each geometric sequence.

55. $a_9 = 8, r = \frac{1}{2}$ **56.** $a_9 = -5, r = -\frac{1}{2}$

57. $a_{11} = -5, r = -\frac{1}{2}$ **58.** $a_9 = -\frac{1}{3}, r = \frac{1}{2}$

59. Writing Describe the similarities and differences between a common difference and a common ratio.

Challenge

60. Banking Copy and complete the table below. Use the geometric mean. Assume compound interest is earned and no withdrawals are made.

Period 1	Period 2	Period 3
$140.00		$145.64
$600.00		$627.49
$25.00		$32.76
$57.50		$60.37
$100.00		$111.98
$250.00		$276.55

Find a_1 for a geometric sequence with the given terms.

61. $a_5 = 112$ and $a_7 = 448$ **62.** $a_9 = \frac{1}{2}$ and $a_{12} = \frac{1}{16}$

63. What is the common ratio in the geometric sequence 4, 10, 25, 62.5, . . . ?

   Ⓐ 0.4   Ⓒ 15

   Ⓑ 2.5   Ⓓ 25

64. The first term of a geometric sequence is 1 and its common ratio is 6. What is the sixth term?

   Ⓕ 31   Ⓗ 7776

   Ⓖ 3176   Ⓘ 46,656

65. Determine by inspection the end behavior of the graph of $y = -2x^3 + 5x - 4$.

   Ⓐ falls to the left, falls to the right: ($\swarrow$, $\searrow$)

   Ⓑ falls to the left, rises to the right: ($\swarrow$, $\nearrow$)

   Ⓒ rises to the left, falls to the right: ($\nwarrow$, $\searrow$)

   Ⓓ rises to the left, rises to the right: ($\nwarrow$, $\nearrow$)

66. What are the asymptotes of the graph of $y = \frac{10}{x-5}$?

   Ⓕ $x = 0, y = 5$ Ⓗ $x = 5, y = 10$

   Ⓖ $x = 5, y = 0$ Ⓘ $x = 10, y = 5$

67. What are the points of discontinuity of $y = \frac{x(2x-1)(x+1)}{(x+5)(x+1)}$?

Apply What You've Learned

MATHEMATICAL
PRACTICES
MP 4, MP 7

Look back at the information on page 563 about Matthew's toy car collection.

a. Explain why a sequence in which the terms increase by the same percent from one term to the next is a geometric sequence.

b. The table from page 563 is shown again below. Consider the values in the second column as a sequence. Find the common ratio and explain what it means.

Year	Value of Toy Car
2009	$96.17
2010	$100.02
2011	$104.02
2012	$108.18
2013	$112.51

c. Let a_1 be the value of the toy car in 1994. What term of the sequence is $96.17?

d. Find the value of the toy car in 1994.

e. Write recursive and explicit formulas for the sequence of car values.

Arithmetic Series

Common Core State Standards

Extends F-IF.A.3 Recognize that sequences are functions, sometimes defined recursively, whose domain is a subset of the integers.

MP 1, MP 2, MP 3, MP 4

Objective To define arithmetic series and find their sums

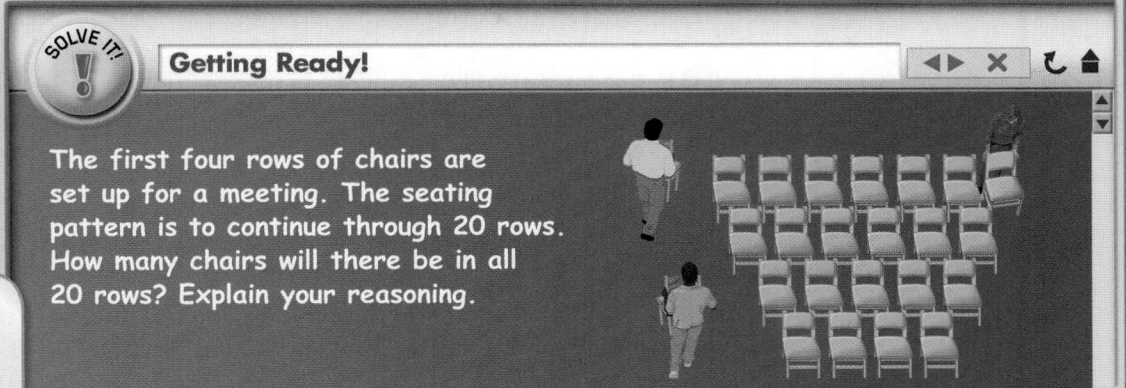

SOLVE IT!

Getting Ready!

The first four rows of chairs are set up for a meeting. The seating pattern is to continue through 20 rows. How many chairs will there be in all 20 rows? Explain your reasoning.

Be sure you understand the problem. How many chairs are in the 20th row?

MATHEMATICAL PRACTICES Just as you found formulas for terms of sequences, you can find formulas for the sums of the terms of sequences.

Lesson Vocabulary
• series
• finite series
• infinite series
• arithmetic series
• limits

Essential Understanding When you know two terms and the number of terms in a finite arithmetic sequence, you can find the sum of the terms.

A **series** is the indicated sum of the terms of a sequence. A **finite series**, like a finite sequence, has a first term and a last term, while an **infinite series** continues without end.

Finite sequence

6, 9, 12, 15, 18

Infinite sequence

3, 7, 11, 15, . . .

Finite series

6 + 9 + 12 + 15 + 18 (The sum is 60.)

Infinite series

3 + 7 + 11 + 15 + . . .

An **arithmetic series** is a series whose terms form an arithmetic sequence (as shown above). When a series has a finite number of terms, you can use a formula involving the first and last term to evaluate the sum.

take note

Property   Sum of a Finite Arithmetic Series

The sum S_n of a finite arithmetic series $a_1 + a_2 + a_3 + \cdots + a_n$ is

$$S_n = \frac{n}{2}(a_1 + a_n)$$

where a_1 is the first term, a_n is the nth term, and n is the number of terms.

Problem 1 Finding the Sum of a Finite Arithmetic Series

What is the sum of the even integers from 2 to 100?

The series $2 + 4 + 6 + \cdots + 100$ is arithmetic with first term 2, last (and 50th) term 100, and common difference 2. The sum is

$$S_{50} = \frac{50}{2}(2 + 100) = 25(102) = 2550.$$

 Got It? 1. a. What is the sum of the finite arithmetic series
$$4 + 9 + 14 + 19 + 24 + \cdots + 99?$$

 b. Reasoning Will the sum of a sequence of even numbers always be an even number? Will the sum of a sequence of odd numbers always be an odd number? Explain.

Problem 2 Using the Sum of a Finite Arithmetic Series

Bonus A company pays a $10,000 bonus to salespeople at the end of their first 50 weeks if they make 10 sales in their first week, and then improve their sales numbers by two each week thereafter. One salesperson qualified for the bonus with the minimum possible number of sales. How many sales did the salesperson make in week 50? In all 50 weeks?

Think

The first week sales were 10.
Sales increased by 2 each week.

The sequence is arithmetic. Use the explicit formula to find the sales in week 50.
Substitute 50 for n, 10 for a_1, and 2 for d. Then simplify.

Use the formula for S_n to find the total sales for all 50 weeks.
Substitute 50 for n, 10 for a_1, and 108 for a_{50}. Then simplify.

Write the answers.

Write

$a_1 = 10$

$d = 2$

$a_n = a_1 + (n - 1)d$
$a_{50} = 10 + (50 - 1)2$
$\quad\quad = 10 + (49)2$
$\quad\quad = 10 + 98 = 108$

$S_n = \frac{n}{2}(a_1 + a_n)$
$S_{50} = \frac{50}{2}(10 + 108)$
$\quad\quad = 25(118) = 2950$

The salesperson made 108 sales in week 50 and 2950 sales in all 50 weeks.

 Got It? 2. The company in Problem 2 has an alternative bonus plan. It pays a $5000 bonus if a new salesperson makes 10 sales in the first week and then improves by *one* sale per week each week thereafter. One salesperson qualified for this bonus with the minimum number of sales. How many sales did the salesperson make in week 50? In all 50 weeks?

You can use the Greek capital letter sigma, Σ, to indicate a sum. With it, you use *limits* to indicate how many terms you are adding. **Limits** are the least and greatest values of n in the series. You write the limits below and above the Σ to indicate the first and last terms of the series.

For example, you can write the series
$3^2 + 4^2 + 5^2 + \cdots + 108^2$ as $\sum_{n=3}^{108} n^2$.

Upper limit: the series ends with $n = 108$.

$$\sum_{n=3}^{108} n^2$$

The explicit formula for each term is n^2.

Lower limit: the series begins with $n = 3$.

For an infinite series, summation notation shows ∞ as the upper limit.

To find the number of terms in a series written in Σ form, subtract the lower limit from the upper limit and add 1.

The number of terms in the series above is $108 - 3 + 1 = 106$.

Problem 3 **Writing a Series in Summation Notation**

Multiple Choice What is summation notation for the series?
$7 + 11 + 15 + \cdots + 203 + 207$

(A) $\displaystyle\sum_{n=1}^{51}(4n + 3)$ (B) $\displaystyle\sum_{n=1}^{50}(4n + 3)$ (C) $\displaystyle\sum_{n=1}^{50}(7n)$ (D) $\displaystyle\sum_{n=1}^{51}(7n)$

Plan

What do you need to write a series in summation notation?
You need an explicit formula for the nth term and the lower and upper limits.

The sequence 7, 11, 15, $\ldots$, 203, 207 is arithmetic with first term $a = 7$ and common difference $d = 4$.

$a_n = a_1 + (n - 1)d$ Use the explicit formula for an arithmetic sequence.

$a_n = 7 + (n - 1)4$ Substitute 7 for a_1, and 4 for d.

$\quad = 4n + 3$ Simplify.

An explicit formula for the nth term is $4n + 3$.

$a_n = 4n + 3$ Use the explicit formula to find the value of n for the term 207.

$207 = 4n + 3$ Substitute 207 for a_n.

$204 = 4n$ Solve for n.

$51 = n$

The upper limit is 51. You can write the series as $\displaystyle\sum_{n=1}^{51}(4n + 3)$. The correct answer is A.

Got It? **3.** What is summation notation for the series?
     a. $-5 + 2 + 9 + 16 + \cdots + 261 + 268$
     b. $500 + 490 + 480 + \cdots + 20 + 10$

take note

Key Concept **Summation Notation and Linear Functions**

If the explicit formula for the nth term in summation notation is a *linear* function of n, then the series is arithmetic. The slope of the linear function is the common difference between terms of the series.

Problem 4 Finding the Sum of a Series

What is the sum of the series written in summation notation?

A $\sum\limits_{n=1}^{70} (5n + 3)$

Since the formula is a linear function of n, the series is arithmetic.

$$a_1 = 5(1) + 3 = 8 \qquad \text{Find } a_1.$$

$$a_{70} = 5(70) + 3 = 353 \qquad \text{Find } a_{70}.$$

$$S_n = \frac{n}{2}(a_1 + a_n) \qquad \text{Use the formula for the sum of a finite arithmetic series.}$$

$$S_{70} = \frac{70}{2}(8 + 353) = 12{,}635 \qquad \text{There are 70 terms, so } n = 70.$$

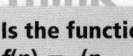

Is the function
$f(n) = (n - 1)^2$
linear?
No; the function
is quadratic.

B $\sum\limits_{n=1}^{7} (n - 1)^2$

This series is not arithmetic. However, you can evaluate by adding the terms.

$$\sum\limits_{n=1}^{7} (n - 1)^2$$

$$= (1 - 1)^2 + (2 - 1)^2 + (3 - 1)^2 + (4 - 1)^2 + (5 - 1)^2 + (6 - 1)^2 + (7 - 1)^2$$

$$= 0 + 1 + 4 + 9 + 16 + 25 + 36 = 91$$

 Got It? **4.** What is the sum of each finite series?

a. $\sum\limits_{n=1}^{40} (3n - 8)$ **b.** $\sum\limits_{n=1}^{4} n^3$ **c.** $\sum\limits_{n=0}^{100} (-1)^n$

On a graphing calculator, you can find the sum of a finite series by using commands from the **LIST** menu.

 Problem 5 Using a Graphing Calculator to Find the Sum of a Series

What is the sum of the series written in summation notation? $\sum\limits_{n=1}^{70} (5n + 3)$

Plan

**What calculator
commands do you
use to find the sum
of a series?**
Use the sum and
sequence commands.

Input the sum command.   Input the sequence command.   Input the formula, N, and the lower and upper limits.

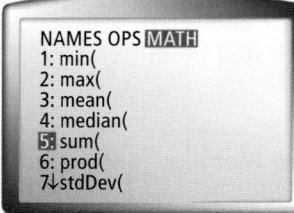

The sum is 12,635.

 Got It? **5.** Use a graphing calculator. What is $\sum\limits_{n=1}^{50} (n^2 - n)$?

Lesson Check

Do you know HOW?

Find the sum of each finite arithmetic series.

1. $4 + 7 + 10 + 13 + 16 + 19 + 22$

2. $10 + 20 + 30 + \cdots + 110 + 120$

Write each arithmetic series in summation notation.

3. $3 + 6 + 9 + 12 + 15 + 18 + 21$

4. $1 + 5 + 9 + \cdots + 41 + 45$

Do you UNDERSTAND?

5. **Vocabulary** What is the difference between an arithmetic sequence and an arithmetic series?

6. **Error Analysis** A student writes the arithmetic series $3 + 8 + 13 + \ldots + 43$ in summation notation as $\sum\limits_{n=3}^{8}(3 + 5n)$. Describe and correct the error.

7. **Reasoning** Is it possible to have more than one arithmetic series with four terms whose sum is 44? Explain.

Practice and Problem-Solving Exercises

A Practice

Find the sum of each finite arithmetic series.   ◀ See Problem 1.

8. $2 + 4 + 6 + 8$

9. $8 + 9 + 10 + \cdots + 15$

10. $5 + 6 + 7 + \cdots + 11$

11. $1 + 4 + 7 + \cdots + 31$

12. $7 + 14 + 21 + \cdots + 105$

13. $(-3) + (-6) + (-9) + \cdots + (-30)$

14. **Grades** A student has taken three math tests so far this semester. His scores for the first three tests were 75, 79, and 83.   ◀ See Problem 2.

    a. Suppose his test scores continue to improve at the same rate. What will be his grade on the sixth (and final) test?

    b. What will be his total score for all six tests?

Write each arithmetic series in summation notation.   ◀ See Problem 3.

15. $4 + 8 + 12 + 16 + 20$

16. $7 + 9 + 11 + \cdots + 21$

17. $5 + 8 + 11 + \cdots + 38$

18. $100 + 90 + 80 + \cdots + 10$

19. $(-3) + (-6) + (-9) + \cdots + (-30)$

20. $105 + 97 + 89 + \cdots + (-71)$

Find the sum of each finite series.   ◀ See Problem 4.

21. $\sum\limits_{n=1}^{5}(2n - 1)$

22. $\sum\limits_{n=1}^{10}(3n - 4)$

23. $\sum\limits_{n=1}^{8}(7 - n)$

24. $\sum\limits_{n=1}^{4} 2^n$

25. $\sum\limits_{n=1}^{9}(-1)^n \cdot 2$

26. $\sum\limits_{n=5}^{10}(20 - n)$

Use a graphing calculator to find the sum of each series.   ◀ See Problem 5.

27. $\sum\limits_{n=1}^{50}(2n - 3)$

28. $\sum\limits_{n=1}^{26}(n^2 - 3n)$

29. $\sum\limits_{n=1}^{10}(-2)^n$

30. $\sum\limits_{n=1}^{20}(n^3 - 10n^2)$

31. $\sum\limits_{n=5}^{73}(-4n + 32)$

32. $\sum\limits_{n=5}^{25}(n^2 - 14n + 32)$

 **33. Think About a Plan** A meeting room is set up with 16 rows of seats. The number of seats in a row increases by two with each successive row. The first row has 12 seats. What is the total number of seats?
- How can you find the number of seats in each row using an explicit formula?
- What is the number of seats in the 16th row?
- How can you find the sum of the seats in 16 rows?

Determine whether each list is a *sequence* or a *series* and *finite* or *infinite*.

34. $1, 2, 4, 8, 16, 32, \ldots$

35. $1, 0.5, 0.25, 0.125, 0.0625$

36. $5 + 10 + \cdots + 25$

37. $-0.5 - 0.25 - 0.125 - \ldots$

38. $\dfrac{4}{3}, \dfrac{7}{3}, \dfrac{10}{3}, \dfrac{13}{3}, \dfrac{16}{3}, \ldots$

39. $2.3 + 4.6 + 9.2 + 18.4$

Each sequence has eight terms. Evaluate each related series.

40. $\dfrac{1}{2}, \dfrac{3}{2}, \dfrac{5}{2}, \ldots, \dfrac{15}{2}$

41. $1, -1, -3, \ldots, -13$

42. $5, 13, 21, \ldots, 61$

43. $-3.5, -1.25, 1, \ldots, 12.25$

44. $1765, 1414, 1063, \ldots, -692$

45. $-13, -14.5, -16, \ldots, -23.5$

 46. Architecture In a 20-row theater, the number of seats in a row increases by three with each successive row. The first row has 18 seats.
- **a.** Write an arithmetic series to represent the number of seats in the theater.
- **b.** Find the total seating capacity of the theater.
- **c.** Front-row tickets for a concert cost $60. After every 5 rows, the ticket price goes down by $5. What is the total amount of money generated by a full house?

47. a. Grocery A supermarket displays cans in a triangle. Write an explicit formula for the sequence of the number of cans.
- **b.** Use summation notation to write the related series for a triangle with 10 cans in the bottom row.
- **c.** Suppose the triangle had 17 rows. How many cans would be in the 17th row?
- **d. Reasoning** Could the triangle have 110 cans? 140 cans? Explain.

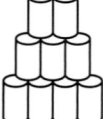

Evaluate each series to the given term.

48. $2 + 4 + 6 + 8 + \ldots$; 10th term

49. $-5 - 25 - 45 - \ldots$; 9th term

50. a. Open-Ended Write two explicit formulas for arithmetic sequences.
- **b.** Write the first five terms of each related series.
- **c.** Use summation notation to rewrite each series.
- **d.** Evaluate each series.

 **Challenge**   **Use the values of a_1 and S_n to find the value of a_n.**

51. $a_1 = 4$ and $S_{40} = 6080$; a_{40}

52. $a_1 = -6$ and $S_{50} = -5150$; a_{50}

Find a_1 for each arithmetic series.

53. $S_8 = 440$ and $d = 6$

54. $S_{30} = 240$ and $d = -2$

55. Evaluate S_{10} for the series $x + (x + y) + (x + 2y) + \dots$

56. Evaluate S_{15} for the series $3x + (3x - 2y) + (3x - 4y) + \dots$

Standardized Test Prep

SAT/ACT

57. Which expression represents the series $14 + 20 + 26 + 32 + 38 + 44 + 50$?

(A) $\displaystyle\sum_{n=2}^{8}(7n - 1)$

(C) $\displaystyle\sum_{n=3}^{8}(6n - 4)$

(B) $\displaystyle\sum_{n=3}^{9}(6n - 4)$

(D) $\displaystyle\sum_{n=8}^{14}(n + 6)$

58. What is the common ratio in the geometric sequence $\frac{9}{2}, 3, 2, \frac{4}{3}, \dots$?

(F) $\frac{3}{2}$

(G) $\frac{9}{2}$

(H) $\frac{2}{3}$

(I) $\frac{27}{2}$

59. Which expression is NOT equivalent to $\sqrt[4]{4n^2}$?

(A) $\left(4n^2\right)^{\frac{1}{4}}$

(B) $2n^{\frac{1}{2}}$

(C) $\left(2|n|\right)^{\frac{1}{2}}$

(D) $\sqrt{2|n|}$

60. The graph shows the inverse of which function?

(F) $y = 3x$

(H) $y = 3^x$

(G) $y = -3^{2x}$

(I) $y = 2^{3x}$

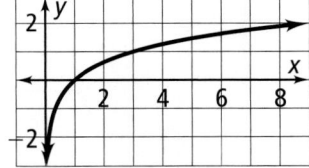

Short Response

61. Solve the equation $x^2 + 10x + 40 = 5$ by completing the square.

Mixed Review

Write an explicit formula for each geometric sequence. Then find the first three terms.

See Lesson 9-3.

62. $a_1 = 1, r = 2$

63. $a_1 = -1, r = -1$

64. $a_1 = 3, r = \frac{3}{2}$

Simplify each rational expression. State any restrictions on the variable.

See Lesson 8-4.

65. $\dfrac{x^2 + 4x + 3}{x^2 - 3x - 4}$

66. $\dfrac{c^2 - 8c + 12}{c^2 - 11c + 30}$

67. $\dfrac{3z^4 + 36z^3 + 60z^2}{3z^3 - 3z^2}$

Get Ready!   **To prepare for Lesson 9-5, do Exercises 68–70.**

Find the common ratio for each geometric sequence.

See Lesson 9-3.

68. $90, -30, 10, \dots$

69. $64, 48, 36, \dots$

70. $-9, 4.5, -2.25, \dots$

Concept Byte

For Use With Lesson 9-5

Geometry and Infinite Series

© **Common Core State Standards**

A-SSE.B.4 Derive the formula for the sum of a geometric series (when the common ratio is not 1), and use the formula to solve problems.

MP 7

You can use geometric figures to model some infinite series.

Activity 1

Geometry Draw a geometric figure to model the series.

$$\frac{1}{2} + \left(\frac{1}{2}\right)^2 + \left(\frac{1}{2}\right)^3 + \cdots + \left(\frac{1}{2}\right)^n + \cdots$$

Draw a square. Shade one half of the square. Then shade one half of the remaining unshaded region. Continue until the square is full.

So the series appears to have a sum of 1.

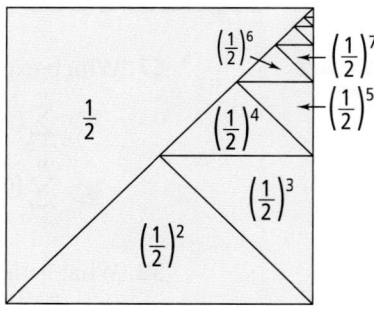

You can write an infinite series from a geometric model.

Activity 2

Geometry Write the series modeled by the trapezoids. Estimate the sum of the series. Explain your reasoning.

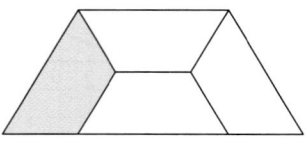 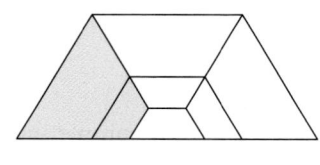 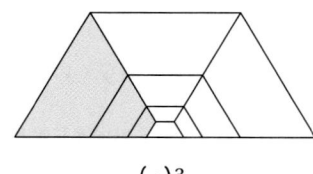

$$\frac{1}{4} \qquad + \qquad \left(\frac{1}{4}\right)^2 \qquad + \qquad \left(\frac{1}{4}\right)^3 + \cdots$$

The shaded region approaches one third of the figure.

So the series $\frac{1}{4} + \left(\frac{1}{4}\right)^2 + \left(\frac{1}{4}\right)^3 + \cdots + \left(\frac{1}{4}\right)^n + \cdots$ appears to have a sum of $\frac{1}{3}$.

Exercises

1. a. Write the series modeled by the figure at the right.
   b. Evaluate the series. Explain your reasoning.

2. Draw a figure to model the series.

$$\frac{1}{5} + \left(\frac{1}{5}\right)^2 + \left(\frac{1}{5}\right)^3 + \cdots + \left(\frac{1}{5}\right)^n + \cdots$$

© **3. Make a Conjecture** Consider the series.

$$\frac{1}{c} + \left(\frac{1}{c}\right)^2 + \left(\frac{1}{c}\right)^3 + \cdots + \left(\frac{1}{c}\right)^n + \cdots, c > 1$$

What is the sum of the series? Explain your reasoning.

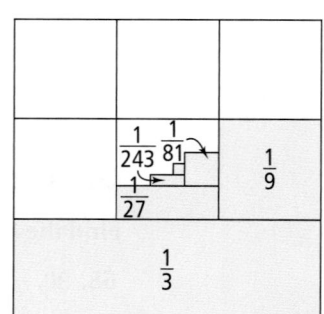

© Common Core State Standards

A-SSE.B.4 Derive the formula for the sum of a geometric series (when the common ratio is not 1), and use the formula to solve problems.

MP 1, MP 2, MP 3, MP 4, MP 5

Objective To define geometric series and find their sums

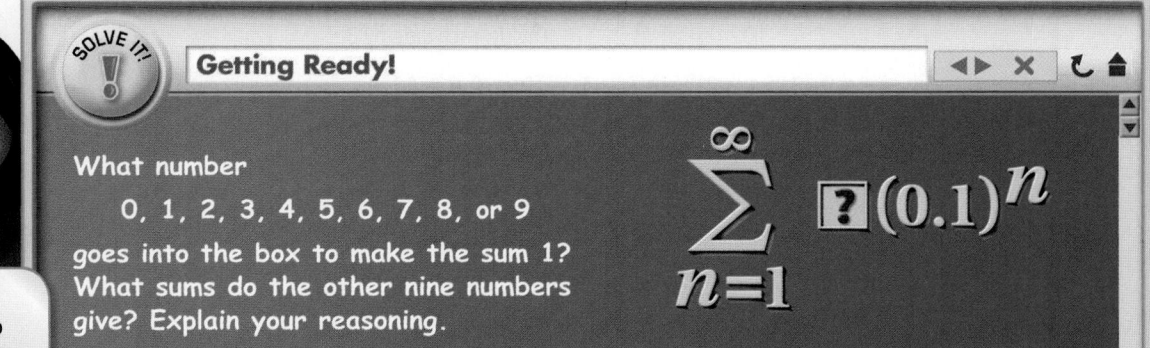

Getting Ready!

What number

0, 1, 2, 3, 4, 5, 6, 7, 8, or 9

goes into the box to make the sum 1? What sums do the other nine numbers give? Explain your reasoning.

$$\sum_{n=1}^{\infty} \boxed{?}(0.1)^n$$

The symbol ∞ means there is no upper limit on the values of n. They go on forever.

MATHEMATICAL PRACTICES

You can write any whole number that has the same digit in every place as the sum of the terms of a geometric sequence. For example,

$$4444 = 4(10)^0 + 4(10)^1 + 4(10)^2 + 4(10)^3$$

Lesson Vocabulary
• geometric series
• converge
• diverge

You can write any rational number as an infinite repeating decimal.

For example, $\frac{47}{90} = 0.5222 \ldots$

Therefore, you can write any rational number as a number plus the sum of an infinite geometric sequence.

$$0.5222 \ldots = 0.5 + 2(0.1)^2 + 2(0.1)^3 + 2(0.1)^4 + \ldots$$

Essential Understanding Just as with finite arithmetic series, you can find the sum of a finite geometric series using a formula. You need to know the first term, the number of terms, and the common ratio.

A **geometric series** is the sum of the terms of a geometric sequence.

take note

Key Concept **Sum of a Finite Geometric Series**

The sum S_n of a finite geometric series $a_1 + a_1 r + a_1 r^2 + \cdots + a_1 r^{n-1}, r \neq 1$, is

$$S_n = \frac{a_1(1 - r^n)}{1 - r}$$

where a_1 is the first term, r is the common ratio, and n is the number of terms.

Problem 1 Finding the Sums of Finite Geometric Series

What is the sum of the finite geometric series?

Plan

What do you need to find the sum?
You need the first term, the common ratio, and the number of terms in the series.

Ⓐ $3 + 6 + 12 + 24 + \cdots + 3072$

The first term is 3. The common ratio is $\frac{6}{3} = \frac{12}{6} = \frac{24}{12} = 2$. The nth term is 3072.

$$a_n = a_1 r^{n-1} \qquad \text{Use the explicit formula.}$$

$$3072 = 3 \cdot 2^{n-1} \qquad \text{Substitute 3 for } a_1, \text{ 2 for } r, \text{ and 3072 for } a_n.$$

$$1024 = 2^{n-1} \qquad \text{Divide each side by 3.}$$

1024 is 2^{10}, so $n - 1 = 10$ and $n = 11$.

$$S_n = \frac{a_1(1 - r^n)}{1 - r} \qquad \text{Use the sum formula.}$$

$$S_{11} = \frac{3(1 - 2^{11})}{1 - 2} \qquad \text{Substitute 3 for } a_1, \text{ 2 for } r, \text{ and 11 for } n.$$

$$= 6141 \qquad \text{Simplify.}$$

The sum of the series is 6141.

Think

When the lower limit on n is not 1, how can you find the number of terms?
The number of terms always equals upper limit $-$ lower limit $+1$.

Ⓑ $\displaystyle\sum_{n=0}^{20} 4\left(\frac{1}{2}\right)^n$

The first term is $a_1 = 4\left(\frac{1}{2}\right)^0 = 4$. The common ratio is $r = \frac{1}{2}$. The lower limit is 0 and the upper limit is 20, so the number of terms is $n = 21$.

$$S_n = \frac{a_1(1 - r^n)}{1 - r} \qquad \text{Use the sum formula.}$$

$$S_{21} = \frac{4\left(1 - \left(\frac{1}{2}\right)^{21}\right)}{1 - \frac{1}{2}} \qquad \text{Substitute 4 for } a_1, \frac{1}{2} \text{ for } r, \text{ and 21 for } n.$$

$$\approx 8 \qquad \text{Use a calculator.}$$

The sum of the series is approximately 8.

 Got It? **1.** What is the sum of the finite geometric series?

    a. $-15 + 30 - 60 + 120 - 240 + 480$

    b. $\displaystyle\sum_{n=1}^{10} 5 \cdot (-2)^{n-1}$

The Soldier's Reasonable Request A famous story involves a soldier who rescues his king in battle. The king grants him any prize "within reason" from the riches of the kingdom. The soldier asks for a chessboard with a single kernel of wheat on the first square, two kernels of wheat on the second square, then four, then eight, and so on for all 64 squares of the chessboard. The king decides that the request is reasonable.

See Problem 2 for the outcome.

 **Problem 2** **Using the Geometric Series Formula**

According to the story on the preceding page, how many total kernels of wheat did the soldier request?

Know	Need	Plan
The amount of wheat in the first 4 squares	The total amount of wheat	Use the sum formula to find the total amount of wheat.

Step 1 Identify the first term, common ratio, and the number of terms.

$$a_1 = 1, r = 2, n = 64$$

Step 2 Use the sum formula.

$$S_n = \frac{a_1(1 - r^n)}{1 - r}$$ Write the sum formula.

$$S_{64} = \frac{1(1 - 2^{64})}{1 - 2}$$ Substitute for a_1, r, and n.

$$= 2^{64} - 1 \approx 1.845 \times 10^{19}$$ Simplify.

There will be approximately 1.845×10^{19} kernels of wheat.

 Got It? **2.** To save money for a vacation, you set aside \$100. For each month thereafter, you plan to set aside 10% more than the previous month. How much money will you save in 12 months?

The Rest of the Story A bushel of wheat contains about a million kernels. The total US output of wheat in a recent year was just over 2.1 billion bushels. How many years of production at that level would it take the United States to produce enough wheat to satisfy the soldier's "reasonable" request?

The terms of a geometric series grow rapidly when the common ratio is greater than 1. Likewise, they diminish rapidly when the common ratio is between 0 and 1. In fact, they diminish so rapidly that an *infinite geometric series* has a finite sum.

take note

Key Concept **Infinite Geometric Series**

An infinite geometric series with first term a_1 and common ratio $|r| < 1$ has a finite sum

$$S = \frac{a_1}{1 - r}.$$

An infinite geometric series with $|r| \geq 1$ does not have a finite sum.

To say that an infinite series $a_1 + a_2 + a_3 + \ldots$, has a sum means that the *sequence of partial sums* $S_1 = a_1$, $S_2 = a_1 + a_2$, $S_3 = a_1 + a_2 + a_3$, $\ldots$, $S_n = a_1 + a_2 + \cdots + a_n$, $\ldots$ **converges** to a number S as n gets very large.

When an infinite series does not converge to a sum, the series **diverges**. An infinite geometric series with $|r| \geq 1$ diverges.

Ⓒ Problem 3 Analyzing Infinite Geometric Series

Does the series *converge* or *diverge*? If it converges, what is the sum?

Ⓐ $1 + \frac{1}{2} + \frac{1}{4} + \ldots$

Think

When does an infinite geometric series converge?
An infinite geometric series converges when the absolute value of the common ratio is less than 1.

$$r = \frac{1}{2} \div 1 = \frac{1}{2}$$

Since $|r| = \left|\frac{1}{2}\right| < 1$, the series converges.

$$S = \frac{a_1}{1-r} = \frac{1}{1 - \frac{1}{2}} = \frac{1}{\frac{1}{2}} = 2$$

Ⓑ $\displaystyle\sum_{n=0}^{\infty} \left(\frac{2}{3}\right)\left(-\frac{5}{4}\right)^n$

Since $|r| = \left|-\frac{5}{4}\right| = \frac{5}{4} > 1$, the series diverges.

Ⓒ ✓ Got It? 3. Does the infinite series *converge* or *diverge*? If it converges, what is the sum?

a. $\frac{1}{2} + \frac{3}{4} + \frac{9}{8} + \ldots$ b. $\frac{1}{3} - \frac{1}{9} + \frac{1}{27} - \frac{1}{81} + \ldots$ c. $\displaystyle\sum_{n=1}^{\infty} \left(\frac{2}{3}\right)^n$

d. **Reasoning** Does every infinite geometric series either converge or diverge? Explain.

✓ Lesson Check

Do you know HOW?

Evaluate each finite geometric series.

1. $\frac{1}{5} + \frac{1}{10} + \frac{1}{20} + \frac{1}{40} + \frac{1}{80}$

2. $9 - 6 + 4 - \frac{8}{3} + \frac{16}{9}$

Determine whether each infinite geometric series *diverges* or *converges*.

3. $1 - \frac{1}{6} + \frac{1}{36} - \frac{1}{216} + \ldots$

4. $\frac{1}{64} + \frac{1}{32} + \frac{1}{16} + \ldots$

Do you UNDERSTAND?  MATHEMATICAL PRACTICES

Ⓒ 5. Error Analysis A classmate uses the formula for the sum of an infinite geometric series to evaluate $1 + 1.1 + 1.21 + 1.331 + \ldots$ and gets -10. What error did your classmate make?

Ⓒ 6. Writing Explain how you can determine whether an infinite geometric series has a sum.

Ⓒ 7. Compare and Contrast How are the formulas for the sum of a finite arithmetic series and the sum of a finite geometric series similar? How are they different?

Practice and Problem-Solving Exercises  MATHEMATICAL PRACTICES

 **Practice**   Evaluate the sum of the finite geometric series.   ◀ See Problem 1.

8. $1 + 2 + 4 + 8 + \cdots + 128$

9. $4 + 12 + 36 + 108 + \cdots + 972$

10. $3 + 6 + 12 + 24 + 48 + \cdots + 768$

11. $-5 - 10 - 20 - 40 - \cdots - 2560$

12. $\sum\limits_{n=1}^{5} 3^n$

13. $\sum\limits_{n=1}^{4} \left(\frac{1}{2}\right)^{n+1}$

14. $\sum\limits_{n=1}^{4} \left(\frac{2}{3}\right)^{n-1}$

15. $\sum\limits_{n=1}^{5} \left(\frac{1}{3}\right)^{n-1}$

16. Financial Planning In March, a family starts saving for a vacation they are planning for the end of August. The family expects the vacation to cost $1375. They start with $125. Each month they plan to deposit 20% more than the previous month. Will they have enough money for their trip? If not, how much more do they need?   ◀ See Problem 2.

Determine whether each infinite geometric series *diverges* or *converges*. If the series converges, state the sum.   ◀ See Problem 3.

17. $1 + \frac{1}{4} + \frac{1}{16} + \ldots$

18. $1 - \frac{1}{2} + \frac{1}{4} - \ldots$

19. $4 + 2 + 1 + \ldots$

20. $1 + 2 + 4 + \ldots$

21. $6 + 18 + 54 + \ldots$

22. $-54 - 18 - 6 - \ldots$

23. $1 - 1 + 1 - \ldots$

24. $1 + \frac{1}{5} + \frac{1}{25} + \ldots$

25. $\frac{1}{4} + \frac{1}{2} + 1 + 2 + \ldots$

Evaluate each infinite geometric series.

26. $1.1 + 0.11 + 0.011 + \ldots$

27. $1.1 - 0.11 + 0.011 - \ldots$

28. $1 - \frac{1}{5} + \frac{1}{25} - \frac{1}{125} + \ldots$

29. $3 + 1 + \frac{1}{3} + \frac{1}{9} + \ldots$

30. $3 + 2 + \frac{4}{3} + \frac{8}{9} + \ldots$

31. $3 - 2 + \frac{4}{3} - \frac{8}{9} + \ldots$

 **Apply**   Determine whether each series is *arithmetic* or *geometric*. Then evaluate the finite series for the specified number of terms.

32. $2 + 4 + 8 + 16 + \ldots$; $n = 10$

33. $2 + 4 + 6 + 8 + \ldots$; $n = 20$

34. $-5 + 25 - 125 + 625 - \ldots$; $n = 9$

35. $6.4 + 8 + 10 + 12.5 + \ldots$; $n = 7$

36. $1 + 2 + 3 + 4 + \ldots$; $n = 1000$

37. $81 + 27 + 9 + 3 + \ldots$; $n = 200$

© **38. Think About a Plan** The height a ball bounces is less than the height of the previous bounce due to friction. The heights of the bounces form a geometric sequence. Suppose a ball is dropped from one meter and rebounds to 95% of the height of the previous bounce. What is the total distance traveled by the ball when it comes to rest?
- Does the problem give you enough information to solve the problem?
- How can you write the general term of the sequence?
- What formula should you use to calculate the total distance?

39. Communications Many companies use a telephone chain to notify employees of a closing due to bad weather. Suppose a company's CEO (Chief Executive Officer) calls four people. Then each of these people calls four others, and so on.
  a. Make a diagram to show the first three stages in the telephone chain. How many calls are made at each stage?
  b. Write the series that represents the total number of calls made through the first six stages.
  c. How many employees have been notified after stage six?

40. Graphing Calculator The graph models the sum of the first n terms in the geometric series with $a_1 = 20$ and $r = 0.9$.
  a. Write the first four sums of the series.
  b. Use the graph to evaluate the series to the 47th term.
  c. Write and evaluate the formula for the sum of the series.
  d. Graph the formula using the window values shown. Use the graph to verify your answer to part (b).

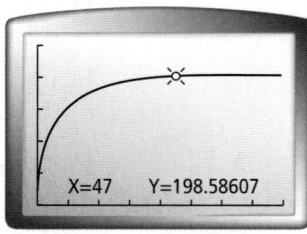

X=47   Y=198.58607

Xmin=0   Ymin=0
Xmax=94   Ymax=250
Xscl=10   Yscl=50

Evaluate each infinite series that has a sum.

41. $\displaystyle\sum_{n=1}^{\infty} \left(\frac{1}{5}\right)^{n-1}$ **42.** $\displaystyle\sum_{n=1}^{\infty} 3\left(\frac{1}{4}\right)^{n-1}$ **43.** $\displaystyle\sum_{n=1}^{\infty} \left(-\frac{1}{3}\right)^{n-1}$ **44.** $\displaystyle\sum_{n=1}^{\infty} 7(2)^{n-1}$ **45.** $\displaystyle\sum_{n=1}^{\infty} (-0.2)^{n-1}$

46. Open-Ended Write an infinite geometric series that converges to 3. Use the formula to evaluate the series.

47. Reasoning Find the specified value for each infinite geometric series.
  a. $a_1 = 12$, $S = 96$; find r **b.** $S = 12$, $r = \frac{1}{6}$; find a_1

48. Writing Suppose you are to receive an allowance each week for the next 26 weeks. Would you rather receive (a) $1000 per week or (b) $.02 the first week, $.04 the second week, $.08 the third week, and so on for the 26 weeks? Justify your answer.

49. The sum of an infinite geometric series is twice its first term.
  a. Error Analysis A student says the common ratio of the series is $\frac{3}{2}$. What is the student's error?
  b. Find the common ratio of the series.

50. Physics Because of friction and air resistance, each swing of a pendulum is a little shorter than the previous one. The lengths of the swings form a geometric sequence. Suppose the first swing of a pendulum has a length of 100 cm and the return swing is 99 cm.
  a. On which swing will the arc first have a length less than 50 cm?
  b. What is the total distance traveled by the pendulum when it comes to rest?

51. Where did the formula for summing finite geometric series come from? Suppose the geometric series has first term a_1 and constant ratio r, so that $S_n = a_1 + a_1 r + a_1 r^2 + \cdots + a_1 r^{n-1}$.
  a. Show that $rS_n = a_1 r + a_1 r^2 + a_1 r^3 + \cdots + a_1 r^n$.
  b. Use part (a) to show that $S_n - rS_n = a_1 - a_1 r^n$.
  c. Use part (b) to show that $S_n = \dfrac{a_1 - a_1 r^n}{1 - r} = \dfrac{a_1(1 - r^n)}{1 - r}$.

52. The function $S(n) = \dfrac{10(1 - 0.8^n)}{0.2}$ represents the sum of the first n terms of an infinite geometric series.

    a. What is the domain of the function?
    b. Find $S(n)$ for $n = 1, 2, 3, \ldots, 10$. Sketch the graph of the function.
    c. Find the sum S of the infinite geometric series.

53. Use the formula for the sum of an infinite geometric series to show that $0.\overline{9} = 1$.
    (*Hint:* $0.\overline{9} = \dfrac{9}{10} + \dfrac{9}{100} + \dfrac{9}{1000} + \ldots$)

Apply What You've Learned

 MATHEMATICAL PRACTICES
MP 2, MP 6

Look back at the information on page 563 about Matthew's sale of cars from his toy car collection. In the Apply What You've Learned in Lesson 9-3, you found the common ratio for the sequence of the toy car values shown in the second column of the table.

Consider the sequence of amounts Matthew received for the 7 toy cars he sold in 7 consecutive years. Let a_1 be the value of the first toy car Matthew sold. Use the following words, numbers, expressions, and equations to complete the sentences below.

sequence	series	$a_n = a_1 \cdot r^{n-1}$	$S_n = \dfrac{a_1(1 - r^n)}{1 - r}$	$S = \dfrac{a_1}{1 - r}$

S_n	a_n	r	$a_1(1.04)^7$	$a_1(1.04)^6$

a_1	6	7	\$67.56	\$80.45

A geometric **a.** ? that represents Matthew's total revenue from the sale of 7 cars is $a_1 + a_1(1.04) + a_1(1.04)^2 + \cdots + $ **b.** ? . To find the sum, use the formula **c.** ? . Substitute 533.62 for **d.** ? , substitute 1.04 for **e.** ? , and substitute **f.** ? for n. Then solve for **g.** ? . The value of the first toy car Matthew sold was **h.** ? .

Pull It **All Together**

Completing the Performance Task

To solve these problems, you will pull together concepts and skills related to sequences and series.

Look back at your results from the Apply What You've Learned sections in Lessons 9-3 and 9-5. Use the work you did to complete the following.

1. Solve the problem in the Task Description on page 563 by determining the years in which Matthew sold the 7 toy cars. Show all your work and explain each step of your solution.

 2. Reflect Choose one of the Mathematical Practices below and explain how you applied it in your work on the Performance Task.

MP 2: Reason abstractly and quantitatively.

MP 4: Model with mathematics.

MP 6: Attend to precision.

MP 7: Look for and make use of structure.

On Your Own

Matthew has another valuable collection of a certain baseball card. He bought his first card in 1995. Since then, the value of the baseball card has increased by the same percent each year. The table below shows the value of the baseball card for the years 2007–2012, as published in a collector's magazine.

Year	Value of Baseball Card
2007	$50.00
2008	$51.00
2009	$52.02
2010	$53.06
2011	$54.12
2012	$55.20

Beginning in 1997, Matthew sold 12 baseball cards, with each sale occurring one year after the previous sale and at the published price.

Find the total revenue Matthew received from the sale of the 12 baseball cards.

Connecting BIG ideas and Answering the Essential Questions

1 Variable

You can define a sequence
- by describing its nth term with a formula using n.
- by stating its first term and a formula that relates the $n - 1$ and nth terms.

2 Equivalence

$a_n = a + (n - 1)d$ and $a_1 = a$, $a_n = a_{n-1} + d$ for $n > 1$ define the same arithmetic sequence, $a, a + d, a + 2d, \ldots$

3 Modeling

You can model a geometric sequence explicitly or recursively. The sum of its first n terms is $\frac{a_1(1 - r^n)}{1 - r}$.

Mathematical Patterns and Arithmetic Sequences (Lessons 9-1 and 9-2)

$a_n = 2 - \frac{3}{4}(n - 1)$ and $a_1 = 2$, so

$a_n = a_{n-1} - \frac{3}{4}$ represents the arithmetic sequence $2, \frac{5}{4}, \frac{2}{4}, -\frac{1}{4}, -1, \ldots$

Mathematical Patterns and Geometric Sequences (Lessons 9-1 and 9-3)

$a_n = 2\left(-\frac{1}{2}\right)^{n-1}$ and $a_1 = 2$, so

$a_n = \left(-\frac{1}{2}\right)a_{n-1}$ represents the geometric sequence $2, -1, \frac{1}{2}, -\frac{1}{4}, \frac{1}{8}, \ldots$

Arithmetic Series (Lesson 9-4)

The sum $S_n = a_1 + a_2 + \cdots + a_n$ of an arithmetic series is $S_n = \frac{n}{2}(a_1 + a_n)$. The sum

$S_6 = 2 + \frac{5}{4} + \frac{2}{4} - \frac{1}{4} - 1 - \frac{7}{4}$

$= 3\left(2 - \frac{7}{4}\right) = \frac{3}{4}.$

Geometric Series (Lesson 9-5)

$S_n = \frac{a_1(1 - r^n)}{1 - r}$ is the sum of the first n terms of a geometric series. If the series is infinite with $|r| < 1$, the sum is $S = \frac{a_1}{1 - r}$.

For the geometric series, $a_1 = 2$, $a_n = \left(-\frac{1}{2}\right)a_{n-1}$,

$S_6 = \frac{2\left(1 - \left(-\frac{1}{2}\right)^6\right)}{1 - \left(-\frac{1}{2}\right)}$, or $\frac{21}{16}$, and

$S = \frac{2}{1 - \left(-\frac{1}{2}\right)} = \frac{4}{3}.$

Chapter Vocabulary

- arithmetic mean (p. 574)
- arithmetic sequence (p. 572)
- arithmetic series (p. 587)
- common difference (p. 572)
- common ratio (p. 580)
- converge (p. 598)

- diverge (p. 598)
- explicit formula (p. 565)
- finite series (p. 587)
- geometric mean (p. 583)
- geometric sequence (p. 580)
- geometric series (p. 595)

- infinite series (p. 587)
- limits (p. 589)
- recursive formula (p. 565)
- sequence (p. 564)
- series (p. 587)
- term of a sequence (p. 564)

Choose the vocabulary term that correctly completes each sentence.

1. When you use Σ to write a series, you can use ___?___ to indicate how many terms you are adding.

2. An ordered list of terms is a ___?___ .

3. If an infinite geometric series ___?___ , then it must have a sum.

4. There is a constant ___?___ between consecutive terms in a geometric sequence.

5. A formula that expresses the nth term of a sequence in terms of n is a(n) ___?___ .

9-1 Mathematical Patterns

Quick Review

A **sequence** is an ordered list of numbers called **terms**.

A **recursive definition** gives the first term and defines the other terms by relating each term after the first term to the one before it.

An **explicit formula** expresses the nth term in a sequence in terms of n, where n is a positive integer.

Example

A sequence has an explicit formula $a_n = n^2$. What are the first three terms of this sequence?

$a_1 = (1)^2 = 1$ Substitute 1 for n and evaluate.

$a_2 = (2)^2 = 4$ Substitute 2 for n and evaluate.

$a_3 = (3)^2 = 9$ Substitute 3 for n and evaluate.

The first three terms are 1, 4, and 9.

Exercises

Find the first five terms of each sequence.

6. $a_n = -2n + 3$

7. $a_n = -n^2 + 2n$

8. $a_n = 2a_{n-1} - 1$, where $a_1 = 2$

9. $a_n = \frac{1}{2} a_{n-1}$, where $a_1 = 20$

Write a recursive definition for each sequence.

10. 5, 22, 39, 56, . . .   **11.** −2, 7, 16, 25, . . .

Write an explicit formula for each sequence.

12. 1, 4, 7, 10, . . .   **13.** 4, 1.5, −1, − 3.5, . . .

9-2 Arithmetic Sequences

Quick Review

In an **arithmetic sequence**, the difference between consecutive terms is constant. This difference is the **common difference**.

For an arithmetic sequence, a is the first term, a_n is the nth term, n is the number of the term, and d is the common difference.

An explicit formula is $a_n = a + (n - 1)d$.

A recursive formula is $a_n = a_{n-1} + d$, with $a_1 = a$.

The **arithmetic mean** of two numbers x and y is the average of the two numbers $\frac{x + y}{2}$.

Example

What is the missing term of the arithmetic sequence 11, ■, 27, . . . ?

arithmetic mean $= \frac{11 + 27}{2} = \frac{38}{2} = 19$

The missing term is 19.

Exercises

Determine whether each sequence is arithmetic. If so, identify the common difference and find the 32nd term of the sequence.

14. 2, 4, 7, 10, . . .   **15.** 3, 18, 33, 48, . . .

16. 7, 10, 13, 16, . . .   **17.** 2, 5, 9, 14, . . .

Find the missing term(s) of each arithmetic sequence.

18. 1, ■, 9, . . .   **19.** 104, ■, 99, . . .

20. −1, ■, 11, . . .   **21.** −4.6, ■, −5.2, . . .

22. −13, ■, ■, ■, −3, . . .   **23.** 2, ■, ■, ■, −0.4, . . .

Write an explicit formula for each arithmetic sequence.

24. −2, 7, 16, 25, . . .   **25.** 62, 59, 56, 53, . . .

9-3 Geometric Sequences

Quick Review

In a **geometric sequence**, the ratio of consecutive terms is constant. This ratio is the **common ratio**.

For a geometric sequence, a is the first term, a_n is the nth term, n is the number of the term, and r is the common ratio.

An explicit formula is $a_n = a \cdot r^{n-1}$.

A recursive formula is $a_n = a_{n-1} \cdot r$, with $a_1 = a$.

The geometric mean of two positive numbers x and y is $\sqrt{xy}$.

Example

What is the sixth term of the geometric sequence that begins 2, 6, 18, . . . ?

$a_1 = 2$ and $r = 6 \div 2 = 3$

$a_6 = 2 \cdot 3^{6-1} = 486$ Substitute 6 for n, 2 for a_1, and 3 for r.

The sixth term is 486.

Exercises

Determine whether each sequence is geometric. If so, identify the common ratio and find the next two terms.

26. $1, \frac{1}{2}, \frac{1}{4}, \frac{1}{8}, \ldots$

27. $1, 3, 5, 7, \ldots$

28. $3, 3.6, 4.32, 5.184, \ldots$

Find the missing term(s) of each geometric sequence.

29. $3, \blacksquare, 12, \ldots$

30. $0.004, \blacksquare, 0.4, \ldots$

31. $-20, \blacksquare, \blacksquare, \blacksquare, -1.25, \ldots$

Write an explicit formula for each geometric sequence.

32. $1, 2, 4, 8, \ldots$

33. $25, 5, 1, \frac{1}{5}, \ldots$

Use an explicit formula to find the 10th term of each geometric sequence.

34. $5, 10, 20, 40, \ldots$ **35.** $-3, 6, -12, 24, \ldots$

9-4 Arithmetic Series

Quick Review

A **series** is the expression for the sum of the terms of a sequence.

An **arithmetic series** is the sum of the terms of an arithmetic sequence. The sum S_n of the first n terms of an arithmetic series is $S_n = \frac{n}{2}(a_1 + a_n)$. You can use a summation symbol, Σ, and lower and upper **limits** to write a series. The lower limit is the least value of n and the upper limit is the greatest value of n.

Example

What is the sum of the arithmetic series?

$2 + 5 + 8 + 11 + 14 + 17 + 20$

$a_1 = 2$, $a_7 = 20$, and $n = 7$.

$S_7 = \frac{7}{2}(2 + 20)$ Substitute 7 for n, 2 for a_1, and 20 for a_7.

$= 77$ Evaluate.

Exercises

Use summation notation to write each arithmetic series for the specified number of terms. Then evaluate the sum.

36. $10 + 7 + 4 + \ldots; n = 5$

37. $50 + 55 + 60 + \ldots; n = 7$

38. $6 + 7.4 + 8.8 + \ldots; n = 11$

39. $21 + 19 + 17 + \ldots; n = 8$

Find the number of terms in each series, the first term, and the last term. Then evaluate the sum.

40. $\displaystyle\sum_{n=1}^{3}(17n - 25)$ **41.** $\displaystyle\sum_{n=2}^{10}\left(\frac{1}{2}n + 3\right)$

9-5 Geometric Series

Quick Review

A **geometric series** is the sum of the terms of a geometric sequence. The sum S_n of the first n terms of a geometric series is $S_n = \frac{a_1(1 - r^n)}{1 - r}, r \neq 1$.

When an infinite series has a finite sum, the series **converges**. When the series does not converge, the series **diverges**.

In a geometric series, when $|r| < 1$, the series converges to $S = \frac{a_1}{1 - r}$. When $|r| \geq 1$, the series diverges.

Example

What is the sum of the geometric series?

$$5 + 10 + 20 + 40 + 80 + 160$$

$n = 6$, $a_1 = 5$, and $r = 10 \div 5 = 2$.

$S_6 = \frac{5(1 - 2^6)}{1 - 2}$ Substitute 6 for n, 5 for a_1, and 2 for r.

$= 315$ Evaluate.

The sum is 315.

Exercises

Evaluate each finite series for the specified number of terms.

42. $1 + 2 + 4 + \ldots ; n = 5$

43. $80 - 40 + 20 - \ldots ; n = 8$

44. $12 + 2 + \frac{1}{3} + \ldots ; n = 4$

Determine whether each infinite geometric series converges or diverges. If the series converges, state the sum.

45. $150 + 30 + 6 + \ldots$

46. $2.2 + 2.42 + 2.662 + \ldots$

47. $-10 - 20 - 40 - \ldots$

48. $\frac{2}{3} + \frac{4}{9} + \frac{8}{27} + \ldots$

Do you know HOW?

Write a recursive definition and an explicit formula for each sequence. Then find a_{12}.

1. 7, 13, 19, 25, 31, . . .

2. 10, 20, 40, 80, 160, . . .

Determine whether each sequence is *arithmetic, geometric,* or *neither.* Then find the tenth term.

3. 23, 27, 31, 35, 39, . . .

4. $-12, -5, 2, 9, 16, \ldots$

5. $-5, 15, -45, 135, -405, \ldots$

6. $\frac{1}{4}, 1, 4, 16, \ldots$

Find the missing term of each arithmetic sequence.

7. 4, ■, 12, . . .

8. -11, ■, 23, . . .

Determine whether each sequence is *arithmetic* or *geometric.* Then identify the common difference or common ratio.

9. 1620, 540, 180, 60, 20, . . .

10. 78, 75, 72, 69, 66, 63, 60, . . .

11. $\frac{3}{32}, \frac{3}{16}, \frac{3}{8}, \frac{3}{4}, \frac{3}{2}, 3, 6, \ldots$

a_1 is the first term of a sequence, r is a common ratio, and d is a common difference. Write the first five terms.

12. $a_1 = 2, r = -2$

13. $a_1 = 3, d = 7$

14. $a_1 = -100, r = \frac{1}{5}$

15. $a_1 = 19, d = -4$

Find the missing term of each geometric sequence.

16. 2, ■, 0.5, . . .

17. 2, ■, 8, . . .

Find the sum of each infinite geometric series.

18. $0.5 + 0.05 + 0.005 + \ldots$

19. $1 - \frac{1}{2} + \frac{1}{4} - \ldots$

20. $6 + 5 + \frac{25}{6} + \ldots$

Determine whether each series is *arithmetic* or *geometric.* Then evaluate the finite series for the specified term number.

21. $2 + 7 + 12 + \ldots ; n = 8$

22. $5000 + 1000 + 200 + \ldots ; n = 5$

23. $1 + 0.01 - 0.98 - \ldots ; n = 5$

24. $2 + 6 + 18 + \ldots ; n = 6$

Find the sum of each series.

25. $\displaystyle\sum_{n=1}^{5} (3n + 1)$

26. $\displaystyle\sum_{n=1}^{8} \frac{2n}{3}$

27. $\displaystyle\sum_{n=4}^{10} (0.8n - 0.4)$

28. $\displaystyle\sum_{n=2}^{6} (-2)^{n-1}$

Do you UNDERSTAND?

29. You have saved $50. Each month you add $10 more to your savings.
   a. Write an explicit formula to model the amount you have saved after n months.
   b. How much have you saved after six months?

30. Open-Ended Write an arithmetic sequence. Then write an explicit formula for it.

31. Reasoning How can you tell if a geometric series converges or diverges? Include examples of both types of series. Evaluate the series that converges.

32. A diamond is purchased for $2500. Suppose its value increases 5% each year.
   a. What is the value of diamond after 8 years?
   b. Writing Explain how you can write an explicit formula for a geometric sequence to answer the question.

Ⓣ Ⓘ Ⓟ Ⓢ   Ⓕ Ⓞ Ⓡ   Ⓢ Ⓤ Ⓒ Ⓒ Ⓔ Ⓢ Ⓢ

Read the question at the right. Then follow the tips to answer the sample question.

TIP 1

Find where y = 0. These are the x-intercepts of the graph.

TIP 2

Check your solutions in the original equation.

The graph below shows the quadratic function $y = 2x^2 + 2x - 4$. Use the graph to find the solutions of $2x^2 + 2x - 4 = 0$.

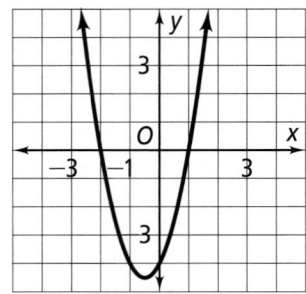

Ⓐ −4 and 0   Ⓒ −1 and 2

Ⓑ −2 and 1   Ⓓ 2 and −1

Think It Through

The x-intercepts of the graph are at $x = -2$ and $x = 1$.

Substitute to verify your answers.

$$2(-2)^2 + 2(-2) - 4$$
$$= 2(4) - 4 - 4$$
$$= 0$$
$$2(1)^2 + 2(1) - 4$$
$$= 2 + 2 - 4$$
$$= 0$$

The correct answer is B.

Vocabulary Builder

As you solve test items, you must understand the meanings of mathematical terms. Match each term with its mathematical meaning.

A. recursive formula

B. limit

C. explicit formula

D. sequence

I. a formula that expresses the nth term in terms of n

II. an ordered list of numbers

III. the least or greatest integer value of n in a series

IV. a formula that gives the first term in a sequence and defines the other terms by relating each term to the one before it

Selected Response

Read each question. Then write the letter of the correct answer on your paper.

1. What is the solution set of the equation $(2x - 4)(x + 6) = 0$?

Ⓐ $\{4, 6\}$ Ⓒ $\{2, -6\}$

Ⓑ $\{-4, 6\}$ Ⓓ $\{-2, -6\}$

2. What are the first five terms of the sequence $a_n = 2n - 1$?

Ⓕ 0, 1, 2, 3, 4   Ⓗ 2, 4, 6, 8, 10

Ⓖ 1, 3, 5, 7, 9   Ⓘ 3, 5, 7, 9, 11

3. What is the common ratio in a geometric series if $a_2 = \frac{2}{5}$ and $a_5 = \frac{16}{135}$?

Ⓐ $\frac{2}{5}$ Ⓒ $\frac{6}{65}$

Ⓑ $\frac{2}{3}$ Ⓓ $\frac{8}{27}$

4. The total area of a sheet of paper can be represented by $27x^3 + 64y^3$. Which factors could represent the length times the width?

F $(3x + 4y)(3x^2 + 4y^2)$

G $(3x + 4y)(9x^2 - 12xy + 16y^2)$

H $(3x - 4y)(9x^2 - 12xy + 16y^2)$

I $(3x + 4y)(3x^2 - 3xy + 4y^2)$

5. The graph below shows the quadratic function $y = x^2 + 2x - 3$. Use the graph to find all the solutions of $x^2 + 2x - 3 = 0$.

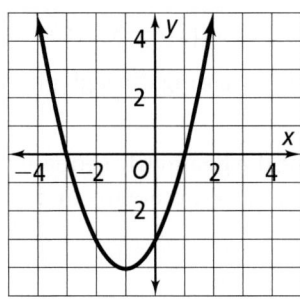

A -3

B -1

C -3 and 1

D 3 and -1

6. The table shows ordered pairs that satisfy the equation $y = -x^2 + 2x + 15$.

x	−3	0	2	3	5
y	0	15	15	12	0

Based on this table, what is the solution set of the equation $-x^2 + 2x + 15 = 0$?

F $\{0, 15\}$

H $\{5, 0\}$

G $\{-3, 15\}$

I $\{-3, 5\}$

7. What is the product of $\dfrac{x^2 + 5x + 4}{(x - 1)(x + 1)}$ and $\dfrac{x^2 - 5x + 6}{x - 2}$?

A $\dfrac{x^2 + 7x + 12}{x - 1}$ for $x \neq 1$

B $\dfrac{x^2 + x - 12}{x - 1}$ for $x \neq -1, 1,$ or 2

C $\dfrac{x^2 + x - 12}{x - 1}$ for $x \neq 1$

D $\dfrac{x^2 + 7x + 12}{x - 1}$ for $x \neq -1, 1,$ or 2

8. What is the sum of the infinite geometric series $\frac{1}{4} + \frac{1}{16} + \frac{1}{64} + \frac{1}{256} + \ldots$?

F $\frac{1}{4}$

H $\frac{1}{2}$

G $\frac{1}{3}$

I 3

9. If $f(x) = 4x^4 - 9$ and $g(x) = 2x^2 + 3$, what is $\left(\frac{f}{g}\right)(x)$?

A $2x^2 - 3$

B $2x + 3$

C $2x - 3$

D $2x^2 + 3$

10. What is the solution of $\log x - \log 3 = 8$?

F 10^8

G 8×10^3

H 3×10^3

I 3×10^8

11. What is $\dfrac{4x^2 - 1}{2x^2 - 5x - 3} \cdot \dfrac{x^2 - 6x + 9}{2x^2 + 5x - 3}$?

A 1

B $x + 3$

C $x - 3$

D $\left(\dfrac{x - 3}{x + 3}\right)$

12. Which is the factored form of $0.81p^2 - 0.09$?

F $(0.9p + 0.045)(0.9p - 0.045)$

G $(0.9p + 0.3)(0.9p - 0.3)$

H $(0.9p + 0.03)(0.9p - 0.03)$

I $(0.9p + 0.81)(0.9p - 0.81)$

13. Which sum is equal to $\dfrac{x^2 + 4x - 3}{x^2 - 9}$?

A $\dfrac{1}{x - 3} + \dfrac{x}{x + 3}$

C $\dfrac{x^2}{x - 3} + \dfrac{4x - 3}{x + 3}$

B $\dfrac{x - 3}{x + 3} + \dfrac{x - 1}{x - 3}$

D $\dfrac{1}{x + 3} + \dfrac{x}{x - 3}$

Constructed Response

14. Marisol wants to start saving money for college. She sees the advertisement below in her local newspaper.

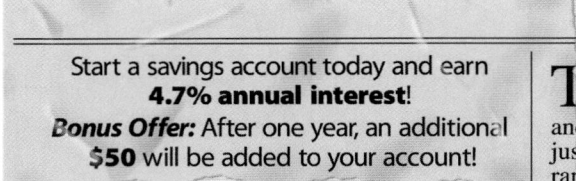

Start a savings account today and earn
4.7% annual interest!
Bonus Offer: After one year, an additional
$50 will be added to your account!

For x dollars in this savings account, $I(x) = 1.047x$ is the value of the account after one year. $B(x) = x + 50$ is the value of the account after the one-year bonus. $(B \circ I)(x)$ models the value of this account after one year of investment time and the one-year bonus. Marisol opens a savings account by depositing $120. What is the value of the account after one year?

15. The area of the parallelogram is 35 square units. What is the value of x?

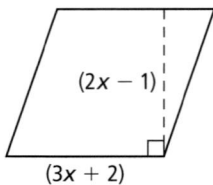

$(2x - 1)$

$(3x + 2)$

16. What is the sum of the following finite geometric series?

$1 + 4 + 16 + 64 + 256$

17. What is the solution to $\sqrt{x - 1} = \sqrt{x} - 1$?

18. Rita works a part-time job at a clothing store and earns $7 per hour. Juan works at another clothing store and earns $6 per hour plus a 10% commission on sales. How many sales, in dollars, would Juan have to make in two hours to earn the same amount as Rita in a two-hour shift?

19. Let $f(x) = x + 1$ and $g(x) = x^2$. What is $(g \circ f)(2)$?

20. What is the factored form of $9x^2 - 4$?

21. Write the equation represented by the graph.

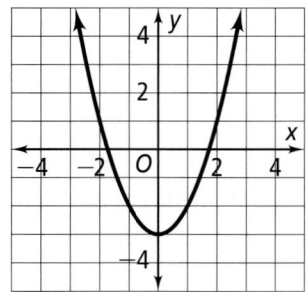

22. What is the graph and absolute value of $-3 + 2i$?

23. What is an equation of the line passing through points $(3, 5)$ and $(7, 1)$?

24. Write an explicit formula for the geometric sequence for which $a_1 = 6$ and $r = \frac{1}{2}$. Then generate the first five terms.

25. What is the inverse of $y = \sqrt{x - 5}$?

Extended Response

26. In a geometric sequence, $a_1 = 2$ and $a_5 = 162$. Explain how to use the geometric mean to find the missing terms a_2, a_3, and a_4.

27. a. Use a graphing calculator to find the points of intersection of the functions $f(x) = x^2 - 2x - 3$ and $g(x) = x^3 - 3x^2 - x + 3$.

b. Explain why the x-coordinates of the points of intersection are the solutions to the equation $f(x) = g(x)$.

Get Ready!

CHAPTER 10

Lesson 4-1 ◖ ## Graphing Quadratic Functions

Graph each function.

1. $y = -x^2$

2. $y = \frac{1}{3}x^2$

3. $y = 2x^2 + 5$

4. $y = x^2 + 6x + 8$

Lesson 4-3 ◖ ## Identifying Quadratic Functions

Determine whether each function is *linear* or *quadratic*. Identify the quadratic, linear, and constant terms.

5. $y = 6x - x^2 + 1$

6. $f(x) = -2(3 + x)^2 + 2x^2$

7. $y = 2x - y - 13$

8. $y = 4x(7 - 2x)$

9. $g(x) = -2x^2 - 3(x - 2)$

10. $y = x - 2(x + 5)$

Lesson 4-6 ◖ ## Completing the Square

Complete the square.

11. $x^2 + 8x + \blacksquare$

12. $x^2 - 5x + \blacksquare$

13. $x^2 + 14x + \blacksquare$

Rewrite each equation in vertex form. Then graph the function.

14. $y = x^2 + 6x + 7$

15. $y = 2x^2 - 4x + 10$

16. $y = -3x^2 + x$

Lesson 4-1 ◖ ## Graphing Quadratic Functions in Vertex Form

Graph each function.

17. $y = 2(x - 3)^2 + 1$

18. $y = -1(x + 7)^2 - 4$

Lesson 2-7 ◖ ## Graphing Absolute Value Functions

Graph each function.

19. $y = 2|x|$

20. $y = |x| + 2$

 ## Looking Ahead Vocabulary

21. The word *radius* is a Latin word for the spoke of a wheel. It is also the source of the word "radio" because electromagnetic rays radiate from a radio in every direction. Why do you think mathematicians use the term radius to label any line segment from the center of a circle to any point on the circle?

22. In geometry, you learned that a *vertex* is typically a corner or point where two lines intersect. The four corners of a square are called vertices. Using this information, what can you conclude about the vertex of a parabola?

CHAPTER 10

Quadratic Relations and Conic Sections

Download videos connecting math to your world.

Interactive! Vary numbers, graphs, and figures to explore math concepts.

The online Solve It will get you in gear for each lesson.

Math definitions in English and Spanish

Online access to stepped-out problems aligned to Common Core

Get and view your assignments online.

Extra practice and review online

Virtual Nerd™ tutorials with built-in support

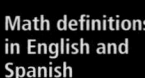
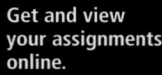
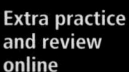
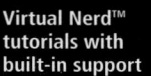

Chapter Preview

Vocabulary

English/Spanish Vocabulary Audio Online:

English	Spanish
center of a circle, *p. 630*	centro de un círculo
circle, *p. 630*	círculo
conic section, *p. 614*	sección cónica
directrix, *p. 622*	directriz
ellipse, *p. 638*	elipse
hyperbola, *p. 645*	hipérbola
radius, *p. 630*	radio
standard form of an equation of a circle, *p. 630*	forma normal de la ecuación de un círculo

BIG ideas

1 Modeling
Essential Question What is the intersection of a cone and a plane parallel to a line along the side of the cone?

2 Equivalence
Essential Question What is the graph of $\frac{x^2}{9} + \frac{y^2}{9} = 1$?

3 Coordinate Geometry
Essential Question What is the difference between the algebraic representations of ellipses and hyperbolas?

 DOMAINS
• Expressing Geometric Properties with Equations
• Interpreting Functions

Common Core Performance Task

Conic Insects

Kenjiro used conic sections to draw a butterfly on a coordinate plane, as shown below. He wants to reproduce the drawing on his graphing calculator.

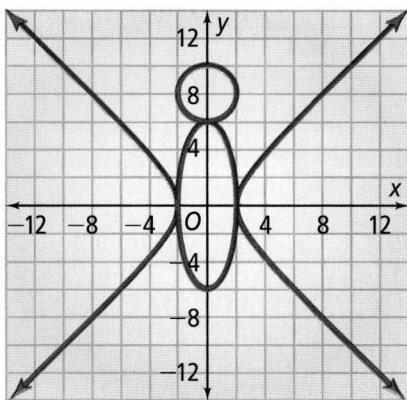

Task Description

Explain how to reproduce the butterfly on a graphing calculator. Provide the equations you should enter and the viewing window you should use so that the graph resembles Kenjiro's drawing as closely as possible.

Connecting the Task to the Math Practices

MATHEMATICAL PRACTICES

As you complete the task, you'll apply several Standards for Mathematical Practice.

- You'll make sense of the given drawing and identify the important features so you can write an equation for the head of the butterfly. (MP 1, MP 2)

- You'll write an equation for the body of the butterfly and explain how you know that your equation is correct. (MP 3)

- You'll work with mathematical terminology as you consider the equation for the wings of the butterfly. (MP 6)

10-1 Exploring Conic Sections

Common Core State Standards

Prepares for G-GPE.A.1 Derive the equation of a circle . . . **Also Prepares for G-GPE.A.2 and G-GPE.A.3**

MP 1, MP 2, MP 3, MP 5

Objective To graph and identify conic sections

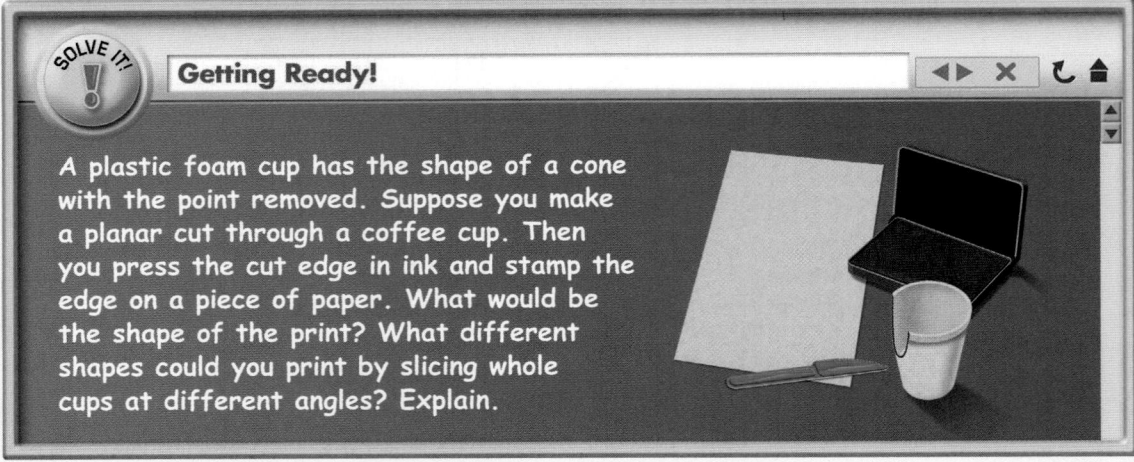

Getting Ready!

A plastic foam cup has the shape of a cone with the point removed. Suppose you make a planar cut through a coffee cup. Then you press the cut edge in ink and stamp the edge on a piece of paper. What would be the shape of the print? What different shapes could you print by slicing whole cups at different angles? Explain.

Lesson Vocabulary
• conic section

In Chapter 4, you studied parabolas. Geometrically, a parabola has the shape of a cross section of a cone that you cut in a particular way. Parabolas form a family of curves that belong to a larger family known as *conic sections*.

Essential Understanding There are four types of curves known as conic sections: parabolas, circles, ellipses, and hyperbolas. Each curve has its own distinct shape and properties.

take note

Key Concept Conic Sections

A **conic section** is a curve you get by intersecting a plane and a double cone. By changing the inclination of the plane, you can get a circle, a parabola, an ellipse, or a hyperbola.

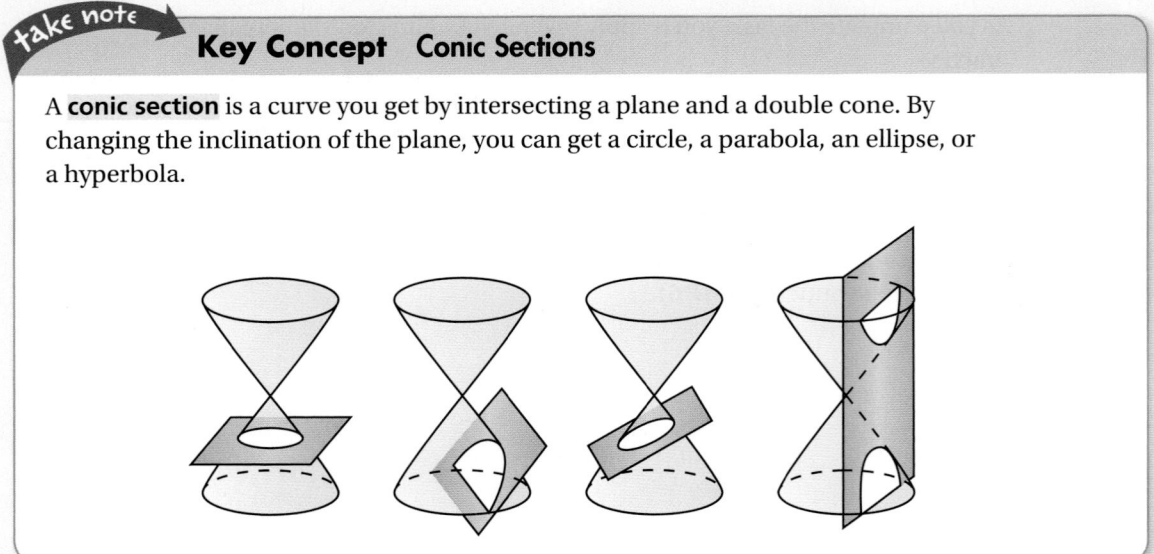

You can use lines of symmetry to graph a conic section.

 **Problem 1** Graphing a Circle

What is the graph of $x^2 + y^2 = 25$? What are its lines of symmetry? What are the domain and range?

Know	Need	Plan
An equation	The lines of symmetry of the graph, and the domain and range of the relation	• Plot points and connect them with a smooth curve. • Look for lines of symmetry on the graph. • Determine the domain and range.

Think

Can you find values of x and y that satisfy the equation?
Yes; find the x- and y-intercepts. Then look for other values of x and y that make the calculations easy.

Make a table of values. Plot the points and connect them with a smooth curve.

x	−5	−4	−3	0	3	4	5
y	0	±3	±4	±5	±4	±3	0

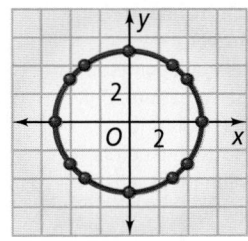

The graph is a circle with radius 5. Its center is the origin. Every line through the center is a line of symmetry.

The domain is the set of real numbers x with $-5 \leq x \leq 5$. The range is the set of real numbers y with $-5 \leq y \leq 5$.

 Got It? **1. a.** What is the graph of $x^2 + y^2 = 9$? What are its lines of symmetry? What are the domain and range?

    b. Reasoning In Problem 1, why is there no point on the graph with x-coordinate 6?

Its many lines of symmetry make a circle a special kind of an *ellipse*. In general, an ellipse has only two lines of symmetry.

 **Problem 2** Graphing an Ellipse

Think

What values should you substitute for x?
Substitute both positive and negative values for x.

What is the graph of $9x^2 + 16y^2 = 144$? What are its lines of symmetry? What are the domain and range?

Make a table of values. Plot the points and connect them with a smooth curve.

x	−4	−3	0	3	4
y	0	±2	±3	±2	0

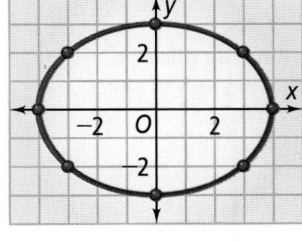

The graph is an ellipse. The center is the origin. The ellipse has two lines of symmetry, the x-axis and the y-axis.

The domain is the set of real numbers x with $-4 \leq x \leq 4$. The range is the set of real numbers y with $-3 \leq y \leq 3$.

 Got It? **2.** What is the graph of $2x^2 + y^2 = 18$? What are its lines of symmetry? What are the domain and range?

Not all conic sections consist of one smooth curve. The hyperbola consists of two separate curves called branches.

Problem 3 Graphing a Hyperbola

What is the graph of $x^2 - y^2 = 9$? What are its lines of symmetry? What are the domain and range?

Make a table of values.

x	−5	−4	−3	−2	−1	0	1	2	3	4	5
y	±4	±2.6	0	—	—	—	—	—	0	±2.6	±4

Think

How will you know which points to connect?
Plot enough points so you see a pattern. Only connect points if you know that the points between them satisfy the equation.

Plot the points and connect them with smooth curves.

The graph is a hyperbola that consists of two branches. Its center is the origin. It has two lines of symmetry, the x-axis and the y-axis.

The domain is the set of real numbers x with $x \le -3$ or $x \ge 3$. The range is the set of real numbers.

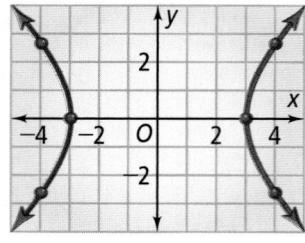

Got It? 3. What is the graph of $x^2 - y^2 = 16$? What are its lines of symmetry? What are the domain and range?

In this chapter, there is a separate lesson for each of the conic sections. You should already be able to identify each curve by its shape and features such as the vertex of a parabola, the center of an ellipse, circle, or hyperbola, and the intercepts of each curve.

Problem 4 Identifying Graphs of Conic Sections

What are the center and intercepts of each conic section? What are the domain and range?

A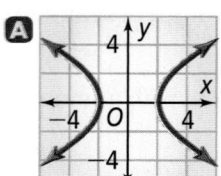

B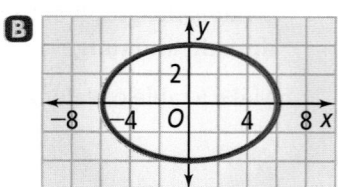

Think

What do you observe from the graph of the hyperbola?
The graph of this hyperbola extends forever but has no x-values between −2 and 2.

The center of the hyperbola is $(0, 0)$. The x-intercepts are $(-2, 0)$ and $(2, 0)$. There are no y-intercepts. The domain is the set of real numbers x with $x \le -2$ or $x \ge 2$. The range is the set of real numbers.

The center of the ellipse is $(0, 0)$. The x-intercepts are $(-6, 0)$ and $(6, 0)$. The y-intercepts are $(0, -4)$ and $(0, 4)$. The domain is the set of real numbers x with $-6 \le x \le 6$. The range is the set of real numbers y with $-4 \le y \le 4$.

Got It? **4.** What are the center and intercepts of the conic section? What are the domain and range?

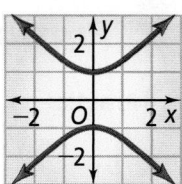

Problem 5 Using Models

Design Two patterns, such as arrays of dots or lines, can overlap to form moiré patterns. In the diagram, what pattern do the intersecting ripples form? Which of these equations is a possible model for the pattern: $x^2 - y^2 = 1$, $x^2 + y^2 = 16$, or $25x^2 + 9y^2 = 225$?

Think

How can you identify a possible model?
Find the type of conic section represented by each equation.

The intersecting ripples form a circle.

The equation $x^2 + y^2 = 16$ represents a conic section with two sets of intercepts, $(\pm 4, 0)$ and $(0, \pm 4)$. Each intercept is 4 units from the center. The equation models a circle.

 Got It? **5.** Unintended moiré patterns cause problems for printers. Describe the unintended pattern. Which equation in Problem 5 is a possible model for each pattern?

a.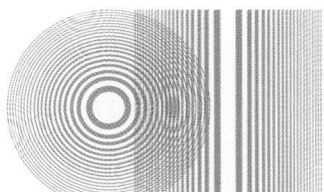

b.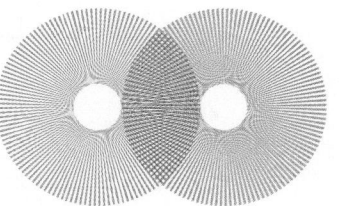

✓ **Lesson Check**

Do you know HOW?

Graph each equation. Find the lines of symmetry, the domain, and the range.

1. $x^2 + 4y^2 = 36$ **2.** $4x^2 - 9y^2 = 36$

Identify the domain and range.

3. 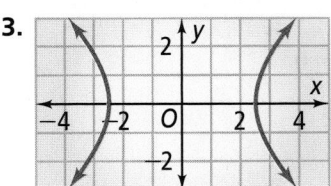   **4.**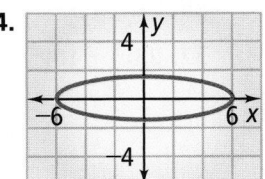

Do you UNDERSTAND?

5. Vocabulary Identify the type of conic section graphed.

a. 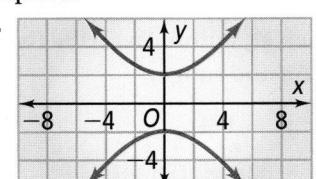   **b.**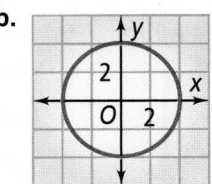

6. Compare and Contrast How is the domain of an ellipse different from the domain of a hyperbola?

Practice and Problem-Solving Exercises

 MATHEMATICAL PRACTICES

See Problems 1, 2, and 3.

 Practice   Graph each equation. Identify the conic section and describe the graph and its lines of symmetry. Then find the domain and range.

7. $3y^2 - x^2 = 25$ **8.** $2x^2 + y^2 = 36$ **9.** $x^2 + y^2 = 16$

10. $3y^2 - x^2 = 9$ **11.** $4x^2 + 25y^2 = 100$ **12.** $x^2 + y^2 = 49$

13. $x^2 - y^2 + 1 = 0$ **14.** $x^2 - 2y^2 = 4$ **15.** $6x^2 + 6y^2 = 600$

16. $x^2 + y^2 - 4 = 0$ **17.** $6x^2 + 24y^2 - 96 = 0$ **18.** $4x^2 + 4y^2 - 20 = 0$

19. $x^2 + 9y^2 = 1$ **20.** $4x^2 - 36y^2 = 144$ **21.** $4y^2 - 36x^2 = 1$

Identify the conic section. Then give the center, intercepts, domain, and range of each graph.

See Problem 4.

22.
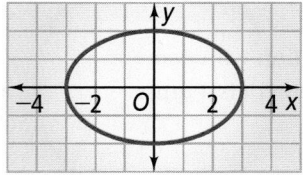

23.
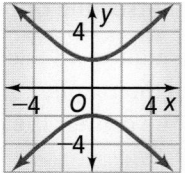

24.
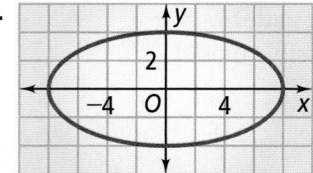

25.
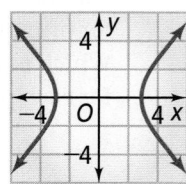

26.
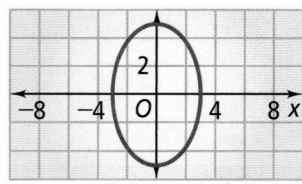

27.
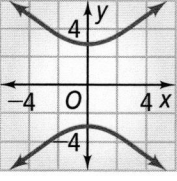

Match each equation with a graph in Exercises 22–27.

See Problem 5.

28. $x^2 - y^2 = 9$ **29.** $4x^2 + 9y^2 = 36$ **30.** $y^2 - x^2 = 4$

31. $x^2 + 4y^2 = 64$ **32.** $25x^2 + 9y^2 = 225$ **33.** $y^2 - x^2 = 9$

 Apply   Graph each equation. Describe the graph and its lines of symmetry. Then find the domain and range.

34. $9x^2 - y^2 = 144$ **35.** $11x^2 + 11y^2 = 44$

36. $-8x^2 + 32y^2 - 128 = 0$ **37.** $25x^2 + 16y^2 - 320 = 0$

38. Think About a Plan The light emitted from a lamp with a shade forms a shadow on the wall. How can you turn the lamp in relation to the wall so that the shadow cast by the shade forms a parabola and a circle?
- How can a drawing or model help you solve this problem?
- Can you form a hyperbola and an ellipse? If so, explain how.

39. a. Writing Describe the relationship between the center of a circle and the axes of symmetry of the circle.

   b. Make a Conjecture Where is the center of an ellipse or a hyperbola located in relation to the axes of symmetry? Verify your conjecture with examples.

Graph each circle with the given radius or diameter so that the center is at the origin. Then write the equation for each graph.

40. radius 6 **41.** radius $\frac{1}{2}$ **42.** diameter 8 **43.** diameter 2.5

Mental Math Each given point is on the graph of the given equation. Use symmetry to find at least one more point on the graph.

44. $(2, -4)$, $y^2 = 8x$ **45.** $(-\sqrt{2}, 1)$, $x^2 + y^2 = 3$

46. $(2, 2\sqrt{2})$, $x^2 + 4y^2 = 36$ **47.** $(-2, 0)$, $9x^2 + 9y^2 - 36 = 0$

48. $(-3, -\sqrt{51})$, $6y^2 - 9x^2 - 225 = 0$ **49.** $(0, \sqrt{7})$, $x^2 + 2y^2 = 14$

STEM 50. Sound An airplane flying faster than the speed of sound creates a cone-shaped pressure disturbance in the air. This is heard by people on the ground as a sonic boom. What is the shape of the path on the ground?

51. Open-Ended Describe any other figures you can see that can be formed by the intersection of a plane and another shape, such as a sphere.

 **Challenge**

52. a. Graph the equation $xy = 16$. Use both positive and negative values for x.
   b. Which conic section does the equation appear to model?
   c. Identify any intercepts and lines of symmetry.
   d. Does your graph represent a function? If so, rewrite the equation using function notation.

53. Graphing Calculator An xy-term has an interesting effect on the graph of a conic section. Sketch the graph of each conic section below using your graphing calculator. (*Hint:* To solve for y, you will need to complete a square.)
   a. $4x^2 + 2xy + y^2 = 9$
   b. $4x^2 + 2xy - y^2 = 9$

Standardized Test Prep

54. Which expression can be simplified to $\frac{x-1}{x-3}$?

Ⓐ $\frac{x^2 - x - 6}{x^2 - x - 2}$ 　　 Ⓑ $\frac{x^2 - 2x + 1}{x^2 + 2x - 3}$ 　　 Ⓒ $\frac{x^2 - 3x - 4}{x^2 - 7x + 12}$ 　　 Ⓓ $\frac{x^2 - 4x + 3}{x^2 - 6x + 9}$

55. Which is the graph of $4x^2 - y^2 = 4$?

Ⓕ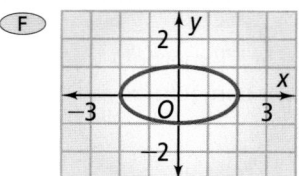

Ⓗ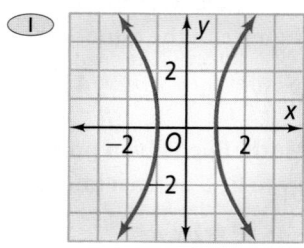

Ⓖ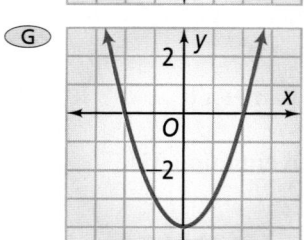

Ⓘ

56. Which product is NOT equal to 13?

Ⓐ $(4 + \sqrt{3})(4 - \sqrt{3})$ 　　　　 Ⓒ $(6 + \sqrt{23})(6 - \sqrt{23})$

Ⓑ $(5 - 2\sqrt{3})(5 + 2\sqrt{3})$ 　　　　 Ⓓ $(7 - \sqrt{6})(7 + \sqrt{6})$

57. Which function represents exponential growth?

Ⓕ $y = 35x^{1.35}$ 　　 Ⓖ $y = 35 \cdot (0.35)^x$ 　　 Ⓗ $y = 35 \cdot (1.35)^x$ 　　 Ⓘ $y = 35 \div (1.35)^x$

58. What is an explicit formula for the sequence 4, 9, 16, 25, 36, . . . ? What is the ninth term in this sequence?

Mixed Review

Determine whether each geometric series *diverges* or *converges*. If the series converges, state the sum.

◀ See Lesson 9-5.

59. $1 + 3 + 9 + \ldots$ 　　　　 **60.** $1 + \frac{4}{3} + \frac{16}{9} + \ldots$ 　　　　 **61.** $\frac{1}{2} + \frac{1}{4} + \frac{1}{8} + \ldots$

Expand each binomial.

◀ See Lesson 5-7.

62. $(x - y)^3$ 　　 **63.** $(p + q)^6$ 　　 **64.** $(x - 2)^4$ 　　 **65.** $(3 - x)^5$

Get Ready! To prepare for Lesson 10-2, do Exercises 66–69.

Make a table of values for each equation. Then graph the equation.

◀ See Lesson 2-7.

66. $y = |x|$ 　　 **67.** $y = |x| + 3$ 　　 **68.** $y = |x - 2|$ 　　 **69.** $y = |x + 1| - 4$

© **Common Core State Standards**

Prepares for G-GPE.A.1 Derive the equation of a circle . . . **Also Prepares for G-GPE.A.2 and G-GPE.A.3**

MP 5

You can use your graphing calculator to graph relations that are not functions.

Example

Graph the ellipse $\frac{x^2}{16} + \frac{y^2}{9} = 1$.

Step 1 Solve the equation for y.

$$\frac{x^2}{16} + \frac{y^2}{9} = 1$$

$$\frac{y^2}{9} = 1 - \frac{x^2}{16}$$

$$y^2 = 9\left(1 - \frac{x^2}{16}\right)$$

$$y = \pm 3\sqrt{1 - \frac{x^2}{16}}$$

Step 2 Enter the equations as $\mathbf{Y_1}$ and $\mathbf{Y_2}$.

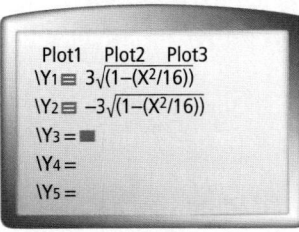

Plot1 Plot2 Plot3
\Y1◼ 3√(1−(X²/16))
\Y2◼ −3√(1−(X²/16))
\Y3 = ◼
\Y4 =
\Y5 =

Step 3 Select a square window.

ZOOM MEMORY
1: ZBOX
2: Zoom In
3: Zoom Out
4: ZDecimal
5: ZSquare
6: ZStandard
7↓ZTrig

Step 4 Graph.

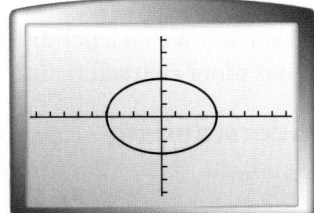

Exercises

Graph each conic section.

1. $x^2 + y^2 = 25$

2. $4x^2 + y^2 = 16$

3. $9x^2 - 16y^2 = 144$

4. $x^2 - y^2 = 3$

5. $\frac{x^2}{4} - \frac{y^2}{9} = 1$

6. $x^2 + \frac{y^2}{4} = 16$

7. a. Graph $y = \sqrt{\frac{81}{4} - x^2}$ and $y = -\sqrt{\frac{81}{4} - x^2}$.
   b. Estimate the x-intercepts and find the y-intercepts.
   c. Adjust the window to $-9.3 \le x \le 9.5$. What are the x-intercepts?
   d. What conic section does the graph represent?

Graph each conic section. Find the x- and y-intercepts.

8. $4x^2 + y^2 = 25$

9. $x^2 + y^2 = 30$

10. $9x^2 - 4y^2 = 72$

© **11. Writing** Explain how to use a graphing calculator to graph $x = |y - 3|$.

© **12. Reasoning** Which conic sections can you graph using only one equation? Explain.

Common Core State Standards

G-GPE.A.2 Derive the equation of a parabola given a focus and directrix.

MP 1, MP 3, MP 4, MP 6

Objective To write the equation of a parabola and to graph parabolas

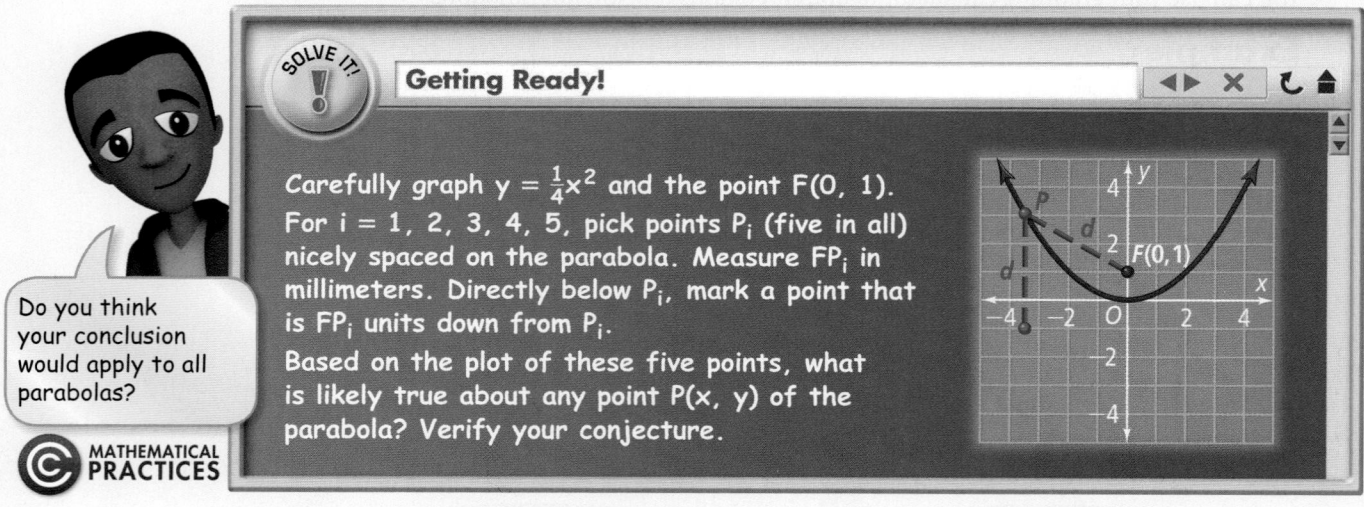

SOLVE IT!

Getting Ready!

Carefully graph $y = \frac{1}{4}x^2$ and the point F(0, 1). For i = 1, 2, 3, 4, 5, pick points P_i (five in all) nicely spaced on the parabola. Measure FP_i in millimeters. Directly below P_i, mark a point that is FP_i units down from P_i.

Based on the plot of these five points, what is likely true about any point P(x, y) of the parabola? Verify your conjecture.

Do you think your conclusion would apply to all parabolas?

MATHEMATICAL PRACTICES

From Chapter 4, you know that a parabola has a vertex and an axis of symmetry. A parabola also has other characteristics.

Essential Understanding Each point of a parabola is equidistant from a point called the *focus* and a line called the *directrix*.

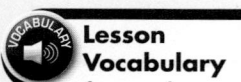

Lesson Vocabulary
- focus of a parabola
- directrix
- focal length

take note

Key Concept Parabola

Definition

A parabola is the set of all points in a plane that are the same distance from a fixed line and a fixed point not on the line.

The fixed point is called the **focus of a parabola**.

The fixed line is called the **directrix**.

The distance between the vertex and the focus is the **focal length** of the parabola.

Graph

axis of symmetry

Focus

directrix

Vertical Parabola

Focus

directrix

axis of symmetry

Horizontal Parabola

In this lesson, you will consider vertical parabolas (each of which has a vertical axis of symmetry and a horizontal directrix) and horizontal parabolas (each of which has a horizontal axis of symmetry and a vertical directrix).

You can find the equation of a vertical parabola with vertex at the origin by using the geometric definition. If you denote the focus by $(0, c)$, the directrix is the line with equation $y = -c$.

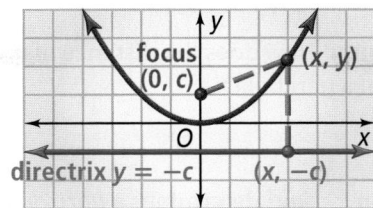

Here's Why It Works Any point (x, y) on the parabola must be equidistant from the focus and the directrix. Use the Distance Formula.

$$\sqrt{(x-0)^2 + (y-c)^2} = \sqrt{(x-x)^2 + (y-(-c))^2} \qquad \text{Distance Formula}$$

$$x^2 + (y-c)^2 = 0^2 + (y+c)^2 \qquad \text{Square each side.}$$

$$x^2 + y^2 - 2cy + c^2 = y^2 + 2cy + c^2 \qquad \text{Expand.}$$

$$x^2 - 2cy = 2cy \qquad \text{Subtract } y^2 \text{ and } c^2 \text{ from each side.}$$

$$x^2 = 4cy \qquad \text{Add } 2cy \text{ to each side.}$$

$$y = \frac{1}{4c}x^2 \qquad \text{Standard quadratic form}$$

Note that the equation has the expected quadratic form $y = ax^2$ for a vertical parabola with vertex at $(0, 0)$. The coefficient $a = \frac{1}{4c}$ determines both the focus $(0, c)$ and the directrix $y = -c$. This is the key to shifting between the algebraic and geometric representations of a parabola.

© **Problem 1** **Parabolas with Equation $y = ax^2$**

Plan

How can you tell if this is a vertical or a horizontal parabola?
The focus and the vertex are on the axis of symmetry. They both lie on the y-axis so the parabola is vertical.

Ⓐ **What is an equation of the parabola with vertex at the origin and focus $(0, 2)$?**

The focus is directly above the vertex.

This is a vertical parabola with vertex at the origin.

The focus is $(0, c)$, so $c = 2$.

$$y = \frac{1}{4c}x^2 = \frac{1}{4(2)}x^2 = \frac{1}{8}x^2$$

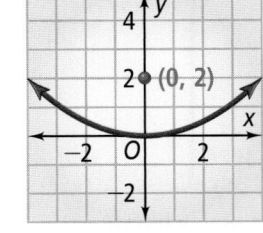

Think

What does the sign of a tell you about the graph?
Since a is negative, the parabola opens downward.

Ⓑ **What are the focus and directrix of the parabola with equation $y = -\frac{1}{12}x^2$?**

This is a vertical parabola with vertex at the origin and $a = -\frac{1}{12}$.

$$a = \frac{1}{4c} = -\frac{1}{12}$$

$$4c = -12$$

$$c = -3$$

Since the vertex is at the origin, knowing c, you can conclude that the focus is the point $(0, -3)$ and the directrix is the line with equation $y = 3$.

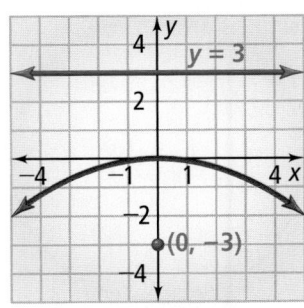

Got It? **1. a.** What is an equation of the parabola with vertex $(0, 0)$ and focus $(0, -1.5)$?

   b. What are the vertex, focus, and directrix of the parabola with equation $y = \frac{x^2}{4}$?

   c. Reasoning How does the distance of the focus from the vertex affect the shape of a parabola?

The quadratic equation $x = ay^2$ determines a *horizontal parabola* with vertex at $(0, 0)$. The coefficient $a = \frac{1}{4c}$ determines both the focus $(c, 0)$ and the directrix $x = -c$.

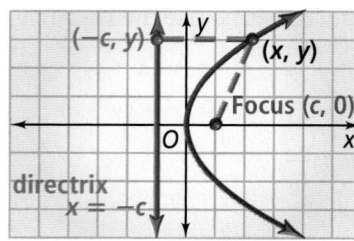

© **Problem 2** **Parabolas with Equation $x = ay^2$**

Plan

How can you tell if this is a vertical or a horizontal parabola?
The directrix is parallel to the *y*-axis, so this is a horizontal parabola.

A What is an equation of a parabola with vertex at the origin and directrix $x = 1.25$?

The directrix lies directly to the right of the vertex.

The parabola is horizontal.

The directrix has equation $x = -c$, so $c = -1.25$. Thus,
$$x = \frac{1}{4c} y^2 = \frac{1}{4(-1.25)} y^2 = -\frac{1}{5} y^2$$

Check for Reasonableness

The graph is reasonable since it opens in the negative direction and $a < 0$.

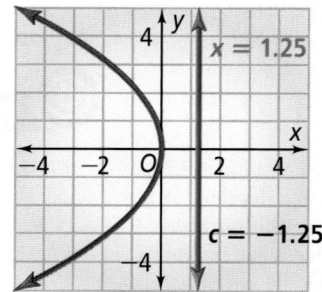

Think

What does the sign of *a* tell you about the graph?
Since *a* is positive, the parabola opens to the right.

B What are the vertex, focus, and directrix of the parabola with equation $x = 0.75y^2$?

This is a horizontal parabola. The vertex is at the origin and $a = 0.75$. Thus,

$$a = \frac{1}{4c} = 0.75$$

$$4c = \frac{1}{0.75}$$

$$c = \frac{1}{3}$$

Knowing c, you can conclude that the focus is the point $\left(\frac{1}{3}, 0\right)$. The directrix is the line with equation $x = -\frac{1}{3}$.

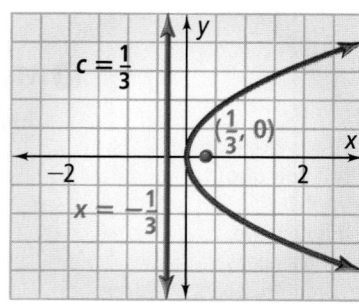

Got It? 2. a. What is an equation of the parabola with vertex at the origin and directrix $x = -\frac{5}{2}$?

b. What are the vertex, focus, and directrix of the parabola with equation $x = -4y^2$?

The geometry of a parabola implies a very important reflective property that gives real-world meaning to the word "focus."

As the diagram of the *parabolic reflector* shows, lines from the focus reflect off the parabola along lines parallel to the axis of symmetry. This is how a flashlight works. Conversely, lines parallel to the axis of symmetry reflect off the parabola directly into the focus. This is how a satellite dish works.

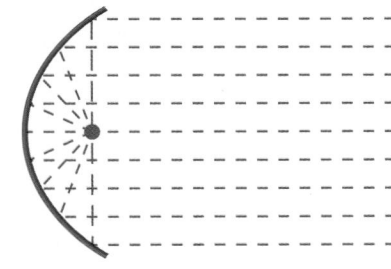

Problem 3 **Using Parabolas to Solve Problems** STEM

Think

What is the shape of the solar reflector?
A cross section is part of a parabola and is 8 ft across.

Solar Reflector **The parabolic solar reflector pictured has a depth of 2 feet at the center. How far from the vertex is the focus? (What is the focal length?)**

Graph the parabola in a coordinate system with vertex $(0, 0)$. The vertical parabola has the form $y = \frac{1}{4c}x^2$. Substitute either the point $(-4, 2)$ or the point $(4, 2)$.

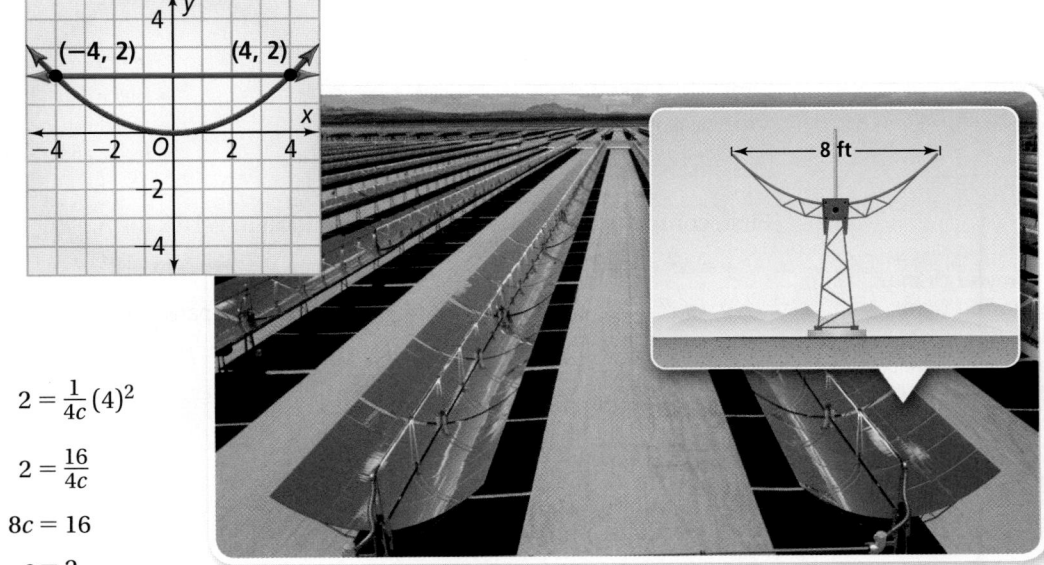

$2 = \frac{1}{4c}(4)^2$

$2 = \frac{16}{4c}$

$8c = 16$

$c = 2$

Therefore the focus is at $(0, 2)$, 2 ft from the vertex.
The focal length is 2 ft.

 Got It? 3. The mirrored reflector of a flashlight is 8 cm across and 4 cm deep. How far from the vertex should the light bulb be positioned?

In Chapter 4, you studied how to translate a parabola from one with vertex $(0, 0)$ to one with vertex (h, k). For such a translation, all of the other features—axis of symmetry, focus, and directrix—translate along with the parabola and its vertex.

take note

Key Concept   Transformations of a Parabola

Vertical Parabola	**Vertex (0, 0)**	**Vertex (h, k)**
Equation	$y = \frac{1}{4c}x^2$	$y = \frac{1}{4c}(x - h)^2 + k$
Focus	$(0, c)$	$(h, k + c)$
Directrix	$y = -c$	$y = k - c$

Horizontal Parabola	**Vertex (0, 0)**	**Vertex (h, k)**
Equation	$x = \frac{1}{4c}y^2$	$x = \frac{1}{4c}(y - k)^2 + h$
Focus	$(c, 0)$	$(h + c, k)$
Directrix	$x = -c$	$x = h - c$

© **Problem 4** **Analyzing a Parabola**

What are the vertex, focus, and directrix of the parabola with equation $y = x^2 - 4x + 8$?

Know	Need	Plan
The equation of the parabola	• vertex • focus • directrix	• Find c, h, and k • Use these values to find the vertex, focus, and directrix.

First, complete the square to get the equation in vertex form.

Think

How can you change the equation to an equivalent form?
Subtract the same value outside the parentheses that you added inside the parentheses.

$y = x^2 - 4x + 8$ Standard form $y = ax^2 + bx + c$

$y = (x^2 - 4x + 4) + 8 - 4$ Add $\left(\frac{1}{2} \cdot -4\right)^2$ inside parentheses; subtract it outside.

$y = (x - 2)^2 + 4$ Vertex form $y = \frac{1}{4c}(x - h)^2 + k$

Note that, in this case, $\frac{1}{4c} = 1$, so $c = 0.25$.

The vertex (h, k) is $(2, 4)$.

The focus $(h, k + c)$ is $(2, 4.25)$.

The directrix $y = k - c$ is $y = 3.75$.

✓ **Got It? 4.** What are the vertex, focus, and directrix of the parabola with equation $y = x^2 + 8x + 18$?

Problem 5 Writing an Equation of a Parabola

Multiple Choice Which is an equation of the parabola with vertex (3, 7) and focus (5, 7)?

Ⓐ $x = \frac{1}{4}(y-7)^2 + 3$

Ⓒ $x = \frac{1}{8}(y-7)^2 + 3$

Ⓑ $y = \frac{1}{8}(x-7)^2 + 3$

Ⓓ $x = \frac{1}{8}(y+7)^2 - 3$

Plan

How do you determine which equation to use?
Use the focus and the vertex to determine the orientation of the parabola.

The focus is to the right of the vertex, so the parabola is horizontal. Also, (h, k) is (3, 7) and $(h + c, k)$ is (5, 7), so $c = 2$. Substitute all this information into the equation for a horizontal parabola, $x = \frac{1}{4c}(y-k)^2 + h$, to get $x = \frac{1}{8}(y-7)^2 + 3$.
The correct answer is C.

 Got It? 5. What is an equation of the parabola with vertex (1, 4) and focus (1, 6)?

 Lesson Check

Do you know HOW?

Write an equation of a parabola with the given information.

1. vertex (0, 0), focus $\left(0, \frac{1}{2}\right)$

2. vertex (3, 2), focus (4, 2)

Find the vertex, the focus, and the directrix of each parabola.

3. $x = \frac{1}{16} y^2$

4. $y = x^2 + 6x + 5$

Do you UNDERSTAND?  **MATHEMATICAL PRACTICES**

Ⓒ **5. Vocabulary** If the vertex of a parabola is 3 units from the focus, how far is the focus from the directrix?

Ⓒ **6. Error Analysis** The vertex of a parabola is at the origin, one unit away from the focus. A student concludes that the equation is $y = \frac{1}{4}x^2$. Identify at least two ways in which the student's equation might be in error.

 Practice and Problem-Solving Exercises  **MATHEMATICAL PRACTICES**

 Ⓐ **Practice** Write an equation of a parabola with vertex at the origin and the given focus. ◀ **See Problem 1.**

7. focus at (6, 0)

8. focus at (0, −4)

9. focus at (0, 7)

10. focus at (−1, 0)

11. focus at (2, 0)

12. focus at (0, −5)

Identify the vertex, the focus, and the directrix of the parabola with the given equation. Then sketch the graph of the parabola. ◀ **See Problems 1 and 2.**

13. $y = 4x^2$

14. $y = -\frac{1}{8}x^2$

15. $x = y^2$

16. $x = \frac{1}{2}y^2$

Write an equation of a parabola with vertex at the origin and the given directrix. ◀ **See Problem 2.**

17. directrix $x = -3$

18. directrix $y = 5$

19. directrix $y = -\frac{1}{3}$

20. directrix $x = 9$

21. directrix $y = 2.8$

22. directrix $x = -3.75$

 **See Problem 3.**

STEM **23. Optics** A cross section of a flashlight reflector is a parabola. The bulb is located at the focus. Suppose the bulb is located $\frac{1}{4}$ in. from the vertex of the reflector. Model a cross section of the reflector by writing an equation of a parabola that opens upward and has its vertex at the origin. What is an advantage of this parabolic design?

Identify the vertex, the focus, and the directrix of the parabola with the given equation. Then sketch the graph of the parabola.

 See Problem 4.

24. $y = x^2 + 4x + 3$ **25.** $y = x^2 - 6x + 11$ **26.** $y = x^2 + 8x + 13$

27. $y = x^2 - 2x - 4$ **28.** $y = x^2 - 8x + 17$ **29.** $y = 2x^2 + 4x - 2$

Write an equation of a parabola with the given vertex and focus.

 See Problem 5.

30. vertex $(4, 1)$, focus $(6, 1)$ **31.** vertex $(0, 3)$, focus $(-8, 3)$

32. vertex $(-5, 4)$, focus $(-5, 0)$ **33.** vertex $(7, 2)$, focus $(7, -2)$

B **Apply**

Identify the vertex, the focus, and the directrix of a parabola with each equation. Then sketch a graph of the parabola with the given equation.

34. $y^2 - 25x = 0$ **35.** $x^2 = -4y$ **36.** $(x - 2)^2 = 4y$

37. $-8x = y^2$ **38.** $y^2 - 6x = 18$ **39.** $x^2 + 24y - 8x = -16$

C **40. Think About a Plan** In some solar collectors, a mirror with a parabolic cross section is used to concentrate sunlight on a pipe, which is located at the focus of the mirror as shown in the diagram. What is an equation of the parabola that models the cross section of the mirror?
• What information can you get from the diagram?
• What information do you need to be able to write an equation that models the cross section of the mirror?

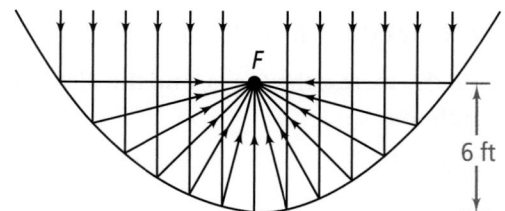

STEM **41. Earth Science** The equation $d = \frac{1}{10}s^2$ relates the depth d (in meters) of the ocean to the speed s (in m/s) at which tsunamis travel. What is the graph of the equation?

Use the information in each graph to write the equation for the parabola.

42.
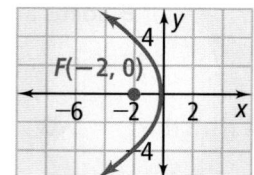

43.
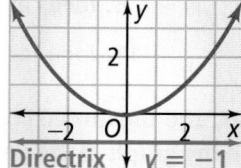

44.
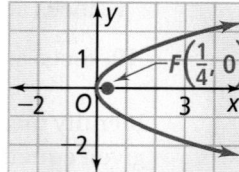

STEM **45. Sound** Broadcasters use a parabolic microphone on football sidelines to pick up field audio for broadcasting purposes. A certain parabolic microphone has a reflector dish with a diameter of 28 inches and a depth of 14 inches. If the receiver of the microphone is located at the focus of the reflector dish, how far from the vertex should the receiver be positioned?

Graph each equation.

46. $y^2 - 8x = 0$

47. $y^2 - 8y + 8x = -16$

48. $2x^2 - y + 20x = -53$

49. $x^2 = 12y$

50. $y = 4(x - 3)^2 - 2$

51. $(y - 2)^2 = 4(x + 3)$

Write an equation of a parabola with vertex at (1, 1) and the given information.

52. directrix $y = -\frac{1}{2}$

53. directrix $x = \frac{3}{2}$

54. focus at $(1, 0)$

 **55. Writing** Explain how to find the distance from the focus to the directrix of the parabola $x = 2y^2$.

 **Challenge**

56. Reasoning Use the definition of a parabola to show that the parabola with vertex (h, k) and focus $(h, k + c)$ has the equation $(x - h)^2 = 4c(y - k)$.

57. a. What part of a parabola is modeled by the function $y = \sqrt{x}$?
  b. State the domain and range for the function in part (a).

58. Proof If the radius and depth of a satellite dish are equal, prove that the radius is four times the focal length.

Standardized Test Prep

SAT/ACT

59. What is the equation of a parabola with vertex at the origin and focus at $\left(0, \frac{5}{2}\right)$?

Ⓐ $x = -\frac{1}{10}y^2$ Ⓑ $x = \frac{1}{10}y^2$ Ⓒ $x = -\frac{1}{10}x^2$ Ⓓ $y = \frac{1}{10}x^2$

60. Use the information in the graph to find the equation for the graph.

Ⓕ $y^2 + 6x = 0$ Ⓗ $x^2 + 6y = 0$

Ⓖ $y^2 - 6x = 0$ Ⓘ $x^2 - 6y = 0$

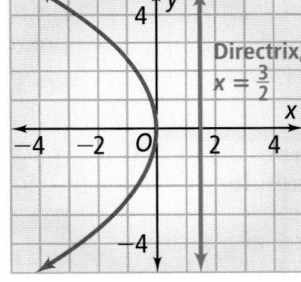

61. Which expression is NOT equivalent to $\left(25x^4y\right)^{\frac{1}{3}}$?

Ⓐ $x\sqrt[3]{25xy}$ Ⓒ $\sqrt[3]{25x^4y}$

Ⓑ $5x\sqrt[3]{xy}$ Ⓓ $\sqrt[6]{625x^8y^2}$

Extended Response

62. Use the properties of logarithms to write log 12 in four different ways. Name each property you use.

Mixed Review

Graph each equation. Identify the conic section and describe the graph and its lines of symmetry. Then find the domain and range.

See Lesson 10-1.

63. $x^2 + y^2 = 64$

64. $x^2 + 9y^2 = 9$

65. $4x^2 - 9y^2 = 36$

Get Ready! To prepare for Lesson 10-3, do Exercises 66–69.

Complete the square.

See Lesson 4-6.

66. $x^2 - 2x + \blacksquare$ **67.** $x^2 + 4x + \blacksquare$ **68.** $x^2 + 10x + \blacksquare$ **69.** $x^2 - 6x + \blacksquare$

Common Core State Standards

G-GPE.A.1 Derive the equation of a circle of given center and radius using the Pythagorean Theorem; complete the square to find the center and radius of a circle given by an equation.

MP 1, MP 3, MP 4, MP 7

10-3 Circles

Objectives To write and graph the equation of a circle
To find the center and radius of a circle and use them to graph the circle

Getting Ready!

In your backyard, there is a square-shaped bare patch in the middle of the grass. You want to put a circular pond in that patch. You also want a circular feeder pond at its upper right as shown in the drawing. What is the radius of the pond? What is the radius of the feeder pond? Explain.

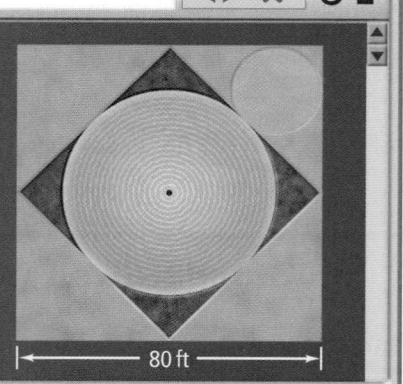

|← 80 ft →|

Try sketching a scale drawing on grid paper.

 **MATHEMATICAL PRACTICES**

Lesson Vocabulary

• circle
• center of a circle
• radius
• standard form of an equation of a circle

A **circle** is the set of all points in a plane that are a distance r from a given point, the **center of a circle**. The distance r is the **radius** of the circle. The use of *distance* in these definitions makes the distance formula

$d = \sqrt{(x_2 - x_1)^2 + (y_2 - y_1)^2}$ a useful tool for describing a circle in the coordinate plane.

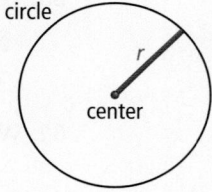

circle

center

Essential Understanding An equation of a circle with center $(0, 0)$ and radius r in the coordinate plane is $x^2 + y^2 = r^2$.

Not every circle has its center at the origin. Suppose a circle with radius r has center (h, k). Then r is the distance from (h, k) to any point (x, y) on the circle.

$r = \sqrt{(x - h)^2 + (y - k)^2}$ Distance formula
$r^2 = (x - h)^2 + (y - k)^2$ Square each side.

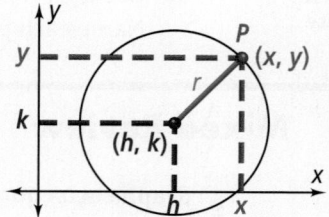

take note

Key Concept   **Standard Form of an Equation of a Circle**

The **standard form of an equation of a circle** with center (h, k) and radius r is
$(x - h)^2 + (y - k)^2 = r^2$.

You can use the center and the radius of a circle to write an equation for the circle.

 Problem 1 Writing an Equation of a Circle

Plan

How do you know which equation to use?

Since this circle is not centered at the origin, use the standard form equation.

What is an equation of the circle with center $(-4, 3)$ and radius 4?

$(x - h)^2 + (y - k)^2 = r^2$ Use the standard form.

$(x - (-4))^2 + (y - 3)^2 = 4^2$ Substitute -4 for h, 3 for k, and 4 for r.

$(x + 4)^2 + (y - 3)^2 = 16$ Simplify.

An equation of the circle is $(x + 4)^2 + (y - 3)^2 = 16$.

Check   Solve the equation for y. Enter both functions into your graphing calculator.

$(x + 4)^2 + (y - 3)^2 = 16$

$(y - 3)^2 = 16 - (x + 4)^2$

$y - 3 = \pm \sqrt{16 - (x + 4)^2}$

$y = 3 \pm \sqrt{16 - (x + 4)^2}$

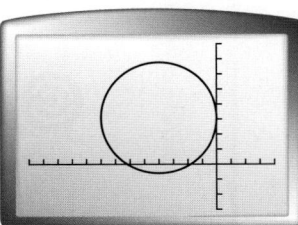

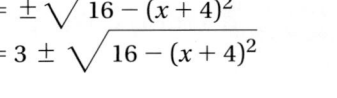 **Got It? 1.** What is an equation of the circle with center $(5, -2)$ and radius 8? Check your answer.

 Problem 2 Using Translations to Write an Equation

What is an equation for the translation of $x^2 + y^2 = 9$ by 4 units left and 3 units up? Draw the graph.

Know	Need	Plan
The original equation that is translated 4 units left and 3 units up	The equation and graph of the translation	• Use the standard form to write the equation of the translation. • Graph the equation.

Think

How does the translation help you draw the graph?

Use the translation to determine the new center coordinates.

$x^2 + y^2 = 9$ Write the given equation.

$(x - (-4))^2 + (y - 3)^2 = 9$ The graph is translated left 4 units and up 3 units.

$(x + 4)^2 + (y - 3)^2 = 3^2$ Simplify inside the parentheses. The form $(x - h)^2 + (y - k)^2 = r^2$ shows the radius r.

Graph the given equation and the translation.

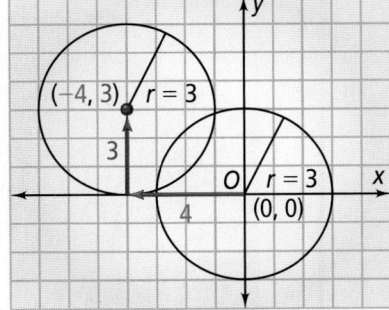

 Got It? 2. What is an equation for each translation?
  a. $x^2 + y^2 = 1$; left 5 units and down 3 units
  b. $x^2 + y^2 = 9$; right 2 units and up 3 units

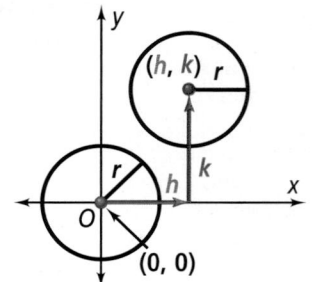

Key Concept Transforming a Circle

take note

You can use the parameter r to stretch or shrink the unit circle $x^2 + y^2 = 1$ to the circle $x^2 + y^2 = r^2$ with radius r.

You can use the parameters h and k to translate the circle $x^2 + y^2 = r^2$ with center $(0, 0)$ to the circle $(x - h)^2 + (y - k)^2 = r^2$ with center (h, k).

Problem 3 Using a Graph to Write an Equation

Multiple Choice Which equation models the circular irrigation field?

Ⓐ $(x - 450)^2 + (y - 500)^2 = 160{,}000$

Ⓑ $(x + 500)^2 + (y + 450)^2 = 160{,}000$

Ⓒ $(x - 450)^2 + (y - 500)^2 = 400$

Ⓓ $(x + 450)^2 + (y + 500)^2 = 400$

Plan

What information do you need to write an equation for the circle?

You need the center and radius of the circle.

According to the photograph, this circular irrigation field has radius 400 and center at the point (450, 500).

$(x - h)^2 + (y - k)^2 = r^2$ Use the standard form.

$(x - 450)^2 + (y - 500)^2 = 400^2$ Substitute the values of h, k, and r from the photograph.

$(x - 450)^2 + (y - 500)^2 = 160{,}000$ Simplify.

The correct answer is A.

Got It? 3. a. What is an equation of the circle for a circular irrigation field that has radius 12 and center $(7, -10)$?

  b. Reasoning Will the graph of every equation of the form $(x - h)^2 + (y - k)^2 = r^2$, where h, k, and r are real numbers, be a circle? Explain your reasoning.

(450, 500)

400 ft

You can find the center and radius of a circle by rewriting the equation in standard form. In some cases, you may need to complete the square.

 Problem 4 **Finding the Center and Radius**

What are the center and radius of the circle with the given equation?

Plan

What do you need to do to the equation to find the center and radius of the circle?
Write the equation in standard form.

A $(x - 16)^2 + (y + 9)^2 = 144$

$(x - 16)^2 + (y - (-9))^2 = 12^2$ Rewrite the equation in standard form.

$h = 16$ $k = -9$ $r = 12$ Find h, k, and r.

The center of the circle is $(16, -9)$. The radius is 12.

B $x^2 + y^2 + 8x - 10y = 8$

$(x^2 + 8x) + (y^2 - 10y) = 8$ Set up to complete the squares.

$(x^2 + 8x + 16) + (y^2 - 10y + 25) = 8 + 16 + 25$ Complete the squares and balance the equation.

$(x + 4)^2 + (y - 5)^2 = 49$ Simplify.

$(x - (-4))^2 + (y - 5)^2 = 7^2$ Rewrite the equation in standard form.

$h = -4$ $k = 5$ $r = 7$ Find h, k, and r.

The center of the circle is $(-4, 5)$. The radius is 7.

Got It? **4.** What are the center and radius of the circle with the given equation?

     a. $(x + 8)^2 + (y + 3)^2 = 121$ **b.** $x^2 + y^2 - 6x + 14y = 8$

You can use the center and the radius to graph a circle.

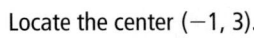 **Problem 5** **Graphing a Circle Using Center and Radius**

Plan

What information do you need to graph a circle?
You need the center and radius of the circle.

What is the graph of $(x + 1)^2 + (y - 3)^2 = 25$?

$(x - (-1))^2 + (y - 3)^2 = 5^2$ Rewrite the equation in standard form.

$h = -1$ $k = 3$ $r = 5$ Identify h, k and r.

center: $(-1, 3)$ radius: $r = 5$ Find the center and the radius of the circle.

                          Locate the center $(-1, 3)$.

                          Draw a circle of radius 5.

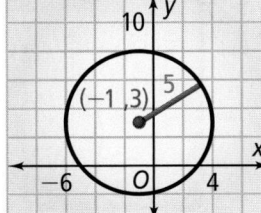

Got It? **5.** What is the graph of $(x - 4)^2 + (y + 2)^2 = 49$?

Lesson Check

Do you know HOW?

Use the given information to write an equation of a circle.

1. center at $(-1, -5)$, radius 2

2. center at $(0, 0)$, radius 6

Write an equation for each translation.

3. $x^2 + y^2 = 121$; up 3 units

4. $x^2 + y^2 = 16$; left 5 units and down 3 units

Do you UNDERSTAND?

 5. Error Analysis A student claims that the circle $(x + 7)^2 + (y - 7)^2 = 8$ is a translation of the circle $x^2 + y^2 = 8$, 7 units right and 7 units down. What is the student's mistake?

 6. Reasoning Let $P(x, y)$ be any point on the circle with center $(0, 0)$ and radius r. Prove that $x^2 + y^2 = r^2$ is an equation for the circle.

Practice and Problem-Solving Exercises

 **Practice**

Write an equation of a circle with the given center and radius. Check your answers.

See Problem 1.

7. center $(0, 0)$, radius 10

8. center $(-4, -6)$, radius 7

9. center $(2, 3)$, radius 4.5

10. center $(-6, 10)$, radius 1

11. center $(1, -3)$, radius 10

12. center $(-1.5, -3)$, radius 2

Write an equation for each translation.

See Problem 2.

13. $x^2 + y^2 = 9$; down 1 unit

14. $x^2 + y^2 = 1$; left 1 unit

15. $x^2 + y^2 = 25$; right 2 units and down 4 units

16. $x^2 + y^2 = 81$; left 1 unit and up 3 units

17. $x^2 + y^2 = 100$; down 5 units

18. $x^2 + y^2 = 49$; right 3 units and up 2 units

19. An archery target has a circular bull's-eye (diameter 24 cm) surrounded by four concentric rings, each with a width of 12 cm. Draw the target in a coordinate plane with center at the origin. Write the equations of the circles that form the boundaries of the different regions of the target.

Write an equation for each circle. Each interval represents one unit.

See Problem 3.

20.

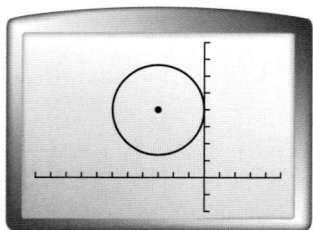

21.

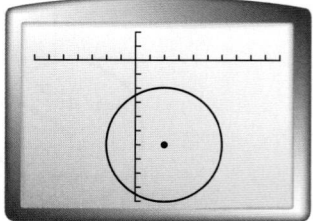

For each equation, find the center and radius of the circle.

See Problem 4.

22. $(x - 1)^2 + (y - 1)^2 = 1$

23. $(x + 2)^2 + (y - 10)^2 = 4$

24. $(x - 3)^2 + (y + 1)^2 = 36$

25. $(x + 3)^2 + (y - 5)^2 = 81$

26. $x^2 + (y + 3)^2 = 25$

27. $(x + 6)^2 + y^2 = 121$

Use the center and the radius to graph each circle.

See Problem 5.

28. $(x + 4)^2 + (y - 4)^2 = 4$

29. $(x - 6)^2 + y^2 = 64$

30. $x^2 + y^2 = 9$

31. $(x + 3)^2 + (y - 9)^2 = 49$

32. $(x - 7)^2 + (y - 1)^2 = 100$

33. $x^2 + (y + 4)^2 = 144$

B Apply

Write the equation of the circle that passes through the given point and has a center at the origin. (*Hint:* You can use the distance formula to find the radius.)

34. $(0, 4)$

35. $(0, -3)$

36. $(-5, 0)$

37. $(\sqrt{3}, 0)$

38. $(4, -3)$

39. $(12, -5)$

40. $(-2, 3)$

41. $(1, -5)$

42. $(-6, -4)$

Ⓒ 43. Think About a Plan Three gears of radii 6 in., 4 in., and 2 in. mesh with each other in a motor assembly as shown to the right. What is the equation of each circle in standard form?
- How can the diagram of the gears in the coordinate plane help you solve this problem?
- How can you write an equation for each circle?

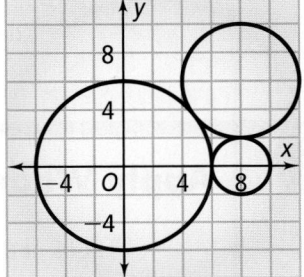

Ⓒ 44. Open-Ended Write two functions that together represent a circle.

Use the given information to write an equation of the circle.

45. radius 7, center $(-6, 13)$

46. area 25π, center $(5, -3)$

47. center $(-2, 7.5)$, circumference 3π

48. center $(1, -2)$, through $(0, 1)$

49. center $(2, 1)$, through $(6, 4)$

50. center $(6, 4)$, through $(2, 1)$

51. translation of $(x - 1)^2 + (y + 3)^2 = 36$, 2 units left and 4 units down

STEM 52. Machinery Three gears, A, B, and C, mesh with each other in a motor assembly. Gear A has a radius of 4 in., B has a radius of 3 in., and C has a radius of 1 in. If the largest gear is centered at $(-7, 0)$, the smallest gear is centered at $(4, 0)$, and Gear B is centered at the origin, what is the equation of each circle in standard form?

Find the center and the radius of each circle.

53. $x^2 + y^2 = 2$

54. $x^2 + (y + 1)^2 = 5$

55. $x^2 + y^2 = 14$

56. $x^2 + (y - 4)^2 = 11$

57. $(x + 5)^2 + y^2 = 18$

58. $(x + 2)^2 + (y + 4)^2 = 50$

59. $(x + 3)^2 + (y - 5)^2 = 38$

60. $x^2 + 2x + 1 + y^2 = 4$

61. $x^2 + y^2 - 6x - 2y + 4 = 0$

62. $x^2 + y^2 - 4y - 16 = 0$

 **Challenge** Graph each pair of equations. Identify the conic section represented by the graph. Then write a single equation for the conic section.

63. $y = 3 + \sqrt{16 - (x - 4)^2}$

$y = 3 - \sqrt{16 - (x - 4)^2}$

64. $y = -2 + \sqrt{x - 3}$

$y = -2 - \sqrt{x - 3}$

 65. Astronomy The table gives the diameters of three planets.

   a. Use a center of $(0, 0)$ to graph a circle that represents the size of each planet.

   b. Write an equation representing the circular cross section through the center of each planet.

66. a. A circle contains the points $(0, 0)$, $(6, 8)$, and $(7, 7)$. Find its equation by solving a system of three equations.

   b. Several parabolas contain the three points of part (a), but only one is described by a quadratic function. What is that function?

Planet	Diameter (miles)
Mercury	3031
Mars	4222
Earth	7926

 ## Apply What You've Learned

MATHEMATICAL PRACTICES
MP 1, MP 2

Look at the drawing of the butterfly from page 613 and use it to answer the following questions.

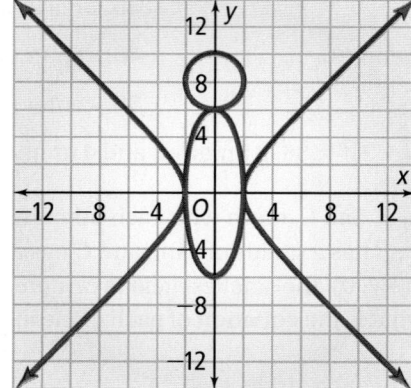

   a. The head of the butterfly appears to be a circle with center on the y-axis. Name two points that the circle passes through.

   b. Explain how you can use your answer to part (a) to find the center and radius of the circle.

   c. Write an equation of the circle. How can you check that your equation is reasonable?

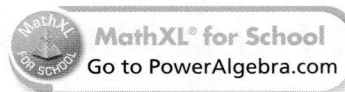
Do you know HOW?

Describe the graph and identify the domain and range for each equation.

1. $y^2 - 2x^2 = 16$

2. $3x^2 + 3y^2 - 12 = 0$

3. $9x^2 - 25y^2 = 225$

4. $36 - 4x^2 - 9y^2 = 0$

Identify the vertex, focus, and directrix of each parabola. Then graph the parabola.

5. $y = 3x^2$

6. $x = 4(y + 2)^2$

7. $y + 1 = (x - 3)^2$

Write an equation for the parabola with the given vertex and focus.

8. vertex $(-5, 4)$; focus $(-5, 0)$

9. vertex $(7, 2)$; focus $(7, -2)$

10. vertex $(0, 0)$; focus $(-7, 0)$

11. vertex $(2, 4)$; focus $(1, 4)$

12. Write an equation that models the graph below.

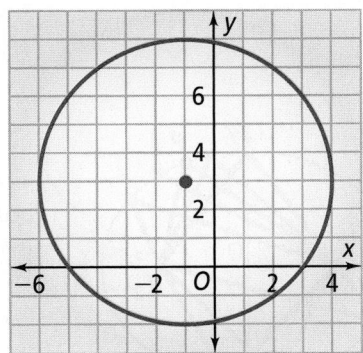

Write an equation in standard form of the circle with the given center and radius.

13. center $(-6, 3)$, radius 8

14. center $(1, 1)$, radius 1.5

Do you UNDERSTAND?

Determine whether each point lies on the graph of the conic section with the given equation.

15. $x^2 + y^2 = 36$
  a. $(-6, 0)$ **b.** $(-2, -\sqrt{3})$ **c.** $(0, \sqrt{2})$

16. $4x^2 - y^2 - 4 = 0$
  a. $(-1, 0)$ **b.** $(2, 2)$ **c.** $(1, 0)$

17. The table below represents points on the graph of a conic section. Identify the conic section.

x	-12	-8	0	12
y	0	± 12	± 16	0

ⓒ 18. Writing Suppose that $x^2 = 4py$ and $y = ax^2$ represent the same parabola. Explain how a and p are related.

ⓒ Reasoning Without graphing, describe how each graph differs from the graph of $y = x^2$.

19. $y = 2x^2$ **20.** $y = -x^2$

21. $y = x^2 + 2$ **22.** $y = \frac{1}{3}x^2$

23. A circle has center $(0, 0)$ and radius 1. Write an equation that represents the translation of the circle 7 units left and 8 units up. Then graph the equation.

Write the standard form of the equation of the circle that passes through the given point and whose center is at the origin.

24. $(-6, 0)$ **25.** $(0, 5)$

26. $(-11, -11)$ **27.** $(-8, 14)$

10-4 Ellipses

Common Core State Standards

G-GPE.A.3 Derive the equations of ellipses . . . given foci, using the fact that the sum or difference of distances from the foci is constant.

MP 1, MP 2, MP 3, MP 4, MP 7

Objectives To write the equation of an ellipse
To find the foci of an ellipse
To graph an ellipse

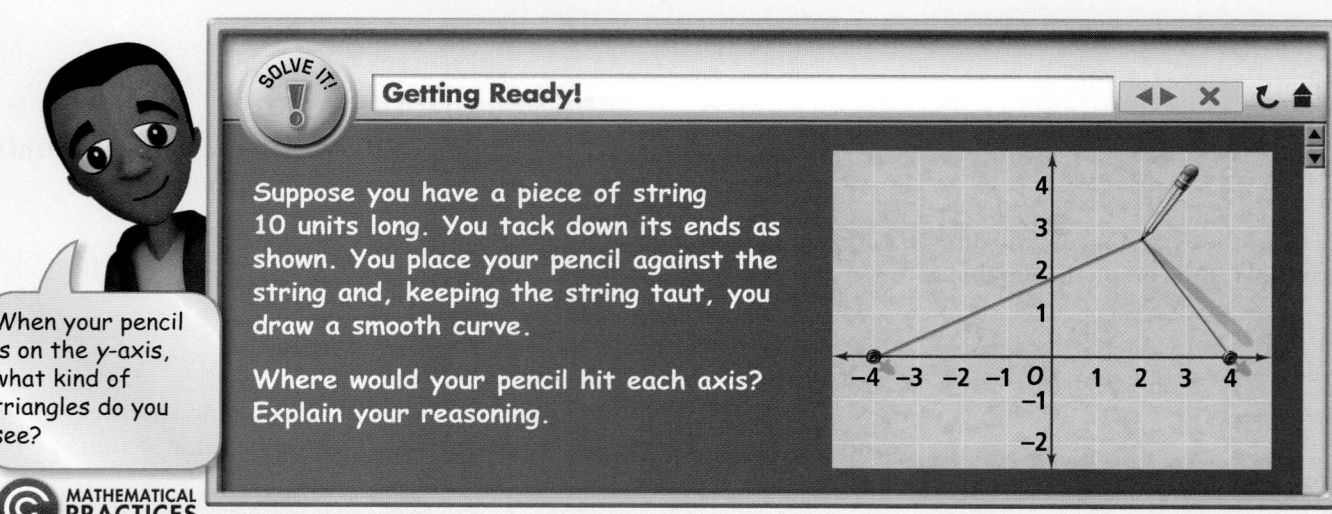

SOLVE IT!

Getting Ready!

When your pencil is on the y-axis, what kind of triangles do you see?

Suppose you have a piece of string 10 units long. You tack down its ends as shown. You place your pencil against the string and, keeping the string taut, you draw a smooth curve.

Where would your pencil hit each axis? Explain your reasoning.

MATHEMATICAL PRACTICES

Lesson Vocabulary
- ellipse
- focus of an ellipse
- major axis
- center of an ellipse
- minor axis
- vertices of an ellipse
- co-vertices of an ellipse

Points on the smooth curve in the Solve It have a total distance of 10 units to the points $(-4, 0)$ and $(4, 0)$. In fact, all of the points on the smooth curve have a total distance of 10 units to the two fixed points. You can describe this smooth curve with an equation.

Essential Understanding A circle is the set of points a fixed distance from one point. An *ellipse* "stretches" a circle in one direction and is the set of points that have a total fixed distance from two points.

take note

Key Concept Ellipse

Definition
An **ellipse** is a set of all points P in a plane such that the sum of the distances from P to two fixed points F_1 and F_2 is a constant k. A **focus of an ellipse** (plural: foci) is one of the two fixed points.

Graph

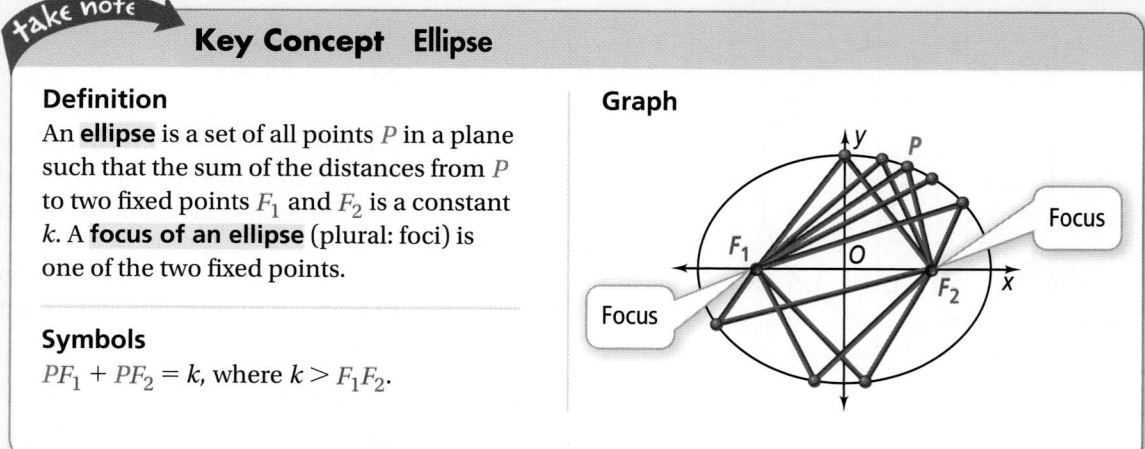

Symbols
$PF_1 + PF_2 = k$, where $k > F_1F_2$.

The **major axis** is the segment that contains the foci and has its endpoints on the ellipse. Its midpoint is the **center of the ellipse**. The **minor axis** is perpendicular to the major axis at the center. The **vertices of an ellipse** (singular: *vertex*) are the endpoints of the major axis. The **co-vertices of an ellipse** are the endpoints of the minor axis.

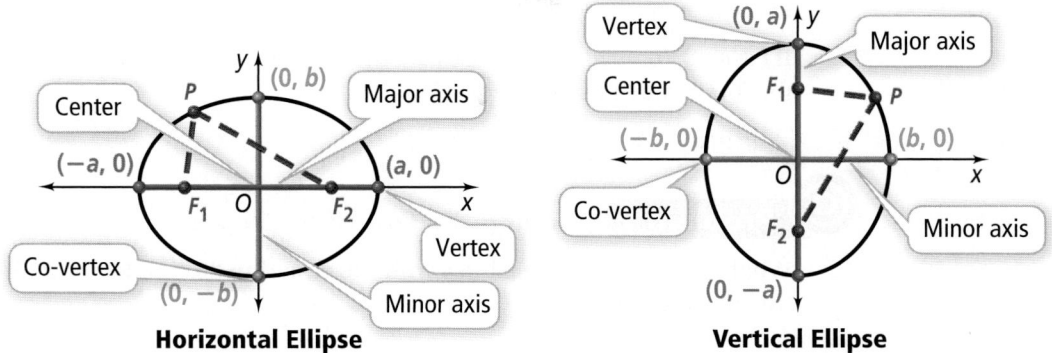

Horizontal Ellipse   **Vertical Ellipse**

take note

Key Concept   Properties of Ellipses with Center (0, 0)

	Horizontal Ellipses	**Vertical Ellipses**
Standard Equation	$\dfrac{x^2}{a^2} + \dfrac{y^2}{b^2} = 1,\ a > b > 0$	$\dfrac{x^2}{b^2} + \dfrac{y^2}{a^2} = 1,\ a > b > 0$
Major Axis	horizontal	vertical
Vertices	$(\pm a, 0)$	$(0, \pm a)$
Co-vertices	$(0, \pm b)$	$(\pm b, 0)$
Foci	$(\pm c, 0)$ on x-axis	$(0, \pm c)$ on y-axis

The length of the major axis is $2a$ and the length of the minor axis is $2b$.
For any point P on an ellipse, $PF_1 + PF_2 = 2a$.

© **Problem 1**   **Writing an Equation of an Ellipse**

Think

What is the orientation of the ellipse?
Since the vertices $(-6, 0)$ and $(6, 0)$ are aligned horizontally, the ellipse is horizontal.

What is an equation in standard form of an ellipse centered at the origin with vertex $(-6, 0)$ and co-vertex $(0, 3)$?

Since one vertex is $(-6, 0)$, the other vertex is $(6, 0)$. The major axis is horizontal.
Since one co-vertex is $(0, 3)$, the other co-vertex is $(0, -3)$. The minor axis is vertical.
So $a = 6$, $b = 3$, $a^2 = 36$, and $b^2 = 9$.

$\dfrac{x^2}{a^2} + \dfrac{y^2}{b^2} = 1$ Standard form of a horizontal ellipse

$\dfrac{x^2}{36} + \dfrac{y^2}{9} = 1$ Substitute for a^2 and b^2.

✓ **Got It?** **1.** What is the equation in standard form of an ellipse centered at the origin with vertex $(0, 5)$ and co-vertex $(2, 0)$?

Since the co-vertex $P(0, b)$ is on the ellipse, $PF_1 + PF_2 = 2a$. If you denote the distance from each focus to the center of the ellipse by c, then a, b, and c are the lengths of the sides of a right triangle, as shown in the ellipse at the right. Thus, the distances from the center to each vertex, to each co-vertex, and to each focus are related by the Pythagorean Theorem: $a^2 = b^2 + c^2$.

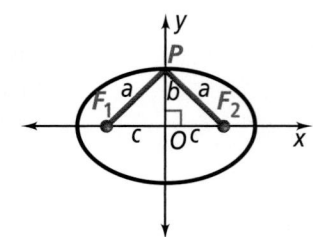

If $(\pm a, 0)$, $(0, \pm b)$, and $(\pm c, 0)$ are the vertices, the co-vertices, and the foci of an ellipse, respectively,

$$c^2 = a^2 - b^2$$

Problem 2 Finding the Foci of an Ellipse

What are the foci of the ellipse with the equation $25x^2 + 9y^2 = 225$? Graph the foci and the ellipse.

Know	Need	Plan
The equation of an ellipse.	The coordinates of the vertices, co-vertices, and foci.	• Write the equation in standard form to find a^2 and b^2. Use $c^2 = a^2 - b^2$ to find c. • Use a, b, and c to graph the ellipse.

$$25x^2 + 9y^2 = 225$$

$$\frac{25x^2}{225} + \frac{9y^2}{225} = 1 \qquad \text{Divide each side by 225.}$$

$$\frac{x^2}{9} + \frac{y^2}{25} = 1 \qquad \text{Simplify to standard form.}$$

Since $25 > 9$ and 25 is with y^2, the major axis is vertical.

$$a^2 = 25 \text{ and } b^2 = 9$$

$$c^2 = a^2 - b^2 = 25 - 9 = 16$$

$$c = \pm 4$$

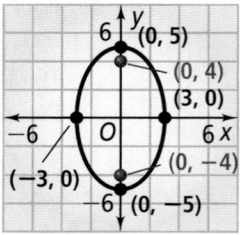

The foci are $(0, 4)$ and $(0, -4)$. Plot points for the vertices, co-vertices, and foci, then graph the ellipse.

  Got It? 2. a. What are the coordinates of the foci of the ellipse with the equation $36x^2 + 100y^2 = 3600$? Graph the ellipse.

   b. Reasoning What happens to the foci as c gets closer to 0? What would the graph of an ellipse be if $c = 0$?

Like parabolas, ellipses have an important reflective property related to their foci: Any line emanating from one focus of an ellipse will reflect off the ellipse directly into the other focus. This property is related to the two-focus definition of an ellipse and can give a new interpretation to the same picture.

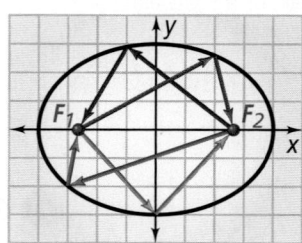

Problem 3 Using the Foci of an Ellipse STEM

Whispering Gallery A room with an elliptical ceiling (called an *ellipsoid*, since it is 3-dimensional) forms a "whispering gallery." Thanks to the reflective property of the ellipse, a whispered message at one focus can be heard clearly by someone standing across the room at the other focus. If the elliptical ceiling has a major axis of 120 feet and a minor axis of 72 feet, how far apart are the foci?

Plan

How can you find the distance between foci, given the major and minor axes?
Find the values of a and b. Then, use a^2 and b^2 to solve for c. The distance between the foci is $2c$.

The major axis has length $2a = 120$, so $a = 60$.

The minor axis has length $2b = 72$, so $b = 36$.

Thus $c = \sqrt{a^2 - b^2} = \sqrt{60^2 - 36^2} = 48$.

The foci are $2c = 96$ feet apart.

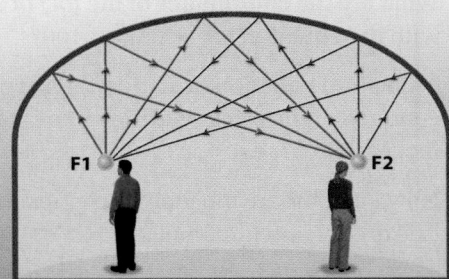

F1   F2

Got It? **3.** How far apart are the foci of an ellipse with a major axis of 26 ft and a minor axis of 10 ft?

Problem 4 Using the Foci of an Ellipse

What is the standard form equation of the ellipse shown?

The foci are on the x-axis, so the major axis is horizontal.

Think

How can you write the equation of an ellipse given a focus and a vertex?
Find the values of a and c. Use a^2 and c^2 to find b^2.

Since $c = 5$ and $a = 8$, $c^2 = 25$ and $a^2 = 64$.

$c^2 = a^2 - b^2$

$25 = 64 - b^2$ Substitute.

$b^2 = 39$ Solve.

$\dfrac{x^2}{a^2} + \dfrac{y^2}{b^2} = 1$ Standard form of a horizontal ellipse

$\dfrac{x^2}{64} + \dfrac{y^2}{39} = 1$ Substitute.

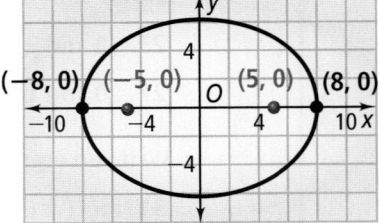

Got It? **4.** What is the standard form equation of an ellipse with foci at $(0, \pm\sqrt{17})$ and co-vertices at $(\pm6, 0)$?

Lesson Check

Do you know HOW?

1. What is an equation in standard form of an ellipse with co-vertices $(0, \pm 6)$ and major axis with length 16?

2. What are the coordinates of the foci of an ellipse with the equation $4x^2 + 25y^2 = 100$?

3. What is an equation in standard form of an ellipse centered at the origin with vertices $(\pm 13, 0)$ and foci $(\pm 12, 0)$?

4. How far apart are the foci of an ellipse with a major axis of 32 ft and minor axis of 14 ft?

Do you UNDERSTAND?

5. **Error Analysis** A student claims that an equation of the ellipse shown is $\frac{x^2}{41} + \frac{y^2}{29} = 1$. Describe the student's error. What is the correct equation in standard form of the ellipse?

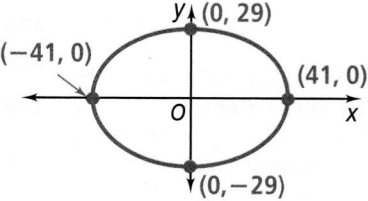

6. **Reasoning** Explain why a circle is a special case of an ellipse.

Practice and Problem-Solving Exercises

 Practice

Write an equation of an ellipse in standard form with center at the origin and with the given vertex and co-vertex listed respectively.   ◀ See Problem 1.

7. $(4, 0), (0, 3)$ 8. $(0, 1), (2, 0)$ 9. $(3, 0), (0, -1)$ 10. $(0, 6), (1, 0)$

11. $(0, -7), (4, 0)$ 12. $(-6, 0), (0, 5)$ 13. $(-9, 0), (0, -2)$ 14. $(0, 5), (-3, 0)$

Find the foci for each equation of an ellipse. Then graph the ellipse.   ◀ See Problem 2.

15. $\frac{x^2}{4} + \frac{y^2}{9} = 1$ 16. $\frac{x^2}{9} + \frac{y^2}{25} = 1$ 17. $\frac{x^2}{81} + \frac{y^2}{49} = 1$ 18. $\frac{x^2}{25} + \frac{y^2}{16} = 1$

19. $\frac{x^2}{64} + \frac{y^2}{100} = 1$ 20. $3x^2 + y^2 = 9$ 21. $x^2 + 4y^2 = 16$ 22. $\frac{x^2}{225} + \frac{y^2}{144} = 1$

Find the distance between the foci of an ellipse. The lengths of the major and minor axes are listed respectively.   ◀ See Problem 3.

23. 40 and 24   24. 30 and 18   25. 10 and 8   26. 16 and 10

27. 20 and 16   28. 18 and 14   29. 36 and 12   30. 8 and 6

Write an equation of an ellipse for the given foci and co-vertices.   ◀ See Problem 4.

31. foci $(\pm 6, 0)$, co-vertices $(0, \pm 8)$ 32. foci $(0, \pm 8)$, co-vertices $(\pm 8, 0)$

33. foci $(\pm 5, 0)$, co-vertices $(0, \pm 8)$ 34. foci $(0, \pm 4)$, co-vertices $(\pm 2, 0)$

35. **Miniature Golf** The figure at the right represents a miniature golf green. The green is elliptical with the tee at one focus and the hole at the other.
   a. How far is the hole from the tee ?
   b. Knowing that the border is elliptical, how should you aim your putt from the tee?

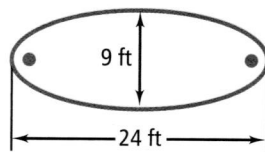

Find the foci for each equation of an ellipse.

36. $4x^2 + 9y^2 = 36$ **37.** $16x^2 + 4y^2 = 64$ **38.** $4x^2 + 36y^2 = 144$

39. $25x^2 + 4y^2 = 100$ **40.** $36x^2 + 8y^2 = 288$ **41.** $25x^2 + 24y^2 = 600$

42. Think About a Plan The open area south of the White House is known as the Ellipse, or President's Park South. It is 902 ft wide and 1058 ft long. Assume the origin is at the center of the President's Park South. What is the equation of the ellipse in standard form?
- How does the length and width of the ellipse relate to the equation?
- What does the center at the origin tell you?
- How can you write the equation of the ellipse in standard form?

43. The eccentricity of an ellipse is a measure of how nearly circular it is. Eccentricity is defined as $\frac{c}{a}$, where c is the distance from the center to a focus and a is the distance from the center to a vertex.
  a. Find the eccentricity of an ellipse with foci $(\pm 9, 0)$ and vertices $(\pm 10, 0)$.
  b. Find the eccentricity of an ellipse with foci $(\pm 1, 0)$ and vertices $(\pm 10, 0)$.
  c. Describe the shape of an ellipse that has an eccentricity close to 0.
  d. Describe the shape of an ellipse that has an eccentricity close to 1.

Write an equation for each ellipse.

44. 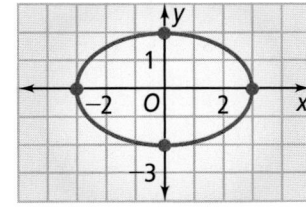   **45.** 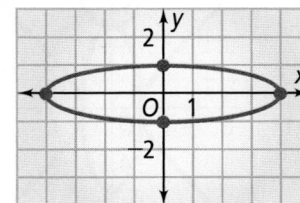   **46.**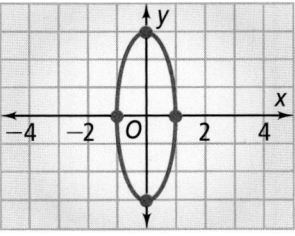

47. Open-Ended Find a real-world design that uses ellipses. Place a coordinate grid over the design and write an equation of the ellipse.

Write an equation of an ellipse in standard form with center at the origin and with the given characteristics.

48. focus $(1, 0)$, width 4   **49.** $a = 5$, $b = 2$, width 10

50. vertex $(-11, 0)$, co-vertex $(0, 9)$ **51.** height 29, width 53

52. focus $(-5, 0)$, co-vertex $(0, -12)$ **53.** $c^2 = 68$, vertex $(0, -18)$

54. focus $(0, 3\sqrt{2})$, height 19   **55.** focus $(2, 0)$, x-intercept 4

56. focus $(0, -5)$, y-intercept 8   **57.** focus $(3, 0)$, x-intercept -6

58. $a = 3$, $b = 2$, width 4   **59.** $a = 2\sqrt{5}$, $b = 3\sqrt{2}$, width $6\sqrt{2}$

STEM 60. Aerodynamics Scientists used the Transonic Tunnel at NASA Langley Research Center, Virginia, to study the dynamics of air flow. The elliptical opening of the Transonic Tunnel is 82 ft wide and 58 ft high. What is an equation of the ellipse?

 **Challenge**

61. Astronomy The sun is at a focus of Earth's elliptical orbit.
  a. Find the distance from the sun to the other focus.
  b. Refer to Exercise 43 for the definition of eccentricity. What is the eccentricity of the orbit?
  c. Write an equation of Earth's orbit. Assume that the major axis is horizontal.

 62. Writing The area of a circle is πr^2. The area of an ellipse is πab. Explain the connection.

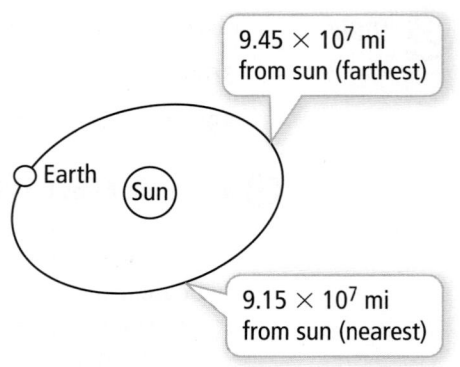

9.45×10^7 mi from sun (farthest)

Earth Sun

9.15×10^7 mi from sun (nearest)

Apply What You've Learned

 MATHEMATICAL PRACTICES
MP 3

In the Apply What You've Learned in Lesson 10-3, you wrote an equation for the head of the butterfly from page 613. Now consider the body of the butterfly.

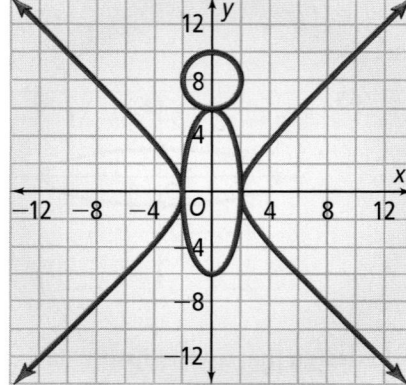

a. The body of the butterfly appears to be an ellipse with center at the origin. What are the vertices and co-vertices of the ellipse?

b. Write an equation of the ellipse.

c. Write an argument to convince someone that your equation of the ellipse is correct.

 **Hyperbolas**

 Common Core State Standards

G-GPE.A.3 Derive the equations of hyperbolas . . . given foci, using the fact that the sum or difference of distances from the foci is constant.

MP 1, MP 2, MP 3, MP 4, MP 5

Objectives To graph hyperbolas
To find and use the foci of a hyperbola

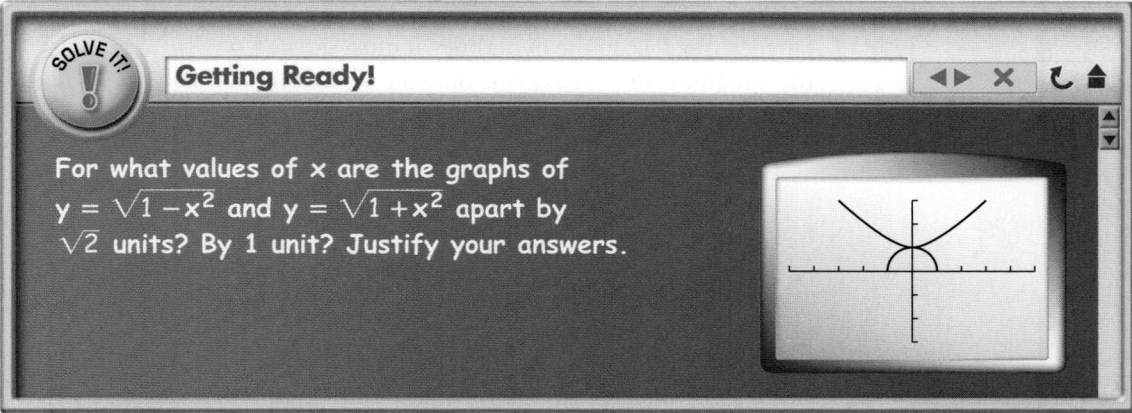

SOLVE IT!

Getting Ready!

For what values of x are the graphs of $y = \sqrt{1 - x^2}$ and $y = \sqrt{1 + x^2}$ apart by $\sqrt{2}$ units? By 1 unit? Justify your answers.

Lesson Vocabulary

- hyperbola
- focus of the hyperbola
- vertex of a hyperbola
- transverse axis
- axis of symmetry
- center of a hyperbola
- conjugate axis

In the Solve It, you saw the top halves of two different conic sections. You can complete each conic section by graphing $y = -\sqrt{1 - x^2}$ and $y = -\sqrt{1 + x^2}$ respectively.

Recall from Lesson 10-1, that you can get a variety of conic sections by slicing the double cone with a plane. Changing the angle at which the plane slices the double cone determines the shape of the curve and whether or not the plane will slice both cones. If the plane is parallel to the axis of the double cone, it slices both cones and the result is a *hyperbola*.

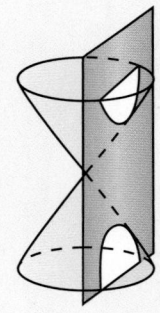

Essential Understanding Like the ellipse, the hyperbola's shape is determined by its distance from two foci.

take note

Key Concept **Hyperbola**

A **hyperbola** is the set of points P in a plane such that the absolute value of the difference between the distances from P to two fixed points F_1 and F_2 is a constant k.

$$|PF_1 - PF_2| = k, \text{ where } k < F_1F_2$$

Each fixed point F is a **focus of the hyperbola**.

Since F_1 and F_2 are the foci of the hyperbola, the long and short segments in each of the 2 colored paths differ in length by k.

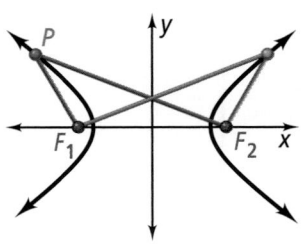

A hyperbola consists of two smooth branches. The turning point of each branch is a **vertex** of the hyperbola. The segment connecting the two vertices is the **transverse axis**, which lies on the **axis of symmetry**. The two foci also lie on the axis of symmetry. The **center of the hyperbola** is the midpoint between the two vertices, which also is the midpoint between the two foci.

Just as for an ellipse, if the foci are $(\pm c, 0)$, the distance between the two foci is $2c$. If the vertices are $(\pm a, 0)$, the distance between the vertices is $2a$.

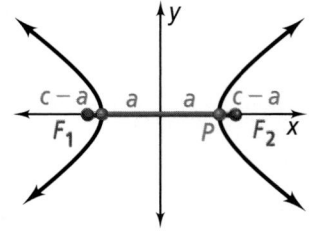

Since vertex P is on the hyperbola, it must satisfy the equation $\left|PF_1 - PF_2\right| = k$, but you can also see that

$$\left|PF_1 - PF_2\right| = \left|[2a + (c - a)] - (c - a)\right|$$
$$= \left|2a + c - a - c + a\right|$$
$$= \left|2a\right| = 2a$$

Therefore, $k = 2a$.

In a standard hyperbola, c is related to a and b by the equation $c^2 = a^2 + b^2$. The length of the **conjugate axis** is $2b$. The transverse and conjugate axes determine a rectangle that lies between the vertices, and the diagonals of that central rectangle determine the asymptotes of the hyperbola. Recall that an asymptote is a line that a graph approaches. The branches of the hyperbola will approach the asymptotes.

take note

Key Concept Properties of Hyperbolas with Center (0, 0)

Horizontal Hyperbola	**Vertical Hyperbola**
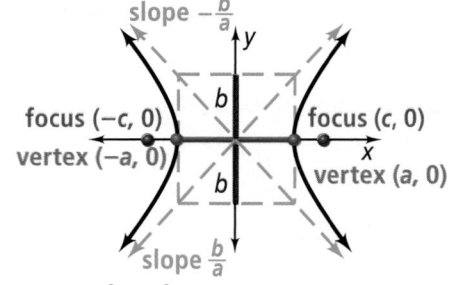	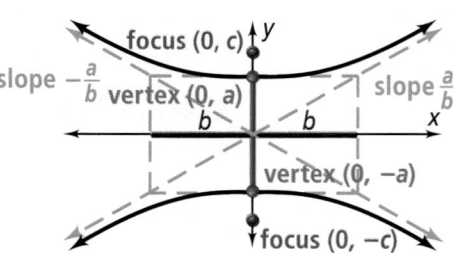
Equation: $\dfrac{x^2}{a^2} - \dfrac{y^2}{b^2} = 1$	Equation: $\dfrac{y^2}{a^2} - \dfrac{x^2}{b^2} = 1$
Transverse axis: Horizontal	Transverse axis: Vertical
Vertices: $(\pm a, 0)$	Vertices: $(0, \pm a)$
Foci: $(\pm c, 0)$, where $c^2 = a^2 + b^2$	Foci: $(0, \pm c)$, where $c^2 = a^2 + b^2$
Asymptotes: $y = \pm\dfrac{b}{a}x$	Asymptotes: $y = \pm\dfrac{a}{b}x$

Because of symmetry, for both the ellipse and a hyperbola, the value of c is half the distance between the two foci.

Problem 1 Writing and Graphing the Equation of a Hyperbola

A hyperbola centered at $(0, 0)$ has vertices $(\pm 4, 0)$ and one focus $(5, 0)$.

A What is the standard-form equation of the hyperbola?

The vertices are $(\pm 4, 0)$, so $a = 4$. One focus is $(5, 0)$, so $c = 5$.

The transverse axis is horizontal.

Use $c^2 = a^2 + b^2$ to find b: $5^2 = 4^2 + b^2$, so $b = 3$.

Write the equation of a horizontal hyperbola in standard form, $\dfrac{x^2}{a^2} - \dfrac{y^2}{b^2} = 1$

$$\dfrac{x^2}{4^2} - \dfrac{y^2}{3^2} = 1 \qquad \text{Substitute values for } a \text{ and } b.$$

$$\dfrac{x^2}{16} - \dfrac{y^2}{9} = 1 \qquad \text{Simplify.}$$

Think

Is the transverse axis horizontal or vertical?
The vertices and focus are on a horizontal line. The transverse axis is horizontal.

B Sketch the hyperbola. Use a graphing calculator to check.

Step 1 Draw the horizontal transverse axis, vertices, and central rectangle. The central rectangle guides the drawing of the graph. It shares a center with the hyperbola and in this case has a height of $2b$ and a width of $2a$. If the hyperbola were vertical the dimensions would be reversed.

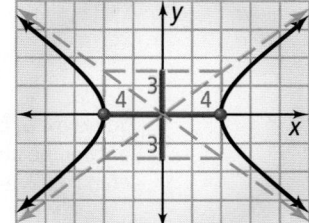

Step 2 Extend the diagonals of the rectangle to show the asymptotes.

Step 3 Sketch the branches from the vertices.

Check Solve for y,

$$\dfrac{x^2}{16} - \dfrac{y^2}{9} = 1$$

$$\dfrac{y^2}{9} = \dfrac{x^2}{16} - 1$$

$$y^2 = 9\left(\dfrac{x^2}{16} - 1\right)$$

$$y = \pm 3\sqrt{\dfrac{x^2}{16} - 1}.$$

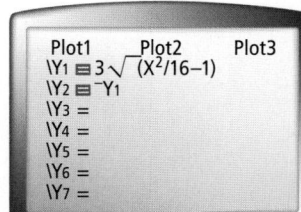

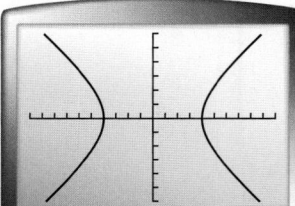

Got It? **1. a.** What is the standard-form equation of the hyperbola with vertices $(0, \pm 4)$ and foci $(0, \pm 5)$?

   b. Sketch the hyperbola. Use a graphing calculator to check.

   c. Reasoning Under what circumstances are the asymptotes of the graph of a hyperbola perpendicular?

Problem 2 Analyzing a Hyperbola from Its Equation

What are the vertices, foci, and asymptotes of the hyperbola with equation
$9y^2 - 7x^2 = 63$? Sketch the graph. Use a graphing calculator to check your sketch.

Think

Write

Write the equation.

$$9y^2 - 7x^2 = 63$$

In standard form, the right side must be 1. Divide each side by 63.

$$\frac{9y^2}{63} - \frac{7x^2}{63} = 1$$

Simplify. Since y^2 has the positive coefficient, the hyperbola is vertical. The vertices and foci are on the y-axis.

$$\frac{y^2}{7} - \frac{x^2}{9} = 1$$

Compare to $\frac{y^2}{a^2} - \frac{x^2}{b^2} = 1$ to find a^2 and b^2.

$a^2 = 7$ and $b^2 = 9$
$a = \pm\sqrt{7}$ $b = \pm 3$

Find c^2. Use $c^2 = a^2 + b^2$.

$c^2 = 7 + 9$, so $c = \pm\sqrt{7 + 9} = \pm 4$

You know a, b, and c. You can answer the questions and draw the graph. $\sqrt{7} \approx 2.65$

Vertices: $(0, \pm\sqrt{7})$, Foci: $(0, \pm 4)$.
Slopes of asymptotes: $m = \pm\frac{\sqrt{7}}{3}$
Asymptotes:
$$y = \pm\frac{\sqrt{7}}{3}x$$

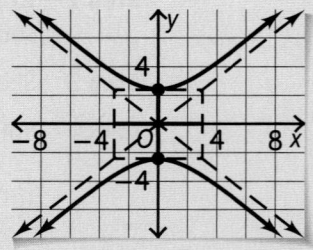

Check

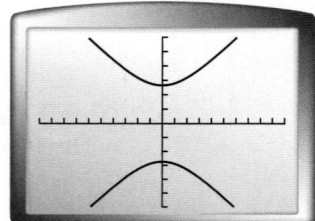

```
 Plot1   Plot2   Plot3
\Y1 ◻ √ (7)√ (X²/9+1)
\Y2 ◻ ⁻Y1
\Y3 =
\Y4 =
\Y5 =
\Y6 =
\Y7 =
```

```
WINDOW
Xmin = −10
Xmax = 10
Xscl = 1
Ymin = −6
Ymax = 6
Yscl = 1
Xres = 1
```

 Got It? 2. What are the vertices, foci, and asymptotes of the hyperbola with equation
$9x^2 - 4y^2 = 36$? Sketch a graph. Use a graphing calculator to check your sketch.

The *reflection property of a hyperbola* is important in optics. As with an ellipse, the reflection property of a hyperbola involves both foci, but only one branch reflects. Any ray on the *external side* of a branch directed at its internal focus will reflect off the branch toward the *external focus*.

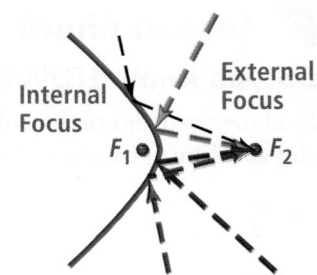

Internal Focus

External Focus

F_1 F_2

© **Problem 3** **Modeling with a Hyperbola** STEM

Communications The graph shows a 2-dimensional view of a satellite dish. The focus is located at F_1, but the receiving device is located on the bottom of the dish at the point F_2. The rays are reflected by the first reflector (the black curve) toward F_1, and then reflected by the second reflector (the blue curve) toward F_2.

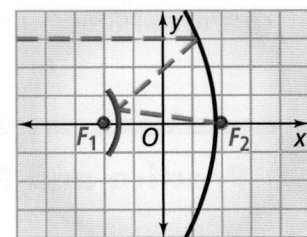

A **What kind of curve is the second reflector? How can you tell?**

The second reflector is a hyperbola because it reflects rays aimed at its internal focus toward its external focus.

B **The vertex of the second reflector is 3 in. from F_1 and 21 in. from F_2. What is an equation for the second reflector? Assume the conic is horizontal and centered at the origin.**

Step 1 Determine the standard-form equation of the conic.
The conic is a horizontal hyperbola centered at the origin.

$$\frac{x^2}{a^2} - \frac{y^2}{b^2} = 1$$

Step 2 Find c.
The distance between the foci is $3 + 21 = 24$ in.
Since c is half this distance, $c = 12$.

Step 3 Find a.
The distance from the internal focus to the vertex of the reflector is 3 in.
So, $c - a = 12 - a = 3$ and $a = 9$.

Step 4 Use c and a to find b^2.

$b^2 = c^2 - a^2$

$\quad = 12^2 - 9^2$ Substitute and simplify.

$\quad = 63$ Simplify.

Step 5 Use a and b^2 to write the equation.

An equation is $\frac{x^2}{81} - \frac{y^2}{63} = 1$.

Got It? **3.** Suppose the vertex of the second reflector in Problem 3 were 4 in. from F_1 and 18 in. from F_2. What is the equation for the second reflector? Assume the conic is horizontal and centered at the origin.

Think

What information does the diagram give up?
It helps you see the relative positions of the reflectors and foci.

Lesson Check

Do you know HOW?

Find the vertices and foci of each hyperbola. Write the slopes of the asymptotes. Then sketch the graph.

1. $\frac{x^2}{36} - \frac{y^2}{25} = 1$

2. $\frac{y^2}{16} - \frac{x^2}{25} = 1$

3. $4y^2 - x^2 = 16$

4. $16x^2 - 25y^2 = 400$

5. What is an equation of a hyperbola with vertices $(\pm 5, 0)$ and focus $(7, 0)$?

Do you UNDERSTAND?

6. Compare and Contrast How is graphing a hyperbola like graphing an ellipse? How is it different?

7. Error Analysis Your friend says that a graph must be a vertical hyperbola because the larger denominator is under the y^2 term. What error did your friend make?

Practice and Problem-Solving Exercises

 Practice

Write an equation of a hyperbola with the given values, foci, or vertices. Assume that the transverse axis is horizontal.

See Problem 1.

8. $a = 3, b = 4$

9. $a = 12, c = 13$

10. $b = 9, c = 10$

11. $a = 7, b = 11$

12. foci $(\pm 13, 0)$, vertices $(\pm 12, 0)$

13. foci $(\pm 3, 0)$, vertices $(\pm 2, 0)$

Find the vertices, foci, and asymptotes of each hyperbola. Then sketch the graph.

See Problem 2.

14. $\frac{y^2}{81} - \frac{x^2}{16} = 1$

15. $\frac{y^2}{49} - \frac{x^2}{64} = 1$

16. $\frac{x^2}{121} - \frac{y^2}{144} = 1$

17. $\frac{x^2}{64} - \frac{y^2}{36} = 1$

18. $\frac{y^2}{25} - \frac{x^2}{100} = 1$

19. $81y^2 - 9x^2 = 729$

20. $4y^2 - 25x^2 = 100$

21. $36x^2 - 8y^2 = 288$

22. $14y^2 - 28x^2 = 448$

STEM 23. Satellite Dish The diagram at the right models a satellite dish and the small reflector inside it. Suppose F_1 and F_2 are 7 meters apart, and F_1 is 1 meter from the vertex of the small reflector. What equation best models the small reflector?

See Problem 3.

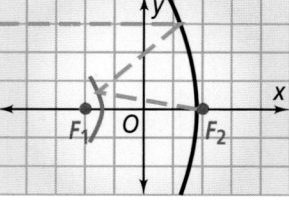

 **Apply**

24. Think About a Plan The path that Voyager 2 made around Jupiter followed one branch of a hyperbola. Find an equation that models the path of Voyager 2 around Jupiter, given that $a = 2,184,140$ km and $c = 2,904,906.2$ km. Use the horizontal model.
- What information do you need to write the equation?
- How can you use the given information to find the information you need?

Write an equation of a hyperbola with the given foci and vertices.

25. foci $(\pm 5, 0)$, vertices $(\pm 3, 0)$

26. foci $(0, \pm 13)$, vertices $(0, \pm 5)$

27. foci $(0, \pm 2)$, vertices $(0, \pm 1)$

28. foci $(\pm \sqrt{5}, 0)$, vertices $(\pm 2, 0)$

Write an equation of a hyperbola from the given information. Assume the center of each hyperbola is (0, 0).

29. Transverse axis is vertical and is 9 units; central rectangle is 9 units by 4 units

30. Perimeter of central rectangle is 16 units; vertices are $(0, 3)$ and $(0, -3)$

31. (Distance from the center of a hyperbola to a focus)$^2 = 96$; endpoints of the transverse axis are at $(-\sqrt{32}, 0)$ and $(\sqrt{32}, 0)$.

 Graphing Calculator Solve each equation for *y*. Graph each relation on your graphing calculator. Use the TRACE feature to locate the vertices.

32. $x^2 - 2y^2 = 4$ **33.** $x^2 - y^2 = 1$ **34.** $3x^2 - y^2 = 2$

Graph each equation.

35. $5x^2 - 12y^2 = 120$ **36.** $16x^2 - 20y^2 = 560$ **37.** $\dfrac{y^2}{20} - \dfrac{x^2}{5} = 1$

STEM **38. Comets** The path of a comet around the sun followed one branch of a hyperbola. Find an equation that models its path around the sun, given that $a = 40$ million miles and $c = 250$ million miles. Use the horizontal model.

ⓒ **39. Open-Ended** Choose two points on an axis to be the vertices of a hyperbola. Choose two other points on the same axis to be the foci. Write the equation of your hyperbola and draw its graph.

ⓒ **40. Error Analysis** On a test, a student found that the foci of the hyperbola with equation $\dfrac{y^2}{100} - \dfrac{x^2}{21} = 1$ were $(0, \pm\sqrt{79})$. The teacher credited the student three points out of a possible five. What did the student do right? What did the student do wrong?

 **41.** The function $y = \sqrt{x^2 - 9}$ represents part of a hyperbola. The tables show the coordinates of several points on the graph.

X	Y₁		X	Y₁
0	ERROR		10	9.5394
1	ERROR		20	19.774
2	ERROR		30	29.85
3	0		40	39.887
4	2.6458		50	49.914
5	4		60	59.925
6	5.1962		70	69.936
X=0			X=10	

a. Explain why ERROR appears for some entries.

b. Describe the relationship between the *x*- and *y*-coordinates as *x* increases.

ⓒ **c. Reasoning** Do you think that the *x*- and *y*-coordinates will ever be equal? Explain.

ⓒ **d. Make a Conjecture** What are the equations of the asymptotes of this hyperbola? Verify your answer by drawing the complete graph.

42. **Air Traffic Control** Suppose you are an air traffic controller directing the pilot of a plane on a hyperbolic flight path. You and another air traffic controller from a different airport send radio signals to the pilot simultaneously. The two airports are 48 km apart. The pilot's instrument panel tells him that the signal from your airport always arrives 100 μs (microseconds) before the signal from the other airport.

   a. Which airport is the plane closer to?

   b. If the signals travel at a rate of 300 m/μs, what is the difference in distances from the plane to the two airports?

   c. Write the equation of the flight path. (*Hint: k = 2a*)

   d. Draw the hyperbola. Which branch represents the flight path?

Apply What You've Learned

MATHEMATICAL
PRACTICES
MP 6

In the Apply What You've Learned in Lessons 10-3 and 10-4, you wrote equations for the head and body of the butterfly. Now consider the curve that creates the wings of the butterfly. Select all of the following that are true. Explain your reasoning.

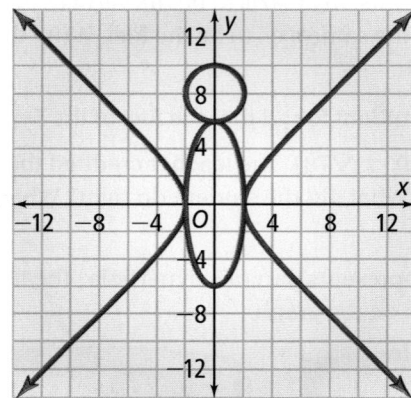

A. The wings of the butterfly appear to be made by a hyperbola with a vertical transverse axis.

B. One vertex of the hyperbola is (2, 0).

C. The foci of the hyperbola are ($\pm c$, 0), where $c > 2$.

D. The conjugate axis of the hyperbola is horizontal.

E. The equation of the hyperbola has the form $\frac{x^2}{a^2} - \frac{y^2}{b^2} = 1$.

F. The equation of the hyperbola has the form $\frac{y^2}{a^2} - \frac{x^2}{b^2} = 1$.

G. The asymptotes of the hyperbola appear to be $y = x$ and $y = -x$, so $a = b$.

10-6 Translating Conic Sections

© **Common Core State Standards**

G-GPE.A.2 Derive the equation of a parabola given a focus and directrix. **Also G-GPE.A.1, F-IF.C.8**

MP 1, MP 3, MP 4, MP 5, MP 7

Objectives To write the equation of a translated conic section
To identify a translated conic section from an equation

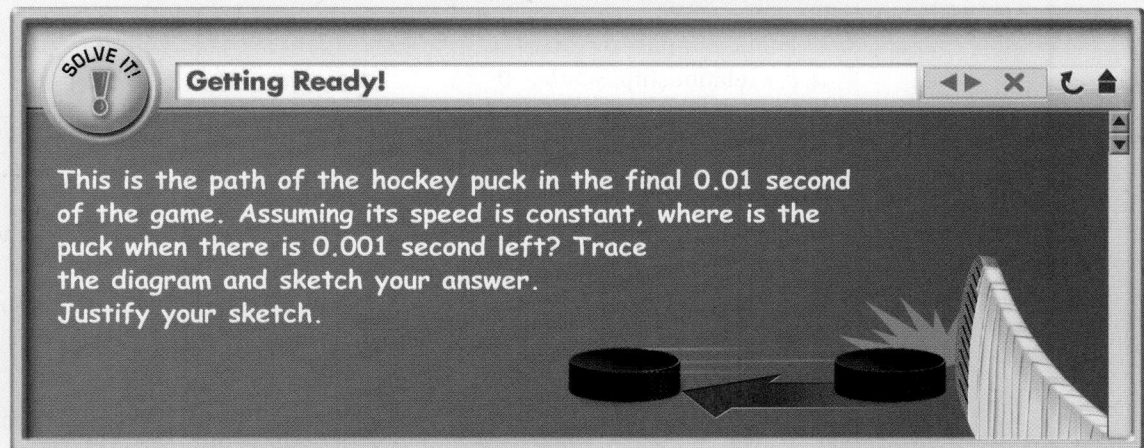

Getting Ready!

This is the path of the hockey puck in the final 0.01 second of the game. Assuming its speed is constant, where is the puck when there is 0.001 second left? Trace the diagram and sketch your answer. Justify your sketch.

In this lesson you will practice translation skills to locate ellipses and hyperbolas when their centers move from $(0, 0)$ to (h, k). You will not need to relearn the geometry of these curves. Each will still depend on the same distances, a, b, and c that relate to their vertices and foci.

Essential Understanding In a relation with an x-y relationship, replacing x by $x - h$ and y by $y - k$ (with $h > 0$ and $k > 0$) translates the graph of the relation h units to the right and k units up.

The summary tables in this lesson are like those from the lesson on parabolas. Notice how each entry in the "Center $(0, 0)$" column relates to the corresponding entry in the "Center (h, k)" column.

take note

Summary   Translating Horizontal Ellipses

Horizontal Ellipse	Center (0, 0)	Center (h, k)
Standard-Form Equation	$\dfrac{x^2}{a^2} + \dfrac{y^2}{b^2} = 1$	$\dfrac{(x - h)^2}{a^2} + \dfrac{(y - k)^2}{b^2} = 1$
Vertices	$(\pm a, 0)$	$(h \pm a, k)$
Co-vertices	$(0, \pm b)$	$(h, k \pm b)$
Foci	$(\pm c, 0)$	$(h \pm c, k)$
a, b, c relationship, $a > b > 0$	$c^2 = a^2 - b^2$	$c^2 = a^2 - b^2$

Summary   Translating Vertical Ellipses

Vertical Ellipse	Center (0, 0)	Center (h, k)
Standard-Form Equation	$\dfrac{x^2}{b^2} + \dfrac{y^2}{a^2} = 1$	$\dfrac{(x - h)^2}{b^2} + \dfrac{(y - k)^2}{a^2} = 1$
Vertices	$(0, \pm a)$	$(h, k \pm a)$
Co-vertices	$(\pm b, 0)$	$(h \pm b, k)$
Foci	$(0, \pm c)$	$(h, k \pm c)$
a, b, c relationship, $a > b > 0$	$c^2 = a^2 - b^2$	$c^2 = a^2 - b^2$

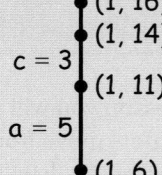 **Problem 1**   **Writing an Equation of a Translated Ellipse**

What is the standard-form equation of an ellipse with vertices (1, 6) and (1, 16), and one focus at (1, 14)? Sketch the ellipse.

Think

Graph the points to find the orientation. The ellipse is vertical with center at (1, 11), halfway between the two vertices.

The vertices are 5 units from the center. The focus is 3 units from the center. Substitute values into $b^2 = a^2 - c^2$.

Write an equation for the vertical ellipse using $h = 1$, $k = 11$, $a^2 = 25$, and $b^2 = 16$.

Sketch the ellipse. Draw a smooth curve through the vertices and co-vertices.

Write

• (1, 16)
• (1, 14)

$c = 3$

• (1, 11)

$a = 5$

• (1, 6)

$a = 5$, so $a^2 = 25$
$c = 3$, so $c^2 = 9$
$b^2 = 25 - 9 = 16$

$$\dfrac{(x - 1)^2}{16} + \dfrac{(y - 11)^2}{25} = 1$$

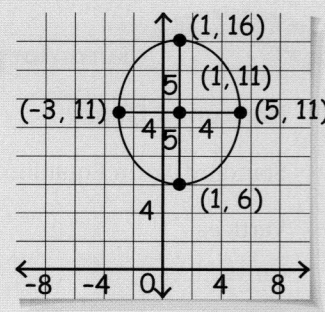

Got It?   **1.** What is the standard-form equation of an ellipse with vertices (2, 3) and (22, 3), and one focus at (6, 3)? Sketch the ellipse.

Summary Translating Horizontal and Vertical Hyperbolas

Horizontal Hyperbola	Center (0, 0)	Center (h, k)
Standard-Form Equation	$\dfrac{x^2}{a^2} - \dfrac{y^2}{b^2} = 1$	$\dfrac{(x-h)^2}{a^2} - \dfrac{(y-k)^2}{b^2} = 1$
Vertices	$(\pm a, 0)$	$(h \pm a, k)$
Foci	$(\pm c, 0)$	$(h \pm c, k)$
Asymptotes	$y = \pm\dfrac{b}{a}x$	$y - k = \pm\dfrac{b}{a}(x - h)$
a, b, c relationship	$c^2 = a^2 + b^2$	$c^2 = a^2 + b^2$

Vertical Hyperbola	Center (0, 0)	Center (h, k)
Standard-Form Equation	$\dfrac{y^2}{a^2} - \dfrac{x^2}{b^2} = 1$	$\dfrac{(y-k)^2}{a^2} - \dfrac{(x-h)^2}{b^2} = 1$
Vertices	$(0, \pm a)$	$(h, k \pm a)$
Foci	$(0, \pm c)$	$(h, k \pm c)$
Asymptotes	$y = \pm\dfrac{a}{b}x$	$y - k = \pm\dfrac{a}{b}(x - h)$
a, b, c relationship	$c^2 = a^2 + b^2$	$c^2 = a^2 + b^2$

As with the ellipse, you can identify the characteristics of a hyperbola just by analyzing its equation.

 Problem 2 Analyzing a Hyperbola from Its Equation

What are the center, vertices, foci, and asymptotes of the hyperbola with equation $\dfrac{(y-1)^2}{25} - \dfrac{(x-3)^2}{144} = 1$? Sketch the graph.

The equation is of the form $\dfrac{(y-k)^2}{a^2} - \dfrac{(x-h)^2}{b^2} = 1$, so the hyperbola is vertical with $h = 3$, $k = 1$, $a^2 = 25$, $b^2 = 144$, and $c^2 = a^2 + b^2 = 25 + 144 = 169$.

Center: $(h, k) = (3, 1)$
Vertices: $(h, k \pm a) = (3, 1 \pm 5)$; $(3, 6)$ and $(3, -4)$
Foci: $(h, k \pm c) = (3, 1 \pm 13)$; $(3, 14)$ and $(3, -12)$

The equations of the asymptotes are $y - 1 = \dfrac{5}{12}(x - 3)$ and $y - 1 = -\dfrac{5}{12}(x - 3)$.

To graph the hyperbola, first graph the vertices and central rectangle. Draw the asymptotes. Then sketch the branches through the vertices and along the asymptotes.

Think

How can you find the asymptotes?
Use the point-slope form of a line to find the equations for the asymptotes.

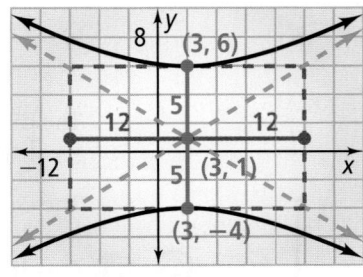

Got It? 2. What are the center, vertices, foci, and asymptotes of the hyperbola with equation $\dfrac{(x-2)^2}{36} - \dfrac{(y+2)^2}{64} = 1$? Sketch the graph.

All equations for conic sections expand to the general equation form

$$Ax^2 + Bxy + Cy^2 + Dx + Ey + F = 0,$$

where A and C are not both equal to zero. If the conic section is horizontal or vertical, $B = 0$ and the general form becomes

$$Ax^2 + Cy^2 + Dx + Ey + F = 0.$$

To locate the center or the two foci of a conic section, you must first convert the general form equation into the standard form for that conic section. This usually involves completing the square at least once and possibly twice.

Ⓒ **Problem 3** **Identifying a Translated Conic Section**

Multiple Choice Which conic section has the equation $4x^2 + y^2 - 24x + 6y + 9 = 0$?

Ⓐ circle; center $(3, -3)$
Ⓒ circle; center $(-3\sqrt{3}, 3\sqrt{3})$
Ⓑ ellipse; foci $(3, -3 - 3\sqrt{3})$ and $(3, -3 + 3\sqrt{3})$
Ⓓ ellipse; foci $(0, 3)$ and $(0, -3)$

Complete the square for the x- and y-terms to write the equation in standard form.

$$4x^2 + y^2 - 24x + 6y + 9 = 0$$

$4x^2 - 24x + y^2 + 6y = -9$	Group the x- and y-terms.
$4(x^2 - 6x) + (y^2 + 6y) = -9$	Factor.
$4(x^2 - 6x + (-3)^2) + (y^2 + 6y + 3^2) = -9 + 4(-3)^2 + 3^2$	Complete the square.
$4(x^2 - 6x + 9) + (y^2 + 6y + 9) = -9 + 36 + 9$	Simplify.
$4(x - 3)^2 + (y + 3)^2 = 36$	Factor.
$\dfrac{4(x - 3)^2}{36} + \dfrac{(y + 3)^2}{36} = 1$	Divide by 36 so the right side is 1.
$\dfrac{(x - 3)^2}{9} + \dfrac{(y + 3)^2}{36} = 1$	Simplify.

Think

How do you complete the square?
Divide the x (or y) coefficient by 2. Square the result.

The equation represents a vertical ellipse. The center is $(3, -3)$. Since $a^2 = 36$, $a = 6$. Since $b^2 = 9$, $b = 3$. Use these values to locate the foci.

$$c^2 = a^2 - b^2$$
$$= 36 - 9$$
$$= 27$$
$$c = 3\sqrt{3}$$

The distance from the center $(3, -3)$ of the vertical ellipse to the foci is $3\sqrt{3}$. The foci are at $(3, -3 - 3\sqrt{3})$ and $(3, -3 + 3\sqrt{3})$.

The correct choice is B.

Ⓒ ✓ **Got It?** **3. a.** Which type of conic section has equation $x^2 + y^2 - 12x + 4y = 8$? What is its center? Sketch the graph.

 b. Reasoning Using as few changes as possible, modify the equation $4x^2 + y^2 - 24x + 6y + 9 = 0$ to make it an equation of a hyperbola.

Problem 4 Modeling With a Conic Section

Navigation A lighthouse is on an island 3 miles from a long, straight shoreline. A boat sails around the island; deliberately following a path that always keeps it twice as far from the shoreline as it is from the lighthouse. What is an equation of the conic section describing the boat's path?

Draw a diagram of the situation with the lighthouse at $(0, 0)$, the shore at the line $x = 3$, and the boat at an arbitrary point (x, y) satisfying the given distance condition.

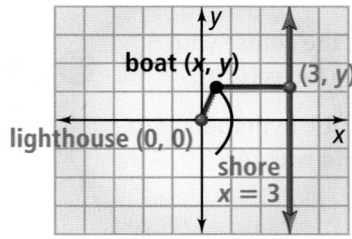

The distance from the boat to the lighthouse is $\sqrt{x^2 + y^2}$ and the distance from the boat to the shore is the horizontal difference $3 - x$. The distance condition translates to:

$$2\sqrt{x^2 + y^2} = 3 - x$$

$$4(x^2 + y^2) = (3 - x)^2 \qquad \text{Square each side.}$$

$$4x^2 + 4y^2 = 9 - 6x + x^2 \qquad \text{Expand.}$$

$$3x^2 + 6x + 4y^2 = 9 \qquad \text{Combine like terms.}$$

$$3(x^2 + 2x + 1) + 4y^2 = 9 + 3(1) \qquad \text{Complete the square.}$$

$$3(x + 1)^2 + 4y^2 = 12 \qquad \text{Simplify.}$$

$$\frac{3(x + 1)^2}{12} + \frac{4y^2}{12} = 1 \qquad \text{Divide each side by 12 so the right side equals 1.}$$

$$\frac{(x + 1)^2}{4} + \frac{y^2}{3} = 1 \qquad \text{Simplify.}$$

This is the standard-form equation for a horizontal ellipse centered at $(-1, 0)$ with major axis of length $2a = 4$ and minor axis of length $2b = 2\sqrt{3}$. Note that $c = \sqrt{a^2 - b^2} = \sqrt{4 - 3} = 1$, so the lighthouse is at one focus of the ellipse.

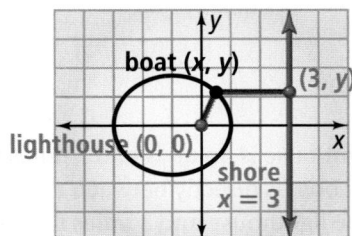

The boat follows an elliptical path modeled by the equation $\frac{(x + 1)^2}{4} + \frac{y^2}{3} = 1$.

 Got It? 4. If the lighthouse were 8 miles from the shore and the boat were to stay 3 times as far from the shore as from the lighthouse, what would be the equation of the conic section describing the boat's path?

Lesson Check

Do you know HOW?

Identify the center, vertices, and foci of the ellipse or hyperbola.

1. ellipse: $\dfrac{(x+7)^2}{225} + \dfrac{(y+1)^2}{144} = 1$

2. hyperbola: $\dfrac{(x-1)^2}{9} - \dfrac{(y-3)^2}{4} = 1$

3. Write the standard-form equation of the ellipse with vertices $(0, -4)$ and $(0, 12)$ and with a focus $(0, 0)$.

4. Write the standard-form equation of the hyperbola with vertices $(-3, 6)$ and $(-3, -8)$ and with foci $(-3, -11)$ and $(-3, 9)$.

Do you UNDERSTAND?

5. **Vocabulary** Which of the conic sections have more than one focus: circle, parabola, ellipse, hyperbola?

6. **Error Analysis** Your friend said that the points $(-14, 1)$ and $(10, 1)$ are the vertices of the graph of the equation $\dfrac{(x-2)^2}{144} - \dfrac{(y+1)^2}{25} = 1$. What error did your friend make?

7. **Reasoning** A student claims that the graph of the equation $x^2 + y^2 + 8x - 10y + 41 = 0$ is a circle with center at $(-4, 5)$ and radius $\sqrt{41}$. Explain the student's error and describe the correct graph.

Practice and Problem-Solving Exercises

 **Practice**

Write the standard-form equation of an ellipse with the given characteristics. Sketch the ellipse.

◀ See Problem 1.

8. vertices $(-5, 1)$ and $(1, 1)$, focus $(-3, 1)$

9. vertices $(3, -1)$ and $(3, -11)$, focus $(3, -4)$

10. vertices $(9, 9)$ and $(9, -5)$, focus $(9, 6)$

11. vertices $(-5, 4)$ and $(8, 4)$, focus $(-4, 4)$

Identify the center, vertices, and foci of each hyperbola.

◀ See Problem 2.

12. $\dfrac{(x+11)^2}{16} - \dfrac{y^2}{9} = 1$

13. $\dfrac{(y-4)^2}{9} - \dfrac{(x-3)^2}{4} = 1$

14. $\dfrac{(y+8)^2}{4} - \dfrac{(x+3)^2}{49} = 1$

Identify each conic section by writing the equation in standard form and sketching the graph. For a parabola, give the vertex. For a circle, give the center and the radius. For an ellipse or a hyperbola, give the center and the foci.

◀ See Problem 3.

15. $x^2 - 8x - y + 19 = 0$

16. $3x^2 + 6x + y^2 - 6y = -3$

17. $y^2 - x^2 + 6x - 4y = 6$

18. $x^2 - 4y^2 - 2x - 8y = 7$

19. $y^2 - 2x - 4y = -10$

20. $x^2 + y^2 - 4x - 6y - 3 = 0$

21. **Navigation** A lighthouse is on an island 4 miles from a long, straight shoreline. When a boat is directly between the lighthouse and the shoreline, it is 1 mile from the lighthouse and 3 miles from the shore. As it sails away from the shore and lighthouse, it continues so that the difference in distances between boat and lighthouse and between boat and shore is always 2 miles.
   a. What conic section models this problem?
   b. What part of the graph does the lighthouse represent? The shoreline?
   c. What equation represents the path of the boat?

◀ See Problem 4.

 **Apply**

© 22. **Think About a Plan** An ellipse has center $(3, 2)$, one vertex $(9, 2)$, and one co-vertex $(3, -1)$. Sketch its graph. Then write its equation.
- How can the sketch help you write the equation?
- What information do you need to write the equation?

© 23. **Reasoning** Use the equation $Ax^2 + Bxy + Cy^2 + Dx + Ey + F = 0$ to identify the shape of the graph that results in each case.
- **a.** $A = C = D = E = 0, B \neq 0, F \neq 0$
- **b.** $A = B = C = D = 0, E \neq 0, F \neq 0$

Sketch each conic section. Then write its equation.

24. A parabola has vertex $(2, -3)$ and focus $(2, 5)$.

25. A hyperbola has center $(6, -3)$, one focus $(6, 0)$, and one vertex $(6, -1)$.

26. **Theater Arts** The director of a stage show asks you to design an elliptical platform. Her sketch shows the platform centered at $(9, 7)$ from the front left corner of the stage. The platform has a 12-ft major axis parallel to the front edge of the stage and extends to within 3 ft of the edge. Write an equation that models the platform.

Write an equation for each graph.

27.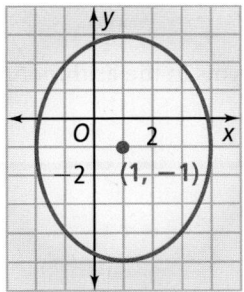

28.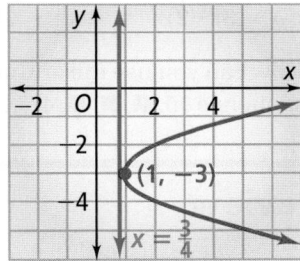

The graph of each equation is to be translated 2 units left and 4 units up. Write each new equation.

29. $(x - 2)^2 + (y + 4)^2 = 16$

30. $\dfrac{(x - 3)^2}{64} + \dfrac{(y - 3)^2}{36} = 1$

31. $y = 2x^2$

32. $9x^2 + 3x + 10 = 16y^2 + 154 + 3x$

Graph each pair of functions. Identify the conic section represented by the graph and write the functions as a single equation in standard form.

33. $y = \sqrt{36 - 4x^2}$
    $y = -\sqrt{36 - 4x^2}$

34. $y = \sqrt{4x^2 - 36}$
    $y = -\sqrt{4x^2 - 36}$

35. $y = 0.5\sqrt{36 - x^2}$
    $y = -0.5\sqrt{36 - x^2}$

© **Challenge** 36. **Open-Ended** On a graphing calculator, create a design using three translated quadratic relations.

37. Astronomy The dimensions of the elliptical orbits of three planets are given in millions of kilometers in the table. The sun is at one focus. The other focus is on the positive x-axis.

a. Write an equation for each orbit and draw the curves on your graphing calculator. (Remember to adjust the viewing window.)

ⓒ **b. Reasoning** Which orbit is most circular? Justify your reasoning.

Planet	a	b
Earth	149.60	149.58
Mars	227.9	226.9
Mercury	57.9	56.6

Standardized Test Prep

SAT/ACT

38. What is the standard form of the equation of the conic given by $2x^2 + 2y^2 + 4x - 12y - 22 = 0$?

Ⓐ $\dfrac{(x+1)^2}{21} - \dfrac{(y-3)^2}{21} = 1$

Ⓒ $\dfrac{(x-3)^2}{21} + \dfrac{(y+1)^2}{21} = 1$

Ⓑ $\dfrac{(x+1)^2}{21} + \dfrac{(y-3)^2}{21} = 1$

Ⓓ $\dfrac{(x-1)^2}{7} + \dfrac{(y+3)^2}{3} = 1$

39. Using a calculator, what are the approximate solutions of $x^2 - 7x + 5 = 0$?

Ⓕ $-0.65, 7.65$ Ⓖ $-7.65, 0.65$ Ⓗ $-1.14, 6.14$ Ⓘ $0.81, 6.19$

40. What is the center of the circle with equation $(x+3)^2 + (y-2)^2 = 49$?

Ⓐ $(3, -2)$ Ⓑ $(-3, 2)$ Ⓒ $(3, 2)$ Ⓓ $(-3, -2)$

Short Response

41. How can you use the arithmetic mean to find the missing terms in the arithmetic sequence 15, ■, ■, ■, 47, ... ?

Mixed Review

Find the foci of each hyperbola. Draw the graph.

◀ See Lesson 10-5.

42. $\dfrac{x^2}{49} - \dfrac{y^2}{36} = 1$

43. $8y^2 - 6x^2 = 72$

44. $4y^2 - 100x^2 = 400$

Solve each equation. Check your answers.

◀ See Lesson 8-6.

45. $\dfrac{1}{3x+1} = \dfrac{1}{x^2 - 3}$

46. $\dfrac{2}{x+2} = \dfrac{6}{x^2 - 4}$

47. $\dfrac{5}{x^2 - x} + \dfrac{3}{x-1} = 6$

Simplify each expression.

◀ See Lesson 7-6.

48. $\ln e$

49. $2\ln e$

50. $\ln e^3$

51. $4\ln e^2$

Get Ready!   **To prepare for Lesson 11-1, do Exercises 52–53.**

Evaluate each expression for the given value of the variable.

◀ See Lesson 1-3.

52. $x + 5x - x - 9; x = -2$

53. $(n-4)^2 + n; n = 5$

Concept Byte
For Use With Lesson 10-6

Common Core State Standards

Extends A-REI.C.7 Solve a simple system consisting of a linear equation and a quadratic equation in two variables algebraically and graphically. **Also A-REI.D.11**

MP 3

Solving Quadratic Systems

In Chapter 3, you solved systems of linear equations algebraically and graphically. You can use the same methods to solve systems of quadratic equations.

Example 1

Solve the system algebraically. $\begin{cases} x^2 - y^2 = 9 \\ x^2 + 9y^2 = 169 \end{cases}$

$x^2 - y^2 = 9$

$\underline{x^2 + 9y^2 = 169}$ Subtract like terms to eliminate the x^2 term.

$-10y^2 = -160$

$y = 4$ or $y = -4$ Solve for y.

$x^2 - (4)^2 = 9$ Substitute the values of y $x^2 - (-4)^2 = 9$

$x^2 = 25$ into the original equations. $x^2 = 25$

$x = 5$ or $x = -5$ Solve for x. $x = 5$ or $x = -5$

The ordered pairs $(5, 4)$, $(-5, 4)$, $(5, -4)$, and $(-5, -4)$ are solutions to the system.

Example 2

Solve the system by graphing. $\begin{cases} x^2 + y^2 = 36 \\ y = (x - 2)^2 - 3 \end{cases}$

$x^2 + y^2 = 36$ Solve the first equation for y.

$y = \pm\sqrt{36 - x^2}$

Graph the equations and find the point(s) of intersection. The solutions are approximately $(-1, 5.9)$ and $(4.6, 3.8)$.

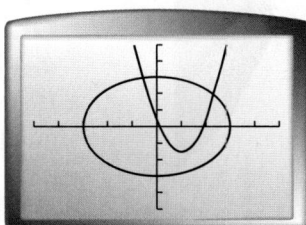

Exercises

Solve each quadratic system.

1. $\begin{cases} x^2 + 64y^2 = 64 \\ x^2 + y^2 = 64 \end{cases}$

2. $\begin{cases} 2x^2 - y^2 = 2 \\ x^2 + y^2 = 25 \end{cases}$

3. $\begin{cases} 9x^2 + 25y^2 = 225 \\ y = -x^2 + 5 \end{cases}$

4. a. Writing The system that consists of $y = -3x + 6$ and $y = x^2 - 4x$ is a linear-quadratic system. How would you solve the system algebraically? Graphically?

   b. Solve the system in part (a).

Identify each system as linear-quadratic or quadratic-quadratic. Then solve.

5. $\begin{cases} y = x - 1 \\ x^2 + y^2 = 25 \end{cases}$

6. $\begin{cases} 9x^2 + 4y^2 = 36 \\ x^2 - y^2 = 4 \end{cases}$

7. $\begin{cases} -x + y = 4 \\ y = x^2 - 4x + 2 \end{cases}$

8. $\begin{cases} 4x^2 + 25y^2 = 100 \\ y = x + 2 \end{cases}$

Pull It **All Together**

Completing the Performance Task

Look back at your results from the Apply What You've Learned sections in Lessons 10-3, 10-4, and 10-5. Use the work that you did to complete the following.

To solve these problems, you will pull together concepts and skills related to conic sections.

1. Solve the problem in the Task Description on page 613 by explaining how to reproduce the butterfly on a graphing calculator. Provide the equations you should enter and the viewing window you should use so that the graph resembles Kenjiro's drawing as closely as possible. Show all your work and explain each step of your solution.

 2. **Reflect** Choose one of the Mathematical Practices below and explain how you applied it in your work.

   MP 1: Make sense of problems and persevere in solving them.

   MP 2: Reason abstractly and quantitatively.

   MP 3: Construct viable arguments and critique the reasoning of others.

   MP 6: Attend to precision.

On Your Own

Kenjiro used conic sections to draw a beetle on a coordinate plane, as shown below. He used a parabola for the antennae. Now he wants to reproduce the drawing on his graphing calculator.

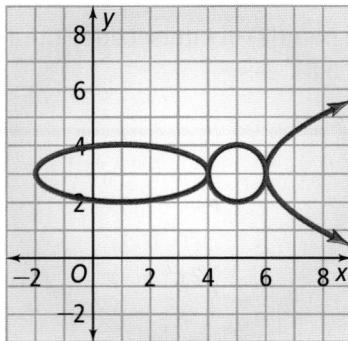

Explain how to reproduce the beetle on a graphing calculator. Provide the equations you should enter and the viewing window you should use so that your beetle resembles Kenjiro's drawing as closely as possible.

Connecting BIG ideas and Answering the Essential Questions

1 Modeling

The intersection of a cone and a plane parallel to the side of a cone is a parabola.

→

Parabolas (Lesson 10-2)

Centered at the origin,
- a parabola has equation $y = ax^2$, or $x = ay^2$.

→

Translating Conic Sections (Lesson 10-6)

Centered at (h, k),
- substitute $x - h$ for x and $y - k$ for y in the original equation for a conic section.

2 Equivalence

$\frac{x^2}{9} + \frac{y^2}{9} = 1$ is an equation of a circle centered at the origin with radius 3. Multiply each side by 9 to get $x^2 + y^2 = 9$.

→

Circles (Lesson 10-3)

Centered at the origin,
- a circle with radius r has equation $x^2 + y^2 = r^2$.

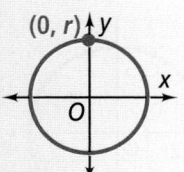

→

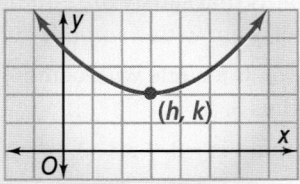

3 Coordinate Geometry

The x^2 and y^2 terms of the algebraic form of an ellipse are both positive. For a hyperbola, one term is negative.

→

Ellipses and Hyperbolas (Lessons 10-4 and 10-5)

Centered at the origin,
- an ellipse has equation $\frac{x^2}{a^2} + \frac{y^2}{b^2} = 1$
- a hyperbola has equation $\frac{x^2}{a^2} - \frac{y^2}{b^2} = 1$ or $\frac{y^2}{a^2} - \frac{x^2}{b^2} = 1$.

→

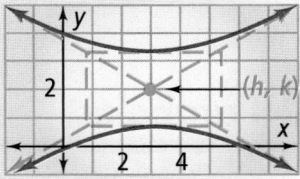

Chapter Vocabulary

- axis of symmetry (p. 646)
- center of a circle (p. 630)
- center of a hyperbola (p. 646)
- center of an ellipse (p. 639)
- circle (p. 630)
- conic section (p. 614)
- conjugate axis (p. 646)
- co-vertices of an ellipse (p. 639)

- directrix (p. 622)
- ellipse (p. 638)
- focal length (p. 622)
- focus of a parabola (p. 622)
- foci of an ellipse (p. 638)
- foci of a hyperbola (p. 645)
- hyperbola (p. 645)
- major axis (p. 639)

- minor axis (p. 639)
- radius (p. 630)
- standard form of an equation of a circle (p. 630)
- transverse axis (p. 646)
- vertices of an ellipse (p. 639)
- vertices of a hyperbola (p. 646)

Fill in the blanks.

1. In the definition of a parabola, a point on the curve is equidistant from the focus and the ___?___ .

2. The vertices of an ellipse are on its ___?___ .

3. $(x - h)^2 + (y - k)^2 = r^2$ is the ___?___ .

4. The distance from a point on a circle to its center is the ___?___ of the circle.

5. The vertices of a hyperbola are on its ___?___ .

10-1 Exploring Conic Sections

Quick Review

A **conic section** is formed by the intersection of a plane and a double cone. Circles, ellipses, parabolas, and hyperbolas are all conic sections.

Example

Graph the equation $x^2 + y^2 = 9$. Identify the conic section, the domain, and the range.

Plot points that satisfy the equation. Connect them with a smooth curve.

The graph is a circle with center $(0, 0)$ and radius 3.

The domain is $-3 \leq x \leq 3$.

The range is $-3 \leq y \leq 3$.

Exercises

Graph each equation. Identify the conic section, any lines of symmetry, and the domain and range.

6. $\dfrac{x^2}{49} + \dfrac{y^2}{121} = 1$ **7.** $x^2 + y^2 = 4$

8. $\dfrac{x^2}{25} - \dfrac{y^2}{4} = 1$ **9.** $x = 2y^2 + 5$

Identify the center and domain and range of each graph.

10. 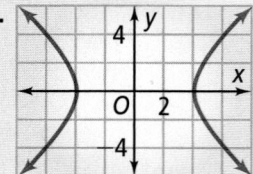   **11.**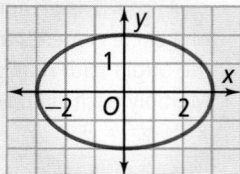

10-2 Parabolas

Quick Review

In a plane, a parabola is the set of all points that are the same distance, c, from a fixed point, the **focus** and a fixed line, the **directrix**.

For $y = ax^2$, if $a > 0$, the parabola opens up, and has focus $(0, c)$ and directrix $y = -c$; if $a < 0$, the parabola opens down, and has focus $(0, -c)$ and directrix $y = c$.

For $x = ay^2$, if $a > 0$, the parabola opens right, and has focus $(c, 0)$ and directrix $x = -c$; if $a < 0$, the parabola opens left, and has focus $(-c, 0)$ and directrix $x = c$. In all cases, $a = \dfrac{1}{4c}$.

Example

Write an equation of a parabola that opens up, with vertex at the origin and focus 1 unit from the vertex.

Since the parabola opens up, use $y = ax^2$. Since the focus is 1 unit from the vertex, $c = 1$.

$$a = \frac{1}{4c} = \frac{1}{4(1)} = \frac{1}{4}$$

An equation for the parabola is $y = \frac{1}{4}x^2$.

Exercises

Write an equation of a parabola with vertex at the origin and the given focus.

12. $(5, 0)$ **13.** $(0, -5)$ **14.** $(0, 6)$

Write an equation of a parabola that opens up, with vertex at the origin and a focus as described.

15. focus is 2.5 units from the vertex

16. focus is $\frac{1}{12}$ of a unit from the vertex

Write an equation of a parabola with the given focus and directrix.

17. focus: $(0, 3)$; directrix: $y = -1$

18. focus: $(-2, 0)$; directrix: $x = 4$

Find the focus and the directrix of the graph of each equation. Sketch the graph.

19. $y = 5x^2$ **20.** $x = 2y^2$ **21.** $x = -\frac{1}{8}y^2$

10-3 Circles

Quick Review

In a plane, a **circle** is the set of all points that are a given distance, the **radius**, r, from a given point, the **center**, (h, k).

Example

Write an equation in standard form of a circle with center $(-3, 4)$ and radius 2.

Use the standard form of the equation of a circle. Substitute -3 for h, 4 for k, and 2 for r.

$$(x - h)^2 + (y - k)^2 = r^2$$
$$(x - (-3))^2 + (y - 4)^2 = 2^2$$
$$(x + 3)^2 + (y - 4)^2 = 4$$

An equation for the circle is $(x + 3)^2 + (y - 4)^2 = 4$.

Exercises

Write an equation in standard form of a circle with the given center and radius.

22. center $(0, 0)$; radius 4

23. center $(8, 1)$; radius 5

Write an equation for each translation of $x^2 + y^2 = r^2$ with the given radius.

24. left 3 units, up 2 units; radius 10

25. right 5 units, down 3 units; radius 8

Find the center and the radius of each circle. Graph each circle. Describe the translation from center $(0, 0)$.

26. $(x - 1)^2 + y^2 = 64$

27. $(x + 7)^2 + (y + 3)^2 = 49$

10-4 Ellipses

Quick Review

An **ellipse** is the set of all points P, where the sum of the distances between P and two fixed points, the **foci**, is constant. The **major axis** contains the foci, and its endpoints are the **vertices of the ellipse**. For $a > b$, there are two standard forms of ellipses centered at the origin. If $\frac{x^2}{a^2} + \frac{y^2}{b^2} = 1$, the major axis is horizontal with vertices $(\pm a, 0)$, foci $(\pm c, 0)$, and co-vertices $(0, \pm b)$. If $\frac{x^2}{b^2} + \frac{y^2}{a^2} = 1$, the major axis is vertical with vertices $(0, \pm a)$, foci $(0, \pm c)$, and co-vertices $(\pm b, 0)$. In either case, $c^2 = a^2 - b^2$.

Example

Write an equation of an ellipse with foci $(\pm 5, 0)$ and co-vertices $(0, \pm 3)$.

Since the foci are $(\pm 5, 0)$, the major axis is horizontal. Since $c = 5$ and $b = 3$, $c^2 = 25$ and $b^2 = 9$. Using the equation $c^2 = a^2 - b^2$, $a^2 = 34$.

An equation of the ellipse is $\frac{x^2}{34} + \frac{y^2}{9} = 1$.

Exercises

Write an equation of an ellipse centered at the origin, satisfying the given conditions.

28. foci $(\pm 1, 0)$; co-vertices $(0, \pm 4)$

29. vertex $(0, \sqrt{29})$; co-vertex $(-5, 0)$

30. focus $(0, 1)$; vertex $(0, \sqrt{10})$

31. foci $(\pm 2, 0)$; co-vertices $(0, \pm 6)$

32. Write an equation of an ellipse centered at the origin with height 8 units and width 16 units.

33. Find the foci of the graph of $\frac{x^2}{4} + \frac{y^2}{9} = 1$. Graph the ellipse.

10-5 Hyperbolas

Quick Review

A **hyperbola** is the set of all points P such that the absolute value of the difference of the distances from P to two fixed points, the **foci**, is constant. There are two standard forms of hyperbolas centered at the origin. If $\frac{x^2}{a^2} - \frac{y^2}{b^2} = 1$, the asymptotes are $y = \pm \frac{b}{a}x$, the **transverse axis** is horizontal with vertices $(\pm a, 0)$, and the foci are $(\pm c, 0)$. If $\frac{y^2}{a^2} - \frac{x^2}{b^2} = 1$, the asymptotes are $y = \pm \frac{a}{b}x$, the transverse axis is vertical with vertices $(0, \pm a)$, and the foci are $(0, \pm c)$. In either case, $c^2 = a^2 + b^2$.

Example

Find the foci of the graph of $\frac{x^2}{25} - \frac{y^2}{9} = 1$.

The equation is in the form $\frac{x^2}{a^2} - \frac{y^2}{b^2} = 1$, so the transverse axis is horizontal; $a^2 = 25$ and $b^2 = 9$.

Using the Pythagorean Theorem to find c,
$c = \sqrt{25 + 9} = \sqrt{34} \approx 5.8$.
The foci, $(\pm c, 0)$, are approximately $(5.8, 0)$ and $(-5.8, 0)$.

Exercises

Find the foci of each hyperbola. Graph the hyperbola.

34. $\frac{x^2}{36} - \frac{y^2}{225} = 1$

35. $\frac{y^2}{400} - \frac{x^2}{169} = 1$

36. $\frac{x^2}{121} - \frac{y^2}{81} = 1$

Write an equation of a hyperbola with the given foci and vertices.

37. foci $(\pm 17, 0)$, vertices $(\pm 8, 0)$

38. foci $(0, \pm 25)$, vertices $(0, \pm 7)$

39. Find an equation that models the hyperbolic path of a spacecraft around a planet if $a = 107{,}124$ km and $c = 213{,}125.9$ km.

10-6 Translating Conic Sections

Quick Review

Substitute $(x - h)$ for x and $(y - k)$ for y to translate graphs of the conic sections.

Example

Identify and describe the conic section represented by the equation $2x^2 + 3y^2 + 4x + 12y - 22 = 0$.

By completing the square, the equation becomes $\frac{(x + 1)^2}{18} + \frac{(y + 2)^2}{12} = 1$, which is an ellipse.

The center is $(-1, -2)$ and the major axis is horizontal.

Using the equation $c^2 = a^2 - b^2$, $c = \sqrt{6}$, so the distance from the center of the ellipse to the foci is $\sqrt{6}$.

Since the ellipse is centered at $(-1, -2)$ and the major axis is horizontal, the foci are located $\sqrt{6}$ to the left and right of this center.

The foci are at $(-1 + \sqrt{6}, -2)$ and $(-1 - \sqrt{6}, -2)$.

Exercises

Write an equation of a conic section with the given characteristics.

40. a circle with center $(1, 1)$; radius 5

41. an ellipse with center $(3, -2)$; vertical major axis of length 6; minor axis of length 4

42. a hyperbola with vertices $(3, 3)$ and $(9, 3)$; foci $(1, 3)$ and $(11, 3)$

Identify the conic section and sketch the graph. If it is a parabola, give the vertex. If it is a circle, give the center and radius. If it is an ellipse or a hyperbola, give the center and foci.

43. $-x^2 + y^2 + 4y - 16 = 0$

44. $x^2 + y^2 + 3x - 4y - 9 = 0$

45. $x^2 + x - y - 42 = 0$

Do you know HOW?

Identify the type of each conic section. Give the center, domain, and range of each graph.

1.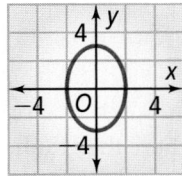

2.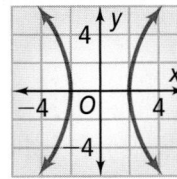

3.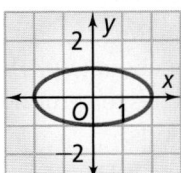

4.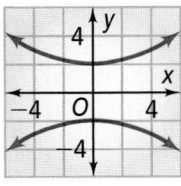

Identify the focus and the directrix of the graph of each equation.

5. $y = 3x^2$

6. $x = -2y^2$

7. $x + 5y^2 = 0$

8. $9x^2 - 2y = 0$

Write an equation of a parabola with its vertex at the origin and the given characteristics.

9. focus at $(0, -2)$

10. focus at $(3, 0)$

11. directrix $x = 7$

12. directrix $y = -1$

For each equation, find the center and radius of the circle. Graph the circle.

13. $(x - 2)^2 + (y - 3)^2 = 36$

14. $(x + 5)^2 + (y + 8)^2 = 100$

15. $(x - 1)^2 + (y + 7)^2 = 81$

16. $(x + 4)^2 + (y - 10)^2 = 121$

Write an equation of an ellipse for each given height and width. Assume that the center of the ellipse is (0, 0).

17. height 10 units; width 16 units

18. height 2 units; width 12 units

19. height 9 units; width 5 units

Find the foci of each ellipse. Then graph the ellipse.

20. $x^2 + \dfrac{y^2}{49} = 1$

21. $4x^2 + y^2 = 4$

Find the foci of each hyperbola. Then graph the hyperbola.

22. $\dfrac{x^2}{64} - \dfrac{y^2}{4} = 1$

23. $y^2 - \dfrac{x^2}{225} = 1$

Write an equation of an ellipse with the given characteristics.

24. center $(-2, 7)$; horizontal major axis of length 8; minor axis of length 6

25. center $(3, -2)$; vertical major axis of length 12; minor axis of length 10

Write an equation of a hyperbola with the given characteristics.

26. vertices $(\pm 3, 7)$; foci $(\pm 5, 7)$

27. vertices $(2, \pm 5)$; foci $(2, \pm 8)$

Identify the conic section represented by each equation. If it is a parabola, give the vertex. If it is a circle, give the center and radius. If it is an ellipse or a hyperbola, give the center and foci. Sketch the graph.

28. $3y^2 - x - 6y + 5 = 0$

29. $4x^2 + y^2 - 16x - 6y + 9 = 0$

Do you UNDERSTAND?

30. Writing Explain how you can tell what kind of conic section a quadratic equation describes without graphing the equation.

31. Reasoning What shape is an ellipse whose height and width are equal?

32. Open-Ended Write an equation of a hyperbola whose transverse axis is on the x-axis.

TIPS FOR SUCCESS

Read the question at the right. Then follow the tips to answer the multiple choice question.

TIP 1

Read the labels on the axes to understand the meaning of a point on the graph.

A stone falls from a 56-foot cliff. The graph shows the height of the stone h, in feet, after t seconds. In about how many seconds does the stone reach the ground?

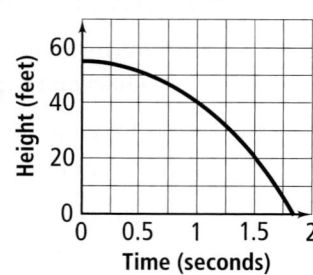

A) 0.9 second
B) 1.0 second
C) 1.5 seconds
D) 1.9 seconds

TIP 2

Use the graph to determine when $h = 0$.

Think It Through

Find the point where the graph crosses the horizontal axis.

The graph crosses the horizontal axis at about $(1.9, 0)$. So the stone reaches the ground in about 1.9 seconds.

The correct answer is D.

Vocabulary Builder

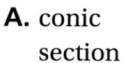

As you solve test items, you must understand the meanings of mathematical terms. Match each term with its mathematical meaning.

A. conic section

B. hyperbola

C. directrix

D. ellipse

E. circle

I. a set of points P in a plane such that the absolute value of the difference between the distances from P to two fixed points F_1 and F_2 is a constant k

II. a set of points P in a plane such that the sum of the distances from P to two fixed points F_1 and F_2 is a constant k

III. the set of all points in a plane that are a distance r from a given point

IV. a curve formed by the intersection of a plane and a double cone

V. the fixed line equidistant with the focus from each point on a parabola

Selected Response

Read each question. Then write the letter of the correct answer on your paper.

1. Which of the following equations represents the graph of a hyperbola with foci at $(5, 0)$ and $(-5, 0)$?

A) $\frac{x^2}{25} - \frac{y^2}{4} = 1$

B) $\frac{x^2}{21} + \frac{y^2}{4} = 1$

C) $\frac{x^2}{21} - \frac{y^2}{4} = 1$

D) $\frac{x^2}{25} + \frac{y^2}{4} = 1$

2. If the equation $y = 4^x$ is graphed, which of the following values of x would produce a point closest to the x-axis?

F) 3
G) 0
H) 1
I) 4

3. An acrobat landed on a teeterboard and launched his partner into the air. The graph below shows the height h of the partner, in yards, at t seconds after the launch.

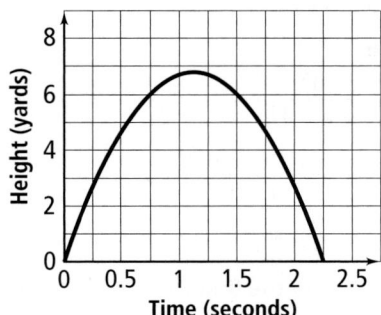

Which value is the best approximation of the maximum height of the partner?

(A) 6.0 yards (C) 6.8 yards

(B) 6.4 yards (D) 7.2 yards

4. The bacteria in a petri dish are growing exponentially with time, as shown in the table below.

Bacteria Growth

Day	Bacteria
0	50
1	150
2	450

Which of the following equations expresses the number of bacteria y present at day x?

(F) $y = (3)^x$

(G) $y = 50 + (3)^x$

(H) $y = 50 \cdot (3)^x$

(I) $y = 150 \cdot (3)^x$

5. Which of the following statements is true about the functions $|-2x|$ and $-2|x|$?

(A) The graphs are the same.

(B) The graph of $-2|x|$ is a reflection of $|-2x|$ across the x-axis.

(C) The graph of $-2|x|$ is a reflection of $|-2x|$ across the y-axis.

(D) The graphs have no similarities.

6. Alex dives from a diving board into a swimming pool. Her distance above the pool, in feet, is given by the equation $h(t) = -16.17t^2 + 13.2t + 33$, where t is the number of seconds after jumping.

What is the height of the diving board?

(F) -16.17 ft

(G) 13.2 ft

(H) 30.03 ft

(I) 33 ft

7. What is the standard form of the equation of the conic section given below?

$$25x^2 - 49y^2 - 1225 = 0$$

(A) $\dfrac{x^2}{49} - \dfrac{y^2}{25} = 1$

(B) $\dfrac{x^2}{49} + \dfrac{y^2}{25} = 1$

(C) $25x^2 - 49y^2 = 1225$

(D) $49x^2 - 25y^2 = 1$

8. Owen threw a ball straight up into the air from an initial height of 5 feet. The graph below shows the height h of the ball, in feet, at t seconds after Owen threw it. Of the following times, when was the ball closest to the ground?

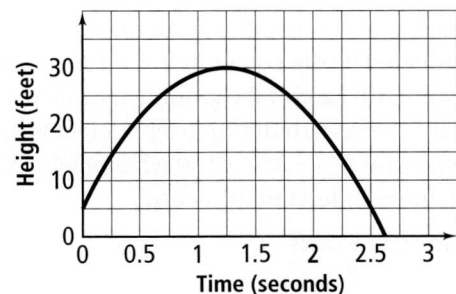

(F) 0.6 second

(G) 1 second

(H) 1.6 seconds

(I) 2 seconds

Constructed Response

9. The graph below shows the height h in feet, of an object t seconds after it is tossed from a building. The table shows the height, in feet, of another object t seconds after it is dropped. How long, in seconds, is the first object that hits the ground in the air? Write your answer to the nearest hundredth.

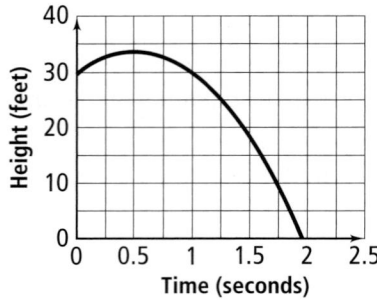

$h(t) = 1.8t^2 - 20t + 26$

t	$h(t)$
0	26
0.5	16.5
1	7.8
1.5	0.05
1.6	−1.4

10. What is the length of the major axis of an ellipse with foci at $(4, 0)$ and $(-4, 0)$, and with a minor axis of length 6?

11. A total of $323 was collected from 40 people to cover the exact cost of their dinners. Some ordered steak at $8.50 per person, and others ordered chicken at $7.50 per person. How many people ordered chicken?

12. The height of an acorn falling from the top of a 45-ft tree is modeled by the equation $h = -16t^2 + 45$. Before the acorn can hit the ground, a squirrel jumps out and intercepts it. If the squirrel's height is modeled by the equation $h = -3t + 32$, at what height, in feet, did the squirrel intercept the acorn?

13. What is the value of x?
$$\frac{10}{x(x-3)} + \frac{4}{x} = \frac{5}{x-3}$$

14. What is the y-value of the focus of the parabola?

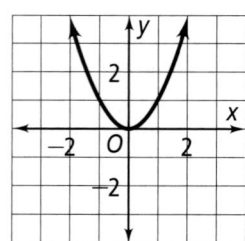

15. Which is the first *incorrect* step in simplifying? Explain.
$$\frac{4}{(x-1)^{-1}(x^2 + 3x - 4)}$$

Step 1: $\dfrac{4(x-1)}{x^2 + 3x - 4}$

Step 2: $\dfrac{4(x-1)}{(x+4)(x-1)}$

Step 3: $\dfrac{4(x-1)}{(x+4)(x-1)} \div \dfrac{x-1}{x-1}$

Step 4: $\dfrac{4}{x+4} \div \dfrac{4}{4} = \dfrac{1}{x}$

16. What is the sum of the first 7 terms of the geometric series below?

1, 2, 4, 8, . . .

17. What are the extraneous roots of the equation $\dfrac{x}{x-1} - \dfrac{2}{x} = \dfrac{1}{x-1}$?

18. Find the zeros of the function $y = x^2 - 2x$. Show your work.

19. What are the coordinates of the foci of the graph of $4x^2 - 24x = 64 - 25y^2$?

20. Which conic section is represented by the equation $x^2 + y^2 = 6x - 14y - 9$?

21. If x is a real number, for what values of x is the equation $(3x - 6)(x - 2)^{-1} = 3$ true?

22. What is the solution of the equation $\sqrt{x + 5} = \sqrt{2x - 4}$?

Extended Response

23. Suppose you put $10,000 in an account that pays 6.5% annual interest compounded continuously. How much will be in the account after one year? After five years?

24. Explain how to graph $y = \frac{1}{2}\sqrt{x + 3} - 3$ by translating the graph of $y = \sqrt{x}$.

25. Find a nonzero value for k such that the equation $kx^2 - 10x + 25 = 0$ has one solution. Show your work.

26. Explain when the function $y = a \cdot b^x$ models exponential growth and when it models exponential decay.

Get Ready!

Skills
Handbook,
page 972

Finding Percent

Write each number as a percent.

1. $\frac{5}{6}$ **2.** $\frac{7}{36}$ **3.** $\frac{48}{52}$ **4.** 0.3056

Skills
Handbook,
page 975

Simplifying Expressions

Simplify each expression.

5. $8 \cdot 7 \cdot 6 \cdot 5 \cdot 4$ **6.** $\frac{52 \cdot 51 \cdot 50}{3 \cdot 2 \cdot 1}$ **7.** $\frac{5 \cdot 4 \cdot 3 \cdot 2 \cdot 1}{3 \cdot 2 \cdot 1 \cdot 2 \cdot 1}$

Lesson 5-7

Expanding Binomials

Use Pascal's Triangle to expand each binomial.

8. $(a + b)^5$ **9.** $(j + 3k)^3$ **10.** $(m + 0.7)^2$

11. $(2 + t)^4$ **12.** $(m + n)^2$ **13.** $(x + 3y)^4$

Lesson 6-1

Finding Real Roots

Find the real square roots of each number.

14. $\frac{1}{100}$ **15.** $\frac{1}{400}$ **16.** $\frac{1}{196}$

17. $\frac{1}{4}$ **18.** $\frac{1}{9}$ **19.** $\frac{1}{576}$

Looking Ahead Vocabulary

20. In driver's education class, students may learn how to drive through a *simulation*. How do you think simulations might be used in a math class?

21. When you describe the likelihood that it will rain tomorrow given that it rained today, you are giving a *conditional probability*. What is the condition in this situation?

22. When you give a value to represent the typical data value in a data set, you are giving a *measure of central tendency* of the data set. What value do you think best represents the following data set? Explain.

$\{1, 3, 3, 3, 4, 10, 20, 30, 40\}$

CHAPTER

11

Probability and Statistics

Download videos connecting math to your world.

Interactive! Vary numbers, graphs, and figures to explore math concepts.

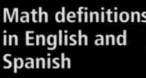

The online Solve It will get you in gear for each lesson.

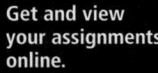

Math definitions in English and Spanish

Online access to stepped-out problems aligned to Common Core

Get and view your assignments online.

Extra practice and review online

Virtual Nerd™ tutorials with built-in support

Chapter Preview

Vocabulary

English/Spanish Vocabulary Audio Online:

English	Spanish
combination, *p. 676*	combinación
conditional probability, *p. 696*	probabilidad condicional
experimental probability, *p. 681*	probabilidad experimental
measure of central tendency, *p. 711*	medida de tendencia central
mutually exclusive events, *p. 689*	sucesos mutuamente excluyentes
normal distribution, *p. 739*	distribución normal
permutation, *p. 675*	permutación
simulation, *p. 682*	simulación
theoretical probability, *p. 683*	probabilidad teórica

BIGideas

1 **Probability**
Essential Question What is the difference between a permutation and a combination?

2 **Probability**
Essential Question What is the difference between experimental and theoretical probability?

3 **Data Collection and Analysis**
Essential Question How are measures of central tendency different from standard deviation?

 DOMAINS
• Conditional Probability and the Rules of Probability
• Making Inferences and Justifying Conclusions
• Use Probability to Make Decisions

Common Core Performance Task

Gender and Handedness

A couple plans to have three children. For each child, the probability that the child is a boy is 0.5 and the probability that the child is a girl is 0.5. And for each child, the probability that the child is left-handed is 0.1. The tree diagram below shows the different orders the couple can have three boys and/or girls.

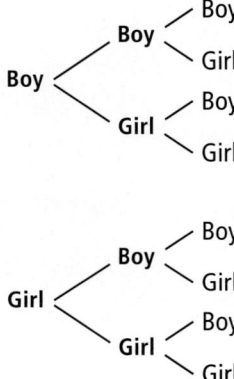

Boy
  Boy
    Boy
    Girl
  Girl
    Boy
    Girl

Girl
  Boy
    Boy
    Girl
  Girl
    Boy
    Girl

Task Description

Find the probability that at least two of the three children will be girls, and that at least one of the three children will be left-handed. (Assume that a child's gender and whether he or she is left- or right-handed are not related in any way.)

Connecting the Task to the Math Practices

MATHEMATICAL PRACTICES

As you complete the task, you'll apply several Standards for Mathematical Practice.

- You'll analyze the task and relate its solution to the information shown in the diagram. (MP 1)

- You'll reason abstractly and quantitatively using the complement of an event and conditional probability. (MP 2)

- You'll use a simulation to find experimental probabilities. (MP 4)

11-1 Permutations and Combinations

Common Core State Standards

S-CP.B.9 Use permutations and combinations to compute probabilities of compound events and solve problems.

MP 1, MP 3, MP 4, MP 6

Objectives To count permutations
To count combinations

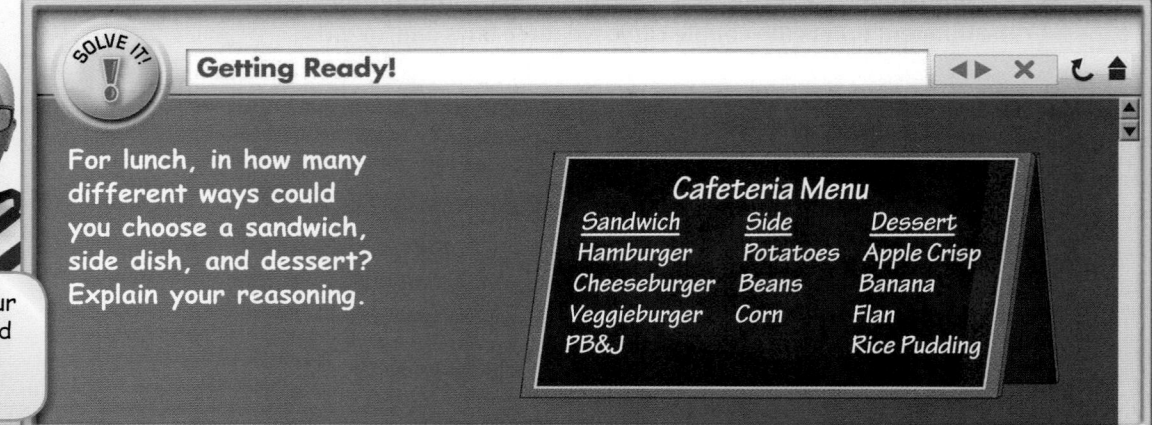

SOLVE IT!

Getting Ready!

For lunch, in how many different ways could you choose a sandwich, side dish, and dessert? Explain your reasoning.

Try starting with your favorite sandwich and find out how many choices you have.

Cafeteria Menu

Sandwich	Side	Dessert
Hamburger	Potatoes	Apple Crisp
Cheeseburger	Beans	Banana
Veggieburger	Corn	Flan
PB&J		Rice Pudding

MATHEMATICAL PRACTICES

It is fairly easy to count the ways you can pick items from a short list. But sometimes you have so many choices that counting the possibilities is impractical.

Essential Understanding You can use multiplication to quickly count the number of ways certain things can happen.

The **Fundamental Counting Principle** describes the method of using multiplication to count.

Lesson Vocabulary
- Fundamental Counting Principle
- permutation
- *n* factorial
- combination

take note

Key Concept   Fundamental Counting Principle

If event M can occur in m ways and is followed by event N that can occur in n ways, then event M followed by event N can occur in $m \cdot n$ ways.

Example 3 pants and 2 shirts give $3 \cdot 2 = 6$ possible outfits.

Here's Why It Works Making a tree diagram, you can see that there are 3 groups of 2 outfits, or $3 \cdot 2 = 6$ outfits, starting with the pants.

You can extend the Fundamental Counting Principle to three or more events.

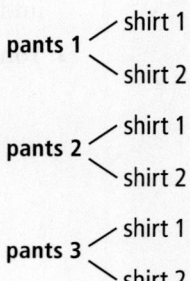

pants 1 — shirt 1
pants 1 — shirt 2

pants 2 — shirt 1
pants 2 — shirt 2

pants 3 — shirt 1
pants 3 — shirt 2

 **Problem 1** Using the Fundamental Counting Principle

Motor Vehicles The photos show Maryland license plates in 2004 and 1912. How many more 2004-style license plates were possible than 1912-style plates?

Think

How many digits are in our number system? How many letters are in our alphabet?
There are 10 digits and 26 letters.

For the 2004 license plates, there were places for three letters and three digits. Number of possible 2004 license plates:

$26 \cdot 26 \cdot 26 \cdot 10 \cdot 10 \cdot 10 = 17{,}576{,}000$

For the 1912 license plates, there were places for four digits. Number of possible 1912 license plates:

$10 \cdot 10 \cdot 10 \cdot 10 = 10{,}000$

$17{,}576{,}000 - 10{,}000 = 17{,}566{,}000$ Find the difference.

There were 17,566,000 more 2004-style license plates possible than 1912-style plates.

 Got It? **1.** In 1966, one type of Maryland license plate had two letters followed by four digits. How many of this type of license plate were possible?

A **permutation** is an arrangement of items in a particular order. Suppose you wanted to find the number of ways to order three items. There are 3 ways to choose the first item, 2 ways to choose the second, and 1 way to choose the third. By the Fundamental Counting Principle, there are $3 \cdot 2 \cdot 1 = 6$ permutations.

Using *factorial* notation, you can write $3 \cdot 2 \cdot 1$ as 3!, read "three factorial." For any positive integer n, **n factorial** is $n! = n(n - 1) \cdot \ldots \cdot 3 \cdot 2 \cdot 1$. Zero factorial is $0! = 1$.

 **Problem 2** Finding the Number of Permutations of *n* Items

Plan

What strategy can you use to help you determine the answer?
Act it out and you will see how many options you have at each step.

In how many ways can you file 12 folders, one after another, in a drawer?

Use the Fundamental Counting Principle to count the number of permutations of 12 items. There are 12 ways to select the first folder, 11 ways to select the next folder, and so on. The total number of permutations is

$12! = 12 \cdot 11 \cdot \ldots \cdot 2 \cdot 1 = 479{,}001{,}600.$

There are 479,001,600 ways to file 12 folders in a drawer.

 Got It? **2.** In how many ways can you arrange 8 shirts on hangers in a closet?

Sometimes you are interested in the number of permutations possible using all of the objects from a set, but just a few at a time. You can still use the Fundamental Counting Principle or factorial notation.

Key Concept Number of Permutations

The number of permutations of n items of a set arranged r items at a time is

$$_nP_r = \frac{n!}{(n-r)!} \text{ for } 0 \le r \le n.$$

Example $_{10}P_4 = \frac{10!}{(10-4)!} = \frac{10!}{6!} = 5040$

Problem 3 Finding $_nP_r$

Track Ten students are in a race. First, second, and third places will win medals. In how many ways can 10 runners finish first, second, and third (no ties allowed)?

Method 1 Use the Fundamental Counting Principle.

$$10 \cdot 9 \cdot 8 = 720$$

Method 2 Use the permutation formula.

There are $n = 10$ runners to arrange taking $r = 3$ at a time.

$$_nP_r = \frac{n!}{(n-r)!} \qquad \text{Use the formula.}$$

$$= \frac{10!}{(10-3)!} \qquad \text{Substitute 10 for } n \text{ and 3 for } r.$$

$$= \frac{10!}{7!} = 720 \qquad \text{Simplify.}$$

There are 720 ways that 10 runners can finish in first, second, and third places.

Got It? **3. a.** In how many ways can 15 runners finish first, second, and third?
  b. Reasoning In Problem 3, is the number of ways for runners to finish first, second, and third the same as the number of ways to finish eighth, ninth, and tenth? Explain.

Plan

If you use the Fundamental Counting Principle, how many numbers will you need to multiply together?
You will multiply 3 numbers together to represent the possibilities of finishing first, second, and third.

Suppose in Problem 3 that the first three runners advance to the championship race. In that case, the order in which the first three runners cross the finish line does not matter. A selection in which order does not matter is a **combination**.

As with permutations, you can use a formula to find the number of combinations of n items chosen r at a time.

Key Concept Number of Combinations

The number of combinations of n items of a set chosen r items at a time is

$$_nC_r = \frac{n!}{r!(n-r)!} \text{ for } 0 \le r \le n.$$

Example $_5C_3 = \frac{5!}{3!(5-3)!} = \frac{5!}{3! \cdot 2!} = \frac{120}{6 \cdot 2} = 10$

 **Problem 4** Finding $_nC_r$

What is $_{13}C_4$, the number of combinations of 13 items taken 4 at a time?

Think

You need the formula for number of combinations. Substitute 13 for n and 4 for r.

Write out the factorial in the numerator to make it easier to divide. Remove common factors.

Write

$$_nC_r = \frac{n!}{r!(n-r)!}$$

$$_{13}C_4 = \frac{13!}{4!(13-4)!}$$

$$= \frac{13!}{4! \cdot 9!}$$

$$= \frac{13 \cdot 12 \cdot 11 \cdot \overset{5}{\cancel{10}} \cdot \cancel{9!}}{\cancel{4} \cdot \cancel{3} \cdot \cancel{2} \cdot 1 \cdot \cancel{9!}} = 715$$

 Got It? 4. What is the value of each expression?

    a. $_8C_3$ **b.** $_9C_2$ **c.** $_{15}C_5$

When determining whether to use a permutation or combination, you must decide whether order is important.

 **Problem 5** Identifying Whether Order Is Important

For each situation, determine whether you should use a permutation or combination. What is the answer to each question?

Plan

How will you solve?
If order is important, use the formula $_nP_r = \frac{n!}{(n-r)!}$ and if order is not important, use the formula $_nC_r = \frac{n!}{r!(n-r)!}$.

A A chemistry teacher divides his class into eight groups. Each group submits one drawing of the molecular structure of water. He will select four of the drawings to display. In how many different ways can he select the drawings?

There is no reason why order is important. Use a combination.

$$_nC_r = \frac{n!}{r!(n-r)!}; \qquad _8C_4 = \frac{8!}{4!(8-4)!} = \frac{8 \cdot 7 \cdot 6 \cdot 5 \cdot \cancel{4!}}{4 \cdot 3 \cdot 2 \cdot 1 \cdot \cancel{4!}} = 70$$

There are 70 ways to select the drawings.

B You will draw winners from a total of 25 tickets in a raffle. The first ticket wins $100. The second ticket wins $50. The third ticket wins $10. In how many different ways can you draw the three winning tickets?

Values of the tickets depend on the order in which you draw them. Order is important. Use a permutation.

$$_nP_r = \frac{n!}{(n-r)!}; \qquad _{25}P_3 = \frac{25!}{(25-3)!} = \frac{25!}{22!} = 25 \cdot 24 \cdot 23 = 13,800$$

There are 13,800 ways you can draw the winning tickets.

 Got It? 5. In Problem 5A, how many ways are possible for the teacher to select and arrange the four drawings from left to right on the wall?

Lesson Check

Do you know HOW?

Evaluate each expression.

1. $_6P_3$ **2.** $_9P_4$ **3.** $_5C_2$ **4.** $_7C_5$

5. Sports How many different nine-player batting orders can be chosen from a baseball team of 16?

Do you UNDERSTAND?

 **6. Vocabulary** Explain the difference between permutations and combinations.

 **7. Reasoning** Use the definition of permutation to show why 0! should equal 1.

 **8. Open-Ended** Describe a situation in which the number of outcomes is given by $_9P_2$.

Practice and Problem-Solving Exercises

 **Practice**

9. You have five shirts and four pairs of pants. How many different ways can you arrange your shirts and pants into outfits?

See Problem 1.

10. To create an entry code for a push-button door lock, you need to first choose a letter and then, three single-digit numbers. How many different entry codes can you create?

11. The prom committee has four sites available for the banquet and three sites for the dance. How many arrangements are possible for the banquet and dance?

Evaluate each expression.

See Problem 2.

12. $5!$ **13.** $10!$ **14.** $13!$ **15.** $5!3!$

16. $\frac{12!}{6!}$ **17.** $5(4!)$ **18.** $\frac{10!}{7!3!}$ **19.** $\frac{15!}{10!5!}$

20. Automobiles You should rotate tires on a car at regular intervals.
　a. In how many ways can four tires be arranged on a car?
　b. If a spare tire is included, how many arrangements are possible?

Evaluate each expression.

See Problem 3.

21. $_8P_1$ **22.** $_8P_2$ **23.** $_8P_3$ **24.** $_8P_4$

25. $_3P_2$ **26.** $_5P_4$ **27.** $_9P_6$ **28.** $_7P_4$

29. Scheduling Fifteen students ask to visit a college admissions counselor. Each scheduled visit includes one student. In how many ways can ten time slots be assigned?

Evaluate each expression.

See Problem 4.

30. $_6C_2$ **31.** $_8C_5$ **32.** $_4C_4$ **33.** $_4C_3$

34. $_7C_3$ **35.** $3\left(_5C_4\right)$ **36.** $_6C_2 + _6C_3$ **37.** $\frac{_7C_4}{_9C_4}$

38. Awards There are eight swimmers in a competition where the top three swimmers advance. In how many ways can three swimmers advance?

For each situation, determine whether to use a permutation or a combination. Then solve the problem.

◀ See Problem 5.

39. How many different teams of 11 players can be chosen from a soccer team of 16?

40. Suppose you find seven equally useful articles related to the topic of your research paper. In how many ways can you choose five articles to read?

41. A salad bar offers eight choices of toppings for a salad. In how many ways can you choose four toppings?

 **Apply**

Assume a and b are positive integers. Determine whether each statement is *true* or *false*. If it is true, explain why. If it is false, give a counterexample.

42. $a! + b! = b! + a!$

43. $a!(b!c!) = (a!b!)c!$

44. $(a + b)! = a! + b!$

45. $(ab)! = a!b!$

46. $(a!)! = (a!)^2$

47. $(a!)^b = a^{(b!)}$

48. Think About a Plan You and your friends are picking up videos at a video store. You have selected 7 videos but will only have time to watch 3 videos together. How many different ways can you select the 3 videos to watch?
- Does the order in which the videos are selected make a difference?
- What formula should you use?

49. Security A car door lock has a five-button keypad. Each button has two numerals. The entry code 21914 uses the same button sequence as the code 11023. How many different five-button patterns are possible? You can use a button more than once.

    Ⓐ 120   Ⓑ 720   Ⓒ 3125   Ⓓ 5555

50. Consumer Issues A consumer magazine rates televisions by identifying two levels of price, five levels of repair frequency, three levels of features, and two levels of picture quality. How many different ratings are possible?

51. Writing In how many ways is it possible to arrange the two numbers a and b in an ordered pair? Explain why such a pair is called an *ordered* pair.

52. Reasoning Determine whether the statement $_nC_r = {_nP_r}$ is *always*, *sometimes*, or *never* true. Explain your reasoning.

53. There are 3!, or 6, arrangements of 3 objects. Consider the number of clockwise arrangements possible for objects placed in a loop, without a beginning or end.

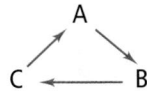   ABC, BCA, and CAB are all parts of one possible clockwise loop arrangement of the letters A, B, and C.

a. Find the number of clockwise loop arrangements possible for letters A, B, and C.
b. Use the diagram at the right to help find the number of loop arrangements possible for A, B, C, and D.
c. Write an expression for the number of clockwise loop arrangements for n objects.

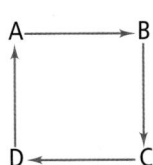

Challenge

54. Data Analysis The bar graph at the right shows the results of 40 responses to a survey.

a. Find the number of possible combinations of five people who squeeze toothpaste from the middle of the tube.

b. Suppose five people are chosen at random from all the people who responded to the survey. How many combinations of five people are possible?

© **55. a.** In how many ways can you choose three flags from a collection of seven different flags?

b. In how many different orders can you arrange three flags?

c. Writing You want to arrange three flags from a group of seven. Explain how you can use $_7C_3 \cdot 3!$ to create the permutation formula.

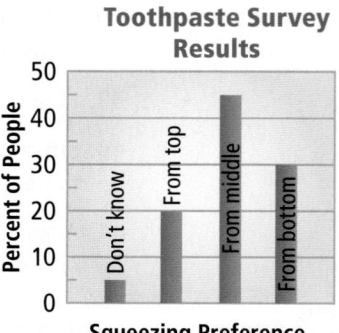

Toothpaste Survey Results

Percent of People — Squeezing Preference (Don't know, From top, From middle, From bottom)

Standardized Test Prep

SAT/ACT

56. What is the value of $_7C_2$?

    Ⓐ 2520   Ⓑ 49   Ⓒ 42   Ⓓ 21

57. What is the complete solution set of $\frac{3}{x^2 - 1} + \frac{4x}{x + 1} = \frac{1.5}{x - 1}$?

    Ⓕ 1, −1   Ⓖ 1, 0.375   Ⓗ 0.375   Ⓘ 0.375, 3

58. Use a calculator to solve $-x^2 - 3x + 7 = 0$. Round to the nearest hundredth.

    Ⓐ −0.76, 4.76   Ⓑ 0.76, 5.76   Ⓒ −1.54, 4.54   Ⓓ −4.54, 1.54

59. What is the center of the circle with equation $(x - 5)^2 + (y + 1)^2 = 81$?

    Ⓕ (5, 1)   Ⓖ (5, −1)   Ⓗ (−5, 1)   Ⓘ (−5, −1)

Short Response

60. What is the sum of the two infinite series $\sum_{n=1}^{\infty} \left(\frac{2}{3}\right)^{n-1}$ and $\sum_{n=1}^{\infty} \left(\frac{2}{3}\right)^{n}$?

Mixed Review

Identify the center, vertices, and foci for each ellipse.   ◀ **See Lesson 10-6.**

61. $\dfrac{(x - 2)^2}{9} + \dfrac{(y - 1)^2}{25} = 1$ **62.** $\dfrac{(x - 1)^2}{49} + \dfrac{(y - 1)^2}{36} = 1$

Factor each expression completely.   ◀ **See Lesson 4-4.**

63. $4x^2 - 8x + 4$ **64.** $-x^2 - 6x - 9$ **65.** $3x^2 - 75$

Get Ready!   To prepare for Lesson 11-2, do Exercises 66–68.

Simplify each expression.   ◀ **See Lesson 11-1.**

66. $10 \cdot 9 \cdot 8 \cdot 7 \cdot 6$ **67.** $\dfrac{8 \cdot 7 \cdot 5 \cdot 6}{4 \cdot 3 \cdot 2 \cdot 1}$ **68.** $\dfrac{7 \cdot 6 \cdot 5 \cdot 4 \cdot 3 \cdot 2 \cdot 1}{4 \cdot 3 \cdot 2 \cdot 1}$

Probability

Common Core State Standards

Prepares for S-IC.A.2 Decide if a specified model is consistent with results from a given data generating process, e.g., using simulation.

MP 1, MP 3, MP 4, MP 5, MP 6

Objective To find the probability of an event using theoretical, experimental, and simulation methods

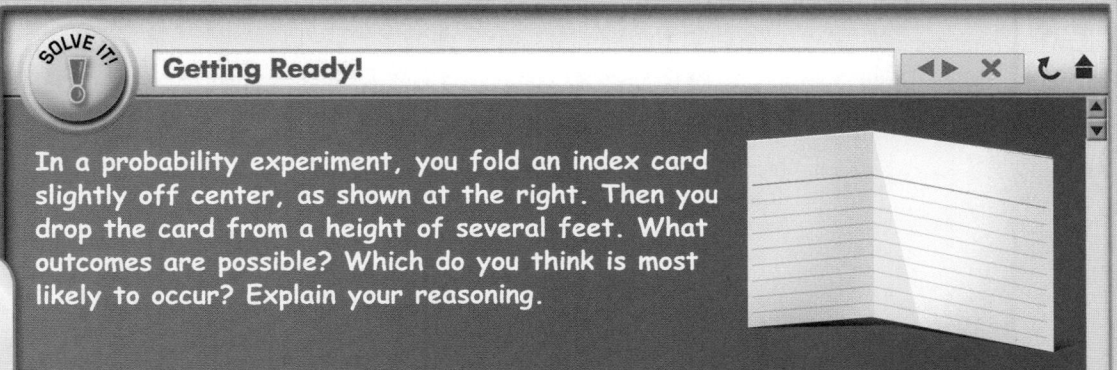

SOLVE IT!

Getting Ready!

In a probability experiment, you fold an index card slightly off center, as shown at the right. Then you drop the card from a height of several feet. What outcomes are possible? Which do you think is most likely to occur? Explain your reasoning.

Try it out! Find out if the results agree with your prediction.

MATHEMATICAL PRACTICES

Probability measures how likely it is for an event to occur.

Essential Understanding The probability of an impossible event is 0 (or 0%). The probability of a certain event is 1 (or 100%). Otherwise, the probability of an event is a number between 0 and 1 (or a percent between 0% and 100%).

When you gather data from observations, you can calculate an *experimental probability*. Each observation is an experiment or a trial.

Lesson Vocabulary
• experimental probability
• simulation
• sample space
• equally likely outcomes
• theoretical probability

take note

Key Concept Experimental Probability

experimental probability of event: $P(\text{event}) = \dfrac{\text{number of times the event occurs}}{\text{number of trials}}$

Problem 1 Finding Experimental Probability

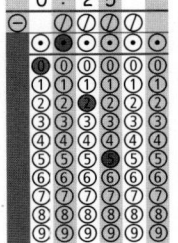

Think

What is a trial? What is an event?
A trial is selecting a vehicle parking in the lot. An event is the vehicle you select being a truck.

Gridded Response Of the 60 vehicles in a teachers' parking lot today, 15 are pickup trucks. What is the experimental probability that a vehicle in the lot is a pickup truck?

$$P(\text{pickup truck}) = \frac{\text{number of pickup trucks}}{\text{number of vehicles}} = \frac{15}{60} = 0.25, \text{ or } 25\%$$

The probability that a vehicle in the lot is a pickup truck is 0.25.

Got It? **1.** A softball player got a hit in 20 of her last 50 times at bat. What is the experimental probability that she will get a hit in her next at bat?

Sometimes actual trials are difficult or unreasonable to conduct. In these situations, you can estimate the experimental probability of an event by using a simulation. A **simulation** is a model of the event.

Problem 2 Using a Simulation

Testing On a multiple-choice test, each item has 4 choices, but only one choice is correct. How can you simulate guessing the answers? What is the probability that you will pass the test by guessing at least 6 of 10 answers correctly?

Plan

How do you simulate guessing one out of four?
You can pick at random from four numbers, specifying that one of them will be the "correct" answer.

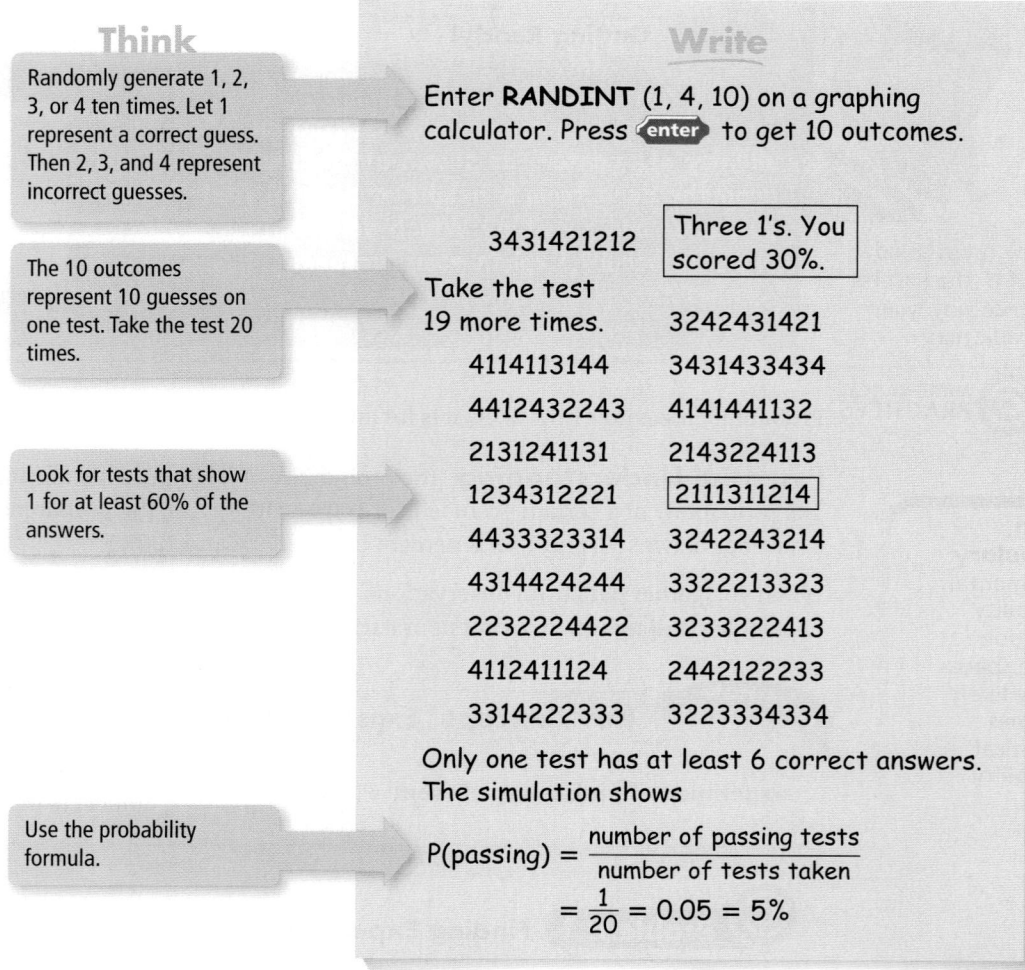

Think

Randomly generate 1, 2, 3, or 4 ten times. Let 1 represent a correct guess. Then 2, 3, and 4 represent incorrect guesses.

The 10 outcomes represent 10 guesses on one test. Take the test 20 times.

Look for tests that show 1 for at least 60% of the answers.

Use the probability formula.

Write

Enter **RANDINT** (1, 4, 10) on a graphing calculator. Press **enter** to get 10 outcomes.

3431421212 — Three 1's. You scored 30%.

Take the test 19 more times.

	3242431421
4114113144	3431433434
4412432243	4141441132
2131241131	2143224113
1234312221	2111311214
4433323314	3242243214
4314424244	3322213323
2232224422	3233222413
4112411124	2442122233
3314222333	3223334334

Only one test has at least 6 correct answers. The simulation shows

$$P(passing) = \frac{number\ of\ passing\ tests}{number\ of\ tests\ taken}$$

$$= \frac{1}{20} = 0.05 = 5\%$$

 Got It? **2.** In Problem 2, what is the probability of passing if a passing score is 50% or better?

The set of all possible outcomes to an experiment or activity is a **sample space**. When each outcome in a sample space has the same chance of occurring, the outcomes are **equally likely outcomes**.

For one roll of a standard number cube, there are six equally likely outcomes in the sample space. You can calculate *theoretical probability* as a ratio of outcomes.

Key Concept Theoretical Probability

If a sample space has n equally likely outcomes and an event A occurs in m of these outcomes, then the **theoretical probability** of event A is $P(A) = \frac{m}{n}$.

Sample space: n outcomes

Event A: m outcomes

 Problem 3 Finding Theoretical Probability

What is the theoretical probability of each event?

Ⓐ getting a 5 on one roll of a standard number cube

There are six equally likely outcomes, 1, 2, 3, 4, 5, and 6. The number 5 occurs one way.

$$P(5) = \frac{1}{6}$$

Ⓑ getting a sum of 5 on one roll of two standard number cubes

There are 36 possible equally likely outcomes. The favorable outcomes are those with a sum of 5.

$$P(\text{sum } 5) = \frac{4}{36} = \frac{1}{9}$$

Plan

How many outcomes are there?
Each cube has six numbers on it, so there are 6 • 6 = 36 outcomes.

Got It? **3. a.** What is the theoretical probability of getting a sum that is an odd number on one roll of two standard number cubes?

 b. Reasoning Without calculating the probability, is it more likely to get an even or odd number on one roll of a standard number cube? Explain.

It can be easier to use *combinatorics* to find theoretical probability rather than listing and counting all the equally likely outcomes. Combinatorics include the Fundamental Counting Principle, and ways to count permutations and combinations.

 Problem 4 Finding Probability Using Combinatorics

What is the theoretical probability of being dealt exactly two 7's in a 5-card hand from a standard 52-card deck?

A standard 52-card deck has 4 suits; hearts, diamonds, clubs, and spades. Each suit contains cards numbered 2 though 10, and an ace, jack, queen, and king.

Think

Should you use permutations or combinations?
Order does not matter. Use combinations.

The number of combinations of two 7's from four 7's = $_4C_2$.

The number of combinations of 3 non-sevens from 48 other cards = $_{48}C_3$.

The number of 5-card hands with two 7's = $_4C_2 \cdot {}_{48}C_3$.

The number of possible 5-card hands = $_{52}C_5$.

$$P(\text{hand with two 7's}) = \frac{_4C_2 \cdot {}_{48}C_3}{_{52}C_5} = \frac{103,776}{2,598,960} \approx 0.0399, \text{ or about } 4\%.$$

Sometimes you can use areas to find a theoretical probability.

Problem 5 **Finding Geometric Probability**

Geometry A batter's strike zone depends on the height and stance of the batter.
What is the geometric probability that a baseball thrown at random within the
batter's strike zone, as shown in the figure below, will be a high-inside strike (one of
the hardest pitches to hit)?

Think

**What are the
favorable outcomes?
All outcomes?**
Favorable outcomes are
points in the high-inside
region. All outcomes are
points in the strike zone.

$$P(\text{high-inside strike}) = \frac{\text{area of high-inside strike zone}}{\text{area of total strike zone}}$$

$$= \frac{4 \cdot 6}{17 \cdot 22}$$

$$\approx 0.064$$

For a baseball thrown at random in the batter's strike zone, the probability that it will be
a high-inside strike is about 6.4%.

Got It? **5.** Suppose a batter's strike zone is 15 in.-by-20 in. and the high-inside strike
zone is 3 in.-by-5 in. What is the probability that a baseball thrown at
random within the strike zone will be a high-inside strike?

Lesson Check

Do you know HOW?

1. What is the experimental probability a quarterback will complete his next pass if he has completed 30 of his last 40 passes?

2. What is the experimental probability a quarterback will complete his next pass if he has completed 36 of his last 45 passes?

Find the theoretical probability of each event when rolling a standard number cube.

3. $P(3)$

4. $P(2 \text{ or } 4)$

Do you UNDERSTAND?

5. **Vocabulary** Explain the difference between experimental probability, theoretical probability, and geometric probability.

6. **Writing** Describe three ways you could simulate answering a true-false question.

7. **Reasoning** Why is a simulation better the more times you perform it?

Practice and Problem-Solving Exercises  MATHEMATICAL PRACTICES

 **Practice**

8. A class tossed coins and recorded 161 heads and 179 tails. What is the experimental probability of heads? Of tails?

See Problem 1.

9. Another class rolled number cubes. Their results are shown in the table. What is the experimental probability of rolling each number?

Number	1	2	3	4	5	6
Occurrences	42	44	45	44	47	46

Graphing Calculator For Exercises 10–12, define a simulation by telling how you represent correct answers, incorrect answers, and the quiz. Use your simulation to find each experimental probability.

See Problem 2.

10. If you guess the answers at random, what is the probability of getting at least two correct answers on a five-question true-or-false quiz?

11. If you guess the answers at random, what is the probability of getting at least three correct answers on a five-question true-or-false quiz?

12. A five-question multiple-choice quiz has five choices for each answer. What is the probability of correctly guessing at random exactly one correct answer? Exactly two correct answers? Exactly three correct answers? (*Hint:* You could let any two digits represent correct answers, and the other digits represent wrong answers.)

A jar contains 30 red marbles, 50 blue marbles, and 20 white marbles. You pick one marble from the jar at random. Find each theoretical probability.

See Problem 3.

13. $P(\text{red})$

14. $P(\text{blue})$

15. $P(\text{not white})$

16. $P(\text{red or blue})$

A bag contains 36 red blocks, 48 green blocks, 22 yellow blocks, and 19 purple blocks. You pick one block from the bag at random. Find each theoretical probability.

17. P(green) **18.** P(purple) **19.** P(not yellow)

20. P(green or yellow) **21.** P(yellow or not green) **22.** P(purple or not red)

23. Games A group of 30 students from your school is part of the audience for a TV game show. The total number of people in the audience is 150. What is the theoretical probability of 3 students from your school being selected as contestants out of 9 possible contestant spots?

 See Problem 4.

Geometry Suppose that a dart lands at random on the dartboard shown at the right. Find each theoretical probability.

See Problem 5.

24. The dart lands in the bull's-eye.

25. The dart lands in a green region.

26. The dart scores at least 10 points.

27. The dart scores less than 10 points.

Width of each ring = *r*.

B Apply

28. Think About a Plan Suppose you roll two standard number cubes. What is the theoretical probability of getting a sum of 7?
- What is the sample space?
- How many outcomes are there?

In a class of 147 students, 95 are taking math (M), 73 are taking science (S), and 52 are taking both math and science. One student is picked at random. Find each probability.

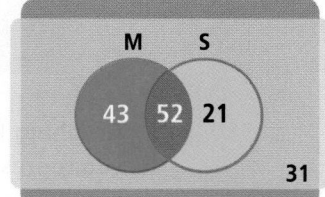

29. P(taking math or science or both)

30. P(not taking math)

31. P(taking math but not science)

32. P(taking neither math nor science)

33. Lottery A lottery has 53 numbers from which five are drawn at random. Each number can only be drawn once. What is the probability of your lottery ticket matching all five numbers in any order?

34. a. Sports Out of four games, team A has won one game and team B has won three games in a championship series. What is the experimental probability that team A wins the next game? That team B wins the next game?
  b. Reasoning Do you think that experimental probability is a good predictor of the winner of the next game? Explain.

35. Writing Explain what you would need to know to determine the theoretical probability of a five-digit postal ZIP code ending in 1.

 **Challenge**

36. Assume that an event is neither certain nor impossible. Then the odds in favor of the event are the ratio of the number of favorable outcomes to the number of unfavorable outcomes.

a. If the odds in favor of the event are a to b, or $\frac{a}{b}$, what is the probability of the event?

b. If the probability of the event is $\frac{a}{b}$, what are the odds in favor of the event?

c. Would you rather play a game in which your odds of winning are $\frac{1}{2}$, or a game in which your probability of winning is $\frac{1}{2}$? Explain.

 ## Apply What You've Learned

 MATHEMATICAL
PRACTICES
MP 1

Look back at the tree diagram on page 673 showing the possible orders in which boys and/or girls can be born into a family with three children. The sample space below lists each outcome in the tree diagram as a group of three letters.

Sample space: {BBB, BBG, BGB, BGG, GBB, GBG, GGB, GGG}

Complete the table by listing the outcomes in the sample space that satisfy each event, and then finding the probability of each event.

Event	Outcomes	Probability
0 of 3 children is a girl.	a. __?__	b. __?__
1 of 3 children is a girl.	c. __?__	d. __?__
2 of 3 children are girls.	e. __?__	f. __?__
3 of 3 children are girls.	g. __?__	h. __?__

11-3 Probability of Multiple Events

Common Core State Standards

S.CP.B.7 Apply the Addition Rule, $P(A \text{ or } B) = P(A) + P(B) - P(A \text{ and } B)$, and interpret the answer in terms of the model. **Also S-CP.A.2, S-CP.A.5**

MP 1, MP 2, MP 3, MP 4, MP 6

Objectives To find the probability of the event A and B
To find the probability of the event A or B

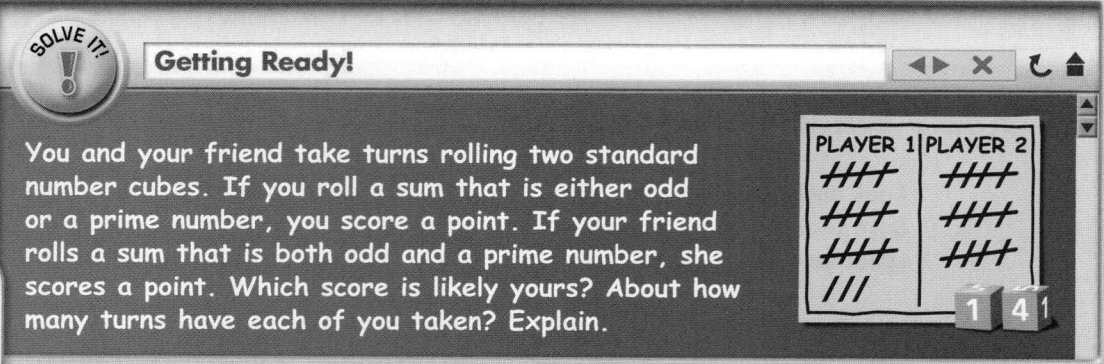

Getting Ready!

You and your friend take turns rolling two standard number cubes. If you roll a sum that is either odd or a prime number, you score a point. If your friend rolls a sum that is both odd and a prime number, she scores a point. Which score is likely yours? About how many turns have each of you taken? Explain.

Make sure you understand the game. What is the difference between the words "or" and "and"?

MATHEMATICAL PRACTICES

You can find the probabilities of multiple events occurring by using the probabilities of the individual events.

Essential Understanding To find the probability of two events occurring together, you have to decide whether one event occurring affects the other event.

When the occurrence of one event affects how a second event can occur, the events are **dependent events**. Otherwise, the events are **independent events**.

Lesson Vocabulary
• dependent events
• independent events
• mutually exclusive events

Problem 1 Classifying Events

Are the outcomes of each trial dependent or independent events?

Think

What must you ask yourself?
Does the first event have any effect on the outcome of the second event?

A Roll a number cube. Then spin a spinner.

The two events do not affect each other. They are independent.

B Pick one flash card, then another from a stack of 30 flash cards.

Picking the first card affects the possible outcomes of picking the second card. The events are dependent.

Got It? **1.** You select a coin at random from your pocket. You replace the coin and select again. Are your selections independent events? Explain.

Multiply to find the probability that two independent events will both occur.

take note

Key Concept Probability of A and B

If A and B are independent events, then $P(A \text{ and } B) = P(A) \cdot P(B)$.

Problem 2 Finding the Probability of Independent Events

Picnic At a picnic there are 10 diet drinks and 5 regular drinks. There are also 8 bags of fat-free chips and 12 bags of regular chips. If you grab a drink and a bag of chips without looking, what is the probability that you get a diet drink and fat-free chips?

Think

Is it important that you don't look?
Yes; probability is based on random events. It is not random if you look.

Event A = picking a diet drink   Event B = picking fat-free chips

A and B are independent. Picking a drink has no effect on picking the chips.

$$P(A \text{ and } B) = P(A) \cdot P(B)$$

$$= \frac{\text{number of diet drinks}}{\text{total number of drinks}} \cdot \frac{\text{number of bags of fat-free chips}}{\text{total number of bags of chips}}$$

$$= \frac{10}{15} \cdot \frac{8}{20} = \frac{4}{15} \approx 0.267, \text{ or } 26.7\%$$

The probability that you get a diet drink and fat-free chips is about 26.7%.

 Got It? 2. In Problem 2, what is the probability that you get a regular drink and regular chips?

Two events that cannot happen at the same time are **mutually exclusive events**. If A and B are mutually exclusive events, then $P(A \text{ and } B) = 0$.

 Problem 3 Mutually Exclusive Events

You roll a standard number cube. Are the events mutually exclusive? Explain.

Think

Can you roll a 2 and a 3 at the same time?
No; just one number comes up on one roll of one number cube.

A rolling a 2 and a 3

You cannot roll a 2 and 3 at the same time. The events are mutually exclusive.

B rolling an even number and a multiple of 3

You can roll a 6—an even number and a multiple of 3—at the same time. The events are not mutually exclusive.

 Got It? 3. You roll a standard number cube. Are the events mutually exclusive? Explain.
   a. rolling an even number and rolling a prime number
   b. rolling an even number and rolling a number less than 2

To find the probability of either event A or event B occuring, you need to determine whether events A and B are mutually exclusive.

take note

Key Concept Probability of A or B

$$P(A \text{ or } B) = P(A) + P(B) - P(A \text{ and } B)$$

If A and B are mutually exclusive events, then $P(A \text{ or } B) = P(A) + P(B)$.

Problem 4 Finding Probability for Mutually Exclusive Events

Languages At your high school, a student can take one foreign language each term. About 37% of the students take Spanish. About 15% of the students take French. What is the probability that a student chosen at random is taking Spanish or French?

Know	Need	Plan
• The percentages of students taking Spanish or French. • Students can take one foreign language at a time.	The probability that a student is taking Spanish or French.	Use the correct formula for $P(A \text{ or } B)$.

"One foreign language each term" means the events are mutually exclusive.

$$P(\text{Spanish or French}) = P(\text{Spanish}) + P(\text{French})$$

$P(A \text{ or } B) = P(A) + P(B)$ for mutually exclusive events.

$$\approx 0.37 + 0.15$$
$$= 0.52$$

The probability that a student chosen at random is taking Spanish or French is about 0.52, or about 52%.

 Got It? **4. a.** In Problem 4, about 9% of the students take Mandarin Chinese. What is the probability that a student chosen at random is taking Spanish, French, or Mandarin Chinese?

b. Reasoning Without knowing the number of students in the school in Problem 4, can you determine which language most students take? Explain.

When two events are *not* mutually exclusive, you need to subtract the probability of the common outcomes to find $P(A \text{ or } B)$.

 Problem 5 Finding Probability

Multiple Choice Suppose you reach into the dish and select a token at random. What is the probability that the token is round or green?

Ⓐ $\frac{2}{9}$　　　Ⓑ $\frac{3}{9}$　　　Ⓒ $\frac{6}{9}$　　　Ⓓ $\frac{8}{9}$

Think

Are the events mutually exclusive?
No; it is possible to have a round *and* green token.

$P(\text{round or green})$

$\quad = P(\text{round}) + P(\text{green}) - P(\text{round and green})$

$= \frac{5}{9} + \frac{3}{9} - \frac{2}{9} = \frac{6}{9}$

The probability of selecting a round or green token is $\frac{6}{9}$, or $\frac{2}{3}$. The correct answer is C.

 Got It? **5.** Suppose you select a token at random from the dish above. What is each probability?

a. the token is square or red　　　**b.** the token is green or square

Lesson Check

Do you know HOW?

A and *B* are independent events. Find *P*(*A* and *B*).

1. $P(A) = \frac{1}{6}$, $P(B) = \frac{2}{5}$ **2.** $P(A) = \frac{9}{20}$, $P(B) = \frac{3}{4}$

C and *D* are mutually exclusive events. Find *P*(*C* or *D*).

3. $P(C) = \frac{2}{5}$, $P(D) = \frac{3}{5}$ **4.** $P(C) = \frac{1}{2}$, $P(D) = \frac{3}{8}$

5. Events *A* and *B* are not mutually exclusive. If $P(A) = \frac{1}{2}$, $P(B) = \frac{1}{4}$, and $P(A \text{ and } B) = \frac{1}{8}$, find $P(A \text{ or } B)$.

Do you UNDERSTAND?

6. Vocabulary Explain the difference between independent events and mutually exclusive events.

7. Error Analysis The weather forecast for the weekend is a 30% chance of rain on Saturday and a 70% chance of rain on Sunday. Your friend says that means there is a 100% chance of rain this weekend. What error did your friend make?

8. Open-Ended Describe two events that are mutually exclusive.

 ## Practice and Problem-Solving Exercises

 **Practice** **Tell whether the outcomes of each trial are dependent events or independent events.**   ◀ **See Problem 1.**

9. A month is selected at random; a number from 1 to 30 is selected at random.

10. A month is selected at random; a day of that month is selected at random.

11. A letter of the alphabet is selected at random; one of the remaining letters is selected at random.

12. The color of a car is selected at random; the type of transmission is selected at random.

Q and *R* are independent events. Find *P*(*Q* and *R*).   ◀ **See Problem 2.**

13. $P(Q) = \frac{1}{4}$, $P(R) = \frac{2}{3}$ **14.** $P(Q) = \frac{12}{17}$, $P(R) = \frac{3}{8}$

15. $P(Q) = 0.6$, $P(R) = 0.9$ **16.** $P(Q) = \frac{1}{3}$, $P(R) = \frac{6}{7}$

17. Reading Suppose you have five books in your book bag. Three are novels, one is a biography, and one is a poetry book. Today you grab one book out of your bag without looking, and return it later. Tomorrow you do the same thing. What is the probability that you grab a novel both days?

Two fair number cubes are rolled. State whether the events are mutually exclusive. Explain your reasoning.   ◀ **See Problem 3.**

18. The sum is a prime number; the sum is less than 4.

19. The numbers are equal; the sum is odd.

20. The product is greater than 20; the product is a multiple of 3.

S and T are mutually exclusive events. Find $P(S \text{ or } T)$.

◀ See Problem 4.

21. $P(S) = \frac{5}{8}, P(T) = \frac{1}{8}$

22. $P(S) = \frac{3}{5}, P(T) = \frac{1}{3}$

23. $P(S) = 12\%, P(T) = 27\%$

24. Population About 30% of the U.S. population is under 20 years old. About 17% of the population is over 60. What is the probability that a person chosen at random is under 20 or over 60?

A standard number cube is tossed. Find each probability.

◀ See Problem 5.

25. $P(3 \text{ or odd})$

26. $P(4 \text{ or even})$

27. $P(\text{even or less than } 4)$

28. $P(\text{odd or greater than } 2)$

29. $P(\text{odd or prime})$

30. $P(4 \text{ or less than } 6)$

Ⓑ Apply 31. Suppose a number from 1 to 100 is selected at random. What is the probability that a multiple of 4 or 5 is chosen?

Ⓒ 32. Think About a Plan A multiple-choice test has four choices for each answer. Suppose you make a random guess on three of the ten test questions. What is the probability that you will answer all three correctly?
  • Is each guess a dependent event or an independent event?
  • What is the probability that a random guess on one question will yield the correct answer?

Statistics The graph at the right shows the types of jobs held by people in the U.S. Find each probability.

33. A person is in a service occupation.

34. A person is in service or sales and office.

35. A person is not in production, transportation, and material moving.

36. A person is neither in service nor in sales and office.

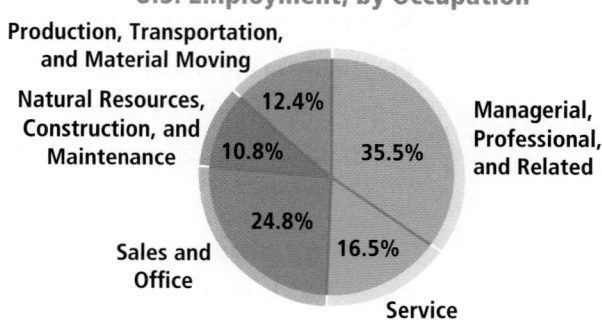

U.S. Employment, by Occupation

Production, Transportation, and Material Moving

Natural Resources, Construction, and Maintenance

12.4%

10.8%

35.5%

Managerial, Professional, and Related

24.8%

16.5%

Sales and Office

Service

Source: U.S. Census Bureau

A jar contains four blue marbles and two red marbles. Suppose you choose a marble at random, and do not replace it. Then you choose a second marble. Find the probability of each event.

37. You select a blue marble and then a red marble.

38. You select a red marble and then a blue marble.

39. One of the marbles you select is blue and the other is red.

40. Both of the marbles you select are red.

For each set of probabilities, determine if the events A and B are mutually exclusive.

41. $P(A) = \frac{1}{2}, P(B) = \frac{1}{3}, P(A \text{ or } B) = \frac{2}{3}$

42. $P(A) = \frac{1}{6}, P(B) = \frac{3}{8}, P(A \text{ or } B) = \frac{13}{24}$

 **Challenge**

43. Two standard number cubes are rolled. What is the probability that the sum is greater than 9 or less than 6?

44. Reasoning Tatyana has $x + 2$ pens in the pocket of her backpack. Samuel has $2x - 1$ pens in the pocket of his backpack.

   a. Tatyana has 2 blue pens. Find the probability that she pulls out a blue pen at random.

   b. Samuel has $x - 3$ blue pens. Find the probability that he pulls out a blue pen at random.

   c. Find the probability that either Tatyana or Samuel pulls out a blue pen at random.

Standardized Test Prep

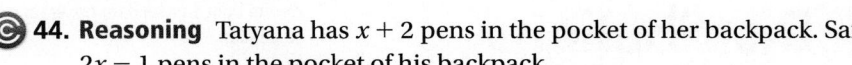

GRIDDED RESPONSE

SAT/ACT

45. A bag contains 5 red marbles, 1 blue marble, 3 yellow marbles, and 2 green marbles. One marble is drawn from the bag. What is the probability that the marble is red or yellow?

46. What is the theoretical probability of getting a 1 or 6 when rolling a standard number cube?

47. The first term of an arithmetic series is 123. The common difference is 12 and the sum 1320. How many terms are in the series?

48. What is the slope of the graph of the equation $6x - 18y = -24$?

49. What is the radius of the circle with equation $x^2 - 4x + y^2 - 21 = 0$?

50. How many five-letter permutations can you form from the letters of the word COMPUTER?

Mixed Review

Find the theoretical probability of each event when rolling a standard number cube.

◀ **See Lesson 11-2.**

51. $P(5)$ **52.** $P(\text{an even number})$ **53.** $P(\text{less than 4})$

Solve each equation. Check each solution.

◀ **See Lesson 8-6.**

54. $\frac{1}{2} - x = \frac{x}{6}$ **55.** $\frac{2}{2x-1} = \frac{x}{3}$ **56.** $\frac{3}{2x} - \frac{2}{3x} = 5$

Solve each equation. Check your answers.

◀ **See Lesson 7-6.**

57. $\ln 2x = 3$ **58.** $\ln x + \ln 2 = 6$ **59.** $\ln x^2 + 1 = 5$

Get Ready! **To prepare for Lesson 11-4, do Exercises 60–62.**

A spinner has four equal sections that are red, blue, green, and yellow. Find each probability for two spins.

◀ **See Lesson 11-3.**

60. $P(\text{blue, then blue})$ **61.** $P(\text{red, then yellow})$ **62.** $P(\text{not yellow, then green})$

Probability Distributions

Common Core State Standards

S-IC.A.2 Decide if a specified model is consistent with results from a given data-generating process, e.g., using simulation.

MP 1

A **probability distribution** is a function that gives the probability of each outcome in a sample space. You can use a frequency table or a graph to show a probability distribution.

The theoretical probability of rolling each number on a standard number cube is the same: $\frac{1}{6}$. It is a **uniform distribution**, a probability distribution that is equal for each event in the sample space. Here is a table and graph of its probability distribution.

Event: Roll	1	2	3	4	5	6
Frequency	1	1	1	1	1	1
Probability	$\frac{1}{6}$	$\frac{1}{6}$	$\frac{1}{6}$	$\frac{1}{6}$	$\frac{1}{6}$	$\frac{1}{6}$

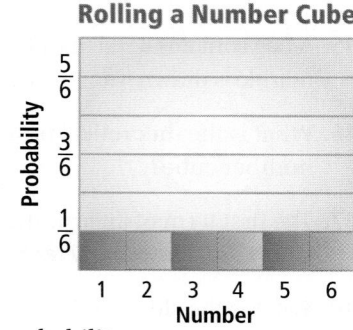

Now, suppose you roll two standard number cubes. You can show the probability distribution for the sum of the numbers by making a frequency table and drawing a graph.

Activity 1

Roll a pair of standard number cubes 36 times. Record the sum for each roll.

1. Copy the frequency table below. Use your data to complete your table.

Event: Sum	2	3	4	5	6	7	8	9	10	11	12
Frequency	■	■	■	■	■	■	■	■	■	■	■
Probability	■	■	■	■	■	■	■	■	■	■	■

2. Copy and complete the graph at the right using your data.

3. Make a graph of the probability distribution for the sums of two number cubes rolled 36 times, based on the *theoretical probabilities* of each sum.

4. a. Reasoning Compare the graphs. Do you think the number cubes you rolled are fair? Explain.

  b. Explain why there are differences, if any, between the theoretical model and the experimental model.

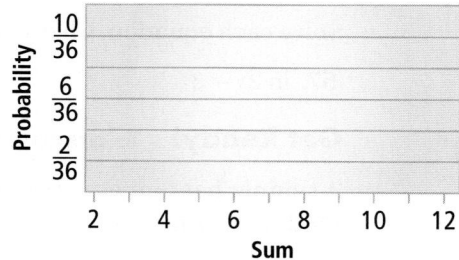

When you can assign numerical values to events, the **cumulative frequency** is the number of times events with values that are less than or equal to a given value occurs. **Cumulative probability** is the probability of events occuring with values that are less than or equal to a given value.

You can use the data you collected in Activity 1 to construct a cumulative probability distribution.

Activity 2

5. Copy and complete the table below. Add the probabilities within each range to find the cumulative probalities.

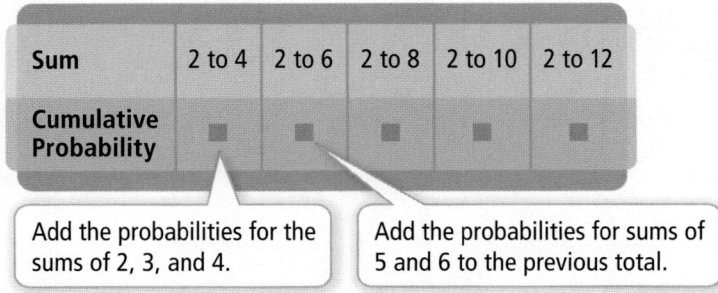

Sum	2 to 4	2 to 6	2 to 8	2 to 10	2 to 12
Cumulative Probability	▪	▪	▪	▪	▪

Add the probabilities for the sums of 2, 3, and 4.

Add the probabilities for sums of 5 and 6 to the previous total.

Ⓒ **6. Reasoning** Explain why the cumulative probability in the last interval is 1.

7. Copy the graph below and complete it using the cumulative probabilites you computed.

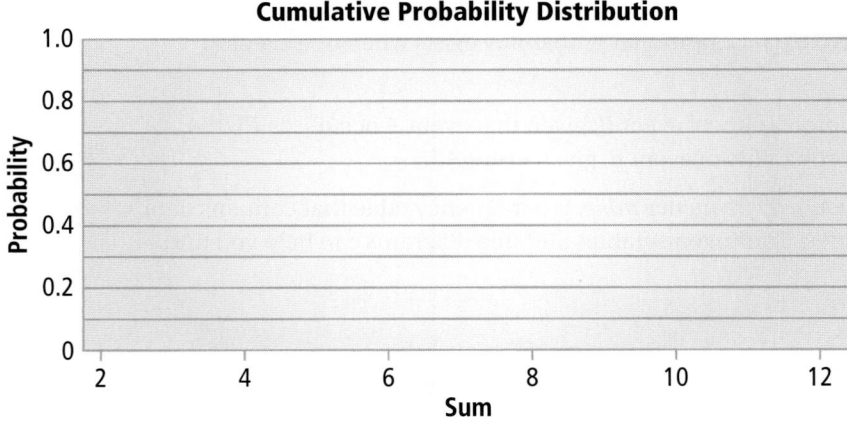

Cumulative Probability Distribution

Exercises

8. a. If you roll a pair of number cubes to model a situation and observe a sum of 7 four times in a row, would you question the model? Explain.

   b. If you observed a sum of 2 four times in a row, would you question the model? Explain.

9. Use a table and a graph to show the probability distribution for the spinner {red, green, blue, yellow}.

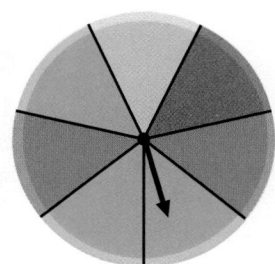

11-4 Conditional Probability

 Common Core State Standards

S-CP.B.6 Find the conditional probability of A given B as the fraction of B's outcomes that also belong to A . . .
Also S-CP.A.1, S-CP.A.3, S-CP.A.4, S-CP.A.5, S-CP.B.8
MP 1, MP 2, MP 3, MP 4, MP 6

Objectives To find conditional probabilities
To use tables and tree diagrams to determine conditional probabilities

SOLVE IT!

Getting Ready!

A great prize is inside Box 1, 2, or 3. You choose Box 1. You are shown that Box 2 contains a rubber chicken. You are given a chance to change your choice. Should you stay with Box 1 or should you change to Box 3? Justify your answer.

This sounds like a great idea for a television game show!

 **MATHEMATICAL PRACTICES**

The probability that an event, *B*, will occur given that another event, *A*, has already occurred is called a **conditional probability**.

 **Lesson Vocabulary**
- conditional probability
- contingency table

Essential Understanding Conditional probability exists when two events are dependent.

You write the conditional probability of event *B*, given that event *A* occurs, as $P(B|A)$. You read $P(B|A)$ as "the probability of event *B*, given event *A*."

A **contingency table**, or *two-way frequency table*, is a frequency table that contains data from two different categories. Contingency tables and tree diagrams can help you find conditional probabilities.

 **Problem 1** Finding Conditional Probability

Education The table shows students by gender and by type of school in 2005. You pick a student at random.

A What is $P(\text{female}\,|\,\text{graduate school})$?

Think

What's the condition?
The student is at a graduate school.

The condition that the person selected is at graduate school limits the sample space to the 3,303,000 graduate students. Of those, 1,954,000 are female.

$P(\text{female}\,|\,\text{graduate school}) = \frac{1954}{3303} \approx 0.59$

Student Genders

	Males (in thousands)	Females (in thousands)
Two-year colleges	1866	2462
Four-year colleges	4324	5517
Graduate schools	1349	1954

SOURCE: U.S. Census Bureau

B What is P(female)?

$$P(\text{F}) = \frac{\text{total number of females}}{\text{total number of students}} = \frac{2462 + 5517 + 1954}{1866 + 2462 + 4324 + 5517 + 1349 + 1954}$$

$$= \frac{9933}{17{,}472} \approx 0.57$$

  Got It? **1. a.** In Problem 1, what is P(Four-year | male)?

b. Reasoning Without calculating, given a student is enrolled in a four-year college, is it more likely for the student to be male or female? Explain.

Problem 2 **Conditional Probability in Statistics**

Multiple Choice Americans recycle increasing amounts through municipal waste collection. The table shows the collection data for 2007. What is the probability that a sample of recycled waste is paper?

Ⓐ 16% Ⓒ 33%

Ⓑ 28% Ⓓ 57%

Municipal Waste Collected (millions of tons)

Material	Recycled	Not Recycled
Paper	45.2	37.8
Metal	7.2	13.6
Glass	3.2	10.4
Plastic	2.1	28.6
Other	21.7	46.3

SOURCE: U.S. Environmental Protection Agency

Think

What's the condition?
The waste sample has to be recycled waste.

The given condition is that the waste is *recycled*. A favorable outcome is that the recycled waste is paper.

$$P(\text{paper} \mid \text{recycled}) = \frac{45.2}{45.2 + 7.2 + 3.2 + 2.1 + 21.7}$$

$$\approx 0.57, \text{ or } 57\%$$

The probability that the recycled waste is paper is about 57%. The correct answer is D.

 Got It? **2. a.** What is the probability that a sample of recycled waste is plastic?

b. What is the probability that a sample of recycled waste is glass?

You can use a formula to find conditional probability.

take note

Key Concept **Conditional Probability**

For any two events A and B with $P(A) \neq 0$,

$$P(B \mid A) = \frac{P(A \text{ and } B)}{P(A)}$$

Using the formula for conditional probability, you can calculate a conditional probability from other probabilities.

Problem 3 **Using the Conditional Probability Formula**

Market Research A utility company asked 50 of its customers whether they pay their bills online or by mail. What is the probability that a customer pays the bill online, given that the customer is male?

Bill Payment

	Online	By Mail
Male	12	8
Female	24	6

Think

To use $P(\text{online}\mid\text{male})$
$= \dfrac{P(\text{male and online})}{P(\text{male})}$,
you need
$P(\text{male and online})$
and $P(\text{male})$.

There are 20 males, and 12 males pay online out of 50 total customers. Substitute and simplify.

Write

$$P(\text{male and online}) = \frac{12}{50}$$

$$P(\text{male}) = \frac{20}{50}$$

$$P(\text{online}\mid\text{male}) = \frac{P(\text{male and online})}{P(\text{male})}$$

$$= \frac{\frac{12}{50}}{\frac{20}{50}}$$

$$= \frac{12}{20} = \frac{3}{5} = 0.6$$

The probability that a customer pays online given that the customer is male is 0.6.

Got It? 3. Researchers asked shampoo users whether they apply shampoo directly to the head, or indirectly using a hand. What is the probability that a respondent applies shampoo directly to the head, given that the respondent is female?

Applying Shampoo

	Directly Onto Head	Into Hand First
Male	2	18
Female	6	24

It follows from $P(B\mid A) = \dfrac{P(A \text{ and } B)}{P(A)}$ that $P(A \text{ and } B) = P(A) \cdot P(B\mid A)$.

You can use this rule along with a tree diagram to find probabilities of dependent events.

 **Problem 4** Using a Tree Diagram

Education A school system compiled the following information from a survey it sent to people who were juniors 10 years earlier.

- **85% of the students graduated from high school.**
- **Of the students who graduated from high school, 90% are happy with their present jobs.**
- **Of the students who did not graduate from high school, 60% are happy with their present jobs.**

What is the probability that a person from the junior class 10 years ago graduated from high school and is happy with his or her present job?

Think

What are the branches at each point?
The tree first branches at "graduated" and "not graduated." Each of these branches at "happy" and "not happy."

Make a tree diagram to help organize the information.
Let G = graduated, NG = not graduated, H = happy with present job, and NH = not happy with present job.

This branch represents the students who did graduate.

Each first branch represents a simple probability $P(G) = 0.85$ and $P(NG) = 0.15$.

This branch represents the students who did not graduate.

Each second branch represents a conditional probability $P(H \mid G) = 0.90$ and $P(NH \mid NG) = 0.40$

```
                    0.90      H
              G
         0.85      0.10   NH

              0.15      0.60   H
         NG
                   0.40
                          NH
```

Think

Which path should you follow?
Follow the path that represents graduates who are happy with their present job.

The blue highlighted path represents $P(G$ and $H)$.

$$P(G \text{ and } H) = P(G) \cdot P(H \mid G)$$
$$= 0.85 \cdot 0.90$$
$$= 0.765$$

The probability that a person from the junior class 10 years ago graduated and is happy with his or her present job is 0.765, or 76.5%.

 Got It? **4.** What is the probability that a student from the junior class 10 years ago in Problem 4 did not graduate and is happy with his or her present job?

Lesson Check

Do you know HOW?

A card is drawn from a standard deck of cards. Find each probability, given that the card drawn is black.

1. $P(\text{club})$ **2.** $P(4)$ **3.** $P(\text{diamond})$

4. The probability that a car has two doors, given that it is red, is 0.6. The probability that a car has two doors *and* is red is 0.2. What is the probability that a car is red?

Do you UNDERSTAND?

5. Reasoning Using the tree diagram in Problem 4, explain why the probabilities on each pair of branches must add up to 1.

6. Open-Ended Describe a situation in which you would use conditional probability to find the answer.

7. Compare and Contrast How are the Fundamental Counting Principle and tree diagrams alike? How are they different?

Practice and Problem-Solving Exercises

 **Practice**

Use the table to find each probability.

8. $P(\text{has diploma})$

9. $P(\text{has diploma and experience})$

10. $P(\text{has experience} \mid \text{has diploma})$

11. $P(\text{has no diploma} \mid \text{has experience})$

See Problems 1 and 2.

Characteristics of Job Applicants

		Has Experience	
		Yes	No
Has High School Diploma	Yes	54	27
	No	5	4

Use the table to find each probability.

12. $P(\text{The recipient is male.})$

13. $P(\text{The degree is a bachelor's.})$

14. $P(\text{The recipient is female, given that the degree is an associate's.})$

15. $P(\text{The degree is } not \text{ an associate's, given that the recipient is male.})$

Projected Number of Degree Recipients in 2010 (thousands)

Degree	Male	Female
Associate's	245	433
Bachelor's	598	858

SOURCE: U.S. National Center for Education Statistics

Use the survey results for Exercises 16 and 17.

16. Find the probability that a respondent has a pet, given that the respondent has had a pet.

17. Find the probability that a respondent has never had a pet, given that the respondent does not have a pet now.

See Problems 3 and 4.

> 39% have a pet now and have had a pet.
>
> 61% do not have a pet now.
>
> 86% have had a pet.
>
> 14% do not have a pet now and have never had a pet.

18. Sports A football team has a 70% chance of winning when it doesn't snow, but only a 40% chance of winning when it snows. Suppose there is a 50% chance of snow. Make a tree diagram to find the probability that the team will win.

19. Make a tree diagram based on the survey results below. Then find P(a female respondent is left-handed) and P(a respondent is both male and right-handed).
- Of all the respondents, 17% are male.
- Of the male respondents, 33% are left-handed.
- Of female respondents, 90% are right-handed.

 **Apply**

20. Suppose A and B are independent events, with $P(A) = 0.60$ and $P(B) = 0.25$. Find each probability.

    a. $P(A \text{ and } B)$ **b.** $P(A \mid B)$

    c. What do you notice about $P(A)$ and $P(A \mid B)$?

    d. Reasoning One way to describe A and B as independent events is *The occurrence of B has no effect on the probability of A*. Explain how the answer to part (c) illustrates this relationship.

21. Think About a Plan A math teacher gives her class two tests. 60% of the class passes both tests and 80% of the class passes the first test. What percent of those who pass the first test also pass the second test?
- What conditional probability are you looking for?
- How can a tree diagram help you solve this problem?

Weather Use probability notation to describe the chance of each event. Let **S, C, W, and R represent sunny, cloudy, windy, and rainy weather, respectively.**

22. cloudy weather   **23.** sunny and windy weather   **24.** rainy weather if it is windy

25. Transportation You can take Bus 65 or Bus 79. You take the first bus that arrives. The probability that Bus 65 arrives first is 75%. There is a 40% chance that Bus 65 picks up passengers along the way. There is a 60% chance that Bus 79 picks up passengers. Your bus picked up passengers. What is the probability that it was Bus 65?

The tree diagram relates snowfall and school closings. Find each probability. Let H, L, O, and C represent heavy snowfall, light snowfall, schools open, and schools closed, respectively.

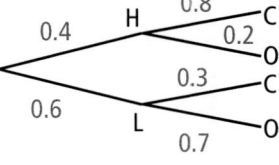

26. $P(C)$ **27.** $P(H \text{ and } O)$ **28.** $P(H \mid C)$

29. $P(L \mid O)$ **30.** $P(L \mid C)$ **31.** $P(H \mid O)$

 **Challenge**

32. a. Writing Explain which branches of the tree diagram at the right represent conditional probabilities. Give a specific example.

    b. Are the event of having a license and the event of being an adult independent events? Justify your answer.

    c. Open-Ended Estimate probabilities for each branch of the tree diagram for your city or town. Then find $P(L)$.

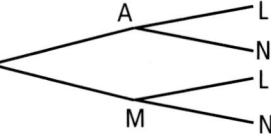

A = adult (21 or older)
M = minor (under 21)
L = licensed driver
N = not licensed to drive

33. Reasoning Sixty percent of a company's sales representatives have completed training seminars. Of these, 80% have had increased sales. Overall, 56% of the representatives (whether trained or not) have had increased sales. Use a tree diagram to find the probability of increased sales, given that a representative has not been trained.

Apply What You've Learned

In the following exercises you will use the idea of the *complement of an event*. The complement of an event *A* is the set of all possible outcomes in the sample space that are not in *A*. For example, if *A* is the event "showing a prime number when rolling a standard number cube", then the sample space is {1, 2, 3, 4, 5, 6}, the event *A* is {2, 3, 5}, and the complement of *A* is {1, 4, 6}. The complement of an event *A* is often denoted "not *A*."

The sum of the probability of an event and its complement is 1. So for an event *A*, $P(A) + P(\text{not } A) = 1$, or $P(\text{not } A) = 1 - P(A)$.

a. Suppose $P(C) = 0.45$. What is $P(\text{not } C)$?

In the Apply What You've Learned in Lesson 11-2, you determined the number of favorable outcomes and calculated the theoretical probability of events related to the problem on page 673.

b. Recall that the sample space of all possible outcomes with respect to gender when having three children is {BBB, BBG, BGB, BGG, GBB, GBG, GGB, GGG}. What is the complement of the event {BBB, BBG, BGG, GGB, GGG}? What is the probability of the complement?

c. Suppose event *D* is "at least one of the children is left-handed." What is the complement of event *D*?

In parts (d) and (e), let *G* be the event that a child is a girl, let *B* be the event that a child is a boy, and let *L* be the event that a child is left-handed.

d. Find $P(G \mid L)$ and $P(L \mid G)$.

e. Find $P(\text{not } L \mid \text{not } G)$.

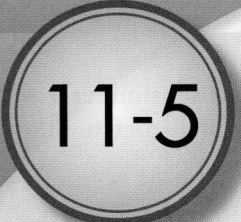

11-5 Probability Models

Common Core State Standards

S-MD.B.6 Students will use probabilities to make fair decisions . . .

S-MD.B.7 Students will analyze decisions using probability concepts . . .

MP 1, MP 3, MP 4

Objective To use probabilities to make fair decisions and analyze decisions

SOLVE IT!

Getting Ready!

Suppose you and your friends are trying to decide who gets to sit in the front seat of the car for a road trip. What are some ways that you and your friends can reach a fair decision? (Assume that none of you are driving.)

Develop a plan for investigating this situation.

MATHEMATICAL PRACTICES

In the Solve It, you may have thought about ways that you have reached fair decisions. In this lesson, you will learn how to use probabilities to make fair decisions.

Essential Understanding You can use probability models to analyze situations and make fair decisions.

Lesson Vocabulary
• probability model

A fair game is a game in which all of the participants have an equal chance of winning. For example, two players take turns rolling a number cube. The first player gets a point if an odd number is rolled, and the second player gets a point if an even number is rolled. Each player has the same probability of scoring a point on each roll. Similarly, a fair decision is based on choices that are equally likely to be chosen.

 Problem 1 Making a Fair Decision

A class of 25 students wants to choose 3 students at random to bring food for a class party. Any set of 3 students should have an equal chance of being chosen. Which of the following strategies will result in a fair decision?

Think

What is required for a decision to be fair?
Each possible outcome must be equally likely.

A The students line up alphabetically, and each one in succession flips a fair coin. The first three students to flip heads bring the food.

This strategy will not result in a fair decision because all students do not have an equal chance of being chosen. Students at the back of the line will probably never get to flip a coin.

B Each student draws a card from a well-shuffled deck of 52 cards. The teacher shuffles a second deck of cards, spreads them out, and draws cards one by one until he matches the cards of three of the students.

Assuming a good shuffle, this strategy gives any group of three students an equal chance of being selected. So this strategy will result in a fair decision.

 Got It? **1.** Two siblings are trying to decide who has to mow the lawn this weekend. They decide to race, and the winner does not have to mow the lawn. Is the result a fair decision? Explain.

For an event to be random, there is no predetermined pattern or bias toward any particular outcome. You can use random numbers to help you make fair decisions.

A random number table contains randomly generated digits from 0 to 9. You can use these numbers to model randomness for sampling purposes. Part of a random number table is shown below. Typically, space is inserted between groups of 5 numbers to help with readability.

Random Number						
87494	39707	20525	95704	48361	27556	34599
14164	15888	24997	82392	08525	47551	37304
61249	08241	16243	18371	03349	91759	53613
67868	56747	73521	05975	40411	49493	70904

 Problem 2 **Using Random Numbers**

A coach wants to select 3 of her 15 basketball players at random to lead warm-ups before practice each week. The coach assigns each player a number from 01 to 15. How can the coach use the random number table to fairly choose the three players?

Step 1 Choose a line of digits from a random number table.

87494 39707 20525 95704 48361 27556 34599

Step 2 Read the digits from the random number table in consecutive pairs until you get the numbers for three of the players. Skip numbers like 87 and 49 because they do not represent any of the 15 players. Also ignore any duplicates that may occur.

87494 39707 20525 95704 48361 27556 34599

The coach chooses the players assigned numbers 07, 04, and 12 to lead warm-ups.

Plan

How do you handle the spaces in the digits?
Ignore the spaces between the digits. For example, the third two-digit number is 43.

 Got It? **2. a.** A teacher wants to organize 10 students into two teams for a math game. The teacher assigns each student a number from 0 to 9. He uses the second line of digits from the random number table above to select the teams. He alternates the assigned team as each student is chosen. Which numbers will be used to create team 1?

b. Reasoning Is this a fair way to determine the teams? Explain.

You can use a **probability model** to assign probabilities to outcomes of a chance process. In Lesson 11-2, you learned that you can use a simulation to estimate the experimental probability of an event. A simulation is an example of a probability model. You can use probability and simulations to make predictions about real-life situations.

© **Problem 3** Modeling with a Simulation

A restaurant gives away 4 different toys in their kids' meals. Each meal contains exactly one toy, and the toys are equally and randomly distributed. About how many kids' meals would a parent expect to have to buy to get all 4 toys?

Know	Need	Plan
You know that toys are randomly distributed in each kids' meal. There is 1 toy in each meal.	A probability model that generates four equally likely events	You can use a spinner with four equal sections to simulate the random choosing of each toy.

Step 1 Spin the spinner and keep track of the results in a frequency table. Continue spinning until you have simulated getting each toy at least once.

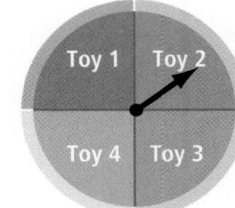

Kids' Meal Simulation

Toy	Tally	Frequency
1	//	2
2	///	3
3	/	1
4	//	2

The results of this trial indicate that you would expect to have to buy $2 + 3 + 1 + 2 = 8$ kids' meals in order to get all 4 different toys.

Think

Why do you need to repeat the simulation?
In general, the number of kids' meals you have to buy to collect all four toys will vary.

Step 2 Repeat the simulation several times.
Suppose that you conduct the simulation 24 more times and the results indicate that you can expect to have to buy the meal the following number of times before you get all 4 toys.

7, 9, 12, 6, 15, 5, 8, 10, 7, 13, 11, 6, 8, 9, 12, 13, 9, 10, 12, 7, 11, 5, 6, and 8.

Step 3 Find the average number of kids' meals needed to get all 4 toys.

$\frac{227}{25} = 9.08$

On average, you will need to buy about 9 kids' meals in order to get all 4 toys.

✓ **Got It?** **3.** Suppose that you are playing a board game for which you must roll a 6 on a number cube before you are able to move your game piece from start. Describe a simulation you can use to predict the number of times you would expect to have to roll the number cube before you can move from start.

You can use contingency tables to determine conditional probabilities and use those probabilities to evaluate decisions.

Problem 4 Using Probability to Analyze Decisions

A pharmaceutical company is testing the effectiveness of a new drug for asthma patients. Out of 160 volunteers who suffer from asthma, 80 are given the drug, and 80 are given a placebo, which has no active ingredients. After 2 weeks, the volunteers are asked if they noticed improvement in their asthma symptoms. The results of the survey are shown in the contingency table at the right.

	Improved	Did not Improve	Totals
Received the Drug	67	13	80
Received the Placebo	24	56	80
Totals	91	69	160

A What is the probability that a volunteer reported noticeable improvement in symptoms given that he received the test drug?

The first row represents the total number of volunteers who received the drug. The number of those volunteers that reported improvements in symptoms is 67.

$$P(\text{improvement} \mid \text{drug}) = \frac{\text{number of volunteers who improved}}{\text{number of volunteers who received the drug}} = \frac{67}{80} = 0.8375$$

B What is the probability that a volunteer received the placebo given that he did not report a noticeable improvement in symptoms?

The second column of data shows the total number of volunteers who did not report improvements in symptoms, 69. The second row represents the total number of volunteers who received a placebo.

$$P(\text{placebo} \mid \text{no improvement}) = \frac{56}{69} \approx 0.8116$$

Think

How can you use what you know to analyze the company's decision?
You can use the probabilities to analyze whether the drug was actually effective.

C The pharmaceutical company decides to produce and distribute this drug. The drug is marketed as an effective way to improve the symptoms of asthma. Based on the results of the test, did the company make a good decision? Explain.

The probabilities calculated above show that about 8 out of 10 people who are given the drug experience improvements in symptoms. Also, about 7 out of 10 who receive the placebo do not experience improvement in symptoms. Based on this study, the new drug appears to be effective at treating asthma symptoms. The company made a good decision.

Got It? 4. The results of another test are shown in the contingency table below. Should the company produce and distribute the new drug? Explain.

	Reported Improvements	Did not Report Improvements	Totals
Received the Drug	23	27	50
Received the Placebo	19	31	50
Totals	42	58	100

Lesson Check

Do you know HOW?

Use the contingency table for Exercises 1 and 2.

	Passed	Failed	Totals
Studied	8	1	9
Did not Study	3	6	9
Totals	11	7	18

1. Find $P(\text{passed} \mid \text{studied})$.

2. Find $P(\text{did not study} \mid \text{failed})$.

Do you UNDERSTAND?

3. Open Ended Give an example of a fair decision and an example of an unfair decision if two brothers are trying to decide who has to wash the dishes.

4. Error Analysis A classmate conducted a simulation to predict how many boxes of cereal he would need to buy to get all 5 prizes. After one trial of the simulation, he concluded that he would need to buy 7 boxes of cereal. What was your classmate's error? How should he conduct the simulation?

5. Vocabulary Look up the definition of simulation in a dictionary or online. How does this definition relate to the concept of simulation in mathematics?

Practice and Problem-Solving Exercises

 **Practice**

For Exercises 6–7, determine whether strategies described result in a fair decision. Explain.

◀ **See Problem 1.**

6. There are 24 students in math class. The teacher wants to choose 4 students at random to come to the board and work a math problem. She writes each student's name on a slip of paper, places them in a hat, and chooses 4 without looking.

7. You and three friends want to choose which two of your group will shovel the snow in the driveway. You are each assigned a number from 1 to 4, and then you spin a spinner to choose the first person. Then that person chooses the second person.

For Exercises 8–9, use the lines from a random number table below.

◀ **See Problem 2.**

84496 18732 60330 19536 58380 52544 48712
01603 48862 18519 29834 90890 69751 20514

8. The advisor of the Good Citizen's club wants to select 4 of its 25 members to raise and lower the flag each day this week. She assigns a two-digit number from 01 to 25 to each student. What are the numbers that correspond to the members who will raise and lower the flag?

9. Camp A coach wants to select 5 of his 16 players at random to help with a youth basketball camp this weekend. He assigns a two-digit number from 01 to 16 to each player. What are the numbers of the players who will help at the camp?

10. Shopping A grocery store is giving away scratch-off tickets to each customer when they spend over $50. There are 3 different discount offers randomly and equally distributed among the scratch-off tickets. What is a simulation you could use to find, on average, how many times a customer would have to spend over $50 in order to get all 3 different discount offers?

◀ **See Problem 3.**

11. Testing The contingency table below shows the number of nursing students who took preparatory class before taking their board exams and the number of students who passed the board exams on their first attempt.

◀ See Problem 4.

	Preparatory Class	No Preparatory Class	Totals
Passed Exams	14	11	25
Did not Pass Exams	3	6	9
Totals	17	17	34

a. What is the probability that a nursing student passed the board exams given that he or she took the preparatory class?
b. What is the probability that a nursing student did not pass the board exams given that he or she did not take the preparatory class?
c. A student decides to take the preparatory class before he takes the board exams. Is this a good decision? Explain.

 **Apply**

12. Community Service There are 24 members in a school's drama club. The advisor wants to randomly select 8 members to help seat patrons prior to a play at a local theater. How can the advisor choose the 8 members fairly? Explain.

Suppose you take a multiple-choice quiz. There are 4 choices for each question. You do not know the answers to the last 5 questions, so you guess the answers. For Exercises 13–14, use the simulation results below, where 1 represents a correct answer and 2, 3, and 4 represent incorrect answers.

31242 41211 34141 41212 23342 23242 13412
11313 42433 32334 31234 13314 41432 23413
42322 14331 12224 12232 31232 22223 31233
11214 33243 33414 21224 34112 43432 14234

13. How many trials of the simulation were conducted? What was the average number of correct answers for these trials?

14. If you need at least 3 correct answers to earn a passing grade, what is the experimental probability of guessing the answers and getting a passing grade based on this simulation?

Ⓒ 15. Think About a Plan A delivery company is evaluating the effectiveness of a defensive driving course. The contingency table at the right displays data about drivers who took the course. Based on these results, the company decides to continue to offer the defensive driving course. Is this a good decision? Explain.

	Took Course	Did not Take Course	Totals
No Major Accidents	3	18	21
At least 1 Major Accident	0	4	4
Totals	3	22	25

• What probabilities do you need to analyze the decision?
• How do you decide whether the course is effective?

 **16. Writing** What role does probability play in decision-making and problem solving? Support your answer with examples.

17. Sports The local football team's field goal kicker has made 16 out of 20 field goal attempts from less than 30 yards so far this season. So, the experimental probability that the kicker will make his next field goal kick is 80%. What simulation could you use to find the average number of field goals he will make if he has three attempts of less than 30 yards in a game?

 Challenge

18. In some contests, the prizes are randomly distributed, but there may be more of one kind of prize than another. Suppose there are 250 tickets in a raffle. There is 1 grand prize, 5 first prizes, and 20 second prizes available. How can you simulate the results of the raffle?

Apply What You've Learned

 MATHEMATICAL PRACTICES
MP 4

The couple from the problem on page 673 conducted a simulation that models having three children. They flipped a coin to determine gender, and used a random number generator to determine handedness. Their results are given in the table below. "H" represents a child being a girl, and "T" represents a child being a boy. The digits 0–8 represent a child being right-handed, and the digit 9 represents a child being left-handed.

H0 H1 H6	T3 H3 T2	H9 T4 T9	H9 H8 H5	T3 H9 T4
T0 T7 H7	H6 H1 H8	H5 H0 T5	H3 T1 T1	T5 H8 T7
H3 T4 H1	H0 T1 H8	T7 T7 T6	T2 T7 H1	T3 H5 T0
T0 H1 H6	H4 T8 H9	T0 H4 T0	H1 H6 T0	T4 T7 H5

Use the simulation results. Choose from the following numbers to complete the sentences below.

6	$\dfrac{3}{10}$	$\dfrac{9}{20}$	4	$\dfrac{1}{5}$

$\dfrac{3}{20}$	20	60	9	3

a. There are __?__ families represented.

b. __?__ families have 2 girls out of 3 children.

c. __?__ families have 3 girls out of 3 children.

d. P(at least 2 girls) is __?__ .

e. P(at least one left-handed) is __?__ .

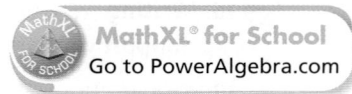

Do you know HOW?

Evaluate each expression.

1. $4!$

2. $6!$

3. $\dfrac{5!}{3!}$

4. $\dfrac{6!}{4!2!}$

5. $_7C_3$

6. $_9C_8$

7. $_5P_2$

8. $_{11}P_9$

9. $_4C_4$

10. $_4P_4$

11. $2\left(_5C_4\right) - {_3}C_2$

12. $3\left(_3P_2\right) + {_3}P_1$

Indicate whether each situation involves a combination or permutation. Then solve.

13. How many ways are there to select five actors from a troupe of nine to improvise a scene?

14. How many different three-student study groups can be formed from a class of 15?

15. Your teacher is looking for a new apartment. There are five apartments available. In how many ways can your teacher inspect the apartments?

Suppose you select a number at random from the sample space {5, 6, 7, 8, 9, 10, 11, 12, 13, 14}. Find each probability.

16. $P(7)$

17. $P(5 \text{ or } 13)$

18. $P(\text{greater than } 10)$

19. $P(\text{multiple of } 30)$

20. $P(\text{less than } 7 \text{ or greater than } 10)$

21. $P(\text{greater than } 6 \text{ and less than } 12)$

22. $P(\text{integer})$

23. $P(\text{less than } 10 \mid \text{less than } 13)$

24. $P(\text{greater than } 8 \mid \text{less than } 11)$

25. $P(\text{greater than } 7 \mid \text{greater than } 12)$

Two standard number cubes are tossed. State whether the events are mutually exclusive. Then find $P(A \text{ or } B)$.

26. A means their sum is 12; B means both are odd.

27. A means they are equal; B means their sum is a multiple of 3.

Do you UNDERSTAND?

Ⓒ 28. Vocabulary Explain the difference between experimental probability and theoretical probability.

Ⓒ 29. Suppose you select a number at random from the set $\{90, 91, 92, \ldots, 99\}$. Event A is selecting a multiple of 2. Event B is selecting a multiple of 3.

 a. Writing Are events A and B mutually exclusive? Are they independent? Explain your answers.

 b. Find $P(A)$ and $P(B)$.

 c. Find $P(A \text{ and } B)$.

 d. Find $P(A \text{ or } B)$.

 e. Find $P(A \mid B)$ and $P(B \mid A)$.

Ⓒ 30. Reasoning Let F and G be mutually exclusive events. Event F occurs more frequently than event G. Write the following in order from least to greatest: $P(F), P(G), P(F \text{ or } G), P(G \mid F)$.

Ⓒ 31. Error Analysis For two events A and B, a student calculates the probabilities shown. Explain how you can tell that the student made a mistake.

$$P(A \text{ and } B) = 0.35$$
$$P(A \mid B) = 0.29$$

Ⓒ 32. Writing A local restaurant owner employs 6 high school students who all want to work the same shift during spring break vacation week. To choose which 2 students will can work the shift, the owner assigns each student employee a number between 1 and 6, and then she rolls a standard number cube twice. The numbers that the number cubes show represent the employees who can work the shift. (If there are doubles, she rolls again.) Is the result a fair decision? Explain.

Analyzing Data

Common Core State Standards

S-MD.B.6 Use probabilities to make fair decisions . . .
MP 1, MP 3, MP 4, MP 6

Objectives To calculate measures of central tendency
To draw and interpret box-and-whisker plots

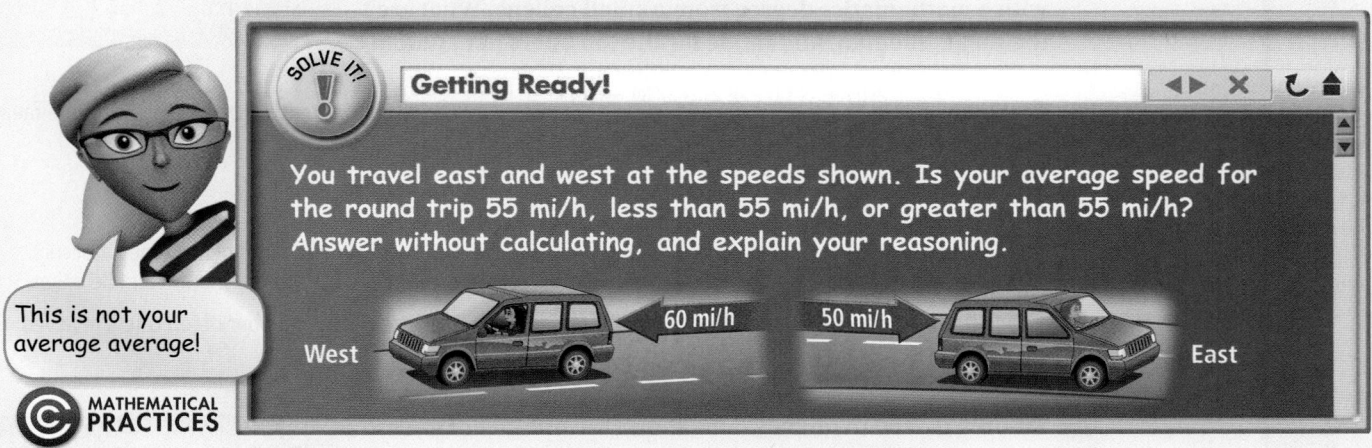

This is not your average average!

MATHEMATICAL PRACTICES

People often refer to the mean as the *average*. The mean is only one of the measures considered the average, a measure of the center of a set of data.

Essential Understanding You can describe and compare sets of data using various statistical measures, depending on what characteristics you want to study.

Statistics is the study, analysis, and interpretation of data. One way to analyze data is by finding a *measure of central tendency*. A **measure of central tendency** indicates the "middle" of the data set. The *mean, median,* and *mode* are the most common measures of central tendency.

Lesson Vocabulary

- measure of central tendency
- mean
- median
- mode
- bimodal
- outlier
- range of a set of data
- quartile
- interquartile range
- box-and-whisker plot
- percentile

Key Concepts   Measures of Central Tendency

Measure	Definition	Example, using 1, 2, 3, 3, 4, 5, 5, 9
Mean	sum of the data values number of data values	$\dfrac{1+2+3+3+4+5+5+9}{8} = 4$
Median	for a data set listed in order: the middle value for an odd number of data values; the mean of the two middle values for an even number of data values	For 1, 2, 3, 3, 4, 5, 5, 9, the middle two values are 3 and 4. The median is their mean, $\dfrac{3+4}{2} = 3.5$.
Mode	the most frequently occurring value(s)	Two modes: In 1, 2, 3, 3, 4, 5, 5, 9, both 3 and 5 occur twice.

A **bimodal** data set has two modes. If a data set has more than two modes, then the modes are probably not statistically useful. If no value occurs more frequently than any other, then there is no mode.

 Problem 1 Finding Measures of Central Tendency

Career The frequency table shows the number of job offers received by each student within two months of graduating with a mathematics degree from a small college. What are the mean, median, and mode for the job offers per student?

Job Offers	0	1	2	3	4
Students	2	2	4	5	2

Think

How do you find the total number of job offers?
Add the products of each number of job offers and the number of students with that many job offers.

Mean: $\bar{x} = \dfrac{2(0) + 2(1) + 4(2) + 5(3) + 2(4)}{15}$

$= \dfrac{33}{15} = 2.2$

The mean is 2.2.

The symbol $\bar{x}$, read "*x bar*," represents the mean.

Median: 0, 0, 1, 1, 2, 2, 2, 2, 3, 3, 3, 3, 3, 4, 4
The median is 2.

List each value the number of times it occurs. Arrange them in order. Find the middle value.

Mode: Five students received 3 job offers each.
The mode is 3.

The mode is the number of job offers received by most students.

Got It? **1.** The frequency table shows the number of trees in the yard of each house on one street. What are the mean, median, and mode for the trees per yard?

Trees	3	4	5	6	7	8
Yards	1	5	7	4	1	2

An **outlier** is a value that is substantially different from the rest of the data in a set. If the data is in one variable, outliers can occur at the "ends." They can be misleading because they can affect measures of central tendency.

 Problem 2 Identifying an Outlier

Multiple Choice Which is an outlier for this data set: 56 65 73 59 98 65 59?

     Ⓐ 42   Ⓑ 65   Ⓒ 98   Ⓓ 59

Think

What should you do first?
Put the numbers in order.

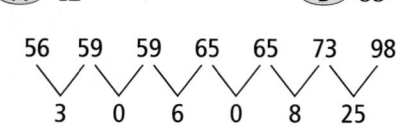

Order the data.

Find differences between adjacent values.

98 appears to be substantially different, so 98 is an outlier. The correct answer is C.

Got It? **2.** Suppose the values in Problem 2 are the data for the situations below. Would you discard the outlier? Explain.
     a. water temperature of a lake at seven locations
     b. the number of customers in a restaurant each night in one week

The **range of a set of data** is the difference between the greatest and least values. If you order data from least value to greatest value, the median divides the data into two parts. The median of each part divides the data further and you have four parts in all. The values separating the four parts are **quartiles**. The **interquartile range** is the difference between the third and first quartiles.

© **Problem 3** Comparing Data Sets

Temperature The table shows average monthly water temperatures for four locations on the Gulf of Mexico. How can you compare the 12 water temperatures from St. Petersburg with the 12 water temperatures from Key West?

Gulf of Mexico Eastern Coast Water Temperatures (°F)

Location	J	F	M	A	M	J	J	A	S	O	N	D
St. Petersburg, Florida	62	64	68	74	80	84	86	86	84	78	70	64
Key West, Florida	69	70	75	78	82	85	87	87	86	82	76	72
Dauphin Island, Alabama	51	53	60	70	75	82	84	84	80	72	62	56
Grand Isle, Louisiana	61	61	64	70	77	83	85	85	83	77	70	65

SOURCE: National Oceanographic Data Center

Know

Water temperatures near the two cities

Need

The means, medians, modes, ranges, and interquartile ranges

Plan

Order the data. Find the means, medians, modes, minimums, maximums, quartiles, range, and interquartile range.

St. Petersburg:

$$\bar{x} = \frac{\begin{array}{c}62 + 64 + 64 + 68 + 70 + 74 + 78 \\ + \ 80 + 84 + 84 + 86 + 86\end{array}}{12}$$

$$= \frac{900}{12} = 75 \text{ (mean water temperature)}$$

Modes: 64, 84, and 86

Min.: 62; Max.: 86; Range: $86 - 62 = 24$

Median $(Q_2) = 76$

62 64 (64 68) 70 (74 78) 80 (84 84) 86 86

Median of lower part $(Q_1) = 66$

Median of upper part $(Q_3) = 84$

Interquartile range:
$Q_3 - Q_1 = 84 - 66 = 18$

Key West:

$$\bar{x} = \frac{\begin{array}{c}69 + 70 + 72 + 75 + 76 + 78 + 82 \\ + \ 82 + 85 + 86 + 87 + 87\end{array}}{12}$$

$$= \frac{949}{12} \approx 79.1 \text{ (mean water temperature)}$$

Modes: 82 and 87

Min.: 69; Max.: 87; Range: $87 - 69 = 18$

Median $(Q_2) = 80$

69 70 (72 75) 76 (78 82) 82 (85 86) 87 87

Median of lower part $(Q_1) = 73.5$

Median of upper part $(Q_3) = 85.5$

Interquartile range:
$Q_3 - Q_1 = 85.5 - 73.5 = 12$

Think

What location has a greater range in water temperature? The range of water temperatures at St. Petersburg is 6°F greater than the range at Key West.

The range and the interquartile range show the temperatures varying less at Key West than at St. Petersburg. Also, the temperatures at Key West are generally higher.

Got It? **3.** How can you compare the 12 water temperatures in Problem 3 from Dauphin Island with the 12 water temperatures from Grand Isle?

A *box-and-whisker plot* uses minimum and maximum values, the median, and the first and third quartiles to display the spread, or variability, in a data set.

take note

Key Concept   Box-and-Whisker Plot

Definition

A **box-and-whisker plot** is a way to display data that uses
- quartiles to bound the center box and
- the minimum and maximum values to form the whiskers.

Graph

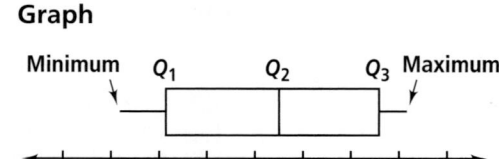

© **Problem 4** **Using a Box-and-Whisker Plot**

How can you use a graphing calculator box-and-whisker plot to find quartiles for the water temperature data of St. Petersburg from Problem 3?

Think

What about the appearance of a box-and-whisker plot might suggest an outlier?
If a "whisker" is much longer than the box, it's endpoint may be an outlier.

Step 1 For St. Petersburg, use **STAT EDIT** to enter the temperature data in **L1**.

Step 2 In **STAT PLOT**, select a box-and-whisker plot. Enter **L1** for the St. Petersburg data. Enter the window values. Draw the box-and-whisker plot.

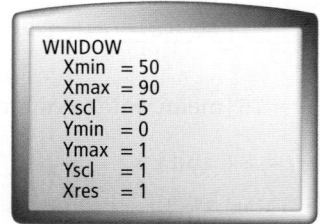
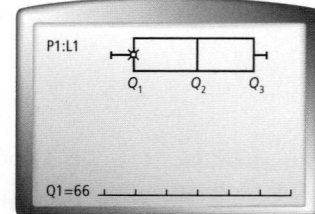

Step 3 Use **TRACE** to find the quartiles: $Q_1 = 66$, $Q_2 = 76$, and $Q_3 = 84$.

© ✓ **Got It?** **4. a.** How can you use graphing calculator box-and-whisker plots to find water temperature quartiles for other Gulf Coast sites in Problem 3?

   b. Reasoning Is a box-and-whisker plot a useful graphical display for data with an outlier? Explain.

A **percentile** is a number from 0 to 100 that you can associate with a value x from a data set. It shows the percent of the data that are less than or equal to x. If x is at the 63rd percentile, then 63% of the data are less than or equal to x.

 **Problem 5** Finding Percentiles

Plan

What should you do first to find percentiles?
Put the data in order.

Testing Here is an ordered list of midterm test scores for a Spanish class. What value is at the 65th percentile?

41	54	61	65	67	73	74
77	77	77	79	80	82	88
89	93	97	98	98	100	

Of the 20 values, 65% fall at or below the value at the 65th percentile.

$$20 \cdot 65\% = 20 \cdot 0.65 = 13$$

13 values fall at or below 82, the value at the 65th percentile.

 Got It? **5.** What are the values at each percentile for the data in Problem 5?

    a. 55th percentile   **b.** 95th percentile

 ## Lesson Check

Do you know HOW?

Identify the outlier in the data set. Then find the mean, median, and mode of the data set when the outlier is included and when it is not.

1. 16 19 21 18 18 54 20 22 23 17

2. 90 100 110 40 98 102 112 90 92

3. Using your results from Exercises 1 and 2, explain which measure of central tendency is most affected by an outlier.

4. Find the values at the 40th and 80th percentiles for the values below.

    58 53 35 60 58 42 57 60 43 44 51 49 58

Do you UNDERSTAND?  MATHEMATICAL PRACTICES

5. Vocabulary Which measure of central tendency would best represent the values below? Explain your reasoning.

    4 1 5 5 6 8 9 5 5 3 2 7 5 5 1

6. Error Analysis A student found the median of the data set below. Explain the student's error. What is the median?

Score	80	85	90	95
Frequency	6	4	10	1

$$\text{Median: } \frac{85+90}{2} = \frac{175}{2} = 87.5$$

 ## Practice and Problem-Solving Exercises  MATHEMATICAL PRACTICES

 **Practice**   Find the mean, median, and mode of each set of values.   ◀ See Problem 1.

7. Time spent on Internet per day (in minutes): 75 68 43 120 65 180 95 225 140

8.

Age (years)	13	14	15	16	17	18	19
Frequency	7	12	18	9	5	4	2

Identify the outlier of each set of values.

See Problem 2.

9. 3.4 4.5 2.3 5.9 9.8 3.3 2.1 3.0 2.9

10. 17 21 19 10 15 19 14 0 11 16

11. Weather The table shows average monthly temperatures of two cities. How can you compare the temperatures?

See Problems 3 and 4.

	J	F	M	A	M	J	J	A	S	O	N	D
Jacksonville, Florida	52.4	55.2	61.1	67.0	73.4	79.1	81.6	81.2	78.1	69.8	61.9	55.1
Austin, Texas	48.8	52.8	61.5	69.9	75.6	81.3	84.5	84.8	80.2	71.1	60.9	51.6

Make a box-and-whisker plot for each set of values.

12. 12 11 15 12 19 20 19 14 18 15 16

13. 120 145 133 105 117 150 130 136 128

Find the values at the 30th and 90th percentiles for each data set.

See Problem 5.

14. 6283 5700 6381 6274 5700 5896 5972 6075 5993 5581

15. 7 12 3 14 17 20 5 3 17 4 13 2 15 9 15 18 16 9 1 6

 **Apply**

Identify the outlier in each data set. Then find the mean, median, and mode of the data set when the outlier is included and when it is not.

16. 947 757 103 619 661 582 626 900 869 728 1001 596 515

17. 87 104 381 215 174 199 233 186 142 228 9 53 117 129

18. 49 57.5 58 49.2 62 22.2 67 52.1 77 99.9 80 51.7 64

19. Think About a Plan Use the water temperature data for the eastern coast of the Gulf of Mexico during the summer months, as shown in the graph below. Find the quartiles by graphing a box-and-whisker plot of the data.

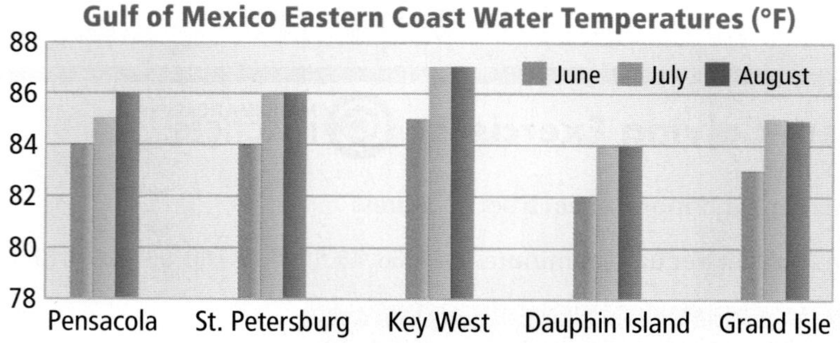

Gulf of Mexico Eastern Coast Water Temperatures (°F)

[Bar graph with y-axis from 78 to 88, legend: June, July, August; x-axis categories: Pensacola, St. Petersburg, Key West, Dauphin Island, Grand Isle]

- What information can you get from the graph?
- How can you use that information to make a box-and-whisker plot?
- How can you find the quartiles using your box-and-whisker plot?

STEM 20. Meteorology On May 3, 1999, 59 tornadoes hit Oklahoma in the largest tornado outbreak ever recorded in the state. Sixteen of these were classified as strong (F2 or F3) or violent (F4 or F5).
  a. Make a box-and-whisker plot of the data for length of path.
  b. Identify the outliers. Remove them from the data set and make a revised box-and-whisker plot.
  © **c. Writing** How does the removal of the outliers affect the box-and-whisker plot? How does it affect the median of the data set?

For Exercises 21–23, use the set of values below.
1 1 1 1 1 1 2 3 5 8 13 21 34 55 89 89 89 89 89 89

21. At what percentile is 1?   **22.** At what percentile is 34?

© **23. Error Analysis** A student claims that 89 is at the 70th percentile. Explain the student's error.

24. Advertising An electronics store placed an ad in the newspaper showing flat-screen TVs for sale. The ad says "Our flat-screen TVs average $695." The prices of the flat-screen TVs are $1200, $999, $1499, $895, $695, $1100, $1300, and $695.
  a. Find the mean, median, and mode of the prices.
  b. Which measure is the store using in its ad? Why did they choose it?
  c. As a consumer, which measure would you want to see advertised? Explain your reasoning.

© **25. Reasoning** Which measure better represents a data set with several outliers—the mean or the median? Justify your answer.

26. The table displays the frequency of scores for one Calculus class on the Advanced Placement Calculus exam. The mean of the exam scores is 3.5.

Score	1	2	3	4	5
Frequency	1	3	f	12	3

  a. What is the value of f in the table?
  b. What is the mode of all of the exam scores?
  c. What is the median of all of the exam scores?

27. Grades Some teachers use a *weighted mean* to calculate grades. Each score is assigned a weight based on its importance. To find a weighted mean, multiply each score by its weight and add the results. For example, a student's final chemistry grade is based on four sources: 30% from lab reports, 10% from quizzes, 25% from the midterm exam, and 35% from the final exam. What is the student's weighted mean given the scores shown?

Lab Reports	82
Quizzes	95
Midterm Exam	76
Final Exam	88

© **Challenge**

28. Reasoning What effect will adding 10 to every value in a data set have on the mean, median, mode, range, and box-and-whisker plot? What will be the effect if you multiply each value by 10?

Major Tornadoes in Oklahoma, May 3, 1999

Length of Path (miles)	Intensity
6	F3
9	F3
4	F2
37	F5
7	F2
12	F3
8	F2
7	F2
15	F4
39	F4
1	F2
22	F3
15	F3
8	F2
13	F3
2	F2

SOURCE: National Oceanic & Atmospheric Administration

29. Track and Field The box-and-whisker plots show the 36 best qualifying distances for the shot put events for men and women during the 2004 Olympics. Compare box-and-whisker plots. Describe any conclusions you can draw about Olympic-level male and female shot-putters.

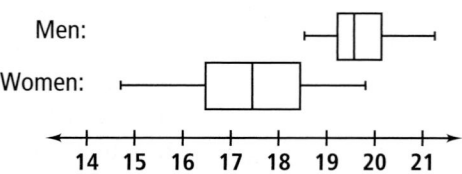

Standardized Test Prep

SAT/ACT

30. Use a calculator to solve $2x^2 - 7x - 5 = 0$. Round answers to the nearest hundredth.

   (A) $-1.56, -4.44$ (B) $-5.44, 1.56$ (C) $-0.61, 4.11$ (D) $-5.56, -1.44$

31. Which function generates the table of values below?

x	-2	-1	0	1	2
y	$\frac{27}{8}$	$\frac{9}{2}$	6	8	$\frac{32}{3}$

   (F) $27\left(\frac{2}{3}\right)^x$ (G) $6\left(\frac{4}{3}\right)^x$ (H) $\left(\frac{8}{3}\right)^x$ (I) $6\left(\frac{3}{4}\right)^x$

32. A homeroom class consists of 6 boys whose last name begins with S, 8 boys whose last name begins with T, 4 girls whose last name begins with S, and 11 girls whose last name begins with T. A student is chosen at random from the class. What is the probability that the student is a girl or has a last name that begins with S?

   (A) $\frac{18}{29}$ (B) $\frac{21}{29}$ (C) $\frac{23}{29}$ (D) $\frac{25}{29}$

Short Response

33. In a library, the probability that a book is a hardback, given that it is illustrated, is 0.40. The probability that a book is hardback *and* illustrated is 0.20. Find the probability that a book is illustrated.

Mixed Review

Of all the respondents to a survey, 59% are girls. Of the girls, 61% read horror stories. Of the boys, 49% read horror stories. Find each probability.

   See Lesson 11-4.

34. P(boy and reads horror stories)   **35.** P(reads horror stories)

Determine whether each sequence is arithmetic. If it is, identify the common difference.

   See Lesson 9-2.

36. $16, 7, -2, \ldots$ **37.** $34, 51, 68, \ldots$ **38.** $2, 2.2, 2.22, \ldots$ **39.** $1, 1, 1, \ldots$

Get Ready! To prepare for Lesson 11-7, do Exercises 40–43.

Find all real square roots of each number.

   See Lesson 6-1.

40. 256   **41.** 0.0081   **42.** $\frac{121}{16}$ **43.** $\frac{361}{25}$

11-7 Standard Deviation

© Common Core State Standards

S-ID.A.4 Use the mean and standard deviation of a data set to fit it to a normal distribution and to estimate population percentages. **Also S-IC.B.6**

MP 1, MP 3, MP 4, MP 5, MP 8

Objectives To find the standard deviation and variance of a set of values
To apply standard deviation and variance

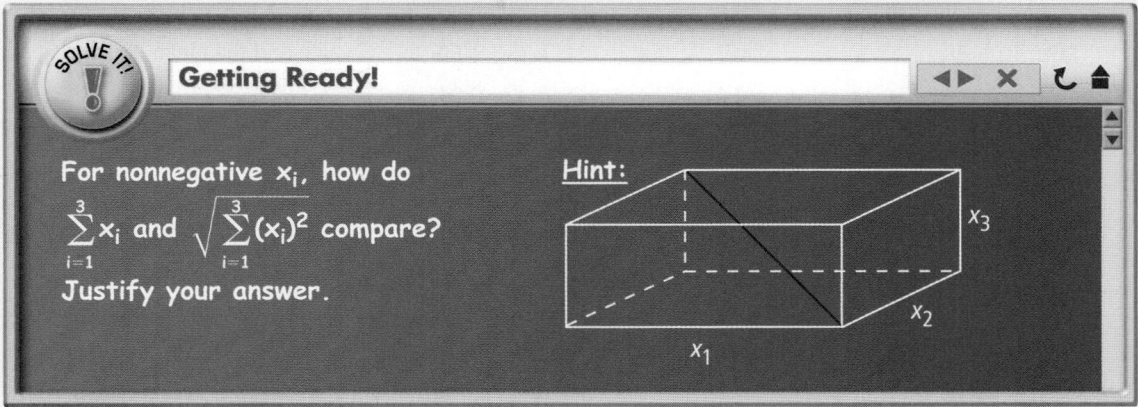

SOLVE IT!

Getting Ready!

For nonnegative x_i, how do

$\sum\limits_{i=1}^{3} x_i$ and $\sqrt{\sum\limits_{i=1}^{3}(x_i)^2}$ compare?

Justify your answer.

Hint:

You learned about summation notation in Chapter 9. To find the mean of a data set, you sum the data values and divide by the number of data values. You can use summation to measure how data deviates from the mean.

Lesson Vocabulary
• measure of variation
• variance
• standard deviation

Essential Understanding Standard deviation is a measure of how far the numbers in a data set deviate from the mean.

In the previous lesson you studied range and interquartile range. Each of these is a **measure of variation**. A measure of variation describes how the data in a data set are spread out.

Variance and **standard deviation** are measures showing how much data values deviate from the mean. The Greek letter σ (sigma) represents standard deviation. σ^2 (sigma squared) is the variance.

take note

Key Concepts **Finding Variance and Standard Deviation**

• Find the mean, $\bar{x}$, of the n values in a data set.
• Find the difference, $x - \bar{x}$, between each value x and the mean.
• Square each difference, $(x - \bar{x})^2$.
• Find the average (mean) of these squares. This is the variance.

$$\sigma^2 = \frac{\sum (x - \bar{x})^2}{n}$$

• Take the square root of the variance. This is the standard deviation.

$$\sigma = \sqrt{\frac{\sum (x - \bar{x})^2}{n}}$$

 **Problem 1** Finding Variance and Standard Deviation

What are the mean, variance, and standard deviation of these values?
6.9 8.7 7.6 4.8 9.0

$$\bar{x} = \frac{6.9 + 8.7 + 7.6 + 4.8 + 9.0}{5} = 7.4 \qquad \text{Find the mean.}$$

Think

How can you organize you work?
Use a table to record the values.

Make a table.

x	$\bar{x}$	$x - \bar{x}$	$(x - \bar{x})^2$
6.9	7.4	−0.5	0.25
8.7	7.4	1.3	1.69
7.6	7.4	0.2	0.04
4.8	7.4	−2.6	6.76
9.0	7.4	1.6	2.56
		Sum	11.30

Find difference between each value and the mean. Square the differences.

Add the squares of the differences.

$$\sigma^2 = \frac{\sum (x - \bar{x})^2}{n} = \frac{11.3}{5} = 2.26 \qquad \text{Find the variance.}$$

$$\sigma = \sqrt{\sigma^2} = \sqrt{2.26} \approx 1.5 \qquad \text{Find the standard deviation.}$$

The mean is 7.4. The variance is 2.26. The standard deviation is about 1.5.

 Got It? **1.** What are the mean, variance, and standard deviation of these values?
52 63 65 77 80 82

 **Problem 2** Using a Calculator to Find Standard Deviation (STEM)

Meteorology The table displays the number of U.S. hurricane strikes by decade from the years 1851 to 2000. What are the mean and standard deviation for this data set?

Decade	1	2	3	4	5	6	7	8	9	10	11	12	13	14	15
Strikes	19	15	20	22	21	18	21	13	19	24	17	14	12	15	14

SOURCE: National Hurricane Center

Think

How do you know you are entering all the data values?
The calculator value for n should match the number of table values.

Step 1 Use **STAT EDIT** to enter the data in list **L1**.

Step 2 In **STAT CALC** select the **1– Var Stats** option.

The mean is 17.6; the standard deviation is about 3.5.

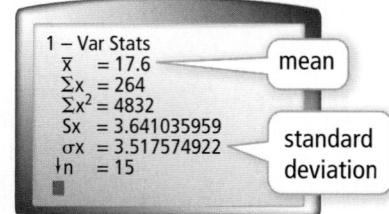

Got It? 2. Meteorology The table displays the number of hurricanes in the Atlantic Ocean from 1992 to 2006. What are the mean and standard deviation?

Year	1	2	3	4	5	6	7	8	9	10	11	12	13	14	15
Number	4	4	3	11	10	3	10	8	8	9	4	7	9	14	5

Source: National Hurricane Center

In a data list, every value falls within some number of standard deviations of the mean. For example, if the mean is 50 and the standard deviation is 10, then a value x with $40 \le x \le 60$ is within one standard deviation of the mean.

Ⓒ Problem 3 Using Standard Deviation to Describe Data STEM

Meteorology Use the U.S. hurricane-strike data from Problem 2. Within how many standard deviations from the mean do all of the values fall?

Know	Need	Plan
The data values, their mean, and their standard deviation	The number of standard deviations from the mean that include all the data	• Draw a number line. • Plot the data values and the mean. • Mark off intervals of 3.5 on either side of the mean.

Think

What is a good way to tell which values lie within each σ interval?
Plotting the values on a number line makes it easy to see the σ intervals.

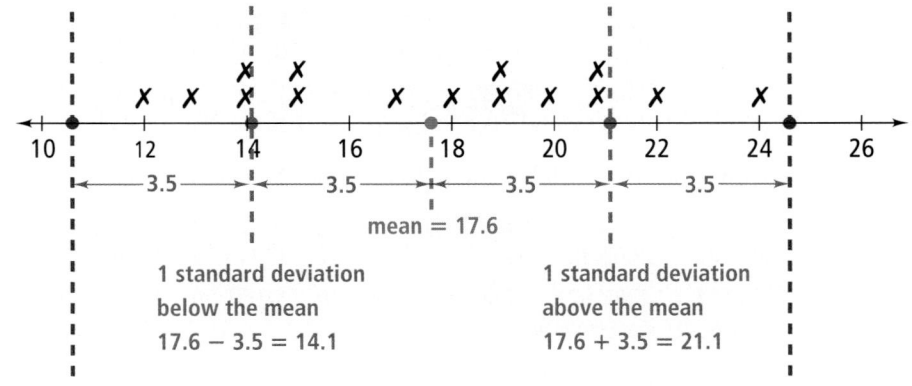

2 standard deviations below the mean
$17.6 - 2(3.5) = 10.6$

2 standard deviations above the mean
$17.6 + 2(3.5) = 24.6$

All of the values fall within two standard deviations of the mean. Hurricane watchers can expect that the number of U.S. hurricane strikes in a decade will probably fall within two standard deviations of the 15-decade mean.

Ⓒ   **Got It? 3. Meteorology** Use the Atlantic Ocean hurricane data from Got It 2.
  a. Within how many standard deviations of the mean do all of the values fall?
  b. Reasoning How might the U.S. Federal Emergency Management Agency (FEMA) use this information?

Lesson Check

Do you know HOW?

1. Find the mean, variance, and standard deviation for the data set.

   5, 15, 9, 3, 12, 8, 13, 6, 18, 11

2. Within how many standard deviations of the mean do all of the data values fall?

   12, 17, 15, 13, 9, 10, 12, 10, 15, 17

Do you UNDERSTAND?

3. **Vocabulary** Explain the difference between *measures of central tendency* and *measures of variation*.

4. **Compare and Contrast** Three data sets each have a mean of 70. Set A has a standard deviation of 10. Set B has a standard deviation of 5. Set C has a standard deviation of 20. Compare and contrast these 3 sets.

5. **Reasoning** What is the effect of an outlier on the standard deviation of a data set?

Practice and Problem-Solving Exercises

 **Practice**   Find the mean, variance, and standard deviation for each data set.   ◄ See Problem 1.

6. 78 90 456 673 111 381 21

7. 13 15 17 18 12 21 10

8. 12 3 2 4 5 7

9. 60 40 35 45 39

Graphing Calculator Find the mean and the standard deviation.   ◄ See Problem 2.

10. The Dow Jones Industrial average for the first 12 weeks of 1988:

1911.31	1956.07	1903.51	1958.22	1910.48	1983.26
2014.59	2023.21	2057.86	2034.98	2087.37	2067.14

11. The Dow Jones Industrial average for the first 12 weeks of 2008:

12800.18	12606.30	12099.3	12207.17	12743.19	12182.13
12348.21	12381.02	12266.39	11893.69	11951.09	11972.25

Determine the whole number of standard deviations from the mean that include all data values.   ◄ See Problem 3.

12. The mean price of the nonfiction books on a best-sellers list is $25.07; the standard deviation is $2.62.
    $26.95, $22.95, $24.00, $24.95, $29.95, $19.95, $24.95, $24.00, $27.95, $25.00

13. The mean length of Beethoven's nine symphonies is 37 minutes; the standard deviation is 12 minutes.
    27 min, 30 min, 47 min, 35 min, 30 min, 40 min, 35 min, 22 min, 65 min

14. Find the standard deviation for each data set. Use the standard deviations to compare each pair of data sets.
    fastest recorded speeds of various large wild cats (miles per hour):
    70 50 30 40 35 30 30 40 15
    fastest recorded speeds of various birds in flight (miles per hour):
    217 106 95 56 65 37 50 31 53 25 25 25

15. **Think About a Plan** Use the data for daily energy usage of a small town during ten days in June. Find the mean and the standard deviation of the data. How many values in the data set fall within one standard deviation from the mean? Within two standard deviations? Within three standard deviations?

51.8 MWh	53.6 MWh	54.7 MWh	51.9 MWh	49.3 MWh
52.0 MWh	53.5 MWh	51.2 MWh	60.7 MWh	59.3 MWh

    • How is the mean of the data set used in the formula for standard deviation?
    • How can a table help you find the standard deviation?
    • How can a graph help you decide how many standard deviations a data value is from the mean?

Income Use the chart at the right for Exercises 16–18.

16. Find the mean income for each year.

17. **Writing** Use the standard deviation for each year to describe how farm income varied from 2001 to 2002.

18. For 2001, the farm incomes of which states are not within one standard deviation of the mean?

19. **a. Data Collection** Make a table showing the number of siblings of each student in your class.
    b. Find the mean and standard deviation of the data.

20. **Energy** The data for daily energy usage of a small town during ten days in January is shown.

83.8 MWh	87.1 MWh	92.5 MWh	80.6 MWh	82.4 MWh
77.6 MWh	78.9 MWh	78.2 MWh	81.8 MWh	80.1 MWh

    a. Find the mean and the standard deviation of the data.
    b. How many values in the data set fall within one standard deviation from the mean? Within two standard deviations? Within three standard deviations?

21. **Error Analysis** One of your friends says that the data below fall within three standard deviations from the mean. Your other friend disagrees, saying that the data fall within six standard deviations from the mean. With whom do you agree? Explain.

Farm Income in Midwestern States (millions of dollars)

State	2001	2002
Iowa	10,653	10,834
Kansas	7979	7862
Minnesota	7537	7478
Missouri	4723	4402
Nebraska	9221	9589
North Dakota	2938	3223
South Dakota	3897	3779

SOURCE: U.S. Department of Agriculture

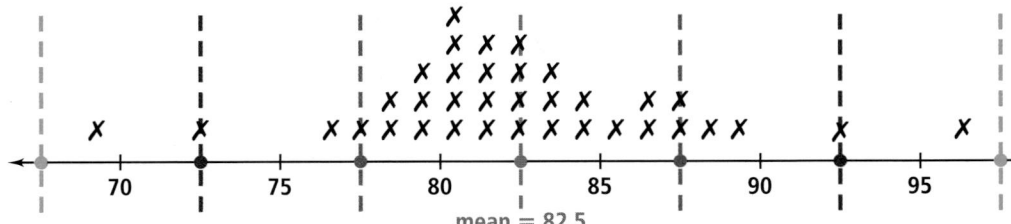

22. a. Use the table to find the range, the mean, and the standard deviation of the ages for each team.

    ⓒ **b. Reasoning** For two data sets, does the set with the greater range necessarily have the greater standard deviation? Support your answer with your results from part (a).

23. a. What effect will adding 10 to every value in a data set have on the standard deviation?

    b. What will be the effect if you multiply each value by 10?

Ages of the Members of Soccer Teams in an Adult League

Men	19	18	21	22	22	23
	23	23	23	22	36	22
	24	21	21	21	21	22
Women	26	31	22	24	20	22
	20	30	25	26	32	30
	23	33	21	27	24	28

Standardized Test Prep

GRIDDED RESPONSE

SAT/ACT

For Exercises 24–25, use the following bowling scores for six members of a bowling team: 175, 210, 180, 195, 208, 196.

24. What is the mean of the scores?

25. What is the standard deviation of the scores?

26. The 30th term of a finite arithmetic series is 4.4. The sum of the first 30 terms is 78. What is the value of the first term of the series?

27. What is the probability of NOT getting a five when rolling a number cube? Write your answer as a fraction reduced to lowest terms.

Mixed Review

Make a box-and-whisker plot for each set of values.

◀ **See Lesson 11-6.**

28. 25, 25, 30, 35, 45, 45, 50, 55, 60, 60

29. 20, 23, 25, 36, 37, 38, 39, 50, 52, 55

Find the center and the radius of each circle.

◀ **See Lesson 10-3.**

30. $(x - 2)^2 + (y + 1)^2 = 36$

31. $(x - 1)^2 + (y - 1)^2 = 4$

Get Ready! **To prepare for Lesson 11-8, do Exercises 32–37.**

Simplify each radical expression.

◀ **See Lesson 6-1.**

32. $\dfrac{1}{\sqrt{4}}$

33. $-\dfrac{1}{\sqrt{9}}$

34. $\dfrac{1}{\sqrt{36}}$

35. $-\dfrac{1}{\sqrt{121}}$

36. $-\dfrac{1}{\sqrt{81}}$

37. $\dfrac{1}{\sqrt{49}}$

Samples and Surveys

Common Core State Standards

S-IC.A.1 Understand statistics as a process for making inferences about population parameters based on a random sample from that population. **Also S-IC.B.3, S-IC.B.4, S-IC.B.6**

MP 1, MP 2, MP 3, MP 4

Objectives To identify sampling methods
To recognize bias in samples and surveys

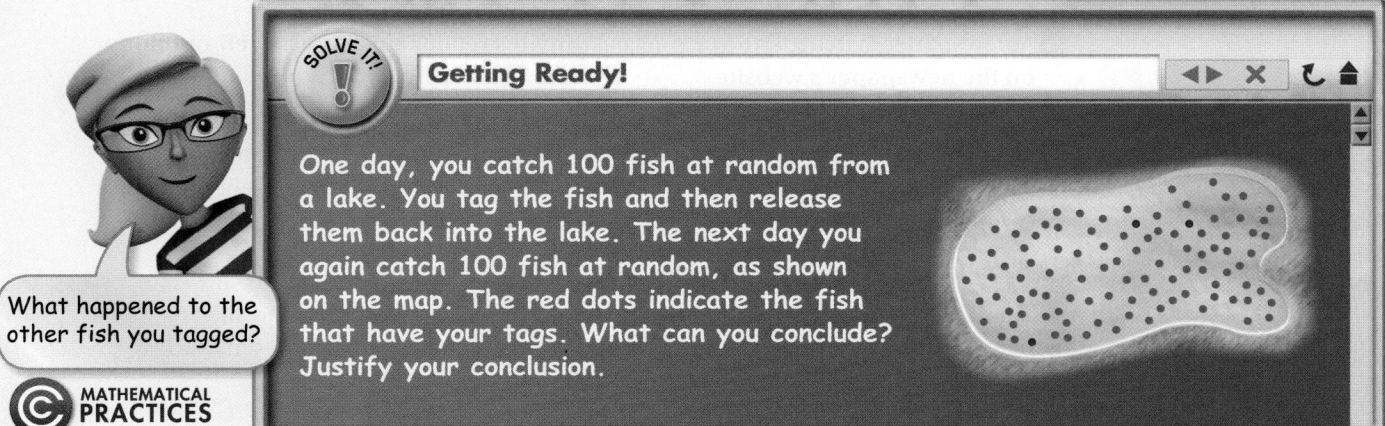

SOLVE IT!

Getting Ready!

One day, you catch 100 fish at random from a lake. You tag the fish and then release them back into the lake. The next day you again catch 100 fish at random, as shown on the map. The red dots indicate the fish that have your tags. What can you conclude? Justify your conclusion.

What happened to the other fish you tagged?

MATHEMATICAL PRACTICES

Lesson Vocabulary
• population
• sample
• convenience sample
• self-selected sample
• systematic sample
• random sample
• bias
• observational study
• controlled experiment
• survey

A **population** is all the members of a set. A **sample** is part of a population. If you determine a sample carefully, the statistics for the sample can be used to make general conclusions about the larger population.

Essential Understanding You can get good statistical information about a population by studying a sample of the population.

Suppose you want to know what percent of all voters in your city favor a tax increase to pay for school improvements. It likely would be impossible to ask an opinion of every voter. So instead you select a sample of the voters to estimate the percentage who favor the idea.

You can define different sample types by the methods used to select them.

Key Concepts **Sampling Types and Methods**

For a **convenience sample**, select any members of the population who are conveniently and readily available.

For a **self-selected sample**, select only members of the population who volunteer for the sample.

For a **systematic sample**, order the population in some way, and then select from it at regular intervals.

In a **random sample**, all members of the population are equally likely to be chosen.

Samples vary in how well they reflect a population. A sample has a *bias* when a part of a population is overrepresented or underrepresented. A **bias** is a systematic error introduced by the sampling method.

 Problem 1 Analyzing Sampling Methods

Public Opinion A newspaper wants to find out what percent of the city population favors a property tax increase to raise money for local parks. What is the sampling method used for each situation? Does the sample have a bias? Explain.

Think

Who are the people in the sample?
The people in the sample are only those who might be selected. In this case, only those who visit the website.

A **A newspaper article on the tax increase invites readers to express their opinions on the newspaper's website.**

This is a self-selected sample. It might have a bias, depending on who visits the website. The people who respond may overrepresent or underrepresent some views. For example, some property owners who are against the tax might organize a campaign to get friends and neighbors to visit the website.

B **A reporter interviews people leaving the city's largest park.**

This is a convenience sample, since it is convenient for the reporter to stay in one place. Because the location is near a park, the sample may overrepresent park supporters and the results will have a bias.

C **A survey service calls every 50th listing from the local phone book.**

This is a systematic sample because the phone listing is ordered alphabetically. The regular sampling interval is every 50 listings. This sample may have a bias if there is some link between people who are listed (or not listed) in a phone book and people who pay property taxes.

  Got It? **1. a.** To survey the eating habits of the community, employees of a local television station interview people visiting a food court in the mall. What sampling method are they using? Does the sample have a bias? Explain.

b. **Reasoning** A poll of every person in the population is a *census*. What is a situation that requires a census instead of a sample?

One way to collect sample information is to perform a study.

 **Key Concepts** **Study Methods**

In an **observational study**, you measure or observe members of a sample in such a way that they are not affected by the study.

In a **controlled experiment**, you divide the sample into two groups. You impose a treatment on one group but not on the other "control" group. Then you compare the effect on the treated group to the control group.

In a **survey**, you ask every member of the sample a set of questions.

A poorly designed study can result in unreliable statistics. You should always analyze a study's methods before making general conclusions about the population.

Problem 2 Analyzing Study Methods

Which type of study method is described in each situation? Should the sample statistics be used to make a general conclusion about the population?

A **Researchers randomly choose two groups from 10 volunteers. Over a period of 8 weeks, one group eats ice cream before going to sleep, and the other does not. Volunteers wear monitoring devices while sleeping, and researchers record dream activity.**

This is an example of a controlled experiment. The statistics for this study are based on such a small sample that the findings are unreliable as a general conclusion.

B **Students in a science class record the height of bean plants as they grow.**

This is an observational study. The statistics may provide a general conclusion about the growth rate of a bean plant. However, soil type, amount of sunlight and water, fertilizer, and other factors could affect the growth rate.

C **Student council members ask every tenth student in the lunch line if they like the cafeteria food.**

This is a survey. The results are not reliable because people waiting in line are more likely to enjoy the cafeteria food than those who brought their lunch from home.

Think

How can you tell if a sample is a random sample?
In a random sample, each group of the same size is equally likely to be chosen.

Got It? **2.** A pharmaceutical company asks for volunteers to test a new drug to treat high blood pressure. Half of the volunteers will be given the drug, and half will be given a placebo. The researcher will monitor the blood pressure of each volunteer. Which type of study method is the researcher using? Should the sample statistics be used to make a general conclusion about the effectiveness of the drug in the larger population? Explain.

Problem 3 Designing a Survey

Sports **During the 2008 Olympic Games, a U.S. swimmer won more medals than any other swimmer in history. What sampling method could you use to find the percent of students in your school who recognize that swimmer from a photograph? What is an example of a survey question that is likely to yield information that has no bias?**

A possible sampling method is to question every 10th student entering school in the morning. This is a systematic sampling. It usually contains the least bias. A possible unbiased survey question is, "Who is pictured in this photograph?".

Think

How do you think of a survey question that has no bias?
Keep it simple. The simplest question is likely to be the least biased.

Got It? **3.** What sampling method could you use to find the percent of residents in your neighborhood who recognize the governor of your state by name? What is an example of a survey question that is likely to yield information that has no bias?

Lesson Check

Do you know HOW?

1. To investigate a community's reading habits, a newspaper conducts a poll from a table near the exit of a history museum.
   a. What is the sampling method?
   b. Does the sampling method have any bias? Explain.

2. A survey asks, "Aren't handmade gifts always better than tacky purchased gifts?" Does this survey question have any bias? Explain.

Do you UNDERSTAND?

3. **Vocabulary** What is the difference between a population and a sample? Give an example of each.

4. **Writing** What does it mean to have an unbiased sample? Why does it matter?

5. **Reasoning** Would a large or small sample tend to give a better estimate of how the total population feels about a topic? Explain.

Practice and Problem-Solving Exercises

 Identify the sampling method. Then identify any bias in each method. ◀ See Problem 1.

6. A supermarket wants to find the percent of shoppers who use coupons. A manager interviews every shopper entering the greeting card aisle.

7. A maintenance crew wants to estimate how many of 3000 air filters in a 30-story office building need replacing. The crew examines five filters chosen at random on each floor of the building.

8. The student government wants to find out how many students have after-school jobs. A pollster interviews students selected at random as they board buses at the end of the school day.

For Exercises 9–11, identify the type of study method described in each situation and explain whether the sample statistics can be used to make a general conclusion about the population. ◀ See Problem 2.

9. A list of students is randomly generated from the school database. Information for every student is entered into the database, and each student has an equally likely chance of being selected. The students selected are asked how much time they spend on household chores each week.

10. The local librarian collects data about the types of books that are checked out so that she can place a new book order accordingly. She records the type of book checked out by every other person each day for three weeks.

11. **Gardening** A gardener tests a new plant food by planting seeds from the same package in the same soil and location. Each plant is given the same amount of water, but one plant is given food and the other is given no food at all. He records the growth and flowering rates of each plant.

12. a. **Energy** What sampling method could you use to find the percent of adults in your community who support building more nuclear power plants? ◀ See Problem 3.
    b. What is an example of a survey question that is likely to yield unbiased information?

 **Apply** A university researcher is studying the effect of watching television on residents of the city. Describe a sampling method that can be used for each population.

13. all teenagers

14. all homeowners

15. all women over the age of 21

16. all children under the age of 13

17. Think About a Plan An online advertisement asks you to participate in a survey. The survey asks how much time you spend online each week. What sampling method is the survey using? Identify any bias in the sampling method.
- What population is likely to see the survey?
- What population is likely to respond to the survey?

18. Entertainment A magazine publisher mails a survey to every tenth person on a subscriber list. The survey asks for three favorite leisure activities. What sampling method is the survey using? Identify any bias in the sampling method.

19. Student government members survey every tenth student who enters the school building and asks whether students favor the school's new dress code. The sample statistics show that 54% favor the new dress code, 42% oppose the dress code, and 4% have no opinion.
- **a.** What is the population?
- **b.** What is the sample?
- **c.** What general conclusion can be made about the population?

20. Compare and Contrast Describe how a convenience sample and a self-selected sample are alike and how they are different.

21. Elections In a recent election, a survey of randomly selected registered voters was conducted to determine which candidate was likely to win. 48% of respondents said that they would vote for candidate A, 46% would vote for candidate B, and 6% were undecided. Based on the sampling results, can you make a general conclusion that it is more likely that candidate A will win the election? Explain.

22. Customer Satisfaction A car dealership conducts a satisfaction survey. They randomly select a sample of 500 customers from a list of 5000 new customers in the past year. Of the 500 surveys sent, 300 are returned. The statistics show that the dealership is achieving a high level of customer satisfaction. Can the owner of the dealership assume this is true overall? Explain.

23. For a class project, a student studies the likelihood that students turn in their homework each day. For each of her classes, she observes the teacher collect homework. She records the number of students who turn in homework, and the number who do not. The resulting data show that 86% of students turned in homework on time and 5% of students did not turn in any homework at all during the week.
- **a.** What type of sampling method was used?
- **b.** What type of study was performed?
- **c.** Can the student use these statistics to make a general conclusion about all students in her school? Explain.

Challenge

24. **Open Ended** The government uses a variety of methods to estimate how the general public is feeling about the economy. A researcher wants to conduct a study to determine whether people who live in his state are representative of the latest government results. What type of study should the researcher use? Explain.

25. In a recent telephone survey, respondents were asked questions to determine whether they supported the new law that required every passenger to wear a seat belt while in a moving vehicle. The first question was, "According to the National Highway Traffic Safety Administration, wearing seat belts could prevent 45% of the fatalities suffered in car accidents. Do you think that everyone should wear safety belts?" Does this question introduce a bias into the survey? Explain.

Standardized Test Prep

SAT/ACT

26. To determine the most popular brands of tea consumed by Americans, a survey is conducted in a busy downtown location at lunchtime. Which of the following is NOT a potential bias in the sampling method?

Ⓐ Urban office employees are not representative of the general population.

Ⓑ The results could be influenced by national brand teas available in the area.

Ⓒ A lunchtime survey does not reflect peoples' tastes at other times of the day.

Ⓓ The survey must include call-in and online responses.

27. Which is the equation for the graph of the circle at the right?

Ⓕ $x^2 + (y - 5)^2 = 16$

Ⓖ $x^2 + (y + 5)^2 = 16$

Ⓗ $(x - 5)^2 + y^2 = 16$

Ⓘ $(x + 5)^2 + y^2 = 16$

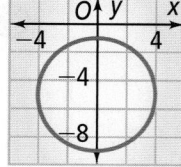

Short Response

28. What is the sum of the infinite geometric sequence? Show your work.

$$\frac{2}{5}, \frac{4}{25}, \frac{8}{125}, \cdots$$

Mixed Review

Find the mean and the standard deviation for each data set.　　　　◀ See Lesson 11-7.

29. 0, 1, 1, 1, 2, 2, 2, 3, 3, 4, 5, 10

30. 1, 1, 2, 2, 3, 4, 5, 6, 8, 9, 10, 10, 12

Find the inverse of each function. Is the inverse a function?　　　　◀ See Lesson 6-7.

31. $f(x) = 2x + 5$

32. $f(x) = x^2$

33. $f(x) = \frac{5x^2}{9}$

34. $f(x) = 3\sqrt{x}$

Get Ready! To prepare for Lesson 11-9, do Exercises 35–38.

Evaluate each expression.　　　　◀ See Lesson 11-1.

35. $_4C_2$

36. $_3C_3$

37. $_5C_2$

38. $_{12}C_7$

11-9 Binomial Distributions

Common Core State Standards

Extends S-CP.B.9 Use permutations and combinations to compute probabilities of compound events and solve problems.

MP 1, MP 2, MP 3, MP 4, MP 5

Objective To find binomial probabilities and to use binomial distributions

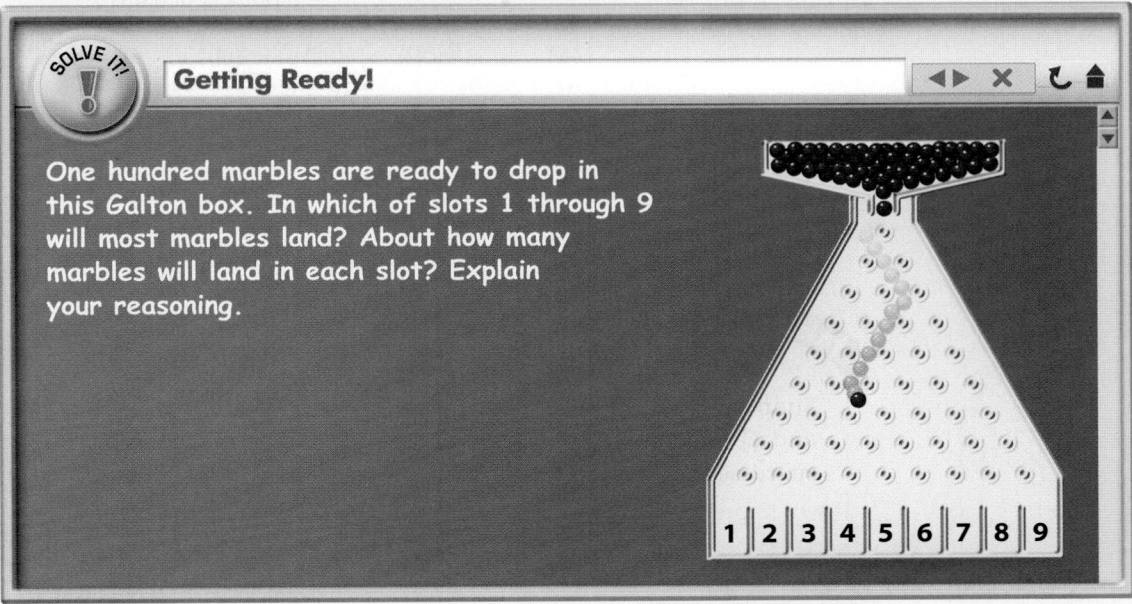

SOLVE IT!

Getting Ready!

One hundred marbles are ready to drop in this Galton box. In which of slots 1 through 9 will most marbles land? About how many marbles will land in each slot? Explain your reasoning.

1 2 3 4 5 6 7 8 9

Lesson Vocabulary
• binomial experiment
• binomial probability
• Binomial Theorem

At each level of a Galton box, a marble can take one of two possible paths.

Essential Understanding You can use binomial probabilities in situations involving two possible outcomes.

take note ▸ **Key Concept** **Binomial Experiment**

A **binomial experiment** has these important features:

• There are a fixed number of trials.
• Each trial has two possible outcomes.
• The trials are independent.
• The probability of each outcome is constant throughout the trials.

Recall from Lesson 11-4 that you can use a tree diagram to find probabilities. The tree diagram on the following page shows different outcomes and probabilities for a basketball player shooting two free throws. It is known that this player is a good shooter, having hit (H) about 90% of the free throws so far this season.

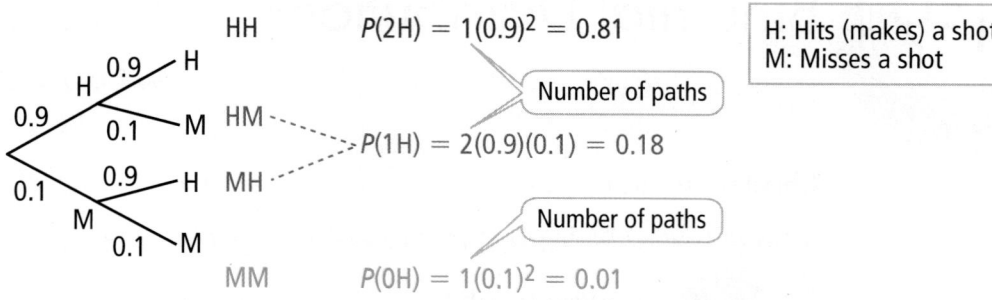

H: Hits (makes) a shot
M: Misses a shot

$P(2H) = 1(0.9)^2 = 0.81$

Number of paths

$P(1H) = 2(0.9)(0.1) = 0.18$

Number of paths

$P(0H) = 1(0.1)^2 = 0.01$

Suppose the player needs to make one of two free throws to win a game. The purple and red labels show $P(2 \text{ hits}) + P(1 \text{ hit}) = 0.81 + 0.18 = 0.99$.

The basketball player shoots 2 free throws—each independent of the other (pressure notwithstanding). The player will succeed on 0, 1, or 2 of them. You can compute the probabilities shown in the tree diagram by using the **binomial probability** formula.

 **Key Concept** **Binomial Probability**

Suppose you have n repeated independent trials, each with a probability of success p and a probability of failure q (with $p + q = 1$). Then the **binomial probability** of x successes in the n trials can be found by the following formula.

$$P(x) = {_nC_x}p^x q^{n-x}$$

 Problem 1 **Using a Formula to Find Probabilities**

Merchandising As part of a promotion, a store is giving away scratch-off cards. Each card has a 40% chance of awarding a prize. Suppose you have five cards. Find the probability that exactly four of the five cards will reveal a prize.

Know
- The number of trials n
- The number of successes x
- The probability of success p

Need
- The probability of failure q
- The probability of picking exactly 4 winning cards

Plan
- Decide that this is binomial probability.
- Find the probability of failure q.
- Use the formula for binomial probability.

Determine if this a binomial experiment.

- The situation involves 5 repeated trials—5 cards selected at random.
- Each trial has two possible outcomes: It is a winner or it is not.
- The probability of success is constant, 0.4, throughout the trials.
- The trials are independent. The outcome of scratching one card does not affect the probability of any of the other cards revealing a prize.

How can you find $_nC_x$ using your calculator?

$_nC_x = \dfrac{n!}{x!(n-x)!}$

On a graphing calculator, use **MATH** and $_nC_r$ in the **PRB** menu.

This is a binomial experiment with $n = 5$, $x = 4$, $p = 0.4$, and $q = 1 - p = 0.6$.

$$P(x) = {}_nC_x p^x q^{n-x}$$
$$P(4) = {}_5C_4(0.4)^4(0.6)^1 \quad \text{Substitute.}$$
$$= 5(0.4)^4(0.6)^1 \quad \text{Evaluate } {}_5C_4.$$
$$\approx 0.08 \quad \text{Simplify.}$$

The probability is about 0.08 that exactly 4 of the five cards will reveal a prize.

 Got It? **1.** What is the probability that the number of cards that reveal a prize is 0? 1? 2? 3? 5?

The Binomial Theorem (Lesson 5-7) says that for every positive integer n,

$$(a + b)^n = P_0a^n + P_1a^{n-1}b + P_2a^{n-2}b^2 + \cdots + P_{n-1}ab^{n-1} + P_nb^n$$

where $P_0, P_1, \ldots, P_n$ are the numbers in the nth row of Pascal's Triangle.

For that row, it is possible to show that $P_i = {}_nC_i$. Thus, you can state the **Binomial Theorem** using combinations.

 take note

Key Concept Binomial Theorem

For every positive integer n,
$$(a + b)^n = {}_nC_0a^n + {}_nC_1a^{n-1}b + {}_nC_2a^{n-2}b^2 + \cdots + {}_nC_{n-1}ab^{n-1} + {}_nC_nb^n$$

© **Problem 2** Expanding Binomials

Use the Binomial Theorem to solve.

A What is the binomial expansion of $(x + y)^5$?

Use the Binomial Theorem with $a = x$, $b = y$, and $n = 5$.

$$(x + y)^5 = {}_5C_0x^5 + {}_5C_1x^4y + {}_5C_2x^3y^2 + {}_5C_3x^2y^3$$
$$+ {}_5C_4xy^4 + {}_5C_5y^5$$
$$= x^5 + 5x^4y + 10x^3y^2 + 10x^2y^3 + 5xy^4 + y^5 \quad \text{Substitute for the } {}_nC_i.$$

Think

Which $_4C_i$ do you use in the third term?
You use $_4C_0$, not $_4C_1$, for the first term. Therefore, use $_4C_2$ in the third term.

B What is the third term of $(2x - 3y)^4$?

The third term of the binomial expansion is ${}_4C_2a^{4-2}b^2$.

$${}_4C_2a^{4-2}b^2 = {}_4C_2(2x)^2(-3y)^2 \quad \text{Substitute } a = 2x \text{ and } b = -3y.$$
$$= 6(4x^2)(9y^2) \quad \text{Evaluate } {}_4C_2.$$
$$= 216x^2y^2 \quad \text{Simplify.}$$

 Got It? **2.** What is the binomial expansion of $(3x + y)^4$?

Now you can apply the Binomial Theorem to binomial probabilities. To find the full probability distribution for a binomial experiment, expand the binomial $(p + q)^n$. For example, suppose you guess on four questions of a five-choice multiple-choice test. For four questions, $n = 4$, P(guessing correctly) $= \frac{1}{5}$, so $p = 0.2$, and $q = 0.8$.

	4 correct		3 correct		2 correct		1 correct		0 correct
$(p + q)^4 =$	$1p^4$	$+$	$4p^3q$	$+$	$6p^2q^2$	$+$	$4pq^3$	$+$	$1q^4$
$=$	$(0.2)^4$	$+$	$4(0.2)^3(0.8)$	$+$	$6(0.2)^2(0.8)^2$	$+$	$4(0.2)(0.8)^3$	$+$	$(0.8)^4$
$=$	0.0016	$+$	0.0256	$+$	0.1536	$+$	0.4096	$+$	0.4096

You can display the distribution of binomial probabilities as a graph.

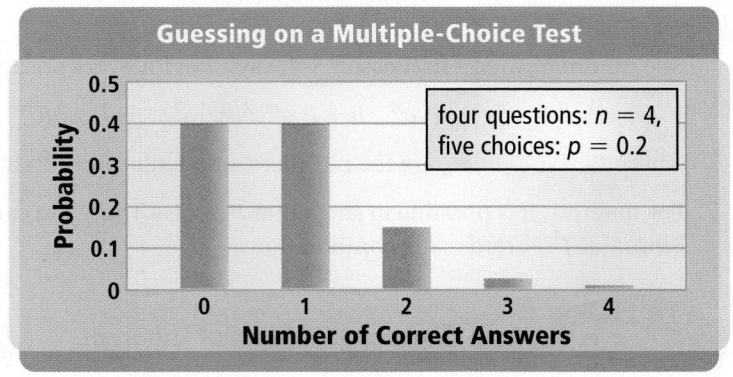

Guessing on a Multiple-Choice Test

four questions: $n = 4$, five choices: $p = 0.2$

Probability vs. *Number of Correct Answers*

Problem 3 Applying Binomial Probability

Manufacturing Each hour at a cell phone factory, Quality Control (QC) tests the durability of four randomly selected phones. If more than one fails, QC rejects the entire production for that hour. If in one hour, 95% of the phones made are acceptable, what is the probability that QC rejects that hour's phone production?

Think

What is a "success" in one trial of this binomial experiment?
Success in this experiment means that a phone fails the test.

Write the binomial expansion of $(p + q)^n$ with $n = 4$, $p = 0.05$, and $q = 0.95$.

	4 fail	3 fail	2 fail	1 fail	0 fail

$$(p + q)^4 = p^4q^0 + 4p^3q^1 + 6p^2q^2 + 4p^1q^3 + p^0q^4$$

$$= (0.05)^4 + 4(0.05)^3(0.95)^1 + 6(0.05)^2(0.95)^2 + 4(0.05)^1(0.95)^3 + (0.95)^4$$

$$\approx 0.000006 + 0.000475 + 0.013538 + 0.171475 + 0.814506$$

Probability (4, 3, or 2 phones fail) $\approx 0.000006 + 0.000475 + 0.013538$

$$\approx 0.014019, \text{ or about } 1.4\%$$

There is about a 1.4% chance that QC will reject the phones produced in the last hour.

Got It? **3.** A multiple-choice quiz has five questions. Each question has four answer choices. If you guess every answer, what is the probability of getting at least three correct?

Lesson Check

Do you know HOW?

Find the probability of x successes in n trials for the given probability of success p on each trial.

1. $x = 2$, $n = 6$, $p = 0.4$

2. $x = 6$, $n = 9$, $p = 0.5$

Find the indicated term of each binomial expansion.

3. fourth term of $(c + d)^6$

4. second term of $(x - 2y)^5$

5. What is the probability of 2 successes in 4 trials of an experiment if the probability of success of one trial is 0.3?

Do you UNDERSTAND?

6. Vocabulary Explain how flipping a coin 10 times meets all of the conditions for a binomial experiment.

7. Error Analysis A student finds the fifth term of the binomial expansion $(j - k)^7$. Describe and correct the error the student made.

$$_nC_5 a^{(n-5)} b^5 = \,_7C_5 j^2 (-k)^5$$
$$= -21 j^2 k^5$$

Practice and Problem-Solving Exercises

 **Practice**

Find the probability of x successes in n trials for the given probability of success p on each trial.

◀ See Problem 1.

8. $x = 3$, $n = 8$, $p = 0.3$

9. $x = 4$, $n = 8$, $p = 0.3$

10. $x = 5$, $n = 10$, $p = 0.5$

11. $x = 5$, $n = 10$, $p = 0.1$

12. Battery Life A calculator contains four batteries. With normal use, each battery has a 90% chance of lasting for one year. What is the probability that all four batteries will last a year?

Expand each binomial.

◀ See Problem 2.

13. $(a + b)^4$

14. $(m + 5n)^3$

15. $(3x + 2y)^5$

16. $(4c - d)^4$

Find the indicated term of each binomial expansion.

17. second term of $(2g + 2h)^7$

18. fifth term of $(x - y)^5$

19. first term of $(e + 3f)^6$

20. eighth term of $(3x - y)^8$

Use the binomial expansion of $(p + q)^n$ to calculate each binomial distribution.

◀ See Problem 3.

21. $n = 6$, $p = 0.3$

22. $n = 6$, $p = 0.5$

23. $n = 6$, $p = 0.9$

24. $n = 8$, $p = 0.45$

Apply Ⓒ 25. **Think About a Plan** One survey found that 80% of respondents eat corn on the cob in circles rather than from side to side. Assume that this sample accurately represents the population. What is the probability that, out of five people you know, at least two of them eat corn on the cob in circles?
  • How can you find the probability that one person eats corn on the cob in circles?
  • How does a probability distribution help you solve the problem?

STEM 26. **Weather** A scientist hopes to launch a weather balloon on one of the next three mornings. For each morning, there is a 40% chance of suitable weather. What is the probability that there will be at least one morning with suitable weather?

Marketing A fruit company guarantees that 90% of the pineapples it ships will ripen within four days of delivery. Find each probability for a case containing 12 pineapples.

27. All 12 are ripe within four days.

28. At least 10 are ripe within four days.

29. No more than 9 are ripe within four days.

Ⓒ 30. **Open-Ended** Describe a situation that the graph might represent.

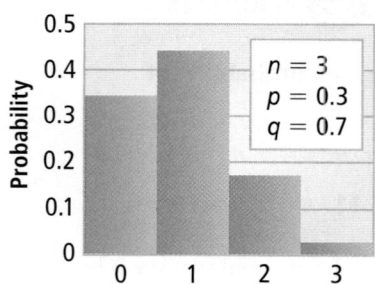

Sociology A study shows that 50% of people in a community watch television during dinner. Suppose you select 10 people at random from this population. Find each probability.

31. P(exactly 5 of the 10 people watch television during dinner)

32. P(exactly 6 of the 10 people watch television during dinner)

33. P(at least 5 of the 10 people watch television during dinner)

Ⓒ 34. **Writing** Explain how a binomial experiment is related to a binomial expansion.

STEM 35. **Quality Control** A company claims that 99% of its cereal boxes have at least as much cereal by weight as the amount stated on the box.
  a. At a quality control checkpoint, one box out of a random sample of ten boxes falls short of its stated weight. What is the probability of this happening due to chance variation in box weights?
  Ⓒ b. **Reasoning** Suppose three of ten boxes fail to have the claimed weight. What would you conclude? Explain.

36. **Basketball** Suppose you make 90% of your free throws and you attempt 3 free throws. Use the Binomial Theorem to calculate each probability.

    a. You do not make any of them.

    b. You only make 1 of them.

    c. You only make 2 of them.

    d. You make all of them.

STEM 37. **Genetics** About 11% of the general population is left-handed. At a school with an average class size of 30, each classroom contains four left-handed desks. Does this seem adequate? Justify your answer.

Ⓒ 38. **Open-Ended** Describe a binomial experiment that can be solved using the expression $_7C_2(0.6)^2(0.4)^5$.

Ⓒ 39. Graph each probability distribution for $(p + q)^3$.

    a. $p = 0.9, q = 0.1$ **b.** $p = 0.45, q = 0.55$

    c. Compare and Contrast How are the graphs in parts (a) and (b) similar? How are they different?

 **Challenge**

Statistics **A multiple-choice test has ten questions. Each question has five choices, with only one correct answer.**

40. Statisticians consider a "rare" event to have less than a 5% chance of occurring. According to this standard, what grades would be rare on this test if you guess? Justify your answer.

41. Design and conduct a simulation to model this situation. Gather results of simulations from your classmates. Do these results confirm the grades you identified as rare in Exercise 40? Explain.

42. **Pascal's Triangle** The nth row of Pascal's triangle has $n + 1$ terms. Find $_8C_4$. What row and term does this value represent in Pascal's Triangle? Use combinations to find the value of the 8th term of the 13th row of Pascal's triangle.

43. **Graphing Calculator** Enter the binomial probability formula as shown. Set the window and table shown. (To get integer values of x, you may need to adjust your window.)

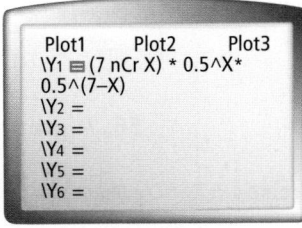 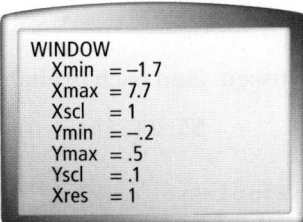 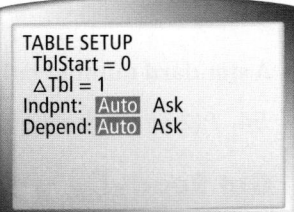

    a. Examine the graph of $y = {}_7C_x(0.5)^x(0.5)^{7-x}$. Describe any symmetry in the graph.

    b. Verify the symmetry by displaying values of the function in table form.

    c. Change the graph to $y = {}_7C_x(0.6)^x(0.4)^{7-x}$. Does this graph have any symmetry? Explain.

Standardized Test Prep

SAT/ACT

44. A survey shows that 60% of adults floss their teeth every day. In a random sample of ten adults, what is the probability that exactly six adults floss every day?

    (A) 11%   (B) 25%   (C) 60%   (D) 100%

45. Which of the statements about the following equation is correct?

$$\frac{b^2 - 4b + 3}{b - 3} = b - 1$$

    (F) The equation is always true.

    (G) The equation is always true, except when $b = 3$.

    (H) The equation is never true.

    (I) The equation is true when $b = 3$.

46. Which is the inverse of $f(x) = (x - 3)^2$?

    (A) $f^{-1}(x) = \dfrac{x^2}{(3x - 1)^2}$ (C) $f^{-1}(x) = \dfrac{1}{(3x - 1)^2}$

    (B) $f^{-1}(x) = \pm \sqrt{x} + 3$ (D) $f^{-1}(x) = \pm \sqrt{x - 3}$

47. If $\log 4 \approx 0.60206$ and $\log 5 \approx 0.69897$, what is the approximate value of $\log 80$?

    (F) 0.2534   (G) 0.2914   (H) 1.903   (I) 11.1835

Extended Response

48. In a geometric sequence, $a_1 = 3$ and $a_4 = 192$. Explain how to find a_2 and a_3.

Mixed Review

Identify any bias in each survey question.   ◀ See Lesson 11-8.

49. Do you agree that replacing that dog park with a beautiful new library would be better for our town?

50. Do you agree with the amendments to Proposition 39?

Find the vertices, foci, and asymptotes of each hyperbola.   ◀ See Lesson 10-5.

51. $\dfrac{y^2}{49} - \dfrac{x^2}{25} = 1$ **52.** $4y^2 - 9x^2 = 36$ **53.** $64y^2 - 36x^2 = 576$

A standard number cube is tossed. Find each probability.   ◀ See Lesson 11-3.

54. $P(2$ or greater than $3)$ **55.** $P(6$ or even$)$ **56.** $P(\text{prime or } 1)$

Get Ready!   **To prepare for Lesson 11-10, do Exercises 57–60.**

Find the mean and standard deviation for each data set.   ◀ See Lessons 11-6 and 11-7.

57. 16, 20, 28, 25, 26, 33, 27, 22, 29, 18   **58.** 81, 78, 79, 80, 76, 88, 83, 90, 87, 76

59. 8.5, 7.9, 8.2, 9.0, 8.3, 9.1, 9.2   **60.** 23.5, 22.4, 25.6, 26.8, 28.1, 22.3, 24.5

11-10 Normal Distributions

© Common Core State Standards

S-ID.A.4 Use the mean and standard deviation of a data set to fit it to a normal distribution and to estimate population percentages. Recognize that there are data sets for which such a procedure is not appropriate . . .

MP 1, MP 3, MP 4

Objective To use a normal distribution

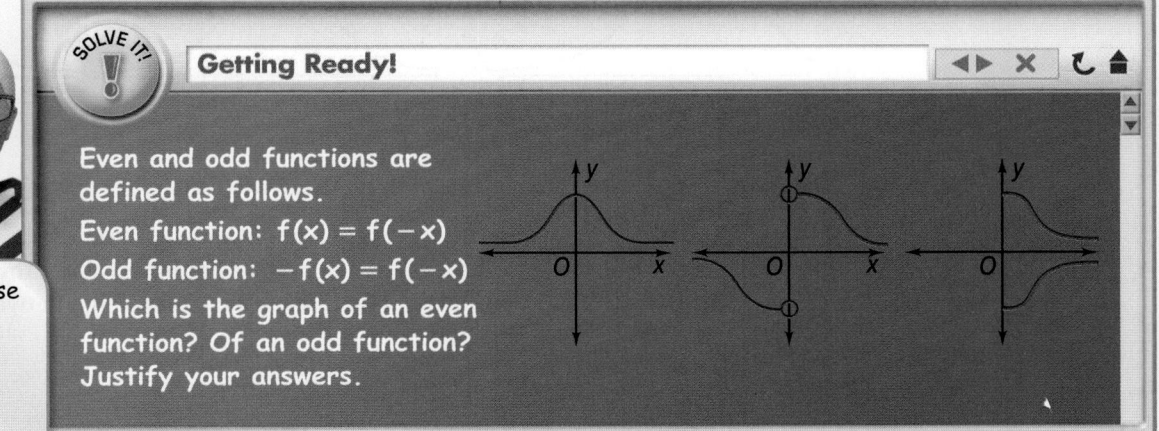

SOLVE IT!

Getting Ready!

Even and odd functions are defined as follows.
Even function: $f(x) = f(-x)$
Odd function: $-f(x) = f(-x)$
Which is the graph of an even function? Of an odd function? Justify your answers.

Try it out. Suppose (2, 2) is a point on $f(x)$. If $f(x)$ is even, what other point is on the graph of $f(x)$?

MATHEMATICAL PRACTICES

A **discrete probability distribution** has a finite number of possible events, or values. The binomial probability distribution you studied in the preceding lesson is a discrete probability distribution.

The events for a **continuous probability distribution** can be any value in an interval of real numbers. If a data set is large, the distribution of its discrete values approximates a continuous distribution.

Essential Understanding Many common statistics (such as human height, weight, or blood pressure) gathered from samples in the natural world tend to have a *normal distribution* about their mean.

A **normal distribution** has data that vary randomly from the mean. The graph of a normal distribution is a normal curve.

Lesson Vocabulary
• discrete probability distribution
• continuous probability distribution
• normal distribution

Key Concept   Normal Distribution

In a normal distribution,
• 68% of data fall within one standard deviation of the mean
• 95% of data fall within two standard deviations of the mean
• 99.7% of data fall within three standard deviations of the mean

A normal distribution has a symmetric bell shape centered on the mean.

Sometimes data are not normally distributed. A data set could have a distribution that is *skewed*, an asymmetric curve where one end stretches out further than the other end. When a data set is skewed, the data do not vary predictably from the mean. This means that the data do not fall within the standard deviations of the mean like normally distributed data, and so it is inappropriate to use mean and standard deviation to estimate percentages for skewed data.

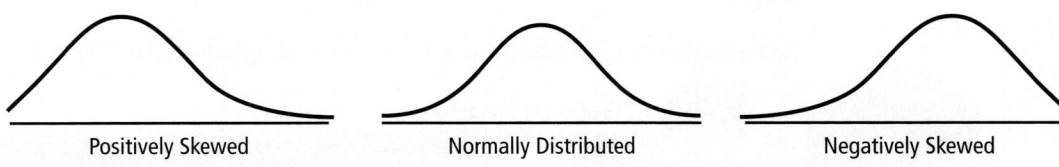

Positively Skewed   Normally Distributed   Negatively Skewed

Problem 1   Analyzing Normally Distributed Data   STEM

Zoology The bar graph gives the weights of a population of female brown bears. The red curve shows how the weights are normally distributed about the mean, 115 kg. Approximately what percent of female brown bears weigh between 100 and 129 kg?

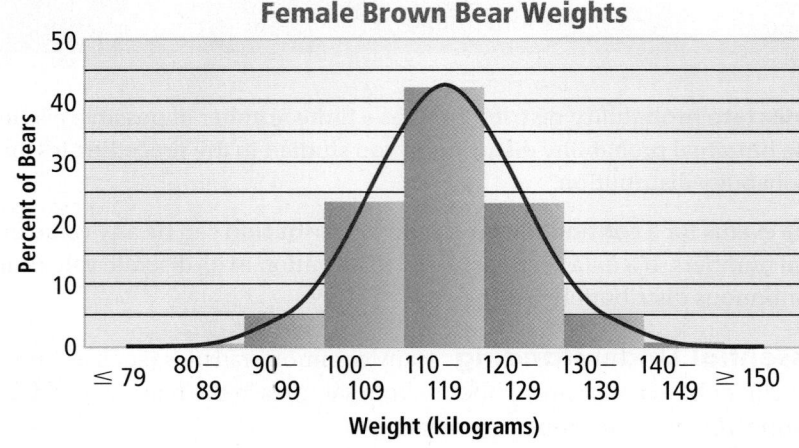

Female Brown Bear Weights

Percent of Bears (y-axis: 0, 10, 20, 30, 40, 50)

Weight (kilograms): ≤ 79, 80–89, 90–99, 100–109, 110–119, 120–129, 130–139, 140–149, ≥ 150

Plan

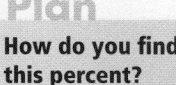

How do you find this percent?
The percents for each bar are based on the same sample population of bears. You can add the percents.

Estimate and add the percents for the intervals 100–109, 110–119, and 120–129.

$$23 + 42 + 23 = 88$$

About 88% of female brown bears weigh between 100 and 129 kg.

✓ **Got It?**   **1. a.** Approximately what percent of female brown bears in Problem 1 weigh less than 120 kg?

       b. The standard deviation in the weights of female brown bears is about 10 kg. Approximately what percent of female brown bears have weights that are within 1.5 standard deviations of the mean?

When data are normally distributed, you can sketch the graph of the distribution using the fact that a normal curve has a symmetric bell shape.

© **Problem 2** Sketching a Normal Curve ⓈTEM

Zoology For a population of male European eels, the mean body length and one positive and negative standard deviation is shown below. Sketch a normal curve showing the eel lengths at one, two, and three standard deviations from the mean.

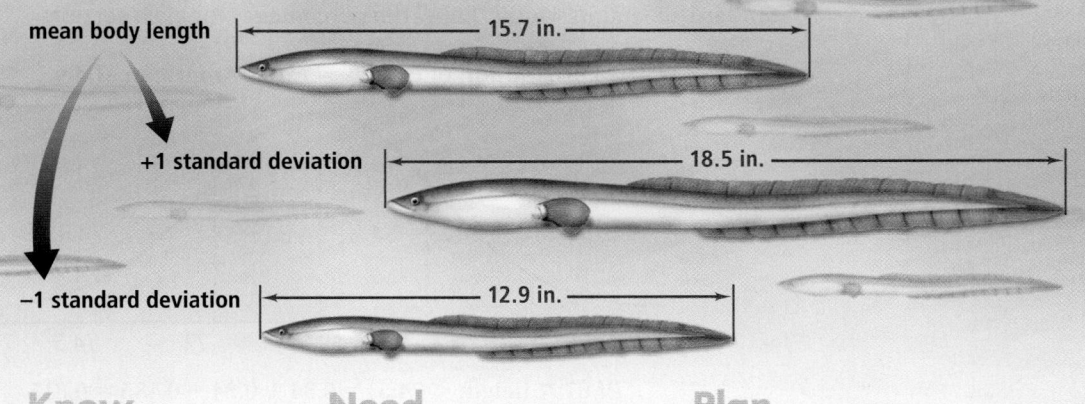

mean body length — 15.7 in.

+1 standard deviation — 18.5 in.

−1 standard deviation — 12.9 in.

Know	Need	Plan
The mean and the standard deviation of the population	Lengths that are one, two, and three standard deviations from the mean	• Multiply the standard deviation by 1, 2, and 3. • Draw vertical lines at the mean ± these values. • Sketch the normal curve.

Think

How high do you draw the curve?
Unless you actually label the vertical scale, it doesn't matter.

Distribution of Body Lengths for Male European Eels

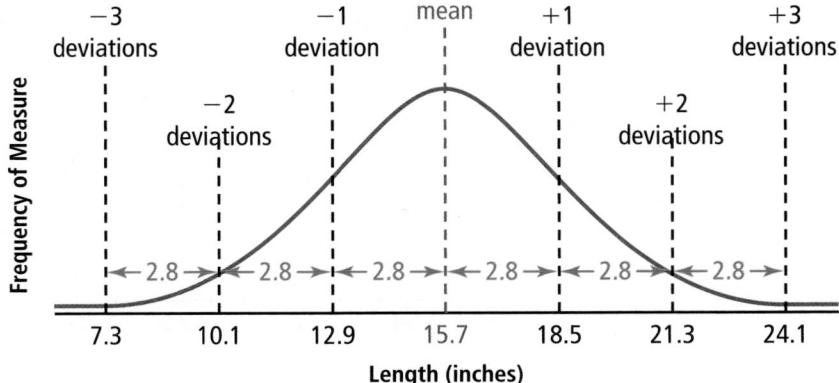

−3 deviations	+3 deviations
−1 deviation	+1 deviation
mean	
−2 deviations	+2 deviations

Frequency of Measure

←2.8→ ←2.8→ ←2.8→ ←2.8→ ←2.8→ ←2.8→

7.3   10.1   12.9   15.7   18.5   21.3   24.1

Length (inches)

✓ **Got It? 2.** For a population of female European eels, the mean body length is 21.1 in. The standard deviation is 4.7 in. Sketch a normal curve showing eel lengths at one, two, and three standard deviations from the mean.

When you show a probability distribution as a bar graph, the height of the bar indicates probability. For a normal distribution, however, the area between the curve and an interval on the *x*-axis represents probability.

 **Problem 3** Analyzing a Normal Distribution

The heights of adult American males are approximately normally distributed with mean 69.5 in. and standard deviation 2.5 in.

Plan

How do you divide the graph of the distribution?
Draw vertical lines at intervals that are one standard deviation wide, on both sides of the mean.

A What percent of adult American males are between 67 in. and 74.5 in. tall?

Draw a normal curve. Label the mean. Divide the graph into sections of standard-deviation widths. Label the percentages for each section.

Distribution of Heights—Adult American Males

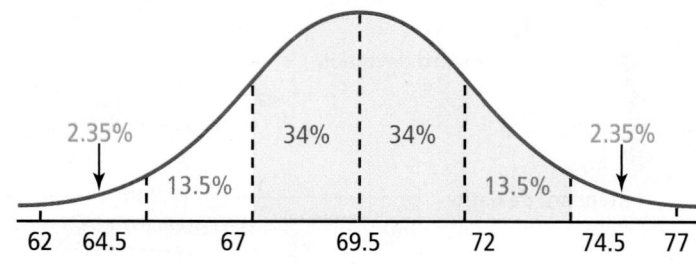

$$P(\,67 < \text{height} < 74.5) = 0.34 + 0.34 + 0.135 = 0.815$$

About 82% of adult American males are between 67 in. and 74.5 in. tall.

B In a group of 2000 adult American males, about how many would you expect to be taller than 6 ft (or 72 in.)?

Because the graph is symmetric about the mean, the right half of the distribution contains 50% of the data. If you subtract everything between 69.5 in. and 72 in. from the right half, only the part of the distribution that is greater than 72 in. remains.

Distribution of Heights—Adult American Males

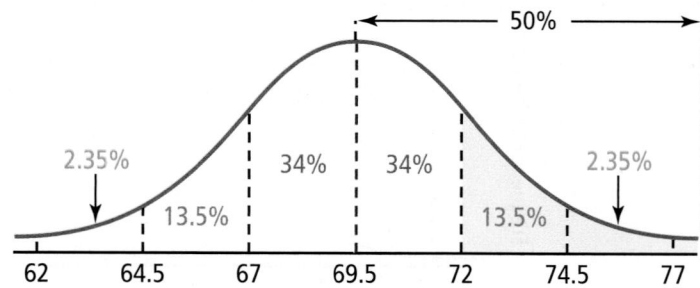

$$P(\text{height} > 72) = 0.50 - 0.34 = 0.16$$

You would expect about 16% of the 2000 adult American males to be taller than 72 in. You would expect about 0.16 · 2000 = 320 to be over 6 ft tall.

  Got It? 3. The scores on the Algebra 2 final are approximately normally distributed with a mean of 150 and a standard deviation of 15.
  a. What percentage of the students who took the test scored above 180?
  b. If 250 students took the final exam, approximately how many scored above 135?
  c. Reasoning If 13.6% of the students received a B on the final, how can you describe their scores? Explain.

Lesson Check

Do you know HOW?

1. Use the graph from Problem 1. What is the approximate percent of female brown bears weighing at least 100 kg?

2. Draw a curve to represent a normally distributed experiment that has a mean of 180 and a standard deviation of 15. Label the *x*-axis and indicate the probabilities.

3. The scores on an exam are normally distributed, with a mean of 85 and a standard deviation of 5. What percent of the scores are between 85 and 95?

Do you UNDERSTAND?

 MATHEMATICAL PRACTICES

4. Vocabulary Why is a normal distribution "normal"?

5. Compare and Contrast How do the mean and median compare in a normal distribution?

6. Reasoning What is the effect on a normal distribution if each data value increases by 10? Justify your answer.

Practice and Problem-Solving Exercises  MATHEMATICAL PRACTICES

 **Practice**

Biology The heights of men in a survey are normally distributed about the mean. Use the graph for Exercises 7–10.

◀ See Problem 1.

7. About what percent of men aged 25 to 34 are 69–71 in. tall?

8. About what percent of men aged 25 to 34 are less than 70 in. tall?

9. Suppose the survey included data on 100 men. About how many would you expect to be 69–71 in. tall?

10. The mean of the data is 70, and the standard deviation is 2.5. Approximately what percent of men are within one standard deviation of the mean height?

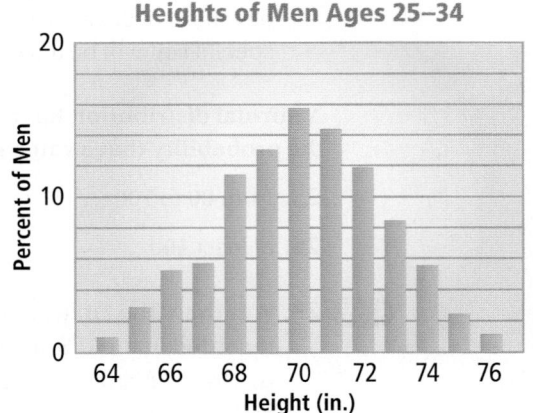

Sketch a normal curve for each distribution. Label the *x*-axis values at one, two, and three standard deviations from the mean.

◀ See Problem 2.

11. mean = 45, standard deviation = 5

12. mean = 45, standard deviation = 10

13. mean = 45, standard deviation = 2

14. mean = 45, standard deviation = 3.5

A set of data has a normal distribution with a mean of 50 and a standard deviation of 8. Find the percent of data within each interval.

◀ See Problem 3.

15. from 42 to 58

16. greater than 34

17. less than 50

18. Think About a Plan The numbers of paper clips per box in a truckload of boxes are normally distributed, with a mean of 100 and a standard deviation of 5. Find the probability that a box will *not* contain between 95 and 105 clips.
- How should you label the vertical lines on the graph of the normal distribution?
- Which parts of the graph are *not* between 95 and 105 clips?

19. a. From the table at the right, select the set of values that appears to be distributed normally.
  b. Using the set you chose in part (a), make a histogram of the values.
  c. Sketch a normal curve over your graph.

20. Writing In a class of 25, one student receives a score of 100 on a test. The grades are distributed normally, with a mean of 78 and a standard deviation of 5. Do you think the student's score is an outlier? Explain.

21. Sports To qualify as a contestant in a race, a runner has to be in the fastest 16% of all applicants. The running times are normally distributed, with a mean of 63 min and a standard deviation of 4 min. To the nearest minute, what is the qualifying time for the race?

22. Agriculture To win a prize at the county fair, the diameter of a tomato must be greater than 4 in. The diameters of a crop of tomatoes grown in a special soil are normally distributed, with a mean of 3.2 in. and a standard deviation of 0.4 in. What is the probability that a tomato grown in the special soil will be a winner?

Set 1	Set 2	Set 3
1	5	5
10	7	6
5	7	9
19	7	1
2	4	1
7	11	5
1	7	11
7	7	1
2	7	10
10	9	4
6	7	2
9	7	8

A normal distribution has a mean of 100 and a standard deviation of 10. Find the probability that a value selected at random is in the given interval.

23. from 80 to 100

24. from 70 to 130

25. from 90 to 120

26. at least 100

27. at most 110

28. at least 80

STEM 29. Weather The table at the right shows the number of tornadoes that were recorded in the U.S. in 2008.
  a. Draw a histogram to represent the data.
  b. Does the histogram approximate a normal curve? Explain.
  c. Is it appropriate to use a normal curve to estimate the percent of tornados that occur during certain months of the year? Explain.

30. Error Analysis In a set of data, the value 332 is 3 standard deviations from the mean and the value 248 is 1 standard deviation from the mean. A classmate claims that there is only one possible mean and standard deviation for this data set. Do you agree? Explain.

31. Reasoning Jake and Elena took the same standardized test, but are in different classes. They both received a score of 87. In Jake's group, the mean was 80 and the standard deviation was 6. In Elena's group, the mean was 76 and the standard deviation was 4. Did either student score in the top 10% of his or her group? Explain.

Month	Tornadoes
1	84
2	147
3	129
4	189
5	461
6	294
7	93
8	101
9	111
10	21
11	20
12	40

32. Manufacturing Tubs of yogurt weigh 1.0 lb each, with a standard deviation of 0.06 lb. At a quality control checkpoint, 12 of the tubs taken as samples weighed less than 0.88 lb. Assume that the weights of the samples were normally distributed. How many tubs of yogurt were taken as samples?

33. Reasoning Describe how you can use a normal distribution to approximate a binomial distribution. Draw a binomial histogram and a normal curve to help with your explanation.

Standardized Test Prep

34. For a daily airline flight between two cities, the number of pieces of checked luggage has a mean of 380 and a standard deviation of 20. On what percent of the flights would you expect from 340 to 420 pieces of checked luggage?

    Ⓐ 34%   Ⓑ 47.5%   Ⓒ 68%   Ⓓ 95%

35. A jar contains 37 pennies, 53 nickels, 29 dimes, and 21 quarters. A coin is drawn at random from the jar. What is the probability that the coin drawn is NOT a quarter?

    Ⓕ $\dfrac{56,869}{2,744,000}$ Ⓖ $\dfrac{3}{20}$ Ⓗ $\dfrac{3}{17}$ Ⓘ $\dfrac{17}{20}$

36. A multiple-choice quiz contains five questions, each with three answer choices. You select all five answer choices at random. What is the best estimate of the probability that you will get at least four answers correct?

    Ⓐ 4.1%   Ⓑ 4.5%   Ⓒ 13.2%   Ⓓ 46.1%

37. Distribution A has 50 data values with mean 40 and standard deviation 2.4. Distribution B has 30 data values with mean 40 and standard deviation 2.8. Which distribution has more data values at or below 40? Show your work.

Mixed Review

Find the probability of x successes in n trials for the given probability of success p on each trial.   ◀ **See Lesson 11-9.**

38. $x = 4, n = 7, p = 0.2$ **39.** $x = 2, n = 9, p = 0.4$ **40.** $x = 6, n = 10, p = 0.3$

Graph each equation. Identify the conic section and describe the graph and its lines of symmetry. Then find the domain and range.   ◀ **See Lesson 10-1.**

41. $x^2 + y^2 = 64$ **42.** $x^2 - y^2 = 9$ **43.** $9x^2 + 25y^2 = 225$

Get Ready!   **To prepare for Lesson 12-1, do Exercises 44–46.**

Write an equation for each horizontal translation of $y = x - 2$. Then graph each translation.   ◀ **See Lesson 2-6.**

44. 1 unit right   **45.** 2 units left   **46.** $\dfrac{3}{4}$ unit left

Concept Byte

For Use With Lesson 11-10

ACTIVITY

Margin of Error

© **Common Core State Standards**

S-IC.B.4 Use data from a sample survey to estimate a population mean or proportion; develop a margin of error through the use of simulation models for random sampling.

MP 1

The mean of a sample may or may not be the mean of the population the sample was drawn from. The **margin of error** helps you find the interval in which the mean of the population is likely to be. The margin of error is based on the size of the sample and the *confidence level* desired.

A 95% confidence level means that the probability is 95% that the true population mean is within a range of values called a **confidence interval**. It also means that when you select many different large samples from the same population, 95% of the confidence intervals will actually contain the population mean.

The means of all the samples follow a normal distribution.

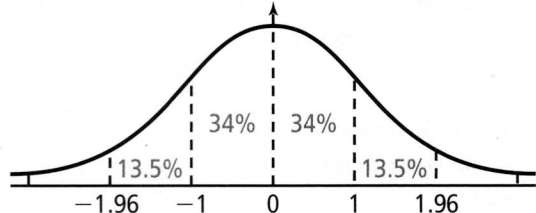

The normal distribution above shows that 95% of values are between -1.96 and 1.96 standard deviations from the mean. To find the margin of error based on the mean of a large set of data at a 95% confidence level, you use the formula $ME = 1.96 \cdot \frac{s}{\sqrt{n}}$, where ME is the margin of error, s is the standard deviation of the sample data, and n is the number of values in the sample. The confidence interval for the population mean μ (pronounced *myoo*) is $\bar{x} - ME \leq \mu \leq \bar{x} + ME$, where $\bar{x}$ is the sample mean.

Activity 1

A grocery store manager wanted to determine the wait times for customers in the express lines. He timed customers chosen at random.

1. What is the mean and stardard deviation of the sample? Round to the nearest tenth of a minute.

2. At a 95% confidence level, what is the approximate margin of error? Round to the nearest tenth of a minute.

3. What is the confidence interval for a 95% confidence level?

4. What is the meaning of the interval in terms of wait times for customers?

Waiting Time (minutes)				
3.3	5.1	5.2	6.7	7.3
7.5	4.6	6.2	5.5	3.6
3.4	3.5	8.2	4.2	3.8
4.7	4.6	4.7	4.5	9.7
5.4	5.9	6.7	6.5	8.2
3.1	3.2	8.2	2.5	4.8

You can also find the margin of error and the confidence interval for a sample proportion. A **sample proportion** $\hat{p}$ is the ratio $\frac{x}{n}$, where x is the number of times an event occurs in a sample of size n.

Activity 2

What is the sample proportion for each situation? Write the ratios as percents rounded to the nearest tenth of a percent.

5. In a poll of 1085 voters selected randomly, 564 favor Candidate A.

6. A coin is tossed 40 times, and it comes up heads 25 times.

To find the margin of error for a sample proportion at a 95% confidence level, use the formula $ME = 1.96 \cdot \sqrt{\frac{\hat{p}(1 - \hat{p})}{n}}$, where ME is the margin of error, $\hat{p}$ is the sample proportion, and n is the sample size. The confidence interval for the population proportion p is $\hat{p} - ME \le p \le \hat{p} + ME$.

Activity 3

Find (a) the sample proportion, (b) the margin of error, and (c) the 95% confidence interval for the population proportion.

7. In a survey of 530 randomly selected high school students, 280 preferred watching football to watching basketball.

8. In a simple random sample of 500 people, 342 reported using social networking sites on the Internet.

Exercises

For Exercises 9–10, find the 95% confidence interval for the population mean or population proportion, and interpret the confidence interval in context.

9. A consumer research group tested the battery life of 36 randomly chosen batteries to establish the likely battery life for the population of same type of battery.

10. In a poll of 720 likely voters, 358 indicate they plan to vote for Candidate A.

11. Data Collection Roll a number cube 30 times. Record the results from each roll. In parts (a) and (b), find the sample proportion, the margin of error for a 95% confidence level, and the 95% confidence interval for the population proportion.

   a. rolling a 2

   b. rolling a 3

   c. Is the 95% confidence intervals for the population proportion about the same for rolling a 2 and for rolling a 3?

   d. Compare your sample proportions to the theoretical proportions for parts (a) and (b). Would you expect the theoretical proportion to be within the confidence intervals you found? Explain.

Battery Life (In Hours)			
63.2	84.6	78.4	85.8
62.1	81.8	63.6	64.2
79.4	75.2	54.1	73.4
66.3	74.5	71.6	60.1
61.2	74.5	72.4	81.3
61.4	83.6	75.6	74.1
68.3	82.2	59.3	47.6
86.2	64.3	72.7	71.8
71.4	63.6	59.6	68.1

Drawing Conclusions from Samples

© Common Core State Standards

S-IC.B.5 Using data from a randomized experiment to compare two treatments; use simulations to decide if differences between parameters are significant.

MP 1

You can compare samples to determine if the difference in mean or proportion for a large population, based on a given confidence level, is significant. If a population is large and there are at least 30 data points in a sample, then the means and proportions can be compared using a normal distribution.

An important measure for normally distributed data is the **z-score,** which indicates the number of standard deviations a value lies above or below the mean of a population. When finding the z-score of a data point of a population, the formula is $z = \frac{x - \mu}{\sigma}$, where x is a data point, μ is the mean of a population, and σ is the standard deviation of the population.

Activity 1

In a given population, the weights of newborns are normally distributed about the mean 3250 g. The standard deviation of the population is 500 g.

1. What is the z-score of a newborn weighing 2500 g?

2. What is the z-score of a newborn weighing 4500 g?

3. What is the probability that a newborn weighs between 2270 g and 4230 g? Use z-scores of the weights and the normal curve.

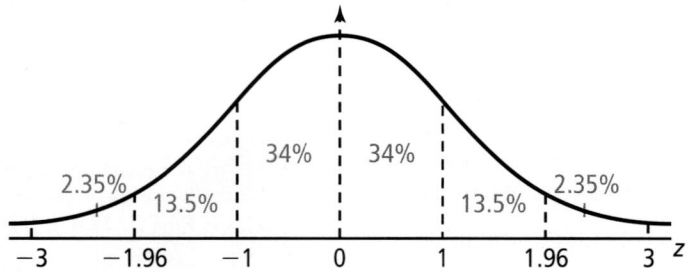

To compare the mean of a sample with the mean of a population, you use the formula $z = \frac{\bar{x} - \mu}{\frac{\sigma}{\sqrt{n}}}$, where $\bar{x}$ is the mean of the sample, μ is the mean of the population, σ is the standard deviation of the population, and n is the sample size. A z-score that is between -1.96 and 1.96 means that at a 95% confidence level, there is not a significant difference between the sample mean and the population mean. A z-score of less than -1.96 or greater than 1.96 indicates that at a 95% confidence level the differences between the sample mean and the population mean is significant and the differences are not simply due to chance.

Activity 2

A company that develops fertilizers wants to know whether either of the two new fertilizers they have in development shows a significant difference in the growth of plants based on a 95% confidence level. The company has data on the growth of bean plants without fertilizers. For a growth period of one month, the population of the beans grown without fertilizers have a mean of 20 cm with a standard deviation of 1 cm.

4. A company researcher chooses 30 plants at random and uses fertilizer A for one month. The researcher finds that after using fertilizer A, the mean of the bean plants' growth is 20.4 cm. What is the z-score for the mean of the sample treated with fertilizer A compared to the population of bean plants without fertilizer?

5. Does fertilizer A meet a 95% confidence level for having growth that is significantly different from growth without fertilizer?

6. To test fertilizer B, the researcher chooses 35 plants at random. The bean plants' growth averages 20.3 cm. What is the z-score for the mean of the sample treated with fertilizer B compared to the population of bean plants without fertilizer?

7. Does fertilizer B meet a 95% confidence level for having growth that is significantly different from growth without fertilizer?

8. Based on these data, would you advise the company to market fertilizer A or fertilizer B? Explain.

To compare the proportion of a sample with the proportion of a population, you use the formula for the z-score for a proportion, $z = \dfrac{\hat{p} - p}{\sqrt{\dfrac{p(1-p)}{n}}}$, where $\hat{p}$ is the sample proportion, p is the population proportion, and n is the sample size. For a 95% confidence level, a z-score between -1.96 and 1.96 means that difference between the sample and the population is not significant. A z-score of less than -1.96 or greater than 1.96 means that the difference in the proportions is significant, and not simply due to chance.

Activity 3

Suppose your teacher accidentally gives you a multiple-choice calculus test, instead of an Algebra 2 test. There are 40 true-false questions, and you and your classmates answer the questions randomly. The probability of getting an answer correct is $\frac{1}{2}$. You can use $\frac{1}{2}$ as the population proportion.

9. Develop a simulation for answering the 40 questions. Record your results.

10. What is the z-score for the sample based on your trials?

11. Compare your results with the results obtained by the rest of the class. At a 95% confidence level, what percentage of the results in the class showed a statistically significant difference from a score you would expect to get by guessing?

Pull It **All Together**

Completing the Performance Task

Look back at your results from the Apply What You've Learned sections in Lessons 11-2, 11-4, and 11-5. Use the work you did to complete the following.

To solve these problems, you will pull together concepts and skills related to probability and statistics.

1. Solve the problem in the Task Description on page 673 by finding the probability that at least two of the three children will be girls and at least one of the children will be left-handed. Show all your work and explain each step of your solution.

2. **Reflect** Choose one of the Mathematical Practices below and explain how you applied it in your work on the Performance Task.

   MP 1: Make sense of problems and persevere in solving them.

   MP 2: Reason abstractly and quantitatively.

   MP 4: Model with mathematics.

On Your Own

A couple plans to have two children. For each child, the probability that the child is a boy is 0.5, the probability that the child is a girl is 0.5 and the probability that the child is left-handed is 0.1.

Use a simulation similar to the one described on page 709 to collect data on at least twenty possible outcomes for the gender and handedness of the couple's two children.

a. Make a table to display the data you collect in the simulation.

b. Use your simulation results to determine the experimental probability that the couple has a boy and a girl, and neither child is left-handed. How does the experimental probability compare to the theoretical probability? Explain.

Chapter Review

Connecting BIG ideas and Answering the Essential Questions

1 Probability
A combination is a collection. A permutation is an ordered collection.

Permutations and Combinations (Lesson 11-1)

For n items chosen r at a time, $0 \le r \le n$,

- $_nP_r = \dfrac{n!}{(n-r)!}$
- $_nC_r = \dfrac{n!}{r!(n-r)!}$

Probability of Multiple Events and Conditional Probability (Lessons 11-3 and 11-4)

If A and B are independent events,
- $P(A \text{ and } B) = P(A) \cdot P(B)$
- $P(A \text{ or } B) = P(A) + P(B)$

The probability of event B, given event A is $P(B \mid A) = \dfrac{P(A \text{ and } B)}{P(A)}$.

2 Probability
You base experimental probability on *past*—and theoretical probability on *possible*—occurrences.

Probability (Lesson 11-2)

Experimental probability:

$P(\text{event}) = \dfrac{\text{number of times the event occurs}}{\text{number of trials}}$

Theoretical probability:

For n equally likely outcomes, if event A occurs in m of these outcomes, then $P(A) = \dfrac{m}{n}$.

Probability Models (Lesson 11-5)

You can use probability models to simulate how equally likely outcomes may occur for actual events.

3 Data Collection and Analysis
Probability concepts can be used to analyze data and make decisions. Standard deviation describes how data spread out from a particular middle (central tendency) value.

Analyzing Data and Standard Deviation (Lessons 11-6 and 11-7)

- $\bar{x}$, the mean, $= \dfrac{\sum x}{n}$
- σ, standard deviation $= \sqrt{\dfrac{\sum(x - \bar{x})^2}{n}}$

Binomial Distributions and Normal Distributions (Lessons 11-9 and 11-10)

In a normal distribution, about 68% (95%) of data are within one (two) standard deviation(s) of the mean.

Chapter Vocabulary

- binomial probability (p. 732)
- conditional probability (p. 696)
- continuous probability distribution (p. 739)
- dependent events (p. 688)
- discrete probability distribution (p. 739)
- equally likely outcomes (p. 682)
- independent events (p. 688)
- interquartile range (p. 713)
- mean (p. 711)
- median (p. 711)
- mode (p. 711)
- mutually exclusive events (p. 689)
- normal distribution (p. 739)
- outlier (p. 712)
- percentile (p. 714)
- probability distribution (p. 694)
- probability model (p. 705)
- random sample (p. 725)
- range of a set of data (p. 713)
- sample (p. 725)
- sample space (p. 682)
- standard deviation (p. 719)
- survey (p. 726)
- variance (p. 719)

Fill in the blanks.

1. A(n) __?__ is part of a population.

2. A(n) __?__ has a value substantially different from other data in the set.

3. A function that gives the probability of each event in a sample space is a(n) __?__ .

4. The __?__ is the simplest measure of variation.

11-1 Permutations and Combinations

Quick Review

If event M can occur in m ways and event N can occur in n ways, then M followed by N can occur in $m \cdot n$ ways. The notation **$n!$ (n factorial)** means $n(n-1) \cdot \ldots \cdot 3 \cdot 2 \cdot 1$. The number of ways to choose r items from a set of n items, without regard to order, is $_nC_r = \frac{n!}{r!(n-r)!}$. The number of ways to choose r items from a set of n items and place those items in some order is $_nP_r = \frac{n!}{(n-r)!}$.

Example

A vacationer making travel preparations chooses three books from a shelf containing 15 books. How many ways are there to choose three books without regard to order? How many ways are there to choose one book for the trip to the destination, one for the stay, and one for the homeward trip?

Ignoring order, there are $_{15}C_3 = \frac{15!}{3!\,12!} = 455$ ways to choose three books.

There are $_{15}P_3 = \frac{15!}{12!} = 2730$ ways to choose three books to read in a particular order.

Exercises

Evaluate each of the following.

5. $3!$

6. $9!$

7. $\frac{4!}{2!}$

8. $\frac{5!}{2!\,2!}$

9. $_7C_2$

10. $_4C_3 + _6C_5$

11. $_6P_2$

12. $_4P_3 + _6P_5$

13. Camping On a camping trip, you bring 12 food items for 4 dinners. For each dinner, you use 3 items. In how many ways can you choose the 3 items for the first dinner? For the second? For the third? For the fourth?

14. Advertising A newspaper ad includes a telephone number 1-555-DIAL VSW. How many seven-letter arrangements are possible for the phone number using the 26 letters of the alphabet if no letter is used more than once? Express your answer using scientific notation.

11-2 Probability

Quick Review

Experimental probability is based on successes during repeated trials, while **theoretical probability** is based on number of occurrences in a **sample space** of equally likely outcomes. When an actual event cannot easily be repeated through numerous trials, a **simulation** can be used to obtain an experimental probability.

Example

What is the probability that you were born on a Thursday?

Since you had an equal chance of being born on any one of the 7 days of the week, the probability that you were born on a Thursday is $\frac{1}{7}$.

Exercises

15. How many possible outcomes are there when a standard number cube is rolled three times?

16. You flipped a coin 70 times and recorded 23 heads. What is the experimental probability of flipping tails?

Find the probability of each event.

17. A standard number cube is rolled and comes up 13.

18. A number picked at random from the numbers 1 through 15 is prime.

19. Writing Suppose you have 20 tiles with the numbers 1 through 20. The theoretical probability that a tile chosen at random is a 5 is $\frac{1}{20}$. If you pick a tile randomly, 20 times, replacing the chosen tile each time, will you get a 5 once? Explain.

11-3 Probability of Multiple Events

Quick Review

For any events A and B,
$P(A \text{ or } B) = P(A) + P(B) - P(A \text{ and } B)$. When the occurrence of one event affects how a second event can occur, the events are **dependent**. When A and B are **independent**, $P(A \text{ and } B) = P(A) \cdot P(B)$. For **mutually exclusive events**, $P(A \text{ and } B) = 0$ so $P(A \text{ or } B) = P(A) + P(B)$.

Example

You roll a standard number cube. Are the events "roll a 1" and "roll an even number" mutually exclusive? Explain.

You cannot roll a 1 and an even number at the same time. The events are mutually exclusive.

Exercises

Classify each pair of events as *dependent* or *independent*.

20. A student in your algebra class is selected at random. One of the remaining students is selected at random.

21. You select a number 1 through 6 by tossing a standard number cube. You select a second number by tossing the number cube again.

Calculate each probability, given that $P(A) = 0.3$, $P(B) = 0.7$, and A and B are independent.

22. $P(A \text{ and } B)$

23. $P(A \text{ or } B)$

11-4 Conditional Probability

Quick Review

The probability that event B will occur, given that A has already occured, is the **conditional probability**
$P(B|A) = \frac{P(A \text{ and } B)}{P(A)}$.

Example

A standard number cube is rolled twice. If the first number rolled is a and the second is b, find $P(a \text{ is even and } b > 2)$ and $P(b \text{ is even} \mid b > 3)$.

Since number cube rolls are independent events,

$$P(a \text{ is even and } b > 2) = P(a \text{ is even}) \cdot P(b > 2)$$
$$= \frac{1}{2} \cdot \frac{2}{3} = \frac{1}{3}$$

$$P(b \text{ is even} \mid b > 3) = \frac{P(b > 3 \text{ and } b \text{ is even})}{P(b > 3)}$$

$$= \frac{P(4 \text{ or } 6)}{P(4 \text{ or } 5 \text{ or } 6)} = \frac{\frac{2}{6}}{\frac{3}{6}} = \frac{2}{3}.$$

Exercises

Calculate each probability, given that $P(A) = 0.3$, $P(B) = 0.7$, and A and B are independent.

24. $P(A|B)$

25. $P(B|A)$

Calculate each probability, given that $P(A) = 0.5$, $P(B) = 0.4$, and $P(A \text{ and } B) = 0.1$.

26. $P(A|B)$

27. $P(B|A)$

28. $P(A \text{ and } B \mid A \text{ or } B)$

11-5 Probability Models

Quick Review

Probability models and simulations with equally likely outcomes can be used to make fair decisions. It is important to simulate the event so that the likelihood of each outcome is represented correctly. Random number tables, number cubes, and coin flips are commonly used to generate the random data in a simulation.

Example

Suppose that there are an equal number of red, green, blue, purple, and orange gumballs in a gumball machine. How many gumballs you would expect to buy before you got a red gumball?

Use random numbers and let red = 1, green = 2, blue = 3, purple = 4, and orange = 5.

27629 73963 08403 31642 08807 03871 92122

You had to buy 8 gumballs before getting a red one. Do several more trials and find the average value.

Exercises

Determine whether the following strategies will result in a fair decision. Explain.

29. Four students are eligible to deliver the morning announcements for the following week. The principal folds the paper in four equal square sections and writes each name in one of the sections. Then she tosses a coin onto the paper. The name closest to the coin will deliver the morning announcements.

30. Sports There are 3 equally talented goalies on your soccer team. Your coach assigns each goalie a number 1–3 and uses a spinner to choose which player will play goalie in each game this season. Assume the players are uninjured and eligible to play the entire season.

31. Reasoning In the gumball example at the left, each gumball costs $.25. Your friend decides to try for the red gumball. Is this a good decision? Explain.

11-6 Analyzing Data

Quick Review

You can use **measures of central tendency** to analyze data. The **mean**, $\bar{x}$, equals the sum of the values divided by the number of values. The **median** is the middle value of a data set in numerical order. The **mode** is the most frequently occurring value. A data value substantially different from the rest of the data is an **outlier**. A **box-and-whisker plot** summarizes information about the **range**, the median, and the first and third **quartiles** of a data set.

Example

Find the mean, median, mode, and range of the following set of numbers, and identify any outliers.

   3, 3, 4, 6, 19

The mean is $\frac{3 + 3 + 4 + 6 + 19}{5} = 7$.

The median is the middle data value, which is 4.

The mode is 3, which occurs twice.

The range is $19 - 3 = 16$.

The value 19 is very different from the others and is an outlier.

Exercises

32. Identify the outlier of this set of values.
   17, 15, 16, 15, 9, 18, 16

Find the mean, median, and mode for each set of values.

33. 1, 1, 3, 3, 5, 5, 6, 7, 9, 9, 9, 10, 10

34. 0, 3, 3, 7, 7, 8, 21, 22, 25

35. 8, 9, 11, 12, 13, 15, 16, 18, 18, 18, 27

36. 11, 6, 9, 4, 19, 10, 15, 2

Find the range, Q_1, and Q_3 for each set of values.

37. 25, 25, 30, 35, 45, 45, 50, 55, 60, 60

38. 20, 23, 25, 36, 37, 38, 39, 50, 52, 55

39. 36, 36, 48, 65, 75, 82, 92, 101

11-7 Standard Deviation

Quick Review

The range of a data set is one **measure of variation**, used to describe the spread of data. Another measure of variation is the **standard deviation**, defined as

$$\sigma = \sqrt{\frac{\sum(x - \bar{x})^2}{n}}$$

where $\bar{x}$ is the mean of the data set and n is the number of values. The **variance** is σ^2.

Example

Find the mean, variance, and standard deviation for the following data values: 1, 3, 4, 6, 8, 11, 23.

The mean is $\bar{x} = \frac{1 + 3 + 4 + 6 + 8 + 11 + 23}{7} = 8$.

The sum of the squares of the differences is

$(-7)^2 + (-5)^2 + (-4)^2 + (-2)^2 + 0^2 + 3^2 + 15^2 = 328$.

So the variance is $\sigma^2 = \frac{328}{7} \approx 46.9$, and the standard deviation is $\sigma \approx \sqrt{46.9} \approx 6.8$.

Exercises

For each pair of data sets, which is likely to have the greater standard deviation?

40. heights of three people
heights of twenty people

41. ages of thirty college students
ages of thirty high school students

42. gas mileages of eighteen sport utility vehicles
gas mileages of eighteen automobiles of various types

Find the mean and the standard deviation for each set of values.

43. 1, 1, 2, 2, 3, 4, 5, 6, 8, 9, 10, 10, 12, 20

44. 15, 17, 19, 20, 14, 23, 12

45. 3.1, 4.5, 7.8, 7.9, 8.0, 9.6, 11.6

11-8 Samples and Surveys

Quick Review

A **sample** is part of a **population**. For a **random sample**, all members of the population are equally likely to be chosen. A **bias** is a systematic error introduced by the sampling method.

Example

Identify any bias in the survey question "Do you think the school day should be extended even longer than it already is?" Explain.

There is bias because the question is leading. It implies that the school day is already too long and should not be extended.

Exercises

Determine if each of the following is a random sample. Explain your answer.

46. The first 50 names in the telephone directory

47. Twelve jurors chosen through examination by opposing lawyers

48. Two class representatives chosen by drawing names from a hat

49. Five newspapers picked on the basis of circulation size

50. The city council is trying to determine if the city's residents support the building of a new parking garage. They poll 200 people at the local bus station. Identify any bias in the sampling method.

11-9 Binomial Distributions

Quick Review

A **binomial experiment** has repeated independent trials with each trial having two possible outcomes. In a binomial experiment with probability of success p and of failure q (so $p + q = 1$), the probability of exactly x successes in n trials is $_nC_x p^x q^{n-x}$. This value is the **binomial probability**. The **Binomial Theorem** says that for every positive integer n,
$(a + b)^n = {}_nC_0 a^n + {}_nC_1 a^{n-1}b + {}_nC_2 a^{n-2}b^2 + \cdots + {}_nC_{n-1}ab^{n-1} + {}_nC_n b^n$.

Example

In a binomial trial, the probability of success is 0.8 for each trial. Find the probability of exactly 4 successes in 7 trials.

$p = 0.8$, $q = 0.2$, $x = 4$, and $n = 7$

$P(4) = {}_7C_4(0.8)^4(0.2)^3$

$\quad\quad = \dfrac{7!}{3!4!}(0.8)^4(0.2)^3$

$\quad\quad \approx 0.115$

The probability of 4 successes in 7 trials is 0.115.

Exercises

For each of the following binomial experiments, state the value of p, the probability of success.

51. A series of coin flips, where success is "heads."

52. A series of number cube rolls, where success is "2 or 4."

In a binomial trial, the probability of success is 0.6 for each trial. Find the probability of each of the following.

53. 13 successes in 24 trials

54. 9 successes in 20 trials

55. 9 successes in 15 trials

56. 6 failures in 12 trials

Use the Binomial Theorem to write each of the following.

57. the third term in the expansion of $(a + b)^7$

58. the sixth term in the expansion of $(a + b)^8$

11-10 Normal Distributions

Quick Review

A **normal distribution** shows data that vary from the mean in a random, continuous manner. The pattern they form is a bell-shaped curve called a normal curve.

Example

Sketch a curve for a normal distribution with mean 10 and standard deviation 4. Label the x-axis at one, two, and three standard deviations from the mean.

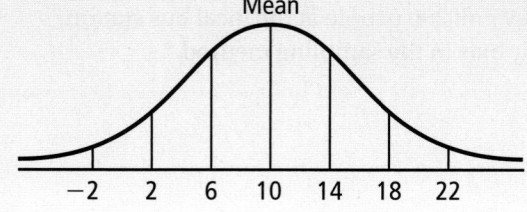

Mean

−2 2 6 10 14 18 22

Exercises

For each of the following, state whether the probability distribution would be *discrete* or *continuous*.

59. distance from an arrow's impact point to the center of the bullseye

60. shoe sizes on a softball team

61. price of a gallon of premium unleaded gasoline at a randomly selected gas station

62. time a customer spends on hold during a call to a computer manufacturer's tech support

63. **Auto Maintenance** Suppose the time required for an auto shop to do a tune-up is normally distributed, with a mean of 102 minutes and a standard deviation of 18 minutes. What is the probability that a tune-up will take more than two hours? Under 66 minutes?

Do you know HOW?

Evaluate each expression.

1. $6!$

2. $_7C_3$

3. $_{11}P_9$

Q **and** *R* **are independent events. Find** $P(Q \text{ and } R)$**.**

4. $P(Q) = 0.5$, $P(R) = 0.4$

5. $P(Q) = \frac{1}{3}$, $P(R) = \frac{3}{8}$

Use the table below for Exercises 6–8.

Age of Respondent	Number of Groups	
	0–4	5 or more
< 30	7	18
≥ 30	12	12

6. Find $P(5 \text{ or more})$.

7. Find $P(5 \text{ or more} \mid \text{age} <30)$.

8. Find $P(\text{age} \geq 30 \mid 0-4)$.

Two standard number cubes are tossed. State whether the events are mutually exclusive.

9. One of the numbers is 1 less than the other. The sum is odd.

10. The sum is greater than 10. Six is one of the numbers.

11. Find Q_1 and Q_3 for this set of values: 36, 38, 42, 47, 51, 56, 62, 69, 70, 74.

12. Open-Ended At a local high school, there are 150 student parking spaces in the parking lot. There are 200 applications for parking permits. Describe a way that the permits can be assigned fairly.

A set of data has a normal distribution with a mean of 29 and a standard deviation of 4. Find the percent of data within each interval.

13. from 25 to 33

14. greater than 29

A newspaper wants to take a poll about which candidate voters prefer for President. Identify any bias in each sampling method.

15. The newspaper interviews people at a political debate.

16. The newspaper calls people selected at random from the local telephone book.

17. At a high school, 30% of the students buy class rings. You select five students at random. Find $P(\text{exactly two buy rings})$ and $P(\text{at least two buy rings})$.

Do you UNDERSTAND?

18. Indicate whether each situation involves a combination or a permuation.
  a. A team of 6 chosen from a class of 36
  b. An 8-digit code chosen for a lock

19. A data set is normally distributed with a mean of 37 and a standard deviation of 8.1. Sketch a normal curve for the distribution. Label the *x*-axis values at one, two, and three standard deviations from the mean.

© 20. Open-Ended A student guesses the answers to three questions on a true-false test. Design and describe a simulation to find the probability that the student guesses at least one of the questions correctly.

© 21. Writing Describe how a situation can have more than one sample space. Include an example.

22. Airline Ticket Pricing The table contains information from a study of the prices of comparable airline tickets. Which sample most likely was greater in size, A or B? Explain.

Sample	Standard deviation
A	$10.81
B	$3.97

Common Core Cumulative Standards Review

 **ASSESSMENT**

Vocabulary Review

As you solve test items, you must understand the meanings of mathematical terms. Match each term with its mathematical meaning.

A. normal distribution

B. standard deviation

C. quartile

D. median

E. mutually exclusive events

I. one of three values that separate a finite data set into 4 equal parts

II. a measure of how much the values in a data set vary from the mean

III. the middle value of a data set

IV. shows data that vary randomly from the mean in a bell-shaped curve

V. events that cannot happen at the same time

Selected Response

Read each question. Then write the letter of the correct answer on your paper.

1. A and B are mutually exclusive events. $P(A) = \frac{1}{3}$ and $P(B) = \frac{1}{2}$. What is $P(A \text{ or } B)$?

ⓐ $\frac{1}{6}$

ⓑ $\frac{2}{3}$

ⓒ $\frac{5}{6}$

ⓓ 1

2. Which of the following relationships is best represented by the graph at the right?

Ⓕ $y = -2^x$

Ⓖ $y = 2(3)^{-x}$

Ⓗ $y = -2(3)^x$

Ⓘ $y = (-6)^x$

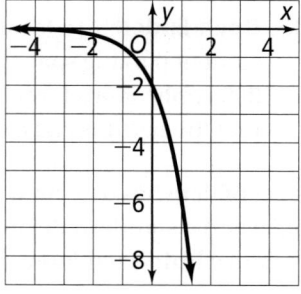

3. Which is the equation $5x - 7y = 25$ written in slope-intercept form?

- Ⓐ $y = \frac{-5}{7}x + 5$
- Ⓑ $y = \frac{5}{7}x - \frac{25}{7}$
- Ⓒ $y = \frac{5}{7}x + 5$
- Ⓓ $y = \frac{7}{5}x + \frac{25}{7}$

4. What is the vertex of the graph of $y = 2x^2 - 4x + 5$?

- Ⓕ $(1, 5)$
- Ⓗ $(1, 3)$
- Ⓖ $(3, 1)$
- Ⓘ $(5, 0)$

5. Which equation has $2 - \sqrt{3}$ as one of its solutions?

- Ⓐ $x^2 + 4x + 1 = 0$
- Ⓑ $x^2 - 4x + 1 = 0$
- Ⓒ $x^2 + 4x - 1 = 0$
- Ⓓ $x^2 - 4x - 1 = 0$

6. The equation for the circle below is $x^2 + y^2 = 9$. If the graph is translated one unit up and two units to the left, what is the new equation?

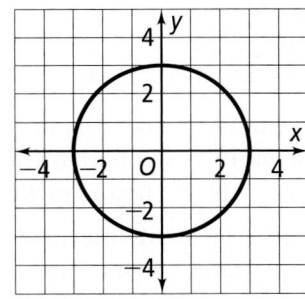

- Ⓕ $(x - 1)^2 + (y + 2)^2 = 9$
- Ⓖ $(x + 1)^2 + (y - 2)^2 = 9$
- Ⓗ $(x - 2)^2 + (y + 1)^2 = 9$
- Ⓘ $(x + 2)^2 + (y - 1)^2 = 9$

7. In six basketball games, you scored the following points per game. What is the approximate standard deviation of points scored?

8 11 14 7 12 18

- Ⓐ 1.0
- Ⓒ 4.0
- Ⓑ 2.0
- Ⓓ 5.0

8. What is the sum of the geometric series $5 + 10 + 20 + 40$?

- Ⓕ $S = \frac{2(1 - 5^4)}{1 - 5}$
- Ⓗ $S = \frac{5(1 - 4^2)}{1 - 4}$
- Ⓖ $S = \frac{5(1 - 2^4)}{1 - 2}$
- Ⓘ $S = \frac{2(1 - 4^5)}{1 - 4}$

9. What is the solution of the system of equations?
$$\begin{cases} 3x - 2y = 8 \\ x + 3y = -1 \end{cases}$$

- Ⓐ $(-1, 2)$
- Ⓒ $(-5, 2)$
- Ⓑ $(7, -22)$
- Ⓓ $(2, -1)$

10. What are the solutions to $9x^2 + 4 = 0$?

- Ⓕ ± 2
- Ⓗ $\pm \frac{2}{3}$
- Ⓖ $\pm \frac{2}{3}i$
- Ⓘ $\pm \sqrt{\frac{2}{3}}$

11. If $f(x) = x^2 - 1$ and $g(x) = |2x + 3|$, which has the greatest value?

- Ⓐ $f(3) + g(3)$
- Ⓒ $f(3) - g(3)$
- Ⓑ $\frac{f(3)}{g(3)}$
- Ⓓ $f(3) \cdot g(3)$

12. If $f(x) = 2x^2$ and $g(x) = 3(x + 1)$, which is an equivalent form of $f(x) + g(x)$?

- Ⓕ $2x^2 + 3x + 1$
- Ⓖ $2x^2 + 3x + 3$
- Ⓗ $2x^2 + 3x - 3$
- Ⓘ $5x^3 + 3$

13. The first term of an arithmetic series is 123. The common difference is 12 and the sum is 1113. How many terms are in the series?

- Ⓐ 7
- Ⓒ 9
- Ⓑ 8
- Ⓓ 10

14. In the equation $y = 2x^2 - x - 21$, which is a value of x when $y = 0$?

- Ⓕ -21
- Ⓗ 3
- Ⓖ $1\frac{1}{2}$
- Ⓘ $3\frac{1}{2}$

Constructed Response

15. What is the maximum value of the objective function $P = 3x + 4y$ within the feasible region described by the constraints at the right?

$$\begin{cases} x \geq 0, \ y \geq 0 \\ x + y \leq 4 \\ 2x + y \leq 5 \end{cases}$$

16. What is the remainder when $x^2 + 3x - 5$ is divided by $x + 3$?

17. For the function $f(x) = x^2 - 2x + 15$, what is the average rate of change in the interval from $x = 1$ to $x = 2$?

18. Solve $\log_7 x = \log_3 10$. Round your answer to the nearest tenth.

19. Evaluate $\displaystyle\sum_{n=1}^{8} \frac{3n}{2}$.

20. For a school play, six 9th graders and six 10th graders volunteer to be ushers. If two ushers are chosen at random by drawing names from a bowl, what is the probability that both ushers will be 10th graders? Write your answer as a fraction.

21. What is the radius of the circle with equation $x^2 - 6x + y^2 - 4y - 12 = 0$? If necessary, round your answer to the nearest hundredth.

22. Suppose x and y vary inversely and $x = 4$ when $y = 9$. What is x when $y = 12$?

23. Students were asked in a survey whether they had been to a movie theater in the last month. The table below shows the results.

	Yes	No
Male	35	17
Female	28	20

What is the probability that a student has not gone to the movies recently, given that the student is a male?

24. Simplify the expression $(2\sqrt{6} - 3)(2\sqrt{6} + 3)$. Show all your work.

25. What is the coefficient of x^2y^4 in the expansion of $(x + 2y)^6$?

26. An employer is selecting 4 out of 30 workers as employees of the month.
   a. Does this situation involve a combination or a permutation? Explain.
   b. How many different selections are possible?

27. Solve the equation $\frac{x}{6} = \frac{x + 4}{9}$. Check your solution. Show your work.

28. State the property or properties used to justify the identity $9 \log 3 - 3 \log 9 = \log 27$.

29. Find all asymptotes of the graph of $y = \frac{3x^2 + 1}{x^2 + 2x - 3}$.

Extended Response

30. Find the vertices, intercepts, asymptotes, and foci of the hyperbola $\frac{x^2}{16} - \frac{y^2}{9} = 1$.

31. Is the series $10{,}000 + 1000 + 100 + 10 + \ldots$ *arithmetic* or *geometric*? Find the sum of the first eight terms.

32. The following data set is a sample of the ages of students in an art school.

13 12 15 18 14 16 18 12 13 14 14 17 15 8 17 16
12 16 14 15 13 13 17 15 14 18 16 12 12 13

Find the mean and standard deviation. Then find the margin of error with a 95% confidence level by using the formula $ME = 1.96\frac{s}{\sqrt{n}}$. Round to the nearest hundredth. Explain what this information tells you about the ages of students in the entire art school.

Get Ready!

Lesson 1-3

Evaluating Expressions

Evaluate $ad - bc$ for the given values of the variables.

1. $a = -1, b = -2, c = 5, d = 4$

2. $a = \frac{1}{2}, b = -1, c = -\frac{2}{3}, d = 2$

3. $a = 2, b = \frac{1}{2}, c = \frac{1}{4}, d = -\frac{1}{8}$

4. $a = -\frac{1}{3}, b = \frac{1}{2}, c = \frac{1}{4}, d = -\frac{2}{3}$

Lesson 3-6

Identifying Matrix Elements

Identify the indicated element.

$$A = \begin{bmatrix} 2 & -1 & 3 \\ 5 & 7 & -9 \\ 4 & 11 & 21 \end{bmatrix}$$

5. a_{23}　　　　**6.** a_{32}　　　　**7.** a_{13}

Lessons 3-2 and 3-6

Solving Systems of Equations

Solve each system.

8. $\begin{cases} -2x + y = -5 \\ 4x + y = -2 \end{cases}$

9. $\begin{cases} 4x - y = -2 \\ -\frac{1}{2}x - y = 1 \end{cases}$

10. $\begin{cases} 3x + y = 5 \\ -x + y = 2 \end{cases}$

11. $\begin{cases} x + y + z = 10 \\ 2x - y = 5 \\ y - z = 15 \end{cases}$

12. $\begin{cases} -x + y + 2z = 16 \\ 2x - 2y - 2z = -16 \\ x + y = 0 \end{cases}$

13. $\begin{cases} -2x + 3y + z = 1 \\ x - 3z = 7 \\ -y + z = -5 \end{cases}$

 Looking Ahead Vocabulary

14. The local museum store sells books, postcards, and gifts. There are different prices for museum members and nonmembers. At the end of each month, the numbers of items sold in each category are recorded in a table, or *matrix*. Make a sketch of what one of these might look like for one month.

15. Suppose you have the twelve tables, one for each month, of the museum's sales in the previous problem. These can be combined using *matrix addition* to determine the total number of items sold in each category during the year. Describe how this is done. Use several examples like the one you made in the previous problem to see if your method works.

CHAPTER 12

Matrices

Download videos connecting math to your world.

Interactive! Vary numbers, graphs, and figures to explore math concepts.

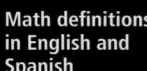
The online Solve It will get you in gear for each lesson.

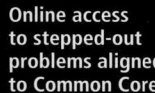
Math definitions in English and Spanish

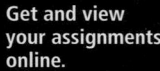
Online access to stepped-out problems aligned to Common Core

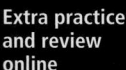
Get and view your assignments online.

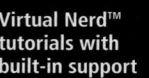 
Extra practice and review online

Chapter Preview

Vocabulary

English/Spanish Vocabulary Audio Online:

English	Spanish
determinant, *p. 784*	determinante
dilation, *p. 802*	dilatación
equal matrices, *p. 767*	matrices equivalentes
image, *p. 801*	imagen
matrix equation, *p. 765*	ecuación matricial
preimage, *p. 801*	preimagen
scalar multiplication, *p. 772*	multiplicación escalar
variable matrix, *p. 793*	matriz variable
zero matrix, *p. 765*	matriz cero

BIG ideas

1 Data Representation
Essential Question How can you use a matrix to organize data?

2 Modeling
Essential Question How can you use a matrix equation to model a real-world situation?

3 Transformations
Essential Question How can a matrix represent a transformation of a geometric figure in the plane?

 DOMAINS
• Vector and Matrix Quantities
• Congruence

Virtual Nerd™ tutorials with built-in support

Common Core Performance Task

Animal Care

Kristi has two pet rabbits. She feeds her rabbits a combination of three different brands of food. She wants to feed the rabbits the correct amount of each brand of food to provide the rabbits with the proper balance of nutrients. Each rabbit requires 8.5 g of protein, 7 g of fat, and 11 g of carbohydrate each day. The amount of each nutrient in one scoop of food, for brands A, B, and C, is shown in the table below.

Nutrient	Brand A	Brand B	Brand C
Protein (g)	2.5	0	5
Fat (g)	2.5	5	2.5
Carbohydrate (g)	1.25	2.5	7.5

Task Description

How many scoops of each type of food create a mixture with the proper nutrition for two rabbits?

Connecting the Task to the Math Practices

As you complete the task, you'll apply several Standards for Mathematical Practice.

- You'll use matrices to organize the data. (MP 1)
- You'll model the problem with a system of linear equations and a matrix equation. (MP 4)
- You'll find the inverse of a 3×3 matrix using a calculator. (MP 5)

Adding and Subtracting Matrices

Common Core State Standards

N-VM.C.8 Add, subtract, and multiply matrices of appropriate dimensions. **Also N-VM.C.10**

MP 1, MP 2, MP 3, MP 4, MP 8

Objective To add and subtract matrices and to solve matrix equations

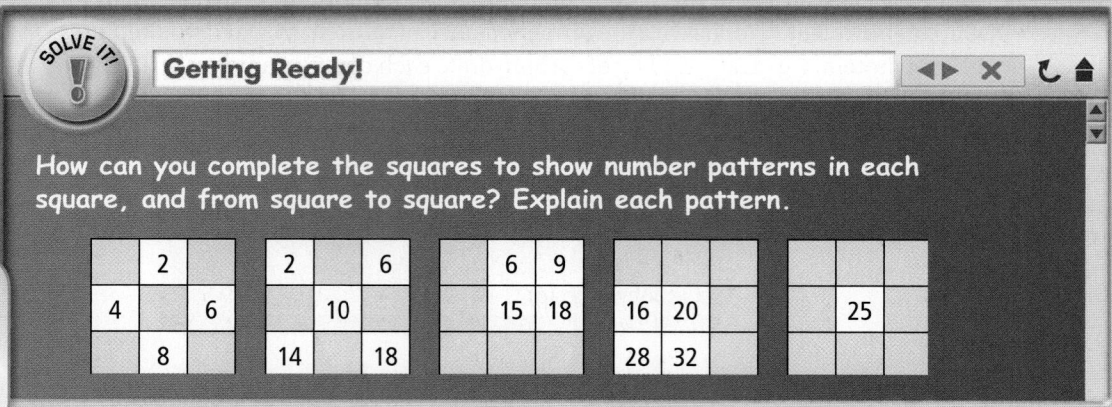

SOLVE IT!

Getting Ready!

How can you complete the squares to show number patterns in each square, and from square to square? Explain each pattern.

If you get stuck, shift your perspective from the patterns in each square to the patterns between squares, or vice versa.

MATHEMATICAL PRACTICES

In Lesson 3-6, you solved a system of equations by expressing it as a single matrix. Now you will learn how to work with more than one matrix at a time.

Essential Understanding You can extend the addition and subtraction of numbers to matrices.

Recall that the *dimensions* of a matrix are the numbers of rows and columns. A matrix with 2 rows and 3 columns is a 2×3 matrix. Each number in a matrix is a *matrix element*. In matrix A, a_{12} is the element in row 1 and column 2.

Sometimes you want to combine matrices to get new information. You can combine two matrices with equal dimensions by adding or subtracting the corresponding elements. **Corresponding elements** are elements in the same position in each matrix.

Lesson Vocabulary
- corresponding elements
- matrix equation
- zero matrix
- equal matrices

Key Concept **Matrix Addition and Subtraction**

To add matrices A and B with the same dimensions, add corresponding elements. Similarly, to subtract matrices A and B with the same dimensions, subtract corresponding elements.

$$A = \begin{bmatrix} a_{11} & a_{12} \\ a_{21} & a_{22} \end{bmatrix} \qquad\qquad B = \begin{bmatrix} b_{11} & b_{12} \\ b_{21} & b_{22} \end{bmatrix}$$

$$A + B = \begin{bmatrix} a_{11} + b_{11} & a_{12} + b_{12} \\ a_{21} + b_{21} & a_{22} + b_{22} \end{bmatrix} \qquad A - B = \begin{bmatrix} a_{11} - b_{11} & a_{12} - b_{12} \\ a_{21} - b_{21} & a_{22} - b_{22} \end{bmatrix}$$

Problem 1 Adding and Subtracting Matrices

Think

To add matrices they need to have the same dimensions. What are the dimensions of C?
C has 2 rows and 3 columns, so it's a 2×3 matrix.

Given $C = \begin{bmatrix} 3 & 2 & 4 \\ -1 & 4 & 0 \end{bmatrix}$ and $D = \begin{bmatrix} 1 & 4 & 3 \\ -2 & 2 & 4 \end{bmatrix}$, what are the following?

A $C + D$

$$\begin{bmatrix} 3 & 2 & 4 \\ -1 & 4 & 0 \end{bmatrix} + \begin{bmatrix} 1 & 4 & 3 \\ -2 & 2 & 4 \end{bmatrix}$$

$$= \begin{bmatrix} 3+1 & 2+4 & 4+3 \\ -1+(-2) & 4+2 & 0+4 \end{bmatrix}$$

$$= \begin{bmatrix} 4 & 6 & 7 \\ -3 & 6 & 4 \end{bmatrix}$$

B $C - D$

$$\begin{bmatrix} 3 & 2 & 4 \\ -1 & 4 & 0 \end{bmatrix} - \begin{bmatrix} 1 & 4 & 3 \\ -2 & 2 & 4 \end{bmatrix}$$

$$= \begin{bmatrix} 3-1 & 2-4 & 4-3 \\ -1-(-2) & 4-2 & 0-4 \end{bmatrix}$$

$$= \begin{bmatrix} 2 & -2 & 1 \\ 1 & 2 & -4 \end{bmatrix}$$

  Got It? **1.** Given $A = \begin{bmatrix} -12 & 24 \\ -3 & 5 \\ -1 & 10 \end{bmatrix}$ and $B = \begin{bmatrix} -3 & 1 \\ 2 & -4 \\ -1 & 5 \end{bmatrix}$, what are the following?

a. $A + B$

b. $A - B$

c. Reasoning Is matrix addition commutative? Explain.

A **matrix equation** is an equation in which the variable is a matrix. You can use the addition and subtraction properties of equality to solve a matrix equation. An example of a matrix equation is shown below.

$$\begin{bmatrix} 1 & 0 & 12 \\ 3 & 5 & 9 \\ 7 & 8 & -2 \end{bmatrix} + A = \begin{bmatrix} 8 & 11 & 9 \\ -5 & 5 & 2 \\ 10 & 7 & 8 \end{bmatrix}$$

 Problem 2 Solving a Matrix Equation

Sports The first table shows the teams with the four best records halfway through their season. The second table shows the full season records for the same four teams. Which team had the best record during the second half of the season?

Records for the First Half of the Season

Team	Wins	Losses
Team 1	30	11
Team 2	29	12
Team 3	25	16
Team 4	24	17

Records for Season

Team	Wins	Losses
Team 1	53	29
Team 2	67	15
Team 3	58	24
Team 4	61	21

Know	Need	Plan
• Records for the first half of the season • Records for the full season	Records for the second half of the season	• Use the equation: first half records + second half records = season records. • Solve the matrix equation.

Step 1 Write 4×2 matrices to show the information from the two tables.

Let A = the first half records
B = the second half records
F = the final records

$$A = \begin{bmatrix} 30 & 11 \\ 29 & 12 \\ 25 & 16 \\ 24 & 17 \end{bmatrix} \quad F = \begin{bmatrix} 53 & 29 \\ 67 & 15 \\ 58 & 24 \\ 61 & 21 \end{bmatrix}$$

Think

What are the dimensions of matrix B?
B will have 4 rows and 2 columns. It is a 4×2 matrix.

Step 2 Solve $A + B = F$ for B.

$B = F - A$

$$B = \begin{bmatrix} 53 & 29 \\ 67 & 15 \\ 58 & 24 \\ 61 & 21 \end{bmatrix} - \begin{bmatrix} 30 & 11 \\ 29 & 12 \\ 25 & 16 \\ 24 & 17 \end{bmatrix} = \begin{bmatrix} 53 - 30 & 29 - 11 \\ 67 - 29 & 15 - 12 \\ 58 - 25 & 24 - 16 \\ 61 - 24 & 21 - 17 \end{bmatrix} = \begin{bmatrix} 23 & 18 \\ 38 & 3 \\ 33 & 8 \\ 37 & 4 \end{bmatrix}$$

Team 2 had the best record (38 wins and 3 losses) during the second half of the season.

 Got It? 2. If $B = \begin{bmatrix} 1 & 6 & -1 \\ 2 & 6 & 1 \\ -1 & -2 & 4 \end{bmatrix}$, $C = \begin{bmatrix} 2 & 0 & 0 \\ -1 & -3 & 6 \\ 2 & 3 & -1 \end{bmatrix}$, and $A - B = C$, what is A?

For $m \times n$ matrices, the additive identity matrix is the **zero matrix** O, or $O_{m \times n}$, with all elements zero. The *opposite*, or *additive inverse*, of an $m \times n$ matrix A is $-A$ where each element is the opposite of the corresponding element of A.

Ⓒ Problem 3 Using Identity and Opposite Matrices

Think

How is this like adding real numbers?
Adding zero leaves the matrix unchanged. Adding opposites give you zero.

What are the following sums?

Ⓐ $\begin{bmatrix} 1 & 2 \\ 5 & -7 \end{bmatrix} + \begin{bmatrix} 0 & 0 \\ 0 & 0 \end{bmatrix}$

$= \begin{bmatrix} 1 + 0 & 2 + 0 \\ 5 + 0 & -7 + 0 \end{bmatrix} = \begin{bmatrix} 1 & 2 \\ 5 & -7 \end{bmatrix}$

Ⓑ $\begin{bmatrix} 2 & 8 \\ -3 & 0 \end{bmatrix} + \begin{bmatrix} -2 & -8 \\ 3 & 0 \end{bmatrix}$

$= \begin{bmatrix} 2 + (-2) & 8 + (-8) \\ -3 + 3 & 0 + 0 \end{bmatrix} = \begin{bmatrix} 0 & 0 \\ 0 & 0 \end{bmatrix}$

Got It? 3. What are the following sums?

a. $\begin{bmatrix} 14 & 5 \\ 0 & -2 \end{bmatrix} + \begin{bmatrix} -14 & -5 \\ 0 & 2 \end{bmatrix}$

b. $\begin{bmatrix} 0 & 0 & 0 \\ 0 & 0 & 0 \end{bmatrix} + \begin{bmatrix} -1 & 10 & -5 \\ 0 & 2 & -3 \end{bmatrix}$

Properties Properties of Matrix Addition

If A, B, and C are $m \times n$ matrices, then

Example	Property
$A + B$ is an $m \times n$ matrix	Closure Property of Addition
$A + B = B + A$	Commutative Property of Addition
$(A + B) + C = A + (B + C)$	Associative Property of Addition
There is a unique $m \times n$ matrix O such that $O + A = A + O = A$	Additive Identity Property
For each A, there is a unique opposite, $-A$, such that $A + (-A) = O$	Additive Inverse Property

Equal matrices have the same dimensions and equal corresponding elements. For example, $\begin{bmatrix} 0.25 & 1.5 \\ -3 & \frac{4}{5} \end{bmatrix}$ and $\begin{bmatrix} \frac{1}{4} & 1\frac{1}{2} \\ -3 & 0.8 \end{bmatrix}$ are equal matrices. You can use the definition of equal matrices to find unknown values in matrix elements.

Problem 4 Finding Unknown Matrix Values

Multiple Choice What values of x and y make the equation true?

$$\begin{bmatrix} 9 & 3x + 1 \\ 2y - 1 & 10 \end{bmatrix} = \begin{bmatrix} 9 & 16 \\ -5 & 10 \end{bmatrix}$$

Ⓐ $x = 3, y = 5$
Ⓑ $x = \frac{17}{3}, y = 5$
Ⓒ $x = 5, y = -2$
Ⓓ $x = 5, y = -3$

Think

How can you solve the equation?
For the two matrices to be equal, the corresponding elements must be equal.

$3x + 1 = 16$	Set corresponding elements equal.
$3x = 16 - 1$	Isolate the variable term.
$3x = 15$	Simplify.
$x = 5$	Solve for x and y.

$2y - 1 = -5$
$2y = -5 + 1$
$2y = -4$
$y = -2$

The correct answer is C.

 Got It? 4. What values of x, y, and z make the following equations true?

a. $\begin{bmatrix} x + 3 & -2 \\ y - 1 & x + 1 \end{bmatrix} = \begin{bmatrix} 9 & -2 \\ 2y + 5 & 7 \end{bmatrix}$

b. $\begin{bmatrix} z & -3 \\ 3x & 0 \end{bmatrix} - \begin{bmatrix} 10 & -4 \\ x & 2y + 6 \end{bmatrix} = \begin{bmatrix} 2 & 1 \\ 8 & 4y + 12 \end{bmatrix}$

Lesson Check

Do you know HOW?

Find each sum or difference.

1. $\begin{bmatrix} 1 & -1 \\ 2 & 3 \end{bmatrix} + \begin{bmatrix} 0 & 2 \\ -4 & 5 \end{bmatrix}$

2. $\begin{bmatrix} 5 & -3 & 7 \\ -1 & 0 & 8 \end{bmatrix} - \begin{bmatrix} 4 & 6 & -1 \\ 2 & 1 & 0 \end{bmatrix}$

Solve each matrix equation.

3. $\begin{bmatrix} 6 & 1 \\ 4 & -2 \end{bmatrix} + X = \begin{bmatrix} 3 & 5 \\ -1 & 9 \end{bmatrix}$

4. $X - \begin{bmatrix} 2 & 0 \\ 5 & -1 \end{bmatrix} = \begin{bmatrix} 4 & 10 \\ 8 & -3 \end{bmatrix}$

Do you UNDERSTAND?

5. **Vocabulary** Are the two matrices equal? Explain.

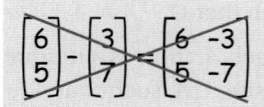

$\begin{bmatrix} \frac{1}{2} & \frac{3}{8} \\ 0.2 & \sqrt[3]{27} \end{bmatrix}$ and $\begin{bmatrix} 0.5 & 0.375 \\ \frac{1}{5} & 3 \end{bmatrix}$

6. **Error Analysis** Describe and correct the error made in subtracting the two matrices.

Practice and Problem-Solving Exercises

MATHEMATICAL PRACTICES

A Practice

Find each sum or difference.

See Problem 1.

7. $\begin{bmatrix} 5 & 4 & 3 \\ 1 & -2 & 6 \end{bmatrix} + \begin{bmatrix} 1 & 1 & 1 \\ 1 & 1 & 1 \end{bmatrix}$

8. $\begin{bmatrix} 2 & 1 & 2 \\ 1 & 2 & 1 \end{bmatrix} - \begin{bmatrix} 2 & 3 & 2 \\ 3 & 2 & 3 \end{bmatrix}$

9. $\begin{bmatrix} 6.4 & -1.9 \\ -6.4 & 0.8 \end{bmatrix} + \begin{bmatrix} -2.5 & -0.4 \\ 5.8 & 8.3 \end{bmatrix}$

10. $\begin{bmatrix} 1.5 & -1.9 \\ 0 & 4.6 \end{bmatrix} - \begin{bmatrix} 8.3 & -3.2 \\ 2.1 & 5.6 \end{bmatrix}$

Solve each matrix equation.

See Problem 2.

11. $\begin{bmatrix} 1 & 2 \\ 2 & 1 \\ -3 & 4 \end{bmatrix} + X = \begin{bmatrix} 5 & -6 \\ 1 & 0 \\ 8 & 5 \end{bmatrix}$

12. $\begin{bmatrix} 2 & 1 & -1 \\ 0 & 2 & 1 \end{bmatrix} - X = \begin{bmatrix} 11 & 3 & -13 \\ 15 & -9 & 8 \end{bmatrix}$

13. $X - \begin{bmatrix} 1 & 4 \\ -2 & 3 \end{bmatrix} = \begin{bmatrix} 5 & -2 \\ 1 & 0 \end{bmatrix}$

14. $X + \begin{bmatrix} 6 & 1 \\ -2 & 3 \end{bmatrix} = \begin{bmatrix} 2 & 0 \\ -3 & 1 \end{bmatrix}$

Find each sum.

See Problem 3.

15. $\begin{bmatrix} 2 & -3 & 4 \\ 5 & 6 & -7 \end{bmatrix} + \begin{bmatrix} 0 & 0 & 0 \\ 0 & 0 & 0 \end{bmatrix}$

16. $\begin{bmatrix} 6 & -3 \\ -7 & 2 \end{bmatrix} + \begin{bmatrix} -6 & 3 \\ 7 & -2 \end{bmatrix}$

Find the value of each variable.

See Problem 4.

17. $\begin{bmatrix} 2 & 2 \\ -1 & 6 \end{bmatrix} - \begin{bmatrix} 4 & -1 \\ 0 & 5 \end{bmatrix} = \begin{bmatrix} x & y \\ -1 & z \end{bmatrix}$

18. $\begin{bmatrix} 2 & 4 \\ 8 & 4.5 \end{bmatrix} = \begin{bmatrix} 4x - 6 & -10t + 5 \\ 4x & 15t + 1.5x \end{bmatrix}$

Find each matrix sum or difference if possible. If not possible, explain why.

$$A = \begin{bmatrix} 3 & 4 \\ 6 & -2 \\ 1 & 0 \end{bmatrix} \qquad B = \begin{bmatrix} -3 & 1 \\ 2 & -4 \\ -1 & 5 \end{bmatrix} \qquad C = \begin{bmatrix} 1 & 2 \\ -3 & 1 \end{bmatrix} \qquad D = \begin{bmatrix} 5 & 1 \\ 0 & 2 \end{bmatrix}$$

19. $A + B$ **20.** $B + D$ **21.** $C + D$ **22.** $B - A$ **23.** $C - D$

ⓒ 24. Think About a Plan The table shows the number of beach balls produced during one shift at two manufacturing plants. Plant 1 has two shifts per day and Plant 2 has three shifts per day. Write matrices to represent one day's total output at the two plants. Then find the difference between daily production totals at the two plants.
- How can you use the number of shifts to find the total daily production totals at each plant?
- What matrix equation can you use to solve this problem?

Beach Ball Production Per Shift

	1-color		3-color	
	Plastic	Rubber	Plastic	Rubber
Plant 1	500	700	1300	1900
Plant 2	400	1200	600	1600

25. Sports The modern pentathlon is a grueling all-day competition. Each member of a team competes in five events: target shooting, fencing, swimming, horseback riding, and cross-country running. Here are scores for the U.S. women at the 2004 Olympic Games.
a. Write two 5×1 matrices to represent each woman's scores for each event.
b. Find the total score for each athlete.

U.S. Women's Pentathlon Scores, 2004 Olympics

Event	Anita Allen	Mary Beth Iagorashvili
Shooting	952	760
Fencing	720	832
Swimming	1108	1252
Riding	1172	1144
Running	1044	1064

Source: Athens 2004 Olympic Games

ⓒ 26. Data Analysis Refer to the table at the right.
a. Add two matrices to find the total number of people participating in each activity.
b. Subtract two matrices to find the difference between the numbers of males and females in each activity.
c. Reasoning In part (b), does the order of the matrices matter? Explain.

U.S. Participation (millions) in Selected Leisure Activities

Activity	Male	Female
Movies	59.2	65.4
Exercise Programs	54.3	59.0
Sports Events	40.5	31.1
Home Improvement	45.4	41.8

Source: U.S. National Endowment for the Arts

ⓒ 27. Writing Given a matrix A, explain how to find a matrix B such that $A + B = 0$.

Solve each equation for each variable.

28. $\begin{bmatrix} 4b + 2 & -3 & 4d \\ -4a & 2 & 3 \\ 2f - 1 & -14 & 1 \end{bmatrix} = \begin{bmatrix} 11 & 2c - 1 & 0 \\ -8 & 2 & 3 \\ 0 & 3g - 2 & 1 \end{bmatrix}$

29. $\begin{bmatrix} 4c & 2 - d & 5 \\ -3 & -1 & 2 \\ 0 & -10 & 15 \end{bmatrix} = \begin{bmatrix} 2c + 5 & 4d & g \\ -3 & h & f - g \\ 0 & -4c & 15 \end{bmatrix}$

30. Find the sum of $E = \begin{bmatrix} 3 \\ 4 \\ 7 \end{bmatrix}$ and the additive inverse of $G = \begin{bmatrix} -2 \\ 0 \\ 5 \end{bmatrix}$.

31. Prove that matrix addition is commutative for 2×2 matrices.

32. Prove that matrix addition is associative for 2×2 matrices.

Standardized Test Prep

SAT/ACT

33. What is the sum $\begin{bmatrix} 5 & 7 & 3 \\ -1 & 0 & -4 \end{bmatrix} + \begin{bmatrix} -7 & 4 & 2 \\ 1 & -2 & -3 \end{bmatrix}$?

Ⓐ The matrices cannot be added.

Ⓑ $\begin{bmatrix} -2 & 11 & 5 \\ 0 & -2 & -7 \end{bmatrix}$ Ⓒ $\begin{bmatrix} 12 & 3 & 1 \\ -2 & 2 & -1 \end{bmatrix}$ Ⓓ $\begin{bmatrix} -35 & 28 & 6 \\ -1 & 0 & 12 \end{bmatrix}$

34. Which arithmetic sequence includes the term 27?

I. $a_1 = 7, a_n = a_{n-1} + 5$ II. $a_n = 3 + 4(n - 1)$ III. $a_n = 57 - 6n$

Ⓕ I only   Ⓖ I and II only   Ⓗ II and III only   Ⓘ I, II, and III

35. Which equation is graphed at the right?

Ⓐ $(x + 3)^2 + (y - 2)^2 = 25$

Ⓑ $(x - 2)^2 + (y + 3)^2 = 25$

Ⓒ $(x + 2)^2 + (y - 3)^2 = 25$

Ⓓ $(x - 3)^2 + (y + 2)^2 = 25$

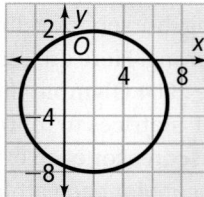

Short Response

36. For a daily airline flight to Denver, the numbers of checked pieces of luggage are normally distributed with a mean of 380 and a standard deviation of 20. What number of checked pieces of luggage is 3 standard deviations above the mean?

Mixed Review

A set of data with a mean of 62 and a standard deviation of 5 is normally distributed. Find the percent of data within each interval.

See Lesson 11-10.

37. from 57 to 67   **38.** greater than 52   **39.** from 62 to 72

Find the slope and y-intercept of each line.

See Lesson 2-3.

40. $y = 2x - 6$ **41.** $3y = 6 + 2x$ **42.** $-x - 2y = 12$ **43.** $y = 5x$

Get Ready!   To prepare for Lesson 12-2, do Exercises 44–45.

Find each sum.

See Lesson 12-1.

44. $\begin{bmatrix} 3 & 5 \\ 2 & 8 \end{bmatrix} + \begin{bmatrix} 3 & 5 \\ 2 & 8 \end{bmatrix} + \begin{bmatrix} 3 & 5 \\ 2 & 8 \end{bmatrix}$

45. $\begin{bmatrix} -4 \\ 7 \end{bmatrix} + \begin{bmatrix} -4 \\ 7 \end{bmatrix} + \begin{bmatrix} -4 \\ 7 \end{bmatrix} + \begin{bmatrix} -4 \\ 7 \end{bmatrix} + \begin{bmatrix} -4 \\ 7 \end{bmatrix}$

Working with Matrices

© Common Core State Standards

N-VM.C.8 Add, subtract, and multiply matrices of appropriate dimensions.

MP 5

MATHEMATICAL PRACTICES

You can use a graphing calculator to work with matrices. First you need to know how to enter a matrix into the calculator.

Example 1

Enter matrix $A = \begin{bmatrix} -3 & 4 \\ 7 & -5 \\ 0 & -2 \end{bmatrix}$ into your graphing calculator.

Select the **EDIT** option of the (matrix) feature to edit matrix **[A]**. Specify a 3×2 matrix by pressing **3** (enter) **2** (enter). Enter the matrix elements one row at a time, pressing (enter) after each element. Then use the (quit) feature to return to the main screen.

```
NAMES MATH  EDIT
1: [A]
2: [B]
3: [C]
4: [D]
5: [E]
```

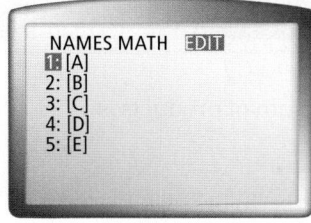

```
MATRIX [A]   3   ×2
[ 0       0        ]
[ 0       0        ]
[ 0       0        ]

1, 1 = 0
```

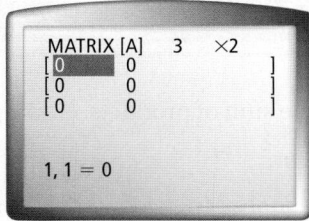

```
MATRIX [A]   3   ×2
[ −3      4        ]
[ 7       −5       ]
[ 0       −2       ]

3, 2 = −2
```

Example 2

Given $A = \begin{bmatrix} -3 & 4 \\ 7 & -5 \\ 0 & -2 \end{bmatrix}$ and $B = \begin{bmatrix} 10 & -7 \\ 4 & -3 \\ -12 & 11 \end{bmatrix}$, find $A + B$ and $A - B$.

Enter both matrices into the calculator. Use the **NAMES** option of the (matrix) feature to select each matrix. Press (enter) to see the sum. Repeat the corresponding steps to find the difference $A - B$.

```
[A] + [B]
      [[ 7      −3      ]
       [ 11     −8      ]
       [ −12    9       ]]
```

Exercises

Find each sum or difference.

1. $\begin{bmatrix} 0 & -3 \\ 5 & -7 \end{bmatrix} - \begin{bmatrix} -5 & 3 \\ 4 & 10 \end{bmatrix}$

2. $\begin{bmatrix} 3 & 5 & -7 \\ 0 & -2 & 0 \end{bmatrix} - \begin{bmatrix} -1 & 6 & 2 \\ -9 & 4 & 0 \end{bmatrix}$

3. $\begin{bmatrix} 3 \\ 5 \end{bmatrix} - \begin{bmatrix} -6 \\ 7 \end{bmatrix}$

4. $[3 \quad 5 \quad -8] + [-6 \quad 4 \quad 1]$

5. $\begin{bmatrix} 17 & 8 & 0 \\ 3 & -5 & 2 \end{bmatrix} - \begin{bmatrix} 4 & 6 & 5 \\ 2 & -2 & 9 \end{bmatrix}$

6. $[-9 \quad 6 \quad 4] + [-3 \quad 8 \quad 4]$

Matrix Multiplication

© Common Core State Standards

N-VM.C.6 Use matrices to represent and manipulate data . . .
N-VM.C.7 Multiply matrices by scalars to produce new matrices . . . **Also N-VM.C.8, N-VM.C.9**

MP 1, MP 2, MP 3, MP 4, MP 8

Objective To multiply matrices using scalar and matrix multiplication

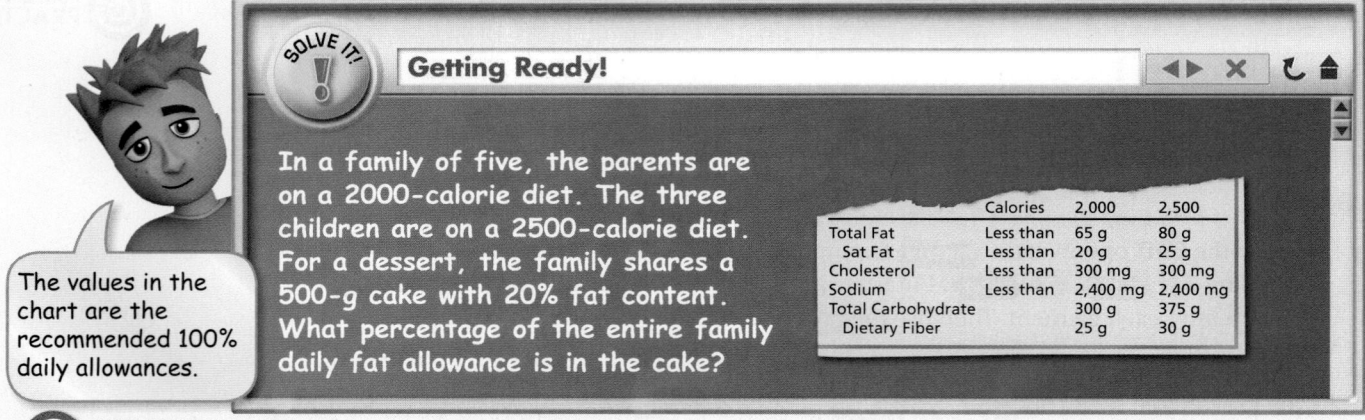

SOLVE IT!

Getting Ready!

In a family of five, the parents are on a 2000-calorie diet. The three children are on a 2500-calorie diet. For a dessert, the family shares a 500-g cake with 20% fat content. What percentage of the entire family daily fat allowance is in the cake?

Calories		2,000	2,500
Total Fat	Less than	65 g	80 g
Sat Fat	Less than	20 g	25 g
Cholesterol	Less than	300 mg	300 mg
Sodium	Less than	2,400 mg	2,400 mg
Total Carbohydrate		300 g	375 g
Dietary Fiber		25 g	30 g

The values in the chart are the recommended 100% daily allowances.

MATHEMATICAL PRACTICES

In the Solve It, you may have found the sum of products. Finding the sum of products is essential to matrix multiplication.

Lesson Vocabulary
• scalar
• scalar multiplication

Essential Understanding The product of two matrices is a matrix. To find an element in the product matrix, you multiply the elements of a row from the first matrix by the corresponding elements of a column from the second matrix. Then add the products.

Before you learn how to multiply two matrices, however, you should learn a simpler type of multiplication. This type of multiplication allows you to scale, or resize, the elements of the matrix.

$$3\begin{bmatrix} 5 & -1 \\ 3 & 7 \end{bmatrix} = \begin{bmatrix} 3(5) & 3(-1) \\ 3(3) & 3(7) \end{bmatrix} = \begin{bmatrix} 15 & -3 \\ 9 & 21 \end{bmatrix}$$

The real number factor (such as 3 in the example) is a **scalar**. Multiplication of a matrix A by a scalar c is **scalar multiplication**. To find the resulting matrix cA, you multiply each element of A by c.

take note

Key Concept   Scalar Multiplication

To multiply a matrix by a scalar c, multiply each element of the matrix by c.

$$A = \begin{bmatrix} a_{11} & a_{12} & a_{13} \\ a_{21} & a_{22} & a_{23} \end{bmatrix} \qquad cA = \begin{bmatrix} ca_{11} & ca_{12} & ca_{13} \\ ca_{21} & ca_{22} & ca_{23} \end{bmatrix}$$

Problem 1 Using Scalar Products

Think

What operation should you do first?
You should first multiply by the scalars, 4 and 3.

If $A = \begin{bmatrix} 2 & 8 & -3 \\ -1 & 5 & 2 \end{bmatrix}$ and $B = \begin{bmatrix} -1 & 0 & 5 \\ 0 & 3 & -2 \end{bmatrix}$, what is $4A + 3B$?

$$4A + 3B = 4\begin{bmatrix} 2 & 8 & -3 \\ -1 & 5 & 2 \end{bmatrix} + 3\begin{bmatrix} -1 & 0 & 5 \\ 0 & 3 & -2 \end{bmatrix}$$

$$= \begin{bmatrix} 8 & 32 & -12 \\ -4 & 20 & 8 \end{bmatrix} + \begin{bmatrix} -3 & 0 & 15 \\ 0 & 9 & -6 \end{bmatrix}$$

$$= \begin{bmatrix} 5 & 32 & 3 \\ -4 & 29 & 2 \end{bmatrix}$$

 Got It? **1.** Using matrices A and B from Problem 1, what is $3A - 2B$?

---

take note

Properties Scalar Multiplication

If A and B are $m \times n$ matrices, c and d are scalars, and O is the $m \times n$ zero matrix, then

Example	Property
cA is an $m \times n$ matrix	**Closure Property**
$(cd)A = c(dA)$	**Associative Property of Multiplication**
$c(A + B) = cA + cB$ $(c + d)A = cA + dA$	**Distributive Properties**
$1 \cdot A = A$	**Multiplicative Identity Property**
$0 \cdot A = O$ and $cO = O$	**Multiplicative Properties of Zero**

 Problem 2 Solving a Matrix Equation With Scalars

Think

Where have you seen problems that look like this before?
You saw problems like this when you solved one variable equations like $2x + 3(5) = 20$.

What is the solution of $2X + 3\begin{bmatrix} 2 & -1 \\ 3 & 4 \end{bmatrix} = \begin{bmatrix} 8 & 5 \\ 11 & 0 \end{bmatrix}$?

$2X + \begin{bmatrix} 6 & -3 \\ 9 & 12 \end{bmatrix} = \begin{bmatrix} 8 & 5 \\ 11 & 0 \end{bmatrix}$ Multiply by the scalar 3.

$2X = \begin{bmatrix} 8 & 5 \\ 11 & 0 \end{bmatrix} - \begin{bmatrix} 6 & -3 \\ 9 & 12 \end{bmatrix}$ Subtract $\begin{bmatrix} 6 & -3 \\ 9 & 12 \end{bmatrix}$ from each side.

$2X = \begin{bmatrix} 2 & 8 \\ 2 & -12 \end{bmatrix}$ Simplify.

$X = \begin{bmatrix} 1 & 4 \\ 1 & -6 \end{bmatrix}$ Multiply each side by $\frac{1}{2}$ and simplify.

 Got It? **2.** What is the solution of $3X - 2\begin{bmatrix} -1 & 5 \\ 7 & 0 \end{bmatrix} = \begin{bmatrix} 17 & -13 \\ -7 & 0 \end{bmatrix}$?

The product of two matrices is a matrix. To find an element in the product matrix, multiply the elements of a row from the first matrix by the corresponding elements of a column from the second matrix. Then add the products.

take note

Key Concept Matrix Multiplication

To find element c_{ij} of the product matrix AB, multiply each element in the ith row of A by the corresponding element in the jth column of B. Then add the products.

$$AB = \begin{bmatrix} a_{11} & a_{12} \\ a_{21} & a_{22} \end{bmatrix} \begin{bmatrix} b_{11} & b_{12} \\ b_{21} & b_{22} \end{bmatrix} = \begin{bmatrix} a_{11}b_{11} + a_{12}b_{21} & a_{11}b_{12} + a_{12}b_{22} \\ a_{21}b_{11} + a_{22}b_{21} & a_{21}b_{12} + a_{22}b_{22} \end{bmatrix}$$

Problem 3 Multiplying Matrices

Think

What relationship must exist between the numbers of elements in a row of A and a column of B?

They must be equal.

If $A = \begin{bmatrix} 2 & 1 \\ -3 & 0 \end{bmatrix}$ and $B = \begin{bmatrix} -1 & 3 \\ 0 & 4 \end{bmatrix}$, what is AB?

Step 1 Multiply the elements in the first row of A by the elements in the first column of B. Add the products and place the sum in the first row, first column of AB.

$$\begin{bmatrix} 2 & 1 \\ -3 & 0 \end{bmatrix} \begin{bmatrix} -1 & 3 \\ 0 & 4 \end{bmatrix} = \begin{bmatrix} -2 & \_ \\ \_ & \_ \end{bmatrix}$$ $2(-1) + 1(0) = -2$

Step 2 Multiply the elements in the first row of A by the elements in the second column of B. Add the products and place the sum in the first row, second column of AB.

$$\begin{bmatrix} 2 & 1 \\ -3 & 0 \end{bmatrix} \begin{bmatrix} -1 & 3 \\ 0 & 4 \end{bmatrix} = \begin{bmatrix} -2 & 10 \\ \_ & \_ \end{bmatrix}$$ $2(3) + 1(4) = 10$

Repeat Steps 1 and 2 with the second row of A to fill in row two of the product matrix.

Step 3 $\begin{bmatrix} 2 & 1 \\ -3 & 0 \end{bmatrix} \begin{bmatrix} -1 & 3 \\ 0 & 4 \end{bmatrix} = \begin{bmatrix} -2 & 10 \\ 3 & \_ \end{bmatrix}$ $(-3)(-1) + 0(0) = 3$

Step 4 $\begin{bmatrix} 2 & 1 \\ -3 & 0 \end{bmatrix} \begin{bmatrix} -1 & 3 \\ 0 & 4 \end{bmatrix} = \begin{bmatrix} -2 & 10 \\ 3 & -9 \end{bmatrix}$ $(-3)(3) + 0(4) = -9$

The product of $\begin{bmatrix} 2 & 1 \\ -3 & 0 \end{bmatrix}$ and $\begin{bmatrix} -1 & 3 \\ 0 & 4 \end{bmatrix}$ is $\begin{bmatrix} -2 & 10 \\ 3 & -9 \end{bmatrix}$.

  Got It? 3. If $A = \begin{bmatrix} 2 & -1 \\ 3 & 4 \end{bmatrix}$ and $B = \begin{bmatrix} -3 & 1 \\ 0 & 2 \end{bmatrix}$, what are the following products?

    a. AB **b.** BA

    c. Reasoning Is matrix multiplication commutative? Explain.

Problem 4 Applying Matrix Multiplication

Sports In 1966, Washington and New York (Giants) played the highest scoring game in National Football League history. The table summarizes the scoring. A touchdown (TD) is worth 6 points, a field goal (FG) is worth 3 points, a safety (S) is worth 2 points, and a point after touchdown (PAT) is worth 1 point. Using matrix multiplication, what was the final score?

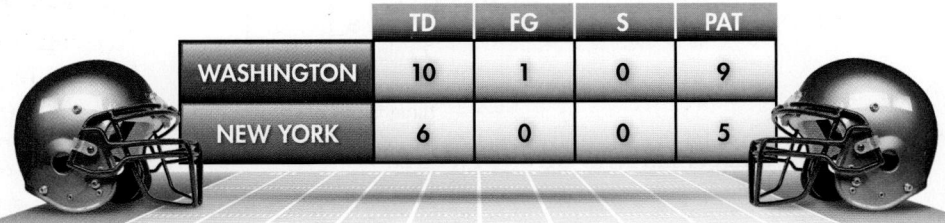

	TD	FG	S	PAT
WASHINGTON	10	1	0	9
NEW YORK	6	0	0	5

Know
- The number of each type of score
- The point value of each score

Need
The scoring summary and point values as matrices

Plan
Multiply the matrices to find each team's final score.

Think

What is the meaning of each number in matrix P?
They are the point values for each type of score.

Step 1 Enter the information in matrices.

$$S = \begin{bmatrix} 10 & 1 & 0 & 9 \\ 6 & 0 & 0 & 5 \end{bmatrix} \qquad P = \begin{bmatrix} 6 \\ 3 \\ 2 \\ 1 \end{bmatrix}$$

Step 2 Use matrix multiplication. The final score is the product SP.

$$SP = \begin{bmatrix} 10 & 1 & 0 & 9 \\ 6 & 0 & 0 & 5 \end{bmatrix} \begin{bmatrix} 6 \\ 3 \\ 2 \\ 1 \end{bmatrix}$$

$$= \begin{bmatrix} 10(6) + 1(3) + 0(2) + 9(1) \\ 6(6) + 0(3) + 0(2) + 5(1) \end{bmatrix} = \begin{bmatrix} 72 \\ 41 \end{bmatrix}$$

Step 3 Interpret the product matrix.

The first row of SP shows scoring for Washington, so the final score was Washington 72, New York 41.

Got It? **4.** There are three ways to score in a basketball game: three-point field goals, two-point field goals, and one-point free throws. In 1994, suppose a high school player scored 36 two-point field goals and 28 free throws. In 2006, suppose a high school player scored 7 three-point field goals, 21 two-point field goals, and 18 free throws. Using matrix multiplication, how many points did each player score?

You can multiply two matrices A and B only if the number of columns of A is equal to the number of rows of B.

Property Dimensions of a Product Matrix

If A is an $m \times n$ matrix and B is an $n \times p$ matrix, then the product matrix AB is an $m \times p$ matrix.

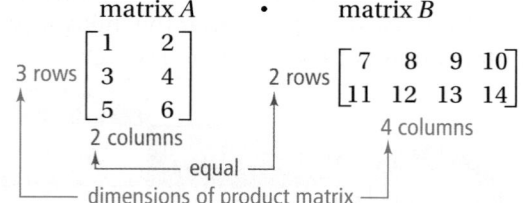

matrix A • matrix B

3 rows $\begin{bmatrix} 1 & 2 \\ 3 & 4 \\ 5 & 6 \end{bmatrix}$ 2 rows $\begin{bmatrix} 7 & 8 & 9 & 10 \\ 11 & 12 & 13 & 14 \end{bmatrix}$

2 columns   4 columns

equal

dimensions of product matrix

Product matrix AB is a 3×4 matrix.

(c) **Problem 5** Determining Whether Product Matrices Exist

Does either product AB or BA exist?

$$A = \begin{bmatrix} -2 & 1 \\ 3 & -2 \\ 0 & 1 \end{bmatrix} \qquad B = \begin{bmatrix} -1 & 0 & 2 & 1 \\ 2 & 0 & 0 & 3 \end{bmatrix}$$

AB BA

$(3 \times 2)(2 \times 4) \; \rightarrow \; 3 \times 4$ product matrix $(2 \times 4)(3 \times 2) \; \rightarrow \;$ no product

equal   Product AB exists.   not equal

✓ **Got It? 5.** Do the following products exist?

$$A = \begin{bmatrix} 1 & 4 \\ -3 & 5 \end{bmatrix} \qquad B = \begin{bmatrix} -1 & 1 \end{bmatrix} \qquad C = \begin{bmatrix} 4 & 2 & 0 \\ 1 & 3 & 5 \end{bmatrix}$$

     a. AB **b.** BA **c.** AC **d.** CA **e.** BC

Matrix multiplication of square $(n \times n)$ matrices has some of the properties of real number multiplication.

Properties Matrix Multiplication

If A, B, and C are $n \times n$ matrices, and O is the $n \times n$ zero matrix, then

Example	Property
AB is an $n \times n$ matrix	**Closure Property**
$(AB)C = A(BC)$	**Associative Property of Multiplication**
$A(B + C) = AB + AC$ $(B + C)A = BA + CA$	**Distributive Property**
$OA = AO = O$	**Multiplicative Property of Zero**

Lesson Check

Do you know HOW?

Let $A = \begin{bmatrix} 3 & -1 \\ 2 & 0 \end{bmatrix}$ and $B = \begin{bmatrix} 1 & 3 \\ -2 & 2 \end{bmatrix}$.

Find each of the following.

1. $2A$

2. $3B - 2A$

3. AB

4. BA

Do you UNDERSTAND?

5. Vocabulary Which type of multiplication, *scalar* or *matrix*, can help you with a repeated matrix addition problem? Explain.

6. Error Analysis Your friend says there is a right order and a wrong order when multiplying A (a 2×4 matrix) and B (a 3×6 matrix). Explain your friend's error.

 Practice and Problem-Solving Exercises

 Use matrices A, B, C, and D. Find each product, sum, or difference.

See Problem 1.

$$A = \begin{bmatrix} 3 & 4 \\ 6 & -2 \\ 1 & 0 \end{bmatrix} \qquad B = \begin{bmatrix} -3 & 1 \\ 2 & -4 \\ -1 & 5 \end{bmatrix} \qquad C = \begin{bmatrix} 1 & 2 \\ -3 & 1 \end{bmatrix} \qquad D = \begin{bmatrix} 5 & 1 \\ 0 & 2 \end{bmatrix}$$

7. $3A$

8. $4B$

9. $-3C$

10. $-D$

11. $A - 2B$

12. $3A + 2B$

13. $4C + 3D$

14. $2A - 5B$

Solve each matrix equation. Check your answers.

See Problem 2.

15. $3\begin{bmatrix} 2 & 0 \\ -1 & 5 \end{bmatrix} - 2X = \begin{bmatrix} -10 & 5 \\ 0 & 17 \end{bmatrix}$

16. $4X + \begin{bmatrix} 1 & 3 \\ -7 & 9 \end{bmatrix} = \begin{bmatrix} -3 & 11 \\ 5 & -7 \end{bmatrix}$

17. $\frac{1}{2}X + \begin{bmatrix} 4 & -3 \\ 12 & 1 \end{bmatrix} = \begin{bmatrix} 2 & 1 \\ 1 & 2 \end{bmatrix}$

18. $5X - \begin{bmatrix} 1.5 & -3.6 \\ -0.3 & 2.8 \end{bmatrix} = \begin{bmatrix} 0.2 & 1.3 \\ -5.6 & 1.7 \end{bmatrix}$

Find each product.

See Problem 3.

19. $\begin{bmatrix} -3 & 4 \\ 5 & 2 \end{bmatrix}\begin{bmatrix} 1 & 0 \\ 2 & -3 \end{bmatrix}$

20. $\begin{bmatrix} 1 & 0 \\ 2 & -3 \end{bmatrix}\begin{bmatrix} -3 & 4 \\ 5 & 2 \end{bmatrix}$

21. $\begin{bmatrix} 0 & 2 \\ -4 & 0 \end{bmatrix}\begin{bmatrix} 0 & 2 \\ -4 & 0 \end{bmatrix}$

22. $\begin{bmatrix} -3 & 5 \end{bmatrix}\begin{bmatrix} -3 \\ 5 \end{bmatrix}$

23. $\begin{bmatrix} -3 & 5 \end{bmatrix}\begin{bmatrix} -3 & 0 \\ 5 & 0 \end{bmatrix}$

24. $\begin{bmatrix} -3 & 5 \end{bmatrix}\begin{bmatrix} 0 & -3 \\ 0 & 5 \end{bmatrix}$

25. $\begin{bmatrix} 0 & -3 \\ 0 & 5 \end{bmatrix}\begin{bmatrix} -3 & 0 \\ 5 & 0 \end{bmatrix}$

26. $\begin{bmatrix} 1 & 0 \\ -1 & -5 \\ 0 & 3 \end{bmatrix}\begin{bmatrix} -1 & 0 \\ 0 & -1 \end{bmatrix}$

27. $\begin{bmatrix} -1 & 3 & -3 \\ 2 & -2 & 1 \end{bmatrix}\begin{bmatrix} 5 \\ 4 \\ 3 \end{bmatrix}$

28. Business A florist makes three special floral arrangements. One uses three lilies. The second uses three lilies and four carnations. The third uses four daisies and three carnations. Lilies cost $2.15 each, carnations cost $.90 each, and daisies cost $1.30 each.

See Problem 4.

a. Write a matrix to show the number of each type of flower in each arrangement.

b. Write a matrix to show the cost of each type of flower.

c. Find the matrix showing the cost of each floral arrangement.

Determine whether the product exists.

◀ See Problem 5.

$$F = \begin{bmatrix} 2 & 3 \\ 6 & 9 \end{bmatrix} \qquad G = \begin{bmatrix} -3 & 6 \\ 2 & -4 \end{bmatrix} \qquad H = \begin{bmatrix} -5 \\ 6 \end{bmatrix} \qquad J = \begin{bmatrix} 0 & 7 \end{bmatrix}$$

29. FG **30.** GF **31.** FH **32.** HG **33.** JH

 **Apply**

© **34. Think About a Plan** A hardware store chain sells hammers for $3, flashlights for $5, and lanterns for $7. The store manager tracks the daily purchases at three of the chain's stores in a 3×3 matrix. What is the total gross revenue from the flashlights sold at all three stores?

Number of Items Sold

	Store A	Store B	Store C
Hammers	10	9	8
Flashlights	3	14	6
Lanterns	2	5	7

- How can you use matrix multiplication to solve this problem?
- What does the product matrix represent?

35. Sports Two teams are competing in a two-team track meet. Points for individual events are awarded as follows: 5 points for first place, 3 points for second place, and 1 point for third place. Points for team relays are awarded as follows: 5 points for first place and no points for second place.
a. Use matrix operations to determine the score in the track meet.

Team	Individual Events			Relays	
	First	Second	Third	First	Second
West River	8	5	2	8	5
River's Edge	6	9	12	6	9

b. Who would win if the scoring were changed to 5 points for first place, 2 points for second place, and 1 point for third place in each individual event and 5 points for first place and 0 points for second place in a relay?

For Exercises 36–43, use matrices D, E, and F. Perform the indicated operations if they are defined. If an operation is not defined, label it *undefined*.

$$D = \begin{bmatrix} 1 & 2 & -1 \\ 0 & 3 & 1 \\ 2 & -1 & -2 \end{bmatrix} \qquad E = \begin{bmatrix} 2 & -5 & 0 \\ 1 & 0 & -2 \\ 3 & 1 & 1 \end{bmatrix} \qquad F = \begin{bmatrix} -3 & 2 \\ -5 & 1 \\ 2 & 4 \end{bmatrix}$$

36. DE **37.** $-3F$ **38.** $(DE)F$ **39.** $D(EF)$

40. $D - 2E$ **41.** $(E - D)F$ **42.** $(DD)E$ **43.** $(2D)(3F)$

© **44. Writing** Suppose A is a 2×3 matrix and B is a 3×2 matrix with elements not all being equal. Are AB and BA equal? Explain your reasoning. Include examples.

For Exercises 45–48, use matrices *P, Q, R, S,* and *I.* Determine whether the two expressions in each pair are equal.

$$P = \begin{bmatrix} 3 & 4 \\ 1 & 2 \end{bmatrix} \qquad Q = \begin{bmatrix} 1 & 0 \\ 3 & -2 \end{bmatrix} \qquad R = \begin{bmatrix} 1 & 4 \\ -2 & 1 \end{bmatrix} \qquad S = \begin{bmatrix} 0 & 1 \\ 2 & 0 \end{bmatrix} \qquad I = \begin{bmatrix} 1 & 0 \\ 0 & 1 \end{bmatrix}$$

45. $(P + Q)R$ and $PR + QR$

46. $(P + Q)I$ and $PI + QI$

47. $(P + Q)(R + S)$ and $(P + Q)R + (P + Q)S$

48. $(P + Q)(R + S)$ and $PR + PS + QR + QS$

Apply What You've Learned

MATHEMATICAL
PRACTICES
MP 1

Look back at the information on page 763 about the daily nutritional requirements of Kristi's pet rabbits. The table listing the content of three brands of rabbit food is shown again below.

Nutrient	Brand A	Brand B	Brand C
Protein (g)	2.5	0	5
Fat (g)	2.5	5	2.5
Carbohydrate (g)	1.25	2.5	7.5

a. Use the values in the rows and columns of the table to write a matrix, *A.* What are the dimensions of matrix *A*?

b. Write a 1×3 matrix *B* to represent the daily nutritional requirements for one rabbit.

c. Write the matrix expression *cB* (where *c* is a constant) that represents the amounts of nutrients needed for two rabbits, and then find the product. Call the product matrix *D.*

Networks

 Common Core State Standards

N-VM.C.6 Use matrices to represent and manipulate data . . .

MP 4

A finite graph is a set of points, called vertices, connected by curves, or paths.

You can use a matrix to describe a finite graph. The digit "1" indicates a path between two vertices or one vertex and itself. The digit "0" indicates that no path exists between two vertices or from one vertex to itself.

Example 1

Write a matrix A to represent the finite graph. Explain the significance of element a_{41}.

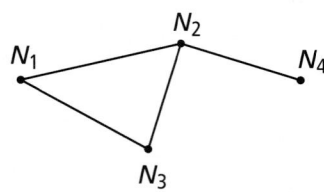

$$A = \begin{array}{c} \\ N_1 \\ N_2 \\ N_3 \\ N_4 \end{array} \begin{array}{cccc} N_1 & N_2 & N_3 & N_4 \\ \left[\begin{array}{cccc} 0 & 1 & 1 & 0 \\ 1 & 0 & 1 & 1 \\ 1 & 1 & 0 & 0 \\ 0 & 1 & 0 & 0 \end{array}\right] \end{array}$$

There is a path from N_2 to N_4.

Element a_{41} is 0. It indicates that there is no path between N_4 and N_1.

Directed graphs are finite graphs that indicate the direction of a path. The directed graph below represents the information in the map.

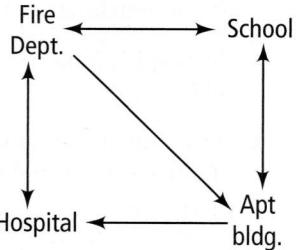

You can use a matrix to represent the information in a directed graph.

Example 2

Write a matrix B to represent the information from the directed graph. Compare elements b_{12} and b_{21}.

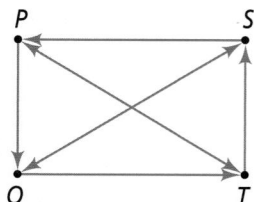

$$B = \begin{array}{c} \\ P \\ Q \\ S \\ T \end{array} \begin{array}{cccc} \text{To} \rightarrow P & Q & S & T \\ \text{From} \rightarrow \\ \left[\begin{array}{cccc} 0 & 1 & 0 & 1 \\ 0 & 0 & 1 & 1 \\ 1 & 1 & 0 & 0 \\ 1 & 0 & 1 & 0 \end{array}\right] \end{array}$$

Element b_{12} is 1 and b_{21} is 0. The path between P and Q is one way, from P to Q.

Example 3

Draw a directed graph to represent the information in the matrix.

$$
C = \begin{array}{c} \text{To} \rightarrow \\ \text{From} \rightarrow A \\ B \\ C \end{array}
\begin{array}{ccc}
A & B & C
\end{array}
\begin{bmatrix}
1 & 1 & 1 \\
1 & 0 & 1 \\
0 & 0 & 0
\end{bmatrix}
$$

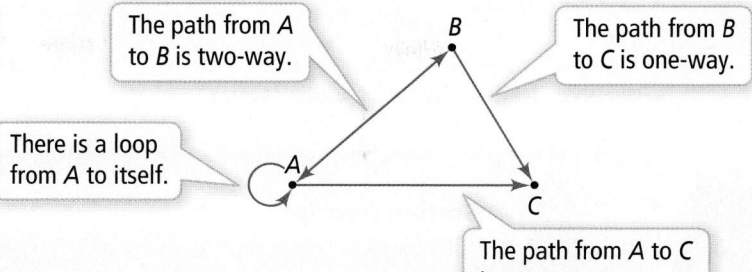

The path from A to B is two-way.

The path from B to C is one-way.

There is a loop from A to itself.

The path from A to C is one-way.

Exercises

Write a matrix to represent each finite or directed graph.

1.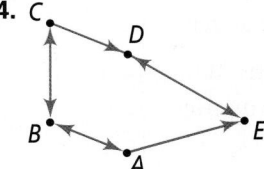

2.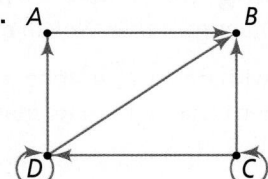

3.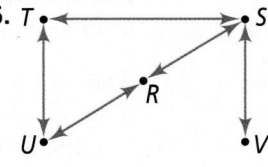

4.

5.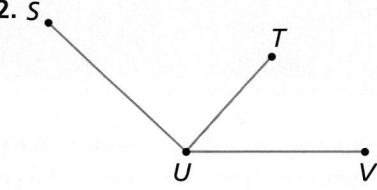

6.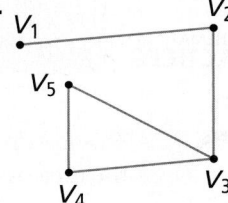

Draw a directed graph to represent the information in each matrix.

7.
$$
\begin{array}{c}
\\ J \\ K \\ L \\ M
\end{array}
\begin{array}{cccc}
J & K & L & M
\end{array}
\begin{bmatrix}
0 & 0 & 0 & 1 \\
0 & 0 & 1 & 1 \\
0 & 1 & 0 & 1 \\
1 & 1 & 1 & 0
\end{bmatrix}
$$

8.
$$
\begin{array}{c}
\\ A \\ B \\ C \\ D
\end{array}
\begin{array}{cccc}
A & B & C & D
\end{array}
\begin{bmatrix}
0 & 0 & 1 & 1 \\
1 & 1 & 0 & 0 \\
0 & 1 & 0 & 1 \\
1 & 0 & 1 & 0
\end{bmatrix}
$$

9.
$$
\begin{array}{c}
\\ N_1 \\ N_2 \\ N_3 \\ N_4
\end{array}
\begin{array}{cccc}
N_1 & N_2 & N_3 & N_4
\end{array}
\begin{bmatrix}
1 & 1 & 1 & 1 \\
0 & 0 & 1 & 1 \\
1 & 0 & 0 & 0 \\
0 & 0 & 1 & 0
\end{bmatrix}
$$

ⓒ **10. Travel** Alice and Becky live on Parkway East, at the intersections of Owens Bridge and Bay Bridge, respectively. Carl and David live on Parkway West, at the intersections of Bay Bridge and Owens Bridge, respectively. Parkway East is a one-way street running east. Parkway West is one-way running west. Both bridges are two-way.
  a. Draw a directed graph indicating road travel between the houses.
  b. Write a matrix T to represent the information in the directed graph.
  c. Writing Calculate T^2. What does the matrix model? Explain.

12-3

Determinants and Inverses

Common Core State Standards

N-VM.C.10 . . . The determinant of a square matrix is nonzero if and only if the matrix has a multiplicative inverse.

N-VM.C.12 Work with 2 × 2 matrices as a transformation of the plane . . .

MP 1, MP 2, MP 3, MP 4, MP 5, MP 6

Objective To find the inverse of a matrix

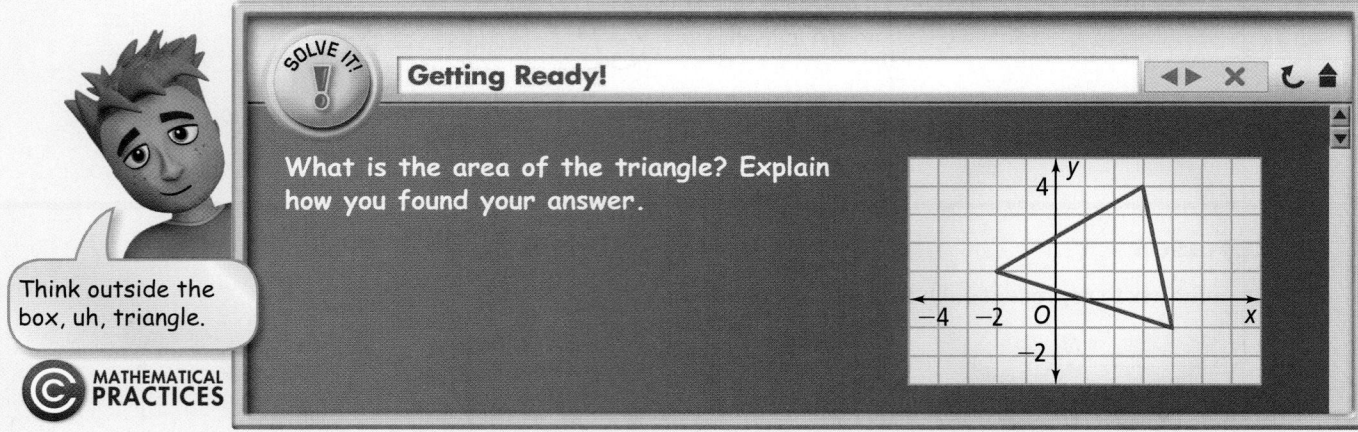

SOLVE IT!

Getting Ready!

What is the area of the triangle? Explain how you found your answer.

Think outside the box, uh, triangle.

MATHEMATICAL PRACTICES

Lesson Vocabulary

- square matrix
- multiplicative identity matrix
- multiplicative inverse matrix
- determinant
- singular matrix

This lesson will prepare you to use matrices to solve problems, including how to find the area of a triangle with vertices anywhere in the coordinate plane.

Essential Understanding The product of a matrix and its *multiplicative inverse matrix* is the *multiplicative identity matrix*. Not all matrices have inverse matrices.

A **square matrix** is a matrix with the same number of rows and columns. While there is a multiplicative identity matrix for any square matrix, not all square matrices have multiplicative inverses.

take note

Key Concepts Identity and Multiplicative Inverse Matrices

For an $n \times n$ matrix, the **multiplicative identity matrix** is an $n \times n$ matrix I, or I_n, with 1's along the main diagonal and 0's elsewhere.

$$I_2 = \begin{bmatrix} 1 & 0 \\ 0 & 1 \end{bmatrix}, \quad I_3 = \begin{bmatrix} 1 & 0 & 0 \\ 0 & 1 & 0 \\ 0 & 0 & 1 \end{bmatrix}, \quad \text{and so forth.}$$

If A and B are square matrices and $AB = BA = I$, then B is the **multiplicative inverse matrix** of A, written A^{-1}.

 **Problem 1** **Determining Whether Matrices are Inverses**

Think

How do you determine whether A and B are inverses?
Find AB and BA. Each product must equal I.

For each of the following, are matrices A and B inverses?

A $A = \begin{bmatrix} 1 & 2 \\ 3 & 4 \end{bmatrix}$ $B = \begin{bmatrix} -2 & 1 \\ \frac{3}{2} & -\frac{1}{2} \end{bmatrix}$

Since $AB = I$ and $BA = I$,
matrices A and B are inverses.

B $A = \begin{bmatrix} 1 & 0 & 2 \\ -2 & 1 & 1 \\ -1 & 1 & 2 \end{bmatrix}$ $B = \begin{bmatrix} -1 & -2 & 2 \\ -3 & -4 & 5 \\ 1 & 1 & -1 \end{bmatrix}$

Since $AB = I$ and $BA = I$,
matrices A and B are inverses.

C $A = \begin{bmatrix} 2 & 4 \\ 2 & 2 \end{bmatrix}$ $B = \begin{bmatrix} 2 & 5 \\ -1 & -3 \end{bmatrix}$

Since $AB \neq I$ (and $BA \neq I$),
matrices A and B are not inverses.

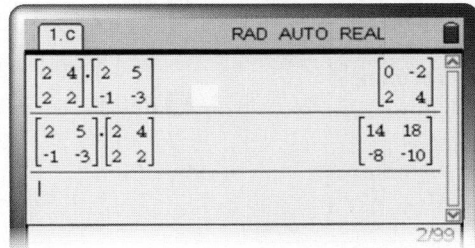

Got It? **1.** For each of the following, are A and B inverses?

a. $A = \begin{bmatrix} 1 & 1 \\ 5 & 4 \end{bmatrix}$ $B = \begin{bmatrix} -4 & 1 \\ 5 & -1 \end{bmatrix}$ **b.** $A = \begin{bmatrix} 3 & 2 \\ 5 & 4 \end{bmatrix}$ $B = \begin{bmatrix} 2 & -1 \\ -\frac{5}{2} & \frac{3}{2} \end{bmatrix}$

c. Reasoning Does the matrix $\begin{bmatrix} 0 & 0 \\ 0 & 0 \end{bmatrix}$ have an inverse? Explain.

Every square matrix with real-number elements has a number associated with it.
The number is its *determinant*. Given $A = \begin{bmatrix} a & b \\ c & d \end{bmatrix}$,

Write	**Read**	**Evaluate**
↓	↓	↓
det A	the determinant of A	$\det \begin{bmatrix} a & b \\ c & d \end{bmatrix} = ad - bc$

Key Concept Determinants of 2 × 2 and 3 × 3 Matrices

The **determinant** of a 2 × 2 matrix $\begin{bmatrix} a & b \\ c & d \end{bmatrix}$ is det $\begin{bmatrix} a & b \\ c & d \end{bmatrix} = ad - bc$.

The determinant of a 3 × 3 matrix $\begin{bmatrix} a_1 & b_1 & c_1 \\ a_2 & b_2 & c_2 \\ a_3 & b_3 & c_3 \end{bmatrix}$ is

$$a_1 b_2 c_3 + b_1 c_2 a_3 + c_1 a_2 b_3 - (a_3 b_2 c_1 + b_3 c_2 a_1 + c_3 a_2 b_1)$$

Visualize the pattern this way: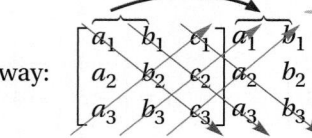

a copy of the first two columns

© **Problem 2** **Evaluating the Determinants of Matrices**

What are the following determinants?

Think

What can you do first to evaluate a 3 × 3 determinant?
Copy the first two columns to the right of the matrix.

$$\begin{bmatrix} 1 & 0 & -2 \\ 0 & 4 & -1 \\ 3 & 5 & 2 \end{bmatrix} \begin{matrix} 1 & 0 \\ 0 & 4 \\ 3 & 5 \end{matrix}$$

A det $\begin{bmatrix} 3 & -1 \\ 2 & 5 \end{bmatrix} = (3)(5) - (-1)(2) = 15 - (-2) = 17$

B det $\begin{bmatrix} 1 & 0 & -2 \\ 0 & 4 & -1 \\ 3 & 5 & 2 \end{bmatrix} = (1)(4)(2) + (0)(-1)(3) + (-2)(0)(5)$
$$- [(3)(4)(-2) + (5)(-1)(1) + (2)(0)(0)]$$
$$= 8 + 0 + 0 - (-24 - 5 + 0)$$
$$= 37$$

Check Use a graphing calculator.

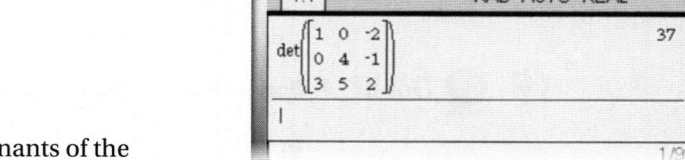

✓ **Got It?** **2.** What are the determinants of the
following matrices?

a. $\begin{bmatrix} 3 & 6 \\ 2 & 5 \end{bmatrix}$

b. $\begin{bmatrix} -2 & 0 \\ 3 & 0 \end{bmatrix}$

c. $\begin{bmatrix} 1 & 0 & 3 \\ 2 & 4 & 6 \\ 5 & -1 & 3 \end{bmatrix}$

You can use determinants to find the areas of polygons. Since all polygons can be divided into triangles, all you need is a way to find the area of a triangle.

take note

Key Concept Area of a Triangle

The area of a triangle with vertices (x_1, y_1), (x_2, y_2), and (x_3, y_3) is

$$\text{Area} = \frac{1}{2} |\det A| \text{ where } A = \begin{bmatrix} x_1 & y_1 & 1 \\ x_2 & y_2 & 1 \\ x_3 & y_3 & 1 \end{bmatrix}$$

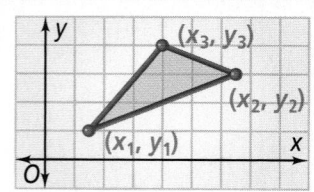

Problem 3 Finding the Area of a Polygon

Land One factor in flood safety along a levee is the area that will absorb water should the levee break. The coordinates shown are in miles. What is the area in the pictured California community?

(1.4, 2.0)

(1.9, 0.4)

(0, 0)

$$A = \begin{bmatrix} x_1 & y_1 & 1 \\ x_2 & y_2 & 1 \\ x_3 & y_3 & 1 \end{bmatrix}$$ Matrix for area formula

$$= \begin{bmatrix} 0 & 0 & 1 \\ 1.9 & 0.4 & 1 \\ 1.4 & 2.0 & 1 \end{bmatrix}$$ Substitute coordinates.

Think

Why must you use absolute value?
A determinant can be positive or negative. Area must be positive.

$\text{Area} = \frac{1}{2} |\det A|$ Area formula

$= 1.62$ Use a calculator to evaluate.

The area of the triangle is 1.62 mi^2.

Check for Reasonableness The area is approximately one half the area of a 1.9 by 2 rectangle. Thus, an area of about 1.6 units^2 is reasonable.

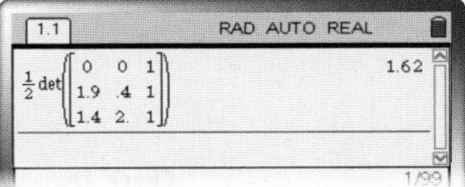

Got It? **3.** What is the area of the triangle with the given vertices?
   a. $(1, 3), (-3, 0), (5, 0)$ **b.** $(1, 3), (5, 8), (9, -1)$

The determinant of a matrix can help you determine whether the matrix has an inverse and, if it exists, to find the inverse.

take note

Key Concept Inverse of a 2 × 2 Matrix

Let $A = \begin{bmatrix} a & b \\ c & d \end{bmatrix}$.

If $\det A = 0$, then A is a **singular matrix** and has no inverse.

If $\det A \neq 0$, then the inverse of A, written A^{-1}, is

$$A^{-1} = \frac{1}{\det A} \begin{bmatrix} d & -b \\ -c & a \end{bmatrix} = \frac{1}{ad - bc} \begin{bmatrix} d & -b \\ -c & a \end{bmatrix}.$$

Problem 4 Finding the Inverse of a Matrix

Does the matrix $A = \begin{bmatrix} -3 & 6 \\ -1 & 3 \end{bmatrix}$ have an inverse? If it does, what is A^{-1}?

Think

Evaluate det A. If $det\ A \neq 0$, the matrix has an inverse.

Find A^{-1}. Switch elements on the main diagonal. Change signs on the other diagonal.

From above, det $A = -3$. For A, $a = -3$, $b = 6$, $c = -1$, and $d = 3$.

Multiply by the scalar and simplify the fractions.

Write

$$\begin{aligned} det\ A &= ad - bc \\ &= (-3)(3) - (6)(-1) \\ &= -9 - (-6) \\ &= -9 + 6 \\ &= -3 \end{aligned}$$
det $A \neq 0$, so A has an inverse.

$$A^{-1} = \frac{1}{det\ A} \begin{bmatrix} d & -b \\ -c & a \end{bmatrix}$$

$$= \frac{1}{-3} \begin{bmatrix} 3 & -6 \\ 1 & -3 \end{bmatrix}$$

$$= \begin{bmatrix} \frac{3}{-3} & \frac{-6}{-3} \\ \frac{1}{-3} & \frac{-3}{-3} \end{bmatrix}$$

$$= \begin{bmatrix} -1 & 2 \\ -\frac{1}{3} & 1 \end{bmatrix}$$

Check Use a graphing calculator.

Method 1

Check that $AA^{-1} = I$.

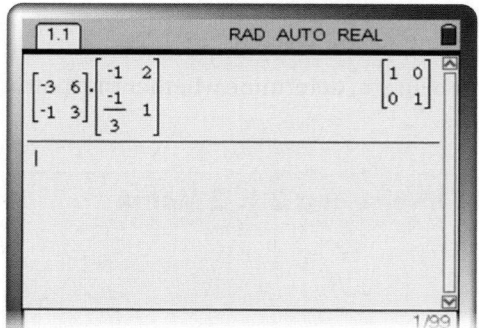

Method 2

Find A^{-1}.

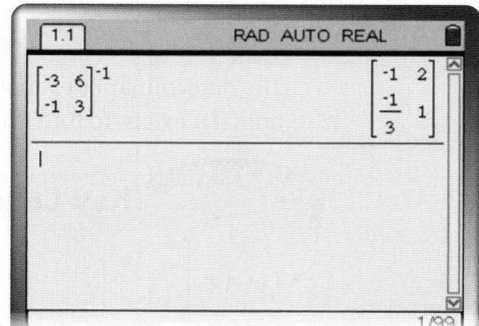

 Got It? 4. Does the matrix have an inverse? If so, what is it?

    a. $A = \begin{bmatrix} 4 & 2 \\ 3 & 2 \end{bmatrix}$ **b.** $B = \begin{bmatrix} 2 & 5 \\ -4 & -10 \end{bmatrix}$ **c.** $C = \begin{bmatrix} 7 & 4 \\ 5 & 3 \end{bmatrix}$

Problem 5 **Encoding and Decoding With Matrices**

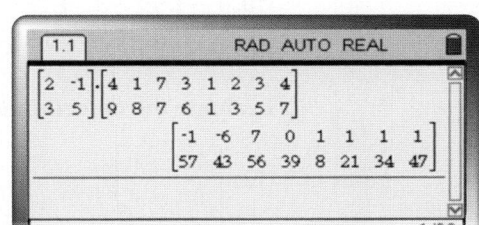

A How can you use matrix multiplication to encode the account number from the credit card?

Step 1 Select a coding matrix. $C = \begin{bmatrix} 2 & -1 \\ 3 & 5 \end{bmatrix}$

Step 2 Place the card information in a matrix with appropriate dimensions for multiplication by the coding matrix.

$A = \begin{bmatrix} 4 & 1 & 7 & 3 & 1 & 2 & 3 & 4 \\ 9 & 8 & 7 & 6 & 1 & 3 & 5 & 7 \end{bmatrix}$

Step 3 Multiply the coding matrix and the information matrix to encode the information. Use a calculator.

$CA = \begin{bmatrix} 2 & -1 \\ 3 & 5 \end{bmatrix}\begin{bmatrix} 4 & 1 & 7 & 3 & 1 & 2 & 3 & 4 \\ 9 & 8 & 7 & 6 & 1 & 3 & 5 & 7 \end{bmatrix}$

$= \begin{bmatrix} -1 & -6 & 7 & 0 & 1 & 1 & 1 & 1 \\ 57 & 43 & 56 & 39 & 8 & 21 & 34 & 47 \end{bmatrix}$

Step 4 The coded account number is
$-1, -6, 7, 0, 1, 1, 1, 1, 57, 43, 56, 39, 8, 21, 34, 47.$

B How do you use a decoding matrix to recover the account number?

Multiply the coded information by the inverse of the coding matrix.

$\begin{bmatrix} 2 & -1 \\ 3 & 5 \end{bmatrix}^{-1}\begin{bmatrix} -1 & -6 & 7 & 0 & 1 & 1 & 1 & 1 \\ 57 & 43 & 56 & 39 & 8 & 21 & 34 & 47 \end{bmatrix} = \begin{bmatrix} 4 & 1 & 7 & 3 & 1 & 2 & 3 & 4 \\ 9 & 8 & 7 & 6 & 1 & 3 & 5 & 7 \end{bmatrix}$

Got It? **5. a.** How can you use matrix multiplication and the coding matrix $\begin{bmatrix} 4 & 8 \\ -2 & 4 \end{bmatrix}$ to encode the credit card account number in Problem 5?

b. How can you use the inverse of the coding matrix to recover the credit card number?

 Lesson Check

Do you know HOW?

Evaluate the determinant of each matrix.

1. $\begin{bmatrix} 4 & -1 \\ 8 & 2 \end{bmatrix}$ **2.** $\begin{bmatrix} 1 & 0 & 0 \\ -1 & 2 & 3 \\ 4 & -1 & 2 \end{bmatrix}$

Find the inverse of each matrix, if it exists.

3. $\begin{bmatrix} 4 & 2 \\ 10 & 5 \end{bmatrix}$ **4.** $\begin{bmatrix} 5 & 2 \\ 7 & 3 \end{bmatrix}$

Do you UNDERSTAND?  **MATHEMATICAL PRACTICES**

5. Error Analysis What mistake did the student make when finding the determinant of $\begin{bmatrix} 2 & 5 \\ -3 & 1 \end{bmatrix}$?

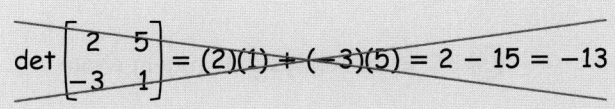

$\det \begin{bmatrix} 2 & 5 \\ -3 & 1 \end{bmatrix} = (2)(1) + (-3)(5) = 2 - 15 = -13$

6. Reasoning Explain why a 2×3 matrix does not have a multiplicative inverse.

Practice and Problem-Solving Exercises

MATHEMATICAL PRACTICES

 **Practice**

Determine whether the matrices are multiplicative inverses. ◄ **See Problem 1.**

7. $\begin{bmatrix} 3 & 2 \\ 4 & 3 \end{bmatrix}, \begin{bmatrix} 3 & -2 \\ -4 & 3 \end{bmatrix}$

8. $\begin{bmatrix} -3 & 7 \\ -2 & 5 \end{bmatrix}, \begin{bmatrix} -5 & 7 \\ -2 & 3 \end{bmatrix}$

9. $\begin{bmatrix} \frac{1}{5} & -\frac{1}{10} \\ 0 & \frac{1}{4} \end{bmatrix}, \begin{bmatrix} 5 & 2 \\ 0 & 4 \end{bmatrix}$

10. $\begin{bmatrix} 1 & 2 & -1 \\ -1.5 & -3 & 1.75 \\ 0 & -1 & 0.5 \end{bmatrix}, \begin{bmatrix} 1 & 0 & 2 \\ 3 & 2 & -1 \\ 6 & 4 & 0 \end{bmatrix}$

11. $\begin{bmatrix} 2 & 2 & 2 \\ -2 & 2 & -2 \\ -2 & -2 & -2 \end{bmatrix}, \begin{bmatrix} 2 & 2 & 2 \\ -2 & 2 & -2 \\ -2 & -2 & -2 \end{bmatrix}$

Evaluate the determinant of each matrix. ◄ **See Problems 2, 3, and 4.**

12. $\begin{bmatrix} 7 & 2 \\ 0 & -3 \end{bmatrix}$

13. $\begin{bmatrix} 6 & 2 \\ -6 & -2 \end{bmatrix}$

14. $\begin{bmatrix} 0 & 0.5 \\ 1.5 & 2 \end{bmatrix}$

15. $\begin{bmatrix} \frac{1}{2} & \frac{2}{3} \\ \frac{3}{5} & \frac{1}{4} \end{bmatrix}$

16. $\begin{bmatrix} -1 & 3 \\ 5 & 2 \end{bmatrix}$

17. $\begin{bmatrix} 5 & 3 \\ -2 & 1 \end{bmatrix}$

18. $\begin{bmatrix} 2 & -1 \\ 5 & -4 \end{bmatrix}$

19. $\begin{bmatrix} -4 & 3 \\ 2 & 0 \end{bmatrix}$

20. $\begin{bmatrix} 1 & 2 & 5 \\ 3 & 1 & 0 \\ 1 & 2 & 1 \end{bmatrix}$

21. $\begin{bmatrix} 1 & 4 & 0 \\ 2 & 3 & 5 \\ 0 & 1 & 0 \end{bmatrix}$

22. $\begin{bmatrix} -2 & 4 & 1 \\ 3 & 0 & -1 \\ 1 & 2 & 1 \end{bmatrix}$

23. $\begin{bmatrix} 2 & 3 & 0 \\ 1 & 2 & 5 \\ 7 & 0 & 1 \end{bmatrix}$

Graphing Calculator Evaluate the determinant of each 3 × 3 matrix.

24. $\begin{bmatrix} 1 & 0 & 0 \\ 0 & 1 & 0 \\ 0 & 0 & 1 \end{bmatrix}$

25. $\begin{bmatrix} 0 & -2 & -3 \\ 1 & 2 & 4 \\ -2 & 0 & 1 \end{bmatrix}$

26. $\begin{bmatrix} 12.2 & 13.3 & 9 \\ 1 & -4 & -17 \\ 21.4 & -15 & 0 \end{bmatrix}$

27. Use the map to determine the approximate area of the Bermuda Triangle.

Determine whether each matrix has an inverse. If an inverse matrix exists, find it.

28. $\begin{bmatrix} 2 & -1 \\ 1 & 0 \end{bmatrix}$

29. $\begin{bmatrix} 2 & 3 \\ 1 & 1 \end{bmatrix}$

30. $\begin{bmatrix} 2 & 3 \\ 2 & 4 \end{bmatrix}$

31. $\begin{bmatrix} 1 & 3 \\ 2 & 0 \end{bmatrix}$

32. $\begin{bmatrix} 6 & -8 \\ -3 & 4 \end{bmatrix}$

33. $\begin{bmatrix} 4 & 8 \\ -3 & -2 \end{bmatrix}$

34. $\begin{bmatrix} -1.5 & 3 \\ 2.5 & -0.5 \end{bmatrix}$

35. $\begin{bmatrix} 1 & -2 \\ 3 & 0 \end{bmatrix}$

36. Error Analysis A student wrote $\begin{bmatrix} 1 & \frac{1}{2} \\ \frac{1}{3} & \frac{1}{4} \end{bmatrix}$ as the inverse of $\begin{bmatrix} 1 & 2 \\ 3 & 4 \end{bmatrix}$. What mistake did the student make? Explain your reasoning.

37. Use the coding matrix in Problem 5 to encode the phone number (555) 358-0001. ◄ **See Problem 5.**

Evaluate each determinant.

38. $\begin{bmatrix} 4 & 5 \\ -4 & 4 \end{bmatrix}$
39. $\begin{bmatrix} -3 & 10 \\ 6 & 20 \end{bmatrix}$
40. $\begin{bmatrix} -\frac{1}{2} & 2 \\ -2 & 8 \end{bmatrix}$
41. $\begin{bmatrix} 6 & 9 \\ 3 & 6 \end{bmatrix}$

42. $\begin{bmatrix} 0 & 2 & -3 \\ 1 & 2 & 4 \\ -2 & 0 & 1 \end{bmatrix}$
43. $\begin{bmatrix} 5 & 1 & 0 \\ 0 & 2 & -1 \\ -2 & -3 & 1 \end{bmatrix}$
44. $\begin{bmatrix} 4 & 6 & -1 \\ 2 & 3 & 2 \\ 1 & -1 & 1 \end{bmatrix}$
45. $\begin{bmatrix} -3 & 2 & -1 \\ 2 & 5 & 2 \\ 1 & -2 & 0 \end{bmatrix}$

Ⓒ **46. Think About a Plan** Use matrices to find the area of the figure at the right.
- What shapes do you know how to find the area of?
- Can the polygon be broken into these shapes?
- How many shapes will you need to break the polygon into?

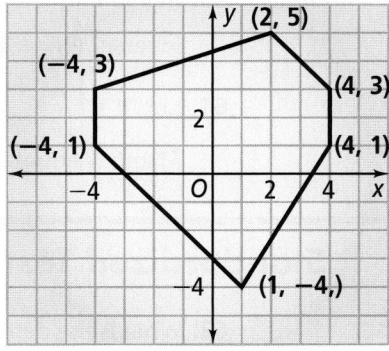

Ⓒ **47. Writing** Suppose $A = \begin{bmatrix} a & b \\ c & d \end{bmatrix}$ has an inverse. In your own words, describe how to switch or change the elements of A to write A^{-1}.

48. If matrix A has an inverse, what must be true?

I. $AA^{-1} = I$ II. $A^{-1}A = I$ III. $A^{-1}I = A^{-1}$

Ⓐ I only   Ⓒ I and II only

Ⓑ II only   Ⓓ I, II, and III

49. Geometry Use matrices to find the area of the figure at the right. Check your result by using standard area formulas.

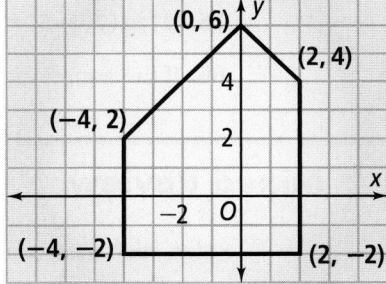

Determine whether each matrix has an inverse. If an inverse matrix exists, find it. If it does not exist, explain why not.

50. $\begin{bmatrix} 1 & 4 \\ 1 & 3 \end{bmatrix}$
51. $\begin{bmatrix} 4 & 7 \\ 3 & 5 \end{bmatrix}$
52. $\begin{bmatrix} -3 & 11 \\ 2 & -7 \end{bmatrix}$
53. $\begin{bmatrix} 2 & 0 \\ 0 & 2 \end{bmatrix}$

54. $\begin{bmatrix} -2 & 1 & -1 \\ 2 & 0 & 4 \\ 0 & 2 & 5 \end{bmatrix}$
55. $\begin{bmatrix} 2 & 0 & -1 \\ -1 & -1 & 1 \\ 3 & 2 & 0 \end{bmatrix}$
56. $\begin{bmatrix} 0 & 0 & 2 \\ 1 & 4 & -2 \\ 3 & -2 & 1 \end{bmatrix}$
57. $\begin{bmatrix} 1 & 2 & 6 \\ 1 & -1 & 0 \\ 1 & 0 & 2 \end{bmatrix}$

58. Writing Evaluate the determinant of each matrix. Describe any patterns.

a. $\begin{bmatrix} 1 & 2 & 3 \\ 1 & 2 & 3 \\ 1 & 2 & 3 \end{bmatrix}$
b. $\begin{bmatrix} -1 & -2 & -3 \\ -3 & -2 & -1 \\ -1 & -2 & -3 \end{bmatrix}$
c. $\begin{bmatrix} 1 & 2 & 3 \\ 2 & 3 & 1 \\ 1 & 2 & 3 \end{bmatrix}$
d. $\begin{bmatrix} -1 & 2 & -3 \\ 2 & -3 & -1 \\ -1 & 2 & -3 \end{bmatrix}$

59. Reasoning For what value of x will matrix A have no inverse? $A = \begin{bmatrix} 1 & 2 \\ 3 & x \end{bmatrix}$

Challenge

60. Reasoning Suppose $A = \begin{bmatrix} a & b \\ c & d \end{bmatrix}$. For what values of a, b, c, and d will A be its own inverse? (*Hint:* There is more than one correct answer.)

61. Let $M = \begin{bmatrix} a & b \\ c & d \end{bmatrix}$ and $N = \begin{bmatrix} e & f \\ g & h \end{bmatrix}$. Prove that the product of the determinants of M and N equals the determinant of the matrix product MN.

Standardized Test Prep

GRIDDED RESPONSE

SAT/ACT

62. What is the determinant of $\begin{bmatrix} -2 & -3 \\ 5 & 0 \end{bmatrix}$?

63. If $A = \begin{bmatrix} 4 & 2 \\ -3 & -1 \end{bmatrix}$, and the inverse of A is $x\begin{bmatrix} -1 & -2 \\ 3 & 4 \end{bmatrix}$, what is the value of x? Enter your answer as a fraction.

64. What is the value of $\frac{6!}{8!}$? Give your answer as a fraction in simplest terms.

65. If $\log(7y - 5) = 2$, what is the value of y?

66. If the equation for a circle is $x^2 + y^2 - 2x + 6y - 6 = 0$, what is its radius?

Mixed Review

Solve each matrix equation.

See Lesson 12-2.

67. $2\begin{bmatrix} -1 & 3 \\ -2 & 0 \end{bmatrix} - 3X = \begin{bmatrix} -8 & -9 \\ -7 & -3 \end{bmatrix}$

68. $2X + 3\begin{bmatrix} 4 & -6 \\ 8 & -3 \end{bmatrix} = \begin{bmatrix} -8 & 20 \\ -16 & 5 \end{bmatrix}$

Evaluate each expression.

See Lesson 11-1.

69. $6!$

70. $9!$

71. $\frac{15!}{5!}$

72. $\frac{12!}{6!3!}$

Get Ready! **To prepare for Lesson 12-4, do Exercises 73–76.**

Solve each system.

See Lesson 3-5.

73. $\begin{cases} x = 5 \\ x - y + z = 5 \\ x + y - z = -5 \end{cases}$

74. $\begin{cases} x - y - z = 9 \\ 3x + 2z = 12 \\ x = y - 2z \end{cases}$

75. $\begin{cases} -x + 2y + z = 0 \\ y = -2x + 3 \\ z = 3x \end{cases}$

76. $\begin{cases} 5x - 4y - 3z = 3 \\ z = y + x \\ x = 3y + 1 \end{cases}$

Do you know HOW?

Use matrices A, B, C, and D. Perform each operation.

$$A = \begin{bmatrix} 3 & 1 \\ 5 & 7 \end{bmatrix} \qquad B = \begin{bmatrix} 4 & 6 \\ 1 & 0 \end{bmatrix}$$

$$C = \begin{bmatrix} -5 & 3 \\ 1 & 9 \end{bmatrix} \qquad D = \begin{bmatrix} 1.5 & 2 \\ 9 & -6 \end{bmatrix}$$

1. $A + C$ **2.** $B - A$

3. $3D$ **4.** BA

5. $C(DB)$ **6.** $(AB)C$

Solve each matrix equation.

7. $X + \begin{bmatrix} -3 & 2 \\ 9 & -7 \end{bmatrix} = \begin{bmatrix} -3 & 5 \\ 4 & -5 \end{bmatrix}$

8. $\begin{bmatrix} 4 & -6 \\ -7 & 2 \end{bmatrix} - X = \begin{bmatrix} -1 & -7 \\ 3 & -2 \end{bmatrix}$

9. $X - \begin{bmatrix} -3 & 2 & -1 \\ 6 & -7 & 8 \end{bmatrix} = \begin{bmatrix} -2 & 3 & 5 \\ 1 & -3 & 7 \end{bmatrix}$

10. $3X + \begin{bmatrix} -2 & 1 \\ 7 & -3 \end{bmatrix} = \begin{bmatrix} 4 & -5 \\ -8 & 9 \end{bmatrix}$

11. $\begin{bmatrix} -3 & 2 \\ 5 & -1 \end{bmatrix} = \begin{bmatrix} 4 & 5 \\ -1 & 3 \end{bmatrix} - \frac{1}{2}X$

Solve each equation for x and y.

12. $\begin{bmatrix} -3 + 2x & 2 \\ 4 & -7y \end{bmatrix} = \begin{bmatrix} x - 4 & 2 \\ 4 & -35 \end{bmatrix}$

13. $\begin{bmatrix} 2x & 3 \\ -3 & -7x + y \end{bmatrix} = \begin{bmatrix} 3x + 2 & 3 \\ -3 & -4x \end{bmatrix}$

Evaluate the determinant of each matrix.

14. $\begin{bmatrix} -5 & 3 \\ 1 & 2 \end{bmatrix}$ **15.** $\begin{bmatrix} 3 & -1 \\ 4 & 2 \end{bmatrix}$

16. $\begin{bmatrix} -3 & 2 & 0 \\ -2 & 1 & 5 \\ -1 & 0 & 3 \end{bmatrix}$ **17.** $\begin{bmatrix} 5 & -1 & 1 \\ -3 & 0 & 2 \\ 7 & -8 & 4 \end{bmatrix}$

Find the inverse of each matrix, if it exists.

18. $\begin{bmatrix} -5 & 2 \\ 3 & -1 \end{bmatrix}$

19. $\begin{bmatrix} 4 & -5 \\ 1 & -6 \end{bmatrix}$

20. $\begin{bmatrix} -1 & 3 & 3 \\ 1 & 5 & 1 \\ 2 & 4 & -3 \end{bmatrix}$

21. $\begin{bmatrix} 3 & -1 & 2 \\ -1 & 0 & 2 \\ 1 & 3 & -1 \end{bmatrix}$

Given the vertices, find the area of each triangle.

22. $(-4, 1)$, $(5, 2)$, and $(2, -3)$

23. $(-2, -3)$, $(-5, 4)$, and $(4, 1)$

Do you UNDERSTAND?

24. Writing How can you decide whether you can multiply two matrices?

25. Open-Ended Write a matrix equation with solution $\begin{bmatrix} 12 & 7 & -3 & 8 \\ 9 & 0 & -11 & 1 \end{bmatrix}$.

26. Reasoning Suppose the product of two matrices has dimensions 4×3. If one of the matrices in the multiplication has dimensions 4×5, what are the dimensions of the other matrix?

27. Sales A store sells three kinds of pencils. The first matrix below shows the prices, in dollars, for each type. The second matrix shows the quantity sold for each type. Explain how you can find the total sales using the two matrices.

$$\begin{array}{c} \text{Type} \\ \begin{array}{ccc} A & B & C \end{array} \\ \begin{bmatrix} 3 & 4 & 2 \end{bmatrix} \end{array} \qquad \begin{array}{c} \text{Type} \\ \begin{array}{c} A \\ B \\ C \end{array} \begin{bmatrix} 20 \\ 10 \\ 15 \end{bmatrix} \end{array}$$

Inverse Matrices and Systems

© **Common Core State Standards**
N-VM.C.8 Add, subtract, and multiply matrices of appropriate dimensions.
MP 1, MP 2, MP 3, MP 4

Objective To solve systems of equations using matrix inverses and multiplication

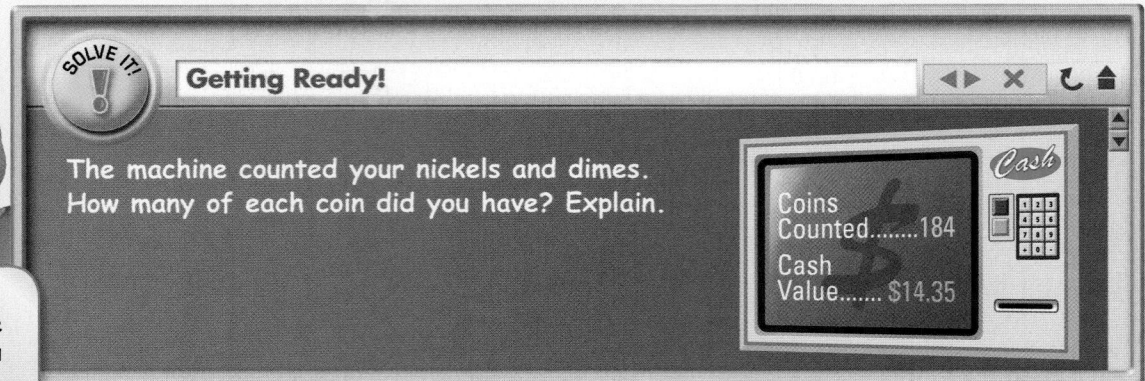

You know how to solve this one! The lesson will give you another method.

© **MATHEMATICAL PRACTICES** In Chapter 3, you used row operations on a matrix to solve a system of equations. Now you will solve systems by solving a matrix equation.

 Lesson Vocabulary
• coefficient matrix
• variable matrix
• constant matrix

Essential Understanding You can solve some matrix equations $AX = B$ by multiplying each side of the equation by A^{-1}, the inverse of matrix A.

If matrix A has an inverse, you can use it to solve the matrix equation $AX = B$. Multiply each side of the equation by A^{-1} to find X.

$$AX = B$$
$$A^{-1}AX = A^{-1}B \quad \text{Multiply each side by } A^{-1}.$$
$$IX = A^{-1}B \quad A^{-1}A = I, \text{ the identity matrix.}$$
$$X = A^{-1}B \quad IX = X$$

© **Problem 1** Solving a Matrix Equation Using an Inverse Matrix

What is the solution of each matrix equation?

A $\begin{bmatrix} 5 & 3 \\ 3 & 2 \end{bmatrix} X = \begin{bmatrix} 1 \\ -3 \end{bmatrix}$

Think

How do you know the equation has a solution?
Check det A. If det $A \neq 0$, you can solve the equation.

Step 1 Evaluate det A and find A^{-1}.

$$\det A = (5)(2) - (3)(3) = 1$$

$$A^{-1} = \frac{1}{\det A}\begin{bmatrix} d & -b \\ -c & a \end{bmatrix} = \frac{1}{1}\begin{bmatrix} 2 & -3 \\ -3 & 5 \end{bmatrix} = \begin{bmatrix} 2 & -3 \\ -3 & 5 \end{bmatrix}$$

Does it matter if you multiply by A^{-1} on the left or right side of A?
Even though
$A^{-1}A = AA^{-1} = I$,
you must multiply each side of the equation by A^{-1} on the left.

Step 2 Multiply each side of the equation by A^{-1}.

$$\begin{bmatrix} 2 & -3 \\ -3 & 5 \end{bmatrix}\begin{bmatrix} 5 & 3 \\ 3 & 2 \end{bmatrix}X = \begin{bmatrix} 2 & -3 \\ -3 & 5 \end{bmatrix}\begin{bmatrix} 1 \\ -3 \end{bmatrix}$$

$$\begin{bmatrix} (2)(5)+(-3)(3) & (2)(3)+(-3)(2) \\ (-3)(5)+(5)(3) & (-3)(3)+(5)(2) \end{bmatrix}X = \begin{bmatrix} (2)(1)+(-3)(-3) \\ (-3)(1)+(5)(-3) \end{bmatrix}$$

$$\begin{bmatrix} 1 & 0 \\ 0 & 1 \end{bmatrix}X = \begin{bmatrix} 11 \\ -18 \end{bmatrix}$$

$$X = \begin{bmatrix} 11 \\ -18 \end{bmatrix}$$

Check

Method 1

Use paper and pencil.

$$\begin{bmatrix} 5 & 3 \\ 3 & 2 \end{bmatrix}X \stackrel{?}{=} \begin{bmatrix} 1 \\ -3 \end{bmatrix}$$

$$\begin{bmatrix} 5 & 3 \\ 3 & 2 \end{bmatrix}\begin{bmatrix} 11 \\ -18 \end{bmatrix} \stackrel{?}{=} \begin{bmatrix} 1 \\ -3 \end{bmatrix}$$

$$\begin{bmatrix} (5)(11)+(3)(-18) \\ (3)(11)+(2)(-18) \end{bmatrix} \stackrel{?}{=} \begin{bmatrix} 1 \\ -3 \end{bmatrix}$$

$$\begin{bmatrix} 1 \\ -3 \end{bmatrix} = \begin{bmatrix} 1 \\ -3 \end{bmatrix} ✔$$

Method 2

Use a calculator.

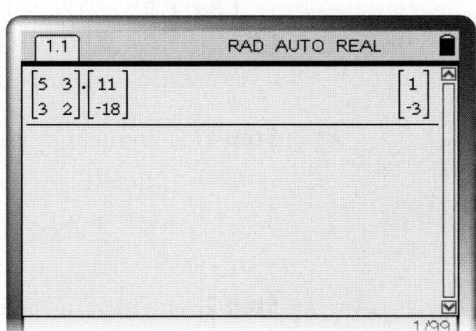

B $\begin{bmatrix} 3 & -9 \\ -2 & 6 \end{bmatrix}X = \begin{bmatrix} 2 \\ 5 \end{bmatrix}$

Evaluate det A.

det $A = (3)(6) - (-2)(-9) = 18 - 18 = 0$.

Matrix A has no inverse. The matrix equation has no solution.

 Got It? **1.** What is the solution of each matrix equation?

a. $\begin{bmatrix} 4 & 3 \\ 2 & 2 \end{bmatrix}X = \begin{bmatrix} -5 \\ 2 \end{bmatrix}$ **b.** $\begin{bmatrix} 7 & 5 \\ 4 & 3 \end{bmatrix}X = \begin{bmatrix} -3 & 0 \\ 1 & 4 \end{bmatrix}$ **c.** $\begin{bmatrix} 2 & 3 \\ 4 & 6 \end{bmatrix}X = \begin{bmatrix} 3 \\ -7 \end{bmatrix}$

You can write a system of equations as a matrix equation $AX = B$, using a **coefficient matrix**, a **variable matrix**, and a **constant matrix**.

System of Equations

$\begin{cases} 2x + 3y = 1 \\ 5x - 2y = 13 \end{cases}$

Matrix Equation

$$\begin{bmatrix} 2 & 3 \\ 5 & -2 \end{bmatrix}\begin{bmatrix} x \\ y \end{bmatrix} = \begin{bmatrix} 1 \\ 13 \end{bmatrix}$$

coefficient matrix, A variable matrix, X constant matrix, B

Problem 2 Writing a System as a Matrix Equation

What is the matrix equation that corresponds to each system?

Ⓐ $\begin{cases} 4x + 7y = 6 \\ -5x + 3y = 1 \end{cases}$

Step 1 Identify the coefficient, variable, and constant matrices.

coefficient matrix, A variable matrix, X constant matrix, B

$$\begin{bmatrix} 4 & 7 \\ -5 & 3 \end{bmatrix} \qquad \begin{bmatrix} x \\ y \end{bmatrix} \qquad \begin{bmatrix} 6 \\ 1 \end{bmatrix}$$

Step 2 Write the matrix equation.

$$\begin{bmatrix} 4 & 7 \\ -5 & 3 \end{bmatrix} \begin{bmatrix} x \\ y \end{bmatrix} = \begin{bmatrix} 6 \\ 1 \end{bmatrix}$$

Ⓑ $\begin{cases} 3a + 5b - 12c = 6 \\ 7b + 2c = 8 \\ 5a = 3c + 1 \end{cases}$

Plan

How is this system different from the one in part A?
There are three variables. Some terms have coefficients of 0, and the third equation has a variable on the right side of the = sign.

Step 1 Rewrite the system so the variables are in the same order in each equation.

$$\begin{cases} 3a + 5b - 12c = 6 \\ 7b + 2c = 8 \\ 5a = 3c + 1 \end{cases} \quad \rightarrow \quad \begin{cases} 3a + 5b - 12c = 6 \\ 7b + 2c = 8 \\ 5a \quad\quad - 3c = 1 \end{cases}$$

Step 2 Identify the coefficient, variable, and constant matrices.

coefficient matrix, A variable matrix, X constant matrix, B

$$\begin{bmatrix} 3 & 5 & -12 \\ 0 & 7 & 2 \\ 5 & 0 & -3 \end{bmatrix} \qquad \begin{bmatrix} a \\ b \\ c \end{bmatrix} \qquad \begin{bmatrix} 6 \\ 8 \\ 1 \end{bmatrix}$$

Step 3 Write the matrix equation.

$$\begin{bmatrix} 3 & 5 & -12 \\ 0 & 7 & 2 \\ 5 & 0 & -3 \end{bmatrix} \begin{bmatrix} a \\ b \\ c \end{bmatrix} = \begin{bmatrix} 6 \\ 8 \\ 1 \end{bmatrix}$$

 Got It? **2.** What is the matrix equation that corresponds to each system?

a. $\begin{cases} 3x - 7y = \quad 8 \\ 5x + y = -2 \end{cases}$ **b.** $\begin{cases} x + 3y + 5z = \quad 12 \\ -2x + \quad y - 4z = -2 \\ 7x - 2y \quad\quad = \quad 7 \end{cases}$ **c.** $\begin{cases} 2x + 3 = 8y \\ -x + y = -4 \end{cases}$

If the coefficient matrix has an inverse, you can use it to find a unique solution to a system of equations.

Problem 3 Solving a System of Two Equations

What is the solution of the system $\begin{cases} 5x - 4y = 4 \\ 3x - 2y = 3 \end{cases}$? Solve using matrices.

Think

Write the system as a matrix equation. Write the coefficient, variable, and constant matrices.

You need to find A^{-1}. Since det $A = 2$, A^{-1} exists.

Multiply each side of the matrix equation by A^{-1} on the left.

Solve for $\begin{bmatrix} x \\ y \end{bmatrix}$ and check.

Write

$$A \quad\quad X \quad = B$$

$$\begin{bmatrix} 5 & -4 \\ 3 & -2 \end{bmatrix} \begin{bmatrix} x \\ y \end{bmatrix} = \begin{bmatrix} 4 \\ 3 \end{bmatrix}$$

$$A^{-1} = \frac{1}{\det A} \begin{bmatrix} -2 & 4 \\ -3 & 5 \end{bmatrix}$$

$$= \frac{1}{(5)(-2) - (3)(-4)} \begin{bmatrix} -2 & 4 \\ -3 & 5 \end{bmatrix}$$

$$= \frac{1}{2} \begin{bmatrix} -2 & 4 \\ -3 & 5 \end{bmatrix}$$

$$= \begin{bmatrix} -1 & 2 \\ -\frac{3}{2} & \frac{5}{2} \end{bmatrix}$$

$$\begin{bmatrix} -1 & 2 \\ -\frac{3}{2} & \frac{5}{2} \end{bmatrix} \begin{bmatrix} 5 & -4 \\ 3 & -2 \end{bmatrix} \begin{bmatrix} x \\ y \end{bmatrix} = \begin{bmatrix} -1 & 2 \\ -\frac{3}{2} & \frac{5}{2} \end{bmatrix} \begin{bmatrix} 4 \\ 3 \end{bmatrix}$$

$$\begin{bmatrix} x \\ y \end{bmatrix} = \begin{bmatrix} (-1)(4) + (2)(3) \\ \left(-\frac{3}{2}\right)(4) + \left(\frac{5}{2}\right)(3) \end{bmatrix} = \begin{bmatrix} 2 \\ \frac{3}{2} \end{bmatrix}$$

The solution is $x = 2$, $y = \frac{3}{2}$.

$5(2) - 4\left(\frac{3}{2}\right) = 4$ ✔

$3(2) - 2\left(\frac{3}{2}\right) = 3$ ✔

Got It? 3. What is the solution of each system of equations? Solve using matrices.

a. $\begin{cases} 9x + 2y = 3 \\ 3x + y = -6 \end{cases}$

b. $\begin{cases} 4x - 6y = 9 \\ -10x + 15y = 8 \end{cases}$

The system $\begin{cases} -6x + 3y = 8 \\ 4x - 2y = 10 \end{cases}$ has coefficient matrix $A = \begin{bmatrix} -6 & 3 \\ 4 & -2 \end{bmatrix}$ with det $A = 0$. There is no inverse matrix and the system has no unique solution. Recall that this means the system either has no solutions (graphs are parallel lines in the 2×2 case) or infinitely many solutions (graphs are the same line in the 2×2 case). For the system above, the lines are parallel.

You can use a graphing calculator to solve a system of three equations.

 Problem 4 Solving a System of Three Equations

Multiple Choice On a new exercise program, your friend plans to do a run-jog-walk routine every other day for 40 min. She would like to burn 310 calories during each session. The table shows how many calories a person your friend's age and weight burns per minute of each type of exercise.

Calories Burned

Running (8 mi/h)	Jogging (5 mi/h)	Walking (3.5 mi/h)
12.5 cal/min	7.5 cal/min	3.5 cal/min

If your friend plans on jogging twice as long as she runs, how many minutes should she exercise at each rate?

(A) run 10, jog 5, walk 25

(C) run 5, jog 10, walk 25

(B) run 30, jog 15, walk 5

(D) run 10, jog 20, walk 10

Step 1 Define the variables.

Let x = number of minutes running.

y = number of minutes jogging.

z = number of minutes walking.

Think

How many equations do you need to solve this problem?

Since there are three variables you need three equations.

Step 2 Write a system of equations for the problem.

$$\begin{cases} 12.5x + 7.5y + 3.5z = 310 \\ x + y + z = 40 \\ 2x = y \end{cases} \rightarrow \begin{cases} 12.5x + 7.5y + 3.5z = 310 \\ x + y + z = 40 \\ 2x - y + 0z = 0 \end{cases}$$

Step 3 Write the system as a matrix equation.

$$\begin{bmatrix} 12.5 & 7.5 & 3.5 \\ 1 & 1 & 1 \\ 2 & -1 & 0 \end{bmatrix} \begin{bmatrix} x \\ y \\ z \end{bmatrix} = \begin{bmatrix} 310 \\ 40 \\ 0 \end{bmatrix}$$

Step 4 Use a calculator. Solve for the variable matrix.

Step 5 Interpret the solution.

Your friend should run for 10 min, jog for 20 min, and walk for 10 min.
The correct answer is D.

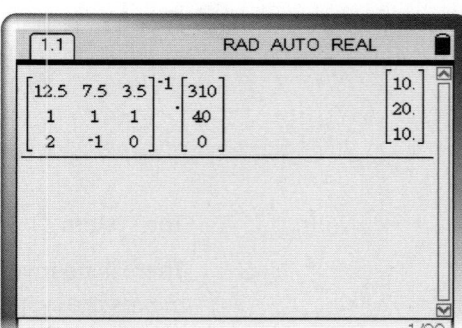

Got It? **4.** After following her exercise program from Problem 4 for a month, your friend plans to increase the calories she burns with each session. She still wants to exercise for 40 min every other day, but now she wants to burn 460 calories during each session. If she only runs and jogs, how many minutes of each exercise type should she do now?

 Lesson Check

Do you know HOW?

Write each system as a matrix equation.

1. $\begin{cases} -6x + 3y = 8 \\ 4x - 2y = 10 \end{cases}$

2. $\begin{cases} 2x + 3y = 12 \\ x - 2y + z = 9 \\ 6y - 4z = 8 \end{cases}$

Solve each system using a matrix equation. Check your answer.

3. $\begin{cases} x + 2y = 11 \\ x + 4y = 17 \end{cases}$

4. $\begin{cases} 2x - 3y = 6 \\ x + y = -12 \end{cases}$

Do you UNDERSTAND?  MATHEMATICAL PRACTICES

5. Error Analysis A student is trying to use the matrix equation below to solve a system of equations. What error did the student make? What matrix equation should the student use?

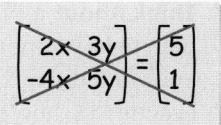

6. Reasoning Explain how to write the matrix equation $\begin{bmatrix} -2 & 3 \\ 4 & 1 \end{bmatrix} \begin{bmatrix} p \\ q \end{bmatrix} = \begin{bmatrix} 2 \\ -5 \end{bmatrix}$ as a system of linear equations.

 Practice and Problem-Solving Exercises  MATHEMATICAL PRACTICES

A **Practice** Solve each matrix equation. If an equation cannot be solved, explain why. ◀ See Problem 1.

7. $\begin{bmatrix} 12 & 7 \\ 5 & 3 \end{bmatrix} X = \begin{bmatrix} 2 & -1 \\ 3 & 2 \end{bmatrix}$

8. $\begin{bmatrix} 0 & -4 \\ 0 & -1 \end{bmatrix} X = \begin{bmatrix} 0 \\ 4 \end{bmatrix}$

 9. $\begin{bmatrix} 5 & 1 & 4 \\ 2 & -3 & -5 \\ 7 & 2 & -6 \end{bmatrix} X = \begin{bmatrix} 5 \\ 2 \\ 5 \end{bmatrix}$

10. $\begin{bmatrix} 6 & 10 & 13 \\ 4 & -2 & 7 \\ 0 & 9 & -8 \end{bmatrix} X = \begin{bmatrix} 84 \\ 18 \\ 56 \end{bmatrix}$

Write each system as a matrix equation. Identify the coefficient matrix, the variable matrix, and the constant matrix. ◀ See Problem 2.

11. $\begin{cases} x + y = 5 \\ x - 2y = -4 \end{cases}$

12. $\begin{cases} y = 3x - 7 \\ x = 2 \end{cases}$

13. $\begin{cases} 3a + 5b = 0 \\ a + b = 2 \end{cases}$

14. $\begin{cases} x + 3y - z = 2 \\ x + 2z = 8 \\ 2y - z = 1 \end{cases}$

15. $\begin{cases} r - s + t = 150 \\ 2r + t = 425 \\ s + 3t = 0 \end{cases}$

16. $\begin{cases} x + 2y = 11 \\ 2x + 3y = 18 \end{cases}$

Solve each system of equations using a matrix equation. Check your answers.  See Problem 3.

17. $\begin{cases} x + 3y = 5 \\ x + 4y = 6 \end{cases}$

18. $\begin{cases} p - 3q = -1 \\ -5p + 16q = 5 \end{cases}$

19. $\begin{cases} 300x - y = 130 \\ 200x + y = 120 \end{cases}$

20. $\begin{cases} x + 5y = -4 \\ x + 6y = -5 \end{cases}$

21. $\begin{cases} 2x + 3y = 12 \\ x + 2y = 7 \end{cases}$

22. $\begin{cases} 2x + 3y = 5 \\ x + 2y = 6 \end{cases}$

23. $\begin{cases} x + y + z = 4 \\ 4x + 5y = 3 \\ y - 3z = -10 \end{cases}$

24. $\begin{cases} 9y + 2z = 18 \\ 3x + 2y + z = 5 \\ x - y = -1 \end{cases}$

25. $\begin{cases} 9y + 2z = 14 \\ 3x + 2y + z = 5 \\ x - y = -1 \end{cases}$

26. Fitness Your classmate is starting a new fitness program. He is planning to ride  See Problem 4. his bicycle 60 minutes every day. He burns 7 Calories per minute bicycling at 11 mph and 11.75 Calories per minute bicycling at 15 mph. How long should he bicycle at each speed to burn 600 calories per hour?

Ⓑ Apply

Ⓒ 27. Think About a Plan Suppose you want to fill nine 1-lb tins with a snack mix. You plan to buy almonds for $2.45/lb, peanuts for $1.85/lb, and raisins for $.80/lb. You want the mix to contain twice as much nuts as raisins by weight. If you spend exactly $15, how much of each ingredient should you buy?
- How many equations do you need to represent this situation?
- How can you represent this system using a matrix equation?

28. Nutrition Suppose you are making a trail mix for your friends and want to fill three 1-lb bags. Almonds cost $2.25/lb, peanuts cost $1.30/lb, and raisins cost $.90/lb. You want each bag to contain twice as much nuts as raisins by weight. If you spent $4.45, how much of each ingredient did you buy?

Solve each system.

29. $\begin{cases} -3x + 4y = 2 \\ x - y = -1 \end{cases}$

30. $\begin{cases} x + 2y = 10 \\ 3x + 5y = 26 \end{cases}$

31. $\begin{cases} x - 3y = -1 \\ -6x + 19y = 6 \end{cases}$

32. $\begin{cases} x = 5 - y \\ 3y = z \\ x + z = 7 \end{cases}$

33. $\begin{cases} -x = -4 - z \\ 2y = z - 1 \\ x = 6 - y - z \end{cases}$

34. $\begin{cases} -b + 2c = 4 \\ a + b - c = -10 \\ 2a + 3c = 1 \end{cases}$

35. $\begin{cases} x + y + z = 4 \\ 4x + 5y = 4 \\ y - 3z = -9 \end{cases}$

36. $\begin{cases} x + y + z = 4 \\ 4x + 5y = 3 \\ y - 3z = -10 \end{cases}$

37. $\begin{cases} -2w + x + y = 0 \\ -w + 2x - y + z = 1 \\ -2w + 3x + 3y + 2z = 6 \\ w + x + 2y + z = 5 \end{cases}$

38. $\begin{cases} -2w + x + y = -2 \\ -w + 2x - y + z = -4 \\ -2w + 3x + 3y + 2z = 2 \\ w + x + 2y + z = 6 \end{cases}$

Solve each matrix equation. If the coefficient matrix has no inverse, write *no unique solution*.

39. $\begin{bmatrix} 1 & 1 \\ 1 & 2 \end{bmatrix}\begin{bmatrix} x \\ y \end{bmatrix} = \begin{bmatrix} 8 \\ 10 \end{bmatrix}$

40. $\begin{bmatrix} 2 & -3 \\ -4 & 6 \end{bmatrix}\begin{bmatrix} a \\ b \end{bmatrix} = \begin{bmatrix} 1 \\ -2 \end{bmatrix}$

41. $\begin{bmatrix} 2 & 1 \\ 4 & 3 \end{bmatrix}\begin{bmatrix} x \\ y \end{bmatrix} = \begin{bmatrix} 10 \\ -2 \end{bmatrix}$

Determine whether each system has a unique solution. If it has a unique solution, find it.

42. $\begin{cases} 20x + 5y = 240 \\ y = 20x \end{cases}$

43. $\begin{cases} 20x + 5y = 145 \\ 30x - 5y = 125 \end{cases}$

44. $\begin{cases} y = 2000 - 65x \\ y = 500 + 55x \end{cases}$

45. $\begin{cases} y = \frac{2}{3}x - 3 \\ y = -x + 7 \end{cases}$

46. $\begin{cases} 3x + 2y = 10 \\ 6x + 4y = 16 \end{cases}$

47. $\begin{cases} x + 2y + z = 4 \\ y = x - 3 \\ z = 2x \end{cases}$

48. Coordinate Geometry The coordinates (x, y) of a point in a plane are the solution of the system $\begin{cases} 2x + 3y = 13 \\ 5x + 7y = 31 \end{cases}$. Find the coordinates of the point.

49. Geometry A rectangle is twice as long as it is wide. The perimeter is 840 ft. Find the dimensions of the rectangle.

Ⓒ **50. Reasoning** Substitute each point $(-3, 5)$ and $(2, -1)$ into the slope-intercept form of a linear equation to write a system of equations. Then use the system to find the equation of the line containing the two points. Explain your reasoning.

Ⓒ **Challenge**   **Solve each matrix equation.**

51. $-2\begin{bmatrix} -2 & 0 \\ 0 & -1 \end{bmatrix} + \begin{bmatrix} 0 & -3 \\ 5 & -4 \end{bmatrix} X + \begin{bmatrix} 0 & -3 \\ 5 & -4 \end{bmatrix} = \begin{bmatrix} 19 & -27 \\ 10 & -24 \end{bmatrix}$

52. $\begin{bmatrix} 0 & -6 \\ 1 & 2 \end{bmatrix} - \begin{bmatrix} 5 & 2 \\ 4 & 3 \end{bmatrix} X - \begin{bmatrix} 2 & -26 \\ 3 & -18 \end{bmatrix} = \begin{bmatrix} 3 & 25 \\ 2 & 24 \end{bmatrix}$

53. $\begin{bmatrix} 7 & -5 & 3 \\ 0 & 1 & 3 \\ 8 & 4 & -2 \end{bmatrix} X + \begin{bmatrix} 5 \\ -9 \\ 0 \end{bmatrix} = \begin{bmatrix} 54 \\ -12 \\ 96 \end{bmatrix}$

54. $\begin{bmatrix} -1 & 0 & 2 \\ -6 & -5 & 0 \\ 1 & 4 & 1 \end{bmatrix} - \begin{bmatrix} -4 & 0 & 2 \\ 0 & 3 & 6 \\ 0 & 5 & 0 \end{bmatrix} X = \begin{bmatrix} -21 & 10 & 26 \\ -54 & 1 & -15 \\ 1 & 4 & -24 \end{bmatrix}$

Ⓒ **Open-Ended**   **Complete each system for the given number of solutions.**

55. infinitely many

$\begin{cases} x + y = 7 \\ 2x + 2y = \blacksquare \end{cases}$

56. one solution

$\begin{cases} x + y + z = 7 \\ y + z = \blacksquare \\ z = \blacksquare \end{cases}$

57. no solution

$\begin{cases} x + y + z = 7 \\ y + z = \blacksquare \\ y + z = \blacksquare \end{cases}$

58. Nutrition A caterer combines ingredients to make a paella, a Spanish fiesta dish. The paella weighs 18 lb, costs $29.50, and supplies 850 g of protein.
  a. Write a system of three equations to find the weight of each ingredient that the caterer uses.
  b. Solve the system. How many pounds of each ingredient did she use?

Paella Nutrition Chart

Food	Cost/lb	Protein/lb
Chicken	$1.50	100 g
Rice	$.40	20 g
Shellfish	$6.00	50 g

Standardized Test Prep

59. Which matrix equation represents the system $\begin{cases} 2x - 3y = -3 \\ -5x + y = 14 \end{cases}$?

Ⓐ $\begin{bmatrix} x \\ y \end{bmatrix}\begin{bmatrix} 2 & -3 \\ -5 & 1 \end{bmatrix} = \begin{bmatrix} -3 \\ 14 \end{bmatrix}$ Ⓒ $\begin{bmatrix} 2 & -3 \\ -5 & 1 \end{bmatrix}\begin{bmatrix} -3 \\ 14 \end{bmatrix} = \begin{bmatrix} x \\ y \end{bmatrix}$

Ⓑ $\begin{bmatrix} 2 & -3 \\ -5 & 1 \end{bmatrix}\begin{bmatrix} x \\ y \end{bmatrix} = \begin{bmatrix} -3 \\ 14 \end{bmatrix}$ Ⓓ $\begin{bmatrix} -3 \\ 14 \end{bmatrix}[x \quad y] = \begin{bmatrix} 2 & -3 \\ -5 & 1 \end{bmatrix}$

60. What is the value of x if $17e^{4x} = 85$?

Ⓕ $\frac{5}{4}$ Ⓖ $\frac{\ln 85}{17 \cdot \ln 4}$ Ⓗ $\frac{\ln 5}{4}$ Ⓘ $\frac{\ln 85 - \ln 17}{\ln 4}$

61. A set of data is normally distributed with a mean of 44 and a standard deviation of 3.2. Which statements are NOT true?
 I. 68% of the values are between 37.6 and 50.4
 II. 13.5% of the values are less than 40.8
 III. 5% of the values are lower than 37.6 or higher than 50.4

  Ⓐ I and II only Ⓒ II and III only

  Ⓑ I and III only Ⓓ I, II, and III

62. How can you write the three equations below as a matrix equation for a system? Explain your steps.
$2x - 3y + z + 10 = 0$
$x + 4y = 2z + 11$
$-2y + 3z + 7 = 3x$

Apply What You've Learned

MATHEMATICAL
PRACTICES
MP 4

In the Apply What You've Learned in Lesson 12-2, you represented quantities given in the problem on page 763 in matrix form. Now, you will use those matrices to write a matrix equation and a system of linear equations that model the problem.

 a. Define a variable for each unknown quantity in the problem. Then write a matrix X, the variable matrix that corresponds to the problem.

 b. Using matrix X from part (a) and matrix D from part (c) of the Apply What You've Learned on page 779, write a matrix equation, $AX = D$.

 c. Find the matrix product AX. Explain how the matrix equation $AX = D$ is equivalent to a system of equations that models the problem.

Geometric Transformations

Common Core State Standards

G-CO.A.5 Given a geometric figure and a rotation, reflection, or translation, draw the transformed figure . . . Specify a sequence of transformations . . . **Also G-CO.A.2, N-VM.C.6, N-VM.C.7, N-VM.C.8**

MP 1, MP 2, MP 3, MP 4

Objective To transform geometric figures using matrix operations

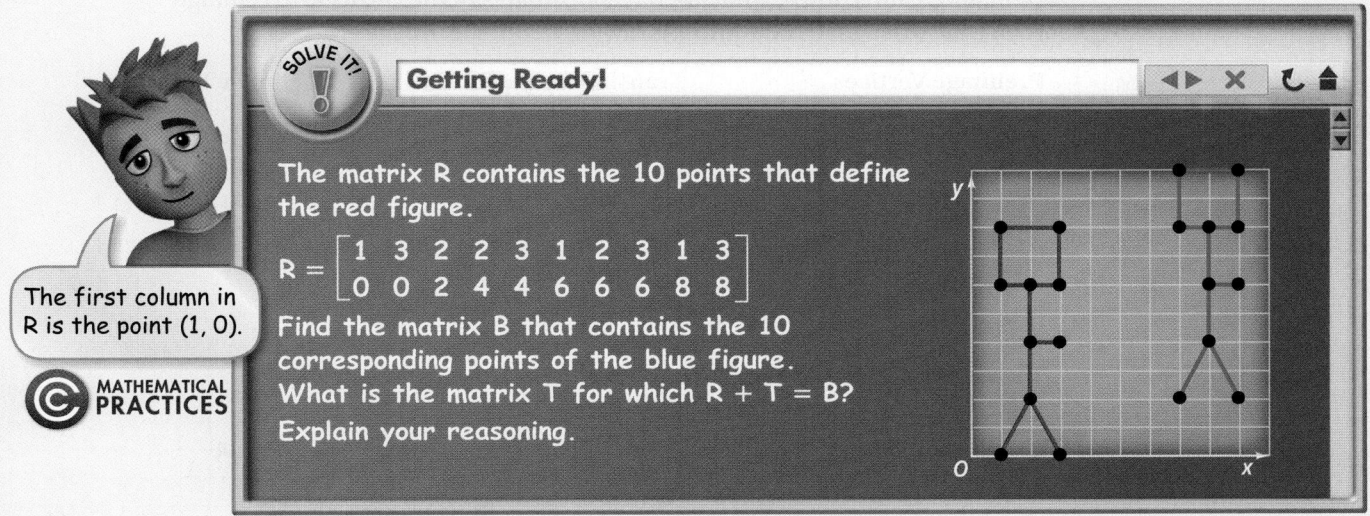

SOLVE IT!

Getting Ready!

The matrix R contains the 10 points that define the red figure.

$$R = \begin{bmatrix} 1 & 3 & 2 & 2 & 3 & 1 & 2 & 3 & 1 & 3 \\ 0 & 0 & 2 & 4 & 4 & 6 & 6 & 6 & 8 & 8 \end{bmatrix}$$

The first column in R is the point (1, 0).

MATHEMATICAL PRACTICES

Find the matrix B that contains the 10 corresponding points of the blue figure. What is the matrix T for which R + T = B? Explain your reasoning.

Matrix *T* in the Solve It *translates* the figure. Other transformations *dilate*, *rotate*, and *reflect* such geometric figures.

Lesson Vocabulary
- image
- preimage
- dilation
- rotation
- center of rotation

Essential Understanding You can multiply a 2×1 matrix representing a point by a 2×2 matrix to rotate the point about the origin or reflect the point across a line.

You can write the *n* points that define a figure as a $2 \times n$ matrix. For example, you can represent the four vertices of kite *ABCD* with the 2×4 matrix shown.

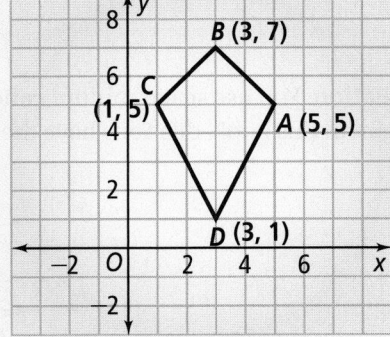

$$\begin{array}{c} x\text{-coordinate} \\ y\text{-coordinate} \end{array} \begin{array}{cccc} A & B & C & D \\ \begin{bmatrix} 5 & 3 & 1 & 3 \\ 5 & 7 & 5 & 1 \end{bmatrix} \end{array}$$

A change to a figure is a transformation of the figure. The transformed figure is the **image**. The original figure is the **preimage**. In the Solve It, the red figure is the preimage. The blue figure is the image.

The transformation of the figure in the Solve It is a translation—moving a figure to a new location without changing its size, shape, or orientation. You can use matrix addition to translate all the vertices of a figure in one step.

Problem 1 Translating a Figure

Kite $ABCD$ has vertices $(5, 5)$, $(3, 7)$, $(1, 5)$, and $(3, 1)$. If you translate it 8 units to the right and 5 units down, what are the coordinates of the vertices of its image $A'B'C'D'$? Use matrix addition. Draw $ABCD$ and its image.

Think

To translate 8 units to the right, what must you do to each x-coordinate?

Add 8 to each x-coordinate to translate 8 units to the right.

Preimage Vertices	Translation Matrix	Image Vertices

$$
\begin{matrix} A & B & C & D \end{matrix}
$$

Add 8 to each x-coordinate.

$$
\begin{matrix} A' & B' & C' & D' \end{matrix}
$$

$$
\begin{bmatrix} 5 & 3 & 1 & 3 \\ 5 & 7 & 5 & 1 \end{bmatrix} + \begin{bmatrix} 8 & 8 & 8 & 8 \\ -5 & -5 & -5 & -5 \end{bmatrix} = \begin{bmatrix} 13 & 11 & 9 & 11 \\ 0 & 2 & 0 & -4 \end{bmatrix}
$$

Subtract 5 from each y-coordinate.

The vertices of the preimage, $A(5, 5)$, $B(3, 7)$, $C(1, 5)$, and $D(3, 1)$ translate to the vertices $A'(13, 0)$, $B'(11, 2)$, $C'(9, 0)$, and $D'(11, -4)$ of the image.

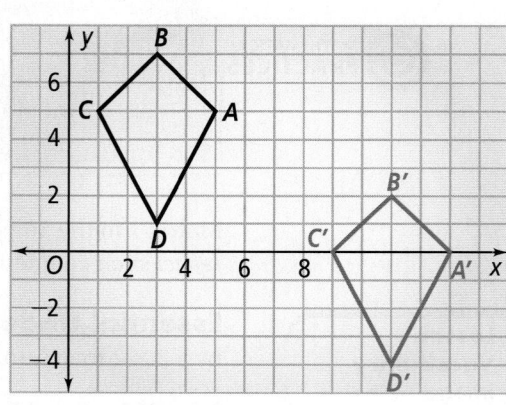

Got It? 1. a. Reasoning How would you translate the kite image $A'B'C'D'$ to the kite preimage $ABCD$?

  b. A pentagon has vertices $(0, -5)$, $(-1, -1)$, $(-5, 0)$, $(1, 3)$, and $(4, 0)$. Use matrix addition to translate the pentagon 3 units left and 2 units up. What are the vertices of the image? Graph the preimage and the image.

You enlarge or reduce a figure with a **dilation**. You use scalar multiplication to dilate a figure with center of dilation at the origin. In this book, dilations have their centers at the origin.

$$
2\begin{bmatrix} A & B & C \\ -1 & 3 & 2 \\ 0 & 2 & -1 \end{bmatrix} = \begin{bmatrix} A' & B' & C' \\ -2 & 6 & 4 \\ 0 & 4 & -2 \end{bmatrix}
$$

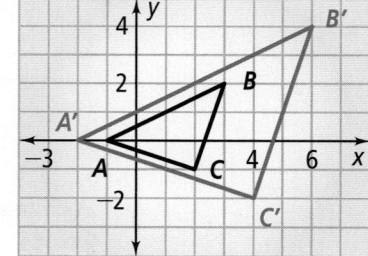

 **Problem 2** Dilating a Figure

Digital Media The width of the digital picture is presently 800 pixels (approximately 11.1 in.). Its height is 600 pixels (approximately 8.3 in.). You want to reduce its width as shown. This will allow the picture to fit on any computer screen without scrolling. Using a dilation, what are the coordinates of the vertices of the reduced image?

Know
- Current picture size
- Dilated picture width

Need
- Scale factor
- Dilated picture height

Plan
- Find the scale factor.
- Write a preimage matrix of the photo coordinates.
- Use scalar multiplication.

Step 1 Find the scale factor.

Dilated picture width: 640 pixels

Current picture width: 800 pixels

Scale factor $= \dfrac{\text{Dilated Width}}{\text{Current Width}} = \dfrac{640}{800}$, or 0.8.

Step 2 Multiply the preimage matrix by the scale factor, 0.8.

$$0.8\begin{bmatrix} 0 & 800 & 800 & 0 \\ 0 & 0 & 600 & 600 \end{bmatrix} = \begin{bmatrix} 0 & 640 & 640 & 0 \\ 0 & 0 & 480 & 480 \end{bmatrix}$$

The coordinates of the vertices of the reduced image are (0, 0), (640, 0), (640, 480), and (0, 480).

Got It? **2.** You are to enlarge a picture by the factor 2. The preimage is 5 in. by 3 in.
  a. Write a matrix of coordinates of the preimage vertices. Make one vertex (0, 0).
  b. What are the coordinates of the vertices of the image? Show the multiplication that you used for the dilation.
  c. **Reasoning** You enlarged the picture by the factor 2. By what factor did you increase its area?

A **rotation** turns a figure about a fixed point—the **center of rotation**. You can multiply a figure's vertex matrix by a rotation matrix to find the vertices of the rotation image. In this book, rotations are counterclockwise about the origin.

The matrix $\begin{bmatrix} 0 & -1 \\ 1 & 0 \end{bmatrix}$ rotates a figure 90°. A 90° rotation followed by another 90° rotation, or

$$\begin{bmatrix} 0 & -1 \\ 1 & 0 \end{bmatrix}\begin{bmatrix} 0 & -1 \\ 1 & 0 \end{bmatrix} = \begin{bmatrix} 0 & -1 \\ 1 & 0 \end{bmatrix}^2 = \begin{bmatrix} -1 & 0 \\ 0 & -1 \end{bmatrix},$$

is a 180° rotation. Rotate another 90° for a 270° rotation.

take note

Properties   Rotation Matrices for the Coordinate Plane

90° Rotation	180° Rotation	270° Rotation	360° Rotation
$\begin{bmatrix} 0 & -1 \\ 1 & 0 \end{bmatrix}$	$\begin{bmatrix} -1 & 0 \\ 0 & -1 \end{bmatrix}$	$\begin{bmatrix} 0 & 1 \\ -1 & 0 \end{bmatrix}$	$\begin{bmatrix} 1 & 0 \\ 0 & 1 \end{bmatrix}$

© **Problem 3** **Rotating a Figure**

Rotate the triangle with vertices $A(1, 1)$, $B(5, 2)$, and $C(-2, 3)$ by the indicated amount. What are the vertices of the image? Graph the preimage and the image in the same coordinate plane.

Plan

How do you rotate the triangle?
Multiply the 2 × 3 triangle matrix by the appropriate rotation matrix to get the 2 × 3 image matrix.

Ⓐ 90°

$$\begin{bmatrix} 0 & -1 \\ 1 & 0 \end{bmatrix}\begin{bmatrix} 1 & 5 & -2 \\ 1 & 2 & 3 \end{bmatrix}$$

$$= \begin{bmatrix} -1 & -2 & -3 \\ 1 & 5 & -2 \end{bmatrix}$$

The vertices of the image are $(-1, 1)$, $(-2, 5)$, and $(-3, -2)$.

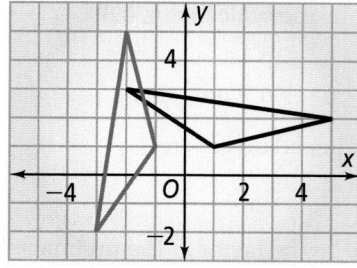

Ⓑ 180°

$$\begin{bmatrix} -1 & 0 \\ 0 & -1 \end{bmatrix}\begin{bmatrix} 1 & 5 & -2 \\ 1 & 2 & 3 \end{bmatrix}$$

$$= \begin{bmatrix} -1 & -5 & 2 \\ -1 & -2 & -3 \end{bmatrix}$$

The vertices of the image are $(-1, -1)$, $(-5, -2)$, and $(2, -3)$.

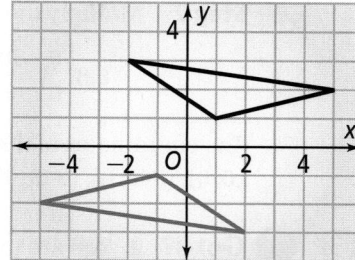

✓ **Got It?** **3.** Rotate the triangle with vertices $D(-3, 0)$, $E(-4, 4)$, and $F(1, 1)$ the indicated amount. What are the vertices of the image? Graph the preimage and the image in the same coordinate plane.
   a. 270°   **b.** 360°

A *reflection* maps a point or figure in the coordinate plane to its mirror image using a specific line as its line of reflection. In this book, the lines of reflection are $y = 0$ (the x-axis), $x = 0$ (the y-axis), $y = x$, and $y = -x$.

take note

Properties   Reflection Matrices for the Coordinate Plane

across x-axis	across y-axis	across $y = x$	across $y = -x$
$\begin{bmatrix} 1 & 0 \\ 0 & -1 \end{bmatrix}$	$\begin{bmatrix} -1 & 0 \\ 0 & 1 \end{bmatrix}$	$\begin{bmatrix} 0 & 1 \\ 1 & 0 \end{bmatrix}$	$\begin{bmatrix} 0 & -1 \\ -1 & 0 \end{bmatrix}$

Problem 4   Reflecting a Figure

Reflect the quadrilateral with vertices $A(2, 1)$, $B(8, 1)$, $C(8, 4)$, and $D(5, 5)$ across the indicated line. What are the vertices of the image? Graph the preimage and the image in the same coordinate plane.

Think

Does it matter what order you list the points in the preimage matrix?
Yes; you should list them in order as you move around the outside of the figure.

A y-axis

$$\begin{bmatrix} -1 & 0 \\ 0 & 1 \end{bmatrix} \begin{bmatrix} 2 & 8 & 8 & 5 \\ 1 & 1 & 4 & 5 \end{bmatrix}$$

$$= \begin{bmatrix} -2 & -8 & -8 & -5 \\ 1 & 1 & 4 & 5 \end{bmatrix}$$

The vertices of the image are $(-2, 1)$, $(-8, 1)$, $(-8, 4)$, and $(-5, 5)$.

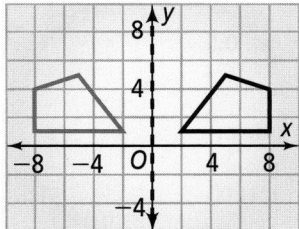

B $y = -x$

$$\begin{bmatrix} 0 & -1 \\ -1 & 0 \end{bmatrix} \begin{bmatrix} 2 & 8 & 8 & 5 \\ 1 & 1 & 4 & 5 \end{bmatrix}$$

$$= \begin{bmatrix} -1 & -1 & -4 & -5 \\ -2 & -8 & -8 & -5 \end{bmatrix}$$

The vertices of the image are $(-1, -2)$, $(-1, -8)$, $(-4, -8)$, and $(-5, -5)$.

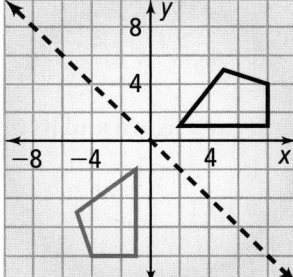

 Got It? **4.** Reflect the quadrilateral with vertices $E(1, 1)$, $F(3, 1)$, $G(6, 4)$, and $H(1, 3)$ across the indicated line. What are vertices of the image? Graph the preimage and the image in the same coordinate plane.

   a. x-axis   **b.** $y = x$

Lesson Check

Do you know HOW?

Use matrices to perform the following transformations on the triangle with vertices $A(1, 1)$, $B(2, 4)$, and $C(4, -1)$. State the coordinates of the vertices of the image.

1. Reduce by a factor of $\frac{1}{2}$.

2. Rotate $270°$.

3. Reflect across the line $y = x$.

Do you UNDERSTAND?

4. **Reasoning** Which transformations, translation, dilation, rotation, or reflection, leave the size of a figure unchanged? Explain.

5. **Writing** Describe two ways that the point $(3, 7)$ can be transformed to the point $(7, 3)$.

6. **Reasoning** What is true about
$$\begin{bmatrix} -3 & 0 \\ 0 & -3 \end{bmatrix}\begin{bmatrix} 1 & -2 & 4 \\ 1 & -1 & 2 \end{bmatrix} \text{ and } -3\begin{bmatrix} 1 & -2 & 4 \\ 1 & -1 & 2 \end{bmatrix}? \text{ Explain.}$$

Practice and Problem-Solving Exercises

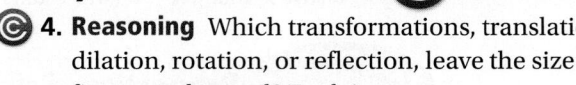

 **Practice**

Use matrix addition to find the coordinates of each image after a translation 3 units left and 5 units up. If possible, graph each pair of figures on the same coordinate plane.

See Problem 1.

7. $A(1, -3)$, $B(1, 1)$, $C(5, 1)$, $D(5, -3)$

8. $G(0, 0)$, $H(4, 4)$, $I(8, 0)$, $J(4, -4)$

9. $J(-10, 2)$, $K(-16, 1)$, $L(12, -5)$

10. $R(9, 3)$, $S(3, 6)$, $T(3, 3)$, $U(6, -3)$

Find the coordinates of each image after the given dilation.

See Problem 2.

11. $\begin{bmatrix} 0 & 2 & 5 & 8 \\ 0 & 4 & 5 & 1 \end{bmatrix}, 2$

12. $\begin{bmatrix} -7 & -3 & 4 \\ -5 & 4 & 0 \end{bmatrix}, 0.5$

13. $\begin{bmatrix} -8 & 2 & 3 & 1 & -2 \\ 6 & 4 & 0 & -4 & 0 \end{bmatrix}, 1.5$

Graph each figure and its image after the given rotation.

See Problem 3.

14. $\begin{bmatrix} 0 & -3 & 5 \\ 0 & 1 & 2 \end{bmatrix}; 90°$

15. $\begin{bmatrix} -1 & 0 & 5 \\ -1 & 5 & 0 \end{bmatrix}; 180°$

16. $\begin{bmatrix} -5 & 6 & 0 \\ -1 & 2 & 4 \end{bmatrix}; 90°$

Find the coordinates of each image after the given rotation.

17. $\begin{bmatrix} 3 & 6 & 3 & 6 \\ -3 & 3 & 3 & -3 \end{bmatrix}; 270°$

18. $\begin{bmatrix} 0 & 4 & 8 & 6 \\ 0 & 4 & 4 & 2 \end{bmatrix}; 360°$

19. $\begin{bmatrix} 1 & 2 & 3 & 4 & 2.5 \\ 3 & 2 & 2 & 3 & 5 \end{bmatrix}; 180°$

Graph each figure and its image after reflection across the given line.

See Problem 4.

20. $\begin{bmatrix} 0 & -3 & 5 \\ 0 & 1 & 2 \end{bmatrix}; y = x$

21. $\begin{bmatrix} -1 & 0 & 5 \\ -1 & 5 & 0 \end{bmatrix}; y\text{-axis}$

22. $\begin{bmatrix} -3 & -5 & -10 \\ 4 & 7 & 1 \end{bmatrix}; x\text{-axis}$

Find the coordinates of each image after reflection across the given line.

23. $\begin{bmatrix} 3 & 6 & 3 & 6 \\ -3 & 3 & 3 & -3 \end{bmatrix}; y = -x$

24. $\begin{bmatrix} 0 & 4 & 8 & 6 \\ 0 & 4 & 4 & 2 \end{bmatrix}; x\text{-axis}$

25. $\begin{bmatrix} 1 & 2 & 3 & 4 & 2.5 \\ 3 & 2 & 2 & 3 & 5 \end{bmatrix}; y = x$

 **Apply**

Geometry Each matrix represents the vertices of a polygon. Translate each figure 5 units left and 1 unit up. Express your answer as a matrix.

26. $\begin{bmatrix} -3 & -3 & 2 & 2 \\ -2 & -4 & -2 & -4 \end{bmatrix}$
  27. $\begin{bmatrix} -3 & 0 & 3 & 0 \\ -9 & -6 & -9 & -12 \end{bmatrix}$
  28. $\begin{bmatrix} 0 & 1 & -4 \\ 0 & 3 & 5 \end{bmatrix}$

For Exercises 29–32, use $\triangle ABC$. Write the coordinates of each image in matrix form.

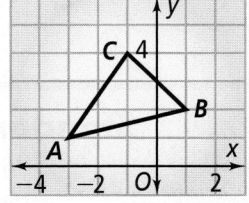

29. a translation 2 units left and 3 units down

30. a dilation half the original size

31. a rotation of 180°

32. a reflection across the x-axis

33. Think About a Plan In an upcoming cartoon, the hero is a gymnast. In one scene he swings around a high bar. Describe the rotation matrices that would be needed so four frames of the movie would show the illustrated motion (below), one frame after the other.
  • What do you need to do first to describe the motion?
  • Can you use just one rotation matrix, or do you need three?

Frame 1	Frame 2	Frame 3	Frame 4
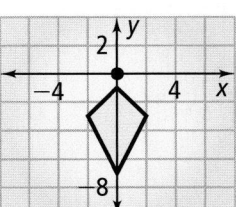	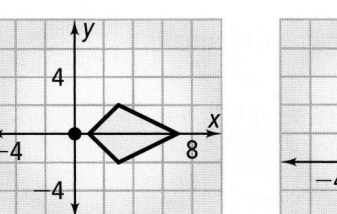	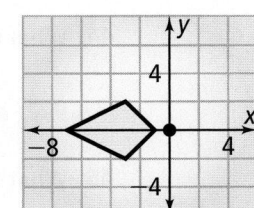	

34. Animation Suppose you want the cartoon of the gymnast in the previous exercise to show two revolutions around the bar. What rotation matrices are needed so eight frames of the movie would show the illustrated motion, one frame after the other.

35. Writing Explain why you might want to represent a transformation as a matrix.

Use matrices to represent the vertices of graph f and graph g. Name each transformation.

36. 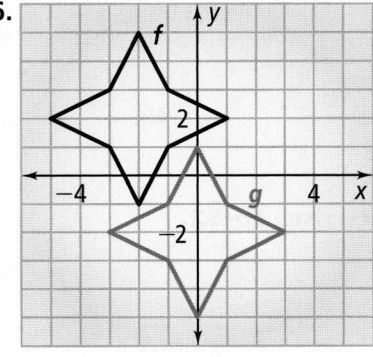 **37.** 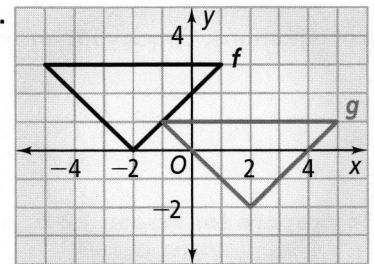 **38.**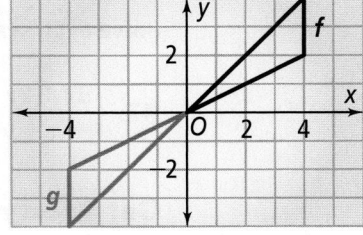

Challenge **Geometry** Each matrix represents the vertices of a transformed polygon. Write a matrix to represent the vertices of the image before each transformation.

39. $\begin{bmatrix} -3 & 0.5 & -5 \\ 0 & 3 & 3 \end{bmatrix}$; dilation of 2

40. $\begin{bmatrix} 3 & 4.5 & 5 & 3.5 \\ 3 & 1.5 & 2 & 4 \end{bmatrix}$; rotation of 90°

Ⓒ **41. Writing** Explain why a reflection of a matrix of points from a function table across the line $y = x$ is equivalent to finding the inverse of the function.

Standardized Test Prep

SAT/ACT

42. What are the coordinates of $X(5, 1)$, $Y(-5, -3)$, and $Z(-1, 3)$ reflected across the line $y = x$?

  Ⓐ $X'(-5, -1)$, $Y'(5, 3)$, $Z'(1, -3)$ Ⓒ $X'(-1, -5)$, $Y'(3, 5)$, $Z'(-3, 1)$

  Ⓑ $X'(1, 5)$, $Y'(-3, -5)$, $Z'(3, -1)$ Ⓓ $X'(5, 1)$, $Y'(-5, -3)$, $Z'(-1, 3)$

43. Given $P = \begin{bmatrix} 4 & 3 & -2 \\ -1 & 0 & 5 \end{bmatrix}$ and $Q = \begin{bmatrix} 3 & -2 & -5 \\ -1 & -2 & -1 \end{bmatrix}$, what is $2P - 3Q$?

  Ⓕ $\begin{bmatrix} 1 & -5 & 3 \\ 0 & -2 & 6 \end{bmatrix}$ Ⓖ $\begin{bmatrix} 17 & 0 & 19 \\ -5 & 6 & 7 \end{bmatrix}$ Ⓗ $\begin{bmatrix} -1 & 12 & 11 \\ 1 & 6 & 13 \end{bmatrix}$ Ⓘ $\begin{bmatrix} 1 & 5 & 3 \\ 0 & 2 & 6 \end{bmatrix}$

44. What is the solution to the matrix equation $\begin{bmatrix} 3 & -1 \\ -1 & 2 \end{bmatrix}\begin{bmatrix} a \\ b \end{bmatrix} = \begin{bmatrix} 7 \\ -9 \end{bmatrix}$?

  Ⓐ $a = 7, b = -9$ Ⓑ $a = 2, b = 1$ Ⓒ $a = \frac{7}{3}, b = \frac{9}{2}$ Ⓓ $a = 1, b = -4$

45. What is the determinant of $\begin{bmatrix} -5 & 4 \\ -9 & 7 \end{bmatrix}$?

  Ⓕ -71 Ⓖ 1 Ⓗ -3 Ⓘ 71

Short Response

46. The results of a college entrance exam are shown at the right. What is the probability that a student's score on the verbal section is from 401 to 514?

Section	Mean	Standard Deviation
Math	505	111
Verbal	514	113

Mixed Review

Solve each system of equations. Check your answers.

See Lesson 12-4.

47. $\begin{cases} 3x + 2y = 5 \\ -x + y = -5 \end{cases}$

48. $\begin{cases} x + 4y + 3z = 3 \\ 2x - 5y - z = 5 \\ 3x + 2y - 2z = -3 \end{cases}$

49. $\begin{cases} x + y + z = -1 \\ y + 3z = -5 \\ x + z = -2 \end{cases}$

Get Ready! **To prepare for Lesson 12-6, do Exercises 50–52.**

Find each product.

See Lesson 12-2.

50. $0.8\begin{bmatrix} 20 \\ 15 \end{bmatrix}$

51. $\begin{bmatrix} 1 & -2 \end{bmatrix}\begin{bmatrix} 2 \\ -5 \end{bmatrix}$

52. $\begin{bmatrix} -3 & -5 \end{bmatrix}\begin{bmatrix} -4 \\ -2 \end{bmatrix}$

© **Common Core State Standards**

N-VM.B.5a Represent scalar multiplication graphically by scaling vectors . . . perform scalar multiplication component-wise. **Also N-VM.A.2, N-VM.A.3, N-VM.B.4, N-VM.B.5b**

MP 1, MP 2, MP 3, MP 4

Objective To use basic vector operations and the dot product

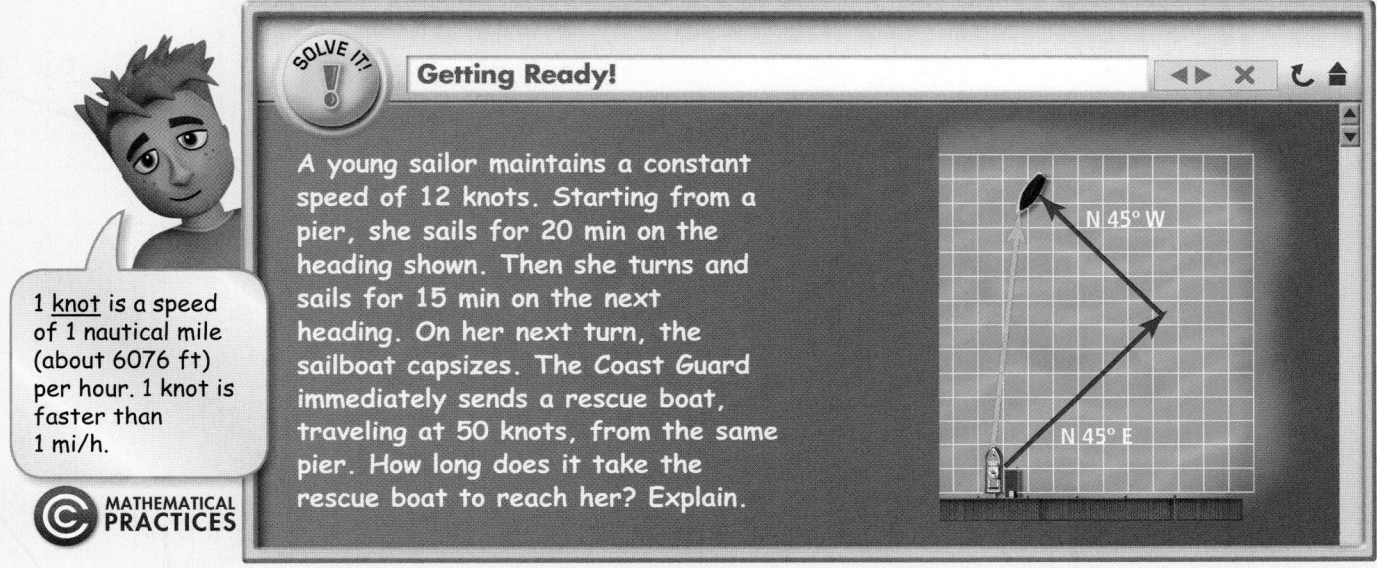

SOLVE IT!

Getting Ready!

A young sailor maintains a constant speed of 12 knots. Starting from a pier, she sails for 20 min on the heading shown. Then she turns and sails for 15 min on the next heading. On her next turn, the sailboat capsizes. The Coast Guard immediately sends a rescue boat, traveling at 50 knots, from the same pier. How long does it take the rescue boat to reach her? Explain.

1 <u>knot</u> is a speed of 1 nautical mile (about 6076 ft) per hour. 1 knot is faster than 1 mi/h.

© **MATHEMATICAL PRACTICES**

In the Solve It, the Coast Guard had to know both distance and direction to rescue the sailor.

Lesson Vocabulary
• vector
• magnitude
• initial point
• terminal point
• dot product
• normal vectors

Essential Understanding A *vector* is a mathematical object that has both *magnitude* (size) and direction.

take note

Key Concept Vectors in Two Dimensions

A vector has magnitude and direction. You can describe a vector as a directed line segment with initial and terminal points. Two such segments with the same magnitude and direction represent the same vector.

$\mathbf{v} = \overrightarrow{PQ}$ where $P = (1, 1)$ and $Q = (3, 4)$ and
$\mathbf{v} = \overrightarrow{RS}$ where $R = (-1, 2)$ and $S = (1, 5)$

represent the same vector.

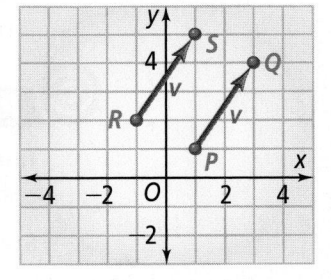

A **vector** has both magnitude and direction. You often use an arrow to represent a vector. The **magnitude** of a vector **v** is the length of the arrow. You can denote it as $|\mathbf{v}|$. You show the direction of the vector by the **initial point** and the **terminal point** of the arrow.

The position of a vector is not important. For this reason, a vector **v** in standard position has initial point $(0, 0)$ and is completely determined by its terminal point (a, b). You can represent **v** in component form as $\langle a, b \rangle$. Use the Pythagorean theorem to find the magnitude of **v**, $|\mathbf{v}| = \sqrt{a^2 + b^2}$.

Ⓒ **Problem 1** Representing a Vector

What is the component form of the vector v = $\overrightarrow{PQ}$ shown here?

Think

For component form, the initial point must be at the origin. You need to move it 1 unit left and 2 units down.

You must move the terminal point in the same way.

The new terminal point is the component form.

Write

$(1 - 1, 2 - 2) = (0, 0)$

$(8 - 1, 5 - 2) = (7, 3)$

$\mathbf{v} = \langle 7, 3 \rangle$

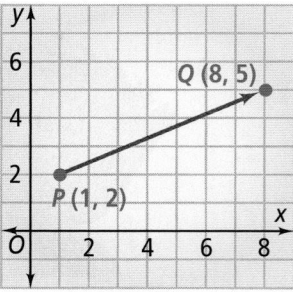

✓ **Got It?** **1.** What are the component forms of the two vectors shown here?

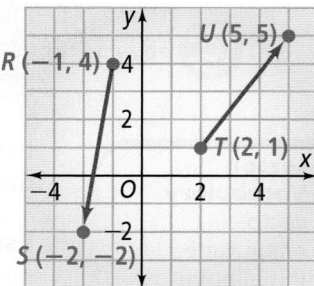

You can also write a vector $\mathbf{v} = \langle a, b \rangle$ in matrix form, $\mathbf{v} = \begin{bmatrix} a \\ b \end{bmatrix}$. By writing in matrix form, you can use matrix transformations to transform a vector.

Ⓒ **Problem 2** Rotating a Vector

Rotate the vector w = $\langle 3, -2 \rangle$ by 90°. What is the component form of the resulting vector?

Think

How can you rotate points in the coordinate plane?
You can multiply by a rotation matrix.

Step 1 Write the vector in matrix form. $\begin{bmatrix} 3 \\ -2 \end{bmatrix}$

Step 2 Multiply the vector by the 90° rotation matrix.

$$\begin{bmatrix} 0 & -1 \\ 1 & 0 \end{bmatrix} \begin{bmatrix} 3 \\ -2 \end{bmatrix} = \begin{bmatrix} 2 \\ 3 \end{bmatrix}$$

Step 3 The resulting vector is $\langle 2, 3 \rangle$.

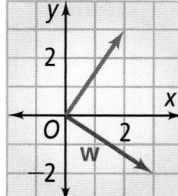

Got It? 2. a. Rotate the vector $\mathbf{v} = \langle -3, 5 \rangle$ by 270°. What is the component form of the resulting vector?

        b. Reasoning What other matrix transformations can you apply to vectors in matrix form?

You can use real number operations to define operations involving vectors.

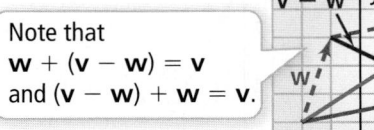 **Properties**   **Operations With Vectors**

Given $\mathbf{v} = \langle v_1, v_2 \rangle$, $\mathbf{w} = \langle w_1, w_2 \rangle$, and any real number k:

$$\mathbf{v} + \mathbf{w} = \langle v_1 + w_1, v_2 + w_2 \rangle$$
$$\mathbf{v} - \mathbf{w} = \langle v_1 - w_1, v_2 - w_2 \rangle$$
$$k\mathbf{v} = \langle kv_1, kv_2 \rangle$$

Note that
$\mathbf{w} + (\mathbf{v} - \mathbf{w}) = \mathbf{v}$
and $(\mathbf{v} - \mathbf{w}) + \mathbf{w} = \mathbf{v}$.

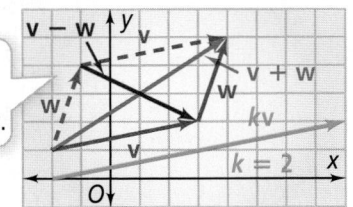

Problem 3   **Adding and Subtracting Vectors**

Let $\mathbf{u} = \langle -2, 3 \rangle$ and $\mathbf{v} = \langle 5, -2 \rangle$. What is $|\mathbf{u} + \mathbf{v}|$, rounded to the nearest hundredth?

To find $\mathbf{u} + \mathbf{v}$, use the tip-to-tail method shown above.

Step 1   Draw $\mathbf{u} = \langle -2, 3 \rangle$ in standard position.

Step 2   At the tip of $\mathbf{u}$, draw $\mathbf{v} = \langle 5, -2 \rangle$ from $(-2, 3)$ to $(3, 1)$.

Step 3   Draw $\mathbf{u} + \mathbf{v}$ to have the initial point of $\mathbf{u}$ and the terminal point of $\mathbf{v}$.

Step 4   Express $\mathbf{u} + \mathbf{v}$ in component form. $\mathbf{u} + \mathbf{v} = \langle 3, 1 \rangle$

Step 5 $|\mathbf{u} + \mathbf{v}| = \sqrt{3^2 + 1^2} = \sqrt{10} \approx 3.16$

Check $\mathbf{u} + \mathbf{v} = \langle -2, 3 \rangle + \langle 5, -2 \rangle = \langle -2 + 5, 3 + (-2) \rangle = \langle 3, 1 \rangle$

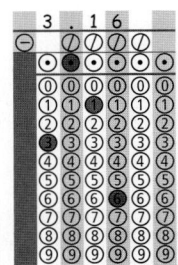

> **Think**
>
> **How do you draw v with initial point (−2, 3)?**
> Use $(-2 + 5, 3 - 2) = (3, 1)$ for the terminal point.

 Got It? 3. Using the vectors given in Problem 3, what is $|\mathbf{u} - \mathbf{v}|$?

Scalar multiplication of a vector by a positive number (other than 1) changes only the magnitude. Multiplication by a negative number (other than −1) changes the magnitude and reverses the direction of the vector.

For $\mathbf{v} = \langle 1, -2 \rangle$ and $\mathbf{w} = \langle 2, 3 \rangle$, what are the graphs of the following vectors?

Plan

How should you start?
Begin by finding the component form of the scaled vectors.

A $\mathbf{v}$ and $3\mathbf{v}$

$3\mathbf{v} = 3\langle 1, -2 \rangle$

$= \langle 3(1), 3(-2) \rangle$

$= \langle 3, -6 \rangle$

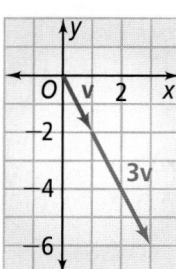

B $\mathbf{w}$ and $-2\mathbf{w}$

$-2\mathbf{w} = -2\langle 2, 3 \rangle$

$= \langle -2(2), -2(3) \rangle$

$= \langle -4, -6 \rangle$

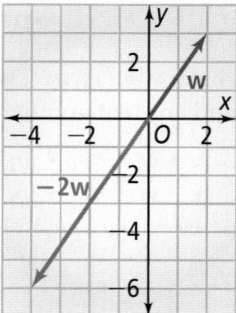

✓ **Got It?** **4.** Given $\mathbf{u} = \langle -2, 4 \rangle$, what are the graphs of the following vectors?

a. $-\mathbf{u}$ **b.** $\frac{1}{2}\mathbf{u}$

If $\mathbf{v} = \langle v_1, v_2 \rangle$ and $\mathbf{w} = \langle w_1, w_2 \rangle$, the **dot product** $\mathbf{v} \cdot \mathbf{w}$ is $v_1 w_1 + v_2 w_2$.
If $\mathbf{v} \cdot \mathbf{w} = 0$, the two vectors are **normal**, or perpendicular, to each other.

 Problem 5 Finding Dot Products

Are the following vectors normal?

Think

How can you check your results?
If the slopes of the lines containing the vectors are negative reciprocals, the vectors are normal.

A $\mathbf{t} = \langle 2, -5 \rangle$, $\mathbf{u} = \langle 7, 3 \rangle$

$\mathbf{t} \cdot \mathbf{u} = (2)(7) + (-5)(3)$

$= 14 + (-15) = -1$

$\mathbf{t}$ and $\mathbf{u}$ are not normal.

Check

$m_{\mathbf{t}} = \dfrac{-5 - 0}{2 - 0} = -\dfrac{5}{2}$

$m_{\mathbf{u}} = \dfrac{3 - 0}{7 - 0} = \dfrac{3}{7}$

not perpendicular ✔

B $\mathbf{v} = \langle 10, -4 \rangle$, $\mathbf{w} = \langle 2, 5 \rangle$

$\mathbf{v} \cdot \mathbf{w} = (10)(2) + (-4)(5)$

$= 20 - 20 = 0$

$\mathbf{v}$ and $\mathbf{w}$ are normal.

Check

$m_{\mathbf{v}} = \dfrac{-4 - 0}{10 - 0} = -\dfrac{2}{5}$

$m_{\mathbf{w}} = \dfrac{5 - 0}{2 - 0} = \dfrac{5}{2}$

perpendicular ✔

✓ **Got It?** **5.** Are the following vectors normal?

a. $\langle -2, 6 \rangle$, $\langle -9, -18 \rangle$ **b.** $\left\langle 3, \frac{5}{6} \right\rangle$, $\left\langle -\frac{10}{9}, 4 \right\rangle$

Lesson Check

Do you know HOW?

Let $P = (-2, 2)$, $Q = (3, 4)$, $R = (-2, 5)$, and $S = (2, -8)$. What are the component forms of the following vectors?

1. $\overrightarrow{PQ}$

2. $\overrightarrow{RS} + \overrightarrow{PQ}$

3. $\overrightarrow{RS} - \overrightarrow{RQ}$

4. $-5\overrightarrow{PR}$

Do you UNDERSTAND?

5. Vocabulary Which of the following vectors has the greatest magnitude? Explain.

$\mathbf{a} = \langle 3, 4 \rangle$ $\qquad$ $\mathbf{b} = \langle -4, 3 \rangle$ $\qquad$ $\mathbf{c} = \langle 4, -3 \rangle$

6. Error Analysis Your friend says that the magnitude of vector $\langle 8, 3 \rangle$ is 4 times that of vector $\langle 2, 3 \rangle$ since 8 is 4 times 2. Explain why your friend's statement is incorrect.

Practice and Problem-Solving Exercises

 Practice

Referring to the graph, what are the component forms of the following vectors?

7. u

8. v

9. w

10. f

11. g

12. h

See Problem 1.

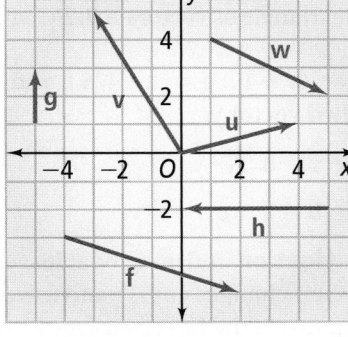

Transform each vector as described. Write the resulting vector in component form.

See Problem 2.

13. $\langle 5, 1 \rangle$; rotate $90°$

14. $\langle -4, 3 \rangle$; rotate $180°$

15. $\langle 0, 2 \rangle$; rotate $270°$

16. $\langle 11, -4 \rangle$; reflect across x-axis

17. $\langle -3, 0 \rangle$; reflect across y-axis

18. $\langle 4, 5 \rangle$; reflect across $y = x$

19. $\langle 4, -3 \rangle$; reflect across $y = -x$

Let $\mathbf{u} = \langle -1, 3 \rangle$, $\mathbf{v} = \langle 2, 4 \rangle$, and $\mathbf{w} = \langle 2, -5 \rangle$. Find the component forms of the following vectors.

See Problems 3 and 4.

20. $\mathbf{u} + \mathbf{v}$

21. $\mathbf{v} + \mathbf{w}$

22. $\mathbf{u} - \mathbf{v}$

23. $\mathbf{u} - \mathbf{w}$

24. $2\mathbf{u}$

25. $-4\mathbf{w}$

26. $\frac{3}{2}\mathbf{v}$

27. $-3\mathbf{v}$

Determine whether the vectors in each pair are normal to each other.

See Problem 5.

28. $\langle 6, -3 \rangle$ and $\langle 2, 4 \rangle$

29. $\langle 8, -4 \rangle$ and $\langle -2, 4 \rangle$

30. $\begin{bmatrix} 1 \\ 8 \end{bmatrix}$ and $\begin{bmatrix} 4 \\ -2 \end{bmatrix}$

31. $\begin{bmatrix} 0.8 \\ -0.6 \end{bmatrix}$ and $\begin{bmatrix} 0.3 \\ 0.4 \end{bmatrix}$

B **Apply**   Let $\mathbf{u} = \begin{bmatrix} -5 \\ 3 \end{bmatrix}$, $\mathbf{v} = \begin{bmatrix} 4 \\ -3 \end{bmatrix}$, and $\mathbf{w} = \begin{bmatrix} 2 \\ 2 \end{bmatrix}$. Find the following vectors.

32. $2\mathbf{u} + 3\mathbf{v}$ **33.** $2\mathbf{v} - 4\mathbf{w}$ **34.** $-\mathbf{u} - \mathbf{w}$ **35.** $-3\mathbf{u} + \mathbf{v} - \frac{1}{2}\mathbf{w}$

C **36. Think About a Plan** A ferry shuttles people from one side of a river to the other. The speed of the ferry in still water is 25 mi/h. The river flows directly south at 7 mi/h. If the ferry heads directly west, what is the ferry's resulting speed?
- How can a sketch help you solve this problem?
- What formula can you use to find the speed?

37. Aviation A twin-engine airplane has a speed of 300 mi/h in still air. Suppose the airplane heads south and encounters a wind blowing 50 mi/h due east. What is the resultant speed of the airplane?

38. Aviation A small airplane lands at a point 216 mi east and 76 mi north of the point from which it took off. How far did the airplane fly?

39. Consider the triangle with vertices at $A(2, 2)$, $B(5, 3)$, and $C(3, 6)$. Express the sides of the triangle as vectors $\overrightarrow{AB}$, $\overrightarrow{BC}$, and $\overrightarrow{CA}$.

Let $\mathbf{a} = \langle 6, -1 \rangle$, $\mathbf{b} = \langle -4, 3 \rangle$, and $\mathbf{c} = \langle 2, 0 \rangle$. Solve each of the following for the unknown vector v.

40. $\mathbf{a} + \mathbf{v} = \mathbf{b}$ **41.** $\mathbf{c} - \mathbf{v} = \mathbf{b}$

42. $\mathbf{v} - \mathbf{b} = \mathbf{a} + \mathbf{c}$ **43.** $\mathbf{a} + \mathbf{b} + \mathbf{c} + \mathbf{v} = (0, 0)$

44. Navigation A fishing boat leaves its home port and travels 150 mi directly east. It then changes course and travels 40 mi due north. How long will the direct return trip take if the boat averages 23 mi/h?

C **45. Writing** Subtract any vector from itself. The result is still a vector, but a unique one. Explain what this vector is, and what it means for vector addition.

C **Reasoning** Do the following properties hold for vectors and scalars? Identify each property and make a diagram to support your answers.

46. $\mathbf{u} + \mathbf{v} = \mathbf{v} + \mathbf{u}$ **47.** $k(\mathbf{u} + \mathbf{v}) = k\mathbf{u} + k\mathbf{v}$

48. $\mathbf{u} - \mathbf{v} = \mathbf{v} - \mathbf{u}$ **49.** $(\mathbf{u} + \mathbf{v}) + \mathbf{w} = \mathbf{u} + (\mathbf{v} + \mathbf{w})$

C **Challenge** **50. Aviation** A helicopter starts at $(0, 0)$ and makes three legs of a flight represented by the vectors $\langle 10, 10 \rangle$, $\langle 5, -4 \rangle$, and $\langle -3, 5 \rangle$, in that order. If another helicopter starts at $(0, 0)$ and flies the same three legs in a different order, would it end in the same place? Justify your answer.

51. Two vectors are parallel if the absolute value of their dot product is equal to the product of their magnitudes. Which of the following vectors are parallel? Which are perpendicular?

$\mathbf{a} = \begin{bmatrix} 0.9 \\ 1.2 \end{bmatrix}$ $\mathbf{b} = \begin{bmatrix} -2 \\ 1.5 \end{bmatrix}$ $\mathbf{c} = \begin{bmatrix} 6 \\ -8 \end{bmatrix}$ $\mathbf{d} = \begin{bmatrix} -4.5 \\ -6 \end{bmatrix}$

52. Given $\mathbf{u} = \langle -4, 3 \rangle$ and $\mathbf{v} = \langle 1, -2 \rangle$, find $\mathbf{w}$ if $\mathbf{u} \cdot \mathbf{w} = 7$ and $\mathbf{v} \cdot \mathbf{w} = -8$.

STEM 53. Physics When an object is not moving, all the forces acting on it must sum to 0. The object is said to be *in equilibrium*. Two cables of different lengths hold a stoplight over an intersection. The force vectors being applied along the two cables are $\langle 20, 18 \rangle$ and $\langle -20, 12 \rangle$. The magnitude of each vector is measured in pounds. A third force vector in this situation is the force due to gravity, and is straight downward. How much does the stoplight weigh?

Apply What You've Learned

MATHEMATICAL PRACTICES
MP 5

Refer to the problem on page 763. In the Apply What You've Learned in Lesson 12-4, you wrote a matrix equation with the coefficient matrix A. Use a graphing calculator to find A^{-1} and det A. Select all of the following that are true. Explain your reasoning.

A. The determinant of A is 78.125.

B. The determinant of A is $\frac{1}{78.125}$.

C. The equation $AX = D$ has infinitely many solutions.

D. The equation $AX = D$ has a unique solution.

E. If A is an $n \times n$ matrix with an inverse, and if X and D are matrices with n rows, then $A^{-1}AX = DA^{-1} = X$.

F. $AA^{-1} = \begin{bmatrix} 1 & 0 & 0 \\ 0 & 1 & 0 \\ 0 & 0 & 1 \end{bmatrix}$

G. $AA^{-1} = \begin{bmatrix} 2 & 0 & 0 \\ 0 & 0.6 & 0 \\ 0 & 0 & 24 \end{bmatrix}$

12

Pull It All Together

Completing the Performance Task

To solve these problems, you will pull together concepts and skills related to matrices.

Look back at your results from the Apply What You've Learned sections in Lessons 12-2, 12-4, and 12-6. Use the work you did to complete the following.

1. Solve the problem in the Task Description on page 763 by finding the number of scoops of each type of food that result in a mixture with the proper nutrition for two rabbits. Be sure to show all your work and explain each step of your solution.

2. **Reflect** Choose one of the Mathematical Practices below and explain how you applied it in your work on the Performance Task.

    MP 1: Make sense of problems and persevere in solving them.

    MP 4: Model with mathematics.

    MP 5: Use appropriate tools strategically.

On Your Own

Refer to the problem presented on page 763. The pet food store offers another brand of rabbit food, Brand D, with the nutrients shown in the table below.

Nutrient	Brand A	Brand B	Brand C	Brand D
Protein (g)	2.5	0	5	3
Fat (g)	2.5	5	2.5	3
Carbohydrate (g)	1.25	2.5	7.5	1.5

Can Kristi still give her rabbits the proper nutrition by using Brand D instead of Brand C? Instead of Brand A? instead of Brand B? Explain your reasoning. If Brand D can be substituted for another brand of rabbit food in the mix, give the number of scoops needed for each brand to yield a mix with the proper nutrition for two rabbits.

12 Chapter Review

Connecting BIG ideas and Answering the Essential Questions

1 Data Representation
You can organize data in a matrix in exactly the same way that you organize data in a rectangular table.

2 Modeling
If you can model a real-world situation with a system of equations, you can represent the system with a matrix equation.

3 Transformations
You can use matrix operations to transform points in a plane:
- addition for translating
- multiplication for rotating and reflecting
- scalar multiplication for dilating.

Adding, Subtracting, and Multiplying Matrices (Lessons 12-1 and 12-2)
To add or subtract matrices, add or subtract corresponding elements.
To multiply two matrices:
$$\begin{bmatrix} a & b \\ c & d \end{bmatrix}\begin{bmatrix} e & f \\ g & h \end{bmatrix} = \begin{bmatrix} ae + bg & af + bh \\ ce + dg & cf + dh \end{bmatrix}$$

Determinants and Inverses (Lesson 12-3)
Let A be an $n \times n$ matrix. If det $A \neq 0$, then A^{-1} exists and $AA^{-1} = A^{-1}A = I_n$ (the $n \times n$ identity matrix).

Geometric Transformations (Lesson 12-5)
$$\begin{bmatrix} 0 & -1 \\ 1 & 0 \end{bmatrix}, \begin{bmatrix} -1 & 0 \\ 0 & -1 \end{bmatrix}, \begin{bmatrix} 0 & 1 \\ -1 & 0 \end{bmatrix}, \text{ and}$$
$$\begin{bmatrix} 1 & 0 \\ 0 & 1 \end{bmatrix} \text{ rotate } 90°, 180°, 270°, \text{ and } 360°.$$

Vectors (Lesson 12-6)
You can add two vectors as matrices, or graphically.

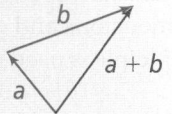

Inverse Matrices and Systems (Lesson 12-4)
The matrix equation $AX = B$ represents a system of linear equations.

A is the coefficient matrix,
X is the variable matrix,
B is the constant matrix.

If det $A \neq 0$, then multiply each side by A^{-1} to find X.
$$A^{-1}AX = A^{-1}B$$
$$X = A^{-1}B$$

Chapter Vocabulary

- center of rotation (p. 804)
- coefficient matrix (p. 793)
- constant matrix (p. 793)
- corresponding elements (p. 764)
- determinant (p. 784)
- dilation (p. 802)
- dot product (p. 812)
- equal matrices (p. 767)
- image (p. 801)
- initial point (p. 809)
- magnitude (p. 809)
- matrix equation (p. 765)
- multiplicative identity matrix (p. 782)
- multiplicative inverse matrix (p. 782)
- normal vectors (p. 812)
- preimage (p. 801)
- rotation (p. 804)
- scalar (p. 772)
- scalar multiplication (p. 772)
- singular matrix (p. 785)
- square matrix (p. 782)
- terminal point (p. 809)
- variable matrix (p. 793)
- vector (p. 809)
- zero matrix (p. 766)

Choose the correct term to complete each sentence.

1. If corresponding elements of matrices are equal, the matrices are __?__ .

2. The additive identity of a matrix is the __?__ .

3. A(n) __?__ consists of a coefficient matrix, a variable matrix, and a constant matrix.

4. An $n \times n$ matrix is called a(n) __?__ .

12-1 Adding and Subracting Matrices

Quick Review

To perform matrix addition or subtraction, add or subtract the corresponding elements in the matrices.

Two matrices are **equal matrices** when they have the same dimensions and corresponding elements are equal. This principle is used to solve a **matrix equation**.

Example

If $A = \begin{bmatrix} 2 & 1 & -2 \\ 1 & 4 & 3 \\ -2 & -1 & 5 \end{bmatrix}$ and $B = \begin{bmatrix} 1 & -2 & 4 \\ -3 & -2 & 1 \\ 0 & 0 & 5 \end{bmatrix}$,

what is $A + B$?

$A + B = \begin{bmatrix} 2+1 & 1+(-2) & -2+4 \\ 1+(-3) & 4+(-2) & 3+1 \\ -2+0 & -1+0 & 5+5 \end{bmatrix}$

$= \begin{bmatrix} 3 & -1 & 2 \\ -2 & 2 & 4 \\ -2 & -1 & 10 \end{bmatrix}$

Exercises

Find each sum or difference.

5. $\begin{bmatrix} 1 & 2 & -5 \\ 3 & -2 & 1 \end{bmatrix} + \begin{bmatrix} -2 & 7 & -3 \\ 1 & 2 & 5 \end{bmatrix}$

6. $\begin{bmatrix} 0 & 2 \\ -4 & -1 \end{bmatrix} - \begin{bmatrix} -5 & 6 \\ -9 & -1 \end{bmatrix}$

Solve each matrix equation.

7. $\begin{bmatrix} 2 & -6 & 8 \end{bmatrix} + \begin{bmatrix} -1 & -2 & 4 \end{bmatrix} = X$

8. $\begin{bmatrix} 7 & -1 \\ 0 & 8 \end{bmatrix} + X = \begin{bmatrix} 4 & 9 \\ -3 & 11 \end{bmatrix}$

Find the value of each variable.

9. $\begin{bmatrix} x-5 & 9 \\ 4 & t+2 \end{bmatrix} = \begin{bmatrix} -7 & w+1 \\ 8-r & 1 \end{bmatrix}$

10. $\begin{bmatrix} -4+t & 2y \\ r & w+5 \end{bmatrix} = \begin{bmatrix} 2t & 11 \\ -2r+12 & 9 \end{bmatrix}$

12-2 Matrix Multiplication

Quick Review

To obtain the product of a matrix and a **scalar**, multiply each matrix element by the scalar. Matrix multiplication uses both multiplication and addition. The element in the ith row and the jth column of the product of two matrices is the sum of the products of each element of the ith row of the first matrix and the corresponding element of the jth column of the second matrix. The first matrix must have the same number of columns as the second has rows.

Example

If $A = \begin{bmatrix} 1 & -3 \\ -2 & 0 \end{bmatrix}$ and $B = \begin{bmatrix} 1 & 4 \\ 0 & 2 \end{bmatrix}$, what is AB?

$AB = \begin{bmatrix} (1)(1)+(-3)(0) & (1)(4)+(-3)(2) \\ (-2)(1)+(0)(0) & (-2)(4)+(0)(2) \end{bmatrix}$

$= \begin{bmatrix} 1 & -2 \\ -2 & -8 \end{bmatrix}$

Exercises

Use matrices A, B, C, and D to find each scalar product and sum, or difference, if possible. If an operation is not defined, label it *undefined*.

$A = \begin{bmatrix} 6 & 1 & 0 & 8 \\ -4 & 3 & 7 & 11 \end{bmatrix}$ $B = \begin{bmatrix} 1 & 3 \\ -2 & 4 \end{bmatrix}$

$C = \begin{bmatrix} -2 & 1 \\ 4 & 0 \\ 2 & 2 \\ 1 & 1 \end{bmatrix}$ $D = \begin{bmatrix} 5 & -2 \\ 3 & 6 \end{bmatrix}$

11. $3A$

12. $B - 2A$

13. AB

14. BA

15. $AC - BD$

16. $4B - 3D$

12-3 Determinants and Inverses

Quick Review

A **square matrix** with 1's along its main diagonal and 0's elsewhere is the **multiplicative identity matrix**, I. If A and X are square matrices such that $AX = I$, then X is the **multiplicative identity matrix** of A, A^{-1}.

You can use a calculator to find the inverse of a matrix. You can find the inverse of a 2×2 matrix

$A = \begin{bmatrix} a & b \\ c & d \end{bmatrix}$ by using its **determinant**.

$$A^{-1} = \frac{1}{\det A}\begin{bmatrix} d & -b \\ -c & a \end{bmatrix} = \frac{1}{ad - bc}\begin{bmatrix} d & -b \\ -c & a \end{bmatrix}$$

Example

What is the determinant of $\begin{bmatrix} 2 & -3 \\ 3 & -4 \end{bmatrix}$?

$$\det \begin{bmatrix} 2 & -3 \\ 3 & -4 \end{bmatrix} = (2)(-4) - (-3)(3)$$
$$= -8 - (-9) = 1$$

Exercises

Evaluate the determinant of each matrix and find the inverse, if possible.

17. $\begin{bmatrix} 6 & 1 \\ 0 & 4 \end{bmatrix}$

18. $\begin{bmatrix} 5 & -2 \\ 10 & -4 \end{bmatrix}$

19. $\begin{bmatrix} 10 & 1 \\ 8 & 5 \end{bmatrix}$

20. $\begin{bmatrix} 1 & 0 & 2 \\ -1 & 0 & 1 \\ -1 & -2 & 0 \end{bmatrix}$

12-4 Inverse Matrices and Systems

Quick Review

You can use inverse matrices to solve some matrix equations and systems of equations. When equations in a system are in standard form, the product of the **coefficient matrix** and the **variable matrix** equals the **constant matrix**. You solve the equation by multiplying both sides of the equation by the inverse of the coefficient matrix. If that inverse does not exist, the system does not have a unique solution.

Example

What is the matrix equation that corresponds to the following system? $\begin{cases} 2x - y = 12 \\ x + 4y = 15 \end{cases}$

Identify $A = \begin{bmatrix} 2 & -1 \\ 1 & 4 \end{bmatrix}$, $X = \begin{bmatrix} x \\ y \end{bmatrix}$, and $B = \begin{bmatrix} 12 \\ 15 \end{bmatrix}$.

The matrix equation is $AX = B$ or $\begin{bmatrix} 2 & -1 \\ 1 & 4 \end{bmatrix}\begin{bmatrix} x \\ y \end{bmatrix} = \begin{bmatrix} 12 \\ 15 \end{bmatrix}$.

Exercises

Use an inverse matrix to solve each equation or system.

21. $\begin{bmatrix} 3 & 5 \\ 6 & 2 \end{bmatrix} X = \begin{bmatrix} -2 & 6 \\ 4 & 12 \end{bmatrix}$

22. $\begin{cases} x - y = 3 \\ 2x - y = -1 \end{cases}$

23. $\begin{bmatrix} 4 & 1 \\ 2 & 1 \end{bmatrix}\begin{bmatrix} x \\ y \end{bmatrix} = \begin{bmatrix} 10 \\ 6 \end{bmatrix}$

24. $\begin{bmatrix} -6 & 0 \\ 7 & 1 \end{bmatrix} X = \begin{bmatrix} -12 & -6 \\ 17 & 9 \end{bmatrix}$

25. $\begin{cases} x + 2y = 15 \\ 2x + 4y = 30 \end{cases}$

26. $\begin{cases} a + 2b + c = 14 \\ b = c + 1 \\ a = -3c + 6 \end{cases}$

12-5 Geometric Transformations

Quick Review

A change made to a figure is a transformation. The original figure is the **preimage**, and the transformed figure is the **image**. A translation slides a figure without changing its size or shape. A **dilation** changes the size of a figure. You can use matrix addition to translate a figure and scalar multiplication to dilate a figure.

You can use multiplication by the appropriate matrix to perform transformations that are specific reflections or **rotations**. For example, to reflect a figure across the y-axis,

multiply by $\begin{bmatrix} -1 & 0 \\ 0 & 1 \end{bmatrix}$.

Example

A triangle has vertices $A(3, 2)$, $B(1, -2)$, and $C(1, 2)$. What are the coordinates after a 90° rotation?

$$\begin{bmatrix} 0 & -1 \\ 1 & 0 \end{bmatrix} \begin{bmatrix} 3 & 1 & 1 \\ 2 & -2 & 2 \end{bmatrix} = \begin{bmatrix} -2 & 2 & -2 \\ 3 & 1 & 1 \end{bmatrix}$$

The coordinates are $(-2, 3)$, $(2, 1)$, and $(-2, 1)$.

Exercises

In matrix form, write the coordinates of each image of the triangle with vertices $A(3, 1)$, $B(-2, 0)$, and $C(1, 5)$.

27. a translation 3 units left and 4 units up

28. a reflection across the y-axis

29. a reflection across the line $y = x$

30. a dilation half the original size

31. a dilation twice the original size

32. a rotation of 270°

12-6 Vectors

Quick Review

A **vector** has both **magnitude** and **direction**. It is a directed line segment that you can describe using a pair of **initial** and **terminal** points. If a vector were in standard position with the initial point at $(0, 0)$, the component form would be $\langle a, b \rangle$ and the magnitude $|v| = \sqrt{a^2 + b^2}$ would give you the length.

Given two vectors $\mathbf{v} = \langle v_1, v_2 \rangle$ and $\mathbf{w} = \langle w_1, w_2 \rangle$, the **dot product** $\mathbf{v} \cdot \mathbf{w}$ is $v_1 w_1 + v_2 w_2$. If the dot product equals 0, then $\mathbf{v}$ and $\mathbf{w}$ are **normal**, or perpendicular, to each other.

Example

Are the vectors $\langle -1, 2 \rangle$ and $\langle 4, 2 \rangle$ normal?

$\langle -1, 2 \rangle \cdot \langle 4, 2 \rangle = (-1)(4) + (2)(2)$

$= -4 + 4 = 0$

The vectors are normal.

Exercises

Let $\mathbf{u} = \langle -3, 4 \rangle$, $\mathbf{v} = \langle 2, 4 \rangle$, and $\mathbf{w} = \langle 4, -1 \rangle$. Write each resulting vector in component form and find the magnitude.

33. $\mathbf{u} + \mathbf{v}$ **34.** $\mathbf{w} - \mathbf{u}$

35. $3\mathbf{u}$ **36.** $-2\mathbf{w} + 3\mathbf{v}$

37. $\frac{1}{2}\mathbf{v} + 3\mathbf{u}$ **38.** $-\mathbf{w} + 3\mathbf{v} + 2\mathbf{u}$

Find the dot product of each pair of vectors and determine whether they are normal.

39. $\langle 4, -3 \rangle$ and $\langle -3, -4 \rangle$

40. $\begin{bmatrix} 1 \\ 7 \end{bmatrix}$ and $\begin{bmatrix} 14 \\ -2 \end{bmatrix}$

Do you know HOW?

Find each sum or difference.

1. $\begin{bmatrix} 4 & 7 \\ -2 & 1 \end{bmatrix} - \begin{bmatrix} -9 & 3 \\ 6 & 0 \end{bmatrix}$

2. $\begin{bmatrix} 4 & -5 & 1 \\ 10 & 7 & 4 \\ 21 & -9 & -6 \end{bmatrix} + \begin{bmatrix} -7 & -10 & 4 \\ 17 & 0 & 3 \\ -2 & -6 & 1 \end{bmatrix}$

Find each product.

3. $\begin{bmatrix} 2 & 6 \\ 1 & 0 \end{bmatrix}\begin{bmatrix} -1 & 5 \\ 3 & 1 \end{bmatrix}$

4. $2\begin{bmatrix} -8 & 5 & -1 \\ 0 & 9 & 7 \end{bmatrix}$

5. $\begin{bmatrix} 0 & 3 \\ -4 & 9 \end{bmatrix}\begin{bmatrix} -4 & 6 & 1 & 3 \\ 9 & -8 & 10 & 7 \end{bmatrix}$

Find the determinant of each matrix.

6. $\begin{bmatrix} 1 & 0 & 0 \\ 0 & 1 & 0 \\ 0 & 0 & 1 \end{bmatrix}$

7. $\begin{bmatrix} 2 & 3 & 0 \\ -1 & 1 & 0 \\ 4 & 2 & 1 \end{bmatrix}$

8. $\begin{bmatrix} 8 & -3 \\ 2 & 9 \end{bmatrix}$

9. $\begin{bmatrix} \frac{1}{2} & -3 \\ 1 & 0 \end{bmatrix}$

Find the inverse of each matrix, if it exists.

10. $\begin{bmatrix} 3 & 8 \\ -7 & 10 \end{bmatrix}$

11. $\begin{bmatrix} 0 & -5 \\ 9 & 6 \end{bmatrix}$

12. $\begin{bmatrix} 3 & 1 & 0 \\ 1 & -1 & 2 \\ 1 & 1 & 1 \end{bmatrix}$

13. $\begin{bmatrix} 1 & 1 & 2 \\ 2 & 1 & 3 \\ 2 & 1 & 1 \end{bmatrix}$

Solve each matrix equation.

14. $\begin{bmatrix} 3 & -8 \\ 10 & 5 \end{bmatrix} - X = \begin{bmatrix} 2 & 8 \\ -1 & 12 \end{bmatrix}$

15. $\begin{bmatrix} 3 & 2 \\ -1 & 5 \end{bmatrix} X = \begin{bmatrix} -10 & -11 \\ 26 & -36 \end{bmatrix}$

16. $2X - \begin{bmatrix} -2 & 0 \\ 1 & 4 \end{bmatrix} = \begin{bmatrix} 5 & 10 \\ -15 & 9 \end{bmatrix}$

Find the area of each triangle with the given vertices.

17. vertices at $(2, 3), (-3, -1), (0, 4)$

18. vertices at $(-2, -3), (5, 0), (-1, 4)$

Parallelogram $ABCD$ has coordinates $A(2, -1)$, $B(4, 3)$, $C(1, 5)$, and $D(-1, 1)$. Write a matrix for the vertices after each transformation.

19. a dilation by a factor of $\frac{2}{3}$

20. a translation 2 units right and 4 units down

21. a rotation of $270°$ 22. a reflection across $y = x$

Let $u = \langle -2, 1 \rangle$, $v = \langle 1, 5 \rangle$, and $w = \langle -1, -3 \rangle$. Find each of the following.

23. $u - v$ 24. $3v$

25. $3w + 2u - 2w$ 26. $3v - 2u$

27. $u \cdot v$ 28. $v \cdot w$

Determine whether each pair of vectors is normal.

29. $\langle 3, -4 \rangle, \langle -8, 6 \rangle$ 30. $\langle 5, -2 \rangle, \langle 3, 4 \rangle$

Do you UNDERSTAND?

31. **Open-Ended** Write a matrix that has no inverse.

32. **Writing** Explain how to determine whether two matrices can be multiplied and what the dimensions of the product matrix will be.

33. **Shopping** A local store is having a special promotion where all movies sell at the same price and all video games sell at another price. Suppose you buy 5 movies and 4 video games for $97.50 and your friend buys 3 movies and 6 video games for $103.50. Write a matrix equation to describe the purchases. Then solve the matrix equation to find the price of a movie and the price of a video game.

34. **Writing** Describe the advantages and disadvantages of writing a vector in matrix form instead of component form.

TIPS FOR SUCCESS

Some problems require you to find the equations of lines.

TIP 1

Use the equation $y = mx + b$, where m represents the slope and b is the y-intercept.

Which matrix equation is represented by the graph below?

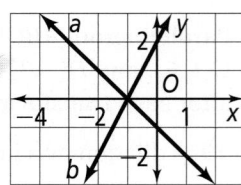

A $\begin{bmatrix} 1 & -1 \\ 2 & -1 \end{bmatrix} \begin{bmatrix} x \\ y \end{bmatrix} = \begin{bmatrix} 1 \\ -2 \end{bmatrix}$

B $\begin{bmatrix} -1 & -1 \\ 1 & -1 \end{bmatrix} \begin{bmatrix} x \\ y \end{bmatrix} = \begin{bmatrix} 1 \\ -2 \end{bmatrix}$

C $\begin{bmatrix} -1 & -1 \\ 2 & -1 \end{bmatrix} \begin{bmatrix} x \\ y \end{bmatrix} = \begin{bmatrix} 1 \\ -2 \end{bmatrix}$

D $\begin{bmatrix} -1 & -1 \\ 2 & -1 \end{bmatrix} \begin{bmatrix} x \\ y \end{bmatrix} = \begin{bmatrix} 2 \\ 1 \end{bmatrix}$

TIP 2

Rewrite the equations as matrices in standard form.

Think It Through

The slope of line a is -1 and its y-intercept is $(0, -1)$.

The equation of line a is $y = -x - 1$.

As a matrix equation in standard form, the equation of line a is

$$\begin{bmatrix} -1 & -1 \end{bmatrix} \begin{bmatrix} x \\ y \end{bmatrix} = \begin{bmatrix} 1 \end{bmatrix}$$

The slope of line b is 2 and its y-intercept is $(0, 2)$.

The equation of line b is $y = 2x + 2$.

As a matrix equation in standard form, the equation of line b is

$$\begin{bmatrix} 2 & -1 \end{bmatrix} \begin{bmatrix} x \\ y \end{bmatrix} = \begin{bmatrix} -2 \end{bmatrix}$$

The correct answer is C.

Vocabulary Review

As you solve test items, you must understand the meanings of mathematical terms. Match each term with its mathematical meaning.

A. image

B. dilation

C. preimage

D. determinant

E. square matrix

I. a matrix with the same number of rows and columns

II. a figure after a transformation

III. a transformation that enlarges or reduces a figure

IV. a real number computed from the elements of a square matrix

V. a figure before a transformation

Selected Response

Read each question. Then write the letter of the correct answer on your paper.

1. If a person walks toward you, and the expression $|13 - 3t|$ represents his or her distance from you at time t, what does the 3 represent?

   A number of steps   C the walking rate

   B total distance   D number of minutes

2. The graph of $y = |x - 1|$ is translated up 4 units and to the right 3 units. Which equation represents the translated graph?

   F $y = |x - 3| + 4$ H $y = |x - 4| - 3$

   G $y = |x - 4| + 4$ I $y = |x + 2| + 4$

3. Which inequality is described by the graph below?

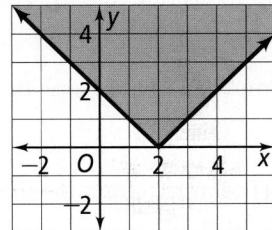

- (A) $y \le |x - 2|$
- (B) $y \ge |x + 2|$
- (C) $y \ge |x - 2|$
- (D) $y \ge |x| + 2$

4. Which of the following is the compound inequality that describes the range of the following function?

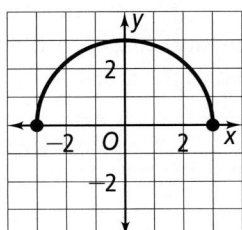

- (F) $-3 < y \le 0$
- (G) $-3 \le y < 3$
- (H) $0 \le y \le 3$
- (I) $5 \le y \le 6$

5. Which system is represented by the graph below?

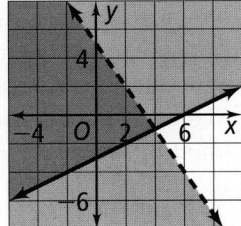

- (A) $\begin{cases} 2y + 6 \ge x \\ y < -\frac{3}{2}x + 5 \end{cases}$
- (C) $\begin{cases} 2y - 6 \ge x \\ y < -\frac{3}{2}x + 5 \end{cases}$
- (B) $\begin{cases} 2y + 6 \ge x \\ y > -\frac{3}{2}x + 5 \end{cases}$
- (D) $\begin{cases} 2y + 6 \ge x \\ -y < \frac{3}{2}x + 5 \end{cases}$

6. The graph below shows a quadratic function. Which of the following equations is represented by the graph?

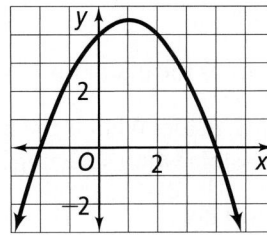

- (F) $y = x^2 - 2x - 8$
- (G) $y = -x^2 + x + 4$
- (H) $y = \frac{1}{2}x^2 + x + 8$
- (I) $y = -\frac{1}{2}x^2 + x + 4$

7. The graph of a quadratic function in the xy-plane opens downward and has x-intercepts at $x = -3$ and $x = 5$. For what x-value is the value of this function greatest?

- (A) $x = -3$
- (C) $x = 2$
- (B) $x = 1$
- (D) $x = 5$

8. The area of a rectangle is $6x^3 - 22x^2 + 23x - 5$. The width is $3x - 5$. What is the length?

- (F) $2x^2 - 4x + 1$
- (G) $2x^2 + 4x - 1$
- (H) $2x^2 + 1$
- (I) $2x^2 - x - 4$

9. Which relation is the inverse of $f(x) = (x - 3)^2$?

- (A) $g(x) = \dfrac{x^2}{(3x - 1)^2}$
- (B) $g(x) = \dfrac{1}{(3x - 1)^2}$
- (C) $g(x) = \pm\sqrt{x} + 3$
- (D) $g(x) = \pm\sqrt{x - 3}$

Constructed Response

10. Let $f(x) = 2x^2 + 3x - 1$ and $g(x) = x - 1$.
Evaluate $(g \cdot f)(2)$.

11. How many roots does the equation $\frac{2}{x^2} + \frac{1}{x} = 0$ have?

12. A box has 10 items inside. What is the number of combinations possible when selecting 3 of the items?

13. What is the value of $\det \begin{bmatrix} 7 & -1 \\ 3 & 2 \end{bmatrix}$?

14. If $\log a = 0.6$, and $\log b = 0.7$, what is $\log a^2 b$?

15. What is the sum of the geometric series below?

$$\sum_{n=1}^{8} 3 \cdot (-2)^{n-1}$$

16. A and B are independent but not mutually exclusive events. If $P(A) = \frac{1}{4}$ and $P(B) = \frac{1}{5}$, what is $P(A \text{ and } B)$?

17. What is the value of x in the solution of the matrix equation below?

$$\begin{bmatrix} 5 & -3 \\ 2 & -1 \end{bmatrix} \begin{bmatrix} x \\ y \end{bmatrix} = \begin{bmatrix} 2 \\ 1 \end{bmatrix}$$

18. Determine the function that is the inverse of $f(x) = 2^{x-1}$.

19. Write the equation for the parabola with a focus of $(3, 0)$ and a directrix $x = -3$.

20. What is the equation of the circle below?

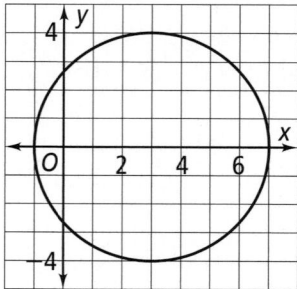

21. Describe the vertical asymptotes and holes for the graph of the function $y = \frac{3x^2 - 2x - 1}{x^2 - 1}$.

22. What is an equation of an ellipse with height 2 meters and width 4 meters? Assume that the center of the ellipse is $(0, 0)$.

23. What are the asymptotes of the graph of $y = \frac{x - 3}{x^2 - 2x - 15}$?

24. Use the binomial theorem to find the third term in the expansion of $(3a - 4)^5$.

Extended Response

25. In a geometric sequence, $a_1 = 3$ and $a_5 = 768$. Explain how to find a_2 and a_3.

26. A dietician wants to prepare a meal with 24 g of protein, 27 g of fat, and 20 g of carbohydrates using the three foods shown in the table.

Food	Protein	Fat	Carbohydrates
A	2 g/oz	3 g/oz	4 g/oz
B	3 g/oz	3 g/oz	1 g/oz
C	3 g/oz	3 g/oz	2 g/oz

a. Set up a matrix equation for the data.
b. Solve the matrix equation.
c. How many ounces of each food are needed?

27. The coach of a high school debate team must choose 4 of the 6 members to represent the team at a state-wide competition. Each of the team members is equally qualified for the competition. Use probability concepts to describe how the coach can make his decision fairly. Describe why your method is fair.

Get Ready!

Lesson 8-3  **Analyzing Graphs of Rational Functions**

Find the vertical asymptotes and holes for the graph of each rational function.

1. $y = \dfrac{2}{x-3}$

2. $y = \dfrac{x+2}{(2x+1)(x-4)}$

Lesson 8-4 **Simplifying Complex Fractions**

Simplify each complex fraction.

3. $\dfrac{\frac{2}{a}}{\frac{1}{b}}$

4. $\dfrac{5+\frac{1}{2}}{2-\frac{1}{5}}$

5. $\dfrac{\frac{3}{c+d}}{2}$

6. $\dfrac{\frac{1}{4}}{\frac{4}{c}}$

7. $\dfrac{\frac{2}{3}}{\frac{6}{c+4}}$

8. $\dfrac{\frac{4}{x}}{\frac{2}{8}}$

9. $\dfrac{3-\frac{1}{2}}{\frac{7}{6}}$

10. $\dfrac{\frac{9}{m-n}}{\frac{3}{2m-2n}}$

Lesson 9-1 **Writing Formulas for Sequences**

Find the next two terms in each sequence. Write a formula for the *n*th term. Identify each formula as *explicit* or *recursive*.

11. $16, 13, 10, 7, \ldots$

12. $-1, -8, -27, -64, -125, \ldots$

Lesson 10-6 **Translating Conic Sections**

Write an equation for each conic section. Then sketch the graph.

13. circle with center at $(1, -4)$ and radius 4

14. ellipse with center at $(2, 5)$, vertices at $(5, 5)$ and $(-1, 5)$, and co-vertices at $(2, 3)$ and $(2, 7)$

15. parabola with vertex at $(0, -3)$ and focus at $(0, 5)$

16. hyperbola with center at $(6, 1)$, one focus at $(6, 6)$, and one vertex at $(6, -2)$

 Looking Ahead Vocabulary

17. If you were to graph the average monthly rainfall for your community for the past 5 years, you would very likely graph a *periodic function*. Why do you think it is called a periodic function?

18. Graph the month-by-month attendance at one of these larger National Parks—The Everglades, Grand Canyon, Yellowstone, Yosemite—for several years. The pattern that results may resemble a *sine curve*. Describe the features of this curve.

CHAPTER 13

Periodic Functions and Trigonometry

Download videos connecting math to your world.

Interactive! Vary numbers, graphs, and figures to explore math concepts.

The online Solve It will get you in gear for each lesson.

Math definitions in English and Spanish

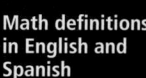

Online access to stepped-out problems aligned to Common Core

Get and view your assignments online.

Extra practice and review online

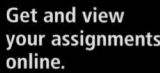
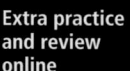

Virtual Nerd™ tutorials with built-in support

Chapter Preview

Vocabulary

English/Spanish Vocabulary Audio Online:

English	Spanish
amplitude, *p. 830*	amplitud
central angle, *p. 844*	ángulo central
cosine, *p. 838*	coseno
cycle, *p. 828*	ciclo
midline, *p. 830*	línea media
period, *p. 828*	período
periodic function, *p. 828*	función periódica
phase shift, *p. 875*	cambio de fase
radian, *p. 844*	radián
sine, *p. 838*	seno
tangent, *p. 868*	tangente
unit circle, *p. 838*	círculo unitario

BIG ideas

1 Modeling

Essential Question How can you model periodic behavior?

2 Function

Essential Question What function has as its graph a sine curve with amplitude 4, period π, and a minimum at the origin?

3 Function

Essential Question If you know the value of $\sin \theta$, how can you find $\cos \theta$, $\tan \theta$, $\csc \theta$, $\sec \theta$, and $\cot \theta$?

 DOMAINS

• Trigonometric Functions
• Interpreting Functions

Common Core Performance Task

Animating a Game

Suzanne is designing a computer game. She uses a coordinate plane to help her design the layout. In the game, a dragonfly will start at the bottom of the circle shown here and move counterclockwise around it. The dragonfly will complete one cycle around the circle in 5 seconds traveling around the circle at a constant rate.

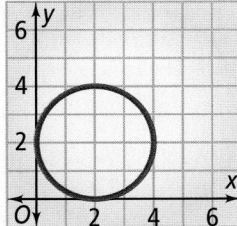

After 8 seconds, a frog will jump out and eat the dragonfly. Suzanne wants to determine the location of the dragonfly when this occurs.

Task Description
Determine the coordinates of the dragonfly when the frog eats it. Round each coordinate to the nearest hundredth.

Connecting the Task to the Math Practices

MATHEMATICAL PRACTICES

As you complete the task, you'll apply several Standards for Mathematical Practice.

- You'll make sense of the given information by making tables and graphs of repeating data. (MP 1, MP 8)

- You'll look for structure in given functions to determine which aspects of the real-world situation they describe accurately. (MP 7)

- You'll write your own functions to model the real-world situation and check your work using technology. (MP 4, MP 5)

13-1 Exploring Periodic Data

Common Core State Standards

F-IF.B.4 For a function that models a relationship between two quantities, interpret key features of graphs . . . and sketch graphs . . . **Also Prepares for F-TF.B.5**

MP 1, MP 2, MP 3, MP 4, MP 6

Objectives To identify cycles and periods of periodic functions
To find the amplitude of periodic functions

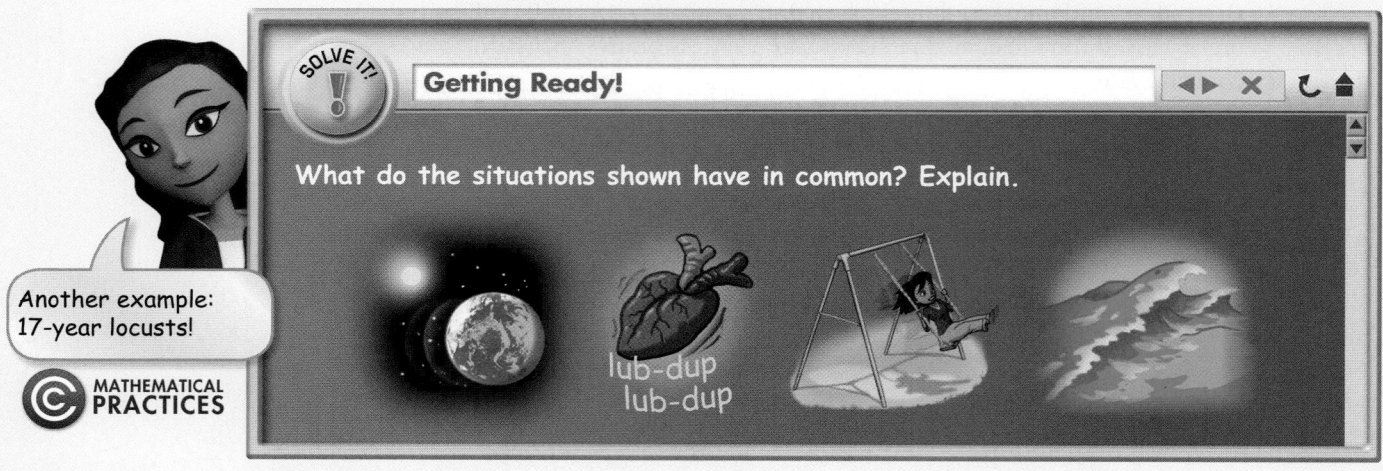

Getting Ready!

What do the situations shown have in common? Explain.

lub-dup
lub-dup

Another example:
17-year locusts!

MATHEMATICAL PRACTICES

Lesson Vocabulary
• periodic function
• cycle
• period
• amplitude

A **periodic function** is a function that repeats a pattern of y-values (outputs) at regular intervals. One complete pattern is a **cycle**. A cycle may begin at any point on the graph of the function. The **period** of a function is the horizontal length—the distance along the x-axis—of one cycle. The x-value in a periodic function often represents time.

Essential Understanding Periodic behavior is behavior that repeats over intervals of constant length.

Problem 1 Identifying Cycles and Periods

Analyze the periodic function below. Identify the cycle in two different ways. What is the period of the function?

Think

Is there a good point at which to start the cycle?
If you start at the maximum value, it is easy to tell when you have completed the cycle.

Begin at any point on the graph. Trace one complete cycle.

The beginning and ending x-values of each cycle determine the period of the function.

One cycle begins at $x = 2$ and ends at $x = 6$; $6 - 2 = 4$, so the period of the function is 4.

Got It? 1. Analyze each periodic function. Identify the cycle in two different ways. What is the period of the function?

a.

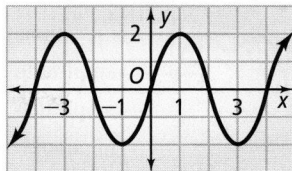

b.

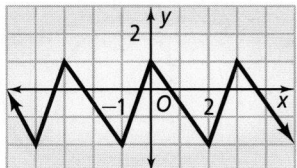

You can analyze the graph of a function to determine if the function is periodic.

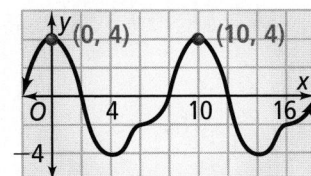 **Problem 2** Identifying Periodic Functions

Is the function periodic? If it is, what is its period?

Think

Do the y-values of the function repeat?
No; there is a repeating pattern but the actual y-values do not repeat.

A

Although the graph shows similar curves, the y-values from one section do not repeat in other sections. The function is not periodic.

B

The pattern of y-values in one section repeats exactly in other sections. The function is periodic.

Find points at the beginning and end of one cycle. Subtract the x-values of the points: $10 - 0 = 10$. The pattern in the graph repeats every 10 units, so its period is 10.

  Got It? 2. Is the function periodic? If it is, what is its period?

a.

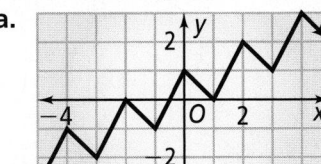

b.

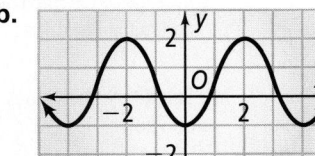

c. **Reasoning** If the period of a function is 4 seconds, how many cycles does it have in a minute? What is the period of a function that has 180 cycles per minute (for example, a point on a spinning wheel)? That has 440 cycles per second (for example, a point on the end of a tuning fork)?

The *amplitude* of a periodic function measures the amount of variation in the function values.

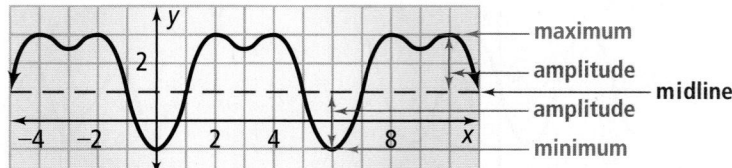

The **midline** is the horizontal line midway between the maximum and minimum values of a periodic function. The **amplitude** is half the difference between the maximum and minimum values of the function.

$$\text{amplitude} = \tfrac{1}{2}(\text{maximum value} - \text{minimum value})$$

Problem 3 Finding Amplitude and Midline of a Periodic Function

What is the amplitude of the periodic function at the right? What is the equation of the midline?

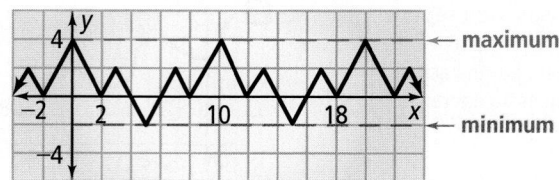

Think	Write
Use the definition of amplitude.	$\text{amplitude} = \tfrac{1}{2}(\text{maximum value} - \text{minimum value})$
Substitute 4 for the maximum and -2 for the minimum.	$= \tfrac{1}{2}[4 - (-2)]$
Subtract within parentheses and simplify.	$= \tfrac{1}{2}(6) = 3$
The midline is the horizontal line through the average of the maximum and minimum values.	$y = \tfrac{1}{2}(\text{maximum value} + \text{minimum value})$
Substitute the values and solve.	$= \tfrac{1}{2}[4 + (-2)]$ $= \tfrac{1}{2}(2) = 1$

 Got It? **3.** What is the amplitude of each periodic function? What is the equation of the midline?

a.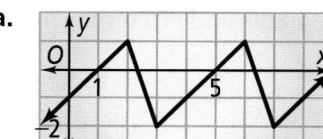

b.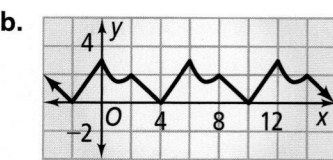

You can model some data with periodic functions. The rotation of a Ferris wheel, the beating of a heart, and the movement of sound waves are all examples of real-world events that generate periodic data.

 Problem 4 Using a Periodic Function to Solve a Problem STEM

Sound Waves Sound is produced by periodic changes in air pressure called sound waves. The yellow graph in the digital wave display at the right shows the graph of a pure tone from a tuning fork. What are the period and the amplitude of the sound wave?

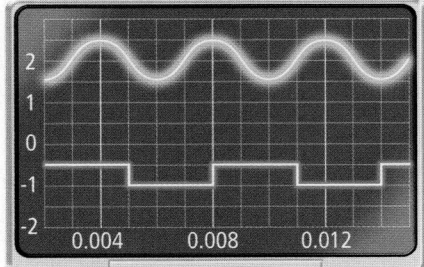

One cycle of the sound wave occurs from 0.004 s to 0.008 s. The maximum value of the function is 2.5, and the minimum value is 1.5.

Plan

How does identifying the cycle help you?
The period is the horizontal length of the cycle. The amplitude is half the vertical length of the cycle.

Find the period.

period = 0.008 − 0.004

= 0.004

Find the amplitude.

amplitude = $\frac{1}{2}(2.5 - 1.5)$

= $\frac{1}{2}(1) = \frac{1}{2}$

The period of the sound wave is 0.004 s. The amplitude is $\frac{1}{2}$.

 Got It? **4.** What are the period, the amplitude, and the equation of the midline of the green graph in the digital wave display in Problem 4?

Lesson Check

Do you know HOW?

Determine if the function *is* or *is not* periodic. If it is, find the period.

1.

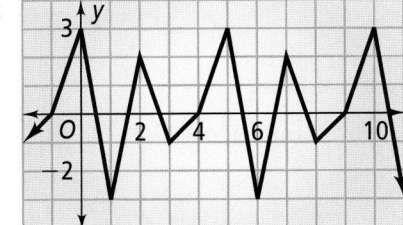

2.

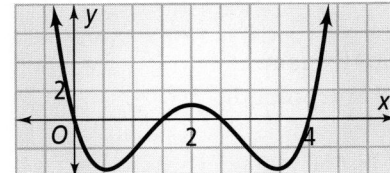

Do you UNDERSTAND? MATHEMATICAL PRACTICES

3. Writing A sound wave can be graphed as a periodic function. Name two more real-world examples of periodic functions.

4. Error Analysis A student looked at the following function and wrote that the amplitude was 2. Describe and correct the student's error.

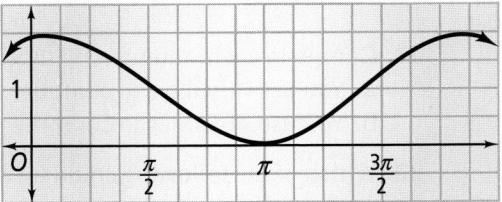

5. Reasoning Suppose *f* is a periodic function. The period of *f* is 5 and $f(1) = 2$. What are $f(6)$ and $f(11)$? Explain your reasoning.

6. A wave has a maximum of 6. If its midline is at $y = 1$, what is its minimum?

Practice and Problem-Solving Exercises  MATHEMATICAL PRACTICES

 Practice

Identify one cycle in two different ways. Then determine the period of the function.

◀ See Problem 1.

7.

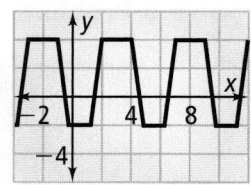

8.

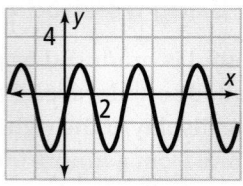

9.

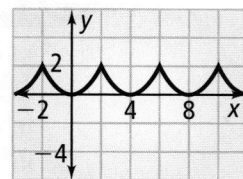

Determine whether each function *is* or *is not* periodic. If it is, find the period.

◀ See Problem 2.

10.

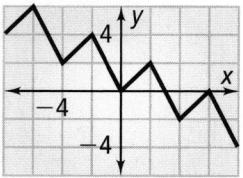

11.

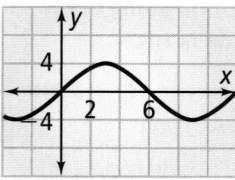

12.

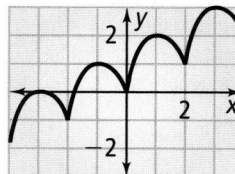

13.

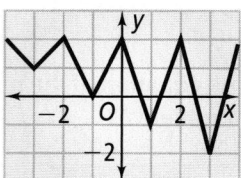

14.

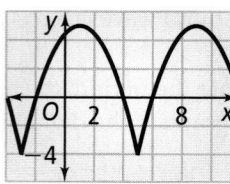

15.

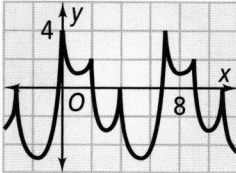

Find the amplitude of each periodic function, and midline.

◀ See Problems 3 and 4.

16.

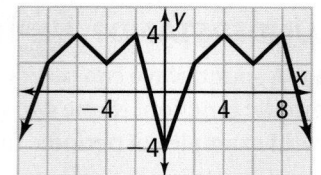

17.

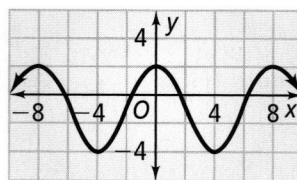

18.

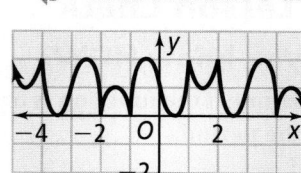

B Apply

Sketch the graph of a sound wave with the given period, amplitude, and midline.

19. period 0.02, amplitude 4, midline 6

20. period 0.005, amplitude 9, midline −5

21. Complete each statement with x or y.
  a. You use ■-values to compute the amplitude of a function.
  b. You use ■-values to compute the period of a function.

22. Which of the following could be represented by a periodic function? Explain.
  a. the average monthly temperature in your community, recorded every month for three years
  b. the population in your community, recorded every year for the last 50 years
  c. the number of cars per hour that pass through an intersection near where you live, recorded for two consecutive work days

23. Writing What do all periodic functions have in common?

24. Think About a Plan

A person's pulse rate is the number of times his or her heart beats in one minute. Each cycle in the graph represents one heartbeat. What is the pulse rate?

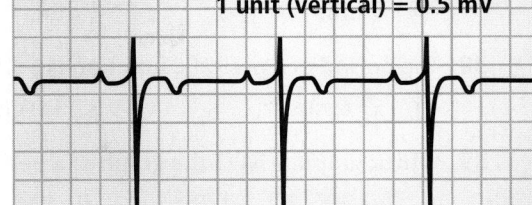

RHYTHM STRIP 1 unit (horizontal) = 0.2 s
1 unit (vertical) = 0.5 mV

- Will you compute the period or the amplitude, or both?
- Does the graph provide information you do NOT need?

25. Health An electrocardiogram (EKG or ECG) measures the electrical activity of a person's heart in millivolts over time. Refer to the graph in the previous exercise.
- **a.** What is the period of the EKG shown above?
- **b.** What is the amplitude of the EKG?

26. Open-Ended Sketch a graph of a periodic function that has a period of 3 and an amplitude of 2.

Find the maximum, minimum, and period of each periodic function. Then copy the graph and sketch two more cycles.

27.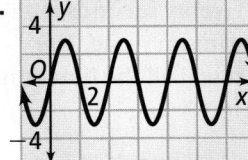

28.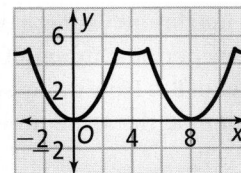

29.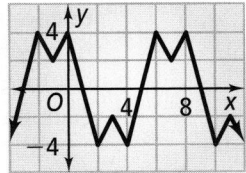

Language Arts Functions that repeat over time are common in everyday life. The English language has many words that stand for common periods of time. State the period of time from which each term derives.

30. annual   **31.** biweekly   **32.** quarterly   **33.** hourly   **34.** circadian

 **Challenge**

35. Suppose g is a periodic function. The period of g is 24, $g(3) = 67$, and $g(8) = 70$. Find each function value.
- **a.** $g(27)$ **b.** $g(80)$ **c.** $g(-16)$ **d.** $g(51)$

36. Calendar A day is a basic measure of time. A solar year is about 365.2422 days. We try to keep our calendar in step with the solar year.
- **a.** If every calendar year has 365 days, by how many days would the calendar year and the solar year differ after 100 years?
- **b.** If every fourth year has an extra "leap" day added, by how many days would the two systems differ after 100 years?
- **c.** If every hundred years the "leap" day is omitted, by how many days would the two systems differ after 100 years?
- **d. Reasoning** Why is it important for the difference between the calendar year and the solar year to be zero?

37. A periodic function goes through 5 complete cycles in 4 min. What is the period of the function?

Ⓐ $\frac{1}{5}$ min   Ⓑ $\frac{1}{4}$ min   Ⓒ 48 s   Ⓓ 75 s

38. The period of a periodic function is 8 s. How many cycles does it go through in 30 s?

Ⓕ $\frac{4}{15}$ cycle   Ⓖ 3.75 cycles   Ⓗ 22 cycles   Ⓘ 240 cycles

39. Which graph is NOT the graph of a periodic function?

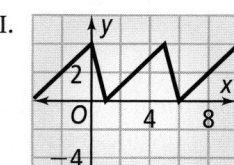

I.   II.   III.

Ⓐ I only   Ⓑ II only   Ⓒ III only   Ⓓ II and III only

40. The amplitude of a periodic function is 2.5 and its minimum value is 0. What is the function's maximum value?

Ⓕ −2.5   Ⓖ 0   Ⓗ 2.5   Ⓘ 5.0

Extended Response

41. Two periodic functions have periods of 6 s and 7 s. A machine records the two functions reaching their maximum values at the same time. Twenty seconds later, the machine records a new periodic function reaching its maximum value. The new function has a period of 8 s. How many seconds after that will all the functions reach their maximum values at the same time? Explain.

Apply What You've Learned

MATHEMATICAL
PRACTICES
MP 1, MP 8

Look back at the given information on page 827. Let $d = f(t)$ be a function that gives the horizontal distance d of the dragonfly from the y-axis after t seconds. Let $h = g(t)$ be a function that gives the height h of the dragonfly above the x-axis after t seconds.

a. Make a table of values for t and d. Graph your data and connect the points with a smooth curve. (*Hint*: Consider times when the dragonfly is at the top or bottom of the circle or at the rightmost point or leftmost point of the circle.)

b. Is $d = f(t)$ periodic? If so, find the period, amplitude, and midline.

c. Make a table of values for t and h. Then graph your data and connect the points with a smooth curve.

d. Is $h = g(t)$ periodic? If so, find the period, amplitude, and midline.

Geometry Review

For Use With Lesson 13-2

Special Right Triangles

@ **Common Core State Standards**

Reviews G-SRT.C.6 Understand that by similarity, side ratios in right triangles . . . lead to definitions of trigonometric ratios for acute angles.

MP 8

In Geometry, you learned about two special right triangles, the 45°-45°-90° triangle and the 30°-60°-90° triangle. The figures at the right summarize the relationships among the lengths of the sides of each triangle.

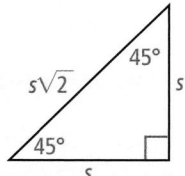
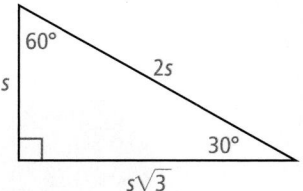

Example 1

Find the missing side lengths in each 45°-45°-90° triangle.

A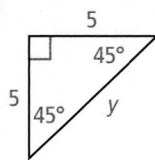

$$y = \sqrt{2} \cdot 5 \qquad\qquad \text{hypotenuse} = \sqrt{2} \cdot \text{leg}$$

$$y = 5\sqrt{2} \qquad\qquad \text{Simplify.}$$

B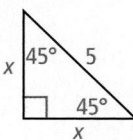

$$5 = \sqrt{2} \cdot x$$

$$x = \frac{5}{\sqrt{2}} = \frac{5\sqrt{2}}{2}$$

Example 2

Find the missing side lengths in the 30°-60°-90° triangle at the right.

$$4 = \sqrt{3} \cdot x \qquad\qquad \text{longer leg} = \sqrt{3} \cdot \text{shorter leg}$$

$$x = \frac{4}{\sqrt{3}} = \frac{4\sqrt{3}}{3} \qquad\qquad \text{Divide and simplify.}$$

$$y = 2x \qquad\qquad \text{hypotenuse} = 2 \cdot \text{shorter leg}$$

$$y = 2 \cdot \frac{4\sqrt{3}}{3} = \frac{8\sqrt{3}}{3} \qquad \text{Substitute } \frac{4\sqrt{3}}{3} \text{ for } x \text{ and simplify.}$$

Exercises

Use the given information to find the missing side length(s) in each 45°-45°-90° triangle. Rationalize any denominators.

1. hypotenuse 1 in. **2.** leg 2 cm **3.** hypotenuse $\sqrt{3}$ ft **4.** leg $2\sqrt{5}$ m

Use the given information to find the missing side lengths in each 30°-60°-90° triangle. Rationalize any denominators.

5. shorter leg 3 in. **6.** longer leg 1 cm **7.** hypotenuse 1 ft **8.** shorter leg $\sqrt{3}$ cm

13-2 Angles and the Unit Circle

 Common Core State Standards

Prepares for F-TF.A.2 Explain how the unit circle . . . enables the extension of trigonometric functions to all real numbers, interpreted as radian measures of angles traversed counterclockwise around the unit circle.

MP 1, MP 2, MP 3, MP 5

Objectives To work with angles in standard position
To find coordinates of points on the unit circle

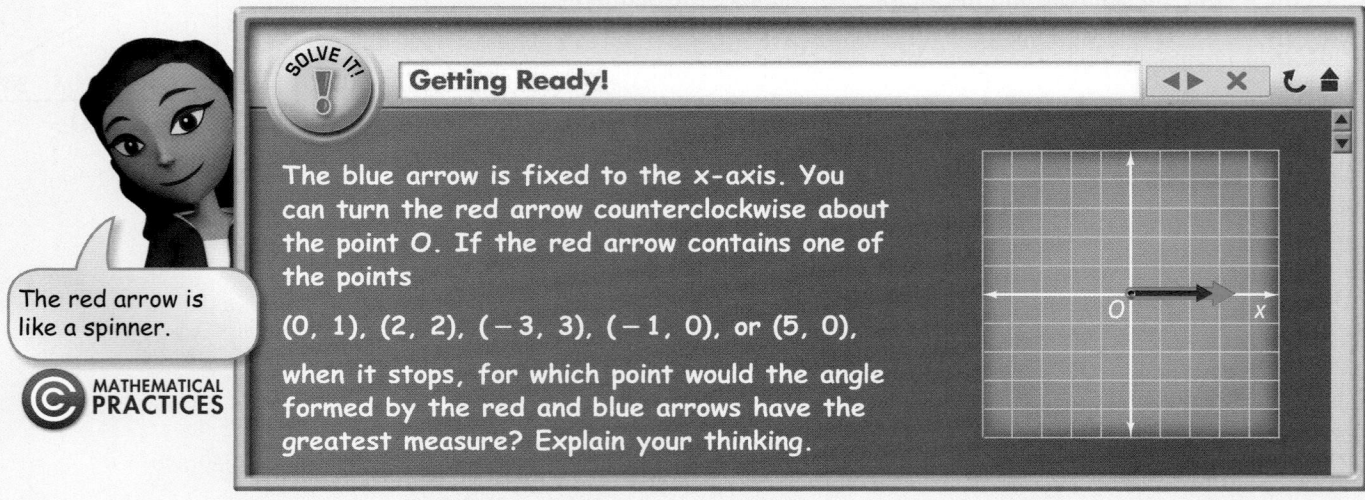

The red arrow is like a spinner.

SOLVE IT!

Getting Ready!

The blue arrow is fixed to the x-axis. You can turn the red arrow counterclockwise about the point O. If the red arrow contains one of the points

(0, 1), (2, 2), (−3, 3), (−1, 0), or (5, 0),

when it stops, for which point would the angle formed by the red and blue arrows have the greatest measure? Explain your thinking.

MATHEMATICAL PRACTICES

Lesson Vocabulary

- standard position
- initial side
- terminal side
- coterminal angles
- unit circle
- cosine of θ
- sine of θ

An angle in the coordinate plane is in **standard position** when the vertex is at the origin and one ray is on the positive *x*-axis. The ray on the *x*-axis is the **initial side** of the angle. The other ray is the **terminal side** of the angle.

The measure of an angle in standard position is the amount of rotation from the initial side to the terminal side.

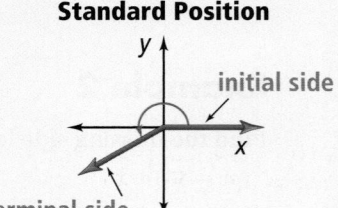

Standard Position

Essential Understanding The measure of an angle in standard position is the input for two important functions. The outputs are the coordinates (called *cosine* and *sine*) of the point on the terminal side of the angle that is 1 unit from the origin.

The measure of an angle is positive when the rotation from the initial side to the terminal side is in the counterclockwise direction. The measure is negative when the rotation is clockwise.

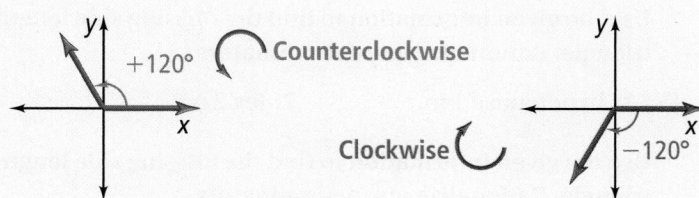

Problem 1 Measuring Angles in Standard Position

What are the measures of each angle?

A

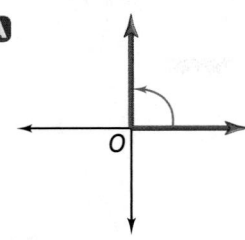

B

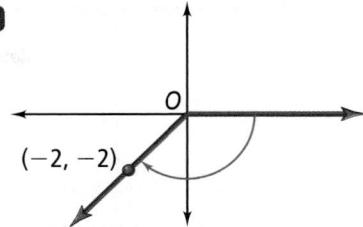

(−2, −2)

Think

How many degrees are in a circle?
There are 360° in a circle, 180° in half of a circle, and 90° in a quarter of a circle.

This angle is a counterclockwise rotation that makes a right angle, so its measure is 90°.

This angle is a clockwise rotation that goes 45° beyond a right angle, so its measure is −135°.

 Got It? 1. What is the measure of the angle shown?

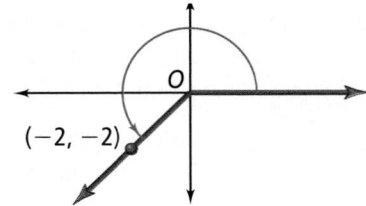

(−2, −2)

Problem 2 Sketching Angles in Standard Position

What is a sketch of each angle in standard position?

A 36°   **B** 315°   **C** − 150°

Think

What is the initial side of the angle?
In standard position, the initial side is always the positive x-axis.

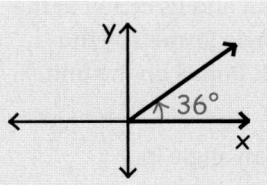

36° Counterclockwise

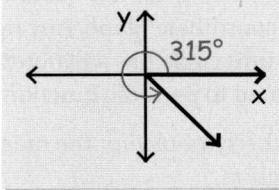

315° Counterclockwise

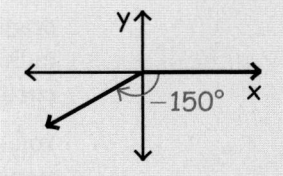

150° Clockwise

 Got It? 2. What is a sketch of each angle in standard position?

     a. 85°   **b.** −320°   **c.** 180°

Two angles in standard position are **coterminal angles** if they have the same terminal side.

Angles in standard position that have measures 135° and −225° are coterminal.

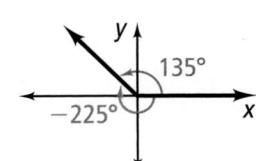

Ⓒ Problem 3 Identifying Coterminal Angles

Multiple Choice Which of the following angles is not coterminal with any of the other three?

A 300°   **B** −60°   **C** 60°   **D** −420°

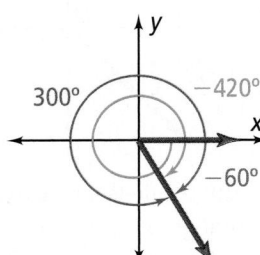

Think

How do you know if two angles are coterminal?
Two angles are coterminal if they differ by a multiple of 360°.

Angles of 300° and −60° are coterminal. An angle of −420° is coterminal with both, since it is a full 360° rotation beyond −60°.

An angle of 60° is not coterminal with any of the other three.

Angles of 300°, −60°, and −420° all have the same terminal side and are coterminal. The 60° angle has a different terminal side. The correct answer is C.

 Got It? **3.** Which angles are coterminal?

a. −315°   **b.** 45°   **c.** 315°   **d.** 405°

In a 360° angle, a point 1 unit from the origin on the terminal ray makes one full rotation about the origin. The resulting circle is a unit circle. The **unit circle** has a radius of 1 unit and its center at the origin of the coordinate plane. Any right triangle formed by the radius of the unit circle has a hypotenuse of 1. Points on the unit circle are related to periodic functions.

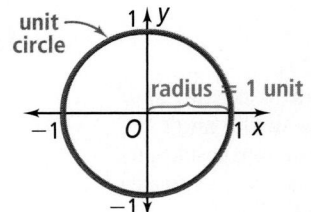

You can use the symbol θ for the measure of an angle in standard position.

take note

Key Concepts   Cosine and Sine of an Angle

Suppose an angle in standard position has measure θ. The **cosine of θ** (cos θ) is the x-coordinate of the point at which the terminal side of the angle intersects the unit circle. The **sine of θ** (sin θ) is the y-coordinate.

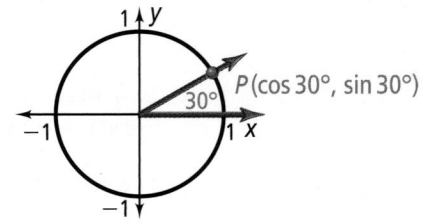

Problem 4 Finding Cosines and Sines of Angles

What are $\cos \theta$ and $\sin \theta$ for $\theta = 90°$, $\theta = -180°$, and $\theta = 270°$?

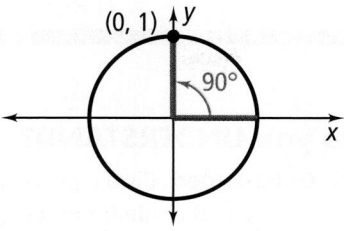

$\cos 90° = 0$
$\sin 90° = 1$

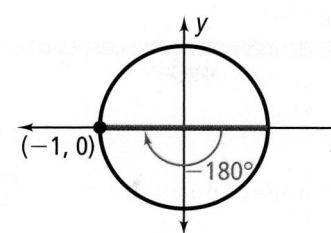

$\cos(-180°) = -1$
$\sin(-180°) = 0$

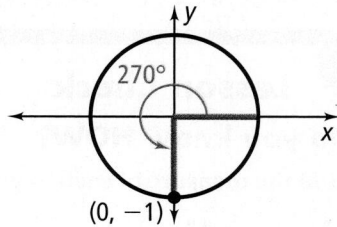

$\cos 270° = 0$
$\sin 270° = -1$

Got It? **4. a.** What are $\cos \theta$ and $\sin \theta$ for $\theta = -90°$, $\theta = 360°$, and $\theta = 540°$?

b. In a triangle, sine and cosine are ratios between side lengths. What ratios produce the values in (a)?

You can find the exact value of sine and cosine for angles that are multiples of 30° or 45°.

Problem 5 Finding Exact Values of Cosine and Sine

What are the cosine and sine of the angle?

A $\theta = 60°$

Know	Need	Plan
An angle	The x- and y-coordinates of the point where the angle intersects the unit circle	• Sketch the angle on the unit circle. • Use the angle to draw a right triangle with one leg on the x-axis.

The cosine of 60° is the length of the shorter leg of the triangle. The sine of 60° is the length of the longer leg of the triangle. In a 30°-60°-90° triangle, the shorter leg is half the hypotenuse and the longer leg is $\sqrt{3}$ times the shorter leg.

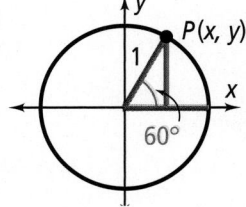

$\cos 60° = x = $ length of shorter leg $= \dfrac{1}{2}$

$\sin 60° = y = $ length of longer leg $= \dfrac{\sqrt{3}}{2}$

B $\theta = 225°$

Draw the angle in standard position to determine the point $P(x, y)$ on the unit circle. P is in the third quadrant, so the signs of x and y will be negative. Form a right triangle with hypotenuse 1. In a 45°-45°-90° triangle, the lengths of the legs of the triangle are $\dfrac{\sqrt{2}}{2}$ times the hypotenuse.

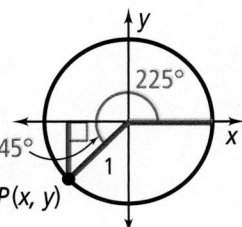

$\cos 225° = x = -$length of leg $= -\dfrac{\sqrt{2}}{2}$ $\sin 225° = y = -$length of leg $= -\dfrac{\sqrt{2}}{2}$

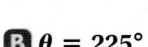

Got It? 5. What are the cosine and sine of the angle?

a. $\theta = -45°$ **b.** $\theta = 150°$

c. Reasoning For an angle θ, can $\cos \theta$ equal $\sin \theta$? Explain.

Lesson Check

Do you know HOW?

Find the measure of each angle in standard position.

1.
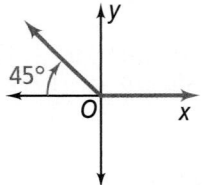

2.
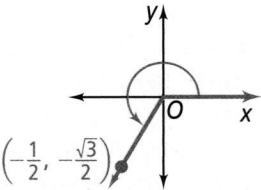

Sketch each angle in standard position. Then find the measure of a coterminal angle.

3. 28° **4.** 325°

 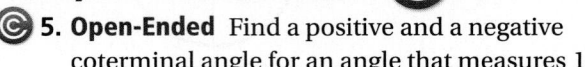
Do you UNDERSTAND?

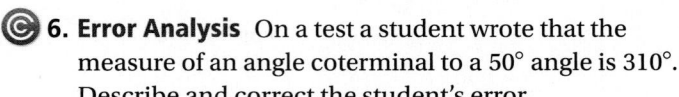

5. Open-Ended Find a positive and a negative coterminal angle for an angle that measures 1485°.

6. Error Analysis On a test a student wrote that the measure of an angle coterminal to a 50° angle is 310°. Describe and correct the student's error.

Practice and Problem-Solving Exercises MATHEMATICAL PRACTICES

 Practice Find the measure of each angle in standard position. ◀ **See Problem 1.**

7.
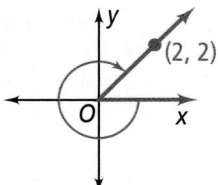
(2, 2)

8.
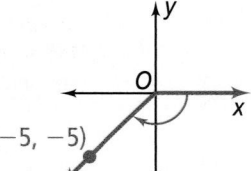
(−5, −5)

9.
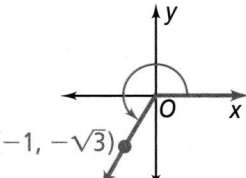
(−1, −√3)

10. $\left(-\frac{\sqrt{3}}{2}, \frac{1}{2}\right)$
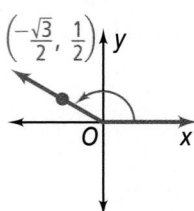

11.
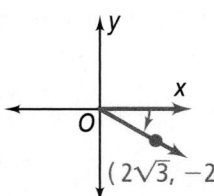
(2√3, −2)

12.
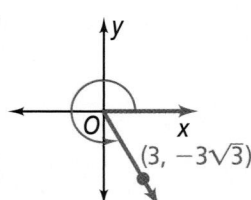
(3, −3√3)

Sketch each angle in standard position. ◀ **See Problem 2.**

13. 40° **14.** −130° **15.** −270° **16.** 120° **17.** 95°

Find the measure of an angle between 0° and 360° coterminal with each given angle. ◀ **See Problem 3.**

18. 385° **19.** 575° **20.** −405° **21.** −356°

22. 500° **23.** −210° **24.** 415° **25.** −180°

Find the exact values of the cosine and sine of each angle. Then find the decimal values. Round your answers to the nearest hundredth.

◀ See Problems 4 and 5.

26.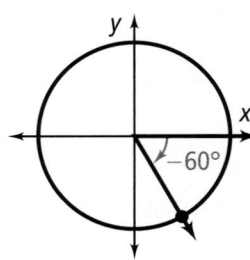

27.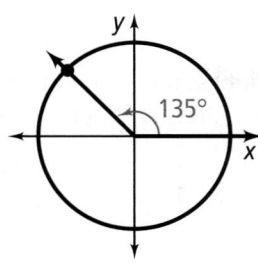

28.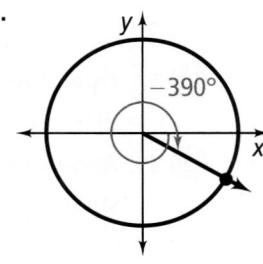

29. $-240°$ **30.** $390°$ **31.** $315°$ **32.** $-30°$ **33.** $-225°$

 **Apply**

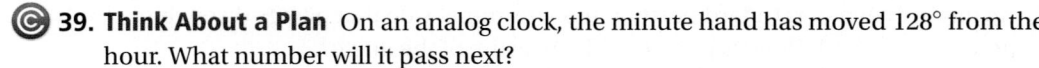

Graphing Calculator For each angle θ, find the values of $\cos \theta$ and $\sin \theta$. Round your answers to the nearest hundredth.

34. $-95°$ **35.** $-10°$ **36.** $154°$ **37.** $90°$ **38.** $210°$

39. Think About a Plan On an analog clock, the minute hand has moved $128°$ from the hour. What number will it pass next?
- How can a drawing help you understand the problem?
- How can you find the number of degrees between every two consecutive numbers?

Open-Ended Find a positive and a negative coterminal angle for the given angle.

40. $45°$ **41.** $10°$ **42.** $-675°$ **43.** $400°$ **44.** $213°$

Determine the quadrant or axis where the terminal side of each angle lies.

45. $150°$ **46.** $210°$ **47.** $540°$ **48.** $-60°$ **49.** $0°$

50. Time The time is 2:46 P.M. What is the measure of the angle that the minute hand swept through since 2:00 P.M.?

51. a. Copy and complete the chart at the right.
    b. Suppose you know that $\cos \theta$ is negative and $\sin \theta$ is positive. In which quadrant does the terminal side of the angle lie?
    c. Writing Summarize how the quadrant in which the terminal side of an angle lies affects the sign of the sine and cosine of that angle.

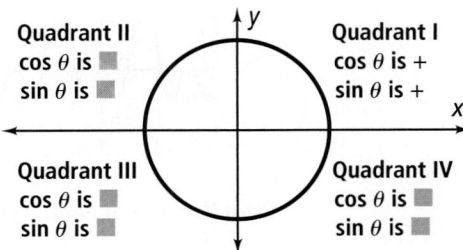

52. a. Graphing Calculator Use a calculator to find the value of each expression: $\cos 40°$, $\cos 400°$, and $\cos (-320°)$.
    b. Reasoning What do you notice about the values you found in part (a)? Explain.

Challenge Sketch each angle in standard position. Use the unit circle and a right triangle to find exact values of the cosine and the sine of the angle.

53. $-300°$ **54.** $120°$ **55.** $225°$ **56.** $-780°$ **57.** $1020°$

58. Open-Ended Find the measures of four angles in standard position that have a sine of 0.5. (*Hint:* Use the unit circle and right triangles.)

59. Reasoning Suppose θ is an angle in standard position and $\cos\theta = -\frac{1}{2}$ and $\sin\theta = -\frac{\sqrt{3}}{2}$. Can the value of θ be $60°$? Can it be $-120°$? Draw a diagram and justify your reasoning.

Standardized Test Prep

SAT/ACT

60. Which angle, in standard position, is NOT coterminal with the others?

     Ⓐ $-570°$ Ⓑ $-170°$ Ⓒ $190°$ Ⓓ $550°$

61. An angle drawn in standard position has a terminal side that passes through the point $(\sqrt{2}, -\sqrt{2})$. What is one possible measure of the angle?

     Ⓕ $45°$ Ⓖ $225°$ Ⓗ $315°$ Ⓘ $330°$

62. An angle of $120°$ is in standard position. What are the coordinates of the point at which the terminal side intersects the unit circle?

     Ⓐ $\left(\frac{1}{2}, \frac{\sqrt{3}}{2}\right)$ Ⓑ $\left(-\frac{1}{2}, \frac{\sqrt{3}}{-2}\right)$ Ⓒ $\left(\frac{-\sqrt{3}}{2}, \frac{1}{2}\right)$ Ⓓ $\left(-\frac{1}{2}, \frac{\sqrt{3}}{2}\right)$

Short Response

63. Use an angle in standard position to find the exact value of $[\sin(-135°)]^2 + [\cos(-135°)]^2$. Show your work.

Mixed Review

Determine whether each function *is* or *is not* periodic. If it is, find the period.  **See Lesson 13-1.**

64. 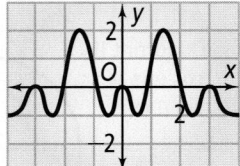   **65.** 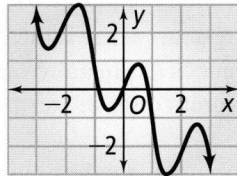   **66.**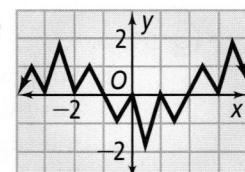

Find the foci of each hyperbola. Draw the graph.   **See Lesson 10-5.**

67. $\dfrac{y^2}{16} - \dfrac{x^2}{4} = 1$ **68.** $\dfrac{y^2}{25} - \dfrac{x^2}{100} = 1$ **69.** $\dfrac{x^2}{36} - \dfrac{y^2}{49} = 1$ **70.** $\dfrac{x^2}{81} - \dfrac{y^2}{64} = 1$

Get Ready! **To prepare for Lesson 13-3, do Exercises 71–74.**

Find the area of a circle with the given radius or diameter. Use 3.14 for π.    **See p. 976.**

71. radius 4 in.   **72.** diameter 70 m   **73.** radius 8 mi   **74.** diameter 3.4 ft

Measuring Radians

 Common Core State Standards
Prepares for F-TF.A.1 Understand radian measure of an angle as the length of the arc on the unit circle subtended by the angle.
MP 1

In the past, you have used degrees to measure angles. When angles are used in periodic functions, they are often measured in larger units called radians.

1. Measure the diameter of a cylinder and calculate its radius. On a piece of string, mark off a "number line" with each unit equal to the radius. Mark at least seven units.

2. Wrap the string around the cylinder. How many radius units are needed to go around the cylinder one time?

3. Use the end of the cylinder to draw a circle on a sheet of paper. Keep the cylinder in place and wrap the string around it on the paper. Mark an arc of the circle equal to one radius unit of length.

4. Remove the cylinder and string. Use paper folding to locate the center of the circle. (Fold the circle onto itself and crease the paper along a diameter. Repeat to get a second diameter.) Draw a central angle that intercepts one radius unit of arc.

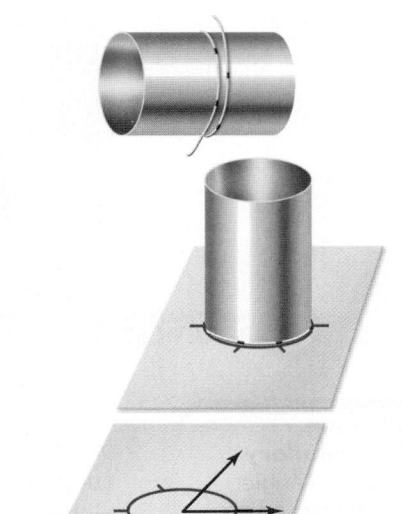

The measure of the angle you drew in Question 4 is 1 radian.

5. Use a protractor to measure the angle from Question 4 in degrees.

6. **Reasoning** The formula $C = 2\pi r$ relates the circumference of a circle C to its radius r. *Exactly* how many radians are in a 360° angle? Explain.

The diagram at the right shows that a rotation of 180° is equivalent to π radians.

7. Find the number of degrees in one radian by dividing 180 by π. How does your answer compare to the measurement you made in Question 5?

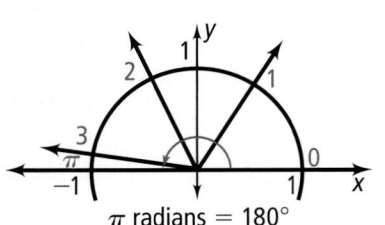

π radians $= 180°$

Exercises

Use the proportion $\frac{d°}{180°} = \frac{r \text{ radians}}{\pi \text{ radians}}$. Find the equivalent degree measure or radian measure.

8. 10° **9.** 45° **10.** 90° **11.** 120° **12.** 270°

13. 310° **14.** 50° **15.** 415° **16.** 170° **17.** 380°

18. $\frac{13\pi}{18}$ radians **19.** $\frac{3\pi}{8}$ radians **20.** $\frac{7\pi}{2}$ radians **21.** $\frac{11\pi}{4}$ radians **22.** $\frac{5\pi}{6}$ radians

13-3 Radian Measure

Common Core State Standards

F-TF.A.1 Understand radian measure of an angle as the length of the arc on the unit circle subtended by the angle.

MP 1, MP 2, MP 3, MP 4, MP 6

Objectives To use radian measure for angles
To find the length of an arc of a circle

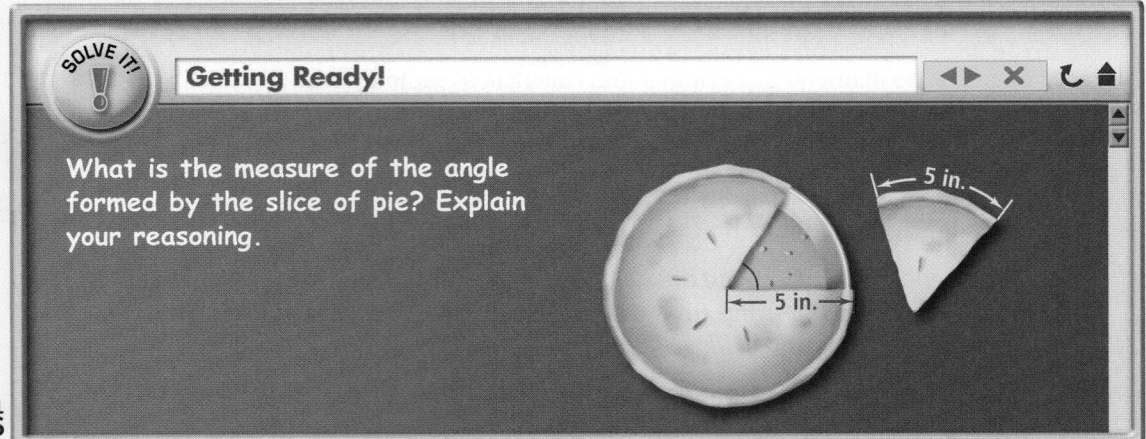

Getting Ready!

What is the measure of the angle formed by the slice of pie? Explain your reasoning.

5 in.

5 in.

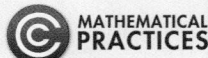

MATHEMATICAL PRACTICES

Lesson Vocabulary
- central angle
- intercepted arc
- radian

A **central angle** of a circle is an angle with a vertex at the center of a circle. An **intercepted arc** is the portion of the circle with endpoints on the sides of the central angle and remaining points within the interior of the angle.

A **radian** is the measure of a central angle that intercepts an arc with length equal to the radius of the circle. Radians, like degrees, measure the amount of rotation from the initial side to the terminal side of an angle.

Essential Understanding An angle with a full circle rotation measures 2π radians. An angle with a semicircle rotation measures π radians.

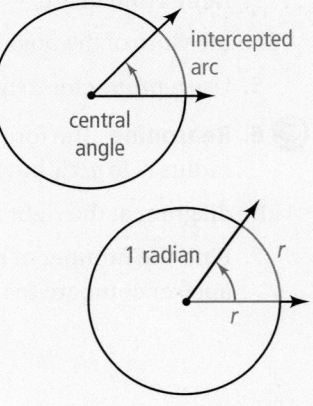

intercepted arc

central angle

1 radian

r

r

Key Concept Proportion Relating Radians and Degrees

You can use the proportion $\frac{d°}{180°} = \frac{r \text{ radians}}{\pi \text{ radians}}$ to convert between radians and degrees.

Here's Why It Works

Because the circumference of a circle is $2\pi r$, there are 2π radians in any circle. Since 2π radians $= 360°$, it follows that π radians $= 180°$. This equality leads to the following *conversion factors* for converting between radian measure and degree measure.

Key Concept   Converting Between Radians and Degrees

To convert degrees to radians, multiply by $\frac{\pi \text{ radians}}{180°}$.

To convert radians to degrees, multiply by $\frac{180°}{\pi \text{ radians}}$.

You can use the conversion factors and dimensional analysis to convert between angle measurement systems.

Problem 1   Using Dimensional Analysis

Think

How do you know which conversion factor to use?
Because radians are in the numerator, use the conversion factor with radians in the denominator.

A What is the degree measure of an angle of $-\frac{3\pi}{4}$ radians?

$$-\frac{3\pi}{4} \text{ radians} = -\frac{3\pi}{4} \text{ radians} \cdot \frac{180°}{\pi \text{ radians}} \quad \text{Multiply by } \frac{180°}{\pi \text{ radians}}.$$

$$= -\frac{3\cancel{\pi}}{\cancel{1}4} \text{ radians} \cdot \frac{\overset{45°}{\cancel{180°}}}{\cancel{\pi \text{ radians}}} \quad \text{Simplify.}$$

$$= -135°$$

An angle of $-\frac{3\pi}{4}$ radians measures $-135°$.

B What is the radian measure of an angle of $27°$?

$$27° = 27° \cdot \frac{\pi \text{ radians}}{180°} \quad \text{Multiply by } \frac{\pi \text{ radians}}{180°}.$$

$$= {}^{3}\cancel{27°} \cdot \frac{\pi \text{ radians}}{20\cancel{180°}} \quad \text{Simplify.}$$

$$= \frac{3\pi}{20} \text{ radians}$$

An angle of $27°$ measures $\frac{3\pi}{20}$ radians.

Got It?   1. What is the degree measure of each angle expressed in radians? What is the radian measure of each angle expressed in degrees? (Express radian measures in terms of π.)

    a. $\frac{\pi}{2}$ radians   **b.** $225°$ **c.** 2 radians   **d.** $150°$

Think

What kind of angle
is π?
It is a straight angle.

Problem 2 Finding Cosine and Sine of a Radian Measure

What are the exact values of cos $\left(\frac{\pi}{4} \text{ radians}\right)$ and sin $\left(\frac{\pi}{4} \text{ radians}\right)$?

$\frac{\pi}{4} = \frac{1}{4}\pi = \frac{1}{4}$ of a straight angle or 45°

Draw the angle on the unit circle.

Complete a 45°-45°-90° triangle. Since the hypotenuse
has length 1, both legs have length $\frac{\sqrt{2}}{2}$

Thus, cos$\left(\frac{\pi}{4} \text{ radians}\right) = \frac{\sqrt{2}}{2}$ and sin$\left(\frac{\pi}{4} \text{ radians}\right) = \frac{\sqrt{2}}{2}$.

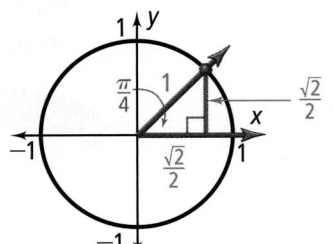

 Got It? **2.** What are the exact values of cos$\left(\frac{7\pi}{6} \text{ radians}\right)$ and
sin$\left(\frac{7\pi}{6} \text{ radians}\right)$?

If you know the radius and the measure in radians of a central angle, you can find the
length of the intercepted arc.

take note

Key Concept   Length of an Intercepted Arc

For a circle of radius r and a central angle of
measure θ (in radians), the length s
of the intercepted arc is $s = r\theta$.

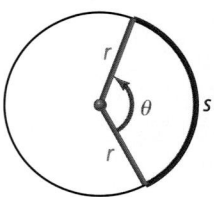

Here's Why It Works The length of the intercepted arc is the same fraction of the
circumference of the circle as the central angle is of 2π. So, $\frac{\theta}{2\pi} = \frac{s}{C}$. Since $C = 2\pi r$, then
$\frac{\theta}{2\pi} = \frac{s}{2\pi r}$. This simplifies to $\theta = \frac{s}{r}$. Multiplying by r results in $s = r\theta$.

 Problem 3 Finding the Length of an Arc

Think

What units will the
length of the arc
have?
Because the radius is in
inches, the arc length will
be in inches too.

Use the circle at the right. What is length s to the nearest tenth?

$s = r\theta$ Use the formula.

$= 3 \cdot \frac{5\pi}{6}$ Substitute 3 for r and $\frac{5\pi}{6}$ for θ.

$= \frac{5\pi}{2}$ Simplify.

≈ 7.9 Use a calculator.

The arc has a length of about 7.9 in.

  Got It? **3. a.** What is length b in Problem 3 to the nearest tenth?
    b. Reasoning If the radius of the circle doubled, how would the
      arc length change?

Problem 4 Using Radian Measure to Solve a Problem

Weather Satellite A weather satellite in a circular orbit around Earth completes one orbit every 2 h. How far does the satellite travel in 1 h?

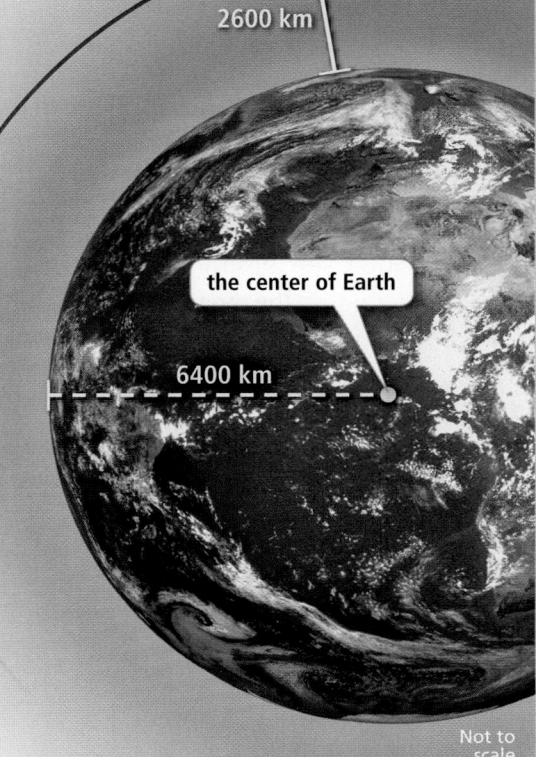

Know

- A complete satellite orbit is 2 h.
- The radius of the Earth is 6400 km.
- The height of the orbit is 2600 km.

Need

The distance that the satellite travels in 1 h

Plan

- Find the angle the satellite travels in 1 h.
- Then use the formula for arc length. $s = r\theta$

Step 1 Find the angle through which the satellite travels in 1 h.

$$\theta = \frac{1}{2} \cdot 2\pi = \pi$$

Step 2 Find the length of the arc.

$$s = r\theta$$
$$= (6400 + 2600)\,\pi$$
$$= 9000\pi$$
$$\approx 28{,}274$$

The satellite travels about 28,000 km in 1 h.

 Got It? **4.** Suppose the satellite orbited 3600 km above Earth's surface and completed an orbit every 4 h. How far would the satellite have travelled in 1 h?

 Lesson Check

Do you know HOW?

1. Find the radian measure of an angle of 300°.

2. Find the degree measure of an angle of $\frac{3\pi}{4}$ radians.

3. Find the length a.

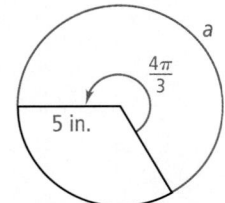

Do you UNDERSTAND? MATHEMATICAL PRACTICES

4. Vocabulary The radius of a circle is 9 cm. A central angle intercepts an arc that is 9 cm. What is the measure of the central angle in radians?

5. Reasoning A certain baker believes that a perfect slice of pie has a central angle of 1 radian. How many "perfect" slices can he get out of one pie?

Practice and Problem-Solving Exercises

 MATHEMATICAL PRACTICES

 Practice

Write each measure in radians. Express your answer in terms of π and as a decimal rounded to the nearest hundredth.

 See Problem 1.

6. $-300°$

7. $150°$

8. $-90°$

9. $-60°$

10. $160°$

11. $20°$

Write each measure in degrees. Round your answer to the nearest degree, if necessary.

12. 3π radians

13. $\frac{11\pi}{10}$ radians

14. $-\frac{2\pi}{3}$ radians

15. -3 radians

16. 1.57 radians

17. 4.71 radians

The measure θ of an angle in standard position is given. Find the exact values of $\cos \theta$ and $\sin \theta$ for each angle measure.

See Problem 2.

18. $\frac{\pi}{6}$ radians

19. $\frac{\pi}{3}$ radians

20. $\frac{\pi}{2}$ radians

21. $-\frac{\pi}{4}$ radians

22. $\frac{2\pi}{3}$ radians

23. $-\frac{\pi}{2}$ radians

24. $\frac{5\pi}{4}$ radians

25. $\frac{7\pi}{6}$ radians

Use each circle to find the length of the indicated arc. Round your answer to the nearest tenth.

See Problem 3.

26.

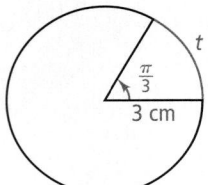

27.

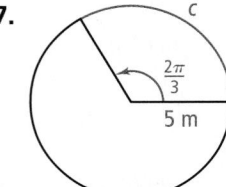

28.

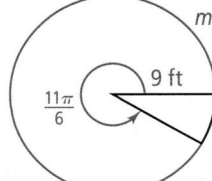

29.

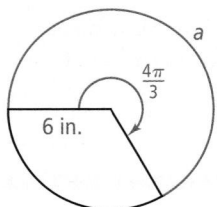

30.

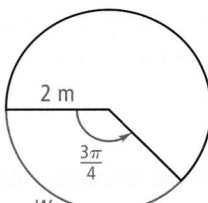

31.

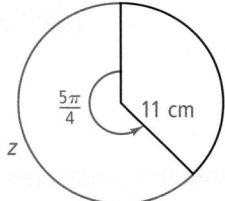

Find the length of each arc.

32.

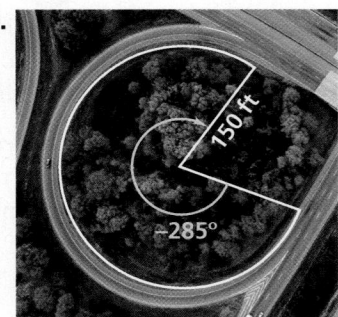

33.

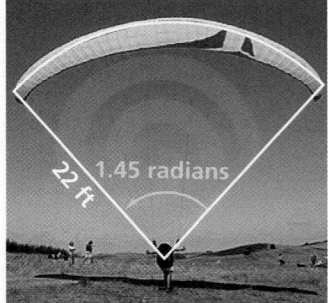

STEM 34. **Space** ◀ **See Problem 4.**

STEM 34. **Space** A geostationary satellite is positioned 35,800 km above Earth's surface. It takes 24 h to complete one orbit. The radius of Earth is about 6400 km.
   a. What distance does the satellite travel in 1 h? 3 h? 2.5 h? 25 h?
   ⓒ **b. Reasoning** After how many hours has the satellite traveled 200,000 km?

 **Apply**

ⓒ 35. **Think About a Plan** Suppose a windshield wiper arm has a length of 22 in. and rotates through an angle of 110°. What distance does the tip of the wiper travel as it moves once across the windshield?
   • Which formula can help you answer this question?
   • Do you need to convert between degrees and radians?

36. **Geography** The 24 lines of longitude that approximate the 24 standard time zones are equally spaced around the equator.
   a. Suppose you use 24 central angles to divide a circle into 24 equal arcs. Express the measure of each angle in degrees and in radians.
   b. The radius of the equator is about 3960 mi. About how wide is each time zone at the equator?
   c. The radius of the Arctic Circle is about 1580 mi. About how wide is each time zone at the Arctic Circle?

Determine the quadrant or axis where the terminal side of each angle lies.

37. $\frac{4\pi}{3}$ radians   38. $-\frac{5\pi}{4}$ radians   39. $-\pi$ radians   40. $\frac{6\pi}{5}$ radians

Draw an angle in standard position with each given measure. Then find the values of the cosine and sine of the angle.

41. $\frac{7\pi}{4}$ radians   42. $-\frac{2\pi}{3}$ radians   43. $\frac{5\pi}{2}$ radians   44. $\frac{7\pi}{6}$ radians

ⓒ 45. **Writing** Two angles are measured in radians. Explain how to tell whether the angles are coterminal without rewriting their measures in degrees.

ⓒ 46. **Open-Ended** Draw an angle in standard position. Draw a circle with its center at the vertex of the angle. Find the measure of the angle in radians and degrees.

47. **Transportation** Suppose the radius of a bicycle wheel is 13 in. (measured to the outside of the tire). Find the number of radians through which a point on the tire turns when the bicycle has moved forward a distance of 12 ft.

ⓒ 48. **Error Analysis** A student wanted to rewrite $\frac{9\pi}{4}$ radians in degrees. The screen shows her calculation. What error did the student make?

49. **Music** A CD with diameter 12 cm spins in a CD player. Calculate how much farther a point on the outside edge of the CD travels in one revolution than a point 1 cm closer to the center of the CD.

50. **Geography** Assume that Earth is a sphere with radius 3960 miles. A town is at latitude 32° N. Find the distance in miles from the town to the North Pole. (*Hint:* Latitude is measured north and south from the equator.)

The given angle θ is in standard position. Find the radian measure of the angle that results after the given number of revolutions from the terminal side of θ.

51. $\theta = \frac{\pi}{2}$; 1 clockwise revolution

52. $\theta = -\frac{2\pi}{3}$; 1 counterclockwise revolution

 53. Reasoning Use the proportion $\dfrac{\text{measure of central angle}}{\text{length of intercepted arc}} = \dfrac{\text{measure of one complete rotation}}{\text{circumference}}$ to derive the formula $s = r\theta$. Use θ for the central angle measure and s for the arc length. Measure the rotation in radians.

Standardized Test Prep

SAT/ACT

54. Which pairs of measurements represent the same angle measures?

I. $240°$, $\frac{7\pi}{6}$ radians II. $135°$, $\frac{3\pi}{4}$ radians III. $150°$, $\frac{5\pi}{6}$ radians

Ⓐ I and II only Ⓑ I and III only Ⓒ II and III only Ⓓ I, II, and III

55. What is the exact value of $\cos\left(\frac{5\pi}{4}\text{ radians}\right)$?

Ⓕ $-\frac{\sqrt{3}}{2}$ Ⓖ $-\frac{\sqrt{2}}{2}$ Ⓗ $-\frac{1}{2}$ Ⓘ $\frac{\sqrt{2}}{2}$

56. Two arcs have the same length. One arc is intercepted by an angle of $\frac{3\pi}{2}$ radians in a circle of radius 15 cm. If the radius of the other circle is 25 cm, what central angle intercepts the arc?

Ⓐ $\frac{3\pi}{2}$ radians Ⓑ $\frac{9\pi}{10}$ radians Ⓒ $\frac{5\pi}{2}$ radians Ⓓ $\frac{5\pi}{3}$ radians

Short Response

57. For a central angle of one radian, describe the relationship between the radius of the circle and the length of the arc.

Mixed Review

Sketch each angle in standard position. ◀ See Lesson 13-2.

58. $15°$ **59.** $-75°$ **60.** $150°$ **61.** $-270°$ **62.** $-85°$

Find the mean and the standard deviation for each set of values. ◀ See Lesson 11-6.

63. 12 13 15 9 16 5 18 16 12 11 15 **64.** 21 29 35 26 25 28 27 51 24 34

Get Ready! To prepare for Lesson 13-4, do Exercises 65–67.

Use the graph. Find each of the following. ◀ See Lesson 13-1.

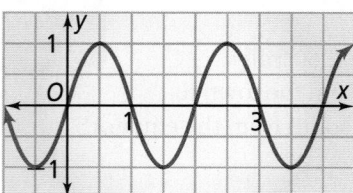

65. the period **66.** the domain **67.** the amplitude **68.** the equation of the midline

13-4

The Sine Function

 Common Core State Standards

F-TF.A.2 Explain how the unit circle . . . enables the extension of trigonometric functions to all real numbers . . . **Also F-IF.B.4, F-IF.C.7e, F-TF.B.5**

MP 1, MP 2, MP 3, MP 4, MP 5

Objectives To identify properties of the sine function
To graph sine curves

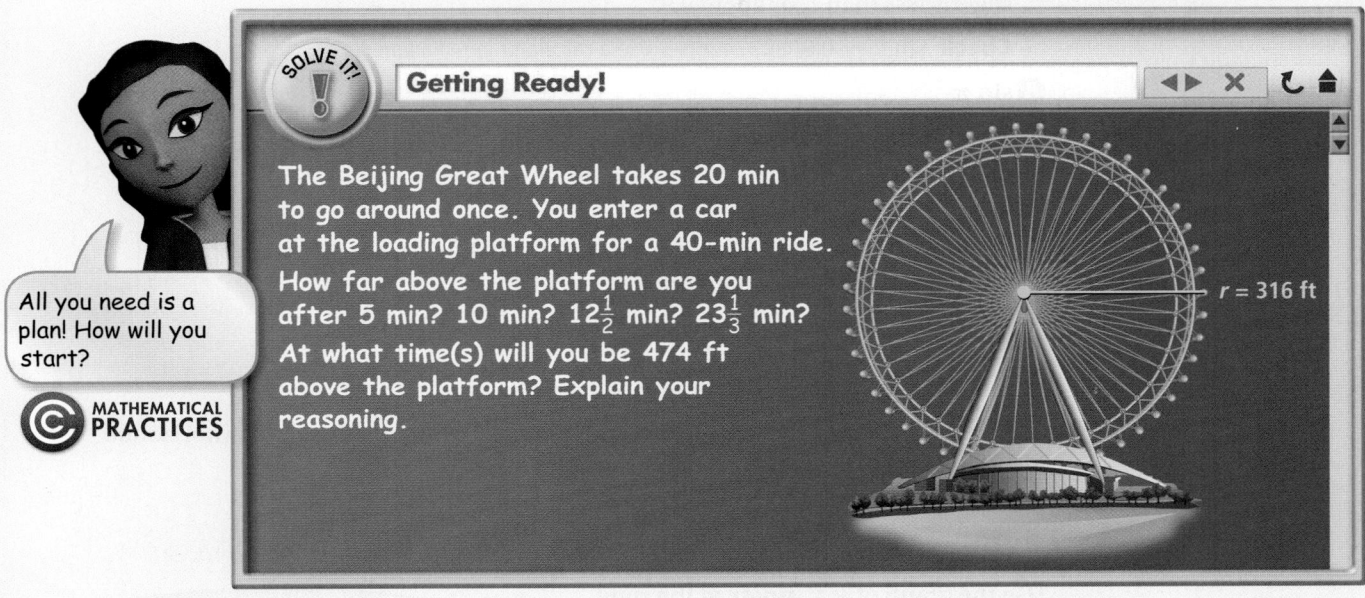

SOLVE IT!

Getting Ready!

The Beijing Great Wheel takes 20 min to go around once. You enter a car at the loading platform for a 40-min ride. How far above the platform are you after 5 min? 10 min? $12\frac{1}{2}$ min? $23\frac{1}{3}$ min? At what time(s) will you be 474 ft above the platform? Explain your reasoning.

r = 316 ft

All you need is a plan! How will you start?

MATHEMATICAL PRACTICES

Lesson Vocabulary
• sine function
• sine curve

The **sine function**, $y = \sin \theta$, matches the measure θ of an angle in standard position with the y-coordinate of a point on the unit circle. This point is where the terminal side of the angle intersects the unit circle.

You can graph the sine function in radians or degrees. In this book, you should use radians unless degrees are specified. For each and every point along the unit circle, the radian measure of the arc has a corresponding sine value. In the graphs below, the points for 1, 2, and 3 radians are marked on the unit circle. The black bars represent the sine values of the points on the circle translated onto the sine graph.

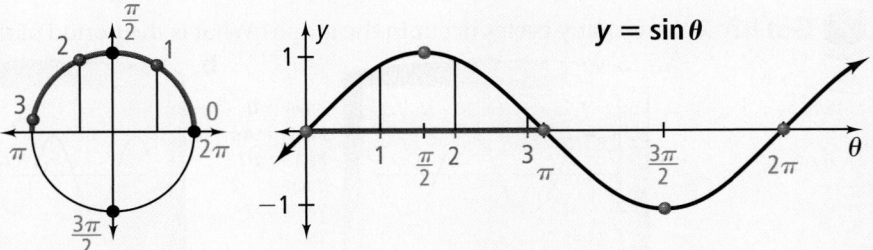

Essential Understanding As the terminal side of an angle rotates about the origin (beginning at 0), its sine value on the unit circle increases from 0 to 1, decreases from 1 to −1, and then increases back to 0.

Problem 1 Estimating Sine Values Graphically

What is a reasonable estimate for each value from the graph? Check your estimate with a calculator.

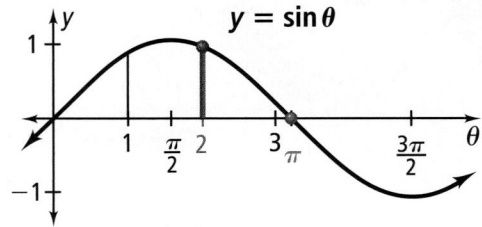

A sin 2

The sine function reaches its maximum value of 1 at $\frac{\pi}{2} \approx 1.57$. The value of the function at 2 is slightly less than 1, or about 0.9.

Think

How accurate should your estimate be?

The y-values range from -1 to 1, so the estimate should be to the nearest tenth.

Check sin 2 ≈ 0.9092974268   Use a calculator in radian mode.

B sin π

The sine function crosses the x-axis at π, so sin π = 0.

Check sin π = 0   Use a calculator in radian mode.

 Got It? **1.** What is a reasonable estimate for each value from the graph above? Check your estimate with a calculator.

  a. sin 3   **b.** $\sin \frac{3\pi}{2}$

The graph of a sine function is called a **sine curve**. By varying the period (horizontal length of one cycle), you get different sine curves.

 Problem 2 Finding the Period of a Sine Curve

Use the graph of $y = \sin 4x$ at the right.

A **How many cycles occur in the graph at the right?**

The graph shows 4 cycles.

B **What is the period of $y = \sin 4x$?**

$$2\pi \div 4 = \frac{\pi}{2}$$ Divide the interval of the graph by the number of cycles.

The period of $y = \sin 4x$ is $\frac{\pi}{2}$.

Plan

How do you find the number of cycles?

Identify the smallest repeating section of the graph and count the number of times it occurs.

Xmin = 0
Xmax = 2π
Xscl = π/2
Ymin = −2
Ymax = 2
Yscl = 1

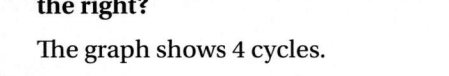

Got It? **2.** How many cycles occur in the graph? What is the period of the sine curve?

a.

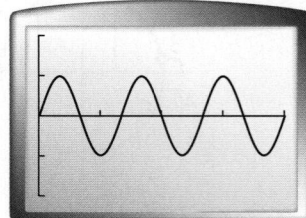

Xmin = 0
Xmax = 4π
Xscl = π/2
Ymin = −2
Ymax = 2
Yscl = 1

b.

Xmin = 0
Xmax = 4π
Xscl = π/2
Ymin = −2
Ymax = 2
Yscl = 1

You can also vary the amplitude of a sine curve.

 Problem 3 **Finding the Amplitude of a Sine Curve**

The graphing calculator screens at the right show four graphs of $y = a \sin x$. Each x-axis shows values from 0 to 2π.

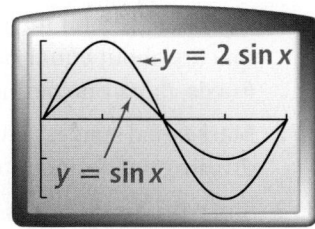

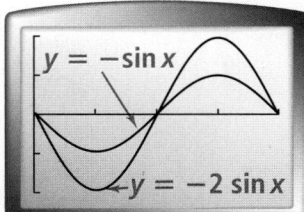

Think

What is the amplitude?
The amplitude is half the difference of the maximum and minimum values of the periodic function.

A What is the amplitude of each sine curve? How does the value of a affect the amplitude?

The amplitude of $y = \sin x$ is 1, and the amplitude of $y = 2 \sin x$ is 2.
The amplitude of $y = -\sin x$ is 1, and the amplitude of $y = -2 \sin x$ is 2.
In each case, the amplitude of the curve is $|a|$.

B How does a negative value of a affect the position of the curve?

When a is negative, the graph is a reflection across the x-axis.

 Got It? **3.** The equation of the graph is of the form $y = a \sin x$. What is the amplitude of the sine curve? What is the value of a?

a.

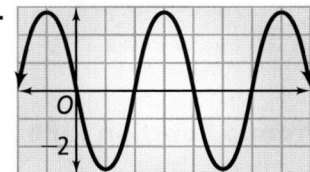

b.

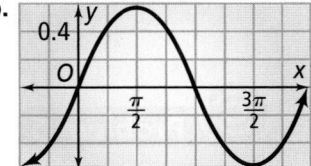

The summary box below lists the properties of sine functions.

take note

Concept Summary Properties of Sine Functions

Suppose $y = a \sin b\theta$, with $a \neq 0$, $b > 0$, and θ in radians.

* $|a|$ is the amplitude of the function.
* b is the number of cycles in the interval from 0 to 2π.
* $\frac{2\pi}{b}$ is the period of the function.

You can use five points equally spaced through one cycle to sketch a sine curve. For $a > 0$, this five-point pattern is *zero-max-zero-min-zero*.

Problem 4 Sketching a Graph

What is the graph of one cycle of a sine curve with amplitude 2, period 4π, midline $y = 0$, and $a > 0$? Using the form $y = a \sin b\,\theta$, what is an equation for the sine curve?

Step 1 Choose scales for the y-axis and the θ-axis that are about equal ($\pi \approx 3$ units). On the θ-axis, mark one period (4π).

Step 2 Mark equal spaces through one cycle by dividing the period into fourths.

Step 3 Since the amplitude is 2, the maximum is 2 and the minimum is -2. Since $a > 0$, the maximum value occurs before the minimum value. Plot the five-point pattern and sketch the curve.

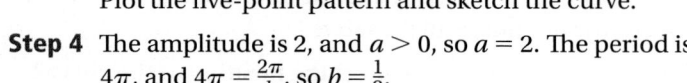

Step 4 The amplitude is 2, and $a > 0$, so $a = 2$. The period is 4π, and $4\pi = \frac{2\pi}{b}$, so $b = \frac{1}{2}$.

An equation for the function is $y = 2 \sin \frac{1}{2}\theta$.

> **Think**
>
> **What do you need to find to write the equation?**
> You need to find a and b.

✓ **Got It?** **4.** What is the graph of one cycle of a sine curve with amplitude 3, period 4π, and $a > 0$? Use the form $y = a \sin b\,\theta$. What is an equation with $a > 0$ for the sine curve?

Problem 5 Graphing From a Function Rule

What is the graph of one cycle of $y = \frac{1}{2} \sin 2\theta$?

Know	**Need**	**Plan**
An equation of the form $y = a \sin b\theta$	The graph of one cycle of the equation	Identify the amplitude and period to find and plot points of the *zero-max-zero-min-zero* pattern.

Step 1 Find the amplitude, number of cycles, and period.

$$|a| = \left|\frac{1}{2}\right| = \frac{1}{2} \text{ and } b = 2, \text{ so it cycles 2 times from 0 to } 2\pi.$$

Period: $\frac{2\pi}{b} = \frac{2\pi}{2} = \pi$

Step 2 Divide the period into fourths. Identify θ-values for the five-point pattern.

$$\pi \div 4 = \frac{\pi}{4} \qquad \text{The } \theta\text{-values are } 0, \frac{\pi}{4}, \frac{\pi}{2}, \frac{3\pi}{4}, \text{ and } \pi.$$

Step 3 Sketch the graph.

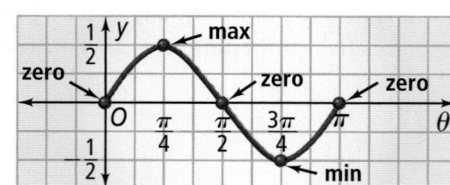

Got It? **5.** What is the graph of one cycle of each sine function?

      a. $y = 1.5 \sin 2\theta$ **b.** $y = 3 \sin \frac{\pi}{2}\theta$

 Problem 6 **Using the Sine Function to Model Light Waves**

Multiple Choice The graphs at the right model waves of red, blue, and yellow light. Which equation best models blue light?

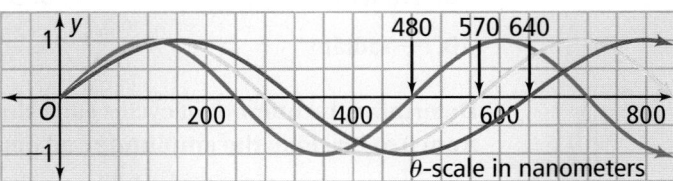

θ-scale in nanometers

  Ⓐ $y = \sin 240\pi\theta$ Ⓑ $y = \sin 480\pi\theta$ Ⓒ $y = \sin \frac{\pi}{480}\theta$ Ⓓ $y = \sin \frac{\pi}{240}\theta$

According to the graph, one blue cycle takes 480 nanometers to complete, so the period is 480.

Think

How can you check if you found the correct value for *b*?
Multiply the value you found for *b* by the number of nanometers where the first cycle ends. The product should be 2π.

To write an equation, first find *b*.

$$\text{period} = \frac{2\pi}{b} \quad \text{Use the relationship between the period and } b.$$

$$480 = \frac{2\pi}{b} \quad \text{Substitute.}$$

$$b = \frac{2\pi}{480} \quad \text{Multiply each side by } \frac{b}{480}.$$

An equation for blue light is $y = \sin \frac{2\pi}{480}\theta$ or $y = \sin \frac{\pi}{240}\theta$. The correct answer is D.

 Got It? **6.** What equation best models red light in Problem 6?

 Lesson Check

Do you know HOW?

1. a. How many cycles does this graph of a sine function have in the interval from 0 to 2π?

   b. What are the amplitude and period?

   c. Write an equation for the function.

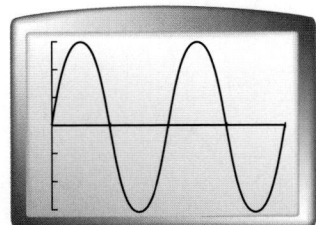

Xmin = 0
Xmax = 2π
Xscl = $\pi/2$
Ymin = -3
Ymax = 3
Yscl = 1

2. Sketch one cycle of the sine curve that has amplitude 2 and period $\frac{\pi}{3}$.

Do you UNDERSTAND?  MATHEMATICAL PRACTICES

3. Vocabulary What is the difference between one cycle and the period of a sine curve?

4. Open-Ended Write a sine function that has a period greater than the period for $y = 5 \sin \frac{\theta}{2}$.

5. Error Analysis A student drew this graph for the function $y = -3 \sin \pi\theta$. Describe and correct the student's errors.

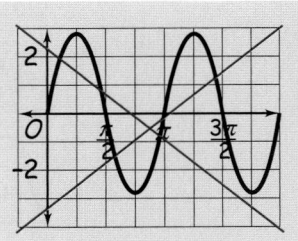

Practice and Problem-Solving Exercises

 MATHEMATICAL PRACTICES

 Practice

Use the graph at the right to find the value of $y = \sin\theta$ for each value of θ.

See Problem 1.

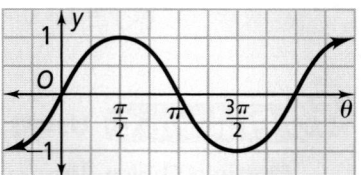

6. $\frac{\pi}{2}$ radians

7. 3 radians

8. 4 radians

9. 5 radians

10. $\frac{3\pi}{2}$ radians

11. $\frac{7\pi}{4}$ radians

Determine the number of cycles each sine function has in the interval from 0 to 2π. Find the amplitude and period of each function.

See Problems 2 and 3.

12.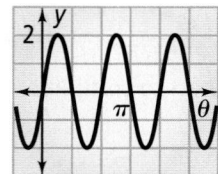

13.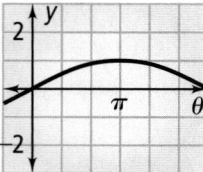

14.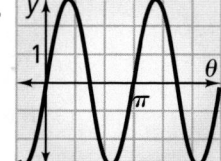

Sketch one cycle of each sine curve. Assume $a > 0$. Write an equation for each graph.

See Problem 4.

15. amplitude 2, period $\frac{2\pi}{3}$

16. amplitude $\frac{1}{3}$, period π

17. amplitude 4, period 4π

18. amplitude 3, period 2π

19. amplitude 1, period 2

20. amplitude 1.5, period 3

Sketch one cycle of the graph of each sine function.

See Problem 5.

21. $y = \sin \pi\theta$

22. $y = \sin 3\theta$

23. $y = -\sin \frac{\pi}{2}\theta$

24. $y = 2 \sin \pi\theta$

25. $y = 4 \sin \frac{1}{2}\theta$

26. $y = -4 \sin \frac{1}{2}\theta$

Find the period of each sine curve. Then write an equation for each sine function.

See Problem 6.

27.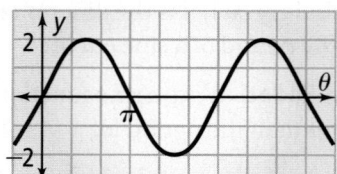

28.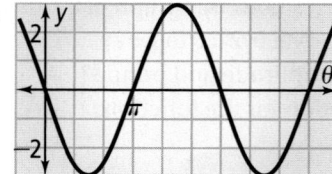

29.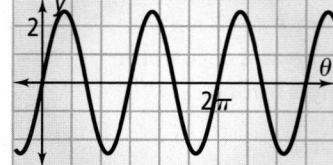

30.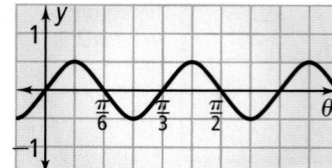

Apply

Determine the number of cycles each sine function has in the interval from 0 to 2π. Find the amplitude and period of each function.

31. $y = \sin \theta$ **32.** $y = \sin 5\theta$ **33.** $y = \sin \pi\theta$

34. $y = 3 \sin \theta$ **35.** $y = -5 \sin \theta$ **36.** $y = -5 \sin 2\pi\theta$

37. Graphing Calculator Graph the functions $y = 3 \sin \theta$ and $y = -3 \sin \theta$ on the same screen. How are the two graphs related? How does the graph of $y = a \sin b\theta$ change when a is replaced with its opposite?

38. Use the formula period $= \frac{2\pi}{b}$ to find the period of each sine function.

    a. $y = 1.5 \sin 2\theta$ **b.** $y = 3 \sin \frac{\pi}{2}\theta$

 39. Think About a Plan The sound wave for the note A above middle C can be modeled by the function $y = 0.001 \sin 880\pi\theta$. Sketch a graph of the sine curve.
- What is the period of the function?
- What is the amplitude of the function?
- How many cycles of the graph are between 0 and 2π?

Find the period and amplitude of each sine function. Then sketch each function from 0 to 2π.

40. $y = -3.5 \sin 5\theta$ **41.** $y = \frac{5}{2} \sin 2\theta$ **42.** $y = -2 \sin 2\pi\theta$

43. $y = 0.4 \sin 3\theta$ **44.** $y = 0.5 \sin \frac{\pi}{3}\theta$ **45.** $y = -1.2 \sin \frac{5\pi}{6}\theta$

 46. Open-Ended Write the equations of three sine functions with the same amplitude that have periods of 2, 3, and 4. Then sketch all three graphs.

47. Music The sound wave for a certain pitch fork can be modeled by the function $y = 0.001 \sin 1320\pi\theta$. Sketch a graph of the sine curve.

 **Challenge**

48. Astronomy In Houston, Texas, at the spring equinox (March 21), there are 12 hours and 9 minutes of sunlight. The longest and shortest day of the year vary from the equinox by 1 h 55 min. The amount of sunlight during the year can be modeled by a sine function.

    a. Define the independent and dependent variables for a function that models the variation in hours of sunlight in Houston.

    b. What are the amplitude and period of the function measured in days?

    c. Write a function that relates the number of days away from the spring equinox to the variation in hours of sunlight in Houston.

    d. Estimation Use your function from part (c). In Houston, about how much less sunlight does February 14 have than March 21?

STEM **Sound** For sound waves, the period and the frequency of a pitch are reciprocals of each other: period $= \frac{\text{seconds}}{\text{cycle}}$ and frequency $= \frac{\text{cycles}}{\text{second}}$. Write an equation for each pitch. Let $\theta =$ time in seconds. Use $a = 1$.

49. the lowest pitch easily heard by humans: 30 cycles per second

50. the lowest pitch heard by elephants: 15 cycles per second

51. the highest pitch heard by bats: 120,000 cycles per second

Find the period and amplitude of each function. Sketch each function from 0 to 2π.

52. $y = \sin(\theta + 2)$ **53.** $y = \sin(\theta - 3)$ **54.** $y = \sin(2\theta + 4)$

Standardized Test Prep

SAT/ACT

55. Which value is NOT the same as the other three values?

   Ⓐ $\sin 100°$ Ⓑ $\sin 80°$ Ⓒ $\sin -80°$ Ⓓ $\sin -260°$

56. What is the amplitude of $y = 3 \sin 4\theta$?

   Ⓕ $\frac{4}{3}$ Ⓖ 3   Ⓗ 4   Ⓘ 2π

57. Which answer choice describes $y = -\sin 2\theta$?

   Ⓐ amplitude -1, period 4π Ⓒ amplitude 1, period π

   Ⓑ amplitude 2, period $-\pi$ Ⓓ amplitude 2π, period 1

58. Which function has a period of 4π and an amplitude of 8?

   Ⓕ $y = -8 \sin 8\theta$ Ⓖ $y = -8 \sin \frac{1}{2}\theta$ Ⓗ $y = 8 \sin 2\theta$ Ⓘ $y = 4 \sin 8\theta$

Short Response

59. Find the value of θ that is between $90°$ and $180°$ such that $\sin \theta = \sin 60°$. Show your work.

Mixed Review

Write each measure in radians. Express the answer in terms of π and as a decimal rounded to the nearest hundredth.

                                                      ◀ See Lesson 13-3.

60. $-80°$ **61.** $150°$ **62.** $-240°$ **63.** $320°$ **64.** $-450°$

65. A poll of teenagers in one town showed that 43% play a team sport. It also   ◀ See Lesson 11-4.
showed that 21% play varsity team sports. Find the probability that a teenager plays varsity sports, given that the teenager plays a team sport.

Get Ready! To prepare for Lesson 13-5, do Exercises 66–69.

Find the x-coordinate of each point on the unit circle at the right.

◀ See Lesson 13-2.

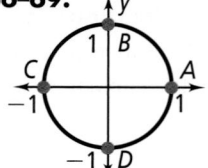

66. A **67.** B **68.** C **69.** D

Do you know HOW?

1. Find the period and amplitude of the periodic function.

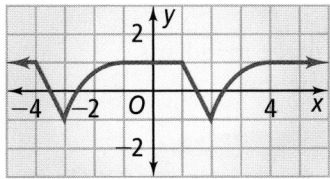

2. Find the measure of the angle in standard position.

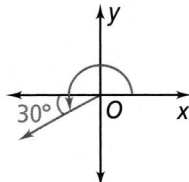

Sketch each angle in standard position.

3. $-150°$

4. $240°$

Write each measure in radians. Express the answer in terms of π and as a decimal rounded to the nearest hundredth.

5. $-180°$

6. $36°$

Write each measure in degrees. Round your answer to the nearest degree if necessary.

7. $\frac{2}{3}\pi$ radians

8. $-\frac{7}{6}\pi$ radians

9. 0.5 radians

10. -2 radians

The measure θ of an angle in standard position is given. Find the exact values of $\cos\theta$ and $\sin\theta$ for each angle measure.

11. $-225°$

12. $120°$

13. $-\frac{4\pi}{3}$ radians

14. $\frac{5\pi}{4}$ radians

15. Find the length of the intercepted arc to the nearest tenth for an arc with a central angle of measure $\theta = \frac{\pi}{3}$ on a circle of radius $r = 10$.

16. Sketch one cycle of a sine function with amplitude 3 and period 2.

17. Find the amplitude, period, and midline of the graph of $y = \frac{1}{4}\sin 3\theta$.

Do you UNDERSTAND?

18. Open-Ended Sketch the graph of a periodic function with a period of 10 and an amplitude of 7.

19. Writing You are given an angle with a positive angle measure in degrees. Describe how you can find an angle coterminal with that angle that also has a positive angle measure in degrees.

20. Reasoning On a merry-go-round, you stand 15 feet from the center while your friend stands 10 feet from the center. How would you find how much further you travel in one revolution than your friend? What is that distance?

21. Reasoning Will two sine functions with the same period but different amplitudes intersect? Explain.

22. Reasoning In the formula $y = a \sin b\theta$, you know how the values a, b, and θ affect the graph of the sine wave.
   a. Hypothesize how the formula would need to change to allow for a sine wave whose midline was above or below the x-axis.
   b. How would it change to show a wave translated left or right?

Concept Byte

For Use With Lesson 13-4

TECHNOLOGY

Graphing Trigonometric Functions

 **Common Core State Standards**

Prepares for F-TF.B.5 Choose trigonometric functions to model periodic phenomena with specified amplitude, frequency, and midline.

MP 5

Activity 1

MATHEMATICAL
PRACTICES

Compare the graphs of $y = \cos x$ from $-360°$ to $360°$ and from -2π to 2π radians.

Step 1 Press **mode** to set the mode to degrees. Adjust the window values. Graph the function.

Step 2 Change the mode to radians. Graph the function.

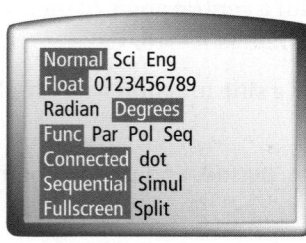

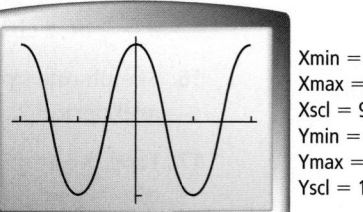

Xmin = −360
Xmax = 360
Xscl = 90
Ymin = −1.2
Ymax = 1.2
Yscl = 1

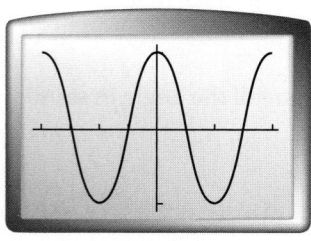

Xmin = −2π
Xmax = 2π
Xscl = $\frac{\pi}{2}$
Ymin = −1.2
Ymax = 1.2
Yscl = 1

The graphs appear to be identical. The function has a period of $360°$ or 2π radians.

Activity 2

Graph the function $y = \sin x$. Find $\sin 30°$ and $\sin 150°$.

Step 1 Set the mode to degrees and adjust the window values as shown.

Step 2 Graph the function. Use the **trace** key to find the y-values when $x = 30$ and $x = 150$.

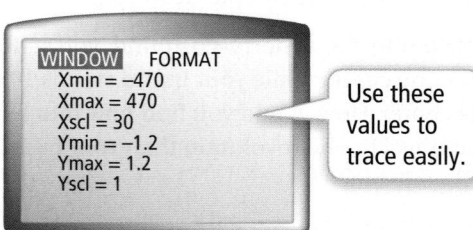

Use these values to trace easily.

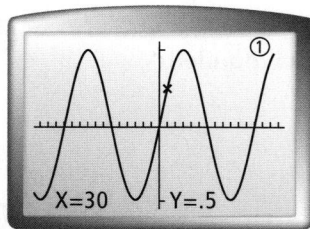

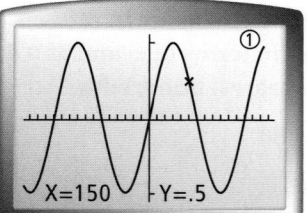

Exercises

Use appropriate window values to identify the period of each function in radians and in degrees. Then evaluate each function at 90°.

1. $y = \cos x$

2. $y = \sin x$

3. $y = \sin 3x$

4. $y = -3 \sin x$

5. $y = \cos (x + 30)$

Ⓒ **Writing** Graph the two functions in the same window. Compare the graphs. How are they similar? How are they different?

6. $y = \sin x, y = \cos x$

7. $y = \sin x, y = \cos\left(x - \frac{\pi}{2}\right)$

8. $y = \sin x, y = \cos\left(x + \frac{\pi}{2}\right)$

The Cosine Function

 Common Core State Standards

F-TF.B.5 Choose trigonometric functions to model periodic phenomena . . . **Also F-IF.B.4, F-IF.C.7e, F-TF.A.2**

MP 1, MP 2, MP 3, MP 4, MP 5

Objectives To graph and write cosine functions
To solve trigonometric equations

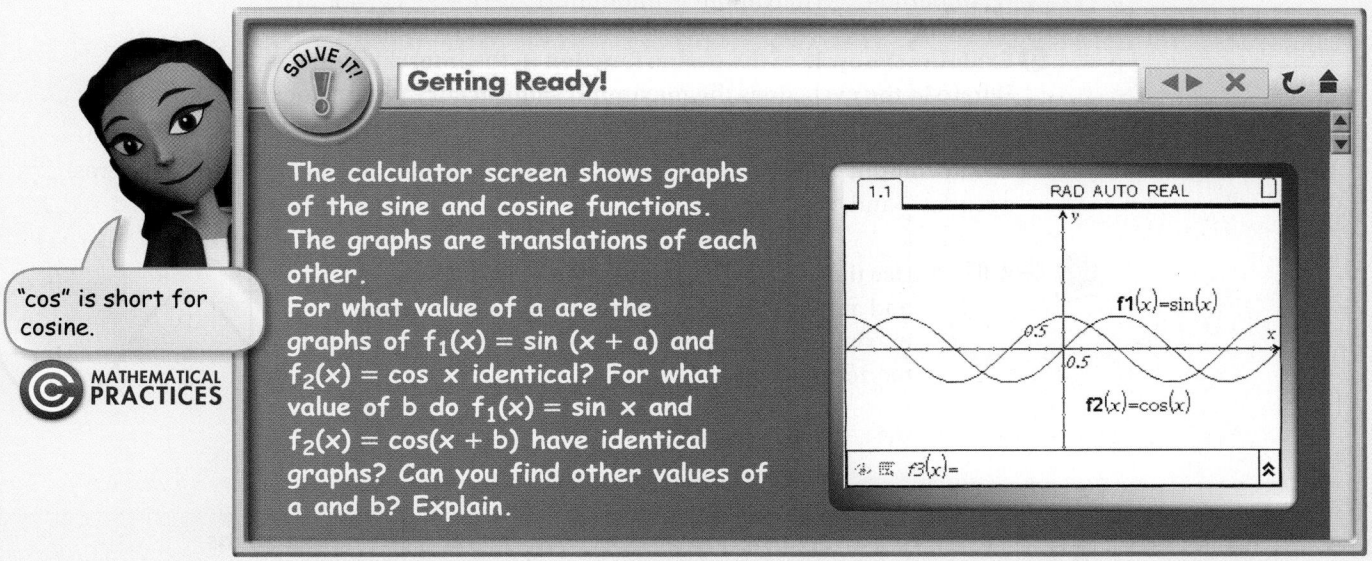

SOLVE IT!

Getting Ready!

The calculator screen shows graphs of the sine and cosine functions. The graphs are translations of each other.
For what value of a are the graphs of $f_1(x) = \sin(x + a)$ and $f_2(x) = \cos x$ identical? For what value of b do $f_1(x) = \sin x$ and $f_2(x) = \cos(x + b)$ have identical graphs? Can you find other values of a and b? Explain.

"cos" is short for cosine.

MATHEMATICAL PRACTICES

1.1   RAD AUTO REAL

$f1(x) = \sin(x)$

$f2(x) = \cos(x)$

$f3(x) =$

Lesson Vocabulary
• cosine function

The **cosine function**, $y = \cos \theta$, matches θ with the x-coordinate of the point on the unit circle where the terminal side of angle θ intersects the unit circle. The symmetry of the set of points $(x, y) = (\cos \theta, \sin \theta)$ on the unit circle guarantees that the graphs of sine and cosine are congruent translations of each other.

Essential Understanding For each and every point along the unit circle the radian measure of the arc has a corresponding cosine value. The colored bars represent the cosine values of the points on the circle translated onto the cosine graph. So as the terminal side of an angle rotates about the origin (beginning at 0°), its cosine value on the unit circle decreases from 1 to −1, and then increases back to 1.

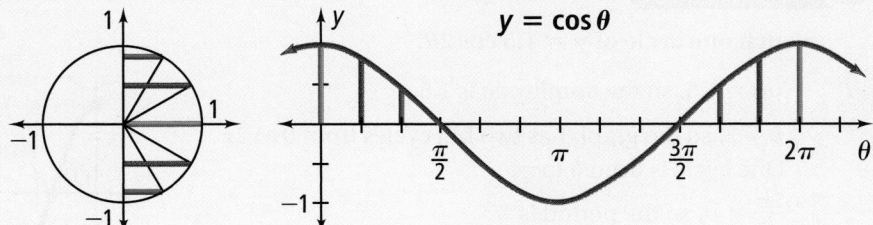

$y = \cos \theta$

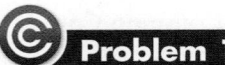 **Problem 1** Interpreting a Graph

A **What are the domain, period, range, and amplitude of the cosine function?**

The domain of the function is all real numbers.

The function goes from its maximum value of 1 to its minimum value of -1 and back again in an interval from 0 to 2π. The period is 2π. The midline is $y = 0$.

The range of the function is $-1 \le y \le 1$.

$$\text{amplitude} = \tfrac{1}{2}(\text{maximum} - \text{minimum}) = \tfrac{1}{2}[1 - (-1)] = 1$$

Think

How do you find a zero of a function?
Zeros are where the graph of a function crosses the x-axis.

B **Examine the cycle of the cosine function in the interval from 0 to 2π. Where in the cycle does the maximum value occur? Where does the minimum occur? Where do the zeros occur?**

The maximum value occurs at 0 and 2π. The minimum value occurs at π. The zeros occur at $\frac{\pi}{2}$ and $\frac{3\pi}{2}$.

 Got It? **1.** Use the graph. What are the domain, period, range, and amplitude of the sine function? Where do the maximum and minimum values occur? Where do the zeros occur?

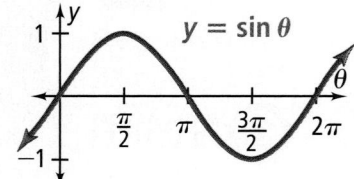

take note **Concept Summary** **Properties of Cosine Functions**

Suppose $y = a \cos b\theta$, with $a \ne 0$, $b > 0$, and θ in radians.

- $|a|$ is the amplitude of the function.
- b is the number of cycles in the interval from 0 to 2π.
- $\frac{2\pi}{b}$ is the period of the function.

To graph a cosine function, locate five points equally spaced through one cycle. For $a > 0$, this five-point pattern is *max-zero-min-zero-max*.

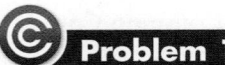 **Problem 2** Sketching the Graph of a Cosine Function

Plan

What should you find to graph the function?
Find the amplitude, cycle, and period.

Sketch one cycle of $y = 1.5 \cos 2\theta$.

$|a| = 1.5$, so the amplitude is 1.5.

$b = 2$, so the graph has two full cycles from 0 to 2π. One cycle is from 0 to π.

$\frac{2\pi}{b} = \pi$, so the period is π.

Divide the period into fourths. Plot the five-point pattern for one cycle. Use 1.5 for the maximum and -1.5 for the minimum. Sketch the curve.

Choose scales for axes that are about equal ($\frac{\pi}{3} \approx 1$).

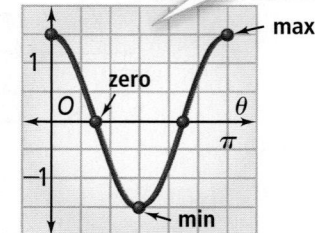

Got It? **2.** Sketch one cycle of $y = 2\cos\frac{\theta}{3}$.

 Problem 3 **Modeling with a Cosine Function** STEM

Oceanography The water level varies from low tide to high tide as shown. What is a cosine function that models the water level in inches above and below the average water level? Express the model as a function of time in hours since 10:30 A.M..

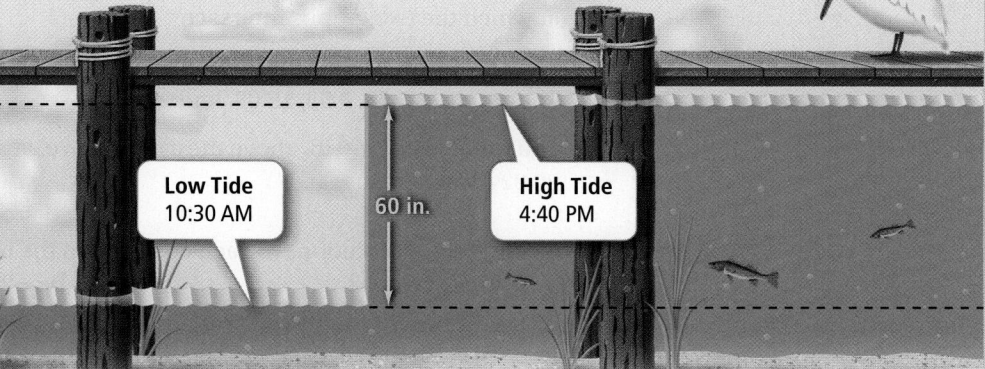

Low Tide
10:30 AM

60 in.

High Tide
4:40 PM

Know
- The difference of the 2 water levels is 60 in.
- The time difference between the low level and the high level is 6 h 10 min.

Need
A cosine function that models the water level as a function of time

Plan
- Find values of a and b.
- Substitute the values of a and b into $y = a\cos b\theta$.

Amplitude is $\frac{1}{2}(60) = 30$. Since the tide is at -30 inches at time zero, the curve follows the *min-zero-max-zero-min* pattern, so $a = -30$.

The cycle is halfway complete after 6 h and 10 min, so the full period is 12 hours and 20 minutes or $12\frac{1}{3}$ hours.

$$12\frac{1}{3} = \frac{2\pi}{b}$$

$$b = \frac{6\pi}{37}$$

So, the function $f(t) = -30\cos\left(\frac{6\pi}{37}t\right)$ models the water level.

 Got It? **3. a.** Suppose that the water level varies 70 inches between low tide at 8:40 A.M. and high tide at 2:55 P.M. What is a cosine function that models the variation in inches above and below the average water level as a function of the number of hours since 8:40 A.M.?

   b. At what point in the cycle does the function cross the midline? What does the midline represent?

You can solve an equation by graphing to find an exact location along a sine or cosine curve.

 **Problem 4** Solving a Cosine Equation

Suppose you want to find the time t in hours when the water level from Problem 3 is exactly 10 in. above the average level represented by $f(t) = 0$. What are all solutions to the equation $-30 \cos\left(\frac{6\pi}{37}t\right) = 10$ in the interval from 0 to 25?

Plan

How can two equations help find the solutions?
The solutions occur where their graphs intersect.

Step 1 Use two equations. Graph $y = 10$ and $y = -30 \cos\left(\frac{6\pi}{37}t\right)$ on the same screen.

Step 2 Use the **INTERSECT** feature to find the points at which the two graphs intersect.

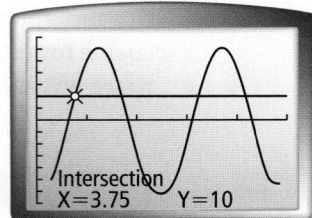

Xmin = 0
Xmax = 25
Xscl = 5
Ymin = −35
Ymax = 35
Yscl = 5

The graphs show four solutions in the interval. They are $t \approx 3.75$, 8.58, 16.08, and 20.92.

The water level is 10 in. above the average level at about 3.75 h, 8.58 h, 16.08 h, and 20.92 h after 10:30 A.M.

Got It? **4.** What are all solutions to each equation in the interval from 0 to 2π?
    a. $3 \cos 2t = -2$ **b.** $-2 \cos \theta = 1.2$
    c. Reasoning In the interval from 0 to 2π, when is $-2 \cos \theta$ less than 1.2? Greater than 1.2?

Lesson Check

Do you know HOW?

Sketch the graph of each function in the interval from 0 to 2π.

1. $y = \cos \frac{1}{2}\theta$ **2.** $y = 2 \cos \frac{\pi}{3}\theta$

Write a cosine function for each description. Assume that $a > 0$.

3. amplitude 3, period 2π **4.** amplitude 1.5, period π

Do you UNDERSTAND? MATHEMATICAL PRACTICES

5. Open-Ended Write a cosine function with amplitude 5 and between 2 and 3 cycles from 0 to 2π.

6. Assume θ is in the interval from 0 to 2π.
    a. For what values of θ is y positive for $y = \cos \theta$?
    b. For what values of θ is y positive for $y = -\sin \theta$?
    c. Reasoning What sine function has the same graph as $y = -3 \cos \frac{2\pi}{3}\theta$?

Practice and Problem-Solving Exercises MATHEMATICAL PRACTICES

A **Practice** Find the period and amplitude of each cosine function. Determine the values of x for $0 \leq x \leq 2\pi$ where the maximum value(s), minimum value(s), and zeros occur.   **◀ See Problem 1.**

7.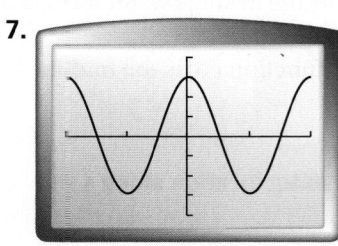

Xmin = −2π
Xmax = 2π
Xscl = π
Ymin = −4
Ymax = 4
Yscl = 1

8.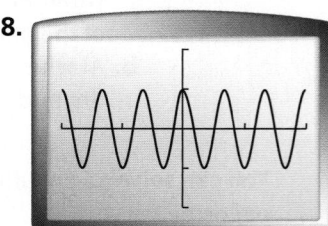

Xmin = −2π
Xmax = 2π
Xscl = π
Ymin = −2
Ymax = 2
Yscl = 1

9.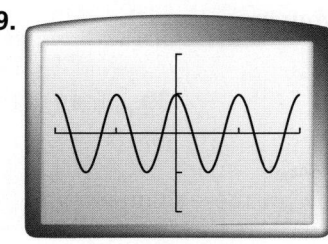

Xmin = -2π
Xmax = 2π
Xscl = π
Ymin = -2
Ymax = 2
Yscl = 1

10.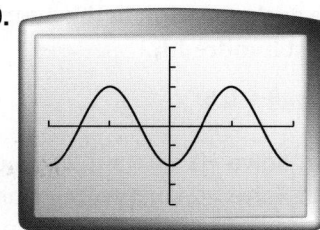

Xmin = -2π
Xmax = 2π
Xscl = π
Ymin = -4
Ymax = 4
Yscl = 1

Sketch one cycle of the graph of each cosine function.   ◀ See Problem 2.

11. $y = \cos 2\theta$ **12.** $y = -3\cos\theta$ **13.** $y = -\cos 3t$ **14.** $y = \cos\frac{\pi}{2}\theta$ **15.** $y = -\cos\pi\theta$

Write a cosine function for each description. Assume that $a > 0$.   ◀ See Problem 3.

16. amplitude 2, period π **17.** amplitude $\frac{\pi}{2}$, period 3   **18.** amplitude π, period 2

Write an equation of a cosine function for each graph.

19.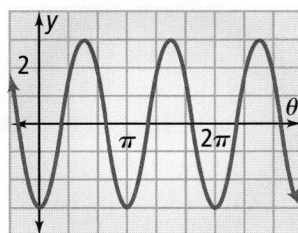

20.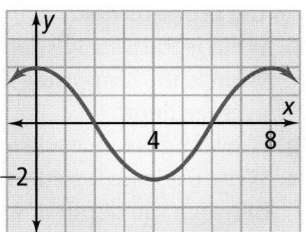

Solve each equation in the interval from 0 to 2π. Round your answer to the nearest hundredth.   ◀ See Problem 4.

21. $\cos 2t = \frac{1}{2}$ **22.** $20\cos t = -8$ **23.** $-2\cos\pi\theta = 0.3$

24. $3\cos\frac{t}{3} = 2$ **25.** $\cos\frac{1}{4}\theta = 1$ **26.** $8\cos\frac{\pi}{3}t = 5$

B  **Apply**   **Identify the period, range, and amplitude of each function.**

27. $y = 3\cos\theta$ **28.** $y = -\cos 2t$ **29.** $y = 2\cos\frac{1}{2}t$ **30.** $y = \frac{1}{3}\cos\frac{\theta}{2}$

31. $y = 3\cos\left(-\frac{\theta}{3}\right)$ **32.** $y = -\frac{1}{2}\cos 3\theta$ **33.** $y = 16\cos\frac{3\pi}{2}t$ **34.** $y = 0.7\cos\pi t$

ⓒ **35. Think About a Plan** In Buenos Aires, Argentina, the average monthly temperature is highest in January and lowest in July, ranging from 83°F to 57°F. Write a cosine function that models the change in temperature according to the month of the year.
  • How can you find the amplitude?
  • What part of the problem describes the length of the cycle?

ⓒ **36. Writing** Explain how you can apply what you know about solving cosine equations to solving sine equations. Use $-1 = 6\sin 2t$ as an example.

Solve each equation in the interval from 0 to 2π. Round your answers to the nearest hundredth.

37. $\sin \theta = 0.6$　　　　**38.** $-3 \sin 2\theta = 1.5$　　　　**39.** $\sin \pi\theta = 1$

40. a. Solve $-2 \sin \theta = 1.2$ in the interval from 0 to 2π.
　　b. Solve $-2 \sin \theta = 1.2$ in the interval $2\pi \le \theta \le 4\pi$. How are these solutions related to the solutions in part (a)?

41. a. Graph the equation $y = -30 \cos\left(\frac{6\pi}{37}t\right)$ from Problem 3.
　　b. The independent variable θ represents time (in hours). Find four times at which the water level is the highest.
　　c. For how many hours during each cycle is the water level above the line $y = 0$? Below $y = 0$?

STEM **42. Tides** The table at the right shows the times for high tide and low tide of one day. The markings on the side of a local pier showed a high tide of 7 ft and a low tide of 4 ft on the previous day.

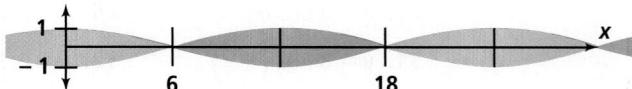

Tide Table	
High tide	4:03 A.M.
Low tide	10:14 A.M.
High tide	4:25 P.M.
Low tide	10:36 P.M.

　　a. What is the average depth of water at the pier? What is the amplitude of the variation from the average depth?
　　b. How long is one cycle of the tide?
　　c. Write a cosine function that models the relationship between the depth of water and the time of day. Use $y = 0$ to represent the average depth of water. Use $t = 0$ to represent the time 4:03 A.M.
　　Ⓒ **d. Reasoning** Suppose your boat needs at least 5 ft of water to approach or leave the pier. Between what times could you come and go?

 **Challenge**

43. Graph one cycle of $y = \cos \theta$, one cycle of $y = -\cos \theta$, and one cycle of $y = \cos(-\theta)$ on the same set of axes. Use the unit circle to explain any relationships you see among these graphs.

STEM **44. Biology** A helix is a three-dimensional spiral. The coiled strands of DNA and the edges of twisted crepe paper are examples of helixes. In the diagram, the y-coordinate of each edge illustrates a cosine function. Write an equation for the y-coordinate of one edge.

 45. a. Graphing Calculator Graph $y = \cos \theta$ and $y = \cos\left(\theta - \frac{\pi}{2}\right)$ in the interval from 0 to 2π. What translation of the graph of $y = \cos \theta$ produces the graph of $y = \cos\left(\theta - \frac{\pi}{2}\right)$?
　　b. Graph $y = \cos\left(\theta - \frac{\pi}{2}\right)$ and $y = \sin \theta$ in the interval from 0 to 2π. What do you notice?
　　Ⓒ **c. Reasoning** Explain how you could rewrite a sine function as a cosine function.

Standardized Test Prep

SAT/ACT

46. Which function has a period of 2π and an amplitude of 4?

(A) $f(x) = 2 \cos 4\theta$ (C) $f(x) = 2 \cos \theta$

(B) $f(x) = 4 \cos 2\theta$ (D) $f(x) = 4 \cos \theta$

47. Which equation corresponds to the graph shown at the right? The screen dimensions are $-4\pi \le x \le 4\pi$ and $-2 \le y \le 2$.

(F) $y = \frac{1}{2} \cos \frac{x}{4}$ (H) $y = \frac{1}{2} \cos 4x$

(G) $y = 2 \cos \frac{x}{4}$ (I) $y = 2 \cos 4x$

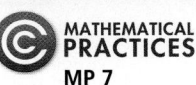

48. Which equation has the same graph as $y = -\cos t$?

(A) $y = \cos(-t)$ (C) $y = \cos(t - \pi)$

(B) $y = \sin(t - \pi)$ (D) $y = -\sin t$

49. How many solutions does the equation $1 = -\sin 2t$ have for $0 \le t \le 2\pi$?

(F) 1   (G) 2   (H) 3   (I) 4

Short Response

50. What are the amplitude and period of $y = -0.2 \cos \frac{\pi}{3}\theta$?

Apply What You've Learned

MATHEMATICAL PRACTICES

MP 7

In the Apply What You've Learned in Lesson 13-1, you considered a function $d = f(t)$ that gives the horizontal distance d of the dragonfly from the y-axis after t seconds, and a function $h = g(t)$ that gives the height h of the dragonfly above the x-axis after t seconds. Refer to the problem on page 827. Choose from the following words, numbers, and equations to complete the sentences below to model $d = f(t)$ and $h = g(t)$ using cosine and sine functions.

2	4	5	π
$\frac{2\pi}{5}$	$\frac{5}{2\pi}$	$\frac{\pi}{2}$	$\frac{\pi}{5}$

a. For the functions $y = a \cos bx$ and $y = a \sin bx$ to have the same amplitude as the functions $d = f(t)$ and $h = g(t)$, a must be equal to __?__ .

b. For the functions $y = a \cos bx$ and $y = a \sin bx$ to have the same period as the functions $d = f(t)$ and $h = g(t)$, b must be equal to __?__ .

13-6 The Tangent Function

Common Core State Standards

F-IF.C.7e Graph . . . trigonometric functions, showing period, midline, and amplitude. **Also F-TF.A.2, F-TF.B.5**

MP 1, MP 2, MP 3, MP 4, MP 5

Objective To graph the tangent function.

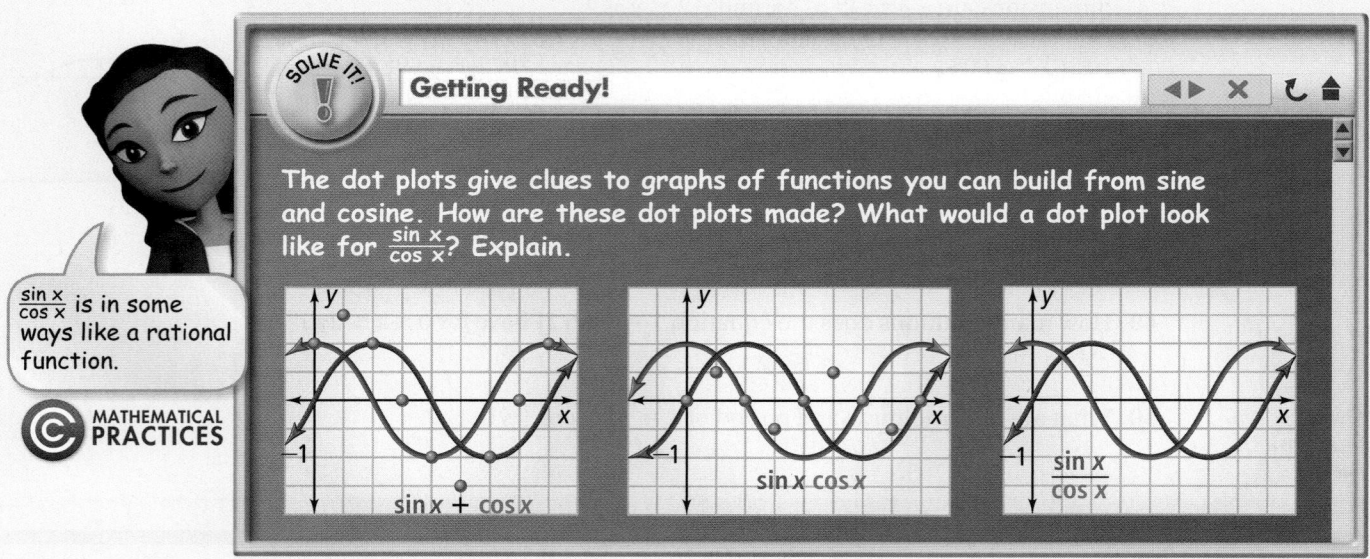

SOLVE IT!

Getting Ready!

The dot plots give clues to graphs of functions you can build from sine and cosine. How are these dot plots made? What would a dot plot look like for $\frac{\sin x}{\cos x}$? Explain.

$\sin x + \cos x$

$\sin x \cos x$

$\frac{\sin x}{\cos x}$

$\frac{\sin x}{\cos x}$ is in some ways like a rational function.

MATHEMATICAL PRACTICES

The tangent function is closely associated with the sine and cosine functions, but it differs from them in three dramatic ways.

Lesson Vocabulary
• tangent of θ
• tangent function

Essential Understanding The tangent function has infinitely many points of discontinuity, with a vertical asymptote at each point. Its range is all real numbers. Its period is π, half that of both the sine and cosine functions. Its domain is all real numbers except odd multiples of $\frac{\pi}{2}$.

take note

Key Concept   Tangent of an Angle

Suppose the terminal side of an angle θ in standard position intersects the unit circle at the point (x, y). Then the ratio $\frac{y}{x}$ is the **tangent of θ,** denoted $\tan \theta$.

In this diagram, $x = \cos \theta$, $y = \sin \theta$, and $\frac{y}{x} = \tan \theta$.

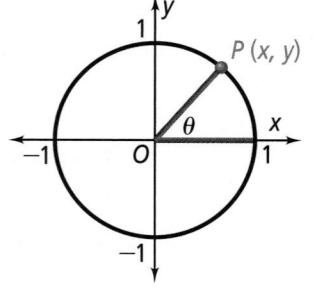

 **Problem 1** Finding Tangents Geometrically

Think

Will a graph help?
Yes; use a graph of the unit circle to visualize the problem.

What is the value of each expression? Do not use a calculator.

A tan π

An angle of π radians in standard position has a terminal side that intersects the unit circle at the point $(-1, 0)$.

$$\tan \pi = \frac{0}{-1} = 0$$

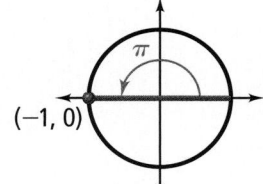

B tan $\left(-\frac{5\pi}{6}\right)$

An angle of $-\frac{5\pi}{6}$ radians in standard position has a terminal side that intersects the unit circle at the point $\left(-\frac{\sqrt{3}}{2}, -\frac{1}{2}\right)$.

$$\tan\left(-\frac{5\pi}{6}\right) = \frac{-\frac{1}{2}}{-\frac{\sqrt{3}}{2}} = \frac{1}{\sqrt{3}} = \frac{\sqrt{3}}{3}.$$

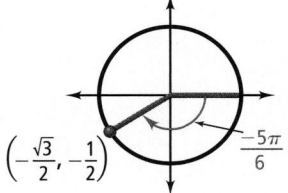

 Got It? **1.** What is the value of each expression? Do not use a calculator.

a. tan $\frac{\pi}{2}$ **b.** tan $\frac{2\pi}{3}$ **c.** tan $\left(-\frac{\pi}{4}\right)$

There is another way to geometrically define tan θ.

The diagram shows the unit circle and the vertical line $x = 1$. The angle θ in standard position determines a point $P(x, y)$.

By similar triangles, the length of the vertical red segment divided by the length of the horizontal red segment is equal to $\frac{y}{x}$. The horizontal red segment has length 1 since it is a radius of the unit circle, so the length of the vertical red segment is $\frac{y}{x}$ or tan θ, which is also the y-coordinate of Q.

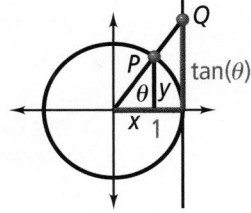

If θ is an angle in standard position and *not* an odd multiple of $\frac{\pi}{2}$, then the line containing the terminal side of θ intersects the line $x = 1$ at a point Q with y-coordinate tan θ.

The graph at the right shows one cycle of the **tangent function**, $y = \tan \theta$, for $-\frac{\pi}{2} < \theta < \frac{\pi}{2}$. The pattern repeats periodically with period π. At $\theta = \pm\frac{\pi}{2}$, the line through P fails to intersect the line $x = 1$, so tan θ is undefined.

$y = \tan \theta$

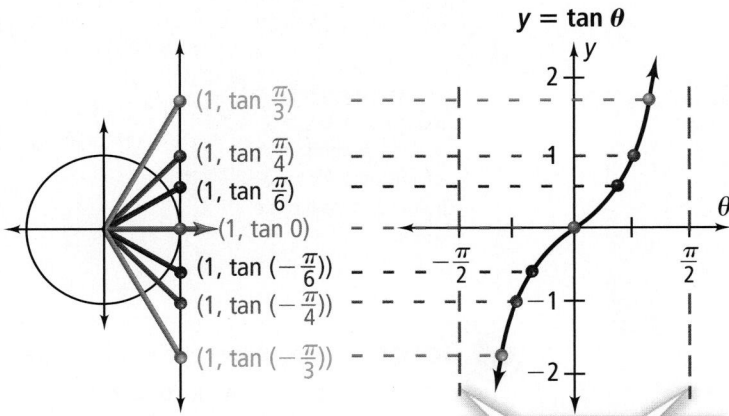

The graph approaches two vertical asymptotes.

Concept Summary   Properties of Tangent Functions

Suppose $y = a \tan b\theta$, with $a \neq 0$, $b > 0$, and θ in radians.

- $\frac{\pi}{b}$ is the period of the function.
- One cycle occurs in the interval from $-\frac{\pi}{2b}$ to $\frac{\pi}{2b}$.
- There are vertical asymptotes at each end of the cycle.

You can use asymptotes and three points to sketch one cycle of a tangent curve. As with sine and cosine, the five elements are equally spaced through one cycle. Use the pattern *asymptote-(−a)-zero-(a)-asymptote*. In the graph at the right, $a = b = 1$.

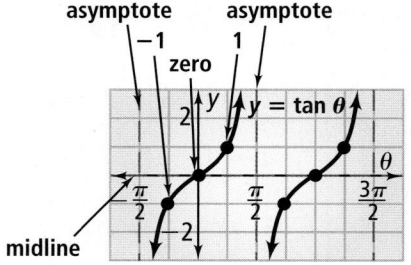

The next example shows how to use the period, asymptotes, and points to graph a tangent function.

 Problem 2 **Graphing a Tangent Function**

Sketch two cycles of the graph of $y = \tan \pi\theta$.

Think	Write
Use the formula for the period. Substitute π for b and simplify.	$\text{period} = \frac{\pi}{b}$ $= \frac{\pi}{\pi} = 1$
One cycle occurs in the interval from $-\frac{\pi}{2b}$ to $\frac{\pi}{2b}$.	$\frac{-\pi}{2b} = \frac{-\pi}{2\pi} = -\frac{1}{2}$ $\frac{\pi}{2b} = \frac{\pi}{2\pi} = \frac{1}{2}$ One cycle is from $-\frac{1}{2}$ to $\frac{1}{2}$.
Asymptotes occur at each end of the cycle.	Asymptotes are at $\theta = -\frac{1}{2}, \frac{1}{2}$, and $\frac{3}{2}$.
Divide the period into fourths and locate 3 points between the asymptotes. Plot the points and sketch the curve.	$\left(-\frac{1}{4}, -1\right)$, $(0, 0)$, and $\left(\frac{1}{4}, 1\right)$ are on the graph. 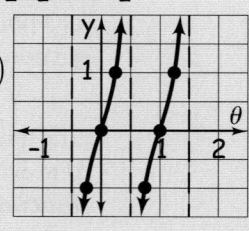

✔ **Got It?** **2.** Sketch two cycles of the graph of each tangent curve.

a. $y = \tan 3\theta, 0 \leq \theta \leq \frac{2\pi}{3}$ **b.** $y = \tan \frac{\pi}{2}\theta, 0 \leq \theta \leq 4$

Problem 3 Using the Tangent Function to Solve Problems ⟨STEM⟩

Design An architect is designing the front facade of a building to include a triangle, similar to the one shown. The function $y = 100 \tan \theta$ models the height of the triangle, where θ is the angle indicated. Graph the function using the degree mode. What is the height of the triangle if $\theta = 16°$? If $\theta = 22°$?

200 ft

Think

How should you graph the function?
"Degree mode" suggests that you use a graphing calculator. Then use **TABLE** to show y values for different θ values.

Step 1 Graph the function.

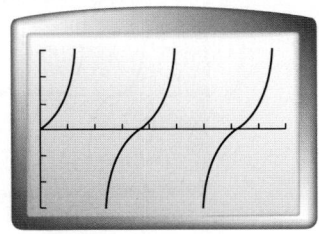

Xmin = 0
Xmax = 470
Xscl = 50
Ymin = −300
Ymax = 300
Yscl = 90

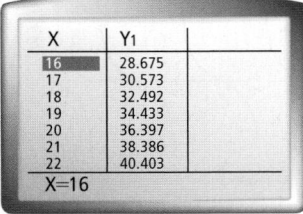

X	Y₁
16	28.675
17	30.573
18	32.492
19	34.433
20	36.397
21	38.386
22	40.403
X=16	

Step 2 Use the **TABLE** feature.

When $\theta = 16°$, the height of the triangle is about 28.7 ft. When $\theta = 22°$, the height of the triangle is about 40.4 ft.

  Got It? 3. a. What is the height of the triangle when $\theta = 25°$?
  b. Reasoning The architect wants the triangle to be at least one story tall. The average height of a story is 14 ft. What must θ be for the height of the triangle to be at least 14 ft?

 Lesson Check

Do you know HOW?

Find each value without using a calculator.

1. $\tan \frac{\pi}{4}$

2. $\tan \frac{7\pi}{6}$

3. $\tan \left(-\frac{\pi}{4} \right)$

4. $\tan \left(-\frac{3\pi}{3} \right)$

Do you UNDERSTAND?  MATHEMATICAL PRACTICES

© **5. Vocabulary** Successive asymptotes of a tangent curve are $x = \frac{\pi}{3}$ and $x = -\frac{\pi}{3}$. What is the period?

© **6. Error Analysis** A quiz contained a question asking students to solve the equation $8 = -2 \tan 3\theta$ to the nearest hundredth of a radian. One student did not receive full credit for writing $\theta = -1.33$. Describe and correct the student's error.

© **7. Writing** Explain how you can write a tangent function that has the same period as $y = \sin 4\theta$.

Practice and Problem-Solving Exercises  MATHEMATICAL PRACTICES

Ⓐ Practice   Find each value without using a calculator. ◀ **See Problem 1.**

8. $\tan(-\pi)$ **9.** $\tan \pi$ **10.** $\tan \frac{3\pi}{4}$ **11.** $\tan \frac{\pi}{2}$

12. $\tan\left(-\frac{7\pi}{4}\right)$ **13.** $\tan 2\pi$ **14.** $\tan\left(-\frac{3\pi}{4}\right)$ **15.** $\tan\left(\frac{3\pi}{2}\right)$

Each graphing calculator screen shows the interval 0 to 2π. What is the period of each graph? ◀ **See Problem 2.**

16.
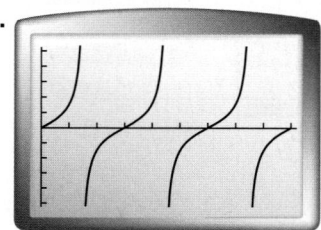

17.
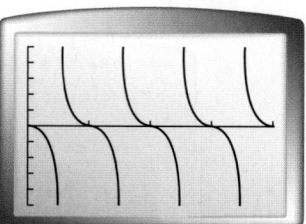

Identify the period and determine where two asymptotes occur for each function.

18. $y = \tan 5\theta$ **19.** $y = \tan \frac{3\theta}{2}$ **20.** $y = \tan 4\theta$ **21.** $y = \tan \frac{2}{3\pi}\theta$

Sketch the graph of each tangent curve in the interval from 0 to 2π.

22. $y = \tan \theta$ **23.** $y = \tan 2\theta$ **24.** $y = \tan \frac{2\pi}{3}\theta$ **25.** $y = \tan(-\theta)$

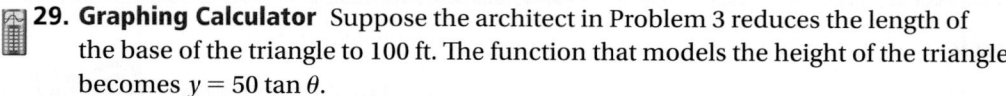 **Graphing Calculator** Graph each function on the interval $0 \le x \le 2\pi$ and ◀ **See Problem 3.**
$-200 \le y \le 200$. Evaluate each function at $x = \frac{\pi}{4}, \frac{\pi}{2},$ and $\frac{3\pi}{4}$.

26. $y = 50 \tan x$ **27.** $y = -100 \tan x$ **28.** $y = 125 \tan\left(\frac{1}{2}x\right)$

29. Graphing Calculator Suppose the architect in Problem 3 reduces the length of the base of the triangle to 100 ft. The function that models the height of the triangle becomes $y = 50 \tan \theta$.
     a. Graph the function on a graphing calculator.
     b. What is the height of the triangle when $\theta = 16°$?
     c. What is the height of the triangle when $\theta = 22°$?

Ⓑ Apply  Identify the period for each tangent function. Then graph each function in the interval from -2π to 2π.

30. $y = \tan \frac{\pi}{6}\theta$ **31.** $y = \tan 2.5\theta$ **32.** $y = \tan\left(-\frac{3}{2\pi}\theta\right)$

Graphing Calculator Solve each equation in the interval from 0 to 2π. Round your answers to the nearest hundredth.

33. $\tan \theta = 2$ **34.** $\tan \theta = -2$ **35.** $6 \tan 2\theta = 1$

 36. a. Open-Ended Write a tangent function.
     b. Graph the function on the interval -2π to 2π.
     c. Identify the period and the asymptotes of the function.

37. Think About a Plan A quilter is making hexagonal placemats by sewing together six quilted isosceles triangles. Each triangle has a base length of 10 in. The function $y = 5 \tan \theta$ models the height of the triangular quilts, where θ is the measure of one of the base angles. Graph the function. What is the area of the placemat if the triangles are equilateral?
- How can a graph of function help you find the height of each triangle?
- How can you find the area of each triangle?
- What will be the last step in your solution?

38. Ceramics An artist is making triangular ceramic tiles for a triangular patio. The patio will be an equilateral triangle with base 18 ft and height 15.6 ft.
a. Find the area of the patio in square feet.
b. The artist uses tiles that are isosceles triangles with base 6 in. The function $y = 3 \tan \theta$ models the height of the triangular tiles, where θ is the measure of one of the base angles. Graph the function. Find the height of the tile when $\theta = 30°$ and when $\theta = 60°$.
c. Find the area of one tile in square inches when $\theta = 30°$ and when $\theta = 60°$.
d. Find the number of tiles the patio will require if $\theta = 30°$ and if $\theta = 60°$.

Use the function $y = 200 \tan x$ on the interval $0° \le x \le 141°$. Complete each ordered pair. Round your answers to the nearest whole number.

39. $(45°, \blacksquare)$ **40.** $(\blacksquare°, 0)$ **41.** $(\blacksquare°, -200)$ **42.** $(141°, \blacksquare)$ **43.** $(\blacksquare°, 550)$

Write an equation of a tangent function for each graph.

44.
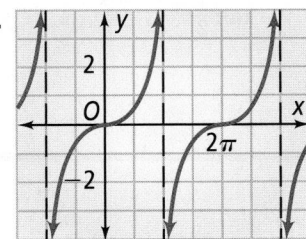

45.
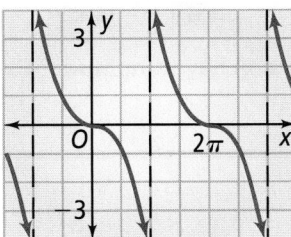

46.
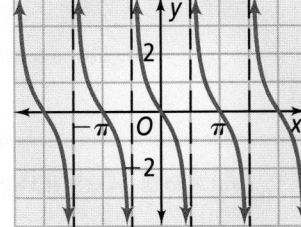

47. Construction An architect is designing a hexagonal gazebo. The floor is a hexagon made up of six isosceles triangles. The function $y = 4 \tan \theta$ models the height of one triangle, where θ is the measure of one of the base angles and the base of the triangle is 8 ft long.
a. Graph the function. Find the height of one triangle when $\theta = 60°$.
b. Find the area of one triangle in square feet when $\theta = 60°$.
c. Find the area of the gazebo floor in square feet when the triangles forming the hexagon are equilateral.

48. a. The graph of $y = \frac{1 - \cos x}{\sin x}$ suggests a tangent curve of the form $y = a \tan bx$. Graph the function using the window $[-3\pi, 3\pi]$ by $[-4, 4]$.
b. What is the period of the curve? What is the value of a?
c. Find the x-coordinate halfway between a removable discontinuity and the asymptote to its right. Find the corresponding y-coordinate.
d. Find an equivalent function of the form $y = a \tan bx$.

Challenge

49. **Geometry** Use the drawing at the right and similar triangles. Justify the statement that $\tan \theta = \frac{\sin \theta}{\cos \theta}$.

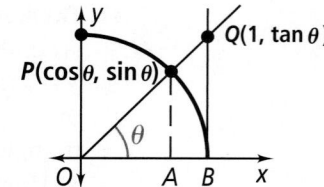

50. **a.** Graph $y = \tan x$, $y = a \tan x$ (with $a > 0$), and $y = a \tan x$ (with $a < 0$) on the same coordinate plane.

   b. Reasoning Recall the pattern of five elements for graphing a tangent function: *asymptote-(−1)-zero-(1)-asymptote*. How does the value of a affect this pattern?

51. **Writing** How many solutions does the equation $x = \tan x$ have for $0 \le x < 2\pi$? Explain.

Standardized Test Prep

52. Which value is NOT defined?

   Ⓐ $\tan 0$ Ⓑ $\tan \pi$ Ⓒ $\tan \frac{3\pi}{2}$ Ⓓ $\frac{1}{\tan \frac{\pi}{4}}$

53. What is the exact value of $\tan \frac{7\pi}{6}$?

   Ⓕ $-\sqrt{3}$ Ⓖ $-\frac{\sqrt{3}}{3}$ Ⓗ $\frac{\sqrt{3}}{3}$ Ⓘ $\sqrt{3}$

54. Which equation does NOT represent a vertical asymptote of the graph of $y = \tan \theta$?

   Ⓐ $\theta = -\frac{\pi}{2}$ Ⓑ $\theta = 0$ Ⓒ $\theta = \frac{\pi}{2}$ Ⓓ $\theta = \frac{3\pi}{2}$

55. Which function has a period of 4π?

   Ⓕ $y = \tan 4\theta$ Ⓖ $y = \tan 2\theta$ Ⓗ $y = \tan \frac{1}{2}\theta$ Ⓘ $y = \tan \frac{1}{4}\theta$

56. Does a tangent function have amplitude? Explain.

Mixed Review

Solve each equation in the interval from 0 to 2π. Round your answer to the nearest hundredth.   🔙 **See Lesson 13-5.**

57. $\cos t = \frac{1}{4}$ 58. $10 \cos t = -2$ 59. $3 \cos \frac{t}{5} = 1$ 60. $5 \cos \pi t = 0.9$

61. Find the mean, median, and mode for the set of values.   🔙 **See Lesson 11-5.**
   9 6 8 1 3 4 5 2 6 8 4 9 12 3 4 10 7 6

Find the 27th term of each sequence.   🔙 **See Lesson 9-2.**

62. 5, 8, 11, . . .   63. 59, 48, 37, . . .   64. −11, −5, 1, . . .   65. 6, −7, −20, . . .

Get Ready!   **To prepare for Lesson 13-7, do Exercises 66–68.**

Identify each horizontal and vertical translation of the parent function $y = |x|$.   🔙 **See Lesson 2-6.**

66. $y = |x - 2| + 5$ 67. $y = |x + 5| - 4$ 68. $y = |x + 2| + 1$

13-7

Translating Sine and Cosine Functions

 Common Core State Standards

F-TF.B.5 Choose trigonometric functions to model periodic phenomena . . .

F-IF.C.7e Graph . . . trigonometric functions, showing period, midline, and amplitude.

MP 1, MP 2, MP 3, MP 4, MP 5, MP 7

Objectives To graph translations of trigonometric functions
To write equations of translations

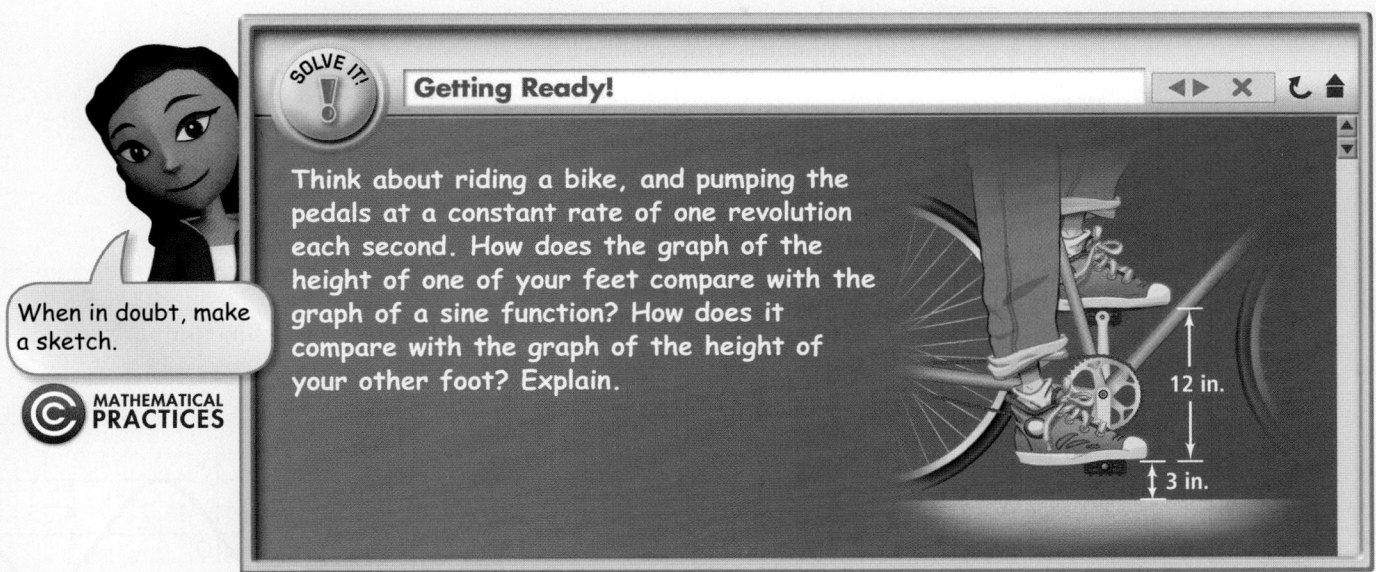

SOLVE IT!

Getting Ready!

◀▶ ✕ ↻ 🔼

Think about riding a bike, and pumping the pedals at a constant rate of one revolution each second. How does the graph of the height of one of your feet compare with the graph of a sine function? How does it compare with the graph of the height of your other foot? Explain.

12 in.

3 in.

When in doubt, make a sketch.

MATHEMATICAL PRACTICES

Recall that for any function f, you can graph $f(x - h)$ by translating the graph of f by h units horizontally. You can graph $f(x) + k$ by translating the graph of f by k units vertically.

Lesson Vocabulary
• phase shift

Essential Understanding You can translate periodic functions in the same way that you translate other functions.

Each horizontal translation of certain periodic functions is a **phase shift**.

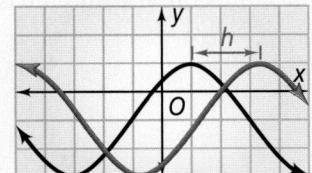

$g(x)$: horizontal translation of $f(x)$
$g(x) = f(x - h)$

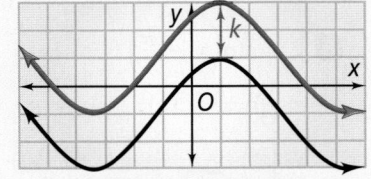

$h(x)$: vertical translation of $f(x)$
$h(x) = f(x) + k$

When $g(x) = f(x - h)$, the value of h is the amount of the shift. If $h > 0$, the shift is to the right. If $h < 0$, the shift is to the left. When $h(x) = f(x) + k$, the value of k is the amount of the midline shift. If $k > 0$, the midline shifts up. If $k < 0$, the midline shifts down.

Problem 1 Identifying Phase Shifts

What is the value of h in each translation? Describe each phase shift (use a phrase such as 3 *units to the left*).

A $g(x) = f(x - 2)$

$h = 2$; the phase shift is 2 units to the right.

B $y = \cos(x + 4)$

$\quad = \cos(x - (-4))$

$h = -4$; the phase shift is 4 units to the left.

✓ **Got It?** **1.** What is the value of h in each translation? Describe each phase shift (use a phrase such as 3 *units to the left*).

    a. $g(t) = f(t - 5)$

    b. $y = \sin(x + 3)$

You can analyze a translation to determine how it relates to the parent function.

 Problem 2 Graphing Translations

Use the graph of the parent function $y = \sin x$. What is the graph of each translation in the interval $0 \le x \le 2\pi$?

A $y = \sin x + 3$

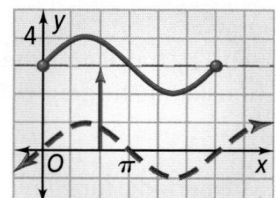

$k = 3$

Translate the graph of the parent function 3 units up. The midline is $y = 3$.

B $y = \sin\left(x - \dfrac{\pi}{2}\right)$

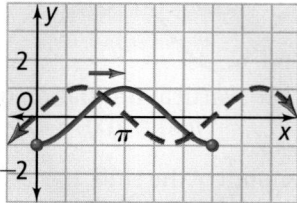

$h = \dfrac{\pi}{2}$

Translate the graph of the parent function $\frac{\pi}{2}$ units to the right.

Got It? **2.** Use the graph of $y = \sin x$ from Problem 2. What is the graph of each translation in the interval $0 \le x \le 2\pi$?

a. $y = \sin x - 2$ **b.** $y = \sin(x - 2)$

c. Which translation is a phase shift?

d. Which translation gives the graph a new midline?

You can translate both vertically and horizontally to produce combined translations.

 Problem 3 **Graphing a Combined Translation**

Use the graph of the parent function $y = \sin x$ in Problem 2. What is the graph of the translation $y = \sin(x + \pi) - 2$ in the interval $0 \le x \le 2\pi$?

Think

What are the translations?
Because π is added to x, the horizontal phase shift is π units left. Because -2 is added to the dependent value, the vertical translation is 2 units down.

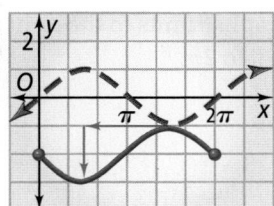

Translate the graph of the parent function 2 units down and π units to the left.

 Got It? **3.** Use the graph at the right of the parent function $y = \cos x$. What is the graph of each translation in the interval $0 \le x \le 2\pi$?

a. $y = \cos(x - 2) + 5$

b. $y = \cos(x + 1) + 3$

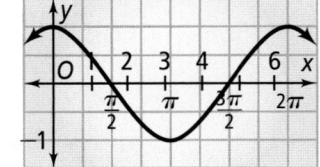

The translations graphed in Problems 2 and 3 belong to the families of the sine and cosine functions.

---

take note

Concept Summary   **Families of Sine and Cosine Functions**

Parent Function	Transformed Function
$y = \sin x$	$y = a \sin b(x - h) + k$
$y = \cos x$	$y = a \cos b(x - h) + k$

- $|a|$ = amplitude (vertical stretch or shrink)
- $\dfrac{2\pi}{b}$ = period (when x is in radians and $b > 0$)
- h = phase shift, or horizontal shift
- k = vertical shift ($y = k$ is the midline)

Problem 4 Graphing a Translation of $y = \sin 2x$

What is the graph of $y = \sin 2\left(x - \frac{\pi}{3}\right) - \frac{3}{2}$ in the interval from 0 to 2π?

Since $a = 1$ and $b = 2$, the graph is a translation of $y = \sin 2x$.

Think

Why should you graph the parent function first?
Once you know the relative dimensions of the curve, you can translate it according to the h- and k-values.

Step 1 Sketch one cycle of $y = \sin 2x$. Use five points in the pattern *zero-max-zero-min-zero*.

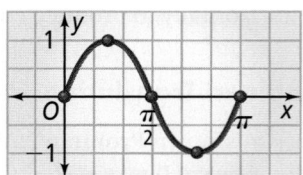

Step 2 Since $h = \frac{\pi}{3}$ and $k = -\frac{3}{2}$, translate the graph $\frac{\pi}{3}$ units to the right and $\frac{3}{2}$ units down. Extend the periodic pattern from 0 to 2π. Sketch the graph.

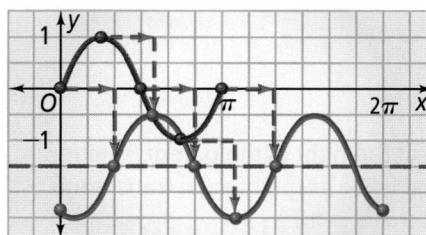

The blue curve above is the graph of $y = \sin 2\left(x - \frac{\pi}{3}\right) - \frac{3}{2}$.

 Got It? 4. What is the graph of each translation in the interval from 0 to 2π?
    a. $y = -3 \sin 2\left(x - \frac{\pi}{3}\right) - \frac{3}{2}$
    b. $y = 2 \cos \frac{\pi}{2}(x + 1) - 3$

You can write an equation to describe a translation.

 Problem 5 Writing Translations

Think

What are a, b, h, and k in $y = a \sin b(x - h) + k$?
$a = b = 1$, $h = 0$, and $k = -\pi$.

What is an equation that models each translation?

A $y = \sin x$, π units down
    π units down means $k = -\pi$.
    An equation is $y = \sin x - \pi$.

B $y = -\cos x$, 2 units to the left
    2 units to the left means $h = -2$.
    An equation is $y = -\cos(x + 2)$.

 **Got It? 5.** What is an equation that models each translation?
    a. $y = \cos x$, $\frac{\pi}{2}$ units up
                            b. $y = 2 \sin x$, $\frac{\pi}{4}$ units to the right

You can write a trigonometric function to model a situation.

 Problem 6 **Writing a Trigonometric Function to Model a Situation** STEM

Temperature Cycles The table gives the average temperature in your town x days after the start of the calendar year ($0 \le x \le 365$). Make a scatter plot of the data. What cosine function models the average daily temperature as a function of x?

Day of Year	16	47	75	106	136	167	198	228	258	289	319	350
Temperature (°F)	33	35	42	52	62	72	77	76	69	58	48	38

Think

Make a scatter plot of the data in the table.

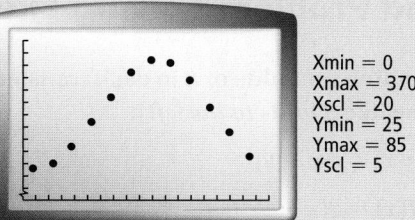

Xmin = 0
Xmax = 370
Xscl = 20
Ymin = 25
Ymax = 85
Yscl = 5

The cosine function has the form $y = a \cos b(x - h) + k$. Find the values a, b, h, and k.

Write

amplitude: $a = \frac{1}{2}(\text{max} - \text{min})$

$= \frac{1}{2}(77 - 33) = 22$

One complete cycle takes 365 days.

period $= \frac{2\pi}{b}$

$365 = \frac{2\pi}{b}$, so $b = \frac{2\pi}{365}$

The maximum point of the curve is (198, 77).

phase shift: $h = 198 - 0 = 198$
vertical shift: $k = 77 - 22 = 55$

Write the function in the form $y = a \cos b(x - h) + k$.

$y = 22 \cos \frac{2\pi}{365}(x - 198) + 55$

To check your answer, graph the function with the scatter plot to see if it is a good fit.

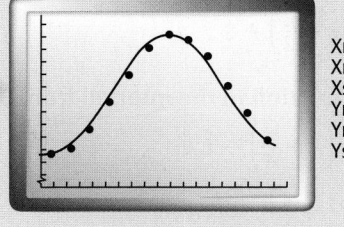

Xmin = 0
Xmax = 370
Xscl = 20
Ymin = 25
Ymax = 85
Yscl = 5

  Got It? **6. a.** Use the model in Problem 6. What was the average temperature in your town 150 days into the year?

b. What value does the midline of this model represent?

c. Reasoning Can you use this model to predict temperatures for next year? Explain your answer.

Lesson Check

Do you know HOW?

1. Graph $y = \sin\left(x + \frac{\pi}{4}\right)$ in the interval from 0 to 2π.

2. Describe any phase shift or vertical shift in the graph of $y = 4\cos(x - 2) + 9$.

3. What is an equation that shifts $y = \cos x$, 3 units up and $\frac{2\pi}{3}$ units to the right?

Do you UNDERSTAND?

4. **Vocabulary** Write a sine function that has amplitude 4, period 3π, phase shift π, and vertical shift -5.

5. **Error Analysis** Two students disagree on the translation for $y = \cos 3\left(x + \frac{\pi}{6}\right)$. Amberly says that it is $\frac{\pi}{2}$ units to the left of $y = \cos 3x$. Scott says that it is $\frac{\pi}{6}$ units to the left of $y = \cos 3x$. Is either student correct? Describe any errors of each student.

Practice and Problem-Solving Exercises

 Determine the value of h in each translation. Describe each phase shift (use a phrase like *3 units to the left*).

See Problem 1.

6. $g(x) = f(x + 1)$

7. $g(t) = f(t + 2)$

8. $f(z) = g(z - 1.6)$

9. $f(x) = g(x - 3)$

10. $y = \sin(x + \pi)$

11. $y = \cos\left(x - \frac{5\pi}{7}\right)$

Use the function $f(x)$ at the right. Graph each translation.

See Problem 2.

12. $g(x) = f(x) + 1$

13. $g(x) = f(x) - 3$

14. $g(x) = f(x + 2)$

15. $g(x) = f(x - 1)$

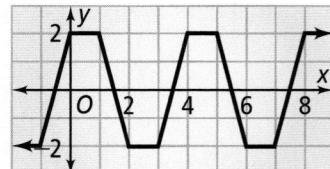

Graph each translation of $y = \cos x$ in the interval from 0 to 2π.

16. $y = \cos(x + 3)$

17. $y = \cos x + 3$

18. $y = \cos x - 4$

19. $y = \cos(x - 4)$

20. $y = \cos x + \pi$

21. $y = \cos(x - \pi)$

Describe any phase shift and vertical shift in the graph.

See Problem 3.

22. $y = 3\sin x + 1$

23. $y = 4\cos(x + 1) - 2$

24. $y = \sin\left(x + \frac{\pi}{2}\right) + 2$

25. $y = \sin(x - 3) + 2$

Graph each function in the interval from 0 to 2π.

26. $y = 2\sin\left(x + \frac{\pi}{4}\right) - 1$

27. $y = \sin\left(x + \frac{\pi}{3}\right) + 1$

28. $y = \cos(x - \pi) - 3$

29. $y = 2\sin\left(x - \frac{\pi}{6}\right) + 2$

Graph each function in the interval from 0 to 2π.

See Problem 4.

30. $y = 3\sin\frac{1}{2}x$

31. $y = \cos 2\left(x + \frac{\pi}{2}\right) - 2$

32. $y = \frac{1}{2}\sin 2x - 1$

33. $y = \sin 3\left(x + \frac{\pi}{3}\right)$

34. $y = \sin 2(x + 3) - 2$

35. $y = 3\sin\frac{\pi}{2}(x - 2)$

Write an equation for each translation.

◀ **See Problem 5.**

36. $y = \sin x$, π units to the left

37. $y = \cos x$, $\frac{\pi}{2}$ units down

38. $y = \sin x$, 3 units up

39. $y = \cos x$, 1.5 units to the right

STEM **40. Temperature** The table below shows water temperatures at a buoy in the Gulf of Mexico on several days of the year.

◀ **See Problem 6.**

Day of Year	16	47	75	106	136	167	198	228	258	289	319	350
Temperature (°F)	71	69	70	73	77	82	85	86	84	82	78	74

a. Plot the data.

b. Write a cosine model for the data.

 **Apply**

Write an equation for each translation.

41. $y = \cos x$, 3 units to the left and π units up

42. $y = \sin x$, $\frac{\pi}{2}$ units to the right and 3.5 units up

ⓒ **43. Think About a Plan** The function $y = 1.5 \sin \frac{\pi}{6}(x - 6) + 2$ represents the average monthly rainfall for a town in central Florida, where x represents the number of the month (January = 1, February = 2, and so on). Rewrite the function using a cosine model.
- How does the graph of $y = \sin x$ translate to the graph of $y = \cos x$?
- What parts of the sine function will stay the same? What must change?

Write a cosine function for each graph. Then write a sine function for each graph.

44.

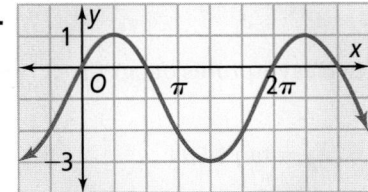

45.

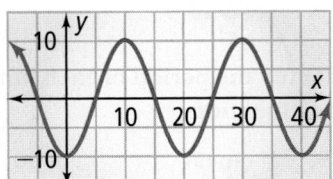

46. The graphs of $y = \sin x$ and $y = \cos x$ are shown at the right.
- **a.** What phase shift will translate the cosine graph onto the sine graph? Write your answer as an equation in the form $\sin x = \cos(x - h)$.
- **b.** What phase shift will translate the sine graph onto the cosine graph? Write your answer as an equation in the form $\cos x = \sin(x - h)$.

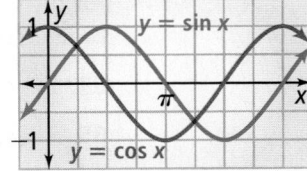

ⓒ **47. a. Open-Ended** Draw a periodic function. Find its amplitude and period. Then sketch a translation of your function 3 units down and 4 units to the left.
- **b. Reasoning** Suppose your original function is $f(x)$. Describe your translation using the form $g(x) = f(x - h) + k$.

48. a. Write $y = 3 \sin(2x - 4) + 1$ in the form $y = a \sin b(x - h) + k$. (*Hint:* Factor where possible.)
- **b.** Find the amplitude, midline, and period. Describe any translations.

Challenge Use a graphing calculator to graph each function in the interval from 0 to 2π. Then sketch each graph.

49. $y = \sin x + x$

50. $y = \sin x + 2x$

51. $y = \cos x - 2x$

52. $y = \cos x + x$

53. $y = \sin (x + \cos x)$

54. $y = \sin (x + 2 \cos x)$

Standardized Test Prep

SAT/ACT

55. Which function is a phase shift of $y = \sin \theta$ by 5 units to the left?

  Ⓐ $y = 5 \sin \theta$ Ⓒ $y = \sin (\theta + 5)$

  Ⓑ $y = \sin \theta + 5$ Ⓓ $y = \sin 5\theta$

56. Which function is a translation of $y = \cos \theta$ by 5 units down?

  Ⓕ $y = -5 \cos \theta$ Ⓗ $y = \cos (\theta - 5)$

  Ⓖ $y = \cos \theta - 5$ Ⓘ $y = \cos (-5\theta)$

57. Which function is a translation of $y = \sin \theta$ that is $\frac{\pi}{3}$ units up and $\frac{\pi}{2}$ units to the left?

  Ⓐ $y = \sin \left(\theta + \frac{\pi}{3} \right) + \frac{\pi}{2}$ Ⓒ $y = \sin \left(\theta - \frac{\pi}{2} \right) + \frac{\pi}{3}$

  Ⓑ $y = \sin \left(\theta + \frac{\pi}{2} \right) + \frac{\pi}{3}$ Ⓓ $y = \sin \left(\theta - \frac{\pi}{3} \right) - \frac{\pi}{2}$

Short Response

58. Find values of a and b such that the function $y = \sin \theta$ can be expressed as $y = a \cos (\theta + b)$.

Mixed Review

Identify the period of each function. Then tell where two asymptotes occur for each function.

See Lesson 13-6.

59. $y = \tan 6\theta$ **60.** $y = \tan \frac{\theta}{4}$ **61.** $y = \tan 1.5\theta$ **62.** $y = \tan \frac{\theta}{6}$

For the given probability of success P on each trial, find the probability of x successes in n trials.

See Lesson 11-8.

63. $x = 4, n = 5, p = 0.2$ **64.** $x = 3, n = 5, p = 0.6$

65. $x = 4, n = 8, p = 0.7$ **66.** $x = 7, n = 8, p = 0.7$

Get Ready! To prepare for Lesson 13-8, do Exercises 67–71.

See p. 973.

Find the reciprocal of each fraction.

67. $\frac{9}{13}$ **68.** $\frac{-5}{8}$ **69.** $\frac{1}{2\pi}$ **70.** $\frac{4m}{15}$ **71.** $\frac{14}{-t}$

Reciprocal Trigonometric Functions

Common Core State Standards

F-IF.C.7e Graph . . . trigonometric functions, showing period, midline, and amplitude.

MP 1, MP 2, MP 3, MP 4, MP 5

Objectives To evaluate reciprocal trigonometric functions
To graph reciprocal trigonometric functions

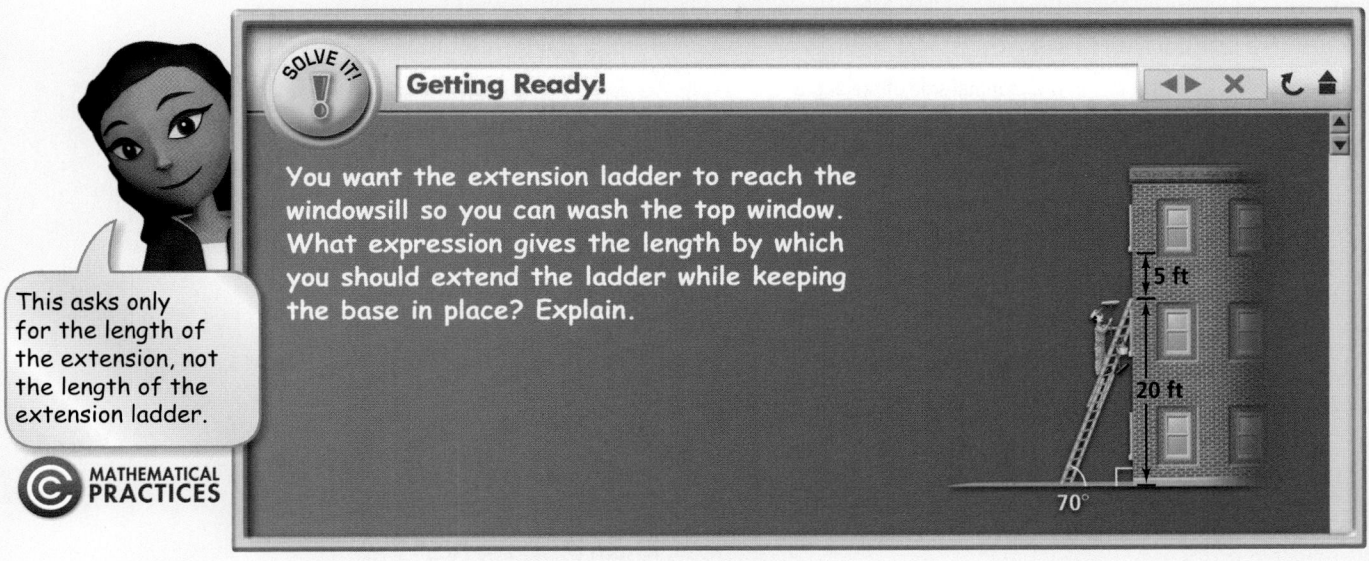

SOLVE IT!

Getting Ready!

You want the extension ladder to reach the windowsill so you can wash the top window. What expression gives the length by which you should extend the ladder while keeping the base in place? Explain.

5 ft

20 ft

70°

This asks only for the length of the extension, not the length of the extension ladder.

MATHEMATICAL PRACTICES

Lesson Vocabulary
• cosecant
• secant
• cotangent

To solve an equation $ax = b$, you multiply each side by the reciprocal of a. If a is a trigonometric expression, you need to use its reciprocal.

Essential Understanding Cosine, sine, and tangent have reciprocals. Cosine and *secant* are reciprocals, as are sine and *cosecant*. Tangent and *cotangent* are also reciprocals.

take note

Key Concept   Cosecant, Secant, and Cotangent Functions

The **cosecant** (csc), **secant** (sec), and **cotangent** (cot) functions are defined using reciprocals. Their domains do not include the real numbers θ that make the denominator zero.

$$\csc \theta = \frac{1}{\sin \theta} \qquad \sec \theta = \frac{1}{\cos \theta} \qquad \cot \theta = \frac{1}{\tan \theta}$$

(cot $\theta = 0$ at odd multiples of $\frac{\pi}{2}$, where tan θ is undefined.)

You can use the unit circle to evaluate the reciprocal trigonometric functions directly. Suppose the terminal side of an angle θ in standard position intersects the unit circle at the point (x, y).

Then $\csc \theta = \frac{1}{y}$, $\sec \theta = \frac{1}{x}$, $\cot \theta = \frac{x}{y}$.

P (x, y)

θ

O   1

x

You can use what you know about the unit circle to find exact values for reciprocal trigonometric functions.

Problem 1 Finding Values Geometrically

What are the exact values of $\cot\left(-\frac{5\pi}{6}\right)$ and $\csc\left(\frac{\pi}{6}\right)$? Do not use a calculator.

Think

Find the point where the unit circle intersects the terminal side of the angle $-\frac{5\pi}{6}$ radians.

Find the exact value of $\cot\left(-\frac{5\pi}{6}\right)$.

Find the point where the unit circle intersects the terminal side of the angle $\frac{\pi}{6}$ radians.

Find the exact value of $\csc\left(\frac{\pi}{6}\right)$.

Write

$$\cot\left(-\frac{5\pi}{6}\right)$$

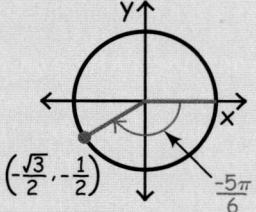

$\left(-\frac{\sqrt{3}}{2}, -\frac{1}{2}\right)$ $\frac{-5\pi}{6}$

$$\cot\left(-\frac{5\pi}{6}\right) = \frac{x}{y}$$

$$= \frac{-\frac{\sqrt{3}}{2}}{-\frac{1}{2}} = \sqrt{3}$$

$$\cot\left(-\frac{5\pi}{6}\right) = \sqrt{3}$$

$$\csc\left(\frac{\pi}{6}\right)$$

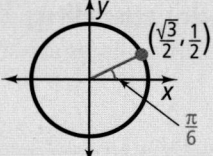

$\left(\frac{\sqrt{3}}{2}, \frac{1}{2}\right)$ $\frac{\pi}{6}$

$$\csc\left(\frac{\pi}{6}\right) = \frac{1}{y}$$

$$= \frac{1}{\frac{1}{2}} = 2$$

$$\csc\left(\frac{\pi}{6}\right) = 2$$

Got It? 1. What is the exact value of each expression? Do not use a calculator.

a. $\csc\frac{\pi}{3}$

b. $\cot\left(-\frac{5\pi}{4}\right)$

c. $\sec 3\pi$

d. Reasoning Use the unit circle at the right to find $\cot n$, $\csc n$, and $\sec n$. Explain how you found your answers.

$\frac{3}{5}$

Use the reciprocal relationships to evaluate secant, cosecant, or cotangent on a calculator, since most calculators do not have these functions as menu options.

Problem 2 Finding Values with a Calculator

What is the decimal value of each expression? Use the radian mode on your calculator. Round to the nearest thousandth.

Think

Can you use the $\sin^{-1}$, $\cos^{-1}$, and $\tan^{-1}$ keys on the calculator for the reciprocal functions?
No; those keys are *inverse functions*, not reciprocal functions.

A sec 2

$$\sec 2 = \frac{1}{\cos 2}$$

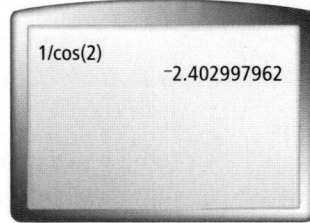

1/cos(2)

　　　　-2.402997962

$\sec 2 \approx -2.403$

C csc 35°

$$\csc 35° = \frac{1}{\sin 35°}$$

To evaluate an angle in degrees in radian mode, use the degree symbol from the ANGLE menu.

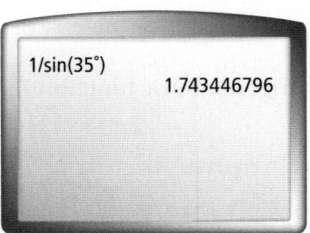

1/sin(35°)

　　　　1.743446796

$\csc 35° \approx 1.743$

B cot 10

$$\cot 10 = \frac{1}{\tan 10}$$

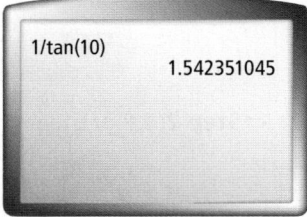

1/tan(10)

　　　　1.542351045

$\cot 10 \approx 1.542$

D cot π

$$\cot \pi = \frac{1}{\tan \pi}$$

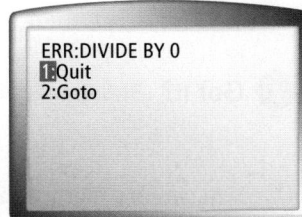

ERR:DIVIDE BY 0
1:Quit
2:Goto

Evaluating cot π results in an error message, because tan π is equal to zero.

Got It? 2. What is the decimal value of each expression? Use the radian mode on your calculator. Round your answers to the nearest thousandth.
a. cot 13
b. csc 6.5
c. sec 15°
d. sec $\frac{3\pi}{2}$
e. **Reasoning** How can you find the cotangent of an angle without using the tangent key on your calculator?

The graphs of reciprocal trigonometric functions have asymptotes where the functions are undefined.

 Problem 3 Sketching a Graph

Think
For what values is csc*x* undefined?
Wherever $\sin x = 0$, its reciprocal is undefined.

What are the graphs of $y = \sin x$ and $y = \csc x$ in the interval from 0 to 2π?

Step 1 Make a table of values.

x	0	$\frac{\pi}{6}$	$\frac{\pi}{3}$	$\frac{\pi}{2}$	$\frac{2\pi}{3}$	$\frac{5\pi}{6}$	π	$\frac{7\pi}{6}$	$\frac{4\pi}{3}$	$\frac{3\pi}{2}$	$\frac{5\pi}{3}$	$\frac{11\pi}{6}$	2π
$\sin x$	0	0.5	0.9	1	0.9	0.5	0	−0.5	−0.9	−1	−0.9	−0.5	0
$\csc x$	—	2	1.2	1	1.2	2	—	−2	−1.2	−1	−1.2	−2	—

Step 2 Plot the points and sketch the graphs.

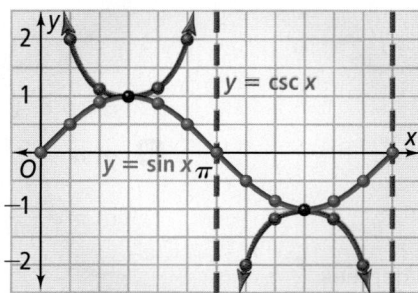

$y = \csc x$ will have a vertical asymptote whenever its denominator ($\sin x$) is 0.

✓ **Got It?** **3.** What are the graphs of $y = \tan x$ and $y = \cot x$ in the interval from 0 to 2π?

You can use a graphing calculator to graph trigonometric functions quickly.

Problem 4 Using Technology to Graph a Reciprocal Function

Plan
How can you find the value?
Use the table feature of your calculator.

Graph $y = \sec x$. What is the value of sec 20°?

Step 1 Use degree mode.
Graph $y = \frac{1}{\cos x}$.

Step 2 Use the **TABLE** feature.
sec 20° ≈ 1.0642

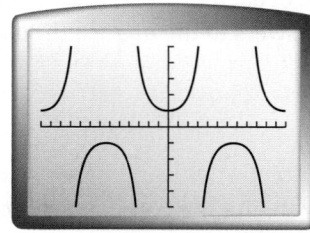

Xmin = −360
Xmax = 360
Xscl = 30
Ymin = −5
Ymax = 5
Yscl = 1

X	Y₁
20	1.0642
21	1.0711
22	1.0785
23	1.0864
24	1.0946
25	1.1034
26	1.1126

X=20

✓ **Got It?** **4.** What is the value of csc 45°? Use the graph of the reciprocal trigonometric function.

You can use a reciprocal trigonometric function to solve a real-world problem.

 **Problem 5** **Using Reciprocal Functions to Solve a Problem**

A restaurant is near the top of a tower. A diner looks down at an object along a line of sight that makes an angle of θ with the tower. The distance in feet of an object from the observer is modeled by the function $d = 601 \sec \theta$. How far away are objects sighted at angles of 40° and 70°?

θ

d

601 ft

Set your calculator to degree mode. Enter the function and construct a table that gives values of d for various angles of θ.

Think

How can you check that your answers are correct?
Multiply the answers by $\cos \theta$. If the answers are correct, then the product is 601.

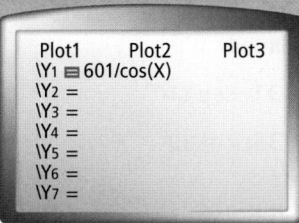

```
Plot1    Plot2    Plot3
\Y1 ▪ 601/cos(X)
\Y2 =
\Y3 =
\Y4 =
\Y5 =
\Y6 =
\Y7 =
```

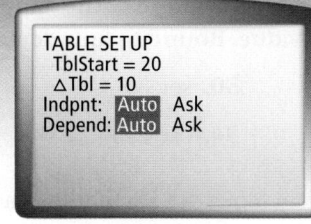

```
TABLE SETUP
 TblStart = 20
 ΔTbl = 10
Indpnt: Auto  Ask
Depend: Auto  Ask
```

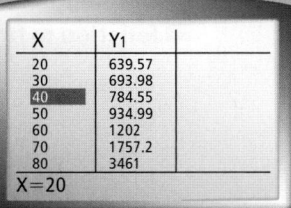

```
  X     Y1
  20    639.57
  30    693.98
  40    784.55
  50    934.99
  60    1202
  70    1757.2
  80    3461
X=20
```

From the table, the objects are about 785 feet away and 1757 feet away, respectively.

 Got It? **5.** The 601 in the function for Problem 5 is the diner's height above the ground in feet. If the diner is 553 feet above the ground, how far away are objects sighted at angles of 50° and 80°?

 Lesson Check

Do you know HOW?

Find each value without using a calculator.

1. $\csc \dfrac{\pi}{2}$

2. $\sec \left(-\dfrac{\pi}{6}\right)$

Use a calculator to find each value. Round your answers to the nearest thousandth.

3. $\csc 1.5$

4. $\sec 42°$

5. An extension ladder leans against a building forming a 50° angle with the ground. Use the function $y = 21 \csc x + 2$ to find y, the length of the ladder. Round to the nearest tenth of a foot.

Do you UNDERSTAND?  **MATHEMATICAL PRACTICES**

© 6. Reasoning Explain why the graph of $y = 5 \sec \theta$ has no zeros.

© 7. Error Analysis On a quiz, a student wrote $\sec 20° + 1 = 0.5155$. The teacher marked it wrong. What error did the student make?

© 8. Compare and Contrast How are the graphs of $y = \sec x$ and $y = \csc x$ alike? How are they different? Could the graph of $y = \csc x$ be a transformation of the graph of $y = \sec x$?

Practice and Problem-Solving Exercises

 MATHEMATICAL PRACTICES

 **Practice**

Find each value without using a calculator. If the expression is undefined, write *undefined*.

◀ See Problem 1.

9. $\sec(-\pi)$　　　**10.** $\csc \frac{5\pi}{4}$　　　**11.** $\cot\left(-\frac{\pi}{3}\right)$　　　**12.** $\sec \frac{\pi}{2}$

13. $\cot\left(-\frac{3\pi}{2}\right)$　　**14.** $\csc \frac{7\pi}{6}$　　　**15.** $\sec\left(-\frac{3\pi}{4}\right)$　　**16.** $\cot(-\pi)$

📱 **Graphing Calculator** Use a calculator to find each value. Round your answers to the nearest thousandth.

◀ See Problem 2.

17. $\sec 2.5$　　　**18.** $\csc(-0.2)$　　　**19.** $\cot 56°$　　　**20.** $\sec\left(-\frac{3\pi}{2}\right)$

21. $\cot(-32°)$　　**22.** $\sec 195°$　　　**23.** $\csc 0$　　　**24.** $\cot(-0.6)$

Graph each function in the interval from 0 to 2π.

◀ See Problem 3.

25. $y = \sec 2\theta$　　**26.** $y = \cot \theta$　　**27.** $y = \csc 2\theta - 1$　　**28.** $y = \csc 2\theta$

📱 **Graphing Calculator** Use the graph of the appropriate reciprocal trigonometric function to find each value. Round to four decimal places.

◀ See Problem 4.

29. $\sec 30°$　　**30.** $\sec 80°$　　**31.** $\sec 110°$　　**32.** $\csc 30°$

33. $\csc 70°$　　**34.** $\csc 130°$　　**35.** $\cot 30°$　　**36.** $\cot 60°$

37. Distance A woman looks out a window of a building. She is 94 feet above the ground. Her line of sight makes an angle of θ with the building. The distance in feet of an object from the woman is modeled by the function $d = 94 \sec \theta$. How far away are objects sighted at angles of 25° and 55°?

◀ See Problem 5.

 **Apply**

© **38. Think About a Plan** A communications tower has wires anchoring it to the ground. Each wire is attached to the tower at a height 20 ft above the ground. The length y of the wire is modeled with the function $y = 20 \csc \theta$, where θ is the measure of the angle formed by the wire and the ground. Find the length of wire needed to form an angle of 45°.
  * Do you need to graph the function?
  * How can you rewrite the function so you can use a calculator?

39. Multiple Representations Write a cosecant model that has the same graph as $y = \sec \theta$.

Match each function with its graph.

40. $y = \frac{1}{\sin x}$　　　　　**41.** $y = \frac{1}{\cos x}$　　　　　**42.** $y = -\frac{1}{\sin x}$

a. 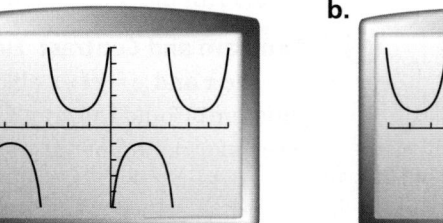　　**b.** 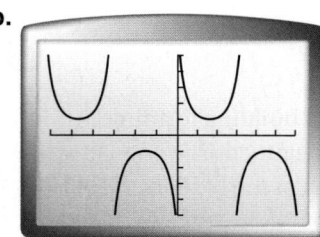　　**c.**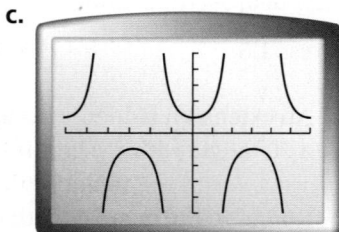

Graph each function in the interval from 0 to 2π.

43. $y = \csc \theta - \dfrac{\pi}{2}$ **44.** $y = \sec \dfrac{1}{4}\theta$ **45.** $y = -\sec \pi\theta$ **46.** $y = \cot \dfrac{\theta}{3}$

47. a. What are the domain, range, and period of $y = \csc x$?
    b. What is the relative minimum in the interval $0 \le x \le \pi$?
    c. What is the relative maximum in the interval $\pi \le x \le 2\pi$?

ⓒ **48. Reasoning** Use the relationship $\csc x = \dfrac{1}{\sin x}$ to explain why each statement is true.
    a. When the graph of $y = \sin x$ is above the x-axis, so is the graph of $y = \csc x$.
    b. When the graph of $y = \sin x$ is near a y-value of -1, so is the graph of $y = \csc x$.

ⓒ **Writing** **Explain why each expression is undefined.**

49. $\csc 180°$ **50.** $\sec 90°$ **51.** $\cot 0°$

52. Indirect Measurement The fire ladder forms an angle of measure θ with the horizontal. The hinge of the ladder is 35 ft from the building. The function $y = 35 \sec \theta$ models the length y in feet that the fire ladder must be to reach the building.

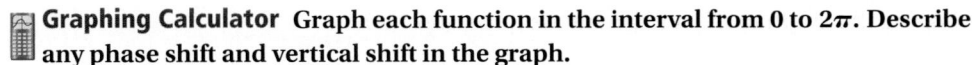

    a. Graph the function.
    b. In the photo, $\theta = 13°$. What is the ladder's length?
    c. How far is the ladder extended when it forms an angle of 30°?
    d. Suppose the ladder is extended to its full length of 80 ft. What angle does it form with the horizontal? How far up a building can the ladder reach when fully extended? (*Hint:* Use the information in the photo.)

ⓒ **53. a.** Graph $y = \tan x$ and $y = \cot x$ on the same axes.
    b. State the domain, range, and asymptotes of each function.
    c. Compare and Contrast Compare the two graphs. How are they alike? How are they different?
    d. Geometry The graph of the tangent function is a reflection image of the graph of the cotangent function. Name at least two reflection lines for such a transformation.

📟 **Graphing Calculator** **Graph each function in the interval from 0 to 2π. Describe any phase shift and vertical shift in the graph.**

54. $y = \sec 2\theta + 3$ **55.** $y = \sec 2\left(\theta + \dfrac{\pi}{2}\right)$ **56.** $y = -2 \sec (x - 4)$

57. $f(x) = 3 \csc (x + 2) - 1$ **58.** $y = \cot 2(x + \pi) + 3$ **59.** $g(x) = 2 \sec \left(3\left(x - \dfrac{\pi}{6}\right)\right) - 2$

ⓒ **60. a.** Graph $y = -\cos x$ and $y = -\sec x$ on the same axes.
    b. State the domain, range, and period of each function.
    c. For which values of x does $-\cos x = -\sec x$? Justify your answer.
    d. Compare and Contrast Compare the two graphs. How are they alike? How are they different?
    e. Reasoning Is the value of $-\sec x$ positive when $-\cos x$ is positive and negative when $-\cos x$ is negative? Justify your answer.

61. a. Reasoning Which expression gives the correct value of csc 60°?

    I. $\sin\left(\left(60^{-1}\right)^\circ\right)$ II. $(\sin 60^\circ)^{-1}$ III. $(\cos 60^\circ)^{-1}$

    b. Which expression in part (a) represents $\sin\left(\frac{1}{60}\right)^\circ$?

 Challenge

62. Reasoning Each branch of $y = \sec x$ and $y = \csc x$ is a curve. Explain why these curves cannot be parabolas. (*Hint:* Do parabolas have asymptotes?)

63. Reasoning Consider the relationship between the graphs of $y = \cos x$ and $y = \cos 3x$. Use the relationship to explain the distance between successive branches of the graphs of $y = \sec x$ and $y = \sec 3x$.

64. a. Graph $y = \cot x$, $y = \cot 2x$, $y = \cot(-2x)$, and $y = \cot\frac{1}{2}x$ on the same axes.

    b. Make a Conjecture Describe how the graph of $y = \cot bx$ changes as the value of b changes.

Apply What You've Learned

Refer to the problem on page 827 and look back at the tables and graphs you made for the functions $d = f(t)$ and $h = g(t)$ in the Apply What You've Learned in Lesson 13-1.

    a. What is a phase shift and vertical translation you can use to transform the function $d = 2\cos\left(\frac{2\pi}{5}t\right)$ that results in the function $d = f(t)$?

    b. Write a function $d = f(t)$ that models the horizontal distance d of the dragonfly from the y-axis after t seconds. Check your function by graphing it on your calculator and comparing the graph to the one you made in Lesson 13-1.

    c. What is a phase shift and vertical translation you can use to transform the function $h = 2\sin\left(\frac{2\pi}{5}t\right)$ that results in the function $h = g(t)$?

    d. Write a function $h = g(t)$ that models the height h of the dragonfly above the x-axis after t seconds. Check your function by graphing it on your calculator and comparing the graph to the one you made in Lesson 13-1.

Completing the Performance Task

Look back at your results from the Apply What You've Learned sections in Lessons 13-1, 13-5, and 13-8. Use the work you did to complete the following.

To solve these problems, you will pull together many concepts and skills related to trigonometric functions.

1. Solve the problem in the Task Description on page 827 to determine the coordinates of the dragonfly when the frog eats it. Round each coordinate to the nearest hundredth. Show all your work and explain each step of your solution.

 2. Reflect Choose one of the Mathematical Practices below and explain how you applied it in your work on the Performance Task.

MP 1: Make sense of problems and persevere in solving them.

MP 4: Model with mathematics.

MP 5: Use appropriate tools strategically.

MP 7: Look for and make use of structure.

MP 8: Look for and express regularity in repeated reasoning.

On Your Own

For another part of Suzanne's computer game, a fish swims at different depths and occasionally jumps out of the water. The circular path of the fish is shown in the graph, where the line $y = 6$ represents the surface of the water. The fish starts at (4, 1), moves counterclockwise around the circle, and completes one cycle in 3 seconds. Suzanne wants to know when the fish will be out of the water.

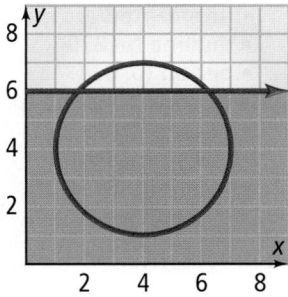

Determine a range of times when the fish will be above the surface of the water during its first cycle. Round times to the nearest hundredth of a second.

Connecting **BIG** ideas and Answering the Essential Questions

1 Modeling
You can use combinations of circular functions (sine and cosine) to model natural periodic behavior.

2 Function
The graph of
$$y = 4 \sin 2\left(x - \frac{\pi}{4}\right) + 4$$
has amplitude 4, period π, midline of $y = 4$, and a minimum at the origin.

3 Function
If you know the value of $\sin \theta$, find an angle with measure θ in standard position on the unit circle to find values of the other trigonometric functions.

Angles, the Unit Circle, and Radian Measure (Lessons 13-2 and 13-3)
One radian is the measure of a central angle of a circle that intercepts an arc of length equal to the radius of the circle.

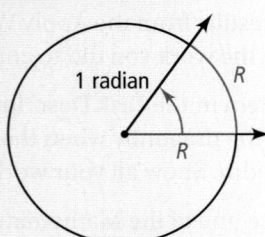

Sine, Cosine, and Tangent Functions (Lessons 13-4, 13-5, and 13-6)

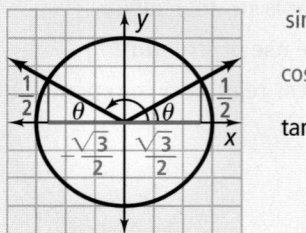

$$\sin \theta = \frac{1}{2}$$
$$\cos \theta = \pm \frac{\sqrt{3}}{2}$$
$$\tan \theta = \frac{\sin \theta}{\cos \theta}$$
$$= \pm \frac{1}{\sqrt{3}}$$

Translating Sine and Cosine Functions (Lesson 13-7)
For the functions
$$y = a \sin b(x - h) + k,$$
and
$$y = a \cos b(x - h) + k,$$

- $|a|$ is the amplitude
- $\frac{2\pi}{b}$ is the period
- h is the phase shift, or horizontal shift
- k is the vertical shift ($y = k$ is the midline)

Reciprocal Trigonometric Functions (Lesson 13-8)
$$\csc \theta = \frac{1}{\sin \theta} = 2$$
$$\sec \theta = \frac{1}{\cos \theta} = \pm \frac{2}{\sqrt{3}}$$
$$\cot \theta = \frac{1}{\tan \theta} = \pm \sqrt{3}$$

Chapter Vocabulary

- amplitude (p. 830)
- central angle (p. 844)
- cosecant (p. 883)
- cosine function (p. 861)
- cosine of θ (p. 838)
- cotangent (p. 883)
- coterminal angle (p. 837)
- cycle (p. 828)

- initial side (p. 836)
- intercepted arc (p. 844)
- midline (p. 830)
- period (p. 828)
- periodic function (p. 828)
- phase shift (p. 875)
- radian (p. 844)
- secant (p. 883)

- sine curve (p. 852)
- sine function (p. 851)
- sine of θ (p. 838)
- standard position (p. 836)
- tangent function (p. 869)
- tangent of θ (p. 868)
- terminal side (p. 836)
- unit circle (p. 838)

Choose the correct term to complete each sentence.

1. The __?__ of a periodic function is the length of one cycle.

2. Centered at the origin of the coordinate plane, the __?__ has a radius of 1 unit.

3. An asymptote of the __?__ occurs at $\theta = \frac{\pi}{2}$, and repeats every π units.

4. A horizontal translation of a periodic function is a(n) __?__ .

5. The __?__ is the reciprocal of the cosine function.

13-1 Exploring Periodic Data

Quick Review

A **periodic function** repeats a pattern of y-values at regular intervals. One complete pattern is called a **cycle**. A cycle may begin at any point on the graph. The **period** of a function is the length of one cycle. The **midline** is the line located midway between the maximum and the minimum values of the function. The **amplitude** of a periodic function is half the difference between its maximum and minimum values.

Example

What is the period of the periodic function?

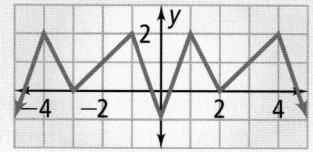

One cycle is 5 units long, so the period of the function is 5.

Exercises

6. Determine whether the function below *is* or *is not* periodic. If it is, identify one cycle in two different ways and find the period and amplitude.

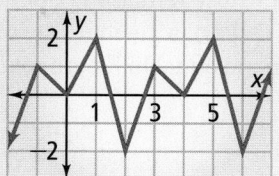

7. Sketch the graph of a wave with a period of 2, an amplitude of 4, and a midline of $y = 1$.

8. Sketch the graph of a wave with a period of 4, an amplitude of 3, and a midline of $y = 0$.

13-2 Angles and the Unit Circle

Quick Review

An angle is in **standard position** if the vertex is at the origin and one ray, the **initial side**, is on the positive x-axis. The other ray is the **terminal side** of the angle. Two angles in standard position are **coterminal** if they have the same terminal side.

The **unit circle** has radius of 1 unit and its center at the origin. The **cosine of θ** (cos θ) is the x-coordinate of the point where the terminal side of the angle intersects the unit circle. The **sine of θ** (sin θ) is the y-coordinate.

Example

What are the cosine and sine of $-210°$?

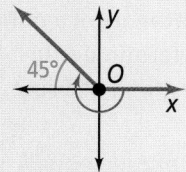

Sketch an angle of $-210°$ in standard position with a unit circle. The terminal side forms a $30°$-$60°$-$90°$ triangle with

hypotenuse = 1, shorter leg = $\frac{1}{2}$, longer leg = $\frac{\sqrt{3}}{2}$

Since the terminal side lies in Quadrant II, $\cos(-210°)$ is negative and $\sin(-210°)$ is positive.

$$\cos(-210°) = -\frac{\sqrt{3}}{2} \text{ and } \sin(-210°) = \frac{1}{2}$$

Exercises

9. Find the measurement of the angle in standard position below.

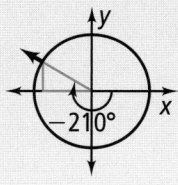

10. Sketch a $-30°$ angle in standard position.

11. Find the measure of an angle between $0°$ and $360°$ coterminal with a $-120°$ angle.

12. Find the exact values of the sine and cosine of $315°$ and $-315°$. Then find the decimal equivalents. Round your answers to the nearest hundredth.

13-3 Radian Measure

Quick Review

A **central angle** of a circle is an angle whose vertex is at the center of a circle and whose sides are radii of the circle. An **intercepted arc** is the portion of the circle whose endpoints are on the sides of the angle and whose remaining points lie in the interior of the angle. A **radian** is the measure of a central angle that intercepts an arc equal in length to a radius of the circle.

Example

What is the radian measure of an angle of $-210°$?

$$-210° = -210° \cdot \frac{\pi}{180°} \text{ radians} = -\frac{7\pi}{6} \text{ radians}$$

Exercises

The measure θ of an angle in standard position is given.

a. Write each degree measure in radians and each radian measure in degrees rounded to the nearest degree.

b. Find the exact values of $\cos \theta$ and $\sin \theta$ for each angle measure.

13. $60°$

14. $-45°$

15. $180°$

16. 2π radians

17. $\frac{5\pi}{6}$ radians

18. $-\frac{3\pi}{4}$ radians

19. Use the circle to find the length of the indicated arc. Round your answer to the nearest tenth.

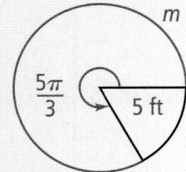

13-4 The Sine Function

Quick Review

The **sine function** $y = \sin \theta$ matches the measure θ of an angle in standard position with the y-coordinate of a point on the unit circle. This point is where the terminal side of the angle intersects the unit circle. The graph of a sine function is called a **sine curve**.

For the sine function $y = a \sin b\theta$, the amplitude equals $|a|$, there are b cycles from 0 to 2π, and the period is $\frac{2\pi}{b}$.

Example

Determine the number of cycles the sine function $y = -7 \sin 3\theta$ has in the interval from 0 to 2π. Find the amplitude and period of each function.

For $y = -7 \sin 3\theta$, $a = -7$ and $b = 3$. Therefore there are 3 cycles from 0 to 2π. The amplitude is $|a| = |-7| = 7$. The period is $\frac{2\pi}{b} = \frac{2\pi}{3}$.

Exercises

Sketch the graph of each function in the interval from 0 to 2π.

20. $y = 3 \sin \theta$

21. $y = \sin 4\theta$

22. Write an equation of a sine function with $a > 0$, amplitude 4, and period 0.5π.

13-5 The Cosine Function

Quick Review

The **cosine function** $y = \cos\theta$ matches the measure θ of an angle in standard position with the x-coordinate of a point on the unit circle. This point is where the terminal side of the angle intersects the unit circle.

For the cosine function $y = a\cos b\theta$, the amplitude equals $|a|$, there are b cycles from 0 to 2π, and the period is $\frac{2\pi}{b}$.

Example

Find all solutions to $5\cos\theta = -4$ in the interval from 0 to 2π. Round each answer to the nearest hundredth.

On a graphing calculator graph the equations $y = -4$ and $y = 5\cos\theta$.

Use the Intersect feature to find the points at which the two graphs intersect. The graph shows two solutions in the interval. They are $\theta \approx 2.50$ and 3.79.

Exercises

Sketch the graph of each function in the interval from 0 to 2π.

23. $y = 2\cos\left(\frac{\pi}{2}\theta\right)$

24. $y = -\cos 2\theta$

25. Write an equation of a cosine function with $a > 0$, amplitude 3, and period π.

Solve each equation in the interval from 0 to 2π. Round your answer to the nearest hundredth.

26. $3\cos 4\theta = -2$

27. $\cos(\pi\theta) = -0.6$

13-6 The Tangent Function

Quick Review

The **tangent** of an angle θ in standard position is the y-coordinate of the point where the terminal side of the angle intersects the tangent line $x = 1$. A **tangent function** in the form $y = a\tan b\theta$ has a period of $\frac{\pi}{b}$. Unlike the graphs of the sine and the cosine, the tangent is periodically undefined. At these points, the graph has vertical asymptotes.

Example

What is the period of $y = \tan\frac{\pi}{4}\theta$? Tell where two asymptotes occur.

$$\text{period} = \frac{\pi}{b} = \frac{\pi}{\frac{\pi}{4}} = 4$$

One cycle occurs in the interval from -2 to 2, so there are asymptotes at $\theta = -2$ and $\theta = 2$.

Exercises

Graph each function in the interval from 0 to 2π. Then evaluate the function at $t = \frac{\pi}{4}$ and $t = \frac{\pi}{2}$. If the tangent is undefined at that point, write *undefined*.

28. $y = \tan\frac{1}{2}t$

29. $y = \tan 3t$

30. $y = 2\tan t$

31. $y = 4\tan 2t$

13-7 Translating Sine and Cosine Functions

Quick Review

Each horizontal translation of certain periodic functions is a **phase shift**. When $g(x) = f(x - h) + k$, the value of h is the amount of the horizontal shift and the value of k is the amount of the vertical shift. $y = k$ is the midline of the graph.

Example

What is an equation for the translation of $y = \sin x$, 2 units to the right and 1 unit up?

2 units to the right means $h = 2$, and 1 unit up means $k = 1$.

An equation is $y = \sin(x - 2) + 1$.

Exercises

Graph each function in the interval from 0 to 2π.

32. $y = \cos\left(x + \frac{\pi}{2}\right)$ **33.** $y = 2\sin x - 4$

34. $y = \sin(x - \pi) + 3$ **35.** $y = \cos(x + \pi) - 1$

Write an equation for each translation.

36. $y = \sin x$, $\frac{\pi}{4}$ units to the right

37. $y = \cos x$, 2 units down

13-8 Reciprocal Trigonometric Functions

Quick Review

The **cosecant** (csc), **secant** (sec), and **cotangent** (cot) functions are defined as reciprocals for all real numbers θ (except those that make a denominator zero).

$$\csc\theta = \frac{1}{\sin\theta} \qquad \sec\theta = \frac{1}{\cos\theta} \qquad \cot\theta = \frac{1}{\tan\theta}$$

Example

Suppose $\sin\theta = -\frac{3}{5}$. Find $\csc\theta$.

$$\csc\theta = \frac{1}{\sin\theta} = \frac{1}{\frac{-3}{5}} = -\frac{5}{3}$$

Exercises

Evaluate each expression. Write your answer in exact form.

38. $\sec(-45°)$ **39.** $\cot 120°$

40. $\csc 150°$ **41.** $\cot(-150°)$

Graph each function in the interval from 0 to 4π.

42. $y = 2\csc\theta$ **43.** $y = \sec\theta - 1$

44. $y = \cot\frac{1}{4}\theta$ **45.** $y = \csc\frac{1}{2}\theta + 2$

13 Chapter Test

Do you know HOW?

Determine whether each function *is* or *is not* periodic. If it is periodic, find the period and amplitude.

1.

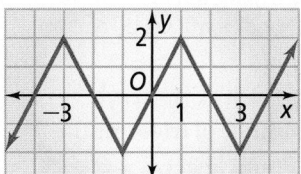

2.

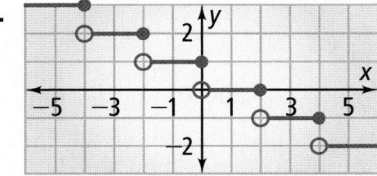

Find the measure of an angle between 0° and 360° coterminal with the given angle.

3. $-32°$ **4.** $-229°$ **5.** $375°$

Write each measure in radians. Express your answer in terms of π and also as a decimal rounded to the nearest hundredth.

6. $-225°$ **7.** $120°$ **8.** $600°$

Write each radian measure in degrees. If necessary, round your answer to the nearest degree.

9. $\dfrac{5\pi}{6}$ **10.** -2.5π **11.** 0.8

12. Using the graph below, determine how many cycles the sine function has in the interval from 0 to 2π. Find the amplitude, period, and midline.

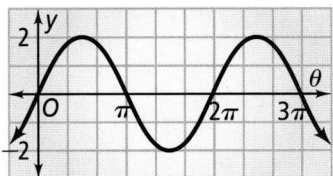

Find the amplitude and period of each function. Then sketch one cycle of the graph of each function.

13. $y = 4\sin(2x)$ **14.** $y = 2\sin(4x)$

Solve each equation in the interval from 0 to 2π. Give an exact answer and an answer rounded to the nearest hundredth.

15. $\cos t = \dfrac{1}{2}$ **16.** $3\tan 2t = \sqrt{3}$

Graph each function in the interval from 0 to 2π.

17. $y = 2\cos x$ **18.** $y = \cos(x + \pi)$

19. $y = -\cos\dfrac{\theta}{\pi}$ **20.** $y = \tan\dfrac{\pi}{3}\theta$

21. $y = \cot x$ **22.** $y = \sec\theta + 1$

23. $y = \csc\dfrac{\theta}{2}$ **24.** $y = \csc(\theta + 1)$

Write an equation for each translation.

25. $y = \cos x$, 7.5 units to the right

26. $y = \sin x$, 3 units to the left, 1.5 units down

Evaluate each expression. Write your answer in exact form. If the expression is undefined, write *undefined*.

27. $\sin 30°$ **28.** $\sin(-330°)$

29. $\sec 270°$ **30.** $\tan(-60°)$

Do you UNDERSTAND?

31. Open-Ended Sketch a function with period 4, amplitude 7, and midline $y = 3$.

32. Writing Explain how to convert an angle measure in radians to an angle measure in degrees. Include an example.

STEM 33. Physics On each swing, a pendulum 18 inches long travels through an angle of $\dfrac{3\pi}{4}$ radians. How far does the tip of the pendulum travel in one swing? Round your answer to the nearest inch.

34. Reasoning What are the steps you take to find the asymptotes of the function $y = \tan(ax + b)$?

TIPS FOR SUCCESS

Some problems ask you to use given results to find the probability of independent events.

TIP 1

Find the number of trials for the experiment.

The table below shows the results of spinning a spinner.

Outcome	Frequency
Orange	8
Green	7
Blue	5

What is the probability of landing on orange and then blue?

Ⓐ $\frac{1}{10}$ Ⓒ $\frac{2}{5}$

Ⓑ $\frac{7}{20}$ Ⓓ $\frac{13}{20}$

TIP 2

Find the number of times the events "landing on orange" and "landing on blue" occur.

Think It Through

The number of trials for the experiment is $8 + 7 + 5 = 20$. Of those, 8 are orange.

$$\frac{8}{20} = \frac{2}{5}$$

The probability of spinning blue is $\frac{5}{20} = \frac{1}{4}$. The probability of spinning orange, then blue is

$$\frac{2}{5} \cdot \frac{1}{4} = \frac{2}{20} = \frac{1}{10}.$$

The correct answer is A.

Vocabulary Review

As you solve test items, you must understand the meanings of mathematical terms. Match each term with its mathematical meaning.

A. amplitude

B. initial side

C. radian

D. terminal side

E. phase shift

I. the measure of a central angle that intercepts an arc equal in length to a radius of the circle

II. the ray not on the x-axis of an angle in standard position

III. a horizontal translation of certain periodic functions

IV. the ray on the x-axis of an angle in standard position

V. half the difference between the minimum and maximum values of a periodic function

Selected Response

Read each question. Then write the letter of the correct answer on your paper.

1. What is the sum of the geometric series
$2 + 4 + 8 + \ldots + 64$?

Ⓐ 30   Ⓒ 126

Ⓑ 62   Ⓓ 252

2. Solve the following equation for x.

$$y = \frac{1}{\sqrt{x+6}}$$

Ⓕ $x = \frac{1}{\sqrt{y-6}}$ Ⓗ $x = \frac{1}{y^2} - 6$

Ⓖ $x = \frac{1}{y^2} + 6$ Ⓘ $x = \frac{1}{y} - 6$

3. Which point is *not* a solution of the inequality $y > 2|x + 3| - 7$?

- (A) $(0, 0)$
- (C) $(1, 1)$
- (B) $(-2, -1)$
- (D) $(-1, 1)$

4. Which of the following equations is an equivalent form of $3x - 4y = 36$ that makes it easy to identify the y-intercept?

- (F) $y = -\frac{3}{4}x - 9$
- (H) $y - 6 = \frac{3}{4}(x + 4)$
- (G) $y + 6 = \frac{3}{4}(x - 4)$
- (I) $y = \frac{3}{4}x - 9$

5. Which point in the feasible region below maximizes the objective function $C = 2x + 3y$?

$$\begin{cases} x \geq 0, y \geq 0 \\ x + y \leq 8 \\ 3x + 2y \leq 18 \end{cases}$$

- (A) $(0, 0)$
- (B) $(2, 6)$
- (C) $(0, 8)$
- (D) $(18, 0)$

6. Which best describes the transformations used to obtain the graph of $y = 3(-x + 3)^3$ from the graph of $y = x^3$?

- (F) reflect across the x-axis, shift left 3 units, stretch by a factor of 3
- (G) reflect across the y-axis, shift right 3 units, stretch by a factor of 3
- (H) reflect across the x-axis, shift right 3 units, stretch by a factor of 3
- (I) reflect across the y-axis, shift left 3 units, stretch by a factor of 3

7. A sixth degree polynomial equation with rational coefficients has roots -1, $2i$, and $1 - \sqrt{5}$. Which of the following cannot also be a root of the polynomial?

    I. 1   II. $-2i$ III. $\sqrt{5}$ IV. $1 - i$

- (A) I only
- (C) III and IV only
- (B) II and III only
- (D) II, III, and IV only

8. Which equation shows an inverse variation?

- (F) $y = 5x$
- (H) $6 = \frac{x}{y}$
- (G) $xy - 4 = 0$
- (I) $y = -4$

9. Which is equivalent to $2^9 = 512$?

- (A) $\log_{512} 2 = 9$
- (C) $\log_2 9 = 512$
- (B) $\log_2 512 = 9$
- (D) $\log_9 512 = 2$

10. What are the roots of $5x^4 - 12x^3 - 11x^2 + 6x = 0$?

- (F) $-1, \frac{5}{2}, 3$
- (H) $0, 1, \frac{5}{2}, 3$
- (G) $-1, 0, \frac{2}{5}, 3$
- (I) $-1, -\frac{2}{5}, 0, 3$

11. Which equation represents a circle with center $(-3, 8)$ and radius 12?

- (A) $(x - 8)^2 + (y + 3)^2 = 144$
- (B) $(x - 8)^2 - (y + 3)^2 = 144$
- (C) $(x + 3)^2 + (y - 8)^2 = 144$
- (D) $(x - 3)^2 - (y - 8)^2 = 144$

12. The table below shows the results of spinning a spinner. What is the probability of the spinner landing on white, then red?

Outcome	Frequency
Red	7
Blue	3
White	5

- (F) $\frac{1}{9}$
- (H) $\frac{7}{18}$
- (G) $\frac{7}{45}$
- (I) $\frac{4}{5}$

13. During a promotional event, two customers at a clothing store between 9 and 10 A.M. will be randomly selected to win a gift certificate. Suppose you and a friend visit the store and there are 19 other customers between 9 and 10 A.M. What is the probability you and your friend will NOT both win the gift certificate?

- (A) $\frac{1}{210}$
- (C) $\frac{2}{21}$
- (B) $\frac{2}{19}$
- (D) $\frac{209}{210}$

14. What is the sixth term in the expansion of $(2x - 3y)^7$?

- (F) $21\,x^2 y^5$
- (G) $-126\,x^2 y^5$
- (H) $-20{,}412\,x^2 y^5$
- (I) $20{,}412\,x^2 y^5$

Constructed Response

15. What is the integer equivalent of i^6?

16. What is the distance of $4 - 5i$ from the origin?

17. To the nearest hundredth, what is the theoretical probability of rolling a 3 on a standard number cube?

18. What is the determinant of $\begin{bmatrix} 5 & -3 \\ 4 & 1 \end{bmatrix}$?

19. A periodic function has an amplitude of 14 and a minimum value of -3. What is its maximum value?

20. Suppose y varies directly with the square of x. If $y = 20$ when $x = 3$, what is $|x|$ when $y = 80$?

21. What is the solution to the equation $7^{2x} = 75$ to the nearest hundredth?

22. The table below shows a family's daily water usage for 2 weeks. Find the standard deviation of the data to the nearest hundredth.

Daily Water Usage (gal)

92.3	81.3
85.3	81.6
89.7	76.9
101.2	94.0
80.3	89.6
91.4	96.3
88.8	102.1

23. If $A = \begin{bmatrix} 3 & -1 & 0 \\ -5 & 4 & 2 \end{bmatrix}$, what is the entry a_{12} of the matrix $3A$?

24. Find the sum of the rational expressions below. What is the coefficient of the x^2 term in the numerator of the sum? $\dfrac{x+1}{x^2+2} + \dfrac{x+1}{3x+6}$

25. Find all asymptotes of the graph of $y = \dfrac{3x^2 - 5x - 2}{x^2 + 2x - 8}$.

26. Using Pascal's Triangle, what is the expansion of $(r - 3)^4$?

$$1$$
$$1 \; 1$$
$$1 \; 2 \; 1$$
$$1 \; 3 \; 3 \; 1$$
$$1 \; 4 \; 6 \; 4 \; 1$$

27. What is the directrix of the graph of $6x = x^2 + 8y + 9$?

28. What is the inverse matrix of $\begin{bmatrix} 2 & 1 \\ -3 & -2 \end{bmatrix}$?

29. Solve $8 + \sqrt{5x + 2} = 10$.

30. If $B = \begin{bmatrix} 2 & -1 & 3 \\ 4 & -8 & 0 \\ 5 & 6 & 9 \end{bmatrix}$ and $C = \begin{bmatrix} 4 & 0 & 7 \\ -3 & 1 & 2 \\ 9 & -5 & 6 \end{bmatrix}$, what is $B + C$?

Extended Response

31. The table shows the values of an investment after the given number of years of continuously compounded interest.

Years	0	1	2	3
Value	$750.00	$780.61	$812.47	$845.62

  a. What is the rate of interest?
  b. Write an equation to model the growth of the investment.
  c. To the nearest year, when will the investment be worth more than $1000?

32. In a geometric sequence, $a_1 = 8$ and $a_4 = 27$. Explain how to find a_7.

Get Ready!

Lesson 4-5 ◆ Solving Quadratic Equations

Solve each equation.

1. $4x^2 = 25$ **2.** $x^2 - 23 = 0$ **3.** $3x^2 = 80$

4. $8x^2 - 44 = 0$ **5.** $0.5x^2 = 15$ **6.** $6x^2 - 13 = 11$

Lesson 6-7 ◆ Finding the Inverse of a Function

For each function f, find f^{-1} and the domain and range of f and f^{-1}.
Determine whether f^{-1} is a function.

7. $f(x) = 5x + 2$ **8.** $f(x) = \sqrt{x + 3}$

9. $f(x) = \sqrt{3x - 4}$ **10.** $f(x) = \frac{5}{x}$

11. $f(x) = \frac{10}{x - 1}$ **12.** $f(x) = \frac{10}{x} - 1$

Lesson 7-5 ◆ Solving Exponential and Logarithmic Equations

Solve each equation.

13. $4^x = \frac{1}{8}$ **14.** $\log 5x + 1 = -1$

15. $7^{3x} = 500$ **16.** $\log 3x + \log x = 9$

17. $\log(4x + 3) - \log x = 5$ **18.** $3^x = 243$

Lessons 13-4, 13-5, and 13-6 ◆ Evaluating Trigonometric Functions

For each value of θ, find the values of $\cos\theta$, $\sin\theta$, and $\tan\theta$. Round your
answers to the nearest hundredth.

19. $48°$ **20.** $-105°$ **21.** $16°$ **22.** $\frac{5\pi}{6}$

Looking Ahead Vocabulary

23. The equation $1 + \tan^2\theta = \sec^2\theta$ is a *trigonometric identity*. Use what you know about identities to make a conjecture about this equation.

24. The Pythagorean Theorem is a special case of the *Law of Cosines*. What do you suppose you will use the Law of Cosines to find?

CHAPTER 14

Trigonometric Identities and Equations

Chapter Preview

Vocabulary

English/Spanish Vocabulary Audio Online:

English	Spanish
Law of Cosines, *p. 936*	Ley de cosenos
Law of Sines, *p. 929*	Ley de senos
trigonometric identity, *p. 904*	identidad trigonométrica
trigonometric ratios for a right triangle, *p. 922*	razones trigonométricas para un triángulo rectángulo

BIG ideas

1 Equivalence
Essential Question How do you verify that an equation involving the variable *x* is an identity?

2 Function
Essential Question A trigonometric function corresponds one number to many, so how can its inverse be a function?

3 Equivalence
Essential Question How do the trigonometric *functions* relate to the trigonometric *ratios* for a right triangle?

 DOMAINS
- Trigonometric Functions
- Similarity, Right Triangles, and Trigonometry

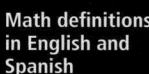
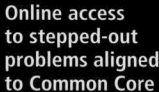
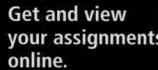
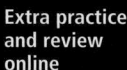
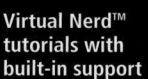

Download videos connecting math to your world.

Interactive! Vary numbers, graphs, and figures to explore math concepts.

The online Solve It will get you in gear for each lesson.

Math definitions in English and Spanish

Online access to stepped-out problems aligned to Common Core

Get and view your assignments online.

Extra practice and review online

Virtual Nerd™ tutorials with built-in support

Common Core Performance Task

Determining the Length of a Zip Line

A crew is setting up a zip line between two towers with support wires, as shown in the figure. They know the heights of the towers and the angles that two of the support wires make with the ground, which is level between the towers.

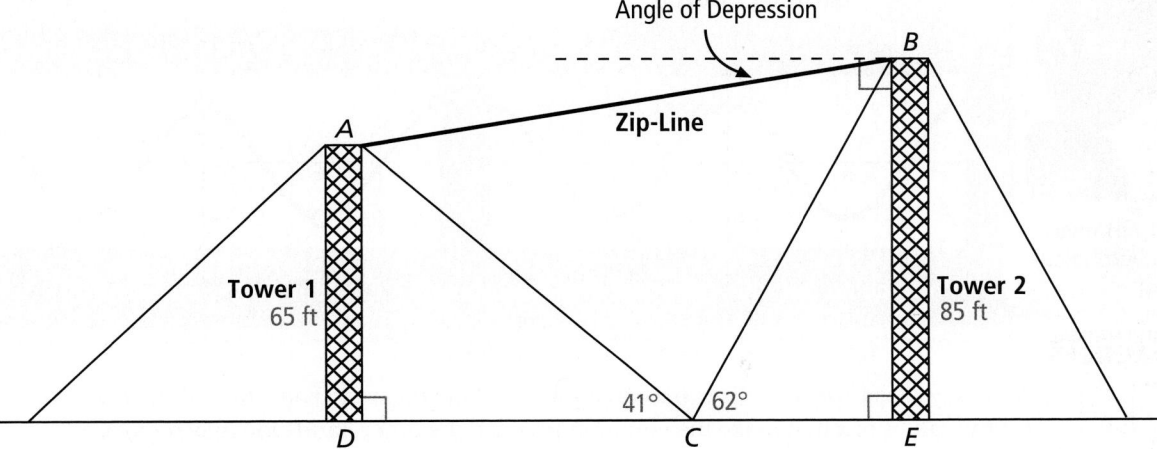

The crew's leader is concerned that the angle of depression of the zip line may be too great, resulting in a ride that is too fast. She wants to know how the length of the zip line will change if the angle of depression is halved. (In this case, the crew would set up a taller Tower 1.)

Task Description

Describe how the length of the zip line will change if its angle of depression is halved. Include the length of each zipline in your answer.

Connecting the Task to the Math Practices

MATHEMATICAL PRACTICES

As you complete the task, you'll apply several Standards for Mathematical Practice.

- You'll analyze the given information and identify relationships among important quantities in a real-world situation. (MP 1, MP 4)

- You'll calculate accurately and efficiently to determine lengths and angle measures. (MP 6)

- You'll look for structure in a geometric figure and apply appropriate properties. (MP 7)

14-1 Trigonometric Identities

© Common Core State Standards

F-TF.C.8 Prove the Pythagorean identity $\sin^2(\theta) + \cos^2(\theta) = 1$ and use it to find $\sin(\theta)$, $\cos(\theta)$, or $\tan(\theta)$, given $\sin(\theta)$, $\cos(\theta)$, or $\tan(\theta)$, and the quadrant of the angle.

MP 1, MP 2, MP 3, MP 4

Objective   To verify trigonometric identities

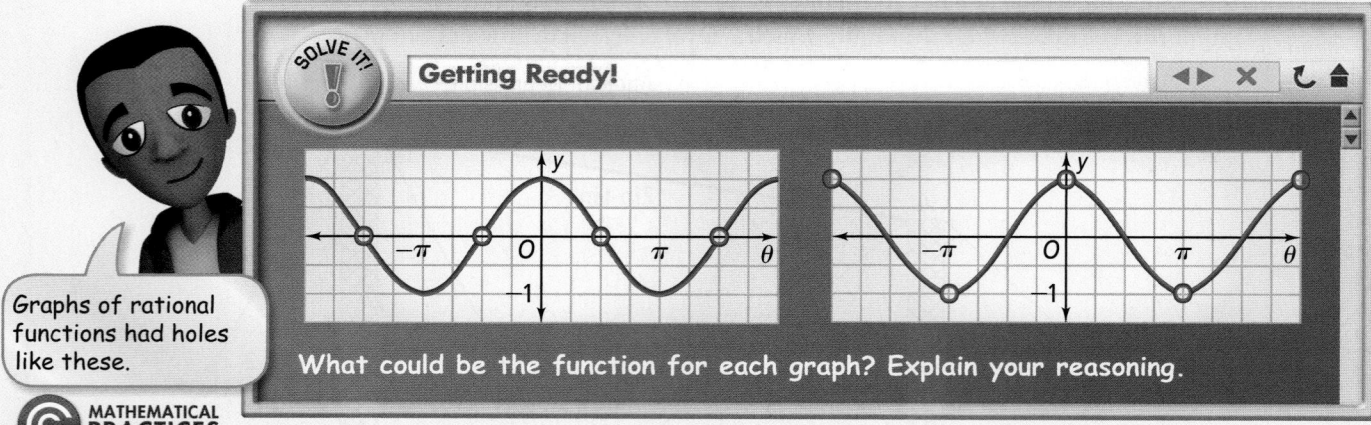

Getting Ready!

Graphs of rational functions had holes like these.

MATHEMATICAL PRACTICES

What could be the function for each graph? Explain your reasoning.

You may recognize $x^2 = 5x - 6$ as an equation that you are to solve to find the few, if any, values of x that make the equation true. On the other hand, you may recognize $\frac{x^5}{x^3} = x^2$ as an *identity*, an equation that is true for all values of x for which the expressions in the equation are defined. (Here, $\frac{x^5}{x^3}$ is not defined for $x = 0$.)

A **trigonometric identity** in one variable is a trigonometric equation that is true for all values of the variable for which all expressions in the equation are defined.

Lesson Vocabulary

• trigonometric identity

Essential Understanding   The interrelationships among the six basic trigonometric functions make it possible to write trigonometric expressions in various equivalent forms, some of which can be significantly easier to work with than others in mathematical applications.

Some trigonometric identities are definitions or follow immediately from definitions.

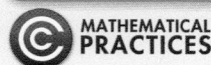

Key Concept   Basic Identities

Reciprocal Identities $\csc \theta = \dfrac{1}{\sin \theta}$ $\sec \theta = \dfrac{1}{\cos \theta}$ $\tan \theta = \dfrac{1}{\cot \theta}$

$\sin \theta = \dfrac{1}{\csc \theta}$ $\cos \theta = \dfrac{1}{\sec \theta}$ $\cot \theta = \dfrac{1}{\tan \theta}$

Tangent Identity $\tan \theta = \dfrac{\sin \theta}{\cos \theta}$ | **Cotangent Identity** $\cot \theta = \dfrac{\cos \theta}{\sin \theta}$

The *domain of validity* of an identity is the set of values of the variable for which all expressions in the equation are defined.

 **Problem 1** Finding the Domain of Validity

Plan

How can an expression be undefined?
An expression could contain a denominator that could be zero or it could contain an expression that is itself undefined for some values.

What is the domain of validity of each trigonometric identity?

A $\cos \theta = \frac{1}{\sec \theta}$.

The domain of $\cos \theta$ is all real numbers. The domain of $\frac{1}{\sec \theta}$ excludes all zeros of $\sec \theta$ (of which there are none) and all values θ for which $\sec \theta$ is undefined (odd multiples of $\frac{\pi}{2}$).

Therefore the domain of validity of $\cos \theta = \frac{1}{\sec \theta}$ is the set of real numbers except for the odd multiples of $\frac{\pi}{2}$.

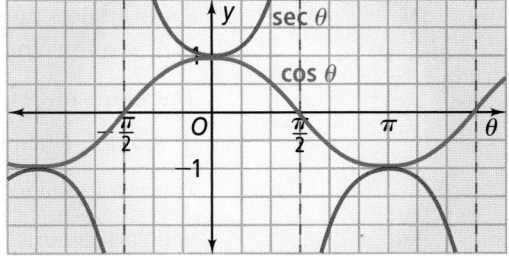

B $\sec \theta = \frac{1}{\cos \theta}$.

The domain of validity is the same as part (a), because $\sec \theta$ is not defined for odd multiples of $\frac{\pi}{2}$, and the odd multiples of $\frac{\pi}{2}$ are the zeros of $\cos \theta$.

 Got It? **1.** What is the domain of validity of the trigonometric identity $\sin \theta = \frac{1}{\csc \theta}$?

You can use known identities to verify other identities. To verify an identity, you can use previously known identities to transform one side of the equation to look like the other side.

 **Problem 2** Verifying an Identity Using Basic Identities

Plan

What identity do you know that you can use?
Look for a way to write the expression on the left in terms of $\sin \theta$ and $\cos \theta$. The identity $\sec \theta = \frac{1}{\cos \theta}$ does the job.

Verify the identity. What is the domain of validity?

A $(\sin \theta)(\sec \theta) = \tan \theta$

$(\sin \theta)(\sec \theta) = \sin \theta \cdot \frac{1}{\cos \theta}$ Reciprocal Identity

$= \frac{\sin \theta}{\cos \theta}$ Simplify.

$= \tan \theta$ Tangent Identity

The domain of $\sin \theta$ is all real numbers. The domains of $\sec \theta$ and $\tan \theta$ exclude all zeros of $\cos \theta$. These are the odd multiples of $\frac{\pi}{2}$. The domain of validity is the set of real numbers except for the odd multiples of $\frac{\pi}{2}$.

B $\frac{1}{\cot \theta} = \tan \theta$

$\frac{1}{\cot \theta} = \frac{1}{\frac{1}{\tan \theta}}$ Definition of cotangent

$= \tan \theta$ Simplify.

The domain of $\cot \theta$ excludes multiples of π. Also, $\cot \theta = 0$ at the odd multiples of $\frac{\pi}{2}$. The domain of validity is the set of real numbers except *all* multiples of $\frac{\pi}{2}$.

 Got It? **2.** Verify the identity $\frac{\csc \theta}{\sec \theta} = \cot \theta$. What is the domain of validity?

You can use the unit circle and the Pythagorean Theorem to verify another identity. The circle with its center at the origin with a radius of 1 is called the unit circle, and has an equation $x^2 + y^2 = 1$.

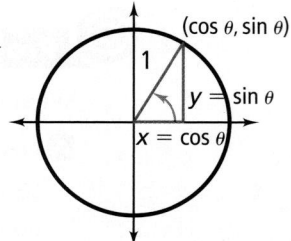

Every angle θ determines a unique point on the unit circle with x- and y-coordinates $(x, y) = (\cos \theta, \sin \theta)$.

Therefore, for every angle θ,

$$(\cos \theta)^2 + (\sin \theta)^2 = 1 \quad \text{or} \quad \cos^2 \theta + \sin^2 \theta = 1.$$

> This form allows you to write the identity without using parentheses.

This is a Pythagorean identity. You will verify two others in Problem 3.

You can use the basic and Pythagorean identities to verify other identities. To prove identities, transform the expression on one side of the equation to the expression on the other side. It often helps to write everything in terms of sines and cosines.

 Problem 3 Verifying a Pythagorean Identity

Plan

With which side should you work?
It usually is easier to begin with the more complicated-looking side.

Verify the Pythagorean identity $1 + \tan^2 \theta = \sec^2 \theta$.

$$1 + \tan^2\theta = 1 + \left(\frac{\sin \theta}{\cos \theta}\right)^2 \qquad \text{Tangent Identity}$$

$$= 1 + \frac{\sin^2 \theta}{\cos^2 \theta} \qquad \text{Simplify.}$$

$$= \frac{\cos^2 \theta}{\cos^2 \theta} + \frac{\sin^2 \theta}{\cos^2 \theta} \qquad \text{Find a common denominator.}$$

$$= \frac{\cos^2 \theta + \sin^2 \theta}{\cos^2 \theta} \qquad \text{Add.}$$

$$= \frac{1}{\cos^2 \theta} \qquad \text{Pythagorean identity}$$

$$= \sec^2 \theta \qquad \text{Reciprocal identity}$$

You have transformed the expression on the left side of the equation to become the expression on the right side. The equation is an identity.

Got It? **3. a.** Verify the third Pythagorean identity, $1 + \cot^2 \theta = \csc^2 \theta$.

b. Reasoning Explain why the domain of validity is not the same for all three Pythagorean identities.

You have now seen all three Pythagorean identities.

Key Concept **Pythagorean Identities**

$$\cos^2 \theta + \sin^2 \theta = 1 \qquad 1 + \tan^2 \theta = \sec^2 \theta \qquad 1 + \cot^2 \theta = \csc^2 \theta$$

There are many trigonometric identities. Most do not have specific names.

 Problem 4 Verifying an Identity

Verify the identity $\tan^2 \theta - \sin^2 \theta = \tan^2 \theta \sin^2 \theta$.

Plan

How do you begin when both sides look complicated?
It often is easier to collapse a difference (or sum) into a product than to expand a product into a difference.

$$\tan^2 \theta - \sin^2 \theta = \frac{\sin^2 \theta}{\cos^2 \theta} - \sin^2 \theta \qquad \text{Tangent identity}$$

$$= \frac{\sin^2 \theta}{\cos^2 \theta} - \frac{\sin^2 \theta \cos^2 \theta}{\cos^2 \theta} \qquad \text{Use a common denominator.}$$

$$= \frac{\sin^2 \theta - \sin^2 \theta \cos^2 \theta}{\cos^2 \theta} \qquad \text{Simplify.}$$

$$= \frac{\sin^2 \theta (1 - \cos^2 \theta)}{\cos^2 \theta} \qquad \text{Factor.}$$

$$= \frac{\sin^2 \theta (\sin^2 \theta)}{\cos^2 \theta} \qquad \text{Pythagorean identity}$$

$$= \frac{\sin^2 \theta}{\cos^2 \theta} \sin^2 \theta \qquad \text{Rewrite the fraction.}$$

$$= \tan^2 \theta \sin^2 \theta \qquad \text{Tangent Identity}$$

✔ **Got It?** **4.** Verify the identity $\sec^2 \theta - \sec^2 \theta \cos^2 \theta = \tan^2 \theta$.

You can use trigonometric identities to simplify trigonometric expressions.

 Problem 5 Simplifying an Expression

What is a simplified trigonometric expression for $\csc \theta \tan \theta$?

Think

Write the expression. Then replace $\csc \theta$ with $\frac{1}{\sin \theta}$.

Replace $\tan \theta$ with $\frac{\sin \theta}{\cos \theta}$.

Simplify.

$\frac{1}{\cos \theta} = \sec \theta$.

Write

$$\csc \theta \tan \theta = \frac{1}{\sin \theta} \cdot \tan \theta$$

$$= \frac{1}{\sin \theta} \cdot \frac{\sin \theta}{\cos \theta}$$

$$= \frac{\sin \theta}{\sin \theta \cos \theta}$$

$$= \frac{1}{\cos \theta}$$

$$= \sec \theta$$

✔ **Got It?** **5.** What is a simplified trigonometric expression for $\sec \theta \cot \theta$?

Lesson Check

Do you know HOW?

Verify each identity.

1. $\tan \theta \csc \theta = \sec \theta$

2. $\csc^2 \theta - \cot^2 \theta = 1$

3. $\sin \theta \tan \theta = \sec \theta - \cos \theta$

4. Simplify $\tan \theta \cot \theta - \sin^2 \theta$.

Do you UNDERSTAND?

 5. Vocabulary How does the identity $\cos^2 \theta + \sin^2 \theta = 1$ relate to the Pythagorean Theorem?

6. Error Analysis A student simplified the expression $2 - \cos^2 \theta$ to $1 - \sin^2 \theta$. What error did the student make? What is the correct simplified expression?

Practice and Problem-Solving Exercises

A Practice   **Verify each identity. Give the domain of validity for each identity.**   ◀ See Problems 1–4.

7. $\cos \theta \cot \theta = \dfrac{1}{\sin \theta} - \sin \theta$ 8. $\sin \theta \cot \theta = \cos \theta$ 9. $\cos \theta \tan \theta = \sin \theta$

10. $\sin \theta \sec \theta = \tan \theta$ 11. $\cos \theta \sec \theta = 1$ 12. $\tan \theta \cot \theta = 1$

13. $\sin \theta \csc \theta = 1$ 14. $\cot \theta = \csc \theta \cos \theta$ 15. $\csc \theta - \sin \theta = \cot \theta \cos \theta$

Simplify each trigonometric expression.   ◀ See Problem 5.

16. $\tan \theta \cot \theta$ 17. $1 - \cos^2 \theta$ 18. $\sec^2 \theta - 1$

19. $1 - \csc^2 \theta$ 20. $\sec^2 \theta \cot^2 \theta$ 21. $\cos \theta \tan \theta$

22. $\sin \theta \cot \theta$ 23. $\sin \theta \csc \theta$ 24. $\sec \theta \cos \theta \sin \theta$

25. $\sin \theta \sec \theta \cot \theta$ 26. $\sec^2 \theta - \tan^2 \theta$ 27. $\dfrac{\sin \theta}{\cos \theta \tan \theta}$

 **B Apply**   **28. Think About a Plan** Simplify the expression $\dfrac{\tan \theta}{\sec \theta - \cos \theta}$.

- Can you write everything in terms of $\sin \theta$, $\cos \theta$, or both?
- Are there any trigonometric identities that can help you simplify the expression?

Simplify each trigonometric expression.

29. $\cos \theta + \sin \theta \tan \theta$ 30. $\csc \theta \cos \theta \tan \theta$

31. $\tan \theta (\cot \theta + \tan \theta)$ 32. $\sin^2 \theta + \cos^2 \theta + \tan^2 \theta$

33. $\sin \theta (1 + \cot^2 \theta)$ 34. $\sin^2 \theta \csc \theta \sec \theta$

35. $\sec \theta \cos \theta - \cos^2 \theta$ 36. $\csc \theta - \cos \theta \cot \theta$

37. $\csc^2 \theta (1 - \cos^2 \theta)$ 38. $\dfrac{\csc \theta}{\sin \theta + \cos \theta \cot \theta}$

39. $\dfrac{\cos \theta \csc \theta}{\cot \theta}$ 40. $\dfrac{\sin^2 \theta \csc \theta \sec \theta}{\tan \theta}$

Express the first trigonometric function in terms of the second.

41. $\sin \theta$, $\cos \theta$

42. $\tan \theta$, $\cos \theta$

43. $\cot \theta$, $\sin \theta$

44. $\csc \theta$, $\cot \theta$

45. $\cot \theta$, $\csc \theta$

46. $\sec \theta$, $\tan \theta$

Verify each identity.

47. $\sin^2 \theta \tan^2 \theta = \tan^2 \theta - \sin^2 \theta$

48. $\sec \theta - \sin \theta \tan \theta = \cos \theta$

49. $\sin \theta \cos \theta (\tan \theta + \cot \theta) = 1$

50. $\dfrac{1 - \sin \theta}{\cos \theta} = \dfrac{\cos \theta}{1 + \sin \theta}$

51. $\dfrac{\sec \theta}{\cot \theta + \tan \theta} = \sin \theta$

52. $\left(\cot \theta + 1 \right)^2 = \csc^2 \theta + 2 \cot \theta$

53. Express $\cos \theta \csc \theta \cot \theta$ in terms of $\sin \theta$.

54. Express $\dfrac{\cos \theta}{\sec \theta + \tan \theta}$ in terms of $\sin \theta$.

Use the identity $\sin^2\theta + \cos^2\theta = 1$ and the basic identities to answer the following questions. Show all your work.

55. Given that $\sin \theta = 0.5$ and θ is in the first quadrant, what are $\cos \theta$ and $\tan \theta$?

56. Given that $\sin \theta = 0.5$ and θ is in the second quadrant, what are $\cos \theta$ and $\tan \theta$?

57. Given that $\cos \theta = -0.6$ and θ is in the third quadrant, what are $\sin \theta$ and $\tan \theta$?

58. Given that $\sin \theta = 0.48$ and θ is in the second quadrant, what are $\cos \theta$ and $\tan \theta$?

59. Given that $\tan \theta = 1.2$ and θ is in the first quadrant, what are $\sin \theta$ and $\cos \theta$?

60. Given that $\tan \theta = 3.6$ and θ is in the third quadrant, what are $\sin \theta$ and $\cos \theta$?

61. Given that $\sin \theta = 0.2$ and $\tan \theta < 0$, what is $\cos \theta$?

 **Challenge**

62. The unit circle is a useful tool for verifying identities. Use the diagram at the right to verify the identity $\sin(\theta + \pi) = -\sin \theta$.
  a. Explain why the y-coordinate of point P is $\sin(\theta + \pi)$.
  b. Prove that the two triangles shown are congruent.
  c. Use part (b) to show that the two blue segments are congruent.
  d. Use part (c) to show that the y-coordinate of P is $-\sin \theta$.
  e. Use parts (a) and (d) to conclude that $\sin(\theta + \pi) = -\sin \theta$.

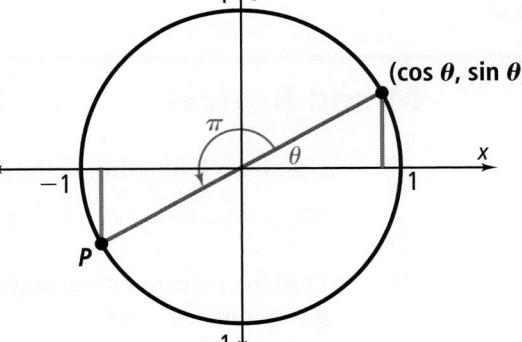

Use the diagram in Exercise 62 to verify each identity.

63. $\cos(\theta + \pi) = -\cos \theta$

64. $\tan(\theta + \pi) = \tan \theta$

Simplify each trigonometric expression.

65. $\dfrac{\cot^2 \theta - \csc^2 \theta}{\tan^2 \theta - \sec^2 \theta}$

66. $(1 - \sin \theta)(1 + \sin \theta)\csc^2 \theta + 1$

67. Physics When a ray of light passes from one medium into a second, the angle of incidence θ_1 and the angle of refraction θ_2 are related by Snell's law: $n_1 \sin \theta_1 = n_2 \sin \theta_2$, where n_1 is the index of refraction of the first medium and n_2 is the index of refraction of the second medium. How are θ_1 and θ_2 related if $n_2 > n_1$? If $n_2 < n_1$? If $n_2 = n_1$?

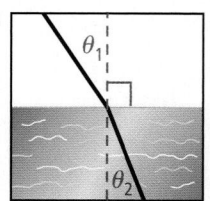

Standardized Test Prep

SAT/ACT

68. Which expression is equivalent to $2 \cot \theta$?

Ⓐ $\dfrac{1}{2 \tan \theta}$　　　Ⓑ $\dfrac{2}{\cot \theta}$　　　Ⓒ $\dfrac{2 \cos \theta}{\sin \theta}$　　　Ⓓ $\dfrac{\sin \theta}{\frac{1}{2} \cos \theta}$

69. Which equation is NOT an identity?

Ⓕ $\cos^2 \theta = 1 - \sin^2 \theta$　　　　　Ⓗ $\sin^2 \theta = \cos^2 \theta - 1$

Ⓖ $\cot^2 \theta = \csc^2 \theta - 1$　　　　　Ⓘ $\tan^2 \theta = \sec^2 \theta - 1$

70. Which expressions are equivalent?

I. $(\sin \theta)(\csc \theta - \sin \theta)$　　　II. $\sin^2 \theta - 1$　　　III. $\cos^2 \theta$

Ⓐ I and II only　　　Ⓑ II and III only　　　Ⓒ I and III only　　　Ⓓ I, II, and III

71. How can you express $\csc^2 \theta - 2 \cot^2 \theta$ in terms of $\sin \theta$ and $\cos \theta$?

Ⓕ $\dfrac{1 - 2 \cos^2 \theta}{\sin^2 \theta}$　　Ⓖ $\dfrac{1 - 2 \sin^2 \theta}{\sin^2 \theta}$　　Ⓗ $\sin^2 \theta - 2 \cos^2 \theta$　　Ⓘ $\dfrac{1}{\sin^2 \theta} - \dfrac{2}{\tan^2 \theta}$

72. Which expression is equivalent to $\dfrac{\tan \theta}{\cos \theta - \sec \theta}$?

Ⓐ $\csc \theta$　　　Ⓑ $\sec \theta$　　　Ⓒ $-\csc \theta$　　　Ⓓ $\tan^2 \theta$

Short Response

73. Show that $(\sec \theta + 1)(\sec \theta - 1) = \tan^2 \theta$ is an identity.

Mixed Review

Graph each function in the interval from 0 to 2π.　　　　　◀ **See Lesson 13-8.**

74. $y = \csc(-\theta)$　　　**75.** $y = -\sec 0.5\,\theta$　　　**76.** $y = -\sec(0.5\,\theta + 2)$　　　**77.** $y = \pi \sec \theta$

Find the measure of an angle between 0° and 360° that is coterminal with the given angle.　　　　　◀ **See Lesson 13-2.**

78. 395°　　　**79.** 405°　　　**80.** −225°　　　**81.** −149°

Get Ready!　**To prepare for Lesson 14-2, do Exercises 82–84.**

For each function f, find f^{-1}.　　　　　◀ **See Lesson 6-7.**

82. $f(x) = x + 1$　　　**83.** $f(x) = 2x - 3$　　　**84.** $f(x) = x^2 + 4$

14-2

Solving Trigonometric Equations Using Inverses

© Common Core State Standards

F-TF.B.6 Understand that restricting a trigonometric function to a domain . . . allows its inverse to be constructed. **Also F-TF.B.7**

MP 1, MP 2, MP 3, MP 4, MP 5

Objectives To evaluate inverse trigonometric functions
To solve trigonometric equations

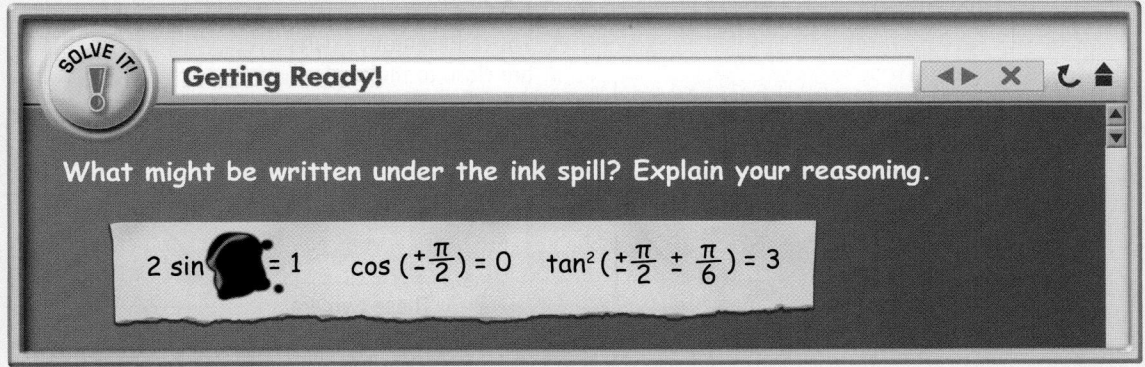

Getting Ready!

What might be written under the ink spill? Explain your reasoning.

$$2 \sin \text{◼} = 1 \qquad \cos\left(\pm\frac{\pi}{2}\right) = 0 \qquad \tan^2\left(\pm\frac{\pi}{2} \pm \frac{\pi}{6}\right) = 3$$

You have seen that inverse functions are useful for solving equations. To solve $x^3 = 5$, the cube root function gives $x = \sqrt[3]{5}$. To solve $x^2 = 5$, however, the square root function does not give both solutions $\sqrt{5}$ and $-\sqrt{5}$.

Because the trigonometric functions are periodic, a trigonometric equation like $\sin\theta = 0$ has infinitely many solutions. (Think of the sine graph.) Any inverse function for $\sin\theta$ must, however, give only one solution.

Essential Understanding To solve some trigonometric equations, you can use an inverse trigonometric function to find one solution. Then you can use periodicity to find all solutions.

Since a function must be single-valued, you define the inverse function for each of sine, cosine, and tangent by inverting only the representative part that has the simplest domain values.

take note

Key Concept	**Inverses of Three Trigonometric Functions**		
		Domain	**Range**
Function	$y = \cos\theta$	$0 \le \theta \le \pi$	$-1 \le y \le 1$
Inverse Function	$\theta = \cos^{-1} x$	$-1 \le x \le 1$	$0 \le \theta \le \pi$
Function	$y = \sin\theta$	$-\frac{\pi}{2} \le \theta \le \frac{\pi}{2}$	$-1 \le y \le 1$
Inverse Function	$\theta = \sin^{-1} x$	$-1 \le x \le 1$	$-\frac{\pi}{2} \le \theta \le \frac{\pi}{2}$
Function	$y = \tan\theta$	$-\frac{\pi}{2} < \theta < \frac{\pi}{2}$	y is any real number
Inverse Function	$\theta = \tan^{-1} x$	x is any real number	$-\frac{\pi}{2} < \theta < \frac{\pi}{2}$

The graphs on the left below show the "representative part" of the function that is inverted. The graphs on the right show the inverse functions.

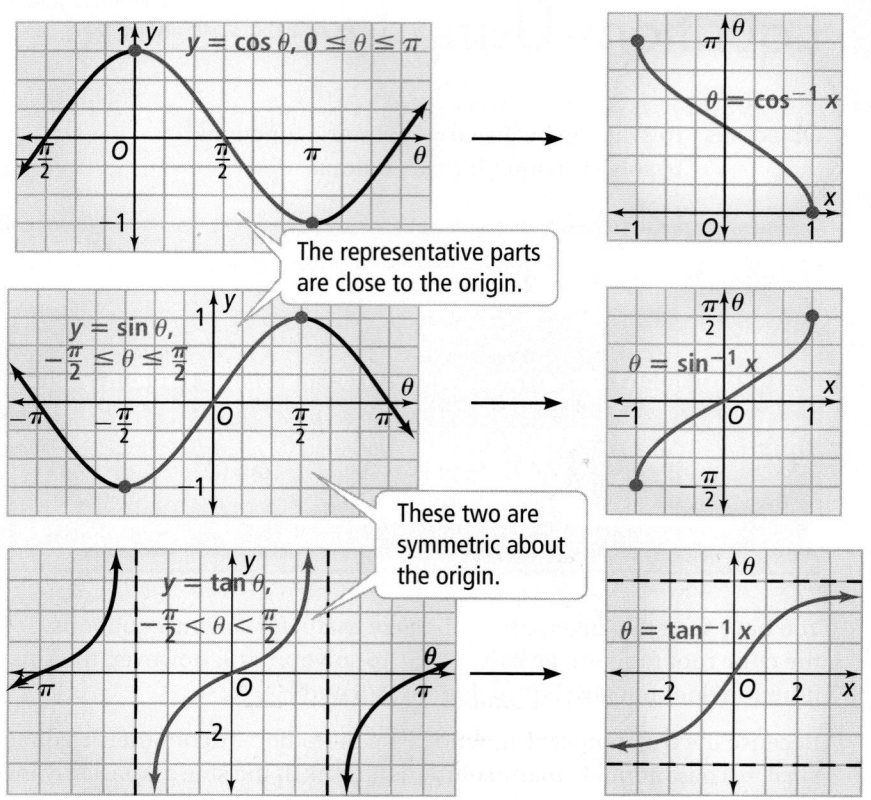

The representative parts are close to the origin.

These two are symmetric about the origin.

The values of inverse trigonometric functions are measures of angles. You can use the unit circle to find the values in either radians or degrees.

© **Problem 1** Using the Unit Circle

Multiple Choice What is $\cos^{-1}\left(\frac{1}{2}\right)$ in degrees?

A −60°   B 30°   C 60°   D 300°

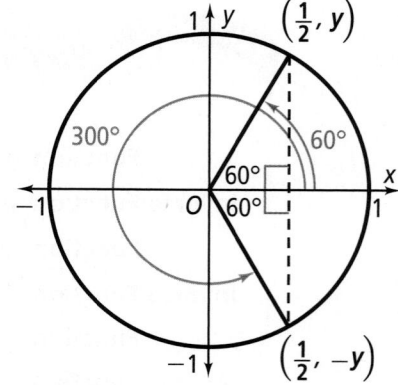

Draw a unit circle and mark each point on the circle that has x-coordinate $\frac{1}{2}$. These points and the origin form 30°-60°-90° triangles.

The simplest domain values for cosine that allow cosine to have values from −1 to 1 are the angles in the top half of the unit circle.

Thus, even though

$$\cos 60° = \cos 300° = \cos(-60°),$$

$\cos^{-1}\left(\frac{1}{2}\right)$ must be 60°. The correct choice is C.

Plan

How does the unit circle help you find angle measures?
The unit circle helps you recall the simplest domain values for a given trigonometric function.

Got It? **1.** Use a unit circle. What is each inverse function value in degrees?

a. $\cos^{-1}\left(-\frac{1}{2}\right)$ **b.** $\sin^{-1}\left(\frac{1}{2}\right)$ **c.** $\tan^{-1} 1$

You can use an inverse trigonometric function and the unit circle to find all angles having a given trigonometric function value.

 Problem 2 Using a Calculator to Find the Inverse of Sine

What are the radian measures of all angles whose sine is -0.9? Solve using an inverse function, a calculator, and the unit circle.

$\sin^{-1}(-0.9) \approx -1.12$ Use $\sin^{-1}$ and a calculator in radian mode.

Think

How do you find the angle in Quadrant III?
From $(x_1, -0.9)$, draw a line perpendicular to the y-axis to find $(x_2, -0.9)$.

The angle must be between $-\frac{\pi}{2}$ and $\frac{\pi}{2}$, so it is in Quadrant IV. The sine function is also negative in Quadrant III, as shown in the figure at the right. So $\pi + 1.12 \approx 4.26$ is another solution.

You can write the radian measures of all the angles whose sine is -0.9 as

$-1.12 + 2\pi n$ and $4.26 + 2\pi n$.

n represents any integer.

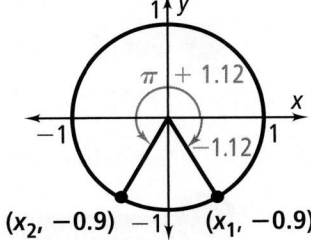

$(x_2, -0.9)$ $(x_1, -0.9)$

 Got It? **2.** What are the radian measures of all angles for each description?
a. angles whose sine is 0.44 **b.** angles whose sine is -0.73

 Problem 3 Using a Calculator to Find the Inverse of Tangent

What are the radian measures of all angles whose tangent is -0.84? Use an inverse function, a calculator, and the unit circle.

$\tan^{-1}(-0.84) \approx -0.70$ Use $\tan^{-1}$ and a calculator in radian mode.

Think

What are the representative angles for tangent?
The representative angles for tangent have values from $-\frac{\pi}{2}$ to $\frac{\pi}{2}$.

The angle must be between $-\frac{\pi}{2}$ and $\frac{\pi}{2}$, so it is in Quadrant IV. The tangent function is also negative in Quadrant II, as shown in the figure at the right. So $\pi - 0.70 \approx 2.44$ is another solution.

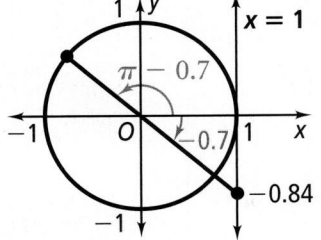

You can write the radian measures of all the angles whose tangent is -0.84 as

$-0.70 + 2\pi n$ and $2.44 + 2\pi n$, or simply as $-0.70 + \pi n$.

  Got It? **3.** What are the radian measures of all angles for each description?
a. angles whose tangent is 0.44 **b.** angles whose tangent is -0.73
c. Reasoning You can also write the radian measures for Problem 3 as $2.44 + \pi n$. Explain why.

In contrast to trigonometric identities, most trigonometric equations are true for only certain values of the variable.

 Problem 4 Solving a Trigonometric Equation

Plan

How do you begin?
You want to isolate the variable θ. First isolate $\cos \theta$. Then use inverse cosine.

What values for θ ($0 \le \theta < 2\pi$) satisfy the equation $4 \cos \theta - 1 = \cos \theta$?

$$4 \cos \theta - 1 = \cos \theta$$

$3 \cos \theta = 1$ Add 1 and $-\cos \theta$ to each side.

$\cos \theta = \frac{1}{3}$ Divide each side by 3.

$\cos^{-1} \frac{1}{3} \approx 1.23$ Use the inverse function to find one value of θ.

Cosine is also positive in Quadrant IV. So another value of θ is $2\pi - 1.23 \approx 5.05$. The two solutions between 0 and 2π are approximately 1.23 and 5.05.

Got It? 4. What values for θ ($0 \le \theta < 2\pi$) satisfy the equation $3 \sin \theta + 1 = \sin \theta$?

Sometimes you can solve trigonometric equations by factoring.

 Problem 5 Solving by Factoring

What are the values for θ that satisfy the equation $2 \cos \theta \sin \theta + \sin \theta = 0$ for $0 \le \theta < 2\pi$?

Think

Write the equation.

Factor.

Use the Zero Product Property.

Solve for $\cos \theta$.

Use the unit circle.

Write

$2 \cos \theta \sin \theta + \sin \theta = 0$

$\sin \theta (2 \cos \theta + 1) = 0$

$\sin \theta = 0$ or
$2 \cos \theta + 1 = 0$

$\sin \theta = 0$ or
$\cos \theta = -\frac{1}{2}$

$\theta = 0, \pi, \frac{2\pi}{3},$ or $\frac{4\pi}{3}$

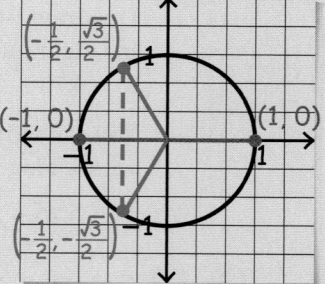

Got It? 5. What are the values for θ that satisfy the equation
$\sin \theta \cos \theta - \cos \theta = 0$ for $0 \le \theta < 2\pi$?

You can use inverses of trigonometric functions to solve problems.

 Problem 6 Using the Inverse of a Trigonometric Function

Energy Conservation An air conditioner cools a home when the outside temperature is above 25°C. During the summer, you can model the outside temperature in degrees Celsius using the function $f(t) = 24 - 8 \cos \frac{\pi}{12} t$, where t is the number of hours past midnight. During what hours is the air conditioner cooling the home?

By graphing, you can find when the graph of $y = f(t)$ is above the graph of $y = 25$, as shown at the right.

You can also solve algebraically.

Plan

When does the air conditioner run?
The air conditioner runs when the temperature $f(t) > 25$.

$24 - 8 \cos \frac{\pi}{12} t = 25$	Set $f(t) = 25$.
$-8 \cos \frac{\pi}{12} t = 1$	Subtract 24.
$\cos \frac{\pi}{12} t = -0.125$	Divide by -8.
$\frac{\pi}{12} t = \cos^{-1}(-0.125)$	Use inverse cosine.
$t = \frac{12}{\pi} \cos^{-1}(-0.125)$	Multiply by $\frac{12}{\pi}$.
$t \approx 6.5$	Evaluate.

The air conditioner comes on about 6.5 h after midnight or 6:30 A.M. By the symmetry of the graph, it goes off about 6.5 h before midnight, or 5:30 P.M.

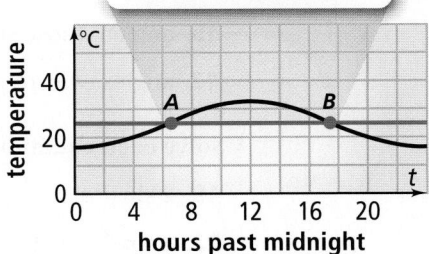

The air conditioner is cooling the home between points A and B.

 Got It? 6. Suppose the air conditioner is set to cool when the temperature is above 26°C. During what hours would the air conditioner run?

 Lesson Check

Do you know HOW?

Use a unit circle. What are the degree measures of all angles with the given sine value?

1. $-\frac{1}{2}$

2. $\frac{\sqrt{2}}{2}$

Solve each equation for θ with $0 \le \theta < 2\pi$.

3. $3 \cos \theta = -2$

4. $\sqrt{2} \cos \theta - \sqrt{2} = 0$

Do you UNDERSTAND?

MATHEMATICAL PRACTICES

5. Writing Compare finding the inverse of $y = 3x - 4$ to finding the inverse of $y = 3 \sin \theta - 4$. Describe any similarities and differences.

6. Error Analysis A student solved the equation $\sin^2 \theta = \frac{1}{2} \sin \theta$, $0 \le \theta < 2\pi$, as shown. What error did the student make?

$$\sin^2 \theta = \frac{1}{2} \sin \theta$$
$$\sin \theta = \frac{1}{2}$$
$$\theta = \frac{\pi}{6} \text{ and } \frac{5\pi}{6}$$

Practice and Problem-Solving Exercises

 MATHEMATICAL PRACTICES

A Practice

Use a unit circle, a 30°-60°-90° triangle, and an inverse function to find the degree measure of each angle.

◀ See Problem 1.

7. angle whose sine is 1

8. angle whose tangent is $\frac{\sqrt{3}}{3}$

9. angle whose sine is $-\frac{\sqrt{3}}{2}$

10. angle whose tangent is $-\sqrt{3}$

11. angle whose cosine is 0

12. angle whose cosine is $-\frac{\sqrt{2}}{2}$

Use a calculator and inverse functions to find the radian measures of all angles having the given trigonometric values.

◀ See Problems 2 and 3.

13. angles whose tangent is 1

14. angles whose sine is 0.37

15. angles whose sine is -0.78

16. angles whose tangent is -3

17. angles whose cosine is -0.89

18. angles whose sine is -1.1

Solve each equation for θ with $0 \leq \theta < 2\pi$.

◀ See Problems 4 and 5.

19. $2 \sin \theta = 1$

20. $2 \cos \theta - \sqrt{3} = 0$

21. $4 \tan \theta = 3 + \tan \theta$

22. $2 \sin \theta - \sqrt{2} = 0$

23. $3 \tan \theta - 1 = \tan \theta$

24. $3 \tan \theta + 5 = 0$

25. $2 \sin \theta = 3$

26. $2 \sin \theta = -\sqrt{3}$

27. $(\cos \theta)(\cos \theta + 1) = 0$

28. $(\sin \theta - 1)(\sin \theta + 1) = 0$

29. $2 \sin^2 \theta - 1 = 0$

30. $\tan \theta = \tan^2 \theta$

31. $\sin^2 \theta + 3 \sin \theta = 0$

32. $\sin \theta = -\sin \theta \cos \theta$

33. $2 \sin^2 \theta - 3 \sin \theta = 2$

34. Energy Conservation Suppose the outside temperature in Problem 6 is modeled by the function $f(t) = 27 - 6 \cos \frac{\pi}{12} t$ instead. During what hours is the air conditioner cooling the house?

◀ See Problem 6.

B Apply

Each diagram shows one solution to the equation below it. Find the complete solution of each equation.

35.

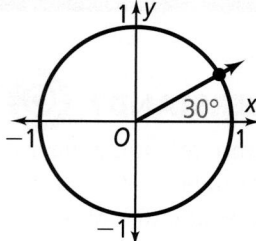

$5 \sin \theta = 1 + 3 \sin \theta$

36.

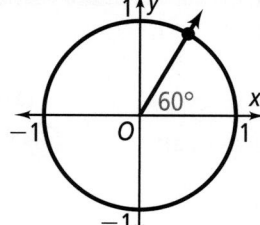

$6 \cos \theta - 5 = -2$

37.

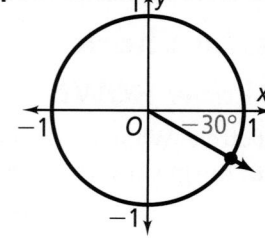

$4 \sin \theta + 3 = 1$

Solve each equation for θ with $0 \leq \theta < 2\pi$.

38. $\sec \theta = 2$

39. $\csc \theta = -1$

40. $\csc \theta = 3$

41. $\cot \theta = -10$

42. **Think About a Plan** The function $h = 25 \sin\left(\frac{\pi}{20}(t - 10)\right) + 34$ models the height h of a Ferris wheel car in feet, t seconds after starting. When will the car first be 30 ft off the ground?
   - What is the inverse function?
   - How can the inverse function help you answer the question?

STEM 43. **Electricity** The function $I = 40 \sin 60\pi t$ models the current I in amps that an electric generator is producing after t seconds. When is the first time that the current will reach 20 amps? -20 amps?

44. **Reasoning** The graphing calculator screen shows a portion of the graphs of $y = \sin \theta$ and $y = 0.5$.
   a. Write the complete solution of $\sin \theta \geq 0.5$.
   b. Write the complete solution of $\sin \theta \leq 0.5$.
   c. **Writing** Explain how you can solve inequalities involving trigonometric functions.

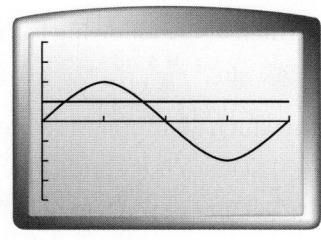

Xmin = 0
Xmax = 2π
Xscl = $\frac{\pi}{2}$
Ymin = −2
Ymax = 2
Yscl = 0.5

Find the complete solution in radians of each equation.

45. $2 \sin^2 \theta + \cos \theta - 1 = 0$

46. $\sin^2 \theta - 1 = \cos^2 \theta$

47. $2 \sin \theta + 1 = \csc \theta$

48. $3 \tan^2 \theta - 1 = \sec^2 \theta$

49. $\sin \theta \cos \theta = \frac{1}{2} \cos \theta$

50. $\tan \theta \sin \theta = 3 \sin \theta$

51. $2 \cos^2 \theta + \sin \theta = 1$

52. $\sin \theta \cot^2 \theta - 3 \sin \theta = 0$

53. $4 \sin^2 \theta + 1 = 4 \sin \theta$

Find the x-intercepts of the graph of each function.

54. $y = 2 \cos \theta + 1$

55. $y = 2 \sin^2 \theta - 1$

56. $y = \cos^2 \theta - 1$

57. $y = \tan^2 \theta - 1$

58. $y = 2 \sin^4 \theta - \sin^2 \theta$

59. $y = 2 \cos^2 \theta - 3 \cos \theta - 2$

60. Find the complete solution of $\sin^2 \theta + 2 \sin \theta + 1 = 0$. (*Hint:* How would you solve $x^2 + 2x + 1 = 0$?)

61. **a.** **Open-Ended** Write three trigonometric equations each with the complete solution $\pi + 2\pi n$.
   b. Describe how you found the equations in part (a).

C Challenge   **Solve each trigonometric equation for θ in terms of y.**

Sample $y = 2 \sin 3\theta + 4$

$\sin 3\theta = \dfrac{y - 4}{2}$

$3\theta = \sin^{-1}\left(\dfrac{y - 4}{2}\right) + 2\pi n, \ 2 \leq y \leq 6$

$\theta = \dfrac{1}{3} \sin^{-1}\left(\dfrac{y - 4}{2}\right) + \dfrac{2\pi}{3} n, \ 2 \leq y \leq 6$

62. $y = \cos 2\theta$

63. $y = 3 \sin (\theta + 2)$

64. $y = -4 \cos 2\pi\theta$

65. $y = 2 \cos \theta + 1$

STEM **66. Tides** One day the tide at a point in Maine could be modeled by $h = 5 \cos \frac{2\pi}{13} t$, where h is the height of the tide in feet above the mean water level and t is the number of hours past midnight. At what times that day would the tide have been each of the following?

a. 3 ft above the mean water level

b. *at least* 3 ft above the mean water level

Standardized Test Prep

SAT/ACT

67. Which of the following is NOT equal to 60°?

Ⓐ $\sin^{-1} \frac{\sqrt{3}}{2}$ Ⓑ $\cos^{-1} \frac{1}{2}$ Ⓒ $\tan^{-1} \sqrt{3}$ Ⓓ $\tan^{-1} \frac{\sqrt{3}}{3}$

68. In which quadrants are the solutions to $\tan \theta + 1 = 0$?

Ⓕ Quadrants I and II   Ⓗ Quadrants II and IV

Ⓖ Quadrants II and III   Ⓘ Quadrants III and IV

69. Which of these angles have a sine of about -0.6?

I. 143.1°   II. 216.9°   III. 323.1°

Ⓐ I and II only   Ⓒ II and III only

Ⓑ I and III only   Ⓓ I, II, and III

70. What are the solutions of $2 \sin \theta - \sqrt{3} = 0$ for $0 \leq \theta < 2\pi$?

Ⓕ $\frac{\pi}{6}$ and $\frac{5\pi}{6}$ Ⓖ $\frac{\pi}{3}$ and $\frac{2\pi}{3}$ Ⓗ $\frac{2\pi}{3}$ and $\frac{4\pi}{3}$ Ⓘ $\frac{4\pi}{3}$ and $\frac{5\pi}{3}$

71. Suppose $a > 0$. Under what conditions for a and b will $a \sin \theta = b$ have exactly two solutions in the interval $0 \leq \theta < 2\pi$?

Ⓐ $a = b$ Ⓑ $b > a$ Ⓒ $a = -b$ Ⓓ $a > b > -a$

Extended Response

72. Solve $2 \sin^2 \theta = -\sin \theta$ for θ with $0 \leq \theta < 2\pi$. Show your work.

Mixed Review

Simplify each expression.   ◀ **See Lesson 14-1.**

73. $\cos^2 \theta \sec \theta \csc \theta$ **74.** $\sin \theta \sec \theta \tan \theta$ **75.** $\csc^2 \theta (1 - \cos^2 \theta)$

76. $\frac{\cos \theta \csc \theta}{\cot \theta}$ **77.** $\frac{\sec \theta}{\cot \theta + \tan \theta}$ **78.** $\frac{\sin \theta + \tan \theta}{1 + \cos \theta}$

Write a cosine function for each description.   ◀ **See Lesson 13-5.**

79. amplitude 4, period 8   **80.** amplitude 3, period 2π **81.** amplitude $\frac{\pi}{4}$, period 3π

Get Ready!   **To prepare for Lesson 14-3, do Exercises 82–84.**

Solve each proportion.   ◀ **See p. 974.**

82. $\frac{x}{7} = \frac{28}{49}$ **83.** $\frac{10}{14} = \frac{15}{x}$ **84.** $\frac{21}{10} = \frac{x}{25}$

14-3

Right Triangles and Trigonometric Ratios

© Common Core State Standards

G-SRT.C.6 Understand that by similarity, side ratios in right triangles . . . lead to definitions of trigonometric ratios for acute angles. **Also G-SRT.C.8**

MP 1, MP 2, MP 3, MP 4, MP 5

Objective To find lengths of sides in a right triangle
To find measures of angles in a right triangle

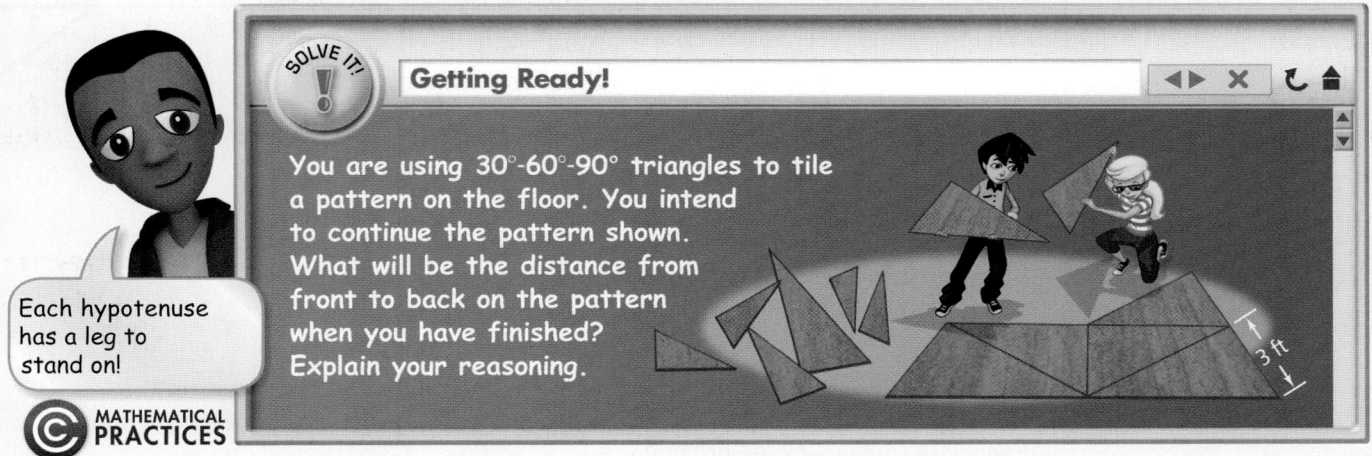

SOLVE IT!

Getting Ready!

You are using 30°-60°-90° triangles to tile a pattern on the floor. You intend to continue the pattern shown. What will be the distance from front to back on the pattern when you have finished? Explain your reasoning.

3 ft

Each hypotenuse has a leg to stand on!

MATHEMATICAL PRACTICES

Lesson Vocabulary
• trigonometric ratios

There is a connection between the trigonometric functions and the right-triangle trigonometric ratios that you may have studied in geometry.

Essential Understanding If you restrict the domain of the trigonometric functions to angle measures between 0° and 90°, the function values are the trigonometric ratios associated with the acute angles of a right triangle.

Dilate the unit circle by the factor r and the terminal side of an angle θ will intersect the circle of radius r in the point $(x, y) = (r\cos\theta, r\sin\theta)$.

Key Concept **Trigonometric Ratios for a Circle**

$$\sin\theta = \frac{y}{r} \qquad \csc\theta = \frac{r}{y}$$

$$\cos\theta = \frac{x}{r} \qquad \sec\theta = \frac{r}{x}$$

$$\tan\theta = \frac{y}{x} \qquad \cot\theta = \frac{x}{y}$$

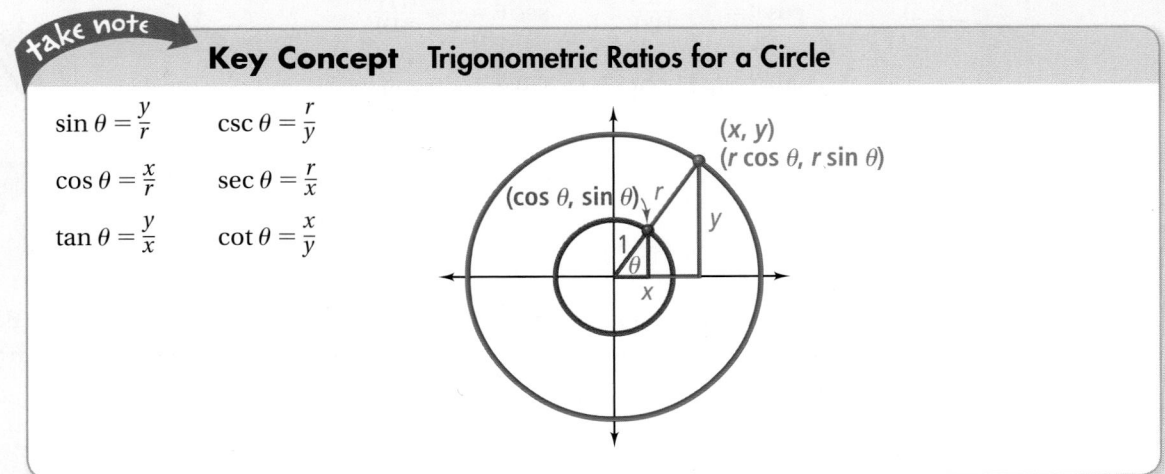

(x, y)
$(r\cos\theta, r\sin\theta)$
$(\cos\theta, \sin\theta)$
r
y
1
θ
x

Problem 1 Trigonometric Values Beyond the Unit Circle

Think

How do you find *r*?
Use the distance formula.

For a standard-position angle determined by the point $(8, -6)$, what are the values of the six trigonometric functions?

First, find the distance r of the point from the origin:

$$r = \sqrt{(8-0)^2 + (-6-0)^2} = 10.$$

Then,

$$\sin \theta = \frac{y}{r} = \frac{-6}{10} = -\frac{3}{5} \qquad \csc \theta = \frac{r}{y} = \frac{10}{-6} = -\frac{5}{3}$$

$$\cos \theta = \frac{x}{r} = \frac{8}{10} = \frac{4}{5} \qquad \sec \theta = \frac{r}{x} = \frac{10}{8} = \frac{5}{4}$$

$$\tan \theta = \frac{y}{x} = \frac{-6}{8} = -\frac{3}{4} \qquad \cot \theta = \frac{x}{y} = \frac{8}{-6} = -\frac{4}{3}$$

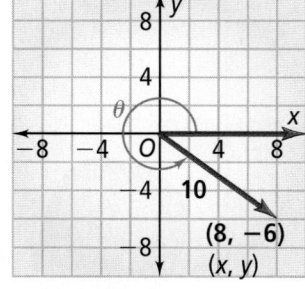

 Got It? 1. For a standard-position angle determined by the point $(-5, 12)$, what are the values of the six trigonometric functions?

If you use only points in the first quadrant, the values of x, y, and r are positive. The values of the trigonometric functions are also positive and are the **trigonometric ratios** for an acute angle θ of a right triangle.

take note ➤ **Key Concept** Trigonometric Ratios for a Right Triangle

If θ is an acute angle of a right triangle, x is the length of the adjacent leg (ADJ), y is the length of the opposite leg (OPP), and r is the length of the hypotenuse (HYP), then the trigonometric ratios of θ are as follows.

$$\sin \theta = \frac{y}{r} = \frac{\text{OPP}}{\text{HYP}} \qquad \csc \theta = \frac{r}{y} = \frac{\text{HYP}}{\text{OPP}}$$

$$\cos \theta = \frac{x}{r} = \frac{\text{ADJ}}{\text{HYP}} \qquad \sec \theta = \frac{r}{x} = \frac{\text{HYP}}{\text{ADJ}}$$

$$\tan \theta = \frac{y}{x} = \frac{\text{OPP}}{\text{ADJ}} \qquad \cot \theta = \frac{x}{y} = \frac{\text{ADJ}}{\text{OPP}}$$

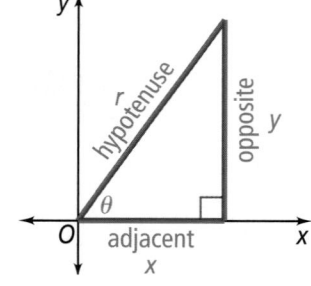

There are many applications of right-triangle trigonometry. Most involve degree measure and require the use of a calculator. Therefore, you will want to set your calculator to *degree mode*.

 **Problem 2** **Finding Distance**

Plan

Which trigonometric ratio do you use?
You know an angle and an *adjacent* side. You want to find the *opposite* side. Use tangent.

The large glass pyramid at the Louvre in Paris has a square base. The angle formed by each face and the ground is 49.7°. How high is the pyramid?

The distance from the center of a side of the pyramid to a point directly below the top of the pyramid is half the length of a side, or 17.5 m.

$$\tan 49.7° = \frac{x}{17.5}$$

$$x = 17.5 \cdot \tan 49.7°$$

$$x \approx 20.6$$

The pyramid is about 20.6 m high.

 Got It? **2.** What is each distance for the Louvre pyramid?
    a. from the center of a side of the base to the top along a lateral face
    b. from a corner of the base to the top

In right triangle trigonometry, the value of one trigonometric ratio determines the values of the others.

 **Problem 3** **Finding Trigonometric Ratios**

Plan

How do you begin?
A diagram will help you see the legs—opposite and adjacent to the angle—and the hypotenuse.

In $\triangle ABC$, $\angle C$ is a right angle and $\sin A = \frac{5}{13}$. What are $\cos A$, $\cot A$, and $\sin B$?

Step 1 Draw a diagram.

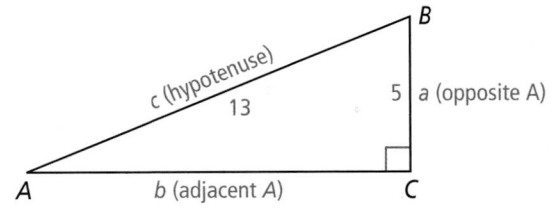

Step 2 Use the Pythagorean Theorem to find b.

$$c^2 = a^2 + b^2$$
$$13^2 = 5^2 + b^2$$
$$169 = 25 + b^2$$
$$144 = b^2$$
$$12 = b$$

Step 3 Write the ratios.

$$\cos A = \frac{\text{ADJ}}{\text{HYP}} = \frac{12}{13} \qquad \cot A = \frac{\text{ADJ}}{\text{OPP}} = \frac{12}{5} \qquad \sin B = \frac{\text{OPP}}{\text{HYP}} = \frac{12}{13}$$

 Got It? **3.** In $\triangle DEF$, $\angle D$ is a right angle and $\tan E = \frac{3}{4}$. What are $\sin E$ and $\sec F$?

If you are given the measures of an acute angle and a side of a right triangle, you can find the lengths of the other two sides.

 Problem 4 Using a Trigonometric Ratio to Solve a Problem

Aviation An airplane's angle of descent into the airport is 3°. If the airplane begins its descent at an altitude of 5000 ft, what is its straight-line distance to the airport?

Know

An airplane is 5000 ft high and starts to descend at an angle of 3° with the horizontal.

Need

The straight-line distance from the airplane to the airport.

Plan

Draw a right triangle to show the known information. Set up a trigonometric ratio that involves the known information and what you want to find.

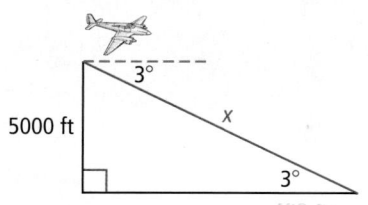

Let x represent the straight-line distance.

$$\sin 3° = \frac{5000}{x} \qquad \sin \theta = \frac{OPP}{HYP}$$

$$x = \frac{5000}{\sin 3°} \qquad \text{Solve for } x.$$

$$\approx 95{,}500 \qquad \text{Use a calculator.}$$

The straight-line distance is about 95,500 ft, or about 18 miles.

 Got It? **4.** If the airplane in Problem 4 begins its descent at an altitude of 4000 feet, what is its straight-line distance to the airport?

Given any two sides in a right triangle, you can use inverse trigonometric functions to find the measures of the acute angles.

 Problem 5 Finding an Angle Measure

Plan

Which trigonometric ratio do you use?
You know the side adjacent to D and the hypotenuse. Use cosine.

In $\triangle DGH$, $\angle H$ is a right angle, $h = 13$, and $g = 5$. What is $m\angle D$?

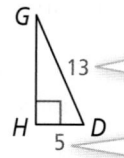

Side h is opposite $\angle H$.

Side g is opposite $\angle G$.

$$\cos D = \frac{5}{13} \qquad \cos D = \frac{ADJ}{HYP}$$

$$m\angle D = \cos^{-1} \frac{5}{13} \quad \text{Solve for } m\angle D.$$

$$\approx 67.38° \qquad \text{Use a calculator.}$$

To the nearest tenth of a degree, $m\angle D$ is 67.4°.

 Got It? **5.** What is $m\angle A$ in each triangle? Use a trigonometric ratio.

a.
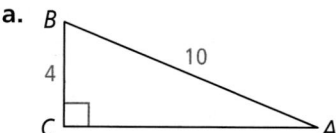

b.
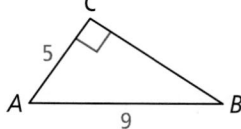

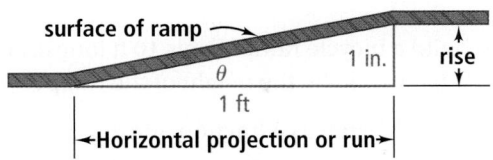 **Problem 6** **Using the Inverse of a Trigonometric Function** **STEM**

Construction You must build a wheelchair ramp so the slope is not more than 1 in. of rise for every 1 ft of run. What is the maximum angle that the ramp can make with the ground, to the nearest tenth of a degree?

surface of ramp
θ
1 in.   rise
1 ft
←Horizontal projection or run→

Let θ = the measure of the angle the ramp makes with the ground.

You know the lengths of the leg opposite and the leg adjacent to the angle you need to find. So, use the tangent ratio.

Think

Does the answer make sense?
The angle should be small for a wheelchair ramp, so the answer makes sense.

$\tan \theta = \dfrac{1}{12}$ Rewrite 1 ft as 12 in.

$\theta = \tan^{-1} \dfrac{1}{12}$ Use the inverse tangent function.

$\theta \approx 4.76$ Use a calculator.

The maximum angle (rounded) that the ramp can make with the ground is 4.8°.

Got It? 6. An entrance to a building is not wheelchair accessible. The entrance is 6 feet above ground level and 30 feet from the roadway.
     a. How long must the ramp be for the slope to meet the regulation of 1 inch of rise for every 1 foot of run?
     b. Reasoning How can you build a ramp to meet the regulation within the space of 30 feet?

Lesson Check

Do you know HOW?

Use the diagram for Exercises 1–3.

1. Write ratios for sin 57°, cos 57°, and tan 57°.

2. If $a = 10$, what is b?

3. Find the values of sin 33°, cos 33°, and tan 33° as fractions and as decimals. Round to the nearest tenth.

4. Find $\sin^{-1} 0.6$ to the nearest tenth of a degree.

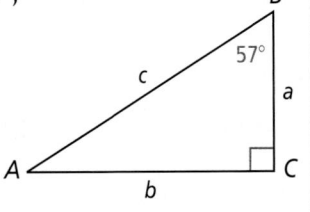

Do you UNDERSTAND? **MATHEMATICAL PRACTICES**

5. Writing In a right triangle, the length of the shortest side is 8.4 m and the length of the hypotenuse is 12.9 m. Show and describe how you would find the acute angle measures.

6. Error Analysis One of the angles in a right triangle measures 0.45 radians. The side opposite the angle measures 4 cm. A student finds the length of the hypotenuse. What mistake does the student make?

$\sin 0.45 = \dfrac{4}{x}$

$x = 4 \sin^{-1} 0.45$

$x \approx 1.87$

Practice and Problem-Solving Exercises

MATHEMATICAL PRACTICES

A Practice

Find the values of the six trigonometric functions for the angle in standard position determined by each point.

◀ See Problem 1.

7. $(-4, 3)$ **8.** $(5, 12)$ **9.** $(1, -5)$ **10.** $(-5, -2)$ **11.** $(-3, \sqrt{7})$

12. You want to build a bicycle ramp that is 10 ft long and makes a 30° angle with the ground. What would be the height of the ramp?

◀ See Problem 2.

13. In $\triangle ABC$, find each value as a fraction and as a decimal. Round to the nearest hundredth.

◀ See Problem 3.

   a. $\sin A$ **b.** $\sec A$ **c.** $\cot A$

   d. $\csc B$ **e.** $\sec B$ **f.** $\tan B$

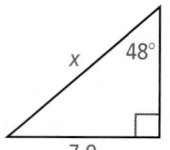

14. In $\triangle GHI$, $\angle H$ is a right angle, $GH = 40$, and $\cos G = \frac{40}{41}$. Draw a diagram and find each value in fraction and in decimal form.

   a. $\sin G$ **b.** $\sin I$ **c.** $\cot G$

   d. $\csc G$ **e.** $\cos I$ **f.** $\sec H$

Find each length x. Round to the nearest tenth.

◀ See Problem 4.

15.

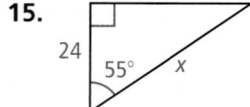

16.

17.

18. Indirect Measurement In 1915, the tallest flagpole in the world stood in San Francisco.

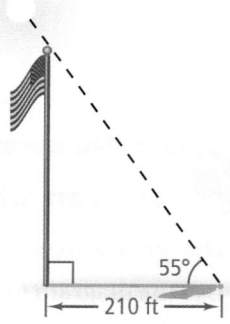

   a. When the angle of elevation of the sun was 55°, the length of the shadow cast by this flagpole was 210 ft. Find the height of the flagpole to the nearest foot.

   b. What was the length of the shadow when the angle of elevation of the sun was 34°?

   c. What do you need to assume about the flagpole and the shadow to solve these problems? Explain why.

In $\triangle ABC$, $\angle C$ is a right angle. Find the remaining sides and angles. Round your answers to the nearest tenth.

◀ See Problem 5.

19. $b = 5$, $c = 10$ **20.** $a = 5$, $b = 6$ **21.** $b = 12$, $c = 15$

22. $a = 8.1$, $b = 6.2$ **23.** $b = 4.3$, $c = 9.1$ **24.** $a = 17$, $c = 22$

STEM 25. Rocket Science An observer on the ground at point A watches a rocket ascend. The observer is 1200 ft from the launch point B. As the rocket rises, the distance d from the observer to the rocket increases.

◀ See Problem 6.

   a. Express $m\angle A$ in terms of d.

   b. Find $m\angle A$ if $d = 1500$ ft. Round your answer to the nearest degree.

   c. Find $m\angle A$ if $d = 2000$ ft. Round your answer to the nearest degree.

Sketch a right triangle with θ as the measure of one acute angle. Find the other five trigonometric ratios of θ.

26. $\sin \theta = \frac{3}{8}$ **27.** $\cos \theta = \frac{7}{20}$ **28.** $\cos \theta = \frac{1}{5}$ **29.** $\tan \theta = \frac{24}{7}$

30. $\sec \theta = \frac{16}{9}$ **31.** $\cot \theta = \frac{5}{4}$ **32.** $\sin \theta = 0.35$ **33.** $\csc \theta = 5.2$

34. Think About a Plan A radio tower has supporting cables attached to it at points 100 ft above the ground. Write a model for the length *d* of each supporting cable as a function of the angle θ that it makes with the ground. Then find *d* when θ = 60° and when θ = 50°.
- Which trigonometric function applies?
- How do you set up the equation?

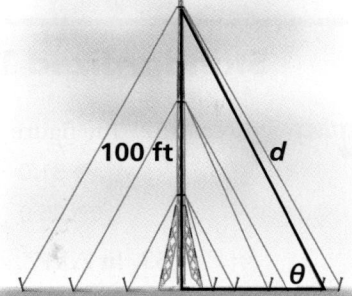

35. Indirect Measurement You are 330 ft from the base of a building. The angles of elevation to the top and bottom of a flagpole on top of the building are 55° and 53°. Find the height of the flagpole.

36. A 150-ft redwood tree casts a shadow. Express the length *x* of the shadow as a function of the angle of elevation of the sun θ. Then find *x* when θ = 35° and θ = 70°.

37. Geometry An altitude inside a triangle forms 36° and 42° angles with two of the sides. The altitude is 5 m long. Find the area of the triangle.

In △*ABC*, ∠*C* is a right angle. Two measures are given. Find the remaining sides and angles. Round your answers to the nearest tenth.

38. $b = 8, c = 17$ **39.** $a = 7, b = 10$ **40.** $m\angle A = 52°, c = 10$

41. $m\angle A = 34.2°, b = 5.7$ **42.** $m\angle B = 17.2°, b = 8.3$ **43.** $m\angle B = 8.3°, c = 20$

44. a. In Problem 5, use the Pythagorean Theorem to find *GH*.
b. Multiple Representations Use a trigonometric ratio to find *GH*.

45. Open-Ended If $\sin \theta = \frac{1}{2}$, describe a method you could use to find all the angles between 0° and 360° that satisfy this equation.

46. Reasoning Show that cos *A* defined as a ratio equals cos θ using the unit circle.

Use the definitions of trigonometric ratios in right △*ABC* to verify each identity.

47. $\sec A = \frac{1}{\cos A}$ **48.** $\tan A = \frac{\sin A}{\cos A}$ **49.** $\cos^2 A + \sin^2 A = 1$

50. Geometry A regular pentagon is inscribed in a circle of radius 10 cm.
a. Find the measure of ∠*C*.
b. Find the length of the diagonal *PS*. (*Hint:* First find *RS*.)

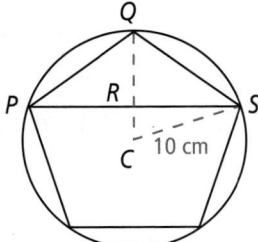

51. The tallest obelisk in Europe is the Wellington Testimonial in Dublin, Ireland. The distance between an angle of 37° from the ground and the top of the obelisk and an angle of 30° from the ground to the top of the obelisk is 25 m. Use these measurements to find the height of the obelisk. Use the diagram at the right to set up some trigonometric equations.

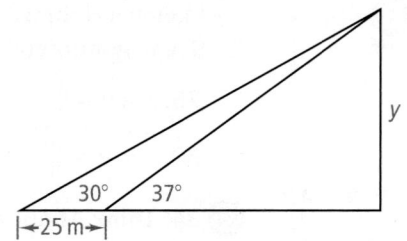

Standardized Test Prep

SAT/ACT

52. The figure at the right is a rectangle. What is the value of x?

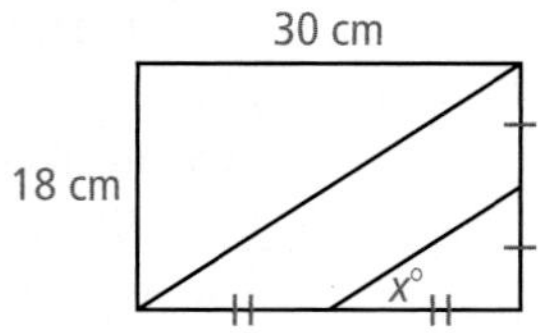

(A) 31.0 (C) 53.1

(B) 36.9 (D) 59.0

30 cm
18 cm

53. In $\triangle XYZ$, $\angle Z$ is a right angle and $\tan X = \frac{8}{15}$. What is $\sin Y$?

(F) $\frac{8}{17}$ (G) $\frac{15}{17}$ (H) $\frac{17}{15}$ (I) $\frac{15}{8}$

54. In the right triangle at the right, $\cos y° = \frac{5}{13}$. If $x + 2z = 7.1$ (z not pictured), what is the value of z?

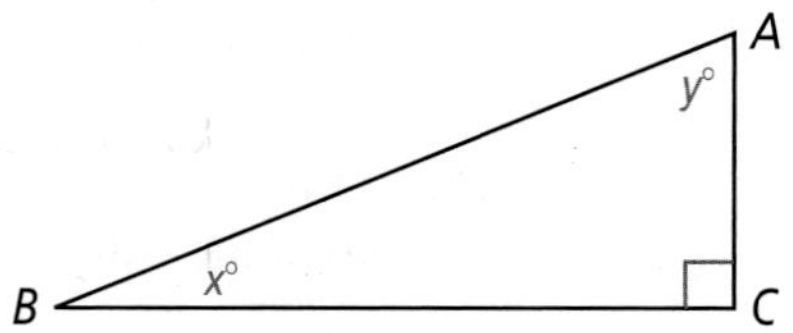

(A) 67.3 (C) −7.76

(B) 22.6 (D) −30.1

55. The sides of a rectangle are 25 cm and 8 cm. What is the measure of the angle formed by the short side and a diagonal of the rectangle?

(F) 17.7° (G) 18.7° (H) 71.3° (I) 72.3°

Short Response

56. Find the measures of the acute angles of a right triangle, to the nearest tenth, if the legs are 135 cm and 95 cm.

Apply What You've Learned

MATHEMATICAL
PRACTICES
MP 1, MP 4

Look back at the figure of the towers, support wires, and zip line on page 903.

a. Write a relationship in $\triangle ADC$ that you can use to find the length of the support wire $\overline{AC}$. Then find the length of $\overline{AC}$ to the nearest hundredth of a foot.

b. Write a relationship in $\triangle ADC$ that you can use to find the length of $\overline{DC}$. Then find the length of $\overline{DC}$ to the nearest hundredth of a foot.

c. Explain how you know the lengths you found in parts (a) and (b) are reasonable.

d. Find the lengths of $\overline{BC}$ and $\overline{EC}$ to the nearest hundredth of a foot.

Do you know HOW?

Verify each identity.

1. $\sin \theta \tan \theta = \sec \theta - \cos \theta$

2. $\tan \theta = \dfrac{\sec \theta}{\csc \theta}$

3. $\dfrac{\sec \theta}{\cos \theta} = 1 + \tan^2 \theta$

4. $\dfrac{\cos \theta}{\sec \theta} = 1 - \dfrac{\sin \theta}{\csc \theta}$

Simplify each trigonometric expression.

5. $\sec \theta \cot \theta$

6. $\sec^2 \theta - 1$

7. $-1 - \cot^2 \theta$

8. $\sin \theta \cot \theta$

9. $1 - \cos^2 \theta$

10. $\dfrac{\sec \theta \sin \theta}{\tan \theta}$

11. $\cos \theta \tan \theta$

12. $\sin \theta + \cos \theta \cot \theta$

Use a unit circle and a 30°-60°-90° triangle to find the degree measures of the angles.

13. angles whose cosecant is 2

14. angles whose secant is -2

15. angles whose tangent is $\sqrt{3}$

16. angles whose cotangent is $-\sqrt{3}$

Find the value of each expression in radians to the nearest thousandth. If the expression is undefined, write *Undefined*.

17. $\cos^{-1}\left(-\dfrac{\pi}{5}\right)$

18. $\sin^{-1} \dfrac{\pi}{10}$

19. $\tan^{-1} 4.35$

20. $\cos^{-1}(-2.35)$

21. $\sin^{-1}\left(-\dfrac{5\pi}{7}\right)$

22. $\tan^{-1}(-1.05)$

23. $\tan^{-1} \dfrac{\pi}{9}$

24. $\sin^{-1}(-0.45)$

Solve each equation for θ with $0 \le \theta < 2\pi$.

25. $2 \cos \theta = -\sqrt{2}$

26. $\sin \theta (\cos \theta + 1) = 0$

27. $\tan^2 \theta - \sqrt{3} \tan \theta = 0$

In $\triangle ABC$, $\angle C$ is a right angle. Find the remaining sides and angles. Round your answers to the nearest tenth.

28. $b = 14, c = 16$

29. $a = 7.9, b = 6.2$

30. $b = 29, c = 35$

31. $a = 6.1, c = 10.2$

32. $a = 10, c = 14$

33. $a = 9, b = 4$

34. $b = 7, c = 12$

35. $b = 11.1, c = 26.3$

Sketch a right triangle with θ as the measure of one acute angle. Find the other five trigonometric ratios of θ.

36. $\sin \theta = \dfrac{5}{7}$

37. $\cos \theta = \dfrac{2}{9}$

38. $\sec \theta = \dfrac{20}{11}$

39. $\csc \theta = \dfrac{8}{3}$

40. $\tan \theta = \dfrac{11}{4}$

41. $\cot \theta = 5$

Do you UNDERSTAND?

42. **Writing** How is solving the trigonometric equation $\tan^2 \theta - 3 \tan \theta + 2 = 0$ similar to solving $x^2 - 3x + 2 = 0$?

43. **Open-Ended** Draw a right triangle. Measure the lengths of two sides, and then find the length of the remaining side without measuring.

44. **Reasoning** Explain why the trigonometric equation $\sin^2 \theta - \sin \theta - 6 = 0$ has no solutions.

45. **Indirect Measure** A man stands at the top of a building and you are standing 45 feet from the building. The angle of elevation to the top of the man's head is 54°, and the angle of elevation to the man's feet is 51°. To the nearest inch, how tall is that man?

14-4 Area and the Law of Sines

© **Common Core State Standards**

G-SRT.D.9 Derive the formula $A = 1/2\ ab \sin (C)$ for the area of a triangle . . .
G-SRT.D.11 Understand and apply the Law of Sine . . .
Also G-SRT.D.10

MP 1, MP 2, MP 3, MP 4

Objectives To find the area of any triangle
To use the Law of Sines

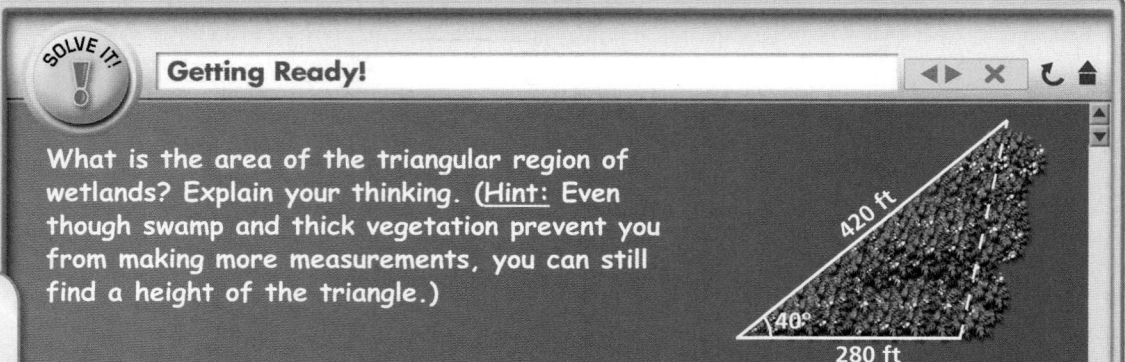

Getting Ready!

What is the area of the triangular region of wetlands? Explain your thinking. (<u>Hint:</u> Even though swamp and thick vegetation prevent you from making more measurements, you can still find a height of the triangle.)

420 ft

40°

280 ft

What information do you need? How will you find it?

© MATHEMATICAL PRACTICES

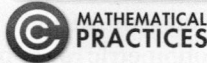

Lesson Vocabulary
• Law of Sines

Recall from geometry that if you know three parts of a triangle then you can sometimes *solve the triangle*; that is, you can determine its complete shape. This is what the congruence statements SAS, ASA, AAS, SSS were all about.

Essential Understanding If you know two angles and a side of a triangle, you can use trigonometry to solve the triangle. If you know two sides and the included angle, you can find the area of the triangle.

The area of a triangle with base b and height h is $\frac{1}{2}bh$. When you don't know h but you do know an angle measure, there may be another way to find the area.

Formula Area of a Triangle

Any $\triangle ABC$ with side lengths a, b, and c, has area

$$\frac{1}{2}bc \sin A = \frac{1}{2}ac \sin B = \frac{1}{2}ab \sin C.$$

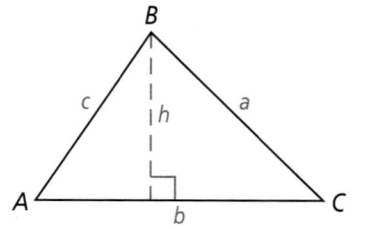

Here's Why It Works The area of the triangle above is $\frac{1}{2}bh$. The altitude h to side AC completes a right triangle. Thus, $\sin A = \frac{h}{c}$, so $h = c \sin A$. Substituting, $\frac{1}{2}bh = \frac{1}{2}bc \sin A$. You can derive $\frac{1}{2}ac \sin B$ and $\frac{1}{2}ab \sin C$ in a similar way.

 **Problem 1** Finding the Area of a Triangle

Gridded Response What is the area of $\triangle ABC$ to the nearest tenth of a square mile?

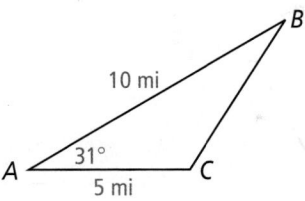

Plan

Can you use the area formula (previous page)?
You need two sides and the included angle—which is what you have here.

In $\triangle ABC$, $b = 5$, $c = 10$, and $m\angle A = 31°$.

$$\text{Area} = \frac{1}{2}\,bc\sin A = \frac{1}{2}(5)(10)\sin 31°$$

$$\approx 12.9$$

The area is about 12.9 mi². Write 12.9 in the grid.

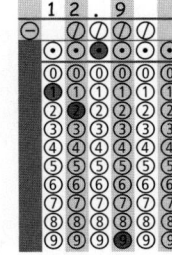

✓ **Got It?** **1.** A triangle has sides of 12 in. and 15 in. The measure of the angle between them is 24°. What is the area of the triangle?

The relationship $\frac{1}{2}\,bc\sin A = \frac{1}{2}\,ac\sin B = \frac{1}{2}\,ab\sin C$ yields an important formula when you divide each expression by $\frac{1}{2}\,abc$. The formula, known as the **Law of Sines**, relates the sines of the angles of a triangle to the lengths of their opposite sides.

take note

Theorem   Law of Sines

In any triangle, the ratio of the sine of each angle to its opposite side is constant. In particular, for $\triangle ABC$, labeled as shown,

$$\frac{\sin A}{a} = \frac{\sin B}{b} = \frac{\sin C}{c}.$$

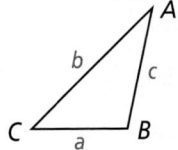

You can use the Law of Sines to find missing measures of any triangle when you know the measures of

- two angles and any side
- two sides and an obtuse angle opposite one of them, or
- two sides and an acute angle opposite one of them, where the length of the side opposite the known acute angle is greater than or equal to the length of the remaining known side.

In Problem 2, you know the measures of two angles and a side (AAS). In Problem 3, you know the measures of two sides and an obtuse angle opposite one of them (SSA with A obtuse).

Problem 2 Finding a Side of a Triangle

In $\triangle PQR$, $m\angle R = 39°$, $m\angle Q = 32°$, and $PQ = 40$ cm. What is RQ?

Think

Write

Draw and label a diagram.

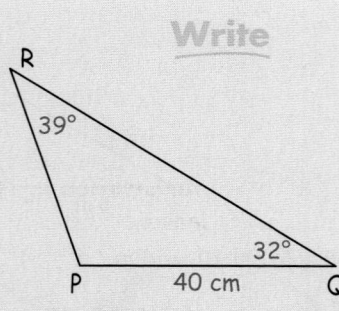

Find the measure of $\angle P$ opposite $\overline{RQ}$.

$$m\angle P = 180° - 39° - 32° = 109°$$

Use the Law of Sines.

$$\frac{\sin 109°}{RQ} = \frac{\sin 39°}{40}$$

Solve for RQ.
Use a calculator.

$$RQ = \frac{40 \sin 109°}{\sin 39°} \approx 60.1 \text{ cm}$$

 Got It? 2. In $\triangle KLM$, $m\angle K = 120°$, $m\angle M = 50°$, and $ML = 35$ yd. What is KL?

Problem 3 Finding an Angle of a Triangle

In $\triangle RST$, $t = 7$, $r = 9$, and $m\angle R = 110°$. What is $m\angle S$?

Plan

How do you proceed?
You have information
that will give you
$m\angle T$. $m\angle T$ will give
you $m\angle S$.

Step 1 Draw and label a diagram.

Step 2 Use the Law of Sines. Find $m\angle T$.

$$\frac{\sin T}{7} = \frac{\sin 110°}{9} \qquad \text{Law of Sines.}$$

$$\sin T = \frac{7 \sin 110°}{9} \qquad \text{Solve for } \sin T.$$

$$m\angle T = \sin^{-1}\left(\frac{7 \sin 110°}{9}\right) \qquad \text{Solve for } m\angle T.$$

$$m\angle T \approx 47° \qquad \text{Use a calculator.}$$

Step 3 Find the measure of $\angle S$.

$$m\angle S \approx 180° - 110° - 47° = 23°$$

 Got It? 3. a. In $\triangle PQR$, $m\angle R = 97.5°$, $r = 80$, and $p = 75$. What is $m\angle P$?
      b. In Problem 3, can you use the Law of Sines to find the heights of the triangle? Explain your answer.

In the SSA case, if the known non-included angle is acute, you have an ambiguous situation. Inverse sine is not able to distinguish whether a second angle is, say, 47° or 133°.

In the SAS and SSS congruence situations, the Law of Sines is not useful because you do not have a known angle paired with a known opposite side. You will find out how to solve these triangles in the next lesson.

Problem 4 Using the Law of Sines to Solve a Problem

Surveying A surveyor locates points *A* and *B* at the same elevation and measures distance and angles as pictured.

Plan

How do you write an equation to solve?
Write a proportion that includes the distance you know, *AB*, and the distance you want, *BC*.

A What is *BC*, the distance from *B* to the summit?

First find $m\angle ABC$ and $m\angle ACB$.

$$m\angle ABC = 180° - 31° = 149°$$
$$m\angle ACB = 180° - 18° - 149° = 13°$$

Now use the Law of Sines with $\triangle ABC$.

$$\frac{\sin A}{BC} = \frac{\sin C}{AB} \qquad \text{Law of Sines}$$

$$\frac{\sin 18°}{BC} = \frac{\sin 13°}{3950} \qquad \text{Substitute.}$$

$$BC = \frac{3950 \sin 18°}{\sin 13°} \qquad \text{Solve for } BC.$$

$$BC \approx 5426 \qquad \text{Simplify.}$$

The distance from *B* to the summit is about 5426 ft.

B What is *CD*, the height of the mountain above points *A* and *B*?

In right $\triangle BCD$, you know *BC* and $m\angle B$. Use the sine ratio.

$$\sin 31° \approx \frac{CD}{5426} \qquad \text{Definition of sine}$$

$$CD \approx 5426 \sin 31° \qquad \text{Solve for } CD.$$

$$CD \approx 2795 \qquad \text{Use a calculator.}$$

The summit is about 2795 ft higher than points *A* and *B*.

Got It? 4. A landscaper sights the top of a tree at a 68° angle. She then moves an additional 70 ft directly away from the tree and sights the top at a 43° angle. How tall is the tree to the nearest tenth of a foot?

Lesson Check

Do you know HOW?

1. A triangle has sides 2.4 and 9.0 and the measure of the angle between those sides is 98°. What is the area of the triangle?

2. In $\triangle PQR$, $m\angle P = 85°$, $m\angle R = 54°$, and $QR = 30$. What is PR?

3. In $\triangle HJK$, $m\angle J = 14°$, $HK = 6$, and $JK = 11$. What is $m\angle H$?

Do you UNDERSTAND?

4. **Vocabulary** Suppose you are given information about a triangle according to SSS, SAS, AAS, and ASA. For which of these can you immediately use the Law of Sines to find one of the remaining measures?

5. **Error Analysis** Suppose you used the Law of Sines and wrote $a = \frac{3 \sin 22°}{\sin 45°}$. Is that the same equation as $a = 3 \sin\left(\frac{22}{45}\right)°$? Explain.

Practice and Problem-Solving Exercises

 **Practice** Find the area of each triangle. Round your answer to the nearest tenth.

See Problem 1.

6.
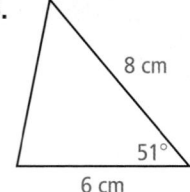
8 cm
51°
6 cm

7.
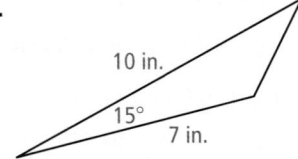
10 in.
15°
7 in.

8.
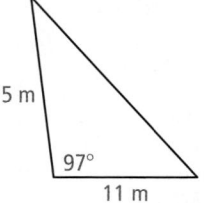
15 m
97°
11 m

Use the Law of Sines. Find the measure x to the nearest tenth.

See Problems 2 and 3.

9.
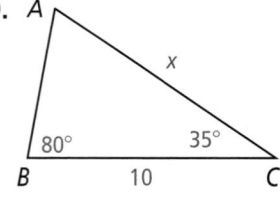
A
x
80°   35°
B   10   C

10.
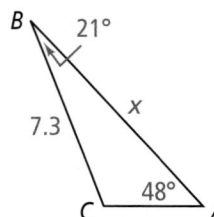
B 21°
7.3 x
48°
C   A

11.
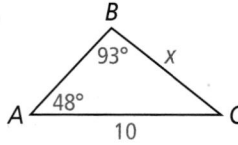
B
93° x
A 48°
10   C

12.
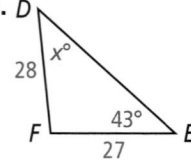
D
28   $x°$
43°
F   27   E

13.
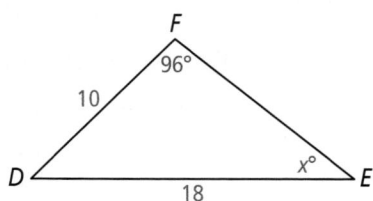
F
96°
10
D $x°$
18   E

14. In $\triangle DEF$, $m\angle F = 43°$, $d = 16$ mm, and $f = 24$ mm. Find $m\angle D$.

15. In $\triangle ABC$, $m\angle A = 52°$, $c = 10$ ft, and $a = 15$ ft. Find $m\angle C$.

16. **Surveying** The distance from you to the base of a tower on top of a hill is 2760 ft. The angle of elevation of the base is 26°. The angle of elevation of the top of the tower is 32°. Draw a diagram. Find to the nearest foot the height of the tower above the top of the hill.

See Problem 4.

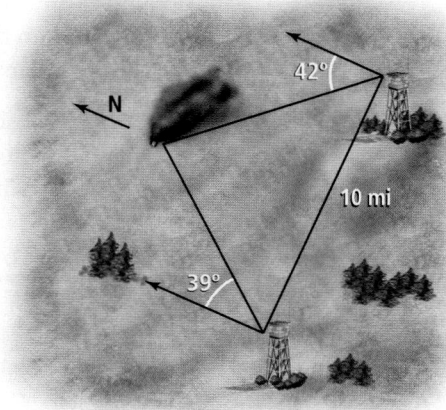

B Apply

Ⓒ 17. Think About a Plan One of the congruent sides of an isosceles triangle is 10 cm long. One of the congruent angles has a measure of 54°. Find the perimeter of the triangle. Round your answer to the nearest centimeter.
- Can drawing a diagram help you solve this problem?
- What information do you need before finding the perimeter?
- How can you find that information?

18. Forestry A forest ranger in an observation tower sights a fire 39° east of north. A ranger in a tower 10 miles due east of the first tower sights the fire at 42° west of north. How far is the fire from each tower?

19. Geometry The sides of a triangle are 15 in., 17 in., and 16 in. The smallest angle has a measure of 54°. Find the measure of the largest angle. Round to the nearest degree.

Find the remaining sides and angles of △DEF.
Round your answers to the nearest tenth.

20. $m\angle D = 54°$, $m\angle E = 54°$, and $d = 20$

21. $m\angle D = 54°$, $e = 8$ m, and $d = 10$

Ⓒ 22. Reasoning In △ABC, $a = 10$ and $b = 15$.
  a. Does the triangle have a greater area when $m\angle C = 1°$ or when $m\angle C = 50°$?
  b. Does the triangle have a greater area when $m\angle C = 50°$ or when $m\angle C = 179°$?
  c. For what measure of $\angle C$ does △ABC have the greatest area? Explain.

Ⓒ 23. Open-Ended Sketch a triangle. Specify three of its measures, then use the Law of Sines to find the remaining measures.

Find the area of △ABC. Round your answer to the nearest tenth.

24. $m\angle C = 68°$, $b = 12.9$, $c = 15.2$

25. $m\angle A = 52°$, $a = 9.71$, $c = 9.33$

26. $m\angle A = 23°$, $m\angle C = 39°$, $b = 14.6$

27. $m\angle B = 87°$, $a = 10.1$, $c = 9.8$

In △ABC, $m\angle A = 40°$ and $m\angle B = 30°$. Find each value to the nearest tenth.

28. Find AC for $BC = 10.5$ m.

29. Find BC for $AC = 21.8$ ft.

30. Find AC for $AB = 81.2$ yd.

31. Find BC for $AB = 5.9$ cm.

32. Measurement A vacant lot is in the shape of an isosceles triangle. It is between two streets that intersect at an 85.9° angle. Each of the sides of the lot that face these streets is 150 ft long. Find the perimeter of the lot to the nearest foot.

Ⓒ 33. a. In the diagram at the right, $m\angle A = 30°$, $AB = 10$, and $BC = BD = 6$. Use the Law of Sines to find $m\angle D$, $m\angle ABD$, and $m\angle ABC$.
  b. Reasoning Notice that two sides and a nonincluded angle of △ABC are congruent to the corresponding parts of △ABD, but the triangles are not congruent. Must △EFG be congruent to △ABD if $EF = 10$, $FG = 6$, and $\angle E \cong \angle A$? Explain.

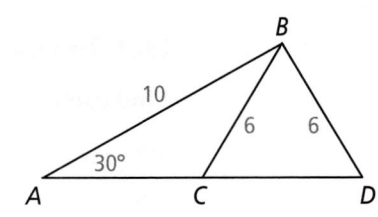

Challenge

34. Sailing Buoys are located in the sea at points *A*, *B*, and *C*. ∠*ACB* is a right angle. *AC* = 3.0 mi, *BC* = 4.0 mi, and *AB* = 5.0 mi. A ship is located at point *D* on $\overline{AB}$ so that m∠*ACD* = 30°. How far is the ship from the buoy at point *C*? Round your answer to the nearest tenth of a mile.

35. Writing Suppose you know the measures of all three angles of a triangle. Can you use the Law of Sines to find the lengths of the sides? Explain.

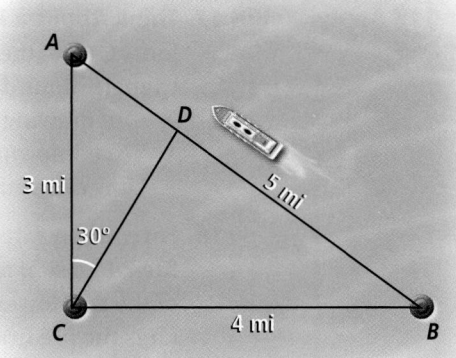

Standardized Test Prep

36. In △*GDL*, m∠*D* = 57°, *DL* = 10.1, and *GL* = 9.4. What is the best estimate for m∠*G*?

   Ⓐ 64°   Ⓑ 51°   Ⓒ 39°   Ⓓ 26°

37. For which set of given information can you compute the area of △*ABC*?

   Ⓕ m∠*C* = 58°, *c* = 23   Ⓗ m∠*C* = 58°, *a* = 43, *c* = 23

   Ⓖ m∠*B* = 26°, *a* = 43   Ⓘ m∠*C* = 26°, *a* = 43, *b* = 23

38. Two points in front of a tall building are 250 m apart. The angles of elevation of the top of the building from the two points are 37° and 13°. What is the best estimate for the height of the building?

   Ⓐ 150 m   Ⓑ 138 m   Ⓒ 83 m   Ⓓ 56 m

Short Response

39. Two sides of a scalene triangle are 9 m and 14 m. The area of the triangle is 31.5 m². Find the measure of one of the angles of the triangle to the nearest tenth of a degree. Show your work.

Mixed Review

Sketch one cycle of the graph of each sine function.   ◀ *See Lesson 13-4.*

40. $y = 4 \sin \theta$ **41.** $y = 4 \sin \pi\theta$ **42.** $y = \sin 4\theta$

Let *u* = (−2, 3), *v* = (1, 4), and *w* = (4, −1). Find the component form of each vector.   ◀ *See Lesson 12-6.*

43. $u + v$ **44.** $v + w$ **45.** $u - v$ **46.** $u - w$

Get Ready! **To prepare for Lesson 14-5, do Exercises 47–50.**   ◀ *See Lesson 14-3.*

Find each angle measure to the nearest tenth of a degree.

47. $\cos^{-1} \frac{3}{5}$ **48.** $\tan^{-1} 0.4569$ **49.** $\sin^{-1} \frac{5}{8}$ **50.** $\tan^{-1} \sqrt{2}$

The Ambiguous Case

© **Common Core State Standards**

G-SRT.D.11 Understand and apply the Law of Sines . . . to find unknown measurements in right and non-right triangles . . .

MP 2

The triangles at the right have one pair of congruent angles and two pairs of congruent sides. But the triangles are not congruent. Notice that the congruent angles are not included by the congruent sides.

When you know the measures of two sides of a triangle and one of the opposite angles, there may be two triangles with those measurements. You can use the Law of Sines to find the other measures for both triangles.

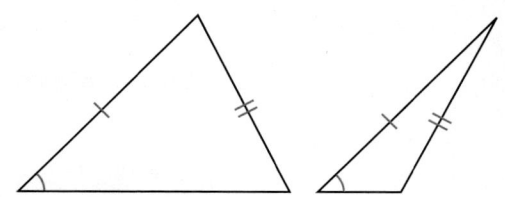

Example

In each $\triangle ABC$ at the right, $m\angle A = 35°$, $a = 11$, and $b = 15$. Find $m\angle B$.

$$\frac{\sin A}{a} = \frac{\sin B}{b} \qquad \text{Law of Sines}$$

$$\frac{\sin 35°}{11} = \frac{\sin B}{15} \qquad \text{Substitute.}$$

$$\sin B = \frac{15 \sin 35°}{11} \qquad \text{Solve for } \sin B.$$

$$m\angle B = \sin^{-1}\left(\frac{15 \sin 35°}{11}\right) \approx 51° \qquad \text{Solve for } m\angle B.\ \text{Use a calculator.}$$

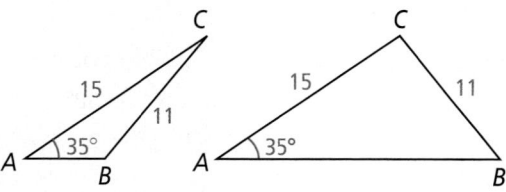

The sine function is also positive in Quadrant II. So another value of $m\angle B$ is about $180° - 51° = 129°$.

Because there are two possible angle measures for $\angle B$, there are two triangles that satisfy the given conditions. In one triangle the angle measures are about $35°$, $51°$, and $94°$. In the other, the angle measures are about $35°$, $129°$, and $16°$.

Exercises

In each $\triangle ABC$, find the measures for $\angle B$ and $\angle C$ that satisfy the given conditions. Draw diagrams to help you decide whether two triangles are possible.

1. $m\angle A = 62°$, $a = 30$, and $b = 32$

2. $m\angle A = 16°$, $a = 12$, and $b = 37.5$

3. $m\angle A = 48°$, $a = 93$, and $b = 125$

4. $m\angle A = 112°$, $a = 16.5$, and $b = 5.4$

5. $m\angle A = 23.68$, $a = 9.8$, and $b = 17$

6. $m\angle A = 155°$, $a = 12.5$, and $b = 8.4$

7. Multiple Choice You can construct a triangle with compass and straightedge when given three parts of the triangle (except for three angles). Which of the following given sets could result in the ambiguous case?

Ⓐ Given: three sides

Ⓑ Given: two sides and an included angle

Ⓒ Given: two sides and a non-included angle

Ⓓ Given: two angles and a non-included side

14-5 The Law of Cosines

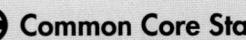
Common Core State Standards

G-SRT.D.10 Prove the Laws of Sines and Cosines and use them to solve problems.
G-SRT.D.11 Understand and apply the Law of Cosines . . . to find unknown measurements in right and non-right triangles . . .
MP 1, MP 2, MP 3, MP 4

Objective To use the Law of Cosines in finding the measures of sides and angles of a triangle

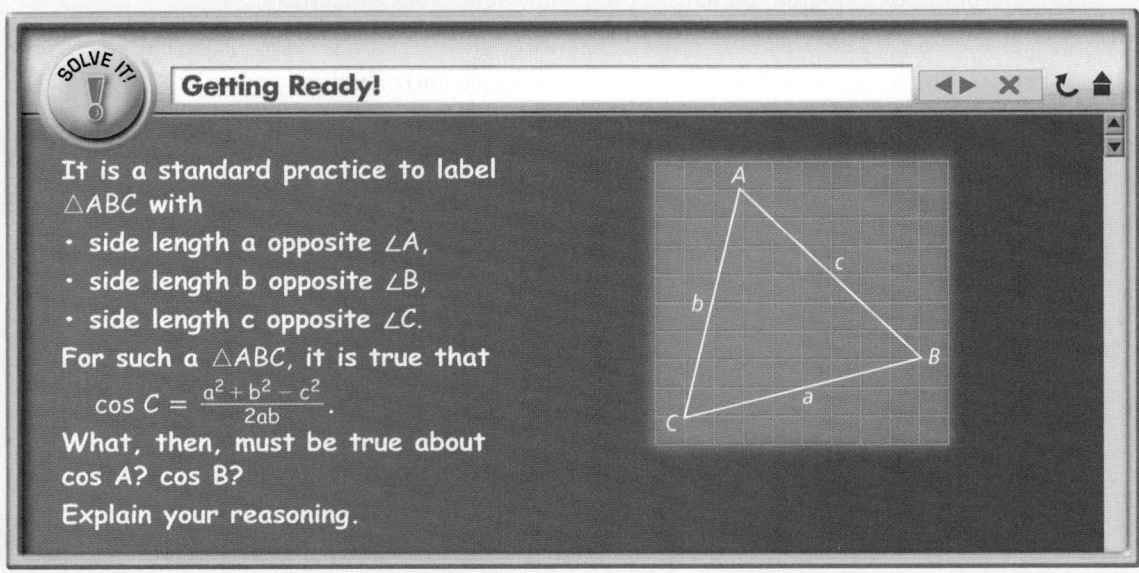

SOLVE IT!

Getting Ready!

It is a standard practice to label △ABC with
• side length a opposite ∠A,
• side length b opposite ∠B,
• side length c opposite ∠C.
For such a △ABC, it is true that
$$\cos C = \frac{a^2 + b^2 - c^2}{2ab}.$$
What, then, must be true about cos A? cos B?
Explain your reasoning.

MATHEMATICAL PRACTICES

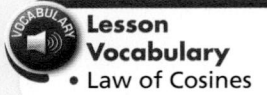

Lesson Vocabulary
• Law of Cosines

The measures of all three sides (SSS) or the measures of two sides and the included angle (SAS) determine a triangle. The Law of Sines does not enable you to solve such a triangle, but the Law of Cosines does.

Essential Understanding If you know the measures of enough parts of a triangle to completely determine the triangle, you can solve the triangle.

The **Law of Cosines** relates the length of a side of any triangle to the measure of the opposite angle.

take note

Theorem   Law of Cosines

In △ABC, let a, b, and c represent the lengths of the sides opposite ∠A, ∠B, and ∠C, respectively.
• $a^2 = b^2 + c^2 - 2bc \cos A$
• $b^2 = a^2 + c^2 - 2ac \cos B$
• $c^2 = a^2 + b^2 - 2ab \cos C$

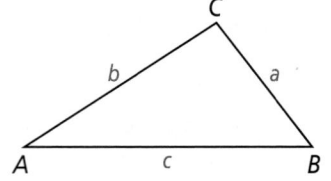

Here's Why It Works

In this $\triangle ABC$ with altitude h, let $AD = x$.

Then $DB = c - x$.

In $\triangle ADC$,

$b^2 = x^2 + h^2$ and

$\cos A = \frac{x}{b}$ or $x = b \cos A$.

In $\triangle CBD$,

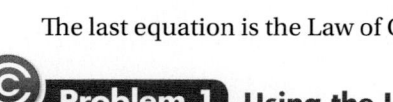

$$a^2 = (c - x)^2 + h^2 \qquad \text{Pythagorean Theorem}$$
$$= c^2 - 2cx + x^2 + h^2 \qquad \text{Square the binomial.}$$
$$= c^2 - 2cx + b^2 \qquad \text{Substitute } b^2 \text{ for } x^2 + h^2.$$
$$= c^2 - 2cb \cos A + b^2 \qquad \text{Substitute } b \cos A \text{ for } x.$$
$$= b^2 + c^2 - 2bc \cos A \qquad \text{Commutative Properties of Addition and Multiplication}$$

> Try it yourself for obtuse $\angle B$.

The last equation is the Law of Cosines.

Problem 1 Using the Law of Cosines to Solve a Problem

Multiple Choice The sailboat race committee wants to lay out a triangular course with a 40° angle between two sides that measure 3.5 mi and 2.5 mi. What will be the approximate length of the third side?

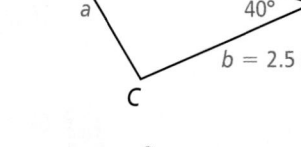

Ⓐ 2.0 mi   Ⓒ 5.1 mi

Ⓑ 2.3 mi   Ⓓ 9.8 mi

This triangle is determined by SAS. Use the form of the Law of Cosines that has a^2 on one side.

Think

Does the answer make sense?
If $3.5 - 2.5 < a$, and $a < 3.5 + 2.5$, the answer makes sense. $a \approx 2.3$, and $1 < 2.3 < 6$ is true, so the answer makes sense.

$$a^2 = b^2 + c^2 - 2bc \cos A$$
$$a^2 = 2.5^2 + 3.5^2 - 2(2.5)(3.5) \cos 40° \qquad \text{Substitute.}$$
$$\approx 5.094 \qquad \text{Use a calculator.}$$
$$a \approx 2.26 \qquad \text{Use a calculator.}$$

The third side of the course will be about 2.3 mi long. The correct choice is B.

 Got It? **1. a.** The lengths of two sides of a triangle are 8 and 10, and the measure of the angle between them is 40°. What is the approximate length of the third side?

     b. Reasoning The measure of the included angle for the course in Problem 1 can be between 0° and 180°. Between what lengths can the length of the third side be? Explain your answer.

You can also use the Law of Cosines with triangles determined by the measures of all three sides (SSS).

Problem 2 Finding an Angle Measure

What is the measure of $\angle C$ in the triangle at the right?
Round your answer to the nearest tenth of a degree.

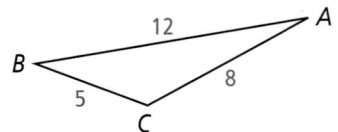

Think

Choose the form of the Law of Cosines that contains $\angle C$.

Substitute and simplify.

Combine like terms.

Solve for $\cos C$.

Solve for $m\angle C$.
Use a calculator.

Write

$c^2 = a^2 + b^2 - 2ab \cos C$

$12^2 = 5^2 + 8^2 - 2(5)(8) \cos C$

$144 = 25 + 64 - 80 \cos C$

$55 = -80 \cos C$

$\cos C = -\dfrac{55}{80}$

$m\angle C = \cos^{-1}\left(-\dfrac{55}{80}\right) \approx 133.4°$

 Got It? 2. The lengths of the sides of a triangle are 10, 14, and 15. What is the measure of the angle opposite the longest side?

Sometimes you need to use the Law of Cosines followed by the Law of Cosines again or by the Law of Sines.

Problem 3 Finding an Angle Measure

Plan

How do you start?
Drawing a diagram makes it easier to see what you know and what you are looking for.

In $\triangle ABC$, $b = 6.2$, $c = 7.8$, and $m\angle A = 45°$. What is $m\angle B$?

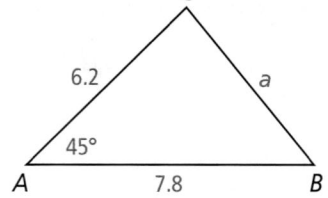

Step 1 Draw a diagram.

Step 2 Find a. Since you cannot find $m\angle B$ directly, use the Law of Cosines to find a.

$a^2 = b^2 + c^2 - 2bc \cos A$

$a^2 = 6.2^2 + 7.8^2 - 2(6.2)(7.8) \cos 45°$　　Substitute.

≈ 30.89　　Simplify.

$a \approx 5.56$　　Solve for a.

Step 3 Use the Law of Sines or the Law of Cosines to find $m\angle B$.

$$\frac{\sin B}{6.2} \approx \frac{\sin 45°}{5.56}$$ Law of Sines

$$\sin B \approx \frac{6.2 \sin 45°}{5.56}$$ Solve for $\sin B$.

$$m\angle B \approx \sin^{-1}\left(\frac{6.2 \sin 45°}{5.56}\right)$$ Solve for $m\angle B$. ($\angle B$ is not obtuse because $b < c$.)

$$\approx 52°$$ Use a calculator.

 Got It? 3. In $\triangle RST$, $s = 41$, $t = 53$, and $m\angle R = 126°$. What is $m\angle T$?

 ## Lesson Check

Do you know HOW?

1. In $\triangle ABC$, $m\angle B = 26°$, $a = 20$ in., and $c = 10$ in. Find b.

2. In $\triangle ABC$, $a = 8$ m, $b = 5$ m, and $c = 10$ m. Find $m\angle A$.

3. In $\triangle KNP$, $k = 21$ cm, $n = 12$ cm, and $m\angle P = 67°$. Find $m\angle N$.

4. In $\triangle WXY$, $w = 7.7$ ft, $x = 6.4$ ft, and $y = 8.5$ ft. Find $m\angle W$.

Do you UNDERSTAND? MATHEMATICAL PRACTICES

5. Writing Explain how you choose between the Law of Sines and the Law of Cosines when finding the measure of a missing angle or side.

6. Error Analysis A student solved for $m\angle C$, for $a = 11$ m, $b = 17$ m, and $c = 15$ m. What was the student's mistake?

$$\cos C = \frac{15^2 - 11^2 - 17^2}{2(11)(17)}$$

$$\cos C \approx -0.495$$

$$C = \cos^{-1}(-0.495) \approx 119.7°$$

 ## Practice and Problem-Solving Exercises  MATHEMATICAL PRACTICES

 **A Practice** Use the Law of Cosines. Find length x to the nearest tenth. ⬤ **See Problem 1.**

7.
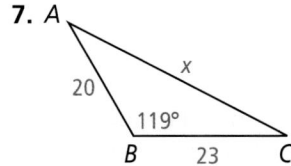

8.

9.

Use the Law of Cosines. Find x to the nearest tenth. ⬤ **See Problem 2.**

10.

11.

12.
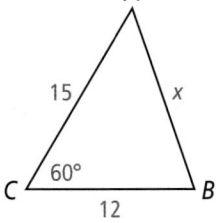

---

13. In $\triangle DEF$, $d = 15$ in., $e = 18$ in., and $f = 10$ in. Find $m\angle F$.

14. In $\triangle ABC$, $a = 20$ m, $b = 14$ m, and $c = 16$ m. Find $m\angle A$.

15. In $\triangle DEF$, $d = 12$ ft, $e = 10$ ft, and $f = 9$ ft. Find $m\angle F$.

Use the Law of Cosines and the Law of Sines. Find x to the nearest tenth.

 See Problem 3.

16.

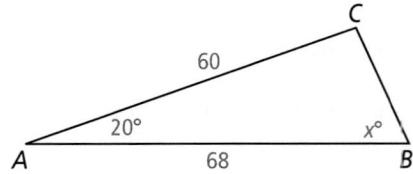

17.

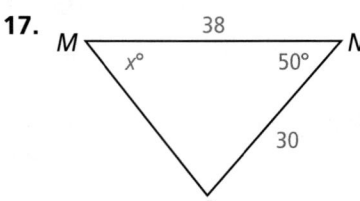

18. In $\triangle ABC$, $b = 4$ in., $c = 6$ in., and $m\angle A = 69°$. Find $m\angle C$.

19. In $\triangle RST$, $r = 17$ cm, $s = 12$ cm, and $m\angle T = 13°$. Find $m\angle S$.

20. In $\triangle DEF$, $d = 20$ ft, $e = 25$ ft, and $m\angle F = 98°$. Find $m\angle D$.

B Apply

For each triangle, write the correct form of the Law of Cosines or the Law of Sines to solve for the measure in red. Use only the information given in blue.

21.

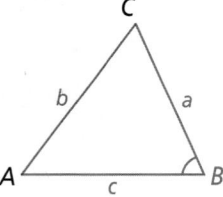

22.

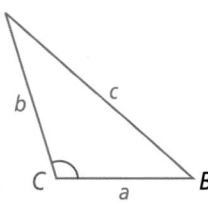

23.

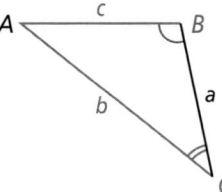

24.

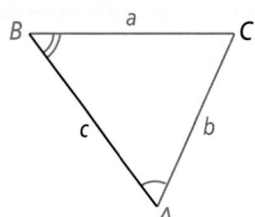

25.

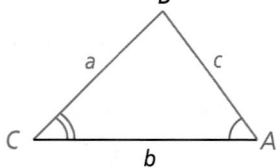

26.

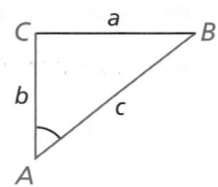

27. Think About a Plan A touring boat was heading toward an island 80 nautical miles due south of where it left port. After traveling 15 nautical miles, it headed 8° east of south to avoid a fleet of commercial fishermen. After traveling 6 nautical miles, it turned to head directly toward the island. How far was the boat from the island at the time it turned?
- Can a diagram help you understand the problem?
- What are you asked to find?
- Which measurements do you need to solve the problem?

28. Sports A softball diamond is a square that is 65 ft on a side. The pitcher's mound is 46 ft from home plate. How far is the pitcher from third base?

Find the remaining sides and angles in each triangle. Round your answers to the nearest tenth.

29.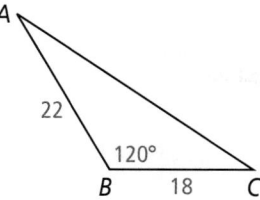

30.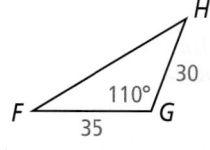

31.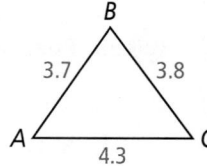

© **32. a. Open-Ended** Sketch a triangle. Specify three of its measures so that you can use the Law of Cosines to find the remaining measures.

    b. Solve for the remaining measures of the triangle.

© **33. Writing** Given the measures of three angles of a triangle, explain how to find the ratio of the lengths of two sides of the triangle.

34. Geometry The lengths of the sides of a triangle are 7.6 cm, 8.2 cm, and 5.2 cm. Find the measure of the largest angle.

35. Navigation A pilot is flying from city A to city B, which is 85 mi due north. After flying 20 mi, the pilot must change course and fly 10° east of north to avoid a cloudbank.

    a. If the pilot remains on this course for 20 mi, how far will the plane be from city B?

    b. How many degrees will the pilot have to turn to the left to fly directly to city B? How many degrees from due north is this course?

In $\triangle ABC$, $m\angle A = 53°$ and $c = 7$ cm. Find each value to the nearest tenth.

36. Find $m\angle B$ for $b = 6.2$ cm.   **37.** Find a for $b = 13.7$ cm.   **38.** Find a for $b = 11$ cm.

39. Find $m\angle C$ for $b = 15.2$ cm.   **40.** Find $m\angle B$ for $b = 37$ cm.   **41.** Find a for $b = 16$ cm.

In $\triangle RST$, $t = 7$ ft and $s = 13$ ft. Find each value to the nearest tenth.

42. Find $m\angle T$ for $r = 11$ ft.   **43.** Find $m\angle T$ for $r = 6.97$ ft.   **44.** Find $m\angle S$ for $r = 14$ ft.

45. Find r for $m\angle R = 35°$.   **46.** Find $m\angle S$ for $m\angle R = 87°$.   **47.** Find $m\angle R$ for $m\angle S = 70°$.

48. Geometry The lengths of the adjacent sides of a parallelogram are 54 cm and 78 cm. The larger angle measures 110°. What is the length of the longer diagonal? Round your answer to the nearest centimeter.

49. Geometry The lengths of the adjacent sides of a parallelogram are 21 cm and 14 cm. The smaller angle measures 58°. What is the length of the shorter diagonal? Round your answer to the nearest centimeter.

© **50. Reasoning** Does the Law of Cosines apply to a right triangle? That is, does $c^2 = a^2 + b^2 - 2ab \cos C$ remain true when $\angle C$ is a right angle? Justify your answer.

 **Challenge**

51. a. Find the length of the altitude to $\overline{PQ}$ in the triangle at the right.

    b. Find the area of $\triangle PQR$.

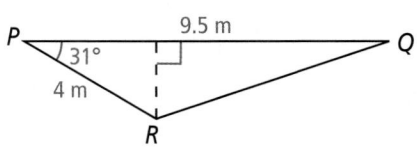

52. Physics A pendulum 36 in. long swings 30° from the vertical. How high above the lowest position is the pendulum at the end of its swing? Round your answer to the nearest tenth of an inch.

 53. Reasoning If you solve for cos A in the Law of Cosines, you get

$$\cos A = \frac{b^2 + c^2 - a^2}{2bc}.$$

   a. Use this formula to explain how cos A can be positive, zero, or negative, depending on how $b^2 + c^2$ compares to a^2.

   b. What does this tell you about $\angle A$ in each case?

Apply What You've Learned

MATHEMATICAL
PRACTICES
MP 6

Look back at the information on page 903 about the zipline. In the Apply What You've Learned in Lesson 14-3, you calculated the lengths of the support wires $\overline{AC}$ and $\overline{BC}$. Choose from the following words, numbers, and angle measures to complete the sentences below.

| Law of Sines | Law of Cosines | 121.6 | 152.9 | 195.4 |

| 49° | 50.5° | 52.5° | 77° | 103° |

Based on the given information in the figure on page 903, you can conclude that $m\angle ACB =$ **a.** ? . Since you know the lengths of $\overline{AC}$ and $\overline{BC}$, you can use the **b.** ? to find the length of $\overline{AB}$. The length of $\overline{AB}$ is approximately **c.** ? feet.

Now you can use the Law of Sines to find $m\angle BAC$. The measure of $\angle BAC$ is approximately **d.** ? . Finally, you can use everything you know about $\triangle ABC$ to conclude that the measure of $\angle ABC$ is approximately **e.** ? .

14-6 Angle Identities

© Common Core State Standards

F-TF.C.9 Prove the addition and subtraction formulas for sine, cosine, and tangent and use them to solve problems.

MP 1, MP 2, MP 3, MP 4, MP 8

Objectives To verify and use angle identities
To verify and use sum and difference identities

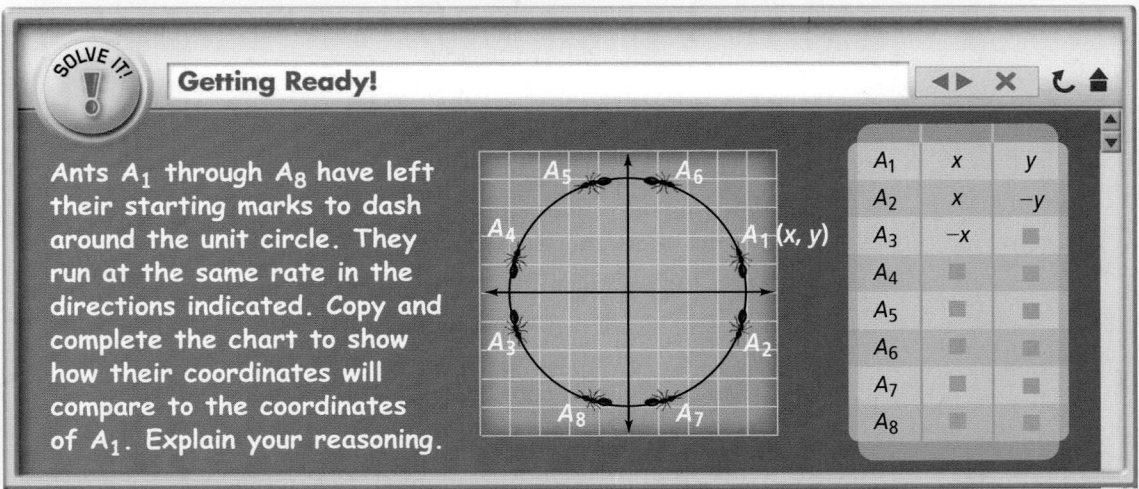

SOLVE IT!

Getting Ready!

Ants A_1 through A_8 have left their starting marks to dash around the unit circle. They run at the same rate in the directions indicated. Copy and complete the chart to show how their coordinates will compare to the coordinates of A_1. Explain your reasoning.

A_1	x	y
A_2	x	$-y$
A_3	$-x$	▪
A_4	▪	▪
A_5	▪	▪
A_6	▪	▪
A_7	▪	▪
A_8	▪	▪

The fact that $(\pm x, \pm y)$ and $(\pm y, \pm x)$ can represent eight different points suggests that you can derive several trigonometric identities directly from the unit circle.

Essential Understanding Several trigonometric identities involve a single angle. Other trigonometric identities involve two angles. No important trigonometric identity is *additive*; for example, $\sin(A + B) \neq \sin A + \sin B$.

take note

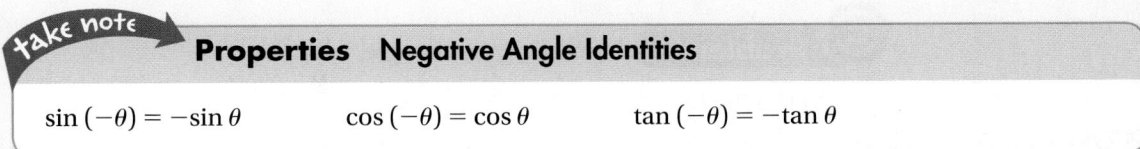

Properties   Negative Angle Identities

$$\sin(-\theta) = -\sin\theta \qquad \cos(-\theta) = \cos\theta \qquad \tan(-\theta) = -\tan\theta$$

Here's Why It Works In the figure at the right, angles θ and $-\theta$ have the same amount of rotation, but the rotations are in opposite directions.

Point Q is a reflection of P across the x-axis. The x-coordinates of P and Q (cosine) are the same and their y-coordinates (sine) are opposites. So $\cos(-\theta) = \cos\theta$ and $\sin(-\theta) = -\sin\theta$.

Similarly, S is the reflection of R across the x-axis. So $\tan(-\theta) = -\tan\theta$.

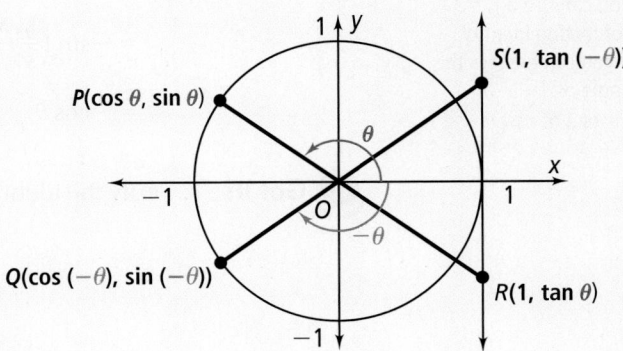

The cosine curve is the sine curve translated $\frac{\pi}{2}$ radians to the left. The cotangent curve is the tangent curve reflected across the x-axis and translated $\frac{\pi}{2}$ radians horizontally.

Identities of another type relate to complementary angles. These are called *cofunction* identities.

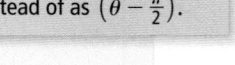

Properties Cofunction Identities

$$\sin\left(\frac{\pi}{2} - \theta\right) = \cos\theta \qquad \cos\left(\frac{\pi}{2} - \theta\right) = \sin\theta \qquad \tan\left(\frac{\pi}{2} - \theta\right) = \cot\theta$$

Here's Why It Works In the figure at the right, θ is a counterclockwise rotation from the positive x-axis and $\frac{\pi}{2} - \theta$ is the same amount of rotation clockwise from the positive y-axis.

Point Q is a reflection of P across the line $y = x$. If (x, y) are the coordinates of P, then (y, x) are the coordinates of Q. So $\cos\left(\frac{\pi}{2} - \theta\right) = \sin\theta$ and $\sin\left(\frac{\pi}{2} - \theta\right) = \cos\theta$.

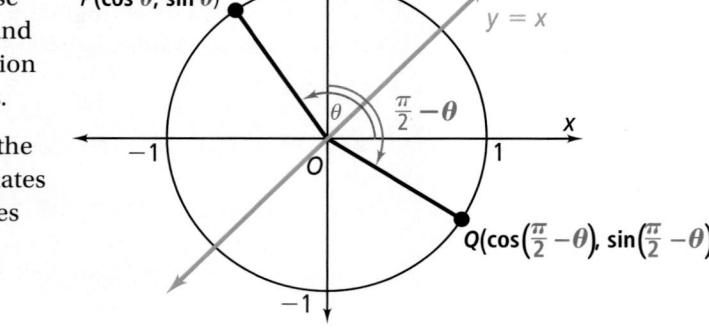

Then, by the Tangent Identity,

$$\tan\left(\frac{\pi}{2} - \theta\right) = \frac{\sin\left(\frac{\pi}{2} - \theta\right)}{\cos\left(\frac{\pi}{2} - \theta\right)}$$

$$= \frac{\cos\theta}{\sin\theta}$$

$$= \cot\theta.$$

 Problem 1 **Verifying an Angle Identity**

Verify the identity $\sin\left(\theta - \frac{\pi}{2}\right) = -\cos\theta$.

$$\sin\left(\theta - \frac{\pi}{2}\right) = \sin\left(-\left(\frac{\pi}{2} - \theta\right)\right) \qquad b - a = -(a - b)$$

$$= -\sin\left(\frac{\pi}{2} - \theta\right) \qquad \sin(-\theta) = -\sin\theta$$

$$= -\cos\theta \qquad \sin\left(\frac{\pi}{2} - \theta\right) = \cos\theta$$

Plan

Can you use a cofunction identity?
You can use a cofunction identity if you can express the angle as $\left(\frac{\pi}{2} - \theta\right)$ instead of as $\left(\theta - \frac{\pi}{2}\right)$.

Got It? 1. Verify the identity $\cos\left(\theta - \frac{\pi}{2}\right) = \sin\theta$.

The cofunction identities were derived using the unit circle. So they apply to an angle θ of any size.

© Problem 2 Deriving a Cofunction Identity

How can you use the definitions of the trigonometric ratios for a right triangle to derive the cofunction identity for sin $(90° - A)$?

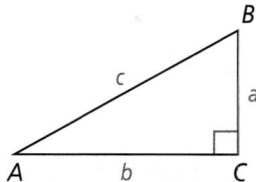

Think

What does 90° − A have to do with a right triangle?
If one acute angle has measure A, the other has measure 90° − A.

In a right triangle, the acute angles are complementary. So $A + B = 90°$ and $B = 90° - A$, where A and B are the measures of acute angles.

$\sin (90° - A) = \sin B$ *A* and *B* are complementary angles.

$\qquad = \dfrac{b}{c}$ Definition of sine in a right triangle

$\qquad = \cos A$ Definition of cosine in a right triangle

✓ Got It? 2. How can you use the definitions of the trigonometric ratios for a right triangle to derive the cofunction identity for sec $(90° - A)$?

You can use angle identities to solve trigonometric equations.

© Problem 3 Solving a Trigonometric Equation

What are all the values that satisfy $\sin \theta = \sin \left(\dfrac{\pi}{2} - \theta \right)$ for $0 \le \theta < 2\pi$?

$\sin \theta = \sin \left(\dfrac{\pi}{2} - \theta \right)$

Plan

Why is it a good idea to get the angles the same?
Once the angles are identical, you can rewrite the equation in terms of one trigonometric function.

$\sin \theta = \cos \theta$ Cofunction Angle Identity

$\dfrac{\sin \theta}{\cos \theta} = 1$ Divide by $\cos \theta$.

$\tan \theta = 1$ Tangent Identity

$\qquad \theta = \tan^{-1} 1$ Solve for one value of θ.

$\qquad \theta = \dfrac{\pi}{4}$

Another solution is $\dfrac{\pi}{4} + \pi$, or $\dfrac{5\pi}{4}$.

© ✓ Got It? 3. a. What are all values that satisfy $\sin \left(\dfrac{\pi}{2} - \theta \right) = \sec \theta$ for $0 \le \theta < 2\pi$?

     b. Reasoning In Problem 3, if θ is not restricted to be between 0 and 2π, can you use the fact that sine is a periodic function to find all values of θ? Explain.

Trigonometric functions are not additive; that is $\cos (A + B) \neq \cos A + \cos B$. It is also true that $\cos (A - B) \neq \cos A - \cos B$.

Properties   Angle Difference Identities

$\sin (A - B) = \sin A \cos B - \cos A \sin B$

$\cos (A - B) = \cos A \cos B + \sin A \sin B$

$\tan (A - B) = \dfrac{\tan A - \tan B}{1 + \tan A \tan B}$

Here's Why It Works   In the figure, angles A, B, and $A - B$ are shown.

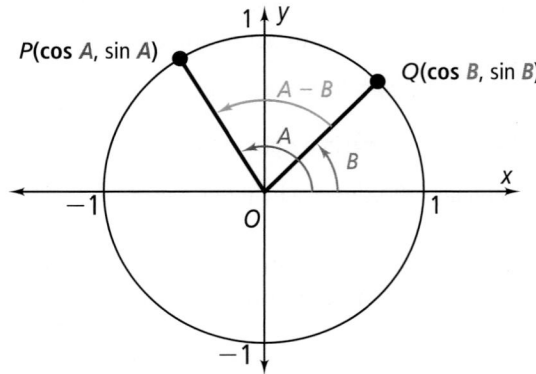

First, use the distance formula to find the square of the distance between P and Q.

$$(PQ)^2 = (x_1 - x_2)^2 + (y_1 - y_2)^2$$
$$= (\cos A - \cos B)^2 + (\sin A - \sin B)^2$$
$$= \cos^2 A - 2 \cos A \cos B + \cos^2 B + \sin^2 A - 2 \sin A \sin B + \sin^2 B$$
$$= 2 - 2 \cos A \cos B - 2 \sin A \sin B \qquad \text{Use the Pythagorean identity } \sin^2 \theta + \cos^2 \theta = 1.$$

Now use the Law of Cosines to find $(PQ)^2$ in $\triangle POQ$.

$$(PQ)^2 = (PO)^2 + (QO)^2 - 2(PO)(QO) \cos(A - B)$$
$$= 1^2 + 1^2 - 2(1)(1) \cos(A - B)$$
$$= 2 - 2 \cos(A - B)$$

The Transitive Property for Equality tells you that the two expressions for $(PQ)^2$ are equal.

$$2 - 2 \cos (A - B) = 2 - 2 \cos A \cos B - 2 \sin A \sin B$$
$$-2 \cos (A - B) = -2 \cos A \cos B - 2 \sin A \sin B \qquad \text{Subtract 2 from each side.}$$
$$\cos (A - B) = \cos A \cos B + \sin A \sin B \qquad \text{Divide each side by } -2.$$

You can also derive an identity for $\sin(A - B)$. Then you can use the Tangent Identity to derive an identity for $\tan(A - B)$.

 Problem 4 **Using an Angle Difference Identity**

What is the exact value of cos 15°?

$$\cos(A - B) = \cos A \cos B + \sin A \sin B \qquad \text{Cosine Angle Difference Identity}$$

$$\cos(60° - 45°) = \cos 60° \cos 45° + \sin 60° \sin 45° \qquad \text{Substitute 60° for } A \text{ and 45° for } B.$$

$$= \frac{1}{2}\left(\frac{\sqrt{2}}{2}\right) + \frac{\sqrt{3}}{2}\left(\frac{\sqrt{2}}{2}\right) \qquad \text{Replace with exact values.}$$

$$= \frac{\sqrt{2}}{4} + \frac{\sqrt{6}}{4} \qquad \text{Simplify.}$$

$$= \frac{\sqrt{2} + \sqrt{6}}{4}$$

So $\cos 15° = \dfrac{\sqrt{2} + \sqrt{6}}{4}$.

Think

How do you know which measures to subtract?
You know exact values for 30°, 60°, 45°, and 90°. Use two measures with a difference of 15°.

Got It? **4.** What is the exact value of $\sin 15°$?

You can use difference identities to derive sum identities.

 Problem 5 **Deriving a Sum Identity**

How can you derive an identity for $\cos(A + B)$? Use the difference identity for $\cos(A - B)$.

$$\cos(A + B) = \cos(A - (-B))$$

$$= \cos A \cos(-B) + \sin A \sin(-B) \qquad \text{Cosine Angle Difference Identity}$$

$$= \cos A \cos B + \sin A (-\sin B) \qquad \text{Negative Angle Identity}$$

$$= \cos A \cos B - \sin A \sin B \qquad \text{Simplify.}$$

Think

How are subtraction and addition related?
Adding a number is the same as subtracting the additive inverse of the number.

Got It? **5.** How can you derive an identity for $\sin(A + B)$? Use the difference identity for $\sin(A - B)$.

---

take note

Properties **Angle Sum Identities**

$$\sin(A + B) = \sin A \cos B + \cos A \sin B$$

$$\cos(A + B) = \cos A \cos B - \sin A \sin B$$

$$\tan(A + B) = \frac{\tan A + \tan B}{1 - \tan A \tan B}$$

Problem 6 Using an Angle Sum Identity

What is the exact value of sin 105°?

Think	Write
Write the Sine Angle Sum Identity.	$\sin(A + B) = \sin A \cos B + \cos A \sin B$
Find two angles that sum to 105° and have exact sine and cosine values. Let $A = 60°$ and $B = 45°$.	$\sin(60° + 45°) = \sin 60° \cos 45° + \cos 60° \sin 45°$
Substitute exact values and multiply.	$= \dfrac{\sqrt{3}}{2}\left(\dfrac{\sqrt{2}}{2}\right) + \dfrac{1}{2}\left(\dfrac{\sqrt{2}}{2}\right)$ $= \dfrac{\sqrt{6}}{4} + \dfrac{\sqrt{2}}{4}$
Simplify.	$= \dfrac{\sqrt{6} + \sqrt{2}}{4}$

 Got It? 6. What is the exact value of tan 105°?

 Lesson Check

Do you know HOW?

1. Verify the identity
   $\sin\left(\frac{\pi}{2} + \theta\right) + \sin\left(\frac{\pi}{2} - \theta\right) = 2\cos\theta$.

2. Solve $\tan\left(\frac{\pi}{2} - \theta\right) = 1$ for $0 \le \theta < 2\pi$.

3. Find the exact value of $\cos(-315)°$.

4. Find the exact value of $\sin(-105)°$.

Do you UNDERSTAND?  **MATHEMATICAL PRACTICES**

5. **Error Analysis** A question on a test asked, "Between 0 and 2π, the equation $-\cos\theta = \cos\theta$ has how many solutions?" A student divided each side by $\cos\theta$ to get $-1 = 1$ and concluded that there are no solutions. What mistake did the student make?

6. **Reasoning** Use an angle difference identity to show that $\sin\left(\frac{\pi}{2} - \theta\right) = \cos\theta$.

 Practice and Problem-Solving Exercises  **MATHEMATICAL PRACTICES**

 **Practice**   Verify each identity.   ◀ **See Problem 1.**

7. $\csc\left(\theta - \frac{\pi}{2}\right) = -\sec\theta$

8. $\sec\left(\theta - \frac{\pi}{2}\right) = \csc\theta$

9. $\cot\left(\frac{\pi}{2} - \theta\right) = \tan\theta$

10. $\csc\left(\frac{\pi}{2} - \theta\right) = \sec\theta$

11. $\tan\left(\theta - \frac{\pi}{2}\right) = -\cot\theta$

12. $\sec\left(\frac{\pi}{2} - \theta\right) = \csc\theta$

Use the definitions of the trigonometric ratios for a right triangle to derive a cofunction identity for each expression.

See Problem 2.

13. $\tan(90° - A)$ **14.** $\csc(90° - A)$ **15.** $\cot(90° - A)$

Solve each trigonometric equation for θ with $0 \le \theta < 2\pi$.

See Problem 3.

16. $\cos\left(\dfrac{\pi}{2} - \theta\right) = \csc\theta$ **17.** $\sin\left(\dfrac{\pi}{2} - \theta\right) = -\cos(-\theta)$ **18.** $\tan\left(\dfrac{\pi}{2} - \theta\right) + \tan(-\theta) = 0$

19. $\tan^2\theta - \sec^2\theta = \cos(-\theta)$ **20.** $2\sin\left(\dfrac{\pi}{2} - \theta\right) = \sin(-\theta)$ **21.** $\tan\left(\dfrac{\pi}{2} - \theta\right) = \cos(-\theta)$

Ⓒ Mental Math Find the value of each trigonometric expression.

See Problems 4, 5, and 6.

22. $\cos 50° \cos 40° - \sin 50° \sin 40°$ **23.** $\sin 80° \cos 35° - \cos 80° \sin 35°$

24. $\sin 100° \cos 170° + \cos 100° \sin 170°$ **25.** $\cos 183° \cos 93° + \sin 183° \sin 93°$

Find each exact value. Use a sum or difference identity.

26. $\cos 105°$ **27.** $\tan 75°$ **28.** $\tan 15°$ **29.** $\sin 75°$ **30.** $\cos 75°$

31. $\tan(-15°)$ **32.** $\sin 225°$ **33.** $\cos 240°$ **34.** $\sin 390°$ **35.** $\cos(-300°)$

Ⓑ Apply

Ⓒ 36. Think About a Plan At exactly $22\frac{1}{2}$ minutes after the hour, the minute hand of a clock is at point P, as shown in the diagram. Several minutes later, it has rotated θ degrees clockwise to point Q. The coordinates of point Q are $(\cos -(\theta + 45°), \sin -(\theta + 45°))$. Write the coordinates of point Q in terms of $\cos\theta$ and $\sin\theta$.

- What trigonometric identities can you use?
- How can you use the diagram to check your answer?

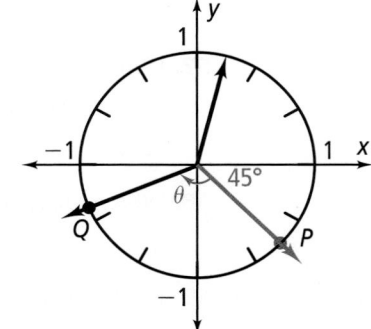

Verify each identity.

37. $\sin(A - B) = \sin A \cos B - \cos A \sin B$

38. $\tan(A - B) = \dfrac{\tan A - \tan B}{1 + \tan A \tan B}$

39. $\tan(A + B) = \dfrac{\tan A + \tan B}{1 - \tan A \tan B}$

40. $\sin\left(x + \dfrac{\pi}{3}\right) + \sin\left(x - \dfrac{\pi}{3}\right) = \sin x$

STEM 41. Gears The diagram at the right shows a gear whose radius is 10 cm. Point A represents a $60°$ counterclockwise rotation of point $P(10, 0)$. Point B represents a θ-degree rotation of point A. The coordinates of B are $(10 \cos(\theta + 60°), 10 \sin(\theta + 60°))$. Write these coordinates in terms of $\cos\theta$ and $\sin\theta$.

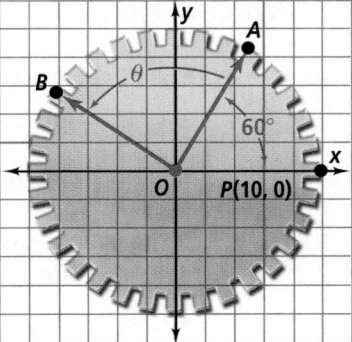

Rewrite each expression as a trigonometric function of a single angle measure.

42. $\sin 2\theta \cos\theta + \cos 2\theta \sin\theta$ **43.** $\sin 3\theta \cos 2\theta + \cos 3\theta \sin 2\theta$ **44.** $\cos 3\theta \cos 4\theta - \sin 3\theta \sin 4\theta$

45. $\cos 2\theta \cos 3\theta - \sin 2\theta \sin 3\theta$ **46.** $\dfrac{\tan 5\theta + \tan 6\theta}{1 - \tan 5\theta \tan 6\theta}$ **47.** $\dfrac{\tan 3\theta - \tan\theta}{1 + \tan 3\theta \tan\theta}$

48. Error Analysis A student tries to show that $\sin(A+B) = \sin A + \sin B$ is true by letting $A = 120°$ and $B = 240°$. Why is the student's reasoning not correct?

$\sin(120° + 240°) = \sin(360°) = 0$

$\sin 120° + \sin 240° = \frac{\sqrt{3}}{2} + \left(-\frac{\sqrt{3}}{2}\right) = 0$

Challenge

49. a. Reasoning A function is *even* if $f(-x) = f(x)$. A function is *odd* if $f(-x) = -f(x)$. Which trigonometric functions are even? Which are odd?

b. Writing Are all functions either even or odd? Explain your answer. Give a counterexample if possible.

Use the sum and difference formulas to verify each identity.

50. $\cos(\pi - \theta) = -\cos\theta$

51. $\sin(\pi - \theta) = \sin\theta$

52. $\sin(\pi + \theta) = -\sin\theta$

53. $\cos(\pi + \theta) = -\cos\theta$

54. $\sin\left(\frac{3\pi}{2} - \theta\right) = -\cos\theta$

55. $\cos\left(\theta + \frac{3\pi}{2}\right) = \sin\theta$

Standardized Test Prep

SAT/ACT

56. Which expressions are equivalent?

   I. $-\tan\left(\frac{\pi}{2} - \theta\right)$ II. $\tan\left(\theta - \frac{\pi}{2}\right)$ III. $\tan\left(-\left(\frac{\pi}{2} - \theta\right)\right)$

   Ⓐ I and II only   Ⓑ II and III only   Ⓒ I and III only   Ⓓ I, II, and III

57. Which expression is equal to $\cos 50°$?

   Ⓕ $\sin 20° \cos 30° + \cos 20° \sin 30°$ Ⓗ $\sin 20° \cos 30° - \cos 20° \sin 30°$

   Ⓖ $\cos 20°\cos 30° + \sin 20° \sin 30°$ Ⓘ $\cos 20°\cos 30° - \sin 20° \sin 30°$

58. Which expression is NOT equivalent to $\cos\theta$?

   Ⓐ $-\sin(\theta - 90°)$ Ⓑ $-\cos(-\theta)$ Ⓒ $\sin(\theta + 90°)$ Ⓓ $-\cos(\theta + 180°)$

Short Response

59. Find an exact value for $\sin 165°$. Show your work.

Mixed Review

Use the Law of Cosines. Find the indicated length to the nearest tenth.

See Lesson 14-5.

60. In $\triangle DEF$, $m\angle E = 54°$, $d = 14$ ft, and $f = 20$ ft. Find e.

61. In $\triangle RST$, $m\angle T = 32°$, $r = 10$ cm, and $s = 17$ cm. Find t.

Write each measure in radians. Express the answer in terms of π and as a decimal rounded to the nearest hundredth.

See Lesson 13-3.

62. $80°$ **63.** $-50°$ **64.** $-15°$ **65.** $70°$ **66.** $190°$

Get Ready! To prepare for Lesson 14-7, do Exercises 67–69.

Complete the following angle identities.

See Lesson 14-6.

67. $\cos(A + B) = \blacksquare$ **68.** $\sin(A + B) = \blacksquare$ **69.** $\tan(A + B) = \blacksquare$

14-7

Double-Angle and Half-Angle Identities

 Common Core State Standards

F-TF.C.9 Prove the addition and subtraction formulas for sine, cosine, and tangent and use them to solve problems.

MP 1, MP 2, MP 3, MP 8

Objectives To verify and use double-angle identities
To verify and use half-angle identities

Getting Ready!

You remove the largest possible hemisphere from the cylinder to form a bowl. For a given radius, r, what is the smallest total surface area possible for the bowl? Explain your thinking.

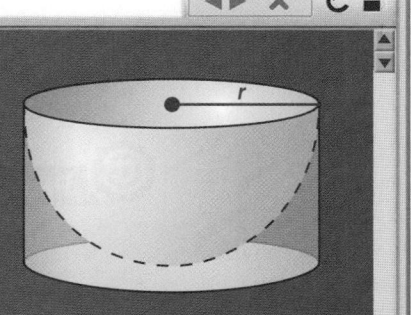

What geometric figures make up the bowl?

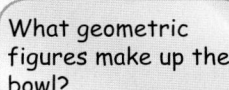 MATHEMATICAL
PRACTICES

If an equation contains two variables, such as radius and height, you can find a special case of the equation by replacing one of the variables with the other variable.

Essential Understanding The *double-angle identities* are special cases of the angle sum identities. Substitute $\frac{\theta}{2}$ for θ in certain double-angle identities and you get the *half-angle identities*.

Properties   Double-Angle Identities

$\cos 2\theta = \cos^2 \theta - \sin^2 \theta$	$\sin 2\theta = 2 \sin \theta \cos \theta$
$\cos 2\theta = 2 \cos^2 \theta - 1$	$\tan 2\theta = \dfrac{2 \tan \theta}{1 - \tan^2 \theta}$
$\cos 2\theta = 1 - 2 \sin^2 \theta$	

Here's Why It Works

Let $\theta = A = B$.

$\cos (A + B) = \cos A \cos B - \sin A \sin B$ Cosine Angle Sum Identity

$\cos (\theta + \theta) = \cos \theta \cos \theta - \sin \theta \sin \theta$ Substitute θ for A and B.

$\cos 2\theta = \cos^2 \theta - \sin^2 \theta$ Simplify.

You can make the same substitution in the other angle sum identities.

Problem 1 Deriving a Double-Angle Identity

How can you derive the identity $\cos 2\theta = 1 - 2\sin^2\theta$?

Use the Pythagorean identity $\sin^2\theta + \cos^2\theta = 1$ to get $\cos^2\theta = 1 - \sin^2\theta$.

$\cos 2\theta = \cos^2\theta - \sin^2\theta$ Cosine Double-Angle Identity

$= (1 - \sin^2\theta) - \sin^2\theta$ Use the Pythagorean identity.

$= 1 - 2\sin^2\theta$ Simplify.

Think

Now what?
You want to replace $\cos^2\theta$. A Pythagorean identity uses both $\cos^2\theta$ and $\sin^2\theta$.

 Got It? 1. How can you derive the identity $\cos 2\theta = 2\cos^2\theta - 1$?

You can use the other angle sum identities to derive double-angle identities for the sine and tangent.

 Problem 2 Using a Double-Angle Identity

What is the exact value of cos 120°? Use a double-angle identity.

$\cos 120° = \cos(2 \cdot 60°)$ Rewrite 120 as (2 · 60).

$= \cos^2 60° - \sin^2 60°$ Cosine Double-Angle Identity

$= \left(\frac{1}{2}\right)^2 - \left(\frac{\sqrt{3}}{2}\right)^2$ Replace with exact values.

$= -\frac{1}{2}$ Simplify.

Plan

Which of the three cosine identities should you use?
You can use any one of them.

 Got It? 2. What is the exact value of sin 120°? Use a double-angle identity.

You can use the double-angle identities to verify other identities.

 Problem 3 Verifying an Identity

Verify the identity $\cos 2\theta = \frac{1 - \tan^2\theta}{1 + \tan^2\theta}$.

$\dfrac{1 - \tan^2\theta}{1 + \tan^2\theta} = \dfrac{1 - \tan^2\theta}{\sec^2\theta}$ Use a Pythagorean identity.

$= \dfrac{1}{\sec^2\theta} - \dfrac{\tan^2\theta}{\sec^2\theta}$ Write as two fractions.

$= \dfrac{1}{\frac{1}{\cos^2\theta}} - \dfrac{\frac{\sin^2\theta}{\cos^2\theta}}{\frac{1}{\cos^2\theta}}$ Express in terms of $\sin\theta$ and $\cos\theta$.

$= \cos^2\theta - \sin^2\theta$ Simplify.

$= \cos 2\theta$ Cosine Double-Angle Identity

Think

Which Pythagorean identity could you use?
You need an identity involving tangent. So use $1 + \tan^2\theta = \sec^2\theta$.

Got lt? 3. Verify the identity $2 \cos 2\theta = 4 \cos^2 \theta - 2$.

There are also half-angle identities for sine, cosine, and tangent.

> **take note**

> ### Properties   Half-Angle Identities
>
> $$\sin \frac{A}{2} = \pm \sqrt{\frac{1 - \cos A}{2}} \qquad \cos \frac{A}{2} = \pm \sqrt{\frac{1 + \cos A}{2}} \qquad \tan \frac{A}{2} = \pm \sqrt{\frac{1 - \cos A}{1 + \cos A}}$$
>
> Choose the positive or negative sign for each radical depending on the quadrant in which $\frac{A}{2}$ lies.

You can use double-angle identities to derive half-angle identities.

Here's Why It Works

Let $\theta = \frac{A}{2}$.

$$\cos 2\theta = 2 \cos^2 \theta - 1 \qquad \text{Cosine Double-Angle Identity}$$

$$\cos 2\left(\frac{A}{2}\right) = 2 \cos^2 \frac{A}{2} - 1 \qquad \text{Substitute } \frac{A}{2} \text{ for } \theta.$$

$$\frac{\cos A + 1}{2} = \cos^2 \frac{A}{2} \qquad \text{Solve for } \cos^2 \frac{A}{2}.$$

$$\pm \sqrt{\frac{\cos A + 1}{2}} = \cos \frac{A}{2} \qquad \text{Take the square root of each side.}$$

Similarly, $\sin \frac{A}{2} = \pm \sqrt{\frac{1 - \cos A}{2}}$ and $\tan \frac{A}{2} = \pm \sqrt{\frac{1 - \cos A}{1 + \cos A}}$.

You can use half-angle identities to find exact trigonometric values.

Problem 4 Using Half-Angle Identities

What is the exact value of each expression? Use the half-angle identities.

A $\sin 15°$

Think

How do you know if the result is positive or negative?
Sketch the angle in a unit circle and determine if its sine is positive or negative in that quadrant.

$$\sin 15° = \sin \left(\frac{30}{2}\right)° \qquad \text{Rewrite 15 as } \frac{30}{2}.$$

$$= \sqrt{\frac{1 - \cos 30°}{2}} \qquad \text{Use the principal square root, since } \sin 15° \text{ is positive.}$$

$$= \sqrt{\frac{1 - \frac{\sqrt{3}}{2}}{2}} \qquad \text{Substitute the exact value for } \cos 30°.$$

$$= \sqrt{\frac{2 - \sqrt{3}}{4}} \qquad \text{Simplify.}$$

$$= \frac{\sqrt{2 - \sqrt{3}}}{2}$$

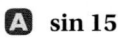

B $\cos 150°$

$$\cos 150° = \cos\left(\frac{300}{2}\right)° \qquad \text{Rewrite 150 as } \tfrac{300}{2}.$$

$$= -\sqrt{\frac{1 + \cos 300°}{2}} \qquad \text{Use the negative square root, since } \cos 150° \text{ is negative.}$$

$$= -\sqrt{\frac{1 + \left(\frac{1}{2}\right)}{2}} \qquad \text{Replace with an exact value.}$$

$$= -\sqrt{\frac{3}{4}} \qquad \text{Simplify.}$$

$$= -\frac{\sqrt{3}}{2} \qquad \text{Simplify.}$$

 Got It? 4. What is the exact value of each expression? Use the half-angle identities.

    a. $\sin 150°$ **b.** $\tan 150°$

© **Problem 5** Using a Half-Angle Identity

Given $\sin\theta = -\frac{24}{25}$ **and** $180° < \theta < 270°$, **what is** $\sin\frac{\theta}{2}$?

Know	Need	Plan
$\sin\theta,\ 180° < \theta < 270°$	$\sin\frac{\theta}{2}$	Find $\cos\theta$ and substitute it into the half-angle identity for sine.

$$\cos^2\theta + \sin^2\theta = 1 \qquad \text{Pythagorean identity}$$

$$\cos^2\theta + \left(-\frac{24}{25}\right)^2 = 1 \qquad \text{Substitute.}$$

$$\cos^2\theta = \frac{49}{25^2} \qquad \text{Solve for } \cos^2\theta.$$

$$\cos\theta = -\frac{7}{25} \qquad \text{Choose the negative square root since } \theta \text{ is in Quadrant III.}$$

Now find $\sin\frac{\theta}{2}$.

Since $180° < \theta < 270°$, then $90° < \frac{\theta}{2} < 135°$ and $\frac{\theta}{2}$ is in Quadrant II.

$$\sin\frac{\theta}{2} = \pm\sqrt{\frac{1 - \cos\theta}{2}} \qquad \text{Half-angle identity}$$

$$= \sqrt{\frac{1 - \left(-\frac{7}{25}\right)}{2}} \qquad \text{Substitute. Choose the positive square root since } \frac{\theta}{2} \text{ is in Quadrant II.}$$

$$= \frac{4}{5} \qquad \text{Simplify.}$$

© **Got It? 5.** Given $\sin\theta = -\frac{24}{25}$ and $180° < \theta < 270°$, what is the exact value of each expression?

    a. $\cos\frac{\theta}{2}$ **b.** $\tan\frac{\theta}{2}$

    c. Reasoning How would your answers change if $270° < \theta < 360°$? Explain.

Lesson Check

Do you know HOW?

1. Use a double-angle identity to find the exact value of $\sin 120°$.

2. Use a half-angle identity to find the exact value of $\sin 90°$.

3. Given $\tan \theta = \frac{3}{2}$ and $180° < \theta < 270°$, find the exact value of each expression.
   a. $\cos 2\theta$
   b. $\sin \frac{\theta}{2}$
   c. $\cos \frac{\theta}{2}$

Do you UNDERSTAND?

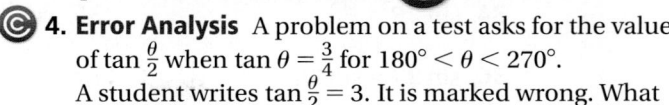

4. **Error Analysis** A problem on a test asks for the value of $\tan \frac{\theta}{2}$ when $\tan \theta = \frac{3}{4}$ for $180° < \theta < 270°$. A student writes $\tan \frac{\theta}{2} = 3$. It is marked wrong. What is the student's mistake?

5. Express $2 \sin 2A \cos 2A$ using only one trigonometric function.

6. **Writing** Explain how to express $-\sqrt{\frac{1 - \cos 5A}{2}}$ as $\sin \theta$, where θ is an expression in terms of A.

Practice and Problem-Solving Exercises

 **Practice**

Use an angle sum identity to derive each double-angle identity.  See Problems 1, 2, and 3.

7. $\sin 2\theta = 2\sin \theta \cos \theta$

8. $\tan 2\theta = \dfrac{2 \tan \theta}{1 - \tan^2 \theta}$

Use a double-angle identity to find the exact value of each expression.

9. $\sin 240°$
10. $\cos 120°$
11. $\tan 120°$
12. $\sin 90°$

13. $\cos 240°$
14. $\tan 240°$
15. $\cos 600°$
16. $\sin 600°$

Use a half-angle identity to find the exact value of each expression. See Problem 4.

17. $\cos 15°$
18. $\tan 15°$
19. $\sin 15°$
20. $\sin 22.5°$

21. $\cos 22.5°$
22. $\tan 22.5°$
23. $\cos 90°$
24. $\sin 7.5°$

Given $\cos \theta = -\frac{4}{5}$ and $90° < \theta < 180°$, find the exact value of each expression. See Problem 5.

25. $\sin \frac{\theta}{2}$
26. $\cos \frac{\theta}{2}$
27. $\tan \frac{\theta}{2}$
28. $\cot \frac{\theta}{2}$

Given $\cos \theta = -\frac{15}{17}$ and $180° < \theta < 270°$, find the exact value of each expression.

29. $\sin \frac{\theta}{2}$
30. $\cos \frac{\theta}{2}$
31. $\tan \frac{\theta}{2}$
32. $\sec \frac{\theta}{2}$

 **Apply**

33. **Think About a Plan** Triangle ABC is a right triangle with right angle C. Show that $\cos^2 \frac{B}{2} = \frac{a + c}{2c}$.
   - What identity will you use?
   - How can you find the ratio or ratios you need to substitute in the identity?
   - What will be your last step in the solution?

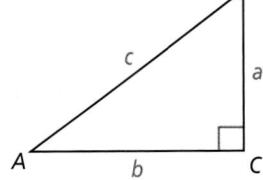

$\triangle RST$ has a right angle at T. Use identities to show that each equation is true.

34. $\sin 2R = \dfrac{2rs}{t^2}$

35. $\cos 2R = \dfrac{s^2 - r^2}{t^2}$

36. $\sin 2S = \sin 2R$

37. $\sin^2 \dfrac{S}{2} = \dfrac{t - r}{2t}$

38. $\tan \dfrac{R}{2} = \dfrac{r}{t + s}$

39. $\tan^2 \dfrac{S}{2} = \dfrac{t - r}{t + r}$

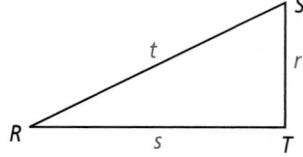

ⓒ 40. Reasoning If $\sin 2A = \sin 2B$, must $A = B$? Explain.

Given $\cos \theta = \dfrac{3}{5}$ and $270° < \theta < 360°$, find the exact value of each expression.

41. $\sin 2\theta$

42. $\cos 2\theta$

43. $\tan 2\theta$

44. $\csc 2\theta$

45. $\sin \dfrac{\theta}{2}$

46. $\cos \dfrac{\theta}{2}$

47. $\tan \dfrac{\theta}{2}$

48. $\cot \dfrac{\theta}{2}$

Use identities to write each equation in terms of the single angle θ. Then solve the equation for $0 \le \theta < 2\pi$.

49. $4 \sin 2\theta - 3 \cos \theta = 0$

50. $2 \sin 2\theta - 3 \sin \theta = 0$

51. $\sin 2\theta \sin \theta = \cos \theta$

52. $\cos 2\theta = -2 \cos^2 \theta$

Simplify each expression.

53. $2 \cos^2 \theta - \cos 2\theta$

54. $\sin^2 \dfrac{\theta}{2} - \cos^2 \dfrac{\theta}{2}$

55. $\dfrac{\cos 2\theta}{\sin \theta + \cos \theta}$

56. a. Write an identity for $\sin^2 \theta$ by using the double-angle identity $\cos 2\theta = 1 - 2\sin^2 \theta$. The resulting identity is called a *power reduction identity*.
b. Find a power reduction identity for $\cos^2 \theta$ using a double-angle identity.

ⓒ 57. Open-Ended Choose an angle measure A.
a. Find $\sin A$ and $\cos A$.
b. Use an identity to find $\sin 2A$.
c. Use an identity to find $\cos \dfrac{A}{2}$.

ⓒ 58. Writing Consider the graph of $y = \sqrt{\dfrac{1 - \cos A}{1 + \cos A}}$. Describe the period and any asymptotes if they exist.

 **Challenge**

Use double-angle identities to write each expression, using trigonometric functions of θ instead of 4θ.

59. $\sin 4\theta$

60. $\cos 4\theta$

61. $\tan 4\theta$

Use half-angle identities to write each expression, using trigonometric functions of θ instead of $\dfrac{\theta}{4}$.

62. $\sin \dfrac{\theta}{4}$

63. $\cos \dfrac{\theta}{4}$

64. $\tan \dfrac{\theta}{4}$

65. Use the Tangent Half-Angle Identity and a Pythagorean identity to prove each identity.
a. $\tan \dfrac{A}{2} = \dfrac{\sin A}{1 + \cos A}$

b. $\tan \dfrac{A}{2} = \dfrac{1 - \cos A}{\sin A}$

Apply What You've Learned

In the Apply What You've Learned in Lesson 14-5, you calculated the length of the zip line in the figure on page 903. Now consider what happens when the angle of depression of the zip line is halved.

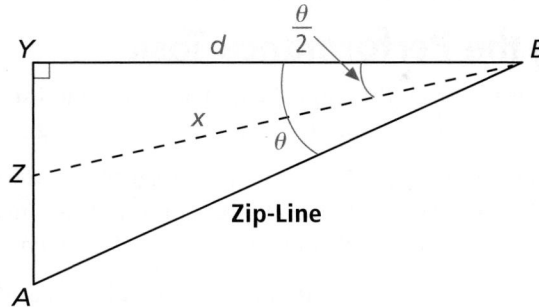

a. In the above figure (which is not drawn to scale), θ is the angle of depression of the zip line. Let d be the perpendicular distance between the towers and let x be the length of the zip line when the angle of depression is halved. Write an equation that shows how $\cos \frac{\theta}{2}$ is related to x and d.

b. Solve the equation you wrote in part (a) for x.

c. Use an identity to rewrite the equation from part (b) so that it involves $\cos \theta$ instead of $\cos \frac{\theta}{2}$.

Pull It **All Together**

Completing the Performance Task

Look back at your results from the Apply What You've Learned sections in Lessons 14-3, 14-5, and 14-7. Use the work you did to complete the following.

To solve these problems, you will pull together concepts and skills related to trigonometric functions.

1. Solve the problem in the Task Description on page 903 by describing how the length of the zip line will change if its angle of depression is halved. Include the length of each zipline in your answer. Show all your work and explain each step of your solution.

 2. **Reflect** Choose one of the Mathematical Practices below and explain how you applied it in your work on the Performance Task.

   MP 1: Make sense of problems and persevere in solving them.

   MP 4: Model with mathematics.

   MP 6: Attend to precision.

   MP 7: Look for and make use of structure.

On Your Own

For their next job, the crew is setting up a zip line between towers on a hill. They know the angles and lengths that are marked in the figure.

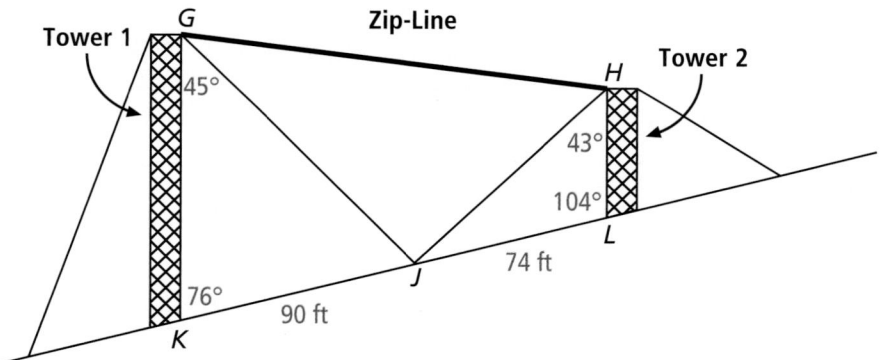

Describe how the length of the zip line will change if its angle of depression is doubled. Include the length of each zipline in your answer.

14 Chapter Review

Connecting BIG ideas and Answering the Essential Questions

1 Equivalence
To verify that an equation in θ is an identity, show that both of its sides have equal values for each possible replacement for θ.

→ **Trigonometric Identities (Lesson 14-1)**

$$2 \tan \theta \cos^2 \theta = \frac{2 \sin \theta \cos^2 \theta}{\cos \theta}$$
$$= 2 \sin \theta \cos \theta$$

→ **Angle Identities, and Double- and Half-Angle Identities. (Lessons 14-6 and 14-7)**

$$\sin(-\theta) = -\sin \theta$$
$$\sin\left(\frac{\pi}{2} - \theta\right) = \cos \theta$$
$$\sin(A + B) = \sin A \cos B - \sin B \cos A$$
$$\sin 2\theta = 2 \sin \theta \cos \theta$$
$$\sin \frac{A}{2} = \pm \sqrt{\frac{1 - \cos A}{2}}$$

2 Function
If the domain of a trigonometric function is appropriately restricted, its inverse is a function.

→ **Inverse Trigonometric Functions (Lesson 14-2)**

$y = \sin \theta$	$0 \le \theta \le \pi$	$\theta = \sin^{-1} x$
$y = \cos \theta$	$-\frac{\pi}{2} \le \theta \le \frac{\pi}{2}$	$\theta = \cos^{-1} x$
$y = \tan \theta$	$-\frac{\pi}{2} < \theta < \frac{\pi}{2}$	$\theta = \tan^{-1} x$

3 Equivalence
The trigonometric function values of θ, $0° < \theta < 90°$, are the trigonometric ratios for a right triangle.

→ **Right Triangles and Trigonometric Ratios (Lessons 14-3)**

$$\sin \theta = \frac{\text{OPP}}{\text{HYP}} = \frac{y}{r}$$
$$\cos \theta = \frac{\text{ADJ}}{\text{HYP}} = \frac{x}{r}$$
$$\tan \theta = \frac{\text{OPP}}{\text{ADJ}} = \frac{y}{x}$$

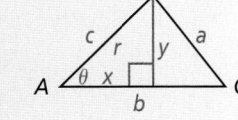

→ **Area, the Law of Sines, and the Law of Cosines (Lessons 14-4 and 14-5)**

Area $\triangle ABC$: $\quad \frac{1}{2} bc \sin A$

Law of Sines: $\quad \dfrac{\sin A}{a} = \dfrac{\sin B}{b} = \dfrac{\sin C}{c}$

Law of Cosines: $\quad a^2 = b^2 + c^2 - 2bc \cos A$

Chapter Vocabulary

- Law of Cosines (p. 936)
- Law of Sines (p. 929)
- trigonometric identity (p. 904)
- trigonometric ratios (p. 920)

Choose the correct term to complete each sentence.

1. You can find the missing measures of any triangle by using the _?_ if you know the measures of two angles and a side.

2. The six ratios of the lengths of the sides of a right triangle are known as the _?_ .

3. If you know the measures of two sides and the angle between them, you can use the _?_ to find missing parts of any triangle.

4. A trigonometric equation that is true for all values except those for which the expressions on either side of the equal sign are undefined is a _?_ .

5. The _?_ can be used to find missing measures of any triangle when you know two sides and the angle opposite one of them.

14-1 Trigonometric Identities

Quick Review

A **trigonometric identity** is a trigonometric equation that is true for all values except those for which the expressions on either side of the equal sign are undefined.

Reciprocal Identities

$$\csc \theta = \frac{1}{\sin \theta} \qquad \sec \theta = \frac{1}{\cos \theta} \qquad \cot \theta = \frac{1}{\tan \theta}$$

Tangent and Cotangent Identities

$$\tan \theta = \frac{\sin \theta}{\cos \theta} \qquad \cot \theta = \frac{\cos \theta}{\sin \theta}$$

Pythagorean Identities

$$\cos^2 \theta + \sin^2 \theta = 1 \qquad 1 + \tan^2 \theta = \sec^2 \theta$$

$$1 + \cot^2 \theta = \csc^2 \theta$$

Example

Simplify the trigonometric expression $\cot \theta \sec \theta$.

$$\cot \theta \sec \theta = \frac{\cos \theta}{\sin \theta} \cdot \sec \theta \qquad \text{Cotangent Identity}$$

$$= \frac{\cos \theta}{\sin \theta} \cdot \frac{1}{\cos \theta} \qquad \text{Reciprocal identity}$$

$$= \frac{1}{\sin \theta} \qquad \text{Simplify.}$$

$$= \csc \theta \qquad \text{Reciprocal identity}$$

Exercises

Verify each identity. Give the domain of validity for each identity.

6. $\sin \theta \tan \theta = \dfrac{1}{\cos \theta} - \cos \theta$

7. $\cos^2 \theta \cot^2 \theta = \cot^2 \theta - \cos^2 \theta$

Simplify each trigonometric expression.

8. $1 - \sin^2 \theta$

9. $\dfrac{\cos \theta}{\sin \theta \cot \theta}$

10. $\csc^2 \theta - \cot^2 \theta$

11. $\cos^2 \theta - 1$

12. $\dfrac{\sin \theta \cos \theta}{\tan \theta}$

13. $\sec \theta \sin \theta \cot \theta$

14-2 Solving Trigonometric Equations Using Inverses

Quick Review

The function $\cos^{-1} x$ is the inverse of $\cos \theta$ with the restricted domain $0 \le \theta \le \pi$. The function $\sin^{-1} x$ is the inverse of $\sin \theta$ with the restricted domain $-\frac{\pi}{2} \le \theta \le \frac{\pi}{2}$, and $\tan^{-1} x$ is the inverse of $\tan \theta$ with the restricted domain $-\frac{\pi}{2} < \theta < \frac{\pi}{2}$.

Example

Solve $2 \cos \theta \sin \theta - \sqrt{3} \cos \theta = 0$ for θ with $0 \le \theta < 2\pi$.

$$2 \cos \theta \sin \theta - \sqrt{3} \cos \theta = 0$$

$\cos \theta (2 \sin \theta - \sqrt{3}) = 0$ Factor.

$\cos \theta = 0$ or $2 \sin \theta - \sqrt{3} = 0$ Zero-Product Property.

$\cos \theta = 0 \qquad \sin \theta = \dfrac{\sqrt{3}}{2}$ Solve for $\cos \theta$ and $\sin \theta$.

$\theta = \dfrac{\pi}{2}$ or $\dfrac{3\pi}{2} \qquad \theta = \dfrac{\pi}{3}$ or $\dfrac{2\pi}{3}$ Use the unit circle.

Exercises

Use a unit circle and 30°-60°-90° triangles to find the value in degrees of each expression.

14. $\sin^{-1}\left(-\dfrac{\sqrt{3}}{2}\right)$ **15.** $\tan^{-1} \sqrt{3}$

16. $\tan^{-1}\left(-\dfrac{\sqrt{3}}{3}\right)$ **17.** $\cos^{-1} \dfrac{\sqrt{3}}{2}$

Use a calculator and inverse functions to find the value in radians of each expression.

18. $\sin^{-1} 0.33$ **19.** $\tan^{-1}(-2)$

20. $\cos^{-1}(-0.64)$ **21.** $\cos^{-1} 0.98$

Solve each equation for $0 \le \theta < 2\pi$.

22. $2 \cos \theta = 1$ **23.** $\sqrt{3} \tan \theta = 1$

24. $\sin \theta = \sin^2 \theta$ **25.** $\sec \theta = 2$

14-3 Right Triangles and Trigonometric Ratios

Quick Review

The six different ratios of the sides of a triangle are know as the **trigonometric ratios** for a right triangle. Those ratios depend on the size of the acute angles in the right triangle.

If θ is an acute angle of a right triangle, x is the length of the adjacent leg (ADJ), y is the length of the opposite leg (OPP), and r is the length of the hypotenuse (HYP), then the trigonometric ratios of θ are as follows.

$$\sin \theta = \frac{y}{r} = \frac{OPP}{HYP} \qquad \csc \theta = \frac{r}{y} = \frac{HYP}{OPP}$$

$$\cos \theta = \frac{x}{r} = \frac{ADJ}{HYP} \qquad \sec \theta = \frac{r}{x} = \frac{HYP}{ADJ}$$

$$\tan \theta = \frac{y}{x} = \frac{OPP}{ADJ} \qquad \cot \theta = \frac{x}{y} = \frac{ADJ}{OPP}$$

Example

In $\triangle ABC$, $\angle C$ is a right angle, $a = 4$ and $c = 9$. What are $\cos A$, $\sin A$, and $\tan A$ in fraction form?

Using the Pythagorean Theorem, $b = \sqrt{65}$.

The ratios are $\cos A = \frac{b}{c} = \frac{\sqrt{65}}{9}$, $\sin A = \frac{a}{c} = \frac{4}{9}$, and $\tan A = \frac{a}{b} = \frac{4}{\sqrt{65}} = \frac{4\sqrt{65}}{65}$.

Exercises

Find the values of the six trigonometric functions for the angle in standard position determined by each point.

26. $(-3, 4)$ **27.** $(-8, -15)$

In $\triangle ABC$, $\angle B$ is a right angle, $AB = 30$, and $\sec A = \frac{5}{3}$. Find each value in fraction and in decimal form.

28. $\cos A$ **29.** $\sin A$

30. $\tan C$ **31.** $\csc C$

In $\triangle FGH$, $\angle G$ is a right angle. Find the remaining sides and angles. Round your answers to the nearest tenth.

32. $f = 3, h = 9$ **33.** $f = 12, g = 20$

34. $g = 55, h = 40$ **35.** $f = 5, h = 4$

Find each length x. Round to the nearest tenth.

36.
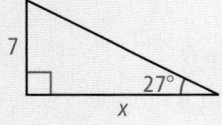

37.
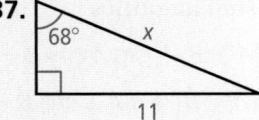

14-4 and 14-5 Law of Sines and Law of Cosines

Quick Review

You can use the Law of Sines and the Law of Cosines to find missing measures of a triangle. For $\triangle ABC$:

The **Law of Sines** states that $\frac{\sin A}{a} = \frac{\sin B}{b} = \frac{\sin C}{c}$.

The **Law of Cosines**

$$a^2 = b^2 + c^2 - 2bc \cos A \qquad b^2 = a^2 + c^2 - 2ac \cos B$$

$$c^2 = a^2 + b^2 - 2ab \cos C$$

Example

In $\triangle ABC$, $m\angle B = 60°$, $a = 12$, and $c = 8$. What is b to the nearest tenth?

$b^2 = 12^2 + 8^2 - 2(12)(8)\cos 60°$ Law of Cosines

$b^2 = 112$ Simplify.

$b \approx 10.6$ Use a calculator.

Exercises

Find the area of each triangle. Round your answers to the nearest hundredth.

38.
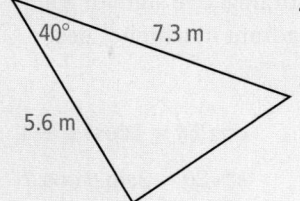

39.
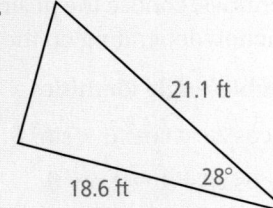

40. In $\triangle LMN$, $m\angle L = 67°$, $m\angle N = 24°$, and $MN = 16$ in. Find LM to the nearest tenth.

41. In $\triangle DEF$, $d = 25$ in., $e = 28$ in., and $f = 20$ in. Find $m\angle F$ to the nearest tenth.

42. In $\triangle GHI$, $h = 8$, $i = 12$, and $m\angle G = 96°$. Find $m\angle I$ to the nearest tenth.

14-6 Angle Identities

Quick Review

Angle identities are used to solve trigonometric equations.

Negative angle identities

$$\sin(-\theta) = -\sin\theta \qquad \tan(-\theta) = -\tan\theta$$
$$\cos(-\theta) = \cos\theta$$

Cofunction identities

$$\sin\left(\frac{\pi}{2} - \theta\right) = \cos\theta \qquad \tan\left(\frac{\pi}{2} - \theta\right) = \cot\theta$$
$$\cos\left(\frac{\pi}{2} - \theta\right) = \sin\theta$$

Angle difference identities

$$\sin(A - B) = \sin A \cos B - \cos A \sin B$$
$$\cos(A - B) = \cos A \cos B + \sin A \sin B$$
$$\tan(A - B) = \frac{\tan A - \tan B}{1 + \tan A \tan B}$$

Angle sum identities

$$\sin(A + B) = \sin A \cos B + \cos A \sin B$$
$$\cos(A + B) = \cos A \cos B - \sin A \sin B$$
$$\tan(A + B) = \frac{\tan A + \tan B}{1 - \tan A \tan B}$$

Example

What is the exact value of $\cos(165°)$?

$$\cos 165° = \cos(120° + 45°)$$
$$= \cos 120° \cos 45° - \sin 120° \sin 45°$$
$$= (-\cos 60°)\cos 45° - \sin 60° \sin 45°$$
$$= -\frac{1}{2} \cdot \frac{\sqrt{2}}{2} - \frac{\sqrt{3}}{2} \cdot \frac{\sqrt{2}}{2}$$
$$= -\frac{\sqrt{2}}{4} - \frac{\sqrt{6}}{4}$$
$$= -\frac{\sqrt{2} + \sqrt{6}}{4}$$

Exercises

Verify each identity.

43. $\cos\left(\theta + \frac{\pi}{2}\right) = -\sin\theta$

44. $\sin^2\left(\theta - \frac{\pi}{2}\right) = \cos^2\theta$

Find the exact value.

45. $\tan 15°$ **46.** $\sin 300°$

47. $\cos 255°$ **48.** $\tan(-75°)$

14-7 Double-Angle and Half-Angle Identities

Quick Review

You can use double-angle and half-angle identities to find exact values of trigonometric expressions. In the half-angle identities, choose the positive or negative sign for each function depending on the quadrant in which $\frac{A}{2}$ lies.

Double-angle identities

$$\cos 2\theta = \cos^2\theta - \sin^2\theta \qquad \cos 2\theta = 2\cos^2\theta - 1$$
$$\cos 2\theta = 1 - 2\sin^2\theta \qquad \sin 2\theta = 2\sin\theta\cos\theta$$
$$\tan 2\theta = \frac{2\tan\theta}{1 - \tan^2\theta}$$

Half-angle identities

$$\sin\frac{A}{2} = \pm\sqrt{\frac{1 - \cos A}{2}} \qquad \tan\frac{A}{2} = \pm\sqrt{\frac{1 - \cos A}{1 + \cos A}}$$
$$\cos\frac{A}{2} = \pm\sqrt{\frac{1 + \cos A}{2}}$$

Example

What is the exact value of $\cos 75°$?

$$\cos 75° = \cos\left(\frac{150°}{2}\right)$$
$$= \sqrt{\frac{1 + \cos 150°}{2}}$$
$$= \sqrt{\frac{1 - \frac{\sqrt{3}}{2}}{2}} = \sqrt{\frac{2 - \sqrt{3}}{4}} = \frac{\sqrt{2 - \sqrt{3}}}{2}$$

Exercises

Use the double-angle identity to find the exact value of each expression.

49. $\sin 120°$ **50.** $\cos 30°$

51. $\tan 300°$ **52.** $\sin 240°$

Do you know HOW?

Simplify each trigonometric expression.

1. $\sin\theta + \cos\theta\cot\theta$ **2.** $\sec\theta\sin\theta\cot\theta$

3. $\cot\theta\,(\tan\theta + \cot\theta)$

Verify each identity.

4. $\sec\theta\sin\theta\cot\theta = 1$

5. $\csc^2\theta - \cot^2\theta = 1$

6. $\sec\theta\cot\theta = \csc\theta$

7. $\sec^2\theta - 1 = \tan^2\theta$

Use a unit circle and 30°-60°-90° triangles to find values of θ in degrees for each expression.

8. $\sin\theta = \dfrac{\sqrt{3}}{2}$ **9.** $\cos\theta = \dfrac{\sqrt{3}}{2}$

10. $\cos\theta = -1$ **11.** $\tan\theta = \sqrt{3}$

Solve each equation for θ with $0 \le \theta < 2\pi$.

12. $4\sin\theta + 2\sqrt{3} = 0$ **13.** $2\cos\theta = 1$

14. $\sqrt{2}\sin\theta - 1 = 0$

In $\triangle ABC$, find each value as a fraction and as a decimal. Round to the nearest hundredth.

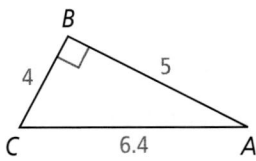

15. $\sin A$ **16.** $\sec A$ **17.** $\cot A$

18. $\csc C$ **19.** $\sec C$ **20.** $\tan C$

In $\triangle DEF$, $\angle F$ is a right angle. Find the remaining sides and angles. Round your answers to the nearest tenth.

21. $e = 6, f = 10$ **22.** $d = 10, e = 12$

23. $e = 21, f = 51$ **24.** $d = 5.5, e = 2.6$

25. Find the area of the triangle.

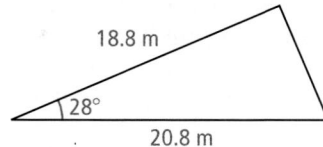

26. In $\triangle ABC$, $m\angle A = 45°$, $m\angle C = 23°$, and $BC = 25$ in. Find AB to the nearest tenth.

27. In $\triangle MNP$, $m\angle N = 45°$, $m = 20$ cm, and $p = 41$ cm. Find n to the nearest tenth.

28. In $\triangle PQR$, $p = 51$ ft, $q = 81$ ft, and $r = 61$ ft. Find $m\angle R$ to the nearest tenth.

29. In $\triangle STU$, $m\angle S = 96°$, $t = 8$ in., and $u = 10$ in. Find $m\angle U$ to the nearest tenth.

Verify each identity.

30. $-\sin\!\left(\theta - \dfrac{\pi}{2}\right) = \cos\theta$ **31.** $\csc\!\left(\theta - \dfrac{\pi}{2}\right) = -\sec\theta$

Solve each trigonometric equation for θ with $0 \le \theta < 2\pi$.

32. $\sin\!\left(\theta - \dfrac{\pi}{2}\right) = \sec\theta$ **33.** $\cot\!\left(\dfrac{\pi}{2} - \theta\right) = \sin\theta$

Use a double-angle identity to find the exact value of each expression.

34. $\sin 60°$ **35.** $\cos 60°$ **36.** $\tan 60°$

Use a half-angle identity to find the exact value of each expression.

37. $\tan 30°$ **38.** $\sin 90°$ **39.** $\cos 180°$

Do you UNDERSTAND?

Ⓒ **40. Writing** Suppose you know the lengths of all three sides of a triangle. Can you use the Law of Sines to find the measures of the angles? Explain.

Ⓒ **41. Open-Ended** Choose an angle measure A. Find $\sin A$ and $\cos A$. Then use the identities to find $\cos 2A$ and $\sin\dfrac{A}{2}$.

Common Core
End-of-Course Assessment

 ASSESSMENT

Complete the following items. For multiple choice items, write the letter of the correct response on your paper. For all other items, show or explain your work.

1. The graph of a quadratic function $f(x)$ is shown below.

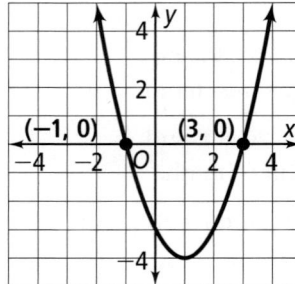

$(-1, 0)$ $(3, 0)$

Use the graph to solve $f(x) < 0$.

- **A** $-1 < x < 3$
- **B** $-1 \le x \le 3$
- **C** $x < -1$ or $x > 3$
- **D** $x \le -1$ or $x > 3$

2. Newton's Law of Universal Gravitation is $F = \dfrac{Gm_1m_2}{r^2}$. Solve this equation for r.

- **F** $r = \sqrt{\dfrac{F}{Gm_1m_2}}$
- **G** $r = \sqrt{\dfrac{Gm_1m_2}{F}}$
- **H** $r = \dfrac{F}{2Gm_1m_2}$
- **I** $r = \dfrac{Gm_1m_2}{2F}$

3. Let $f(x) = x^3 - 4x^2 + 9x$ and let $g(x) = 6x^3 + x^2 - 5x - 12$. What is $f(x) - g(x)$?

- **A** $-5x^3 - 5x^2 + 14x + 12$
- **B** $-5x^3 - 3x^2 + 4x - 12$
- **C** $7x^3 - 3x^2 + 4x - 12$
- **D** $-5x^4 - 5x^3 + 14x^2 + 12x$

4. Let $f^{-1}(x) = 2x + 3$. What is the solution of $f(x) = f^{-1}(x)$?

- **F** $x = -1$ or $x = -2$
- **G** $x = -3$
- **H** $(x, y) = (-1, -2)$
- **I** $(x, y) = (-3, -3)$

5. Which is a simpler form of $\dfrac{\sqrt{5}}{3 - \sqrt{2}}$?

- **A** $\dfrac{\sqrt{10}}{3\sqrt{2} - 2}$
- **B** $\dfrac{5}{3\sqrt{5} - 10}$
- **C** $\dfrac{3\sqrt{5} - 10}{7}$
- **D** $\dfrac{3\sqrt{5} + \sqrt{10}}{7}$

6. What is the product of $(2 + 5i)$ and $(4 + 3i)$?

- **F** $8 + 15i$
- **G** $8 + 26i$
- **H** $-7 + 15i$
- **I** $-7 + 26i$

7. Multiply $\dfrac{x^3}{x^2 - 4} \cdot \dfrac{5x + 10}{10x}$.

- **A** $\dfrac{5x}{4}$
- **B** $\dfrac{x^2}{2(x - 2)}$
- **C** $\dfrac{x^2(x + 2)}{2(x^2 - 4)}$
- **D** $\dfrac{5x^3}{10x(x - 2)}$

8. Which is a simpler form of the complex fraction $\dfrac{\frac{1}{b} + c}{b + \frac{1}{c}}$?

- **F** 1
- **G** $\dfrac{c}{b}$
- **H** $\left(\dfrac{1}{b} + c\right)^2$
- **I** $(1 + c)(b + 1)$

9. What is the sum of the x-intercepts of the graph of the quadratic function $y = x^2 - 4x - 12$?

- **A** 6
- **B** 4
- **C** -1
- **D** -4

10. What is the equation of a parabola with the following characteristics?

Axis of symmetry: $x = -3$

Range: all real numbers less than or equal to 4

- (F) $y = -(x - 4)^2 - 3$
- (H) $y = -(x + 3)^2 + 4$
- (G) $y = (x - 4)^2 - 3$
- (I) $y = (x + 3)^2 + 4$

11. The graph of a degree 4 polynomial function with integer zeros is shown below.

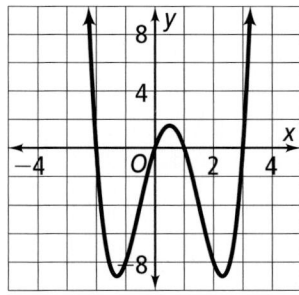

What is the equation of the polynomial function?

- (A) $y = x^4 - 6x^3 + 11x^2 - 6x$
- (B) $y = x^4 - 2x^3 - 5x^2 + 6x$
- (C) $y = x^4 - 2x^3 + x^2 + 3x$
- (D) $y = x^4 + 2x^3 - 5x^2 - 6x$

12. Which function is best represented by the graph below?

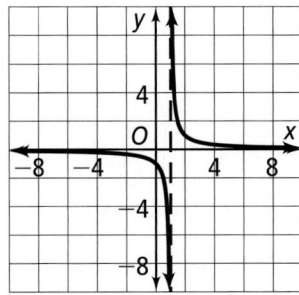

- (F) $y = \dfrac{1}{x - 1}$
- (H) $y = \dfrac{x}{x - 1}$
- (G) $y = \dfrac{1}{x + 1}$
- (I) $y = \dfrac{x}{x + 1}$

13. How many distinct real roots does the equation $x^4 + 3x^3 - 4x = 0$ have?

- (A) 1
- (B) 2
- (C) 3
- (D) 4

14. Which function best represents the graph?

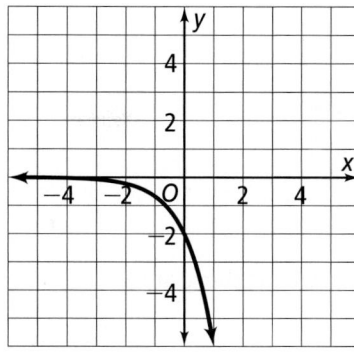

- (F) $f(x) = 2 \cdot 3^{-x}$
- (G) $f(x) = -2 \cdot 3^x$
- (H) $f(x) = 2 \cdot 3^x$
- (I) $f(x) = -2 \cdot 3^{-x}$

15. Consider the piecewise defined function graphed below.

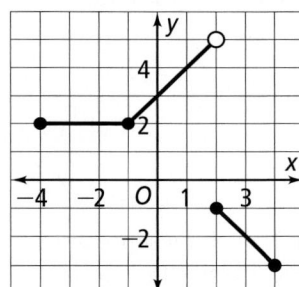

What is the equation for the piecewise defined function?

- (A) $f(x) = \begin{cases} 2, \text{ if } -2 \le x < -1 \\ x + 3, \text{ if } -1 \le x < 2 \\ -x + 1, \text{ if } 2 \le x \le 4 \end{cases}$

- (B) $f(x) = \begin{cases} 2, \text{ if } -4 \le x \le -1 \\ x + 3, \text{ if } -1 < x \le 2 \\ -x + 1, \text{ if } 2 < x \le 4 \end{cases}$

- (C) $f(x) = \begin{cases} 2x, \text{ if } -4 \le x < -1 \\ x + 3, \text{ if } -1 \le x < 2 \\ -x + 1, \text{ if } 2 \le x \le 4 \end{cases}$

- (D) $f(x) = \begin{cases} 2x, \text{ if } -4 \le x < -1 \\ x + 3, \text{ if } -1 \le x < 2 \\ -x - 1, \text{ if } 2 \le x \le 4 \end{cases}$

16. The graph of a rational function is shown below.

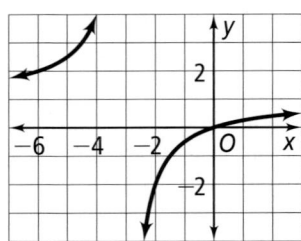

Which function best represents the graph?

F. $f(x) = \dfrac{3}{x-1}$

G. $f(x) = \dfrac{1}{x+3}$

H. $f(x) = \dfrac{3x}{x-1}$

I. $f(x) = \dfrac{x}{x+3}$

17. Consider the polynomial function
$f(x) = -2x^4 + 8x^3 + 4x^2 - 3$. What is the end behavior of the graph?

A. down and down

B. down and up

C. up and up

D. up and down

18. If $f(x) = (x+2)^2 - 1$, what is the largest possible domain of f so that its inverse is also a function?

F. $x \geq -2$ H. $x \geq 0$

G. $x \geq -1$ I. $x \geq 2$

19. Solve $\dfrac{3}{2x+10} + \dfrac{5}{4} = \dfrac{7}{x+5}$ for x.

A. $-\dfrac{50}{11}$ C. $-\dfrac{9}{5}$

B. $-\dfrac{34}{10}$ D. $-\dfrac{3}{5}$

20. Solve $\sqrt{x-2} - 7 = -4$ for x.

F. 5   H. 18

G. 11   I. 25

21. What is the x-coordinate of the vertex of the graph of $f(x) = 2x^2 + 4x - 6$?

A. -6 B. -1 C. 1   D. 4

22. The horizontal asymptote of the graph of $y = \dfrac{4x-4}{2x-6}$ is $y = t$ for a real number t. What is the value of t?

F. 1   G. 2   H. 3   I. 4

23. Graph $f(x) = |2x+6| - 1$.

24. The graph of $y = x^2$ is shown below.

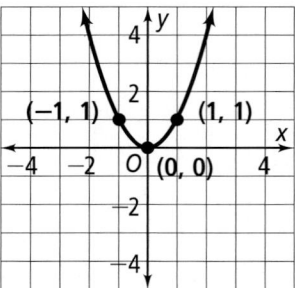

Use transformations to graph $y = -x^2 - 3$.

25. Consider the graph of the function $f(x) = 2(4)^x$. Explain how the graph of the function $g(x) = -2(4)^x + 3$ can be obtained from the graph of $f(x)$.

26. Let $f(x) = \dfrac{4}{x-1}$.

a. Determine $f^{-1}(x)$. Show or explain your work.

b. Find $f(f^{-1}(x))$ and $f^{-1}(f(x))$. Show your work.

c. How are the domain and range of f and f^{-1} related?

27. Consider the expression $\left(\dfrac{r^{3m}}{r^{-m}t^{4n}}\right)^{\frac{1}{n}} \cdot \left(\dfrac{r^{\frac{1}{n}}}{t^{\frac{2}{m}}}\right)^{-m}$.

a. Simplify the expression so that r and t are only written once. Show your work.

b. Using your answer from part (a), evaluate the expression when $m = 1$, $n = 2$, and $t = -3i$. Show your work.

c. For what values of r will the expression you found in part (b) be a real number? Explain your answer.

28. A company needs to ship bags of golf balls that contain 690 golf balls, plus or minus 6 golf balls. If x represents the actual number of golf balls, which inequality can represent this situation?

Ⓐ $|x + 6| \geq 690$

Ⓑ $|x - 6| \leq 690$

Ⓒ $|x + 690| \geq 6$

Ⓓ $|x - 690| \leq 6$

29. A boat took 4 h to make a trip downstream with a current of 6 km/h. The return trip against the same current took 10 h. How far did the boat travel?

Ⓕ 48 km   Ⓖ 84 km   Ⓗ 160 km   Ⓘ 196 km

30. What are all the complex solutions of $x^2 - 4x = -5$?

Ⓐ $x = -1, x = 5$

Ⓑ $x = 1, x = 3$

Ⓒ $x = 2 + i, x = 2 - i$

Ⓓ $x = 2 + 3i, x = 2 - 3i$

31. The function below can be used to find the total amount $C(x)$ an electric company charges a customer who uses x kilowatt-hours (kWh) in a month.

$$C(x) = \begin{cases} 0.07275x + 6.00, \text{ if } 0 \leq x \leq 400 \\ 0.05535x + 35.10, \text{ if } x > 400 \end{cases}$$

If a customer uses 546 kWh in a month, what is the total amount charged?

Ⓕ $45.72   Ⓖ $65.32   Ⓗ $78.28   Ⓘ $111.04

32. Simplify $\dfrac{r^{\frac{1}{2}}}{r^{-\frac{1}{4}}}$.

Ⓐ $-r^{\frac{1}{4}}$ Ⓑ $-r^2$ Ⓒ $r^{\frac{1}{8}}$ Ⓓ $r^{\frac{3}{4}}$

33. The graph of a quadratic function, $y = ax^2 + bx + c$ passes through the points shown. What is the axis of symmetry of the parabola?

Ⓕ $x = -2$

Ⓖ $x = -1$

Ⓗ $x = 1$

Ⓘ $x = 2$

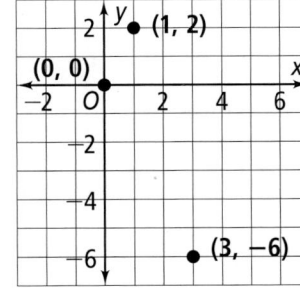

34. What is the end behavior of the graph of the polynomial function $f(x) = -2x^5 + x^4 + 3x^3 - x + 1$?

Ⓐ down and up

Ⓑ up and up

Ⓒ up and down

Ⓓ down and down

35. The principal amount invested in an account with 1.5% interest compounded continuously is $500. The equation $A(x) = 500e^{0.015x}$ can be used to find the balance in the account after x years. To the nearest year, in how many years will the account have a balance of $820?

Ⓕ 2 years   Ⓗ 72 years

Ⓖ 33 years   Ⓘ 109 years

36. The graph of the exponential equation $y = 2^x$ is reflected across the y-axis and moved down 1 unit. What is the equation of the resulting graph?

Ⓐ $y = 2^{-x-1}$ Ⓒ $y = 2^{-x} - 1$

Ⓑ $y = -2^{x-1}$ Ⓓ $y = -2^x - 1$

37. The function $C(x) = \dfrac{10}{2x^2 + 1}$ can be used to find the concentration $C(x)$ in mg/L of a certain drug in the bloodstream of a patient x hours after the injection is given. In approximately how many hours after the injection will the concentration of the drug be 1.3 mg/L?

Ⓕ 0.5 h   Ⓗ 1.8 h

Ⓖ 0.7 h   Ⓘ 2.3 h

38. The half-life of radium-226 is about 1,600 years. After 4,000 years what percentage of a sample of radium-226 remains?

Ⓐ 2.5%   Ⓒ 40.0%

Ⓑ 17.7%   Ⓓ 75.8%

39. Solve $8.2(3^{2x-4}) - 11 = 557.1$. Round your answer to the nearest tenth.

Ⓕ 1.8   Ⓖ 2.9   Ⓗ 3.5   Ⓘ 3.9

40. An exponential function is represented in the table below.

x	f(x)
−2	12
−1	6
0	3
1	1.5

Which equation best represents the function?

ⓐ $f(x) = 3\left(2^{-x}\right)$ ⓒ $f(x) = 2^{-x} + 3$

ⓑ $f(x) = 3\left(2^x\right)$ ⓓ $f(x) = 2^x + 3$

41. What is the range of the graph of $f(x) = -ab^x$ if $a > 0$ and $b > 1$?

ⓕ $f(x) \leq 0$ ⓗ $f(x) \geq a$

ⓖ $f(x) \leq a$ ⓘ All real numbers

42. The characteristics of function $f(x) = ax^n$ are shown below.

Domain: All real numbers

Range: $x \leq 0$

Symmetric with respect to the y-axis

What must be true about the values of a and n?

ⓐ $a < 0$ and n is even ⓒ $a > 0$ and n is even

ⓑ $a < 0$ and n is odd ⓓ $a > 0$ and n is odd

43. A train leaves a city traveling due north. A car leaves the city at the same time traveling due west. The car is traveling 15 mi/h faster than the train. After 2 h they are approximately 150 mi apart. What is the speed of the train?

ⓕ 30 mi/h ⓗ 60 mi/h

ⓖ 45 mi/h ⓘ 75 mi/h

44. A high school sold 800 tickets for a soccer game. Three types of tickets were sold, adult, student and child. There were four times as many adult tickets sold as child tickets. And there were 62 more student tickets sold than adult tickets. How many adult tickets were sold?

ⓐ 82 ⓑ 123 ⓒ 328 ⓓ 384

45. Let $f(x) = 3x + 5$ and let $g(x) = x^2 + 2x$. What is $f(-3) \cdot g(-3)$?

ⓕ −32 ⓗ 9

ⓖ −12 ⓘ 60

46. The volume of a square pyramid with a height equal to four less than the length of a side of the base is given by $V(x) = \frac{1}{3}\left(x^3 + 8x^2 + 16x\right)$ where x is the height in cm. If the length of a side of the base is 9 cm, what is the volume of the pyramid?

ⓐ 135 cm³ ⓒ 507 cm³

ⓑ 405 cm³ ⓓ 1,521 cm³

47. A quadratic function is represented in the table below.

x	f(x)
1	−13
2	−3
3	3
4	5
5	3

Which equation best represents the function?

ⓕ $f(x) = -2\left(x - 4\right)^2 + 5$

ⓖ $f(x) = -2\left(x - 3\right)^2 + 3$

ⓗ $f(x) = 2\left(x - 4\right)^2 + 5$

ⓘ $f(x) = 2\left(x - 3\right)^2 + 3$

48. Find the x-value of the solution to the following system of equations.

$$\begin{cases} 3x + y = -3 \\ x + y = 1 \end{cases}$$

ⓐ −2 ⓒ $\frac{3}{5}$

ⓑ −1 ⓓ 3

49. Solve $4\left(3^x\right) = 26$ for x.

ⓕ 0.3 ⓗ 1.7

ⓖ 1.3 ⓘ 2.2

50. The amount of cesium-137 remaining after x years in an initial sample of 200 milligrams can be found using the equation $C(x) = 200e^{-0.02295x}$. In approximately how many years will the sample contain 120 milligrams of cesium-137?

   Ⓐ 13   Ⓑ 22   Ⓒ 26   Ⓓ 39

51. Graph the solution set of the following system of inequalities.
$$\begin{cases} x - 3y \le 6 \\ 2x + y > 5 \end{cases}$$

52. Simplify the expression. Show your work.
$$\sqrt{16x^2y^{12}}$$

53. What is the vertex of the graph of $f(x) = a|bx - 1| + c$? Explain your answer.

54. A company produces two types of doghouses, regular and deluxe. A regular doghouse requires 7 hours to build and 3 hours to paint. A deluxe doghouse requires 11 hours to build and 4 hours to paint. The company employs 5 builders and 2 painters. Each employee can work a maximum of 40 hours.
  a. Write a system of inequalities that can be used to find the number of each type of doghouse built in a week. Define the variables you use in your system.
  b. Graph the solution set of your system of inequalities from part (a). Label each line in your graph.
  c. A regular doghouse sells for $100. A deluxe doghouse sells for $200. How many of each can be built, painted, and sold in one week to maximize sales?

55. Consider the function $f(x) = \frac{1}{x}$.
  a. Graph $f(x)$.
  b. Explain how the graph of $g(x) = \frac{4}{x+2}$ compares to the graph of $f(x)$.
  c. What is the horizontal asymptote (if any) of the graph of $g(x)$?
  d. What is the vertical asymptote of the graph of $g(x)$? Explain how this relates to the domain of $g(x)$.

56. Consider the recursive model shown below.
$$\begin{cases} a_1 = 5 \\ a_{n+1} = a_n - 7 \end{cases}$$

What is an explicit formula for this sequence?

  Ⓕ $a_n = -7 + 5n$

  Ⓖ $a_n = 5 - 7n$

  Ⓗ $a_n = -7 + 5(n - 1)$

  Ⓘ $a_n = 5 - 7(n - 1)$

57. An arch in the shape of the upper half of an ellipse supports a bridge that spans a distance of 80 ft. The maximum height of the arch is 30 ft. To the nearest tenth of a foot, what is the height of the arch 28 ft from the center?

  Ⓐ 14.4 ft   Ⓒ 28.1 ft

  Ⓑ 21.4 ft   Ⓓ 29.7 ft

58. A scientist wants to study the affects of a new medication on acne. Which type of study would give the most reliable results?

  Ⓕ Controlled experiment

  Ⓖ Observational study

  Ⓗ Survey

  Ⓘ Random sample

59. Suppose scores on an entry exam are normally distributed. The exam has a mean score of 140 and a standard deviation of 20. What is the probability that a person who took the test scored between 120 and 160?

  Ⓐ 14%   Ⓒ 68%

  Ⓑ 40%   Ⓓ 95%

60. What is $\cos \theta$ when $\sin \theta = \frac{3}{5}$ and θ is in Quadrant II?

  Ⓕ $-\frac{4}{5}$ Ⓗ $\frac{2}{5}$

  Ⓖ $-\frac{2}{5}$ Ⓘ $\frac{4}{5}$

61. An equation of an ellipse is $9(x+9)^2 + 4(y+4)^2 = 36$. What is the y-coordinate of the center of the ellipse?

(A) -9 (B) -4 (C) 4 (D) 9

62. What is the determinant of the matrix?

$$\begin{bmatrix} 1 & 3 & -1 \\ 1 & 2 & 1 \\ -2 & -5 & -4 \end{bmatrix}$$

(F) -8 (H) 0

(G) -4 (I) 4

63. Write the expression as a single logarithm.

$4\log_3 x + \log_3 y - 2\log_3 z$

(A) $\log_3 \dfrac{x^4 y}{z^2}$ (C) $\log_3 (4x + y - 2z)$

(B) $\dfrac{\log_3 x^4 y}{\log_3 z^2}$ (D) $\log_3 (x^4 + y - z^2)$

64. A computer manufacturing company sampled two different parts and tested for defects. The results are shown in the table below.

	Part A	Part B
Defective	14	33
Not defective	266	312

What is the probability that if a Part B is randomly chosen, it is defective?

(F) 5.28%   (H) 9.57%

(G) 5.71%   (I) 10.58%

65. The graph of the hyperbola $\dfrac{(x-2)^2}{25} - \dfrac{(y-3)^2}{9} = 1$ is shown at the right.

How does the graph of $\dfrac{(x-2)^2}{9} - \dfrac{(y-3)^2}{25} = 1$ differ from this graph?

(A) The asymptotes are less steep.

(B) The foci become $(-1, 3)$ and $(5, 3)$.

(C) The vertices become $(-1, 3)$ and $(5, 3)$.

(D) The transverse axis becomes vertical.

66. What is $64°$ in radians? Round your answer to the nearest hundredth.

(F) 1.12   (H) 10.19

(G) 5.63   (I) 402.12

67. A set of data has a normal distribution with a mean of 72 and a standard deviation of 6. What percent of data is greater than 84?

(A) 84%   (C) 13.5%

(B) 50%   (D) 2.35%

68. An employee's initial salary is \$30,000. The person receives a 5% raise at the end of each year. What is the formula for the term s_n which represents the salary at the beginning of the nth year?

(F) $s_n = 30{,}000 + 1.05n$

(G) $s_n = 30{,}000 + 5(n - 1)$

(H) $s_n = 30{,}000(1.05)^{n-1}$

(I) $s_n = 30{,}000(1.05)^n$

69. Use the Change of Base Formula to approximate the value of $\log_2 3.2$ to the nearest tenth.

(A) 0.2   (C) 1.7

(B) 0.8   (D) 9.2

70. If $B = \begin{bmatrix} -2 & 1 \\ 4 & -1 \end{bmatrix}$, what is B^{-1}?

(F) $\begin{bmatrix} -0.5 & 1 \\ 0.25 & -1 \end{bmatrix}$ (H) $\begin{bmatrix} 2 & -1 \\ -4 & 1 \end{bmatrix}$

(G) $\begin{bmatrix} 0.5 & 0.5 \\ 2 & 1 \end{bmatrix}$ (I) $\begin{bmatrix} 4 & -1 \\ -2 & 1 \end{bmatrix}$

71. Which expression is equivalent to $(\sin \theta)(\sec \theta)$?

(A) $\cos \theta$ (C) $\sin \theta$

(B) $\tan \theta$ (D) $\csc \theta$

72. The magnitude M of an earthquake can be found using the equation $M(x) = \log\left(\dfrac{x}{0.001}\right)$ where x represents the seismograph reading of the earthquake in mm. An earthquake has a magnitude of 6.2. What is the seismograph reading of the earthquake in mm?

(F) 0.0062   (H) 1.014

(G) 0.0008   (I) 1584.9

73. Which function has a period of 4π and an amplitude of 6?

Ⓐ $y = -6 \sin 8\theta$

Ⓑ $y = 6 \sin 2\theta$

Ⓒ $y = 3 \sin 6\theta$

Ⓓ $y = -6 \sin \frac{1}{2}\theta$

74. Which equation represents a circle with center $(-4, -6)$ and radius 6?

Ⓕ $(x - 4)^2 + (y - 6)^2 = 36$

Ⓖ $(x + 4)^2 + (y + 6)^2 = 36$

Ⓗ $(x + 4)^2 + (y + 6)^2 = 6$

Ⓘ $(x - 4)^2 + (y - 6)^2 = 6$

75. What is the exact value of $\tan 240°$?

Ⓐ $\dfrac{\sqrt{2}}{2}$ Ⓒ 1

Ⓑ $\dfrac{\sqrt{3}}{3}$ Ⓓ $\sqrt{3}$

76. Multiply $\begin{bmatrix} 4 & -1 \\ 0 & 5 \end{bmatrix} \cdot \begin{bmatrix} 1 & 3 \\ -6 & 1 \end{bmatrix}$.

Ⓕ $\begin{bmatrix} 4 & 14 \\ -24 & 11 \end{bmatrix}$ Ⓗ $\begin{bmatrix} 10 & -30 \\ 11 & 5 \end{bmatrix}$

Ⓖ $\begin{bmatrix} 4 & -3 \\ 0 & 5 \end{bmatrix}$ Ⓘ $\begin{bmatrix} 10 & 11 \\ -30 & 5 \end{bmatrix}$

77. Consider the vectors **u** and **v** below.

  a. Show the addition of the two vectors graphically. Label your answer **w**.

  b. Using your answer from part (a), find $-0.5\mathbf{w}$.

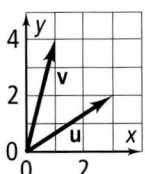

78. Solve for x. Show or explain your work.

$2 \ln 4x + 5 = 8$

79. A pendulum initially swings through an arc that is 20 inches long. On each swing, the length of the arc is 0.85 of the previous swing.

  a. Write a recursive model of geometric decay to represent the sequence of lengths of the arc of each swing. Let $p_1 = 20$.

  b. Rewrite your model from part (a) using an explicit formula.

  c. What is the approximate total distance the pendulum has swung after 11 swings? Show your work.

  d. What is the total distance, approximately, that the pendulum has swung when it stops? Show your work.

80. The equation of an ellipse is $4x^2 + 9y^2 + 8x - 54y + 49 = 0$.

  a. Write the equation in standard form. Show your work.

  b. What are the foci and vertices of the ellipse? Show your work or explain your answer.

  c. Graph the ellipse. Label the center of the ellipse on your graph.

81. Consider the following system of equations.

$$\begin{cases} x + 2z = -1 \\ y - 2z = 2 \\ 2x + y + z = 1 \end{cases}$$

  a. Represent the system of equations using the matrix equation $AX = B$.

  b. Find the determinant of the matrix A.

  c. Solve the equation from part (a). If it cannot be solved, use your result from part (b) to explain why.

82. Consider the function $f(x) = 2 \cos(4x)$.

  a. What are the period and amplitude of the graph of $f(x)$?

  b. Graph $f(x)$ over two periods.

  c. Solve $f(x) = 0.5$ algebraically. Show your work and give your answer in radians.

Skills Handbook

Percents and Percent Applications

Percent means "per hundred." Find fraction, decimal, and percent equivalents by replacing one symbol for *hundredths* with another.

Example 1

Write each number as a percent.

a. $0.082 = 8.2\%$

Move the decimal point two places to the right and write a percent sign.

b. $\frac{3}{5} = \frac{60}{100} = 60\%$

Write the fraction as hundredths. Then replace the hundredths with a percent sign.

c. $1\frac{1}{6} = \frac{7}{6} = 1.1666\overline{6} = 116.\overline{6}\%$

First, use $7 \div 6$ to write $1\frac{1}{6}$ as a decimal.

Example 2

Write each percent as a decimal.

a. $50\% = 0.50 = 0.5$

Move the decimal point two places to the left and drop the percent sign.

b. $\frac{1}{2}\% = 0.5\% = 00.5\% = 0.005$

Example 3

Use an equation to solve each percent problem.

a. What is 30% of 12?

$n = 0.3 \times 12$

$n = 3.6$

b. 18 is 0.3% of what?

$18 = 0.003 \times n$

$\frac{18}{0.003} = \frac{0.003n}{0.003}$

$6000 = n$

c. What percent of 60 is 9?

$n \times 60 = 9$

$60n = 9$

$n = \frac{9}{60} = 0.15 = 15\%$

Exercises

Write each decimal as a percent and each percent as a decimal.

1. 0.46   **2.** 1.506   **3.** 0.007   **4.** 8%   **5.** 103.5%   **6.** 3.3%

Write each fraction or mixed number as a percent.

7. $\frac{1}{4}$ **8.** $\frac{3}{8}$ **9.** $\frac{2}{3}$ **10.** $\frac{4}{9}$ **11.** $1\frac{3}{20}$ **12.** $\frac{1}{200}$

Use an equation to solve each percent problem. Round your answer to the nearest tenth, if necessary.

13. What is 25% of 50?

14. What percent of 58 is 37?

15. 120% of what is 90?

16. 8 is what percent of 40?

17. 15 is 75% of what?

18. 80% of 58 is what?

Operations With Fractions

To add or subtract fractions, use a common denominator. The common denominator is the least common multiple of the denominators.

Example 1

Simplify $\frac{2}{3} + \frac{3}{5}$.

$\frac{2}{3} + \frac{3}{5} = \frac{2}{3} \cdot \frac{5}{5} + \frac{3}{5} \cdot \frac{3}{3}$ For 3 and 5, the least common multiple is 15.

$= \frac{10}{15} + \frac{9}{15}$ Write $\frac{2}{3}$ and $\frac{3}{5}$ as equivalent fractions with denominators of 15.

$= \frac{19}{15}$ or $1\frac{4}{15}$ Add the numerators.

Example 2

Simplify $5\frac{1}{4} - 3\frac{2}{3}$.

$5\frac{1}{4} - 3\frac{2}{3} = 5\frac{3}{12} - 3\frac{8}{12}$ Write equivalent fractions.

$= 4\frac{15}{12} - 3\frac{8}{12}$ Write $5\frac{3}{12}$ as $4\frac{15}{12}$ so you can subtract the fractions.

$= 1\frac{7}{12}$ Subtract the fractions. Then subtract the whole numbers.

To multiply fractions, multiply the numerators and multiply the denominators. You can simplify by using a greatest common factor.

Example 3

Simplify $\frac{3}{4} \cdot \frac{8}{11}$

Method 1 $\frac{3}{4} \cdot \frac{8}{11} = \frac{24}{44} = \frac{24 \div 4}{44 \div 4} = \frac{6}{11}$ **Method 2** $\frac{3}{4} \cdot \frac{\cancel{8}^{2}}{11} = \frac{6}{11}$

Divide 24 and 44 by 4, their greatest common factor.   Divide 4 and 8 by 4, their greatest common factor.

To divide fractions, use a reciprocal to change the problem to multiplication.

Example 4

Simplify $3\frac{1}{5} \div 1\frac{1}{2}$

$3\frac{1}{5} \div 1\frac{1}{2} = \frac{16}{5} \div \frac{3}{2}$ Write mixed numbers as improper fractions.

$= \frac{16}{5} \cdot \frac{2}{3}$ Multiply by the reciprocal of the divisor.

$= \frac{32}{15}$ or $2\frac{2}{15}$ Simplify.

Exercises

Perform the indicated operation.

1. $\frac{3}{5} + \frac{4}{5}$ **2.** $\frac{1}{2} + \frac{2}{3}$ **3.** $4\frac{1}{2} + 2\frac{1}{3}$ **4.** $5\frac{3}{4} + 4\frac{2}{5}$ **5.** $\frac{2}{3} - \frac{3}{7}$

6. $5\frac{1}{2} - 3\frac{2}{5}$ **7.** $7\frac{3}{4} - 4\frac{4}{5}$ **8.** $3\frac{4}{5} \cdot 10$ **9.** $2\frac{1}{2} \cdot 3\frac{1}{5}$ **10.** $6\frac{3}{4} \cdot 5\frac{2}{3}$

11. $\frac{1}{2} \div \frac{1}{3}$ **12.** $\frac{6}{5} \div \frac{3}{5}$ **13.** $8\frac{1}{2} \div 4\frac{1}{4}$ **14.** $\frac{8}{9} - \frac{2}{3}$ **15.** $5\frac{1}{4} \cdot 8$

Ratios and Proportions

A *ratio* is a comparison of two quantities by division. You can write *equal ratios* by multiplying or dividing each quantity by the same nonzero number.

Ways to Write a Ratio
$a : b \quad a \text{ to } b \quad \frac{a}{b} \ (b \neq 0)$

Example 1

Write $3\frac{1}{3} : \frac{1}{2}$ as a ratio in simplest form.

$$3\frac{1}{3} : \frac{1}{2} \rightarrow \frac{3\frac{1}{3}}{\frac{1}{2}} = \frac{20}{3} \text{ or } 20 : 3$$

$\times 6$
$\times 6$

In simplest form, both terms should be integers. Multiply by the common denominator, 6.

A rate is a ratio that compares different types of quantities. In simplest form for a rate, the second quantity is one unit.

Example 2

Write **247 mi in 5.2 h** as a rate in simplest form.

$$\frac{247 \text{ mi}}{5.2 \text{ h}} = \frac{47.5 \text{ mi}}{1 \text{ h}} \text{ or } 47.5 \text{ mi/h}$$

$\div 5.2$
$\div 5.2$

Divide by 5.2 to make the second quantity one unit.

A proportion is a statement that two ratios are equal. You can find a missing term in a proportion by using the cross products.

Cross Products of a Proportion
$$\frac{a}{b} = \frac{c}{d} \ \rightarrow \ ad = bc$$

Example 3

The Copy Center charges \$2.52 for 63 copies. At that rate, how much will the Copy Center charge for 140 copies?

$$\begin{array}{l} \text{cost} \rightarrow \\ \text{copies} \rightarrow \end{array} \quad \frac{2.52}{63} = \frac{c}{140} \qquad \text{Set up a proportion.}$$

$$2.52 \cdot 140 = 63c \qquad \text{Use cross products.}$$

$$c = \frac{2.52 \cdot 140}{63} \qquad \text{Solve for } c.$$

$$= 5.6 \text{ or } \$5.60$$

Exercises

Write each ratio or rate in simplest form.

1. 15 to 20   **2.** $85 : 34$ **3.** 38 g in 4 oz   **4.** 375 mi in 4.3 h   **5.** $\frac{84}{30}$

Solve each proportion. Round your answer to the nearest tenth, if necessary.

6. $\frac{a}{5} = \frac{12}{15}$ **7.** $\frac{21}{12} = \frac{14}{x}$ **8.** $8 : 15 = n : 25$ **9.** $2.4 : c = 4 : 3$ **10.** $\frac{17}{8} = \frac{n}{20}$

11. $\frac{13}{n} = \frac{20}{3}$ **12.** $5 : 7 = y : 5$ **13.** $\frac{0.4}{3.5} = \frac{5.2}{x}$ **14.** $\frac{4}{x} = \frac{7}{6}$ **15.** $4 : n = n : 9$

16. A canary's heart beats 130 times in 12 s. Use a proportion to find about how many times its heart beats in 50 s.

Simplifying Expressions With Integers

To add two numbers with the same sign, *add* their absolute values. The sum has the same sign as the numbers. To add two numbers with different signs, find the *difference* between their absolute values. The sum has the same sign as the number with the greater absolute value.

Example 1

Add.

a. $-8 + (-5) = -13$

b. $-8 + 5 = -3$

c. $8 + (-5) = 3$

To subtract a number, add its opposite.

Example 2

Subtract.

a. $4 - 7 = 4 + (-7)$
$= -3$

b. $-4 - (-7) = -4 + 7$
$= 3$

c. $-4 - 7 = -4 + (-7)$
$= -11$

The product or quotient of two numbers with the same sign is positive. The product or quotient of two numbers with different signs is negative.

Example 3

Multiply or divide.

a. $(-3)(-5) = 15$

b. $-35 \div 7 = -5$

c. $24 \div (-6) = -4$

Example 4

Simplify $2^2 - 3(4 - 6) - 12$.

$2^2 - 3(4 - 6) - 12 = 2^2 - 3(-2) - 12$
$= 4 - 3(-2) - 12$
$= 4 - (-6) - 12$
$= 4 + 6 - 12 = -2$

Order of Operations

1. Perform any operation(s) inside grouping symbols.
2. Simplify any terms with exponents.
3. Multiply and divide in order from left to right.
4. Add and subtract in order from left to right.

Exercises

Simplify each expression.

1. $-4 + 5$

2. $12 - 12$

3. $-15 + (-23)$

4. $4 - 17$

5. $-5 - 12$

6. $3 - (-5)$

7. $-8 - (-12)$

8. $-19 + 5$

9. $(-7)(-4)$

10. $-120 \div 30$

11. $(-3)(4)$

12. $75 \div (-3)$

13. $(-6)(15)$

14. $(18)(-4)$

15. $-84 \div (-7)$

16. $-2(1 + 5) + (-3)(2)$

17. $-4(-2 - 5) + 3(1 - 4)$

18. $20 - (3)(12) + 4^2$

19. $\frac{-15}{-5} - \frac{36}{-12} + \frac{-12}{-4}$

20. $5^2 - 6(5 - 9)$

21. $(-3 + 2^3)(4 + \frac{-42}{7})$

Area and Volume

The *area* of a plane figure is the number of square units contained in the figure.
The *volume* of a space figure is the number of cubic units contained in the figure.
Formulas for area and volume are listed on page 693.

Example 1

Find the area of each figure.

a.
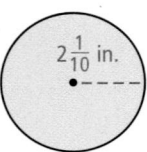

$A = \pi r^2$

$\approx \frac{22}{7} \cdot \left(\frac{21}{10}\right)^2$

$= \frac{693}{50} = 13\frac{43}{50}$ in. ^{2}

b.
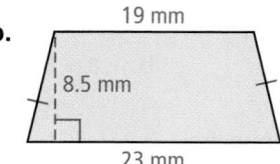

$A = \frac{1}{2}(b_1 + b_2)h$

$= \frac{1}{2}(19 + 23) \cdot 8.5$

$= 178.5$ mm^2

Example 2

Find the volume of each figure.

a.
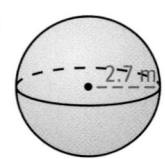

$V = \frac{4}{3}\pi r^3$

$\approx \frac{4}{3} \cdot 3.14 \cdot 2.7^3$

$= 82.40616 \approx 82.4 m^3$

b.
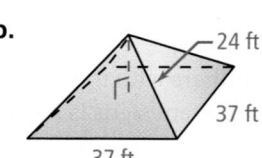

$V = \frac{1}{3}Bh$

$= \frac{1}{3}(37^2) \cdot 24$

$= 10,952$ ft^3

Exercises

Find the exact area of each figure.

1.
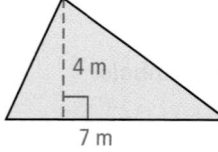

2.
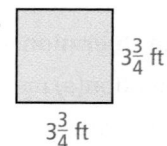

3.
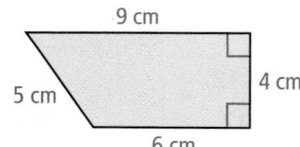

4.
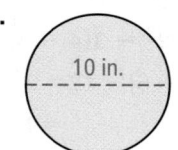

Find the exact volume of each figure.

5.
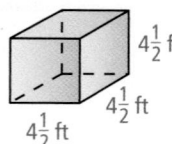

6.
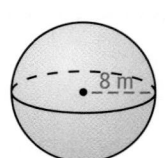

7.
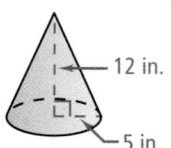

8.
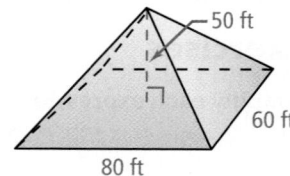

9. Find the area of a triangle with a base of 17 in. and a height of 13 in.

10. Find the volume of a rectangular box 64 cm long, 48 cm wide, and 58 cm high.

11. Find the surface area of the cube in Exercise 5.

The Coordinate Plane, Slope, and Midpoint

The *coordinate plane* is formed when two perpendicular number lines intersect at a point called the origin, forming four quadrants.

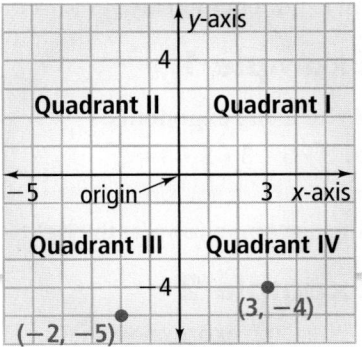

Example 1

In which quadrant would you find each point?

a. $(3, -4)$ Move 3 units right and 4 units down. The point is in Quadrant IV.

b. $(-2, -5)$ Move 2 units left and 5 units down. The point is in Quadrant III.

To find the slope of a line on the coordinate plane, choose two points on the line and use the slope formula.

Example 2

Find the slope of each line.

a.
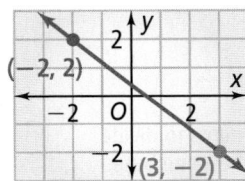

$$m = \frac{y_2 - y_1}{x_2 - x_1}$$
$$= \frac{2 - (-2)}{-2 - 3}$$
$$= \frac{4}{-5} \text{ or } -\frac{4}{5}$$

b.
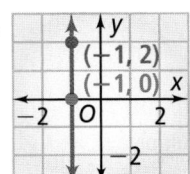

$$m = \frac{y_2 - y_1}{x_2 - x_1}$$
$$= \frac{2 - 0}{-1 - (-1)} = \frac{2}{0}$$

Since you cannot divide by zero, this line has an undefined slope.

If (x_m, y_m) is the midpoint of the segment joining (x_1, y_1) and (x_2, y_2), then $x_m = \frac{x_1 + x_2}{2}$ and $y_m = \frac{y_1 + y_2}{2}$.

Example 3

Find the coordinates of the midpoint of the segment with endpoints $(-2, 5)$ and $(6, -3)$.

$\frac{-2 + 6}{2} = 2$ and $\frac{5 + (-3)}{2} = 1$ so the midpoint is $(2, 1)$.

Exercises

In which quadrant would you find each point? Graph each point on a coordinate plane.

1. $(3, 2)$ **2.** $(-4, 3)$ **3.** $(2, -3)$ **4.** $(4, -2)$ **5.** $(-4, -5)$ **6.** $(-1, -3)$

Find the slope of each line.

7.
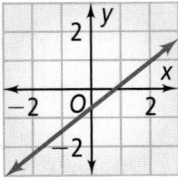

8.
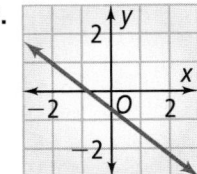

9.
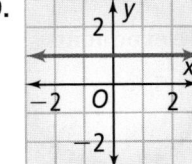

10. the line containing $(-3, 4)$ and $(2, -6)$

11. the line containing $(25, 40)$ and $(100, 55)$

Find the midpoint of the segment with the given endpoints.

12. $(-4, 4), (2, -5)$ **13.** $(3, 3), (7, -6)$ **14.** $(-1, -8), (0, -3)$ **15.** $(3, 4), (2, -6)$

Operations With Exponents

An exponent indicates how many times a number is used as a factor.

Example 1

Write using exponents.

a. $3 \cdot 3 \cdot 3 \cdot 3 \cdot 3 = 3^5$

b. $a \cdot a \cdot b \cdot b \cdot b \cdot b = a^2 b^4$

$2^n = \blacksquare$	$10^n = \blacksquare$
$2^2 = 4$	$10^2 = 100$
$2^1 = 2$	$10^1 = 10$
$2^0 = 1$	$10^0 = 1$
$2^{-1} = \frac{1}{2}$	$10^{-1} = \frac{1}{10}$
$2^{-2} = \frac{1}{4}$	$10^{-2} = \frac{1}{100}$

The patterns shown at the right indicate that $a^0 = 1$ and that $a^{-n} = \frac{1}{a^n}$.

Example 2

Write each expression so that all exponents are positive.

a. $a^{-2}b^3 = \frac{1}{a^2} \cdot b^3 = \frac{b^3}{a^2}$

b. $x^3 y^0 z^{-1} = x^3 \cdot 1 \cdot \frac{1}{z} = \frac{x^3}{z}$

You can simplify expressions that contain powers with the same base.

Example 3

Simplify each expression.

a. $b^5 \cdot b^3 = b^{5+3}$ Add exponents to multiply
$= b^8$ powers with the same base.

b. $\dfrac{x^5}{x^7} = x^{5-7}$ Subtract exponents to divide
$= x^{-2} = \dfrac{1}{x^2}$ powers with the same base.

You can simplify expressions that contain parentheses and exponents.

Example 4

Simplify each expression.

a. $\left(\dfrac{ab}{n}\right)^3 = \dfrac{a^3 b^3}{n^3}$ Raise each factor in the parentheses to the third power.

b. $(c^2)^4 = c^{2 \cdot 4} = c^8$ Multiply exponents to raise a power to a power.

Exercises

Write each expression using exponents.

1. $x \cdot x \cdot x$

2. $x \cdot x \cdot x \cdot y \cdot y$

3. $a \cdot a \cdot a \cdot a \cdot b$

4. $\dfrac{a \cdot a \cdot a \cdot a}{b \cdot b}$

Write each expression so that all exponents are positive.

5. c^{-4}

6. $m^{-2}n^0$

7. $x^5 y^{-7} z^{-3}$

8. $ab^{-1}c^2$

Simplify each expression. Use positive exponents.

9. $d^2 d^6$

10. $\dfrac{a^5}{a^2}$

11. $\dfrac{c^7}{c}$

12. $\dfrac{n^3}{n^6}$

13. $\dfrac{a^5 b^3}{ab^8}$

14. $(3x)^2$

15. $\left(\dfrac{a}{b}\right)^4$

16. $\left(\dfrac{xz}{y}\right)^6$

17. $(c^3)^4$

18. $\left(\dfrac{x^2}{y^5}\right)^3$

19. $(u^4 v^2)^3$

20. $(p^5)^{-2}$

21. $\dfrac{(2a^4)(3a^2)}{6a^3}$

22. $(x^{-2})^3$

23. $(mg^3)^{-1}$

24. $g^{-3}g^{-1}$

25. $\dfrac{(3a^3)^2}{18a}$

26. $\dfrac{c^3 d^7}{c^{-3} d^{-1}}$

Factoring and Operations With Polynomials

Example 1

Perform each operation.

a. $(3y^2 - 4y + 5) + (y^2 + 9y)$

$= (3y^2 + y^2) + (-4y + 9y) + 5$ To add, group like terms.

$= 4y^2 + 5y + 5$

b. $(n + 4)(n - 3)$

$= n(n) + n(-3) + 4(n) + 4(-3)$ Distribute n and 4.

$= n^2 - 3n + 4n - 12$ Combine like terms.

$= n^2 + n - 12$

To factor a polynomial, first find the greatest common factor (GCF) of the terms. Then use the distributive property to factor out the GCF.

Example 2

Factor $6x^3 - 12x^2 + 18x$.

$6x^3 = 6 \cdot x \cdot x \cdot x; -12x^2 = 6 \cdot (-2) \cdot x \cdot x; 18x = 6 \cdot 3 \cdot x$ List the factors of each term. The GCF is $6x$.

$6x^3 - 12x^2 + 18x = 6x(x^2) + 6x(-2x) + 6x(3)$ Use the distributive property to factor out $6x$.

$= 6x(x^2 - 2x + 3)$

When a polynomial is the product of two binomials, you can work backward to find the factors.

$$x^2 + bx + c = (x + \blacksquare)(x + \blacksquare)$$

The *sum* of these numbers must equal b.
The *product* of these numbers must equal c.

Example 3

Factor $x^2 - 13x + 36$.

Choose numbers that are factors of 36. Look for a pair with the sum -13.

The numbers -4 and -9 have a product of 36 and a sum of -13. The factors are $(x - 4)$ and $(x - 9)$. So, $x^2 - 13x + 36 = (x - 4)(x - 9)$.

Factors	Sum
$-6 \cdot (-6)$	-12
$-4 \cdot (-9)$	-13

Exercises

Perform the indicated operations.

1. $(x^2 + 3x - 1) + (7x - 4)$

2. $(5y^2 + 7y) - (3y^2 + 9y - 8)$

3. $4x^2(3x^2 - 5x + 9)$

4. $-5d(13d^2 + 7d + 8)$

5. $(x - 5)(x + 3)$

6. $(n - 7)(n - 2)$

Factor each polynomial.

7. $a^2 - 8a + 12$

8. $n^2 - 2n - 8$

9. $x^2 + 5x + 4$

10. $3m^2 - 9$

11. $y^2 + 5y - 24$

12. $s^3 + 6s^2 + 11s$

13. $2x^3 + 4x^2 - 8x$

14. $y^2 - 10y + 25$

Scientific Notation and Significant Digits

In *scientific notation*, a number has the form $a \times 10^n$, where n is an integer and $1 \le a < 10$.

Example 1

Write 5.59×10^6 in standard form.

$5.59 \times 10^6 = 5\,590\,000 = 5,590,000$

A positive exponent indicates a value greater than 1.
Move the decimal point six places to the right.

Example 2

Write 0.0000318 in scientific notation.

$0.0000318 = 3.18 \times 10^{-5}$

Move the decimal point to create a number between 1 and 10.
Since the original number is less than 1, use a negative exponent.

When a measurement is in scientific notation, all the digits of the number between 1 and 10 are *significant digits*. When you multiply or divide measurements, your answer should have as many significant digits as the least number of significant digits in any of the numbers involved.

Example 3

Multiply $(6.71 \times 10^8 \text{ mi/h})$ and $(3.8 \times 10^4 \text{ h})$.

$(6.71 \times 10^8 \text{ mi/h})(3.8 \times 10^4\,h) = (6.71 \cdot 3.8)(10^8 \cdot 10^4)$ Rearrange factors.

three significant digits   two significant digits

$= 25.498 \times 10^{12}$ Add exponents when multiplying powers of 10.

$= 2.5498 \times 10^{13}$ Write in scientific notation.

$\approx 2.5 \times 10^{13} \text{mi}$ Round to two significant digits.

Exercises

Change each number to scientific notation or to standard form.

1. 1,340,000   **2.** 6.88×10^{-2} **3.** 0.000775   **4.** 0.0072   **5.** 1.113×10^5

6. 8.0×10^{-4} **7.** 1895   **8.** 2.3×10^3 **9.** 123,400   **10.** 7.985×10^4

Write each product or quotient in scientific notation. Round to the appropriate number of significant digits.

11. $(1.6 \times 10^2)(4.0 \times 10^3)$ **12.** $(2.5 \times 10^{-3})(1.2 \times 10^4)$ **13.** $(4.237 \times 10^4)(2.01 \times 10^{-2})$

14. $\dfrac{7.0 \times 10^5}{2.89 \times 10^3}$ **15.** $\dfrac{1.4 \times 10^4}{8.0 \times 10^2}$ **16.** $\dfrac{6.48 \times 10^6}{3.2 \times 10^5}$

17. $(1.78 \times 10^{-7})(5.03 \times 10^{-5})$ **18.** $(7.2 \times 10^{11})(5 \times 10^6)$ **19.** $(8.90 \times 10^8) \div (2.36 \times 10^{-2})$

20. $(3.95 \times 10^4) \div (6.8 \times 10^8)$ **21.** $(4.9 \times 10^{-8}) \div (2.7 \times 10^{-2})$ **22.** $(3.972 \times 10^{-5})(4.7 \times 10^{-4})$

The Pythagorean Theorem and the Distance Formula

In a right triangle, the sum of the squares of the lengths of the legs is equal to the square of the length of the hypotenuse. Use this relationship, known as the Pythagorean Theorem, to find the length of a side of a right triangle.

The Pythagorean Theorem

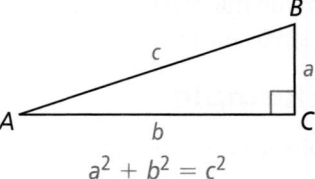

$$a^2 + b^2 = c^2$$

Example 1

Find m in the triangle below, to the nearest tenth.

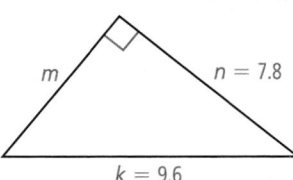

$$m^2 + n^2 = k^2$$
$$m^2 + 7.8^2 = 9.6^2$$
$$m^2 = 9.6^2 - 7.8^2 = 31.32$$
$$m = \sqrt{31.32} \approx 5.6$$

To find the distance between two points on the coordinate plane, use the distance formula.

The distance d between any two points (x_1, y_1) and (x_2, y_2) is

$$d = \sqrt{(x_2 - x_1)^2 + (y_2 - y_1)^2}$$

Example 2

Find the distance between $(-3, 2)$ and $(6, -4)$.

$$d = \sqrt{(6 - (-3))^2 + (-4 - 2)^2}$$
$$= \sqrt{9^2 + (-6)^2}$$
$$= \sqrt{81 + 36}$$
$$= \sqrt{117}$$
$$\approx 10.8$$

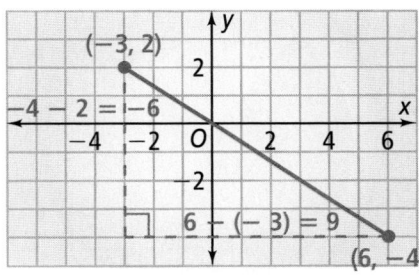

Thus, d is about 10.8 units.

Exercises

In each problem, a and b are the lengths of the legs of a right triangle and c is the length of the hypotenuse. Find each missing length. Round your answer to the nearest tenth.

1. c if $a = 6$ and $b = 8$

2. a if $b = 12$ and $c = 13$

3. b if $a = 8$ and $c = 17$

4. c if $a = 10$ and $b = 3$

5. a if $b = 100$ and $c = 114$

6. b if $a = 12.0$ and $c = 30.1$

Find the distance between each pair of points, to the nearest tenth.

7. $(0, 0), (4, -3)$

8. $(-5, -5), (1, 3)$

9. $(-1, 0), (4, 12)$

10. $(-4, 2), (4, -2)$

11. $(0, 15), (17, 0)$

12. $(-8, 8), (8, 8)$

13. $(-1, 1), (1, -1)$

14. $(-2, 9), (0, 0)$

15. $(-5, 3), (4, 3)$

16. $(2, 1), (3, 4)$

17. $(3, -2), (3, 5)$

18. $(5, 4), (-3, 1)$

Bar and Circle Graphs

Sometimes you can draw different graphs to represent the same data, depending on the information you want to share. A *bar graph* is useful for comparing amounts; a *circle graph* is useful for comparing percents.

Example

Display the 2007 data on immigration to the United States in a bar graph and a circle graph.

To make a circle graph, first find the *percent* of the data in each category. Then express each percent as a decimal and multiply by 360° to find the size of each *central angle*.

Africa $\rightarrow$ $\quad \dfrac{89.3}{1003.7} \approx 0.09$ or 9%
Total $\rightarrow$

$0.09 \times 360° \approx 32°$

Draw a circle and use a protractor to draw each central angle.

Immigration to the United States, 2007

Place of Origin	Immigrants (1000's)
Africa	89.2
Asia	359.4
Europe	120.8
North America	331.7
South America	102.6

Source: Department of Homeland Security

To make a bar graph, place the categories along the bottom axis. Decide on a scale for the side axis. An appropriate scale would be 0–400, marked in intervals of 100. For each data item, draw a bar whose height is equal to the data value.

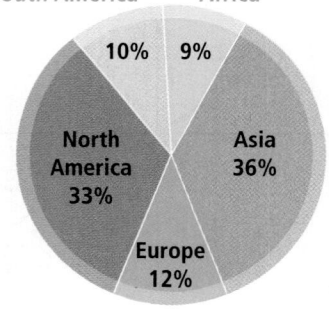

Immigration to the United States, 2007

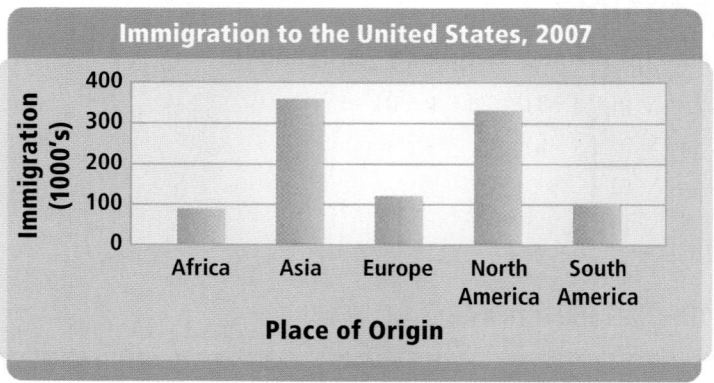

Exercises

Display the data from each table in a bar graph and a circle graph.

1. **NASA Space Shuttle Expenses, 2000**

Operation	Millions of Dollars
Orbiter, integration	698.8
Propulsion	1,053.1
Mission, launch operations	738.8
Flight operations	244.6
Ground operations	510.3

Source: U.S. National Aeronautics and Space Administration

2. **Cable TV Revenue, 2006**

	Millions of Dollars
Airtime	4,566
Basic service	42,918
Pay-per-view, premium services	13,322
Installation	729
Other	27,188

Source: U.S. Census Bureau

Descriptive Statistics and Histograms

For numerical data, you can find the *mean,* the *median,* and the *mode.*

Mean　　　　The sum of the data values in a data set divided by the number of data values

Median　　　The middle value of a data set that has been arranged in increasing or decreasing order. If the data set has an even number of values, the median is the mean of the middle two values.

Mode　　　　The most frequently occurring value in a data set

Example 1

Find the mean, median, and mode for the following data set.　　　5　7　6　3　1　7　9　5　10　7

Mean　　　　$\dfrac{5 + 7 + 6 + 3 + 1 + 7 + 9 + 5 + 10 + 7}{10} = 6$

Median　　　5, 7, 6, 3, 1, 7, 9, 5, 10, 7　　Rearrange the numbers from least to greatest.

　　　　　　1, 3, 5, 5, 6, 7, 7, 7, 9, 10　　The median is the mean of the two middle numbers, 6 and 7.

　　　　　　The median is $\dfrac{6 + 7}{2} = 6.5$.

Mode　　　　The most frequently occurring data value is 7.

The frequency of a data value is the number of times it occurs in a data set.
A *histogram* is a bar graph that shows the frequency of each data value.

Example 2

Use the survey results to make a histogram for the cost of a movie ticket at various theaters.

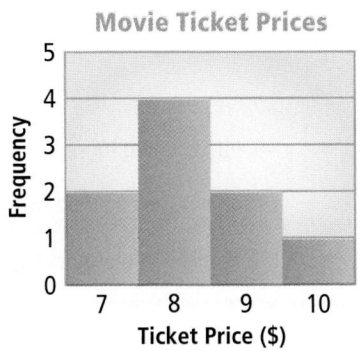

Exercises

Find the mean, the median, and the mode of each data set.

1. −3 4 5 5 −2 7 1 8 9

2. 0 0 1 1 2 3 3 5 3 8 7

3. 2.4 2.4 2.3 2.3 2.4 12.0

4. 1 1 1 1 2 2 2 3 3 4

5. 1.2 1.3 1.4 1.5 1.6 1.7 1.8

6. −4 −3 −2 −1 0 1 2 3 4

Make a histogram for each data set.

7. 7 4 8 6 6 8 7 7 5 7

8. 73 75 76 75 74 75 76 74 76 75

Operations With Rational Expressions

A *rational expression* is an expression that can be written in the form $\frac{\text{polynominal}}{\text{polynominal}}$, where the denominator is not zero. A rational expression is in simplest form if the numerator and denominator have no common factors except 1.

Example 1

Write the expression $\frac{4x + 8}{x + 2}$ in simplest form.

$\frac{4x + 8}{x + 2} = \frac{4(x + 2)}{x + 2}$ Factor the numerator.

$\phantom{\frac{4x + 8}{x + 2}} = 4$ Divide out the common factor $x + 2$.

To add or subtract two rational expressions, use a common denominator.

Example 2

Simplify $\frac{x}{2y} + \frac{x}{3y}$.

$\frac{x}{2y} + \frac{x}{3y} = \frac{x}{2y} \cdot \frac{3}{3} + \frac{x}{3y} \cdot \frac{2}{2}$ The common denominator of $3y$ and $2y$ is $6y$.

$\phantom{\frac{x}{2y} + \frac{x}{3y}} = \frac{3x}{6y} + \frac{2x}{6y}$

$\phantom{\frac{x}{2y} + \frac{x}{3y}} = \frac{5x}{6y}$ Add the numerators.

To multiply rational expressions, first find and divide out any common factors in the numerators and the denominators. Then multiply the remaining numerators and denominators. To divide rational expressions, first use a reciprocal to change the problem to multiplication.

Example 3

Simplify $\frac{40x^2}{21} \div \frac{5x}{14}$.

$\frac{40x^2}{21} \div \frac{5x}{14} = \frac{40x^2}{21} \cdot \frac{14}{5x}$ Change dividing by $\frac{5x}{14}$ to multiplying by the reciprocal, $\frac{14}{5x}$.

$\phantom{\frac{40x^2}{21} \div \frac{5x}{14}} = \frac{8 \; \cancel{40x^2} \, 1}{3 \; \cancel{21}} \times \frac{\cancel{14} \, 2}{\cancel{5x} \, 1}$ Divide out the common factors 5, x, and 7.

$\phantom{\frac{40x^2}{21} \div \frac{5x}{14}} = \frac{16x}{3}$ Multiply the numerators ($8x \cdot 2$). Multiply the denominators ($3 \cdot 1$).

Exercises

Write each expression in simplest form.

1. $\frac{4a^2b}{12ab^3}$ **2.** $\frac{5n + 15}{n + 3}$ **3.** $\frac{x - 7}{2x - 14}$ **4.** $\frac{28c^2(d - 3)}{35c(d - 3)}$

Perform the indicated operation.

5. $\frac{3x}{2} + \frac{5x}{2}$ **6.** $\frac{3x}{8} + \frac{5x}{8}$ **7.** $\frac{5}{h} - \frac{3}{h}$ **8.** $\frac{6}{11p} - \frac{9}{11p}$ **9.** $\frac{3x}{5} - \frac{x}{2}$

10. $\frac{13}{2x} - \frac{13}{3x}$ **11.** $\frac{7x}{5} + \frac{5x}{7}$ **12.** $\frac{5a}{b} + \frac{3a}{5b}$ **13.** $\frac{7x}{8} \cdot \frac{32x}{35}$ **14.** $\frac{3x^2}{2} \cdot \frac{6}{x}$

15. $\frac{8x^2}{5} \cdot \frac{10}{x^3}$ **16.** $\frac{7x}{8} \cdot \frac{64}{14x}$ **17.** $\frac{16}{3x} \div \frac{5}{3x}$ **18.** $\frac{4x}{5} \div \frac{16}{15x}$ **19.** $\frac{x^3}{8} \div \frac{x^2}{16}$

Reference

Table 1 **Measures**

	United States Customary	**Metric**
Length	12 inches (in.) = 1 foot (ft) 36 in. = 1 yard (yd) 3 ft = 1 yard 5280 ft = 1 mile (mi) 1760 yd = 1 mile	10 millimeters (mm) = 1 centimeter (cm) 100 cm = 1 meter (m) 1000 mm = 1 meter 1000 m = 1 kilometer (km)
Area	144 square inches (in.^{2}) = 1 square foot (ft^2) 9 ft^2 = 1 square yard (yd^2) 43,560 ft^2 = 1 acre (a) 4840 yd^2 = 1 acre	100 square millimeters (mm^2) = 1 square centimeter (cm^2) 10,000 cm^2 = 1 square meter (m^2) 10,000 m^2 = 1 hectare (ha)
Volume	1728 cubic inches (in.^{3}) = 1 cubic foot (ft^3) 27 ft^3 = 1 cubic yard (yd^3)	1000 cubic millimeters (mm^3) = 1 cubic centimeter (cm^3) 1,000,000 cm^3 = 1 cubic meter (m^3)
Liquid Capacity	8 fluid ounces (fl oz) = 1 cup (c) 2 c = 1 pint (pt) 2 pt = 1 quart (qt) 4 qt = 1 gallon (gal)	1000 milliliters (mL) = 1 liter (L) 1000 L = 1 kiloliter (kL)
Weight or Mass	16 ounces (oz) = 1 pound (lb) 2000 pounds = 1 ton (t)	1000 milligrams (mg) = 1 gram (g) 1000 g = 1 kilogram (kg) 1000 kg = 1 metric ton
Temperature	32°F = freezing point of water 98.6°F = normal human body temperature 212°F = boiling point of water	0°C = freezing point of water 37°C = normal human body temperature 100°C = boiling point of water

	Customary Units and Metric Units	
Length	1 in. = 2.54 cm 1 ft ≈ 0.305 m 1mi ≈ 1.61 km	1 cm ≈ 0.39 in. 1 m ≈ 3.28 ft 1 km ≈ 0.62 mi
Area	1 acre = 0.40 ha	1 ha ≈ 2.47 acres
Capacity	1 qt ≈ 0.95 L	1 L ≈ 1.06 qt
Weight and Mass	1 oz ≈ 28.4 g 1 lb ≈ 0.45 kg	1 g ≈ 0.035 oz 1 kg ≈ 2.205 lb

Time

60 seconds (s) = 1 minute (min) 60 minutes = 1 hour (h) 24 hours = 1 day (d) 7 days = 1 week (wk)	4 weeks (approx.) = 1 month (mo) 365 days = 1 year (yr) 52 weeks (approx.) = 1 year	12 months = 1 year 10 years = 1 decade 100 years = 1 century

Table 2 **Reading Math Symbols**

Symbols	Words
$\cdot$, $\times$	multiplication sign, times
$\pm$	plus or minus positive or negative
$=$	equals
$\stackrel{?}{=}$	equals?
$\approx$	is approximately equal to
$\neq$	is not equal to
$<$	is less than
$>$	is greater than
$\leq$	is less than or equal to
$\geq$	is greater than or equal to
$\cong$	is congruent to
$\sim$	is similar to
$(\ )$	parentheses for grouping
$[\ ]$	brackets for grouping
$\{\ \}$	braces for a set
$\%$	percent
$|a|$	absolute value of a
$-a$	opposite of a
$a:b; \frac{a}{b}$	ratio of a to b
$\frac{1}{a}, a^{-1}, a \neq 0$	reciprocal of a
a^n	nth power of a
a^{-n}	$\frac{1}{a^n}, a \neq 0$
$\sqrt{a}$	nonnegative square root of a
$\sqrt[n]{a}$	nth root of a (nonnegative if n even)
$°$ as in $a°$	degree(s)
$\circ$ as in $f \circ g$	composition of functions
π	pi, an irrational number, approximately equal to 3.14
e	an irrational number approximately equal to 2.72
i	the imaginary number $\sqrt{-1}$
$a + bi, b \neq 0$	a complex number
∞	infinity
$\sum$	sigma, summation
σ	sigma, standard deviation
σ^2	variance
$\overleftrightarrow{AB}$	line through points A and B
$\overrightarrow{AB}$	vector AB

Symbols	Words
$\overline{AB}$	segment with endpoints A and B
AB	length of $\overline{AB}$; distance between points A and B
$\angle A$	angle A
$m\angle A$	measure of angle A
$\triangle ABC$	triangle ABC
(x, y)	ordered pair
$x_1, x_2, \ldots$	specific values of the variable x
$y_1, y_2, \ldots$	specific values of the variable y
$\bar{x}$	mean of data values x_i
$f(x)$	f of x; the function value at x
f^{-1}	function inverse
$\log$	logarithm
$\ln$	natural logarithm
$\begin{bmatrix} a & b \\ c & d \end{bmatrix}$	matrix
a_{mn}	element in mth row, nth column of matrix A
A^{-1}	inverse of matrix A
$\begin{vmatrix} a & b \\ c & d \end{vmatrix}$	determinant of a matrix
$\det A$	determinant of matrix A
$n!$	n factorial
$_nC_r$	combinations of n things chosen r at a time
$_nP_r$	permutations of n things arranged r at a time
$P(\text{event})$	probability of the event
$P(A|B)$	probability of event A, given event B
$\sin A$	sine of $\angle A$
$\cos A$	cosine of $\angle A$
$\tan A$	tangent of $\angle A$
$\csc A$	cosecant of $\angle A$
$\sec A$	secant of $\angle A$
$\cot A$	cotangent of $\angle A$
$\wedge$	raised to a power (in a spreadsheet formula)
$*$	multiply (in a spreadsheet formula)
$/$	divide (in a spreadsheet formula)
$\ldots$	and so on

Properties and Formulas

Order of Operations
1. Perform any operation(s) inside grouping symbols.
2. Simplify any terms with exponents.
3. Multiply and divide in order from left to right.
4. Add and subtract in order from left to right.

The Pythagorean Theorem
In a right triangle, the sum of the squares of the lengths of the legs is equal to the square of the length of the hypotenuse.

$a^2 + b^2 = c^2$.

The Distance Formula
The distance d between any two points (x_1, y_1) and (x_2, y_2) is $d = \sqrt{(x_2 - x_1)^2 + (y_2 - y_1)^2}$.

The Midpoint Formula
The midpoint M of a line segment with endpoints $A(x_1, y_1)$ and $B(x_2, y_2)$ is $\left(\dfrac{x_1 + x_2}{2}, \dfrac{y_1 + y_2}{2}\right)$.

Chapter 1 Expressions, Equations, and Inequalities

Closure
For all real numbers a and b, $a + b$ and $a \cdot b$ are real numbers.

The Associative Properties
For all real numbers a, b, and c:

$(a + b) + c = a + (b + c)$
$(a \cdot b) \cdot c = a \cdot (b \cdot c)$

The Commutative Properties
For all real numbers a and b:

$a + b = b + a$ and $a \cdot b = b \cdot a$

The Identity Properties
For every real number a:
$a + 0 = a$ and $0 + a = a$ $a \cdot 1 = a$ and $1 \cdot a = a$
0 is the additive identity.   1 is the multiplicative identity.

The Inverse Properties
For every real number a:

$a + (-a) = 0$ and $a \cdot \dfrac{1}{a} = 1$ $(a \neq 0)$

The Distributive Properties
For all real numbers a, b, and c:

$a(b + c) = ab + ac$ $(b + c)a = ba + ca$
$a(b - c) = ab - ac$ $(b - c)a = ba - ca$

Multiplication
Let a represent a real number.
Multiplication by 0: $0 \cdot a = 0$.
Multiplication by -1: $-1 \cdot a = -a$

Opposites
Let a and b represent real numbers.
Opposite of a Sum: $-(a + b) = -a + (-b) = -a - b$
Opposite of a Difference: $-(a - b) = -a + b = b - a$
Opposite of a Product: $-(ab) = -a \cdot b = a \cdot (-b)$
Opposite of an Opposite: $-(-a) = a$

Properties of Equality
Assume a, b, and c represent real numbers.

Reflexive: $a = a$
Symmetric: If $a = b$, then $b = a$.
Transitive: If $a = b$ and $b = c$, then $a = c$.
Substitution: If $a = b$, then you can replace a with b and vice versa.
Addition: If $a = b$, then $a + c = b + c$.
Subtraction: If $a = b$, then $a - c = b - c$.
Multiplication: If $a = b$, then $ac = bc$.
Division: If $a = b$ and $c \neq 0$, then $\dfrac{a}{c} = \dfrac{b}{c}$.

Properties of Inequality
Let a, b, and c represent real numbers.

Transitive: If $a > b$ and $b > c$, then $a > c$.
Addition: If $a > b$, then $a + c > b + c$.
Subtraction: If $a > b$, then $a - c > b - c$.
Multiplication: If $a > b$ and $c > 0$, then $ac > bc$.
                 If $a > b$ and $c < 0$, then $ac < bc$.
Division: If $a > b$ and $c > 0$, then $\dfrac{a}{c} > \dfrac{b}{c}$.
                 If $a > b$ and $c < 0$, then $\dfrac{a}{c} < \dfrac{b}{c}$.

Chapter 2 Functions, Equations, and Graphs

Direct Variation
$y = kx$ or $\dfrac{y}{x} = k$, where $k \neq 0$.

Slope of a Line Containing (x_1, y_1) and (x_2, y_2)
$$\text{slope} = \frac{\text{vertical change (rise)}}{\text{horizontal change (run)}} = \frac{y_2 - y_1}{x_2 - x_1},$$
where $x_2 - x_1 \neq 0$

Point-Slope Equation of a Line
The equation of the line through point (x_1, y_1) with slope m is $y - y_1 = m(x - x_1)$.

Function Families

Assume a, k, and h are positive numbers.

Parent	$y = f(x)$
Reflection across x-axis	$y = -f(x)$

Vertical stretch ($a > 1$)	$y = af(x)$
Vertical shrink ($0 < a < 1$)	

Translation
horizontal to left by h	$y = f(x + h)$
horizontal to right by h	$y = f(x - h)$
vertical up by k	$y = f(x) + k$
vertical down by k	$y = f(x) - k$

Chapter 4 Quadratic Functions and Equations

Quadratic Functions

Parent	$y = x^2$
Reflection across x-axis	$y = -x^2$

Stretch ($a > 1$)	$y = ax^2$
Shrink ($0 < a < 1$)	

Translation
horizontal by h	$y = (x - h)^2 + k$
vertical by k	

Vertex Form	$y = a(x - h)^2 + k$
Standard Form	$y = f(x) = ax^2 + bx + c$

The graph is a parabola that opens up
if $a > 0$ and down if $a < 0$.
The vertex is (h, k) (Vertex Form) and
$\left(-\frac{b}{2a}, f\left(-\frac{b}{2a}\right)\right)$ (Standard Form).
The axis of symmetry is $x = h$ (Vertex Form)
and $x = -\frac{b}{2a}$ (Standard Form).

Factoring Perfect-Square Trinomials

$a^2 + 2ab + b^2 = (a + b)^2$
$a^2 - 2ab + b^2 = (a - b)^2$

Factoring a Difference of Two Squares

$a^2 - b^2 = (a + b)(a - b)$

Multiplication Property of Square Roots

For any numbers $a \geq 0$ and $b \geq 0$, $\sqrt{ab} = \sqrt{a} \cdot \sqrt{b}$.

Division Property of Square Roots

For any numbers $a \geq 0$ and $b > 0$, $\sqrt{\frac{a}{b}} = \frac{\sqrt{a}}{\sqrt{b}}$.

Zero-Product Property

If $ab = 0$, then $a = 0$ or $b = 0$.

The Quadratic Formula

If $ax^2 + bx + c = 0$, then $x = \frac{-b \pm \sqrt{b^2 - 4ac}}{2a}$

Discriminant

The discriminant of a quadratic equation in the form
$ax^2 + bx + c = 0$ is $b^2 - 4ac$.

$b^2 - 4ac > 0 \Rightarrow$ two real solutions
$b^2 - 4ac = 0 \Rightarrow$ one real solution
$b^2 - 4ac < 0 \Rightarrow$ two complex solutions

Square Root of a Negative Real Number

For any positive number a,
$\sqrt{-a} = \sqrt{-1 \cdot a} = \sqrt{-1} \cdot \sqrt{a} = i\sqrt{a}$.
Example: $\sqrt{-5} = i\sqrt{5}$
Note that
$(\sqrt{-5})^2 = (i\sqrt{5})^2 = i^2(\sqrt{5})^2 = -1 \cdot 5 = -5$ (not 5).

Chapter 5 Polynomials and Polynomial Functions

End Behavior of a Polynomial Function

The end behavior of a polynomial function of degree n
with leading term ax^n:

a	n	end behavior
positive	even	up and up
positive	odd	down and up
negative	even	down and down
negative	odd	up and down

Factor Theorem

The expression $x - a$ is a linear factor of a polynomial
if and only if the value a is a zero of the related
polynomial function.

Remainder Theorem

If you divide a polynomial $P(x)$ of degree $n \geq 1$ by $x - a$,
then the remainder is $P(a)$.

Factoring a Sum or Difference of Cubes

$a^3 + b^3 = (a + b)(a^2 - ab + b^2)$
$a^3 - b^3 = (a - b)(a^2 + ab + b^2)$

Rational Root Theorem

Let $P(x) = a_n x^n + a_{n-1} x^{n-1} + \cdots + a_1 x + a_0$ be a
polynomial with integer coefficients.
Integer roots of $P(x) = 0$ must be factors of a_0.
Rational roots have reduced form $\frac{p}{q}$ where p is an
integer factor of a_0 and q is an integer factor of a_n.

Conjugate Root Theorems

Suppose $P(x)$ is a polynomial with *rational* coefficients.
If $a + \sqrt{b}$ is an irrational root with a and b rational, then
$a - \sqrt{b}$ is also a root.

Suppose $P(x)$ is a polynomial with *real* coefficients.
If $a + bi$ is a complex root with a and b real, then $a - bi$ is
also a root.

Fundamental Theorem of Algebra

If $P(x)$ is a polynomial of degree $n \geq 1$, then $P(x) = 0$ has exactly n roots, including multiple and complex roots.

Binomial Theorem

For every positive integer n, $(a + b)^n =$
$P_0 a^n + P_1 a^{n-1} b + P_2 a^{n-2} b^2 + \cdots + P_{n-1} ab^{n-1} + P_n b^n$
where $P_0, P_1, \ldots, P_n$ are the numbers in the nth row of Pascal's Triangle.

Chapter 6 Radical Functions and Rational Exponents

Properties of Exponents

For any nonzero number a and any integers m and n,

$a^0 = 1$ $(ab)^n = a^n b^n$

$\dfrac{a^m}{a^n} = a^{m-n}$ $a^m \cdot a^n = a^{m+n}$

$a^{-n} = \dfrac{1}{a^n}$ $(a^m)^n = a^{mn}$

           $\left(\dfrac{a}{b}\right)^n = \dfrac{a^n}{b^n}$

nth Roots of nth Powers

For any real number a,

$\sqrt[n]{a^n} = \begin{cases} a & \text{if } n \text{ is odd} \\ |a| & \text{if } n \text{ is even} \end{cases}$

Combining Radical Expressions: Products

If $\sqrt[n]{a}$ and $\sqrt[n]{b}$ are real numbers, then $\sqrt[n]{a} \cdot \sqrt[n]{b} = \sqrt[n]{ab}$.

Combining Radical Expressions: Quotients

If $\sqrt[n]{a}$ and $\sqrt[n]{b}$ are real numbers and $b \neq 0$,

then $\dfrac{\sqrt[n]{a}}{\sqrt[n]{b}} = \sqrt[n]{\dfrac{a}{b}}$

Properties of Rational Exponents

If the nth root of a is a real number and m is an integer, then
$a^{\frac{1}{n}} = \sqrt[n]{a}$ and $a^{\frac{m}{n}} = \sqrt[n]{a^m} = \left(\sqrt[n]{a}\right)^m$. If m is negative, $a \neq 0$.

Composition of Inverse Functions

If f and f^{-1} are inverse functions, then
$(f^{-1} \circ f)(x) = x$ and $(f \circ f^{-1})(x) = x$ for x in the domains of f and f^{-1}, respectively.

Radical Functions

	Square Root	nth Root
Parent	$y = \sqrt{x}$	$y = \sqrt[n]{x}$
Reflection across x-axis	$y = -\sqrt{x}$	$y = -\sqrt[n]{x}$
Stretch ($a > 1$) Shrink ($0 < a < 1$)	$y = a\sqrt{x}$	$y = a\sqrt[n]{x}$
Translation horizontal by h vertical by k	$y = \sqrt{x - h} + k$	$y = \sqrt[n]{x - h} + k$

Chapter 7 Exponential and Logarithmic Functions

Exponential Functions

Parent, $b > 0$, $b \neq 1$	$y = b^x$
Reflection across x-axis	$y = -b^x$
Stretch ($a > 1$) Shrink ($0 < a < 1$)	$y = ab^x$
Translation horizontal by h vertical by k	$y = b^{x-h} + k$

Continuously Compounded Interest

$A(t) = P \cdot e^{rt}$, where $A(t)$ represents the total, P represents the principal, r represents the interest rate, and t represents time in years.

Logarithmic Functions

	Base b	Base e
Parents, $b > 0$, $b \neq 1$	$y = \log_b x$	$y = \ln x$
Reflection across x-axis	$y = -\log_b x$	$y = -\ln x$
Stretch ($a > 1$) Shrink ($0 < a < 1$)	$y = a \log_b x$	$y = a \ln x$
Translation horizontal by h vertical by k	$y = \log_b (x - h) + k$	$y = \ln (x - h) + k$

Properties of Logarithms

For any positive numbers m, n, and b where $b \neq 1$
Product Property: $\log_b mn = \log_b m + \log_b n$
Quotient Property: $\log_b \dfrac{m}{n} = \log_b m - \log_b n$
Power Property: $\log_b m^n = n \log_b m$

Change of Base Formula

For any positive numbers, m, b, and c, with
$b \neq 1$ and $c \neq 1$, $\log_b m = \dfrac{\log_c m}{\log_c b}$.

Chapter 8 Rational Functions

Inverse Variation

$xy = k$, $y = \dfrac{k}{x}$, or $x = \dfrac{k}{y}$, where $k \neq 0$.

Combined Variation

z varies jointly with x and y: $z = kxy$
z varies jointly with x and y and inversely with w: $z = \dfrac{kxy}{w}$
z varies directly with x and inversely with the product wy: $z = \dfrac{kx}{wy}$

Reciprocal Functions

Parent	$y = \dfrac{1}{x}$, $x \neq 0$
Reflection across x-axis	$y = -\dfrac{1}{x}$, $x \neq 0$
Stretch ($a > 1$) Shrink ($0 < a < 1$)	$y = \dfrac{a}{x}$, $x \neq 0$
Translation horizontal by h vertical by k	$y = \dfrac{a}{x - h} + k$, $x \neq h$
Asymptotes	$y = k$ (horiz.), $x = h$ (vert.)

Chapter 9 Sequences and Series

Arithmetic Mean of Two Numbers

$\frac{x+y}{2}$

Arithmetic Sequence

A recursive definition for an arithmetic sequence with a starting value a and a common difference d has two parts:

$a_1 = a$: initial condition

$a_{n+1} = a_n + d$, for $n \geq 1$: recursive formula

An explicit definition for this sequence is the formula:

$a_n = a + (n-1)d$ for $n \geq 1$.

Geometric Sequence

A recursive definition for a geometric sequence with a starting value a and a common ratio r has two parts:

$a_1 = a$: initial condition

$a_{n+1} = a_n \cdot r$, for $n \geq 1$: recursive formula

An explicit definition for this sequence is the formula:

$a_n = ar^{n-1}$, for $n \geq 1$.

Sum of a Finite Arithmetic Series

The sum S_n of a finite arithmetic series

$a_1 + a_2 + a_3 + \cdots + a_n$ is $S_n = \frac{n}{2}(a_1 + a_n)$

where a_1 is the first term, a_n is the nth term, and n is the number of terms.

Sum of a Finite Geometric Series

The sum S_n of a finite geometric series

$a_1 + a_1 r + a_1 r^2 + \cdots + a_1 r^{n-1}$ is $S_n = \frac{a_1(1 - r^n)}{1 - r}$

where a_1 is the first term, r is the common ratio, and n is the number of terms.

Sum of an Infinite Geometric Series

An infinite geometric series with $|r| < 1$ converges to the sum S given by the following formula:

$S = \frac{a_1}{1 - r}$.

Chapter 10 Quadratic Relations and Conic Sections

Parabolas

Vertical	Vertex $(0, 0)$	Vertex (h, k)
Equation	$y = \frac{1}{4c} x^2$	$y = \frac{1}{4c}(x - h)^2 + k$
Focus	$(0, c)$	$(h, c + k)$
Directrix	$y = -c$	$y = -c + k$
Horizontal	Vertex $(0, 0)$	Vertex (h, k)
Equation	$x = \frac{1}{4c} y^2$	$x = \frac{1}{4c}(y - k)^2 + h$
Focus	$(c, 0)$	$(c + h, k)$
Directrix	$x = -c$	$x = -c + h$

Circles, radius $= r$

	Center $(0, 0)$	Center (h, k)
Equation	$x^2 + y^2 = r^2$	$(x - h)^2 + (y - k)^2 = r^2$

Ellipses

Horizontal, $a > b$	Center $(0, 0)$	Center (h, k)
Equation	$\frac{x^2}{a^2} + \frac{y^2}{b^2} = 1$	$\frac{(x - h)^2}{a^2} + \frac{(y - k)^2}{b^2} = 1$
Vertices	$(\pm a, 0)$	$(\pm a + h, k)$
Co-Vertices	$(0, \pm b)$	$(h, \pm b + k)$
Foci, $c^2 = a^2 - b^2$	$(\pm c, 0)$	$(\pm c + h, k)$
Major axis	$y = 0$	$y = k$
Minor axis	$x = 0$	$x = h$

Vertical, $a > b$	Center $(0, 0)$	Center (h, k)
Equation	$\frac{x^2}{b^2} + \frac{y^2}{a^2} = 1$	$\frac{(x - h)^2}{b^2} + \frac{(y - k)^2}{a^2} = 1$
Vertices	$(0, \pm a)$	$(h, \pm a + k)$
Co-Vertices	$(\pm b, 0)$	$(\pm b + h, k)$
Foci, $c^2 = a^2 - b^2$	$(0, \pm c)$	$(h, \pm c + k)$
Major axis	$x = 0$	$x = h$
Minor axis	$y = 0$	$y = k$

Hyperbolas

Horizontal, $a > b$	Center $(0, 0)$	Center (h, k)
Equation	$\frac{x^2}{a^2} - \frac{y^2}{b^2} = 1$	$\frac{(x - h)^2}{a^2} - \frac{(y - k)^2}{b^2} = 1$
Vertices	$(\pm a, 0)$	$(\pm a + h, k)$
Foci, $c^2 = a^2 + b^2$	$(\pm c, 0)$	$(\pm c + h, k)$
Transverse axis	$y = 0$	$y = k$
Asymptotes	$y = \pm \frac{b}{a} x$	$y = \pm \frac{b}{a}(x - h) + k$

Vertical, $a > b$	Center $(0, 0)$	Center (h, k)
Equation	$\frac{y^2}{a^2} - \frac{x^2}{b^2} = 1$	$\frac{(y - k)^2}{a^2} - \frac{(x - h)^2}{b^2} = 1$
Vertices	$(0, \pm a)$	$(h, \pm a + k)$
Foci, $c^2 = a^2 + b^2$	$(0, \pm c)$	$(h, \pm c + k)$
Transverse axis	$x = 0$	$x = h$
Asymptotes	$y = \pm \frac{a}{b} x$	$y = \pm \frac{a}{b}(x - h) + k$

Chapter 11 Probability and Statistics

Fundamental Counting Principle
If event M can occur in m ways and is followed by event N that can occur in n ways, then event M followed by event N can occur in $m \cdot n$ ways.

Number of Permutations
The number of permutations of n items of a set arranged r items at a time is

$$_nP_r = \frac{n!}{(n-r)!} \text{ for } 0 \leq r \leq n.$$

Number of Combinations
The number of combinations of n items of a set chosen r items at a time is

$$_nC_r = \frac{n!}{r!(n-r)!} \text{ for } 0 \leq r \leq n.$$

Probability of *A* and *B*
If A and B are independent events, then
$P(A \text{ and } B) = P(A) \cdot P(B)$.

Probability of *A* or *B*
$P(A \text{ or } B) = P(A) + P(B) - P(A \text{ and } B)$
If A and B are mutually exclusive events, then
$P(A \text{ or } B) = P(A) + P(B)$.

Conditional Probability
For any two events A and B with $P(A) \neq 0$, the probability of event B, given event A, is:

$$P(B|A) = \frac{P(A \text{ and } B)}{P(A)}$$

Mean, Variance, and Standard Deviation
Mean: $\bar{x} = \dfrac{x_1 + x_2 + x_3 + \cdots + x_n}{n}$

Variance: $\sigma^2 = \dfrac{\sum(x - \bar{x})^2}{n}$

Standard deviation: $\sigma = \sqrt{\dfrac{\sum(x - \bar{x})^2}{n}}$

Binomial Probability
For repeated independent trials, each with a probability of success p and a probability of failure q (with $p + q = 1$), the probability of x successes in n trials is
$P(x) = {_nC_x}p^x q^{n-x}$.

Binomial Theorem Using Combinations
For every positive integer n, use the combinations formula $_nC_r$ to expand $(a + b)^n$:

$(a + b)^n = {_nC_0}a^n + {_nC_1}a^{n-1}b + {_nC_2}a^{n-2}b^2 +$
$\qquad \cdots + {_nC_{n-1}}ab^{n-1} + {_nC_n}b^n$

Chapter 12 Matrices

Properties of Matrix Addition
If A, B, and C are $m \times n$ matrices, then

Closure Property:	$A + B$ is an $m \times n$ matrix
Commutative Property:	$A + B = B + A$
Associative Property:	$(A + B) + C = A + (B + C)$
Identity Property:	There is a unique $m \times n$ matrix O such that $O + A = A + O = A$
Inverse Property:	For each A, there is a unique opposite, $-A$, such that $A + (-A) = O$

Properties of Scalar Multiplication
If A and B are $m \times n$ matrices, c and d are scalars, and O is the $m \times n$ zero matrix, then

Closure Property:	cA is an $m \times n$ matrix
Associative Property:	$(cd)A = c(dA)$
Distributive Property:	$c(A + B) = cA + cB$ $(c + d)A = cA + dA$
Identity Property:	$1 \cdot A = A$
Property of Zero:	$0 \cdot A = O$ and $cO = O$

Properties of Matrix Multiplication
If A, B, and C are $n \times n$ matrices and O is the $n \times n$ zero matrix, then

Closure Property:	AB is an $n \times n$ matrix
Associative Property:	$(AB)C = A(BC)$
Distributive Property:	$A(B + C) = AB + AC$ $(B + C)A = BA + CA$
Property of Zero:	$OA = AO = O$

Determinants of 2 × 2 and 3 × 3 Matrices
The determinant of a 2×2 matrix $\begin{bmatrix} a & b \\ c & d \end{bmatrix}$ is $ad - bc$.

The determinant of a 3×3 matrix $\begin{bmatrix} a_1 & b_1 & c_1 \\ a_2 & b_2 & c_2 \\ a_3 & b_3 & c_3 \end{bmatrix}$ is

$a_1 b_2 c_3 + b_1 c_2 a_3 + c_1 a_2 b_3 - (a_3 b_2 c_1 + b_3 c_2 a_1 + c_3 a_2 b_1)$

Inverse of a 2 × 2 Matrix
If $A = \begin{bmatrix} a & b \\ c & d \end{bmatrix}$ and $\det A \neq 0$,

then the inverse of A is

$$A^{-1} = \frac{1}{\det A}\begin{bmatrix} d & -b \\ -c & a \end{bmatrix} = \frac{1}{ad - bc}\begin{bmatrix} d & -b \\ -c & a \end{bmatrix}.$$

Chapter 13 Periodic Functions and Trigonometry

Convert Between Radians and Degrees
Use the proportion $\frac{d°}{180°} = \frac{r \text{ radians}}{\pi \text{ radians}}$ to convert between radians and degrees.

To convert degrees to radians, multiply by $\frac{\pi \text{ radians}}{180°}$.

To convert radians to degrees, multiply by $\frac{180°}{\pi \text{ radians}}$.

Length of an Intercepted Arc
For a circle of radius r and a central angle of measure θ (in radians), the length s of the intercepted arc is $s = r\theta$.

Sine and Cosine Functions

	Sine	Cosine
Parents	$y = \sin x$	$y = \cos x$
Reflection across x-axis	$y = -\sin x$	$y = -\cos x$
Amplitude $\lvert a \rvert$	$y = a \sin x$	$y = a \cos x$
Period $\frac{2\pi}{b}$, $b > 0$	$y = \sin bx$	$y = \cos bx$
Translation horizontal by h vertical by k	$y = \sin(x - h) + k$	$y = \cos(x - h) + k$

Tangent Function

Parent	$y = \tan x$
Reflection across x-axis	$y = -\tan x$
Period $\frac{\pi}{b}$	$y = \tan bx$
Translation horizontal by h vertical by k	$y = \tan(x - h) + k$
Asymptotes ($\tan bx$)	$x = n\frac{\pi}{2b}$, n odd

Chapter 14 Trigonometric Identities and Equations

Basic Identities
Reciprocal Identities:

$\csc\theta = \frac{1}{\sin\theta}$ $\sec\theta = \frac{1}{\cos\theta}$ $\tan\theta = \frac{1}{\cot\theta}$

$\sin\theta = \frac{1}{\csc\theta}$ $\cos\theta = \frac{1}{\sec\theta}$ $\cot\theta = \frac{1}{\tan\theta}$

Tangent Identity:

$\tan\theta = \frac{\sin\theta}{\cos\theta}$

Cotangent Identity:

$\cot\theta = \frac{\cos\theta}{\sin\theta}$

Pythagorean Identities
$\cos^2\theta + \sin^2\theta = 1$ $1 + \tan^2\theta = \sec^2\theta$ $\cot^2\theta + 1 = \csc^2\theta$

Area of a Triangle
In $\triangle ABC$ with a, b, and c the lengths of the sides opposite $\angle A$, $\angle B$, and $\angle C$, respectively,

Area $\triangle ABC = \frac{1}{2}bc \sin A = \frac{1}{2}ac \sin B = \frac{1}{2}ab \sin C$.

Law of Sines
In $\triangle ABC$ with a, b, and c the lengths of the sides opposite $\angle A$, $\angle B$, and $\angle C$, respectively,

$\frac{\sin A}{a} = \frac{\sin B}{b} = \frac{\sin C}{c}$.

Law of Cosines
In $\triangle ABC$ with a, b, and c the lengths of the sides opposite $\angle A$, $\angle B$, and $\angle C$, respectively,

$a^2 = b^2 + c^2 - 2bc \cdot \cos A$
$b^2 = a^2 + c^2 - 2ac \cdot \cos B$
$c^2 = a^2 + b^2 - 2ab \cdot \cos C$

Negative Angle Identities
$\sin(-\theta) = -\sin\theta$ $\cos(-\theta) = \cos\theta$ $\tan(-\theta) = -\tan\theta$

Cofunction Angle Identities
$\sin\left(\frac{\pi}{2} - \theta\right) = \cos\theta$ $\cos\left(\frac{\pi}{2} - \theta\right) = \sin\theta$ $\tan\left(\frac{\pi}{2} - \theta\right) = \cot\theta$

Angle Difference Identities
$\sin(A - B) = \sin A \cos B - \cos A \sin B$
$\cos(A - B) = \cos A \cos B + \sin A \sin B$
$\tan(A - B) = \frac{\tan A - \tan B}{1 - \tan A \tan B}$

Angle Sum Identities
$\sin(A + B) = \sin A \cos B + \cos A \sin B$
$\cos(A + B) = \cos A \cos B - \sin A \sin B$
$\tan(A + B) = \frac{\tan A + \tan B}{1 - \tan A \tan B}$

Double-Angle Identities
$\cos 2\theta = \cos^2\theta - \sin^2\theta$ $\sin 2\theta = 2\sin\theta\cos\theta$

$\cos 2\theta = 2\cos^2\theta - 1$ $\tan 2\theta = \frac{2\tan\theta}{1 - \tan^2\theta}$

$\cos 2\theta = 1 - 2\sin^2\theta$

Half-Angle Identities

$\sin\frac{A}{2} = \pm\sqrt{\frac{1 - \cos A}{2}}$

$\cos\frac{A}{2} = \pm\sqrt{\frac{1 + \cos A}{2}}$

$\tan\frac{A}{2} = \pm\sqrt{\frac{1 - \cos A}{1 + \cos A}}$

Formulas of **Geometry**

You will use a number of geometric formulas as you work through your algebra book. Here are some perimeter, area, and volume formulas.

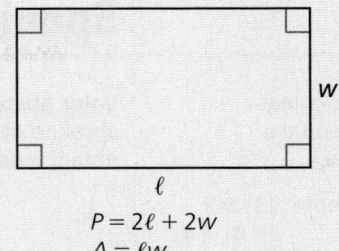

$P = 2\ell + 2w$
$A = \ell w$

Rectangle

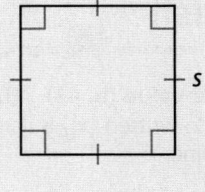

$P = 4s$
$A = s^2$

Square

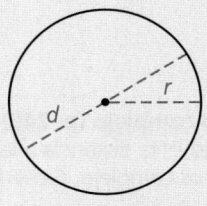

$C = 2\pi r$ or $C = \pi d$
$A = \pi r^2$

Circle

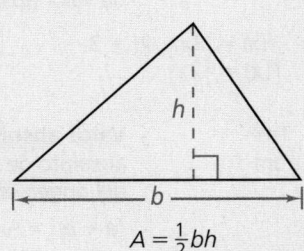

$A = \frac{1}{2}bh$

Triangle

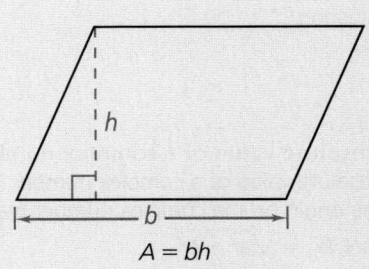

$A = bh$

Parallelogram

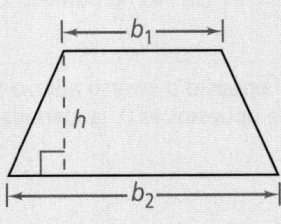

$A = \frac{1}{2}(b_1 + b_2)h$

Trapezoid

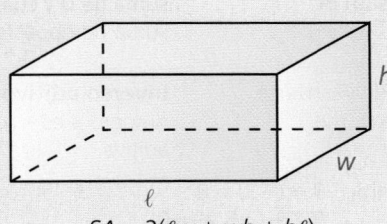

$SA = 2(\ell w + wh + h\ell)$
$V = Bh$
$V = \ell wh$

Right Prism

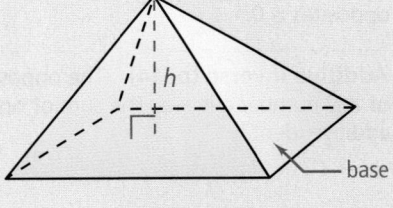

$V = \frac{1}{3}Bh$

Pyramid

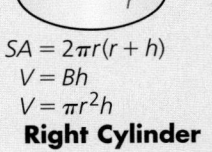

$SA = 2\pi r(r + h)$
$V = Bh$
$V = \pi r^2 h$

Right Cylinder

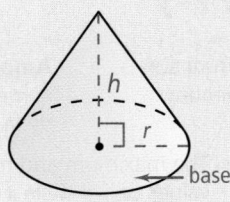

$V = \frac{1}{3}Bh$
$V = \frac{1}{3}\pi r^2 h$

Right Cone

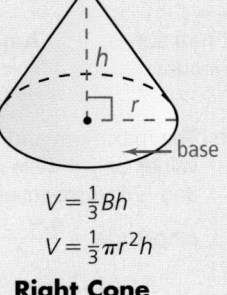

$SA = 4\pi r^2$
$V = \frac{4}{3}\pi r^3$

Sphere

English/Spanish Illustrated **Glossary**

English

Spanish

A

Absolute value (p. 41) The absolute value of a real number, x, written $|x|$, is its distance from zero on the number line.

Valor absoluto de un número real (p. 41) El valor absoluto de un número real, x, escrito como $|x|$, es su distancia desde cero en la recta numérica.

Example $|3| = 3$
$|-4| = 4$

Absolute value function (p. 107) A function of the form $f(x) = |mx + b| + c$, where $m \neq 0$, is an absolute value function.

Función de valor absolute (p. 107) Una función de la forma $f(x) = |mx + b| + c$, donde $m \neq 0$, es una función de valor absoluto.

Example $f(x) = |3x - 2| + 3$
$f(x) = |2x|$

Absolute value of a complex number (p. 249) The absolute value of a complex number is its distance from the origin on the complex number plane. In general, $|a + bi| = \sqrt{a^2 + b^2}$.

Valor absoluto de un número complejo (p. 249) El valor absoluto de un número complejo es la distancia a la que está del origen en el plano de números complejo. Generalmente, $|a + bi| = \sqrt{a^2 + b^2}$.

Example $|3 - 4i| = \sqrt{3^2 + (-4)^2} = 5$

Additive identity (p. 14) The additive identity is 0. The sum of 0 and any number is that number. The sum of opposites is 0.

Identidad aditiva (p. 14) La identidad aditiva es 0. La suma de 0 y cualquier número es ese mismo número. La suma de opuestos es 0.

Additive inverse (p. 14) The opposite or additive inverse of any number a is $-a$. The sum of opposites is 0, the additive identity.

Inverso aditivo (p. 14) El opuesto o inverso aditivo de un número a es $-a$. La suma de opuestos es 0, la identidad aditiva.

Example $3 + (-3) = 0$
$5.2 + (-5.2) = 0$

Algebraic expression (p. 5) An algebraic expression is a mathematical phrase that contains one or more variables.

Expresión algebraica (p. 5) Una expresión algebraica es una frase matemática que contiene una o más variables.

Example $2x + 3$
$z - y$

Amplitude (p. 830) The amplitude of a periodic function is half the difference between the maximum and minimum values of the function.

Amplitud (p. 830) La amplitud de una función periódica es la mitad de la diferencia entre los valores máximo y mínimo de la función.

Example The maximum and minimum values of $y = 4 \sin x$ are 4 and -4, respectively.
amplitude $= \dfrac{4 - (-4)}{2} = 4$

English

Arithmetic mean (p. 574) The arithmetic mean, or average, of two numbers is their sum divided by two.

Example The arithmetic mean of 12 and 15 is $\dfrac{12 + 15}{2} = 13.5$.

Arithmetic sequence (p. 572) An arithmetic sequence is a sequence with a constant difference between consecutive terms.

Example The arithmetic sequence 1, 5, 9, 13, . . . has a common difference of 4.

Arithmetic series (p. 587) An arithmetic series is a series whose terms form an arithmetic sequence.

Example $1 + 5 + 9 + 13 + 17 + 21$ is an arithmetic series with six terms.

Asymptote (p. 435) An asymptote is a line that a graph approaches as x or y increases in absolute value.

Example The function $y = \dfrac{x + 2}{x - 2}$ has $x = 2$ as a vertical asymptote and $y = 1$ as a horizontal asymptote.

Axis of symmetry (pp. 107,194) The axis of symmetry is the line that divides a figure into two parts that are mirror images.

Example

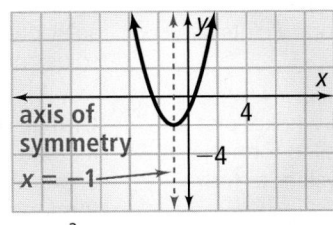

$y = x^2 + 2x - 1$

Spanish

Media aritmética (p. 574) La media aritmética, o promedio, de dos números es su suma dividida por dos.

Secuencia aritmética (p. 572) Una secuencia aritmética es una secuencia de números en la que la diferencia entre dos números consecutivos es constante.

Serie aritmética (p. 587) Una serie aritmética es una serie cuyos términos forman una progresión aritmética.

Asíntota (p. 435) Una asíntota es una recta a la cual se acerca una gráfica a medida que x o y aumentan de valor absoluto.

Eje de simetría (pp. 107,194) El eje de simetría es la recta que divide una figura en dos partes que son imágenes una de la otra.

B

Bias (p. 726) A bias is a systematic error introduced by the sampling method.

Bimodal (p. 712) A bimodal data set has two modes.

Example {1, 2, 3, 3, 4, 5, 6, 6} mode = 3 and 6

Sesgo (p. 726) El sesgo es un error sistemático introducido por medio del método de muestreo.

Bimodal (p. 712) Un conjunto bimodal de datos tiene dos modas.

English

Spanish

Binomial experiment (p. 731) A binomial experiment is one in which the situation involves repeated trials. Each trial has two possible outcomes (success or failure), and the probability of success is constant throughout the trials.

Experimento binomial (p. 731) Un experimento binomial es un experimento que requiere varios ensayos. Cada ensayo tiene dos resultados posibles (éxito o fracaso), y la probabilidad de éxito es constante durante todos los ensayos.

Binomial probability (p. 732) In a binomial experiment with probability of success p and probability of failure q, the probability of x successes in n trials is given by $_nC_x p^x q^{n-x}$.

Probabilidad binomial (p. 732) En un experimento binomial con una probabilidad de éxito p y una probabilidad de fracaso q, la probabilidad de x éxitos en n ensayos se expresa con $_nC_x p^x q^{n-x}$.

Example Suppose you roll a standard number cube and that you call rolling a 1 a success. Then $p = \frac{1}{6}$ and $q = \frac{5}{6}$. The probability of rolling nine 1's in twenty rolls is $_{20}C_9 \left(\frac{1}{6}\right)^9 \left(\frac{5}{6}\right)^{11} \approx 0.0022$.

Binomial Theorem (pp. 327, 733) For every positive integer n, $(a + b)^n = P_0 a^n + P_1 a^{n-1}b + P_2 a^{n-2}b^2 + \cdots + P_{n-1}ab^{n-1} + P_n b^n$ where $P_0, P_1, \ldots, P_n$ are the numbers in the row of Pascal's Triangle that has n as its second number.

Teorema binomial (pp. 327, 733) Para cada número entero positivo n, $(a + b)^n = P_0 a^n + P_1 a^{n-1}b + P_2 a^{n-2}b^2 + \cdots + P_{n-1}ab^{n-1} + P_n b^n$, donde $P_0, P_1, \ldots, P_n$ son los números de la fila del Triángulo de Pascal cuyo segundo número es n.

Example $(x + 1)^3 = {}_3C_0(x)^3 + {}_3C_1(x)^2(1)^1 + {}_3C_2(x)^1(1)^2 + {}_3C_3(1)^3 = x^3 + 3x^2 + 3x + 1$

Boundary (p. 114) A boundary of the graph of a linear inequality is a line in the coordinate plane. It separates the solutions of the inequality from the nonsolutions. Points of the line itself may or may not be solutions.

Límite (p. 114) Un límite de la gráfica de una desigualdad lineal es una línea en el plano de coordenadas. Ésta separa las soluciones de la desigualdad de las no soluciones. Las soluciones pueden ser o no puntos de la línea.

Box-and-whisker plot (p. 714) A box-and-whisker plot is a method of displaying data that uses quartiles to form the center box and the maximum and minimum values to form the whiskers.

Gráfica de cajas (p. 714) Una gráfica de cajas es un método para mostrar datos que utiliza cuartiles para formar una casilla central y los valores máximos y mínimos para formar los conectores.

Example

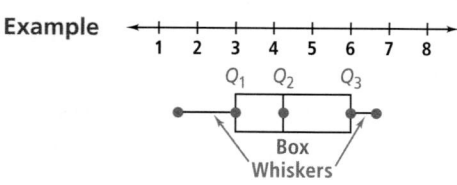

Branch (p. 508) Each piece of a discontinuous graph is called a branch.

Rama (p. 508) Cada segmento de una gráfica discontinua se llama rama.

Example

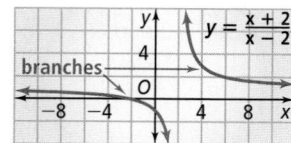

English

Center of a circle (p. 630) The center of a circle is the point that is the same distance from every point on the circle.

Center of an ellipse (p. 639) The center of an ellipse is the midpoint of the major axis.

Center of rotation (p. 804) A center of rotation is the fixed point of a rotation.

Example

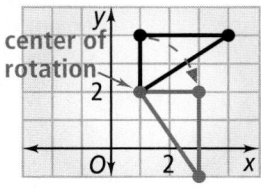

Central angle (p. 844) A central angle of a circle is an angle whose vertex is at the center of a circle.

Example

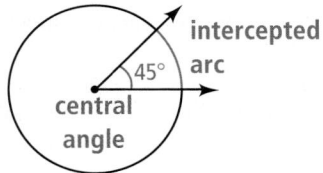

Change of Base Formula (p. 464) $\log_b M = \frac{\log_c M}{\log_c b}$, where M, b, and c are positive numbers, and $b \neq 1$ and $c \neq 1$.

Example $\log_3 8 = \frac{\log 8}{\log 3} \approx 1.8928$

Circle (p. 630) A circle is the set of all points in a plane at a distance r from a given point. The standard form of the equation of a circle with center (h, k) and radius r is $(x - h)^2 + (y - k)^2 = r^2$.

Example

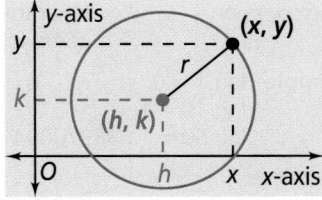

Coefficient (p. 20) The numerical factor in a term.

Example The coefficient of $-3k$ is -3.

Spanish

Centro de un círculo (p. 630) El centro de un círculo es el punto que está situado a la misma distancia de cada punto del círculo.

Centro de una elipse (p. 639) El centro de una elipse es el punto medio entre los dos ejes mayores.

Centro de rotación (p. 804) Un centro de rotación es el punto fijo de una rotación.

Ángulo central (p. 844) El ángulo central de un círculo es un ángulo cuyo vértice está situado en el centro del círculo.

Fórmula de cambio de base (p. 464) $\log_b M = \frac{\log_c M}{\log_c b}$, donde M, b y c son números positivos y $b \neq 1$ y $c \neq 1$.

Círculo (p. 630) Un círculo es el cojunto de todos los puntos situados en un plano a una distancia r de un punto dado. La forma normal de la ecuación cuyo centro es (h, k) y cuyo radio es r es $(x - h)^2 + (y - k)^2 = r^2$.

Coeficiente (p. 20) El factor numérico de un término.

English

Spanish

Coefficient matrix (p. 793) When representing a system of equations with a matrix equation, the matrix containing the coefficients of the system is the coefficient matrix.

Matriz de coeficientes (p. 793) Al representar un sistema de ecuaciones con una ecuación de matriz, la matriz que contiene los coeficientes del sistema es la matriz de coeficientes.

Example
$$\begin{cases} x + 2y = 5 \\ 3x + 5y = 14 \end{cases}$$

coefficient matrix $\begin{bmatrix} 1 & 2 \\ 3 & 5 \end{bmatrix}$

Combination (p. 676) Any unordered selection of r objects from a set of n objects is a combination. The number of combinations of n objects taken r at a time is

$$_nC_r = \frac{n!}{r!(n-r)!} \text{ for } 0 \le r \le n.$$

Combinación (p. 676) Cualquier selección no ordenada de r objetos tomados de un conjunto de n objetos es una combinación. El número de combinaciones de n objetos, cuando se toman r objetos cada vez, es

$$_nC_r = \frac{n!}{r!(n-r)!} \text{ para } 0 \le r \le n.$$

Example The number of combinations of seven items taken four at a time is

$$_7C_4 = \frac{7!}{4!(7-4)!} = 35.$$

There are 35 ways to choose four items from seven items without regard to order.

Combined variation (p. 501) A combined variation is a relation in which one variable varies with respect to each of two or more variables.

Variación combinada (p. 501) Una variación combinada es una relación en la que una variable varía con respecto a cada una de dos o más variables.

Example $y = kx^2 \sqrt{z}$

$z = \frac{kx}{y}$

Common difference (p. 572) A common difference is the difference between consecutive terms of an arithmetic sequence.

Diferencia común (p. 572) La diferencia común es la diferencia entre los términos consecutivos de una progresión aritmética.

Example The arithmetic sequence 1, 5, 9, 13, . . . has a common difference of 4.

Common logarithm (p. 453) A common logarithm is a logarithm that uses base 10. You can write the common logarithm $\log_{10} y$ as $\log y$.

Logaritmo común (p. 453) El logaritmo común es un logaritmo de base 10. El logaritmo común $\log_{10} y$ se expresa como $\log y$.

Example $\log 1 = 0$
$\log 10 = 1$
$\log 50 = 1.698970004 \ldots$

Common ratio (p. 580) A common ratio is the ratio of consecutive terms of a geometric sequence.

Razón común (p. 580) Una razón común es la razón de términos consecutivos en una secuencia geométrica.

Example The geometric sequence 2.5, 5, 10, 20, . . . has a common ratio of 2.

Visual **Glossary**

English

Spanish

Conic section (p. 614)   A conic section is a curve formed by the intersection of a plane and a double cone.

Sección cónica (p. 614)   Una sección cónica es una curva que se forma por la intersección de un plano con un cono doble.

Example

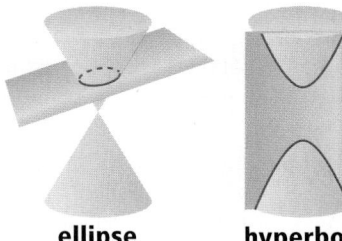

ellipse   **hyperbola**

Conjugate axis (p. 646)   The conjugate axis for the hyperbola $\frac{x^2}{a^2} - \frac{y^2}{b^2} = 1$, $a > b > 0$, is the segment from $(0, -b)$ to $(0, b)$. For $\frac{y^2}{a^2} - \frac{x^2}{b^2} = 1$, the conjugate axis is the segment from $(-b, 0)$ to $(b, 0)$.

Eje conjugado (p. 646)   El eje conjugado de la hipérbola $\frac{x^2}{a^2} - \frac{y^2}{b^2} = 1$, $a > b > 0$, es el segmento desde el punto $(0, -b)$ hasta el punto $(0, b)$. Para $\frac{y^2}{a^2} - \frac{x^2}{b^2} = 1$, el eje conjugado es el segmento desde el punto $(-b, 0)$ hasta el punto $(b, 0)$.

Conjugate Root Theorem (p. 314)   If $P(x)$ is a polynomial with rational coefficients, then the irrational roots of $P(x) = 0$ occur in conjugate pairs. That is, if $a + \sqrt{b}$ is an irrational root with a and b rational, then $a - \sqrt{b}$ is also a root. If $P(x)$ is a polynomial with real coefficients, then the complex roots of $P(x) = 0$ occur in conjugate pairs. That is, if $a + bi$ is a complex root with a and b real, then $a - bi$ is also a root.

Teorema de raíces conjugadas (p. 314)   Si $P(x)$ es un polinomio con coeficientes racionales, entonces las raíces irracionales de $P(x) = 0$ ocurren en pares conjugados. Es decir, si $a + \sqrt{b}$ es una raíz irracional donde a y b son racionales, entonces $a - \sqrt{b}$ también es una raíz. Si $P(x)$ es un polinomio con coeficientes reales, entonces las raíces complejas de $P(x) = 0$ ocurren en los pares conjugados. Es decir, si $a + bi$ es una raíz compleja donde a y b son reales, entonces $a - bi$ también es una raíz.

Conjugates (p. 314)   Number pairs of the form $a + \sqrt{b}$ and $a - \sqrt{b}$ are conjugates.

Conjugados (p. 314)   Los pares de números con la forma $a + \sqrt{b}$ y $a - \sqrt{b}$ son conjugados.

Example $5 + \sqrt{3}$ and $5 - \sqrt{3}$ are conjugates.

Consistent system (p. 137)   A system of linear equations is consistent if it has at least one solution.

Sistema consistente (p. 137)   Un sistema de ecuaciones lineales es consistente si tiene por lo menos una solución.

Constant (p. 5)   A constant is a quantity whose value does not change.

Constante (p. 5)   Una constante es una cantidad cuyo valor no cambia.

Constant matrix (p. 793)   When representing a system of equations with a matrix equation, the matrix containing the constants of the system is the constant matrix.

Matriz de constantes (p. 793)   Al representar un sistema de ecuaciones con una ecuación matricial, la matriz que contiene las constantes del sistema es la matriz de constantes.

Example $\begin{cases} x + 2y = 5 \\ 3x + 5y = 14 \end{cases}$

constant matrix $\begin{bmatrix} 5 \\ 14 \end{bmatrix}$

Constant of proportionality (p. 341) If $y = ax^b$ describes y as a power function of x, then y varies directly with, or is proportional to, the bth power of x. The constant a is the constant of proportionality.

Constante de proporcionalidad (p. 341) Si $y = ax^b$ describe a y como una potencia de la función de x, entonces y varía directamente con, o es proporcional a, la b^{ma} potencia de x. La constante a es la constante de proporcionalidad.

Constant of variation (p. 68) The constant of variation is the ratio of the two variables in a direct variation and the product of the two variables in an inverse variation.

Constante de variación (p. 68) La constante de variación es la razón de dos variables en una variación directa y el producto de las dos variables en una variación inversa.

Example In $y = 3.5x$, the constant of variation k is 3.5. In $xy = 5$, the constant of variation k is 5.

Constant term (p. 20) A constant term is a term with no variables.

Término constante (p. 20) Un término constante es un término que no tiene variables.

Constraint (p. 157) Constraints are restrictions on the variables of the objective function in a linear programming problem. *See* **Linear programming.**

Restriccion (p. 157) Las restricciones son limitaciones a las variables de una función objetiva en un problema de programación lineal. *Ver* **Linear programming.**

Continuous graph (p. 516) A graph is continuous if it has no jumps, breaks, or holes.

Gráfica continua (p. 516) Una gráfica es continua si no tiene saltos, interrupciones o huecos.

Continuous probability distribution (p. 739) A continuous probability distribution has as its events any of the infinitely many values in an interval of real numbers.

Distribución de probabilidad continua (p. 739) Una distribución de probabilidad continua tiene como sucesos a cualquiera del número infinito de valores en un intervalo de números reales.

Continuously compounded interest (p. 446) When interest is compounded continuously on principal P, the value A of an account is $A = Pe^{rt}$.

Interés compuesto continuo (p. 446) En un sistema donde el interés es compuesto continuamente sobre el capital P, el valor de A de una cuenta es $A = Pe^{rt}$.

Example Suppose that $P = \$1200$, $r = 0.05$, and $t = 3$. Then
$$A = 1200e^{0.05 \cdot 3}$$
$$= 1200(2.718 \ldots)^{0.15}$$
$$\approx 1394.20$$

Controlled experiment (p. 726) In a controlled experiment, you divide the sample into two groups. You impose a treatment on one group but not the other "control" group. Then you compare the effect on the treated group to the control group.

Experimento controlado (p. 726) En un experimento controlado, se divide la muestra en dos grupos. Uno de los grupos se manipula y el otro grupo "controlado" se mantiene en su estado original. Luego se comparan el estado del grupo manipulado y el estado del grupo controlado.

Convenience sample (p. 725) In a convenience sample you select any members of the population who are conveniently and readily available.

Muestra de conveniencia (p. 725) En una muestra de conveniencia se selecciona a cualquier miembro de la población que está convenientemente disponible.

Visual Glossary

English

Converge (p. 598)   An infinite series
$a_1 + a_2 + \cdots + a_n + \cdots$ converges if the sum
$a_1 + a_2 + \cdots + a_n$ gets closer and closer to a real number
as n increases.

Example $1 + \frac{1}{2} + \frac{1}{4} + \frac{1}{8} + \cdots$ converges.

Coordinate space (p. 164)   Coordinate space is a three-dimensional space where each point is described uniquely using an ordered triple of numbers.

Example

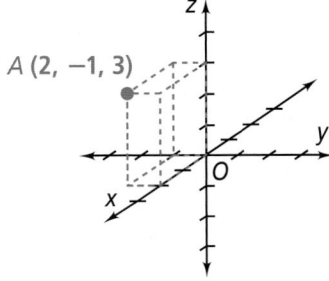

$A\ (2,\ -1,\ 3)$

Correlation (p. 92)   A correlation indicates the strength of a relationship between two data sets.

Correlation coefficient (p. 94)   The correlation coefficient, r, indicates the strength of the correlation. The closer r is to 1 or -1, the more closely the data resembles a line and the more accurate your model is likely to be.

Corresponding elements (p. 764)   Corresponding elements are elements in the same position in each matrix.

Cosecant function (p. 883)   The cosecant (csc) function is the reciprocal of the sine function. For all real numbers θ
except those that make $\sin \theta = 0$, $\csc \theta = \frac{1}{\sin \theta}$.

Example   If $\sin \theta = \frac{5}{13}$, then $\csc \theta = \frac{13}{5}$.

Spanish

Convergir (p. 598)   Una serie infinita
$a_1 + a_2 + \cdots + a_n + \cdots$ es convergente si la suma
$a_1 + a_2 + \cdots + a_n$ se aproxima cada vez más a un número
real a medida que el valor de n incrementa.

Espacio de coordenadas (p. 164)   Un espacio de coordenadas es un espacio tridimensional en el cual cada punto es definido de manera única por una tripleta ordenada de números.

Correlación (p. 92)   Una correlación indica la fuerza de una relación entre dos conjuntos de datos.

Coeficiente de correlación (p. 94)   El coeficiente de correlación, r, indica la fuerza de la correlación. Mientras más cerca está r de 1 ó -1, más se parecen los datos a una línea y será más probable que tu modelo sea preciso.

Elementos correspondientes (p. 764)   Los elementos correspondientes son elementos que se encuentran en la misma posición de cada matriz.

Función cosecante (p. 883)   La función cosecante (csc) se define como el recíproco de la función seno. Para todos los números reales θ, excepto aquéllos para los que $\sin \theta = 0$,
$\csc \theta = \frac{1}{\sin \theta}$.

English

Spanish

Cosine function, Cosine of θ (pp. 838, 861) The cosine function, $y = \cos \theta$, matches the measure θ of an angle in standard position with the x-coordinate of a point on the unit circle. This point is where the terminal side of the angle intersects the unit circle. The x-coordinate is the cosine of θ.

Función coseno, Coseno de θ (pp. 838, 861) La función coseno, $y = \cos \theta$, empareja la medida θ de un ángulo en posición estándar con la coordenada x de un punto en el círculo unitario. Este es el punto en el que el lado terminal del ángulo interseca al círculo unitario. La coordenada x es el coseno de θ.

Example

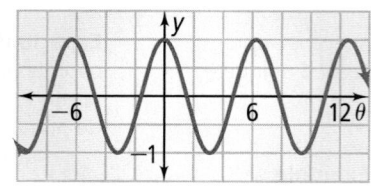
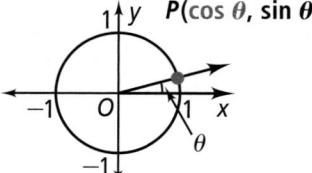

Cotangent function (p. 883) The cotangent (cot) function is the reciprocal of the tangent function. For all real numbers θ except those that make $\tan \theta = 0$, $\cot \theta = \frac{1}{\tan \theta}$.

Función cotangente (p. 883) La función cotangente (cot) es el recíproco de la función tangente. Para todos los números reales θ, excepto aquéllos para los que $\tan \theta = 0$, $\cot \theta = \frac{1}{\tan \theta}$.

Example If $\tan \theta = \frac{5}{12}$, then $\cot \theta = \frac{12}{5}$.

Coterminal angle (p. 837) Two angles in standard position are coterminal if they have the same terminal side.

Ángulo coterminal (p. 827) Dos ángulos que están en posición normal son coterminales si tienen el mismo lado terminal.

Example

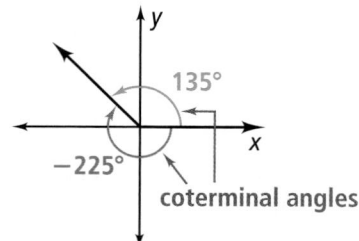

Angles that have measures 135° and −225° are coterminal.

Co-vertices (p. 639) The endpoints of the minor axis of an ellipse are the co-vertices of the ellipse.

Covértices (p. 639) Los puntos de intersección entre una elipse y los ejes menores son los covértices de la elipse.

Example

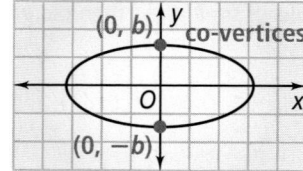

Cumulative probability (p. 695) Probability over a continuous range of events is cumulative probability.

Probabilidad acumulativa (p. 695) La probabilidad que existe a lo largo de una serie continua de sucesos es la probabilidad acumulativa.

English

Cycle (p. 828) A cycle of a periodic function is an interval of x-values over which the function provides one complete pattern of y-values.

Spanish

Ciclo (p. 828) El ciclo de una función periódica es un intervalo de valores de x de los cuales la función produce un patrón completo de valores de y.

Example

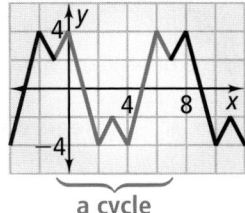

a cycle

D

Decay factor (p. 436) In an exponential function of the form $y = ab^x$, b is the decay factor if $0 < b < 1$.

Factor de decremento (p. 436) En una función exponencial de la forma $y = ab^x$, b es el factor de decremento si, $0 < b < 1$.

Example In the equation $y = 0.3^x$, 0.7 is the decay factor.

Degree of a monomial (p. 280) The degree of a monomial in one variable is the exponent of the variable.

Grado de un monomio (p. 280) El grado de un monomio en una variable es el exponente de la variable.

Degree of a polynomial (p. 280) The degree of a polynomial is the greatest degree among its monomial terms.

Grado de un polinomio (p. 280) El grado de un polinomio es el grado mayor entre los términos de monomios.

Example $P(x) = x^6 + 2x^3 - 3$ degree 6

Dependent events (p. 688) Two events are dependent if the occurrence of one event affects the probability of the second event.

Sucesos dependientes (p. 688) Cuando el resultado de un suceso influye en la probabilidad de que ocurra el segundo suceso, los dos sucesos son dependientes.

Example You have a bag with red and blue marbles. You draw one marble at random and then another without replacing the first. The colors drawn are dependent events. A red marble on the first draw changes the probability for each color on the second draw.

Dependent system (p. 137) A system of equations that does not have a unique solution is a dependent system.

Sistema dependiente (p. 137) Un sistema de ecuaciones es dependiente cuando no tiene una solución única.

Example $\begin{cases} y = 2x + 3 \\ -4x + 2y = 6 \end{cases}$ represents two equations for the same line, so it has many solutions. It is a dependent system.

English

Dependent variable (p. 63)   If a function is defined by an equation using the variables x and y, where y represents output values, then y is the dependent variable.

Spanish

Variable dependiente (p. 63)   Si una función es definida por una ecuación que usa las variables x e y, donde y representa valores de salida, entonces y es la variable dependiente.

Example $y = 2x + 1$
y is the dependent variable.

Descartes' Rule of Signs (p. 315)   Let $P(x)$ be a polynomial with real coefficients written in standard form.
– The number of positive real roots of $P(x) = 0$ is either equal to the number of sign changes between consecutive coefficients of $P(x)$ or is less than that by an even number;
– The number of negative real roots of $P(x) = 0$ is either equal to the number of sign changes between consecutive coefficients of $P(-x)$ or is less than that by an even number. (Count multiple roots according to their multiplicity.)

Regla de los signos de Descartes (p. 315)   Sea $P(x)$ un polinomio con coeficientes reales escritos en forma normal.
– El número de raíces positivas reales de $P(x) = 0$ es igual al número de cambios de signos entre coeficientes consecutivos de $P(-x)$ o es menor que eso en un número par;
– El número de raíces negativas reales de $P(x) = 0$ es igual al número de cambios de signos entre coeficientes consecutivos de $P(-x)$ o es menor que eso en un número par. (Cuenta las raíces múltiples según su multiplicidad).

Determinant (p. 784)   The determinant of a square matrix is a real number that can be computed from its elements according to a specific formula.

Determinante (p. 784)   El determinante de una matriz cuadrada es un número real que se puede calcular a partir de sus elementos por medio de una fórmula específica.

Example   The determinant of $\begin{bmatrix} 3 & -2 \\ 5 & 6 \end{bmatrix}$ is
$3(6) - 5(-2) = 28$.

Difference of cubes (p. 297)   A difference of cubes is an expression of the form $a^3 - b^3$. It can be factored as $(a - b)(a^2 + ab + b^2)$.

Diferencia de dos cubos (p. 297)   La diferencia de dos cubos es una expresión de la forma $a^3 - b^3$. Se puede factorizar como $(a - b)(a^2 + ab + b^2)$.

Example $x^3 - 27 = (x - 3)(x^2 + 3x + 9)$

Difference of two squares (p. 220)   A difference of two squares is an expression of the form $a^2 - b^2$. It can be factored as $(a + b)(a - b)$.

Diferencia de dos cuadrados (p. 220)   La diferencia de dos cuadrados es una expresión de la forma $a^2 - b^2$. Se puede factorizar como $(a + b)(a - b)$.

Example $25a^2 - 4 = (5a + 2)(5a - 2)$
$m^6 - 1 = (m^3 + 1)(m^3 - 1)$

Dilation (p. 802)   A dilation is a transformation that can change the size of a figure. When the center of the dilation is the origin, you can use scalar multiplication to find the coordinates of the vertices of an image.

Dilatación (p. 802)   Una dilatación es una transformación que puede cambiar el tamaño de una figura. Cuando el centro de dilatación está en el origen, se hallan las coordenadas de los vértices de la imagen por medio de la multiplicación de escalar.

Example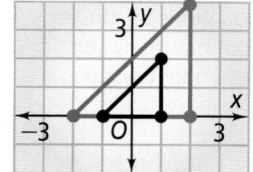

English

Direct variation (p. 68)   A linear function defined by an equation of the form $y = kx$, where $k \neq 0$, represents direct variation.

Example $y = 3.5x$, $y = 7x$, $y = -\frac{1}{2}x$

Directrix (p. 622)   The directrix of a parabola is the fixed line used to define a parabola. Each point of the parabola is the same distance from the focus and the directrix.

Example

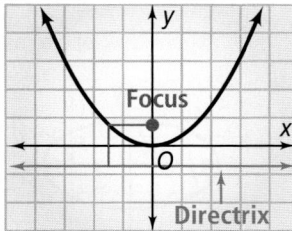

Discontinuous graph (p. 516)   A graph is discontinuous if it has a jump, break, or hole.

Discrete probability distribution (p. 739)   A discrete probability distribution has a finite number of Possible events.

Discriminant (p. 242)   The discriminant of a quadratic equation in the form $ax^2 + bx + c = 0$ is the value of the expression $b^2 - 4ac$.

Example $3x^2 - 6x + 1$
$$\text{discriminant} = (-6)^2 - 4(3)(1)$$
$$= 36 - 12 = 24$$

Diverge (p. 598)   An infinite series diverges if it does not converge.

Example $1 + 2 + 4 + 8 + \cdots$ diverges.

Domain (p. 61)   The domain of a relation is the set of all inputs, or x-coordinates, of the ordered pairs.

Examples   In the relation {(0, 1), (0, 2), (0, 3), (0, 4), (1, 3), (1, 4), (2, 1)}, the domain is {0, 1, 2}. In the function $f(x) = x^2 - 10$, the domain is all real numbers.

Spanish

Variación directa (p. 68)   Una función lineal definida por una ecuación de la forma $y = kx$, donde $k \neq 0$, representa una variación directa.

Directriz (p. 622)   La directriz de una parábola es la recta fija con que se define una parábola. Cada punto de la parábola está a la misma distancia del foco y de la directriz.

Gráfica discontinua (p. 516)   Una gráfica es discontinua si tiene un salto, interrupción o hueco.

Distribución de probabilidad discreta (p. 739)   Una distribución de probabilidad discreta tiene un número finito de sucesos posibles.

Discriminante (p. 242)   El discriminante de una ecuación cuadrática en la forma $ax^2 + bx + c = 0$ es el valor de la expresión $b^2 - 4ac$.

Divergir (p. 598)   Una serie infinita es divergente si no es convergente.

Dominio (p. 61)   El dominio de una relación es el conjunto de todos los valores de entrada, o coordenadas x, de los pares ordenados.

English

Dot product (p. 812) Given vectors $\mathbf{v} = \langle v_1, v_2 \rangle$ and $\mathbf{w} = \langle w_1, w_2 \rangle$, the dot product $\mathbf{v} \cdot \mathbf{w}$ is the quantity $v_1 w_1 + v_2 w_2$.

Spanish

Producto escalar (p. 812) Dados los vectores $\mathbf{v} = \langle v_1, v_2 \rangle$ y $\mathbf{w} = \langle w_1, w_2 \rangle$, el producto escalar $\mathbf{v} \cdot \mathbf{w}$ es la suma $v_1 w_1 + v_2 w_2$.

E

Ellipse (p. 638) An ellipse is the set of points P in a plane such that the sum of the distances from P to two fixed points $F1$ and $F2$ is a given constant k. The standard form of the equation of an ellipse with its center at the origin is $\frac{x^2}{a^2} + \frac{y^2}{b^2} = 1$ if the major axis is horizontal and $\frac{x^2}{b^2} + \frac{y^2}{a^2} = 1$ if the major axis is vertical, where $a > b$.

Elipse (p. 638) Una elipse es el conjunto de puntos P situados en un plano tal que la suma de las distancias entre P y dos puntos fijos F_1 y F_2 es una constante dada k. La forma normal de la ecuación de una elipse con su centro en el origen es $\frac{x^2}{a^2} + \frac{y^2}{b^2} = 1$ si el eje mayor es horizontal y $\frac{x^2}{b^2} + \frac{y^2}{a^2} = 1$ si el eje mayor es vertical, donde $a > b$.

Example

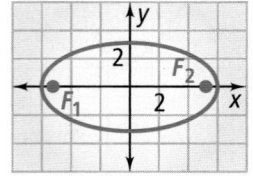

$$\frac{x^2}{36} + \frac{y^2}{9} = 1$$
$$F_1 = (-3\sqrt{3}, 0), \; F_2 = (3\sqrt{3}, 0)$$

End behavior (p. 282) End behavior of the graph of a function describes the directions of the graph as you move to the left and to the right, away from the origin.

Comportamiento extremo (p. 282) El comportamiento extremo de la gráfica de una función describe las direcciones de la gráfica al moverse a la izquierda y a la derecha, apartándose del origen.

Equal matrices (p. 767) Equal matrices are matrices with the same dimensions and equal corresponding elements.

Matrices equivalentes (p. 767) Dos matrices son equivalentes si y sólo si tienen las mismas dimensiones y sus elementos correspondientes son iguales.

Example Matrices A and B are equal.

$$A = \begin{bmatrix} 2 & 6 \\ \frac{9}{3} & 1 \end{bmatrix} \quad B = \begin{bmatrix} \frac{6}{3} & 6 \\ 3 & \frac{-13}{-13} \end{bmatrix}$$

Equally likely outcomes (p. 682) Equally likely outcomes are events in a sample space that have the same chance of occurring.

Resultados igualmente probables (p. 682) Resultados igualmente probables son sucesos en un espacio muestral con la misma probabilidad de ocurrir.

Equation (p. 26) An equation is a statement that two algebraic expressions are equal.

Ecuación (p. 26) Una ecuación es un enunciado que describe dos expresiones algebraicas iguales.

Equivalent systems (p. 144) Equivalent systems are systems that have the same solution(s).

Sistemas equivalentes (p. 144) Sistemas equivalentes son sistemas que tienen la misma solución o las mismas soluciones.

English

Evaluate (p. 19) To evaluate an algebraic expression, substitute a number for each variable in the expression. Then simplify using the order of operations.

Example When $x = 2$ and $y = -1$,
$2x + 3y$ evaluates to 1.

Expand (p. 326) To expand the power of a binomial, multiply as needed, then write the polynomial in standard form.

Example
$$(x + 4)^3 = (x + 4)(x + 4)^2$$
$$= (x + 4)(x^2 + 8x + 16)$$
$$= x^3 + 8x^2 + 16x + 4x^2 + 32x + 64$$
$$= x^3 + 12x^2 + 48x + 64$$

Experimental probability (p. 681) The experimental probability of an event is the ratio
$$\frac{\text{number of times the event occurs}}{\text{number of trials}}.$$

Example Suppose a basketball player has scored 19 times in 28 attempts at a basket. The experimental probability of the player's scoring is
$P(\text{score}) = \frac{19}{28} \approx 0.68$, or 68%.

Explicit formula (p. 565) An explicit formula expresses the nth term of a sequence in terms of n.

Example Let $a_n = 2n + 5$ for positive integers n. If $n = 7$, then
$a_7 = 2(7) + 5 = 19$.

Exponential decay (p. 435) Exponential decay is modeled by a function of the form $y = ab^x$ with $0 < b < 1$.

Exponential equation (p. 469) An exponential equation contains the form b^{cx}, with the exponent including a variable.

Example
$$5^{2x} = 270$$
$$\log 5^{2x} = \log 270$$
$$2x \log 5 = \log 270$$
$$2x = \frac{\log 270}{\log 5}$$
$$2x \approx 3.4785$$
$$x \approx 1.7392$$

Spanish

Evaluar (p. 19) Para evaluar una expresión algebraica, sustituye cada variable de la expresión con un número. Luego, simplifica usando el orden de operaciones.

Expandir (p. 326) Para expandir la potencia de un binomio, multiplica como sea necesario. Luego, escribe el polinomio en forma normal.

Probabilidad experimental (p. 681) La probabilidad experimental de un suceso es la razón
$$\frac{\text{number of times the event occurs}}{\text{number of trials}}.$$

Fórmula explícita (p. 565) Una fórmula explícita expresa el n-ésimo término de una progresión en función de n.

Decaimiento exponencial (p. 435) El decaimiento exponencial se expresa con una función $y = ab^x$ donde $0 < b < 1$.

Ecuación exponencial (p. 469) Una ecuación exponencial tiene la forma b^{cx}, y su exponente incluye una variable.

English

Spanish

Visual Glossary

Exponential function (p. 434) The general form of an exponential function is $y = ab^x$, where x is a real number, $a \neq 0$, $b > 0$, and $b \neq 1$. When $b > 1$, the function models exponential growth with growth factor b. When $0 < b < 1$, the function models exponential decay with decay factor b.

Función exponencial (p. 434) La forma general de una función exponencial es $y = ab^x$, donde x es un número real, $a \neq 0$, $b > 0$ y $b \neq 1$. Cuando $b > 1$, la función representa un incremento exponencial con factor de incremento b. Cuando $0 < b < 1$, la función representa el decremento exponencial con factor de decremento b.

Example

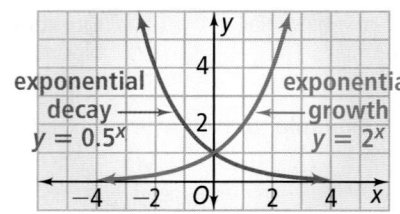

Exponential growth (p. 435) Exponential growth is modeled by a function of the form $y = ab^x$ with $b > 1$.

Crecimiento exponencial (p. 435) El crecimiento exponencial se expresa con una función de la forma $y = ab^x$ donde $b > 1$.

Extraneous solution (p. 42) An extraneous solution is a solution of an equation derived from an original equation but it is not a solution of the original equation.

Solución extraña (p. 42) Una solución extraña es una solución de una ecuación derivada de una ecuación dada, pero que no satisface la ecuación dada.

Example
$$\sqrt{x - 3} = x - 5$$
$$x - 3 = x^2 - 10x + 25$$
$$0 = x^2 - 11x + 28$$
$$0 = (x - 4)(x - 7)$$
$$x = 4 \text{ or } 7$$

The number 7 is a solution, but 4 is not, since $\sqrt{4 - 3} \neq 4 - 5$.

F

Factor Theorem (p. 289) The expression $x - a$ is a linear factor of a polynomial if and only if the value of a is a root of the related polynomial function.

Teorema de factores (p. 289) La expresión $x - a$ es un factor lineal de un polinomio si y sólo si el valor de a es una raíz de la función polinomial con la que se relaciona.

Example The value 2 makes the polynomial $x^2 + 2x - 8$ equal to zero. So, $x - 2$ is a factor of $x^2 + 2x - 8$.

Factoring (p. 216) Factoring is rewriting an expression as the product of its factors.

Descomposición factorial (p. 216) Descomponer en factores es el proceso de escribir de nuevo una expresión como el producto de sus factores.

Example expanded form   factored form
$$x^2 + x - 56 \qquad (x + 8)(x - 7)$$

Feasible region (p. 157) In a linear programming problem, the feasible region contains all the values that satisfy the constraints on the objective function.

Región factible (p. 157) En un problema de programación lineal, la región factible contiene todos los valores que satisfacen las restricciones de la función objetiva.

English

Finite Series (p. 587) A finite series is a series with a finite number of terms.

Focal length (p. 622) The focal length of a parabola is the distance between the vertex and the focus.

Focus (plural: foci) of a hyperbola (p. 645) A hyperbola is the set of all points P in a plane such that the difference of the distances from P to two fixed points is constant. Each of the fixed points is a focus of the hyperbola.

Focus (plural: foci) of a parabola (p. 622) A parabola is the set of all points in a plane that are the same distance from a fixed line and a fixed point not on the line. The fixed point is the focus of the parabola.

Focus (plural: foci) of an ellipse (p. 638) An ellipse is the set of all points P in a plane such that the sum of the distances from P to two fixed points is constant. Each of the fixed points is a focus of the ellipse.

Frequency table (p. 694) A frequency table is a list of the outcomes in a sample space and the number of times each outcome occurs.

Function (p. 62) A function is a relation in which each element of the domain corresponds with exactly one element in the range.

Example The relation $y = 3x^3 - 2x + 3$ is a function. $f(x) = 3x^3 - 2x + 3$ is the same relation written in function notation.

Function notation (p. 63) If f is the name of a function, the function notation $f(x)$ shows the function name f and also represents the range value $f(x)$ for the domain value x. You read the function notation $f(x)$ as "f of x" or "a function of x." Note that $f(x)$ does *not* mean "f times x."

Example When the value of x is 3, $f(3)$, read "f of 3," represents the value of the function at 3.

Function rule (p. 63) A function rule represents an output value in terms of an input value.

Fundamental Counting Principle (p. 674) The Fundamental Counting Principle is a tool that you can use to quickly count the number of ways certain things can happen.

Spanish

Serie finita (p. 587) Una serie finita es una serie con un número finito de términos.

Distancia focal (p. 622) La distancia focal de una parábola es la distancia entre el vértice y el foco.

Foco de una hipérbola (p. 645) Una hipérbola es el conjunto de puntos P en un plano tal que la diferencia de las distancias desde P hasta dos puntos fijos es constante. Cada uno de los puntos fijos es el foco de la hipérbola.

Foco de una parábola (p. 622) Una parábola es el conjunto de todos los puntos en un plano con la misma distancia desde una línea fija y un punto fijo que no permanece en la línea. El punto fijo es el foco de la parábola.

Foco de una elipse (p. 638) Una elipse es el conjunto de todos los puntos P en un plano en el cual la suma de las distancias desde P hasta dos puntos fijos es constante. Cada uno de estos puntos fijos es un foco de la elipsis.

Tabla de frecuencias (p. 694) Una tabla de frecuencias es una lista de los resultados de un espacio muestral y el número de veces que cada resultado ocurre.

Función (p. 62) Una función es una relación en la que cada elemento del dominio corresponde exactamente con un elemento del rango.

Notación de una función (p. 63) Si f es el nombre de una función, la notación de la función $f(x)$ indica el nombre de la función y también representa el valor del rango $f(x)$ para el valor del dominio x. La función de la notación $f(x)$ se lee "f de x" o "una función de x." Observa que $f(x)$ *no* significa "f por x".

Regla de función (p. 63) Una regla de función representa un valor de salida en función a un valor de entrada.

Principio básico de conteo (p. 674) El principio básico de conteo es una herramienta que se puede utilizar para hacer un conteo rápido del número de formas en que pueden ocurrir ciertas cosas.

English

Spanish

Fundamental Theorem of Algebra (p. 320) If $P(x)$ is a polynomial of degree $n \geq 1$ with complex coefficients, then $P(x) = 0$ has at least one complex root.

Teorema fundamental de álgebra (p. 320) Si $P(x)$ es un polinomio de grado $n \geq 1$ con coeficientes complejos, entonces $P(x) = 0$ tiene por lo menos una raíz compleja.

Example $P(x) = 3x^3 - 2x + 3$ is of degree 3, so $P(x) = 0$ has at least one complex root.

 G

Geometric mean (p. 583) The geometric mean of any two positive numbers is the positive square root of the product of the two numbers.

Media geométrica (p. 583) La media geométrica de dos números positivos es la raíz cuadrada positiva del producto de los dos números.

Example The geometric mean of 12 and 18 is $\sqrt{12 \cdot 18} \approx 14.6969$.

Geometric sequence (p. 580) A geometric sequence is a sequence with a constant ratio between consecutive terms.

Secuencia geométrica (p. 580) Una secuencia geométrica es una secuencia con una razón constante entre términos consecutivos.

Example The geometric sequence 2.5, 5, 10, 20, 40 . . . , has a common ratio of 2.

Geometric series (p. 595) A geometric series is the sum of the terms in a geometric sequence.

Serie geométrica (p. 595) Una serie geométrica es la suma de términos en una progresión geométrica.

Example One geometric series with five terms is $2.5 + 5 + 10 + 20 + 40$.

Greatest common factor (p. 218) The greatest common factor (GCF) of an expression is the common factor of each term of the expression that has the greatest coefficient and the greatest exponent.

Máximo factor común (p. 218) El máximo factor común de una expresión es el factor común de cada término de la expresión que tiene el mayor coeficiente y el mayor exponente.

Example The GCF of $4x^2 + 20x - 12$ is 4.

Greatest integer function (p. 90) The greatest integer function corresponds each input x to the greatest integer less than or equal to x.

Función del entero mayor (p. 90) La función del entero mayor relaciona cada entrada x con el entero mayor que es menor o igual a x.

Growth factor (p. 436) In an exponential function of the form $y = ab^x$, b is the growth factor if $b > 1$.

Factor de incremento (p. 436) En una función exponencial de la forma $y = ab^x$, b es el factor de incremento si $b > 1$.

Example In the exponential equation $y = 2^x$, 2 is the growth factor.

 H

Half-plane (p. 114) A half-plane is the set of points in a coordinate plane that are on one side of the boundary of the graph of a linear inequality.

Semiplano (p. 114) Un semiplano es el conjunto de puntos de un plano de coordenadas que están a un lado del límite de la gráfica de desigualdad lineal.

English

Spanish

Hyperbola (p. 645)   A hyperbola is a set of points P in a plane such that the difference between the distances from P to the foci F_1 and F_2 is a given constant k. $|PF_1 - PF_2| = k$ The standard form of an equation of a hyperbola centered at $(0, 0)$ is $\frac{x^2}{a^2} - \frac{y^2}{b^2} = 1$ if the transverse axis is horizontal and $\frac{y^2}{a^2} - \frac{x^2}{b^2} = 1$ if the transverse axis is vertical.

Hipérbola (p. 645)   Una hipérbola es un conjunto de puntos P en un plano tal que la diferencia entre las distancias de P a los focos F_1 y F_2 es una constante k dada. $|PF_1 - PF_2| = k$ La forma normal de la ecuación de una hipérbola centrada en $(0, 0)$ es $\frac{x^2}{a^2} - \frac{y^2}{b^2} = 1$, si el eje transversal es horizontal, y $\frac{y^2}{a^2} - \frac{x^2}{b^2} = 1$, si el eje transversal es vertical.

Example

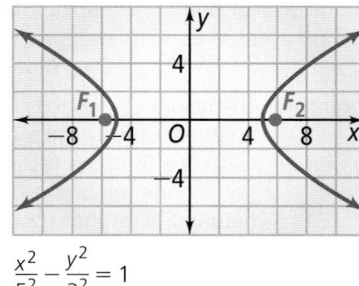

$$\frac{x^2}{5^2} - \frac{y^2}{3^2} = 1$$

I

***i* (p. 248)**   The imaginary number i is the principal square root of -1.

***i* (p. 248)**   El número imaginario i es la raíz cuadrada principal de -1.

Example $i = \sqrt{-1}$ and $i^2 = -1$.

Identity (p. 28)   An equation that is true for every value of the variable is an identity.

Identidad (p. 28)   Una ecuación que es verdadera para cada valor de la variable es una identidad.

Image (p. 801)   An image is a figure obtained by a transformation of a preimage.

Imagen (p. 801)   Una imagen es la figura que resulta después de que la preimagen sufre una transformación.

Example

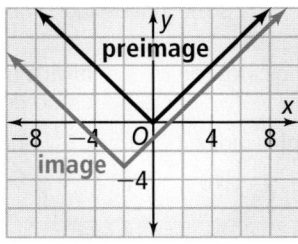

Imaginary number (p. 249)   An imaginary number is any number of the form $a + bi$, where a and b are real numbers and $b \neq 0$.

Número imaginario (p. 249)   Un número imaginario es cualquier número de la forma $a + bi$, donde a y b son números reales y $b \neq 0$.

Example $2 + 3i$
$7i$
i

Imaginary unit (p. 248)   The imaginary unit i is the complex number whose square is -1.

Unidad imaginaria (p. 248)   La unidad imaginaria i es el número complejo cuyo cuadrado es -1.

English

Spanish

Inconsistent system (p. 137)   A system of equations that has no solution is an inconsistent system.

Sistema incompatible (p. 137)   Un sistema incompatible es un sistema de ecuaciones para el cual no hay solución.

Example $\begin{cases} y = 2x + 3 \\ -2x + y = 1 \end{cases}$ is a system of parallel lines, so it has no solution. It is an inconsistent system.

Independent events (p. 688)   When the outcome of one event does not affect the probability of a second event, the two events are independent.

Sucesos independientes (p. 688)   Cuando el resultado de un suceso no altera la probabilidad de otro, los dos sucesos son independientes.

Example The results of two rolls of a number cube are independent. Getting a 5 on the first roll does not change the probability of getting a 5 on the second roll.

Independent system (p. 137)   A system of linear equations that has a unique solution is an independent system.

Sistema independiente (p. 137)   Un sistema de ecuaciones lineales que tenga una sola solución es un sistema independiente.

Example $\begin{cases} x + 2y = -7 \\ 2x - 3y = 0 \end{cases}$ has the unique solution $(-3, -2)$. It is an independent system.

Independent variable (p. 63)   If a function is defined by an equation using the variables x and y, where x represents input values, then x is the independent variable.

Variable independiente (p. 63)   Si una función es definida por una ecuación con las variables x e y, donde x representa los valores de entrada, entonces x es la variable independiente.

Example $y = 2x + 1$
x is the independent variable.

Index (p. 362)   With a radical sign, the index indicates the degree of the root.

Índice (p. 362)   Con un signo de radical, el índice indica el grado de la raíz.

Example index 2   index 3   index 4
$$\sqrt{16} \qquad \sqrt[3]{16} \qquad \sqrt[4]{16}$$

Infinite series (p. 587)   An infinite series is a series with infinitely many terms.

Serie infinita (p. 587)   Una serie infinita es una serie con un número infinito de términos.

Initial point (p. 809)   The initial point of a vector is the endpoint (not the tip) of a vector arrow.

Punto de inicio (p. 809)   El punto de inicio de un vector es el extremo (no la punta) de una flecha vectorial.

English

Spanish

Initial side (p. 836) When an angle is in standard position, the initial side of the angle is given to be on the positive x-axis. The other ray is the terminal side of the angle.

Lado inicial (p. 836) Cuando un ángulo está en posición normal, el lado inicial del ángulo se ubica en el eje positivo de las x. El otro rayo, o semirrecta, forma el lado terminal del ángulo.

Example

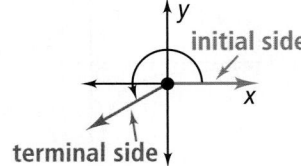

Intercepted arc (p. 844) An intercepted arc is the portion of a circle whose endpoints are on the sides of a central angle of the circle and whose remaining points lie in the interior of the angle.

Arco interceptado (p. 844) Un arco interceptado es la porción de un círculo cuyos extremos quedan sobre los lados de un ángulo central del círculo y cuyos puntos restantes quedan en el interior del ángulo.

Example

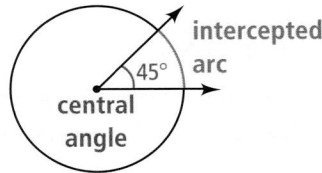

Interquartile range (p. 713) The interquartile range of a set of data is the difference between the third and first quartiles.

Intervalo intercuartil (p. 713) El rango intercuartil de un conjunto de datos es la diferencia entre el tercero y el primer cuartiles.

Example The first and third quartiles of the data set {2, 3, 4, 5, 5, 6, 7, 7} are 3.5 and 6.5. The interquartile range is $6.5 - 3.5 = 3$.

Inverse function (p. 405) If function f pairs a value b with a then its inverse, denoted f^{-1}, pairs the value a with b. If f^{-1} is also a function, then f and f^{-1} are inverse functions.

Funcion inversa (p. 405) Si la función f empareja un valor b con a, entonces su inversa, cuya notación es f^{-1}, empareja el valor a con b. Si f^{-1} también es una función, entonces f y f^{-1} son funciones inversas.

Example If $f(x) = x + 3$, then $f^{-1}(x) = x - 3$.

Inverse operations (p. 27) Inverse operations are operations that undo each other.

Operaciones inversas (p. 27) Operaciones inversas son operaciones que se cancelan mutuamente.

Inverse relation (p. 405) If a relation pairs element a of its domain with element b of its range, the inverse relation "undoes" the relation and pairs b with a. If (a, b) is an ordered pair of a relation, then (b, a) is an ordered pair of its inverse.

Relación inversa (p. 405) Si una relación empareja el elemento a de su dominio con el elemento b de su rango, la relación inversa "deshace" la relación y empareja b con a. Si (a, b) es un par ordenado de una relación, entonces (b, a) es un par ordenado de su inversa.

Visual **Glossary**

English

Spanish

Inverse variation (p. 498)   An inverse variation is a relation represented by an equation of the form $xy = k$, $y = \frac{k}{x}$, or $x = \frac{k}{y}$, where $k \neq 0$.

Variación inversa (p. 498)   Una variación inversa es una relación representada por la ecuación $xy = k$, $y = \frac{k}{x}$, ó $x = \frac{k}{y}$, donde $k \neq 0$.

Example

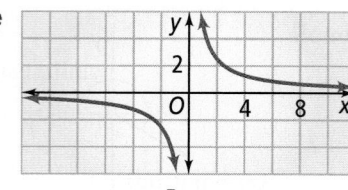

$xy = 5$, or $y = \frac{5}{x}$

J

Joint variation (p. 501)   A joint variation is a relation in which one variable varies directly with respect to each of two or more variables.

Variación conjunta (p. 501)   Una variación conjunta es una relación en la cual el valor de una variable varía directamente con respecto a cada una de dos o más variables.

Example $z = 8xy$
$T = kPV$

L

Law of Cosines (p. 936)   In $\triangle ABC$, let a, b, and c represent the lengths of the sides opposite $\angle A$, $\angle B$, and $\angle C$, respectively. Then
$a^2 = b^2 + c^2 - 2bc \cos A$,
$b^2 = a^2 + c^2 - 2ac \cos B$, and
$c^2 = a^2 + b^2 - 2ab \cos C$

Ley de cosenos (p. 936)   En $\triangle ABC$, sean a, b y c las longitudes de los lados opuestos a $\angle A$, $\angle B$ y $\angle C$, respectivamente. Entonces
$a^2 = b^2 + c^2 - 2bc \cos A$,
$b^2 = a^2 + c^2 - 2ac \cos B$ y
$c^2 = a^2 + b^2 - 2ab \cos C$

Example

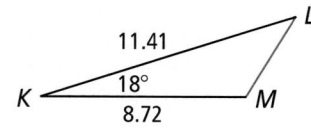

$LM^2 = 11.41^2 + 8.72^2 - 2(11.42)(8.72) \cos 18°$
$LM^2 = 16.9754$
$LM = 4.12$

Law of Sines (p. 929)   In $\triangle ABC$, let a, b, and c represent the lengths of the sides opposite $\angle A$, $\angle B$, and $\angle C$, respectively. Then $\frac{\sin A}{a} = \frac{\sin B}{b} = \frac{\sin C}{c}$.

Ley de senos (p. 929)   En $\triangle ABC$, sean a, b y c las longitudes de los lados opuestos a $\angle A$, $\angle B$ y $\angle C$, respectivamente. Entonces $\frac{\text{sen } A}{a} = \frac{\text{sen } B}{b} = \frac{\text{sen } C}{c}$.

Example

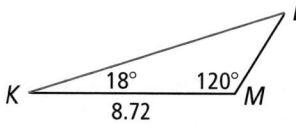

$m\angle L = 180 - (120 + 18) = 42°$

$$\frac{KL}{\sin 120°} = \frac{872}{\sin 42°}$$

$$KL = \frac{872 \sin 120°}{\sin 42°}$$

$$KL = 11.26$$

English

Spanish

Like radicals (p. 374)   Like radicals are radical expressions that have the same index and the same radicand.

Radicales semejantes (p. 374)   Los radicales semejantes son expresiones radicales que tienen el mismo índice y el mismo radicando.

Example $4\sqrt[3]{7}$ and $\sqrt[3]{7}$ are like radicals.

Like terms (p. 21)   Like terms have the same variables raised to the same powers.

Términos semejantes (p. 21)   Los términos semejantes tienen las mismas variables elevadas a las mismas potencias.

Limits (p. 589)   Limits in summation notation are the least and greatest integer values of the index n.

Límites (p. 589)   Los límites en notación de sumatoria son el menor y el mayor valor del índice n en números enteros.

Example

$$\text{limits} \nearrow \overset{3}{\underset{n=1}{\Sigma}} (3n + 5)$$

Line of best fit (p. 94)   The trend line that gives the most accurate model of related data is the line of best fit.

Recta de mayor aproximación (p. 94)   La línea de tendencia que representa con mayor precisión los datos relacionado es la recta de mayor aproximación.

Linear equation (p. 75)   A linear equation in two variables is an equation that can be written in the form $ax + by = c$. *See also* **Standard form of a linear equation.**

Ecuación lineal (p. 75)   Una ecuación lineal de dos variables es una ecuación que se puede escribir de la forma $ax + by = c$. *Ver también* **Standard form of a linear equation.**

Example $y = 2x + 1$ can be written as $-2x + y = 1$.

Linear function (p. 75)   A function whose graph is a line is a linear function. You can represent a linear function with a linear equation.

Función lineal (p. 75)   Una función cuya gráfica es una recta es una función lineal. La función lineal se representa con una ecuación lineal.

Example

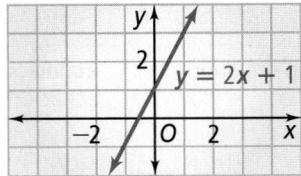

Linear inequality (p. 114)   A linear inequality is an inequality in two variables whose graph is a region of the coordinate plane that is bounded by a line.

Desigualdad lineal (p. 114)   Una desigualdad lineal es una desigualdad de dos variables cuya gráfica es una región del plano de coordenadas delimitado por una recta.

Example

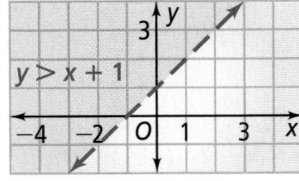

$y > x + 1$

English   Spanish

Linear programming (p. 157)   Linear programming is a method for finding a minimum or maximum value of some quantity, given a set of constraints.

Programación lineal (p. 157)   Programación lineal es un método para hallar el valor mínimo y máximo de una cantidad que se expresa como un conjunto de limitaciones.

Example   Restrictions $x \geq 0$, $y \geq 0$, $x + y \leq 7$, and $y \leq -2x + 8$
Objective function: $B = 2x + 4y$
Evaluate $B = 2x + 4y$ at each vertex.
The minimum value of B occurs when $x = 0$ and $y = 0$. The m aximum value of B occurs when $x = 0$ and $y = 7$.

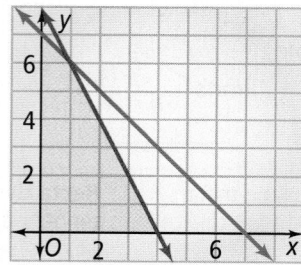

Linear system (p. 134)   A linear system is a set of two or more linear equations that use the same variables.

Sistema lineal (p. 134)   Un sistema lineal es un conjunto de dos o más ecuaciones lineales con las mismas variables.

Example

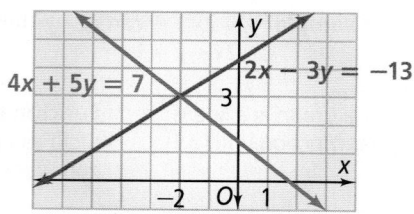

Literal equation (p. 29)   A literal equation is an equation that uses more than one letter as a variable.

Ecuación literal (p. 29)   Una ecuación literal es una ecuación en la cual más de una letra expresa una variable.

Logarithm (p. 451)   The logarithm base b of a positive number x is defined as follows: $\log_b x = y$, if and only if $x = b^y$.

Logaritmo (p. 451)   La base del logaritmo b de un número positivo x se define como $\log_b x = y$, si y sólo si $x = b^y$.

Example $\log_2 8 = 3$
$\log_{10} 100 = \log 100 = 2$
$\log_5 5^7 = 7$

English

Spanish

Logarithmic equation (p. 471) A logarithmic equation is an equation that includes a logarithm involving a variable.

Ecuación logarítmica (p. 471) Una ecuación logarítmica es una ecuación que incluye un logaritmo con una variable.

Example $\log_3 x = 4$

Logarithmic function (p. 454) A logarithmic function is the inverse of an exponential function.

Función logarítmica (p. 454) Una función logarítmica es la inversa de una función exponencial.

Example

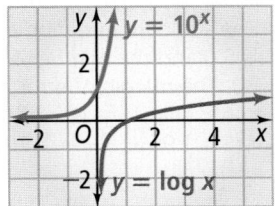

Logarithmic scale (p. 453) A logarithmic scale is a scale that uses the logarithm of a quantity instead of the quantity itself.

Escala logarítmica (p. 453) Una escala logarítmica es una escala que usa el logaritmo de una cantidaden vez de la cantidad misma.

M

Magnitude (p. 809) The magnitude of a vector **v** is the length of the arrow.

Magnitud (p. 809) La magnitud de un vector **v** es la longitud de la flecha.

Major axis (p. 639) The major axis of an ellipse is the segment that contains the foci of the ellipse and has endpoints on the ellipse.

Eje mayor (p. 639) En una elipsis, el eje mayor es el segmento que contiene los focos de la elipsis y tiene puntos extremos sobre la elipsis.

Example

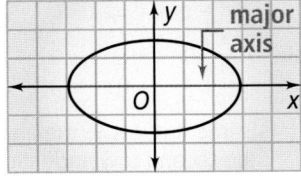

Mapping diagram (p. 60) A mapping diagram describes a relation by linking elements of the domain with elements of the range.

Mapa (p. 60) Un mapa describe una relación al unir los elementos del dominio con los elementos del rango.

Example Domain Range

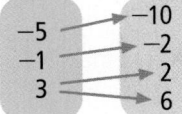

English

Margin of error (p. 746) The distance from the sample mean or sample proportion that is used to create a confidence interval for the population mean or the population proportion. For a 95% confidence level, $ME = 1.96 \cdot \frac{s}{\sqrt{n}}$, where ME is the margin of error, s is the standard deviation of the sample data, and n is the number of values in the sample.

Spanish

Margen de error (p. 746) La distancia desde la media de una muestra o desde la proporción de una muestra que se usa para crear el intervalo de confianza para la media o proporción de una población. Para un nivel de confianza de 95%, $ME = 1.96 \cdot \frac{s}{\sqrt{n}}$, siendo ME el margen de error, s la desviación estándar de los datos de la muestra, y n el número de valores en la muestra.

Example The standard deviation of a sample is 5.0 and the number of trials is 30. The margin of error at a 95% confidence level is
$$ME = 1.96 \cdot \frac{50}{\sqrt{30}} \approx 1.79.$$

Matrix (p. 174) A matrix is a rectangular array of numbers written within brackets.

Matriz (p. 174) Una matriz es un conjunto de números encerrados en corchetes y dispuestos en forma de rectángulo.

Example $A = \begin{bmatrix} 1 & -2 & 0 & 10 \\ 9 & 7 & -3 & 8 \\ 2 & -10 & 1 & -6 \end{bmatrix}$

The number 2 is the element in the third row and first column. A is a 3×4 matrix.

Matrix element (p. 174) Every item listed in a matrix is an element of the matrix. An element is identified by its position in the matrix.

Elemento matricial (p. 174) Cada cifra de una matriz es un elemento de la matriz. El elemento se identifica según la posición que ocupa en la matriz.

Example $A = \begin{bmatrix} 1 & -2 & 0 & 10 \\ 9 & 7 & -3 & 8 \\ 2 & -10 & 1 & -6 \end{bmatrix}$

Element a_{21} is 9, the element in the second row and first column.

Matrix equation (p. 765) A matrix equation is an equation in which the variable is a matrix.

Ecuación matricial (p. 765) Una ecuación matricial es una ecuación en que la variable es una matriz.

Example

Solve $X + \begin{bmatrix} 3 & -2 \\ 5 & 1 \end{bmatrix} = \begin{bmatrix} 4 & 0 \\ 0 & 3 \end{bmatrix}$

$X = \begin{bmatrix} 4 & 0 \\ 0 & 3 \end{bmatrix} - \begin{bmatrix} 3 & -2 \\ 5 & 1 \end{bmatrix} = \begin{bmatrix} 1 & 2 \\ -5 & 2 \end{bmatrix}$

Maximum value (p. 195) The maximum value of a function $y = f(x)$ is the greatest y-value of the function. It is the y-coordinate of the highest point on the graph of f.

Valor máximo (p. 195) El valor máximo de una función $y = f(x)$ es el valor más alto de y de la función. Es la coordenada y del punto más alto de la gráfica de f.

English

Mean (p. 711) The sum of the data values divided by the number of data values is the mean. *See also* **Arithmetic mean.**

Example {1, 2, 3, 3, 6, 6}
$$\text{mean} = \frac{1 + 2 + 3 + 3 + 6 + 6}{6}$$
$$= \frac{21}{6} = 3.5$$

Measures of central tendency (p. 711) The mean, the median, and the mode are each central values that help describe a set of data. They are called measures of central tendency.

Example {1, 2, 3, 3, 4, 5, 6, 6}
mean = 3.75
median = 3.5
modes = 3 and 6

Measure of variation (p. 719) Measures of variation, such as the range, the interquartile range, and the standard deviation, describe how the data in a data set are spread out.

Median (p. 711) The median is the middle value in a data set. If the data set contains an even number of values, the median is the mean of the two middle values.

Example {1, 2, 3, 3, 4, 5, 6, 6}
$$\text{median} = \frac{3 + 4}{2} = \frac{7}{2} = 3.5$$

Midline (p. 830) The horizontal line through the average of the maximum and minimum values.

Example

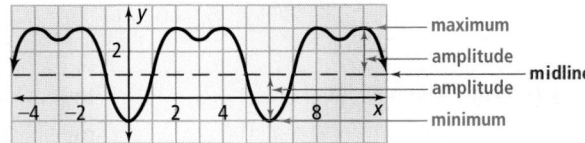

Minor axis (p. 639) The minor axis of an ellipse is the segment that is perpendicular to the major axis at its midpoint and has endpoints on the ellipse.

Example

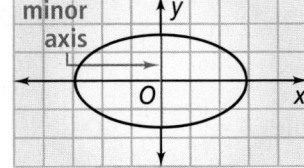

Spanish

Media (p. 711) La suma de los valores de datos dividida por el número de valores de datos sumados es la media. *Ver también* **Arithmetic mean.**

Medidas de tendencia central (p. 711) La media, la mediana y la moda son los valores centrales que facilitan la descripción de un conjunto de datos. A estos valores se les llama medidas de tendencia central.

Medida de dispersión (p. 719) Las medidas de dispersión, tal como el rango, el intervalo intercuartil y la desviación típica, describen cómo se dispersan los datos en un conjunto de datos.

Mediana (p. 711) La mediana es el valor situado en el medio en un conjunto de datos. Si el conjunto de datos contiene un número par de valores, la mediana es la media de los dos valores del medio.

Línea media (p. 830) Recta horizontal que pasa a través de la media de los valores máximos y mínimos.

Eje menor (p. 639) En una elipsis, el eje menor es el segmento perpendicular al eje mayor en su punto medio y que tiene puntos extremos sobre la elipsis.

English

Minimum value (p. 195) The minimum value of a function $y = f(x)$ is the least y-value of the function. It is the y-coordinate of the lowest point on the graph of f.

Mode (p. 711) The mode is the most frequently occurring value (or values) in a set of data.

Monomial (p. 280) A monomial is either a real number, a variable, or a product of real numbers and variables with whole number exponents.

Multiple zero (p. 291) If a linear factor is repeated in the complete factored form of a polynomial, the zero related to that factor is a multiple zero.

Multiplicative identity (p. 14) The multiplicative identity is 1. The product of 1 and any number is that number. The product of reciprocals is 1.

Multiplicative identity matrix (p. 782) For an $n \times n$ square matrix, the multiplicative identity matrix is an $n \times n$ square matrix I, or $I_{n \times n}$, with 1's along the main diagonal and 0's elsewhere.

Multiplicative inverse (p. 14) The reciprocal or multiplicative inverse of any nonzero number a is $\frac{1}{a}$. The product of reciprocals is 1, the multiplicative identity.

Multiplicative inverse of a matrix (p. 782) If A and X are $n \times n$ matrices, and $AX = XA = I$, then X is the multiplicative inverse of A, written A^{-1}.

Spanish

Valor mínimo (p. 195) El valor mínimo de una función $y = f(x)$ es el valor más bajo de y de la función. Es la coordenada y del punto más bajo de la gráfica de f.

Moda (p. 711) La moda es el valor o valores que ocurren con mayor frecuencia en un conjunto de datos.

Monomio (p. 280) Un monomio es un número real, una variable o un producto de números reales y variables cuyos exponentes son números enteros.

Cero múltiplo (p. 291) Si un factor lineal se repite en la forma factorizada completa de un polinomio, el cero relacionado con ese factor es un cero múltiplo.

Identidad multiplicativa (p. 14) La identidad multiplicativa es 1. El producto de 1 y cualquier otro número es ese número. El producto del recíproco es 1.

Matriz de identidad multiplicativa (p. 782) Para una matriz cuadrada $n \times n$, la matriz de identidad multiplicativa es la matriz cuadrada I de $n \times n$, o $I_{n \times n}$, con unos por la diagonal principal y ceros en los demás lugares.

Inverso multiplicativo (p. 14) El recíproco o inverso multiplicativo de cualquier número a, que no sea cero, es $\frac{1}{a}$. El producto de recíprocos es 1, la identidad multiplicativa.

Inverso multiplicativo de una matriz (p. 782) Si A y X son matrices $n \times n$, y $AX = XA = I$, entonces X es el inverso multiplicativo de A, expresado como A^{-1}.

Example $\{1, 2, 3, 3, 4, 5, 6, 6\}$
The modes are 3 and 6.

Example $1, x, 2z, 4ab^2$

Example The zeros of the function
$P(x) = 2x(x - 3)^2(x + 1)$ are 0, 3,
and -1. Since $(x - 3)$ occurs twice
as a factor, 3 is a multiple zero.

Example $I_{2 \times 2} = \begin{bmatrix} 1 & 0 \\ 0 & 1 \end{bmatrix}$, $I_{3 \times 3} = \begin{bmatrix} 1 & 0 & 0 \\ 0 & 1 & 0 \\ 0 & 0 & 1 \end{bmatrix}$

Example $5 \times \frac{1}{5} = 1$

Example $A = \begin{bmatrix} 2 & 1 \\ 4 & 0 \end{bmatrix}$, $X = \begin{bmatrix} 0 & \frac{1}{4} \\ 1 & \frac{1}{2} \end{bmatrix}$

$AX = \begin{bmatrix} 1 & 0 \\ 0 & 1 \end{bmatrix} = I$, so $X = A^{-1}$

English

Spanish

Multiplicity (p. 291) The multiplicity of a zero of a polynomial function is the number of times the related linear factor is repeated in the factored form of the polynomial.

Multiplicidad (p. 291) La multiplicidad de un cero de una función polinomial es el número de veces que el factor lineal relacionado se repite en la forma factorizada del polinomio.

Example The zeros of the function
$P(x) = 2x(x - 3)^2(x + 1)$ are 0, 3,
and -1. Since $(x - 3)$ occurs twice as
a factor, the zero 3 has multiplicity 2.

Mutually exclusive events (p. 689) When two events cannot happen at the same time, the events are mutually exclusive. If A and B are mutually exclusive events, then $P(A \text{ or } B) = P(A) + P(B)$.

Sucesos mutuamente excluyentes (p. 689) Cuando dos sucesos no pueden ocurrir al mismo tiempo, son mutuamente excluyentes. Si A y B son sucesos mutuamente excluyentes, entonces $P(A \text{ or } B) = P(A) + P(B)$.

Example Rolling an even number E and
rolling a multiple of five M on a
standard number cube are
mutually exclusive events.

$$P(E \text{ or } M) = P(E) + P(M)$$
$$= \frac{3}{6} + \frac{1}{6}$$
$$= \frac{4}{6}, \text{ or } \frac{2}{3}$$

n factorial (n!) (p. 675) For any positive integer n, n factorial is $n(n - 1) \cdot \cdots \cdot 3 \cdot 2 \cdot 1$. Zero factorial $(0!) = 1$.

n factorial (n!) (p. 675) Para cualquier entero n, n factorial es $n(n - 1) \cdot \cdots \cdot 3 \cdot 2 \cdot 1$. El cero factorial $(0!) = 1$.

Example $4! = 4 \cdot 3 \cdot 2 \cdot 1 = 24$

nth root (p. 361) For any real numbers a and b, and any positive integer n, if $a^n = b$, then a is an nth root of b.

raíz n-ésima (p. 361) Para todos los números reales a y b, y todo número entero positivo n, si $a^n = b$, entonces a es la n-ésima raíz de b.

Example $\sqrt[5]{32} = 2$ because $2^5 = 32$.
$\sqrt[4]{81} = 3$ because $3^4 = 81$.

Natural base exponential function (p. 446) A natural base exponential function is an exponential function with base e.

Función exponencial con base natural (p. 446) Una función exponencial con base natural es una función exponencial con base e.

Natural logarithmic function (p. 478)   A natural logarithmic function is a logarithmic function with base e. The natural logarithmic function, $y = \ln x$, is $y = \log_e x$. It is the inverse of $y = e^x$.

Función logarítmica natural (p. 478)   Una función logarítmica natural es una función logarítmica con base e. La función logarítmica natural, $y = \ln x$, es $y = \log_e x$. Ésta es la función inversa de $y = e^x$.

Example

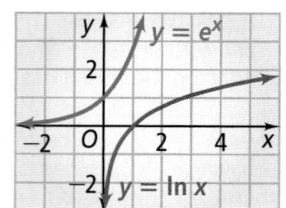

$\ln e^3 = 3$
$\ln 10 \approx 2.3026$
$\ln 36 \approx 3.5835$

Non-removable discontinuity (p. 516)   A non-removable discontinuity is a point of discontinuity that is not removable. It represents a break in the graph of f where you cannot redefine f to make the graph continuous.

Discontinuidad irremovible (p. 516)   Una discontinuidad irremovible es un punto de discontinuidad que no se puede remover. Representa una interrupción en la gráfica f donde no se puede redefinir f para volverla una gráfica continua.

Normal distribution (p. 739)   A normal distribution shows data that vary randomly from the mean in the pattern of a bell-shaped curve.

Distribución normal (p. 739)   Una distribución normal muestra, con una curva en forma de campana, datos que varían alcatoriamento respecto de la media.

Example

Distribution of Test Scores

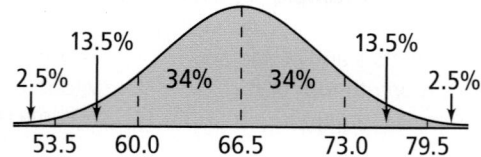

In a class of 200 students, the scores on a test were normally distributed. The mean score was 66.5 and the standard deviation was 6.5. The number of students who scored greater than 73 percent was about 13.5% + 2,5% of those who took the test.
16% of 200 = 32
About 32 students scored 73 or higher on the test.

Normal vectors (p. 812)   Normal vectors are perpendicular vectors. Their dot product is 0.

Vectores normales (p. 812)   Los vectores normales son vectores perpendiculares. El producto escalar es 0.

Numerical expression (p. 5)   A numerical expression is a mathematical phrase that contains numbers and operation symbols.

Expresión numérica (p. 5)   Una expresión numérica es una expresión matemática compuesta de números y símbolos de operación.

English

Objective function (p. 157) In a linear programming model, the objective function is a model of the quantity that you want to make as large or as small as possible. *See* **Linear programming.**

Observational study (p. 726) In an observational study, you measure or observe members of a sample in such a way that they are not affected by the study.

One-to-one function (p. 408) A one-to-one function is a function for which each *y*-value in the range corresponds to exactly one *x*-value in the domain. A one-to-one function f has an inverse f^{-1} that is also a function.

Opposite (p. 14) The opposite or additive inverse of any number a is $-a$. The sum of opposites is zero, the additive identity.

Example $3 + (-3) = 0$
$5.2 + (-5.2) = 0$

Ordered triples (p. 164) Ordered triples of the form (x, y, z) represent the location of a point in coordinate space.

Example $(2, 4, 5)$
$(0, 1, 2)$
$(0, 0, 0)$

Outlier (p. 712) An outlier is a value substantially different from the rest of the data in a set.

Example The outlier in the data set
$\{56, 64, 73, 59, 98, 65, 59\}$ is 98.

Parabola (p. 194) A parabola is the graph of a quadratic function. It is the set of all points P in a plane that are the same distance from a fixed point F, the focus, as they are from a line d, the directrix.

Spanish

Función objetiva (p. 157) En un modelo de programación lineal, la función objetiva es un modelo de la cantidad que se quiere aumentar o disminuir cuanto sea posible. *Ver* **Linear programming.**

Estudio de observación (p. 726) En un estudio de observación, se miden u observan a los miembros de una muestra de tal manera que no les afecte el estudio.

Función uno a uno (p. 408) Una función uno a uno es una función donde cada valor *y* que se encuentra en el rango corresponde exactamente a un valor *x* en el dominio. Una función uno a uno f tiene un inverso f^{-1} que también es una función.

Opuesto (p. 14) El opuesto o inverso aditivo de cualquier número a es $-a$. La suma de opuestos es cero, la identidad aditiva.

Tripletas ordenadas (p. 164) Las tripletas ordenadas de la forma (x, y, z) representan la ubicación de un punto en el espacio de coordenadas.

Valor extremo (p. 712) Un valor extremo es un valor considerablemente diferente al resto de los datos de un conjunto.

Parábola (p. 194) La parábola es la gráfica de una función cuadrática. Es el conjunto de todos los puntos P situados en un plano a la misma distancia de un punto fijo F, o foco, y de la recta d, o directriz.

Example

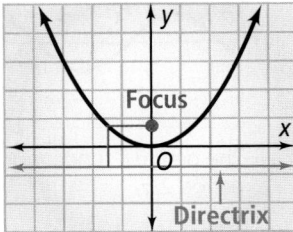

Parallel lines (p. 85) Parallel lines are coplanar lines that do not intersect. In the coordinate plane, parallel lines have the same slope.

Rectas paralelas (p. 85) Rectas paralelas son líneas coplanares que no se intersecan. En un plano de coordenadas, las rectas paralelas tienen la misma pendiente.

Parent function (p. 99) A parent function is the simplest form of a set of functions that form a family.

Función elemental (p. 99) Una función madre es la mínima expresión de un conjunto de funciones que forma una familia.

Example $y = x$ is the parent function for the functions of the form $y = x + k$.

Pascal's Triangle (p. 327) Pascal's Triangle is a triangular array of numbers in which the first and last number is 1. Each of the other numbers in the row is the sum of the two numbers above it.

Triángulo de Pascal (p. 327) El Triángulo de Pascal es una distribución triangular de números en la cual el primer número y el último número son 1. Cada uno de los otros números en la fila es la suma de los dos números de encima.

Example **Pascal's Triangle**

```
            1
          1   1
        1   2   1
      1   3   3   1
    1   4   6   4   1
  1   5  10  10   5   1
```

Percentiles (p. 714) A percentile is a number from 0 to 100 that you can associate with a value x from a data set. It shows the percent of the data that are less than or equal to x.

Percentiles (p. 714) Un percentil es un número de 0 a 100 que se puede asociar con un valor x de un conjunto de datos. Éste muestra el porcentaje de los datos que son menores o iguales a x.

Perfect square trinomial (p. 219) A perfect square trinomial is a trinomial that is the square of a binomial.

Trinomio cuadrado perfecto (p. 219) Un trinomio cuadrado perfecto es un trinomio que es el cuadrado de un binomio.

Example perfect square   binominal
          trinominal   square

$$16x^2 - 24x + 9 = (4x - 3)^2$$

Period (p. 828) The period of a periodic function is the horizontal length of one cycle.

Período (p. 828) El período de una función periódica es el intervalo horizontal de un ciclo.

Example

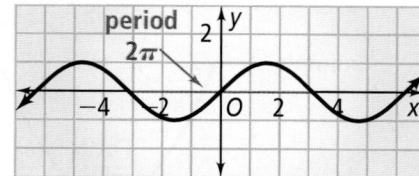

The periodic function $y = \sin x$ has period 2π.

English

Periodic function (p. 828)   A periodic function repeats a pattern of y-values at regular intervals.

Example

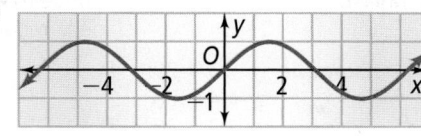

$$y = \sin x$$

Permutation (p. 675)   A permutation is an arrangement of items in a particular order. The number of permutations of n objects taken r at a time is $_nP_r = \frac{n!}{(n - r)!}$ for $1 \leq r \leq n$.

Example $_8P_5 = \frac{8!}{(8 - 5)!}$

$$= \frac{8 \cdot 7 \cdot 6 \cdot 5 \cdot 4 \cdot 3!}{3!}$$

$$= 8 \cdot 7 \cdot 6 \cdot 5 \cdot 4$$

$$= 6720$$

Perpendicular lines (p. 85)   Perpendicular lines are lines that intersect to form right angles. In the coordinate plane, perpendicular lines have slopes with product -1.

Phase shift (p. 875)   A horizontal translation of a periodic function is a phase shift.

Example

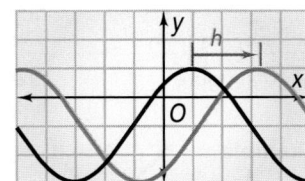

$g(x)$: horizontal translation of $f(x)$
$$g(x) = f(x - h)$$

Piecewise function (p. 90)   A piecewise function has different rules for different parts of its domain.

Point of discontinuity (p. 516)   A point of discontinuity is the x-coordinate of a point where the graph of $f(x)$ is not continuous.

Example $f(x) = \frac{2}{x - 2}$ has a point of discontinuity at $x = 2$.

Spanish

Función periódica (p. 828)   Una función periódica repite un patrón de valores y a intervalos regulares.

Permutación (p. 675)   Una permutación es la disposición de objetos en un orden determinado. El número de permutaciones de n objetos seleccionados r veces es $_nP_r = \frac{n!}{(n - r)!}$ para $1 \leq r \leq n$.

Rectas perpendiculares (p. 85)   Rectas perpendiculares son rectas que se intersecan y forman ángulos rectos. En un plano de coordenadas, las rectas perpendiculares tienen pendientes cuyo producto es -1.

Cambio de fase (p. 875)   Una traslación horizontal de una función periódica es un cambio de fase.

Función de fragmentos (p. 90)   Una función de fragmentos tiene reglas diferentes para diferentes partes de su dominio.

Punto de discontinuidad (p. 516)   Un punto de discontinuidad es la coordenada x de un punto donde la gráfica de $f(x)$ no es continua.

English

Point-slope form (p. 81) The point-slope form of an equation of a line is $y - y_1 = m(x - x_1)$, where m is the slope of the line and (x_1, y_1) is a point on the line.

Example $y - 3 = 2(x - 1)$
$y + 4 = 5(x - 2)$
$y - 2 = 3(x + 2)$

Polynomial (p. 280) A polynomial is a monomial or the sum of monomials.

Example $3x^3 + 4x^2 - 2x + 5$
$8x$
$x^2 + 4x + 2$

Polynomial function (p. 280) A polynomial in the variable x defines a polynomial function of x.

Example $P(x) = a_n x^n + a_{n-1} x^{n-1} - 1 + \cdots + a_1 x + a_0$ is a polynomial function, where n is a nonnegative integer and the coefficients $a_n, \ldots, a_0$ are real numbers.

Population (p. 725) A population is the members of a set.

Power function (p. 341) A power function is a function of the form $y = a \cdot x^b$, where a and b are nonzero real numbers.

Preimage (p. 801) The preimage is the original figure before a transformation.

Example

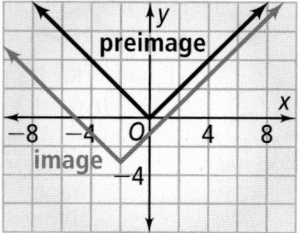

Principal root (p. 361) When a number has two real roots, the positive root is called the principal root. A radical sign indicates the principal root. The principal root of a negative number a is $i\sqrt{|a|}$.

Example The number 25 has two square roots, 5 and -5. The principal square root, 5, is indicated by $\sqrt{25}$ or $25^{\frac{1}{2}}$.

Spanish

Forma punto-pendiente (p. 81) La forma punto-pendiente de una ecuación lineal es $y - y_1 = m(x - x_1)$, donde m es la pendiente de la recta y (x_1, y_1) es un punto de la recta.

Polinomio (p. 280) Un polinomio es un monomio o la suma de dos o más monomios.

Función polinomial (p. 280) Un polinomio en la variable x define una función polinomial de x.

Población (p. 725) Una población está compuesta por los miembros de un conjunto.

Función de potencia (p. 341) Una función de potencia es una función de la forma $y = a \cdot x^b$, donde a y b son números reales diferentes de cero.

Preimagen (p. 801) La preimagen es la figura original antes de sufrir una transformación.

Raíz principal (p. 361) Cuando un número tiene dos raíces reales, la raíz positiva es la raíz principal. El signo del radical indica la raíz principal. La raíz principal de un número negativo a es $i\sqrt{|a|}$.

English

Probability distribution (p. 694)   A probability distribution is a function that tells the probability of each outcome in a sample space.

Spanish

Distribución de probabilidades (p. 694)   Una distribución de probabilidades es una función que señala la probabilidad de que cada resultado ocurra en un espacio muestral.

Example

Roll	Fr.	Prob.
1	5	0.125
2	9	0.225
3	7	0.175
4	8	0.2
5	8	0.2
6	3	0.075

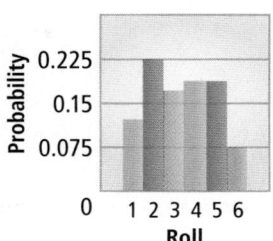

The table and graph both show the experimental probability distribution for the outcomes of 40 rolls of a standard number cube.

Probability model (p. 705)   A mathematical representation of a situation in which probabilities are assigned to outcomes.

Modelo de probabilidad (p. 705)   Representación matemática de una situación en la que se asignan probabilidades a los resultados.

Example   A restaurant gives a randomly selected toy with each child's meal. There are 5 different toys. Getting a certain toy has a probability of $\frac{1}{5}$. A probability model could be a random number table where 0 and 1 represent the first toy, 2 and 3 represent the second toy, and so on. Getting a 0 or a 1 has the probability of $\frac{1}{5}$.

Pure imaginary number (p. 249)   If $a = 0$ and $b \neq 0$, the number $a + bi$ is a pure imaginary number.

Número imaginario puro (p. 249)   Si $a = 0$ y $b \neq 0$, el número $a + bi$ es un número imaginario puro.

Q

Quadratic equation (p. 226)   A quadratic equation is one that can be written in the standard form $ax^2 + bx + c = 0$, where $a \neq 0$.

Ecuación cuadrática (p. 226)   Una ecuación cuadrática es una ecuación que se puede expresar en forma normal como $ax^2 + bx + c = 0$, donde $a \neq 0$.

Example $2x^2 + 3x + 1 = 0$

Quadratic Formula (p. 240)   The Quadratic Formula is $x = \frac{-b \pm \sqrt{b^2 - 4ac}}{2a}$. It gives the solutions to the quadratic equation $ax^2 + bx + c = 0$.

Fórmula cuadrática (p. 240)   La fórmula cuadrática es $x = \frac{-b \pm \sqrt{b^2 - 4ac}}{2a}$. Ésta da las soluciones a la ecuación cuadrática $ax^2 + bx + c = 0$.

Example   If $-x^2 + 3x + 2 = 0$, then

$$x = \frac{-3 \pm \sqrt{(3)^2 - 4(-1)(2)}}{2(-1)}$$

$$= \frac{-3 \pm \sqrt{17}}{-2}$$

English	Spanish

Quadratic function (p. 194) A quadratic function is a function that you can write in the form $f(x) = ax^2 + bx + c$ with $a \neq 0$.

Función cuadrática (p. 194) Una función cuadrática es una función que puedes escribir como $f(x) = ax^2 + bx + c$ con $a \neq 0$.

Example

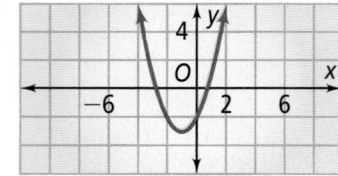

$$y = x^2 + 2x - 2$$

Quantity (p. 5) A mathematical quantity is anything that can be measured or counted.

Cantidad (p. 5) Una cantidad matemática es cualquier cosa que se puede medir o contar.

Quartile (p. 713) Quartiles are values that separate a finite data set into four equal parts. The second quartile (Q_2) is the median of the data. The first and third quartiles (Q_1 and Q_3) are the medians of the lower half and upper half of the data, respectively.

Cuartil (p. 713) Los cuartiles son valores que separan un conjunto finito de datos en cuatro partes iguales. El segundo cuartil (Q_2) es la mediana de los datos. Los cuartiles primero y tercero (Q_1 y Q_3) son las medianas de la mitad superior e inferior de los datos, respectivamente.

Example $\{2, 3, 4, 5, 5, 6, 7, 7\}$

$$Q_1 = 3.5$$
$$Q_2 \text{ (median)} = 5$$
$$Q_3 = 6.5$$

 R

Radian (p. 844) $\dfrac{a°}{180°} = \dfrac{r \text{ radians}}{\pi \text{ radians}}$

Radián (p. 844) $\dfrac{a°}{180°} = \dfrac{r \text{ radianes}}{\pi \text{ radianes}}$

Example $60° \rightarrow \dfrac{60}{180} = \dfrac{x}{\pi}$

$$x = \dfrac{60\pi}{180}$$
$$= \dfrac{\pi}{3}$$

Thus, $60° = \dfrac{\pi}{3}$ radians.

Radical equation (p. 390) A radical equation is an equation that has a variable in a radicand or has a variable with a rational exponent.

Ecuación radical (p. 390) La ecuación radical es una ecuación que contiene una variable en el radicando o una variable con un exponente racional.

Example $(\sqrt{x})^3 + 1 = 65$

$$x^{\frac{3}{2}} + 1 = 65$$

Radical function (p. 415) A radical function is a function that can be written in the form $f(x) = a\sqrt[n]{x - h} + k$, where $a \neq 0$. For even values of n, the domain of a radical function is the real numbers $x \geq h$. *See also* **Square root function.**

Función radical (p. 415) Una función radical es una función quepuede expresarse como $f(x) = a\sqrt[n]{x - h} + k$, donde $a \neq 0$. Para n par, el dominio de la función radical son los números reales tales que $x \geq h$. *Ver también* **Square root function.**

Example $f(x) = \sqrt{x - 2}$

English

Radicand (p. 362)   The number under a radical sign is the radicand.

Example   The radicand in $3\sqrt[4]{7}$ is 7.

Radius (p. 630)   The radius r of a circle is the distance between the center of the circle and any point on the circumference.

Example

Random sample (p. 725)   In a random sample, all members of the population are equally likely to be chosen as every other member.

Example   Let the set of all females between the ages of 19 and 34 be the population. A random selection of 900 females between those ages would be a sample of the population

Range (p. 61)   The range of a relation is the set of all outputs or y-coordinates of the ordered pairs.

Example   In the relation {(0, 1), (0, 2), (0, 3), (0, 4), (1, 3), (1, 4), (2, 1)}, the range is {1, 2, 3, 4}. In the function $f(x) = |x - 3|$, the range is the set of real numbers greater than or equal to 0.

Range of a set of data (p. 713)   The range of a set of data is the difference between the greatest and least values.

Example   The range of the set {3.2, 4.1, 2.2, 3.4, 3.8, 4.0, 4.2, 2.8} is $4.2 - 2.2 = 2$.

Rational equation (p. 542)   A rational equation is an equation that contains a rational expression.

Rational exponent (p. 382)   If the nth root of a is a real number and m is an integer, then $a^{\frac{1}{n}} = \sqrt[n]{a}$ and $a^{\frac{m}{n}} = \sqrt[n]{a^m} = \left(\sqrt[n]{a}\right)^m$. If m is negative, $a \neq 0$.

Example $4^{\frac{1}{3}} = \sqrt[3]{4}$

$5^{\frac{3}{2}} = \sqrt{5^3} = \left(\sqrt{5}\right)^3$

Spanish

Radicando (p. 362)   La expresión que aparece debajo del signo radical es el radicando.

Radio (p. 630)   El radio r de un círculo es la distancia entre el centro del círculo y cualquier punto de la circunferencia.

Muestra aleatoria (p. 725)   En una muestra aleatoria, la probabilidad de ser seleccionado es igual para todos los miembros.

Rango (p. 61)   El rango de una relación es el conjunto de todas las salidas posibles, o coordenadas y, de los pares ordenados.

Rango de un conjunto de datos (p. 713)   El rango de un conjunto de datos es la diferencia entre el valor máximo y el valor mínimo de los datos.

Ecuación racional (p. 542)   Una ecuación racional es una ecuación que contiene una expresión racional.

Exponente racional (p. 382)   Si la raíz n-ésima de a es un número real y m es un número entero, entonces $a^{\frac{1}{n}} = \sqrt[n]{a}$ y $a^{\frac{m}{n}} = \sqrt[n]{a^m} = \left(\sqrt[n]{a}\right)^m$. Si m es negativo, $a \neq 0$.

Visual Glossary

Rational expression (p. 527) A rational expression is the quotient of two polynomials.

Expresión racional (p. 527) Una expresión racional es el cociente de dos polinomios.

Rational function (p. 515) A rational function $f(x)$ can be written as $f(x) = \frac{P(x)}{Q(x)}$, where $P(x)$ and $Q(x)$ are polynomial functions. The domain of a rational function is all real numbers except those for which $Q(x) = 0$.

Función racional (p. 515) Una función racional $f(x)$ se puede expresar como $f(x) = \frac{P(x)}{Q(x)}$, donde $P(x)$ y $Q(x)$ son funciones de polinomios. El dominio de una función racional son todos los números reales excepto aquéllos para los cuales $Q(x) = 0$.

Example

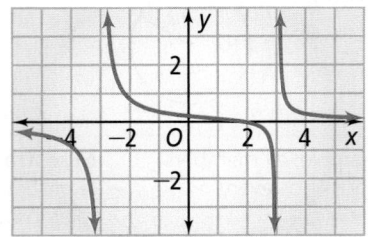

The function $y = \frac{x-2}{x^2-9}$ is a rational function with three branches separated by asymptotes $x = -3$ and $x = 3$.

Rational Root Theorem (p. 312) Let $P(x) = a_n x^n + a_{n-1} x^{n-1} + \cdots + a_1 x + a_0$ be a polynomial with integer coefficients.
Then there are a limited number of possible roots of $P(x) = 0$:
–Integer roots must be factors of a_0;
–Rational roots must have reduced form p/q where p is an integer factor of a_0 and q is an integer factor of a_n.

Teorema de la Raíz Racional (p. 312) Sea $P(x) = a_n x^n + a_{n-1} x^{n-1} + \cdots + a_1 x + a_0$ un polinomio con enteros como coeficientes.
Entonces hay un número limitado de raíces posibles para $P(x) = 0$:
–Las raíces enteras deben ser factores de a_0;
–Las raíces racionales deben ser de forma simplificada p/q, donde p es un factor entero de a_0 y q es un factor entero de a_n.

Example The polynomial equation
$10x^3 + 6x^2 - 11x - 2 = 0$ has leading coefficient 10 (with factors $(\pm 1, \pm 2, \pm 5, \pm 10)$ and constant term -2 (with factors ± 1 and ± 2). Its only possible rational roots are
$\pm 1, \pm 2, \pm \frac{1}{2}, \pm \frac{1}{5},$
$\pm \frac{2}{5}, \pm \frac{1}{10}.$

Rationalize the denominator (p. 369) To rationalize the denominator of an expression, rewrite it so there are no radicals in any denominator and no denominators in any radical.

Racionalizar el denominador (p. 369) Para racionalizar el denominador de una expresión, ésta se escribe de modo que no haya radicales en ningún denominador y no haya denominadores en ningún radical.

Example $\frac{1}{\sqrt{2}} = \frac{1}{\sqrt{2}} \times \frac{\sqrt{2}}{\sqrt{2}} = \frac{\sqrt{2}}{2}$

English

Reciprocal (p. 14) The reciprocal or multiplicative inverse of any nonzero number a is $\frac{1}{a}$. The product of reciprocals is 1, the multiplicative identity.

Example $5 \times \frac{1}{5} = 1$

Reciprocal function (p. 507) A reciprocal function belongs to the family whose parent function is $f(x) = \frac{1}{x}$ where $x \neq 0$. You can write a reciprocal function in the form $f(x) = \left(\frac{a}{x} - h\right) + k$, where $a \neq 0$ and $x \neq h$.

Example $f(x) = \frac{1}{2x + 5}$

$p(v) = \frac{3}{v} + 5$

Recursive formula (p. 565) A recursive formula defines the terms in a sequence by relating each term to the ones before it.

Example Let $a_n = 2.5a_{n-1} + 3a_{n-2}$.

If $a_5 = 3$ and $a_4 = 7.5$, then

$a_6 = 2.5(3) + 3(7.5) = 30$.

Reduced row echelon form (p. 177) A matrix that represents the solution of a system is in reduced row echelon form. The leading 1 in each row has 0's elsewhere in its column.

Reflection (p. 101) A reflection flips the graph of a function across a line, such as the x- or y-axis. Each point on the graph of the reflected function is the same distance from the line of reflection as is the corresponding point on the graph of the original function.

Example

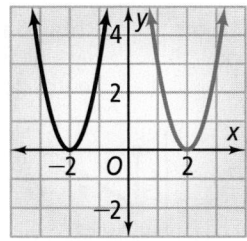

Relation (p. 60) A relation is a set of ordered pairs.

Example $\{(0, 1), (0, 2), (0, 3), (0, 4), (1, 3)\}$

Spanish

Recíproco (p. 14) El recíproco o inverso multiplicativo de un número distinto de cero a es $\frac{1}{a}$. El producto de recíprocos es 1, la identidad multiplicativa.

Función recíproca (p. 507) Una función recíproca pertenece a la familia cuya función madre es $f(x) = \frac{1}{x}$ donde $x \neq 0$. Se puede escribir una función recíproca como $f(x) = \left(\frac{a}{x} - h\right) + k$, donde $a \neq 0$ y $x \neq h$.

Fórmula recursiva (p. 565) Una fórmula recursiva define los términos de una secuencia al relacionar cada término con los términos que lo anteceden.

Forma reducida fila-escalón (p. 177) Una matriz que representa la solución de un sistema está en forma reducida fila-escalón. El 1 principal en cada fila tiene ceros en otras partes de la columna.

Reflexión (p. 101) Una reflexión voltea la gráfica de una función sobre una línea, como el eje de las x o el eje de las y. Cada punto de la gráfica de la función reflejada está a la misma distancia del eje de reflexión que el punto correspondiente en la gráfica de la función original.

Relación (p. 60) Una relación es un conjunto de pares ordenados.

Relative maximum (minimum) (p. 291) A relative maximum (minimum) is the value of the function at an up-to-down (down-to-up) turning point.

Máximo (minimo) relativo (p. 291) El máximo (mínimo) relativo es el valor de la función en un punto de giro de arriba hacia abajo (de abajo hacia arriba).

Example

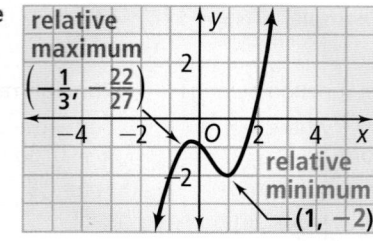

Remainder Theorem (p. 307) If you divide a polynomial $P(x)$ of degree $n > 1$ by $x - a$, then the remainder is $P(a)$.

Teorema del residuo (p. 307) Si divides un polinomio $P(x)$ con un grado $n > 1$ por $x - a$, el residuo es $P(a)$.

Example If $P(x) = x^3 - 4x^2 + x + 6$
is divided by $x - 3$, then the remainder is
$P(3) = 3^3 - 4(3)^2 + 3 + 6 = 0$ (which
means that $x - 3$ is a factor of $P(x)$).

Removable discontinuity (p. 516) A removable discontinuity is a point of discontinuity, a, of function f that you can remove by redefining f at $x = a$. Doing so fills in a hole in the graph of f with the point $(a, f(a))$.

Discontinuidad removible (p. 516) Una discontinuidad removible es un punto de discontinuidad a en una función f que se puede remover al redefinir f en $x = a$. Al hacer esto, se llena un hueco en la gráfica f con el punto $(a, f(a))$.

Root (p. 232) A root of a function is the input value for which the value of the function is zero. A root of an equation is a value that makes the equation true. *See also* **Zero of a function.**

Raíz (p. 232) La raíz de una función es el valor de entrada para el cual el valor de la función es cero. La raíz de una ecuación es un valor que hace verdadera la ecuación. *Ver también* **Zero of a function.**

Example -2 and 3 are roots of the function
$f(x) = (x + 2)(x - 3)$ and the
equation $(x + 2)(x - 3) = 0$.

Rotation (p. 804) A rotation is a transformation that turns a figure about a fixed point called the center of rotation.

Rotación (p. 804) Rotación es una transformación que hace girar una figura alrededor de un punto fijo llamado centro de rotación.

Example

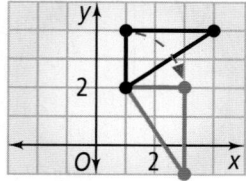

Row operation (p. 176) A row operation on an augmented matrix is any of the following: switch two rows, multiply a row by a constant, add one row to another.

Operación de fila (p. 176) Una operación de fila en una matriz ampliada es cualquiera de las siguientes opciones: el intercambio de dos filas, la multiplicación de una fila por una constante o la suma de dos filas.

English

Sample (p. 725) A sample from a population is some of the population.

Example Let the set of all males between the ages of 19 and 34 be the population. A random selection of 900 males between those ages would be a sample of the population.

Sample proportion (p. 747) The ratio $\hat{p}$ compares x to n where x is the number of times an event occurs and n is the sample size. $\hat{p} = \frac{x}{n}$.

Example In a taste test, 120 persons sampled two types of cola; 40 people preferred cola A. The sample proportion is $\frac{40}{120}$, or $\frac{1}{3}$.

Sample space (p. 682) The set of all possible outcomes of an experiment is called the sample space.

Example When you roll a number cube, the sample space is {1, 2, 3, 4, 5, 6}.

Scalar (p. 772) A scalar is a real number factor in a special product, such as the 3 in the vector product 3**v**.

Scalar multiplication (p. 772) Scalar multiplication is an operation that multiplies a matrix A by a scalar c. To find the resulting matrix cA, multiply each element of A by c.

Example
$$2.5\begin{bmatrix} 1 & 0 \\ -2 & 3 \end{bmatrix} = \begin{bmatrix} 2.5(1) & 2.5(0) \\ 2.5(-2) & 2.5(3) \end{bmatrix}$$
$$= \begin{bmatrix} 2.5 & 0 \\ -5 & 7.5 \end{bmatrix}$$

Scatter plot (p. 92) A scatter plot is a graph that relates two different sets of data by plotting the data as ordered pairs. You can use a scatter plot to determine a relationship between the data sets.

Spanish

Muestra (p. 725) Una muestra de una población es una parte de la población.

Proporción de una muestra (p. 747) La razón $\hat{p}$ compara x a n, siendo x el número de veces que sucede un evento y n el tamaño de la muestra. $\hat{p} = \frac{x}{n}$.

Espacio muestral (p. 682) El espacio muestral es el conjunto de todos los resultados posibles de un suceso.

Escalar (p. 772) Un escalar es un factor que es un número real en un producto especial, como el 3 en el producto vectorial 3**v**.

Multiplicación escalar (p. 772) La multiplicación escalar es la que multiplica una matriz A por un número escalar c. Para hallar la matriz cA resultante, multiplica cada elemento de A por c.

Diagrama de puntos (p. 92) Un diagrama de puntos es una gráfica que relaciona dos conjuntos de datos presentando los datos como pares ordenados. El diagrama de puntos sirve para definir la relación entre conjuntos de datos.

Example

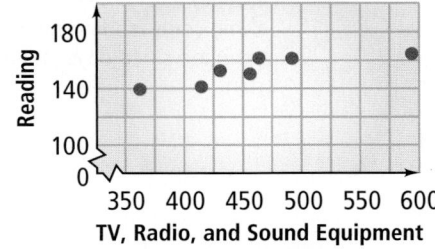

Dollars Spent Per Capita on Entertainment

Source: U.S. Bureau of Labor Statistics

English

Secant function (p. 883) The secant (sec) function is the reciprocal of the cosine function. For all real numbers θ except those that make $\cos \theta = 0$, $\sec \theta = \frac{1}{\cos \theta}$.

Example If $\cos \theta = \frac{5}{13}$, then $\sec \theta = \frac{13}{5}$.

Self-selected sample (p. 725) In a self-selected sample you select only members of the population who volunteered for the sample.

Sequence (p. 564) A sequence is an ordered list of numbers.

Example 1, 4, 7, 10, . . .

Series (p. 587) A series is the sum of the terms of a sequence.

Example The series $3 + 6 + 9 + 12 + 15$ corresponds to the sequence 3, 6, 9, 12, 15. The sum of the series is 45.

Simplest form of a radical expression (p. 368) A radical expression with index n is in simplest form if there are no radicals in any denominator, no denominators in any radical, and any radicand has no nth power factors.

Simplest form of a rational expression (p. 527) A rational expression is in simplest form if its numerator and denominator are polynomials that have no common divisor other than 1.

Example $\dfrac{x^2 - 7x + 12}{x^2 - 9} = \dfrac{(x - 4)(x - 3)}{(x + 3)(x - 3)} = \dfrac{x - 4}{x + 3}$, where $x \neq -3$

Simulation (p. 682) A simulation is a model that imitates one or more events.

Example Suppose a weather forecaster predicts a 50% chance of rain for the next three days. You can use three coins landing heads up to simulate three days in a row of rain.

Spanish

Función secante (p. 883) La función secante (sec) es el recíproco de la función coseno. Para todos los números reales θ, excepto aquéllos para los que $\cos \theta = 0$, $\sec \theta = \frac{1}{\cos \theta}$.

Muestra de voluntarios (p. 725) En una muestra de voluntarios se seleccionan sólo a los miembros de la población que se ofrecen voluntariamente para ser parte de la muestra.

Progresión (p. 564) Una progresión es una sucesión de números.

Serie (p. 587) Una serie es la suma de los términos de una secuencia.

Mínima expresión de una expresión radical (p. 368) Una expresión radical con índice n está en su mínima expresión si no tiene radicales en ningún denominador ni denominadores en ningún radical y los radicandos no tienen factores de potencia.

Forma simplificada de una expresión racional (p. 527) Una expresión racional se encuentra en su mínima expresión si su numerador y su denominador son polinomios que no tienen otro divisor aparte de 1.

Simulación (p. 682) Una simulación es un modelo que imita uno o más sucesos.

English

Spanish

Sine curve (p. 852)   A sine curve is the graph of a sine function.

Sinusoide (p. 852)   Sinusoide es la gráfica de la función seno.

Example

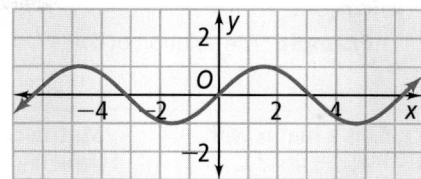

Sine function, Sine of θ (pp. 838, 851)   The sine function, $y = \sin\theta$, matches the measure θ of an angle in standard position with the y-coordinate of a point on the unit circle. This point is where the terminal side of the angle intersects the unit circle. The y-coordinate is the sine of θ.

Función seno, Seno de θ (pp. 838, 851)   La función seno, $y = \sin\theta$, empareja la medida θ de un ángulo en posición estándar con la coordenada y de un punto en el círculo unitario. Este es el punto en el que el lado terminal del ángulo interseca al círculo unitario. La coordenada y es el seno de θ.

Example

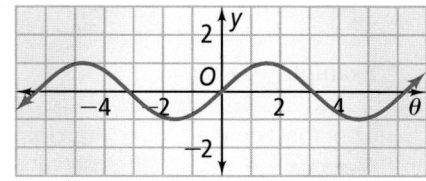

Singular matrix (p. 785)   A singular matrix is a square matrix with no inverse. Its determinant is 0.

Matriz singular (p. 785)   Una matriz singular es una matriz al cuadrado que no tiene inverso. El determinante de la matriz es 0.

Slope (p. 74)   The slope of a non-vertical line is the ratio of the vertical change to the horizontal change between points. You can calculate slope by finding the ratio of the difference in the y-coordinates to the difference in the x-coordinates for any two points on the line. The slope of a vertical line is undefined.

Pendiente (p. 74)   La pendiente de una línea no vertical es la razón del cambio vertical al cambio horizontal entre puntos. Puedes calcular la pendiente al hallar la razón de la diferencia de la coordenada y y la diferencia de la coordenada x para dos puntos cualesquiera de la línea. La pendiente de una línea vertical es indefinida.

Example   The slope of the line through points $(-1, -1)$ and $(1, -2)$ is

$$\frac{-2 - (-1)}{1 - (-1)} = \frac{-1}{2} = -\frac{1}{2}.$$

Slope-intercept form (p. 76)   The slope-intercept form of an equation of a line is $y = mx + b$, where m is the slope and b is the y-intercept.

Forma pendiente-intercepto (p. 76)   La forma pendiente-intercepto de una ecuación lineal es $y = mx + b$, donde m es la pendiente y b es el intercepto en y.

Example $y = 8x + 2$

$y = -x + 1$

$y = -\frac{1}{2}x - 14$

Solution of a system (p. 134)   A solution of a system is a set of values for the variables that makes all the equations true.

Solución de un sistema (p. 134)   Una solución de un sistema es un conjunto de valores para las variables que hace que todas las ecuaciones sean verdaderas.

English	Spanish

Solution of an equation (p. 27)   A solution of an equation is a number that makes the equation true.

Solución de una ecuación (p. 27)   Una solución de una ecuación es cualquier número que haga verdadera la ecuación.

Example   The solution of $2x - 7 = -12$ is $x = -2.5$.

Square matrix (p. 782)   A square matrix is a matrix with the same number of columns as rows.

Matriz cuadrada (p. 782)   Una matriz cuadrada es la que tiene la misma cantidad de columnas y filas.

Example   Matrix A is a square matrix.

$$A = \begin{bmatrix} 1 & 2 & 0 \\ -1 & 0 & -2 \\ 1 & 2 & 3 \end{bmatrix}$$

Square root equation (p. 390)   A square root equation is a radical equation in which the radical has index 2.

Ecuación de raíz cuadrada (p. 390)   Una ecuación de raíz cuadrada es una ecuación radical en la cual el radical tiene índice 2.

Example $\sqrt{x} = 4$

Square root function (p. 415)   A square root function is a function that can be written in the form $f(x) = a\sqrt{x - h} + k$, where $a \neq 0$. The domain of a square root function is all real numbers $x \geq h$.

Función de raíz cuadrada (p. 415)   Una función de raíz cuadrada es una función que puede ser expresada como $f(x) = a\sqrt{x - h} + k$, donde $a \neq 0$. El dominio de una función de raíz cuadrada son todos los números reales tales que $x \geq h$.

Example $f(x) = 2\sqrt{x - 3} + 4$

Standard deviation (p. 719)   Standard deviation is a measure of how much the values in a data set vary, or deviate, from the mean, $\bar{x}$. To find the standard deviation, follow five steps:

- Find the mean of the data set.
- Find the difference between each data value and the mean.
- Square each difference.
- Find the mean of the squares.
- Take the square root of the mean of the squares. This is the standard deviation.

Desviación típica (p. 719)   La desviación típica denota cuánto los valores de un conjunto de datos varían, o se desvían, de la media, $\bar{x}$. Para hallar la desviación típica, se siguen cinco pasos:

- Se halla la media del conjunto de datos.
- Se calcula la diferencia entre cada valor de datos y la media.
- Se eleva al cuadrado cada diferencia.
- Se halla la media de los cuadrados.
- Se calcula la raíz cuadrada de la media de los cuadrados. Ésa es la desviación típica.

Example $\{0, 2, 3, 4, 6, 7, 8, 9, 10, 11\}$

$\bar{x} = 6$

standard deviation $= \sqrt{12} \approx 3.46$

Standard form of a circle (p. 630)   *See* **Circle**.

Forma normal de un círculo (p. 630)   *Ver* **Circle**.

Example $(x - 3)^2 + (y - 4)^2 = 4$

English

Standard form of a linear equation (p. 82)   The standard form of a linear equation is $Ax + By = C$, where A, B, and C are real numbers, and A and B are not *both* zero.

Example   In standard form, the equation
$$y = \frac{4}{3}x - 1 \text{ is}$$
$$4x + (-3)y = 3.$$

Standard form of a polynomial function (p. 281)   The standard form of a polynomial function arranges the terms by degree in descending numerical order. A polynomial function, $P(x)$, in standard form is $P(x) = a_n x^n + a_{n-1}x^{n-1} + \cdots + a_1 x + a_0$, where n is a nonnegative integer and $a_n, \ldots, a_0$ are real numbers.

Example $2x^3 - 5x^2 - 2x + 5$

Standard form of a quadratic function (p. 202)   The standard form of a quadratic function is $f(x) = ax^2 + bx + c$ with $a \neq 0$.

Example $f(x) = 2x^2 + 5x + 2$

Standard position (p. 836)   An angle in the coordinate plane is in **standard position** when the vertex is at the origin and one ray is on the positive x-axis.

Example

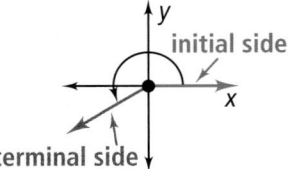
initial side

terminal side

Step function (p. 90)   A step function pairs every number in an interval with a single value. The graph of a step function can look like the steps of a staircase.

Sum of cubes (p. 297)   The sum of cubes is an expression of the form $a^3 + b^3$. It can be factored as $(a + b)(a^2 - ab + b^2)$.

Example $x^3 + 27 = (x + 3)(x^2 - 3x + 9)$

Survey (p. 726)   In a survey, you ask every member of a sample the same set of questions.

Spanish

Forma normal de una ecuación lineal (p. 82)   La forma normal de una ecuación lineal es $Ax + By = C$, donde A, B y C son números reales, y A y B no son cero *ambos*.

Forma normal de una función polinomial (p. 281)   La forma normal de una función polinomial organiza los términos por grado en orden numérico descendiente. Una función polinomial, $P(x)$, en forma normal es $P(x) = a_n x^n + a_{n-1}x^{n-1} + \cdots + a_1 x + a_0$, donde n es un número entero no negativo y $a_n, \ldots, a_0$ son números reales.

Forma normal de una función cuadrática (p. 202)   La forma normal de una función cuadrática es $f(x) = ax^2 + bx + c$ CON $a \neq 0$.

Posición estándar (p. 836)   Un ángulo en el plano de coordenadas se encuentra en **posición estándar** si el vértice se encuentra en el origen y una semirrecta se encuentra en el eje x positivo.

Función escalón (p. 90)   Una función escalón empareja cada número de un intervalo con un solo valor. La gráfica de una función escalón se puede parecer a los peldaños de una escalera.

Suma de dos cubos (p. 297)   La suma de dos cubos es una expresión de la forma $a^3 + b^3$. Se puede factorizar como $(a + b)(a^2 - ab + b^2)$.

Encuesta (p. 726)   En una encuesta, se le hace a cada miembro de una muestra la misma serie de preguntas.

English

Spanish

Synthetic division (p. 306) Synthetic division is a process for dividing a polynomial by a linear expression $x - a$. You list the standard-form coefficients (including zeros) of the polynomial, omitting all variables and exponents. You use a for the "divisor" and add instead of subtract throughout the process.

División sintética (p. 306) La división sintética es un proceso para dividir un polinomio por una expresión lineal $x - a$. En este proceso, escribes los coeficientes de forma normal (incluyendo los ceros) del polinomio, omitiendo todas las variables y todos los exponentes. Usas a como "divisor" y sumas, en vez de restar, a lo largo del proceso.

Example

$$\begin{array}{r|rrrrr} -3 & 2 & 5 & 0 & -2 & -8 \\ & & -6 & 3 & -9 & 33 \\ \hline & 2 & -1 & 3 & -11 & 25 \end{array}$$

Divide $2x^4 + 5x^3 - 2x - 8$ by $x + 3$. $2x^4 + 5x^3 - 2x - 8$ divided by $x + 3$ gives $2x^3 - x^2 + 3x - 11$ as quotient and 25 as remainder.

System of equations (p. 134) A system of equations is a set of two or more equations using the same variables.

Sistema de ecuaciones (p. 134) Un sistema de ecuaciones es un conjunto de dos o más ecuaciones que contienen las mismas variables.

Example $\begin{cases} 2x - 3y = -13 \\ 4x + 5y = 7 \end{cases}$

Systematic sample (p. 725) In a systematic sample you order the population in some way, and then select from it at regular intervals.

Muestra sistemática (p. 725) En una muestra sistemática se ordena la población de cierta manera y luego se selecciona una muestra de esa población a intervalos regulares.

 T

Tangent function, Tangent of θ (pp. 868, 869) The tangent function, $y = \tan\theta$, matches the measure θ, of an angle in standard position with the y/x ratio of the (x, y) coordinates of a point on the unit circle. This point is where the terminal side of the angle intersects the unit circle. y/x is the tangent of θ.

Función tangente, Tangente de θ (pp. 868, 869) La función tangente, $y = \tan\theta$, empareja la medida θ, de un ángulo en posición estándar con la razón y/x de las coordenadas (x, y) de un punto en el círculo unitario. Este es el punto en el que el lado terminal del ángulo interseca al círculo unitario. y/x es la tangente de θ.

Example

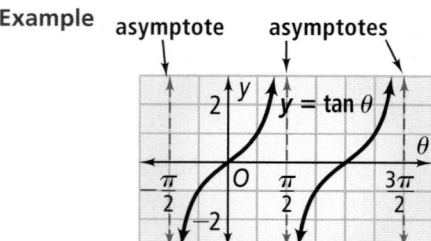 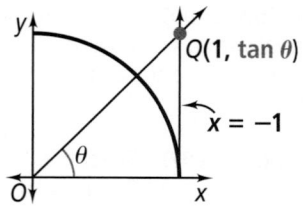

Term of a sequence (p. 564) Each number in a sequence is a term.

Término de una progresión (p. 564) Cada número de una progresión es un término.

Example 1, 4, 7, 10, . . .
The second term is 4.

English

Term of an expression (p. 20) A term is a number, a variable, or the product of a number and one or more variables.

Example The expression $4x^2 - 3y + 7.3$ has 3 terms.

Terminal point (p. 809) The terminal point of a vector is the tip (not the endpoint) of a vector arrow.

Terminal side (p. 836) *See* **Initial side.**

Test point (p. 115) A test point is a point that you pick on one side of the boundary of the graph of a linear inequality. If the test point makes the inequality true, then all points on that side of the boundary are solutions of the inequality. If the test point makes the inequality false, then all points on the other side are solutions.

Theoretical probability (p. 683) If a sample space has n equally likely outcomes, and an event A occurs in m of these outcomes, then the theoretical probability of event A is $P(A) = \frac{m}{n}$.

Example Use the set {1, 4, 9, 16, 25, 36, 49, 64, 81, 100}. The probability that a number selected at random is greater than 50 is $P(A) = \frac{3}{10} = 0.3$.

Transformation (p. 99) A transformation of a function $y = af(x - h) + k$ is a change made to at least one of the values a, h, and k. The four types of transformations are dilations, reflections, rotations, and translations.

Example $g(x) = 2(x - 3)$ is a transformation of $f(x) = x$.

Translation (p. 99) A translation shifts the graph of the parent function horizontally, vertically, or both without changing its shape or orientation.

Example

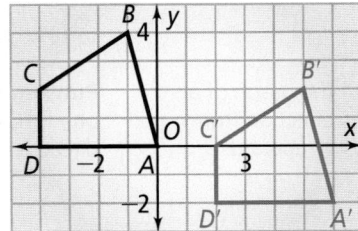

Spanish

Término de una expresión (p. 20) Un término es un número, una variable o el producto de un número y una o más variables.

Punto terminal (p. 809) El punto terminal de un vector es la punta (no el extremo) de una flecha vectorial.

Lado terminal (p. 836) *Ver* **Initial side.**

Punto de prueba (p. 115) Un punto de prueba es un punto que escoges a un lado del límite de la gráfica de una desigualdad lineal. Si el punto de prueba hace que la desigualdad sea verdadera, entonces todos los puntos en ese límite son soluciones de la desigualdad. Si el punto de prueba hace que la desigualdad sea falsa, entonces todos los puntos del otro lado del límite son soluciones.

Probabilidad teórica (p. 683) Si un espacio muestral tiene n resultados con la misma probabilidad de ocurrir, y ocurre un suceso A en m de estos resultados, entonces la probabilidad teórica del suceso A es $P(A) = \frac{m}{n}$.

Transformación (p. 99) Una transformación de una función $y = af(x - h) + k$ es un cambio que se le hace a por lo menos uno de los valores a, h y k. Hay cuatro tipos de transformaciones: dilataciones, reflexiones, rotaciones y traslaciones.

Traslación (p. 99) Una traslación desplaza la gráfica de la función madre horizontalmente, verticalmente o en ambas direcciones, sin cambiar su forma u orientación.

English

Spanish

Transverse axis (p. 646) The transverse axis of a hyperbola is the segment that is on the line containing the foci and has endpoints on the hyperbola.

Eje transversal (p. 646) El eje transversal de una hipérbola es el segmento que se encuentra sobre la línea que contiene los focos y tiene sus puntos extremos sobre la hipérbola.

Example

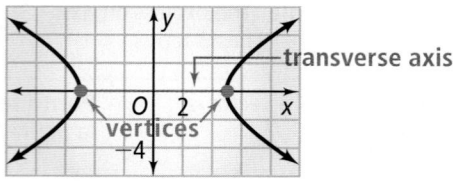

Trend line (p. 93) A trend line is a line that approximates the relationship between two variables, or data sets, of a scatter plot.

Línea de tendencia (p. 93) Una línea de tendencia es una línea que aproxima la relación entre dos variables o conjuntos de datos de un diagrama de dispersión.

Example

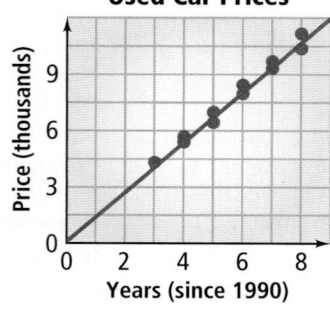

Used Car Prices

Trigonometric identity (p. 904) A trigonometric identity in one variable is a trigonometric equation that is true for all values of the variable for which both sides of the equation are defined.

Identidad trigonométrica (p. 904) Una identidad trigonométrica en una variable es una ecuación trigonométrica que es verdadera para todos los valores de la variable para los cuales se definen los dos lados de la ecuación.

Example $\tan \theta = \frac{\sin \theta}{\cos \theta}$

Trigonometric ratios (p. 920) If θ is an acute angle of a right triangle, x is the length of the adjacent leg (ADJ), y is the length of the opposite leg (OPP), and r is the length of the hypotenuse (HYP), then the trigonometric ratios of θ are

$\sin \theta = \frac{y}{r} = \frac{OPP}{HYP}$ $\csc \theta = \frac{r}{y} = \frac{HYP}{OPP}$

$\cos \theta = \frac{x}{r} = \frac{ADJ}{HYP}$ $\sec \theta = \frac{r}{x} = \frac{HYP}{ADJ}$

$\tan \theta = \frac{y}{x} = \frac{OPP}{ADJ}$ $\cot \theta = \frac{x}{y} = \frac{ADJ}{HYP}$

Razones trigonométricas (p. 920) Si θ es un ángulo agudo de un triángulo, x es la longitud del cateto adyacente (ADJ), y es la longitud del cateto opuesto (OPP) y r es la longitud de la hipotenusa (HYP), entonces las razones trigonométricas son:

$\sin \theta = \frac{y}{r} = \frac{OPP}{HYP}$ $\csc \theta = \frac{r}{y} = \frac{HYP}{OPP}$

$\cos \theta = \frac{x}{r} = \frac{ADJ}{HYP}$ $\sec \theta = \frac{r}{x} = \frac{HYP}{ADJ}$

$\tan \theta = \frac{y}{x} = \frac{OPP}{ADJ}$ $\cot \theta = \frac{x}{y} = \frac{ADJ}{HYP}$

Turning point (p. 282) A turning point of the graph of a function is a point where the graph changes direction from upwards to downwards or from downwards to upwards.

Punto de giro (p. 282) Un punto de giro de la gráfica de una función es un punto donde la gráfica cambia de dirección de arriba hacia abajo o vice versa.

English

Uniform Distribution (p. 694)   A uniform distribution is a probability distribution that is equal for each event in the sample space.

Unit circle (p. 838)   The unit circle has a radius of 1 unit and its center is at the origin of the coordinate plane.

Example

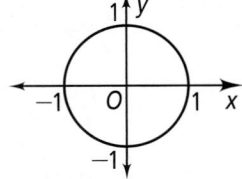

Value (p. 5)   The value of a quantity is its measure or the number of items that you count.

Variable (p. 5)   A variable is a symbol, usually a letter, that represents one or more numbers.

Variable matrix (p. 793)   When representing a system of equations with a matrix equation, the matrix containing the variables of the system is the variable matrix.

Example $\begin{cases} x + 2y = 5 \\ 3x + 5y = 14 \end{cases}$

variable matrix $\begin{bmatrix} X \\ Y \end{bmatrix}$

Variable quantity (p. 5)   A variable quantity can have values that vary.

Variance (p. 719)   Variance is the square of the standard deviation. $\sigma^2 = \frac{\left(\sum (x - \bar{x})^2 \right)}{n}$.

Vector (p. 809)   A vector is a mathematical object that has both magnitude and direction.

Vertex (p. 107)   A vertex of a function is a point where the function reaches a maximum or a minimum value.

Spanish

Distribución uniforme (p. 694)   Una distribución uniforme es una distribución de probabilidad que es igual para cada suceso en el espacio muestral.

Círculo unitario (p. 838)   El círculo unitario tiene un radio de 1 unidad y el centro está situado en el origen del plano de coordenadas.

Valor (p. 5)   El valor de una cantidad es su medida o el número de datos que cuentas.

Variable (p. 5)   Una variable es un símbolo, generalmente una letra, que representa uno o más valores.

Matriz variable (p. 793)   Al representar un sistema de ecuaciones con una ecuación de matricial, la matriz que contenga las variables del sistema es la matriz variable.

Cantidad variable (p. 5)   Una cantidad variable puede tener valores que varían.

Varianza (p. 719)   La varianza es el cuadrado de la desviación estándar. $\sigma^2 = \frac{\left(\sum (x - \bar{x})^2 \right)}{n}$.

Vector (p. 809)   Un vector es un objeto matemático que tiene tanto magnitud como dirección.

Vértice (p. 107)   El vértice de una función es el punto donde la función alcanza un valor máximo o mínimo.

Visual **Glossary**

English

Spanish

Vertex form of a quadratic function (p. 194) The vertex form of a quadratic function is $f(x) = a(x - h)^2 + k$, where $a \neq 0$ and (h, k) is the coordinate of the vertex of the function.

Forma del vértice de una función cuadrática (p. 194) La forma vértice de una función cuadrática es $f(x) = a(x - h)^2 + k$, donde $a \neq 0$ y (h, k) es la coordenada del vértice de la función.

Example $f(x) = x^2 + 2x - 1 = (x + 1)^2 - 2$
The vertex is $(-1, -2)$.

Vertex of a parabola (p. 194) The vertex of a parabola is the point where the function for the parabola reaches a maximum or a minimum value. The parabola intersects its axis of symmetry at the vertex.

Vértice de una parábola (p. 194) El vértice de una parábola es el punto donde la función de la parábola alcanza un valor máximo o mínimo. La parábola y su eje de simetría se intersecan en el vértice.

Example

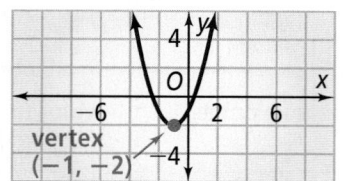

The vertex of the quadratic function
$y = x^2 + 2x - 1$ is $(-1, -2)$.

Vertical compression (p. 102) A vertical compression reduces all *y*-values of a function by the same factor between 0 and 1.

Compresión vertical (p. 102) Una compresión vertical reduce todos los valores de *y* de una función por el mismo factor entre 0 y 1.

Vertical stretch (p. 102) A vertical stretch multiplies all *y*-values of a function by the same factor greater than 1.

Estiramiento vertical (p. 102) Un estiramiento vertical multiplica todos los valores de *y* por el mismo factor mayor que 1.

Vertical-line test (p. 62) You can use the vertical-line test on the graph of a relation to tell whether the relation is a function. If a vertical line passes through more than one point on the graph of a relation, then the relation is *not* a function.

Prueba de la recta vertical (p. 62) Puedes usar la prueba de la línea vertical en la gráfica de una relación para saber si la relación es una función. Si una línea vertical pasa por más de un punto de la gráfica de la relación, entonces la relación *no* es una función.

Example

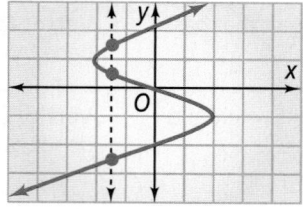

This relation is not a function.

Visual **Glossary**

English

Spanish

Vertices of a hyperbola (p. 646) The endpoints of the transverse axis of a hyperbola are the vertices of the hyperbola.

Vértices de una hipérbola (p. 646) Los dos puntos de intersección de la hipérbola y su eje mayor son los vértices de la hipérbola.

Example

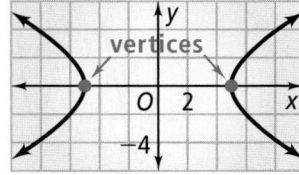

Vertices of an ellipse (p. 639) The endpoints of the major axis of an ellipse are the vertices of the ellipse.

Vértices de una elipse (p. 639) Los dos puntos de intersección de la elipse y su eje mayor son los vértices de la elipse.

Example

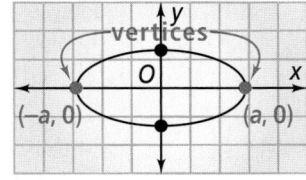

X

x-intercept, y-intercept (p. 76) The point at which a line crosses the *x*-axis (or the *x*-coordinate of that point) is an *x*-intercept. The point at which a line crosses the *y*-axis (or the *y*-coordinate of that point) is a *y*-intercept.

Intercepto en *x*, intercepto en *y* (p. 76) El punto donde una recta corta el eje *x* (o la coordenada *x* de ese punto) es el intercepto en *x*. El punto donde una recta cruza el eje *y* (o la coordenada *y* de ese punto) es el intercepto en *y*.

Example

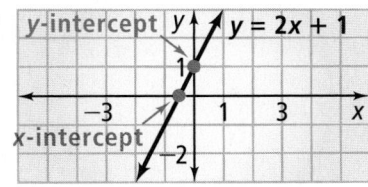

The *x*-intercept of $y = 2x + 1$ is
$\left(-\frac{1}{2}, 0\right)$ or $-\frac{1}{2}$.
The *y*-intercept of $y = 2x + 1$ is $(0, 1)$
or 1.

Z

Zero matrix (p. 766) The zero matrix O, or $O_{m \times n}$, is the $m \times n$ matrix whose elements are all zeros. It is the additive identity matrix for the set of all $m \times n$ matrices.

Matriz cero (p. 766) La matriz cero, O, o $O_{m \times n}$, es la matriz $m \times n$ cuyos elementos son todos ceros. Es la matriz de identidad aditiva para el conjunto de todas las matrices $m \times n$.

Example $\begin{bmatrix} 1 & 4 \\ 2 & -3 \end{bmatrix} + O = \begin{bmatrix} 1 & 4 \\ 2 & -3 \end{bmatrix}$

Zero of a function (p. 226) A zero of a function $f(x)$ is any value of x for which $f(x) = 0$.

Cero de una función (p. 226) Un cero de una función $f(x)$ es cualquier valor de x para el cual $f(x) = 0$.

Example

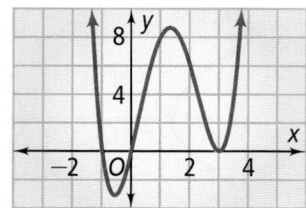

Zero-Product Property (p. 226) If the product of two or more factors is zero, then one of the factors must be zero.

Propiedad del cero del producto (p. 226) Si el producto de dos o más factores es cero, entonces uno de los factores debe ser cero.

Example $(x - 3)(2x - 5) = 0$
$x - 3 = 0$ or $2x - 5 = 0$

z-score (p. 748) The z-score of a value is the number of standard deviations that the value is from the mean.

Puntaje z (p. 748) El puntaje z de un valor es el número de desviaciones normales que tiene ese valor de la media.

Example $\{0, 2, 3, 4, 6, 7, 8, 9, 10, 11\}$
$\bar{x} = 6$
standard deviation $= \sqrt{12} \approx 3.46$
For 8, z-score $= \dfrac{8 - 6}{\sqrt{12}} \approx 0.58$.

Selected Answers

Chapter 1

Get Ready! pp. 1 1. 0 **2.** -2 **3.** -2.09 **4.** 8.05
5. $-\frac{3}{4}$ **6.** $\frac{11}{12}$ **7.** $10\frac{7}{10}$ **8.** $3\frac{1}{2}$ **9.** -42 **10.** 72 **11.** 9
12. -9.8 **13.** $-3\frac{1}{3}$ **14.** $-5\frac{1}{2}$ **15.** $-4\frac{2}{3}$ **16.** $-\frac{3}{4}$
17. -21 **18.** 7.35 **19.** $-\frac{1}{6}$ **20.** $-\frac{3}{5}$ **21.** -20 **22.** 8
23. 0.97 **24.** -5 **25.** 55 **26.** 3 **27.** because the placement of the parentheses changes the order of operations **28.** 3 **29.** 3 terms **30.** Calculate the answer numerically. **31.** $\frac{3}{n-3}$

Lesson 1-1   pp. 4–10

Got It? 1. The pattern shows a center square and a yellow square added to each side with the number of squares per side increasing by one.

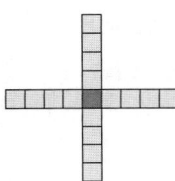

2. 52 tiles **3. a.** $12 **b.** $20 **c.** The number of platys must be a whole number whereas the length of fish can be a fraction or a decimal.
Lesson Check 1. add 35 **2.** rotate 90° clockwise
3.

Input	Process Column	Output
1	2(1)	2
2	2(2)	4
3	2(3)	6
4	2(4)	8
⋮	⋮	⋮
n	2(n)	2n

4.

Input	Process Column	Output
1	3(1)	3
2	3(2)	6
3	3(3)	9
4	3(4)	12
⋮	⋮	⋮
n	3(n)	3n

5. Answers may vary. Sample: Look for the same type of change between consecutive figures.
6. Answers may vary. Sample: Tables of values and pictorial representations are both convenient ways to organize data and discover patterns. Tables give more

detail. Pictorial representations are visual. **7.** No; the output is $\frac{1}{2}$ the input for all values except the first (Input: 3; Output: 2).
Exercises 9. Base of 3 squares with the number of squares increasing vertically by one on each of the outer squares of the base.

11. One square, then 2^2 or 4 squares, then 3^2 or 9 squares, then 4^2 or 16 squares. In general, the number of squares is $n \times n$ or n^2.

13. $2n$

Input	Process Column	Output
1	2(1)	2
2	2(2)	4
3	2(3)	6
4	2(4)	8
⋮	⋮	⋮
n	2(n)	2n

15. $4n - 1$

Input	Process Column	Output
1	4(1) − 1	3
2	4(2) − 1	7
3	4(3) − 1	11
4	4(4) − 1	15
⋮	⋮	⋮
n	4(n) − 1	4n − 1

17. 7; 8; $n + 2$
19. Output = Input + 1

Input	Process Column	Output
1	(1) + 1	2
2	(2) + 1	3
3	(3) + 1	4
4	(4) + 1	5
5	(5) + 1	6
⋮	⋮	⋮
n	(n) + 1	n + 1

21. Output = Input − 1

Input	Process Column	Output
1	(1) − 1	0
2	(2) − 1	1
3	(3) − 1	2
4	(4) − 1	3
5	(5) − 1	4
⋮	⋮	⋮
n	(n) − 1	$n − 1$

23. 40 **25.** add 6 or $6n$; 30, 36, 42 **27.** add 3, then add 4, then add 5, and so on; 21, 28, 36 **29.** multiply by 3; 243, 729, 2187 **31.** The black square and dot each move clockwise one block
33. 9216 in.^{3} **35.** $n + 10$, where n is the number of months **37.** 21; $4n + 1$ **39.** −13; $7 − 4n$; or $−4n + 7$
41. Answers may vary. Sample: Jesse will not grow at the same rate between the ages of 15 and 20 as he has during the 4 years prior to age 15. **43.** D **45. a.** Each number is a result of the division of the previous number by 2. **b.** $36 \div 2 = 18$, $18 \div 2 = 9$, $9 \div 2 = 4.5$, so 4.5 is the first noninteger number. **46.** 1.9 **47.** −3.8 **48.** 27
49. 0 **50.** −0.4 **51.** 7 **52.** 50% **53.** 25% **54.** 33.33%
55. 140% **56.** 172% **57.** 123%

Lesson 1-2   pp. 11–17

Got It? 1. rational numbers
2.

$$\frac{1}{3} \quad 1.\overline{4} \quad \sqrt{3}$$

3. a. $\sqrt{26} < 6.25$ or $6.25 > \sqrt{26}$ **b.** $a < c$; a will be to the left of c on the number line.
4. a. Distr. Prop.
  b. $a + [3 + (−a)]$
      $= a + [(−a) + 3]$ Comm.
      $= [a + (−a)] + 3$ Assoc.
      $= 0 + 3$ Inverse
      $= 3$ Identity
Lesson Check 1. Answers may vary. Sample: the number of times a cricket chirps **2.** Answers may vary. Sample: the change in number of people on a bus after a stop **3.** Answers may vary. Sample: the outdoor temperature in tenths of a degree **4.** Inv. Prop. of Add.
5. Assoc. Prop. of Mult. **6.** multiplicative inverse **7.** Both properties result in the original term; 0 is the additive identity, whereas 1 is the multiplicative identity. **8.** The equation illustrates the Comm. Prop. of Add. **9.** Answers may vary. Sample: $\sqrt{2}$ is not a rational number because it cannot be written as a quotient of integers.
Exercises 11. y, natural numbers; p, rational numbers
13.

15.

17.

19.

21.

23. $>$ **25.** $<$ **27.** $>$ **29.** $>$ **31.** $>$ **33.** $<$
35. Distr. Prop. **37.** Assoc. Prop. of Mult. **39.** Ident. Prop. of Add. **41–48.** Answers may vary. Samples are given. **41.** −5 **43.** $−1\frac{1}{4}$ **45.** $1\frac{2}{3}$ **47.** 4 **49.** $\sqrt{50}$ in. × $\sqrt{50}$ in. × $\sqrt{50}$ in. **51.** natural numbers **53.** irrational numbers **55.** irrational numbers **57.** 8, 1, $\frac{1}{3}$, $−\sqrt{2}$, −3
59. 5.73, $\frac{1}{4}$, −0.06, $−3\sqrt{3}$, −17 **61.** Answers may vary. Sample: 7 **63.** Answers may vary. Sample: $\sqrt{2}$ and $\sqrt{2}$ **65.** Answers may vary. **67.** Answers may vary.

69. $5(x + 2y − 7)$ **71.** No; $\frac{1}{0}$ is undefined. **73.** H

Lesson 1-3   pp. 18–24

Got It? 1. H **2.** $150 − 2d$, with $d =$ the number of days **3. a.** 18 **b.** Yes; the numerator will become $2x^2 − y^2$, not $2x^2 − 2y^2$. **4.** Let $x =$ the number of two-point shots, $y =$ the number of three-point shots, $z =$ the number of one-point free throws, $2x + 3y + 1z$; 42 points **5. a.** $−3j^2 − 7k + 5j$
b. $12a − 53b$
Lesson Check 1. $\frac{2 + b}{3}$ **2.** $4k + m$ **3.** 12 **4.** 13
5. −5 **6.** −5 **7.** The student did not distribute the −1. $3p^2q + 2p − (5q + p − 2p^2q) = 3p^2q + 2p − 5q − p + 2p^2q = 5p^2q + p − 5q$ **8.** A constant is a term with no variables, whereas a coefficient is the numerical factor in a term. **9.** Answers may vary. Sample: Both algebraic expressions and numerical expressions represent a quantity using numbers, operations and grouping symbols. An algebraic expression includes variables when representing a quantity. Examples: numerical expression: $3 + 6(5 − 2)$; algebraic expression: $2z + 3z(6 + 5z)$.
Exercises 11. $8(x + 3)$ **13.** $130 − 10w$, with $w =$ number of weeks **15.** $250 − 60w$, with $w =$ number of weeks **17.** −16 **19.** −12 **21.** 4 ft **23.** 1600 ft
25. $1331 **27.** $1610.51 **29.** Let $x =$ the number of 3-run home runs and $y =$ the number of 2-run hits; $3x + 2y$; 14 **31.** $2s + 5$ **33.** $6a + 3b$ **35.** $−0.5x$
37. $4g − 2$ **39.** 3 **41.** 37 **43.** 10 **45.** $\frac{\$84}{m}$
47. $\frac{5x^2}{2}$ **49.** y **51.** $−2x^2 + 2y^2$ **53.** $8.5x − 15$ **55.** No; John did not use the opposite of a sum correctly; $−(x + y) + 3(x − 4y)$; $−x − y + 3x − 12y$; $2x − 13y$ **57.** Distr. Prop. **59.** Opposite of a Difference

61. Answers may vary. Sample:

$$2(b-a) + 5(b-a)$$
$$= (2+5)(b-a) \quad \text{Distr. Prop.}$$
$$= 7(b-a) \quad \text{Add.}$$
$$= 7b - 7a \quad \text{Distr. Prop.}$$

Lesson 1-4   pp. 26–32

Got It? 1. $\frac{3}{2}$ **2.** -1 **3.** 40 m $\times$ 120 m **4. a.** never
b. always **5. a.** $C = K - 273$ **b.** always
Lesson Check 1. 23.2 **2.** -90 **3.** 12
4. $k = \frac{1}{2}(r - 15)$ **5.** $k = \frac{1}{3}(z + 6)$
6. $k = -\left(\frac{1}{6}\right)(h + 14)$ **7.** To find a solution of an
equation means to find the value of the variable that
makes the equation true. **8.** Four buses are not enough.
The number of buses must be a whole number, so round
the number of buses to 5. **9.** The 2nd line is incorrect;
subtract 10 from both sides: $12x = -12\ x = -1$
Exercises 11. -81 **13.** 14 **15.** 8 **17.** -5
19. $-\frac{1}{9}$ **21.** $\frac{3}{2}$ **23.** -6 **25.** 0 **27.** 300 mi/h; 600 mi/h
29. sometimes **31.** sometimes **33.** $h = \frac{2A}{b}$ **35.** $w = \frac{V}{\ell h}$
37. $x = \frac{c}{a+b}$, $a \neq -b$ **39.** $x = 2(m + n) + 2$ **41.** 1.5
43. $\frac{23}{3}$, or $7\frac{2}{3}$ **45.** 34° and 56° **47.** $b_2 = \frac{2A}{h} - b_1$
49. $v = \frac{h + 5t^2}{t}$ **51.** $r_2 = \frac{Rr_1}{r_1 - R}$ **53.** 40°, 140°
55. $x = \frac{3b + 2c - 5}{b - c}$, $\frac{b°}{c}$ **57.** $x = \frac{4a - 3bc}{aq - 5bp}$, $5bp \neq aq$
59. $x = \frac{10c}{a}$, $a \neq 0$ **61.** Let $c =$ number of swim days;
$3c = 82 + c$; 41 days **63.** No; $n = \frac{s}{1-s}$ **not** $\frac{s}{s-1}$
65. 264 ft

Lesson 1-5   pp. 33–40

Got It? 1. $\frac{x}{3} \leq 15$
  2. $x \leq -8$

3. more than 32 songs **4.** always
5. a. $x \geq 2$ and $x < 6$

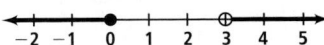

b. sometimes; The compound inequality is true when
$x = 5$ and not true when $x = 7$.
6. a. $w < -3$ or $w > \frac{8}{7}$

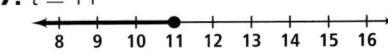

b. $x < -1$ or $x > 3$

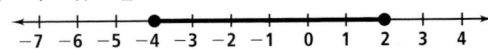

Lesson Check 1. $R \geq J$ **2.** $w \geq 40$ and $w < 74$

3. $x \leq -2$

4. $1 < x < \frac{9}{5}$

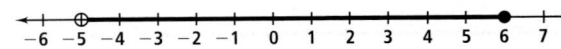

5. $x \leq 0$ or $x > 3$

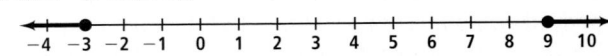

6. Answers may vary. Sample: $5 < 6$, but $-5 > -6$.
7. The transitive, addition and subtraction properties of
inequality are similar to the properties of equality. The
multiplication and division properties differ. Multiplying or
dividing each side of an inequality by a negative number
reverses the direction of the inequality symbol.
8. Answers may vary. Sample: $3x + 5 < 3(x + 5)$
9. No; Answers may vary. Sample: $2x < x + 1$ and
$x + 1 > 3$
Exercises 11. $8x \geq 25$ **13.** $\frac{x}{12} \leq 6$
15. $k > -9$

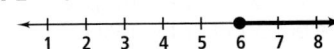

17. $t \leq 11$

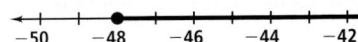

19. $y \leq -6$

21. $m < 10$

23. $w > 6$

25. The longest side is less than 21 cm. **27.** at most 40
students **29.** always **31.** never **33.** sometimes
35. sometimes
37. $-4 \leq x \leq 2$

39. $-5 < x \leq 6$

41. all real numbers

43. $x \leq -3$ or $x \geq 9$

45. $z \geq 6$

47. $x \geq -48$

49. no solution **51.** 98 **53.** $2 < AB < 6$ **55.** The classmate reversed the direction of the $\geq$ symbol to $\leq$ incorrectly. The correct answer is $y \leq -20$. **57.** Distr. Prop.; arithmetic; Subtr. Prop. of Inequality; Mult. Prop. of Inequality

59. $-1 < x < 8$

61. $x < -2$ or $x > 2$

63. Answers may vary. Sample: $-3x + 1 > 4$
65. Answers may vary. Sample: $2x + 4 \leq 0$ or $-3x - 3 \leq 0$
67. D **69.** D **71.** $7a + 5$ **72.** $-2x + 14y$
73. $\frac{b}{12} + 1$ **74.** $1.61 - 0.1k$ **75.** 4
76. no solution **77.** $\frac{9}{10}$ **78.** -20

Lesson 1-6   pp. 41–48

Got It?

1. $\frac{2}{3}, -2$

2. $-7, -11$

3. -1 **4.** $-\frac{4}{3} \leq x \leq 4$

5. a. $x < -5$ or $x > 1$

b. The graph will have two closed circles with an arrow extending to the left of one and to the right of the other. **6.** $|h - 52.5| \leq 0.5$
Lesson Check 1. $-4, 4$ **2.** $-12, 4$ **3.** $-\frac{6}{5}$
4. $-11 < x < 9$

5. $x \leq -1$ or $x \geq 4$

6. A solution of an eq. is extraneous if it is a solution to a derived eq., but is not a solution to the original eq.
7. when the number is positive or 0 **8.** Answers may vary. Sample: $d < -5$ and $5d > 25$ **9.** Answers may vary. Sample: An absolute value equation or inequality represents two equations or inequalities; each equation or inequality is solved in the same manner as a linear equation or inequality.
Exercises 11. $-8, 8$ **13.** $-\frac{5}{3}, 3$ **15.** no solution
17. $-7, 17$ **19.** $-\frac{3}{2}$ **21.** $\frac{3}{2}$ **23.** $-1, \frac{3}{2}$

25. $0 < y < 18$

27. $-2 < x < 6$

29. $-3\frac{1}{2} \leq w \leq \frac{1}{2}$

31. $x < -12$ or $x > 6$

33. $y \leq -9$ or $y \geq 15$

35. $x \leq -3$ or $x \geq 4$

37. $|h - 1.4| \leq 0.1$ **39.** $|C - 27.5| \leq 0.25$
41. $|m - 1250| \leq 50$ **43.** no solution **45.** $-\frac{14}{3}, \frac{16}{3}$
47. no solution **49.** $\frac{11}{8}$ **51.** $-\frac{71}{36}$ **53.** $|c - 28.75| \leq$ 0.25; 0.25; $28.50 \leq c \leq 29.00$ **55.** $|x| < 4$
57. $-6 \leq x \leq 8\frac{2}{3}$

59. all real numbers

61. all real numbers

63. $x \leq -8.4$ or $x \geq 9.6$

65. $-5 < x < 11$

67. The graph of $|x| < a$ is the set of all points on the number line that lie between a and $-a$. The graph of $|x| > a$ has two parts; the left part consists of the points to the left of $-a$, and the right part consists of the points to the right of a. **69.** $|t - 350| \leq 5$ **71.** $|t - 15| \leq$ 30 **73.** $|x - 9.55| \leq 0.02$; $9.53 \leq x \leq 9.57$
75. never; absolute value is nonnegative **77.** sometimes; $|5| = 5$ but $|-5| \neq -5$ **79.** sometimes; $|-4 + 2| \neq -4 + 2$ **81.** The "3" in the second set of equations should be "-3."

$$-4x + 1 < -3$$
$$-4x < -4$$
$$x > 1 \ not \ x > -\frac{1}{2}$$

83. $\frac{ab + d}{c}, \frac{-ab + d}{c}$, $c \neq 0$, $ab \geq 0$
85. $(-6 \leq x \leq -5)$ or $(5 \leq x \leq 6)$

87. $x \geq \frac{5}{2}$

89. Use *and* if the absolute value is less than a value and use *or* if the absolute value is greater than a value.

91. 0 **93.** 0.04

94. $y < 6$

95. $s < \frac{2}{15}$

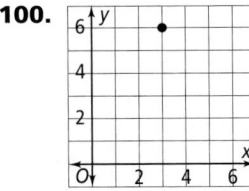

96. $a > 4$

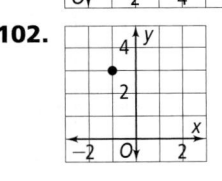

97. Each figure has 4 more squares than the previous figure.

98. Each figure n has n more circles than the previous figure.

99.

100.

101.

102.

Chapter Review pp. 50–52

1. solution of the equation **2.** absolute value
3. reciprocal **4.** compound inequality **5.** add 5; *25, 30, 35* **6.** add 1; 7, 8, 9 **7.** 12; $n + 8$ **8.** 76; $19n$ **9.** $20n$
10. irrational numbers **11.** rational numbers, integers
12. rational numbers, integers, whole numbers, natural number **13.** real numbers, rational numbers
14. $-\sqrt{60} > -8$ or $-8 < -\sqrt{60}$ **15.** $5 < \sqrt{32}$ or $\sqrt{32} > 5$ **16.** Inv. Prop. of Mult. **17.** Assoc. Prop. of Mult. **18.** 114 **19.** $5b$ **20.** 11 **21.** 6

22. $z \leq \frac{2}{5}$

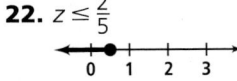

23. $x > 2$

24. no solution
25. $x \leq \frac{3}{2}$ or $x > 6$

26. 10 cm, 6 cm **27.** 1 **28.** no solution **29.** $x = -8$ or $x = -12$ **30.** no solution
31. $-\frac{1}{3} \leq x \leq \frac{5}{3}$

32. $y < 0$ or $y > 18$

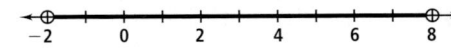

33. $-\frac{18}{7} \leq x \leq \frac{18}{7}$

34. $x < -14$ or $x > 10$

35. $|x - 43.6| \leq 0.1$

Chapter 2

Get Ready! p. 57 1. $6s$ **2.** $4a + b$ **3.** $xy - y + x$
4. $1.5g$ **5.** 0 **6.** $3b - 2c - 2$ **7.** $6f - 5d$ **8.** $3h + 3g$
9. $-2z + 5$ **10.** $2g - 4dg - 12d$ **11.** $8v - 6$
12. $7t - 3st - 5s$ **13.** -56 **14.** 80 **15.** -10
16. -24 **17.** 1075 **18.** 5 **19.** -1.75 **20.** 1.5 **21.** 20
22. 2 **23.** 5 **24.** 4 **25.** $-2 < x < 8$

26. $a \leq 0$

27. $x > -1$

28. $x < -4$ or $x > \frac{10}{3}$

29. $-\frac{1}{2} \leq d \leq \frac{25}{4}$

30. $-24 \leq f \leq 18$

31. Answers may vary. Sample: the Civil War, the Great Depression, the Louisiana Purchase **32.** Answers may vary. Sample: From 1 to 2 years of age; a person has usually stopped growing by age 30, but a baby is still growing at age 1. **33.** Answers may vary. Sample: The image is a reflection, left to right, of what other people see; the size is the same. **34.** Answers may vary. Sample: An inequality determines the limit of a value, or a boundary, for the solution on the number line.

Lesson 2-1 — pp. 60–67

Got It?

1. Let Jan = 1, Feb = 2, Mar = 3, and Apr = 4.

Input		Output
1	→	69
2	→	70
3	→	75
4	→	78

$\{(1, 69), (2, 70), (3, 75), (4, 78)\}$

x Month	y Temperature (°F)
1	69
2	70
3	75
4	78

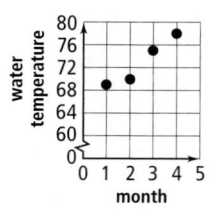

2. domain: $\{-3, 0, 2, 9, 23\}$, range: $\{-99, -18, 0, 7, 14\}$ **3. a.** no **b.** yes **c.** In a mapping diagram for a relation that is not a function, there is at least one element in the domain that has more than one arrow originating from it. In a mapping diagram for a function, each element in the domain has at most one arrow originating from it. **4.** b and c **5. a.** 9 **b.** 1 **c.** −19
6. Let x = number of bottles purchased and C = total cost; $C(x) = 1.19x$; $17.85
Lesson Check 1. domain: $\{0, 3, 4\}$, range: $\{-2, 1, 2, 4\}$
2. domain: $\{-4, -3, 0, 4\}$, range: $\{-4, -3, 0, 4\}$
3. no **4.** yes **5.** Yes; a relation is any set of pairs of input and output values. No; a function is a relation in which each element of the domain is paired with exactly one element of the range. **6.** *Every* vertical line does not need to intersect a function. Rewrite as: "In a function, every vertical line must intersect the graph in *at most* one point." **7.** A horizontal-line test checks the pairing of one element of the range with one or more elements of the domain. A function can have a pairing of one element of the range with *one or more* elements of the domain. A horizontal-line test cannot determine whether a relation is a function.
Exercises 9. domain: $\{1, 2, 3, 4, 5, 6\}$, range: $\{6, 7, 8, 9, 11\}$ **11.** yes **13.** yes **15.** yes
17. 71; (4, 71) **19.** −15; (9, −15) **21.** −2; (3, −2)
23. −132; (−11, −132) **25.** $C(m) = 4.52 + 0.12m$; $34.52 **27.** 13.5 cm² **29.** domain: all real numbers, range: $y \geq 0$; yes **31.** ≈4849 cm³
33. a. 109.4 **b.** 10.4 **c.** −11.1 **d.** −7.2
35. $f(x) - g(x) = (3x - 21) - (3x + 21)$
$= 3x - 21 - 3x - 21 = -42$

37. No; each $x > \frac{7}{3}$ is paired with two y values.
39. a. yes **b.** No; 6 would be paired with both 2.5 and 3.
41. H **43.** 1.9, $\sqrt{3}$, $\frac{5}{4}$, −1.2 **44.** $\frac{2}{3}$, $-\frac{20}{3}$ **45.** −13, 15
46. $x > -3$ **47.** $x \leq \frac{3}{2}$ **48.** $-\frac{3}{2} < x < \frac{3}{2}$ **49.** $x \geq -3$
50. $\frac{1}{4}x$ **51.** $-\frac{1}{2}x$ **52.** $20x$

Lesson 2-2 — pp. 68–73

Got It? 1. a. yes; −7, $y = -7x$ **b.** no **2. a.** yes; $-\frac{5}{3}$
b. yes; $\frac{1}{9}$ **3.** 60 **4. a.** 280 **b.** No; if $y^2 = kx^2$, then $y = \pm\sqrt{kx}$. So, $\frac{y}{x}$ could be $+\sqrt{k}$ for one pair of values and $+\sqrt{k}$ for another pair. Then y would not vary directly with x.
5. a. 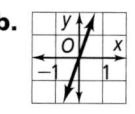 **b.**

Lesson Check 1. $y = -\frac{1}{2}x$ **2.** $\frac{3}{2}$ **3.** $\frac{5}{4}$ **4.** Answers may vary. Sample: Two variables are directly related when the ratio of the output to the input is a constant value.
5. For a direct variation, $y = kx$ where k is the constant of variation. If $x = 0$, then $y = 0$ and the graph of $y = kx$ passes through the origin. **6.** Answers may vary. Sample: $y = -8x$.
Exercises 7. yes; 7, $y = 7x$ **9.** no **11.** yes; 12
13. yes; −2 **15.** no **17.** yes; 6 **19.** −3 **21.** $\frac{6}{7}$ **23.** 21
25. 4 min **27.**

x	y
−1	3
1	−3
2	−6

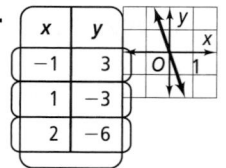

29.

x	y
−1	−1
1	1
2	2

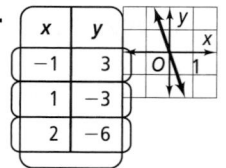

31. yes; $k = \frac{2}{3}$, $y = \frac{2}{3}x$ **33.** no
35. $y = 2x$ 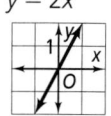 **37.** $y = -4.5x$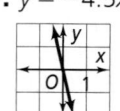
39. $y = \frac{3}{5}x$ 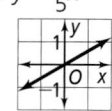 **41.** $y = \frac{2}{7}x$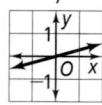

43. 0.625 **45.** 0.225 **47.** First, it does not say that y varies directly with x. Second, every direct variation includes the point (0, 0), so x cannot be determined because k could be any value.
49. Answers may vary. Sample: $y = 3.2x$

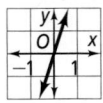

51. Answers may vary. Sample: If y varies directly with x^2, and $y = 2$ when $x = 4$, then $y = \frac{81}{8}$ when $x = 9$.
53. $c = 0$, $a \neq 0$, $b \neq 0$
55. y is divided by 7; $y = kx$, so if x is divided by 7, $y = k\left(\frac{x}{7}\right)$ or $\frac{1}{7}$ the original value of y.
57. 1091 **59.** 0 **61.** -5

62.

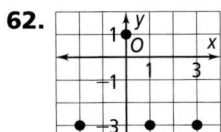

domain: $\{-2, 0, 1, 3\}$; range: $\{-3, 1\}$

63.

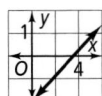

domain: $\{4, 7\}$; range: $\{-1, 0\}$

64.

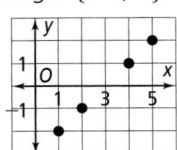

domain: $\{1, 2, 4, 5\}$; range: $\{-2, -1, 1, 2\}$

65.

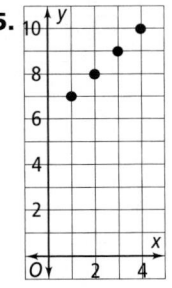

domain: $\{1, 2, 3, 4\}$; range: $\{7, 8, 9, 10\}$

66. $8n$; 40, 48, 56 **67.** $7 - 2n$; $-3, -5, -7$
68. $12(13 - n)$; 96, 84, 72 **69.** $15(n + 1)$; 90, 105,120 **70.** $\frac{17}{3}$; 7; $\frac{23}{3}$; $\frac{29}{3}$ **71.** -3.2; -2; -1.4; 0.4
72. -5; 1; 4; 13 **73.** -9; -8; -7.5; -6

Lesson 2-3 pp. 74–80

Got It? 1. a. -1 **b.** 1 **c.** undefined **d.** $\frac{1-4}{8-5} = \frac{-3}{3} = -1 = \frac{3}{-3} = \frac{4-1}{5-8}$ **2. a.** $y = 6x + 5$
b. $y = -\frac{1}{2}x - 3$ **c.** No; any two points on a line can be used to calculate the slope.

3. a. $y = -\frac{3}{2}x + 9$; $-\frac{3}{2}$; (0, 9)
b. $y = -\frac{7}{5}x - 7$; $-\frac{7}{5}$; (0, -7)

4. $y = \frac{4}{7}x - 2$

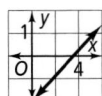

Lesson Check 1. $y = \frac{1}{2}x + 1$ **2.** $y = \frac{4}{3}x + \frac{1}{3}$ **3.** -1
4. 1 **5.** The y-intercept of a line is the point at which the line crosses the y-axis. The x-intercept is the point at which the line crosses the x-axis. **6.** Since division by zero is undefined, the slope of a vertical line that passes through (a, b) and (a, c), $\frac{c-b}{0}$, is undefined. **7.** She subtracted the x-coordinates in the wrong order. The x- and y-coordinates of each point must be subtracted consistently.

Exercises 9. -2 **11.** $\frac{4}{11}$ **13.** 1 **15.** 0 **17.** $y = 3x + 2$
19. $y = \frac{5}{6}x + 12$ **21.** $y = -5x - 7$ **23.** $y = \frac{3}{2}x + \frac{7}{2}$; $\frac{3}{2}$, $\left(0, \frac{7}{2}\right)$ **25.** $y = -\frac{4}{3}x + \frac{5}{6}$; $-\frac{4}{3}$, $\left(0, \frac{5}{6}\right)$ **27.** $y = 7$; 0, (0, 7)

29.

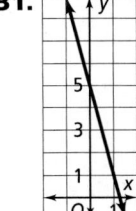

31.

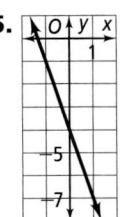

33.

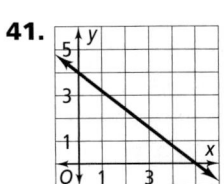

35.

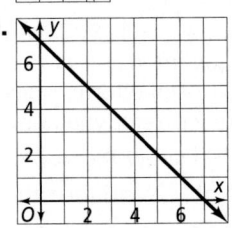

37.

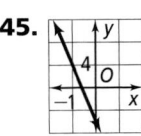

39.

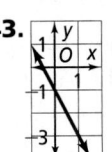

41.

43.

45.

47. 0; (0, 3) **49.** $-\frac{1}{4}$; (0, 3) **51.** undefined slope; no y-intercept **53.** $-\frac{1}{2}$; $\left(0, -\frac{5}{2}\right)$ **55.** $-\frac{A}{B}$; $\left(0, \frac{C}{B}\right)$
57. a. 1 **b.** 1 **c.** 1 **d.** 1 **e.** Any two points on a line can be used to find the slope of the line.
59. $-\frac{5}{13}$ **61.** $\frac{15}{2}$

Lesson 2-4   pp. 81–88

Got It? 1. $y + 1 = -3(x - 7)$ **2. a.** $y - 7 = \frac{7}{5}x$
b. $y = \frac{7}{5}(x + 5)$; Either point can be used to put the equation of the line in point-slope form.
3. $-91x + 10y = 36$
4. (0, −2), (4, 0);   **5. a.**

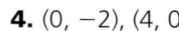
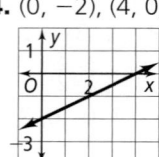

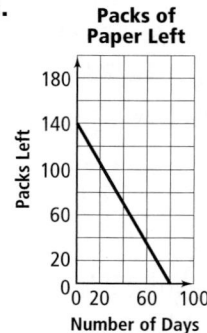

Packs of Paper Left

b. $7x + 4y = 560$ **c.** 87.5 **6. a.** $y = -2x + 6$
b. $y = -\frac{3}{2}x + 6$

Lesson Check 1. $y = -3x - 1$ **2.** $y = \frac{1}{2}x + 2$
3. (0, 6), (2, 0)

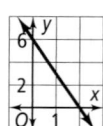

4. $3x + y = -1$ **5.** $3x + 2y = -9$ **6. a.** point-slope
b. slope-intercept **c.** standard **d.** point-slope
7. Point-slope form; since the x-intercept is the point where y is zero, you know the point on the line, $(x, 0)$, and you know the slope. **8.** $-\frac{b}{a}$ **9.** No; one line has a slope of -2 and the other line has a slope of $-\frac{1}{2}$. $-\frac{1}{2}$ is the reciprocal of -2, not the *negative* reciprocal.
Exercises 11. $y - 12 = \frac{5}{6}(x - 22)$ **13.** $y + 2 = 0$
15. $y - 2 = 5x$ **17.** Answers may vary. Sample:
$y = \frac{5}{4}(x - 1)$ or $y - 5 = \frac{5}{4}(x - 5)$ **19.** Answers may vary. Sample: $y + 1 = -\frac{4}{3}x$ or $y + 5 = -\frac{4}{3}(x - 3)$
21. Answers may vary. Sample: $y - 9 = -\frac{7}{5}(x - 1)$
or $y - 2 = -\frac{7}{5}(x - 6)$ **23.** $7x + y = -9$
25. $-42x + 10y = 79$

27. (0, −2), (−5, 0)   **29.** (0, 2), $\left(\frac{14}{5}, 0\right)$

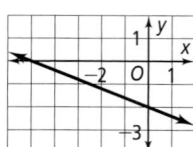
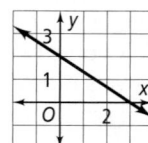

31. $y = -2.5x + 20$

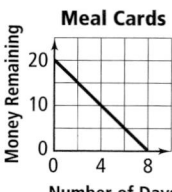

Meal Cards

33. $y = \frac{5}{2}x + \frac{17}{2}$ **35.** $y = \frac{1}{3}x + \frac{5}{3}$

37.   **39.**

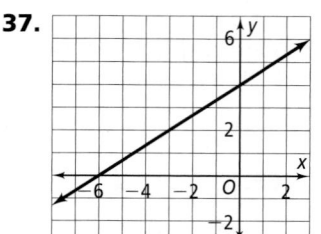
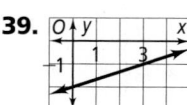

41.

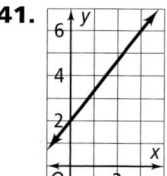

43. $y + 4 = \frac{7}{5}(x + 3)$ or $y + \frac{1}{2} = \frac{7}{5}\left(x + \frac{1}{2}\right)$
45. $y = \frac{3}{4}x + 3$ **47.** $y = -\frac{3}{2}x - \frac{1}{2}$
49. a. $y - 12 = -\frac{4}{3}(x + 3)$

b. $y + 4 = -\frac{4}{3}(x - 9)$ **c.** They have the same standard form: $4x + 3y = 24$.
51. $y = -\frac{3}{2}x - 1$

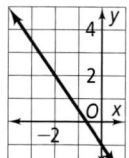

53. yes
55. The eq. of the line connecting (1, 3) to (−2, 6) is $y = -x + 4$. The eq. of the line connecting (1, 3) to (3, 5) is $y = x + 2$. The slopes are neg. reciprocals so the lines are perpendicular. Therefore, by def. of a rt. triangle, it is a rt. triangle.

Lesson 2-5
pp. 92–98

Got It?
1. a. strong negative correlation

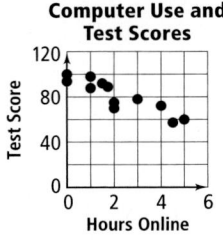

Computer Use and Test Scores

b. about $170 **2.** Answers may vary. Sample:
$y = 3575x + 19354$
3. $y = 0.09x + 2.44$, where 1997 is year 0; $4.96

Lesson Check
1. strong positive correlation **2.** no correlation

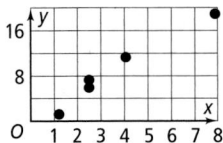
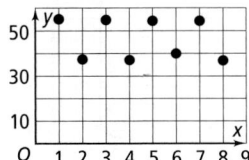

3. strong positive correlation

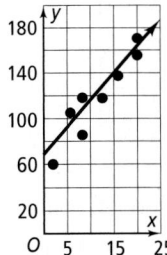

4. Plot the data points in a scatter plot to determine the correlation. The closer the data points fall along a line with a positive or negative slope, the stronger the correlation. **5.** No; answers may vary. Sample: A trend line is determined by using two pts. close to the line drawn through the data sets of the scatter plot. The line of best fit is the most accurate of the trend lines because it uses all the data pts. **6.** The slope of the trend line or line of best fit is positive for data pts. with positive correlation and negative for data pts. with negative correlation. The constant of variation for a direct variation is positive for data pts. with positive correlation.

Exercises
7. strong negative correlation

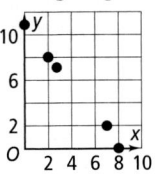

9. Answers may vary. Sample: $y = -0.7x - 4$
11. Answers may vary. Sample: $y = 4.47x + 33.31$
13. 6,055,359 tonnes **15.** no; Answers may vary.
17. yes
19. a.

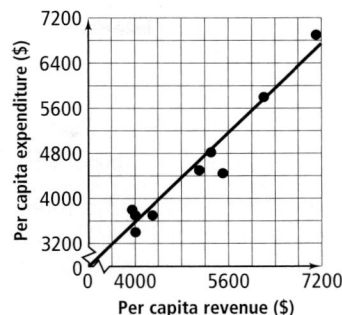

b. about $2506 **c.** about $5610 **d.** Answers may vary. Sample: Yes; expenditure would be predicted to be between $5300 and $5400.
21. G
23.
$$(y - 1) = \frac{2}{3}(x + 1)$$
$$(-3 - 1) = \frac{2}{3}(a + 1)$$
$$-4 = \frac{2}{3}a + \frac{2}{3}$$
$$\frac{-14}{3} = \frac{2}{3}a$$
$$-7 = a$$

24.

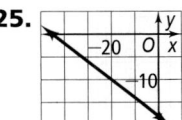

25.

26.

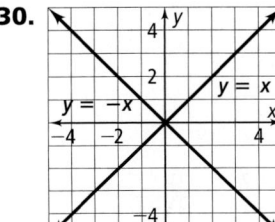

27. $-2x + y = 2$ **28.** $x + y = 0$ **29.** $y = 2$
30.

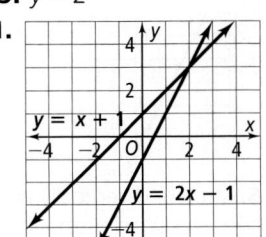

31.

32.

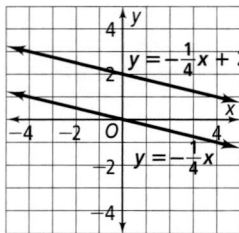

Lesson 2-6   pp. 99–106

Got It? 1. a. Each output for $y = 2x - 3$ is three less than the corresponding output for $y = 2x$. The graph of $y = 2x - 3$ is the graph of $y = 2x$ translated down three units.

b.

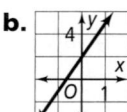

2. $f\left(x + \frac{1}{2}\right)$ **3.** $h(x) = -3x - 3$

4. a.

x	y
−5	$\frac{2}{3}$
−2	$\frac{2}{3}$
0	−1
3	$\frac{1}{3}$
5	$-\frac{2}{3}$

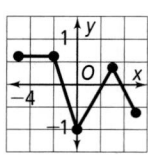

b. Sometimes; Answers may vary. Sample: switching the order of a horizontal translation and a reflection in the y-axis will change the resulting graph, but switching the order of a horizontal and vert. translation will not.
5. a. $g(x) = 2x - 3$ **b.** $g(x) = f(x + 4) - 2$; translated left 4 units and translated down 2 units
Lesson Check 1. translated 6 units up **2.** compressed vertically by a factor of 0.25 **3.** translated 4 units to the rt.
4. reflected over y-axis
5. translated 1 unit to the left and 2 units down

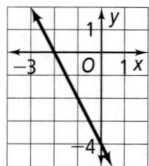

6. stretched vertically by a factor of 2 and translated 1 unit up

7. $g(x)$ is the graph of $h(x)$ translated 2 units up

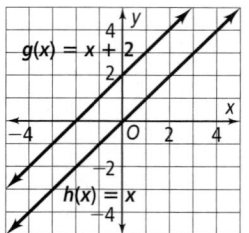

8. Answers may vary. Sample: $f(x) = x$, $f(x - 2) = f(x) - 2$ **9.** $f(x) = -x - 2$; $g(x) = f(-x) = x - 2$
Exercises
11. The function is $y = x$ translated 4.5 units up.

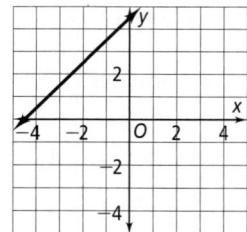

13.

x	f(x) + 3
−2	6
0	4
1	1
3	2

15.

x	f(x) + 4
−3	5
−1	2
1	4
4	7

17. $y = f(x) + 4$
19. translated rt. 4 units   **21.** translated left 3 units

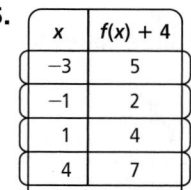

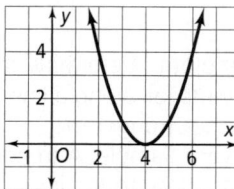

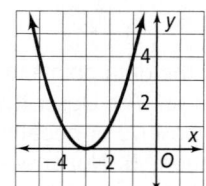

23. $g(x) = -x - 1$ **25.** $g(x) = -2x + 4$
27. $y = 2x$ **29.** $y = \frac{1}{4}x$ **31.** $g(x) = -0.5x$
33. vertically compressed by a factor of $\frac{1}{4}$ and translated down 2 units
35. translate to the right 10 s
37. $f(x) = -\frac{1}{3}x - 1$; $g(x) = \frac{1}{3}x + 1$; $g(x) = -f(x)$

41. translated 6 units down   **43.** translated 4 units up

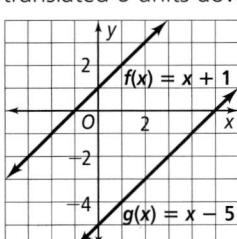

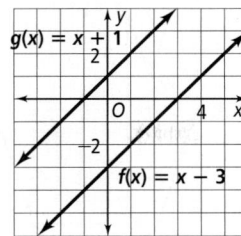

45. The first two steps are incorrect; the transformations should be: shift 1 unit left, vertically stretch by a factor of 2, and shift 3 units down.

47. 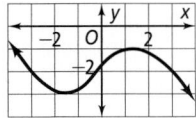   **49.**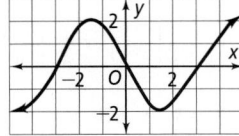

51. D **53.** A
55. $y = -15.82x + 914.59$
56. $-2, 8$ **57.** $-12, 11$ **58.** $-3, \frac{21}{5}$

Lesson 2-7   pp. 107–113

Got It?

1. a.
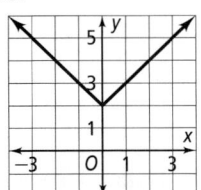

vertex at $(0, 2)$; translated up 2 units from the parent function
b. No; transformations of this form move the vertex up or down along the axis of symmetry, so the axis stays the same.

2.
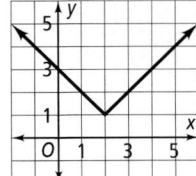

3. a. 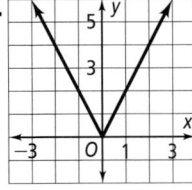   **b.**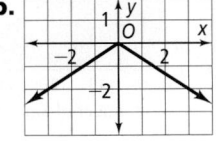

4. $(1, -3)$; $x = 1$; translated 1 unit to the rt., vertically stretched by a factor of 2, then reflected over the x-axis and translated down 3 units **5.** $y = \frac{1}{4}|x - 2| - 1$

Lesson Check 1. $(-4, -3)$; $x = -4$ **2.** $(-3, 9)$; $x = -3$
3. vert. stretch **4.** vert. stretch **5.** Yes; you can determine the position of a graph of an absolute value function by identifying the vertex, axis of symmetry and the transformation of the absolute value parent function. Answers may vary. Sample: $y = -\frac{1}{2}|x + 3| - 5$; vertex $(-3, -5)$; axis of symmetry, $x = -3$; translated 3 units to the left, vertically compressed by a factor of $\frac{1}{2}$, then reflected over the x-axis and translated down 5 units.
6. Answers may vary. Sample: $y = |x + 1| - 2$ and $y = -|x + 1| - 2$ **7.** $y = |x|$ is the same as $y = x$ when $x \geq 0$ and is the reflection of $y = x$ across the x-axis when $x < 0$.

Exercises

9.

x	y
−2	1
−1	0
0	−1
1	0
2	1

11.

x	y
−4	2
−3	1
−2	0
−1	1
0	2

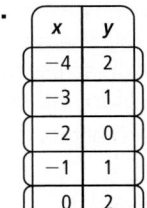

13.

x	y
−7	2
−6	1
−5	0
−4	1
−3	2

15.

x	y
−8	1
−7	0
−6	−1
−5	0
−4	1

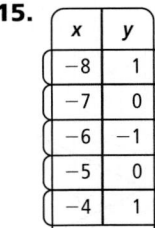

17.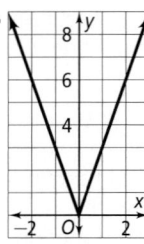

19.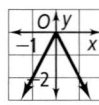

vertically stretched by a factor of 2 and reflected across the x-axis

vertically stretched by a factor of 3

21.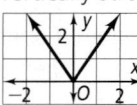

vertically stretched by a factor of $\frac{3}{2}$

23. $(-2,-4)$; $x = -2$; translate 2 units to the left and 4 units down **25.** $(-6, 0)$; $x = -6$; translate 6 units to the left and vertically stretch by a factor of 3 **27.** $(5, 0)$; $x = 5$; translate 5 units to the rt. and reflect across the x-axis **29.** $y = -2|x - 5| + 1$

31. 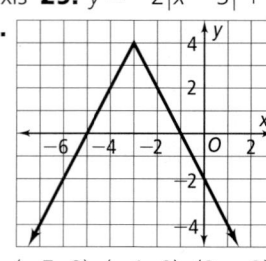   **33.**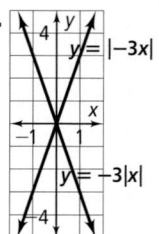

$(-5, 0), (-1, 0), (0, -2)$

The graphs are not identical; one is the reflection across the x-axis of the other.

35. a. Answers may vary. Sample: reflection across the x-axis, vert. compression by a factor of $\frac{1}{2}$, translation down $\frac{1}{2}$ unit, translation rt. 6 units

b. No; changing the order of the transformations can change the graph.

37. 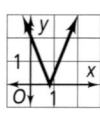   **39.** 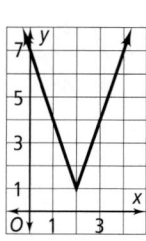   **41.**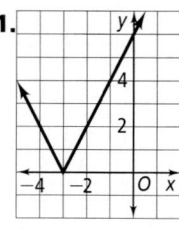

43. 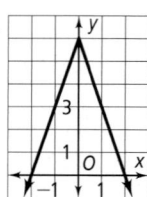   **45. a.**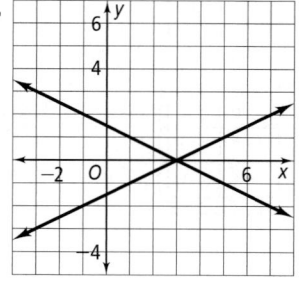

b. No; $f(x) = g(x)$ only for $x = 3$.

47.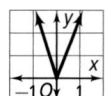

49.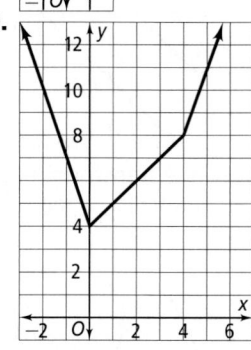

51. C **53.** A **55.** $y = x + 1$ **56.** $y = -\frac{1}{2}x + 2$

57. $g(x) = -x - 7$ **58.** $g(x) = -2x - 6$

59. $g(x) = -4 - x$ **60.** Answers may vary. Sample: $y = \frac{4}{5}x + 1$ **61.** Answers may vary. Sample: $y = -\frac{4}{5}x + 8$

62. 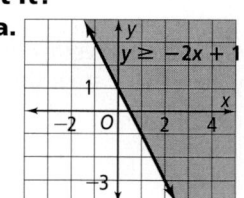   **63.**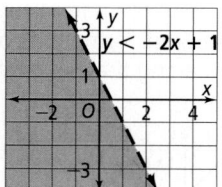

$p \le 1.25$ $t > 13$

64.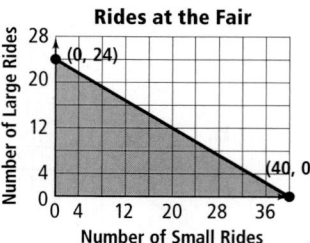

$t \le -3$

Lesson 2-8   pp. 114–120

Got It?

1. a.

$y \ge -2x + 1$

b.

$y < -2x + 1$

2. a.

Rides at the Fair

(0, 24)

(40, 0)

Number of Large Rides

Number of Small Rides

b. The number of rides cannot be neg.

3.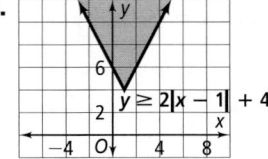
$y \geq 2|x - 1| + 4$

4. a. $y > -|x + 4| + 3$ **b.** No; when you solve the ineq. for y, you multiply both sides by -1. This changes the ineq. sign from $>$ to $<$.

Lesson Check

1.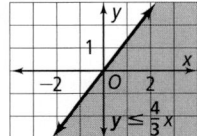
$y \leq \frac{4}{3}x$

2.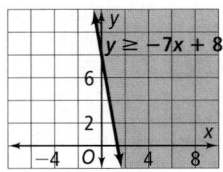
$y \geq -7x + 8$

3.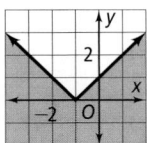

4.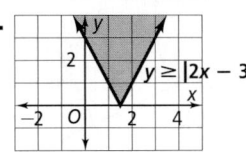
$y \geq |2x - 3|$

5. No; the boundary consists of points where *equality* holds, while the shaded region consists of points where the *inequality* holds. **6.** Graphing a linear inequality in two variables includes first graphing the boundary line, which is a linear eq. in two variables, and then shading the half-plane. **7.** No; $\left(\frac{3}{4}, 0\right)$ does not satisfy the inequality because $2.25 > 3$ is false.

Exercises

9.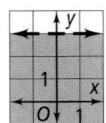

11.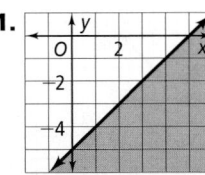

13.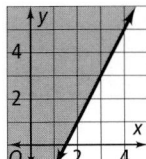

15.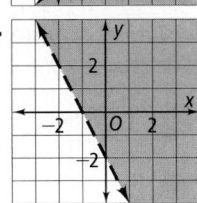

17. a. $y \geq 20x$ if $x \leq 6$; $y \geq 15x$ if $x > 6$
b.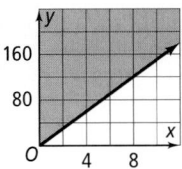

19.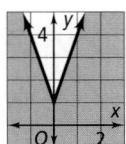

21.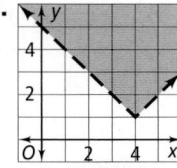

23.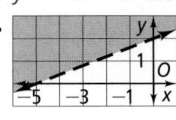

25.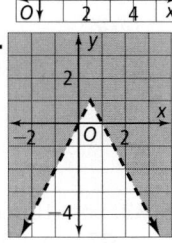

27. $y < -x - 2$ **29.** $2y \geq |2x + 6|$

31. 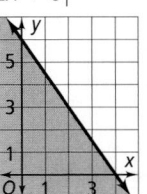 **33.** 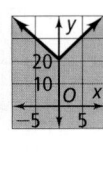 **35.**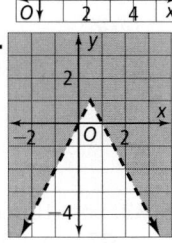

37.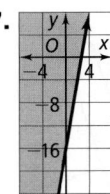

39. $x > -3$ **41.** $y \geq -2x + 4$
43. $y < -|x - 4|$ **45.** C
47. when the origin lies on the boundary line

49.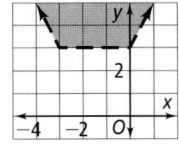

51.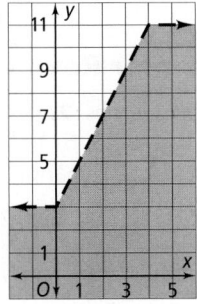

53. I

55. let c = amnt. of a commission,
let s = amnt. of a sale
$$c = ks$$
$$(\$48,000) = k(\$800,000)$$
$$0.06 = k$$
$$c = 0.06 (\$650,000) = \$39,000$$
(OR sltn. by another appropriate method)

56.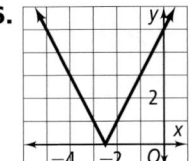

57.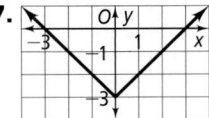

58.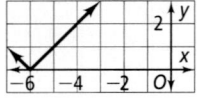

59.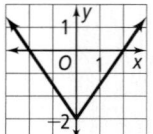

60.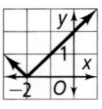

61.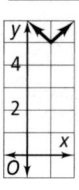

62. no **63.** yes; 100 **64.** yes; −5 **65.** no
66. yes; 3 **67.** no **68.** yes; −10 **69.** no
70. strong neg. correlation

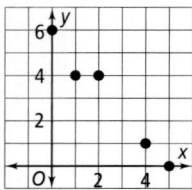

71. no correlation

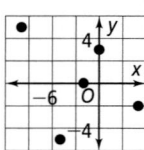

72–74.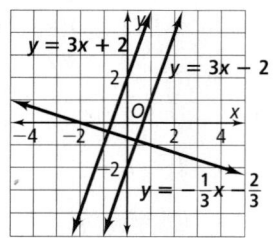

Chapter Review   pp. 122–126

1. sometimes **2.** point-slope **3.** yes; domain:
$\{-10, -6, 5, 6, 10\}$, range: $\{2, 3, 4, 7\}$ **4.** no; domain:
$\{1, 3, 4, 10\}$, range: $\{5, 6, 8, 12\}$ **5.** no; domain:
$\left\{-2, -\frac{3}{2}, -1, \frac{1}{2}, 1, 2, 3\right\}$, range: $\left\{-\frac{7}{2}, -\frac{1}{2}, 0, \frac{1}{2}, \frac{3}{2}, 2, \frac{5}{2}\right\}$

6. yes; domain: $\left\{-2, -1, \frac{1}{2}, 3\right\}$, range: $\{2\}$ **7.** 6, 4.5, 1

8. $-3\frac{3}{4}, -3\frac{3}{16}, -1\frac{7}{8}$ **9.** no **10.** no **11.** yes; 1; $y = x$

12. −4; 1.2 **13.** $\frac{10}{3}$; −1 **14.** $\frac{7}{2}$; $-1\frac{1}{20}$ **15.** $-\frac{4}{3}$; 0.4

16. $-\frac{2}{5}$ **17.** $\frac{7}{6}$ **18.** $\frac{2}{3}$ **19.** $-\frac{4}{9}$ **20.** $y = -3x + 4$

21. $y = \frac{1}{2}x + 6$

22. $y = 2x - \frac{3}{2}$

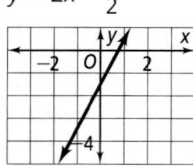

23. $y = \frac{2}{3}x + 3$

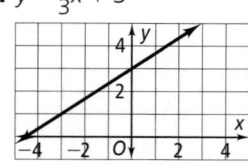

24. $y = -x + 5$

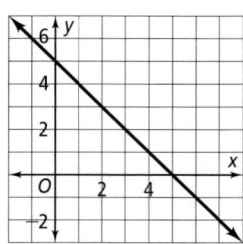

25. $y = -\frac{1}{3}x + \frac{5}{3}$

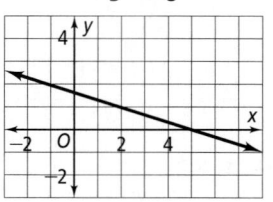

26. $y = -3(x - 4)$; $3x + y = 12$
27. $y + 1 = 5(x - 1)$; $5x - y = 6$
28. $y + 7 = -\frac{7}{3}(x - 3)$; $7x + 3y = 0$
29. $y - 3 = 2(x - 2)$; $2x - y = 1$
30. a. $y = -\frac{1}{2}x + 7$ **b.** $y = 2x - 13$

c. $y = -\frac{1}{2}x + 7$

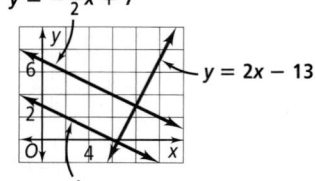

$y = 2x - 13$

$y = -\frac{1}{2}x + 3$

31.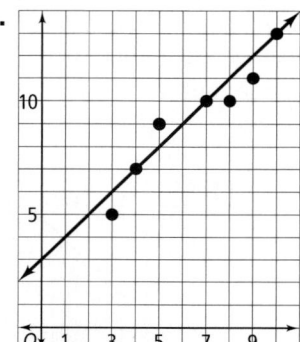

strong pos. correlation; Answers may vary.
Sample: $y = x + 3$; 18

32.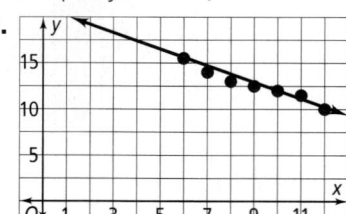

strong neg. correlation; Answers may vary.
Sample: $y = -0.9x + 21$; 7.5

33.

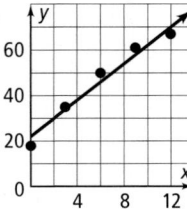

strong pos. correlation; Answers may vary.
Sample: $y = 4x + 22$; 82

34. $y = f(x + 2) - 7$ **35.** $y = -f(x - 5)$

36. $y = f(-x) + 3$ **37.** translated 4 units down

38. vertically stretched by a factor of 12, translated 2 units up **39.** vertically stretched by a factor of 2, reflected across the y-axis, reflected across the x-axis

40. $y = |x - 2| + 4$ **41.** $y = |x + 3|$

42. $y = |x - 5| + 2$ **43.** $y = |x - 4| + 1$

44.

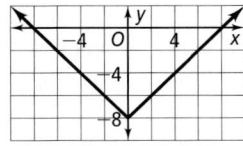

45. 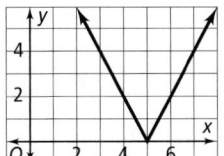   **46.**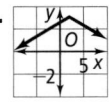

47. 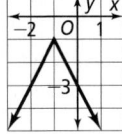   **48.** $(4, 0)$; $x = 4$

49. $(0, 2)$; $x = 0$

50. 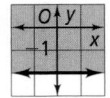   **51.**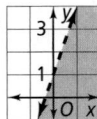

52. 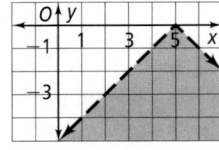   **53.**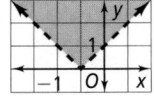

54. a. Answers may vary. Sample: $x + 3y \le 15$

   b. Answers may vary. Sample: domain:
    $\{0, 1, 2, 3, 4, 5, 6, 7, 8, 9, 10, 11, 12, 13, 14, 15\}$,
    range: $\{0, 1, 2, 3, 4, 5\}$

   c.

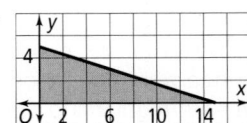

55. Answers may vary. Sample: $y \le -|x| - 1$

Chapter 3

Get Ready! p. 131 1. 28 **2.** 33 **3.** $-\frac{15}{2}$ **4.** 15

5. $y = \frac{1}{2}x - \frac{5}{2}$ **6.** $y = -2x - 3$ **7.** $y = 5x + 16$

8. $y = 3x - 7$ **9.** $y = \frac{2}{5}x - \frac{3}{2}$ **10.** $y = 4x + 11$

11. $y = -6x - 8$ **12.** $y = -3x + 18$

13. 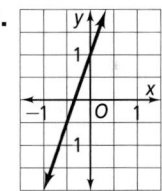   **14.**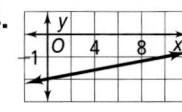

15. 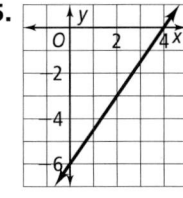   **16.**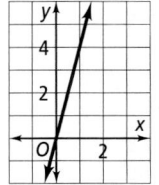

17. 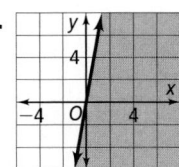   **18.**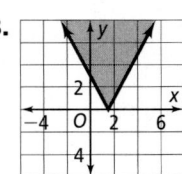

19. 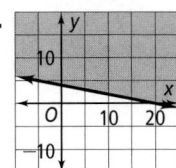   **20.**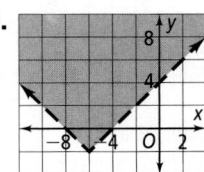

21. Answers may vary. Samples: Rocky Mountains, Appalachian Mountains **22.** Answers may vary. Sample: Your actions are consistent with your words when your actions show what you are saying. For example, if you say you are happy and you are laughing or smiling. **23.** 15 books or more; 15 books or more but less than 19, i.e., 15, 16, 17, or 18 books

Lesson 3-1   pp. 134–141

Got It? 1. $(2, -1)$ **2. a.** Spiny Dogfish: 59.5 cm; Greenland: 55.75 cm **b.** Each species of shark has a maximum total length; growth rates decrease with increase in age. **3.** in the yr 1990; about 1,100,000 **4. a.** inconsistent **b.** independent **c.** dependent

Lesson Check

1. $(2, 1)$ **2.** $(2, 0)$

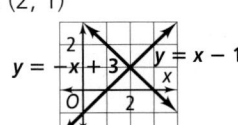   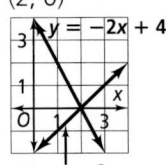

3. 2 pens; 4 pencils **4.** No; an independent system has a unique solution whereas an inconsistent system has no solution.

5. Answers may vary. Sample: $\begin{cases} y = 2x + 1 \\ y = 2x - 3 \end{cases}$

6. Independent; if the slope of one equation is the negative reciprocal of the slope of the other equation, the lines are perpendicular and intersect at a unique point.

Exercises 7–11. How solutions are determined may vary (graphing or using a table).

7. (3, 1)

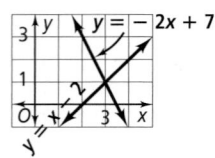

9. (−2, 4)

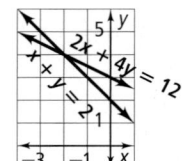

11. no solution

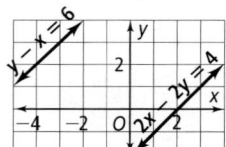

13. 2 small; 4 large
15. Models may vary. Sample: Use 0 for 1970.

$\begin{cases} y = 0.22x + 67.5 \\ y = 0.15x + 75.507 \end{cases}$

Around 2085, the quantities will be equal.
17. dependent **19.** inconsistent **21.** independent
23. dependent **25.** independent **27.** dependent
29. infinitely many solutions **31.** no solution

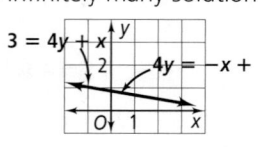 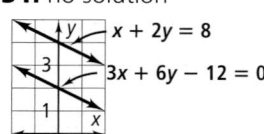

33. $\left(\dfrac{28}{5}, \dfrac{26}{5}\right)$

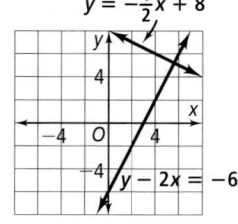

35. inconsistent **37.** inconsistent

39.

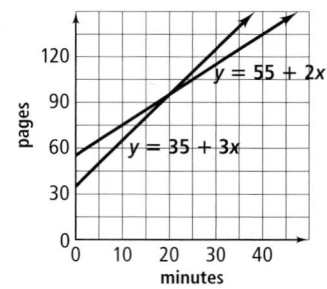

After 20 min you and your friend will have read the same number of pages.
41. My friend did not extend the table of values far enough. Scrolling down will show that when $x = 4$, then $Y1 = Y2 = -2$. So, the system has a solution, $(4, -2)$.
43. An independent system has one solution. The slopes are different, but the y-intercepts could be the same. An inconsistent system has no solution. The slopes are the same and the y-intercepts are different. A dependent system has an infinite number of solutions. The slopes and y-intercepts are the same. **45.** sometimes **47.** never
49. Answers may vary. Sample: $5x + 2y = 5$
51. They are equivalent eqs. **53.** A **55.** C

Lesson 3-2   pp. 142–148

Got It? 1. (−2.5, 2.5) **2.** $.95 per download; $5.50 one-time registration fee **3.** (4, 0) **4. a.** (−2, 3) **b.** Yes; the solution (−5, 2) is a solution to both eqs. in the system, so substituting $y = 2$ into either equation will result in $x = -5$. **5. a.** no solution; The eq. is always false. **b.** infinite number of solutions; The eq. is always true.

Lesson Check 1. (1, 2) **2.** (−6, −6) **3.** (2, 1)
4. (5, −3) **5.** $\left(-\dfrac{1}{5}, \dfrac{19}{5}\right)$ **6.** (2, 1)
7. Answers may vary. Sample:

$\begin{cases} 4x - 3y = -2 \\ 3x - 2y = -1 \end{cases}$

$\begin{cases} -8x + 6y = 4 \\ 9x - 6y = -3 \end{cases}$

8. In the substitution method of solving a system of equations, you first solve one equation for one of the variables. Then substitute for this variable in the other equation and solve for the other variable. In the elimination method, you create an equivalent system of equations that contain a pair of additive inverses so that you can eliminate one variable and solve for the remaining variable.
9. Let r = number of regular cups of coffee and c = number of large cups of coffee. First, $r + c = 5$: because a total of 5 cups of coffee were purchased. Second, $r + 1.5c = 6$: because each regular cup of coffee is $1, each large cup is $1.50, and the total spent is $6. Then, solve the system of equations using elimination by

subtracting the first equation from the second to eliminate r and solve for c. $c = 2$; 2 large cups

Exercises 11. $(-2, 4)$ **13.** $(0.75, 2.5)$ **15.** $(8, -1)$
17. $(-2, -5)$ **19.** seven \$1-bills; eight \$5-bills
21. 3 vans and 2 sedans **23.** $(2, 4)$ **25.** $(2, -2)$
27. $(4, 1)$ **29.** $(1, 1)$ **31.** infinite number of solutions;
$\{(x, y)\,|-2x + 3y = 13\}$ **33.** $(3, 2)$ **35.** $(5, 4)$
37. $\left(\frac{20}{17}, \frac{19}{17}\right)$ **39.** $(4, 1)$ **41.** no solution
43. 10 deliveries **45.** $(4, -3)$ **47.** $(-3, 4)$
49. $(300, 150)$ **51.** $(0.5, 0.25)$
53. Error in 5th line: $-4(-7 - x) = 28 + 4x$ not
$-28 - 4x$; Lines 5–9 should be: $3x + 28 + 4x = 14$;
$7x = -14$; $x = -2$; $y = -7 - (-2)$; $y = -5$
55. Answers may vary. Sample:
$\begin{cases} -3x + 4y = 12 \\ 5x - 3y = 13 \end{cases}$, $(8, 9)$
57. In determining whether to use substitution or elimination to solve an equation, look at the equations to determine if one is solved or can be easily solved for a particular variable. If that is the case, substitution can easily be used. Otherwise, elimination might be easier.
59. Substitution; the second equation is solved for y; $(-7, -26)$ **61.** Elimination; substitution would be difficult since no coefficient is 1 in the original system. Dividing the first equation by 3 and dividing the second equation by 5 results in an equivalent system where y would be eliminated from the system if the equations were subtracted; $(-1, -3)$
63. yes; -40 degrees **65.** 0 **67.** 2 **69.** 6 **71.** 4

Lesson 3-3   pp. 149–155

Got It? 1. $(4, 1)$, $(5, 0)$, $(6, 0)$, $(7, 0)$

2.
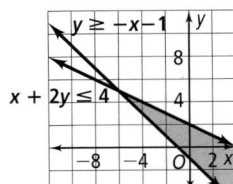

3. 5 meats and no vegetables; 4 meats and 1 or 2 vegetables; 3 meats and 2, 3, or 4 vegetables; 2 meats and 3, 4, 5, or 6 vegetables; 1 meat and 4 − 8 vegetables; no meat 5 − 10 vegetables

4. $y > 2|x - 1|$
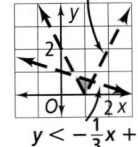

Lesson Check

1.
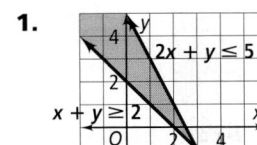

2.
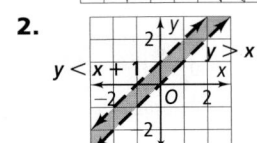

3.
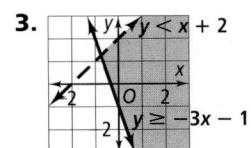

4. 0 h TV and 1, 2, or 3 h football; 1 h TV and 1 or 2 h football; or 2 h TV and 1 h football **5.** Intersection; the solution of two inequalities is the overlap or the intersection of the graphs of the individual inequalities. **6.** The graphical solution of a system of inequalities consists of the overlap or intersection of the individual half-planes and corresponding boundary lines (either dotted or solid). The graphical solution of a system of equations includes only the intersection of the lines, not the half-planes. **7.** For each inequality, the wrong half-plane has been shaded. The half-plane below $y = \frac{1}{2}x - 1$ should be shaded and the half-plane above $y = -3x + 3$ should be shaded. Also, both boundary lines should be dashed because the inequalities are $<$ and $>$.

Exercises 9. $(0, 0)$, $(0, 1)$, $(0, 2)$, $(0, 3)$, $(0, 4)$, $(0, 5)$, $(0, 6)$, $(0, 7)$, $(1, 0)$, $(1, 1)$, $(1, 2)$, $(1, 3)$, $(1, 4)$, $(1,5)$, $(1, 6)$, $(2, 0)$, $(2, 1)$, $(2, 2)$, $(2, 3)$, $(2, 4)$, $(2, 5)$, $(3, 3)$, $(3, 4)$

11.
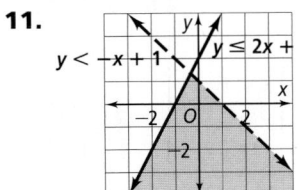

13.
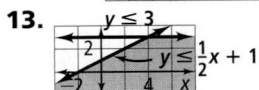

15.
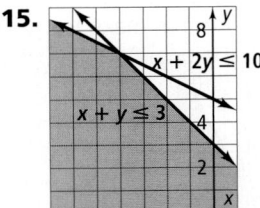

17.
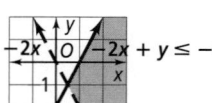
$y > -2x$ $-2x + y \le -2$

19. no solution
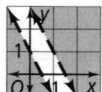

21. Let $r =$ number of rose plants and $t =$ number of tulip plants.
$t + r \ge 50$
$r \le 80$
Because the number of plants must be a whole number, only the points in the overlap that represent whole numbers are solutions of the problem.

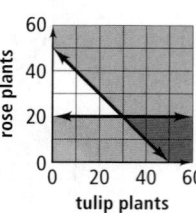
rose plants / tulip plants

23.
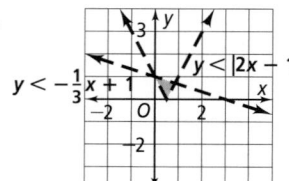
$y < -\frac{1}{3}x + 1$ $y < |2x - 1|$

25.
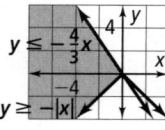
$y \le -\frac{4}{3}x$
$y \ge -|x|$

27.
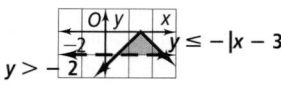
$y > -2$ $y \le -|x - 3|$

29.
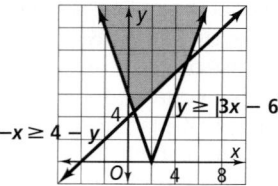
$-x \ge 4 - y$ $y \ge |3x - 6|$

31. (0, 4), (0, 5), (0, 6), (1, 3), (1, 4), (1, 5), (2, 3), (2, 4); the sum of the servings must be greater than or equal to 4 and less than or equal to 6.

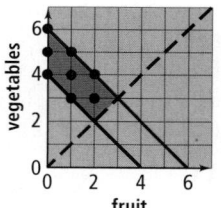
vegetables / fruit

33. Answers may vary. Sample: $\begin{cases} x < 5 \\ y \ge 1 \end{cases}$
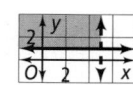

35. Use test pts. that are not on either of the boundary lines and that make the calculations as easy as possible (e.g., the origin). **37.** A, B **39.** A, B **41.** B, C **43.** A **45.** A

47.
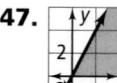

49.
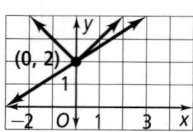
(0, 2)

51.
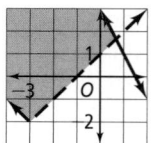

53. $y > |x - 1| + 1$
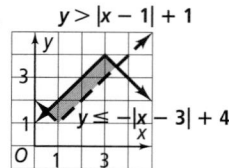
$y \le -|x - 3| + 4$

55. $\begin{cases} y \ge |x| - 2 \\ y \le -|x| + 2 \end{cases}$

57. $\begin{cases} y \le 4 \\ y \ge 0 \\ y \le 2x \\ y \ge 2x - 8 \end{cases}$

59. C **61.** B **63.** $(-9, -26)$ **64.** $\left(\frac{23}{14}, -\frac{13}{14}\right)$
65. no solution **66.** $(-2, -1)$ **67.** $(-1, 2)$
68. $\left(-\frac{4}{7}, \frac{1}{14}\right)$ **69–72.** Answers may vary. Samples are given for each exercise. **69.** (0, 3) **70.** (0, 3)
71. (2, −1) **72.** (1, −1)

Lesson 3-4   pp. 157–162

Got It? 1. a. P has a maximum value of 7.5 at (0, 2.5). **b.** Yes; Answers may vary. Sample: $P = 5$ has the same (maximum) value at all four vertex points. $P = x + 2y$ has maximum value 5 at R and S. **2.** 100 T-shirts and 10 sweatshirts.

Lesson Check

1.
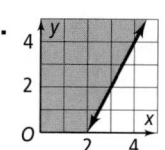

2.
(graph with y and x axes)

3.
$x + 2y \le 10$
$x \ge 1$ $y \ge 2$

4.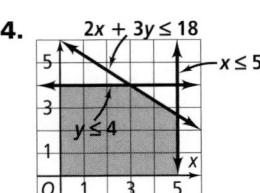

$2x + 3y \le 18$
$x \le 5$
$y \le 4$

5. (0, 0), (0, 4), (5, 0), (5, 4)

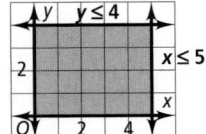

$y \le 4$
$x \le 5$

6. (0, 8), (3, 5), (0, 5)

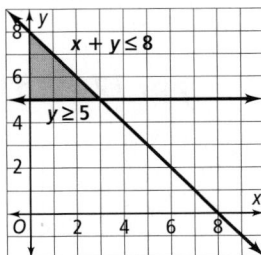

$x + y \le 8$
$y \ge 5$

7. Constraints are limits or restrictions on the variables in the objective function in a linear programming problem. These constraints are written as linear inequalities.

8. Linear programming is an extension of solving linear inequalities. For each, you are given constraints represented by linear inequalities that are graphed. All the points in the overlapping region are solutions, but linear programming problems are usually looking for maximum or minimum values of some quantity modeled with an objective function.

9. Answers may vary. Sample: $\begin{cases} y \le x \\ y \le -x + 4 \\ 0 \le y \le 1 \end{cases}$

$P = 2x + 3y$, $P(0, 0) = 0$, $P(1, 1) = 5$, $P(3, 1) = 9$, $P(4, 0) = 8$; maximum value of P is 9 at (3, 1)

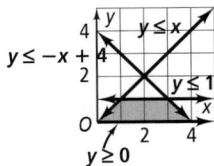

$y \le -x + 4$
$y \le x$
$y \le 1$
$y \ge 0$

Exercises

11.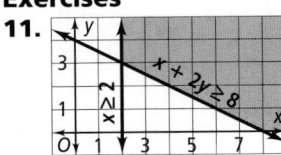

$x \ge 2$
$x + 2y \ge 8$

vertices: (8, 0), (2, 3); minimized at (8, 0)

13. Let s = number of Spruce trees and m = number of Maple trees.

a. $\begin{cases} 30s + 40m \le 2100 \\ 600s + 900m \le 45,000 \\ s \ge 0, m \ge 0 \end{cases}$

b. $P = 650s + 300m$

c.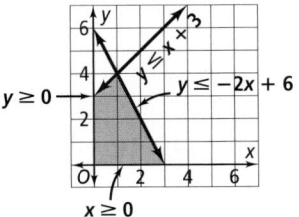

vertices: (0, 0), (0, 50), (30, 30), (70, 0)

d. 70 spruce trees and 0 maple trees

15. He is not considering the constraint $y \le x + 3$; maximize when $P = 11$ at (1, 4)

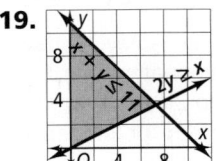

$y \le x + 3$
$y \ge 0$
$y \le -2x + 6$
$x \ge 0$

17.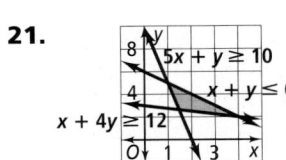

$x + 2y \le 9$
$3x + y \le 7$

vertices: (0, 0), (1, 4), (0, 4.5), $\left(\frac{7}{3}, 0\right)$; maximized when $P = 6$ at (1, 4)

19.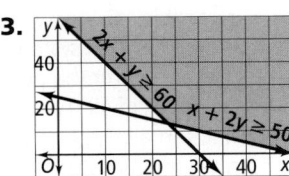

$x + y \le 11$
$2y \ge x$

vertices: (0, 0), $\left(7\frac{1}{3}, 3\frac{2}{3}\right)$, (0, 11); maximized when $P = 29\frac{1}{3}$ at $\left(7\frac{1}{3}, 3\frac{2}{3}\right)$.

21.

$5x + y \ge 10$
$x + y \le 6$
$x + 4y \ge 12$

vertices: $\left(\frac{28}{19}, \frac{50}{19}\right)$, (4, 2) (1, 5); minimized when $C = 67,370$ at $\left(\frac{28}{19}, \frac{50}{19}\right)$

23.

$2x + y \ge 60$
$x + 2y \ge 50$

vertices: (0, 60), $\left(23\frac{1}{3}, 13\frac{1}{3}\right)$, (50, 0); minimized when $x = 23\frac{1}{3}$ and $y = 13\frac{1}{3}$; Round to (23, 14) and (24, 13); (24, 13) gives a minimum cost of $261

25. C

27.

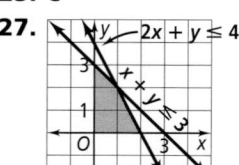

vertices: (0, 0), (2, 0), (0, 3), (1, 2)

28. $y < -2x + 8$

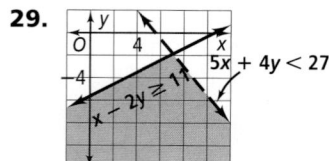

29.

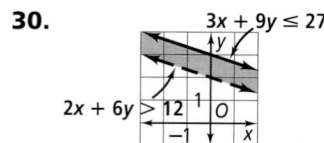

30.

$3x + 9y \le 27$

$2x + 6y > 12$

31. 1 **32.** −34 **33.** 24 **34.** 65 **35.** (0, 6), (−3, 0)
36. (0, 4), (18, 0) **37.** (0, −1), (1, 0)

Lesson 3-5   pp. 166–173

Got It? 1. (4, 2, −3) **2. a.** (4, −1, 2) **b.** Answers may
vary. Sample: Yes; you can choose to eliminate either x, y,
or z resulting in a system of equations in 2 variables.
3. a. (2, 1, −4) **b.** No; in Step 1 we solved for x in terms
of y only. Therefore, once we found the value of y we
could have substituted that value into the equation we
wrote in Step 1 and solved for x without ever finding the
z-value. **4.** 50 T-shirts, 50 polo shirts, and 100 rugby shirts
Lesson Check 1. (5, −3, −2) **2.** (6, 0, −2)
3. (0, 3, 4) **4.** (2, 1, −5) **5.** Answers may vary. Sample:
Substitution is the best method to use when one of the
equations can be solved easily for one variable. **6.** Answers
may vary. Sample: (0, 0, 0) is a unique solution to a system
of three variables. The planes intersect at one common point.
When a system has no solution, no point lies in all three
planes. **7.** No solution since no point lies in all three planes.
The three planes are parallel. **8.** infinitely many solutions
Exercises 9. (4, 2, −3) **11.** (2, 1, −5) **13.** $\left(\frac{1}{2}, -3, 1\right)$
15. (1, −4, 3) **17.** (4, −1, 2) **19.** $\left(-\frac{10}{13}, -\frac{2}{13}, \frac{4}{13}\right)$

21. (8, −4, 2) **23.** (−2, −1, −3) **25.** (0, 1, 7)
27. (5, −2, 0) **29.** (1, 3, 2) **31.** $m\angle P = 32°$;
$m\angle Q = 96°$; $m\angle R = 52°$ **33.** (8, 1, 3)
35. $\left(\frac{1}{2}, 2, -3\right)$ **37.** no solution **39.** (2, 4, 6)
41. (0, 2, −3)
43. Answers may vary. Sample: Solution is (1, 2, 3).
$$\begin{cases} x + y + z = 6 \\ 2x - y + 2z = 6 \\ 3x + 3y + z = 12 \end{cases}$$

45. Let E, F, and V represent the number of edges, faces,
and vertices, respectively. From the first statement,
$E = \frac{5}{2}F$. From the second statement, $V = \frac{5}{3}F$. From the
third statement, $V + F = E + 2$. Solving this system of 3
equations yields $E = 30$, $F = 12$, and $V = 20$.

Lesson 3-6   pp. 174–181

Got It? 1. 17
2. a. $\begin{bmatrix} -4 & -2 & | & 7 \\ 3 & 1 & | & -5 \end{bmatrix}$ **b.** $\begin{bmatrix} 4 & -1 & 2 & | & 1 \\ 0 & 1 & 5 & | & 20 \\ 2 & 1 & 0 & | & 7 \end{bmatrix}$

3. $\begin{cases} 2x = 6 \\ 5x - 2y = 1 \end{cases}$
4. a. (1, 2) **b.** elimination; you use the same steps to
solve **5.** $\left(1, \frac{1}{2}, 3\right)$
Lesson Check 1. 2×1 **2.** 2×4
3. $\begin{bmatrix} 3 & 5 & | & 0 \\ 1 & 1 & | & 2 \end{bmatrix}$ **4.** $\begin{bmatrix} 1 & 3 & -1 & | & 2 \\ 1 & 0 & 2 & | & 8 \\ 0 & 2 & -1 & | & 1 \end{bmatrix}$

5. 16 **6.** a_{21} is 0, the element in row 2, column 1. a_{12}
is −9, the element in row 1 and column 2. **7.** Answers
may vary. Sample: The entry fee to a school play is $2
for adults. Jamie paid a total of $8 for 4 student entry fees
and 2 adult entry fees. What is the student entry fee?
Exercises 9. 1 **11.** 8
13. $\begin{bmatrix} 3 & 2 & | & 16 \\ 0 & 1 & | & 5 \end{bmatrix}$ **15.** $\begin{bmatrix} 1 & -1 & 1 & | & 150 \\ 2 & 0 & 1 & | & 425 \\ 0 & 1 & 3 & | & 0 \end{bmatrix}$

17. $\begin{bmatrix} 1 & -1 & 1 & | & 0 \\ 1 & -2 & -1 & | & 5 \\ 2 & -1 & 2 & | & 8 \end{bmatrix}$ **19.** $\begin{cases} 5x + y = -3 \\ -2x + 2y = 4 \end{cases}$

21. $\begin{cases} 2x + y + z = 1 \\ x + y + z = 2 \\ x - y + z = -2 \end{cases}$ **23.** $\begin{cases} 5x + 2y + z = 5 \\ 4x + y + 2z = 8 \\ x + 3y - 6z = 2 \end{cases}$

25. (−1, 0) **27.** (4, 6) **29.** (2, 3)

31. $10,000 at 4% and $15,000 at 6%;
Let x = amount invested at 4% and
y = amount invested at 6%.
$$\begin{cases} x + y = 25{,}000 \\ 0.04x + 0.06y = 1300 \end{cases}$$
$$\begin{bmatrix} 1 & 1 & | & 25000 \\ 0.04 & 0.06 & | & 1300 \end{bmatrix} = \begin{bmatrix} 1 & 0 & | & 10000 \\ 0 & 1 & | & 15000 \end{bmatrix}$$
33. (3, 1,1) **35.** (35, −22, −16) **37.** (1, 1, 1, 1)
39. (2, 3) **41.** 1 qt. of red paint: $7.75; 1 qt. of yellow
paint: $5.75 **43.** Answers may vary. Sample: 0; 0
45. (8, 2) **47.** $\left(\frac{1}{8}, -\frac{1}{17}\right)$ **49.** G
51. $x \le -\frac{3}{2}$;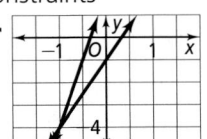
52. $x \ge -35$;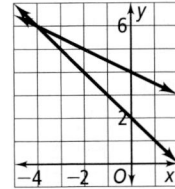
53. $x \ge 4$;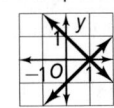
54. $\frac{15}{2}, -\frac{9}{2}$ **55.** 10, −10 **56.** 10, −6 **57.** $y = 2x$
58. $y = \frac{1}{3}x$

Chapter Review   pp. 183–186

1. independent system **2.** Linear programming;
constraints
3. 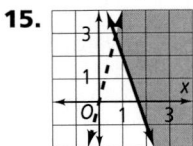 independent; (−1, −4)
4. dependent **5.** inconsistent **6.** dependent
7. independent; (−4, 6)   **8.** independent; (1, 0) v
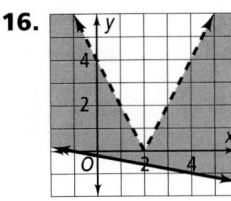
9. 3 pens **10.** (−1, −2) **11.** (0, −5) **12.** (−2, 3)
13. inconsistent; no solution **14.** 1 serving of roast beef
and 2 servings of mashed potatoes
15.
16.

17.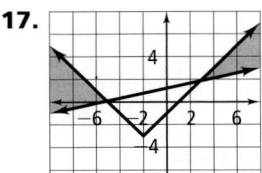
18.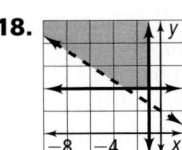
19. 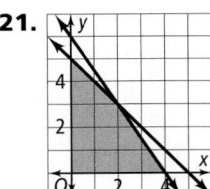 Let r = amount of regular coffee and
d = amount of decaffeinated coffee
$$\begin{cases} r + d \le 10 \\ r \ge 3d, r \ge 0, d \ge 0 \end{cases}$$
20. vertices: (4, 0) and (2, 3);
$C = 4$ is minimized at (4, 0).
21. vertices: (0, 0), (4, 0), (2, 3), (0, 5);
$P = 25$ is maximized at (0, 5).
22. 50 chef's salads and 50 Caesar salads
23. (1, 3, −2) **24.** (−4, 1, −5) **25.** (6, 0, −2)
26. no solution **27.** $\left(\frac{1}{2}, \frac{1}{4}\right)$ **28.** (1, −1)
29. (2, −4, 6) **30.** (5, 2, −3)

Chapter 4

Get Ready! p. 191 1. 6 **2.** 4
3. $-2 < x < 6$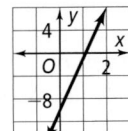
4. $y \le -\frac{5}{4}$ or $y \ge \frac{9}{4}$
5. $y = 9x - 10$

6. $y = \frac{1}{2}x + 8$

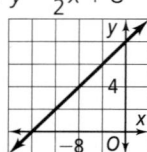

7. translated 4 units to the right and 2 units up
8. translated 10 units to the left and 3 units down
9. $(10, -1)$ **10.** $(-6, -6)$ **11.** Answers may vary.
Sample: application forms, registration forms, tests
12. Answers may vary. Sample: monsters, ghosts, tooth
fairy **13.** writing

Lesson 4-1   pp. 194–201

Got It?

1. a.

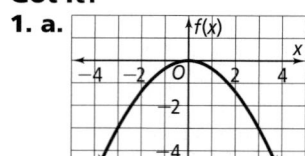

b. If a is a negative number, the parabola will open
downward. There will be a maximum value for y at the
vertex of the parabola.
2. a. translated 3 units up

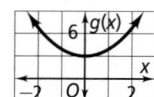

b. translated 1 unit to the left

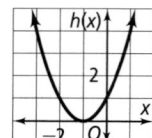

3. vertex: $(-1, 4)$; axis of symmetry: $x = -1$; maximum:
4; domain: all real numbers, range: $y \le 4$ **4.** stretch by
the factor 2, translate 2 units to the left and 5 units
down.
5. $f(x) = -\frac{2}{9}(x - 2)^2 + 7$

Lesson Check

1.

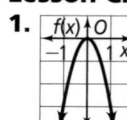

2. minimum **3.** $y = -2(x - 0)^2 + 35$ **4.** when $a > 0$
5. No; a must be > 0 or < 0. **6.** $y = (x + 6)^2$ is the
graph of $y = x^2$ translated 6 units to the left and has a
minimum at $(-6, 0)$; $y = (x - 6)^2 + 7$ is the graph of
$y = x^2$ translated 6 units to the right and 7 units up, with
a minimum at $(6, 7)$.

Exercises

7.

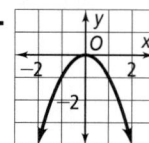

9.

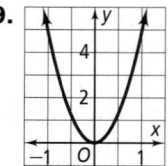

11.

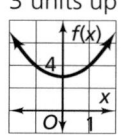

13.

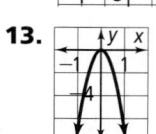

15. translated
3 units up

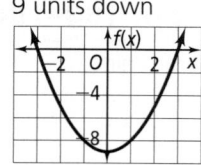

17. translated
6 units down

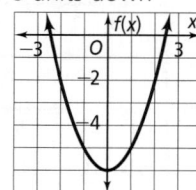

19. translated
9 units down

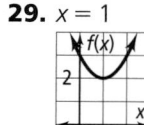

21. translated
1.5 units up

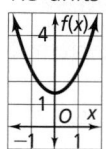

23. vertex: $(-20, 0)$; axis of symmetry: $x = -20$;
maximum: 0; domain: all real numbers, range: $y \le 0$
25. vertex: $(-5.5, 0)$; axis of symmetry: $x = -5.5$;
minimum: 0; domain: all real numbers, range: $y \ge 0$
27. vertex: $(4, -25)$; axis of symmetry: $x = 4$;
maximum: -25; domain: all real numbers, range:
$y \le -25$
29. $x = 1$ **31.** $x = 2$ **33.** $x = 1$

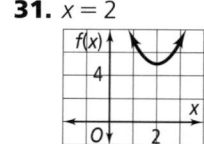

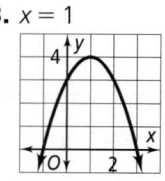

35. $y = (x - 2)^2 + 5$ **37.** $y = -\frac{1}{2}(x + 4)^2 + 2$
39. 1000 chips; $20
41. similar: same vertex $(-1, -2)$ and open upward,
same domain (all real numbers), same range ($y \ge -2$),
same y-intercept, $(0, 1)$; different: $y = 3|x + 1| - 2$ is
an absolute value function with x-intercepts
$\left(-\frac{1}{3}, 0\right)$ and $\left(-\frac{5}{3}, 0\right)$, and $y = 3(x + 1)^2 - 2$ is a
quadratic function with x-intercepts $\left(-1 \pm \sqrt{\frac{2}{3}}, 0\right)$

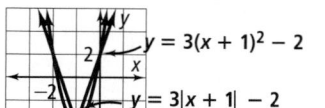

43. similar: same vertex $(-3, 0)$ and open upward, same domain (all real numbers), same range $(y \geq 0)$, same x-intercept, $(-3, 0)$; different: $y = |x + 3|$ is an absolute value function with y-intercept $(0, 3)$, and $y = (x + 3)^2$ is a quadratic function with y-intercept $(0, 9)$

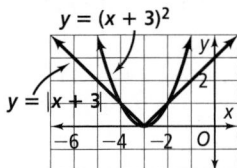

45. stretch vertically by a factor of 2, reflect across the x-axis, translate 1 unit to the left and 1 unit up

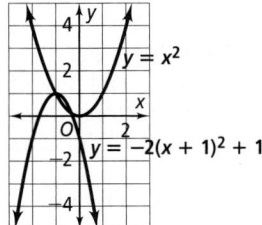

47. a. $10; 9; -1$ **b.** $9; 6; -3$ **c.** $6; 1; -5$
d. The rate of change decreases at a greater rate.
e. Yes; the rates of change increase as you move away from the origin on the negative x-axis.

49. $y = -7(x - 1)^2 + 2$
51. $y = -7x^2 + 5$
53. Answers may vary. Sample: $y = (x + 10)^2 - 4$
55. Answers may vary. Sample:
   $k = -2, a = 3; y = 3(x - 1)^2 - 2$
57. Answers may vary. Sample:
   $a = -6, k = 35; y = -6(x + 1)^2 + 35$
59. a. $ah^2 + k$ **b.** when $h = 0$
61. $y = \frac{1}{2}(x + 3)^2$ **63.** $y = -\frac{1}{4}(x - 4)^2$
65. $y = -4(x + 3)^2$ **67.** G

69. $2x + 2y = 225$
   $2y = 225 - 2x$
   $y = \frac{225}{2} - x$
   $A = xy = x\left(\frac{225}{2} - x\right)$
   $A = -x^2 + 112.5x$
Graph the function. There is a max. at about $(56.25, 3164.06)$, so the max. area is about 3164.06 ft^2 and the length of each side is 56.25 ft.

70. $(3, 2)$ **71.** $(-10, 6)$ **72.** $(1, 0, 3)$
73. $(0, 0)$ **74.** $(-1, 0)$ **75.** $(5, 0)$

Lesson 4-2   pp. 202–208

Got It? 1. vertex: $\left(-\frac{2}{3}, 7\frac{1}{3}\right)$; axis of symmetry: $x = -\frac{2}{3}$; maximum: $7\frac{1}{3}$; range: $y \leq 7\frac{1}{3}$

2.

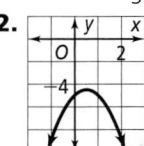

3. $y = -(x - 2)^2 - 1$ **4. a.** 4 ft **b.** because the y-intercept is $(0, 0)$

Lesson Check 1. vertex: $(0, -4)$; axis of symmetry: $x = 0$; minimum: -4

2.

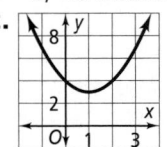

3.

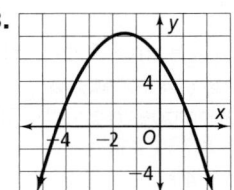

4. $y = (x - 1)^2 + 8$ **5.** $y = -\left(x - \frac{3}{2}\right)^2 + \frac{5}{4}$
6. Error in calculation of x. The correct calculation is:
$x = \frac{-(-4)}{2(2)} = 1$
$y = 2(1) - 4(1) - 3$
$ = 2 - 4 - 3$
$ = -5$
Vertex: $(1, -5)$

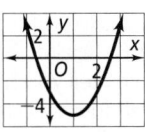

7. The vertex of a function written in vertex form can easily be determined. It is (h, k) where $f(x) = a(x - h)^2 + k$. The vertex of a function in standard form is $\left(\frac{-b}{2a}, f\left(\frac{-b}{2a}\right)\right)$ where $f(x) = ax^2 + bx + c$.

Exercises 9. vertex: $(1, 2)$; axis of symmetry: $x = 1$; maximum: 2; range: $y \leq 2$ **11.** vertex: $(1, 6)$; axis of symmetry: $x = 1$; maximum: 6; range: $y \leq 6$
13. vertex: $\left(-\frac{3}{4}, 5\frac{1}{8}\right)$; axis of symmetry: $x = -\frac{3}{4}$; maximum: $5\frac{1}{8}$; range: $y \leq 5\frac{1}{8}$ **15.** vertex: $\left(-\frac{1}{2}, \frac{1}{4}\right)$; axis of symmetry: $x = -\frac{1}{2}$; maximum: $\frac{1}{4}$; range: $y \leq \frac{1}{4}$

17.

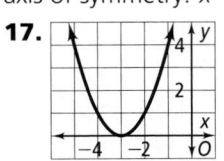

19.

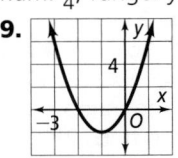

21.

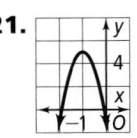

23.

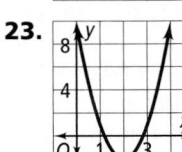

25.

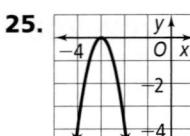

27. $y = (x + 1)^2 + 4$ **29.** $y = 2\left(x - \frac{5}{4}\right)^2 + \frac{71}{8}$

31. $y = \frac{9}{4}\left(x + \frac{2}{3}\right)^2 - 2$

33.

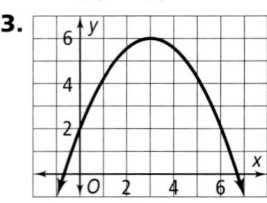

35.

37. 4 cm × 9 cm × 9 cm **39.** $b = -6$; $c = 5$

41. $a = 1$; $c = -2$ **43. a.** The projectile represented by the equation goes higher by 28 feet. **b.** equation: $t = 0.27$ s and $t = 3.73$ s; table: $t = 0.38$ s and $t = 2.62$ s

45. (0, 3) **47.** (0, −54) **49.** $a = -6$, $b = 24$

51. $a = 3$, $b = -12$

53.

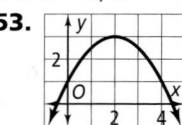

Lesson 4-3   pp. 209–214

Got It? 1. $y = -3x^2 + x$ **2a.** Rocket 2 **b.** Rocket 1: D: $0 \le t \le 9.4$, R: $0 \le h \le 352.6$; Rocket 2: D: $0 \le t \le 12$, R: $0 \le h \le 580$ **c.** The domains tell you how many seconds the rockets were in the air. The domains are different because the rockets were in the air for different amounts of time.
3. $y = -0.329x^2 + 9.798x + 15.571$; 88.5°F at 2:53 P.M. (although the meteorologist's prediction is 89° at 3 P.M.)
Lesson Check 1. $y = -2x^2 + 3x - 1$
2. $y = 2x^2 + 6x + 7.5$ **3.** $y = -2x^2 + 10x - 13.5$
4. Answers may vary. Sample: A rough plot of the data will indicate whether the data are collinear (linear regression) or non-collinear where the data follows a curve (quadratic regression). **5.** A parabola that opens up always attains greater values than one that opens down. **6.** y is not a function of x since for one value of x, "3," there are 2 values of y, "4" and "0."
Exercises 7. $y = -x^2 + 3x - 4$ **9.** $y = 2x^2 - x + 3$
11. $y = x^2 - 6x + 3$ **13.** $y = x^2 + 2x$
15. $y = -x^2 + x - 2$ **17. a.** $y = -16x^2 + 33x + 46$, where x is the number of seconds after release and y is the height in ft **b.** 28.5 ft **c.** about 63 ft **19.** yes; $y = -2x^2 + 3x + 5$ **21.** yes; $y = 0.625x^2 - 1.75x + 1$
23. $y = 0.005x^2 - 1.95x + 120$; 66 mm
25. a. $y = -0.004x^2 + 0.859x + 27.53$ **b.** Answers may vary. Sample: domain: integers from −10 to 17; range: whole numbers from 18 to 42 **c.** the year 2003

d. The year 2022; the year is outside the domain of the data pts. **27. a.** (3, 5) **b.** 3; substitute x- and y-values in the general form of a quadratic, then solve the resulting linear system for the coefficients.

Lesson 4-4   pp. 216–223

Got It? 1. a. $(x + 10)(x + 4)$ **b.** $(x - 5)(x - 6)$
c. $-(x + 2)(x - 16)$ **2. a.** $7(n^2 - 3)$ **b.** $9(x + 2)(x - 1)$
c. $4(x^2 + 2x + 3)$ **3. a.** $(x + 1)(4x + 3)$
b. $(x - 2)(2x - 3)$ **c.** No; $2x^2 + 2x + 2 = 2(x^2 + x + 1)$, there are no real factors of a and c whose product is 1 and whose sum is 1. **4.** $(8x - 1)^2$
5. $(4x - 9)(4x + 9)$
Lesson Check 1. $(x + 4)(x + 2)$ **2.** $(x - 12)(x - 1)$
3. $(x - 9)(x + 9)$ **4.** $(5y - 6)(5y + 6)$ **5.** $(y - 3)^2$
6. $(2x - 1)^2$ **7.** 5x **8.** $4a^2$ **9.** 6 **10.** 7h **11.** No; the middle term is not twice the product of the square root of the end terms. **12.** For $a \ne 1$, look for two factors whose sum is b and whose product is ac. For $a = 1$, look for two factors whose sum is b and whose product is c.
13. $a^2 - 2ab + b^2 - 25$ Group the first 3 terms.
    $= \left(a^2 - 2ab + b^2\right) - 25$
    $= (a - b)^2 - 5^2$
    $= (a - b - 5)(a - b + 5)$
Exercises 15. $(x + 2)(x + 3)$ **17.** $(x + 2)(x + 8)$
19. $(x + 2)(x + 20)$ **21.** $-(x - 1)(x - 12)$
23. $(x - 4)(x - 6)$ **25.** $(x - 4)(x - 9)$
27. $-(x - 4)(x + 5)$ **29.** $(c - 7)(c + 9)$
31. $-(t - 11)(t + 4)$ **33.** 5b; $5b(5b - 4)$
35. 5; $5(t + 1)(t - 2)$ **37.** 9; $9(3p^2 - p + 2)$
39. $(x - 8)(2x - 3)$ **41.** $(m - 3)(2m - 5)$
43. $(x - 12)(2x - 3)$ **45.** $(y + 4)(5y - 8)$
47. $(x + 1)^2$ **49.** $(k - 9)^2$

51. cannot be factored; 8 is not a perfect square and there are no positive factors of 32 that have a sum of 16.
53. $(x - 2)(x + 2)$ **55.** cannot be factored; This is a sum of squares, not a difference of squares.
57. $(5x - 1)$ cm by $(5x - 1)$ cm **59.** $2(3z + 2)(3z - 2)$
61. $16(2t + 1)(2t - 1)$ **63.** $3(y + 5)(y + 3)$
65. $3(x + 1)(x - 9)$ **67.** $2(x - 5)(2x - 1)$
69. $-\left(\frac{1}{4}s - 1\right)\left(\frac{1}{4}s + 1\right)$
71. The third line should be $x(2x - 5) - (2x - 5)$, and the final line should be $(x - 1)(2x - 5)$. **73.** y; $y(y - 1)$
75. 10; $10(x - 3)(x + 3)$ **77.** 2; $2(x^2 - 37x + 6)$ **79.** D
81. Answers may vary. **83.** $(0.5t + 0.4)(0.5t - 0.4)$
85. $(x + 12)(x - 3)$ **87.** $(2x + 9)(3x + 14)$
89. Factor the GCF, $4x^2$, from the terms to get $4x^2(x^2 + 6x + 8)$. Look for numbers whose product is 8 and whose sum is 6. The numbers 4 and 2 work. The complete factorization is $4x^2(x + 4)(x + 2)$.

91. $(2x - 5y)(2x + 5y)\left(4x^2 + 25y^2\right)$

93. $(x - 8)(x + 3)$ **95.** B **97. a.** By entering the given lists into a graphing calculator and then calculating the quadratic regression, you get $h = -16t^2 + 22t + 3$ as the quadratic model for the ball's height as a function of time.

b. $h = -16t^2 + 22t + 3$

$h = -[8t(2t - 3) + 1(2t - 3)]$

$h = -(2t - 3)(8t + 1)$

98. $y = -0.149x^2 + 5.171x + 16.971$ **99.** penny: 2.5g, nickel: 5g, dime: 2.3g

100. 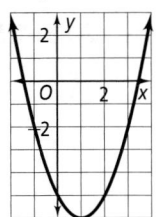 **101.**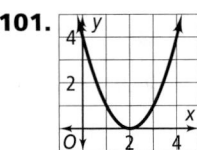

102.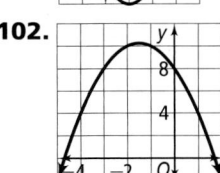

Algebra Review p. 225 1. $3\sqrt{2}$ **3.** $-4\sqrt{2}$ **5.** $\frac{-\sqrt{91}}{13}$

7. $-10\sqrt{2}$ **9.** 108 **11.** $|xy|$ **13.** $-\frac{|x|\sqrt{35}}{5}$ **15.** $\frac{5\sqrt{14}}{7}$

Lesson 4-5 pp. 226–231

Got It? 1. 3, 4 **2.** 3, $\frac{1}{4}$ **3.** -6, 4 **4. a.** $53\frac{1}{3}$ m; $21\frac{1}{3}$ m; answers may vary. Sample: domain: $0 \le x \le 60$, range: $0 \le y \le 30$ **b.** No; domains and ranges are constrained by real-world limits.

Lesson Check 1. 3, -3 **2.** -4, -9 **3.** $-\frac{2}{3}$, 1
4. 4.372, -1.372 **5.** 2.608, -2.108 **6.** -1; since $y = 0$ when $x = 5$, substitute these values into the equation to find b. **7.** when the coefficients are integers and a recognizable pattern of factoring is evident **8.** One solution: when the table's range consists of zero and all positive numbers or zero and all negative numbers. No solution: when the table does not include zero and the y-values are either all positive or all negative numbers

Exercises 9. -4, -2 **11.** -1, $\frac{3}{2}$ **13.** -2, -1 **15.** 0, 4
17. 0, 4 **19.** 3, 8 **21.** -0.78, 1.28 **23.** 4, -10
25. 0.8, -1 **27.** -1.67, -1.5 **29.** -0.94, 2.34
31. -1, 0.25 **33.** -1.46, 5.46 **35.** -1.16, 2.16
37. 3 in. **39.** about 3.6 ft **41.** Answers may vary.
Samples are given: **a.** $x^2 - 8x + 15 = 0$
b. $x^2 + x - 6 = 0$ **c.** $x^2 + 7x + 6 = 0$ **43.** $-\frac{3}{2}$, $-\frac{2}{3}$
45. -4, $\frac{5}{2}$ **47.** -1, 4 **49.** -4, 0 **51.** 4.37, -1.37

53. -1, $\frac{10}{3}$ **55.** $(0, -2)$, $(2, 2)$ **57.** Solve $(x - 4)(x - 6) = 0$ to find that the zeros of $y = x^2 - 10x + 24$ are 4 and 6. Average 4 and 6 to get 5. This is the x-coordinate of the vertex. Substitute 5 for x in $x^2 - 10x + 24$ to find that -1 is the y-coordinate of the vertex. The vertex is $(5, -1)$.

59. a. 2.45m **b.** ≈ 1.3s **61.** H
63. reflection across the x-axis, followed by a vertical translation 2 units up, and stretched by a factor of 3

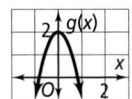

Lesson 4-6 pp. 233–239

Got It? 1. a. $\sqrt{5}$, $-\sqrt{5}$ **b.** $\sqrt{2}$, $-\sqrt{2}$
2. 42 in. $\times$ 67.2 in. **3.** 2, 12 **4. a.** 9 **b.** No; $\left(\frac{b}{2}\right)^2 = \frac{b^2}{4}$, which is a function of b. **5.** $\frac{1}{2} \pm \frac{\sqrt{13}}{2}$

6. $y = \left(x + \frac{3}{2}\right)^2 - \frac{33}{4}$; vertex: $\left(-\frac{3}{2}, -\frac{33}{4}\right)$; y-intercept: $(0, -6)$

Lesson Check 1. 6, -6 **2.** 3, -3 **3.** 1 **4.** 25 **5.** 4
6. 36 **7.** 2500 **8.** 256 **9.** First, you rewrite the eq. to get all terms with x on one side. Then, you find $\left(\frac{b}{2}\right)^2$ and add it to both sides of the eq. Then, you factor the resulting trinomial.

10. $x^2 + 12x + 5 = 3$

$x^2 + 12x = -2$ — Rewrite to get all terms with x on one side of the eq.

$\left(\frac{12}{2}\right)^2 = 6^2 = 36$ — Find $\left(\frac{b}{2}\right)^2 = 36$.

$x^2 + 12x + 36 = -2 + 36$ — Add 36 to each side.

$(x + 6)^2 = 34$ — Factor the trinomial.

11. Your friend should also have subtracted 49; $(x^2 - 14x + 49) + 36 - 49 = (x - 7)^2 - 13$

Exercises 13. 2, -2 **15.** $\frac{5}{3}$, $-\frac{5}{3}$ **17.** $2\sqrt{2}$, $-2\sqrt{2}$
19. -4, -2 **21.** -1, 3 **23.** -4, 3 **25.** $-\frac{4}{5}$, $\frac{2}{5}$
27. $-\frac{10}{3}$, $\frac{2}{3}$ **29.** $\frac{1}{4}$ **31.** 100 **33.** 4 **35.** $6 \pm \sqrt{29}$
37. $1 \pm \sqrt{6}$ **39.** $5 \pm \sqrt{13}$ **41.** $3 \pm \sqrt{11}$
43. $-\frac{5}{4} \pm \frac{1}{4}\sqrt{37}$ **45.** $-\frac{3}{5} \pm \frac{\sqrt{21}}{5}$
47. $y = 2(x - 2)^2 - 7$ **49.** $y = (x + 2)^2 - 11$
51. $y = -(x - 2)^2 + 3$ **53.** 10, -10 **55.** 22, -22
57. 18, -18 **59.** 1, -1 **61.** 84, -84
63. $\frac{-5 \pm \sqrt{37}}{2}$ **65.** $\frac{1 \pm \sqrt{21}}{2}$ **67.** $\frac{2 \pm \sqrt{10}}{3}$
69. $\frac{-3 \pm \sqrt{41}}{8}$ **71.** $\frac{1}{3}$, $-\frac{2}{3}$ **73.** $-3 \pm \sqrt{7}$
75. a. $-.01(x - 59)^2 + 36.81$; 36.81 ft **b.** 7.65 ft
c. about 120 ft **77.** $\frac{-a \pm a\sqrt{13}}{6}$

79. $-\frac{3}{2a}$, $-\frac{1}{2a}$, $a \neq 0$ **81.** $-\frac{2}{3a}$, $\frac{5}{2a}$, $a \neq 0$

83. $y = -4\left(x + \frac{5}{8}\right)^2 + \frac{73}{16}$; $\left(-\frac{5}{8}, \frac{73}{16}\right)$

85. $y = -\frac{1}{5}(x - 2)^2 + 3$; $(2, 3)$ **87.** G

89. $x^2 - 9 = -8x$

$\quad x^2 + 8x = 9$ Move the variables to the left side and the constant to the right by using the Add. Prop. of Eq.

$\quad \left(\frac{8}{2}\right)^2 = 4^2 = 16$ Find $\left(\frac{b}{2}\right)^2 = 16$.

$\quad x^2 + 8x + 16$ Add 16 to each
$\quad = 9 + 16$ side.

$\quad (x + 4)^2 = 25$ Factor left side. Simplify right side.

$\quad x + 4 = \pm 5$ Take the square root of each side.

$\quad x = -4 \pm 5$ Add -4 to each side.

$\quad x = -9, 1$ Simplify.

90. $\frac{1}{2}$, 1 **91.** -4, 1 **92.** 8, $-\frac{2}{3}$

93. yes; $y = \frac{1}{2}x^2 + \frac{7}{2}x + 9$ **94.** yes;

$y = -\frac{1}{2}x^2 + x + 2$ **95.** yes; $y = 3x^2 - 5x + 2$

96. $(2, 0)$ **97.** $(3, 1)$ **98.** $(3, 1)$ **99.** 24 **100.** 84

Lesson 4-7   pp. 240–247

Got It? 1. a. -2 **b.** $-2 \pm \sqrt{7}$ **2. a.** $10.74 **b.** Yes; a neg. profit means more money was spent than earned. **3. a.** no real solutions **b.** two real solutions **4.** Yes;

$b^2 - 4ac = (85)^2 - 4(-16)\left(-109\frac{11}{12}\right) = 190\frac{1}{3}$.

The discriminant is pos. So the eq. has two real solutions.

Lesson Check 1. $\frac{5 \pm \sqrt{53}}{2}$ **2.** $\frac{-3 \pm \sqrt{61}}{2}$ **3.** $3, -\frac{1}{2}$
4. no real solutions **5.** -32; no real solutions **6.** 273; two real solutions **7.** 0; one real solution **8.** $k = \pm 6$ for one real solution; $k > 6$ or $k < -6$ for two real solutions
9. Answers may vary. Sample: The discriminants of eqs. with one real solution are all zero and thus equal, but the solutions may or may not be equal. An example is $x^2 - 8x + 16$ and $x^2 - 4x + 4$. Each has a discriminant of zero, but the solutions are 4 and 2. **10.** Yes; the eqs. can share common factors such as for $x^2 + 2x - 8$ where the discriminant is 36 and the solutions are 2 and -4, and $x^2 - 4x + 4$ where the discriminant is zero and the solution is 2.

Exercises 11. 1, 3 **13.** $-\frac{7}{2}$, 1 **15.** -5 **17.** $\frac{3 \pm \sqrt{5}}{2}$
19. $\frac{2 \pm \sqrt{10}}{3}$ **21.** 1, 4 **23.** \$16.34 **25.** -4; no real solutions **27.** 0; one **29.** 169; two **31.** 1; two
33. 0; one **35.** -23; no real solutions **37.** no
39. 2.29 in. $\times$ 15.71 in. **41.** $-\frac{1}{6}$, 1 **43.** -2.49, 0.89
45. -0.19, 2.69 **47.** 1, 10 **49.** $-\frac{3}{2}, \frac{1}{2}$ **51.** -1.70, 4.70
53. -8.47, 0.47 **55.** 1.47, -7.47 **57.** about 1.89 s

59. one **61.** two **63.** two **65.** two **67. a.** k such that $|k| < 12$ **b.** 12 or -12 **c.** k such that $|k| > 12$
69. a. $x^2 = 100\pi$ **b.** 17.72 cm
71. Answers may vary. Sample: $x^2 + 5x + 3 = 0$
73. 0, $\pm \sqrt{5}$ **75.** -5, 1 **77.** The absolute value of
$\frac{\sqrt{b^2 - 4ac}}{2a}$ is the distance from the axis of symmetry to the x-intercepts, if the discriminant is nonnegative.
79. 3 **81.** 15 **82.** -2, 10 **83.** $\frac{2 \pm \sqrt{2}}{2}$ **84.** $\frac{3 \pm \sqrt{41}}{2}$
85. $9z^2 + 3z$ **86.** $4x + k$ **87.** $2y - 8x$
88. $2\sqrt{17}$ **89.** 5 **90.** 13

Lesson 4-8   pp. 248–255

Got It? 1. a. $2i\sqrt{3}$ **b.** $5i$ **c.** $i\sqrt{7}$ **d.** $8i \neq -8$
2. a. 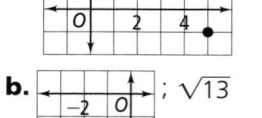 ; $\sqrt{26}$

b. 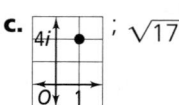 ; $\sqrt{13}$ **c.** ; $\sqrt{17}$

3. a. $4 - i$ **b.** $-2 + 7i$ **c.** $12i$ **d.** $18i$ **4. a.** -21
b. $23 - 2i$ **c.** 41 **5. a.** $\frac{7}{25} - \frac{26}{25}i$ **b.** $-\frac{1}{6} - \frac{2}{3}i$
c. $\frac{15}{113} - \frac{112}{113}i$ **6. a.** $5(x + 2i)(x - 2i)$
b. $(x + 9i)(x - 9i)$ **7. a.** $\frac{1 \pm i\sqrt{23}}{6}$
b. $2 \pm i$

Lesson Check 1. $5i\sqrt{3}$ **2.** 5 **3.** $(x + 4i)(x - 4i)$
4. $7 - 3i$ **5.** $13 - 6i$ **6.** The add. inv. of a complex number, $a + bi$, is the opposite of the complex number, or $-a - bi$. The complex conjugate of a complex number, $a + bi$, is the real part plus the opposite of the imaginary part of the complex number, or $a - bi$. **7.** error in the sign of the last term of the first line, which carries through to the end of the calculation; the line should be: " . . .
$= 16 + 28i - 28i - 49i^2$
$= 16 + 49$
$= 65.$ "

Exercises 9. $i\sqrt{7}$ **11.** $9i$
13. 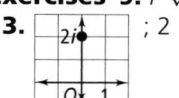 ; 2   **15.** 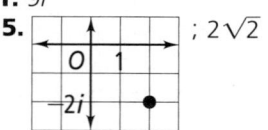 ; $2\sqrt{2}$

17.  ; $3\sqrt{5}$ **19.** $1 - 7i$ **21.** $10 + 6i$

23. $9 + 58i$ **25.** -36 **27.** $-\frac{2}{5} - \frac{3}{5}i$ **29.** $\frac{8}{17} + \frac{19}{17}i$
31. $\frac{8}{13} + \frac{12}{13}i$ **33.** $(x + 5i)(x - 5i)$
35. $3(s + 5i)(s - 5i)$ **37.** $(2b + i)(2b - i)$

39. $-1 \pm i\sqrt{2}$ **41.** $1 \pm i\frac{\sqrt{10}}{2}$ **43.** $2 \pm i$

45. a. A: -5; B: $3 + 2i$; C: $2 - i$; D: $3i$; E: $-6 - 4i$; F: $-1 + 5i$ **b.** A: 5; B: $-3 - 2i$; C: $-2 + i$; D: $-3i$; E: $6 + 4i$; F: $1 - 5i$ **c.** A: -5; B: $3 - 2i$; C: $2 + i$; D: $-3i$; E: $-6 + 4i$; F: $-1 - 5i$ **d.** A: 5; B: $\sqrt{13}$; C: $\sqrt{5}$; D: 3; E: $2\sqrt{13}$; F: $\sqrt{26}$ **47.** $-5, 5$ **49.** $-1 + 5i$

51. $8 - 2i$ **53.** $6 + 10i$ **55.** $10 + 11i$ **57.** trapezoid **59.** $\frac{1}{26} + \frac{3}{52}i$ **61.** sum: 2, product: 3

63. sum: $\frac{3}{2}$, product: $\frac{3}{2}$ **65.** Answers may vary. Sample:

$x^2 - 4x + 29 = 0$ **67.** $x = -7, y = 3$

69. $x = -7, y = -3$ **71.** all nonzero numbers x and y such that $|x| = |y|$ **73.** B **75.** A

77. $\dfrac{-3 \pm \sqrt{41}}{4}$ **78.** $\dfrac{-1 \pm \sqrt{17}}{8}$ **79.** $\dfrac{-7 \pm \sqrt{17}}{2}$

80. 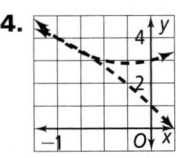 ; axis of symmetry: $x = -1$

81. 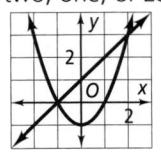 ; axis of symmetry: $x = 4$

82. ; axis of symmetry: $x = 1$

83. $y = 3x - 4$ **84.** $y = -0.5x - 2$
85. $y = -7x + 10$ **86.** $y = 2x + 8$

87. 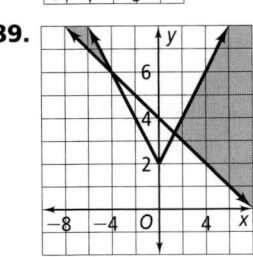 **88.** no solution

89.

Got It? 1. $(-3, 0)$, $(-2, 1)$ **2.** $(-5, 0)$, $(1, 6)$
3. a. $(0, 5)$, $(2, 1)$ **b.** no solution
4. a. 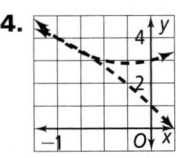 **b.** infinite, one, or none

Lesson Check 1. $(1, 2)$, $(2, 3)$ **2.** $(1, -1)$, $(2, 0)$

3. $(2, -5)$, $\left(-\frac{4}{3}, \frac{25}{9}\right)$

4. 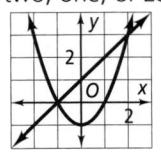 **5.**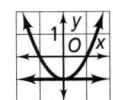

6. For each system of eqs., linear or quadratic, to solve the system you need to find the pt. (or pts.) of intersection or, in the case of inequalities, the regions of intersection. A linear system of eqs. can have one, infinite, or no solutions, whereas a quadratic systems of eqs. can have one, two, infinite, or no solutions.
7. a. two, one, or zero

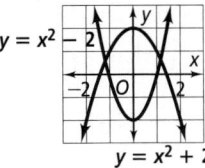

b. two, one, or zero

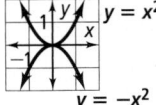
$y = x^2 + 2$

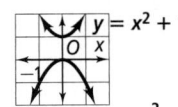

c. four, three, two, one, or zero

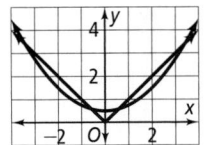 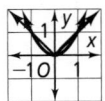

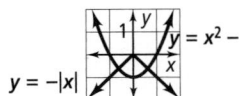 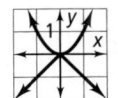 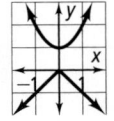

Exercises

9. (0, 1), (4, 9);

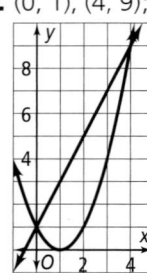

11. $(0, 1), \left(-\frac{5}{2}, 6\right)$;

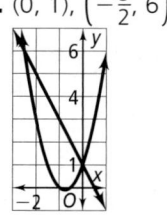

13. $\left(\dfrac{-3 + \sqrt{17}}{2}, \dfrac{-11 + \sqrt{17}}{2}\right), \left(\dfrac{-3 - \sqrt{17}}{2}, \dfrac{-11 - \sqrt{17}}{2}\right)$
$\approx (0.56, -3.44), (-3.56, -7.56)$

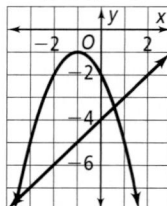

15. (3, 7), (−2, 2) **17.** (1, −2) **19.** $(-3 + \sqrt{6}, -1 + \sqrt{6}), (-3 - \sqrt{6}, -1 - \sqrt{6})$ **21.** (0, −1)

23. $(0, -3), \left(\frac{1}{3}, -\frac{31}{9}\right)$ **25.** no solution

27.

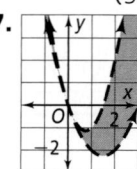

29. width = 20.45 in. and length = 21.45 in.; or width = 6.55 in. and length = 7.55 in.

31. (8.42, −5.42), (−1.42, 4.42) **33.** $\left(-1, -\frac{3}{2}\right)$

35. (0, −4), (2, −2)

37.

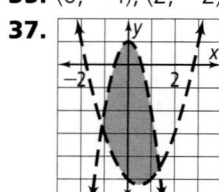

39.

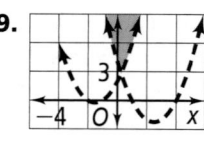

41. (0, −1), (1, 0) **43.** (10, 68), (−3, 16)

45. $(-8, -16), \left(-\frac{4}{3}, 4\right)$ **47. a.** $0 < p < 25$

b. 13 **49.** no solution **51.** $\left(\frac{1}{2}, \frac{7}{2}\right)$

53.

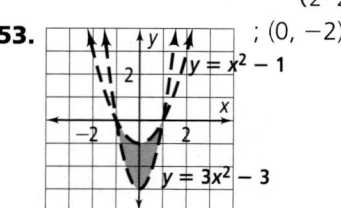

; (0, −2)

55.

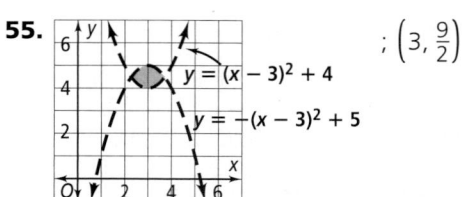

; $\left(3, \frac{9}{2}\right)$

57. never; $x^2 + c \neq x^2 + d$

59. always; $\left(\dfrac{-a - b}{2}, \dfrac{a^2 - 2ab + b^2}{2}\right)$

61. $\sqrt{5} - 1$ units **63.** F

65. $x = \dfrac{-b \pm \sqrt{b^2 - 4ac}}{2a}$

$x = \dfrac{-(5) \pm \sqrt{(5)^2 - 4(-3)(4)}}{2(-3)}$

$x = \dfrac{5 \pm \sqrt{73}}{6}$

66. $-4 + 3i$ **67.** $7 + 7i$ **68.** $3 + 3i$ **69.** $-1, -\frac{3}{2}$

70. 1, 3 **71.** $\frac{3}{5}$ **72.** $y = -(k - 2)^2 + 10$

73. $y = (x + 3)^2 - 8$ **74.** $y = 2(n - 2)^2 - 11$

75. $11q$ **76.** $2a^2b + ab^2$ **77.** $-y^2 + 2y$

Chapter Review pp. 267–272

1. standard **2.** discriminant **3.** complex **4.** vertex: (−2, −6); axis of symmetry: $x = -2$; minimum: −6; domain: all real numbers; range: $y \geq -6$ **5.** vertex: (3, 2); axis of symmetry: $x = 3$; maximum: 2; domain: all real numbers; range: $y \leq 2$ **6.** vertex: (1, 5); axis of symmetry: $x = 1$; minimum: 5; domain: all real numbers; range: $y \geq 5$ **7.** vertex: (−9, −4); axis of symmetry: $x = -9$; minimum: −4 domain: all real numbers; range: $y \geq -4$

8.

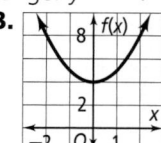

translation 4 units up

9.

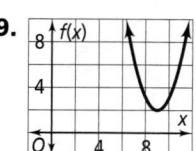

translation 9 units to the right and 2 units up

10.

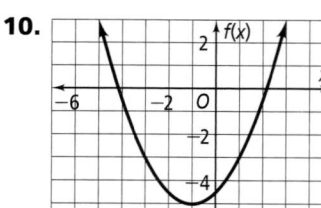

vert. compression by a factor of $\frac{1}{2}$, translation 1 unit to the left and 5 units down

11. $y = 2(x - 2)^2 + 1$ **12.** $y = \left(-\frac{1}{3}\right)(x + 5)^2 + 4$

13.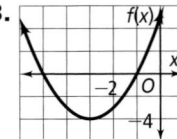

14.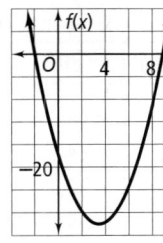

15.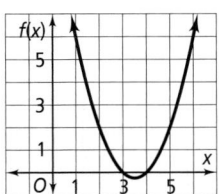

16.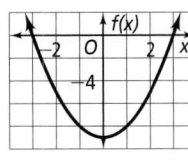

17. $f(x) = 4(x - 1)^2 - 2$ **18.** $f(x) = (x - 4)^2 - 4$

19. $f(x) = 8\left(x + \frac{1}{2}\right)^2 - 14$ **20.** $f(x) = -2\left(x + \frac{3}{2}\right)^2 + \frac{29}{2}$

21. 1s; 25 ft **22.** $y = x^2 - 6x + 5$

23. $y = -2x^2 + 8x - 8$ **24.** $y = x^2 + 3x - 18$

25. $y = -0.5x^2 + 2.5x - 7$

26. $y = -0.0043x^2 + 0.3521x + 0.3691$

27. $(x - 6)(x - 2)$ **28.** $(3x - 4)(x + 5)$

29. $-2(2x - 1)(x - 3)$ **30.** $(x + 10)(x + 4)$

31. $(x - 7)^2$ **32.** $(3x + 5)^2$ **33.** $4(3x - 2)(3x + 2)$

34. $(5x - 2)(5x + 2)$ **35.** $6x$; $6x(x - 4)$

36. 7; $-7(2x^2 + 7)$ **37.** $-2, 6$ **38.** $-2, \frac{7}{2}$

39. $-4, 2$ **40.** $-9, 2$

41. 1, -2.6;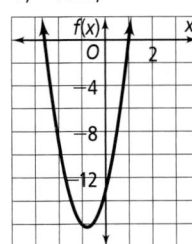

42. 1.345, -3.345;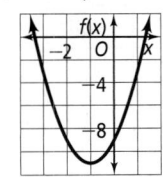

43. 1.618, -0.618;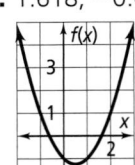

44. 3.236, -1.236;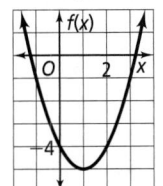

45. 2, 4 **46.** no real solutions **47.** 4.56, 0.44 **48.** 2, 4

49. ± 2 **50.** $\pm\sqrt{5}$ **51.** ± 3 **52.** $\pm 2\sqrt{3}$ **53.** 9 **54.** $\frac{9}{4}$

55. $-4 \pm \sqrt{10}$ **56.** $5 \pm \sqrt{38}$ **57.** $-1, \frac{1}{3}$ **58.** $1 \pm i\sqrt{3}$

59. $\frac{-3 \pm i\sqrt{91}}{2}$ **60.** 1, $-\frac{3}{4}$ **61.** 1, $-\frac{8}{3}$ **62.** 3 **63.** 4, -1

64. 1.744, -0.344 **65.** 164; two **66.** -3; none

67. 0; one **68.** 233; two **69.** 10.2736 ft × 16.5472 ft

70. $2i\sqrt{6}$ **71.** $-3 + i\sqrt{2}$ **72.** $-50 + 40i$

73. $6 + 4i\sqrt{6}$ **74.** $3 + 9i$ **75.** $13 + 20i$ **76.** $21 - 25i$

77. $-12 - 15i$ **78.** $-3 - 2i$ **79.** $-\frac{1}{2} - \frac{1}{2}i$ **80.** $\pm 3i$

81. $\frac{1}{5} \pm \frac{2}{5}i$ **82.** $2 \pm i\sqrt{6}$ **83.** $\frac{-4 \pm i\sqrt{26}}{7}$

84. $(7, -6), (-2, 12)$ **85.** $(5, -27), (-2, 8)$

86. $(-5, 37), (3, -27)$;

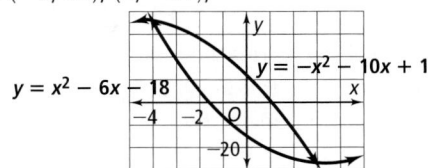

87. $(6.32, 15.64), (-3.32, -3.64)$;

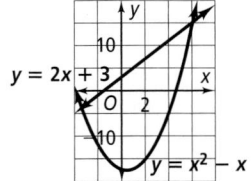

88.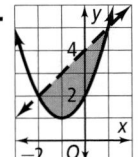

89.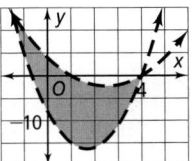

Chapter 5

Get Ready! p. 277

1.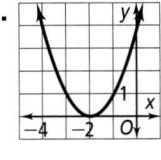

2.

3.

4. $y = x^2 + 3x - 4$ **5.** $y = x^2 - 2x + 1$

6. $y = -x^2 - x + 12$ **7.** 0.25, -1 **8.** $-6.39, 4.39$

9. $-6.38, 0.38$ **10.** $-4, 5$ **11.** $-9, 3$ **12.** 1, 2

13. 24; two real solutions **14.** 0; one real solution

15. 0; one real solution **16.** south **17.** The highest pt. in Maine may be lower than the highest pt. in the United States. The relative maximum of a graph for a given region is the maximum for that region only, whereas the maximum of the graph may be greater than or equal to the relative maximum for the region.
18. $4x^2 + 4x + 1$

Lesson 5-1   pp. 280–287

Got It? 1. a. $5x^4 + 3x^3 - x$; quartic trinomial
b. $-4x^5 + 2x^2 + 13$; quintic trinomial **2.** up and down
3. a. end behavior: up and down; two turning points $(0.33, -2.15)$ and $(1, -2)$; decreases from $-\infty$ to $\frac{1}{3}$, increases from $\frac{1}{3}$ to 1, and decreases from 1 to ∞

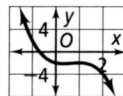

b. end behavior: down and up; no turning points; increases from $-\infty$ to ∞

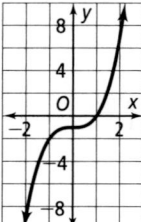

4. a. degree: 4 **b.** Answers may vary. Sample: $y = x^5$
Lesson Check 1. cubic monomial **2.** quadratic trinomial **3.** $5x^2 + 7x + 3$ **4.** $9x - 3$ **5.** up and down
6. Yes; the graph of a linear binomial or linear monomial is a straight line; $f(x) = 2x$ **7.** The graph of $y = 4x^3 + 4$ has no turning points, *not* one turning point.
Exercises 9. $-3x + 5$; linear binomial
11. $x^4 - x^3 + x$; quartic trinomial **13.** $3a^3 + 5a^2 + 1$; cubic trinomial **15.** $12x^4 + 3$; quartic binomial
17. $-2x^3$; cubic monomial **19.** $-x^4 + 3x^2$; quartic binomial **21.** up and up **23.** down and up **25.** down and down **27.** up and down **29.** up and down **31.** up and up
33. end behavior: up and down; two turning pts. $(-0.51, 1.12)$ and $(0.36, 4.12)$; decreases from $-\infty$ to -0.51, increases from -0.51 to 0.36, and decreases from 0.36 to ∞ **35.** end behavior: down and up; no turning pts.; increases from $-\infty$ to ∞ **37.** end behavior: down and up; no turning pts.; increases from $-\infty$ to ∞ **39.** 3
41. $-4a^4 + a^3 + a^2$; quartic trinomial
43. $6x^2$; quadratic monomial **45.** $-9d^3 - 13$; cubic binomial **47.** negative; 3 **49.** positive; 4

51. For $f(x) = x^3 - 3x^2 - 2x - 6$,

x	f(x)	1st diff	2nd diff	3rd diff
0	−6			
		−4		
1	−10		0	
		−4		6
2	−14		6	
		2		6
3	−12		12	
		14		6
4	2		18	
		32		
5	34			

For $f(x) = ax^3 + bx^2 + cx + d$,

x	f(x)	1st diff	2nd diff	3rd diff
0	d			
		$a + b + c$		
1	$a + b + c + d$		$6a + 2b$	
		$7a + 3b + c$		$6a$
2	$8a + 4b + 2c + d$		$12a + 2b$	
		$19a + 5b + c$		$6a$
3	$27a + 9b + 3c + d$		$18a + 2b$	
		$37a + 7b + c$		$6a$
4	$64a + 16b + 4c + d$		$24a + 2b$	
		$61a + 9b + c$		
5	$125a + 25b + 5c + d$			

53. a.

x	y	1st diff	2nd diff
−2	8		
		−6	
−1	2		4
		−2	
0	0		4
		2	
1	2		4
		6	
2	8		

b.

x	y	1st diff	2nd diff
−2	20		
		−15	
−1	5		10
		−5	
0	0		10
		5	
1	5		10
		15	
2	20		

c.

x	y	1st diff	2nd diff
−2	18		
		−15	
−1	3		10
		−5	
0	−2		10
		5	
1	3		10
		15	
2	18		

d.

x	y	1st diff	2nd diff
−2	28		
		−21	
−1	7		14
		−7	
0	0		14
		7	
1	7		14
		21	
2	28		

e.

x	y	1st diff	2nd diff
−2	29		
		−21	
−1	8		14
		−7	
0	1		14
		7	
1	8		14
		21	
2	29		

f.

x	y	1st diff	2nd diff
−2	23		
		−18	
−1	5		14
		−4	
0	1		14
		10	
1	11		14
		24	
2	35		

Second differences of quadratic functions are constant.
55. missing values: y: 0, −6, −4; first differences: −6, 2
57. −35; Let $y = 2x^3 + bx^2 + cx + 7$. Evaluate
$f(1) = 7$ and $f(2) = 9$ to find a system of equations
for b and c. $b = −5$ and $c = 3$, so $f(−2) = −35$.

Lesson 5-2   pp. 288–295

Got It? 1. $x(x − 4)(x + 3)$
2. 0, 3, −5;

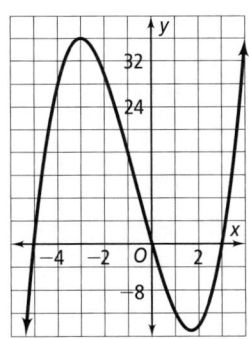

3. a. $f(x) = x^2 − 9$ **b.** $P(x) = x^3 − 3x^2 − 9x + 27$

c.

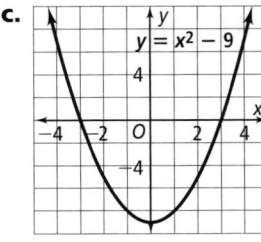 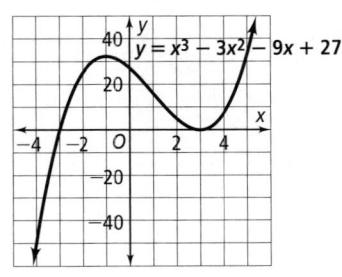

Both graphs have x-intercepts of 3 and −3. The quadratic
has up and up end behavior and one turning pt., and the
cubic has down and up end behavior and two turning pts.

4. 0 is a zero of multiplicity 1, the graph looks close to
linear at $x = 0$; 2 is a zero of multiplicity 2, the graph
looks close to quadratic at $x = 2$. **5.** relative maximum:
$(−0.86, 3.13)$; relative minimum: $(0.64, −2)$ **6.** 2.28 in.³
Lesson Check 1. 0, 6 **2.** −4, 5 **3.** −12, 7, 9
4. $f(x) = x^3 − x$ **5.** $h(x) = x^4 + 4x^3 − 26x^2 − 60x + 225$
6. Error in writing the factors: a function that has zeros at 3
and −1 has factors of $x − 3$ and $x + 1$ *not* $x + 3$ and
$x − 1$, so $f(x) = x^2 − 2x − 3$ *not* $x^2 + 2x − 3$.
Exercises 7. $x(x + 5)(x + 2)$ **9.** $x(x − 7)(x + 3)$
11. $x(x + 4)^2$
13. 1, −2;   **15.** 0, −5, 8;

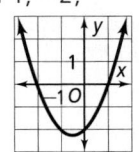   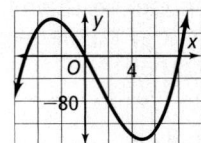

17. −1, 1, 2;

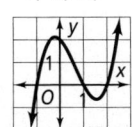

19. $y = x^3 − 18x^2 + 107x − 210$ **21.** $y = x^3 +$
$9x^2 + 15x − 25$ **23.** $y = x^3 + 2x^2 − x − 2$
25. $y = x^4 − 5x^3 + 6x^2$ **27.** −3 (multiplicity 3)
29. −1, 0, $\frac{1}{2}$ **31.** 4 (multiplicity 2) **33.** $−\frac{3}{2}$, 1
(multiplicity 2) **35.** relative maximum: $(−3.19, 24.19)$;
relative minimum: $(0.52, −1.38)$ **37.** relative maximum:
$(2.15, 12.32)$; relative minimum: $(−0.15, −12.32)$
39. a. $\ell = 16 − 2x$; $w = 12 − 2x$; $h = x$
b. $V = x(16 − 2x)(12 − 2x)$
c.   194 in.³, 2.26 in.

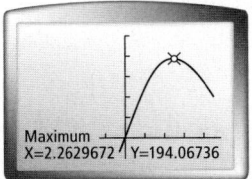

41. $y = −2x(x + 5)(x − 4)$ **43.** 1 ft increase in each
dimension **45.** $V = 12x^3 − 27x$ **47.** relative maximum:
$(2.53, 10.51)$; relative minimum: $(5.14, −7.14)$; $\frac{3}{2}$, 4, 6
49. no relative maximum; relative minimum: $(−1, −1)$;
−2, 0 **51.** Answers may vary. Sample: The linear
factors can be determined by examining the x-intercepts
of the graph. **53.** −1, 4, $\frac{3}{2}$ **55.** $y = x^4 − 1$

Lesson 5-3   pp. 296–302

Got It? 1. a. ± 1, $\pm 2i$ **b.** 0, 2, 3 **2. a.** ± 2, $\pm 2i$
b. 0, -4, 2 **c.** 2, $-1 \pm i\sqrt{3}$ **3. a.** -1.84
b. The second method seems to be a more reliable way to find the solutions because you do not risk missing a pt. of intersection. **4.** 7, 8, 9
Lesson Check 1. $(x - 6)(x + 3)$
2. $(x - 3)(x^2 + 3x + 9)$ **3.** $(x^2 + 4)(x + 3)$
4. $(x - 2)(x + 2)(x^2 + 2)$ **5.** $-4, \frac{1}{2}$ **6.** $-2, 0, 1$
7. a. difference of squares **b.** sum of cubes **c.** difference of cubes **d.** difference of squares **8.** Graphing; imaginary numbers don't exist on the x-axis. **9.** Method 1: Graph $y = x^6 - x^2$. Find the zeros for the real solutions.

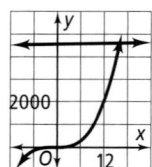

Method 2: Factor and solve x for $x^6 - x^2 = 0$.
$x^2(x^4 - 1) = x^2(x^2 - 1)(x^2 + 1) =$
$x^2(x - 1)(x + 1)(x^2 + 1) = 0$
$x = 0, \pm 1$

Exercises 11. 10, $-5 \pm 5i\sqrt{3}$ **13.** $\frac{1}{4}, \frac{-1 \pm i\sqrt{3}}{8}$

15. $\frac{1}{3}, -\frac{5}{2}$ **17.** 4, $-2 \pm 2i\sqrt{3}$ **19.** $-\frac{1}{2}, \frac{1 \pm i\sqrt{3}}{4}$
21. ± 2 **23.** $\pm\sqrt{2}, \pm 3i$ **25.** $-2, 1, 5$ **27.** 0, 1
29. 0, -1, -2 **31.** 0, -0.5, 1.5 **33.** 1, 7 **35.** -2, 5
37. 16 yrs old; $x^2(x + 2) = 3x + 4560$;

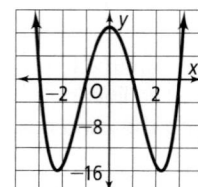

39. 0, $5 \pm 2\sqrt{3}$ **41.** 0, $\frac{5 \pm 5\sqrt{2}}{2}$ **43.** $\frac{4}{3}, \frac{-2 \pm 2i\sqrt{3}}{3}$
45. $1.9(1 \pm i)$, $-1.9(1 \pm i)$ **47.** 0, ± 1, ± 2 **49.** -1, $\pm i$
51. 2 ft × 3 ft × 6 ft **53.** 5 m
55. ± 3, ± 1; $y = (x - 1)(x + 1)(x - 3)(x + 3)$;

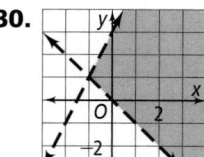

57. Answers may vary.
59. Answers may vary. Sample:
$$f(x) = 4x(x + 12)\left(x - \frac{1}{4}\right)\left(x - \frac{1}{6}\right)$$
$$p(x) = x(x + 12)(4x - 1)(6x - 1)$$

61. C **63.** B **65.** $3(x - 4)(x - 2)$ **66.** $2x(x + 3)^2(x - 3)$
67. $x^2(x - 5)(x + 1)$ **68.** -2, 6 **69.** ± 6
70. $-\frac{1}{2}$, 3 **71.** 12 **72.** $-\frac{1}{5}$

Lesson 5-4   pp. 303–310

Got It? 1. $3x - 8$, R 0 **2. a.** yes; $P(x) = (x + 5)(x^4 - 1)$
b. $(x + 2)(3x + 1)$ **3.** $x^2 + 7x - 8$, R 0 **4.** width: $(x + 1)$ in.; height: $(x + 2)$ in.; length: $(x + 3)$ in. **5.** 0
Lesson Check 1. $2x + 3$, R 5 **2.** $x^2 + 2x + 5$
3. $x^2 + x - 2$ **4.** $4x^2 + x - 6$, R 6
5. $9x^2 + 12x + 40$, R 120 **6.** $x - a$ is a factor of $P(x)$.
7. The polynomials need to be written in standard form since the leading coefficient of both polynomials determines the leading term of the quotient.
8. Answers may vary. Check student's work.
Exercises 9. $x - 8$ **11.** $x^2 + 4x + 3$, R 5
13. $3x^2 + 3x + 2$ **15.** $x - 10$, R 40 **17.** no
19. yes **21.** $x^2 + 4x + 3$ **23.** $x^2 - 11x + 37$, R -128
25. $x + 1$, R 4 **27.** $x^2 - 3x + 9$
29. $y = (x + 1)(x + 3)(x - 2)$
31. width $= x$; length $= x + 3$; height $= x - 2$
33. 0 **35.** 12 **37.** 10 **39.** 0 **41.** The constant term of the dividend is missing and the divisor is -1 *not* 1:
$x^3 - x^2 - 2x = (x + 1)(x^2 - 2x) = x(x + 1)(x - 2)$
43. $x + 2$ **45.** $x^3 - 3x^2 + 12x - 35$, R 109
47. $x + 4$ **49.** no **51.** yes **53.** yes **55.** no
57. $x^3 - x^2 + 1$ **59.** $x^3 + 7x + 5$
61. $x^3 - 2x^2 - x + 6$ **63. a.** $x + 1$ **b.** $x^2 + x + 1$
c. $x^3 + x^2 + x + 1$ **d.** $(x - 1)(x^4 + x^3 + x^2 + x + 1)$
65. $x + 2i$ **67.** D **69.** A **71.** 0, -1 **72.** 0, 1
73. -5, 0, 5 **74.** $\frac{-3 \pm \sqrt{17}}{2}$ **75.** $-1 \pm \sqrt{3}$
76. 1, $-\frac{5}{7}$ **77.** $\frac{5 \pm \sqrt{5}}{2}$ **78.** $3 \pm \sqrt{2}$ **79.** $\frac{-7 \pm \sqrt{5}}{2}$
80.

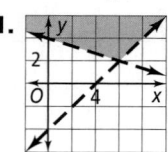

81.

82.

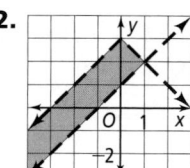

83. 24 **84.** 5 **85.** $23 - 11i$

Lesson 5-5   pp. 312–317

Got It? 1. $\frac{2}{3}$ **2.** 2, −1, $−\frac{3}{2}$ **3.** 3 + 2i

4. $P(x) = x^4 − 14x^3 + 69x^2 − 194x + 208$ **5. a.** There are three or one positive real roots and one negative real root. The graph confirms one negative and one positive real root. **b.** Real roots can be confirmed graphically because they are x-intercepts. Complex roots cannot be confirmed graphically because they have an imaginary component.

Lesson Check 1. ±1, ±2 **2.** ±1, ±2, ±3, ±6, $±\frac{1}{2}$, $±\frac{3}{2}$ **3.** ±1, ±2, ±3, ±4, ±6, ±12, $±\frac{1}{3}$, $±\frac{2}{3}$, $±\frac{4}{3}$

4. $P(x) = x^2 − 14x + 45$ **5.** $P(x) = x^3 + 4x^2 + 4x + 16$
6. Answers may vary. Samples: 1 + 2i, 1 − 2i; $1 + \sqrt{2}$, $1 − \sqrt{2}$ **7. a.** never; 5 does not divide 8 evenly **b.** always; −2 divides 8 evenly **8.** Complex number roots come in pairs; if −4i is a root, so is 4i.

Exercises 9. ±1; no rational roots **11.** ±1, ±2, ±2, ±4, $±\frac{1}{2}$; no rational roots **13.** ±1, ±2, ±3, ±4, ±6, ±12, $±\frac{1}{4}$, $±\frac{1}{2}$, $±\frac{3}{4}$, $±\frac{3}{2}$; no rational roots **15.** ±1, ±2, ±5, ±10, $±\frac{1}{7}$, $±\frac{2}{7}$, $±\frac{5}{7}$, $±\frac{10}{7}$; no rational roots **17.** ±1, ±2, ±5, ±10, $±\frac{1}{2}$, $±\frac{5}{2}$, $±\frac{1}{5}$, $±\frac{2}{5}$, $±\frac{1}{10}$; no rational roots
19. $14 + \sqrt{2}$, 6i **21.** $\sqrt{3}$, $5 + \sqrt{11}$
23. $P(x) = x^2 + 24x + 135$ **25.** $P(x) = x^2 − 18x + 90$
27. $P(x) = x^4 − 10x^3 + 294x^2 − 1690x + 21{,}125$
29. $P(x) = x^4 − 58x^3 + 1290x^2 − 13{,}066x + 51{,}545$
31. two or no positive real roots; one negative real root
33. no rational roots **35.** no rational roots **37.** no rational roots **39.** $P(x) = x^4 + 3x^3 + 207x^2 + 675x − 4050$
41. $P(x) = x^4 + 6x^3 + 27x^2 − 366x − 518$ **43.** Error in second line, sign of second term; the line should be: $P(−1) = −x^3 + x^2 − x + 1$. Since there are three sign changes in $P(−x)$, there are three or one negative real roots.
45. height: 5 ft; bases: 10 ft, 14 ft
47. Answers may vary. Samples: **a.** $x − 1 − \sqrt{2} = 0$
b. $x^2 − 2(1 + \sqrt{2})x + (1 + \sqrt{2})^2 = 0$ **c.** −1
49. Answers may vary. Sample: You cannot use the Conjugate Root Theorem for irrational roots unless the equation has rational coefficients.

Lesson 5-6   pp. 319–324

Got It? 1. 0, 1, −5, 2 **2. a.** −1, 2, $\frac{1 ± i\sqrt{23}}{4}$
b. i. A 5th degree polynomial function has four, two, or no turning pts. Three turning pts. are visible, so there must be a fourth one. This will turn the graph back across the x-axis. **ii.** The Fundamental Thm. of Algebra states

---

there will be five roots, and the Conjugate Root Thm. requires pairs of irrational or complex roots. Only two zeros appear in the graph, so there are three zeros remaining. Of the remaining roots, either there are three real roots, or one real and two complex roots. Either way, there is at least one real root that does not appear in the graph.
Lesson Check 1. four roots **2.** fourteen roots
3. 5, ±4i **4.** 0, 2, ±i **5.** By the Fundamental Thm. of Algebra, polynomial equation of degree n has exactly n roots. **6.** Answers may vary. Sample: $y = x^4 + 8x^2 + 16$ **7.** Use synthetic division to test for and factor out linear factors until a quadratic factor is obtained. Then use the Quadratic Formula if the quadratic factor cannot be factored further.
Exercises 9. −1, ±2i **11.** −1, 2, 4 **13.** 2, $±\sqrt{3}$
15. 0, ±3, ±i **17.** 3, ±i **19.** 2, $±\sqrt{3}$ **21.** ±2, ±i
23. −6, ±i **25.** ±4, $\frac{−1 ± i\sqrt{3}}{2}$ **27.** five complex roots; one, three, or five real roots; possible rational roots: ±1, ±2, ±3, ±6, ±9, ±18 **29.** six complex roots; zero, two, four, or six real roots; possible rational roots: $±\frac{1}{4}$, $±\frac{1}{2}$, $±\frac{3}{4}$, ±1, $±\frac{3}{2}$, ±2, ±3, ±4, ±6, ±8, ±12, ±24 **31.** −2, $±\sqrt{5}$ **33.** −2, $\frac{4}{3}$, 3
35. 3, $−1 ± i\sqrt{2}$ **37.** $−\frac{1}{2}$, −1, ±3 **39.** 3 bridges
41. sometimes **43.** always **45.** Answers may vary. Sample: $y = x^4 + 3x^2 + 2$
47. Given any polynomial eq. of odd degree $n ≥ 1$, the eq. has exactly n roots. Since imaginary roots occur in pairs, a polynomial of odd degree n will have an even number of imaginary roots and thus an odd number of real roots. So, any odd degree polynomial eq. with real coefficients has at least one real root.
49. 5th degree; rational zero:

$$−\frac{5}{6}(x − \sqrt{2})(x + \sqrt{2})(x − \sqrt{3})(x + \sqrt{3})(x + \frac{5}{6})$$

$$= x^5 + \frac{5}{6}x^4 − 5x^3 − \frac{25}{6}x^2 + 6x + 5.$$

51. G **53.** Substitute (2, −2) into both inequalities to see if the pt. satisfies both inequalities. If it does, then (2, −2) is a solution of the system. If one or both inequalities are not satisfied by the pt.(2, −2), then (2, −2) is not a solution of the system.
54. $x^4 + 6x^3 + 14x^2 + 24x + 40 = 0$
55. $3 ± 2\sqrt{2}$ **56.** $\frac{−5 ± i\sqrt{47}}{4}$
57. $\frac{3 ± i\sqrt{23}}{4}$ **58.** $f(x) = −x^2 + 2x + 3$
59. $f(x) = 2x^2 + 24x + 75$ **60.** $x^3 + 3x^2 + 3x + 1$
61. $x^3 − 9x^2 + 27x − 27$ **62.** $x^4 − 8x^3 + 24x^2 − 32x + 16$ **63.** $x^2 − 2x + 1$ **64.** $x^3 + 15x^2 + 75x + 125$
65. $−x^3 + 12x^2 + 48x + 64$

Lesson 5-7 pp. 326–330

Got It? 1. $a^8 + 8a^7b + 28a^6b^2 + 56a^5b^3 + 70a^4b^4 + 56a^3b^5 + 28a^2b^6 + 8ab^7 + b^8$ **2. a.** $16x^4 - 96x^3 + 216x^2 - 216x + 81$ **b.** If you express 11 as $(10 + 1)$ and calculate the powers using Pascal's triangle, it will be the coefficients.

Lesson Check 1. $x^3 + 3x^2a + 3xa^2 + a^3$
2. $x^5 - 10x^4 + 40x^3 - 80x^2 + 80x - 32$
3. $4x^2 + 16x + 16$ **4.** $27a^3 - 54a^2 + 36a - 8$
5. a. yes **b.** yes **c.** no **6.** The coefficients for the expansion of $(a + b)^n$ are equal to the numbers in the nth row of Pascal's Triangle, respectively. **7.** 13; $n + 1$

Exercises 9. $a^4 + 8a^3 + 24a^2 + 32a + 16$
11. $x^3 - 15x^2 + 75x - 125$ **13.** $x^{10} + 20x^9 + 180x^8 + 960x^7 + 3360x^6 + 8064x^5 + 13{,}440x^4 + 15{,}360x^3 + 11{,}520x^2 + 5120x + 1024$ **15.** $b^9 + 27b^8 + 324b^7 + 2268b^6 + 10{,}206b^5 + 30{,}618b^4 + 61{,}236b^3 + 78{,}732b^2 + 59{,}049b + 19{,}683$
17. $a^4 + 12a^3b + 54a^2b^2 + 108ab^3 + 81b^4$
19. $65{,}536 - 131{,}072x + 114{,}688x^2 - 57{,}344x^3 + 17{,}920x^4 - 3584x^5 + 448x^6 - 32x^7 + x^8$
21. $27a^3 - 189a^2 + 441a - 343$
23. $81y^4 - 1188y^3 + 6534y^2 - 15{,}972y + 14{,}641$
25. a. 6 **b.** 489,888 **27.** $135x^4$ **29.** $625b^8$ **31.** The challenge of the Binomial Theorem occurs when there is a coefficient with the x. However, it is much more efficient to use the Binomial Theorem than FOIL when expanding a binomial that is raised to a high power. **33.** $x^{20} + 40x^{18} + 720x^{16} + 7680x^{14} + 53{,}760x^{12} + 258{,}048x^{10} + 860{,}160x^8 + 1{,}966{,}080x^6 + 2{,}949{,}120x^4 + 2{,}621{,}440x^2 + 1{,}048{,}576$ **35.** $a^5 - 5a^4b^2 + 10a^3b^4 - 10a^2b^6 + 5ab^8 - b^{10}$ **37.** $256x^4 - 1792x^3y + 4704x^2y^2 - 5488xy^3 + 2401y^4$
39. $4096x^{18} + 12{,}288x^{15}y^2 + 15{,}360x^{12}y^4 + 10{,}240x^9y^6 + 3840x^6y^8 + 768x^3y^{10} + 64y^{12}$
41. $125a^3 + 150a^2b + 60ab^2 + 8b^3$ **43.** $-32y^{10} + 80y^8x - 80y^6x^2 + 40y^4x^3 - 10y^2x^4 + x^5$ **45.** Answers may vary. Sample: Since one of the terms is negative $(-y)$ and it is alternately raised to odd and even powers; the term is negative when raised to an odd power and positive when raised to an even power.
47. $-29{,}113 + 17{,}684i$
49. $\left(x^{14} - 21x^{10} + 35x^6 - 7x^2\right) + i\left(-7x^{12} + 35x^8 - 21x^4 + 1\right)$ **51.** $\frac{1}{64}$
53. $(-1 + i\sqrt{3})^3 = -1 + 3i\sqrt{3} + 9 - 3i\sqrt{3} = 8$
55. G **57.** Let c_a = the first company's cost per month and let c_b = the second company's cost per month: $c_a = 2.25t + 7.95$ and $c_b = 2.75t$

$$c_a = c_b$$
$$2.25t + 7.95 = 2.75t$$
$$7.95 = 0.5t$$
$$15.9 = t$$

The cost will be equal after 15.9 hours of use.

58. $-3, -1, \dfrac{-3 \pm i\sqrt{11}}{2}$ **59.** $1, \pm i, \pm 3i$
60. $-4, \dfrac{-3 \pm i\sqrt{7}}{4}$ **61.** $-1, 1, 2, 7$ **62.** $-18 + 43i$
63. $600i$ **64.** -2 **65.** $\frac{7}{5} + \frac{31}{5}i$ **66.** $2x^3 + 5x^2 - x + 9$; cubic polynomial of 4 terms **67.** $-7x^2 + 4x + 1$; quadratic trinomial **68.** $12x^4 - 3x^3 - 9x^2 + x - 8$; quartic polynomial of 5 terms

Lesson 5-8 pp. 331–338

Got It? 1. $y = 1.667x^3 + 1.3 \times 10^{-12}x^2 - 4.667x + 5$ **2.** 22.52 billion lbs **3.** Answers may vary. Sample: The cubic model would fit the data better than the linear model because of the $(n + 1)$ Pt. Principle. Both models have down and up end behavior and increasing growth. The cubic shows slowing growth followed by rapidly increasing growth.
4. a. $y = 0.269867411x - 3.919692952$

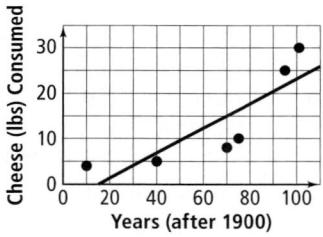

b. 1980: 17.7 lbs; 2000: 23.07 lbs; 2012: 26.31 lbs; most confident for the yrs 1980 and 2000, since they are within the domain of the data set; least confident for the yr 2012, since it is outside the domain of the data set
Lesson Check 1. linear **2.** quadratic **3.** cubic
4. quartic **5.** interpolation since the data point is within the domain of the data set **6.** yes, since the four pts. pass the vertical-line test, a cubic function will fit the pts.; $y = -x^3 - 3x^2 - 3x$ **7.** cubic model; the closer R^2 is to 1, the better the fit
Exercises 9. $y = \frac{1}{2}x - 3$ **11.** $y = -0.929x^2 + 7.786x + 4$ **13.** $y = x^2 - 6x + 1$ **15.** $y = 2x^3 + x^2 - 4x + 6$ **17.** (where x = yrs after 1900) quadratic: $y = -1.25 \times 10^{-4}x^2 - 0.003x + 2.804$, cubic: $y = -8.33 \times 10^{-6}x^3 + 0.002x^2 - 0.190x + 8.142$; cubic; cubic **19.** linear: $y = -0.057x + 19.93$, quadratic: $y = -0.025x^2 + 0.14x + 19.595$; quadratic; quadratic
21. 1950: 2.60%; 1988: 1.23%; 2010: 0.35%

23. January: 19.714 millions of barrels/day; March: 19.8 millions of barrels/day; October: 18.535 millions of barrels/day **25.** cubic: $y = 10.25x^3 + 5x^2 - 2.25x - 8.2$; quartic: $y = 2.042x^4 + 10.25x^3 - 4.042x^2 - 2.25x - 4$; quartic, $(R^2 = 1)$ **27.** $y = -0.275x^4 + 0.85x^3 - 4.025x^2 - 8.15x + 7$ **29.** $y = 0.0611511911x^3 - 0.9276466231x^2 + 6.184642324x + 1.750778723$; $R^2 = 0.9994739763$; good fit **31.** $y = 0.111x^4 - 45.618x^3 + 6997.73x^2 - 476,931.355x + 12,185,696.59$ **33.** A quadratic model would be more appropriate, given the real world context. According to the cubic model, there would be a negative number of students enrolled in the course in the year 2024.
35. a. −0.48; −0.75

b.

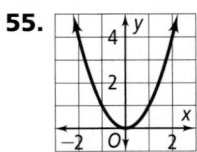

A linear model seems to be most appropriate.

c. Answers may vary. Sample: $y = -0.4464x + 57.77$
d. 4.2% **e.** No; although R^2 is close to 1, the model is not realistic since it predicts that the percentage will eventually become 0, and then negative.

37. $y = \frac{1}{8}(x^2 - 4)^2$

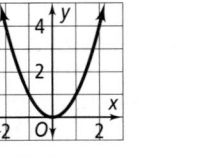

39. 1 **41.** $-\frac{7}{8}$
43. $32x^5 + 240x^4 + 720x^3 + 1080x^2 + 810x + 243$ **44.** $1331x^3 - 363x^2 + 33x - 1$
45. $4096 - 6144x + 3456x^2 - 864x^3 + 81x^4$
46. $64 + 432x + 972x^2 + 729x^3$
47. $|x - 8| < 1$ **48.** $\left|x - \frac{3}{8}\right| \le \frac{1}{8}$
49. $|y - 2.8| < 1.1$ **50.** $|t - 750| < 250$
51. $s = \sqrt{A}$ **52.** $\ell = \frac{P}{2} - w$ **53.** $r = \frac{C}{2\pi}$ **54.** $b = \frac{A}{h}$
55.

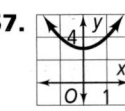

56.

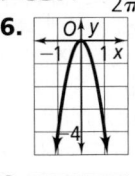

57.

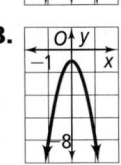

58.

Lesson 5-9   pp. 339–345

Got It? 1. $y = 2(x + 3)^3 - 4$ **2.** $1 - \sqrt[3]{2}$
3. a. Answers may vary. Sample: $y = x^4 - 6x^3 + x^2 - 6x$ **b.** Yes; $-f(x)$ is the function reflected across the x-axis, so the zeros will stay the same. **4.** 972 kW
Lesson Check 1. −2 **2.** 3 **3.** $\frac{1}{3}$ **4.** No; a power function is of the form $y = ax^b$, where y varies directly with the bth power of x. **5.** $y = x^3$ has end behavior of down and up with no turning pt. Thus, at most, there is one real root. **6.** Both $y = x^3$ and $y = 4x^3$ pass through the origin, have the same end behavior of down and up, and no turning pts. $y = 4x^3$ is $y = x^3$ stretched vertically by a factor of 4.
Exercises 7. $y = -3(x - 1)^3 + 2$
9. $y = -(x + 5)^3 - 1$ **11.** $y = -3\left(x + \frac{1}{2}\right)^3 + \frac{3}{4}$
13. $\frac{8}{3}$ **15.** $-\frac{2}{15}$ **17.** $1 - \frac{1}{2}\sqrt[3]{20}$ **For Exercises 19–24, answers may vary. Samples: 19.** $x^4 - x^3 - x^2 - x - 2$ **21.** $x^4 - 2x^3 - 2x^2 - 2x - 3$
23. $x^4 + 5x^3 + 5x^2 + 5x + 4$ **25.** $38.4 \approx 38$ slices
27. 90 lb·ft²/s² **29.** Yes; using parent function $y = x^2$, stretch vertically by a factor of 2, then translate 5 units up and 3 units to the right. **31.** Yes; using parent function $y = x^2$, translate 9 units down and 4 units to the right.
33. reflection across the x-axis, vert. stretch by a factor of 2, translation 1 unit up and 1 unit to the right
35. vert. stretch by a factor of 3, translation 2 units down and 1 unit to the right **37.** reflection across the x-axis, translation 2 units up and 4 units to the right
39. 40 lb·ft²/s² **41.** Some quartic polynomials have four x-intercepts and cannot be written in that form; $y = x^4 - 20x^2 + 64$; $y = x^4 - 5x^2 + 4$.
43. 150 watts **45.** B
47. $y = (x - 2)^2 - 1$
$= x^2 - 4x + 4 - 1$
$= x^2 - 4x + 3$
48. $y = -2x^3 + 3x^2 - x - 2$ **49.** $y = 3x^3 - 5x - 3$
50. $y = -\frac{4}{5}x + \frac{16}{5}$ **51.** $y = -3x + 5$ **52.** yes **53.** no
54. $x^2(x^8 + 1)$ **55.** $(x - y)(x + y)(x^2 + y^2)$
56. $13x^3y^6(13x^3y^6 - 1)$

Chapter Review   pp. 347–352

1. D **2.** B **3.** C **4.** A **5.** $y = -x^4 + 12$; quartic binomial; down and down **6.** $y = x^2 - x + 7$; quadratic trinomial; up and up **7.** $y = -x^4 + 2x^3 + 3x^2 - 6x + 12$; quartic polynomial of five terms; down and down
8. $y = x^3 + 2x^2 - 4x + 8$; cubic polynomial of four terms; down and up **9.** $y = x^4 - 3x^3 + 3x^2 + 10$; quartic polynomial of four terms; up and up **10.** 3

11. If n is even there are an odd number of turning points; if n is odd there are an even number of turning points.
12. $f(x) = x^3 - 4x^2 - 11x - 6$ **13.** $f(x) = x^3 - x^2 - 2x$ **14.** $f(x) = x^3 - 6x^2 + 11x - 6$
15. $f(x) = x^3 - 3x^2 - 6x + 8$ **16.** 0, -2 (multiplicity 3)
17. 2 (multiplicity 2), -2 (multiplicity 2) **18.** 0, $-\frac{1}{2}$, 1
19. 5, -2 (multiplicity 2) **20.** relative maximum: (0.8672, -1.9351); relative minimums: (0, -3), (2.8828, -12.1704); zeros: $x = -0.5992$, $x = 3.7115$
21. relative maximum: (-0.8441, 9.3023); relative minimum: (0.7108, -0.0964); zeros: $x = -1.6180$, $x = 0.6180$, $x = 0.8$ **22.** relative minimum: (1, -4); zeros: $x = -0.2491$, $x = 1.6633$
23. relative maximum: (-0.4142, -3.3432); relative minimum: (2.4142, -14.6569); zero: $x = 4$ **24.** 3, 8
25. $-\frac{1}{2}$ **26.** 0, $\frac{-1 \pm \sqrt{37}}{2}$ **27.** $\frac{2 \pm i\sqrt{2}}{2}$
28. no real roots; **29.** 2.3949;

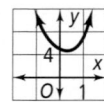   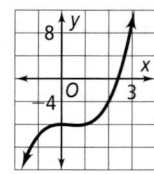

30. 4.87 in. $\times$ 2.87 in. $\times$ 2.87 in. **31.** $x^2 + 6x + 9$
32. $2x^2 + x - 3$, R 1 **33.** yes **34.** no **35.** $x^2 - 1$
36. $2x^2 - 6x + 2$, R -20 **37.** $5x^2 + 18x + 36$, R 12
38. -14 **39.** 2 **40.** $\pm 1, \pm 2, \pm 3, \pm 6$
41. $\pm 1, \pm 2, \pm\frac{1}{3}, \pm\frac{2}{3}$ **42.** $\pm 1, \pm 2, \pm 3, \pm 4, \pm 6, \pm 12,$ $\pm\frac{1}{4}, \pm\frac{1}{2}, \pm\frac{3}{4}, \pm\frac{3}{2}$ **43.** $\pm 1, \pm 7, \pm\frac{1}{3}, \pm\frac{7}{3}$ **44.** -3
45. -5 **46.** 1, -4, $-\frac{1}{2}$ **47.** 1, -2, $-\frac{2}{3}$ **48.** $1 + i$
49. $5 - \sqrt{3}$, $\sqrt{2}$ **50.** $3i$, $-7i$ **51.** $-2 - \sqrt{11}$, $-4 + 6i$
52. $y = x^2 - 17x + 70$ **53.** $y = x^3 + 3x^2 + 25x + 75$
54. $y = x^2 - 12x + 37$ **55.** $y = x^4 - 4x^3 - 10x^2 + 68x - 80$ **56.** one positive real zero; two or no negative real zeros **57.** two or no positive real zeros; one negative real zero **58.** four, two, or no positive real zeros; no negative real zeros **59.** two or no positive real zeros; two or no negative real zeros **60.** 3 **61.** 4 **62.** 5 **63.** 6
64. 1, $-3 \pm \sqrt{7}$ **65.** 2, $\pm\sqrt{5}$ **66.** 1, $\frac{1 \pm i\sqrt{15}}{4}$
67. -3, 6, $\frac{1 \pm \sqrt{5}}{2}$ **68.** 9 **69.** 1, 8, 28, 56, 70, 56, 28, 8, 1
70. 16 **71.** 105 **72.** $x^3 + 27x^2 + 243x + 729$
73. $b^4 + 8b^3 + 24b^2 + 32b + 16$
74. $27a^3 + 27a^2 + 9a + 1$ **75.** $x^3 - 15x^2 + 75x - 125$ **76.** $x^3 - 6x^2y + 12xy^2 - 8y^3$
77. $243a^5 + 1620a^4b + 4320a^3b^2 + 5760a^2b^3 + 3840ab^4 + 1024b^5$ **78.** $x^6 + 6x^5 + 15x^4 + 20x^3 + 15x^2 + 6x + 1$ **79.** $64x^6 - 192x^5 + 240x^4 - 160x^3 + 60x^2 - 12x + 1$ **80.** 108 **81.** $6a^2c^2$

82. $y = 3.5x^2 - 4.5x + 5$
83. $y = 2.082999x - 2.475234$; $y = 0.086232x^2 + 0.008929x + 5.963724$; $y = -0.002554x^3 + 0.178307x^2 - 0.913645x + 8.205128$; cubic is best fit since $R^2 = 1$.
84. $y = -5.8667x^3 + 120.5333x^2 - 629.2667x + 1421$; $1097.2 \approx 1097$ **85.** $y = -(x - 2)^3 + 1$
86. $y = 6(x + 3)^3$ **87.** Answers may vary. Sample: $y = x^4 - 10x^3 + 25x^2 - 10x + 24$ **88.** $y = 0.3x^5 + 3$

Chapter 6

Get Ready! p. 357 **1.** domain: $\{1, 2, 3, 4\}$, range: $\{2, 3, 4, 5\}$ **2.** domain: $\{1, 2, 3, 4\}$, range: $\{2\}$
3. domain: all real numbers, range: $y \geq -8$ **4.** domain: all real numbers, range: $y \geq 3$
5. 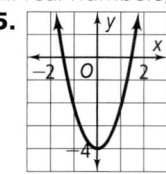   **6.**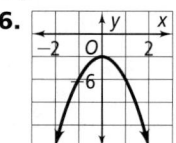

7.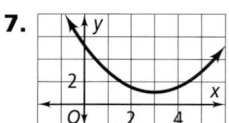

8. $3y^2 - 14y + 8$ **9.** $49a^2 - 100$
10. $x^3 + 4x^2 - 15x - 18$ **11.** -2, 7 **12.** $\frac{5}{2}$, 3
13. -4, $\frac{2}{3}$ **14.** $\frac{1}{2}$ **15.** $\pm\frac{7}{2}$ **16.** $\pm\sqrt{7}$ **17.** Yes; it is a better deal to first take 50% off the shirt and then use the $10 coupon. **18.** A "one-to-one function" is a function where there is exact correspondence of every element of the domain with exactly one element of the range.
19. the non-negative root

Lesson 6-1   pp. 361–367

Got It? **1. a.** 0; -1; 2 **b.** ± 0.1; no real square root; $\pm\frac{6}{11}$ **c.** Any negative number multiplied by itself an even number of times will always be positive. Therefore, there can be no real nth roots (where n is even) for a negative number b. **2. a.** -3 **b.** no real root **c.** 7 **d.** no real root
3. a. $9x^2$ **b.** a^4b^5 **c.** $|x^3|y^4$ **4.** 0; 100
Lesson Check **1.** ± 5 **2.** ± 0.4 **3.** no real root
4. $3|b|$ **5.** $a^4|b^9|$ **6.** $-5a$ **7.** 16 has two real fourth roots, ± 2. **8.** The real roots of a number are the positive and negative (but not imaginary) roots of the number; the principal root of a number is the nonnegative root of the number. **9.** n is odd.

Exercises **11.** ± 0.07 **13.** $\pm\frac{8}{13}$ **15.** 0.5 **17.** 0.07

19. none **21.** $\pm\frac{10}{3}$ **23.** 0.5 **25.** -3 **27.** $3y^2$ **29.** $2y^2$
31. ± 10 **33.** ± 0.5 **35.** about 0.8 in. **37. a.** about
79.01 ft **b.** about 44.44 ft **39.** $\frac{1}{3}$ **41.** $\frac{1}{4}$ **43.** Answers
may vary. Sample: $\sqrt[3]{-8x^6}$, $-\sqrt[4]{16x^8}$, $\sqrt[5]{-32x^{10}}$
45. always; x^2 is always nonnegative **47.** some; they are
equal for $x = -1, 0, 1$ **49.** even: $|m|$; odd: m
51. even: $|m^3|$; odd: m^3 **53.** 48
55. a diagonal of a square with side 5 **57.** G
59. System: $-35 = (-3)^3a + (-3)^2b + (-3)c + d$,
$1 = (0)^3a + (0)^2b + (0)c + d$, $3 = (2)^3a + (2)^2b +$
$(2)c + d$, $7 = (4)^3a + (4)^2b + (4)c + d$ (OR equivalent
system); solution: $a = 0.35, b = -1.85, c = 3.3, d = 1$,
cubic polynomial: $y = 0.35x^3 - 1.85x^2 + 3.3x + 1$.

60. $y = (x + 2)^3 + 3$ **61.** $y = \frac{1}{2}x^3 - 2$ **62.** $1, \frac{3}{4}$
63. $\frac{5 \pm i\sqrt{11}}{6}$ **64.** $\frac{11}{6}$ **65.** $2x^3y^3$ **66.** $\frac{ac}{3}$ **67.** $\frac{4}{x^2}$

Lesson 6-2   pp. 367–373

Got It? 1. a. No; the indexes are different. **b.** Yes; $\sqrt[5]{10}$
2. $4x^2\sqrt[3]{2x}$ **3.** $15x^3y^3\sqrt{7y}$ **4. a.** $5|x|$ **b.** yes;
$\frac{3x^2\sqrt{2x}}{x\sqrt{2x}} = 3x$ **5. a.** $\frac{\sqrt[3]{175xy}}{5y}$ **b.** D; there is no y in
the expression.

Lesson Check 1. $\sqrt{10}$ **2.** $-3\sqrt[3]{4}$ **3.** Not possible, the
indexes are different. **4.** not possible; $\sqrt{-4}$ is not a real
number. **5.** $\sqrt[3]{3x}$ **6.** $x^2\sqrt{3x}$ **7.** $2x\sqrt[3]{4x}$ **8.** $x \le 0$; for
$x \le 0$, $-4x^3 \ge 0$ and $\sqrt{-4x^3}$ is real. **9.** error in line 1:
$\frac{\sqrt[7]{x^5}}{\sqrt[4]{x^2}} \ne 7^{-4}\sqrt{\frac{x^5}{x^2}}$

Exercises 11. 4 **13.** not possible **15.** 5 **17.** 6
19. $2x\sqrt{5x}$ **21.** $5x^2\sqrt{2x}$ **23.** $3y^3\sqrt[3]{2y}$ **25.** $-5x^2y\sqrt[3]{2y^2}$
27. $-2xy\sqrt[5]{xy^2}$ **29.** $8y^3\sqrt{5y}$ **31.** $40x|y|\sqrt{3}$
33. $-2x^2y\sqrt[3]{30x}$ **35.** $4xy^2\sqrt[3]{y}$ **37.** 10 **39.** $2x^2y^2\sqrt{2}$
41. $\frac{2\sqrt[3]{x^2y}}{x}$ **43.** $\frac{\sqrt{2x}}{2}$ **45.** $\frac{\sqrt[3]{4x}}{2}$ **47.** $\frac{\sqrt[4]{250}}{5}$ **49.** $\frac{\sqrt{15y}}{5y}$
51. $\frac{\sqrt[3]{150ab^2c}}{5a}$ **53.** 6 cm^2 **55.** about 212 mi/h
57. $5\sqrt{10}$ **59.** $3x^6y^5\sqrt{2y}$ **61.** $10 + 7\sqrt{2}$ **63.** $\frac{|x|\sqrt{10y}}{2y^2}$
65. $\frac{\sqrt[3]{3x^2}}{3x}$ **67.** $\frac{\sqrt[3]{2xy^2}}{xy}$ **69.** 4 g/cm^3 **71.** Check students'
work. **73.** always **75.** sometimes **77.** $2\sqrt{5}$
79. $a = -2c, b = -6d$ **81.** H **83.** F **85.** $11|a^{45}|$
86. $9c^{24}d^{32}$ **87.** $4a^{27}$ **88.** $2y^5$ **89.** $y^2 - 4y + 16$,
R -128 **90.** $6a^2 - 5a + 4$ **91.** 25 **92.** 25 **93.** $\frac{121}{4}$
94. $\frac{121}{4}$ **95.** $\frac{3}{5} + \frac{1}{5}i$ **96.** $\frac{10}{13} - \frac{15}{13}i$ **97.** $\frac{16}{17} - \frac{4}{17}i$
98. $-\frac{7}{74} - \frac{5}{74}i$

Lesson 6-3   pp. 374–380

Got It? 1. a. The indexes are different. You cannot
combine the expressions. **b.** $7x\sqrt{xy}$ **c.** $2\sqrt[5]{3x^2}$
2. a. about 84.9 in. **b.** The length of the diagonal of a
square of side 6 can be found using the Pythagorean
Thm. to be $\sqrt{6^2 + 6^2} = \sqrt{72}$. Using this information
you can calculate the perimeter of the window and
simplify the expression at the end. **3.** $6\sqrt[3]{2}$
4. $46 + 16\sqrt{5}$ **5. a.** 24 **b.** 1 **6. a.** $-\sqrt{21} - \sqrt{35}$
b. $\frac{1}{3}(12x + 4x\sqrt{6})$ **c.** after rationalizing; When the
numerator is multiplied by the conjugate of the
denominator it is more convenient if $\sqrt{8}$ is not yet
simplified.
Lesson Check 1. $12\sqrt{6}$ **2.** cannot combine **3.** $3\sqrt{3x}$
4. $7\sqrt{3}$ **5.** 13 **6.** $75 + 34\sqrt{5}$ **7.** $-16 - 3\sqrt{2}$
8. a. not like radicals **b.** like radicals; $9\sqrt{3xy}$ **c.** not like
radicals **9.** They are alike in that you can also use the
FOIL method and Distr. Prop. to multiply binomial radical
expressions; they are different in that you cannot multiply
like radicands together if they do not have the same
index.
Exercises 11. $4\sqrt[3]{3}$ **13.** $-2\sqrt{x}$ **15.** $5\sqrt[3]{x^2}$
17. $33\sqrt{2}$ **19.** $7\sqrt{2}$ **21.** $9\sqrt[3]{3} - 6\sqrt[3]{2}$ **23.** $8 + 4\sqrt{5}$
25. $63 - 38\sqrt{2}$ **27.** $49 + 12\sqrt{13}$ **29.** 14 **31.** -40
33. $-2 + 2\sqrt{3}$ **35.** $13 + 7\sqrt{3}$ **37.** 140.3 in.^{2}
39. $8\sqrt{3}$ **41.** $5\sqrt{3} - 4\sqrt{2}$ **43.** $-2\sqrt[3]{2}$
45. $-11 + \sqrt{21}$ **47.** $84 + 24\sqrt{6}$ **49.** 2 **51.** $4x\sqrt{3}$
53. Answers may vary. Sample: Without simplifying first,
you must estimate three square roots and then add the
estimates. If they are first simplified, then they can be
combined as $13\sqrt{2}$. Then only one square root need be
estimated. **55.** Answers may vary. Sample:
$(\sqrt{7} + 2)(\sqrt{7} - 2), (2\sqrt{2} + \sqrt{5})(2\sqrt{2} - \sqrt{5})$
57. $2\sqrt{3} - \sqrt{2}$ **59.** $11|x| - 3|x|\sqrt{11}$
61. $\frac{3\sqrt{5} + 2\sqrt{3}}{3}$ **63.** $\frac{x + 5\sqrt[4]{x^3}}{x}$ **65.** $-\frac{1}{2}$
67. $a = 0$ and $b \ge 0$, or $b = 0$ and $a \ge 0$ **69.** 13
71. $\frac{15}{7}$ **73.** 9 **74.** $3\sqrt[3]{2}$ **75.** $\frac{2\sqrt[3]{x^2}}{x}$ **76.** 4 **77.** 6 **78.** $2x$
79. $7x^2\sqrt{2}$ **80.** $x\sqrt{15}$ **81.** $15x^2$ **82.** $2, -1 \pm i\sqrt{3}$
83. $-10, 5 \pm 5i\sqrt{3}$
84. $\frac{1}{5}, \frac{-1 \pm i\sqrt{3}}{10}$ **85.** $\sqrt{7}$ (multiplicity 2), $-\sqrt{7}$
(multiplicity 2) **86.** $\frac{2\sqrt{5}}{5}$ (multiplicity 2), $-\frac{2\sqrt{5}}{5}$
(multiplicity 2) **87.** $\pm\frac{1}{3}, \pm\frac{1}{3}i$ **88.** x^6 **89.** p^5q^5
90. 2^9 or 512 **91.** 3^3 or 27

Lesson 6-4   pp. 381–388

Got It? 1. a. 8 **b.** 11 **c.** 6 **2. a.** $\frac{\sqrt[8]{w^3}}{w}$, $\sqrt[5]{w}$ **b.** $x^{\frac{3}{4}}, y^{\frac{4}{5}}$
c. If m is negative, a is in the denominator and $\frac{1}{a}$ is
undefined when $a = 0$. **3. a.** The length of a Venusian

year is about 0.61 Earth years. **b.** The length of a Jovian year is about 12.76 Earth years. **4. a.** $\sqrt[4]{27}$ **b.** $\sqrt[6]{x^5}$ **c.** $\sqrt[6]{16,807}$ **5. a.** $\frac{1}{8}$ **b.** 8 **c.** $\frac{1}{2187}$ **6. a.** $\frac{1}{2x^5}$ **b.** $27x^8\sqrt{x^4y^3}$

Lesson Check 1. 5 **2.** 5 **3.** $\frac{1}{125}$ **4.** $\frac{1}{128}$ **5.** $\sqrt[4]{11^3}$ **6.** $\frac{\sqrt{x}}{x}$ **7.** $(1 + \sqrt{2})$ or any nonzero number times $(1 + \sqrt{2})$ **8.** error in third line, second term; $5\left(5^{\frac{1}{2}}\right) = 5^{\frac{3}{2}}$. The third and fourth lines should be: $\dfrac{20 - 5^{\frac{3}{2}}}{20 - 5\sqrt{5}}$

9. $(-64)^{\frac{1}{3}} = \sqrt[3]{-64} = -4$ and $-64^{\frac{1}{3}} = -\sqrt[3]{64} = -4$; $(-64)^{\frac{1}{2}} = \sqrt{-64}$, is not a real number, but $-64^{\frac{1}{2}} = -\sqrt{64} = -8$ is a real number.

Exercises 11. 3 **13.** 10 **15.** $7\sqrt{3}$ **17.** 3 **19.** $\sqrt[9]{x}$ **21.** $\sqrt[7]{x^2}$ or $(\sqrt[7]{x})^2$ **23.** $\frac{1}{\sqrt[8]{y^9}}$ or $\frac{1}{(\sqrt[8]{y})^9}$ **25.** $\sqrt{x^3}$ or $(\sqrt{x})^3$ **27.** $(-10)^{\frac{1}{2}}$ **29.** $(7x)^{\frac{3}{2}}$ **31.** $a^{\frac{2}{3}}$ **33.** $c^{\frac{1}{2}}$ **35.** ≈ 72.8 m **37.** ≈ 7.9 m **39.** $\sqrt[12]{6^7}$ **41.** $\sqrt[10]{5^7}$ **43.** $\frac{\sqrt[3]{4}}{2}$ **45.** $\frac{\sqrt[6]{7776}}{6}$ **47.** 4 **49.** 4 **51.** $\frac{1}{16}$ **53.** 64 **55.** $\frac{1}{x^2}$ **57.** $\frac{x^{\frac{1}{3}}}{3x}$ **59.** $-\frac{3}{x^3}$ **61.** $\frac{y^4}{x^3}$ **63.** $\frac{1}{x}$ **65.** x^3y^9 **67.** about 78%; 61%; 37% **69.** -7 **71.** 64 **73.** 2,097,152 **75.** $-\frac{1}{81}$ **77.** 125 **79.** $x^{\frac{1}{2}}$ **81.** $x^{\frac{3}{10}}$ **83.** $x^{\frac{1}{6}}y^{\frac{1}{4}}$ **85.** $\frac{4x^7}{9y^9}$ **87.** $\frac{2x^2}{3y^3}$

89. a. $(\sqrt{x})^4 = \sqrt{x} \cdot \sqrt{x} \cdot \sqrt{x} \cdot \sqrt{x} = x \cdot x = x^2$, so $\sqrt[4]{x^2} = \sqrt{x}$. **b.** $\sqrt[4]{x^2} = (x^2)^{\frac{1}{4}} = x^{\frac{2}{4}} = x^{\frac{1}{2}} = \sqrt{x}$ **91.** 49 **93.** $x^{2\pi}$ **95.** $3^{\sqrt{2}}$ **97.** 33.13 mi/h **99.** 12 **101.** 3

Lesson 6-5   pp. 390–397

Got It? 1. 6 **2.** 5, -11 **3.** 37,500,000 m³ **4. a.** 10 **b.** when you raise each side of an equation to a power **5.** 9

Lesson Check 1. 12 **2.** 27 **3.** $\frac{1}{25}$ **4.** 4 **5.** 1 **6.** 512 **7.** 3; The solution of 3 yields a negative value for $x - 6$, but the right side of the equation ($\sqrt{3(3)}$) cannot be negative. **8.** Solving square root equations is different from solving absolute value equations in that you use a different technique to isolate the variable. In square root equations, you square each side. In absolute value equations, you write two new equations and solve both. Solving square root equations is similar to solving absolute value equations in that both can introduce extraneous solutions.

Exercises 9. 16 **11.** 22 **13.** 5 **15.** 4 **17.** $\frac{2}{3}$ **19.** -29, 25 **21.** 78 **23.** 0 **25.** about 4 in. **27.** 1 **29.** 3 **31.** $-3, -4$ **33.** 1 **35.** 3 **37.** 1 **39.** -2 **41.** 1 **43.** 5 **45.** $10\sqrt[4]{3}$ or about 13.16 cm **47.** 5 **49.** 8

51. 5 **53.** 1 **55.** 9, -7 **57.** 9 **59.** $x = 4$ is a solution, but $x = 1$ is an extraneous solution. **61.** Answers may vary. Sample: $\sqrt{x - 3} = \sqrt{3x + 5}$ **63.** C **65.** 0, 2 **67.** 0 **69.** $\sqrt{6}$ **71.** $\sqrt{10}$ **73.** B **75.** D

Lesson 6-6   pp. 398–404

Got It? 1. $(f + g)(x) = 2x^2 + x + 5$, domain: all real numbers; $(f - g)(x) = 2x^2 - x + 11$, domain: all real numbers **2.** $(f \cdot g)(x) = 9x^3 - 30x^2 - 23x - 4$, domain: all real numbers; $\left(\frac{f}{g}\right)(x) = x - 4$, domain: all real numbers except $x = -\frac{1}{3}$ **3.** 4 **4.** Let $D(x) = $ cost after applying the 15% store discount, $E(x) = $ cost after applying the 20% employee discount, and $x = $ cost of items. Then $D(x) = 0.85x$ and $E(x) = 0.80x$.
a. $(E \circ D)(x) = 0.68x$ **b.** $(D \circ E)(x) = 0.68x$
c. The total discounts are the same.

Lesson Check 1. $3x^3 - 2x^2 + 3x - 2$ **2.** $-x^2 + 3x - 3$ **3.** $3x^2 + 1$ **4.** $x^2 + 3x - 1$ **5.** $x^2 - 3x + 3$ **6.** $-x^2 + 3x - 3$ **7.** Answers may vary. Sample: $f(x) = 3x^2 + 1, g(x) = 2x + 1; (f \circ g)(x) = 12x^2 + 12x + 4; (g \circ f)(x) = 6x^2 + 3$ **8.** Answers may vary. Sample: $f(x) = 2x, g(x) = 0.5x; f(g(x)) = x$

Exercises 9. $x^2 + 7x + 5$; domain: all real numbers **11.** $x^2 - 7x - 5$; domain: all real numbers **13.** $\frac{7x + 5}{x^2}$; domain: all real numbers except $x = 0$ **15.** $2 - x + \frac{1}{x}$; domain: all real numbers except $x = 0$ **17.** $\frac{1}{x} + x - 2$; domain: all real numbers except $x = 0$ **19.** $2x - x^2$; domain: all real numbers except $x = 0$ **21.** $2x^2 + 2x - 4$; domain: all real numbers **23.** $-2x^2 + 2$; domain: all real numbers **25.** $2x + 3$; domain: all real numbers except $x = 1$ **27.** 8 **29.** 20 **31.** 8 **33.** $4a$ **35.** $4a^2 + 4$ **37.** 25 **39.** 9 **41.** 0.25 **43.** $a^2 - 3$ **45. a.** $f(x) = 0.95x$ **b.** $g(x) = x - 200$ **c.** $1225 **d.** $1235 **47.** $x^2 - x + 7$; domain: all real numbers **49.** $x^2 - 5x - 3$; domain: all real numbers **51.** $-x^2 + 5x + 13$; domain: all real numbers **53.** $4x^2 - 14x + 3$; domain: all real numbers **55.** $2x^3 - x^2 - 11x + 10$; domain: all real numbers **57.** $\frac{2x + 5}{x^2 - 3x + 2}$; domain: all real numbers except $x = 1$ and 2 **59.** Substitute $5995x$ for y; $79,850 **61. a.** $g(x)$ is the bonus earned when x is the amount of sales over $5000. $h(x)$ is the excess sales over $5000. **b.** $(g \circ h)(x)$; you first need to find the excess sales over $5000 to calculate the bonus. **63.** 1 **65.** 0 **67.** 8 **69.** -2 **71. a.** ≈ 1963; The area after 2 seconds is about 1963 in.² **b.** ≈ 7854 in.² **73.** $x - 2; x - 2$ **75.** $x - 3; x - 6$ **77.** $\frac{x^2 + 5}{2}; \frac{x^2 + 10x + 25}{4}$

79. $x^7 - x^6 - 16x^5 + 10x^4 + 85x^3 - 25x^2 - 150x$; domain: all real numbers **81.** $\frac{x-3}{x^2+2x}$; domain: all real numbers except $x = 0, -2, \sqrt{5}$, and $-\sqrt{5}$ **83.** 2
85. $8a + 4h$ **87.** H **89.** Look at the 5th number in Row 7 of Pascal's triangle to find the coefficient of the x^3y^4 term in the expansion of $(x + y)^7$.
$35(3x)^3(-y)^4 = 945x^3y^4$, so 945 is the coefficient.
90. 1 **91.** -3 **92.** 4 **93.** 3 **94.** 2 **95.** 3

96. $x^8 + 32x^7 + 448x^6 + 3584x^5 +$
$17{,}920x^4 + 57{,}344x^3 + 114{,}688x^2 + 131{,}072x +$
$65{,}536$ **97.** $x^6 + 6x^5y + 15x^4y^2 + 20x^3y^3 + 15x^2y^4 +$
$6xy^5 + y^6$ **98.** $16x^4 - 32x^3y + 24x^2y^2 - 8xy^3 + y^4$
99. $128x^7 - 1344x^6y + 6048x^5y^2 - 15{,}120x^4y^3 +$
$22{,}680x^3y^4 - 20{,}412x^2y^5 + 10{,}206xy^6 - 2187y^7$
100. $59{,}049 - 65{,}610x + 29{,}160x^2 - 6480x^3 +$
$720x^4 - 32x^5$ **101.** $1024x^5 - 1280x^4y + 640x^3y^2 -$
$160x^2y^3 + 20xy^4 - y^5$ **102.** $x^8 + 4x^7 + 6x^6 +$
$4x^5 + x^4$ **103.** $x^{12} + 12x^{10}y^3 + 60x^8y^6 + 160x^6y^9 +$
$240x^4y^{12} + 192x^2y^{15} + 64y^{18}$

104. no solution

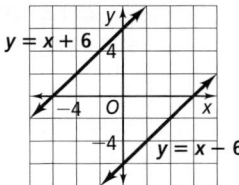

105. (2, 2)

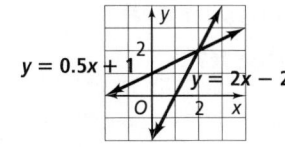

106. (1, 1)

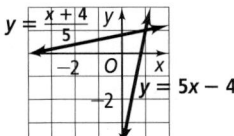

Lesson 6-7   pp. 405–412

Got It?

1. a.

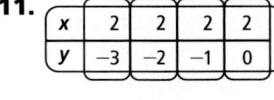

b. t is a function; the inverse of t is not a function; there are 2 y-values for one x-value **2.** $y = \frac{x}{2} - 4$

3.

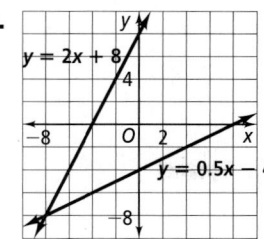

4. a. domain: all real numbers; range: all real numbers
b. $g^{-1}(x) = -\frac{1}{4}x + \frac{3}{2}$ **c.** domain: all real numbers; range: all real numbers **d.** Yes; for each x in the domain of g^{-1}, there is only one value of y in the range. **5.** $v = \sqrt{19.6d}$;
21.7 m/s **6. a.** $g^{-1}(x) = \frac{4 - 2x}{x}$ **b.** 0 is not in the domain of g^{-1} so $(g \circ g^{-1})(0)$ does not exist. **c.** 0
Lesson Check 1. $f^{-1}(x) = \frac{x-3}{4}$; yes
2. $f^{-1}(x) = \pm\sqrt{x+1}$; no **3.** $f^{-1}(x) = -1 \pm \sqrt{x}$; no
4. a. $h^{-1}(x) = -\frac{1}{x} - 2$ **b.** -2.25 **c.** 0 **5.** no; yes
6. 2, 5 **7.** Answers may vary. Samples: $f(x) = 2x + 1$ and
$g(x) = x - 2$; $f(x) = x^2$ and $g(x) = x + 1$
Exercises
9.

x	0	1	2	3
y	1	2	3	4

11.

x	2	2	2	2
y	-3	-2	-1	0

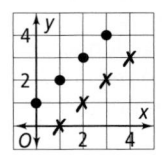

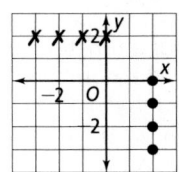

13. $y = \frac{1}{2}x + \frac{1}{2}$; yes **15.** $y = \pm\sqrt{\frac{5-x}{2}}$; no

17. $y = \pm\sqrt{\frac{x+5}{3}}$; no **19.** $y = \frac{4 \pm \sqrt{x}}{3}$; no

21.

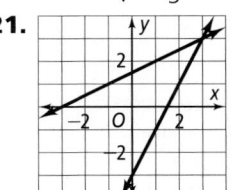

23.

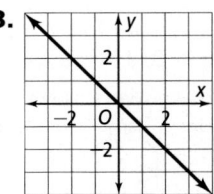

25.

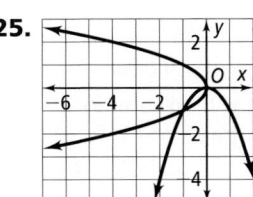

27.

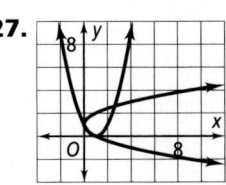

29.

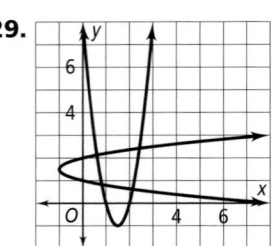

31. $f^{-1}(x) = x^2 + 5$, $x \geq 0$, domain of f: $x \geq 5$, range of f: $y \geq 0$, domain of f^{-1}: $x \geq 0$, range of f^{-1}: $y \geq 5$; f^{-1} is a function **33.** $f^{-1}(x) = \frac{3 - x^2}{2}$, $x \geq 0$, domain of f: $x \leq \frac{3}{2}$, range of f: $y \geq 0$, domain of f^{-1}: $x \geq 0$, range of f^{-1}: $y \leq \frac{3}{2}$; f^{-1} is a function **35.** $f^{-1}(x) = \pm \sqrt{1 - x}$, domain of f: all real numbers, range of f: $y \leq 1$, domain of f^{-1}: $x \leq 1$, range of f^{-1}: all real numbers; f^{-1} is not a function **37. a.** $r = \sqrt[3]{\frac{3V}{4\pi}}$; yes **b.** 20.29 ft **39.** -10

41. d **43.** $f^{-1}(x) = \pm\sqrt[4]{x}$; no **45.** $f^{-1}(x) = \pm \sqrt{\frac{2x + 8}{3}}$; no

47. $f^{-1}(x) = \frac{x^2 - 6x + 10}{2}$, $x \geq 3$; yes **49.** -1

51. $f^{-1}(x) = x^2$, $x \leq 0$, domain of f: $x \geq 0$, range of f: $y \leq 0$, domain of f^{-1}: $x \leq 0$, range of f^{-1}: $y \geq 0$; f^{-1} is a function **53.** $f^{-1}(x) = 3 - x^2$, $x \geq 0$, domain of f: $x \leq 3$, range of f: $y \geq 0$, domain of f^{-1}: $x \geq 0$, range of f^{-1}: $y \leq 3$; f^{-1} is a function **55.** $f^{-1}(x) = \pm \sqrt{2x}$, domain of f: all real numbers, range of f: $y \geq 0$, domain of f^{-1}: $x \geq 0$, range of f^{-1}: all real numbers; f^{-1} is not a function **57.** $f^{-1}(x) = \pm\sqrt{x} + 4$, domain of f: all real numbers, range of f: $y \geq 0$, domain of f^{-1}: $x \geq 0$, range of f^{-1}: all real numbers; f^{-1} is not a function

59. $f^{-1}(x) = \pm\frac{1}{\sqrt{x}} - 1$, domain of f: $x \neq -1$, range of f: $y > 0$, domain of f^{-1}: $x > 0$, range of f^{-1}: $y \neq -1$; f^{-1} is not a function **61.** $f^{-1}(x) = \left(\frac{3}{x}\right)^2$, $x \geq 0$, domain of f: $x > 0$, range of f: $y > 0$, domain of f^{-1}: $x > 0$, range of f^{-1}: $y > 0$; f^{-1} is a function

63. a–b. Answers may vary. Samples are given.

a.
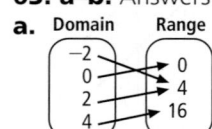

b.
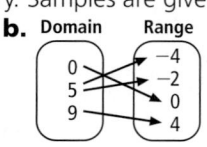

65. $h = s\sqrt{2}$; $s = \frac{h\sqrt{2}}{2} = 3\sqrt{2} \approx 4.2$ in. **67. a.** The horizontal line test tells you if there is more than one x-value for every y-value. Since the graph of f^{-1} interchanges the x and y values of f, if f passes the horizontal line test, f^{-1} will pass the vertical line test and it will be a function. **b.** no **69.** $f^{-1}(x) = x^3 + 5$; yes **71.** $f^{-1}(x) = 2 + \sqrt[3]{x}$; yes

73. $f^{-1}(x) = \pm\sqrt[4]{\frac{5x}{6}}$; no **75.** C **76.** F **77.** B

79. $2x + 7$ **80.** $-x - 10$ **81.** $-\frac{3}{2}x + 11$

82. $2x^2 + 28x$ **83.** 32 **84.** $2x + 28$ **85.** -2

86. no real root **87.** 3 **88.** -3 **89.** -3

90. 0.4 **91.** 30 **92.** 0.05

93.
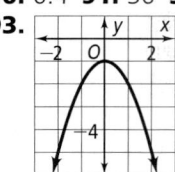

94.
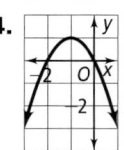

95.
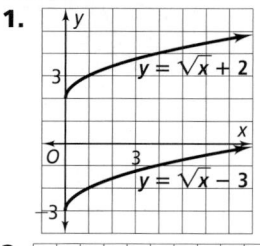

Lesson 6-8   pp. 414–420

Got It?

1.
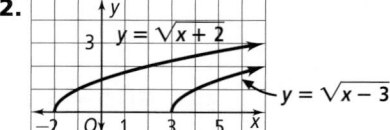

2.
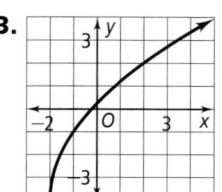

3.
    4. 1999   **5.**
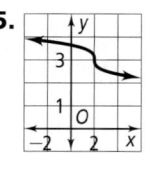

6. a. $y = \sqrt[3]{8x + 32} - 2$ is the graph of $y = 2\sqrt[3]{x}$ translated 4 units to the left and 2 units down.
b. $y = 9|x + 2|$; the graph of $y = 9|x + 2|$ is the graph of $y = 9|x|$ translated 2 units to the left; You are rewriting the function so that x has a coefficient of 1.

Lesson Check

1.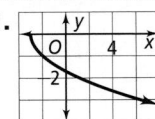

2.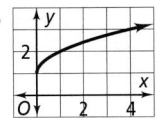

3. $y = 2\sqrt{x-1}$; the graph of $y = 2\sqrt{x}$ translated 1 unit to the right **4.** $y = 2\sqrt[3]{x+2}$; the graph of $y = 2\sqrt[3]{x}$ translated 2 units to the left **5.** When $|a| < 1$, a will vertically compress $y = a\sqrt{x}$ and when $|a| > 1$, a will vertically stretch $y = a\sqrt{x}$; this is similar to its effect on other functions. **6.** $g(x)$ is the reflection of $f(x)$ across the x-axis and again across $x = -1$.

Exercises

7.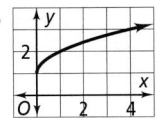

9.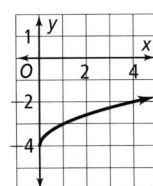

11.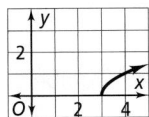

13.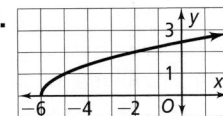

15.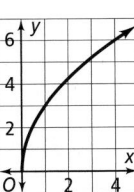

17.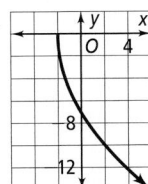

19. 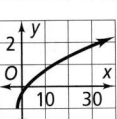   **21.** 147 **23.** −1

25.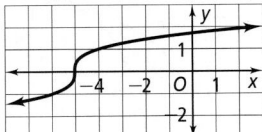

27.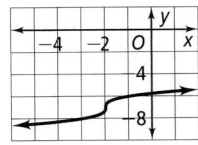

29.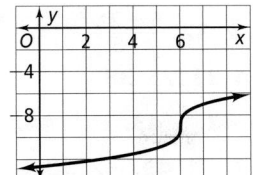

31. $y = 3\sqrt{x-1}$; the graph of $y = 3\sqrt{x}$ translated 1 unit to the right **33.** $y = -4\sqrt{x+4}$; the graph of $y = -4\sqrt{x}$ translated 4 units to the left
35. $y = 5\sqrt{x+5} - 3$; the graph of $y = 5\sqrt{x}$ translated 5 units to the left and 3 units down
37. ≈ 16.44 ft; ≈ 29.22 ft
39. 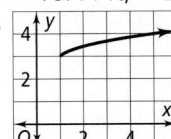   domain: $x \geq 1$, range: $y \geq 3$

41. a. $y = \sqrt{x-2} - 2$ **b.** domain: $x \geq 2$, range: $y \geq -2$ **c.** No; the function pairs the number 3 with the number −1, which is not a non-negative real number.
43. a. $y = 5\sqrt{x-4} - 1$; the graph of $y = 5\sqrt{x}$, translated 4 units to the right and 1 unit down
45. $y = -2\sqrt[3]{x - \frac{1}{4}}$; the graph of $y = -2\sqrt[3]{x}$, translated $\frac{1}{4}$ unit to the right **47.** $y = 10 - \frac{1}{3}\sqrt[3]{x+3}$; the graph of $y = -\frac{1}{3}\sqrt[3]{x}$, translated 3 units to the left and 10 units up
49. $\frac{1}{3}$ **51.** 0, 1, 9

53. a. 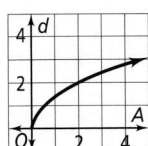   **b.** $15\sqrt{2}$ in. ≈ 21.2 in.

55. $y = -\sqrt{8}\sqrt{x - \frac{3}{4}}$; the graph of $y = -\sqrt{8x}$, translated $\frac{3}{4}$ unit to the right; domain: $x \geq \frac{3}{4}$, range: $y \leq 0$
57. $y = -\sqrt{12}\sqrt{x + \frac{3}{2}} - 3$; the graph of $y = -\sqrt{12x}$, translated $\frac{3}{2}$ units to the left and 3 units down; domain: $x \geq -\frac{3}{2}$, range: $y \leq -3$
59. for all odd positive integers

Chapter Review   pp. 422–426

1. radicand **2.** radical functions **3.** rational exponent
4. composite function **5.** 5 **6.** 0.7 **7.** −2 **8.** −2
9. $9|x|$ **10.** $4x^2$ **11.** $2|x^3|$ **12.** $0.2x$ **13.** $\frac{x^2}{2}$ **14.** $5x^2y^3$
15. 3 **16.** −7 **17.** 4 **18.** $4x^2$ **19.** $30y$ **20.** 4 **21.** $3xy$
22. $\frac{3|x|}{y^2}$ **23.** $\frac{2\sqrt{3}}{3}$ **24.** $\frac{\sqrt{3x}}{8}$ **25.** $\frac{y\sqrt[3]{150x}}{10x^2}$ **26.** $22\sqrt{3}$
27. $26\sqrt{5x}$ **28.** $x\sqrt[3]{2}$ **29.** $14 + 7\sqrt{2}$ **30.** −6

31. $100 + 10\sqrt{6} - 10\sqrt{3} - 3\sqrt{2}$ **32.** $\frac{5 + 2\sqrt{5}}{5}$
33. $\frac{9 + 3\sqrt{2}}{7}$ **34.** 5 **35.** 3 **36.** 4 **37.** 25 **38.** x
39. $-2y^3$ **40.** $81x^2y^4$ **41.** $\frac{1}{x^3y^6}$ **42.** $\frac{1}{x}$ **43.** x^3y^6 **44.** -1
45. 15 **46.** 5 **47.** 10, -8 **48.** 2, -1 **49.** -2 **50.** 0, 16
51. 0, 36 **52.** 9.05 W **53.** $x^2 + x - 20$; domain: all real
numbers **54.** $x^2 - x - 12$; domain: all real numbers
55. $x^3 - 4x^2 - 16x + 64$; domain: all real numbers
56. $x + 4$; domain: all real numbers except $x = 4$ **57.** 50
58. 5 **59.** 23 **60.** $5a^2 + 3$ **61.** $D(C(x)) = 0.5x - 0.5$,
$C(D(x)) = 0.5x - 1$; use the coupon after the store discount.
62. $f^{-1}(x) = \pm\sqrt{\frac{x + 8}{2}}$; no **63.** $f^{-1}(x) = 5 - \frac{1}{3}x$; yes
64. $f^{-1}(x) = x^2 - 6, x \geq 0$; yes **65.** $f^{-1}(x) = \frac{3 \pm \sqrt{x}}{2}$; no

66.

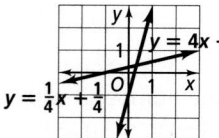

domain of f: all real
numbers, range of f: all
real numbers, domain of
f^{-1}: all real numbers, range
of f^{-1}: all real numbers

67. domain of f: all real numbers, range of
f: $y \geq 0$; domain of f^{-1}: $x \geq 0$, range of f^{-1}: all real
numbers

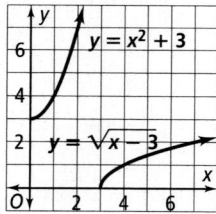

68. domain of f: $x \geq 3$, range of f: $y \geq 0$, domain of
f^{-1}: $x \geq 0$, range of f^{-1}: $y \geq 3$

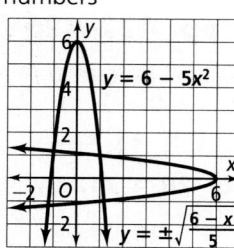

69. domain of f: all real numbers, range of
f: $y \leq 6$, domain of f^{-1}: $x \leq 6$, range of f^{-1}: all real
numbers

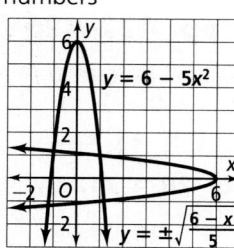

70. $s = \sqrt[3]{V}$; 4 ft

71. domain: $x \geq 0$, range: $y \geq -5$

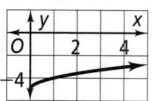

72. domain: $x \geq -8$, range: $y \geq 0$

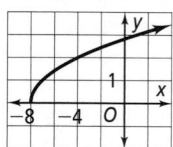

73. domain: $x \geq 0$, range: $y \geq 9$

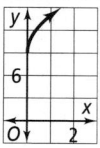

74. domain: $x \geq 4$, range: $y \leq 0$

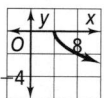

75. domain: all real numbers, range: all real numbers

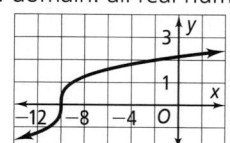

76. domain: all real numbers, range: all real numbers

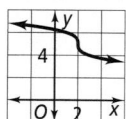

77. $y = 3\sqrt{x - 3} + 4$; the graph of $y = 3\sqrt{x}$ translated
3 units to the right and 4 units up **78.** $y = -6\sqrt{x - 4}$;
the graph of $y = -6\sqrt{x}$ translated 4 units to the right
79. $y = 2\sqrt[3]{x + 3}$; the graph of $y = 2\sqrt[3]{x}$ translated
3 units to the left **80.** $y = \frac{1}{2}\sqrt{x - 4} + 6$; the graph of
$y = \frac{1}{2}\sqrt{x}$ translated 4 units to the right and 6 units up
81. no solution   **82.** 6

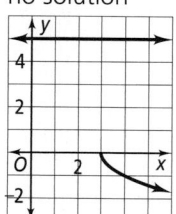   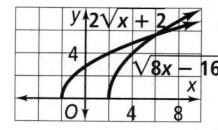

Chapter 7

Get Ready! p. 431 **1.** 0.1; 10; 1000 **2.** $\frac{4}{9}$; 1; $\frac{9}{4}$
3. $-\frac{1}{625}$; $-\frac{1}{25}$; -1 **4.** $-\frac{1}{3}$; -1; -3

5. 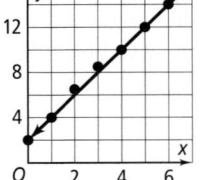 ; $y = 2x + 2$

6. 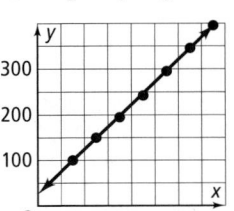 ; $y = 25x + 25$

7. $y = x^2$

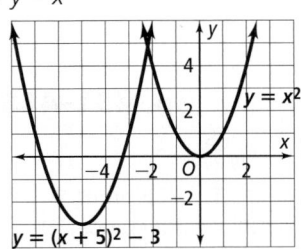

8. $y = x^3$

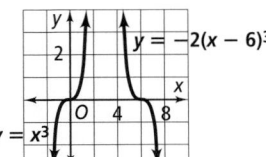

9. x^2 **10.** $16x^4$ **11.** $y = \pm\sqrt{\dfrac{10 - x}{2}}$; no
12. $y = -4 + \sqrt[3]{x + 1}$; yes **13.** decrease
14. exponential **15.** no

Lesson 7-1   pp. 434–441

Got It?

1. a. 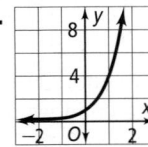   **b.**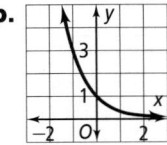

c. 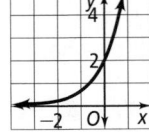   **d.** domain: all real numbers, range: $y > 0$; y-intercept: $(0, a)$ where $y = ab^x$

2. a. exponential growth; 3 **b.** exponential decay; 11
c. exponential growth; 2000 **3.** $593.84 **4. a.** after 8 yrs
b. after 11 yrs; then the account contains $1710.34.
5. a. ≈ 3 **b.** No; the function is asymptotic to the x-axis.
Lesson Check 1. decay; 10 **2.** growth; 0.75

3. growth; 1 **4.** decay; 1

5. 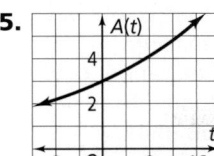   **6.**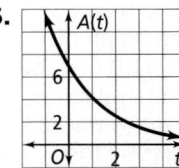

7. If $a > 0$ and $b > 1$, then the function represents exponential growth; if $a > 0$ and $0 < b < 1$, then the function represents exponential decay. **8. a.** quadratic; degree 2 with $3x^2$ as the leading term **b.** exponential; the equation is of the form $y = ab^x$ **c.** linear; degree 1 with x as the leading term **d.** exponential; the equation is of the form $y = ab^x$ **9.** $0.3 < 1$, so 0.3 is the decay factor

Exercises

11. 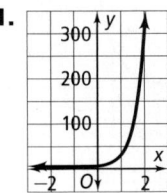   **13.**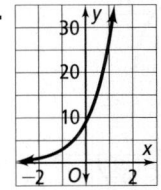

15. 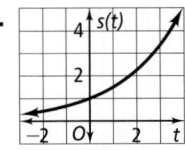   **17.**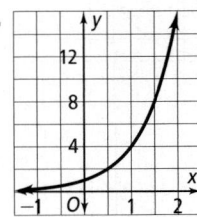

19. exponential decay; 2 **21.** exponential decay; 0.8
23. exponential growth; 0.45 **25.** exponential
decay; 1 **27.** $y = 120{,}000(1.012)^x$; 143,512
29. a. $y = 72(\frac{1}{2})^x$ **b.** 2.25 in. **31. a.** about 5.6%
b. about 0.0017% **33.** Answers may vary. Sample:
$y = 59.5(0.6)^x$ **35.** 6 **37.** 0.45 **39.** 0.999 **41.** 2
43. C **45.** B; The graph shows a decreasing function, which eliminates A. The y-values are all positive, which eliminates C. **47.** G **49.** G

Lesson 7-2   pp. 442–450

Got It?

1. reflects across the x-axis; compresses by a factor of 0.5

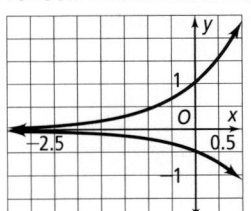

2. a. translate 2 units to the left; the *y*-intercept becomes 16
b. Stretch the graph of $y = (0.25)^x$ by a factor of 5 and translate the graph of $y = 5 \cdot 0.25^x$ 5 units up
3. a. about 31.9 min **b.** No; a hot coffee cannot cool below room temperature. So, to use exponential data, it is important to translate the data by 68 units.
4. $e^8 \approx 2980.957987$; three methods: use the e^x key, $x = 8$; graph $y = e^x$ and find y for $x = 8$; or use the table of values for $y = e^x$ and find y for $x = 8$
5. about $4475
Lesson Check 1. stretch by a factor of 2 and reflection across the *x*-axis **2.** compress by a factor of $\frac{1}{2}$ **3.** translate 5 units to the right **4.** translate 3 units up **5.** yes **6.** no; $2000e^{0.05t} \neq 1000(e^{0.04t} + e^{0.06t})$

Exercises

7. 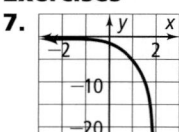   **9.**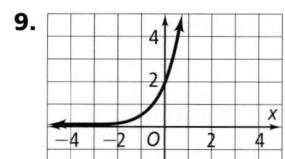

11. 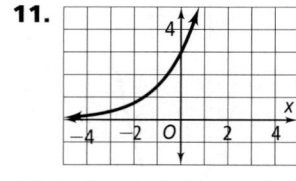   **13.**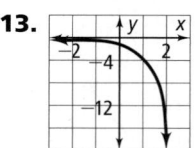

15. 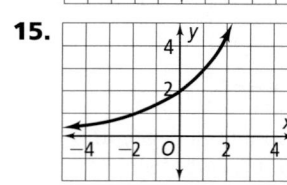   **17.**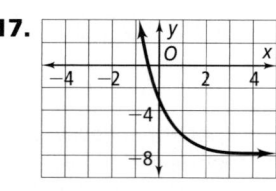

19. 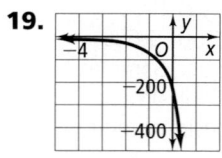   **21.**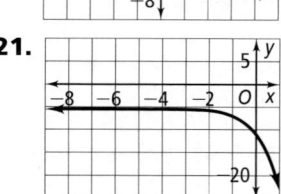

23. 403.4288 **25.** 1 **27.** 15.1543 **29.** $448.30
31. $6168.41 **33.** graph is a shift of the parent function 2 units to the left and 1 unit up
35. 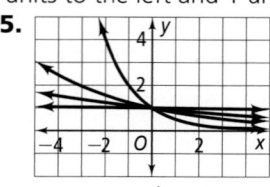   As the value of *b* approaches 1, the graph comes closer to being a straight line.

37. $y = 24\left(\frac{1}{2}\right)^{\frac{1}{5730}x}$; 0.64 mg **39.** $y = -3^x$;
$y = -3^{x-8} + 2$ **41.** $y = -3\left(\frac{1}{3}\right)^x$;
$y = -3\left(\frac{1}{3}\right)^{x+15} - 1$ **43. a.** about 8 names; about 20

names **b.** Graphically, it will never happen; the graph has $y = 25$ as an asymptote. (In reality, you would be close to knowing all the names in about 21 days.) **c.** Answers may vary. Sample: My learning rate might be higher since I can learn names quickly. **45.** G **47.** H
49. $A(t) = Pe^{rt}$
$\qquad \$8000 = Pe^{(0.06)(4)}$
$$P = \frac{\$8000}{e^{(0.06)(4)}}$$
$\qquad P = \$6293.02$
50. exponential growth; 23 **51.** exponential growth; 3
52. exponential decay; 2 **53.** exponential growth; 5
54. $6\sqrt{5}$ **55.** $-\sqrt[3]{4}$ **56.** $5(\sqrt{3} + \sqrt{5})$
57. $2(\sqrt[4]{2} + \sqrt[4]{8})$ **58.** $\sqrt{3}$ **59.** $11\sqrt{7}$
60. $f^{-1}(x) = \frac{x+1}{4}$; yes **61.** $f^{-1}(x) = x^{\frac{1}{7}}$; yes
62. $f^{-1}(x) = \left(\frac{x-1}{5}\right)^{\frac{1}{3}}$; yes

Lesson 7-3 pp. 451–458

Got It? 1. a. $\log_6 36 = 2$ **b.** $\log_{\frac{2}{3}} \frac{8}{27} = 3$

c. $\log_3 1 = 0$ **2. a.** 3 **b.** $\frac{5}{2}$ **c.** $-\frac{5}{6}$ **3.** ≈ 16 times
4. a. domain: $x > 0$; range: all real numbers; no *y*-intercept; vertical asymptote: $x = 0$

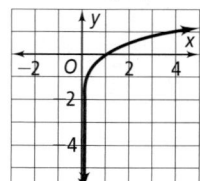

b.

x	$2^y = x$	*y*
−1	$2^y = -1$	undefined
0	$2^y = 0$	undefined
1	$2^y = 1$	0
2	$2^y = 2$	1

5. a. translates the graph of the parent function 3 units to the right and 4 units up; The asymptote changes from $x = 0$ to $x = 3$. The domain changes from $x > 0$ to $x > 3$. The range remains all real numbers. **b.** stretch the graph of the parent function by a factor of 5; The asymptote, domain, and the range remain the same.
Lesson Check 1. $\log_5 25 = 2$ **2.** $\log_4 64 = 3$
3. $\log_3 243 = 5$ **4.** $\log_5 25 = 2$ **5.** 3 **6.** 1 **7.** 2 **8.** −2
9. a. no **b.** yes **c.** yes **d.** no **10.** Choose a few points on the graph of $y = 6^x$, reverse their coordinates, and plot them. **11.** $y = \log_2 (x + 4)$ translates the graph of $y = \log_2 x$ 4 units to the left. Asymptote changes from $x = 0$ to $x = -4$. Domain changes from $x > 0$ to $x > -4$. Range remains the same.

Exercises 13. $\log 1000 = 3$ **15.** $\log \frac{1}{10} = -1$
17. $\log_{\frac{1}{2}} 4 = -2$ **19.** $\log 0.01 = -2$ **21.** $\frac{1}{2}$ **23.** $\frac{3}{2}$
25. $\frac{1}{2}$ **27.** 2 **29.** 1 **31.** 3 **33.** The earthquake in Chile was about 39.81 times more intense. **35.** The earthquake in Missouri was about 10 times more intense.
36–39.

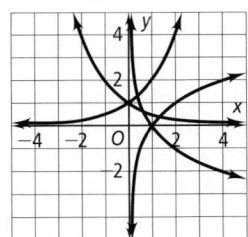

41. translate the graph 2 units to the right **43.** translate the graph 2 units to the left and 1 unit down
45. $\approx 3.16 \times 10^{-9}$ **47.** $10^{-4} = 0.0001$ **49.** $4^0 = 1$
51. $2^{-1} = \frac{1}{2}$ **53.** $10^1 = 10$ **55.** -2 **57.** 7
59. $(2x + 1)^5 = (a + b)$ **61.** $y = 4^x$ **63.** $y = 10^x$
65. $y = 10^x - 1$ **67.** $y = 2^{x-2}$
69.

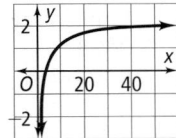

71.

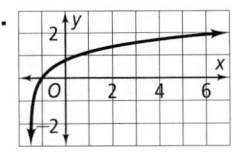

73. domain $x > 0$, range: all real numbers **75.** domain $x > 3$, range: all real numbers **77.** $4 = \log_3 (81)$
79. $8 = \log_6 (a + 1)$ **81.** 3 **83.** -2 **85.** D **87.** C

Lesson 7-4 pp. 462–468

Got It? 1. a. $\log_4 15x^2$ **b.** 1 **2. a.** $\log_3 2 + 3\log_3 5 - \log_3 37$ **b.** $2 + 5 \log_3 x$ **3. a.** $\frac{5}{3}$ **b.** ≈ 2.085
4. Substance B; $\log 2$; $-\log[H^+_B] + \log[H^+_B] = \log 2$
Lesson Check 1. $\log_4 16$ **2.** $\log_6 6$ **3.** $\log_3 x - \log_3 y$
4. $2 \log m + 5 \log n$ **5.** $\frac{1}{2}\log_2 x$ **6. a.** Product Prop. and Power Prop. **b.** Quotient Prop. **7.** 0.00001 **8.** Answers may vary. Samples: $\log 150 = \log 25 + \log 6$
Exercises 9. $\log 14$ **11.** $\log 972$ **13.** $\log \frac{m^4}{n}$
15. $\log_6 5x$ **17.** $\log_3 32xy$ **19.** $2 + \log_7 x + \log_7 y + \log_7 z$ **21.** $2 \log a$ **23.** $2 \log_3 2 + 2 \log_3 x$
25. $2 \log a + 3 \log b - 4 \log c$ **27.** $1 + \frac{1}{2}\log_8 3 + \frac{5}{2}\log_8 a$ **29.** $1 + 4 \log m - 2 \log n$ **31.** ≈ 1.2
33. ≈ 1.43 **35.** ≈ 3.631 **37.** ≈ 3.183 **39.** -2 **41.** 1
43. 2 **45.** Yes, because the loudness of the sound is 102 dB.
47. The coefficient $\frac{1}{2}$ is missing in $\log_4 s$;
$$\log_4 \sqrt{\frac{t}{s}} = \frac{1}{2}\log_4 \frac{t}{s}$$
$$= \frac{1}{2}(\log_4 t - \log_4 s)$$
$$= \frac{1}{2}\log_4 t - \frac{1}{2}\log_4 s$$

49. The log of a product is equal to the sum of the logs. $\log(MN) = \log M + \log N$. **51.** false; $\frac{1}{2}\log_3 3 = \log_3 3^{\frac{1}{2}}$, not $\log_3 \frac{3}{2}$ **53.** false; $\log_b \frac{x}{y} = \log_b x - \log_b y$
55. false; $\log_4 7 - \log_4 3 = \log_4 \frac{7}{3}$ not $\log_4 4$.
57. $\log_x \frac{2\sqrt{y}}{z^3}$ **59.** $\log_b \frac{\sqrt[3]{x^2}\ \sqrt[4]{y^3}}{z^5}$ **61.** $\log s + \frac{1}{2}\log 7 - 2 \log t$ **63.** $3 \log m - 4 \log n + 2 \log p$ **65.** $\frac{1}{2}\log_b x + \frac{2}{3}\log_b y - \frac{2}{5}\log_b z$ **67.** $\frac{1}{2}\log(x + 2) + \frac{1}{2}\log(x - 2) - 2 \log(x + 3)$ **69.** $\frac{\log 8}{\log 3}$ **71.** $\frac{\log 3.3}{\log 9}$ **73.** A 1.0 magnitude star is about 2.5 times brighter than a 2.0 magnitude star.
75. $\frac{1}{2}\log x + \frac{1}{4}\log 2 - \log y$
77. $\frac{1}{2}\log_7 (r + 9) - 2 \log_7 s - \frac{1}{3}\log_7 t$ **79.** 0 **81.** I
83. $\log 18 = \log \frac{36}{2} = \log 36 - \log 2$;
　　　　Quotient Prop.
　　　$= \log 2 \cdot 9 = \log 2 + \log 9$;
　　　　Product Prop.
　　　$= \log 324^{\frac{1}{2}} = \frac{1}{2}\log 324$;
　　　　Power Prop.
　　　$= \log 2 \cdot 3^2 = \log 2 + 2 \log 3$;
　　　　Product and Power Prop.

84. $\log_7 49 = 2$ **85.** $\log_8 \frac{1}{4} = -\frac{2}{3}$
86. $-3 = \log_5 \frac{1}{125}$ **87.** ± 8 **88.** $\frac{64}{7}$ **89.** 2
90. $x^3 + 5x^2 - 3x - 15$ **91.** $x^4 + 17x^2 + 16$
92. $x^4 - 2x^3 - 2x^2 + 14x - 35$ **93.** 2 **94.** 3 **95.** $\frac{1}{3}$

Lesson 7-5 pp. 469–476

Got It? 1. $\frac{4}{9}$ **2. a.** ≈ 1.5122 **b.** because the terms cannot be written with a common base **3. a.** ≈ 0.8588
b. ≈ 1.2114 **4.** ≈ 13.51 yrs **5.** 1.45 **6.** 200
Lesson Check 1. 2 **2.** ≈ 3.6439 **3.** 25 **4.** 2000
5. The log bases are not equal.
$\log_2 x = 2 \log_3 9$
$\log_2 x = \log_3 9^2$
$\log_2 x = 4$
　$x = 2^4$
　$x = 16$
6. Yes; $5^x = 0$ has no solution.

Exercises 7. 3 **9.** 1 **11.** $\frac{4}{5}$ **13.** 2 **15.** 1.5850
17. 3 **19.** 0.9534 **21.** 0.2720 **23.** 0.5690
25. 4.7027 **27.** 6 **29.** 0.64 **31.** about the yr 2012
33. $\frac{\sqrt{10}}{10}$ or about 0.3162 **35.** 10,000 **37.** $\sqrt{10}$ or ≈ 3.1623 **39.** 2 **41.** $100{,}000\sqrt{5}$ or $\approx 223{,}606.8$

43. $\frac{1}{4}$ **45.** 7 **47. a.** 18.9658 **b.** 18.9658 **c.** Answers may vary. Sample: You don't have to use the Change of Base Formula with the base-10 method, but there are fewer steps with the base-2 method. **49.** ≈ 7.6 *yrs* **51.** 3 **53.** 3 **55.** -2 **57.** $-\frac{1}{2}$ **59.** Answers may vary. Sample: $\log x = 1.6$; $x \approx 39.81$ **61.** 143.6 **63. a.** top up: 10^{-5} W/m² top down: $10^{-2.5}$ W/m² **b.** 99.68% **65.** 625 **67.** 10 **69.** 1.5 **71.** 2.7944 **73.** 500 **75.** $114.\overline{3}$ **77.** $x = y = 2$ **79.** $-2, 5$ **81.** 1 **83 a.** bassoon, guitar, harp, violin, viola, cello **b.** bassoon, guitar, harp, cello, bass **c.** harp, violin **d.** harp **85.** 333 **87.** 4

Lesson 7-6   pp. 478–483

Got It? 1. a. $\ln 175$ **b.** $\ln \frac{x}{4}$ **c.** $\ln 5x^3y^2$ **2. a.** e^2, or about 7.39 **b.** $\frac{-5 \pm e^2}{2}$, or about 0.8 or -4.13 **c.** $\frac{e^2}{6}$, or about 1.23 **3. a.** $\ln 2 + 2$, or about 4.48 **b.** $-\ln 10$, or about -2.3 **c.** $\frac{\ln 10}{3}$, or about 0.77 **4. a.** No; the maximum velocity of 5.4 km/s is less than the 7.7 km/s needed for a stable orbit. **b.** Yes; if, R could be changed so that $V > 7.7$.
Lesson Check 1. $\ln 81$ **2.** $\ln 1.8$ **3.** $\ln 12$ **4.** $-\ln 4$ **5.** ≈ 10.9 **6.** ≈ 14.4 **7.** ≈ 7.39 **8.** ≈ -0.718
9. error in 3rd line: $4x = 5$
        should be: $4x = e^5$
              $x = \frac{e^5}{4}$; $x \approx 37.1$
10. No; $\ln 5$ has base e and $\log_2 10$ has base 2.

Exercises 11. $\ln 125$ **13.** $\ln 4$ **15.** $\ln \frac{\sqrt[3]{xy}}{z^4}$ **17.** $\ln 40,960$
19. $\ln 1$ **21.** 0.135 **23.** ± 11.588 **25.** ± 2.241
27. 1488.979 **29.** ≈ 2.890 **31.** ≈ 1.242 **33.** ≈ 2.401
35. 0 **37.** ≈ 2.2 **39.** at least 25 s **41.** $\approx 11,552$ yrs
43. $\frac{1}{4}$ **45.** 83 **47.** 2 **49.** 10 **51.** $\frac{1}{2}$ **53.** ≈ 301 days
55. never **57.** 10.8 **59.** ≈ 19.8 h **61.** 78.342
63. Because the function is simplified in the beginning and the sq. root of the exponential function is not calculated.
65. a. ≈ 43 *min*
b. $t = -\frac{1}{0.041} \ln\left(\frac{T - 72}{164}\right)$

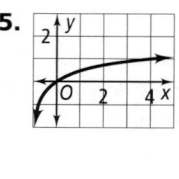

Temperature (°F)	225	200	175	150	125	100	75
Minutes Later	1.7	6.0	11.3	18.1	27.6	43.1	97.6

67. 4 **69.** 0.2975 **71.** 3 **72.** 4 **73.** 2.846
74. 0.272 **75.** $3333.\overline{3}$ **76.** 1.002 **77.** 9.0×10^{-5}
78. $y = \frac{x - 7}{5}$; yes **79.** $y = \sqrt[3]{\frac{x - 10}{2}}$; yes
80. $y = \pm \sqrt{5 - x}$; no **81.** $y = \frac{x - 2}{3}$; yes **82.** 10
83. 15 **84.** $\frac{6}{5}$

Chapter Review   pp. 487–490

1. exponential decay; exponential growth **2.** asymptote **3.** logarithm; natural logarithm function **4.** continuously compounded interest **5.** natural logarithmic function **6.** exponential growth; (0, 1) **7.** exponential growth; (0, 2) **8.** exponential growth; (0, 0.2) **9.** exponential decay; (0, 3) **10.** exponential growth; $\left(0, \frac{25}{7}\right)$
11. exponential growth; (0, 0.0015) **12.** exponential decay; (0, 2.25) **13.** exponential decay; (0, 0.5)
14. $y = 12,500(0.91)^x$; \$7800 **15.** $y = 50(1.03)^x$; \$58
16. The parent graph $y = 2^x$ is stretched by a factor of 5, translated 1 unit to the left, and 3 units up. **17.** The parent graph $y = \left(\frac{1}{3}\right)^x$ is reflected across the x-axis, stretched by a factor of 2, and translated 2 units to the right. **18.** \$1100.76 **19.** \$291.91 **20.** 0.0498
21. 0.3679 **22.** 148.4132 **23.** 0.6065 **24.** $2 = \log_6 36$
25. $-3 = \log_2 0.125$ **26.** $3 = \log_3 27$
27. $-3 = \log 0.001$ **28.** 6 **29.** -2 **30.** -5 **31.** 0
32.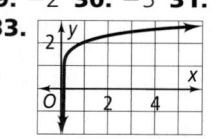

33.

34.

35.

36. The parent graph $y = \log_4 x$ is stretched by a factor of 3 and translated 1 unit to the left.
37. The parent graph $y = \ln x$ is reflected across the x-axis and translated 2 units up. **38.** $\log 24$; Product Prop.
39. $\log_2 \frac{5}{3}$; Quotient Prop. **40.** $\log_3 7x^4$; Power and Product Prop. **41.** $\log \frac{x}{y}$; Quotient Prop. **42.** $\log \frac{5}{x^2}$; Power and Quotient Prop. **43.** $\log_4 x^5$; Power and Product Prop. **44.** $2 \log_4 x + 3 \log_4 y$; Product and Power Prop. **45.** $\log 4 + 4 \log s + \log t$; Product and Power Prop. **46.** $\log_3 2 - \log_3 x$; Quotient Prop. **47.** $2 \log(x + 3)$; Power Prop. **48.** $3 \log_2 2 + 3 \log_2 (y - 2)$; Power and Product Prop. **49.** $2 \log z - \log 5$; Power and Quotient Prop. **50.** ≈ 2.8 **51.** ≈ 2.1 **52.** 0.75 **53.** 3.2619

54. 4.6542 **55.** 1.3652 **56.** 3.3333 **57.** 8 **58.** 50
59. 7.6256×10^{12} **60.** 0.9307 **61.** 0.6599
62. 0.6658 **63.** 3.0589 **64.** $\approx 18.2\ h$ **65.** ≈ 0.83
66. ≈ 2.26 **67.** ≈ 4.31 **68.** ≈ 0.54 **69.** ≈ 3.77
70. ≈ 6.03 **71.** $\approx 3.4\%$

Chapter 8

Get Ready! p. 495 1. $\frac{4}{3}$; -4 **2.** $-\frac{2}{3}$; 2 **3.** $-\frac{10}{3}$; 10
4. $-\frac{16}{7}$; $\frac{48}{7}$ **5.** $(x + 3)(x - 2)$ **6.** $(4x + 5)(x + 3)$
7. $(3x - 5)(3x + 5)$ **8.** $(x - 6)^2$ **9.** $(3x + 4)(x + 2)$
10. $(x - 3)(x - 2)$ **11.** 1, -8 **12.** -6, -8 **13.** 4, 2
14. 0, $-\frac{2}{3}$ **15.** 8, $\frac{1}{2}$ **16.** 15, -2 **17.** Answers may vary.
Sample: Inverse is used when one quantity increases as the
other quantity decreases.
18. Answers may vary. Sample:

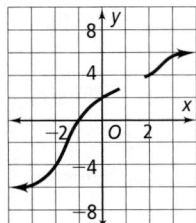

Lesson 8-1   pp. 498–505

Got It? 1. a. direct; $y = 40x$ **b.** inverse; $y = \frac{8}{x}$
c. neither **2. a.** $y = -\frac{56}{x}$
b.   **c.** -28

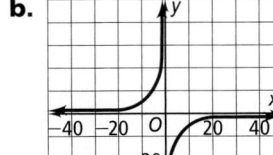

3. a. $t = \frac{225}{n}$ **b.** 9 students **4.** 23 bags
5. a. 4018 joules **b.** 12 m; No, you need not
calculate PE to find the height. Substitute the mass
and height of the first diver, and the mass of
the second diver in $PE = mgh$ and set the two
expressions equal. Solve the equation for h to calculate
the height of the second diver.
Lesson Check 1. inverse; $y = \frac{6}{x}$ **2.** direct; $y = 5x$
3. In direct variation, two positive quantities either
increase together or decrease together. In an
inverse variation, as one quantity increases, the other
quantity decreases and vice versa. **4.** p varies directly
with q, r, and t and inversely with s. **5.** d varies
directly with the cube root of r and inversely with
the square of t.

Exercises 7. neither **9.** inverse; $y = \frac{0.3}{x}$
11. $y = -\frac{1300}{x}$; -130 **13.** $y = \frac{5}{x}$; $\frac{1}{2}$

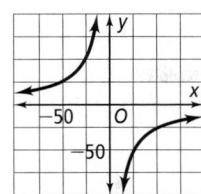   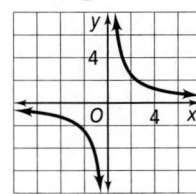

15. $y = \frac{250}{x}$; 25   **17.** $y = -\frac{5}{3x}$; $-\frac{1}{6}$

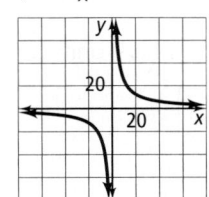   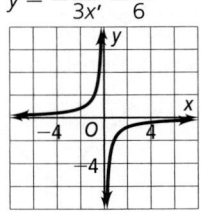

19. a. $s = 2.5m$ **b.** 100 muffins **21. a.** $PE = 2gh$
b. 2 m **23.** $F = \frac{km}{d^2}$; $m = \frac{Fd^2}{k}$ **25. a.** $V = \frac{nRT}{P}$
b. ≈ 76.58 L **c.** ≈ 20 moles **27.** $z = 10xy$; 360
29. 10 **31.** $18\frac{2}{3}$ **33.** 18 **35.** $\frac{1}{4}$ **37.** 2.5 **39.** 2.625
41. Div. by zero is undefined. **43.** Answers may vary.
Sample: Quadruple the volume and leave the radius
constant, halve the radius and leave the volume constant,
multiply the volume by 16 and double the radius, and
multiply the volume and radius by $\frac{1}{4}$. **45.** G **47.** H
49. $\frac{e^5}{4} \approx 37.1$ **50.** $3e^4 \approx 163.79$ **51.** $\frac{e^2}{8} \approx 0.92$
52. $-90x^2$ **53.** $84x^2$ **54.** $10x^2 y^3 \sqrt{2y}$
55. $y = |x|$ translated 2 units up

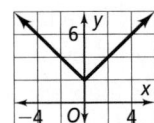

56. $y = |x|$ translated 2 units to the left

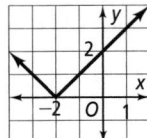

57. $y = |x|$ translated 3 units down

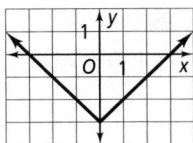

58. $y = |x|$ translated 3 units to the rt.

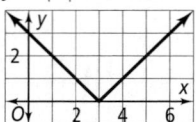

59. $y = |x|$ translated 4 units to the left and 5 units down

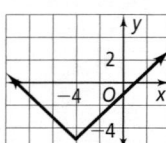

60. $y = |x|$ translated 10 units to the rt. and 7 units up

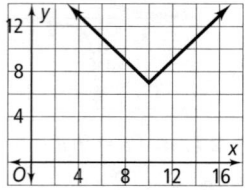

Lesson 8-2   pp. 507–514

Got It?

1. a.

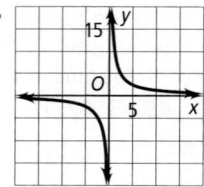

no x- or y-intercept; horizontal asymptote: $y = 0$; vertical asymptote: $x = 0$; domain: all real numbers except $x = 0$, range: all real numbers except $y = 0$

b. Yes; because all the functions have similar graphs.

2. a. $y = \frac{1}{2x}$ is a shrink of the graph of $y = \frac{1}{x}$ by a factor of $\frac{1}{2}$. **b.** $y = \frac{2}{x}$ is a stretch of the graph of $y = \frac{1}{x}$ by a factor of 2. **c.** $y = -\frac{1}{2x}$ is a reflection across the x-axis and a shrink of the graph of $y = \frac{1}{x}$ by a factor of $\frac{1}{2}$.

3.

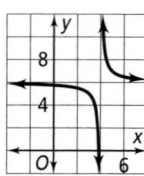

domain: all real numbers except $x = 4$, range: all real numbers except $y = 6$

4. $y = \frac{2}{x-1} - 4$ **5. a.** $C = \frac{1200}{n}$; domain: whole numbers from 1 to 312; 160 students **b.** $C = \frac{1200}{n-30}$; Domain: whole numbers from 1 to 282; 190 students

Lesson Check

1.

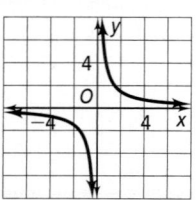

2. $y = \frac{1}{x}$ translated 5 units up **3.** $y = \frac{1}{x}$ reflected across the x-axis and stretched by a factor of 4 **4.** horizontal asymptote: $y = -7$, vertical asymptote: $x = -2$
5. shrink of the graph of $y = \frac{1}{x}$ by a factor of $\frac{1}{2}$

6. Answers may vary. Sample: $y = -\frac{2}{x}$ **7.** For $y = \frac{2}{x}$: stretch if $|a| > 1$ and shrink if $0 < |a| < 1$

Exercises

9.

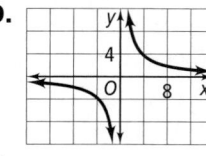

no x- or y-intercept; horizontal asymptote: $y = 0$, vertical asymptote: $x = 0$; domain: all real numbers except $x = 0$, range: all real numbers except $y = 0$

11.

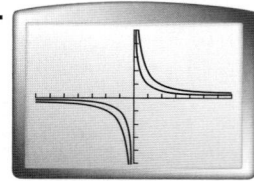

no x- or y-intercept; horizontal asymptote: $y = 0$, vertical asymptote: $x = 0$; domain: all real numbers except $x = 0$, range: all real numbers except $y = 0$

13.

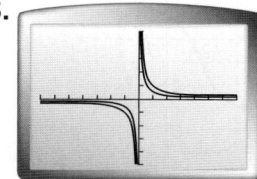

stretch by a factor of 2

15.

compression by a factor of 0.5

compression by a factor of 0.75

17.

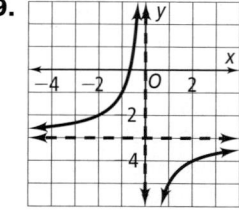

19.

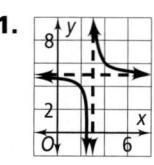

domain: all real numbers except $x = 0$, range: all real numbers except $y = -3$

21.

domain: all real numbers except $x = 3$, range: all real numbers except $y = 4$

23. 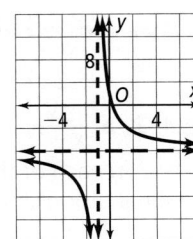 domain: all real numbers except $x = -1$, range: all real numbers except $y = -8$

25. 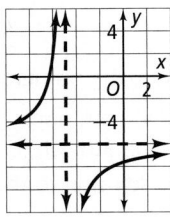 domain: all real numbers except $x = -5$, range: all real numbers except $y = -6$

27. $y = \dfrac{2}{x + 2} + 3$ **29.** 7.67 ft

33. 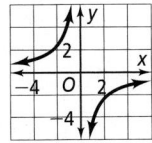 **35.**

37. Answers may vary. Sample: The graph of the translation looks similar to the graph of $y = \frac{1}{x}$, so knowing the asymptotes helps to position the translation; check students' work.

39. 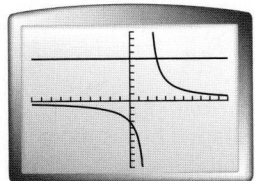 ; (3, 6)

41. 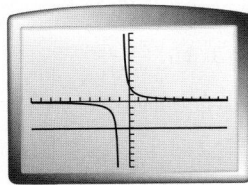 ; (−1.75, −4)

43. a. $m = \dfrac{10,000}{g}$

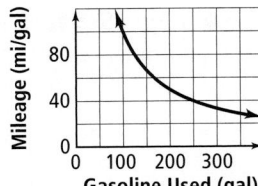

b. $m = \dfrac{10,000}{g - 50}$ **c.** 25 mi/gal; 28.57 mi/gal

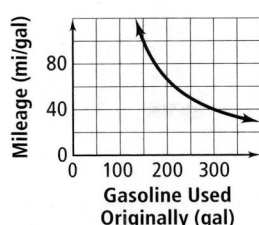

45. The branches of $y = \frac{1}{x^2}$ are in Quadrants I and II. The branches of $y = \frac{1}{x}$ are in Quadrants I and III. The graphs intersect at (1, 1). The graph of $y = \frac{1}{x^2}$ is closer to the x-axis for $x > 1$, and the graph of $y = \frac{1}{x}$ is closer to the y-axis for $0 < x < 1$. **47.** $y = \frac{16}{x}$, $y = -\frac{16}{x}$

Lesson 8-3   pp. 515–523

Got It? 1. a. domain: all real numbers except $x = 4$ and $x = -4$; points of discontinuity: non-removable at $x = 4$ and $x = -4$; no x-intercept, y-intercept: $\left(0, -\frac{1}{16}\right)$
b. domain: all real numbers; no points of discontinuity; x-intercepts: (1, 0) and (−1, 0), y-intercept: $\left(0, -\frac{1}{3}\right)$
c. domain: all real numbers except $x = -2$ and $x = -1$; points of discontinuity: non-removable at $x = -2$, removable at $x = -1$; no x-intercept, y-intercept: $\left(0, \frac{1}{2}\right)$ **2.**
a. $x = 1$ and $x = -3$ **b.** $x = -3$ **c.** no vertical asymptotes **3. a.** $y = -2$ **b.** $y = 0$ **c.** no horizontal asymptote

4.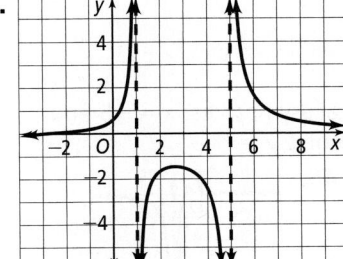

5. a. 4 gal **b.** No, because the graph changes when $y_1 = 0.8$ and intersects the graph of $y_2 = \frac{2 + (0.1)x}{2 + x}$ at $x \approx 0.6$. So, to have 80% orange juice, about 0.6 gal should be added.
Lesson Check 1. $x = -5$ and $x = -4$ **2.** $x = 9$ and $x = -2$ **3.** $x = -1$ **4.** $x = \frac{1}{3}$ and $x = 2$ **5.** $x = -5$
6. $x = -2$ and $x = -3$ **7.** $x = 1$
8. $x = 1$ and $x = -3$

9. 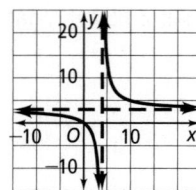 **10.**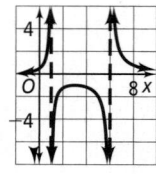

11. the function is undefined at $x = 1$ and $x = -3$

12. degree 2; function is discontinuous at 2 values of x

Exercises 13. domain: all real numbers except $x = 0$ and $x = 2$; points of discontinuity: non-removable at $x = 0$ and $x = 2$; no x- or y-intercept **15.** domain: all real numbers except $x = \pm 1$; pts. of discontinuity: non-removable at $x = -1$, removable at $x = 1$; no x-intercept; y-intercept: $(0, 3)$ **17.** vertical asymptote at $x = -2$

19. vertical asymptotes at $x = -\frac{3}{2}$ and $x = 1$

21. hole at $x = -2$ **23.** $y = 0$ **25.** $y = 1$ **27.** $y = 0$

29. 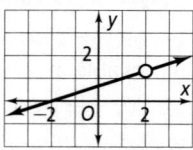 **31.**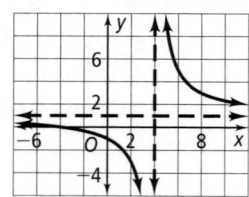

33.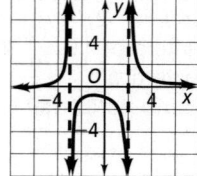

35. 900 ml **37.** vertical asymptote at $x = -2$

39. 6 free throws

41. correct answer: vertical asymptotes: $x = -5$ and $x = -1$, horizontal asymptote: $y = 1$

43. 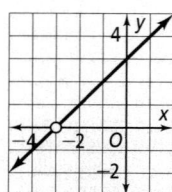 **45.**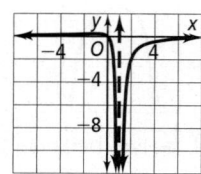

47. Answers may vary. Sample: There is no value of x for which the denominator equals 0.

49. Answers may vary. Samples: **a.** $y = \frac{x^2 - 7x + 12}{x^2 + 2x - 3}$

b. $y = \frac{x + 4}{x^2 - 3x}$ **c.** $y = \frac{3(x + 1)^2}{x^2 - 4}$ **51.** 8 **53.** $\frac{2}{3}$

Lesson 8-4 pp. 527–533

Got It? 1. a. $-\frac{4x}{y}$; $x \neq 0$, $y \neq 0$ **b.** $\frac{x + 4}{x - 3}$; $x \neq 2$ or 3

c. $-\frac{4}{x + 3}$; $x \neq \pm 3$ **2.** $\frac{2(x + 1)}{(x + 4)^2}$; $x \neq \pm 4$ **3. a.** $\frac{2x}{x - 1}$; $x \neq 1, -1, -4, 0,$ or 3 **b.** 6 restrictions; 2 in each of the original denominators, and 2 in the denominator of the reciprocal of the second rational expression. **4.** a square

Lesson Check 1. $\frac{z - 3}{2(z + 3)}$; $z \neq -3$ **2.** $\frac{3}{x}$; $x \neq 0$ or 1

3. $\frac{3(x + 5)}{x + 3}$; $x \neq -3, -6,$ or 2

4. $-\frac{x + 6}{x + 2}$; $x \neq -6, -2, 2, 3,$ or 5 **5.** Yes; the numerator and denominator are polynomials with no common factor. **6.** No; $x = 2$ will make the denominator of $\frac{x}{x - 2}$ 0, so $x = 2$ is not a solution. There is no solution to the eq.

7. Length $= \frac{2(a + 8)}{a + 5}$, $-10 < a < -5$, $a \neq -8$

Exercises 9. $\frac{1}{2x - 1}$; $x \neq 0$ or $\frac{1}{2}$ **11.** $7 - z$; $z \neq -7$

13. $-\frac{x + 4}{x - 5}$; $x \neq 5$ or 3 **15.** $\frac{xy^5}{4}$; $x \neq 0$, $y \neq 0$

17. $-\frac{4(x + 6)}{3(3x + 8)}$; $x \neq 3$ or $-\frac{8}{3}$ **19.** 1; $x \neq -2, -1, 2,$ or 3

21. $\frac{y}{2x^2}$; $x \neq 0$, $y \neq 0$ **23.** 1; $y \neq -2$ or 4 **25.** $\frac{4(y - 3)}{y(y + 5)}$; $y \neq 2, -5,$ or 0 **27.** $\frac{x - 8}{x - 10}$; $x \neq -3$ or 10

29. $\frac{y(y + 3)}{12(y + 4)}$; $x \neq 0$, $y \neq -4$ or 3

31. $R_{cylinder} = \frac{V_{cylinder}}{SA_{cylinder}} = \frac{rh}{2(r + h)}$; $R_{cube} = \frac{V_{cube}}{SA_{cube}} = \frac{s}{6}$; if $r = h = s$, then $R_{cylinder} = \frac{r}{4}$ and $R_{cube} = \frac{r}{6}$. $R_{cylinder} > R_{cube}$. The cylindrical shaped box is more efficient. If $s = h = 2r$ (diameter), then $R_{cylindrical} = R_{cube}$. The boxes are equally efficient.

33. $\frac{18x}{(x + 9)(x + 3)}$; $x \neq -9, -3,$ or 3 **35.** $\frac{x + 1}{x - 1}$; $x \neq -\frac{1}{2}, \frac{1}{2}, 1,$ or -2 **37.** They are equally efficient.

39. never **41.** never **43.** 2; $x \neq -3$ or 1

45. a. $2x^n + 1$ **b.** 2 is a factor of $2x^n$, so $2x^n$ is even and $2x^n + 1$ is odd. **47.** $\frac{-3a^2b^2}{4}$; $a \neq 0$, $a \neq b$, $b \neq 0$

49. $\frac{(x + 1)(x + 5)}{(x - 3)(x + 4)}$; $x \neq 3, -3, -4, 1,$ or -5 **51.** H

53. $-x \log 3 = \log \frac{1}{243}$

$$-x = \frac{\log \frac{1}{243}}{\log 3}$$

$$-x = -5$$

$$x = 5$$

54. hole at $x = 3$ **55.** vertical asymptotes at $x = -\frac{2}{3}$ and $x = -1$ **56.** hole at $x = 4$, vertical asymptote at $x = -3$ **57.** 3 **58.** -5 **59.** $\frac{3}{2}$ **60.** $\frac{3}{4}$ **61.** 49 **62.** 168 **63.** 2 **64.** $\frac{17}{38}$ **65.** $\frac{19}{75}$ **66.** $\frac{11}{72}$ **67.** $\frac{137}{180}$

Lesson 8-5   pp. 534–541

Got It? 1. a. $2(x + 2)(x - 3)$
b. $(x - 1)(x - 2)^2(x + 4)$ **2. a.** $\frac{x + 2}{x}$, $x \neq 1$ or 0
b. $\frac{2(x - 1)}{x^2 - 4}$; $x \neq \pm 2$ **c.** Yes, however the denominator could have to be factored more and there would be additional, incorrect limitations on x. **3. a.** $\frac{x - 2}{x - 1}$, $x \neq 1$ or 2 **b.** $\frac{x^2 - x - 4}{x^2 + 6x + 5}$; $x \neq -5$ or -1 **4. a.** $\frac{x^2 y}{x + y}$
b. $\frac{(x - 1)^2}{2x}$; $x \neq 0, -2$, or ± 1 **5.** Option 1 still gives the better combined mpg since Option 3 gives 18.46 mpg.

Lesson Check 1. $\frac{2a - 10}{3a - 5}$; $a \neq \frac{5}{3}$ **2.** $\frac{6x - 11}{x^2 - 4}$; $x \neq \pm 2$
3. $\frac{-11m}{3m + 6}$; $m \neq -2$ **4.** $\frac{-4(2b - 5)}{(b - 4)(b + 4)(b - 2)}$; $b \neq 2$ or ± 4
5. error in finding a common denominator:

$$\frac{1 + \frac{1}{x}}{\frac{3}{x}} = \frac{\frac{x + 1}{x}}{\frac{3}{x}}$$

$$= \frac{x + 1}{x} \cdot \frac{x}{3}$$

$$= \frac{x + 1}{3}$$

6. Answers may vary. Sample: $\frac{x^2 - 1}{x^2 - 6x + 5}$, $\frac{x^2 + 6x + 5}{x^2 - 25}$

Exercises 7. $9(x + 2)(2x - 1)$ **9.** $5(y + 4)(y - 4)$
11. $\frac{1}{x}$; $x \neq 0$ **13.** $\frac{-3}{x}$; $x \neq 0$ **15.** $\frac{xy + 8y + 4}{2xy^2}$; $x \neq 0, y \neq 0$ **17.** $\frac{y - 6}{2(y + 2)}$; $y \neq -2$
19. $\frac{-x + 6}{(x - 3)(x + 3)}$; $x \neq \pm 3$ **21.** $\frac{-2x(x + 3)}{(x - 2)(x - 1)(x + 1)}$; $x \neq \pm 1$ or 2 **23.** $\frac{15}{28}$ **25.** $\frac{b}{9}$ **27.** $\frac{3x}{2 + xy}$ **29.** $\frac{3}{x - 6}$
31. $\frac{3x - 8}{4x^2}$; $x \neq 0$ **33.** $\frac{7x - 17}{(x - 3)(x + 3)}$; $x \neq \pm 3$
35. $\frac{x(3x^2 + x - 1)}{x^2 - 2}$; $x \neq \pm\sqrt{2}$ **37.** 3.84 in. **39.** Yes;
when you add, subtract, multiply, or divide rational expressions you get another rational expression. The restriction is that you must divide by a nonzero rational expression. **41.** $\frac{3x + 2y}{7x - 5y}$ **43.** x **45. a.** $\frac{2}{3}$ **b.** $\frac{3}{5}$ **c.** $\frac{2}{3}$ **d.** $\frac{1}{3}$
47. a. ≈ 1.18 ohms **b.** 6 ohms, 6 ohms, 3 ohms
49. G **51.** F

Lesson 8-6   pp. 542–548

Got It? 1. a. 1 **b.** 0 **2. a.** ≈ 4.47 m/h **b.** The direction of wind affects the speed (rate) of the bike. Since the speed is inversely related to time, change in speed will lead to change in time. Since there is no wind, the speed of the bike will remain same to and from the store, hence the time to and from the store will remain the same. **3.** $0.\overline{27}$

Lesson Check 1. 5 **2.** -1 **3.** -2 **4.** 310 mi/h
5. LCD was not found. The correct answer is

$$\frac{35 + 9x}{7x} = \frac{28(7)}{7x}, x \neq 0$$
$$9x = 161$$
$$x = \frac{161}{9} = 17.\overline{8}$$

6. Answers may vary. Sample: $\frac{2}{x - 3} + \frac{1}{x + 3} = \frac{5x}{x^2 - 9}$
7. Answers may vary. Sample: (1) Substitute the solution into the original equation. (2) Check to see if the solution is in the domain of the graph of the original equation.
Exercises 9. 10 **11.** 2 **13.** -1, 12 **15.** ≈ -1.45, ≈ 1.65 **17.** -3, -2 **19.** 1 **21.** 0.6 **23.** 1.5 **25.** 1.75 **27.** ± 2 **29.** ≈ 1.69, ≈ -0.44 **31.** $E = mc^2$ **33.** $c = \pm\sqrt{a^2 - b^2}$
35. $B = \pm\sqrt{\frac{2Vm}{r^2 q}}$ **37.** $1\frac{5}{7}$ h **39.** 4 test scores **41. a.** \$2250
b. $\frac{15,000}{24 + x}$ (3.60) **c.** $2250 - \frac{15,000}{24 + x}$ (3.60) **d.** ≈ 32.7 mpg
43. 3 **45.** no solution **47.** no solution **49.** no solution
51. 1, $-\frac{2}{3}$ **53.** Answers may vary. **55.** Answers may vary. **57.** D **59.** B

Chapter Review   pp. 553–556

1. simplest form **2.** combined variation **3.** complex fraction **4.** point of discontinuity **5.** branch **6.** 12
7. $y = \frac{72}{x}$ **8.** $y = 6x$ **9.** $z = \frac{7}{4}xy$; 56 **10.** $z = \frac{4x}{y}$; 2

11. 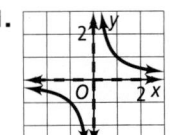 no x- or y-intercept; vert. asymptote: $x = 0$, horizontal asymptote: $y = 0$

12. 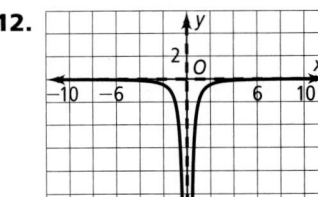 no x- or y-intercept; vert. asymptote: $x = 0$, horizontal asymptote: $y = 0$

13.

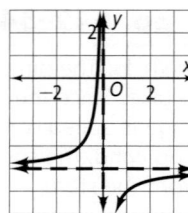

x-intercept: $(-0.25, 0)$, no y-intercept; vert. asymptote: $x = 0$, horizontal asymptote: $y = -4$

14.

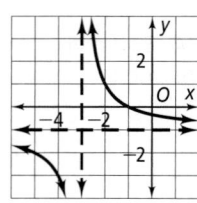

x-intercept: $(-1, 0)$, y-intercept: $(0, -\frac{1}{3})$; vert. asymptote: $x = -3$, horizontal asymptote: $y = -1$

15. $y = \frac{4}{x} + 3$ **16.** $y = \frac{4}{x-2} + 2$ **17.** $y = \frac{4}{x+3} - 4$

18. $y = \frac{4}{x-4} - 3$

19. pts. of discontinuity: $x = -2, 1$;

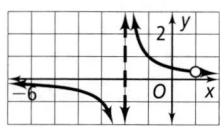

vert. asymptote: $x = -2$, horizontal asymptote: $y = 0$; hole at $x = 1$

20. $1, -1$

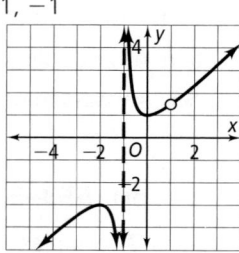

vert. asymptote: $x = -1$; hole at $x = 1$

21. no pts. of discontinuity

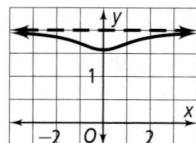

horizontal asymptote: $y = 2$

22.

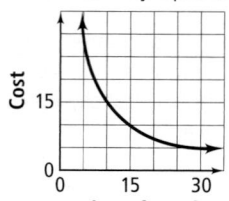

$\approx 31{,}056$ headsets

Cost / Number of Headsets (thousands)

23. $\frac{x+5}{x+4}$; $x \neq -4$ or -5 **24.** $\frac{(x-1)(x+1)}{x+3}$; $x \neq -4, -3,$ or 6 **25.** $\frac{(2x-1)(x+1)}{x+4}$; $x \neq -4, -1,$ or 0

26. $\frac{r}{3}$, where r is the radius **27.** $\frac{3(3x-4)}{(x-2)(x+2)}$; $x \neq \pm 2$

28. $\frac{-x^2 + 3x + 2}{x(x+1)(x-1)(x+3)}$; $x \neq \pm 1, 0,$ or -3

29. $\frac{2(x-1)}{3x-1}$ **30.** $\frac{1}{4(x+y)}$ **31.** -1 **32.** no solution

33. $-12, 9$ **34.** you: 10 mi/h friend: 8 mi/h

Chapter 9

Get Ready! p. 561 1. 9, 11, 13, 15 **2.** 1, 6, 11, 16
3. 0.9, 1.1, 1.3, 1.5 **4.** $-2, -7, -12, -17$
5. $3\frac{1}{3}, 7\frac{1}{3}, 11\frac{1}{3}, 15\frac{1}{3}$ **6.** $-12, -15, -18, -21$ **7.** subtract
5; $-11, -16, -21$ **8.** mult. by 2; 16, 32, 64 **9.** alternate
subtract 9 and add 1; $-7, -6, -15$ **10.** add 3; 19, 22, 25
11. $\frac{4}{3}$ **12.** $\frac{3}{4}$ **13.** $\frac{5}{3}$ **14.** $\frac{5}{18}$ **15.** Answers may vary.
Sample: $f(x) = 2x - 1$; 1, 3, 5, 7, 9 **16.** Answers may
vary. Sample: $g(x) = 1 - 2x$; $-1, -3, -5, -7, -9$; yes;
common difference: -2 **17.** Answers may vary. Sample:
$h(x) = 5(2)^x$; 10, 20, 40, 80, 160; yes; common ratio: 2

Lesson 9-1 pp. 564–571

Got It? 1. 147 **2. a.** $a_1 = 1$ and $a_n = na_{n-1}$
b. $a_1 = 1$ and $a_n = a_{n-1} + n^2$ **3. a.** $a_n = n^2 - 1$; 399
b. To find the nth term using an explicit formula, you
simply substitute for n in the formula. To find the nth
term using a recursive definition may require many
iterations. **4.** 18 months
Lesson Check 1. 2, 7, 12, 17, 22 **2.** $-1, 0, 3, 8, 15$
3. $a_1 = 3$ and $a_n = 2a_{n-1}$ **4.** $a_n = 2 + 3n$ **5.** A recursive
formula defines the terms in a sequence by relating each term
after the first term to the one before it and requires that the
previous term be known to find a given term. An example of a
recursive formula for the sequence 8, 4, 2, 1, $\ldots$ is $a_1 = 8$
and $a_n = \frac{1}{2}a_{n-1}$. An explicit formula describes the nth term
of a sequence using the variable n and only requires the
number of the term to be known. An example of an explicit
formula for the sequence 1, 3, 5, 7, $\ldots$ is $a_n = 2n - 1$.
6. The "$+1$" in $a_n = 3n + 1$ is incorrect for the sequence
1, 4, 7, 10, $\ldots$. The correct explicit formula is
$a_n = -2 + 3n$.
Exercises 7. 5, 8, 11, 14, 17, 20 **9.** $\frac{1}{2}, 1, \frac{3}{2}, 2, \frac{5}{2}, 3$
11. 2, 10, 24, 44, 70, 102 **13.** $-\frac{1}{2}, 3, \frac{25}{2}, 31, \frac{123}{2}, 107$
15. $a_1 = 80$ and $a_n = a_{n-1} - 3$ **17.** $a_1 = 0$ and
$a_n = a_{n-1} + (n+1)$ **19.** $a_1 = 100$ and $a_n = \frac{1}{10}a_{n-1}$

21. $a_1 = 4$ and $a_n = -2a_{n-1}$ **23.** $a_1 = 1$ and $a_n = a_{n-1} + n^2$ **25.** $a_n = 3n + 1$; 31 **27.** $a_n = \frac{n-6}{2}$; 2
29. $a_n = n^2 + 1$; 101 **31.** $a_n = 3^{n-1}$; 19,683
33. 5 **35.** $\frac{5}{16}$ **37.** $\frac{9}{1024}$ **39.** -47 **41.** $-\frac{9}{8}$ **43.** recursive;
3, 9, 21, 45, 93 **45.** explicit; $-24, -21, -16, -9, 0$
47. explicit; $-6, -18, -38, -66, -102$ **49.** 25, 36, 49, 64
51. $\frac{16}{5}, \frac{25}{6}, \frac{36}{7}, \frac{49}{8}$ **53.** \$140 **55.** 20, 23; $a_n = 3n + 2$,
explicit OR $a_n = a_{n-1} + 3$; $a_1 = 5$, recursive
57. 216, 343; $a_n = n^3$, explicit
59. 144, 169; $a_n = (n + 6)^2$, explicit OR
$a_n = a_{n-1} + 2n + 11$, $a_1 = 49$, recursive **61.** $-1, -\frac{1}{2}$;
$a_n = \frac{-32}{2^n}$, explicit OR $a_n = \frac{a_{n-1}}{2}$, $a_1 = -16$, recursive
63. $-11, -19$; $a_n = 29 - 8n$, explicit OR
$a_n = a_{n-1} - 8$, $a_1 = 21$, recursive **65. a.** 25 boxes
b. 110 boxes **c.** 9 levels **67.** $a_n = 10 \cdot 2^{n-1}$
69. $a_n = 1 + 4(n - 1)$ **71.** 34.9 **73.** 2.19 **75.** 36.5
76. 2 **77.** 4 **78.** -5 **79.** -1 **80.** 1 **81.** 2
82. subtract 2; $-2, -4, -6$
83. add 17; 185, 202, 219 **84.** add $\frac{3}{7}$; $\frac{17}{7}, \frac{20}{7}, \frac{23}{7}$

Lesson 9-2   pp. 572–577

Got It? 1. a. not arithmetic **b.** arithmetic **2. a.** 93
b. 95, 110 **3. a.** 115 **b.** yes, use the formula for arithmetic
mean and solve for a_7, $a_7 = 2a_6 - a_5$ **4.** 65 seats
Lesson Check 1. 56 **2.** 87 **3.** 13 **4.** 39 **5.** In an
arithmetic sequence, the diff. between any two
consecutive terms is always the same number. **6.** Answers
may vary. Sample: 2, 4, 8, 16, 32, . . .
Exercises 7. yes; 10 **9.** yes; 3 **11.** yes; 4 **13.** 127
15. 240 **17.** 12.5 **19.** -7 **21.** 13 **23.** 7.5 **25.** \$135
27. 18 **29.** 36 **31.** 2 **33.** The student multiplied
the third term by 2 instead of adding 2. The correct
answer is 6. **35.** 120 **37.** 1.1 **39.** 0
41. $a_n = 2 + 2(n - 1)$; $a_n = a_{n-1} + 2$, $a_1 = 2$
43. $a_n = -5 + 1(n - 1)$; $a_n = a_{n-1} + 1$, $a_1 = -5$
45. $a_n = -5 + 1.5(n - 1)$; $a_n = a_{n-1} + 1.5$, $a_1 = -5$
47. $a_n = 1 + \frac{1}{3}(n - 1)$; $a_n = a_{n-1} + \frac{1}{3}$, $a_1 = 1$
49. $a_n = 27 - 12(n - 1)$; $a_n = a_{n-1} - 12$, $a_1 = 27$
51. Answers may vary. Sample: An advantage of a recursive
formula is that only the preceding term must be known to
find the next term; a disadvantage is that many calculations
may be required to find a term. An advantage of an explicit
formula is that it is easy to find any term. Use the recursive
formula when the previous term and common diff. are
known. Use the explicit formula when the term number and
common diff. are known. **53.** $-4, -10, -16$
55. $-8, -17, -26$ **57.** 17, 17, 17 **59.** $-12.5, -8, -3.5$
61. \$5055 **63.** 21st term **65.** 54 **67.** $a_1 = -1$, $d = 3$

69. $a_1 = 52$, $d = -10$ **71.** $a_1 = -100.5$, $d = 22$
73. $9k + 32$ **75.** D

77.
$$\frac{3}{(x-1)(x+1)} + \frac{4x(x-1)}{(x-1)(x+1)} = \frac{1.5(x+1)}{(x-1)(x+1)}, x \neq \pm 1$$
$$3 + 4x^2 - 4x = 1.5x + 1.5$$
$$4x^2 - 5.5x + 1.5 = 0$$
$$x^2 - \frac{11}{8}x + \frac{3}{8} = 0$$
$$(x - 1)\left(x - \frac{3}{8}\right) = 0$$
$$x = \frac{3}{8}$$
(Reject $x = 1$ because 1 is not in the domain.)
78. recursive; $-2, -7, -12, -17, -22$
79. explicit; 6, 18, 36, 60, 90 **80.** explicit; 0, 3, 8, 15, 24
81. recursive; $-121, -108, -95, -82, -69$
82. $y - 3 = \frac{8}{3}x$ or $y - 11 = \frac{8}{3}(x - 3)$
83. $y - 6 = 4(x - 4)$ or $y - 30 = 4(x - 10)$
84. $y - 10 = 8(x - 1)$ or $y - 42 = 8(x - 5)$
85. $r = \frac{\sqrt[3]{6\pi^2 V}}{2\pi}$ **86.** 32 **87.** 625 **88.** -81

Lesson 9-3   pp. 580–586

Got It? 1. a. yes; $a_1 = 2$, $r = 2$ **b.** no **c.** yes; $a_1 = 2^3$,
$r = 2^4$ **2.** 6 or -6 **3. a.** explicit; it is easier to use
because only one calculation is needed. **b.** about 16.8 cm,
about 4 cm **4.** ± 60
Lesson Check 1. no **2.** yes; 2 **3.** 729 **4.** 0.0064
5. The third term would be the geometric mean of 5
and 80 which is 20. Since a is pos. and r^2 is always
pos., the third term, ar^2, cannot be neg.
6. For both the arithmetic mean and the geometric mean,
the middle term of any three consecutive terms can be
determined using the first and last of the three terms. The
arithmetic mean is the sum of the first and last terms
divided by 2, whereas the geometric mean is the square
root (or its opposite) of the product of the first and the
last terms.
Exercises 7. yes; 2 **9.** yes; -2 **11.** yes; 0.4
13. yes; $-\frac{1}{3}$ **15.** yes; 1.5 **17.** yes; 6 **19.** 6561
21. 0.078125 **23.** $\frac{-3}{2048}$ **25.** about 656.1 g; about
182.5 g; about 96.2 g
27. ± 1530 **29.** ± 1.5 **31.** ± 6 **33.** $a_n = 100(-20)^{n-1}$;
(100, -2000, 40,000, $-800,000$, 16,000,000
35. $a_n = 1024(0.5)^{n-1}$; 1024, 512, 256, 128, 64
37. $a_n = 10(-1)^{n-1}$; 10, -10, 10, -10, 10 **39.** arithmetic;
125, 150 **41.** geometric; -80, 160 **43.** neither; 25, 36
45. 7.5, 22.5, 67.5 or -7.5, 22.5, -67.5
47. $-6.64, -11.02, -18.30$ or 6.64, -11.02, 18.30
49. about 74.3 mi **51.** 768 **53.** 3×4^{19} or
824,633,720,832 **55.** 4 **57.** 10

59. Both the common diff. and the common ratio are used to find the next term in a sequence, but a common diff. is added and a common ratio is multiplied. **61.** 7 **63.** B **65.** C **67.** $x \neq -1, -5$; there's a hole in the graph at $x = -1$. There's a vert. asymptote at $x = -5$.

Lesson 9-4   pp. 587–593

Got It? 1. a. 1030 **b.** Yes; no; the sum of any number of even numbers is always even. The sum of an odd number of odd numbers is odd, but the sum of an even number of odd numbers is even. **2.** 59 sales; 1725 sales

3. a. $\sum_{n=1}^{40}(-12 + 7n)$ **b.** $\sum_{n=1}^{50}(510 - 10n)$ **4. a.** 2140

b. 100 **c.** 1 **5.** 41,650

Lesson Check 1. 91 **2.** 780 **3.** $\sum_{n=1}^{7}3n$

4. $\sum_{n=1}^{12}(-3 + 4n)$ **5.** An arithmetic sequence is a list of numbers for which successive numbers have a common difference. **6.** The lower limit should not be 3, it should be one and the expression $5n - 2$ should be in parentheses. The correct summation notation is $\sum_{n=0}^{8}(3 + 5n)$. **7.** Yes; $44 = 2(a_1 + a_4)$, so any combination of a_1 and a_4 with a sum of 22 is a possible series.

Exercises 9. 92 **11.** 176 **13.** −165 **15.** $\sum_{n=1}^{5}4n$

17. $\sum_{n=1}^{12}(2 + 3n)$ **19.** $\sum_{n=1}^{10}(-3n)$ **21.** 25 **23.** 20

25. −2 **27.** 2400 **29.** 682 **31.** −8556 **33.** 432 seats **35.** sequence; finite **37.** series; infinite **39.** series; finite **41.** −48 **43.** 35 **45.** −146 **47. a.** $a_n = n + 1$

b. $\sum_{n=1}^{9}(n + 1)$ **c.** 18 cans **d.** No; no; 13 rows have 104 cans, 14 rows have 119 cans, 15 rows have 135 cans, and 16 rows have 152 cans. The number of rows would not be an integer for 110 cans or 140 cans. **49.** −765 **51.** 300 **53.** 34 **55.** $10x + 45y$ **57.** C **59.** B

61. $\left(\frac{b}{2}\right)^2 = \left(\frac{10}{2}\right)^2 = 25$
$$x^2 + 10x + 25 = -35 + 25$$
$$(x + 5)^2 = -10$$
$$x + 5 = \pm i\sqrt{10}$$
$$x = -5 \pm i\sqrt{10}$$

62. $a_n = 2^{n-1}$; 1, 2, 4 **63.** $a_n = -1(-1)^{n-1}$; −1, 1, −1
64. $a_n = 3\left(\frac{3}{2}\right)^{n-1}$; 3, $\frac{9}{2}$, $\frac{27}{4}$ **65.** $\frac{x + 3}{x - 4}$; $x \neq 4$, $x \neq -1$
66. $\frac{c - 2}{c - 5}$; $c \neq 5$, $c \neq 6$ **67.** $\frac{z^2 + 12z + 20}{z - 1}$; $z \neq 1$,
$z \neq 0$ **68.** $-\frac{1}{3}$ **69.** $\frac{3}{4}$ **70.** $-\frac{1}{2}$

Lesson 9-5   pp. 595–601

Got It? 1. a. 315 **b.** −1705 **2.** about $2138.43 **3. a.** diverges **b.** converges; $\frac{1}{4}$ **c.** converges; 2 **d.** Yes; if $|r| < 1$, the series converges. If $|r| \geq 1$, the series diverges.

Lesson Check 1. $\frac{31}{80}$ **2.** $\frac{55}{9}$ **3.** converges **4.** diverges **5.** Since $r = 1.1 > 1$, the series diverges and does not have a sum. **6.** An infinite geometric series has a sum only when the series converges, which is when $|r| < 1$. **7.** The sum of a finite arithmetic series is $S_n = \frac{n}{2}(a_1 + a_n)$.

The sum of finite geometric series is $S_n = \frac{a_1(1 - r^n)}{1 - r}$.

The formulas are similar in that each sum requires the first term and the number of terms in the series. The formulas are different in that the sum of a finite arithmetic series needs the last term, while the sum of a finite geometric series needs the common ratio.

Exercises 9. 1456 **11.** −5115 **13.** $\frac{15}{32}$ **15.** $\frac{121}{81}$

17. converges; $\frac{4}{3}$ **19.** converges; 8 **21.** diverges; no sum **23.** diverges; no sum **25.** diverges; no sum **27.** 1 **29.** $\frac{9}{2}$

31. $\frac{9}{5}$ **33.** arithmetic; 420 **35.** geometric; about 96.47 **37.** geometric; about 121.5

39. a.

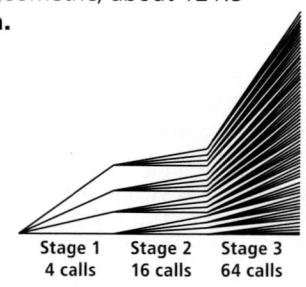

Stage 1	Stage 2	Stage 3
4 calls	16 calls	64 calls

b. $4 + 16 + 64 + 256 + 1024 + 4096$
c. 5460 employees **41.** $\frac{5}{4}$ **43.** $\frac{3}{4}$ **45.** $0.8\overline{3}$ **47. a.** $\frac{7}{8}$
b. 10 **49. a.** Answers may vary. Sample: The student used $r - 1$ instead of $1 - r$ in the formula for the sum of an infinite geometric series. **b.** $\frac{1}{2}$

51. a. $rS_n = r(a_1 + a_1r + \cdots + a_1r^{n-1}) = a_1r +$
$a_1r^2 + \cdots + a_1r^n$
b. $S_n - rS_n = a_1 + a_1r + a_1r^2 + \cdots + a_1r^{n-1}$
$- a_1r - a_1r^2 - \cdots - a_1r^{n-1} - a_1r^n$
$= a_1 - a_1r^n$
c. $S_n - rS_n = a_1 - a_1r^n$
$S_n(1 - r) = a_1 - a_1r^n$
$S_n = \frac{a_1 - a_1r^n}{1 - r} = \frac{a_1(1 - r^n)}{1 - r}$

53. $a_1 = \frac{9}{10}$, $r = \frac{1}{10}$; $S = \frac{\frac{9}{10}}{1 - \frac{1}{10}} = 1$

Chapter Review   pp. 603–606

1. limits **2.** sequence **3.** converges **4.** common ratio
5. explicit formula **6.** 1, −1, −3, −5, −7
7. 1, 0, −3, −8, −15 **8.** 2, 3, 5, 9, 17 **9.** 20, 10, 5, 2.5, 1.25 **10.** $a_n = a_{n-1} + 17, a_1 = 5$ **11.** $a_n = a_{n-1} + 9,$ $a_1 = -2$ **12.** $a_n = 3n - 2$ **13.** $a_n = 6.5 - 2.5n$ **14.** no
15. yes; $d = 15, a_{32} = 468$ **16.** yes; $d = 3, a_{32} = 100$
17. no **18.** 5 **19.** 101.5 **20.** 5 **21.** −4.9
22. −10.5, −8, −5.5 **23.** 1.4, 0.8, 0.2
24. $a_n = -2 + 9(n - 1)$ **25.** $a_n = 62 - 3(n - 1)$
26. yes; $r = \frac{1}{2}; \frac{1}{16}, \frac{1}{32}$ **27.** no **28.** yes;
$r = 1.2; 6.2208, 7.46496$ **29.** ±6 **30.** ±0.04
31. ±10, −5, ±2.5 **32.** $a_n = 2^{n-1}$
33. $a_n = 25\left(\frac{1}{5}\right)^{n-1}$ **34.** 2560 **35.** 1536
36. $\sum_{n=1}^{5}(13 - 3n); 20$ **37.** $\sum_{n=1}^{7}(45 + 5n); 455$
38. $\sum_{n=1}^{11}(4.6 + 1.4n); 143$ **39.** $\sum_{n=1}^{8}(23 - 2n); 112$
40. 3; −8, 26; 27 **41.** 9; 4, 8; 54 **42.** 31 **43.** $53\frac{1}{8}$
44. $14\frac{7}{18}$ **45.** converges; $S = 187.5$ **46.** diverges
47. diverges **48.** converges; $S = 2$

Chapter 10

Get Ready! p. 611

1.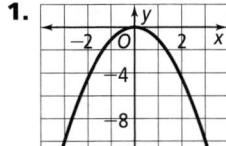
2.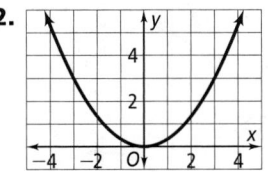
3.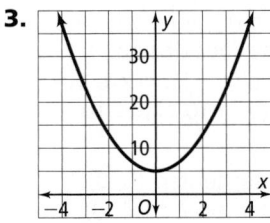
4.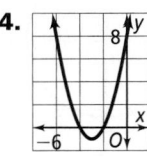

5. quadratic; $-x^2, 6x, 1$ **6.** linear; none, $-12x, -18$
7. linear; none, $x, -\frac{13}{2}$ **8.** quadratic; $-8x^2, 28x,$ none
9. quadratic; $-2x^2, -3x, 6$ **10.** linear; none, $-x, -10$
11. 16 **12.** $\frac{25}{4}$ **13.** 49

14. $y = (x + 3)^2 - 2$
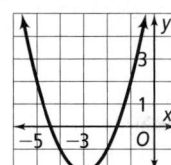

15. $y = 2(x - 1)^2 + 8$
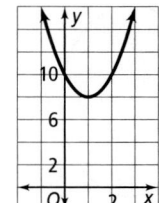

16. $y = -3\left(x - \frac{1}{6}\right)^2 + \frac{1}{12}$
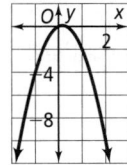

17.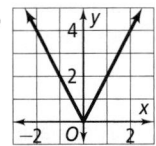
18.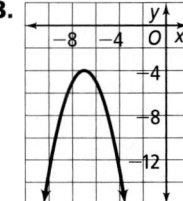

19.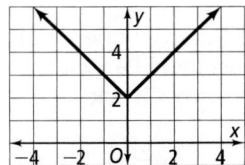
20.

21. The radius of a circle is the distance from the center of the circle to any pt. on the circle. The radius extends in every direction from the center and ends on the circle. All radii of the same circle are equal. **22.** The vertex of a parabola is the lowest or highest pt. of a parabola; it is the pt. where the parabola changes direction.

Lesson 10-1   pp. 614–621

Got It?
1. a. 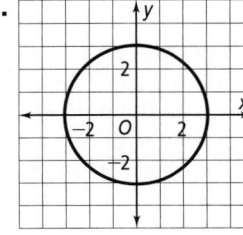   circle: center (0,0); radius 3; lines of sym.: every line through the origin; domain: $-3 \le x \le 3$, range: $-3 \le y \le 3$

b. 6 is outside the domain of x.

2.

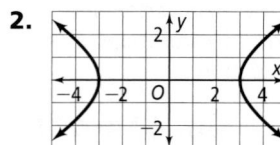

ellipse: center (0,0); lines of sym.: x-axis and y-axis; domain: $-3 \leq x \leq 3$, range: $-3\sqrt{2} \leq y \leq 3\sqrt{2}$

3.

hyperbola: center (0,0); lines of sym.: x-axis and y-axis; domain: $x \leq -4$ or $x \geq 4$, range: all real numbers

4. center of hyperbola: (0, 0); no x-intercepts, y-intercepts: (0, 1), (0, −1); domain: all real numbers, range: $y \leq -1$ or $y \geq 1$ **5. a.** Ellipse; the eq. $9x^2 + 25y^2 = 225$ represents a conic section with two sets of intercepts, (±3, 0) and (0, ±5). Since the intercepts are not equidistant from the center, the eq. models an ellipse.
b. Hyperbola; the eq. $x^2 - y^2 = 1$ represents a conic section with one set of intercepts, (±1, 0), so the eq. must model a hyperbola.

Lesson Check

1.

lines of sym.: x-axis and y-axis; domain: $-6 \leq x \leq 6$, range: $-3 \leq y \leq 3$

2.

lines of sym.: x-axis and y-axis; domain: $x \leq -3$ or $x \geq 3$, range: all real numbers

3. domain: $x \leq -2.5$ or $x \geq 2.5$, range: all real numbers
4. domain: $-6 \leq x \leq 6$, range: $-1.5 \leq y \leq 1.5$
5. a. hyperbola **b.** circle **6.** Answers may vary. Sample answer: The domain of an ellipse is an interval between two real numbers, such as $-a \leq x \leq a$. The domain of a hyperbola is two intervals, such as $x \leq -a$ or $x \geq a$, if there are x-intercepts, or all real numbers if there are no x-intercepts.

Exercises

7.

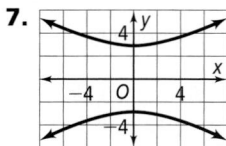

hyperbola; center: (0, 0); no x-intercepts, y-intercepts: $\left(0, \pm\frac{5\sqrt{3}}{3}\right)$; lines of sym.: x-axis and y-axis; domain: all real numbers, range: $y \leq -\frac{5\sqrt{3}}{3}$ or $y \geq \frac{5\sqrt{3}}{3}$

9.

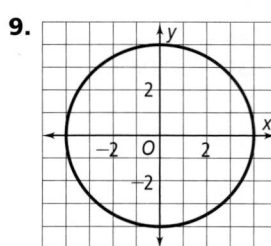

circle; center: (0, 0); radius: 4; x-intercepts: (±4, 0), y-intercepts: (0, ±4); infinitely many lines of sym.; domain: $-4 \leq x \leq 4$, range: $-4 \leq y \leq 4$

11.

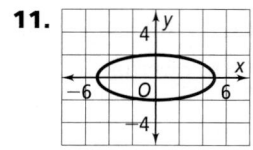

ellipse; center: (0, 0); x-intercepts: (±5, 0), y-intercepts: (0, ±2); lines of sym.: x-axis and y-axis; domain: $-5 \leq x \leq 5$, range: $-2 \leq y \leq 2$

13.

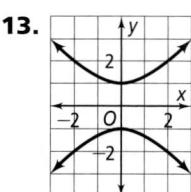

hyperbola; center: (0, 0); no x-intercepts, y-intercepts: (0, ±1); lines of sym.: x-axis and y-axis; domain: all real numbers, range: $y \leq -1$ or $y \geq 1$

15.

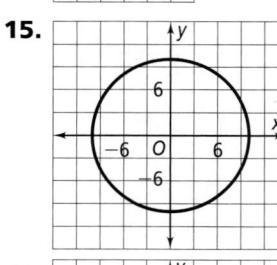

circle; center: (0, 0); radius: 10; x-intercepts: (±10, 0), y-intercepts: (0, ±10); infinitely many lines of sym.; domain: $-10 \leq x \leq 10$, range: $-10 \leq y \leq 10$

17.

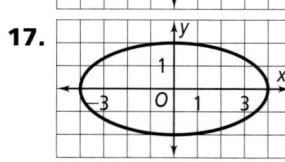

ellipse; center: (0, 0); x-intercepts: (±4, 0), y-intercepts: (0, ±2); lines of sym.: x-axis and y-axis; domain: $-4 \leq x \leq 4$, range: $-2 \leq y \leq 2$

19.

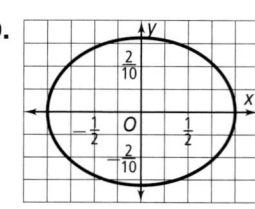

ellipse; center: (0, 0); x-intercepts: (±1, 0), y-intercepts: $\left(0, \pm\frac{1}{3}\right)$; lines of sym.: x-axis and y-axis; domain: $-1 \leq x \leq 1$, range: $-\frac{1}{3} \leq y \leq \frac{1}{3}$

21. 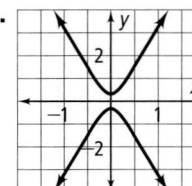 hyperbola; center: $(0, 0)$; no x-intercepts, y-intercepts: $\left(0, \pm\frac{1}{2}\right)$; lines of sym.: x-axis and y-axis; domain: all real numbers, range: $y \le -\frac{1}{2}$ or $y \ge \frac{1}{2}$

23. hyperbola; center: $(0, 0)$; no x-intercepts, y-intercepts: $(0, \pm 2)$; domain: all real numbers, range: $y \le -2$ or $y \ge 2$ **25.** hyperbola; center: $(0, 0)$; x-intercepts: $(\pm 3, 0)$, no y-intercepts; domain: $x \le -3$ or $x \ge 3$, range: all real numbers **27.** hyperbola; center: $(0, 0)$; no x-intercepts, y-intercepts: $(0, \pm 3)$; domain: all real numbers, range: $y \le -3$ or $y \ge 3$ **29.** 22

31. 24 **33.** 27

35. 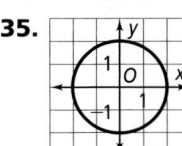 circle; center: $(0, 0)$; radius: 2; x-intercepts: $(\pm 2, 0)$, y-intercepts: $(0, \pm 2)$; infinitely many lines of sym.; domain: $-2 \le x \le 2$, range: $-2 \le y \le 2$

37. 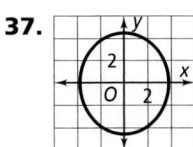 ellipse; center: $(0, 0)$; x-intercepts: $\left(\pm\frac{8\sqrt{5}}{5}, 0\right)$, y-intercepts: $(0, \pm 2\sqrt{5})$; lines of sym.: x-axis and y-axis; domain: $-\frac{8\sqrt{5}}{5} \le x \le \frac{8\sqrt{5}}{5}$, range: $-2\sqrt{5} \le y \le 2\sqrt{5}$

39. a. All lines in the plane that pass through the center of a circle are axes of sym. of the circle. **b.** The axes of sym. of an ellipse intersect at the center of the ellipse. The same is true for a hyperbola. This can be confirmed using, for example, $4x^2 + 9y^2 = 36$ and $4x^2 - 9y^2 = 36$.

41. 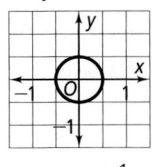
$x^2 + y^2 = \frac{1}{4}$

43. 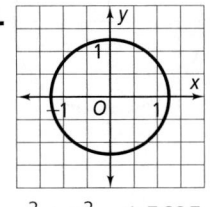
$x^2 + y^2 = 1.5625$

45. Sample: $(\sqrt{2}, 1)$ **47.** Sample: $(2, 0)$ **49.** $(0, -\sqrt{7})$
51. Answers may vary.

53. a. 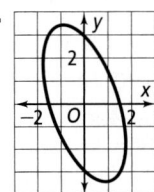 **b.**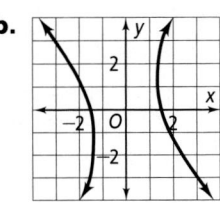

55. I **57.** H **59.** diverges **60.** diverges **61.** converges
62. $x^3 - 3x^2y + 3xy^2 - y^3$

63. $p^6 + 6p^5q + 15p^4q^2 + 20p^3q^3 + 15p^2q^4 + 6pq^5 + q^6$ **64.** $x^4 - 8x^3 + 24x^2 - 32x + 16$
65. $243 - 405x + 270x^2 - 90x^3 + 15x^4 - x^5$

66.

x	-2	-1	0	1	2
y	2	1	0	1	2

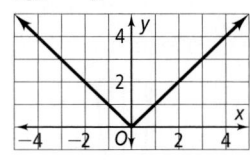

67.

x	-2	-1	0	1	2
y	5	4	3	4	5

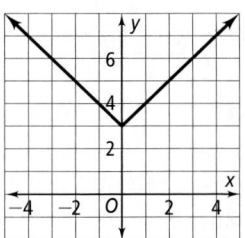

68.

x	0	1	2	3	4
y	2	1	0	1	2

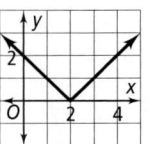

69.

x	-3	-2	-1	0	1
y	-2	-3	-4	-3	-2

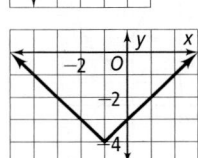

Lesson 10-2 pp. 622–629

Got It? 1. a. $y = -\frac{1}{6}x^2$ **b.** vertex: $(0, 0)$; focus: $(0, 1)$; directrix: $y = -1$ **c.** As the distance between the vertex and focus increases, the width of the parabola increases.
2. a. $x = \frac{1}{10}y^2$ **b.** vertex: $(0, 0)$; focus: $\left(-\frac{1}{16}, 0\right)$; directrix: $x = \frac{1}{16}$ **3.** 1 cm **4.** vertex: $(-4, 2)$; focus: $\left(-4, 2\frac{1}{4}\right)$; directrix: $y = 1\frac{3}{4}$ **5.** $y = \frac{1}{8}(x - 1)^2 + 4$

Lesson Check 1. $y = \frac{1}{2}x^2$ **2.** $x = \frac{1}{4}(y - 2)^2 + 3$
3. vertex: $(0, 0)$; focus: $(4, 0)$; directrix: $x = -4$
4. vertex: $(-3, -4)$; focus: $(-3, -3.75)$; directrix: $y = -4.25$ **5.** 6 units **6.** With the focus one unit away from the vertex of a parabola at the origin, $c = \pm 1$. Given this information, the student cannot tell whether the parabola opens in the vert. direction, with one of the eqs. $y = \frac{1}{4}x^2$ or $y = -\frac{1}{4}x^2$, or whether the parabola opens in the horizontal direction, with one of the eqs. of $x = \frac{1}{4}y^2$ or $x = -\frac{1}{4}y^2$.

Exercises 7. $x = \frac{1}{24}y^2$ **9.** $y = \frac{1}{28}x^2$ **11.** $x = \frac{1}{8}y^2$

13. vertex: $(0, 0)$;

focus: $\left(0, \frac{1}{16}\right)$;

directrix: $y = -\frac{1}{16}$

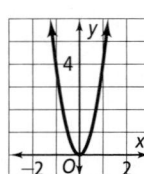

15. vertex: $(0, 0)$;

focus: $\left(\frac{1}{4}, 0\right)$;

directrix: $x = -\frac{1}{4}$

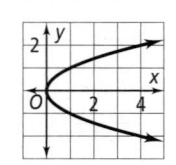

17. $x = \frac{1}{12}y^2$ **19.** $y = \frac{3}{4}x^2$ **21.** $y = -\frac{5}{56}x^2$ **23.** Answers may vary. Sample: $y = x^2$. The light produced by the bulb will reflect off the parabolic mirror in parallel rays.

25. vertex: $(3, 2)$;

focus: $\left(3, \frac{9}{4}\right)$;

directrix: $y = \frac{7}{4}$

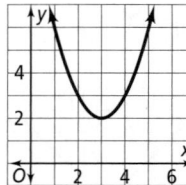

27. vertex: $(1, -5)$;

focus: $\left(1, -4\frac{3}{4}\right)$;

directrix: $y = -5\frac{1}{4}$

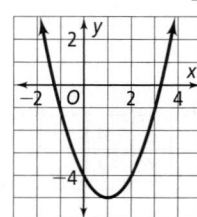

29. vertex: $(-1, -4)$;

focus: $\left(-1, -3\frac{7}{8}\right)$;

directrix: $y = -4\frac{1}{8}$

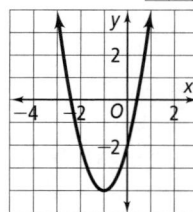

31. $x = -\frac{1}{32}(y - 3)^2$ **33.** $y = -\frac{1}{16}(x - 7)^2 + 2$

35. vertex: $(0, 0)$; focus: $(0, -1)$; directrix: $y = 1$

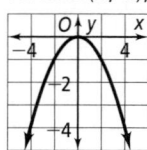

37. vertex: $(0, 0)$;
focus: $(-2, 0)$;
directrix: $x = 2$

39. vertex: $(4, 0)$;
focus: $(4, -6)$;
directrix: $y = 6$

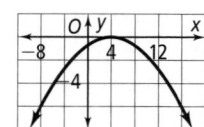

41.

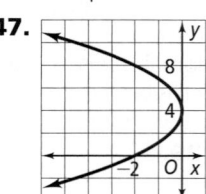

43. $y = \frac{1}{4}x^2$ **45.** 3.5 in.

47.

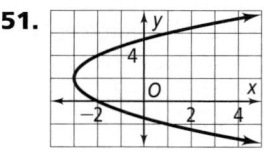

49.

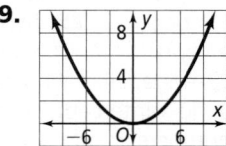

51.

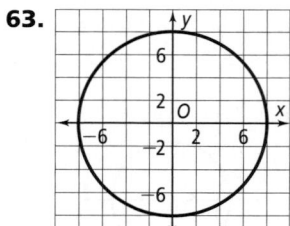

53. $x = -\frac{1}{2}(y - 1)^2 + 1$

55. Answers may vary. Sample: Write the eq. in the form $x = \dfrac{1}{4\left(\frac{1}{8}\right)}y^2$. The distance from the focus to the directrix is $2\left(\frac{1}{8}\right)$, or $\frac{1}{4}$. **57. a.** the top half of the parabola, $y^2 = x$ **b.** domain: $x \geq 0$, range: $y \geq 0$ **59.** D **61.** B

63.

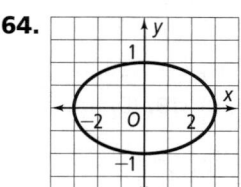

circle: center $(0, 0)$, radius 8; x-intercepts: $(\pm 8, 0)$, y-intercepts: $(0, \pm 8)$; infinitely many lines of sym.; domain: $-8 \leq x \leq 8$, range: $-8 \leq y \leq 8$

64.

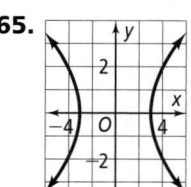

ellipse: center $(0, 0)$; x-intercepts: $(\pm 3, 0)$, y-intercepts: $(0, \pm 1)$; lines of sym.: x-axis and y-axis; domain: $-3 \leq x \leq 3$, range: $-1 \leq y \leq 1$

65.

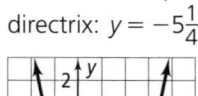

hyperbola: center $(0, 0)$; x-intercepts $(\pm 3, 0)$, no y-intercept; lines of sym.: x-axis and y-axis; domain: $x \leq -3$ or $x \geq 3$, range: all real numbers

66. 1 **67.** 4 **68.** 25 **69.** 9

Lesson 10-3 pp. 630–636

Got It? 1. $(x - 5)^2 + (y + 2)^2 = 64$ **2. a.** $(x + 5)^2 + (y + 3)^2 = 1$ **b.** $(x - 2)^2 + (y - 3)^2 = 9$
3. a. $(x - 7)^2 + (y + 10)^2 = 144$ **b.** Yes; the values h and k determine the position of the circle and r determines the size. **4. a.** center $(-8, -3)$, radius 11
b. center $(3, -7)$, radius $\sqrt{66}$
5.

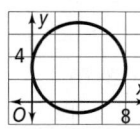

Lesson Check 1. $(x + 1)^2 + (y + 5)^2 = 4$
2. $x^2 + y^2 = 36$ **3.** $x^2 + (y - 3)^2 = 121$
4. $(x + 5)^2 + (y + 3)^2 = 16$ **5.** The circle with equation $(x + 7)^2 + (y - 7)^2 = 8$ is a translation of the circle with equation $x^2 + y^2 = 8$ as 7 units left and 7 units up, not right and down. **6.** If $P(x, y)$ is one of the pts. $(r, 0)$, $(-r, 0)$, $(0, r)$, or $(0, -r)$, subst. shows that $x^2 + y^2 = r^2$. If $P(x, y)$ is any other pt. on the circle, drop a perpendicular $\overline{PK}$ from P to K on the x-axis. $\triangle OPK$ is a rt. triangle with legs of lengths $|x|$ and $|y|$ and with hypotenuse of length r. By the Pythagorean Thm., $|x|^2 + |y|^2 = r^2$, so $x^2 + y^2 = r^2$.

Exercises 7. $x^2 + y^2 = 100$ **9.** $(x - 2)^2 + (y - 3)^2 = 20.25$ **11.** $(x - 1)^2 + (y + 3)^2 = 100$
13. $x^2 + (y + 1)^2 = 9$ **15.** $(x - 2)^2 + (y + 4)^2 = 25$
17. $x^2 + (y + 5)^2 = 100$
19.

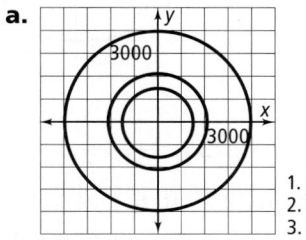

; $x^2 + y^2 = 144$, $x^2 + y^2 = 576$, $x^2 + y^2 = 1296$, $x^2 + y^2 = 2304$, $x^2 + y^2 = 3600$

21. $(x - 2)^2 + (y + 6)^2 = 16$ **23.** center $(-2, 10)$, radius 2 **25.** center $(-3, 5)$, radius 9 **27.** center $(-6, 0)$, radius 11
29.

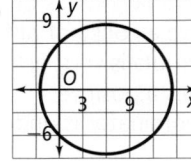

31.

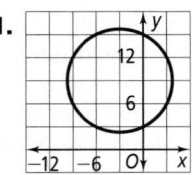

33.

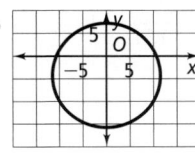

35. $x^2 + y^2 = 9$ **37.** $x^2 + y^2 = 3$ **39.** $x^2 + y^2 = 169$
41. $x^2 + y^2 = 26$ **43.** $x^2 + y^2 = 36$, $(x - 8)^2 + (y - 6)^2 = 16$, $(x - 8)^2 + (y)^2 = 4$ **45.** $(x + 6)^2 + (y - 13)^2 = 49$ **47.** $(x + 2)^2 + (y - 7.5)^2 = 2.25$
49. $(x - 2)^2 + (y - 1)^2 = 25$ **51.** $(x + 1)^2 + (y + 7)^2 = 36$ **53.** center $(0, 0)$, radius $\sqrt{2}$ **55.** center $(0, 0)$, radius $\sqrt{14}$ **57.** center $(-5, 0)$, radius $3\sqrt{2}$
59. center $(-3, 5)$, radius $\sqrt{38}$ **61.** center $(3, 1)$, radius $\sqrt{6}$

63.

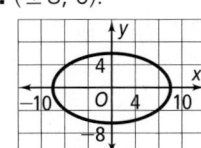

circle; $(x - 4)^2 + (y - 3)^2 = 16$

65. a.

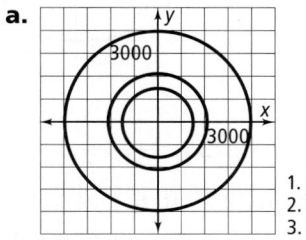

1. Mercury
2. Mars
3. Earth

b. Earth: $x^2 + y^2 = 15,705,369$
Mars: $x^2 + y^2 = 4,456,321$
Mercury: $x^2 + y^2 = 2,296,740$

Lesson 10-4 pp. 638–644

Got It? 1. $\dfrac{x^2}{4} + \dfrac{y^2}{25} = 1$
2. a. $(\pm 8, 0)$.

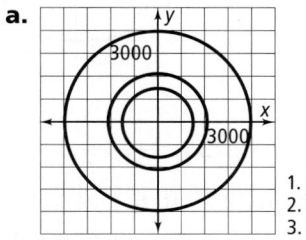

b. The vertex and co-vertex approach the same distance from the center of the ellipse; a circle
3. 24 ft **4.** $\dfrac{x^2}{36} + \dfrac{y^2}{53} = 1$

Lesson Check 1. $\dfrac{x^2}{64} + \dfrac{y^2}{36} = 1$ **2.** $(\pm \sqrt{21}, 0)$
3. $\dfrac{x^2}{169} + \dfrac{y^2}{25} = 1$ **4.** $6\sqrt{23}$ ft ≈ 28.77 ft **5.** The student used a and b instead of a^2 and b^2; $\dfrac{x^2}{1681} + \dfrac{y^2}{841} = 1$
6. The eq. of an ellipse with center at the origin is $\dfrac{x^2}{a^2} + \dfrac{y^2}{b^2} = 1$. For a circle, the major axis and the minor axis are of equal length such that $a = b = r$. Thus, by subst., $\dfrac{x^2}{r^2} + \dfrac{y^2}{r^2} = 1$ or $x^2 + y^2 = r^2$.

Exercises 7. $\frac{x^2}{16} + \frac{y^2}{9} = 1$ **9.** $\frac{x^2}{9} + y^2 = 1$

11. $\frac{x^2}{16} + \frac{y^2}{49} = 1$ **13.** $\frac{x^2}{81} + \frac{y^2}{4} = 1$

15. $(0, \pm\sqrt{5})$ **17.** $(\pm4\sqrt{2}, 0)$

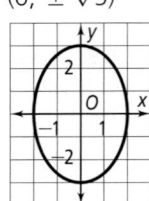 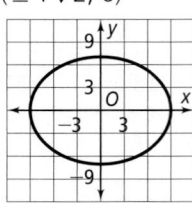

19. $(0, \pm6)$ **21.** $(\pm2\sqrt{3}, 0)$

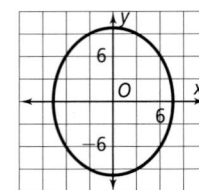 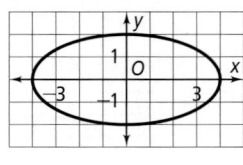

23. 32 **25.** 6 **27.** 12 **29.** $24\sqrt{2}$ **31.** $\frac{x^2}{100} + \frac{y^2}{64} = 1$

33. $\frac{x^2}{89} + \frac{y^2}{64} = 1$ **35. a.** about 22.25 ft **b.** Due to the reflective prop. of an ellipse, you can aim your putt at any part of the border. The ball will reflect off the border and go directly into the hole. **37.** $(0, \pm2\sqrt{3})$ **39.** $(0, \pm\sqrt{21})$ **41.** $(0, \pm1)$ **43. a.** 0.9 **b.** 0.1 **c.** The shape is close to a circle. **d.** The shape is close to a line segment.

45. $\frac{x^2}{16} + y^2 = 1$ **49.** $\frac{x^2}{25} + \frac{y^2}{4} = 1$

51. $\frac{x^2}{702.25} + \frac{y^2}{210.25} = 1$ **53.** $\frac{x^2}{256} + \frac{y^2}{324} = 1$

55. $\frac{x^2}{16} + \frac{y^2}{12} = 1$ **57.** $\frac{x^2}{36} + \frac{y^2}{27} = 1$ **59.** $\frac{x^2}{20} + \frac{y^2}{18} = 1$

61. a. 3×10^6 min **b.** about 0.016

c. $\frac{x^2}{8.649 \times 10^{15}} + \frac{y^2}{8.64675 \times 10^{15}} = 1$

Lesson 10-5   pp. 645–652

Got It? 1. a. $\frac{y^2}{16} - \frac{x^2}{9} = 1$

b. 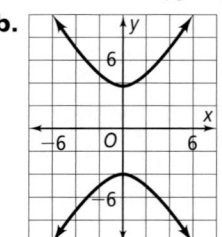   **c.** when $a = b$

2. vertices: $(\pm2, 0)$; foci: $(\pm\sqrt{13}, 0)$; asymptotes: $y = \pm\frac{3}{2}x$

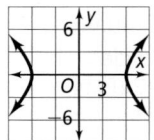

3. $\frac{x^2}{49} - \frac{y^2}{72} = 1$

Lesson Check

1. vertices: $(\pm6, 0)$; foci: $(\pm\sqrt{61}, 0)$; slopes of asymptotes: $\pm\frac{5}{6}$

2. vertices: $(0, \pm4)$; foci: $(0, \pm\sqrt{41})$; slopes of asymptotes: $\pm\frac{4}{5}$

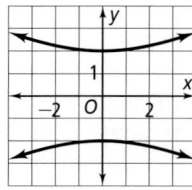 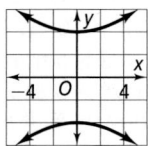

3. vertices: $(0, \pm2)$; foci: $(0, \pm2\sqrt{5})$; slopes of asymptotes: $\pm\frac{1}{2}$

4. vertices: $(\pm5, 0)$; foci: $(\pm\sqrt{41}, 0)$; slopes of asymptotes: $\pm\frac{4}{5}$

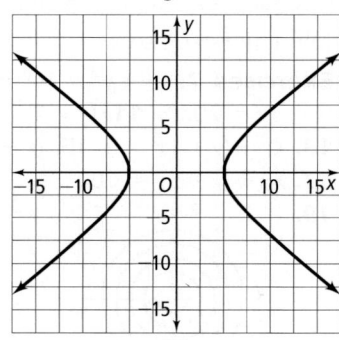

5. $\frac{x^2}{25} - \frac{y^2}{24} = 1$ **6.** Answers may vary. Sample: Similarities—Both have two axes of sym. that intersect at the center of the figure and two foci that lie on the same line as the two "principal" vertices. Differences— An ellipse consists of pts. whose distances from the foci have a constant sum, whereas a hyperbola consists of pts. whose distances from the foci have a constant diff. **7.** Answers may vary. Sample: A hyperbola is vert. or horizontal depending on whether it has a positive coefficient not because the larger denominator is under the y^2 term.

Exercises 9. $\frac{x^2}{144} - \frac{y^2}{25} = 1$ **11.** $\frac{x^2}{49} - \frac{y^2}{121} = 1$

13. $\frac{x^2}{4} - \frac{y^2}{5} = 1$

15. vertices: $(0, \pm 7)$; foci: $(0, \pm\sqrt{113})$; asymptotes: $y = \pm\frac{7}{8}x$

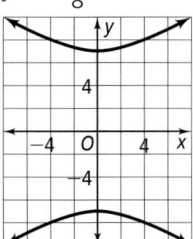

17. vertices: $(\pm 8, 0)$; foci: $(\pm 10, 0)$; asymptotes: $y = \pm\frac{3}{4}x$

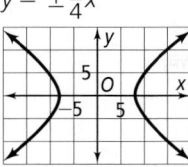

d. $y = x, y = -x$

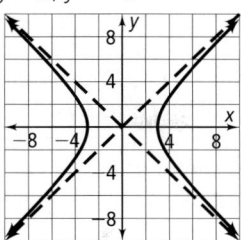

19. vertices: $(0, \pm 3)$; foci: $(0, \pm 3\sqrt{10})$; asymptotes: $y = \pm\frac{1}{3}x$

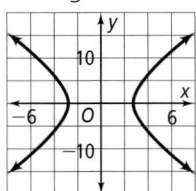

21. vertices: $(\pm 2\sqrt{2}, 0)$; foci: $(\pm 2\sqrt{11}, 0)$; asymptotes: $y = \pm\frac{3\sqrt{2}}{2}x$

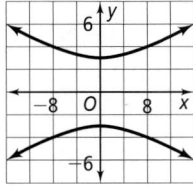

Lesson 10-6   **pp. 653–660**

Got It?

1. $\frac{(x-12)^2}{100} + \frac{(y-3)^2}{64} = 1$;

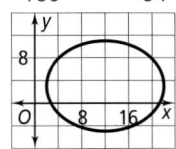

2. center $(2, -2)$; vertices: $(-4, -2), (8, -2)$; foci: $(-8, -2), (12, -2)$; asymptotes: $y + 2 = \pm\frac{4}{3}(x - 2)$

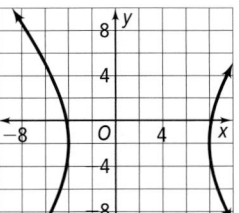

23. $x^2 - \frac{y^2}{6} = 1$ **25.** $\frac{x^2}{9} - \frac{y^2}{16} = 1$

27. $y^2 - \frac{x^2}{3} = 1$ **29.** $\frac{y^2}{20.25} - \frac{x^2}{4} = 1$

31. $\frac{x^2}{32} - \frac{y^2}{64} = 1$

33. $y = \pm\sqrt{x^2 - 1}$; $(\pm 1, 0)$ **35.**

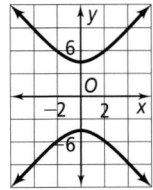

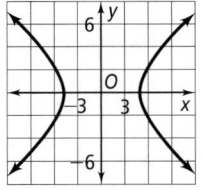

3. a. circle with center $(6, -2)$ and radius $4\sqrt{3}$

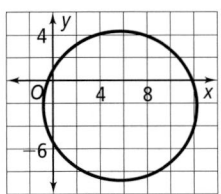

37.

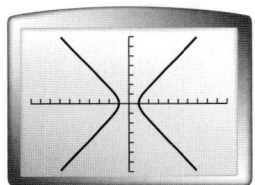

b. Replace $+y^2$ with $-y^2$ to get a new eq., $4x^2 - y^2 - 24x + 6y + 9 = 0$. The standard eq. of the hyperbola is $\frac{(x-3)^2}{4.5} - \frac{(y-3)^2}{18} = 1$.

4. $\frac{(x+1)^2}{9} + \frac{y^2}{8} = 1$

39. Answers may vary.

41. a. For the x-values in those rows, the value of $x^2 - 9$ is neg., so $\sqrt{x^2 - 9}$ is not a real number. **b.** As x increases, y increases, but the diff. between x and y gets closer to zero. **c.** No; for positive values of x greater than 3, $x = \sqrt{x^2}$ and $\sqrt{x^2} \neq \sqrt{x^2 - 9}$.

Lesson Check 1. center $(-7, -1)$; vertices: $(-22, -1)$, $(8, -1)$; foci: $(-16, -1), (2, -1)$ **2.** center $(1, 3)$; vertices: $(4, 3), (-2, 3)$; foci: $(1 \pm \sqrt{13}, 3)$ **3.** $\frac{x^2}{48} + \frac{(y-4)^2}{64} = 1$

4. $\dfrac{(y+1)^2}{49} - \dfrac{(x+3)^2}{51} = 1$ **5.** ellipse and hyperbola

6. Your friend used the center $(-2, 1)$ instead of $(2, -1)$. The vertices are $(-10, -1)$ and $(14, -1)$. **7.** The student didn't write the standard-form equation correctly. The standard-form equation is $(x+4)^2 + (y-5)^2 = 0$. This is an equation of a circle with center at $(-4, 5)$ and radius 0. Since the radius is 0, the graph is a single point, $(-4, 5)$.

Exercises

9. $\dfrac{(x-3)^2}{21} + \dfrac{(y+6)^2}{25} = 1$

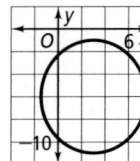

11. $\dfrac{(x-1.5)^2}{42.25} + \dfrac{(y-4)^2}{12} = 1$

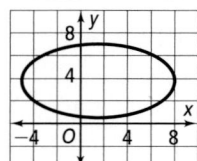

13. center: $(3, 4)$; vertices: $(3, 1)$, $(3, 7)$; foci: $(3, 4 \pm \sqrt{13})$

15. $y = (x-4)^2 + 3$; parabola; vertex: $(4, 3)$

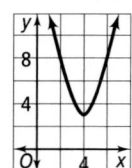

17. $(y-2)^2 - (x-3)^2 = 1$; hyperbola; center: $(3, 2)$, foci: $(3, 2 \pm \sqrt{2})$;

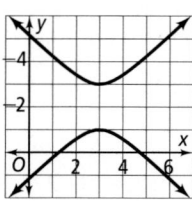

19. $x = \frac{1}{2}(y-2)^2 + 3$; parabola; vertex: $(3, 2)$

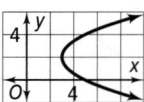

21. a. hyperbola **b.** one focus; the other focus

c. with the center at the origin, $x^2 - \dfrac{y^2}{3} = 1$

23. a. hyperbola **b.** horizontal line

25.

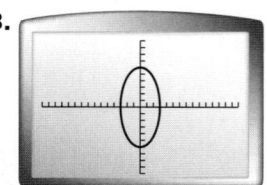

$\dfrac{(y+3)^2}{4} - \dfrac{(x-6)^2}{5} = 1$

27. $\dfrac{(x-1)^2}{9} + \dfrac{(y+1)^2}{16} = 1$ **29.** $x^2 + y^2 = 16$

31. $y = 2(x+2)^2 + 4$

33.

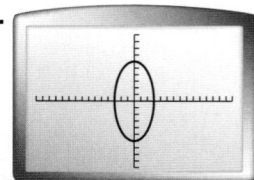

ellipse; $\dfrac{x^2}{9} + \dfrac{y^2}{36} = 1$

35.

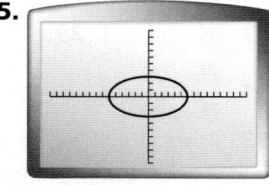

ellipse; $\dfrac{x^2}{36} + \dfrac{y^2}{9} = 1$

37. a. Earth: $\dfrac{x^2}{(149.60)^2} + \dfrac{y^2}{(149.58)^2} = 1$;

Mars: $\dfrac{x^2}{(227.9)^2} + \dfrac{y^2}{(226.9)^2} = 1$;

Mercury: $\dfrac{x^2}{(57.9)^2} + \dfrac{y^2}{(56.6)^2} = 1$

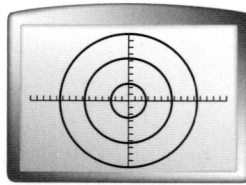

```
WINDOW FORMAT
Xmin = -379.0322...
Xmax = 379.03225...
Xscl = 25
Ymin = -250
Xmax = 250
Yscl = 25
```

b. Earth: $\frac{a}{b}$ is closest to 1 **39.** I **41.** Let a_1, a_2, and a_3 represent the missing terms in the arithmetic sequence: 15, a_1, a_2, a_3, 47. a_2 is the arithmetic mean of 15 and 47, so $a_2 = \frac{15+47}{2} = 31$. Likewise, $a_1 = \frac{15+a_2}{2} = \frac{15+31}{2} = 23$, and $a_3 = \frac{a_2+47}{2} = \frac{31+47}{2} = 39$. The missing terms are 23, 31, and 39.

42. foci: $(\pm\sqrt{85}, 0)$ **43.** foci: $(0, \pm\sqrt{21})$

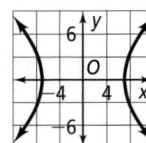 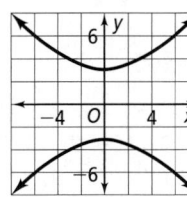

44. 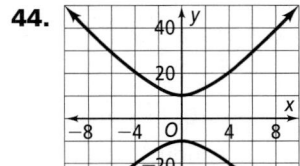 foci: $(0, \pm 2\sqrt{26})$

45. $\dfrac{3\pm\sqrt{17}}{2}$ **46.** 5 **47.** $\dfrac{9\pm\sqrt{201}}{12}$ **48.** 1 **49.** 2 **50.** 3 **51.** 8 **52.** -19 **53.** 6

Chapter Review   pp. 663–666

1. directrix **2.** major axis **3.** standard form of an eq. of a circle **4.** radius **5.** transverse axis

6. 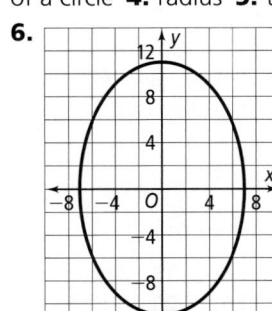 ellipse; lines of sym.: x-axis and y-axis; domain: $-7 \le x \le 7$, range: $-11 \le y \le 11$

7. 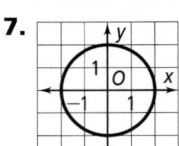 circle; lines of sym.: every line through the center; domain: $-2 \le x \le 2$, range: $-2 \le y \le 2$

8. 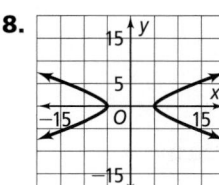 hyperbola; lines of sym.: x-axis and y-axis; domain: $x \le -5$ or $x \ge 5$, range: all real numbers

9. 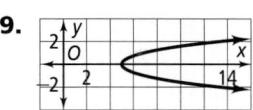 parabola; line of sym.: x-axis; domain: $x \ge 5$, range: all real numbers

10. center $(0, 0)$; domain: $x \le -4$ or $x \ge 4$, range: all real numbers **11.** center $(0, 0)$; domain: $-3 \le x \le 3$, range: $-2 \le y \le 2$ **12.** $x = \frac{1}{20}y^2$ **13.** $y = -\frac{1}{20}x^2$

14. $y = \frac{1}{24}x^2$ **15.** $y = \frac{1}{10}x^2$ **16.** $y = 3x^2$

17. $y = \frac{1}{8}x^2 + 1$ **18.** $x = -\frac{1}{12}y^2 + 1$

19. focus: $\left(0, \frac{1}{20}\right)$, directrix: $y = -\frac{1}{20}$

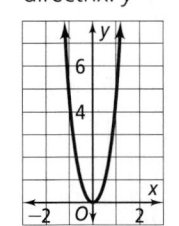

20. focus: $\left(\frac{1}{8}, 0\right)$, directrix: $x = -\frac{1}{8}$

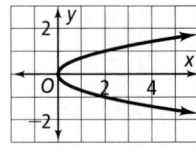

21. focus: $(-2, 0)$, directrix: $x = 2$

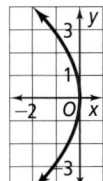

22. $x^2 + y^2 = 16$ **23.** $(x-8)^2 + (y-1)^2 = 25$
24. $(x+3)^2 + (y-2)^2 = 100$
25. $(x-5)^2 + (y+3)^2 = 64$
26. center $(1, 0)$, radius 8

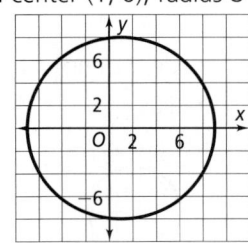

circle with radius 8 translated 1 unit to the rt.

27. center $(-7, -3)$, radius 7

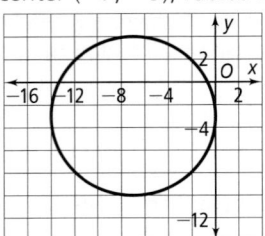

circle with radius 7 translated 7 units to the left and 3 units down

28. $\frac{x^2}{17} + \frac{y^2}{16} = 1$ **29.** $\frac{x^2}{25} + \frac{y^2}{29} = 1$ **30.** $\frac{x^2}{9} + \frac{y^2}{10} = 1$

31. $\frac{x^2}{40} + \frac{y^2}{36} = 1$ **32.** $\frac{x^2}{64} + \frac{y^2}{16} = 1$

33. foci: $(0, \pm\sqrt{5})$ **34.** foci: $(\pm 3\sqrt{29}, 0)$

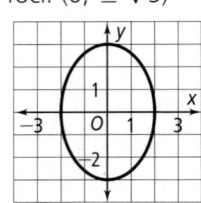   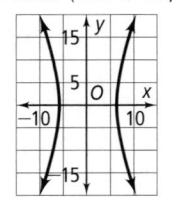

35. foci: $(0, \pm\sqrt{569})$ **36.** foci: $(\pm\sqrt{202}, 0)$

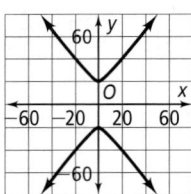   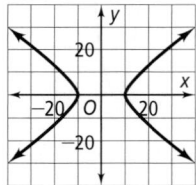

37. $\frac{x^2}{64} - \frac{y^2}{225} = 1$ **38.** $\frac{y^2}{49} - \frac{x^2}{576} = 1$

39. $\frac{x^2}{1.148 \times 10^{10}} - \frac{y^2}{3.395 \times 10^{10}} = 1$

40. $(x - 1)^2 + (y - 1)^2 = 25$

41. $\frac{(x-3)^2}{4} + \frac{(y+2)^2}{9} = 1$

42. $\frac{(x-6)^2}{9} - \frac{(y-3)^2}{16} = 1$

43. hyperbola; center $(0, -2)$, foci: $(0, -2 \pm 2\sqrt{10})$ **44.** circle; center $\left(-\frac{3}{2}, 2\right)$, radius $\frac{\sqrt{61}}{2}$

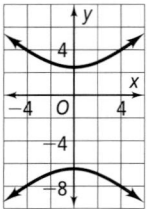   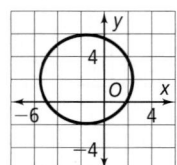

45. parabola; vertex: $\left(-\frac{1}{2}, -\frac{169}{4}\right)$

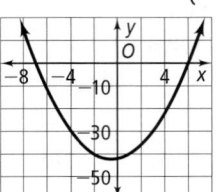

Chapter 11

Get Ready!   p. 671

1. $83.\overline{3}\%$ **2.** $19.\overline{4}\%$ **3.** $\approx 92.308\%$ **4.** 30.56%
5. 6720 **6.** 22,100 **7.** 10 **8.** $a^5 + 5a^4b + 10a^3b^2 + 10a^2b^3 + 5ab^4 + b^5$ **9.** $j^3 + 9j^2k + 27jk^2 + 27k^3$
10. $m^2 + 1.4m + 0.49$ **11.** $16 + 32t + 24t^2 + 8t^3 + t^4$ **12.** $m^2 + 2mn + n^2$ **13.** $x^4 + 12x^3y + 54x^2y^2 + 108xy^3 + 81y^4$ **14.** $\pm\frac{1}{10}$ **15.** $\pm\frac{1}{20}$
16. $\pm\frac{1}{14}$ **17.** $\pm\frac{1}{2}$ **18.** $\pm\frac{1}{3}$ **19.** $\pm\frac{1}{24}$ **20.** In a math class, when actual trials are difficult to conduct, you can find experimental probability by using a simulation which is a model of one or more events. **21.** It rained today. **22.** The mean, $12.\overline{6}$; the data are fairly evenly distributed around the mean which makes the mean the best representation of the data given.

Lesson 11-1   pp. 674–680

Got It? 1. 6,760,000 **2.** 40,320 **3a.** 2730 **b.** Yes; because $n = 10$ and $r = 3$ in the formula $_nP_r$ for both cases. **4a.** 56 **b.** 36 **c.** 3003 **5.** 1680
Lesson Check 1. 120 **2.** 3024 **3.** 10 **4.** 21
5. 4,151,347,200 **6.** A permutation is an arrangement of items in a particular order; order is important. An arrangement in which order does not matter is a combination. **7.** $_nP_r = \frac{n!}{(n-r)!}$; substituting $n = r$, we get $_nP_n = \frac{n!}{(n-n)!} = \frac{n!}{0!}$; but $_nP_n = n! = \frac{n!}{1}$; substituting values again, we get $\frac{n!}{1} = \frac{n!}{(n-n)!}$, and so $0! = 1$.

Exercises 9. 20 **11.** 12 **13.** 3,628,800 **15.** 720
17. 120 **19.** 3003 **21.** 8 **23.** 336 **25.** 6 **27.** 60,480
29. 10,897,286,400 **31.** 56 **33.** 4 **35.** 15 **37.** $\frac{5}{18}$
39. combination; 4368 **41.** combination; 70
43. True because of the Assoc. Prop. of Mult.
45. False; answers may vary. Sample: $(3 \cdot 2)! = 6! = 720$ and $3! \cdot 2! = 6 \cdot 2 = 12$
47. False; answers may vary. Sample: $(3!)^2 = 6^2 = 36$ and $3^{(2!)} = 3^2 = 9$ **49.** C **51.** Two ways, because order matters. **53a.** 2 **b.** 6

c. $(n-1)!$ **55. a.** 35 **b.** 6 **c.** $_7C_3 = \frac{7!}{3!4!}$,
so $_7C_3 \cdot 3! = \frac{7!}{4!}$, which is the permutation formula for
$_7P_3$. **57.** H **59.** G **61.** center: (2, 1); vertices: (2, 6),
(2, −4); co-vertices: (5, 1), (−1, 1); foci: (2, 5), (2, −3)
62. $(x-1)^2 + (y-1)^2 = 36$ is a circle (not an ellipse)
with center (1, 1) and radius 6. **63.** $4(x-1)^2$
64. $-(x+3)^2$ **65.** $3(x-5)(x+5)$ **66.** 30,240
67. $\frac{4}{5}$ **68.** 210

Lesson 11-2   pp. 681–687

Got It? 1. 0.40 or 40% **2.** 0.20 or 20% **3a.** $\frac{1}{2}$ **b.** The
likelihood of getting an even or odd is the same, i.e. $\frac{1}{2}$.
4. $\frac{48}{2,598,960}$ or 0.0000184689 or $\approx 0.00185\%$
5. 0.05 or 5%
Lesson Check 1. 0.75 or 75% **2.** 0.80 or 80%
3. $\frac{1}{6}$ **4.** $\frac{1}{3}$ **5.** Experimental probabilities are calculated on
the basis of data from an experiment, actual or
simulated. Given equally likely outcomes, the basis for
calculating theoretical probability is being able to
determine the no. of ways that an event can occur
within these outcomes. Comparisons of measures such
as length and area are the basis of geometric
probability. **6.** Answers may vary. Samples: Flip a coin;
generate random numbers on a calculator; roll a die with
odd numbers as true and even numbers as false.
7. Because you are averaging over more samples, you
are getting a more accurate average.
Exercises 9. the number 1: $\frac{21}{134} \approx 15.7\%$; the number
2: $\frac{11}{67} \approx 16.4\%$; the number 3: $\frac{45}{268} \approx 16.8\%$; the
number 4: $\frac{11}{67} \approx 16.4\%$; the number 5: $\frac{47}{268} \approx 17.5\%$; the
number 6: $\frac{23}{134} \approx 17.2\%$ **11.** Answers may vary. Sample:
Toss 5 coins. Keep a tally of the times three or more heads
are tossed. (A head represents a correct answer.) Do this
100 times. The total number of tally marks, as a percent,
gives the experimental probability. The simulated
probability should be about 50%. **13.** $\frac{3}{10}$, or 30%
15. $\frac{4}{5}$, or 80% **17.** $\frac{48}{125}$, or 38.4%
19. $\frac{103}{125}$, or 82.4%
21. $\frac{77}{125}$, or 61.6% **23.** $\frac{_{30}C_3 \cdot {}_{120}C_6}{_{150}C_9} \approx 0.17879 \approx 17.9\%$
25. $\frac{5}{8}$, or 62.5% **27.** $\frac{3}{4}$, or 75% **29.** $\frac{116}{147} \approx 78.9\%$
31. $\frac{43}{147} \approx 29.3\%$ **33.** 1 chance in 2,869,685 or
$\approx 0.00003485\%$ **35.** if there are any restrictions on the
last digit of a ZIP code

Lesson 11-3   pp. 688–693

Got It? 1. Independent; the number of coins is the same
after the coin is replaced. **2.** 0.20, or 20% **3a.** Not
mutually exclusive; 2 is a prime number and an even
number. **b.** Mutually exclusive; there is no even number
less than 2 in the roll of a number cube. **4a.** 0.61, or
61% **b.** Yes; the percentage of students tells which
language is chosen by more students. **5a.** $\frac{5}{9}$ **b.** $\frac{5}{9}$

Lesson Check 1. $\frac{1}{15}$, or $6.\overline{6}\%$ **2.** $\frac{27}{80}$, or 33.75%
3. 1, or 100% **4.** $\frac{7}{8}$, or 87.5% **5.** $\frac{5}{8}$, or 62.5%
6. Events A and B are independent if the outcomes of A
do not affect the outcomes of B. The events are mutually
exclusive if A and B cannot occur at the same time. For
independent events, $P(A \text{ and } B) = P(A) \cdot P(B)$. For
mutually exclusive events, $P(A \text{ and } B) = 0$. For any events,
$P(A \text{ or } B) = P(A) + P(B) - P(A \text{ and } B)$. **7.** Since these are
not mutually exclusive events, $P(A \text{ and } B) \neq 0$. The
student should have multiplied to get the correct answer,
which is 0.21 or 21%.
Exercises 9. independent **11.** dependent **13.** $\frac{1}{6}$
15. 0.54 **17.** $\frac{9}{25}$ **19.** mutually exclusive; if the numbers
are equal, then the sum is even **21.** $\frac{3}{4}$ **23.** 39% **25.** $\frac{1}{2}$
27. $\frac{5}{6}$ **29.** $\frac{2}{3}$ **31.** $\frac{2}{5}$ **33.** 14.5% **35.** 87.4% **37.** $\frac{4}{15}$
39. $\frac{8}{15}$ **41.** not mutually exclusive **43.** $\frac{4}{9}$ **45.** $\frac{8}{11}$ **47.** 8
49. 5 **51.** $\frac{1}{6}$ **52.** $\frac{1}{2}$ **53.** $\frac{1}{2}$ **54.** $\frac{3}{7}$ **55.** $-\frac{3}{2}$, 2 **56.** $\frac{1}{6}$
57. $\frac{1}{2}e^3 \approx 10.04$ **58.** $\frac{1}{2}e^6 \approx 201.71$ **59.** $\pm e^2 \approx \pm 7.39$
60. $\frac{1}{16}$ **61.** $\frac{1}{16}$ **62.** $\frac{3}{16}$

Lesson 11-4   pp. 696–702

Got It? 1a. ≈ 0.57355 or $\approx 57.355\%$ **b.** Female; there
are more females enrolled. **2a.** ≈ 0.026448 or $\approx 2.64\%$
b. ≈ 0.040302 or $\approx 4.03\%$ **3.** 0.2 **4.** 9%

Lesson Check 1. $\frac{1}{2}$ **2.** $\frac{1}{13}$, or 7.7% **3.** 0% **4.** 50%
5. The sum of the probability of an event happening and
the probability of an event not happening is 1. Each branch
represents either the event happening or the event not
happening. **7.** Answers may vary. Sample: You can use
both to determine the number of ways a sequence of
events can occur. A tree diagram can represent all
outcomes for a given situation. If there are many branches,
it may be easier to use the Fundamental Counting Principle
to find the number of outcomes.
Exercises 9. 0.6 **11.** ≈ 0.085 **13.** ≈ 0.682
15. ≈ 0.709 **17.** $\approx 23\%$

19.

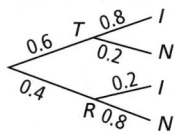

M = male
F = female
R = right-handed
L = left-handed

$P(L|F) = 10\%$, $P(M \text{ and } R) \approx 11.4\%$

21. 75% **23.** $P(S \text{ and } W)$ **25.** $\frac{2}{3}$, or 66.67%

27. 0.08, or 8% **29.** 0.84 **31.** 0.16

33.

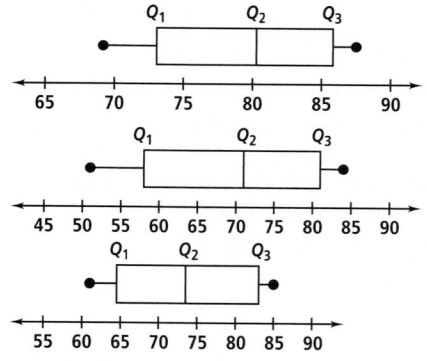

T = representative that completed training seminars
R = representative that didn't complete a training seminar
I = representative with increased sales
N = representative without increased sales

$P(I|N) = 0.2$

Lesson 11-5   pp. 703–709

Got It? 1. Answers may vary. Sample answer: No, it is not likely that both siblings have an equal chance of winning the race. **2. a.** 1, 6, 8, 9, 3 **b.** Yes, each student has an equal chance of being selected for either team. **3.** Answers may vary. Sample answer: Roll the cube until you get a 6. Keep track of the results. Repeat several times and take the average number of rolls needed. **4.** Answers may vary. Sample answer: No, almost as many volunteers who received the placebo reported improvement as received the drug. Fewer than half of those who received the drug reported improvement.

Lesson Check 1. about 0.89 **2.** about 0.86 **3.** Answers may vary. Sample answer: Flipping a coin to decide who has to wash the dishes is a fair decision. Arm wrestling to see who has to wash the dishes might be unfair if one brother is stronger than the other. **4.** Answers may vary. Sample answer: He only conducted 1 trial of the simulation, which is not enough to arrive at an accurate prediction. He should conduct the simulation at least 25 times and find the average number of boxes needed. **5.** Answers may vary. Sample answer: A simulation is an imitation or way of acting something out. In a mathematical simulation, a probability model is used to act out a situation that would be difficult or impractical to actually perform.

Exercises 7. Answers may vary. Sample answer: This will not result in a fair decision because the first person chooses the second person and might favor someone over someone else. **9.** 01, 05, 16, 03, 08 **11. a.** about 0.82 **b.** about 0.35 **c.** Sample answer: Yes, a high percentage of students who took the class passed the board exams on their first attempt so the class appears to be

beneficial. **13.** 28 trials; about 1.14 correct answers per trial **15.** Answers may vary. Sample answer: Yes, the defensive driving course appears to be very effective and should be offered again. None of the drivers who took the course were involved in a major accident in the previous year. **17.** Answers may vary. Sample answer: Use a graphing calculator to generate random integers from 1 to 5. Let the integers 1, 2, 3, and 4 represent a made field goal, and let 5 represent a missed field goal. Generate random integers in groups of 3 to simulate the attempts in the next game. Perform the simulation at least 20 or 25 times and find the average number of field goals made. **19.** A **21.** C **23.** 0.35 **24.** 0.52 **25.** 0.7 **26.** 18

Lesson 11-6   pp. 711–718

Got It? 1. mean: 5.25, median: 5, mode: 5 **2a.** Yes; it is unlikely that the water temperature of a lake would change by 25 degrees. **b.** No; 98 would represent the busiest night of the week and it may relate to a weekly event. **3.** Dauphin Island: mean: $69.08\overline{3}$, mode: 84, range: 33, $Q_1 = 58$, median: 71, $Q_3 = 81$, interquartile range: 23; Grand Isle: mean: $73.41\overline{6}$, modes: 61, 70, 77, 83, 85, range: 24, $Q_1 = 64.5$, median: 73.5, $Q_3 = 83$, interquartile range: 18.5; The range and the interquartile range show the temperatures varying less at Grand Isle than at Dauphin Island. Also, the temperatures at Grand Isle are generally higher. **4a.** Use STAT PLOT, select a box-and-whisker plot. Enter data for the three remaining Gulf Coast sites. Enter the window values. Draw the box-and-whisker plots. Use TRACE on the plot to find quartiles Q_1, Q_2 and Q_3.

b. Yes, a box-and-whisker plot uses minimum and maximum values, the median, and the first and third quartiles to display the variability in a data set. **5a.** 79 **b.** 98

Lesson Check 1. outlier: 54; outlier included: mean: 22.8, median: 19.5, mode: 18; outlier not included: mean: $19.\overline{3}$, median: 19, mode: 18 **2.** outlier: 40; outlier included: mean: $92.\overline{6}$, median: 98, mode: 90; outlier not included: mean: 99.25, median: 99, mode: 90 **3.** the mean because the sum of the data values is affected and

the mean depends on the sum **4.** 40%: 49 and below; 80%: 58 and below **5.** the mean; when data are somewhat sym, the best representation is the mean **6.** The error is in how to calculate the median. The median is the middle value or the 11th value which is 90.
Exercises 7. mean: 112.$\overline{3}$, median: 95, mode: none
9. 9.8 **11.** Jacksonville: mean: 67.991$\overline{6}$, mode: none, range: 29.2, $Q_1 = 58.15$, median: 68.4, $Q_3 = 78.6$, interquartile range: 20.45; Austin: mean: 68.58$\overline{3}$, mode: none, range: 36, $Q_1 = 56.85$, median: 70.5, $Q_3 = 80.75$, interquartile range: 23.9; the range and the interquartile range show the temperatures varying less at Jacksonville than at Austin.

13.

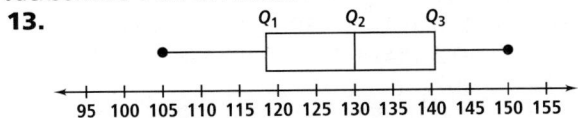

95 100 105 110 115 120 125 130 135 140 145 150 155

15. 5; 17 **17.** outlier: 381; outlier included: mean: ≈ 161.214, median: 158, mode: none; outlier not included: mean: ≈ 144.308, median: 142, mode: none

19.

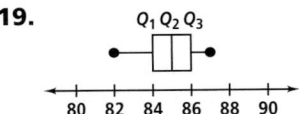

80   82   84   86   88   90

21. 30th **23.** 89 is at the 100th percentile, since 100% of the values are less than or equal to 89. **25.** The median; a few outliers can heavily influence the mean without drastically affecting the median. **27.** 83.9
29. Answers may vary. Sample: The range for women's shot put is greater than that for men's. The men are more consistent, as indicated by the shorter box and whiskers. Overall the men tend to throw farther. **31.** G

33. $P(H|I) = 0.40$, $P(H \text{ and } I) = 0.20$

$$P(H|I) = \frac{P(H \text{ and } I)}{P(I)}$$

$$0.40 = \frac{0.20}{P(I)}$$

$$P(I) = 0.50$$

34. 0.20 **35.** 0.56 **36.** yes; −9 **37.** yes; 17 **38.** no
39. yes; 0 **40.** ± 16 **41.** ± 0.09 **42.** ± $\frac{11}{4}$ **43.** ± $\frac{19}{5}$

Lesson 11-7   pp. 719–724

Got It? 1. $\bar{x} = 69.8\overline{3}$, $\sigma^2 = 115.1389$, $\sigma = 10.7303$
2. $\bar{x} = 7.2\overline{6}$, $\sigma = 3.316$ **3a.** within 3 standard deviations of the mean **b.** FEMA can expect that the no. of hurricanes for a 15-year period will fall within 3 standard deviations of the mean.
Lesson Check 1. $\bar{x} = 10$, $\sigma^2 = 19.8$, $\sigma = 4.45$
2. within 2 standard deviations of the mean **3.** Measures of central tendency are specific data pts. which give a summary of the middle of the data set, whereas the measures of variation give a summary of the variation of

the data set within the range of distribution. **4.** Standard deviation measures how widely spread the data values are. If the data pts. are close to the mean, the standard deviation is small; if the data pts. are far from the mean, the standard deviation is large. The data pts. of Set B are closer to the mean of 70 than the data pts. of Sets A and C; likewise, the data pts. of Set A are closer to 70 than the data pts. of Set C. **5.** The effect of an outlier on the standard deviation is to increase the standard deviation.
Exercises 7. $\bar{x} \approx 15.1$, $\sigma^2 \approx 12.4$, $\sigma \approx 3.5$
9. $\bar{x} = 43.8$, $\sigma^2 = 75.76$, $\sigma \approx 8.7$ **11.** $\bar{x} \approx 12320.00$, $\sigma \approx 273.71$ **13.** 3 standard deviations **15.** $\bar{x} = 53.8$, $\sigma \approx 3.4$; 1σ: 7; 2σ: 9; 3σ: 10 **17.** Overall farm income increased slightly, but there was less variability among the states in 2002. The income in 2001 clustered more tightly around the mean. (2001: $\sigma_x \approx 2679$, 2002: $\sigma_x \approx 2758$)
21. Your first friend; one standard deviation encompasses all values within one standard deviation above and below the mean. The graph shows that all values are within 3 standard deviations of the mean. **23. a.** no change to σ
b. σ increases by a factor of 10 **25.** 13 **27.** $\frac{5}{6}$

28.

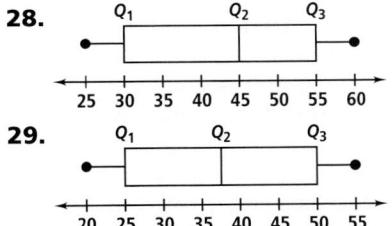

25   30   35   40   45   50   55   60

29.

Q_1 Q_2 Q_3

20   25   30   35   40   45   50   55

30. center (2, −1); radius 6 **31.** center (1, 1); radius 2
32. $\frac{1}{2}$ **33.** $-\frac{1}{3}$ **34.** $\frac{1}{6}$ **35.** $-\frac{1}{11}$ **36.** $-\frac{1}{9}$ **37.** $\frac{1}{7}$

Lesson 11-8   pp. 725–730

Got It? 1a. convenience sample; yes; since the location is at the food court in the mall, the sample may over-represent food court or fast food supporters. **b.** Answers may vary. Sample: population data for the US census
2. Controlled study; If other factors of the volunteers are random, like age, gender, and overall health, are known, the results can be used to make a general conclusion.
3. Answers may vary. Sample: Use a systematic sample. Go to every fifth house in your neighborhood. State the first and last names of the governor and ask a household member to identify the named person. A possible unbiased survey question is, "Who is this person?".
Lesson Check 1a. convenience sample **b.** Yes; since the location is near the exit of a history museum, the sample may over represent people who enjoy learning history and the results will have a bias. **2.** Yes; the question is leading and loaded. It suggests the person wants a particular answer. **3.** All members of the set are the population. A sample is a subset of the population.

Answers may vary. Sample: population: students in a high school; sample: students who like to snowboard
4. It is important to have as little error as poss. in a sample, thus giving an unbiased sample. An unbiased sample is more representative of an entire population.
5. A large sample size would give a better estimate. The size of the sample is important to the reliability of the sample.
Exercises 7. systematic sampling; no bias **9.** Survey; the statistics can be used to make a general conclusion about the population because the sample is randomly generated, and the survey question does not introduce a bias into the study. **11.** Controlled experiment; the statistics from this study can be used to make a general conclusion about the effectiveness of the plant food for this particular plant type as compared with giving no plant food at all. **13.** Answers may vary. Sample: Convenience sampling; interview students at a local high school.
15. Answers may vary. Sample: Self-selected sampling; a newspaper article invites females over the age of 21 to call the paper and express their opinions.
17. self-selected sampling; biased because only those who spend time online will respond. **19. a.** all students at the school **b.** every tenth student who enters the school building the day of the survey **c.** Answers may vary. Sample: A little over half of students favor the new dress code.
21. Answers will vary. Sample: No, because you would have to assume that all registered voters will actually vote on Election Day. **23. a.** convenience sample
b. observational study **c.** Answers may vary. Sample: The statistics do not necessarily represent the school population because a random sample was not used to conduct the study. **25.** Yes, the question is leading the respondent to a particular desired answer, and it gives statistics that may elicit a strong reaction. Also, it requires the respondent to answer a question about whether a person *should* wear a safety belt, which may not necessarily influence whether they support the law.
27. G **29.** $\bar{x} \approx 2.83$, $\sigma \approx 2.54$ **30.** $\bar{x} \approx 5.62$, $\sigma \approx 3.67$
31. $y = \frac{1}{2}(x - 5)$; yes **32.** $y = \pm\sqrt{x}$; no
33. $y = \pm\sqrt{\frac{9x}{5}}$; no **34.** $y = \frac{x^2}{9}$, $x \geq 0$; yes **35.** 6
36. 1 **37.** 10 **38.** 792

Lesson 11-9   pp. 731–738

Got It?
1. $P(0) = 0.07776$; $P(1) = 0.2592$; $P(2) = 0.3456$; $P(3) = 0.2304$; $P(5) = 0.01024$
2. $81x^4 + 108x^3y + 54x^2y^2 + 12xy^3 + y^4$
3. ≈ 0.1035, or about 10.4%
Lesson Check 1. ≈ 0.3110, or $\approx 31.10\%$
2. ≈ 0.1641, or $\approx 16.41\%$ **3.** $20c^3d^3$ **4.** $-10x^4y$

5. 0.2646, or 26.46% **6.** Answers may vary. Sample: A binomial experiment has three important features: **a.** The situation involves repeated trials; flipping a coin 10 times has 10 trials. **b.** Each trial has two possible outcomes; in this case, heads or tails. **c.** The probability of success is constant throughout the trials; the trials of flipping a coin, are independent. **7.** The student wrote "5" instead of "4". It should be: $_nC_{(5-1)}a^{n-4}b^4 = {_7C_4}j^3(-k)^4 = 35j^3k^4$

Exercises 9. ≈ 0.1361, or $\approx 13.61\%$
11. ≈ 0.0015, or $\approx 0.15\%$
13. $a^4 + 4a^3b + 6a^2b^2 + 4ab^3 + b^4$
15. $243x^5 + 810x^4y + 1080x^3y^2 + 720x^2y^3 + 240xy^4 + 32y^5$ **17.** $896g^6h$ **19.** e^6
21. $P(0) \approx 0.1176$, $P(1) \approx 0.3025$, $P(2) \approx 0.3241$, $P(3) \approx 0.1852$, $P(4) \approx 0.0595$, $P(5) \approx 0.0102$, $P(6) \approx 0.0007$
23. $P(0) \approx 0.000001$, $P(1) \approx 0.000054$, $P(2) \approx 0.0012$, $P(3) \approx 0.0146$, $P(4) \approx 0.0984$, $P(5) \approx 0.3543$, $P(6) \approx 0.5314$
25. 0.99328 **27.** ≈ 0.2824 **29.** ≈ 0.1109
31. ≈ 0.2461 **33.** ≈ 0.6230 **35a.** 0.0914 **b.** The probability that three boxes would be underweight is 0.0001. You can conclude that there might be a malfunction in the machinery or that the company's claim may be false. **37.** The probability of a group of 30 students having 4 or fewer left-handed students is about 77.05%. This means that more than three quarters of the classes will have enough left-handed desks; 4 is an adequate no.
39a. $P(0) = 0.001$, $P(1) = 0.027$, $P(2) = 0.243$, $P(3) = 0.729$

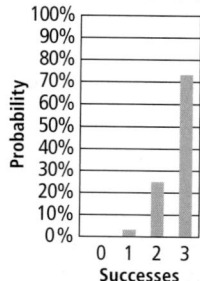

b. $P(0) = 0.166375$, $P(1) = 0.408375$, $P(2) = 0.334125$, $P(3) = 0.091125$

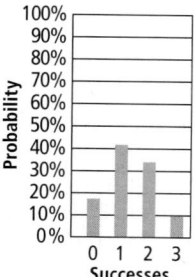

c. The probabilities of each graph sum to 1; $P(0) + P(1) + P(2) + P(3) = 1$. The probabilities of part (a) increase with increasing success numbers; the maximum probability occurring at $P(3)$. The probabilities of part (b) peak with a maximum at $P(1)$ and then decrease with increasing success numbers. **41.** Answers may vary.

43. a. The graph is sym. about the line $x = 3.5$.

b.

x	y
0	0.0078
1	0.0547
2	0.1641
3	0.2734
4	0.2734
5	0.1641
6	0.0547
7	0.0078

c. No; the bulge in the graph has shifted rt.

Lesson 11-10   pp. 739–745

Got It? 1a. 71%   **b.** 88%

2.

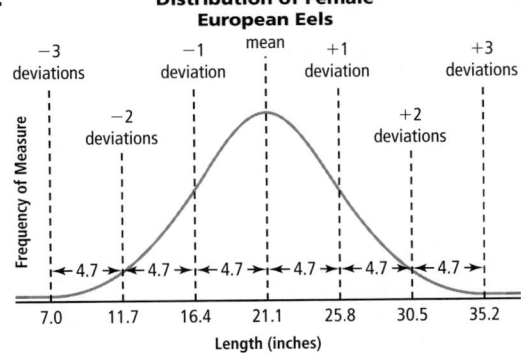

Distribution of Female European Eels

3a. 2.5%   **b.** 210 students   **c.** The students that received a B had scores between 165 and 180.

Lesson Check 1. 94%

2.

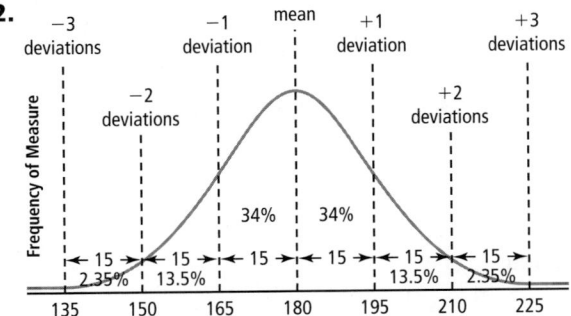

3. 47.5%   **4.** Normal distribution means that most of the examples in a data set are close to the mean; the distribution of the data is within 1, 2, or 3 standard deviations of the mean. **5.** The mean and median are equivalent in a normal distribution. **6.** mean increases by 10: the bell curve is translated 10 units to the rt.; standard deviation and shape of the distribution do not change since each data value increases by the same amount.

Exercises 7. ≈43%   **9.** ≈43 men

11.

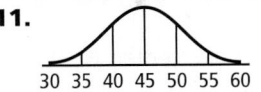

30 35 40 45 50 55 60

13.

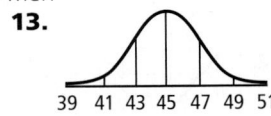

39 41 43 45 47 49 51

15. 68%   **17.** 50%   **19a.** Set 2

b. and c.

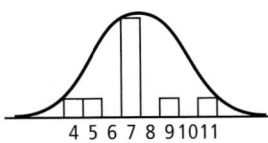

4 5 6 7 8 9 10 11

21. 59 min   **23.** 47.5%   **25.** 81.5%   **27.** 84%

29a.

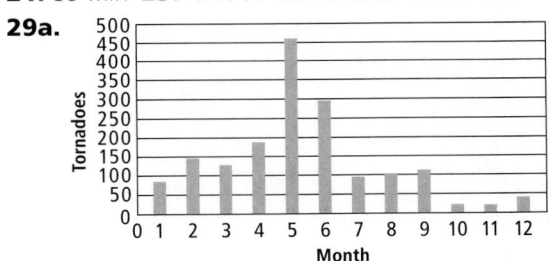

b. No; the curve is skewed to the left. **c.** No, mean and standard deviation are appropriate only for measuring normally distributed data. **31.** Yes; Elena scored within the top 10% of her group. Her score is 2.75 standard deviations above the mean, which places her in the top 1%. Jake did not score in the top 10%. His score is 1.16 standard deviations above the mean, or at the 88th percentile. **33.** A binomial distribution has a finite no. of probabilities, which sum to 1 and are a subset of a larger normal distribution. For example, using $n = 6$, $p = 0.5$, the binomial distribution probabilities are $P(0) \approx 0.0156$, $P(1) \approx 0.0938$, $P(2) \approx 0.2344$, $P(3) \approx 0.3125$, $P(4) \approx 0.2344$, $P(5) \approx 0.0938$, $P(6) \approx 0.0156$.

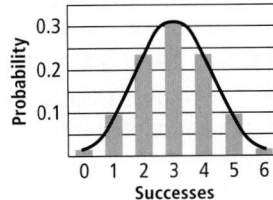

35. | 37. For Distribution A with 50 data values, 25 values are at or below 40, which is the mean. For Distribution B with 30 data values, 15 values are at or below the mean 40. So Distribution A has more values at or below 40. **38.** 0.02867 **39.** 0.1612 **40.** 0.03676

41.

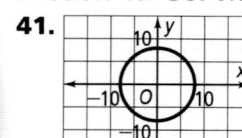

circle; center: (0, 0), radius: 8; lines of sym.: all lines through the center; domain: $-8 \le x \le 8$, range: $-8 \le y \le 8$

42.

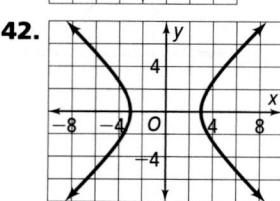

hyperbola; center: (0, 0), foci: $(\pm 3\sqrt{2}, 0)$; lines of sym.: $x = 0$, $y = 0$; domain: $x \le -3$ or $x \ge 3$; range: all real numbers

43.

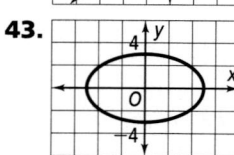

ellipse; center: (0, 0), foci: $(\pm 4, 0)$; lines of sym.: $x = 0$, $y = 0$; domain: $-5 \le x \le 5$, range: $-3 \le y \le 3$

44. $y = x - 3$;

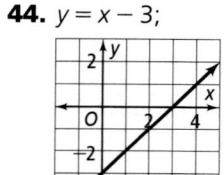

45. $y = x$;

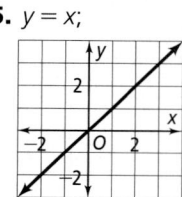

46. $y = x - \frac{5}{4}$;

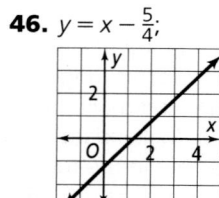

Chapter Review   pp. 751–756

1. sample **2.** outlier **3.** probability distribution **4.** range of a set of data **5.** 6 **6.** 362,880 **7.** 12 **8.** 30 **9.** 21 **10.** 10 **11.** 30 **12.** 744 **13.** 220; 84; 20; 1 **14.** 3.315312×10^9 **15.** 216 **16.** $\frac{47}{70}$ **17.** 0 **18.** $\frac{2}{5}$ **19.** Not necessarily; you may pick a 5 zero times, one time, or more than once. Each time you pick, the prob. that it will be a 5 is $\frac{1}{20}$. **20.** dependent **21.** independent **22.** 0.21 **23.** 0.79 **24.** 0.3 **25.** 0.7 **26.** $\frac{1}{4}$ **27.** $\frac{1}{5}$ **28.** $\frac{1}{8}$ **29.** This will not necessarily result in a fair decision, because the principal may aim at a particular name, which means that not all students have an equally likely chance of being chosen. **30.** Yes, this will result in a fair decision, because the probabilities of each goalie being chosen are the same. **31.** Answers may vary. **32.** 9 **33.** mean: 6,

median: 6, mode: 9 **34.** mean: $10.\overline{6}$, median: 7, modes: 3 and 7 **35.** mean: 15, median: 15, mode: 18 **36.** mean: 9.5, median: 9.5, mode: none **37.** range: 35; $Q_1 = 30$; $Q_3 = 55$ **38.** range: 35; $Q_1 = 25$; $Q_3 = 50$ **39.** range: 65; $Q_1 = 42$; $Q_3 = 87$ **40.** heights of 3 people **41.** ages of thirty college students **42.** gas mileage of 18 automobiles of various types **43.** $\bar{x} \approx 6.64$, $\sigma \approx 5.12$ **44.** $\bar{x} \approx 17.14$, $\sigma \approx 3.52$ **45.** $\bar{x} = 7.5$, $\sigma \approx 2.67$ **46.** not a random sample; they will all begin with the letter "a" **47.** not a random sample; the lawyers will choose jurors that are likely to support their side **48.** random sample; all students have an equal chance to be chosen **49.** not a random sample; the five with the largest (or smallest) circulation size will be picked **50.** People at the bus station may be less likely to own a car and therefore less likely to be in favor of a new garage. **51.** $\frac{1}{2}$ **52.** $\frac{1}{3}$
53. ≈ 0.14 **54.** ≈ 0.0710 **55.** ≈ 0.2066 **56.** ≈ 0.1766 **57.** $21a^5b^2$ **58.** $56a^3b^5$ **59.** continuous **60.** discrete **61.** discrete **62.** continuous **63.** 16%; 2.5%

Chapter 12

Get Ready!   p. 761

1. 6 **2.** $\frac{1}{3}$ **3.** $-\frac{3}{8}$ **4.** $\frac{7}{72}$ **5.** -9 **6.** 11 **7.** 3 **8.** $\left(\frac{1}{2}, -4\right)$
9. $\left(-\frac{2}{3}, -\frac{2}{3}\right)$ **10.** $\left(\frac{3}{4}, \frac{11}{4}\right)$ **11.** $(7, 9, -6)$ **12.** $(0, 0, 8)$
13. $(7, 5, 0)$

Lesson 12-1   pp. 764–770

Got It?

1a. $\begin{bmatrix} -15 & 25 \\ -1 & 1 \\ -2 & 15 \end{bmatrix}$ **b.** $\begin{bmatrix} -9 & 23 \\ -5 & 9 \\ 0 & 5 \end{bmatrix}$

c. Yes; it does not matter in which order you add matrices.

2. $A = \begin{bmatrix} 3 & 6 & -1 \\ 1 & 3 & 7 \\ 1 & 1 & 3 \end{bmatrix}$ **3a.** $\begin{bmatrix} 0 & 0 \\ 0 & 0 \end{bmatrix}$ **b.** $\begin{bmatrix} -1 & 10 & -5 \\ 0 & 2 & -3 \end{bmatrix}$

4a. $x = 6$, $y = -6$ **b.** $x = 4$, $y = -3$, $z = 2$

Lesson Check

1. $\begin{bmatrix} 1 & 1 \\ -2 & 8 \end{bmatrix}$ **2.** $\begin{bmatrix} 1 & -9 & 8 \\ -3 & -1 & 8 \end{bmatrix}$ **3.** $\begin{bmatrix} -3 & 4 \\ -5 & 11 \end{bmatrix}$ **4.** $\begin{bmatrix} 6 & 10 \\ 13 & -4 \end{bmatrix}$

5. Yes; the elements in each of the corresponding positions are equal.

6. The elements were not subtracted. The correct answer is $\begin{bmatrix} 6 \\ 5 \end{bmatrix} - \begin{bmatrix} 3 \\ 7 \end{bmatrix} = \begin{bmatrix} 3 \\ -2 \end{bmatrix}$

Exercises

7. $\begin{bmatrix} 6 & 5 & 4 \\ 2 & -1 & 7 \end{bmatrix}$ **9.** $\begin{bmatrix} 3.9 & -2.3 \\ -0.6 & 9.1 \end{bmatrix}$ **11.** $\begin{bmatrix} 4 & -8 \\ -1 & -1 \\ 11 & 1 \end{bmatrix}$

13. $\begin{bmatrix} 6 & 2 \\ -1 & 3 \end{bmatrix}$ **15.** $\begin{bmatrix} 2 & -3 & 4 \\ 5 & 6 & -7 \end{bmatrix}$

17. $x = -2, y = 3, z = 1$ **19.** $\begin{bmatrix} 0 & 5 \\ 8 & -6 \\ 0 & 5 \end{bmatrix}$ **21.** $\begin{bmatrix} 6 & 3 \\ -3 & 3 \end{bmatrix}$

23. $\begin{bmatrix} -4 & 1 \\ -3 & -1 \end{bmatrix}$ **25a.** $\begin{bmatrix} 952 \\ 720 \\ 1108 \\ 1172 \\ 1044 \end{bmatrix} ; \begin{bmatrix} 760 \\ 832 \\ 1252 \\ 1144 \\ 1064 \end{bmatrix}$

b. Allen: 4996; Iagorashvili: 5052
27. Matrix B would have the same dimensions as A. Its elements would be the opposites of the corresponding elements in A.
29. $c = \frac{5}{2}, d = \frac{2}{5}, f = 7, g = 5, h = -1$

31. Consider any two 2×2 matrices, $A = \begin{bmatrix} a & b \\ c & d \end{bmatrix}$ and $B = \begin{bmatrix} w & x \\ y & z \end{bmatrix}$. By the definition of matrix addition and the Comm. Prop. of Add.

$A + B = \begin{bmatrix} a & b \\ c & d \end{bmatrix} + \begin{bmatrix} w & x \\ y & z \end{bmatrix} = \begin{bmatrix} a+w & b+x \\ c+y & d+z \end{bmatrix}$

$\qquad = \begin{bmatrix} w+a & x+b \\ y+c & z+d \end{bmatrix} = \begin{bmatrix} w & x \\ y & z \end{bmatrix} + \begin{bmatrix} a & b \\ c & d \end{bmatrix}$

$\qquad = B + A$

33. B **35.** B **37.** 68% **38.** 97.5% **39.** 47.5%
40. 2, −6 **41.** $\frac{2}{3}$, 2 **42.** $-\frac{1}{2}$, −6 **43.** 5, 0

44. $\begin{bmatrix} 9 & 15 \\ 6 & 24 \end{bmatrix}$ **45.** $\begin{bmatrix} -20 \\ 35 \end{bmatrix}$

Lesson 12-2   pp. 772–779

Got It?

1. $\begin{bmatrix} 8 & 24 & -19 \\ -3 & 9 & 10 \end{bmatrix}$ **2.** $\begin{bmatrix} 5 & -1 \\ \frac{7}{3} & 0 \end{bmatrix}$ **3a.** $\begin{bmatrix} -6 & 0 \\ -9 & 11 \end{bmatrix}$

b. $\begin{bmatrix} -3 & 7 \\ 6 & 8 \end{bmatrix}$ **c.** No; explanations may vary. Sample: For

the matrices in parts (a) and (b), $AB = \begin{bmatrix} -6 & 0 \\ -9 & 11 \end{bmatrix}$ and

$BA = \begin{bmatrix} -3 & 7 \\ 6 & 8 \end{bmatrix}$, so $AB \neq BA$. **4.** player from 1994: 100 pts., player from 2006: 81 pts. **5a.** no **b.** yes
c. yes **d.** no **e.** yes

Lesson Check

1. $\begin{bmatrix} 6 & -2 \\ 4 & 0 \end{bmatrix}$ **2.** $\begin{bmatrix} -3 & 11 \\ -10 & 6 \end{bmatrix}$ **3.** $\begin{bmatrix} 5 & 7 \\ 2 & 6 \end{bmatrix}$ **4.** $\begin{bmatrix} 9 & -1 \\ -2 & 2 \end{bmatrix}$
5. Scalar; repeated matrix addition is repeated addition of each element of the matrix, which is the same as scalar multiplication of the matrix. **6.** The product of two

matrices A and B exists only if the number of columns of A is equal to the number of rows of B. Since A is a 2×4 matrix with 4 columns and B is a 3×6 matrix with 3 rows and $4 \neq 3$, the product AB does not exist. Likewise, since $6 \neq 2$, the product BA does not exist.

Exercises

7. $\begin{bmatrix} 9 & 12 \\ 18 & -6 \\ 3 & 0 \end{bmatrix}$ **9.** $\begin{bmatrix} -3 & -6 \\ 9 & -3 \end{bmatrix}$ **11.** $\begin{bmatrix} 9 & 2 \\ 2 & 6 \\ 3 & -10 \end{bmatrix}$

13. $\begin{bmatrix} 19 & 11 \\ -12 & 10 \end{bmatrix}$ **15.** $\begin{bmatrix} 8 & -2.5 \\ -1.5 & -1 \end{bmatrix}$ **17.** $\begin{bmatrix} -4 & 8 \\ -22 & 2 \end{bmatrix}$

19. $\begin{bmatrix} 5 & -12 \\ 9 & -6 \end{bmatrix}$ **21.** $\begin{bmatrix} -8 & 0 \\ 0 & -8 \end{bmatrix}$ **23.** $[34 \quad 0]$

25. $\begin{bmatrix} -15 & 0 \\ 25 & 0 \end{bmatrix}$ **27.** $\begin{bmatrix} -2 \\ 5 \end{bmatrix}$ **29.** yes **31.** yes **33.** yes
35a. River's Edge: 99 pts.; West River: 97 pts. **b.** West River

37. $\begin{bmatrix} 9 & -6 \\ 15 & -3 \\ -6 & -12 \end{bmatrix}$ **39.** $\begin{bmatrix} 17 & -24 \\ -33 & -7 \\ 69 & -18 \end{bmatrix}$ **41.** $\begin{bmatrix} 34 & -1 \\ 6 & -13 \\ -7 & 16 \end{bmatrix}$

43. $\begin{bmatrix} -90 & 0 \\ -78 & 42 \\ -30 & -30 \end{bmatrix}$ **45.** yes **47.** yes

Lesson 12-3   pp. 782–790

Got It? 1a. yes **b.** yes **c.** No; no matrix that is multiplied by the zero matrix will give an identity matrix.
2a. 3 **b.** 0 **c.** −48 **3a.** 12 units^2 **b.** 28 units^2

4a. yes; $\begin{bmatrix} 1 & -1 \\ -\frac{3}{2} & 2 \end{bmatrix}$ **b.** no **c.** yes; $\begin{bmatrix} 3 & -4 \\ -5 & 7 \end{bmatrix}$

5a. 88, 68, 84, 60, 12, 32, 52, 72, 28, 30, 14, 18, 2, 8, 14, 20 **b.** Multiply the coded information by the inverse of the coding matrix: $\begin{bmatrix} 4 & 1 & 7 & 3 & 1 & 2 & 3 & 4 \\ 9 & 8 & 7 & 6 & 1 & 3 & 5 & 7 \end{bmatrix}$

Lesson Check 1. 16 **2.** 7 **3.** does not exist

4. yes; $\begin{bmatrix} 3 & -2 \\ -7 & 5 \end{bmatrix}$

5. The student did not subtract correctly.
$\det \begin{bmatrix} 2 & 5 \\ -3 & 1 \end{bmatrix} = (2)(1) - (-3)(5) = 2 - (-15)$
$\qquad = 2 + 15 = 17$
6. A 2×3 matrix does not have a multiplicative inverse because it is not a square matrix. The number of rows must equal the number of columns for a multiplicative inverse to be possible.
Exercises 7. yes **9.** yes **11.** no **13.** 0 **15.** $-\frac{11}{40}$
17. 11 **19.** −6 **21.** −5 **23.** 106 **25.** 6 **27.** 466,250 mi^2

29. yes; $\begin{bmatrix} -1 & 3 \\ 1 & -2 \end{bmatrix}$ **31.** yes; $\begin{bmatrix} 0 & \frac{1}{2} \\ \frac{1}{3} & -\frac{1}{6} \end{bmatrix}$

33. yes; $\begin{bmatrix} -\dfrac{1}{8} & -\dfrac{1}{2} \\ \dfrac{3}{16} & \dfrac{1}{4} \end{bmatrix}$ **35.** yes; $\begin{bmatrix} 0 & \dfrac{1}{3} \\ -\dfrac{1}{2} & \dfrac{1}{6} \end{bmatrix}$

37. 2, 10, 10, 6, 9, 55, 15, 15, 9, 20 **39.** −120 **41.** 9
43. −3 **45.** 1 **47.** Answers may vary. Sample: Form a new matrix by switching the element in row 1, column 1 with the element in row 2, column 2. Then replace the other two elements with their opposites. Finally, divide each element by the determinant of the original matrix. **49.** 38 units²

51. yes; $\begin{bmatrix} -5 & 7 \\ 3 & -4 \end{bmatrix}$ **53.** yes; $\begin{bmatrix} 0.5 & 0 \\ 0 & 0.5 \end{bmatrix}$

55. yes; $\begin{bmatrix} 0.4 & 0.4 & 0.2 \\ -0.6 & -0.6 & 0.2 \\ -0.2 & 0.8 & 0.4 \end{bmatrix}$

57. no inverse because the determinant equals zero

59. 6 **61.** $MN = \begin{bmatrix} ae + bg & af + bh \\ ce + dg & cf + dh \end{bmatrix}$
det $MN = (ae + bg)(cf + dh) - (af + bh)(ce + dg)$
$\quad = acef + adeh + bcfg + bdgh$
$\qquad - acef - adfg - bceh - bdgh$
$\quad = adeh + bcfg - adfg - bceh$
Also, det $M \cdot$ det $N = (ad - bc)(eh - fg)$
$\qquad\qquad\qquad = adeh - adfg - bceh + bcfg.$
So, det $M \cdot$ det $N =$ det MN

63. $\dfrac{1}{2}$ **65.** 15 **67.** $\begin{bmatrix} 2 & 5 \\ 1 & 1 \end{bmatrix}$ **68.** $\begin{bmatrix} -10 & 19 \\ -20 & 7 \end{bmatrix}$ **69.** 720
70. 362,880 **71.** $1.08972864 \times 10^{10}$ **72.** 110,880
73. no solution **74.** (6, 0, −3) **75.** (3, −3, 9)
76. (−2, −1, −3)

Lesson 12-4   pp. 792–800

Got It?
1a. $\begin{bmatrix} -8 \\ 9 \end{bmatrix}$ **b.** $\begin{bmatrix} -14 & -20 \\ 19 & 28 \end{bmatrix}$

c. Since matrix A has no inverse, the eq. has no solution.

2a. $\begin{bmatrix} 3 & -7 \\ 5 & 1 \end{bmatrix}\begin{bmatrix} x \\ y \end{bmatrix} = \begin{bmatrix} 8 \\ -2 \end{bmatrix}$

b. $\begin{bmatrix} 1 & 3 & 5 \\ -2 & 1 & -4 \\ 7 & -2 & 0 \end{bmatrix}\begin{bmatrix} x \\ y \\ z \end{bmatrix} = \begin{bmatrix} 12 \\ -2 \\ 7 \end{bmatrix}$

c. $\begin{bmatrix} 2 & -8 \\ -1 & 1 \end{bmatrix}\begin{bmatrix} x \\ y \end{bmatrix} = \begin{bmatrix} -3 \\ -4 \end{bmatrix}$

3a. (5, −21) **b.** no solution **4.** run: 32 min; jog: 8 min
Lesson Check
1. $\begin{bmatrix} -6 & 3 \\ 4 & -2 \end{bmatrix}\begin{bmatrix} x \\ y \end{bmatrix} = \begin{bmatrix} 8 \\ 10 \end{bmatrix}$ **2.** $\begin{bmatrix} 2 & 3 & 0 \\ 1 & -2 & 1 \\ 0 & 6 & -4 \end{bmatrix}\begin{bmatrix} x \\ y \\ z \end{bmatrix} = \begin{bmatrix} 12 \\ 9 \\ 8 \end{bmatrix}$

3. (5, 3) **4.** (−6, −6) **5.** The student did not separate the coefficient matrix and the variable matrix. The matrix

eq. should be written as $\begin{bmatrix} 2 & 3 \\ -4 & 5 \end{bmatrix}\begin{bmatrix} x \\ y \end{bmatrix} = \begin{bmatrix} 5 \\ 1 \end{bmatrix}$.

6. Use matrix multiplication to combine the coefficient matrix and the variable matrix into a product matrix. Then set the first element in the product matrix equal to the first element in the constant matrix and set the second element in the product matrix equal to the second element in the constant matrix. The result will be a system of equations.;
$\quad -2p + 3q = 2$
$\quad 4p + q = -5$
Exercises

7. $\begin{bmatrix} -15 & -17 \\ 26 & 29 \end{bmatrix}$ **9.** $\begin{bmatrix} \dfrac{29}{31} \\ -\dfrac{66}{217} \\ \dfrac{34}{217} \end{bmatrix}$ **11.** $\begin{bmatrix} 1 & 1 \\ 1 & -2 \end{bmatrix}\begin{bmatrix} x \\ y \end{bmatrix} = \begin{bmatrix} 5 \\ -4 \end{bmatrix}$;

coefficient matrix: $\begin{bmatrix} 1 & 1 \\ 1 & -2 \end{bmatrix}$, variable matrix: $\begin{bmatrix} x \\ y \end{bmatrix}$,

constant matrix: $\begin{bmatrix} 5 \\ -4 \end{bmatrix}$ **13.** $\begin{bmatrix} 3 & 5 \\ 1 & 1 \end{bmatrix}\begin{bmatrix} a \\ b \end{bmatrix} = \begin{bmatrix} 0 \\ 2 \end{bmatrix}$; coefficient

matrix: $\begin{bmatrix} 3 & 5 \\ 1 & 1 \end{bmatrix}$, variable matrix: $\begin{bmatrix} a \\ b \end{bmatrix}$, constant matrix: $\begin{bmatrix} 0 \\ 2 \end{bmatrix}$

15. $\begin{bmatrix} 1 & -1 & 1 \\ 2 & 0 & 1 \\ 0 & 1 & 3 \end{bmatrix}\begin{bmatrix} r \\ s \\ t \end{bmatrix} = \begin{bmatrix} 150 \\ 425 \\ 0 \end{bmatrix}$; coefficient

matrix: $\begin{bmatrix} 1 & -1 & 1 \\ 2 & 0 & 1 \\ 0 & 1 & 3 \end{bmatrix}$, variable matrix: $\begin{bmatrix} r \\ s \\ t \end{bmatrix}$,

constant matrix: $\begin{bmatrix} 150 \\ 425 \\ 0 \end{bmatrix}$

17. (2, 1) **19.** $\left(\dfrac{1}{2}, 20\right)$ **21.** (3, 2) **23.** (2, −1, 3)
25. (1, 2, −2) **27.** 2.5 lb of almonds, 3.5 lb of peanuts, and 3 lb of raisins **29.** (−2, −1) **31.** (−1, 0) **33.** (5, 0, 1)
35. (1, 0, 3) **37.** (1, 1, 1, 1) **39.** (6, 2) **41.** (16, −22)
43. (5.4, 7.4) **45.** (6, 1) **47.** (2, −1, 4) **49.** length = 280 ft,

width = 140 ft **51.** $\begin{bmatrix} -3 & 2 \\ -5 & 8 \end{bmatrix}$ **53.** $\begin{bmatrix} 10 \\ 3 \\ -2 \end{bmatrix}$ **55.** 14

57. Answers may vary. Sample: $y + z = 0$; $y + z = 1$
59. B **61.** A

Lesson 12-5   pp. 801–808

Got It? 1a. Subtract 8 from each x-coordinate and add 5 to each y-coordinate.

b. $\begin{bmatrix} 0 & -1 & -5 & 1 & 4 \\ -5 & -1 & 0 & 3 & 0 \end{bmatrix} + \begin{bmatrix} -3 & -3 & -3 & -3 & -3 \\ 2 & 2 & 2 & 2 & 2 \end{bmatrix}$

$= \begin{bmatrix} -3 & -4 & -8 & -2 & 1 \\ -3 & 1 & 2 & 5 & 2 \end{bmatrix}$; (−3, −3), (−4, 1), (−8, 2),

(−2, 5), (1, 2)

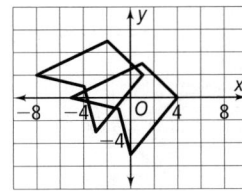

2. Answers may vary. Samples:

a. $\begin{bmatrix} 0 & 5 & 5 & 0 \\ 0 & 0 & 3 & 3 \end{bmatrix}$

b. $2\begin{bmatrix} 0 & 5 & 5 & 0 \\ 0 & 0 & 3 & 3 \end{bmatrix} = \begin{bmatrix} 0 & 10 & 10 & 0 \\ 0 & 0 & 6 & 6 \end{bmatrix}$;
(0, 0), (10, 0), (10, 6), (0, 6)

c. 4

3a. (0, 3), (4, 4), (1, −1); **b.** (−3, 0), (−4, 4), (1, 1);

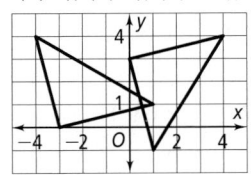 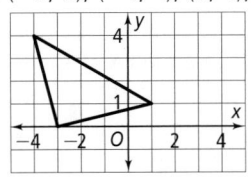

4a. (1, −1), (3, −1), (6, −4), (1, −3);

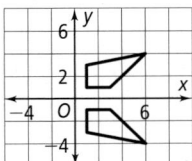

b. (1, 1), (1, 3), (4, 6), (3, 1);

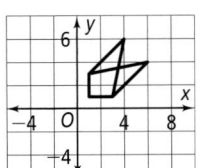

Lesson Check 1. $A'\left(\frac{1}{2}, \frac{1}{2}\right)$, $B'(1, 2)$, $C'\left(2, -\frac{1}{2}\right)$
2. $A'(1, -1)$, $B'(4, -2)$, $C'(-1, -4)$ **3.** $A'(1, 1)$,
$B'(4, 2)$, $C'(-1, 4)$ **4.** Translations, rotations and
reflections leave the size of the figure unchanged.
Translation moves the figure to a new location. Rotation
turns the figure about a fixed pt. Reflection maps a figure
in the coordinate plane to its mirror image using a specific
line as its mirror. **5.** Answers may vary. Sample: reflection
across $y = x$; translation 4 units to the right and 4 units
down
6. They are equal.
$$\begin{bmatrix} -3 & 0 \\ 0 & -3 \end{bmatrix}\begin{bmatrix} 1 & -2 & 4 \\ 1 & -1 & 2 \end{bmatrix} = -3\begin{bmatrix} 1 & 0 \\ 0 & 1 \end{bmatrix}\begin{bmatrix} 1 & -2 & 4 \\ 1 & -1 & 2 \end{bmatrix}$$
$$= -3\begin{bmatrix} 1 & -2 & 4 \\ 1 & -1 & 2 \end{bmatrix}$$

Exercises 7. (−2, 2), (−2, 6), (2, 6), (2, 2);

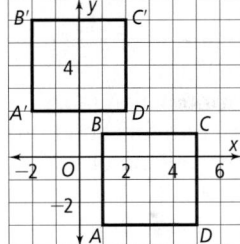

9. (−13, 7), (−19, 6), (9, 0);

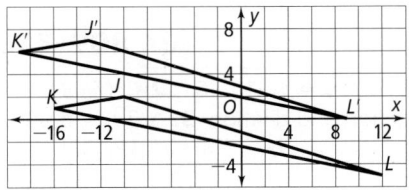

11. (0, 0), (4, 8), (10, 10), (16, 2)
13. (−12, 9), (3, 6), (4.5, 0), (1.5, −6), (−3, 0)
15.

17. (−3, 3), (3, −6), (3, −3), (−3, −6)
19. (−1, −3), (−2, −2), (−3, −2), (−4, −3), (−2.5, −5)
21.

23. (3, −3), (−3, −6), (−3, −3), (3, −6)
25. (3, 1), (2, 2), (2, 3), (3, 4), (5, 2.5)

27. $\begin{bmatrix} -8 & -5 & -2 & -5 \\ -8 & -5 & -8 & -11 \end{bmatrix}$ **29.** $\begin{bmatrix} -5 & -1 & -3 \\ -2 & -1 & 1 \end{bmatrix}$

31. $\begin{bmatrix} 3 & -1 & 1 \\ -1 & -2 & -4 \end{bmatrix}$ **33.** Apply a 90° rotation matrix

$\begin{bmatrix} 0 & -1 \\ 1 & 0 \end{bmatrix}$ three times to determine the image matrix for
each frame. The fourth application of the 90° rotation matrix
would show the gymnast at the starting position of Frame 1.

37. $f\colon \begin{bmatrix} -5 & -2 & 1 \\ 3 & 0 & 3 \end{bmatrix}$, $g\colon \begin{bmatrix} -1 & 2 & 5 \\ 1 & -2 & 1 \end{bmatrix}$ translation

39. $\begin{bmatrix} -1.5 & 0.25 & -2.5 \\ 0 & 1.5 & 1.5 \end{bmatrix}$

41. Answers may vary. Sample: The reflection of a matrix of pts. from a function table across the line $y = x$ interchanges the values of y and x in the function table. Finding the inverse of the matrix of pts. of a function from a function table also results in the interchanging of the values of y and x.

43. H **45.** G **47.** $(3, -2)$ **48.** $(1, -1, 2)$ **49.** $(0, 1, -2)$

50. $\begin{bmatrix} 16 \\ 12 \end{bmatrix}$ **51.** [12] **52.** [22]

Lesson 12-6   pp. 809–815

Got It? 1. $u = \langle 3, 4 \rangle$; $v = \langle -1, -6 \rangle$ **2a.** $\langle 5, 3 \rangle$
b. translation, reflection and dilation **3.** $\sqrt{74} \approx 8.60$
4a. 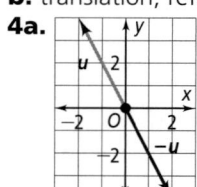   **b.**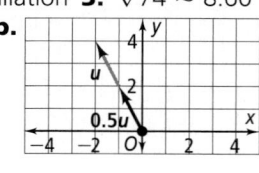

5a. not normal **b.** normal
Lesson Check 1. $\langle 5, 2 \rangle$ **2.** $\langle 9, -11 \rangle$ **3.** $\langle -1, -12 \rangle$
4. $\langle 0, -15 \rangle$ **5.** The magnitudes of vectors **a**, **b**, and **c** are the same: 5. **6.** Although the x-component of $\langle 8, 3 \rangle$ is 4 times the x-component of $\langle 2, 1 \rangle$, the y-component and the magnitude of $\langle 8, 3 \rangle$ are not 4 times those of $\langle 2, 1 \rangle$, $3 \neq 4 \times 1$ and $\sqrt{73} \neq 4 \times \sqrt{5}$.
Exercises 7. $\langle 4, 1 \rangle$ **9.** $\langle 4, -2 \rangle$ **11.** $\langle 0, 2 \rangle$ **13.** $\langle -1, 5 \rangle$
15. $\langle 2, 0 \rangle$ **17.** $\langle 3, 0 \rangle$ **19.** $\langle 3, -4 \rangle$ **21.** $\langle 4, -1 \rangle$
23. $\langle -3, 8 \rangle$ **25.** $\langle -8, 20 \rangle$ **27.** $\langle -6, -12 \rangle$ **29.** not normal **31.** normal **33.** $\langle 0, -14 \rangle$ **35.** $\langle 18, -13 \rangle$
37. about 304 mi/h **39.** $\overrightarrow{AB} = \langle 3, 1 \rangle$, $\overrightarrow{BC} = \langle -2, 3 \rangle$, $\overrightarrow{CA} = \langle -1, -4 \rangle$ **41.** $\langle 6, -3 \rangle$ **43.** $\langle -4, -2 \rangle$
45. $v - v = \langle 0, 0 \rangle$; $\langle 0, 0 \rangle$, the zero vector, is the additive identity for the set of all vectors and $-v$ is the additive inverse of any given vector **v**; so $v + \langle 0, 0 \rangle = v$ and $v + (-v) = \langle 0, 0 \rangle$.
47. yes; Distributive Prop.

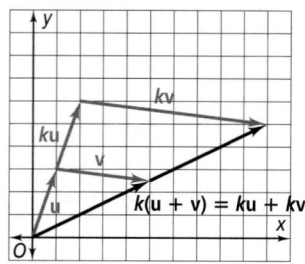

49. yes; Assoc. Prop. of Add.

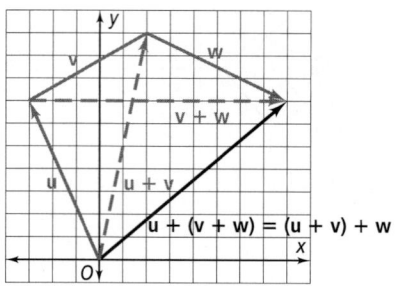

51. a and **d** are parallel; **a** and **b** are perpendicular; **b** and **d** are perpendicular

Chapter Review   pp. 817–820

1. equal matrices **2.** zero matrix **3.** matrix equation
4. square matrix

5. $\begin{bmatrix} -1 & 9 & -8 \\ 4 & 0 & 6 \end{bmatrix}$ **6.** $\begin{bmatrix} 5 & -4 \\ 5 & 0 \end{bmatrix}$ **7.** [1   -8   12]

8. $\begin{bmatrix} -3 & 10 \\ -3 & 3 \end{bmatrix}$ **9.** $x = -2$, $w = 8$, $r = 4$, $t = -1$

10. $t = -4$, $y = \frac{11}{2}$, $r = 4$, $w = 4$

11. $\begin{bmatrix} 18 & 3 & 0 & 24 \\ -12 & 9 & 21 & 33 \end{bmatrix}$ **12.** undefined **13.** undefined

14. $\begin{bmatrix} -6 & 10 & 21 & 41 \\ -28 & 10 & 28 & 28 \end{bmatrix}$ **15.** $\begin{bmatrix} -14 & -2 \\ 43 & -7 \end{bmatrix}$

16. $\begin{bmatrix} -11 & 18 \\ -17 & -2 \end{bmatrix}$ **17.** 24; $\begin{bmatrix} \frac{1}{6} & -\frac{1}{24} \\ 0 & \frac{1}{4} \end{bmatrix}$

18. 0; does not exist

19. 42; $\begin{bmatrix} \frac{5}{42} & -\frac{1}{42} \\ -\frac{4}{21} & \frac{5}{21} \end{bmatrix}$ **20.** 6; $\begin{bmatrix} \frac{1}{3} & -\frac{2}{3} & 0 \\ -\frac{1}{6} & \frac{1}{3} & -\frac{1}{2} \\ \frac{1}{3} & \frac{1}{3} & 0 \end{bmatrix}$

21. $\begin{bmatrix} 1 & 2 \\ -1 & 0 \end{bmatrix}$ **22.** $(-4, -7)$ **23.** $\begin{bmatrix} 2 \\ 2 \end{bmatrix}$ **24.** $\begin{bmatrix} 2 & 1 \\ 3 & 2 \end{bmatrix}$

25. no unique solution **26.** no unique solution

27. $\begin{bmatrix} 0 & -5 & -2 \\ 5 & 4 & 9 \end{bmatrix}$ **28.** $\begin{bmatrix} -3 & 2 & -1 \\ 1 & 0 & 5 \end{bmatrix}$ **29.** $\begin{bmatrix} 1 & 0 & 5 \\ 3 & -2 & 1 \end{bmatrix}$

30. $\begin{bmatrix} 1.5 & -1 & 0.5 \\ 0.5 & 0 & 2.5 \end{bmatrix}$ **31.** $\begin{bmatrix} 6 & -4 & 2 \\ 2 & 0 & 10 \end{bmatrix}$ **32.** $\begin{bmatrix} 1 & 0 & 5 \\ -3 & 2 & -1 \end{bmatrix}$

33. $\langle -1, 8 \rangle$; about 8.1 **34.** $\langle 7, -5 \rangle$; about 8.6
35. $\langle -9, 12 \rangle$; 15 **36.** $\langle -2, 14 \rangle$; about 14.1
37. $\langle -8, 14 \rangle$; about 16.1 **38.** $\langle -4, 21 \rangle$; about 21.4
39. 0; normal **40.** 0; normal

Chapter 13

Get Ready! p. 825

1. vert. asymptote: $x = 3$ **2.** vert. asymptotes:
$x = -\frac{1}{2}$ and $x = 4$ **3.** $\frac{2b}{a}$ **4.** $\frac{55}{18}$ **5.** $\frac{3}{2(c+d)}$ **6.** $\frac{c}{16}$
7. $\frac{c+4}{9}$ **8.** $\frac{16}{x}$ **9.** $\frac{15}{7}$ **10.** 6 **11.** 4, 1; $a_n = 19 - 3n$,
explicit or $a_1 = 16$, $a_n = a_{n-1} - 3$, recursive
12. $-216, -343$; $a_n = -n^3$, explicit
13. $(x - 1)^2 + (y + 4)^2 = 16$;

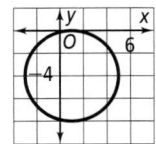

14. $\frac{(x-2)^2}{9} + \frac{(y-5)^2}{4} = 1$;

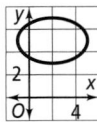

15. $y = \frac{1}{32}x^2 - 3$;

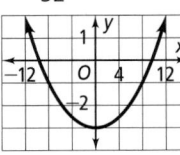

16. $\frac{(y-1)^2}{9} - \frac{(x-6)^2}{16} = 1$;

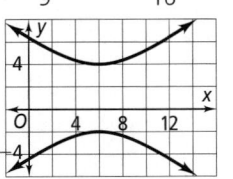

17. Answers may vary. Sample: Similar data tends to recur after a certain period has lapsed. In this case, 12 months.

Lesson 13-1 pp. 828–834

Got It? 1a. from $x = -3$ to $x = 1$ or from
$x = 0$ to $x = 4$; 4 **b.** from $x = -4$ to $x = -1$ or from
$x = 0$ to $x = 3$; 3 **2a.** no **b.** yes; 4 **c.** 15 cycles;
$\frac{1}{3}$ s; $\frac{1}{440}$ s **3a.** 1.5; $y = -0.5$ **b.** 1.5; $y = 0.5$
4. period: 0.006; amplitude: 0.25; $y = -0.75$
Lesson Check 1. periodic; 5 **2.** no **3.** Answers may
vary. Sample: hands of a clock, phases of the moon
4. The amplitude is not 2, but $\frac{2}{2} = 1$. **5.** $f(6) = f(11) = 2$;
for any x, $f(x + 5)$ will always equal $f(x)$ because the
period is 5. **6.** -4
Exercises 7. $x = -2$ to $x = 3$, $x = 2$ to $x = 7$; 5
9. $x = 0$ to $x = 4$, $x = 2$ to $x = 6$; 4 **11.** periodic; 12
13. not periodic **15.** periodic; 7 **17.** 3; $y = -1$

19.

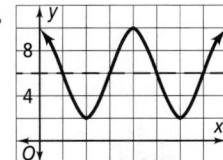

1 unit on the x-axis is 0.005 s.
21. a. y **b.** x **23.** repeating of a pattern at regular
intervals **25. a.** 1 s **b.** 1.5 mV
27. 3, -3, 4;

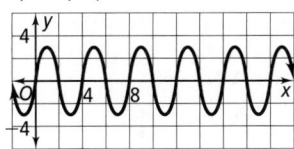

29. 4, -4, 8;

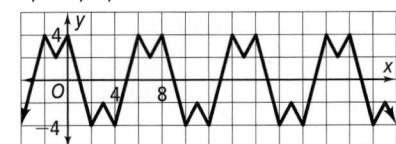

31. 2 weeks **33.** 1 hr **35. a.** 67 **b.** 70 **c.** 70 **d.** 67
37. C **39.** B **41.** 64 s; The first two functions are at
the beginning of their cycles together every $6 \cdot 7 = 42$
seconds: 42, 84, 126, . . . The third function is at the
beginning of its cycle every 8 seconds, starting at $(42 + 20)$
seconds: 62, 70, 78, 86, 94, 102, 110, 118, 126, . . .
The three functions are all at the beginning of their cycles
at 126 seconds, which is 64 seconds after the third
function achieves its first maximum.

Geometry Review p. 835

1. $\frac{\sqrt{2}}{2}$ in. **3.** $\frac{\sqrt{6}}{2}$ ft **5.** hypotenuse: 6 in., longer leg:
$3\sqrt{3}$ in. **7.** shorter leg: $\frac{1}{2}$ ft, longer leg: $\frac{\sqrt{3}}{2}$ ft

Lesson 13-2 pp. 836–842

Got It? 1. 225°
2a. 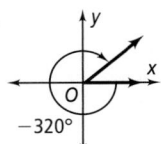 **b.** **c.**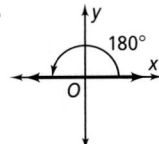

3. $-315°, 45°, 405°$
4a. $\cos(-90°) = 0$, $\sin(-90°) = -1$; $\cos(360°) = 1$,
$\sin(360°) = 0$; $\cos(540°) = -1$, $\sin(540°) = 0$
b. $\cos-90° = \frac{0}{1} = 0$, $\sin-90° = \frac{-1}{1} = -1$
$\cos 360° = \frac{1}{1} = 1$, $\sin 360° = \frac{0}{1} = 0$
$\cos 540° = \frac{-1}{1} = -1$, $\sin 540° = \frac{0}{1} = 0$

5a. $\frac{\sqrt{2}}{2}, -\frac{\sqrt{2}}{2}$ **b.** $-\frac{\sqrt{3}}{2}, \frac{1}{2}$ **c.** Yes; for example, when $\theta = 45°$, $\sin \theta = \cos \theta$.

Lesson Check 1. 135° **2.** 240°

3. 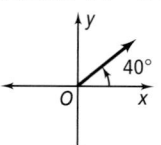 ; −332° **4.** 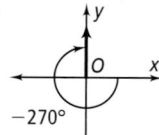 ; −35°

5. Answers may vary. Sample: 45° and −315° **6.** The measure of the coterminal angle is not 310°; the measure of the coterminal angle is 50° − 360° = −310°.

Exercises 7. −315° **9.** 240° **11.** −30°

13. 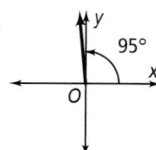 **15.**

17.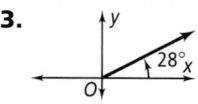

19. 215° **21.** 4° **23.** 150°

25. 180° **27.** $-\frac{\sqrt{2}}{2}, \frac{\sqrt{2}}{2}$; −0.71, 0.71

29. $-\frac{1}{2}, \frac{\sqrt{3}}{2}$; −0.50, 0.87 **31.** $\frac{\sqrt{2}}{2}, -\frac{\sqrt{2}}{2}$, 0.71, −0.71 **33.** $-\frac{\sqrt{2}}{2}, \frac{\sqrt{2}}{2}$; −0.71, 0.71 **35.** 0.98, −0.17 **37.** 0.00, 1.00 **39.** 5

41–43. Answers may vary. Samples:

41. 370°, −350° **43.** 40°, −320° **45.** II

47. negative x-axis **49.** positive x-axis

51a.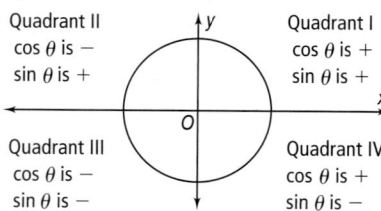

Quadrant II	Quadrant I
cos θ is −	cos θ is +
sin θ is +	sin θ is +
Quadrant III	Quadrant IV
cos θ is −	cos θ is +
sin θ is −	sin θ is −

b. II **c.** If the terminal side of an angle is in Quadrants I or II, then the sine of the angle is positive. If the terminal side of an angle is in Quadrants I or IV, then the cosine of the angle is positive.

53. 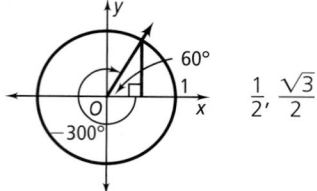 $\frac{1}{2}, \frac{\sqrt{3}}{2}$

55. 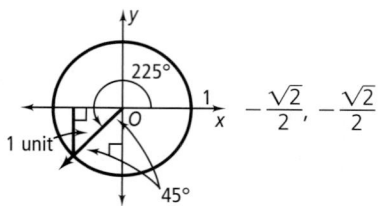 $-\frac{\sqrt{2}}{2}, -\frac{\sqrt{2}}{2}$

57. 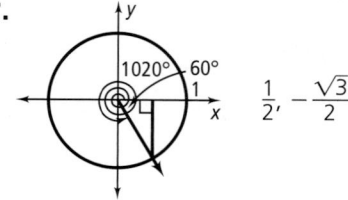 $\frac{1}{2}, -\frac{\sqrt{3}}{2}$

59. No; yes; if the sine and cosine are both negative, the angle is in Quadrant III. 60° is in Quadrant I and −120° is in Quadrant III;

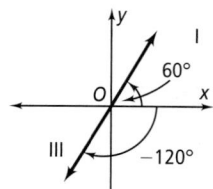

61. H

63.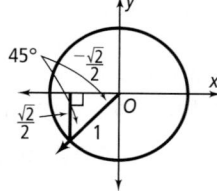

The terminal side forms an angle of 45° with the negative x-axis, so: $\sin(-135°) = -\frac{\sqrt{2}}{2}$ and $\cos(-135°) = -\frac{\sqrt{2}}{2}$. Then $[\sin(-135°)]^2 + [\cos(-135°)]^2 = \left(-\frac{\sqrt{2}}{2}\right)^2 + \left(-\frac{\sqrt{2}}{2}\right)^2 = \frac{2}{4} + \frac{2}{4} = \frac{4}{4} = 1$.

64. periodic; 3 **65.** not periodic **66.** periodic; 6 **67.** (0, 2√5), (0, −2√5); **68.** (0, 5√5), (0, −5√5);

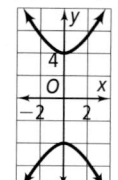

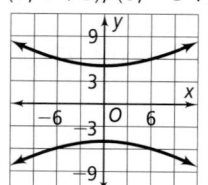

69. $(\sqrt{85}, 0)$, $(-\sqrt{85}, 0)$;

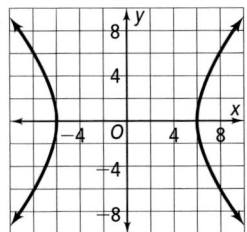

70. $(\sqrt{145}, 0)$, $(-\sqrt{145}, 0)$;

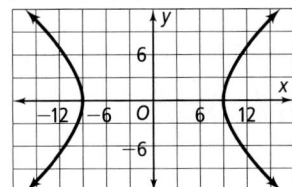

71. 50.24 in.^{2} **72.** 3846.5 m^2 **73.** 200.96 mi^2
74. 9.0746 ft^2

Lesson 13-3   pp. 844–850

Got It? 1a. 90° **b.** $\frac{5\pi}{4}$ radians **c.** $\frac{360°}{\pi} \approx 114.59°$

d. $\frac{5\pi}{6}$ radians **2.** $-\frac{\sqrt{3}}{2}$, $-\frac{1}{2}$ **3a.** 6.3 in. **b.** Arc length
would also double. **4.** $\approx$ 15,708 km
Lesson Check 1. $\frac{5\pi}{3}$ radians $\approx$ 5.24 radians **2.** 135°
3. $\frac{20\pi}{3} \approx$ 20.94 in. **4.** 1 radian **5.** 6 "perfect" slices
Exercises 7. $\frac{5\pi}{6}$, 2.62 **9.** $-\frac{\pi}{3}$, -1.05 **11.** $\frac{\pi}{9}$, 0.35
13. 198° **15.** $-172°$ **17.** 270° **19.** $\frac{1}{2}$, $\frac{\sqrt{3}}{2}$
21. $\frac{\sqrt{2}}{2}$, $-\frac{\sqrt{2}}{2}$ **23.** 0, -1 **25.** $-\frac{\sqrt{3}}{2}$, $-\frac{1}{2}$ **27.** 10.5 m
29. 25.1 in. **31.** 43.2 cm **33.** $\approx$31.9 ft **35.** $\approx$42.2 in.
37. III **39.** negative x-axis

41.

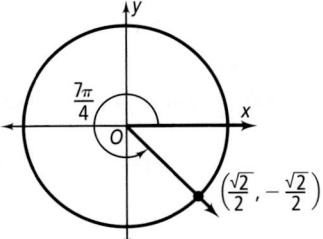

0.71, -0.71

43.

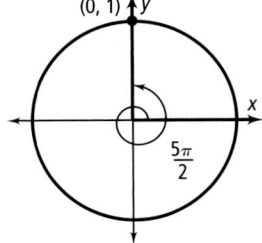

0.00, 1.00

45. If two angles measured in radians are coterminal, the
difference of their measures will be evenly divisible by 2π.
47. $\approx$11 radians **49.** $\approx$6.3 cm **51.** $-\frac{3\pi}{2}$ radians
53. $\frac{\theta}{s} = \frac{2\pi}{2\pi r}$
$\quad\frac{\theta}{s} = \frac{1}{r}$
$\quad\theta r = s$
$\quad\quad s = \theta r$
55. G **57.** For a central angle of 1 radian, the length of
the intercepted arc is the length of the radius.

58. 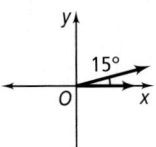   **59.**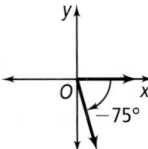

60. 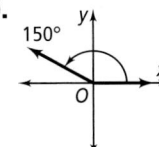   **61.**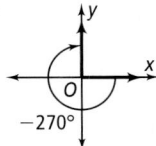

62.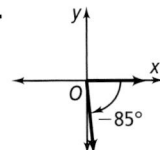

63. mean $\approx$ 12.9, s.d. $\approx$ 3.53 **64.** mean $= 30$,
s.d. $\approx$ 8.09 **65.** 2 **66.** all real numbers **67.** 1
68. $y = 0$

Lesson 13-4   pp. 851–858

Got It? 1a. $\approx$ 0.1411; estimates may vary. **b.** -1
2a. 2; 2π **b.** 3; $\frac{4\pi}{3}$ **3a.** 3; -3 **b.** 0.6; 0.6

4.

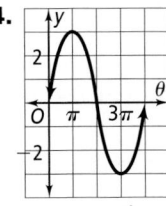

$y = 3 \sin \frac{1}{2}\theta$

5a. 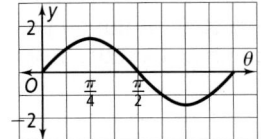   **b.**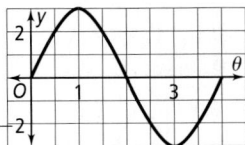

6. $y = \sin \frac{\pi}{320}\theta$

Lesson Check 1a. 2 **b.** 3; π **c.** $y = 3 \sin 2\theta$

2.

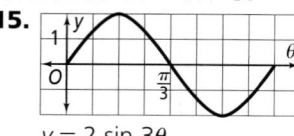

3. One cycle of a sine function is an interval on the x-axis with length equal to the period. The period is the length of one cycle. **4.** Answers may vary. Sample: $y = 5 \sin \frac{\theta}{3}$

5. The amplitude is 3, but since $a < 0$, the graph is reflected across the x-axis. Also, the period is 2, not π.

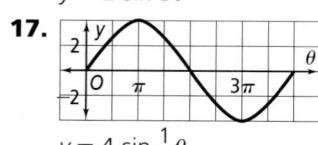

Exercises 7. ≈ 0.1 **9.** ≈ -1 **11.** ≈ -0.7 **13.** $\frac{1}{2}$; 1, 4π

15.

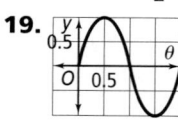

$y = 2 \sin 3\theta$

17.

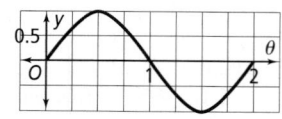

$y = 4 \sin \frac{1}{2}\theta$

19.

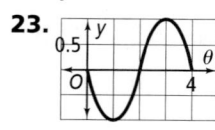

$y = \sin \pi\theta$

21.

23.

25.

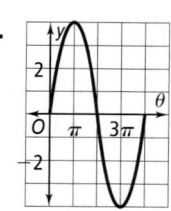

27. 2π; $y = 2 \sin \theta$ **29.** π; $y = \frac{5}{2} \sin 2\theta$ **31.** 1; 1, 2π
33. π; 1, 2 **35.** 1; 5, 2π

37.

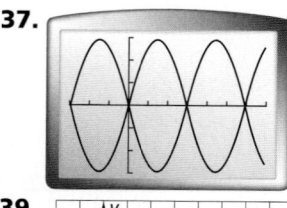

They are reflections of each other across the x-axis. When a is replaced by its opposite, the graph is a reflection of the original graph across the x-axis.

39.

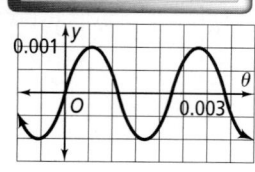

41. π, $\frac{5}{2}$;

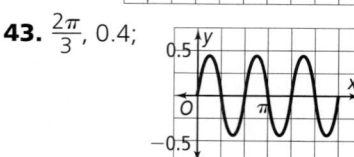

43. $\frac{2\pi}{3}$, 0.4;

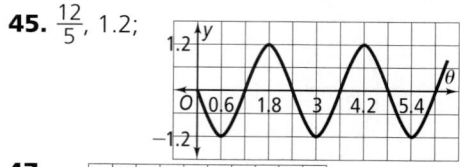

45. $\frac{12}{5}$, 1.2;

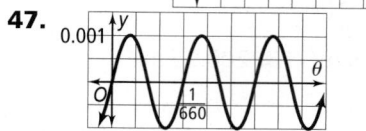

47.

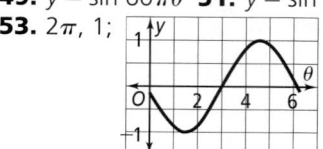

49. $y = \sin 60\pi\theta$ **51.** $y = \sin 240{,}000\pi\theta$
53. 2π, 1;

55. C
57. C
59. 120°; consider the point where a 60° angle intersects the unit circle. Reflect this point across the y-axis. The image is the intersection of a 120° angle and the unit circle. These two points have the same y-coordinate. Therefore $\sin 120° = \sin 60°$.

60. $-\frac{4\pi}{9}$ radians, -1.40 radians **61.** $\frac{5\pi}{6}$ radians, 2.62 radians **62.** $-\frac{4\pi}{3}$ radians, -4.19 radians

63. $\frac{16\pi}{9}$ radians, 5.59 radians **64.** $-\frac{5\pi}{2}$ radians, -7.85 radians **65.** $\approx 49\%$ **66.** 1 **67.** 0 **68.** -1 **69.** 0

Lesson 13-5   pp. 861–867

Got It? 1. domain: all real numbers; period: 2π; range: $-1 \le y \le 1$; amplitude: 1 sine: max at $\frac{\pi}{2}$; min at $\frac{3\pi}{2}$; zeros at 0, π, 2π

2.

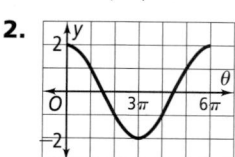

3a. $f(t) = -35 \cos \left(\frac{4\pi}{25}t\right)$ **b.** The function would cross the midline at 3 hours, 7 minutes, 30 seconds. The midline represents average water level. **4a.** 1.15, 1.99, 4.29, 5.13 **b.** 2.21, 4.06 **c.** $0 \le \theta < 2.21$ and $4.06 < \theta \le 2\pi$; $2.21 < \theta < 4.06$

Lesson Check

1. 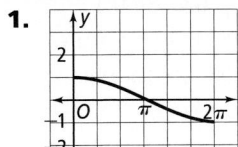 **2.**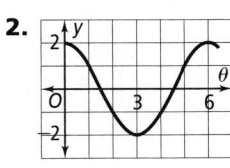

3. $y = 3 \cos \theta$ **4.** $y = 1.5 \cos 2\theta$ **5.** Answers may vary. Sample: $y = 5 \cos \left(\frac{5}{2}\theta\right)$ **6a.** $0 \le \theta < \frac{\pi}{2}$, $\frac{3\pi}{2} < \theta \le 2\pi$
b. $\pi < \theta < 2\pi$ **c.** $y = 3 \sin \left(\frac{2\pi}{3}x - \frac{\pi}{2}\right)$

Exercises 7. 2π, 3; max: 0, 2π; min: π; zeros: $\frac{\pi}{2}, \frac{3\pi}{2}$
9. π, 1; max: 0, π, 2π; min: $\frac{\pi}{2}, \frac{3\pi}{2}$; zeros: $\frac{\pi}{4}, \frac{3\pi}{4}, \frac{5\pi}{4}, \frac{7\pi}{4}$

11. 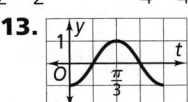 **13.**

15.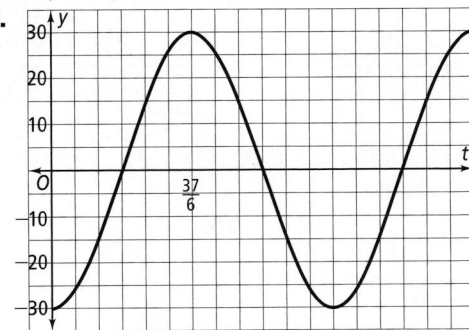

17. $y = \frac{\pi}{2} \cos \frac{2\pi}{3} \theta$ **19.** $y = -3 \cos 2\theta$
21. 0.52, 2.62, 3.67, 5.76
23. 0.55, 1.45, 2.55, 3.45, 4.55, 5.45 **25.** 0.00
27. 2π, $-3 \le y \le 3$, 3 **29.** 4π, $-2 \le y \le 2$, 2
31. 6π, $-3 \le y \le 3$, 3 **33.** $\frac{4}{3}$, $-16 \le y \le 16$, 16
35. $y = 70 + 13 \cos \frac{\pi}{6}(x - 1)$ where x represents the months of the year with January as 1, February as 2, March as 3, etc. **37.** 0.64, 2.50
39. 0.50, 2.50, 4.50

41a.

b. 4:40 P.M.; 5:00 A.M. (next day); 5:20 P.M. (next day); 5:40 A.M. (2 days after time 0) **c.** 6 h 10 min; 6 h 10 min
43. On the unit circle, the x-values of $-\theta$ are equal to the x-values of θ, so $\cos(-\theta) = \cos \theta$. $-\cos \theta$ is the opposite

of $\cos \theta$, so these graphs are reflections of each other across the x-axis.

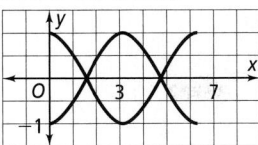

45. a. 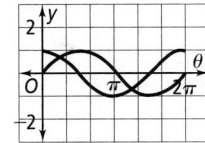 **b.**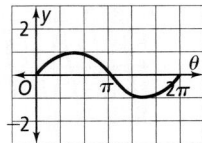

shift of $\frac{\pi}{2}$ units to the right   They are the same.
c. To write a sine function as a cosine function, replace sin with cos and replace θ with $\theta - \frac{\pi}{2}$.
47. F **49.** G

Lesson 13-6   pp. 868–874

Got It? 1a. not defined **b.** $\sqrt{3}$ **c.** -1
2a. 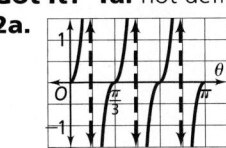 **b.**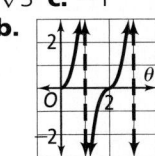

3a. ≈ 46.6 ft **b.** $\approx 8°$
Lesson Check 1. 1 **2.** $\frac{\sqrt{3}}{3}$ **3.** -1 **4.** 0 **5.** $\frac{2\pi}{3}$ **6.** The student found 3θ instead of θ. Divide each side of the equation $3\theta = -1.33$ by 3 to get $\theta = -0.44$.
7. $y = \tan 2\theta$; the period of the function $y = \sin 4\theta$ is $\frac{\pi}{2}$.
For a tangent function to have the same period, $\frac{\pi}{2}$, b must equal 2.
Exercises 9. 0 **11.** undefined **13.** 0 **15.** undefined
17. $\frac{\pi}{2}$ **19.** $\frac{2\pi}{3}$; $\theta = -\frac{\pi}{3}$ and $\theta = \frac{\pi}{3}$ **21.** $\frac{3\pi^2}{2}$; $\theta = -\frac{3\pi^2}{4}$ and $\theta = \frac{3\pi^2}{4}$

23. 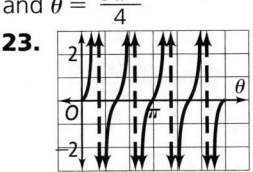 **25.**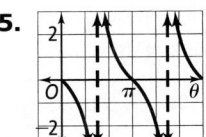

27.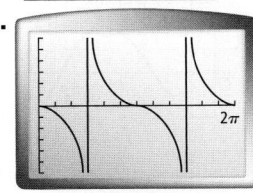

-100, undefined, 100

29a.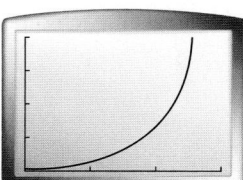

b. ≈ 14.3 ft
c. ≈ 20.2 ft

31. $\frac{2\pi}{5}$;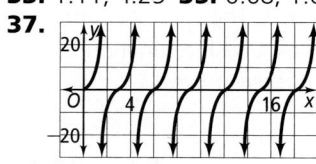

33. 1.11, 4.25 **35.** 0.08, 1.65, 3.22, 4.79

37.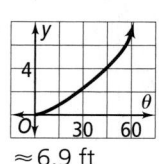

$150\sqrt{3}$ in.^{2} ≈ 260 in.^{2}

39. 200 **41.** 135 **43.** 70 **45.** $y = -\tan\left(\frac{1}{2}x\right)$

47a.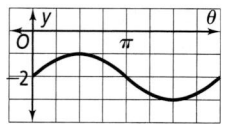

b. ≈ 27.7 ft^2
c. ≈ 166.3 ft^2

≈ 6.9 ft

49. Answers may vary. Sample: Triangles *OAP* and *OBQ* both share the angle θ and each triangle has a right angle, so they are similar by AA. $\frac{\sin\theta}{\cos\theta} = \frac{AP}{OA} = \frac{BQ}{OB} = \frac{\tan\theta}{1}$. Thus $\frac{\sin\theta}{\cos\theta} = \tan\theta$. **51.** 2; for $0 \le x < 2\pi$, *x* is nonnegative and there are only 2 sections of the graph of the tangent function on or above the *x*-axis. **53.** H **55.** I **57.** 1.32, 4.97 **58.** 1.77, 4.51 **59.** 6.15 **60.** 0.44, 1.56, 2.44, 3.56, 4.44, 5.56 **61.** mean ≈ 5.9, median = 6, modes = 4 and 6 **62.** 83 **63.** −227 **64.** 145 **65.** −332 **66.** 2 units to the right and up 5 units **67.** 5 units to the left and down 4 units **68.** 2 units to the left and up 1 unit

Lesson 13-7   pp. 875–882

Got It? 1a. 5; 5 units to the right **b.** −3; 3 units to the left

2a. 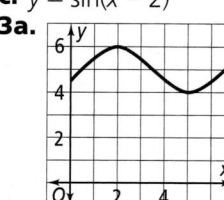   **b.**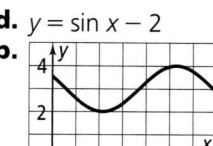

c. $y = \sin(x - 2)$ **d.** $y = \sin x - 2$

3a. 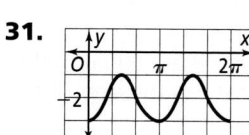   **b.**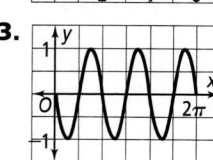

4a. 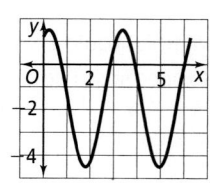   **b.**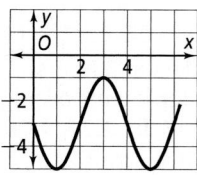

5a. $y = \cos x + \frac{\pi}{2}$ **b.** $y = 2\sin\left(x - \frac{\pi}{4}\right)$ **6a.** 69.9°F
b. the average of the highest and lowest temperatures
c. Yes; data can be extrapolated to calculate for next year.
Lesson Check
1.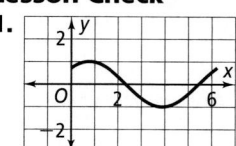

2. phase shift: 2 units to the right; vertical shift: 9 units up
3. $y = \cos\left(x - \frac{2\pi}{3}\right) + 3$ **4.** Answers may vary.
Sample: $y = 4\sin\frac{2}{3}(x - \pi) - 5$ **5.** Scott is correct;
$y = a\cos b(x - h) + k = \cos 3\left(x + \frac{\pi}{6}\right)$ where $h = -\frac{\pi}{6}$.
The phase shift is $\frac{\pi}{6}$ units to the left of $y = \cos 3x$.
Exercises 7. −2; 2 units to the left **9.** 3; 3 units to the right **11.** $\frac{5\pi}{7}$; $\frac{5\pi}{7}$ units to the right

13.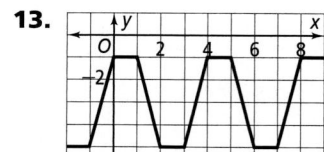

15. 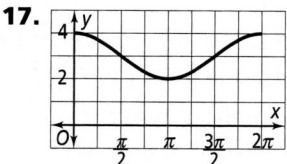   **17.**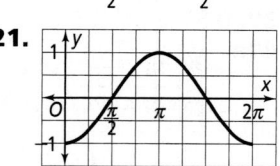

19. 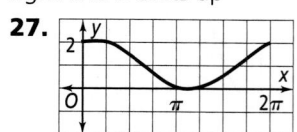   **21.**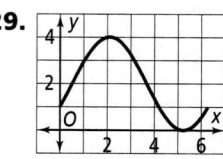

23. 1 unit to the left and 2 units down **25.** 3 units to the right and 2 units up

27. 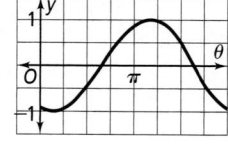   **29.**

31.   **33.**

35.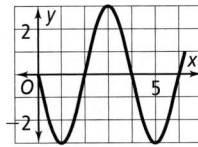

37. $y = \cos x - \frac{\pi}{2}$ **39.** $y = \cos(x - 1.5)$ **41.** $y = \cos(x + 3) + \pi$ **43.** $y = 1.5 \cos\left[\frac{\pi}{6}(x - 6) - \frac{\pi}{2}\right] + 2$

45. $y = -10 \cos\frac{\pi}{10}x$; $y = 10 \sin\left(\frac{\pi}{10}x - \frac{\pi}{2}\right)$

49.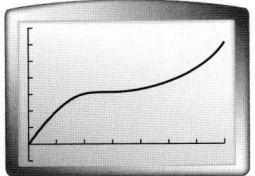

51.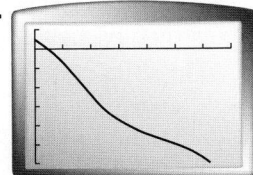

53.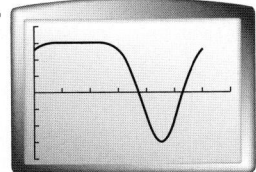

55. C **57.** B **59.** $\frac{\pi}{6}$; $\theta = -\frac{\pi}{12}, \frac{\pi}{12}$ **60.** 4π; $\theta = -2\pi, 2\pi$

61. $\frac{2\pi}{3}$; $\theta = -\frac{\pi}{3}, \frac{\pi}{3}$ **62.** 6π; $\theta = -3\pi, 3\pi$ **63.** 0.0064

64. 0.3456 **65.** ≈ 0.136 **66.** ≈ 0.198 **67.** $\frac{13}{9}$ **68.** $-\frac{8}{5}$

69. 2π **70.** $\frac{15}{4m}$ **71.** $-\frac{t}{14}$

Lesson 13-8   pp. 883–890

Got It? 1a. $\frac{2\sqrt{3}}{3}$ **b.** -1 **c.** -1 **d.** $\frac{3}{4}, \frac{5}{4}, \frac{5}{3}$ by the definition of a unit circle, the length of the hypotenuse of the right triangle is 1; by the Pythag. Thm., the length of the unlabeled leg is $\frac{4}{5}$. So the triangle is similar to a 3-4-5 right triangle. **2a.** ≈ 2.16 **b.** ≈ 4.649 **c.** ≈ 1.035 **d.** undefined **e.** use $\frac{\cos x}{\sin x}$

3.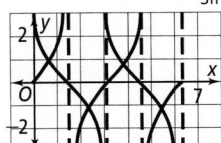

4. ≈ 1.4142 **5.** about 860 ft away and 3185 ft away

Lesson Check 1. 1 **2.** $\frac{2\sqrt{3}}{3}$ **3.** ≈ 1.003 **4.** ≈ 1.346

5. 29.4 ft **6.** $y = 5 \sec \theta = \frac{5}{\cos \theta}$; there is no value of θ that will make $\frac{5}{\cos \theta}$ equal to zero. **7.** The student found the reciprocal of $(1 + \cos 20°) = \frac{1}{1 + \cos 20°} \approx 0.5155$. The answer should be: $\sec 20° + 1 = \frac{1}{\cos 20°} + 1 \approx 1.0642 + 1 \approx 2.0642$. **8.** The graphs have the same period and range. The domain of $y = \sec x$ is all real numbers except $n\pi + \frac{\pi}{4}$ (where n is an integer), which are its asymptotes. The domain of $y = \csc x$ is all real numbers except $\frac{n\pi}{2}$ (where n is an integer), which are its asymptotes. The graph of $y = \csc x$ can be obtained as a translation of $y = \sec\left(x - \frac{\pi}{4}\right)$ of the parent function $y = \sec x$.

Exercises 9. -1 **11.** $\frac{-\sqrt{3}}{\sqrt{3}}$ **13.** 0 **15.** $-\sqrt{2}$

17. ≈ -1.248 **19.** ≈ 0.675 **21.** ≈ -1.6 **23.** undefined

25.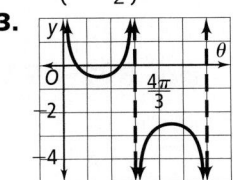

27.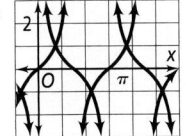

29. 1.1547 **31.** -2.9238 **33.** 1.0642 **35.** 1.7321

37. ≈ 104 ft and ≈ 164 ft **39.** Answers may vary. Sample: $y = \csc\left(\theta + \frac{\pi}{2}\right)$ **41.** C

43.

45.

47a. domain: all real numbers except multiples of π, range: $y \geq 1$ or $y \leq -1$; period: 2π **b.** 1 **c.** -1

49. $\csc 180°$ is undefined because $\sin 180° = 0$ and $\csc \theta = \frac{1}{\sin \theta}$. **51.** $\cot 0°$ is undefined because $\sin 0° = 0$ and $\cot \theta = \frac{\cos \theta}{\sin \theta}$.

53a.

b. The domain of $y = \tan x$ is all real numbers except odd multiples of $\frac{\pi}{2}$, where its asymptotes occur. The domain of $y = \cot x$ is all real numbers except multiples of π, where its asymptotes occur. The range of both functions is all real numbers. **c.** The graphs have the same period and range. Their asymptotes are shifted $\frac{\pi}{2}$ units.

d. Answers may vary. Sample: $x = \frac{\pi}{4}$, $x = \frac{3\pi}{4}$

55. 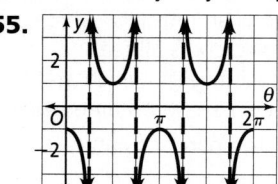 $\frac{\pi}{2}$ units to the left

57. 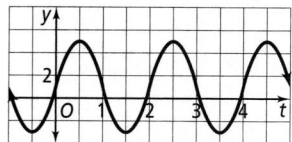 2 units to the left and 1 unit down

59. $\frac{\pi}{6}$ units to the right and 2 units down

61a. II **b.** I

63. $y = \cos 3x$ cycles 3 times for each cycle of $y = \cos x$. Thus, for each cycle of $y = \sec x$, $y = \sec 3x$ cycles 3 times, and each cycle of $y = \sec 3x$ is $\frac{1}{3}$ as wide as one cycle of $y = \sec x$.

Chapter Review pp. 892–896

1. period **2.** unit circle **3.** tangent function
4. phase shift **5.** secant function
6. periodic; from 0 to 4 or from 4 to 6; 4; 2
7. Answers may vary. Sample:

8.

9. −225°

10.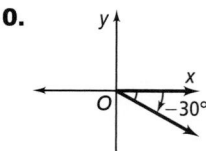

11. 240° **12.** $\sin (315°) = -\frac{\sqrt{2}}{2} \approx -0.71$, $\cos (315°) = \frac{\sqrt{2}}{2} \approx 0.71$; $\sin (-315°) = \frac{\sqrt{2}}{2} \approx 0.71$, $\cos (-315°) = \frac{\sqrt{2}}{2} \approx 0.71$ **13a.** $\frac{\pi}{3}$ **b.** $\frac{1}{2}$, $\frac{\sqrt{3}}{2}$

14a. $-\frac{\pi}{4}$ **b.** $\frac{\sqrt{2}}{2}$, $-\frac{\sqrt{2}}{2}$ **15a.** π **b.** $-1, 0$

16a. 360° **b.** 1, 0 **17a.** 150° **b.** $-\frac{\sqrt{3}}{2}$, $\frac{1}{2}$

18a. −135° **b.** $-\frac{\sqrt{2}}{2}$, $-\frac{\sqrt{2}}{2}$
19. 26.2 ft
20.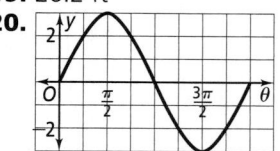

21.

22. $y = 4 \sin 4\theta$
23.

24.

25. $y = 3 \cos 2\theta$ **26.** 0.58, 1.00, 2.15, 2.57, 3.72, 4.14, 5.29, 5.71 **27.** 0.70, 1.30, 2.70, 3.30, 4.70, 5.30
28.

0.41, 1

29.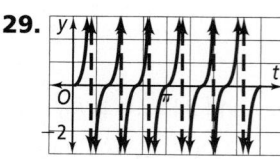

−1, undefined

30.

2, undefined

31.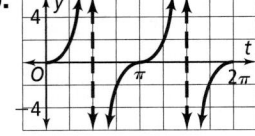

undefined, 0

32.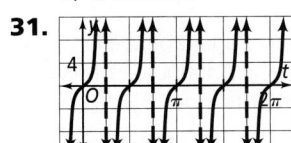

33.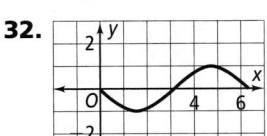

34.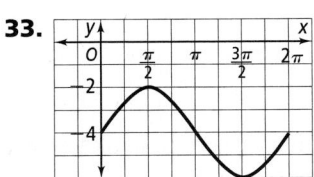

35.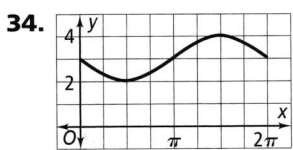

36. $y = \sin\left(x - \frac{\pi}{4}\right)$ **37.** $y = \cos x - 2$ **38.** $\sqrt{2}$

39. $-\frac{\sqrt{3}}{3}$ **40.** 2 **41.** $\sqrt{3}$

42.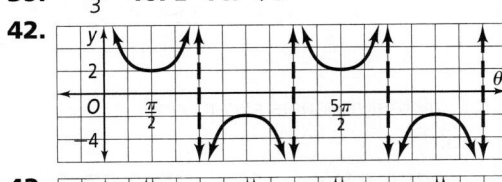

43.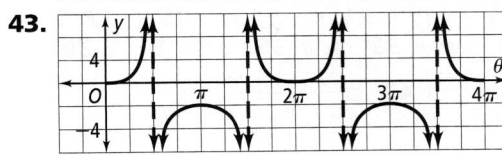

44.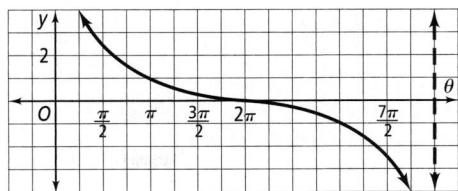

45.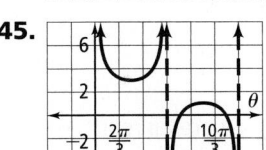

Chapter 14

Get Ready! p. 901

1. $x = \pm\frac{5}{2}$ **2.** $x = \pm\sqrt{23}$ **3.** $x = \pm4\sqrt{\frac{5}{3}}$ **4.** $x = \pm\sqrt{\frac{11}{2}}$
5. $x = \pm\sqrt{30}$ **6.** $x = \pm2$ **7.** $f^{-1}(x) = \frac{x-2}{5}$; domain of
f and *range of* f^{-1}: all real numbers, range of f and
domain of f^{-1}: all real numbers; yes **8.** $f^{-1}(x) = x^2 - 3$;
domain of f and *range of* f^{-1}: all real numbers ≥ -3,
domain of f^{-1}: all real numbers; range of f: all real

numbers ≥ 0; yes **9.** $f^{-1}(x) = \frac{x^2 + 4}{3}$; domain of
f and *range of* f^{-1}: all real numbers $\geq \frac{4}{3}$, domain of f^{-1}:

all real numbers; range of f: all real numbers ≥ 0; yes
10. $f^{-1}(x) = \frac{5}{x}$; domain of f and range of f^{-1}: all real
numbers except 0, domain of f^{-1} and range of f: all real
numbers except 0; yes **11.** $f^{-1}(x) = \frac{10}{x} + 1$; domain of
f and range of f^{-1}: all real numbers except 1, domain of
f^{-1} and range of f: all real numbers except 0; yes

12. $f^{-1}(x) = \frac{10}{x+1}$; domain of f and range of f^{-1}: all real
numbers except 0, domain of f^{-1} and range of f: all real
numbers except -1; yes **13.** $x = -\frac{3}{2}$ **14.** $x = 0.002$
15. $x = 1.0646$ **16.** $x = 18257.4$ **17.** $x = 0.00003$
18. $x = 5$ **19.** 0.67; 0.74; 1.11 **20.** -0.26; -0.97; 3.73
21. 0.96; 0.28; 0.29 **22.** -0.87; 0.50; -0.58
23. Answers may vary. Sample: The eq. is true for all
values of θ for which $\tan^2 \theta$ and $\sec^2 \theta$ are defined.
24. Answers may vary. Sample: the lengths of the sides
of rt. triangles

Lesson 14-1 pp. 904–910

Got It? 1. all real numbers except multiples of π

2. $\frac{\csc \theta}{\sec \theta} = \frac{\left(\frac{1}{\sin \theta}\right)}{\left(\frac{1}{\cos \theta}\right)} = \frac{\cos \theta}{\sin \theta} = \cot \theta$; all real numbers except

multiples of $\frac{\pi}{2}$

3a. $1 + \cot^2 \theta = 1 + \left(\dfrac{\cos \theta}{\sin \theta}\right)^2$

$$= 1 + \dfrac{\cos^2 \theta}{\sin^2 \theta}$$

$$= 1 + \dfrac{1 - \sin^2 \theta}{\sin^2 \theta}$$

$$= 1 + \dfrac{1}{\sin^2 \theta} - \dfrac{\sin^2 \theta}{\sin^2 \theta}$$

$$= 1 + \csc^2 \theta - 1$$

$$= \csc^2 \theta$$

b. No; the domains of $\sin \theta$ and $\cos \theta$ are all real numbers, but the domains of $\tan \theta$, $\cot \theta$, $\sec \theta$, and $\csc \theta$ have restrictions.

4. $\sec^2 \theta - \sec^2 \theta \cos^2 \theta$

$$= \left(\dfrac{1}{\cos \theta}\right)^2 - \left(\dfrac{1}{\cos \theta}\right)^2 \cos^2 \theta$$

$$= \dfrac{1}{\cos^2 \theta} - \dfrac{1}{\cos^2 \theta} \cdot \cos^2 \theta$$

$$= \dfrac{1}{\cos^2 \theta} - \dfrac{\cos^2 \theta}{\cos^2 \theta}$$

$$= \dfrac{1 - \cos^2 \theta}{\cos^2 \theta}$$

$$= \dfrac{\sin^2 \theta}{\cos^2 \theta}$$

$$= \tan^2 \theta$$

5. $\csc \theta$

Lesson Check

1. $\tan \theta \csc \theta$

$$= \dfrac{\sin \theta}{\cos \theta} \cdot \dfrac{1}{\sin \theta}$$

$$= \dfrac{1}{\cos \theta}$$

$$= \sec \theta$$

2. $\csc^2 \theta - \cot^2 \theta$

$$= \left(\dfrac{1}{\sin \theta}\right)^2 - \left(\dfrac{\cos \theta}{\sin \theta}\right)^2$$

$$= \dfrac{1}{\sin^2 \theta} - \dfrac{\cos^2 \theta}{\sin^2 \theta}$$

$$= \dfrac{1 - \cos^2 \theta}{\sin^2 \theta}$$

$$= \dfrac{\sin^2 \theta}{\sin^2 \theta}$$

$$= 1$$

3. $\sin \theta \tan \theta$

$$= \sin \theta \cdot \dfrac{\sin \theta}{\cos \theta}$$

$$= \dfrac{\sin^2 \theta}{\cos \theta}$$

$$= \dfrac{1 - \cos^2 \theta}{\cos \theta}$$

$$= \dfrac{1}{\cos \theta} - \dfrac{\cos^2 \theta}{\cos \theta}$$

$$= \sec \theta - \cos \theta$$

4. $\tan \theta \cot \theta - \sin^2 \theta$

$$= \tan \theta \, \dfrac{1}{\tan \theta} - \sin^2 \theta$$

$$= \dfrac{\tan \theta}{\tan \theta} - \sin^2 \theta$$

$$= 1 - \sin^2 \theta$$

$$= \cos^2 \theta$$

5. Answers may vary. Sample: Letting a and b be the legs, and c the hypotenuse of a right triangle, the Pythagorean Theorem states that $a^2 + b^2 = c^2$. Dividing both sides by c^2, then $\dfrac{a^2}{c^2} + \dfrac{b^2}{c^2} = \left(\dfrac{a}{c}\right)^2 + \left(\dfrac{b}{c}\right)^2 = 1$. Calling the angle between a and c θ, then $\sin \theta = \dfrac{b}{c}$ and $\cos \theta = \dfrac{a}{c}$. By substitution, $\cos^2 \theta + \sin^2 \theta = 1$. **6.** wrong calculation: $2 - \cos^2 \theta = 2 - (1 - \sin^2 \theta) = 2 - 1 + \sin^2 \theta = 1 + \sin^2 \theta$

Exercises

7. $\cos \theta \cot \theta$

$$= \cos \theta \left(\dfrac{\cos \theta}{\sin \theta}\right)$$

$$= \dfrac{1 - \sin^2 \theta}{\sin \theta}$$

$$= \dfrac{1}{\sin \theta} - \sin \theta; \text{ all real numbers except multiples of } \pi$$

9. $\cos \theta \tan \theta$

$$= \cos \theta \left(\dfrac{\sin \theta}{\cos \theta}\right) = \sin \theta; \text{ all real numbers except odd}$$

multiples of $\dfrac{\pi}{2}$

11. $\cos \theta \sec \theta$

$$= \cos \theta \left(\dfrac{1}{\cos \theta}\right) = 1; \text{ all real numbers except odd}$$

multiples of $\dfrac{\pi}{2}$

13. $\sin \theta \csc \theta$

$$= \sin \theta \left(\dfrac{1}{\sin \theta}\right) = \dfrac{\sin \theta}{\sin \theta} = 1; \text{ all real numbers except}$$

multiples of π

15. $\csc \theta - \sin \theta$

$$= \dfrac{1}{\sin \theta} - \sin \theta$$

$$= \dfrac{1 - \sin^2 \theta}{\sin \theta}$$

$$= \dfrac{\cos^2 \theta}{\sin \theta}$$

$$= \cot \theta \cos \theta; \text{ all real numbers except odd}$$

multiples of $\dfrac{\pi}{2}$

17. $\sin^2 \theta$ **19.** $-\cot^2 \theta$ **21.** $\sin \theta$ **23.** 1 **25.** 1 **27.** 1
29. $\sec \theta$ **31.** $\sec^2 \theta$ **33.** $\csc \theta$ **35.** $\sin^2 \theta$ **37.** 1 **39.** 1

41. $\pm \sqrt{1 - \cos^2 \theta}$ **43.** $\pm \dfrac{\sqrt{1 - \sin^2 \theta}}{\sin \theta}$
45. $\pm \sqrt{\csc^2 \theta - 1}$

47. $\sin^2 \theta \tan^2 \theta = \sin^2 \theta \left(\dfrac{\sin^2 \theta}{\cos^2 \theta} \right)$

$$= (1 - \cos^2 \theta) \left(\dfrac{\sin^2 \theta}{\cos^2 \theta} \right)$$

$$= \dfrac{\sin^2 \theta - \sin^2 \theta \cos^2 \theta}{\cos^2 \theta}$$

$$= \dfrac{\sin^2 \theta}{\cos^2 \theta} - \dfrac{\sin^2 \theta \cos^2 \theta}{\cos^2 \theta}$$

$$= \tan^2 \theta - \sin^2 \theta$$

49. $\sin \theta \cos \theta (\tan \theta + \cot \theta)$

$$= \sin \theta \cos \theta \left(\dfrac{\sin \theta}{\cos \theta} + \dfrac{\cos \theta}{\sin \theta} \right)$$

$$= \dfrac{\sin^2 \theta \cos \theta}{\cos \theta} + \dfrac{\cos^2 \theta \sin \theta}{\sin \theta}$$

$$= \sin^2 \theta + \cos^2 \theta = 1$$

51. $\dfrac{\sec \theta}{\cot \theta + \tan \theta}$

$$= \dfrac{\dfrac{1}{\cos \theta}}{\dfrac{\cos \theta}{\sin \theta} + \dfrac{\sin \theta}{\cos \theta}} \cdot \dfrac{\sin \theta \cos \theta}{\sin \theta \cos \theta}$$

$$= \dfrac{\sin \theta}{\cos^2 \theta + \sin^2 \theta} = \dfrac{\sin \theta}{1} = \sin \theta$$

53. $\dfrac{1 - \sin^2 \theta}{\sin^2 \theta}$

55. $\sin^2 \theta + \cos^2 \theta = 1$

$(0.5)^2 + \cos^2 \theta = 1$

$0.25 + \cos^2 \theta = 1$

$\cos^2 \theta = 1 - 0.25$

$\cos^2 \theta = 0.75$

$\cos \theta = \pm \sqrt{0.75}$

Since θ is in the first quadrant, $\cos \theta$ is positive;

$\cos \theta = 0.866025404$

$\tan \theta = \dfrac{\sin \theta}{\cos \theta}$

$$= \dfrac{0.5}{0.866025404}$$

$$= 0.577350269$$

57. $\sin^2 \theta + \cos^2 \theta = 1$

$\sin^2 \theta + (-0.6)^2 = 1$

$\sin^2 \theta + 0.36 = 1$

$\sin^2 \theta = 1 - 0.36$

$\sin^2 \theta = 0.64$

$\sin \theta = \pm \sqrt{0.64}$

Since θ is in the third quadrant, $\sin \theta$ is negative; $\sin \theta = -0.8$

$\tan \theta = \dfrac{\sin \theta}{\cos \theta}$

$$= \dfrac{-0.8}{-0.6}$$

$$= 1.333333333$$

59. $\tan \theta = \dfrac{\sin \theta}{\cos \theta}$, $\sin^2 \theta + \cos^2 \theta = 1$, which can be rewritten as $\sin^2 \theta = 1 - \cos^2 \theta$

$1.2 = \dfrac{\sin \theta}{\cos \theta}$

$1.2^2 = \dfrac{\sin^2 \theta}{\cos^2 \theta}$

$1.44 \left(\cos^2 \theta \right) = \sin^2 \theta$

$1.44 \left(\cos^2 \theta \right) = 1 - \cos^2 \theta$

$1.44 \left(\cos^2 \theta \right) + \cos^2 \theta = 1$

$2.44 \left(\cos^2 \theta \right) = 1$

$\cos^2 \theta = \dfrac{1}{2.44}$

$\cos^2 \theta = 0.409836066$

$\cos \theta = \pm \sqrt{0.409836066}$

Since θ is in the first quadrant, $\cos \theta$ is positive; $\cos \theta = 0.640184400$

$\tan \theta = \dfrac{\sin \theta}{\cos \theta}$

$1.2 = \dfrac{\sin \theta}{0.640184400}$

$\sin \theta = 0.76822128$

61. $\sin^2 \theta + \cos^2 \theta = 1$

$(0.2)^2 + \cos^2 \theta = 1$

$0.04 + \cos^2 \theta = 1$

$\cos^2 \theta = 1 - 0.04$

$\cos^2 \theta = 0.96$

$\cos \theta = \pm \sqrt{0.96}$

Since $\sin \theta$ is positive and $\tan \theta$ is negative, θ is in the fourth quadrant, so $\cos \theta$ is positive; $\cos \theta = 0.97979590$

63. $\cos(\theta + \pi) = |\cos \theta|$, but is also in Quadrant III and is negative, so $\cos(\theta + \pi) = -\cos \theta$ **65.** 1

67. If $n_2 > n_1$, then $\theta_1 > \theta_2$; if $n_2 < n_1$, then $\theta_1 < \theta_2$; if $n_2 = n_1$, then $\theta_2 = \theta_1$. **69.** H **71.** F

73. By the Difference of Squares Property and the second Pythagorean Identity: $(\sec \theta + 1)(\sec \theta - 1) = \sec^2 \theta - 1$

$$= \tan^2 \theta$$

74.
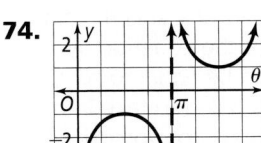

75.

76.

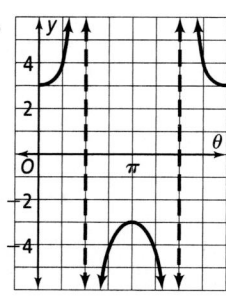

77.

78. 35° **79.** 45° **80.** 135° **81.** 211°
82. $f^{-1}(x) = x - 1$ **83.** $f^{-1}(x) = \frac{x+3}{2}$
84. $f^{-1}(x) = \pm\sqrt{x-4}$

Lesson 14-2   pp. 911–918

Got It? 1a. 120° **b.** 30° **c.** 45° **2a.** 0.46 + 2πn and
2.69 + 2πn **b.** −0.82 + 2πn and 3.96 + 2πn
3a. 0.41 + 2πn and 3.56 + 2πn, or just 0.41 + πn
b. −0.63 + 2πn and 2.51 + 2πn, or just −0.63 + πn
c. $\tan(\theta + \pi) = \tan\theta$ **4.** $\frac{11\pi}{6}$ and $\frac{7\pi}{6}$ **5.** $\frac{\pi}{2}$ and $\frac{3\pi}{2}$
6. The air conditioner comes on about 7 hours after
midnight, 7 A.M., and goes off about 7 hours before
midnight, 5 P.M.
Lesson Check 1. −30° + 360° · n and 210° + 360° · n
2. 60° + 360° · n and 120° + 360° · n **3.** 2.30, 3.98
4. 0 **5.** Answers may vary. Sample: To find the inverse of
$y = 3x - 4$, you interchange x and y and solve for y:
$x = 3y - 4$, $y = \frac{x+4}{3}$. Replace y with $f^{-1}(x)$ to find
$f^{-1}(x) = \frac{x+4}{3}$. To find the inverse of $y = 3\sin\theta - 4$, you
interchange θ and y and solve for $\sin y$ and then solve for
y: $\theta = 3\sin y - 4$, $\sin y = \frac{\theta+4}{3}$ and $y = \sin^{-1}\left(\frac{\theta+4}{3}\right)$.
Replace y with $f^{-1}(\theta)$ to find $f^{-1}(\theta) = \sin^{-1}\left(\frac{\theta+4}{3}\right)$.
The procedure for finding the inverse is the same; for
$y = 3\sin\theta - 4$ you will also use the inverse sine function.
6. The student divided both sides of the equation by
$\sin\theta$, which in the given interval can be equal to zero.
There is an error in that the student failed to take into
account the fact that division by zero is not possible.
Exercises 7. 90° + n · 360° **9.** 240° + n · 360°
and 300° + n · 360° **11.** 90° + n · 360° and 270° +
n · 360°, or just 90° + n · 180° **13.** 0.79 + πn, or just
$\frac{\pi}{4}$ + πn **15.** −0.89 + 2πn and 4.04 + 2πn
17. 2.67 + 2πn and 3.62 + 2πn **19.** $\frac{\pi}{6}, \frac{5\pi}{6}$ **21.** $\frac{\pi}{4}, \frac{5\pi}{4}$

23. 0.46, 3.61 **25.** no solution **27.** $\frac{\pi}{2}, \pi, \frac{3\pi}{2}$
29. $\frac{\pi}{4}, \frac{3\pi}{4}, \frac{5\pi}{4}, \frac{7\pi}{4}$ **31.** 0, π **33.** $\frac{7\pi}{6}, \frac{11\pi}{6}$ **35.** 30° +
n · 360° and 150° + n · 360° **37.** 210° + n · 360° and
330° + n · 360° **39.** $\frac{3\pi}{2}$ **41.** 3.04, 6.18 **43.** 0.0028 s;
0.019 s **45.** 0 + 2πn, $\frac{2}{3}\pi$ + 2πn, $\frac{4}{3}\pi$ + 2πn
47. $\frac{\pi}{6}$ + 2πn, $\frac{5\pi}{6}$ + 2πn, $\frac{3\pi}{2}$ + 2πn
49. $\frac{\pi}{6}$ + 2πn, $\frac{5\pi}{6}$ + 2πn, $\frac{\pi}{2}$ + πn
51. $\frac{\pi}{2}$ + 2πn, $\frac{7\pi}{6}$ + 2πn, $\frac{11\pi}{6}$ + 2πn
53. $\frac{\pi}{6}$ + 2πn, $\frac{5\pi}{6}$ + 2πn **55.** $\frac{\pi}{4}$ + $\frac{\pi n}{2}$ **57.** $\frac{\pi}{4}$ + $\frac{\pi n}{2}$
59. $\frac{2\pi}{3}$ + 2πn, $\frac{4\pi}{3}$ + 2πn **61a.** Answers may vary.
Sample: cos θ = −1, 2 cos θ = −2, 3 cos θ = −3
b. Start with cos θ = −1, and then multiply both sides of
the eq. by any nonzero number.
63. $\theta = \sin^{-1}\left(\frac{y}{3}\right) - 2$ **65.** $\theta = \cos^{-1}\left(\frac{y-1}{2}\right)$ **67.** D
69. C **71.** D **73.** cot θ **74.** $\tan^2\theta$ **75.** 1 **76.** 1
77. sin θ **78.** tan θ **79.** $y = 4\cos\frac{\pi}{4}\theta$
80. $y = 3\cos\theta$ **81.** $y = \frac{\pi}{4}\cos\frac{2}{3}\theta$ **82.** −4 **83.** 21
84. $52\frac{1}{2}$

Lesson 14-3   pp. 919–926

Got It? 1. $\sin\theta = \frac{12}{13}$, $\cos\theta = -\frac{5}{13}$, $\tan\theta = -\frac{12}{5}$,
$\csc\theta = \frac{13}{12}$, $\sec\theta = -\frac{13}{5}$, $\cot\theta = -\frac{5}{12}$
2a. 27.1 m **b.** 32.3 m **3.** $\sin E = \frac{3}{5}$, $\sec F = \frac{5}{3}$
4. ≈76,430 ft ≈ 14.5 mi **5a.** 23.58° **b.** 56.25° **6a.** 72 ft
b. Answers may vary. Sample: Build the ramp in
3 sections, each of which is 24 ft, and with landings
between sections.
Lesson Check 1. $\sin 57° = \frac{b}{c}$, $\cos 57° = \frac{a}{c}$, $\tan 57° = \frac{b}{a}$
2. 15.4 **3.** $\sin 33° = \frac{a}{c} = 0.5$, $\cos 33° = \frac{b}{c} = 0.8$,
$\tan 33° = \frac{a}{b} = 0.6$ **4.** 36.9° **5.** Answers may vary.
Sample: Using the inverse of cosine, you can find the
acute angle between the shortest side and the
hypotenuse, $\theta = \cos^{-1}\left(\frac{8.4}{12.9}\right) \approx 49.4°$. Because the
triangle is a right triangle, the remaining acute angle is
≈ 90° − 49.4° = 40.6°. **6.** The student confuses $\sin^{-1}\theta$
with $\frac{1}{\sin\theta}$. He or she should have divided by sin 0.45.
$x = \frac{4}{\sin 0.45} \approx 9.20$ cm
Exercises
7. $\sin\theta = \frac{3}{5}$, $\cos\theta = -\frac{4}{5}$, $\tan\theta = -\frac{3}{4}$,
$\csc\theta = \frac{5}{3}$, $\sec\theta = -\frac{5}{4}$, $\cot\theta = -\frac{4}{3}$
9. $\sin\theta = -\frac{5\sqrt{26}}{26}$, $\cos\theta = \frac{\sqrt{26}}{26}$, $\tan\theta = -5$,
$\csc\theta = -\frac{\sqrt{26}}{5}$, $\sec\theta = \sqrt{26}$, $\cot\theta = -\frac{1}{5}$

11. $\sin \theta = \frac{\sqrt{7}}{4}$, $\cos \theta = -\frac{3}{4}$, $\tan \theta = -\frac{\sqrt{7}}{3}$,
$\csc \theta = \frac{4\sqrt{7}}{7}$, $\sec \theta = -\frac{4}{3}$, $\cot \theta = -\frac{3\sqrt{7}}{7}$

13a. $\frac{15}{17} \approx 0.88$ **b.** $\frac{17}{8} \approx 2.13$ **c.** $\frac{8}{15} \approx 0.53$

d. $\frac{17}{8} \approx 2.13$ **e.** $\frac{17}{15} \approx 1.13$ **f.** $\frac{8}{15} \approx 0.53$ **15.** 41.8

17. 25.2 **19.** $a \approx 8.7$, $m\angle A = 60.0°$, $m\angle B = 30.0°$
21. $a = 9.0$, $m\angle A \approx 36.9°$, $m\angle B \approx 53.1°$ **23.** $a \approx 8.0$,
$m\angle A \approx 61.8°$, $m\angle B \approx 28.2°$ **25a.** $m\angle A = \cos^{-1}\left(\frac{1200}{d}\right)$
b. 37° **c.** 53°

27.

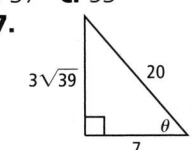

$\sin \theta = \frac{3\sqrt{39}}{20}$, $\tan \theta = \frac{3\sqrt{39}}{7}$, $\csc \theta = \frac{20\sqrt{39}}{117}$,
$\sec \theta = \frac{20}{7}$, $\cot \theta = \frac{7\sqrt{39}}{117}$

29.

$\sin \theta = \frac{24}{25}$, $\cos \theta = \frac{7}{25}$, $\csc \theta = \frac{25}{24}$,
$\sec \theta = \frac{25}{7}$, $\cot \theta = \frac{7}{24}$

31.

$\sin \theta = \frac{4\sqrt{41}}{41}$, $\cos \theta = \frac{5\sqrt{41}}{41}$, $\tan \theta = \frac{4}{5}$,
$\csc \theta = \frac{\sqrt{41}}{4}$, $\sec \theta = \frac{\sqrt{41}}{5}$

33.

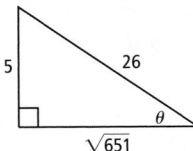

$\sin \theta = \frac{5}{26}$, $\cos \theta = \frac{\sqrt{651}}{26}$, $\tan \theta = \frac{5\sqrt{651}}{651}$
$\sec \theta = \frac{26\sqrt{651}}{651}$, $\cot \theta = \frac{\sqrt{651}}{5}$

35. 33.4 ft **37.** 20.3 m² **39.** $c \approx 12.2$, $m\angle A \approx 35.0°$,
$m\angle B \approx 55.0°$ **41.** $a \approx 3.9$, $c \approx 6.9$, $m\angle B = 55.8°$
43. $a \approx 19.8$, $b \approx 2.9$, $m\angle A = 81.7°$ **45.** Using inverse
sine, you can find that $\theta = 30°$. Since sine is positive in the
first and second quadrants, another solution is 150°. All the
solutions would be $30° + n \cdot 360°$ and $150° + n \cdot 360°$.

47. $\sec A = \frac{c}{b} = \frac{1}{\left(\frac{b}{c}\right)} = \frac{1}{\cos A}$

49. $\cos^2 A + \sin^2 A = \left(\frac{b}{c}\right)^2 + \left(\frac{a}{c}\right)^2$
$= \frac{b^2 + a^2}{c^2} = 1$

53. G **55.** I

Lesson 14-4 pp. 928–934

Got It? 1. 36.6 in.² **2.** 31.0 yd **3a.** 68.4° **b.** yes;
$\frac{\sin T}{\text{height}} = \frac{\sin 90°}{9}$; height $\approx 9 \sin 47° \approx 6.6$ **4.** 104.7 ft

Lesson Check 1. ≈ 10.7 square units **2.** ≈ 19.8
3. $\approx 26.3°$ or $\approx 153.7°$ **4.** AAS, ASA **5.** No; For $\frac{\sin 22°}{\sin 45°}$
you find the sine of each numerator and denominator,
$\sin 22°$ and $\sin 45°$; for $\sin\left(\frac{22°}{45°}\right)$ you find the sine of the
quotient of $\left(\frac{22°}{45°}\right)$.

Exercises 7. 9.1 in.² **9.** 10.9 **11.** 7.4 **13.** 33.5°
15. 31.7° **17.** 32 cm **19.** 66° **21.** $m\angle E \approx 40.3°$,
$m\angle F \approx 85.7°$, $f \approx 12.3$ m **25.** 44.4 **27.** 49.4
29. 28.0 ft **31.** 4.0 cm **33a.** 56.4°, 93.6°, 26.4° **b.** No;
$\triangle EFG$ could be congruent to $\triangle ABC$ instead of $\triangle ABD$.
35. No; you need at least one side in order to set up a
proportion you can then solve.
37. I
39. $A = \frac{1}{2} ab \sin C$
$\sin C = \frac{2(A)}{ab} = \frac{2(31.5)}{9(14)} = 0.5$
$m\angle C = \sin^{-1} 0.5 = 30°$
So, the measure of the included angle for the given
sides is 30° or 150°.

40.

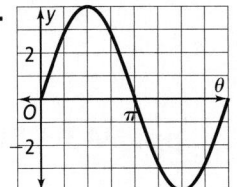

41.

42.

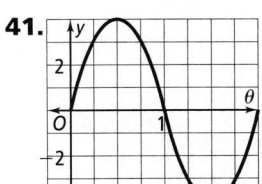

43. $\langle -1, 7 \rangle$ **44.** $\langle 5, 3 \rangle$ **45.** $\langle -3, -1 \rangle$ **46.** $\langle -6, 4 \rangle$
47. 53.1° **48.** 24.6° **49.** 38.7° **50.** 54.7°

Lesson 14-5   pp. 936–942

Got It? 1a. 6.4

b. 1 mi to 6 mi;
$a^2 = 2.5^2 + 3.5^2 - 2(2.5)(3.5) \cos A$
$a^2 = 18.5 - 17.5 \cos A$;
if $A = 0°$, then $\cos A = 1$ and $a = 1$; if $A = 180°$,
then $\cos A = -1$ and $a = 6$. **2.** 75.3° **3.** 30.7°

Lesson Check 1. ≈ 11.85 in. **2.** $\approx 52.4°$ **3.** $\approx 34.1°$
4. $\approx 60.3°$ **5.** Use the Law of Sines when you have two
sides and a non-included angle or two angles and a side;
use the Law of Cosines when you have two sides and an
included angle or three sides. **6.** The denominator should
be negative. The answer should be:

$$\cos C = \frac{15^2 - 11^2 - 17^2}{-2(11)(17)} \approx 0.495$$

$$C = \cos^{-1}(0.495) \approx 60.3°$$

Exercises 7. 37.1 **9.** 13.7 **11.** 27.0 **13.** 33.7° **15.** 47.2°
17. 50.8 **19.** 27.0° **21.** $b^2 = a^2 + c^2 - 2ac \cos B$
23. $\frac{\sin B}{b} = \frac{\sin C}{c}$ **25.** $\frac{\sin C}{c} = \frac{\sin A}{a}$ **27.** ≈ 59.1 nautical
miles **29.** $b \approx 34.7$, $m\angle A \approx 26.7°$, $m\angle C \approx 33.3°$
31. $m\angle A \approx 56.1°$, $m\angle B \approx 70.0°$, $m\angle C \approx 53.9°$

33. For any two side lengths a and b, the ratio $\frac{a}{b}$ is equal to the
ratio $\frac{\sin A}{\sin B}$, which can be found since A and B are given.

35a. ≈ 45.4 mi **b.** 14.4° left; 4.4° west of north
37. 11.0 cm **39.** 27.0° **41.** 13.0 cm **43.** 21.5°
45. 8.3 ft **47.** 79.6° **49.** 18 cm
51. a. 2.1 m
   b. 9.8 m²
53. a. $\cos A > 0$ if $b^2 + c^2 > a^2$;
   $\cos A = 0$ if $b^2 + c^2 = a^2$;
   $\cos A < 0$ if $b^2 + c^2 < a^2$
b. acute $\triangle$ if $\cos A > 0$; right $\triangle$ if $\cos A = 0$;
obtuse $\triangle$ if $\cos A < 0$

Lesson 14-6   pp. 943–950

Got It?
1. $\cos\left(\theta - \frac{\pi}{2}\right) = \cos\left(-\left(\frac{\pi}{2} - \theta\right)\right)$
$$= \cos\left(\frac{\pi}{2} - \theta\right)$$
$$= \sin\theta$$

2. $\sec(90° - A) = \dfrac{1}{\cos(90° - A)} = \dfrac{1}{\sin\theta} = \csc\theta$
   $\sec(90° - A) = \csc\theta$

3a. 0, π **b.** yes; πn
4. $\dfrac{\sqrt{6} - \sqrt{2}}{4}$

5. $\sin(A + B) = \sin(A - (-B))$
$$= \sin A \cos(-B) - \cos A \sin(-B)$$
$$= \sin A \cos B - \cos A(-\sin B)$$
$$= \sin A \cos B + \cos A \sin B$$

6. $-2 - \sqrt{3}$

Lesson Check
1. $\sin\left(\frac{\pi}{2} + \theta\right) + \sin\left(\frac{\pi}{2} - \theta\right)$
$$= \sin\left(\frac{\pi}{2} - (-\theta)\right) + \sin\left(\frac{\pi}{2} - \theta\right)$$
$$= \cos(-\theta) + \cos\theta$$
$$= \cos\theta + \cos\theta$$
$$= 2\cos\theta$$

2. $\frac{\pi}{4}, \frac{5\pi}{4}$ **3.** $\frac{\sqrt{2}}{2}$ **4.** $-\dfrac{\sqrt{2} + \sqrt{6}}{4}$

5. There are 2 solutions, $\frac{\pi}{2}$ and $\frac{3\pi}{2}$, between 0 and 2π
because: $-\cos\theta = \cos\theta$
      $2\cos\theta = 0$
      $\cos\theta = 0; \theta = \frac{\pi}{2}, \frac{3\pi}{2}$

6. $\sin\left(\frac{\pi}{2} - \theta\right) = \sin\frac{\pi}{2}\cos\theta - \cos\frac{\pi}{2}\sin\theta$
$$= (1)\cos\theta - (0)\sin\theta$$
$$= \cos\theta$$

Exercises

7. $\csc\left(\theta - \frac{\pi}{2}\right) = \dfrac{1}{\sin\left(\theta - \frac{\pi}{2}\right)}$
$$= \dfrac{1}{\sin\left(-\left(\frac{\pi}{2} - \theta\right)\right)}$$
$$= \dfrac{1}{-\sin\left(\frac{\pi}{2} - \theta\right)}$$
$$= \dfrac{1}{-\cos\theta}$$
$$= -\sec\theta$$

9. $\cot\left(\frac{\pi}{2} - \theta\right) = \dfrac{\cos\left(\frac{\pi}{2} - \theta\right)}{\sin\left(\frac{\pi}{2} - \theta\right)}$
$$= \dfrac{\sin\theta}{\cos\theta}$$
$$= \tan\theta$$

11. $\tan\left(\theta - \frac{\pi}{2}\right) = \tan\left(-\left(\frac{\pi}{2} - \theta\right)\right)$
$$= -\tan\left(\frac{\pi}{2} - \theta\right)$$
$$= -\cot\theta$$

13. $\tan(90° - A) = \cot A$ **15.** $\cot(90° - A) = \tan A$
17. $\frac{\pi}{2}, \frac{3\pi}{2}$ **19.** π **21.** $\frac{\pi}{2}, \frac{3\pi}{2}$ **23.** $\frac{\sqrt{2}}{2}$ **25.** 0
27. $-\sqrt{3} - 2$ **29.** $\dfrac{\sqrt{2} + \sqrt{6}}{4}$
31. $-2 + \sqrt{3}$ **33.** $-\frac{1}{2}$ **35.** $\frac{1}{2}$
37. $\sin(A - B) = \cos\left[\frac{\pi}{2} - (A - B)\right]$
$$= \cos\left[\left(\frac{\pi}{2} - A\right) + B\right]$$
$$= \cos\left(\frac{\pi}{2} - A\right)\cos B - \sin\left(\frac{\pi}{2} - A\right)\sin B$$
$$= \sin A \cos B - \cos A \sin B$$

39. $\tan(A+B) = \dfrac{\sin(A+B)}{\cos(A+B)}$

$= \dfrac{\sin A \cos B + \cos A \sin B}{\cos A \cos B - \sin A \sin B}$

$= \dfrac{\frac{\sin A \cos B + \cos A \sin B}{\cos A \cos B}}{\frac{\cos A \cos B - \sin A \sin B}{\cos A \cos B}}$

$= \dfrac{\frac{\sin A \cos B}{\cos A \cos B} + \frac{\cos A \sin B}{\cos A \cos B}}{\frac{\cos A \cos B}{\cos A \cos B} - \frac{\sin A \sin B}{\cos A \cos B}}$

$= \dfrac{\tan A + \tan B}{1 - \tan A \tan B}$

41. $(5\cos\theta - 5\sqrt{3}\sin\theta,\ 5\sin\theta + 5\sqrt{3}\cos\theta)$
43. $\sin 5\theta$ **45.** $\cos 5\theta$ **47.** $\tan 2\theta$
49. a. even: cosine, secant; odd: sine, cosecant, tangent, cotangent

b. No; answers may vary. Sample:
$y = \sin x - \cos x$. For $x = \frac{\pi}{4}$, $f(x) = \sin\frac{\pi}{4} - \cos\frac{\pi}{4} = 0$, and $f(-x) = \sin\left(-\frac{\pi}{4}\right) - \cos\left(-\frac{\pi}{4}\right) = -\sqrt{2}$. Because $f(x) \neq f(-x)$, and $-f(x) \neq f(-x)$, the function is neither even nor odd.

51. $\sin(\pi - \theta) = \sin\pi\cos\theta - \cos\pi\sin\theta$
$= 0 - (-1)\sin\theta = \sin\theta$

53. $\cos(\pi + \theta) = \cos\pi\cos\theta - \sin\pi\sin\theta$
$= (-1)\cos\theta - 0 = -\cos\theta$

55. $\cos\left(\theta + \frac{3\pi}{2}\right) = \cos\theta\cos\frac{3\pi}{2} - \sin\theta\sin\frac{3\pi}{2}$
$= \cos\theta(0) - \sin\theta(-1) = \sin\theta$

57. I
59. $\sin(165°) = \sin(15°)$
$= \sin(45° - 30°)$
$= \sin 45°\cos 30° - \cos 45°\sin 30°$
$= \dfrac{\sqrt{2}}{2} \cdot \dfrac{\sqrt{3}}{2} - \dfrac{\sqrt{2}}{2} \cdot \dfrac{1}{2}$
$= \dfrac{\sqrt{6}}{4} - \dfrac{\sqrt{2}}{4} = \dfrac{\sqrt{6} - \sqrt{2}}{4}$

60. ≈ 16.34 ft **61.** ≈ 10.0 cm **62.** $\frac{4\pi}{9}$ and 1.40
63. $-\frac{5\pi}{18}$ and -0.87 **64.** $-\frac{\pi}{12}$ and -0.26
65. $\frac{7\pi}{18}$ and 1.22 **66.** $\frac{19\pi}{18}$ and 3.32
67. $\cos A \cos B - \sin A \sin B$
68. $\sin A \cos B + \cos A \sin B$ **69.** $\frac{\tan A + \tan B}{1 - \tan A \tan B}$

Lesson 14-7   pp. 951–957

Got It?
1. $\cos 2\theta = \cos^2\theta - \sin^2\theta$
$= \cos^2\theta - (1 - \cos^2\theta)$
$= \cos^2\theta - 1 + \cos^2\theta$
$= 2\cos^2\theta - 1$

2. $\frac{\sqrt{3}}{2}$ **3.** $2\cos 2\theta = 2(2\cos^2\theta - 1) = 4\cos^2\theta - 2$
4a. $\frac{1}{2}$ **b.** $-\frac{\sqrt{3}}{3}$
5a. $-\frac{3}{5}$ **b.** $-\frac{4}{3}$ **c.** If $270° < \theta < 360°$,
$135° < \frac{\theta}{2} < 180°$ and $\frac{\theta}{2}$ is also in Quadrant II. The answers will remain the same.
Lesson Check 1. $\frac{\sqrt{3}}{2}$ **2.** 1 **3a.** $-\frac{5}{13}$ **b.** $\sqrt{\frac{13 + 2\sqrt{13}}{26}}$
c. $-\sqrt{\frac{13 - 2\sqrt{13}}{26}}$

4. The student did not correctly determine in which quadrant $\frac{\theta}{2}$ will be. If $180° < \theta < 270°$, $90° < \frac{\theta}{2} < 135°$, then $\frac{\theta}{2}$ is in Quadrant II and the tangent will be negative. **5.** $\sin 4A$

6. $\sin\frac{5A}{2} = -\sqrt{\frac{1 - \cos 5A}{2}}$ if $360° < 5A < 450°$, $180° < \frac{5A}{2} < 225°$ and the sine is negative in Quadrant III.

Exercises
7. $\sin 2\theta = \sin(\theta + \theta)$
$= \sin\theta\cos\theta + \cos\theta\sin\theta$
$= 2\sin\theta\cos\theta$

9. $-\frac{\sqrt{3}}{2}$ **11.** $-\sqrt{3}$ **13.** $-\frac{1}{2}$ **15.** $-\frac{1}{2}$ **17.** $\frac{\sqrt{2 + \sqrt{3}}}{2}$
19. $\frac{\sqrt{2 - \sqrt{3}}}{2}$ **21.** $\frac{\sqrt{2 + \sqrt{2}}}{2}$ **23.** 0 **25.** $\frac{3\sqrt{10}}{10}$ **27.** 3
29. $\frac{4\sqrt{17}}{17}$ **31.** -4

33. $\cos B = 2\cos^2\frac{B}{2} - 1$
$2\cos^2\frac{B}{2} = \cos B + 1$
$\cos^2\frac{B}{2} = \frac{\cos B + 1}{2}$
Since $\cos B = \frac{a}{c}$,
$\cos^2\frac{B}{2} = \frac{\frac{a}{c} + 1}{2} = \frac{a + c}{2c}$.

35. $\cos 2R = \cos^2 R - \sin^2 R$
$= \left(\frac{s}{t}\right)^2 - \left(\frac{r}{t}\right)^2$
$= \frac{s^2}{t^2} - \frac{r^2}{t^2}$
$= \frac{s^2 - r^2}{t^2}$

37. $\sin^2\frac{S}{2} = \left(\sin\frac{S}{2}\right)^2$
$= \left(\pm\sqrt{\frac{1 - \cos S}{2}}\right)^2$
$= \frac{1 - \cos S}{2} = \frac{1 - \frac{r}{t}}{2}$
$= \frac{1}{2} - \frac{r}{2t} = \frac{t - r}{2t}$

39. $\tan^2 \frac{S}{2} = \left(\tan \frac{S}{2}\right)^2$

$\qquad = \left(\pm \sqrt{\frac{1-\cos S}{1+\cos S}}\right)^2 = \frac{1-\cos S}{1+\cos S} = \frac{1-\frac{r}{t}}{1+\frac{r}{t}}$

$\qquad = \frac{t-r}{t+r}$

41. $-\frac{24}{25}$ **43.** $\frac{24}{7}$ **45.** $\frac{\sqrt{5}}{5}$ **47.** $-\frac{1}{2}$

49. $\cos\theta(8\sin\theta - 3) = 0$; $\frac{\pi}{2}, \frac{3\pi}{2}$, 0.384, 2.757

51. $\cos\theta(2\sin^2\theta - 1) = 0$; $\frac{\pi}{2}, \frac{3\pi}{2}, \frac{\pi}{4}, \frac{3\pi}{4}, \frac{5\pi}{4}, \frac{7\pi}{4}$

53. 1 **55.** $\cos\theta - \sin\theta$

59. $4\sin\theta\cos\theta(\cos^2\theta - \sin^2\theta)$

61. $\dfrac{4\tan\theta(1-\tan^2\theta)}{\tan^4\theta - 6\tan^2\theta + 1}$

63. $\pm\sqrt{\dfrac{1}{2} \pm \dfrac{1}{2}\sqrt{\dfrac{1}{2} + \dfrac{1}{2}\cos\theta}}$

65. a. $\tan\frac{A}{2} = \pm\sqrt{\frac{1-\cos A}{1+\cos A}}$

$\qquad = \pm\sqrt{\frac{1-\cos A}{1+\cos A} \cdot \frac{1+\cos A}{1+\cos A}}$

$\qquad = \pm\sqrt{\frac{1-\cos^2 A}{(1+\cos A)^2}}$

$\qquad = \pm\sqrt{\frac{\sin^2 A}{(1+\cos A)^2}}$

$\qquad = \frac{\sin A}{1+\cos A}$

Since $\tan\frac{A}{2}$ and $\sin A$ have the same sign wherever $\tan\frac{A}{2}$ is defined, only the positive sign occurs.

67. G **69.** I **71.** $\frac{\sqrt{2}}{2}$ **72.** $\frac{\sqrt{3}}{2}$ **73.** $\sqrt{3}$ **74.** about 4.1; 12 **75.** 2; 4 **76.** 45.2 **77.** 26.6 **78.** 57.6

Chapter Review   pp. 959–962

1. Law of Sines **2.** trig. ratios **3.** Law of Cosines **4.** trig. ident. **5.** Law of Sines **6.** $\sin\theta\tan\theta = \sin\theta\frac{\sin\theta}{\cos\theta} = \frac{\sin^2\theta}{\cos\theta} = \frac{1-\cos^2\theta}{\cos\theta} = \frac{1}{\cos\theta} - \cos\theta$; domain of validity: all real numbers except odd multiples of $\frac{\pi}{2}$

7. $\cos^2\theta\cot^2\theta = \cos^2\theta\frac{\cos^2\theta}{\sin^2\theta} = \frac{\cos^2\theta(1-\sin^2\theta)}{\sin^2\theta} = \frac{\cos^2\theta - \cos^2\theta\sin^2\theta}{\sin^2\theta} = \cot^2\theta - \cos^2\theta$; domain of validity: all real numbers except 0 and multiples of π
8. $\cos^2\theta$ **9.** 1 **10.** 1 **11.** $-\sin^2\theta$ **12.** $\cos^2\theta$ **13.** 1
14. $-60°$ **15.** $60°$ **16.** $-30°$ **17.** $30°$ **18.** 0.34
19. -1.11 **20.** 2.27 **21.** 0.20 **22.** $\frac{\pi}{3}, \frac{5\pi}{3}$ **23.** $\frac{\pi}{6}, \frac{7\pi}{6}$

24. $0, \frac{\pi}{2}, \pi$ **25.** $\frac{\pi}{3}, \frac{5\pi}{3}$ **26.** $\sin\theta = \frac{4}{5}, \cos\theta = -\frac{3}{5}$, $\tan\theta = -\frac{4}{3}, \csc\theta = \frac{5}{4}, \sec\theta = -\frac{5}{3}, \cot\theta = -\frac{3}{4}$

27. $\sin\theta = -\frac{15}{17}, \cos\theta = -\frac{8}{17}, \tan\theta = \frac{15}{8}, \csc\theta = -\frac{17}{15}$, $\sec\theta = -\frac{17}{8}, \cot\theta = \frac{8}{15}$ **28.** $\frac{3}{5}$, 0.6 **29.** $\frac{4}{5}$, 0.8

30. $\frac{3}{4}$, 0.75 **31.** $\frac{5}{3}$, 1.$\overline{6}$ **32.** $g \approx 9.5, \angle F \approx 18.4$, $\angle H \approx 71.6$ **33.** $h = 16, \angle F \approx 36.9, \angle H \approx 53.1$
34. $f \approx 37.7, \angle F \approx 43.3, \angle H \approx 46.7$
35. $g \approx 6.4, \angle F \approx 51.3, \angle H \approx 38.7$ **36.** 13.7
37. 29.4 **38.** 13.14 m² **39.** 92.12 ft² **40.** 7.1 in.
41. 43.9° **42.** 52.2°

43. $\cos\left(\theta + \frac{\pi}{2}\right) = \cos\theta\cos\frac{\pi}{2} - \sin\theta\sin\frac{\pi}{2}$

$\qquad = \cos\theta \times 0 - \sin\theta \times 1 = -\sin\theta$

44. $\sin^2\left(\theta - \frac{\pi}{2}\right) = \left[\sin\left(\theta - \frac{\pi}{2}\right)\right]^2$

$\qquad = \left[\sin\theta \cos\frac{\pi}{2} - \cos\theta \sin\frac{\pi}{2}\right]^2$

$\qquad = [\sin\theta \times 0 - \cos\theta \times 1]^2$

$\qquad = (-\cos\theta)^2 = \cos^2\theta$

45. $2 - \sqrt{3}$ **46.** $-\frac{\sqrt{3}}{2}$ **47.** $\frac{\sqrt{2}-\sqrt{6}}{4}$ **48.** $-2-\sqrt{3}$

49. $\frac{\sqrt{3}}{2}$ **50.** $\frac{\sqrt{3}}{2}$ **51.** $-\sqrt{3}$ **52.** $-\frac{\sqrt{3}}{2}$

Skills Handbook

p. 972 1. 46% **3.** 0.7% **5.** 1.035 **7.** 25%
9. 66.$\overline{6}$% **11.** 115% **13.** 12.5 **15.** 75 **17.** 20%
p. 973 1. $1\frac{2}{5}$ **3.** $6\frac{5}{6}$ **5.** $\frac{5}{21}$ **7.** $2\frac{19}{20}$ **9.** 8 **11.** $1\frac{1}{2}$
13. 2 **15.** 42
p. 974 1. 3 to 4 **3.** 19 g in 2 oz **5.** $\frac{14}{5}$ **7.** 8 **9.** 1.8
11. 1.95 **13.** 45.5 **15.** ± 6
p. 975 1. 1 **3.** -38 **5.** -17 **7.** 4 **9.** 28 **11.** -12
13. -90 **15.** 12 **17.** 19 **19.** 9 **21.** -10
p. 976 1. 14 m² **3.** 30 cm² **5.** $91\frac{1}{8}$ ft³ **7.** 100π in.³
9. 110.5 in.² **11.** $121\frac{1}{2}$ ft²
p. 977 1. I **3.** IV **5.** III **7.** $\frac{4}{5}$ **9.** 0 **11.** $\frac{1}{5}$ **13.** $\left(5, -\frac{3}{2}\right)$
15. $\left(\frac{5}{2}, -1\right)$
p. 978 1. x^3 **3.** $a^4 b$ **5.** $\frac{1}{c^4}$ **7.** $\frac{x^5}{y^7 z^3}$ **9.** d^8 **11.** c^6
13. $\frac{a^4}{b^5}$ **15.** $\frac{a^4}{b^4}$ **17.** c^{12} **19.** $u^{12}v^6$ **21.** a^3 **23.** $\frac{1}{mg^3}$
25. $\frac{a^5}{2}$
p. 979 1. $x^2 + 10x - 5$ **3.** $12x^4 - 20x^3 + 36x^2$

5. $x^2 - 2x - 15$ **7.** $(a - 6)(a - 2)$ **9.** $(x + 4)(x + 1)$
11. $(y + 8)(y - 3)$ **13.** $2x(x^2 + 2x - 4)$

p. 980 1. 1.34×10^6 **3.** 7.75×10^{-4} **5.** 111,300
7. 1.895×10^3 **9.** 1.234×10^5 **11.** 6.4×10^5
13. 8.52×10^2 **15.** 17.5 **17.** 8.95×10^{-12}
19. 3.77×10^{10} **21.** 1.8×10^{-6}

p. 981 1. 10 **3.** 15 **5.** 54.7 **7.** 5 **9.** 13 **11.** 22.7
13. 2.8 **15.** 9 **17.** 7

p. 982 1.

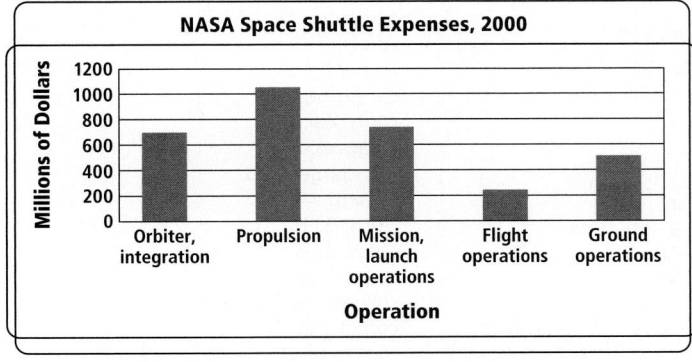

NASA Space Shuttle Expenses, 2000

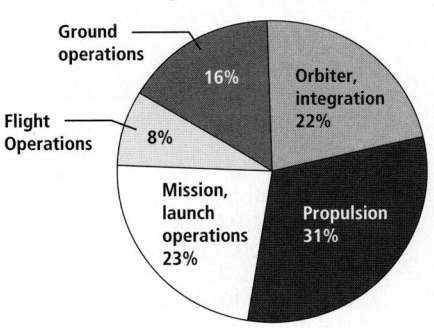

NASA Space Shuttle Expenses, 2000

p. 983 1. $3.\overline{7}$; 5; 5 **3.** $3.9\overline{6}$; 2.4; 2.4 **5.** 1.5; 1.5;
no mode

7.

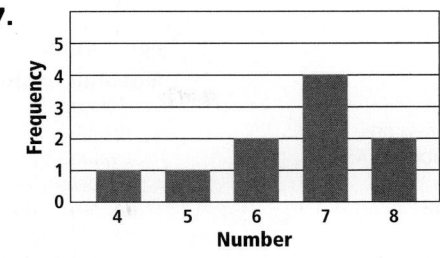

p. 984 1. $\frac{a}{3b^2}$ **3.** $\frac{1}{2}$ **5.** $4x$ **7.** $\frac{2}{h}$ **9.** $\frac{x}{10}$ **11.** $\frac{74x}{35}$
13. $\frac{4x^2}{5}$ **15.** $\frac{16}{x}$ **17.** $\frac{16}{5}$ **19.** $2x$

Index

Index

arithmetic sequences, 572, 604
atmospheric pressure, 475, 513
for binomial probability, 732, 734
brightness of stars, 467
for centripetal force, 372
Change of Base, 464
circumference of a circle, 15, 17
for conditional probability, 697, 753
converting between radians and
    degrees, 844
for density, 372
direct variation function, 68
for distance, 408
earthquake intensity, 453
electric current, 16
error of margin for drilling a hole, 48
for expanding a binomial, 327
experimental probability of an event,
    681
explicit, 565, 567, 604, 605
generating mathematical patterns,
    564, 565, 567
for geometric sequences, 565, 566,
    567
for geometric series, 597, 606
harmonic mean, 540
for height as a function of time, 344
hourly wage, 548
Ideal Gas Law, 504
independent events, 753
interest, 446, 488
inverses of, 408
for kinetic energy, 343, 344
mass energy equivalence, 493
maximum flow of water in a pipe, 395
mean, 711, 754
measuring bacteria populations, 482
median, 711
mode, 711
mutually exclusive events, 689, 753
number of combinations, 676
number of permutations, 676
perimeter of a rectangle, 28
for planetary motion, 383
point-slope form, 81
potential energy, 502
probability of A and B, 688, 753
probability of A or B, 689, 753
quadratic, 240–248
radioactive to nonradioactive carbon,
    387
radius of a circle, 414
radius of a sphere, 365
recursive, 565, 566, 604, 605
resistance, 540
slope, 81, 84
solving for one variable, 142, 184
sound, measuring, 466, 475
standard deviation, 711, 719
sum of arithmetic series, 587, 605
sum of geometric series, 595, 606

surface area, 66, 276, 531
surface area of a cylinder, 53
tapered cylinders, 547
temperature conversions, 29, 410
for time as a function of acceleration,
    371
variance, 719
for velocity, 372, 404, 480
for volume, 67, 292, 309, 365, 392,
    410, 421, 426, 531
wind chill, 387
wind power, 327

fractions, complex, 536, 537

frequency, cumulative, 695

frog-jumping competition, 228

function(s). *See also* equation(s)
    absolute value, 90, 107–113, 125,
        126
    adding, 398, 399
    as Big Idea, 122, 133, 182, 183, 266,
        267, 346, 347, 422, 486, 487, 552,
        553, 892, 958, 959
    composition of, 399, 400–401, 408,
        409
    continuous, 516
    cosecant, 883
    cosine, 875–882, 895
    cotangent, 883
    cube root, 417
    cubic, 283–284, 339–340
    defined, 62
    dependent variable in, 63
    discontinuous, 516
    discrete, 437
    dividing, 398, 399
    domain of, 62, 398, 399, 408, 414,
        425, 434, 435, 515, 516
    exponential. *See* exponential functions
    family of, 99–106, 125
    graphing quadratic, 194–201
    graphing trigonometric, 860, 886
    greatest integer, 90
    identifying, 60–65
    independent variables in, 63
    input of the, 63
    inverse. *See* inverse functions
    linear. *See* linear functions
    logarithmic. *See* logarithmic functions
    maximum and minimum values, 158,
        185, 195, 291, 292
    monomial, 352
    multiplying, 398, 399
    natural logarithmic, 478–483
    objective, 157, 185
    one-to-one, 408
    operations with, 398–404, 425
    parent. *See* Parent Function
    periodic. *See* periodic function
    piecewise, 90–91
    polynomial. *See* polynomial functions

power, 341
quadratic. *See* quadratic functions
quartic, 341
radical, 414–420
rational. *See* rational functions
reciprocal. *See* reciprocal functions
reciprocal trigonometric, 883–890,
    896
rewriting by completing the square,
    233–239
secant, 883
simplest form of, 99, 125
sine, 851–858, 875–882, 894
square root, 414–420, 426
step, 90
subtracting, 398, 399
transformations. *See* transformations
translations. *See* translations
trigonometric, 860, 886
vertical-line test, 62–63
zeros of. *See* zero(s)

function notation, 62, 63, 407

function rule, 63

Fundamental Counting Principle, 674,
    675

Fundamental Theorem of Algebra,
    319–324, 351

G

Galton box, 731

GCF (greatest common factor), 218,
    297

geography, 849

geometric
    mean, 583, 605
    probability, 684
    series, 595–601, 606
    transformations, 801–808, 820

geometric sequences, 580–586
    analyzing, 581
    arithmetic vs., 583
    defined, 580
    formula for, 565, 566, 567, 605
    geometric series, 595–601, 606
    identifying, 580–581

Geometry as Big Idea, 958, 959

Geometry exercises, 17, 30, 31, 39, 52,
    66, 73, 88, 154, 173, 180, 213,
    222, 238, 246, 294, 301, 308, 309,
    329, 366, 379, 410, 411, 426, 449,
    570, 577, 684, 686, 789, 799, 807,
    808, 874, 889, 925, 933, 941

Geometry Review
    Special Right Triangles, 825

STAT PLOT feature, 459, 460, 477, 714
sum of a series, 590
systems of equations, 795
TABLE feature, 140, 202, 227, 437, 871
tangent function, 871
TBLSET feature, 470, 472
Tmax feature, 413
Tmin feature, 413
TRACE feature, 506
transformations, 110
trigonometric functions, 860, 886
VALUE option, 163
VARS feature, 413, 460
vertex form, 236
Xmax feature, 413
Xmin feature, 413
YLIST feature, 477
ZERO option, 163, 227, 299
zeros of polynomial function, 321
ZOOM feature, 460

Graphing Conic Sections, 621

Graphing Trigonometric functions, 860

Greatest Common Factor (GCF), 218, 297

Greatest Integer Function, 90

Gridded Response
exercises, 32, 48, 56, 73, 130, 148, 173, 190, 208, 247, 276, 317, 338, 356, 380, 388, 430, 476, 483, 494, 523, 560, 571, 601, 610, 636, 670, 681, 693, 724, 811, 815, 929, 942
problems, 27, 175, 242, 307, 400, 447, 520, 574, 760, 790, 824, 900

growth, exponential, 434–441, 488

growth factor, 435, 436, 488

guess and check, 286, 312

H

half-angle identities, 951–957, 962

half-plane, 114

Here's Why It Works, 674, 928
angle difference identities, 946
area of a triangle, 928
Change of Base Formula, 464
cofunction identities, 944
double-angle identities, 951
Fundamental Counting Principle, 674
half-angle identities, 953
inequalities, 34
Law of Cosines, 937
length of an intercepted arc, 846
logarithms, 462
negative angle identities, 943
parabolas, 623
point-slope form, 81
quadratic function, 203

relating radians and degrees, 845
Remainder Theorem, 307
sum and differences of cubes, 298
vertical in-line test, 62

Homework Online, 7–10, 15–17, 22–24, 30–32, 38–40, 46–48, 65–67, 71–73, 78–80, 86–88, 96–98, 104–106, 111–113, 118–120, 138–140, 146–148, 153–154, 160–162, 171–173, 179–181, 199–201, 206–207, 212–214, 217–220, 221–223, 229–231, 237–239, 245–247, 253–255, 262–264, 293–295, 301–302, 308–309, 316–317, 322–324, 329–330, 335–337, 343–345, 364–366, 371–373, 378–380, 386–388, 395–397, 402–404, 410–412, 418–420, 439–440, 447–449, 456–458, 466–467, 473–476, 481–483, 503–505, 512–513, 521–523, 531–532, 539–540, 546–548, 569–571, 575–576, 584–585, 591–593, 599–601, 618–619, 627–629, 634–636, 642–644, 658–660, 678, 685–686, 691–692, 700–701, 715–716, 722, 728, 735, 743, 768, 777, 778, 788, 789, 797, 798, 806, 813, 832, 840, 841, 848, 849, 856, 864, 865, 872, 880, 881, 888, 908, 916, 924, 932, 939, 940, 948, 949, 955

horizontal
asymptotes, 518, 554
ellipse, 639
line, 75, 414
translation, 100–101, 102, 108, 415

Horse Hollow Wind Energy Center, 342

hyperbola, 645–652
analyzing, 648
axes of, 646
branches of, 616, 646, 649
center of, 646, 666
conic sections, 614
defined, 645, 666
equation of, 647, 648, 655–656
foci of, 645, 666
graphing, 616, 647
horizontal, 655
reflection property, 649
translations, 655
vertical, 655
vertices of, 645, 646

I

i, **imaginary number,** 248, 249, 272

Iberian lynx, 438

identity(ies)
additive, 14, 767
of angles, 943–956, 962

cofunction, 944, 945, 962
cotangent, 904, 960
domain of validity, 904
equations as, 28, 29, 52
multiplicative, 782, 819
Pythagorean, 906, 960
reciprocal, 904, 960
tangent, 904, 947, 960
trigonometric, 904–910, 960
verifying, 905, 906, 952–953
writing without parentheses, 906

image, 801, 820

imaginary
axis, 249, 250
numbers, 248, 249, 272
solutions to quadratic equations, 252, 272
unit, 248, 249

inconsistent system, 137

independent
events, 688, 689, 753
system, 137, 184
variable, 63

index of the radical expression, 362, 423

industrial design, 531

industry, 548

inequality(ies)
absolute-value, 41–48, 117, 152
compound, 36–37, 43, 52
exponential, 484–485
graphing, 33, 35, 114–120, 126
linear, 114, 115, 117, 149–155, 166, 185
logarithmic, 484–485
polynomial. *See* polynomial equations
properties of, 34
quadratic, 256–257, 261, 272
rational, 550–551
real numbers as a solution, 36, 52
solving, 33–40
solving, as Big Idea, 49, 50, 133, 182, 183, 421, 422
systems of, 157, 166, 184, 185
writing, 33, 34, 117

infinite
geometric series, 594, 598
series, 587

initial
point, 809, 820
side of angles, 836, 894

integers, 12

intercepted arc, 844, 845, 895

interdisciplinary
agriculture, 222, 746
archaeology, 448, 481
architecture, 234, 375, 592, 871
astronomy, 467, 636, 644, 857

Sum of a Finite Arithmetic Series, 595
Tangent of an Angle, 868
Theoretical Probability, 683
Transformations of a Parabola, 626
Transforming a Circle, 632
Translation of the Parabola, 197
Trigonometric Ratios for a Circle, 919
Trigonometric Ratios for a Right
   Triangle, 920
Variables and Expressions, 5
Variance and Standard Deviation, 719
Vectors in Two Dimensions, 809
Vertex Principle of Linear
   Programming, 158
Vertical Asymptotes of Rational
   Functions, 517
Writing and Graphing Inequalities, 33

Know/Need/Plan problems, 20, 69, 77,
   82, 94, 117, 136, 151, 205, 284,
   289, 313, 320, 391, 400, 445, 471,
   502, 511, 597, 615, 626, 631, 640,
   690, 713, 721, 732, 766, 803, 839,
   847, 854, 863, 922, 954

L

language arts, 833

Law
   of Cosines, 936–942, 961
   of Sines, 928–934, 961

Least Common Denominator (LCD),
   535, 537

Least Common Multiple (LCM), 534–
   535

length
   of an intercepted arc, 845, 846
   sides of triangles, 928–932, 935, 938,
   939

Lesson Check, 7, 15, 22, 30, 37, 45, 64,
   71, 78, 86, 96, 103, 111, 118, 138,
   145, 152, 160, 171, 179, 198, 206,
   212, 221, 229, 237, 244, 253, 261,
   285, 293, 300, 308, 315, 322, 328,
   335, 342, 364, 370, 378, 385, 394,
   401, 409, 418, 439, 447, 456, 465,
   473, 480, 503, 512, 521, 530, 539,
   545, 568, 575, 583, 591, 598, 617,
   627, 634, 642, 650, 658, 678, 691,
   700, 722, 728, 735, 743, 768, 777,
   787, 798, 806, 813, 831, 840, 846,
   855, 864, 861, 880, 887, 908, 915,
   923, 932, 939, 948, 955

like radicals, 374, 424

like terms, 21, 52

limits, 589, 605

line(s). *See also* linear equations
   boundary, 107, 114, 115, 126
   horizontal, 75, 414

intercept of, 76
parallel, 81, 85, 124
perpendicular, 81, 85, 124
slope of, 74, 75, 124
vertical, 75, 107, 414
writing equations of, 83
x-intercept, 76, 289
y-intercept, 76

linear data, 215

linear equation(s)
   defined, 75
   direct variation, 68–73, 123
   graphing, 77, 83, 84, 124
   line of best fit, 94–95
   matrix representation of, 174–178
   modeling, 92–98
   for parallel lines, 85
   for perpendicular lines, 85
   Piecewise Function, 90–91
   point-slope form, 81–82, 83, 124
   slope formula, 74
   slope-intercept form, 77, 83, 124
   solving using calculators, 178
   solving using matrices, 174–178, 186
   standard form, 82–83, 124
   systems of. *See* linear systems
   for a trend line, 94
   writing, 76

linear factors, 288, 289

linear functions, 74–80
   defined, 75
   graphs of, 124
   slope-intercept form of, 76

linear inequality(ies), 149–155
   defined, 114
   solving by graphing, 115, 117, 150–
    151, 185
   solving using tables, 149–150
   systems of, 166, 185

linear polynomial, 281

linear programming, 157–162
   activity, 163
   constraints in, 157, 185
   defined, 157
   vertex principle of, 158

linear-quadratic system, 258–264
   solving by graphing, 259
   solving by substitution, 259

linear regression, 94, 136, 352

linear regression (LinReg), 94

linear system(s)
   absolute-value, 152
   classifying, 137
   consistent, 137, 184
   defined, 134, 184
   dependent, 137, 184
   equivalent, 142, 144, 168
   inconsistent, 137, 184

independent, 137, 184
of inequalities, 157, 184
linear term, 281
with no unique solution, 145, 166,
   184
solving algebraically, 142–155, 184
solving by elimination, 144, 184
solving by graphing, 134–141, 150,
   166, 168
solving by substitution, 142–143, 169,
   184
solving with calculators, 178
solving with matrix equations, 174–
   178
solving with tables, 134–141, 149–150

line of best fit, 94, 95, 125

LIST feature, 590

literal equation, 29

logarithm(s)
   base ten, 453, 463
   Change of Base Formula, 464
   common, 453, 489
   defined, 451
   evaluating, 452
   expanding, 463
   natural, 478–483, 490
   properties of, 462–468, 472, 489
   simplifying, 463
   using for exponential models, 477

logarithmic
   expressions, 451, 478–479
   inequalities, 484–485
   scale, 453, 465

logarithmic equation(s)
   defined, 490
   natural, 479
   solving, 469–476

logarithmic function(s)
   define, 454
   families of, 455
   graphing, 454–455
   as inverses, 451–458, 489
   natural, 478, 490
   translations, 455

long division of polynomials, 302–304

look for a pattern, 522

look for key words, 34, 72

Looking Ahead Vocabulary, 1, 57, 131,
   191, 277, 357, 431, 495, 561, 611,
   671, 761, 825, 901

M

magnitude, 809, 820

major axis of an ellipse, 639, 665

make a drawing, 188

Multiplicative Property of Zero, 773, 776

multiplicity of a zero, 291

multi-step equations, 27

music, 143, 476, 849, 857

mutually exclusive events, 689, 690, 753

My Math Video, 3, 59, 133, 196, 279, 359, 433, 497, 563, 613, 673, 763, 827, 903

N

The (n + 1) Point Principle, 332, 333, 352

natural
    logarithmic equation, 478–479
    logarithms, 478–483, 490
    numbers, 12

natural base exponential functions, 446

natural logarithmic function, 478

negative
    angle identities, 943, 962
    numbers, 21
    square root, 248

Networks, 780–781

Newton's Law of Cooling, 483

n factorial ($n!$), 675, 752

non-mutually exclusive events, 690

non-removable discontinuity, 516

normal
    curve, 741
    vectors, 812

normal distribution, 739–745
    analyzing, 742
    defined, 744, 756
    sketching a normal curve, 741

notation
    alternative for radicals, 381
    factorial, 675
    function, 62, 63, 407
    summation, 589, 590, 605

nth root, 361–366, 423

nth term of a sequence, 565

number(s)
    of combinations, 676
    complex. See complex number(s)
    imaginary, 249, 272
    integers, 12
    irrational, 12
    natural, 12
    of permutations, 676
    rational, 12, 377
    real. See real numbers

roots of. *See* roots of numbers
    simplifying, 249
    whole, 12

number cubes, 694–695

number line, 13

numerical expression, 5

O

objective function, 157, 185

oblique asymptotes, 524–525

observational study, 727

oceanography, 440, 863

one-step equations, 27

one-to-one function, 408

online activities. *See* Dynamic Activities; Homework Online; MathXL for School; My Math Video; PowerAlgebra.com; Problems Online; Solve It!; vocabulary, Vocabulary Audio Online

Open-Ended exercises, 8, 9, 24, 40, 47, 72, 105, 126, 127, 138, 140, 147, 154, 160, 173, 179, 181, 187, 200, 213, 222, 224, 230, 254, 262, 273, 286, 294, 302, 311, 317, 323, 365, 372, 379, 385, 387, 396, 403, 427, 440, 449, 457, 475, 491, 505, 512, 513, 526, 531, 539, 545, 548, 557, 570, 579, 585, 592, 600, 607, 619, 635, 643, 651, 660, 667, 678, 691, 700, 701, 707, 710, 730, 736, 737, 757, 791, 799, 821, 833, 840, 841, 842, 849, 855, 857, 859, 864, 881, 898, 909, 927, 933, 941, 956, 963

operations
    with complex numbers, 250
    with functions, 398–404, 425
    inverse, 27
    with rational expressions, 528, 534, 535, 536
    row, 176, 185

opposites
    additive inverse, 14
    defined, 14
    of a difference, 21
    of an opposite, 21
    of a product, 21
    of real numbers, 14
    simplifying algebraic expressions, 21
    of a sum, 21

ordered
    pairs, 60, 110, 121–122, 123, 164
    triples, 164, 167

outliers, 712, 754

P

packaging design, 286

parabola(s), 622–629
    axis of symmetry, 194, 624
    conic sections and, 614
    defined, 194, 622, 664
    directrix, 622, 664
    equation of, 209, 623–624, 627
    focal length, 622, 664
    graphing, 194, 197, 268
    maximums and minimums, 195
    points on, 622–623
    properties of, 194, 268
    transformations, 195, 626
    translations, 197
    vertex form, 194, 196, 198

parallel lines, 81, 85, 124

parameters, 266

parametric equations, 413

Parent Function
    absolute value, 107, 108
    defined, 99, 125
    exponential functions, 444
    logarithmic functions, 455
    quadratic, 194
    radical functions, 415
    reciprocal functions, 509

Pascal, Blaise, 327

Pascal's Triangle, 326–330

patterns, 4–9. *See also* sequences
    expressing with algebra, 5–6, 51
    formulas to generate, 564, 565, 567
    identifying, 4, 51
    mathematical, 564–571, 604
    Moiré, 617

percentile
    defined, 715
    finding, 715

perfect square trinomial
    defined, 220
    factoring, 219, 220, 234–235, 297

period
    defined, 828
    of functions, 828, 893
    of sine curve, 852
    of tangent function, 869

periodic
    cycle, 828–829
    data, 828–834, 894

periodic function(s)
    amplitude of, 830
    cycles of, 828–829
    defined, 828, 893
    identifying, 829

permutations, 674–680
    defined, 675

Q

Math Symbols, 986
Measures, 985
Properties and Formulas, 987–992

reflection matrix, 804

reflection(s)
absolute value functions, 108
defined, 101, 125
of ellipse, 640
exponential functions, 434, 444
geometric, 801, 805, 820
of hyperbola, 649
logarithmic functions, 455
quadratic functions, 195
reciprocal function, 509

Reflexive Property of Equality, 26

regression
cubic, 331–334
exponential, 459
linear, 94–95, 333
logarithmic, 459
polynomial, 331–334
quadratic, 211, 331

relation(s), 60–65
defined, 60, 123
domain of, 61, 62, 123
graphing, 60–61, 406–407
inverse, 405–413
mapping diagram, 60–61
range of, 61, 62, 123
table of values, 60–61

Remainder Theorem, 307, 349

removable discontinuity, 516

Review
Square Roots and Radicals, 225
Properties of Exponents, 360
Special Right Triangles, 835

right triangles
side lengths of, 920, 922
special, 835
trigonometric ratios for, 919–926

roots of numbers
cube, 361, 362, 417
nth, 361–366, 423
principal, 361, 381, 423
real, 362–363
square. See Square root(s)
writing equations from, 232

roots of polynomial equations
Conjugate Root Theorem, 350
Descartes' Rule of Signs, 315, 350
determining the number of, 319–322
finding by graphing, 299
identifying, 314
irrational, 314, 350
theorems of, 312, 313, 350
writing equations from, 232

rotation
center of, 804

of matrices, 801, 804, 820
measures of angles, 836
of vectors, 810

row operation, 176, 185

S

sample(s), 725–730
bias in, 751, 755
convenience, 725
defined, 725, 755
random, 725, 755
self-selected, 725
systematic, 725

sample proportion, 747

sample space
defined, 682
equally likely, 682, 752

scalar multiplication, 772–773, 802, 811, 812, 818

scalars, 772, 773–774

scatter plots, 92–93, 125

science, 466, 584

secant function, 883, 897

seismology, 474

self-selected sample, 725

sequences
arithmetic, 572–577, 604
defined, 564, 604
explicit formulas, 565, 567, 604, 605
Fibonacci Sequence, 578
finite, 587
geometric, 580–586, 605
infinite, 587
nth term, 565
recursive formula, 565, 566, 604, 605
terms of, 564, 568

series
analyzing, 598
arithmetic, 587–595, 605
defined, 587, 604, 605
finite, 587, 595, 596
geometric, 594, 595–601, 606
infinite, 587, 594, 598
sum of a, 589, 590

Short Response exercises,
end of chapter problems, 56, 130, 190, 276, 356, 430, 494, 560, 610, 670, 760, 824, 900, 966
end of lesson problems, 10, 17, 24, 67, 80, 88, 98, 106, 113, 155, 162, 181, 201, 231, 255, 264, 287, 302, 324, 345, 373, 397, 404, 420, 450, 458, 468, 505, 514, 533, 541, 586, 593, 620, 644, 652, 660, 680, 687, 702, 718, 730, 745, 770, 779, 800,

808, 842, 850, 858, 867, 874, 882, 910, 926, 934, 950, 957

show your work, 54

shrink. *See* compression

sigma
standard deviation, 719
summation, 589

simplest form
absolute value functions, 107
defined, 527
of functions, 99, 125
of radical expressions, 368
of rational expressions, 527, 535, 536, 555
writing expressions in, 385

simplifying
expressions, 21, 52
imaginary numbers, 249
logarithms, 463
numbers, 249
problem solving strategy, 12, 18, 19, 21, 23, 24, 25, 26, 28, 35, 36, 42, 49, 51, 52, 53, 63, 64, 69, 70, 76, 82, 84, 101, 124, 128, 167, 169, 170, 176, 177, 182, 204, 225, 236, 240, 241, 242, 244, 249, 250, 251, 252, 254, 256, 271, 272, 286, 290, 297, 300, 304, 321, 328, 330, 342, 349, 354, 360, 365, 366, 367, 368, 369, 370, 371, 372, 373, 375, 376, 377, 378, 379, 382, 384, 385, 386, 387, 388, 389, 391, 392, 393, 394, 403, 404, 417, 422, 423, 424, 425, 426, 430, 436, 441, 447, 453, 463, 465, 466, 469, 472, 478, 480, 481, 490, 493, 494, 501, 502, 505, 510, 516, 517, 527, 528, 531, 532, 534, 536, 537, 538, 539, 540, 542, 543, 555, 556, 565, 573, 574, 577, 581, 588, 596, 597, 631, 633, 640, 647, 648, 649, 652, 656, 657, 907, 908
radical expressions, 363, 368–370, 376, 423
rational exponents, 381–388
rational expressions, 528

simulations, 682, 731, 752

sine, of angles, 838, 839, 845, 894

sine curve, 852, 895, 944

sine function, 851–858
families of, 877
graphing, 851, 852–854
inverse, 913
modeling light waves, 855
properties of, 853, 894
radian measures, 851
translations, 875, 882, 896, 944
unit circles and, 851

Skills Handbook
Area and Volume, 972

Index

Vertex Principle of Linear Programming, 158, 185

vertical
asymptotes, 518, 554
ellipse, 639
line, 75, 107, 414
translation, 102, 108, 109, 125, 195, 415

Vertical-line test, 62–63, 414

vocabulary
Chapter Vocabulary, 50, 122, 183, 267, 347, 422, 487, 553, 751, 817, 893
exercises, 15, 22, 30, 45, 64, 71, 78, 86, 138, 145, 152, 160, 171, 179, 198, 221, 229, 235, 237, 285, 293, 300, 315, 322, 328, 335, 342, 370, 378, 394, 409, 439, 456, 461, 465, 512, 530, 557, 568, 591, 617, 627, 658, 678, 685, 691, 707, 710, 715, 722, 728, 735, 743, 768, 777, 813, 848, 855, 871, 880, 908, 932
Lesson Vocabulary, 4, 11, 18, 26, 33, 41, 60, 68, 74, 81, 91, 99, 107, 114, 125, 134, 142, 157, 166, 174, 194, 202, 209, 216, 226, 234, 241, 249, 259, 280, 288, 296, 303, 312, 319, 326, 331, 339, 361, 367, 374, 390, 398, 405, 414, 434, 442, 451, 462, 469, 478, 498, 515, 527, 534, 542, 564, 572, 580, 587, 595, 614, 622, 630, 638, 645, 674, 681, 688, 696, 711, 719, 725, 739, 764, 772, 782, 792, 801, 809, 829, 836, 844, 851, 861, 868, 875, 883, 904, 919, 928, 936
Looking Ahead Vocabulary, 57, 131, 191, 277, 431, 495, 561, 611, 671, 761, 825, 901
Vocabulary Audio Online, 2, 58, 132, 192, 278, 358, 432, 495, 562, 612, 672, 762, 826, 902
Vocabulary Builder, 54, 128, 188, 274, 758, 822, 899, 959

W

Whispering Gallery, 641

whole numbers, 12

words modeling algebraic expressions, 18–19

work backwards, 362

writing
equations, 74–80, 83, 124, 232, 452
exercises, 16, 17, 24, 25, 31, 32, 39, 47, 48, 53, 72, 89, 96, 97, 105, 112, 120, 127, 140, 145, 147, 154, 171, 179, 180, 187, 207, 213, 222, 224, 245, 273, 294, 302, 310, 311, 317, 329, 336, 345, 353, 372, 379, 411, 413, 418, 427, 460, 461, 466, 474, 477, 482, 484, 491, 503, 505, 512, 513, 522, 540, 547, 557, 576, 585, 598, 600, 607, 621, 629, 636, 644, 661, 667, 679, 680, 685, 686, 701, 709, 717, 723, 728, 736, 744, 752, 757, 769, 778, 781, 789, 790, 791, 806, 807, 814, 821, 831, 833, 841, 849, 859, 860, 865, 871, 874, 889, 898, 915, 917, 923, 927, 934, 939, 941, 950, 956, 963
expressions, 20, 385
functions, 110, 451–458
inequalities, 33, 34, 117
technical writing, 525
Think/Write problems, 6, 35, 101, 108, 144, 168, 176, 198, 220, 234, 243, 252, 259, 300, 328, 364, 368, 376, 384, 417, 437, 465, 519, 529, 538, 543, 566, 582, 588, 648, 654, 677, 682, 698, 786, 795, 830, 870, 879, 884, 907, 914, 930, 938, 948
translations, 877

X

x-axis, 101, 102, 164, 195, 197, 226, 256, 435

x-coefficient, 175

x-coordinate, 61, 62, 74, 123, 124, 203, 416

x-intercept, 76, 243, 289, 291, 319, 348

Xmax feature, 413

Xmin feature, 413

xy-coordinate plane, 164

Y

y-axis, 101, 102, 164

y-coefficient, 175

y-coordinate, 61, 62, 74, 123, 124, 203

y-intercept, 76

YLIST feature, 477

Z

z-axis, 164

zero(s)
additive identity, 13
multiplication by, 21
multiplicative inverse and, 13
multiplicative property of, 773, 776
multiplicity of, 291
of polynomial functions, 288, 289, 348
properties of, 13, 226, 270, 289, 773
of quadratic equation, 226, 270
of quadratic function, 226
of quartic functions, 341
as a real number, 13
of transformed cubic function, 339–340

ZERO option, 163, 227, 299

Zero-Product Property, 226, 270, 288, 289, 349

zoology, 440, 740, 741

ZOOM feature, 460

z-score, 748

Acknowledgments

Staff Credits

The people who made up the High School Mathematics team—representing composition services, core design digital and multimedia production services, digital product development, editorial, editorial services, manufacturing, marketing, and production management—are listed below.

Emily Allman, Dan Anderson, Scott Andrews, Christopher Anton, Carolyn Artin, Michael Avidon, Margaret Banker, Charlie Bink, Niki Birbilis, Suzanne Biron, Beth Blumberg, Tim Breeze-Thorndike, Kyla Brown, Rebekah Brown, Judith Buice, Sylvia Bullock, Stacie Cartwright, Carolyn Chappo, Christia Clarke, Mary Ellen Cole, Tom Columbus, Andrew Coppola, AnnMarie Coyne, Bob Craton, Nicholas Cronin, Patrick Culleton, Damaris Curran, Steven Cushing, Sheila DeFazio, Cathie Dillender, Emily Dumas, Patty Fagan, Frederick Fellows, Jorgensen Fernandez, Mandy Figueroa, Suzanne Finn, Sara Freund, Matt Frueh, Jon Fuhrer, Andy Gaus, Mark Geyer, Mircea Goia, Andrew Gorlin, Shelby Gragg, Ellen Granter, Jay Grasso, Lisa Gustafson, Toni Haluga, Greg Ham, Marc Hamilton, Chris Handorf, Angie Hanks, Scott Harris, Cynthia Harvey, Phil Hazur, Thane Heninger, Aun Holland, Amanda House, Chuck Jann, Linda Johnson, Blair Jones, Marian Jones, Tim Jones, Gillian Kahn, Matthew Keefer, Brian Keegan, Jim Kelly, Jonathan Kier, Jennifer King, Tamara King, Elizabeth Krieble, Meytal Kotik, Brian Kubota, Roshni Kutty, Mary Landry, Christopher Langley, Christine Lee, Sara Levendusky, Lisa Lin, Wendy Marberry, Dominique Mariano, Clay Martin, Rich McMahon, Eve Melnechuk, Cynthia Metallides, Hope Morley, Christine Nevola, Michael O'Donnell, Michael Oster, Ameer Padshah, Stephen Patrias, Jeffrey Paulhus, Jonathan Penyack, Valerie Perkins, Brian Reardon, Wendy Rock, Marcy Rose, Carol Roy, Irene Rubin, Hugh Rutledge, Vicky Shen, Jewel Simmons, Ted Smykal, Emily Soltanoff, William Speiser, Jayne Stevenson, Richard Sullivan, Dan Tanguay, Dennis Tarwood, Susan Tauer, Tiffany Taylor-Sullivan, Catherine Terwilliger, Mark Tricca, Maria Torti, Leonid Tunik, Ilana Van Veen, Lauren Van Wart, John Vaughan, Laura Vivenzio, Samuel Voigt, Kathy Warfel, Don Weide, Laura Wheel, Eric Whitfield, Sequoia Wild, Joseph Will, Kristin Winters, Allison Wyss, Dina Zolotusky

Additional Credits: Michele Cardin, Robert Carlson, Kate Dalton-Hoffman, Dana Guterman, Narae Maybeth, Carolyn McGuire, Manjula Nair, Rachel Terino, Steve Thomas

Illustration

Stephen Durke: 574; **Phil Guzy:** 596, 597; **Rob Schuster:** 4, 5, 11, 18, 26, 33, 39, 41, 48, 60, 68, 74, 81, 84, 99, 107, 114, 116, 134, 142, 143, 149, 157, 165, 166, 168, 171, 174, 194, 202, 207, 216, 226, 233, 240, 258, 280, 288, 294, 296, 303, 308, 312, 326, 331, 367, 374, 375, 381, 390, 395, 398, 405, 414, 429, 434, 449, 451, 469, 498, 515, 522, 527, 534, 542, 547, 564, 566, 567, 570, 571, 572, 580, 587, 595, 609, 614, 617, 619, 630, 638, 641, 653, 865; **Ted Smykel:** 209; **Pearson Education:** 596, 597; **Judi Pinkham:** 230; **Pronk&Associates:** 12, 362, 399, 462, 589; **XNR Productions:** 788

Technical Illustration

Aptara, Inc.; GGS Book Services

Photographs

Every effort has been made to secure permission and provide appropriate credit for photographic material. The publisher deeply regrets any omission and pledges to correct errors called to its attention in subsequent editions.

Unless otherwise acknowledged, all photographs are the property of Pearson Education, Inc.

Photo locators denoted as follows: Top (T), Center (C), Bottom (B), Left (L), Right (R), Background (Bkgd)

Cover
JL Klein & ML Hubert/Biosphoto

Front Matter
ix, **x** Peter Mason/Getty Images; **xii** Jeff Greenberg/PhotoEdit, Inc.
28 (T) BL Images Ltd/Alamy Images; **39** (TR) Richard Wahlstrom/Workbook/Jupiter Images/Getty Images; **45** (TR) UPI Photo/Roger Williams/NewsCom; **61** (TR, TCR, CR, CC) Jupiter Images/Brand X/Alamy, (TC) Roberto Mettifogo/Getty Images; **84** (BCR) William Harader, (BR) Zen Shui/SuperStock; **135** (CR) Doug Perrine/Peter Arnold Inc./PhotoLibrary Group, Inc./Getty Images, (TCR) Paul Nicklen/National Geographic Image Collection; **159** (TCR) Andy Crawford/©DK Images, (TCR) Getty Images, (TC) Steve Gorton/©DK Images; **164** (BR) Image Source/Getty Images; **198** (T) Design Pics Inc/Alamy; **205** (TR) Jeff Greenberg/PhotoEdit, Inc.; **228** (TR) ©Harvey Lloyd/Getty Images, (TCR) Andy Harmer/Photo Researchers, Inc.; **234** (TR) Rolf Hicker Photography/Alamy Images; **306** (BR) James Baigrie/Botanica/Jupiter Images/Getty Images; **333** (T) Andre Gallant/Getty Images, (TC) D. Hurst/Alamy, (TCR) Mark Sytes/Alamy, (TR) Peter Cade/Getty Images; **342** AF/Fotolia; **375** Wave Royalty Free/Alamy; **383** (TR) Detlev van Ravenswaay/Photo Researchers, Inc.; **392** (BC) Bob Llewellyn **408** (T) Bob Krist/Corbis; **438** (TR) John Cancalosi/Alamy Images; **453** (CR) Earth Imaging/Getty Images; **467** (BR) Jerry Lodriguss/Science Photo Library/Photo Researchers, Inc.; **476** (TR) Dave King/©DK Images; **480** (TR) JPL/NASA; **502** (TR) Chase Jarvis (R) Corbis Super RF/Alamy; **513** (TCR) NASA; **544** (TR) JPL/NASA; **578** (CR) ©DK Images, (L) Bob Gibbons/Alamy Images, (R) John Glover/Alamy Images, (CL) Peter Anderson/©DK Images; **582** (T) Thomas J. Peterson/Alamy Images; **625** (B) Hank Morgan/Photo Researchers, Inc.; **632** (B) Guido Alberto Rossi/Tips Images/Tips Italia Srl a socio unico/Alamy; **641** (C) Museum of Science and Industry; **675** (T) Ron Chapple Stock; **684** (C) Koji Aoki/Aflo/Getty Images; **775** (TR, TL) iStockphoto; **803** (TC) Wolfgang Spunbarg/PhotoEdit, Inc.; **847** (CR) European Space Agency/Science Photo Library/Photo Researchers, Inc., (TCR) Steve Gorton/©DK Images; **848** (BL) David Zimmerman/Getty Images, (BR) Fnalphotos/Dreamstime LLC; **887** (TR) ART on FILE/Corbis; **889** (CR) Demetrio Carrasco/©DK Images; NewsCom; **921** (TR) age fotostock/SuperStock; **931** (C) mediacolor's/Alamy Images.